PREFACE

Our twentieth century world is changing rapidly. Important changes have been made in the law of business. These are presented in this Sixth Edition of BUSINESS LAW PRINCIPLES AND CASES in new chapters and in many new and expanded topics within chapters on traditional subjects.

Consumer Protection

The interests of the consumer are being increasingly recognized by federal and state legislation and by administrative regulation. The importance of this area of the law is recognized by Chapter 8, Consumer Protection, which embraces important provisions of the Uniform Consumer Credit Code and the federal Consumer Credit Protection Act. Bait advertising, games of chance as promotional devices, seals of approval, home solicitation sales, referral sales, mail order transactions, credit cards, balloon payments, preservation of consumer defenses, collection methods, protection of credit standing, mutual funds, and consumer remedies are some of the topics in this new chapter.

The following topics are examples of those pertaining to consumer protection which are incorporated in other chapters: unordered goods, disclosure in a separate statement for an installment loan, fine print in contracts, domination by seller, unequal bargaining power, credit insurance, unconscionable and oppressive contracts, consumer protection rescission, and waiver of defenses in secured credit sales.

Environmental Law

Society increasingly recognizes the social importance of the conservation of natural resources and of the protection of our physical environment. Man's desire to obtain an unpolluted environment is becoming crystallized into a right, as set forth in Chapter 7, Environmental Law and Community Planning.

Administrative Agencies

The importance of administrative agencies, particularly those on the federal level, continues to grow. The special character of these agencies is recognized in Chapter 6. Consideration is given to the administrator's power, the pattern of administrative procedure, and the finality of administrative determination.

Franchises

Numerous questions raised by the recent tremendous growth of franchising operations necessitate an understanding of the basic principles of the law involved. These are considered in Chapter 47.

Computers and Other New Topics

The impact of data processing, computers, and retrieval systems is recognized in such topics as defamation by computer, computer programs as property, and computers and corporate management.

Antidiscrimination legislation affects several areas of business law, as reflected by topics dealing with businesses serving the public (restaurants, common carriers of passengers, and hotels and motels), employment, deeds, leases, and insurance.

Numerous other topics include: wiretapping and electronic surveillance; national data banks, notaries public, transfer of title in self-service stores; condominiums; and no-fault insurance.

UCC and UCCC

The rapid growth in the number of court decisions under the Uniform Commercial Code since the publication of the Fifth Edition has necessitated an expanded presentation of the law in such areas as sales, commercial paper, and secured transactions. More evident in the opinions too is the influence of the UCC on contracts in general. An appendix includes the complete Official Text of the Uniform Commercial Code.

The Uniform Consumer Credit Code has been adopted in several states. Regardless of the number of additional states that adopt the UCCC, this uniform act is having a definite influence on state legislation concerning consumer credit practices. Chapter 14, Legality and Public Policy, and Chapter 8, Consumer Protection, incorporate provisions of the UCCC.

Social Forces

The unique treatment of social forces in the prior editions is continued in this Sixth Edition. In Chapter 2, Law As an Expression of Social Forces, the specific objectives of the law are discussed against the background of the general objective of creating, maintaining, and restoring order, stability, and justice. The student also learns to think of the law as an evolutionary process and as a synthesis of prior law.

Authoritative

The material in this edition has been made up-to-date through an examination of professional publications in the field, new federal legislation, administrative agency regulations, and every reported decision of the federal courts, the state supreme courts, and the intermediate state courts.

Reference is made by the footnotes to uniform statutes, model acts, and restatements of the law as well as to recent cases. In addition to the UCC and UCCC, the uniform statutes and model acts cited pertain to arbitration, anatomical gifts, gifts to minors, aeronautics, fraudulent conveyances, vendor and purchaser risks, disposition of unclaimed property, partnerships, limited partnerships, business corporations, probate, and simultaneous deaths.

R.A.A.

W.A.K.

CONTENTS

1 Legal Rights and the Agencies for Their Enforcement

Law has developed because men and society have wanted relationships between men, and between men and government, to conform to certain standards. Each person has desired to know what conduct he could reasonably expect from others as well as what conduct others could reasonably expect from him so that he could make decisions intelligently in terms of his legal rights and obligations. The rules or laws adopted for this purpose have expressed the social, economic, and moral standards and aspirations of society.

NATURE OF LEGAL RIGHTS AND THE LAW

Law consists of the entire body of principles that govern conduct and the observance of which can be enforced in courts. If there were no man-made law, no doubt many persons would be guided by principles of moral or natural law. Most people would act in accordance with the dictates of conscience, the precepts of right living that are a part of religion, and the ethical concepts that are generally accepted in the community. Those who would choose to act otherwise, however, would constitute a serious problem for society. Man-made law is necessary, therefore, to provide not only rules of conduct but also the machinery and procedures for enforcing right conduct, for punishing wrongful acts, and for settling disputes that arise even when both parties are motivated by good intentions.

§ 1:1. What Are Legal Rights? What are legal rights? And who has them? In answering these questions, we tend to make the mistake of thinking of the present as being characteristic of what was and what will be. But consider the evolution of the concept of the "rights of man" and the right of privacy.

(1) The "Rights of Man" Concept. Our belief in the American way of life and in the concepts on which our society or government is based should not obscure the fact that at one time there was no American way of life and that the concept of man possessing rights recognized by government was the fruit of more than a revolution—it was a product of creation. While many religious leaders, philosophers, and poets spoke of the rights of man and of the dignity of man, rulers laughed at such pretensions and held man tightly in a society based on status. If he were a nobleman, he had the rights of a nobleman of his degree. If he were a warrior, he had the rights of a warrior. If a slave, he had very few rights at all. In each case the law saw only status; rights attached not to a man but to his status.

In the course of time, serfdom displaced slavery in much of the Western world. Eventually feudalism disappeared and, with the end of the Thirty Years War, the modern society of nations began to emerge. Surely one might say that in such a "new order" man had legal rights. No, not as a man but only as a subject. Even when the English colonists settled in America, they brought with them not the rights of men but the rights of British subjects. Even when the colonies were within one year of war, the Second Continental Congress presented to King George III the Olive Branch Petition which beseeched the king to recognize the colonists' rights as Englishmen. For almost a year the destiny of the colonies hung in the balance with the colonists unable to decide between remaining loyal to the Crown, seeking to obtain recognition of their rights as Englishmen (a "status" recognition), or doing something else.

Finally, the ill-advised policies of George III and the eloquence of Thomas Paine's Common Sense tipped the scales and the colonies spoke on July 4, 1776, not in the terms of the rights of English subjects but in terms of the rights of man existing independently of any government. Had the American Revolution been lost, the Declaration of Independence would have gone rattling down the corridors of time with many other failures. But the American Revolution was won, and the new government that was established was based upon "man" as the building block rather than upon "subjects." Rights of man replaced the concept of rights of subjects. With this transition the obligations of a king to his faithful subjects were replaced by the rights of man existing without regard to will or authority of any kind. Since then, America has been going through additional stages of determining what is embraced by the concept of "rights of man."

(2) The Right of Privacy. Today everyone recognizes that there is a right of privacy. Before 1890, however, this right did not exist in American law. Certainly the men who wrote the Declaration of Independence and the Bill of Rights Amendments to the Constitution were conscious of rights. How can we explain that the law did not recognize a right of privacy until a full century later?

The answer is that at a particular time people worry about the problems which face them. Note the extent of the fears and concern of the framers of the Bill of Rights Amendments to the Constitution. The Fourth Amendment states, "The right of the people to be secure in their persons, houses, papers, and effects, against unreasonable searches and seizures, shall not be violated, and no Warrants shall issue, but upon probable cause, supported by Oath or affirmation, and particularly describing the place to be searched, and the persons or things to be seized." The man of 1790 was afraid of a recurrence of the days of George III.

The framers of the Fourth Amendment declared what we today would regard as a segment of privacy—protection from police invasion of privacy.

The man of 1790 just was not concerned with invasion of privacy by a private person. While a snooping person could be prosecuted to some extent under a Peeping Tom Statute, this was a criminal liability. The victim could not sue for damages for the invasion of his privacy.

If we are honest with history, all that we can say is that modern man thinks highly of his privacy and wants it to be protected. And, knowing that the law is responsive to the wishes of society, we can also say that the right is protected by government. But note that we should go no further than to say that it is a right which society wishes to protect at the present time. If circumstances arise in our national life of such a nature that privacy will hamper or endanger national defense, we can expect that the "right" of privacy will be limited or modified. We should therefore approach problems relating to rights with an open mind, realizing that there are only such legal rights as we the people, through our legal system, choose to recognize.

(a) WIRETAPPING AND ELECTRONIC SURVEILLANCE. It is a violation of federal statute to tap or intercept telephone conversations, even when authorized by state law, and evidence of illegally-overheard conversations or evidence discovered by virtue of the information contained in such conversations may not be admitted in either state or federal courts.[1] Electronic surveillance and wiretapping, whether by officers or private persons, is a federal crime;[2] and damages may be recovered by any person whose communications are intercepted, disclosed, or used in violation of the statute.[3]

(b) NATIONAL DATA BANKS. Various proposals have been made for the formation of national or central data banks which, in effect, would keep detailed records of each person, enterprise, and region. It is apparent that for the purpose of determining the needs of the nation, such detailed information would be of great value. For example, what are the facts about environmental pollution, the patterns of crime, the problems of automobile insurance? Before anything can be done about our national problems, we must have facts. But those same facts that would be useful for solving our national problems could also lead to the curtailment of the right of privacy. We would then need to solve the problem of improper use of the facts by those in control of the computerized data banks or by those having access to that information.

From one standpoint requiring the disclosure of endless information to the government destroys the concept of privacy. From another point of view, it is merely the recognition that privacy, as in the case of all legal rights,

---

[1] Lee v Florida, 392 US 378. The prohibition extends to picking up conversations electronically by microphone or induction coil, even though the pickup device is in a public place outside of where the defendant is talking and no trespass or entry into private property is involved. Katz v United States, 389 US 347.

[2] Title III Omnibus Crime Control and Safe Streets Act of 1968, § 802, 18 USC § 2511.

[3] § 802, 18 USC § 2520.

is limited. The national data bank problem is basically one of whether the concept of privacy should apply to a situation to which it had never applied, nor could apply, until the national population became larger, before the computer came into existence, and government had abandoned the laissez-faire policy of former years.

§ **1:2. What Is the Law?** The expression, "a law," is ordinarily used in connection with a statute enacted by a state legislature or the Congress of the United States, such as an act by the federal Congress to extend the benefits of old-age insurance. All of the principles that make up law, however, are not laws adopted by legislative bodies.

Constitutional law includes the constitutions in force in the particular area or territory. In each state, two constitutions are in force, the state constitution and the national constitution.

Statutory law includes statutes adopted by the lawmakers. Each state has its own legislature and the United States has the Congress, both of which enact laws. In addition, every city, county, or other subdivision has some power to adopt ordinances which, within their sphere of operation, have the same binding effect as legislative acts.

Of great importance are the *administrative regulations,* such as rules of the Securities and Exchange Commission and the National Labor Relations Board. The regulations promulgated by national and state administrative agencies generally have the force of statute and are therefore part of "the law."

Law also includes principles that are expressed for the first time in court decisions. This is *case law.* For example, when a court must decide a new question or problem, its decision becomes a *precedent* and stands as the law for that particular problem in the future. This rule that a court decision becomes a precedent to be followed in similar cases is the *doctrine of stare decisis.*

In England, common or community law developed in the centuries following the Norman Conquest in 1066. This *common law* was a body of unwritten principles that were based on customs and usages of the community. These principles were recognized and enforced by the courts. By the time the colonies were founded in America, the English common law had become a definite, established body of principles and was brought to the New World to become the basis for the law of the colonies and of virtually all of the states.

Law also includes treaties made by the United States, and proclamations and orders by the President of the United States or by other public officials.

§ **1:3. Uniform State Laws.** To secure uniformity as far as possible, the National Conference of Commissioners on Uniform State Laws, composed of representatives from all the states, has drafted statutes on various business subjects for adoption by the states. The most outstanding of such laws is the Uniform Commercial Code (UCC).[4] The Code regulates the fields of sales of goods; commercial paper, such as checks; secured transactions in personal property; and particular aspects of banking, letters of credit, warehouse receipts, bills of lading, and investment securities.

National uniformity has also been brought about in some areas of consumer protection by the adoption of the federal Consumer Credit Protection Act (CCPA), Title I of which is popularly known as the Truth in Lending Act.[5] A Uniform Consumer Credit Code (UCCC) has been proposed and is now before the states for adoption. To the extent that it is adopted, it will complement the Uniform Commercial Code and expand the scope of consumer protection now afforded under the federal statutes and existing state laws.[6]

§ 1:4. Classifications of Law. Law is classified in many ways. For example, *substantive law,* which defines the substance of legal rights and liabilities, is contrasted with *procedural law,* which specifies the procedure that must be followed in enforcing those rights and liabilities. The following additional classifications will prove useful:

(1) Law and Equity. Law is frequently classified as being "law" or "equity." During the early centuries following the Norman Conquest, it was common for subjects of the English Crown to present to the King petitions requesting particular favors or relief that could not be obtained in the ordinary courts of law. The extraordinary or special relief granted by the chancellor, to whom the King referred such matters, was of such a nature as was dictated by principles of justice and equity. This body of principles was called *equity.* While originally applied by separate courts, today the same court usually administers both "law" and "equity."

(2) Classification Based upon Historical Sources. Law is sometimes classified in terms of its source as the *civil law,* which comes from the Roman civil law, and the *common law,* which is based upon the English common law or the common law that has developed in the states of the United States.

The *law merchant,* which was recognized by early English merchants, has been absorbed to a large extent by the common law. During the centuries that the common law was developing in England, merchants of different nations, trading in all parts of the world, developed their own sets of rules to govern their business transactions. Much of our modern business law relating to commercial paper, insurance, credit transactions, and partnerships originally developed in the law merchant.

---

[4] The Code has been adopted in every state except Louisiana. It has also been adopted in the Virgin Islands and for the District of Columbia.

[5] 15 USC § 1601 et seq., and 18 USC § 891 et seq.

[6] As of July, 1974, the Uniform Consumer Credit Code had been adopted in Colorado, Idaho, Indiana, Kansas, Oklahoma, Utah, and Wyoming. See Ch. 8.

AGENCIES FOR ENFORCEMENT OF LEGAL RIGHTS

Legal rights are meaningless unless they can be enforced. Agencies for law enforcement may be classified as private or public.

§ 1:5. Private Agencies. Because of the rising costs, delays, and complexities of litigation, businessmen often seek to determine disputes out of court.

(1) Arbitration. By the use of *arbitration* a dispute is brought before one or more arbitrators who make a decision which the parties have agreed to accept as final. This procedure first reached an extensive use in the field of commercial contracts. Arbitration today is encouraged as a means of avoiding expensive litigation and easing the workload of courts.[7] Arbitration is now favored by law [8] where once it was viewed with hostility. Arbitration enables the parties to present the facts before trained experts because the arbitrators are familiar with the practices that form the background of the dispute. Parties to a contract which is to be in effect for some time may specify in the contract that any dispute shall be submitted to arbitrators to be selected by the parties.

A Uniform Arbitration Act has been adopted in a number of states.[9] Under this Act and similar statutes, the parties to a contract may agree in advance that all disputes arising thereunder will be submitted to arbitration. In some instances the contract will name the arbitrators for the duration of the contract. Frequently the parties provide their own remedy against failure to abide by the award of the arbitrators. The parties may execute a mutual indemnity bond by which each agrees to indemnify the other for any loss caused by his failure to carry out the arbitration award.

The growth of arbitration has been greatly aided by the American Arbitration Association not only in the development of standards, procedures, and forms for arbitration, but also by the creation of panels of qualified arbitrators from which the parties to a contract may select those who will settle their dispute.

(2) Reference to Third Person. An out-of-court determination of disputes under construction contracts is often made under a term of the contract that any dispute shall be referred to the architect in charge of the construction and that his decision shall be final.

Increasingly, other types of transactions provide for a third person or a committee to decide rights of persons. Thus, employees and an employer may have agreed as a term of the employment contract that claims of employees under retirement and pension plans shall be decided by a designated board or committee. The seller and buyer may have selected a third person to

---

[7] Tepper Realty Co. v Mosaic Tile Co. (DC SD NY) 259 F Supp 688.

[8] California State Council of Carpenters v Superior Court, 11 Cal App 3d 144, 89 Cal Rptr 625.

[9] The 1955 version of the Uniform Arbitration Act has been adopted in Alaska, Arizona, Illinois, Indiana, Maine, Maryland, Massachusetts, Michigan, Minnesota, Nevada, Texas, and Wyoming. The earlier 1925 version of the Act is in force in North Carolina, Pennsylvania, Utah, and Wisconsin.

determine the price to be paid for goods. Ordinarily the parties agree that the decision of such a third person or board shall be final and that no appeal or review may be had in any court.[10] In most cases, the referral situation involves the determination of a particular fact in contrast to arbitration which seeks to end a dispute.

§ 1:6. Courts. A *court* is a tribunal established by government to hear and decide matters properly brought before it, giving redress to the injured or enforcing punishment against wrongdoers, and to prevent wrongs. A *court of record* is one whose proceedings are preserved in an official record. A *court not of record* has limited judicial powers; its proceedings are not recorded, at least not officially.

Each court has inherent power to establish rules necessary to preserve order in the court or to transact the business of the court. An infraction of these rules or the disobedience to any other lawful order, as well as a willful act contrary to the dignity of the court or tending to pervert or obstruct justice, may be punished as *contempt of court.*

Each court is empowered to decide certain types or classes of cases. This power is called *jurisdiction.* A court may have original or appellate jurisdiction, or both. A court with *original jurisdiction* has the authority to hear a controversy when it is first brought into court. A court having *appellate jurisdiction,* on the other hand, has authority to review the judgment of an inferior court.

The jurisdiction of a court may be general as distinguished from limited or special. A court having *general jurisdiction* has power to hear and decide all controversies involving legal rights and duties. A court of *limited* or special *jurisdiction* has authority to hear and decide only those cases that fall within a particular class, such as cases in which the amounts involved are below a specified sum (see Appendix 1).

Courts are frequently classified in terms of the nature of their jurisdiction. A *criminal court* is one that is established for the trial of crimes, which are regarded as offenses against the public. A *civil court,* on the other hand, is authorized to hear and decide issues involving private rights and duties and also noncriminal public matters. In like manner, courts are classified into equity courts, juvenile courts, probate courts, and courts of domestic relations upon the basis of their limited jurisdiction.

§ 1:7. Other Public Agencies. Government provides a system by which the rights of the parties under the law can be determined and enforced. Generally the instrumentality of government by which this is accomplished is a court; the process involved is an action or a lawsuit. In modern times a suit for a declaratory judgment has been added as an alternative to the traditional type of lawsuit. Administrative agencies have also been created to enforce law and to determine rights within certain areas. These court procedures are discussed further in Appendix 2.

---

[10] Bruner v Mercantile National Bank, (Tex Civ App) 455 SW2d 323.

QUESTIONS AND CASE PROBLEMS

1. (a) What is law?
   (b) Why has law developed?
   (c) What is the difference between law and a "law"?
2. Statutory law, which is law enacted by a legislative body (Congress, state legislature, city council), is probably the type of law best known by most people. Identify and explain each of the other types of law.
3. What does each of the following abbreviations stand for?
   (a) UCC (b) UCCC (c) CCPA
   Note: To avoid confusion in the use of the first two abbreviations, it is suggested that UCC be identified as "U double-C" and UCCC as "U triple-C."
4. A state statute provides that no person shall be allowed to work in specified occupations for more than eight hours a day. Is this a substantive or procedural law?
5. Are legal rights static? Support your answer either by tracing the evolution of the concept of the rights of man or by contrasting the legal questions raised by electronic surveillance and national data banks.
6. (a) What is the procedure for settling a dispute by arbitration?
   (b) What is the advantage of this procedure?

2 Law As an Expression of Social Forces

OBJECTIVES OF THE LAW

The purpose of law is to provide order, stability, and justice. Thus viewed, the law consists of relatively fixed rules which regulate conduct according to the morality of the community. Proper conduct, as determined by the community, should be allowed or required; improper conduct should be prohibited. Law, then, is a social institution. It is not an end unto itself but is an instrumentality for obtaining social justice.

§ 2:1. Law as Social Justice. Many factors and institutions have made their contribution in the molding of concepts of justice. Home and school training, religion, enlightened self-interest, social and business groups, and the various media of modern communication and entertainment all play a part. For example, various organizations such as chambers of commerce,[1] better business bureaus, informal groups of businessmen, trade groups, and conferences have emphasized what is ethical in business by stressing fair competition and service to the community. In turn, these organizations and groups have helped to bring about the adoption of statutes that modify the law to reflect the changed business ethics.

It would be a mistake, however, to assume that justice is a universal value which means the same to all people in all ages. Each individual's concept of justice varies in terms of his personality, his training, and his social and economic position. Justice has different meanings to the employer and the employee, to the millionaire and the pauper, to the industrial worker and the farmer, to the retired person and the young married adult, to the progressive and the conservative, or to the professor and the student! For this reason special interest groups attempt to modify the law so that it will be more favorable to the members of those groups. To the extent that such modifications are gained at the expense of the rights of the members of other groups, the law fails in its purpose of achieving justice for all. This is but one evidence of the fact that the law is no better than the human beings who make it, interpret it, and enforce it. Absolute justice is unattainable by

[1] The Business-Consumer Relations Code, adopted by the Chamber of Commerce of the United States in 1970, states in part: "We reaffirm the responsibility of American business to protect the health and safety of consumers in the design and manufacture of products and the provision of consumer services. This includes action against harmful side effects on the quality of life and the environment arising from technological progress."

human beings, but that is no reason why society should ever relent in its efforts to attain as high a level of substantial justice as is humanly possible.

When we consider a rule of law only as it exists today, it may appear just as arbitrary as the rule that twelve inches make one foot. The reason may be that we fail to understand the purpose of the law; or we may not be sufficiently familiar with all sides of the problem to recognize that the rule is just in the sense that it is the best rule that could be devised under the circumstances.

§ 2:2. Specific Objectives of the Law. The objectives of the Constitution of the United States are included in its preamble. Important statutes frequently include a statement of their objectives. In many instances, however, the objective of the law is not stated or it is expressed in very general terms. Whether stated or not, each law has an objective; and it is helpful in understanding the nature and purpose of the law to know what the objectives of our various laws are.

In the following enumeration the more important specific objectives of the law are discussed against the background of our understanding of the general objective of creating, maintaining, and restoring order, stability, and justice.[2]

(1) Protection of the State. A number of laws are designed to protect the existing governments, both state and national. Laws condemning treason, sedition, and subversive practices are examples of society taking measures to preserve governmental systems. Less dramatic are the laws that impose taxes to provide for the support of those governments.

(2) Personal Protection. At an early date, laws developed to protect the individual from being injured or killed. The field of criminal law is devoted to a large extent to the protection of the person. In addition, under civil law a suit can be brought to recover damages for the harm done by such acts. For example, a grossly negligent driver of an automobile who injures a pedestrian is subject to a penalty imposed by the state in the form of imprisonment or a fine, or both. He is also liable to the injured person for the payment of damages, which may include not only medical and hospital costs but also loss of time from work and mental anguish. Over a period of time the protection of personal rights has broadened to protect reputation and privacy and to protect contracts and business relations from malicious interference by outsiders. (See § 2:7, Nature and Purpose of Cases, and p. 20, Korn v Rennison.)

It is a federal offense knowingly to injure, intimidate, or interfere with anyone exercising a basic civil right (such as voting), taking part in any federal government program, or receiving federal assistance. Interference with attendance in a public school or college, with participation in any state or local governmental program, with service as a juror in a state court, or

---

[2] For a fuller treatment of the social forces, see Ronald A. Anderson, *Social Forces and the Law* (Cincinnati: South-Western Publishing Co., 1969).

with the use of any public facility (common carrier, hotel, or restaurant) is likewise prohibited when based on race, color, religion, or national origin discrimination.[3]

Protection of the person is expanding to protect the "economic man." Laws prohibiting discrimination in employment, in furnishing hotel accommodations and transportation, and in commercial transactions and the sale of property represent an extension of the concept of protecting the person. When membership in a professional association, a labor union, or a trade or business group has economic importance to its members, an applicant cannot be arbitrarily excluded from the membership, nor may a member be expelled without notice of the charge against him and an opportunity to be heard.[4]

(3) Protection of Public Health, Safety, and Morals. The law seeks to protect the public health, safety, and morals in many ways. Laws relating to quarantine, food inspection, and compulsory vaccination are designed to protect the public health. Laws regulating highway speeds and laws requiring fire escapes or guard devices around moving parts of factory machinery are for the safety of the public. Laws prohibiting the sale of liquor to minors and those prohibiting obscenity protect the morals of the public.

(4) Property Protection. Just as both criminal and civil laws have developed to protect the individual's physical well-being, such laws also have developed to protect one's property from damage, destruction, and other harmful acts. If a thief steals an automobile, he is liable civilly to the owner of the automobile for its value and is criminally responsible to the state.

(5) Title Protection. Because of the importance of ownership of property, one of the objectives of the law has been to protect the title of an owner to his property so that he remains the owner until it is clearly proved that he has transferred the title to someone else. Thus, if property is stolen, the true owner may recover it from the thief. He may even recover his property from a person who purchased it in good faith from the thief.

(6) Freedom of Personal Action. In the Anglo-American stream of history, man's desires for freedom from political domination gave rise to the American Revolution, and the desire for freedom from economic domination gave rise to the free enterprise philosophy. Today we find freedom as the dominant element in the constitutional provisions for the protection of freedom of religion, press, and speech, and also in such laws as those against trusts or business combinations in restraint of trade by others. (See p. 21, Engel v Vitale.)

This right of freedom of personal action, however, cannot be exercised by one person in such a way that it interferes to an unreasonable extent

---

[3] Civil Obedience Act of 1968, PL 90-284, 19 USC § 245.

[4] Silver v New York Stock Exchange, 373 US 341; Cunningham v Burbank Board of Realtors, 262 Cal App 2d 211, 68 Cal Reptr 653.

with the rights of others. Freedom of speech, for example, does not mean freedom to speak or write a malicious, false statement about another person's character. In effect, this means that one person's freedom of speech must be balanced with another person's right to be free from defamation of character or reputation.

(7) Freedom of Use of Property. Closely related to the objective of protection of freedom of action is that of protecting the freedom of the use of property. This freedom is achieved by prohibiting, restraining, or penalizing acts of others that would hamper the reasonable use of property by its owner.

Absolute freedom of this kind would permit its owner to make any use he chose of his property—even in a way that would harm others, to sell it at any price he desired, or to make any disposition of it that he wished. Such freedom is not recognized today, for everywhere we find some limitation of the right of the owner of property to do as he pleases with it.

The law prohibits an owner from using his property in such a way as to injure another or another's property. Further, zoning laws may limit the use of his land. Building restrictions in a deed may restrict the type of building that the owner may construct on his land. Fire laws and building codes may specify details of construction of his building. Labor laws may require that he equip a business building with safety devices. Likewise, an antipollution law restricts the freedom of the owner of property to use it in any way that he desires.

(8) Enforcement of Intent. The law usually seeks to enforce the intent of the contracting parties. This objective is closely related to the concept that the law seeks to protect the individual's freedom of action. For example, if a person provides by his will for the distribution of his property when he dies, the law will generally allow the property to pass to the persons intended by the deceased owner. The law will likewise seek to carry out the intention of the parties to a business transaction. To illustrate, if you and an electrician agree that he shall rewire your house for $200, the law will ordinarily enforce that contract because that is what was intended by both parties.

The extent to which the intent of one person or of several persons will be carried out has certain limitations. Sometimes the intent is not effective unless it is manifested by a particular written formality. For example, a deceased person may have intended that his friend should receive his house, but in most states that intent must be shown by a written will signed by the deceased owner. Likewise, in some cases the intent of the parties may not be carried out because the law regards the purpose of the intent as illegal or otherwise improper.

(9) Protection from Exploitation, Fraud, and Oppression. Many rules of law have developed in the courts and many statutes have been enacted to protect certain groups or individuals from exploitation or oppression by others. (See p. 22, Falcone v Middlesex County Medical Society.) Thus, the law developed that a minor (a person under legal age) could set aside his contract, subject to certain exceptions, in order to give the minor an opportunity to avoid a bad bargain.

Persons who buy food that is packed in tin cans are given certain rights against the seller and the manufacturer. Since they cannot see the contents, buyers of such products need special protection against unscrupulous canners. The consumer is also protected by laws against adulteration and poisons in foods, drugs, and household products because he would ordinarily be unable to take care of himself. Laws prohibiting unfair competition and discrimination, both economic and social, are also designed to protect from oppression.

For the purpose of brevity, "oppression" is used here to include not only conscious wrongdoing by another but also cases of hardship or misfortune where consequences to the victim may be regarded as extreme or oppressive.

(10) Furtherance of Trade. Society may seek to further trade in a variety of ways, as by establishing a currency as a medium of payment; by recognizing and giving legal effect to installment sales; by adopting special rules for checks, notes, and similar instruments so that they can be widely used as credit devices and substitutes for money; or by enacting laws to mitigate the harmful effects of alternating periods of depression and inflation.

Laws that have been considered in connection with other objectives may also serve to further trade. For example, laws protecting against unfair competition have this objective, as well as the objective of protecting certain classes from exploitation by others.

(11) Creditor Protection. Society seeks to protect the rights of creditors and to protect them from dishonest or fraudulent acts of debtors. Initially creditors are protected by the law which declares that contracts are binding and which provides the machinery for the enforcement of contracts, and by the provision of the federal Constitution that prohibits states from impairing the obligation of contracts. Further, creditors may compel a debtor to come into bankruptcy in order to settle his debts as far as his property permits. If the debtor has concealed his property or transferred it to a friend in order to hide it from his creditors, the law permits the creditors to claim the property for the payment of the debts due them.

(12) Debtor Rehabilitation. Society has come to regard it as unsound that debtors should be ruined forever by the burden of their debts. The passing centuries have seen the debtor's prison abolished. Bankruptcy laws have been adopted to provide the debtor with a means of settling his debts as best he can and then starting upon a new economic life. In times of widespread depression the same objective has been served by special laws that prohibit the foreclosure of mortgages and regulate the amount of the judgments that can be entered against mortgage debtors.

(13) Stability. Stability is particularly important in business transactions. When you buy a house, for example, you not only want to know the exact meaning of the transaction under today's law but you also hope that the transaction will have the same meaning in the future. When the businessman invests money, he desires the law to remain the same as it was when he acted.

Because of the objective of stability, the courts will ordinarily follow former decisions unless there is some valid reason to depart from them. When no former case directly bears on the point involved, the desire for stability will influence the courts to reach a decision that is a logical extension of some former decision or which follows a former decision by analogy rather than to strike off on a fresh path and to reach a decision unrelated to the past. Thus, stability is achieved through continuity based on the assumption that many problems of today and tomorrow will be basically the same as those that were settled yesterday.

(14) Flexibility. If stability were an absolute objective of the law, the cause of justice would often be thwarted. The reason that originally gave rise to a rule of law may have ceased to exist.[5] The rule then appears unjust because it reflects a concept of justice that is outmoded or obsolete. For example, capital punishment, which one age believed just, has been condemned by another age as unjust. We must not lose sight of the fact that the rule of law under question was created to further the sense of social justice existing at that time; but our concepts of justice may change.

The law itself may be flexible in that it makes provision for changes in rules to meet situations that cannot be anticipated or for which an explicit set of rules cannot be developed satisfactorily in advance. (See p. 24, Williams v Indiana.) Our constitutions state the procedures for their amendment. Such changes in constitutional law are purposely made difficult in order to serve the objective of stability, but they are possible when the need for change is generally recognized by the people of the state or nation.

Changes by legislative action in federal and state statutes and local ordinances are relatively easier to make. Furthermore, some statutes recognize the impossibility of laying down in advance a hard and fast rule that will do justice in all cases. The typical modern statute, particularly in the field of regulation of business, will therefore contain "escape clauses" by which a person can escape from the operation of the statute under certain circumstances. Thus, a rent control law may impose a rent ceiling—that is, a maximum above which landlords cannot charge; but it may also authorize a greater charge when special circumstances make it just to allow such exception, as when the landlord has made expensive repairs to the property or when his taxes have increased materially.

---

[5] "It is revolting to have no better reason for a rule of law than that so it was laid down in the time of Henry IV. It is still more revolting if the grounds upon which it was laid down have vanished long since, and the rule simply persists from blind imitation of the past." Holmes, Collected Papers 187 (1920).

"The law must be stable, but it must not stand still." Roscoe Pound, *Introduction to the Philosophy of Law* (Connecticut: Yale University Press, 1922).

The rule of law may be stated in terms of what a reasonable or prudent man would do. Thus, whether you are negligent in driving your automobile is determined in court by whether you exercised the same degree of care that a prudent man would have exercised had he been driving your car under the circumstances in question. This is a vague and variable standard as to how you must drive your car, but it is the only standard that is practical. The alternative would be a detailed motor code specifying how you should drive your car under every situation that might arise, a code that obviously could not foresee every possibility and which certainly would be too long for any driver to know in every detail by memory.

(15) Practical Expediency. Frequently the law is influenced by what is practical or expedient in the situation. In some of these situations, the law will strive to make its rules fit the business practices of society. For example, a signature is frequently regarded by the law as including a stamping, printing, or typewriting of a name, in recognition of the business practice of "signing" letters and other instruments by mechanical means. A requirement of a handwritten signature would impose a burden on business that would not be practically expedient.

§ 2:3. Conflicting Objectives. As we have seen, the specific objectives of the law sometimes conflict with each other. When this is true, the problem is one of social policy, which in turn means a weighing of social, economic, and moral forces to determine which objective should be furthered. Thus, we find a conflict at times between the objective of the state seeking protection from the conduct of individuals or groups and the objective of freedom of action by those individuals and groups.

Thus, while protection of the freedom of the individual urges the utmost freedom of religious belief, society will impose limitations on religious freedom where it believes such freedom will cause harm to the public welfare. (See p. 25, United States v Kuch.) Thus, state laws requiring vaccination against smallpox were enforced against the contention that this violated religious principles. Similarly, parents failing to provide medical care for a sick child will be held guilty of manslaughter if the child dies, even though the parents sincerely believed as a matter of religious principle that medical care was improper. In contrast, when the harm contemplated is not direct or acute, religious freedom will prevail, so that a compulsory child education law will not be enforced against Amish parents who as a matter of religion were opposed to state education.[6]

As another example, the objective of protecting title may conflict with the objective of furthering trade. Consider again the example of the stolen property that was sold by the thief to one who purchased it for value and in good faith, without reason to know that the goods had been stolen. If we are to further the objective of protecting the title to the property, we will conclude that the owner can recover the property from the innocent

---

[6] Wisconsin v Yoder, 406 US 205 (high school student).

purchaser. This rule, however, will discourage trade, for people will be less willing to buy goods if they run the risk that the goods were stolen and may have to be surrendered. If we instead think only of taking steps to encourage buying and selling, we will hold that the buyer takes a good title because he acted in good faith and paid value. If we do this, we then destroy the title of the original owner and obviously abandon our objective of protecting title to property. As a general rule, society has followed the objective of protecting title. In some instances, however, the objective of furthering trade is adopted by statute and the buyer is given good title, as in certain cases of commercial paper (notes, drafts, and checks) or of the purchaser from a regular dealer in other people's goods.

GROWTH OF LAW

§ 2:4. Law as an Evolutionary Process. At any given time the law may appear to be static. And, in fact, a number of legal principles have remained unchanged for centuries. But many rules of law have changed and are continuing to change.

Let us consider an example of this type of change. When the economy was patterned on a local community unit in which everyone knew each other and each other's product, the concept of "let the buyer beware" expressed a proper basis on which to conduct business. Much of the early law of the sales of goods was predicated on this philosophy. In today's economy, however, with its emphasis on interstate, national, and even international activities, the buyer has little or no direct contact with the manuafcturer or seller, and the packaging of articles makes their presale examination impossible. Under the circumstances the consumer must rely on the integrity of others to an increasing degree. Gradually practices that were tolerated and even approved in an earlier era have been condemned, and the law has changed to protect the buyer by warranties when his own caution can no longer protect him.

Moreover, new principles of law are being developed to meet the new situations that have arisen. Every new invention and every new business practice introduces a number of situations for which there is no satisfactory rule of law. For example, how could there have been a law governing the liability of a food canner to the consumer before canning was invented? How could there have been a law relating to stocks and bonds before those instruments came into existence? How could there have been a law with respect to the liability of radio and television broadcasters before such methods of communication were developed? This pattern of change will continue as long as man strives for better ways to achieve his desires.

§ 2:5. Law as a Synthesis. Law as a synthesis may be illustrated by the law as it relates to contracts for the sale of a house. Originally such a contract could be oral—that is, merely spoken words with nothing in writing to prove that there was such a contract. Of course, there was the practical question of proof—that is, whether the jury would believe that there was such a contract—but no rule said that the contract must be in writing. This situation made it possible for a witness in court to swear falsely that Jones had agreed to sell his house for a specified sum. Even though Jones had not made such an agreement, the jury might believe the false witness and Jones would have to give up his house on terms to which he had not agreed. To help prevent such a miscarriage of justice, a statute was passed in England in 1677 declaring that contracts for the sale of houses had to be evidenced by a writing.

This law ended the evil of persons lying that there was an oral agreement for the sale of a house, but was justice finally achieved? Not always, for cases arose in which Jones did in fact make an oral agreement to sell his land to Smith. Smith would take possession of the land and would make valuable improvements at great expense and effort, and then Jones would have Smith thrown off the land. Smith would defend on the ground that Jones had orally agreed to sell the land to him. Jones would then say, "Where is the writing that the statute requires?" To this, Smith could only reply that there was no writing. No writing meant no enforceable legal agreement; and therefore Smith lost the land, leaving Jones with the land and all the improvements that Smith had made. That certainly was not just. What then?

Gradually the law courts developed the rule that in spite of the fact that the statute required a writing, the courts would enforce an oral contract for the sale of land when the buyer had gone into possession and made valuable improvements of such a nature that it would be difficult to determine what amount of money would be required to make up the loss if he were to be put off the land.

Thus, the law passed through three stages: (1) The original concept that all land contracts could be oral. Because the perjury evil arose under this rule of law, society swung to (2) the opposite rule that no such contract could be oral. This rule gave rise to the hardship case of the honest buyer under an oral contract who made extensive improvements. The law then swung, not back to the original rule, but to (3) a middle position, combining both (1) and (2), that is, combining the element of the written requirement as to the ordinary transaction but allowing oral contracts in the special cases to prevent hardship.

This example is also interesting because it shows the way in which the courts "amend" the law by decision. The flat requirement of the statute was "eroded" by decisions and by exceptions created by the courts in the interest of furthering justice.

§ 2:6. Perspective. As you study the rules of law in the chapters that follow, consider each rule in relationship to its social, economic, and moral background. Try to determine the particular objective of each important rule. To the extent that you are able to analyze law as the product of man striving for justice in society, you will have a greater insight into the law itself, the world in which you live, the field of business, and the mind of man.

CASE STUDY

§ 2:7. Nature and Purpose of Cases. Following the text in each chapter are cases for analysis and study. They illustrate how certain principles of law are applied in lawsuits by our courts. The information for each case is presented in three parts: (1) the heading, (2) the facts of the case, and (3) the opinion. In this explanation the first case, Korn v Rennison, p. 20, will be used as an example.

(1) ***Heading.*** The heading of the case consists of the title and the source.

(a) TITLE. The title of the case usually consists of the names of the parties to the action. In the illustrative case Korn, as plaintiff, sued Rennison (and others) as defendants.

The title of an appealed case may not reveal who the plaintiff was in the original or lower court or who the defendant was. When the action is started in the lower court, the first party named is the plaintiff and the second is the defendant. When the case is appealed, the name of the party who takes the appeal may appear first on the records of the higher court, so that if the defendant takes the appeal, the original order of the names of the parties is then reversed.

(b) SOURCE. The second part of the heading gives the source of the opinion. The opinion is found in "21 Conn Supp 400, 156 A2d 476." This means that the opinion is found in the 21st volume of the Connecticut Supplement (Conn Supp) reporter beginning at page 400, and that it is also found in the Atlantic (A) sectional reporter [7] in volume 156 of the second series beginning at page 476.

(2) ***Facts.*** The paragraph in smaller type following the heading is a summary of the facts of the case, which provides a background for an understanding and analysis of the opinion. Read the statement of facts for Korn v Rennison. Keep in mind the principles of law that you studied in the chapter. Then read the opinion carefully to see how the court made its decision, what it decided, and whether it agrees with what you thought would be decided.

(3) ***Opinion.*** The opinion of the court includes the name of the judge, excerpts from the reasoning of the court, and the judgment.

(a) JUDGE. At the beginning of the opinion is the name of the judge who wrote it. The opinion in the first case was written by Judge Alcorn. If the case has been appealed, the judge who wrote the opinion is speaking for the entire court, unless otherwise indicated. In cases at the trial level, normally one [8] judge is disposing of the case, as in the Korn case.

The letter or letters following the name of the judge indicate his rank or title. J. stands for Judge or Justice. (JJ. is the plural form.) Other abbreviations include C.J. for Chief Justice or Circuit Judge, D.J. for District

---

[7] See Appendix 3, footnote 1, for sectional reporters.

[8] In some instances a case at the trial stage is disposed of by three judges instead of one.

Judge, P.J. for Presiding Judge or President Judge, and C. for Chancellor or Commissioner.

(b) Body of the Opinion. The material following the judge's name is quoted from the opinion of the court. Words enclosed in brackets [ ] did not appear in the original opinion but have been added to explain a legal term, to identify a party, or to clarify a statement. Ellipses (three or four periods) are used to indicate that something has been omitted that is not pertinent to the point of law in which we are concerned at this time.

Decisions vary in length from less than a page to more than a hundred pages, and opinions frequently involve several points of law. Each case in this book has been carefully edited so that the excerpts reprinted here will be convenient for student use.

The edited opinion in Korn v Rennison consists of three paragraphs. In the first paragraph the judge indicates that more than a half-century ago the existence of a right of privacy was recognized by some as a matter of common or nonstatutory law. In the second paragraph he brings the subject down to date, pointing out the present state of the law and the social and scientific factors which influenced the growth of the law. The last paragraph points out the conflict of interests that are involved; and a further recognition of the growth of the law is made, the trend being in favor of a right of privacy. The case then ends with the dismissal of the objection to the plaintiff's claim. The theory is that there is a common-law right of privacy, and consequently it is no defense to say there is no such right.

Opinions do not follow a standard pattern of organization; but usually the well-written opinion will carefully examine the arguments presented by all parties and then explain why the court accepts or rejects those arguments in whole or in part. In this process the opinion may discuss the opinion of the lower court, the decisions in similar cases in other courts, and material from other sources.[9]

(c) Judgment. The case is concluded with a statement of the court's decision. If the case has been appealed and the court agrees with the lower court, the decision may simply be "Judgment affirmed" or a similar expression. If the appellate court disagrees, the decision may be expressed as "Judgment reversed." "Case remanded" means that the case is returned to the lower court to proceed further in harmony with the appellate court's decision. In lower court cases when the judgment is on a narrow issue, the judgment of the court may be limited to "Objection sustained" or "Objection dismissed."

A judge of the court who disagrees with the majority may simply declare as part of the record that he dissents; or he may file a dissenting opinion, as occurred in the case on page 22.

[9] See Appendix 3, "How to Find the Law."

§ 2:8. Checklist for Case Study. The questions in the following checklist will serve as a guide for the analysis of each case. It should be understood, however, that not every case will provide answers to all of these questions.

1. ***Court.*** In what court was the action brought originally, and which court filed the opinion being studied?
2. ***Parties.*** Who were the parties to the action? Were they the parties to the original transaction, or were they strangers such as creditors?
3. ***Purpose of the Action.*** What was the relief or remedy sought in the action?
4. ***Action Appealed from.*** What was done in the lower court which the appellant deemed wrong and from which he appealed?
5. ***Arguments of the Parties.*** What were the arguments made by the respective parties?
6. ***Decision of the Court.*** What did the court decide?
7. ***Basis for Decision.*** On what authority or ground did the court base its decision? Was is common law, decision, statute, Restatement of the Law, text, logic, or the personal belief of the court?
8. ***Appraisal of the Decision.*** What social objectives are advanced by the decision? What social obejctives are hindered or defeated by the decision? Is the decision socially desirable? Is it practical in application? Does it give rise to any dangers?

CASES FOR CHAPTER 2

Korn v Rennison

21 Conn Supp 400, 156 A2d 476 (1959)

The substance of the complaint was that through an arrangement and agreement between Rennison and other defendants, a photograph of Korn, the plaintiff, was published for advertising purposes in the defendant newspaper without the knowledge, consent, or permission of the plaintiff and in violation of her personal liberties and private rights. As a result, the defendants received monetary benefits and advantages while the plaintiff received none and was subjected to ridicule, embarrassment, vexation, and humiliation. The plaintiff, a minor, brought this action by her mother to recover damages.

ALCORN, J. . . . The defendants argue that . . . a right [of privacy] was not recognized at common law and therefore, in the absence of statute, it cannot exist in Connecticut today. When Samuel D. Warren and Louis D. Brandeis first gave form and substance to the right of privacy in 1890, it was one objective of their discussion in 4 Harvard Law Review 193 to demonstrate that the right found support in common-law principles. Underlying their reasoning is the premise that the common law is not static and its protecting arm does not become immobilized from lack of precedent.

In the years intervening since the right was thus defined, a constantly increasing number of jurisdictions have recognized its independent existence. Press, photography, radio, and television represent elements in constantly changing conditions which impinge upon individual privacy. With the environmental changes of modern living has grown the need that man's inner nature and feelings as well as his body and possessions receive the protection of the law. Hence, the right of privacy has become established in nearly half the states. . . .

The line to be drawn between reasonable demands of individual privacy and public interest in legitimate news is not always easy to define, but the boundary is more readily perceived in the case of commercial advertising. . . . No case decided within the last fifteen years has been found in which the existence of a right of privacy has been denied. Decisions which originally denied the right have, with apparently a single exception, since been overruled, modified, or altered by statute. Rhode Island appears to stand alone as an unqualified precedent for denying a recovery in damages for an invasion of the right of privacy. . . .

[Objection of defendants dismissed.]

Engel v Vitale

370 US 421 (1962)

The New York State education program provided for a voluntary nondenominational prayer in public schools. This was attacked as a violation of the freedom of religion guaranteed by the First Amendment.

BLACK, J. . . . [A school board directed] the following prayer to be said aloud by each class in the presence of a teacher at the beginning of each school day:

"Almighty God, we acknowledge our dependence upon Thee, and we beg Thy blessings upon us, our parents, our teachers and our Country."

This daily procedure was adopted on the recommendation of the State Board of Regents, a governmental agency created by the State Constitution to which the New York Legislature has granted broad supervisory, executive, and legislative powers over the State's public school system. These state officials composed the prayer which they recommended and published as a part of their "Statement on Moral and Spiritual Training in the Schools," saying: "We believe that this Statement will be subscribed to by all men and women of good will, and we call upon all of them to aid in giving life to our program." . . .

We think that the constitutional prohibition against laws respecting an establishment of religion must at least mean that in this country it is no part of the business of government to compose official prayers for any group of the American people to recite as a part of a religious program carried on by government. . . .

By the time of the adoption of the Constitution, our history shows that there was a widespread awareness among many Americans of the dangers of a union of Church and State. These people knew, some of them from bitter personal experience, that one of the greatest dangers to the freedom of the individual to worship in his own way lay in the government's placing its official stamp of approval upon one particular kind of prayer or one particular form of religious services. They knew the anguish, hardship, and bitter strife that could come when zealous religious groups struggled with one another to obtain the government's stamp of approval from each King, Queen, or Protector that came to temporary power. The Constitution was intended to avert a part of this danger by leaving the government of this country in the hands of the people rather than in the hands of any monarch. But this safeguard was not enough. Our Founders were no more willing to let the content of their prayers and their privilege of praying whenever they pleased be influenced by the ballot box than they were to let these vital matters of personal conscience depend upon the succession of monarchs. The First Amendment was added to the Constitution to stand as a guarantee that neither the power nor the prestige of the Federal Government would be used to control, support, or influence the kinds of prayer the American people can say—that the people's religions must not be subjected to the pressures of government for change each time a new political administration is elected to office. Under that Amendment's prohibition against governmental establishment of religion, as reinforced by the provisions of the Fourteenth Amendment, government in this country, be it state or federal, is without power to prescribe by law any particular form of prayer which is to be used as an official prayer in carrying on any program of governmentally sponsored religious activity. . . .

It is true that New York's establishment of its Regents' prayer as an officially approved religious doctrine of that State does not amount to a total establishment of one particular religious sect to the exclusion of all others—that, indeed, the governmental endorsement of that prayer seems relatively insignificant when compared to the governmental encroachments upon religion which were commonplace 200 years ago. To those who may subscribe to the view that because the Regents' official prayer is so brief and general there can be no danger to religious freedom in its governmental establishment, however, it may be appropriate to say in the words of James Madison, the author of the First Amendment:

"It is proper to take alarm at the first experiment on our liberties. . . . Who does not see that the same authority which can establish Christianity, in exclusion of all other Religions, may establish with the same ease any particular sect of Christians, in exclusion of all other Sects? That the same authority which can force a citizen to contribute three pence only of his property for the support of any one establishment, may force him to conform to any other establishment in all cases whatsoever?" . . .

[School prayer held unconstitutional.]

STEWART, J. (dissenting) . . . With all respect, I think the Court has misapplied a great constitutional principle. I cannot see how an "official religion" is established by letting those who want to say a prayer say it. On the contrary, I think that to deny the wish of these school children to join in reciting this prayer is to deny them the opportunity of sharing in the spiritual heritage of our Nation. . . .

At the opening of each day's Session of this Court we stand, while one of our officials invokes the protection of God. Since the days of John Marshall our Crier has said, "God save the United States and this Honorable Court." Both the Senate and the House of Representatives open their daily Sessions with prayer. Each of our Presidents . . . has upon assuming his office asked for the protection and help of God. . . .

One of the stanzas of "The Star-Spangled Banner," made our National Anthem by Act of Congress in 1931, contains the verse: ". . . And this be our motto 'In God is our Trust.' "

In 1954 Congress added a phrase to the Pledge of Allegiance to the Flag so that it now contains the words "one Nation *under* God indivisible, with liberty and justice for all." In 1952 Congress enacted legislation calling upon the President each year to proclaim a National Day of Prayer. Since 1865 the words "IN GOD WE TRUST" have been impressed on our coins.

Countless similar examples could be listed, but there is no need to belabor the obvious. It was all summed up by this Court just ten years ago in a single sentence: "We are a religious people whose institutions presuppose a Supreme Being." Zorach v Clauson, 343 US 306, 313. . . .

I do not believe that this Court, or the Congress, or the President has by the actions and practices I have mentioned established an "official religion" in violation of the Constitution. And I do not believe the State of New York has done so in this case. What each has done has been to recognize and to follow the deeply entrenched and highly cherished spiritual traditions of our Nation—traditions which come down to us from those who almost two hundred years ago avowed their "firm Reliance on the Protection of divine Providence" when they proclaimed the freedom and independence of this brave new world.

I dissent.

Falcone v Middlesex County Medical Society

34 NJ 582, 170 A2d 791 (1961)

Dr. Falcone was admittedly a licensed and qualified physician and surgeon, holding degrees from a Philadelphia school and from the College of Medicine of the University of Milan, who practiced surgery and obstetrics. He met all the requirements of the bylaws of the Middlesex County Medical Society. The Society, however, refused him membership on the ground that it had an unwritten rule requiring that every applicant have four years of study in a medical school recognized by the American Medical Association. Dr. Falcone did not meet this requirement since the Philadelphia school was not AMA-approved and, although the University of Milan was so approved, the course was not four years. Dr. Falcone brought suit against the Society for refusing to admit him to membership.

JACOBS, J. . . . The Society's declaration of his ineligibility and its refusal to admit him to membership have had seriously adverse economic and professional effects on Dr. Falcone. He was a member of the medical staffs of the Middlesex General Hospital and St. Peter's General Hospital in New Brunswick but was dropped because they, like other hospitals in the area, require that their staff physicians be members of the County Medical Society. It seems entirely evident that Dr. Falcone cannot successfully continue his practice of surgery and obstetrics or properly serve his surgical and obstetric patients without the use of local hospital facilities; he testified that in order to earn a livelihood it is necessary "to belong to the local society" for "otherwise, you cannot use the hospitals." The virtual monopoly which the Society possesses in fact over the use of local hospital facilities results from the well-known interrelationship between the County Society, the State Medical Society, the American Medical Association, and the Joint Commission on Accreditation of Hospitals. . . .

Over thirty years ago Professor Chafee, in his discussion of nonprofit associations, pointed to the distinction between the customary social and fraternal organizations on the one hand and trade unions and professional societies on the other hand; he noted that whereas exclusion or expulsion from a social or fraternal organization may result in little more than hurt feelings, exclusion or expulsion from a trade union or a professional society may result, as here, in deprivation of the invaluable opportunity "to earn a livelihood." . . . In a more recent discussion addressed specially to medical societies, the editors of the Yale Law Journal, after pointing out that exclusion or expulsion from a local medical society results, as a practical matter, in the deprivation of hospital facilities, descriptively noted that "nonmembership amounts to a partial revocation of licensure to practice medicine." 63 Yale LJ 953. . . .

We are here concerned with . . . an organization, membership in which may . . . be viewed as "an economic necessity"; in dealing with such an organization, the court must be particulary alert to the need for truly protecting the public welfare and advancing the interests of justice by reasonably safeguarding the individual's opportunity for earning a livelihood while not impairing the proper standards and objectives of the organization. . . .

When courts originally declined to scrutinize admission practices of membership associations, they were dealing with social clubs, religious organizations, and fraternal associations. Here the policies against judicial intervention were strong, and there were no significant countervailing policies. When the courts were later called upon to deal with trade and professional associations exercising virtually monopolistic control, different factors were involved. The intimate personal relationships which pervaded the social, religious, and fraternal organizations were hardly in evidence and the individual's opportunity of earning a livelihood and serving society in his chosen trade or profession appeared as the controlling policy consideration. . . .

It must be borne in mind that the County Medical Society is not a private voluntary membership association with which the public has little or no concern. It is an association with which the public is highly concerned and which engages in activities vitally affecting the health and welfare of the people. . . . Through its interrelationships, the County Medical Society possesses, in fact, a virtual monopoly over the use of local hospital facilities. As a result it has power, by excluding Dr. Falcone from membership, to preclude him from successfully continuing in his practice of obstetrics and surgery and to restrict patients who wish to engage him as an obstetrician or surgeon in their freedom of choice of physicians. Public policy strongly dictates that this power should not be unbridled but should be viewed judicially as a fiduciary power to be exercised in reasonable and lawful manner for the advancement of the interests of the medical profession and the public generally. . . .

In the light of all of the foregoing, the effort of the County Society to apply its unwritten requirement of four years' attendance at an AMA approved medical college so as to exclude Dr. Falcone from membership, must be viewed as patently arbitrary and unreasonable and beyond the pale of the law. When the County Society engages in action which is designed to advance medical science or elevate professional standards, it should and will be sympathetically supported. When, however, as here, its action . . . runs strongly counter to the public policy of our State and the true interests of justice, it should and will be stricken down. . . .

[Admission ordered.]

Williams v Indiana

— Ind —, 307 NE2d 457 (1974)

A police broadcast stated that a named motel had been robbed by two men using a sawed off shotgun. The men were reported fleeing in an automobile travelling northwestwardly. Police officers hearing this report assumed that the robbers were seeking to escape to Chicago and went to the nearest intersection of the road leading to that city. They saw a car which they thought might contain the suspects. They trailed the car to another intersection where the better lighting gave a better view of the driver. The police then stopped the car. After it was stopped, the police saw a shotgun in the back of the car and a man attempting to hide on the back seat. The men in the car where arrested and prosecuted for robbery of the motel. They claimed that the evidence of what was learned when their car was stopped could not be admitted at the trial because they had been stopped without a search warrant. This contention was rejected by the trial court and the men were convicted. They appealed.

ARTERBURN, C.J. . . . The sole contention is that the initial stopping of the Appellants' car was unlawful and that, therefore, the fruits of this unlawful seizure must be excluded from the trial. . . .

The legal question that confronts us, to be very specific, is: did the police officers have the right to stop the motorist on the basis of the suspicion created by the meager facts received over the radio and the police officers' calculations from those facts? After the stopping of the Appellants' car, it became immediately apparent without a search, but from open observation (the shotgun and the passenger hiding in the car) that probable cause existed for the arrest of the Appellants. If the stopping was legal, then all that followed was legal. . . . The question is "whether the facts known . . . at the time he (a police officer) stopped the car were sufficient to warrant a man of reasonable caution in the belief that an investigation was appropriate." . . .

In fact, this case presents squarely to us the question whether or not under similar circumstances a roadblock could be set up at certain points where it has reasonably been calculated that fleeing robbers might be apprehended. Justice Jackson of the United States Supreme Court, dissenting from the approval of a seizure and search, realized and noted the problem, commenting as follows:

"If we assume, for example, that a child is kidnapped and the officers throw a roadblock about the neighborhood and search every outgoing car, it would be a drastic and undiscriminating use of the search. The officers might be unable to show probable cause for searching any particular car. However, I should candidly strive hard to sustain such an action, executed fairly and in good faith, because it might be reasonable to subject travelers to that indignity if it was the only way to save a threatened life and detect a vicious crime. But I should not strain to sustain such a roadblock and universal search to salvage a few bottles of bourbon and catch a bootlegger." Brinegar v United States (1948), 338 US 160 at 183. . . . However, the suggestion by Justice Jackson that the right to stop depends upon the enormity of the crime creates an uncertain and hazardous standard for police officers to follow.

In Terry v Ohio (1968), 392 US 1, . . . the United States Supreme Court had before it a situation in which a police officer with thirty (30) years experience on a particular beat became suspicious of the actions of two men who repeatedly and alternately made numerous round-trip strolls past a store window. The officer accosted these men when they were conferring with a third man with whom they had previously conferred during their strolls. In a brief "pat down" or "frisk" the officer discovered concealed weapons on two of the men. In upholding this particular "search and seizure" the Supreme Court said that:

". . . in justifying the particular intrusion the police officer must be able to point to specific and articulable facts which, taken together with rational inferences from those facts, reasonably warrant that intrusion. The scheme of the Fourth Amendment becomes meaningful only when it is assured that at some point the conduct of those charged with enforcing the laws can be subjected to the more detached, neutral scrutiny of a judge who must evaluate the reasonableness of a particular search or seizure in light of the particular circumstances. And in making that assessment it is imperative that the facts be judged against an objective standard: would the facts available to the officer at the moment of the seizure . . . "warrant a man of reasonable caution in the belief" that the action taken was appropriate? . . .

Our society has a right to protect itself. What is "unreasonable" under the Fourth Amendment is a function of the totality of conditions existing within our society at any moment in history. Social interests under the police power should give law officers the right to stop users of the highways to check, for instance, their right to use the highway or to check the vehicles for safety standards. . . .

Similarly, we have the searches of passengers boarding airplanes. . . . Such procedures have been very effective in deterring "hijacking," and insofar as our limited observation reveals have met with the traveling public's approval.

We offer the following hypothetical: At a party of, say, twenty or so persons a valuable diamond ring is discovered to be missing from the person of one of the guests. Absent any more information, there would not be probable cause to detain one specific individual from among the persons present, but would it be unreasonable to detain *all* the persons present? A distinction may exist between what is a reasonable restraint of an individual and what is a reasonable restraint of an identifiable group. The interference with citizen liberty described in the above situations may be rationalized on the basis that although there is not probable cause for suspicion of one specific person, probable cause does exist as to an identifiable group (e.g.) those persons using the highways at a certain time and certain place in the aftermath of a crime, those persons boarding airplanes, those persons at the party.

It has been said that constitutional interpretation must conform to the changes which progress has wrought in our society since the adoption of the Constitution. The classic formulation is that the Chief Justice Marshall's: ". . . we must never forget that it is a constitution we are expounding . . . a constitution, intended to endure for ages to come, and, consequently, to be adapted to the various crises of human affairs." . . .

The automobile has made an alteration in our way of life unforeseen and unforeseeable by the Founding Fathers. It is our duty to be rational and sensible in our constitutional interpretation so that modern society is not damaged or injured by an irrational and unrealistic refusal to recognize the necessities brought about by these changes. The primary purpose of government is the protection of society. An instrument should not be so interpreted as to thwart that main objective.

If the police officers under the facts before us had observed the incriminating evidence inside the car while it was parked on the roadside, there would be no question here as to the right of the officers to arrest the driver and the occupant and to make a further search. . . .

As we previously stated, the question before us is whether or not suspicion such as the officers had in this case is a sufficient basis for the stopping, of an automobile upon the public highway. We believe that it is, and that such pronouncement is a reasonable interpretation of constitutional rights which are rights that belong to the public [the State] as well as to a defendant in a criminal case. Courts have to balance out the rights and have done so in the past. . . .

[Judgment affirmed.]

United States v Kuch

(DC Dist Col) 288 F Supp 439 (1968)

Kuch was indicted for violating the federal Marihuana Tax Act which taxed licensed sellers and prohibited the sale or transfer by an unlicensed person of marihuana or LSD. She defended on the ground of religious freedom. She was an ordained minister of the Neo-American

Church and claimed that she was providing the drug for use in the religious services.

GESELL, D.J. . . . The Neo-American Church was incorporated in California in 1965 as a nonprofit corporation. It claims a nationwide membership of about 20,000. At its head is a Chief Boo Hoo. Defendant Kuch is the primate of the Potomac, a position analogized to bishop. She supervises the Boo Hoos in her area. There are some 300 Boo Hoos throughout the country. In order to join the church a member must subscribe to the following principles:

(1) Everyone has the right to expand his consciousness and stimulate visionary experience by whatever means he considers desirable and proper without interference from anyone;

(2) The psychedelic substances, such as LSD, are the true Host of the Church, not drugs. They are sacramental foods, manifestations of the Grace of God, of the infinite imagination of the Self, and therefore belong to everyone;

(3) We do not encourage the ingestion of psychedelics by those who are unprepared.

Building on the central thesis of the group that psychedelic substances, particularly marihuana and LSD, are the true Host, the Church specifies that "it is the Religious *duty* of all members to partake of the sacraments on regular occasions." . . .

The dividing line between what is, and what is not, a religion is difficult to draw. . . . Obviously this question is a matter of delicacy and courts must be ever careful not to permit their own moral and ethical standards to determine the religious implications of beliefs and practices of others. Religions now accepted were persecuted, unpopular and condemned at their inception.

. . . There is need to develop a sharper line of demarkation between religious activities and personal codes of conduct that lack spiritual import. Those who seek the constitutional protections for their participation in an establishment of religion and freedom to practice its beliefs must not be permitted the special freedoms this sanctuary may provide merely by adopting religious nomenclature and cynically using it as a shield to protect them when participating in antisocial conduct that otherwise stands condemned. In a complex society where the requirements of public safety, health and order must be recognized, those who seek immunity from these requirements on religious grounds must at the very least demonstrate adherence to ethical standards and a spiritual discipline.

The defendant has sought to have the Church designated a religion primarily by emphasizing that ingestion of psychedelic drugs brings about a religious awareness and sharpens religious instincts. There was proof offered that the use of psychedelic drugs may, among other things, have religious implications. Various writings on the subject were received in evidence and testimony was taken from two professors, not members of the Church but having theological interest in the subject, who had themselves taken drugs experimentally and had studied religious manifestations of psychedelic drug ingestion. . . .

Assuming . . . that the Neo-American Church is a genuine religion and that Kuch subscribes fully to its doctrines and thus may invoke the full constitutional guarantees for free religious expression, her contentions are still without merit. The Constitution protects the right to have and to express beliefs. It does not blindly afford the same absolute protection to acts done in the name of or under the impetus of religion. . . .

Defendant misconceives the Constitution and the decisions when she claims in effect an unbridled right to practice her beliefs. The public interest is paramount and if properly determined the Congress may inhibit or prevent acts as opposed to beliefs even where those acts are in accord with religious convictions or beliefs. If individual religious conviction permits one to act contrary to civic duty, public health and the criminal laws of the land, then the right to be let alone in one's belief with all the spiritual peace it guarantees would be destroyed in the resulting breakdown of society. There is abroad among some in the land today a view that the individual is free to do anything he wishes.

A nihilistic, agnostic and anti-establishment attitude exists. These beliefs may be held. They may be expressed but where they are antithetical to the interests of others who are not of the same persuasion and contravene criminal statutes legitimately designed to protect society as a whole, such conduct should not find any constitutional sanctuary in the name of religion or otherwise. . . .

. . . The Court concludes that under any common sense view of undisputed facts the full enforcement of the statute here involved is necessary in the public interest and the unintended but obvious restrictions on the practices of defendant's church are wholly permissible.

There is substantial evidence that the use of marihuana creates a health hazard, is often the first step toward serious drug addiction in the progression to heroin, and is frequently associated with the commission of non-drug crimes, often crimes of violence. While all its effects are still unknown and the reactions of users differ, depending on emotional, psychological and frequency-of-use factors, the drug marihuana may often predispose to antisocial behavior and precipitate psychotic episodes. Among other reactions, hallucinations and delusions, impairment of judgment and memory, and confusion and delirium are common. Among chronic users, extremely violent aggressive conduct is manifested. Medical experts, narcotic experts, law enforcement officials, psychologists and proponents of freer marihuana use are not in accord but there is a very substantial body of opinion among individuals in each of these categories which supports the implications of marihuana use summarized above.

. . . To except the members of the Neo-American Church from the regulation of this drug, as Kuch requests, would not amount to some slight exception that would in no way interfere with the purposes of the Marihuana Tax Act. On the contrary, it would permit anyone to violate the law by paying the Church membership fee. The number of marihuana cases in this Court suggests that there are many who would quickly take out membership and the Act would soon be a nullity. . . .

As part of her motion to dismiss the indictment on religious grounds, defendant has also made what may be broadly described as the "peyote" argument. The claim is that she is denied equal protection in the constitutional sense because members of another religion are permitted under the narcotic laws to use peyote, a similar and at least as harmful an hallucinatory drug.

In People v Woody, 61 Cal 2d 716, 40 Cal Rptr 69, 394 P2d 813 (1964), the California Supreme Court broadly applied the tests of Sherbert v Verner, 374 US 398, 83 S Ct 1790, 10 L Ed 2d 965 (1963), and held that a state statute prohibiting the unauthorized use of peyote could not constitutionally be applied to a member of the Native American Church. The Native American Church, made up of from 30,000 to 250,000 American Indians, had a "long history" of the use of peyote. The court found that:

"Although peyote serves as a sacramental symbol similar to bread and wine in certain Christian churches, it is more than a sacrament. Peyote constitutes in itself an object of worship; prayers are directed to it much as prayers are devoted to the Holy Ghost. On the other hand, to use peyote for nonreligious purposes is sacrilegious. . . ." 40 Cal Rptr 69 at 73, 394 P2d 813 at 817.

Against the "virtual inhibition of the practice of defendants' religion" imposed by the state statute, the California court balanced the state's interest in enforcing the statute in order to determine whether that interest was so "compelling" as to necessitate "an abridgment of defendants' First Amendment right." The court found that the record did not support "the state's chronicle of harmful consequences of the use of peyote" and held in favor of an exemption for the defendant members of the Native American Church.

Defendant asserts that marihuana is less harmful, or no more harmful, than peyote and that under the reasoning in Woody, she is entitled to an exemption from the Marihuana Tax Act. This Court, however, is not bound by decisions of the California Supreme Court. While it may appear incongruous that the court found, on the one hand, that the state had not shown that peyote had harmful consequences and yet found, on the other hand, that peyote "engenders hallucinatory symptoms similar to those produced in cases of schizophrenia, dementia praecox, or paranoia"—that problem is not before the Court. The concern here is to analyze the scheme and effects of the federal statutes under which Kuch has been indicted.

The Commissioner of Food and Drugs has exempted peyote, when used by the Native American Church, from regulation under the Drug Abuse Control Amendments to the Federal Food, Drug and Cosmetic Act. 21 USC § 360a (f)(1). . . .

The Court must assume that the FDA [Food and Drug Administration] in granting the peyote exemption acted within its delegated authority. . . . As to marihuana, Congress, rather than delegating responsibility to the FDA, itself determined that there was a clear hazard to health in the use of the drug. That this legislative determination still has validity and a wholly rational basis is demonstrated by the materials submitted to the Court at the hearing on the motion of which the Court takes judicial notice. It is not the function of the Court to go any further behind this legislative determination as to marihuana. . . .

. . . These laws, enacted to preserve public safety, health and order, will be enforced. On the proofs before the Court the statutes are unrelated to the suppression of religion or religious beliefs and there is no denial of defendant's rights under the Constitution of the United States.

[Statute sustained.]

QUESTIONS AND CASE PROBLEMS

1. What is the general purpose of law?
2. Of the specific objectives of the law, which do you consider to be the most important? Why?
3. (a) When specific objectives of the law conflict in a given situation, which objective prevails?
   (b) Are creditor protection and debtor rehabilitation conflicting specific objectives of the law?
4. (a) How can law be dynamic if stability is one of its specific objectives?
   (b) How do some statutes provide for "built-in" flexibility?
5. Sometimes the development of the law seems to follow a zig-zag course. What is the explanation?
6. When O'Brien was prosecuted for burning his draft card, he raised the defense that the right of free speech gave him the privilege to express his disapproval of the draft and of the war in this manner. Was he correct? [United States v O'Brien, 391 US 367]
7. The City of Columbia, South Carolina, provided for the fluoridation of the city water supply. Hall claimed that this deprived him of his constitutional right to drink unfluoridated water since there was no other water supply, and further attacked the validity of the plan on the ground that dental cavities are not contagious and therefore a public health problem did not exist. Was he correct? [Hall v Bates, Mayor of Columbia, 247 SC 511, 148 SE2d 345]
8. Two high school girls on the Ann Arbor Union High School tennis team wished to enter the interscholastic tennis matches to represent their school. The Michigan High School Athletic Association regulations prohibited competition between boys and girls. The girls brought a suit against the State Board of Education to prevent enforcing this regulation. Was the regulation valid? [Morris v Michigan State Board of Education (CA6 Mich) 472 F2d 1207]

9. Briney owned an unused farmhouse. Annoyed with repeated stealing of personal property from the house, he set up a loaded shotgun so that anyone who entered through the front door would be shot in the legs. There was nothing to indicate the presence of the gun. Katko was a stranger who had been sentenced to 60 days in jail for stealing private property from a building. He was paroled for good behavior. Without any permission from Briney, Katko entered the farmhouse. When he opened the door, the gun went off and he was struck in the legs. He sued Briney for the injuries which he sustained. The jury returned a verdict of $20,000 compensatory damages and $10,000 punitive damages. Briney appealed on the grounds that he was not liable because a property owner can protect his property from being stolen by a trespasser. Was he correct? [Katko v Briney, (Iowa), 183 NW2d 657]

3 Criminal Law and Business

In order to preserve our freedom and to protect the rights that give meaning to that freedom, society imposes certain limitations that apply to everyone through rules of law and government. Three areas of the law that determine whether conduct is wrongful are contract law, criminal law, and the law of torts.

A claim based upon contract law arises, for example, when an employee sues his employer for failing to pay him his proper wages, or when a beneficiary brings suit on a life insurance policy. Contract law in general is discussed in Part 3. Special types of contracts, such as those for sales and insurance, constitute the subject matter of several other parts that follow.

Criminal law is the subject of discussion in this chapter, and the law of torts is discussed in Chapter 4.

GENERAL PRINCIPLES

A *crime* is a violation of the law that is punished as an offense against the state or government. Ordinarily the victim of a crime receives no benefit from the criminal prosecution of a defendant. California, Massachusetts, and New York, however, have statutes providing for varying degrees of financial indemnification to persons injured by criminal acts.

§ **3:1. Classification of Crimes.** Crimes may be classified (1) in terms of the source of the law prohibiting them, (2) in terms of their seriousness, or (3) in terms of their nature.

(1) Source of Criminal Law. Crimes are classified in terms of their origin as common-law and statutory crimes. Some offenses that are defined by statute are merely declaratory of the common law. Each state has its own criminal law, although a general pattern among the states may be observed.

(2) Seriousness of Offense. Crimes are classified in terms of their seriousness as treason, felonies, and misdemeanors. *Treason* is defined by the Constitution of the United States, which states that "Treason against the United States, shall consist only in levying War against them, or in adhering to their Enemies, giving them Aid and Comfort." [1]

---

[1] Art. III, § 3.

Felonies include the other more serious crimes, such as arson, homicide, and robbery, which are punishable by confinement in prison or by death.[2] Sometimes a statute may convert an act, previously a minor offense, into a felony.

Crimes not classified as treason or felonies are *misdemeanors*. Reckless driving, weighing and measuring goods with scales and measuring devices that have not been inspected, and disturbing the peace by illegal picketing are generally classified as misdemeanors. An act may be a felony in one state and a misdemeanor in another.

(3) Nature of Crimes. Crimes are also classified in terms of the nature of the misconduct. *Crimes mala in se* include acts that are inherently vicious or, in other words, that are naturally evil as measured by the standards of a civilized community. *Crimes mala prohibita* include those acts that are wrong merely because they are declared wrong by some statute, such as a law. (See p. 39, United States v Jackson.)

(4) Federal Crimes. With the rise of modern interstate transportation and communication, local or state law often is inadequate to cope with criminal conduct, so many federal statutes have been adopted. If criminal activity crosses state lines, it obviously comes under the federal law. Thus, knowingly shipping a stolen car from one state to another is clearly a violation of the federal Dyer Act which makes it a crime to ship a car in interstate commerce knowing that it is stolen. The fact that the interstate aspect is merely a fragment of a total criminal plan does not exclude the federal law prohibiting parking in certain locations.

§ 3:2. Basis of Criminal Liability. A crime generally consists of two elements: (1) an act or omission, and (2) a mental state. In the case of some crimes, such as the illegal operation of a business without a license, it is immaterial whether the act causes harm to others. In other cases the defendant's act must be the sufficiently direct cause of harm to another in order to impose criminal liability, as in the case of unlawful homicide. (See p. 40, Pennsylvania v Root.)

Mental state does not require an awareness or knowledge of guilt. In most crimes it is sufficient that the defendant voluntarily did the act that is criminal, regardless of motive or evil intent. In some instances a particular mental state is required, such as the necessity that a homicide be with malice aforethought to constitute murder. In some cases it is the existence of a specific intent that differentiates the crime committed from other offenses, as an assault with intent to kill is distinguished by that intent from an ordinary assault or an assault with intent to rob.

§ 3:3. Parties to a Crime. Two or more parties may directly or indirectly contribute to the commission of a crime. At common law participants in the commission of a felony are sometimes known as *principals* and *accessories.*

---

[2] People v Beasley, 370 Mich 242, 121 NW2d 457.

(1) Principals. Principals may be divided into two classes: (1) *principals in the first degree,* who actually engage in the perpetration of the crime, and (2) *principals in the second degree,* who are actually or constructively present and aid and abet in the commission of the act. For example, a person is a principal in the second degree if he assists by words of encouragement, stands ready to assist or to give information, or keeps watch to prevent surprise or capture.

The distinction as to degree is frequently abolished by statute so that all persons participating in a crime are principals.

(3) Accessories. Accessories to a crime are also divided into two classes, accessories before the fact and accessories after the fact. An *accessory before the fact* differs from a principal in the second degree only by reason of his absence from the scene of the act. An *accessory after the fact* is a person who knowingly assists one who has committed a felony. Thus, a person is an accessory after the fact if, after the commission of the crime and with intent to assist a felon, he gives warning to prevent arrest or shelters or aids in an escape from imprisonment.

§ **3:4. Responsibility for Criminal Acts.** In some cases certain classes of persons are not fully responsible for their criminal acts. These include (1) minors, (2) insane persons, (3) intoxicated persons, and (4) corporations.

(1) Minors. Some states have legislation fixing the age of criminal responsibility of minors. At common law, when a child is under the age of seven years, the law presumes him to be incapable of committing a crime; after the age of fourteen he is presumed to have capacity as though he were an adult; and between the ages of seven and fourteen, no presumption of law arises and it must be shown that the minor has such capacity. The existence of capacity cannot be presumed from the mere commission of the act.

(2) Insane Persons. An insane person is not criminally responsible for his acts. There is a conflict of opinion over what constitutes such insanity as to excuse a person legally from the normal consequence of his acts. All courts, however, agree that intellectual weakness alone is not such insanity.

A test commonly applied is the *right-and-wrong test.*[3] The responsibility of the defendant is determined in terms of his ability to understand the nature of his act and to distinguish right from wrong in relation to it.

Some courts also use the *irresistible-impulse test,* the theory of which is that although the defendant may know right from wrong, if he acts under an uncontrollable impulse because of an unsound state of mind caused by disease of any nature, he has not committed a voluntary act and is not

---

[3] A statute which adopts the right-and-wrong test does not violate the federal Constitution. Minnesota v Rawland, 294 Minn 17, 199 NW2d 774.

criminally responsible. If the mental instability is not caused by disease, the irresistible-impulse test is not applied.

In many jurisdictions the right-and-wrong test and the irresistible-impulse test have been replaced by the rule stated in the Model Penal Code of the American Law Institute that "A person is not responsible for criminal conduct if at the time of such conduct as a result of mental disease or defect he lacks substantial capacity to appreciate the wrongfulness of his conduct or to conform his conduct to the requirements of the law." [4]

When insanity takes the form of delusions or hallucinations, the defendant is not legally responsible when the imagined facts, if they were true, would justify or excuse the act.

(3) Intoxicated Persons. Involuntary intoxication relieves a person from criminal responsibility; voluntary intoxication generally does not. An exception to this rule is made in the case of a crime requiring specific intent when the accused was so intoxicated that he was incapable of forming such intent.[5]

(4) Corporations. The modern tendency is to hold corporations criminally responsible for their acts. A corporation may also be held liable for crimes based upon the failure to act. In some instances, the crime may be defined by statute in such a way that it requires or is interpreted as requiring a living "person" to commit the crime, in which case a corporation cannot be held criminally liable.

Certain crimes, such as perjury, cannot be committed by corporations. It is also usually held that crimes punishable only by imprisonment or corporal punishment cannot be committed by corporations. If the statute imposes a fine in addition to or in lieu of imprisonment or corporal punishment, a corporation may be convicted for the crime. Thus a corporation may be fined for violating the federal antitrust law by conspiring or combining to restrain interstate commerce. A corporation may be fined for committing criminal manslaughter when death has been caused by the corporation's failure to install safety equipment required by statute.

§ 3:5. Prevention of Crimes. The usual method employed to prevent crimes is punishment. (See p. 41, Carnley v Cochran.) This may take the form of fines, imprisonment, or other penalties. In most states a life sentence is imposed on the third or fourth felony conviction.[6] The legislatures may prescribe any punishment for crime, subject to federal constitutional provisions that prohibit "excessive fines" and "cruel and unusual punishments."

---

[4] United States v Brawner, (CA Dist Col) 471 F2d 969 (overruling Durham v United States, 94 US App DC 228, 214 F2d 862, and retaining the definition of mental disease or defect as including "any abnormal condition of the mind which substantially affects mental or emotional processes and substantially affects behavior controls.").

[5] People v Reynolds, 27 Ill 2d 523, 190 NE2d 301.

[6] Cooper v Texas, (Tex Crim App) 492 SW2d 545.

A jury cannot be constitutionally given an uncontrolled discretion to fix punishment at life imprisonment or death.[7]

An indigent defendant who is unable to pay any money obligation imposed by a court, whether a criminal fine or an order for support and lying-in expenses incurred with respect to an illegitimate child, cannot be imprisoned but must be allowed to make payments in reasonable installments.[8]

§ **3:6. Treatment of the Accused Party.** The great concern of the law for the protection of the accused party from government persecution is reflected in the recent decisions of the Supreme Court relating to the rights of the person accused of crime. His right to be warned when arrested that what he states may be admitted as evidence against him, his right to be informed that he may remain silent and that he has the right to counsel, the necessity of appointing counsel for the indigent defendant before trying him for any offense for which he may be imprisoned,[9] and various other rights are all based on the premise that the defendant is to be assumed innocent until shown to be guilty and that in his contest with the government, he must be protected from any possible unfairness or oppression.

When evidence is obtained by police officers illegally without a search warrant, it is not admissible in court. (See p. 42, Katz v United States.) Here the fear is that the officers will falsely plant incriminating evidence in order to obtain a conviction of the defendant. As a counterargument, it can be said that if the incriminating evidence is in fact found, the law should not be required to shut its eyes to its existence.

SECURITY FROM BUSINESS CRIMES

The field of criminal law as it affects business security includes larceny; receiving stolen goods; robbery; burglary; embezzlement; arson; obtaining goods by false pretenses; using false weights, measures, or labels; using bad checks, swindles and confidence games, counterfeit money, or the mails for the purpose of defrauding another; forgery; criminal libel; lotteries; and riots and civil disorders.

§ **3:7. Larceny.** *Larceny* is the wrongful or fraudulent taking and carrying away by any person of the personal property of another, with a fraudulent intent to deprive the owner of his property. The place from which the property is taken is generally immaterial, although by statute the offense is sometimes subjected to a greater penalty when property is taken from a particular kind of building, such as a warehouse. Shoplifting is a common form of larceny.

At common law a distinction was made between grand and petty larceny on the basis of the value of the property taken. In some states this distinction has been abolished. Where it continues, the effect of the distinction may be to make the offense a felony in the case of grand larceny, rather than a misdemeanor.

---

[7] Furman v Georgia, 408 US 238.

[8] Pennsylvania v Cliff, 451 Pa 427, 304 A2d 158.

[9] Argersinger v Hamlin, 407 US 25.

At common law a defendant taking property of another with the intent to return it was not guilty of larceny. This has been changed in some states so that a person who "borrows" a car for a joyride is guilty of larceny, theft, or some other statutory offense.[10] Statutes in many states penalize as larceny by trick the use of any device or fraud by which the wrongdoer obtains the possession of, or title to, personal property from the true owner. In some states all forms of larceny and robbery are consolidated in a statutory crime of theft. At common law there was no single offense of theft.

The concept of property which may be the subject of larceny has been expanded. For example, the theft of computer programs constitutes larceny. One half of the states have statutes punishing the theft of trade secrets as larceny.[11]

The fact that the person from whom the thief has taken the personal property is not the owner does not constitute a defense to the prosecution of the thief for larceny.[12]

The National Motor Vehicle Theft Act makes it a federal crime to transport a stolen motor vehicle in interstate commerce or to deal therein.[13] This statute is broadly interpreted so that an automobile is "stolen" whenever there is any unlawful taking with an intent to deprive the owner of his rights. Thus, an automobile is "stolen" within the federal statute when the defendant rents it by producing a credit card and a driver's license which have been stolen and impersonates the true owner of the license and the card.[14]

§ 3:8. Robbery. At common law *robbery* was the unlawful taking of personal property of any value from the possession or from the presence of another by means of force or by putting the possessor in fear. It differed from larceny primarily in the necessity of the use of force or fear, so that a pickpocket whose act of stealing was unknown to his victim committed larceny but not robbery.

In most states there are special penalties for various forms of aggravated robbery, such as robbery by use of a deadly weapon.

§ 3:9. Burglary. At common law *burglary* was the breaking and entering in the nighttime of the dwelling house of another, with the intent to commit a felony. While one often thinks of a burglary as stealing property, any felony would satisfy the definition. The offense was aimed primarily at protecting the habitation and thus illustrates the social objective of protection of the person, in this case the persons living or dwelling in the building.

Modern statutes have eliminated many of the requirements of the common-law definition so that it is immaterial when or where there is an entry to commit a felony, and the elements of breaking and entering are frequently omitted. Under some statutes the offense is aggravated and the

---

[10] Oregon v Eyle, 236 Ore 199, 388 P2d 110.
[11] New Jersey Statutes Annotated, 2A:119-5.3 et seq.
[12] New Jersey v Leicht, 124 NJ Super 127, 305 A2d 78.
[13] 18 USC §§ 2312, 2313.
[14] United States v Ellis, (CA8 Mo) 428 F2d 818.

penalty is increased in terms of the place where the offense is committed, such as a bank building, freight car, or warehouse. Related statutory offenses have also been created, such as the crime of possessing burglar's tools.

§ **3:10. Arson.** At common law *arson* was the willful and malicious burning of the dwelling-house of another. As such, it was designed to protect human life, although the defendant was guilty if there was a burning even though no one was actually hurt. In most states arson is a felony so that if someone in fact is killed in the resulting fire, the offense is murder by application of the felony-murder rule, under which a homicide, however unintended, occurring in the commission of a felony is automatically classified as murder.

In virtually every state a special offense of *burning to defraud insurers* has been created by statute, such burning not constituting arson when the defendant burns his own house to collect on his fire insurance, since the definition of arson required that the dwelling house be that of another person. In many states it is now arson to burn any building owned by another, even though it is not a dwelling.

§ **3:11. Receiving Stolen Goods.** The crime of *receiving stolen goods* is the receiving of goods which have been stolen, with knowledge of that fact, and with the intent to deprive the owner of them.[15] It is immaterial that the goods were received from a person who was not the person who stole them,[16] such as another receiver of the goods or an innocent middleman, and it is likewise immaterial that the receiver does not know the identity of the owner or the thief.

§ **3:12. Embezzlement.** *Embezzlement* is the fraudulent conversion of property or money owned by another by a person to whom it has been entrusted, as in the case of an employee.[17] It is a statutory crime designed to cover the case of unlawful takings that were not larceny because the wrongdoer did not take the property from the possession of another, and which were not robbery because there was neither a taking nor the use of force or fear.

It is immaterial whether the defendant received the money or property from the victim or from a third person. Thus, an agent commits embezzlement when he receives and keeps payments from third persons which he should remit to his principal, even though the agent is entitled to retain part of such payments as his commissions.[18]

Today every jurisdiction has not only a general embezzlement statute but also various statutes applicable to particular situations, such as embezzlement by trustees, employees, and government officials.

Statutes in many states provide that when an owner gives a contractor money which is intended to be used to pay various persons for work done in connection with the building being constructed for the owner but the

---

[15] McCoy v Indiana, 241 Ind 104, 170 NE2d 43.
[16] Connecticut v Cohn, 24 Conn Supp 232, 189 A2d 508.
[17] New Jersey v Daly, 38 NJ 1, 182 A2d 861.
[18] Sherman v Mississippi, 234 Miss 775, 108 So2d 205.

contractor does not use the money for that purpose, he commits a special form of larceny or embezzlement or an offense often called *misapplication of trust funds.* A statute making such conduct criminal is constitutional as against the contention that to imprison a contractor for not paying his bills amounts to constitutionally prohibited imprisonment for debt.[19]

Generally the fact that the defendant intends to return the property or money which he embezzles, or does in fact do so, is no defense.[20] However, as a practical matter an embezzler returning what he has taken will ordinarily not be prosecuted because the owner will not desire to testify against him.

§ **3:13. Obtaining Goods by False Pretenses.** In almost all of the states, statutes are directed against obtaining money or goods by means of false pretenses. (See p. 44, California v Randono.) These statutes vary in detail and scope. Sometimes the statutes are directed against particular forms of deception, such as using bad checks.

§ **3:14. False Weights, Measures, and Labels.** Cheating, defrauding, or misleading the public by the use of false, improper, or inadequate weights, measures, and labels is a crime. Numerous federal and state regulations have been adopted on this subject.[21]

§ **3:15. Swindles and Confidence Games.** The act of a person who, intending to cheat and defraud, obtains money or property by trick, deception, fraud, or other device, is an offense known as a *swindle* [22] or *confidence game.* False or bogus checks and spurious coins are frequently employed in swindling operations directed toward the man engaged in business.

§ **3:16. Counterfeit Money.** It is a federal crime to make, to possess with intent to pass, or to pass counterfeit coins, bank notes, or obligations or other securities of the United States. Legislation has also been enacted against the passing of counterfeit foreign securities or notes of foreign banks.

The various states also have statutes prohibiting the making and passing of counterfeit coins and bank notes. These statutes often provide, as does the federal statute, a punishment for the mutilation of bank notes or the lightening or mutilation of coins.

§ **3:17. Use of Mails to Defraud.** Congress has made it a crime to use the mails to further any scheme or artifice to defraud. To constitute the offense, there must be (1) a contemplated or organized scheme or artifice to defraud or to obtain money or property by false pretenses, and (2) the mailing or the causing of another to mail a letter, writing, or pamphlet for the purpose of executing or attempting to execute such scheme or artifice. Illustrations

---

[19] Washington v McDonald, 1 Wash App 592, 463 P2d 174.
[20] Clark v Delaware, (Del) 287 A2d 660.
[21] See § 14:16 et seq., and § 23:5.
[22] State v Wells, 265 Minn 212, 121 NW2d 68.

of schemes or artifices that come within the statute are false statements to secure credit, circulars announcing false cures for sale, false statements to sell stock in a corporation, and false statements as to the origin of a fire and the value of the destroyed goods for the purpose of securing indemnity from an insurance company. Federal law also makes it a crime to use a telegram to defraud.

§ **3:18. Lotteries.** There are three elements to a lottery: (1) a payment of money or something of value for the opportunity to win (2) a prize (3) by lot or chance.[23] If these elements appear, it is immaterial that the transaction appears to be a legitimate form of business, or advertising, or that the transaction is called by some name other than a lottery.

The sending of a chain letter through the mail is generally a federal offense, both as a mail fraud and as an illegal lottery, when the letter solicits contributions or payments for a fraudulent purpose.

§ **3:19. Forgery.** *Forgery* consists of the fraudulent making or material altering of an instrument, such as a check, which apparently creates or changes a legal liability of another. The instrument must have some apparent legal efficacy to constitute forgery.[24]

Ordinarily forgery consists of signing another's name with intent to defraud. It may also consist of making an entire instrument or altering an existing one. It may result from signing a fictitious name or the offender's own name with the intent to defraud.

When the nonowner of a credit card signs the owner's name on a credit card invoice, such an act is a forgery. In most states a special statute makes it a crime to fraudulently use a credit card. In such a case the prosecuting attorney may choose either to prosecute the defendant for violation of the forgery statute or the special credit card statute.[25]

§ **3:20. Criminal Libel.** A person who falsely defames another without legal excuse or justification may be subject to criminal liability as well as civil liability.[26] *Criminal libel* is based upon its tendency to cause a breach of the peace. Under some statutes, however, the offense appears to be based upon the tendency to injure another.

No publication or communication to third persons is required in the case of criminal libel. The offense is committed when the defendant communicates the libel directly to the person libeled as well as when he makes it known to third persons.

---

[23] Maine v Bussiere, 155 Maine 331, 154 A2d 702.

[24] Although the Uniform Commercial Code does not contain any provisions relating to crimes, if the defendant is indicted for forgery of a check, which is a form of commercial paper regulated by the Code, reference will be made to the Code to determine whether the writing in question is a check. Faulkner v Alaska, 445 P2d 815.

[25] Coleman v Alabama, 290 Ala 349, 276 So2d 589.

[26] Commonwealth v Acquaviva, 187 Pa Super 550, 145 A2d 407.

The truth of the statement is a defense in civil libel. In order to constitute a defense to criminal libel, the prevailing view requires that a proper motive on the part of the accused be shown and proof that the statement is true.

In a number of states, slander generally or particular kinds of slander have been made criminal offenses by statute.

§ 3:21. Riots and Civil Disorders. Damage to property in the course of a riot or civil disorder is ordinarily a crime to the same extent as though only one wrongdoer were involved. That is, there is larceny, or arson, and so on, depending on the nature of the circumstances, without regard to whether one person or many are involved. In addition, the act of assembling as a riotous mob and engaging in civil disorders is generally some form of crime in itself, without regard to the destruction or theft of property, whether under common-law concepts of disturbing the peace or under modern antiriot statutes.[27]

A state may make it a crime to riot or to incite to riot, although a statute relating to inciting must be carefully drawn to avoid infringing constitutionally protected free speech.[28]

---

[27] United States v Matthew, (CA Dist Col) 419 F2d 1177.
[28] Louisiana v Douglas, (La) 278 So2d 485.

CASES FOR CHAPTER 3

United States v Jackson

(CA5 Tex) 451 F2d 281 (1971)

The Mercantile Bank of Dallas was holding municipal bonds which had been paid and were to be destroyed. Before this was done, the bonds were apparently stolen. Sixty-five thousand dollars of these bonds were later deposited by Jackson in the Texas Bank and Trust Company with the instructions to collect the amount due and then put the money into a new account which Jackson had just opened under the name of Ed Lee Robbins. Thereafter, Jackson telephoned from Oklahoma to the bank in Dallas to inquire if his account had been opened. Jackson was told that it would be necessary to sign some additional forms. Jackson then left Oklahoma to go to Texas. On his arrival he was arrested by FBI agents. He was prosecuted for violating the Federal Wire Fraud Act by making the telephone call from Oklahoma to Texas.

RONEY, C.J. . . . The single legal point of defendant's argument . . . is that the telephone call from Tulsa, Oklahoma, to Dallas, Texas, was not an act prohibited by [the federal statute]. He argues that the call was merely made for the purpose of inquiring about the opening of defendant's bank account. He says that this was a legitimate call between client and his bank and had nothing to do with an alleged fraudulent scheme, if one existed.

Defendant's conviction stands or falls on the determination of whether or not the telephone call was made for the purpose of "executing such scheme or artifice."

The Wire Fraud Statute does not require that the scheme be successful, or even that the victim be deceived. It need only be shown that there was a scheme and that interstate wires were "used as a step in the execution of the scheme." . . .

The evidence shows that Jackson's telephone call was a part of the scheme from its inception. Before he left the Texas Bank and Trust Company on May 23rd, Jackson told Mr. Robert Houston that he traveled and that he would be calling. Since Jackson would be unable to withdraw any of the proceeds of the stolen municipal bonds until they had been cashed and his account had been opened, it was impossible for him to consummate his scheme without ascertaining whether or not the money was in his account. This information was indispensable to complete the execution of the scheme. It could have been obtained by a personal visit to the bank, or by an intrastate telephone call, without violating this law. But it was not. Defendant's call was made in interstate commerce and thus ran afoul of the federal law. . . .

[Conviction affirmed.]

Pennsylvania v Root

403 Pa 571, 170 A2d 310 (1961)

Root was challenged to an illegal auto race at night on a public highway. While the challenger was doing 70 to 90 miles an hour in a 50-mile-an-hour no-passing zone, he crossed the dividing line in attempting to pass Root, struck an oncoming truck, and was killed. Root was prosecuted for involuntary manslaughter. From a conviction, Root appealed.

JONES, C.J. . . . While precedent is to be found for application of the tort law concept of "proximate cause" in fixing responsibility for criminal homicide, the want of any rational basis for its use in determining criminal liability can no longer be properly disregarded. When proximate cause was first borrowed from the field of tort law and applied to homicide prosecutions in Pennsylvania, the concept connoted a much more direct causal relation in producing the alleged culpable result than it does today. Proximate cause, as an essential element of a tort founded in negligence, has undergone in recent times, and is still undergoing, a marked extension. More specifically, this area of civil law has been progressively liberalized in favor of claims for damages for personal injuries to which careless conduct of others can in some way be associated. To persist in applying the tort liability concept of proximate cause to prosecutions for criminal homicide after the marked expansion of *civil* liability of defendants in tort actions for negligence would be to extend possible *criminal* liability to persons chargeable with unlawful or reckless conduct in circumstances not generally considered to present the likelihood of a resultant death. . . .

Legal theory which makes guilt or innocence of criminal homicide depend upon such accidental and fortuitous circumstances as are now embraced by modern tort law's encompassing concept of proximate cause is too harsh to be just. . . .

In this case, the conduct of the defendant was not the proximate cause of the decedent's death as a matter of law. . . .

The deceased was aware of the dangerous condition created by the defendant's reckless conduct in driving his automobile at an excessive rate of speed along the highway but, despite such knowledge, he recklessly chose to swerve his car to the left and into the path of an oncoming truck, thereby bringing about the head-on collision which caused his own death.

To summarize, the tort liability concept of proximate cause has no proper place in prosecutions for criminal homicide and more direct causal connection is required for conviction. . . . In the instant case, the defendant's reckless conduct was not a sufficiently direct cause of the competing driver's death to make him criminally liable therefor. . . .

[Conviction reversed.]

EAGEN, J. (dissenting) . . . If the defendant did not engage in the unlawful race and so operate his automobile in such a reckless manner, this accident would never have occurred. He helped create the dangerous event. He was a vital part of it. The victim's acts were a natural reaction to the stimulus of the situation. The race, the attempt to pass the other car and forge ahead, the reckless speed, all of these factors the defendant himself helped create. He was part and parcel of them. That the victim's response was normal under the circumstances, that his reaction should have been expected and was clearly foreseeable, is to me beyond argument. That the defendant's recklessness was a substantial factor is obvious. All of this, in my opinion, makes his unlawful conduct a direct cause of the resulting collision. . . .

Acts should be judged by their tendency under the known circumstances, not by the actual intent which accompanies their performance. Every day of the year, we read that some teen-agers, or young adults, somewhere in this country, have been killed or have killed others, while racing their automobiles. Hair-raising, death-defying, law-breaking rides, which encompass "racing," are the rule rather than the exception, and endanger not only the participants, but also every motorist and passenger on the road. To call such . . . [conduct] unlikely to result in death, is to ignore the cold and harsh reality of everyday occurrences. . . .

1 Wharton, Criminal Law and Procedure § 68 [Anderson Edition] (1957), speaking of causal connection, says: "A person is only criminally liable for what he has caused, that is, there must be a causal relationship between his act and harm sustained for which he is prosecuted. It is not essential to the existence of a causal relationship that the ultimate harm which has resulted was foreseen or intended by the actor. It is sufficient that the ultimate harm is one which a reasonable man would foresee as being reasonably related to the acts of the defendant." Section 295, in speaking about manslaughter, says: "When homicide is predicated upon the negligence of the defendant, it must be shown that his negligence was the proximate cause or a contributing cause of the victim's death. It must appear that the death was not the result of misadventure, but the natural and probable result of a reckless or culpably negligent act. To render a person criminally liable for negligent homicide, the duty omitted or improperly performed must have been his personal duty, and the negligent act from which death resulted must have been his personal act, and not the act of another. But he is not excused because the negligence of someone else contributed to the result, when his act was the primary or proximate cause and the negligence of the other did not intervene between his act and the result."

Professor Joseph Beale, late renowned member of the Harvard Law School faculty, in an article entitled, The Proximate Consequence of an Act, 33 HarvLRev 633, 646, said, "Though there is an active force intervening after defendant's act, the result will nevertheless be proximate if the defendant's act actually caused the intervening force. In such a case the defendant's force is really continuing in active operation *by means of the force it stimulated into activity*." . . .

But, says the majority opinion, these are principles of tort law and should not in these days be applied to the criminal law. But such has been the case since the time of Blackstone. . . .

Carnley v Cochran

(Fla) 118 So2d 629 (1960)

Carnley was convicted of forgery and was sentenced to a term of 6 months to 10 years under a Florida statute authorizing an indeterminate sentence within specified minimum and maximum limitations. He brought a suit against Cochran, the Director of the Corrections Division, seeking release on the ground that the statute was unconstitutional and violated the prohibition of the Florida constitution against "indefinite imprisonment."

THORNAL, J. . . . In . . . ancient . . . centuries . . . a basic concept of punishment for the commission of crime was retribution. It was thought that if an individual violated the laws prescribed for the governance of the community he should compensate in kind, whether physical or material, as a retributive punishment for the offense which he had committed. So it was that . . . God instructed Moses:

> And if any mischief follow, then thou shalt give life for life,
> Eye for eye, tooth for tooth, hand for hand, foot for foot,
> Burning for burning, wound for wound, stripe for stripe.
>
> *Exodus 21:23-25*

This concept of retributive justice . . . continues to influence the thinking of many.

With the passage of time, and especially during the current century, penologists and sociologists have arrived at the conclusion that retribution, in and of itself, is unjustifiable as the sole and only objective of punishment for crime.

An enlightened society is rapidly coming to the view that the results to be accomplished by a sentence in a criminal matter are twofold, to wit: (1) deterrence, and (2) rehabilitation. . . .

The currently accepted guide to a sentence in a criminal matter is that it should be sufficiently severe to deter the particular offender and others similarly conditioned from committing other breaches of the criminal law. Nevertheless, it should be sufficiently flexible to permit opportunity to consider the individual involved in order to take advantage of every possibility for rehabilitation. . . .

The sentencing judge must evaluate the qualities and potentials of the individual before him in the light of his judicial responsibility to the community. . . .

The so-called indeterminate sentence . . . makes possible a more flexible opportunity for rehabilitation. It constantly holds out to the individual law violator the incentive to minimize his term of imprisonment. It offers him every chance to re-establish himself as a useful member of society, provided he has the courage and ambition to accomplish this desirable result. . . .

[Relief denied.]

Katz v United States

389 US 347 (1967)

Katz was suspected of making bets by telephone. FBI agents placed an electronic listening device on the top of the roof of a public telephone booth and recorded statements made by Katz into the phone. These recordings of his half of the telephone conversations were admitted in evidence at a trial in spite of his objections. He was convicted of placing bets by phone and appealed.*

STEWART, J. . . . The petitioner [Katz raises two] questions. . . .

"A. Whether a public telephone booth is a constitutionally protected area so that evidence obtained by attaching an electronic listening recording device to the top of such a booth is obtained in violation of the right to privacy of the user of the booth.

"B. Whether physical penetration of a constitutionally protected area is necessary before a search and seizure can be said to be violative of the Fourth Amendment to the United States Constitution."

We decline to adopt this formulation of the issues. In the first place, the correct solution of Fourth Amendment problems is not necessarily promoted by incantation of the phrase "constitutionally protected area." Secondly, the Fourth Amendment cannot be translated into a general constitutional "right to privacy." That Amendment protects individual privacy against certain kinds of governmental intrusion. . . . But the protection of a person's *general* right to privacy—his right to be let alone by other people—is, like the protection of his property and of his very life, left largely to the law of the individual States.

The Government contends, however, that the activities of its agents in this case should not be tested by Fourth Amendment requirements, for the surveillance technique they employed involved no physical penetration of the telephone booth from which the petitioner placed his calls. It is true that the absence of such penetration was at one time thought to foreclose further Fourth Amendment inquiry, Olmstead v United States, 277 US 438, 457, 464, 466, . . . ; for that Amendment was thought to limit only searches and seizures of tangible property. But . . . we have since departed from the narrow view on which that decision rested. . . . Once . . . it is recognized that the Fourth Amendment protects people—and not simply "areas"—against unreasonable searches and seizures, it becomes clear that the reach of that Amendment cannot turn upon the presence or absence of a physical intrusion into any given enclosure.

. . . The Government's activities in electronically listening to and recording the petitioner's words violated the privacy upon which he justifiably relied while using the telephone booth and thus constituted a "search and seizure" within the meaning of the Fourth Amendment. The fact that the electronic device employed to achieve that end did not happen to penetrate the wall of the booth can have no constitutional significance.

---

* See p. 3 concerning electronic surveillance.

The question remaining for decision, then, is whether the search and seizure conducted in this case complied with constitutional standards. In that regard, the Government's position is that its agents acted in an entirely defensible manner: They did not begin their electronic surveillance until investigation of the petitioner's activities had established a strong probability that he was using the telephone in question to transmit gambling information to persons in other states, in violation of federal law. Moreover, the surveillance was limited, both in scope and in duration, to the specific purpose of establishing the contents of the petitioner's unlawful telephonic communications. The agents confined their surveillance to the brief periods during which he used the telephone booth, and they took great care to overhear only the conversations of the petitioner himself. . . .

The Government urges that, because its agents . . . did no more here than they might properly have done with prior judicial sanction, we should retroactively validate their conduct. That we cannot do. It is apparent that the agents in this case acted with restraint. Yet the inescapable fact is that this restraint was imposed by the agents themselves, not by a judicial officer. They were not required, before commencing the search, to present their estimate of probable cause for detached scrutiny by a neutral magistrate. They were not compelled, during the conduct of the search itself, to observe precise limits established in advance by a specific court order. Nor were they directed, after the search had been completed, to notify the authorizing magistrate in detail of all that had been seized. In the absence of such safeguards, this Court has never sustained a search upon the sole ground that officers reasonably expected to find evidence of a particular crime and voluntarily confined their activities to the least intrusive means consistent with that end. Searches conducted without warrants have been held unlawful "notwithstanding facts unquestionably showing probable cause," . . . for the Constitution requires "that the deliberate, impartial judgment of a judicial officer . . . be interposed between the citizen and the police. . . ." . . . "Over and again this Court has emphasized that the mandate of the [Fourth] Amendment requires adherence to judicial processes" . . . and that searches conducted outside the judicial process, without prior approval by judge or magistrate, are per se unreasonable under the Fourth Amendment—subject only to a few specifically established and well-delineated exceptions. . . .

The Government . . . urges . . . that surveillance of a telephone booth should be exempted from the usual requirement of advance authorization by a magistrate upon a showing of probable cause. We cannot agree. Omission of such authorization "bypasses the safeguards provided by an objective predetermination of probable cause, and substitutes instead the far less reliable procedure of an after-the-event justification for the . . . search, too likely to be subtly influenced by the familiar shortcomings of hindsight judgment." . . .

Wherever a man may be, he is entitled to know that he will remain free from unreasonable searches and seizures. The government agents here ignored "the procedure of antecedent justification . . . that is central to the Fourth Amendment," a procedure that we hold to be a constitutional precondition of the kind of electronic surveillance involved in this case. Because the surveillance here failed to meet that condition, and because it led to the petitioner's conviction, the judgment must be reversed.

BLACK, J. (dissenting) . . . The Fourth Amendment says that "The right of the people to be secure in their persons, houses, papers, and effects, against unreasonable searches and seizures, shall not be violated, and no Warrants shall issue, but upon probable cause, supported by Oath or affirmation, and particularly describing the place to be searched, and the persons or things to be seized."

The first clause protects "persons, houses, papers, and effects, against unreasonable searches and seizures. . . ." These words connote the idea of tangible things with size, form, and weight, things capable of being searched, seized, or both. The second clause of the Amendment still further establishes its Framers' purpose to limit its protection to tangible things by providing that no warrants shall issue but those "particularly describing the place to be searched, and the person or things to be seized." A conversation overheard by eavesdropping, whether by plain snooping or wiretapping, is not tangible and, under the normally accepted meanings of the words, can neither be searched nor seized. In addition the language of the second clause indicates that the Amendment refers to something not only tangible so it can be seized but to something already in existence so it can be described. Yet the Court's interpretation would have the Amendment apply to overhearing future conversations which by their very nature are nonexistent until they take place. How can one "describe" a future conversation, and, if one cannot, how can a magistrate issue a warrant to eavesdrop one in the future? It is argued that information showing what is expected to be said is sufficient to limit the boundaries of what later can be admitted into evidence; but does such general information really meet the specific language of the Amendment which says "particularly describing?" Rather than using language in a completely artificial way, I must conclude that the Fourth Amendment simply does not apply to eavesdropping.

Tapping telephone wires, of course, was an unknown possibility at the time the Fourth Amendment was adopted. But eavesdropping (and wiretapping is nothing more than eavesdropping by telephone) was . . . "an ancient practice which at common law was condemned as a nuisance. 4 Blackstone, Commentaries 168. In those days the eavesdropper listened by naked ear under the eaves of houses or their windows, or beyond their walls seeking out private discourse." . . . There can be no doubt that the Framers were aware of this practice, and if they had desired to outlaw or restrict the use of evidence obtained by eavesdropping, I believe that they would have used the appropriate language to do so in the Fourth Amendment. . . .

I do not deny that common sense requires and that this Court often has said that the Bill of Rights' safeguards should be given a liberal construction. This principle, however, does not justify construing the search and seizure amendment as applying to eavesdropping or the "seizure" of conversations. The Fourth Amendment was aimed directly at the abhorred practice of breaking in, ransacking and searching homes and other buildings, and seizing people's personal belongings without warrants issued by magistrates. The Amendment deserves, and this Court has given it, a liberal construction in order to protect against warrantless searches of buildings and seizures of tangible personal effects. But until today this Court has refused to say that eavesdropping comes within the ambit of Fourth Amendment restrictions. . . .

Since I see no way in which the words of the Fourth Amendment can be construed to apply to eavesdropping, that closes the matter for me. In interpreting the Bill of Rights, I willingly go as far as a liberal construction of the language takes me, but I simply cannot in good conscience give a meaning to words which they have never before been thought to have and which they certainly do not have in common ordinary usage. I will not distort the words of the Amendment in order to "keep the Constitution up to date" or "to bring it into harmony with the times." It was never meant for this Court to have such power, which in effect would make us a continuously functioning constitutional convention. . . .

The Fourth Amendment protects privacy only to the extent that it prohibits unreasonable searches and seizures of "persons, houses, papers and effects." No general right is created by the Amendment so as to give this Court the unlimited power to hold unconstitutional everything which affects privacy. . . .

California v Randono

32 Cal App 3d 164, 108 Cal Rptr 326 (1973)

Randono and Dreyer were partners. They owned two bars and restaurants—Feliciano's and the Saddleback Inn. Saddleback Inn was headed for bankruptcy. The partners decided to take advantage of this situation by ordering $20,000 worth of liquor on credit to be charged to the Saddleback Inn with the intent of immediately transferring the liquor to Feliciano's without paying for it. This was done and one of the partners was then prosecuted for theft by false pretenses.

KERRIGAN, A.J. . . . The trial court specifically found that the defendant was guilty of theft by false pretenses. To support a false pretenses conviction, it must be shown that the defendant made a false pretense or representation with intent to defraud the owner of his property, and that the owner was in fact defrauded, in that he relied on the false representation in parting with his property. . . .

The Attorney General contends that the evidence also supports conviction of larceny by trick or device. We disagree. Larceny by trick or device is the appropriation of property, the possession of which was fraudulently acquired; obtaining property by false pretenses is the fraudulent or deceitful acquisition of both title and possession. . . . Where one is induced to sell property through another's false representations, if the seller intends to pass only possession at the time of sale, the buyer commits the offense of larceny by trick or device, but if the seller intends to pass title, the buyer commits the offense of obtaining property by false pretenses. . . .

. . . In the absence of evidence to the contrary, we must presume that defendant's suppliers intended . . . to convey title to defendant or the Saddleback on delivery of the liquor. Consequently, the offense, if any, must have been theft by false pretenses. . . .

There is no dispute as to the element of actual fraud. . . .

Nor is there any question about the reliance element. Reliance may be inferred from all the circumstances. . . . The only reasonable inference to be drawn from delivery of 334 cases of liquor under invoices marked with prices and terms of payment is that the dealers expected to be paid, and relied on that expectation in making the deliveries.

The false pretense may consist in any act, word, symbol, or token calculated and intended to deceive. It may be either express or implied from words or conduct. . . . The trial court adopted the prosecution's theory, that the false representations consisted of defendant's implied promise to pay for the ordered liquor, with the intention not to perform. Such a promise is a false or fraudulent representation or pretense within the meaning of . . . the Penal Code. . . .

Defendant ordered the liquor from wholesale suppliers. There is no evidence of any facts or circumstances that would suggest to any of the dealers that the orders were out of the ordinary. When goods are ordered by one dealer from another in the ordinary course of business, the law will imply a promise to pay. . . .

The alternative is to suppose that the dealers intended the $20,000 worth of liquor as gifts. Any such presumption would fly in the face of reason and experience. The invoices, which include both price and terms of payment, contradict any inference of donative intent. . . .

Dreyer testified that he and defendant agreed to order the liquor and not to pay for it; that the liquor was removed from the Saddleback to Feliciano's and hidden behind a wall built for that purpose. His testimony was corroborated by three witnesses. . . .

[Penal Code] Section 484 provides: "Every person . . . who shall knowingly and designedly, by any false or fraudulent representation or pretense, defraud any other person of money, labor or real or personal property, . . . is guilty of theft." . . .

Defendant's position is that to construe the words "representation or pretense" to include silence is counter to the fair import of those words. . . .

But defendant's false representation was not manifested by silence; it was manifested by his conduct in ordering the liquor. Nothing in section 484 requires that the false pretense be expressed in words; conduct is sufficient if it is calculated to mislead. . . .

[Conviction affirmed.]

QUESTIONS AND CASE PROBLEMS

1. What is the objective of the rule of law that an irresistible impulse to commit a crime does not excuse criminal liability when the mental instability is not the result of disease?

2. Wolfe gave some counterfeit money to Ballinger, telling her that the bills were counterfeit and that she should go "downtown" to pass them and that,

being New Year's Eve, it was a good time to pass them. Ballinger thereafter spent two of the bills and attempted to destroy the balance. Wolfe was arrested and prosecuted for passing counterfeit obligations of the United States with the intent to defraud. He raised the defense that he could not be guilty as Ballinger was told that the money was counterfeit. Decide. [United State v Wolfe, (CA7 Ill) 307 F2d 798 cert den 372 US 945]

3. Morse was convicted of forging the name "Hillyard Motors" as the drawer of a check. He appealed on the ground that signing such a name had no legal effect, and that therefore he was not guilty of forgery. Decide. [Washington v Morse, 38 Wash 2d 927, 234 P2d 478]
4. Swanson wanted to procure a loan from the Lincoln Bank. He falsely represented to the bank that he owned 629 head of cattle when in fact he owned only 80. The bank made a loan to him of approximately $3,000 and credited his account with this amount. Before Swanson drew any money from the bank, the bank's agent learned of the falsity of Swanson's representation. Swanson thereafter drew out by check the amount of the loan. Swanson was then prosecuted by the state for obtaining property by false pretenses. He defended on the ground that he had not actually drawn any money from the bank until after the bank, through its agent, knew of the fraud and that since the bank took no steps to prevent the money from going out thereafter, it was in effect the bank's own negligence that made it sustain loss. Was this a valid defense? [Nebraska v Swanson, 179 Neb 693, 140 NW2d 618]
5. Socony Mobil Oil Co. ran a telephone bingo game series. The gasoline station dealers purchased the bingo cards from Socony and gave them free to anyone requesting them, whether a customer or not. It was not possible to play the game without a card. A cash prize was awarded the winner. The State of Texas brought an injunction action against Socony to stop this on the ground that it was a lottery. Socony raised the defense that since no value or consideration was given by the persons participating in the bingo games, it was not a lottery. Decide. [Texas v Socony Mobil Oil Co., (Tex Civ App) 386 SW2d 169]
6. Krehbiel was the manager of a vacuum cleaning company. In order to promote sales, he and the company adopted a plan by which any purchaser of a vacuum cleaner who gave the name of a prospective customer would receive $25 if the named person thereafter purchased a vacuum cleaner. The Attorney General of Oklahoma brought an action against the manager and the company to stop the plan on the ground that it was a lottery under a statute which declared that "Every person who sets up, promotes, or engages in any plan by which goods or anything of value is sold to a person, firm, or corporation for a consideration and upon the further consideration that the purchaser agrees to secure one (1) or more persons to participate in the plan by respectively making a similar purchase or purchases and in turn agreeing to secure one (1) or more persons likewise to join in said plan, each purchaser being given the right to secure money, credits, goods, or something of value, depending upon the number of persons joining in the plan, shall be held to have set up and promoted a lottery." Decide. [Krehbiel v Oklahoma, (Okla) 378 P2d 768]

7. Koonce entered a gas station after it was closed for the night. By means of force, he removed the cash box from a soft drink vending machine. He was prosecuted for burglarizing a "warehouse." Was he guilty? [Koonce v Kentucky, (Ky) 452 SW2d 822; Shumate v Kentucky, (Ky) 433 SW2d 340]
8. Tauscher was prosecuted for embezzlement. It was shown that while claiming to act as agent, he, without authority, had drawn a check on his employer's bank account and kept the proceeds of the check for his own use. Was he guilty of embezzlement? [Oregon v Tauscher, 227 Ore 1, 360 P2d 764]
9. Dumont was prosecuted for obtaining merchandise by using a stolen credit card and signing a sales slip with the name of the card holder. Dumont was prosecuted under a general criminal law statute that classified the offense as a felony. Dumont claimed that this statute had been superseded by a later statute specifically applying to the unlawful use of credit cards, under which the offense was merely a misdemeanor, and that she could not be prosecuted under the earlier forgery statute. Was she correct? [Oregon v Dumont, 3 Ore App 189, 471 P2d 847]
10. Rapp opened a checking account under an assumed name. He then issued worthless checks on that account using the assumed name. He was prosecuted for uttering forged instruments. Was he guilty? {Rapp v Florida, (Fla App), 274 So2d 18]
11. A New York statute declares that possession of a firearm is not a felony if it is kept "in a place of business." Santiago drove a taxicab in New York City. The taxicab company assigned the cab to him. He kept his receipts in a cigar box, along with an automatic pistol. He was prosecuted for the illegal possession of firearms. He raised the defense that the pistol was kept "in a place of business." Was this a valid defense? [New York v Santiago, 343 NY S2d 805]
12. Westman pleaded guilty to the larceny of a minibike. The bike was worth approximately $250 in 1969 when it was new. It was stolen in 1971. If the bike had a value in 1971 of over $100, Westman was guilty of a felony. If the value was not over $100, the crime would be a misdemeanor. Was Westman guilty of a felony? [Michigan v Westman, — Mich App —, 220 NY2d 169]

4 The Law of Torts and Business

GENERAL PRINCIPLES

A *tort* is a private injury or wrong arising from a breach of a duty created by law. It is often defined as a wrong independent of contract. Most torts, although not all, involve moral wrongs, but not all moral wrongs are torts.

Tort law includes harm to the person, as well as damage to property caused negligently or intentionally. In some instances, liability is imposed merely because the activity of the wrongdoer is so dangerous that it is deemed proper that he should pay for any harm that has been caused.

§ 4:1. Tort, Crime, and Breach of Contract. A crime is a wrong arising from a violation of a public duty, whereas a tort is a wrong arising from a violation of a private duty. An act may be both a crime and a tort as in the case of the theft of an automobile.

Although the state recognizes both crimes and torts as wrongs, it attaches different consequences to them. In the case of a crime, the state brings the action to enforce a prescribed penalty or punishment. On the other hand, when an act or omission is a tort, the state allows an action for redress by the injured party.

The wrongs or injuries caused by a breach of contract arise from the violation of an obligation or duty created by consent of the parties. A tort arises from the violation of an obligation or duty created by law. The same act may be both a breach of contract and a tort. For example, when an agent exchanges property instead of selling it as directed by his principal, he is liable for breach of contract and for the tort of conversion.

§ 4:2. Basis of Tort Liability. The mere fact that a person is hurt or harmed in some way does not mean that he can sue and recover damages from the person causing the harm. There must exist a recognized basis for liability.

(1) Voluntary Act. The defendant must be guilty of a voluntary act or omission. Acts that are committed or omitted by one who is confronted with sudden peril or pressing danger not of his own making are considered as having been committed or omitted involuntarily.

(2) Intent. Whether intent to do an unlawful act or intent to cause harm is required as a basis for tort liability depends upon the nature of the act involved. Liability is imposed for some torts even though the person committing the tort acted in complete ignorance of the nature of his act and without any intent to cause harm. Thus, a person going on land that does not belong to him is liable for the tort of trespass unless he has permission from the owner.

In the case of other torts, such as assault, slander, malicious prosecution, or interference with contracts, it is necessary for the plaintiff to show that there was an intent on the part of the defendant to cause harm or at least the intent to do an act which a reasonable man would anticipate as likely to cause harm.

(3) Motive. As a general rule, motive is immaterial except as it may be evidence to show the existence of intent. In most instances any legal right may be exercised even with bad motives, and an act that is unlawful is not made legal by good motives.

(4) Proximate Cause. In order to fix legal responsibility upon one as a wrongdoer, it is necessary to show that the injury was the proximate result of his voluntary act. Whether an act is the proximate cause of an injury is usually a question of fact for the jury to determine.

§ 4:3. Liability-Imposing Conduct. In the more elementary forms intentional harm involves wrongs, such as an assault; a battery; intentionally causing mental distress; and intentional wrongs directed against property, such as stealing another's automobile, cutting timber from his land, or setting his house on fire. Note that most of these "elementary" torts are also crimes. Somewhat more complex are the torts of fraud, slander and libel, the invasion of privacy, and the intentional interference with contract rights or business relations of others.

Many of the torts just specified did not exist 100 to 150 years ago. In terms of liability, the action for wrongful death did not exist until created by statute in the middle of the last century. Prior to that time, the common-law rule that death extinguished all claims was followed.

§ 4:4. Absolute Liability. In some areas of the law, liability for harm exists without regard to whether there was any negligence or intention to cause harm. For example, in most states when a contractor blasts with dynamite and debris is hurled onto the land of another, the landowner may recover damages from the contractor even though the contractor had used due care, and therefore was not negligent, and did not intend to cause the landowner any harm by committing an intentional trespass on his land.

By this concept of absolute liability, society is in effect taking a middle position between (a) liability based on moral fault and (b) illegality. That is, society is saying that the activity is so dangerous to the public that liability must be imposed even though no fault is present. Yet society will not go so far as to say that the activity is so dangerous that it must be outlawed.

Instead, the compromise is made to allow the activity but make it pay its injured victims regardless of the circumstances under which the injuries were sustained. Statutes are expanding the area of absolute liability.

(1) Industrial Activity. There is generally absolute liability for harm growing out of the storage of inflammable gas and explosives in the middle of a populated city; crop dusting, where the chemical used is dangerous to life and the dusting is likely to be spread by the wind; factories emitting dangerous fumes, smoke, and soot in populated areas. By statute, the concept of absolute liability has been extended to certain areas of industrial activity, the social justification being that the industry that benefits from the activity and which can the better procure insurance against loss or which can shift the incidence of economic loss to the consuming public should be required to bear the loss as a cost of doing business rather than the person who is harmed. This philosophy underlies workmen's compensation in which the liability of the employer is not predicated upon his fault but upon the fact that the accident or occupational disease is employment-related. Child labor statutes frequently provide for absolute liability when harm arises from a violation of their provisions.

In the United States there is no common-law liability for the non-negligent spread or origination of fire. This rule has been changed by statutes, such as those imposing liability when locomotives are not equipped with spark arresters or when a prairie fire is intentionally started during a dry period. By decision or statute, approximately one fourth of the states have imposed the standard of absolute liability upon aircraft for damage caused to persons or property on the ground.[1]

(2) Consumer Protection. Pure foods statutes may impose absolute liability upon the seller of foods in favor of the ultimate consumer who is harmed by them. Decisions and statutes have imposed to a certain extent a pseudo-absolute liability on the manufacturer of goods.

§ **4:5. Negligence.** The widest range of tort liability today arises in the field of *negligence,* which exists whenever the defendant has acted with less care than would be exercised by a reasonable man under the circumstances. More specifically stated, the defendant has failed to exercise that degree of care which a reasonable man would exercise under the circumstances, and such negligence is the proximate cause of harm to a person or property.

(1) The Imaginary Reasonable Man. The reasonable man whose behavior is made the standard is an imaginary man. In a given case which is tried before a jury, the reasonable man becomes the model man as he appears to the composite or combined minds of the jurors.

This reasonable man is not any one of the jurors nor an average of what the jurors would do. The law is not concerned with what the jurors would

[1] Adler's Quality Bakery, Inc. v Gaseteria, Inc., 32 NJ 55, 159 A2d 97.

do in a like situation, for it is possible that they may be more careful or less careful than the abstract reasonable man. Likewise it is not what is done in the community, for the community may live above or below the standard of the reasonable man.

(2) Variable Character of the Standard. By definition, the standard is a variable standard for it does not tell you specifically in any case what should have been done. This flexibility is confusing to everyone in the sense that you never know the exact answer in any borderline case until after the lawsuit is over. From the standpoint of society, however, this very flexibility is desirable because it is obviously impossible to foresee every possible variation in the facts that might arise and even more impossible to keep such a code of conduct up-to-date. Imagine how differently the reasonable man must act while driving today's automobile on today's superhighways than he did when he drove a Model-T more than a half century ago.

(3) Duty of Care. A person is under a duty to act carefully with respect to those persons or things which are likely to be within the area in which they might be affected by his conduct.

At one time the zone of duty to exercise care was narrower when the question involved the negligence of a seller or a manufacturer. For a time it was held that the only person to whom a manufacturer or vendor owed any duty was his own purchaser. If the purchaser was injured because of the negligence of the manufacturer or vendor in making the product, the purchaser could sue the vendor; but if someone else was injured, there was no liability. This rule has gradually been abandoned so that the manufacturer or seller is liable to third persons whom he should have foreseen would be injured by his negligence.

A person is under a duty of care to other persons whose presence he should reasonably anticipate, but by common law he is not under a duty to anticipate the presence of persons unlawfully on his property. The owner of the land cannot make his land unsafe for trespassers for the purpose of injuring them, as by setting spring guns.

(4) Degree of Care. The degree of care required of a person is that which an ordinarily prudent man would exercise under similar circumstances. It does not mean such a degree of care as would have prevented the harm from occurring, nor is it enough that it is just as much care as everyone else exercises. Nor is it sufficient that one has exercised the degree of care which is customary for persons in the same kind of work or business, or that one has employed the methods customarily used. If one is engaged in services requiring skill, the care, of course, must measure up to a higher standard. The degree of care exercised must be commensurate with the danger that would probably result if such care were lacking.[2] In all cases it is the

---

[2] Friese v Boston Consolidated Gas Co., 324 Mass 623, 88 NE2d 1.

diligence, care, and skill that can be reasonably expected under the circumstances. Whether one has exercised that degree of care which is required under the circumstances is a question that is determined by the jury.

(5) Contributory Negligence. Generally, one cannot recover for injuries caused by another's negligence if his own negligence has contributed to the injury. The plaintiff's negligence, however, must be a proximate cause of the injury; that is, it must contribute to the injury in order to defeat recovery.

In this connection there has developed a doctrine variously called the *doctrine of last clear chance,* the *humanitarian doctrine,* or the *doctrine of discovered peril.* Under this doctrine, although the plaintiff is negligent, the defendant is held liable if he had the last clear chance to avoid the injury. In such a case the theory is that the plaintiff's negligence is not the proximate cause and therefore does not contribute to the injury.

When the plaintiff is guilty of contributory negligence, he is ordinarily denied recovery without regard to whether the defendant was more negligent than he. The common law does not recognize comparative degrees of negligence, nor does it try to apportion the injury to the two parties in terms of the degree of their respective fault. As an exception to these principles, a number of states provide that the plaintiff's negligence does not bar his recovery but merely reduces the amount which he recovers in proportion to the degree or extent of his own negligence.

(6) Proof of Negligence. The plaintiff ordinarily has the burden of proving that the defendant did not exercise reasonable care. In some instances, however, it is sufficient for the plaintiff to prove that the injury was caused by some thing that was within the control of the defendant. If injury ordinarily results from such an object only when there is negligence, the proof of these facts is prima facie proof that the defendant was negligent. This is expressed by the maxim *res ipsa loquitur* (the occurrence or thing speaks for itself). The burden of proving that the plaintiff was contributorily negligent is upon the defendant.

§ 4:6. Division of Liability. In some instances, when two or more defendants have caused harm to the plaintiff or his property, it is difficult or impossible to determine just what damage was done by each. For example, automobile No. 1 strikes automobile No. 2, which is then struck by automobile No. 3. Ordinarily, it is impossible to determine how much of the damage to automobile No. 2 was caused by each of the other cars. Similarly, a tract of farm land down the river may be harmed because two or more factories have dumped industrial wastes into the river. It is not possible to determine how much damage each of the factories has caused the farm land.

By the older view, a plaintiff was denied the right to recover from any of the wrongdoers in these situations. The courts followed the theory that a plaintiff is not entitled to recover from a defendant unless the plaintiff can prove what harm was caused by that defendant. The modern trend of the cases is to hold that all of the defendants are jointly and severally liable for the total harm sustained by the plaintiff. (See p. 64, Maddux v Donaldson.) A variation of this trend permits the plaintiff to divide the total damage by the number of defendants and to recover that fraction of his total loss from each defendant.

(1) Liability for Act of Another. A person who commits a wrong is liable even though he employs another to do the actual harm. Thus, a person sending a messenger boy to leave a package in a building is liable for the resulting harm when the package contains a bomb. In some instances, an innocent party may also be liable for the act of another. Thus, an employer, although free of fault, may be liable for the harm caused by his employee.

§ **4:7. Who May Sue.** In some torts the wrongdoer's act gives not only the immediate victim the right to sue but also persons standing in certain relationships to the victim. Thus, under certain circumstances a husband can sue for an injury to his wife, or a parent can sue for an injury to the child. In a wrongful death action the surviving group (typically the spouse, child, and parents of the person who has been killed) have a right to sue the wrongdoer for such death.

§ **4:8. Immunity from Liability.** In certain instances, conduct that would otherwise impose tort liability upon a person does not do so because he has some immunity which shields him. This concept has a parallel in the field of contract law where certain persons, such as those under legal age, may avoid their contracts. There is also a parallel in the field of criminal law where persons who are deemed insane are not punishable for acts which would otherwise be criminal.

(1) Governments. Governments are generally immune from tort liability. This rule has been eroded by decision and in some instances by statutes, such as the Federal Tort Claims Act, which, subject to certain exceptions, permits the recovery of damages for property, personal injury, or death action claims arising from the negligent act or omission of any employee of the United States under such circumstances that the United States, "if a private person, would be liable to the claimant in accordance with the law of the place where the act or omission occurred."

Public officers, when acting within the sphere of their discretion, and higher public executive officials are personally immune from tort liability.

(2) Minors. All persons are not equally liable for torts. A minor of tender years, generally under 7, cannot be guilty of negligence or contributory negligence. Between the ages of 7 and 14, a minor is presumed to have capacity to commit a tort, although the contrary may be shown.[3] Above

---

[3] Piechalak v Liberty Trucking Co., 58 Ill App 2d 289, 208 NE2d 379.

14 years, no distinction is made in terms of age. A minor who drives a motorcycle or an automobile on the public highway must observe the same standard of care as an adult.

In many states statutes impose liability upon parents for property damage up to a stated maximum caused by the child, without regard to whether the parent was at fault or negligent in any way.[4]

*(3) **Family Relationships.*** At common law no suit could be brought by a husband against his wife and vice versa. By statute this immunity has been abolished as to torts involving property. The immunity continues in most states with respect to personal torts, whether intentional or negligent, although some two fifths of the states now allow personal tort actions between spouses. The trend of judicial decisions rejects the argument that the allowance of such suits would open the door to fraud and collusion between spouses when one of them is insured. A similar immunity exists between parent and child in most states with respect to personal tort claims.

*(4) **Charities.*** Charities were once exempt from tort law. For example, a hospital could not be held liable for the negligent harm to a patient caused by its staff or employees. Within the last three decades this immunity has been rejected in nearly two thirds of the states. It is quite likely that in the coming years it will be repudiated generally.

SECURITY FROM BUSINESS TORTS

In business dealings several kinds of torts may occur, such as defamation, embracing slander and libel; intentional causing of mental distress; false imprisonment; fraud; disparagement of goods and slander of title; infringement of trademarks, patents, and copyrights; unfair competition; wrongful interference with business relations and contracts; and combining to divert trade, trespass, and violence.

§ **4:9. Intentional Causing of Mental Distress.** When the defendant commits an act which by itself is a tort, there is ordinarily recovery for the mental distress which he causes thereby. That is, mental suffering is merely an element of the damages sustained by an injured party for an assault. The question arises whether there is liability when the actor says things to the plaintiff or does acts for the purpose of causing him emotional disturbance or distress and the plaintiff does suffer such emotional distress, perhaps even to the point of becoming physically ill from the experience.

At common law words by themselves have been held not to give rise to any liability, unless they were defamatory. Likewise, conduct designed to cause distress was not actionable. With the turn of the century, and particularly in the last quarter century, recovery has been allowed in a number of cases in which no ordinary or traditional form of tort was committed and the common element in these cases was that the defendant had willfully

---

[4] LaBonte v Federal Mutual Insurance Co., 159 Conn 252, 268 A2d 663.

subjected the plaintiff to unnecessary emotional disturbance. This result was reached when the common carrier or the hotel insulted a patron; a collection agency used unreasonable means of collection designed to harass the debtor; an outrageous practical joke was played upon the plaintiff, or his personal or physical condition was purposely exploited by such joke; the corpse of a close relative was concealed, mistreated, or interference made with the burial; or the defendant engaged in a steady campaign to intimidate a critic of the defendant's product, including illegal electronic eavesdropping.[5]

Statements made to humiliate the plaintiff because of his race, creed, or national origin will impose liability for the emotional distress caused thereby and for any physical illness which results therefrom. Generally the theory on which recovery is allowed in these cases is clouded by efforts to bring the case within the standard patterns of liability. Occasionally a court frankly recognizes that it is imposing liability merely because mental distress was intentionally caused.

§ **4:10. False Imprisonment.** False imprisonment is the intentional, unprivileged detaining of a person without his consent. It may take the extreme form of kidnapping. At the other extreme, a shopper who is detained in the store manager's office and questioned as to shoplifting is the victim of false imprisonment where there is no reasonable ground for believing that the shopper was a thief. False imprisonment also includes detention under an official arrest when there is no legal justification for that arrest.

(1) ***Detention.*** Any detention at any place by any means for any duration of time is sufficient. Stone walls are not required to make a false imprisonment. If a bank robber holds a bank teller at gun point for the purpose of preventing him from attacking the other robbers or from escaping, there is a detention. Also there is a detention when the shopper is stopped by the store detectives and not allowed to leave.

(2) ***Consent and Privilege.*** By definition, no false imprisonment occurs when the person detained consents thereto. For example, when a merchant without any justification detains a person on the suspicion of shoplifting, such detention is not a false imprisonment if the victim consents to it without any protest. If the merchant has reasonable ground for believing that the victim had been guilty of shoplifting, the action of the merchant is not false imprisonment even though the victim is detained under protest and does not consent thereto. Statutes in some states give merchants a privilege to detain persons reasonably suspected of shoplifting. This privilege protects the merchant not only with respect to detention within the store for questioning but also protects the merchant when the shopper is turned over to the police under a formal arrest.[6]

---

[5] Nader v General Motors Corp., 25 NY2d 560, 255 NE2d 765.

[6] Jacques v Sears, Roebuck & Co., 30 NY2d 466, 334 NYS2d 632, 285 NE2d 871.

When the merchant acts in a reasonable way in the exercise of his privilege, he cannot be held liable for damages for false imprisonment or on any other ground even though the victim is thereafter acquitted when tried for the crime of shoplifting.

§ 4:11. Fraud. A person is entitled to be protected from fraud and is entitled to recover damages for the harm caused by fraud. (See p. 65, Barylski v Andrews.) For the purpose of tort law, fraud has the same scope and meaning as fraud for the purpose of avoiding a contract, with the important exception that in tort law damages must be sustained by the plaintiff in addition to his reliance on the false statement.[7]

There is a significant difference in damages recoverable. If the defendant is guilty of fraud in connection with the contract, the plaintiff may recover punitive damages in addition to the ordinary compensatory damages that would be allowed in an action for breach of contract. (See p. 66, Midwest Supply, Inc. v Waters.)

§ 4:12. Defamation-Slander. Reputation is injured by *defamation,* which is a publication tending to cause one to lose the esteem of the community.[8] *Slander* is a form of actionable defamation consisting of the publication or communication to another of false spoken words or gestures.[9] Liability for slander is imposed to provide security of reputation.

(1) Damages. Whether the plaintiff must actually prove that he was injured by the slander depends upon the nature of the defamatory matter. Words that charge another with the commission of a crime involving moral turpitude and infamous punishment; that impute a disease at the present time that will exclude one from society; or that have a tendency to injure one in his business, profession, or occupation are regarded by the law as *actionable per se* because from common experience it is known that damages occur as a natural sequence of the communication of such words.[10] If defamatory matter is actionable per se, the plaintiff is not required to prove actual damage sustained in consequence of the slander. Otherwise he must do so and, if he cannot prove injury, he is not entitled to recover damages.

Under some statutes the damages recoverable may be reduced if no actual malice was present and if a retraction is properly made.[11]

An accusation of shoplifting is slanderous per se as it involves a charge which is basically larceny, and thus comes within the rule that the defamed person may recover damages for defamation when accused of a crime even though no exact damages are shown. It is sufficient that the accusation would convey to an ordinary man that the plaintiff had been accused of

---

[7] See p. 48.
[8] Restatement of the Law of Torts, § 559.
[9] § 568(2).
[10] § 570.
[11] Werner v S. Cal. Associated Newspapers, 35 Cal 2d 121, 216 P2d 825.

shoplifting even though the language was not as explicit as might be required of an indictment in a criminal prosecution for the offense.

*(2) **Privilege.*** Under certain circumstances no liability arises when false statements are published and cause damages. An *absolute privilege* exists in the case of public officers who, in the performance of their duties, should have no fear of possible liability for damages.[12]

Other circumstances may afford a *qualified* or *conditional privilege.*[13] A communication made in good faith upon a subject in which the party communicating has an interest, or in reference to which he has a right, is priviledged if made to a person having a corresponding interest or right, although it contains matter which, without this privilege, would be slanderous. Thus, a person, in protecting his interests, may in good faith charge another with the theft of his watch. A mercantile agency's credit report is privileged when made to an interested subscriber in good faith in the regular course of its business.[14] In some states a manager or other person in charge of a store has a qualified privilege; that is, he is not liable in damages for making an accusation of shoplifting if he acted in a reasonable manner in seeking to ascertain the facts. If he did not act in a reasonable manner or acted with malice, he is liable for damages to the person unjustly accused.[15] When a client falsely tells his attorney that a customer owes him money, such statement is not slander even though it is wrong. (See p. 67, Williams v Gulf Coast Collection Agency Company.)

*(3) **Malice.*** It is frequently said that there must be "malice" in order to constitute slander. This is not, however, malice in fact, but merely malice in law, which exists when the speaker is not privileged to make his defamatory statements.

§ 4:13. Defamation—Libel. Another wrong against the security of business relations takes the form of written defamation. This is known as *libel.* Although usually in writing, it may be in print, picture, or in any other permanent, visual form.[16] For example, to construct a gallows in front of another's residence is libelous.

The elements necessary to maintain an action for libel are the same as for slander. In the case of libel, however, it is not necessary, as a general rule, to allege and prove damages because damages will be presumed.[17] In other words, all forms of libel are actionable per se.

There is a conflict of authority as to the classification of defamatory statements made over the radio or television. Some courts treat such statements as libelous when read from a written script and slanderous when not.

---

[12] R § 585 et seq.
[13] §§ 593 to 598.
[14] Petition of Retailers Commercial Agency, Inc., 342 Mass 515, 174 NE2d 376.
[15] Southwest Drugs Stores v Garner, (Miss) 195 So2d 837.
[16] § 568(1).
[17] § 569.

Other courts regard the broadcasting as slander without regard to whether there was a script.

In the heat of argument, people will often say things that are exaggerated. Generally such words will be so general that they do not come within the slander per se rule. This means that the plaintiff is not entitled to recover damages unless he can show how and to what extent he was harmed by the statements. Thus, the statement of an agent of an employer that the bargaining agent for the union and the union shop steward were "gangsters" was not slander per se; it was so general a statement that it did not charge the defendant with any particular crime for which the plaintiff could be prosecuted, nor did it come within the area of slander per se. It was merely vituperation which did not impose liability in the absence of proof that it caused the plaintiff actual damage.[18]

§ **4:14. Defamation by Computer.** A person's credit standing or reputation may be damaged because a computer contains erroneous information relating to him. When the computer is part of a data bank system and the erroneous information is supplied to third persons, that could be more than merely annoying and could be damaging. Will the data bank operator or service company be held liable to the person so harmed? There does not appear to be any reported decision on this point, but it is believed that if the operator or the company has exercised reasonable care to prevent errors and to correct errors, there will not be any liability on either the actual programmer-employee operating the equipment or the management providing the computer service. Conversely, if negligence or an intent to harm is shown, existing principles of law would sustain the liability of the persons involved for what might be given a distinctive name of *defamation by computer*. It might be that liability could be avoided by supplying the person to whom the information relates with a copy of any printout of information which the data bank supplies to third persons, as this would tend to show good faith on the part of the management of the data bank operation and a reasonable effort to keep the information accurate.

Liability for defamation by computer may arise under the federal Fair Credit Reporting Act of 1970 when the person affected is a consumer. The federal Credit Card Act of 1970 further protects from defamation by computer. These acts, which are not limited to situations involving computers, are discussed in Chapter 8 on consumer protection.

§ **4:15. Disparagement of Goods and Slander of Title.** In the transaction of business one is entitled to be free from interference by means of malicious false claims or statements made by others in respect to the quality or the title of his property.[19] Actual damages must be proved by the plaintiff to have proximately resulted from the false communication by the defendant

---

[18] Williams v Rutherford Freight Lines, Inc., 10 NC App 348, 179 SE2d 319.

[19] §§ 624 and 626; Cunningham v Simpson, 1 Cal 3d 301, 81 Cal Rptr 855, 461 P2d 39.

to a third person. The plaintiff must show that in consequence thereof the third person has refrained from dealing with the plaintiff.

§ **4:16. Infringement of Trademarks.** A *trademark* is a word, name, device, symbol, or any combination of these, used by a manufacturer or seller to distinguish his goods from those of other persons. When the trademark of a particular person is used or substantially copied by another, it is said that the trademark is infringed. The owner of the trademark may sue for damages and enjoin its wrongful use.

A person who by fraudulent statements obtains the registration of a trademark in the Federal Patent Office is liable for the damages which such false registration causes anyone.

§ **4:17. Infringement of Patents.** A grant of a *patent* entitles the patentee to prevent others for a period of 17 years from making, using, or selling the particular inventions.[20] Anyone so doing without the patentee's permission is guilty of a patent infringement.

An infringement exists, even though all the parts or features of an invention are not copied, if there is a substantial identity of means, operation, and result between the original and new devices. In the case of a process, however, all successive steps or their equivalent must be copied. In the case of a combination of ingredients, the use of the same ingredients with others constitutes an infringement, except when effecting a compound essentially different in nature.

§ **4:18. Infringement of Copyrights.** A wrong similar to the infringement of a patent is the infringement of a copyright. A *copyright* is the right given by statute to prevent others for a limited time from printing, copying, or publishing a production resulting from intellectual labor. The right exists for a period of 28 years and can be renewed for another period of 28 years.

Infringement of copyright in general consists of copying the form of expression of ideas or conceptions. There is no copyright in the idea or conception itself, but only in the particular way in which it is expressed. In order to constitute an infringement, the production need not be reproduced entirely nor be exactly the same as the original. Reproduction of a substantial part of the original, although paraphrased or otherwise altered, constitutes an infringement; but appropriation of only a word or single line does not.

One guilty of infringement of copyright is liable to the owner for damages and profits, or only damages, which are to be determined by the court. The owner is also entitled to an injunction to restrain further infringement.

§ **4:19. Unfair Competition.** Unfair competition is unlawful and the person injured thereby may sue for damages or for an injunction to stop the practice, or he may report the matter to a trade commission or other agency.[21]

---

[20] As to patentability of computer programs, see p. 338.
[21] See p. 73.

It is unfair competition to imitate signs, store fronts, advertisements and packaging of goods of a competitor.[22] Thus, when one adopts a box of distinctive size, shape, and color in which to market candy, and a competitor copies the same style, form, and dress of the package, the latter may be enjoined from so doing and in some cases may be liable for damages.

Every similarity to a competitor, however, is not necessarily unfair competition. For example, the term "downtown" is merely descriptive, so the Downtown Motel cannot obtain an injunction against the use of the name Downtown Motor Inn, because a name that is merely descriptive cannot be exclusively appropriated or adopted.[23] As an exception, if the descriptive word has been used by a given business for such a long time as to be identified with the business in the public mind, a competitor cannot use that name.

The goodwill that is related to a trade name is an important business asset; and there is a judicial trend in favor of protecting a trade name from a competitor's use of a similar name, not only when such use is intentionally deceptive but also when it is merely confusing to the public.[24]

Historically the law was only concerned with protecting competitors from unfair competition by their rivals. Under consumer protection statutes most states now give protection to the consumer who is harmed by the unfair competitive practices.[25]

§ **4:20. Combinations to Divert Trade.** Business relations may be disturbed by a combination to keep third persons from dealing with another who is the object of attack. Such a combination, resulting in injury, constitutes an actionable wrong known as *conspiracy* if the object is unlawful, or if a lawful object is procured by unlawful means.

If the object of a combination is to further lawful interest of the association, no actionable wrong exists so long as lawful means are employed. For example, when employees are united in a strike, they may peacefully persuade others to withhold their patronage from the employer. On the other hand, all combinations to drive or keep away customers or prospective employees by violence, force, threats, or intimidation are actionable wrongs. To illustrate, a combination is usually treated as an unlawful conspiracy for which damages may be recovered when the customers are threatened and for this reason withdraw their patronage.

Labor laws make some combinations unfair labor practices, while other combinations to divert trade are condemned as illegal trusts.[26]

§ **4:21. Wrongful Interference with Business Relations.** One of the fundamental rights of an individual is to earn his living by selling his labor or

---

22 R § 741.

23 Region v Downtowner of Ft. Worth, (Tex Civ App) 420 SW2d 809.

24 Metropolitan Life Insurance Co. v Metropolitan Insurance Co., (DC ND Ill) 180 F Supp 682, affirmed, 277 F2d 896 CA7.

25 See Ch. 8.

26 See Ch. 5.

by engaging in trade or business. A wrongful interference with this liberty is a tort for which damages may be recovered and which, in some cases, may be restrained by an injunction.

The right to conduct one's business is, nevertheless, subject to the rights of others. Hence, the injuries suffered by one in business through legitimate competition give no right of redress.[27] It has been considered wrongful interference, however, if one destroys the business of another for a malicious purpose, even though legal means are used.[28]

§ 4:22. Interference with Contract. The tort law relating to interference with contracts and other economic relationships has increased greatly in recent years as a result of the law's seeking to impose upon the marketplace higher ethical standards to prevent the oppression of victims of improper practices. In general terms, when the defendant interferes with and brings about the breach of a contract between a third person and the plaintiff, the circumstances may be such that the plaintiff has an action in tort against the defendant for interfering with his contractual relations. Likewise, the plaintiff may have such a claim for the defendant's interfering with performance by the plaintiff of his contract.

The mere fact that the defendant's voluntary conduct has the effect of interfering with the plaintiff's contract does not establish that the defendant is liable to the plaintiff. For example, when the defendant is acting for what the law regards as his own legitimate economic end, the fact that there results a breach of contract between a third person and the plaintiff does not impose liability on the defendant.

Any lawful contract may be the heart of an action for interference with contractual relations. It is immaterial whether it relates to the performance of personal services or labor.

(1) Contracts Terminable at Will. The fact that a contract is terminable at will does not deprive it of the right to protection from interference. While by hypothesis it is true that the other contracting party could terminate the agreement whenever he chose, there may be no reason to believe that he would have terminated the agreement in the absence of the action or urging of the defendant. In such case the defendant has interfered with the great likelihood that the third person would continue to perform for the benefit of the plaintiff, as he had originally agreed to do.

If a bill collector causes an employee to lose his job, the collector is liable for damages for such interference with the debtor's employment contract.[29]

(2) Prospective Contracts. In addition to protecting existing contracts from intentional interference, tort liability results from acts intentionally committed to prevent the making of a contract.

---

[27] R § 708.
[28] § 709.
[29] Long v Newby, (Alaska) 488 P2d 719.

To illustrate, an action may be brought for slander of title when the malicious false statements of the defendant as to the plaintiff's ownership of property scares a buyer away and prevents the plaintiff from making a sale. Increasingly the concept of protection from interference with expected economic gain has been expanded to protect prospective or possible contracts relating to all subjects.

*(3) **Requirement of Malice.*** There is no liability for interference with contractual relations unless such interference is malicious. The term "malicious" is misleading because it may mean either (a) acting with actual malice, that is, the desire to harm for the sheer sake of causing harm, or (b) the infliction of harm only as a matter of competition in order to advance the actor's personal interest, rather than to inflict injury on the plaintiff for its own sake. The fact that the defendant knows that he is harming the plaintiff by his actions is not the test of whether the defendant is liable for the harm caused the plaintiff, for the defendant may still be not liable when he is acting to further his own interests, even though he is well aware that by doing so he will interfere with the plaintiff's contract. The problem is even more acute when a striking labor union acts for the purpose of advancing its own interests and does so by intentionally interfering with the performance of the plaintiff-employer's contracts, as by striking and making it impossible for him to fill such contracts.

The legitimate self-interest, the existence of which protects the defendant from liability, may be a duty on the part of the defendant to act to protect others. Accordingly, an officer of a corporation or an employee is not liable for inducing a breach of contract if in good faith he persuades the corporation to refuse to recognize the contract, when it is his responsibility to give such advice and he honestly believes that there is no existing contract or that there is a valid defense to the contract. (See p. 69, Wilson v McClenny.)

§ 4:23. Violence. Statutes in many states impose upon counties and cities liability for harm caused by rioting mobs.[30] Some statutes extend only to property damage, but others impose liability for personal injuries or death. The statute may define the term "mob" although ordinarily it does not do so. A police officer who kills or injures someone in the performance of his duties is not a "mob" within the meaning of the statutes here considered. Some statutes are so drafted that liability is imposed only when the mob shows or evidences an intent to punish or exercise "correctional power" over its victim.

The term "property" in a mob violence statute generally applies only to tangible property and does not authorize recovery for loss of profits or goodwill resulting from business interruption.[31] Under a statute or ordinance

---

[30] Roy v Hampton, 108 NH 51, 226 A2d 870.

[31] A & B Auto Stores v Newark, 103 NJ Super 559, 248 A2d 258.

which refers to liability for property "injured or destroyed," it is generally sufficient to show that the property was stolen or looted, although there is some authority to the contrary. The fact that the government was unable to prevent the harm or damage is no defense to liability under such statutes.

§ **4:24. Trespass to the Person.** *Trespass to the person* consists of any contact with the victim's person to which he has not consented. It thus includes what is technically described as a battery. It likewise includes an assault in which the victim apprehends the commission of a battery, but he is in fact not touched, and includes false imprisonment. There is liability also for intentionally causing mental stress that results in physical harm to or illness of the victim.[32]

As an aspect of the freedom of the person from unreasonable interference, the law has come to recognize and give constitutional protection to a *right of privacy*. This right is most commonly invaded in one of the following ways: (1) invasion of physical privacy, as by planting a microphone in a person's home; (2) giving unnecessary publicity to personal matters of the plaintiff's life, such as his financial status or his past career; (3) false public association of the plaintiff with some product or principle, such as indicating that he endorses a product or is in favor of a particular law, when such is not the fact; or (4) commercially exploiting the plaintiff's name or picture, as using them in advertising without his permission.

§ **4:25. Trespass to Land.** A *trespass to land* consists of any unpermitted entry below, on, across, or above land. This rule is modified to permit the proper flight of aircraft above the land so long as it does not interfere with a proper use of the land.

§ **4:26. Trespass to Personal Property.** An illegal invasion of property rights with respect to property other than land constitutes a *trespass to personal property* when done negligently or intentionally. When done in good faith and without negligence, there is no liability, in contrast with the case of trespass to land when good faith is not a defense.

Negligent damage to personal property, as in the case of negligent collision of automobiles, imposes liability for harm done. Intentional damage to personal property will impose liability for the damage done and also may justify exemplary or punitive damages.

Conversion occurs when personal property is taken by the wrongdoer and kept from its true owner or prior possessor. Thus a bank clerk commits conversion when he takes money from the bank. Conversion is thus seen to be the civil side of the crimes relating to stealing. The good faith of the converter, however, is not a defense, and an innocent buyer of stolen goods is liable for damages for converting them.[33]

---

[32] Tate v Canonica, 180 Cal App 2d 898, 5 Cal Rptr 28.
[33] McRae v Bandy, 270 Ala 12, 115 So2d 479.

CASES FOR CHAPTER 4

Maddux v Donaldson

362 Mich 425, 108 NW2d 33 (1961)

Maddux was injured when the car in which she was riding was hit by a skidding truck driven by Donaldson, and then by the car following the truck. Maddux sued Donaldson for injuries caused by both collisions. Donaldson claimed that he could only be sued for those injuries which Maddux could show were caused by him and not for the total amount of damages. Because Maddux could not show what part of her injuries were caused by Donaldson, the trial court dismissed the action. Maddux appealed.

SMITH, J. . . . This is one of the most baffling of our current legal problems, critical because of the extensive use of expressways upon which large numbers of cars travel at high speeds in close proximity to one another. . . . What we have is injury to plaintiffs resulting from the independent and tortious acts of two tort-feasors.

There is authority, in this situation, that plaintiff must separate the injuries, ascribing some to one tort-feasor and the balance to the other, much as a housewife separates the colored and the white goods before laundering. Such authority concludes that if plaintiff cannot make such differentiation, he cannot recover from either. This type of decision is well illustrated by the case of Adams v Hall, 1829, 2 Vt 9. In this case an owner of sheep suffered loss to his flock through the depredations of two dogs. The owners he sued jointly. It was shown at the trial, however, that they were not joint owners. In addition, there was no testimony as to which dog killed which sheep. In approving a [dismissal of the action] it was held that neither owner was liable for the actions of the other's dog, merely because they "did the mischief in company."

However defensible such a result may have been in this and cases similar in principle in an agrarian economy shortly after the American Revolution (and even this is open to question), we do not regard it as precedent governing the liability of automobile owners in what are known as "chain collisions" on today's highways. It should be unnecessary to spell out the differences between the social problems presented or the judicial policies involved in their solution. When we impose upon an injured plaintiff the necessity of proving which impact did which harm in a chain collision situation, what we are actually expressing is a judicial policy that it is better that a plaintiff, injured through no fault of his own, take nothing, than that a tortfeasor pay more than his theoretical share of the damages accruing out of a confused situation which his wrong has helped to create. . . .

It is our conclusion that if there is competent testimony, adduced either by plaintiff or defendant, the injuries are factually and medically separable, and that the liability for all such injuries and damages, or parts thereof, may be allocated with reasonable certainty to the impacts in turn, the jury will be instructed accordingly and mere difficulty in so doing will not relieve the triers of the facts of this responsibility. This merely follows the general rule that "where the independent concurring acts have caused distinct and separate injuries to the plaintiff, or where some reasonable means of apportioning the damages is evident, the courts generally will not hold the tort-feasors jointly and severally liable."

But if, on the other hand, the triers of the facts conclude that they cannot reasonably make the division of liability between the tort-feasors, this is the point where the road of authority divides. Much ancient authority, not in truth precedent, would say that the case is now over, and that plaintiff shall take nothing. Some modern courts, as well, hold that this is merely the case of the marauding dogs and the helpless sheep relitigated in the setting of a modern highway. The conclusion is erroneous. . . .

Here, then, is the essence of the problem—Where is the likelihood of injustice? We think it is in denying the blameless victim of traffic chain collision any recovery whatever. We perceive no reason why his tort-feasors should escape liability because of the very complexity of the injury created by their wrong. . . .

[Judgment reversed and new trial ordered.]

BLACK, J. (concurring in reversal). Until now the Michigan rule has been settled. Where two or more wrongdoers separately cause the plaintiff to suffer an unknown or uncertain part or portion of the damages he has shown, each—hitherto—stood responsible to the plaintiff only for the harm caused by his tort, however difficult it may have been to establish the same. . . .

Now we affirm that, where the trier or triers of fact find they cannot ascertain the amount of damages each wrongdoer has inflicted, then such trier or triers are authorized to assess the plaintiff's damages against any one or all of such wrongdoers on the ground that the latter have—in law—participated in the infliction of "a single, indivisible injury." . . .

Barylski v Andrews

(Mo App) 439 SW2d 536 (1969)

Bert Andrews and his wife owned a home which had been seriously damaged by fire in 1953. They repaired the house, covering the burnt portions in the basement with sheetrock and white paint. In 1958 they sold the house to Barylski and his wife without informing them of the fire damage. Mrs. Andrews told the buyers that the house was "in fine condition." When Barylski and his wife discovered the fire damage four years later, they sued Andrews and his wife. From a judgment in favor of the plaintiffs for $1,500, the defendants appealed.

NORMILE, S.J. . . . [When the house was first shown to the plaintiffs,] the house was newly painted, had new hardwood floors and a built-in kitchen. . . .

Appellants urged that . . . it was not shown that an intentional misrepresentation of a material fact was made by the defendants to the plaintiffs and . . . there was no duty on defendants' part to mention the previous fire damage to the house in the absence of inquiry by the plaintiffs.

Fraud is never presumed but must be established by evidence, and the burden of proof is on the party who charges fraud. . . . However, it is not necessary that the elements be established by direct testimony but may be established by facts and circumstances. . . .

The tendency of modern decisions is not to extend, but to restrict the rule requiring diligence and similar rules, such as *caveat emptor,* and the rule granting immunity for dealers' talk; to condemn the falsehood of the fraud-feasor rather than the credulity of his victim. . . .

Was there a representation? In determining this question, we must consider not only the statement by Betty Andrews that "The house is in fine condition," but also the actions of both defendants in concealing the condition of the home and the failure of both to disclose this to the plaintiffs. . . . "A representation is not confined to words or positive assertions; it may consist as well of deeds, acts, or artifices of a nature calculated to mislead another and thereby to allow the fraud-feasor to obtain an undue advantage over him. . . . If he fails to disclose an intrinsic circumstance that is vital to the contract, knowing that the other party is acting upon the presumption that no such fact exists, it would seem quite as much a fraud as if he had expressly denied it, or asserted the reverse, or used any artifice to conceal it, or to call off the buyer's attention from it." . . .

. . . The seriously burned condition of the home . . . was concealed by the painting, papering, plastering, and wallboarding. . . . The plaintiffs could not have been charged with knowledge of this condition. In fact, it was so well concealed that it was not discovered until four years after the purchase of the home. . . .

. . . The acts of both defendants in covering and painting the burned and charred sills, joists, timbers, and other interior areas did affirmatively suppress and cover up the truth and withdrew the plaintiffs' attention from the real facts. The statement of defendant, Betty Andrews, that "The house is in fine condition" also tended affirmatively to cover up or disguise the truth and to distract the plaintiffs' attention from the real facts as to the condition of the home. In this case, the silence of the defendants as to the fire damage related to a material matter known to them. Their duty to speak out arose from their superior knowledge which was not within the fair and reasonable reach of the plaintiffs. . . .

Assuming a false representation by the defendants by their concealment of the condition of the home and by the statement of one defendant designed to suppress the truth, was the resulting false representation material? . . .

Defendants knew of the fire, of the condition of the house, and of the plaintiffs' ignorance of this condition. It is obvious that they intended that plaintiffs purchase the house under this misapprehension. The plaintiffs were obviously ignorant of the concealment of this latent defect. They obviously relied on the truth of the representations as to condition by making the purchase. They were entitled to rely on this representation since the truth was not readily ascertainable to them where a latent defect was involved, and they lacked equal facilities for learning the truth concerning the condition of the house. Thus, all the elements of a fraud were demonstrated and the case was properly submitted to the jury who found in favor of the plaintiffs.

Appellant urges that the Court erred in giving plaintiffs' verdict-directing instruction. However, the only argument made under this point in appellants' brief was that the defendants had repaired the house to make it liveable rather than with an intent to defraud, and that all the evidence was that the house remained structurally safe. In this case, the issue of "fraudulent intent" was for the jury to determine. . . . The structural safety of the house is not relevant where its burned condition, though covered, very materially affected its value. . . .

[Judgment affirmed.]

Midwest Supply, Inc. v Waters

— Nev —, 510 P2d 876 (1973)

Waters advertised that he possessed expertise in tax matters. Relying on such advertising, Midwest Supply had Waters prepare its federal income tax return. Waters had a new employee prepare the return. The new employee was not qualified and the tax return was defective. Midwest was required to pay additional taxes and sued Waters for damages. The jury returned a verdict in favor of Midwest for compensatory damages and also for $100,000 of punitive damages. Judgment was entered on this verdict and Waters appealed.

GUNDERSON, J. . . . Attracted by public advertisements, respondents contacted appellants in 1966 to ascertain if they might file amended personal and partnership income tax returns, relocating to respondents Wallace Waters and Margaret Waters a larger share of an investment tax credit from business equipment purchased in 1964. In February of 1967, appellants prepared for respondents original tax returns for 1966, and nine amended tax returns for 1963, 1964, and 1965. Such returns claimed refunds for taxes previously paid. Although the amended returns showed that the partnership had disposed of the business equipment in 1965, the refund claims were predicated on investment tax credit attributable to that equipment.

At the time, the Internal Revenue Code required repayment of any investment tax credit previously claimed, if the equipment was not retained for the prescribed qualifying period. Hence, after respondents improperly received refunds that appellants erroneously caused them to claim, an Internal Revenue Service audit resulted in assessment to respondents of additional taxes. Enforced collection procedures for these additional taxes, including the filing of tax liens, and numerous levies on wages and bank accounts, caused severe hardship to respondents.

1. Appellants contend the trial court erred in instructing the jury as to fraud because there was no evidence that appellants intentionally misled respondents when undertaking to prepare their tax returns. We disagree. The record contains evidence of willful and wanton misrepresentations, in appellants' advertising and in their internal business practices, specifically aimed at deceiving the members of the public who might rely on appellants for tax expertise.

In their public advertising, appellants "guaranteed accurate tax preparation," stating that they would prepare "complete returns—$5 up." Thereby, appellants suggested their employees' expertise in preparing all types of tax returns.

Despite this, they made no effort to hire employees with even rudimentary skill in accounting or in the preparation of tax returns. Appellants sometimes administered to new employees a 72-hour course in tax return preparation, but apparently even this minimal training was not a prerequisite to serving the public. The temporary employee who prepared respondents' tax returns had been employed in construction work for several years prior to his employment with appellants, and had received no formal training in the preparation of tax returns, either prior to or during his employment with appellants.

Appellants' manual instructed their office managers to counter inquiries concerning the qualifications of employees by saying that "[the company] has been preparing taxes for 20 years." The manual further instructed office managers not to refer to an employee as a "specialist or tax expert," but never to correct news reporters or commentators if they referred to employees in this manner.

In our view, such evidence supports a determination of fraud. "The suppression of a material fact which a party is bound in good faith to disclose is equivalent to a false representation, since it constitutes an indirect representation that such fact does not exist." . . .

3. Finally, appellants contend the jury's award of $100,000 punitive damages was actuated by passion and prejudice.

Our law authorizes punitive damages in proper cases to punish and deter culpable conduct. . . . The amount appropriate to these purposes, which lies in the discretion of the court, need bear no fixed relationship to the compensatory damages awarded. . . . At trial, appellants' net worth was established at six million dollars. The jury was properly instructed, and under the circumstances of this case, we do not find the jury's award of punitive damages excessive. . . .

[Judgment affirmed.]

Williams v Gulf Coast Collection Agency Co.

(Mo App) 493 SW2d 367 (1973)

Williams had a Standard Oil credit card. Through some mistake the Gulf Coast Collection Agency told its attorney that Williams was delinquent and that the attorney should bring suit against Williams. When Williams learned of this, he sued Gulf Coast and claimed that the false statement as to his account was libel per se, which would entitle him to recover damages without actual proof of injury. The court dismissed his case. He appealed.

Dowd, C.J. . . . Plaintiff had sued the defendant for libel per se because of a letter sent by defendant to a lawyer. This letter stated that plaintiff's credit card account with Standard Oil Division of American Motor Company was delinquent and that the plaintiff had not been willing to work out a reasonable schedule of payment. The letter then authorized the lawyer to begin legal action against the plaintiff. Gulf Coast also sent copies of this letter to the plaintiff and to Standard Oil.

The defendant's records were in error, however, and plaintiff's account was actually paid in full. Three months before Gulf Coast sent the letter to the lawyer, Standard Oil had written plaintiff informing him that defendant had been told to discontinue collection action and that plaintiff should disregard any further collection efforts by Gulf Coast. One month after its first letter to the plaintiff, Standard Oil again wrote him, apologizing for the errors in handling his account.

As stated, plaintiff's petition alleged libel per se. The Missouri statute defining libel reads: "A libel is the malicious defamation of a person made public by any printing, writing, sign, picture, representation or effigy tending to provoke him to wrath or expose him to public hatred, contempt or ridicule, or to deprive him of the benefits of public confidence and social intercourse. . . ." . . .

The controlling words in this section are "malicious defamation," and it must be shown that words constitute a defamation before the court will apply the public hatred, contempt feature. . . . "Defamation includes the idea of calumny, aspersion by lying; the injury of another's reputation in that way. To defame is to speak evil of one maliciously, to dishonor, to render infamous." . . .

. . . We do not believe the words in the defendant's letter constitute libel per se under the controlling words "malicious defamation." . . . No reasonable construction of the published words here, taken by themselves, can be said to be malicious defamation so as to constitute libel per se. . . .

. . . . It is not libel per se to publish of one that he owes a debt which is long past due where that charge does not affect the person in his business, vocation, or profession. . . .

We, therefore, hold that defendant's letter did not constitute libel per se. . . .

[Judgment affirmed.]

Sears, Roebuck & Co. v Stiffel Co.

376 US 225 (1964)

Stiffel manufactured a floor lamp which it patented. After this lamp became popular, Sears, Roebuck & Co. made an identical lamp, which they then sold successfully at a lower price. Stiffel sued Sears for an injunction claiming that his patents had been infringed and that Sears was guilty of unfair competition. The District Court held the patents invalid but granted an injunction. Sears appealed.

BLACK, J. . . . The District Court, after holding the patents invalid for want of invention, went on to find as a fact that Sears' lamp was "a substantially exact copy" of Stiffel's and that the two lamps were so much alike, both in appearance and in functional details, "that confusion between them is likely, and some confusion has already occurred." On these findings the court held Sears guilty of unfair competition, enjoined Sears "from unfairly competing with [Stiffel] by selling or attempting to sell pole lamps identical to or confusingly similar to" Stiffel's lamp, and ordered an accounting to fix profits and damages resulting from Sears' "unfair competition."

The Court of Appeals affirmed. . . . That court held that to make out a case of unfair competition under Illinois law, there was no need to show that Sears had been "palming off" its lamps as Stiffel lamps; Stiffel had only to prove that there was a "likelihood of confusion as to the source of the products"—that the two articles were sufficiently identical that customers could not tell who had made a particular one. . . .

The grant of a patent is the grant of a statutory monopoly. . . .

When the patent expires, the monopoly created by it expires, too, and the right to make the article—including the right to make it in precisely the shape it carried when patented—passes to the public. . . .

Obviously a state could not, consistently with the Supremacy Clause of the Constitution, extend the life of a patent beyond its expiration date or give a patent on an article which lacked the level of invention required for federal patents. To do either would run counter to the policy of Congress of granting patents only to true inventions, and then only for a limited time. Just as a state cannot encroach upon the federal patent laws directly, it cannot, under some other law, such as that forbidding unfair competition, give protection of a kind that clashes with the objectives of the federal patent laws.

In the present case the "pole lamp" sold by Stiffel has been held not to be entitled to the protection of either a mechanical or a design patent. An unpatentable article, like an article on which the patent has expired, is in the public domain and may be made and sold by whoever chooses to do so. What Sears did was to copy Stiffel's design and to sell lamps almost identical to those sold by Stiffel. That it had every right to do under the federal patent laws. That Stiffel originated the pole lamp and made it popular is immaterial. . . . To allow a state by use of its law of unfair competition to prevent the copying of an article which represents too slight an advance to be patented would be to permit the state to block off from the public something which federal law has said belongs to the public. The result would be that while federal law grants only . . . 17 years' protection to genuine inventions, . . . states could allow perpetual protection to articles too lacking in novelty to merit any patent at all under federal constitutional standards. This would be too great an encroachment on the federal patent system to be tolerated. . . .

Of course, there could be "confusion" as to who had manufactured these nearly identical articles. But mere inability of the public to tell two identical articles apart is not enough to support an injunction against copying or an award of damages for copying that which the federal patent laws permit to be copied. . . . Because of the federal patent laws a state may not, when the article is unpatented and uncopyrighted, prohibit the copying of the article itself or award damages for such copying. . . . The judgment below did both and in so doing gave Stiffel the equivalent of a patent monopoly on its unpatented lamp. That was error, and Sears is entitled to a judgment in its favor. . . .

[Judgment reversed.]

Wilson v McClenny

262 NC 121, 136 SE2d 569 (1964)

Before a new corporation, Gateway Life Insurance Co., was formed, an agreement was made between the plaintiff (Wilson) and the defendants (McClenny and others) that the plaintiff should be the president of Gateway and the defendants should be the other officers and directors and that all should acquire certain amounts of stock. The plaintiff was hired by the corporation as president in consequence of this agreement but on a yearly contract. When the contract came up for renewal, the directors who had signed this agreement and the other directors voted against renewal of the contract because the plaintiff had a serious drinking problem and had voluntarily committed himself to an institution for inebriates for 21 days. The plaintiff sued the defendants in tort because, as directors, they had interfered with his contract by voting against its renewal when, in fact, his drinking had not interfered with the conduct of the business. From a judgment against Wilson, he appealed.

SHARP, J. . . . Plaintiff's second cause of action is in tort for the wrongful interference by defendants with the contractual relation existing between him and Gateway. . . . "The overwhelming weight of authority in this nation is that an action in tort lies against an outsider who knowingly, intentionally, and unjustifiably induces one party to a contract to breach it to the damage of the other party. . . ."

The contract here was for one year only, but it is a fair inference that both plaintiff and Gateway expected it to be renewed from year to year as long as plaintiff was able to perform his duties. . . . Defendants here are not *outsiders*. They are all stockholders and directors of Gateway. As stockholders, they had a financial interest in the corporation; as directors, they owed it fidelity and the duty to use due care in the management of its business. . . . As either directors or stockholders, they were privileged purposely to cause the corporation not to renew plaintiff's contract as president if, in securing this action, they did not employ any improper means and if they acted in good faith to protect the interests of the corporation. In other words, because of their financial interest and fiduciary relationship they had a qualified privilege to interfere with contractual relations between the corporation and a third party. . . . To hold otherwise, "would tend to hinder directors of a corporation from acting on their judgment for the interest of their corporation." . . .

Directors . . . may not be subjected to liability for acting on the assumption that it might prejudice the corporation to retain as president a man with a drinking problem who had been committed to a State institution as an inebriate. Plaintiff offered no evidence tending to show that the defendants abused their privilege as directors.

The question whether plaintiff's use of alcohol had *actually* rendered him unfit to perform his duties or prejudiced the business of Gateway is not determinative of the [plaintiff's] cause of action. An error in judgment about this would not impose liability upon the directors. . . .

[Judgment affirmed.]

QUESTIONS AND CASE PROBLEMS

1. What is the objective of each of the following rules of law?

(a) In some areas of law, liability for harm exists without regard to whether there was any negligence or intention to cause harm.

(b) Geographical and descriptive names cannot ordinarily be adopted as trademarks.

2. Burdett repaired a neon sign on the restaurant of Cinquanta. They disagreed whether Cinquanta or his insurance company should pay for the work. Burdett and some friends went to the restaurant and ordered an expensive meal for which they refused to pay. A heated argument followed in which Burdett stated to Cinquanta, "I don't like doing business with crooks. You're a deadbeat. You've owed me $155 for three or four months. You're crooks." Cinquanta sued Burdett for slander but did not show in what way he had been damaged by these remarks. Burdett claimed that he was not liable for slander in the absence of proof of any damages as his remarks were not slanderous per se. Decide. [Cinquanta v Burdett, 154 Colo 37, 388 P2d 779]
3. Anheuser-Busch holds a trademark registry for the names of Budweiser and Bud as applied to beer which it manufactures and sells under the slogan, "Where there's life . . . there's Bud." It spent millions of dollars advertising with this slogan. Chemical Corporation of America manufactured a combined floor wax and insecticide which is marketed under the slogan of "Where there's life . . . there's bugs." In addition, there was a similarity between the pattern, background, and stage settings of the television commercials employed by both companies. Anheuser-Busch sued for an injunction to prevent the use of such a slogan. The defendant objected on the ground that the parties were not in competing business. Should the injunction be issued? [Chemical Corp. v Anheuser-Busch, (CA5 Fla) 306 F2d 433, cert den 372 US 965]
4. The Attorney General of the State of Washington informed the news media that a proceeding had been started by him against a dealer because of alleged violations of the State Consumer Protection Act. The dealer sued the State claiming that this was libelous. Decide. [Gold Seal Chinchillas, Inc. v Washington, 69 Wash 2d 828, 420 P2d 698]
5. Henry Niederman was walking on a center city pavement with his small son. An automobile driven by Brodsky went out of control, ran up on the sidewalk, and struck a fire hydrant, a litter pole and basket, a newsstand, and Niederman's son. The car did not touch Niederman, but the shock and fright caused damage to his heart. He sued Brodsky for the harm that he sustained as the result of Brodsky's negligence. Brodsky defended on the ground that he was not liable because he had not touched Niederman. Was this a valid defense? [Niederman v Brodsky, 436 Pa 401, 261 A2d 84]
6. Catalano ran a gasoline service station which was licensed by the State of New York to conduct inspections of motor vehicles. Capital Cities Broadcasting Corporation prepared and televised a "news special" on the subject of the difficulty of obtaining an automobile inspection. It sent an on-the-spot interviewer and photographer to Catalano's station. Catalano, believing that the interviewer was a customer, told her that he could not inspect her automobile because the space in the station was filled with cars being repaired but that, as soon as one of the car stalls was empty, he would take the interviewer's car. This discussion was recorded by the interviewer by means of a concealed tape recorder; but before it was televised, it was edited by eliminating the explanation given by Catalano and thus merely broadcasted his flat refusal to inspect the car. Catalano claimed that this caused him a loss of business and sued Capital for damages. Was it liable? [Catalano v Capital Cities Broadcasting Corp. 313 NYS2d 52]

7. Giles, a guest at a Pick Hotel, wanted to remove his brief case from the right-hand side of the front seat of his auto. To support himself while so doing, he placed his left hand on the center door pillar of the right-hand side of the car. The hotel bellboy closed the rear door of the car without noticing Giles' hand. One of Giles' fingers was smashed by the closing of the door and thereafter had to be amputated. Giles sued the Pick Hotels Corp. Was he entitled to recover? [Giles v Pick Hotels Corp. (CA6 Mich) 232 F2d 887]
8. A statute required that air vent shafts on hotel roofs have parapets at least 30 inches high. Edgar Hotel had parapets only 27 inches high. Nunneley was visiting a registered guest at the Edgar Hotel. She placed a mattress on top of a parapet. When she sat on the mattress, the parapet collapsed and she fell into the air shaft and was injured. She sued the hotel, claiming that its breach of the statute as to the height of the parapets constituted negligence. Decide. [Nunneley v Edgar Hotel, 36 Cal 2d 493, 225 P2d 497]
9. Carrigan, a district manager of Simples Time Recorder Company, was investigating complaints of mismanagement of the Jackson office of the company. He called at the home of Hooks, the secretary of that office. She expressed the opinion that part of the trouble was caused by stealing of parts and equipment by McCall, another employee. McCall was later discharged and sued Hooks for slander. Was she liable? [Hooks v McCall, (Miss) 272 So2d 925]
10. Morris insured his automobile with the South Texas Lloyds. He drove it to a local grocery store and parked on the grocery store lot, leaving the keys in the ignition. While he was in the store, Jones drove the car away without permission and wrecked it. Lloyds paid the loss to Morris and then sued Jones to recover the money which it had paid Morris. Jones denied liability on the grounds that (1) a statute prohibited leaving ignition keys in an unattended vehicle parked on a street, and (2) Morris had been negligent in leaving his keys in the car on the parking lot. Were these defenses valid? [South Texas Lloyds v Jones, (La App) 273 So2d 853]
11. *A*, *B*, and *C* owned land. They did some construction work on their land which prevented the free flow of surface water and caused a flooding of land owned by *D*. *D* sued *A* for the damage caused his land by the flooding. *A* claimed that *D* could not hold him liable for any damage since *D* could not prove how much of the total damage had been caused by *A*, and how much by *B* and *C*, and that in any event, *A* could not be liable for more than ⅓ of the total damage sustained by *D*. Decide. [See Thorson v Minot, (ND) 153 NW2d 764]

5 Government Regulation

The wisdom of whether government should regulate business or whether the free forces of competition should be relied upon to solve a problem presents questions which lie within the domain of disciplines in economics, political science, humanities, and related areas. The problems of government regulation today are primarily what to regulate and how to do it.

§ 5:1. Power to Regulate. The states, by virtue of their police power, may regulate business in all of its aspects so long as they do not impose an unreasonable burden on interstate commerce or any activity of the federal government. The federal government may impose any regulation upon any phase of business that is required by "the economic needs of the nation." [1]

For the most part, there are no significant constitutional limitations on the power of government, state or federal, to regulate business. As long as the regulation applies uniformly to all members within the same class, it is likely that it will be held valid.[2]

§ 5:2. Regulation of Production, Distribution, and Financing. In order to protect the public from harm, government may establish health and purity standards for food, drugs, and cosmetics, and protect consumers from false advertising and labeling. Without regard to the nature of the product, government may regulate business with respect to what materials may be used, the quantity of a product that may be produced or grown, and the price at which the finished product is to be sold. Government may also engage in competition with private enterprises or own and operate an industry.

Under its commerce power the federal government may regulate all methods of interstate transportation and communication, and a like power is exercised by each state over its intrastate traffic. The financing of business is directly affected by the national government in creating a national currency and in maintaining a federal reserve bank system. State and other national laws may also affect financing by regulating the contracts and documents used in financing, such as bills of lading and commercial paper.

---

[1] American Power & Light Co. v SEC, 329 US 90.

[2] See Ronald A. Anderson, *Government and Business* (3d ed; Cincinnati: South-Western Publishing Co., 1966), Ch. 4.

§ 5:3. Regulation of Competition. The federal government, and the states in varying degrees, prohibit unfair methods of competition. Frequently a commission is established to determine, subject to review by the courts, whether a given practice comes within the general class of unfair methods of competition. In other instances the statute specifically defines the practice that is condemned.

The Congress has declared "unlawful" all "unfair methods of competition" and has created a Federal Trade Commission to administer the law. The FTC has held that it is unfair to use certain schemes to obtain customers, such as making gifts to employees for their influence, making gifts offering so-called "free" articles or services, offering benefits of memberships in a fictitious society or a fictitious membership in a given society, offering pretended guaranties, offering pretended "free trial" offers, offering pretended "valuable" premiums, making offers without intention to supply the goods, making fake demonstrations, securing signatures by trick, and lotteries.

In the current decade a shift of emphasis is taking place in appraising methods of doing business. Instead of harm to competitors being the sole consideration, the effect upon the consumer is being given increasing recognition. Many practices that were condemned earlier only because they would harm a competitor by diverting customers from him are now condemned because such practices prevent the customer from obtaining his money's worth.

The FTC has also condemned the practice of using harassing tactics, such as coercion by refusing to sell, boycotting, discrimination, disparagement of a competitor or his products, enforcing payment wrongfully, cutting off or restricting the market, securing and using confidential information, spying on competitors, and inducing breach of customer contracts. Another form of unfair competition that has been condemned is misrepresentation by appropriating business or corporate names, simulating trade or corporate names, appropriating trademarks, simulating the appearance of a competitor's goods, simulating a competitor's advertising, using deceptive brands or labels, and using false and misleading advertising.

In many states, statutes prevent price wars by prohibiting the sale below cost of goods generally or of particular kinds of goods.[3]

§ 5:4. Regulation of Prices. Governments, both national and state, may regulate prices. This may be done directly by the lawmaker, that is, the Congress or the state legislature, or it may be delegated to an administrative office or agency. There is a conflict of authority as to whether private persons may participate in the determination of price. Thus, the state courts disagree as to whether the fair trade laws may constitutionally bind nonsigners.

The federal Clayton Act of 1914, applicable to interstate and foreign commerce, prohibits price discrimination between different buyers of commodities "where the effect of such discrimination may be substantially to

---

[3] Avella v Almac's, Inc., 100 RI 195, 211 A2d 665.

lessen competition or tend to create a monopoly in any line of commerce." (See p. 80, Moore v Mead's Fine Bread Co.)

Discrimination is expressly permitted when it can be justified on the basis of: (a) difference in grade, quality, or quantity involved; (b) the cost of the transportation involved in making the sale; or (c) when the sale is made at the lower price in good faith in order to meet competition.

The Robinson-Patman Act of 1936 permits price differentials based on differences in methods or quantities. Price differentials are also permitted because of the deterioration of goods or when the seller in good faith is making a close-out sale of a particular line of goods. The Robinson-Patman Act reaffirms the right of a seller to select his customers and to refuse to deal with anyone he chooses so long as he acts in good faith and not for the purpose of restraining trade.

The federal law prohibits the furnishing of advertising or other services that, when rendered to one purchaser but not another, will have the effect of granting the former a price discrimination or lower rate. It is made illegal for a seller to accept any fee or commission in connection with the sale except for services actually rendered and unless his services are equally available to all on the same terms. The act makes either the giving or the receiving of any illegal price discrimination a criminal offense.

§ 5:5. Prevention of Monopolies and Combinations. To protect the public from monopolies and combinations in restraint of trade, almost all of the states have enacted antitrust statutes.

The federal antitrust act, known as the Sherman Act,[4] is applicable to both sellers and buyers. It provides that [§ 1] "Every contract, combination in the form of a trust or otherwise, or conspiracy, in restraint of trade or commerce among the several states, or with foreign nations, is declared to be illegal. [§ 2] Every person who shall monopolize, or attempt to monopolize, or combine or conspire with any other person or persons to monopolize any part of the trade or commerce among the several states, or with foreign nations, shall be deemed guilty of a misdemeanor.[5] (See p. 81, Mandeville Island Farms v American Crystal Sugar Co.)

The punishment fixed for the violation of either of these provisions is a fine not exceeding $50,000, or imprisonment not exceeding one year, or both. In addition to this criminal penalty, the law provides for an injunction to stop the unlawful practice and permits the victim of such practices to sue the wrongdoers and recover from them three times the damages that he has sustained.

(1) The Rule of Reason and Industrial Giants. The general approach of the Supreme Court of the United States to the trust problem has

---

[4] This Act has been amended by the Clayton Act, the Federal Trade Commission Act, the Shipping Act, and other legislation.

[5] 15 USC, Ch. 1, §§ 1 and 2.

been that an agreement is not automatically or per se to be condemned as a restraint of interstate commerce merely because it creates a power or a potential to monopolize interstate commerce. It is only when the restraint actually imposed is unreasonable that the practice is unlawful.

Under Section 2 of the Act one man or corporation may violate the law if he or it monopolizes or attempts to monopolize interstate commerce. To some extent the question of bigness, at least when it results from merger, has been met by Congress by amending Section 7 of the Clayton Act to provide that a merger of corporations doing interstate business shall be illegal when the effect of the acquisition by one corporation of all or any part of the assets of the other "may be substantially to lessen competition, or to tend to create a monopoly."[6]

(2) Price-Fixing. *Horizontal price-fixing,* that is, agreements between persons performing similar economic functions, such as agreements between manufacturers or between distributors, is illegal under the federal law without regard to whether the price so fixed is reasonable or fair. *Vertical resale price agreements,* that is, agreements made between a manufacturer and his distributor or distributors, a distributor and his dealer or dealers, and so on, are generally valid.[7]

Price-fixing agreements otherwise invalid are not made valid by the fact that they may have been intended to protect, or that they do have the effect of protecting, consumers. Thus the federal antitrust law is violated by an agreement of manufacturers that they will not raise the price above a specified maximum, and also by an agreement made by a hospital subscription plan and druggists that the latter would sell drugs to participating hospitals at fixed prices.[8]

(3) Stock and Director Control. The federal Clayton Act prohibits the purchase by a corporation of the stock of another corporation engaged in interstate or foreign commerce when the effect is to lessen competition substantially, or when it restrains commerce or tends to create a monopoly. (See p. 82, US v du Pont.)

The Clayton Act does not prohibit the holding of stock in competing corporations by the same person. Although it prohibits the director of one corporation from being a director of another competing corporation engaged in commerce if either corporation has assets in excess of $1 million, this prohibition is not effective in checking the monopoly potential of interlocking private shareholding.

(4) Tie-in Sales and Exclusive Dealer Agreements. The federal Clayton Act of 1914, applicable to interstate and foreign commerce, prohibits

---

[6] 15 USC § 18.

[7] The validity of the contract is distinct from the question of whether third persons are bound thereby. State courts disagree as to whether nonsigners are bound by such contracts.

[8] Blue Cross v Virginia, 211 Va 180, 176 SE2d 439.

the *tie-in sale* or *tie-in lease* by which the person buying or renting goods agrees that with such goods he will only use other material sold or leased by the other party. The Act also prohibits *exclusive dealer agreements* by which a dealer agrees not to handle a competitor's articles. These tie-in and exclusive dealer arrangements are not absolutely prohibited, but only when their effect "may be substantially to lessen competition or tend to create a monopoly in any line of commerce." By virtue of this qualification, a provision that a person leasing machinery shall use only the materials furnished by the lessor is a lawful restriction if the nature of the materials and the machine are such that the machine will not operate properly with the materials produced or offered by any other person. When the materials furnished by any other competitor would be equally satisfactory, however, the agreement is illegal. Thus, an agreement that the lessee of office machinery should use only the paper sold by the lessor for that type of office machine was illegal when it was shown that any other seller could supply paper of suitable quality.

The restriction on the tie-in and exclusive dealer agreements is limited by the right of a seller to state the terms on which he will deal in bona fide transactions not in restraint of trade. There has also been a judicial trend to approve such agreements when the seller did not hold a dominant position in the market.

However, when the seller lends the buyer money on condition that the buyer purchase all of his requirements from the lender, there is a tie-in which violates the antitrust laws, although there is no evidence as to the position of the lender in the credit extension market.[9]

(5) Refusal to Deal. A combination of manufacturers, distributors, and retailers, acting in concert to deprive a single merchant of goods which he needs to compete effectively, is a group boycott in violation of the Sherman Antitrust Act.[10]

(6) Exceptions to the Antitrust Law. By statute or decision, associations of exporters, marine insurance associations, farmers' and dairymen's cooperatives, and labor unions are exempt from the Sherman Antitrust Act with respect to agreements between their members. Under certain circumstances a minimum resale price maintenance agreement is also exempt. Congress has also authorized freight pooling and revenue division agreements between railroad carriers, provided the approval of the Interstate Commerce Commission (ICC) is obtained.

By virtue of statutory exemptions, traffic and trust agreements otherwise prohibited by the antitrust law may be made by ocean carriers, and interstate carriers and telegraph companies may consolidate upon obtaining the approval of the government commission having jurisdiction over them. The

[9] Fortner Enterprises v United States Steel, 394 US 495.
[10] Klor's v Broadway-Hale Stores, 359 US 207.

Newspaper Preservation Act of 1970 grants an antitrust exemption to operating agreements entered into by newspapers to prevent financial collapse.

§ 5:6. Regulation of Employment. Basically the parties are free to make an employment contract on any terms they wish, but by statute employment is subject to certain limitations. Thus, persons under a certain age cannot be employed at certain kinds of labor. Statutes commonly specify minimum wages and maximum hours which the employer must observe. A state may also require employers to pay employees' wages for the time that they are away from work for the purpose of voting.

(1) Fair Labor Standards Act. By this statute, which is popularly known as the Wage and Hour Act, Congress provides that, subject to certain exceptions, persons working in interstate commerce or in an industry producing goods for interstate commerce must be paid not less than $2.10 an hour; and they cannot be employed for more than 40 hours a week unless they are paid time and a half for overtime. The Act prohibits the employment of children under the age of 14 years. It permits the employment of children between the ages of 14 and 16 years in all industries, except mining and manufacturing, under certain prescribed conditions. This Act has been followed by a number of states in regulating those phases of industry not within the reach of the federal statute.

(2) Hours of Service Act. Congress provides in this Act that an employee engaged in moving trains must be given a specified number of off hours after having worked a specified number of hours. For every 14-hour tour of continuous duty, he must be given 12 consecutive off hours. Employees whose duties are to receive and transmit orders by telephone or telegraph for moving trains can be employed up to 12 hours in any 24 when one work shift is employed. If there are two shifts, the maximum is 9 hours. In case of an emergency, the work hours may be extended.

(3) Public Contracts Act. Whenever a contract to manufacture or furnish materials, supplies, and equipment for the United States exceeds $10,000 in amount, the Walsh-Healey Act requires that the contract specify that the contractor shall pay minimum wages and overtime pay, shall not employ child labor, and shall observe standards set by the Act or by the Secretary of Labor of the United States.

(4) Public Works Contracts Act. When a building is constructed or repaired for the United States for more than $2,000, the Davis-Bacon Act requires that the contractor agree to pay his laborers and mechanics not less than the prevailing rate of wages as determined by the Department of Labor. It is made a federal crime for an employer, or an employee with power to hire and fire, to require any employee on public works construction to return or "kickback" to him any part of the employee's wages.

(5) Fair Employment Practices Acts. With some exceptions, employers of 15 or more persons are forbidden to discriminate as to compensation and other privileges, and conditions of employment against any person because of race, religious creed, color, sex, or national origin, or because of age.[11] (See p. 83, Griggs v Duke Power Co.)

The federal Civil Rights Act of 1964 does not require that every employee be treated the same as every other. It does not prohibit the testing or screening of applicants or employees for the purpose of determining whether a person is qualified to be hired, or promoted, or given a wage increase, or given special training. The Act has no effect upon the employer's right to establish compensation scales, providing for bonus pay and incentive pay, or paying different rates in different geographic areas. The employer may also recognize seniority status, whether voluntarily or as part of a collective bargaining agreement.

The federal Civil Rights Act expressly declares that an employer is not required to readjust the "balance" of his payroll in order to include any particular percentage of each race, creed, and sex as his employees. When he hires new employees, the only obligation upon him is to refrain from discriminating as to each applicant.

(6) Sex Discrimination. An employer cannot discriminate on the basis of sex. An employer may not hire on the basis of a stereotype pattern of what is woman's work and what is man's work. Women, therefore, cannot be excluded from working as bartenders and men cannot be excluded from working as airline cabin attendants. Indirect discrimination against sex is also prohibited, as when the employer establishes height and weight specifications for job applicants but such requirements have no bearing on the performance of the work and their effect is to exclude women from the job.

The equality of the sexes is literally applied so that a law is unconstitutional when it gives to women a protection or an advantage which it does not give to men performing the same work. (See p. 85, Eslinger v Thomas.) Likewise, it is a discriminatory labor practice to allow women overtime pay which is denied men, to allow women seniority rights which are not available to men on the same terms, to prohibit women from working at jobs which involve the lifting of heavy weights, and to prohibit long hair for male employees without imposing the same restriction on female employees.

§ **5:7. Labor Representation.** Statutes generally declare the right of employees to form unions and require employers to deal with the union as the bargaining representative of their employees.

(1) Machinery to Enforce Collective Bargaining. To protect the rights of workers to unionize and bargain collectively, the federal government

---

[11] Federal Civil Rights Act of 1964, Title VII. In some states and cities, statutes and ordinances make similar provision. The federal Anti-Age Discrimination Act prohibits such discrimination only as to persons between 40 and 65 years of age.

created the National Labor Relations Board (NLRB). The NLRB determines the proper collective bargaining unit and eliminates unfair practices by which the employer and the unions might interfere with the rights of the employees.

(2) Selection of Bargaining Representative. Generally there is an election by secret ballot to select the bargaining representative of the employees within a particular collective bargaining unit.

(3) Equal Representation of All Employees. Any union selected by the majority of the workers within the unit is the exclusive representative of all the employees in the unit for the purpose of bargaining with respect to wages, hours of employment, or other conditions of employment. Whether or not all the workers are members of the representative union is immaterial for, in any case, this union is the exclusive representative of every employee. It is unlawful for an employee, either a member or a nonmember of the union, to attempt to make a contract directly with the employer. Except as to grievances, every worker must act through the representative union with respect to his contract of employment. At the same time the union is required to represent all workers fairly, nonmembers as well as members. It is unlawful for the union, in bargaining with the employer, to discriminate in any way against any of the employees. The union cannot use its position as representative of all workers to further its interests as a union.

§ 5:8. Unfair Labor Practices. The labor laws prohibit certain practices as unfair and authorize an agency, such as the NLRB, to conduct proceedings to stop such practices.

(1) Unfair Employer Practices. The federal law declares that it is an unfair labor practice for an employer to interfere with unionization, to discriminate against any employee because of his union activities, or to refuse to bargain collectively.

(2) Unfair Union Practices. The federal law declares it to be an unfair labor practice for a union to interfere with employees in forming their unions or in refraining from joining a union; to cause an employer to discriminate against an employee because he belongs to another union or no union; to refuse to bargain collectively; and under certain circumstances to stop work or refuse to work on materials or to persuade others to stop work.

(3) Procedure for Enforcement. Under the National Labor Relations Act the NLRB issues a complaint whenever it is claimed that an unfair labor practice has been committed. The complaint informs the party of the charges made against him and notifies him to appear at a hearing. At the hearing the General Counsel of the board acts as a combination of prosecuting attorney and referee, charged with the duty of presenting the case on behalf of the complainant and of seeing that the hearing is properly conducted.

After the hearing the board makes finding of fact and conclusions of law and either dismisses the complaint or enters an order against the party to stop the unfair labor practices "and to take such affirmative action including reinstatement of employees with or without back pay, as will effectuate the policy of the Act. . . ."

§ **5:9. Union Organization and Management.** In order to insure the honest and democratic administration of unions, Congress adopted the Labor-Management Reporting and Disclosure Act of 1959 to regulate unions operating in or affecting interstate commerce.

The Act protects the rights of union members within their unions by guaranteeing equality, the right to vote on specified matters, and the right to information on union matters and contracts. It also protects members from interference with the enjoyment of these rights.

§ **5:10. Social Security.** The federal Social Security Act establishes a single federal program of aid to the needy aged, the blind, and the disabled. This is called the Supplemental Security Income Program (SSI). Payments are administered directly by the Department of Health, Education, and Welfare.[12]

The states also have plans of assistance for the unemployed, aged, and disabled. The federal law encourages the making of payments under state programs in addition to those received under the federal program. Such additional programs are called State Supplemental Payments (SSP). State plans typically establish an administrative board or agency with which claims for assistance are filed by persons coming within the category to be benefited by the statute. If the board approves a claim, assistance is given to the applicant in the amount specified by the statute for the number of weeks or other period of time designated by the statute.

Federal law allows a state which elects to supplement the SSI payments with an SSP program to choose whether it will retain control over the administration of such supplements or delegate that responsibility to HEW.

Unemployment compensation laws generally deny the payment of benefits when the employee was discharged for good cause, when he abandoned work without cause, failed or refused to seek or accept an offer of suitable employment, or when the unemployment was the result of a labor dispute.

[12] California League of Senior Citizens, Inc. v Brian, 35 Cal App 3d 443, 110 Cal Rptr 809. This system of centralized and unified federal administration replaces the prior Social Security system under which the federal government made grants to states which administered aid under four different programs.

CASES FOR CHAPTER 5

Moore v Mead's Fine Bread Co.

348 US 115 (1955)

Moore ran a bakery in Santa Rosa, New Mexico. His business was wholly intrastate. Mead's Fine Bread Company, his competitor, engaged in an interstate business. Mead cut the price of bread in half in Santa Rosa but made no price cut in any other place in New Mexico or any other state. As a result of this price

cutting, Moore was driven out of business. Moore then sued Mead for damages for violation of the Clayton and Robinson-Patman Acts. Mead claimed that the price cutting was purely intrastate and, therefore, did not constitute a violation of the federal statutes. A judgment was entered for Moore in the District Court but was reversed by the Court of Appeals. Moore filed a petition to review the reversal.

DOUGLAS, J. . . . For some months petitioner [Moore] and respondent [Mead's Fine Bread Co.] were in competition in Santa Rosa. There is evidence that, on the threat of petitioner to move his bakery to another town, the local Santa Rosa merchants agreed to purchase petitioner's products exclusively. Respondent, labeling that action a boycott, cut the wholesale price of bread in Santa Rosa from 14 cents to 7 cents for a pound loaf and from 21 cents to 11 cents for a pound-and-a-half loaf. The Mead companies did not cut the prices of bread in any other town; and respondent did not cut its prices of bread in Farwell, Texas.

The price war continued from September 1948, to April 1949, and as a result petitioner was forced to close his business. . . .

. . . Respondent is engaged in commerce, selling bread both locally and interstate. In the course of such business, it made price discriminations, maintaining the price in the *interstate* transactions and cutting the price in the *intrastate* sales. The destruction of a competitor was plainly established, as required by the amended § 2(a) of the Clayton Act; and the evidence to support a finding of purpose to eliminate a competitor, as required by § 3 of the Robinson-Patman Act, was ample. . . .

. . . The practices in the present case are also included within the scope of the anti-trust laws. We have here an interstate industry increasing its domain through outlawed competitive practices. The victim, to be sure, is only a local merchant; and no interstate transactions are used to destroy him. But the beneficiary is an interstate business; the treasury used to finance the warfare is drawn from interstate, as well as local, sources which include not only respondent but also a group of interlocked companies engaged in the same line of business; and the prices on the interstate sales, both by respondent and by the other Mead companies, are kept high while the local prices are lowered. If this method of competition were approved, the pattern for growth of monopoly would be simple. As long as the price warfare was strictly intrastate, interstate business could grow and expand with impunity at the expense of local merchants. The competitive advantage would then be with the interstate combines, not by reason of their skills or efficiency but because of their strength and ability to wage price wars. The profits made in interstate activities would underwrite the losses of local price-cutting campaigns. No instrumentality of interstate commerce would be used to destroy the local merchant and expand the domain of the combine. But the opportunities afforded by interstate commerce would be employed to injure local trade. Congress, as guardian of the Commerce Clause, certainly has power to say that those advantages shall not attach to the privilege of doing an interstate business. . . .

It is, we think, clear that Congress by the Clayton Act and Robinson-Patman Act barred the use of interstate business to destroy local business, outlawing the price cutting employed by respondent. . . .

[Judgment reversed.]

Mandeville Island Farms v American Crystal Sugar Co.

334 US 219 (1948)

Three California sugar refiners agreed among themselves to pay California sugar-beet farmers a uniform price for their crops. The refined sugar would be sold by the refiners in interstate markets. Mandeville Island Farms, a sugar-beet farmer, sued American Crystal Sugar Co., one of the refiners, for treble damages under the Sherman Act. From a judgment for Mandeville, the sugar company appealed.

RUTLEDGE, J. . . . The refiners controlled the seed supply and the only practical market for beets grown in northern California. When the new contracts were offered to the farmers, they had the choice of either signing or abandoning sugar-beet farming. . . . Because beet prices were determined for the three seasons with reference to the combined returns of the three refiners, the prices received by petitioners for those seasons were lower than if respondent, the most efficient of the three, had based its prices on separate returns. . . .

[The respondent claimed that the growing, purchasing, and refining of sugar beets were local activities and not within the reach of the Sherman Act, which applied only to transactions in interstate commerce, and that no illegal practice occurred in the subsequent interstate distribution of the refined sugar.]

. . . The broad form of respondent's argument cannot be accepted. It is a reversion to conceptions formerly held but no longer effective to restrict either Congress' power . . . or the scope of the Sherman Act's coverage. The artificial and mechanical separation of "production" and "manufacturing" from "commerce," without regard to their economic continuity, the effects of the former two upon the latter, and the varying methods by which the several processes are organized, related, and carried on in different industries, or indeed within a single industry, no longer suffices to put either production or manufacturing and refining processes beyond reach of Congress' authority or of the statute. . . .

. . . The inquiry whether the restraint occurs in one phase or another, interstate or intrastate, of the total economic process is now merely a preliminary step. . . . The vital question becomes whether the effect is sufficiently substantial and adverse to Congress' paramount policy . . . to constitute a forbidden consequence. If so, the restraint must fall; and the injuries it inflicts upon others become remediable under the act's prescribed methods, including the treble damage provision.

. . . It is clear that the agreement is the sort of combination condemned by the act, even though the price-fixing was by purchasers and the persons specially injured under the treble damage claim are sellers, not customers or consumers. . . .

. . . The statute does not confine its protection to consumers, or to purchasers, or to competitors, or to sellers. Nor does it immunize the outlawed acts because they are done by any of these. . . . The act is comprehensive in its terms and coverage, protecting all who are made victims of the forbidden practices by whomever they may be perpetrated. . . .

Nor is the amount of the nation's sugar industry which the California refiners control relevant, so long as control is exercised effectively in the area concerned.

. . . Under the facts characterizing this industry's operation and the tightening of controls in this producing area by the new agreements and understandings, there can be no question that their restrictive consequences were projected substantially into the interstate distribution of the sugar. . . .

[Judgment affirmed.]

United States v E. I. du Pont de Nemours & Co.

353 US 586 (1957)

From 1917 to 1919, du Pont acquired a 23 percent stock interest in General Motors. During the following years, General Motors bought substantially all its automotive finishes and fabrics from du Pont. In 1949 the United States claimed the effect of the stock acquisition had been to lessen competition in interstate commerce on the theory that the sales to General Motors had not been the result of successful competition but were the result of the stock ownership, and therefore such stock ownership violated the Clayton Act. The United States brought an action against du Pont, General Motors, and others. From a decision in their favor, the United States appealed.

BRENNAN, J. . . . Section 7 is designed to arrest in its incipiency not only the substantial lessening of competition from the acquisition by one corporation of the whole or any part of the stock of a competing corporation, but also to arrest in their incipiency restraints or monopolies in a relevant market which, as a reasonable probability, appear at the time of suit likely to result from the acquisition by one corporation of all or any part of the stock of any other corporation. The section is violated whether or not actual restraints or monopolies, or the substantial lessening of competition, have occurred or are intended. Acquisitions solely for investment are excepted, but only if, and so long as, the stock is not used by voting or otherwise to bring about, or in attempting to bring about, the substantial lessening of competition. . . .

We hold that any acquisition by one corporation of all or any part of the stock of another corporation, competitor or not, is within the reach of the section whenever the reasonable likelihood appears that the acquisition will result in a restraint of commerce or in the creation of a monopoly of any line of commerce. Thus, although du Pont and General Motors are not competitors, a violation of the section has occurred if, as a result of the acquisition, there was at the time of suit a reasonable likelihood of a monopoly of any line of commerce. . . .

General Motors . . . accounts annually for upwards of two fifths of the total sales of automotive vehicles in the Nation. . . . du Pont supplied 67 percent of General Motors' requirements for finishes in 1946 and 68 percent in 1947. In fabrics du Pont supplied 52.3 percent of requirements in 1946, and 38.5 percent in 1947. Because General Motors accounts for almost one half of the automobile industry's annual sales, its requirements for automotive finishes and fabrics must represent approximately one half of the relevant market for these materials. Because the record clearly shows that quantitatively and percentagewise du Pont supplies the largest part of General Motors' requirements, we must conclude that du Pont has a substantial share of the relevant market.

We agree with the trial court that considerations of price, quality, and service were not overlooked by either du Pont or General Motors. Pride in its products and its high financial stake in General Motors' success would naturally lead du Pont to try to supply the best. But the wisdom of this business judgment cannot obscure the fact, plainly revealed by the record, that du Pont purposely employed its stock to pry open the General Motors market to entrench itself as the primary supplier of General Motors' requirements for automotive finishes and fabrics.

Similarly, the fact that all concerned in high executive posts in both companies acted honorably and fairly, each in the honest conviction that his actions were in the best interests of his own company and without any design to overreach anyone, including du Pont's competitors, does not defeat the Government's right to relief. It is not requisite to the proof of a violation of § 7 to show that restraint or monopoly was intended.

The statutory policy of fostering free competition is obviously furthered when no supplier has an advantage over his competitors from an acquisition of his customer's stock likely to have the effects condemned by the statute. We repeat, that the test of a violation of § 7 is whether, at the time of suit, there is a reasonable probability that the acquisition is likely to result in the condemned restraints. The conclusion upon this record is inescapable that such likelihood was proved as to this acquisition. . . .

[Judgment reversed.]

Griggs v Duke Power Co.

401 US 424 (1971)

Griggs and other blacks were employed in the labor department of the Duke Power Company. They sought promotion to higher paying departments of their employer but could not obtain promotion because the employer had established promotion standards of (1) high school education, and (2) satisfactory scores on two professionally prepared aptitude tests. The tests were not designed to measure ability to perform the work in the particular department to which they sought promotion. Griggs and other employees brought a class action under Title VII of the Federal Civil Rights Act of 1964, claiming that the promotion criteria discriminated against them because of race. The Court of Appeals held that there was no prohibited discrimination even though white workers apparently obtained better scores on the tests because of having obtained a better public school education.

BURGER, C.J. . . . In 1955 the Company instituted a policy of requiring a high school education for initial assignment to any department except Labor. . . .

The Company added a further requirement for new employees on July 2, 1965. . . . To qualify for placement in any but the Labor

Department it became necessary to register satisfactory scores on two professionally prepared aptitude tests, as well as to have a high school education. . . . In September 1965 the Company began to permit incumbent employees who lacked a high school education to qualify for transfer from Labor or Coal Handling to an "inside" job by passing two tests—the Wonderlic Personnel Test, which purports to measure general intelligence, and the Bennett Mechanical Comprehension Test. Neither was directed or intended to measure the ability to learn to perform a particular job or category of jobs. The requisite scores used for both initial hiring and transfer approximated the national median for high school graduates. . . .

. . . The Court of Appeals noted . . . that there was no showing of a racial purpose or invidious intent in the adoption of the high school diploma requirement or general intelligence test and that these standards had been applied fairly to whites and Negroes alike. It held that, in the absence of a discriminatory purpose, use of such requirements was permitted by the Act. In so doing, the Court of Appeals rejected the claim that because these two requirements operated to render ineligible a markedly disproportionate number of Negroes, they were unlawful under Title VII unless shown to be job related. . . .

The objective of Congress in the enactment of Title VII is plain from the language of the statute. It was to achieve equality of employment opportunities and remove barriers that have operated in the past to favor an identifiable group of white employees over other employees. Under the Act, practices, procedures, or tests neutral on their face, and even neutral in terms of intent, cannot be maintained if they operate to "freeze" the status quo of prior discriminatory employment practices.

The Court of Appeals' opinion . . . agreed that, on the record in the present case, "whites register far better on the Company's alternative requirements" than Negroes. . . . This consequence would appear to be directly traceable to race. . . . Because they are Negroes, petitioners have long received inferior education in segregated schools. . . . What is required by Congress is the removal of artificial, arbitrary, and unnecessary barriers to employment when the barriers operate invidiously to discriminate on the basis of racial or other impermissible classification. . . .

. . . The Act proscribes not only overt discrimination but also practices that are fair in form, but discriminatory in operation. The touchstone is business necessity. If an employment practice which operates to exclude Negroes cannot be shown to be related to job performance, the practice is prohibited.

On the record before us, neither the high school completion requirement nor the general intelligence test is shown to bear a demonstrable relationship to successful performance of the jobs for which it was used. Both were adopted, as the Court of Appeals noted, without meaningful study of their relationship to job-performance ability. Rather, a vice president of the Company testified, the requirements were instituted on the Company's judgment that they generally would improve the overall quality of the work force.

The evidence, however, shows that employees who have not completed high school or taken the tests have continued to perform satisfactorily and make progress in departments for which the high school and test criteria are now used. The promotion record of present employees who would not be able to meet the new criteria thus suggests the possibility that the requirements may not be needed even for the limited purpose of preserving the avowed policy of advancement within the Company. . . .

The Court of Appeals held that the Company had adopted the diploma and test requirements without any "intention to discriminate against Negro employees." . . . But good intent or absence of discriminatory intent does not redeem employment procedures or testing mechanisms that . . . are unrelated to measuring job capability.

The Company's lack of discriminatory intent is suggested by special efforts to help the undereducated employees through Company financing of two-thirds the cost of tuition for high school training. But Congress directed the thrust of the Act to the *consequences* of employment practices, not simply the motivation. More than that, Congress has placed on the employer the burden of showing that any given requirement must have a manifest relationship to the employment in question. . . .

The Company contends that its general intelligence tests are specifically permitted by § 703(h) of the Act. That section authorizes the use of "any professionally developed ability test" that is not "designed, intended *or used* to discriminate because of race. . . ." (Emphasis added.)

The Equal Employment Opportunity Commission, having enforcement responsibility, has issued guidelines interpreting § 703(h) to permit only the use of job-related tests. . . .

Nothing in the Act precludes the use of testing or measuring procedures; obviously they are useful. What Congress has forbidden is giving these devices and mechanisms controlling force unless they are demonstrably a reasonable measure of job performance. Congress has not commanded that the less qualified be preferred over the better qualified simply because of minority origins. Far from disparaging job qualifications as such, Congress has made such qualifications the controlling factor, so that race, religion, nationality, and sex become irrelevant. What Congress has commanded is that any tests used must measure the person for the job and not the person in the abstract.

[Judgment reversed.]

Eslinger v Thomas

(CA4 SC) 476 F2d 225 (1973)

Victoria Eslinger was a student in law school. She applied for a job as a page in the South Carolina Senate. Her application was refused because she was a female. She brought suit claiming that she had been denied her civil rights. The suit was dismissed and she appealed.

WINTER, C.J. . . . The district court found that, at the time plaintiff sought employment, pages were usually college students and a large number were law students at the University of South Carolina Law School. Pages performed various duties assigned by senators, the clerk and other employees of the senate, including running errands, both personal and official, for senators, preparation and distribution of Acts, proofreading, indexing, bookkeeping, obtaining food and drink for the senators, assisting with committee records, relaying messages to senators, attending committee meetings, acting as assistants and helpers to clerks of various committees, and otherwise taking care of senators' needs.

Pages are temporary employees; they work only for the months the senate is in session. The positions are quite attractive to students. Although they are not overpaid, working hours are not long, working hours may be adjusted to suit the convenience of the employee, and pages have the opportunity to view the lawmaking process and to meet state officials.

Suit was filed in February, 1971. Several months thereafter, the South Carolina Senate adopted Resolution S. 525, establishing new classifications and duties of part-time employees formerly known as pages. Under this resolution, females may be employed as "clerical assistants" and "committee attendants," but not as "Senate pages." As a condition of employment, a female is also required to furnish a written statement from her parent or guardian assuming responsibility for her transportation, safety and supervision to and from her local residence and the senate and at her local residence. At the time of trial, three women had been employed pursuant to this resolution, but plaintiff did not apply for such employment, insisting on her right to be a "Senate page." . . .

. . . The district court determined that the custom of the South Carolina Senate to deny females positions as pages, prior to the adoption of Resolution S.525, denied plaintiff her "Constitutional right to seek employment and be employed." The district court concluded, however, that the constitutional rights of female citizens were not violated by the superseding provisions of S.525, and that the prohibition against females running personal errands for senators (one practical effect of the resolution) was not shown to be "arbitrary or wanting in rational justification." . . .

A federal cause of action based on sex-discrimination has no deep common-law roots; rather, it emerges from recent enlightened approaches to what constitutes equal protection of the laws under the fourteenth amendment. . . .

. . . Plaintiff's challenge to the employment practices of the South Carolina Senate is grounded primarily on the equal protection clause of the fourteenth amendment. She urges us to find sex a "suspect classification," which would require "close judicial scrutiny" of a governmental action based upon such a classification. . . .

Until recently an argument that a classification based upon sex violated the equal protection clause bore little chance of success. However, in Reed v Reed, 404 US 71 . . . (1971), the Court struck down a classification based upon sex, holding invalid an Idaho statute which gave a mandatory preference to a male over a female for appointment as administrator of an estate when both were equally qualified and within the same entitlement class. . . .

When we apply the test of *Reed,* we are compelled to conclude that S.525 denies equal protection. The "public image" of the South Carolina Senate and of its members is obviously a proper subject of state concern. Apparently, the South Carolina Senate felt that certain functions performed by pages on behalf of senators, e.g. running personal errands, driving senators about in their autos, packing their bags in hotel rooms, cashing personal checks for senators, etc., were "not suitable under existing circumstances for young ladies and may give rise to the appearance of impropriety." Resolution S.525, n. 2, *supra.* In their brief, defendants argue that "[i]n placing this restriction upon female pages, the Senate is merely attempting to avoid placing one of its employees in a conceivably damaging position, protecting itself from appearing to the public that an innocent relationship is not so innocent, and maintaining as much public confidence while conducting the business of the people of South Carolina as possible."

We find this rationale unconvincing. It rests upon the implied premise, which we think false, that "[o]n the one hand, the female is viewed as a pure, delicate and vulnerable creature who must be protected from exposure to criminal influences; and on the other, as a brazen temptress, from whose seductive blandishments the innocent male must be protected. Every woman is either Eve or Little Eva—and either way, she loses." Johnson and Knapp, Sex Discrimination By Law: A Study in Judicial Perspective, 46 N.Y.U.L.Rev. 675, 704—5 (1971). . . . We have only to look at our own female secretaries and female law clerks to conclude that an intimate business relationship, including traveling on circuit, between persons of different sex presents no "appearance of impropriety" in the current age, graduated as we are from Victorian attitudes. We note also that South Carolina has had female senators. While the record does not reflect their ages, the association of female senator with male page has not given rise to a sufficient "appearance of impropriety" to require legislative regulation which is the reverse of S.525. In short, present societal attitudes reject the notion that, in most forms of business endeavor, free association between the sexes is to be limited, regulated and restricted because of a difference in sex.

The requirements of S.525 of a written statement from the female's parent or guardian assuming responsibility for her transportation, safety and well-being and for her "strict supervision" stand on no firmer ground. Adult females, or nearly adult females, are no longer chattels of their husbands or parents. If they are tendered and accept special protection or special courtesies, there is no violation of right; but unwelcome special protection, especially denial of employment opportunity, foisted upon them is counter to modern law and modern social thinking. . . .

Since we can find no "fair and substantial" relation between the object of S.525 (combatting the "appearance of impropriety") and the ground of difference (sex) upon which the classification rests, we reverse with regard to the denial of declaratory and injunctive relief and remand the case for further proceedings. . . .

[Judgment reversed on the equal protection issue.]

QUESTIONS AND CASE PROBLEMS

1. What is the objective of each of the following rules of law?
   (a) Horizontal price-fixing is illegal under the federal law without regard to whether the price fixed is fair and reasonable.

(b) Farmers' and dairymen's cooperatives are exempt by statute from the operation of the Sherman Antitrust Act.

2. The Delco Cleaners and Dyers did business in Delaware County. The name Delco was a contraction of the name of the county. A suit was brought to enjoin the use of the name "Delco" by another local concern calling itself the "Delco Valet Service." Decide. [Berberian v Ferm, 166 Pa Super 108, 70 A2d 394]

3. The Winsted Hosiery Co. labeled mixed woolen articles as "natural wool," "Australian wool," and other similar terms that did not indicate the mixed nature of the article. The Federal Trade Commission ordered the company to stop the practice of using a "wool" label to describe a mixed article on the ground that it was an unfair trade practice. The company defended on the ground that all other manufacturers understood that the label was not to be taken as true and that the competitors of the company were not deceived. Was this a valid defense? [Federal Trade Commission v Winsted Hosiery Company, 258 US 483]

4. A manufacturer, The White Motor Co., gave each of its dealers an exclusive right to sell its product within a specified territory. The United States claimed that this was an illegal restraint of trade. White replied that the division of territory between its dealers was a marketing necessity because each dealer had to be protected within his territory against the competition of the other White dealers so that he would be free to concentrate on competing with the dealers of other companies. Was the White dealership plan a restraint of trade? [The White Motor Co. v United States, 372 US 253]

5. The El Paso Natural Gas Company acquired the stock and assets of the Pacific Northwest Pipe Line Company. El Paso, although not a California enterprise, supplied over half of the natural gas used in California; all the other natural gas was supplied by California sources. No gas was sold in California by Pacific Northwest, although it was a strong experienced company within the Northwest area and had attempted several times to enter the California market. United States claimed that the acquisition of Pacific by El Paso constituted a violation of § 7 of the Clayton Act, as amended, because the effect would be to remove competition between the two companies within California. The defense was raised that (a) California was not a "section" of the country within the Clayton Act, and (b) the sale of natural gas was not a line of commerce, and (c) the acquisition did not lessen competition when there had not been any prior sales by Pacific within the area. Decide. [United States v El Paso Natural Gas Co., 376 US 651]

6. Kinney Shoe Company and the Brown Shoe Company proposed to merge by giving the Kinney stockholders shares of the Brown Shoe Company stock in exchange for their shares. By dollar value, Brown was the third largest seller of shoes in the United States and fourth largest manufacturer. Kinney was the eighth largest seller and owned and operated the largest independent chain of family shoe stores in the nation. It was claimed that the merger would not lessen competition as Kinney manufactured less than ½ percent of shoes in the United States and Brown produced about 4 percent. Decide. [Brown Shoe Company v United States, 370 US 294]

7. The Nevada Fair-Trade Act validated contracts to maintain minimum resale prices and declared that other persons "whether [or] not a party to such contract" were bound thereby. The Bulova Watch Company brought an action against Zale-Las Vegas, Inc., a jewelry store, for selling below the price established by a fair-trade agreement between Bulova and the Ginsburg Jewelry Company. Zale-Las Vegas defended on the ground that it was not a party to that contract and that the statute binding it by that contract was unconstitutional. Decide. [Zale-Las Vegas, Inc. v Bulova Watch Co., 80 Nev 483, 396 P2d 683]

8. Sun Oil sells gasoline retail in its own gas stations, as well as selling gas to independently-owned gas stations. In selling to one independent, it gave that independent a price cut to enable it to meet the competition of other independent gas stations. The Federal Trade Commission claimed this was an unlawful price discrimination. Sun Oil defended on the ground that the price cut was made as authorized by the statute "in good faith to meet an equally low price of a competitor." Was this defense valid? [Federal Trade Commission v Sun Oil Co., 371 US 505]

9. A New Jersey statute provides that no rebates, allowances, concessions, or benefits shall be given, directly or indirectly, so as to permit any person to obtain motor fuel from a retail dealer below the posted price or at a net price lower than the posted price applicable at the time of the sale. An action was brought by Fried, a retail gasoline dealer, to prevent the enforcement of the statute. He claimed that it was invalid because it was discriminatory in that it related only to the sale of gasoline and that it denied due process by regulating the price. Was the law constitutional? [Fried v Kervick, 34 NJ 68, 167 A2d 380]

10. A Nevada statute required that at all gas stations a sign should be displayed on each pump setting forth the price of the gasoline and certain other information as to taxes and brand. The sign was to be not less than 7 inches high and 8 inches wide nor larger than 12 inches by 12 inches. The statute prohibited any other signs showing prices on the premises. The Redman Petroleum Corporation maintained proper signs on its pumps but also had large signs near the side of the road. There was no claim that any fraud or price-cutting was involved. The signs by the road stated information that conformed to the information of the signs on the pumps. Redman claimed that a substantial sum of money had been invested in these signs by the side of the road and that they had been used for over ten years. Redman claimed that the statute was unconstitutional. Was Redman correct? [Nevada v Redman Petroleum Corp., 77 Nev 163, 360 P2d 842]

11. Collier sued Roth for damages for violating a state Unfair Milk Sales Practices Act. He claimed that he was entitled to recover treble damages. The statute declared that, "Any person who is injured in business or property by reason of another person's violation of any provision [of the statute] may intervene in the suit for injunction . . . against the other person or he may bring a separate action and recover three times the actual damages sustained as a result of the violation, together with the cost of the suit, or he may sue to enjoin the violation. . . ." Was Collier entitled to treble damages? [Collier v Roth, (Mo App) 468 SW2d 57]

6 Administrative Agencies

§ **6:1. Introduction.** Large areas of the American economy are governed by federal administrative agencies created to carry out the general policies specified by Congress. A contract must be in harmony with public policy not only as declared by Congress and the courts but also as applied by the appropriate administrative agency. For example, a contract to market particular goods might not be prohibited by any statute or court decision but it may still be condemned by the Federal Trade Commission as an unfair method of competition. When the proper commission has made its determination, a contract not in harmony therewith, such as a contract of a carrier charging a higher or a lower rate than that approved by the Interstate Commerce Commission, would be illegal. Other federal administrative agencies include the Civil Aeronautics Board, the Federal Communications Commission, the Federal Maritime Commission, the Federal Power Commission, the National Labor Relations Board, and the Securities and Exchange Commission. The law governing these agencies is known as *administrative law*.

State administrative agencies may also affect business and the citizen, because state agencies may have jurisdiction over fair employment practices, workmen's compensation claims, and the renting of homes and apartments.

§ **6:2. Uniqueness of Administrative Agencies.** The structure of government common in the states and the national government is a division into three branches—executive, legislative, and judicial—with the lawmaker selected by popular vote and with the judicial branch acting as the superguardian to prevent either the executive or the legislative branch from exceeding the proper spheres of their respective powers. In contrast, members of administrative agencies are ordinarily appointed (in the case of federal agencies, by the President of the United States with the consent of two thirds of Congress), and the major agencies combine legislative, executive, and judicial powers in that they make the rules, police the community to see that the rules are obeyed, and sit in judgment to determine whether there have been violations.

Although an appeal to the courts may be taken from a regulation or ruling by an administrative agency, the agency is for practical purposes not subject to control by the courts. The subject matter involved is ordinarily so technical and the agency is clothed with such discretion that courts will not reverse agency action unless it can be disapproved as arbitrary and capricious. Very few agency decisions are reversed on this ground. Administrative action is not held to be arbitrary or capricious merely because the judge would have decided the matter otherwise, because the administrative action is new or strange to the law, or because the administrative action causes someone to lose money.

§ 6:3. The Administrator's Powers. For brevity the administrative agency is referred to in this discussion as the *administrator,* whether in fact he is one person or a multiperson commission or panel.

(1) Legislative Powers. The modern administrator has the power to make the laws that regulate the segment of life or industry entrusted to his care. (See p. 97, United States v Howard.) There once was a great reluctance to accept the fact that the administrator made the law, because by our constitutional doctrine only the lawmaker, the Congress or the state legislature, can make laws. It therefore seemed an improper transfer or delegation of power for the lawmaker to set up a separate body or agency and give to it the power to make the laws.

The same forces that led society initially to create the administrator caused society to clothe the administrator with the power to make the laws. Practical expediency gradually prevailed in favor of the conclusion that if we want the administrator to do a job, we must give him the power sufficiently extensive to do so; and we must take the practical approach and ignore the theoretical objection that when we authorize him to do the job, we are in fact telling him to make the law which governs the area that he regulates.

In the early days of administrative regulation, the legislative character of the administrative rule was not clearly perceived, largely because the administrator's sphere of power was so narrow that he was, in effect, merely a thermostat. That is, the lawmaker told him when to do what, and all that the administrator did was to act in the manner in which he had been programmed. For example, the cattle inspector was told to take certain steps when he determined that the cattle had hoof-and-mouth disease. Here it was clear that the lawmaker had set the standard, and the administrator merely "swung into action" when the specified fact situation existed. There is this same pattern of thermostat regulation in the case of tariff legislation, which has authorized the President of the United States to make certain changes to the tariff when he finds that certain facts exist, such as a foreign country discriminating against United States goods, or a certain disparity as to labor costs between the foreign and American goods.

The next step in the growth of the administrative power was to authorize the cattle inspector to act when he found that cattle had a contagious disease, leaving it to him to formulate a rule or guide as to what diseases were contagious. Here again, the discretionary and legislative aspect of the administrator's conduct was obscured by the belief that the field of science would define "contagious," leaving no area of discretionary decision to the administrator.

Today's health administrator may be authorized to make such rules and regulations for the protection or improvement of the common health as it deems desirable. In this respect, it is making the "health law" by its rules. In regulating various economic aspects of national life, the administrator is truly the lawmaker.

Gradually, the courts have come to recognize, or at least to tolerate, the entrusting of a certain job to an agency without doing more than stating to the agency the policy that the administrator should seek to advance, or the goal or objective that he should seek to attain. (See p. 98, American Trucking Association v United States.) Thus, it has been sufficient for a legislature to authorize an administrator to grant licenses "as public interest, convenience, or necessity requires;" "to prohibit unfair methods of competition;" to regulate prices so that they "in [the administrator's] judgment will be generally fair and equitable;" to prevent "profiteering;" "to prevent the existence of intercorporate holdings, which unduly or unnecessarily complicate the structure [or] unfairly or inequitably distribute voting power among security holders;" and to renegotiate government contracts to prevent "excessive profits."

(2) Executive Powers. The modern administrator has executive power to investigate and to require persons to appear as witnesses, and to produce papers for any reason coming within his sphere of operation. Thus, the administrator may investigate in order to police the area subject to his control to see if there is any violation of the law or of its rules generally, to determine whether there is a need for the adoption of additional rules, to ascertain the facts with respect to a particular suspected or alleged violation, and to determine whether its decisions are being obeyed.

The Federal Antitrust Civil Process Act of 1962 is an outstanding example of the extent to which administrative investigation is authorized. The Act provides that upon written demand to a corporation, association, or partnership, the production of documents can be compelled to provide the Department of Justice with information to determine whether there is sufficient ground to bring a civil antitrust suit against the enterprise so directed. Similar powers are possessed by the Federal Trade Commission, the Federal Maritime Commission, the National Science Foundation, the Treasury Department, the Department of Agriculture, the Department of the Army, the Department of Labor, and the Veterans Administration.

The power to investigate is a continuing power, with the result that the administrative agency can, in effect, put the party on probation and require periodic reports to show whether the party has complied with the law.[1]

(3) Judicial Powers. The modern administrator may be given power to sit as a court and to determine whether there have been any violations of the law or of its regulations. Thus the National Labor Relations Board

---

[1] United States v Morton Salt Co., 338 US 632.

determines whether there has been a prohibited unfair labor practice, the Federal Trade Commission will act as a court to determine whether there is unfair competition, and so on. Here there is the theoretical objection that a nonjudicial body is making decisions that should only be made by a court.

When the administrator sits as a judge as to the violation of a regulation that it has made, there is also the element that the "judge" is not impartial because it is trying the accused for violating "its" law rather than "the" law. There is also the objection that the administrator is determining important rights but does so without a jury, which seems inconsistent with the long-established emphasis of our history upon the sanctity of trial by jury. In spite of these theoretical and psychological objections to the administrator's exercise of judicial power, such exercise is now firmly established.

Accepting as a fact that the administrator can make judicial determinations, the question arises as to whether he must proceed exactly as a court, following all of the procedure of a court.

§ 6:4. Pattern of Administrative Procedure. At the beginning of the era of modern regulation of business, the administrator was, to a large extent, a minor executive or police officer charged with the responsibility of enforcing the laws applicable to limited fact situations. The health officer empowered to condemn and destroy diseased cattle was typical. In view of the need for prompt action and because of the relative simplicity of the fact determination to be made, it was customary for him to exercise summary powers; that is, upon finding cattle which he believed diseased, he would have them killed immediately without delaying to find their true owner or without holding a formal hearing to determine whether they were in fact diseased.

Today, the exercise of summary powers is the exceptional case. Now it is permitted mainly in connection with the fraudulent use of the mails or the sending of such improper matter as lottery tickets or obscene matter through the mails, the enforcement of navigation regulations and tax laws, and the exercise of the police power in order to protect the public health and safety. As the regulation of business assumes the aspect of economic rather than health or safety regulation, the need for immediate action by the administrator diminishes, if not disappears, when the administrator acts to determine whether particular conduct comes within the scope of a regulation or whether there has been a violation thereof. Accordingly, concepts of due process generally require that some notice be given those who will be adversely affected and that some form of hearing be held at which they may present their case. As a practical matter, also, the more complicated the nature of the determinations to be made, the longer the period of investigation and deliberation required.

(1) Preliminary Steps. It is commonly provided that either a private individual aggrieved by the conduct of another or the administrator on his own motion may present a complaint. This complaint is served on the alleged wrongdoer, and he is given opportunity to file an answer. There may be other phases of pleading between the parties and the administrator, but eventually the matter comes before the administrator to be heard. After a hearing, the administrator makes a decision and enters an order either dismissing the complaint or directing the adverse party to do or not to do certain acts. This order is generally not self-executing and, in order to enforce it, provision is generally made for an application by the administrator to a court. Sometimes the converse is provided, so that the order of the administrator becomes binding upon the adverse party unless he appeals to a court within a stated period for a review of the order.

The complaint filing and prehearing stage of the procedure may be more detailed. In many of the modern administrative statutes, provision is made for an examination of the informal complaint by some branch of the administrator to determine whether it presents a case coming within the scope of the administrator's authority. It is also commonly provided that an investigation be made by the administrator to determine whether the facts are such to warrant a hearing of the complaint. If it is decided that the complaint is within the jurisdiction of the administrator and that the facts appear to justify it, a formal complaint is issued and served on the adverse party, and an answer is filed by him as above stated.

With the rising complexity of the subjects regulated by administrative agencies, the trend is increasingly in the direction of greater preliminary examination upon the basis of an informal complaint.

Cutting across these procedures are the practical devices of informal settlement and consent decrees. In many instances, the alleged wrongdoer will be willing to change his practices or his conduct upon being informally notified that a complaint has been made against him. It is therefore sound public relations, as well as expeditious handling of the matter, for the administrator to inform the alleged wrongdoer of the charge made against him prior to the filing of any formal complaint in order to give him the opportunity to settle the matter voluntarily. A matter that has already gone into the formal hearing stage may also be terminated by agreement, and a stipulation or consent decree may be filed setting forth the terms of the agreement.

A further modification of this general pattern is made in the case of the Interstate Commerce Commission. Complaints received by the Commission are referred to the Bureau of Informal Cases, which endeavors to secure an amicable adjustment with the carrier. If this cannot be done, the complainant is notified that it will be necessary to file a formal complaint. At this stage of the proceedings, the parties can expedite the matter by agreeing that the case may be heard on the pleadings alone. In this case, the complainant files a pleading or memorandum to which the defendant files an answering memorandum, the plaintiff then filing a reply or rebuttal memorandum. If the parties do not agree to this procedure, a hearing is held after the pleadings have been filed.

(2) The Administrative Hearing. In order to satisfy the requirements of due process, it is generally necessary for the administrator to give notice and to hold a hearing. A significant difference between the administrator's hearing and a court hearing is that there is no right of trial by jury before an administrator. For example, a workmen's compensation board may pass on a claim without any jury. The absence of a jury does not constitute a denial of due process. The theory is that a new right unknown to the common law has been created, and the right to a jury trial exists only where it was recognized at the common law.

The law could have taken the position that whenever a person is brought before any tribunal, he is entitled to have the facts determined by a jury. But the law "froze" the right to trial by jury as it existed in pre-Revolutionary days. Consequently, if there was no right of jury trial in 1775, there is no right of trial by jury today. Since the wide array of government regulation of business today was unknown in 1775, we have the consequence that a great area of twentieth century economic life is determined without a jury. If I wish to sue you for $100, you would be entitled to a trial by jury; but if I am complaining before an administrator, you are not entitled to a jury trial, even though his determination or regulation may cost you a million dollars. The inconsistency in the net result in these two situations is not regarded as having any legal importance.

Another significant difference between an administrative hearing and a judicial hearing is that the administrator may be authorized to make a determination first and then hold a hearing afterwards to verify his result, as contrasted with a court which must have the trial before it makes a judgment. This has important practical consequences in that when the objecting party seeks a hearing after the administrator has acted, he has the burden of proof and the cost of going forward. In consequence of this, the result is that fewer persons go to the trouble of seeking such a hearing. This, in turn, reduces the amount of hearing and litigation in which the administrator becomes involved, with the resultant economy of money and personnel from the government's standpoint.

In some instances the administrator may even establish standards that have the effect of barring a hearing unless there is compliance with such standards. This is an illustration both of the "lawmaking" power, that is, determining who shall be entitled to a hearing, as well as the extent to which a person is entitled to a "court-form" hearing.

When it is sought to obtain an exception from an administrative regulation, the moving party has the burden of proof.[2]

As a general rule, an administrator is not bound by the rules of evidence used in courts, such as the hearsay evidence rule, but may hear any information, leaving it to his experience and judgment to evaluate properly what he hears. The hearsay evidence rule was formed by the courts largely for the purpose of preventing juries from being misled by hearsay. Since the administrator does not act with a jury, the reason for excluding the jury-prejudicing evidence ceases to exist and therefore the exclusionary rule is abandoned. A notable exception is the Federal National Labor Relations Act

[2] City of Mattoon v Illinois Environmental Protection Agency, 11 Ill App 2d 271, 296 NE2d 383.

of 1947, which limits the National Labor Relations Board to hearing only that which would be admissible as evidence in the federal district courts. Originally, the Board was permitted to hear any evidence, not bound by the rules of evidence; but it was felt by the critics of the Board that it was being improperly influenced by hearsay evidence, and that the way to remedy the situation was to return to the old rule of excluding hearsay evidence.

(3) Constitutional Limitations on Investigation. For the most part the constitutional guarantee against unreasonable search and seizure does not afford much protection against the investigation of an administrator, since that guarantee does not apply in the absence of an actual seizure. That is, a subpoena to testify or to produce records cannot be opposed on the ground that it is a search and seizure, as the constitutional protection is limited to cases of actual search and seizure rather than the obtaining of information by compulsion.

The protection afforded by the guarantee against self-incrimination is likewise narrow, for it cannot be invoked (1) as to records which by law must be kept by the person subject to investigation (see p. 99, Shapiro v United States); (2) as to corporate records even though the officer or employee of the corporation in producing them may be producing evidence that would incriminate him; and (3) the protection of the Constitution may be denied when a sufficient immunity from future prosecution is given to the person who is compelled to present evidence that incriminates him.

§ 6:5. Finality of Administrative Determination. Basic to the Anglo-American legal theory is that no one, not even a branch of the government, is above the law. Thus, the growth of powers of the administrative agency was frequently accepted or tolerated on the theory that the administrative agency could not go too far because the courts would review the administrative action. The typical modern statute provides that an appeal may be taken from the administrative action by any person in interest or any person aggrieved. When the question decided by the administrator was a question of law, the court on appeal will reverse the administrator if the court disagrees with him. (See p. 99, Social Security Board v Nierotko.) In contrast, if the controversy turns on a question of fact, a mixed question of law or fact, or value judgments based upon the facts, a court will accept the conclusion of the administrator as final. The net result is that the determination by the administrative agency will, in most cases, be final.

(1) Factors Limiting Court Review. There are two procedural reasons why administrative appeals are frequently lost: (a) absence of standing to appeal, and (b) failure to exhaust the administrative remedy.

Illustrative of the former, the party that appeals (the appellant) may lose because the regulatory statute does not indicate that he may sue. As an example of the latter, if the appellant has not allowed the proceeding before the administrator to take its full course, generally he cannot take an appeal. Thus, an employer contending that the National Labor Relations

Board had no jurisdiction over him cannot enjoin it from proceeding with an unfair labor practice hearing as a means of appealing from the board's decision that it had jurisdiction to proceed with the matter. The rule requiring the exhaustion of the administrative remedy is based in part on fairness to the administrator (namely, that he should be given full opportunity to dispose of the case before an appeal is taken) and in part upon the concept of practical expediency that it would impose an unreasonable burden upon the courts by increasing the number of cases which they would be required to hear if any disgruntled party before an administrator could take an appeal at any point of the proceeding.

(2) Discretion of the Administrator. The greatest limitation upon court review of the administrative action is the rule that a matter involving discretion will not be reversed in the absence of an error of law, or a clear abuse, or the arbitrary or capricious exercise of discretion.[3] (See p. 101, Moog Industries v Federal Trade Commission.) The courts reason that since the administrator was appointed because of his expert ability, it would be absurd for the court that is manifestly unqualified technically to make a decision in the matter to step in and determine whether the administrator made the proper choice. As has been said by the Supreme Court with reference to the Securities Exchange Commission: "The very breadth of the statutory language precludes a reversal of the Commission's judgment save where it has plainly abused its discretion in these matters. . . . Such an abuse is not present in this case.

". . . The Commission's conclusion here rests squarely in that area where administrative judgments are entitled to the greatest amount of weight by appellate courts. It is the product of administrative experience, appreciation of the complexities of the problem, realization of the statutory policies, and responsible treatment of the uncontested facts. It is the type of judgment which administrative agencies are best equipped to make and which justifies the use of the administrative process. . . . Whether we agree or disagree with the result reached, it is an allowable judgment which we cannot disturb."[4]

And with reference to the Federal Communications Commission, the court has declared that ". . . it is the Commission, not the courts, which must be satisfied that the public interest will be served by renewing the license. And the fact that we might not have made the same determination on the same facts does not warrant a substitution of judicial for administrative discretion since Congress has confided the problem to the latter."[5] Similarly, a city commissioner of water pollution will not be ordered to enforce the city's water pollution ordinance when the commissioner in the exercise of his discretion has concluded that there was no violation.[6]

---

[3] Colton v Berman, 21 NY2d 322, 287 NYS2d 47.

[4] Securities and Exchange Commission v Chenery Corporation, 332 US 194, 209-9.

[5] Federal Communications Commission v WOKO, 329 US 223, 229.

[6] Ohio v Locher, 30 Ohio 2d 190, 283 NE2d 164.

The frequent reference of the courts to what would be done if action of the administrator was found to be "arbitrary or capricious" is somewhat misleading because it suggests that there is a wide area in which the court does actively review the administrative action. As a practical matter, the action of the administrator is rarely found to be arbitrary or capricious. As long as the administrator has apparently conducted himself properly, the fact that the court disagrees with his conclusion does not make that conclusion arbitrary or capricious. The fact that the administrative decision will cause a person to lose money is not proof that the action of the administrator was arbitrary. The judicial attitude is that for protection from laws and regulations which are unwise, improvident, or out of harmony with a particular school of thought, the people must resort to the ballot box and not to the court.

Thus, it is sufficient that the administrator had a reasonable basis for his action and a court will not attempt a "second guess" as to "complex criteria" with which an administrative agency is "intimately familiar."[7]

An administrative regulation will be held invalid as arbitrary when, as in the case of an environmental protection control, it requires expensive equipment to guard against a very unlikely risk, particularly when other simpler and less expensive devices are available.[8]

In order to give the individual a direct pathway to his government, the office of Ombudsman for Business has been created within the Department of Commerce. This official is patterned after the Swedish Ombudsman and the British Parliamentary Commission for Administration. He has authority to receive grievances and complaints and to initiate appropriate action.

---

[7] King v Alaska State Housing Authority, (Alaska) 512 P2d 887.

[8] Kesler & Sons Construction Co. v Utah State Division of Health, 30 Utah 2d 90, 513 P2d 1017.

CASES FOR CHAPTER 6

United States v Howard

352 US 212 (1957)

The Congress made it a federal crime to transport fish in interstate commerce from a state if such transportation was "contrary to the law of the state." Howard transported fish from Florida. No Florida statute made it unlawful, but such transportation violated a rule of the Florida Game and Fresh Water Fish Commission. Howard was convicted for violating the federal statute. She claimed that she had not violated the statute because no Florida "law" prohibited such transportation.

REED, J. . . . The sole question presented is whether Rule 14.01 of the Commission's regulations, . . . is a "law" of the State of Florida as that term is used in the Federal Act.

This Court has repeatedly ruled, in other circumstances, that orders of state administrative agencies are the law of the State. . . . In *Grand Trunk R. Co.* v. *Indiana R. Comm'n*, 221 U.S. 400, 403, the Court stated that: "the order [of the Indiana Railroad Commission] . . . is a law of the State within the meaning of the contract clause of the Constitution. . . ." And in *Lake Erie & W. R. Co.* v. *Public Utilities Comm'n*, 249 U.S. 422, 424, it was said that an order of the state public utilities commission "being legislative in its nature . . . is a state law within the meaning of the Constitution of the United States and the laws of Congress regulating our jurisdiction." A similar statement may be found in *Arkadelphia Co.* v. *St. Louis S. W. R. Co.,* 249 U.S. 134, 141. . . .

Appellee argues that the rules of the Florida Commission are so subject to change that they lack sufficient substance and permanence to be the "law" of Florida. We need not decide now whether a state agency could make a rule of such a temporary nature and so unaccompanied by the procedural niceties of rule making that the declaration should not be considered the law of the State for purposes of a statute such as the Black Bass Act. . . .

Accordingly we hold that the phrase "law of the State," as used in this Act, is sufficiently broad to encompass the type of regulation used in Florida. . . .

[Conviction sustained.]

American Trucking Associations v United States

344 US 298 (1953)

The practice developed for owners of trucks who drive their loaded trucks from one point to another to hire themselves and their trucks out to a common carrier so that the return trip would not be made with empty trucks. The Interstate Commerce Commission concluded that these one-trip rentals made it possible for the carriers to operate in part without satisfying the requirements otherwise applicable to them. In order to stop this, the Commission adopted a set of rules which provided that trucks could not be rented by a carrier for less than thirty days. A number of suits were brought to prevent the enforcement of these rules on the ground that they were not authorized by the Interstate Commerce Act and their enforcement would cause financial loss and hardship.

REED, J. . . . All agree that the rules . . . abolish trip-leasing. Unfortunate consequences are predicted for the public interest because the exempt owner-operator will no longer be able to hire himself out at will—in sum, that the industry's ability to serve a fluctuating demand will suffer and transportation costs accordingly go up. It is the Commission's position that the industry and the public will benefit directly because of the stabilization of conditions of competition and rate schedules, and that in fact the continued effectiveness of the Commission's functions under the Motor Carrier Act is dependent on regulation of leasing and interchange. Needless to say, we are ill equipped to weigh such predictions of the economic future. Nor is it our function to act as a super-commission. So we turn to the legal considerations so strongly urged on us.

. . . All urge upon us the fact that nowhere in the Act is there an express delegation of power to control, regulate or affect leasing practices, and it is further insisted that in each separate provision of the Act granting regulatory authority there is no direct implication of such power. Our function, however, does not stop with a section-by-section search for the phrase "regulation of leasing practices" among the literal words of the statutory provisions. As a matter of principle, we might agree with appellants' contentions if we thought it a reasonable canon of interpretation that the draftsmen of acts delegating agency powers, as a practical and realistic matter, can or do include specific consideration of every evil sought to be corrected. But no great acquaintance with practical affairs is required to know that such prescience, either in fact or in the minds of Congress, does not exist. . . . Its very absence, moreover, is precisely one of the reasons why regulatory agencies such as the Commission are created, for it is the fond hope of their authors that they bring to their work the expert's familiarity with industry conditions which members of the delegating legislatures cannot be expected to possess. . . .

Moreover, we must reject at the outset any conclusion that the rules as a whole represent an attempt by the Commission to expand its power arbitrarily; there is clear and adequate evidence of evils attendant on trip-leasing. The purpose of the rules is to protect the industry from practices detrimental to the maintenance of sound transportation services consistent with the regulatory system. Sections 216(b) and 218(a) of the Act, for instance, require the filing of a just and reasonable rate schedule by each common carrier, and the violation of these rates and the demoralization of rate structures generally are a probable concomitant of current leasing practices. Section 204(a)(2) requires the Commission to impose rules relating to safety of operation for vehicles and drivers. These are likewise threatened by the unrestricted use of nonowned equipment by the common carriers. And the requirements of continuous service . . . of observance of authorized routes and termini . . . and the prohibitions of rebates [all matters expressly governed by the Interstate Commerce Act] also may be ignored through the very practices here proscribed. . . .

We hold then that the promulgation of these rules for authorized carriers falls within the Commission's power, despite the absence of specific reference to leasing practices in the Act. . . . This result . . . is foreshadowed . . . by *United States* v. *Pennsylvania R. Co.,* 323 U.S. 612. That case validated an order requiring railroads to lease cars to a competing carrier by sea, in spite of the inability of the Commission to ground its action on some specific provision of the Act. . . . This Court pointed to the fact that the "unquestioned power of the Commission to require establishment of [through] routes would be wholly fruitless, without the correlative power to abrogate the Association's rule which prohibits the interchange." . . .

[Regulation sustained.]

Shapiro v United States

335 US 1 (1948)

Shapiro was a wholesaler of fruit and produce. The Price Administrator acting under the federal Emergency Price Control Act subpoenaed him to produce his business records. Under protest of constitutional privilege he furnished the records. He was later prosecuted for making illegal tie-in sales contrary to the Emergency Price Control Regulations. The evidence on which the prosecution was based was obtained from information found in the records that he had been required to produce before the administrator. He claimed that he was entitled to immunity from prosecution for any matter arising out of those records. His claim of privilege was overruled and he was convicted. He appealed from the conviction.

VINSON, C.J. . . . The Circuit Court of Appeals ruled that the records which petitioner was compelled to produce were records required to be kept by a valid regulation under the Price Control Act; that thereby they became public documents, as to which no constitutional privilege against self-incrimination attaches.

. . . The language of the statute and its legislative history, viewed against the background of settled judicial construction of the immunity provision, indicate that Congress required records to be kept as a means of enforcing the statute and did not intend to frustrate the use of those records for enforcement action by granting an immunity bonus to individuals compelled to disclose their required records to the Administrator. . . .

"The physical custody of incriminating documents does not of itself protect the custodian against their compulsory production. The question still remains with respect to the nature of the documents and the capacity in which they are held. It may yet appear that they are of a character which subjects them to the scrutiny demanded and that the custodian has voluntarily assumed a duty which overrides his claim of privilege. . . . The principle applies not only to public documents in public offices, but also to *records required by law to be kept in order that there may be suitable information of transactions which are the appropriate subjects of governmental regulation and the enforcement of restrictions validly established. There the privilege, which exists as to private papers, cannot be maintained.*" . . .

[Conviction affirmed.]

Social Security Board v Nierotko

327 US 358 (1946)

The National Labor Relations Board may order the reinstatement of an improperly discharged employee and direct that the employer pay him the "back pay" that he lost during the period of his wrongful discharge. The benefits obtained under another statute, the Social Security Act, are affected by the amount of wages received by an employee. In this case, the question arose whether the back pay awarded by the National Labor Relations Board should

be regarded as "wages" for the purpose of the Social Security Act and whether the employee should be regarded as having been employed during the period from the date of his wrongful discharge until his reinstatement under the order of the Board.

REED, J. . . . The respondent, Joseph Nierotko, was found by the National Labor Relations Board to have been wrongfully discharged for union activity by his employer, the Ford Motor Company, and was reinstated by that Board in his employment with directions for "back pay" for the period February 2, 1937, to September 25, 1939. The "back pay" was paid by the employer on July 18, 1941. Thereafter Nierotko requested the Social Security Board to credit him in the sum of the "back pay" on his Old-Age and Survivor's Insurance account with the Board. In conformity with its minute of formal general action of March 27, 1942, the Board refused to credit Nierotko's "back pay" as wages. . . .

Wages are the basis for the administration of federal old-age benefits. . . . Only those who earn wages are eligible for benefits. The periods of time during which wages were earned are important and may be crucial on eligibility. . . .

[Under the act] "wages" means all remuneration for employment. . . .

Surely the "back pay" is "remuneration." . . .

An argument against [this] is the contrary ruling of the governmental agencies which are charged with the administration of the Social Security Act. Their competence and experience in this field command us to reflect before we decide contrary to their conclusion. The first administrative determination was apparently made in 1939 by an Office Decision of the Bureau of Internal Revenue on the problem of whether "back pay" under a Labor Board order was wages subject to tax under . . . the Social Security Act which the Bureau collects. The back pay was held not to be subject as wages to the tax because no service was performed, the employer had tried to terminate the employment relationship, and the allowance of back pay was discretionary with the Labor Board. . . . This position is maintained by the Social Security Board by minute of March 27, 1942. It is followed by the National Labor Relations Board which at one time approved the retention by the employer of the tax on the employees' back pay for transmission to the Treasury Department as a tax on wages and later reversed its position on the authority of the Office Decision to which reference has just been made. . . .

The Office Decision seems to us unsound. . . . There is nothing . . . which supports the idea that the "back pay" award differs from other pay. . . .

But it is urged by petitioner that the administrative construction on the question of whether "back pay" is to be treated as wages should lead us to follow the agencies' determination. There is a suggestion that the administrative decision should be treated as conclusive. . . .

The Social Security Board and the Treasury were compelled to decide, administratively, whether or not to treat "back pay" as wages and their expert judgment is entitled, as we have said, to great weight. . . . However, . . . such decisions are only conclusive as to properly supported findings of fact. . . . Administrative determinations must have a basis in law and must be within the granted authority. Administration, when it interprets a statute so as to make it apply to particular circumstances, acts as a delegate to the legislative power. Congress might have declared that "back pay" awards under the Labor Act should or should not be treated as wages. Congress might have delegated to the Social Security Board to determine what compensation paid by employers to employees should be treated as wages. Except as such interpretive power may be included in the agencies' administrative functions, Congress did neither. An agency may not finally decide the limits of its statutory power. That is a judicial function. Congress used a well understood word—"wages"—to indicate the receipts which were to govern taxes and benefits under the Social Security Act. There may be borderline payments to employees on which courts would follow administrative determination as to whether such payments were or were not wages under the act.

We conclude, however, that the Board's interpretation of this statute to exclude back pay goes beyond the boundaries of administrative routine and the statutory limits. This is a ruling which excludes from the ambit of the Social Security Act payments which we think were included by Congress. It is beyond the permissible limits of administrative interpretation. . . .

Moog Industries v Federal Trade Commission

355 US 411 (1958)

Moog Industries was ordered to stop certain pricing practices by the Federal Trade Commission. It raised the objection that its competitors were also guilty of the same practices and that Moog would be ruined if it were required to stop the practices without also requiring its competitors to stop such practices. The Commission rejected this argument. Moog appealed.

Opinion by the Court . . . In view of the scope of administrative discretion that Congress has given the Federal Trade Commission, it is ordinarily not for courts to modify ancillary features of a valid Commission order. This is but recognition of the fact that in the shaping of its remedies within the framework of regulatory legislation, an agency is called upon to exercise its specialized, experienced judgment. Thus, the decision as to whether or not an order against one firm to cease and desist from engaging in illegal price discrimination should go into effect before others are similarly prohibited depends on a variety of factors peculiarly within the expert understanding of the Commission. Only the Commission, for example, is competent to make an initial determination as to whether and to what extent there is a relevant "industry" within which the particular respondent competes and whether or not the nature of that competition is such as to indicate identical treatment of the entire industry by an enforcement agency. Moreover, although an allegedly illegal practice may appear to be operative throughout an industry, whether such appearances reflect fact and whether all firms in the industry should be dealt with in a single proceeding or should receive individualized treatment are questions that call for discretionary determination by the administrative agency. It is clearly within the special competence of the Commission to appraise the adverse effect on competition that might result from postponing a particular order prohibiting continued violations of the law. Furthermore, the Commission alone is empowered to develop that enforcement policy best calculated to achieve the ends contemplated by Congress and to allocate its available funds and personnel in such a way as to execute its policy efficiently and economically.

The question, then, of whether orders such as those before us should be held in abeyance until the respondents' competitors are proceeded against is for the Commission to decide. . . . If the Commission has decided the question, its discretionary determination should not be overturned in the absence of a patent abuse of discretion. . . .

[Judgment against Moog.]

QUESTIONS AND CASE PROBLEMS

1. Woodham held a license as insurance agent. He was notified to appear in person or by counsel at a hearing to be held by Williams, the State Insurance Commissioner, for the purpose of determining whether Williams should revoke Woodham's license because of improper practices as agent. Woodham appeared at the hearing and testified in his own behalf. He did not make any objection that what he was asked would incriminate him. Williams revoked Woodham's license. Woodham appealed and claimed, among other grounds, that the proceeding before Williams was invalid because Woodham had not been warned that what he would say could be used against him. Were the proceedings valid? [Woodham v Williams, (Fla App) 207 So2d 320]
2. The New York City charter authorizes the New York City Board of Health to adopt a health code and declares that it "shall have the force and effect of

law." The Board adopted a Code in 1964 that provided for the fluoridation of the public water supply. A suit was brought to enjoin the carrying out of this program on the ground that it was unconstitutional and that money could not be spent to carry out such a program in the absence of a statute authorizing such expenditure. It was also claimed that the fluoridation program was unconstitutional because there were other means of reducing tooth decay; fluoridation was discriminatory in that it benefited only children; it unlawfully imposed medication on the children without their consent; and fluoridation "is or may be" dangerous to health. Was the Code provision valid? [Paduano v City of New York, 257 NYS2d 531]

3. A federal statute provides that when a contract between the government and a contractor provides for the determination of a dispute by a federal department head or agency, the decision "shall be final and conclusive unless the same is fraudulent or capricious or arbitrary or so grossly erroneous as necessarily to imply bad faith, or is not supported by substantial evidence." Bianchi contracted with the government to build a water tunnel. The contract contained a standard provision for additional compensation in the event of "changed conditions." The contractor claimed that conditions discovered after the work was begun constituted "changed conditions" and claimed additional compensation. In accord with a provision of the contract, he submitted this claim first to the contracting officer and then to the Board of Claims and Appeals of the Corps of Engineers. Both rejected his claim. Six years thereafter Bianchi sued in the Court of Claims claiming that he was entitled to additional compensation and that he was not bound by the decision of the contracting officer and of the Board of Claims because their decisions were "capricious or arbitrary or so grossly erroneous as necessarily to imply bad faith, or were not supported by substantial evidence." In this proceeding, a substantial amount of new evidence was heard and a decision made in favor of the contractor. The United States appealed. Decide. [United States v Bianchi, 373 US 709]

4. Ordinarily the testimony of a witness at a trial in one case is not admissible as evidence in the trial of a different case involving different parties. *W*, a workman, was injured and filed a workmen's compensation claim. He testified before the compensation board with respect to his injuries. He thereafter died and his widow began a new proceeding before the board to recover damages for his death under the workmen's compensation statute. At the trial of this second case, brought by the widow, the testimony of the deceased husband in the first case was offered in evidence. Should it have been admitted? [Welch v Essex County, 6 NJS 422, 68 A2d 787]

5. The state insurance commissioner was authorized to regulate advertising by insurance companies. A bill was introduced in the legislature affecting insurance companies. One of the companies circulated printed matter in opposition to the proposed law. The state insurance commissioner began to investigate this printed matter on the ground that it was advertising. The insurance company claimed that he did not have jurisdiction to do so. Decide. [See Ex partie Allstate Ins. Co., 248 SC 550, 151 SE2d 849]

7 Environmental Law and Community Planning

PREVENTION OF POLLUTION

The law of the past was aimed at protecting individual property rights. As society changed from rural and agricultural to urban and industrialized, new laws were needed to prevent the pollution of the environment.

§ 7:1. Introduction. Today American society accepts the fact that there must be some limitation upon freedom of action if an environment fit for life is to be maintained. Moreover, a government may require a property owner to install devices at his own expense to prevent an environmental pollution. (See p. 117, Freeman v Contra Costa County Water District.)

§ 7:2. Inadequacy of the Prior Law. The law as it had developed down to the middle of the twentieth century was not adequate to cope with the problems of pollution. The principles of law that had developed were designed to compensate the plaintiff for harm to him. If the plaintiff could show that the polluted air was taking the paint off his house or killing his crops, he might be entitled to relief because he had then shown that he had sustained a specific harm distinct from the harm to the members of the public at large.

Prior to the adoption of recent statutes, the act of polluting the air was not unlawful and, therefore, the district attorney or the attorney general would not have any basis for complaining against the air pollution. Anti-pollution statutes have begun to change this rule of the common law so as to outlaw pollution and to authorize action by government officials and by individual private persons. When a statute does not expressly give the private person the right to sue for judicial relief because of pollution, the common-law rule still bars suit in most jurisdictions. Thus, a group of citizens protesting a rezoning because of the harm that it would cause a bay has been denied standing to object to possible water pollution as the protesting committee would not sustain any harm distinct from that suffered by the public at large.[1]

Even when the plaintiff could show that his property was harmed, he might lose his case by being unable to show that it was the defendant who was the cause of the harm. For example, if there were 10 factories in the

[1] Save the Bay Committee, Inc. v Mayor of the City of Savannah, 227 Ga 436, 181 SE2d 351.

vicinity of the plaintiff's house which were all polluting the air with industrial fumes and the plaintiff sued any one of them, he would have the almost impossible task of proving that it was the fumes from that particular factory which caused the damage. The defendant factory would contend that it was the conduct of the other nine.

If the plaintiff sued all of the factories at one time, he could probably obtain an injunction against all of them; but it was not until the twentieth century was one third underway that the plaintiff would be permitted as a procedural matter to join all the factories in one action—such joinder being earlier prohibited on the ground that each factory had acted independently of the others.

Recovery of money damages for the harm done was virtually impossible because the law required the plaintiff to show how much of his total damage had been caused by which wrongdoer. Thus, if the smoke from two factories caused the paint to peel from the plaintiff's house, he was required to show how much of this was attributable to the smoke of each factory. The law had not yet developed the concept that many courts now apply in automobile collision cases of making each driver jointly and severally liable for the total harm when the exact harm caused by him cannot be determined.

The net result of all of this was that down to almost the present decade the law gave little or no assistance in the fight against pollution when the plaintiff could not show that he had sustained any actual harm from the pollution or where two or more persons or factories had polluted the same environment.

§ 7:3. Federal Environmental Protection. A number of federal statutes provide for research into the effect of the environment upon man and the economy. Congress has adopted the National Environmental Policy Act of 1969 [2] and the Water and Environmental Quality Improvement Act of 1970.[3] Congress has also provided for the study of health hazards caused by pollution,[4] and for informing the public of the significance of the environment and the problems involved.[5]

Congress has provided the means for regulating pesticides and ordering their removal from the market if shown to present an unreasonable adverse effect on man or on the environment, after taking into account social, economic, and environmental costs and benefits.[6] The Federal Trade Commission has requested the manufacturers of household detergents to state on their label whether the product is biodegradable, meaning whether the

---

[2] PL 91-190, 83 Stat 852, 42 USC § 4321 et seq. Among other things, this Act creates a Council on Environment Quality as part of the executive branch of the national government.

[3] PL 91-224, 84 Stat 91.

[4] Heart Disease, Cancer, Stroke and Kidney Disease Amendments of 1970, PL 91-515, 84 Stat 1297, § 501.

[5] Environmental Education Act, PL 91-516, 84 Stat 1312.

[6] Federal Insecticide, Fungicide, and Rodenticide Act (FIFRA), 7 USC § 135 et seq. This Act was rewritten by the Federal Environmental Pesticide Control Act of 1972, PL 92-516, 86 Stat 973, but still retains its original name.

suds and foam will be eliminated by natural biological action in breaking down the chemistry of the detergents into simpler compounds.

§ **7:4. Environmental Impact Statements.** Environmental protection legislation typically requires that any activity which might have a significant effect upon the environment be supported by an environmental impact statement. Whenever any bill is proposed in Congress and whenever any federal action significantly affecting the quality of the human environment is undertaken, a statement must be prepared as to the environmental impact of the action.[7] (See p. 118, National Resources Defense Council, Inc. v Morton.)

If an agency deems that an environmental impact statement (EIS) is unnecessary, it must file a statement in support of this conclusion.[8]

The environmental impact statement required by NEPA (National Environmental Policy Act) is to be made by the particular agency which has the overall responsibility for the project. When one government agency handles the granting of funds for a project but another agency is the one which is actually involved in the work and which has the expertise required for the preparation of the impact statement, the statement should be prepared by the latter agency.

The environmental impact statement must contain a thorough discussion of all reasonable alternatives.[9]

An urban renewal project is a major federal action significantly affecting the quality of the human environment and the NEPA, therefore, requires consideration of the environmental impact at every important stage in the decision-making processes concerning the project.[10]

A multi-family condominium is a major action significantly affecting the environment and must therefore be supported by an environmental impact statement.[11]

When an agency of the national government makes a significant financial contribution to a new major field of technology, as the production of nuclear fuel for use in electrical power plants, the agency must prepare an impact statement on the theory that there is no distinction between requiring an impact statement for a new plant and requiring such a statement for the development of a new technology which will require the construction of many new plants.[12]

---

[7] PL 9-190, 83 Stat 853, § 102; 42 USC § 4332.

[8] Arizona Public Service Co. v Federal Power Commission, (CA Dist Col) 483 F2d 1775.

[9] Environmental Defense Fund, Inc. v Froehlke, (CA8 Ark) 473 F2d 346, 350. "[This] insures that agency officials will be acquainted with the tradeoffs which will have to be made if any particular line of action is chosen."

[10] Businessmen Affected v District of Columbia City Council, (DC Dist Col) 339 F Supp 793.

[11] Loveless v Yantis, 82 Wash 2d 754, 513 P2d 1023.

[12] Scientists' Institute for Public Information, Inc. v Atomic Energy Commission, (CA Dist Col AEC) 481 F2d 1079 (holding that the Atomic Energy Commission was required to prepare a statement for the LMFBR—Liquid Metal Fast Breeder Reactor).

NEPA does not authorize federal courts to make appraisals and comparisons of technical engineering matters to determine what would be best for the environment.[13]

Many states have laws which follow the same pattern as the federal statute.[14]

§ 7:5. Air Pollution. The federal Clean Air Act [15] (as amended and supplemented by the Air Quality Act of 1967 [16]), the Clean Air Amendments of 1970,[17] and the National Motor Vehicles Emissions Standards Act [18] provide for establishing standards to reduce pollution from automobiles, airplanes, and fuel consumption, and require the automobile industry to produce "a substantially pollution-free" automobile engine.

Acting under the authority of the Clean Air Act, the Department of Health, Education, and Welfare has divided the country into *atmosphere areas* for the purpose of applying air controls. The federal Air Pollution Control Administration regulates automobile exhausts. The federal Aviation Administration makes similar regulations for aircraft.

§ 7:6. Noise Pollution. The term "noise pollution" refers to the imposition upon the air of excessive noise. The prior law had developed some protection for a landowner from noise damage. By this law the use of a sound truck or loudspeaker for advertising purposes can be restrained when its noise unreasonably interferes with the use of the neighboring land. Excessive noise from a drive-in theater may be enjoined.[19] When the flight of planes from an airport creates such an unreasonable noise and vibration as to interfere greatly with the use and enjoyment of neighboring land, the landowner may be entitled to an injunction to stop the use of the airport or to change the particular flight pattern. In any case, damages may be recovered for the loss of value of the neighboring land. Such deprivation of value is also generally considered a taking of property so as to require compensation to be made under eminent domain.[20]

The need for protection from noise pollution was not appreciated prior to the expanded use of commercial jet aircraft in the 1960's. While one can regard the protection from noise pollution as an extension of the earlier concept of public nuisance, the prior law does not provide any suitable guide for the solution of present-day cases and it is misleading to look to the prior law.[21]

---

[13] Burleigh v Calloway, (DC Hawaii) 362 F Supp 121.

[14] See, for example, Eastlake Community Council v Roanoke Associates, Inc., 82 Wash 2d 475, 513 P2d 36.

[15] 42 USC § 1857 et seq.

[16] PL 90-148, 81 Stat 485.

[17] PL 91-604, 84 Stat 1676.

[18] 42 USC § 1857f-1 et seq.

[19] Guarina v Bogart, 407 Pa 307, 180 A2d 557.

[20] Griggs v Allegheny County, 369 US 84.

[21] One writer has taken the position that protection from air pollution by noise is embraced within the Preamble of the United States Constitution, in its statement "to assure domestic tranquillity." If one gives proper value to the adjective "domestic" and

The Noise Control Acts of 1970 and 1972 declare a federal policy to promote for all Americans an environment free from noise that jeopardizes their health and welfare.[22] The administrator of EPA [23] is given authority to establish noise emission standards for equipment, motors, and engines. Similar standards may be set for airplanes, railroads, and motor carriers in cooperation with the Secretary of Transportation, the Federal Aviation Administration, and other appropriate agencies.

The EPA administrator may require that equipment bear a label showing compliance with the noise emission standards adopted under the authority of the federal statutes.[24]

The states regulate the noise created by automobiles, motorcycles, and other motor vehicles. When local noise pollution control laws conflict with the federal regulations on the same subject or impose an unreasonable restriction on interstate commerce, the local control is invalid. (See p. 119, Burbank v Lockheed Air Terminal, Inc.) A state may not prohibit the local landing of commercial supersonic transport aircraft, because this would interfere with federal control of interstate commerce.[25]

§ 7:7. Water Pollution. The discharge of refuse into navigable water is prohibited by the River and Harbors Appropriation Act of 1899,[26] and the Federal Water Pollution Control Act amendments of 1972.[27] The federal law prohibiting dumping of waste in navigable waters is violated even though it is not shown that navigation was affected thereby.[28] The federal statutes have been supplemented by federal administrative regulations establishing standards for water quality and guidelines for the design, operation, and maintenance of water waste treatment facilities. The Water Pollution Control Act amendments of 1972 [29] provide for grants for research and construction of water treatment works.

As part of the Saline Water Conversion Act of 1970, provision is made for the development of methods for converting chemically contaminated water into water for beneficial consumptive uses.[30]

Nearly one half of all the water used in the United States is for the purpose of cooling and condensing in connection with industrial uses. The temperature of the water is raised thereby; and when such heated water is

---

bears in mind the era in which the framers of the Constitution lived, it is apparent that "domestic tranquillity" meant to the framers what "law and order" means to the average person today. Furthermore, it is absurd to find that the framers were thinking of a pollution by noise that would develop when the factory system arose and railroads were invented in the next century, and when automobiles and airplanes were invented two centuries later.

22 PL 91-604, 84 Stat 1676; PL 92-574, 86 Stat 1234, 42 USC § 4901.

23 The Environmental Protection Agency is a federal agency established under the Reorganization Plan No. 3 of 1970.

24 PL 92-574, 86 Stat 1234, § 8(a).

25 Opinion of the Justices, (Mass) 271 NE2d 354.

26 § 13, 33 USC § 407.

27 § 101 et seq., 33 USC § 1251 et seq.

28 United States v United States Steel Corp., (CA7 Ind) 482 F2d 439.

29 PL 92-500, 86 Stat 816.

30 42 USC § 1959 et seq.

dumped in a natural stream or water supply, it has a harmful effect similar in many cases to the dumping of organic wastes. Some steps for the prevention of thermal pollution have been made by federal legislation.[31]

§ 7:8. **Waste Disposal.** Waste disposal is to a large degree an aspect of water pollution because of the extent to which waste is dumped into rivers and lakes. It is also an aspect of air pollution through the burning of waste accumulated in open dumping. Various federal statutes seek solutions for the problems involved: the Solid Waste Disposal Act,[32] the Resource Recovery Act of 1970, and Materials Policy Act of 1970.[33] The latter Act seeks to reduce the solid waste problems by encouraging the recycling of such wastes, reprocessing them so that they are usable again for either the same or some other purpose; to promote greater initiative on the part of the states and local communities in meeting the problems; and to encourage the local construction of pilot waste disposal plants utilizing modern technical knowledge. Federal programs are under the guidance of the Secretary of Health, Education, and Welfare (HEW).

The Marine Protection, Research, and Sanctuaries Act of 1972 prohibits dumping in the ocean waste or matter which contains active chemical, biologic, or radioactive agents. The Act also prohibits transporting such materials from the United States for the purpose of dumping in the ocean. The Secretary of Commerce, after consultation with specified agencies, may designate particular areas of the ocean as sanctuaries and then seek to obtain international treaties protecting such areas.[34]

State laws seek to reduce the problem of waste disposal by requiring recycling or reuse of various products. (See p. 121, American Can Co. v Oregon Liquor Control Commission.)

§ 7:9. **Regulation by Administrative Agencies.** For the most part the law against pollution is a matter of the adoption and enforcement of regulations by administrative agencies, such as the federal EPA. Administrative agency control is likely to increase in the future because of the difficulty and technical nature of the problems involved, and because of the interrelationship of pollution problems and nonpollution problems. For example, the problem of disposing of solid wastes presents a phase of the problem of conserving natural resources through the recycling and reuse of waste products. It is estimated that 360 million tons of solid waste are generated annually in the United States and that this amount will double by 1980. The cost of removing and disposing of this waste is $4.5 billion annually. The solid waste problem is a major problem in urban development apart from the pollution aspect.

As further illustration of the interrelationship of problems, it is estimated that the national need for electrical energy has doubled every 10 years since

---

[31] Water Pollution Prevention and Control Act of 1972, 33 USC § 1254(t), 1313(g), (h), 1326.

[32] 42 USC § 3251 et seq.

[33] PL 91-512, 84 Stat 1227.

[34] PL 92-532, 86 Stat 1052.

1945. It is generally believed that the production of electrical energy by nuclear reactor plants is the most likely means of producing the electricity that America will need in the future. This method of production also has the advantage that it causes less air pollution than any other method of producing electricity. Such plants, however, utilize substantial quantities of water for cooling. When water is returned to its source, its temperature has been raised, thus increasing the problem of thermal pollution, although it is claimed that advanced models of reactors have overcome this objection.

It is also likely that there will be increasing cooperative effort made by both government and industry to achieve desired goals.[35]

§ **7:10. Litigation.** The right to bring a private lawsuit to recover damages or to obtain an injunction against pollution will continue. The prior law will probably be changed by giving an individual the right to bring an antipollution suit even though he cannot show that he has sustained any harm different than that sustained by any other member of the general public. For example, the Clean Air Amendments Act of 1972,[36] the Water Pollution Prevention and Control Act of 1972,[37] and the Noise Control Act [38] authorize a private suit by "any person" in a federal district court to stop a violation of the air, water, and noise pollution standards. "The courts have been increasingly willing to recognize the right of organizations to sue on behalf of their members. . . . Some courts have held that organizations have standing to represent their members' interest even without any organization interest being involved." [39]

A private person does not always have the right to sue for violation of an environmental protection control. In some instances the right to sue is restricted to a particular government agency. For example, the right to sue for a violation of the Federal Water Pollution Act is vested exclusively in the administrator of the Environmental Protection Agency. A private citizen or property owner cannot bring suit against an alleged polluter for violating this Act, as distinct from proving that the conduct of the defendant constituted a nuisance affecting the plaintiff.[40] Likewise, an action brought for a violation of the Marine Protection, Research, and Sanctuaries Act of 1972 is brought by the Attorney General of the United States on his own initiative or at the request of the Secretary of Commerce.[41]

It is likely that there will be an increase in antipollution suits brought by a state against defendants who have acted in another state. A complaining

---

[35] See Standard Lime & Refractories Co. v Department of Environmental Resources, 2 Pa Commonwealth Court 434, 279 A2d 383. "Common sense would seem to dictate a conference between representatives of the [business and the government department] to settle their differences, if for no other reason than to help reduce an already overloaded court calendar."

[36] PL 91-604, 84 Stat 1676, § 304.

[37] PL 92-500, 86 Stat 888 § 505, 33 USC § 1365.

[38] PL 92-574, 86 Stat 1243, 42 USC § 4911.

[39] Undergraduate Student Association v Peltason, (DC ND Ill) 359 F Supp 320.

[40] Higginbotham v Barrett, (CA5 Ga) 473 F2d 745.

[41] PL 92-532, 86 Stat 1052, § 303(d).

state may bring suit against citizens of another state to stop pollution harm to the citizens of the plaintiff state. For example, a complaining state, such as California, may bring an action against residents, natural persons, or corporations of Utah on the ground that the conduct of the latter constitutes an unlawful pollution which harms persons in California. Such an action will ordinarily be brought in a federal court of the state in which the defendants reside, in order to obtain an impartial tribunal and one which can enforce its decision.

Illustrative of this type of action, the state of Texas could bring an action in the federal district court for the District of New Mexico against residents of New Mexico to enjoin them from using a chlorinated camphene pesticide on their ranches, which was allegedly carried by rain water into an interstate river that was the water supply for a number of cities in Texas, thereby polluting the water supply.[42]

In any case it is reasonable to expect that courts will not take an active part in the solution of pollution problems. It is likely that they will defer to the decisions on these technical problems made or to be made by the appropriate administrative agency.[43] As evidence of judicial reluctance to become involved in pollution problems, the United States Supreme Court has refused to exercise the jurisdiction given it by the Constitution to hear an original action brought by a state against nonresidents to stop pollution, on the ground that no federal question was involved and that its entertaining of the suit was undesirable because of the scientific questions involved in determining whether there was pollution, that any legal questions involved were "bottomed on state law," and that administrative agencies and commissions, both state and international, were already devoting attention to the particular pollution problem.[44]

Courts will be particularly likely to avoid pollution litigation when the matter before them is merely a small segment of the total pollution problem involved so that the exercise of jurisdiction by a court would hamper or disrupt the work of administrative agencies and study groups.

---

[42] Texas v Pankey, (CA10 NM) 441 F2d 236. The action could ordinarily also be brought in a state or federal court situated in the complaining state. While jurisdiction can be obtained over the nonresident defendant by service under modern long-arm statutes, suits in the courts of the complaining state have the practical disadvantage of requiring a second proceeding in the defendant's state to enforce the judgment obtained in the complaining state. An action could also be brought in a state court in the defendant's state, but this raises the danger of that court's being partial to its local resident. Theoretically, a complaining state could bring an antipollution proceeding as an original action in the Supreme Court of the United States; but in the absence of some strong federal question, that court will refuse to exercise original jurisdiction and will not take any part in the controversy until an appeal has been taken from a lower court decision. See footnote 44.

[43] Boomer v Atlantic Cement Co., 26 NY2d 219, 309 NYS2d 312, 257 NE2d 870.

[44] Ohio v Wyandotte Chemicals Corp., 401 US 493 (Ohio sought to enjoin Canadian, Michigan, and Delaware corporations from dumping mercury into tributaries of Lake Erie, which allegedly polluted that lake which was used by parts of Ohio as a water supply).

§ 7:11. Criminal Liability. In many states criminal proceedings to impose a fine are provided to punish violation of the environmental protection regulations.[45] Antipollution statutes may make it a crime to cause improper pollution. Under such statutes, it is no defense that the defendant did not intend to violate the law or was not negligent.

The fact that the defendant operated his business in the customary way and did not produce any greater amount of pollution than other similar enterprises is not a defense to a prosecution for polluting the environment.[46]

COMMUNITY PLANNING

§ 7:12. Restrictive Covenants in Private Contracts. In the case of private planning, a real estate developer will take an undeveloped tract or area of land, map out on paper an "ideal" community, and then construct the buildings shown on the plan. These he will then sell to private purchasers. The deeds by which he transfers title will contain restrictive covenants that obligate the buyers to observe certain limitations as to the use of their property, the nature of buildings that will be maintained or constructed on the land, and so on.

Frequently a buyer will purchase a lot in an undeveloped tract in the expectation that the seller is going to develop the area in a particular way. Such expectations do not bind the seller and he may change his plans unless the carrying out of those plans was made an express part of the contract with the buyer.[47]

§ 7:13. Public Zoning. Public community planning is generally synonymous with zoning. By *zoning* a city adopts an ordinance imposing restrictions upon the use of the land. The object of zoning is to insure an orderly physical development of the regulated area. In effect, zoning is the same as the restrictive covenants with the difference as to the source of their authority.

Zoning is always based upon a legislative enactment. In most cases this is an ordinance of a local political subdivision, such as a municipality or a county ordinance, as distinguished from a statute adopted by a state legislature or the United States Congress.[48] A local zoning ordinance may be supplemented or reinforced by a general state statute, such as a statute that makes it a crime to violate a local zoning ordinance.

Zoning is to be distinguished from building regulations, although the distinction between the two is not always apparent. For example, a requirement that there be at least four feet of clear space between a building wall and a boundary line is regarded as a zoning requirement, whereas a law requiring that the walls of the building be built of fireproof material is regarded as a building regulation. Both of these requirements, however, have the common element of concern for others. The property owner must maintain a four-foot

---

[45] Delaware v Getty Oil Co., (Del Super) 305 A2d 327.

[46] Ohio River Sand Co. v Kentucky, (Ky) 467 SW2d 347.

[47] Japanese Gardens Mobile Estates, Inc. v Hunt, (Fla App) 261 So2d 193.

[48] In some states the legislative enactment of a local political subdivision is called a "resolution."

setback for the benefit of the community—the passage of light and air is facilitated; in case of fire there is less likelihood of fire spreading if buildings are separated by a substantial space; in case of police or fire emergency it will be possible to cut across the lot instead of going around the block; and the building will probably be aesthetically more attractive if set off by space. The building regulation that seeks to protect from fire is likewise community-oriented in that the neighborhood is less likely to be destroyed by fire if each building is in itself not of a flammable construction.

(1) Validity of Zoning. In terms of social forces, zoning represents the subordination of the landowner's right to use his property as he chooses to the interests of the community at large. Zoning is held constitutional as an exercise of the police power as long as the zoning regulation bears a reasonable relation to health, morals, safety, or general welfare.

A zoning regulation may require that any meeting place must provide parking space for one car for every five seats in the place of assembly. This is a reasonable restriction on private property designed to prevent the overcrowding of highways which results from lack of parking facilities. Overcrowding would have a harmful effect on highway traffic and on the maintenance of fire and police protection.[49]

A zoning ordinance may restrict trailer homes to specified trailer parks.[50] Such a provision bars the owner of a tract of land from placing his own trailer on the land. (See p. 122, City of Colby v Hurtt.) A zoning ordinance may constitutionally exclude gas stations from downtown shopping areas.[51] Zoning laws may seek to limit population density by limiting the number of dwelling units which may be included in a high-rise apartment by fixing a ratio of surrounding land to units.[52]

The fact that the use authorized by zoning is not the most profitable to the owner does not affect the validity of the zoning. That is, the fact that a landowner could make more money if his land were zoned to permit a business use does not render unconstitutional a zoning ordinance which restricts the land to a noncommercial use.[53]

The refusal of a building permit because of a zoning law is not in itself a denial of equal protection.[54] If, however, it can be shown that all persons of a particular race or group were denied permits while others were granted permits under the same circumstances, the refusal of a permit based on such discrimination is a violation of rights protected by the federal Constitution.[55] The application to a church of zoning restrictions which prevent it from

[49] Trustees v Swift, 183 Pa Super 219, 130 A2d 240.

[50] Minnesota v Larson, 292 Minn 296, 195 NW2d 180.

[51] Pure Oil Division of Union Oil Co. v Northville, 27 Mich App 42, 183 NW2d 303.

[52] Frankel v Atlantic City, 124 NJ Super 420, 307 A2d 615.

[53] Edge v Moraine City, 58 OO2d 499, 283 NE2d 219.

[54] Brosten v Scheeler, (DC ND Ill) 360 F Supp 608.

[55] Yick Wo v Hopkins, 118 US 356.

parking buses on its property does not violate the constitutional guarantee of freedom of religion.[56]

A landowner does not have a vested right in the continuance of the zoning ordinance in force when he purchased his land. Consequently, an owner cannot complain when a subsequent amendment of the zoning ordinance imposes additional restrictions on the future use of his land.[57]

Just as restrictive covenants in a deed may become unenforceable because of a change in the nature of the area, a zoning classification may become invalid for the same reason.

(2) Nonconforming Use. When the use to which the land is already being put when the zoning ordinance goes into effect is in conflict with the zoning ordinance, such use is described as a *nonconforming use.* For example, when a zoning ordinance was adopted which required a setback of 25 feet from the boundary line, an already existing building that was only set back 10 feet was a nonconforming use.[58]

The nonconforming use represents one of the major problems involved in zoning. A nonconforming use has a constitutionally protected right to continue.[59] That is, a business or activity which is in itself lawful cannot be wiped out by a zoning ordinance even though it is in conflict with the zoning pattern. Thus, a grocery store already in existence cannot be ordered away when the area is zoned as residential. The hope of the zoners is that the conforming use will disappear. This tends to be a very slow process because the effect of the zoning restriction is to give the nonconforming use a monopoly advantage, and its economic life tends to be extended thereby.

If the nonconforming use is discontinued, it cannot be resumed. The right to make a nonconforming use may thus be lost by abandonment; as when the owner of a garage stops using it for a garage and uses it for storing goods, a return to the use of the property as a garage will be barred by abandonment.[60] Zoning ordinances commonly provide that when a nonconforming use is discontinued for a period of time, such as one year, such discontinuance is evidence of an intention to abandon or is in itself sufficient to terminate the right to resume the nonconforming use.[61]

(3) Variance. The administrative agency charged with the enforcement of the zoning ordinance may generally grant a *variance.* This permits the

---

[56] East Side Baptist Church v Klein, 175 Colo 168, 487 P2d 549.

[57] Citizens Bank and Trust Co. v Park Ridge, 5 Ill App 3d 77, 282 NE2d 751.

[58] United Cerebral Palsy Ass'n v Zoning Board of Adjustment, 382 Pa 67, 114 A2d 331.

[59] Exceptions to this rule are beginning to appear. National Advertising Co. v Monterey County, 1 Cal 3d 875, 83 Cal Rptr 577, 464 P2d 33. The nonconforming use concept is ignored when a safety law is involved, such as a building code designed to prevent fire. Bakersfield v Miller, 4 Cal 2d 93, 48 Cal Rptr 889, 410 P2d 393.

[60] Marchese v Norristown Borough Zoning Board of Adjustment, 2 Pa Commonwealth Court 84, 277 A2d 176.

[61] Jahn v Patterson, 23 App Div 2d 688, 257 NYS2d 639.

owner of the land to use it in a specified manner inconsistent with the zoning ordinance. (See p. 123, Stokes v Jacksonville.) The agency will ordinarily be reluctant to permit a variance when neighboring property owners object because, to the extent that variation is permitted, the basic plan of the zoning ordinance is defeated. Likewise, the allowance of an individual variation may result in such inequality as to be condemned by the courts as *spot zoning.* In addition, there is the consideration of practical expediency that if variances are readily granted, every property owner will request a variance and thus flood the agency with such requests.

In any case a variance will ordinarily be refused when the proposed use for which the variance is sought is one that would be harmful to the public or which would be an illegal use without regard to the zoning restriction.

§ 7:14. Federal Legislation. Federal legislation in the area of community planning is largely directed toward research and financial aid to cities and housing projects. A series of national housing acts of 1948, 1954, 1956, and 1961 has been followed by the Demonstration Cities and Metropolitan Development Act of 1966 [62] and the Housing and Urban Development Act of 1970.[63]

The executive branch of the national government has been expanded by the creation of a Department of Housing and Urban Development (HUD).

The Coastal Zone Management Act of 1972 [64] provides financial assistance to states in protecting coastal zones from overpopulation and to preserve and protect the natural resources of the coast. The Rural Development Act of 1972 [65] amends a number of earlier laws relating to farming and makes additional provision for protection from fire and flood and for the furthering of research for education with the objective of raising the standards of rural life and thereby discouraging the steady population shifts from farm to city.

§ 7:15. Eminent Domain. The power of eminent domain plays an important role in community planning because it is the means by which the land required for housing, redevelopment, and other projects may be acquired. Eminent domain has not become important in the area of environmental law, although it is always present as a possible alternative on the theory that a government-owned plant would be more concerned with protection of the environment.

(1) Public Purpose. When property is taken by government by eminent domain, it must be taken for a public purpose. The taking of property for a private purpose is void as a deprivation of property without due process of law.

Whether the purpose of the taking is public is a question for the courts to determine. The courts are not bound by the declaration in a statute that

---

[62] 42 USC § 1416 et seq.
[63] PL 91-609, 84 Stat 1770.
[64] PL 92-419, 86 Stat.
[65] PL 92-583, 86 Stat 1280, 16 USC § 1451 et seq.

a particular purpose shall be deemed a public purpose when in fact it is a private purpose. As a practical matter, however, a declaration by the lawmaker, particularly by Congress, that a taking is a public purpose will generally be given great respect by the courts.[66] With the widening of the concept of "public purpose," the possibility of a conflict between the lawmaker and the courts as to whether a particular taking is for a public purpose becomes increasingly unlikely.

Property is taken for a public purpose when it is taken for use by the government, as land taken for a courthouse, employing "public" in the sense of "government." Historically, this was the only "public purpose." Today, property is deemed taken for a public purpose when the members of the public at large may use the property thereafter, as a "public" parking garage, the term "public" here being used to refer to people at large rather than to the government. The fact that a charge is made does not destroy the "public" character of an activity. Consequently, land taken for a highway is taken for a public purpose even though the highway is a turnpike that charges tolls for its use. Land is also taken for a public purpose even though particular individuals will receive the benefit of its taking. For example, the taking of land for a low-cost housing project is deemed a public purpose even though it will only benefit the small percentage of the total public who are occupants of the project.

The taking of land for the redevelopment of a blighted area is a public purpose.

It does not appear that there are any constitutional limitations upon the determination that land requires development. In the early days of redevelopment, the land taken was a slum area that was obviously deteriorated. From this beginning redevelopment logically expanded to permit the taking of areas that were likely to become slums. The fact that in this process individual buildings are taken by the government although they are in good condition, does not render the taking unlawful as it is within the discretion of government to determine whether to proceed on a structure-by-structure basis or on the basis of a broad sweep of the blighted area. The fact that individual buildings in the area are not themselves blighted nor used for residential purposes does not require the adoption of a "piecemeal approach" nor prevent reaching the conclusion that "the entire area needed redesigning so that a balanced, integrated plan could be developed for the region." [67] Recent authority holds that redevelopment is not necessarily linked to slum elimination or prevention but permits the taking by eminent domain of vacant, unimproved nonurban land which is standing idle because the title to the land is held by numerous owners. The theory is that communities should eliminate "stagnant and unproductive" conditions of land, and for that purpose they may use the power of eminent domain in order to "serve the health, welfare, social and economic interests, and sound growth of the community." [68]

---

[66] United States v Welch, 327 US 546.
[67] Berman v Parker, 348 US 26.
[68] Levin v Bridgewater Township Committee, 57 NJ 506, 274 A2d 1.

Redevelopment and other public welfare projects are generally managed by independent authorities or agencies, rather than by the government itself. Thus, a state will not ordinarily undertake land redevelopment, but the state legislature will adopt a law creating a municipal redevelopment authority or authorize the creation of local redevelopment authorities. This has the advantage of administrative agency control by experts as discussed in Chapter 6.

Another reason why independent "authorities" are created for redevelopment and other projects is that such an authority may be authorized to issue bonds to finance its operations. Such indebtedness does not constitute a debt of any government within the meaning of a constitutional limitation on debt. Consequently, the indebtedness of a state housing authority is not subject to the constitutional limitation on the debt of the state.[69]

(2) What Constitutes a Taking? In the early days of limited government action, there was ordinarily no question of whether land had been taken. With the advent of the twentieth century, government may engage in activities that affect a landowner without actually taking his land. If such activity is deemed a "taking," the property owner is entitled to compensation. In order to protect the property owner and to prevent hardship to him, the courts have expanded the concept of "taking" to embrace activity which excludes the property owner from his property or substantially lessens its value. Thus, land is deemed "taken" for the purpose of requiring compensation when it is submerged by the backflood of water resulting from the construction of a hydroelectric power plant and dam.

There is authority that pollution by a municipal sewage works, as the result of which water had an offensive odor and was unfit for irrigation because the sewage would clog the irrigation pumps, constitutes a taking by eminent domain for which compensation must be made.[70]

(3) Excess Condemnation. *Excess condemnation* is the taking by eminent domain of property in excess of that actually needed for the public improvement. In some instances, the excess is taken to provide a buffer around the improvement so that undesirable uses are not made of the land neighboring the improved area.[71] Excess condemnation is also sustained when the excess represents fragments or remnants of land that would have little value to the owner. In some instances excess condemnation is sustained on the ground that the taking of an entire tract will be less expensive to the government than paying damages for taking only part of the tract. The reasoning is that the part of the tract remaining has so little value that the government will have paid practically the entire tract value in order to obtain the part.[72]

---

[69] Maine State Housing Authority v Depositors Trust Co. (Maine) 278 A2d 699.

[70] Walla Walla v Conkey, 6 Wash App2d 6, 492 P2d 589.

[71] People ex rel v Lagiss, 223 Cal App2d 23, 35 Cal Rptr 554.

[72] People ex rel v Superior Court and Rodoni, 68 Cal App 2d 206, 436 P2d 342, 65 Cal Rptr 342.

The problem of excess condemnation is frequently present in redevelopment projects. Customarily the proper authority will take a large area of land, put low-cost housing projects on part, set aside part for parks, playgrounds, and streets; and then sell the balance of the land remaining to private purchasers subject to restrictions as to use. The imposition of these restrictions makes the excess land a buffer for the redeveloped area and is accordingly held valid although in excess of actual needs.

CASES FOR CHAPTER 7

Freeman v Contra Costa County Water District

18 Cal App 3d 404, 95 Cal Rptr 852 (1971)

The Contra Costa County Water District adopted a regulation that any customer who had an auxiliary water supply on his land, such as a well, must install at his own expense a device to prevent such auxiliary water from polluting the water of the Water District. The device cost $35.00. Residents of the county claimed the regulation was unconstitutional. The court sustained the regulation of the respondent Water District. The residents appealed.

CHRISTIAN, A.J. . . . Each of the appellants maintains on his property a well from which water is drawn for such purposes as gardening and car-washing. Although appellants had not connected their well water systems to the pipes of the district's public system, the district threatens to terminate service until the affected householders agree to have installed, at their own expense, a "double check valve assembly," designed to prevent water from the auxiliary supply from "backing up" into and contaminating the public water supply. . . .

The record shows without contradiction that contamination of a water system can occur if there is a physical connection between the public system and auxiliary water supply, such as where the two systems are connected by pipes, or where the auxiliary water is "impounded" (e.g., in a swimming pool or fish pond) and an ordinary garden hose from the public water supply is allowed to lie in water from the auxiliary system. In the latter situation a temporary loss of pressure can result in contaminated water being drawn into the public system.

Protection against this risk can be provided by installing in the consumer's water meter box a device which prevents a backward flow of water. . . . Health and Safety Code section 203 provides that the State Department of Public Health "shall examine and may prevent the pollution of sources of public domestic water . . . supply." The department may "adopt and enforce rules and regulations" for this purpose. . . . Pursuant to these statutes, the department adopted administrative regulations designed to prevent contamination or pollution of any public water supply as a result of "actual *or* potential cross-connections" with auxiliary water supplies. . . . A protective device is required to be installed on any premises receiving water from the public water system and containing an auxiliary water supply, regardless of whether the auxiliary water supply is connected to the public water system. . . . The regulations specify various types of protective devices, depending on the "degree of hazard" involved; where the auxiliary and public water supplies are not connected, the protective device required is a "double check valve assembly," which is what respondent desires. . . . Pursuant to the foregoing state regulations, respondent adopted its own regulations providing for discontinuance of water service to any consumer who failed to install the required device.

Appellants contend that the requirement that they install a protective device constitutes a taking of property which must be compensated. They argue that they have the right to take water from their wells and that respondent's demand infringes on their right to use their property as they wish. This contention confuses an exercise of the police power with an exercise of the power of eminent domain; "the constitutional guaranty of just compensation attached to an exercise of the power of eminent domain does not extend to the state's exercise of its police power. . . . It cannot be denied that prevention of water pollution is a legitimate governmental objective, in furtherance of which the police power may be exercised. Appellants argue, however, that it is unreasonable to require them to install a protective device when their water well is not connected to the domestic water supply. Therefore, it is argued, there is no possibility of contamination and the danger that respondent seeks to protect is "imagined and speculative." But the state need not wait until the public safety has actually suffered injury; it may take reasonable steps to protect a public water supply from potential cross-connections that may create a substantial hazard of contamination. Otherwise respondent, or the Department of Public Health, would have the burdensome job of continuous inspection of all premises which possessed auxiliary water supplies to insure that no cross-connections had been made, accidentally or otherwise. It is not unreasonable or oppressive to require appellants to install a $35 device to protect against a potential danger of water contamination. . . .

[Judgment affirmed.]

Natural Resources Defense Council, Inc. v Morton

(CA Dist Col) 458 F2d 827 (1972)

Morton, the U.S. Secretary of the Interior, announced that the United States proposed to sell certain offshore oil lands. The Director of the Bureau of Land Management prepared an environmental impact statement. An injunction against the proposed governmental action was obtained by the Natural Resources Defense Council which claimed that the environmental impact statement was not adequate. The Government moved to dismiss the injunction.

LEVENTHAL, C.J. . . . Oil pollution is the problem most extensively discussed in the Statement and its exposition of unavoidable adverse environmental effects. . . .

. . . The [District] Court found that the Statement failed to provide the "detailed statement" required by NEPA [National Environmental Policy Act] of environmental impact and alternatives. The Court stated:

> . . . The defendants only superficially discussed the alternatives listed in their Final Impact Statement, and they failed to discuss in detail the environmental impacts of the alternatives they listed in the statement. The Court does not wish to give the impression that it believes the alternatives are better than the proposed lease sale, but it believes that these alternatives must be explored and discussed thoroughly in order to comport with the intent and requirements of . . . NEPA. . . .

Congress contemplated that the Impact Statement would constitute the environmental source material for the information of the Congress as well as the Executive, in connection with the making of relevant decisions, and would be available to enhance enlightenment of —and by—the public. The impact statement provides a basis for (a) evaluation of the benefits of the proposed project in light of its environmental risks, and (b) comparison of the net balance for the proposed project with the environmental risks presented by alternative courses of action. . . .

. . . A sound construction of NEPA . . . requires a presentation of the environmental risks incident to reasonable alternative courses of action. The agency may limit its discussion of environmental impact to a brief statement, when that is the case, that the alternative course involves no effect on the environment, or that their effect, briefly described, is simply not significant. . . .

We think the Secretary's Statement erred in stating that the alternative of elimination of oil import quotas was entirely outside its cognizance. Assuming, as the Statement puts it, that this alternative "involves complex factors and concepts, including national security, which are beyond the scope of this statement," it does not follow that the Statement should not present the environmental effects of that alternative.

While the consideration of pertinent alternatives requires a weighing of numerous matters, such as economics, foreign relations, national security, the fact remains that, as to the ingredient of possible adverse environmental impact, it is the essence and thrust of NEPA that the pertinent Statement serve to gather in one place a discussion of the relative environmental impact of alternatives.

The Government also contends that the only "alternatives" required for discussion under NEPA are those which can be adopted and put into effect by the official or agency issuing the statement. The Government seeks to distinguish the kind of impact statement required for a major Federal action from that required with a legislative proposal. . . .

When the proposed action is an integral part of a coordinated plan to deal with a broad problem, the range of alternatives that must be evaluated is broadened. While the Department of the Interior does not have the authority to eliminate or reduce oil import quotas, such action is within the purview of both Congress and the President, to whom the impact statement goes. The impact statement is not only for the exposition of the thinking of the agency, but also for the guidance of these ultimate decisionmakers, and must provide them with the environmental effects of both the proposal and the alternatives, for their consideration along with the various other elements of the public interest. . . .

. . . The discussion of environmental effects of alternatives need not be exhaustive. What is required is information sufficient to permit a reasoned choice of alternatives so far as environmental aspects are concerned. As to alternatives not within the scope of authority of the responsible official, reference may of course be made to studies of other agencies—including other impact statements. Nor is it appropriate, as Government counsel argues, to disregard alternatives merely because they do not offer a complete solution to the problem. If an alternative would result in supplying only part of the energy that the lease sale would yield, then its use might possibly reduce the scope of the lease sale program and thus alleviate a significant portion of the environmental harm attendant on offshore drilling. . . .

The mere fact that an alternative requires legislative implementation does not automatically establish it as beyond the domain of what is required for discussion, particularly since NEPA was intended to provide a basis for consideration and choice by the decisionmakers in the legislative as well as the executive branch. . . .

. . . In this as in other areas, the functions of courts and agencies, rightly understood, are not in opposition but in collaboration, toward achievement of the end prescribed by Congress. So long as the officials and agencies have taken the "hard look" at environmental consequences mandated by Congress, the court does not seek to impose unreasonable extremes or to interject itself within the area of discretion of the executive as to the choice of the action to be taken.

Informed by our judgment that discussion of alternatives may be required even though the action required lies outside the Interior Department, the Secretary will, we have no doubt, be able without undue delay to provide the kind of reasonable discussion of alternatives and their environmental consequences that Congress contemplated.

[Motion denied.]

Burbank v Lockheed Air Terminal, Inc.
411 US 624 (1973)

The City of Burbank, California, adopted an ordinance prohibiting the nighttime takeoffs of jet aircraft between 10 P.M. and 7 A.M. Lockheed Air Terminal owned and operated the Hollywood-Burbank Airport. It sued Burbank to prevent the enforcement of the ordinance.

DOUGLAS, J. . . . The Federal Aviation Act of 1958, . . . as amended by the Noise Control Act . . . and the regulations under it, . . . provides in part, "The United States of America is declared to possess and exercise complete and exclusive national sovereignty in the airspace of the United States. . . ." By § 1348 the Administrator of the Federal Aeronautics Act (FAA) has been given broad authority to regulate the use of the navigable airspace, "in order to insure the safety of aircraft and the efficient utilization of such airspace . . ." and "for the protection of persons and property on the ground. . . ."

. . . The District Court found: "The imposition of curfew ordinances on a nationwide basis would result in a bunching of flights in those hours immediately preceding the curfew. This bunching of flights during these hours would have the twofold effect of increasing an already serious congestion problem and actually increasing, rather than relieving, the noise problem by increasing flights in the period of greatest annoyance to surrounding communities. Such a result is totally inconsistent with the objectives of the federal statutory and regulatory scheme." It also found "the imposition of curfew ordinances on a nationwide basis would cause a serious loss of efficiency in the use of the navigable airspace." . . .

The Noise Control Act of 1972, . . . amending § 611 of the Federal Aviation Act, also involves the Environmental Protection Agency (EPA) in the comprehensive scheme of federal control of the aircraft noise problem. Under the amended § 611(b)(1) the FAA, after consulting with EPA, shall provide "for the control and abatement of aircraft noise and sonic boom, including the application of such standards and regulations in the issuance, amendment, modification, suspension or revocation of any certificate authorized by this title." Section 611(b)(2) as amended provides that future certificates for aircraft operations shall not issue unless the new aircraft noise requirements are met. . . .

. . . The pervasive nature of the scheme of federal regulation of aircraft noise . . . leads us to conclude that there is pre-emption. . . . "Federal control is intensive and exclusive. Planes do not wander about in the sky like vagrant clouds. They move only by federal permission, subject to federal inspection, in the hands of federally certified personnel and under an intricate system of federal command. The moment a ship taxis onto a runway it is caught up in an elaborate and detailed system of controls." . . .

. . . Control of noise is of course deep-seated in the police power of the States. Yet the pervasive control vested in EPA and in FAA under the 1972 Act seems to us to leave no room for local curfews or other local controls. . . . The ultimate remedy for aircraft noise which plagues many communities and tens of thousands of people is not known. The procedures under the 1972 Act are underway. In addition, the Administrator has imposed a variety of regulations relating to takeoff and landing procedures and runway preferences. The Federal Aviation Act requires a delicate balance between safety and efficiency . . . and the protection of persons on the ground. . . . Any regulations adopted by the Administrator to control noise pollution must be consistent with the "highest degree of safety." . . . The interdependence of these factors requires a uniform and exclusive system of federal regulation if the congressional objectives underlying the Federal Aviation Act are to be fulfilled.

If we were to uphold the Burbank ordinance and a significant number of municipalities followed suit, it is obvious that fractionalized control of the timing of take-offs and landings would severely limit the flexibility of the FAA in controlling air traffic flow. The difficulties of scheduling flights to avoid congestion and the concomitant decrease in safety would be compounded. In 1960 the FAA rejected a proposed restriction on jet operations at the Los Angeles airport between 10 p.m. and 7 a.m. because such restrictions could "create critically serious problems to all air transportation patterns." . . . The complete FAA statement said: "The proposed restriction on the use of the airport by jet aircraft between the hours of 10 p.m. and 7 a.m. under certain surface wind conditions has also been reevaluated and this provision has been omitted from the rule. The practice of prohibiting the use of various airports during certain specific hours could create critically serious problems to all air transportation patterns. The network of airports throughout the United States and the constant availability of these airports are essential to the maintenance of a sound air transportation system. The continuing growth of public acceptance of aviation as a major force in passenger transportation and the increasingly significant role of commerical aviation in the nation's economy are accomplishments which cannot be inhibited if the best interest of the public is to be served. It was concluded therefore that the extent of relief from the noise problem which this provision must have achieved would not have compensated the degree of restriction it would have imposed on domestic and foreign Air Commerce."

This decision, announced in 1960, remains peculiarly within the competence of the FAA, supplemented now by the input of the EPA. We are not at liberty to diffuse the powers given by Congress to FAA and EPA by letting the States or municipalities in on the planning. If that change is to be made, Congress alone must do it.

[Enforcement of ordinance enjoined.]

American Can Co. v Oregon Liquor Control Commission

(Ore App) 517 P2d 691 (1973)

The state of Oregon adopted a law, commonly called the "bottle bill," which prohibited the use of nonreturnable containers for beverages and required returnable glass bottles. The American Can Company brought an action against the Oregon Liquor Control Board and sought to have the statute declared unconstitutional. From a decision sustaining the law, American Can appealed.

TANZER, J. . . . The primary legislative purpose of the bottle bill is to cause bottlers of carbonated soft drinks and brewers to package their products for distribution in Oregon in returnable, multiple-use deposit bottles toward the goals of reducing litter and solid waste in Oregon and reducing the injuries to people and animals due to discarded "pull tops."

. . . The evidence . . . demonstrated that the consumption of malt beverages and soft drinks had increased greatly in the United States in recent years, and that a large part of this increase could be attributed to the use of convenient "one-way" packages, including both cans and nonreturnable bottles. Plaintiffs assert that nonreturnable containers are essential to the existence of national and regional beer markets, and that nonreturnable containers are also essential to the continued existence of soft drink enterprises. The nonreturnable containers were shown to have provided economies in the packaging and distribution of soft drinks and beer by eliminating the cost of shipping the containers both ways, thus causing an increase in feasible shipping distances and enlarging the market each manufacturer could cover. Among the effects of the bottle bill, plaintiffs' witnesses predicted, would be a substantial reduction in Oregon sales of soft drinks packaged outside Oregon, and impairment of the ability of distant brewers to compete in the Oregon market. The bottle bill would necessitate substantial changes in the structure of the industries involved in the manufacturing and merchandising of beer and soft drinks. . . .

The Oregon legislature was persuaded that the economic benefit to the beverage industry brought with it deleterious consequences to the environment and additional cost to the public. The aggravation of the problems of litter in public places and solid waste disposal and the attendant economic and esthetic burden to the public outweighed the narrower economic benefit to the industry. Thus the legislature enacted the bottle bill. . . .

As with every change of circumstance in the market place, there are gainers and there are losers. Just as there were gainers and losers, with plaintiffs apparently among the gainers, when the industry adapted to the development of nonreturnable containers, there will be new gainers and losers as they adapt to the ban. The economic losses complained of by plaintiffs in this case are essentially the consequences of readjustment of the beverage manufacturing and distribution systems to the older technology in order to compete in the Oregon market. . . .

Economic loss restricted to certain elements of the beverage industry must be viewed in relation to the broader loss to the general public of the state of Oregon which the legislature sought, by enactment of the bottle bill, to avoid. The availability of land and revenues for solid waste disposal, the cost of litter collection on our highways and in our public parks, the depletion of mineral and energy resources, the injuries to humans and animals caused by discarded pull tops, and the esthetic blight on our landscape, are all economic, safety and esthetic burdens of great consequence which must be borne by every member of the public. The legislature attached higher significance to the cost to the public than they did to the cost to the beverage industry and we have no cause to disturb that legislative determination. . . .

We find that the bottle bill in all of its aspects is reasonably calculated to achieve legitimate state objectives under the police power. . . . The ban on pull tops is reasonably calculated to diminish the injuries to people who step on them and to animals who eat them at pasture as well as to reduce the litter which they create. The placing of a monetary value on beverage containers and its attendant encouragement for people to return them instead of discarding them by the roadside or in other public places or throwing them into the garbage is reasonably calculated to diminish the amount of solid waste and the amount of litter with which the state is required to deal. . . .

The fact that other containers may also create litter and solid waste does not invalidate the legislature's intent to deal with this species of solid waste and litter. . . . "It is no requirement of equal protection that all evils of the same genus be eradicated or none at all." . . . "Evils in the same field may be of different dimensions and proportions, requiring different remedies. Or so the legislature may think. Or the reform may take one step at a time, addressing itself to the phase of the problem which seems most acute to the legislative mind. The legislature may select one phase of one field and apply a remedy there, neglecting the others." . . .

. . . We hold the bottle bill to be a valid exercise of Oregon's police power. . . .

[Judgment affirmed.]

City of Colby v Hurtt

212 Kan 113, 509 P2d 1142 (1973)

The City of Colby prohibited placing a mobile home within the city limits except in a mobile home park or community. Hurtt owned a mobile home. He requested permission from the city to place this home on a tract of land owned in the city by his father. Permission was refused because of the ordinance. In spite of this refusal, Hurtt placed his home on his father's land. He was then prosecuted and convicted in the police court for violating the ordinance.

FATZER, C.J. . . . It is the rule of law in this jurisdiction relating to reasonableness of zoning ordinances that a court may not substitute its judgment for that of the governing body. . . .

"In actions of this nature courts are limited to passing on the reasonableness of the action taken by the county commissioners. The plaintiff in such an action has the burden of establishing his cause of action by a preponderance of the evidence, and it is incumbent upon those attacking the action of the governing body to show the unreasonableness of such action. A court may not substitute its judgment for that of the governing body and should not declare the action of the governing body unreasonable unless clearly compelled to do so by the evidence. . . ."

. . . The ordinance under consideration bears a substantial relationship to public health, safety, and general welfare.

Mobile homes are used for residences but they possess special characteristics which warrant their separate regulation. They involve potential hazards to public health if not properly located and supplied with utilities and sanitary facilities. Mobile homes scattered promiscuously throughout the residential district of a city might well stunt its growth and certainly stifle development of an area for residential purposes. . . .

The appellant next contends the ordinance violates his right to the use and enjoyment of his property and constitutes a taking of his property without due process of law. The point is not well taken. The ordinance was a proper exercise of the police power in protecting the public health, safety, and general welfare of the citizens of the city of Colby. . . .

"Regulations are not unconstitutional merely because they operate as a restraint upon private rights of persons or property, or will result in a loss to individuals. The infliction of such loss is not a deprivation of property without due process of law—the exertion of the police power upon objects lying within its scope in a proper and lawful manner is due process of law. Hence, the police power may be exerted as a restraint upon private rights of persons or to regulate the use of property, and where appropriate or necessary, prohibit the use of property for certain purposes in aid of the public safety and general welfare, and constitutional limitations form no impediment to its exercise where the regulation is reasonable and bears a fair relationship to the object sought to be attained. . . ." . . . [Conviction affirmed.]

Stokes v Jacksonville

(Fla App) 276 So2d 200 (1973)

Bond owned a house in the city of Jacksonville in a section which was zoned for 1-family residences. He and other property owners wished to change the zoning to commercial. The city refused to rezone the property.

RAWLS, A.C.J. . . . Seven lots comprising a little more than one acre of land are involved. . . .

At present, Cassat Avenue is the dividing line in this specific area between commercial development to the west and a residential area to the east. Cassat Avenue is predominantly an automotive oriented artery where sizable investments have been made by automobile dealers. The east-west street on the northern boundary of the subject property is Post Street (a four-lane highway) which becomes Normandy Boulevard (a six-lane thoroughfare) after crossing the western side of Cassat Avenue. A Standard Oil service station is located on the corner of Post Street and Cassat Avenue directly to the north of Lots 102 and 103. Located diagonally across Cassat Avenue from the subject property is a Shell service station and directly west across Cassat Avenue is situated an American Oil Co. service station. So, three out of the four corners of the intersection of Cassat Avenue and Normandy Boulevard-Post Street are now occupied by service stations. In addition, directly across Cassat Avenue from this acre parcel is located a "Super Burger" restaurant, a fish market, House of Trophies business, a billiard parlor, and a cocktail lounge.

This record is replete with evidence that the subject property is not suitable for single family residential zoning [because of excessive noise and fumes from auto traffic]. . . .

Experts adduced by the landowners testified at length as to the unsuitability of the subject property to be used for residential purposes or for apartments or institutions. . . .

Zoning ordinances, like all other legislative acts, are presumed valid. However, in order for a zoning ordinance to be valid it must have some substantial relationship to the promotion of the public health, safety, morals or general welfare. The manifest weight of evidence—actually, the overwhelming evidence—is that the subject property is not suitable for single family residential purposes. But, says the City, the requested zoning classification will increase the traffic volume in this area, and thus under the police power, it is our prerogative to deny the landowners the right to use their property for the purposes for which it is best suited. Such argument will not hold water.

These residents purchased their homes many years ago in a relatively quiet residential area. The sovereign, not the landowners, determined that it was in the public's welfare to expand a two-lane highway into a six-lane thoroughfare continuously traversed by noisy, smoke and fume emissioning behemoths which rendered their residences almost uninhabitable. It was the sovereign, not the subject landowners that granted to the property owners directly across Cassat Avenue the right to develop intense commercial usage of their property without regard to increased vehicular traffic. And it was the sovereign, not the subject landowners, that permitted a service station to the north, and a service station to the northwest, and a service station to the west. These landowners are so surrounded by commercial activity that they must have an empathy with General Custer in his last stand. In short, the sovereign, by its past activities, has changed the character of this immediate neighborhood, and having done so, now refuses to recognize that which it created. . . . " 'Where changed conditions created a situation where the zoning of appellant's property is so unreasonable as to constitute a taking of his property,' then the courts are justified in striking down the arbitrary zoning classification." . . .

The constitutional right of the owner of property to make legitimate use of his lands may not be curtailed by unreasonable restrictions under the guise of police power. The owner will not be required to sacrifice his rights absent a substantial need for restrictions in the interest of public health, morals, safety or welfare. If the zoning restriction exceeds the bounds of necessity for the public welfare, they must be stricken as an unconstitutional invasion of property rights. The zoning restriction, as applied to the facts adduced herein, is invalid in that it exceeds the bounds of necessity for the public welfare and was therefore arbitrary.

[Rezoning ordered.]

QUESTIONS AND CASE PROBLEMS

1. "Smoke, fumes, and noise from public utilities and power plants are not to be condemned as nuisances merely because some harm is sustained from their activity by a particular plaintiff." Objective(s)?
2. Shearing was a homeowner in Rochester. The City burned trash on a nearby tract of land. Fires burned continuously on open ground, not in an incinerator, at times within 800 yards of the plaintiff's house. The smoke and dirt from the fires settled on the house of the plaintiff and on those of other persons in the area. The plaintiff sued to stop the continuance of such burning and to recover damages for the harm done to his home. Decide. [Shearing v Rochester, 51 Misc 2d 436, 273 NYS2d 464]
3. The Belmar Drive-In Theatre Co. brought an action against the Illinois State Toll Highway Commission because the bright lights of the toll road station interfered with the showing of motion pictures at the drive-in. Decide. [Belmar Drive-In Theatre Co. v Illinois State Toll Highway Commission, 34 Ill 2d 544, 216 NE2d 788]
4. Mayfield operated an unfenced automobile junkyard. This was a crime under the ordinances of the Town of Clayton. The Town brought an action against Mayfield to stop the operation of the junkyard and to compel him to remove the accumulated junk. The Town presented evidence showing that the junk served as a breeding ground for mosquitoes, that young children were likely to be attracted to the junkyard and be harmed, and that the combustible nature of the junk constituted a fire hazard. Mayfield testified that he intended to burn the old cars. The evidence indicated that this would create a large quantity of smoke. Decide. [Town of Clayton v Mayfield, 82 NM 596, 485 P2d 352]
5. A zoning ordinance of the City of Dallas, Texas, prohibited the use of property in a residential district for gasoline filling stations. Lombardo brought an action against the City to test the validity of the ordinance. He contended that the ordinance violated the rights of the owners of property in such districts. Do you agree with this contention? [Lombardo v City of Dallas, 124 Tex 1, 73 SW2d 475]
6. Causby owned a chicken farm. The United States Air Force maintained an air base nearby. The flight of heavy bombers and fighter planes frightened the Causbys and the chickens. Although flying at proper altitude, the planes would appear to be so close as to barely miss striking the trees on the farm. The lights of the planes lit up the farm at night. The noise and the lights so disturbed the chickens that Causby abandoned the chicken business. He claimed compensation from the United States. Decide. [United States v Causby, 328 US 256]

7. The Urban Redevelopment Law of Oregon authorized the condemning of blighted urban areas and the acquisition of the property by the Housing Authority by eminent domain. Such part of the land condemned as was not needed by the Authority could be resold to private persons. Foeller and others owned well-maintained buildings within the Vaughn Street area that was condemned under this statute by the Portland Housing Authority as "physically substandard and economically deteriorated." The plaintiffs brought an action to have the statute declared unconstitutional. Decide. [Foeller v Housing Authority of Portland, 198 Ore 205, 256 P2d 752]

8. An action was brought to determine whether a condominium building could be constructed on a particular tract of land. The deed to the land permitted only single-family dwellings and prohibited apartment houses and further declared that the property could only be used by white persons. Did these restrictions bar a condominium building? [Callahan v Weiland, 291 Ala 183, 279 So2d 451]

9. In the course of generating electricity in its atomic-energy-powered plant, the Jersey Central Power & Light Company took cold water from a river to cool its condensers. This raised the temperature of the water, which was then discharged into a nearby creek. On January 28, 1972, the river water temperature was under 40°F and the creek temperature was over 50°F. The electric company shut down its generators on that date; consequently, the river water was not heated by the condensers. When the cold water was dumped into the warm creek, the temperature change killed fish in the creek. The State of New Jersey sued the electric company to recover a statutory penalty for violating the prohibition against placing "any hazardous, deleterious, destructive or poisonous substance" in waters of the state. The electric company claimed that the water which it discharged did not come within the statute. Was the electric company liable for the penalty? [New Jersey v Jersey Central Power & Light Co., 125 NJ Super 97, 308 A2d 671]

10. The Stallcups lived in a rural section of the state. In front of their house ran a relatively unused unimproved public county road. Wales Trucking Co. transported concrete pipe from the plant where it was made to a lake where the pipe was used to construct a water line to bring water to a nearby city. In the course of four months Wales made 825 trips over the road carrying from 58,000 to 72,000 pounds of pipe per trip and making the same number of empty return trips. The heavy use of the road by Wales cut up the dirt and made it like ashes. The Stallcups sued Wales for damages caused by the deposit of dust on their house and for the physical annoyance and discomfort caused by the dust. Wales defended on the ground that it had not been negligent and that its use of the road was not unlawful. Decide. [Wales Trucking Co. v Stallcup, (Tex Civ App) 465 SE2d 44]

8 Consumer Protection

§ **8:1. Introduction.** Consumer grievances, particularly of those in the low income brackets, have been listed as one of the 12 major areas of grievances leading to civil disorders and riots. Among the particular abuses have been "surprise" terms in transactions, exorbitant credit prices, the ability of a finance company to repossess goods that were fully paid for because of a default as to goods purchased later, and the inability to raise as against finance companies and banks the defenses that the goods purchased were defective. These situations have indicated to many persons a need for economic consumer protection aimed at eliminating such hardships and providing the consumer with practical remedies against improper sales and credit transactions and deceptive practices.[1]

At present, only a rather small segment of the credit world is governed by consumer protection legislation, but it would appear that such protection will expand greatly within the next few decades and particular attention must be paid thereto by the man in business.[2]

Generally consumer protection statutes have broader range than the Uniform Commercial Code and expressly extend to leases, contracts for services and improvements, and loans. State laws condemn in varying terms conduct harmful to consumers.[3]

---

[1] The National Consumer Act (NCA) defines *consumer* as "a person other than an organization who seeks or acquires business equipment for use in his business, or real or personal property, services, money, or credit for personal, family, household or agricultural purposes." NCA § 1.301(8). This definition includes a small business sole proprietor and thus goes beyond the ordinary image of a consumer.

Consumer protection is not limited to the protection of persons of limited education or economic means. This is clearly seen in Weisz v Parke-Bernet Galleries, Inc. (NY Civil Court), 67 Misc 2d 1077, 325 NYS2d 576. There it was held that the seller art gallery was liable for breach of warranty where paintings sold by it proved to be forgeries and the fact that there had been an announcement that the sale was subject to the conditions in the catalog, one of which was a warranty disclaimer, did not bind a person not having actual knowledge of the provision.

[2] Additional protection for consumers who are servicemen is provided by the Soldiers' and Sailors' Civil Relief Act, 50 USC App §§ 501-548.

[3] Consumer Protection Law for the City of New York outlaws "unconscionable trade practices," which it defines as "any act or practice in connection with the sale, lease, rental, or loan, or in connection with the offering for sale, lease, rental, or loan of any consumer goods or services, or in the extension of consumer credit, or in the collection of consumer debts, which unfairly takes advantage of the lack of knowledge, ability, experience or capacity of a consumer. . . ." Administrative Code, Ch. 64, § 2203A-2.0.

In a number of states, special statutes establish standards for particular products.[4]

Under compulsion of the National Traffic and Motor Vehicle Safety Act of 1966,[5] "Every manufacturer of motor vehicles or tires shall furnish notification of any defect in any motor vehicle or motor vehicle equipment produced by such manufacturer which he determines, in good faith, relates to motor vehicle safety, to the purchaser . . . of such motor vehicle or motor vehicle equipment, within a reasonable time after such manufacturer has discovered such defect." [6]

§ **8:2. Who Is a Consumer?** Some difficulties are encountered if one approaches the wide spectrum of situations in terms of a "consumer." For example, one does not usually think of a borrower or an investor as a "consumer." The pedestrian run over when your car goes out of control is not ordinarily regarded as a consumer. There is in all these situations, however, a common denominator of protecting someone from a hazard from which he cannot by his own action protect himself.

Product safety is discussed in Chapter 26, and pollution in Chapter 7.[7] This chapter deals with protection of the person as a consumer, a borrower, and an investor.

§ **8:3. Advertising.** Statutes commonly prohibit fraudulent advertising,[8] but most advertising regulations are entrusted to an administrative agency, such as the Federal Trade Commission (FTC), which is authorized to issue orders to stop false, misleading advertising.[9] (See p. 147, J. B. Williams Co. v Federal Trade Commission.)

(1) Deception. Under consumer protection laws deception in advertising, rather than fraud, is the significant element.[10] This is a shift of social point of view. That is, instead of basing the law in terms of fault of the actor (Did he with evil intent make a false statement?), the law is concerned with the problem of the buyer who is likely to be misled by statements made without regard to whether the defendant had any evil intent. (See p. 148, Federal Trade Commission v Colgate-Palmolive Co.)

The good faith of an advertiser or the absence of intent to deceive is immaterial as the purpose of false advertising legislation is to protect the

---

[4] Pennsylvania Uniform Standards Code for Mobile Homes of May 9, 1972, PL No. 69, 35 PS §§ 1655.1 to 1655.10.

[5] 15 USC §§ 1381 et seq, 1402(a).

[6] 15 USC § 1402(a); see also, General Motors Corp. v Volpe, (DC) 321 F Supp 1112 (where General Motors attempted, unsuccessfully, to enjoin the enforcement of this Act).

[7] A new loose-leaf service on "consumerism" embraces air, water, and noise pollution within the concept of "consumer protection."

[8] Kelley v Duling Enterprises, Inc., 84 SD 427, 172 NW2d 727.

[9] 15 USC §§ 45, 52.

[10] Myerson v Lentini Brothers Moving & Storage Co. Inc., 41 App Div 2d 818, 342 NYS2d 445.

consumer rather than to punish the advertiser.[11] The sale of an automobile with its odometer set back to show about one half of its actual mileage is a violation of a consumer protection statute even though the salesman acting for the seller did not know that this had been done.[12]

An advertiser must not deceive by overstating the durability of his product, as by using such terms as "everlasting" and "indestructable." In some instances products are designed to wear out in a short period of time (*planned obsolescence*). Consumer protection of the future will cope with the questions of enforcing minimal durability standards and of giving the consumer accurate information as to the durability of the product he buys.

It is improper to advertise that one brand of sugar has a superior nutritional value over competing brands when in fact all refined sugars are essentially identical in composition and food value; or to advertise in such a way as to convey the impression that the advertised sugar was adopted by a national athletic league as the "official sugar" because of superior quality and nutritional value, when the choice was based solely on its lower cost.[13]

The FTC requires that an advertiser maintain a file containing the data claimed to support an advertising statement as to the safety, performance, efficacy, quality, or comparative price of an advertised product. The FTC can require the advertiser to produce this material. If it is in the interest of the consumer, the Commission can make this information public, except to the extent that it contains trade secrets or matter which is privileged.

(2) Corrective Advertising. When an enterprise has made false and deceptive statements in its advertising, the Federal Trade Commission may require that a new advertisement be made in which the former statements are contradicted and the truth stated. For example, a manufacturer of sugar who advertised that his brand of sugar would give "strength, energy, and stamina to everyone" was required to advertise that "actually [the sugar] is not a specific or unique source of strength, energy, and stamina. No sugar is, because what you need is a balanced diet and plenty of rest and exercise." [14]

Corrective advertising required by the Federal Trade Commission is also called *retractive* advertising. In addition, the Federal Trade Commission may require that the retractive advertising include a statement in large capital letters: "THIS ADVERTISMENT IS PUBLISHED PURSUANT TO ORDER OF THE FEDERAL TRADE COMMISSION."

§ 8:4. Seals of Approval. Many commodities are sold or advertised with a sticker or tag stating that the article has been approved or is guaranteed by some association or organization. Ordinarily, when a product is thus sold,

---

[11] New York v Colorado State Christian College, 346 NYS2d 482, 32 NY2d 356, 298 NE2d 637.

[12] In re Brandywine Volkswagen, Ltd., (Del Super) 306 A2d 24.

[13] In re Amstar Corp. Consent decree, FTC Docket 8887.

[14] FTC Docket 8887.

it will in fact have been approved by some testing laboratory and will probably have proven adequate to meet ordinary consumer needs. A seller who sells with a seal of approval of a third person makes an express warranty that the product has been so approved, so that he is liable for breach of an express warranty if the product was in fact not approved. In addition, the seller would ordinarily be liable for fraud if the statement were not true.

In many instances a buyer who relies on a seal of approval is merely relying on the probability that someone better qualified than he has made what was probably a better examination of the product than he could have made. This is true in the case of the Underwriters' Laboratory (UL), a private laboratory which tests the products of over 12,000 manufacturers for fire, casualty, and electrical safety. Similarly, the Nationwide Consumer Testing Institute, Inc., is a private laboratory testing a limited number of products according to fire, safety, and performance standards. Manufacturers in several industries have formed testing associations to test the safety of their respective products, such as the American Gas Association for gas appliances, the Outdoor Power Equipment Institute for lawnmowers, and the Power Tool Institute for power tools.

(1) Nonapproving Testing. Some organizations merely test and report their findings, leaving the consumer to draw his own conclusions. Examples in this area are Consumers Union and Consumers' Research, which are not supported by industry and make extensive tests of competing products and report the results of such tests in their magazines and annual booklets under the names of *Consumer Reports* and *Consumer Bulletin.*

(2) Refund or Replacement. In some instances, such as in the case of approval by the *Good Housekeeping* and *Parents'* magazines, the magazine promises to refund the purchase price or to replace the purchased article should it prove defective (within 30 days after purchase in the case of *Parents' Magazine*).

The *Good Housekeeping* testing is limited to those products which are advertised in the magazine, and testing is conducted primarily to determine that the advertising statements are true. The testing by the *Parents' Magazine* is to determine whether the products that are advertised in the magazine "are suitable for families with children."

In terms of contract law principles, it would appear that the obligation of the approving magazine or organization under a "refund or replace" clause goes no further than to refund or replace; that is, there is no liability of the approving magazine or organization for damages, whether personal or property, which the consumer may sustain in consequence of the defective condition of the item. There is authority, however, that if the consumer sustains personal injuries, he may recover from a negligently approving magazine or association for his injuries.

If the consumer-buyer sues the seller, a contract provision limiting the buyer's rights to refund or replacement is "prima facie unconscionable" insofar as a claim for personal injuries is involved.[15]

§ 8:5. Labels and Packaging. Closely related to the regulation of advertising is the regulation of labels and marking of products. Various federal statutes are designed to give the consumer accurate information about the product, while others require warnings as to dangers of use or misuse. State consumer protection may prohibit the use of such terms as "jumbo," "giant," "full," which tend to exaggerate the amount of the commodity in a package.

Federal statutes that protect the consumer from being misled by labels or by packaging methods include the Fair Packaging and Labeling Act; the Fur Products Labeling Act, the Wool Products Labeling Act; the federal Cigarette Labeling and Advertising Act; the Food, Drug, and Cosmetic Act; the Wholesome Meat Act; the Wholesome Poultry Products Act; and the Flammable Fabrics Act. The last three statutes seek to protect the consumer from personal harm as well as economic loss.

Labels must be evaluated in light of the ordinary meaning which would be conveyed thereby to the ordinary consumer. Hence, it is improper to label food as "all meat" or "all beef" if the product contains any other element, without regard to whether the alien element makes the food more nutritious.[16]

When a product such as a floor covering adhesive is as explosive as gasoline, it is not sufficient for the manufacturer to label the product as "inflammable" and to specify "caution." The Federal Hazardous Substances Labeling Act of 1960 and the Illinois Hazardous Substances Labeling Act require that such a product be labelled "danger" and "extremely flammable." [17]

The manufacturer may be required to attach to his product a plate stating the capacity of the product, such as the maximum number of persons that a boat can safely accommodate.[18]

The Fair Packaging and Labeling Act applies generally to consumer goods and requires that a product bear a label stating (1) the identity of the product; (2) the name and place of business of the manufacturer, packer, or distributor; (3) the net quantity of the contents; and (4) the net quantity of a serving when the number of servings is stated. The Act gives to the FTC and the Department of Health, Education, and Welfare (HEW) authority to add additional requirements with respect to (1) the use of terms describing packages, such as "large"; (2) the use of "cents-off" or "savings" claims; (3) requiring the disclosure of information as to ingredients in the

---

[15] § 2-719(3).

[16] Federation of Homemakers v Hardin, (DC Dist Col) 328 F Supp 181 (condemning frankfurter label of "all meat" as misleading when 15 percent of bulk was nonmeat, and therefore prohibited by the federal Wholesome Meat Act even though the Secretary of Agriculture had approved such use of the label).

[17] Murray v Wilson Oak Flooring Co. Inc., (CA7 Ill) 475 F2d 129.

[18] J. I. Duncan v Monark Boat Co., (Fla App) 281 So2d 382.

case of nonfoods; [19] and (4) preventing the deceptive partial filling of packages. The disclosure of the name and address of the manufacturer, packer, or distributor of the product is initially important to the consumer who may be purchasing in reliance upon the fact that the product came from a particular source. In the event that the consumer has a product liability claim, this information as to the source is important so that the consumer knows against whom suit can be brought other than his own seller.

Administrative regulations have been adopted to avoid deception by such descriptions as "cents-off," "introductory offer," and "economy size." [20]

§ 8:6. Selling Methods. Consumer protection statutes prohibit the use of improper and deceptive selling methods. (See p. 149, Colorado v Gym of America, Inc.) A Uniform Consumer Sales Practices Act has been adopted in Kansas, Ohio, and Utah. The 1964 version of the Uniform Deceptive Trade Practices Act was adopted in Delaware, Illinois, Maine, and Oklahoma. A 1966 revision of that act was adopted in Colorado, Georgia, Hawaii, Minnesota, Nebraska, New Mexico, and Ohio.

(1) Disclosure of Transaction Terms. The federal law requires the disclosure of all interest charges for loans, points paid for granting the loan, and similar charges. These must be set forth as an annual percentage rate so that the borrower can see just how much the loan costs him during a year.[21] If lenders advertise, certain information must be set forth in the ad.

If sellers advertise their willingness to sell on credit, they cannot state merely the monthly installment that will be due. They also give the consumer additional information: (a) the total cash price; (b) the amount of the down payment required; (c) the number, amounts, and due dates of payments; and (d) the annual percentage rate of the credit charges.[22]

In various ways consumer protection statutes seek to protect the consumer from surprise or unbargained for terms and from unwanted contracts.[23] In the more extreme cases of surprise transactions and terms, the consumer would be protected by the traditional law relating to fraud. Delay and the cost and difficulty of proving a "fraud" case or defense often reduced this right to little value.

---

[19] Such disclosure is required with respect to foods by the Food, Drug, and Cosmetic Act.

[20] A Food and Drug Administration regulation applies to consumer foods. A Federal Trade Commission regulation applies to nonfood household commodities.

[21] Consumer Credit Protection Act, 15 USC §§ 1605, 1606, 1636; Regulation Z adopted by the Federal Reserve Board of Governors, § 226.5. "The avowed purpose of the Consumer Protection Act was to 'assure a meaningful disclosure of credit terms so that the consumer will be able to compare more readily the various credit terms available to him and avoid the uninformed use of credit.' The Act is remedial in nature, designed to remedy what Congressional hearings revealed to be unscrupulous and predatory creditor practices throughout the nation." N. C. Freed Co. Inc. v Board of Governors of Federal Reserve System, (CA2 NY) 473 F2d 1210.

[22] Regulation Z § 226.10.

[23] UCC § 2-316 is in effect a forerunner of such antisurprise protection in requiring that a disclaimer of certain warranties be conspicuous.

The Motor Vehicle Information and Cost Savings Act requires the disclosure to the buyer of various elements in the cost of an automobile.[24] The Act prohibits selling an automobile without informing the buyer that the odometer has been reset below the true mileage. A buyer who is caused loss by odometer fraud may recover from the seller three times his actual loss or $1,500, whichever is greater.[25]

(a) FOUR-INSTALLMENT RULE. Whenever a sale or contract provides for payment in four or more installments it is subject to the Truth in Lending Act. This is so even though no service or finance charge is added because of the installment pattern of paying. (See p. 152, Mourning v Family Publications Service, Inc.)

(2) Home Solicitation Sales. A number of statutes are aimed at the evils involved in home solicitation sales. The typical remedy is to give the buyer a chance to think things over and then decide that he does not want his purchase after all. The NCA gives borrowers and buyers three days in which to set aside a sale or loan over $50 and requires the seller or lender to give a conspicuous written notice of the right to rescind.[26] This is a reasonably good remedy for the consumer against the "hit-and-run" salesman, provided the consumer knows that he has the remedy available and has not paid in full. In some instances the home solicitation salesman brings the store to the home where the buyer cannot afford to pay cash in a store and lacks the credit standing to deal with a store on a credit basis. In such cases, the consumer either does not want to or cannot "afford" to set aside his contract of purchase. Consequently, if there is any evil or hardship in the transaction, some other remedy must be found.

(a) MECHANICS OF CONSUMER CANCELLATION. Problems arise as to how to inform the buyer of his right to cancel and how he is to exercise this right. Generally the contract must contain a notice of the right to cancel set forth in a conspicuous manner.

(b) REFUND ON CANCELLATION. When a consumer-purchaser of goods or services avoids a home solicitation contract as authorized by the UCCC, the seller may retain from any down payment a cancellation fee of 5 percent of the cash price.[27] In contrast, when a debtor rescinds a transaction under the federal Truth in Lending Act, "he is not liable for any finance or other charge, and any security interest given by [him] becomes void upon such a rescission. Within 10 days after receipt of a notice of rescission, the

---

[24] 15 USC § 1901 et seq.

[25] PL 92-513, 86 Stat 947, §§ 403, 409.

[26] NCA § 2.501 et seq.

[27] UCCC § 2.504. In states where the UCCC is in force, this 5 percent provision would displace the provision of the UCC stated in the text (see § 27:22), where the buyer is a "consumer" within the scope of the UCCC.

creditor shall return to the [consumer] any money or property given as earnest money, down payment, or otherwise. . . ."[28]

(3) Referral Sales. The technique of giving the buyer a price reduction for customers referred by him to the seller is theoretically lawful. In effect, it is merely paying the buyer a "commission" for the promotion by him of other sales. In actual practice, however, the referral sales technique is often accompanied by fraud or by exorbitant pricing, so that consumer protection laws variously condemn referral selling.

Illustrative of the fraud aspect, the credit-seller may falsely represent to the buyer that the product will not cost him anything because of the referral system when the seller in fact knows that this is unlikely to happen. The referral system of selling has been condemned as "unconscionable" under the UCC,[29] and is expressly prohibited by the UCCC.[30]

In some states a sale of goods on the referral plan of giving the buyer a price reduction for every prospective buyer referred to the seller constitutes the sale of a security within the local blue-sky law;[31] and when the seller is not licensed to sell securities, the sale is void. In some states it is condemned as an unfair trade practice or lottery.[32] In other jurisdictions referral selling is held not a lottery on the theory that the buyer must use skill and judgment in preparing referral lists, and therefore the matter is not solely dependent on chance and is not a lottery.[33]

(4) Mail-Order Transactions. Some statutes are designed to protect consumers from improper practices by sellers and insurance companies dealing through the mail.[34] The federal statute aimed at preventing use of the mails to defraud furnishes consumer protection if the method of operation comes within that statute. Frequently, the out-of-state enterprise, although it does not intend to defraud the local consumer and therefore does not violate the federal statute, is merely poorly organized so that it is unable to perform its obligations. Ordinarily the amount involved will not be sufficiently great to make it practical to sue the foreign enterprise for breach of its contract. If the foreign enterprise has become insolvent, this is manifestly so.[35]

It is frequently a violation of a consumer protection act to make a direct mail sales solicitation by notifying each person that he has won a contest

---

[28] CCPA § 125(b), 15 USC § 1635(b).

[29] New York v I.T.M., 52 Misc 2d 39, 275 NYS2d 303.

[30] UCCC § 2.411.

[31] Yoder v So-Soft of Ohio, Inc., 94 OL Abs 353, 30 OO2d 566, 202 NE2d 329.

[32] Wesware, Inc. v Texas, (Tex Civ App) 488 SW2d 844.

[33] Braddock v Family Finance Corp., 95 Idaho 256, 506 P2d 824.

[34] California v United National Life Insurance Co., 66 Cal 2d 577, 58 Cal Rptr 599, 427 P2d 199.

[35] Note that if the consumer has paid in advance by check, it is most likely that his check will be held by a holder in due course, against whom the consumer cannot assert the defense of failure of consideration.

which in fact was never conducted, and informing him that by paying a nominal charge the "prize" which he has won will be sent to him.[36]

§ 8:7. Credit Cards. Today's credit card may cover travel and entertainment, as in the case of the cards issued by American Express, or a particular group of commodities, as in the case of a gasoline credit card; or it may be a general-purpose card, covering the purchase of any kind of goods or services. In the case of credit cards issued by banks, the bank may also assure the person cashing a check for the holder that the check will be honored for an amount not exceeding some specified amount, such as $100.

(1) Unauthorized Use. The unsolicited distribution of credit cards to persons who have not applied for them is prohibited.

A card holder is not liable for the unauthorized use of his credit card for more than $50. In order to impose liability up to that amount, the issuer of the card must show that (a) the credit card is an accepted card,[37] (b) the issuer has given the holder adequate notice that he may be held liable in such case, (c) the issuer has furnished the holder with a self-addressed, prestamped notification to be mailed by the card holder in the event of the loss or theft of the credit card, (d) the issuer has provided a method by which the user of the card can be identified as the person authorized to use it,[38] and (e) the unauthorized use occurs before the card holder has notified the issuer that an unauthorized use of the card has occurred or may occur as a result of loss, theft, or otherwise. Even though the federal statute permits the imposition of liability up to $50 for the unauthorized use of a credit card when these conditions have been satisfied, courts may refuse to allow the issuer to recover when the person dealing with the unauthorized possessor of the card was negligent in assuming that the possessor was the lawful holder and in failing to take steps to identify such possessor.[39]

The issuer of a credit card cannot avoid the $50 limitation by suing the owner of the lost card on the theory that the owner had been negligent in the care of the card, which led to its being lost and which in turn made possible its unauthorized use.[40]

§ 8:8. Contract Terms. Consumer protection legislation does not ordinarily affect the right of the parties to make a contract on such terms as they choose. It is customary, however, to prohibit the use of certain clauses which, it is believed, bear too harshly on the debtor or which have too great a

---

[36] Kugler v Market Development Corp., 124 NJ Super 314, 306 A2d 489.

[37] A credit card is "accepted" when "the card holder has requested and received or has signed or has used, or authorized another to use [it], for the purpose of obtaining money, property, labor, or services on credit." CCPA § 103(1).

[38] Regulation Z of the Board of Governors of the Federal Reserve § 226.13(d), as amended, provides that the identification may be by "signature, photograph, or fingerprint on the credit card or by electronic or mechanical confirmation."

[39] Lechmere Tire & Supply v Burwick (Mass), 277 NE2d 503.

[40] National Commercial Bank & Trust Co. v Malik, 72 Misc 2d 865, 339 NYS2d 605.

potential for exploitive abuse by a creditor. For example, the UCCC prohibits provisions authorizing the confessing of judgment against the debtor.[41]

Methods of computing charges and billing methods are frequently regulated. This is done to prevent the creditor from adding back into the contract an element or a charge that could not have been included in the original contract or from enforcing a contract which was different from that bargained for by the consumer.

(1) Unconscionability. To some extent, consumer protection has been provided under the UCC by those courts which hold that the "unconscionability" provision protects from "excessive" or "exorbitant" prices when goods are sold on credit, and that this provision invalidates a clause requiring that a buyer bring any lawsuit against the seller in a state which bears no reasonable relationship to the transaction or to the parties.[42]

(2) Assignment of Wages. State statutes variously restrict or prohibit the assignment of wages for the payment of debt. The UCCC prohibits the consumer from making an absolute assignment of wages as payment, or as security for the payment, of the amount due by him under a sale, lease, or loan agreement. He may, however, make an agreement for the deduction of installment payments from his salary as long as he has the power to revoke the agreement when he chooses.[43]

(3) Form of Contract. Consumer protection laws commonly regulate the form of the contract, requiring that certain items be specifically listed, that payments under the contract be itemized and indicate the allocation to principal, interest, insurance, and so on. Generally certain portions of the contract or all of the contract must be printed in type of a certain size and a copy of the contract must be furnished the buyer. Such statutory requirements are more demanding than the statute of frauds section of the UCC. It is frequently provided that the copy furnished the consumer must be completely filled in. Back-page disclaimers are void if the front page of the contract does not call attention to the presence of such terms.[44]

Under some statutes a person is not bound as a "buyer" and cannot be sued on a retail installment sales contract unless he is named both in the body of the contract as a buyer and signs it in that capacity. If he is not a buyer but a "cosigner" to assist or accommodate the actual buyer, some states require that he sign a separate "cosigner's statement" in a form prescribed by the statute.[45]

---

[41] UCCC §§ 2.415, 3.407.

[42] See § 14:6.

[43] UCCC §§ 2.410, 3.403. As to the garnishment of wages, see § 43:20.

[44] The same conclusion is reached under the UCC on the ground that such a back page disclaimer of a warranty is not "conspicuous," and therefore does not satisfy the requirements of UCC §§ 2-316(2), 1-201(10). Hunt v Perkins Machine Co., 352 Mass 535, 226 NE2d 228. A front page disclaimer is also invalid if not conspicuous. Woodruff v Clark County Farm Bureau Cooperative Association, (Ind) 286 NE2d 188.

[45] R. S. Boston Co. v Chapman, 131 Ill App 2d 385, 266 NE2d 767.

When a consumer protection statute requires that "every retail installment contract must contain the names of the seller and of the buyer," a person is not bound when he signs on the buyer's second line but is not named in the contract.[46]

(4) Limitation of Credit. Various laws may limit the ability to borrow money or purchase on credit. In some states it is prohibited to make "open end" loan mortgages by which the mortgage secures a specified debt and such additional loans as may thereafter be made. Some statutes prohibit liquor distillers from selling to retailers on credit in order to avoid the economic control of the retailers by the distillers.[47]

In some states consumer protection is afforded by placing a time limit on smaller loans.[48]

§ **8:9. Payments.** Under the UCCC, when a consumer sale or lease is made, the consumer may pay only by check. If he pays with any other kind of commercial paper, such as a promissory note, anyone who knows that a consumer transaction was involved cannot be a holder in due course.[49] Thus, if the consumer gives the seller a promissory note, a finance company or a bank taking the note from the seller with knowledge that it is consumer paper cannot be a holder in due course. This has the practical effect of declaring that the consumer may assert against such transferee any defenses which he has against the seller. By paying with a check, the consumer has the added margin of protection of being able to stop payment, which is a practical way of asserting a claim against the seller or of exercising any right of consumer cancellation.

(1) Progressive Application of Payments. Consumer legislation may provide that when a consumer makes a payment on an open charge account, the payment must be applied to pay the oldest items. The result is that, should there be a default at a later date, any right of repossession of the creditor is limited to the later unpaid items. This outlaws a contract provision by which, upon the default of the buyer at a later date, the seller could assert the right to repossess all purchases that had been made at any prior time. Such a provision is outlawed by the UCCC [50] and may be unconscionable under the UCC.[51]

(2) Balloon Payments. Installment contracts sometimes provide for a payment, usually the final payment, which may be substantially larger than the usual or average installment under the contract. Sometimes the purpose of requiring such a payment is to impose on the debtor a greater obligation

---

[46] Logan Furniture Mart, Inc. v Davis, 8 Ill App 3d 150, 289 NE2d 228.
[47] Re Parkway Distributing Co., 204 Pa Super 514, 206 A2d 660.
[48] Abrams v Commercial Credit Plan, Inc., 120 Ga App 520, 197 SE2d 384.
[49] UCCC § 2.403.
[50] § 2.409(1).
[51] Williams v Walker-Thomas Furniture Co., (CA Dist Col) 350 F2d 445.

than he can perform, with the result that the debtor is almost certain to go into default and entitle the creditor to repossess the collateral. The UCCC seeks to outlaw this practice by providing that whenever a payment balloons out to more than double the average of earlier scheduled payments, the debtor has a right to refinance that payment on terms no less favorable to him than those of the original transaction. That is, the creditor must extend further credit rather than claim that the debt is in default.[52]

Regulation Z of the Federal Reserve Board, adopted under the CCPA, provides that "if any payment is more than twice the amount of an otherwise regularly scheduled equal payment, the creditor shall identify the amount of such payment by the term 'balloon payment' and shall state the conditions, if any, under which that payment may be refinanced if not paid when due." [53]

(3) Acceleration of Payment. The ability of a creditor to accelerate payment of the balance due upon default has worked great hardship where the default was trivial in nature or where in fact there was no default. Although the right to accelerate payments upon default is permitted under both the UCC and the UCCC, the former seeks to impose some limitation on the power to accelerate by providing that a power of the creditor to accelerate "at will" or "when he deems himself insecure" must be exercised in good faith,[54] and the UCCC requires the refund of unearned credit charges when the due date has been accelerated.[55]

Some debtor protection laws require that the debtor be in default for a minimum period of time or with respect to a minimum number of installment payments before the balance of the debt can be accelerated.

§ 8:10. Preservation of Consumer Defenses. Consumer protection legislation generally prohibits the consumer from waiving the benefit of any provision of a statute designed for his protection. If he does so, the waiver is void but the transaction otherwise binds the consumer. Some courts hold a waiver of defense is invalid on the ground that it violates public policy. (See p. 151, Fairfield Credit Corp. v Donnelly.)

(1) Prohibition of Waiver of Defenses Against Assignee. Statutes commonly prohibit a buyer from agreeing that he will not assert against the seller's assignee any defense which he could have asserted against the seller.[56] Some statutes take a modified position and permit barring the buyer if, when notified of the assignment, he fails to inform the assignee of his defense against the seller.

---

[52] UCCC §§ 2.405, 3.402.

[53] Regulation Z § 226.8(b)(3).

[54] UCC § 1-208.

[55] UCCC § 2.210(8). "If the maturity is accelerated for any reason and judgment is obtained, the buyer is entitled to the same rebate as if payment had been made on the date judgment is entered."

[56] John Deere Industrial Equipment Co. v Delphia, 266 Ore 116, 511 P2d 386 (refusing to apply the statute to the purchase of heavy farm equipment).

(2) Assertion of Defenses Against Holder of Commercial Paper. Consumer protection statutes often permit the buyer to assert the defense of failure of consideration as against the seller's transferee of the commercial paper signed by the buyer to finance the sale, even though by ordinary rules of law, such transferee would be a holder in due course against whom such defense could not be asserted. In some states this result is achieved expressly by preserving the defenses of the buyer. In other states the statutes go further and declare that "consumer paper" is not negotiable.

The UCCC contains alternative provisions as to the effect of a consumer's defense against a transferee of commercial paper. By Alternative A the transferee is subject to all defenses of the consumer under a consumer sale or lease,[57] which in effect destroys the concept of holder in due course as to the paper involved in such transactions. It is immaterial whether the consumer has purported to waive his defenses as against the transferee.[58]

Under Alternative B a provision waiving defenses against the assignee is given effect by application of the principle of estoppel. That is, if the assignee of the seller or lessor gives the consumer written notice of the assignment and the consumer then gives the assignee written notice of the facts giving rise to his claim or defense within three months after such notice, the assignee is subject to such claims or defenses.[59]

Neither alternative applies when the sale or lease is primarily for an agricultural purpose.

§ 8:11. Credit, Collection, and Billing Methods. Consumer protection statutes sometimes provide for the licensing of persons selling on credit; selling particular kinds of goods, such as automobiles, or home improvements and services; or lending money. When such licensing is required, procedures are established for suspending or revoking the license of a licensee who seriously violates the statute. Such suspension or revocation is attractive from the standpoint of the consumer in that ordinarily the expense and burden of such a proceeding is borne by an administrative agency or a licensing commission, with the consumer appearing merely in the role of a complaining witness rather than as the plaintiff in a court action. Likewise, since the suspension or loss of a license will put the licensee out of business, at least temporarily, it is a punishment or sanction that is much more to be feared than merely being required to pay the injured consumer a refund or to pay a fine to the government.

(1) Collection Methods. In 1930, the FTC began to take steps to prevent scare tactics in debt collection. In 1965, it promulgated, and in 1968 amended, "Guides Against Deceptive Debt Collection." Bar associations have adopted similar guidelines.[60]

---

[57] Note that this includes "services" as well as "goods." UCCC § 2.105(3), (5).

[58] § 2.404, Alternative A.

[59] § 2.404, Alternative B.

[60] See Commercial Lawyers Conference v Grant, 65 Misc 2d § 97, 318 NYS2d 966, referring to the guidelines of the New York City Bar Association.

Unreasonable methods of debt collection are often expressly prohibited by statute or are held by courts to constitute an unreasonable invasion of privacy.[61] Statutes generally prohibit sending bills in such form that they give the impression that a lawsuit has been initiated against the consumer and that the bill is legal process or a warrant issued by the court.[62] The CCPA prohibits the use of extortionate methods of loan collection.[63] A creditor may be prohibited from informing the employer of the debtor that the latter owes him money.[64]

When the seller made telephone calls to the buyer and the buyer's relatives and made obscene, threatening, and malicious statements which caused the buyer to become physically ill, the seller was liable for the tort of intentional mental disturbance. In order to give rise to such liability, "the conduct must be more than mere insults, indignities, threats, and annoyances and must be so shocking and outrageous to exceed all reasonable bounds of decency." [65]

(2) Small Claims Procedures. In a number of states small claims courts are created or compulsory arbitration is provided to reduce the cost and the delay of enforcing small claims.

Some procedures are designed so that a party may proceed without any attorney if he so desires.

A small claims court appeal provision is unconstitutional when it is provided that a party cannot be represented by an attorney in the small claims court and cannot take an appeal which would entitle him to a hearing with representation by an attorney without filing an appeal bond or making a deposit, as payment of such premium or the making of such deposit deprives the party of his property prior to any hearing.[66]

(3) Repossession and Deficiency Liability. The UCCC provides that in the case of a consumer credit sale under $1,000, the seller must choose between repossessing the goods upon a default in the payment of installments and suing the buyer for the balance of the purchase price due. That is, the seller cannot repossess the goods because of a default of the buyer, resell the goods, and then hold the buyer liable for any deficiency that remains because the proceeds from the resale cannot pay the balance due. If the contract price is over $1,000, the UCCC does not prevent the seller

[61] Guthridge v Pen-Mod, Inc., (Del Super) 239 A2d 709.

[62] Florida Stat §§ 817.561, 817.751.

[63] Perez v United States, 402 US 146.

[64] Commercial Lawyers Conference v Grant, 318 NYS2d 966.

[65] Callarama v Associates Discount Corp., 69 Misc 2d 287, 329 NYS2d 711.

[66] Brooks v Small Claims Court, 8 Cal App 3d 661, 105 Cal Rptr 785, 504 P2d 1249. The court commented on the fact that small claims were predominantly asserted by merchants against individual defendants with the consequence that the statutory prohibition against representation by lawyers worked to the disadvantage of the individual debtors because the institutional plaintiffs' representative, although not an attorney, would acquire skill through repetition.

from repossessing and reselling the goods and then obtaining a deficiency judgment.[67]

When there is a loan rather than a sale, however, and property of the debtor is put up as collateral, there is no limitation on the right of the creditor to take possession of the collateral, sell it, and then obtain a judgment against the debtor for the amount remaining due after the application of the sale proceeds to the debt. Under the UCC a secured creditor, whether a lender or a seller, has this right to obtain a deficiency judgment in all cases.[68]

§ 8:12. Protection of Credit Standing and Reputation. In many instances one party to a transaction wishes to know certain things about the other party. This situation arises when a person purchases on credit or applies for a loan, a job, or a policy of insurance. Between two and three thousand private credit bureaus gather such information on borrowers, buyers, and applicants for sale to interested persons.

The Fair Credit Reporting Act (FCRA) of 1970 [69] seeks to afford protection from various abuses that may arise. FCRA applies only to consumer credit, which is defined as credit for "personal, family, and household" use, and does not apply to business or commercial transactions.

The Fair Credit Reporting Act applies only to reports made in a business-world setting, and does not apply to reports which are made by a child adoption agency in connection with an adoption.[70]

Likewise the Fair Credit Reporting Act was designed to protect consumers in their personal or consumer capacity, and hence does not apply when a consumer has applied for commercial credit, as by making an application to lease property for business purposes.[71]

(1) Informing the Applicant. When employment is refused an applicant on the basis of a bureau report, or when a consumer is refused credit or charged at a higher rate, or when a consumer is refused insurance because of a credit report, the user of the report must give the applicant the name and address of the bureau furnishing the report.[72] If the information is not a report furnished by a bureau, as in the case in which the persons given as references by the applicant have been contacted directly, it is necessary to inform the applicant that such information was the basis or part of the basis for the action taken on his application and to inform the applicant that he is entitled to request a summary of the nature of the information.

---

[67] UCCC § 5.103.

[68] UCC § 9-504(2).

[69] PL 91-508, 15 USC § 1681 et seq. adding Title VI to the Consumer Credit Protection Act.

[70] Porter v Talbot Perkins Children's Services, (DC SD NY) 355 F Supp 174.

[71] Sizemore v Bambi Leasing Corp., (DC ND Ga) 360 F Supp 252.

[72] CCPA § 615(a), 15 USC § 1681(m).

(2) Privacy. A report on a person based on personal investigation and interviews, called an *investigative consumer report,* may not be made without informing the person investigated and advising him of his right to discover the results of the investigation.[73] Bureaus are not permitted to disclose information to persons not having a legitimate use for it. It is a federal crime to obtain or to furnish a bureau report for an improper purpose.

On request a bureau must tell a consumer the names and addresses of persons to whom it has made a credit report during the previous six months. It must also tell him when requested which employers were given such a report during the previous two years.

(3) Protection from False Information. Much of the information obtained by bureaus is based on statements made by persons, such as neighbors, when interviewed by the bureau's investigator. Sometimes the statements are incorrect. Quite often they would constitute hearsay evidence and would not be admissible in a legal proceeding. Nevertheless, they will go on the records of the bureau without further verification and will be furnished to a client of the bureau who will tend to regard them as accurate and true.

A person has a limited right to request an agency to disclose to him the information that it has in its files. In general he may learn the nature and substance of the information possessed by the bureau. The right to know does not extend to medical information. It is not required that the bureau identify the persons giving its information to its investigators. The bureau is not required to give the applicant a copy of, nor to permit him to see, its file.

(a) CORRECTION OF ERROR. When a person claims that the information of the bureau is erroneous, the bureau must take steps within a reasonable time to determine the accuracy of the disputed item. It is not required to do so, however, if the bureau has reasonable grounds for believing that the objection is frivolous and irrelevant. If it determines that the information is erroneous, it must give notice of the correction to anyone to whom it had sent a credit report in the preceding six months or for employment in the preceding two years. If the bureau and the applicant do not reach an agreement as to the disputed item, the applicant may give the bureau a written statement of his version of the matter. The bureau must supply a copy of this statement when it furnishes any subsequent report, and on request must send copies of the statement to persons to whom it has already sent a report within the time limitations stated above.

In some instances a stubborn insistence of management on the accuracy of its computers and its clerks has been held to constitute a denial of due process, where such attitude made it impossible for a customer to make any fair presentation of his story before gas or electric services were discontinued.[74]

---

[73] § 606, 15 USC § 1681(d).

[74] Turner v Rochester Gas and Electric Corp., 345 NYS2d 421.

(b) Elimination of Stale Items. Adverse information obtained by investigation cannot be given to a client after 3 months unless verified to determine that it is still valid. Most legal proceedings cannot be reported by a bureau after 7 years. A bankruptcy proceeding cannot be reported after 14 years.[75] Information based on a public record must be up-to-date, or the applicant must be notified that information based on the public record is being furnished. This is designed to eliminate the danger that the bureau will not have been aware of the latest developments in the matter. In many instances cases are settled out of court without any formal notation being made thereof on the court record, with the consequence that if the bureau or anyone else relied only on the court record, there would appear to be an outstanding claim or unpaid judgment in existence.

(c) Inadequacy of Prior Law. In some instances the person harmed by false information could sue the informant for damages for the tort of interference with economic relations or defamation. Ordinarily the injured party cannot recover under either theory because as a practical matter he will not be able to prove that the defendant acted with malice, and in the absence of malice the informant is protected from liability by a qualified privilege. (See p. 153, Bartels v Retail Credit Co.)

§ **8:13. Expansion of Consumer Protection.** Various state laws aimed at preventing fraudulent sales of corporate securities, commonly called blue-sky laws, have been adopted. It was not until the 1930's, however, that federal legislation was adopted. These statutes are discussed in Chapter 51 on corporate stock.

(1) Mutual Funds. Because it is extremely difficult for the small investor to learn all the facts material to the value of a given security, mutual funds have proved very popular in the last two decades. The individual investor will purchase shares in the mutual fund, and the fund in turn will make investments in the securities of various enterprises. The great advantage to the individual is that the problem of investment guidance is passed from his shoulders to those of the investment counselors of the fund. Another advantage to the small investor is that mutual funds will accept for investment sums of money that are relatively small and which ordinarily could not be invested directly in stocks and bonds.

By the Investment Company Act Amendments of 1970,[76] restrictions are imposed by the federal government to prevent mutual funds from overcharging investors for the services they render. If a fund pays an excessive amount to its investment counselor, the dissatisfied investor in the fund or the Securities Exchange Commission may sue the counselor to recover the improper excess portion of the fee.

---

[75] These time limitations do not apply to an application for a loan or for life insurance of $50,000 or more or for employment at a salary of $20,000 a year or more.

[76] PL 91-547, 84 Stat 1413.

When an investor makes a long-term contract with a fund by which he agrees to invest a particular amount for each of a specified number of years, such as $1,000 in each of 10 years, the various charges were often deducted from the payment in the first year. If the investor decided to cancel or withdraw from the mutual fund before the expiration of the 10 years, he lost the amount of such charges.[77] Under the federal law such *front-end loading* is regulated to protect the investor. The fund cannot allocate more than 50 percent of the total charges against the payment made by the investor in the first year. If it charges this maximum amount, the investor is given a varying right of rescission. For example, if he rescinds within 45 days after notice from the fund custodian of the charges to be made, he is entitled to the return of the value of his account and of all amounts charged for administration expenses.

(2) Real Estate Development Sales.

(a) DEVELOPMENT STATEMENT. Anyone promoting the sale of a real estate development which is divided into fifty or more parcels of less than five acres each must file with the Secretary of Housing and Urban Development a *development statement* setting forth significant details of the development specified by the federal Land Sales Act.[78]

(b) PROPERTY REPORT. When anyone buys or rents one of the parcels in the subdivision, a *property report* must be given to him. This is a condensed version of the development statement filed with the Secretary of HUD. This report must be given to the prospective customer more than 48 hours before he signs the contract to buy or lease.

(c) RESCISSION. If the development statement is not filed with the Secretary, the sale or renting of the real estate development may not be promoted through the channels of interstate commerce nor by use of the mail.

If the property report is given to the prospective buyer or tenant less than 48 hours before he signs a contract to buy or lease, or after he has signed, he has 48 hours in which to avoid his contract. If he never receives the property report, he may avoid the contract and there is no statutory limitation on the time in which he must act.

(3) Insurance. The states have made extensive regulation of insurance companies by establishing standards for their financial structure as by

---

[77] In the case of some funds, the investor can purchase directly from the fund and no sales charge is made. In contrast with such funds, commonly called no-load funds, when an investor buys shares of other funds, he pays a commission in order to compensate the brokers and salesmen involved in the transaction. These charges are now regulated by the National Association of Securities Dealers, Inc., subject to supervision by the federal Securities Exchange Commission.

[78] PL 90-448, 82 Stat 590, 15 USC § 1701 et seq.

regulating the reserves which must be maintained in order to assure policyholders that there will be sufficient funds with which to pay policy claims. In the case of a foreign insurance company doing business within a state, the company is commonly required to deposit a substantial sum with a local state official to hold available for the payment of policies issued to persons living within the state.

Statutes often seek to protect the policyholder or applicant from misconduct of insurance agents and brokers. Apart from requiring their licensing, statutes may make certain conduct illegal. For example, it is commonly a crime, called *twisting,* for an insurance salesman to induce a policyholder to cancel his existing policy and change to another company when the policyholder is not benefited from the change and the objective of the salesman is merely to obtain the commissions that the second company will pay him for selling its policy. In some states payments to an insurance broker are declared to be as effective as though made to the insurance company,[79] even though the broker is not the agent of the insurer; thus protecting the customer from the failure of the broker, whether accidental or intentional, to send the money to the insurance company.

(4) Service Contracts. The UCCC treats a consumer service contract the same as a consumer sale of goods if payment is made in installments or a credit charge is made and the amount financed does not exceed $25,000.[80] It defines "services" broadly as embracing work, specified privileges, and insurance provided by a noninsurer. The inclusion of "privileges" makes the UCCC apply to contracts calling for payment on the installment plan or including a financing charge for transportation, hotel and restaurant accommodations, education, entertainment, recreation, physical culture, hospital accommodations, funerals, and similar accommodations. A person sells services and is subject to the UCCC to the extent indicated when he undertakes to furnish the services personally or have someone else furnish them.

Some states have adopted statutes requiring that any present payments for future funeral services or goods must be deposited in a bank account or similar depository to be held for the benefit of the customer. A contract which does not provide for such deposit is void as being against public policy.[81]

The mere extension of credit to the consumer of services does not bring the transaction under the UCCC. That is, the fact that a doctor does not require immediate payment from his patient does not make it a transaction within the UCCC. If, however, the doctor and the patient make an agreement calling for payment by specified installments or with a financing charge added to the amount due, the transaction would be subject to the UCCC.[82]

---

[79] Zak v Fidelity-Phenix Insurance Co., 58 Ill App 2d 341, 208 NE2d 29.

[80] UCCC § 2.104(1). Credit card transactions are exempted unless the person selling the services and the consumer expressly agree that the transaction is subject to the UCCC. § 2.104(2)(a).

[81] Whaley v Holly Hills Memorial Park, Inc., — Tenn App —, 490 SW2d 532.

[82] Official Comment to § 2.105(3).

Closely related to the exploitation of consumers by charging excessive prices is the practice of charging for unperformed services. To some extent such practice is condemned.

(5) Protection of the Indigent. The current growth of consumer protectionism cannot be fully understood without recognizing a companion element of protection of the indigent. Both of these elements—protection of the consumer and protection of the indigent—stem from the social force of protection of the person. Protection of the indigent long existed in the form that a criminal court judge had authority, if he chose, to appoint counsel to represent an indigent defendant who did not have an attorney. In 1963 this right of the trial judge was elevated to a duty, so that it became a constitutionally protected right of the accused to have an attorney appointed for him at public expense when he was charged with a serious offense and was unable to pay for a private attorney.[83] In 1972 the Supreme Court expanded this duty to require the appointment of an attorney whenever the sentence could impose any jail confinement, regardless of how short its duration.[84]

The concept of protection of the indigent has been expanded so that the recipient of welfare payments is entitled to a hearing before such payment may be terminated on the ground of the recipient's disqualification.[85] Likewise, a state welfare law may not exclude from receiving benefits aliens generally or aliens who have not resided within the state for a long time, such as 15 years. Such exclusion is unconstitutional as a denial of the equal protection of the laws to which both citizen and alien are entitled.[86] Likewise, a durational residence requirement as a qualification for admission to a government housing project is unconstitutional as a denial of equal protection of the law.[87]

§ 8:14. Consumer Remedies. The theoretical right of the consumer to sue or to assert a defense is often of little practical value to the consumer because of the small size of the amount involved and the high cost of litigation. Consumer protection legislation has sought to provide special remedies.

(1) Government Agency Action. The UCCC provides for an administrator who will in a sense police business practices to insure comformity with the law.[88] This is not regarded by some as an improvement and has

---

[83] Gideon v Wainwright, 372 US 335. There is some authority that a court should appoint an attorney to represent an indigent civil defendant. Hotel Martha Washington Management v Swinick, (App Div 2d) 322 NYS2d 139. Indigent parents defending a child custody action are entitled to court-appointed counsel at the state's expense. Crist v Division of Youth and Family Services, 128 NJ Super 402, 320 A2d 203.

[84] Argersinger v Hamlin, 407 US 25.

[85] Goldberg v Kelly, 397 US 254.

[86] Graham v Richardson, 403 US 365.

[87] King v New Rochelle Municipal Housing Authority, (CA2 NY) 442 F2d 646.

[88] UCCC § 6.103-6.116.

been criticized on the ground of the danger that the administrator may be creditor-oriented, and the debtor might as a consequence be deprived of protection in many cases when it is a question of policy or discretion as to what action, if any, should be taken by the administrator.[89]

(2) Action by Attorney General. A number of states provide that the state attorney general may bring an action on behalf of a particular group of consumers to obtain cancellation of their contracts and restitution of whatever they had paid. Many states permit the attorney general to bring an action to enjoin violating the consumer protection statute.[90] For example, when an enterprise advertises that it is engaged in providing particular services but in fact it cannot lawfully furnish such services because it is not licensed, it is guilty of false advertising and may be enjoined from continuing to so advertise.[91]

Consumer protection statutes aimed at false advertising authorize buyers to cancel their purchases and obtain the refund of the purchase price paid. Ordinarily the Attorney General is authorized to bring an action to enjoin the improper conduct and to impose some penalty for past misconduct.

Consumer protection statutes commonly give the Attorney General the authority to seek a voluntary discontinuance of improper practices. If this fails, he is authorized to obtain an injunction from a court.

(3) Action by Consumer. Some consumer protection statutes provide that a consumer who is harmed by a violation of the statutes may sue the wrongdoing enterprise to recover a specified penalty or that he may bring a class action. Consumer protection statutes are often designed to rely on private litigation as an aid to enforcement of the statutory provisions.[92] The Consumer Protection Safety Act of 1972 authorizes "any interested person" to bring a civil action to enforce a consumer product safety rule and certain orders of the Food, Drug, and Consumer Protection Agency (FDCPA).[93] Courts are inclined to permit consumers to bring a class action for the reason that the amounts involved will ordinarily be so small that it would not be practical for individual consumers to bring separate actions. Otherwise, defendants could violate the law without fear of being sued for their conduct.[94] But in some cases the individual consumer cannot bring any action, and enforcement of the law is entrusted exclusively to an administrative agency.

---

[89] Furthermore, this opens the door to all the other problems involved in the regulation of business by administrative agencies.

[90] New York v Bevis Industries, Inc., 314 NYS2d 60.

[91] State Board of Architecture v Kirkham, Michael & Associates, Inc., (ND) 179 NW2d 409.

[92] Jones v Seldon's Furniture Warehouse, Inc., (DC ED Va) 357 F Supp 886.

[93] PL 92-573, 86 Stat 1207, § 23.

[94] Riley v New Rapids Carpet Center, 61 NJ 218, 294 A2d 7.

§ 8:15. Civil and Criminal Penalties. The seller or lender engaging in improper consumer practices may be subject to civil penalties and criminal punishment. In some instances the laws in question are the general laws applicable to improper conduct, while in other cases the laws are specifically aimed at the particular consumer practices.

Illustrative of the applicability of the general law, a contractor who falsely stated to a homeowner that certain repairs needed on the roof of her home cost, with labor and materials, $650 when in fact it was only $200 was guilty of the crime of obtaining money by false pretenses.[95]

Under the Truth in Lending Act each periodic statement which violates the disclosure requirements subjects the creditor to a separate claim for damages, as against the contention that there could only be one recovery per customer.[96]

Consumer protection statutes of the disclosure type generally provide that the creditor cannot enforce the obligation of the debtor if the specified information is not set forth in the contract, without regard to whether the statute expressly declares that a nonconforming contract shall be invalid or nonenforceable.[97]

---

[95] Harrick v Maine, 159 Me 499, 196 A2d 101.
[96] Thomas v Myers-Dickson Furniture Co., (CA5 Ga) 479 F2d 740.
[97] Carter v Seaboard Finance Co., 33 Cal 2d 564, 203 P2d 758.

CASES FOR CHAPTER 8

J. B. Williams Co. v Federal Trade Commission

(CA6 FTC) 381 F2d 884 (1967)

The J. B. Williams Co. manufactured Geritol in liquid and tablet form. Through the Parkson Advertising Agency, Williams advertised its product as a corrective for "tired blood." The advertising gave the impression that a person who was tired, run-down, irritable, or nervous had an iron deficiency and that Geritol would cure the deficiency. The Federal Trade Commission concluded that this was false advertising and ordered it to stop. Williams and the advertising agency filed a petition in court to set aside the order of the Commission.

CELEBREZZE, C.J. . . . The question presented by this appeal is whether Petitioners' advertising of a product, Geritol, for the relief of iron deficiency anemia, is false and misleading so as to violate . . . the Federal Trade Commission Act. . . .

The Commission's Order requires that not only must the Geritol advertisements be expressly limited to those persons whose symptoms are due to an existing deficiency of one or more of the vitamins contained in the preparation, or due to an existing deficiency of iron, but also the Geritol advertisements must affirmatively disclose the negative fact that a great majority of persons who experience these symptoms do not experience them because they have a vitamin or iron deficiency; that for the great majority of people experiencing these symptoms, Geritol will be of no benefit. Closely related to this requirement is the further requirement of the Order that the Geritol advertisements refrain from representing that the symptoms are generally reliable indications of iron deficiency. . . .

The Commission's finding that the Geritol advertisements create a false and misleading impression on the public by taking common or universal symptoms and representing these symptoms as generally reliable indications of iron deficiency or iron deficiency anemia, is supported by substantial evidence. . . .

The medical evidence on this issue is conflicting and the question is not one which is susceptible to precise statistical analysis. The evidence presented a range estimated by the doctors to be from 1 percent to 10 percent of the people in this country with iron deficiency or iron deficiency anemia. It is clear that the incidence of iron deficiency anemia is higher in women than in men. . . .

While the advertising does not make the affirmative representation that the majority of people who are tired and run-down are so because of iron deficiency anemia and the product Geritol will be an effective cure, there is substantial evidence to support the finding of the Commission that most tired people are not so because of iron deficiency anemia, and the failure to disclose this fact is false and misleading because the advertisement creates the impression that the tired feeling is caused by something which Geritol can cure. . . .

[FTC order sustained.]

FTC v Colgate-Palmolive Co.

380 US 374 (1965)

The Colgate-Palmolive Company ran a television commercial to show that its shaving cream "Rapid Shave" could soften even the toughness of sandpaper. The commercial showed what was described as the sandpaper test. Actually what was used was a sheet of Plexiglas on which sand had been sprinkled. The FTC claimed that this was a deceptive practice. The advertiser contended that actual sandpaper would merely look like ordinary colored paper and that Plexiglas had been used to give the viewer an accurate visual representation of the test. The FTC issued an order to stop the commercial. The Court of Appeals reversed this order.

WARREN, C.J. . . . The Commission found that the undisclosed use of a plexiglass substitute for sandpaper was [a] material misrepresentation that was a deceptive act separate and distinct from [any] misrepresentation concerning Rapid Shave's underlying qualities. Even if the sandpaper could be shaved just as depicted in the commercials, the Commission found that viewers had been misled into believing they had seen it done with their own eyes. As a result of these findings the Commission entered a cease-and-desist order against the respondents [Colgate and the advertiser]. . . .

. . . The Commission expressed the view that without this visible proof of Rapid Shave's moisturizing ability some viewers might not have been persuaded to buy the product. . . .

. . . When the Commission was created by Congress in 1914, it was directed by § 5 to prevent "[u]nfair methods of competition in commerce." Congress amended the Act in 1938 to extend the Commission's jurisdiction to include "unfair or deceptive acts or practices in commerce"—a significant amendment showing Congress' concern for consumers as well as for competitors. It is important to note the generality of these standards of illegality. . . .

This statutory scheme necessarily gives the Commission an influential role in interpreting § 5 and in applying it to the facts of particular cases arising out of unprecedented situations. Moreover, as an administrative agency which deals continually with cases in the area, the Commission is often in a better position than are courts to determine when a practice is "deceptive" within the meaning of the Act. . . .

We accept the Commission's determination that the commercials involved in this case contained three representations to the public: (1) that sandpaper could be shaved by Rapid Shave; (2) that an experiment had been conducted which verified this claim; and (3) that the viewer was seeing this experiment for himself. . . . For the purposes of our review, we can assume that the first two representations were true; the focus of our consideration is on the third, which was clearly false. The parties agree that § 5 prohibits the intentional misrepresentation of any fact which would constitute a material factor in a purchaser's decision whether to buy. They differ, however, in their conception of what "facts" constitute a "material factor" in a purchaser's decision to buy. Respondents submit, in effect, that the only material facts are those which deal with the substantive qualities of a product. The Commission, on the other hand, submits that the misrepresentation of *any* fact so long as it materially induces a purchaser's decision to buy is a deception prohibited by § 5.

The Commission's interpretation of what is a deceptive practice seems more in line with the decided cases than that of respondents. . . .

We agree with the Commission . . . that the undisclosed use of plexiglass in the present commercials was a material deceptive practice. . . . Respondents claim that it will be impractical to inform the viewing public that it is not seeing an actual test, experiment or demonstration, but we think it inconceivable that the ingenious advertising world will be unable, if it so desires, to conform to the Commission's insistence that the public be not misinformed. If, however, it becomes impossible or impractical to show simulated demonstrations on television in a truthful manner, this indicates that television is not a medium that lends itself to this type of commercial, not that the commercial must survive at all costs. . . .

[Judgment reversed.]

Colorado v Gym of America, Inc.

177 Colo 97, 493 P2d 660 (1972)

The Attorney General of Colorado brought an action against Gym of America to stop certain selling practices which he claimed were prohibited by the Colorado Consumer Protection Act. Gym of America claimed that the statute was unconstitutional because such terms as "advertise," "bait-and-switch," "disparagement," and "tie-in sales" were too vague and that the state lacked power to regulate the practices in question. The trial court held the statute unconstitutional. The Attorney General appealed.

PRINGLE, C.J. . . . First, it was alleged that the appellee [Gym of America] refused to comply with the terms of its advertised offers when customers agreed to purchase services at the reduced rates. Second, it was claimed that appellee informed those who were interested in the advertised health course that the advertised terms would be available only to those who would agree to thereafter become regular and paying club members. Third, it was contended that appellee stated to those who responded to the advertisements that club privileges on terms as advertised would not be available as the offered membership was too short in duration to be of benefit, but that a membership of a much longer period of time would be helpful. Fourth, it was alleged that after potential customers had been told over the telephone that they had received a "free" $60 health club membership, they were advised by Gym of America that this membership was not available independently and only applied as a discount on a regular membership. . . .

We note that this statute is concerned with proscribing certain kinds of specific *future* conduct. As such, the statute provides sanctions of purely prospective effect, such as the restraining orders, injunctions, and assurances of discontinuance. . . . This, of course, means that when the attorney general seeks an injunction he is not demanding that the defendant be punished with a penal sanction, but rather that the defendant be restrained from acting unlawfully in the future. It is unnecessary that such a statute provide absolutely precise warning before its equitable sanctions are applied. . . . The adjudication itself provides notice to the defendant, and is prospective in its application. The result is that the defendant is provided with the explicit terms of the decree or order to tell him what practices are allowed without incurring penalties. Therefore, . . . a statute such as this whose sanctions are injunctions or assurances of discontinuance need not be as precise as a statute where the sanction is penal or criminal. . . .

The question before the Court now is whether the four challenged phrases—"advertise," "bait and switch," "disparagement," and "tie-in sales," as used in the Consumer Protection Act are so vague as to render their meaning unintelligible to people affected by them. We believe that all four terms are not unconstitutionally vague.

First, with respect to "advertise," it is asserted that because the statute's definition section only defines "advertisement," the derivative meaning of the verb "advertise" is impossible to ascertain. This argument is not valid. . . . Clearly, the word "advertise" is but the verbal form of the noun "advertisement." What the statutory definition of the noun encompasses must by common sense apply to the verbal form of the noun when used in the same statute. . . . In this statute, the meaning of "advertise" can and must be determined by reference to the definition of "advertisement" found in Section 1(10). . . .

The statute's "bait and switch" terminology is attacked on the ground that it has no commonly understood meaning and is therefore unconstitutionally vague. This argument must fall for several reasons. First, Section 2(1)(a)(o)(i) *specifically defines* "bait and switch" advertising as advertising which "consists of an attractive but insincere offer to sell a product or service which the seller in truth does not intend or desire to sell." Second, "bait and switch" advertising and selling techniques have long been recognized in the legal literature and have long been subject to equitable sanctions. . . .

The use of the term "disparagement" in the statute is attacked. . . . It may be true that the Colorado Consumer Protection Act does not specifically define "disparagement" anywhere, but, in our view, the word "disparagement" has such a common meaning that to define it would be an exercise in redundancy. The legal literature contains many instances of the use of the word "disparagement" when dealing with forbidden trade practices. . . .

In Electrolux [Corp. v Val Worth, Inc., 6 NY 2d 556, 190 NYS2d 977, 164 NE2d 197] the New York Court of Appeals enjoined a sales promotion scheme whereby a business firm first advertised a product at a very attractive price in order to invite inquiry, then disparaged or "knocked" the product when members of the public made inquiry, and finally offered another item for sale which was more expensive than the first but which seemed like a "bargain" in comparison to the disparaged product that was originally advertised. This deceptive use of advertising as a lure to sell other nonadvertised products or services is exactly the kind of trade practice which the Colorado Consumer Protection Act and the Uniform Deceptive Trade Practices Act . . . prohibit. This is also the "disparagement" that Gym of America is accused of engaging in when it allegedly told members of the public that club privileges on terms as advertised would not be available because the advertised terms were too short in duration to be of any benefit to their health, while an expensive membership of a longer period of time would be quite helpful.

Appellee's last contention concerning the statute's purported vagueness is that the Act's "tie-in sales" language is too ambiguous and uncertain to meet due process requirements. This argument must also fall for several reasons. The Colorado Consumer Protection Act specifically defines "tie-in sales" to mean an "undisclosed condition to be met prior to selling the advertised product or service." . . . Furthermore, the concept of a "tie-in sale" is not new to the law as its practice has long been prohibited by the antitrust laws. . . . These guideposts, added to the fact that a "tie-in sale," like "disparagement," and "bait and switch" tactics, is not a new or unfamiliar term to most business enterprises, leads us to conclude that its use in the Colorado Consumer Protection Act does establish a standard against which one's business and trade activities can be tested. There is a definite background of experience and precedent to illuminate the meaning of the words employed in the statute. No one would reasonably be misled thereby.

The trial court's second basis for declaring the Act unconstitutional is that the statute is an "attempted exercise of power in excess of that which a state may lawfully do under its police powers." We disagree, and find that the legislature acted well within the police power of the state when it enacted the Colorado Consumer Protection Act. . . .

. . . Reasonable state restraints are part of the price we must pay for an ordered society. The corollary to this is that the unrestricted privilege to engage in business or to conduct it as one pleases is not guaranteed by the constitution. . . . Were it otherwise, the public's welfare might often become the forgotten orphan of commercial expediency.

The right to regulate in the name of the police power is especially clear when the legislative intent is to regulate commercial activities and practices which, because of their nature, may prove injurious, offensive, or dangerous to the public. . . . And this police power relates not only to the public's physical or mental health and safety, but also to public *financial safety*. There is a necessary residuum of power which the state possesses to safeguard the interests of its people, and pursuant to this power laws may be passed to protect the public from financial loss . . . and to abate evils which are deemed to arise from the pursuit of business. . . .

. . . It is apparent to this Court that the deceptive trade practices which are the subject matter of the statute under attack in this case injuriously affect both honest business men and consumers. When consumers are induced to purchase inferior merchandise or services as a result of misleading solicitations, when the public is attracted to business concerns on the basis of statements falsely announcing the existence of products which are in fact nonexistent, and when citizens discover that the product they have acquired carries with it a set of obligations which they did not intend to purchase, it is clear that the state's general and financial welfare is thereby aggrieved. To protect the public from such deceptive practices by enjoining their use is a proper and commendable exercise of the legislature's police powers. . . .

[Judgment reversed.]

Fairfield Credit Corp. v Donnelly

158 Conn 543, 264 A2d 547 (1969)

Donnelly purchased a television set on credit from D.W.M. Advertising, Inc. He also contracted for service on the set. D.W.M. assigned the contract to the Fairfield Credit Corporation. D.W.M. went out of existence and the service contract was never performed. Fairfield sued Donnelly for the balance due on the purchase price. Donnelly raised the defense that the service contract had never been performed. Fairfield claimed that this defense could not be asserted against it because the sales contract contained a waiver of defenses. The trial judge held that the plaintiff was entitled to recover the reasonable value of the set. From a judgment for Fairfield, Donnelly appealed.

KING, C.J. . . . The service contract, although contained in a separate writing, is not independent of the instalment contract. The parties did not assent to the two contracts separately but treated them as a single whole. . . . The service contract was delivered with the television set and is supported by the same consideration as is the instalment contract, that is, the defendants' promise, made in the instalment contract, to pay $1210.95. The plaintiff had actual knowledge of the existence of the service contract. . . . D.W.M., had there been no assignment to the plaintiff, could not have enforced the instalment contract in the face of its material breach of the service contract, which . . . was inextricably connected with the instalment contract. . . . In other words, D.W.M. could not have prevailed in an action such as this to recover the unpaid balance of the contract price.

Ordinarily an assignee of a contract takes it subject to all defenses which might have been asserted against the assignor. . . . Thus, without more, there would be no question that the plaintiff would not be able to enforce this contract against the defendants.

The plaintiff claims, however, that it is not subject to any of the defenses which could have been asserted against D.W.M., including the breach of the service contract, because of the following language, in fine print, on the reverse side of the instalment contract: "The Buyer will settle all claims against the named Seller (the assignor) directly with such Seller and will not assert or use as a defense any such claim against the assignee."

Such a provision is generally referred to as a waiver of defense clause and is specifically dealt with in the Uniform Commercial Code [§] 9-206(1), which provides that, "subject to any statute or decision which establishes a different rule for buyers or lessees of consumer goods, an agreement by a buyer or lessee that he will not assert against an assignee any claim or defense which he may have against the seller or lessor is enforceable by an assignee who takes his assignment for value, in good faith and without notice of a claim or defense, except as to defenses of a type which may be asserted against a holder in due course of a negotiable instrument under article 3. . . ."

The statute quoted above has specifically made effective a waiver of defense clause in favor of an assignee of a contract not involving a sale or lease of "consumer goods," as defined in [UCC §] 9-109(1). But the statute takes no position on whether such a clause constitutes a valid waiver by the buyer in a transaction involving consumer goods. . . .

We see no reason why the plaintiff, in taking an assignment of a contract under the circumstances here, should be able to recover against the buyer where the seller could not. If a seller carries out his contract obligations, either he or the assignee can recover against the buyer for any default in performance on his part. . . .

While we have not heretofore had occasion to consider the validity of such a waiver of defense clause, it has been the subject of judicial consideration in a number of states. The decisions have not been entirely in accord. . . . We consider that the better rule is that set forth in cases such as Unico v Owen, 50 NJ 101, 124, 232 A2d 405, which holds that such a clause . . . is void as against public policy. . . .

. . . It has become increasingly clear that the policy of our state is to protect purchasers of consumer goods from the impositions of overreaching sellers. . . . There can be no question that there exists in Connecticut a very strong public policy in favor of protecting purchasers of consumer goods and that for a court to enforce a waiver of defense clause in a consumer-goods transaction would be contrary to that policy. . . .

. . . The plaintiff, as assignee of the instalment contract, stands in the shoes of its assignor, D.W.M., and has no greater rights of recovery in this action than D.W.M. would have had if there had been no assignment and D.W.M. had been the plaintiff.

The complaint in this action is based solely on the instalment contract, and the sole relief claimed is the balance owing under that contract. For the reasons hereinbefore stated, D.W.M. could not have recovered the balance owing under the instalment sales contract, and the plaintiff, as the assignee of D.W.M., is equally disabled from recovery of the balance owing under the contract. . . .

[Judgment reversed.]

Mourning v Family Publications Service, Inc.

411 US 356 (1973)

Acting under the Truth in Lending Act, the Federal Reserve Board adopted a Regulation Z. Among other things, this Regulation declared that whenever a consumer agreed to pay in more than four installments, the person dealing with him was subject to the Truth in Lending Act. The Family Publications Service sold a magazine to Leila Mourning but failed to disclose the information required by the federal Act although payment was to be made by her in 30 monthly installments. Family Publications claimed that the four-installment rule of Regulation Z was invalid and that the federal Truth in Lending Act could not apply to it because it did not make any extra charge for the making of installment payments.

BURGER, C.J. . . . Passage of the Truth-in-Lending Act in 1968 culminated several years of congressional study and debate as to the propriety and usefulness of imposing mandatory disclosure requirements on those who extend credit to consumers in the American market. By the time of passage, it had become abundantly clear that the use of consumer credit was expanding at an extremely rapid rate. . . .

The Truth-in-Lending Act was designed to remedy the problems which had developed. . . . This purpose was . . . "to assure a meaningful disclosure of credit terms so that the consumer will be able to compare more readily the various credit terms available to him and avoid the uninformed use of credit." . . .

. . . Congress determined to lay the structure of the Act broadly and to entrust its construction to an agency with the necessary experience and resources to monitor its operation. Section 105 delegated to the Federal Reserve Board broad authority to promulgate regulations necessary to render the Act effective. . . .

In addition to granting to the Board the authority normally given to administrative agencies to promulgate regulations designed to "carry out the purposes" of the Act, Congress specifically stated: "These regulations may contain such classifications, differentiations, or other provisions, and may provide for such adjustments and exceptions for any class of transactions, as in the judgment of the Board are necessary or proper . . . to prevent circumvention or evasion [of the Act], or to facilitate compliance therewith." . . .

One means of circumventing the objectives of the Truth-in-Lending Act, as passed by Congress, was that of "burying" the cost of credit in the price of goods sold. Thus in many credit transactions in which creditors claimed that no finance charge had been imposed, the creditor merely assumed the cost of extending credit as an expense of doing business, to be recouped as part of the price charged in the transaction. Congress was well aware, from its extensive studies, of the possibility that merchants could use such devices to evade the disclosure requirements of the Act. The Committee hearings are replete with suggestions that such manipulation would render the Act a futile gesture in the case of goods normally sold by installment contract. Opponents of the bill contended that the reporting provisions would actually encourage merchants who had formerly segregated their credit costs not to do so. They predicted that the effect of the Act would thus be to reduce the amount of information available to the consumer, a result directly contrary to that which was intended. . . .

. . . The Board's objective in promulgating the [four-installment] rule was to prevent the Act from fulfilling the prophecy which its opponents had forecast. . . .

. . . In delegating rule making authority to the Board, Congress emphasized the Board's authority to prevent such evasion. . . .

. . . We see no reason to doubt the Board's conclusion that the rule will deter creditors from engaging in the conduct which the Board sought to eliminate. The burdens imposed on creditors are not severe, when measured against the evils which are avoided. . . .

The Truth-in-Lending Act reflects a transition in congressional policy from a philosophy of let-the-buyer-beware to one of let-the-seller-disclose. By erecting a barrier between the seller and the prospective purchaser in the form of hard facts, Congress expressly sought "to . . . avoid the uninformed use of credit." . . . The Four-Installment Rule serves to insure that the protective disclosure mechanism chosen by Congress will not be circumvented.

That the approach taken may reflect what respondent views as an undue paternalistic concern for the consumer is beside the point. The statutory scheme is within the power granted to Congress under the Commerce Clause. It is not a function of the courts to speculate as to whether the statute is unwise or whether the evils sought to be remedied could better have been regulated in some other manner.

[Judgment reversed and remanded.]

POWELL, J. (dissenting) I would affirm the judgment of the Court of Appeals on the ground that there was no extension of consumer credit within the meaning of the Truth in Lending Act. . . .

Clearly the Act applies only to transactions involving the extension of credit. . . .

The transaction before the Court may well have been a credit transaction, but it was *not respondent* that extended the credit. Petitioner obligated herself to pay in advance for the magazines she was to receive. The contract required petitioner to pay equal installments over a 30-month period, but respondent was obligated only to provide magazines over 60 months. In effect petitioner paid every month for two months' worth of magazines. Until the last magazine had been delivered, petitioner would have paid for more magazines than she received. Thus, the contract called for the extension of credit by petitioner to respondent. For this reason it was not an "extension of consumer credit" within the meaning of the Act. . . .

Bartels v Retail Credit Co.

185 Neb 304, 175 NW2d 292 (1970)

Bartels applied for life insurance to the Northwestern Mutual Life Insurance Company

and to the Surety Life Insurance Company. These companies requested information on Bartels from the Retail Credit Company, a merchantile reporting agency. It made a report indicating that Bartels was an excessive drinker. Because of this he was refused life insurance and the Farmers Insurance Group cancelled his automobile insurance. Bartels sued the Retail Credit Company for damages for defamation. From a judgment for Bartels, Retail Credit appealed.

SPENCER, J. . . . The reports were privileged and not subject to an action for defamation. . . .

. . . Reports of mercantile agencies, published in good faith and based upon probable cause, are subject to a qualified or conditional privilege, and ordinarily are not subject to an action for defamation. . . . We are of the opinion that reports made by a mercantile agency to an interested subscriber should be conditionally privileged. A publication loses its character as privileged and is actionable if it is motivated by express or actual malice or if there is such a gross disregard of the rights of the person injured as is equivalent to malice in fact. . . .

The defendant argues: "The reason for the privilege granted in connection with a retail credit report is obvious. It is the necessity of the service of mercantile agencies to the business world and the fact that without the qualified privilege, such agencies would be unable to function properly and business and industry would ultimately suffer the consequences because reports on their proposed customers would either not be obtainable or would be long delayed."

We recognize the need for the services of mercantile agencies, but we must not lose sight also of the need to protect an individual from the secret destruction of his good name and reputation. Users of reports of mercantile agencies usually have utmost confidence in the accuracy of such reports and act accordingly. Consequently, the privilege granted to such agencies must be a qualified one. The privilege must be predicated upon the premise that the reporting agency will exercise all reasonable care to ascertain the facts. Such reports must be compiled with regard to the effect the report will have upon the rights of the subject of the report. To be privileged, a mercantile agency's representatives must act impartially and in good faith, carefully evaluating all information before disseminating any defamatory statements to its subscribers. This requires them to make a thorough and complete investigation and to fully and accurately report information only from reliable sources. An erroneous or careless report serves no purpose except to substantially damage the subject of the report, and when once the report is published, the damage has been done and very little can be done to correct it. . . .

[Judgment reversed because of improper instructions given by the trial court to the jury on other issues.]

QUESTIONS AND CASE PROBLEMS

1. What is the object of each of the following rules of law:
   (a) Back-page disclaimers are void if the front page of the contract does not call attention to the presence of such terms.
   (b) A consumer's waiver of a statute designed for his protection is void, but the transaction otherwise binds the consumer.
2. Greif obtained credit cards from Socony Mobil Oil Co. for himself and his wife. The card specified, "This card is valid unless expired or revoked. Named holder's approval of all purchases is presumed unless written notice of loss or theft is received." Later Greif returned his card to the company, stating that he was canceling it, but that he could not return the card in his wife's possession because they had separated. Subsequently Socony sued Greif for purchases made by the wife on the credit card in her possession. He defended on the ground that he had canceled the credit card contract. Decide. [Socony Mobil Oil Co. v Greif, 10 App Div 2d 119, 197 NYS2d 522]

3. Wilke was contemplating retiring. In response to an advertisement, he purchased from Coinway 30 coin-operated testing machines. He purchased these because Coinway's representative stated that, by placing these machines at different public places, Wilke could obtain supplemental income. This statement was made by the representative although he had no experience as to the cost of servicing such machines or their income-producing potential. The operational costs of the machines by Wilke exceeded the income. Wilke sued Coinway to rescind the contract for fraud. Wilke defended on the ground that the statements made were merely matters of opinion and did not constitute fraud. Was Wilke entitled to rescission? [Wilke v Coinway, Inc., 257 Cal App 2d 126, 64 Cal Rptr 845]

4. On loans made by Test, who ran a pawn shop, he charged 10 percent per month whereas the maximum interest rate allowed was 10 percent per year. Test used the excess charges to defray overhead costs—storage, paper work, and insurance. Test did not make any profit from such charges but made his profit from the resale of pawned articles that were not redeemed by their owners. Miller borrowed money from Test and later claimed that the transactions were usurious because of the "overhead" charges. Was he correct? [Miller v Test, 243 Ark 694, 421 SW2d 345]

5. Clairol is a manufacturer of hair dyes. In order to save packaging costs and for advertising purposes, it sold to jobbers for resale to beauty parlors and beauty schools bottles of dyes in cartons containing six bottles marked "Professional Use Only." Cody's Cosmetics, a discount retailer, procured and broke the six packs and sold the bottles individually to the general public. Clairol's products would deteriorate with time when exposed to light. Cody's displayed the individual bottles in open bins exposed to bright store lighting and sold some bottles after the product life date placed on the bottles by Clairol had expired. Clairol sought to enjoin as unfair competition the sale of its hair dyes by Cody's in the manner above described. Was it entitled to an injunction? [Clairol v Cody's Cosmetics, 353 Mass 385, 231 NE2d 912]

6. Yoder' wife obtained a divorce from him. The divorce decree directed that he pay $200 to the attorney for his wife. Yoder was unemployed and was not able to make this payment. In accordance with the local statute, he was arrested and jailed because of such nonpayment. He applied for a writ of habeas corpus. Decide. [Yoder v County of Cumberland, (Maine) 278 A2d 379]

7. Jordan purchased a stereo from Montgomary Ward & Co. on credit in reliance on the statement in the seller's catalog that the purchase could be charged and no payment would be required until several months later. It was not disclosed that the credit charge was computed by the seller from the date of purchase and not from the later date when payment was due. Jordan claimed that this violated the federal Truth in Lending Act, which requires a disclosure of financing terms in advertising and further provides that "any creditor who fails in connection with any consumer credit transaction to disclose to any person any information required under this Act to be disclosed to that person is liable to that person in an amount equal to . . . twice the amount of the finance charges . . . except that liability under this paragraph shall not be less than $100 nor greater than $1,000." The seller

contended that Jordan could not bring suit. Decide. [Jordan v Montgomery Ward & Co., (CA8 Minn) 442 F2d 78]

8. A New York statute authorized a buyer to cancel a home-solicited sale by giving written notice within three days. Becerra went to the office of Nu Dimensions Figure Salons and signed a contract to take a course of 190 weight-reducing sessions. The contract declared that "buyer specifically acknowledges and understands that the sum promised to be paid herein shall be paid whether or not buyer avails herself of the sessions purchased." When Becerra got home she decided that she did not want the course and notified Nu Dimensions that she cancelled her contract. Was she entitled to do so? [Nu Dimensions Figure Salons v Becerra, (NY Civil Court) 340 NYS2d 268]

9. Romain sold educational materials on a house-to-house sales basis, catering to minority groups and persons of limited education and economic means. The materials were sold at a price approximately two and a half times the reasonable market value of the materials if they were fit for their intended purpose, but there was evidence that much of it was practically worthless. Kugler, the Attorney General, brought a class-action suit on behalf of all customers of Romain to declare their contracts invalid. Decide. [Kugler v Romain, 58 NJ 522, 279 A2d 640]

10. The Consumer Protection Law of 1969 for the city of New York created the office of Commissioner of Consumer Affairs and authorized the Commissioner to adopt regulations outlawing "unconscionable trade practices." He adopted a regulation by which a creditor, or an agency on his behalf, was prohibited from informing a debtor's employer that money was owed by the employee unless a judgment had been obtained by the creditor. This regulation was adopted in the belief that there had been widespread harassment of employees by notifying their employers, with the result that employees frequently paid nonmeritorious claims for fear of losing their jobs. The Commercial Lawyers Conference brought an action against Grant, the Commissioner of Consumer Affairs, to enjoin enforcement of the regulation on the ground that it interfered with a creditor's freedom of speech. Decide. [Commercial Lawyers Conference v Grant, 318 NYS2d 966]

11. Applicants for low-cost housing constructed and maintained by the New Rochelle Municipal Housing Authority were required to wait from 3 to 10 years for an apartment because of the scarcity of such apartments. In order to give preference to local residents, the Authority required that at least one member of a family applying for housing must have been a resident of New Rochelle for 5 continuous years. King moved from North Carolina to New Rochelle and applied for housing. Her application was rejected because she did not satisfy the 5-year residence requirement. Was she improperly excluded? [King v New Rochelle Municipal Housing Authority, (CA2 NY) 442 F2d 646]

9 Nature and Classes of Contracts

§ 9:1. Introduction. Practically every personal business activity involves a contract—an enrollment in college, the purchase of a color TV on the installment plan, the rental of an apartment. Similarly, in each transaction relating to the acquisition of raw materials, their manufacture, and the distribution of the finished products by businesses, a contract that defines the relationship and the rights and obligations of the parties is involved.

Essential to free enterprise in our economic system is the protection of rights created by contracts. Each party to a contract is legally obligated to observe the terms of the agreement, and government generally cannot impair those obligations.

§ 9:2. Definition of Contract. A contract is a binding agreement.[1] By one definition "a *contract* is a promise or a set of promises for the breach of which the law gives a remedy, or the performance of which the law in some way recognizes as a duty."[2] Contracts arise out of agreements; hence, a contract is often defined as "an agreement creating an obligation."[3]

Generally a contract is an exchange of promises or assents by two or more persons, resulting in an obligation to do or to refrain from doing a particular act, which obligation is recognized or enforced by law. A contract may also be formed when a promise is made by one person in exchange for the act or the refraining from the doing of an act by another.

The substance of the definition of a contract is that by mutual agreement or assent the parties create legally enforceable duties or obligations that had not existed before. If a party to a contract does not discharge his obligation, the usual legal remedy is the awarding of damages to the other party through court action.

§ 9:3. Subject Matter of Contracts. The subject matter of a contract may relate to the performance of personal services, such as contracts of employment to work on an assembly line in a factory, to work as a secretary in

[1] The UCC defines "contract" to mean "the total legal obligation which results from the parties' agreement as affected by [the Code] and any other applicable rules of law," UCC § 1-201(11).

[2] Restatement, Contracts, § 1; Mag Construction Co. v McLean County, (ND) 181 NW2d 718.

[3] H. Liebes & Co. v Klengenberg, (CA9 Cal) 23 F2d 611.

an office, to sing on television, or to build a house. The contract may provide for the transfer of the ownership of property, such as a house (real property) or an automobile (personal property), from one person to another. A contract may also call for a combination of these things. For example, a builder may contract to supply materials and do the work involved in installing the materials, or a person may contract to build a house and then transfer the house and the land to the buyer.

§ **9:4. Parties to a Contract.** A person who makes a promise is the *promisor,* and the person to whom the promise is made is called the *promisee.* If the promise is binding, it imposes upon the promisor a duty or obligation and he may be called the *obligor.* The promisee who can claim the benefit of the obligation is also called the *obligee.* The parties to a contract are said to stand in privity with each other, and the relationship between them is termed *privity of contract.*

In written contracts parties may be referred to as "party of the first part" and "party of the second part." Frequently, however, they are given special names that serve better to identify each party. For example, the parties to a contract by which one person agrees that another may occupy his house upon the payment of money are called landlord and tenant, or lessor and lessee, and the contract between them is known as a lease. Other parties have their distinctive names, such as vendor and vendee, for the parties to a sales contract; shipper and carrier, for the parties to a transportation contract; insurer and insured, for the parties to an insurance policy.

A party to a contract may be an individual, a partnership, a corporation, or a government. A person may act for himself, or he may act on behalf of another. There may be one or more persons on each side of the contract. In some cases there are three-sided contracts, as in the case of a credit card, in which there are the company issuing the card, the holder of the card, and the business furnishing goods and services in reliance on the credit card.

In addition to the original parties to the contract, other persons may have rights or duties with respect to it. For example, one party may to some extent assign his rights under the contract to a third person. Again, the contract may have been made for the benefit of a third person, as in a life insurance contract, and the third party (the beneficiary) is permitted to enforce the contract.

§ **9:5. How a Contract Arises.** A contract is based upon an agreement. An agreement arises when one person, the *offeror,* makes an offer and the person to whom the offer is made, the *offeree,* accepts. There must be both an offer and an acceptance. If either is lacking, there is no contract.[4]

An offeror may make an offer to a particular person because he wants only that person to do what he has in mind. On the other hand, he may make the offer to the public at large because he does not care by whom

---

[4] Milanko v Jensen, 404 Ill 261, 88 NE2d 857.

1

THIS AGREEMENT is made on June 8, 1975, between John D. Segal, 2628 Dawes Lane, Springfield, Illinois, the party of the first part, and Glen W. Buswell, 788 Ackley Road, Springfield, Illinois, the party of the second part. 2

The party of the first part agrees [here state what he agrees to do; as: to install aluminum triple-track storm windows in the home of the party of the second part at (address) by (date) in accordance with the specifications attached hereto.] 3

The party of the second part agrees [here state what he agrees to do, as: to pay the party of the first part $_______ upon the satisfactory completion of the work.] 4

John D. Segal
Glen W. Buswell 5

Contract

Note that this contract includes the important items of information: (1) the date, (2) the name and address of each party, (3) the promise or consideration of the seller, (4) the promise or consideration of the buyer, and (5) the signatures of the two parties.

Some contracts and other legal documents must be notarized in the manner explained in § 16:7.

something is done so long as it is done. The latter case arises, for example, when a reward is offered to the public for the return of lost property.

It is frequently said that a meeting of the minds is essential to an agreement or a contract. Modern courts do not stress the meeting of the minds, however, because in some situations the law finds an agreement even though the minds of the parties have not in fact met.

The real test, therefore, is not whether the minds of the parties met, but whether under the circumstances one party was reasonably entitled to believe that there was an offer and the other to believe that there was an acceptance.[5]

---

[5] Restatement, Contracts, § 20, Comment a; Markmann v H. A. Bruntjen Co., 249 Minn 281, 81 NW2d 858.

§ 9:6. Intent to Make a Binding Agreement. Because a contract is based on the consent of the parties and is a legally-binding agreement, it follows that there must be an intent to enter into an agreement which is binding. Although an agreement appears on its face to be a final agreement, it may be shown to be "noncontractual" by its own terms (see p. 167, Pappas v Hauser) or by the subject matter of the agreement and the surrounding circumstances.

When the elements of a contract exist there is a binding contract, even though there is no express statement that the parties are making a contract, that a promise is made, or that something is consideration for a promise. Consequently, where the subcontractors on a construction job were threatening to quit work because they were afraid the contractor would not pay them, the owner became bound by a contract to pay them when he told the subcontractors, "Don't do that. I'll see that you get your money," and "Don't worry about it"; as against the contention that there was no contract because the owner had not stated that he promised to pay the subcontractors.[6]

§ 9:7. Working Arrangements. Working arrangements between parties are sometimes not regarded as "contracts" because it was in fact not the intention of the parties to be so bound thereby that suit could be brought for nonperformance. For example, where a city agreed to provide firefighting protection for an area adjoining the city in order to protect the city from the hazard of the spread of an outlying fire, there was no contract, even though persons in the outlying area made money donations or payments in exchange for such fire protection.[7]

When a working arrangement is part of a clearly contractual relationship, the transaction remains a binding contract because the purpose of the working arrangement is merely to provide flexibility to a contract. Consequently, a contract by which a bank agrees to accept the assignment of such contracts from a dealer as the bank shall deem "acceptable" remains a contract, even though theoretically the bank could refuse to find any contract acceptable. Likewise, a contract to pay commissions to a sales agent on a specified sliding scale on orders under one-quarter million dollars and to pay on larger orders such compensation as shall be agreed to remains a binding contract obligating the employer to pay the agent reasonable compensation for orders over one-quarter million dollars, as against the contention that there was no contract because the parties might never agree to the compensation to be paid on the large orders.

In these latter two situations the fact that there is an underlying business relationship makes it reasonable to conclude that there is a contract and the theoretical objections that could be raised are overcome by the fact that the persons involved want to stay in business, and therefore can be depended upon to act in good faith to carry out their "arrangement" in a way which will be mutually satisfactory and profitable.

---

[6] Carvitto v Ryle, (Mo App) 495 SW2d 109.

[7] Miller v City of St. Joseph, (Mo App) 485 SW2d 688.

§ 9:8. Statistical Projections. Many transactions contemplate future events or benefits. For example, a person may obtain a life insurance policy which pays a certain amount of income per month when he retires; or he might deposit money in a bank and receive a certificate of deposit on which he will receive interest; or he might take a particular job because of the pension plan benefits offered by that employer. In the course of negotiation or discussion leading up to a contract, one party to a transaction may show the other party various charts, tables, and statistical projections into the future to show the actual dollar value of the particular transaction to the other party. It is a question of intent to what extent such matter is merely illustrative and to what extent it is part of the contract. If it is merely illustrative and there is no element of fraudulent deception, there is no liability when the subsequent facts are different than had been projected or estimated. If it is part of the contract, then if there is a difference between the projection and the subsequent reality, there is a breach of contract and liability will be imposed accordingly.

§ 9:9. Enclosed Printed Matter. Frequently a contract is mailed or delivered by one party to the other in an envelope which contains additional printed matter. Similarly, when goods are purchased, the buyer often receives with the goods a manufacturer's manual and various pamphlets. What effect do all these papers have upon the contract?

(1) Incorporation of Other Statement. The contract itself may furnish the key to the answer. Sometimes the contract will expressly refer to and incorporate into the contract the terms of the other writing or printed statement. For example, a warehouse contract may expressly state that it covers the "goods" of the customer, but instead of listing the goods, the contract will continue by following the words "goods of the customer" with the words "as set forth in Schedule A which is delivered to the buyer with this contract." Frequently such a schedule will be stapled or otherwise attached to the contract itself. Or the contract may say that the customer will be charged at the rates set forth in the approved tariff schedule posted on the premises of the warehouse, and may continue with the words, "a copy of which is attached hereto and made part of this contract."

In all of these instances, it is clear that the intent of the parties was to include the other writing in the contract; and such intent will be given that effect.

(2) Exclusion of Other Statement. As the opposite of incorporation, the contract may declare that there is nothing outside of the contract. This means that either there never was anything else or that any prior agreement was merely a preliminary step which is finally cancelled out or erased and the contract in its final form is stated in the writing. For example, the seller of goods may state in his contract that no statements as to the goods had been made to the buyer and that the written contract contains all of the terms of the sale. Such an exclusion clause will ordinarily be given effect according to its terms.

In a strict sense an exclusion clause is unnecessary because if there is a written contract, it will ordinarily be regarded as the entire contract and anything outside of that contract will be ignored. As a practical matter, however, the exclusion clause has value in that some situations arise when it is not quite clear whether the writing is the entire contract or whether the situation is to be treated as though the writing had expressly stated that the earlier terms were incorporated into the contract. In order to avoid uncertainty and make clear the intent of the parties, a provision stating that the writing is the total and exclusive contract has practical value.

(3) Reduction of Contract Terms. The effect of accompanying or subsequently delivered printed matter may be to reduce the terms of the written contract. That is, one party may have had a better bargain under the original contract. In this case the accompanying matter will generally be ignored if it is not shown that the party who would be harmed has agreed that it be part of the contract. (See p. 168, Adamick v Ferguson-Florissant School District.) If a contract has already been made and the accompanying matter seeks to reduce the rights of one party, as when the manufacturer's manual reduces the rights which the buyer would otherwise have, such reduced writing has no effect. A contract once made cannot be changed by unilateral action; that is, by the action of one party or one side to the contract.

§ 9:10. Formal and Simple Contracts. Contracts are classified in terms of their form as (a) contracts under seal, (b) contracts of record, and (c) simple contracts. The first two classes are formal contracts.[8]

(1) Contracts under Seal. A *contract under seal* is executed by affixing a seal or by making an impression upon the paper or upon some tenacious substance, such as wax, attached to the instrument. Although at common law an impression was necessary, the courts now treat various signs or marks to be the equivalent of a seal.[9] To illustrate, most states hold that there is a seal if a person's signature or a corporation's name is followed by a scroll or scrawl, the word "seal," or the letters "L.S." [10]

Two or more persons may use the same seal. When one signer affixes a seal, the subsequent signers, if they deliver the instrument, are presumed to have adopted the seal "unless extrinsic circumstances show a contrary intention." [11]

---

[8] R § 7. The Restatement, Contracts, includes commercial paper (Part IV of this text) in the class of formal contracts.

[9] R § 96. A dot or period following a signature is not sufficient as a seal. Vaccaro v Andresen, (Dist Col App) 201 NE2d 26.

[10] Stern v Lieberman, 307 Mass 77, 29 NE2d 839.

[11] R §§ 98, 99.

A contract under seal is binding at common law solely because of its formality. In some states this has been changed by statute. The Uniform Commercial Code abolishes the law of seals for the sale of goods.[12] In some states the law of seals has been abolished generally without regard to the nature of the transaction involved.[13]

(2) Contracts of Record. One form of *contract of record* arises when one acknowledges before a proper court that he is obligated to pay a certain sum unless a specified thing is done or not done. For example, a party who has been arrested may be released on his promise to appear in court and may bind himself to pay a certain sum in the event that he fails to do so.[14] An obligation of this kind is known as a *recognizance.*

(3) Simple Contracts. All contracts other than contracts of record and contracts under seal are called *simple contracts* or informal contracts, without regard to whether they are oral or written.[15]

§ 9:11. Express and Implied Contracts. Simple contracts may be classified in terms of the way in which they are created, as express contracts and implied contracts.

(1) Express Contracts. An *express contract* is one in which the parties have made oral or written declarations of their intentions and of the terms of the transaction.

(2) Implied Contracts. An *implied contract* (or, as sometimes stated, a contract implied in fact) is one in which the evidence of the agreement is not shown by words, written or spoken, but by the acts and conduct of the parties.[16] Such a contract arises, for example, when one person, without being requested to do so, renders services under circumstances indicating that he expects to be paid for them, and the other person, knowing such circumstances, accepts the benefit of those services.[17] An implied contract cannot arise when there is an existing express contract on the same subject.[18] Likewise, no contract is implied when the relationship of the parties is such that by a reasonable interpretation the performance of services or the supplying of goods was intended as a gift.

---

[12] UCC § 2-203. See the UCC Appendix.

[13] Lake Shore Management Co. v Blum, 92 Ill App 2d 47, 235 NE2d 366.

[14] Modern Finance Co. v Martin, 311 Mass 509, 42 NE2d 533.

[15] R § 11.

[16] Capital Warehouse Co. v McGill-Warner-Farnham Co., 276 Minn 108, 148 NW2d 31. Contracts of this nature may be more accurately described as contracts "expressed" by conduct, as distinguished from contracts expressed in words. It is more common, however, to refer to these contracts as implied.

[17] Martin's Estate, 261 Iowa 630, 155 NW2d 401; Smith v Sypret's Estate, (Mo) 421 SW2d 9.

[18] Moser v Milner Hotels, 6 NJ 278, 78 A2d 393.

In terms of effect, there is no difference between an implied contract and an express contract. The difference relates solely to the manner of proving the contract.[19] (See p. 168, First National Bank v Glenn.) Consequently, when a member of a family group renders ordinary household services to another member of the group, it is presumed that the services are rendered gratuitously unless the claimant can prove that there was an express contract to pay for them or that the services were extraordinary in character. In the absence of such proof, no contract is implied and no recovery is allowed for such services.[20]

When a plumber, in repairing a sewer pipe for a homeowner, found other pipes in need of replacement and so informed the homeowner and proceeded to replace such pipes with her knowledge and without any objection, a contract was implied from the conduct of the parties.[21]

The fact that an agreement can be implied does not necessarily mean that it can be enforced. If the agreement must be in writing to be binding,[22] such as a promise to pay the debt of another, the "implied contract" cannot be enforced in the absence of a sufficient writing.[23] Although a contract is implied in fact, it is necessary that the facts evidence an agreement of the parties.[24]

While conduct is often significant in showing the existence or the meaning of a contract, it is unwise to neglect making an express contract in the hope that a court will find that conduct has given rise to a contract. The reason is that the court might not regard prior conduct as giving rise to a contract obligation. (See p. 169, Hix v Tuloso-Midway Independent School District.)

§ 9:12. Valid and Voidable Contracts and Void Agreements. Another classification of contracts is in terms of their enforceability or validity.

(1) Valid Contracts. A *valid contract* is an agreement that is binding and enforceable. It has all of the essential requirements stated in § 9:16.

(2) Voidable Contracts. A *voidable contract* is an agreement that is otherwise binding and enforceable but, because of the circumstances surrounding its execution or the capacity of one of the parties, it may be rejected at the option of one of the parties.[25] For example, one who has been forced to sign an agreement against his will may in some instances avoid liability on the contract.[26]

---

[19] Plumbing Shop v Pitts, 67 Wash 2d 514, 408 P2d 382.
[20] Stewart v Brandenberg, (Ky) 383 SW2d 122.
[21] Richardson v J. C. Flood Co., (Dist Col App) 190 A2d 259.
[22] See § 15:2.
[23] First Pasadena State Bank v Marquette, (Tex Civ App) 425 SW2d 450.
[24] Armour Rentals, Inc. v General State Authority, 4 Pa Com Ct 517, 287 A2d 862.
[25] R § 13.
[26] See § 13:10.

(3) Void Agreements. A *void agreement* is without legal effect. Thus, an agreement that contemplates the performance of an act prohibited by law is usually incapable of enforcement; hence it is void.[27] Likewise, it cannot be made binding by later approval or ratification.[28]

§ 9:13. Executed and Executory Contracts. Contracts may be classified in terms of the extent to which they have been performed as executed contracts and executory contracts.

(1) Executed Contracts. An *executed contract* is one that has been completely performed. In other words, an executed contract is one under which nothing remains to be done by either party. A contract may be executed at once, as in the case of a cash sale; or it may be executed or performed in the future.

(2) Executory Contracts. In an *executory contract* something remains to be done. For example, if a utility company agrees to furnish electricity to another party for a specified period of time at a stipulated price, the contract is executory. If the entire price is paid in advance, the contract is still deemed executory; although, strictly speaking, it is executed on one side and executory on the other.

Whether a contract is executory determines in some cases whether it can be set aside by a minor or a trustee in bankruptcy of a party. That is, if it is executed, it cannot be set aside; if it is executory, it can.[29]

§ 9:14. Bilateral and Unilateral Contracts. In making an offer the offeror is in effect extending a promise to do something, such as to pay a sum of money, if the offeree will do what the offeror requests. If the offeror extends a promise and asks for a promise in return and if the offeree accepts the offer by making the promise, the contract is called a *bilateral contract* because one promise is given in exchange for another. Thus, each party is bound by the obligation to perform his promise, and there is said to be a mutuality of obligations.

In contrast, the offeror may agree to obligate himself only when something is done by the offeree. Since only one party is obligated to perform after the contract has been made, this kind of contract is called a *unilateral contract*. This is illustrated by the case of the reward for the return of lost property because the offeror does not care for a mere promise by members of the public that they will try to return the lost property. The offeror wants the property, and he promises to pay anyone who returns the property.

---

[27] See § 15:1. Although the distinction between a void agreement and a voidable contract is clear in principle, there is frequently confusion because some courts regard a given transaction as void while others regard it as merely voidable.

[28] Seafarer's Welfare Plan v George E. Light Boat Storage, Inc., (Tex Civ App) 402 SW2d 231.

[29] Wagstaff v Peters, 203 Kan 108, 453 P2d 120.

When the property is returned, his offer is accepted, a contract arises, and the offeror is bound by his agreement. The offeree has nothing more to do because he returned the property called for by the offer. No mutuality of obligations exists in a unilateral contract since the offeree has performed all that is required of him.

§ **9:15. Quasi Contracts.** Under certain circumstances the law imposes an obligation to pay for a benefit received as though a contract had actually been made. This will be done in a limited number of situations in order to attain an equitable or just result.[30] (See p. 170, Continental Forest Products, Inc. v Chandler Supply Co.) For example, when a homeowner permits repairs to be made on his home with the knowledge that they are being made by a stranger who would expect to be paid for such repairs, there is a quasi-contractual duty to pay for the reasonable value of the improvements in order to avoid the homeowner's unjust enrichment at the expense of the repairman.[31] In order to distinguish this type of obligation from a true contract which is based upon the agreement of the parties, the obligation is called a *quasi contract.*

While the objective of the quasi contract is to do justice, one must not jump to the conclusion that a quasi contract will arise every time there is an injustice. The mere fact that someone has benefited someone else and has not been paid will not necessarily give rise to a quasi contract. (See p. 172, Callano v Oakwood Park Homes Corp.) Likewise, no quasicontractual obligation arises when the plaintiff merely confers upon the defendant a benefit to which the defendant was already entitled.

(1) Unexpected Cost. The fact that performance of the contract proves more difficult or more expensive than had been expected does not entitle a party to extra compensation when there was no misrepresentation as to the conditions that would be encountered or the events that would occur and particularly when the party complaining is experienced with the particular type of contract and the problems which are likely to be encountered.[32] That is, the contractor is not entitled to a quasicontractual recovery for the extra expense on the theory that he had conferred a greater benefit than had been contemplated.

§ **9:16. Essential Elements of a Contract.** The requirements of a contract are: (1) an agreement, (2) between competent parties, (3) based upon the genuine assent of the parties, (4) supported by consideration, (5) made for a lawful objective, and (6) in the form required by law, if any. These elements will be considered in the chapters that follow.

---

[30] Dorsey v Delaware, (Del) 301 A2d 516.

[31] Pascall's v Dozier, 219 Tenn 45, 407 SW2d 150.

[32] Knight Bros. Inc. v Nebraska, 189 Neb 64, 199 NW2d 720.

CASES FOR CHAPTER 9

Pappas v Hauser *

(Iowa) 197 NW2d 607 (1972)

A movement was organized to build a Charles City College. Hauser and others signed pledges to contribute to the college. The college failed financially and Pappas was appointed receiver to collect and liquidate the assets of the college corporation. He sued Hauser for the amount due on his pledge.

UHLENHIPP, J. . . . The original pledge form stated, "It is my intention to contribute the sum of $—— to the College Founder's Fund." The form also recited, "This is a statement of intention and expectation and shall not constitute a legal obligation and shall not be legally binding in any way." . . .

. . . The college promoters discovered that they could not obtain credit on the original pledge form. After consideration, they redrafted the form by dropping the statement that the pledge was not a legal obligation and by making the form read "I/we intend to subscribe to the College Founder's Fund the sum of —— Dollars." . . .

. . . Bruno approached . . . Hauser for a pledge. . . . The redrafted pledge form was then in use. Before Hauser signed the pledge form, he and Bruno had a discussion about its meaning. [It was agreed that when Hauser asked]: "What if I should die, have a financial reversal or the College should fail?" Mr. Bruno said, "this is only an intent and not binding and if anything like this should happen you just forget it." . . .

Hauser did not pay his pledge and the receiver commenced the present action against him to have the pledge declared obligatory. . . .

. . . A subscription by which a person for a consideration *binds himself to pay* is a contract. . . . The first issue is whether Hauser "bound himself to pay." . . .

[It was agreed that when Hauser] asked what would happen if he died, had a financial reversal, or the college failed, Bruno answered that the pledge was only a letter of intent and not binding and if anything like that happened "just forget it." This . . . indicates that the pledge was not intended to be obligatory.

The receiver is correct that Hauser also stated at trial at the time he signed the pledge he intended to pay. We have no doubt Hauser did intend to pay; the pledge says so. But that conclusion does not answer the question before us. The question is, was that intention to pay *to be obligatory*?

This is not one of those cases in which a writing is intended as a nullity or a sham. The problem here relates to the *meaning* of a writing which was intended to be effective. We have no doubt the participants intended the pledge to be effective. But effective as what—as a legal obligation or as a nonobligatory declaration of what Hauser planned to do? . . . We think the pledge was intended not legally obligatory. . . .

Three possible pledge forms may be considered. The first one is the original pledge. That form was clear and certain that a legal obligation was not intended; the form so stated. The second possible form is on the other extreme. When the college promoters discovered they could not obtain credit on the original pledge form, they could have drafted a form which was clear and certain that a legal obligation was in fact intended: "I hereby subscribe" or "I promise to pay" or an expression of like import. But the promoters did not adopt such a form. Instead, they took a middle course and drafted a third possible form: "I/we intend to subscribe" and "I intend to pay [] Monthly," etc. What does "intend" mean? . . .

. . . "Care should be taken not to attach promissory and contractual effect to what was at the time merely an expression of intention concerning future action"; . . . "The expression of an *intention* to do a thing, is not a *promise* to do it." . . . "A declaration of intention to act in a certain way, which does not show that

* The structure or anatomy of a judicial opinion is considered in § 2:8. See also § 2:9. Checklist for Case Study.

the party who makes such declaration promises to act in such way, or intends to incur a legal liability obliging him to act in such way, is not an offer which can be accepted so as to make a contract." . . .

We conclude that the pledge is not obligatory . . . [and] deny liability.

[Judgment reversed.]

Adamick v Ferguson-Florissant School District

(Mo App) 483 SW2d 629 (1972)

The School District mailed a teaching contract to Adamick. In the same envelope there was a copy of the school calendar. Adamick and other teachers later brought an action against the school to prevent it from holding classes on three specified dates not listed on the calendar. The District defended on the ground that the calendar could be changed by the District.

CLEMENS, J. . . . The critical issue is whether the calendar is part of the teachers' contract and thus not subject to change without the teachers' consent.

For financial reasons school did not start as scheduled and the district issued a revised calendar by which there were several changes in days of school attendance. . . .

. . . The teachers contend the original school calendar is an integral part of their contract which the district could not change unilaterally. Conversely, the district contends the contract itself is the complete agreement, that the original calendar was merely the announcement of the district's school attendance plan, and changing it by the revised calendar was but a matter of discretionary management.

The general law of contracts applies in the construction of teachers' contracts. . . . Under certain circumstances several documents may be read as a single contract. However, each case the teachers cite involved an actual reference on the face of the contract to a set of rules or an explanatory document which is thereby made a part of the contract. There is no such reference here. Therefore, the cases cited by the teachers are not persuasive.

The intention of the parties must govern the interpretation and construction of a contract. . . . [A contract] "should be interpreted and read in the light of the circumstances of the parties at the time." . . . The contract was mailed at a time when all parties knew there was a substantial possibility the district's voters would not pass a new tax rate and some sort of schedule disruption was likely; the letter of transmittal mentioned the financial crisis. It cannot reasonably be presumed that the school board—well aware of its precarious financial situation—intended to lock itself into a rigid attendance schedule fixed by contract.

Moreover, the contract itself states that the teacher is hired to teach "such number of days as the board of education establishes." If the parties intended to fix the work schedule by contract, this clause is meaningless; the quoted language contemplates unilateral action on the part of the board. We cannot ignore this express language and say the parties intended it to be of no effect.

. . . The calendar did not become a part of the contract. . . .

[Relief denied.]

First National Bank v Glenn

132 Ill App 2d 322, 270 NE2d 493 (1973)

Glenn owned and operated the Seminole Bus Company. The First National Bank held a chattel mortgage on the buses. Stoberl ran a gas and service station. Glenn and Stoberl made an agreement that if Glenn would buy all his gas and have all his repairs made at Stoberl's, he could park his buses at Stoberl's without charge. Because of illness, Glenn stopped running the bus business. He stored the buses at Stoberl's station. Some time thereafter the bank sued Stoberl for possession of the buses. He defended on the ground that he was holding the buses for storage charges under agreement for storage with the bank.

DEMPSEY, J. . . . Leonard Brody, a vice-president of the bank and the bank's sole witness at the trial, testified that the bank did not receive the October and November mortgage installments due from Glenn, and early in December learned that he was ill and that the vehicles were stored at Stoberl's service station. Brody and another official of the bank visited the station. Stoberl informed them that he needed the space occupied by the buses and wished to have them removed. On December 23, 1966, the bank wrote a letter asking him to prepare the vehicles for winter and saying that it would like to work out an arrangement "wherein we will guarantee payment of reasonable storage charges from this point on." Stoberl winterized the buses and the bank paid him $200.00.

During the succeeding months, the parties conducted discussions concerning a possible agreement for the storage charges. Stoberl demanded $7.50 a day for each bus but later reduced this to $4.50 a day. On March 9, 1967, he served a five-day notice for unpaid rent and followed this up with an eviction action in the Circuit Court. However, he dismissed this action and on March 21, 1967, his attorney received a letter from the bank saying that it would be willing to pay $200.00 a month and would be willing to negotiate a settlement for past due rent. No definite agreement was reached. . . .

. . . Stoberl contends that the evidence was sufficient to establish that the dealings between him and the bank constituted a contract implied in law under which the bank was bound to pay reasonable storage charges for the buses parked on his premises.

An implied contract is an obligation created by law independent of an agreement of the parties. It arises out of the acts and conduct of the parties—out of circumstances from which the intent to contract can be inferred. . . .

Such a contract was found to exist in Shaw v. Blessman, 67 Ill. App. 2d 242, 213 N.E.2d 784 (1966). There, the plaintiff, without any express agreement, permitted the defendants to use her trailer for storage purposes. The defendants accepted the benefits of the trailer under such conditions that its use could not have been presumed to be gratuitous. The court determined that out of such acceptance and use there arose a promise implied in law that the defendants would make reasonable rental payments.

In the present case there was no express agreement between Stoberl and the bank, but the evidence discloses that the bank recognized that some compensation was due for storage. Although Brody testified that the bank felt no obligation to pay storage charges, and although a promise to settle is not necessarily a promise to pay . . . it must have been obvious to officials of the bank either from Stoberl's telephone call in October 1966 or when they called upon him in December, that he expected to be compensated monetarily for keeping the vehicles at his station. While there was no meeting of the minds thereafter as to the amount, the failure to agree on a specific sum cannot relieve the bank of the obligation to pay Stoberl for the use of his premises. The law, therefore, will imply a contract so that he may receive reasonable rental.

It may be argued that inasmuch as Glenn did not pay a specific amount for parking the buses, the bank should not be obliged to do so. However, Stoberl was entitled to rely upon the profits he derived from the continuous sale of gasoline, oil and repair work as rent. From the time the bank asserted authority over the buses, Stoberl received only $200.00—and this for preparing them against cold weather damage. This amount cannot be considered as payment in full for the privilege of using his property for several months.

. . . The case will be remanded so that the court may determine . . . the reasonable compensation due Stoberl for storage of the buses. . .

[Reversed and action remanded.]

Hix v Tuloso-Midway Independent School District

(Tex Civ App) 489 SW2d 706 (1973)

Hix was employed as a teacher by the Tuloso-Midway Independent School District. He started work in 1962 under a contract which was renewed each year for another year. In 1968 the contract was not renewed and he brought suit against the District on the theory that there was an obligation to renew his contract in the absence of any ground for discharge. Judgment was entered for the District and Hix appealed.

BISSETT, J. . . . Plaintiff . . . contends that the School District had in effect an express teacher contract renewal policy by virtue of the 1958 published set of Policies, which contained the following statement: "We also have a continuing contract in this school which means if satisfactory work is being done the contracts are automatically extended for one year." That set of Policies was revised in 1960. The Policies were again revised in 1963 and in 1965. The above quoted "continuing contract" provision contained in the 1958 set of Policies does not appear in any of the published Policies of 1960, 1963 or 1965. Plaintiff first became aware of the 1958 policy provision with respect to "continuing contracts" in the fall of 1962. He knew, however, that such tenure provision had been eliminated from the 1960, 1963, and 1965 revisions.

All of the contracts between plaintiff and the School District were in writing. None of them contained any provision for a continuing contract, renewal thereof, or tenure. There was no discussion at any time between plaintiff and the Board of Trustees (or with the Superintendent) of official policies regarding continuing contracts. No official of the School District ever represented to plaintiff that a policy providing for tenure existed. Plaintiff did not, after discovering the continuing contract provision in the 1958 set of Policies, discuss the same with anybody representing the School District. No member of the Board of Trustees, the Superintendent, or any other representative of the School District, ever led plaintiff to believe that any official tenure policy was in effect. Plaintiff was never induced by anyone to sign a teaching contract in the belief that a "continuing contract" policy existed in his favor.

The attorney for the School District, in a letter, dated May 2, 1968, addressed to the State Commissioner of Education, stated: "The policy then and now is to reward satisfactory work by extending their (teachers') contracts, but this has been done by action of the Board each March." Plaintiff says that this statement is proof of a *de facto* tenure policy that clearly implies promise of continued employment. We do not agree. The published school board Policies in effect at all times pertinent to this appeal never expressed anything indicating that it would renew any teacher contract when it expired; furthermore, such policies expressly limited the term of teachers' contracts to two years. The mere fact that a teacher has been rehired each year for a period of years does not constitute any evidence that the School District had impliedly contracted with the teacher to renew the contract every year. Successive renewals of a teacher's contract with admissions by school representatives that such renewals were the reward for satisfactory work does not constitute evidence of *de facto* tenure policy of the school district, or of any implied agreement on the part of the school district that a teacher has a contractual right of renewal so long as the work performed is satisfactory.

. . . No evidence is presented that plaintiff and the Board of Trustees impliedly agreed or had a mutually explicit understanding that plaintiff's last contract would be renewed upon expiration thereof. . . .

[Judgment affirmed.]

Continental Forest Products, Inc. v Chandler Supply Co.

95 Idaho 739, 518 P2d 1201 (1974)

Chandler Supply Company ordered two carloads of lumber from North America Millwork. Continental Forest Products acknowledged the Chandler orders which apparently had been taken to that company when Barker of North America left and went to work for Continental Forest. Chandler assumed that Continental was filling its orders on behalf of North America. He kept the lumber but informed Continental that he had ordered it from North America. North America owed Chandler approximately $6,000 which Chandler expected to set off against the purchase price of its new order. Chandler offered to pay North America the purchase price of the lumber less the $6,000. North America refused to accept payment because the money for the lumber was owed to Continental. Continental, however, demanded full payment without any deduction for the $6,000 owed by North America. Continental sued Chandler and obtained a judgment against

Chandler for the full purchase price of the lumber without any deduction for the $6,000 debt due by North America. Chandler appealed.

BAKES, J. . . . This was Chandler's first order for plywood from North America Millwork, although it had transacted a considerable volume of other lumber business with North America Millwork between December, 1968, and July, 1969. . . .

. . . It is not entirely clear how Continental received Chandler's orders sent to North America. Apparently Ed Barker left his employment with North America and commenced brokering for Continental and gave the orders to Continental. . . .

. . . The trial . . . court discussed the relationship between Continental and Chandler and found that "the very least we have was an implied agreement or quasi contract."

Basically the courts have recognized three types of contractual arrangements. . . . First is the express contract wherein the parties expressly agree regarding a transaction. . . . Secondly, there is the implied in fact contract wherein there is no express agreement but the conduct of the parties implies an agreement from which an obligation in contract exists. . . . The third category is called an implied in law contract, or quasi contract. However, a contract implied in law is not a contract at all, but an obligation imposed by law for the purpose of bringing about justice and equity without reference to the intent or the agreement of the parties and, in some cases, in spite of an agreement between the parties. . . . It is a noncontractual obligation that is to be treated procedurally *as if* it were a contract, and is often referred to as quasi contract, unjust enrichment, implied in law contract or restitution. . . . "The promise is purely fictitious and unintentional, originally implied to circumvent rigid common-law pleading. It was invoked . . . to create one 'for the purpose of bringing about justice without reference to the intention of the parties.' . . ." . . .

In this case it is clear that there is neither an express nor an implied in fact contract since there was [no intention] by Chandler . . . to enter into a contract with Continental. . . . However, we agree with the trial court that under the peculiar circumstances of this case, the third type of contract, implied in law or quasi contract, exists obligating Chandler to pay for the materials which he received. However, the problem which arises is determining the amount of recovery to which Continental is entitled.

As the essence of a contract implied in law lies in the fact that the defendant has received a benefit which it would be inequitable for him to retain, it necessarily follows that the measure of recovery in a quasi-contractual action is not the actual amount of the enrichment, but the amount of the enrichment which, as between the two parties it would be unjust for one party to retain. . . . In the instant case we feel that the enrichment which Chandler "unjustly received" was the value of the plywood shipped less the trade set off which Chandler had against North America Millwork and which he would have been entitled to take had the transaction been completed the way Chandler had intended and attempted to complete it. Chandler had a right to deal exclusively with North America and use his trade set off as part of the purchase price. Chandler should not be deprived of this set off in view of the way that Continental became involved in this transaction. . . .

. . . If any party was responsible for the situation present in this case, it was Continental. Although it is not entirely clear from the record, it would appear that Barker breached the fiduciary duty which he owed to his employer North America Millwork by taking the Chandler purchase orders to Continental. Continental then, wittingly or unwittingly, took advantage of that breach of a fiduciary relationship and filled the orders, apparently without inquiry concerning the status of North America Millwork, the existence of a trade debt, the situation behind Barker's taking the purchase orders to Continental, or notifying Chandler that it was attempting to take over the North America transactions. Under these circumstances we feel that it would not be unjust to require Chandler to pay only that amount which he would have had to pay to North America had the transaction gone the way Chandler had intended and attempted to have it go.

Judgment should be entered for Continental against Chandler in the amount of the principal claim less the amount of the North America Millwork trade debt which Chandler had. . . .

[Judgment reversed and remanded.]

Callano v Oakwood Park Homes Corp.

91 NJ Super 105, 219 A2d 332 (1966)

Pendergast made a contract to buy a new home from the Oakwood Park Homes Corp. and then made a contract with Callano to plant shrubbery on the lot. Callano planted the shrubbery. Shortly thereafter Pendergast died. Oakwood canceled Pendergast's contract for the purchase of the home. Callano then sued Oakwood for the amount due for the shrubbery. From a judgment in favor of Callano, Oakwood appealed.

COLLESTER, J. . . . The single issue is whether Oakwood is obligated to pay plaintiffs for the reasonable value of the shrubbery on the theory of quasi-contractual liability. Plaintiffs contend that defendant was unjustly enriched when the Pendergast contract to purchase the property was canceled and that an agreement to pay for the shrubbery is implied in law. . . .

. . . Quasi or constructive contracts, are a class of obligations which are imposed or created by law without regard to the assent of the party bound, on the ground that they are dictated by reason and justice. They rest solely on a legal fiction and are not contract obligations at all in the true sense, for there is no agreement; but they are clothed with the semblance of contract for the purpose of the remedy. . . .

In cases based on quasi-contract liability, the intention of the parties is entirely disregarded, while in cases of express contracts and contracts implied in fact the intention is of the essence of the transaction. The duty which thus forms the foundation of a quasi-contractual obligation is frequently based on the doctrine of unjust enrichment. It rests on the equitable principle that a person shall not be allowed to enrich himself unjustly at the expense of another. . . .

The key words are *enrich* and *unjustly*. To recover on the theory of quasi-contract, the plaintiffs must prove that defendant was enriched, *viz.*, received a benefit, and that retention of the benefit without payment therefor would be unjust.

It is conceded by the parties that the value of the property, following the termination of the Pendergast contract, was enhanced by the reasonable value of the shrubbery at the stipulated sum of $475. However, we are not persuaded that the retention of such benefit by defendant before it sold the property to [a new buyer] was inequitable or unjust. . . .

In the instant case the plaintiffs entered into an express contract with Pendergast and looked to him for payment. They had no dealings with defendant, and did not expect remuneration from it when they provided the shrubbery. No issue of mistake on the part of plaintiffs is involved. Under the existing circumstances we believe it would be inequitable to hold defendant liable. Plaintiff's remedy is against Pendergast's estate, since they contracted with an expected payment to be made by Pendergast when the benefit was conferred. . . .

Recovery on the theory of quasi-contract was developed under the law to provide a remedy where none existed. Here, a remedy exists. Plaintiffs may bring their action against Pendergast's estate. We hold that under the facts of this case defendant was not unjustly enriched and is not liable for the value of the shrubbery.

[Judgment reversed.]

QUESTIONS AND CASE PROBLEMS

1. State the specific objective(s) of the law (from the list in Chapter 2, pages 10-15) illustrated by the following quotation: "A person shall not be allowed to enrich himself unjustly at the expense of another."

Note: As you study the various rules of law in this chapter and the chapters that follow, consider each rule in relationship to its social, economic, and moral background. Try to determine the particular objective(s) of each important rule. To the extent that you are able to analyze law as the product of man striving for justice in society, you will have a greater insight into the law itself, the world in which you live, the field of business, and the mind of man.

2. Lombard insured his car under a theft policy that required the insurer to repair damages to the car when stolen or to pay the money equivalent of the damages. Lombard's car was stolen, and he and the insurance adjuster agreed as to what repairs should be made. The adjuster then took the car to General Auto Service, Inc. to make the repairs. When the insurance company was unable to pay for the repairs, General Auto Service sued Lombard because he had received the benefit of the contract. Was he liable for the repair bill? [General Auto Service, Inc. v Lombard, (La) 151 So2d 536]

3. Tetrauld made a written agreement to sell his land to Bauer. Tetrauld died. Bauer claimed that after agreement for the sale of the land had been made, they had orally agreed that Tetrauld would give the land to Bauer for his past services instead of selling it to him. Monroe, who was administering the estate of Tetrauld, objected to changing the written contract. A Montana statute provided that a "contract in writing may be altered by a contract in writing or by an executed oral agreement, and not otherwise." Was the oral agreement barred by this statute? [Bauer v Monroe, 117 Mont 306, 158 P2d 485]

4. Mrs. Herbert, the owner of an orchard, and Cantor, to whom she had leased the orchard, desired to borrow money so that a crop could be grown by the tenant. Part of the money required by them was loaned by the Pinnacle Packing Co. and the Medford National Bank. The loan agreement stated that the lenders would "furnish" the money and that when the crops were sold, there would be deducted a sufficient amount "to repay the advances made by [the lenders] before any payments would be made to the borrowers." There was no express provision in the agreement that the borrowers would repay the money. No oral agreement to repay was made by either borrower. Pinnacle Packing Co. then sued Herbert to recover the amount of the money advanced. She defended on the ground that she had not expressly agreed to repay the money borrowed. Decide. [Pinnacle Packing Co. v Herbert, 157 Ore 96, 70 P2d 31]

5. McNulty signed a contract with the Medical Service of District of Columbia, Inc. The contract, which was on a printed form prepared by the corporation, concluded with the clause: "In witness whereof, the party of the first part has caused its corporate seal to be hereunto affixed and these presents to be signed by its duly authorized officers and the party of the second part has hereunto set his hand and seal the day and year first above written." The contract had been sent to McNulty, who signed and sealed it, and then returned it to the corporation. The latter signed but did not seal it, and then sent an executed copy of the contract to the plaintiff without referring to the lack of a seal. When McNulty sued on the contract, the corporation claimed that it was an unsealed contract because it had not been sealed by both parties. Was it correct? [McNulty v Medical Service of District of Columbia, (MC App Dist Col) 176 A2d 783]

6. Martha Parker reared Louis Twiford as a foster son from the time he was 6 or 7 years of age. He lived with her until he was 27 years of age when he married and moved into another house. During the next few years Martha was very ill, and Louis took care of her. She died; and Louis made a claim against Waterfield, her executor, for the reasonable value of the services he had rendered. Was he entitled to recover? [Twiford v Waterfield, 240 NC 582, 83 SE2d 548]
7. A state statute required the County Board of Commissioners to advertise their proceedings in a newspaper. The *Greensburg Times* published the notices for the commissioners. The commissioners later refused to pay the newspaper on the ground that they had not executed a written contract with the newspaper on behalf of the county. Decide. [Board of Commissioners v Greensburg Times, 215 Ind 471, 19 NE2d 459]
8. *A* rented a building from *B* under a long-term lease. *A* contracted with *C* for the installation of an air-conditioning unit in such a way that it could not be removed. *B* had no knowledge of the installation. When *A* did not pay for the work, *C* sued *B* on the ground that *C* had improved *B*'s property and that *B* would be unjustly enriched if not required to pay for the benefit he received. Was *C* entitled to recover the reasonable value of the installation from *B*? [See Kemp v Majestic Amusement Co., 427 Pa 429, 234 A2d 846]
9. William was a certified public accountant. He did all the accounting work for his wife, Frances. William and Frances were divorced but remained friendly. William continued to perform the accounting services as before and also for North Star Motors, a business operated by the brother of Frances. When Frances sued William on a promissory note, he counterclaimed for compensation for his accounting services rendered to his ex-wife and her brother on the theory that an implied contract arose to pay him for such services. Was he entitled to recover on the counterclaim? [Ryan v Ryan, — Del Super —, 298 A2d 343]
10. *A* sued *B*. *A* claimed that because of certain conduct *B* was under a quasi-contractual liability to pay *A* a sum of money spent by *A* in performing certain work. *B* claimed that he could not be liable because he had never made any agreement with *A* to do the work nor to pay him any sum of money. Was this a valid defense? [See Minnesota Avenue, Inc. v Automatic Packages, Inc., 211 Kan 461, 507 P2d 268]
11. *A* made a contract to construct a house for *B*. Subsequently, *B* sued *A* for breach of contract. *A* raised the defense that the contract was not binding because it was not sealed. Is this a valid defense? [See Cooper v G.E. Construction Co., 116 Ga App 690, 158 SE2d 305]
12. The State of North Dakota provided by statute for the distribution among the counties of the state of money paid to the state as motor vehicle registration fees. On the basis of wrong advice by the state's attorney general, the fund was distributed among the counties in an improper manner and nothing remained. Stark County, North Dakota, as a result did not receive the full amount to which it was entitled. Part of the money it should have received was paid to other counties. Stark County sued the State of North Dakota, claiming that the state had a quasi-contractual duty to pay the county the amount which it should have been paid. Decide. [Stark County v State of North Dakota, (ND) 160 NW2d 101]

10 The Agreement

THE OFFER

An *offer* expresses the willingness of the offeror to enter into a contractual agreement regarding a particular subject. It is a promise which is conditional upon an act, a forbearance, or a return promise that is given in exchange for the promise or its performance.

§ **10:1. Requirements of An Offer.** An offer must meet the tests of (1) contractual intention, (2) definiteness, and (3) communication to the offeree.

(1) Contractual Intention. To constitute an offer, the offeror must intend to create a legal obligation or it must appear that he intends to do so. When there is neither such intention nor the appearance of such intention, it makes no difference whether the offeree takes any action concerning the offer. The following are examples of a lack of contractual intention on the part of the offeror.

(a) SOCIAL INVITATIONS. Ordinary invitations to social affairs are not "offers" in the eyes of the law. The acceptance of a social invitation, such as an invitation to go to dinner, does not give rise to a legally binding agreement or contract.

(b) OFFERS MADE IN JEST OR EXCITEMENT. If an offer is made in obvious jest, the offeree cannot accept it and then sue the offeror for breach of the agreement. Here the offeree, as a reasonable person, should realize that no contract is intended and therefore no contract arises even though the offeror speaks words which, if seriously spoken, could be accepted and result in a contract. Likewise, an extravagant offer of a reward made in the heat of excitement cannot be acted upon as a valid offer.

It is not always obvious or apparent to the offeree when the offer is made in jest or under excitement. If it is reasonable under the circumstances for the offeree to believe that the offer was made seriously, a contract is formed by the offeree's acceptance. (See p. 192, Lucy v Zehmer.)

(c) INVITATIONS TO NEGOTIATE. The first statement made by one of two persons is not necessarily an offer. In many instances there may be preliminary discussion or an *invitation* by one party to the other *to negotiate* or talk business.

Ordinarily, when a seller sends out circulars or catalogs listing prices, he is not regarded as making an offer to sell at those prices but as merely indicating that he is willing to consider an offer made by a buyer on those terms. The reason for this rule is in part the practical consideration that since a seller does not have an unlimited supply of any commodity, he cannot possibly intend to make a contract with everyone who sees his circular. The same principle is applied to merchandise that is displayed with price tags in stores or store windows and to most advertisements. A "for sale" advertisement in a newspaper is merely an invitation to negotiate and is not an offer which can be accepted, even though the seller has only one of the particular item advertised.[1]

The circumstances may be such, however, that even a newspaper advertisement constitutes an offer. Thus, the seller made an offer when he advertised specific items that would be sold at a clearance sale at the prices listed and added the words "first come, first served." [2]

Quotations of prices, even when sent on request, are likewise not offers in the absence of previous dealings between the parties or the existence of a trade custom which would give the recipient of the quotation reason to believe that an offer was being made to him. Whether a price quotation is to be treated as an offer or merely an invitation to negotiate is a question of fact as to the intent of the party making such quotations.[3] Although the businessman is not bound by his quotations and price tags, he will as a matter of goodwill ordinarily make every effort to deliver the merchandise at those prices.[4]

In some instances, it is apparent that an invitation to negotiate and not an offer has been made. When construction work is done for the national government, for a state government, or for a political subdivision, statutes require that a printed statement of the work to be done be published and circulated. Contractors are invited to submit bids on the work, and the statute generally requires that the bid of the lowest responsible bidder be accepted. Such an invitation for bids is clearly an invitation to negotiate, both from its nature and from the fact that it does not specify the price to be paid for the work. The bid of each contractor is an offer, and there is no contract until the government accepts one of these bids. This procedure of advertising for bids is also commonly employed by private persons when a large construction project is involved. (See p. 193, Olson v Beacham.)

In some cases the fact that material terms are missing serves to indicate that the parties were merely negotiating and that an oral contract had not been made.[5] When a letter or printed promotional matter of a party leaves many significant details to be worked out later, the letter or printed

---

[1] O'Keefe v Lee Callan Imports, Inc., 128 Ill App 2d 410, 262 NE2d 758.

[2] Lefkowitz v Great Minneapolis Surplus Store, Inc., 251 Minn 188, 86 NW2d 689.

[3] Jaybe Construction Co. v Beco, Inc., 3 Conn Cir 406, 216 A2d 208.

[4] Meridian Star v Kay, 207 Miss 78, 41 So2d 746. Statutes prohibiting false or misleading advertising may also require adherence to advertised prices.

[5] Rabb v Public National Insurance Co., (CA6 Ky) 243 F2d 940.

matter is merely an invitation to negotiate and is not an offer which may be accepted and a contract thereby formed.[6]

(d) STATEMENT OF INTENTION. In some instances a person may make a statement of his intention but not intend to be bound by a contract. For example, when a lease does not expressly allow the tenant to terminate the lease because of a job transfer, the landlord might state that should the tenant be required to leave for that reason, the landlord would do his best to find a new tenant to take over the lease. This declaration of intention does not give rise to a binding contract, and the landlord cannot be held liable for a breach of contract should he fail to obtain a new tenant or should he not even attempt to do so.

(e) AGREEMENTS TO MAKE A CONTRACT AT A FUTURE DATE. No contract arises when the parties merely agree that at a future date they shall consider making a contract or shall make a contract on terms to be agreed upon at that time.[7] In such a case, neither party is under any obligation until the future contract is made. Thus, a promise to pay a bonus or compensation to be decided upon after three months is not binding.[8]

(f) SHAM TRANSACTIONS. Sometimes what appears to be a contract is entered into for the purpose of deceiving a third person or a government examiner. For example, when a bank does not hold sufficient assets to meet the deposit reserve ratio established by the Federal Reserve Bank, a friend of the bank may sign a promissory note payable to the bank so that the bank would appear to hold more assets than it actually does. Such a sham transaction cannot be enforced between the parties.[9] That is, the bank cannot enforce the note against the maker because the bank knew that it was never intended to be a binding transaction.

§ 10:2. Definite Offer. An offer, and the resulting contract, must be definite and certain.[10] If an offer is indefinite or vague or if an essential provision is lacking, no contract arises from an attempt to accept it.[11] The reason is that the courts cannot tell what the parties are to do. Thus, an offer to conduct a business for such time as should be profitable is too vague to be a valid offer. The "acceptance" of such an offer would not result in a contract that could be enforced. A promise to give an injured employee "suitable" employment that he was "able to do" is too vague to be a binding contract.[12]

---

[6] Edmunds v Houston Lighting & Power Co. (Tex Civ App) 472 SW2d 797.

[7] Bogert Construction Co. v Lakebrink, (Mo App) 404 SW2d 779; Walker v Keith, (Ky) 382 SW2d 198.

[8] Sandeman v Sayres, 51 Wash 2d 539, 314 P2d 428.

[9] United States v Aetna Cas. & Surety Co., (CA8 Neb) 480 F2d 1095.

[10] R § 32 Southwest Fabricating and Welding Co. v Jones, (La App) 190 So2d 529.

[11] Williamson v Miller, 231 NC 722, 58 SE2d 743; Wm. Muirhead Construction Co. v Housing Authority of Durham, 1 NC App 181, 160 SE2d 542.

[12] Bonnevier v Dairy Cooperative Association, 227 Ore 123, 361 P2d 262.

The offer and contract may be made definite by reference to another writing, as when the parties agreed that the written lease which was to be executed by them should be the standard form of lease with which both were familiar.

If part of a divisible contract provides for the execution of a future agreement pertaining to certain matters and that part by itself is too vague to be binding, such a provision does not alter the enforceability of other parts of the same contract that are otherwise binding.[13] A *divisible contract* consists of two or more parts and calls for corresponding performances of each part by the parties.

Although an offer must be definite and certain, not all of its terms need be expressed. Some of the terms may be implied. For example, an offer "to pay fifty dollars for a watch" does not state the terms of payment. A court would consider that cash payment was to be made upon delivery of the watch. The offer and contract may also be made definite by reference to another writing,[14] or by referring to the prior dealings of the parties and to trade practices.

§ **10:3. Exceptions to Definiteness.** As exceptions to the requirement of definiteness, the law has come to recognize certain situations where the practical necessity of doing business makes it desirable to have a "contract," yet the situation is such that it is either impossible or undesirable to adopt definite terms in advance. Thus, the law recognizes binding contracts in the following situations, although at the time that the contract is made there is some element which is not definite:

(1) Cost-Plus Contracts. Cost-plus contracts are valid as against the contention that the amount to be paid is not definite when the contract is made. Such contracts protect the contractor by enabling him to enter into a contract without setting up extraordinary reserves against cost contingencies that may arise.[15]

(2) Requirements and Output Contracts. Contracts by which a supplier agrees in advance to sell its entire future output to a particular buyer or by which a buyer agrees to buy all of its needs or requirements from a particular supplier are valid, as discussed in § 23:4, even though at the time of contracting the amount of goods to be covered by the contract is not known.

A contract by which the buyer agrees to purchase its fuel oil requirements for its electricity generating system from the seller is binding, even though the buyer was free to purchase natural gas which could be used as well as oil in the buyer's system; as against the contention that the contract was not

---

[13] Fincher v Belk-Sawyer, (Fla App) 127 So2d 130.
[14] Emerman v Baldwin, 186 Pa Super 561, 142 A2d 440.
[15] US Steel Corp. v United States, (Ct Claims) 367 F2d 399.

binding and was illusory because there was no obligation on the part of the buyer to purchase any quantity from the seller.[16]

(3) Services as Needed. An enterprise may desire to be assured that the services of a given person, customarily a professional man or a specialist, will be available when needed. It is thus becoming valid to make a contract with him to supply such services as in his opinion will be required, although this would appear to be subject to the two evils of not being definite and of giving such person the choice of doing nothing if he so chooses.[17] (See p. 194, Griswold v Heat Incorporated.)

(4) Indefinite Duration Contracts. Contracts with no specific time limit are valid. The law meets the objection that there is a lack of definiteness by interpreting the contract as being subject to termination at the election of either party. This type of contract is used most commonly in employment and in sales transactions.

(5) Open-Term Sales Contracts. Contracts for the sale of goods are valid even though the price or some other term remains open and must be determined at a future date. This is discussed further in § 23:5(3).

(6) Current Market Price. An agreement is not too indefinite to enforce because it does not state the exact price to be paid but specifies that the price shall be that prevailing on a recognized market or exchange. Thus, a provision in a lease is sufficiently definite to be binding when it specifies that if the lease were renewed, the rental should be that of similar properties at the time of renewal.[18]

(7) Standard Form Contracts. In some instances, what would appear to be too vague to be a binding agreement is given the effect of a contract because it is clear that the parties had a particular standard or printed form in mind so that the terms of that standard form fill out the agreement of the parties. Thus, an agreement to lease real estate is binding when the agreement of the parties specified that a particular standard form of lease was to be used.[19] Likewise, an agreement to insure property does not fail to be binding because the terms are not stated, because the law will regard the parties as having intended that the standard form of insurance contract used by the insurance company should govern.

(8) First Refusal Contract. The owner of property may agree to give to the other contracting party a first right to refuse to buy in the event

[16] City of Lakeland v Union Oil Co., (DC Fla) 352 F Supp 758.

[17] Under such contracts the duty to act in good faith supplies the protection found in most contracts in the "usual rules as to certainty and definiteness." McNussen v Graybeal, 141 Mont 571, 405 P2d 447.

[18] George Y. Worthington & Son Management Corp. v Levy, (Dist Col App) 204 A2d 334.

[19] Emerman v Baldwin, 186 Pa Super 561, 142 A2d 440.

that the owner offers the property for sale. A contract conferring such a *preemptive right* or right of first refusal is binding (as against the contention that it is not definite because it does not specify the terms of the subsequent sale), for the parties recognize that the offer made by a third person will supply those details.[20]

(9) Joint Venture Participation. When two or more persons or enterprises pool resources in order to obtain a government contract, agreements as to the manner of dividing the work or profits between them may be enforced even though they are dependent upon future negotiation.[21] In effect, the law is influenced by the practical consideration that from the nature of the activity it would be impossible or impractical to make the agreements between the parties more specific until the government contract was awarded.

§ 10:4. Communication of Offer to the Offeree. The offer must be communicated directly to the offeree [22] by the offeror. Until the offer is made known to the offeree, he does not know that there is something which he can accept. Sometimes, particularly in the case of unilateral contracts, the offeree performs the act called for by the offeror without knowing of the offer's existence. Thus, without knowing that a reward is offered for the arrest of a particular criminal, a person may arrest the criminal. If he learns thereafter that a reward had been offered for the arrest, he cannot recover the reward in most states.[23]

TERMINATION OF THE OFFER

An offer gives the offeree power to bind the offeror by contract. This power does not last forever, and the law specifies that under certain circumstances the power shall be terminated.

§ 10:5. Effect and Methods. Once the offer is terminated, the offeree cannot revive it. If he attempts to accept the offer after it has been terminated, his act is meaningless, unless the original offeror is willing to regard the "late acceptance" as a new offer which he then accepts.

Offers may be terminated in any one of the following ways: (1) revocation of the offer by the offeror, (2) lapse of time, (3) rejection of offer by offeree, (4) counteroffer by offeree, (5) death or disability of either party, and (6) subsequent illegality.

§ 10:6. Revocation of the Offer by the Offeror. Ordinarily the offeror can revoke his offer before it is accepted. If he does so, the offeree cannot create a contract by accepting the revoked offer.[24] Thus, the bidder at an auction

---

[20] Brownies Creek Collieries v Asher Coal Mining Co. (Ky App) 417 SW2d 249.

[21] Air Technology Corp. v General Electric Co., 347 Mass 613, 199 NE2d 538.

[22] Farrell v Neilson, 43 Wash 2d 647, 263 P2d 264.

[23] With respect to the offeror, it should not make any difference as a practical matter whether the services were rendered with or without knowledge of the existence of the offer. Only a small number of states have adopted this view, however.

[24] Merritt Land Corp. v Marcello, RI 291 A2d 263.

sale may withdraw (revoke) his bid (offer) before it is accepted. The auctioneer cannot thereafter accept that bid.

An ordinary offer may be revoked at any time before it is accepted, even though the offeror had expressly promised that the offer would be good for a stated period which had not yet expired, or even though he had expressly promised the offeree that he would not revoke the offer before a specified later date.

(1) What Constitutes a Revocation. No particular form of words is required to constitute a revocation. Any expression indicating that the offer is revoked or the communication of information inconsistent with a continuation of the offer is sufficient. A notice sent to the offeree that the property which is the subject of the offer has been sold to a third person is a revocation of the offer. An order for goods by a customer, which is an offer by him to purchase at certain prices, is revoked by a notice to the seller of the cancellation of the order, provided such notice is communicated before the order is accepted.

(2) Communication of Revocation. A revocation of an offer is ordinarily effective only when it is made known to the offeree. Until it is communicated to him, directly or indirectly, he has reason to believe that there is still an offer which he may accept; and he may rely on this belief.

Except in a few states, a letter or telegram revoking an offer made to a particular offeree is not effective until received by the offeree.[25] It is not a revocation at the time it is written by the offeror nor even when it is mailed or dispatched. A written revocation is effective, however, when it is delivered to the offeree's agent,[26] or to the offeree's residence or place of business, under such circumstances that the offeree would be reasonably expected to be aware of its receipt.

It is ordinarily held that there is a sufficient "communication" of the revocation when the offeree learns indirectly of the offeror's intent to revoke. This is particularly true when the seller-offeror, after making a written offer to sell land to the offeree, sells the land to a third person, and the offeree, who indirectly learns of such sale, necessarily realizes that the seller cannot perform his offer and therefore must be deemed to have revoked it.

If the offeree accepts an offer before it is effectively revoked, a valid contract is created. Thus there may be a contract when the offeree mails or telegraphs his acceptance without knowing that a letter of revocation has been mailed to him.

When an offer is made to the public it may usually be revoked in the same manner in which it was made. For example, an offer of a reward that is made to the general public by an advertisement in a newspaper may be revoked in the same manner. A member of the public cannot recover the amount of the reward by thereafter performing the act for which the reward

[25] L. & E. Wertheimer v Wehle-Hartford Co., 126 Conn 30, 9 A2d 279.
[26] Hogan v Aluminum Lock Shingle Corp., 214 Ore 218, 329 P2d 271.

was originally offered. This exception is made to the rule requiring communication of revocation because it would be impossible for the offeror to communicate the fact that he revokes his offer to every member of the general public who knows of his offer. The public revocation of the public offer is effective even though it is not seen by the person attempting to accept the original offer.

(3) Option Contracts. An *option contract* is a binding promise to keep an offer open for a stated period of time or until a specified date.[27] The offeror cannot revoke his offer if he has received consideration, that is, has been paid, for his promise to keep the offer open. If the owner of a house gives a prospective purchaser a 60-day written option to purchase the property at $25,000 and the customer pays the owner a sum of money, such as $500, the owner cannot revoke the offer within the 60-day period. Even though he expressly tells the purchaser within that time that the option contract is revoked, the purchaser may exercise the option; that is, he may accept the offer.

Under an option contract there is no obligation on the offeree to exercise the option.[28] If the option is exercised, the money paid to obtain the option is ordinarily, but not necessarily, applied as a down payment. If the option is not exercised, the offeror keeps the money paid him.

An option exists only when the option holder has the right to determine whether he shall require the performance called for by the option. If the agreement states that the "option" may be exercised only with the consent of the other party, it is not an option even though so called by the agreement.[29]

If a promise is described by the parties as an "option" but no consideration is given, the promise is subject to revocation as though it were not described as an "option." [30] In those jurisdictions in which the seal retains its common-law force, however, the option contract is binding on the offeror if it is set forth in a sealed writing, even though he does not receive any payment for his agreement.

Frequently an option contract is combined with a lease of real estate or personal property. Thus, a tenant may rent a building for a number of years by an agreement which gives him the option of purchasing the building for a specified amount at the end of the lease.

An option contract is to be distinguished from a preemptive right or first refusal contract under which a person is given the right to buy if the owner chooses to sell but the holder of such right cannot require the owner to sell, as would be the case in an option contract.[31]

---

[27] Davison v Rodes, (Mo App) 299 SW2d 591; Diggs v Siomporas, 248 Md 677, 237 A2d 725.

[28] State ex rel. v Howald, (Mo) 315 SW2d 786.

[29] Owen v Staib, (Ky) 307 SW2d 758.

[30] McPhail v L. S. Starrett Co., (CA1 Mass) 257 F2d 388.

[31] Bennett Veneer Factors, Inc. v Brewer, 73 Wash 2d 849, 441 P2d 128.

An *option*, when supported by consideration, is a contract to keep an offer open for a specified period of time.[32] Generally the consideration given for an option is the payment of a sum of money. In the case of employee stock options the consideration is the agreement of the employee to work for the employer corporation for a certain period of time.[33]

(4) Firm Offers. As another exception to the rule that an offer can be revoked at any time before acceptance, statutes in some states provide that an offeror cannot revoke an offer prior to its expiration when he has made a *firm offer,* that is, an offer in writing which states that it is to be irrevocable for a stated period.[34] This doctrine of firm offers applies to a merchant's written offer for the sale of goods, but with a maximum of three months on its duration.[35] (See p. 195, Coronis Associates v Gordon Construction Co.)

(5) Detrimental Reliance. There is growing authority that where the offeree relies on the offer, the offeror is obligated to keep the offer open for a reasonable time after such action has been taken by the offeree.

(6) Revocation of Offer of Unilateral Contract. Since the offer of a unilateral contract can be accepted only by performing the act called for, it theoretically follows that there is no acceptance until that act is fully performed by the offeree and that the offeror is free to revoke his offer even though the offeree has partly performed and has expended time and money. To avoid this hardship, a number of courts hold that after the offeree has done some substantial act toward acceptance, the offeror cannot revoke the offer until after the lapse of a reasonable time in which the offeree could have completed performance.[36]

§ 10:7. Counteroffer by Offeree. Ordinarily if *A* makes an offer, such as to sell a used automobile for $1,000, and *B* makes an offer to buy at $750, the original offer is terminated.[37] *B* is in effect saying, "I refuse your original offer, but in its place I make a different offer." Such an offer by the offeree is known as a *counteroffer*. In substance, the counteroffer presupposes a rejection of the original offer. In some instances, however, circumstances may show that both parties knew and intended that the offeree's response was not to be regarded as a definite rejection of the original offer but merely as further discussion or as a request for further information.

Counteroffers are not limited to offers that directly contradict the original offers. Any departure from, or addition to, the original offer is a counteroffer even though the original offer was silent as to the point changed

[32] Steel v Eagle, 207 Kan 146, 483 P2d 1063.
[33] Langer v Iowa Beef Packers, Inc., (CA8 Iowa) 420 F2d 365.
[34] Jarka Corp. v Hellenic Lines, (CA2 NY) 182 F2d 916.
[35] UCC § 2-205.
[36] Marchiondo v Schack, 78 NMex 440, 432 P2d 405.
[37] Goodwin v Eller, 127 Colo 529, 258 P2d 493.

or added by the counteroffer.[38] For example, when the offeree stated that he accepted and added that time was of the essence, the "acceptance" was a counteroffer when the original offer had been silent on that point.[39]

A counteroffer is by definition an offer and, if the original offeror (who is now the offeree) accepts it, a binding contract results.[40]

§ 10:8. Rejection of Offer by Offeree. If the offeree rejects the offer and communicates this rejection to the offeror, the offer is terminated, even though the period for which the offeror agreed to keep the offer open has not expired. It may be that the offeror is willing to renew the offer; but unless he does so, there is no offer for the offeree to accept.[41]

The fact that the offeree replies to the offeror without accepting the offer does not constitute a rejection when it is apparent that the failure to accept at that time was not intended as a rejection. For example, when the seller on receiving an order from a customer sent a reply that he would send a "formal confirmation" of the order as soon as the seller received confirmation from his source of supply that the goods were available, the reply of the seller was not a rejection of the offer made by the customer.

§ 10:9. Lapse of Time. When the offer states that it is open until a particular date, the offer terminates on that date if it has not been accepted.[42] This is particularly so where the offeror declares that the offer shall be void after the expiration of the specified time. Such limitations are strictly construed. For example, it has been held that the buyer's attempt to exercise an option one day late had no effect.[43]

If the offer does not specify a time, it will terminate after the lapse of a reasonable time. What constitutes a "reasonable" time is to be determined by what a reasonable man in the position of the offeree would believe was satisfactory to the offeror.[44] Conversely, it does not mean a time which is desired by the offeree.

A reasonable time depends upon the circumstances of each case; that is, upon the nature of the subject matter, the nature of the market in which it is sold, the time of the year, and other factors of supply and demand. If the commodity is perishable in nature or fluctuates greatly in value, the reasonable time will be much shorter than if the commodity or subject matter is a staple article. An offer to sell a harvested crop of tomatoes would expire within a very short time. When a seller purports to accept an offer after it has

---

[38] Wycoff Realty Co. v Grover, 198 Kan 139, 422 P2d 943.

[39] Cheston L. Eshelman Co. v Friedberg, 214 Md 123, 133 A2d 68.

[40] V-1 Oil Co. v Anchor Petroleum Co., 8 Utah 2d 349, 334 P2d 760.

[41] Nabob Oil Co. v Bay State Oil & Gas Co., 208 Okla 296, 255 P2d 513.

[42] Conrad Milwaukee Corp. v Wasilewski, 30 Wis 2d 481, 141 NE2d 240.

[43] Watts v Teagle, 124 Ga App 726, 185 SE2d 803. (Buyer was given an option on February 19. He attempted to exercise it on August 19. The option stated that it expired 180 days from its date when it would "become void and of no force and effect.")

[44] Central Investment Corp. v Container Advertising Co., 28 Colo App 184, 471 P2d 647.

lapsed by the expiration of time, the seller's acceptance is merely a counter-offer and does not create a contract unless that offer is accepted by the buyer.[45]

An option must be exercised within the time specified, whether or not it expressly declares that time is of the essence.[46] If no time is specified, it must be exercised within a reasonable time.[47]

An option can only be exercised by doing that which is specified in the option contract by the specified date. If the option contract requires payment or a tender of payment by a specified date, the option cannot be exercised by giving notice of intent to exercise before that date but actually not making tender of payment until three days after the date.[48]

§ 10:10. Death or Disability of Either Party. If either the offeror or the offeree dies or becomes insane before the offer is accepted, it is automatically terminated.

§ 10:11. Subsequent Illegality. If the performance of the contract becomes illegal after the offer is made, the offer is terminated. Thus, if an offer is made to sell alcoholic liquors but a law prohibiting such sales is enacted before the offer is accepted, the offer is terminated.

ACCEPTANCE OF THE OFFER

Once the offeror expresses or appears to express his willingness to enter into a contractual agreement with the offeree, the latter is in a position to accept the offer.

§ 10:12. Freedom of Offeree. Ordinarily the offeree may refuse to accept an offer. Certain partial exceptions exist.

(1) Public Utilities and Places of Public Accommodation. These are under a duty to serve any fit person. Consequently, when a fit person offers to register at a hotel, that is, offers to hire the room, the hotel has the obligation to accept his offer and enter into a contract for the renting of the room. This is a partial exception to the general rule because there is not an absolute duty to accept on the part of the hotel unless the person is fit and the hotel has space available.

(2) Antidiscrimination. When offers are solicited from members of the general public, an offer may generally not be rejected because of the race, nationality, religion, or color of the offeror. If the solicitor of the offer is willing to enter into a contract to rent, sell, or employ, as the case may be, antidiscrimination laws compel him to accept an offer from any otherwise fit person.

---

[45] 22 West Main Street, Inc. v Boquszewski, 34 App Div 2d 358, 311 NYS2d 565.
[46] Mathews v Kingsley, (Fla) 100 So2d 445.
[47] Baker v Brennan, 419 Pa 222, 213 A2d 362.
[48] Wilson v Ward, 155 Cal App 2d 390, 317 P2d 1018.

§ 10:13. Nature of the Acceptance. An *acceptance* is the assent of the offeree to the terms of the offer. No particular form of words or mode of expression is required, but there must be a clear expression that the offeree agrees to be bound by the terms of the offer. In the absence of a contrary requirement in the offer, an acceptance may be indicated by an informal "O.K.," by a mere affirmative nod of the head, or, in the case of an offer of a unilateral contract, by performing the act called for.

While the acceptance of an offer may be shown by conduct, it must be very clear that the offeree intended to accept the offer. To illustrate the strictness that is often applied, a contractor requested a bid from a subcontractor. The subcontractor made a bid. The contractor then made a bid to the owner on the basis of the subcontractor's bid and also told the subcontractor to proceed with preliminary planning. It was held that this conduct did not constitute an acceptance of the subcontractor's bid, with the result that the subcontractor could revoke the bid.[49]

(1) Unqualified Acceptance. The acceptance must be absolute and unconditional. It must accept just what is offered. If the offeree changes any term of the offer or adds any new term, he does not accept the offer because he does not agree with what was offered.

Where the offeree does not accept the offer exactly as made, the addition of any qualification to the acceptance constitutes a counteroffer and no contract arises unless such counteroffer is accepted by the offeror.[50]

An acceptance that states what is implied by law, however, does not add a new term within this rule. Thus, a provision in an acceptance that payment must be made in cash will usually not be deemed to introduce a new term since a cash payment is implied by law in the absence of a contrary provision. Likewise, an acceptance otherwise unconditional is not impaired by the fact that an additional matter is requested as a favor rather than being made a condition or term of the acceptance. Accordingly, there is an effective acceptance when the buyer, upon accepting, simply requests additional time in which to complete the transaction.

(a) CLERICAL MATTERS. A provision in an acceptance relating to routine or mechanical details of the execution of a written contract will usually not impair the effect of the acceptance.[51] An acceptance by a buyer of an offer to sell real estate is effective even though it contains a request that the title be conveyed to a third person.[52]

(b) APPROVAL OF THIRD PERSON. An acceptance is not effective as such when it adds a condition or requirement that the transaction be approved by a third person. Consequently, there was no acceptance when the offeree

[49] K. L. House Constr. Co., Inc. v Watson, 84 NMex 783, 508 P2d 592.
[50] C. Iber & Sons, Inc. v Grimmett, 108 Ill App 2d 443, 248 NE2d 131.
[51] Carver v Britt, 241 NC 538, 85 SE2d 888.
[52] Wallerius v Hare, 200 Kan 578, 438 P2d 65.

replied that he would have his attorney prepare a contract and expressed the "assurance that we will work out this matter with you subject to such points as our attorney brings up." [53]

§ 10:14. Who May Accept. An offer may be accepted only by the person to whom it is directed. If anyone else attempts to accept it, no agreement or contract with that person arises. (See p. 195, Grieve v Mullaly.)

If the offer is directed not to a specified individual but to a particular class, it may be accepted by anyone within that class. If the offer is made to the public at large, it may be accepted by any member of the public at large who has knowledge of the existence of the offer.

§ 10:15. Manner of Acceptance. The acceptance must conform to any conditions expressed in the offer concerning the manner of acceptance. If the offeror specifies that the acceptance must be written, an oral acceptance is ineffective. If the offeror calls for an acceptance by a specified date, a late acceptance has no effect. When an acceptance is required by return mail, it is usually held that the letter of acceptance must be mailed the same day that the offer was received by the offeree. If the offer specifies that the acceptance be made by the performance of an act by the offeree, he cannot accept by making a promise to do the act but must actually perform it.

A person accepting an offer must comply with any conditions as to the manner of acceptance specified by the offeror. Ordinarily, if the offeree departs from the terms of the offer, there is no acceptance.

As a qualification to this strict rule, when the offeror actually receives notice of the acceptance from the offeree, there is an acceptance even though the communication had not been made in the manner specified by the offeror.[54]

When an offer, a buyer's order on a printed form supplied by the seller, declares that it shall not be binding upon the seller until accepted by the seller and that such acceptance may only be made by signing by the seller or his representative, there is never any acceptance of the buyer's offer when the seller does not sign the order form; and the fact that the seller ordered goods from the manufacturer to fill the buyer's order does not constitute an acceptance.[55]

Unless the offer is clear that a specified manner of acceptance is exclusive, a manner of acceptance indicated by the offeror will be interpreted as merely a suggestion and the offeree's entering upon the performance of the contract will be an acceptance when the offeror has knowledge that the offeree is doing so.[56]

---

[53] Wagner v Rainier Mfg. Co., 230 Ore 531, 371 P2d 74.

[54] University Realty & Development Co. v Omid-Graf, Inc., 19 Ariz App 488, 508 P2d 747. (Lease provided for notice by registered mail of the tenant's exercise of option to renew the lease. It was held that there was a sufficient acceptance of the option offer when the tenant delivered the notice by hand instead of registered mail.)

[55] Antonucci v Stevens Dodge, Inc., (NY Civil Court) 340 NYS2d 979.

[56] Allied Steel and Conveyors, Inc. v Ford Motor Co., (CA6 Miss) 277 F2d 907.

An order or offer to buy goods for prompt or current shipment may be accepted by the seller either by promptly making the shipment or promising to do so.[57] When shipment of goods is claimed to constitute an acceptance of the buyer's order, the seller must notify the buyer of such acceptance within a reasonable time.[58]

When a person accepts services offered by another with the expectation that he will receive compensation, the acceptance of the services without any protest constitutes an acceptance of the offer and a contract exists for the payment of such services. It is immaterial that this conduct was not expressed in words, as the conduct showed the intent of the parties.[59]

(1) Silence as Acceptance. In most cases the silence of the offeree and his failure to act cannot be regarded as an acceptance. (See p. 196, Phelan v Everlith.) Ordinarily the offeror is not permitted to frame his offer in such a way as to make the silence and inaction of the offeree operate as an acceptance. In the case of prior dealings between the parties, as in a record or book club, the offeree may have a duty to reject an offer expressly, and his silence may be regarded as an acceptance.

In transactions relating to the sale of goods, silence is in some instances treated as an acceptance when the parties are both merchants.[60]

(2) Unordered Goods and Tickets. When a seller writes to a person with whom the seller has not had any prior dealings that, unless notified to the contrary, he will send specified merchandise to be paid for at specified prices, or sends the merchandise directly to that person, there is no acceptance if the offeree ignores the offer and does nothing. The silence of the person receiving the letter or the merchandise is not intended by him as an acceptance, and the sender as a reasonable man should recognize that none was intended.

This rule applies to all kinds of goods, books, magazines, and tickets sent to a person through the mail when he has not ordered them and does not use them. The fact that he does not return them does not mean that he accepts them; that is, the offeree is neither required to pay for nor return the goods or other items. A practical solution to the problem is for the recipient of the unordered goods to write, "Return to Sender" on the unopened package and put the package back into the mail without any additional postage.

The Postal Reorganization Act of 1970 provides that the person who receives unordered mailed merchandise has the right "to retain, use, discard, or dispose of it in any manner he sees fit without any obligation whatsoever to the sender." [61] It provides further that any unordered merchandise that

---

[57] UCC § 2-206(1)(b).
[58] UCC § 2-206(2).
[59] Swingle v Myerson, 19 Ariz App 607, 509 P2d 738.
[60] See § 23:5(2)(b).
[61] Federal Postal Reorganization Act § 3009.

is mailed must have attached to it a clear and conspicuous statement of the recipient's rights to treat the goods in this manner.

The mailing of unordered merchandise, other than a free sample conspicuously marked as such, or of a bill for its payment constitutes an unfair method of competition and an unfair trade practice. The distribution of unsolicited goods as part of a scheme to use the mail to defraud violates federal statutes. The payment of money orders made payable to a sender of unsolicited goods may be forbidden.[62]

*(3) **Insurer's Delay in Acting on Application.*** The delay of an insurance company in acting upon an application for insurance generally does not constitute an acceptance.[63] A few courts have held that an acceptance may be implied from the company's failure to reject the application promptly, that there is accordingly a binding contract and the application cannot be rejected. This is particularly true when the applicant has paid the first premium and the insurer fails to return it.[64] Some decisions attain the same practical result by holding the insurer liable for tort if, through its unjustified delay in rejecting the application, the applicant remains unprotected by insurance and then, in the interval, suffers loss that would have been covered by the insurance if it had been issued.[65]

§ **10:16. Communication of Acceptance.** If the offeree accepts the offer, must he notify the offeror that he accepts? The answer depends upon the nature of the offer. When communication is required, the acceptance must be communicated directly to the offeror or his agent. A statement made to a third person is not effective as an acceptance of the offer.

*(1) **Communication of Acceptance in a Bilateral Contract.*** If the offer pertains to a bilateral contract, an acceptance is not effective unless communicated to the offeror. Until the offeree makes known that he agrees to perform in the future, there is no way for the offeror to know whether the offeree accepts the offer or not.

*(2) **Communication of Acceptance in a Unilateral Contract.*** If the offeror makes an offer of a unilateral contract, communication of acceptance is ordinarily not required. In such a case, the offeror calls for a completed or accomplished act. If that act is performed by the offeror with knowledge of the offer, the offer is accepted without any further action by way of notifying the offeree. As a practical matter there will eventually be some notice to the offeror because the offeree who has performed the act will ask the offeror to carry out his promise.

---

[62] Antonucci v Stevens Dodge, Inc., (NY Civil Court) 340 NYS2d 979.

[63] Weaver v West Coast Life Insurance Co., 99 Mont 296, 42 P2d 729.

[64] Snyder v Redding Motors, 131 Cal App 2d 416, 280 P2d 811.

[65] St. Paul F. & M. Insurance Co. v Creach, 199 Okla 372, 186 P2d 641; *Contra:* La Favor v American National Insurance Co., 279 Minn 5, 155 NW2d 286.

(3) Communication of Acceptance in a Guaranty Contract. The general rule that notification of acceptance is not necessary in cases of an offer requesting the performance of an act is not applied in many states when the offer calls for the extension of credit to a buyer in return for which the offeror promises to pay the debt if it is not paid.[66] To illustrate, an uncle may write to a local merchant that if the merchant allows his nephew to purchase goods on credit, the uncle will pay the bill if the nephew does not. The uncle makes an offer of a unilateral contract because he has not asked for a promise by the merchant to extend credit but for the act of extending credit. If the merchant extends the credit, he is doing the act which the uncle calls for by his offer. If the general rule governing acceptances applied, the performance of this act would be a complete acceptance and would create a contract. In the guaranty case, however, another requirement is added, namely, that within a reasonable time after extending credit, the merchant must notify the uncle.

(4) Communication of the Exercise of an Option. Since an option contract binds the offeror to hold an offer open and to refrain from revoking it, the same principles which govern the communication of the acceptance of an offer generally apply to the exercise of an option. This means that there must be a clear and unequivocal expression of the intention of exercising the option. Conduct that is ambiguous or which is as consistent with non-exercise of the option as it is with its exercise is not sufficient.[67]

§ 10:17. Acceptance by Mail or Telegraph. When the offeree conveys his acceptance by mail or telegraph, questions may arise as to the right to use such means of communication and as to the time when the acceptance is effective.

(1) Right to Use Mail or Telegraph. Express directions of the offeror, prior dealings between the parties, or custom of the trade may make it clear that only one method of acceptance is proper. For example, in negotiations with respect to property of rapidly fluctuating value, such as wheat or corporation stocks, an acceptance sent by mail may be too slow. When there is no indication that mail or telegraph is not a proper method, an acceptance may be made by either of those instrumentalities without regard to the manner in which the offer was made.

In former years there was authority for the proposition that an offer could only be accepted by the same means by which the offer was communicated, or it would not be effective until actually received by the offeror.

---

[66] Electric Storage Battery Co. v Black, 27 Wis 2d 366, 134 NW2d 481. Some courts take the view that this type of case is an exception and that notice is essential to complete the contract itself. Others take the view that the failure to give notice is a condition subsequent that discharges the contract which was created when credit was given.

[67] Northcutt v McPherson, 81 NMex 743, 473 P2d 357.

This view is being gradually abandoned. The trend of the modern decisions supports the following provision of the Uniform Commercial Code relating to sales of personal property: "Unless otherwise unambiguously indicated by the language or circumstances, an offer to make a [sales] contract shall be construed as inviting acceptance in any manner and by any medium reasonable in the circumstances."[68]

(2) When Acceptance by Mail or Telegraph Is Effective. If the offeror specifies that an acceptance shall not be effective until received by him, the law will respect the offeror's wish. If there is no such provision and if acceptance by letter is proper, a mailed acceptance takes effect when the acceptance is properly mailed. The letter must be properly addressed to the offeror, and any other precaution that is ordinarily observed to insure safe transmission must be taken. If it is not mailed in this manner, the acceptance does not take effect when mailed, but only when received by the offeror.

The rule that a properly mailed acceptance takes effect at the time it is mailed is applied strictly. The rule applies even though the acceptance letter never reaches the offeror.

An acceptance sent by telegraph takes effect at the time that the message is handed to the clerk at the telegraph office, unless the offeror specifies otherwise or unless custom or prior dealings indicate that acceptance by telegraph is improper.

(3) Proof of Acceptance by Mail or Telegraph. How can the time of mailing be established, or even the fact of mailing in the case of a destroyed or lost letter? A similar problem arises in the case of a telegraphed acceptance. In either case the problem is not one of law but one of fact, that is, a question of proving the case to the jury. The offeror may testify in court that he never received an acceptance, or he may claim that the acceptance was sent after the offer had been revoked. The offeree or his stenographer may then testify that the letter was mailed at a particular time and place. The offeree's case will be strengthened if he can produce postal receipts for the mailing and delivery of a letter sent to the offeror, although these of course do not establish the contents of the letter. Ultimately the case goes to the jury, or to the judge if a jury trial has been waived, to determine whether the acceptance was made at a certain time and place.

(4) Payment and Notice by Mail Distinguished from Acceptance. The preceding principles relate to the acceptance of an offer. When a contract exists and the question is whether a notice has been given or a payment has been made under the contract, those principles do not necessarily apply. Thus the mailing of a check is not the payment of a debt as of the time and place of mailing.

---

[68] UCC § 2-206(1).

Contracts, however, will often extend the "mailed acceptance" rule to payment and giving notice. Thus insurance contracts commonly provide that the mailing of a premium is a sufficient "payment" of the premium to prevent the policy from lapsing for nonpayment of the premium. Likewise, an insurance policy provision requiring that notice of loss be given to the insurer is generally satisfied by a mailing of the notice without actual proof that the notice was received.[69]

§ 10:18. Acceptance by Telephone. Ordinarily acceptance of an offer may be made by telephone unless the circumstances are such that by the intent of the parties or the law of the state no acceptance can be made or contract arise in the absence of a writing.

§ 10:19. Auction Sales. At an auction sale the statements made by the auctioneer to draw forth bids are merely invitations to negotiate. Each bid is an offer, which is not accepted until the auctioneer indicates that a particular offer or bid is accepted. Usually this is done by the fall of the auctioneer's hammer, indicating that the highest bid made has been accepted.[70] As a bid is merely an offer, the bidder may withdraw his bid at any time before it is accepted by the auctioneer.

Ordinarily the auctioneer may withdraw any article or all of the property from the sale if he is not satisfied with the amounts of the bids that are being made. Once he has accepted a bid, however, he cannot cancel the sale. In addition, if it had been announced that the sale was to be made "without reserve," the goods must be sold to the person making the highest bid regardless of how low that may be.

---

[69] Falconer v Mazess, 403 Pa 165, 168 A2d 558.

[70] "Where a bid is made while the auctioneer's hammer is falling in acceptance of a prior bid, the auctioneer may in his discretion reopen the bidding or declare the goods sold under the bid on which the hammer is falling." UCC § 2-328(2).

CASES FOR CHAPTER 10

Lucy v Zehmer

196 Va App 493, 84 SE2d 516 (1954)

Zehmer discussed selling a farm to Lucy. After some discussion of a first draft of a contract, Zehmer and his wife signed a paper stating: "We hereby agree to sell to W. O. Lucy the Ferguson Farm complete for $50,000.00, title satisfactory to buyer." Lucy agreed to purchase the farm on these terms. Thereafter the Zehmers refused to transfer title to Lucy and claimed that they had made the contract for sale as a joke. Lucy brought an action for specific performance of the contract. From a judgment for the Zehmers, Lucy appealed.

BUCHANAN, J. . . . The defendants insist that the evidence was ample to support their contention that the writing sought to be enforced was prepared as a bluff or dare to force Lucy to admit that he did not have $50,000; that the whole matter was a joke; . . . and no binding contract was ever made between the parties. . . .

The appearance of the contract, the fact that it was under discussion for forty minutes or more before it was signed; Lucy's objection to the first draft because it was written in the singular, and he wanted Mrs. Zehmer to sign it also; the rewriting to meet that objection and the signing by Mrs. Zehmer; the discussion of what was to be included in the sale, the provision for the examination of the title, the completeness of the instrument that was executed, the taking possession of it by Lucy with no request or suggestion by either of the defendants that he give it back, are facts which furnish persuasive evidence that the execution of the contract was a serious business transaction rather than a casual, jesting matter as defendants now contend. . . .

If it be assumed, contrary to what we think the evidence shows, that Zehmer was jesting about selling his farm to Lucy and that the transaction was intended by him to be a joke, nevertheless the evidence shows that Lucy did not so understand it but considered it to be a serious business transaction and the contract to be binding on the Zehmers as well as on himself. The very next day he arranged with his brother to put up half the money and take a half interest in the land. The day after that he employed an attorney to examine the title. The next night, Tuesday, he was back at Zehmer's place and there Zehmer told him for the first time, Lucy said, that he wasn't going to sell and he told Zehmer, "You know you sold that place fair and square." After receiving the report from his attorney that the title was good, he wrote to Zehmer that he was ready to close the deal.

Not only did Lucy actually believe, but the evidence shows he was warranted in believing, that the contract represented a serious business transaction and a good faith sale and purchase of the farm.

In the field of contracts, as generally elsewhere, "We must look to the outward expression of a person as manifesting his intention rather than to his secret and unexpressed intention. 'The law imputes to a person an intention corresponding to the reasonable meaning of his words and acts.' " . . .

The mental assent of the parties is not requisite for the formation of a contract. If the words or other acts of one of the parties have but one reasonable meaning, his undisclosed intention is immaterial. . . .

[Judgment reversed and action remanded.]

Olson v Beacham

(ND) 102 NW2d 125 (1960)

Beacham and McElroy advertised for bids for the installation of a cooling system in a building they owned. Olson submitted the lowest bid, but the owners accepted the slightly higher bid of another contractor. Olson sued the owners for breach of contract. From a judgment in favor of the owners, Olson appealed.

SATHRE, C.J. . . . It is the contention of the plaintiff that having submitted the lowest bid . . . a contract resulted between the parties, and that failure on the part of the defendants to accept plaintiff's bid constituted a breach of contract resulting in damages to the plaintiff. . . .

The defendants in advertising for bids stated. . . : "The owner reserves the right to reject any or all bids when such rejection is in the interest of the owner. . . ."

The plaintiff in his bid stipulated: "The undersigned, as bidder, hereby proposes, and if this proposal is accepted, agrees to enter into a contract." . . .

The defendants did not accept the bid of the plaintiff. . . . They clearly had the right under the terms of their advertisement for bids and instruction to bidders to accept or reject any of the bids that might be submitted. The plaintiff recognized the right of the owners and stated . . . he would enter into a contract . . . *if the defendants accepted his bid.* The defendants having rejected the bid of the plaintiff were under no obligation to him and they had the right to determine for themselves which bid submitted would be to their best interest. The plaintiff was aware of this fact when he submitted his bid. The advertisement of the defendants for bids was merely an invitation for offers and was not an offer to accept any particular bid. The advertisement could result in a contract only upon acceptance of a bid submitted by a bidder. . . .

[Judgment affirmed.]

Griswold v Heat Incorporated

108 NH 119, 229 A2d 183 (1967)

Heat Incorporated made an agreement with Griswold, an accountant, by which it agreed to pay him $200 a month for rendering such accounting services "as he, in his sole discretion, may render." When the corporation refused to pay on the ground that the agreement was so indefinite that it was not binding, Griswold sued for damages.

LAMPRON, J. . . . When Heat was incorporated in New Hampshire in 1956, its stockholders and directors were Kretschmar, Harris, and the defendant Illig, each holding 500 shares. Its business, the distribution of heating equipment and boilers, was based in Nashua and operated by Kretschmar, as Harris and Illig had businesses of their own, the former in Portland, Maine, the latter in Fitchburg, Massachusetts.

Plaintiff Griswold, a certified public accountant, was associated with Heat from its beginning. He installed its accounting system, kept the stock book records, the records of meetings of the directors and the stockholders, counseled and advised on bookkeeping and accounting procedures, and on the financial operation of the company. The Trial Court found that Griswold is a 78-year old man with a life expectancy in excess of the remainder of the contract in dispute, who is somewhat deaf, has sciatica, but is alert, moves briskly and he presently is still active in his profession as a certified accountant as a member of a large Portland firm of accountants.

When Kretschmar died in May, 1957, the corporation bought his 500 shares of stock. The remaining stockholders, Harris and Illig, because of their own full time interests, agreed to continue Heat only if a manager could be obtained and if Griswold agreed to continue to serve the corporation as he had in the past. This was arranged and thereafter Griswold, who became the holder of one share of stock, served as director, assistant treasurer, clerk, and continued as financial advisor to the corporation. For these services Griswold received $300 per month, which was reduced to $100 per month in 1960, when Heat had financial reverses, and continued at that rate until January 1, 1964.

Prior to December 2, 1963, Harris notified Illig that he was interested in disposing of his stock in Heat to him. On that date Harris transferred his shares to Illig who became owner of 998 of the 1,000 shares outstanding. Mrs. Illig owning one share and Griswold the other. Illig testified that in connection with this purchase he was desirous that Griswold continue to serve Heat in the same manner as he had in the past and that Griswold agreed to do so for $200 per month which Illig agreed to pay. Both Harris and Griswold, who with Illig then constituted the board of directors of Heat, testified that was the agreement between Illig and Griswold. . . .

Defendants take the position that Griswold's promise by its terms gives the plaintiff such an option in regard to the performance required of him as to render his promise illusory. . . .

Does Griswold's promise or obligation "for such services as he, in his sole discretion, may render" constitute sufficient consideration for Heat's promise to pay him $200 per month for 5 years in accordance with the terms of their agreement?

It has long been the rule in this state that "the proper interpretation of a contract is that which will make it speak the intention of the parties at the time it was made." . . . It follows that in construing the written agreement of these parties, all of its provisions, its subject matter, the situation of the parties at the time, and the object intended to be effected will be considered in arriving at the sense of the words they used. . . .

There was evidence that the nature of the services rendered by Griswold to Heat from its origin in 1956 to December 2, 1963, the date of the agreement, were well known to both Griswold and Illig. The latter testified that on the above date when he purchased Harris' interest, he wanted Griswold to continue to serve the corporation as "he had over the years." He asked Griswold if he was willing to continue in "this fashion," at $200 a month and Griswold said he would. The latter testified that Illig agreed to pay him $200 per month for his "usual services" the nature of which was known to Illig. This insight of the object intended to be effected by the agreement is an important factor in determining the sense of the words used therein by these parties. . . .

The course of conduct of the parties for the first year following their agreement is further evidence "of their common understanding of the meaning of their contract and the result they expected to accomplish thereby." . . . The Trial Court properly found that "the plaintiff during the year 1964 performed approximately the same services as he had previously performed and was paid by the corporation for the entire twelve months." Griswold was paid $200 per month as provided for by the agreement. During that period Illig owned all of the shares of Heat except two, one owned by his wife, the other by Griswold. The three of them constituted the board of directors.

Since this agreement was made by businessmen, it is reasonable to assume that it was made for business reasons and was intended to have business efficacy. . . . It should be so construed. . . . In all such business undertakings an obligation of good faith is implied. . . . An interpretation which makes the agreement fair and reasonable will be preferred to one which leads to harsh and unreasonable results. . . . Similarly "an interpretation that would place one party at the mercy of another should, if at all possible, be avoided." . . .

Construing the language of the agreement in the light of all the criteria previously mentioned, we hold that the provision "for such services as he (Griswold), in his sole discretion, may render" obligated Griswold to render some services to Heat and imposed on him the duty to exercise good faith in the determination of their amount. . . . We further hold that these obligations . . . were sufficient [to support] Heat's promises in the agreement. . . .

The plaintiff is entitled to recover on the contract.

Coronis Associates v Gordon Construction Co.

90 NJ Super 69, 216 A2d 246 (1966)

Gordon, a contractor, requested bids on structural steel from various suppliers. Coronis submitted an offer by letter. The letter said nothing as to the duration or revocability of the offer made therein. He later withdrew the offer. In a lawsuit by Coronis against Gordon, Gordon counterclaimed for damages for breach of contract on the ground that Coronis could not revoke his offer. From a judgment in favor of Coronis, Gordon appealed.

COLLESTER, J.A.D. . . . Prior to the enactment of the Uniform Commercial Code an offer not supported by consideration could be revoked at any time prior to acceptance. . . . The drafters of the Code recognized that the common-law rule was contrary to modern business practice and possessed the capability to produce unjust results. . . . The response was § 2-205 . . . which reverses the common-law rule and states: "An offer by a merchant to buy or sell goods in a *signed writing which by its terms gives assurance that it will be held open* is not revocable, for lack of consideration, during the time stated or if no time is stated for a reasonable time . . ." (Emphasis added) Coronis' letter [making the offer] contains no terms giving assurance it will be held open. We recognize that just as an offeree runs a risk in acting on an offer before accepting it, the offeror runs a risk if his offer is considered irrevocable. . . . In their comments to § 2-205 of the Code the drafters anticipated these risks and stated: "However, despite settled courses of dealing or usages of the trade whereby firm offers are made by oral communication and relied upon without more evidence, such offers remain revocable under this Article since authentication by a writing is the essence of this section." Uniform Commercial Code ([§] 2-205), comment, par. 2.

We think it clear that plaintiff's writing does not come within the provisions of § 2-205 of a "signed writing which by its terms gives assurance that it will be held open." . . .

[Judgment affirmed as to counterclaim.]

Grieve v Mullaly

211 Cal 77, 293 P 619 (1930)

The Mullaly brothers sent Grieve a signed written statement that "we . . . agree to lease [certain specified land] for a period of three

years with privilege of one more year to J. D. Grieve of Davis, Cal." Grieve sold his rights under this writing to Adams. Adams tendered to the Mullaly brothers a formal lease for them to sign. The lease named Adams as the tenant. The Mullaly brothers refused to sign the lease. A suit was brought against the brothers. From a judgment in their favor, an appeal was taken.

WASTE, C.J. . . . In legal effect, the writing [sent to Grieve by the Mullaly brothers] was no more than an offer. . . .

. . . The writing . . . in no way bound Grieve, and it in no way bound defendants until accepted. It amounted to an offer to Grieve to enter into a lease. It is elementary that . . . an offer to contract is not assignable; it being purely personal to the offeree. In this case the offer was made to Grieve. The evidence does not disclose any acceptance by him. Adams attempted to accept the offer, not as the agent or representative of Grieve, but in his own right. This is conclusively shown by the fact that Adams tendered to the Mullalys a lease for their signatures, naming him, Adams, as lessee. . . .

[Judgment affirmed.]

Phelan v Everlith

22 Conn Supp 377, 173 A2d 601 (1961)

Everlith obtained a one-year liability policy of insurance from the insurance company's agent, Phelan. Prior to the expiration of the year, Phelan sent Everlith a renewal policy covering the next year, together with a bill for the renewal premium. The bill stated that the policy should be returned promptly if the renewal was not desired. Everlith did not return the policy or take any other action relating to the insurance. Phelan sued for the renewal premium.

WISE, J. . . . The only dealings the parties had with each other [were] the issuance of the original policy in January, 1959, and the alleged renewal policy. There had been no prior dealings between them. The defendant never made an application for the renewal of the policy; never ordered it or asked that it be renewed; never indicated that he wanted it renewed; nor indicated an acceptance of the renewal; nor was any part of the premium paid by the defendant.

The fundamental and basic requisites that there must be an offer and an acceptance to make a valid contract have been applied to insurance contracts. . . . A renewal policy is a separate contract, independent of the original policy, requiring its own elements of offer and acceptance. . . . The unsolicited issuance of a renewal policy prior to the expiration of the original policy is but a proposal or an offer to insure. . . .

An express acceptance of an offer of renewal is not always necessary but may be implied under some circumstances. A familiar illustration of this is where, in accordance with prior dealings between the parties, the agent writes and delivers a policy to his customer prior to the expiration date and bills him for the premium upon the assumption that in the absence of notice to the contrary the policy will be accepted and the premium paid as in the past. Here, failure of the customer to notify the agent to the contrary will signify the customer's implied acceptance of the policy and his promise to pay the premium within a reasonable time. However, the doctrine that in view of a general custom among insurance agents to renew the insurance of their policyholders without request, a failure by the insured to reject the renewal is tantamount to its acceptance may not be availed of unless the custom is established and it is shown that the party relying thereon knew of it and there had been a course of dealings between the parties from which it could be implied that the policyholders silence or failure to reject the offer would be regarded as an acceptance. . . . Applying these principles to the instant case, it is clear that there was no acceptance by the defendant of the renewal policy.

Only in a single instance, which occurred in January, 1959, had the plaintiff issued a policy to the defendant. Never had he previously renewed a policy for the defendant. A single transaction does not establish a course of conduct or course of dealing. There had been no course of dealing between the parties which would lead the plaintiff to think that defendant's silence would result in the renewal of the policy, nor was there anything in the conduct on the part of the defendant to lead the plaintiff to believe that the policy would be renewed.

In the absence of circumstances from which an acceptance may be implied, an acceptance will not be presumed from a mere failure to decline a proposal. . . .

[Judgment for defendant.]

QUESTIONS AND CASE PROBLEMS

1. What objective of the law (from the list in Chapter 2, page 10) is illustrated by each of the following quotations?
   (a) "Economic life would be most uncertain . . . if we did not have the assurance that contracts once made would be binding."
   (b) An offer is terminated by the lapse of a reasonable time when no time has been stated.
2. The Willis Music Co. advertised a television set at $22.50 in the Sunday newspaper. Ehrlich ordered a set, but the company refused to deliver it on the ground that the price in the newspaper ad was a mistake. Ehrlich sued the company. Was it liable? Reason? [Ehrlich v Willis Music Co., 93 Ohio App 246, 113 NE2d 252]
3. Laseter was employed by Pet Dairy Products Co. When he was injured at work, Pet promised to continue to employ him and to give him light work. Pet later discharged him, and he sued Pet for breach of contract. Was he entitled to recover? [Laseter v Pet Dairy Products Co., (CA4 SC) 246 F2d 747]
4. Owen wrote to Tunison asking if Tunison would sell his store for $6,000. Tunison replied, "It would not be possible for me to sell unless I received $16,000 cash." Owen replied, "Accept your offer." Tunison denied that there was a contract. Decide. [Owen v Tunison, 131 Maine 42, 158 A 926]
5. Ranch owned land. Bentzen and Ranch entered into an "agreement for warranty deed" which provided for the sale of the property to Bentzen, with the purchase price to be paid $1,000 down and the balance "payable by future agreement on or before" a specified date. Thereafter Bentzen sued Ranch for breach of contract and to enforce the contract. Decide. [Bentzen v Ranch, 78 Wyo 158, 320 P2d 440]
6. A buyer sent an offer in the form of a written contract signed by him to the seller on January 15. The seller signed the contract and delivered it to his attorney on January 17. On January 17 the buyer mailed a letter to the seller revoking his offer. The seller received this letter on January 19 but the seller's lawyer sent the signed contract to the buyer on January 22. The buyer refused to perform the contract and the seller sued for damages for its breach. Was the buyer liable? [Kendel v Pontious, (Fla App) 244 So2d 543]
7. The Canonie Construction Company sent Dayhuff a signed paper reading: "Field Purchase Order CANONIE CONSTRUCTION COMPANY . . . To Jack R. Dayhuff . . . Haul sand [for a highway construction project] as required. Approximately 35,000 to 50,000 cubic yards 0.95 per ton scaled." Thereafter Canonie gave the hauling work to the Gibson Coal Company. Dayhuff sued Canonie on the grounds that the purchase order form gave

him the right to do all the hauling for the specified construction job. Was he correct? [Dayhuff v Canonie Construction Co., — Ind App —, 283 NE2d 425]

8. The United Steelworkers, a labor union, and O'Neal Steel, Inc., an employer were negotiating a collective bargaining labor contract. As they neared agreement, the employer submitted to the union a final written contract. The union representative signed the contract contingent upon the omission of paragraph 18 relating to strikes. Was the employer bound by the contract? [United Steelworkers v O'Neal Steel, Inc., (DC ND Ala) 321 F Supp 235]

9. The Great A. & P. Tea Co. rented a store from Geary. On February 25 the company wrote Geary offering to execute a lease for an additional year, commencing on May 1. At 10:30 a.m. on March 7, Geary wrote a letter containing a lease for the additional year and accepting the offer. On the same day at 1:30 p.m. the company mailed Geary a letter stating that it withdrew the offer to execute the new lease. Each party received the other's letter the following day. Was there an effective acceptance of the offer to make a lease? [Geary v Great A. & P. Tea Co., 366 Ill 625, 10 NE2d 350]

10. *A* manufactured electric meters and voltage regulators. *B* sent an order to *A* for such equipment but specified that *B*'s representative inspect the meters at *A*'s plant. *A* agreed to sell the equipment to *B* but objected to plant inspection and sent some equipment without being so inspected. *B* accepted the equipment and sent additional orders which he accepted although there had not been any plant inspection. *A* sued *B* for the purchase price. Can *B* raise the defense that there was no contract because the parties never agreed as to plant inspection? [Midwest Engineering & Constr. Co. v Electric Regulator Corp., (Okla) 435 P2d 89]

11. *A* sent *B* a letter stating "you have a 30-day option in which to purchase my car for $2000.00." *A* claimed that he could not exercise the option because the option was not binding as *A* had not received anything for it. Was *A* correct? [Mobil Oil Corp. v Wroten, (Del Ch) 303 A2d 698]

12. The owner of a business made an offer to sell an interest in the business for a specified price. The buyer wrote back agreeing to the terms of the offer and stating that payment would be made in thirty days after the transaction was completed. Was the owner bound by a contract with the buyer? [Sossamon v Littlejohn, 241 SC 478, 129 SE2d 124]

13. *A* owned land. He signed a contract agreeing to sell the land but reserving the right to take the hay from the land until the following October. He gave the contract form to *B*, a broker. *C*, a prospective buyer, agreed to buy the land and signed the contract but crossed out the provision as to the hay crop. Was there a binding contract between *A* and *C*? [Koller v Flerchinger, 73 Wash 2d 857, 441 P2d 126]

11 Contractual Capacity

§ 11:1. Introduction. All persons do not have the same legal capacity to make a contract. In some cases the legal capacity of a person has no relation to his actual ability. A person who is 17 years old, for example, may have just as much ability to make a contract as an older person. Nevertheless, he is ordinarily under a legal incapacity. In other cases, such as those involving insane persons, the legal incapacity is based upon the inability to understand the consequences of the particular transaction.

Persons whose legal capacity is or may be restricted include minors, insane persons, intoxicated persons, convicts, and aliens. Such a limitation on married women is now largely historical. The restrictions on the contractual powers of corporations are discussed in Chapter 50.

Every party to a contract is presumed to have contractual capacity until the contrary is shown.[1] The fact that a person does not understand a contract does not mean that he lacks contractual capacity.

§ 11:2. Executory and Executed Contracts. When a person's legal capacity is restricted, his rights may depend upon the extent to which his contract has been performed. In an *executory contract,* performance by either party or by both parties is incomplete. The incomplete performance by a party may be partial or total. An *executed contract* is one that has been completely performed by both parties.

§ 11:3. Minors. At common law any person, male or female, under twenty-one years of age was a *minor* (or an infant). At common law, minority ended the day before the 21st birthday. The "day before the birthday" rule is still followed,[2] but the 21 years has been reduced to 18 years in two-thirds of the states and to 19 in a few. Some states provide for determination of minority upon marriage and some specify that the minority of girls shall terminate sooner than that of boys.[3]

---

[1] Kruse v Coos Head Timber Co., 248 Ore 294, 432 P2d 1009.

[2] In determining eligibility for old-age benefits under the Social Security Act and according to the regulations of the Internal Revenue Service, a person is considered as having reached the required age on the day before the specified birthday.

[3] A statute may constitutionally provide for the termination of minority at an earlier age for girls than for boys, as against the contention that such a distinction constitutes a discrimination because of sex and denies equal protection. Stanton v Stanton, Utah 2d, 517 P2d 110. Contra: Bassett v Bassett, (Okla App) 521 P2d 434.

§ 11:4. Minor's Right to Avoid Contracts. With exceptions that will be noted later, a contract made by a minor is voidable [4] at his election.[5] If the minor desires, he may perform his voidable contracts. The adult party to the contract, however, cannot avoid the contract on the ground that the minor could do so if he wished. Until the minor avoids the contract, the adult party is bound by it.

The fact that a minor can avoid his contract explains why stores and dealers will often insist that the parents of a minor sign any contract made with him. A parent or other adult who joins in the contract with the minor is personally bound and must perform even though the minor could or does set it aside as to himself.[6]

(1) Minor's Misrepresentation of Age. Statutes in some states prevent a minor from avoiding his contract if he has fraudulently misrepresented his age. In the absence of such a statute, however, his fraud generally does not affect his right to avoid the contract when sued for its breach, although there is some authority that in such case he must pay for any damage to, or deterioration of, the property he received under the contract. If the minor is suing to recover what he had paid or given the other party, his fraud in misrepresenting his age may bar him from obtaining any relief.

In any case, the other party to the contract may avoid it because of the minor's fraud. There is a conflict of authority, however, as to whether the other party may sue the minor for damages because of the minor's fraud. Recovery is denied in some jurisdictions on the ground that to allow the other party damages for the minor's misrepresentation of his age would in effect deny the minor the right to avoid the contract. Elsewhere recovery is allowed because a minor, although he may avoid his contracts, is liable for his misconduct.

(2) Time for Avoidance. A minor's contract, whether executed or not, ordinarily can be disaffirmed or avoided by the minor at any time during minority or for a reasonable time after becoming of age. What is a reasonable time is a question of fact to be determined in the light of all the surrounding circumstances. (See p. 208, Eastern Airlines Inc. v Stuhl.) After the expiration of a reasonable time following the attainment of majority, the minor ratifies (approves) the contract by his failure to avoid the contract within that time; but in some states an express affirmance is necessary to make a wholly executory contract binding.

In some states, statutes declare that a minor's debt is not binding unless there is some act of ratification after attaining majority. This reverses the

---

[4] In some jurisdictions the appointment of an agent or an attorney by a minor is void rather than voidable. There is no reason why this exception should be made, and there is a tendency to eliminate it.

[5] If the minor dies, the personal representative of his estate may avoid a contract which the minor could have avoided.

[6] The fact that a minor's older brother who is over 21 is with the minor when a purchase is made and takes part in the transaction does not affect the right of the minor to avoid the transaction. Cadigan v Strand Garage, 351 Mass 703, 221 NE2d 468.

pattern of the common law under which the burden would be on the minor to disaffirm the obligation.[7]

As an exception to the right to disaffirm a contract during minority, a minor cannot fully avoid a conveyance or transfer of land made by him until he reaches his majority. Prior to that time, he may partially avoid the conveyance to the extent that he may retake possession of the land and enjoy its use or rent it to others, but he cannot set aside the transfer of title until he is 21.

§ 11:5. What Constitutes Avoidance. Avoidance or disaffirmance of a contract by a minor may be made by any expression of an intention to repudiate the contract. If the minor does an act inconsistent with the continuing validity of the contract, that is deemed a disaffirmance. Thus, when a minor conveyed property to *A* and later, on reaching majority, made a conveyance of the same property to *B*, the second conveyance was deemed an avoidance of the first.

There is a conflict of authority as to whether a minor must disaffirm an executory contract on attaining majority. Some courts hold that he is bound by the contract if he fails to disaffirm it, while others hold that the minor is not bound by an executory contract until he affirms it after attaining his majority. If the contract has been executed by the other contracting party, as by delivering property to the minor, the retention of such property by the minor after he attains majority will generally be regarded as a ratification or affirmance of the contract by him even though the contract is executory as to performance of the minor's obligation.

§ 11:6. Restitution by Minor upon Avoidance. When a minor avoids his contract, must he return what he has received? What happens if what he received has been spent, used, damaged, or destroyed? When the minor has in his possession or control the consideration received by him, or any part of it, he must return it or offer to do so before he can require the other party to undo the contract and set things back to their original position, or as it is called, to restore the *status quo ante*.

When a minor disaffirms his contract, he must avoid all of it. He cannot keep part of the contract and reject the balance. Although the minor must make this restitution if he can, the right to disaffirm his contract is not affected by the fact that he no longer has the money or property to return, or that the property has been damaged. In those states which follow the general rule, the minor can thus refuse to pay for what he has received or he can get back what he has paid or given, even though he himself does not have anything to return or returns the property in a damaged condition. There is, however, a trend which would limit this rule. (See p. 208, Porter v Wilson.)

If the seller improperly refuses to return the purchase price to the minor, the minor in excused from making the useless gesture of returning the goods, which he knows the seller will not accept. And a minor does not lose the

---

[7] Missouri v Davis, (Mo App) 488 SW2d 305.

effect of his disaffirmance by the fact that, having attained majority, he uses the goods temporarily for 2 months while the lawsuit over his disaffirmance is still pending.[8]

This absolute right is limited in some states where a minor must restore what he received or its money equivalent before he can disaffirm the contract. In those states, if he cannot make such restoration, he is denied the right to disaffirm.[9] Many states require the minor to pay for any damage to the returned property if the minor had falsely represented his age when he obtained the property.

When a minor wishes to avoid an insurance contract, he can recover everything that he has paid without regard to whether the insurance company had made any payments to him. The unfairness of this rule has led some jurisdictions to limit the recovery of the minor to the amount of the premiums paid by him in excess of the actual cost of his protection during the time the policy was in force. In some states the minor is by statute denied the right to avoid a life insurance policy on his own life.

§ 11:7. Recovery of Property by Minor upon Avoidance. When the minor avoids his contract, the other contracting party must return all the money or property of the minor that he has received, or the money equivalent of property which he cannot return. (See p. 209, O'Brien v Small.) A minor who avoids his sale or trade of personal property cannot recover that property, however, from a third person to whom the other party to the contract has transferred it.[10]

§ 11:8. Ratification. A minor's voidable contract becomes binding upon him when he ratifies or approves it. Of necessity, the minor can only ratify a contract when he is no longer a minor. He must have attained his majority or his "ratification" would itself be regarded as voidable in order to protect the minor. In contrast, a minor can usually avoid a contract at any time during minority.

Ratification may consist of any expression that indicates an intention to be bound by the contract. In some states a written ratification or declaration of intention is required. An acknowledgment by the minor that a contract had been made during his minority, without any indication of an intention to be bound thereby, is not a ratification.

The making of payments after attaining majority may constitute a ratification. Many courts, however, refuse to recognize payment as ratification in the absence of further evidence of an intent to ratify, an express statement of ratification, or an appreciation by the minor that such payment might constitute a ratification.[11]

---

[8] Adams v Barcomb, 125 Vt 380, 216 A2d 648.

[9] Wheeless v Endora Bank, Ark, 509 SW2d 532. In a few states this limitation is imposed by statute on minors over a certain age. Clark v Stites, 89 Idaho 191, 404 P2d 339.

[10] UCC § 2-403(1).

[11] Bronx Savings Bank v Conduff, 78 N Mex 216, 430 P2d 374.

In addition to ratification based on statements or promises, ratification may be found in the conduct of the minor. If after attaining majority the minor fails to disaffirm an executed contract within a reasonable time, the contract is deemed ratified.[12] If the minor acquired property under his contract and after reaching majority makes a use or disposition of the property inconsistent with disaffirmance, he will also be deemed to have ratified the contract.

§ 11:9. Contracts for Necessaries. A minor is liable for the reasonable value of necessaries that are supplied to him by another person at the minor's request. This exception differs from the others that follow in that the minor is ordinarily not bound by the terms of his contract. In the case of necessaries he is usually required to pay only the reasonable value of what the seller actually delivers and which the minor receives. This duty of the minor is called a quasicontractual liability.[13] It is a duty which the law imposes upon the minor rather than one which he has created by his contract.

Originally necessaries were limited to those things absolutely necessary for the sustenance and shelter of the minor. Thus limited, the term would extend only to the most simple foods, clothing, and lodging. In the course of time, the rule was relaxed to extend generally to things relating to the health, education, and comfort of the minor. Thus, the rental of a house used by a married minor, his wife, and child, is a necessary. And services reasonably necessary to obtaining employment by a minor, such as assistance from an employment agency, have been held to be necessaries. (See p. 209, Gastonia Personnel Corp. v Rogers.) The rule has also been relaxed to hold that whether an item is a necessary in a particular case depends upon the financial and social status, or station in life, of the minor. The rule as such does not treat all minors equally. To illustrate, college education may be regarded as necessary for one minor but not for another, depending upon their respective stations in life.

Property other than food or clothing acquired by a minor is generally not regarded as a necessary. Although this rule is obviously sound in the case of jewelry and property used for pleasure, the same view is held even though the minor is self-supporting and uses the property in connection with his work, as tools of his trade, or an automobile which he must have to go to and from work. The more recent decisions, however, hold that property used by the minor for his support is a necessary. Thus, it has been held that a tractor and farm equipment were necessaries for a married minor who supported his family by farming.[14]

It is likely that necessaries will in time come to mean merely what is important by contemporary standards. Thus, a court in considering the right of a secured creditor to obtain an injunction against disposition of the collateral noted the fact that the "great majority of items repossessed at

---

12 See § 9:14 as to what constitutes an executed contract.
13 See § 9:16 as to quasicontractual liability generally.
14 Williams v Buckler, (Ky) 264 SW2d 279.

residential locations are appliances such as television sets, refrigerators, stoves and sewing machines, and furniture of all kinds." The court then referred to these as "items which under modern living standards are somewhat akin to necessities of life." [15]

Money loaned to a minor is ordinarily not classified as a necessary, even though the minor thereafter purchases necessaries with the borrowed money. An exception is made when the lender advances money for that express purpose and makes certain that the minor purchases necessaries with the money. In such a case the minor must pay the lender the amount of the loan.

If the minor is adequately supplied with necessaries or if those purchased by him are excessive in quantity or too expensive, the courts hold that such purchases are not necessaries and that the contracts are voidable by the minor without liability for the reasonable value of the goods purchased.

§ 11:10. Contracts That Minors Cannot Avoid. Because of the complexities involved with avoiding contracts, several statutes in various states specify those contracts which minors cannot avoid.

(1) Education Loans. Statutes in many states prohibit a minor from disaffirming a loan made for obtaining a higher education.[16]

(2) Medical Care. Statutes sometimes provide that a minor may consent to medical care or treatment. The consent of the minor's parent or guardian is not then required.[17]

(3) Experienced Minor. In order to prevent the minor from using the shield of his minority as a sword to injure others, some states, either by decision or statute, hold that when a minor engages in a business or employment and operates in the same manner as a person having legal capacity, he will not be permitted to set aside contracts arising from that business or employment. (See p. 210, Pankas v Bell.)

(4) Court-Approved Contract. In some states permission of the court may be obtained for a minor to execute a contract. When this permission is obtained and the contract is made, it is fully binding upon the minor. In this manner, a minor may execute a binding contract for professional performances on the stage, in the movies, or on television.

(5) Contracts in Performance of Legal Duty. A minor cannot avoid a contract which the law specifically requires or that provides for the performance of an act which he is legally bound to do. If the law authorizes a minor to make an enlistment contract with a branch of the armed forces, he cannot avoid it on the ground of minority. Many states require that a person file a bond when he brings certain kinds of lawsuits or takes an

[15] Chrysler Credit Corp. v Waegele, 29 Cal App 3d 681, 105 Cal Rptr 914.
[16] New York Education Law, § 281.
[17] Pennsylvania, 35 PS, § 10101.

appeal. If a minor brings such an action or takes an appeal and executes the necessary bond, he cannot avoid liability on the bond on the ground that he is a minor.

If property of a father is held in the name of his minor child under an agreement that it is to be conveyed or sold in a particular manner, a conveyance by the son cannot be avoided by him. Here the transaction by the minor is in performance of the duty imposed upon him by his agreement with his father, and the law will not permit the minor to set the contract aside. In this type of case, the minor has no direct interest in the transaction but in a sense is acting as the agent for the father.

(6) Veterans. In most states, statutes permit veterans who are minors to make binding contracts of certain types, particularly those concerning the purchase of a home.

(7) Bank Accounts. By statute in some states a minor may open a bank account in his own name, and all acts of the minor with respect to the account are binding upon him as though he had attained majority.

(8) Stock Transfers. By statute it is sometimes provided that when a minor transfers shares of stock, the transfer shall be as binding as though he were an adult with respect to anyone not knowing that he is a minor.

§ 11:11. Liability of Parent for Minor's Contract. Ordinarily a parent is not liable on a contract executed by a minor child. The parent may be liable, however, if the child is acting as the agent of the parent in executing the contract.[18] If the parent has neglected the child, the parent is liable to a third person for the reasonable value of necessaries supplied by that person to the child.[19] If a parent joins in a contract with a minor, as when the parent acts as a cosigner, the parent is liable on his own undertaking and remains bound by his contract even though the minor avoids the contract as to himself.

If the minor on disaffirming a contract for the sale of goods returns them to the seller in their original condition and the seller then discharges the minor from his contract and from the installment note which he signed, the parent of the minor and any other person who signed to assist the minor is likewise discharged.[20]

§ 11:12. Insane Persons. If a party to an agreement is insane, he lacks capacity and his contract is either voidable or void. In order to constitute insanity within the meaning of this rule, the party must be so deranged mentally that he does not know that he is making a contract or that he does not understand the consequences of what he is doing. If he lacks such understanding, the cause of his mental condition is immaterial. It may be

[18] See § 42:5.
[19] See § 40:11.
[20] Allen v Small, (Vt) 271 A2d 840.

idiocy, senile dementia, lunacy, imbecility, or such excessive use of alcoholic beverages or narcotics as to cause mental impairment.

If at the time the party makes the contract he understands the nature of his action and its consequences, it is immaterial that he has certain delusions or insane intervals, or that he is eccentric. As long as the contract is made in a lucid interval and is not affected by any delusions, it is valid.

(1) Effect of Insanity. If a party to a contract is insane, he may generally avoid his contracts in the same manner as a minor.[21] Upon the removal of the disability, that is, upon his becoming sane, he may either ratify or disaffirm the contract. If a proper court has appointed a guardian for the insane person, the contract may be ratified or disaffirmed by the guardian. If the insane person dies, his personal representative or heirs may also affirm or disaffirm the contract made by him.

As in the case of minors, the other party to the contract has no right to disaffirm the contract merely because the insane party has the right to do so.

(2) Exceptions. There are several exceptions to the rule that the contracts of an insane person are voidable:

(a) EXISTENCE OF GUARDIAN. It is commonly provided that when a court has appointed a guardian for the insane person, the latter cannot make any contract whatever and an agreement made by him is therefore void.

(b) NECESSARIES. An insane person has a quasicontractual liability to pay the reasonable value of necessaries supplied to him, his wife, or his children.

(c) BENEFICIAL CONTRACT. If the contract was fair, reasonable, and advantageous to the insane person, a substantial number of states hold that he may not avoid the contract when the other party acted without knowledge of the incompetence and in good faith, and it would be impossible to restore the status quo ante.

§ 11:13. Intoxicated Persons. The capacity of a party to contract and the validity of his contract are not affected by the fact that he was drunk at the time of making the contract so long as he knew that he was making a contract. The fact that the contract was foolish and that he would not have made it had he been sober does not make the contract voidable unless it can be shown that the other party purposely caused the person to become drunk in order to induce him to enter into the contract.

If the degree of intoxication is such that the person does not know at the time that he is making a contract, the contract is voidable. The situation is the same as though he were so insane at the time that he did not know what he was doing. Upon becoming sober, the person may avoid or rescind the contract if he so desires. An unreasonable delay in taking steps to set

[21] Davis v Colorado Kenworth Corp., 156 Colo 98, 396 P2d 958.

aside a known contract entered into while intoxicated, however, may bar the intoxicated person from asserting this right.

The fact that the use or possession of the intoxicating liquor by the contracting party was illegal does not bar him from avoiding his contract because of intoxication.[22] The fact that a person is an alcoholic does not in itself establish that he lacks capacity to make a binding contract.[23]

As in the case of a minor, a drunkard is bound by a contract that carries out an obligation or duty imposed by law. He is also required to pay for the reasonable value of all necessaries that are furnished to him.

If a person has been declared by a court to be a habitual drunkard or if a guardian has been appointed for him because of his inability to care for his property, the drunkard is under a continuing disability with respect to making contracts. The statutes which provide for the appointment of a guardian or the adjudication of the status of the drunkard generally specify that after the court has acted, the drunkard has no power to make a contract even when he is sober.

§ **11:14. Convicts.** The capacity to contract of a person convicted of a major criminal offense (a felony or treason) varies from state to state. In some states he may make a valid transfer of his property. In others, he is under either partial or total disability. When there is a disability, it generally exists only during the period of imprisonment.[24]

§ **11:15. Aliens.** An *alien* is a national or subject of a foreign country. Originally aliens were subject to many disabilities. These have been removed in most instances by treaty between the United States and the foreign country, under which each nation agrees to give certain rights to the citizens of the other. Generally an alien's right to make a contract is recognized.[25]

If this country is at war with a nation of which an alien is a subject, he is termed an *enemy alien* without regard to whether he assists his country in the prosecution of the war. An enemy alien is denied the right to make new contracts or to sue on existing ones; but if he is sued, he may defend the action. Contracts made by him, even though made before the war began, will at least be suspended during the war. In some instances, if the contract calls for continuing services or performance, the war terminates the contract.

§ **11:16. Married Women.** At common law a married woman could not make a binding contract. Her agreements were void, rather than voidable, even when she lived apart from her husband. Consequently, she could not ratify an agreement after the removal of the disability by the death of her husband.

---

[22] Hutson v Hutson, 239 Miss 413, 123 So2d 550.

[23] Olsen v Hawkins, 90 Idaho 28, 408 P2d 462.

[24] "Civil death" statutes depriving prisoners of their civil rights have been adopted in one-fourth of the states. Some courts hold these statutes to be unconstitutional. Delorme v Pierce Freightlines Co., (DC D Ore) 353 F Supp 258.

[25] A state cannot restrict or prohibit the employment of aliens in private or public employment. Truax v Raich, 239 US 33; Purdy & Fitzpatrick v California, 79 Cal Rptr 77, 456 P2d 645.

The common-law disability of a married woman has almost been abolished by statute in practically all the states.[26] There are still a few restrictions in some jurisdictions, mainly in instances where the wife might be unduly influenced by the husband. If is probable that these will disappear in the near future.

[26] United States v Yazell, 382 US 341.

CASES FOR CHAPTER 11

Eastern Airlines, Inc. v Stuhl

(NY Civil Court) 65 Misc 2d 901, 318 NYS2d 996 (1970) affirmed 68 Misc 2d 269, 327 NYS2d 752

Stuhl was 20 years of age. He gave checks to Eastern Airlines. These checks were not honored by the bank. Eastern Airlines sued him on the checks. In his answer filed in the lawsuit five months after he attained majority,* he disaffirmed the contract for which the checks had been given.

KASSAL, J. . . . Addressing the defense of disaffirmance, the court concludes that the same is not a valid defense herein since it had not been exercised within a reasonable time after the defendant attained his majority. The defendant attained his majority on April 21, 1964, but he did not disaffirm these checks until September 26, 1964, a period more than five months thereafter.

Some of the considerations which lead to the conclusion that this was not a reasonable period are these: The five months hiatus, the said disaffirmance did not occur until asserted as a defense in legal action, the fact that the defendant is not truly an "infant" in the moral or business concept of this principle since he had admittedly been actively involved in various and numerous business enterprises for at least three years prior thereto or from his 17th birthday on.

Obviously, these all add up to a person who had more than sufficient mental capacity and his disaffirmance, five months after attaining his majority, with regard to the issuance of checks in his twentieth year, should not under these circumstances be considered a disaffirmance within a reasonable period. In the court's opinion, some of the elements that should be considered in determining a reasonable period for a disaffirmance are the business experience, awareness and general acumen of the said infant. We have, in this instance, an example of a very world-wise man attempting, by the device of invoking a disaffirmance, to avail himself of a "free ride" both literally and figuratively.

[Judgment for airline.]

* *Authors' Comment:* At the time the above case arose and was decided, 21 years was the age of majority.

Porter v Wilson

106 NH 270, 209 A2d 730 (1965)

Roy Wilson was an orphan 17 years of age. His aunt retained Porter as attorney to have herself appointed guardian for Roy. Porter later sued Roy to recover $760 as the fee agreed to by Roy for legal services rendered prior to the appointment of the guardian. Roy refused to pay the sum on the ground that he was a minor and had disaffirmed the contract. From a judgment in favor of Roy, Porter appealed.

KENISON, C.J. . . . In Hall v Butterfield, 59 N.H. 354, it was held that the minor was required to pay the value of any benefit derived by him under the contract. The common-law rule that a minor was liable for necessaries was thus extended to require the minor to make restitution to the extent that he received a benefit under the contract. "The right to recover for necessaries is given because the infant has derived a benefit therefrom. . . . If benefit obtained by the infant is the test in one case, why not make it the test in all cases? This has been made the test in the case of lunatics and persons *non compos mentis,* and it should be applied in the case of infants. The true rule is that the contract of an infant or lunatic, whether executed or executory, cannot be rescinded or avoided without restoring to the other party the consideration received, or allowing him to recover compensation for all the benefit conferred upon the party seeking to avoid the contract." . . .

Admittedly the benefit rule represents a minority doctrine, but it has received approval of those who have given the matter serious consideration. . . . We have advanced from the concept of necessaries to the concept that an infant is liable to make restitution for the benefit he receives whether or not classed as necessaries. . . .

The long and short of the matter is that an infant may disaffirm his contracts but he is liable in an action for restitution for the benefit he has received whether or not the benefit is described as necessaries. Legal services in connection with the guardianship of a minor are clearly a benefit to the minor. The defendant is not liable for what he agreed to pay for legal services or the amount charged him but he is liable . . . for the benefit of the legal services he received in such reasonable amount as the Trial Court may determine. . . .

[Judgment reversed and action remanded.]

O'Brien v Small

101 Ohio App 408, 122 NE2d 701 (1954)

Peggy O'Brien purchased a 1952 Hudson automobile from Small when she was a minor. Part of the purchase price was a trade-in of a 1941 Oldsmobile, and part was furnished by a note and a chattel mortgage. Several months later the finance company repossessed the automobile when installment payments were not made. O'Brien then sued Small to set aside the contract and to obtain the refund of what money had been paid on the contract. Small raised the defense that the purchase of the 1952 Hudson had in fact been made by Peggy's adult husband with his money and that the title to the automobile had been placed in Peggy's name. From a judgment for the minor, Small appealed.

SKEEL, J. . . . [The court first held that the lower court should have submitted to the jury the question whether the minor or her husband had been the other party to the contract with the automobile dealer.]

. . . There is evidence in the record tending to show that the money paid in cash on the purchase of the Hudson automobile, or at least part of it, was the property of Charles O'Brien. This issue should have been submitted to the jury under proper instructions from the court. A minor in disaffirming an executed sale is entitled to recover back only such property as was that of the minor, and which the minor parted with in the transaction. Whether or not the Oldsmobile which was turned in was the property of the plaintiff, or her husband, was also an issue in the case. . . .

. . . It is a well recognized principle of law that an infant is bound by and cannot disaffirm an obligation imposed by law. . . . Funds expended for sales tax . . . , fees expended to secure from the county clerk a certificate of title to a motor vehicle, and for the transfer of automobile license plates, are obligations of the purchaser and are imposed by law. The court was therefore in error in instructing the jury that money paid to the defendant to defray such obligations could be recouped by an infant in disaffirming the purchase of an automobile. . . .

The right of an infant upon the disaffirmance of the purchase of personal property is to receive back that which the infant parted with as consideration for the contract. If the plaintiff was the owner of the property in the Oldsmobile, then upon disaffirmance she would be entitled to have the Oldsmobile returned to her, or, if the other party to the contract has put it beyond his power to return the automobile, then the value thereof would be the basis of recovery. . . .

[Judgment reversed and action remanded.]

Gastonia Personnel Corporation v Rogers

276 NC 279, 172 SE2d 19 (1970)

Bobby Rogers, 19, married, quit school, and looked for work. He agreed with the Gastonia

Personnel Corporation, an employment agency, that if he obtained employment through it, he would pay a stated commission. Rogers obtained work through the agency but refused to pay the agreed commission of $295 for which he denied liability on the ground of infancy. From a judgment in favor of Rogers, the agency appealed.

BOBBITT, C.J. . . . Under the common law persons, whether male or female, are classified and referred to as *infants* until they attain the age of twenty-one years. . . .

"By the fifteenth century it seems to have been well settled that an infant's bargain was in general void at his election (that is voidable), and also that he was liable for necessaries." . . .

In accordance with this ancient rule of the common law, this Court has held an infant's contract, unless for "necessaries" or unless authorized by statute, is voidable by the infant, at his election, and may be disaffirmed during infancy or upon attaining the age of twenty-one. . . .

"Necessaries . . . embrace boarding; for shelter is as necessary as food and clothing. They have also been extended so as to embrace schooling and nursing. . . . In regard to the quality of the clothes and the kind of food &c., a restriction is added, that it must appear that the articles were suitable to the infant's degree and estate." . . .

[The court noted a number of statutes which had limited the ability of a minor to disaffirm his contracts.]

. . . Without awaiting additional statutory changes, . . . it seems appropriate that this common-law rule, which is rooted in decisions made by judges centuries ago, should be modified at least to the extent set forth below. . . .

In general, our prior decisions are to the effect that the "necessaries" of an infant, his wife, and child, include only such necessities of life as food, clothing, shelter, medical attention, etc. In our view, the concept of "necessaries" should be enlarged to include such articles of property and such services as are reasonably necessary to enable the infant to earn the money required to provide the necessities of life for himself and those who are legally dependent upon him. . . .

The evidence before us tends to show that defendant, when he contracted with plaintiff, was nineteen years of age, . . . married, a high school graduate, within "a quarter or 22 hours" of obtaining his degree in applied science, and capable of holding a job at a starting annual salary of $4,784.00. To hold, as a matter of law, that such a person cannot obligate himself to pay for services rendered him in obtaining employment suitable to his ability, education, and specialized training, enabling him to provide the necessities of life for himself, his wife and his expected child, would place him and others similarly situated under a serious economic handicap.

In the effort to protect "older minors" from improvident or unfair contracts, the law should not deny to them the opportunity and right to obligate themselves for articles of property or services which are reasonably necessary to enable them to provide for the proper support of themselves and their dependents. The minor should be held liable for the reasonable value of articles of property or services received pursuant to such contract. . . .

[Judgment reversed and action remanded.]

Pankas v Bell

413 Pa 494, 198 A2d 312 (1964)

Bell, aged 20 years and 7 months, went to work in the beauty parlor of Pankas and agreed that when he left the employment, he would not work in or run a beauty parlor business within a ten-mile radius of downtown Pittsburgh, Pennsylvania, for a period of two years. Contrary to this provision, Bell and another employee of Pankas opened up a beauty shop three blocks from his shop and advertised themselves as former employees of Pankas. Pankas sued Bell to stop the breach of the noncompetition or restrictive covenant. Bell claimed that he was not bound because he was a minor when he had agreed to the covenant. From a decision for Pankas, Bell appealed.

JONES, J. . . . The issue [is] not one of the liability of a minor for a breach of his contract but whether a minor should be . . . permitted to repudiate his contract without restoring what he had received and, if restoration cannot be made, without being enjoined from making use of the information he had gained from his employment by the plaintiff to the latter's damage. The [lower] court held that the minor should be enjoined "from making use of that information, in violation of his agreement made at the time when he desired and obtained employment, and upon the faith of which he obtained the information and acquaintance" and the court further observed: "No man would engage the services of an infant if he could not impose the same condition for his own protection against the use of his formulas, trade secrets, and lists of customers that he could exact of an adult." . . .

In the case at bar, we need not nor do we decide that a contract for the employment of a minor is an exception to the general rule that the contracts of minors are voidable. What we do determine is that, although this contract is voidable, the minor should not be permitted to utilize any benefits, training, or knowledge derived from such contract to the damage and detriment of his former employer. As a practical matter, to hold otherwise would deter the employment of minors because no person would care to run the risk of employing a person who could not only avoid the contract but also utilize that which he has derived from the contract to compete with his former employer.

Behind the rule rendering voidable the contracts of a minor is the very laudable purpose of the law to protect minors from contracts which may be disadvantageous to them and to protect them "against their own lack of discretion and against the snares of designing persons" . . . . This "protective cloak" is to safeguard the interests of the minor; it is not to be employed as a vehicle whereby the minor is enabled to practice unconscionable business methods. It is a shield for defense, not a sword for offense. In enjoining this minor from using to his own benefit and to the detriment of his former employer that which he has gained from his former employment, we declare that, even though the contract is voidable, the minor is prohibited from exploiting that which he gained from the contract and that equity should restrain such exploitation.

There is no evidence of any fraud or overreaching on Pankas' part, the contract as a whole was beneficial to Bell, and Bell should be enjoined from exploiting that which he gained from his employment by Pankas. . . .

[Decree affirmed.]

QUESTIONS AND CASE PROBLEMS

1. (a) What is the objective of the rule of law that when a minor avoids a contract, he usually cannot recover his property if the other party has transferred it to a third person who did not know of the minority and purchased the property for value?
   (b) How is the evolutionary nature of the law illustrated by the changes in the definition of a minor's necessaries?
2. Saccavino made a contract with Carl Gambardella, then 15 years of age, and Carl's parents, that he would train Carl to be a horse rider and that he would receive in return a share of Carl's earnings from exhibitions and racing. When Saccavino sued on the contract years later, Carl claimed that it was void. Was he correct? [Saccavino v Gambardella, 22 Conn Supp 168, 164 A2d 304]
3. Martinson executed a note payable to Matz. At the time Martinson was drunk. The next day he was told that he had signed the note. Five years later, Martinson's wife told Matz's attorney that Martinson would not pay the note as he was drunk at the time he executed the note. Matz brought suit on the note two years after that. Could he recover? [Matz v Martinson, 127 Minn 262, 149 NW 370]
4. South Dakota, as in many other states, establishes a lesser degree of duty owed by the driver of an automobile to a nonpaying guest passenger than

to a paying passenger. Bruce Boyd was a passenger in an automobile driven by Roger Alguire, aged eighteen. Bruce paid 50 cents toward gasoline expenses at Roger's insistence. There was an accident in which Roger was killed and Bruce was injured. Bruce sued Roger's estate. Floyd, the administrator of Roger's estate, claimed that since Roger was a minor, if there was a contract between Roger and Bruce for the latter to "pay" for his transportation, it was not binding. Bruce, therefore, was merely a guest, in which case a lower duty was owed to him and Bruce would not be able to recover on the facts of the case. Was Bruce a fare-paying passenger or a guest? [Boyd v Alguire, 82 SD 684, 153 NW2d 192]

5. On February 28, 1958, Alice Sosik signed a note promising to make certain payments to Conlon. She later sued to have the note set aside on the ground that she lacked mental capacity. A letter from a physician was presented which stated that he had examined her on July 3, 1959, and that she "is suffering from a chronic mental illness and is totally incapable of managing her affairs." Was she entitled to set the note aside? [Sosik v Conlon, 91 RI 439, 164 A2d 696]

6. A minor girl had a guardian who had been appointed for her estate. She was about to be married and applied to the court for permission to use $3,000 of her estate for the wedding reception for some 100 guests and $1,000 more for furniture. Her estate consisted of money paid to her guardian from an action to recover damages for her father's death. Was she entitled to make such expenditures? [In re Anonymous, 44 Misc 2d 1082, 252 NYS2d 946]

7. Mary McCoy, a married woman, sold land that she owned to Niblick. Her husband did not sign the contract. Niblick moved onto the property before a deed was delivered and made improvements. Later Mary sought to set the contract aside. A Pennsylvania statute provided that a married woman had the same right as an unmarried woman to sell or dispose of her property but that she could not execute a deed to the property without having her husband sign the deed. Who was entitled to the property? [McCoy v Niblick, 221 Pa 123, 70 A 577]

8. *A*, who appeared to be over 21 years of age, purchased an automobile from *B*. He later informed *B* that he was under 21 and avoided the contract. *A* gave as his explanation that there were certain defects in the car. *B* claimed that these defects were trivial. Assuming that the defects were trivial, could *A* avoid the contract? [Rose v Sheehan Buick, (Fla App) 204 So2d 903]

9. In 1936 Palmer was adjudicated incompetent. In 1942 he was adjudicated competent. In 1952 he purchased policies of fire insurance from the Lititz Mutual Insurance Co. The property insured was destroyed by fire. The company refused to pay on the policies on the ground that Palmer was insane when he applied for and obtained the insurance. Was this a valid defense? [Palmer v Lititz Mutual Insurance Co., (DC WD SC) 113 F Supp 857]

10. Gary Muniz, a minor, purchased a dune buggy from Jones. When Gary's father learned of the purchase, he ordered Gary to take the dune buggy back to Jones or dispose of it. While taking the buggy back to Jones Gary was involved in an accident. The father's insurer denied liability on the basis that Gary was not the owner of the dune buggy at the time of the collision because he had avoided the contract. Was the insurer correct? [St. Paul Fire & Marine Ins. Co. v Muniz, Ariz App, 504 P2d 546]

12 Genuineness of Assent

§ **12:1. Introduction.** An agreement is the result of an offer and an acceptance by competent parties. The enforceability of a contract based upon an agreement may be affected, however, because a mistake was made by either or both of the parties or because the assent of one of the parties was obtained through fraud, undue influence, or duress.

MISTAKES

The law does not treat all mistakes the same. Some have no effect whatever; others make the agreement voidable or unenforceable. Mistakes may be unilateral or mutual (bilateral).

§ **12:2. Unilateral Mistake.** Ordinarily a unilateral mistake regarding a fact does not affect the contract unless the agreement states that it shall be void if the fact is not as believed, or unless the mistake is known to or should be recognized by the other party. Similarly, the fact that a party enters into a contract on the basis of incorrect information does not enable him to avoid the contract when the other party to the contract did not know, cause, or have reason to know that a mistake was being made.[1]

A unilateral mistake of law or as to expectations does not have any effect upon the contract. The courts refuse to recognize ignorance of the law as an excuse. If they did, the unscrupulous could avoid their contracts at will by saying that they did not understand the law.

Contrary to the rule that a unilateral mistake has no effect, an exception is made in the case of government construction work. Here a contractor who makes a unilateral mistake in the computation of his bid may retract his bid even though it has been accepted. (See p. 228, Balaban-Gordon Co., Inc. v Brighton Sewer District.)

If one party knows that the other party has made a mistake, the mistaken party is entitled to rescind the contract. In determining whether the offeree knew that the offeror was making a mistake, it is significant that the mistaken offer was not substantially different from the price ordinarily charged or from offers made by other bona fide bidders.[2]

---

[1] Milton J. Werscher Co. v V. E. Machinery Co., 212 Ore 26, 500 P2d 696.
[2] W. C. James, Inc. v Phillips Petroleum Co., (DC D Colo) 347 F Supp 381.

(1) Negligent Mistake As to Nature of Paper. When a party makes a negligent mistake as to the nature of a paper, he is bound according to its terms. For example, when the printed form for applying for a loan to a corporation contained a guaranty by the president of the corporation of the corporate debt, the president signing the application without reading it was bound by this guaranty, even though he did not know it was in the application and the application was headed merely "application for credit." [3] A unilateral mistake as to the provision of a contract, for example, is ordinarily not an excuse from liability of the party who signed the contract without reading it or who only "half read" it before signing.[4]

(2) Mistakes as to Releases. An insurance claimant is bound by the release given by her to the insurance company when at most there was a unilateral mistake on her part as to its meaning resulting from her own carelessness in reading the release.[5]

When a release is given and accepted in good faith, it is initially immaterial that the releasor or both of the parties were mistaken as to the seriousness or possible future consequences of a known injury or condition. If the release covers all claims "known and unknown," the courts following the common-law view hold that the releasor is bound even though there were other injuries of which the releasor was unaware because the effects of the unknown injuries had not yet appeared. Thus, a person involved in an automobile collision cannot seek to recover damages for injuries after having given a release of all claims; as against the contention that he was not bound by his release because he had made a mistake and the injuries which he had sustained proved to be more serious than expected when the release was executed.[6] This is so even when the injured person relies on the insurer's agent for advice. (See p. 230, Walsh v Campbell.) Some courts avoid this conclusion, however, by refusing to give the release effect when the releasor was mistaken as to his injuries.[7]

(3) Identity of Other Party. When the parties deal face to face, a contract is not affected by the fact that one party may be mistaken as to the identity of the other.[8] When the mistake as to the identity of a party is induced by trick or deception of that party, however, the contract is voidable and may be set aside by the deceived party.

(a) OBJECTIVE VERSUS SUBJECTIVE TEST. A different question arises when the parties do not deal face to face. The courts differ as to the effect of such a mistake, influenced by whether they follow the modern objective test of "appearances to a reasonable man" or the old subjective test of

---

[3] Hofmann Co. v Meisner, 17 Ariz App 263, 497 P2d 83.

[4] Dunlap v Warmack-Fitts Steel Co., (CA 8 Ark) 370 F2d 876.

[5] Thomas v Erie Insurance Exchange, 229 Md 332, 182 A2d 823.

[6] Fieser v Stinnett, 212 Kan 26, 509 P2d 1156.

[7] Ranta v Rake, 91 Idaho 376, 421 P2d 747.

[8] Ludwinska v John Hancock Mutual Life Insurance Co., 317 Pa 577, 178 A28.

"meeting of the minds." The objective test is better because the seller, for example, is always in a position to make a credit examination and, if he makes a mistake, it is his own fault. Furthermore, it is illogical to require a buyer to send an inquiring letter to the seller to verify that the seller really knows who the buyer is and intends to make the contract with him. Thus, there is the possibility of a binding contract between an impostor and the person with whom he deals.

§ 12:3. Mutual Mistake. When both parties make the same mistake of fact, the agreement is void. When the mutual or bilateral mistake is one of law, the contract generally is binding. Thus, the fact that both parties to a lease mistakenly believed that the leased premises could be used for boarding animals does not give the tenant a right to rescind the lease for mutual mistake of law, the theory being that in the eyes of the law the parties knew what the zoning regulations allowed.[9] A few courts have refused to follow this rule, and in several states statutes provide that a mutual mistake of law shall have the same vitiating effect as a mutual mistake of fact. A bilateral mistake with respect to expectations ordinarily has no effect on the contract unless the realization of those expectations is made a condition of the contract.

(1) Possibility of Performance. An agreement is void if there is a mutual mistake as to the possibility of performing the agreement. Assume that *A* meets *B* downtown and makes a contract to sell to *B* his automobile, which both believe is in *A's* garage. Actually the automobile was destroyed by fire an hour before the agreement was made. Since this fact is unknown to both parties, there is a mutual mistake as to the possibility of performing the contract, and the agreement is void.[10]

(2) Identity of Subject Matter. An agreement is void if there is a mutual mistake as to the identity of the subject matter of the contract. (See p. 231, Ouachita Air Conditioning, Inc. v Pierce.) For example, if a buyer and seller discuss the sale of an electrical transformer, but one is thinking of a one-phase transformer and the other is thinking of a three-phase transformer, there is no contract.

The same result could be obtained by applying the rule that a contract must be certain in all of its material terms. If the contract does not specify which type of transformer is being purchased, an essential term is lacking and there is no contract.

(3) Collateral Matters. When a mutual mistake occurs as to a collateral matter, it has no effect on the contract thereafter executed. For example, where the plaintiff asks the fire insurer to issue a policy to protect her if there were no existing policy which protected her, and both she and

---

[9] Hoff v Sander, (Mo App) 497 SW2d 651.

[10] UCC § 2-613 (sale of goods).

the insurance company wrongly believed that there was no other policy, the policy which was issued to her was not void because of the mutual mistake that there was no other policy. The mistake was as to a collateral matter; there was no concealment, as the insured had given the insurer all the information which she possessed and the insurer then concluded that the applicant was not already covered; and the circumstances made it clear that the policy had not been issued on the express condition that it was binding only if there were no other policy protecting the applicant.[11]

§ 12:4. Misrepresentation. Suppose that one party to a contract makes a statement of fact which is false but that he does so innocently without intending to deceive the other party. Can the other party set aside the contract on the ground that he was misled by the statement? It is often held he cannot. In certain instances, however, the law protects the deceived person by permitting him to avoid the contract.

Equity will permit the rescission of the contract when the innocent misstatement of a material fact induces another to make the contract. If the deceived person is a defendant in an action at law, it is generally held that he cannot use as a defense the fact of innocent deception by the plaintiff. There is a tendency, however, for the law courts to adopt the rule of equity. For example, it may be possible for an insurance company to avoid its policy because of an innocent misstatement of a material fact by the applicant. Contracts between persons standing in confidential relationships, such as guardian and ward or parent and child, can be set aside for the same reason.

When a person gives an expert opinion for the purpose of guiding a third person in a business transaction, in which both the expert and the third person are financially interested, there is an ordinary tort duty upon the expert to exercise due care in making his statements. Consequently, when he negligently, although innocently, misrepresents the facts, he is liable to the third person. (See p. 232, Maxey v Quintana.) For example, when a bank that contemplates lending money to a small business informs the federal Small Business Administration (SBA) that the business is in good financial condition, whereupon the SBA guarantees the repayment of the loan which the bank makes to the small business, the bank owes a duty to the SBA to exercise due care in making its statements. If the bank is negligent in misrepresenting the credit condition of the small business, such misrepresentation, although innocently made, is a defense which the SBA may raise when sued by the bank on its guaranty.[12]

§ 12:5. Concealment. Generally one party cannot set aside a contract because the other party failed to volunteer information which the complaining party would desire to know. Ordinarily a failure to inform the other party of something which he would like to know is not fraudulent. For example, where a

[11] Hanover Ins. Co. v Hoch, (Tex Civ App) 469 SW2d 717 (CA5 Tex).

[12] First National Bank v Small Business Administration, (CA5) 429 F2d 280. In effect, this is a type of malpractice rather than a fraud liability.

seller and buyer entered into a settlement agreement of their differences, it was not fraudulent for the seller to fail to inform the buyer that the seller would not do any further business with the buyer, the buyer believing that their business relationship would continue if the dispute were put out of the way by the settlement agreement.[13] If *A* does not ask *B* any questions, *B* is not under any duty to make a full statement of material facts.

There is developing in the law a duty on the seller to inform the buyer of some particular fact of which the buyer is not likely to have knowledge and because of its unusual character would not be likely to inquire of the seller. For example, the owner of a house must inform the prospective buyer that several years before there had been a severe fire in the house, even though the house at the time of sale was structurally sound and had been repaired shortly after the fire so that no signs of fire damage were visible. The failure to disclose such information was held to constitute fraud entitling the buyer to recover damages from the seller.

By this trend the seller of property must disclose to the buyer any defect of which he has knowledge when the circumstances are such that it is not reasonable to expect the buyer to learn the true condition for himself. Silence of the seller in such a case is held to be fraudulent concealment. This rule has been the law in Louisiana for many years in consequence of its civil law background. Under the Louisiana statute "the seller, who knows the vice of the thing he sells and omits to declare it" is liable to the buyer for the refund of the purchase price, damages, and a reasonable attorney's fee. Under this rule it has been held that where a house was subject to flooding from a neighboring river, the seller was required to volunteer that fact to his buyer and where there was no such disclosure, the buyer could cancel the contract and obtain the recovery authorized by the statute.[14]

Similarly, in transactions between banks there seems to be a growing concept of a duty to disclose information which one bank should foresee would be desired by another bank even though the latter had not specifically requested the information.[15]

Likewise, an owner is liable if he does not inform a contractor of subsoil difficulties known to the owner which the contractor will encounter in the performance of a contract. The fact that the owner includes in the contract a provision requiring the contractor to make an examination of the "site of the work" does not alter the obligation of the owner to inform the contractor of nonapparent subsoil conditions.[16]

(1) Confidential Relationship. If *A* and *C* stand in a confidential relationship, such as that of attorney and client, *A* has a duty to reveal anything

[13] Southwest E & T Suppliers, Inc. v American Enka Corp., (CA5 Tex) 463 F2d 1165.

[14] Ford v Broussard, (La App) 248 So2d 629.

[15] Lehigh Valley Trust Co. v Central National Bank, (CA5 Tex) 409 F2d 989.

[16] City of Salinas v Souza & McCue Constr. Co., 66 Cal App 2d 217, 57 Cal Rptr 357, 424 P2d 921.

that is material to *C's* interests, and his silence is given the same effect as though he had knowingly made a false statement that there was no material fact to be told *C*. In such a case *C* can avoid the contract.

(2) Disclosure in Installment Loan. The form on page 219 illustrates the disclosures required by the Consumer Credit Protection Act (CCPA) in an installment loan statement. It appears as Exhibit E in the pamphlet, "What You Should Know About Federal Reserve Regulation Z," prepared by the Board of Governors of the Federal Reserve System.

(3) Fine Print. An intent to conceal may be present when a printed contract or document contains certain clauses in such fine print that it is reasonable to believe that the other contracting party will never take the time nor be able to read such information.

Originally it was probably likely that such fine print was purposely used to conceal from the reader what was stated in the fine print. Today it may more likely be the result of the desire to save paper costs. There is also an element of avoiding "customer shock." If you wish to rent a house and are asked to sign a 10-page printed lease, you might hesitate to rent from that particular landlord. When, however, he hands to you one large folded sheet printed in small type, you do not have the same "customer shock" because you do not realize that all of the 10 pages of material have been squeezed onto the one large folded sheet. Also the seller may wish to avoid the asking of many questions by its customers, and does so by putting the question-provoking provisions in such small print that the customer overlooks them.

In some instances the legislature has outlawed certain fine-print contracts. Statutes commonly declare that insurance policies may not be printed in type of smaller size than designated by the statute. Consumer protection statutes designed to protect the credit buyer frequently require that particular clauses be set in large type. When a merchant selling goods under a written contract disclaims the obligation that goods be fit for their normal use, the Uniform Commercial Code requires the waiver to be set forth in "conspicuous" writing [17] which is defined as requiring "a term or clause . . . [to be] so written that a reasonable person against whom it is to operate ought to have noticed it. A printed heading in capitals . . . is conspicuous. Language in the body of a form is 'conspicuous' if it is in larger or other contrasting type or color. . . ." [18]

There is a growing trend to treat a fine-print clause as not binding upon the party who would be harmed thereby, without considering whether fraud was involved. This conclusion may be legalistically justified on the basis that the person prejudiced by the clause did not know of its existence and could not reasonably be expected to have known of its existence, and therefore the fine-print clause was not one of the terms agreed to by the parties.

---

[17] UCC § 2-316(2).

[18] § 1-201(10).

DISCLOSURE STATEMENT OF LOAN

BORROWERS (NAMES AND ADDRESSES): **LENDER:** **LOAN NO.**________ **Date**________

(STREET ADDRESS)

(CITY) (STATE) (ZIP)

TOTAL OF PAYMENTS	**FINANCE CHARGE**	AMOUNT FINANCED	**ANNUAL PERCENTAGE RATE:**	CREDIT LIFE INSURANCE CHARGE	DISABILITY INSURANCE CHARGE	PROPERTY INSURANCE CHARGE
$	$	$	%	$	$	$

PAYABLE IN:	DUE DATE OF PAYMENTS			AMOUNT OF PAYMENTS			RECORDING FEE
CONSECUTIVE MONTHLY INSTALLMENTS	FIRST:	OTHERS: SAME DAY OF EACH MONTH	FINAL:	FIRST: $	OTHERS: $	FINAL: $	$

INSURANCE

PROPERTY INSURANCE, if written in connection with this loan, may be obtained by borrower through any person of his choice. If borrower desires property insurance to be obtained through the creditor, the cost will be $________ for the term of the credit.

CREDIT LIFE AND DISABILITY INSURANCE is not required to obtain this loan. No charge is made for credit insurance and no credit insurance is provided unless the borrower signs the appropriate statement below:

(a) The cost for Credit Life Insurance alone will be $________ for the term of the credit.

(b) The cost for Credit Life and Disability Insurance will be $________ for the term of the credit.

I desire Credit Life and Disability Insurance.	I desire Credit Life Insurance only.	I DO NOT want Credit Life or Disability Insurance.
(Date) (Signature)	(Date) (Signature)	(Date) (Signature)

REBATE FOR PREPAYMENT IN FULL. If the loan contract is prepaid in full by cash, a new loan, refinancing or otherwise before the final installment date, the borrower shall receive a rebate of precomputed interest computed under the Rule of 78's.

DEFAULT CHARGE. [The creditor should set forth the amount, or method of computing the amount, of any default, delinquency, or similar charges payable in the event of late payments.]

SECURITY

DESCRIPTION

A. ☐ This Loan is Secured By a Security Agreement of Even Date covering..........

The Security Agreement will secure future or other indebtedness and will cover after-acquired property.

☐ Motor Vehicle(s): Make: .... Serial No: ....

☐ Household Goods & Appliances of the following description: ....

☐ Other: (Describe) ....

B. ☐ This Loan is Unsecured.

I ACKNOWLEDGE RECEIPT OF A COPY OF THIS STATEMENT.

Witness: .... Borrower: ....

This form is intended solely for purposes of demonstration. It is not the only format which will permit a creditor to comply with disclosure requirements.

Moreover, the supplier of the form containing the fine-print clause should have realized that the victim of the clause would not know nor have reason to know of its existence. As a practical matter, the conclusion is justified by the consideration that the fine-print clause ordinarily appears in a standard printed form of contract prepared by the enterprise and offered to one who has an inferior bargaining position, such as a consumer, and is offered on a "take-it-or-leave-it" basis.

Where air carriers seek to limit liability, such limitations have been held not effective when obscurely set forth in fine print.[19]

Although the Uniform Commercial Code does not establish any general rule governing all fine-print situations, it is likely that the Code concept of "conspicuous" will be applied by courts increasingly in the future, so that no provision in a contract will be deemed a part of the bargain unless the provision is conspicuous or otherwise called to the attention of the other contracting party. Thus, it will be held that a provision which is in fine print, is under a misleading title or heading, or is buried in many unrelated provisions, was not agreed to by the parties and is not binding upon the party who did not know of its existence.[20]

Similarly, it has been held that the buyer was not bound by a fine-print provision in invoices accompanying deliveries of the goods, which provision obligated the buyer to pay the seller's attorney's fees and collection costs and expenses, where the buyer's president had never read the provision and no employee was authorized to make any agreement as to such matters and the invoices were signed by the employee of the buyer who was nearest to the door at the time of delivery.[21]

*(4) **Active Concealment.*** Concealment may be more than the passive failure to volunteer information. It may consist of a positive act of hiding information from the other party by physical concealment, or it may consist of furnishing the wrong information. Such conduct is generally classified and treated as fraud.

§ **12:6. Fraud.** *Fraud* exists when a person makes a misrepresentation of a material fact, known to him to be untrue or made with reckless indifference as to whether it is true, with the intention of causing the other party to enter into a contract, and the other party is entitled to rely thereon and enters into the contract. Conduct that is unethical but which does not satisfy these elements is not fraud. (See p. 233, Houston Oilers, Inc. v Neely.) When one party to the contract is guilty of fraud, the contract is voidable as against the wrongdoer and may be set aside by the injured party.

---

[19] Owens v Italia Societa per Azione, (NY Civil Court) 70 Misc 2d 719, 334 NYS2d 789.

[20] K & S Oil Well Service, Inc. v Cabot Corp. Inc., (Tex Civ App) 491 SW2d 733.

[21] Spanish Fork Packing Co. v House of Fine Meats, Inc., 29 Utah 2d 312, 508 P2d 1186.

In most states the degree of proof as to fraud is the same as in any other civil case, namely that of proving the disputed fact by a preponderance of the evidence. In a minority of states, a higher degree of proof is required, and fraud must be established by clear and convincing evidence.[22]

Some elements of fraud are given a liberal interpretation by the courts. For convenience the following discussion refers to fraudulent statements, but any kind of communication may be involved. The misrepresentation may also be made by conduct as well as by words.

Fraud is not easy to define because the law tries to balance its desire to protect the injured person from the act of the wrongdoer and its unwillingness to protect the careless person from the consequences of his own neglect.

(1) Mental State. The speaker must intend to deceive. This means that he must either know or believe that what he is saying is false and must intend to mislead, or that he is recklessly indifferent as to whether what he says is true or not. The deceiver must intend that the injured party rely upon the statement and be deceived.

(2) Misstatement of Fact. A misstatement of a past or present fact is an essential element of fraud. A statement that a painting is the work of Rembrandt when the speaker knows that it is the work of an art student in a neighboring school, is such a misstatement.

An intentional misrepresentation of the nature of the transaction between the parties is fraudulent. A person is guilty of fraud when he falsely makes another believe that the contract to be signed is not a contract but is a receipt or a petition.

(3) Misstatement of Intention. A misstatement of intention can constitute fraud when a promise is made by a person who does not intend to keep it.[23] To illustrate, a customer purchases goods from a merchant on credit and agrees to pay for them in sixty days. If the customer does not intend to pay for the goods and he does not do so, he is guilty of fraud in misstating his intention. Suppose that the customer had purchased the goods, intending to pay for them, but he discovered later that he was unable to do so or decided later not to pay for them. In that event he would not be guilty of fraud. In any case, however, he would be liable for a breach of contract to pay as he had promised.

Likewise, it is fraud for a franchisor to make false statements as to what it would do for franchisees where the franchisor lacked the capacity and had no intention of keeping the promises.[24]

---

[22] Loyola Federal Savings and Loan Association v Trenchcraft, 17 Md 646, 303 A2d 432.

[23] Snow v Howard Motors, 3 Conn Cir 702, 223 A2d 409.

[24] Headrick v Mut. Supply Co., (Colo App) 497 P2d 701 (franchisor falsely "represented itself to be a financially strong company which, by means of its capable personnel and mass merchandising methods, could support relatively inexperienced franchisees by supplying them with management advice and balanced inventories at competitive prices").

(4) Misstatement of Opinion or Value. Ordinarily a misstatement of opinion or value is not regarded as fraudulent on the theory that the person hearing the statement recognizes or should recognize that it is merely the speaker's personal view and not a statement of fact.

A promotional or sales talk statement as to future events is not fraud. Thus, a statement by a motion picture distributor to a theatre owner that a given picture "should be a 'blockbuster'" does not constitute fraud.[25] However, when the speaker has expert knowledge or information not available to the other and he should realize that his listener relies upon his expert opinion, a misstatement by him of his opinion or of value, if intentionally made, amounts to fraud. By this view a statement of a party having superior knowledge may be regarded as a statement of fact even though it would be considered as opinion if the parties were dealing on an equal basis.[26]

(5) Misstatement of Law. A misstatement of law is treated in the same manner as a misstatement of opinion or value. Ordinarily the listener is regarded as having an opportunity of knowing what the law is, an opportunity equal to that of his speaker, so that he is not entitled to rely on what the speaker tells him. When the speaker has expert knowledge of the law or represents that he has such knowledge, however, his misstatement can be the basis of fraud.

(6) Materiality of Misstatement. Does it make any difference if the misstatement concerns a trivial matter, or must it be something that a reasonable man would regard as material? Generally the misstatement must pertain to a material matter. The Restatement of the Law of Contracts, however, adopts the view that any statement, whether material or not, constitutes fraud if all the other elements are present.[27]

(7) Investigation Before Relying on Statement. If the injured person has available the ready means of determining the truth, as by looking at something in front of him, he cannot rely on the false statement. The fact that he relies on the other person or that he is too busy to examine or read a document before signing it does not protect him. He takes the risk that a paper will state what he thinks it does when he signs it without reading it. When an illiterate person or one physically unable to read signs a paper without having it explained or read to him, he is ordinarily bound by its contents. As a limitation on this rule, however, some courts hold that the negligence of the injured party is not a bar to a claim for damages when the wrongdoer takes active steps to conceal the truth, as by substituting one paper for another and falsely informing the injured party as to the nature of the paper. (See p. 234, Bob Wilson, Inc. v Swann.)

---

[25] Twentieth Century Fox Distributing Corp. v Lakeside Theatres, Inc., (La App) 267 So2d 225.

[26] Vokes v Arthur Murray, (Fla) 212 So2d 906.

[27] Restatement, Contracts, § 471, Comment (i).

Likewise, it has been held that when the seller of a house, in reply to the questions of the buyer, knowingly makes false statements that the house has been repaired and did not leak, the buyer may recover damages for fraud as against the contention that the buyer was barred because he had not investigated the truth of the seller's statement.[28]

If an examination by the injured person does not reveal the defect, or if the injured person cannot be expected to understand what he sees because of its technical nature, or if a simple examination is not available, the injured person may rely on the statements of the other party and raise the issue of fraud when he learns that they are false. A misrepresentation made to prevent further inquiry also constitutes fraud.[29]

(8) Reliance and Damage. A person can complain of the misrepresentation of another only if he was misled by it and acted in reliance on it. If *A* says that his house is in good condition when it is infested with termites but *B* does not buy the house, *B* cannot complain that *A's* statement was false since *B* cannot show that he was harmed in any way. Even if *B* purchased the house, he cannot recover from *A* when it can be shown that *B* knew there were termites and purchased the property anyway or that he did not care because he intended to tear down the house and erect a new building.

When a person seeks to avoid a contract for fraud, it is theoretically immaterial whether the defrauded person is damaged in the sense that he can show a definite financial loss as the result of the fraud. As a practical matter, however, the defrauded person would probably not raise the question if he did not suffer some damage. If the injured person wishes to sue the wrongdoer for damages, as distinguished from avoiding the contract, then he must show that he has sustained a definite loss or injury and the money value thereof.

(9) Who May Complain. The wrongdoer is liable only to the person he intended to deceive. Ordinarily a fraudulent statement is made directly by the wrongdoer to his intended victim. Suppose, however, that unknown to the speaker a third person overhears him or looks at a letter containing his false statement. Can that third person complain of the speaker's fraud when he thereafter relies upon it? Since the speaker did not intend to harm the third person, no liability results.

This rule does not require that the speaker make the misrepresentation directly to the intended victim. If the speaker makes a public announcement, any member of the public defrauded can bring an action against him. As an illustration, if *A*, in organizing a corporation, issues a prospectus that falsely describes the corporation and its financial status, any person who purchases the stock in reliance on that false prospectus may sue *A*.

---

[28] Steadman v Turner, 84 NMex 738, 507 P2d 799.
[29] Rummer v Throop, 38 Wash 2d 624, 231 P2d 313.

When the speaker gives false information to one person intending that it will be communicated to another whom he hopes to deceive, the latter person may sue for fraud.

(10) Use of Assumed Name. The use of an assumed name is not necessarily fraudulent or unlawful. It is such only when the impostor assumes the name of another person or makes up a name for the purpose of concealing his identity from persons to whom he owes money or a duty, or to avoid arrest, or for the purpose of deceiving the person with whom he is dealing, or of imitating the name of a competitor.

In the absence of any intent to evade or deceive by the use of the assumed name, it is lawful for a person to go by any name he chooses, although other persons may refuse to deal with him unless he uses his actual name. If a person makes a contract in an assumed or fictitious name or in a trade name, he will be bound by his contract because that name was in fact intended to identify him.[30]

(a) CHANGE OF NAME. In most states a person may obtain a decree of court officially changing his name upon filing a petition with the court, setting forth the reason for the desired change and satisfactory proof that there is no fraudulent or criminal purpose in effecting the change. In addition, a person's name may be changed as an incident to being adopted; and a woman's name is changed by marriage and may be changed by divorce.

(b) FICTITIOUS NAME REGISTRATION. If a person or a group of persons, other than a corporation, does business under a fictitious name, a statement must generally be filed in a specified government office setting forth the names and addresses of the persons actually owning or operating the business, together with the name, address, and nature of the business. Violation of such a statute is made a crime and, if the statute expressly so declares, prevents the enterprise from bringing suit on a business contract so long as the name is not registered. No violation generally exists, however, when the other contracting party knows the identity of the persons doing business under the unregistered fictitious name.

(11) Fraud as a Tort. Apart from its effect upon the validity of the contract, the fraud of one party is a tort or civil wrong upon the injured party. The injured party may bring a tort action, in which he may recover the money damages that he has sustained as the result of the fraudulent statement.[31]

§ 12:7. Undue Influence. An aged parent may entrust all his business affairs to his son; an invalid may rely on his nurse; a client may follow implicitly whatever his attorney recommends. The relationship may be such that for

[30] Weikert v Logue, 121 Ga App 171, 173 SE2d 268.
[31] See § 4:12.

practical purposes the one person is helpless in the hands of the other. In such cases, it is apparent that the parent, the invalid, or the client is not in fact exercising his free will in making a contract suggested by the son, nurse, or attorney, but it merely following the will of the other person. Such relationships are called *confidential relationships*. Because of the great possibility that the person dominating the other will take advantage of him, the law presumes that the dominating person exerts *undue influence* upon the other person whenever the dominating person obtains any benefit from a contract made by the dominated person. The contract is then voidable and may be set aside by the other person unless the dominating person can prove that no advantage was taken by him.

The class of confidential relationships is not well-defined. It includes the relationships of parent and child, guardian and ward, physician and patient, attorney and client, and any other relationship of trust and confidence in which one party exercises a control or influence over another.

In some states, however, the mere fact that there is a close blood relationship, such as parent and child, does not constitute a confidential fiduciary relationship.[32]

Whether undue influence exists is a difficult question for the court (ordinarily the jury) to determine. The law does not regard every "influence" as undue. Thus, a nagging wife may drive a man to make a contract, but that is not ordinarily regarded as undue influence. Persuasion and argument are not in themselves undue influence.

An essential element of undue influence is that the person making the contract does not exercise his own free will in so doing. In the absence of a recognized type of confidential relationship, such as that between parent and child, the courts are likely to take the attitude that the person who claims to have been dominated was merely persuaded and consequently there was no undue influence.

(1) Domination by Seller. In some instances the domination of the market or of the buyer by a particular seller may make the agreement with a buyer illegal as a violation of the federal antitrust law.

(2) Unequal Bargaining Power. Sometimes the party with the weaker bargaining power has no practical choice although, as far as the rule of law is concerned, his contract is binding as the voluntary act of a free adult person.

Underlying the traditional concept of the law of contracts is the belief that a person can go elsewhere to contract and therefore when he makes a given contract, his contract is necessarily voluntary. But "going elsewhere" may be meaningless when better terms cannot be obtained elsewhere because the entire industry does business on the basis of the terms in question, or when the particular person cannot obtain better terms elsewhere because of his inferior economic standing or bargaining position.

---

[32] Nelson's Estate, 132 Ill App 2d 740, 270 NE2d 65.

When the condition of relative immobility of either party exists, the tendency is to find that the party might be oppressed or exploited and the social forces which oppose such a result come into play.

In some instances the bargaining scales are sought to be balanced by rules of construction. Thus, an insurance contract is strictly construed against the insurer because it is regarded as a standardized "contract of adhesion" prepared by the insurer to which the insured must adhere if he wants to obtain any insurance.

In some areas statutes have been adopted to create equality of bargaining power, such as the Uniform Commercial Code's provision that establishes higher standards for merchants as compared with casual sellers, and the rights given to labor by the labor-management relations statutes. To these may be added the statute permitting exporters to combine for the purpose of the exporting trade so that they can meet the competition of foreign dealers, such privilege creating an exception to the federal antitrust law under which such combinations in foreign commerce would be prohibited.

§ 12:8. Duress. A person can show *duress* if a threat of violence or other harm deprives him of his free will. Whether other persons of similar mentality, physical health, experience, education, and intelligence would have been similarly affected may influence the jury in determining whether the victim had in fact been deprived of his free will. The threat may be directed against a third person who is a near relative of the intimidated person making the contract. Thus, a threat to injure one's parent, child, husband, wife, brother, aunt, grandchild, or son-in-law will be duress if the effect is to prevent the intimidated person from exercising his own free will.

Generally a threat of economic loss, such as a threat to prevent a contractor from securing further credit necessary to obtain building materials, is not regarded as duress. Some courts have held it to be duress when so serious a loss as burning down his house threatened the victim if he did not agree that he in fact was not exercising a free choice when he made the contract. (See p. 235, Austin Instrument, Inc. v Loral Corp.) In any case, in order to prove duress by business or economic compulsion, it is necessary to show that the victim would suffer irreparable loss for which he could not adequately recover, if at all, by suing the wrongdoer. Where the plaintiff leased equipment essential to production and the lessor without justification increased the rental price four times and brought an action to recover possession of equipment, whereupon the plaintiff paid an additional sum of $2,000 to stop such repossession, the plaintiff may recover the $2,000 together with punitive damages from the lessor.[33]

A threat to prosecute a person or a member of his family for a crime is usually held to constitute duress without regard to whether the person is guilty of the crime or not. However, a threat to resort to civil litigation

[33] Aztec Sound Corp. v Western States Leasing Co., — Colo App —, 510 P2d 897.

made in the belief that there is a right to sue is not duress even though the belief is unfounded.

The fact that the threatening party has the right to do that which he threatens to do does not mean that there is no duress. For example, where a corporate employer threatens to fire an employee if the employee does not sell his stock in the corporation to the employer, there is duress although the employment was terminable at will and the discharge of the employee would not constitute a breach of contract. Because of such duress, the agreement of the employee to sell to the employer could be rescinded by the employee.[34]

There is authority that it is duress to induce a person to make a payment or to execute a promissory note by threatening to break a contract if he does not do so, when such breach of contract would cause him substantial loss.[35]

§ **12:9. Remedies.** Mistake, fraud, undue influence, and duress may make the agreement voidable or, in some instances, void. The following remedies are then available.

(1) Rescission. If the contract is voidable, it can be rescinded or set aside by the party who has been injured or of whom advantage has been taken. If he does not elect to avoid it, however, the contract is valid and binding. In no case can the other party, the wrongdoer, set aside the contract and thus profit by his own wrong. If the agreement is void, neither party can enforce it and no act of avoidance is required by either party to set the contract aside.

If the injured party elects to rescind the contract, he is entitled to recover anything that he has paid or given the other in performance of the contract. If the injured party has received any money or property from the wrongdoer, he must return it as a condition to rescission. If restoration is not possible, as when the injured party has spent the money or consumed the property that he has received, or has sold the property to a third person, or has received personal services under the contract, the injured party is generally barred from rescinding the contract.

When a contract is voidable, the right to rescind the contract is lost by any conduct that is inconsistent with an intention to avoid it. For example, when a party realizes that there has been a mistake but continues with the performance of the contract, his right to avoid the contract because of the mistake is lost.[36] Likewise, it is generally held that a contract, although procured by duress, may be ratified by the victim of the duress as by his adhering to the terms of the contract or making claims to benefits arising

---

[34] Laemmar v J. Walter Thompson Co., (CA7 Ill) 435 F2d 680 (stock was subject to an option of the corporation to repurchase when employment ended).

[35] Grad v Roberts, 19 App Div 2d 718, 242 NYS2d 462.

[36] Dayton v Gibbons & Reed Co., 12 Utah 2d 296, 365 P2d 801.

therefrom.[37] The right to rescind the contract is lost if the injured party, with full knowledge of the facts, affirms the transaction, or when, with such knowledge, he fails to object to the guilty party within a reasonable time. In determining whether a reasonable time has expired, the court considers whether the delay benefited the injured party, whether a late avoidance of the contract would cause unreasonable harm to the guilty person, and whether avoidance would harm intervening rights of third persons acquired after the original transaction.

When the contract has resulted in the transfer of property from the guilty person to the victim, the latter also loses the right to rescind if, with knowledge of the true situation, he retains and uses the property, sells it to another, or uses it after the guilty person refuses to take it back.

(2) Damages. If the other party was guilty of a wrong, such as fraud, as distinguished from making an innocent mistake, the injured party may sue him for damages caused by such a wrong. In the case of the sale of goods, the aggrieved party may both rescind and recover damages;[38] but in other contracts, he must choose one. For example, a person rescinding a contract other than a sale of goods because of fraud cannot also recover damages for the fraud.

(3) Reformation of Contract by Court. When the result of a mutual mistake is that a writing does not correctly state the agreement made by the parties, either party can have the court reform the contract to express the intended meaning.[39] Under modern procedures a person may generally sue on the contract as though it had been reformed and recover if he establishes that he is entitled to reformation of the contract and that there has been a breach of the contract as reformed. Thus, instead of first suing to reform an insurance policy and then bringing a second suit on the policy as reformed, most jurisdictions permit the plaintiff to bring one action in which he may prove his case as to reformation and also his case as to the breach of the contract as reformed.

---

[37] Gallon v Lloyd-Thomas Co. (CA8 Mo) 264 F2d 821.

[38] UCC § 2-721. See also § 2-720, providing that, unless a contrary intent clearly appears, an expression of "rescission" of a sale contract will not be treated as a renunciation or discharge of a claim in damages for a prior breach.

[39] Kear v Hausmann, 152 Neb 512, 41 NW2d 850.

CASES FOR CHAPTER 12

Balaban-Gordon Company, Inc. v Brighton Sewer District

41 App Div 2d 246, 342 NYS2d 435 (1973)

The Brighton Sewer District planned to construct two sewage treatment plants. It advertised for bids. Balaban-Gordon Company was the low bidder with a bid of approximately two and one-third million dollars, which was approximately one-half million dollars less than the next bid. Balaban-Gordon had misinterpreted the construction specifications and failed to include

in its bid the cost of certain equipment. Balaban-Gordon notified the sewer district that it was withdrawing its bid because of this mistake. The sewer district refused to let it do so.

SIMONS, J. . . . The case turns on whether this is the type of mistake which justifies relief by rescission. . . . The exercise of ordinary care may not be interpreted narrowly. . . . Each case must be considered on its own facts. . . .

The parties are in agreement that relief is available where the mistake is clerical or arithmetical. . . . In such a case, the mistaken bid does not express the true intention of the bidder. If he were to recompute the bid or if another person were to do so, the obvious error would be discovered and corrected. Its existence may be objectively determined. . . .

On the other hand, it is commonly recognized that a bidder will not be relieved from an error in a value judgment in estimating the requirements or costs necessary to fulfill a contract. . . . Mistakes of this type are inherent business risks assumed by contractors in all bidding situations. If the specifics of the job were recalculated by the bidder, his bid would be the same, for these estimates do not involve oversights. They represent subjective judgments deliberately made with respect to the requirements of the job. Another person calculating the bid might or might not make the same "mistake," depending upon his mental evaluation of the work to be performed. . . .

The appellant claims that the error must be considered one of these two types, either clerical and arithmetical, or an error of judgment, relief by rescission being available in the former case but not in the latter. Since the incorrect interpretation of the specifications was not clerical or arithmetical appellant claims that respondent should be held to the bid and liable. . . . Unfortunately, not all mistakes made by contractors are categorized so easily. Applying the reasoning of the two types of mistakes to the facts of this case illustrates the difficulty. If respondent's representatives were to recompute its bid, they doubtless would interpret the specifications the same way. In that sense, the bid accurately represented the contract respondent was willing to make. . . . Nevertheless, the error was objectively discoverable. Another contractor computing the bid would not, and in fact no others did, make the same mistake in interpretation and in that sense the bid did not represent the bid intended because respondent was working under a misapprehension with respect to the particulars called for by the specifications. Reasonable care probably dictated that respondent should have asked the engineers to clarify the meaning of the ambiguous specifications (at least one other bidder did so), but respondent's failure to investigate should not prevent it from obtaining relief.

. . . Manifestly, rescission may be allowed more readily for a mistake made by a bidder which is objectively established and which does not evolve from an inherent risk of business. Even though the mistake is the product of negligence on the part of the bidder, relief should be granted because the assurance exists from the objective proof that the transaction is free from mischief. This satisfies a fundamental purpose of the public bidding statutes.

The error in this case did not pertain to an evaluation of risks or estimation of requirements or costs by the bidder and the effect of the mistake was verifiable in much the same way as a clerical error, . . . the impossibility of performance . . . or an arithmetical error. . . . That being the case, it should be excused and rescission granted. In these days of multi-million dollar construction contracts, the public interest requires stability in bidding of public contracts under rules that protect against chicane and overreaching. Nevertheless, little is to be gained if a contractor is forced to perform a contract at an extravagant loss or the risk of possible bankruptcy. If a mistake has been made under circumstances justifying relief, the municipality should not be allowed to enforce the bargain. Its remedy to avoid loss is to award the contract to the next bidder or assume the responsibility of rebidding.

The judgment granting respondent rescission of its bid and cancelling the bond should therefore be affirmed.

Walsh v Campbell

130 Ga App 194, 202 SE2d 657 (1973)

The automobile of Mr. and Mrs. Walsh was struck by the automobile of Campbell. Mrs. Walsh was injured. Campbell had no insurance. Mrs. Walsh notified the State Farm Insurance Company with which she had uninsured motorist coverage. Neff, the adjuster for State Farm told her that the maximum amount which could be paid under the policy was $107.95. This was not true but Mrs. Walsh relied on Neff's statements and released her claim on receiving that amount. Thereafter Mrs. Walsh learned that the coverage of the policy was greater than represented and she repudiated the release and demanded a greater payment. State Farm insisted that the release was binding. The Walshes sued Campbell and State Farm. From a judgment in favor of State Farm, they appealed.

HALL, P.J. . . . Appellants allege that they did not read the pertinent provision of the policy, which was at all relevant times in their possession, nor did they read the release before executing it at their home before the adjuster arrived to pick it up. Both appellants are now and were at all pertinent times able to read and write.

Subsequent to these events, Mrs. Walsh continued to have difficulties with her neck, requiring costly treatment and finally surgery. Eventually an attorney was consulted, the release was attempted to be repudiated, and the settlement amount plus interest was tendered back to State Farm which declined to accept it. . . .

In the trial court, State Farm was granted summary judgment on the basis of the release, and this appeal followed.

Appellants' contentions on appeal are . . . that the court below erred in giving effect to the release because in obtaining it State Farm misrepresented the coverage of the uninsured motorist provision of appellants' policy, and in failing to read it for themselves appellants were justified by a confidential or fiduciary relationship which they enjoyed with State Farm by virtue of having done business for some years with that company and by virtue of State Farm's reassuring advertising implying that it would take care of its insureds. They urge that the signing of the release was prompted by the adjuster's misrepresentation that it was merely a formality allowing State Farm to recover over against Campbell, and by their own unilateral mistake of Mrs. Walsh's injuries. They additionally argue that Mrs. Walsh should not be barred by the release because in payment for her execution of it she received no recompense for personal injuries. . . .

. . . Plaintiffs assert that two items were misrepresented to them: the coverage of their policy and the contents of the release—neither of which they read for themselves. Under Georgia law, absent special circumstances plaintiffs may attack a contract in a court of law on grounds of fraud only where they have exercised due diligence in protecting themselves, instead of merely relying blindly upon representations of another later claimed to have been false. . . . The same rule requiring diligence applies where plaintiff alleges no fraud but a mutual mistake of fact . . . and it applies in the specific situation in which plaintiff claims that what was misrepresented to him was the contents of a contract which he could have read for himself but failed to read. . . . "Where from all the allegations of the pleader it appears that he showed no diligence in ascertaining the nature of the contract he signed, neither a court of law nor equity will relieve him of the consequences." . . .

Though claiming that the agent falsely represented that $107.95 was the maximum amount payable, appellants in their brief . . . state here that Mrs. Walsh asked Mr. Neff for payment under the policy provision *only* of an amount for auto repairs and her husband's lost time from work. It was in response to this request that he quoted the figure of $107.95. On her deposition, Mrs. Walsh was asked whether she had ever pressed Mr. Neff on the question of whether that was all he would pay, or whether she had ever demanded more. Her answers were negative. Review of the record fails to uncover any indication that either of the appellants ever even asked whether personal injuries were compensable to any extent under the uninsured motorist provision of their policy. . . .

Plaintiffs could have studied their own policy, and chose not to do so. They could have scrutinized the release and learned that it was more than merely an instrument allowing State Farm to seek recovery against Campbell. They chose not to do so. Under the decisions and reasoning set out above, they may not now make the opposite choice, unless they had some specific right to rely upon the adjuster's representations without using diligence in their own behalf. To meet this point, the Walshes argue that they enjoyed a confidential relationship with State Farm. . . .

A confidential relationship . . . exists where one party is able "to exercise a controlling influence over the will, conduct, and interest of another; or where, from similar relationship of mutual confidence the law requires the utmost good faith. . . ." The posture of an insured making a claim against his own insurer does not fall within this definition but is one of antagonistic interests.

. . . We note the general rule that the mere insured-insurer relationship will not place fiduciary responsibilities upon the insurer. . . .

. . . The mere fact that one reposes great trust and confidence in another does not serve to create a confidential relationship . . .; nor will a past course of dealings between the parties serve to do so. . . . Even though appellants claim that State Farm seductively advertised that "Like a good neighbor, State Farm is there," this does not change the relationship. For that matter, under Georgia law one does not have a confidential relationship with his "good neighbor." While such advertising may be of dubious accuracy, we nevertheless rule that it does not create a confidential relationship. . . .

[Judgment affirmed.]

Ouachita Air Conditioning, Inc. v Pierce

(La App) 270 So2d 595 (1972)

Ouachita Air Conditioning Company installed an Amana condenser in Pierce's home to replace the York condenser of his air conditioning system. Pierce did not pay for the replacement condenser and Ouachita sued him for the purchase price. He raised the defense that he was not liable because of a mutual mistake of fact.

HALL, J. . . . Defendant's home was equipped with a four-ton York air conditioning system which had originally been engineered and installed by Ballard's, a York distributor. The unit was not cooling properly so defendant called a Mr. Walters, who had been servicing the unit and who was with Ballard's at the time the unit was installed. Walters said he was no longer in the air conditioning repair business and suggested that defendant contact Mr. Lawler, who is president of Ouachita Air Conditioning, Inc. Defendant checked with Ballard's and was informed that Lawler formerly worked for that company when they were installing air conditioners. Defendant then called Lawler and asked him to come out and check the unit and repair it.

Lawler handled Amana air conditioning units and advertised generally as an Amana dealer but this fact was never communicated by Lawler to defendant.

Upon checking defendant's unit, Lawler found that one of the two two-ton compressors was burned out and needed replacing and the other compressor was not working properly. That night Lawler telephoned defendant and suggested that the two compressors be replaced with one four-ton condensing unit. Lawler quoted defendant a price and in answer to defendant's inquiry, assured defendant that the new unit carried a five-year warranty. Defendant agreed to the price and instructed Lawler to go ahead and install the new unit which Lawler advised was on order and should arrive in a few days. The brand name of the new unit was never mentioned. Defendant never stated that he was expecting a York unit to be installed and Lawler never advised defendant he intended to install an Amana unit.

When the new unit arrived, Lawler installed it at plaintiff's home replacing the two York compressors which he removed from the premises. That evening defendant observed that the new unit installed was an Amana unit and he immediately telephoned Lawler and told him that he was expecting a York unit and did not want any brand other than York. Some discussion and negotiations were had between Lawler and defendant about getting a York unit in place of the Amana but they could not agree on the extra cost, particularly as to who should bear the additional installation expense. Defendant made other arrangements and had a new York unit installed and asked Lawler to pick up the Amana unit which he refused to do. This suit followed.

Plaintiff takes the position that it entered into a contract with defendant for the sale and installation of a four-ton condensing unit of unspecified brand at an agreed price and that plaintiff fulfilled its end of the contract by installing a new unit equivalent to the old one and capable of performing the required mechanical function. Plaintiff contends that if there was error or mistake on the part of defendant as to the brand of unit to be installed such error was unilateral and was unknown to plaintiff and cannot serve as the basis for invalidating the contract. . . .

Defendant contends that there was never a completed contract or sale between the parties because there was never a meeting of the minds as to the object of the sale. . . . Defendant further contends that if there was a completed contract it is subject to rescission for error as to the substance or object. . . .

There is nothing in the evidence to indicate that either party acted other than in complete good faith and the testimony of both Lawler and Pierce was straightforward and frank. The evidence supports a finding that Lawler honestly believed that since no brand was specified the agreement was simply for a four-ton condensing unit which would do a job equivalent to the one being replaced. The evidence equally supports a finding that Pierce honestly believed that since they were discussing replacement of a major component part of a complete York system, then the replacement unit would be of the same brand. This belief on the part of defendant was entirely reasonable in view of the fact that he was put in contact with plaintiff through a York serviceman and a York distributor and Lawler was recommended as being experienced in repairing York units.

. . . In this instance the contract of sale was never perfected because there was no . . . agreement as to the thing or object. Otherwise stated, there was error of fact as to the thing or object which vitiated consent. . . .

. . . There was error of fact as to the quality of the object, that is, the manufacturer of the unit, and that this quality was a principal cause of making the contract from defendant's standpoint. While the seller did not have actual knowledge that this was a principal cause or motive it should be presumed that he knew it from the nature of the transaction. . . . Although Lawler was in good faith, when he was confronted with a complete York system in which a major component needed replacing he should have been aware that without anything being said to the contrary, the buyer would expect replacement with the same brand of unit. The trial court was correct in setting aside the sale and rejecting plaintiff's demands. . . .

[Judgment affirmed.]

Authors' Comment: This case was decided in a non-UCC jurisdiction but it rests on general principles of contract law. These principles would be recognized in a UCC state as they have not been displaced by the UCC (UCC § 1-103) and would be recognized generally in situations not governed by the Uniform Commercial Code.

Maxey v Quintana

84 NM 38, 499 P2d 356 (1972)

Maxey purchased a house from Quintana. Dailey was the real estate agent. Daily innocently but wrongly stated that the property was subject to a VA mortgage. Actually it was subject to an FHA mortgage. The interest payments under an FHA mortgage were greater than under a VA mortgage. Maxey was required to pay the greater amount of interest. He did so and then sued Quintana to recover the difference between the interest payments under the two kinds of mortgages. Quintana defended on the ground that the misrepresentation had not been intentionally made and that therefore

damages could not be recovered. From a judgment in favor of Quintana, Maxey appealed.

Wood, C.J. . . . The basis of this contention involves the difference between rescission of a contract and damages for fraud or deceit in connection with the contract. Rescission may be effected without regard to the good faith with which a misrepresentation is made. . . . To recover damages for fraud or deceit, the misrepresentation must be knowingly or recklessly made with intent to deceive. . . .

Ham v Hart, 58 N.M. 550, 273 P2d 748 (1954) states: ". . . we can see no difference in the principle involved in an action at law for damages and a suit in equity for rescission. . . ." Thus, under Ham v Hart, supra, in a suit for damages, it was immaterial whether the defendant acted honestly and in good faith. . . .

Hockett v Winks, 82 N.M. 597, 485 P2d 353 (1971) states: ". . . insofar as the opinion in Ham v Hart, supra, held that the principle of equity applicable to the rescission of contracts is applicable in the tort of deceit (or fraud and deceit as it is sometimes called), undertook to modify the essential elements of the tort of deceit, or sought to create a new tort predicated upon the stated principle of equity, we disavow and hereby overrule that opinion."

Hockett v Winks, supra, made it clear that New Mexico law retains the distinction between the proof required for rescission and the proof required to obtain damages for fraud or deceit. Dailey relies on Hockett v Winks, supra, in contending that "negligent misrepresentation" provides no basis for relief.

This contention, in our opinion, extends the decision in Hockett v Wings, supra, beyond the words used by our New Mexico Supreme Court. The language used states three things—(1) the elements of the tort of fraud or deceit have not been modified, (2) whether a defendant acted honestly and in good faith *is* material to the tort of fraud or deceit, and (3) there is no damage action based solely on facts under which there may be a rescission.

Here, we deal with the claim that misrepresentations occurred and that the misrepresentations were negligently made to plaintiffs' damage. In our opinion neither Ham v Hart, supra, nor Hockett v Winks, supra, addressed themselves to this situation. This situation involves neither rescission nor the tort of fraud or deceit.

Where a plaintiff is so circumstanced that he cannot or does not wish to rescind, and cannot meet the proof required for the tort of fraud or deceit, is he without a remedy for damages caused by a misrepresentation short of fraud? . . .

. . . [Formerly] various courts held that . . . , negligent misrepresentation was not included in the action for fraud or deceit . . . and that the wrong of negligent misrepresentation was without a remedy. . . . Several . . . courts . . . have carried over the negligence action itself from tangible injuries to economic loss, and have allowed recovery in such an action. This position has prevailed, and the negligence action is now generally allowed for negligent misrepresentation, even though it caused only pecuniary harm. . . ." . . .

We hold that negligent misrepresentation is an action upon which relief can be granted, that it is a tort determined by the general principles of the law of negligence and that it is an action separate from the action of fraud or deceit. . . .

[Judgment reversed and action remanded.]

Houston Oilers, Inc. v Neely

(CA10 Okla) 361 F2d 36 (1966)

On December 1, 1964, Neely, a senior in college, made a contract to play the following year for the Houston Oilers professional football team. It was agreed orally that the making of this contract would be kept secret so that Neely would appear to be eligible for a postseason college game. Neely then received a better offer from the Dallas Cowboys and after college went to play for them. Houston sought an injunction against Neely. Neely claimed that the contract with Houston could not be enforced by Houston because of its fraud in stating that the contract would be effective on January 2, 1965, and then in filing the contract with the League Commissioner before that time in violation of the agreement to keep the execution of the contract secret

so as to make him appear eligible for the post-season college football game. From a decision in Neely's favor, Houston appealed.

PICKETT, C.J. . . . Neely was over the age of 21 years, and it is stipulated that he had "special, exceptional, unique knowledge, skill, and ability as a football player." He was competent to enter into a valid contract to perform these services exclusively for a designated person or organization, and upon agreeing to so limit his services, he was subject . . . to be enjoined from performing them for anyone else. . . .

. . . The essence of Neely's contentions . . . is that the contracts are unenforceable because Houston falsely represented that the effective date of the agreement would be January 2, 1965, and that Houston's filing of the contract copies with the Commissioner was a violation of its promise to keep the matter secret. The trial court was of the opinion that these alleged misrepresentations constituted fraud in the inducement of the contract which would subject it to rescission. As has been heretofore stated, each contract specifically provides otherwise. Neely does not say that he was so naive that he did not know his eligibility for further intercollegiate football competition would be destroyed when he signed a professional football contract and received the bonus money. . . . The purpose of secrecy surrounding the execution of the contracts was not to preserve Neely's eligibility, but rather to prevent his ineligibility from becoming known. . . .

Neely, a bright young man, ably advised by his father-in-law, knew exactly what he wanted. With commendable foresight, he sought not only a favorable contract, but also a business arrangement extending beyond his football days. Houston, through its president, undertook to meet this requirement. Neely, after consulting his wife and father-in-law, . . . accepted Houston's final proposal, which he characterized as a "fine offer." Unexpectedly Dallas arrived on the scene, and Neely found another bidder for his services. He welcomed this new opportunity, and apparently plans were set in motion designed to convince him that he could ignore the existing agreements with Houston. . . .

There is insufficient evidence to sustain a finding of material misrepresentation on the part of Houston amounting to fraud which would affect the validity of the contracts. It is true that Neely testified that it was his understanding that the contracts were not to become effective until after the game on January 2. The contracts, however, provided otherwise, and we are not at liberty to rewrite them. Furthermore, the letter of employment, . . . and the $25,000 bonus check which was delivered upon the execution of the contracts, were all dated December 1, 1964. . . .

While it is not contended here that Houston did not have a legal right to sign Neely to a professional player's contract, it is urged that when Houston participated in a scheme to conceal that fact for the purpose of permitting an ineligible player to participate in a postseason game, it was such deceit upon others that a court of equity should not intervene to assist in the enforcement of the contract. With this argument we cannot agree. It is neither unlawful nor inequitable for college football players to surrender their amateur status and turn professional at any time. Neely was free to bind himself to such a contract on December 1, 1964, as he would have been after January 2, 1965. Nor was Houston under any legal duty to publicize the contract or to keep it secret. Its agreement to keep secret that which it had a legal right to keep secret cannot be considered inequitable or unconscionable. . . .

[Judgment reversed and action remanded with instructions to grant the injunction.]

Bob Wilson, Inc. v Swann

(Dist Col App) 168 A2d 198 (1960)

Swann traded in his old car and purchased a used car from Bob Wilson, Inc. The latter's President, Lenoff, wrote down the terms of the sale on a top sheet and then requested Swann to sign the top sheet and the sheets underneath, stating that they were duplicates. Lenoff thereafter had Swann acknowledge each of the sheets before a notary public and write in the margin of each sheet, "We have read this contract; it is correct and complete." Swann did not read the

contract and did not see that the copies had additional interest and charges totaling $613.20 which he was required to pay. He sued the company for overcharging him. From a judgment in his favor, the company appealed.

QUINN, A.J. . . . It is settled that one who refrains from reading a contract and in conscious ignorance of its terms voluntarily assents thereto will not be relieved from his bad bargain. The question whether the same risk falls upon a person who has been disarmed by fraud has not received uniform treatment. The approach taken by some jurisdictions denies redress where the party victimized neglected available means to discover the duplicity. Other courts, adopting what commentators regard as the better view, afford relief where misrepresentation has induced a party to forego the ordinary precaution of investigation. The fact that by so doing the party exercised less vigilance than most people would have employed under the circumstances does not protect the wrongdoer.

We need not consider here whether appellee Swann was unreasonable in trusting Lenoff's representations and in failing to insist on an examination of the papers before signing. In Stern v Moneyweight Scale Co., (1914), 42 App DC 162, the United States Court of Appeals for the District of Columbia ruled that fraud constituted a good defense to a contract which appellee's salesman had misrepresented despite appellant's apparent lack of good judgment in accepting the former's word without question. Such misconduct has also served as a basis for setting aside a contract, and, we believe, warrants a recovery at law. The record shows that Lenoff deliberately sought to mislead Swann and was successful in the attempt. Appellant may not shield itself from the consequences of its agent's deception by saying that Swann should not have been fooled.

[Judgment affirmed.]

Austin Instrument, Inc. v Loral Corporation
29 NY2d 124, 324 NYS2d 22, 272 NE2d 533 (1971)

Loral was awarded a $6 million contract by the United States Navy for the production of radar sets. To perform this contract, Loral required 40 precision-gear component parts. It advertised for bids on these parts and let a subcontract to Austin to supply 23 of the gear parts. In the following year Loral was awarded a second Navy contract. Austin declared that it would not make further deliveries under its subcontract unless Loral agreed to a price increase, both as to parts already delivered and parts to be delivered and also unless Loral gave Austin a subcontract under the second Navy contract for all 40 component gear parts. Loral did not want to increase the prices under the original contract and wished to let subcontracts for parts under the second Navy contract on the basis of individual subcontracts for each part with the lowest bidder thereon. Loral communicated with 10 manufacturers of precision gears but could find none that could supply gears in time to perform its contract with the Navy. Loral then agreed to the price increase in connection with the first Navy contract and awarded Austin the subcontract for all 40 parts under the second Navy contract. After performance of the contracts was completed, Austin sued Loral for the balance due under the contracts. Loral sued Austin to recover the amount of the price increase on the theory that such increase had been agreed to under economic duress. The lower court dismissed Loral's claim and it appealed.

FULD, C.J. . . . A contract is voidable on the ground of duress when it is established that the party making the claim was forced to agree to it by means of a wrongful threat precluding the exercise of his free will. . . . The existence of economic duress or business compulsion is demonstrated by proof that "immediate possession of needful goods is threatened" . . . or, more particularly, in cases such as the one before us, by proof that one party to a contract has threatened to breach the agreement by withholding goods unless the other party agrees to some further demand. . . . However, a mere threat by one party to breach the contract by not delivering the required items, though wrongful, does not in itself constitute economic duress. It must also appear that the threatened party could not obtain the goods from another source of supply and that the ordinary remedy of an action for breach of contract would not be adequate.

We find without any support in the record the conclusion reached by the courts below that Loral failed to establish that it was the victim of economic duress. On the contrary, the evidence makes out a classic case, as a matter of law, of such duress.

It is manifest that Austin's threat—to stop deliveries unless the prices were increased—deprived Loral of its free will. As bearing on this, Loral's relationship with the Government is most significant. . . . Its contract called for staggered monthly deliveries of the radar sets, with clauses calling for liquidated damages and possible cancellation on default. Because of its production schedule, Loral was, in July, 1966, concerned with meeting its delivery requirements in September, October and November, and it was for the sets to be delivered in those months that the withheld gears were needed. Loral had to plan ahead, and the substantial liquidated damages for which it would be liable, plus the threat of default, were genuine possibilities. Moreover, Loral did a substantial portion of its business with the Government, and it feared that a failure to deliver as agreed upon would jeopardize its chances for future contracts. . . . It was perfectly reasonable for Loral, or any other party similarly placed, to consider itself in an emergency, duress situation. . . .

Loral . . . also had the burden of demonstrating that it could not obtain the parts elsewhere within a reasonable time, and . . . it met this burden. The 10 manufacturers whom Loral contacted comprised its entire list of "approved vendors" for precision gears, and none was able to commence delivery soon enough. As Loral was producing a highly sophisticated item of military machinery requiring parts made to the strictest engineering standards, it would be unreasonable to hold that Loral should have gone to other vendors, with whom it was either unfamiliar or dissatisfied, to procure the needed parts. . . . Loral "contacted all the manufacturers whom it believed capable of making these parts" . . . and this was all the law requires.

It is hardly necessary to add that Loral's normal legal remedy of accepting Austin's breach of the contract and then suing for damages would have been inadequate under the circumstances, as Loral would still have had to obtain the gears elsewhere. . . . In other words, Loral actually had no choice, when the prices were raised by Austin, except to take the gears at the "coerced" prices and then sue to get the excess back. . . .

In sum, the record before us demonstrates that Loral agreed to the price increases in consequence of the economic duress employed by Austin. Accordingly, the matter should be remanded to the trial court for a computation of its damages. . . .

[Judgment reversed and action remanded.]

QUESTIONS AND CASE PROBLEMS

1. What is the objective of each of the following rules of law?
   (a) One party generally cannot set aside a contract because the other party failed to volunteer information which the complaining party would desire to know.
   (b) In certain close relationships that are regarded as confidential, it is presumed that a contract which benefits the dominating person was obtained by undue influence, and he has the burden of proving the contrary.
2. Tucker purchased an automobile from Central Motors, relying on the representation that it was the latest model available. The sale was completed on February 9. On February 10, Tucker learned that the representation that the automobile was the latest model was false. He continued to drive the car; and after having driven it in excess of one thousand miles, he

demanded on April 7 that the purchase be set aside for fraud. Decide. [Tucker v Central Motors, 220 La 510, 57 So2d 40]

3. An agent of Thor Food Service Corp. was seeking to sell Makofske a combination refrigerator-freezer and food purchase plan. Makofske was married and had three children. After being informed of the eating habits of Makofske and his family, the agent stated that the cost of the freezer and food would be about $95 to $100 a month. Makofske carefully examined the agent's itemized estimate and made some changes to it. Makofske then signed the contract and purchased the refrigerator-freezer. The cost proved to be greater than the estimated $95 to $100 a month, and Makofske claimed that the contract had been obtained by fraud. Decide. [Thor Food Service Corp. v Makofske, 28 Misc 2d 872, 218 NYS2d 93]

4. Roberts, an educated person, purchased real estate from Morrison. Roberts merely "half-read" the contract which she signed. As a result, she did not notice the provision in the contract with respect to interest on the unpaid portion of the purchase price. She refused to pay the interest specified in the contract. Morrison sued her. Could he recover? [Morrison v Roberts, 195 Ga 45, 23 SE2d 164]

5. Jacobs purchased an automobile from Lowell Perkins Agency. She traded in her old car. For some reason she incorrectly believed that she would not be required to pay any sales tax on the purchase of the new car. Lowell asked her to pay $86 to $87 for the tax in addition to the purchase price. She refused to do so and sued to recover her traded-in car. [Lowell Perkins Agency, Inc. v Jacobs, 250 Ark 952, 469 SW2d 89]

6. A corporation had forfeited its charter and plans were under way to sell its business to a buyer. *A* was a major stockholder of the corporation and was concerned because he had become liable on leases of equipment used by the corporation and hoped that the leases could be transfered to the new business, which would then assume payment of the rentals. *B* held a judgment against the corporation and was about to use legal process to enforce the judgment against the equipment which had been leased to and was used by the corporation. *A* promised *B* that *A* would pay the judgment to *B* if *B* would drop the execution against the leased equipment and the corporate assets. *A* did not keep his promise. *B* sued *A* who raised the defense that he had made the promise because of economic duress and therefore was not liable. Was he correct? [Blumenthal v Heron, 261 Md 234, 274 A2d 636]

7. The highway department of the state of Washington advertised for bids for the construction of a section of highway. J. J. Welcome & Sons Construction Company submitted a bid. Thereafter Welcome sent the highway commission a telegram stating that item (1) in the bid was changed from $210,000 to $295,000. Western Union made a mistake and the telegram as delivered to the highway commission made it a change from 210 to 285 thousand dollars. Welcome was the lowest responsible bidder and its bid was accepted by the highway commission at a total figure of $6,560,049.65. The next lowest bidder was approximately one-quarter million dollars higher. Welcome learned that its bid was accepted and that the correction telegram was erroneous. Welcome requested that the contract be increased by $10,000 to rectify the mistake made by Western Union and pointed out that this would not injure the state

nor any other bidder because the next lowest bidder was still so much more than Welcome's bid. Was Welcome entitled to reformation to correct the mistake? [J. J. Welcome & Sons Construction Co. v Washington, 6 Wash App 2d 985, 497 P2d 953]

8. DeMeo rented a building from Horn. DeMeo was represented by an attorney who prepared the lease. The terms of the lease showed that DeMeo intended to make a particular use of the building which would require alterations necessitating a building permit. Horn knew that the building permit could not be obtained because the building was located in an urban renewal area and was to be demolished but said nothing to DeMeo. The lease recited that "the agreement was entered into after full investigation, neither party relying upon any statement or representation not embodied in this agreement made by the other." When DeMeo learned that he could not obtain the building permit he sued Horn for (1) rescission of the contract, (2) recovery of the down payment made on the lease, and (3) damages for fraud. What, if any, relief is DeMeo entitled to? [DeMeo v Horn, 70 Misc 2d 339, 334 NYS2d 22]

9. *A* claimed that he was entitled to payment of a specified sum under a contract which he had with *B*. *B* denied this liability. *A* threatened to sue *B* if he would not agree to pay the claimed amount. *B* promised to pay the claimed amount. He failed to keep his promise and *A* sued *B* on this later promise for the greater amount. *B* defended on the ground that the promise was not binding because it was obtained by duress. Was this defense valid? [Eggleston v Humble Pipe Line Co., (Tex Civ App) 482 SW2d 909]

10. *A* claimed that *B* owed him money. *A* was under the impression that *B* did not have much money. On the basis of this impression, *A* made a settlement agreement with *B* for a nominal amount. When *A* later learned that *B* was in fact reasonably wealthy, *A* sought to set the agreement aside. Was he entitled to do so? [Myers v Bernard, 38 App Div 2d 619, 326 NYS2d 279]

11. A dealer induced a distributor to sell to him on credit by telling the distributor that the dealer expected to inherit money which he would invest in the business. The dealer did not inherit any money. The distributor claimed that the dealer had been guilty of fraud. Was this correct? [United Fire & Cas. Co. v Nissan Motor Corp., — Colo —, 433 P2d 769]

12. The state of North Dakota, through the Bank of North Dakota, sold county industrial development revenue bonds to the State Security Bank. Thereafter Security State Bank sued to set aside the contract on the ground that it was prohibited by statute from purchasing such bonds in excess of 5% of its capital and the contract to purchase the bonds represented more than 5%. Was it entitled to set aside the contract? [Security State Bank v North Dakota, (ND) 181 NW2d 225]

13 Consideration

§ 13:1. Definition of Consideration. To constitute a contract, the agreement must meet requirements in addition to genuine mutual assent by competent parties. Ordinarily one of these requirements is consideration, but the exceptions to this requirement are increasing.

Consideration is what a promisor demands and receives as the price for his promise. A promise usually is binding upon a person only when he has received consideration.[1] It must be something to which the promisor is not otherwise entitled, and it must be what the promisor specifies as the price for his promise. (See p. 251, Colorado National Bank v Bohm.)

The fact that the promisor incidentally obtains a benefit does not make the benefit consideration for his promise when he had not bargained specifically for that benefit. For example, the Federal Aviation Administration planned to conduct high altitude tests of supersonic planes. To win public support for the program, the agency declared that it would pay all property damage caused by sonic boom. Some property owners who had commenced an action to enjoin the testing then stopped prosecuting the action. Other owners did not bring any action. Thereafter the owners of damaged property sued the government claiming that the declaration that damages would be paid constituted a binding contract. It was held that there was no contract because the promise to pay damages was not the price for forebearing to sue even though it might well have induced such action.[2]

Although some cases define consideration in terms of benefit to the promisor or detriment to the promisee, it is immaterial whether benefit or detriment is present. The essential element is that the act or thing which is done or promised has been specified by the promisor as the price to be paid in order to obtain his promise. (See p. 252, Baehr v Penn-O-Tex Oil Corporation.)

In view of the fact that consideration is the price paid for the promise, it is unimportant who pays that price as long as it has been agreed that it should be paid in that way. For example, consideration may be the extending of credit to a third person, as extending credit to the corporation of which the promisor is a stockholder or to a husband in return for the promise of his wife to pay the debt.[3]

---

[1] Hanson v Central Show Printing Co., 256 Iowa 1221, 130 NW2d 654.
[2] Kirk v United States, (CA10 Okla) 451 F2d 690.
[3] State Bank of Arthur v Sentel, 10 Ill App 3d 86, 293 NE2d 444.

And when one person puts up property as security for a loan made to a third person, such furnishing of security is consideration although it came from the property owner and not from the debtor.[4]

A promise to make a gift, or a promise to do or not to do something without receiving consideration, is unenforceable; but an executed gift or a performance without consideration cannot be rescinded for lack of consideration.

If the contract is bilateral, each party to the contract is a promisor and must receive consideration to make his promise binding. A unilateral contract has only one promisor, and the performance of the act which he called for is the consideration for his promise.

Consideration is sometimes qualified or described as "valuable consideration." This is done to distinguish it from the so-called "good consideration," that is, the love and affection existing between near relatives. In most states good consideration is not consideration at all but is merely a matter of inducement in the making of the promise. Moral obligation is likewise not consideration.[5]

§ 13:2. Binding Character of Promise. To constitute consideration, the promise must be binding, that is, it must impose a liability or create a duty. Suppose that a coal company promises to sell to a factory all the coal which it orders at a specified price, and that the factory agrees to pay that price for any coal which it orders from the coal company. The promise of the factory is not consideration because it does not obligate the factory to buy any coal from the coal company.

If, however, the factory promises to purchase all the coal it requires for a specified period and the coal dealer agrees to supply it at a specified price per ton, there is a valid contract according to most courts. It is true that it cannot be known beforehand how much coal will be ordered. The factory may have a strike or a fire and not operate at all during the year, and therefore require no coal. Moreover, the factory might convert to oil. In spite of these possibilities, such a contract is usually regarded as valid.

Although a contract must impose a binding obligation, it may authorize one or either party to terminate or cancel the agreement under certain circumstances or upon giving notice to the other party. The fact that the contract may be terminated in this manner does not make the contract any less binding prior to such termination.

In some instances where it is manifest that a particular act is impossible to perform, a promise to do that act is not consideration. If there is a possibility that the performance can be made, the consideration is valid.

§ 13:3. Promise to Perform Existing Obligations. Ordinarily, a promise to do, or the performance of, what one is already under legal obligation to do is

---

[4] Carlisle v Commodore Corporation, 15 NC App 620, 190 SE2d 703.

[5] C — v W —, (Tex Civ App) 480 SW2d 474.

not consideration. It is immaterial whether the legal obligation is based upon contract, upon the duties pertaining to an office held by the promisor, or upon statute or general principles of law. This rule is based on the theory that in such instances the promisor receives nothing for his promise since he was entitled to the conduct called for without paying anything extra.

For example, a promise to pay a stated sum of money to a police officer for making an arrest in the line of duty is unenforceable since the promisor receives only that which he has a right to demand without making any promise. If the act requested is above and beyond the call of duty, however, the performance of that act will make the promise binding.

Similarly, a promise to refrain from doing what one has no legal right to do is not consideration.

(1) Completion of Contract. When a contractor refuses to complete a building unless the owner promises him a payment or bonus in addition to the sum specified in the original contract, and the owner promises to make that payment, the question arises whether the owner's promise is binding. Most courts hold that the second promise of the owner is without consideration. A few courts hold that the promise is binding on the theory that the first contract was mutually rescinded and that a second contract, including the promise to pay the bonus, was agreed upon. Some courts hold the promise enforceable on the theory that the contractor has given up his right of election (a) to perform or (b) to abandon the contract and pay damages.

The courts holding that there is no consideration for the second promise make an exception when there are extraordinary circumstances caused by unforeseeable difficulties or mistakes and when the additional amount demanded by the contractor is reasonable for the extra work done by him.[6] They do so usually upon the theory that the first contract was discharged because of an implied condition that the facts would be or would continue to be as supposed by the parties and that the completion of the contract was the consideration for the new promise. Generally, however, unanticipated difficulty or expense, such as a strike or price increase, does not affect the liabilities of the parties. Such risks one takes in making a contract in the same sense that when one buys a coat or a house, he takes the risk that he may not like it as much as he thought he would.

If the promise of the contractor is to do something that is neither expressly nor impliedly a part of the first contract, then the promise of the other party is binding. For example, if a bonus of $1,000 is promised in return for the promise of a contractor to complete the building at a date earlier than that specified in the original agreement, the promise to pay the bonus is binding.

---

[6] Pittsburgh Testing Laboratory v Farnsworth & Chambers Co., (CA10 Okla) 251 F2d 77.

(2) Compromise and Release of Claims. The rule that doing or promising to do what one is bound to do is not consideration applies to a part payment made in satisfaction of an admitted debt. For example, if one person owes another $100, the promise of the latter to take $50 in full payment is not binding upon him and will not prevent him from demanding the remainder later because the partial payment by the debtor is not consideration.

This rule has been severely criticized because it seems unfair to permit the creditor to go back on his promise even though the debtor does owe him the money. In some instances it has been changed by statute or by court decision. Some courts treat the transaction as a binding gift of the remainder on the part of the creditor. Other courts seize the slightest opportunity to find some new consideration.

If the debtor pays before the debt is due, there is, of course, consideration since on the day when payment was made, the creditor was not entitled to demand any payment. Likewise, if the creditor accepts some article, even of slight value, in addition to the part payment, the agreement is held to be binding.

If there is a bona fide dispute as to the amount owed or whether any amount is owed, a payment by the debtor of less than the amount claimed by the creditor is consideration for the latter's agreement to release or settle the claim. As under the rule governing forbearance, it is generally regarded as sufficient if the claimant believes in his claim. Conversely, if the claimant knows that his claim does not have any merit and he is merely pressing it in order to force the other party to make some payment to buy peace from the annoyance of a lawsuit, the settlement agreement based on the part payment is not binding.

When parties to a contract in a good-faith effort to meet the business realities of a situation agree to a reduction of contract terms, there is some authority that the promise of the one party to accept the lesser performance by the other is binding even though technically the promise to render the lesser performance is not consideration because the obligor was already obligated to render the greater performance. Thus a landlord's promise to reduce the rent was binding when the tenant could not pay the original rent and the landlord preferred to have the building occupied even though receiving a smaller rental.[7] When the contract is for the sale of goods, any modification made by the parties to the contract is binding without regard to the existence of consideration for the modification.

(3) Part-Payment Checks. The acceptance and cashing of a check for part of a debt releases the entire debt when the check bears a notation that it is intended as final or full payment and the total amount due is disputed or unliquidated.[8] It probably has this same effect even though the debt is not disputed or unliquidated.[9]

---

[7] Haun v Corkland, 55 Tenn App 292, 399 SW2d 518.

[8] Miller v Montgomery, 77 N Mex 766, 427 P2d 275.

[9] UCC § 3-408. Official Comment, point 2. See also § 1-107, generally, and § 2-209(1) as to the sale of goods.

In some jurisdictions this principle is applied without regard to the form of payment, it being required only that the part payment was in fact received and accepted as discharging the obligation.[10] The California Civil Code, Sec. 1541, provides: "An obligation is extinguished by a release therefrom given to the debtor by the creditor, upon a new consideration, or in writing, with or without new consideration." If the notation that the acceptance of the check constitutes final payment is in print which the court regards as too small, it may not be binding in the absence of evidence that the notation was actually seen by the creditor receiving the check.[11]

*(4) **Composition of Creditors.*** In a *composition of creditors,* the various creditors of one debtor mutually agree to accept a fractional part of their claims in full satisfaction thereof. Such agreements are binding and are supported by consideration.[12] When creditors agree to extend the due date on their debts, the promise of each creditor to forbear is likewise consideration for the promise of the other creditors to forbear.[13]

§ 13:4. Present Versus Past Consideration. Since consideration is what the promisor states must be received for his promise, it must be given after the promisor states what he demands. Past consideration is not valid. When one person performs some service for another without the latter's knowledge or without an understanding that compensation is to be paid, a promise made later to pay for such services is not supported by consideration and is unenforceable. A promise by an employee to refrain from competing with his employer must be supported by consideration when the employment relationship already exists and the employee was not subject to any such restriction under that contract.[14]

A promise made by an employee to refrain from competing with his employer after he leaves the employment is not binding because consideration is lacking when the promise was made after the employee had begun working, as the hiring of the employee could not be consideration for the employee's promise, as it would be past consideration.[15]

*(1) **Moral Obligation.*** Some courts hold that when benefits are obtained by fraud or under circumstances that create a moral obligation, a promise to compensate by the person benefited is supported by consideration. When one promises to pay a debt that was unenforceable because of his minority, or that is barred by the statute of limitations, or that has been discharged in bankruptcy, the promise is binding.[16] There must be clear proof, however, that a subsequent promise was in fact made.

---

10 Rivers v Cole Corp., 209 Ga 406, 73 SE2d 196 (local statutes).
11 Kibler v Frank L. Garrett & Sons, Inc., 73 Wash 2d 523, 439 P2d 416.
12 Massey v Del-Valley Corp., 46 NJ Super 400, 134 A2d 802.
13 Vinylast Corp. v Gordon, — Ill App 2d —, 295 NE2d 523.
14 Mastrom v Warren, 18 NC App 199, 196 SE2d 528.
15 Timenterial, Inc. v Dagata, 29 Conn Supp 180, 277 A2d 512.
16 Port Finance Co. v Daigle, (La App) 236 So2d 256.

The better theory is that the new promise is a waiver of the bar or defense to the action and that no consideration is necessary.

To constitute a promise to pay a debt discharged by bankruptcy, the promise must be clear and must reasonably identify the discharged debt. Thus, a promise "to pay debts" does not revive a debt barred by a bankruptcy discharge where it was not clear whether this meant such debts as would be incurred after the bankruptcy discharge or embraced the earlier debts which had been discharged.[17]

(2) Complex Transaction Rule. Applying the rule that past consideration is not consideration, care must be taken to distinguish between the situation in which the consideration is in fact past and the situation in which the earlier consideration and the subsequent promises were all part of one complex transaction. For example, when an assignment is made and thereafter a third person guarantees the payment of the assigned claim, the earlier transaction may or may not be consideration which will make binding the promise of the guarantor. If the original assignment and the subsequent guarantee are merely parts of a "single transaction" and were all in the contemplation of the parties when the assignment was agreed to, then the prior assignment is consideration for the subsequent guarantee.[18]

In contrast, if the guaranty was not contemplated at the time of the original contract but is merely an afterthought or later development, the earlier assignment would not serve as consideration for the guarantor's promise. Consequently, if there is no new consideration for that promise, it is not binding on the guarantor.

§ 13:5. Forbearance as Consideration. In most cases consideration consists of the performance of an act or the making of a promise to act. But consideration may also consist of *forbearance,* which is refraining from doing an act, or a promise of forbearance. In other words, the promisor may desire to buy the inaction of the other party or his promise not to act.

The waiving or giving up of any right, legal or equitable, can be consideration for the promise of another. Thus, the relinquishment of a right in property, of a right to sue for damages, or of a homestead right will support a promise given in return for it.

When the creditor agrees to extend the time for paying his debt in return for the debtor's promise of a high return of interest, the agreement to extend is consideration for the promise to pay the higher rate of interest.[19]

When a supplier has the right to terminate the contract with the dealer selling its products, the promise of the supplier to refrain from revoking the contract with the dealer is consideration for the dealer's agreement to reduce the commissions taken by him on the resale of the supplier's products.[20]

---

[17] Van Schaack v Moody, 3 Ill App 3d 43, 278 NE2d 145.

[18] Mazzella v Lupinachi, (NY Civil Court) 70 Misc 2d 458, 333 NYS2d 775.

[19] Bloch v Fedak, 210 Kan 63, 499 P2d 1052.

[20] Mattlage Sales, Inc. v Howard Johnson's Wholesale Division, Inc., 39 App Div 2d 958, 333 NYS2d 491.

The right that is surrendered in return for a promise may be a right against a third person or his property, as well as one against the promisor or his property.

As under the rule governing compromises, forbearance to assert a claim is consideration when the claim has been asserted in good faith, even though it is without merit. In the absence of such a belief, forbearance with respect to a worthless claim is not consideration.[21]

Where a father gave the owner of a bulldozer a promissory note to cover the damages done to the bulldozer by his son, the owner's giving up his claim against the father in return for the note constituted consideration for the note even though the owner did not establish that his claim against the father was valid.[22]

Forbearance is not consideration unless it is the price for the promise. The mere fact that some act is done, as the giving of a promissory note, and thereafter the creditor does nothing, does not establish that the forbearance was the price for the making of the promissory note. At the same time such an intent may be inferred from the circumstances and it is not necessary that there be an express declaration or a statement that a promise is made in consideration of the forbearance of the creditor.[23]

§ 13:6. Adequacy of Consideration. Ordinarily the courts do not consider the adequacy of the consideration given for a promise. In the absence of fraud or other misconduct, the courts usually will not interfere to make sure that each side is getting a fair return.[24]

The fact that the consideration supplied by one party is slight when compared with the burden undertaken by the other party is immaterial, as it is a matter for the parties to decide when they make their contract whether each is getting an adequate return.[25] The courts leave each person to his contract and do not seek to reappraise the value that he has placed upon the consideration which he has received. The fact that the consideration given may seem small to other persons or to a reasonable man does not, in the absence of fraud, affect the validity of the contract.

(1) Wisdom of Contract. As a corollary of the concept that the court will not consider the adequacy of consideration, the ordinary rule is that the validity of a contract does not depend upon whether it is a wise or sensible contract. As long as the parties have capacity and there has been genuine assent to the terms of the contract, the court is not concerned with the actual terms of the contract.[26]

The foregoing is not always followed and courts are increasingly monitoring contracts to invalidate those which are unreasonable or unwise. Such

---

[21] In re Stolkin, (CA7 Ill) 471 F2d 1331.

[22] Andrews v Williams, (La) 281 So2d 120.

[23] Boymer v Birmelin, (Fla App) 227 So2d 358.

[24] Cook v American States Ins. Co., — Ind App 2d —, 275 NE2d 832.

[25] Kirshner v Spinella, 73 Misc 2d 962, 343 NYS2d 298.

[26] Tsiolis v Hatterscheidt, 85 SD 568, 187 NW2d 104.

exceptions most frequently arise by virtue of consumer protection statutes or the application of the concept of unconscionability.[27]

(2) Forbearance. If forbearance is called for by the promisor as the price of his promise, it is not material whether the parties agree that the forbearance should be for a long or a short time. The promisee must forbear for the period called for by the promisor, and the law will not attempt to say whether that period is adequate consideration for the promise.

When no specific period of forbearance is stated, the promisee is under a duty to forbear for a reasonable time. If, however, there is no duty to forbear for any period at all, as when the promisee merely agrees to forbear as long as he wishes, there is no consideration since the promisor has not bought anything with his promise.

(3) Failure of Expectations. The fact that what the party obtains in return for his promise is not as advantageous to him as he had expected does not mean that there is an absence or a failure of consideration. Consequently, when an investor obtained the shares of stock which he sought, the contract was fully performed and the fact that the stock proved worthless did not constitute a failure of consideration.[28]

The fact that a club member does not make use of his club privileges does not constitute a lack of consideration for his promise to become a member and to pay for his membership.[29]

§ 13:7. Exceptions to Adequacy of Consideration Rule. Some exceptions to the rule that the courts will not weigh the consideration are discussed in the following paragraphs.

(1) Unconscionability. An excessively hard bargain obtained by a seller of goods at the expense of a small buyer with weak purchasing power has been held to constitute unconscionability,[30] although such a conclusion is merely another way of stating that the consideration received by the buyer was not adequate.

(2) Statutory Exception. In a few states, statutes require that the consideration be adequate, or fair or reasonable, in order to make a contract binding.

Adequacy of the consideration may be questioned in computing tax liability. For example, when it is claimed that the taxable balance of a decedent's estate should be reduced by the amount owed a given creditor, such debt may be deducted only to the extent that the decedent had received

[27] See § 14:6.

[28] Molina v Largosa, (Hawaii) 51, 507, 465 P2d 293.

[29] Sorensen Health Studio v McCoy, 261 Iowa 891, 156 NW2d 341.

[30] Toker v Westerman, 113 NJ Super 452, 274 A2d 78. See also American Home Improvement, Inc. v MacIver, 105 NH 435, 201 A2d 886.

an equivalent value from the creditor. Thus, if the decedent owed the creditor $1,000 for property that was worth $200, only the sum of $200 could be deducted in computing the value of the estate. This determination for tax purposes, however, does not affect the validity of the creditor's contract.

(3) Evidence of Fraud. The smallness of the consideration may be evidence of fraud.[31] Suppose that *R* sells a $15,000 house to *E* for $500. It might be a perfectly innocent transaction in which *R* virtually makes a gift in return for the nominal payment. Since *R*, as the owner of his house, could give it away, nothing prevents his "selling" it at such a low figure. The transaction, however, may be of a different nature. It may be that *E* has defrauded *R* into believing that the property is worthless, and *R* therefore sells it for $500. Or there may be collusion between *R* and *E* to transfer the property in order to hide it from creditors of *R*. The smallness of the consideration does not mean that the transaction is necessarily made in bad faith or for a fraudulent purpose; but if other evidence indicates fraud, the smallness of the consideration corroborates that evidence.

(4) Exchange of Different Quantities of Identical Units. A promise to pay a particular amount of money or to deliver a particular quantity of goods in exchange for a promise to pay or deliver a greater amount or quantity of the same kind of money or goods at the same time and place is not adequate consideration.[32] If I promise to pay you $50 in exchange for your promise to pay me $100 under such circumstances, my promise is not regarded as adequate consideration for your promise, and your promise therefore is not binding upon you.[33]

If there is a difference between the nature of the units promised by the two parties, the law will find that there is consideration and will not ask whether the consideration is adequate. A promise to pay $60 in return for a promise to pay one penny would not be supported by consideration if both amounts of money are current legal tender. On the other hand, a promise to pay $60 in Revolutionary currency in return for one penny of current money or a promise to pay $60 of current money for a coin collector's penny would be supported by consideration since in each case the units are not equivalent.

(5) Equitable Relief. When a plaintiff seeks equitable relief, such as the specific performance of a contract, the courts will generally refuse to assist the plaintiff unless he has given valuable or substantial consideration for his rights.[34]

---

[31] Woods v Griffin, 204 Ark 514, 163 SW2d 322.

[32] R § 76(c).

[33] Note that this is similar to the rule that payment of part of a debt which is due is not consideration for the granting of an extension as to the balance. Shepherd v Erickson, (Tex Civ App) 416 SW2d 450.

[34] Karolkiewicz' Estate v Kary, 100 Ill App 2d 350, 241 NE2d 471.

§ 13:8. Exceptions to Requirements of Consideration. Ordinarily, a promise is not binding unless supported by consideration. There are certain exceptions to this rule.

(1) Voluntary Subscriptions. When charitable enterprises are financed by voluntary subscriptions of a number of persons, the promise of each one is generally enforceable. For example, when a number of people make pledges or subscriptions for the construction of a church, for a charitable institution, or for a college, the subscriptions are binding.

The theories for sustaining such promises vary. One view is that the promise of each subscriber is consideration for the promises of the others. This view is not sound because the promises are not given in exchange for each other. Another view is that the liability of the promisor rests upon a promissory estoppel [35] because obligations have been incurred in reliance upon the promise. Still another view treats such a subscription as an offer of a unilateral contract which is accepted by creating liabilities or making expenditures. Under this theory the promise would be revocable until some act is performed. It is also held by some courts that the acceptance of a subscription carries an implied promise creating an obligation to perform in accordance with the offer.

The real answer is that in these cases consideration is lacking according to the technical standards applied in ordinary contract cases. Nevertheless, the courts enforce such promises as a matter of public policy.

(2) Commercial Paper. The fact that there was no consideration for commercial paper, such as a check or promissory note, or that the consideration was illegal or had failed, may be raised against an ordinary holder of the paper. Such defenses may not be raised against persons acquiring the paper in the course of ordinary business transactions. The result is that the commercial paper may be enforceable even though no consideration was given.

(3) Sealed Instruments. At common law consideration was not necessary to support a promise under seal. In a state which gives the seal its original common-law effect, a gratuitous promise or a promise to make a gift is enforceable when it is set forth in a sealed instrument.

In some states a promise under seal must be supported by consideration, just as though it did not have a seal. Other states take a middle position and hold that the presence of a seal is prima facie proof that there is consideration to support the promise. This means that if nothing more than the existence of the sealed promise is shown, it is deemed supported by consideration. The party making the promise, however, may prove that there was no consideration. If he does, the promise is not binding upon him.

Even in those states in which the contract under seal is binding, the courts of equity will refuse to grant special relief, such as specifically

[35] See § 13:8(7).

enforcing the contract, if there is not a fair or reasonable consideration for the promise.

*(4) **Debts of Record.*** No consideration is necessary to support obligations of record, such as a court judgment. These obligations are enforceable as a matter of public policy.

*(5) **State Statutes.*** Under statutes in some states no consideration is necessary in order to make certain written promises binding. The Model Written Obligations Act, which has been adopted only in Pennsylvania, provides that no release (or promise) made and signed by the person releasing (or promising) shall be "invalid or unenforceable for lack of consideration, if the writing also contains an additional express statement, in any form of language, that the signer intends to be legally bound" by his promise.

*(6) **Uniform Commercial Code.*** Consideration is not required for (a) a merchant's written firm offer as to goods, stated as irrevocable for a fixed time not over three months; [36] (b) a written discharge of a claim for an alleged breach of a commercial contract; [37] or (c) an agreement to modify a contract for the sale of goods.[38]

*(7) **Promissory Estoppel.*** Some courts enforce promises that are not supported by consideration upon the *doctrine of promissory estoppel.* By this doctrine, if a person makes a promise to another and that other person acts upon that promise, the promisor is barred from setting up the absence of consideration in order to avoid his promise. The enforcement of the promise, even though there is no consideration, is deemed proper when the promisor should reasonably expect to induce and does induce action or forbearance of a definite and substantial character on the part of the promisee and when "injustice can be avoided only by enforcement of the promise." The doctrine of promissory estoppel, although conflicting with the basic requirement of consideration, is being given wider recognition as a means of attaining justice. (See p. 253, Hoffman v Red Owl Stores, Inc.)

Promissory estoppel differs from consideration in that the reliance of the promisee is not the bargained for response sought by the promisor. To be consideration, it would be necessary that the promisor specified or requested reliance as the price of his making his promise. By contrast, in the promissory estoppel there is no such specification or request by the promisor; but the promisor, as a reasonable man, should recognize that his action will lead the promisee to rely on the promise and that the promisee will sustain substantial harm if the promise is not performed.[39]

The doctrine of promissory estoppel is not applied when no promise is made and one party merely takes a chance on future developments. Nor

---

36 See § 10:6(4).
37 UCC § 1-107.
38 § 2-209(1).
39 Day v Mortgage Insurance Corp., 91 Idaho 605, 428 P2d 524.

does it apply when it is made clear that certain conditions must be met before any obligation will arise and the claimant fails to meet those conditions, such as making payment in advance.[40] Likewise, since promissory estoppel is based on the ground that there has been reliance on a promise, there must be a communication of the promise to the promisee, in the same sense that an offer must be communicated to an offeree.[41]

Promissory estoppel is also applied by some courts to require an offeror to hold an offer open for a reasonable time even though there is no consideration to do so and although the firm offer concept is not applicable. Thus, when a subcontractor makes a bid to a general contractor and recognizes that the general contractor will rely thereon in making his bid for the construction job, in some states the subcontractor is barred from revoking his offer until a reasonable time has elapsed in which the contractor may accept the offer of the subcontractor.[42] (See p. 254, Constructors Supply Co. v Bostrom Sheet Metal Works, Inc.)

The doctrine of promissory estoppel is not applied merely because a promise is not performed. Thus an employer cannot be held liable to an injured employee on this theory, even though the employer dissuaded third persons from taking a collection for the employee by stating that this was unnecessary and promising that he would take care of the employee for life but thereafter failing to do so.[43]

§ **13:9. Legality of Consideration.** The law will not permit persons to make contracts that violate the law. Accordingly, a promise to do something which the law prohibits or a promise to refrain from doing something which the law requires is not valid consideration and the contract is illegal. This subject is further discussed in Chapter 14.

§ **13:10. Failure of Consideration.** When a promise is given as consideration, the question arises as to whether the promisor will perform his promise. If he does not perform his promise, the law describes the default as a "failure of consideration." (See p. 255, Sanitary Linen Service Co. v Alexander Proudfoot Co.) This is a misnomer since the failure of the promisor is one of performance, not of consideration.

The fact that a contract is under seal does not prevent proof that the consideration for the contract had failed. This does not contradict or impeach the writing but merely proves that the writing has never been performed.[44]

(1) Disappointment. The fact that performance of the contract by the other party does not have the results that one hoped for does not mean that there is a failure of consideration. (See p. 256, Association of Army and Navy Stores v Young.) For example, when one buys a store building in a real estate development, he obviously does so in the expectation that he will obtain a

[40] Corbit v J. I. Case Co., 66 Wash 2d 30, 424 P2d 290.
[41] Hilton v Alexander & Baldwin, 66 Wash 2d 30, 400 P2d 772.
[42] Drennan v Star Paving Co., 51 Cal. 2d 409, 333 P2d 757.
[43] Overlock v Central Vermont Public Service Corp., 126 Vt 549, 237 A2d 356.
[44] Hensel v U.S. Electronic Corp., (Del) 251 A2d 828.

large volume of trade by virtue of his location. It may be that this will not occur because of the continuing of earlier purchasing patterns of the public. While the buyer of the store building is disappointed, there has not been any failure of consideration with respect to the contract by which he agreed to purchase the store building from its owner.

CASES FOR CHAPTER 13

Colorado National Bank v Bohm

(CA9 Cal) 286 F2d 494 (1961)

Gertrude Sears financed the business of her son, Joseph. As evidence of the debt, the son and his wife signed a promissory note for $25,000 payable to the order of the mother. The mother requested Alfred Bohm to sign the note as co-maker. He agreed to do so on the express condition that he would not be liable for the payment of the note. Gertrude died some time later. The Colorado National Bank was named as her executor and demanded payment of the note from Bohm. He raised the defense that there was no consideration for his note. From a judgment in his favor, the bank appealed.

ORR, C.J. . . . The note was in the amount of $25,000. It was dated December 6, 1956, and payable to the order of Mrs. Gertrude Tenderich Sears. The note was signed by Joseph S. Tenderich, son of Mrs. Sears, Elizabeth S. Tenderich, his wife, and appellee Alfred O. L. Bohm, as co-makers. Mrs. Sears is now deceased, and appellant is the executor of her estate. Appellee is a citizen of California; appellant is a citizen of Colorado; Mrs. Sears and her son and daughter-in-law were also citizens of Colorado at the time of the events described herein.

In October, 1956, appellee Bohm was the owner of an alfalfa mill situate[d] near Mason, Nevada. He had been for many years a friend of Mrs. Gertrude Tenderich Sears, a woman of considerable wealth. At a meeting held in Denver, Colorado, in October of 1956 appellee, Mrs. Sears, and her son Joseph reached an agreement that Mrs. Sears would finance Joseph in the operation of a milling business, using the alfalfa mill owned by appellee as a base of operations. Mrs. Sears would furnish Joseph with $40,000, $15,000 of which would be paid to appellee for a lease of said alfalfa mill to Joseph with option to purchase, and $25,000 of which would be used by Joseph as operating capital. The $25,000 would be represented by a promissory note to be signed by Joseph and appellee.

Thereafter the note in suit was prepared. . . .

Mrs. Sears died on May 11, 1957, having made no demand for payment of any of the amounts due on said promissory note. No payment of interest or principal having been made, appellant filed the instant suit for the accelerated full amount against appellee on July 10, 1958. Appellee's answer alleged an agreement between Mrs. Sears and him to the effect that he was not to be held liable on the note. At the trial appellee testified as follows: Mrs. Sears asked him if he would sign the note as a favor to her so as to give Joseph an added sense of responsibility; appellee replied that he was not interested in financing Joseph, to which Mrs. Sears replied that she only wanted him to sign as an incentive to Joseph, and she said, "Fred, I will never ask you or call on you for paying this note or any part of that note." Appellee then agreed to help her and signed the note, but only after she reassured him that she would never call on him to pay any of the note.

The trial court found (1) that there was no consideration for appellee's execution of the note, (2) that appellee signed the note solely for the accommodation of the payee Mrs. Sears, or of the payee and appellee's co-makers, and (3) that appellee signed and delivered the note conditionally, the condition being that he would never be held liable thereon.

. . . As between the original parties, parol evidence is always admissible to show want or failure of consideration. . . . Such evidence does not contradict or vary the terms of the note but impeaches the consideration necessary to make the note enforcible. . . . Appellant contends that this rule does not apply here because there was consideration for the note in the form of both detriment to the promisee and benefit to the promisor; the alleged detriment to Mrs. Sears was the $25,000 she paid out in connection with the note, and the benefit to appellee was the $15,000 he received for the lease and option under the other half of the transaction and the fact that the $25,000 was to be used to operate his mill, from which operation he was to receive rent. The error in appellant's argument in this respect is that it fails to recognize the fundamental common law principle that consideration must be *bargained for*—it must be the thing which the parties agree shall be given in exchange for the promise. . . . The alleged benefits to appellee and detriment to Mrs. Sears could have been consideration for appellee's promise had they been bargained for and intended as such. However, this was not the case, and therefore said benefits and detriment are not consideration. "The mere presence of some incident to a contract which might, under certain circumstances, be upheld as a consideration for a promise, does not necessarily make it the consideration for the promise in that contract. To give it that effect, it must have been offered by one party, and accepted by the other, as one element of the contract." . . . From appellee's conversation with Mrs. Sears it is clear that his signature of the note was given solely in exchange for her promise that he would not be held liable on the note; hence there was no consideration which could make this note enforcible against appellee.

The parol evidence was admissible. The trial court accepted it as true. It is sufficient to sustain the findings.

[Judgment affirmed.]

Baehr v Penn-O-Tex Oil Corporation

258 Minn 533, 104 NW2d 661 (1960)

Kemp leased a gas filling station from Baehr. Kemp, who was heavily indebted to the Penn-O-Tex Oil Corporation, transferred to it his right to receive payments on all claims. When Baehr complained that the rent was not paid, he was finally assured by the corporation that the rent would be paid to him. Baehr did not sue Kemp for the overdue rent but later sued the corporation. From a judgment for the defendant, the plaintiff appealed.

LOEVINGER, J. . . . There was an unequivocal assurance given that the rents would be paid. This cannot be anything but a promise.

However, the fact that a promise was given does not necessarily mean that a contract was made. It is clear that not every promise is legally enforceable. Much of the vast body of law in the field of contracts is concerned with determining which promises should be legally enforced. On the one hand, in a civilized community men must be able to assume that those with whom they deal will carry out their undertakings according to reasonable expectations. On the other hand, it is neither practical nor reasonable to expect full performance of every assurance given, whether it be thoughtless, casual, and gratuitous, or deliberately and seriously made.

The test that has been developed by the common law for determining the enforceability of promises is the doctrine of consideration. This is a crude and not altogether successful attempt to generalize the conditions under which promises will be legally enforced. Consideration requires that a contractual promise be the product of a bargain. However, in this usage, "bargain" does not mean an exchange of things of equivalent, or any, value. It means a negotiation resulting in the voluntary assumption of an obligation by one party upon condition of an act or forbearance by the other. Consideration thus insures that the promise enforced as a contract is not accidental, casual, or gratuitous, but has been uttered intentionally as the result of some deliberation, manifested by reciprocal bargaining or negotiation. In this view, the requirement of consideration is no mere technicality, historical anachronism, or arbitrary formality. It is an attempt to be as reasonable as we can in deciding which promises constitute contracts. . . .

Consideration, as essential evidence of the parties' intent to create a legal obligation, must be something adopted and regarded by the parties as such. Thus, the same thing may be consideration or not, as it is dealt with by the parties. In substance, a contractual promise must be of the logical form: "If . . . [consideration is given] . . . then I promise that. . . ." Of course, the substance may be expressed in any form of words, but essentially this is the logical structure of those promises enforced by the law as contracts.

Applying these principles to the present case, it appears that although defendant's agent made a promise to plaintiff, it was not in such circumstances that a contract was created. . . .

There is no evidence that either of the parties took defendant's assurances seriously or acted upon them in any way. There was, therefore, no consideration. . . .

[Judgment affirmed.]

Hoffman v Red Owl Stores, Inc.

26 Wis 2d 683, 133 NW2d 267 (1965)

Hoffman wanted to acquire a franchise as a Red Owl Grocery Store, Red Owl being a corporation that maintained a system of chain stores. The agent of Red Owl informed Hoffman and his wife that if they would sell their bakery in Wautoma, acquire a certain tract of land in Chilton, another city, and put up a specified amount of money, he would be given a franchise as desired. Hoffman sold his business, acquired the land in Chilton, but was never granted a franchise. He and his wife sued Red Owl, which raised the defense that there had only been an assurance that Hoffman would receive a franchise but no promise supported by consideration and therefore no binding contract to give him a franchise. From a judgment in the Hoffmans' favor, Red Owl appealed.

CURRIE, C.J. . . . The development of the law of promissory estoppel "is an attempt by the courts to keep remedies abreast of increased moral consciousness of honesty and fair representations in all business dealings." . . .

The Restatement avoids use of the term "promissory estoppel," and there has been criticism of it as an inaccurate term. . . . Use of the word "estoppel" to describe a doctrine upon which a party to a lawsuit may obtain affirmative relief offends the traditional concept that estoppel merely serves as a shield and cannot serve as a sword to create a cause of action. . . .

Because we deem the doctrine of promissory estoppel, as stated in Sec. 90 of Restatement, 1 Contracts, as one which supplies a needed weapon which courts may employ in a proper case to prevent injustice, we endorse and adopt it.

The record here discloses a number of promises and assurances given to Hoffman by Lukowitz in behalf of Red Owl upon which plaintiffs relied and acted upon to their detriment. . . .

There remains for consideration the question of law raised by defendants that agreement was never reached on essential factors necessary to establish a contract between Hoffman and Red Owl. Among these were the size, cost, design, and layout of the store building; and the terms of the lease with respect to rent, maintenance, renewal, and purchase options. This poses the question of whether the promise necessary to sustain a cause of action for promissory estoppel must embrace all essential details of a proposed transaction between promisor and promisee so as to be the equivalent of an offer that would result in a binding contract between the parties if the promisee were to accept the same.

Originally the doctrine of promissory estoppel was invoked as a substitute for consideration rendering a gratuitous promise enforceable as a contract. . . . In other words, the acts of reliance by the promisee to his detriment provided a substitute for consideration. If promissory estoppel were to be limited to only those situations where the promise giving rise to the cause of action must be so definite with respect to all details that a contract would result were the promise supported by consideration, then the defendants' instant promises to Hoffman would not meet this test. However, Sec. 90 of Restatement, 1 Contracts, does not impose the requirement that the promise giving rise to the cause of action must be so comprehensive in scope as to meet the requirements of an offer that would ripen into a contract if accepted by the promisee. Rather the conditions imposed are:

(1) Was the promise one which the promisor should reasonably expect to induce action or forbearance of a definite and substantial character on the part of the promisee?

(2) Did the promise induce such action or forbearance?

(3) Can injustice be avoided only by enforcement of the promise? . . .

We conclude that injustice would result here if plaintiffs were not granted some relief because of the failure of defendants to keep their promises which induced plaintiffs to act to their detriment. . . .

[Judgment affirmed on this phase of the case.]

Constructors Supply Co. v Bostrom Sheet Metal Works, Inc.

— Minn —, 190 NW2d 71 (1971)

Constructors Supply Company submitted a bid to construct a laboratory building for the University of Minnesota. Its calculations were based in part on the bid that it had earlier obtained from the Bostrom Sheet Metal Works for the performance of the ventilation work. Constructors was awarded the construction contract. Bostrom then withdrew its bid to Constructors. Constructors was required to make a new subcontract for the ventilation work which it did for a greater amount than Bostrom's bid price. Constructors then sued Bostrom for the loss which it had caused. Bostrom defended on the ground that its bid was merely an offer which had never been accepted and therefore could be revoked by it. Judgment was entered for Constructors. Bostrom appealed.

NELSON, J. . . . The main issues are (1) whether the doctrine of promissory estoppel is applicable to bind a subcontractor to the bid it offers to a prime contractor who does not finally accept that bid but relies on it by incorporating it into the prime bid which it submits; and (2) whether the evidence justifies the application of promissory estoppel in the case at bar.

In granting judgment for plaintiff, the trial court based its decision on the bidding practices of the construction industry in the area. It was brought out at trial that subcontractors and contractors customarily negotiate on the telephone in submitting their bids. The subcontractors itemize their various costs by computing them from the plans and specifications of the project, and when they come up with final figures, they submit them as bids to the prime contractors who use these bids in arriving at their own bids. At times a subcontractor himself has subcontracted various items of the project on which he wishes to bid, and he must receive bids from his subcontractors before he can submit a complete figure to the prime contractors. This whole process usually culminates on the day that the prime bids are due on the project. Much telephoning and hurried activity takes place between the prime contractors and subcontractors in an effort to prepare bids before the prime bid deadline. It was also brought out at trial that subcontractors customarily agree to be bound by the bids they submit to prime contractors and that prime contractors act in reliance on these bids when they submit their own bids to the owner.

Taking these practices into account, the trial court found that plaintiff relied on defendant's bid for the ventilation work in submitting the prime mechanical bid. The trial court concluded that the doctrine of promissory estoppel was properly applicable in the circumstances and entitled plaintiff to recover the damages it sustained as a result of defendant's refusal to perform the work at its original bid price. We affirm.

The doctrine of promissory estoppel, or as it is sometimes called, justifiable reliance, . . . has been characterized by some courts as a species of or substitute for consideration. . . .

There is a split of authority among the courts which have considered the applicability of the doctrine to the situation at hand. Defendant relies on that line of authority which holds that promissory estoppel does not apply to make a subcontractor's bid irrevocable where the prime contractor has not accepted the bid, even though the prime contractor may have relied on the bid by using it in its own bid. . . .

Contrary to the above . . . is the line of authority, cited by plaintiff, which applies promissory estoppel to the construction bidding situation, not . . . as a doctrine which adds an essential contract element to the facts, but as one providing an independent basis of enforcement of the contract based on the facts of bidding procedure, the division of risks between the prime contractor and subcontractor, and an attempt to allow the system of bidding to operate with a minimum of injustice. . . .

It appears to us that in the instant case the proof establishes that plaintiff received a clear and definite offer from defendant; that defendant could expect plaintiff to place substantial reliance on the offer; that plaintiff reasonably relied thereon to its detriment by using defendant's bid in preparing its own prime bid, . . . and that defendant's withdrawal caused plaintiff financial detriment. We must therefore conclude that plaintiff established a cause of action based on promissory estoppel and the trial court could properly apply the doctrine in order to grant relief. . . .

[Judgment affirmed.]

Sanitary Linen Service Co. v Alexander Proudfoot Co.

(CA5 Fla) 435 F2d 292 (1971)

Alexander Proudfoot Company was in the business of devising efficiency systems for industry. It undertook to devise such a system for the Sanitary Linen Service Company. Sanitary claimed that the system failed to effect the promised savings and sued Alexander to get back the money which it had paid. Judgment was entered for Sanitary; Alexander appealed.

BELL, C.J. . . . Proudfoot was to supply a "worthwhile installation of schedule and method improvements designed to provide greater control over utilization of man and machine hours and to effect operating economies." The purpose of the schedule or system, according to Proudfoot's negotiator, was to ferret out and recover lost time in all phases of production, delivery and office work in Sanitary's operations. The benefit would accrue to Sanitary in the form of reduced manpower thus resulting in payroll savings. . . .

The gathering of the data and development of the schedule fell behind and Sanitary's management became restless to see some results. Proudfoot's man in charge of the project reassured Sanitary that savings were just around the corner and that they were going to recommend very shortly that 26 persons be eliminated in the ironing department of the Miami plant. On June 5, 1964 this installation was actually accomplished and the people discharged. Proudfoot's former employees who were on the job at the time admitted at the trial that at the time they had not really worked out a schedule and that without it, the layoff would not achieve the desired result. Shortly after the layoff the plant had to operate at longer hours to get out the necessary production. Employee complaints followed. With the approval of Proudfoot's employees, the 26 persons were rehired. Similar difficulty occurred at the Orlando plant. In sum, as the district court found, former employees of Proudfoot, witnesses for Sanitary at the trial, testified that they were unable to develop an over-all schedule plan that would develop a continuous flow and eliminate lost time.

In July the installation manager was discharged by Proudfoot and new personnel placed on the job in an effort to develop a workable program or installation. Further studies were made and plans and forms drawn up, but no further "installations" were attempted. On October 9, 1964, after having collected $74,200, and spent the contemplated time on the Sanitary job, Proudfoot discontinued its efforts. Several contracts were made after this in an effort to have Proudfoot perform. The parties, however, broke off negotiations and this suit followed.

Originally Sanitary was suing on a theory of breach of express or implied warranty in that the savings promised by Proudfoot did not occur. The district judge found that there was no express promise to effect savings and that there is no implied warranty in a contract for services. He did find, albeit in a rather unspecified way, that Sanitary did not receive what they bargained for, i.e., workable system. He then awarded damages to Sanitary in the nature of restitution. According to the court, they paid for a service which they did not get and thus were entitled to have their money back. . . .

In the final analysis, the question presented is whether a scheduling installation was devised for Sanitary and made operative. After a careful study of the record we conclude, as did the district court, that no scheduling installation as contemplated in the agreement was ever devised or furnished to Sanitary. Thus, as Proudfoot did not produce what they contracted to do, there was a failure of consideration. . . .

[Judgment for plaintiff.]

Association of Army and Navy Stores v Young

296 Ky 61, 176 SW2d 136 (1943)

The Association of Army and Navy Stores gave a price discount to customer members of the Association. The Association agreed to list Young's store as a member store, and Young agreed to pay the Association a percentage of the sales made at its store to Association customer members plus a fixed monthly charge of $2.50. No new customers purchased at Young's store. He refused to pay the Association the monthly charge on the ground that the consideration for the contract had failed. The Association sued Young. The court entered a judgment in favor of Young and the Association appealed.

THOMAS, J. . . . An unexecuted contract is valid and supported by sufficient consideration when there are mutual promises to be performed by each party, the promise of the one being a consideration for the promise of the other. . . .

The mutual promises of the respective parties to the contract upon which this action is based are: That plaintiff agreed with defendant to advertise his store among and with its consumer customers to whom it paid five percent of the amount of their purchases as an inducement for them to patronize defendant's store. It indisputably proved that it did so advertise, not only directly with its consumer members, but also in the publication and distribution of its monthly bulletins or pamphlets. It did not agree in its contract to confine its terms to the acquisition of new customers by defendant, through the process of its operations. In consideration of that indisputably established compliance of plaintiff's promise, defendant agreed to pay to it the items sued for which he never did. . . .

But it is argued . . . that inasmuch as defendant . . . received no new customers from the consumer group after the contract was executed, there was a failure of consideration which relieved him from performing his contract promises. . . . But that argument overlooks the fact that even though there were no new customers acquired by defendant yet plaintiff's efforts in performing its part of the contract was not without possible benefit to defendant. The old customers of defendant who were members of the consumer group might for various reasons cease to continue as such, but which would most likely be prevented by plaintiff's promise to pay them 5% of the amount of their purchases from defendant, thus inducing them to continue to patronize defendant when they might not have otherwise done so. . . .

[Judgment reversed.]

QUESTIONS AND CASE PROBLEMS

1. What is the objective of each of the following rules of law?
   (a) An executed gift or a performance that has been rendered without consideration cannot be rescinded for lack of consideration.
   (b) In the absence of fraud, the adequacy of consideration is usually immaterial.
2. Husted made a down payment on a contract to purchase most of the assets of a corporation. He was not able to complete the purchase and forfeited the down payment. Fuller, who in effect owned, controlled, and was the corporation, stated that he felt an obligation to Husted to see that he got his down payment back and promised that he would give him a promissory

note covering the amount of the down payment. He failed to do so. Husted sued Fuller for breach of his promise to deliver such a note. Fuller claimed that his promise was not binding on him. Decide. [Husted v Fuller, (CA7 Ill) 361 F2d 187]

3. Irene Dewein studied nursing. She did not enter that profession, however, but went to live with and take care of her parents. This she did for 27 years, during which time the father was invalided until his death in 1948. In 1957 the mother died after being frequently bedridden for a period of 2 years. In October, 1956, Irene's brother Edward had said to her, "Sis, I am so grateful you are taking care of mother, and I am certainly going to see you are taken care of for life. You deserve it. Don't worry about the future. I am going to see you are taken care of." The brother died in 1959 without having made any provision in his will for Irene. She sued his estate for the value of her services for 27 years. Decide. [Dewein v Dewein's Executors, 30 Ill App 2d 446, 174 NE2d 875]

4. When Helen Suske sued John Straka on a promissory note that he had given her, he raised the defense that his note was a gift and that he had not received any consideration for it. She claimed that at the time John was obligated to her in several ways and that such obligations constituted consideration. It was claimed that he had promised to marry the plaintiff, that he owed the plaintiff for room rent and money loaned to him, and that he had caused her some inconvenience. Was the note binding? [Suske v Straka, 229 Minn 408, 39 NW2d 745]

5. *A* owed money to a bank. *A* had a bank account in the bank, and under the loan agreement the bank could repay itself the amount of the loan from the bank deposit. When *A* died, his widow was made his executrix. She signed a note individually and, as executrix, promised to pay the bank the amount of *A*'s debt. She did this in return for the bank's promise not to deduct *A*'s debt from his bank account. When the bank sued her on her note, she raised the defense that there was no consideration for it. Was this a valid defense? [Jeter v Citizens National Bank, (Tex Civ App) 419 SW2d 916]

6. A prospective buyer of a house told the real estate broker to hire a contractor to inspect the building for termites. A contractor agreed to do so for $35, but he made a negligent inspection and failed to detect the presence of termites. The buyer sued the contractor for the loss caused by the contractor's negligence. The contractor defended on the ground that he had not charged much for the job. Was this a valid defense? [Mayes v Emery, 3 Wash App 2d 315, 475 P2d 124]

7. Sears, Roebuck & Co. promised to give Forrer "permanent employment." Forrer sold his farm at a loss in order to take the job. Shortly after commencing work, he was discharged by Sears which claimed that the contract could be terminated at will. Forrer claimed that promissory estoppel prevented Sears from terminating the contract. Was he correct? [Forrer v Sears, Roebuck & Co., 36 Wis 2d 388, 153 NW2d 587]

8. Fedun rented a building to Gomer who did business under the name of Mike's Cafe. Later, Gomer was about to sell out the business to Brown and requested Fedun to release him from his liability under the lease. Fedun agreed

to do so. Brown sold out shortly thereafter. The balance of the rent due by Gomer was not paid, and Fedun sued Mike's Cafe on the rent claim. Could he collect after having released Gomer? [Fedun v Mike's Cafe, 204 Pa Super 356, 204 A2d 776]

9. Steve Clark was a member of the Marine Corps. He held a World Service Life Insurance policy. It did not contain any war risk or aviation exclusion clauses. Brumell, an agent of the Prudential Insurance Company, persuaded him to drop this policy on the promise that he would obtain a similar policy from the Prudential Company which likewise would not have any war risk or aviation clauses. The policy which Prudential issued did contain such clauses and thereafter Steve was killed in Vietnam when his helicopter crashed and burned. The Prudential Insurance Company paid his parents as beneficiaries of the policy and then demanded the return of the money on the basis that payment had been made by mistake. They refused to return the money. Were they entitled to retain it? [Prudential Ins. Co. v Clark (CA5 Fla) 456 F2d 932]

10. Allen owned land which was being developed. Her brother, Norburn, wrote to the vice-president of Investment Properties of Asheville, Inc., stating that "this is to certify that I will stand personally liable" for the land preparation expenses. When Investment Properties sued him on this guaranty, he raised the defense that he did not receive any consideration for his promise and therefore it was not binding. Was this a valid defense? [Investment Properties of Asheville, Inc. v Norburn, 281 NC 300, 188 SE2d 342]

11. Youngman went to work for the Nevada Irrigation District. The superintendent promised him that he would receive a specified pay increase in April of each year. When he did not receive the increase he sued the District. He claimed that he had relied on the promise that he would receive such increase and that accordingly the promise was binding. Was he correct? [Youngman v Nevada Irrigation District, — Cal 3d —, 74 Cal Rptr 398, 449 P2d 462]

12. *A* was employed by *B* for some time. At *B*'s request *A* signed a paper stating that *A* would not work for any competitor of *B* for 5 years after *A* left *B*'s employ. Was this contract binding on *A*? [Engineering Associates, Inc. v Pankow, — NC —, 150 SE2d 56]

14 Legality and Public Policy

GENERAL PRINCIPLES

Viewed from the standpoint of the parties to the contract, a contract is a matter of the agreement of the parties. But the contract does not exist in a vacuum and therefore it must satisfy certain standards which society imposes. The agreement of the parties must satisfy all the rules relating to a contract and then in addition it must satisfy the standards relating to legality and public policy. Negatively stated, the agreement will not be a valid contract if it is illegal or contrary to public policy.

§ **14:1. Effect of Illegality.** An agreement is illegal when either its formation or performance is a crime or a tort, or is opposed to public policy. Ordinarily an illegal agreement is void.

When an agreement is illegal, the parties are usually regarded as not entitled to the aid of the courts. If the illegal agreement has not been performed, neither party can sue the other to obtain performance or damages. If the agreement has been performed, neither party can sue the other for damages or to set it aside. (See p. 277, Miller v Radikopf.)

(1) Exceptions. The following are exceptions to the general rule that the court will not aid the parties to an unlawful agreement:

(1) When the law which the agreement violates is intended for the protection of one of the parties, that party may seek relief. For example, when, in order to protect the public, the law forbids the issuance of securities or notes by certain classes of corporations, a person who has purchased them may recover his money.

(2) When the parties are not equally guilty or, as it is said, are not *in pari delicto*, the one less guilty is granted relief when public interest is advanced by so doing. For example, when a statute is adopted to protect one of the parties to a transaction, as a usury law adopted to protect borrowers, the person to be protected will not be deemed to be *in pari delicto* with the wrongdoer when he enters into a transaction which is prohibited by the statute.

(3) An exception may also exist when the illegality is collateral or incidental, as when one of the parties has not obtained a government permit or license necessary to performance of the contract.

(4) When one person has entrusted another with money or property to be used for an illegal purpose, the first person usually may change his mind and recover the money or property provided it has not been spent for the illegal purpose. Thus, money entrusted to an agent for use as a bribe of a third person may be recovered from the agent before it is so used.

As an extension of this rule, if bets were held by a stakeholder and either of the bettors repudiates the bet, the stakeholder must return his bet to him and would be liable if he paid that money to the other bettor. When the act of betting is itself made a crime, some states deny the bettor the right to recover his bet from the stakeholder.[1]

§ **14:2. Partial Illegality.** An agreement may involve the performance of several promises, some of which are illegal and some legal. The legal parts of the agreement may be enforced, provided that they can be separated from the parts which are illegal. The same rule applies when the consideration is illegal in part. The rule is not applied, however, to situations in which the illegal act or consideration is said to taint and strike down the entire agreement.

When there is an indivisible promise to perform several acts, some of which are illegal, the agreement is void. Also when there is a single promise to do a legal act, supported by several considerations, some of which are illegal, the agreement cannot be enforced.

If a contract is susceptible of two interpretations, one legal and the other illegal, the court will assume that the legal meaning was intended unless the contrary is clearly indicated.

§ **14:3. Disguised Transactions.** Frequently parties to an illegal contract will seek to disguise the transaction. Thus, a lender desiring to obtain usurious interest from a private consumer will enter into two transactions: (1) a loan at a lawful rate of interest, and (2) the sale of some property, such as an automobile at an excessive price, the excess in the price constituting an additional payment for making the loan. If the loan transaction and the sales transaction are looked at separately, there is nothing unlawful. Each element of the operation is lawful by itself. The law, however, will look at the entire transaction as a composite and recognize that in fact a usurious loan has been made. Similarly, when a business is sold to a buyer who does not have the license necessary to operate the business, the requirement of a license cannot be evaded by calling the buyer an employee of the seller. (See p. 278, Schara v Thiede.)

§ **14:4. Crimes and Civil Wrongs.** An agreement is illegal and therefore void when it calls for the commission of any act that constitutes a crime. To illustrate, one cannot enforce an agreement by which the other party is to commit

[1] Some courts require that a person repudiating his bet do so before the event which was the subject of the bet has occurred. Other courts permit the recovery of the bet from the stakeholder as long as demand is made prior to payment of the money to the other bettor, even though the event which was the subject of the bet has occurred.

an assault, to steal property, to burn a house, to print a libelous article, or to kill a person.

An agreement that calls for the commission of a civil wrong is also illegal and void. Examples are agreements to damage the goods of another, to slander a third person, to defraud another, or to infringe another's patent, trademark, or copyright. Thus, an agreement for *A's* orchestra to use the name of *B*, a skilled musician, is illegal as a fraud upon the public when *B* is not actually to appear with the orchestra. The use of his name would give the impression that the orchestra was conducted by him.

§ 14:5. Good Faith and Fairness. In addition to the limiting factors of illegality and being contrary to public policy, the law is evolving toward requiring that contracts be neither unfair nor manifest bad faith. Affirmatively stated, it is now required that contracts be fair and be made in good faith. The law is becoming increasingly concerned with whether *A* has utilized a superior bargaining power or superior knowledge to obtain better terms from *B* than *A* would otherwise have obtained.

In the case of goods, the seller must act in good faith, which is defined as to merchant sellers as "honesty in fact and the observance of reasonable commercial standards of fair dealing in the trade."[2]

The burden or duty of exercising good faith is also given statutory recognition in the federal Automotive Dealers' Day in Court Act, providing that "an automobile dealer may bring suit against [an] automobile manufacturer . . . [to] recover the damages by him sustained . . . by reason of the failure of said automobile manufacturer . . . to act in good faith in performing or complying with any of the terms or provisions of the franchise [which has been given by the manufacturer to the dealer] or in terminating, canceling, or not renewing the franchise with said dealer, provided that in any such suit the manufacturer shall not be barred from asserting in defense of any such action the failure of the dealer to act in good faith."[3] By the definition in Section (1)(e) of the Act, "good faith" is significantly stated to mean "the duty of each party to any franchise, and all officers, employees, or agents thereof to act in a fair and equitable manner toward each other so as to guarantee the one party freedom from coercion, intimidation, or threats of coercion or intimidation from the other party: provided that . . . persuasion . . . or argument shall not be deemed to constitute a lack of good faith."[4]

---

[2] See UCC § 2-103(1)(b) as to good faith. Higher standards are also imposed on merchant-sellers by other provisions of UCC. See § 2-314, as to warranties; § 2-603, as to duties with respect to rightfully rejected goods; and § 2-509(3), as to the transfer of risk of loss. While the provisions of the Code above noted do not apply to contracts generally, there is a growing trend of courts to extend Article 2 of the Code, which relates only to the sale of goods, to contract situations generally, on the theory that it represents the latest restatement of the law of contracts made by expert scholars and the legislators of the land.

[3] 15 USC § 1222. Several states have adopted similar laws applicable to franchises generally.

[4] 15 USC § 1221(e).

§ 14:6. Unconscionable and Oppressive Contracts. In a number of instances the law holds that contracts or contract clauses will not be enforced because they are too harsh or oppressive to one of the two parties. This principle is most commonly applied to invalidate a clause providing for the payment by one party of a large penalty if he breaks his contract or a provision declaring that a party shall not be liable for the consequences of his negligence. This principle is extended in connection with the sale of goods to provide that "if the court . . . finds the contract or any clause of the contract to have been unconscionable at the time it was made, the court may refuse to enforce the contract, or it may enforce the remainder of the contract without the unconscionable clause, or it may so limit the application of any unconscionable clause as to avoid any unconscionable result." [5] (See p. 278, Williams v Walker-Thomas Furniture Co.)

In order to bring the unconscionability provision into operation, it is not necessary to prove that fraud was practiced.[6] When there is a grossly disproportionate bargaining power between the parties so that the weaker or inexperienced party "cannot afford to risk confrontation" with the stronger party but "just signs on the dotted line," courts will hold that "grossly unfair terms obtained by the stronger party are void as contrary to public policy.[7]

Under the UCCC a particular clause or an entire agreement relating to a consumer credit sale, a consumer lease, or a consumer loan is void when such provision or agreement is unconscionable.[8] If the debtor waives any of his rights under the UCCC in making a settlement agreement with the seller or lender, such waiver is likewise subject to the power of the court as to unconscionability.[9]

§ 14:7. Social Consequences of Contracts. The social consequences of a contract are an important element today in determining its validity and the power of government to regulate it. These social consequences of a contract are related to the concept of unconscionability, although the latter concept would seem to be concerned with the effect of the contract as between the parties, whereas social consequences have a broader concern for the effect of the particular contract and other similar contracts upon society in general.

(1) The Private Contract in Society. The law of contracts, originally oriented to private relations between private individuals, is moving from the

---

[5] UCC § 2-302(1). The Code as adopted in California and North Carolina omits the unconscionability section. In Lazan v Huntington Town House, Inc., 69 Misc 2d 1017, 332 NYS2d 270 (1969), affirmed 69 Misc 2d 1019, 330 NYS2d 751, the court held that the plaintiff who had rented a hall in a building was entitled to recover his deposit where timely notice of cancellation was given and there was no evidence that the defendant would suffer any damages from the cancellation. "The court finds that the agreement itself is reasonable and fair, but the court finds that the enforcement of the agreement is unreasonable and even unconscionable so as to bring it within the purview of § 2-302 of the UCC."

[6] Jones v Star Credit Corp., 59 Misc 2d 189, 298 NYS2d 264.

[7] Shell Oil Co. v Marinello, 63 NJ 402, 307 A2d 598.

[8] UCCC § 5.108.

[9] § 1.107.

field of bilateral private law to multiparty societal considerations. This concept that no man is an island unto himself is recognized by the Supreme Court in holding that private contracts lose their private and "do-not-touch" character when they become such a common part of our way of life that society deems it necessary to regulate them.

The same view that private matters become a public concern underlies the regulation of membership in and expulsion from professional societies and labor unions. The theory is that the position they occupy in today's economic pattern takes them out of the category of fraternal or social organizations, which must be left to themselves and, to the contrary, clothes them with such a character as justifies their regulation. The same concept underlies the requirement that procedures established by trade organizations and associations be fair.

The significance of the socioeconomic setting of the contract is seen in the minimum wage law decisions. The Supreme Court at first held such laws unconstitutional as an improper interference with the rights of two adult contracting parties. Thereafter it changed its point of view to sustain such laws because of the consequences of substandard wages upon the welfare of the individual, society, and the nation.

This reevaluation of old standards is part of the general move to make modern law more "just." Difficulties arise, however, when each court considers itself free to decide as it chooses, ignoring the social force favoring stability.

(2) The n Factor. With the expansion of the concepts of "against public policy" and "unconscionability" on the one hand, and government regulation of business on the other, the importance of a given contract to society becomes increasingly significant in determining the validity of the contract as between the parties. Less and less are courts considering a contract as only a legal relationship between *A* and *B*. More and more the modern court is influenced in its decision by the recognition of the fact that the contract before the court is not one in a million but is one *of* a million. That is, *n*, or the number of times this particular contract is likely to arise, is considered by the modern court.

For example, *J* makes a contract with *K* that is of the same nature as one that *M* makes with *N*. Also, the insurance policy that the insurer *J* makes with insured *K* is similar to the insurance policy which insurer *M* makes with *N*, and so on. A like similarity or industry-wide pattern is seen in the case of the bank loan made by bank *O* to borrower *P*, by bank *Q* to borrower *R*, and so on.

The appreciation that a particular contract is merely one of many has not only influenced the courts in the interpretation of such contracts but has also been held to justify regulation of the contract by government. The view has been adopted that "when a widely diffused public interest has become enmeshed in a network of multitudinous private arrangements, the authority of the state 'to safeguard the vital interests of its people' . . . is not to be gainsaid by abstracting one such arrangement from its public context and treating it as though it were an isolated private contract constitutionally immune from impairment." [10]

§ 14:8. Illegality in Performing Contract. When a contract is otherwise legal, the fact that one of the parties in performing his part of the contract commits illegal acts not contemplated by the other party does not ordinarily prevent the wrongdoer from recovering on the contract. In some instances, however, the wrong may be regarded as so serious that the wrongdoer is punished by denying him the right to recover on the agreement which he has performed. (See p. 279, McConnell v Commonwealth Pictures Corp.)

AGREEMENTS AFFECTING PUBLIC POLICY

Agreements that interfere with public service or the duties of public officials, obstruct legal process, or discriminate against members of minority groups are considered detrimental to public welfare, and as such are not enforceable.

§ 14:9. Agreements Injuring Public Service. An agreement that tends to interfere with the proper performance of the duties of a public officer—whether legislative, administrative, or judicial—is contrary to public policy and void. Thus, an agreement to procure the award of a public contract by corrupt means is not enforceable. Other examples are agreements to sell public offices, to procure pardons by corrupt means, or to pay a public officer more or less than his legal fees or salary.

One of the most common agreements within this class is the *illegal lobbying agreement*. This term is used to describe an agreement by which one party is to use bribery, threats of a loss of votes, or any other improper means to procure or prevent the adoption of particular legislation by a lawmaking body, such as Congress or a state legislature. Such agreements are clearly contrary to the public interest since they interfere with the workings of the democratic process. They are accordingly illegal and void.

Some courts hold illegal all agreements to influence legislation, regardless of the means contemplated or employed. Other courts adopt the better rule that such agreements are valid in the absence of the use of improper influence or the contemplation of using such influence. According to the latter courts, since any person has the right to state his case to the lawmaker in the hope of influencing his action, it is proper for a person to retain and pay an agent or attorney to present his case to the lawmaker. So long as no improper inducement or threat is to be made to the lawmaker and the agent is to confine himself to stating the facts of the case, leaving it to the free will of the lawmaker to decide for himself, no illegality is present.

§ 14:10. Agreements Involving Conflicts of Interests. Various statutes prohibit government officials from being personally interested, directly or indirectly, in any transaction entered into by such officials on behalf of the

[10] East New York Savings Bank v Hahn, 326 US 230, 232.

government. Thus, a procurement officer purchasing trucks for his government may not purchase the trucks from a corporate automobile agency in which he holds a substantial block of stock. Violation of such a statute may impose a criminal liability on the officer and may make the contract unenforceable against the government.[11]

§ 14:11. Agreements Obstructing Legal Process. Any agreement intended to obstruct or pervert legal processes is contrary to public interest and therefore void. Agreements that promise to pay money in return for the abandonment of the prosecution of a criminal case, for the suppression of evidence in any legal proceeding, for initiating litigation, or for the perpetration of any fraud upon the court are therefore void.

An agreement to pay an ordinary witness more than the regular witness fee allowed by law or a promise to pay him a greater amount if the promisor wins the lawsuit is void. The danger here is that the witness will lie in order to help his party win the case.

Contracts providing for the arbitration of disputes are generally recognized as valid by modern decisions and statutes. Earlier cases held such agreements void as interfering with the jurisdiction of the courts.

(1) Selection of the Court. Contracts representing a substantial obligation will generally contain a provision for dispute settlement and tribunal selection. Sometimes it will be specified that any dispute shall be referred to arbitrators. In some instances it will be specified that any lawsuit must be brought in the courts of a particular state. Such provision will ordinarily be held valid as an aspect of the parties' freedom of contract to agree on such terms as they choose.[12]

Where the obvious purpose of the tribunal designation provision is to erect a hurdle against being sued, the provision will be held void when the parties are not in an equal bargaining position. Thus, it has been held that where the contract of the seller of prefabricated homes specified that any suit brought against the seller by a buyer must be brought in a third state which had no relationship to either the consumer buyer, the seller, or to the performance of the contract, the provision was void as unconscionable because it was clearly aimed at discouraging litigation by the consumer purchaser.[13]

Ordinarily a suit on a contract may be brought in any jurisdiction in which service can be effected. When one of the contracting parties does business in many states, he may include in his contracts a provision that suit may only be brought against him in a court of his home state. When a statute in another state expressly requires that the plaintiff sue in that state, rather than the defendant's home state, it will be held that the statutory

---

[11] United States v Mississippi Valley Generating Co., 364 US 520.

[12] Reeves v Chem Industrial Co., 95 Or 262, 495 P2d 729 (sustaining designation of courts of Ohio under a contract between an Oregon plaintiff and an Ohio defendant).

[13] Paragon Homes v Langlois, (NY) 4 UCCRS 16; Paragon Homes v Crace, (NY) 4 UCCRS 19.

provision for suit in the other state establishes a public policy which invalidates a contract provision requiring that suit be brought in a different state.[14] When a sale of goods is involved, a provision limiting suit to a state which has no relation to either the plaintiff or the defendant is void as unconscionable because it is obviously an attempt to erect a barrier against the bringing of suit.[15]

depends on state laws

§ 14:12. Sunday Laws. Under the English common law an agreement or contract could be executed on any day of the week. Today, however, most states have statutes that prohibit to some extent the making or performance of contracts on Sunday. The terms of the statutes vary greatly from state to state. The statutes may expressly declare agreements void if they are made on Sunday or if they call for performance on Sunday, or they may prohibit the sale of merchandise on Sunday.[16] They may prohibit only "servile" or manual labor, prohibit "worldly employment," or prohibit labor or business or one's "ordinary calling." Under a provision of the last type, one could legally enter into an agreement or do work outside of his regular calling.

(1) Works of Charity and Necessity. Sunday laws expressly provide that they do not apply to works of charity or necessity. *Works of charity* include those acts that are involved in religious worship or in aiding persons in distress. In general a *work of necessity* is an act which must be done at the time in order to be effective in saving life, health, or property.

The "necessity" exception to Sunday laws is generally liberally interpreted so as to permit sales where a contrary conclusion would cause serious economic loss or inconvenience. Thus, it has been held that the necessity exception permitted an auto parts dealer to sell a water pump to a motorist traveling through the state when his water pump broke down.[17]

Some courts hold that having a car washed on Sunday at a commercial carwash is a work of necessity because the motor vehicle code requires that certain parts of the car, as the windshield, be kept clean. Other courts hold that this does not make carwashing on Sunday a work of necessity.[18]

When an offer is made on Sunday but the acceptance is not made until the next day, the agreement is valid because in law it is made on the weekday when it is accepted.[19] When a preliminary oral agreement is made on Sunday but the parties intend that a formal written contract be prepared by their attorneys during the week, the contract so prepared is not a Sunday contract.[20] If a contract is made on Sunday, some courts hold that it can be

---

[14] Johnson Acoustics, Inc. v P. J. Carlin Constr. Co., 29 Conn Supp 457, 292 A2d 273.

[15] UCC § 2-302.

[16] McGowan v Maryland, 366 US 420; Braunfeld v Brown, 366 US 599.

[17] Daffron v Georgia, 229 Ga 337, 190 SE2d 37.

[18] New York v Seuss, (NY City Court) 63 Misc 2d 813, 313 NYS2d 552.

[19] Isenberg v Williams, 306 Mass 86, 27 NE2d 726.

[20] Wasserman v Roach, 336 Mass 564, 146 NE2d 909.

ratified on another day. Other courts, however, hold the contrary on the ground that the contract was illegal when made, and therefore is void and cannot be ratified.[21]

(2) Sunday as Termination Date. When the last day on which payment may be made is a Sunday, it is commonly provided by statute that it may be made on the following business day. In the absence of statute, however, the time is not extended because the last day falls on a Sunday.[22]

§ 14:13. Illegal Discrimination Contracts. A contract that a property owner will not sell his property to a member of a given race cannot be enforced because it violates the Fourteenth Amendment to the federal Constitution.[23] Hotels and restaurants may not deal with their customers on terms that discriminate because of race, religion, color, national origin, or sex.[24]

GAMBLING CONTRACTS

The legislatures of the last century adopted many laws making gambling illegal. When there is such a statute, a gambling agreement is not binding. Even without a statutory prohibition, many gambling agreements are held not binding as contrary to public policy.

§ 14:14. Wagers and Lotteries. Largely as a result of the adoption of antigambling statutes, wagers or bets are generally illegal. Private lotteries involving the three elements of prize, chance, and consideration, or similar affairs of chance, also are generally held illegal. Raffles are usually regarded as lotteries. Sales promotion schemes calling for the distribution of property according to chance among the purchasers of goods are held illegal as lotteries, without regard to whether the scheme is given the name of a guessing contest, raffle, or gift. (See p. 280, Seattle Times Co. v Tielsch.) Giveaway plans and games are lawful as long as it is not necessary to buy anything or to give anything of value in order to participate.[25] If participation is "free," the element of consideration is lacking and there is no lottery.

In some states the public policy against gambling is so strong that suit cannot be brought for a gambling debt even though the debt arose in a foreign jurisdiction in which the debt was lawful.[26]

In many states public lotteries (lotteries run by a state government) have been legalized by statute.

---

[21] R § 539; Sauls v Stone, (Ala) 241 So2d 836.

[22] Torlai v Lee, 270 Cal App 2d 854, 76 Cal Rptr 239.

[23] Shelley v Kraemer, 334 US 1.

[24] Federal Civil Rights Act of 1964, 42 USC § 2000a et seq.; Katzenbach v McClung, 379 US 294; Heart of Atlanta Motel v United States, 379 US 241.

[25] Federal Communications Commission v American Broadcasting Co., 347 US 284.

[26] Hilton of San Juan, Inc. v Lateano, 6 Conn Cir 680, 305 A2d 538.

§ **14:15. Transactions in Futures.** A person may contract to deliver in the future goods which he does not own at the time he makes the agreement. The fact that the seller does not have the goods at the time the contract is made, or that he intends to obtain securities by buying them on margin rather than paying cash in full, does not affect the legality of the transaction. If, however, the parties to the sale and purchase intend that delivery shall not be made but merely that one party shall pay the other the difference between the contract price and market price on the date set for delivery, the transaction is a gambling contract or wager upon the future market price and the contract is illegal and void. Generally, an undisclosed intention of either party or both parties that actual delivery should not be made does not affect the validity of the transaction. Furthermore, it is the intent at the time of the making of the contract which governs. Accordingly, a contract is not rendered illegal because the parties agree later that, instead of actual delivery, a payment representing the market price differential shall be made.

REGULATION OF BUSINESS

§ **14:16. Introduction.** Local, state, and national laws regulate a wide variety of business activities and practices. A businessman violating such regulations may under some statutes be subject to a fine or criminal prosecution, or under others to an order to cease and desist entered by an administrative agency or commission.

Whether an agreement made in connection with business conducted in violation of the law is binding or void depends upon how strongly opposed the public policy is to the prohibited act. Some courts take the view that the agreement is not void unless the statute expressly so specifies. In some instances, as in the case of the failure to register a fictitious name under which the business is done, the statute expressly preserves the validity of the contract by permitting the violator to sue on a contract made while illegally conducting business after his name is registered as required by the statute.

§ **14:17. Statutory Regulation of Contracts.** In order to establish uniformity or to protect one of the parties to a contract, statutes frequently provide that contracts of a given class must follow a statutory model or must contain specified provisions. For example, statutes commonly specify that particular clauses must be included in insurance policies in order to protect the persons insured and their beneficiaries. Others require that contracts executed in connection with credit buying and loans contain particular provisions designed to protect the debtor, as by specifying that he may pay off his debt at an earlier date or buy back within a specified period the property that has been used as security.

Consumer protection legislation gives the consumer the right to change his mind and to rescind his contract in certain situations. It may be required that any written contract signed by the consumer in such a situation shall inform the consumer of his right to rescind. Laws relating to truth in lending, installment sales, and home improvement contracts commonly require that an installment sale contract must specify the cash price, the down payment, the trade-in value if any, the cash balance, the insurance costs, the interest and finance charges.

When the statute imposes a fine or imprisonment for violation, the court should not hold that the contract is void since that would increase the penalty which the legislature had imposed. If a statute prohibits the making of certain kinds of contracts or imposes limitations on the contracts that can be made, the attorney general or other government official may generally be able to obtain an injunction or court order to stop the parties from entering into a prohibited kind of contract.

§ 14:18. Licensed Callings or Dealings. Statutes frequently require that a person obtain a license, certificate, or diploma before he can practice certain professions, such as law or medicine, or carry on a particular business or trade, such as that of a real-estate broker, peddler, stockbroker, hotelkeeper, or pawnbroker. If the requirement is imposed to protect the public from unqualified persons, an agreement to engage in such a profession or business without having obtained the necessary license or certificate is void. Thus, an agreement with an unlicensed physician for services cannot be enforced by him.

On the other hand, a license may be imposed solely as a revenue measure by requiring the payment of a fee for the license. In that event an agreement made in violation of the statute by one not licensed is generally held valid. The contract may also sometimes be held valid when it is shown that no harm has resulted from the failure to obtain a permit to do the work contemplated by the particular contract. Similarly, the fact that a building code required a contractor to obtain an amended building permit when the original cost estimates were exceeded was merely a technical requirement and the contractor was not barred from enforcing the contract because he had failed to obtain such permit.[27]

It is likewise frequently held that the absence of a license cannot be raised as to transactions between persons who should all be licensed, such as dealers, when the purpose of the license requirement is not to protect such persons as against each other but to protect the public generally against such persons.

§ 14:19. Fraudulent Sales. Statutes commonly regulate the sale of certain commodities. Scales and measures of grocers and other vendors must be checked periodically, and they must be approved and sealed by the proper official. Certain articles must be inspected before they are sold. Others must be labeled in a particular way to show their contents and to warn the public of the presence of any dangerous or poisonous substance. Since these laws are generally designed for the protection of the public, transactions in violation of such laws are void.

[27] Gensler v Larry Barrett, Inc., 7 Cal 3d 695, 103 Cal Rptr 247, 499 P2d 503.

When the aim of the law is to raise revenue by requiring the payment of a fee, the violation merely makes the wrongdoer liable for the penalty imposed by the law but does not make the transaction void.

§ 14:20. Administrative Agencies. Large areas of the American economy are governed by federal administrative agencies created to carry out the general policies specified by Congress. A contract must be in harmony with public policy not only as declared by Congress and the courts but also as applied by the appropriate administrative agency. For example, a contract to market particular goods might not be prohibited by any statute or court decision but may still be condemned by the Federal Trade Commission as an unfair method of competition. When the proper commission has made its determination, a contract not in harmony therewith, such as a contract of a carrier charging a higher or a lower rate than that approved by the Interstate Commerce Commission, is illegal.

CONTRACTS IN RESTRAINT OF TRADE

Agreements in restraint of trade constitute a particular segment of agreements which are contrary to public policy. To some extent these agreements are expressly condemned by statute, in which case this kind of agreement is not binding because it is illegal.

§ 14:21. Effect of Agreement. An agreement that unreasonably restrains trade is illegal and void on the ground that it is contrary to public policy. Such agreements take many forms, such as a combination to create a monopoly or to obtain a corner on the market, or an association of merchants to increase prices. In addition to the illegality of the agreement based on general principles of law, statutes frequently declare monopolies illegal and subject the parties to such agreements to various civil and criminal penalties.[28] In some instances, however, the law expressly authorizes combined action.

§ 14:22. Agreements Not to Compete. When a going business is sold, it is commonly stated in the contract that the seller shall not go into the same or a similar business again within a certain geographical area, or for a certain period of time, or both. In early times such agreements were held void since they deprived the public of the service of the person who agreed not to compete, impaired the latter's means of earning a livelihood, reduced competition, and exposed the public to monopoly.[29] To the modern courts the question is whether under the circumstances the restriction imposed upon one party is reasonable to protect the other party. If the restriction is reasonable, it is valid.[30]

A similar problem arises when an employee agrees with his employer that he will not compete with the employer should he leave his employment.

[28] Sherman Antitrust Act, 15 USC §§ 1-7; Clayton Act, 15 USC §§ 12-27; Federal Trade Commission Act, 15 USC §§ 41 to 58.

[29] Alger v Thatcher, 19 Pick 51, 36 (Mass) 51.

[30] R § 516(a); Jewel Box Stores Corp. v Morrow, 272 NC 659, 158 SE2d 840.

Restrictions to prevent such competition are held valid when reasonable and necessary to protect the interest of the employer.[31] For example, a provision that a doctor employed by a medical clinic would not practice medicine for one year within a 50-mile radius of the city in which the clinic was located is reasonable and will be enforced.[32]

While the validity of an employee's restrictive covenant is generally determined in terms of whether its restraint is greater than is required for the reasonable protection of the employer, some courts use a broader test of whether the contract is fair to the employer, the employee, and the public.[33]

In the absence of the sale of a business or the making of an employment contract, an agreement not to compete is void as a restraint of trade and a violation of the antitrust law.[34] Likewise, a promise to refrain from competing made by an employee to the person by whom he is already employed is not supported by consideration and is not binding for that reason as well.[35]

When a restriction on competition as agreed to by the parties is held invalid because its scope as to time or geographical area is too great,[36] there is a conflict of authority as to the action to be taken by the court. Some courts apply the "blue pencil" rule and trim the covenant down to a scope which they deem reasonable and require the parties to abide by that revision.[37] Other courts hold that this is rewriting the contract for the parties, which courts ordinarily cannot do, and refuse to revise the covenant, holding that the covenant is totally void and that the contract is to be applied as though it did not contain any restrictive covenant.[38]

§ 14:23. Resale Price Maintenance Agreements. Under antitrust legislation an agreement between a manufacturer and distributor or between a distributor and dealer that the latter should not resell below a specified minimum price was void.[39] Congress and many of the states have adopted statutes, called *fair trade acts,* which change this rule and sustain the validity of such agreements when they relate to trademark or brand-name articles.[40]

---

[31] R § 516(f); Carl Coiffure, Inc. v Mourlot, (Tex Civ App) 410 SW2d 209.

[32] Hall v Willard & Woolsey, PSC, (Ky) 471 SW2d 316.

[33] E. P. I. of Cleveland v Basler, 12 Ohio App 2d 16, 230 NE2d 552 (holding that a covenant not to compete within a 200-mile radius of a city was unreasonable and not binding when the employer generally did business only within a 60-mile radius and did not operate regularly in 91 percent of the territory within the 200-mile radius).

[34] Hayes v Parklane Hosiery Co., 24 Conn Supp 218, 189 A2d 522.

[35] Wilmar, Inc. v Liles, 13 NC App 71, 185 SE2d 278.

[36] The nature of the business is an important factor in determining what geographic area is reasonable. It is apparent that some businesses, such as building maintenance, will necessarily operate in a limited area. See, for example, Kunz v Bock, (Iowa) 163 NW2d 442.

[37] Extine v Williamson Midwest, 176 Ohio 403, 200 NE2d 297.

[38] Brown v Devine, 240 Ark 838, 402 SW2d 669.

[39] Miles Medical Co. v Park, 220 US 373.

[40] The state acts apply only to intrastate sales. The federal statute applies to interstate sales and permits resale price maintenance agreements when such agreements are lawful in the state in which the goods are to be resold or into which they are to be sent.

The federal statute and many state laws apply not only to those who are parties to the price maintenance agreement but also to anyone having knowledge of the agreement who thereafter in the course of regular business resells the article under its trade name or mark.[41]

There is a conflict of authority as to whether the giving of trading stamps is a violation of a fair trade act.[42]

§ 14:24. Selling Below Cost. Because of the expense involved in detecting violations of fair trade agreements and of enforcing such agreements by litigation, together with the inability in many states to bind third persons by such agreements, a majority of the states have adopted statutes prohibiting selling "below cost" for the purpose of harming competition. Such laws have generally been held constitutional, as against the contention that "below cost" is too vague.

§ 14:25. Middleman Protection. A middleman may make an agreement with his customer which seeks to prevent the customer from bypassing the middleman in dealing directly with the middleman's source of supply. Such a restriction is held invalid as a restraint of trade when the middleman no longer has any interest that requires such protection. (See p. 281, Garelick v Leonardo.)

§ 14:26. Definition. A person is guilty of *usury* when he lends money that is to be repaid unconditionally and he specifies a rate of interest which is greater than that allowed by statute. In determining whether a transaction is usurious, the court will look through the form of the transaction to determine whether there is in fact a loan on which excessive interest is charged.[43]

The charging of excessive interest by the lender of money has long been condemned by usury statutes. In contrast with an illegal agreement which is partially binding, generally only the usurious part is not binding and the lender is generally subject to some penalty.

---

[41] Miller-Tydings Act, 50 Stat 693, 15 USC § 1; McGuire Act, 66 Stat 632, 15 USC § 45.

[42] Statutes governing price maintenance agreements commonly provide that the parties to such contracts may recover damages from third persons who sell the article below the agreement price or may obtain an injunction to compel the observance of that price. Approximately one third of the states hold that such laws are valid and bind both the parties to such agreements and nonsigners; that is, persons who did not join in the agreements but had knowledge thereof. Olin Mathieson Chemical Corp. v Ontario Store, 9 Ohio 2d 67, 223 NE2d 592. In contrast, slightly more than one third of the states hold that the agreements bind only the parties to them and cannot constitutionally bind nonsigners even though so provided by statute. Olin Mathieson Chemical Corp. v Francis, 134 Colo 160, 301 P2d 139; Shakespeare Co. v Lippman's Tool Shop Sporting Goods Co., 334 Mich 109, 54 NW2d 268. In approximately one third of the states resale price maintenance agreements are invalid and bind no one.

[43] Alt v Bailey, 211 Miss 547, 52 So2d 283; Modern Pioneers Insurance Co. v Nandin, 103 Ariz 125, 437 P2d 658.

(1) Maximum Contract and Legal Rates. Most states prohibit by statute the taking of more than a stated annual rate of interest. These statutes provide a *maximum contract rate* of interest— commonly 8 or 10 percent— which is the highest annual rate that can be exacted or demanded under the law of a given state. It is usually recoverable only when there is an agreement in writing to pay that amount. A federal statute limits interest charges to servicemen to 6 percent a year on obligations incurred before entering the service.[44]

The fact that the lender is a national bank does not exempt it from state usury laws. For example, a national bank in Alabama was subject to the usury laws of Alabama and the provisions of the Alabama Small Loan Act which prohibits compound interest. Consequently, there was a prohibited compounding of interest when the national bank in connection with its credit cards charged interest on interest and the bank therefore forfeited the right to any interest as specified by the Alabama law.[45]

All states provide for a legal rate of interest. When there is an agreement for interest to be paid but no rate is specified or when the law implies a duty to pay interest, as on judgments, the *legal rate* is applied. In most states the legal rate of interest is 6 percent per year.

§ 14:27. Special Situations. The deduction by the lender of all of the interest in advance as a discount [46] from the nominal amount of the loan does not constitute usury even though the amount of interest collected represents a rate of interest in excess of that permitted by law. Neither are the usury statutes violated by contracts that provide for the payment of the annual interest charge at the maximum rate in several installments, such as quarterly or monthly.

Usually state statutes permit small loan associations, pawnbrokers, and similar licensed moneylenders to charge a higher rate of interest than is permissible in ordinary business transactions. The reason is that a much greater risk is involved.

A borrower is commonly required to pay some penalty, such as an additional month's interest, when he pays a debt before maturity. Such a payment is generally regarded as not usurious.[47]

When the lender is entitled to repayment of principal and the maximum rate of interest, the transaction is made usurious if in addition he is to receive a percentage of any profit that may be made by the borrower.[48]

In recent years the interest maximums permitted have increased. Under the Uniform Consumer Credit Code (UCCC), the maximum rate on home

---

[44] Soldiers and Sailors' Civil Relief Act, § 206, 50 App USC § 526.

[45] Partain v First National Bank, (CA5 Ala) 467 F2d 167.

[46] The term "discount" refers to the deduction of interest in advance so that the amount received by the borrower is the face of the loan less the amount of the interest or discount.

[47] Reichwein v Kirschenbaum, 98 RI 340, 201 A2d 918.

[48] American Insurers Life Insurance Co. v Regnold, 243 Ark 906, 423 SW2d 551.

mortgages is, with certain exceptions, 18 percent. In the case of consumer credit sales, the UCCC permits interest up to 36 percent per year on the first $300, 21 percent per year on the next $700, and 15 percent per year on the excess over $1,000, or an alternative of 18 percent per year on the entire amount, plus additional charges, such as for insurance.[49] In the case of revolving charge accounts a maximum interest rate of 2 percent per month is authorized by the UCCC on the first $500 and 1½ percent on the excess.[50]

When the debt is accelerated the creditor is entitled to the principal and interest up to the time of acceleration but is not allowed unearned interest.[51]

*(1) **Service Charges.*** Service charges and placement fees are ordinarily added to the express interest in order to determine whether a loan is usurious.[52]

The addition of a recording charge of one or a few dollars does not make the transaction usurious where the amount so charged was the amount specified by statute.[53]

*(2) **Late Charges and Budget Account Charges.*** Courts differ as to the effect of a late payment charge. Some hold that the character of a loan must be determined when the loan is initially made. The fact that at a later date a late payment charge is added does not change the character of the transaction at the time that it was made. These courts hold that the late payment charge is to be ignored in determining the total amount of interest charged. In other states late charges are regarded as interest on the theory that they are payments due because money was not repaid, with the consequence that unless a late charge satisfies the usury law requirement, the lender is subject to the usury statute penalties.[54]

When a seller budgets the purchase and adds a charge to the unpaid balance due by the customer, some courts hold that such charge is subject to the usury law. [55] Other courts hold that the charge is not subject to the usury law because it is merely a variation of the time-price differential.[56] These courts also hold that it is immaterial whether the charge account pattern is an in-house program conducted by the seller for his own customers only, or whether there is a central financing agency which handles accounts for a number of participating merchants.[57]

The "previous balance" method of determining finance charges is proper without regard to whether the unpaid balance on which the finance charge is

---

[49] UCCC §§ 2.201, 2.202.

[50] UCCC § 2.207.

[51] Atlas Financial Corp. v Ezrine, — App Div 2d —, 345 NYS2d 36.

[52] Gangadean v Flori Investment Co., 106 Ariz 245, 474 P2d 1006.

[53] Berrien v Avco Financial Services, Inc., 123 Ga App 862, 182 SE2d 708 affirmed 127 Ga App 584, 194 SE2d 337.

[54] Thrift Funds of Baton Rouge, Inc. v Jones, (La) 274 So2d 150.

[55] Wisconsin v J. C. Penney Co., 48 Wis 2d 125, 179 NW2d 641.

[56] See § 15:30.

[57] Kass v Central Charge Service, Inc., (Dist Col App) 304 A2d 632.

imposed is the balance at the beginning or the end of the period or is an average daily balance.[58]

*(3) **Points.*** In times of relative scarcity of money, it is common for lenders to make a charge for the making of a loan. This is commonly called giving or paying "points" to the lender. It is a fee or charge of one or more percentages of the principal amount of the loan. It is collected by the lender at the time the loan is made and is in the nature of a bonus, premium, or service charge for effecting the loan. Points are distinct from interest, but both must be added together to determine whether the loan is usurious. In computing this total, the points are to be prorated over the years in the life of the loan.[59] Were this not done, the loan would often be usurious as to the first year.

§ 14:28. Credit Insurance. The lender, in addition to charging the maximum interest rate, may require the borrower to buy life insurance payable to the lender for the amount of the loan. If the lender in some manner retains or receives part of the premiums paid for the insurance, with the result that the interest on the loan plus the share of the premiums total more than the maximum interest which could be charged, the transaction is usurious.[60]

Consumer protection statutes in some states prohibit the lender or seller from requiring that the debtor obtain insurance through the lender or seller, or prohibit the lender or seller from receiving directly or indirectly for his own use any part of a payment made by the debtor for insurance premiums.

The Uniform Consumer Credit Code permits the making of such tied-in sales of insurance as long as the premiums charged do not exceed those permitted by the appropriate state commissioner of insurance[61] or as long as the amount is not so great as to be deemed unconscionable.[62]

§ 14:29. Effect of Usury. The effect of an agreement that violates the usury laws differs in the various states. In some states the entire amount of interest is forfeited.[63] In other states the recovery of only the excess is denied. In still others, the agreement is held to be void.[64] If the interest has been paid, the states differ as to whether the borrower recovers merely the amount of the interest paid or whether he recovers two[65] or three times that amount as a penalty.

---

[58] Federated Dept. Stores, Inc. v Pasco, (Fla App) 275 So2d 46.

[59] B. F. Saul Co. v West End Park North, 250 Md 707, 246 A2d 591.

[60] Cochran v Alabama, 270 Ala 440, 119 So2d 339.

[61] UCCC § 4.112.

[62] §§ 4.106, 5.108, 6.111. In view of the high premiums generally allowed by state insurance commissioners in the types of transactions here considered, it has been commented by some that the provisions of the UCCC do not provide any significant protection to the debtor.

[63] Service Loan & Finance Corp. v McDaniel, 115 Ga App 548, 154 SE2d 823.

[64] Curtis v Securities Acceptance Corp., 166 Neb 815, 91 NW2d 19.

[65] Petersen v Philco Finance Corp., 91 Idaho 644, 428 P2d 961, 15-59.

In some states a lender who charges more than twice the lawful rate of interest forfeits both interest and principal, thus cancelling any balance due and also requiring him to return to the debtor any payments which had been made by him.[66] The debtor is limited to recovering the statutory penalty and unless authorized by statute may not recover compensatory or punitive damages.[67]

In some states a special consumer protection statute governs the effect of usury in an installment contract. In contrast with the penalty ordinarily imposed by the usury statutes of permitting the debtor to recover interest or double or treble the amount of interest, some consumer protection statutes declare the original transaction void and permit the debtor to recover both principal and interest which have been paid and bar the creditor from recovering any of the unpaid debt. Under such a statute it has been held that where the creditor loaned money to the debtor and paid a gas station for gas purchased by the debtor on credit, the transaction for the repayment of the cash and the gas bills was usurious where the debtor agreed to pay $6.00 for every $5.00, the debtor agreeing to pay in installments, which brought him within the scope of the Installment Repayment Small Loan and Consumer Act.[68]

§ **14:30. Credit Sale Price.** Usury statutes generally do not apply to sales made on credit, such as installment sales,[69] whether of goods (see p. 282, Equipment Finance, Inc. v Grannas) or real estate. This rule is based on the narrow definition of usury as the charging of more than the lawful rate of interest on a loan. According to the law, when goods are sold on credit or on the installment plan, the seller does not lend money to the buyer but agrees that he is to be paid by the buyer later or at stated times rather than at the time of sale. Since no loan is made, the usury law does not apply and the seller is free to sell for cash at one price and on time at a different price that is much higher and which would be usurious if the usury law applied.

Similarly, when a person buys a house on time, the transaction is not usurious simply because the price is greater than the seller would have demanded for a cash sale and the difference is more than the maximum interest that could have been charged on the cash price.[70]

A few states hold that the time price differential is subject to the usury law [71] or have amended their usury laws or have adopted statutes to regulate the differential between cash and time prices that may be charged by the seller. Such statutes, however, are sometimes limited to sales by retailers to consumers or apply only to sales under a stated dollar maximum. In any

---

66 Lafferty v A. E. M. Developers and Builders Company, (Tex Civ App) 483 SW 2d 279.

67 Moretto v Sussman, (Fla App) 274 So2d 259.

68 Smashed Ice v Lee, 86 SD 658, 200 NW2d 236.

69 Nazarian v Lincoln Finance Co., 77 RI 497, 78 A2d 7.

70 Howell v Mid-State Homes, Inc., 13 Ariz App 371, 476 P2d 892.

71 Lloyd v Gutgsell, 175 Neb 775, 124 NW2d 198.

case, the price differential credit sale is held to be a usurious transaction when it is in fact a loan of money that is disguised as a sale for the purpose of avoiding the usury law.

Many states have adopted retail installment sales laws which apply whenever the sale price is to be paid in installments and the seller retains a security interest in the goods. These laws frequently fix a maximum for the time-price differential,[72] thereby remedying the situation created by the fact that the price differential is not subject to the usury laws.

When the credit seller informs the buyer that the purchase will be financed by a particular bank and the original credit sale contract requires the buyer to pay the credit balance directly to the bank, the transaction is not a sale on credit under which the time-price differential is not subject to the usury law, but is instead a loan by the bank to the buyer even though the transaction is not in the form of a sale and the claim of the bank against the buyer for the unpaid balance is subject to the usury law.[73]

§ 14:31. Corporations and Usury. In many states corporations are prohibited from raising the defense of usury. A loan is not regarded as usurious even though it is made to a corporation which is organized for the purpose of borrowing the money when the lender refuses to make the loan to an individual and suggests that he form a corporation so that higher interest may be charged than would be lawful on a loan to a natural person.[74]

---

[72] See, for example, Singer Co. v Gardner, 121 NJ Super 261, 296 A2d 562 (imposing a 10% limitation).

[73] National Bank of Commerce v Thomsen, 80 Wash 2d 406, 495 P2d 332.

[74] McNellis v Merchants National Bank and Trust Co., (CA 2d) 390 F2d 239.

CASES FOR CHAPTER 14

Miller v Radikopf

— Mich App —, 214 NW2d 897 (1974)

Miller and Radikopf sold Irish sweepstakes tickets. They received two free tickets for every twenty they sold. They made an agreement for dividing winnings on their tickets. One of the tickets won approximately one-half million dollars. Radikopf kept all the money. Miller sued him for his share of the winnings. Judgment was entered for Radikopf. Miller appealed.

PER CURIAM . . . Plaintiff first contends that the possession of a lottery ticket and the winning of a lottery prize is not in itself illegal and therefore contrary to public policy. It is true that receiving a lottery award voluntarily paid, is not prohibited. . . . The general policy of this state against the holding of lotteries . . . would be seriously compromised, however, if lottery winners were allowed to successfully bring suit for their prizes. Although the Court will not interfere where a lottery prize is voluntarily given the winner, public policy demands that courts not give support to the maintenance of lotteries in this state by allowing prize winners judicial process to collect their winnings. . . .

Plaintiff next contends that the 1970 constitutional amendment . . . and the Lottery Act [of] 1972, . . . establishing a state run lottery in Michigan under that amendment, evinces a public policy in favor of the allowance of lotteries. Section 37 of that act, . . . however, specifically exempts the lottery established under that act from the application of other laws concerning lotteries. This specific exemption implies that other lotteries are to remain prohibited by those statutes. This is especially true since the state lottery has as its purpose the raising of revenue for the state, and it would seem incongruous that the Legislature would allow private lotteries to compete with the public lottery and thereby reduce the revenues earned for the state. We therefore hold that the state lottery . . . is the only legal lottery conducted in this state, and that the maintenance of other lotteries is contrary to statute and public policy.

[Judgment affirmed.]

Schara v Thiede

58 Wis 489, 206 NW2d 129 (1973)

Thiede was a licensed tavern owner. Schara wished to purchase the business but he did not have a license. To enable Schara to run the business under Thiede's license, the parties executed an agreement by which Schara was described as running the business as manager for Thiede for the balance of the period of Thiede's license, after which Thiede was to lease the business to Schara. Thiede refused to execute the lease and Schara brought an action against him for breach of his agreement to lease the business. From a judgment for Schara, Thiede appealed.

HEFFERNAN, J. . . . The contract on its face discloses no illegality. It provides merely for the employment of Schara as the manager of Thiede's tavern until June 30, 1970, with Schara to receive a one year lease of the premises thereafter on the condition that the premises remain licensed to operate as a tavern. Taken literally, the contract was legal, and a breach of its conditions by either party could render the other liable for damages.

Despite the facial legality of an agreement, parol evidence is admissible to show that a writing valid on its face is a mere cover for an illegal transaction. . . .

The evidence adduced at trial established that the written contract had little similarity to the parties' actual agreement as they understood it. Both Schara and Thiede . . . testified that there was never any intention that the operator of the tavern act as "manager" for Thiede. On the contrary, the parties contemplated that . . . Schara would operate the tavern as his own business and that the agreement was a lease and a contract of employment.

While they denied that they knew that the arrangement was illegal, all parties to the contract recognized that the agreement was a subterfuge to cover the fact that . . . Schara [was] operating the tavern without a proper license. The agreement, as understood by the parties, was in violation of secs. 176.04 and 176.05, Stats., insofar as it involved the operation of the tavern . . . without having first obtained a proper license.

Thiede relies upon the illegality of the contract to defeat Schara's claim for damages. . . .

"The general rule is that . . . a court will not aid either party to an illegal agreement, whether executory or executed, but leaves the parties where it finds them." Schara does not deny the illegality of the agreement, but argues that the illegal provisions are severable and that the remainder of the agreement, including Thiede's promise to execute a one-year lease on July 1, 1970, is enforceable. The principle of severability may be applicable even though a portion of a contract may be tainted with illegality. . . .

The rule, however, gives no comfort to the plaintiff in this case, for his right to the one-year lease was expressly conditioned upon his faithful performance as "manager" pursuant to the illegal agreement. Schara clearly relies upon the past performance of an illegal transaction and, accordingly, cannot expect relief from the courts.

[Judgment reversed.]

Williams v Walker-Thomas Furniture Co.

(CA Dist Col) 350 F2d 445 (1965)

The Walker-Thomas Furniture Co. sold furniture on credit under contracts which contained a provision that a customer did not own his purchase as long as any balance on any purchase remained due. It sold goods to Williams. At the time when the balance of her account was $164, Walker-Thomas Furniture

Co. sold her a $514 stereo set with knowledge that she was supporting herself and seven children on a government relief check of $218 a month. From 1957 to 1962 Williams had purchased $1,800 worth of goods and made payments of $1,400. When she stopped making payments in 1962, Walker-Thomas sought to take back everything she had purchased since 1957. From a judgment in favor of Walker-Thomas, Williams appealed.

WRIGHT, J. . . . The notion that an unconscionable bargain should not be given full enforcement is by no means novel. In Scott v United States, 79 U.S. (12 Wall) 443, 445 (1870), the Supreme Court stated: "If a contract be unreasonable and unconscionable, but not void for fraud, a court of law will give to the party who sues for its breach damages, not according to its letter, but only such as he is equitably entitled to." Since we have never adopted or rejected such a rule, the question here presented is actually one of first impression.

Congress has recently enacted the Uniform Commercial Code, which specifically provides that the court may refuse to enforce a contract which it finds to be unconscionable at the time it was made. 28 D.C. Code § 2—302 (Supp. IV 1965). The enactment of this section, which occurred subsequent to the contracts here in suit, does not mean that the common law of the District of Columbia was otherwise at the time of enactment, nor does it preclude the court from adopting a similar rule in the exercise of its powers to develop the common law for the District of Columbia. In fact, in view of the absence of prior authority on the point, we consider the congressional adoption of § 2—302 persuasive authority for following the rationale of the cases from which the section is explicitly derived. Accordingly, we hold that where the element of unconscionability is present at the time a contract is made, the contract should not be enforced.

Unconscionability has generally been recognized to include an absence of meaningful choice on the part of one of the parties together with contract terms which are unreasonably favorable to the other party. Whether a meaningful choice is present in a particular case can only be determined by consideration of all the circumstances surrounding the transaction. In many cases the meaningfulness of the choice is negated by a gross inequality of bargaining power. The manner in which the contract was entered is also relevant to this consideration. Did each party to the contract, considering his obvious education or lack of it, have a reasonable opportunity to understand the terms of the contract, or were the important terms hidden in a maze of fine print and minimized by deceptive sales practices? Ordinarily, one who signs an agreement without full knowledge of its terms might be held to assume the risk that he has entered a one-sided bargain. But when a party of little bargaining power, and hence little real choice, signs a commercially unreasonable contract with little or no knowledge of its terms, it is hardly likely that his consent, or even an objective manifestation of his consent, was ever given to all the terms. In such a case the usual rule that the terms of the agreement are not to be questioned should be abandoned and the court should consider whether the terms of the contract are so unfair that enforcement should be withheld. . . .

Because the trial court and the appellate court did not feel that enforcement could be refused, no findings were made on the possible unconscionability of the contracts in [this case]. Since the record is not sufficient for our deciding the issue as a matter of law, the [case is] remanded to the trial court for further proceedings.

So ordered.

McConnell v Commonwealth Pictures Corp.

7 NY2d 465, 166 NE2d 482, 199 NYS2d 483 (1960)

Commonwealth Pictures Corp. agreed to pay McConnell $10,000 and a specified commission if he could persuade Universal Pictures Company to give Commonwealth the distribution rights on its pictures. Without the knowledge of either Universal or Commonwealth, McConnell obtained the distribution rights by paying an agent of Universal the $10,000 Commonwealth paid McConnell. McConnell thereafter sued Commonwealth for the agreed commission.

From a judgment in favor of McConnell, Commonwealth appealed.

DESMOND, C.J. . . . [The lower court] said that, since the agreement sued upon—between plaintiff and defendant—was not in itself illegal, plaintiff's right to be paid for performing it could not be defeated by a showing that he had misconducted himself in carrying it out. The court found a substantial difference between this and the performance of an illegal contract. We take a different view. Proper and consistent application of a prime and long-settled public policy closes the doors of our courts to those who sue to collect the rewards of corruption.

New York's policy has been frequently and emphatically announced in the decisions. "It is the settled law of this State (and probably of every other State) that a party to an illegal contract cannot ask a court of law to help him carry out his illegal object, nor can such a person plead or prove in any court a case in which he, as a basis for his claim, must show forth his illegal purpose. . . . The money plaintiff sues for was the fruit of an admitted crime and 'no court should be required to serve as paymaster of the wages of crime.' "

. . . It is true that some of the leading decisions . . . were in suits on intrinsically illegal contracts, but the rule fails of its purpose unless it covers a case like the one at bar. . . .

We are not working here with narrow questions of technical law. We are applying fundamental concepts of morality and fair dealing not to be weakened by exceptions. So far as precedent is necessary, we can rely on Sirkin v Fourteenth Street Store, 124 App Div 384, 108 NYS 830 . . . and Reiner v North American Newspaper Alliance, 259 NY 250, 181 NE 564, 83 ALR 23. . . . Sirkin is the case closest to ours and shows that, whatever be the law in other jurisdictions, we in New York deny awards for the corrupt performance of contracts even though in essence the contracts are not illegal. Sirkin had sued for the price of goods sold and delivered to defendant. Held to be good was a defense which charged that plaintiff seller had paid a secret commission to an agent of defendant purchaser. There cannot be any difference in principle between that situation and the present one where plaintiff (it is alleged) contracted to buy motion-picture rights for defendant but performed his covenant only by bribing the seller's agent. In the Reiner case (supra), likewise, the plaintiff had fully performed the services required by his agreement with the defendant but was denied a recovery because his performance had involved and included "fraud and deception" practiced not on defendant but on a third party. . . .

Perhaps this application of the principle represents a distinct step beyond Sirkin and Reiner . . . in the sense that we are here barring recovery under a contract which in itself is entirely legal. But if this be an extension, public policy supports it. We point out that our holding is limited to cases in which the illegal performance of a contract originally valid takes the form of commercial bribery or similar conduct and in which the illegality is central to or a dominant part of the plaintiff's whole course of conduct in performance of the contract. . . .

[Judgment reversed.]

Seattle Times Company v Tielsch

80 Wash App 2d 502, 495 P2d 1366 (1972)

The Seattle Times ran a football forecasting contest, called "Guest-Guesser." The Seattle Chief of Police claimed this was illegal as a lottery. The Times brought a declaratory judgment action to determine the legality of the contest. The court held the contest was a lottery and the Seattle Times appealed.

ROSELLINI, J. . . . The result of a football game may depend upon weather, the physical condition of the players and the psychological attitude of the players. It may also be affected by sociological problems between and among the members of a football team. The element of chance is an integral part of the game of football as well as the skill of the players.

The lure of the "Guest-Guesser" contest is partially the participant's love of football, partially the challenge of competition and partially the hope enticingly held out, which is often false or disappointing, that the participant will get something for nothing or a great deal for a very little outlay. . . .

The elements of a lottery are prize, consideration and chance. . . .

The appellant maintains that chance is not a dominant element in football forecasting contests. . . . The trial court found to the contrary upon that evidence, and we think the finding is justified. The appellant's expert statistician who testified at the trial did not state that chance plays no part in the outcome of such a contest or even that it does not play a dominant role. He merely testified that such a contest is not one of "pure chance." Pure chance he defined as a 50-50 chance. He acknowledged that a contestant who consistently predicted the outcome of 14 out of 20 games correctly would be a "highly skilled" contestant. . . .

. . . Where a contest is multiple or serial, and requires the solution of a number of problems to win the prize, the fact that skill alone will bring contestants to a correct solution of a greater part of the problems does not make the contest any the less a lottery if chance enters into the solution of another lesser part of the problems and thereby proximately influences the final result. . . .

Our research has revealed only one case involving a football forecasting game and the game there was a "pool," that is, a gambling game wherein wagers were placed. The Superior Court of Pennsylvania held that it was a lottery. What is most relevant in the case for our consideration here is the court's discussion of the element of chance in forecasting the result of football games. That court said: It is true that for an avid student of the sport of football the chance taken is not so great as for those who have little interest in the game. However, it is common knowledge that the predictions even among these so-called "experts" are far from infallible. Any attempt to forecast the result of a single athletic contest, be it football, baseball, or whatever, is fraught with chance. This hazard is multiplied directly by the number of predictions made. The operators of the scheme involved in this case were well cognizant of this fact for the odds against a correct number of selections were increased from 5 to 1 for three teams picked up to 900 to 1 for fifteen teams. Commonwealth v Laniewski, 173 Pa Super 245, 249, 98 A2d 215, 217 (1953).

The trial court in the instant case recognized the same basic realities attendant upon the enterprise of football game-result forecasting. We are convinced that it correctly held that chance, rather than skill, is the dominant factor in the Times' "Guest-Guesser" contest. The very name of the contest conveys quite accurately the promoter's as well as the participants' true concept of the nature of the contest.

We conclude that the contest, however harmless it may be in the opinion of the participants and the promoters, is a lottery. . . .

[Judgment against Seattle Times.]

Garelick v Leonardo

105 RI 142, 250 A2d 354 (1969)

Garelick made a contract with the Narragansett Brewing Co. to purchase from January, 1953, to December 31, 1957, all of the latter's spent wet grain, a by-product of the brewing process. Garelick then made a contract by which all such grain purchased by him from Narragansett for the period December 28, 1953, through December 31, 1957, inclusive, would be resold to Leonardo. The latter contract specified that "during the period of this Agreement and for a period of five (5) years after the expiration hereof the Buyers will not directly or indirectly purchase spent wet grain from Narragansett." Garelick claimed that Leonardo violated this five-year restriction and sued for damages for such breach and for a court order requiring Leonardo to comply with the restriction. From a decision in Leonardo's favor, Garelick appealed.

ROBERTS, C.J. . . . The sole issue before the court then was whether Leonardo's purchases of grain from Farmers Feed after December 31, 1957, the terminal date of his contract with Garelick, constituted a violation of a valid restraint that would warrant the assessment of damages. . . .

. . . The trial justice concluded that the first period of restraint contemplated in the restrictive covenant was in fact the period of time in which Garelick had an exclusive contract with Narragansett for the purchase of grain, and it is conceded that during this period the agreement was not breached by Leonardo. It was the opinion of the trial justice that the second period of restraint extended over a period of five years, beginning December 31, 1957, which marked the termination, not only of Leonardo's contract with Garelick, but also Garelick's contract with Narragansett.

. . . . The trial justice did not err in holding that the restrictive covenant under consideration was, as to the time element, divisible. . . .

. . . Where restrictive covenants contained in an agreement are divisible, the restraints set out therein will be valid to the extent that they are reasonably necessary for the protection of the interest of the person for whose benefit they are intended, are not unreasonably restrictive of the rights of the person who is so restrained, and are not contrary to public policy. . . .

The question then is whether the restriction upon Leonardo's purchase of grain from Narragansett for a period of five years following December 31, 1957, was unreasonable and, therefore, an illegal restraint of trade that the court will not enforce. 2 Restatement, Contracts. . . . Section 515 suggests that a restraint of trade is unreasonable if it "(a) is greater than is required for the protection of the person for whose benefit the restraint is imposed, or (b) imposes undue hardship upon the person restricted, or . . . (c) is based on a promise to refrain from competition and is not ancillary either to a contract for the transfer of goodwill or other subject of property or to an existing employment or contract of employment." . . . The restraint imposed during the five-year period following December 31, 1957 . . . was greatly in excess of that required for the protection of Garelick and, if enforced, would impose undue hardship upon Leonardo. It is clear from the factual situation disclosed here that as of December 31, 1957, Garelick's contract with Narragansett for the purchase of all of the grain produced by it had terminated and consequently it had no interest to protect during the ensuing five-year period. Obviously, the restraint was designed to protect Garelick's source of supply which he had contracted to deliver to Leonardo: but once that contract had expired, Garelick was left with no interest or right that the enforcement of the . . . restraint would protect.

Obviously, to enforce the . . . restraint would work considerable hardship on Leonardo, who, now unable to obtain the grain from Garelick, would be forbidden to seek such grains as he needed in his business from Narragansett or from Farmers Feed, which now had a contract with Narragansett to take the grain it produced. In the circumstances we find that the restraint—imposed upon Leonardo by the terms of the contract prohibiting him from purchasing grain from Narragansett for a period of five years after the termination of Garelick's contract with Narragansett—was unreasonable, constitutes an illegal restraint, and will not be enforced. . . .

[Judgment affirmed.]

Equipment Finance, Inc. v Grannas

207 Pa Super 363, 218 A2d 81 (1966)

Grannas and his partner purchased heavy equipment from Aggregates Equipment on credit, agreeing to pay in 36 monthly installments including a "credit service charge" of $11,713.44. Aggregates assigned the contract and security agreement to a finance company, Equipment Finance, which later sued Grannas and his partner when they stopped paying the installments. Grannas and his partner raised the defense that the credit service charge was usurious. From a judgment adverse to them, Grannas and his partner appealed.

JACOBS, J. The narrow point of law presented in this appeal is whether or not the [Pennsylvania] Usury Statute applies to a sale of heavy machinery on credit when a finance company . . . purchases from the seller of the machinery the security agreement and accompanying note given by the buyer to the seller. . . .

For purposes of this appeal, it is sufficient to point out that buyer and seller executed a security agreement dated July 9, 1956, covering the rock crushing equipment which seller sold to buyer. The security agreement clearly delineated each component of the selling price. It showed an unpaid cash price of $65,075.28, which included an insurance charge of $2,099.28 and a $5 filing fee. It showed a time balance of $76,788.72, arrived at by adding a "credit service charge" of $11,713.44 to the unpaid cash price. It set forth the terms under which the time balance was to be paid, viz., 36 monthly installments of $2,133.02 each, beginning August 9, 1956. Seller assigned this security agreement and buyer's accompanying note to finance company in return for the unpaid cash price, less insurance and filing charges. Buyer made each month's payment to finance company for 33 months but refused to pay the final three installments, tendering instead a check for $396.92, which it alleged was the entire balance due at the time the thirty-fourth payment was demanded in May, 1959. It contended that the credit service charge of $11,713.44 was usurious and that all it was obliged to pay was 6 percent interest per annum on the declining balance of the unpaid cash price, leaving $396.92 due.

Appellants [Grannas and his partner] would have us hold that certain sections of Article 9 of the Uniform Commercial Code . . . show the intention of the legislature to make this transaction a loan, requiring an application of the Usury Statute. We cannot agree.

The [Pennsylvania] Usury Statute . . . provides: "The lawful rate of interest for a loan or use of money in all cases where no express contract shall have been made for a less rate, shall be 6 percent per annum. . . ."

Courts in this jurisdiction have consistently said that this act does not apply to a bona fide sale of goods on credit. Such sales are the result of a decision by a buyer to purchase property on credit at a higher price than he would pay if he paid cash. There is no loan or use of money on the part of the buyer. . . .

"Of course, all sale or lease contracts which extend credit are, to a certain extent, akin to the making of loans, but where a greater charge is exacted in the case of a sale on credit than in a cash sale, it is included in the selling price of the article. It being uniformly held that sellers are free to contract with buyers as to the terms and conditions of sales, the financing of sales of merchandise by the extension of credit has never been considered subject to the prohibition of usury or to regulations applicable to banking and loan transactions."

A careful review of the testimony and of the law of Pennsylvania satisfies us that prior to the Code this transaction would not be regarded as usurious. We agree with the jury's conclusion that even though a finance company was involved, taking an assignment of the security agreement, the primary purpose of this transaction was the purchase of goods and was not an occasion or pretext for a loan.

With the law thus established, the only inquiry remaining for us is to consider appellants' argument that Article 9 of the Code changes the law since a security agreement was executed here. We think not. . . .

. . . Nowhere in this Article, which is a comprehensive scheme for the regulation of security interests in personal property, is any attempt made to regulate financing charges. This buyer agreed to pay a higher price for the rock crushing equipment for the privilege of buying it on credit and using it while paying it off. He elected to enter into this financing agreement rather than attempting to secure a loan through a bank for reasons not here our concern. Neither Article 9 of the Code nor the public policy arguments advanced by appellants convince this court that we should or can change the financial agreement these businessmen entered into. The latter arguments are more properly addressed to the legislature which has imposed restrictions to cover certain financing situations, as in the Small Loan Act, . . . the Consumer Discount Company Act . . . , and the Motor Vehicle Sales Finance Act. . . . [In the absence of] legislative action to regulate the financing of large commercial transactions between businessmen, we will leave these businessmen, who are presumed to know what they are doing when they consummate equipment purchase agreements, to their bargain.

[Judgment affirmed.]

QUESTIONS AND CASE PROBLEMS

1. The Rhode Island Grocers Association held an annual exhibition. As an added feature to attract public interest, arrangements were made with the Transocean Air Lines for a drawing of a door prize for a free round trip to Hawaii for two. Any spectator attending the exhibition could participate in the drawing by filling out a card with his name and address. Was this a lottery? [Finch v Rhode Island Grocers Association, 93 RI 323, 175 A2d 177]
2. Costello held a license as a professional engineer in New York, Maryland, Illinois, and New Mexico, but he was not licensed in New Jersey. He did consulting engineering work for a New Jersey licensed architect in designing a city swimming pool. When Costello was not paid in full for his services, he sued the architect, who claimed that Costello was not allowed to recover because he did not have a license in New Jersey to render the services for which he claimed compensation. Was he entitled to recover? [Costello v Schmidlin, (CA3 NJ) 404 F2d 87]
3. Las Vegas Hacienda, Inc., advertised that it would pay $5,000 to anyone shooting a hole in one on its golf course. Gibson, who paid the fee of 50 cents, made a hole in one. The golf course corporation refused to pay the $5,000. When Gibson sued for breach of contract, it raised the defense that the contract was an illegal gambling contract and could not be enforced even though gambling as such was legalized in the state. Decide. [Las Vegas Hacienda, Inc. v Gibson, 77 Nev 25, 359 P2d 85]
4. Colonial Stores was looking for someone to build a store in the city and lease it to Colonial. McArver and Gerukos agreed between themselves that they would obtain options to buy some land for a store site and resell the options to a third person who would build a store and lease it to Colonial. All of this was successfully done, but Gerukos kept all of the profits from the transaction. When McArver sued him for his share of the profits, Gerukos raised the defense that McArver could not recover because a statute required that all real estate brokers and salesmen be licensed and McArver did not have such a real estate license. Was this defense valid? [McArver v Gerukos, 265 NC 413, 144 SE2d 277]
5. Burgess, a salesman for Bowyer, failed to turn over to Bowyer an indefinite amount of money collected by him. In order to avoid a criminal prosecution of Burgess by Bowyer, Burgess and his brother-in-law entered into a contract with the employer by which they agreed to pay Bowyer $5,000 if full restitution was not made. No restitution was made, and Bowyer sued Burgess and his brother-in-law on the contract for $5,000. Was he entitled to recover? [Bowyer v Burgess, 54 Cal 2d 97, 4 Cal Rptr 521, 351 P2d 793]
6. Ellis borrowed money from Small and executed a series of six promissory notes payable with the maximum rate of interest. The notes contained an acceleration clause by virtue of which, upon the borrower's default, the lender could declare the entire balance of the debt to be due, together with the contract rate of interest. By virtue of such acceleration, the creditor would be receiving more than the maximum rate since the borrower would have had the money for the shorter period only and not for the original period for which he bargained. Were the notes usurious? [Small v Ellis, 90 Ariz 194, 367 P2d 234]

7. A Virginia statute required builders and persons doing construction work to obtain a license and imposed a fine for failing to do so. F. S. Bowen Electric Co. installed equipment in a building being constructed by Foley. Bowen had not obtained a license. When Foley did not pay Bowen, the latter sued Foley for the money due. Could he recover? [F. S. Bowen Electric Co. v Foley, 194 Va 92, 72 SE2d 388]

8. James owned property in Virginia Beach. He wanted to sell it for $29,000. Kidd wanted to buy the property but could not obtain financing. Finally Brothers agreed to buy the property from James for $28,000 and to resell it to Kidd for $29,000. No cash was paid on the resale to Kidd and Kidd gave Brothers a promissory note for $29,000, payable in 120 monthly installments. In computing the payment schedule, interest at 8% per annum was added to the purchase price. The legal rate of interest under the Virginia Usury Statute was 6%. Kidd claimed that the usury statute was violated by the resale transaction. Was he correct? [Kidd v Brothers, 212 Va 197, 183 SE2d 140]

9. Smith was employed as a salesman for Borden, Inc., which sold food products in 63 counties in Arkansas, 2 counties in Missouri, 2 counties in Oklahoma, and 1 county in Texas. The contract with Smith prohibited him from competing with Borden after leaving its employ. Smith left Borden and went to work for a competitor, Lady Baltimore Foods. Working for this second employer, Smith sold in three counties of Arkansas. He had sold in two of these counties while he worked for Borden. Borden brought an injunction action against Smith and Lady Baltimore to enforce the anti-competitive covenant in Smith's former contract. Was Borden entitled to the injunction? [Borden, Inc. v Smith, 252 Ark 295, 478 SW2d 744]

10. A person borrowed money and executed a promissory note for the loan. The note called for the payment of interest at a usurious rate. Under the local law this made the note void. The lender sued on the note. When the borrower raised the defense that the note was void because of usury, the creditor asserted that he was only claiming the amount of interest which could be lawfully claimed and that therefore the usury aspect was eliminated and he could recover on the note. Was he correct? [Yakutsk v Alfino, — App Div 2d —, 349 NYS2d 718]

11. *A* was employed by *B*. *A* embezzled money from *B*. When his crime was discovered, he promised *B* that he would repay the money which he had taken. He did not do so. *B* sued *A* for breach of his promise. Can *B* recover? [Gallaher Drug Co. v Robinson, 13 Ohio Misc 216, 232 NE2d 668]

15 Form of Contract

As a practical matter, every important contract should be written. In the first place, when the agreement is written, each party knows just what he is agreeing to. Second, the writing assures both parties that at a future date there will be less chance of disagreement as to what has been agreed upon. Third, it eliminates the possibility that either party to the contract can effectively deny having made the contract.

§ 15:1. Oral Contracts Are Generally Valid. Generally a contract is valid whether it is written or oral. By statute, however, some contracts must be evidenced by a writing. Such statutes are designed to prevent the use of the courts for the purpose of enforcing certain oral agreements or alleged oral agreements. It does not apply when an oral agreement has been voluntarily performed by both parties.

Apart from statute, the parties may agree that their oral agreement is not to be binding until a formal written contract is executed,[1] or the circumstances of the transaction may show that such was their intention.[2] Conversely, they may agree that their oral contract is binding even though a written contract is to be executed later. (See p. 301, Elkader Co-operative Co. v Matt.) Similarly, the failure to sign and return a written contract does not establish that there is no contract as there may have been an earlier oral contract.[3] If one of the parties, with the knowledge or approval of the other contracting party, undertakes performance of the contract before it is reduced to writing, it is generally held that the parties intended to be bound from the moment the oral contract was made.

difficulty in determining definiteness

In order for the prior oral agreement to be a binding contract, it must satisfy the requirement of definiteness.[4] If it does not, that not only means that there is no binding oral contract, but it also lends support to the view that the oral negotiations were not intended to be a contract and that there should not be any contract until a definite written contract has been signed.

§ 15:2. Contracts That Must Be Evidenced by a Writing. Ordinarily a contract, whether oral or not, is binding if the existence and terms of the contract can be established to the satisfaction of the trier of fact, ordinarily the jury. In some instances a statute, commonly called a *statute of frauds* [5] requires

[1] Pacific Coast Joint Stock Land Bank v Jones, 14 Cal 2d 8, 92 P2d 390.

[2] Scheck v Francis, 26 NY2d 466, 311 NYS2d 841, 260 NE2d 493.

[3] Osguthorpe v Anschutz Land and Livestock Co., (CA10 Utah) 456 F2d 996.

[4] Alpen v Chapman, (Iowa) 179 NW2d 585.

[5] The name is derived from the original English Statute of Frauds and Perjuries, which was adopted in 1677 and became the pattern for similar legislation in America.

that certain kinds of contracts be evidenced by a writing or they cannot be enforced. This means that either (1) the contract itself must be in writing and signed by both parties, or (2) there be a sufficient written memorandum of the oral contract signed by the person being sued for breach of contract.

Ordinarily an offer may be either written, oral, or expressed by conduct. Even when the contract must be evidenced by a writing under the statute of frauds, the offer which leads up to the contract may be oral. As an exception, statutes regulating the letting of government contracts may require that bids by contractors, the offers, be written and signed.[6]

(1) An Agreement That Cannot Be Performed Within One Year After the Contract Is Made. A writing is required when the contract by its terms cannot be performed within one year after the date of the agreement.[7] Thus, an oral contract made in March to work as management consultant from May 1 of that year to April 30 of the following year was not binding because of the statute of frauds.[8]

The year runs from the time of the making of the oral contract rather than from the date when performance is to begin.[9] In computing the year, the day on which the contract was made is excluded. The year begins with the following day and ends at the close of the first anniversary of the day on which the agreement was made.[10]

The statute of frauds does not apply if it is possible under the terms of the agreement to perform the contract within one year. Thus, a writing is not required when no time for performance is specified and the performance will not necessarily take more than a year. In this case it would be possible to perform the contract within a year, and the statute is inapplicable without regard to the time when performance is begun or completed. A promise to

---

The seventeenth section of that statute governed the sale of goods, and its modern counterpart is § 2-201 of the Uniform Commercial Code, discussed in Chapter 23. The fourth section of the English statute provided the pattern for American legislation with respect to contracts other than for the sale of goods described in this section of the chapter. The English statute was repealed in 1954, except as to land sale and guaranty contracts. The American statutes remain in force, but the liberalization by UCC § 2-201 of the pre-Code requirements with respect to contracts for the sale of goods may be regarded as a step in the direction of the abandonment of the statute of frauds concept.

When the English Statute of Frauds was adopted, the parties to a lawsuit were not permitted to testify on their own behalf, with the result that a litigant had difficulty in disproving perjured testimony of third persons offered as evidence on behalf of the adverse party. The Statute of Frauds was repealed in England partly because it was felt that it permitted the assertion of a "technical" defense as a means of avoiding just obligations and partly on the ground that with parties in interest now having the right to testify there is no longer the need for a writing to protect the parties from perjured testimony of third persons. Azevedo v Minister, 86 Nev 576, 471 P2d 661.

[6] A. A. B. Electric, Inc. v Stevenson Public School District, 5 Wash App 887, 491 P2d 684.

[7] Loncope v Lucerne-in-Maine Community Assn., 127 Maine 282, 143 A64; Peters v Hubbard, 242 Ark 839, 416 SW2d 300.

[8] Hanan v Corning Glass Works, 35 App Div 2d 697, 314 NYS2d 804.

[9] Lund v E. D. Etnyre & Co., 103 Ill App 2d 158, 242 NE2d 611.

[10] Nickerson v Harvard College, 298 Mass 484, 11 NE2d 444.

do an act or upon or until the death of a person does not require a writing, even though that event may not occur until more than a year from the time the agreement is made.

When the contract calls not for a single act but for continuing services to run indefinitely into the future, the statute of frauds is applicable. For example, a business contract to pay an agent a commission for new customers procured by the agent for as long as such customers continue to purchase contemplates acts that may performed beyond the statutory year, and a writing is therefore required. An oral promise to pay a bonus of a specified percentage of the employer's gross annual sales does not come within the statute nor require a writing, even though the amount of the bonus cannot be determined until after the year has expired.[11]

The one-year statute of frauds applies to oral contracts of employment.[12] In most states a writing is not required if the contract may or must be fully performed within a year by one of the contracting parties. By this view, a loan made today to be repaid in three years does not come within the statute because the performance of the lender necessarily takes place within the year. In a minority of states, the statute is applicable as long as performance by one of the parties may be made after the period of a year.

When the work contemplated by the oral contract has been performed, the employer cannot avoid liability under the contract because it was oral. Thus, an employee who has worked until the age of 65 under an oral contract of employment is entitled to recover the retirement benefits specified by the oral contract as against the contention that the contract was not binding because it did not satisfy the requirements of the statute of frauds.[13]

If a contract of indefinite duration is terminable by either party at will, the statute of frauds is not applicable since the contract may be terminated within a year.[14]

(2) An Agreement to Sell or a Sale of Any Interest in Real Property. All contracts to sell and sales of land, buildings, or interests in land, such as mortgages which are treated as such an interest, must be evidenced by a writing.

The statute applies only to the agreement between the owner and purchaser, or between their agents. It does not apply to other or collateral agreements, such as those which the purchaser may make in order to raise the money to pay for the property, or to agreements to pay for an examination or search of the title of the property. Similarly, a partnership agreement to deal in real estate is generally not required for that reason to be in writing. The statute ordinarily does not apply to a contract between a real estate agent and one of the parties to the sales contract employing him.[15]

---

[11] White Lighting Co. v Wolfson, 68 Cal 2d 336, 66 Cal Rptr 697, 438 P2d 345.
[12] Pursell v Wolverine-Pentronix, Inc., 44 Mich App 2d 416, 205 NW2d 504.
[13] Ortega v Kimbell Foods, Inc., (CA10 NMex) 462 F2d 421.
[14] Clarke Floor Machine Co. v De Vere Chemical Co., 9 Wis 2d 517, 101 NW2d 655.
[15] Bleakley v Knights of Columbus, 26 Conn Supp 192, 216 A2d 643.

Thus, a promise by a broker to pay a sum of money to the owner of land if he will sell it to a prospective buyer is not within the statute of frauds.[16]

The statute of frauds does not require that a collateral contract, such as an agreement to make certain repairs, be evidenced by a writing.[17]

A contract for the sale of sand, coal, or oil without any specification as to its location, such as "ten tons of grade A sand," is merely a contract to sell personal property and not the sale of an interest in land.[18] Such a contract must satisfy the requirements of the Uniform Commercial Code as to a sale of goods.

(3) A Promise to Answer for the Debt or Default of Another. When *A* promises *C* to pay *B's* debt to *C* if *B* does not do so, *A* is promising to answer for the debt of another. Such a promise must usually be evidenced by a writing to be enforceable.[19] Thus, the oral promise of the president of a corporation to pay the debts owed by the corporation to its creditors if they will not sue the corporation does not bind the president, even though he is a major shareholder of the corporation and would be indirectly benefited by the forbearance of the creditors.[20]

If the promise is made directly to the debtor that the promisor will pay the creditor of the debtor what is owed him, the statute of frauds is not applicable. In contrast, if the promisor makes the promise to the creditor, it comes within the category of a promise made for the benefit of another and must therefore be evidenced by a writing which satisfies the statute of frauds.

(a) PRIMARY PURPOSE EXCEPTION. The fact that a particular promise is made to the creditor and is therefore a promise to answer for the debt of another does not mean that the statute of frauds will necessarily bar enforcement if the promise is oral. If that promise was made primarily for the benefit of the promisor, rather than for the benefit of the debtor, an exception to the statute of frauds is recognized and the promise is not affected by the statute of frauds. It may be enforced even though it is oral. (See p. 301, R. H. Freitag v Boeing Airplane Co.)

No writing is required when the debt incurred is the debt of the person promising to pay, even though a third person designated by the promisor benefits thereby.[21] Thus, if *A* buys on his own credit from *C* and directs that *C* deliver the goods to *B*, *A* is not promising to pay the debt of *B* but is incurring his own debt.[22] Likewise, when a son arranged with a nursing home to take care of his mother, the nursing home could enforce his oral contract

---

[16] Povetz v Alea, 6 Conn Cir 486, 276 A2d 451.

[17] Ward Cook, Inc. v B-OK, Inc., 261 Ore 227, 493 P2d 136.

[18] Morgan v Jackson Ready-Mix Concrete, 247 Miss 863, 157 So2d 772.

[19] Restatement, Contracts, §§ 180-191; Marshall v Bellin, 27 Wis 2d 88, 133 NW2d 751.

[20] Mid-Atlantic Appliances v Morgan, 194 Va 324, 73 SE2d 385.

[21] Highland Park v Grant-MacKenzie Co., 366 Mich 430, 115 NW2d 270.

[22] Gillhespy v Bolema Lumber and Building Supplies, 5 Mich App 351, 146 NW2d 666.

since he was the other contracting party and his promise to the home was a promise to pay his own debt, rather than that of his mother.[23]

A question of interpretation may arise as to whether the words of one person, written or not, constitute a promise to answer for or guarantee of the debt of another. Where the treasurer of a corporation wrote a letter to a wholesaler in which he said that he personally guaranteed the corporation and then later claimed that this was merely a recommendation and not a guaranty of payment of the corporation's debts, the terms of the entire letter must be examined in order to determine whether the officer had guaranteed payment of the debts.[24]

(4) A Promise by the Executor or Administrator of a Decedent's Estate to Pay a Claim Against the Estate from His Personal Funds. The personal representative (executor or administrator) has the duty of winding up the affairs of a deceased person, paying the debts from the proceeds of the estate and distributing any balance remaining. The executor or administrator is not personally liable for the claims against the estate of the decedent. If the personal representative promises to pay the decedent's debts from his own money, however, the promise cannot be enforced unless it is evidenced by a writing that complies with the terms of the statute.

If the personal representative makes a contract on behalf of the estate in the course of administering the estate, a writing is not required since the representative is then contracting on behalf of the estate and not on his own behalf. Thus, if he employs an attorney to settle the estate or makes a burial contract with an undertaker, no writing is required.

(5) A Promise Made in Consideration of Marriage. If a person makes a promise to pay a sum of money or to give property to another in consideration of marriage or a promise to marry, the agreement must be evidenced by a writing.[25] This provision of the statute of frauds is not applicable to ordinary mutual promises to marry, and it is not affected by the statutes in some states that prohibit the bringing of any action for breach of promise of marriage.

(6) A Sale of Goods. When the contract price for goods is $500 or more, the contract must ordinarily be evidenced by a writing as described in Chapter 23.

(7) Miscellaneous Statutes of Fraud. In a number of states, special statutes require other agreements to be in writing or evidenced by a writing. Thus, a statute may provide that an agreement to name a person as beneficiary in an insurance policy must be evidenced by a writing.[26]

---

[23] Metheany v Waite, 6 Ariz App 9, 429 P2d 501.

[24] Hardware Wholesalers, Inc. v Heath, 10 Ill App 3d 337, 293 NE2d 721.

[25] Koch v Koch, 95 NJ Super 546, 232 A2d 157; Miller v Greene, (Fla) 104 So 2d 457.

[26] Washington v Pottinger, 17 App Div 2d 836, 233 NYS2d 78.

l Code contains three statutes of fraud relating ty: (1) goods;[27] (2) securities, such as stocks sonal property other than goods and securities.[29] s with brokers relating to the sale of land are also frauds.[30]

andum. The statute of frauds requires a writing for come within its scope. This writing may be a note istinguished from a contract. It may be in any form se is to serve as evidence of the contract.

xcept in the case of a sale of goods, the note or memo- n all the material terms of the contract so that the court what was agreed.[31] Thus, it is insufficient if the contract partly written.[32] An ordinary check is not a sufficient en it bears the notation "payment land" but contains no r lacks any material term.[34] The subject matter must be within the writing itself or in other writings to which it refers. t sufficient which does not identify the land which is the contract.[35] Thus, a writing which does not contain any descrip- d does not satisfy the statute of frauds.[36]

states a description of real estate by street number, city or state, is not sufficient; the writing must show the lot and block the property as well as name the city or county and the state.[37] writing does not contain a description which satisfies the statute the land may not be identified by parol evidence.[38]

me states an exception is made to the general rule and it is not that the writing set forth the consideration or terms of payment.[39] It is t necessary that the writing specifically state a term that would be implied, as that the price therein is to be paid in "cash." (See p. 302, Klymyshyn v Szarek.)

The note or memorandum may consist of one writing or instrument or of separate papers, such as letters or telegrams, or of a combination of such papers.[40]

---

27 UCC § 2-201.

28 UCC § 8-319.

29 UCC § 1-206.

30 Osborne v Huntington Beach Union High School District, 5 Cal App 3d 510, 85 Cal Rptr 793.

31 R § 207, 209; Irvine v Haniotis, 208 Okla 1, 252 P2d 470.

32 Forsyth v Brillhart, 216 Md 437, 140 A2d 904.

33 Lewis v Starlin, 127 Mont 474, 267 P2d 127.

34 Monaco v Levy, 12 App Div 2d 790, 209 NY2d 555.

35 Wadsworth v Moe, 53 Wis 2d 620, 193 NW2d 645.

36 Reifenrath v Hansen, 190 Neb 50, 206 NW2d 42.

37 Martin v Seigel, 35 Wash 2d 223, 212 P2d 107.

38 Dunlap-Swain Tire Co., Inc. v Simmons, (Tex Civ App) 450 SW2d 378.

39 Botello v Misener-Collins Co., (Tex) 469 SW2d 793. This is the law under the UCC with respect to contracts for the sale of goods. UCC § 2-201.

40 Vachon v Tomascak, 155 Conn 52, 230 A2d 5.

Separate writings cannot be considered together unless they are linked, either by express reference in each writing to the other or by the fact that each writing clearly deals with the same subject matter. Conversely, when the papers go no further than to show that they deal with similar subject matters, the papers cannot be integrated. For example, a signed memorandum relating to the sale of unidentified land and an unsigned deed could not be deemed one writing for the purpose of the statute of frauds because at most each only showed that it related to a real estate transaction and did not show that they both related to the same transaction and neither writing referred to the other.[41]

It is not necessary that the writing be addressed to the other contracting party [42] or to any person, nor is it necessary that the writing be made with the intent to create a writing to satisfy the statute of frauds.[43] When a corporation made an oral contract of employment with an employee, the minutes of the corporation reciting the adoption of a resolution to employ the employee (which minutes were signed by the president of the corporation) together with the salary check paid the employee constituted a sufficient writing to satisfy the statute of frauds.[44]

The memorandum may be made at the time of the original transaction or at a later date. It must, however, ordinarily exist at the time a court action is brought upon the agreement.

*(2) **Signature.*** The note or memorandum must be signed by the party sought to be charged or his agent.[45] A letter from an employer setting forth the details of an oral contract of employment satisfies the statute of frauds in a suit brought by the employee against the employer, as the writing was signed by the party "sought to be charged." [46] If the employer had sued the employee in such case, the employer's letter would not satisfy the statute of frauds as it would not be signed by the employee.

It should be noted that a contrary rule exists in some states in regard to contracts for the sale of land. Either because of special language in the statute, or because of the rather extraordinary view that "the party to be charged" necessarily means the vendor, these courts hold not only that the vendor must sign the writing regardless of who the defendant is in the suit, but also that the vendor's signature is sufficient to bind the vendee.

Some states require that the authorization of an agent to execute a contract coming within the statute of frauds must also be in writing. In the case of an auction, it is the usual practice for the auctioneer to be the agent of both parties for the purpose of signing the memorandum. If the seller himself acts as auctioneer, however, he cannot sign as agent for the buyer.

---

[41] Young v McQuerrey, (Hawaii) 508 P2d 1051.
[42] Boswell v Rio de Oro Uranium Mines, Inc., 68 NM 457, 362 P2d 991.
[43] Bunbury v Krauss, 41 Wis 2d 522, 164 NW2d 473.
[44] Jennings v Ruidoso Racing Association, 79 NM 114, 441 P2d 42.
[45] R §§ 210, 211.
[46] Dailey v Transitron Overseas Corp., (DC SD Tex) 349 F Supp 797.

An exception is made in some situations when the contract is between merchants and involves the sale of goods.[47]

The fact that an officer or employee is acting on behalf of a corporation does not remove the transaction from the statute of frauds. Consequently, when the statute of frauds requires written authorization for an agent, the corporate officer or employee must have such authorization or the writing which he signs on behalf of the corporation does not satisfy the statute of frauds.[48]

The signature may be made at any place on the writing, although in some states it is expressly required that the signature appear at the end of the writing. The signature may be an ordinary one or any symbol that is adopted by the party as his signature. It may consist of initials, figures, or a mark. When a signature consists of a mark made by a person who is illiterate or physically incapacitated, it is commonly required that the name of the person be placed upon the writing by someone else, who may be required to sign the instrument as a witness. A person signing a trade or an assumed name is liable to the same extent as though he signed in his own name. In the absence of a local statute that provides otherwise, the signature may be made by pencil, as well as by pen, or by typewriter, by print, or by stamp.

A telegram sent by the seller to the buyer is a writing signed by the seller for the purpose of a statute of frauds where the telegram bears the seller's name placed thereon by the telegraph company.[49]

§ 15:4. Effect of Noncompliance. The majority of states hold that a contract which does not comply with the statute of frauds is voidable. A small minority of states hold that such an agreement is void. Under either view, if an action is brought to enforce the contract, the defendant can raise the objection that it is not evidenced by a writing.[50] No one other than the defendant, or his successor in interest, however, can make the objection. Thus, an insurance company cannot refuse to pay on its policy on the ground that the insured did not have any insurable interest in the insured property because he did not have a writing relating to the property that satisfied the statute of frauds.[51]

(1) Part Performance. In some cases, when a writing is not made as required by the statute, the courts will nevertheless enforce the agreement if there has been a sufficient part performance to make it clear that a contract existed.[52] In other instances the court will not enforce the contract but will permit a party to recover the fair value of work and improvements that he has made in reliance upon the contract. This situation arises when a

---

[47] See Ch. 23.
[48] Besinger v National Tea Co., 111 Ill App 3d 589, 275 NE2d 226.
[49] Yaggy v B. V. D. Co., 7 NC App 590, 173 SE2d 496.
[50] Austin & Bass Builders, Inc. v Lewis, (Mo) 359 SW2d 711.
[51] Commercial Union Insurance Co. v Padrick Chevrolet, (Fla) 196 So2d 235.
[52] Casper v Frey, 152 Neb 441, 41 NW2d 363.

tenant improves the land while in possession under an oral lease which cannot be enforced because of the statute of frauds.[53] The situation also arises when a buyer of land under an oral agreement enters into possession of the land. If the purchaser has made valuable improvements to the land, the courts will commonly enforce the oral agreement.

In order for part performance to take an oral contract out of the statute of frauds, the performance must be such as is clearly referable to the terms of the contract. Where this is not so, conduct claimed to be part performance does not establish the oral contract. For example, where the plaintiff claimed that in return for managing and working the defendant's sugar beet operations on certain land for three years he would have the privilege of conducting a cattle feeding operation thereon, the fact that the plaintiff gave up his job and moved his family to the defendant's land and spent much time and effort to learn about the defendant's business did not constitute part performance which would remove the oral cattle feeding agreement from the statute of frauds.[54]

Ordinarily the performance of personal services does not constitute such part performance as will take the case out of the statute of frauds, except in extraordinary cases when the value of the services cannot be measured by money.[55] In any case, evidence as to part performance must be clear and convincing.[56]

(2) Promissory Estoppel. When the facts show that the buyer has relied on the oral contract to such an extent that the doctrine of promissory estoppel would be applicable, the promisor will not be permitted to raise the defense of the statute of frauds.[57]

Before the court dispenses with the need for a writing, it must find that there has been such reliance upon the existence of the oral contract that it would be grossly unfair to refuse to enforce the contract. The mere fact that the promisee relies on the oral contract, however, does not in itself make the oral contract binding.

(3) Recovery of Value Conferred. In most instances a person who is prevented from enforcing a contract because of the statute of frauds is nevertheless entitled to recover from the other party the value of any services or property furnished or money given under the contract. Recovery is based not upon the terms of the contract but upon the quasicontractual obligation of the other party to restore to the plaintiff what he has received in order to prevent his unjust enrichment at the plaintiff's expense.[58]

There is, however, a division of authority as to whether a real estate broker may recover for the value of his services in procuring a buyer under

---

[53] Dale v Fillenworth, 282 Minn 7, 162 NW2d 234.
[54] Buettner v Nostdahl, (ND) 204 NW2d 187.
[55] Crosby v Strahan's Estate, 78 Wyo 302, 324 P2d 492.
[56] Star Dinette & Appliance Co. v Savran, 104 RI 665, 248 A2d 69.
[57] "Moore" Burger, Inc. v Phillips Petroleum Co., (Tex) 492 SW2d 934.
[58] Stuesser v Ebel, 19 Wis 2d 591, 120 NW2d 679.

an oral brokerage agreement in states which require that such agreements be in writing. Recovery is commonly denied [59] on the theory that the real estate broker can be expected to know that his contracts must be in writing and that, as he makes such contracts constantly, it is unlikely that a broker would not appreciate his legal position when he acts under an oral contract. In substance it is held that protecting the public at large from unethical brokers making false claims under alleged oral contracts outweighs the necessity for protecting the occasional broker from oppression at the hands of an unethical customer refusing to recognize an oral contract.

The performance of services for which one is periodically paid is generally regarded as not taking out of the statute an oral contract that cannot be performed in one year. Such performance and payment do not indicate anything more than an agreement to render the services that were rendered and to compensate for them. Furthermore, the person performing the services is in fact paid for what he has done, and therefore he does not sustain any unusual hardship if the alleged oral contract is not enforced.[60]

When a third person is sued for tortious interference with a contract, he cannot defend on the ground that the contract was oral, and thus was not enforceable under the statute of frauds, for the reason that had the defendant not interfered the parties may have voluntarily performed their oral contract.[61]

§ 15:5. Parol Evidence Rule. Can a written contract be contradicted by the testimony of witnesses? The general rule is that spoken words, that is, *parol evidence,* will not be allowed to modify or contradict the terms of a written contract which is complete on its face unless there is clear proof that because of fraud, accident, or mistake the writing is not in fact the contract or the complete or true contract.[62] This is called the *parol evidence rule.* It refers to words spoken before or at the time the contract was made.[63]

To illustrate, assume that *L,* the landlord who is the owner of several new stores in the same vicinity, discusses leasing one of them to *T* (tenant). *L* considers giving *T* the exclusive rights to sell soft drinks and stipulating in the leases with the tenants of the other stores that they cannot do so. *L* and *T* then execute a detailed written lease for the store. The lease makes no provision with respect to an exclusive right of *T* to sell soft drinks. Thereafter *L* leases the other stores to *A, B,* and *C* without restricting them as to the sale of soft drinks, which they then begin to sell, causing *T* to lose money. *T* sues *L,* claiming that the latter has broken his contract by which *T* was to have an exclusive right to sell soft drinks. *L* defends on the ground that the lease, which is the contract, contains no such provision. *T* replies that there

---

[59] Augustine v Trucco, 124 Cal App 2d 229, 268 P2d 780.

[60] Rowland v Ewell, (Fla) 174 So2d 78.

[61] Daugherty v Kessler, 264 Md 281, 286 A2d 95.

[62] Ray v Eurice & Bros., 201 Md 115, 93 A2d 272; U.S.F. & G. Co. v Olds Bros. Lumber Co., 102 Ariz 366, 430 P2d 128.

[63] Mays v Middle Iowa Realty Corp., 202 Kan 712, 452 P2d 279.

was a prior oral understanding to that effect. Will the court permit *T* to prove that there was such an oral agreement?

On the facts as stated, if nothing more is shown, the court will not permit such parol evidence to be presented. The operation of this principle can be understood more easily if the actual courtroom procedure is followed. When *T* sues *L*, his first step will be to prove that there is a contract between them. Accordingly, *T* will offer in evidence the written lease between *T* and *L*. *T* will then take the witness stand and begin to testify about an oral agreement giving him an exclusive right. At that point *L*'s attorney will object to the admission of the oral testimony by *T* because it would modify the terms of the written lease. The court will then examine the lease to see if it appears to be complete; and if the court decides that it is, the court will refuse to allow *T* to offer evidence of an oral agreement. The only evidence before the court then will be the written lease. *T* will lose because nothing is in the written lease about an exclusive right to sell soft drinks.

If a written contract appears to be complete, the parol evidence rule prohibits its alteration not only by oral testimony but also by proof of other writings or memorandums made before or at the time the written contract was executed. An exception is made when the written contract refers to and identifies other writings or memorandums and states that they are to be regarded as part of the written contract. In such a case, it is said that the other writings are integrated or incorporated by reference.

(1) Reason for the Parol Evidence Rule. The parol evidence rule is based on the theory that either (a) there never was an oral agreement or (b) if there was, the parties purposely abandoned it when they executed their written contract. Some courts enforce the parol evidence rule strictly in order to give stability to commercial transactions. (See p. 303, Evans v Borkowski.)

(2) Conflict Between Oral and Written Contracts. Initially, when there is a conflict between the prior oral contract and the later written contract, the variation is to be regarded as (1) a mistake, which can be corrected by reformation, or (2) an additional term in the written contract, which is not binding because it was not part of the agreement. Illustrative of the latter, when a customer and a warehouse made a storage contract over the telephone and nothing was said as to the warehouse's limitation of liability, a limitation-of-liability clause appearing in the printed contract mailed to the customer was not binding upon him.[64]

In view of the fact that a reasonable man in the twentieth century should anticipate that the formal contract will contain many provisions not mentioned in the brief oral negotiating, as in the case of a life insurance contract, courts are very likely to find that any additional term in the formal written contract has either been authorized because anticipated or has been accepted or ratified because the person receiving the printed form has not

---

[64] Dececchis v Evers, 54 Del 99, 174 A2d 463.

repudiated the contract or objected to the term in particular or has performed or accepted performance under the contract. To prevent a loss of rights, it is therefore important to read a formal contract thoroughly and to make prompt objection to any departure from or addition to the original oral contract if such variation is not acceptable.

(3) Liberalization of Parol Evidence Rule. The strictness of the parol evidence rule has been relaxed in a number of jurisdictions. A trend is beginning to appear which permits parol evidence as to the intention of the parties when the claimed intention is plausible from the face of the contract even though there is no ambiguity. There is likewise authority that parol evidence is admissible as to matters occurring before the execution of the contract in order to give a better understanding of what the parties meant by their written contract.[65]

§ 15:6. When the Parol Evidence Rule Does Not Apply. The parol evidence rule may not apply in certain cases, which are discussed in the following paragraphs.

(1) Incomplete Contract. The parol evidence rule necessarily requires that the written contract sum up or integrate the entire contract. If the written contract is on its face or is admittedly not a complete summation, the parties naturally did not intend to abandon the points upon which they had agreed but which were not noted in the contract; and parol evidence is admissible to show the actual agreement of the parties.[66]

A contract may appear on its face to be complete and yet not include everything the parties agreed upon. It must be remembered that there is no absolute standard by which to determine when a contract is complete. All that the court can do is to consider whether all essential terms of the contract are present, that is, whether the contract is sufficiently definite to be enforceable, and whether it contains all provisions which would ordinarily be included in a contract of that nature.

The fact that a contract is silent as to a particular matter does not mean that it is incomplete, for the law may attach a particular legal result (called *implying a term*) when the contract is silent. In such a case, parol evidence which is inconsistent with the term that would be implied cannot be shown. For example, when the contract is silent as to the time of payment, the obligation of making payment concurrently with performance by the other

---

[65] Hohenstein v S.M.H. Trading Corp., (CA5 Ga) 382 F2d 530. This is also the view followed by UCC § 2-202(a) which permits terms in a contract for the sale of goods to be "explained or supplemented by a course of dealing or usage of trade . . . or by course of performance." Such evidence is admissible not because there is an ambiguity but "in order that the true understanding of the parties as to the agreement may be reached." Official Code Comment to § 2-202.

It has also been held that UCC § 1-205 permits proof of trade usage and course of performance with respect to non-Code contracts even though there is no ambiguity. Chase Manhattan Bank v First Marion Bank, (CA5 Fla) 437 F2d 1040.

[66] Johnson Hill's Press, Inc. v. Nasco Industries, 33 Wis 2d 545, 148 NW2d 9.

party is implied, and parol evidence is not admissible to show that there was an oral agreement to make payment at a different time.

(2) Ambiguity. If a written contract is not clear in all its provisions, parol evidence may generally be admitted to clarify the meaning. This is particularly true when the contract contains contradictory measurements or descriptions, or when it employs symbols or abbreviations that have no general meaning known to the court. Parol evidence may also be admitted to show that a word used in a contract has a special trade meaning or a meaning in the particular locality that differs from the common meaning of that word.

The fact that the parties disagree as to the meaning of the contract does not mean that it is ambiguous.[67] Some courts have departed from requiring strict ambiguity and permit parol evidence whenever it is not unreasonably inconsistent with the writing. This is done to throw further light on the intent of the parties and in effect permits parol evidence of anything which is plausible. (See p. 303, Delta Dynamics, Inc. v Arioto.)

(3) Fraud, Accident, or Mistake. A contract apparently complete on its face may have omitted a provision which should have been included. This situation may easily arise in modern times when parties tentatively agree to a draft of a contract which is then typewritten or printed. Frequently people will sign the final copy without adequate attention, assuming that it is a true copy of the earlier draft. It may be that the final copy is not a true copy because one of the parties fraudulently deceived the other into believing that it was a complete copy; because a stenographer or printer, in making the final copy, accidentally omitted a provision; or because a similar accident or mistake had occurred. For these reasons, it is important to read a final contract just as carefully as a preliminary draft and to compare the two before signing.

If, however, the final copy is not a true copy in that it omits a provision because of fraud, accident, or mistake, and this fact is proved to the satisfaction of the court, it is proper to show by oral testimony what the terms of the omitted provision were.[68]

(4) Conduct of Parties. The parol evidence rule does not prevent either party from showing by parol evidence that he was fraudulently induced to execute the contract or that the other party to the contract has not performed his obligation.

Likewise, when suit is brought to recover damages for misrepresentation as to what was covered by the plant's insurance policy, parol evidence is admissible to show what statements were made.[69] This does not contradict the terms of the contract, which would be prohibited by the parol evidence

---

[67] Southern Construction Co. v United States, (Court of Claims) 364 F2d 439.
[68] Snipes Mountain Co. v Benz Bros. & Co., 162 Wash 334, 298 P714.
[69] Vernon Fire & Cas. Ins. Co. Thatcher, (Ind App) 285 NE2d 660.

rule, but merely shows that the defendant said that the contract was something which it was not.

(5) ***Existence or Modification of Contract.*** The parol evidence rule prohibits only the contradiction of a complete written contract. It does not prohibit proof that an obligation under the contract never existed because a condition precedent was not satisfied [70] or that the contract was thereafter modified or terminated. Thus, parol evidence may be admitted to show that a construction contract was not to be binding unless and until the contractor procured a 100 percent construction loan.[71]

Written contracts commonly declare that contracts can only be modified by a writing. In the case of construction contracts, it will ordinarily be stated that no payment will be made for extra work unless there is a written order from the owner or architect calling for such extra work. If the parties proceed in disregard of such a clause requiring a writing, it may be shown by parol evidence that they have done so and the contract will be modified accordingly. Consequently, when a contractor performs extra work upon the oral request of the owner, he may recover therefor because the oral request of the owner was a waiver by him of the written contract provision.[72]

(a) NONBINDING CHARACTER OF FORMAL CONTRACT. Persons often sign documents which look like binding contracts but parol evidence is admitted by the court to show that the parties never really intended to be bound by a contract. Frequently, there is present an element of high pressure selling in which one party is reluctant to sign but only does so when assured that the paper is not a binding contract. When the court holds that parol evidence is admissible to show this and then holds that the paper that looks like a contract is not binding, it is in substance providing a form of consumer protection.

(b) MODIFICATION OF CONTRACT. To return to the illustration of the store lease by *L* to *T* and the alleged oral agreement of an exclusive right to sell soft drinks, three situations may arise. It may be claimed that the oral agreement was made (a) before the execution of the final written lease; (b) at the same time as the execution of the written lease; or (c) subsequent to the execution of the written lease. The parol evidence rule only prohibits the proof of the oral agreement under (a) and (b). It is not applicable to (c), for it can be shown that subsequent to the execution of the contract the parties modified the contract, even though the original contract was in writing and the subsequent modification was oral. Clear proof of the later agreement is required.[73]

When it is claimed that a contract is modified by a later agreement, consideration must support the modifying agreement except in the case of a

---

[70] Perry v Little, (Tex Civ App) 377 SW2d 765.

[71] Sheldon Builders v Trojan Towers, 225 Cal App 2d 781, 63 Cal Rptr 425.

[72] Harrington v McCarthy, 91 Idaho 307, 420 P2d 790.

[73] Finocchiaro v D'Amico, 8 NJ Super 29, 73 A2d 260.

contract for the sale of goods.[74] In any case, if the parties have performed the part of the contract that is modified, it is immaterial that there was no consideration for the agreement for such modification.[75]

(6) Collateral Contract. The parol evidence rule only applies with respect to the written contract of the parties. If they have made two contracts, one written and the other oral, the parol evidence rule does not bar proof of the oral contract. Difficulty arises in determining in fact whether there are two separate contracts or whether there was merely one contract which was written and the oral agreement is asserted in violation of the parol evidence rule in the effort to contradict or bypass the written contract. (See p. 304, Southern Guaranty Ins. Co. v Rhodes.)

§ 15:7. Certification by Notary Public. Various legal papers are sworn to or affirmed before a notary public, and the notary public then certifies what has occurred. The *notary public* is commissioned to administer such an oath or affirmation. Sometimes the use of a notary public is required by the other party to the transaction or contract, as when an insurance company requires that the policyholder make a written statement of his claim and swear to the truth of the statement before a notary public. Sometimes the use of a notary public is required by statute as a condition to recording a particular contract or instrument in the public records; that is, the law will not permit the recording of the paper unless it has been acknowledged before a notary public or other oath-administering official. A notary public is commonly employed when it is necessary to give notice to a party on commercial paper, such as a promissory note, that there has been a default in payment.

(1) Form. The form of the certification of the notary public varies, depending upon whether the notary merely recites what he has been told or vouches for something that he has done—as when he recites that he sent notices to parties of commercial paper, or vouches for something of which he has knowledge—as when he states that "before me appeared John Jones, to me personally known, and in my presence did sign the above document," thus vouching that it was John Jones who appeared and that it was John Jones who signed the paper.

The certification by a notary public is not part of the contract or other paper in a strict sense. It is merely an additional formal aspect which for one reason or another may be necessary or desirable.

(2) False Certification. A notary public who makes a false certification is liable for any loss caused thereby.[76]

---

[74] UCC § 2-209(1).

[75] Eluschuk v Chemical Engineers Termite Control, 246 Cal App 2d 463, 54 Cal Rptr 711.

[76] Thomas v Mississippi for Use of Thorp Finance Corp., 251 Miss 648, 171 So2d 303.

In order to afford greater protection against false certification by notaries, statutes commonly require that a person on becoming a notary public must file with the government a bond by which a surety or insurance company promises that if any person is harmed by a false certification of the notary, the company will pay the damages that person sustains. The employer of a notary public may be liable for the negligence of the notary which causes harm to a third person, to the same extent that an employer would be liable for the negligence of any other employee.[77]

[77] Transamerica Insurance Co. v Valley National Bank, 11 Ariz App 121, 462 P2d 814.

CASES FOR CHAPTER 15

Elkader Cooperative Company v Matt

(Iowa) 204 NW2d 873 (1973)

Matt, a farmer, made an agreement with Elkader Cooperative Company to deliver to it 15,000 bushels of corn. The agreement was made by telephone and Matt was to stop at the office of the Cooperative and sign a written contract. He never signed the written contract and sold the corn to another buyer at a higher price. The Cooperative then sued him for breach of the oral contract to sell the corn to it at the contract price. Matt raised the defense that there was no contract because he had never signed the written contract. From a judgment for Elkader, Matt appealed.

LEGRAND, J. . . . Matt makes two contentions in this court: (1) the trial court should have sustained his motion for a directed verdict on the ground the Cooperative introduced no evidence that the oral agreement between the Cooperative and Matt was to be a contract, as distinguished from mere negotiation preliminary to the execution of a written contract, and (2) the trial court should have instructed the jury on the significance of the parties' intention as to whether the oral agreement or the writing was to be the contract. The statute of frauds is not involved in the appeal.

I. We hold Matt was not entitled to a directed verdict. It is generally held an oral agreement may be enforceable, even though the parties contemplate that it be reduced to writing and signed, if it is complete as to its terms and has been finally agreed to. Under such circumstances the writing is merely an expression of a contract already made. On the other hand, the parties may intend that obligation should arise *only* upon the signing of a written instrument embodying the terms they have tentatively agreed to. . . .

The intention of the parties is decisive on this issue—did they *intend* the oral agreement to be binding or not? This fact question is dependent upon all the circumstances present in the particular case. . . .

On the record before us, there were circumstances justifying a finding [that] the oral agreement was to bind the parties. There were opposing facts which would sustain a contrary conclusion. As the trial court correctly held, this made out a jury case, and Matt was not entitled to a directed verdict. . . .

[Judgment reversed and action remanded.]

R. H. Freitag Mfg. Co. v Boeing Airplane Co.

55 Wash 2d 334, 347 P2d 1074 (1959)

Boeing Airplane Co. contracted with Pittsburgh-Des Moines Steel Co. for the latter to construct a supersonic wind tunnel. R. H. Freitag Mfg. Co. sold material to York-Gillespie Co., which subcontracted to do part of the work. In order to persuade Freitag to keep supplying materials on credit, Boeing and the principal contractor both assured Freitag that he would be paid. Freitag was not paid by the subcontractor

and then sued Boeing and the contractor. They defended on the ground that the assurances given Freitag were not written. From a judgment in favor of the defendants, the plaintiff appealed.

ROSELLINI, J. . . . It is conceded that the Statute of Frauds . . . renders unenforceable any special promise to answer for the debt, default, or misdoings of another. However, this court has recognized and followed the very widely accepted doctrine that, where the leading purpose of the promisor is not to aid the third person in getting credit but to secure a benefit for himself, he will be considered a debtor himself, rather than a surety, and the statute will not apply. . . .

"The purpose of [the statute] was not to effectuate, but to prevent, wrong. It does not apply to promises in respect to debts created at the instance and for the benefit of the promisor, but only to those by which the debt of one party is sought to be charged upon and collected from another. . . .

It is so obviously just that a promisor receiving no benefits should be bound only by the exact terms of his promise, that this statute requiring a memorandum in writing was enacted. Therefore, whenever the alleged promisor is an absolute stranger to the transaction, and without interest in it, courts strictly uphold the obligations of this statute. But cases sometimes arise in which, though a third party is the original obligor, the primary debtor, the promisor has a personal, immediate and pecuniary interest in the transaction, and is therefore himself a party to be benefited by the performance of the promisee. In such cases the reason which underlies and which prompted this statutory provision fails, and the courts will give effect to the promise." . . .

The allegations of the complaint in this instance are ample to support a finding that the assurances of Pittsburgh and Boeing were given to secure a benefit to themselves, a technically satisfactory and expeditious construction of the needed parts, and there is no allegation to show that they had any motive or purpose to benefit York-Gillespie. . . .

[Judgment reversed.]

Klymyshyn v Szarek

29 Mich App 638, 185 NW2d 820 (1971)

Szarek orally agreed to sell an apartment building to Klymyshyn. Klymyshyn made a deposit of $500, for which Szarek gave him a receipt. Szarek later claimed that the oral contract was not binding because the receipt did not satisfy the statute of frauds. From a judgment for Klymyshyn, Szarek appealed.

MCGREGOR, J. . . . Plaintiff agreed to purchase the premises, . . . and defendants gave the following document to him:

> "May 2, 1969
>
> Received from Mr. Stephan Klymyshyn the sum of $500.00 as deposit to purchase apt. at 20001 Conant, for $94,000.00.
>
> (signed) Alex Szarek and Elsie Szarek"

Defendants claim that a preliminary agreement was to be prepared and executed by the parties which would further define the terms of the transaction, and additional terms not agreed upon when the receipt was executed. Defendants' principal contentions are that the document as described above is insufficient to satisfy the statute of frauds, in that the essential terms, *e.g.*, whether for cash or credit, are not defined, and that the time for performance is not specified. . . .

Our courts have indicated a continuing "disposition 'to liberalize its interpretation of the statute of frauds.' " . . . In the case of Duke v Miller (1959), 355 Mich 540, 542, 543, 94 NW2d 819, a similar action for specific performance was instituted, and the only memorandum of the agreement in plaintiff's bill of complaint was as follows:

> "Detroit, Mich., Sept. 24, 1957.
>
> Received of Mr. Newell Duke $150.00 DOLLARS as Down Payment on Lot 109 on Fenkel.
>
> Balance $4,350
>
> $150.00
>
> [s] Ray Miller"

The trial court therein had granted the defendant's motion to dismiss, on the ground that the agreement could not be specifically enforced because the memorandum failed to meet the requirements of the statute of frauds, in that it did not specify the time for payment of the balance and the time for closing the transaction. The Supreme Court was not impressed by the defendant's allegations and reversed the trial court, holding that when a contract is silent as to the time for performance or payment, and absent any expression of a contrary intent, the law will presume a reasonable time.

Furthermore, the Court was not concerned that the contract did not mention the terms of payment of the balance of the purchase price, in that, absent a contrary intention on the face of the instrument, the terms were to be for cash. The Court then went on to say: "Indulgence of that presumption [payment for cash] or inference does not amount to the court's making a new contract for the parties or varying its terms, but merely gives effect to what it is reasonable to assume the parties intended when no contrary intention appears on the face of the instrument." . . .

We find the trial court here was correct in its ruling that the memorandum satisfied the statute of frauds.

[Reversed on other grounds.]

Evans v Borkowski

139 So2d 472 (Fla 1962)

Evans made a written contract to buy property from Borkowski. Under the sales contract the buyer was to make payment in certain installments prior to the delivery of the deed. When the buyer could not make payments on time, the parties entered into a new written agreement, the buyer persuading the seller to do so by orally promising him that he would pay interest on late payments. He was late in making the payments and paid the interest under protest. The buyer later sued the seller to recover the interest payments. From a judgment in the seller's favor, the buyer appealed.

STURGIS, J. . . . Parol testimony is inadmissible to vary, contradict, or add to the terms of a written instrument. . . . "The [parol evidence rule] . . . obviously enables the judge to head off the difficulty at its source, not by professing to decide any question as to the credibility of the asserted oral variation, but by professing to exclude the evidence from the jury altogether. . . ." It . . . rests upon a rational foundation of experience and policy and is essential to the certainty and stability of written obligations. . . .

The seller insists that the buyer made the alleged parol agreement as an inducement to him to accept [the new agreement]. . . . By the same token, it is evident that the parol agreement, if any, was part and parcel of the [new agreement] and as such is inadmissible in evidence.

We deem it in order to note that our holding is based upon what we deem to be well-settled principles of law which have been established as the result of the dictates of experience and wisdom which takes into account the fact that when in conflict, written transactions must prevail over parol transactions; that stability and order compel that course. In so holding, we recognize that under this rule it is inevitable that there will be instances where, as appears to be the case here, an unsuspecting person will accept in good faith the promise of a dissembler and reap the consequences of ill-placed trust. It is regretful that the advantages of maintaining the rule outweigh the disadvantages occasionally suffered by such circumstances. . . .

[Judgment reversed.]

Delta Dynamics, Inc. v Arioto

69 Cal 2d 525, 72 Cal Rptr 785, 446 P2d 785 (1968)

Delta Dynamics developed a trigger lock as a safety device on firearms. It gave Arioto and his partners, doing business as Pixey Distributing Co., the right to distribute the lock for five years; and Pixey agreed to sell a specified number of such locks in each year. The agreement stated: "Should Pixey fail to distribute in any one year the minimum number of devices to be distributed, . . . this agreement shall be subject to termination by Delta on thirty days' notice." The contract also provided that "in the event of breach of this agreement by either

party, the party prevailing in any action for damages or enforcement of the terms of this agreement shall be entitled to reasonable attorneys' fees." Pixey failed to order the contract minimum in the first year. Delta sued Arioto and his partners for breach of contract.

The defendants claimed that suit could not be brought for damages for not ordering the quota on the theory that the only remedy for such breach was that Delta could terminate the contract. At the trial Pixey offered testimony to show that the parties had understood that the termination provision was intended as the sole remedy. Counsel for the defendants called one of the partners and asked, "During the negotiations that culminated in the execution of this contract between your company and Delta Dynamics, was there any conversation or discussion as to what would happen as far as Pixey Distributing Co. is concerned if they failed to meet the minimum quota set up in that contract?" Counsel for Delta objected to this question on the ground that it called for the admission of parol evidence. Counsel for the defendants stated that the contract was ambiguous and that the purpose of the testimony was to show the intention of the parties. The trial judge sustained the objection to the parol evidence, and a judgment was entered in favor of Delta. Arioto and his partners appealed.

TRAYNOR, C.J. . . . Pixey contends . . . that the termination clause made Delta's right to terminate the contract Delta's exclusive remedy for Pixey's failure to meet the annual quota and that the trial court erred in refusing to admit extrinsic evidence offered to prove that the termination clause had that meaning.

"The test of admissibility of extrinsic evidence to explain the meaning of a written instrument is not whether it appears to the court to be plain and unambiguous on its face, but whether the offered evidence is relevant to prove a meaning to which the language of the instrument is reasonably susceptible." To determine whether offered evidence is relevant to prove such a meaning, the court must consider all credible evidence offered to prove the intention of the parties. "If the court decides, after considering this evidence, that the language of a contract, in the light of all the circumstances, is 'fairly susceptible of either of the two interpretations contended for . . .' extrinsic evidence to prove either of such meanings is admissible." . . .

In the present case the parties may have included the termination clause to spell out with specificity the condition on which Delta would be excused from further performance under the contract, or to set forth the exclusive remedy for a failure to meet the quota in any year, or for both such purposes. That clause is therefore reasonably susceptible of the meaning contended for by Pixey, namely, that it expresses the parties' determination that Delta's sole remedy for Pixey's failure to meet a quota was to terminate the contract. There is nothing in the rest of the contract to preclude that interpretation. It does not render meaningless the provision for the recovery of attorneys' fees in the event of an action for damages for breach of the contract, for the attorneys' fees provision would still have full effect with respect to other breaches of the contract. Accordingly, the trial court committed prejudicial error by excluding extrinsic evidence offered to prove the meaning of the termination clause contended for by Pixey. The judgment must therefore be reversed. . . .

Southern Guaranty Ins. Co. v Rhodes

46 Ala App 454, 243 So2d 717 (1971)

Rhodes had an automobile collision and liability policy which was issued by the Southern Guaranty Insurance Company. By an amendment to the policy, an exclusion was made so that it did not apply to any automobile driven by the insured's son, James L. Rhodes. In 1968 the father purchased a 1968 Pontiac for James and sought to obtain liability insurance for him and the new car. The father discussed such insurance with the agent for Southern Guaranty. Thereafter the Southern Guaranty policy was amended to provide liability and collision coverage for the 1968 Pontiac but no change was made to the clause excluding James and the father remained the named insured in the policy. James was in a collision while driving that Pontiac and sued Southern Guaranty.

It raised the defense that the policy expressly excluded liability as to James. He replied that he was not suing on the written policy but on a separate and distinct oral contract of insurance which provided liability coverage for him. The insurer asserted that the parol evidence rule prevented proof of any such oral contract because in fact there was no separate contract to cover the son by insurance and the son by suing on an alleged oral contract was merely trying to contradict the exclusion in the written policy, which the parol evidence rule prevented. From a judgment against Southern Guaranty, it appealed.

WRIGHT, J. . . . The principle of the parol evidence rule is that if parties negotiate . . . the details of a contract, and integrate such negotiations into a single instrument, all other indicia of the negotiations on the subject are legally immaterial for the purpose of determining what are the terms of their act. This principle does not prohibit negotiation of more than one agreement at the same time, nor that one agreement may be reduced to writing and another be oral. If such agreements are clearly collateral, separate and distinct as to subject matter there is no problem presented. They are two separate contracts and are to be considered as such. The oral contract is admissible and enforceable, not as an exception to the parol evidence rule, but as a separate jural act. However, if from a consideration of the negotiations, acts, statements and surrounding circumstances, it appears that it was the intent of the parties that the ultimate written instrument would embody the whole of the transaction, and fully cover the subject of negotiation, there can be no collateral or separate oral agreement on the same subject.

Therefore, we must determine from the conduct and language of the parties, the surrounding circumstances and the written instrument, whether it was the intent of the parties that the written instrument embody all of the prior negotiations and represent the final jural act, or whether it represented only a part thereof and it was intended there be an additional, collateral and separate oral agreement. . . .

The surrounding circumstances at the time of the negotiations between the parties herein was that appellee had purchased a policy of insurance from appellant some months previously. That policy provided initial liability coverage on two automobiles, one of which was ordinarily driven by appellee's son. Upon discovery of the bad driving record of the son, by amendment to the policy, coverage was excluded on the car usually driven by the son, and the son was excluded from any coverage under the policy.

Several months later, appellee purchased another car to be driven by the son. Appellee requested insurance, both liability and collision on the new car and upon the son as driver. Appellee states that appellant's agent told him he would provide such coverage but at a substantially higher premium. Appellee further states that he informed the agent he wanted such a policy regardless of cost and that the agent informed him that he was so covered.

Appellant's agent, to the contrary, stated he informed appellee he could not provide such coverage to the son as a driver with appellant's company, but could secure coverage from a substandard company at an extremely high premium. The agent further stated that appellee then informed him that he could not afford such premium but to go ahead and cover the car under his existing policy. Shortly thereafter, an amendment to appellee's policy was delivered to appellee, together with a nominal additional premium charge. The amendment showed liability and collision coverage on the new automobile. Appellee paid the additional premium, and the accident by the son subsequently occurred.

We consider the above testimony concerning the oral negotiation so it may be compared with the writing, to determine if the writing was intended to cover the subject of the negotiations.

The comparison is made with certain established tests applied to the oral agreement: (1) Is it in form a collateral one; (2) It must not contradict express or implied provisions of the written contract; (3) It must be one that parties would not ordinarily be expected to embody in the writing. . . .

We conclude that the oral agreement sued upon here meets none of the above conditions. It cannot be considered collateral in form as the complaint clearly indicates that the oral contract sued upon is identical with the written policy as amended, except for coverage of appellee's son as a driver. The premium alleged and shown to be paid was that charged for the written contract. There was no other premium paid. The property insured is the same.

The oral contract expressly contradicts the provisions of the written contract in that the written contract excluded appellee's son as an insured driver. . . .

Surely it cannot be contended that the oral agreement would meet condition (3). Such oral contract as appellee sues upon would ordinarily, even certainly, be expected to be embodied in the subsequent written policy. . . . "Insurance policies are notoriously complete, and therefore presumably contain the entire agreement of the parties thereto. . . ." It is customary for persons purchasing and selling insurance to expect the policy to embody their complete agreement.

It must be concluded from the evidence that the oral contract sued upon was not collateral, separate and distinct from the . . . written policy, . . . and thus was not an oral contract valid as of the time of loss complained of, which the jury could consider in arriving at its verdict. . . .

[Reversed and action remanded.]

QUESTIONS AND CASE PROBLEMS

1. State the specific objective(s) of the following rule of law: "Parol evidence is not admissible for the purpose of modifying a written contract when that evidence relates to an agreement made before or at the time that the written contract was executed."

2. Davis went to work for Monorail, Inc. At the time his employment was discussed, Wenner-Gren promised Davis that if Monorail did not pay his salary to him, Wenner-Gren would see that Alwac International, Inc., a corporation which Wenner-Gren controlled, would pay the salary. After 2½ years of employment, Monorail stopped paying his salary whereupon Davis sued Alwac and Wenner-Gren. Wenner-Gren raised the defense that it was not liable because of the statute of frauds. Was it correct? [Davis v Alwac International, Inc., (Tex Civ App) 369 SW2d 797]

3. Aratari obtained a franchise from the Chrysler Corp. to engage in business as an automobile dealer in Rochester, New York. A written franchise contract was executed between the parties identifying the location of the dealer in the city. Aratari later claimed that when the franchise agreement was being negotiated, it had been agreed that Chrysler Corp. would move him to a better location in the city. Was Chrysler liable for damages for having failed to keep this promise? [Aratari v Chrysler Corp., 35 App Div 2d 1077, 316 NYS2d 680]

4. Williams promised to give her cousin, Robinson, her home in her will if he would leave his home and take care of her for the balance of her life. He did so but Williams did not give the property to him by her will. He sued for breach of the oral contract to give him the property. Did the statute of frauds bar his claim? [Williams v Robinson, 251 Ark 1002, 476 SW2d 1]

5. Burgess signed a paper which stated that Eastern Michigan University had a 60-day option to purchase Burgess' home. The writing acknowledged receipt of "one dollar" and "other valuable consideration." Thereafter, Burgess revoked the option. The University claimed that the option could not be revoked because of the recital of consideration. It further claimed that the revocation was not effective under the statute of frauds because it was orally made. It was admitted that in fact Burgess had not received a dollar nor any valuable consideration as recited. Was Burgess bound by a contract? [Board of Control of Eastern Michigan University v Burgess, 45 Mich App 183, 206 NW2d 256]

6. Toups owed money to Ace Ready-Mix Concrete. Toups agreed to haul sand and gravel for Ace, who agreed to reduce the debt owed it by a third person by the amount it owed Toups. Thereafter, Toups claimed payment for the work which he performed in hauling sand and gravel. Ace defended on the ground that it had already credited the amount due Toups against the debt of the third person as agreed to by him. Toups claimed this oral agreement was not binding because it was an oral promise to answer for the debt of a third person and was therefore condemned by the statute of frauds. Was he correct? [Toups v Ace Ready-Mix Concrete, Inc., (La App) 267 So2d 255]

7. Lawrence loaned money to Moore. He died without repaying the loan. Lawrence claimed that when he mentioned the matter to Moore's widow, she promised to pay the debt. She did not do so and Lawrence sued her on her promise. Does she have any defense? [Moore v Lawrence, 252 Ark 759, 480 SW2d 941]

8. Nancy Nelms insured her life and named Betty Murdock as beneficiary. After her death it was claimed that Nelms had made someone else the beneficiary. A written change of beneficiary form which appeared to have been signed by Nelms was offered as evidence that Nelms had changed the beneficiary. The form was acknowledged before a notary public and recited that Nelms had "personally appeared" before the notary public and under oath had acknowledged the change of beneficiary. Other evidence was offered to show that Nelms had not in fact appeared before the notary public at any time. The defense was raised that the notary's statement that Nelms had appeared before him was conclusive and could not be contradicted. Was this correct? [Murdock v Nelms, 212 Va 639, 186 SE2d 46]

16 Interpretation of Contracts

RULES OF CONSTRUCTION AND INTERPRETATION

The terms of a contract should be clearly stated and all important terms should be included. If they are not, the parties might interpret the terms differently. When such differences cannot be resolved satisfactorily by the parties and the issues are brought into court, certain principles of construction and interpretation are applied.

An understanding of the rules discussed in the following paragraphs should help contracting parties to avoid many of the difficulties that may arise when a contract is not drafted carefully.

§ **16:1. Intention.** A contract is to be enforced according to its terms. The court must examine the contract to determine and give effect to what the parties intended, provided their objective is lawful.[1] It is the intention of the parties as expressed in the contract that must prevail.[2] (See p. 318, Keyworth v Industrial Sales.)

A secret intention of one party that is not expressed in the contract has no effect.[3] A party to a contract will ordinarily not be allowed to state what he meant by the words he used, for the test is what a reasonable man would have believed that he intended by those words.[4] For example, when a person guaranteed payment, it could not be shown that he had secretly intended not to do so.[5] A court should not remake a contract for the parties under the guise of interpreting it. Therefore, if the contract is so vague or indefinite that the intended performance cannot be determined, the contract cannot be enforced.

No particular form of words is required and any words manifesting the intent of the parties are sufficient.[6] In the absence of proof that a word has a peculiar meaning or that it was employed by the parties with a particular meaning, a common word is given its ordinary meaning (see p. 319, Kelly v Terrill) and a technical word is given its ordinary technical meaning.[7]

A word will not be given its literal meaning when it is clear that the parties did not intend such a meaning. For example, "and" may be substituted for "or," "may" for "shall," and "void" for "voidable," and vice versa, when it is clear that the parties so intended.

---

[1] Stevens v Fanning, 59 Ill App 2d 285, 207 NE2d 136.
[2] Firestone Tire & Rubber Co. v United States, (Ct Cl) 444 F2d 547.
[3] Leitner v Breen, 51 NJ Super 31, 143 A3d 256.
[4] Minmar Builders v Beltway Excavators, (Dist Col App) 246 A2d 784.
[5] State Bank of Albany v Hickey, 29 App Div 2d 993, 288 NYS2d 980.
[6] Shaw v E. I. duPont DeNemours & Company, 126 Vt 206, 226 A2d 903.
[7] Reno Club v Young Investment Co., 64 Nev 312, 182 P2d 1011.

Rules of grammatical construction and punctuation may be employed to throw light on the intention of the parties, but they are ignored when they clearly conflict with the intention of the parties.

The surrounding circumstances and purposes of an agreement will often show what the parties intended, even though their words are not explicit. For example, where a husband, as part of a divorce settlement, agreed to maintain insurance on his life for the benefit of his minor child, his obligation would be interpreted as meaning to obtain and maintain the insurance until the child had attained his majority, as against the contention that the obligation was not binding because it said nothing as to how long the policy should be maintained.[8]

§ 16:2. Whole Contract. The provisions of a contract must be construed as a whole.[9] This rule is followed even when the contract is partly written and partly oral, but this principle does not apply when an oral agreement must be excluded according to the parol evidence rule.[10] Every word of a contract is to be given effect if reasonably possible.

When several writings (whether letters, telegrams, or memorandums) are executed as part of one transaction, either at the same time or at different times, they are all to be construed as a single writing when it can be determined that that was the intent of the parties.[11]

The objective of viewing the contract in its entirety is not only to make every term of the contract effective but also to understand the objective of the parties in light of the particular transaction involved. (See p. 321, Gulf Shores Leasing Corp. v Avis Rent-A-Car System, Inc.)

(1) Errors and Omissions. Clerical errors and omissions are ignored and the contract is read as the parties intended, provided the errors or omissions are not so material or do not raise such a conflict as to make it impossible to determine the intent of the parties.[12]

(2) Divisible Contract. When a contract contains a number of provisions or performances to be rendered, the question arises as to whether the parties intended merely a group of separate contracts or whether it was to be a "package deal" so that complete performance of every provision of the contract was essential.[13] (See p. 320, Arrow Gas Co. v Lewis.)

§ 16:3. Conditions. In most bilateral contracts the performance of each party is dependent upon the performance by the other party and each party is bound to render his performance. In some contracts an event gives rise to the obligation to perform or affects the existence of an obligation to

[8] Carothers v Carothers, 260 Ore 99, 488 P2d 1185.

[9] Archibald v Midwest Paper Stock Co., (Iowa) 176 NW2d 761.

[10] See § 15:5.

[11] Charpentier v Welch, 74 Idaho 242, 259 P2d 814.

[12] As to the extent to which parol evidence may be employed to explain the meaning of terms and to show the intent of the parties, see § 15:6.

[13] John v United Advertising, Inc., 165 Colo 193, 439 P2d 53.

perform, but there is no obligation on either party to cause the event to occur. For example, under a contract which obligates a roofer to put on a new roof if the roof which he has just installed should leak, the leaking of the roof is an event which gives rise to the obligation to put on a new roof, but manifestly, there is no obligation on the roofer to cause the original roof to leak.

(1) Conditions Precedent. A condition or obligation-triggering event may be described as a *condition precedent* because it precedes the existence of the obligation. In the preceding illustration the leaking of the new roof was a condition precedent to the obligation to install a replacement roof.

A contract between a contractor and a government may contain a condition precedent that the contract shall not be binding unless the proper fiscal officer of the government indorses on the contract a certification that sufficient money is held to make the payments required by the contract.[14]

(2) Conditions Subsequent. The parties may specify that the contract shall terminate when a particular event occurs or does not occur. If government approval is required, the parties may specify that the contract shall not bind them if the government approval cannot be obtained.[15]

A contract for the purchase of land may contain a condition subsequent which cancels the contract if the buyer is not able to obtain a zoning permit to use the building for a particular purpose. When the satisfaction of a condition is dependent upon acts to be taken by one of the contracting parties, he must act within the time specified, if any, or within a reasonable time if none is specified. For example, in the zoning permission situation the buyer must make application for the zoning permission within a reasonable time after the contract is made.[16]

§ 16:4. Contradictory Terms. When a contract is partly printed or typewritten and partly written and the written part conflicts with the printed or typewritten part, the written part prevails. When there is a conflict between a printed part and a typewritten part, the latter prevails.[17] When there is a conflict between an amount or quantity expressed both in words and figures, as on a check, the amount or quantity expressed in words prevails.[18]

When it is possible to give a contract two interpretations and one is lawful and the other unlawful, it is assumed that the lawful interpretation was intended by the parties. Similarly, an interpretation that is fair is preferred over one that will work an unjust hardship or cause one of the parties to forfeit valuable rights.

---

[14] Kooleraire Service and Installation Corp. v Board of Education, 28 NY2d 101, 320 NYS2d 46.

[15] Security Nat. Life Ins. Co. v Pre-Need Camelback Plan, Inc., 19 Ariz App 580, 509 P2d 652.

[16] Battistelli v Corso, 30 Conn Supp 135, 304 A2d 676.

[17] Green Valley Foundation v O'Brien, 78 Wash 2d 245, 473 P2d 844.

[18] Guthrie v National Homes Corp., (Tex) 394 SW2d 494.

(1) Strict Construction Against Drafting Party. An ambiguous contract is interpreted more strictly against the party who drafted it. Thus, printed forms of a contract, such as insurance policies, which are supplied by one party to the transaction, are interpreted against him and in favor of the other party when two interpretations are reasonably possible.[19] If the contract of insurance is clear and unambiguous, however, it will ordinarily be enforced according to its terms, particularly when the insured is a large corporation acting with competent legal advice.[20]

The rule that an ambiguity in a contract is interpreted against the person who prepared the contract is not applied when the other party knew what the preparing party intended. Consequently, although regulations which form part of the employment contract were ambiguous as to whether an employee had an absolute right of reinstatement upon the conclusion of a leave of absence, the fact that the employer had prepared the regulations did not require the conclusion that they should be interpreted against the employer, so as to give the employee a right of reinstatement where the employee knew that the employer regarded this as not granting an absolute right to reinstatement.[21]

§ 16:5. Implied Terms. Although a contract should be explicit and provide for all reasonably foreseeable events, it is not necessary that every provision be set forth. In some cases a term may be implied in the absence of an express statement to the contrary. (See p. 322, Perkins v Standard Oil Co.)

An obligation to pay a certain sum of money is implied to mean payment in legal tender. Likewise, in a contract to perform work there is an implied promise to use such skill as is necessary for the proper performance of the work.[22] In a "cost-plus" contract there is an implied undertaking that the costs will be reasonable and proper. When a note representing a loan is extended by agreement, an implied promise to pay interest during the extension period arises when nothing about interest is stated by the parties.[23] When payment is made "as a deposit on account," it is implied that if the payment is not used for the purpose designated, the payment will be returned to the person who made the deposit.[24] When the contract for work to be done does not specify the exact amount to be paid for the work, the law will imply an obligation to pay the reasonable value for such work.[25]

If a law requires that certain standards be observed, an implied term of the contract is that the standards have been satisfied. For example, when a builder sells a new house, there is an implied condition that every room has the floor-to-ceiling space required by the applicable building code, so that

---

[19] Holmstrom v Mutual Benefit Health & Accident Ass'n, 139 Mont 426, 364 P2d 1065.

[20] Eastcoast Equipment Co. v Maryland Casualty Co., 207 Pa Super 383, 218 A2d 91.

[21] Hamann v Crouch, 211 Kan 852, 508 P2d 568.

[22] Previews, Inc. v Everets, 326 Mass 333, 94 NE2d 267.

[23] Hackin v First National Bank, 101 Ariz 350, 419 P2d 529.

[24] Wilcox v Atkins, (Fla App) 213 So2d 879.

[25] New Mexico v Fireman's Fund Indemnity Co., 67 NMex 360, 355 P2d 291.

there is a breach of contract when in the fact the space in the recreation room was nine inches less than the building code requirement.[26]

A local custom or trade practice, such as that of allowing 30 days' credit to buyers, may form part of the contract when it is clear that the parties intended to be governed by this custom or trade practice or when a reasonable man would believe that they had so intended. Local custom and trade usage may be shown not only to interpret particular words of an existing contract but also to determine whether there was a contract by showing what intent was manifested by the parties, as when it was claimed that the offeree had so acted after receiving the offer that his conduct, when viewed in the light of local custom and usage, showed an intention to accept the offer.[27]

When a written contract does not specify the time for performance, a reasonable time is implied and parol evidence is not admissible to establish a different time for performance.[28]

A term will not be implied in a contract when the court concludes that the silence of the contract on the particular point was intentional.[29]

§ **16:6. Conduct and Custom.** The conduct of the parties in carrying out the terms of a contract may be considered in determining just what they meant by the contract. When performance has been repeatedly tendered and accepted without protest, neither party will be permitted to claim that the contract was too indefinite to be binding. For example, when a travel agent made a contract with a hotel to arrange for "junkets" to the hotel, any claim that it was not certain just what was intended must be ignored when some 80 junkets had already been arranged and paid for by the hotel at the contract price without any dispute as to whether the contract obligation was satisfied.[30]

The conduct of parties is admissible to show the meaning of the contract as viewed in the way the parties perform thereunder. Moreover, when the conduct of the parties is inconsistent with the original written contract, proof of such conduct may justify concluding that the parties had orally modified the original agreement.[31]

Custom and usage in the trade may be proven in order to show the meaning in which terms were employed by the parties. Thus, the meaning of "adverse weather conditions" to the farming-food processing industry may be shown in order to establish the meaning of that term in a farmer's supply contract.[32]

---

[26] Denice v Spotwood I. Quinby, Inc., 248 Md 428, 237 A2d 4.

[27] Industrial Electric-Seattle, Inc. v Bosko, 67 Wash 2d 783, 410 P2d 10.

[28] Johnson v Landa, 10 Mich App 152, 159 NW2d 165.

[29] Glass v Mancuso, (Mo) 444 SW2d 467.

[30] Casino Operations, Inc. v Graham, 86 Nev 764, 476 P2d 953; see UCC § 2-208(1) as to course of performance in the interpretation of contracts for the sale of goods and UCC § 1-105 as to both Code and non-Code transactions.

[31] Wilson v Kauffman, — Ind App —, 296 NE2d 432.

[32] Stender v Twin City Foods, Inc., 82 Wash 2d 250, 510 P2d 221.

§ 16:7. Avoidance of Hardship. When there is ambiguity as to the meaning of a contract, a court will avoid the interpretation that gives one contracting party an unreasonable advantage over the other [33] or which causes a forfeiture of a party's interest.[34] When there is an inequality of bargaining power between the contracting parties, courts will sometimes classify the contract as a *contract of adhesion* in that it was offered on a "take-it-or-leave-it" basis by the stronger party,[35] and the court will interpret the contract as providing what appeared reasonable from the standpoint of the weaker bargaining party.[36]

In some instances, if hardship cannot be avoided in this manner, the court may hold that the contract or a particular provision is not binding because it is unconscionable or contrary to public policy. The extent to which this protection is available is uncertain, and as a general rule a party is bound by his contract even though it proves to be a bad bargain.

When a contract gives one party the power to terminate it on notice, he may exercise that power at any time and for any reason. It is possible, however, that in order to avoid oppression to the other party, limitations may be developed on the right to terminate. Thus, one court has held that when a dealer had to make a substantial investment to qualify for an exclusive franchise, such action by the dealer barred the manufacturer from terminating the franchise before the dealer had had the opportunity to recover his investment, even though the franchise gave each party an unlimited right to terminate on notice.[37]

§ 16:8. The Absent Term. What is the effect of the absence of a provision on a particular matter? It must first be determined whether the silence of the contract is intentional or is an accidental omission. Sometimes it will be obvious that the silence was not accidental. For example, a contract to deliver 10 tons of coal on the first Monday of January, February, and March, would obviously be interpreted as meaning just that and it would not be said that the contract was incomplete or ambiguous because it did not say anything about other months. Here the intent of the parties is clear even though it did not say "January, February, and March only" or "January, February, and March and no other months."

Assume, however, that a coal delivery contract purports to sell 50 tons of coal and then states that 10 tons shall be delivered on the first Monday of January, February, and March. Here it is clear that there are 20 more tons to be delivered but the contract says nothing as to that. In this

---

[33] Pettibone Wood Manufacturing Co. v Pioneer Construction Co., 203 Va 152, 122 SE2d 885.

[34] Equitable Life & Casualty Insurance Co. v Rutledge, 9 Ariz App 551, 454 P2d 869.

[35] Hamilton v Stockton Unified School District, 245 Cal App 2d 944, 54 Cal Rptr 463.

[36] Gray v Zurich Insurance Co., 54 Cal Rptr 104, 419 P2d 168.

[37] Clausen & Sons, Inc. v Theo. Hamm Brewing Co., (CA8 Minn) 395 F2d 388.

case, the silence of the contract is not an intentional exclusion but is a defect in the contract.

When it is concluded that the omission of a term is a defect, what is the legal result? Generally the result will be one of the following.

(1) Implied Term. In some omission cases the law will imply a term to fill up the omission. Thus, when there is a promise to pay $100, it will be implied that $100 in cash is intended.

(2) Parol Evidence. The omission may be regarded as making the contract ambiguous and justifying the admission of parol evidence to determine what was actually intended. (See p. 323, Smith v Smith.) If the parol evidence shows the parties have in fact agreed on the matter not covered by the written contract, the obligation of the parties will be interpreted as a blend or composite of the written contract and the oral terms. If the parol evidence is so vague or lacking that it cannot be said what the parties intended, the case will ordinarily be disposed of in the next category.

(3) No Contract. If a term is omitted from the contract and the omission is not cured by either the implication of a term under (1) or by the introduction of parol evidence under (2), the court may conclude that there is no contract. That is, although the parties obviously sought to agree on something, they had failed to express that intention with sufficient clarity so as to enforce it. Thus, a contract to sell coal without stating any quantity would probably be held to be no contract at all but merely a formal statement of a price or quotation. In some cases the statute of frauds may compel the conclusion that there is no contract when a term is omitted. If the written contract is for the sale of land, the statute of frauds would bar enforcing the contract because the writing does not state the material terms of the contract when nothing more is stated in the contract to identify what land.

(4) Strict Enforcement of Contract. If the omitted matter does not relate to the primary obligation or heart of the contract, it is likely that the omission has no effect on the contract and instead of concluding that there is no contract under (3), the contract will be enforced to its exact letter. For example, if a contract requires a contractor to build a building by August 1, and says nothing about an extension of time in the event of destruction by accidental fire, the contractor is not given any extra time nor any extra compensation when the construction is so destroyed. That is, the contract called for a completed building by August 1 and that is what the contractor must produce or he has broken his contract. Many modern contracts will meet this particular situation by requiring the contractor to maintain fire insurance on the construction and by allowing him an extension of time if there is fire damage for which he is not at fault. If, however, the contract is silent as to such matters, the contractor must perform according to the letter of the contract.

CONFLICT OF LAWS

Since we have 50 state court systems and the federal court system, questions sometimes arise as to what law will be applied by a court. *Conflict of laws* is that branch of law which determines which body of law shall apply.

§ **16:9. State Courts.** It is important to distinguish between the state in which the parties are domiciled or have their permanent home, the state in which the contract is made, and the state in which the contract is to be performed. The state in which the contract is made is determined by finding the state in which the last act essential to the formation of the contract was performed. Thus, when an acceptance is mailed in one state to an offeror in another state, the state of formation of the contract is the state in which the acceptance is mailed if the acceptance becomes effective at that time.[38]

If acceptance by telephone is otherwise proper, the acceptance takes effect at the place where the acceptance is spoken into the phone.[39] Thus, an employment contract is made in the state in which the applicant telephoned his acceptance, and consequently, that state has jurisdiction over his claim to workmen's compensation even though injuries were sustained in another state.[40]

If an action on a contract made in one state is brought in a court of another state, an initial question is whether that court will lend its aid to the enforcement of a foreign (out-of-state) contract. Ordinarily suit may be brought on a foreign contract. But, if there is a strong contrary local policy, recovery may be denied even though the contract was valid in the state where it was made.[41]

The capacity of a natural person to make a contract is governed by the place of contracting; a corporation's capacity to do so is determined by the law of the state of incorporation. The law of the state where the contract is made determines whether it is valid in substance and satisfies requirements as to form. Matters relating to the performance of the contract, excuse or liability for nonperformance, and the measure of damages for nonperformance are generally governed by the law of the state where the contract is to be performed.[42]

Ordinarily the enforceability of a contract, as distinguished from its general validity, is governed by the law of the state where it is made. At times the courts of one jurisdiction refuse to enforce foreign contracts because, although lawful by the law of the jurisdiction where the contract was made or was to be performed, there is a dominant local public policy which bars enforcing the foreign claim or a claim based on a foreign transaction. The fact that a contract requires or contemplates the performance of an act in

---

[38] Goldman v Parkland of Dallas, 7 NC App 400, 173 SE2d 15. As to acceptance by mailing, see § 10:17.

[39] Linn v Employers Reinsurance Corporation, 392 Pa 58, 139 A2d 638.

[40] Travelers Insurance Co. v Workmen's Compensation Appeals Board, 68 Cal 2d 7, 64 Cal Rptr 440, 434 P2d 992.

[41] Windt v Lindy, 169 Tenn 210, 84 SW2d 99.

[42] Scudder v Union National Bank, 91 US 406.

another state which would be illegal if performed in the state where the contract was made does not make the contract illegal in the absence of a dominant, local public policy opposed to such a contract.

When a lawsuit is brought on a contract, the *law of the forum,* that is, of the court in which the action is brought, determines the procedure and the rules of evidence.[43]

Whether there is any right that can be assigned is determined by the law of the state which determines whether the contract is substantively valid. The formal validity of the assignment is determined by the law of the state in which the assignment is made.

(1) Center of Gravity. There is a growing acceptance of the rule that, in place of the rigid or mechanical standards described above, a contract should be governed by the law of the state that has the most significant contacts with the transaction, to which state the contract may be said to gravitate.[44]

(3) Specification by the Parties. It is common for the more important contracts to specify that they shall be governed by the law of a particular state. When this is done, it is generally held that if the contract is lawful in the designated state, it will be enforced in another state and interpreted according to the law of the designated state, even though a contrary result would be reached if governed by the law of the state in which the suit is brought. Whenever a transaction is governed by the Uniform Commercial Code, the parties may agree that their rights and duties shall be governed by the law of any state or nation which "bears a reasonable relation" to the transaction.[45]

§ **16:10. Federal Courts.** When the parties to a contract reside in different states and an action is brought on the contract in a federal court because of their different citizenship, the federal court must apply the same rules of conflict of laws that would be applied by the courts of the state in which the federal court is sitting.[46] Thus, a federal court in Chicago deciding a case involving parties from Indiana and Wisconsin must apply the same rules of conflict of laws as would be applied by the courts of Illinois. The state law must be followed by the federal court in such a case whether or not the federal court agrees with the state law.[47]

---

[43] In contract actions it is generally held that whether a claim is barred by the statute of limitations is determined by the law of the forum. There is a division of authority as to whether a statute of frauds relates to the substance of the contract, the law of the place of making then governing, or whether it is a question of procedure, the law of the forum then governing.

[44] Baffin Land Corp. v Monticello Motor Inn, 70 Wash 2d 893, 425 P2d 623.

[45] UCC § 1-105(1).

[46] Erie R.R. Co. v Tompkins, 304 US 64.

[47] John Hancock Mutual Life Insurance Co. v Tarrence, (CA6 Ky) 244 F2d 86.

MULTIPLE PARTIES

When more than two persons are involved in the same contract, questions may arise as to the nature of the rights or the liabilities created by the contract.

§ 16:11. Joint, Several, and Joint and Several Contracts. When two or more persons are on either side of a contract, an additional question of interpretation may arise, as it may be necessary to determine whether the contract is (1) joint, (2) several, or (3) joint and several.

(1) Joint Contracts. A *joint contract* is one in which two or more persons jointly promise to perform an obligation. If *A, B,* and *C* sign a contract stating "we jointly promise" to do a particular act, the obligation is the joint obligation of *A, B,* and *C.* In the absence of an express intent to the contrary, a promise by two or more persons is generally presumed to be joint and not several.[48]

Each of two or more joint promisors is liable for the entire obligation, but an action must be brought against all who are living and within the jurisdiction of the court. If one of the promisors dies, the surviving promisors remain bound to perform the contract unless it was personal in character and required the joint action of all the obligors for its performance. If the deceased obligor had received a benefit from the contract, a court of equity will also hold his estate liable for the performance of the contract.

Generally the release by the promisee of one or more of the joint obligors releases all.

(2) Several Contracts. *Several contracts* arise when two or more persons separately agree to perform the same obligation even though the separate agreements are set forth in the same instrument.

If *A, B,* and *C* sign a contract stating "we severally promise" or "each of us promises" to do a particular act or to pay a specified sum of money, the three signers are severally bound to perform or to pay; that is, each signer is individually bound.

In many jurisdictions persons liable on related causes of action can be sued at one time. Since the liability of each obligor to a several contract is by definition separate or distinct, the release of one or more of the obligors by the promisee does not release the others.

(3) Joint and Several Contracts. A *joint and several contract* is one in which two or more persons are bound both jointly and severally. If *A, B,* and *C* sign a contract stating "we, and each of us, promise" (or "I promise") to pay a specified sum of money, they are jointly and severally bound. The obligee may treat the claim either as a joint claim or as a group of separate claims. He may bring a suit against all at the same time or

[48] Mintz v Tri-County Natural Gas Co., 259 Pa 477, 103 A285.

against one at a time. The plaintiff may also sue any number of the severally liable parties instead of suing them either singly or all at one time.

CASES FOR CHAPTER 16

Keyworth v Industrial Sales Co.

241 Md 453, 217 A2d 253 (1966)

Keyworth was employed by Industrial Sales Co. In the course of employment, he was injured by Israelson. Industrial Sales made a contract with Keyworth to pay him $100 per week until he was able to return to normal work but specified that such payments would be paid back to Industrial Sales from any recovery that Keyworth would obtain in a lawsuit against Israelson, such payments to be made to Industrial Sales upon the "successful conclusion of the case." Keyworth obtained a recovery in the action against Israelson of $16,600 but refused to make any payment to Industrial Sales because he believed that he had not recovered enough and therefore there was not a "successful conclusion of the case." Industrial Sales sued Keyworth. From a judgment in favor of Industrial Sales, Keyworth appealed.

OPPENHEIMER, J. . . . Keyworth contends that whether or not his personal injury case resulted in a "successful conclusion" . . . is a matter to be determined by a jury. . . .

The construction of a written contract . . . is ordinarily for the determination of the court. . . . The questions here are whether the written agreement is susceptible of a clear and definite understanding, and what effect, if any, is to be given to Keyworth's interpretation of it. . . .

"We may note first that the theory of 'objective law' of contracts has been almost universally adopted by this time. The written language embodying the terms of an agreement will govern the right and liabilities of the parties, irrespective of the intent of the parties at the time they entered into the contract. . . ." ". . . The test of a true interpretation of an offer or acceptance is not what the party making it thought it meant or intended it to mean, but what a reasonable person in the position of the parties would have thought it meant." . . .

In this case Keyworth's deposition as to what he thought the phrase "successful conclusion" of the litigation meant is not the test, nor does his interpretation cast doubt or create an ambiguity, if the language used is clear and definite. . . . There was "a clear indication that the parties to the agreement looked to the creation of a fund consisting of the proceeds of the verdict or settlement resulting from the third-party action; and that [Keyworth] was to receive the proceeds and was to use them, in part, for the repayment of the advances made by the employer. . . . We think the agreement between the employer and Keyworth, construed in the light of the facts and circumstances, meant that the source of the monies to be refunded would be the monies actually paid by the third party defendants . . . and that these monies were to be held as security for the repayment."

On the undisputed facts, Keyworth, as a result of his litigation, received a total of $16,600. His out-of-pocket expenses and losses came to $10,361.55, but this total included $7,057.15 for loss in salary, which, while a proper item in his claim for damages, was more than covered by the $7,200 which the employer advanced him, on the basis of the salary he had been receiving. As the order of the equity court in connection with the distribution of the fund shows, even after the repayment to the employer's workmen's compensation insurance carrier, . . . the repayment of the $7,200 to the employer, and the payment of $5,000 as counsel fee to Keyworth's attorneys, there was a residue for Keyworth of $686.82. . . .

. . . There was no legal obligation of any kind on the employer to make the advances. Under the agreement, Keyworth received money in lieu of salary to which he was not entitled but which he needed. The employer obviously wished to have Keyworth return to his employment when he was able to do so. Keyworth was placed under no requirement to return the money unless his litigation produced the funds necessary to do so, and the employer was given no right to demand repayment except upon the same condition. There was no reason for Keyworth not to repay, as long as he did not have to do so except through the creation of the fund, and no reason for the employer to waive repayment if Keyworth, through the litigation, received enough to cover the amounts he had gratuitously received. This, under the circumstances, was the obvious meaning of the agreement. The test of whether or not the litigation was successfully concluded on the facts before us is not whether Keyworth was satisfied or dissatisfied with what he received, but whether the net amount which he recovered was enough to cover the advances which the employer had made to him. The amount Keyworth received as a result of the litigation, even after deduction of the amounts of the claims which had priority, was more than sufficient for that purpose. The clear meaning of the agreement, on the facts, is that the litigation was successfully concluded. . . .

[Judgment affirmed.]

Kelly v Terrill

132 Ill App 2d 238, 268 NE2d 885 (1971)

Kelly made a contract to purchase a home from the Terrills. He made a down payment or deposit of $1,500 on a total purchase price of $26,000. The contract stated that the deposit would be refunded to Kelly if he was not able to obtain a loan of $25,000 within 14 days. Kelly was unable to obtain such a loan although an application for a loan of $23,700 was approved and Kelly had assets of his own of approximately $9,000. Kelly demanded the return of his deposit. The Terrills refused to return the deposit because Kelly could have paid the purchase price by using the smaller loan and his own assets. The Terrills also claimed that the act of applying for a loan of $23,700 estopped Kelly from enforcing the $25,000 loan provision. Kelly sued for the return of his deposit. From a judgment for Kelly, the Terrills appealed.

ABRAHAMSON, J. . . . [The contract provided that] "Performance by Buyer is contingent upon their ability to procure an FHA loan or other financing in the amount of $25,000.00 within 14 days of the date hereof. Unless a mortgage loan in this amount is made available after diligent effort, this contract shall be considered null and void and Buyers shall be entitled to a refund of all sums paid hereunder."

The plaintiff testified that he visited a bank in Chicago on July 10 and asked for a loan of $25,000.00 but was refused. He then contacted the Hinsdale Federal Savings and Loan Association but was also unable to obtain a $25,000.00 loan from them. On July 12, 1967, the plaintiff submitted a written application to Hinsdale Federal for a loan of $23,700.00 on the property wherein he listed assets owned by him of approximately $8850.00. On July 27, Hinsdale informed the plaintiff that his loan application for $23,700.00 was approved and forwarded the mortgage documents to him to be signed.

. . . The plaintiff telephoned William Terrill, one of the defendants, and advised him that he could not obtain a $25,000.00 mortgage . . .

The defendants contend that the plaintiff, by his conduct, waived his right to insist upon a $25,000.00 loan and that he should be estopped from asserting the failure to obtain that amount when the evidence showed he had sufficient assets to purchase the home. In support of this contention, the defendants argue that "the clear intent of the contract provision relating to financing is to insure that the Buyer has enough money to close the sale." It is elementary contract law, however, that the intention of the parties must be ascertained, if possible, from the language employed in the contract itself and, where there is no ambiguity, from such language alone. . . . If the intention of the parties can be ascertained from the agreement itself, rules of construction have no application and the court should not consider extrinsic facts to determine that intention. . . .

The language employed in the contract before us is clear and unambiguous. Unless the plaintiff was able to procure a loan of $25,000.00 within 14 days after "diligent effort" the contract was null and void and he was entitled to a refund of his . . . deposit. This being so, the financial condition of the plaintiff was of no significance. . . .

The theory of estoppel, also urged by the defendants, has no application to the facts of this case. . . . "Estoppel . . . arises whenever one by his conduct, affirmative or negative, intentionally or through culpable negligence, induces another to believe and have confidence in certain material facts, and the latter having the right to do so, relies and acts thereon, and is as a reasonable and inevitable consequence, misled, to his injury." . . .

There is absolutely no evidence to indicate that the plaintiff at any time induced the defendants to believe he would purchase their home even if he could not obtain a $25,000.00 mortgage. His application for a loan of a lesser amount, communicated only to the lending institution, was neither a waiver of his rights under the contract or such conduct as would estop him from asserting those rights. . . .

[Judgment affirmed.]

Arrow Gas Co. v Lewis

71 NMex 232, 377 P2d 655 (1962)

Richard and Ruby Lewis owned separate tracts of land, designated as Section 1 and Section 18, which they leased to Gailey and Sredanovich. The lease specified that the Lewises would convey to the tenants a one-half interest in the land if the tenants or lessees developed water on the land suitable for irrigation. The tenants developed such a water supply on Section 18 but not on Section 1. Arrow Gas Co. acquired the interest of the lessees and claimed that it was entitled to a one-half interest in Section 18. The Lewises contended that Arrow was not entitled to any interest in the land because the lessees had not developed nor made any effort to develop water on Section 1. From a judgment in favor of the Lewises, Arrow appealed.

CHAVEZ, J. . . . The lease agreement provides:

"It is agreed and understood that the purpose of this Lease is to develop the above described area for irrigation purposes and that the consideration passing from [lessees] to [lessors] for this Lease is the development of water or the effort of [lessees] to develop water upon said premises for irrigation purposes. The [lessors] recognize the value to them of exploration for water to be used for irrigation.

"It is agreed and understood between the parties hereto that in the event that water is developed in sufficient quantities and quality for irrigation purposes that [lessors] shall convey to [lessees] one-half of the above described premises; the division shall be made at the time it is determined that water of sufficient quantity and quality for irrigation purposes has been developed, and such division shall be made upon an equitable basis. . . ." . . .

This brings us to the question of whether the lessees, Gailey and Sredanovich, upon developing water in Section 18, acquired a one-half interest in the lands covered by the lease, or at least a one-half interest in Section 18 where water was developed. . . .

The next question is whether the lease agreement is severable. . . .

In determining whether or not a contract is divisible, the governing principle is the manifested intention of the parties in view of the nature of the contract, that is, their intention to have performance of the contract in parts and have the performance of a part on one side the price or exchange of a corresponding part on the other. . . .

We hold that the intention of the parties is clearly expressed in the lease agreements, i.e., the development of water for irrigation purposes and the vesting of an interest in the land upon its having been determined that water has been developed. It is clear from the evidence presented in the trial that the lessees executed their part of the agreements with respect to Section 18. It is uncontradicted that the well developed by lessees was adequate to provide water of sufficient quantity and quality to irrigate that section, or such part of it as is practicable to farm by irrigation. This performance by lessees entitled them to . . . an undivided one-half interest in Section 18. This is true even though lessees made no effort to develop a water supply in Section 1 because the lease agreements are severable. Under their express terms, the parties assented separately to several things in a single contract. The performance by the lessees in developing water on Section 18 is the separate consideration for the corresponding performance provided for in the lease agreements on the part of appellees.

[Judgment reversed.]

Gulf Shores Leasing Corp. v Avis Rent-A-Car System, Inc.

(CA5 La) 441 F2d 1385 (1971)

Avis Rent-A-Car System gave Southwestern Automotive Leasing Corporation (SALCO) a car and truck rental franchise for three Louisana cities in 1961. The licensing agreement gave each party the right to terminate with or without cause for a certain period of time and further provided that "five years from the date licensee first became an Avis System licensee, . . . licensor may terminate . . . only with cause. . . ." SALCO was not successful and by common consent the franchise rights were transferred in 1964 to Gulf Shores Leasing Corp. In 1968 Avis notified Gulf that it was terminating the license held by Gulf without cause. Gulf claimed that Avis could only terminate for cause because five years had elapsed from the date of the original franchise agreement and brought suit to prevent termination. From a judgment for Avis, an appeal was taken by Gulf.

DAVIS, J. . . . The main question is whether Avis terminated the Gulf Shores licenses within five years after the latter company first became an Avis system licensee within the meaning of the termination provision. The license agreement signed by Gulf Shores was [dated] August 1, 1964, which, in Avis' view, is the commencement of the five-year period, and therefore the January 1969 termination was timely. Gulf Shores, on the other hand, would have us look to the assignment documents which it contends gave it status as an Avis licensee not on August 1, 1964 (their effective date) but as of the time in November 1961 when SALCO first became an Avis licensee; under this theory, Avis' right to terminate without cause expired in November 1966. . . .

We hold . . . Avis' reading of the termination clause is correct. . . .

First, for the assignments. These papers ("Agreements of Assignment and Assumption") conveyed all of SALCO's "right, title, and interest" in its licenses to Gulf Shores, and the latter's claim is that one of the "rights" it received was its predecessor's nearly three years of operation, as a credit toward the five-year period during which the license could be terminated without cause. However, we think that the assignment, as a whole, cannot be squared with this interpretation. Obviously, the appellant had no status whatsoever in the Avis system until the assignment, and one would have to look to the terms of that instrument for the commencement point of its rights. Significantly, there is a specific clause (paragraph 6) providing that "the parties hereto agree that the effective date of said agreement between Licensor [Avis] and Licensee [Gulf Shores] as assignee shall *for all purposes* be August 1, 1964." (emphasis added) Gulf Shores attempts to overcome the apparent import of this sentence, which is reinforced by the italicized phrase, by stressing the words "as assignee." Its construction is that its status as assignee became effective August 1, 1964, but that its status as licensee which is controlling under the termination clause of the license, relates back to November 1961 when SALCO got its franchises. In the face of the all-inclusive phrase, "for all purposes," this is far too much weight to put upon the inclusion of the simple description, "as assignee," in paragraph 6. The dominant tenor of the provision is that August 1, 1964 is the crucial time for all purposes and any exception from that rule would have to have a solid and firm footing, not the mere speculative inference which can conceivably (but not readily) be drawn from the neutral characterization, "as assignee," which appears on its face to do no more than describe how Gulf Shores first entered the Avis system. Moreover, appellant signed the assignment forms in the space calling expressly for the "Name of New Licensees." Since Gulf Shores is thus unqualifiedly denominated the *new* licensee in the assignment itself, it is very hard to consider it as nevertheless standing in every respect in the shoes of the former licensee, especially in view of the specific terms of paragraph 6; it would be even more difficult to read the bare words, "as assignee," as somehow implicitly recognizing appellant's status as the "old" licensee at a time well before the effective date of the instrument under which Gulf Shores joined the Avis organization. . . .

This treatment of the new licensee does not seem unreasonable on its face. The five-year span is a probationary period in which Avis can evaluate the licensee's performance and determine whether it should become a permanent member of the system. Avis could well believe that, for the clause to serve that function, it must apply separately to each new licensee without any "tacking" of a prior licensee's period of operation. In this instance, for example, since SALCO's performance was obviously deemed unsatisfactory, it would not be commercially unreasonable for Avis to want to deny Gulf Shores credit for that prior operation. "Business contracts must be construed with business sense, as they naturally would be understood by intelligent men of affairs." And apart from the facts of this or any particular case, Avis could adopt a universal policy, reflected in its form license agreements, that (at least until the franchise had been in effect for five years) assignees should not hold a preferred status over wholly new operators. . . .

[Judgment affirmed.]

Perkins v Standard Oil Co.

235 Ore 7, 383 P2d 107 (1963)

Standard Oil made a jobbing or wholesale dealership contract with Perkins which limited him to selling Standard's products and required Perkins to maintain certain minimum prices. Standard Oil had the right to approve or disapprove of Perkins' customers. In order to be able to perform under this contract, Perkins had to make a substantial money investment, and his only income was from the commissions on the sales of Standard's products. Standard Oil made some sales directly to Perkins' customers. When Perkins protested, Standard Oil pointed out that the contract did not contain any provision making his rights exclusive. Perkins sued Standard Oil to compel it to stop dealing with his customers. From a decision in Standard's favor, Perkins appealed.

ROSSMAN, J. . . . The contract authorized the plaintiff [Perkins] to sell without Standard's written consent "on a nonexclusive basis" the products which Standard consigned to him but only to service stations or consuming accounts. Standard's written consent was required before the plaintiff could sell to any other account. The plaintiff promised in the contract to use his "best efforts to promote the sale of products consigned hereunder" and to sell a specified minimum amount during each year. . . . The plaintiff was required to deliver to Standard a complete list of the names and addresses of all his distributors and submit to it the names of any new potential distributors. . . .

The plaintiff claims that the contract by its very nature contains an implied condition that Standard would not solicit business directly from his (plaintiff's) customers. Standard protests that such an implied condition would be contrary to the express terms of the contract since the latter (1) provides that the plaintiff was authorized to sell Standard's products only "on a nonexclusive basis" and (2) reserved to Standard the "right to select its own customers." Plaintiff proposes a more restricted interpretation. . . . He concedes that the contract reserved to Standard the right to sell to any new accounts which it found, and to accept or reject any new accounts which he (the plaintiff) might obtain, but he insists that it does not permit Standard to solicit accounts which it had approved as his customers. . . .

In order to be successful in his business and to comply with the terms of his contract, the plaintiff was obliged to make substantial investments in storage facilities, delivery trucks, and other equipment. He was also obliged to hire employees. He was required to use his "best efforts" to promote the sale of Standard's products. Only if he sold Standard's products exclusively could it be said that he was using his best efforts to promote their sale. It is clear, then, that the contract limited his dealership to Standard products. Plaintiff was also required to sell a minimum quantity of other designated Standard petroleum products. If he at any time failed to sell the minimum quantity, Standard was at liberty to terminate its contract with him. Plaintiff's compensation was based exclusively on the sales he made to customers, which he secured through his own efforts. No compensation was available for the plaintiff if he obtained customers for Standard who bought directly from it. Nor does the contract obligate Standard to compensate him for sales made directly by Standard to plaintiff's customers. . . . . . . A condition must be implied that Standard would not solicit customers which had been obtained through plaintiff's efforts. The interpretation of the contract for which Standard contends would leave plaintiff and others in a position similar to his completely at the mercy of Standard. . . .

"We cannot accept [Standard's] construction of its meaning. An intention to make so one-sided an agreement is not readily to be inferred. . . .

"In every contract there is an implied covenant that neither party shall do anything that will have the effect of destroying or injuring the right of the other party to receive the fruits of the contract, which means that in every contract there exists a covenant of good faith and fair dealing." . . .

The implication of a condition finds support in many circumstances. . . . Plaintiff's only source of return on his substantial investments in the business was the sales he made to his customers. If Standard was at liberty to solicit as direct customers, as it contends, . . . plaintiff was in a state of economic servility; we do not believe that the parties intended such a result at the time the contract was signed. . . .

The contract before us is obviously a form contract prepared by Standard. It is a contract of "adhesion" in the sense that it is a take-it-or-leave-it whole. Such contracts are regarded by some authorities as anachronistic or inconsistent with real freedom of contract. At least they should be construed with an awareness of the inequality of the bargainers. . . .

[Judgment reversed.]

Smith v Smith

4 Wash App 608, 484 P2d 409 (1971)

F. Smith and his wife were divorced. As part of the divorce settlement, an agreement was executed by which the husband contracted to provide support for his son, Mackey, as long as the latter was a full-time college student. The father claimed that this obligation ended when the son was out of college for a two-year interval and when the son married. The son claimed that neither of these facts affected the obligation to provide support after he returned to college for those months when he was in fact a full-time college student.

ARMSTRONG, J. . . . That portion of the settlement agreement which is disputed reads as follows: The plaintiff [husband] agrees to pay to the defendant [wife], as Trustee for Mackey F. Smith, the sum of $150.00 per month, for his support, education and maintenance, for each and every calendar month or any portion thereof, in which the said Mackey F. Smith attends as a full time student any university, college, school, professional school, or other institution of higher learning, which sum shall be paid on the first day of each and every month in which the said Mackey F. Smith attends said educational institution as a full time student. However, for the months in which there are less than ten (10) days of school scheduled in said month, then, for that month, plaintiff shall pay a proportionate amount of the monthly support only. . . .

At the time of the divorce in January, 1964, Mackey F. Smith, the only child of the parties, was 20 years of age and had attended college for approximately two and one-half years. He continued in school until December, 1966, at which time he temporarily left school and became employed. Mackey celebrated his 25th birthday and was married during June, 1968.

The present dispute developed when the appellant, Frankland Smith, petitioned the divorce court for a clarification or, in the alternative, for modification of the divorce decree. The husband asserted that the parties intended the child support provisions to apply only while the son was a continuous student at some institution of higher learning; that when the son discontinued his studies as a full-time student between December of 1966 and February of 1969, the husband's obligation of support was thereby permanently terminated because the contract had been abandoned. The husband also contended that the child support payments were not to continue after the son was married. The settlement agreement was silent on both points. . . .

At the trial, the court decided that it was not necessary to receive any testimony as to the intentions of the parties because the contract was complete and unambiguous. . . .

We shall first consider whether the contract of the parties was so complete and unambiguous on its face that the court was warranted in holding that the written instrument was intended to be the final integrated agreement of the parties. The plaintiff husband contends that it is silent in two important respects: (1) Whether the contract was applicable only as long as the son remained a full-time student on a continuous basis and (2) whether the contract was intended to be effective after the marriage of the son. The trial court held that these omissions did not make the contract ambiguous. In effect, the court held that the omissions were irrelevant and immaterial and the writing constituted the complete integration of the agreement of the parties. We cannot agree.

Parol evidence is generally admissible where it does not tend to contradict the terms of the contract, but merely to supply an omission which is relevant and material to the performance of the contract. Under such circumstances the written contract would not contain the entire agreement of the parties and to that extent would be ambiguous as to the intention of the parties. . . . This contract was silent as to the length of time the father would be required to support his son in college and whether it continued in effect two years after the adult son had withdrawn from full time college attendance. Where a contract is silent as to time of duration, it will be implied that performance was intended to take place within a reasonable time. What constitutes a reasonable time is a question of fact which is dependent upon the subject matter of the contract, the situation of the parties, their intention and the circumstances attending the performance of the contract. . . .

If we were to assume that this contract was complete on its face and that time was not relevant and material to its interpretation, the father's obligation to pay support might continue for an unlimited number of years while the son attended "as a full time student any university, college, school, professional school or institution of higher learning." Such a result appears to be unreasonable.

On a retrial the court shall receive parol evidence to ascertain whether the contract contains all of the terms agreed upon by the parties. In the event that no time limit was considered by the parties, the court should determine what would constitute a reasonable time for the father to support his son under all of the circumstances of this case. The court should also consider whether the contract was abandoned by the fact that the son terminated his full-time college attendance for a period of two years.

[Reversed and remanded for a new trial.]

QUESTIONS AND CASE PROBLEMS

1. Fincher was employed by Belk-Sawyer Co. as fashion coordinator for the latter's retail stores. The contract of employment specified her duties as fashion coordinator and also provided for additional services of Fincher to be thereafter agreed upon in connection with beauty consultation and shopping services to be established at the stores. After Fincher had been employed as fashion coordinator for several months, Belk-Sawyer Co. refused to be bound by the contract on the ground that it was too indefinite. Was it bound? [Fincher v Belk-Sawyer Co., (Fla App) 127 So2d 130]

2. Avril, a Pennsylvania corporation, agreed to sell certain cleaning products to Center Chemical Co. at a discount of 45 percent for 20 years and gave Center the exclusive right to sell such products in Florida. Four years later, Center stopped purchasing from Avril, which then sued it for breach of contract. Did the law of Pennsylvania or the Florida law determine the damages which could be recovered? [Center Chemical Co. v Avril, (CA5 Fla) 392 F2d 289]

3. *A* and *B* signed a printed form of agreement by which it appeared that *A* promised to sell and *B* promised to buy certain land. On the blank lines

of the printed form, there was a typewritten provision that *B* had an option to purchase the land. Could *A* sue *B* for breach of contract if *B* did not buy the land? [Welk v Fainbarg, 255 Cal App 2d 269, 63 Cal Rptr 127]

4. Holland, doing business as the American Homes Co., sold Sandi Brown a set of kitchenware on the installment plan. When she stated that she did not have the money to make the monthly payments, it was agreed that Holland would put it on the layaway plan for her. Thereafter Holland and American Homes Co. sued her for the purchase price. She claimed that she had not become the owner of the kitchenware by the transaction which, if true, meant that she could not be sued for the purchase price. She offered witnesses who testified that a layaway plan did not make the goods become the property of the customer but merely put them away where they would not be sold to other customers and that the goods did not become the property of a buyer until the buyer claimed and made payment for the goods within a specified time. Holland objected to the admission of this evidence. Decide. [Holland v Brown, 15 Utah 2d 422, 394 P2d 77]

5. McGill and his grandson, Malo, made an agreement by which the former would live with the latter and receive support and maintenance in return for deeding to the grandson the house of the former. After a number of years, the grandfather left the house because of the threats and physical violence of the grandson. There was no complaint of lack of support and maintenance. Had the grandson broken the contract? [McGill v Malo, 23 Conn Supp 447, 184 A2d 517]

6. All the shareholders of Continental Title Company signed an agreement giving the Stewart Title Company the option to purchase "all" of their shares for a quarter million dollars. The option contract specified that notice of its exercise was to be given to the chairman of the board of the Continental Title Company. The Stewart Title Company notified one of the stockholders, Herbert, that it exercised the option to purchase his 350 shares, paying for them the prorated portion of a quarter million dollars. Herbert refused to sell. A lawsuit was brought against him and evidence was offered that the executives of Stewart understood that they were obtaining an option to purchase the stock of the Continental shareholders one by one. There was no evidence that this belief was communicated to anyone else. Was Herbert required to sell his shares to Stewart? [Stewart Title Company v Herbert, 6 Cal App 3d 957, 85 Cal Rptr 654]

7. Axford rented land from Shellhart. The lease gave the lessee the option to purchase the leased property "any time during the term of this lease or its extension for the sum of $12,000. This option may be exercised at any time prior to December 1, 1969 by giving the Lessors at least 30 days notice in writing of Lessee's intention to so exercise said option." Could the lessee exercise the option by giving notice without paying the purchase price at the same time? [Shellhart v Axford, (Wyo) 485 P2d 1031]

8. Physicians Mutual Insurance Company issued a policy covering the life of Ruby Brown. The policy declared that it did not cover any deaths resulting from "mental disorder, alcoholism, or drug addiction." Ruby was killed when she fell while intoxicated. The insurance company refused to pay because of the quoted provision. Her executor, Savage, sued the insurance company. Did it have a defense? [Physicians Mut. Ins. Co. v Savage, — Ind App —, 296 NE2d 165]

9. Carolina Plywood Distributors was a corporation. It purchased building materials from Clear Fir Sales Company. The president of Carolina wrote a letter to Clear Fir which in part stated, "Please accept this letter as my personal guarantee for the purchases of Carolina Plywood Distributors through December 31, 1970. If we are continuing to do business at that time, we will be glad to renew this guarantee." The debt of Carolina was not paid and Clear Fir sued Carolina and its president. Clear Fir claimed that the quoted letter guaranteed the debt of the corporation. The president defended on the ground that Clear Fir had never accepted his offer of guaranty and therefore he was not bound. Was this defense valid? [Clear Fir Sales Co. v Carolina Plywood Distributors, Inc., 13 NC App 429, 185 SE2d 737]

10. Ern-Roc Homes, a builder, guaranteed that its homes would have no seepage of water into the basement "through the foundation walls." Water entered the basement of the home purchased by Gomes by passing through a door installed in the basement wall, level with the ground in back of the house. The water caused extensive damage in the house. Gomes sued Ern-Roc Homes claiming that there was a breach of the builder's guaranty. Was Gomes correct? [Gomes v Ern-Roc Homes, Inc., (NY Civil Court) 72 Misc 2d 410, 339 NYS2d 401]

11. Carolina Pipeline Co. made a contract in 1956 to supply Carolina Ceramics with natural gas. The contract contained the following provision for price increases: "In the event that the Commodity Charge for gas as purchased by Seller from Transcontinental Gas Pipeline Company is increased above or decreased below 24.0 cents per MCF, or the commodity charge for gas as purchased by Seller from the Southern Natural Gas Company is increased above or decreased below 18.5 cents per MCF, the amount of such increases or decreases shall be added to or subtracted from, as the case may be, the price of gas to Buyer as set forth herein." The gas sold by Pipeline to Ceramics was obtained from Southern. Pipeline notified Ceramics on October 25, 1961, that the price was raised by reason of an increase by Southern of its price. From that time on, Pipeline raised its price every time Southern raised its price. During this time Transcontinental did not change its rates. Ceramics paid the increased rate but later sued Pipeline, claiming that it had been overcharged because the charges to it were based upon the prices of Southern. Its theory was that since there were two sources of supply, the increase of the resale price could not be made on the basis of the price of only one supplier. Ceramics offered parol evidence to show what the parties had intended by the contract. Was this evidence admissible? [Carolina Ceramics, Inc. v Carolina Pipeline Co., 251 SC 151, 161 SE2d 179]

17 Third Persons and Contracts

In some situations a third person will claim that he can assert rights with respect to a contract made by two other persons. This may be a third-party beneficiary contract, an assignment, or a novation. The first two of these are discussed in this section. Novation is discussed in § 17:8(2).

THIRD-PARTY BENEFICIARY CONTRACTS

§ **17:1. Definition.** Ordinarily *A* and *B* will make a contract that concerns only them. They, however, may make a contract by which *B* promises *A* that *B* will make a payment of money to *C*. If *B* fails to perform his promise, *C*, who is not the original promisee, may enforce it against *B*, the promisor. Such an agreement is a *third-party beneficiary contract*.

A life insurance contract is a third-party beneficiary contract, since the insurance company promises the insured to make payment to the beneficiary. Such a contract entitles the beneficiary to sue the insurance company upon the insured's death even though the insurance company never made any agreement directly with the beneficiary.[1] Similarly, when a building owner was obligated to furnish heat to a neighboring building and sold his building to a buyer who agreed to furnish heat to the neighboring building, the owner of the latter, as a third-party beneficiary of that contract, could enforce the buyer's promise to furnish heat.[2]

(1) Termination of Contract. If the third-party beneficiary has accepted the contract or changed his position in reliance on it, the original parties generally cannot thereafter rescind the contract so as to release the obligation to the third party beneficiary.[3] (See p. 335, Bass v Hancock Mutual Life Ins. Co.) The contract, however, may expressly reserve the power of the original parties to make such modification or rescission,[4] or the third party may consent to such a change.

---

[1] Walker Bank & Trust Co. v First Security Corp., 9 Utah 2d 215, 341 P2d 944.

[2] Nicholson v 300 Broadway Realty Corp., 7 NY2d 240, 196 NYS2d 945.

[3] Blackard v Monarch's Manufacturers and Distributors, 131 Ind App 514, 169 NE2d 735.

[4] A common form of reservation is the life insurance policy provision by which the insured reserves the right to change the beneficiary. § 142 of the 1967 tentative draft Restatement of Contracts 2d provides that the promisor and promisee may modify their contract and affect the right of the third-party beneficiary thereby unless the agreement expressly prohibits this or the third-party beneficiary has changed his position in reliance on the promise or has manifested assent to it.

§ 17:2. Incidental Beneficiaries Distinguished. Although the right of a third-party beneficiary to sue is now generally recognized, not everyone who benefits from the performance of a contract between others is such a beneficiary.[5] (See p. 336, McDonald Construction Co. v Murray.) If a city makes a contract with a contractor to pave certain streets, property owners living along those streets will naturally receive a benefit from the performance. This fact, however, does not confer upon them the status of third-party beneficiaries. Accordingly, the property owners cannot sue the contractor if he fails to perform. The courts reason that such beneficiaries are only incidentally benefited. The city contracted for the streets to further the public interest, not primarily to benefit individual property owners.[6]

When it is not clear whether a contract was intended to benefit a third person, it is generally held that he cannot enforce the contract.[7]

§ 17:3. Limitations on Third-Party Beneficiary. While the third-party beneficiary rule gives the third person the right to enforce the contract, it obviously gives him no greater rights than the contract provides. Otherwise stated, the third-party beneficiary must take the contract as he finds it. If there is a limitation or restriction, he cannot ignore it but is bound thereby. Thus, a promise to purchase stock could not be enforced by a third-party beneficiary where the obligation was subject to the condition that certain events occur and those events had not taken place.[8]

ASSIGNMENTS

Under a contract a party may have both rights and duties. Can he transfer or sell his rights to another person? Can he transfer his duties to another person?

A builder may contract to build a house. He may then find that he needs money which he can only procure by obtaining a loan from a bank. The bank demands security. Can he assign to the bank his right to receive payment from the owner under the contract? The situation may also arise that the contractor is unable to perform the contract and wants to substitute another builder to do the actual building. Can this be done? The problem considered here is whether the contractor can make a voluntary assignment of his rights or a delegation of his duties under the contract.

§ 17:4. Definition. Generally an *assignment* is a transfer by a party to a contract of some or all of his rights under the contract to a person not a party to the contract. The party making the assignment is the *assignor,* and the person to whom the assignment is made is the *assignee.* An assignee may generally sue in his own name as though he were a party to the original contract.[9] In many states a partial assignee may sue provided he makes the holders of the remaining fractional parts of the obligation coparties to the action.

---

[5] Lynn v Rainey, (Okla) 400 P2d 805.
[6] R § 147.
[7] Ison v Daniel Crisp Corp., 145 WVa 786, 122 SE2d 553.
[8] Rotermund v U.S. Steel Corp., (CA8 Mo) 474 F2d 1139.
[9] Bush v Eastern Uniform Co., 356 Pa 298, 51 A2d 731.

§ 17:5. Form of Assignment. Generally an assignment may be expressed in any form.[10] Any acts or any words, whether written or spoken, that show an intention to transfer or assign will be given the effect of an assignment.[11] Statutes, however, may require that certain kinds of assignments be in writing or be executed in a particular form.[12] This requirement is common in respect to statutes limiting the assignment of claims to wages.

An assignment is a completed transfer, not a contract. It is therefore immaterial whether or not there is any consideration. An assignment may be made as a gift, although it is usually part of a business transaction.

In a contract to make an assignment, which is executory as far as the assignor is concerned (as contrasted with an assignment, which is executed), there must be consideration as in any other contract.

§ 17:6. Assignment of Rights to Money. A person entitled to receive money, such as payment for the price of goods or for work done under a contract, may generally assign that right to another person.[13] (See p. 337, du Pont de-Bie v Vrendenburgh.) A claim or cause of action against another person may be assigned.[14] A contractor entitled to receive payment from the owner can assign that right to the bank as security for a loan, or he can assign it to anyone else. The fact that the assigned right represents money not yet due does not prevent the application of this rule so long as the contract itself exists at the time of the assignment.[15] Similarly, a person entitled to receive payments of money under a contract of employment may ordinarily assign his right to future wages.

It is frequently held that a claim is assignable if it survives the death of a party.[16]

(1) Nonexisting Contracts. If the contract is not in existence at the time the assignment is made, the attempt to assign money due on the contract in the future does not have the effect of a legal assignment. If the assignment has been supported by consideration, however, a court of equity will compel the assignor to make a transfer when the money is due.

(2) Restrictions upon Assignment. A contract provision prohibiting an assignment may be in either of two forms: (1) a condition that if the contract is assigned, the contract shall be void; or (2) a personal agreement by a party that he will not assign the contract. In a given case it is essential to determine which form of clause is in the contract. If it is the

---

10 R § 157.

11 Buck v Illinois National Bank & Trust Co., 79 Ill App 2d 101, 223 NE2d 167.

12 Assignments that do not become legally effective for certain technical reasons, such as failure to record as required by a local statute, may often be enforced in equity.

13 Adler v Kansas City Springfield and Memphis R.R. Co., 92 Mo 242, 4 SW 917.

14 Atoka, Inc. v Thornton, (Tex Civ App) 477 SW2d 333.

15 The UCC provisions concerning secured transactions do not apply to an absolute assignment of money due or to become due for future services or construction work. UCC § 9-104(f); Lyon v Ty-Wood Corp., 212 Pa Super 69, 239 A2d 819.

16 Travelers Ins. Co. v Turner, 211 Va 552, 178 SE2d 503.

condition form, the making of a prohibited assignment makes the contract void and the assignee acquires no interest. If it is the personal agreement or covenant form, the assignment is effective and the assignee acquires the assignor's interest. If the obligor, the other contracting party, chooses, he may sue the assignor for damages for having made the prohibited assignment. If he does not do so, he waives his rights to damages. When the obligor has waived his right to object to the making of a prohibited assignment, no one else can question the validity of the assignee's interest. For example, when the assignee of a contract for the purchase of property takes out fire insurance on the property, the insurance company cannot claim that he does not have any interest in the property because the antiassignment was violated.[17]

As a practical matter, any antiassignment clauses are generally included in a form supplied by the obligor. Therefore, if there is any ambiguity as to the meaning of the contract, it is to be construed strictly against the obligor. This means that unless it is very clear that a condition against assignment was intended, the courts will favor the personal agreement or covenant view. As an additional reason for reaching this conclusion, courts will avoid forfeitures whenever possible. If the antiassignment clause is a condition, all rights under the contract are forfeited by the making of the assignment. If it is merely a promise or covenant not to assign, liability of the assignor arises because of the assignment but no rights are forfeited.

There is a division of authority as to the effect of a prohibition in a contract against its assignment.[18] In some jurisdictions, if a right to money is otherwise assignable, the right to transfer cannot be restricted by the parties to the contract. Such a restriction is regarded in those states as contrary to public policy because it places a limitation on the assignor's right of property. In other states such a prohibition is recognized as valid[19] on the theory that the parties to the original contract may include such a provision if they choose to do so. In any event, a prohibition against assignment must be clearly expressed and any uncertainty is resolved in favor of assignability.[20]

Rights under contracts for the sale of goods may be assigned, "unless otherwise agreed," except when the assignment would materially change the performance of the other party. Unless the circumstances indicate the contrary, a prohibition of the assignment of "the contract" is to be construed only as prohibiting a delegation of the obligation to perform.[21]

Statutes may validly prohibit the assignment of rights to money. Contractors who build public works are frequently prohibited from assigning money due or money that will become due under the contract. In some states

---

[17] Belge v Aetna Cas. and Surety Co., 39 App Div 2d 295, 334 NYS2d 185.

[18] In some jurisdictions only a clause declaring that an assignment cannot be made is held to bar an assignment.

[19] Masterson v Sine, 68 Cal 2d 222, 65 Cal Rptr 545, 436 P2d 561.

[20] Detroit Greyhound Employees Federal Credit Union v Aetna Life Insurance Co., 381 Mich 683, 167 NW2d 274.

[21] UCC § 2-210(2), (3).

wage earners are prohibited from assigning their future wages, or the law limits the percentage of their wages that can be assigned. In some instances an assignment of wages is lawful, but the assignment must be a separate instrument complete in itself and not be included in the body of any other instrument. The purpose of such a provision is to protect employees from signing printed forms containing "hidden" wage assignment clauses.

§ 17:7. Assignment of Rights to a Performance. When the right of the obligee under the contract is a right to receive a performance by the other party, he may assign his right, provided the performance required of the other party to the contract will not be materially altered or varied by such assignment.[22]

When the obligee is entitled to assign his right, he may do so by his unilateral act. There is no requirement that the obligor consent or agree.[23] Likewise, the act of assigning does not constitute a breach of the contract,[24] unless the contract specifically declares so.

(1) Assignment Increasing Burden of Performance. When the assigning of a right would increase the burden of the obligor in performing, the assignment is ordinarily not permitted. To illustrate, if the assignor has the right to buy a certain quantity of a stated article and to take such property from the seller's warehouse, this right to purchase can be assigned. If, however, the sales contract stipulated that the seller should deliver to the buyer's premises and the assignee lived or had his place of business a substantial distance from the assignor's place of business, the assignment would not be given effect. In this case, the seller would be required to give a performance different from that which he contracted to make.

(2) Personal Satisfaction. A similar problem arises when the goods to be furnished must be satisfactory to the personal judgment of the buyer. Since the seller only contracted that his performance would stand or fall according to the buyer's judgment, the buyer may not substitute the judgment of his assignee.

(3) Personal Services. An employer cannot assign to another the employer's right to have an employee work for him. The relationship of employer and employee is so personal that the right cannot be assigned.[25] The performance contracted for by the employee was to work for a particular employer at a particular place and at a particular job. To permit an assignee to claim the employee's services would be to change that contract.

§ 17:8. Delegation of Duties. A *delegation of duties* is a transfer of duties by a party to a contract to another person who is to perform them in his

---

22 R § 151.
23 General Electric Credit Corp. v Security Bank, (Dist Col App) 244 A2d 920.
24 Earth Products Co. v Oklahoma City, (Okla) 441 P2d 399.
25 Folquet v Woodburn Public Schools, 146 Ore 339, 29 P2d 554.

stead. Under certain circumstances a contracting party may obtain someone else to do the work for him. When the performance is standardized and nonpersonal so that it is not material who performs, the law will permit the delegation of the performance of the contract. In such cases, however, the contracting party remains liable for the default of the person doing the work just as though the contracting party himself had performed or attempted to perform the job.[26] If the contract expressly prohibits delegation, such delegation of duties is prohibited.

If the performance by the promisor requires his personal skill or is a performance in which his credit standing or the other party's confidence in his ability was material in selecting him, delegation of performance is prohibited. A doctor or an artist hired to render a particular service cannot delegate the performance of that duty to another. For example, when a patient contracts with a medical specialist, the specialist must take care of the patient. If the specialist, without justification, leaves the patient in the care of a resident physician, the specialist is liable for breach of his contract. He is not excused on the ground that the resident used reasonable care under the circumstances, because the patient by contracting with a specialist was entitled to receive a specialist's care and not merely the reasonable care of a resident.[27]

(1) Intention to Delegate Duties. A question of interpretation arises as to whether an assignment of "the contract" is only an assignment of the rights of the assignor or is both an assignment of those rights and a delegation of his duties. The trend of authority is to regard such a general assignment as both a transfer of rights and delegation of duties. (See p. 338, Radley v Smith.)

With respect to contracts for the sale of goods, "An assignment of 'the contract' or of 'all my rights under the contract' or an assignment in similar general terms is an assignment of rights and, unless the language or the circumstances (as in an assignment for security) indicate the contrary, it is a delegation of performance of the duties of the assignor and its acceptance by the assignee constitutes a promise by him to perform the duties. This promise is enforceable by either the assignor or the other party to the original contract." [28]

When the contract states that the performance may be rendered by a named party, "his heirs and assigns," it is clear that the duty may be performed by another. For example, when the exclusive right to sell particular land was given to a named broker, "his heirs and assigns," the contract could be performed after the death of the broker by the broker's executor, the latter hiring a licensed real estate agent to perform the services.[29]

---

[26] Brown v Bowers Construction Co., 236 NC 462, 73 SE2d 147.
[27] Alexandridis v Jewett, (CA1 Mass) 388 F2d 829.
[28] UCC § 2-210(4).
[29] Phoenix Title & Trust Co. v Grimes, 101 Ariz 182, 416 P2d 979.

(2) Novation. One who is entitled to receive performance under a contract may agree to release the person who is bound to perform and to permit another person to take his place. When this occurs, it is not a question of merely assigning the liability under the contract but is really one of abandoning the old contract and substituting in its place a new contract. This change of contract is called a *novation.* For example, if *A* and *B* have a contract, they, together with *C,* may agree that *C* shall take *B's* place. If this is done, there is a novation. *B* is then discharged from his contract, and *A* and *C* are bound by the new contract. It must be shown, however, that a novation was intended.[30]

(3) Continuing Liability of Assignor. In the absence of a contrary agreement, such as a novation, an assignor continues to be bound by his obligations under the original contract. Thus, the fact that a buyer assigns his rights to goods under a contract does not terminate his liability to make payment to the seller.[31]

§ 17:9. Partial Assignment. Suppose that a contractor is entitled to receive $2,000 from the party for whom he is constructing a garage. Assume further that the contractor wishes to pay the supplier of cement by assigning to him $500 of the $2,000 which the contractor will receive from the owner. If such a partial transfer could be made, the owner might find himself sued by the contractor for $1,500 and by the materialman for $500. The owner would thus be subjected to the expense and inconvenience of two lawsuits. To avoid this inconvenience and burden to the obligor, all parties must be joined in the action.[32]

§ 17:10. Defenses and Setoffs. The assignee's rights rise no higher than those of the assignor.[33] If the obligor (the other party to the original contract) could successfully defend against a suit brought by the assignor, he will also prevail against the assignee. (See p. 339, Associates Loan Co. v Walkers.)

The assigning of a right does not free it from any defense or setoff to which the right would be subject if it were still held by the assignor.[34] The fact that the assignee has given value for the assignment does not give the assignee any immunuity from defenses which the other party, the obligor, could have asserted against the assignor.[35] The assignee acquires his rights subject to any limitations thereon. Consequently, if the contract contained

[30] Chastain v Cooper & Reed, 152 Tex 322, 257 SW2d 422. In some states, a new contract between the original parties is likewise called a novation. Hudson v Maryland State Housing Co., 207 Md 320, 114 A2d 421.

[31] Greenbrier Homes v Cook, 1 Mich App 326, 136 NW2d 27.

[32] State Bank of Sheridan v Heider, 139 Ore 185, 9 P2d 117.

[33] R § 167; Harrison Mfg. Co. v Philip Rothman & Son., 336 Mass 625, 147 NE2d 155; Ledman v G.A.C. Finance Corp., (Dist Col App) 213 A2d 246.

[34] National Surety Corp. v Algernon Blair, Inc., 114 Ga App 30, 150 SE2d 256.

[35] National Commercial Bank & Trust Co. v Malik, 72 Misc 2d 865, 339 NYS2d 605.

an arbitration clause which bound the assignor, the assignee is bound by that clause when he seeks to enforce his assigned right.[36]

The only way in which the assignee can protect himself is to ask the obligor whether he has any defense or setoff or counterclaim against the assignor. If the obligor states that he has none or makes a declaration of no setoff, he is estopped (barred) from contradicting his statement; and in most cases he is not permitted to prove a defense, setoff, or counterclaim based on facts existing prior to the time of his statement to the assignee.[37]

§ **17:11. Notice of Assignment.** An assignment, if otherwise valid, takes effect the moment it is made. It is not necessary that the assignee or the assignor give notice to the other party to the contract that the assignment has been made. It is highly desirable, however, that the other party be notified as soon as possible after the making of the assignment because, if notice is not given, the assigned right may be impaired or possibly destroyed.

(1) Defenses and Setoffs. Notice of an assignment prevents the obligor from asserting against the assignee any defense or setoff arising after such notice with respect to a matter not related to the assigned claim. If the matter relates to the assigned claim, the fact of notice does not affect the right of the obligor to assert against the assignee any defense or setoff that would have been available were he sued by the assignor.

For example, *O* owns two lots of ground, No. 1 and No. 2. *O* makes two separate contracts with *C*, a paving contractor, to pave these two lots. *C* assigns to *A* his right to be paid for lot No. 1 before he has performed that contract, and *A* notifies *O* of the assignment. After making the assignment, *C* paves both lots but does a poor job on each. When *A* sues *O* for the contract price for lot No. 1, *O* claims a setoff for the damages suffered by him because of the poor work on lots No. 1 and No. 2. The poor work defense with respect to lot No. 1 is obviously related to the claim for the contract price for paving lot No. 1. That defense or setoff may therefore be asserted by *O* against *A*, without regard to when the paving was done or when notice of the assignment was given to *O*.

In contrast, the claim of *O* for damages because of the poor work done on lot No. 2 is not related to the claim that was assigned to *A*. Consequently, the giving of notice of the assignment to *O* cut off the right of *O* to assert against *A* any claim which would thereafter arise with respect to an unrelated matter. Since *O* knew of the assignment of the lot No. 1 contract claim before there was any breach as to lot No. 2, *O* cannot assert his defense with respect to lot No. 2 against *A*.[38]

---

[36] Blum's, Inc. v Ferro Union Corp., 36 App Div 2d 584, 318 NYS2d 414 affirmed 29 NYS2d 689, 325 NYS2d 418, 274 NE2d 751.

[37] Harrison v Galilee Baptist Church, 427 Pa 247, 234 A2d 314.

[38] UCC § 9-318(1); Dickerson v Federal Deposit Insurance Corp., (Fla App) 244 So2d 748.

(2) Discharge. Until the obligor knows that there has been an assignment, he is legally entitled to pay to or perform for the assignor just as though there were no assignment. Such payment or performance is a complete discharge of his obligation under the contract; but in such a case the assignee could proceed against the assignor to require him to account for what he had received. If the assignee has given the obligor notice of the assignment, however, the obligor cannot discharge his obligation to the assignee by making a payment to or a performance for the assignor.[39]

If the debtor, knowing of the assignment, pays the assignor, the assignee may sue either the assignor or the debtor.[40] The payment by the latter with knowledge of the existence of the assignment does not discharge his debt, and the assignor is deemed to have received payment from the debtor on behalf of the assignee.

The notice here considered must relate to the particular claim against the defendant. Thus, knowledge that a business enterprise was obtaining refinancing on the basis of its accounts receivable was not a notice to the debtor of one of the accounts that that account had been assigned to the lending agency.[41]

(3) Priority. If a person assigns the same right to two different assignees, the question arises as to which assignee has obtained the right. By the American rule, the assignee taking the first assignment prevails over the subsequent assignees.[42]

§ 17:12. Warranties of Assignor. When the assignment is made for a consideration, the assignor is regarded as impliedly warranting that the right he assigns is valid, that he is the owner of the claim which he assigns, and that he will not interfere with the assignee's enforcement of the obligation. He does not warrant that the other party will pay or perform as required.

---

39 Olshan Lumber Co. v Bullard, (Tex Civ App) 395 SW2d 670; Lincoln Rochester Trust Co. v S. C. Marasco Steel, Inc., 66 Misc 2d 295, 320 NYS2d 864.

40 Van Waters & Rogers, Inc. v Interchange Resources, Inc., 14 Ariz App 414, 484 P2d 26.

41 Commercial Savings Bank v G & J Wood Products Co., Inc., 46 Mich App 133, 207 NW2d 401.

42 Some states adopt the English view by which the assignee first giving notice to the obligor is entitled to the payment. Under this rule, however, the first assignee may recover the payment made to the subsequent assignee if the latter knew of the prior assignment when he acquired his rights. This right of the prior assignee under the English rule is restricted to suit against the subsequent assignee and does not give him the right to sue the obligor.

CASES FOR CHAPTER 17

Bass v John Hancock Mut. Life Ins. Co.

10 Cal 3d 792, 112 Cal Rptr 195, 518 P2d 1147 (1974)

Pursuant to the Ford Motor Company's contract with the United Automobile Workers (UAW), Ford obtained from John Hancock Mutual Life Insurance Company a group insurance policy in 1964 covering the Ford employees. In 1964 Bass was employed by Ford. He notified Ford that he did not wish to be under the group plan. In 1967, Ford made a

new contract with UAW and obtained a new group policy covering all employees. Ford assumed that Bass did not want to be covered by this new group policy and paid no premiums to the insurance company to cover him. Bass was killed in an automobile accident in 1968 and his beneficiary sued the insurance company. It raised the defense that any coverage of Bass by the 1967 policy had been terminated when Ford failed to pay the premiums with respect to Bass. From a judgment for the insurer, the beneficiary of the policy appealed.

BURKE, J. . . . Bass evidently waived coverage under a 1964 group plan offered by his employer, Ford Motor Company, despite the fact that such insurance was offered free of charge to all employees.

In October 1967, the Ford union contract was renegotiated. . . . As part of the new contract, the Hancock plan was amended . . . to provide for increased benefits. Although three years had passed since Bass had refused coverage, neither Ford nor Hancock solicited Bass' desires with respect to the 1967 plan. . . .

It seems evident to us that a waiver which occurred in 1964 is not necessarily controlling with respect to rights under a 1967 insurance program. . . . Bass was a third party beneficiary under the Ford-UAW union contract and the Ford-Hancock group insurance program, and as such he initially acquired valuable rights to insurance coverage. . . . Although the rights of a third party beneficiary may be voluntarily waived or disclaimed . . . the burden is on the party claiming the waiver ". . . to prove it by clear and convincing evidence that does not leave the matter to speculation, and 'doubtful cases will be decided against a waiver. . . .'" . . .

We may assume that the contract rights which Bass acquired under the 1964 insurance program were, as the trial court found, unequivocally and voluntarily waived or disclaimed by him. . . . The record contains no evidence whatever that Bass subsequently relinquished the new rights to coverage which accrued to him in 1967 by reason of the renegotiation of Ford's labor contract and the amendment of the Hancock group plan. . . . Yet in the absence of a renewed rejection or disclaimer from Bass, or other "clear and convincing" indicium of waiver, we must conclude that Bass retained his group insurance rights under the 1967 plan.

Defendant Hancock contends that even if Bass did not waive his rights to coverage, plaintiff's cause of action would be against Ford rather than Hancock, since Ford paid Hancock no premiums on Bass' account. To the contrary, nonpayment of premiums may have constituted a breach of *Ford's* obligations to Hancock, but would not affect the right of Bass (or plaintiff) to enforce coverage which Hancock agreed to extend to *all* Ford employees. (. . . An employee who otherwise satisfies the conditions of a group plan may maintain an action against the insurer as a third-party beneficiary. . . . The same reasoning would apply, of course, to the employee's beneficiaries.) In a series of recent cases we have held that the employer is the agent of the insurer in performing the duties of administering group insurance policies, including the payment of premiums, and that accordingly the insurer shares responsibility for the employer's mistakes. . . . We see no reason to deviate from this principle in the instant case. Indeed, we note that Hancock's own representative admitted at trial that if a Ford employee were not included in the calculation of premiums by reason of clerical error or mistake, Hancock would nevertheless honor his claim under the group policy and backcharge Ford for the unpaid premiums.

In the instant case, Ford's "mistake" was in assuming that Bass had rejected coverage under the 1967 group plan, without verifying that fact with Bass himself. We think that this kind of mistake is one for which Hancock should share responsibility despite the nonpayment of premiums.

[Judgment reversed and action remanded.]

McDonald Construction Co. v Murray

5 Wash App 68, 485 P2d 626 (1971)

Murray owned a building. He contracted with the McDonald Construction Company to make an addition to the building. Queen Anne News, Inc., was to be a tenant in the new addition. The contract required completion of the work within 75 days. It took 239 days to complete. Murray and Queen Anne News sued McDonald for the damages caused by the delay.

The lower court entered judgment for Murray but dismissed Queen Anne News from the action. McDonald appealed.

JAMES, J. . . . The trial judge found as a fact that Queen Anne News, Inc. was not a party to the construction contract and that its only relationship to the transaction was as a prospective tenant for the premises McDonald undertook to construct. Consequently, Queen Anne News was dismissed from the action.

Queen Anne News claims that the delay in completion of the premises caused it to lose anticipated profits. It asserts a right to recover from McDonald upon the legal theory that it was a third-party beneficiary of the construction contract.

A third-party beneficiary is one who, though not a party to the contract, will nevertheless receive direct benefits therefrom. In determining whether or not a third-party beneficiary status is created by a contract, the critical question is whether the benefits flow directly from the contract or whether they are merely incidental, indirect or consequential. . . . An incidental beneficiary acquires no right to recover damages for non-performance of the contract. Restatement of Contracts, § 147 (1932). "It is not sufficient that the performance of the promise may benefit a third person, but that it must have been entered into for his benefit, or at least such benefit must be the direct result of performance and so within the contemplation of the parties." . . . "The question whether a contract is made for the benefit of a third person is one of construction. The intention of the parties in this respect is determined by the terms of the contract as a whole construed in the light of the circumstances under which it was made." . . . Such "intent" is not a desire or purpose to confer a benefit upon the third person, nor a desire to advance his interests, but an intent that the promisor shall assume a direct obligation to him. . . .

Queen Anne News points out that the evidence established that McDonald was aware of the fact that it was to become the Murrays' tenant when the addition to the Murrays' building was completed. Queen Anne News argues that the Murrays' intent, together with McDonald's knowledge thereof, is sufficient to afford the News the status of a third-party beneficiary.

We do not agree. Any benefit which Queen Anne News could assert would be derived from the intervening tenancy agreement which it had with the Murrays. Queen Anne News derived no direct benefit from the construction contract and consequently had no right of action against McDonald because of McDonald's breach of performance. The trial judge did not err in dismissing Queen Anne News' cross-complaint.

[Judgment affirmed.]

du Pont de-Bie v Vrendenburgh

(CA4 Md) 1057 (1974)

As part of the divorce proceedings between John and Faith Vrendenburgh, a separation agreement was executed under which John agreed to pay periodical sums of money provided Faith had complied with the provisions of the agreement. Faith assigned her right to payment under this agreement to Alexis I. du Pont de-Bie. He brought suit against John and Faith to collect the amount due under the assignment. The lower court entered judgment for him for all money which had become due down to the date of the assignment but refused to enter judgment for him for money becoming due after the assignment. John and Faith appealed.

PER CURIAM . . . In regard to the assignment by appellee's former wife of her rights under the separation agreement, the District Court held that such assignment conveyed rights to only those sums which had accrued at the date of the assignment. The Court suggested, as a basis for such finding, (a) that since the obligations of appellee's wife under the separation agreement were personal in nature, installments to become due in the future under such agreement could not be assigned, and (b) that since installments under the separation agreement were payable to appellee's wife only as long as she remained alive, appellant failed to meet his burden of proving that the wife was still alive as of the date of the judgment. We find unpersuasive these reasons for denial of appellant's right to judgment for all sums accruing under the separation agreement up to the date of the judgment. The general rule, of course, is that executory contracts for personal services or involving a relationship of confidence are not assignable. It is equally well established, though, that the right to receive money due *or to become due* under an existing contract may be assigned, even though the contract, itself, may not be assignable because it involves personal services. The fact that an assignor has obligations as well as rights under a bilateral contract, and that the obligations cannot be assigned, does not prevent him from assigning his rights. Of course, if appellee's former wife had failed to perform her obligations under the agreement, the proof of such failure would have been a valid defense to this part of appellant's counterclaim.

The appellee contends, however, that the burden rested on the appellant to establish that the former wife met the conditions on which the continuance of payments rested, i.e., that the former wife was alive at the time the sums to be paid by the appellee accrued. The separation agreement did provide, in the relevant part, that payments to the wife "shall cease and terminate immediately upon the death of either Husband or Wife." This, of course, did condition the continuation of the payments to the ex-wife on the latter's continued existence. But the vice in appellee's argument is with reference to the burden of proof in this connection. . . . There is a presumption of the continuation of life. Under this presumption, a person shown to have been alive at a given time is presumed to remain alive until the contrary is shown by some sufficient proof or, in the absence of such proof, until a different presumption arises. The existence of such presumption shifts the burden of proving a person's death to the party who relies on such death. In this case, appellee's former wife was shown to be alive as recently as 1971 when she executed the amendment to the assignment, and thus must be presumed to be alive in the absence of any contrary showing by the appellee. Appellant is entitled to judgment on the assignment for all sums which had accrued at the date of the District Court's final order.

. . . The judgment of the district court is affirmed in part, and reversed in part, and the case is remanded with instructions to the district court for the entry of judgment in accordance with the foregoing opinion.

[Judgment affirmed.]

Radley v Smith

6 Utah 2d 314, 313 P2d 465 (1957)

Smith, who owned the Avalon Apartments, sold individual apartments under contracts that required each purchaser to pay $15 a month extra for hot and cold water, heat, refrigeration, taxes, and fire insurance. Smith assigned his interest in the apartment house and under the various contracts to Roberts. She failed to pay the taxes on the building. Radley and other tenants sued Smith and Roberts to compel them to pay the taxes. The action was dropped as to Smith. From a judgment against Roberts, she appealed.

CROCKETT, J. . . . The first of defendant's contentions is that the trial court erred in finding she had assumed any of the duties and obligations arising under the contracts between Smith and the plaintiffs. She maintains that in purchasing Smith's interest she was acquiring only the right to collect payments from the plaintiffs and that she had no intention of assuming the burdens of the contracts. While it is no doubt possible for a party to become the assignee of the rights under a contract without becoming responsible for the duties, the question whether a purported assignment of an entire contract includes such assumption depends upon its terms and the intent of the parties. Whenever uncertainty or ambiguity exists with respect thereto, it is proper for the court to consider all the facts and circumstances, including the words and actions of the parties forming the background of the transaction.

It appears that the defendant had available Smith's contracts which set forth the corresponding rights and duties of the parties, and expressly stated that the provisions would bind the "successors and assigns." She, therefore, knew of the services required of the seller and in fact initially accepted and performed those responsibilities, and further, accepted the $15 per month which the contract recited was to pay for them, and for the payment of taxes.

Applicable to this situation is the rule of construction stated in § 164 (1) of the Restatement of Contracts:

"Where a party to a bilateral contract, which is at the time wholly or partially executory on both sides, purports to assign the whole contract, his action is interpreted, in the absence of circumstances showing a contrary intention, as an assignment of the assignor's rights under the contract and a delegation of the performance of assignor's duties."

There is nothing in this case to affirmatively indicate anything other than that defendant was to assume the responsibilities of the seller under the contracts and the trial court's finding with respect to that issue must therefore be affirmed. . . .

[Judgment affirmed.]

Associates Loan Co. v Walkers

76 NMex 520, 416 P2d 529 (1966)

The Walkers purchased on trial a mechanical water softener from Partin. He represented that the use of the softener would increase the milk production at the Walkers' dairy, and the purchase price could be paid for through such increased production. Partin assigned his contract with the Walkers to Associates Loan Co. When Associates sued the Walkers for the money due under the contract, the Walkers raised the defense that the mechanical water softener did not work as represented. From a judgment for the defendants, Associates appealed.

SPIESS, J. . . . The defense, in substance, is that Partin and Walkers agreed that there would be no sale and the contract would not be effective unless after trial the water softener served to increase Walkers' milk production. This agreement was made orally at the time, or prior to the signing of the written contract. Walkers contend that the oral agreement created a condition precedent to the written contract becoming a valid obligation.

It is further asserted that since the condition failed, the contract did not come into existence. . . .

It is first contended that the transaction falls within the Uniform Commercial Code, and in accordance with its provisions an assignee takes an assigned chose in action subject only to such equities and defenses between the debtor and assignee as are specified in UCC § 9-318(1). . . . It is argued that the equities or defenses so specified do not include the type of defense interposed by Walkers. Therefore, the trial court was in error in permitting Walkers to raise the defense against Associates.

The cited section is as follows: "(1) Unless an account debtor has made an enforceable agreement not to assert defenses or claims arising out of a sale as provided in Section 9-206 . . . the rights of an asignee are subject to (a) all the terms of the contract between the account debtor and assignor and any defense or claim arising therefrom; and (b) any other defense or claim of the account debtor against the assignor which accrues before the account debtor receives notification of the assignment."

The contract involved here does not contain an agreement under which the account debtor[s], Walkers, have precluded themselves from asserting defenses arising out of the sale as against assignee. Consequently, this phase of the Code is not involved. It is apparent that the section quoted makes no substantial change in the law as it existed prior to the adoption of the Uniform Commercial Code. See Anderson's Uniform Commercial Code, Vol. 2, page 602, and Secured Transactions under the Uniform Commercial Code, Coogan, Hogan and Vagts, Vol. 2, p. 1599.

The fundamental rule of law, unchanged by the quoted section of the Uniform Commercial Code, is that an assignee of a chose in action acquires by virtue of his assignment nothing more than the assignor had, any and all equities and defenses which could have been raised by the debtor against the assignor are available to the debtor against the assignee. . . .

If the contract in Partin's hands was subject to a condition precedent under which it was not to become effective until the happening of a contingency, upon assignment the assignee took the contract subject to the same condition. The trial court correctly held that the defense raised by Walkers was available against the assignee, Associates. . . .

[Judgment affirmed.]

QUESTIONS AND CASE PROBLEMS

1. Rexroad contracted with the City of Assaria to improve certain streets within the city. The contract specified that "the contractor shall be liable for all damages to buildings . . . located outside the construction limits (and shall) make amicable settlement of such damage claims. . . ." Anderson, whose house was damaged by the construction work, sued Rexroad for the damages. The latter defended on the ground that Anderson did not have any agreement with him and had not given him any consideration. Decide. [Anderson v Rexroad, 175 Kan 676, 266 P2d 320]

2. McGilco, a building contractor, applied to the Great Southern Savings & Loan Ass'n for a loan to pay for the paving work in the Park Crest Village Development. This paving was done by Stephens. Great Southern agreed to lend the money to McGilco but failed to do so. McGilco did not pay Stephens. Stephens then sued Great Southern for the breach of its contract to lend money to McGilco. Was Stephens entitled to recover in this action? [Stephens v Great Southern Savings & Loan Ass'n, (Mo App) 421 SW2d 332]

3. The City of Moab owed Holder for construction work. Holder assigned his claim against the City to Cooper. Cooper gave the City notice that the claim had been assigned to him and demanded payment. The City refused to pay Cooper but paid Holder instead. Cooper sued Holder for such payment. Was Cooper entitled to recover? [Cooper v Holder, 21 Utah 2d 40, 440 P2d 15]

4. Enos had a policy of insurance with the Franklin Casualty Insurance Company providing for the payment of all reasonable hospitalization expenses up to $500 for each person injured while a passenger in, or upon entering or leaving, the insured's automobile. Wagner, a guest in the automobile, was injured in a highway accident. She was treated by Dr. Jones, who then sued the insurer to obtain payment. Decide. [Franklin Casualty Insurance Company v Jones, (Okla) 362 P2d 964]

5. The City of New Rochelle Humane Society made a contract with the City of New Rochelle to capture and impound all dogs running at large. Spiegler, a minor, was bitten by some dogs while in the school yard. She sued the School District of New Rochelle and the Humane Society. With respect to the Humane Society, she claimed that she was a third party beneficiary of the contract that the Society had made with the City and could therefore sue it for its failure to capture the dogs by which she had been bitten. Was she entitled to recover? [Spiegler v School District, 39 Misc 2d 946, 242 NYS2d 430]

6. Ewin Engineering Corporation owed money to Girod. The latter borrowed money from the Deposit Guaranty Bank & Trust Co. and assigned to it as security for the loan the claim he held against Ewin. The bank immediately notified Ewin of the assignment. Thereafter Ewin paid Girod the balance due him. Ewin then notified the bank that it had paid Girod in full and that it refused to recognize the assignment. The bank sued Ewin. Could it recover? [Ewin Engineering Corp. v Deposit Guaranty Bank & Trust Co., 216 Miss 410, 62 So2d 572]

7. A buyer purchased goods on credit from a seller. Unknown to the buyer, the seller assigned to a finance company his right to the purchase price. Thereafter the buyer, without knowledge of the assignment, returned the

goods to the seller who accepted them and cancelled the buyer's debt. The finance company sued the buyer for the purchase price which had been assigned to it and claimed that it was not bound by the act of the seller. Was the finance company entitled to recover the purchase price from the buyer? [Peoples Finance & Thrift Co. v Landes, 28 Utah 2d 392, 503 P2d 444]

8. Tennefos Construction Company did highway construction work for the North Dakota Highway Department. Alexander supplied them with fill for the construction. Alexander owed money to Rheault who supplied him with oil and fuel. Rheault would not supply Alexander further unless payment of his debts was guaranteed. It was finally agreed that when Tennefos paid for the fill, the checks would be made payable to the order of Rheault and Alexander. Was there an assignment to Rheault? [Rheault v Tennefos Constr. Co., (ND) 189 NW2d 626]

9. Hardin County entered into a contract with Pettigrew & Finney Contracting Co. to install air conditioning in a building owned by the county. The contractor, with the New Amsterdam Casualty Co., executed a performance bond and a labor and material bond naming the county as obligee. By the labor and material bond, the contractor and its surety promised to pay for all labor and materials used in performing the contract. The contractor then subcontracted all nonelectrical work in the project to T. O. Morris. Morris obtained equipment and materials from Air Temperature, Inc. The latter was not paid and it brought suit against Morris, the contractor, and the surety. Neither the contractor nor the surety had any direct dealings with Air Temperature. At the time when Air Temperature furnished the goods to Morris, Air Temperature did not know that the contractor and the surety had executed bonds and Air Temperature had not acted in reliance on the existence of any bonds. Were the contractor and the surety liable to Air Temperature? [Air Temperature Inc. v Morris, (Tenn App) 469 SW2d 495]

10. *A* purchased *B*'s business. *A* orally agreed to pay the business debts of *B*. *C* had sold goods to *B* for *B*'s store but had not been paid. *C* sued *A*. *A* raised the defense that he was not liable because there was no writing for his promise to pay *B*'s debt and the statute of frauds made an oral promise to pay the debt of another unenforceable. Was this a valid defense? [Campbell v Hickory Farms of Ohio, 258 SC 563, 190 SE2d 26]

11. Hudgens purchased a used car from Mack, a dealer. Mack falsely informed Hudgens that the car was in good condition when, in fact, it needed extensive repairs. Mack also refused to live up to his 30-day guarantee when the car was brought back within a few days after the sale. The day following the sale Mack had assigned the contract to Universal C.I.T. Credit Corp. When Hudgens refused to pay on the contract, he was sued by Universal. Hudgens claimed the right to set aside the contract for fraud. Was he entitled to do so? [Universal C.I.T. Credit Corp. v Hudgens, 234 Ark 668, 356 SW2d 658]

18 Discharge of Contracts

A contract is usually discharged by the performance of the terms of the agreement, but termination may also occur by later agreement, impossibility of performance, operation of law, or acceptance of breach.

§ **18:1. Introduction.** In most cases the parties perform their promises and the contract is discharged by performance of its terms. If a dispute arises as to whether there has been performance, the party claiming that he has performed has the burden of proving that fact.

§ **18:2. Discharge by Performance.**

(1) ***Payment.*** When payment is required by the contract, performance consists of the payment of money or, if accepted by the other party, the delivery of property or the rendering of services.

Payment by commercial paper, such as a check, is ordinarily a conditional payment. A check merely suspends the debt until it is presented for payment. If payment is then made, the debt is discharged; if not paid, suit may be brought on either the debt or the check.[1]

(a) APPLICATION OF PAYMENTS. If a debtor owes more than one debt to the creditor and pays him money, a question may arise as to which debt has been paid. If the debtor specifies the debt to which his payment is to be applied and the creditor accepts the money, the creditor is bound to apply the money as specified.[2] Thus, if the debtor specifies that a payment is made for a current purchase, the creditor may not apply the payment to an older balance.[3]

If the debtor does not specify the application to be made, the creditor may apply the payment to any one or more of the debts in such manner as he chooses.[4] As between secured and unsecured claims, the creditor is free to apply the payment to the unsecured claim. The creditor, however, must apply the payment to a debt that is due as contrasted with one which is not yet due. He cannot apply a payment to a claim that is illegal or invalid; but

[1] UCC § 3-802(1)(b).
[2] S. S. Silberblatt, Inc. v United States, (CA5 Tex) 353 F2d 545.
[3] Fuqua v Moody & Clary Co., (Tex Civ App) 462 SW2d 321.
[4] Swift & Co. v Kelley, (Miss) 214 So2d 460.

he may apply the payment to a claim which cannot be enforced because it is barred by the statute of limitations and, according to some authority, to a claim that cannot be enforced for want of a writing required by the statute of frauds.

The fact that payment of one of the debts has been guaranteed by a third person ordinarily does not affect the right of the debtor or creditor to apply a payment to the discharge of either the guaranteed debt or an unguaranteed debt. This is subject to certain exceptions, as when the guarantor has supplied the money with which the payment is made, in which case it must be applied to the discharge of the guaranteed debt,[5] particularly when the creditor knows that the money was so supplied.

If neither the debtor nor the creditor has made any application of the payment, application will be made by the court. There is a division of authority, however, whether the court is to make such application as will be more favorable to the creditor [6] or the debtor. The courts tend to favor the latter view when the rights of third persons are involved, such as the rights of those furnishing the money for the payment.[7] In some instances the court will apply the payment to the oldest outstanding debt.[8]

(b) Record of Application. Ordinarily the application of payment is made by a notation on a payment check or a statement in a covering letter mailed by the debtor. When the creditor makes the application, it is likely that there will be a receipt which will acknowledge the payment and specify the application.

The application of payment may be made orally provided there is a communication of the application made to the other party. In contrast, if the creditor merely receives a payment but never makes any notation of the application made by him or communicates that application to the debtor, it will be held that no application has been made by the creditor.[9]

(2) Time of Performance. When the date or period of time for performance is stipulated, performance should be made on that date or in that time period. (See p. 358, Creasy v Tincher.) It may usually occur later than the date, however, unless the nature or terms of the contract indicate clearly that time of performance is vital, as in the case of contracts for the purchase or sale of property of a fluctuating value.[10] When time is vital, it is said to be "of the essence." [11]

Ordinarily, time is not of the essence.[12] Performance within a reasonable time is sufficient, and if no time is specified, an obligation to perform

---

[5] Sorge Ice Cream & Dairy Co. v Wahlgren, 200 Wis 2d 220, 137 NW2d 118.

[6] Winfield Village v Reliance Insurance Co., 64 Ill App 2d 253, 212 NE2d 10.

[7] As to sureties generally, see Ch. 36.

[8] Michigan v Vandenburg Electric Co., 343 Mich 87, 72 NW2d 216.

[9] Camp v Nokes, 250 Ark 819, 467 SW2d 730.

[10] Mercury Gas & Oil Corp. v Rincon Oil & Gas Corp., 79 NMex 537, 445 P2d 958.

[11] Restatement, Contracts, § 276; Roos v Lassiter, (CA1 Tex) 188 F2d 427.

[12] Kingery Constr. Co. v Scherbarth Welding, Inc., 186 Neb 653, 185 NW2d 857.

within a reasonable time will be implied. (See p. 359, Robinson v Commercial Contractors, Inc.)

In the case of the sale of property, time will not be regarded as of the essence when there has not been any appreciable change in the market value or condition of the property and when the person who delayed does not appear to have done so for the purpose of speculating on a change in market value.[13]

Statutes may provide that a contract shall not be forfeited because of a provision making time of the essence when the complaining party is not harmed by the delay and has been fully compensated. Time can be made of the essence by imposing a time limitation on performance. For example, where a sign contractor was obligated to repair any damage to the sign within 24 normal wǒrking hours after notice of damage, time was of the essence in the making of repairs.[14]

In some contracts the time of performance is conditional, that is, it depends upon the happening of a particular event, the failure of a certain event to happen, or the existence of a certain fact. If the condition is not fulfilled, the promisor has no obligation to perform. To illustrate, a fire insurance policy does not impose any duty for performance on the insurance company until there is a loss within the coverage of the contract. Thus, there may be no performance by the company during the life of the contract.

(3) Tender of Performance. An offer to perform is known as a *tender*. If performance requires the doing of an act, a tender that is refused will discharge the party offering to perform. If performance requires the payment of a debt, however, a tender that is refused does not discharge the obligation.[15] But it stops the running of interest charges and prevents the collection of court costs if the party is sued, providing the tender is kept open and the money is produced in court.

A *valid tender of payment* consists of an unconditional offer of the exact amount due on the date when due or an amount from which the creditor may take what is due without the necessity of making change. It is unnecessary for the debtor to produce the money, however, if the creditor informs him in advance that he will not accept it. The debtor must offer *legal tender* or, in other words, such form of money as the law recognizes as lawful money and declares to be legal tender for the payment of debts. The offer of a check is not a valid tender of payment since a check is not legal tender. A tender of part of the debt is not a valid tender.[16]

A tender of less than the total amount due has no legal effect unless the creditor accepts it. In addition to the amount owed the debtor must tender all accrued interest and any costs to which the creditor is entitled.[17] If the

---

[13] Cline v Hullum, (Okla) 435 P2d 152.
[14] Federal Sign Co. v Fort Worth Motors, (Tex Civ App) 314 SW2d 878.
[15] R § 415.
[16] Kuhn v Hamilton, (ND) 138 NW2d 604.
[17] Smith v Gen Co. Corp., 11 Ill App 3d 106, 296 NE2d 25.

debtor tenders less than the amount due, the creditor may refuse the offer without affecting his rights in any way. If he accepts it, the question then arises whether it is accepted as a payment on account or in full payment of balance due.

§ 18:3. Adequacy of Performance.

(1) Substantial Performance. If the plaintiff in good faith substantially performed the contract, he can sue the other party for payment. He then recovers the contract price subject to a counterclaim for the damages caused the other party by the plaintiff's failure to perform to the letter of the contract.[18]

This rule is most frequently applied in actions on building contracts.[19] Thus, if a contractor undertakes to erect a building for $30,000 but the work that he does is not exactly according to specifications in certain minor respects, he may still sue for the amount due on the contract. Assume that it would cost the owner $500 to correct the defects in the contractor's work. The contractor could recover $30,000 minus $500. The owner would then have $500 with which to have the defects corrected so that he would have his building at the original price of $30,000.

If, however, the defect is of such a nature that it cannot be remedied without rebuilding or materially injuring a substantial part of the building, the measure of damages is the difference between the value of the building as constructed and the value it would have had if it had been built according to the contract.[20]

This *rule of substantial performance* applies only when the departures from the contract or the defects are not made willfully.[21] If the contractor makes a substantial willful departure from the contract, he is in default and cannot recover from the other party to the contract.[22]

Similarly, when a highway contractor encounters unexpected rock formation, he may not complete the easy parts of a highway and refuse to perform the difficult part, and then seek recovery for the work done at the unit price provided for in the contract.[23]

When the nature of the breach of contract is not such that it can be measured by the amount required to correct or complete performance or when the amount performed by the contractor is less than substantial, damages are also held to be the difference between the value which the property would have if the contract had been performed completely and its value with the contract partly performed. Furthermore, in the case of large construction contracts when the total value of the partial performance is large compared to the damages sustained through incomplete or imperfect

[18] Gamble v Woodlea Construction Co., 246 Md 260, 228 A2d 243.
[19] See, for example, Collins v Baldwin, (Okla) 405 P2d 74.
[20] Baker Pool Co. v Bennett, (Ky) 411 SW2d 335.
[21] Lautenbach v Meredith, 240 Iowa 166, 35 NW2d 870.
[22] Deck v Hammer, 7 Ariz App 466, 440 P2d 1006.
[23] Lagrange Construction, Inc. v Kent Corp., 88 Nev 301, 496 P2d 766.

performance, the courts tend to ignore whether or not the breach was intentional on the part of the contractor.

(2) Satisfaction of Promise or Third Person. When the agreement requires that the promisor perform an act to the satisfaction, taste, or judgment of the other party to the contract, the courts are divided as to whether the promisor must so perform as to satisfy the promisee or whether it is sufficient that he perform in a way that would satisfy a reasonable man under the circumstances. When personal taste is an important element, the courts generally hold that the performance is not sufficient unless the promisee is actually satisfied,[24] although in some instances it is insisted that the dissatisfaction be shown to be in good faith and not merely to avoid paying for the work that has been done.[25] The personal satisfaction of the promisee is generally required under this rule when one promises to make clothes, to write a novel, or to paint a portrait to the satisfaction of the other party.

There is a similar division of authority when the subject matter involves the fitness or mechanical utility of the property. With respect to things mechanical and to routine performances, however, the courts are more likely to hold that the promisor has satisfactorily performed if a reasonable man should be satisfied with what was done.[26]

When a building contract requires the contractor to perform the contract to the "satisfaction" of the owner, the owner generally is required to pay if a reasonable man would be satisfied with the work of the contractor.[27]

In contrast, when a building owner makes a contract for painting and paperhanging, and the contract specifies that "work will be completed in the best workmanship manner by union skillful craftsmen," the work is properly performed when it conforms to the standards specified and the owner cannot avoid liability on the ground that he in fact was not satisfied with the work.[28]

When performance is to be approved by a third person, the tendency is to apply the reasonable-man test of satisfaction, especially when the third person has wrongfully withheld his approval or has become incapacitated.

When work is to be done subject to the approval of an architect, engineer, or other expert, ordinarily his determination is final and binding upon the parties in the absence of fraud.[29]

---

[24] Wolff v Smith, 303 Ill App 413, 25 NE2d 399.

[25] Commercial Mortgage & Finance Corp. v Greenwich Savings Bank, 112 Ga App 388, 145 SE2d 249; American Oil Co. v Carey, (DC ED Mich) 246 F Supp 773.

[26] R § 265.

[27] A few states hold that the owner is not liable if in fact he is not satisfied, but his dissatisfaction must be in good faith. Hood v Meininger, 377 Pa 342, 105 A2d 126. Likewise, when a party to a contract is required to furnish a surety bond "acceptable" to the other contracting party, the sufficiency of a bond is to be determined by an objective test of reasonableness. Weisz Trucking Co. v Wohl Construction, 13 Cal App 3d 256, 91 Cal Rptr 489.

[28] Grimpel v Hochman, (NY Civil Court) 74 Misc 2d 39, 343 NYS2d 507.

[29] Joseph Davis, Inc. v Merritt-Chapman & Scott Corp., 27 App Div 2d 114, 276 NYS2d 479.

§ 18:4. Guarantee of Performance.

(1) Obligor's Guarantee. It is common for an obligor to guarantee his performance. Thus, a builder may guarantee for one year that the workmanship will be satisfactory. This means that even though the owner has accepted the building as satisfactory, he will have the right to recover damages from the builder should some defect become known or develop within a year as the result of bad workmanship. Such a guarantee does not relieve the builder of liability to which he would otherwise be subject. For example, when he has not installed the proper 20-year roof he cannot claim that the running of a year bars the recovery of damages for breach of performance.[30]

(2) Third Person's Guarantee. The guarantee may be made by a third person. Thus, a surety company may guarantee to the owner that a contractor will perform his contract. In such case, it is clear that the obligation of the surety is an addition to the liability of the contractor and does not take the place of such liability.

The fact that the owner might have protected himself by obtaining a guarantee of a surety but failed to do so is not a defense which the contractor can raise when the owner asserts a claim against him for nonperformance. The fact that the owner might have reduced or mitigated his damages by obtaining a suretyship guarantee does not affect his right to recover full damages from the contractor.

§ 18:5. Consumer Protection Rescission. Contrary to the basic principle of contract law that a contract between competent adults is a binding obligation, consumer protection legislation is introducing into the law a new concept of giving the consumer a chance to think things over and to rescind the contract. Thus the federal Consumer Credit Protection Act (CCPA) gives a debtor the right to rescind a credit transaction within three days when the transaction would impose a lien upon his home,[31] but he cannot rescind a first mortgage.[32]

The same concept of rescission to protect the consumer is found in the provision of the Uniform Consumer Credit Code, which gives a customer three days in which to avoid any contract for goods or services made in his

---

[30] A. W. Therrien Co. Inc. v H. K. Ferguson Co., (CA1 NH) 470 F2d 912.

[31] CCPA § 125; 15 USC § 1635(a),(e), although it would appear that this section has been to a large extent canceled by the regulation of the Federal Reserve Board permitting the debtor to waive his right of rescission. Regulation Z, § 226.9(e), 12 CFR 226. Likewise the statute does not permit a home buyer to avoid a lien created in the financing of his purchase. If the creditor does not inform the debtor of his right to rescind at the time of the transaction or make the other disclosures required by federal law, the time within which the debtor may rescind is extended until such disclosures are made. § 226.9(a).

[32] 15 USC § 1635(e). This exception is explained in terms of the statute's objective to protect from anticonsumer practices as to second mortgages, although the statutory requirements imposed on the second mortgages would also permit the rescission of a mortgage executed to refinance an exempt first mortgage.

home by the personal solicitation of the seller or the seller's agent.[33] The seller must inform the buyer of his right to cancel; and if he fails to do so, the right of the buyer to cancel continues and is not terminated by the expiration of the three days.[34]

Under the UCCC the debtor may ordinarily rescind a home solicitation sale of goods or services. Some local statutes, however, are limited to particular transactions. The Michigan and Pennsylvania statutes, for example, permit the homeowner to rescind a home improvement sale. Other statutes permit a buyer to rescind any installment sale. The Federal Trade Commission is considering the merits of a regulation giving the consumer three business days to avoid any home-solicited sale exceeding $10.

§ 18:6. Discharge by Agreement. A contract may be terminated by the operation of one of its provisions or by a subsequent agreement.

(1) Provision of Original Contract. The contract may provide that it shall terminate upon the happening of a certain event, such as the destruction of a particular building, or upon the existence of a certain fact, even though the intended performance by one party or both parties has not been completed.[35]

A contract may also provide that either party or both parties can terminate it upon giving a particular notice, such as a 30-day notice, as in the case of an employment contract or a sale with an option to return, or that one party may terminate the contract if he is not satisfied with the performance of the other.[36] The UCC permits the parties to a contract for the sale of goods to agree that the buyer may return the goods and cancel the contract.[37] Notice to terminate must be clear and definite.[38]

When a contract provides for a continuing performance but does not specify how long it shall continue, it is terminable at the will of either party, with the same consequence as though it had expressly authorized termination upon notice.[39]

(2) Rescission by Agreement. The parties to a contract may agree to undo the contract and place each one in his original position by returning any property or money that had been delivered or paid.[40] It is said that they agree to rescind the contract or that there is a *mutual rescission.* Ordinarily no formality is required for rescission; and an oral rescission, or conduct evidencing such an intent, may terminate a written contract. An oral rescission is ineffective, however, in the case of a sale of an interest in land; for,

---

[33] UCCC § 2.502. The seller may retain a cancellation fee of 5 percent of the cash price but not exceeding the amount of the cash down payment. § 2.504.

[34] § 2.503.

[35] R § 396.

[36] Ard Dr. Pepper Bottling Co. v Dr. Pepper Co., (CA5 Fla) 202 F2d 372.

[37] UCC § 2-326.

[38] Shaw v Beall, 70 Ariz 4, 215 P2d 233; Purnell v Atkinson, 248 Ark 401, 451 SW2d 734.

[39] Pearson v Youngstown Sheet & Tube Co., (CA7 Ind) 332 F2d 439.

[40] R § 406.

in such a case, the purpose of the rescission is to retransfer the interest in land. Accordingly, the retransfer or rescission must satisfy the same formalities of the statute of frauds as are applied to the original transfer.[41]

A mutual rescission works a final discharge of the contract in the absence of an express provision in the rescission agreement providing for the later revival of the original contract. Consequently, when there is a mutual rescission of a sales contract following a fire which destroyed the seller's factory, the contract is not revived by the subsequent rebuilding of the factory.[42] If an agreement is voidable because of the fraud of one of the parties, the aggrieved or complaining party may obtain a decree from the court rescinding the contract.[43] This is distinct, however, from rescission based on the agreement of the parties.

(3) Waiver. A term of a contractual obligation is discharged by *waiver* when one party fails to demand performance by the other party or to object when the other party fails to perform according to the terms of the contract.[44] Unlike rescission, a waiver does not return the parties to their original positions; it leaves the parties where they are at the time.

(4) Substitution. The parties may decide that their contract is not the one they want. They may then replace it with another contract. If they do so, the original contract is discharged by *substitution.*[45]

It is not necessary that the parties expressly state that they are making a substitution. Whenever they make a new contract that is clearly inconsistent with a former contract, the court will assume that the earlier contract has been superseded by the latter. Since the new contract must in itself be a binding agreement, it must be supported by consideration.[46] The agreement modifying the original contract may be expressed by words or by conduct, but in any event, it is essential that an agreement to modify be found.[47]

(5) Novation. In a novation, as explained in Chapter 17, the original contract may be discharged by the new contract.[48] When a party's liability under a contract is discharged by a novation, he cannot thereafter sue to enforce a contract or to recover damages for its breach.[49]

(6) Accord and Satisfaction. In lieu of the performance of an obligation specified by a contract, the parties may agree to a different performance.[50]

---

41 § 407.

42 Goddard v Ishikawajima-Harima Heavy Industries Co., 27 Misc 2d 863, 287 NYS2d 901.

43 Binkholder v Carpenter, 260 Iowa 297, 152 NW2d 593.

44 Nelson v Cross, 152 Neb 197, 40 NW2d 663; Fehl-Haber v Nordhagen, 59 Wash 2d 7, 365 P2d 607.

45 R § 418.

46 Better Taste Popcorn Co. v Peters, 124 Ind App 319, 114 NE2d 817.

47 Fast v Kahan, 206 Kan 682, 481 P2d 958.

48 R § 425 et seq.; see § 17:8(2).

49 Christ v Christ, (La App) 251 So2d 197.

50 Mrs. Tucker's Sales Co. v Frosted Foods, Inc., (La App) 68 So2d 219.

Such an agreement is called an *accord.* When the accord is performed or executed, there is an *accord and satisfaction,* which discharges the original obligation.[51] An accord is not binding until the satisfaction is made. Either party may therefore revoke an accord agreeing upon the payment to be made before it has been made.[52]

When the performance of one party under the accord and satisfaction consists of paying a sum of money smaller than that claimed by the other party, there frequently must be a bona fide dispute as to the amount due or the accord and satisfaction must be supported by independent consideration.[53]

(7) Release. A person who has a contract claim or any other kind of claim against another may agree to give up or release his claim against the other. This may be done by delivering a writing which states that the claim is released. At common law, this writing destroyed or extinguished the releasor's claim, with the consequence that a release of one obligor would also discharge a joint obligor. To avoid this result, a releasor will today often execute a written promise not to sue the adverse party. Such a *covenant not to sue* is binding and bars suit against the adverse party but does not bar the one who makes the covenant from suing other persons.

Ordinarily there will be a preliminary agreement to deliver a written release or covenant not to sue for which payment will be made. Generally the preliminary agreement is not a binding contract because it is contemplated that the obligee shall not be bound until he has delivered the writing and has been paid.

§ 18:7. Discharge by Impossibility. Impossibility of performance refers to external or extrinsic conditions as contrasted with the obligor's personal inability to perform. Thus, the fact that a debtor cannot pay his debt because he does not have the money does not present a case of impossibility.

Likewise, riots, shortages of materials, and similar factors usually do not excuse the promisor from performing his contract.[54] The fact that the seller who sold property not owned by him has not been able to purchase it from its owner does not excuse him from his obligation to his buyer.[55] The fact that it will prove more costly to perform the contract than originally contemplated,[56] or that the obligor has voluntarily gone out of business, does not constitute impossibility which excuses performance. No distinction is made in this connection between acts of nature, man, or governments. (See p. 359, Transatlantic Finance Corp. v United States.)

Frequently this problem is met by a provision of the contract that expressly excuses a contractor or provides for extra compensation in the

[51] Long v Weiler, (Mo App) 395 SW2d 234.

[52] Harrison v Gooden, (CA1 NH) 439 F2d 1070.

[53] UCC § 3-408. See also § 2-209(1) as to sales of goods, and § 1-107 generally. Probably no dispute is required when a check which states that it is in full settlement of a claim is accepted.

[54] Hein v Fox, 126 Mont 514, 254 P2d 1076.

[55] Crag Lumber Co. v Croffot, 144 Cal App 2d 755, 301 P2d 952.

[56] P & Z Pacific, Inc. v Panorama Apartments, Inc., (CA9 Ore) 372 F2d 759.

event of certain unforeseen or changed conditions. A party seeking to excuse himself by, or to claim the benefit of, such a clause has the burden of establishing the facts that justify its application.

Interference with the performance of a contract by fire does not excuse performance. Consequently, when a contractor is constructing a building and it is destroyed by fire, he must rebuild the building at his own expense or the expense of his insurer. The fire does not excuse him from performing his contract.[57]

The fact that legal proceedings prevent performance of the contract or make performance more expensive does not constitute impossibility so as to discharge the contract when the law has not changed, when it was foreseeable that there might be a legal proceeding and that it would have the particular result if existing rules of law were applied to the facts of the case. Thus, when an open-air sandblasting subcontractor causes sand damage to machinery on the plaintiff's neighboring land and is by injunction required to take specific precautions to stop such harm, the subcontractor is not excused from performing the sandblasting contract because of such additional expense. There was no impossibility since the subcontractor should have foreseen that the original method of operation could result in injury and that an action might be brought to enjoin such operation and could result in the granting of an injunction.[58]

When the condition or event that is claimed to have made performance impossible is the result of foreseeable wartime conditions, a party is not excused because of the occurrence of such condition or event. By failing to have made express provision therefor in the contract, he must be regarded as having assumed that risk.[59]

(1) Destruction of Particular Subject Matter. When the parties contract expressly for or with reference to a particular subject matter, the contract is discharged if the subject matter is destroyed through no fault of either party.[60] When a contract calls for the sale of a wheat crop growing on a specific parcel of land, the contract is discharged if that crop is destroyed by blight.

On the other hand, if there is merely a contract to sell a given quantity of a specified grade of wheat, the seller is not discharged because his wheat crop is destroyed by blight. The seller makes an absolute undertaking.

(2) Change of Law. A contract is discharged when its performance is made illegal by a subsequent change in the law of the state or country in which the contract is to be performed.[61] Thus, a contract to construct a nonfireproof building at a particular place is discharged by the adoption

---

[57] Midwest Lumber Co. v Dwight E. Nelson Constr. Co., 188 Neb 308, 196 NW2d 377.

[58] Savage v Kiewit, 249 Ore 147, 432 P2d 519.

[59] Aristocrat Highway Displays, Inc. v Stricklin, 68 Cal App 2d 788, 157 P2d 880.

[60] R § 457.

[61] R § 458; Cinquegrano v T. A. Clarke Motors, 69 RI 28, 30 A2d 859.

of a zoning law prohibiting such a building within that area. Mere inconvenience or temporary delay caused by the new law, however, does not excuse performance.

An employee is excused from his obligation under an employment contract when he is drafted for military service.[62]

(3) Death or Disability. When the contract obligates a party to perform an act that requires personal skill or which contemplates a personal relationship with the obligee or some other person, the death or disability of the obligor, obligee, or other person (as the case may be) discharges the contract,[63] as when a newspaper cartoonist dies before the expiration of his contract.[64] If the act called for by the contract can be performed by others or by the promisor's personal representative, however, this rule does not apply.

The death of the person to whom personal services are to be rendered also terminates the contract when the death of that person makes impossible the rendition of the services contemplated. Thus, a contract to employ a person as the musical director for a singer terminates when the singer dies.[65]

When the contract calls for the payment of money, the death of either party does not affect the obligation. If the obligor dies, the obligation is a liability of his estate. If the obligee dies, the right to collect the debt is an asset of his estate. The parties to a contract may agree, however, that the death of either the obligee [66] or the obligor shall terminate the debt. In the latter case, the creditor can obtain insurance on the life of the debtor so that while he loses the debt upon the debtor's death, he is paid by the proceeds of the insurance on the debtor's life.

(4) Act of Other Party. There is in every contract "an implied covenant of good faith and fair dealing" in consequence of which a promisee is under an obligation to do nothing that would interfere with performance by the promisor.[67] When the promisee prevents performance or otherwise makes performance impossible, the promisor is discharged from his contract.[68] Thus, a subcontractor is discharged from his obligation when he is unable to do the work because the principal contractor refuses to deliver to him the material, equipment, or money as required by the subcontract. When the default of the other party consists of failing to supply goods or services, the duty may rest upon the party claiming a discharge of the contract to show that he could not have obtained substitute goods or services elsewhere, either because they were not reasonably available or were not acceptable under the terms of the contract.[69]

---

[62] Autry v Republic Productions, 30 Cal 2d 144, 180 P2d 888.

[63] R § 459; Kowal v Sportswear by Revere, 351 Mass 541, 222 NE2d 778.

[64] Segar v King Features Syndicate, 262 App Div 221, 128 NYS2d 542.

[65] Farnon v Cole, 259 Cal App 2d 855, 66 Cal Rptr 673.

[66] Woods v McQueen, 195 Kan 380, 404 P2d 955.

[67] Colwell Co. v Hubert, 248 Cal App 2d 567, 56 Cal Rptr 753.

[68] Burke v N. P. Clough, 116 Vt 448, 78 A2d 483.

[69] As to the requirement of mitigating damages generally, see § 19:2(1).

The conduct of a party which excuses performance by the other contracting party may be a failure to cooperate with him, as when a contractor failed to cooperate with the cement subcontractor in a manner required by the subcontract in that he failed to prepare the construction sites for the pouring of concrete, to vibrate the concrete properly after it had been poured, and to give the subcontractor a proper voice in the planning of the concrete mix formula.[70]

When the conduct of the other contracting party does not make performance impossible but merely causes delay or renders performance more expensive, the contract is not discharged; but the injured party is entitled to damages for the loss that he incurs.

As part of a party's obligation to do nothing that will interfere with performance by the other contracting party is the duty of an owner or the government to furnish proper building specifications to a construction contractor and to act promptly in correcting them when they are found to be erroneous. If the owner or government delays unreasonably in correcting the specifications, it is responsible to the contractor for the loss thereby caused him.[71]

Acts of third parties do not constitute an excuse for failing to perform a contract. (See p. 361, La Gasse Pool Construction Co. v Fort Lauderdale.)

A promisor is not excused from his contract when it is his own act which has made performance impossible. Consequently, when a data service contracted with a bank to keypunch all its daily operations and to process the cards, the bank was not excused from its obligation under the contract by the fact that it converted to magnetic tapes and installed its own computers. Accordingly the bank could not ignore its contract. It could terminate the contract with the data service, however, by giving the notice required by the contract.[72] Similarly, an employment contract between a corporation and a shareholder in that corporation is not discharged by the voluntary dissolution of the company.[73]

§ 18:8. Economic Frustration. In order to protect from the hardship imposed by the strict principles relating to impossibility, some courts excuse performance on the ground of *economic frustration* as distinguished from impossibility. (See p. 362, Garner v Ellingson.) The effect of this view is to substitute "impracticability" for "impossibility," and to regard performance as impracticable, and therefore excused, when it can only be done at an excessive and unreasonable cost.[74] The doctrine of economic or commercial frustration has been held to excuse the delivery of oil to the plaintiff's farm house when high snowdrifts blocked the road and exposed the defendant's delivery truck to great risk if it attempted to make the oil delivery.[75]

---

[70] Concrete Specialities v H. C. Smith Construction., (CA10 Wyo) 423 F2d 670.
[71] Luria Bros. v United States, (Ct Claims) 369 F2d 701.
[72] Brown v American Bank of Commerce, 79 NMex 222, 441 P2d 751.
[73] Martin v Star Publishing Co., 50 Del 181, 126 A2d 238.
[74] Schmeltzer v Gregory, 266 Cal App 2d 420, 72 Cal Rptr 194.
[75] Whelan v Griffith Consumers Co., (Dist Col App) 170 A2d 229.

And when property is leased in order to use the building for a particular purpose, some courts hold that the lease is discharged when the building burns down, on the theory that the purpose of the lease has been frustrated.[76]

In some instances, the concept of commercial frustration has been extended to permit the setting aside of a transaction when it does not have the income tax consequences contemplated by the parties.[77]

The doctrine of economic or commercial frustration is a very modern inroad into the strict concept of the common law that a party is bound by the contract which he has made and that the fact that an uncontemplated turn of events makes the contract undesirable is not an excuse for failing to perform. The fact that because of greater costs, a real estate developer cannot complete construction with the money obtained by a given loan does not constitute an "impossibility" which excuses him from any of his contractual obligations.[78]

§ 18:9. Temporary Impossibility. Ordinarily a temporary impossibility has either no effect on the obligation to perform of the party who is affected thereby, or at most suspends his duty to perform so that the obligation to perform is revived upon the termination of the impossibility. If, however, performance at that later date would impose a substantially greater burden upon the obligor, some courts excuse him from performing at that time.[79]

(1) Weather. Acts of God, such as tornadoes, lightning, and sudden floods, usually do not terminate a contract even though they make performance difficult or impossible. Thus, weather conditions constitute a risk that is assumed by a contracting party in the absence of a contrary agreement. Consequently, extra expense sustained by a contractor because of weather conditions is a risk which the contractor assumes in the absence of an express provision that he is entitled to additional compensation in such case.[80]

Modern contracts commonly contain a "weather" clause, which either expressly grants an extension for delays caused by weather conditions or expressly denies the right to any extension of time or additional compensation because of weather condition difficulties. Some courts hold that abnormal weather conditions excuse what would otherwise be a breach of contract. Thus, nondelivery of equipment has been excused when the early melting of a frozen river made it impossible to deliver the equipment.[81]

---

[76] Jones v Fuller-Garvey Corp., (Alaska) 386 P2d 838. In some jurisdictions, this result is reached by statute authorizing the termination of the lease in such a case. At common law the destruction of the building did not discharge the obligation of the tenant.

[77] Walker v Continental Life & Accident Co., (CA9 Ariz) 445 F2d 1072.

[78] White Lakes Shopping Center, Inc. v Jefferson Standard Life Ins. Co., 208 Kan 121, 490 P2d 609.

[79] Pacific Trading Co. Inc. v Mouton Rice Milling Co., (CA8 Ark) 184 F2d 141.

[80] Banks Construction Co. v United States, (Ct Claims) 364 F2d 357.

[81] Merl F. Thomas Sons, Inc. v Alaska, (Alaska) 396 P2d 76.

§ **18:10. Discharge by Operation of Law.** In certain situations the law provides for the discharge of a contract, such as when the contract has been altered, has been destroyed by the obligee, is subject to bankruptcy proceedings, or exceeds the statutes of limitations.

(1) Alteration. A written contract, whether under seal or not, may be discharged by alteration.[82] To have this effect, (a) it must be a *material alteration,* that is, it must change the nature of the obligation; (b) it must be made by a party to the contract, because alterations made by a stranger have no effect; (c) it must be made intentionally, and not through accident or mistake; and (d) it must be made without the consent of the other party to the contract.[83] For example, when one party to an advertising contract, without the consent of the other party, added "at a monthly payment basis," thus making the rate of payment higher, the advertiser was discharged from any duty under the contract.[84]

There is no discharge of the contract by alteration when the term added is one which the law would imply, for in such a case the change is not material. Consequently, when a written contract for the sale of a business was modified by adding the statement that it included the goodwill of the business, there was no "alteration" because the sale of the goodwill would be an implied term of the sale of the business.[85]

(2) Destruction of the Contract. The physical destruction of a written contract may be a discharge of the contract. When the person entitled to performance under a sealed instrument destroys the writing with the intent to terminate the liability of the obligor, the latter's liability is discharged.[86] In any case, the physical destruction of the writing may be evidence of an intention to discharge the obligation by mutual agreement.[87]

(3) Merger. In some instances contract rights are merged into or absorbed by a greater right. When an action is brought upon a contract and a judgment is obtained by the plaintiff against the defendant, the contract claim is merged into the judgment.

(4) Bankruptcy. Most debtors may voluntarily enter into a federal court of bankruptcy or be compelled to do so by creditors. The trustee in bankruptcy then takes possession of the debtors' property and distributes it as far as it will go among his creditors. After this is done, the court grants the debtor a discharge in bankruptcy if it concludes that he had acted honestly and had not attempted to defraud his creditors.

---

[82] The definition and effect of alteration in the case of commercial paper has been modified by UCC § 3-407.

[83] Restatement, Contracts, §§ 434-437.

[84] National Railways Advertising Co. v E. L. Bruce Co., 143 Ark 292, 220 SW 48.

[85] Lynn Tucker Sales, Inc. v LeBlanc, 323 Mass 721, 84 NE2d 127.

[86] R § 432.

[87] Reed's Estate, (Mo) 414 SW2d 283.

Even though all creditors have not been paid in full, the discharge in bankruptcy is a bar to the subsequent enforcement of their ordinary contract claims against the debtor. The cause of action or contract claim is not destroyed, but the bankruptcy discharge bars a proceeding to enforce it.[88] Since the obligation is not extinguished, the debtor may waive the defense of discharge in bankruptcy by promising later to pay the debt. Such a waiver is governed by state law. In a few states such waiver must be in writing.

(5) Statutes of Limitations. Statutes provide that after a certain number of years have passed, a contract claim is barred. Technically, this is merely a bar of the remedy and does not destroy the right or cause of action. A few states hold that the statute bars the right as well as the remedy and that there is accordingly no contract after the lapse of the statutory period.

The time limitations provided by the state statutes of limitations vary widely. The period usually differs with the type of contract—ranging from a relatively short period for open accounts (ordinary customers' charge accounts), usually 3 to 5 years; to a somewhat longer period for written contracts, usually 5 to 10 years; to a maximum period for judgments of record, usually 10 to 20 years. In the case of a contract for a sale of goods, the time period is 4 years.[89]

The statute of limitations begins to run the moment that the cause of action of the plaintiff arises, that is, when he is first entitled to bring suit. When the party entitled to sue is under a disability, such as insanity, at the time the cause of action arises, the period of the statute does not begin to run until the disability is removed. When a condition or act prevents the period of the statute of limitations from running, it is said to *toll the running of the statute.*

Statutes of limitations do not run against governments because it is contrary to public policy that the rights of society generally, as represented by the government, should be prejudiced by the failure of the proper governmental officials to take the necessary action to enforce the claims of the government.

The defense of a statute of limitations may be waived by the debtor.[90] The waiver must ordinarily be an express promise to pay or such an acknowledgment of the existence of the debt that the law can imply from the acknowledgment a promise to pay the debt. In some states the promise or acknowledgment must be in writing. Part payment of the principal or interest is also regarded as a waiver of the bar of the statute and revives the debt.

(6) Contract Limitation. Some contracts, particularly insurance contracts, contain a time limitation within which suit may be brought. This is,

---

[88] Earl v Liberty Loan Corp., (La App) 193 So2d 280.
[89] UCC § 2-725(1).
[90] R § 86.

in effect, a private statute of limitations created by agreement of the parties.[91] (See p. 363, State Bank of Viroqua v Capitol Indemnity Corp.) The parties to a sale of goods may by their original agreement reduce the period to not less than one year, but they may not in this manner extend it beyond four years.[92]

§ 18:11. Discharge by Acceptance of Breach. There is a *breach of contract* whenever one party or both parties fail to perform the contract. A contract is discharged by breach if, when one party breaks the contract, the other party accepts the contract as ended. When a breach occurs, however, the injured party is not required to treat the contract as discharged. Since the contract bound the defaulting party to perform, the injured party may insist on the observance of the contract and resort to legal remedies. When the aggrieved party chooses to treat the other party's breach as terminating the contract, he must give unequivocal notice to the other party that he no longer considers the contract to be in effect.[93]

A breach of a part of a divisible contract is not a breach of the entire contract.

A breach does not result in the discharge of a contract when the term broken is not sufficiently important.[94] A term of a contract that does not go to the root of the contract is a *subsidiary term.* When there is a failure to perform such a term, the agreement is not terminated,[95] but the defaulting party may be liable for damages for its breach.

In addition to the effect of a breach as such, the occurrence of a breach also excuses the injured party from his performance if it is conditioned or dependent upon the defaulter's performance of his obligation.[96]

(1) Renunciation. When a party to a contract declares in advance of the time for performance that he will not perform, the other party may (a) ignore this declaration and insist on performance in accordance with the terms of the contract, (b) accept this declaration as an *anticipatory breach* and sue the promisor for damages, or (c) accept the declaration as a breach of the contract and rescind the contract. It is for the injured party to determine what he wishes to do when the other party has made a renunciation.

The same rule applies when one party to the contract insists on a clearly unwarranted interpretation of the contract, since this indicates that he refuses to abide by the contract as it stands.

If the promisee does not elect to rescind the agreement, the contract continues in force; and his remedy is damages for breach either at once or at the time of performance specified by the contract.

---

[91] Proc v Home Insurance Co., 17 NY2d 239, 270 NYS2d 412, 217 NE2d 136.
[92] UCC § 2-725(1).
[93] Dunkley Surfacing Co. v George Madsen Construction Co., 285 Minn 415, 173 NW2d 420.
[94] C. C. Leonard Lumber Co. v Reed, 314 Ky 703, 236 SW2d 961.
[95] R § 274.
[96] K & G Constr. Co. v Harris and Brooks, 223 Md 305, 164 A2d 451.

(2) Incapacitating Self. Another form of anticipatory breach occurs when the promisor makes it impossible for himself to perform his obligation. Under such circumstances, the promisee is entitled to treat the contract as discharged. For example, when one party who is bound by the terms of the contract to turn over specific bonds, stocks, or notes to another party transfers them to a third party instead, the promisee may elect to treat the contract as discharged; or he may hold the promisor accountable for nonperformance when the time for performance arrives. The same is true when one agrees to sell specific goods to another person and then sells them to a third person in violation of his original contract.

CASES FOR CHAPTER 18

Creasy v Tincher

154 WVa 18, 173 SE2d 332 (1970)

The Tinchers signed a contract to sell land to Creasy. The contract specified that the sales transaction was to be completed in 90 days. At the end of the 90 days, Creasy requested an extension of time. The Tinchers refused to grant an extension and stated that the contract was terminated. Creasy sued the Tinchers to compel specific performance of the agreement. From a judgment for the Tinchers, Creasy appealed.

CAPLAN, J. . . . Paragraph 4 [of the sales agreement] provides: "This sale shall be completed and all necessary papers executed and delivered within *90 days* from the date of acceptance hereof by Seller, which date is set forth on the reverse side hereof."

The Tinchers accepted the plaintiff's offer by executing the agreement on August 10, 1966. Thereafter, the plaintiff employed an attorney, Walton Shepherd, to examine the title of the subject real estate. As a result of his examination Mrs. Creasy was advised that one-half of the minerals under one of the tracts had been acquired by the Tinchers by a tax deed and that some corrective action should be taken to clear any cloud that might be created by such deed. On a later occasion Mr. Shepherd referred to this matter as a "minor" defect in the title.

Mrs. Creasy testified that upon learning of the tax deed she related this matter to Mr. Burgess who indicated that he would discuss it with the Tinchers' attorney. Mr. Burgess testified that he was unable to contact their attorney during the ninety-day period referred to in the contract. Nothing further was done by the parties. . . .

. . . The time expressed in the agreement in which the contract shall be consummated is of the essence of the agreement. The language used is clear and unequivocal. It provides that the sale shall be completed within ninety days from the date of acceptance by the seller. [A] contract need not include the words "time is of the essence." In determining this question the general rules of construction are applied. . . . If the language is clear and unambiguous it is to be applied. . . . Here, we believe, the language clearly shows the intention of the parties. . . .

The plaintiff, although denying that time was of the essence of the agreement, says that her failure to perform within the ninety-day period was prompted by the refusal of the sellers to offer her a good and marketable title as provided in the agreement. She asserts that she was thereby relieved of any obligation to have acted within the prescribed period. Thus, we are presented with the question of whether the plaintiff, in these circumstances, is entitled to an order requiring the defendants to specifically perform under the agreement.

Pertinent to the resolution of this question is Paragraph 8 of the agreement which reads: "Seller will, upon tender of the unpaid balance of the purchase price, convey the said property to purchaser by apt and proper deed. . . ." This provision makes it incumbent upon the buyer, the plaintiff, to make a tender of the unpaid balance of the purchase price before the seller is obligated to deliver the deed. This she did not do, either during or after the ninety-day period. . . .

[Judgment affirmed.]

Robinson v Commercial Contractors, Inc.

6 Conn Cir 393, 274 A2d 160 (1970)

The Olin Mathieson Company hired commercial contractors to demolish a building. Robinson made a contract with Commercial to purchase the brick from the demolished building. No specific time for the removal of the brick by Robinson was stated. Commercial bulldozed a large quantity of the brick into the basement in order to fill the excavation. Robinson sued Commercial for breach of contract for not giving him sufficient time in which to remove the brick. Judgment was entered for Robinson and Commercial appealed.

CASALE, J. . . . The trial court reached the following conclusions: The parties entered into a contract for the acquisition by the plaintiff of 150 to 200 loads of brick for $4000. No completion date was agreed on by the parties. A reasonable period of time was necessary to allow the plaintiff to remove the purchased brick from the demolition site. The plaintiff was denied the opportunity of removing the brick purchased. The defendant used much of the brick contracted for to fill the basement, at a great saving to the defendant. The contract was broken by the defendant.

. . . The only conclusion . . . pursued in argument is the conclusion that the plaintiff was denied a reasonable time by the defendant to remove more brick from the demolition site. . . .

It has long been settled law that where no time is specified for the fulfilment of a contract it must be carried out within a reasonable time. . . . The next question is, what constitutes reasonable time?

What is a reasonable time is usually a question of fact under all the circumstances. . . . "What constitutes a reasonable time within which an act is to be performed where a contract is silent upon the subject depends on the subject matter of the contract, the situation of the parties, their intention and what they contemplated at the time the contract was made, and the circumstances attending the performance." . . .

. . . The defendant argues that the plaintiff had approximately sixty days to remove brick from the demolition site and that that period constituted a reasonable time for him to have removed all the brick to which he was entitled. The finding states the plaintiff removed brick from October, 1964, to late December, 1964; on the whole record, it is questionable whether he did in fact have sixty days. Whatever the number of days, however, there is nothing in the finding indicating how many days in that period there was brick on the ground available for removal by the plaintiff; nor is there anything in the finding indicating how many days were unsuitable for brick removal because of weather conditions. The defendant was in charge of the demolition of the building. The progress of the demolition work could determine to a large extent when and in what quantity brick would be available on the ground for removal by the plaintiff.

The subordinate facts found by the trial court indicate that the defendant refused the plaintiff brick; that the defendant had bulldozed good brick into the basement and had used brick for fill purposes; that the plaintiff had complained to the defendant about the lack of brick; and that he was unable to take more than twenty-five loads "because of the action of the defendant."

The trial court was justified in the conclusion that the plaintiff was denied reasonable time to remove the purchased brick from the demolition site. . . .

[Judgment affirmed.]

Transatlantic Financing Corp. v United States

(CA Dist Col) 363 F2d 312 (1966)

The Transatlantic Financing Corp. made a contract with the United States to haul a cargo of wheat from the United States to a safe port in Iran. The normal route lay through the Suez Canal. As the result of the nationalization of the Canal by Egypt and the subsequent

international crisis which developed, the Canal was closed and it was necessary for Transatlantic to go around Africa to get to the destination. It then sued for additional compensation because of the longer route on the theory that it had been discharged from its obligation to carry to Iran for the amount specified in the contract because of "impossibility." From a judgment in favor of the United States, Transatlantic appealed.

WRIGHT, J. . . . It is now recognized that "A thing is impossible in legal contemplation when it is not practicable; and a thing is impracticable when it can only be done at an excessive and unreasonable cost." . . . Restatement, Contracts § 454 (1932); Uniform Commercial Code (U.L.A.) § 2-615, comment 3. The doctrine ultimately represents the ever-shifting line, drawn by courts hopefully responsive to commercial practices and mores, at which the community's interest in having contracts enforced according to their terms is outweighed by the commercial senselessness of requiring performance. . . . First, a contingency—something unexpected—must have occurred. Second, the risk of the unexpected occurrence must not have been allocated either by agreement or by custom. Finally, occurrence of the contingency must have rendered performance commercially impracticable. . . . Unless the court finds these three requirements satisfied, the plea of impossibility must fail.

The first requirement was met here. It seems reasonable, where no route is mentioned in a contract, to assume the parties expected performance by the usual and customary route at the time of contract. Since the usual and customary route from Texas to Iran at the time of contract was through Suez, closure of the Canal made impossible the expected method of performance. But this unexpected development raises rather than resolves the impossibility issue, which turns additionally on whether the risk of the contingency's occurrence had been allocated and, if not, whether performance by alternative routes was rendered impracticable.

Proof that the risk of a contingency's occurrence has been allocated may be expressed in or implied from the agreement. Such proof may also be found in the surrounding circumstances, including custom and usages of the trade. . . . The contract in this case does not expressly condition performance upon availability of the Suez route. Nor does it specify "via Suez" or, on the other hand, "via Suez or Cape of Good Hope." Nor are there provisions in the contract from which we may properly imply that the continued availability of Suez was a condition of performance. Nor is there anything in custom or trade usage, or in the surrounding circumstances generally, which would support our constructing a condition of performance. The numerous cases requiring performance around the Cape when Suez was closed . . . indicate that the Cape route is generally regarded as an alternative means of performance. So the implied expectation that the route would be via Suez is hardly adequate proof of an allocation to the promisee of the risk of closure. . . .

If anything, the circumstances surrounding this contract indicate that the risk of the Canal's closure may be deemed to have been allocated to Transatlantic. We know or may safely assume that the parties were aware, as were most commercial men with interests affected by the Suez situation . . . that the Canal might become a dangerous area. No doubt the tension affected freight rates, and it is arguable that the risk of closure became part of the dickered terms. Uniform Commercial Code § 2-615, comment 8. We do not deem the risk of closure so allocated, however. Foreseeability or even recognition of a risk does not necessarily prove its allocation. . . .

Parties to a contract are not always able to provide for all the possibilities of which they are aware, sometimes because they cannot agree, often simply because they are too busy. Moreover, that some abnormal risk was contemplated is probative but does not necessarily establish an allocation of the risk of the contingency which actually occurs. In this case, for example, nationalization by Egypt of the Canal Corporation and formation of the Suez Users Group did not necessarily indicate that the Canal would be blocked even if a confrontation resulted. The surrounding circumstances do indicate, however, a willingness by Transatlantic to assume abnormal risks, and this fact should legitimately cause us to judge the impracticability of performance by an alternative route in stricter terms than we would were the contingency unforeseen.

We turn then to the question whether occurrence of the contingency rendered performance commercially impracticable under the circumstances of this case. The goods shipped were not subject to harm from the longer, less temperate Southern route. The vessel and crew were fit to proceed around the Cape. Transatlantic was no less able than the United States to purchase insurance to cover the contingency's occurrence. If anything, it is more reasonable to expect owner-operators of vessels to insure against the hazards of war. They are in the best position to calculate the cost of performance by alternative routes (and therefore to estimate the amount of insurance required), and are undoubtedly sensitive to international troubles which uniquely affect the demand for and cost of their services.

The only factor operating here in appellant's favor is the added expense, allegedly \$43,972.00 above and beyond the contract price of \$305,842.92, of extending a 10,000 mile voyage by approximately 3,000 miles. While it may be an overstatement to say that increased cost and difficulty of performance never constitute impracticability, to justify relief there must be more of a variation between expected cost and the cost of performing by an available alternative than is present in this case, where the promisor can legitimately be presumed to have accepted some degree of abnormal risk, and where impracticability is urged on the basis of added expense alone.

We conclude, therefore, as have most other courts considering related issues arising out of the Suez closure, that performance of this contract was not rendered legally impossible. . . .

[Judgment affirmed.]

La Gasse Pool Constr. Co. v Fort Lauderdale

(Fla App) 288 So2d 273 (1974)

La Gasse Pool Construction Company made a contract with the city of Fort Lauderdale to renovate and resurface a swimming pool. When the work was almost completely performed, vandals damaged the pool. The contractor did the work over again and billed the city for the additional work. The contractor sued the city. Judgment was entered in favor of the city and the contractor appealed.

DOWNEY, J. . . . Where the work done by a contractor, pursuant to a contract for the repair of an existing structure, is damaged during the course of the repair work, but the existing structure is not destroyed, upon whom does the loss fall where neither contractor nor owner is at fault?

The general rule is that under an indivisible contract to build an entire structure, loss or damage thereto during construction falls upon the contractor, . . . the theory being that the contractor obligated himself to build an entire structure and absent a delivery thereof he has not performed his contract. If his work is damaged or destroyed during construction he is still able to perform by rebuilding the damaged or destroyed part; in other words, doing the work over again.

In the case of contracts to repair, renovate, or perform work on existing structures, the general rule is that total destruction of the structure of res which is the subject matter of the contract, without fault of either the contractor or owner, excuses performance by the contractor and entitles him to recover for the value of the work done. . . . The rationale of this rule is that the contract has an implied condition that the structure will remain in existence so the contractor can render performance. Destruction of the structure makes performance impossible and thereby excuses the contractor's nonperformance. But where the building or structure to be repaired is not destroyed, but the contractor's work is damaged so that it must be redone, performance is still possible, and it is the contractor's responsibility to redo the work so as to complete his undertaking. In other words, absent impossibility of performance or some other reason for lawful nonperformance, the contractor must perform his contract. Any loss or damage to his work during the process of repairs which can be rectified is his responsibility. The reason for allowing recovery without full performance in the case of total destruction (i.e., impossibility of performance) is absent where the structure remains and simply requires duplicating the work.

In the case at bar the damage to the inside of the pool required the contractor to redo a portion of his work already completed. Unfortunately, that was his responsibility as the pool remained intact and performance by him was not rendered impossible. . . .

[Judgment affirmed.]

Garner v Ellingson

18 Ariz App 181, 501 P2d 22 (1972)

Garner leased a building from Ellingson. Garner applied to the city for a building permit to repair the building so that it could be used as a theater and bookstore. The city refused to issue the permit unless a sprinkler system was installed in the rented building and in an adjacent building which was also owned by Ellingson. Garner was willing to install the sprinkler system in the building which he rented but Ellingson refused to install it in his adjacent building. Garner repudiated the lease and sued for the return of the prepaid rent. He claimed that the lease was not binding because of commercial frustration. From a judgment for Ellingson, Garner appealed.

CASE, J. . . . The dispositive question before us on appeal is whether performance under the lease agreement was "commercially frustrated" by the required structural changes to the demised and adjacent premises so as to relieve all parties of their obligations under the lease. We would answer in the affirmative. . . .

. . . "It is well settled that when, due to circumstances beyond the control of the parties the performance of a contract is rendered impossible, the party failing to perform is exonerated." . . .

It should be noted that the doctrine of commercial frustration is not necessarily limited to strict impossibility, but includes impracticability caused by extreme or unreasonable difficulty or expense. . . .

. . . "The question in cases involving frustration is whether the equities of the case, considered in the light of sound public policy, require placing the risk of a disruption or complete destruction of the contract equilibrium on defendant or plaintiff under the circumstances of a given case . . . and the answer depends on whether an unanticipated circumstance, the risk of which should not be fairly thrown on the promisor, has made performance vitally different from what was reasonably to be expected. . . ."

. . . "The purpose of a contract is to place the risks of performance upon the promisor, and the relation of the parties, terms of the contract, and circumstances surrounding its formation must be examined to determine whether it can be fairly inferred that the risk of the event that has supervened to cause the alleged frustration was not reasonably foreseeable. If it was foreseeable there should have been provision for it in the contract, and the absence of such a provision gives rise to the inference that the risk was assumed." . . .

The doctrine of frustration has been severely limited to cases of extreme hardship so as not to diminish the power of parties to contract, and, in addition, the courts in applying the doctrine have required proof from the party seeking to excuse himself that the supervening frustrating event was not reasonably foreseeable. . . .

In the present case, we must determine whether the requirement to install a sprinkler system was a reasonably foreseeable event which the appellants should have contemplated. The appellees argue strenuously that possible repair to the demised premises was foreseeable and the order of the City should not excuse appellants from their obligation under the lease merely because performance was more expensive. They also urge that a proper interpretation of the lease indicates that lessee is responsible for structural changes.

Appellants, on the other hand, assert the proposition that the appellees, as landlord, are responsible for any structural changes and that under the lease there is no obligation on appellants.

Both arguments are persuasive and if, indeed, our only concern was with the leased premises, we would be obligated to hold that possible structural repairs were reasonably foreseeable. We are not faced with that problem, however.

The facts clearly show that appellants were willing to repair the demised premises. Our primary concern is the question of which parties' obligation, if either, it was to repair the adjacent premises.

In the present case, the undemised premises to be repaired were not even part of the same premises, but were adjacent to the demised premises. We find no authority or logic which would place a duty on a lessee to foresee possible repairs to a premises which were not a subject of a lease. The disputed repairs involved a premises not included in the lease agreement and we find no evidence to show that either of the parties contemplated, or should have reasonably foreseen, that repairs would be needed to a premises not a subject of the lease agreement. If this fact had been known, it seems unlikely that a lease agreement would have been reached. The lease was for one year only, and it is uncontroverted that the sprinkler system in both premises would accrue to appellees at the end of the lease term. There is no indication that this was contemplated by either of the parties.

We do not believe that the duty to repair under these given facts was placed on either of the parties, but rather we hold that the government-imposed repairs on the undemised premises was an event not reasonably foreseen by either of the parties and that the extreme impracticability of performing these repairs so frustrated the value of the agreement between the parties so as to render the lease agreement worthless. . . .

[Judgment reversed.]

State Bank of Viroqua v Capitol Indemnity Corp.

61 Wis 2d 699, 214 NW2d 42 (1974)

The State Bank of Viroqua obtained a bankers blanket bond from the Capitol Indemnity Corporation to protect it from loss by forgery. The bond required that the bank give the insurer notice of any loss at "the earliest practicable moment." DeLap borrowed money from the bank by means of paper on which he forged the name of Mellem. This was learned in October 1969. In October 1970 an agent of Capitol was discussing the bond with the bank. The bank then realized for the first time that the bond covered the DeLap forgery loss. Fifteen days later the bank notified Capitol of that claim. Capitol denied liability because of the delay. The bank sued Capitol. From a judgment in favor of Capitol, the bank appealed.

HALLOWS, C.J. . . . The trial court held the giving of notice 15 months after discovery of the forgery was too late as a matter of law and constituted noncompliance with the contract unless excusable. . . .

The bank claims error on the theory that the language in the bond requiring notice to be given at "the earliest practicable moment" means within a reasonable time under all the circumstances and such circumstances in this case consist of the uncertainty of coverage, the lack of a forfeiture clause and the lack of prejudice to Capitol Indemnity because of the delay.

. . . Most courts have regarded the notice of loss provision as a condition precedent even though the contract does not expressly say so or contain a forfeiture clause and have held that noncompliance will defeat recovery on the bond. The rationale behind the majority rule is to give the earliest opportunity to the surety to investigate, minimize and recoup losses while the time is ripe for such purpose, and to give the surety a reasonable opportunity to protect its rights. Under this view, the failure to comply with the condition precedent to liability vitiates the insured's claim regardless of whether or not prejudice to the surety resulted from the delay or the relative carelessness of the insured in giving notice or the insured's ignorance of coverage under the bond.

. . . We hold that where the giving of timely notice is required by the Bankers Blanket Bond prior to the maturity of the liability of the insurer, such requirement is a condition precedent in fact to liability whether or not expressly so stated and is to be enforced as written whether or not its importance is emphasized by further language that noncompliance works a forfeiture or voids the policy.

Ignorance of policy provisions or a belief that coverage is questionable is no excuse for failure to give notice of loss under the Bankers Blanket Bond. In case of questionable coverage, notice of loss to the insurance company would start the investigative process in motion and resolve the uncertainty of coverage. As for ignorance of coverage, a bank should know its business and the ordinary terms of standard insurance contracts applying to banking business. The existence of such ignorance on the part of a bank would seem to be inexcusable and unreasonable.

The fact that Capitol Indemnity was not prejudiced is irrevelant. The contract language requiring timely notice of loss is designed to prevent prejudice or harm to the insurer. It is a fact of life in the insurance field that a timely notice of loss is important. It is a notice of loss that starts the investigation by the insurance company while the evidence is fresh and gatherable. Insurers are entitled to contract for this protection.

[Judgment affirmed.]

QUESTIONS AND CASE PROBLEMS

1. What is the objective of each of the following rules of law?
   (a) When a construction contract is substantially performed in good faith, the contractor may recover the contract price less damages caused the other party by shortcomings in his performance.
   (b) Impossibility of performance that arises subsequent to the making of the contract ordinarily does not excuse the promisor from his obligations.
2. Coastal Water Co. gave a promissory note to Davis Meter and Supply Co. for $17,662.61. Thereafter Coastal made payments of $4,500 to Davis Meter. Nothing was said as to what accounts were to be credited with these payments. Davis applied some of his money to two items on Coastal's account, leaving a credit balance of $3,023.55. Davis then sued Coastal for $17,662.61 on the note that had become due but was not paid. Coastal claimed that the amount of the note should be reduced by $3,023.55. Davis said that it was holding this as a reserve against future purchases to be made by Coastal. Was it entitled to do so? [Davis Meter and Supply Co. v Coastal Water Co., (DCD SC) 266 F Supp 887]
3. Brown loaned money to Halvorson, a relative, with the understanding that if Brown should die before the money was repaid, the loan was canceled. The loan was not paid by the time Brown died and Fabre, the executor of the estate of Brown, sued Halvorson for the amount of the debt. Was he entitled to recover? [Fabre v Halvorson, 250 Ore 238, 441 P2d 640]
4. A contractor was engaged in open-air sandblasting. The sand caused damage to machinery on neighboring land. A court injunction was obtained against the contractor requiring him to take precautions to prevent such damage. He claimed that it was impossible for him to perform his contract for sandblasting and that he was discharged from his obligation. Was he correct? [Savage v Kiewit, 249 Ore 147, 432 P2d 519]
5. *A* leased a trailer park to *B*. At the time, sewage was disposed of by a septic tank system which was not connected with the public sewage system. *B* knew this and the lease declared that *B* had examined the premises and that *A* made no representation or guarantee as to the condition of the premises. Some time thereafter, the septic tank system stopped working properly and the county public health department notified *B* that he was required to connect the sewage system with the public sewage system or else close the trailer

park. *B* did not want to pay the additional cost involved in connecting with the public system. *B* claimed that he was released from the lease and was entitled to a refund of the deposit which he had made. Was he correct? [Glenn R. Sewell Sheet Metal v Loverde, 70 Cal 2d 666, 75 Cal Rptr 889, 451 P2d 721]

6. Maze purchased 50 shares of stock in the Union Savings Bank, but he did not pay the full purchase price. Maze was later discharged in bankruptcy. Thereafter he was sued for the balance of the purchase price due. Decide. [Burke v Maze, 10 Cal App 206, 101 P 438]

7. Warren and Geraldine Bates, husband and wife, were about to be divorced. They made a written agreement that Warren would pay Geraldine $50 a month until their younger child attained the age of 18 years and that in consideration thereof Geraldine released Warren from all property claims. The agreement did not say that it was binding upon Warren's estate. Upon his death it was claimed by his second wife that the obligation to make the monthly payments terminated with his death. Decide. [Hutchings v Bates, (Tex Civ App) 393 SW2d 338]

8. Banks Construction Co. made a contract with the United States for construction work in connection with an air force base. Because of abnormally large rainfall, the job site was flooded and the contractor was put to extra expense. Banks then sued the United States for the extra cost that it had thus incurred. United States claimed that Banks was bound by the original contract terms. Decide. [Banks Construction Co. v United States, (Ct Claims) 364 F2d 357]

9. Claterbaugh was the owner and president of the Madison Park Appliance and Furniture, Inc. Acting in his individual capacity and without naming Madison Park or indicating that he was acting as its agent, Claterbaugh borrowed money from Hayes. A few days later Claterbaugh made another loan from Hayes in the same manner and gave Hayes a promissory note of the corporation for the total of both loans. Later a payment was made on the loans by a money order in the name of Madison Park. Later, when Hayes sued Claterbaugh for the loans, the latter claimed that there had been a novation by which the corporation was substituted in his place. Was he correct? [Hayes v Clatterbaugh, (La App) 140 So2d 737]

10. John B. Robeson Associates was given a contract to direct sales for the lots in a new cemetery, the Gardens of Faith, Inc. Robeson guaranteed a minimum of $700,000 gross sales in excess of cancellations per year. The contract specified that quarterly in the second year and semiannually in the third year "the quota attained by Robeson will be reviewable by the cemetery, with the right in the cemetery to terminate this contract at its option if Robeson has substantially failed to attain guaranteed quota." In the first year Robeson exceeded the quota. In each of the first two quarters of the second year, Robeson fell under the quota. This was discussed with Gardens of Faith, but the contract was not terminated. Robeson adopted new selling methods and sales increased substantially in the last two quarters so that the annual sales for the second year were only slightly below the agreed quota. The cemetery then elected to terminate the contract. Was it entitled to do so? [John B. Robeson Associates, Inc. v Gardens of Faith, 226 Md 215, 172 A2d 529]

19 Breach of Contract and Remedies

REMEDIES FOR BREACH OF CONTRACT

When a contract obligation is not performed, it is said that the party who has failed to act has broken his contract. The other party is given certain legal remedies for such breach.

§ **19:1. Introduction.** There are three remedies for breach of contract, one or more of which may be available to the injured party: (1) the injured party is always entitled to bring an action for damages; (2) in some instances he may rescind the contract; (3) in some instances he may bring a suit in equity to obtain specific performance.[1]

§ **19:2. Damages.** Whenever a breach of contract occurs, the injured party is entitled to bring an action for damages to recover such sum of money as will place him in the same position as he would have been in if the contract had been performed.[2] If the defendant has been negligent in performing the contract, the plaintiff may sue for the damages caused by the negligence. Thus, a person contracting to drill a well for drinking water can be sued for the damages caused by his negligently drilling the well so as to cause the water to become contaminated.[3]

(1) Mitigation of Damages. The injured party is under a duty to *mitigate the damages* if reasonably possible.[4] That is, he must not permit the damages to increase if he can prevent them from doing so by reasonable efforts. He may thus be required to stop performance on his part of the contract when he knows that the other party is in default. To illustrate, when an architect agreed to prepare preliminary drawings and to complete working drawings and specifications but the other party repudiated the contract upon the completion of the preliminary drawings, the architect could not recover for his services after the repudiation in preparing the working drawings and specifications.[5]

---

[1] As discussed in Appendix 1, local practice must be checked to determine the form of action and the court in which these actions are to be brought. In some states, the action will be an action in assumpsit (upon contract) or an equity action; while in many others, it will be merely a civil action.

[2] White v Metropolitan Merchandise Mart, 48 Del 526, 107 A2d 892.

[3] Sasso v Ayotte, 155 Conn 25, 235 A2d 636.

[4] Coury Bros. Ranches v Ellsworth, 103 Ariz 515, 446 P2d 458.

[5] Wetzel v Rixse, 93 Okla 216, 220 P 607. This principle does not prevent the plaintiff from recovering for the loss of profits that he could reasonably be expected to have made in the performance of the contract; it only limits the extent to which he can recover for expenses incurred in the performance of the contract.

In the case of the breach of an employment contract by an employer, the employee is required to seek other similar employment and the wages earned or which could have been earned from the other similar employment must be deducted from the damages claimed.

If there is nothing which the injured party can reasonably do to reduce damages, there is by definition no duty to mitigate damages. For example, when a leasing company broke its contract to supply a specified computer and auxiliary equipment by delivering a less desirable computer and the specified computer and equipment could not be obtained elsewhere by the customer, the customer was entitled to recover full damages.[6]

The doctrine of mitigation of damages will not be applied to deprive a plaintiff of a benefit to which he would otherwise be entitled. For example, if suit is brought for causing the breach of a contract to lease certain equipment from the plaintiff, the plaintiff was free to lease other equipment to third persons, as against the contention that the plaintiff should have leased the equipment covered by the broken lease and thereby reduced the damages sustained by its breach.[7]

(2) Measure of Damages. When the injured party does not sustain an actual loss from the breach of the contract, he is entitled to a judgment of a small sum, such as one dollar, known as *nominal damages*. If the plaintiff has sustained actual loss, he is entitled to a sum of money that will, so far as possible, compensate him for that loss; such damages are termed *compensatory damages*.

Ordinarily only compensatory damages are recoverable for breach of contract. This is so even though the breach was intentional.[8] The fact that damages cannot be established with mathematical certainty is not a bar to their recovery. All that is required is reasonable certainty and the trier of fact is given a large degree of discretion in determining the damages.[9]

When the contract is to purchase property, the damages are generally the difference between the contract price and the market price. The theory is that if the market price is greater, the buyer has sustained the loss of the indicated price differential because he must purchase in the general market instead of obtaining the property from the defendant. When the contract is to sell property, the loss incurred on its resale represents basically the damages for the breach.

In business activities and construction contracts, the damages for the contractor are initially the loss of profits;[10] while to the other contracting party, the damages sustained upon breach by the contractor are primarily any extra cost in having someone else render the performance.[11]

---

[6] I.O.A. Leasing Corp. v Merle Thomas Corp., 260 Md 243, 272 A2d 1.

[7] Seaboard Music Co. v Germano, 24 Cal App 3d 618, 101 Cal Rptr 255.

[8] Graham v Turner, (Tex Civ App) 472 SW2d 831.

[9] Reynolds Metals Co. v Electric Smith Constr. Equipment Co., 4 Wash 2d 695, 483 P2d 880.

[10] C. C. Hauff Hardware, Inc. v Long Mfg. Co., 260 Iowa 30, 148 NW2d 425.

[11] Crowe v Holloway Development Corp., 114 Ga App 856, 152 SE2d 913.

When a contractor delays in completing the performance of a contract, the injured party may generally recover the cost of renting other premises or goods. For example, when a contractor is late in completing the construction of a potato cellar, the injured person is entitled to recover the fair rental value of another cellar for the period of the delay, together with the cost of transporting the potatoes to the alternate place of storage.[12]

As a general rule, damages sought that are in excess of actual loss for the purpose of punishing or making an example of the defendant cannot be recovered in actions for breach of contract;[13] such damages are known as *punitive damages* (or exemplary damages).

Damages may not be recovered for loss caused by remote injuries unless the plaintiff, at the time the contract was executed, had informed the defendant of the existence of facts that would have given the defendant reason to foresee that his breach of the contract would cause such loss.[14] What constitutes remote loss for which there can be no recovery depends largely upon the facts of each case. Recovery is likewise not allowed as to losses that are not clearly related to the defendant's breach.

Damages must be proved. A plaintiff may not be awarded damages, even for an admitted breach, without proof of the loss that has been caused by such breach.[15] Ordinarily damages representing annoyance or mental anguish may not be recovered for breach of contract.[16]

The plaintiff must establish that the defendant's breach of contract was the cause of the loss which he sustained. Consequently, the fact that an airport broke the terms of its contract by not allowing free parking to patrons of the airport restaurant did not make the airport liable for the drop in the restaurant revenues when there was no evidence showing that the drop in restaurant revenues had been caused by the denial of free parking, as distinguished from a general decline in travel, repairs being made to the airport, and any other cause.[17]

Mere temporal concurrence, that is, the circumstance that in the same period of time the defendant acted wrongly and the plaintiff sustained loss does not establish a causal relationship between the defendant's act and the plaintiff's loss.

(3) Present and Future Damages. The damages recoverable on a breach of a contract may also be analyzed in terms of whether the plaintiff has already maintained the loss in question or will do so in the future. If the plaintiff was required to buy or rent elsewhere, he is ordinarily entitled to recover the cost thereof as an element of damages. When damages relate

---

[12] Olson v Quality-Pak Co., (Idaho) 469 P2d 45.

[13] Hess v Jarboe, 201 Kan 705, 443 P2d 294.

[14] Wilkins v Grays Harbor Community Hospital, 71 Wash 2d 178, 427 P2d 716.

[15] B. & B. Farms, Inc. v Matlock's Fruit Farms, 73 Wash 2d 146, 437 P2d 178 (recovery of lost profits denied for lack of evidence).

[16] Jankowski v Mazzotta, 7 Mich App 483, 152 NW3d 49.

[17] Wheelmakers, Inc. v City of Flint, 47 Mich 2d 434, 209 NW2d 444.

to future loss, the plaintiff is entitled to recover if he can establish the amount of such future loss, such as the loss of future profits, with reasonable certainty.[18] Mathematical precision is not required; but if the plaintiff cannot establish future loss items with reasonable certainty, they cannot be recovered.

(4) Interest. The right to interest has been considered in Chapter 14 as a term of a contract. Distinct from such interest, the law allows the recovery of interest as an element of damages. Generally interest runs from the date when an obligation is due if the amount at the time is liquidated, meaning definite and specific. If the amount due the plaintiff is not liquidated, interest runs only from the date that judgment is entered in his favor.[19]

§ 19:3. Liquidated Damages. The parties may stipulate in their contract that a certain amount shall be paid in case of default. This amount is known as *liquidated damages*. The provision will be enforced if the amount specified is not excessive [20] and if the contract is of such a nature that it would be difficult to determine the actual damages.[21] (See p. 375, Stein v Bruce.) For example, it is ordinarily very difficult, if not impossible, to determine what loss the owner of a building under construction suffers when the contractor is late in completing the building. It is therefore customary to include a liquidated damages clause in a building contract, specifying that the contractor is required to pay a stated sum for each day of delay. When a liquidated damages clause is held valid, the injured party cannot collect more than the amount specified by the clause; and the defaulting party is bound to pay that much damages once the fact is established that he is in default and has no excuse for his default. (See p. 377, Oregon v DeLong Corp.)

A provision that a paving contractor shall pay the city $210 for every day's delay in the performance of a highway paving contract costing more than $1.5 million is valid as a liquidated damages clause.[22]

If the liquidated damages clause calls for the payment of a sum which is clearly unreasonably large and unrelated to the possible actual damages that might be sustained, the clause will be held void as a *penalty*.[23]

Whether damages can be readily determined within the meaning of the above rule is to be determined as of the time the parties make their contract, rather than at the later date when the damages have been sustained.[24]

§ 19:4. Limitation of Liability. A party to a contract generally may include a provision that he shall not be liable for its breach generally, or for a breach

---

[18] Schafer v Sunset Packing Co., 256 Ore 539, 474 P2d 529.

[19] Kayell Development Co., Ltd. v Carney, 4 Colo App 548, 480 P2d 857.

[20] Gruschus v C. R. Davis Contracting Co., 75 NM 649, 409 P2d 500; Blount v Smith, 12 Ohio 41, 231 NE2d 301.

[21] Massey v Love, (Okla) 478 P2d 948; UCC § 2-718(1); Mellor v Budget Advisors, (CA7 Ill) 415 F2d 1218 (recognizing the Code provision in a nonsales transaction).

[22] Dave Gustafson & Co. Inc. v South Dakota, 83 SD 160, 156 NW2d 185.

[23] Rothenberg v Follman, 19 Mich App 383, 172 NW2d 845.

[24] Hutchison v Tompkins, (Fla) 259 So2d 129.

that is due to a particular cause. Common illustrations of such clauses are the seller's statement that he is not liable beyond the refund of the purchase price or the replacement of defective parts, or a construction contract provision that the contractor shall not be liable for delays caused by conduct of third persons. Generally such provisions are valid; but there is a growing trend to limit them or to hold them invalid when it is felt that because of the unequal bargaining power of the contracting parties, the surrender of a right to damages for breach by the other is oppressive or unconscionable.

When the provision is expanded so as to free the contracting party from liability for his own negligence, the provision is sometimes held void as contrary to public policy. This is particularly likely to be the result when the party in question is a public utility, which is under the duty to render the performance or to provide the service in question in a nonnegligent way. (See p. 378, Fedor v Mauwehu Council.)

The fact that a limitation of liability limits or destroys the liability of one party for his nonperformance does not mean that there is no binding contract between the parties (as against the contention that if one party may break the contract without being liable in damages, he in fact is not bound by any contract and hence the other party should not be bound either). There is a binding contract between the supplier of natural gas and its customer even though the supplier declares that while it would make "reasonable provision to insure a continuous supply," it does not insure a continuous supply of gas, will not be responsible for interruptions beyond its control, and "assumes no obligation whatever regarding the quantity and quality of gas delivered . . . or the continuity of service." [25]

§ 19:5. Rescission upon Breach. The injured party may also have the right to treat the contract as discharged. When one party commits a material breach of a contract the other party may rescind the contract because of such breach, although in some situations the right to rescind may be governed or controlled by civil service statutes or similar regulations or by an obligation to submit the matter to arbitration or to a grievance procedure. (See p. 379, Pennel v Pond Union School District.)

quasi-contractual theory

If the injured party exercises the right to rescind after he has performed or paid money due under the contract, he may recover the value of the performance rendered or the money paid. He sues, not on the express contract, but on a quasi contract which the law implies in order to compel the wrongdoer to pay for what he has received and to keep him from profiting by his own wrong.

---

[25] Texas Gas Utilities Co. v Barrett, (Tex) 460 SW2d 409. It would appear that the same consideration of practical expediency that has led the law to sustain output and requirements contracts and to trust to the good faith needs of businessmen for the definition of contract obligations, rather than insisting upon precise contract terms, is tending to favor limitation of liability clauses even though, if given literal effect, they would seem to permit a party to ignore his contract without any legal consequence. This is subject to the qualifications or exceptions noted in the first paragraph of this subsection, in order to protect a person in an inferior bargaining position.

The rescinding party must restore the other party to his original position as far as circumstances will permit, and he must rescind the entire contract. If he cannot make restoration because of his own acts, he cannot rescind the contract. Thus, a buyer who has placed a mortgage on property purchased by him cannot rescind the sales contract because he cannot return the property the way he received it.[26]

The party who takes the initiative in rescinding the contract acts at his risk that he has proper cause to do so. If he does not have proper cause, he is guilty of a breach of the contract.

§ 19:6. Specific Performance. Under special circumstances the injured party may seek the equitable remedy of *specific performance* to compel the other party to carry out the terms of his contract. The granting of this relief is discretionary with the court and will be refused (a) when the contract is not definite;[27] (b) when there is an adequate legal remedy; (c) when it works an undue hardship or an injustice on the defaulting party or the consideration is inadequate;[28] (d) when the agreement is illegal, fraudulent, or unconscionable;[29] or (e) when the court is unable to supervise the performance of such acts,[30] as when services of a technical or complicated nature, such as the construction of a building, are to be rendered.[31] The right to specific performance is also lost by unreasonable delay in bringing suit.[32]

As a general rule, contracts for the purchase of land will be specifically enforced.[33] Each parcel of land is unique and the payment of money damages would only enable the injured person to purchase a similar parcel of land but not the particular land specified in the contract.

Specific performance of a contract to sell personal property generally cannot be obtained. Money damages are deemed adequate on the basis that the plaintiff can purchase identical goods. Specific performance will be granted, however, when the personal property has a unique value to the plaintiff or when the circumstances are such that identical articles cannot be obtained in the market. Thus, specific performance is granted of a contract to sell articles of an unusual age, beauty, unique history, or other distinction, as in the case of heirlooms, original paintings, old editions of books, or relics.[34] Specific performance is also allowed a buyer in the case of a contract to sell shares of stock essential for control of a close corporation,[35]

[26] Bennett v Emerald Service, 157 Neb 176, 59 NW2d 171.

[27] D. M. Wright Builders, Inc. v Bridgers, 2 NC App 662, 163 SE2d 642.

[28] Hodge v Shea, 295 SC 601, 168 SE2d 82.

[29] Tuckwiller v Tuckwiller, (Mo) 413 SW2d 274.

[30] R §§ 358, 359, 367, 368, 370, 371; Rachon v McQuitty, 125 Mont 1, 229 P2d 965.

[31] Northern Delaware Industrial Development Corp. v E. W. Bliss Co., (Del) 245 A2d 431.

[32] Sofio v Glissmann, 156 Neb 610, 57 NW2d 176.

[33] R § 360; Wilkinson v Vaughn, (Mo) 419 SW2d 1.

[34] R § 361.

[35] In a close corporation the stock is owned by a few individuals, and there is no opportunity for the general public to purchase shares.

having no fixed or market value, and not being quoted in the commercial reports or sold on a stock exchange.

Ordinarily contracts for the performance of personal services will not be specifically ordered, both because of the difficulty of supervision by the courts and because of the restriction of the Thirteenth Amendment of the Federal Constitution prohibiting involuntary servitude except as criminal punishment. In some instances, a court will issue a negative injunction which prohibits the defendant from rendering a similar service for anyone else. This may indirectly have the effect of compelling the defendant to work for the plaintiff.

§ **19:7. Waiver of Breach.** The fact that one party has broken a contract does not necessarily mean that there will be a lawsuit or a forfeiture of the contract. For practical business reasons one party may be willing to ignore or waive the breach. When it is established that there has been waiver of a breach, the party waiving the breach cannot take any action on the theory that the contract was broken. The waiver in effect erases the past breach and the contract continues as though the breach had not existed. (See p. 380, Harrison v Puga.)

(1) Scope of Waiver. The waiver of a breach of contract only extends to the matter waived. It does not show any intent to ignore other provisions of the contract. For example, when a contractor is late in completing the construction of a building but the owner waives his objection to the lateness and permits the contractor to continue and finish the construction, such waiver as to time does not waive the obligation of the contractor to complete the building according to the plans and specifications. Only the time of performance requirement has been waived.[36]

(2) Reservation of Right. It may be that the party waiving the breach is willing to accept the defective performance or breach but he does not wish to surrender any claim for damages for the breach. For example, the buyer of coal may need a shipment of coal so badly that he is forced to accept it although it is defective, yet at the same time he does not wish to give up his right to claim damages from the seller because the shipment was defective. In such a case, the aggrieved party should accept the tendered performance with a reservation of rights. In the above illustration the buyer would in effect state that he had accepted the coal but reserved his right to damages for nonconformity to the contract.[37] Frequently the buyer will express the same thought by stating that he accepts the coal without prejudice to his right to damages for nonconformity or that he accepts under protest.

The acceptance under reservation described above may be oral. It is preferable for practical reasons that it be in writing. In many cases the practical procedure is to make the declaration orally as soon as possible and then send a confirming letter. When the matter is sufficiently important, it is also

[36] Ryan v Thurmond, (Tex Civ App) 481 SW2d 199.
[37] UCC § 1-207.

desirable to have the wrongdoer countersign or make a written acknowledgement of the reservation letter.

(3) Waiver of Breach as Modification of Contract. When the contract calls for continuing performance, such as making a delivery of goods or the payment of an installment on the first of each month, the acceptance of a late delivery or a late payment may have more significance than merely waiving a claim for damages because of the lateness. If there are repeated breaches and repeated waivers, the circumstances may show that the parties had modified their original contract. For example, the contract calling for performance on the first of the month may have been modified to permit performance in the first week of the month. When there is a modification of the contract, neither party can go back to the original contract without the consent of the other.

(a) ANTIMODIFICATION CLAUSE. Modern contracts commonly specify that the terms of a contract shall not be deemed modified by waiver as to any breaches. This means that the original contract remains as agreed to and either party may therefore return to and insist upon compliance with the original contract. In order to do this, notice must be given to the other party that in the future the terms of the contract will be insisted upon. For example, where the insurance company followed the pattern of accepting the late payment of insurance premiums it could not declare a policy lapsed for failure to pay the premiums within the required time without first notifying the insured that it was going to insist on compliance with the terms of the policy contract.[38]

§ 19:8. Reformation of Contract. When a written contract does not correctly state what has been agreed to and its correction cannot be obtained by voluntary cooperation, a court will order the correction of the contract when it is clear that a reforming or *reformation* of the contract should be made. In some instances reforming the contract is the first step in showing that the contract which was actually made has been broken by the defendant. For example, assume that *A* owns two houses at 510 and 512 N. Main Street. Assume that he obtains a fire insurance policy on 510 but by mistake the policy refers to 512. Thereafter 510 is destroyed by fire and the insurance company refuses to pay the loss on the theory that it did not insure 510 but insured 512. At this point *A* would ask the court (1) to reform the insurance contract to show that there was in fact insurance on 510, and (2) to award damages to *A* because of the insurer's breach of its contract as to 510.

TORT LIABILITY TO THIRD PERSONS

When a party to a contract fails to perform his obligation, a third person may be harmed. If the third person cannot bring suit as a third party beneficiary, he might seek to recover damages on a theory of tort liability.

[38] Continental Casualty Co. v Union Camp Corp., 230 Ga 8, 195 SE2d 417.

§ 19:9. Tort Liability to Third Person for Nonperformance. By the general rule a total failure to perform a contract does not confer upon a third person a right to sue for tort.[39]

(1) Discharge of Obligee's Duty. An exception is made to the general rule when the obligee, that is, the other party to the contract who will receive the benefit of performance, owes a duty to the third person or the general public, and the performance by the contractor will discharge that duty. Here the breach of the duty by the contractor gives rise to a tort liability in favor of the injured third person against the contractor. To illustrate, the operator of an office building owes the duty to third persons of maintaining its elevators in a safe operating condition. In order to discharge this duty, the building management may make a contract with an elevator maintenance contractor. If the latter fails to perform its contract and a third person is injured because of the defective condition of an elevator, the third person may sue the elevator maintenance contractor for the damages sustained.

(2) Partial Performance. Confusion exists in the law as to the classification to be made of conduct involved when the contracting party has entered upon the performance of the contract but omits some act or measure in consequence of which harm is sustained by a third person. The problem is the same as that involved in determining whether the negligent actor who omits a particular precaution has "acted" negligently or has been guilty of a negligent "omission." In many of the older cases, the courts disposed of the matter by stating that no tort arose when a third person was injured by the breach of a contract between other persons.

A strong factor in favor of no tort liability is the vast, unlimited, and unpredictable liability that a contrary rule would impose. Some courts have not deemed this factor controlling, however, and have held water companies liable in such situations on the theory that having erected hydrants and having entered upon the performance of the contract to supply water, they caused property owners to rely on the appearance of the availability of adequate water and were therefore liable to them if that appearance was not lived up to, as by failing to maintain proper pressure or to keep hydrants in working condition.

§ 19:10. Tort Liability to Third Person for Improper Performance. When one person contracts to perform a service for another person and his defective or improper performance causes harm to a third person, such third person may sue the contractor. This is at least true when the performance of the contract would discharge an obligation or duty which is owed to the injured plaintiff by the person dealing with the contractor. By the older rule of contract law, only the person who had contracted for the services could sue when the services were improperly performed. (See p. 380, A. E. Investment Corp. v Link Builders.)

---

[39] Resort to a tort theory of liability is unnecessary if the aggrieved person is entitled to recover as a third party beneficiary of the contract.

When the contractor fails to perform properly his contract for repairs or alterations, there is a conflict of authority as to whether he is liable to a third person who is injured as the result thereof. For example, suppose that an automobile repairman negligently repairs the brakes of an automobile with the result that it does not stop in time when driven by the owner and runs into a pedestrian. Can the pedestrian sue the repairman for tort damages?

By the older view, the injured plaintiff was automatically barred because he was not a party to the contract with the repairman. The modern view, however, emphasizes the fact that the person who makes a poor repair of the brakes is launching a dangerous instrumentality on the highway just as much as the manufacturer who manufactures an automobile with defective brakes. Both should recognize that their negligence will expose persons on the highway to an unreasonable risk of foreseeable harm. The modern view accordingly holds the negligent repairman liable to the injured third person.

A party to a contract is, of course, directly liable to a third person injured by his negligence in the course of performing the contract. For example, when a contractor used a heavy pile driver close to very old neighboring buildings without taking various precautions to protect them from vibration damage, the contractor was liable to the owners of such houses for the vibration damages caused by his negligence.[40]

[40] Dussell v Kaufman Construction Co., 398 Pa 369, 157 A2d 740.

CASES FOR CHAPTER 19

Stein v Bruce

(Mo App) 366 SW2d 732 (1963)

Stein, as buyer, and Bruce, as seller, made a contract for the sale of land located in Pennsylvania for $19,000. The contract required an initial down payment of $1,900, which was made. Later Stein paid Bruce $1,000 to extend the final settlement date of the contract until the end of the year. Stein did not go through with the sale, whereupon Bruce resold the land to another person for $19,000 within less than one year. After the final performance date of the original sales contract, Bruce kept the $2,900 paid by Stein, claiming that he was entitled thereto because the contract specified that "time is hereby agreed to be the essence of the agreement" and that "should the buyer fail to make settlement as herein provided, the sum or sums paid on account are to be retained by the seller, either on account of the purchase money, or as compensation for the damages and expenses he has been put to in his behalf, as the seller may elect." Stein sued for the return of the $2,900. From a decision adverse to Stein, she appealed.

CROSS, J. . . . Plaintiff . . . argues that . . . the sum named in the contract as liquidated damages is unreasonably large and that it must therefore be considered as a penalty and void. Under such findings, plaintiff insists, she would be entitled to recover of defendants the entire "down payment" of $2900. The contract in question was executed in Pennsylvania and the land was located in that state. All the parties to the contract lived in Pennsylvania. Therefore, our determination of the instant question depends upon whether the down payment in issue is held to be liquidated damages or a penalty under law applicable in the State of Pennsylvania. . . .

The term "liquidated damages" signifies the damages, the amount of which the parties to a contract stipulate and agree, when the contract is entered into, shall be paid in case of breach. As distinguished from liquidated damages, a penalty is a sum inserted in a contract, not as a measure of compensation for its breach, but rather as a punishment for default, or by way of security for actual damages which may be sustained by reason of nonperformance, and it involves the idea of punishment. . . .

In determining whether contractual provisions are to be interpreted as providing for liquidated damages or for a penalty, the courts have enumerated various tests, criteria and factors to be considered. . . .

"The name by which such a clause may be called is but of slight weight, and the controlling elements are the intention of the parties and the special circumstances of the case. . . . The question is to be determined 'by the intention of the parties, drawn from the words of the whole contract, examined in the light of its subject matter and its surroundings; and that in this examination we must consider the relation which the sum stipulated bears to the extent of the injury which may be caused by the several breaches provided against, the ease or difficulty of measuring a breach of damages, and such other matters as are legally or necessarily inherent in the transaction.' . . . Real estate transactions, involving breaches in performance, are peculiarly within that class of cases where the measure of damages is difficult to ascertain. It is for that very reason that the practice has developed of inserting in sales agreements a sum certain, agreed to by the parties, as the amount which will be considered as compensation for a breach in performance. This may be the amount of the deposit or hand money, or it may be a sum in a lesser or greater amount, depending upon the consideration involved. Generally, we have held that where a purchaser repudiates an agreement of sale of real estate containing a provision for liquidated damages, the vendor is entitled to the sum agreed upon as liquidated damages. . . . Where the obligation to purchase has been repudiated, especially where new construction is involved, the vendor usually has the continuing obligation of paying interest on any construction loan, insurance, taxes, broker's commission, maintenance charges, and utilities until the property is actually sold." . . .

The clear language of the contract and the circumstances surrounding the transaction import that the parties intended to stipulate for the retention of the down payment sum as liquidated damages and not as a penalty. That they so intended is strongly supported by the fact that the sale of real estate was the subject matter of the contract. "Damages rising from a breach of a contract for the purchase or sale of real estate are usually so uncertain and difficult of ascertainment that the tendency of the courts generally has been to sustain covenants of the parties liquidating the damages in such cases, unless they are unconscionable or grossly disproportionate to the injury provided against". . . .

"Of all facts difficult to establish, however, the value of land is one of the most difficult; in many neighborhoods sales of land are not frequent and no two persons will precisely agree as to the value thereof. Covenants of the parties liquidating the damages in such cases, when not unconscionable, will be enforced by the courts." Under the foregoing principles of law which govern our deliberations, we must assume that the actual damages resulting from the breach of the real estate sales contract in this case are uncertain in amount and difficult to ascertain or prove, particularly since there is nothing in the contract that furnishes a guide for the determination of damages. Therefore, it will be our duty to hold that the stipulated sum is for liquidated damages *unless we determine it to be unreasonable in amount as a forecast of probable damages and disproportionate to the amount of damages that could probably result from the breach.* We next consider that question.

The amount stipulated in the contract as liquidated damages to be forfeited in event of its breach is the sum of $1,900—exactly 10 percent of the purchase price. It is not, as plaintiff assumes, the sum of $2,900. The sum of $1,000 paid . . . three months after the contract was executed did not represent a stipulated down payment nor was it stipulated to be a sum representing liquidated damages. That sum was paid to defendants as consideration for the extension of time granted for performing the contract—the price of forbearance on the part of defendants from declaring a forfeiture on the part of the purchaser at the termination of the original three month contract period.

We do not believe that an amount representing 10 percent of the total purchase price is an unreasonable provision for liquidated damages in this case, or that it is disproportionate to the probable damages defendants suffered by the breach of the contract. It is apparent from the record that defendants had engaged real estate agents to sell the property and that the sale was effected through them. It is a reasonable inference that defendants were obligated by contract to pay those agents a commission for selling the real estate, that the commission was in fact paid, and further, that it represented a substantial portion of the 10 percent down payment retained after the breach. Furthermore, defendants were burdened by the contract for almost four months. During that interim their property was necessarily "off the market." They were constrained by the contract to reject all other offers of purchase, and forego any opportunity presented to sell it for a higher price. Meanwhile, they were subject to the outlay of money for maintenance of the property and for any continuing obligation such as interest, insurance, taxes, maintenance charges, and utilities. Additionally, defendants were deprived of the use of their money and the opportunity of its investment.

We find ample precedent in Pennsylvania cases for ruling that 10 percent of the purchase price is a reasonable stipulation of liquidated damages. . . . Plaintiff cites certain sections of . . . Pennsylvania's Uniform Commercial Code which applies only to the sale of personal property. We reject them as authority on the issue in this case arising from the sale of real estate. . . .

[Judgment affirmed.]

Oregon v DeLong Corporation

9 Ore App 550, 495 P2d 1215 (1972)

The Oregon Highway Commission made a contract with the DeLong Corporation for the construction of the major components of a bridge across the Columbia River. The contract specified that $2,000 would be paid for each day's delay. DeLong abandoned the contract. The Highway Commission then had a second contractor finish the work. This was finished 476 days after the original completion date. The State then sued DeLong for damages for breach of the contract and for $2,000 for each day's delay. The State claimed that because of the delay, it lost approximately $1.4 million in bridge tolls, ferry operations, and a state bridge subsidy. Judgment was entered in favor of the state for breach of the contract and for liquidated damages of $2,000 x 476 days of delay. DeLong appealed.

FORT, J. . . . We consider first whether plaintiff was entitled to the liquidated damage award for the delay in the completion of work following its termination of the DeLong contract by the state. We recognize initially that in law a provision of a contract is not converted from a penalty to liquidated damages simply by so denominating it. . . .

. . . "Where the amount of loss or harm that has been caused by a breach is uncertain and difficult of estimation in money, experience has shown that the estimate of a court or jury is no more likely to be exact compensation than is the advance estimate of the parties themselves. Further, the enforcement of such agreements saves the time of courts, juries, parties, and witnesses and reduces the expense of litigation. . . ."

". . . In determining whether any particular stipulation is to be regarded as one fixing a penalty, or whether it really liquidates the damages, . . . the situation must be appraised as of the time when the contract was effected, and not as it appears at some other time. . . . The court should consider all of the circumstances which surrounded the parties, together with the ease or difficulty of measuring the breach in damages. A comparison of the size of the stipulated sum not only with the value of the subject-matter of the contracts, but also with the probable consequences of the breach as they appeared when the contract was executed may be helpful. . . .

. . . When the actual damages in case of a breach of the contract must necessarily be speculative, uncertain, and incapable of definite ascertainment, the stipulated sum will be regarded as liquidated damages, and may be recovered as such without proof of actual damages, unless the language of the contract shows, or the circumstances under which it was made indicate, a contrary intention of the parties, or it so manifestly exceeds the actual injury suffered as to be unconscionable. . . . Where the damages are uncertain and speculative, the presumption ordinarily is that the parties have taken that into consideration in making the contract, and have agreed upon a definite sum to be paid in case of a breach, in order to put the question beyond dispute and controversy and to avoid the difficulty of proving actual damages. . . .

"It is also to be noticed that some of the former antipathy to these provisions, which inclined courts at times to construe them as stipulations for a penalty, is moderating." . . .

" 'The later rule . . . is to look with candor, if not with favor, upon such provisions in contracts when deliberately entered into between parties who have equality of opportunity for understanding and insisting upon their rights, as promoting prompt performance of contracts and because adjusting in advance, and amicably, matters the settlement of which through courts would often involve difficulty, uncertainty, delay and expense.' " . . .

Here the difficulty inherent in determining and proving actual damages for delay prior to completion of the bridge is apparent, as for example in determining the net loss of revenue which would have been derived had the bridge been in operation. This is particularly true when the validity of the liquidated damage provision must be determined as of the time the contract was entered into, rather than at the time of completion. . . . That the amount of liquidated damages claimed does not unconscionably exceed the actual injury suffered is seen from the testimony relating to the claimed losses from the ferry operation, absence of toll revenues, and deprivation of the Washington state subsidy.

We think it clear that the challenged provision was correctly viewed as one for liquidated damages, and not as a penalty. . . .

[Judgment affirmed.]

Fedor v Mauwehu Council

21 Conn Supp 38, 143 A2d 466 (1958)

Charles Fedor, a minor, went to a summer camp. His father signed an agreement as a condition to his being admitted to the camp that the minor would not make any claim against the camp for any injury. When Charles was injured at the camp, he sued the camp claiming that the injury was caused by the camp's negligence. It raised the defense that the waiver agreement barred the suit. From a decision for the camp, Charles appealed.

McDONALD, J. . . . Generally speaking, agreements exempting parties from liability for their own negligence are not favored by the law and, if possible, are construed so as not to confer immunity from liability. . . . This general policy against construing agreements of the type involved here so as to confer immunity from liability for negligence is especially desirable in cases where a relationship once entered upon involves a status requiring of one party greater responsibility than that of the ordinary person and where the parties have not equal bargaining power and one party must either accept what is offered or be deprived of the relation. Certain language in defendant's [brief] . . . would appear to a certain extent to indicate the applicability of the foregoing language to the facts of this case—notably where defendant argues: "If this meritorious function [summer camp] is to be kept within the financial means of the greatest number of boys, some concession must be made. The concession in this case was the waiver of liability provision in the camp contract for which has been substituted a personal accident insurance policy to protect the boys and their parents from unfortunate casualties. These were the only terms available to the plaintiff and his parents and they accepted them readily."

In other words, low-income families desiring to take advantage of the opportunity to give their sons the advantages of a Boy Scout camp have no choice other than to sign a waiver absolving the camp from liability for acts of negligence of those responsible for the safety and lives of their sons. In this situation, the language of the court in Parillo v Housing Authority . . . seems particularly in point, where it is stated (16 Conn Supp at page 107): "It can hardly be said to be in the public interest to countenance a policy which would deprive families of low income, otherwise eligible, of the opportunity to obtain dwelling accommodations expressly made available for them by the use of public funds unless they consented to assume the risks flowing from the negligence of the authority in carrying on its operations."

We must bear in mind this general public policy against agreements exempting parties from liability for their own negligence when we consider whether the alleged waiver is binding. . . .

It is doubtful that either the mother or father of this minor plaintiff had the power or authority to waive his rights against the defendant arising out of acts of negligence on the part of the defendant. . . .

[Judgment reversed.]

Pennel v Pond Union School District

29 Cal App 3d 832, 105 Cal Rptr 817 (1973)

Pennel was a first-grade teacher in the Pond Elementary School. She signed a contract to teach the fourth grade for one year. She claimed that she had been coerced into signing the contract and when the school term began she did not come to school but claimed to be ill. The school superintendent decided that she was not ill and discharged her. She brought an action to compel her reinstatement. The lower court refused to order Pennel's reinstatement and she appealed.

FRANSON, A.J. . . . A mutual rescission requires an intent to rescind on the part of both parties. . . . "A rescission by consent may be implied from the acts of the parties. The giving of notice and the conduct of the parties thereafter may amount to rescission by their mutual consent. Moreover, where a rescission on the part of one party is implied by his refusal to comply with the contract, and the other party acquiesces therein, a rescission by consent is effected." . . .

At no time did appellant expressly repudiate or refuse to comply with her contract, and we are unable to find any substantial evidence from which it can be implied that she intended to rescind the contract. Her statements and conduct at the time her performance was due were to the contrary. To have an implied abandonment the acts and conduct relied on must be positive, unequivocal, and inconsistent with the contract. . . .

Viewing the matter solely as one of contract law, it would appear the trial judge determined that respondent had the right to *unilaterally* rescind the contract by reason of appellant's breach in not showing up to teach on the first two days of school. A party to a contract may rescind if there is a material breach by the other party. . . . Under contract principles, the failure to appear at school to teach on the first two days of the school year, absent a legitimate excuse such as illness, well may constitute a material breach justifying a unilateral rescission by the school district, especially in the light of appellant's conduct during the summer months. Unquestionably the opening days of school are important in establishing the teacher-student relationship for the coming year and a slight breach of the contract at the outset may justify termination if it indicates future difficulty in obtaining performance. . . . We hold that the matter of a school board's unilateral termination of a teacher's contract by reason of the teacher's behavior during the school year is not governed by general contract law but, rather, by the Education Code provisions governing administrative procedures for dismissal of teachers. . . .

The judgment is reversed, and the trial court is directed to enter a judgment ordering respondent board to pay to appellant the sum of $8,500, representing her salary for the 1969-1970 school year, plus costs; in addition, respondent is to pay statutory interest on appellant's salary measured from the date each increment was due and payable under her teaching contract. . . .

Harrison v Puga

4 Wash App 52, 480 P2d 247 (1971)

Puga assigned a contract in order to transfer his interest in a cable television enterprise to a corporation to be formed with the Harrisons if, among other things, he was paid $20,000 by June 20, 1967. Partial payments were made of $5,000 on March 27 and $2,500 on July 30, 1967. On December 13, 1967, Puga notified Harrison that the agreement was terminated. The Harrisons sued him for breach of contract. From a judgment for the Harrisons, Puga appealed.

HOROWITZ, Acting C.J. . . . Plaintiffs claim . . . that defendant waived the June 20, 1967 deadline on payment requirements by requesting and accepting payments from plaintiffs after June 20, 1967; that in the absence of a clause making time of the essence or providing for forfeiture, defendant could not legally forfeit the contract without prior notice giving plaintiffs a reasonable opportunity to perform; and that the failure to give such a notice is a breach of contract. We agree with these contentions.

When a contract payee accepts late payments without objection as to their timeliness, he impliedly leads the payor to believe that late payments will be accepted and thus waives the time for payment condition specified in the contract. . . . Accordingly, a contract payee cannot . . . without prior reasonable notice to the payor enforce due date provisions in the contract so as to claim a forfeiture. This is all the more true when the contract neither contains a clause making time of the essence nor a clause providing for forfeiture in the event of breach. . . .

[Judgment affirmed.]

A. E. Investment Corp. v Link Builders, Inc.

62 Wis 2d 479, 214 NW2d 764 (1974)

The More-Way Development Company contracted with Link to construct a building. DeQuardo, Robinson, Crouch & Associates, Inc., were the architects who designed the building. After the building was constructed, A. E. Investment Corporation rented a part of the building. Because of the negligence of the architects, the building settled. The Investment Corporation was forced to leave the building because of this condition. It then sued the architects for the economic loss sustained thereby. The architects filed a demurrer to the complaint. The lower court overruled the demurrer. The defendant architects appealed.

HEFFERNAN, J. . . . It was alleged that the architect was negligent in its failure to adequately supervise the construction, in that it failed to determine the nature and condition of the subsoil prior to and during construction. It was also alleged that, in view of the subsoil conditions, the plans were negligently drawn because they did not provide for the construction of a floor that was necessary to accommodate the plaintiff's business enterprise.

It was alleged that the defendant knew that the building would be used as a commercial store and the plaintiff would therein operate a supermarket. It was alleged that, as the direct and proximate result of the negligence, the floor space leased to the plaintiff began to settle, damage was caused to the walls, the floor became uneven, and eventually the premises became untenantable. . . .

. . . The defendant defines the question . . . as being whether the defendant had a "duty to protect the subtenant plaintiff's future economic interests from loss allegedly resulting from a condition of the building." It responds to that question only by attempting to show that an architect owes no duty to a person with whom he is not in privity of contract. As a consequence, the defendant relies on the narrow argument that it has no responsibility for any economic loss to the plaintiff because it has no duty to the plaintiff at all and no responsibility to be answerable for any damages, irrespective of the nature of the loss. . . .

We believe that the narrow concept of duty relied on by the defendant architect has long been discarded in Wisconsin law. The duty of any person is the obligation of due care to refrain from any act which will cause foreseeable harm to others even though the nature of that harm and the identity of the harmed person or harmed interest is unknown at the time of the act. . . . " . . . Once an act has been found to be negligent, we no longer look to see if there was a duty to the one who was in fact injured.". . .

In the instant case . . . the defendant's alleged failure to properly take into account the condition of the subsoil when designing and supervising the construction of the building was an act or omission that would foreseeably cause some harm to someone. The duty was to refrain from such act or omission. Where, as here, it is alleged that the architect knew the purpose for which the building was being constructed, it was clearly foreseeable that a future tenant of the building was within the ambit of the harm. Hence, the harm to the particular plaintiff was foreseeable, although under the methodology of this court, it is not necessary that either the person harmed or the type of harm that would result be foreseeable. The act or omission in the face of foreseeable harm was negligence. . . .

Under Wisconsin negligence law, architects may be liable to third parties with whom they are not in privity of contract. The lack of privity does not constitute a policy reason for not imposing liability where negligence is shown to be a substantial factor in occasioning the harm.

The defendant also argues that, since an architect is a professional, his paramount duty is to his client, and that, if no duty is breached in connection with the architect-client relationship, there is no responsibility to third parties. We disagree with the argument that a professional can exonerate himself from liability for a negligent act which will foreseeably cause harm to third parties, merely because his client does not object. The very essence of a profession is that the services are rendered with the understanding that the duties of the profession cannot be undertaken on behalf of a client without an awareness and a responsibility to the public welfare. The entire ambit of state regulations as they apply to the profession of architecture is intended, not solely for the protection of the person with whom the architect deals, but for the protection of the world at large. Professionalism is the very antithesis to irresponsibility to all interests other than those of an immediate employer.

In the instant case, however, if, as it is alleged, the defendant architect negligently designed or permitted the erection of an unsuitable or unstable structure, it was hardly acting in the interests of its client, whether that client has seen fit to complain or not. . . .

[Judgment affirmed.]

QUESTIONS AND CASE PROBLEMS

1. What is the objective of each of the following rules of law?
   (a) A party injured by a breach of contract is under a duty to mitigate the damages as far as is reasonably possible.
   (b) Specific performance of certain contracts is granted as an equitable remedy.

2. Kuznicki made a contract for the installation of a fire detection system by Security Safety Corp. for $498. The contract was made one night and canceled at 9:00 a.m. the next morning. Security then claimed one third of the purchase price from Kuznicki by virtue of a provision in the contract that "in the event of cancellation of this agreement . . . the owner agrees to pay 33⅓ percent of the contract price, as liquidated damages." Was Security Safety entitled to recover the amount claimed? [Security Safety Corp. v Kuznicki, 350 Mass 157, 213 NE2d 866]

3. Scheppel, a furniture dealer, received a telephone order on March 9 for furniture subject to the condition that it be delivered to the customer's home by March 23. Scheppel telephoned the factory, which gave the ordered furniture to a motor carrier, Arkansas-Best Freight System, with directions to use Cline Motor Freight for the last leg of the shipment. A different carrier was used, and for some unknown reason the furniture was not delivered in time and the customer canceled his order. Scheppel then sued Arkansas-Best for loss of the profit on the canceled sale to his customer. Decide. [Scheppel v Arkansas-Best Freight System, 117 Ill App 2d 60, 254 NE2d 280]

4. Brewer, who operated a lounge, contracted to give Roberts the right to place amusement machines therein. When Brewer sought to exclude the machines, Roberts sued for specific performance, which Brewer opposed on the ground that specific performance would require the court to supervise the lounge to see that the machines were allowed in it. Decide. [Roberts v Brewer, (Tex Civ App) 371 SW2d 424]

5. Avril agreed to sell certain cleaning products to Center Chemical Co. at a 45 percent discount for 20 years and gave Center an exclusive franchise to sell such products in Florida. If Center did not make specified monthly minimum purchases, Avril could restrict or terminate Center's exclusive rights. The contract provided for periodic readjustment of prices to meet market conditions. Four years later Center stopped purchasing from Avril, which then sued for breach of contract, claiming that it was entitled to recover for the loss of profits which it would have received in the remaining 16 years of the contract. It offered evidence of what the sales and profits had been the first 4 years. Was it entitled to recover profits for the remaining 16 years? [Center Chemical Co. v Avril, (CA5 Fla) 392 F2d 289]

6. Melodee Lane Lingerie Co. was a tenant in a building that was protected against fire by a sprinkler and alarm system maintained by the American District Telegraph Co. Because of the latter's fault, the controls on the system were defective and allowed the discharge of water into the building, which damaged Melodee's property. When Melodee sued A.D.T., it raised the defense that its service contract limited its liability to 10 percent of the annual service charge made to the customer. Was this limitation valid? [Melodee Lane Lingerie Co. v American District Telegraph Co., 18 NY2d 57, 271 NYS2d 937, 218 NE2d 661]

7. *A*, who had contracted to build a house for *B*, departed from the specifications at a number of points. It would cost approximately $1,000 to put the house in the condition called for by the contract. *B* sued *A* for $5,000 for breach of contract and emotional disturbance caused by the breach. Decide. [Jankowski v Mazzotta, 7 Mich App 483, 152 NW2d 49]

8. Dankowski contracted with Cremona to perform construction work on a house for $5,060 and to make a down payment of $2,500. When the work was about 80 percent completed, Dankowski refused to permit Cremona to do any further work because the work done was defective. Cremona brought suit for breach of contract. It was found that the defects in the work could be remedied at a cost of $500 and that Cremona had spent $4,167.26 in performance of the contract. He was awarded damages of $4,167.26 less the $500 necessary for repairs and less the down payment of $2,500, making damages of $1,167.26. The owner appealed. Decide. [Dankowski v Cremona, (Tex Civ App) 352 SW2d 334]

9. Contrary to its subscription contract, the Southern Bell Telephone & Telegraph Co. failed to list the trade name of Scheinuk The Florist, Inc. in the white pages of the phone directory and only listed it in the yellow pages. In order to offset this omission, Scheinuk spent $508 in advertising. He sued the telephone company for damages of $25,147.53, which he asserted was the loss sustained in the 13-month period before the new directory was published. He showed that he was the second largest florist in New Orleans with a mailing list of 20,000 customers, doing approximately 95 percent of its business over the phone. Scheinuk showed that his loss of gross profits during the 13-month period was $2,912.81. He claimed that since florists in the city had a general increase of business of 11.4 percent, the amount of $16,726.72 was the gross profit on the income from sales he would have received if he had been properly listed and thus able to increase at the same rate. He also estimated that he would lose $5,000 in the future as the result of the past omission. The trial judge, hearing the case without a jury, allowed Scheinuk damages of $2,008. To what amount was he entitled? [Scheinuk The Florist, Inc. v Southern Bell Tel. & Tel. Co., (La App) 128 So2d 683]

10. Brown made a contract to sell a motel to the Gulf South Capital Corp. Nothing was said in the contract about paying off any mortgage or other claims against the land. When Gulf delivered the down payment the check specified that all mortgage and other claims against the land above a stated amount were to be removed or paid off by the seller. Brown returned this check and contracted to sell the same motel to another person. Gulf sued Brown for breach of contract. Decide. [Gulf South Capital Corp. v Brown, (Miss) 183 So2d 802]

11. Protein Blenders, Inc. made a contract with Gingerich to buy from his stock of a small corporation. When the buyer refused to take and pay for the stock, Gingerich sued for specific performance of the contract on the ground that the value of the stock was unknown and could not be readily ascertained because it was not sold on the general market. Was he entitled to specific performance? [Gingerich v Protein Blenders, Inc., 250 Iowa 646, 95 NW2d 522]

12. Crommelin was a candidate in a primary election seeking ultimate election to the United States Congress. He made a contract for televising two political speeches with the Montgomery Independent Telecasters. The television company refused to allow him to make the scheduled telecasts. He lost the primary election and then sued for breach of contract, claiming damages consisting of the money that he had spent for campaign expenses and the salary which he would have received as a congressman. [Crommelin v Montgomery Independent Telecasters, 280 Ala 391, 194 So2d 548]

20 Personal Property

GENERAL PRINCIPLES

Property includes the rights of any person to possess, use, enjoy, and dispose of a thing. It is not necessary that all of these rights be held by the same person at one time.

§ **20:1. Basic Property Concepts.** *Property* means the rights and interests which one has in anything subject to ownership, whether that thing be movable or immovable, tangible or intangible, visible or invisible. A right in a thing is property, without regard to whether such right is absolute or conditional, perfect or imperfect, legal or equitable.

§ **20:2. Personal Property.** *Personal property* consists of (1) things which are tangible and movable, such as furniture and books; and (2) claims and debts, which are called *choses in action.* Common forms of choses in action are insurance policies, stock certificates, bills of lading, and evidences of indebtedness, such as notes.

Personal property can be defined indirectly as including all property that is neither real property nor a lease of real property. *Real property* means all rights and interests of indefinite duration in land and things closely pertaining to land, such as trees and buildings.

(1) Expanding Concept of Personal Property. New types of personal property have developed. Thus, gas and water are generally regarded by courts as "property" for the purpose of criminally prosecuting persons who tap water mains and gas pipes and thus obtain water and gas without paying.

The modern techniques of sound and image recording have led to the necessity of giving protection against copying and competition. Federal and state statutes provide for the copyright protection of musical compositions and create new crimes of record and tape piracy.[1]

The theft of papers on which computer programs are written is larceny or "theft of property" under a statute which defines "property" as including "all writings, of every description, provided such property possesses any ascertainable value," even though the exact value of such programs cannot be determined.[2]

---

[1] PL 92-140, 85 Stat 391, 17 USC §§ 1, 5, 20, 101; Pennsylvania, Act of January 10, 1972, PL 872, 18 PS § 1878.1.

[2] Handcock v Texas, (Tex Crim App) 402 SW2d 906.

The problem of keeping the definition of "property" up-to-date is also seen when an employee is prosecuted for embezzlement when he draws a check on his employer's account with which to pay his own bills. Although embezzlement is the conversion of "property" entrusted by the owner to an employee or agent, and although no property is entrusted to the employee drawing such checks as he has not received any actual money or funds from the employer, it is generally held that the employee is guilty of embezzlement in such case. In some states it is held that the employee does not commit embezzlement, the theory being that only property which can be the subject of larceny, i.e., tangible personal property, can be the subject of embezzlement.[3]

With modern transplanting of organs, the question arises as to whether human organs are personal property. Society has assumed the "ownership" potential of human organs by the Uniform Anatomical Gift Act.

§ 20:3. Limitations on Ownership. When one has all possible existing rights in and over a thing, he is said to have *absolute ownership*. The term "absolute," however, is somewhat misleading, for one's rights in respect to the use, enjoyment, and disposal of a thing are subject to certain restrictions, such as the following:

(1) Rights of Government. All property is subject to the right of the government to compel the owner to give up a part for public purposes. This *power to tax* is an inherent right of sovereign states. By another power, called the *police power,* the government can adopt reasonable rules and regulations in respect to the use and enjoyment of property for the protection of the safety, health, morals, and general welfare of the community. This police power is in substance the power to govern for the common good. Zoning laws that restrict the use of property within specified areas may be adopted under this power.

Private property is also subject to the right of the government to take it for public purposes. This right of *eminent domain* may also be exercised by certain corporations, such as railroads and public utilities. Constitutional provisions require that fair compensation be paid the owner when property is taken by eminent domain.[4] Such provisions do not apply when there is merely a loss of value caused by the use of the police power.

(2) Rights of Creditors. Property is subject to the rights of one's creditors. It may be taken by judicial proceedings to satisfy just claims against the owner or his estate. A person cannot dispose of his property in any way so as to defeat the rights of his creditors.

(3) Rights of Others. The law restricts the use and enjoyment of property in that the owner is not allowed to use it unreasonably in a way that will

---

[3] Oregon v Tauscher, 227 Ore 1, 360 P2d 764.

[4] Board of Commissioners v Gardner, 57 NMex 478, 260 P2d 682.

injure other members of society. What is reasonable or unreasonable use of property by the owner depends upon the circumstances in a particular situation. (See p. 400, Fontainebleau Hotel Corp. v Forty-Five Twenty-Five, Inc.) For example, even though it is essential that a city dispose of trash, it may not do so by burning it at a city dump in open fires which burn and smoke continuously within a short distance of private homes, with the smoke and dirt from the fires settling on such homes; in such case, the conduct of the city was a nuisance which would be stopped by injunction and damages would be awarded to the complaining property owners and the fact that the defendant was a city did not exempt it from the prohibition against using property so as not to harm others.[5]

§ 20:4. Liability for Use of Personal Property. Ordinarily an owner is not liable for harm sustained by someone else merely because the owner's personal property was involved. Thus, the owner of an automobile generally is not liable to a third person who is run into by a thief driving the automobile. This conclusion is reached even though the owner did not take every possible precaution against theft. For example, a transportation firm which left the ignition keys in its airport limousine was not liable when a boy of 14 years of age attempted to steal the car and, in so doing, ran into and injured another person. The transportation company had no reason to foresee that the limousine would be stolen or that the thief would then drive in such a way as to cause harm.[6]

ACQUIRING TITLE TO PERSONAL PROPERTY

Title to personal property may be acquired in any of a variety of ways by the voluntary action of the owner or by the operation of law.

§ 20:5. Introduction. In this chapter the following methods will be discussed: copyrights, patents, and trademarks; accession; confusion; gifts; lost property; transfer by nonowner; occupation; escheat; and judgments.

§ 20:6. Copyrights, Patents, and Trademarks. Under its constitutional authority, Congress has adopted copyright and patent right laws to further the arts and sciences by granting artists and inventors exclusive rights in the product of their mental labors.

(1) Common-Law Copyright. At common law an author or compiler of data who did not make his work public had a right that no one could use his work without his permission. This is called a common-law copyright. It is closely related to the concept of privacy as is seen from the fact that

[5] Shearing v Rochester, 51 Misc 2d 436, 273 NYS2d 464.

[6] Canavin v Wilmington Transportation Co., 208 Pa Super 506, 223 A2d 902. Statutes frequently make it a crime to leave an automobile with keys in the ignition. When such a statute is violated, some courts hold that the person leaving the keys is liable for the damages sustained by the third person with whom the fleeing thief has a collision.

the common-law copyright is destroyed when a publication is made. Publication does not mean printing, but means any communication to others under such circumstances as to justify the belief that it was made known with the intent that it be common property.[7] Thus, anyone is free to copy material not covered by a copyright when its creator had distributed it publicly.[8]

A person having a conversation with someone has the right to repeat that conversation in a book, as against the contention of the other party, or someone on his behalf, that the conversation is subject to a common-law copyright which prevents literary use being made of the conversation without the consent of both parties.[9]

(2) Statutory Copyright. Federal statutes authorize a copyright that is not destroyed by publication. Under the federal statutes a *copyright* is a grant to an author giving him the exclusive right to possess, make, publish, and sell copies of his intellectual productions, or to authorize others to do so, for a period of 28 years, with the privilege of a renewal and an extension for an additional term of 28 years. A copyright may be secured for lists of addresses, books, maps, musical compositions, motion pictures, and similar productions, provided the work is an original expression of an idea. The copyright laws protect against the intentional copying of the manner in which an idea is expressed. Copyright protection was extended to sound recordings in 1971.

Works of domestic origin exported to foreign countries that have ratified the Universal Copyright Convention may use the internationally accepted copyright symbol © in place of or in addition to the word "Copyright" or its abbreviation. Note the form of the copyright notice on the back of the title page of this book.

The right to intellectual publication exists in respect to expressed ideas whether or not they are entirely original, new, or meritorious, as long as they are the result of independent and mental labor.

There is no right in an idea that is voluntarily communicated. Thus, if *A* discloses to *B* an idea that *A* has for a play or a sales promotion program, *A* is not entitled to payment from *B* when *B* uses that idea unless there is a contract between the parties that *B* should make such payment.[10]

(3) Right of Privacy. To some extent a right of privacy may afford protection against exploitation similar to that of the common-law copyright. When a person is a public figure, however, his public life is generally not protected by either a common-law copyright or a right of privacy. When a person dies, his family may not object to publicity or artistic works relating to the dead person. The theory of the law is that only the dead person

[7] Carpenter Foundation v Oakes, 26 Cal App 3d 784, 103 Cal Rptr 368.

[8] Columbia Broadcasting System, Inc. v DeCosta, (CA1 RI) 377 F2d 315 (creator of "Have Gun Will Travel" had made public distribution of cards bearing the uncopyrighted phrase and therefore could not recover damages for misappropriation of the phrase by the television network program).

[9] Hemingway's Estate v Random House, 53 Misc 2d 462, 279 NYS2d 51.

[10] Blaustein v Burton, 9 Cal App 3d 161, 88 Cal Rptr 319.

could have objected to the invasion of his privacy, and that ordinarily those who survive him cannot claim that their privacy is being invaded by the publicity given to the person who had died. Consent to publicity removes any restriction based on a common-law copyright or a right of privacy.

(4) Patents. A *patent* is a grant to one who has given physical expression to an idea, giving him the exclusive right to make, use, and sell, and to authorize others to make, use, and sell the invention for a period of 17 years. A patent is not renewable. The invention must be a new and useful art, machine, or composition of matter not previously known and used.

The law of patents is evolving to provide protection for computer programs.[11] Initially, such patents were denied on the theory that a program merely represented "thinking." The commercial necessity of protecting programs has led to the adoption of the view that a program may be patented when something more than mere thinking is shown. This is not a satisfactory rule of law, and corrective legislation is now pending in Congress.

If a thing is not patented or if the patent has expired, anyone may make, use, or sell it without the permission of or any payment to the original designer or creator.[12]

(5) Trademarks. A trademark is "any word, name, symbol, or device or combination thereof adopted and used by a manufacturer or merchant to identify his goods to distinguish them from those manufactured or sold by others."[13]

By Federal statute, a trademark can be registered by its owner or user. This entitles him to the exclusive use of the trademark for 20 years. A person using a trademark without the permission of the registered owner may be sued by the owner for damages.[14]

In order to be registered, a trademark must be distinctive. Ordinarily a name or symbol which is merely descriptive of the article or the name of a city or a geographic area cannot be registered as a trademark. An exception to this statement is made when the particular words have been used for so long that to the public at large they now identify the particular product and its origin. When the descriptive or geographic terms have acquired such a *secondary* meaning, they may be registered as a trademark. (See p. 400, Bardahl Oil Co. v Atomic Oil Co.)

§ 20:7. Accession. Property may be acquired by *accession,* that is, by means of an addition to or an increase of the thing that is owned, as in the case of produce of land or the young of animals. As a general rule, repairs and

---

[11] Application of Bernhart, 57 US Court of Customs and Patent Appeals, 417 F2d 1395.

[12] Plastic and Metal Fabricators, Inc. v Roy, 163 Conn 257, 303 A2d 725.

[13] 15 USC § 1127.

[14] 15 USC § 1125(a).

additions become a part of the article that is repaired or modified.[15] (See p. 402, Texas Hydraulic & Equipment Co. v Associates Discount Corp.) Likewise, when materials are furnished to another to be manufactured into an article, title to the finished article is in the owner of the materials. If the manufacturer, however, adds a large proportion of other materials, title will then usually vest in him.

A more difficult problem arises when a change in property is made against the wishes or at least without the consent of the owner. In such a case, the gaining of property by accession depends upon whether the act was done intentionally and willfully, or unintentionally and innocently.

To illustrate, when a stolen car is retaken on behalf of the owner, the car owner is entitled to keep a new engine which had been put into the car on the basis that the engine had become part of the car by accession. A good faith purchaser of the car may take from the car a sun visor, seat covers, and a gas tank which he added to the car on the basis that these items are not owned by the previous owner.[16]

In other instances the courts determine whether title has passed by accession on the basis of whether or not the labor and materials of the trespasser have changed the property into a different specie. Another rule frequently used is that title does not change by accession even though the former value of the goods has been changed, so long as there is no loss of identity. Under this rule the owner of the original material may follow it and seize it in its new shape or form, regardless of the alteration which it has undergone, so long as he can prove the identity of the original material. The factor that influences the courts in applying one or the other rule is the desire to attain as fair a result as possible under the circumstances.

These rules merely relate to the right of the original owner to obtain the return of the property taken from him. They do not relate to his right to sue the person taking the property. Under other rules of property and tort law, the person taking the owner's property from him, however innocently, is liable for money damages representing the value of the property. If the taking is not innocently done, punitive damages may also be recovered by the owner.

§ 20:8. Confusion. Personal property may be acquired when the property of two persons becomes intermingled under such circumstances that one owner forfeits his right in his goods. Under this *doctrine of confusion of goods,* if a person willfully and wrongfully mixes his own goods with those of another so as to render them indistinguishable, he loses his part of the property and the innocent party acquires title to the total mass.

The doctrine of confusion does not apply (1) when the mixture is by consent of the parties; (2) when the mixture is made without fraudulent intent, as by accident or mistake; or (3) when the goods that have been mixed

---

15 Bozeman Mortuary Ass'n v Fairchild, 253 Ky 74, 68 SW2d 756.

16 Farm Bureau Mutual Automobile Ins. Co. v Moseley, 47 Del 256, 90 A2d 485.

are of equal kind and grade, as in the case of oil, tea, and wheat. In these cases each owner is entitled to his proportionate share of the mixture.

§ **20:9. Gifts.** Title to personal property may be transferred by the voluntary act of the owner without receiving anything in exchange, that is, by *gift.* The person making the gift, the *donor,* may do so because of things which the recipient of the gift, the *donee,* has done in the past or which he is expected to do in the future, but such matters of inducement are not deemed consideration so as to alter the "free" character of the gift.

A donor may make a gift of a fractional interest in property, as when he purchases stock and has it registered in the name of himself and of the donee.[17]

(1) Inter Vivos Gifts. The ordinary gift that is made between two living persons is an *inter vivos gift.* For practical purposes the rule is that the gift takes effect upon the donor's expressing an intention to transfer title and making delivery, subject to the right of the donee to divest himself of title by disclaiming the gift within a reasonable time after learning that it has been made. Since there is no consideration for a gift, an intended donee cannot sue for breach of contract, and the courts will not compel the donor to complete the gift.

The fact that the donee is willing to return the gift if needed by the donor does not destroy the effect of a gift, where such return would be at the option of the donee and the donor did not have any right to compel the return.[18]

The circumstance that the donee agrees to make a particular use of the given property does not require the conclusion that there was no gift. Consequently, where the mother made a gift to her daughter of a joint bank account, the fact that it was labeled "reserve account" and that the daughter agreed to keep the account intact in case the money should be needed by her mother did not destroy the effect of the gift which had been made, so that upon the mother's death the representative of her estate could not claim any interest in the account as against the daughter.[19]

(a) INTENT. The intent "to make" a gift requires an intent to transfer title at that time. In contrast, an intent to confer a benefit at a future date is not a sufficient intent to create any right in the intended donee. A gift may be made subject to a condition, such as graduation, but the condition must be expressed. Thus, it may be shown that the owner of shares of stock retained such control over the stock that there was no gift even though the shares were registered in the name of the owner's wife and she received and kept the dividends on the stock, the owner proving that the transfer was made to the wife for convenience and that he did not intend that she should receive more than the dividends.[20]

---

[17] Bunt v Fairbanks, 81 SD 255, 134 NW2d 1.
[18] Trautt's Estate, 10 Ill App 2d 953, 295 NE2d 293.
[19] Hitchcock's Estate, (Mo App) 483 SW2d 617.
[20] Jenkins v Jenkins, (Miss) 278 So2d 446.

(b) DELIVERY. The delivery of a gift may be a *symbolic delivery,* as by the delivery of means of control of property, such as keys to a lock or ignition keys to an automobile, or by the delivery of papers that are essential to or closely associated with ownership of the property, such as documents of title or ship's papers. The delivery of a symbol is effective as a gift if the intent to make a gift is established; as contrasted with merely giving the recipient of the token temporary access to property, as for example, until the deliveror comes back from the hospital.[21]

A gift may be made by delivering a deed or an assignment to the donee. Thus, *A* may give his television set to *B* by delivering to *A* a signed and sealed writing which declares that *A* gives the set to *B*. This sealed writing is called a deed and would be used when the subject of the gift is a thing. If the subject of the gift is a claim, an assignment would be used. For example, if *C* was owed $100 by *D, C* could make a gift of that money to *E* by giving him a writing saying that he assigned to *E* his claim against *D*. The fact that a deed is used instead of an assignment, or vice versa, is unimportant as the courts will carry out the intent of making a gift regardless of what the document is called.

A gift may be made by depositing money in the bank account of an intended donee. If the account is a joint account in the names of two persons, a deposit of money in the account by one person may or may not be a gift to the other. Parol evidence is generally admissible to show whether there was an intention to make a gift.

When a savings account passbook is essential to the withdrawal of money from a savings account, parents do not make a gift to a minor child when they open a savings account in his name but keep possession of the passbook. Under such circumstances there was no delivery, actual or symbolic, to the son so that the parents remained the owner of the money in the savings account and were entitled thereto upon the son's death.[22] Similarly, no gift of a certificate of deposit is established when the bank would not have permitted the withdrawal of the money represented by the certificate without the consent of the alleged donor.[23]

The essential element of delivery is the relinquishment of control over the property. If the owner retains control, there is no delivery. Hence, the fact that property is placed in a jointly-owned safe deposit box does not make the sharer of the box a co-owner of the property. Consequently, upon the death of the person depositing the property, the other party does not become the owner merely because the box was rented by them as "joint tenants with the right of survivorship." This term is narrowly construed to relate only to the use of the box and not to the ownership of its contents.[24]

Ordinarily the fact that the donee uses the gift negligently does not make the donor liable to a third person injured by the donee. Thus, a mother who

---

[21] Schilling v Waller, 243 Md 271, 220 A2d 580.
[22] Ruffalo v Savage, 252 Wis 175, 31 NW2d 175.
[23] Porterfield v Porterfield's Estate, 253 Ark 1073, 491 SW2d 48.
[24] Wilson's Estate, 404 Ill 207, 88 NE2d 662.

buys an automobile for her adult son is not liable to a person injured by the son's driving, even though the mother knew that her son was an inebriate and drug addict.[25]

(c) DONOR'S DEATH. If the donor dies before doing what is needed to make an effective gift, the gift fails. An agent or the executor or administrator of the donor cannot thereafter perform the missing step on behalf of the donor. For example, in a state where a transfer of title to a motor vehicle could not be made without a transfer of the title certificate, that transfer must be made while the donor is living and cannot be made after his death by his executor.[26]

(2) Gifts Causa Mortis. A *gift causa mortis* is made when the donor, contemplating his imminent and impending death, delivers personal property to the donee with the intent that the donee shall own it if the donor dies. This is a conditional gift, and the donor is entitled to take the property back (a) if he does not die; (b) if he revokes it before he dies; (c) if the donee dies before the donor does.

(3) United States Government Savings Bonds. United States Government savings bonds are issued under a Treasury regulation which specifies that they are payable only to the registered owner and may be transferred only in the manner authorized by the regulation. They may only be surrendered to the United States Government and reissued to the donee; the owner cannot make a direct gift to the donee.[27]

(4) Uniform Gifts to Minors Act. Most states have adopted the Uniform Gifts to Minors Act,[28] which provides an additional method for making gifts to minors of money and of registered and unregistered securities. Under the Act a gift of money may be made by an adult to a minor by depositing it with a broker or a bank in an account in the name of the donor or another adult or a bank with trust powers "as custodian for [name of minor] under the [name of state] Uniform Gifts to Minors Act." If the gift is a registered security, the donor registers the security in a similar manner. If the security is unregistered, it must be delivered by the donor to another adult or a trust company accompanied by a written statement signed by the donor and the custodian, in which the donor sets forth that he delivers the described property to the custodian for the minor under the uniform act and in which the custodian acknowledges receipt of the security.[29]

Under the uniform Act the custodian is in effect a guardian of the property for the minor, but he may use it more freely and is not subject to the

[25] Estes v Gibson, (Ky) 257 SW2d 604.

[26] Varvaris v Varvaris, 255 Iowa 800, 124 NW2d 163.

[27] O'Dell v Garrett, 82 NMex 240, 478 P2d 568.

[28] The Uniform Gifts to Minors Act was originally proposed in 1956. It was revised in 1965 and again in 1966. One of these versions, often with minor variations, has been adopted in every state except Georgia and Louisiana. It has been adopted for the Virgin Islands and the District of Columbia.

[29] Uniform Gifts to Minors Act (UGMA), § 2.

many restrictions applicable to a true guardian. When property is held by a custodian for the benefit of a minor under the Uniform Gifts to Minors Act, the custodian has discretionary power to use the property for the "support, maintenance, education and benefit" of the minor but the custodian may not use the custodial property for his personal benefit.[30] The gift is final and irrevocable for tax and all other purposes upon complying with the procedure of the Act. The property can be transferred by the custodian to a third person free from the possibility that a minor donee might avoid the transfer.

(5) Conditional Gifts. A gift may be made on condition, such as "This car is yours when you graduate" or "This car is yours unless you drop out of school." The former gift is subject to a *condition precedent,* and the latter to a *condition subsequent.* That is, the condition to the first gift must be satisfied before any gift or transfer of title takes place, while the satisfaction of the second condition operates to destroy or divest a transfer of title that had taken place. Ordinarily, no condition is recognized unless it is expressly stated; but some courts regard an engagement ring as a conditional gift, particularly if the girl is the one who breaks or causes the breaking of the engagement.[31] Other gifts made by the man in contemplation of marriage are not regarded as conditional.

(6) Anatomical Gifts. The Uniform Anatomical Gift Act[32] permits anyone 18 years or older to make a gift of his body or any part or organ to take effect upon his death. The gift may be made to a school, a hospital, an organ bank, or a named patient. Such a gift may also be made, subject to certain restrictions by the spouse, adult child, parent, adult brother or sister, or guardian of a deceased person.[33] Independently of the Act, a living person may make a gift, while living, of part of his body, as in the case of a blood transfusion or a kidney transplant.

§ 20:10. Lost Property. Personal property is *lost* when the owner does not know where it is located but intends to retain title or ownership to it. The person finding lost property does not acquire title but only possession. Ordinarily the finder of lost property is required to surrender the property to the true owner when the latter establishes his ownership. Meanwhile the finder is entitled to retain his possession as against everyone else.[34]

Without a contract with the owner or a statute so providing, the finder of lost property is not entitled to a reward or to compensation for his services.

(1) Finding in Public Place. If the lost property is found in a public place, such as a hotel, under such circumstances that to a reasonable man it

[30] Schwartz's Estate, 449 Pa 112, 295 A2d 600.

[31] Goldstein v Rosenthal, (NY Civil Court) 56 Misc 2d 311, 288 NYS2d 503.

[32] This Act has been adopted in every state except California, Kentucky, Louisiana, Massachusetts, and Nebraska. It has been adopted for the District of Columbia. California and Louisiana have local statutes substantially similar to the Uniform Act.

[33] Uniform Anatomical Gift Act, §§ 2, 3.

[34] Toledo Tr. Co. v Simmons, 52 Ohio App 373, 3 NE2d 661.

would appear that the property had been intentionally placed there by the owner and that he is likely to recall where he left it and to return for it, the finder is not entitled to possession of the property but must give it to the proprietor or manager of the public place to keep it for the owner.[35] This exception does not apply if it appears that the property was not intentionally placed where it was found, because in such case it is not likely that the owner will recall having left it there.

(2) Finding on Private Property. When property is found in a private home by an outsider, such as a repairman or a contractor, the owner of the home is entitled to possession of the property, until the true owner establishes his right thereto. Where small boys trepassing in a junkyard found a glass jar containing approximately $13,000 the owner of the yard was entitled to possession of the "find" as against the small boys.[36]

In contrast, some courts permit the finder to retain the property when the identity of the owner is unknown, as long as the finder was lawfully on the premises where he found the property. For example, where a contractor, in building a recreation room, found approximately $5,000 in currency hidden behind a wooden block on the floor of a cabinet-type sink, the contractor was entitled to keep the money, as against the claim of the owner of the building.[37]

(3) Statutory Change. In some states, statutes have been adopted permitting the finder to sell the property or claim it as his own if the owner does not appear within a stated period of time. In such a case the finder is required to give notice, as by newspaper publication, in order to attempt to reach the owner.

(4) Multiple Finders. When two or more persons find property they are equally entitled to the rights of a finder. Consequently, when a statute gives a finder the ownership of the found property when not claimed by the true owner, three persons "finding" the property are each entitled to a ⅓ share when it is not claimed by the owner.[38]

§ **20:11. Transfer by Nonowner.** Ordinarily a sale or other transfer by one who does not own the property will pass no title. No title is acquired by theft. The thief acquires possession only; and if he makes a sale or gift of the property to a third person, the latter accordingly only acquires the possession of the property.[39] The true owner may reclaim the property from the

---

[35] Jackson v Steinberg, 186 Ore 129, 200 P2d 376.

[36] Bishop v Ellsworth, 91 Ill App 2d 386, 234 NE2d 49.

[37] Hurley v Niagara Falls, 30 App Div 2d 93, 289 NYS2d 889, affirmed 29 NY2d 687, 306 NYS2d 689, 254 NE2d 915. (No distinction is to be made in terms of the nature of the property or whether it is buried or hidden above the ground.)

[38] Edmonds v Ronella, 73 Misc 2d 598, 342 NYS2d 408.

[39] Barry Industries, Inc. v Aetna Cas. & Surety Co., (Dist Col App) 302 A2d 61.

thief or from his transferee, or he may sue them for the conversion of his property and recover the value of the stolen property.[40]

In some states this rule is fortified by statutes which declare that the title to an automobile cannot be transferred, even by the actual owner, without a delivery of a properly-indorsed title certificate. The states that follow the common law do not make the holding of a title certificate essential to the ownership of an automobile, although as a matter of police regulation the owner must obtain such a certificate.

As an exception to the rule that a nonowner cannot transfer title, an agent, who does not own the property but who is authorized to sell it, may transfer the title of his principal. Likewise, certain relationships create a power to sell and transfer title, such as a pledge or an entrustment. An owner of property may also be barred or estopped from claiming that he is still the owner when he had done such acts as deceive an innocent buyer into believing that someone else was the owner or had authority to sell.

§ **20:12. Occupation of Personal Property.** Title to personal property may be acquired under certain circumstances by *occupation,* that is, by taking and holding possession of the property.

(1) Wild Animals. Wild animals, living in a state of nature, are not owned by any individual. Title to them is held by the state, as sovereign, in a trustee-like capacity for the public. In the absence of restrictions imposed by game laws, the person who acquires dominion or control over a wild animal becomes its owner. What constitutes sufficient dominion or control varies with the nature of the animal and all the surrounding circumstances. If the animal is killed, tied, imprisoned, or otherwise prevented from going at its will, the hunter exercises sufficient dominion or control over the animal and becomes the owner.

If the wild animal, subsequent to its capture, should escape and return to its natural state, it resumes the status of a wild animal. The first captor thereby loses his title, and a new hunter can acquire title to the animal by capture.

As a qualification to the ordinary rule, the exception developed that if the animal is killed or captured on the land of another while the hunter is guilty of trespassing, that is, if he is upon the land without the permission of the owner, the animal when killed or captured does not belong to the hunter but to the landowner.

(a) GAME LAWS. Generally state game laws narrow the common-law rights by establishing closed seasons during which the hunter is not permitted to capture the game. A federal statute similarly protects migratory birds which fly across national boundaries. Violation of these statutes is punishable by fine or imprisonment or both.

---

[40] Farm Bureau Mutual Automobile Insurance Co. v Moseley, 47 Del 256, 90 A2d 485.

In most states the game laws widen the common-law right in certain instances. It is sometimes provided that when game is started on the land on which a person is lawfully hunting, he may follow the game onto neighboring land. This right of hot pursuit is sometimes given to any person with a hunting license, but in other instances it is limited to farmers who are hunting.

(b) POLLUTION DAMAGE TO WILD ANIMALS. When a business enterprise pollutes the environment and such pollution causes the death of wildlife, some courts allow the state to bring a suit against the polluter to recover damages for destruction of the wildlife. Other courts deny recovery by the state. (See p. 403, North Dakota v Dickinson Cheese Co.)

(2) ***Abandoned Personal Property.*** Personal property is deemed abandoned when the owner relinquishes possession of it with the intention to disclaim title to it. Yesterday's newspaper which is thrown out in the trash is abandoned personal property. Title to abandoned property may be acquired by the first person who obtains possession and control. A person becomes the owner the moment he takes possession of the abandoned personal property.

When the owner of property flees in the face of an approaching peril, the fact that he leaves property without taking it does not constitute an abandonment of the property, as an abandonment occurs only when the leaving of the property is a truly voluntary act of the owner. Consequently, paintings which an owner left in his apartment when he fled from approaching enemy armies were not abandoned and the ownership of the fleeing owner was therefore not affected.[41]

§ 20:13. Escheat. Difficult questions arise in connection with unclaimed property. In the case of personal property, the practical answer is that the property will probably disappear after a period of time, or it may be sold for unpaid charges, as by a carrier, hotel, or warehouse. A growing problem arises with respect to unclaimed corporate dividends, bank deposits, insurance payments, and refunds. It has been estimated that every year a billion dollars of such intangibles become due and owing to persons who never claim them. Most states have a statute providing for the *escheat* of such unclaimed property to the state government. A number of states have adopted the Uniform Disposition of Unclaimed Property Act.[42] The state in which the person entitled to payment resides is the state which is entitled to acquire the ownership of intangible claims by escheat.[43]

---

[41] Menzel v List, 49 Misc 2d 300, 267 NYS2d 804.

[42] The 1954 version of the Act was adopted in Alabama, Arizona, California, Florida, Idaho, Illinois, Indiana, Louisiana, Maryland, Oregon, South Carolina, South Dakota, Utah, Vermont, Virginia, Washington, and West Virginia. A revision of the Act was made in 1966, and this revised form has been adopted in Iowa, Minnesota, Montana, Nebraska, New Mexico, Oklahoma, Rhode Island, and Wisconsin.

[43] Western Union Telegraph Co. v Pennsylvania, 369 US 71.

§ 20:14. Judgments. The entry of a judgment ordinarily has no effect upon the title to personal property owned by the judgment debtor. Exceptions arise when (1) the purpose of entering the judgment is to determine title to the property as against the whole world, or (2) the action is brought to recover the value of converted personal property. In the latter case the payment of the judgment entered against the converter for the value of the goods transfers title to him as though there had been a voluntary sale.[44]

MULTIPLE OWNERSHIP OF PERSONAL PROPERTY

§ 20:15. Introduction. All interests in a particular object of property may be held in *severalty*, that is, by one person alone. Ownership in severalty also exists when title is held in the form of "*A* or *B*," as the use of the word "or" is inconsistent with co-ownership.[45]

Several persons may have concurrent interests in the same property, and the relative interests of co-owners as between themselves may differ. For example, when the owner of a bank account causes the bank to add the name of another person to the account so that either may draw checks on the account, both the original and the new owner are co-owners of the account as far as the bank is concerned. As between themselves, however, they may in fact be co-owners or the one whose name is added may merely be an agent for the other. In the latter case, while the agent has the right to withdraw money, he cannot keep the money for himself.

The forms of multiple ownership include: (1) tenancy in common, (2) joint tenancy, (3) tenancy by entirety, and (4) community property.

§ 20:16. Tenancy in Common. A *tenancy in common* is a form of ownership by two or more persons. The interest of a tenant in common may be transferred or inherited, in which case the taker becomes a tenant in common with the others. This tenancy is terminated only when there is a partition, giving each a specific portion, or when one person acquires all of the interests of the co-owners.

§ 20:17. Joint Tenancy. A *joint tenancy* is another form of ownership by two or more persons. A joint tenant may transfer his interest to a third party, but this destroys the joint tenancy. In such a case the remaining joint tenant becomes a tenant in common with the third person who has acquired the interest of the other joint tenant.

Upon the death of a joint tenant, the remaining tenants take the share of the deceased, and finally the last surviving joint tenant takes the property as a holder in severalty.[46]

When a surviving joint tenant receives the share of the predeceasing joint tenant by virtue of survivorship, the survivor does not "inherit" from the joint tenant and therefore is not subject to any estate or inheritance tax in

---

[44] Some courts hold that title passes to the converter upon the mere entry of a judgment against him although it has not yet been paid. In contrast, others hold that title passes only upon payment of the judgment to the plaintiff.

[45] Jenkins v Meyer, (Mo) 380 SW2d 315.

[46] Clausen v Warner, 118 Ind App 340, 78 NE2d 551.

states that follow the common law.[47] In some states, however, statutes have been adopted that subject the surviving tenant to the same tax as though he had inherited the fractional share of the predeceasing tenant.

(1) Statutory Change. Statutes in many states have modified the common law by adding a formal requirement to the creation of a joint tenancy with survivorship. At common law such an estate would be created by a transfer of property to "*A* and *B* as joint tenants." Under these statutes it is necessary to add the words "with right of survivorship," or similar words, if it is desired to create a right of survivorship.[48] If there is no right of survivorship, the transfer does not create a joint tenancy. Thus, a certificate of deposit issued only in the name of "*A* or *B*" does not create a joint tenancy because it does not refer to a survivor.[49]

Joint tenancy statutes permit the owner of property to transfer it directly to himself and another to obtain the advantage of survivorship without the necessity of an intermediate transfer to a strawman.[50]

Courts do not favor joint tenancy and will construe a transfer of property to several persons to be a tenancy in common whenever possible. Statutes in many states have abolished or modified joint tenancy, especially as to survivorship.

(2) Bank Accounts. The deposit of money in a joint account constitutes a gift of a joint ownership interest in the deposit of money when that is the intent of the depositor. The mere fact that money is deposited in a joint account does not in itself establish that there was such a gift, particularly where the evidence indicates that the deposits were made in the joint account "solely for the convenience of enabling either of the parties to draw therefrom for family purposes." [51] (See p. 403, Weaver's Estate v Lock.) When the joint account is merely an agency device, the account agent is not entitled to use any part of the deposit as his own money.

(a) STATUTORY CHANGE. A bank account may be transferred by gift to another person or to a co-account owner when there is an intent to make a gift and a delivery. Thus, it has been held that when the owner of a savings account changes the account to a joint account and informs the other account "owner" that it is a gift to her and delivers the savings book to her, there is an effective gift, even though the donor retains the right to withdraw from the account.[52]

Statutes in many states regulate the deposit of money in bank accounts in two names. For the most part these statutes are designed to protect the bank from suit by one of the account owners when the bank honors

---

[47] Calvert v Wallrath, (Tex) 457 SW2d 376.
[48] Nunn v Keith, 289 Ala 518, 268 So2d 792.
[49] Dalton v Eyestone, 240 Ark 1032, 403 SW2d 730.
[50] Milliken v First Nat Bank, (Me) 290 A2d 889.
[51] Stewart v Stewart, 228 Ga 517, 186 SE2d 746.
[52] Astravas v Petronis, — Mass —, 280 NE2d 183.

a check or withdrawal made by the other. In some instances the statute also regulates the rights between the co-owners, as by stating that the surviving account owner is the owner of the balance standing in the account, thus eliminating the necessity of proving that there was an intent to make a gift to him of the money on deposit.[53]

§ **20:18. Tenancy by Entirety.** At common law a *tenancy by entirety* (or tenancy by the entireties) was created when property was transferred to husband and wife in such a manner that it would create a joint tenancy if transferred to other persons, not husband and wife.[54] It differs from joint tenancy, however, in that the right of survivorship cannot be extinguished and one tenant alone cannot convey his interest to a third person, although in some jurisdictions he may transfer his right to share the possession and the profits. This form of property holding is popular in common-law jurisdictions because creditors of one of the spouses cannot reach the property while both are living. Only a creditor of both the husband and the wife under the same obligation can obtain execution against the property. Moreover, the tenancy by entirety is in effect a substitute for a will since the surviving spouse acquires the complete property interest upon the death of the other. There may be other reasons, however, why each spouse should make a will.

Generally a tenancy by the entirety is created by the mere fact that property is transferred to two persons who are husband and wife, even though it is not expressly stated that such a tenancy is thereby created, unless, of course, it is expressly stated that a different tenancy is created. This type of tenancy may also be created by either husband or wife. Thus, when a husband opens a bank account in the name of himself and his wife, or the survivor of them, and either the husband or wife may make withdrawals, a tenancy by the entirety is created as to any money that is deposited in the account, even though all deposits are made by the husband.

If the grantees are not lawfully married to each other, a tenancy by the entireties does not arise. However, the fact that a tenancy by the entireties was intended is often held a sufficient indication that there was to be survivorship, with the result that on the death of one spouse the share of the dying spouse passes to the other by survivorship. (See p. 404, Lopez v Lopez.)

In many states the granting of an absolute divorce converts a tenancy by the entireties into a tenancy in common.

§ **20:19. Community Property.** In some states property acquired during the period of marriage is the *community property* of the husband and wife. Some statutes provide for the right of survivorship; others provide that half of the property of the deceased husband or wife shall go to the heirs, or permit such half to be disposed of by will. It is commonly provided that property acquired by either spouse during the marriage is prima facie

---

[53] Wszolek's Estate, 112 NH 310, 295 A2d 444.

[54] Hoffman v Nerwell, 249 Ky 270, 60 SW2d 607.

community property, even though title is taken in the spouse's individual name, unless it can be shown that it was obtained with property possessed by that spouse prior to the marriage.[55]

[55] Lovelady v Loughridge, 204 Okla 186, 228 P2d 358.

CASES FOR CHAPTER 20

Fontainebleau Hotel Corp. v Forty-Five Twenty-Five, Inc.

(Fla) 114 So2d 357 (1959)

The Eden Roc and the Fontainebleau are neighboring hotels in Miami Beach, Florida. Fontainebleau proposed to construct a 14-story annex to its building on its land. This construction would block the view of the Atlantic Ocean for persons in the Eden Roc Hotel. The Forty-Five Twenty-Five, Inc., which was the owner of Eden Roc, brought an action against the Fontainebleau Hotel Corp. to prevent the construction of the annex. From a decision against the construction, Fontainebleau appealed.

PER CURIAM. . . . This is indeed a novel application of the maxim *sic utere tuo ut alienum non laedas*. This maxim does not mean that one must never use his own property in such a way as to do any injury to his neighbor. . . . It means only that one must never use his property so as not to injure the lawful *rights* of another. . . . "It is well settled that a property owner may put his own property to any reasonable and lawful use, so long as he does not thereby deprive the adjoining landowner of any right of enjoyment of his property *which is recognized and protected by law, and so long as his use is not such a one as the law will pronounce a nuisance*." [Emphasis supplied.]

No American decision has been cited . . . in which it has been held that—in the absence of some contractual or statutory obligation—a landowner has a legal right to the free flow of light and air across the adjoining land of his neighbor. Even at common law, the landowner has no legal right, in the absence of an easement or uninterrupted use and enjoyment for a period of 20 years, to unobstructed light and air from the adjoining land. . . .

There being, then, no legal right to the free flow of light and air from the adjoining land, it is universally held that where a structure serves a useful and beneficial purpose, it does not give rise to a cause of action, either for damages or for an injunction under the maxim *sic utere tuo ut alienum non laedas*, even though it causes injury to another by cutting off the light and air and interfering with the view that would otherwise be available over adjoining land in its natural state, regardless of the fact that the structure may have been erected partly for spite. . . .

We see no reason for departing from this universal rule. If, as contended on behalf of plaintiff, public policy demands that a landowner in the Miami Beach area refrain from constructing buildings on his premises that will cast a shadow on the adjoining premises, an amendment of its comprehensive planning and zoning ordinance, applicable to the public as a whole, is the means by which such purpose should be achieved. (No opinion is expressed here as to the validity of such an ordinance, if one should be enacted pursuant to the requirements of law.) . . . But to change the universal rule—and the custom followed in this state since its inception—that adjoining landowners have an equal right under the law to build to the line of their respective tracts and to such a height as is desired by them (in the absence, of course, of building restrictions or regulations) amounts, in our opinion, to judicial legislation. . . .

[Judgment reversed.]

Bardahl Oil Co. v Atomic Oil Co.

(CA10 Okla) 351 F2d 148 (1965)

Atomic Oil Company sold an oil product for automobiles under the name of SAV-MOTOR. It registered the name under the Lanham Trademark Act of 1946. Bardahl Oil Company sold an oil additive under the name

of SAVOIL. Atomic Oil sued Bardahl for an injunction and damages, claiming that SAVOIL infringed the registration of SAVMOTOR. Bardahl defended on the ground that the registration of SAVMOTOR under the Act was improper and that the public did not associate the mark with Atomic Oil. An injunction was granted. Bardahl appealed.

PHILLIPS, C.J. . . . On September 23, 1958, Atomic filed its application in the United States Patent Office for the registration of the trade-mark "Savmotor." In the photostat of the trade-mark in the file wrapper of the Patent Office application, the trade-mark appears in black and white. The mark is for an oil concentrate or oil additive. On the can in which the concentrate or additive is sold commercially, the mark has a red background. At the upper portion of the mark there is an atomic bomb burst design in white in the shape of a mushroom. On this white burst, in large black letters, appears "Savmotor." Below the burst appear the words, in black, "Oil Concentrate." Below that, in rather large white letters, appear the words "Motor Protection." Following that, appear the words "Product of Atomic Oil Company of Oklahoma Tulsa, Oklahoma," and at the base of the mark, on a black background, appear the words, in white, "Cars . Trucks . Tractors . Diesels." The mark was registered on January 12, 1960, as No. 691,152 under the Lanham Trade-Mark Act of 1946. The atomic bomb burst design does not appear on that trade-mark. However, on December 24, 1958, Atomic filed an application for an additional trade mark. It is substantially the same as the earlier trade-mark, except it contains in black and white the bomb burst design, with the words "Savmotor" and "Motor Oil Additive" imposed thereon in white letters. On March 15, 1960, the last-mentioned mark was granted Atomic as an additional trade mark, No. 694,445. In the registered marks, instead of "Oil Concentrate" the words used are "Oil Additive."

In 1962, the Bardahl Companies began selling, in a green can, a product of the same basic material as the Atomic product. At the top of the design of the Bardahl product, imposed on the green background, are the words, in white, "Scientifically Formulated Oil Stabilizer." Below that appears a white shield, and on that shield appear in red the letters "SAV," then a representation of a drop of oil, followed by the letters "IL." Below the shield, on a green background, appear the words, "Reduces Oil Consumption of Engines" and the words "Cars, Tractors, Trucks, Diesels." On the other side of the can, on the green background appear the letters "SAV," the representation of a drop of oil, and the letters "IL" and below that directions for use and a statement of the characteristics and functions of the Bardahl product. Among other things claimed is that it "reduces oil burning in high-mileage cars—stops embarrassing exhaust smoke, controls piston blow-by and plug fouling—while providing proper lubrication and reducing engine wear." On the side of the can, in fairly large white letters on the green background, appear the words "Bardahl Oil Company, St. Louis 20, Mo. Authorized Blender for Bardahl Manufacturing Corporation, Seattle 7, Washington."

The trial court found that the Atomic marks were descriptive words and devices and not entitled to registration under the Lanham Trade-mark Act of 1946; and it further found that the Atomic marks had acquired a secondary meaning in Missouri, Oklahoma, and Texas, and that there was a likelihood of confusion between the two marks.

The trial court granted an injunction against the Bardahl Companies, restraining them from selling their product with the mark "SAVOIL" thereon in the States of Missouri, Texas and Oklahoma. It awarded Atomic $1,485 for contempt of court for violation of the preliminary injunction which it had granted, but denied an accounting for profits or damages, on the ground that there had been no showing of fraud or intent to palm off the Bardahl product as the product of Atomic. From that judgment, both plaintiffs and defendants below have appealed.

Atomic claims that the injunction should have embraced all of the states in which it was doing business, and that it should have been awarded damages. The Bardahl Companies contend that Atomic's marks were merely descriptive and that there was no proof of a secondary meaning, even in the States of Missouri, Oklahoma and Texas.

A mark, which, when applied to the goods of the person claiming the mark, is merely descriptive of the characteristics or qualities or of the use or functions of the goods cannot be registered.

The word "save" means to protect—to preserve or guard from injury. Webster's New International Dictionary, 2d Ed. Unabridged, p. 2223. The word, here, clearly means to save the motor or protect the motor of automotive engines by improving the quality of the motor oil. Of course, as applied to the products here involved, "motor" means an automotive engine. It seems perfectly clear to us that the word "Savmotor" is descriptive of the qualities and the functions of the products and was not entitled to registration under the Lanham Act.

To acquire a secondary meaning, descriptive words must "have been used so long and so exclusively by one producer with reference to his" goods or articles "that, in that trade and to that branch of the purchasing public, the word or phrase [has] come to mean that the article" is "his product."

. . . "The application of this doctrine of secondary meaning requires that not merely 'a subordinate meaning' but 'the primary significance of the term in the minds of the consuming public . . . is not the product but the producer.' "

. . . "To establish a secondary meaning for an article it must be shown that the design is a mark of distinction identifying the source of the article and that purchasers are moved to buy it because of its source."

We have carefully examined the evidence and find no proof, whatever, that Atomic's marks had come to identify in the minds of the purchasers thereof Atomic as the manufacturer or producer of the products to which Atomic's marks were affixed. . . .

[Reversed and remanded.]

Texas Hydraulic & Equipment Co. v Associates Discount Corp.

(Tex Civ App) 414 SW2d 199 (1967)

Lane bought a dump truck on credit. The Texas Hydraulic replaced the body and hoist on the truck. Lane failed to make the payments for the truck and Associates Discount sought to foreclose on the truck. Texas Hydraulic objected that it owned the hoist and dump body which it had added to the truck. The lower court held that ownership of the body and hoist had passed to Lane and was subject to the claim of the finance company. Texas Hydraulic appealed.

PHILLIPS, C.J. . . . Appellant contends that the dump body and hoist had not become a part of the truck by accession. In this connection he points to testimony to the effect that the body and hoist, although welded to the body of the truck, can be cut off with a torch, leaving no damage to the body. On the other hand, appellee calls our attention to testimony that the dump truck had a body or hoist at the time it was originally sold, that it was not a dump truck without a dump bed and that the new dump body had been welded, and in addition bolted, to the bed of the truck.

There was ample evidence for the trial court to find that the dump body and hoist had become part of the truck by accession. . . .

It is undisputed that appellant, in making the transaction with C. H. Lane whereby the dump body and hoist were attached to the truck by welding, did not have any character of written contract with Lane, a chattel mortgage, or any other agreement which in any way purported to make the sale conditional. Nor was there any attempt to retain title to the dump body and hoist in appellant Texas Hydraulics.

Instead, the evidence given by appellant's own witness indicated that an absolute sale and transfer of the dump body and hoist was made at the time of delivery of the truck to Lane after the dump body and hoist had been welded on. Appellant had refused to release possession of the dump body and hoist until satisfactory arrangements had been made for their payment which clearly evidenced the fact that appellant was aware that delivery of the truck with the hoist and bed was a significant step in its transaction with Lane.

Upon being advised by appellant that he could not have the truck with the dump body and hoist until payment had been made, Lane informed appellant that he was expecting an insurance company to pay some money because of the damage done to the old dump body and hoist which had been removed. Appellant then made inquiry directly to the insurance company about its position, and upon receiving the promise from the insurance company that it would pay the money on the old dump body and hoist jointly to appellant and to Lane, appellant released possession of the truck, dump body and hoist to Lane and delivered the same to him, taking a delivery receipt.

Appellant relied on and accepted the promise of a third party . . . for payment before making delivery of the truck, dump body and hoist to Lane, and that, coupled with delivery and the complete absence of any attempt by appellant to enter into a written conditional sales contract, or to retain a chattel mortgage lien on the chattels sold by it clearly indicate that appellant considered the sale to be complete at the time of delivery. . . .

[Judgment affirmed.]

North Dakota v Dickinson Cheese Company, Inc.

(ND) 200 NW2d 59 (1972)

In the process of manufacturing cheese, the Dickinson Cheese Company discharged whey into the Heart River in North Dakota. This violated the North Dakota Antipollution Act. It caused the death of some 36,000 pounds of fish. North Dakota sued Dickinson and its plant manager for the damage. Judgment was entered for the defendants. The State appealed.

STRUTZ, C.J. . . . The sole question before us on this appeal is whether the State of North Dakota, as represented by the State Game and Fish Department, has such property rights in fish, while they are in the river in a free state, that the invasion of those property rights by the defendants will support an action for damages.

Fish swimming in streams of the State are *ferae naturae*. . . .

Ownership of and title to fish while they are in such state of freedom is in the State for the purpose of regulating the enjoyment, use, possession, disposition, and conservation thereof for the benefit of the people. . . .

The regulatory power of the State extends not only to the taking of its fish but also over the waters inhabited by the fish. . . .

It has been held that the power to protect fish and game is an inherent attribute of the State's sovereign power. . . .

It has been held that although the law provides that the ownership of fish, while they are in a state of freedom, is in the State for the purposes of regulation of their taking and conservation, the interest of the State in fish running wild in the streams of the State is that of a sovereign, and not that of an owner. . . .

As sovereign, the State has the power to determine when and under what conditions fish running wild may be taken and thus reduced to ownership, but it does not have such property interest in the fish while they are in a wild state sufficient to support a civil action for damages for the destruction of those fish which have not been reduced to possession. . . .

Did the . . . "Antipollution Act" bestow upon the State of North Dakota the power to maintain an action for monetary damages for the unlawful killing of fish in the wild state? We think not. That [law] was enacted to give to the State the power to control, prevent, and abate the pollution of surface waters in the State. It gives to the State of North Dakota, through its Water Pollution Control Board, acting jointly with the State Health Council, the authority to adopt, amend, or repeal rules, regulations, and standards of quality of the waters of the State, and it fixes penalties for the violation thereof. It does not give to the State ownership sufficient to support a civil action for damages against one who unlawfully pollutes a stream and thus causes the destruction of fish while they are running wild in such water. . . .

[Judgment affirmed.]

Weaver's Estate v Lock

75 Ill App 2d 227, 220 NE2d 321 (1966)

Jean Weaver opened a joint bank account in her name and the name of her daughter, Mary Lock. When Jean died the court administering Jean's estate treated the account balance as part of Jean's estate. Mary claimed the balance and appealed.

SMITH, J. . . . In 1957, Jean Weaver established a savings account with the Marine Bank and gave a power of attorney to her daughter-in-law, Mary B. Weaver, authorizing her to draw checks on the account and to endorse and deposit checks. Mary Weaver exercised her authority when Mrs. Weaver was hospitalized in 1958. In 1960, Mrs. Weaver cancelled the power of attorney and converted the savings account to a joint tenancy account with her daughter, Mary Lock. Both signed the usual joint tenancy bank card. In January 1962, she converted this account into a joint tenancy with her son, Bill Weaver, both signing the joint tenancy card. In September 1962, she restored the same account to a joint tenancy with Mary Lock, both signing the card. Mrs. Weaver was hospitalized twice in 1964, the second time being her last. She suffered a stroke about October 15, and was unable to communicate as a result of paralysis. She was then 77 years old. On November 24, Mary Lock was appointed conservator. Jean Weaver died December 23, 1964. Mary Lock filed her inventory after the death of Jean Weaver and listed the savings account as "now the property of Mary W. Lock." Objections to the final report and to this item were filed by an heir. The objections were sustained. There is no doubt but that the funds originally were those of Jean Weaver.

The understanding creation of a joint tenancy bank account creates a presumption of a gift to the survivor and such presumption can be overcome only by clear and convincing evidence that no gift was intended. . . . Clear and convincing evidence is that quantum of proof which leaves no reasonable doubt in the mind of the trier of fact of the truth of the fact in issue. . . . Where the account is created for the convenience of the decedent, the donative intent is rebutted. . . . Where the evidence shows clearly and convincingly that the donative intent was present and the survivor was to be the ultimate recipient, the right of survivorship will be enforced. . . . In the light of these principles, we turn to the evidence.

The objector, Bill Weaver, testified that when his mother asked him to sign the joint tenancy card, he asked "why" and she said, "I am frequently ill and I can't get out and I sometimes need money to pay bills and I want you to go and do it for me." He suggested to her that he could get her money and she said, "I don't think you will; it is my money and I am only doing it so that if I am unable to get out someone can do this for me." Mary Lock testified: "The first person that suggested that I had some right to this money was Mr. Hoffman at the bank. It was news to me. . . . Mr. Hoffman wanted to put it in my name and my husband's. I said no, she is not gone, she may not go. My mother never told me she put the money in the bank in order [that] it would be mine when she died. She never told me that." It seems clear to us that the presumption of donative intent, be it treated as engendered by the mother-daughter relationship or by the agreement or by both, is thus clearly and effectively negated. The frequent changes suggest a fitting pattern of convenience and indicate no intention of an ultimate gift to the other joint tenant. . . . It is clear that no present gift of an interest in the fund was intended and, further, none of the successive joint tenants even thought so. The judgment of the trial court was correct.

[Judgment affirmed.]

Lopez v Lopez

250 Md 491, 243 A2d 588 (1968)

Alejo Lopez was married to Soledad. While still married to her, he married Helen in 1946. In 1947 and 1952 two parcels of real estate were conveyed to Alejo and Helen "his wife, as tenants by the entireties." Soledad divorced Alejo in 1954 and a week later Alejo remarried Helen. Alejo was killed in an accident. Helen claimed both tracts of land by survivorship. The court held that Helen was the sole owner of the two parcels. An appeal was taken by the beneficiaries of the trust created by Alejo's will.

SINGLEY, J. . . . The first parcel was conveyed in 1947 to "Alejo Lopez and Helen Lopez, his wife, as tenants by the entirety, the survivors of them . . ."; the second parcel was deeded in 1952 to the "party(ies) of the second part ["Alejo L. Lopez and Helen G. Lopez, his wife"] . . . as Tenants by the Entirety."

Alejo's and Helen's marriage was clearly invalid prior to the second ceremony in 1954. The beneficiaries claim that both parcels were owned solely by Alejo Lopez at the time of his death and that title should have passed to the trust under his will. They argue that title to properties conveyed to parties as husband and wife, when there was no valid marriage relationship, should be vested in the party who provided the consideration, in this case Alejo. Helen, while admitting that tenancies by the entirety were not created, contends that an intent to create rights of survivorship has been shown, sufficient to vest title in Helen, as the survivor of Alejo.

In our view, Helen must prevail. We are here dealing with deeds which convey property to the grantees as husband and wife. Had they been validly married, a tenancy by the entirety would have been created. . . . However, a tenancy by the entirety can only be created when the parties stand in relationship of husband and wife at the time of the grant to them . . . . Absent such a relationship, the attempt to create a tenancy by the entirety fails. Generally, in the case of a deed conveying property to grantees as husband and wife who are in fact not married, there is a presumption favoring tenancies in common, but this presumption will yield to the showing of a contrary intent. . . . In the instant case, we regard Alejo's attempt to take title as tenants by the entirety as a sufficient showing of his intention to create a right of survivorship, and the presumption favoring a tenancy in common must yield to a joint tenancy. . . .

. . . A subsequent marriage does not convert a joint tenancy or a tenancy in common into a tenancy by the entirety. . . .

[Judgment affirmed.]

QUESTIONS AND CASE PROBLEMS

1. Carol and Robert, both over 21, became engaged. Robert gave Carol an engagement ring. He was killed in an automobile crash before they were married. His estate demanded that Carol return the ring. Was she entitled to keep it? [Cohen v Bayside Federal Savings and Loan Ass'n, 62 Misc 2d 738, 309 NYS2d 980]
2. Adele Barret purchased corporate stock jointly in her name and the name of her niece, Mary Oliver, with the right of survivorship. When Adele died, the persons who received her estate claimed that the taxes on the estate should be paid proportionately by Mary since she was benefiting from the death of Adele. Decide. [Barret's Estate, (Fla App) 137 So2d 587]
3. Hughes and Kay were not married, but property was deeded to them as "husband and wife." Subsequently they brought an action to determine their rights in the property. What type of tenancy was created by the deed? [Hughes v Kay, 194 Ore 519, 242 P2d 788]
4. The owner of an investment account certificate issued by a savings and loan association directed the association to name him and the church of which he was a member "as joint tenants with right of survivorship." When the owner opened the account he had signed a signature card. The association did not require a new signature card after being told to add the church as a co-owner, and no representative of the church ever signed any card or other document. Interest payments on the certificate were made to the original owner until his death and the church never knew of the transaction until the original owner died. The executor of the original owner then brought action against the church to determine the owner of the certificate. Was the church entitled to the certificate? [Wantuck v United Savings and Loan Association, (Mo) 461 SW2d 692]
5. Brogden acquired a biblical manuscript in 1945. In 1952 he told his sister Lucy that he wanted Texas A. & M. College to have this manuscript. He

dictated a note so stating and placed it with the manuscript. He made some effort to have an officer of the college come for the manuscript. In 1956 he delivered the manuscript to his sister, stating that he was afraid that someone would steal it. Later in the year he told a third person that he was going to give the manuscript to the college. In 1957 he was declared incompetent. In 1959 the sister delivered the manuscript to the college. In April, 1960, Brogden died, and his heirs, Bailey and others, sued Harrington and other officers of the college to have the title to the manuscript determined. Decide. [Harrington v Bailey, (Tex Civ App) 351 SW2d 946]

6. Lyons and his wife had a savings account in a bank in the names of "E. L. Lyons or Mrs. E. L. Lyons." Both husband and wife signed a signature card agreeing to the rules and regulations of the bank. Did this create a tenancy by the entireties? [Lyons' Estate, (Fla) 90 So2d 39]
7. In 1922 John Vlcek and Julia were married in Europe. He came alone to the United States and lived with Matilda. In 1948 property was purchased by them and the deed made the transfer to "Stephen and Matilda Vlcek." Stephen died in 1958. The two women and their children claimed the property. Who was entitled? [Vlcek v Vlcek, 42 App Div 2d 308, 346 NYS2d 893]
8. Henry Larson delivered a check to his son, Clifford, for $8,500. The check bore the notation "As Loan." Some time later the son asked the father what he should do about the loan. Henry wrote Clifford a note in broken English saying "Keep it No Return." Henry died and the cancelled check with the notation "As Loan" was found among his papers. Henry's administratrix sued Clifford for repayment of the loan. Did he have any defense? [Larson's Estate, 71 Wash 2d 349, 428 P2d 558]
9. Land was conveyed to Mattie Moring and Richard Roundtree as joint tenants with the right of survivorship. Mattie mortgaged the land to D.A.D., Inc., without the consent or knowledge of Richard. D.A.D. brought a foreclosure action on the mortgage. Mattie died. Was D.A.D. entitled to enforce the mortgage (a) as to all of the land, (b) as to Mattie's one-half interest, (c) as to none of the land? [D.A.D., Inc. v Moring, (Fla App) 218 So2d 451]
10. Semple conveyed land to William Thompson and his brother A. C. Thompson, as "tenants by the entireties." A C. Thompson died and his personal representative, the Pennsylvania Bank and Trust Company, claimed that the Semple deed had created a tenancy in common. William claimed that it had created a joint tenancy and that he was accordingly entitled to all of the land by survivorship. Was he correct? [Pennsylvania Bank and Trust Co. v Thompson, 432 Pa 262, 247 A2d 771]
11. Frank Stamets opened a savings account in the First National Bank. The account stood in the name of "Frank Stamets or Lena Stamets," Lena being being his sister. The signature, which was signed by Frank only, stated that the account was owned by Frank and Lena as joint tenants with the right of survivorship. All the money deposited was Frank's. The signature card was never signed by Lena. On Frank's death, Lena claimed the bank account. The estate of Frank claimed it on the ground that Lena had never signed the signature card. Decide. [Stamets' Estate, 260 Iowa 93, 148 NW2d 468]

21 Bailments

GENERAL PRINCIPLES

Many instances arise in which the owner of personal property entrusts it to another. A person checks his coat at a restaurant or loans his car to a friend. He delivers a watch to a jeweler for repairs,[1] takes furniture to a warehouse for storage, or delivers goods to an airline for shipment. The delivery of property under such circumstances is a bailment.

§ **21:1. Definition.** A *bailment* is the legal relation that arises whenever one person delivers possession of personal property to another person under an agreement or contract by which the latter is under a duty to return the identical property to the former or to deliver it or dispose of it as agreed.[2] The person who turns over the possession of the property is the *bailor.* The person to whom he gives the possession is the *bailee.*

§ **21:2. Elements of Bailment.** Because of the complex nature of bailment it is often necessary to break it down into specific categories in order to obtain a clear understanding of each element. The following list provides a discussion of each element in detail.

(1) Agreement. The bailment is based upon an agreement.[3] Technically the bailment is the act of delivering the property to the bailee and the relationship existing thereafter. The agreement that precedes this delivery is an agreement to make a bailment rather than the actual bailment. Generally this agreement will contain all the elements of a contract so that the bailment transaction in fact consists of (a) a contract to bail and (b) the actual bailing of the property. Ordinarily there is no requirement that the contract of bailment be in writing.[4]

The statute of frauds does not apply to a bailment agreement. If there is a written agreement, the parol evidence rule is applicable to the agreement if complete. If the written agreement is not complete, the missing terms may be proven by parol evidence.[5]

(2) Personal Property. The subject of a bailment may be any personal property of which possession may be given. Real property cannot be bailed.

---

[1] Dick v Reese, 90 Idaho 447, 412 P2d 315.

[2] Sullivant v Penn. Fire Insurance Co., 223 Ark 721, 268 SW2d 372.

[3] Greenberg v Shoppers' Garage, Inc., 329 Mass 31, 105 NE2d 839.

[4] In some states, however, a writing or recording of the bailment agreement may be necessary to protect the interest of the bailor.

[5] Russom v INA, (CA6 Tenn) 421 F2d 985.

*(3) **Bailor's Interest.*** The bailor is usually the owner of the property, but ownership by him is not required. It is sufficient that the bailor have physical possession. Thus, an employee may be a bailor in leaving his employer's truck at a garage. Whether possession is lawful or not is immaterial. A thief, for example, may be a bailor.

*(4) **Bailee's Interest.*** Title to the property does not pass to the bailee, and he cannot sell the property to a third person unless the bailee is also an agent to make such a sale. If he attempts to do so, his act only transfers possession and the owner may recover the property from the third person.

The bailor may cause third persons to believe that the bailee is the owner of the bailed property. If he does so, he may be estopped to deny that the bailee is the owner as against persons who have relied on the bailor's representations. As a further exception, if the bailee is a dealer in goods of the kind entrusted to him by the bailor, a sale by the bailee to a buyer in ordinary course of business will pass the bailor's title to the buyer.

*(5) **Delivery and Acceptance.*** The bailment arises when, pursuant to the agreement of the parties, the property is delivered to the bailee and accepted by him as subject to the bailment agreement. (See p. 417, Theobald v Satterthwaite.) Thus, no bailment arises when an employee leaves his tools in his workbench overnight, particularly where the employee had been informed by the employer that the latter would not be responsible for any loss of tools.[6]

Delivery may be actual, as when the bailor physically hands a book to the bailee. Or it may be a *constructive delivery,* as when the bailor points out a package to the bailee who then takes possession of it.

*(6) **Return of Specific Property.*** A bailment places a duty upon the bailee to return the specific property that was bailed or to deliver or dispose of it in the manner directed by the bailor. If a person has an option of paying money or of returning property other than that which was delivered to him, there is generally no bailment. Thus, when a farmer delivers wheat to a grain elevator that gives him a receipt and promises to return either the wheat or a certain amount of money upon presentation of the receipt, the relationship is not a bailment.[7] The importance of this distinction lies in the fact that when the relationship is not a bailment but some other relationship, such as a sale, the risk of loss will ordinarily be on the warehouse if the property is damaged or destroyed; whereas, if it is a bailment, the bailor would ordinarily bear the loss.

(a) BAILMENT OF FUNGIBLE GOODS. In the case of the bailment of *fungible goods,* such as grain and oil, where any one unit or quantity is

[6] Collins v Boeing Co., 4 Wash App 705, 483 P2d 1282.

[7] In some states, however, statutes declare that the relationship between the farmer and the grain elevator is a bailment and not a sale. United States v Haddix & Sons, Inc., (CA6 Mich) 415 F2d 584.

exactly the same as any other unit or quantity, the law treats the transaction as a bailment when there is an obligation to return only an equal quantity of goods of the same description as the goods originally delivered. Thus, an agreement by a grain elevator receiving 1,000 bushels of Grade A wheat from a farmer to return to him on demand 1,000 bushels of Grade A wheat gives rise to a bailment even though there is no agreement that the identical wheat delivered by the farmer is to be returned to him.

An "identical return" bailment might be made in some cases, as when a farmer has developed some experimental seed which he desires to be returned to him. Ordinarily, however, the grain that a farmer delivers to the elevator will be a recognized commercial variety so that the elevator is likely to have, or is likely to receive thereafter, identically similar grain from other farmers, in which case the warehouse will not ordinarily undertake to return to any one customer the identical grain delivered by that customer to the elevator but merely an equivalent quantity of grain.

(b) Option to Purchase. In an option to purchase, the transaction is a bailment, with the rights and liabilities of the parties being determined on that basis, until the bailee exercises the option. Theoretically this is inconsistent with the definition of bailment because it contradicts the obligation of the bailee to return the identical property.

The bailment with an option to purchase may sometimes be used in connection with credit sales, in which case the "rental" payments by the bailee (who is actually the buyer) will be calculated in terms of the amount due on the balance of the purchase price; and upon exercising the option to purchase, the bailee-buyer will be required to pay any unpaid balance of the purchase price.[8]

§ 21:3. Classifications of Bailments. Bailments are classified as ordinary and extraordinary. *Extraordinary bailments* are those in which the bailee is given unusual duties and liabilities by law, as in the case of bailments in which a motel or a common carrier is the bailee. *Ordinary bailments* include all other bailments.

Bailments may or may not provide for compensation to the bailee. Upon that basis they may be classified as *contract bailments* and *gratuitous bailments*. Contract bailments are those mutually agreed upon. If a minor rightfully cancels a purchase and offers to return the goods to the seller but the latter wrongly refuses to accept the goods, the minor, while still in possession of the goods, is a gratuitous bailee.[9]

Bailments may also be classified as for the (1) sole benefit of the bailor, as when a farmer gratuitously transports another's produce to the city; (2) sole benefit of the bailee, as when a person borrows the automobile of a friend; or (3) benefit of both parties (mutual-benefit bailment), as when

---

[8] This is a secured transaction which is regulated by Article 9 of the UCC (see Ch. 35).

[9] Loomis v Imperial Motors, 88 Idaho 74, 396 P2d 467.

one rents a power tool. A mutual-benefit bailment also arises when a prospective buyer of an automobile leaves his present car with the dealer so that the latter may test and make an appraisal of it for a contemplated trade-in.[10]

§ 21:4. Constructive Bailments. When one person comes into possession of personal property of another without the owner's consent, the law treats the possessor as though he were a bailee. Sometimes this relationship is called a *constructive bailment*. It is thus held that a person who finds lost property must treat that property as if he were a bailee.

A police officer taking possession of stolen goods is deemed a bailee for the true owner. A seller who has not yet delivered the goods to his buyer is treated as the bailee of the goods if title has passed to the buyer. Similarly, a buyer who is in possession of goods, the title to which has not passed to him, is a bailee.

Likewise, when an armored car service left a money bag with a bank by mistake the bank became a constructive bailee under a gratuitous bailment.[11]

§ 21:5. Renting of Space Distinguished. The renting of space in a locker or building does not give rise to a bailment by the placing of goods by the renter in the space when under the rental agreement he has the exclusive right to use the space. In such a case, putting property into the space does not constitute a delivery of the goods into the possession of the owner of the space. On this basis, there is no bailment in a self-service parking lot when the car owner parks his car, retains the key, and his only contact with any parking lot employee is upon making payment when leaving the lot. In such situations the car owner merely rents the space for parking. (See p. 419, Rhodes v Pioneer Parking Lot, Inc.)

The practical consequence of this conclusion is that if the car is damaged or if it disappears, the car owner cannot recover damages from the parking lot management unless the owner can show some fault on the part of the parking lot.[12] If the transaction were a bailment, the owner of the car would establish a prima facie right to recover by proving the fact of the bailment and that there was a loss.

If the parking lot is a locked enclosure with a guard to whom the patron must surrender a parking ticket received on entering the lot and pay any parking fee that is not yet paid, a modern trend regards the transaction as a bailment.[13] The theoretical objection to this view is that the lot does not have full dominion and control over the car since it cannot move the car because the patron has retained possession of the keys. At the same time, since it has the power to exclude others from the car, it is "realistic" to treat the parking lot as a bailee and hold it to a bailee's standard of care.

---

[10] Sampson v Birkeland, 63 Ill App 2d 178, 211 NE2d 139.
[11] Armored Car Service, Inc. v First National Bank, (Fla App) 144 So2d 431.
[12] Wall v Airport Parking Co., 41 Ill 2d 506, 244 NE2d 190.
[13] Liberty Mutual Insurance Co. v Meyers Brothers Operations, Inc., (NY Civil Court) 315 NYS2d 196.

§ 21:6. Bailment of Contents of Container. It is a question of the intention of the parties, as that appears to a reasonable person, whether the bailing of a container also constitutes a bailment of articles contained in it; that is, whether a bailment of a truck is a bailment of articles in the truck, whether a bailment of a coat is a bailment of articles in the pockets of the coat, and so on. When the contained articles are of a nature that are reasonably or normally to be found in the container, they are regarded as bailed in the absence of an express disclaimer. If the articles are not of such a nature and their presence in the container is unknown to the bailee, there is no bailment of such articles. Consequently, the parking of a car which constituted a bailment was not a bailment of valuable drawings and sporting equipment which were on the back seat but which were not visible from outside the car.[14]

§ 21:7. Duties and Liabilities of the Bailee.

(1) Performance. If the bailment is based upon a contract, the bailee must perform his part of the contract and is liable to the bailor for any loss arising out of his failure to do so. If the bailment is for repair, the bailee is under the duty to make the repairs properly. The fact that the bailee uses due care does not excuse him for failing to perform according to his contract. (See p. 418, Baena Brothers v Welge.)

A repairman to whom property, such as an automobile, is entrusted is both a bailee and a contracting party. Consequently, in addition to his obligation to care for the property as a bailee, he must perform his duties as a contracting party. When he undertakes to repair, some courts find an implied warranty that the repair will be effective. Should the repairman fail to repair properly, the bailor who uses the property with knowledge that it had not been effectively repaired, will be barred from claiming for damages sustained through injury arising from such use. For example, when the bailor was aware of the fact that the automobile repairman had failed to repair the brakes, the bailor could be barred by his contributory negligence from recovering damages from the repairman for an injury sustained when the automobile could not be stopped because of the defective brakes and struck a utility pole.[15]

(2) Care of the Property. The bailee is under a duty to care for the property entrusted to him. If the property is damaged or destroyed, the bailee is liable for the loss (a) if the harm was caused in whole or in part by the bailee's failure to use reasonable care under the circumstances, or (b) if the harm was sustained during unauthorized use of the property by the bailee. Otherwise the bailor bears the loss. Thus, if the bailee was exercising due care and was making an authorized use of the property, the bailor must bear the loss of or damage to the property caused by an act of a third person, whether willful or negligent, by an accident or occurrence for which no one

---

[14] Cerreta v Kinney Corp., 50 NJ Super 514, 142 A2d 917.
[15] Bereman v Burdolski, 204 Kan 162, 460 P2d 567.

is at fault, or by an act of God. In this connection the term *act of God* means a natural phenomenon that it is not reasonably foreseeable, such as a sudden flood or lightning.

Some courts hold that in the automobile parking lot situation the operator of the lot has the duty to exercise ordinary care for the protection of the automobile regardless of whether the relationship is a bailment or some other relationship, such as a leasing of space or the granting of a license to use the parking lot.[16]

(a) STANDARD OF CARE. The standard for ordinary bailments is reasonable care under the circumstances, that is, the degree of care which a reasonable person would exercise in the situation in order to prevent the realization of reasonably foreseeable harm. The significant factors in determining what constitutes reasonable care in a bailment are the time and place of making the bailment, the facilities for taking care of the bailed property, the nature of the bailed property, the bailee's knowledge of its nature, and the extent of the bailee's skill and experience in taking care of goods of that kind.

The bailee is not an insurer of the safety of the property, even though he assures the bailor that he will take good care of the property;[17] and he is not liable when there is no proof of his negligence as a cause of the harm nor of his unauthorized use of the property.

(b) CONTRACT MODIFICATION OF LIABILITY. A bailee's liability may be expanded by contract. A provision that he assumes absolute liability for the property is binding, but there is a difference of opinion as to whether a stipulation to return the property "in good condition" or "in as good condition as received" has the effect of imposing such absolute liability. An ordinary bailee may limit his liability, except for his willful conduct, by agreement or contract; but modern cases hold that a specialized commercial bailee, such as an auto parking garage, cannot limit its liability for either its willful or negligent conduct.[18]

By definition a limitation of liability must be a term of the bailment contract before any question arises as to whether it is binding. Thus, a limitation contained in a receipt mailed by a bailee after receiving a coat for storage is not effective to alter the terms of the bailment as originally made.[19]

(c) INSURANCE. In the absence of a statute or contract provision, a bailee is not under any duty to insure for the benefit of the bailor the property entrusted to his care.[20]

---

[16] Equity Mutual Insurance Co. v Affiliated Parking, Inc., (Mo) 448 SW2d 909.

[17] Peacock Motor Co. v Eubanks, (Fla) 145 So2d 498.

[18] In some states, statutes expressly prohibit certain kinds of paid bailees from limiting their liability. Universal Cigar Corp. v The Hertz Corp., 55 Misc 2d 284 NYS2d 337.

[19] Fisher v Herman, (NY Civil Court) 63 Misc 2d 44, 310 NYS2d 270.

[20] Commodity Credit Corp. v American Equitable Assurance Co., 198 Ark 1160, 133 SW2d 433.

(3) Unauthorized Use. The bailee is liable for conversion, just as though he stole the property, if he uses the property without authority or uses it in any manner to which the bailor had not agreed. Ordinarily he will be required to pay compensatory damages, although punitive damages may be inflicted when the improper use was deliberate and the bailee was recklessly indifferent to the effect of his use upon the property.

(4) Return. The bailee is under a duty to return the identical property which is the subject of the bailment or to deliver it as directed. The redelivery to the bailor or delivery to a third person must be made in accordance with the terms of the contract as to time, place, and manner. When the agreement between the parties does not control these matters, the customs of the community govern.

Special statutes may protect the lessor of personal property, as by making it a special criminal offense for the lessee to convert rented property. The statute may create a presumption or inference to aid in the prosecution of the wrongdoer, similar to the presumption created in the case of a bad-check law. For example, a statute may declare that it is prima facie evidence of intent to defraud for a person renting property to sign the rental agreement or lease with a name other than his own or to fail to return the property to its owner within 10 days after being personally served with a written demand for it. In some states it is a crime to abandon or conceal rented goods, such as an automobile.[21]

The bailee is excused from delivery when the goods are lost, stolen, or destroyed without his fault. If his fault or neglect has caused or contributed to the loss, however, he is liable. To illustrate, certain goods are destroyed by a flood while in the possession of the bailee. If the bailee could have protected the goods from the flood by taking reasonable precautions, the bailee is liable.

The bailee is excused from the duty to return the goods when they have been taken from him under process of law. To illustrate, if the police seize the property as stolen goods, the bailee is no longer under a duty to return the goods to the bailor.

If the bailee has a lien on the property, he is entitled to keep possession of the property until he has been paid the claim on which the lien is based.

§ 21:8. Burden of Proof. When the bailor sues the bailee, the bailor has the burden of proving that the bailee was at fault and that such fault was the proximate cause of the loss. (See p. 420, Axelrod v Wardrobe Cleaners, Inc.) A prima facie right of the bailor to recover is established, however, by proof that the property was delivered by the bailor to the bailee and thereafter could not be returned or was returned in a damaged condition. If the loss was caused by fire or theft, the bailee need show only the cause of the loss; and the bailor does not recover from the bailee unless the bailor is able to

---

[21] New Jersey v Madewell, 63 NJ 506, 309 A2d 201.

prove affirmatively that the bailee was negligent and that such negligence contributed to or caused the loss.[22]

§ **21:9. Rights of the Bailor.** If the bailor is obligated to render a service to the bailee, his failure to do so will ordinarily bar the bailor from recovering compensation from the bailee. Consequently, where a customer rented a typewriter from a typewriter-renting business and the business agreed to keep the typewriter in good working condition, the business was not entitled to recover rental payments when the typewriter did not work and the business could not put it in good working condition.[23]

(1) Rights Against the Bailee. The bailor may sue the bailee for breach of contract if the goods are not redelivered to the bailor or delivered to a third person as specified by the bailment agreement. He may also maintain actions for negligence, willful destruction, and unlawful retention or conversion of the goods. Actions for unlawful retention or conversion can be brought only after the bailor is entitled to possession.

When the bailee obtains possession of the goods by fraudulently inducing the bailor to make the bailment, the bailee is guilty of conversion. For example, where a television service man fraudulently told a customer that he wanted to take the set from the customer's home to the shop of the repairman's employer in order to show the employer how badly prior repairs had been made by another employee of the employer, but the actual purpose was to obtain and keep possession of the set until the customer paid improper service charges, the conduct of the repairman constituted a conversion and the customer may recover from the employer the value of the set and may also recover punitive damages of three times the value of the set.[24]

The fact that the bailment contract stipulates that the bailee shall return the goods in good condition, reasonable wear and tear excepted, is generally regarded as not changing the rules as to incidence of loss. Thus, the bailor, as in the ordinary case, bears the risk of loss from fire of unknown origin; and the bailee is not made an insurer against fire by the inclusion of such terms in the bailment contract.[25]

(2) Rights Against Third Persons. The bailor may sue third persons damaging or taking the bailed property from the bailee's possession, even though the bailment is for a fixed period that has not expired. In such a case

---

[22] This is the majority view. The minority courts are influenced by the consideration that fire or theft loss may often be the result of the bailee's negligence and that in any case the bailee has the means of protecting the property and superior means of knowing just what happened. By these courts the bailee should be required to prove freedom from negligence as well as the fact that the loss was caused by fire or theft. Threlkeld v Breaux Ballard, 296 Ky 344, 177 SW2d 157.

[23] Royal McBee Corp. v Bryant, (Dist Col App) 217 A2d 603.

[24] Schaffner v Pierce, 347 NYS2d 411.

[25] Edward Hines Lumber Co. v Purvine Logging Co., 240 Ore 60, 399 P2d 893.

the bailor is said to recover damages for injury to his *reversionary interest,* that is, the right which he has to regain the property upon the expiration of the period of the bailment.

§ 21:10. Duties and Liabilities of Bailor.

(1) Condition of the Property. In a mutual-benefit bailment for hire, the bailor is under a duty to furnish goods reasonably fit for the purpose contemplated by the parties. If the bailee is injured or if his property is damaged because of the defective condition of the bailed property, the bailor may be liable. If the bailment is for the sole benefit of the bailee, the bailor is under a duty to inform the bailee of those defects of which he is actually aware, but he is not under any duty to look for defects. If the bailee is harmed by a defect that was known to the bailor, the bailor is liable for damages. If the bailor receives a benefit from the bailment, he must not only inform the bailee of known defects, but he must also make a reasonable investigation to discover defects. The bailor is liable for the harm resulting from defects which would have been disclosed had he made such an examination, in addition to those which were known to him from an unknown defect.

If the defect would not have been revealed by a reasonable examination, the bailor, regardless of the classification of the bailment, is not liable for harm which results.

In any case the bailee, if he knows of the defective condition of the bailed property, is barred by his contributory negligence or assumption of risk if, in spite of that knowledge, he makes use of the property and sustains injury because of its condition.

(a) HARM TO BAILEE'S EMPLOYEE. When harm is caused a bailee's employee because of the negligence of the bailor, the latter is liable to the employee of the bailee, even though the employee did not have any direct dealings or contractual relationship with the bailor.

(b) BAILOR'S IMPLIED WARRANTY. In many cases the duty of the bailor is described as an implied warranty that the goods will be reasonably fit for their intended use. Apart from an implied warranty, the bailor may expressly warrant the condition of the property, in which event he will be liable for the breach of the warranty to the same extent as though he had made a sale rather than a bailment of the property.

With the modern rise of car and equipment renting, there is beginning to appear a new trend in cases that extends to the bailee and third persons the benefit of an implied warranty by the bailor that the article is fit for its intended use and will remain so, as distinguished from merely that it was reasonably fit, or that it was fit at the beginning of the bailment, or that the property was free from defects known to the bailor or which reasonable investigation would disclose. (See p. 421, Cintrone v Hertz Truck Leasing & Rental Service.)

The significance of analysis on the basis of warranty lies in the fact that warranty liability may exist even though the bailor was not negligent.[26]

When a used car is loaned to a prospective buyer to "test drive," there is no implied warranty that it is fit for use although the dealer as bailor will be liable for negligence if he failed to exercise reasonable care to discover any defect in the car,[27] or failed to disclose to the buyer any defect of which he had knowledge. When the bailee has reason to know that the bailor has purchased, rather than manufactured, the equipment he is renting to the bailee and that the bailor has no special knowledge with respect to the equipment, a warranty of fitness for purpose may be disclaimed by the bailment agreement.[28]

(2) Repair of the Property. Under a rental contract the bailor has no duty to make repairs that are ordinary and incidental to the use of the goods bailed. The bailee must bear the expense of such repairs, in the absence of a contrary contract provision. If, however, the repairs required are of an unusual nature or if the bailment is for a short period of time, the bailor is required to make the repairs unless they were caused by the negligence or fault of the bailee.

§ 21:11. Liability to Third Persons. When the bailee injures a third person with the bailed property, as when a bailee runs into a third person while he is driving a rented automobile, the bailee is liable to the third person to the same extent as though the bailee were the owner of the property. When the bailee repairs bailed property, he is liable to third persons who are injured in consequence of the negligent way in which he has made the repair. Conversely, the bailee is not liable to a third person who is injured by a thief who steals the bailed property from the bailee even though the theft was possible because the bailee was negligent.

The bailor is ordinarily not liable to a third person. (See p. 423, Dukes v McGimsey.) Unless the bailee is acting as the employee or agent of the bailor, a fault or negligence of the bailee is not imputed to the bailor.

The bailor is liable, however, to the injured third person: (1) if the bailor has entrusted a dangerous instrumentality to one whom he knew was ignorant of its dangerous character; (2) if the bailor has entrusted an instrumentality such as an automobile to one whom he knows to be so incompetent or reckless that injury of third persons is a foreseeable consequence; (3) if

---

[26] United Airlines, Inc. v Johnson Equipment Co., (Fla App) 227 So2d 528 (sustaining right of plaintiff to a new trial on the warranty theory, although the first trial on the theory of negligence had ended with a verdict in favor of the defendant, that is, with the conclusion that the defendant was not negligent. The commercial lessor may also be liable on the strict tort theory). See § 26:3(2) and § 26:18.

[27] Smith v Mooers, 206 Va 307, 142 SE2d 473.

[28] Northwest Collectors, Inc. v Gerritsen, 74 Wash 2d 690, 446 P2d 197. (The lessee selected the supplier, and the particular goods were then purchased from that supplier by the bailor under an agreement that the bailor would rent the goods to the bailee.) Note that if the bailment is actually a plan of selling on installment payments to the bailee, a disclaimer of warranties must satisfy the requirements of a disclaimer provision in a sales contract under Article 2 of the Uniform Commercial Code.

the bailor has entrusted property with a defect that causes harm to the third person when the circumstances are such that bailor would be liable to the bailee if the latter were injured because of the defect; [29] or (4) if the bailee is using the bailed article, such as driving an automobile, as the bailor's employee and in the course of his employment.

A number of states have enacted statutes by which a person granting permission to another to use his automobile automatically becomes liable for any negligent harm caused by the person to whom he has entrusted the automobile. That is, permissive use imposes liability on the owner or provider for the permittee's negligence. In some states the statute is limited to cases where the permittee is under a specified age, such as 16 years. Under some statutes the owner is only liable with respect to harm sustained while the permittee is using the automobile for the purpose for which permission was granted. The fact that a lessee under a long-term lease may be embraced within the term of "owner" for the purpose of a motor vehicle statute does not affect the tort liability of the owner if such liability otherwise exists.

Under what is called the *family purpose doctrine,* some courts hold that when the bailor supplies a car for the use of his family, or members thereof, he is liable for the harm caused by a member of the family while negligently driving the car. Other jurisdictions reject this doctrine and refuse to impose liability on the bailor of the automobile unless there is an agency relationship between him and the driver.

[29] Huckabee v Bell & Howell, Inc., 102 Ill App 2d 429, 243 NE2d 317 (employee of bailee).

CASES FOR CHAPTER 21

Theobald v Satterthwaite

30 Wash 2d 92, 190 P2d 714 (1948)

Theobald went to the beauty parlor operated by Satterthwaite. She left her fur coat in the outer reception room. When she returned to the reception room, she found that the coat had been stolen. She then sued Satterthwaite for the value of the coat. From a judgment in Theobald's favor, the defendant appealed.

MALLERY, C.J. . . . Theobald had patronized the shop on a number of occasions previous to the day in question and knew the arrangements of the rooms. On a previous occasion she had inquired of appellant, Satterthwaite, if the reception room was a safe place to leave her coat and had been assured that it was safe. Nothing had been stolen from the reception room in twenty years of operation, and the hooks in that room were the only places provided for customers on which to hang their wraps. There was no bell or warning device on the door that sounded when it was opened. A thief could see into the reception room and if a garment hung there, could open the door, take it off the hook, and leave without being seen from the operating room.

On December 24, 1946, . . . Theobald came into the beauty shop by appointment to get a permanent wave. She sat in the reception room with her fur coat on until the appellant . . . invited her into the operating room. Whereupon she removed her coat, which was natural and expected, for the period while receiving her permanent wave. She hung it on a hook provided for wraps in the reception room. [The appellant was not] aware that she had worn her fur coat on that day. When Satterthwaite had finished the work on respondent's hair, respondent went into the reception room to get her coat and found that it had been stolen. An alarm was given and the police were called, but to no avail. She valued the coat at $300 for which amount the lower court gave her judgment upon the theory that the [appellant was bailee] of the coat and had been negligent in caring for it because of having furnished an unsafe place to leave it.

The [appellant contends that she is] not liable because there was no bailment. Respondent contends that there was a bailment and relies upon the rule in Bunnell v Stern, 122 NY 539, 25 NE 910. . . . In that case a lady had gone to a clothing store by buy a coat. In order to try on a new garment, she took off her coat and laid it down in the presence of store attendants some distance away from the mirror she used in her fitting. Of this the store employees had knowledge. After her fitting she returned for her coat and found it gone. The court said: "Under these circumstances we think that it became their duty to exercise some care for the plaintiff's cloak because she had laid it aside with their invitation and with their knowledge and, without question or notice from them, had put it in the only place she could." . . .

While we are not inclined to view the element of delivery in any technical sense, still we think there can be no delivery unless there is change of possession of an article from one person to another. . . . One who takes off a garment and deposits it in his own presence as one would do in a restaurant retains the power of surveillance and control in himself, and the burden of care is not transferred with regard to such an article because the operators of the restaurant have not knowingly received the exclusive possession and dominion over it. In the instant case the respondent may not have had an adequate opportunity for surveillance; nevertheless she had not transferred control of it to the appellant by a delivery, and [appellant was] unaware that a valuable fur coat had been left in the reception room.

We therefore agree with the appellant's contention that there was no bailment in this case because there was no change of possession of the coat and hence no delivery. It follows that, in the absence of a bailment, the appellants owed the respondent no duty of care or were not negligent in failing to guard it effectively.

[Judgment for plaintiff reversed.]

Baena Brothers v Welge

3 Conn Cir 67, 207 A2d 749 (1964)

Welge owned a sofa and chair which Baena Brothers agreed to reupholster and to reduce the size of the arms. The work was not done according to the agreement, and the furniture when finished had no value to Welge and was not accepted by him. Baena then sued him for the contract price. Welge counterclaimed for the value of the furniture. From a judgment in favor of Welge on both issues, Baena appealed.

PRUYN, J. . . . The arms on the sofa and chair had been slimmed to such an extent that the overhang of the arms which the defendant desired—and an overhang appeared on the floor sample—had been entirely eliminated, thereby altering the style of the furniture from colonial to modern. The plaintiff knew the purposes for which the furniture, when reupholstered and slimmed, was intended. The furniture as delivered was not reasonably fit for the purposes for which it was intended, did not conform to the contract, and had no value to the defendant. . . .

The facts in the case before us bring it within the doctrine of . . . "a bailment where work and labor, care and pains, are to be performed or bestowed upon the thing delivered to the bailee. The parties to a bailment of this character—one for their mutual benefit—enter into a contract, express or implied or both, by which the bailee engages to perform the agreed services and return the thing bailed in its altered or repaired form and the bailor in return for the services of the bailee agrees to pay him the agreed upon compensation. In a contract of this character there are certain implied obligations of the bailee which the law attaches to the contract in the absence of express provision in the contract to the contrary: One, that the thing which the bailee agrees to alter or repair, when so altered or repaired, shall be reasonably fit for the purpose intended, or capable of the use intended, and of which purpose or use the bailee shall know. . . . Another, that the bailee shall exercise ordinary care in the performance of the service he agrees to do in relation to the thing bailed." . . . The plaintiff broke the contract of bailment: the alterations were not in accordance with the contract; the furniture was not reasonably fit for the purpose intended, of which the plaintiff was aware. The defendant . . . was under no obligation to pay for it.

Where the bailee has deviated from the bailor's instructions in altering the thing bailed, with the result that it has lost its value to the bailor and is worthless to him, as in the instant case, and has been abandoned to the bailee, the bailor may sue . . . for the value of the property. . . . "In determining this value, it is generally sufficient to show the money value of the goods in the market at that time. . . . Where an article does not, however, have a market value, or in the case of goods having a special and peculiar value to the owner, then full compensation requires that he recover 'the value to him based on his actual money loss, all the circumstances and conditions considered, resulting from his being deprived of the property, not including, however, any sentimental or fanciful value he may for any reason place upon it.' " . . .

[Judgment affirmed.]

Rhodes v Pioneer Parking Lot, Inc.

(Tenn), 501 SW2d 569 (1973)

Rhodes parked his car on the self-service, park-and-lock lot of Pioneer Parking Lot, Inc. The car was later stolen from the lot by an unknown thief. Rhodes sued the parking lot on the theory that it had breached its duty as a bailee. The parking lot defended on the ground that it was not a bailee. Judgment was entered for the plaintiff, and Pioneer Parking Lot appealed.

LEECH, S.J. . . . The ticket received by appellee when he parked his car contained the following language: "NOTICE THIS CONTRACT LIMITS OUR LIABILITY—READ IT, WE RENT SPACE ONLY. No bailment is created and we are not responsible for loss of or damage to, car or contents. This ticket is sold subject to space being available and is not transferable." A sign posted on the lot [stated] "CARS WITHOUT VALIDATED TICKET WILL BE TOWED AWAY."

There are no restrictions or controls over entry or departure of vehicles or people to and from the parking lot. Moreover, there has never been any attendant to service or look after this lot. Although there is but one entrance which is also the exit, there are no cashiers on this lot.

On October 8, 1969 at about 12:00 o'clock noon, the plaintiff drove his 1968 Chevrolet Camaro onto the defendant's parking lot. At the entrance to this parking lot there is a ticket meter. Plaintiff placed fifty cents in the meter and the meter returned to him the previously set out ticket. Plaintiff then drove his car further into the lot and without any direction or supervision parked it himself; removed the keys from the ignition; placed his ticket on the dash in accordance with the instructions; and locked his car and left the lot keeping his keys himself. Subsequently, plaintiff returned to the parking lot to find that his car had been stolen. His car was later found in a stripped condition and as a result he brought this suit to recover the value of his car.

The trial judge found that the stipulated facts made out a bailor-bailee relationship between plaintiff and defendant and that plaintiff was entitled to recover the value of the car.

The only issue before this Court is whether the relationship between plaintiff and defendant constituted a bailment, so as to permit plaintiff to recover damages for the failure of defendant to redeliver plaintiff's car on demand.

A bailment is the delivery of personalty to another for a particular purpose or on mere deposit, on a contract express or implied, that after the purpose has been fulfilled, it shall be redelivered to the person who delivered it, or otherwise dealt with according to his direction or kept until he reclaims it. . . .

The creation of a bailment in the absence of an express contract requires that possession and control over the subject matter pass from the bailor to the bailee. In order to constitute a sufficient delivery of the subject matter there must be a full transfer, either actual or constructive, of the property to the bailee so as to exclude it from the possession of the owner and all other persons and give to the bailee, for the time being, the sole custody and control thereof. . . .

In parking lot and parking garage situations, a bailment is created where the operator of the lot or garage has knowingly and voluntarily assumed control, possession, or custody of the motor vehicle; if he has not done so, there may be a mere license to park or a lease of parking space. . . . [Courts have] found a bailment where possession of the vehicle was actually surrendered to an attendant. Another factor used to determine whether the operator of the lot has assumed control is the surrender of the keys by the motorist to the operator. . . . Moreover, in [some cases] the necessary possession and control were found where the car could not be taken from the parking garage without the presentation of a parking ticket and payment of the parking fee to an attendant-cashier. . . .

In the case at bar, however, we find no evidence to justify a finding that the plaintiff delivered his car into the custody of the defendant, nor do we find any act or conduct upon the defendant's part which would justify a reasonable person believing that an obligation of bailment had been assumed by the defendant. To the contrary, the facts show that the plaintiff at no time left his car in defendant's possession and control. Plaintiff paid the designated parking fee by depositing the money in the ticket meter. He drove his car into the parking lot, undirected and unsupervised by defendant, and chose a parking space within the lot suitable to himself. Plaintiff then parked and locked the car, retaining the key. At no time did plaintiff come into contact with any of defendant's employees, nor was plaintiff required to contact an employee of the defendant on taking his car from the parking lot. It necessarily follows, therefore, that there was no bailor-bailee relationship established between the plaintiff and the defendant.

However, plaintiff argues that the statement "CARS WITHOUT VALIDATED TICKETS WILL BE TOWED AWAY" would lead the average person to believe that there would be some supervision of the vehicle while it was parked in the lot, and that such was sufficient to create an implied contract of bailment. We disagree. The clear meaning of the statement is that cars in the parking lot would be checked for the sole purpose of enforcing payment of the parking fee and not that the parking lot operator was exercising dominion over all vehicles parked on the lot, especially where as in the case at bar the parking fee was paid. . . .

[Judgment reversed.]

Axelrod v Wardrobe Cleaners, Inc.

(La App) 289 So2d 847 (1974)

Axelrod took home draperies to Wardrobe Cleaners to be dry cleaned. The head of the drapery department examined the draperies to determine if they were strong enough to be cleaned. He accepted the drapes from Axelrod. The colors of the drapes were ruined in the process of dry cleaning and Axelrod sued Wardrobe Cleaners for the damages. From a judgment in favor of Axelrod, Wardrobe Cleaners appealed.

STOULIG, J. . . . George Pringle, head of defendant's drapery department, called at the Axelrod home on August 16, 1972 to inspect the dining room draperies for dry-cleaning purposes. He was in the Axelrod home for 30 minutes, during which time he inspected both the lining and the drapery material itself. . . .

Having satisfied himself the fabric had sufficient strength to withstand cleaning, Pringle accepted the drapes. His unqualified acceptance was an implied assurance to the plaintiff-customer that the drapes could withstand the cleaning process to which they would be subjected. It created the relationship of a bailment for hire between the parties, thereby imposing upon the defendant the duty of diligent care. . . .

The unconditional acceptance for cleaning, coupled with the defendant's admission that the damage occurred while the drapes were in its custody, establishes a prima facie case of negligence against defendant and thrust upon it the burden of exculpating itself from fault or lack of due care in handling the plaintiff's property. In other words, it must prove that it acted as a prudent bailee. . . .

The owner of Wardrobe Cleaners, Inc., Pete Kissgen, Jr., . . . explained [that] with the many new imported fabrics now in use, it is difficult to predict how the dyes will react to the cleaning process. In this case he stated the draperies could not be pretested for colorfastness because if the dyes did run the fabric would be ruined in the test area. It is acknowledged that the defendant was not equipped to chemically test the fabric for colorfastness. However, if any doubt existed in defendant's mind as to the advisibility of dry-cleaning these drapes, as a prudent bailee it should have either subjected them to additional tests or refused to accept them.

[Judgment affirmed.]

Cintrone v Hertz Truck Leasing & Rental Service

45 NJ 434, 212 A2d 769 (1965)

Contract Packers rented a truck from Hertz Truck Leasing. Packers' employee, Cintrone, was injured while riding in the truck, being driven by his helper, when the brakes of the truck did not function properly and the truck crashed. Cintrone sued Hertz. From a judgment in favor of Hertz, Cintrone appealed.

FRANCIS, J. . . . Under the lease the trucks were kept at Contract Packers' premises but Hertz agreed to service, repair, and maintain them. . . .

The failure of the brakes at the time of the accident was not chargeable to negligence on defendant's part. Plaintiff seeks a reversal of the adverse judgment, however, on the ground that the contractual relationship between Hertz and his employer gave rise to an implied continuing promissory warranty by Hertz that the truck in question was fit for the purposes for which plaintiff's employer rented it, *i.e.*, operation and transportation of goods on the public highways. . . .

It the relationship in the present case between Contract Packers and Hertz were manufacturer or dealer and purchaser, an implied warranty of fitness for operation on the public highway would have come into existence at the time of the sale. . . .

There is no good reason for restricting such warranties to sales. Warranties of fitness are regarded by law as an incident of a transaction because one party to the relationship is in a better position than the other to know and control the condition of the chattel transferred and to distribute the losses which may occur because of a dangerous condition the chattel possesses. These factors make it likely that the party acquiring possession of the article will assume it is in a safe condition for use and therefore refrain from taking precautionary measures himself. . . .

In this connection it may be observed also that the comment to the warranty section of the Uniform Commercial Code speaks out against confining warranties to sales transactions. The comment says: "Although this section is limited in its scope and direct purpose to warranties made by the seller to the buyer as part of a contract of sale, the warranty sections of this Article are not designed in any way to disturb those lines of case law growth which have recognized that warranties need not be confined either to sales contracts or to the direct parties to such a contract. They may arise in other appropriate circumstances such as in the case of bailments for hire, whether such bailment is itself the main contract or is merely a supplying of containers under a contract for the sale of their contents. . . ." See Comment, [UCC §] 2-313. . . .

"The expansion of enterprises engaged solely in bailment for hire seems to justify increasing imposition of absolute warranties, at least to the extent that they would be imposed upon a seller of similarly used goods. In addition, reliance is greater than in the typical sale, for it is generally true that the bailee for hire spends less time shopping for the article than he would in selecting like goods to be purchased, and since the item is not one he expects to own, he will usually be less competent in judging its quality."

A sale transfers ownership and possession of the article in exchange for the price; a bailment for hire transfers possession in exchange for the rental and contemplates eventual return of the article to the owner. By means of a bailment parties can often reach the same business ends that can be achieved by selling and buying. The goods come to the user for the time being, and he benefits by their use and enjoyment without the burdens of becoming and remaining the owner. The owner-lessor benefits by receiving the rent for the temporary use. . . .

We may take judicial notice of the growth of the business of renting motor vehicles, trucks and pleasure cars. . . . The offering to the public of trucks and pleasure vehicles for hire necessarily carries with it a representation that they are fit for operation. This representation is of major significance because both new and used cars and trucks are rented. In fact, . . . the rental rates are the same whether a new or used vehicle is supplied. In other words, the lessor in effect says to the customer that the representation of fitness for use is the same whether the vehicle supplied is new or old. From the standpoint of service to the customer, therefore, the law cannot justly accept any distinction between the obligation assumed by a U-drive-it company whether the vehicle is new or old when rented. The nature of the business is such that the customer is expected to, and in fact must, rely ordinarily on the express or implied representation of fitness for immediate use. . . . To illustrate, if a traveler comes into an airport and needs a car for a short period and rents one from a U-drive-it agency, when he is "put in the driver's seat," his reliance on the fitness of the car assigned to him for the rental period whether new or used usually is absolute. In such circumstances the relationship between the parties fairly calls for an implied warranty of fitness for use, at least equal to that assumed by a new car manufacturer. The content of such warranty must be that the car will not fail mechanically during the rental period.

In the case before us, it is just as obvious that when a company like Contract Packers rents trucks for limited or extended periods for use in its occupation of transportation of goods, it too relies on the express or implied representation of the person in the business of supplying vehicles for hire, that they are fit for such use. . . .

When the implied warranty or representation of fitness arises, . . . it continues for the agreed rental period. The public interests involved are justly served only by treating an obligation of that nature as an incident of the business enterprise. The operator of the rental business must be regarded as possessing expertise with respect to the service life and fitness of his vehicles for use. That expertise ought to put him in a better position than the bailee to detect or to anticipate flaws or defects or fatigue in his vehicles. Moreover, as between bailor for hire and bailee, the liability for flaws or defects not discoverable by ordinary care in inspecting or testing ought to rest with the bailor just as it rests with a manufacturer who buys components containing latent defects from another maker, and installs them in the completed product, or just as it rests with a retailer at the point of sale to the consumer. . . .

The warranty or representation of fitness is not dependent upon existence of Hertz' additional undertaking to service and maintain the trucks while they were leased. That undertaking serves particularly to instill reliance in Contract Packers upon mechanical operability of the trucks throughout the rental period. But the warranty or representation that the vehicles will not fail for that period sprang into existence on the making of the agreement to rent the trucks, and was an incident thereof, irrespective of the service and maintenance undertaking. . . .

In this developing area of the law, we perceive no sound reason why a distinction in principle should be made between the sale of a truck to plaintiff's employer by a manufacturer, and a lease for hire of the character established by the evidence. . . .

[Judgment reversed and new trial ordered.]

Authors' Note. California has imposed strict tort liability (see p. 49) on the commercial lessors of motor vehicles, thereby achieving independently of the warranty concept a result similar to that reached in the Cintrone case on the basis of a warranty concept. [Price v Shell Oil Co., 2 Cal 3d 245, 85 Cal Rptr 178, 466 P2d 722]

Dukes v McGimsey

(Tenn App), 500 SW2d 448 (1972)

Virginia McGimsey loaned her auto to Terry to whom she was then engaged and did later marry. At the time of lending the car, Terry was 18, had recently been discharged from the Army, and Virginia knew that he did not have a driver's license. Some time thereafter, Terry became intoxicated and while driving Virginia's car, ran into Edgar Dukes. Dukes sued Terry and Virginia. From a judgment in favor of Dukes, Virginia appealed.

MATHERNE, J. . . . "The general rule is that one who turns his automobile over to one under the influence of an intoxicant, or to one addicted to the use of intoxicants to excess, or to a driver who is known to the party loaning the car to be a reckless or negligent or otherwise incompetent driver, is charged with negligence." . . .

The only proof presented by the plaintiffs that the defendant owner of the automobile, Virginia McGimsey, violated the foregoing rule is the fact Terry Shumate was extremely drunk at the time of the collision, and the fact Terry Shumate did not have a driver's license. The plaintiffs presented no proof that Terry Shumate was drunk or drinking when he obtained possession of the automobile from Virginia McGimsey; no proof that Terry Shumate was addicted to the excessive use of intoxicants; no proof that Terry Shumate was a reckless or negligent driver; and no proof of any other incompetence on the part of Terry Shumate either physical or mental.

. . . The mere fact [that] the borrower is unlicensed does not render the owner of an automobile liable for the negligence of the borrower where such fact has no causal connection with the injury or damage. The proof fails to establish the cause of the collision was in any manner due to the failure of Terry Shumate to have a driver's license. We conclude, under the proof, the cause of the collision was the drunken state of the defendant Terry Shumate, and not in any way the lack of a driver's license or the lack of the ability to drive an automobile absent the element of intoxication.

The question then becomes whether, under the facts, the defendant owner of the automobile can be held liable for the damages resulting from the intoxicated condition of Terry Shumate.

The plaintiffs rely upon the case of Sadler v Draper (1959), 46 TennApp 1, 326 SW2d 148, wherein the agent of the owner of an automobile loaned the vehicle to one Crenshaw. In describing the borrower of the automobile, Judge Felts summarized as follows: "There is little or no dispute in the evidence that Crenshaw was incompetent, reckless, an habitual drunkard, and without a driver's license; and that Foxall (agent) was well acquainted with Crenshaw, a cousin of his, and knew that Crenshaw was unfit to be entrusted with an automobile; and the evidence was that Crenshaw had been drinking all day and was under the influence of liquor when Foxall (agent) loaned him the car."

Under those facts the Court in *Sadler* was clearly justified in finding negligent entrustment of an automobile. . . .

The facts in the case at bar as herein summarized do not support, nor allow, the application of the rule so as to render the owner Virginia McGimsey negligent in the entrustment of her automobile to the codefendant Terry Shumate.

. . . No prima facie case of negligent entrustment was made. The plaintiff has the burden of proving negligent entrustment of an automobile. The authorities herein cited will not permit an inference of negligent entrustment by the mere proof that the borrower was drunk at the time of the collision, or by the mere proof the borrower did not have a driver's license. The plaintiff must go further and prove those conditions . . . on the one hand; and prove the lack of a driver's license was a causal factor on the other. . . .

[Judgment reversed.]

QUESTIONS AND CASE PROBLEMS

1. Harris, who owned a commercial fishing boat, contracted with Deveau to install radar equipment in the boat. Deveau temporarily loaned Harris some radar equipment, and Harris put out to sea on a fishing trip. When he returned, the borrowed radar equipment was found ruined by salt water. Deveau sued Harris for the damage to the equipment. Apparently the sea water had entered when heavy seas broke a window. Was Harris liable for the damage? [Harris v Deveau, (Alaska) 385 P2d 283]
2. The Hawkeye Specialty Co. had a contract to supply the United States with bolts that were heat-chemically treated to protect against corrosion. Hawkeye sent a quantity of untreated bolts to Bendix Corporation under a contract by which Bendix was to treat the bolts as required by Hawkeye's contract with the United States. What was the relationship between Hawkeye and Bendix with respect to the bolts thus delivered? [Hawkeye Specialty Co. v Bendix Corporation, (Iowa) 160 NW2d 341]
3. Lewis put a paper bag containing $3,000 in cash in a railroad station coin-operated locker. After the period of the coin rental expired, a locker company employee opened the locker, removed the money, and because of the amount, surrendered it to the police authorities, as was required by the local law. When Lewis demanded the return of the money from Aderholdt, the police property clerk, the latter required Lewis to prove his ownership to the funds because there were circumstances leading to the belief that the money had been stolen by Lewis. He sued the police property clerk and the locker company. Was the locker company liable for breach of duty as a bailee? [Lewis v Aderholdt, (CA Dist Col App) 203 A2d 919]
4. Taylor parked his automobile in a garage operated by the Philadelphia Parking Authority and paid a regular monthly charge therefor. There was a written agreement between them which provided: "The Authority shall have the right to move the applicant's automobile to such location as it may deem necessary in order to facilitate the most effective use of the parking space on the roof. Ignition keys must be left in the automobile at all times." It was thereafter agreed between the parties that Taylor could retain the ignition key at all times and lock the auto in order to protect the valuable merchandise which he carried in his car. Taylor brought the car into the garage, locked it, and left with the keys. The car was missing when he returned. He sued the parking Authority on the theory that it had breached a duty as bailee. The Authority claimed that it was not a bailee. Was the Authority correct? [Taylor v Philadelphia Parking Authority, 398 Pa 9, 156 A2d 525]
5. King owned a credit card issued by the Air Travel Company. It was lost or stolen and King reported it. Thereafter Jackson presented the credit card to the Hertz Corporation office at the Newark, New Jersey, airport. By impersonating King and forging his name, Jackson rented a car from Hertz. Jackson failed to return the car and sometime thereafter had a collision with Zuppa. Zuppa sued Hertz under a statute which had the effect of imposing liability on Hertz for harm to third persons by any bailee of a Hertz automobile. Was Jackson a bailee? [Zuppa v Hertz Corp., 111 NJ Super 419, 268 A2d 364]
6. Morse, who owned a diamond ring, valued at $2,000, took the ring to Homer's, Inc., to sell for him. Homer placed the ring in the window display

of his store. There was no guard or grating across the opening of the window inside his store. There was a partitioned door that was left unlocked. On two former occasions Homer's store had been robbed. Several weeks after Morse left his ring, armed men robbed the store and took several rings from the store window, including Morse's ring. He sued Homer, who defended on the ground that he was not liable for the criminal acts of others. Decide. [Morse v Homer's, Inc., 295 Mass 606, 4 NE2d 625]

7. Nutrodynamics delivered a quantity of loose pills that it manufactured to Ivers-Lee for the latter to place them in foil packages and then in shipping containers suitable for delivery to customers of Nutrodynamics. Approximately 193 cartons of packaged pills were finished and in Ivers-Lee's possession when Beck brought a suit against Nutrodynamics and directed the sheriff to attach the pills in the possession of Ivers-Lee. Ivers-Lee had not been paid for its work in packaging. It claimed the right to keep the goods until paid but nevertheless surrendered them to the sheriff. Was it entitled to any claim on the goods in the hands of the sheriff? [Beck v Nutrodynamics, Inc., 77 NJ Super 448, 186 A2d 715]
8. O'Donnell was driving his father's automobile when he had a collision with a car driven by Collins and a car driven by Ebel. In the resulting lawsuit, O'Donnell asserted against Collins a claim for the total amount of the damage to his father's car. Collins claimed that O'Donnell could not recover for the damage since it was not his car. Decide. [Ebel v Collins and O'Donnell, 47 Ill App 2d 327, 198 NE2d 552]
9. Osell, who held a private pilot's license, rented an airplane from Hall. While attempting to land the plane, he flew through a cloud formation, although he could have avoided doing so. In turning out of the clouds, he struck a hillside and wrecked the plane. Flying through clouds under these circumstances was a violation of the federal civil air regulations. Hall sued Osell for the destruction of the plane. Decide. [Hall v Osell, 102 Cal App 2d 849, 228 P2d 293]
10. The State of New York loaned without charge a sand loading machine to the Village of Catskill. Hood was employed by the Village and, while using the loader as part of his work, was injured because the drive chain, which was worn and out of alignment, caught his leg. He sued the State of New York for the damages he sustained. The State produced evidence that the machine had been serviced shortly before the accident and that it was then in good working order. Was Hood entitled to recover? [Hood v New York, (Court of Claims of New York) 48 Misc 2d 43, 264 NYS2d 134]
11. Gregg sold his motorcycle. The buyer loaned it back to him. When the buyer later requested the motorcycle, Gregg sold it to a third person. Was Gregg guilty of a crime? [New Mexico v Gregg, 83 NMex 397, 492 P2d 1260]
12. Joan took driving lessons at the A-North Shore Driving School. Later the school loaned her an automobile and took her for her state driving test. Crowley was the state examiner. Joan drove into a signal box on the side of the road. Crowley was seriously injured. He sued the driving school. Was it liable? [Crowley v A-North Shore Driving School, 19 Ill App 3d 1035, 313 NE2d 200]

22 Special Bailments and Documents of Title

A special bailment relation, rather than an ordinary bailment, arises when goods are stored in a warehouse, or delivered to a merchant to sell for the owner, or delivered to a carrier to be transported. In some instances a hotelkeeper may have a bailee's liability. Some of these special bailees issue a document of title, such as a warehouse receipt or bill of lading, on receiving goods from the bailor.

WAREHOUSEMEN

A warehouseman is a specialized type of bailee who ordinarily gives the bailor a document of title or warehouse receipt in exchange for the goods.

§ **22:1. Definition.** A person engaged in the business of storing the goods of others for compensation is a *warehouseman.* A *public warehouseman* holds himself out generally to serve the public without discrimination.

An enterprise which stores boats outdoors on land is a "warehouseman" since it is "engaged in the business of storing goods for hire," as against the contention that the storage was out-of-doors and not in a warehouse or similar structure.[1]

§ **22:2. Rights and Duties of Warehousemen.** The common-law rights and duties of a warehouseman, in the absence of modification by statute, are in the main the same as those of a bailee in an ordinary mutual-benefit bailment.[2] (See p. 436, Brace v Salem Cold Storage, Inc.)

The public warehouseman has a lien against the goods for reasonable charges.[3] It is a *specific lien* in that it attaches only to the property with respect to which the charges arose and cannot be asserted against other property of the same owner in the possession of the warehouseman. The warehouseman, however, may make a lien carry over to other goods by noting on the receipt for one lot of goods that a lien is also claimed thereon for charges as to other goods.[4] The warehouseman's lien for storage charges may be enforced by sale after due notice has been given to all persons who

---

[1] Fireman's Fund American Ins. Co. v Capt. Fowler's Marina, Inc., (DCD Mass) 343 F Supp 347.

[2] UCC § 7-204; Belland v American Auto Insurance Co., (Dist Col App) 101 A2d 517. The Uniform Commercial Code does not change the prior rule by which when loss by fire is shown, the burden is upon the warehouseman to disprove negligence. Canty v Wyatt Storage Corp., 208 Va 161, 156 SE2d 582.

[3] UCC § 7-209(1).

[4] § 7-209(1).

claim any interest in the property stored. When a person is not a warehouseman he may not assert a warehouseman's lien.[5]

Most states have passed warehouse acts defining the rights and duties of the warehouseman and imposing regulations as to charges and liens, bonds for the protection of patrons, the maintenance of storage facilities in a suitable and safe condition, inspections, and general methods of transacting business.

§ 22:3. Warehouse Receipts. A *warehouse receipt* is a written acknowledgment by a warehouseman that certain property has been received for storage from a named person. It also sets forth the terms of the contract of storage. The warehouse receipt is a document of title because the person lawfully holding the receipt is entitled to the goods or property represented by the receipt. Certain details describing the transaction must be included, but beyond this no particular form for a warehouse receipt is required.

The receipt can be issued only if goods have actually been received by the warehouseman. If a receipt is issued without the goods having been received, the warehouseman is liable to a good-faith purchaser of the receipt for the loss he sustains thereby. The issuance of a receipt when goods have not been received by the warehouseman is also a crime in many states.

§ 22:4. Rights of Holders of Warehouse Receipts. A warehouse receipt in which it is stated that the goods received will be delivered to the depositor, or to any other specified person, is a *nonnegotiable warehouse receipt*; but a receipt in which it is stated that the goods received will be delivered to the bearer, or to the order of any person named in such receipt, is a *negotiable warehouse receipts.*[6]

The transfer of negotiable warehouse receipts is made by delivery or by indorsement and delivery. It is the duty of the warehouseman to deliver the goods to the holder of a negotiable receipt and to cancel such receipt before making delivery of the goods. The surrender of a nonnegotiable receipt is not required.

If the person who deposited the goods with the warehouse did not own the goods or did not have the power to transfer title to them, the holder of the warehouse receipt is subject to the title of the true owner.[7] Accordingly, when goods are stolen and delivered to a warehouse and a receipt is issued for them, the owner prevails over the holder of the receipt.[8]

The transferee of a warehouse receipt is given the protection of certain warranties from his immediate transferor; namely, that the instrument is genuine, that its transfer is rightful and effective, and that the transferor has no knowledge of any facts that impair the validity or worth of the receipt.[9]

---

[5] Silver Bowl, Inc. v Equity Metals, Inc., 93 Idaho 487, 464 P2d 926.

[6] § 7-104.

[7] § 7-503(1).

[8] § 7-503(1).

[9] § 7-507. These warranties are in addition to any that may arise between the parties by virtue of the fact that the transferor is selling the goods represented by the receipt to the transferee. See Chapter 26 as to sellers' warranties.

§ 22:5. Field Warehousing. Ordinarily, stored goods are placed in a warehouse belonging to the warehouseman. The owner of goods, such as a manufacturer, may keep the goods in his own storage room or building, however, and have a warehouse company take control of the room or building. When the warehouseman takes exclusive control of the property, it may issue a warehouse receipt for the goods even though they are still on the premises of the owner. Such a transaction has the same legal effect with respect to other persons and purchasers of the warehouse receipt as though the property were in the warehouse of the warehouseman. This practice is called *field warehousing* since the goods are not taken to the warehouse but remain "in the field."

The purpose is to create warehouse receipts which the owner of the goods is able to pledge as security for loans.[10] The owner could, of course, have done this by actually placing the goods in a warehouse, but this would have involved the expense of transportation and storage.

§ 22:6. Limitation of Liability of Warehousemen. A warehouseman may limit liability by a provision in the warehouse receipt specifying the maximum amount for which he will be liable. This privilege is subject to two qualifications: (1) the customer must be given the choice of storing the goods without such limitation if he pays a higher storage rate, and (2) the limitation must be stated as to each item or unit of weight. A limitation is in proper form when it states that the maximum liability for a piano is $1,000 or that the maximum liability per bushel of wheat is a stated amount. Conversely, there cannot be a blanket limitation of liability, such as "maximum liability $50," when the receipt covers two or more items.[11] General contract law determines whether a limitation clause is a part of the contract between the warehouseman and his customer. (See p. 437, Birmingham Television Corp. v Water Works.)

FACTORS

§ 22:7. Definition. A *factor* is a special type of bailee who sells goods consigned to him as though he were the owner of the goods. The device of entrusting a person with the possession of property for the purpose of sale is commonly called *selling on consignment.* The owner who seeks or consigns the goods for sale is the *consignor*. The person or agent to whom they are consigned is the *consignee*; he may also be known as a commission merchant. His compensation is known as a *commission* or *factorage.* The property remains the property of the owner, and the consignee acts as his agent to pass title to the buyer.[12]

Factoring as defined above has to a large degree been displaced, except with respect to the sale of livestock, by other methods of doing business. Today one is more likely to find the seller selling the goods on credit to a

[10] Heffron v Bank of America, (CA9 Cal) 113 F2d 239.

[11] Modelia v Rose Warehouse, (NY) 5 UCCRS 1004.

[12] If the factor guarantees payment to the consignor, he is called a *del credere factor.*

middleman with the latter having the right to return goods not sold, the seller then assigning his account receivable. Or the seller may store the goods in a warehouse or place them on board a carrier and then effect a sale by delivering the warehouse receipts or bills of lading rather than by sending the goods to a factor. The condemnation of consignment selling, when used as a means of restraining trade,[13] has given additional reason for abandoning the selling on consignment in favor of other patterns.

§ 22:8. Effect of Factor Transaction. Since a factor is by definition authorized by the consignor to sell the goods entrusted to him, such a sale will pass the title of the consignor to the purchaser. Before the factor makes the sale, the goods belong to the consignor; but in some instances creditors of the factor may ignore the consignor and treat the goods as though they belonged to the consignee.[14] If the consignor is not the owner, as when a thief delivers stolen goods to the factor, a sale by the factor is an unlawful conversion. It is constitutional, however, to provide that the factor who sells in good faith in ignorance of the rights of other persons in the goods he sells is protected from liability and cannot be treated as a converter of the goods,[15] as would be the case in the absence of such a statutory immunity.[16]

COMMON CARRIERS

Common carriers are bailees with respect to the property which they carry as freight. They typically issue documents of title or bills of lading for such property.

§ 22:9. Definition. A *carrier* is one who undertakes the transportation of goods, regardless of the method of transportation or the distance covered. The *consignor* or shipper is the person who delivers goods to the carrier for shipment. The *consignee* is the person to whom the goods are shipped and to whom the carrier should deliver the goods.

A carrier may be classified as (1) a *common carrier,* which holds itself out as willing to furnish transportation for compensation without discrimination to all members of the public who apply,[17] assuming that the goods to be carried are proper and that facilities of the carrier are available; (2) a *contract carrier,* which transports goods under individual contracts; or (3) a *private carrier,* such as a truck fleet owned and operated by an industrial firm. The common carrier law applies to the first, the bailment law to the second, and the law of employment to the third.

The unlicensed carriage of goods for hire on one trip makes a person guilty of violating a law requiring a special permit or license from the state to operate as a common carrier.[18]

---

[13] Simpson v Union Oil Co., 377 US 13.

[14] UCC § 2-326.

[15] Montana Meat Co. v Missoula Livestock Auction Co., 125 Mont 66, 230 P2d 955.

[16] Sig Ellingson & Co. v De Vries, (CA8 Minn) 199 F2d 677.

[17] P.U.C. v Johnson Motor Transport, 147 Maine 138, 84 A2d 142.

[18] State v Logan, (Mo) 411 SW2d 86.

§ **22:10. Freight Forwarders.** A *freight forwarder* accepts freight from shippers ordinarily in less-than-carload lots, combines such freight into carloads, and delivers them as carloads to a carrier for shipment to a particular point where the carload lots are separated and the items carried to their respective destinations. A freight forwarder does not own or operate any of the transportation facilities. Freight forwarders in some jurisdictions are subject to the same government regulations as common carriers.

§ **22:11. Bills of Lading.** When the carrier accepts goods for shipment or forwarding, it ordinarily issues to the shipper a *bill of lading* [19] in the case of land or marine transportation or an *airbill* [20] for air transportation. This instrument, which is a document of title, is both a receipt for the goods and a contract stating the terms of carriage. Title to the goods may be transferred by a transfer of the bill of lading made with that intention.

With respect to intrastate shipments, bills of lading are governed by the Uniform Commercial Code.[21] Interstate transportation is regulated by the federal Bills of Lading Act.[22]

A bill of lading is a *negotiable bill of lading* when by its terms the goods are to be delivered to bearer or to the order of a named person.[23] Any other bill of lading, such as one that consigns the goods to a specified person, is a nonnegotiable or *straight bill of lading.*[24]

(1) Contents of Bill of Lading. The form of the bill of lading is regulated in varying degrees by administrative agencies.[25]

As against a bona fide transferee of the bill of lading, a carrier is bound by the recitals in the bill as to the contents, quantity, or weight of goods.[26] This means that the carrier must produce the goods which are described, even though they had not existed, or pay damages for failing to do so. This rule is not applied if facts appear on the face of the bill that should keep the transferee from relying on the recital.

(2) Negotiability. The person to whom a bill of lading has been negotiated acquires the direct obligation of the carrier to hold possession of the goods for him according to the terms of the bill of lading as fully as if the carrier had contracted with him, and ordinarily he acquires the title to the bill and the goods it represents. The rights of the holder of a negotiable bill

---

[19] In order to avoid the delay of waiting for a bill of lading mailed to the destination point from the point where the goods were received by the carrier, UCC § 7-305(1) authorizes the carrier at the request of the consignor to provide for the issuance of the bill at the destination rather than the receipt point.

[20] UCC § 1-201(6).

[21] Article 7.

[22] Title 49, USC § 81 et seq.

[23] UCC § 7-104(1)(a).

[24] § 7-104(2). Interstate Commerce Commission regulations applicable to rail shipments require nonnegotiable bills to be printed on white paper and negotiable bills on yellow paper.

[25] The UCC contains no provision regulating the form of the bill of lading.

[26] UCC § 7-301(1).

are not affected by the fact (a) that the former owner of the bill had been deprived of it by misrepresentation, fraud, accident, mistake, duress, undue influence, loss, theft, or conversion; or (b) that the goods had already been surrendered by the carrier or had been stopped in transit.[27]

The rights of the holder of a bill of lading are subject to the title of a true owner of the goods who did not authorize the delivery of the goods to the carrier. For example, when a thief delivers the goods to the carrier and then negotiates the bill of lading, the title of the owner of the goods prevails over the claim of the holder of the bill.[28]

(3) Warranties. The transferee for value of either a negotiable or non-negotiable bill of lading acquires from his transferor, in the absence of any contrary provision, the benefit of implied warranties (a) that the bill of lading is genuine, (b) that its transfer is rightful and is effective to transfer the goods represented thereby, and (c) that the transferor has no knowledge of facts that would impair the validity or worth of the bill of lading.[29]

§ 22:12. Rights of Common Carriers. A common carrier of goods has the right to make reasonable and necessary rules for the conduct of its business. It has the right to charge such rates for its services as yield it a fair return on the property devoted to the business of transportation, but the exact rates charged are regulated by the Interstate Commerce Commission in the case of interstate carriers and by state commissions in the case of intrastate carriers. As an incident of the right to charge for its services, a carrier may charge *demurrage:* a charge for the detention of its cars or equipment for an unreasonable length of time by either the consignor or consignee.

As security for unpaid transportation and service charges, a common carrier has a lien on goods that it transports. The carrier's lien also secures demurrage charges, the costs of preservation of the goods, and the costs of sale to enforce the lien.[30] The lien of a carrier is a specific lien. It attaches only to goods shipped under the particular contract, but includes all of the shipment even though it is sent in installments. Thus, when part of the shipment is delivered to the consignee, the lien attaches to the portion remaining in possession of the carrier.

§ 22:13. Duties of Common Carrier. A common carrier is generally required (1) to receive and carry proper and lawful goods of all persons who offer them for shipment; (2) to furnish facilities that are adequate for the transportation of freight in the usual course of business, and to furnish proper storage facilities for goods awaiting shipment or awaiting delivery after shipment; (3) to follow the directions given by the shipper; (4) to load and

---

[27] § 7-502(2).

[28] § 7-503(1).

[29] UCC § 7-507; Federal Bills of Lading Act (FBLA), 49 USC §§ 114, 116. When the transfer of the bill of lading is part of a transaction by which the transferor sells the goods represented thereby to the transferee, there will also arise the warranties that are found in other sales of goods.

[30] UCC § 7-307(1); FBLA, 49 USC § 105.

unload goods delivered to it for shipment (in less-than-carload lots in the case of railroads), but the shipper or consignee may assume this duty by contract or custom; (5) to deliver the goods to the consignee or his authorized agent, except when custom or special arrangement relieves the carrier of this duty.

Goods must be delivered at the usual place for delivery at the specified destination. When goods are shipped under a negotiable bill of lading, the carrier must not deliver the goods without obtaining possession of the bill properly indorsed. When goods are shipped under a straight bill of lading, the carrier is justified in delivering to the consignee, unless notified by the shipper to deliver to someone else. If the carrier delivers the goods to the wrong person, it is liable for breach of contract and for the tort of conversion.

§ 22:14. Liabilities of Common Carrier. When goods are delivered to a common carrier for immediate shipment and while they are in transit, the carrier is absolutely liable for any loss or damage to the goods unless it can prove that it was due solely to one or more of the following excepted causes: (a) act of God, or a natural phenomenon that is not reasonably foreseeable; (b) act of public enemy, such as the military forces of an opposing government, as distinguished from ordinary robbers; (c) act of public authority, such as a health officer removing goods from a truck; (d) act of the shipper, such as fraudulent labeling or defective packing; or (e) inherent nature of the goods, such as those naturally tending to spoil or deteriorate.

Unusually heavy rains do not constitute an act of God even though flood conditions are created thereby, for the reason that rains and even heavy rains are not unexpectable. Consequently, a common carrier is liable for loss caused by delay resulting from such flood conditions.[31]

When a carrier claims the benefit of an excepted cause, it must show that the excepted cause was the sole cause of the harm. Consequently, where the carrier was negligent when confronted with a flood condition, it was liable even though the flood was an act of God, the carrier being negligent in failing to move the goods of the shipper from a lower level track to higher ground.[32]

(1) Carrier's Liability for Delay. A carrier is liable for losses caused by its failure to deliver goods within a reasonable time.[33] Thus, the carrier is liable for losses arising from a fall in price or a deterioration of the goods caused by its unreasonable delay. The carrier, however, is not liable for every delay. Risks of ordinary delays incidental to the business of transporting goods are assumed by the shipper.

---

[31] Southern Pacific Co. v Loden, 19 Ariz App 460, 508 P2d 347.

[32] St. Louis-San Francisco Rwy. Co. v Ozark White Lime Co., 177 Ark 1018, 9 SW2d 17.

[33] Seaboard Air Line R.R. Co. v Lake Region Packing Ass'n, (Fla App) 211 So2d 25.

(2) Liability of Initial and Connecting Carriers. When goods are carried over the lines of several carriers, the initial and the final carrier, as well as the carrier on whose line the loss is sustained, may be liable to the shipper or the owner of the goods; but only one payment may be obtained.

(3) Limiting Liability. In the absence of a constitutional or statutory prohibition, a carrier generally has the right to limit its liability by contract. A clause limiting the liability of the carrier is not enforceable unless consideration is given for it, usually in the form of a reduced rate, and provided further that the shipper is allowed to ship without limitation of liability if he chooses to pay the higher or ordinary rate.[34]

A carrier may by contract relieve itself from liability for losses not arising out of its own negligence. A carrier accepting freight for shipment outside the state cannot require the shipper to agree that it will not be liable for losses occurring on the line of a connecting carrier.

A common carrier may make an agreement with the shipper as to the value of the property. If the amount is reasonable, such an agreement will usually bind the shipper whether or not the loss was due to the carrier's fault.

Limitation of liability is governed by the Carriage of Goods by Sea Act, in the case of water carriers,[35] and by the Warsaw Convention in the case of international air transportation. By the Warsaw Convention, liability is limited to a stated amount. Its provisions apply both to regular commercial flights and to charter flights. Under the latter, transportation details are arranged by an association which charters a flight with the airline and then makes individual arrangements with association members for such flights, with the airline delivering individual tickets to each passenger. When the airline is also the actual operator of the plane, there is no practical difference between a voyage charter flight and an ordinary scheduled commercial flight.[36]

(4) Notice of Claim. The bill of lading and applicable government regulations may require that a carrier be given notice of any claim for damages or loss of goods within a specified time, generally not less than nine months. A provision in the tariff limiting the time for such notice is not binding on a consignee who has not received a copy of the bill of lading. (See p. 439, Wells & Coverly v Red Star Express.)

(5) Liability for Baggage. A common carrier of passengers is required to receive a reasonable amount of baggage. Its liability in this respect is the same as the liability of a carrier of goods. If the passenger retains custody of his baggage, the carrier is liable only for lack of reasonable care or willful misconduct on the part of its agents and employees. Limitations on baggage liability are commonly authorized by law and are binding upon passengers even though unknown to them.

---

[34] UCC § 7-309(2).
[35] Aluminious Pozuelo, Ltd. v S. S. Navigator, (CA2 NY) 407 F2d 152.
[36] Block v Compagnie Nationale Air France, (CA5 Ga) 386 F2d 323.

HOTEL-KEEPERS

A hotelkeeper has a bailee's liability with respect to property specifically entrusted to his care. With respect to property in the possession of the guest, the hotelkeeper has supervisory liability.

§ 22:15. Definitions.

(1) Hotelkeeper. The term *hotelkeeper* is used by the law to refer to an operator of a hotel, motel, or tourist home, or to anyone else who is regularly engaged in the business of offering living accommodations to all transient persons.[37] In the early law he was called an innkeeper or a tavern-keeper.

(2) Guests. The essential element in the definition of *guest* is that he is a transient. He need not be a traveler or come from a distance. A person living within a short distance of the hotel who engages a room at the hotel and remains there overnight is a guest.

§ 22:16. Guest Relationship Duration. The relationship of guest and hotel-keeper does not begin until a person is received as a guest by the hotel-keeper.[38] The relationship terminates when the guest leaves or when he ceases to be a transient, as when he arranges for a more or less permanent residence at the hotel. The transition from the status of guest to the status of boarder or lodger must be clearly indicated. It is not established by the mere fact that one remains at the hotel for a long period, even though it runs into months.

A person who enters a hotel at the invitation of a guest or attends a dance or a banquet given at the hotel is not a guest.[39] Similarly, the guest of a registered occupant of a motel room who shares the room with the occupant without the knowledge or consent of the management is not a guest of the motel, since there is no relationship between that person and the motel.[40]

§ 22:17. Discrimination. Since a hotel is by definition an enterprise holding itself out to serve the public, it follows that members of the public, otherwise fit, must be accepted as guests. If the hotel refuses accommodations for an improper reason, it is liable for damages, including exemplary damages. A guest has been held entitled to recover punitive damages when improperly ejected under circumstances indicating an intentional and willful disregard of the guest's rights.[41]

A hotel may also be liable under a civil rights or similar statutory provision, and it may also be guilty of a crime. By virtue of the federal Civil

[37] A person furnishing the services of a hotelkeeper has the status of such even though the word "hotel" is not used in the business name. Lackman v Department of Labor and Industries, (Wash) 471 P2d 82.

[38] Langford v Vandaveer, (Ky) 254 SW2d 498.

[39] Moody v Kenny, 153 La 1007, 97 So 21.

[40] Langford v Vandaveer, (Ky) 254 SW2d 498.

[41] Milner Hotels v Brent, 207 Miss 892, 43 So2d 654.

Rights Act of 1964, neither a hotel nor its concessionaire can discriminate against patrons or segregate them on the basis of race, color, religion, or national origin. The federal Act is limited to discrimination for the stated reasons and does not in any way interfere with the right of the hotel to exclude those who are unfit persons to admit because they are drunk or criminally violent, nor persons who are not dressed in the manner required by reasonable hotel regulations applied to all persons. When there has been improper discrimination or segregation or it is reasonably believed that such acts may occur, the federal Act authorizes the institution of proceedings in the federal courts for an order to stop such prohibited practices.

§ **22:18. Liability of Hotelkeeper.** In the absence of a valid limitation, the hotelkeeper is generally an insurer of the safety of goods of a guest.[42] As exceptions, the hotelkeeper is not liable for loss caused by an act of God, a public enemy, act of public authority, the inherent nature of the property, or the fault of the guest.

In most states, statutes limit or provide a method for limiting the liability of a hotelkeeper.[43] The statutes may limit the extent of liability, reduce the liability of the hotelkeeper to that of an ordinary bailee, or permit him to limit his liability by contract or by posting a notice of the limitation.[44] Some statutes relieve the hotelkeeper from liability when directions for depositing valuables with the hotelkeeper are posted on the doors of the rooms occupied and the guest fails to comply with the directions. When a statute permits a hotel receiving valuables for deposit in its safe deposit box to limit its liability to the amount specified in the agreement signed by the guest, such limitation binds the guest even though the loss was caused by negligence on the part of the hotel.[45]

Even when there is no such limitation on the liability of a hotel, it is not liable for more than the value of the guest's property and is not liable for consequential harm that may flow from the loss of the property. (See p. 440, Morse v Piedmont Hotel Co.)

§ **22:19. Lien of Hotelkeeper.** The hotelkeeper is given a lien on the baggage of his guests for the agreed charges or, if no express agreement was made, the reasonable value of the accommodations furnished. Statutes permit the hotelkeeper to enforce his lien by selling the goods at public sale.[46] The lien of the hotelkeeper is terminated by (1) the guest's payment of the hotel's charges, (2) any conversion of the guest's goods by the hotelkeeper, and

---

[42] Zurich Fire Insurance Co. v Weil, (Ky) 259 SW2d 54.

[43] Kelly v Milner Hotels, 176 Pa Super 316, 106 A2d 636.

[44] Goodwin v Georgian Hotel Co., 197 Wash 173, 84 P2d 681.

[45] Kalpakian v Oklahoma Sheraton Corp., (CA10 Okla) 398 F2d 243.

[46] There is authority that the hotelkeeper's lien may not be exercised unless the guest is given an impartial judicial hearing and that it is unconstitutional as a denial of due process to permit the hotelkeeper to hold or sell the guest's property without such a hearing. Klim v Jones, (DC ND Cal) 315 F Supp 109.

(3) surrender of the goods to the guest. In the last situation an exception is made when the goods are given to the guest for temporary use.

§ **22:20. Boarders or Lodgers.** To those persons who are permanent boarders or lodgers, rather than transient guests, the hotelkeeper owes only the duty of an ordinary bailee of their personal property under a mutual-benefit bailment.

A hotelkeeper has no common-law right of lien on property of his boarders or lodgers, as distinguished from his guests, in the absence of an express agreement between the parties. In a number of states, however, legislation giving a lien to a boardinghouse or a lodginghouse keeper has been enacted.

CASES FOR CHAPTER 22

Brace v Salem Cold Storage, Inc.

146 WVa 180, 118 SE2d 799 (1961)

Brace and his brother delivered cabbage to the Salem Cold Storage Company for refrigerated storage. The cabbage was later returned to them in a damaged condition. They sued Salem on the ground that through its negligence it had failed to keep the cabbage at a proper temperature. The jury returned a verdict in favor of the plaintiffs, but the trial judge set the verdict aside on the ground that the negligence of the warehouseman had not been established and that therefore the verdict in favor of the plaintiffs was not proper. The plaintiffs appealed from this action.

CALHOUN, J. . . . The liability of a warehouseman for negligence is stated in Code, 1931, 47-5-21, as follows: "A warehouseman shall be liable for any loss or injury to the goods caused by his failure to exercise such care in regard to them as a reasonably careful owner of similar goods would exercise; but he shall not be liable, in the absence of an agreement to the contrary, for any loss or injury to the goods which could not have been avoided by the exercise of such care." Statutes of this nature are merely declaratory of the common law. . . .

"It is well settled that when goods are stored in a warehouse, the relation of bailor and bailee, with its correlative rights and duties, is created between the depositor or owner of the goods and the warehouseman. The warehouseman is a bailee for hire." . . .

"Where goods in cold storage are damaged, the burden of proof of negligence of the warehouseman rests on the depositor or owner of the goods. The depositor or owner is not necessarily required, however, to show specific acts of negligence causing the damage. It is generally held that where the owner shows that the goods were in good condition at the time they were delivered to the cold-storage warehouse, and that they were returned in a damaged condition from a cause not inherent in the goods themselves, the owner has made out a prima facie case, and it is incumbent on the warehouseman to account for the injury to the goods in some manner consistent with the exercise of due care on his part, unless the damage is of such nature as to result from natural causes, or deterioration, or internal defects without fault on the part of the warehouseman. If the evidence of the warehouseman gives an explanation of the injury which is consistent with reasonable care on his part, the bailor must show positive negligence on the part of the coldstorage operator." . . .

The defendant was not an insurer of the cabbage stored in its cold storage warehouse, but was required to exercise only ordinary care. It was, nevertheless, required to employ the skill and peculiar knowledge requisite to the operation of the business in which it was engaged. In order to recover in this action, it was incumbent upon the plaintiffs to establish negligence on the part of the defendant, and that such negligence caused the damage to the cabbage. In a case such as this, if the owner of the goods proves that the goods when placed in the cold storage warehouse were in good condition and that, when demanded within a reasonable time, they were in a damaged condition, there may be cast upon the defendant warehouseman thereby a burden of going forward with the evidence, in accordance with principles previously stated herein; but the ultimate burden of proof remains upon the plaintiff throughout the trial to establish his case by a preponderance of the evidence. . . .

"When the evidence is conflicting, or when the facts, though undisputed, are such that reasonable men may draw different conclusions from them, the question of negligence is for the jury." . . . "As in other cases, the question whether the damage to or loss of perishable property in a cold-storage warehouse is due to the negligence of the warehouseman is one for determination by the jury, where there is substantial evidence on which to submit such issue." . . . [The Court then considered the conflicting testimony as to the warehouseman's negligence.] On the whole case, we feel that the facts bearing both upon the right to recover and upon the amount of the verdict were peculiarly for jury determination; and that the trial court would not have been warranted in setting aside the verdict on the ground of insufficiency of evidence to support such verdict. . . .

The judgment . . . is reversed, the verdict of the jury is reinstated, and judgment for the plaintiffs . . . is rendered in this court.

Code Comment: The provision of the West Virginia Statute cited in the opinion is virtually identical with UCC Sec. 7-204 stating the duty of care of a warehouseman. The same result would be reached under the Code.

Birmingham Television Corp. v Water Works

— Ala —, 290 So2d 636 (1974)

The Birmingham Television Corporation stored some equipment with Harris Warehouse Company. A water main in the city burst. The warehouse was flooded. The television corporation sued the water works and the warehouse. The warehouseman raised the defense that the action was not commenced within nine months after notice was given of the damage, as was expressly required by the terms of the warehouse receipt. The television corporation claimed that the provision was not binding because it was on the back of the receipt. Summary judgment was entered in favor of the warehouse. The television corporation appealed.

BLOODWORTH, J. . . . The sole issue on this appeal is whether or not the trial court was correct in granting a motion for summary judgment in favor of the appellees based upon the warehouse receipt provision limiting the time within which action may be maintained by the appellant against the appellees for damages to the bailed goods. We conclude that the trial court erred herein and reverse and remand. . . .

. . . (The nine-month limitation appears at the bottom of the copy hereinabove set forth under the heading "NOTICE OF CLAIM AND FILING OF SUIT—Sec. 12.") Motion for summary judgment was granted, whereupon appellant appealed. The Water Works is not a party to this appeal.

Appellant [argues that] nine months is unreasonable as a matter of law, . . . that the trial court erred in holding appellant to be bound by the nine-month limitation because there was no evidence that the provision was specifically called to appellant's attention, [and] that appellant cannot be charged with knowledge of the contract terms. . . .

. . . We think there existed for the jury's determination a genuine issue of fact as to whether the conditions of bailment set forth on the reverse side of the warehouse receipt were accepted by the appellant-bailor so as to become part of the bailment contract. . . .

"*Such special provision* in a contract of bailment *limiting bailee's liability,* to be effective, *must be known to, or brought to the notice of, the bailor, and be assented to by him.* . . . A disclaimer of liability can only become effective if brought to the bailor's knowledge. . . .

"More specifically, to the case at bar, the rule of modern authorities is that the bailor is not chargeable with notice of special provisions diminishing liability of the bailee which appear upon something not apparently related to the bailment contract itself or given to the bailor ostensibly as a ticket of identification of the bailed property, unless called to his attention or known to him. . . . Accordingly when appellant-bailor delivered 'possession, custody and control' of his automobile to appellee-bailee 'for a reward'—i.e. compensation for its safe-keeping—there was imposed on appellee the duty to exercise reasonable care to protect the property and upon request, within the terms of the contract when the condition of the bailment shall have been terminated, to redeliver it to the appellant. For negligent breach of this duty there was consequent liability.

"The receipt by appellant of the 'ticket' did not bind him to recitals of the disclaimer of liability on its reverse side unless known to him or brought to his notice or attention, thereby bringing such provision within and making it part of the terms of the bailment. . . .

Reviewing the facts in the instant case in light of the above stated principles, we find that a genuine issue of fact exists as to whether the terms on the reverse side of the warehouse receipt were accepted by the appellant-bailor and thereby became a part of the contract of bailment. Neither the motion for summary judgment nor appellees' pleas state whether the terms set forth on the reverse side of the warehouse receipt (which purport to materially modify both the common-law rights and obligations of bailor and bailee as well as the statutory provisions respecting limitation of actions) were called to the appellant's attention and were accepted by it.

Nor do we think that such knowledge on appellant's part can be presumed from the issuance of the warehouse receipt itself. The front of the warehouse receipt appears to be just that—a receipt identifying the bailed goods and listing charges—nothing more. No part of the contract appears on the face of the receipt. No notation appears on the face of the receipt advising the bailor to "see reverse side." Nothing on the face of the receipt in any way gives notice that the receipt is a contract of bailment which materially alters the rights of the parties.

. . . The bailor, *unless his attention is called to the fact that such conditions are intended as a part of the contract, is not charged with notice, where he has no actual knowledge, of provisions limiting liability which appear upon something not apparently related to the contract itself, or given to the bailor ostensibly for some other purpose.* There is authority which justifies the rule on the ground, among others, that the bailee, if he wishes to qualify his contract, should do so in an unmistakable manner, and *it is not reasonably to be expected, nor is the bailor required to anticipate, that important terms of a contract will be found upon what is accepted merely as a means of identification or for some other purpose which to a reasonable man would not appear to be germane to the agreement itself.*" . . .

We further note that appellant did not sign the purported contract of bailment on the reverse side of the warehouse receipt; nor is there anything in the record to reflect that appellant orally acknowledged and accepted these terms and conditions as being the contract of bailment.

Appellees argue that appellant's act of leaving the goods with the appellees constituted an acceptance of the terms on the reverse side of the warehouse receipt. . . .

While the acts of a party may under some circumstances be such as to constitute an acceptance of a contract, surely such could not be the case unless the acting party is shown to have had knowledge of the contract. Certainly, it would be unreasonable to interpret the act of tendering goods for bailment as an acceptance of specific contract terms where the bailor is not shown to have had knowledge or notice of the existence of said contract terms. . . . In the usual circumstances, the tendering of goods creates only a common law bailment.

. . . Appellees aver that the delivery of the receipts containing the purported contract *followed* appellant's depositing the equipment for storage. An act which precedes notice of the contract (assuming only for purposes of argument such receipt did give appellant notice) cannot be reasonably interpreted as an acceptance of said contract. . . .

Nor can appellant's subsequent retention of the receipt be interpreted as an acceptance of the terms and conditions on the reverse side. . . .

" 'Where, however, the bailor receives and retains the ticket without knowing that it contained any special terms or conditions and without his attention being called to that fact, and on the assumption that the ticket was merely a token or means of identifying his property, the majority of cases hold that such retention of the ticket does not constitute an acceptance of the terms therein and so he is not bound by the provisions for limited liability, on the theory that the minds of the parties never met: hence, the special contract was never entered into. The mere fact that the bailor examined the ticket sufficiently to know that there was printed matter thereon, and had opportunity to examine it critically, and had capacity to understand the meaning of it still does not make him chargeable with notice of the special provisions therein, for he is under no legal duty to read such matter, since, as has been stated, the ticket is considered primarily as a token or means of identification which is to be surrendered when the property is redelivered.' "

It is thus that we hold only that, under the facts of this cause as they appear in the record at this early stage of the proceedings, we cannot say that as matter of law appellant accepted the terms and conditions on the reverse side of the warehouse receipt as part of the contract of bailment. At the very least, it appears to be a question of fact for the jury as to whether or not appellant had actual notice or under the circumstances should be charged with notice, of the terms and conditions on the reverse side of the warehouse receipt, most notably the requirement that suit be brought within nine months rather than the usual six years.

Having concluded that there exists at least one genuine issue of fact for the jury's determination, we find it unnecessary to consider the other issues argued on this appeal.

We, therefore, conclude that the trial court erred in granting the motion for summary judgment in favor of appellees. . . .

[Judgment reversed and action remanded.]

Wells & Coverly v Red Star Express

62 Misc 2d 269, 306 NYS2d 710 (1969)

Irwin sold to Wells & Coverly merchandise that was shipped to the buyer by Red Star Express, a motor carrier. The goods never arrived. Wells & Coverly sued Red Star, which raised the defense that it had not been given notice of the loss within nine months as required by the tariff or regulations on file with the appropriate governmental agency and as required by the bill of lading that Red Star had issued on receiving the goods. Wells & Coverly moved for summary judgment.

CARDAMONE, J. . . . The plaintiff (consignee) has moved for summary judgment against the carrier on the loss in transit of two cartons of clothing shipped to the plaintiff clothing store by Harry Irwin, Inc., (shipper) on August 3, 1967, amounting to the sum of $990.20.

The two cartons of clothing were delivered to the defendant, Red Star Express Lines of Auburn, Inc., for delivery to the plaintiff, Wells & Coverly, Inc., a retail men's clothing store in Syracuse, New York, but the defendant trucking company failed to deliver the cartons to the plaintiff. Notice was given on August 3, 1967, by the defendant to Harry Irwin, Inc. that the said cartons had been lost. The plaintiff paid Irwin the full amount of $990.20 and has sought to recover this amount from the defendant, Red Star. The defendant admits (in its Statement dated January 7, 1969) that it had delivered to it the two cartons of clothing, that it did not make the delivery, and that it had given notice to Harry Irwin, Inc. that the cartons had been lost and that it had, since August 3, 1967, actual knowledge of this loss.

In opposition to the motion for summary judgment, the defendant claims that the bill of lading is subject to the applicable motor carrier classification or tariff. The terms of the tariff, filed with the appropriate regulatory agency, set forth as a condition precedent to recovery the requirement that claims must be filed, in writing, with the carrier within nine months after a reasonable time for delivery has elapsed. The defendant alleges that the plaintiff is bound by the terms of the bill of lading and the requirements of the applicable tariff and that it failed to file the required written notice within nine months.

The simple question is whether such tariff is binding on the plaintiff herein so as to defeat its motion for summary judgment, despite the defendant's admitted knowledge of the loss.

If this transaction is governed by the applicable provisions of the Uniform Commercial Code, the plaintiff is a person entitled to delivery by the defendant (UCC 7-403) and all of the provisions of the Uniform Commercial Code are subject to the tariff which has been filed (UCC 7-103). The questions then remaining would be whether the written proof of loss was filed by the plaintiff within the nine month period specified in the tariff and whether such nine month period was a reasonable limitation; if so, summary judgment should be granted to the plaintiff; if not, summary judgment should be granted to the defendant.

The rule of law construing the validity of the shortening of periods of limitation in a variety of commercial transactions is governed by a standard of reasonableness. This standard considers the provisions of the contract, the circumstances of its performance and the bargaining positions of the parties. . . . Generally, where there is an effective reduction in a time limitation, the parties in litigation were both parties to the contract and had an opportunity to bargain with one another regarding its termination. Even so, the courts have considered some limitations unenforceable as being unreasonable. The plaintiff here is not a party to the contract and had no opportunity to bargain as to this limitation of time. Thus, under the general rule, such a limitation of time would be unenforceable insofar as this plaintiff is concerned. . . .

This Court has concluded, however, that the facts here do not bring this transaction within the provisions of the Uniform Commercial Code. A careful analysis of all of the papers lead to the conclusion that the goods in question were never delivered by the defendant carrier to the plaintiff at its place of business in Syracuse. Similarly, and as a logical corollary, the bill of lading was never delivered to the plaintiff, either. The carrier is required to tender such bill of lading to the consignee when the shipment is delivered. . . . Not having received the goods or the bill of lading, this Court concludes that the plaintiff was not bound by the terms thereof.

Finally, the defendant admits that: (1) it did not make the delivery to the plaintiff; (2) it gave notice to the shipper that the cartons had been lost; (3) since August 3, 1967, it has had actual knowledge of the fact of its loss of the cartons which were to have been delivered to the plaintiff. On basic equitable principles, it is impractical to charge the plaintiff here with a duty to search the applicable tariff in order to ascertain the existence of a time limitation. It is more reasonable to impose the burden on the defendant carrier, who has knowledge of such time limitation, requiring it, once it had knowledge of the loss, to serve a clear, distinct, and unequivocal notice on the plaintiff fixing the time within which the plaintiff is required to prepare and file a written claim. . . . Having neither tendered the bill of lading nor served such a notice on the plaintiff, the defendant cannot be heard to complain now that it did not receive a written notice of a loss which it caused itself and of which it had knowledge.

This record presents no questions of fact the solution of which should await a trial. Accordingly, plaintiff's motion for summary judgment is granted with costs.

Morse v Piedmont Hotel Co.

110 Ga App 509, 139 SE2d 133 (1964)

Morse, a jewelry salesman, was a guest in the Piedmont Hotel. He entrusted a sample case to a bellboy of the hotel to place on the airport bus of an independent taxicab company. At some point between the hotel and the airport the sample case disappeared. The guest's employer was paid for the loss by his insurer, but the insurer then canceled the policy as to Morse and Morse was then fired by the employer. No other insurance company would cover him as a jewelry salesman, with the result that he was unable to get another job as such, although he had been a jewelry salesman for 40 years. This shock induced a heart attack that confined him

at home for several months. Morse then sued both the hotel and the taxicab company for the earnings that he had lost, claiming $100,000; and damages for pain and suffering, claiming $25,000. From a judgment for the defendants, Morse appealed.

HALL, J. . . . The plaintiff relies on the decision in G. C. G. Jewelry Manufacturing Corp. v Atlanta Baggage & Cab Co., 109 Ga App 469, 136 SE 419, another case which arose out of the loss of the jewelry sample case which allegedly caused the damages the plaintiff sues for in the present case. There the plaintiff's employer sued the defendant cab company as a bailee for the loss of the sample case, and this court held the petition set forth a cause of action. That was an action for property damages caused by the bailee's negligence, for which a bailee is clearly liable. . . . The decision does not support the present action against allegedly negligent bailees, which seeks damages for the plaintiff's inability, resulting from the theft of the jewelry sample case, to obtain insurance covering him as a jewelry salesman and the consequent loss of his employment and earning capacity in this occupation and physical and mental pain and suffering.

In this petition the only duty allegedly owed to the plaintiff and breached by the defendants is the duty to protect the property the plaintiff entrusted to the defendants. The only damages that the plaintiff claims to have resulted to him from this alleged breach of duty are consequent to the loss of an insurance company which had to compensate the plaintiff's employer for its loss of the stolen jewelry case. For such indirect damages the law does not allow recovery. . . .

Generally a person is not liable for the unintentional invasion of the interest of another in his contractual or employment relationships with third persons. The rights or interests of the plaintiff which he alleges have been damaged —the interest in retaining insurance protection and the interest in his employment—he had by virtue of relations with others than the defendants in this case. The petition does not show that the plaintiff had property rights in his relationships with the insurance company, or his employer, but such interests of the plaintiff as were damaged inhered in these relationships. The law does not place upon these defendants the duty to protect these interests of the plaintiff against unintentional invasion. . . .

[Judgment affirmed.]

QUESTIONS AND CASE PROBLEMS

1. Johnston, a guest in a hotel operated by the Mobile Hotel Co., entrusted his property to the hotel. During the night the property was stolen from the hotel in spite of the careful protection given the property by the hotel. Johnston sued the hotel, which claimed it was not liable because the robbers were public enemies and that fact excused the hotel. Was this defense valid? [Johnston v Mobile Hotel Co., 27 Ala App 145, 167 So 595; cert den 232 Ala 175, 167 So 596]
2. Norvell took certain trunks containing samples to the St. George Hotel. The hotelkeepers knew that the sample trunks belonged to J. R. Torrey & Co. The trunks were retained to secure payment of Norvell's unpaid board bill under an alleged statutory right. The statute gave any hotelkeeper a "specific lien upon all property or baggage deposited with them for the amount of the charges against them or their owners if guests at such hotel." J. R. Torrey & Co. brought an action against the owners of the hotel to recover for a wrongful detention of the trunks. Was it entitled to judgment? [Torrey v McClellan, 17 Tex Civ App 371, 43 SW 64]
3. Evers owned and operated a warehouse. De Cecchis phoned and inquired as to the rates and then brought furniture in for storage. Nothing was said at any time about any limitation of the liability of Evers as a warehouseman. A warehouse receipt was mailed to De Cecchis several days later. The receipt

contained a clause that limited liability to $50 per package stored. Was the limitation of liability binding on De Cecchis? [De Cecchis v Evers, 54 Del 99, 174 A2d 463]

4. The J. C. Trucking Co., Inc., was engaged under contracts to transport dress material from New York City to dressmaking establishments in New Haven, Hartford, and Bridgeport, Connecticut, and then to transport the finished dresses back to New York City. Dresses that were being carried to Ace-High Dresses, Inc., were stolen from the trucking company. Ace-High Dresses sued the trucking company and claimed that the latter was liable for the loss as a common carrier. Was it a common carrier? [Ace-High Dresses v J. C. Trucking Co., 122 Conn 578, 191 A 536]

5. Dovax Fabrics, Inc. had been shipping goods by a common carrier, G & A Delivery Corp., for over a year, during which all of G & A's bills to Dovax bore the notation, "Liability limited to $50 unless greater value is declared and paid for. . . ." Dovax gave G & A three lots of goods, having a total value of $1,799.95. A truck containing all three was stolen that night, without negligence on the part of G & A. Should Dovax recover from G & A (a) $1,799.95, (b) $150 for the three shipments, or (c) nothing? [Dovax Fabrics, Inc. v G & A Delivery Corp., (NY Civil Ct) 4 UCCRS 492]

6. McCarley sued the Foster-Milburn Co., a medical manufacturing company. He claimed that there was jurisdiction to bring the lawsuit because Foster was doing business within the state through an agent, Obergfel. Foster supplied Obergfel with a product called *Westsal,* made by a subsidiary of Foster. Obergfel was to sell this product directly to doctors. He also sold products produced by other medical manufacturers. Obergfel solicited orders from doctors, sold in his own name, incurred all expenses, made all collections, and after deducting his commissions, remitted the balance to Foster. Foster shipped the *Westsal* to Obergfel, who warehoused it and then reshipped it to the purchasers. If Obergfel was not an agent of Foster, the suit was not properly brought. Was Obergfel the agent of Foster? [McCarley v Foster-Milburn Co., (DC WD NY) 93 F Supp 421]

7. Vanguard Transfer Co. ran a moving and storage business. It obtained an insurance policy from the St. Paul Fire & Marine Insurance Co. covering goods which it had "accepted at the warehouse for storage." Dahl rented a room in Vanguard's building. Both Dahl and Vanguard had keys to the room. Dahl was charged a flat monthly rental for the room and could keep any property there which he desired. Vanguard did not make any record of the goods which Dahl brought to the warehouse. There was a fire in the warehouse and Dahl's property was destroyed. He sued the insurance company. Was it liable? [Dahl v St. Paul & Marine Insurance Co., 36 Wis 2d 420, 153 NW2d 624]

8. David Crystal sent merchandise by Ehrlich-Newmark Trucking Co. The truck with Crystal's shipment of goods was hijacked in New York City. Crystal sued Ehrlich-Newmark for the loss. It defended on the ground that it was not liable because the loss had been caused by a public enemy. Was this defense valid? [David Crystal, Inc. v Ehrlich-Newmark Trucking Co., Inc., (NY Civil Ct) 314 NYS2d 559]

9. The patron of a motel opened the bedroom window at night and went to sleep. During the night a prowler pried open the screen, entered the room, and stole property of the guest. The patron sued the motel. The motel raised the contentions that it was not responsible for property in the possession of the guest and that the guest had been contributorily negligent in opening the window. Under what circumstances could the patron recover damages? [Buck v Hankin, 217 Pa Super 262, 269 A2d 344]

10. The Utah Public Service Commission granted a contract carrier permit to the Salt Lake Transportation Company to transport passengers between the Salt Lake airport for four principal airlines and the three leading hotels in the city. The Realty Purchasing Company and various hotels and taxicab companies objected to the granting of the permit on the ground that the company performed a taxicab service and was therefore a common carrier. Decide. [Realty Purchasing Co. v Public Service Commission, 9 Utah 2d 375, 345 P2d 606]

11. Wells Fargo wished to operate an armored car service in Nebraska and applied to the state Railway Commission for permission to solicit business from all persons desiring to ship cash, letters, books, and data processing materials. The Commission granted it a license as a contract carrier. Was it a contract carrier? [Wells Fargo Armored Service Corp. v Bankers Dispatch Corp., 186 Neb 263, 182 NW2d 648]

12. Flores stored his furniture with Didear Van & Storage Company. The storage charges were not kept up-to-date and a notice dated April 15 was sent to Flores stating that the goods would be sold for nonpayment of storage charges if the charges were not paid on or before April 24. Didear sold the furniture. Flores thereafter sued Didear for conversion. Could Flores recover? [Flores v Didear Van & Storage Co., (Tex Civ App) 489 SW2d 406]

13. Olson stored a Persian rug with Security Van Lines. Nothing was said to her as to liability for moth damage. Ten days thereafter, Security Van Lines sent her a warehouse receipt for the rug. The receipt contained a provision stating that the warehouseman was not liable for moth damage. While in the possession of Security, the rug was damaged greatly by moths. Olson sued Security for the value of the rug. It raised the defense that it was not liable because of the warehouse receipt provision. Was this provision a valid defense? [Olson v Security Van Lines, Inc., (La App) 297 So2d 647]

23 Nature and Form of Sales

NATURE AND LEGALITY

The most common business transactions involve the sale and purchase of goods, that is, items of tangible personal property, such as food, clothing, and books. The law of sales is a fusion of the law merchant, the common law of England, and former statutes as modified and codified by Article 2 of the Uniform Commercial Code.

§ **23:1. Definition.** A *sale of goods* is a present transfer of title to movable personal property in consideration of a payment of money, an exchange of other property, or the performance of services.[1] The consideration in a sale, regardless of its nature, is known as the *price*; it need not be money. The parties to a sale are the person who owns the goods and the person to whom the title is transferred. The transferor is the seller or vendor, and the transferee is the buyer or vendee. If the price is payable wholly or partly in goods, each party is a seller insofar as the goods he is to transfer are concerned.

When a free item is given with the purchase of other goods, it is the purchasing of the other goods which is the price for the "free" goods and hence the transaction as to the free goods is a sale.[2]

§ **23:2. Sale Distinguished.** A sale is an actual present transfer of title. If there is a transfer of a lesser interest than ownership or title, the transaction is not a sale.

*(1) **Bailment.*** A bailment is not a sale because only possession is transferred to the bailee. The bailor remains the owner.

Since a bailment is distinct from a sale, the common practice of leasing equipment and automobiles on a long-term basis would have the effect of making bailment law applicable to many transactions that would otherwise be governed by the law of sales. There is a trend in the law, however, to hold the bailor to the same responsibilities as a seller. Likewise, statutes applicable to "owners" may define that term to include lessees under long-term leases.[3]

*(2) **Gift.*** There can be no sale without consideration, or a price. A gift is a gratuitous transfer of the title of property.

---

1 De Mers v O'Leary, 126 Mont 528, 254 P2d 1080; Com. v Kayfield, (Pa) 40 D&C 2d 689.

2 Sheppard v Revlon, Inc., (Fla App) 267 So2d 662.

3 The New York Vehicle & Traffic Law defines "owner" to include a lessee renting an automobile for more than 30 days. Aetna Casualty & Surety Co. v World Wide Rent-A-Car, Inc., 28 App Div 2d 286, 284 NYS2d 807.

*(3) **Contract to Sell.*** When the parties intend that title to goods will pass at a future time and they make a contract providing for that event, a *contract to sell* is created.[4]

*(4) **Option to Purchase.*** A sale, a present transfer of title, differs from an *option to purchase.* The latter is neither a transfer of title nor a contract to transfer title but a power to require a sale to be made at a future time.[5]

*(5) **Conditional Sale.*** A *conditional sale* customarily refers to a "condition precedent" transaction by which title does not vest in the purchaser until he has paid in full for the property purchased. This was formerly a common type of sale used when personal property was purchased on credit and payment was to be made in installments. This transaction is now classified as a secured transaction under Article 9 of the UCC.

*(6) **Furnishing of Labor or Services.*** A contract for personal services is to be distinguished from a sale of goods even when some transfer of personal property is involved in the performing of the services. For example, the contract of a repairman is a contract for services even though in making the repairs he may supply parts necessary to perform his task. The supplying of such parts is not regarded as a sale because it is merely incidental to the primary contract of making repairs, as contrasted with the purchase of goods, such as a television set, with the incidental service of installation.

Similarly, when a surgical pin is inserted in the bone as part of hospitalization, the transaction as to the pin cannot be isolated and treated as a sale but is merely part of a broad contract for services. And an agreement by an artist to make a painting on a television program and donate the painting as part of a charitable drive is an agreement to render services and not a contract for sale of goods.[6]

In four fifths of the states, statutes limit the liability of hospitals and blood banks for harm resulting from transfusions to cases in which negligence of the defendant is shown.[7]

§ 23:3. Subject Matter of Sales. The subject matter of a sale is anything that is movable when it is identified as the subject of the transaction.[8] The subject matter may not be (1) investment securities, such as stocks and bonds, the sale of which is regulated by Article 8 of the UCC; (2) choses in action, such as insurance policies and promissory notes, since they are assigned or

---

[4] UCC § 2-106(1).

[5] Western Helicopter Operations v Nelson, 118 Cal App 2d 359, 257 P2d 1025.

[6] National Historic Shrines Foundation v Dali, (NY) 4 UCCRS 71.

[7] A statute declaring the nonliability of hospitals and blood banks supplying blood for a transfusion is constitutional as against the contention that it deprives one of due process and equal protection. McDaniel v Baptist Memorial Hospital, (CA6 Tenn) 469 F2d 230 (refusing to impose strict tort liability).

[8] UCC § 2-105(1). It may also include things which are attached to the land, such as those consisting of (a) timber or minerals or buildings or materials forming part of buildings if they are to be removed or severed by the seller, and (b) other things attached to land to be removed by either party. § 2-107.

negotiated rather than sold, or which, because of their personal nature, are not transferable in any case; or (3) real estate, such as a house, factory, or farm.

Most goods are tangible and solid, such as an automobile or a chair. But goods may also be fluid, as oil or gasoline. Goods may also be intangible, as natural gas and electricity. (See p. 456, Helvey v Wabash County REMC.) The UCC does not apply to the sale of a business.[9]

(1) Nonexistent and Future Goods. Generally a person cannot make a present sale of nonexistent or future goods or goods that he does not own. He can make a contract to sell such goods at a future date; but since he does not have the title, he cannot transfer that title now. For example, an agreement made today that all the fish caught on a fishing trip tomorrow shall belong to a particular person does not make him the owner of those fish today.

When the parties purport to effect a present sale of future goods, the agreement operates only as a contract to sell the goods.[10] Thus, a farmer purporting to transfer the title today to the future crop would be held subject to a duty to transfer title to the crop when it came into existence. If he did not keep the promise, he could be sued for breach of contract; but the contract would not operate to vest the title in the buyer automatically.

§ 23:4. Law of Contracts Applicable. A sale is a voluntary transaction between two parties. Accordingly, most of the principles that apply to contractual agreements in general are equally applicable to a sale. Modern marketing practices, however, have modified the strict principles of contract law, and this approach to the problem is carried into the UCC. Thus, a sales contract can be made in any manner; and it is sufficient that the parties by their conduct recognize the existence of a contract, even though it cannot be determined when the contract was made, and generally even though one or more terms are left open.[11]

In some instances the UCC treats all buyers and sellers alike. In others, it treats merchants differently than it does the occasional or casual buyer or seller; in this way the UCC recognizes that the merchant is experienced in his field and has a specialized knowledge of the relevant commercial practices.[12]

(1) Offer. Contract law as to offers is applicable to sales except that an offer by a merchant cannot be revoked, even though there is no consideration to keep the offer open, if the offer expresses an intention that it will not

---

[9] Field v Golden Triangle Broadcasting, Inc., 451 Pa 410, 305 A2d 689 (two radio stations together with their assets).

[10] § 2-105(2).

[11] § 2-204. This provision of the UCC is limited by requiring that there be "a reasonably certain basis for giving an appropriate remedy."

[12] § 2-104(1).

be revoked, is made in writing, and is signed by the merchant.[13] The expressed period of irrevocability, however, cannot exceed three months. If nothing is said as to the duration of the offer, this irrevocability continues only for a reasonable time.

(2) Acceptance. The UCC redeclares the general principle of contract law that an offer to buy or sell goods may be accepted in any manner and by any medium which is reasonable under the circumstances, unless a specific manner or medium is clearly indicated by the terms of the offer or the circumstances of the case.[14]

(a) ACCEPTANCE BY SHIPMENT. Unless otherwise clearly indicated, an order or other offer to buy goods that are to be sent out promptly or currently can be accepted by the seller either by actually shipping the goods, as though a unilateral contract offer had been made; or by promptly promising to make shipment, as though a bilateral contract, that is, an exchange of promises, had been offered.[15] If acceptance is made by shipping the goods, the seller must notify the buyer within a reasonable time that the offer has been accepted in this manner.[16]

(b) ADDITIONAL TERMS IN ACCEPTANCE. Unless it is expressly specified that an offer to buy or sell goods must be accepted just as made, the offeree may accept a contract but at the same time propose an additional term. This new term, however, does not become binding unless the offeror thereafter consents to it. Consequently, when the buyer sends an order which the seller acknowledges on his own printed form, any additional material term in the seller's printed form that is not in the buyer's order form or which is not implied by custom or prior dealings is merely regarded as an additional term that may or may not be accepted by the buyer. That is, the order is deemed "accepted" in spite of the addition of this new material term, but the new term does not become part of the contract until it in turn is accepted by the buyer. (See p. 457, Application of Doughboy Industries, Inc.)

The acceptance by the buyer may be found either in his express statement, orally or in writing, that he accepts the additional term; or it may be deduced from his conduct, as when he accepts the goods with knowledge that the additional term has been made.

In a transaction between merchants, the additional term becomes part of the contract if that term does not materially alter the offer and no objection is made to it.[17] If this additional term in the seller's form of acknowledgment operates solely to his advantage, however, it is a material term which must be accepted by the buyer to be effective.

---

[13] § 2-205.

[14] § 2-206(1)(a).

[15] § 2-206(1)(b).

[16] § 2-206(2).

[17] § 2-207; Application of Doughboy Industries, Inc., 17 App Div 2d 216, 233 NYS2d 488.

*(3) **Determination of Price.*** The price for the goods may be expressly fixed by the contract, or the parties may merely indicate the manner of determining price at a later time.[18] A sales contract is binding even though it calls for a specified price "plus extras" but does not define the extras, which it leaves for future agreement.[19]

When persons experienced in a particular industry make a contract without specifying the price to be paid, the price will be determined by the manner which is customary in the industry. Consequently, where the parties knew that the custom of the industry was to pay for sugar beets at a later date on the basis of the sugar content of the beets supplied and of the selling price of sugar for the current year, a contract for the sale of a crop of sugar beets is not void because it does not specify a price and the price will be determined according to the industry custom.[20]

Ordinarily, if nothing is said as to price, the buyer is required to pay the reasonable value of the goods. The reasonable price is generally the market price, but not necessarily, as when the market price is under the control of the seller. When the contract did not fix the price of potatoes, the buyer was obligated to pay the reasonable price for potatoes at the place and time of delivery, and the federal-state market news reports for that city on the day after the potatoes were delivered were evidence of such reasonable price.[21]

In recent years there has been an increase in use of the "cost plus" formula for determining price. Under this form of agreement the buyer pays the seller a sum equal to the cost to the seller of obtaining the goods plus a specified percentage of that cost.

The contract may expressly provide that one of the parties may determine the price, in which case he must act in good faith in so doing.[22] Likewise, the contract may specify that the price shall be determined by some standard or by a third person. If for any reason other than the fault of one of the parties the price cannot be fixed in the manner specified, the buyer is required to pay the reasonable value for the goods unless it is clear that the parties intended that if the price were not determined in the manner specified, there would be no contract. In the latter case the buyer must return the goods and the seller refund any payment made on account. If the buyer is unable to return such goods, he must pay their reasonable value at the time of delivery.

*(4) **Output and Requirement Contracts.*** Somewhat related to the open-term concept concerning price is that involved in the output and requirement contracts in which the quantity which is to be sold or purchased is not a specific quantity but is such amount as the seller should produce

---

[18] UCC § 2-305.

[19] Silver v Sloop Silver Cloud, (DC SD NY) 259 F Supp 187.

[20] California Lettuce Growers v Union Sugar Co., 45 Cal 2d 474, 289 P2d 785.

[21] Lamberta v Smiling Jim Potato Co., (US Dept of Agriculture) 25 AD 1181, 3 UCCRS 981.

[22] Good faith requires that the party in fact act honestly and, in the case of a merchant, also requires that he follow reasonable commercial standards of fair dealing which are recognized in the trade. UCC §§ 1-201(19), 2-103(b).

or the buyer should require. Although this introduces an element of uncertainty, such sales contracts are valid. To prevent oppression, they are subject to two limitations: (a) the parties must act in good faith; and (b) the quantity offered or demanded must not be unreasonably disproportionate to prior output or requirements or to a stated estimate.[23] (See p. 458, Romine, Inc. v Savannah Steel Co.)

When the sales contract is a continuing contract, as one calling for periodic delivery of fuel, but no time is set for the life of the contract, the contract runs for a reasonable time but may be terminated on notice by either party unless otherwise agreed.[24]

*(5) **Seals.*** A seal on a contract or on an offer of sale has no effect. Thus, in determining whether there is consideration or if the statute of limitations is applicable, the fact that there is a seal on the contract is ignored.[25]

*(6) **Usage of Trade and Course of Dealing.*** Established usages or customs of trade and prior courses of conduct or dealings between the parties are to be considered in connection with any sales transaction. In the absence of an express term excluding or "overruling" the prior pattern of dealings between the parties and the usages of the trade, it is to be concluded that the parties contracted on the basis of the continuation of those patterns of doing business. More specifically, the patterns of doing business as shown by the prior dealings of the parties and usages of the trade enter into and form part of their contract and may be looked to in order to find what was intended by the express provisions of the contract and to supply otherwise missing terms. (See p. 459, In re Boone Livestock Co.)

*(7) **Implied Conditions.*** The field of implied conditions under contract law is broadened to permit the release of a party from obligation under a sales contract when performance has been made commercially impracticable, as distinguished from impossible: (a) by the occurrence of a contingency, the nonoccurrence of which was a basic assumption on which the contract was made; or (b) by compliance in good faith with any applicable domestic or foreign governmental regulation or order, whether or not it is later held valid by the courts.[26] "A severe shortage of raw materials or of supplies due to a contingency such as war, embargo, local crop failure, unforeseen shutdown of major sources of supply, or the like, which either causes a marked increase in cost or altogether prevents the seller from securing supplies necessary to his performance, is within the contemplation" of this provision of the UCC.[27]

---

[23] UCC § 2-306(1).

[24] UCC § 2-309(2); Sinkoff Beverage Co. v Schlitz Brewing Co., 51 Misc 2d 446, 273 NYS2d 364.

[25] UCC § 2-203.

[26] UCC § 2-615(a). If under the circumstances indicated in the text the seller is totally disabled from performing, he is discharged from his contract. If he is able to produce some goods, he must allocate them among customers, but any customer may reject the contract and such fractional offer. § 2-615(b), § 2-616.

[27] § 2-615, Official Comment, point 4.

(8) Modification of Contract. A departure is made from the general principles of contract law in that an agreement to modify the contract for the sale of goods is binding even though the modification is not supported by consideration.[28]

(9) Parol Evidence Rule. The parol evidence rule applies to the sale of goods with the slight modification that a writing is not presumed or assumed to represent the entire contract of the parties unless the court specifically decides that it does. If the court so decides, parol evidence is admissible to show what the parties meant by their words but cannot add additional terms to the writing. If the court decides that the writing was not intended to represent the entire contract, the writing may be supplemented by parol proof of additional terms so long as such terms are not inconsistent with the original written terms.[29]

A sales contract, although written, may be modified by an oral agreement except to the extent that a writing is required by the statute of frauds. Even when the sales contract specifies that there cannot be an oral modification, the conduct of the parties may be such that there is a waiver of such prohibition and an oral modification is then binding.[30]

(10) Fraud and Other Defenses. The defenses that may be raised in a suit on a sales contract are in general the same as on any other contract. When one party is defrauded, he may cancel the transaction and recover what he has paid or the goods that he has delivered, together with damages for any loss which he has sustained. If title was obtained by the buyer by means of his fraud, the title is voidable by an innocent seller while the goods are still owned by the buyer and the sale may be set aside.

If the sales contract or any clause in it was unconscionable when made, a court may refuse to enforce it, as discussed in Chapter 14.

§ 23:5. Illegal Sales. Certain conditions must exist for a sale to be considered illegal.

(1) Illegality at Common Law. At common law a sale is illegal if the subject matter is itself bad. The transaction may also be illegal even though the subject matter of the sale may be unobjectionable in itself, as when the agreement provides that the goods that are sold shall be employed for some unlawful purpose or when the seller assists in the unlawful act. To illustrate, when the seller falsely brands goods, representing them to be imported, to assist the buyer in perpetrating a fraud, the sale is illegal. The mere fact, however, that the seller has knowledge of the buyer's unlawful purpose does not, under the general rule, make the sale illegal unless the purpose is the commission of a serious crime.

---

[28] § 2-209(1).

[29] § 2-202; Hunt Foods and Industries v Doliner, 49 Misc 2d 246, 267 NYS2d 364.

[30] C.I.T. Corp. v Jonnet, 419 Pa 435, 214 A2d 620.

(2) Illegality Under Statutes. Practically every state has legislation prohibiting certain sales when they are not conducted according to the requirements of the statutes. Thus, a statute may require that a particular class of goods, such as meat, be inspected before a legal sale can be made. In addition to statutes which invalidate the sale, a number of statutes make it a criminal act or impose a penalty for making a sale under certain circumstances. Statutes commonly regulate sales by establishing standards as to grading, size, weight, and measure, and by prohibiting adulteration.

In addition to the restrictive state statutes, federal legislation regulates the sale of goods in interstate commerce. The federal Food, Drug, and Cosmetic Act, for example, prohibits the interstate shipment of misbranded or adulterated foods, drugs, cosmetics, and therapeutic devices. A product which does not carry adequate use instructions and warnings is deemed "misbranded" for the purpose of the statutes.[31] Other statutes, such as those designed to regulate competition, further protect the consumer from fraud.

States may prohibit the making of sales on Sunday either generally or as to particular commodities or classes of stores. Such laws do not violate any guarantee of religious freedom nor deprive persons of the equal protection of the laws. In some instances, however, a Sunday closing law may be unconstitutional because it is too vague.[32]

(3) Effect of Illegal Sale. An illegal sale or contract to sell cannot be enforced. This rule is based on public policy. As a general rule, courts will not aid either party in recovering money or property transferred pursuant to an illegal agreement. Relief is sometimes given, however, to an innocent party to an unlawful agreement. For example, if one party is the victim of a fraudulent transaction. he may recover what he has transferred to the other party even though the agreements between them arose out of some illegal scheme.

§ 23:6. Bulk Transfer. Whenever a merchant is about to transfer a major part of his materials, supplies, merchandise, or other inventory, not in the ordinary course of business, advance notice of the transfer must be given to his creditors in accordance with Article 6 of the Uniform Commercial Code. The essential characteristic of businesses subject to Article 6 is that they sell from inventory or a stock of goods,[33] as contrasted with businesses which render services. If the required notice is not given, the creditors may reach the sold property in the hands of the transferee and also in the hands of any subsequent transferee who knew that there had not been compliance with the UCC or who did not pay value.[34] This is designed to protect creditors of a merchant from the danger that he may sell all of his inventory, pocket the money, and then disappear, leaving them unpaid. The protection

[31] United States v Sullivan, 332 US 689.
[32] Minnesota v Target Stores, 279 Minn 447, 156 NW2d 908.
[33] Silco Automatic Vending Co. v Howells, 105 NJ Super 511, 253 A2d 480.
[34] UCC § 6-101 et seq.

given to creditors by the bulk transfer legislation is in addition to the protection which they have against their debtor for fraudulent transfers or conveyances, and the remedies that can be employed in bankruptcy proceedings.

Ordinarily, the transferee who receives the goods does not become liable for the debts of his transferor merely because the requirements of Article 6 have not been satisfied. If the transferee has mixed the transferred goods with his own goods so that it is not possible to identify the transferred goods, the transferee is personally liable for debts of the transferor. (See p. 460, Cornelius v J & R Motor Supply Corp.)

The fact that there has been noncompliance with Article 6 of the UCC regulating bulk transfers, however, does not affect the validity of a bulk sale of goods as between the immediate parties to the transfer since Article 6 is operative only with respect to the rights of creditors of the seller.[35]

FORMALITY OF THE SALES CONTRACT

In order to afford protection from false claims, sales of goods above a certain amount, subject to certain exceptions, must be evidenced by a writing.

§ **23:7. Amount.** The statute of frauds provision of the Uniform Commercial Code applies whenever the sales price is $500 or more.[36] If the total contract price equals or exceeds this amount, the law applies even though the contract covers several articles, the individual amounts of which are less than $500, provided the parties intended to make a single contract rather than a series of separate or divisible contracts. In the latter case, if each contract is for less than $500, no writing is required.

§ **23:8. Nature of the Writing Required.** To be effective, the writing evidencing the sales contract must meet certain requirements.

(1) Terms. The writing need only give assurance that there was a transaction. Specifically it need only indicate that a sale or contract to sell has been made and state the quantity of goods involved. Any other missing terms may be shown by parol evidence in the event of a dispute.[37]

(2) Signature. The writing must be signed by the person who is being sued or his authorized agent. The signature must be placed on the writing with the intention of authenticating the writing. It may consist of initials or be printed, stamped, or typewritten as long as made with the necessary intent.

When the transaction is between merchants, an exception is made to the requirement of signing. The failure of a merchant to repudiate a confirming letter sent him by another merchant binds him just as though he had signed the letter or other writing.[38] This ends the evil of a one-sided

---

[35] Macy v Oswald, 198 Pa Super 435, 182 A2d 94.
[36] UCC § 2-201.
[37] § 2-201(1).
[38] § 2-201(2). The confirming letter must be sent within a reasonable time after the transaction, and the receiving merchant must give written notice of his objection thereto within ten days after receiving the confirming letter.

writing under which the sender of the letter was bound, but the receiver could safely ignore the transaction or could hold the sender as he chose.

The provision as to merchants makes it necessary for a merchant buyer or merchant seller to watch his mail and to act promptly if he is not to be bound by a contract for sale with respect to which he has signed no writing. It deprives the party who fails to reject the confirmation of the defense of the statute of frauds.[39]

(3) Time of Execution. The required writing may be made at any time at or after the making of the sale. It may even be made after the contract has been broken or a suit brought on it, since the essential element is the existence of written proof of the transaction when the trial is held. Accordingly, when the buyer writes in reply to the seller, after a 45-day delay, and merely criticizes the quality of some of the goods, the conduct of the buyer is a confirmation.[40]

(4) Particular Writings. The writing may be a single writing, or it may be several writings considered as a group. Formal contracts, bills of sale, letters, and telegrams are common forms of writings that satisfy the requirement. Purchase orders, cash register receipts, sales tickets, invoices, and similar papers generally do not satisfy the requirements as to a signature, and sometimes they do not specify any quantity or commodity.

§ 23:9. Effect of Noncompliance. A sales agreement that does not comply with the statute of frauds is not enforceable, nor can the noncomplying agreement be raised as a defense.[41] The defense that a sales contract does not satisfy the requirements may be waived, however, and the contract then enforced as though the statute of frauds had been satisfied.

When the question is whether there has been a sale or a bailment, the fact that there is a writing under the statute of frauds is evidence indicating that the transaction was a sale. Conversely, the fact that an automobile dealer did not execute either a bill of sale or a memorandum satisfying the requirement of a writing was evidence which confirmed the contention of the car owner that he had not sold his automobile to the dealer but had entrusted it to him for resale. The result was that the dealer was the owner's agent or bailee, and the dealer was therefore guilty of embezzlement when he did not account to the owner for the proceeds from the resale of the car.[42]

§ 23:10. When Proof of Oral Contract Is Permitted. The absence of a writing does not always bar proof of a sales contract.

(1) Receipt and Acceptance. An oral sales contract may be enforced if it can be shown that the goods were delivered by the seller and were

---

[39] Reich v Helen Harper, (NY) 3 UCCRS 1048.

[40] Reich v Helen Harper, (NY) 3 UCCRS 1048.

[41] UCC § 2-201(1). However, the contract itself is not unlawful and may be voluntarily performed by the parties.

[42] Benefield v Alabama, 5 Ala Crim Div 4, 246 So2d 479.

received and accepted by the buyer. Consequently, when the buyer purchases and receives goods on credit, the seller may sue for the purchase price even though the total is $500 and there is no writing, for the reason that the receipt and acceptance of the goods by the buyer took the contract out of the statute of frauds.[43] Both a receipt and an acceptance by the buyer must be shown. If only part of the goods have been received and accepted, the contract may be enforced only insofar as it relates to those goods received and accepted.[44]

The buyer's receipt of the goods may be symbolic, as in the case of the seller's transfer of a covering bill of lading to the buyer.

When the goods are delivered at the buyer's direction to a third person who accepts the goods, the oral contract of the buyer is taken out of the statute of frauds. Consequently, a broker's oral contract is taken out of the statute when, following his instructions, the goods are delivered to the broker's customer and are then accepted by the customer.[45]

(2) ***Payment.*** An oral contract may be enforced if the buyer has made full payment. In the case of part payment for divisible units of goods, a contract may be enforced only with respect to goods for which payment has been made and accepted.[46] When the goods are not divisible, as in the case of an automobile, the part payment takes the entire contract out of the statute of frauds.[47]

There is some uncertainty under this rule as to the effectiveness of "payment" by check or a promissory note executed by the buyer. Under the law of commercial paper a check or note is conditional payment when delivered, and it does not become absolute until the instrument is paid. The earlier decisions held that the delivery of a negotiable instrument was not such a payment as would make the oral contract enforceable unless it was agreed at that time that the instrument was to be accepted as absolute, and not conditional, payment. A modern contrary view, which is influenced by the fact that businessmen ordinarily regard the delivery of a check or note as "payment," holds that the delivery of such an instrument is sufficient to make the oral contract enforceable.[48]

When the buyer has negotiated or assigned to the seller a commercial paper that was executed by a third person and the seller has accepted the instrument, a payment has been made within the meaning of the statute of frauds.

---

[43] Gardner and Beedon Co. v Cooke, — Ore —, 513 P2d 758.

[44] UCC § 2-201(3)(c).

[45] Dairyman's Cooperative Creamery Ass'n v Leipold, 34 Cal App 3d 184, 109 Cal Rptr 753.

[46] § 2-201(3(c).

[47] Lockwood v Smigel, 18 Cal App 3d 800, 96 Cal Rptr 289; Cohn v Fisher, 118 NJ Super 286, 287 A2d 222.

[48] Cohn v Fisher, 118 NY Super 286, 287 A2d 222. The Restatement of Contracts, § 205, adopts this view. It would appear that the draftsmen of the UCC are also in favor of this view, for the comment to § 2-201 states that "part payment may be made by money or check, accepted by the seller."

(3) Nonresellable Goods. No writing is required when the goods are specifically made for the buyer and are of such an unusual nature that they are not suitable for sale in the ordinary course of the seller's business. (See p. 461, LTV Aerospace Corp. v Bateman.) For example, when 14 rolling steel doors were tailor-made by the seller for the buyer's building and were not suitable for sale to anyone else in the ordinary course of the seller's business, and could only be sold as scrap, the oral contract of sale was enforceable.[49]

Under this exception an oral contract for the sale of wall mirrors to be cut to size and installed in a new hotel could be enforced as the special measurements of the mirrors made them unsuitable for sale to others in the ordinary course of the seller's business, and a writing was therefore not required.[50] In order for the nonresellable goods exception to apply, however, the seller must have made a substantial beginning in manufacturing the goods or, if he is a middleman, in procuring them, before receiving notice of a repudiation by the buyer.[51]

(4) Judicial Admission. No writing is required when the person alleged to have made the contract voluntarily admits in the course of legal proceedings that he has done so.

§ 23:11. Non-Code Local Requirements. In addition to the UCC requirement as to a writing, other statutes may impose requirements. For example, consumer protection legislation commonly requires the execution of a detailed contract and the giving of a copy thereof to the consumer. The result is that even though the Code requirements have been satisfied, the buyer may still be able to avoid the transaction for noncompliance with some other statutory requirement.

§ 23:12. Bill of Sale. Regardless of the requirement of the statute of frauds, the parties may wish to execute a writing as evidence or proof of the sale. Through custom this writing has become known as a *bill of sale*; but it is neither a bill nor a contract. It is merely a receipt or writing signed by the seller in which he recites that he has transferred the title of the described property to the buyer.

In many states provision is made for the public recording of bills of sale when goods are left in the seller's possession. In the case of the sale of certain types of property, a bill of sale may be required in order to show that the purchaser is the lawful owner. Thus, some states require the production of a bill of sale before the title to an automobile will be registered in the name of the purchaser.

A bill of sale may serve as evidence of an intent to transfer title to an automobile. Thus, the fact that a car dealer failed to execute an assignment

---

[49] Walter Balfour & Co. v Lizza & Sons, (NY) 6 UCCRS 649.

[50] Distribu-Dor, Inc. v Karadanis, 11 Cal App 3d 463, 90 Cal Rptr 231.

[51] UCC § 2-201(3)(a).

of the title certificate to a used car did not prevent the buyer of the used car from acquiring title when the seller delivered a bill of sale to the buyer.[52]

[52] Cochran v Harris, 123 Ga App 212, 180 SE2d 290.

CASES FOR CHAPTER 23

Helvey v Wabash County REMC

— Ind App —, 278 NE2d 608 (1972)

Wabash County REMC supplied electricity. It supplied current of 135 volts which caused damage to the household appliances of Helvey. These appliances were rated to use only 110 volts. Helvey sued Wabash County REMC more than four years after the harm was sustained. Wabash County REMC raised the defense that the suit was barred by the four-year statute of limitations applied by the Uniform Commercial Code to causes of action arising from sales. Helvey claimed that this statute was not applicable because it applied only to "goods" and the defendant was a supplier of "electricity." From a judgment for Wabash, Helvey appealed.

ROBERTSON, J. . . . In order for the Uniform Commercial Code statute of limitations to apply, electricity must possess the following qualities:

"(1) 'Goods' means all things (including specially manufactured goods) which are movable at the time of identification to the contract for sale other than the money in which the price is to be paid, investment securities . . . and things in action. . . . (2) Goods must be both existing and identified before any interest in them can pass. . . ." [UCC § 2-105]

Helvey is of the opinion that electrical energy is not a transaction in goods but rather a furnishing of a service, which would make [a six-year] statute of limitations applicable. . . .

Helvey concedes that electricity is legally considered to be personal property, that it is subject to ownership, and that it may be bartered and sold. . . . We further note that electricity may be stolen . . . and taxed. . . .

It is necessary for goods to be (1) a thing; (2) existing, and (3) movable, with (2) and (3) existing simultaneously. We are of the opinion that electricity qualifies in each respect. Helvey says it is not movable and in this respect we do not agree, if for no other reason than the monthly reminder from the electric company of how much current has passed through the meter. Logic would indicate that whatever can be measured in order to establish the price to be paid would be indicative of fulfilling both the existing and movable requirements of goods.

We further take note that one of the [principal] underlying purposes in adoption of the Uniform Commercial Code is "to make uniform the law among the various jurisdictions." [UCC § 1-102(2)(c)] With this in mind, we rely upon the authority of Gardiner v Philadelphia Gas Works (1964), 413 Pa 415, 197 A2d 612, wherein natural gas was determined to be goods within the scope of the Uniform Commercial Code, therefore, the four-year statute of limitations was applicable.

Helvey further argues that electricity not being goods under the purview of the Uniform Commercial Code, [was "service" and] the . . . six-year statute of limitations necessarily applies. . . .

. . . We believe that Helvey attaches too strained a definition to the word ["service,"] as well as its use in the authorities he cites. . . . An appropriate definition of the word "service" has been defined as:

"We have for definition not 'service' in the abstract, nor in its general sense, but 'merchandising service,' and that of a limited character: 'utility merchandising service.' 'Merchandise' (the verb) means to trade, buy and sell articles of commerce. It connotes both the act of buying and selling and the thing bought or sold." [citing case] While this case is directed to sales of appliances by a utility, we believe the definition is equally befitting the sale of its principal product. . . .

[Judgment affirmed.]

Application of Doughboy Industries, Inc.

17 App Div 2d 216, 233 NYS2d 488 (1962)

Doughboy Industries, Inc., as the buyer under a sales contract, began a proceeding against Pantasote, as the seller, pertaining to the arbitration of a question arising under the contract. Doughboy objected to the arbitration on the theory that the parties had never agreed to arbitrate and filed a petition to obtain a stay of the arbitration proceeding. The application for a stay of arbitration was refused, and Doughboy appealed.

BREITEL, J. . . . This case involves a conflict between a buyer's order form and a seller's acknowledgment form, each memorializing a purchase and sale of goods. The issue arises on whether the parties agreed to arbitrate future disputes. The seller's form had a general arbitration provision. The buyer's form did not. The buyer's form contained a provision that only a signed consent would bind the buyer to any terms thereafter transmitted in any commercial form of the seller. The seller's form, however, provided that silence or a failure to object in writing would be an acceptance of the terms and conditions of its acknowledgment form. The buyer never objected to the seller's acknowledgment, orally or in writing. In short, the buyer and seller accomplished a legal equivalent to the irresistible force colliding with the immovable object. . . .

Of interest in the case is that both the seller and buyer are substantial businesses—a "strong" buyer and a "strong" seller. This is not a case of one of the parties being at the bargaining mercy of the other. . . .

Recognizing, as one should, that the businessmen in this case acted with complete disdain for the "lawyer's content" of the very commercial forms they were sending and receiving, the question is what obligation ought the law to attach to the arbitration clause. . . . Of course, if the two commercial forms are given effect, they cancel one another. . . .

As a matter of law, there was no agreement to arbitrate. . . .

But the problem of conflicting commercial forms is one with which there has been much concern before this, and a new effort at rational solution has been made. The new solution would yield a similar result. The Uniform Commercial Code . . . provides:

"§ 2-207 Additional Terms in Acceptance or Confirmation

"(1) A definite and seasonable expression of acceptance or a written confirmation which is sent within a reasonable time operates as an acceptance even though it states terms additional to or different from those offered or agreed upon, unless acceptance is expressly made conditional on assent to the additional or different terms.

"(2) The additional terms are to be construed as proposals for addition to the contract. Between merchants such terms become part of the contract unless: (a) the offer expressly limits acceptance to the terms of the offer; (b) they materially alter it; or (c) notification of objection to them has already been given or is given within a reasonable time after notice of them is received.

"(3) Conduct by both parties which recognizes the existence of a contract is sufficient to establish a contract for sale although the writings of the parties do not otherwise establish a contract. In such case the terms of the particular contract consist of those terms on which the writings of the parties agree, together with any supplementary terms incorporated under any other provisions of this Act."

While this new section is not in its entirety in accordance with New York law in effect when the events in suit occurred . . . , in its particular application to the problem at hand it is quite useful. The draftsman's comments to Section 2-207 are in precise point . . . Thus, it is said:

"3. Whether or not additional or different terms will become part of the agreement depends upon the provisions of subsection (2). If they are such as materially to alter the original bargain, they will not be included unless expressly agreed to by the other party. If, however, they are terms which would not so change the bargain they will be incorporated unless notice of objection to them has already been given or is given within a reasonable time.

"6. If no answer is received within a reasonable time after additional terms are proposed, it is both fair and commercially sound to assume that their inclusion has been assented to. Where clauses on confirming forms sent by both parties conflict, each party must be assumed to object to a clause of the other conflicting with one on the confirmation sent by himself. As a result the requirement that there be notice of objection which is found in subsection (2) is satisfied and the conflicting terms do not become a part of the contract. The contract then consists of the terms originally expressly agreed to, terms on which the confirmations agree, and terms supplied by this Act, including subsection (2)."

On this exposition, the arbitration clause, whether viewed as a material alteration under subsection (2), or as a term nullified by a conflicting provision in the buyer's form, would fail to survive as a contract term. In the light of the New York cases, at least, there can be little question that an agreement to arbitrate is a material term, one not to be injected by implication, subtlety or inveiglement. And the conclusion is also the same if the limitation contained in the offer (the buyer's purchase order) is given effect, as required by subsection 2(a) of the new section.

Accordingly, the order denying petitioner-appellant buyer's motion to stay arbitration should be reversed, on the law, with costs to petitioner-appellant and the motion should be granted. . . .

Romine, Inc. v Savannah Steel Co.

117 Ga App 353, 160 SE2d 659 (1968)

Romine, a contractor, had a construction contract with the government. Savannah Steel Co. contracted to supply Romine with the steel required for the construction. Because of an error in the government specifications, the amount of steel actually needed was less than one tenth of the amount of the estimate on which Romine and Savannah had relied. Savannah sued Romine for breach of the requirements contract. The trial judge entered a summary judgment in favor of Savannah Steel, from which Romine appealed.

JORDAN, P.J. . . . Savannah Steel Co., Inc. brought suit against Romine, Inc., to recover an alleged balance due of $3,788.04 on a contract to supply the defendant with its steel requirements in performing a contract with the United States Government. The defendant, Romine, Inc., admitted a portion of the indebtedness, but contends that the amount of $2,725 on a purchase order submitted to the plaintiff as the cost of all reinforcing steel for concrete paving, is not alone determinative of the amount due for such steel requirements, and claims a credit of $2,474 for steel not required, shipped, or delivered. The trial judge considered the pleadings and depositions, granted a summary judgment for the plaintiff in the full amount sought, and simultaneously denied the motion of the defendant for a summary judgment. The defendant appeals from this order.

3. If a court determines as a matter of law that a provision of a contract is unconscionable when made, it may, among other things, so limit the application of any unconscionable provision to avoid an unconscionable result. [UCC Sec.] 2-302. See discussion, Anderson's Uniform Commercial Code, Vol. 1, pp. 146-150. This provision is not designed, however, merely to relieve a party of a bad bargain. Ibid., p. 148.

4. Where a term is used in a contract which is intended to cover the requirements of the buyer as may occur in good faith, no quantity unreasonably disproportionate to any stated estimate may be tendered or demanded. [UCC Sec.] 2-306. The agreed estimate is to be regarded as a center around which the parties intend the variation to occur. See Uniform Commercial Code, 1962 Official Text with Comments, published by The American Law Institute and Uniform Conference of Commissioners on Uniform State Laws, p. 75, Comment 4. The cited provision is applicable regardless of the character of the seller or buyer. See Anderson, supra, Vol. 1, p. 164. It would seem to follow logically that where the quantity actually delivered and accepted to meet the requirements of the buyer is unreasonably disproportionate to the estimated requirements, the lot price for the estimated total requirements is not a lot price for the actual requirements, although it may serve to establish a unit price therefor. . . .

5. Applying the foregoing principles to the case at bar, where a contractor furnishes a steel supplier with the drawings and specifications

on a proposed construction contract with the United States Government, and the supplier estimates the steel requirements, and furnishes the contractor with a written proposal to furnish, among other items, the necessary reinforcing steel for "concrete paving (15½ tons) —$2,725," and the contractor, upon the award of the construction contract, submits a purchase order to the supplier for "all reinforcing required for concrete pavement, except for dowel pins, including support accessories 2725," which the supplier purports to fulfil, the intent of the parties is to be gathered from a consideration of both documents, and the order for "all" at the stated price of "$2,725" is to be construed as conditioned upon the recognized estimate of 15½ tons, in the absence of anything to the contrary appearing in the documents, or otherwise. In brief, that part of the proposal showing "15½ tons" is not without meaning in construing the contract. Actually, both the purchase order and the proposal are deficient in many respects unless explained by the requirements of the government contract on which the proposal and order are based. Construed in this manner, the amount of $2,725 is the "quid pro quo" for "all" of the steel required in terms centering around "15½ tons" and the intent of the parties cannot be enlarged upon to the extent of limiting the total price to $2,725 if the amount of steel, as required and delivered, is grossly disproportionate to 15½ tons, either above or below such stated amount. Under such circumstances the monetary consideration due the supplier under the contract is for determination based on all the steel actually furnished in terms of the price per ton at the rate of 15½ tons for $2,725.

6. It is obvious from the record before this court that the estimate of steel requirements as shown in the contract is grossly disproportionate to the actual requirements, and that this situation arose as the result of a mistake without fault of either party. The drawings and specifications prepared by the government made it appear that reinforcing steel would be required for 3,438 square yards of concrete paving, but the government informed the contractor and the contractor notified the supplier that this was not true, as only 316 square yards required reinforcing steel. In fact, the remainder was unacceptable if constructed with reinforcing steel. The supplier apparently delivered the steel as required for 316 square yards of paving and the claimed credit of $2,474 by the defendant for 3,122 square yards not requiring steel appears to be an apportionment on this basis. But there is no evidence to show what steel was actually delivered by the supplier in terms of actual weight to support a computation of the amount due on a price per ton basis as the true consideration under the construction placed on the contract in the preceding division of this opinion. Thus, while the result may be substantially the same when there is proof of the amount of steel actually delivered, this issue is not resolved by the record before this court.

7. Under these circumstances the amount actually due the plaintiff is still in issue even though the plaintiff is entitled to judgment in some amount, and it was error for the trial judge to grant a summary judgment for the plaintiff in the full amount claimed, but he did not err in refusing to grant a summary judgment for the defendant.

Judgment affirmed on the refusal of a summary judgment for the defendant; reversed on the grant of a summary judgment for the plaintiff.

In re Boone Livestock Co.

US Dept of Agriculture, 27 AD 475, 5 UCCRS 498 (1968)

Boone Livestock Co. was in the business of buying and selling cattle. It purchased cattle and resold them, specifying to its customers that the cattle weighed certain amounts, whereas these amounts were the weights at which the cattle had been purchased by Boone from its suppliers increased by arbitrary amounts. It was claimed that these weights were false, and a proceeding was brought against Boone.

Flavin, Judicial Officer. This is a disciplinary proceeding under the Packers and Stockyards Act, 1921, as amended and supplemented (7 USC § 181 et seq.), instituted by a complaint filed November 17, 1965, by the Director, Packers and Stockyards Division (presently the Packers and Stockyards Administration),

Consumer and Marketing Service, United States Department of Agriculture. . . .

The complaint filed herein alleges, in part, that respondent "during the period from, on, or about January 14, 1965, through, on, or about June 5, 1965, purchased livestock for its own account in Alabama, Florida, Mississippi, and Texas" at listed or stated weights "and, on the dates of said purchases or within a few days thereafter, knowingly sold such livestock for its own account on a weight basis, in commerce, to various persons, at false and incorrect weights which respondent obtained by adding an arbitrary number of pounds to the purchase weights." Specific instances of such practice are then set forth in the complaint. . . .

It is clear from the record that the weight of the livestock involved herein sold by respondent and listed on its invoices to the purchasers thereof was comprised of, and resulted from, the addition of an arbitrary figure or number of pounds, usually a total of 1,000 pounds or more per sale, to the weight at which respondent purchased such live stock. . . .

Respondent makes much of the fact that it made no affirmative statements or representations during negotiations with its customers or on the invoices that the stated or listed weight in each transaction was its purchase weight. However, in view of the prevailing custom, practice or "usage of trade," no affirmative representation was needed to make respondent's purchase weights a part or term of the contracts involved. See § 1-205 of Uniform Commercial Code. . . . On the contrary, it would be incumbent upon respondent expressly to provide otherwise in its sales contracts with its customers. In other words, respondent had a duty to speak or to alter the prevailing custom by specific contract terms if it wished to sell the livestock involved at other than its purchase weights. Rather than doing so, respondent sold the cattle at other than its purchase weights without contracting to do so or so informing its customers while aware that such customers assumed and believed that they were purchasing the livestock on the basis of respondent's purchase weights. Also, no other assumption would be reasonable in view of the circumstances of the sales, that is, purchase of the livestock while they were in transit with no additional weighing to determine contract weight. Respondent's contentions that the sale weight in each of the transactions involved was an agreed arbitrary weight between respondent and the buyer, or merely a weight at which respondent was willing to sell the livestock or a reasonable weight subject to the buyer's approval are all without foundation and negatived by the custom in the industry, the testimony of respondent's customers, and the statements of respondent's president. . . .

[Disciplinary order entered against Boone.]

Cornelius v J & R Motor Supply Corp.

(Ky) 468 SW2d 781 (1971)

Costello owned an automobile accessory and appliance business. He purchased goods for his inventory from J & R Motor Supply Corporation. Costello sold his business to Cornelius before paying for the purchases from J & R. Cornelius mixed the Costello inventory with his own so that the two could not be identified. J & R and another creditor claimed that Cornelius was liable for the amount of the bills owed by Costello because the sale of the business had been made without complying with Article 6 of the Uniform Commercial Code. The court held that Cornelius was personally liable for plaintiff's claims. Cornelius appealed.

STEINFELD, J. . . . The questions before us are whether personal judgments were proper, the amounts for which judgments should have been entered if plaintiffs below prevail and whether filing of the claims in the bankruptcy proceeding precluded the creditors from prosecuting the suits.

[UCC §] 6-104 declares that ". . . a bulk transfer subject to this article is ineffective against any creditor . . . unless: (a) The transferee requires the transferor to furnish a list of his existing creditors . . ." prepared as statutorily required. [UCC §] 6-105 provides:

". . . any bulk transfer subject to this article . . . is ineffective against any creditor of the transferor unless at least ten days before he takes possession of the goods or pays for them, whichever happens first, the transferee gives notice of the transfer in the manner and to the persons hereafter provided [UCC §] 6-107. . . ."

The intent of the Bulk Sales Law is to protect the rights of all creditors existing at the time of the transfer. . . .

We now approach the question of whether a personal judgment was authorized. We believe the act did not so contemplate except under special circumstances. . . . The ordinary bulk sales statute " . . . merely makes it (the sale) voidable against both parties for the benefit of creditors." With respect to section 6-104 the Official Code Comments state: "Any such creditor or creditors may therefore disregard the transfer and levy on the goods as still belonging to the transferor, or a receiver representing them can take them by whatever procedure the local law provides." The status of the buyer is as a trustee or receiver for the benefit of creditors of the seller existing at the time of the sale. The rule is well expressed in Southwestern Drug Corp. v McKesson & Robbins, 141 Tex 284, 172 SW2d 485, 155 ALR 1056 (1943):

"Failure of the purchaser to comply with the Bulk Sales Law fixes his liability as that of a receiver, and he becomes bound to see that the property, or its value, is applied to the satisfaction of claims of the creditors of the seller. In other words, he becomes a trustee, charged with the duties and liabilities of a trustee. Under the law he is charged with liability only to the extent of the value of the property received by him, and his liability is to all of the creditors pro rata. . . . However, if a purchaser or receiver disposes of or converts to his own use property acquired in violation of the Bulk Sales Law, placing it beyond the reach of creditors, he will be held personally liable for the value thereof. . . .

. . . Since the purchasers so commingled the merchandise that it could not be segregated personal liability ensued. . . .

The Bulk Sales Law is not new in this state. The provisions of the present act are quite similar to our earlier one. Therefore the teachings of cases decided before the enactment of the Uniform Commercial Code are helpful. . . .

"Stated generally, a purchaser in violation of the Bulk Sales Act acquires no rights in the property purchased as against the creditors of the seller.

His status is generally considered, the statute sometimes expressly so providing, to be that of a trustee or receiver for the benefit of all the creditors of the seller, existing at the time of transfer. . . .

The liability as a trustee or receiver is to all the creditors pro rata. . . ."

. . . The appellees were entitled to judgment merely for their pro rata share determined on the basis of the creditors existing when the sale was consummated. . . . Also see 2 Anderson's Uniform Commercial Code, page 199 which points out that the existing, as distinguished from future creditors, are to share. . . .

The judgment is reversed for proceedings consistent herewith.

LTV Aerospace Corp. v Bateman

(Tex Civ App) 492 SW2d 703 (1973)

The LTV Aerospace Corporation manufactured all-terrain vehicles for use in Southeast Asia. LTV made an oral contract with Bateman under which it would supply the packing cases needed for overseas shipment. Bateman made substantial beginnings in the production of packing cases following LTV's specifications. LTV thereafter stopped production of its vehicles and refused to take delivery of the cases. When sued for breach of contract, LTV raised the defense that there was no writing to satisfy the statute of frauds. From a judgment for Bateman, LTV appealed.

McKay, J. . . . In December, 1969, appellant circulated a detailed invitation to bid so as to find a local supplier who could manufacture the shipping containers or crates to specifications and in quantities to 8,000 containers. The containers were to be delivered on a periodic basis to be specified by appellant to fit its production schedule.

Appellee in December, 1969, received from a third party a copy of the invitation to bid, and later in that month submitted a detailed written bid to appellant. Negotiations between appellee and representatives of appellant followed and after some oral changes on both specifications and price an agreement was reached and the bid was accepted by appellant. The exact terms of the agreement were disputed at the trial.

Appellee in January, 1970, employed workmen, purchased raw materials, plant equipment and facilities and began building shipping containers or crates, the first being delivered about January 20, 1970.

In March, 1970, appellee received a written purchase order from appellant, dated January 7, 1970, requesting delivery of 900 containers of the type and at the price previously agreed. Some crates had already been delivered and accepted by appellant before the purchase order was received by appellee about March 17, 1970.

In September, 1970, appellee received an amended or revised purchase order changing and reducing the quantity of containers from 900 to 653, the number 653 being the number of containers which had already been delivered and paid for. The new purchase order also requested production of 450 container bottoms only at a price then specially agreed upon. These bottoms were manufactured, delivered and paid for.

No additional containers or bottoms were ordered or built, and appellant's Tyler plant subsequently ceased operations.

The record shows that appellant did not sign appellee's written bid, which was amended and later orally changed, and appellee did not sign either of appellant's purchase orders. . . .

The contract which appellee seeks to enforce involves sale and purchase of shipping containers of the value of substantially more than $500. Appellant did not sign appellee's written bid. Therefore, it must be determined whether the contract here is governed by Subsection (c)(1) of sec. 2.201, UCC, as specially manufactured goods for appellant and not suitable for sale to others in the ordinary course of appellee's business. We hold that the contract is so governed.

These shipping crates or containers were manufactured by appellee to detailed specifications required by appellant, and they were to be used for shipping overseas an all-terrain vehicle manufactured by appellant. They were not suitable for sale to others in the ordinary course of appellee's business. The record discloses that appellee had made a substantial beginning in manufacture of the goods, and it was done for appellant's benefit before any notice of repudiation was given or received. The contract was not rendered unenforceable by the statute because it falls under an exception under which the statute of frauds need not be complied with. Appellant's first three points are overruled. Rose Acre Farms, Inc. v L. P. Cavett Co. of Indiana, 279 NE2d 280 (Ind App 1st Dist, 1972); 1 Anderson, Uniform Comm. Code, sec. 2-201.46; Ann Statute of Frauds—Manufactured Goods, 25 ALR2d 692.

Appellant claims that there is a writing which satisfies the requirements of subsection (a), and that it is the purchase order, and therefore subsection (c)(1) cannot apply. Subsection (a) requires "some writing sufficient to indicate that a contract for sale has been made between the parties and *signed by the party against whom enforcement is sought* . . . ." Emphasis ours. The issuing of a purchase order for 900 crates or containers, unsigned by appellee against whom it is sought to be enforced, is not such a writing as will satisfy subsection (a). . . .

[Judgment affirmed.]

QUESTIONS AND CASE PROBLEMS

1. Suburban Gas Heat of Kennewick sold propane gas for domestic consumption. As the result of its negligence in supplying propane gas mixed with water, there was an explosion which caused damage to Kasey. When Kasey sued to enforce the liability of Suburban Gas Heat as a seller, Suburban raised the defense that it was engaged in furnishing a public service and not in the sale of personal property within the meaning of the Uniform Sales

Act. Was Suburban correct? [Kasey v Suburban Gas Heat of Kennewick, Inc., 60 Wash 2d 468, 374 P2d 549]

2. Crocker printed and distributed Christmas cards. At certain intervals such cards which could not be sold would be destroyed. Crocker's employees took a large quantity of Christmas cards for that purpose to McFaddin who ran a dump and salvage operation. Persons bringing material to McFaddin would pay one fee for material that could be salvaged by him and a higher fee if instructions were given to destroy the material. When Crocker's employees took the Christmas cards to McFaddin, nothing was said as to the disposition to be made of them and only a salvage fee was paid. Later, Crocker learned that McFaddin had resold the cards. He sued McFaddin, claiming that McFaddin could not make such a sale because the transaction between Crocker and McFaddin was a bailment. McFaddin defended on the ground that the transaction was a sale, an abandonment, or a gift, and that in any instance McFaddin could sell the property and otherwise treat it as his own. Decide. [H. S. Crocker Co. v McFaddin, 148 Cal App 2d 639, 307 P2d 429]

3. Berger did business under the name of Warren Freezer Food Co. A consumer named Vernon made a contract for the purchase of a large quantity of freezer items, under which it was agreed that Warren Freezer would keep Vernon's food in its freezer, Vernon would take a portion of the order each week and would make a weekly installment payment, which would be applied to the note that Vernon had signed for the total bill. When Vernon would call for a part of the order of food, each item was individually wrapped in plain paper. When Vernon requested delivery, the individual packages were put into cardboard boxes on the exterior of which was a statement of the gross and net weight of the total contents and the defendant's name and place of business. Berger was prosecuted for violating the Michigan statute against "misbranding," which statute declared that an article was misbranded "if in package form" and the package did not show the true net weight. Was Berger guilty of violating this statute? [Michigan v Berger, 7 Mich App 695, 153 NW2d 161]

4. The Tober Foreign Motors, Inc., sold an airplane to Skinner on installments. Later it was agreed that the monthly installments should be reduced in half. Thereafter Tober claimed that the reduction agreement was not binding because it was not supported by consideration. Was this claim correct? [Skinner v Tober Foreign Motors, Inc., 345 Mass 429, 187 NE2d 669]

5. Members of the Colonial Club purchased beer from outside the state and ordered it sent to the Colonial Club. The club then kept it in the club refrigerator and served the beer to its respective owners upon demand. The club received no compensation or profit from the transaction. The club was indicted for selling liquor unlawfully. Decide. [North Carolina v Colonial Club, 154 NC 177, 69 SE 771]

6. A customer purchased furniture from a dealer. The furniture selected by the customer was not in stock, and the dealer loaned the customer some furniture to use until the selected furniture was delivered. An item of the loaned furniture collapsed and injured the customer. The customer sued the dealer three years and four months later. The dealer defended on the ground that

the non-Code two-year statute of limitations had expired. The customer claimed that there was a sale and that accordingly suit could be brought within the four-year period authorized by the UCC § 2-725. Decide. [Garfield v Furniture Fair-Hanover, 113 NJ Super 509, 274 A2d 325]

7. Gallick sold sugar to Castiglione with knowledge that the latter intended to use it in the illegal manufacture of liquor. The buyer did not pay the purchase price. Gallick then sued him for the purchase price. Castiglione defended on the ground that the contract was illegal. Decide. [Gallick v Castiglione, 2 Cal App 2d 716, 38 P2d 858]

8. Fallis farmed about 550 acres. He made an oral contract to sell and deliver to Grains 5,000 bushels of soybeans at $2.54 per bushel. Shortly thereafter, Grains sent Fallis a written contract signed by Grains. Fallis did not sign the contract and did not return it. When he failed to deliver the soybeans under the contract, he was sued for the breach thereof by Grains. He raised the defense of the Statute of Frauds. Grains claimed that the Statute of Frauds was not applicable because Fallis had not rejected the written contract that had been sent to him. Decide. [Grains v Fallis, 239 Ark 962, 395 SW2d 555]

9. Hess entered into a contract to supply Hazle Township with "100 tons more or less" of crushed gravel. Hess delivered 6,000 tons and claimed that the Township was required to pay for that amount by virtue of the language quoted above. Was Hess correct? [J. A. & W. A. Hess, Inc. v Hazle Township, 9 Pa Commonwealth Ct 409, 305 A2d 404]

10. The state of Minnesota prohibited the sale of glue to minors in order to protect them from the brain-damaging consequences of glue sniffing. In violation of this statute Warren sold glue to Ricken, a minor. Zerby, his minor friend, sniffed the glue and was killed by the fumes. Suit was brought against Warren who raised the defenses of contributory negligence and assumption or risk. Were these defenses valid? [Zerby v Warren, 297 Minn 134, 210 NW2d 58]

11. Crown Central Petroleum Corporation, a refinery, orally agreed to supply Davis, an independent dealer, with 1.2 million gallons of gas a month. Because of the oil shortage Crown refused to deliver the gas as promised. Davis sued Crown. Was Crown liable? [Davis v Crown Central Petroleum Corp., (CA4 NC) 483 F2d 1014]

24 Risk and Property Rights

§ 24:1. **Types of Problems.** In most sales transactions the buyer receives the proper goods, makes payment, and the transaction is thus completed; however, several types of problems may arise—(1) problems pertaining to damage to goods, (2) those resulting from creditors' claims, and (3) problems relating to insurance. These problems usually can be avoided if the parties make express provisions concerning them in their sales contract. When the parties have not specified by their contract what results they desire, however, the rules stated in this chapter are applied by the law.

(1) Damage to Goods. If the goods are damaged or totally destroyed without any fault of either the buyer or the seller, must the seller bear the loss and supply new goods to the buyer; or is it the buyer's loss, so that he must pay the seller the price even though he now has no goods or has only damaged goods? [1] The fact that there may be insurance does not diminish the importance of this question, for the answer to it determines whose insurer is liable and the extent of that insurer's liability.

(2) Creditors' Claims. Creditors of a delinquent seller may seize the goods as belonging to the seller, or the buyer's creditors may seize them on the theory that they belong to the buyer. In such cases the question arises whether the creditors are correct as to who owns the goods. The question of ownership is also important in connection with the consequence of a resale by the buyer, or the liability for or the computation of certain kinds of taxes, and the liability under certain registration and criminal law statutes.[2]

(3) Insurance. Until the buyer has received the goods and the seller has been paid, both the seller and buyer have an economic interest in the sales transaction.[3] The question arises as to whether either or both have enough

---

[1] UCC § 2-509.

[2] UCC § 2-401, as to when title passes.

[3] See UCC § 2-501(1)(a), and note also that the seller may have a security interest by virtue of the nature of the shipment or the agreement of the parties. The buyer also acquires a special property right in the goods that entitles him to reclaim the goods on the seller's insolvency if payment of all or part of the purchase price has been made in advance. § 2-502.

interest to entitle them to insure the property involved, that is, whether they have an insurable interest.[4]

§ **24:2. Nature of the Transaction.** The answer to be given to each of the questions noted in the preceding section depends upon the nature of the transaction between the seller and the buyer. Sales transactions may be classified according to (1) the nature of the goods and (2) the terms of the transaction.

(1) Nature of Goods. The goods may be (a) existing and identified goods or (b) future goods.

(a) EXISTING AND IDENTIFIED GOODS. *Existing goods* are physically in existence and owned by the seller. When particular goods have been selected by either the buyer or seller, or both of them, as being the goods called for by the sales contract, the goods are described as *identified goods.* If the goods are existing and identified, it is immaterial whether the seller must do some act or must complete the manufacture of the goods before they satisfy the terms of the contract.

(b) FUTURE GOODS. If the goods are not both existing and identified at the time of the sales transaction, they are *future goods.* Thus, goods are future goods when they are not yet owned by the seller, when they are not yet in existence, or when they have not been identified.

(2) Terms of the Transaction. Ordinarily the seller is only required to make shipment, and the seller's part is performed when he hands over the goods to a carrier for shipment to the buyer. The terms of the contract, however, may obligate the seller to deliver the goods at a particular place, for example, to make delivery at destination. The seller's part of the contract then is not completed until the goods are brought to the destination point and there tendered to the buyer. If the transaction calls for sending the goods to the buyer, it is ordinarily required that the seller deliver the goods to a carrier under a proper *contract for shipment* to the buyer. Actual physical *delivery at destination* is only required when the contract expressly states so.

Instead of calling for the actual delivery of goods, the transaction may relate to a transfer of the document of title representing the goods. For example, the goods may be stored in a warehouse, the seller and the buyer having no intention of moving the goods, but intending that there should be a sale and a delivery of the warehouse receipt that stands for the goods. Here the obligation of the seller is to produce the proper paper as distinguished

---

[4] To insure property, a person must have such a right or interest in the property that its damage or destruction would cause him financial loss. When he would be so affected, he is said to have an insurable interest in the property. The ownership of personal property for the purpose of insurance is determined by the law of sales. Motors Insurance Corp. v Safeco Insurance Co., (Ky) 412 SW2d 584.

from the goods themselves. The same is true when the goods are represented by any other document of title, such as a bill of lading issued by a carrier.

As a third type of situation, the goods may be stored with, or held by, a third person who has not issued any document of title for the goods, but the seller and buyer intend that the goods shall remain in that bailee's hands, the transaction being completed without any delivery of the goods themselves or of any document of title.

§ 24:3. Risk, Rights, and Insurable Interest in Particular Transactions. The various kinds of goods and terms may be combined in a number of ways. Only the six more common types of transactions will be considered in relationship to the time when risk, rights, and insurable interest are acquired by the buyer. The first three types pertain to existing and identified goods; the last three, to future goods.

Keep in mind that the following rules of law apply only in the absence of a contrary agreement by the parties concerning these matters.

(1) Existing Goods Identified at Time of Contracting.

(a) NO DOCUMENTS OF TITLE. If the seller is a merchant, the risk of loss passes to the buyer when he receives the goods from the merchant; if a nonmerchant seller, the risk passes when the seller makes the goods available to the buyer. Thus, the risk of loss remains longer on the merchant seller, a distinction which is made on the ground that the merchant seller, being in the business, can more readily protect himself against such continued risk.

The title to existing goods identified at the time of contracting, when no document of title (such as a warehouse receipt or a bill of lading) is involved, passes to the buyer at the time and place of contracting. (See p. 479, Moffit v Hieby.)

When it is agreed that the buyer will not take the goods, a helicopter, until the seller has given the buyer instructions as to use, the risk of loss remains upon the seller until the instruction obligation has been performed. Consequently, when the buyer is in the helicopter which is being flown by an employee of the seller who is giving instruction to the buyer, the risk of loss has not yet passed to the buyer and, therefore, was borne by the seller when the helicopter crashed while on the instructional flight.[5]

When testing or operating of installed goods is part of the seller's obligation, the risk of loss will generally remain on the seller until such obligation has been performed. (See p. 482, Wilke v Cummins Diesel Engines.)

When the buyer becomes the owner of the goods, he has an insurable interest in them. Conversely, the seller no longer has an insurable interest unless he has reserved a security interest to protect his right to payment.[6]

---

[5] Ellis v Bell Aerospace, (DC Ore) 315 F Supp 221.

[6] Secured transactions are discussed in Chapters 35 and 36.

The operation of the rule that title is transferred at the time of the transaction applies even though a local statute requires the registration of the transfer of title. Thus, the transfer of title of an automobile is complete as between the parties, in the absence of a contrary intention, when the agreement is made to sell or transfer the title to a specific car, even though the delivery of a title certificate as required by law has not been made.[7] For example, when the parties intend a sale of an automobile and unconditional possession of it is given to the buyer, the buyer becomes the owner and the car is no longer "owned" or "held for sale" by the seller within the meaning of his insurance policy, even though the title certificate has not been executed.[8] In some states, however, it is expressly declared by statute that no title is transferred in the absence of a delivery of the certificate of title.[9]

The fact that "title" has not been transferred to a motor vehicle because of a statute making the issuance of a title certificate essential for that purpose does not affect the transfer of the risk of loss as between the seller and buyer.[10] Likewise, the fact that the buyer pays with a check that is subsequently dishonored does not affect the transfer of title tor him.[11]

(2) Existing Goods Identified at Time of Contracting, Represented by Negotiable Document of Title. Here the buyer has an insurable interest in the goods at the time and place of contracting; but he does not ordinarily become subject to the risk of loss nor acquire the title until he receives delivery of the document.[12]

(3) Existing Goods Identified at Time of Contracting, Held by Bailee, Without Document of Title. Here the goods owned by the seller are held by a warehouseman, garageman, repairman, or other bailee, but there is no document of title and the sales contract does not call for a physical delivery of the goods—the parties intending that the goods should remain where they are. In such a case the answers to the various problems are the same as in situation (1), page 467, except that the risk of loss does not pass to the buyer, but remains with the seller until the bailee acknowledges that he is holding the goods in question for the buyer.

(4) Future Goods.

(a) MARKING FOR BUYER. If the buyer sends an order for goods to be manufactured by the seller or to be filled by him from inventory or by

---

[7] Transportation Equipment Co. v Dabdoub, (La) 69 So2d 640.

[8] Motors Insurance Corp. v Safeco Insurance Co., (Ky) 412 SW2d 584.

[9] Schroeder v Zykan, (Mo) 255 SW2d 105.

[10] Park County Implement Co. v Craig, (Wyo) 397 P2d 800.

[11] Gross v Powell, 288 Minn 386, 181 NW2d 113.

[12] Express provision is made for the case of a nonnegotiable document and other factual variations. UCC § 2-509(2)(c), § 2-503(4). When delivery of a document is to be made, the seller may send the document through customary banking channels as well as make a tender in person or by an agent. § 2-503(5)(b). Even though the form of the document of title is such that title is retained by the seller for security purposes, the risk of loss nevertheless passes to the buyer.

purchases from third persons, one step in the process of filling the order is the seller's act of marking, tagging, labeling, or in some way doing an act for the benefit of his shipping department or for himself to indicate that certain goods are the ones to be sent or delivered to the buyer under contract. This act of unilateral identification of the goods is enough to give the buyer a property interest in the goods and gives him the right to insure them.[13] Neither risk of loss nor title passes to the buyer at that time, however, but remains with the seller who, as the continuing owner, also has an insurable interest in the goods. Thus, neither title nor liability passes to the buyer until some other event, such as a shipment or delivery, occurs.

The parties may by their agreement delay the transfer of title until a later date, as by specifying that title shall not pass until payment is made or until the goods arrive at their destination. This retention of title by the seller is for the purpose of security only and the buyer nevertheless acquires an insurable interest upon identification. (See p. 479, Silver v Sloop Silver Cloud.)

(b) CONTRACT FOR SHIPMENT TO BUYER. In this situation the buyer has placed an order for future goods to be shipped to him, and the contract is performed by the seller when he delivers the goods to a carrier for shipment to the buyer. Under such a contract the risk of loss and title pass to the buyer when the goods are delivered to the carrier, that is, at the time and place of shipment. After that happens, the seller has no insurable interest unless he has reserved a security interest in the goods.[14]

The fact that a shipment of goods is represented by a bill of lading or an airbill issued by the carrier, and that in order to complete the transaction it will be necessary to transfer that bill to the buyer, does not affect these rules or bring the transaction within situation (3), page 468.

A provision for the inspection or testing of the goods by the buyer or by a third person at the buyer's place of business, at a building site, or at a place where the goods are to be installed may have the effect of delaying the transfer of the risk of loss to the buyer until the time when the goods are inspected or tested and approved as conforming.

(c) CONTRACT FOR DELIVERY AT DESTINATION. When the contract requires the seller to make delivery of future goods at a particular destination point, the buyer acquires a property right and an insurable interest in the goods at the time and place they are marked or shipped; but the risk of loss and the title do not pass until the carrier tenders or makes the goods available at the destination point. The seller retains an insurable interest until that time; and if he has a security interest in the goods, he continues to retain that interest until the purchase price has been paid.

The preceding information concerning six types of sales transactions is summarized in the table on the following page.

---

[13] UCC § 2-501(1)(b). Special provision is made as to crops and unborn young animals. § 2-501(1)(c).

[14] The reservation of a security interest by the seller does not affect the transfer of the risk to the buyer.

<table>
<tr><th>Nature of Goods</th><th>Terms of Transaction</th><th>Transfer of Risk of Loss to Buyer</th><th>Transfer of Title to Buyer</th><th>Acquisition of Insurable Interest by Buyer *</th></tr>
<tr><td rowspan="3">Existing Goods Identified at Time of Contracting</td><td>1. Without document of title</td><td>Buyer's receipt of goods from merchant seller; tender of delivery by nonmerchant seller
Sec. 2-509(3)</td><td>Time and place of contracting
Sec. 2-401(3)(b)</td><td>Time and place of contracting
Sec. 2-501(1)(a)</td></tr>
<tr><td>2. Delivery of document of title only</td><td>Buyer's receipt of negotiable document of title
Sec. 2-509(2)(a)</td><td>Time and place of delivery of document by seller
Sec. 2-401(3)(a)</td><td>Time and place of contracting
Sec. 2-501(1)(a)</td></tr>
<tr><td>3. Goods held by bailee, without document of title</td><td>Time of bailee's acknowledgment of buyer's right to possession
Sec. 2-509(2)(b)</td><td>Time and place of contracting
Sec. 2-401(3)(b)</td><td>Time and place of contracting
Sec. 2-501(1)(a)</td></tr>
<tr><td rowspan="3">Future Goods</td><td>4. Marking for buyer</td><td>No transfer</td><td>No transfer</td><td>At time of marking
Sec. 2-501(1)(b)</td></tr>
<tr><td>5. Contract for shipment to buyer</td><td>Delivery of goods to carrier
Sec. 2-509(1)(a)</td><td>Time and place of delivery of goods to carrier
Sec. 2-401(2)(a)</td><td>Time and place of delivery to carrier or of marking for buyer
Sec. 2-501(1)(b)</td></tr>
<tr><td>6. Contract for delivery at destination</td><td>Tender of goods at destination
Sec. 2-509(1)(b)</td><td>Tender of goods at destination
Sec. 2-401(2)(b)</td><td>Time and place of delivery to carrier or of marking for buyer
Sec. 2-501(1)(b)</td></tr>
</table>

* The seller retains an insurable interest in the goods as long as he has a security interest in them. When the buyer acquires an insurable interest, he also acquires a special property in the goods, less than title, which entitles him to certain remedies against the seller.

§ **24:4. Self-Service Stores.** In the case of goods sold in a self-service store, the reasonable interpretation of the agreement of the parties is that the store by its act of putting the goods on display on the shelves makes an offer to sell such goods for cash and confers upon a prospective customer a license to carry the goods to the cashier in order to make payment, thus effecting the transfer of title or sale. On this rationale, no warranty liability of the store arises prior to the buyer's payment.[15]

Likewise, any act of removing the goods from the store without making payment, even though with the connivance of the cashier, constitutes larceny or shoplifting.[16]

§ 24:5. Automobiles. In general, preexisting motor vehicle registration statutes have not been expressly affected by the adoption of the UCC. Consequently, in some states title to a motor vehicle does not pass unless there is a transfer of title within the scope of the UCC and also unless the formalities imposed by the state motor vehicle registration act are satisfied.

In some states the proper execution or indorsement and delivery of a title certificate is an essential element to the transfer of title to a motor vehicle; while in other states, following the common-law view or influence, such a document is merely evidence of a transfer of title but is not an essential element of effecting transfer. In the latter states, a transfer of title may occur when the parties agree that the automobile "belongs" to the other party even though nothing has been done with respect to the title certificate.[17] In such a state, when the purchased automobile has been delivered to the buyer on a cash and trade-in sale, the ownership passes to the buyer for the purpose of his insurance contract at the time of delivery even though the title papers are to be executed and the cash balance paid on the following day.[18] In most states the pre-Code motor vehicle statute remains in force to determine the location of "ownership" for the purpose of imposing tort liability or determining the coverage of liability insurance.[19]

§ 24:6. Damage or Destruction of Goods. In the absence of a contrary agreement,[20] damage to or the destruction of the goods affects the transaction as follows:

(1) Damage to Identified Goods Before Risk of Loss Passes. When goods that were identified at the time the contract was made are damaged or destroyed without the fault of either party before the risk of loss has passed, the contract is avoided if the loss is total. If the loss is partial or if the goods have so deteriorated that they do not conform to the contract, the buyer has the option, after inspection of the goods, (a) to treat the contract as avoided, or (b) to accept the goods subject to an allowance or

---

[15] A contrary view is beginning to be recognized by which the sale occurs when the buyer takes the item from the shelf. The fact that the buyer can return the item to the shelf is regarded under this view as being a "return" by the buyer who thereby transfers back to the seller the title which had already passed to the buyer when he selected the item.

[16] Connecticut v Boyd, 5 Conn Cir 648, 260 A2d 618.

[17] UCC § 2-401; Metropolitan Auto Sales Corp v Koneski, 252 Md 145, 249 A2d 141.

[18] Motors Insurance Corp v Safeco Insurance Co., (Ky) 412 SW2d 584.

[19] Nationwide Mutual Insurance Co. v Hayes, 276 NC 620, 174 SE2d 511.

[20] UCC § 2-303.

deduction from the contract price. In either case the buyer cannot assert any claim against the seller for breach of contract.[21]

When the buyer makes an effective rejection of nonconforming goods and the goods are then stolen before the seller has come for them, the buyer is not liable for the value of the stolen goods, unless the seller can establish that the buyer was negligent in caring for the goods after their rejection. (See p. 480, Graybar Electric Co. v Shook.)

When the seller agrees to maintain the goods, a television antenna, he does not obligate himself to replace the goods when damaged by lightning.[22]

A provision in a credit sale agreement that the buyer will at all times keep the goods fully insured against loss is not a "contrary agreement" within the UCC so as to shift the loss to the buyer at an earlier time.[23]

(2) Damage to Identified Goods After Risk of Loss Passes. If partial damage or total destruction occurs after the risk of loss has passed, it is the buyer's loss. It may be, however, that the buyer will be able to recover the amount of the damages from the person in possession of the goods or from a third person causing the loss.

(3) Damage to Unidentified Goods. So long as the goods are unidentified, no risk of loss has passed to the buyer. If any goods are damaged or destroyed during this period, it is the loss of the seller. The buyer is still entitled to receive the goods for which he contracted. If the seller fails to deliver the goods, he is liable to the purchaser for the breach of his contract. The only exception arises when the parties have expressly provided in the contract that destruction of the seller's supply shall be deemed a release of the seller's liability or when it is clear that the parties contracted for the purchase and sale of part of the seller's supply to the exclusion of any other possible source of such goods.

(4) Reservation of Title or Possession. When the seller reserves title or possession solely as security to make certain that he will be paid, the risk of loss is borne by the buyer if the circumstances are such that he would bear the loss in the absence of such reservation.

§ 24:7. Sales on Approval and with Right to Return. A sales transaction may give the buyer the privilege of returning the goods. In a *sale on approval,* the sale is not complete until the buyer approves. A *sale or return* is a completed sale with the right of the buyer to return the goods and thereby set aside the sale. The agreement of the parties determines whether the sale is an approval or with return; but if they have failed to indicate their intention, it is a sale on approval if the goods are purchased for use, that is,

---

[21] § 2-613.
[22] Lair Distributing Co. v Crump, 48 Ala App 72, 261 So2d 904.
[23] Hayward v Postma, 31 Mich App 720, 188 NW2d 31.

by a consumer, and a sale or return if purchased for resale, that is, by a merchant.[24]

(1) Sale on Approval. In the absence of a contrary agreement, title and risk of loss remain with the seller under a sale on approval. Use of the goods by the buyer consistent with the purpose of trial is not an election or approval by him. There is an approval, however, if he acts in a manner that is not consistent with a reasonable trial, or if he fails to express his choice within the time specified or within a reasonable time if no time is specified. If the goods are returned, the seller bears the risk and the expense involved.[25] Since the buyer is not the "owner" of the goods while they are on approval, his creditors cannot reach them.[26]

(2) Sale or Return. In a sale or return, title and risk of loss pass to the buyer as in the case of an ordinary or absolute sale. In the absence of a contrary agreement, the buyer under a sale or return may return all of the goods or any commercial unit thereof. A *commercial unit* is any article, group of articles, or quantity which commercially is regarded as a separate unit or item, such as a particular machine, a suite of furniture, or a carload lot.[27] The goods must be substantially in their original condition, and the option to return must be exercised within the time specified by the contract or within a reasonable time if none is specified. The return under such a contract is at the buyer's risk and expense.[28] As long as the goods are in the buyer's possession under a sale or return contract, his creditors may treat the goods as belonging to him.[29]

The delivery of goods to an agent for sale is not a sale and return. Therefore, when the owner of an automobile leaves it with a dealer to obtain an offer of purchase which the owner would then be required to approve in order to effect the sale, there is no "sale or return" and creditors of the dealer have no claim against the automobile.[30]

(3) Consignment Sale. A consignment or a sale on consignment is merely an authorization or agency to sell. It is not a sale on approval or a sale with right to return. Since the relationship is an agency, the consignor, in the absence of some contrary contract restriction, may revoke the agency at will and take possession of his property by any lawful means.[31] If such repossession of the goods constitutes a breach of his contract with the

---

[24] § 2-326(1). An "or return" provision is treated as a sales contract for the purpose of applying the statute of frauds, and cannot be established by parol evidence when it would contradict a sales contract indicating an absolute sale. § 2-326(4).

[25] § 2-327(1).

[26] § 2-326(2).

[27] § 2-105(6).

[28] § 2-327(2).

[29] § 2-326(2); Guardian Discount Co. v Settles, 114 Ga App 418, 151 SE2d 530.

[30] Allgeier v Campisi, 117 Ga App 105, 159 SE2d 458.

[31] Parks v Atlanta News Agency, 115 Ga App 842, 156 SE2d 137.

consignee, the consignor is liable to the consignee for damages for breach of contract.

Whether goods are sent to a person as buyer or on consignment to sell for the seller is a question of the intention of the parties.[32] In some instances the creditors of the consignee may treat the goods held by the consignee on consignment as though they belonged to him, thereby ignoring and destroying the consignor's ownership.

§ **24:8. Sale of Fungible Goods.** *Fungible goods* are goods of a homogeneous nature that they may be sold by weight or measure. They are goods of which any unit is from its nature or by commercial usage treated as the equivalent of any other unit.[33] Wheat, oil, coal, and similar bulk commodities are fungible goods since, given a mass of the same grade or uniformity, any one bushel or other unit of the mass will be exactly the same as any other bushel or similar unit.

Title to an undivided share or quantity of an identified mass of fungible goods may pass to the buyer at the time of the transaction, making the buyer an owner in common with the seller.[34] For example, when a person sells to another 600 bushels of wheat from his bin which contains 1,000 bushels, title to 600 bushels passes to the buyer at the time of the transaction, giving him a 6/10ths undivided interest in the mass as an owner in common. The courts in some states, however, have held that the title does not pass until a separation of the purchased share has been made.

§ **24:9. Sale of Undivided Shares.** The problem of the passage of title to a part of a larger mass of fungible goods is distinct from the problem of the passage of title when the sale is made of a fractional interest without any intention to make a later separation. In the former case the buyer is to become the exclusive owner of a separated portion. In the latter case he is to become a co-owner of the entire mass. Thus, there may be a sale of a part interest in a radio, an automobile, or a flock of sheep.[35]

§ **24:10. Auction Sales.** When goods are sold at an auction in separate lots, each lot is a separate transaction, and title to each passes independently of the other lots.[36] Title to each lot passes when the auctioneer announces by the fall of the hammer or in any other customary manner that the auction is completed as to that lot.[37]

§ **24:11. Reservation of a Security Interest.** The seller may fear that the buyer will not pay for the goods. The seller could protect himself by insisting that the buyer pay cash immediately. This may not be practical for geographic

[32] Donich v U.S.F.&G. Co., 149 Mont 79, 423 P2d 298.
[33] UCC § 1-201(17).
[34] § 2-105(4).
[35] § 2-403(1).
[36] § 2-328(1).
[37] § 2-328(2).

or business reasons. The seller may then give credit but protect himself by retaining a security interest in the goods.

(1) ***Bill of Lading.*** The seller may retain varying degrees of control over the goods by the method of shipment. Thus, the seller may ship the goods to himself in the buyer's city, receiving from the carrier the bill of lading for the goods.[38] In such a case the buyer cannot obtain the goods from the carrier since the shipment is not directed to him, as in the case of a straight bill of lading, or because he does not hold the bill of lading, if it is a negotiable or order bill. The seller's agent in the buyer's city can arrange for or obtain payment from the buyer and then give him the documents necessary to obtain the goods from the carrier.

If the goods are sent by carrier under a negotiable bill of lading to the order of the buyer or has agent, the seller may also retain the right of possession of the goods by keeping possession of the bill of lading until he receives payment.[39]

(2) ***C.O.D. Shipment.*** In the absence of an extension of credit, a seller has the right to keep the goods until paid, but he loses this right if he delivers possession of the goods to anyone for the buyer. However, when the goods are delivered to a carrier, the seller may preserve his right to possession by making the shipment C.O.D., or by the addition of any other terms indicating an intention that the carrier should not surrender the goods to the buyer until the buyer has made payment. Such a provision has no effect other than to keep the buyer from obtaining possession until he has made payment. The C.O.D. provision does not affect the problem of determining whether title or risk of loss has passed.

Under a C.O.D. shipment the carrier acts as an agent for the shipper. If it accepts a check from the consignee and the check is not honored by the bank on which it is drawn, the carrier is liable to the shipper for the amount thereof.

§ 24:12. Effect of Sale on Title. As a general rule, a person can sell only such interest or title in goods as he possesses. If the property is subject to a bailment, a sale by the bailor is subject to the bailment. Similarly, the bailee can only transfer his right under the bailment, assuming that the bailment agreement permits his right to be assigned or transferred. The fact that the bailee is in possession does not give him the right to transfer the bailor's title.

Moreover, a thief or finder generally cannot transfer the title to property since he can only pass that which he has, namely the possession but not the title.[40] In fact, the purchaser from the thief not only fails to obtain title

---

[38] § 2-505.
[39] § 2-505(1)(a).
[40] Coomes v Drinkwalter, 181 Neb 450, 149 NW2d 60.

but also becomes liable to the owner as a converter of the property even though he made the purchase in good faith.

A thief cannot pass good title to a stolen automobile. The owner may recover the automobile from the subpurchaser although the latter buys in good faith and pays value.[41] The fact that the negligence or the act of the owner contributed to or facilitated the theft does not stop the true owner from asserting his title.

The buyer of stolen goods must surrender them to the true owner even though he had acted in good faith, had given value, had been shown a forged bill of sale, and had been falsely told that the certificate of title to the goods, an automobile, was being held by a bank as security for the financing of the original purchase of the automobile by the seller.

In some states it is expressly declared by statute that a buyer of stolen goods does not acquire title as against the true owner even though he purchases in good faith.[42]

There are certain instances, however, when either because of the conduct of the owner or the desire of society to protect the bona fide purchaser for value, the law permits a greater title to be transferred than the seller possessed.

(1) Sale by Entrustee. If the owner entrusts his goods to a merchant who deals in goods of that kind, the latter has the power to transfer the entruster's title to anyone who buys from him in the ordinary course of business. (See p. 483, Medico Leasing Co. v Smith.)

When a dealer obtains goods from a wholesaler in violation of the latter's instructions to his employees that no sales should be made to the dealer, the dealer is to be deemed an entrustee and therefore may pass the wholesaler's title to a buyer in ordinary course. The fact that the wholesaler's employees had violated the duty owed to the employer did not entitle him to recover the property from the buyer in ordinary course.[43]

It is immaterial why the goods were entrusted to the merchant. Hence, the leaving of a watch for repair with a jeweler who sells new and second-hand watches would give the jeweler the power to pass the title to a buyer in the ordinary course of business.[44] Goods in inventory have a degree of "negotiability" so that the ordinary buyer, whether a consumer or another merchant, buys the goods free of the ownership interest of the person entrusting the goods to the seller.[45] The entrustee is, of course, liable to the owner for damages caused by the entrustee's sale of the goods and is guilty of some form of statutory offense or embezzlement.

If the entrustee is not a merchant, but merely a prospective customer trying out an automobile, there is no transfer of title to the buyer of the

---

[41] Reynoldsburg Motor Sales, Inc. v City of Columbia, 32 Ohio App 2d 271, 61 OO2d 310, 289 NE2d 909.

[42] Stohr v Randle, 81 Wash 2d 881, 505 P2d 1281.

[43] Humphrey Cadillac & Oldsmobile Co. v Sinard, 85 Ill App 2d 64, 229 NE2d 365.

[44] UCC § 2-403(2), (3). There is authority that in order for this section to apply, the merchant status of the entrustee must be known both to the entruster and the purchaser. Atlas Auto Rental Corp. v Weisberg, 54 Misc 2d 168, 281 NYS2d 400.

[45] UCC § 2-403(1); Mattek v Malofsky, 42 Wis 2d 16, 165 NW2d 406.

car from the entrustee.[46] Likewise, there is no transfer of title when a bailee, who is not a seller of goods of that kind, sells the property of a customer. (See p. 485, Gallagher v Unenrolled Motor Vessel River Queen.)

(2) Consignment Sale. A manufacturer or distributor may send goods to a dealer for sale to the public with the understanding that the manufacturer or distributor is to remain the owner, and the dealer in effect is to act as his agent. When the dealer maintains a place of business at which he deals in goods of the kind in question under a name other than that of the consigning manufacturer or distributor, the creditors of the dealer may reach the goods as though they were owned by him.[47]

(3) Estoppel. The owner of property may estop himself from asserting that he is the owner and denying the right of another person to sell the property. A person may purchase a product and have the bill of sale made out in the name of a friend to whom he then gives possession of the product and the bill of sale. He might do so in order to deceive his own creditors or to keep other persons from knowing that he made the purchase. If the friend should sell the product to a bona fide purchaser who relies on the bill of sale as showing that the friend was the owner, the true owner is estopped or barred from denying the friend's apparent ownership or his authority to sell.

(4) Powers. In certain circumstances, persons in possession of someone else's property may sell the property. This arises in the case of pledgees, lienholders, and some finders who, by statute, may have authority to sell the property to enforce their claim or when the owner cannot be found.

(5) Negotiable Documents of Title. By statute, certain documents of title, such as bills of lading and warehouse receipts, have been clothed with a degree of negotiability when executed in proper form.[48] By virtue of such provisions, the holder of a negotiable document of title directing delivery of the goods to him or his order, or to bearer, may transfer to a purchaser for value acting in good faith such title as was possessed by the person leaving the property with the issuer of the document. In such cases, it is immaterial that the holder had not acquired the document in a lawful manner.

(6) Recording and Filing Statutes. In order to protect subsequent purchasers and creditors, statutes may require that certain transactions be recorded or filed and may provide that if that is not done, the transaction has no effect against a purchaser who thereafter buys the goods in good

---

[46] Atlas Auto Rental Corp. v Weisberg, 54 Misc 2d 168, 281 NYS2d 400.

[47] UCC § 2-326(3). The manufacturer or dealer may protect himself from this under Article 9 of the Code, or by complying with any local statute that protects him in such case.

[48] § 7-502(2).

faith from the person who appears to be the owner or against the execution creditors of such an apparent owner. Thus, if a seller retains a security interest in the goods sold to the buyer but fails to file a financing statement in the required manner, the purchaser appears to be the owner of the goods free from any security interest and subsequent bona fide purchasers or creditors of the buyer can acquire title from him free of the seller's security interest.

(7) Voidable Title. If the buyer has a voidable title, as when he obtained the goods by fraud, the seller can rescind the sale while the buyer is still the owner. If, however, the buyer resells the property to a bona fide purchaser before the seller has rescinded the transaction, the subsequent purchaser acquires valid title.[49] It is immaterial whether the buyer having the voidable title had obtained title by fraud as to his identity, or by larceny by trick, or that he had paid for the goods with a bad check, or that the transaction was a cash sale and the purchase price has not been paid.[50]

(8) Goods Retained by Seller. When the seller after making the sale is permitted to retain possession of the goods, he has the power to transfer the title to a buyer in the ordinary course of business. Such permitted retention is an entrusting within the sale by entrustee rule described in (1), page 476. The purpose is to protect the second purchaser, on the ground that he had the right to rely on the apparent ownership of his seller.

(a) PROTECTION OF SELLER. As will be discussed in connection with the remedies of the parties, a seller who is lawfully in possession of property that he has sold may resell it to a second purchaser if the first purchaser is in default in the payment of the purchase price. Here the object of the statute is not to protect the second purchaser but to enable the seller to remedy the situation created by the first purchaser's default.

(b) PROTECTION OF CREDITORS OF SELLER. The continued possession of goods by the seller after their sale is generally deemed evidence that the sale was a fraud upon creditors, that is, that the sale was not a bona fide actual transfer of title but was merely a device to place the title out of the reach of the creditors of the seller. When the sale is fraudulent by local law, creditors of the seller may treat the sale as void and may have the property put up for sale on execution as though the property still belonged to the seller. The retention of possession by a merchant seller is declared not fraudulent, however, when made in good faith in the current course of business and when it does not exceed a period of time which is commercially reasonable.[51] For example, the fact that the merchant retains possession until transportation of the goods is arranged is not fraudulent as to creditors.

[49] § 2-403(1).
[50] § 2-403(1)(a) to (d).
[51] § 2-402(2).

CASES FOR CHAPTER 24

Moffitt v Hieby

149 Tex 161, 229 SW2d 1005 (1950)

Mrs. Hieby sold growing grapefruit to Moffitt. The written contract specified: "All terms of this agreement have been reduced to writing herein." The contract provided for the harvesting of the crop nine weeks later and stated: "Seller agrees that if harvesting is paid by buyer, it is to be charged to seller's account." The crop was damaged by the failure of Mrs. Hieby to care for and water the orchards after making the sale. Moffitt refused to take the grapefruit. Mrs. Hieby sued him for damages for the breach of the contract. From a judgment for the plaintiff, the defendant appealed.

HARVEY, J. . . . The agreement entered into by the parties appears on its face to be an executed contract. . . .

Inasmuch as title to the grapefruit on the trees passed to the buyer as of the date of the contract, with a consequent delivery thereof made in the orchards, and there was nothing on the part of the seller that remained to be done in the matter, there was no implied obligation on the part of the seller to water the orchards or perform any other act with reference thereto. Had the parties so desired and had so agreed, it would have been quite easy for them to have inserted a stipulation in the contract to the effect that the seller should do whatever might have been deemed advisable under the circumstances with reference to the care to be taken of the orchards, as well as in regard to any other matters. This they did not do, and there is no occasion for the courts to add to the contract as made by them. . . .

[Judgment for plaintiff affirmed.]

HART, J. (dissenting) . . . The defendants pleaded that the breach of the implied obligation of the plaintiff to care for the orchards, resulting in the failure of the fruit to reach normal or full size, was a material breach of the contract which released the defendants from the obligation to harvest and pay for the fruit. . . .

Assuming the facts to be as pleaded and testified to by the defendants and their witnesses, an obligation should be implied in fact that the seller would, after the date of the contract, with reasonable diligence and prudence continue to water and otherwise properly care for the orchards so that the fruit would attain the size and quality which would normally be expected. Otherwise, it seems apparent that the intention of the parties would not be accomplished but, on the other hand, would be defeated. The contract discloses on its face that the buyer would be permitted a period of more than two months in which to gather the fruit and that the seller would pay the expense of harvesting. Aside from their right to enter the orchards for the purpose of gathering the fruit, the buyers were given no control over the orchards; and it would follow that if the trees were to be watered and otherwise cared for, this would have to be done by the seller. Regardless of whether, as a matter of law, the title to the grapefruit had passed to the buyers, the seller, since she remained in charge of the orchards, should be under an obligation implied in fact (assuming the defendant's testimony to be true) to care for the orchards so that the fruit would normally develop and not be rendered unfit for the purposes for which the defendants were buying it.

Code Comment: The same decision and the same dissent would be made under the Code.

Silver v Sloop Silver Cloud

(DC SD NY) 259 F Supp 187 (1966)

LeConte contracted to build a sloop for Silver for $27,750. The sloop was to be built in Holland and brought to New York. Clause 3 of the contract stated that "title to the vessel hereby ordered shall not pass to the purchaser until the entire purchase price and any extra or additional charges have been paid in full or security acceptable to builder given therefor, and builder has delivered its bill of sale. . . ." When the sloop was brought to New York, LeConte tendered the sloop to Silver and claimed $3,309 for extras. A dispute arose over whether the sloop had been properly constructed.

Silver brought an action to obtain possession of the sloop and claimed that he was entitled to it because title had passed to him.

TENNEY, B.J. . . . Plaintiff alleges that under § 2-401(2)(b) of the UCC, where the contract requires delivery at destination, title passes on tender of the goods. This would be true except that the section cited prefaces this statement with the phrase "unless otherwise explicitly agreed." Clause 3 of the May 24, 1965 contract has been previously set forth in full. I hold that this clause fulfills the requirement of the UCC that an explicit statement can alter the title-passing provision. Plaintiff's argument that Clause 3 contravenes the statutory provisions of the UCC is without merit. He argues that the contract clause relating to passing of title cannot contravene the provisions of the statute. Obviously, the provision does not conflict with the statute since the section specifically allows the parties to determine when title shall pass.

Plaintiff further alleges that title to future goods passes to the buyer when they are "shipped, marked or otherwise designated by the seller as goods to which the contract refers," under UCC § 2-501(1)(b). This argument is erroneous. The Section states nothing as to passing of title; it only sets forth the manner in which identification of the goods to the contract will be made, thus giving the buyer a "special property" and an insurable interest in the goods. These are not the equivalent of placing title in the buyer. UCC § 2-401(1) provides that title cannot pass prior to identification; it does *not* provide that title must pass once the goods are identified. Therefore, under these provisions, plaintiff has not established that title has passed. . . .

Plaintiff further states that the contract for extras must be considered as a contract independent of the agreement of May 24, 1965, and that since plaintiff has paid the original purchase price of $27,750.00 he is entitled to "SILVER CLOUD." The contract provides, however, that the price of the sloop is $27,750.00 *plus extras*. Even though this was left to future agreement, according to plaintiff, this does not mean that the "plus extras" term is not a part of the contract. Indeed, § 2-305 of the UCC provides that a contract for sale can be concluded even though the price is not settled. The agreement of October 1965 can only be considered as a modification of the original contract under UCC § 2-209. It would be highly inaccurate to consider a contract for the extras to be considered separately from the contract of sale. Further, Clause 3 of the original agreement provides that title shall not pass until the full price is paid including "any extra or additional charges." It would be patently incorrect to conclude that the parties did not contemplate the cost of extras as part of the original contract. . . .

[Judgment for defendant.]

Graybar Electric Co. v Shook

283 NC 213, 195 SE2d 514 (1973)

Shook ordered three reels of burial cable from Graybar Company for use in construction work. By mistake, two of the three reels which were sent were aerial cable, although each carton was marked "burial cable." Shook accepted the one reel of proper cable and rejected the two nonconforming reels. Because of their size they were left on the ground at the construction site and Graybar was notified of the rejection. Graybar did not collect the cable. Shook attempted to return the cable but could not do so because there was a strike of truck drivers. About four months later the two reels of cable were stolen by unidentified persons. Graybar sued Shook for the purchase price. Graybar claimed that after the rejection was made by Shook, it had been agreed that Shook would return the nonconforming reels to Graybar. From a judgment for Shook, Graybar appealed.

HIGGINS, J. . . . The parties admitted the following: (1) The defendant placed an order with the plaintiff for three reels of burial (underground) cable to be delivered at Six Run Grocery Store, a rural community sixteen miles south of Clinton. (2) On April 6 the plaintiff delivered one reel of burial cable and, by mistake, delivered two reels of aerial cable. The aerial cable was totally unsuited to the defendant's use. Defendant notified the plaintiff of the mistake and received a request that the nonconforming reels be returned. Here the parties disagree. The plaintiff contends the defendant contracted to make the return. The defendant contends he agreed to contact a trucking company and request that it pick up and return the nonconforming reels. The defendant's request was turned down by three different trucking concerns on account of a strike in the trucking industry.

As the defendant's underground cable work progressed beyond the Six Run Grocery Store, the defendant left the nonconforming cable at the store and so notified the plaintiff. The evidence discloses that the cable was stored directly beside the grocery store building near the owner's dwelling in a space which the defendant rented for storage purposes. "The area where the cable was stored was well lighted at all times."

On July 20, 1970, the defendant discovered that one of the reels had been stolen and the following day notified the plaintiff. On that day, also, the defendant contacted a garage operator who promised to pick up the remaining reel and store it in his garage some distance from Six Run. However, before the transfer, the second reel was stolen. The defendant so notified the plaintiff.

The court, upon the disputed facts, found the defendant had not entered into a contract to return the nonconforming cable. A finding supported by evidence "must be accepted as final truth upon the appeal to the Supreme Court." . . . When findings of fact sufficient to determine the entire controversy are made by the court, failure to find other facts is not error. . . . The plaintiff's claim, therefore, that it was prejudiced by the court's failure to make requested findings is not error. The court's actual findings determined the entire controversy.

The plaintiff, having made the error of delivering the nonconforming goods on a moving job in the country, was entitled to notice of the nonconformity sufficient to enable it to repossess the nonconforming goods. The plaintiff was given prompt notice but delayed action for more than three months. The cable was stolen from the defendant's regular storage space where the plaintiff had delivered it. Evidence is lacking that a safer storage space was available. The defendant's workmen moved on, leaving the cable and the responsibility for its safety on the owner.

The plaintiff, failing in its efforts to establish a contract on the part of the defendant to return the shipment, however, contends in the alternative that [UCC §] 2-602(2)(b) . . . required the defendant to exercise reasonable care in holding the rejected goods pending the plaintiff's repossession and removal and that the defendant failed to exercise the required care in storage.

Actually, the plaintiff made an on the spot delivery at a store and dwelling in the country. The defendant's work force was stringing underground cable along the highway and the crew was in continual movement. Obviously the crew could not be expected to carry with it two thousand pounds of useless cable and was within its rights placing the cable in its regular storage space and notifying the plaintiff of the place of storage. Both parties realized that cable weighing almost a ton would require men and a truck to remove it. Also both parties assumed that the danger of theft from a well lighted store area was a minimal risk. The property itself was a poor candidate for larceny. The cable was permitted to remain where the plaintiff knew it was located for more than three months. The plaintiff, therefore, had ample opportunity to repossess its property.

The Uniform Commercial Code emphasizes promptness and good faith. The prospective purchaser may exercise a valid right to reject and even if he takes possession, responsibility expires after a reasonable time in which the owner has opportunity to repossess. "Where a tender or delivery of goods so fails to conform to the contract as to give a right of rejection the risk of their loss remains on the seller until cure or acceptance." [UCC §] 2-510(1). The defendant did not accept the aerial cable. According to the evidence and the court's findings, the defendant acted in accordance with the request of the owner in attempting to facilitate the return of that which the defendant rejected. The plaintiff with full notice of the place of storage which was at the place of delivery did nothing but sleep on its rights for more than three months.

The superior court was fully justified in the findings of fact, conclusions of law, and in the judgment dismissing the action. The judgment of the Court of Appeals affirming the superior court was correct. . . .

[Judgment affirmed.]

Wilke v Cummins Diesel Engines

252 Md 611, 250 A2d 886 (1969)

Wilke purchased a generator from Cummins Diesel Engines, subject to field tests after delivery and installation at a job site where Wilke was engaged in construction work as a subcontractor on certain facilities. Cummins delivered the generator in August, long before needed. The next spring, in hooking it up, Wilke found it severely damaged from water frozen in its cooling system. He notified Cummins, who removed and repaired it and billed Wilke for the repairs. Wilke sued Cummins to recover possession. Judgment was for Cummins. Wilke appealed.

SINGLEY, J. . . . William F. Wilke, Inc. (Wilke), the appellant here and plaintiff below, is a mechanical contractor who was a subcontractor on a job involving the construction of certain facilities for the United States Government at Aberdeen Proving Ground. The performance of the contract required, among other things, that Wilke supply and install an emergency diesel-powered generator in conformance with government specifications. After a discussion with representatives of Cummins Diesel Engines, Inc. (Cummins), the appellee here and defendant below, Wilke received a quotation from them dated 14 July 1965. On 3 August 1965, Wilke issued a purchase order for an emergency diesel generator "in strict compliance with plans and specifications . . . $13,300. *This price includes all requirements as set forth in paragraph 39.22* [the portion of the government specifications which dealt with the emergency diesel generator] *except subparagraphs k and l*" [which dealt with the fuel oil storage tank, the cleaning and painting of such tanks, and oil pipe and fittings]. (Emphasis added)

The job progressed with agonizing slowness, and by August, 1966, was only 50 percent complete. Although it was far too early to install the generator, Cummins was anxious to deliver it to the job site and did so on 17 August 1966. It was delivered by Cummins' truck, unloaded by Wilke's crane, and placed on a permanent base which had been prepared for it. At the time of delivery, the generator was lacking two starting batteries. When asked how Cummins' representative explained the absence of the batteries, Wilke's foreman at the job answered: "He said the batteries were not in the machine because he did not want us to start it or fool with it. His statement was, 'This is my baby until I start it and turn it over to you.' " This testimony was not challenged by Cummins. Also missing were the maintenance and operating instruction manuals that were included in the specifications. . . .

The job continued to move at a snail's pace, and until the spring of 1967 the generator sat on its base enclosed in a housing intended to protect it from the weather since it was designed to operate out of doors. When Wilke started to hook up the generator, it was discovered that the water in its cooling system had frozen during the previous winter and that the engine had been severely damaged.

Wilke notified Cummins of the damage, and Cummins, after an investigation, decided that repairs could not be made on the job site. The generator was picked up by Cummins and taken away to be repaired. There were no discussions between the parties as to the responsibility for the repairs prior to their completion. On 9 June, Cummins sent Wilke a bill for $2,231.20 for the work and conditioned return of the generator on the payment of the bill. On 19 June, Wilke instituted an action of replevin, and on the same day, Cummins sent Wilke a corrected bill in the amount of $2,798.27. The generator was returned to the job site where Cummins supervised the electrical installation, start-up, and field tests. In April of 1968, the replevin action was tried without a jury by the Superior Court of Baltimore City which, on 8 April 1968, entered judgment absolute in favor of Cummins for the return of the property or, alternatively, for

$2,798.27, one cent damages, and costs. It is from this judgment that Wilke has appealed.

The court below concluded the "title did pass at the time of delivery of the machine, and that the tests which were to be made thereafter were not a condition to the passing of title" and that "the implication is that when someone in this kind of business (Cummins) is told that it is necessary that [the generator] be put into operation, these circumstances justify Cummins' conclusion that they have an implied order to repair . . . [which] carries with it the responsibility of payment for the repairs before the machine can be released from the custody of the repairman." . . .

One of the more startling differences between the UCC and the [Uniform] Sales Act is the UCC's adoption of the flexible contractual approach instead of following the more rigid concept of title to which the Sales Act adhered. . . .

The Official Comment to UCC § 2-101 . . . puts it this way:

"The arrangement of the present Subtitle is in terms of contract for sale and the various steps of its performance. The legal consequences are stated as following directly from the contract and action taken under it without resorting to the idea of when property or title passed or was to pass as being the determining factor. *The purpose is to avoid making practical issues between practical men turn upon the location of an intangible something, the passing of which no man can prove by evidence and to substitute for such abstractions proof of words and actions of a tangible character.*" . . . (Emphasis added)

. . . In the absence of a delivery of conforming goods, the risk of damage remained with Cummins, the seller, notwithstanding the delivery of the generator to the job site, the receipt of payment from Wilke, and some eight months' delay in start-up. . . .

The narrow issue here is, whether Cummins made a "delivery" of goods which conformed to the contract. . . . Wilke's purchase order specifically incorporated the government specifications, which consisted of two and a half pages of single-spaced typescript which detailed the field tests to be performed prior to acceptance by the government. . . .

The delivery of the generator to the job site, while identifying the goods to the contract, did not amount to a delivery of goods or the performance of obligations conforming to the contract. It could not constitute such a delivery and performance until the generator had been installed, started up, and field tests completed to the satisfaction of the government. Until then, risk of loss remained with Cummins regardless of where title may have stood.

While it is conceivable that a negligent act could be postulated which would have made it possible to hold Wilke responsible for the cost of repairing the damage, such a course of conduct is absent here. The generator, when delivered, was completely enclosed and had been delivered in an inoperable condition so that no one could "start it or fool with it" until it was "turned over" to Wilke. On these facts, the judgment in Cummins' favor was clearly erroneous.

[Judgment reversed.]

Medico Leasing Co. v Smith

(Okla) 457 P2d 548 (1969)

Medico Leasing Co. owned a used Buick automobile which it delivered to Smith, a used car dealer, to find a buyer. Smith sold it to Wessel Buick Co., which sold it to Country Cousins Motors, which sold it to the Carters. When Smith failed to pay Medico, the latter brought an action of replevin against the Carters in which the other dealers were made additional defendants. The claim of Medico was dismissed, and damages were awarded the Carters and Country Cousins on cross-petitions. Medico appealed.

HODGES, J. . . . The principal issue presented by this appeal is the trial court's ruling that the defendant, Wessel Buick Co., was a "buyer in the ordinary course of business" in good faith as defined by Sections 1-201(9) and 2-403(2) of the Oklahoma Uniform Commercial Code when they . . . purchased the automobile from defendant Smith, a used car dealer, to whom plaintiff had entrusted possession of the car. The trial court found that Wessel Buick acquired sufficient legal title even though the sale was made without the actual transfer of the automobile's Certificate of Title, and therefore the defendants, Carters and Country Cousins Motors, were entitled to damages for the wrongful taking.

The evidence shows substantially the following facts: Plaintiff corporation was engaged in the business of leasing various items of equipment and had leased a 1962 Buick automobile for a period of two years. Subsequent to the termination of the lease, the car was offered for sale by means of advertising in the newspaper. In answer to the ad, the defendant Smith telephoned the treasurer of the corporation, hereinafter referred to as Raskin, who had placed the ad and informed him that he could sell the car. Raskin informed Smith that he could have the car to show to a prospect; however, he did not give Smith the certificate of title. Smith, testifying for the plaintiff, contradicted the testimony of Raskin in that he stated that the only instructions he got from Raskin was that he wanted $2,200.00 for the car. Raskin was later warned by the president of plaintiff corporation to be careful of Smith. Smith was engaged in the used car business and had been for some time prior to this transaction. This fact was known to both the president of the corporation and to Raskin. In addition to showing the car to the prospect, Smith took the car to defendant Wessel Buick Co., sold it to them, and retained the money himself. Some three weeks following the sale, Smith gave Raskin a check for $600.00 with the notation thereon, "Partial payment 62 Buick, hold for cashiers check." Raskin testified that he accepted this check on the date that it bears. This check was never cashed, however, as there were insufficient funds deposited in the bank to cover it.

Some time following the sale of the car to defendant Wessel, an employee of Wessel, designated as the title clerk, called Smith for the certificate of title and was informed by him that the certificate had been left with her previously. Subsequent to that conversation, the clerk again contacted Smith and was informed that he did not have the certificate but that he would try to get it. Not receiving the certificate, the clerk made application to the Tax Commission for a lost certificate of title and in time received it. Prior to making application for lost title, defendant Wessel sold the Buick to the defendant Country Cousins Motors, who subsequently sold the car to defendants W. C. and Dorene Carter.

Meanwhile, plaintiff had not received any money for its car and, further, could not find the car. Through the Tax Commission it traced the ownership registration of the car and found it to be in the possession of W. C. and Dorene Carter. Plaintiff then filed a suit in replevin, posted bond, took possession of the car from the Carters and sold it to a third party.

Plaintiff does not contest the fact that Smith is their agent, but they maintain that he . . . did not have title to the automobile or authority to convey title. They assert that Smith could not convey any better title than he had, and as he had no title, none was conveyed. It is further asserted by plaintiff that defendant Wessel was not a buyer in good faith as required by our Uniform Commercial Code, because they purchased the car without a certificate of title under facts and circumstances which would have put an ordinarily prudent businessman on inquiry.

The provisions of the Code pertinent to the issues in this case are in part set out:

"[UCC §] 2-403(2) Any entrusting of possession of goods to a merchant who deals in goods of that kind gives him power to transfer all rights of the entruster to a buyer in the ordinary course of business.

"[UCC §] 1-201(9) "Buyer in ordinary course of business means a person who in good faith and without knowledge that the sale to him is in violation of the ownership rights or security interest of a third party in the goods buys in ordinary course from a person in the business of selling goods of that kind but does not include a pawnbroker. 'Buying' may be for cash or by exchange of other property or on secured or unsecured credit and includes receiving goods or documents of title under a preexisting contract for sale but does not include transfer in bulk or as security for or in total or partial satisfaction of a money debt."

The "entruster" in the instant case, the plaintiff, had good title to the Buick, which was a used car. The one to whom the automobile was entrusted, Smith, as a used car dealer, is a "merchant who deals in goods of that kind" within the meaning of the statute. Smith was known by the plaintiff to be a used car dealer. . . .

. . . The question then arises as to whether Wessel was a buyer in good faith when they purchased the car without a certificate of title.

It has long been held by this court that a certificate of title to an automobile issued under the motor vehicle act is not a muniment of title which establishes ownership, but is merely intended to protect the public against theft and to facilitate recovery of stolen automobiles and otherwise aid the state in enforcement of its regulation of motor vehicles. . . . This rule was not changed with the passage of the Uniform Commercial Code. Under Sec. 1-201(15) the certificate of title of an automobile is not listed as a "document of title." It was not necessary for the defendant Smith to deliver the certificate of title before he conveyed ownership of the Buick automobile, and the absence of a certificate does not invalidate the sale or prevent title from passing. . . .

. . . There was no proof that any defendant knew of any limitation of title or should have known prior to or at the time of purchase of the Buick automobile. We find the action of the trial court in sustaining the demurrers was proper.

[Judgment affirmed.]

Gallagher v Unenrolled Motor Vessel River Queen

(CA5 Tex) 475 F2d 117 (1973)

Smith operated a marina and sold and repaired boats. Gallagher rented a stall at the marina at which he kept his vessel, the River Queen. Without any authorization, Smith sold the vessel to Courtesy Ford. Gallagher sued Courtesy Ford for the vessel. Judgment was entered in favor of Gallagher and an appeal was taken.

PER CURIAM:

Plaintiffs sued to recover possession of their 38-foot pleasure motor boat, RIVER QUEEN, which one defendant, a marina operator, had sold to the other defendants. Judgment was entered for plaintiff against the purchasers on the finding that the marina operator had no right to sell the plaintiff's vessel, and against the marina operator in favor of the purchasers who had paid for the boat which they could not keep.

The purchasers appeal on the ground that they acquired all rights to RIVER QUEEN under Section 2-403(b) of the Uniform Commercial Code . . . which provides: "(b) Any entrusting of possession of goods to a merchant who deals in goods of that kind gives him power to transfer all rights of the entruster to a buyer in ordinary course of business." We find no error in the District Court's conclusion that ". . . Plaintiffs did not entrust the vessel River Queen to Defendant Smith as a merchant within the meaning of Section 2-403 of the Uniform Commercial Code. Plaintiffs rented a stall at Defendant Smith's marina to keep this vessel. This defendant operated several businesses at this one location. His business of renting stalls for vessels was separate and apart from his business as a boat repair. By inference, the Court concluded that the renting of stalls was also separate and apart from his business as a boat merchant. The River Queen was kept at this marina pursuant to [oral] rental contract."

[Judgment affirmed.]

QUESTIONS AND CASE PROBLEMS

1. A buyer purchased furniture on credit and made a number of payments thereafter. When he stopped making payments, the seller claimed the right to repossess the furniture on the theory that it had been sold on approval and that the buyer had never manifested his approval. Was the seller correct? [Gantman v Paul, 203 Pa Super 158, 199 A2d 519]

2. *B* purchased nationally advertised camping equipment from *S* for $1,000 and paid *S* with a bad check. *B* immediately resold the goods to *C* for $200. *C* had asked *B* if he had a bill of sale or a receipt for the goods. *B* had stated that he did not. *S* sued *C* to recover the goods. Decide. [Hollis v Chamberlin, 243 Ark 201, 419 SW2d 116]

3. *B* purchased a used automobile from *A* with a bad check. *B* then took the automobile to an auction in which the automobile was sold to *C*, who had no knowledge of the prior history of the automobile. When *B*'s check was dishonored, *A* brought suit against *C* to reclaim the automobile. Was he entitled to do so? [Greater Louisville Auto Auction, Inc. v Ogle Buick, Inc., (Ky) 387 SW2d 17]

4. Eastern Supply Co. purchased lawn mowers from the Turf Man Sales Corp. The purchase order stated on its face "Ship direct to 30th & Harcum Way, Pitts., Pa." Turf Man delivered the goods to Helm's Express, Inc. for shipment and delivery to Eastern at the address in question. Did title pass on delivery of the goods to Helm or upon their arrival at the specified address? [In re Eastern Supply Co., 21 (Pa) D&C 2d 128, 107 Pitts Leg J 451]

5. Di Lorenzo had possession of certain goods that belonged to Wolf, a dealer in household furniture. The goods were destroyed by fire. Not knowing of this, the parties made an agreement for the sale of the goods. The dealer brought an action against Di Lorenzo. Decide. [Wolf v Di Lorenzo, 22 Misc 323, 49 NYS 191]

6. Lieber had possession of military souvenirs that he had obtained while on active duty in the Armed Forces of the United States in World War II. Many years later his chauffeur stole the souvenirs and sold them to a dealer, Mohawk Arms, which purchased in good faith. Lieber located the souvenirs and sued Mohawk Arms. Did it have a defense? [Lieber v Mohawk Arms, Inc., 64 Misc 2d 206, 314 NYS2d 510]

7. Burke fraudulently induced Cavanaugh Bros. to sell him a horse. Three months later Burke sold the horse to Porell, a bona fide purchaser. Cavanaugh sued Porell to obtain the horse on the theory that because of Burke's fraud he never obtained title and Cavanaugh Bros. still owned the horse. Decide. [Porell v Cavanaugh Bros., 69 NH 364, 41 A 860]

8. Atlas Auto Rental Corp., which rented automobiles to the public, would sell its used cars from time to time. It permitted Schwartzman, a prospective buyer, to test drive a two-year old station wagon. Before Schwartzman left with the car, he gave Atlas a check which was later returned by the drawee bank marked "No funds." Schwartzman and the car disappeared. Schwartzman apparently sold the car to Weisberg, a licensed automobile wrecker and junk dealer for $300. Weisberg did not obtain a bill of sale or a title certificate from Schwartzman. Weisberg resold the automobile on the same day for $1,200. Atlas sued Weisberg for converting the automobile. Weisberg raised the defense that he was protected by the UCC. Was he correct? [Atlas Auto Rental Corp. v Weisberg, (NY Civil Court) 54 Misc 2d 168, 281 NYS2d 400]

9. Coburn bought cattle from Regan and paid for them with a check at the time of sale. The parties agreed that Regan would hold the cattle for a few days. The day before Coburn was to take the cattle, Regan sold them to

Drown who gave him a check at that time. After Regan took the check but before Drown had taken possession of the cattle, Regan told Drown that Coburn had purchased the cattle. Drown took the cattle. Coburn sued Drown for their value. Decide. [Coburn v Drown, 114 Vt 158, 40 A2d 528]

10. The Auburn Motor Co. sold five automobiles to Levasseur of Rhode Island to be shipped C.O.D. via the Adams Express Co. from Indiana to Providence, Rhode Island. While the goods were in transit, Levasseur borrowed money from the New England Auto Insurance Co. to pay for the cars and executed a mortgage on the cars to secure payment of the loan. On the day the cars were received, Levasseur transferred one of them to the Whitten Motor Vehicle Co. The Whitten company sold the car to Andrews. In an action brought by the New England Auto Investment Co. against Andrews, the defendant alleged that the mortgage was invalid and contended that the Auburn Motor Co. had retained title and right of possession. Do you agree with this contention? [New England Auto Investment Co. v Andrews, 47 RI 299, 132 A 883]

11. Hargo Woolen Mills manufactured woolen cloth. In doing this, use was made of card waste. This was supplied to Hargo by a waste dealer, the Shabry Trading Company. Shabry delivered 24 bales of waste to Hargo which Hargo did not wish to use as it had an adequate supply. To save storage and transportation costs, it was agreed to leave the excess bales in the possession of Hargo and that if Hargo should use any of them, it would notify Shabry and make payment for such bales. Hargo owed money to Meinhard-Commercial Corporation. It began a court procedure by which a receiver was appointed to take possession of the assets of Hargo. The receiver seized the 24 bales of waste which had been delivered to Hargo by Shabry. Shabry claimed these bales. Was it entitled to them? [Meinhard Commercial Corp. v Hargo Woolen Mills, (NH) 300 A2d 321]

25 Obligation and Performance

DUTIES AND PERFORMANCE OF PARTIES

§ 25:1. **Basic Obligation.** Each party to a sales contract is bound to perform according to its terms. Each is likewise under the duty to exercise good faith in its performance and to do nothing that would impair the expectation of the other party that the contract will be duly performed.

(1) Good Faith. "Every contract or duty . . . imposes an obligation of good faith in its performance or enforcement." [1] The UCC defines good faith as meaning "honesty in fact in the conduct or transaction concerned." [2] In the case of the merchant seller or buyer of goods, the Code carries the concept of good faith further and imposes the additional requirement that the merchant seller or buyer observe "reasonable commercial standards of fair dealing in the trade." [3] (See p. 498, Umlas v Acey Oldsmobile, Inc.)

§ 25:2. **Conditions Precedent to Performance.** In the case of a cash sale not requiring the physical moving of the goods, the duties of the seller and buyer are concurrent. Each one has the right to demand that the other perform at the same time. That is, as the seller hands over the goods, the buyer theoretically must hand over the purchase money. If either party refuses to act, the other party has the right to withhold his performance.[4] In the case of a shipment contract, there is a time interval between the performances of the parties; the seller will have performed his part of the contract by delivering the goods to the carrier; but the buyer's obligation will not arise until he has received and accepted the goods.

The duty of a party to a sales contract to perform his part of the contract may be subject to a *condition precedent,* that is, by the terms of the contract he is not required to perform until some event occurs or until some act is performed. Quite commonly the condition precedent is performance by the other party. Thus, a contract may provide that the seller shall deliver merchandise but that the buyer must first pay for it in full. Under this contract the duty of the seller to deliver the merchandise is subject to the condition precedent of payment in full by the buyer. If the buyer never performs his part of the contract, the duty of the seller under that contract never arises.

---

[1] UCC § 1-203.
[2] § 1-201(19).
[3] § 2-103(1)(b).
[4] UCC §§ 2-507, 2-511.

If there is a promise that the condition precedent shall happen or be performed, the promisee may treat nonperformance as a breach of contract and claim damages of the other party for failing to bring about the fulfillment of the condition.

To illustrate the distinction between a mere condition precedent and a contractual obligation to obtain the satisfaction of the condition precedent, a buyer might order goods to be manufactured but because of outstanding patents the contract specifies that the obligation of the manufacturer is dependent upon the buyer's securing the permission or license of the patent holder. This would create a condition precedent so that the manufacturer's failure to manufacture would be excused if the buyer did not obtain the license. The contract might specify instead that the buyer undertakes or agrees to obtain the license for the manufacturer. The buyer's failure to obtain the license is a breach of contract by the buyer, which not only excuses the manufacturer from performance but also entitles him to recover damages from the buyer for the buyer's failure to perform his obligation. The manufacturer in such case can recover the profits that he could have made had the transaction with the buyer been completed, together with any expenses he may have already incurred in preparing to perform the contract.

§ 25:3. Seller's Duty to Deliver. It is the seller's duty to make "delivery," [5] which does not refer to a physical delivery but merely means that the seller must permit the transfer of possession of the goods to the buyer. That is, the seller makes the goods available to the buyer. The delivery must be made in accordance with the terms of the sale or contract to sell.[6]

There is no violation of the Automobile Dealers Day in Court Act when the automobile manufacturer stops manufacturing a particular line of cars, even though the manufacturer may have bound itself by contract to supply such cars. In such case the manufacturer is liable for damages for breach of contract but it has not violated the federal statute.[7]

(1) Place, Time, and Manner of Delivery. The terms of the contract determine whether the seller is to send the goods or the buyer is to call for them, or whether the goods must be transported by the seller to the buyer, or whether the transaction is to be completed by the delivery of documents without the movement of the goods. In the absence of a provision in the contract or a contrary course of performance or usage of trade, the place of delivery is the seller's place of business, if he has one; otherwise, it is his residence. If, however, the subject matter of the contract consists of identified goods that are known by the parties to be in some other place, that place is the place of delivery. Documents of title may be delivered through customary banking channels.[8]

---

[5] Permalum Window & Awning Mfg. Co. v Permalum Mfg. Co., (Ky) 412 SW2d 863.

[6] UCC § 2-301.

[7] Buono Sales, Inc. v Chrysler Motors Corp., (CA2 NJ) 449 F2d 715.

[8] § 2-308.

When a method of transportation called for by the contract becomes unavailable or commercially impracticable, the seller must make delivery by means of a commercially reasonable substitute if available and the buyer must accept such substitute.[9] This provision is applicable when a shipping strike makes impossible the use of the specified means of transportation.[10]

If the seller is required to send the goods but the agreement does not provide for the time of sending them, he must send the goods within a reasonable time. An effectual tender or offer of delivery by the seller must be made at a reasonable hour.[11] The same rule applies to a demand for possession of the goods by the buyer. What constitutes a reasonable hour is to be determined in view of the circumstances of each case.

(2) Quantity Delivered. The buyer has the right to insist that all the goods be delivered at one time. If the seller delivers a smaller quantity than that stipulated in the contract, the buyer may refuse to accept the goods. In the case of a divisible contract, if the buyer accepts or retains part of the goods with knowledge of the seller's intention to deliver no more, the buyer must pay the proportionate price representing the items or units which he has received; if the contract is not divisible, he must pay the full contract price. If the goods are used or disposed of by the buyer before he learns of the seller's intention, the buyer is only required to pay the fair value of the goods he has received.

(a) Delivery in Installments. The buyer is under no obligation or duty to accept delivery of goods by installments unless the contract contemplates such deliveries [12] or unless the circumstances are such as to give rise to the right to make delivery in lots.[13]

When the contract provides for delivery and payment by installments, a difficult problem is presented when the seller fails to make a proper delivery or when the buyer fails to pay for one or more installments. For example, *A* agrees to sell 6,000 tons of coal to *B* to be delivered in three equal monthly installments. In the first month *A* delivers only the first 150 tons. The courts in some states hold that the buyer must accept the remaining installments, although he is entitled to damages for the deficiency in the short delivery. Other states take the view that time is of the essence in such contracts and that a failure to deliver a particular installment goes to the root of the contract, entitling the buyer to cancel the entire transaction.

There is a breach of the entire contract whenever the seller's default as to one or more installments substantially impairs the value of the whole

---

9 § 2-514(1).

10 Caruso-Rinella-Battaglia Co. v Delano Corp., (US Dept of Agriculture) 25 AD 1028, 3 UCCRS 863.

11 UCC § 2-503(1)(a).

12 § 2-307.

13 § 2-307. This situation would arise whenever it is physically impossible because of the buyer's limited facilities or commercially impractical for any reason for the seller to make complete delivery.

contract.[14] Whether the breach of contract is so material that it justifies the injured party in refusing to carry out the remaining terms of the contract and suing for damages for breach of the entire contract, or whether the breach applies only to the defective or missing installments so that the buyer is only entitled to damages as to them, depends on the terms of the contract and the circumstances of the case. (See p. 499, Continental Grain Co. v Simpson Feed Co.)

If payment is to be made for each installment, the delivery of each installment and the payment for each installment are conditions precedent to the respective duties of the buyer to accept and of the seller to deliver subsequent installments.[15]

(3) Delivery to Carrier. When the seller is required to or may send the goods to the buyer but the contract does not require him to make a delivery at a particular destination, the seller, in the absence of a contrary agreement, must put the goods in the possession of a proper carrier and make such contract for their transportation as is reasonable in view of the nature of the goods and other circumstances of the case. For example, if the goods require refrigeration and the risk of loss passes to the buyer on delivery to the carrier, the seller must contract with the carrier to provide the necessary refrigeration.

The seller must also obtain and promptly deliver or tender in properly indorsed form any document, such as a bill of lading, that is required by the buyer in order to obtain possession of the goods. The seller must likewise promptly notify the buyer of the shipment.[16] If the seller fails to notify the buyer or to make a proper contract of carriage, the buyer may reject the goods when material delay or loss is caused by such breach.[17] Consequently, in the preceding refrigerated-goods case, if the seller did not arrange for refrigeration and this caused the goods to spoil in transit, the buyer could reject the goods, even though the risk of loss had passed to the buyer on delivery to the carrier; but he would not be able to reject the goods if they spoiled because of improper refrigeration when the seller had initially made a proper contract for refrigeration with the carrier.

(4) Delivery at Destination. If the contract requires the seller to make delivery at a destination point, the seller must make a proper tender of the goods at that point. If any documents that are necessary to obtain possession of the goods are issued by a carrier, the seller must also tender such documents.[18]

---

[14] UCC § 2-612(3). The buyer, however, may waive the breach and he is deemed to reinstate the contract if he accepts a nonconforming installment without seasonably notifying the seller that he cancels the contract, or if he sues with respect only to past installments, or if he demands the delivery of future installments.

[15] Restatement of Contracts, § 272, Illus. 1.

[16] UCC § 2-504.

[17] § 2-504.

[18] § 2-503(3).

(5) Cure of Defective Tender. The seller or vendor has the right to *cure,* or remedy, a defective tender by making a second tender or delivery after the first has been properly rejected by the buyer because it did not conform to the contract. If the time for making delivery under the contract has not expired, the seller need only give the buyer seasonable (timely) notice of his intention to make a proper delivery within the time allowed by the contract, and he may then do so. If the time for making the delivery has expired, the seller is given an additional reasonable time in which to make a substitute conforming tender if he so notifies the buyer and if he had acted reasonably in making the original tender, believing that it would be acceptable.[19]

These rules apply only when goods are offered by the seller in performance of the contract and they are rejected by the buyer as nonconforming. If the buyer has accepted the goods, the question of whether the seller may make repairs or replace with other goods in order to cure some defect is not a question of curing the defective tender, for by definition there has been a breach of the contract and the question is then analyzed as a cure of breach rather than a cure of tender.

§ **25:4. Buyer's Duty to Accept Goods.** It is the duty of the buyer to accept the delivery of proper goods.

(1) Right to Examine Goods. Unless otherwise agreed, the buyer, when tender of the goods is made, has the right before payment for or acceptance of the goods to inspect them at any reasonable place or time and in any reasonable manner to determine whether they meet the requirements of the contract.[20] A C.O.D. term, however, bars inspection before payment unless there is an agreement to the contrary.[21]

A court must be realistic in appraising the sufficiency of a buyer's opportunity to inspect and should not hold that the buyer has accepted when, because of the technical or complex nature of the goods, the buyer cannot determine whether they are satisfactory until he makes use of them. Consequently, the buyer of a new automobile is not deemed to have accepted it simply because he could have taken it for a "spin around the block" when, in driving it home instead, the transmission ceased to function less than a mile from the dealer's showroom and after a few minutes of driving.[22]

(2) What Constitutes Acceptance of Goods. Acceptance ordinarily is an express statement by the buyer that he accepts or approves the goods. It may also consist of conduct which expresses such an intent, such as the failure to object within a reasonable period of time or the use of the goods in such a way as would be inconsistent with a rejection of them by the

[19] § 2-508.
[20] § 2-513(1).
[21] § 2-513(3)(a).
[22] Zabriskie Chevrolet v Smith, 99 NJ Super 441, 240 A2d 195.

buyer.[23] A buyer accepts the goods when he makes continued use and does not attempt to return the goods until after 14 months.[24]

A buyer accepts an automobile when he signs a contract stating that he accepts it "in good order" and drives it to his home.[25] A buyer, of course, accepts the goods when he modifies them, because such action is inconsistent with the continued ownership of the goods by the seller. Consequently, when the purchaser of a truck installed a hoist and dump bed on it, such action was inconsistent with ownership by the seller, and the buyer therefore became liable for the contract price of the truck.[26]

When a construction contractor orders equipment from a seller and installs it in a building which he is constructing, the act of installing the equipment in the building is an act inconsistent with the seller's ownership and is therefore an acceptance of the goods. (See p. 501, United States for the Use of Fram Corp. v Crawford.)

While the continued use of goods or the making of successive installment payments is strong evidence that the buyer has accepted the goods, that is not the case when the buyer made such use of the goods or made such payments in reliance on the seller's assurance that defects could be remedied. Thus, when a buyer of hauling trailers, upon complaining that they sagged when loaded, was assured by the seller that the defect in the trailers could be corrected by repairs which the seller would make, there was no acceptance of them arising from the fact that the buyer thereafter made regular payments and used them for over 12 months and over 50,000 miles.[27]

*(3) **Effect of Acceptance on Breach.*** Acceptance of the goods by the buyer does not discharge the seller from liability in damages or other legal remedy for breach of any promise or warranty in the contract to sell or the sale. But the seller is not liable if, after acceptance of the goods, the buyer fails to give notice of the breach of any promise or warranty within a reasonable time after the buyer knows or ought to know of the breach.[28]

§ 25:5. Buyer's Duty to Pay. The buyer is under a duty to pay for the goods at the contract rate for any goods accepted.[29] In the absence of a contrary provision, payment must be made in cash and must be made concurrently with receipt of the goods; and, conversely, payment cannot be required before that time.[30]

---

23 UCC § 2-606(1).

24 Chaffin v Bittinsky, 126 Vt 218, 227 A2d 296.

25 Rozmus v Thompson's Lincoln-Mercury Co., 209 Pa Super 120, 224 A2d 782.

26 Park County Implement Co. v Craig, (Wyo) 397 P2d 800.

27 Trailmobile Division of Pullman, Inc. v Jones, 118 Ga App 472, 164 SE2d 346.

28 UCC § 2-607(2), (3). This section rejects the view that acceptance of the goods is a waiver of any claim for damages.

29 §§ 2-301, 2-607(1).

30 § 2-310(a). If delivery under the contract is to be made by a delivery of document of title, payment is due at the time and place at which the buyer is to receive the document regardless of where the goods are to be received. § 2-310(c).

A buyer is not required to pay for partial or installment deliveries unless the contract so requires. (See p. 501, Cameras for Industry v I. D. Precision Components Corp.) If delivery by lots is proper and the price can be apportioned, however, the buyer must pay for each lot as delivered.[31]

The seller may accept a commercial paper, such as a check, in payment of the purchase price. This form of payment, unless the parties expressly agree otherwise, is merely a conditional payment, that is, conditional upon the instrument's being honored and paid. If the instrument is not paid, it ceases to be payment of the purchase price and the seller is then an unpaid seller.[32] Refusal of payment by check does not affect the rights of the parties under the sales contract as long as the seller gives the buyer a reasonable time in which to procure the legal tender with which to make payment.[33]

The parties may agree to a sale on credit. This may be done for each sale individually or for sales generally, as in the case of a charge account in a department store. When a sale is made on credit, the parties may include special provisions to protect the seller.

Tender or offer of the purchase price has the same effect as actual payment in imposing upon the seller the duty to make delivery. If the seller fails to make delivery when a proper tender of payment is made, he is in default under the contract.

It must also be remembered that if the seller is in default, the buyer may cancel the contract.

(1) Escrow Payment. The escrow payment provides a form of security. This technique can be employed where one party is unwilling to act until the other party pays while the payor is unwilling to pay until the other party acts. For example, the goods which the seller is selling to the buyer may be in the warehouse of a supplier in a distant city. If the buyer would pay the seller in advance, the buyer would then be taking a number of risks which he might not wish to assume. The same would be true if the seller would obtain and deliver the goods before he was paid. In such a case the parties could agree that the buyer would deposit the purchase price in an escrow account in a bank, with instructions to the bank to pay the money to the seller when proper papers were submitted by the seller to the bank showing that the goods had been sent to the buyer, or to return the money to the buyer if the seller had not performed within a specified time.

When money is so deposited with a bank or other third person under such an agreement, it is commonly called an escrow deposit and the fund so deposited must be maintained as a separate or distinct fund.

§ 25:6. Duties Under Particular Terms. A sale may be as simple as a face-to-face exchange of money and goods, but it frequently involves a more complicated pattern, with some element of tansportation, generally by a

---

[31] UCC § 2-307.
[32] § 2-511.
[33] Silver v Sloop Silver Cloud, (DC SD NY) 259 F Supp 187.

common carrier. This, in turn, generally results in the addition of certain special terms to the sales transaction.

*(1) **FOB.*** The term FOB or "free on board," may be used with reference to the seller's city, or the buyer's city, or an intermediate city, as in the case of a transshipment. It may also be used with reference to a named carrier, such as FOB a specified vessel, car, or other vehicle. In general, an FOB term is to be construed as requiring delivery to be made at the FOB point, as contrasted with merely a shipment to that point,[34] and as imposing upon the seller the risk and expense involved in getting the goods to the designated place or on board the specified carrier.[35]

Where goods are sent FOB the seller's plant, the buyer is required to pay for the goods although they were damaged by freezing while in transit as the risk of loss had passed from the seller to the buyer upon delivery to the carrier.[36]

Likewise, where the seller of unassembled prefabricated homes transported the homes to the building site at his own expense and the sale was made by the seller "FOB building site," the title to the goods passed at the building site within the state of Kansas. Therefore, the Kansas sales tax law applied to the transaction. (See p. 502, Custom Built Homes Co. v Kansas State Commission of Revenue.)

*(2) **CIF.*** The term CIF indicates that the payment by the buyer is a lump sum covering the cost (selling price) of the goods, insurance on them, and freight to the specified destination of the goods. The CIF term imposes upon the seller the obligation of putting the goods in the possession of a proper carrier, or loading and paying for the freight, or procuring the proper insurance, of preparing an invoice of the goods and any other document needed for shipment, and of forwarding all documents to the buyer with commercial promptness.[37]

Under a CIF contract the buyer bears the risk of loss after the goods have been delivered to the carrier.[38] He must pay for the goods when proper documents representing them are tendered to him, which in turn means that he is not entitled to inspect the goods before paying for them, unless the contract expressly provides for payment on or after the arrival of the goods.[39]

---

[34] See p. 491. When a port is selected as the FOB point for an imported article, the price is frequently described as the price POE or "port of entry."

[35] UCC § 2-319(1).

[36] Storz Brewing Co. v Brown, 154 Neb 204, 47 NW2d 407.

[37] § 2-320(1), (2). The term C & F or CF imposes the same obligations and risks as a CIF term with the exception of the obligation as to insurance. Under a CF contract, the seller completes his performance by delivery of the goods to the carrier and by proper payment of the freight charges on the shipment, whereupon title and risk of loss pass to the buyer. Amco Transworld Inc. v M/V Bambi, (DC SD Tex) 257 F Supp 215.

[38] UCC § 2-320(2)(c). The CIF and CF contracts may be modified to place the risk of deterioration during shipment on the seller by specifying that the price shall be based on the arrival or "out turn" quality, or by having the seller warrant the condition or quality of the goods on their arrival. § 2-321(2).

[39] § 2-320(4), 2-321(3).

(3) Ex-ship. If the contract provides for delivery ex-ship, the seller bears the risk of loss until the goods have left the ship's tackle or have otherwise been properly unloaded. He must discharge all liens arising from the transportation of the goods and must furnish the buyer with such documents or instructions as enable him to obtain the goods from the carrier.[40]

(4) No Arrival, No Sale. When goods are sent under such a term, the seller bears the risk of loss during transportation; but if the goods do not arrive, he is not responsible to the buyer for in such case there is no sale. The buyer is protected in that he is only required to pay for the goods if they arrive.

The "no arrival, no sale" contract requires the seller to ship proper conforming goods and to tender them on their arrival if they do arrive. He must, of course, refrain from interfering with the arrival of the goods.[41]

§ 25:7. Adequate Assurance of Performance. Whenever a party to the sales transaction has reason to believe that the other party may not perform his part of the contract, he may make a written demand upon the other party for adequate assurance that he will in fact perform his contract. For example, when goods are to be delivered at a future date or in installments over a period of time, the buyer may become fearful that the seller will not be able to make the future deliveries required. The buyer may in such case require assurance from the seller that the contract will be performed.[42]

(1) Form of Assurance. The person upon whom demand for assurance is made must give "such assurance of due performance as is adequate under the circumstances of the particular case."[43] The exact form of assurance is not specified. If the party on whom demand is made has an established reputation, his reaffirmance of his contract obligation and a statement that he will perform may be sufficient to assure a reasonable man that it will be performed. In contrast, the person's reputation or economic position at the time may be such that there is no assurance that there will be a proper performance in the absence of a guarantee by a third person or the furnishing of security by way of a pledge or other device to protect the demanding party against default.[44]

(2) Failure to Give Assurance. The party on whom demand is made may state he will not perform; that is, he repudiates the contract. In contrast with a flat repudiation, the party upon whom demand is made may fail to reply or may give only a feeble answer that is not sufficient to assure a

---

[40] § 2-322(2).

[41] § 2-324(a).

[42] § 2-609(1). Between merchants the reasonableness of the grounds for insecurity is determined according to commercial standards. § 2-609(2).

[43] § 2-609(4).

[44] Between merchants the adequacy of any assurance is determined according to commercial standards. UCC § 2-609(2).

reasonable man that performance will be made. The failure to provide adequate assurance within 30 days after receiving the demand, or a lesser time when 30 days would be unreasonable, constitutes a repudiation of the contract.[45]

ASSIGNMENT OF SALES CONTRACTS

The assignment of a sales contract by either party ordinarily does not affect the obligations of the original seller and buyer. The seller and the buyer are each bound by the same obligations as before.

§ 25:8. Effect of Assignment. If the buyer is the assignor, there may be a modification of the original contract as by specifying that the seller is to deliver the goods to the buyer's assignee. The printed form used by the seller usually will specify that if the seller assigns the contract, the buyer agrees to pay the assignee.

When, as is generally the case, the seller and a finance company have an agreement that the seller's contracts with buyers shall be assigned to the finance company, the printed form of the seller will commonly name the finance company as assignee. Such a form is often supplied to the seller by the finance company. It may be provided, however, that the individual buyers shall continue to make payments to the seller with the latter making periodic payments of lump sums to the finance company.

§ 25:9. Obligation of Seller's Assignee as to Performance. Ordinarily an assignment by a seller is merely a way of converting the seller's account receivable or contract rights into immediate cash and does not represent an undertaking by the assignee to perform the contract. When the seller has more contracts than he can handle or is going out of business, however, the assignment of a contract may be intended to delegate to his assignee the performance of the contract.

An assignee of the seller is not liable to the buyer for a breach of the assigned contract by the original seller, particularly when the assignee is not bound to render any performance. For example, the finance company to which the seller has assigned a credit contract is not liable for breach of warranty.[46]

§ 25:10. Defenses of Buyer Against Seller's Assignee. Ordinarily the assignee of the seller is subject to any defense which the buyer would have against the seller. Credit sales contracts commonly provide, however, that the buyer agrees not to assert against the seller's assignee any claim which he could assert against the seller. This makes the contract much more attractive to the assignee by, in effect, making it "negotiable" and giving the assignee the greater assurance that he will be legally entitled to collect the face amount

---

[45] § 2-609(4). This enables the adverse party to take steps at an earlier date to protect himself against the default of the other party, as by making substitute contracts to replace the repudiated contracts.

[46] Pendarvis v General Motors Corp., (NY) 6 UCCRS 457.

of the contract. Such a provision is generally valid, as far as the UCC is concerned,[47] although in a given state there may be an additional local non-Code consumer protection statute which declares such a waiver clause invalid generally or as applied to consumer goods, or when notice of the assignment is not given to the buyer. (See p. 503, D. P. C. Corp. v Jobson.)

[47] UCC § 9-206(1).

CASES FOR CHAPTER 25

Umlas v Acey Oldsmobile, Inc.

(NY Civil Court) 62 Misc 2d 819, 310 NYS2d 147 (1970)

Umlas made a contract to buy a new automobile from Acey Oldsmobile. He was allowed to keep his old car until the new car was delivered. The sales contract gave him a trade-in value on the old car of $650, but specified that it would be reappraised when it was actually brought in to the dealer. When Umlas brought the trade-in to the dealer, an employee of Acey took it for a test drive and told Acey that it was worth from $300 to $400. Acey stated to Umlas that the trade-in would be appraised at $50. Umlas refused to buy from Acey and purchased from another dealer who appraised the trade-in at $400. Umlas sued Acey for breach of contract. Acey defended on the ground that its conduct was authorized by the reappraisal clause.

SANDLER, J. . . . Underlying plaintiff's law suit is the charge . . . that the reappraisal was not done in good faith.

The defendant interposed a counterclaim for an amount just in excess of $300.00 that is totally without any semblance of merit, and that was obviously designed to harass the plaintiff by removing the case from the Small Claims Part of this Court.

I find as a fact that defendant's employee did state to plaintiff that he had reappraised plaintiff's car in the amount of $50.00 . . . and that this valuation was not made in good faith.

The critical legal question thus becomes whether the provision of the form order, under which defendant reserved the right to reappraise the used car allowance at the time of delivery where delivery is deferred, implies that the right of reappraisal is to be exercised in good faith. I conclude as a matter of law that good faith is an essential implied condition for the exercise of the right of reappraisal. See Uniform Commercial Code, 1-201, 2-103; c.f. 2-305.

To hold otherwise would mean that the order agreement, and the promises exchanged therein, was intended to be wholly illusory until delivery had been completed. Such a construction would make a travesty of an agreement that evoked from the plaintiff, as it was intended to, the following substantial reliance: a down playment, suspension for a period of his right to acquire a car elsewhere, and the securing of a bank loan. . . .

In reaching the above conclusion, I do not wish to be understood as doubting the legitimate considerations prompting the provision in question when the delivery of the car is to be deferred. Obviously, the buyer's car may suffer some deterioration during the intervening period. . . .

But the fact that the clause represents a reasonable response to a practical problem does not obscure the reality that it is open to, and indeed lends itself to, serious and recurrent abuse. In the presence of a potential buyer, searching for the optimum price for his used car, a dealer may well be disposed to place a generous value on the used car, realizing that he could later renegotiate the figure when his bargaining position was immensely strengthened.

For it is surely clear that when a buyer has signed an order for a particular car of a certain color and with special accessories, has made a cash downpayment, has secured a bank loan, and has arrived in his somewhat worn old car ready to receive a resplendent new vehicle, his ability to resist a new less-favorable deal is at a very low ebb indeed.

Surely, it is no surprise that defendant's witness acknowledged that used car allowances are often lowered at the delivery date. And although no testimony was presented directly, it is surely a fair surmise that instances in which used cars are found to have a higher value at the delivery date would represent extraordinary phenomena in the annals of any car dealer.

In evaluating the appropriate remedy for the kind of breach presented, I have considered that the arrangement of circumstances in this very common situation presents car dealers with a powerful inducement to place high values on used cars when attempting to land the order and low values when the physical presence of the new car after an intervening period has substantially reduced the purchasers' resistance. Car dealers should be encouraged to withstand this temptation. . . .

The plaintiff, like any purchaser under the circumstances, was entitled to a good faith valuation of his car on the delivery date.

In the absence of any good faith reappraisal by the defendant, the only valuation by the defendant is that fixed at the time of the original order, and I find that to be controlling.

Accordingly, I find for the plaintiff in the sum of $270.00 with interest from December 1, 1969.

Continental Grain Co. v Simpson Feed Co.

(DC ED Ark) 102 F Supp 354; affirmed (CA8 Ark) 199 F2d 284 (1952)

The Continental Grain Co., a grain dealer, made a contract with the Simpson Feed Co., a grain elevator company, to purchase approximately five carloads of soybeans, delivery to be made from October 1 to November 30 at seller's option, with the buyer to furnish the seller shipping instructions as each of the cars was loaded. On October 30, the first car was loaded and shipping instructions given by the buyer the same day. The next day a second car was loaded, but instructions were not given until after 48 hours. The seller refused to accept such delayed instructions and canceled the contract. The buyer then purchased four carloads of soybeans in the market and brought suit for the difference between the market and the contract price.

LEMLEY, D.J. . . . "The failure to make punctual payment may be material or trivial according to the circumstances. We must know the cause of the default, the length of the delay, the needs of the vendor, and the expectations of the vendee. If the default is the result of accident or misfortune, if there is a reasonable assurance that it will be promptly repaired, and if immediate payment is not necessary to enable the vendor to proceed with performance, there may be one conclusion. If the breach is willful, if there is no just ground to look for prompt reparation, if the delay has been substantial, or if the needs of the vendor are urgent so that timely performance is imperiled, in these and in other circumstances, there may be another conclusion. Sometimes the conclusion will follow from all the circumstances as an inference of law to be drawn by the judge; sometimes, as an inference of fact to be drawn by the jury."

In the Restatement of the Law of Contracts, Section 275, it is said that the factors to be considered in measuring the materiality of a breach of such contract include the following: (1) the extent to which the injured party will obtain the substantial benefits which he could reasonably have anticipated; (2) the extent to which the injured party may be adequately compensated in damages for lack of complete performance; (3) the greater or less hardship on the party failing to perform in terminating the contract; (4) the willful, negligent, or innocent behavior of the party failing to perform, and (5) the greater or less uncertainty that the party failing to perform will perform the remainder of the contract. In the following section, 276, of the Restatement, it is stated that in mercantile contracts performance at the time agreed upon is important, and if the delay of one party is considerable, "having reference to the nature of the transaction and the seriousness of the consequences," and is not justified by the conduct of the other party, the latter need not perform further.

Assuming that the conduct of the plaintiff with respect to the second carload of soybeans amounted to a breach of its contract, nevertheless, when such breach is viewed in the light of the above-mentioned factors, we believe that, as a matter of law, it was insubstantial and did not have the effect of relieving the defendant of its obligation to perform its contract further, either with respect to the 2,000 bushels of soybeans loaded on October 31 or as to the remaining 6,000 bushels, which were never loaded.

While it appears that the parties contemplated that deliveries were to be made in installments and paid for separately, no particular number of installments or times for shipment were specified, and the defendant had the right, had it seen fit to do so, to tender all of the beans either on the first or the last day of the contract period. Plaintiff had no right to insist on delivery of any part of the beans prior to November 30. As a matter of fact, no beans were loaded until October 30, approximately six weeks after the contract was entered into and almost at the end of the first month of the contract period. The fact that the defendant was given approximately two and one-half months from the date of the contract to complete delivery, coupled with the fact that it did not undertake to perform until the month of October was practically gone, demonstrates to our mind that neither party was in a particular hurry with respect to these deliveries, and that time was not of the essence of the contract, except to the extent that the defendant was obligated to complete its deliveries by the end of November. At the time of the assumed breach, twenty-eight days of the month remained.

There is no suggestion that the plaintiff's delay in furnishing shipping instructions manifested any inability on its part to perform its contractual obligations, or that it evidenced any intent on its part to repudiate the contract or to abandon further performance under it, and there is no evidence that the defendant so construed it. On the contrary, the undisputed evidence is that on and after November 2 plaintiff advised the defendant that it intended to perform fully and urged the defendant to do likewise, even going so far as to offer it an extension of time within which to complete deliveries.

Defendant sustained no substantial damages as a result of the plaintiff's delay, nor did it run the risk of future damage. The marked rise in the price of soybeans between September 14 and November 2 gave it a considerable margin of safety had the market begun to fall, which it did not do. Moreover, defendant was under contract to furnish beans to others at even lower prices than that at which it had contracted with the plaintiff. The only damages that the defendant could have suffered as a result of the plaintiff's delay, under the evidence in this case, would have been demurrage on the car, or the expense of unloading it, and interest for two days on the money which it had tied up in the second carload of beans. The plaintiff, on the other hand, as a result of the defendant's refusal to perform further has sustained damages to the extent of several thousand dollars.

There is no showing here that the plaintiff's delay was either willful or negligent. Its explanation that it spent the 48 hours in obtaining clearances, from New Orleans, and that as soon as such clearances were obtained it furnished the defendant shipping instructions, is unchallenged.

Under such circumstances we do not feel that any reasonable man, in the exercise of fair and impartial judgment, could conclude that plaintiff's delay was such a material breach as to justify the defendant in canceling the contract either in whole or in part.

[Judgment for plaintiff.]

Code Comment: The same decision would be made under the Code since on the analysis of the facts as made by the court it would reach the conclusion that the breach of the buyer as to one installment did not "substantially impair the value of the whole contract," the latter being the test for determining whether breach as to an installment causes a breach of the whole contract. UCC § 2-612(3). A further element supporting this conclusion under the Code is the fact that the buyer volunteered an assurance of performance without waiting for the seller to demand it of him, as he could do under UCC § 2-609.

United States for the Use of Fram Corp. v Crawford

(CA5 Ga) 443 F2d 611 (1971)

Crawford, who was constructing a building for the United States Navy, purchased fuel equipment from Fram Corp. and installed the equipment in the building. Fram sued for the purchase price. Crawford claimed that he had not accepted the equipment because it was defective. From a judgment for Crawford, Fram appealed.

AINSWORTH, C.J. . . . The contract price for the fuel filter/separator units was $55,564.20. Floyd Crawford admitted at the trial that of that sum, $6,298.50 had not been paid. There was no testimony to the contrary. The appellees maintain that they are excused from further payment by the deficiencies in Fram's performance on the contract. Fram contends, to the contrary, that the Trial Judge should have directed a verdict in its favor on its claim for the $6,298.50. We sustain Fram's contention.

It is undisputed that Fram furnished the eighteen fuel filter/separator units called for by the contract, and that Crawford received and installed all eighteen units. Section 2-607 of the Uniform Commercial Code . . . provides . . . : "The buyer must pay at the contract rate for any goods accepted." Acceptance of goods occurs when the buyer "does any act inconsistent with the seller's ownership." Georgia UCC § 2-606 (1)(c). No case is reported in which the Georgia courts have had occasion to interpret section 2-606(1)(c). Courts in other jurisdictions, interpreting the same section of the Uniform Commercial Code, have held that installation by the buyer of heavy equipment supplied by the seller is an act inconsistent with the seller's ownership. See Marbelite Company v City of Philadelphia, 1966, 208 Pa Super 256, 222 A2d 443 (traffic signal equipment); Park County Implement Co. v Craig, Wyo. 1964, 397 P2d 800 (hoist and dump bed on vehicle). We believe that the Georgia courts, confronted with the same issue in the instant case, would give section 2-606(1)(c) the same construction. A buyer who has accepted goods may under certain conditions revoke his acceptance. Georgia UCC § 2-608. However, once Crawford had accepted and installed the units supplied in place on the Albany site, any subsequent attempt at revocation was ineffective. . . .

[Judgment reversed and action remanded.]

Cameras for Industry v I. D. Precision Components Corp.

49 Misc 2d 1044, 268 NYS2d 860 (1966)

Cameras for Industry made a contract to purchase component parts from Precision Components Corp. for use in the manufacture of security camera systems. When full deliveries were not made under the purchase orders, Cameras brought suit against Precision. The case, by agreement of the parties, was referred to a special referee to determine if there had been a breach of the contract.

MAZUR, Special Referee . . . By purchase orders dated March 1, 1963, and March 19, 1963, certain specified parts were ordered. The March 1 purchase order provided for an April 10, 1963, delivery date, while the March 19 purchase order provided for a delivery date of five to six weeks, or before, with a promise of partial shipment during the week of April 8. Both orders provided that time was of the essence and that partial shipments would be accepted. It is conceded that these orders were placed by plaintiff and were accepted by the defendant.

Apparently on April 9, 1963, and at various dates thereafter, up to and including April 26, 1963, partial shipments were made, with a total invoice value of $1,748.73. After that date, however, no further deliveries were made by the defendant to the plaintiff.

Plaintiff's insistence on timely delivery appears to have been occasioned by the fact that it had schedules to meet in its own production.

According to plaintiff's version of the facts, when it appeared that there would not be timely fulfillment of its orders, one of its representatives visited defendant's plant and discovered that plaintiff's work had been taken off the machines in favor of other jobs. However, so frantic was he for delivery, that he requested shipment of anything available, whether in finished or unfinished state, so that plaintiff could utilize whatever parts were usable. There appears to be some indication that at least part of the shipments were not usable.

Defendant's version of what happened is in direct contravention to plaintiff's testimony. According to defendant, it refused to fulfill the balance of the orders because plaintiff failed to pay for the partial shipments, and because plaintiff had been complaining that the tolerances and finishes were not in strict accordance with its specifications. It is defendant's contention that it was justified in halting production by plaintiff's attempt to vary its previously submitted specifications by requiring tolerances and finishes out of line with the original price estimates. . . .

Since the transaction herein took place prior to September 27, 1964, the effective date of the Uniform Commercial Code, it is governed by the appropriate provisions of Article 5 of the Personal Property Law, (Uniform Sales Act) now repealed. . . . Naturally, the seller is excused from performance if its failure is due to the acts of the buyer, or a refusal by the buyer to perform on his part. . . .

Partial deliveries do not obligate a buyer to make partial payments. The fact that the contracts herein provided that partial deliveries would be accepted merely obligated the buyer to accept shipments in a manner he would not otherwise be bound to do . . . but did not, without more, obligate it to make advance payments. . . .

It is obvious that the refusal by the seller herein to further perform the contracts was occasioned not as a result of anything the buyer did or omitted to do, but rather as a result of seller's realization either that it had made an unprofitable bargain or that it could use its machines more profitably. A buyer is entitled to expect full performance of a deal as made, and this is what the plaintiff herein did not get. Plaintiff is, therefore, entitled to recover for damages ensuing by defendant's delay in performing and refusing to complete deliveries. . . .

Code Comment: The same decision would be made under the Code as there was no evidence that the sales contract provided for delivery by lots and that the price could be apportioned to the respective lots. The general rule under the Code, by which a buyer is not required to pay for partial or installment deliveries when the contract does not so require, would therefore apply. UCC § 2-307.

Custom Built Homes Co. v Kansas State Commission of Revenue

184 Kan 31, 334 P2d 808 (1959)

Custom Built Homes purchased unassembled prefabricated houses from Page-Hill in Minnesota to be delivered by the seller "F.O.B. building site . . . Kansas." The seller brought the houses to the building site in sections by tractor-trailor, where he would unhitch the trailer and unload the shipment. Kansas taxed Custom Built on the sale. Custom Built raised the defense that there was no sale within the state of Kansas. From a judgment in favor of Kansas, Custom Built appealed.

SCHROEDER, J. . . . When did title pass? The parties recognize this to be the determinative question in this lawsuit.

Appellant seizes upon the finding of the trial court that title to the prefabricated exterior and interior sections passed to the appellant at the time the hooks of the Page-Hill crane were removed from such sections. . . . The sections were nailed to the foundation at the time the hooks were removed and had thus become permanently affixed to and had become a part of the real estate prior to the passing of title to the appellant.

Further argument by the appellant inferentially proceeds on the theory that title to a prefabricated house unit cannot pass in parts at different times, but of necessity under the contract must pass *in toto* at a specific time in accordance with the intention of the parties.

Appellant argues that title to the prefabricated roof and ceiling sections did not pass until such sections had become permanently affixed to and had become a part of the real estate. This is based upon testimony that initially these sections were unloaded by a separate stationary crane furnished by Page-Hill in much the same fashion as the exterior and interior wall panels. . . .

Appellant also contends that the trial court erred as to the time title passed to the loose materials since it failed to amplify such finding by stating what percentage these loose items bore to the entire unit, and further in failing to make a finding as to the time title to all of these units of a prefabricated house as a whole was contemplated to pass from Page-Hill to the appellant under the sales contract. . . .

The initial letters, "F.O.B." frequently found in contracts for goods to be shipped stand for the words "free on board." In commercial practice these words have a well-defined meaning, and, as applied to the sale of merchandise destined for shipment, mean that such goods are to be put into the hands of the carrier at the point of shipment free of expense to the buyer. . . .

" 'Where the contract provides for a sale f.o.b. the point of destination, the title is generally held not to pass, in the absence of a contrary intention between the parties, until the goods have been delivered at the point designated.' " . . .

In our opinion "F.O.B. building site in Wyandotte County, Kansas," has a clear and unambiguous meaning. Applied to the facts in this case as to each prefabricated house unit under the contract it means free on board the semi-trailer at the building site in Stony Point Heights Addition, Wyandotte County, Kansas. No contrary intention between the parties to the sales contract appearing from the face of the instrument, title to the merchandise passed upon delivery to the appellant (buyer) free on board the semi-trailer at the building site in Wyandotte County, Kansas. . . .

. . . As to each prefabricated house unit under the contract title passed upon delivery to the appellant—the time at which the tractor was unhooked from the semi-trailer loaded with the merchandise parked at the building site. On the issues here this is practically equivalent to the trial court's conclusion that title to portions of the merchandise passed when it was unloaded from the semi-trailer. The ultimate conclusion of the trial court that the merchandise occupied the status of tangible personal property at the time title passed to the appellant resulted in a correct decision.

[Judgment affirmed.]

Code Comment: This case was decided under the prior Uniform Sales Act but the same decision would be made under UCC § 2-319(1).

D. P. C. Corp. v Jobson

15 App Div 2d 861, 224 NYS2d 772 (1962)

Jobson purchased an automobile from Reynolds Motors, Inc. Reynolds assigned the contract to D. P. C. Corporation, a finance company. D. P. C. sued Jobson for the balance due on the purchase price. Jobson claimed that there had been a breach of warranty. D. P. C. claimed that this defense could not be raised against it because the sales contract stated that no defense could be raised against an assignee of the contract. A local non-UCC statute provided that an assignee was subject to defenses available against his assignor if he did not give notice to the buyer of the fact that the assignment had been made and that he was not so subject if he gave notice of the assignment and did not receive any return notice of any defense within ten days thereafter. Judgment was entered against Jobson and he appealed.

PER CURIAM: The plaintiff, as assignee of a conditional sales contract covering an automobile sold to the defendant-appellant by the respondent Reynolds Motors, Inc., brought this action for the unpaid balance of the purchase price. The defendant-appellant interposed an answer setting up a counterclaim for a breach of warranty against the plaintiff and Reynolds Motors, Inc., joining the latter as a party to the action upon the counterclaim. Upon motion of Reynolds Motors, Inc., the counterclaim was dismissed as to it. This was erroneous. The interposition of the counterclaim against the assignee up to the amount of the assignee's demand was authorized [although] the conditional sales contract contained a provision to the effect that the buyer agreed "not to set up any claim or defense arising out of the sale against such Seller as a defense, counterclaim or offset to any action by any assignee for the unpaid balance of the purchase price."

However this provision of the contract was not enforceable against the appellant in the absence of a showing by the assignee that it had received "no notice of the facts giving rise to the claim or defense within ten days after . . . [it mailed] to the buyer . . . notice of the assignment," together with the statutory notice specified in subdivision 9 of section 302 of the Personal Property Law. It does not appear that any such notice had ever been given to the appellant by the plaintiff assignee. . . .

[Judgment reversed.]

QUESTIONS AND CASE PROBLEMS

1. A computer manufacturer promoted the sale of a digital computer as a "revolutionary breakthrough." It made a contract to deliver one of these computers to a buyer. It failed to deliver the computer and explained that its failure was caused by unanticipated technological difficulties. Was this an excuse for nonperformance by the seller? [United States v Wegematic Corp., (CA2 NY) 360 F2d 674]
2. International Minerals and Metals Corporation contracted to sell Weinstein scrap metal to be delivered within 30 days. Later the seller informed the buyer that it could not make delivery within that time. The buyer agreed to an extension of time, but no limiting date was set. Within what time must the seller perform? [International Minerals and Metals Corp. v Weinstein, 236 NC 558, 73 SE2d 472]
3. Fleet purchased an ice cream freezer and compressor unit from Lang. Thereafter Fleet disconnected the compressor and used it to operate an air conditioner. When sued for the purchase price of the freezer and compressor unit, Fleet claimed that he had not accepted the goods. Was he correct? [Lang v Fleet, 193 Pa Super 365, 165 A2d 258]
4. George A. Ohl & Co. made a contract "to sell to A. J. Ellis a No. 5 press . . . for the sum of $680." The press was known by both parties to be stored in the factory of another company. The agreement contained no stipulation as to the place of delivery, and there was no usage of the trade governing the question. In an action brought by Gruen, assignee of Ellis, against the Ohl company, the place of delivery was a point of contention. Decide. [Gruen v George A. Ohl & Co., 81 NJL 626, 80 A 547]
5. Price agreed to purchase two barge-loads of coal from Brown. The coal was delivered on barges of the buyer on the Green River at or near Mining City, Kentucky, in accordance with the agreement. The buyer, after being given an opportunity to inspect the coal, hooked onto the barges and transported them up the river to Bowling Green, several miles away. During subsequent litigation the buyer contended that he had not accepted the coal. Do you agree? [Brown v Price, 207 Ky 8, 268 SW 590]
6. The Spaulding & Kimball Co. ordered from the Aetna Chemical Co. 75 cartons of window washers. The buyer received them and sold about a third to its customers. The buyer later refused to pay for them, claiming that the quality was poor. The seller sued for the price, claiming that the goods had been accepted. Decide. [Aetna Chemical Co. v Spaulding & Kimball Co., 98 Vt 51, 126 A 582]

7. The Tri-Bullion Smelting & Development Co. agreed to sell, and Jacobsen to buy, the seller's output of zinc concentrates for a two-year period. A year and a half later, the Tri-Bullion Co. closed its mine and notified Jacobsen that it would make no further deliveries. Jacobsen refused to pay for the last shipment. Jacobsen sued the Tri-Bullion Co. The defendant contended that the plaintiff had breached the contract by failure to pay for the goods delivered. Do you agree? [Tri-Bullion Smelting & Development Co. v Jacobsen, 147 CCA 454, 233 F 646]
8. The seller sold goods to a township. Under the state law governing townships, it was not possible for the township to make immediate payment of any bill presented to it. To the contrary, it was necessary that a bill be presented to the township auditor and approved by him before payment could be made. The seller claimed that the township was obligated to pay for the goods upon delivery. Decide. [J. C. Georg Service Corp. v Summit, 28 App Div 2d 578, 279 NYS2d 674]
9. Pittman purchased a Ford Galaxie from Perry Ford Co. The car caught on fire because of defective wiring. Pittman sued Ford Motor Co. for breach of warranty. Ford Motor Co. raised the defense that it had excluded liability in the manner authorized by the UCC (Sec. 2-316). Pittman objected that this section only applied to "sellers," and Perry Ford was the seller. Ford Motor Co. countered that Perry was merely its agent so that Ford Motor Co. was the actual seller of the Ford. Was Ford Motor Co. the seller? [Ford Motor Co. v Pittman, (Fla App) 227 So2d 246]
10. The Rock Glen Salt Co. agreed to sell to Segal of Massachusetts some bags of salt. It obtained from the Watkins Salt Co., New York, the bags of salt ordered by Segal and 15 barrels of salt ordered by another customer. The bags and barrels of salt were placed in a car and shipped to Boston. The bill of lading for the entire shipment was made out to the seller, and indorsed and sent to Segal, who was notified by the carrier of the arrival of the car. In an action brought by the salt company against Segal to recover the purchase price, he contended that (a) he could accept the salt in the bags and reject the salt in the barrels or (b) reject the entire shipment. What is your opinion? [Rock Glen Salt Co. v Segal, 229 Mass 115, 118 NE 239]

26 Warranties and Other Product Liabilities

GENERAL PRINCIPLES

When goods prove defective or cause harm, a question arises as to whether anyone is liable to the person harmed for the loss which he has sustained. The answer in some instances is based on general common law rules. In other instances, it is based upon the Uniform Commercial Code or new liability concepts.

§ **26:1. Introduction.** A seller or manufacturer may be liable for the loss caused to another because of the condition or malperformance of his product (1) when he has made an express guarantee; or (2) an express warranty; or (3) an implied warranty arises by operation of law; or tort liability is imposed because of the defendant's (4) fraud, (5) negligence, or (6) strict tort responsibility. When liability (1) is involved, the question of the relative rights of the parties is governed by general principles of contract law; when liability under (2) or (3), namely warranties, is involved, liability is governed by Article 2 of the Uniform Commercial Code. When either (4), (5), or (6) is involved, the parties are governed by general principles of tort law. Both the general principles of contract law as to the guarantee and the tort law as to the latter concepts remain in force and have not been displaced by the Uniform Commercial Code.[1]

The concurrent existence of these different theories is in part the result of historical accident. The importance of each lies in the fact that a plaintiff might be barred or denied recovery under one theory but may be able to recover under another theory. Likewise, in some instances the measure of damages under one theory will be different than under another.

The modern theories of product liability mentioned above have in effect destroyed the common-law concept of caveat emptor or "let the buyer beware."

The view has been expressed that the rule of caveat emptor presupposes that the buyer is on an equal footing with the seller and that he relies on his own reasoning and judgment in entering into the contract.[2] This assumption in effect heralds the disappearance of the doctrine of caveat emptor in most cases when a merchant seller or a product of modern technocracy is involved, because in such situations it is increasingly likely that the seller and

---

[1] UCC § 1-103.

[2] Vernali v Centrella, 28 Conn Supp 476, 266 A2d 200.

buyer will not be on the same footing and that the buyer cannot depend on his own judgment.

When one couples the product liability rules with the rules provided by consumer protection statutes and agencies, it is apparent that the twentieth century may be said to have adopted the rule of "let the seller beware."

§ 26:2. The Interest Protected. When a product is defective, harm may be caused to (1) person, (2) property, or (3) commercial or economic interests. Under (1) the buyer of the product may be injured when the truck he has purchased goes out of control and plunges down the side of a hill. Third persons may also be injured, such as other passengers in the car, bystanders, or the driver of another car. The defective car may also cause injury to a total stranger who seeks to rescue one of the victims. Property damage under (2) is sustained when the buyer's truck is damaged when it plunges down the slope. The car of the other driver may be damaged or a building into which the runaway truck careens may be damaged. Commercial and economic interests of the buyer (3) are affected by the fact that the truck is defective. Even if no physical harm is sustained, the fact remains that the truck is not as valuable as it would have been, and the buyer who has paid for the truck on the basis of the value it should have had has been deprived of some of his money to the extent that he is not getting what he bargained for. If the buyer is required to rent a truck from someone else or loses his opportunity to haul freight for compensation, the fact that the truck was defective causes him economic or commercial loss.

Assuming that suit is brought by a proper plaintiff, almost every state today permits recovery for personal or property damage under every theory of product liability. The same is true with respect to economic loss when suit is brought for breach of warranty, fraud, or negligence. However, about one half of the states which permit strict tort recovery refuse to extend it to allow recovery for commercial loss. There is every reason to believe that by the end of the century recovery for all forms of harm will be permitted under all theories of product liability.

The objective of providing product safety goes beyond the boundaries of the law of sales and enters the area of consumer and employee protection.

(1) Consumer Protection. The Consumer Product Safety Act of 1972 [3] created an independent federal agency with broad power to establish safety regulations for all food, drugs, and common household products. The purpose of this agency, the Food, Drug, and Consumer Protection Agency (FDCPA), is to protect the consumer from physical injury, adulteration, misbranding, and illegal distribution of products.

(2) Employee Protection. The Federal Occupational Safety and Health Act [4] authorizes the Secretary of Labor to establish job safety standards

[3] PL 92-573, 86 Stat 1207, 15 USC § 2051 et seq.
[4] 29 USC § 651 et seq.

and creates an agency under him known as the Occupational Safety and Health Administration (OSHA).

§ **26:3. Who May Sue and Be Sued.**

(1) The Plaintiff. The law is moving to the conclusion that anyone harmed because of an "improper" product may sue whoever is in any way responsible. Only a half century ago, the circle of liability was narrowly drawn so that only a buyer could sue his seller or only a person negligently using a product could be sued for the tort damage thereby caused. Thus, a suit for a breach of warranty could only be brought by a plaintiff against a person with whom he was in privity; that is, the other party to the sales contract by which the plaintiff purchased the article. If the plaintiff was not a party to the contract with the defendant, he could not sue for breach of warranty. When suit was brought for negligence, the remote plaintiff who had been injured by the product was likewise barred from suing the seller or the manufacturer of the product. This rule has generally been abolished.[5] The modern rule is that whenever the manufacturer, as a reasonable man, should foresee that if he is negligent, a particular class of persons will be injured by his product, the manufacturer is liable to an injured member of that class without regard to whether such plaintiff purchased from him or from anyone, as in the case of a person injured by something which was given to him or to a bystander.

The UCC expressly abolishes the requirement of privity to a limited extent by permitting a suit for breach of warranty to be brought against the seller by members of the buyer's family, his household, and his guests, with respect to personal injury sustained by them.[6]

Privity is not required under the French law recognized in Louisiana, and the warranty liability of the manufacturer runs with the product.[7] There is no requirement that the strict tort liability plaintiff be in privity with the defendant. Historically the strict tort liability doctrine began as a means of avoiding the privity limitation that formerly existed on warranty liability. In jurisdictions that have abandoned the requirement of privity in warranty cases, the distinction between warranty liability and strict tort liability ceases.

As an application of the principle that privity of contract is not required in strict tort, the manufacturer of water meters who sold the meters to a

---

[5] Admiral Oasis Hotel Corp. v Home Gas Industries, Inc., 68 Ill App 2d 297, 216 NE2d 282.

[6] UCC § 2-318. Note that this does not cover property loss which the beneficiary might sustain, Kenney v Sears, Roebuck & Co., 355 Mass 604, 246 NE2d 649, and that it does not extend to employees of the buyer nor such third persons as pedestrians. The UCC expressly leaves open for local state law to determine whether the requirement of privity is abolished further than declared by the UCC. California and Utah have not adopted this section because it is more restrictive than pre-Code law in those states.

Under the UCC the guests must be guests in the buyer's home, but some jurisdictions have ignored this limitation.

[7] Media Production Consultants, Inc. v Mercedes-Benz of North America, Inc., 262 La 80, 262 So2d 377 (non-Code).

city water system was held to be liable to a homeowner whose home was damaged when a defective water meter broke. To impose liability, it was sufficient that the defendant knew that the product would be used under such circumstances and that, if defective, harm would be caused to persons in the position of the plaintiff.[8]

In order for a nonprivity plaintiff to come within the scope of UCC § 2-318, it is necessary that the use of the goods by such third person be foreseeable. When a consumer who bought a dining room table rented his home and furnishings to a third party, the use of the dining room table by the tenant was not foreseeable as there was no reason to foresee that the buyer would be renting anything. Consequently, when the tabletop fell down and injured the tenant's wife, she could not recover from the seller under the authority of § 2-318 because she was not an expected user.[9]

In a few states the existence of the requirement of privity still remains and some states take a straddle position of requiring privity when economic loss is involved. The greatest inroad in the concept of privity of contract has been made where the plaintiff has been personally injured as contrasted with economically harmed. Motivated by the social force that places protection of the person of the individual above that of property rights, the law has been more willing to extend the field of liability to aid the plaintiff who has been physically injured by the runaway tractor than the plaintiff who was not able to use the tractor that he purchased and was required to rent another tractor, thereby sustaining an economic rather than a physical loss.[10]

The law is moving toward allowing recovery for harm without regard to whether it is injury to person, damage to property, or economic loss, and without regard to the existence of privity between the parties.

(a) SUBPURCHASERS. When privity is not required for suit, subpurchasers, that is, customers of the buyer, may sue the original seller from whom their seller purchased his goods. Thus, the purchaser of a can of soup from the corner grocery store can sue the distributor from whom the store purchased the can. When privity is required, the customer can only sue the store from which he made the purchase.

By the modern rule the lack of privity between the defendant and plaintiff is ignored when it was contemplated that members of the plaintiff's class would ultimately buy the property in question.[11]

With the rise of modern mass marketing it became apparent that the contemplated user of goods, the consumer, constituted a broader class than

---

[8] Rosenau v New Brunswick, 51 NJ 130, 238 A2d 169.

[9] Barry v Ivarson, Inc., (Fla App) 249 So2d 44 (indicating that a decision against the tenant could also rest on the ground that privity of contract was required except to the extent abandoned by UCC § 2-318 and that such section did not apply to tenants of a buyer and hence did not abolish the requirement of privity as to a tenant).

[10] Note that this distinction is also made by UCC § 2-318 in allowing recovery by the persons named for personal injuries sustained by them.

[11] Griffith v Byers Constr. Co., 212 Kan 65, 510 P2d 198.

the actual buyers and that a concept, namely privity, which would only protect buyers and not consumers did not satisfy the needs of the modern situation.[12]

(b) EMPLOYEES. Most states permit employees to sue a remote party, as a manufacturer of the product or machine purchased by the employer of the injured employee. For example, where flame-resistant clothing is sold to the employer for the personal safety of his employees and the employer is told that it is "flameproof," an employee may sue for breach of warranty.[13]

Some courts refuse to recognize warranty liability in such case and recovery by an employee is then dependent upon his being able to prove negligence of the manufacturer or to establish the basis for strict tort liability. When privity is required to sustain a warranty suit, the employee of a subpurchaser cannot sue the original seller, so that the employee of the buyer of a house cannot sue the distributor who sold the garage door to a subcontractor who installed it in the house which was then purchased by the plaintiff's employer.[14]

(c) BYSTANDERS. Historically a bystander, that is, a third person who was not a buyer from the defendant nor a subpurchaser from anyone, could not recover from a defendant in a product liability suit. This limitation has been abandoned when the buyer is able to establish the negligence of the defendant.

In some states the courts have ignored privity of contract when the injured person was a member of the public or a stranger at large, by adopting a doctrine of strict tort liability which makes a manufacturer liable to one who is harmed or sustains property loss because of a defect in the product when such defect makes use of the product dangerous to the user or to persons or property in the vicinity.[15] Thus, a strict tort liability action may be brought by the driver or passenger of a second car when it has a collision with a first car because of a defect in the steering mechanism[16] or brakes of the first car; or there is a collision because of a defective driving shaft in the first car; or the bystander was injured by a runaway vehicle which started by itself because of an accelerator or transmission defect or a short circuit. A bystander may sue the manufacturer of a defective shotgun shell which bursts the gun barrel and the manufacturer of a defective beer keg which exploded; and a neighbor may sue the manufacturer of a propane gas tank which exploded. There is also a trend to allow recovery by the "stranger" for breach of warranty. (See p. 534, Guarino v Mine Safety Appliance Co.)

---

[12] Maynard v General Electric Co., (DC WVa) 350 F Supp 949.
[13] Froysland v Leef Bros., Inc., 293 Minn 201, 197 NW2d 656.
[14] Verddier v Neal Blun Co., 128 Ga App 321, 196 SE2d 469.
[15] Mitchell v Miller, 26 Conn Supp 142, 214 A2d 694.
[16] Codling v Paglia, 32 NY2d 330, 345 NYS2d 461, 298 NE2d 622.

Privity of contract is not required in strict tort and is being abandoned generally as courts recognize that the problem is one of how to allocate the loss for accidents rather than a commercial problem of contractual responsibility.[17] The trend increasingly is to base liability upon the foreseeability of the harm sustained by the injured person rather than upon the existence of a contract between the defendant and the injured person.[18]

There is a growing trend to eliminate the requirement of privity when the plaintiff suing the manufacturer is a third person injured by the defective product—such as a bystander, pedestrian, or driver of the other car, or a garage mechanic working on the car—when such third person is injured because of a defect in the car produced by the manufacturer.[19]

(2) The Defendant. The stating of who may be sued is the other side of the coin of stating who may sue. For example, the statement that a subpurchaser may sue the remote manufacturer implies that a manufacturer may be sued by a remote subpurchaser.

(a) SELLER. A person selling goods may be sued by his buyer on any theory of product liability applicable to the facts. It is immaterial whether the seller sells at wholesale or retail. It is important, however, whether the seller deals in goods of the kind in question. If he does, he is classified as a "merchant" and is held to a higher degree of responsibility for the product than one who is merely making a casual sale.

When privity is required, the seller is subject to product liability suit only by his buyer.

(b) MANUFACTURER. There is little difference today between the product liability of a manufacturer and a seller. This logically follows from the fact that the manufacturer is also a seller in that he sells his manufactured goods to a distributor, wholesaler, or other outlet, and is thus the first seller of the finished product.

Two factors may contribute to imposing a higher responsibility on the manufacturer. First, the manufacturer is generally a merchant in that the goods which he sells are those which he has been manufacturing for some time, that is, goods in which he deals. Secondly, the manufacturer is the best able to detect or guard against hazards. This is particularly true in an age of complex products and opaque packaging. The manufacturer is the only one who really knows what is going into the product.

---

[17] Elmore v American Motors Corp., 70 Cal 2d 578, 75 Cal Rptr 652, 451 P2d 84.

[18] Mack Trucks v Jet Asphalt and Rock Co., 246 Ark 99, 437 SW2d 459.

[19] Connolly v Hagi, 24 Conn Supp 198, 188 A2d 884; Darryl v Ford Motor Co., (Tex) 440 SW2d 630. Contra: Berzon v Don Allen Motors, 23 App Div 2d 530, 256 NYS2d 643 (holding that the passengers in an automobile which was struck by a truck made by the manufacturer and sold by the dealer to the defendant-driver cannot sue the manufacturer and dealer on the ground of an implied warranty relating to the braking system of the vehicle made and sold by them).

The retailer may sue the manufacturer for breach of the implied warranty of merchantability.[20]

(c) MANUFACTURER OF COMPONENT PART. Many items of goods in today's market place are not made entirely by one manufacturer. Thus, the harm may be caused in a given case by a defect in a component part of the finished product. The fact that the part of the total product containing the defective part which caused the plaintiff's harm was made by another manufacturer is not a defense to a defendant who is sued for breach of warranty or for strict tort liability. If the purchase of the component part was made from a reputable supplier and there was no prior history of complaints or defects with respect to that part, such circumstances would show the absence of negligence or of fraud on the part of the defendant when product liability is asserted on such grounds.

When a buyer purchases equipment from a dealer who assembles it as specified from parts supplied by the manufacturer, the manufacturer is not liable to an employee of the buyer who is injured because of the absence of a protective shield when the manufacturer had manufactured such a shield but the buyer had not purchased it.[21]

It is not clear whether the supplier of the component part is liable on strict tort to the person ultimately harmed. Strict tort liability of the supplier of the component part has been denied by some courts [22] but sustained by others.

A person injured while on a golf course when an automobile that was parked on the club parking lot became "unparked" and ran downhill can sue the manufacturer of the defective parking unit of the car.

The buyer of an automobile may sue the component part manufacturer for negligence and breach of warranty.[23]

*(3) **Advertising.*** In many instances recovery by the buyer against the remote manufacturer or seller is based on the fact that the defendant had advertised directly to the public and therefore made a warranty to the purchasing consumer of the truth of his advertising. Thus, the purchaser of an automobile can sue the remote manufacturer when the purchaser has relied on mass media advertising that the car was trouble free, economical, and built with high quality workmanship.[24] (See p. 535, Hamon v Digliani.)

When advertising brochures make statements as to the capacity of the goods, such statements constitute express warranties and bind the manufacturer to the ultimate consumer. And when a distributor distributes the

---

[20] Redman Industries v Binkey, 49 Ala App 595, 274 So2d 621.

[21] Willeford v Mayrath Co., 7 Ill App 3d 357, 287 NE2d 502.

[22] Goldberg v Kollsman Instrument Corp., 12 NY2d 432, NYS2d 592, 191 NE2d 81, 240. City of Franklin v Badger Ford Truck Sales, Inc., 58 Wis 2d 641, 207 NW2d 866.

[23] Clark v Bendix Corp., 42 App Div 2d 727, 345 NYS2d 662.

[24] Inglis v American Motors Corp., 3 Ohio 2d 132, 209 NE2d 583.

brochures with his name stamped thereon, he adopts the statements and is bound by them as warranties.[25]

Although advertising by the manufacturer to the consumer is often a reason for not requiring privity when the consumer sues the manufacturer, the absence of advertising by the manufacturer does not bar such action by the buyer.[26]

(4) Direct Sales Contact. In many instances recovery is allowed by a buyer against a remote manufacturer because there have been direct dealings between them which justify regarding the buyer and the manufacturer as being in privity, as against the contention that the buyer was only in privity with the local dealer from whom he bought the product. For example, where the manufacturer enters into direct negotiations with the ultimate buyer in any phase of the manufacturing or financing of the transaction, the sale will probably be treated as though it were made directly by the manufacturer to the ultimate purchaser even though for the purpose of record keeping the transaction is treated as a sale by the manufacturer to a dealer and by that dealer to the ultimate purchaser. Thus, when the dealer arranges a meeting between the representative of the manufacturer and the customer, and the customer makes the purchase price check payable directly to the manufacturer, and the manufacturer sends the goods directly to the customer, the manufacturer is in effect the seller and no question of privity is involved.[27] Likewise, recovery may be allowed when the consumer mails to the manufacturer a warranty registration card which the manufacturer had packed with the manufactured article.

EXPRESS WARRANTIES

A warranty may be express or implied. Both have the same legal effect and operate as though the seller had made an express guarantee.

§ 26:4. Definition. An *express warranty* is a part of the basis for the sale; that is, the buyer has purchased the goods on the reasonable assumption that they were as stated by the seller. Thus, a statement by the seller with respect to the quality, capacity, or other characteristic of the goods is an express warranty. To illustrate, the seller may say: "This cloth is all wool," "This paint is for household woodwork," or "This engine can produce 50 horsepower." The good faith of a warranty defendant is immaterial.[28]

§ 26:5. Form of Express Warranty. No particular form of words is necessary to constitute an express warranty. A seller need not state that he makes a warranty nor in fact even intend to make a warranty.[29] It is sufficient that the seller assert a fact that becomes a part or term of the bargain or

[25] Hawkins Construction Co. v Mathews Co., Inc., 190 Neb 546, 209 NW2d 643.
[26] Lonzrick v Republic Steel Corp., 6 Ohio 2d 227, 35 OO2d 404, 218 NE2d 185.
[27] Marion Power Shovel v Huntsman, 246 Ark 149, 437 SW2d 784.
[28] Geohagan v General Motors Corp., — Ala —, 279 So2d 436.
[29] UCC § 2-313(2).

transaction between the parties. It is not necessary that the seller make an express statement, for the express warranty may be found in his conduct. Accordingly, if the buyer asks for a can of outside house paint and the seller hands him a can of paint, the seller's conduct expresses a warranty that the can contains outside house paint.

The seller's statement may be written or printed, as well as oral. The words on the label of a can and in a newspaper ad for "boned chicken" constitute an express warranty that the can contains chicken that is free of bones.[30]

A statement about the goods may also bind the seller even though it was actually made by the manufacturer, as in the case of a label placed by the latter on a can of household paint. Here the seller is bound by an express warranty even though the buyer selected the can of paint from a shelf and without comment paid for it. The seller, by exposing the can to sale with the manufacturers' label appearing on it, has in effect adopted that label as his own statement and it therefore constitutes an express warranty by the seller.

Statements in the seller's advertising material as to the performance characteristics of the goods can constitute express warranties, but in a given case these will be excluded when the buyer signs a written contract which states that it is the entire contract, conspicuously excludes all warranties not set forth therein, and calls upon the buyer to read the contract before he signs it.[31]

§ 26:6. Time of Making Express Warranty. It is immaterial whether the express warranty is made at the time of or after the sale. No separate consideration is required for the warranty when it is part of a sale. If a warranty is made after the sale, no consideration is required since it is regarded as a modification of the sales contract.[32]

§ 26:7. Seller's Opinion or Statement of Value. "An affirmation merely of the value of goods or a statement purporting to be merely the seller's opinion or commendation of the goods does not create a warranty." [33] A purchaser, as a reasonable man, should not believe such statements implicitly, and therefore he cannot hold the seller to them should they prove false. Thus, "sales talk" by a seller that "this is the best piece of cloth in the market" or that glassware "is as good as anyone else's" is merely an opinion which the buyer cannot ordinarily treat as a warranty.

Likewise, statements of the seller that his product is of good quality and that the buyer will be pleased with the results are merely "sales talk" or opinions and not express warranties.[34] Thus, a statement by a drugstore clerk to the prospective purchaser of hair dye that the customer "would get very

---

[30] Lane v Swanson, 130 Cal App 2d 210, 278 P2d 723.

[31] Pennsylvania Gas Co. v Secord Brothers, Inc., 73 Misc 2d 1031, 343 NYS2d 256.

[32] UCC § 2-313. Official Comment, point 7.

[33] § 2-313(2).

[34] Olin Mathieson Chemical Corp. v Moushon, 93 Ill App 2d 280, 235 NE2d 263.

fine results" with a particular dye was merely a matter of opinion and not a warranty that the buyer would not suffer an adverse skin reaction from the dye.[35]

It is probable, however, that the UCC will permit an exception to be made, as under the prior law, when the circumstances are such that a reasonable man would rely on such a statement. If the buyer has reason to believe that the seller is possessed of expert knowledge of the conditions of the market and the buyer requests his opinion as an expert, the buyer would be entitled to accept as a fact the seller's statement as to whether a given article was the best obtainable; and the statement could be reasonably regarded as forming part of the basis of the bargain of the parties. Thus, a statement by a florist that bulbs are of first-grade quality may be a warranty.[36]

IMPLIED WARRANTIES

Whenever a sale of goods is made, certain warranties are implied unless they are expressly excluded. The scope of these warranties may differ in terms of whether the seller is a merchant or a casual seller.

§ 26:8. Definition. An *implied warranty* is one that was not made by the seller but which is implied by the law. In certain instances the law implies or reads a warranty into a sale although the seller did not make it. That is, the implied warranty arises automatically from the fact that a sale has been made; as compared with express warranties, which arise because they form part of the basis on which the sale has been made.

The fact that express warranties are made does not exclude implied warranties; and when both express and implied warranties exist, they should be construed as consistent with each other and as cumulative if such construction is reasonable. In case it is unreasonable to construe them as consistent and cumulative, an express warranty prevails over an implied warranty as to the same subject matter, except in the case of an implied warranty of fitness for a particular purpose.[37] When there is an express warranty as to a particular matter, it is unnecessary to find an implied warranty relating thereto.[38]

§ 26:9. Warranties of All Sellers. A distinction is made between a merchant seller and the casual seller. There is a greater range of warranties in the case of the merchant seller.

(1) Warranty of Title. Every seller, by the mere act of selling, makes a warranty that his title is good and that the transfer is rightful.[39] A warranty of title may be specifically excluded, or the circumstances may be such as to

---

35 Carpenter v Alberto Culver Co., 28 Mich App 399, 184 NW2d 547.

36 Diepeveen v Vogt, 27 NJ Super 254, 99 A2d 329.

37 UCC § 2-317.

38 Inglis v American Motors Corp., 3 Ohio 2d 132, 209 NE2d 583.

39 UCC § 2-312(1)(a). A warranty of title, as well as a warranty of freedom from encumbrances, which arises when a sale is made, is not classified as an implied warranty by the UCC even though it is in the nature of an implied warranty.

prevent the warranty from arising. The latter situation is found when the buyer has reason to know that the seller does not claim to hold the title or that he is claiming to sell only such right or title as he or a third person may have.[40] For example, no warranty of title arises when the seller makes the sale in a representative capacity, such as a sheriff, an auctioneer, or an administrator of a decedent's estate. Likewise, no warranty arises when the seller makes the sale as a pledgee or mortgagee.

There is a breach of the implied warranty of title when the goods are seized by the police as having been stolen, such seizure casting such a cloud on the title of the buyer that there is a breach of the warranty without regard to the outcome of the police seizure.[41]

When an auction is advertised to sell cattle owned by a named farmer on his land but the auction is not held because of insufficient bidders, whereupon the farmer made a direct sale to a prospective bidder, a warranty of title and freedom from encumbrance arose and imposed liability upon the farmer when the buyer was compelled to pay an encumbrance to retain possession.[42]

(2) Warranty Against Encumbrances. Every seller by the mere act of selling makes a warranty that the goods shall be delivered free from any security interest or any other lien or encumbrance of which the buyer at the time of the sales transaction had no knowledge.[43] Thus, there is a breach of warranty when the automobile sold to the buyer is already subject to an outstanding encumbrance that had been placed on it by the original owner and which was unknown to the buyer at the time of the sale.[44]

This warranty refers to the goods only at the time they are delivered to the buyer and is not concerned with an encumbrance which existed before or at the time the sale was made. For example, a seller may not have paid in full for the goods which he is reselling and the original supplier may have a lien on the goods. The seller may resell the goods while that lien is still on them, and his only duty is to pay off the lien before he delivers the goods to the buyer.

(3) Warranty of Conformity to Description, Sample, or Model. When the contract is based in part on the understanding that the seller will supply goods according to a particular description or that the goods will be the same as the sample or a model, the seller is bound by an express warranty that the goods shall conform to the description, sample, or model.[45] Ordinarily a *sample* is a portion of a whole mass that is the subject of the transaction, while a *model* is a replica of the article in question. The mere

---

[40] § 2-312(2).

[41] American Container Corp. v Hanley Trucking Corp., 111 NJ Super 322, 268 A2d 313.

[42] Fields v Sugar, 251 Ark 1062, 476 SW2d 814.

[43] § 2-312(1)(b).

[44] Kruger v Bibi (NY) 3 UCCRS 1132.

[45] UCC § 2-313(1)(b),(c).

fact that a sample is exhibited in the course of negotiations does not make the sale a sale by sample, as there must be an intent manifested that the sample be part of the basis of contracting.[46]

A dealer selling an automobile without disclosing that it had been in a wreck and saying that it was a "demonstrator" car and "like new" is liable to the buyer for the latter's loss as the goods do not conform to the description.[47]

(4) Warranty of Fitness for a Particular Purpose. If the buyer intends to use the goods for a particular or unusual purpose, as contrasted with the ordinary use for which they are customarily sold,[48] the seller makes an implied warranty that the goods will be fit for the purpose when the buyer relies on the seller's skill or judgment to select or furnish suitable goods, and when the seller at the time of contracting knows or has reason to know the buyer's particular purpose and his reliance on the seller's judgment.[49] For example, where a farmer relied on the sales representative in purchasing feed for his cattle, a particular purpose warranty arose.[50] Where a government representative inquired of the seller whether the seller had a tape suitable for use on the government's NCR 304 computer system, there arose an implied warranty, unless otherwise exluded, that the tape furnished by the seller was fit for that purpose.[51]

The fact that the seller did not intend to make a warranty of fitness for a particular purpose is immaterial. Parol evidence is admissible to show that the seller had knowledge of the buyer's intended use.[52]

Where the seller did not know that the buyer was purchasing cattle for breeding purposes, no implied warranty arose that the cattle sold were fit for that purpose. Consequently, there was no breach of warranty when the cattle were in fact infected with bruccellosis, which made them unfit for breeding although it did not make the beef unfit for human consumption.[53]

No warranty of fitness for a particular purpose arises when the buyer makes an independent test of the product and purchases on the basis of that test rather than on the basis of the seller's recommendation.[54]

(5) Second Collision Injury. When an automobile is in a collision there is frequently a secondary consequence as when the driver is thrown

---

[46] Sylvia Coal Co. v Mercury Coal & Coke Co., 151 WVa 818, 156 SE2d 1.

[47] King v O'Rielly Motor Co., 16 Ariz App 518, 494 P2d 718.

[48] Price Brothers Lithographic Co. v American Packing Co., (Mo) 381 SW2d 830.

[49] UCC § 2-315. This warranty applies to every seller, but as a matter of fact it will probably always be a merchant seller who has such skill and judgment that the Code provision would be applicable. In contrast, when a seller of coal has had no experience in the selection of coal for the manufacture of coke, no implied warranty of fitness for that purpose arises. Sylvia Coal Co. v Mercury Coal & Coke Co., 151 WVa 818, 156 SE2d 1.

[50] Boehm v Fox, (CA10 Kan) 473 F2d 445.

[51] Appeals of Reeves Soundcraft Corp., (ASBCA) 2 UCCRS 210.

[52] General Electric Co.'s Appeal, (US Dept Interior, Board of Contract Appeals) ID 95, 3 UCCRS 510.

[53] Fear Ranches, Inc. v Berry, (CA10 NMex) 470 F2d 905.

[54] Valiga v National Food Co., 58 Wis 2d 232, 206 NW2d 377.

forward and strikes the steering wheel. This consequential effect is sometimes called a *second collision.* In some cases the harm caused by the second collision is increased because of the design of the automobile. Can product liability be based on this design?

Courts have been reluctant to recognize as a "defect" a design detail which magnifies or enhances the consequence of the collision because such second collision cause was not a cause of the original occurrence. When the harm-causing condition is obvious, it is likely that courts will refuse to allow the recovery of damages for second collision harm. For example, the fact that a steering wheel is not padded does not impose liability on the manufacturer even though the driver is seriously injured when the impact of a collision throws him forward and his face hits the uncovered steering wheel.

In contrast, when the defect is not obvious, the courts will tend to impose second collision damage liability. For example, where in addition to striking the steering wheel, the horn cap flew off and exposed sharp metal prongs on which the driver was severely cut, the manufacturer has been held liable for the injury so inflicted. Likewise, the manufacturer has been held liable where the gas tank of the car was so weakly attached to the car that it sheared off when there was a low-speed rear-end collision and threw gasoline into the car, causing the fire death of its occupants.

(a) DUPLICATING WARRANTIES. When the buyer's particular purpose is also the ordinary purpose for which the goods are used, the buyer is protected by a double warranty in most cases. When the seller is a merchant, the implied warranty of merchantability arises. When the conditions specified as to a warranty of fitness for a particular purpose have been satisfied, that warranty also arises. Ordinarily there is no advantage to the buyer in having such double protection. If, however, he has disclaimed the warranty of merchantability, such protection has value because he may still assert a breach of the warranty of fitness for a particular purpose.[55]

§ 26:10. Additional Implied Warranties of Merchant Seller.

(1) Warranty Against Infringement. Unless otherwise agreed every seller who is a merchant regularly dealing in goods of the kind which he has sold warrants that the goods shall be delivered free of the rightful claim of any third person by way of patent or trademark infringement or the like.[56]

(2) Warranty of Merchantability or Fitness for Normal Use. A merchant seller who makes a sale of goods in which he customarily deals [57] makes an implied warranty of merchantability.[58] The warranty is in fact a

[55] Tennessee Carolina Transportation, Inc. v Strick Corporation, 283 NC 423, 196 SE2d 711.

[56] UCC § 2-312(3).

[57] This includes the seller of food or drink to be consumed on the premises or to be taken out. UCC § 2-314(1).

[58] § 2-314(1).

group of warranties, the most important of which is that the goods are fit for the ordinary purposes for which they are sold. Consequently, when the seller of ice-making and beverage-vending machines is a merchant of such machines, an implied warranty of fitness for use arises.[59] Also included are implied warranties as to the general or average quality of the goods, and their packaging and labeling.[60]

The implied warranty of merchantability relates to the condition of the goods at the time the seller is to perform under the contract. Once the risk of loss has passed to the buyer, there is no warranty as to the continuing merchantability of the goods unless such subsequent deterioration or condition is proof that the goods were in fact not merchantable when the seller made delivery.

A seller is not protected from warranty liability by the fact that he took every possible step to make the product safe. Similarly, it is no defense that the defendant could not have known of or discovered the dangerous character of the product, for warranty liability is not merely an assurance that the defendant has exercised due care but is an undertaking or guarantee that the product is fit for use.[61]

§ 26:11. Warranties in Particular Sales. Particular types of sales may involve special considerations.

(1) Sale of Food or Drink. The sale of food or drink, whether to be consumed on or off the seller's premises, is a sale and, when made by a merchant, carries the implied warranty that the food is fit for its ordinary purpose, that is, human consumption.[62]

The UCC does not end the conflict between courts applying the foreign-natural test and those applying the reasonable-expectation test. The significance of the two is that in the first test a buyer cannot recover as a matter of law when he is injured by a "natural" substance in the food, such as a cherry pit in a cherry pie; whereas under the reasonable-expectation test, it is necessary to make a determination of fact, ordinarily by the jury, to determine whether the buyer could reasonably expect the object in the food.[63] It is, of course, necessary to distinguish the foregoing situations from those in which the preparation of the food contemplates the continued presence of some element that is not removed, such as prune stones in cooked prunes. The reasonable-expectation test is to be applied in determining whether a restaurant is liable to a patron who broke a tooth on an olive pit.[64] (See p. 538, Webster v Blue Ship Tea Room.)

---

[59] S.F.C. Acceptance Corp. v Ferree, (Pa) 39 D&C2d 225.

[60] UCC § 2-314(2). Other implied warranties on the part of a merchant may also arise from a course of dealing or usage of trade. § 2-314(3).

[61] Green v American Tobacco Co., (CA5 Fla) 325 F2d 673.

[62] § 2-314(1),(2)(c).

[63] Hunt v Ferguson-Paulus Enterprises, 243 Ore 546, 415 P2d 13.

[64] Hochberg v O'Donnell's Restaurant, Inc., (Dist Col App) 272 A2d 846.

The buyer of food that is unwholesome, as in the case of a customer purchasing a spoiled sandwich at a lunch counter, may recover either on strict tort or breach of warranty theory.[65]

Warranty liability extends to any harm resulting from the nonconformity of the goods and is not limited to personal injuries. For example, the economic loss sustained when seeds for plants fail to grow and mature properly may be a breach of the implied warranty of fitness.[66]

(2) Sale of Article Under Patent or Trade Name. The sale of a patented or trade-name article is treated with respect to warranties in the same way as any other sale. If the seller is a merchant selling goods of the kind in question, the ordinary merchant's warranty of merchantability arises even though the parties have described the goods by a patent number or trade name. The fact that the sale is made on the basis of the patent or trade name does not bar the existence of a warranty of fitness for a particular purpose when the circumstances giving rise to such a warranty otherwise exist. It is a question of fact, however, whether the buyer relied on the seller's skill and judgment when he made the purchase. That is, if the buyer asked for a patent- or trade-name article and insisted on it, it is apparent that he did not rely upon the seller's skill and judgment and therefore the factual basis for an implied warranty of fitness for the particular purpose was lacking.[67] If the necessary reliance upon the seller's skill and judgment is shown, however, the warranty arises in that situation.

For example, where a computer and nine items of hardware were purchased by trade name and number upon the recommendation of the computer company to provide the buyer with a computer-based record-keeping system, the fact that the equipment was ordered by trade name and number did not show that the buyer was purchasing at its risk. The circumstances showed the sale was made in reliance on the seller's skill and with appreciation of the buyer's problems. The sale of the particular equipment to the buyer was made as constituting the equipment needed by the buyer. Under such circumstances a warranty of the fitness of the equipment for such purposes was to be implied.[68]

The seller of automobile parts is not liable for breach of the implied warranty of their fitness when the parts were ordered by catalog number for use in a specified vehicle and the seller did not know that the lubrication system of the automobile had been changed by the buyer so as to make the parts ordered unfit for use.[69]

(3) Sale on Buyer's Specifications. When the buyer furnishes the seller with exact specifications for the preparation or manufacture of goods, the

[65] Wachtel v Rosol, 159 Conn 496, 271 A2d 84.

[66] Economy Mills of Elwell, Inc. v Motorists Mut. Ins. Co., 8 Mich App 451, 154 NW2d 659.

[67] UCC § 2-315, Official Comment, point 5.

[68] Sperry Rand Corp. v Industrial Supply Corp., (CA5 Fla) 337 F2d 363.

[69] Mennella v Schork, 49 Misc 2d 449, 267 NYS2d 428.

same warranties arise as in the case of any other sale of such goods by the particular seller. No warranty of fitness for a particular purpose can arise, however, since it is clear that the buyer is purchasing on the basis of his own decision and is not relying on the seller's skill and judgment.

In sales made upon the buyer's specifications, no warranty against infringement is impliedly made by the merchant seller; and conversely, the buyer in substance makes a warranty to protect the seller from liability should the seller be held liable for patent violation by following the specifications of the buyer.[70]

(4) Sale of Secondhand or Used Goods. No warranty arises as to fitness of used property for ordinary use when the sale is made by a casual seller. If made by a merchant seller, such a warranty may sometimes be implied. Prior to the UCC a number of states followed the rule that no warranty arose in connection with used or secondhand goods, particularly automobiles and machinery;[71] whereas some courts found a warranty of fitness for ordinary use in the sale of secondhand goods, particularly airplanes and heavy farm equipment. It is likely that this conflict will continue under the UCC.[72]

(5) Goods for Animals. There is a trend to hold that goods intended for animals are covered by the same warranties that cover goods intended for human consumption. Thus, it has been held that an implied warranty arises that animal vaccines are fit for their intended use.[73]

DISCLAIMER OF WARRANTIES

The seller and the buyer may agree that there shall be no warranties. In some states this is limited in terms of public policy or consumer protection.

§ **26:12. Validity of Disclaimer.** Warranties may be disclaimed by agreement of the parties,[74] subject to the limitation that such a provision must not be unconscionable.[75] It is proper for the jury to consider the purchase price in determining the scope of the warranty of fitness, as where coal was bought for one-half (or less) the price of standard coal.[76]

---

[70] UCC § 2-312(3).

[71] Kilborn v Henderson, 37 Ala App 173, 65 So2d 533.

[72] See UCC § 2-314, Official Comment, point 3.

[73] Chandler v Anchor Serum Co., 198 Kan 571, 426 P2d 82. The absence of any qualification in the UCC in terms of the character of the intended user of the goods should be regarded as supporting this conclusion.

[74] The term *disclaimer* refers to the consensual agreement of the parties which constitutes an express term of their contract. *Exclusion of warranties* may refer to any conduct which excludes warranties, and embraces not only disclaimers but also exclusion by examination and by custom or course of doing. *Modification of warranties* is often misused to refer to a partial disclaimer.

[75] UCC §§ 2-316(1), 2-302(1). A distinction must be made between holding that the circumstances do not give rise to a warranty, thus precluding warranty liability, and holding that the warranty which would otherwise arise has been excluded or surrendered by the contract of the parties.

[76] Sylvia Coal Co. v Mercury Coal & Coke Co., 151 WVa 818, 156 SE2d 1.

If a warranty of fitness [77] is excluded or if it is modified in writing, it must be conspicuous in order to make certain that the buyer will be aware of its presence.[78] If the implied warranty of merchantability is excluded, the exclusion clause must expressly mention the word "merchantability" and it must be conspicuous. (See p. 539, Hunt v Perkins Machinery Co.)

A disclaimer provision is made conspicuous by printing it under a conspicuous heading, but in such case the heading must indicate that there is an exclusion or modification of warranties. Conversely, a heading cannot be relied upon to make such a provision "conspicuous" when the heading is misleading and wrongfully gives the impression that there is a warranty, as a heading stating "Vehicle Warranty," when in fact the provision that follows contains a limitation of warranties.[79] And a disclaimer that is hidden in a mass of printed material handed to the buyer is not conspicuous and is not effective to exclude warranties.[80]

A disclaimer of warranty made orally may be ignored where the seller has given the impression that it is not serious.[81]

§ 26:13. Particular Provisions. Such a statement as "there are no warranties which extend beyond the description on the face hereof" excludes all implied warranties of fitness.[82] Implied warranties are excluded by the statement of "as is," "with all faults," or other language which in normal common speech calls attention to the warranty exclusion and makes it clear that there is no implied warranty.[83] For example, an implied warranty that a steam heater would work properly in the buyer's dry cleaning plant was effectively excluded by provisions that "the warranties and guarantees herein set forth are made by us and accepted by you in lieu of all statutory or implied warranties or guarantees, other than title. . . . This contract contains all agreements between the parties and there is no agreement, verbal or otherwise, which is not set down herein," and the contract contained only a "one year warranty on labor and material supplied by [seller]." [84] A statement that a particular warranty or remedy contained in the contract is "in lieu of all other warranties expressed or implied" is effective to exclude all implied warranties of fitness.[85]

In order for a disclaimer of warranties to be a binding part of an oral sales contract, the disclaimer must be called to the attention of the buyer.

---

[77] By the letter of the Code, the text statement is applicable to any warranty of fitness, see UCC § 2-316(2), although by the Official Comment to § 2-316, point 4, it would appear to be only the warranty of fitness for a particular purpose.

[78] As to the definition of "conspicuous," see UCC § 1-201(10).

[80] Ford Motor Co. v Pittman, (Fla App) 227 So2d 246.

[79] Mack Trucks v Jet Asphalt and Rock Co., 246 Ark 99, 437 SW2d 459.

[81] Weisz v Parke-Bernet Galleries, Inc., (NY Civil Court) 67 Misc 2d 1077, 325 NYS2d 576.

[82] UCC § 2-316(2).

[83] § 2-316(3)(a).

[84] Thorman v Polytemp, (NY) 2 UCCRS 772.

[85] Construction Aggregate Corp. v Hewitt-Robins, (CA7 Ill) 404 F2d 505.

These provisions as to exclusions of warranties apply to leases of personal property that in substance are sales.[86]

When the goods are sold by description and sample, the implied warranties and conformity thereto are not excluded by the fact that the sale was made "as is" and that the contract disclaims all warranties, whether express or implied, and the use of descriptions, samples, or models, as conformity to the description and sample go so clearly to the essence of the bargain that the disclaimer will not be regarded as applicable to them.[87] In Louisiana a non-Code rule is followed that even though a thing is sold "as is" such provision does not negate the seller's fundamental warranty that the thing sold is fit for its intended use.[88]

§ **26:14. Exclusion of Warranties by Examination of Goods.** There is no implied warranty with respect to defects in goods that an examination should have revealed when the buyer before making the final contract has examined the goods, or a model or sample, or has refused to make such examination.[89]

The examination of the goods by the buyer does not exclude the existence of an express warranty [90] unless it can be concluded that the buyer thereby learned of the falsity of the statement claimed to be a warranty, with the consequence that such statement did not in fact form part of the bargain.

§ **26:15. Post-Sale Disclaimer.** Frequently the statement excluding or modifying warranties appears for the first time in a written contract sent to confirm or memorialize the oral contract made earlier; or it appears in an invoice, a bill, or an instruction manual delivered to the buyer at or after the time that he receives the goods. Such post-sale disclaimers have no effect on warranties that arose at the time of the sale.[91] Likewise, an oral, express warranty made by the salesman is not excluded by a disclaimer of oral warranties made on the back of the credit sale printed form which was not called to the buyer's attention.[92]

An exclusion of warranties in a manufacturer's manual given to the buyer after the sale is not binding on a buyer because it is not a term of the sales contract.[93] If the buyer would assent to the post-sale disclaimer, however, it would be effective as a modification of the sales contract.

OTHER THEORIES OF PRODUCT LIABILITY

§ **26:16. Negligence.** Another basis for recovering damages from the seller is his negligence. Independently of the UCC, a person injured through the

[86] Sawyer v Pioneer Leasing Corp., 244 Ark 943, 428 SW2d 46.
[87] Mobile Housing, Inc. v Stone, (Tex Civ App) 490 SW2d 611.
[88] McLain v Cuccia, (La App) 259 So2d 337 (non-Code).
[89] UCC § 2-316(3)(b).
[90] Capital Equipment Enterprises, Inc. v North Pier Terminal Co., 117 Ill App 2d 264, 254 NE2d 542.
[91] Admiral Oasis Hotel Corp. v Home Gas Industries, Inc., 68 Ill App 2d 297, 216 NE2d 282.
[92] Sellman Auto, Inc. v McCowan, 89 Nev 353, 513 P2d 1228.
[93] Rehurek v Chrysler Credit Corp., (Fla App) 262 So2d 452.

use or condition of personal property may be entitled to sue the manufacturer for the damages which he sustains, on the theory that the defendant was negligent in the preparation or manufacture of the article, or in the preparation of instructions as to proper use or warning as to dangers. In this respect, a manufacturer is responsible for having the knowledge of an expert in his line of production [94] and must therefore take reasonable steps to guard against the dangers that would be apparent to an expert.

There is no duty on the seller to test a product which he purchases from a reputable manufacturer if he has no reason to believe that there may be a defect. Statutes, however, sometimes impose upon dealers, as in the case of automobiles, the duty to make tests.[95]

(1) Violation of Government Safety Regulation. If the manufacturer or the seller violates a statute or an applicable administrative regulation, such violation is often held to be evidence of negligence or to constitute negligence in itself (negligence per se). The consequence is that when such breach is the cause of the harm, negligence liability may be enforced. Thus, a manufacturer has been held liable for negligence when an explosion occurred, possibly because of inadequate warning. The manufacturer failed to distribute toluol (methylbenzene) in bright red containers, in violation of a statute so requiring. The violation of such a safety statute was negligence per se.[96]

§ **26:17. Fraud.** The UCC expressly preserves the pre-Code law as to fraud,[97] with the consequence that a person defrauded by false statements made by the seller or the manufacturer with knowledge that such statements were false, or with reckless indifference as to their truth, will generally be able to recover damages for the harm sustained because of such misrepresentation.

(1) Consumer Protection. In many instances consumer protection regulations will provide the consumer with protection from deceptive conduct, as distinguished from conduct which is actually fraudulent.

§ **26:18. Strict Tort Liability.** Another and separate basis for recovering damages is the theory of strict tort liability. Independently of the UCC, a manufacturer or distributor of a defective product is liable to a person who is injured by the product when such injury is foreseeable, without regard to whether the person injured is a purchaser, a consumer, or a third person such as a bystander or a pedestrian. This concept is not one of absolute liability; that is, it must first be shown that there was a defect in the product. It is like warranty liability in that the defendant is liable from the fact that his defective product caused harm, that it is immaterial that no negligence

[94] Moren v Samuel M. Langston Co., 96 Ill App 2d 133, 237 NE2d 759.
[95] Glynn Plymouth v Davis, 120 Ga App 475, 170 SE2d 848.
[96] Johnson v Chemical Supply Co., 38 Wis 2d 194, 156 NW2d 455.
[97] UCC § 1-103.

is shown, and that it is no defense that the defect was in a component part purchased from another manufacturer.[98]

A plaintiff does not set forth a claim for strict tort liability when he merely avers that the defendant represented that his product "offered unprecedented safety" as such a statement was merely sales talk or opinion which could not be used as the basis for a strict tort liability claim.[99]

COMPARISON OF PRODUCT LIABILITY THEORIES

In a given case the plaintiff must determine which theories are available to him. If two or more may be asserted, the plaintiff will consider which theory is most advantageous to him. This generally means whether a given theory will entitle the plaintiff to a greater amount of damages or whether an action brought on a particular theory would be subject to a defense which would bar recovery on other theories.

§ 26:19. Cumulative Liabilities. The theories of product liability are not mutually exclusive. Thus, a given set of facts may give rise to two or more theories of liability. For example, where a rock-crushing machine was dangerous to workmen because an unguarded rotating axle projected from the machine, it was held that there was (1) liability for breach of the express warranty that the machine was safe, (2) liability for breach of the implied warranty of fitness for the particular purpose of crushing rock, and (3) liability for strict tort.[100]

In many instances it will not make any difference to anyone whether there is only one basis of product liability or several. In some instances it may be important. For example, a warranty liability is barred if injury is sustained in the fifth year after the delivery of the goods for the reason that the statute of limitations as to warranty claims runs from the date of delivery of the goods and not from the later date when injury is sustained. In contrast, the statute of limitations applicable to strict tort generally runs from the date of the injury so that an injured plaintiff probably would have two years after the date of his injury in which to sue. Thus, the plaintiff injured in the fifth year could bring suit for strict tort in the sixth and seventh years although he would be barred from suing on either an express or an implied warranty. In such a situation it is obviously highly important to the plaintiff that he has the right to recover in strict tort.

---

[98] The concept of strict tort liability was judicially declared in Greenman v Yuba Power Products, 59 Cal 2d 57, 27 Cal Rptr 697, 377 P2d 897. It was also declared by and is often identified as Restatement of Torts 2d § 402A. In some jurisdictions the term "products liability" is used to refer to the strict tort theory of liability. Willeford v Mayrath, 7 Ill App 3d 357, 287 NE2d 502.

"The doctrine of strict liability is hardly more than what exists under implied warranty when stripped of the contract doctrines of privity, disclaimer, requirements of notice of defect, and limitations through inconsistencies with express warranties." Shepard v Alexian Brothers Hospital, Inc., 33 Cal App 3d 606, 109 Cal Rptr 132.

[99] Hoffman v A. B. Chance Co., (DC Pa) 339 F Supp 1385, amended 346 F Supp 991.

[100] Bindel v Iowa Mfg. Co., (Iowa) 197 NW2d 552.

In some states strict tort does not cover economic loss whereas warranty does. In such a state the truck buyer who lost profits because he could not use his truck would seek to establish warranty liability of the defendant rather than strict tort.

It is rare that a product liability suit will be based on fraud, because of the difficulty of establishing the mental state of the defendant essential to the liability, namely, that he knew that his statements were false or that he was recklessly indifferent to whether they were true or not. Negligence actions, although common, present the problem of proving just what the defendant did and in showing that what he did fell below the standard of what a reasonable man would have done. In an era of mass production it has become increasingly difficult to show just what was done by the defendant as to any one item of goods.

Both warranty and strict tort liability make the plaintiff's case easier by freeing him from showing what the defendant did. It is sufficient that the plaintiff establish that there was a "defective" condition of the product which proximately caused his harm. As between warranty and strict tort, the absence of the requirement of privity or of notice of the defect and the possible inapplicability of concepts of disclaimer generally make recovery on strict tort theory an easier matter, assuming that such theory is recognized by the particular court; but this distinction tends to disappear as courts expand the concept of warranty liability to match strict tort liability. (See p. 540, Kassab v Central Soya.)

It is to be remembered that a seller or manufacturer may by the express terms of his contract assume a liability broader than would arise without such an express undertaking. For example, where a skin cream was sold in a jar and carton which stated that the cream was chemically pure and absolutely safe, such statements constituted express warranties binding both the manufacturer and the seller; and the statement that it was safe was an absolute undertaking that it was safe for everyone, as distinguished from merely an implied warranty of fitness which would be subject to an exception of a particular allergy of a plaintiff.[101]

§ **26:20. Nature of the Transaction.** Warranty liability arises only when there has been a sale or a commercial leasing of goods. Fraud liability and negligence liability may arise without regard to the nature of the transaction involving the plaintiff or the defendant.

The strict tort liability concept may be applied whenever there is any transfer of possession of goods, whether the transaction is a sale, a free distribution of samples, or a commercial leasing of goods.[102] Neither the strict tort liability concept nor the UCC warranties apply, however, to transactions that are regarded as the sale of services, although a modern trend appears to extend the sale-of-goods concepts to service transactions.

---

[101] Spiegel v Saks 34th Street, 43 Misc 2d 1065, 252 NYS2d 852; affirmed 26 App Div 2d 660, 272 NYS2d 972.

[102] Price v Shell Oil Co., 2 Cal 3d 245, 85 Cal Rptr 178, 466 P2d 722.

Consumer protection laws frequently treat contracts for services the same as contracts for the sale of goods. If one views the situation from the standpoint of the buyer, many of the reasons which give rise to the modern law of product liability also urge the extension of those concepts to service contracts. It is probable that this will occur in time. Contracts to render computer services have in several instances been interpreted as sales contracts.

An intermediate step in the direction of eliminating the distinction between services and goods insofar as warranties are concerned has been taken by holding that the sale of electricity was a service but that it was nevertheless subject to warranties.[103] When the transaction is a service contract or a hybrid of a supplying of materials and the rendition of services, liability must rest either upon breach of contract, fraud, or negligence and ordinarily neither warranty nor strict tort liability can arise. Thus, the concept of strict tort liability does not extend to services, such as the professional services rendered by an optometrist in fitting contact lenses, and this conclusion is not altered by the fact that the business is conducted on a large-scale advertising basis with standardized techniques.[104] Likewise, it is generally held that neither a sales warranty nor strict tort [105] liability arises in connection with materials or equipment used in connection with medical care or treatment.

§ 26:21. Improper Product.

(1) Defect. The mere fact that harm is sustained by using the defendant's product does not impose liability under any theory. There must be some defect in the product which was caused or not removed by the defendant. If the product is defective when it leaves the control of the defendant, this element of product liability is satisfied.

There is a conflict of authority as to whether the strict tort liability defect must be such as to make the product "dangerously defective" [106] to the consumer or whether it is sufficient that the product was in fact defective and that the defect caused harm.[107]

(2) Design. Is a product defective because it could have been designed better? At present neither negligence nor warranty liability can be based on the fact that the product could have been designed so that it would have been safer, whether this would have prevented the occurrence of any harm or would have reduced the extent of injury when harm occurred. At present the law does not require that a product be "accident-proof" or "other-party proof," and a manufacturer or seller is not liable merely because his product could have been constructed in a way that would have made its use less

---

[103] Buckeye Union Fire Ins. Co. v Detroit Edison Co., 38 Mich App 325, 196 NW2d 316.

[104] Barbee v Rogers, (Tex) 425 SW2d 342.

[105] Magrine v Krasnica, 94 NJ Super 228, 227 A2d 539; affirmed 100 NJ Super 223, 241 A2d 637.

[106] Restatement of Torts, 2d § 402A.

[107] Cronin v J. B. E. Olson Corp., 8 Cal 3d 121, 104 Cal Rptr 433, 501 P2d 1153; Glass v Ford Motor Co., 123 NJ Super 599, 304 A2d 562.

dangerous or which would have protected the user from the mistakes of other persons, such as other drivers. Thus, the fact that an automobile would be less subject to crushing the driver when involved in a collision if steel side rails were welded to the automobile frame does not in itself impose liability on the manufacturer for failing to use such a design. Administrative regulations have imposed higher standards of safety.

As in the ordinary tort case, there is no liability when harm is not foreseeable. For example, when the law requires that a particular product be used with a safety device, the manufacturer of the product is not negligent when the product is used without the safety device required by law. Thus, the manufacturer of grinding wheels had the right to anticipate that the danger of injury from flying fragments of the wheel would be reduced or eliminated by the use of a protective shield as was required by law and was therefore not under any obligation to make the wheels "accident-proof" when used without a protective shield.[108]

The fact that a manufacturer expects that a safety device will be added to his product does not protect him from strict tort liability when in fact it is not added and the product is therefore unreasonably dangerous to the user.[109]

The warranty of fitness for ordinary use is likewise broken if the product lacks those safety devices which are necessary to make the use of the product reasonably safe.[110]

(3) ***Malfunction.*** The fact that the product doesn't work or does not work properly may constitute a breach of an implied warranty of fitness for ordinary use or for a particular purpose or an express warranty as to performance.

A malfunction of the product is not sufficient to impose liability for negligence or strict tort. For example, the fact that the steering wheel failed to control the car or the brakes failed to hold does not alone establish that there was a defect. When, however, the circumstances are such that there is no logical explanation for the malfunctioning other than a defect in the product, many courts will permit the jury to infer that there was a defect. A few courts bypass this inference by holding that the unexplained malfunction of the defendant's product is sufficient to impose liability upon him. As products become more technical and complex in character, and the jury therefore increasingly dependent upon the testimony of experts as to what happened, it is likely that courts will increasingly permit product liability recovery merely upon proof that the product did not function the way it was intended to work.

When the product is destroyed so that it is impossible to make a post-accident examination to determine whether there was a defect, there is an

---

[108] Bravo v Tiebout, 40 Misc 2d 558, 243 NYS2d 335; affirmed 272 NYS2d 689.
[109] Wheeler v Standard Tool and Mfg. Co., (DC SD NY) 359 F Supp 298.
[110] Grant v National Acme Co., (DC Mich) 351 F Supp 972.

increasing tendency of the courts to find that malfunction before or at the time of the accident is sufficient evidence of a defect or that the mere fact of malfunctioning was a sufficient basis for a recovery, although the plaintiff could not prove that there was a defect. For example, when the evidence establishes a malfunctioning of the steering wheel of an automobile which caused the automobile to cross into the other lane and strike the oncoming plaintiff, it will generally be held that the "defect" element is satisfied when the lane-crossing car is destroyed by a fire following the collision or is so badly damaged that an examination of the steering mechanism is useless.

In many instances it is sufficient to establish that the malfunctioning of the product was the cause of the harm, without specifically establishing why the product malfunctioned. For example, in the case of the product car crossing into the wrong lane, the product plaintiff will not be required to prove why the steering wheel permitted the product car to cross lanes. It is sufficient that the evidence establish that the car was in the same or substantially the same condition as when it left the possession and control of the defendant and that the evidence does not establish that there was some other cause for the improper behavior of the product car which would explain why it crossed into the wrong lane.

*(4) **Foreseeable Misuse.*** A product is "defective" for the purpose of the product liability principles when it is not safe to use in either the way the product was intended to be used or when misused for a purpose not intended by the defendant but which was reasonably foreseeable by him. For example, a hammer used for driving metal pins in metal must have a greater strength than a hammer used in driving nails in wood. A hammer manufactured and sold as a carpenter's hammer is therefore not fit for use as a metal-pin-driving hammer. However, when there is a widespread misuse of carpenter's hammers for driving metal pins, a manufacturer is subject to product liability if his product does not meet the needs of both the foreseeable misuse as well as the intended use of his product. In such a case the manufacturer has been held subject to strict tort liability when a carpenter's hammer chipped while being misused for driving a metal pin and the flying chip destroyed an eye of the user.

§ 26:22. Instructions and Warnings. When the proper manner of use is part of the common knowledge of man and the dangers are obvious, there is ordinarily no duty to furnish instructions as to use or to furnish with warnings as to any dangers. To illustrate, there is no necessity of supplying instructions as to how to use a kitchen knife or any obligation to warn the user of the danger of being cut. If the product is not a common object, instructions may be essential to enable the user to know how to use it. In such case the product alone without the necessary instructions would not satisfy the warranty of fitness for normal use embraced within the warranty of merchantability nor the warranty of fitness for a particular purpose. Furthermore, if use of the product without instructions would expose the user or bystanders to an unreasonable risk of harm, the absence of instructions would make the product defective so as to impose liability for negligence or strict tort upon the defendant.

Moreover, the instructions with the product are in a sense a "product" in themselves so that there is liability for unfit or defective instructions. For example, when a product is sold that is to be installed by the consumer, the written instructions which accompany the appliance create an implied warranty that it will be fit for the ordinary purpose for which it is used and will be safely operable when it is installed in accordance with such instructions. That is to say, if a manufacturer furnishes instructions as to the manner in which his product is to be used, the consumer is entitled to think that when so used, it will not injure him. Conversely, a manufacturer furnishing instructions for the use of the property warrants the product as fit for that use but not for use in any other manner, particularly when the product is dangerous when used improperly, as in the case of a gas heater which is likely to generate excessive carbon monoxide if not installed and vented properly.[111]

The same considerations that apply to instructions also apply to warnings as to limitations on the capacity of the product or warnings as to its use.

In some instances instructions and warnings must be designed to be attached to the product. For example, if may be necessary to attach a warning plate or tag to protect the actual user; for example, the employee of the buyer. Merely informing the employer or providing him with a printed manual which the employee might never see will not be sufficient. In contrast, a seller of drugs in advertising their use to physicians may give instructions and warnings in language that doctors will understand, although patients will not.

Various state and federal statutes regulate the subject of instructions and warnings as to certain kinds of products, such as drugs, explosives, and inflammable products. If a defendant fails to furnish the proper instructions and warnings, he may be liable for violation of such a statute as well as subject to product liability for the harm caused. If a seller knows that a buyer is purchasing for resale and the product is not "packaged" in the manner required by law for a lawful resale, the seller would be guilty of a breach of the implied warranty of merchantability.[112]

When a supplier who has designed a product expressly for use by the buyer has reason to foresee that harm will arise if he fails to warn that the product may explode when used in the manner intended by the parties, the supplier is liable in strict tort when an explosion occurring in making

---

[111] Reddick v White Consolidated Industries, (DC SD Ga) 295 F Supp 243.

[112] Frequently the reselling buyer will require a seller to make an express warranty as to compliance of the product with government regulations, so that any violation of the government regulation constitutes a breach of the express warranty. The breach of the government standard is often sufficient to establish negligence liability of the defendant and to establish the defective character of the product both for negligence and strict tort liability.

a test run of the product under the seller's supervision injured one of the buyer's employees and killed another. The defendant supplier was familiar with the buyer's processes and had measured the temperatures in the buyer's ovens which were used in printing fabrics. The supplier had designed a special coating compound to be used in such process, which product was composed of two ingredients, one of which had a flashpoint within the range of the buyer's drying and fusing ovens. The two ingredients were supplied in separate containers and then combined at the buyer's plant to make the test run by the supplier. The supplier did not give any warning as to the identity or characteristics of the explosive ingredient nor of the fact that it could explode in the buyer's ovens. The court held that strict tort liability arose because of such failure to warn.[113]

Where a product was seriously dangerous because of the danger of ejection of a part, a warning printed on a card which came with the product is inadequate and the manufacturer is liable for failing to attach a warning plate to the product to assure that whoever would use the product would be warned.[114]

§ 26:23. Disclaimer of Liability. A party may disclaim warranty liability under a sale or commercial leasing if the requirements of the UCC § 2-316 are satisfied. As an exception to this statement, a few states hold that such a disclaimer is contrary to public policy and may not be given effect when there is a substantial inequality in the bargaining power of the seller and the buyer.[115]

In any case, a disclaimer included in a contract by the defendant will be strictly interpreted against the defendant and not given wider application than is required by its terms. For example, when a sales contract disclaims the seller's liability for breach of warranty, it will not have any effect on product liability based on theories other than warranty. That is, a disclaimer of warranty liability does not disclaim product liability based on fraud, negligence, or strict tort.

(1) Limitation of Remedy. A manufacturer or seller will often seek to avoid the question of the validity of a disclaimer of warranties by limiting the buyer's remedies rather than purporting to disclaim all warranty liability. This is commonly done by declaring that the warranty liability shall be limited to refunding the cost of the product or replacing the defective parts. In terms of dollars recovered by the injured plaintiff, there is no great

---

[113] Patch v Stanley Works, (CA2 Conn) 448 F2d 483.

[114] Saum v Venick, 33 Ohio App 2d 11, 62 OO2d 49, 293 NE2d 313.

[115] Henningsen v Bloomfield Motors, 32 NJ 358, 161 A2d 69. When warranty liability is disclaimed as between the parties, the seller will ordinarily be free of warranty liability to a third person, such as a subpurchaser or a bystander.

When the defendant is negligent, a disclaimer of liability will often be held invalid as contrary to public policy, particularly when the sale relates to consumer goods which the buyer is purchasing for consumer use as contrasted with a merchant purchasing for resale. When the defendant would otherwise be liable for strict tort, a disclaimer of liability made by the buyer does not bind the buyer nor any third person injured by the product.

difference between declaring that the plaintiff shall not recover anything or that he shall recover only a few dollars. For example, consider situations in which a defective electric fan causes a fire that burns down a house, or a boiler safety valve fails to function and a destructive explosion occurs.

When personal injury is sustained in consequence of the breach of a warranty, the UCC declares that a limitation on the remedy is prima facie unconscionable.[116] This means that the "refund or replace" provision has no effect as against a plaintiff who is personally injured unless the defendant can show that in fact the limitation was not unconscionable. As a practical matter, a defendant will never be able to do this in the ordinary consumer situation so that for all practical purposes the UCC can be regarded as declaring such a provision void when a person sustains personal injury.

§ **26:24. Cause of Harm.** The harm sustained by the product liability plaintiff must have been "caused" by the defendant. Here the concepts are the same as in the case of "proximate" in tort liability, without regard to whether suit is brought for negligence or on the theory of strict tort liability or breach of warranty.

If a plaintiff cannot establish that the goods were in the harm-causing condition when they left the possession and control of the defendant, the plaintiff has failed to show that the defendant caused his harm. In some instances the plaintiff will be aided in proving this by the circumstances of the case, as where a product is sold in a factory-sealed container and thereafter explodes. In such a case it will ordinarily be concluded that there was a defect which made it explode and that the defect was sealed into the product before it had left the factory.

§ **26:25. Existence of Middleman.** In many product liability situations the product is distributed or resold by a middleman as a dealer. The question then arises whether a defendant manufacturer is shielded from liability to the ultimate purchaser or a third person if it is the act or omission of the middleman which made the product defective.

If the act of the middleman makes the product defective, the manufacturer is not liable when there is no reason to foresee such negligence. To illustrate, if the mechanic of the car dealer tightens the steering mechanism of an automobile but does so in an improper way which causes a cable to snap and this thereafter makes the car go out of control, the manufacturer is not liable for this intervening act.

If the manufacturer expects or depends upon the middleman to make the product safe for use, there is no negligence liability when the middleman fails to make the car safe if the manufacturer had no reason to foresee that there would be such a failure. Consequently, negligence liability of the manufacturer or supplier to the ultimate customer does not arise when the manufacturer or supplier believes or has reason to believe that an intermediate distributor or processor is to complete processing or is to take further steps

---

[116] UCC § 2-719(3).

that will remove an otherwise foreseeable danger.[117] Accordingly, although the supplier of unfinished pork to a retailer should realize that it might contain trichinae and be dangerous to the ultimate consumers, he is not liable to an ultimate consumer who contracts trichinosis when the retailer in purchasing the unfinished pork told the supplier that he would finish processing it, which would destroy any trichinae, and the supplier did not know or have reason to know that the retailer failed to do so.

When the circumstances are such that a manufacturer would be liable in strict tort to a person injured because of a defect, however, the duty to take steps to avoid the harm is absolute, and liability cannot be avoided by delegating the function of checking or repairing to a distributor or dealer. More specifically, when there is a defect in an automobile for which the manufacturer would be liable on the strict tort theory, he cannot avoid liability to the injured customer by shifting to the local distributor or dealer the function of making the final inspection and repairs to new cars.

§ 26:26. Accident and Misconduct of Plaintiff. Ordinarily no product liability arises when the harm is the result of accident. Thus, a seller or manufacturer is not liable for negligence or for breach of warranty of fitness when the harm is caused not by a defect in the goods but by an accident or the conduct of the buyer. Consequently, there is no liability based on negligence or breach of warranty when the buyer of a rotary power lawnmower is injured by the mower when he slipped on a slope of grass and his foot slid under the protective guard which he had raised from 3 to 3¼ inches above the ground.[118]

The defendant is generally not liable on any theory of product liability when the harm was caused by the plaintiff's misuse of the product [119] or his voluntary use of the product with knowledge that it was defective. For example, where a television set smoked and sparked and turned itself on, the seller was not liable for the loss sustained when the set caught fire after it had been shut off for the night and the fire destroyed the buyer's house, as the conduct of the buyer in using the set in spite of the sparks and smoke, and in failing to unplug the set at night, constituted such conduct on his part as barred recovery for the consequences of the defective condition of the set.[120]

Ordinarily, however, the plaintiff is not barred from recovering because he was negligent in failing to examine the product to see if it was defective. Likewise, there is no implied warranty that a child will not be killed by eating roach poison, since the roach poison is sold as a poison and need only be fit for the purpose for which it was to be used.[121]

---

[117] Schneider v Suhrmann, 8 Utah 2d 35, 327 P2d 822.

[118] Myers v Montgomery Ward & Co., 253 Md 282, 252 A2d 855.

[119] No strict tort product liability arises when the product is used in a manner contrary to the instructions given by the defendant. Procter & Gamble Mfg. Co. v Langley, (Tex Civ App) 422 SW2d 773.

[120] Erdman v Johnson Brothers Radio and Television Co., 260 Md 190, 271 A2d 744.

[121] Rumsey v Freeway Manor Minimax, (Tex Civ App) 423 SW2d 387.

When the plaintiff is an employee of the buyer, many courts will permit strict tort recovery by the employee against the manufacturer when the employee is injured by heavy power equipment even though the danger was obvious. For example, a large cutter was dangerously designed because the area of the cutting jaws was not guarded, so that it was obvious that someone falling in front of the cutter could easily lose a hand if, in attempting to catch hold of something, he would put his hand into the cutting area. When an employee's foot slipped and he fell toward the machine and his hand entered the cutting area and he was injured, it was held that the manufacturer was liable in strict tort even though the danger was obvious —the court refusing to hold that by working near or with the defective equipment supplied by an employer, an employee was barred from recovering on the theory that he had assumed the risk of an obvious danger.

§ 26:27. Notice of Defect.

*(1) **Breach of Warranty.*** When a buyer seeks to recover from his seller for breach of warranty, he must establish that he gave the seller notice of the defect within a reasonable time after he discovered or should have discovered the defect.[122]

If the warranty suit is not brought by the plaintiff against his immediate seller, this notice requirement is not applicable.

*(2) **Tort Liabilities.*** When the product liability plaintiff sues for fraud, negligence, or strict tort, there is no requirement that notice was given to the defendant of the existence of the defect.

Ordinarily the facts are such that the strict tort liability plaintiff is generally a subpurchaser or a third person so that he could not have given notice of any defect prior to his injury. For example, the buyer of an automobile could be required to give notice to the seller that the brakes of the car were defective; but it is obvious that a bystander who is run over when the brakes fail to hold would not know in advance of being run over that there was any defect, or the identity of the car which would run over him, or the identity of the manufacturer who should be notified, and so on.

122 UCC § 2-607(3).

CASES FOR CHAPTER 26

Guarino v Mine Safety Appliance Co.

25 NY2d 460, 306 NYS2d 942, 255 NE2d 173 (1969)

Rooney was a city sewer engineer. While at work he was overcome by sewer gas and died when his gas mask failed to function. The mask was made by the Mine Safety Appliance Company. Guarino and other construction workers attempted to rescue Rooney and were killed by the gas. A suit was brought for the death of Guarino and the others on the theory that Mine Safety had broken the implied warranty of fitness for intended purpose and that the rescue death of Guarino and the others was part of

the harm caused by the breach of warranty and for which Mine Safety was therefore liable. From the judgment for Guarino, Mine Safety appealed.

JASEN, J. . . . This appeal presents for our review the "danger invites rescue" doctrine.

In New York the rescue doctrine had its historical genesis in Eckert v Long Is. R. R. Co. (43 NY 502 [1871]), which stated that the plaintiff's intestate, who was killed while attempting to rescue a child on the railroad tracks, was not to be found contributorily negligent unless acting rashly or recklessly. The purpose of the doctrine, we said, was to prevent a plaintiff from being found contributorily negligent, as a matter of law, when he voluntarily placed himself in a perilous situation to prevent another from suffering serious injury. . . .

In these actions plaintiffs seek application of the "danger invites rescue" doctrine to a situation where a breach of warranty endangers a person so as to invite rescue by a third party. It is significant to note that all of the cases that have invoked the rescue doctrine since it was first promulgated by this court have been negligence actions. This is, we believe, the first instance in which the doctrine has been invoked in an action where . . . the wrong complained of has been breach of warranty.

We do not believe that the theory of the action, whether it be negligence or breach of warranty, is significant where the doctrine of "danger invites rescue" applies. A breach of warranty and an act of negligence are both clearly wrongful acts. Both terms are synonymous as regards fixation of liability, differing primarily in their requirements of proof.

. . . The rescue doctrine should be applied when "one party *by his culpable act* has placed another person in a position of imminent peril which invites a third person, the rescuing plaintiff, to come to his aid."

Moreover . . . "[a] breach of warranty . . . is not only a violation of the sales contract out of which the warranty arises but it is a tortious wrong." . . .

Here the defendant committed a culpable act against the decedent Rooney, by manufacturing and distributing a defective oxygen-producing mask. . . . By virtue of this defendant's culpable act, Rooney was placed in peril, thus inviting his rescue by the plaintiffs who were all members of Rooney's sewage treatment crew. There was no time for reflection when it became known that Rooney was in need of immediate assistance in the dark tunnel some 30 to 40 feet below the street level. These plaintiffs responded to the cries for help in a manner which was reasonable and consistent with their concern for each other as members of a crew. To require that a rescuer answering the cry for help make inquiry as to the nature of the culpable act that imperils someone's life would defy all logic.

"[T]hese judgments . . . rest fundamentally on the rescue doctrine, a concept unaffected by the exact label put upon the wrong which created the danger to the imperiled victim. For the same reason, the rescuer's status as a user or non-user of the defective instrumentality is not directly relevant to our analysis. It is enough that the plaintiffs attempted to rescue a user with respect to whom a breach of warranty or 'tortious wrong' had been committed." . . .

We conclude that a person who by his culpable act, whether it stems from negligence or breach of warranty, places another person in a position of imminent peril, may be held liable for any damages sustained by a rescuer in his attempt to aid the imperilled victim. . . .

[Judgment affirmed.]

Hamon v Digliani

148 Conn 710, 174 A2d 294 (1961)

Hamon purchased Lestoil, a household detergent, from Digliani. She was severely burned by it and sued the seller and its manufacturers, the Lestoil Corporation and the Adell Chemical Company. The manufacturers had extensively promoted the product by television, radio, and newspapers, stating that it could be used safely for household and cleaning tasks and that it was "the all-purpose detergent—for all household cleaning and laundering." The manufacturers defended on the ground that Hamon had

not purchased the bottle of Lestoil from them. From a judgment in their favor, Hamon appealed.

MURPHY, A.J. . . . Within recent years, numerous cases have arisen in other jurisdictions in which the courts have extended breach of warranty law to encompass a right of action against the manufacturer for breach of either an express or an implied warranty of his product and have eliminated privity of contract as an element essential to recovery. . . .

The representation made by a manufacturer on the packages of its detergent [has been] held to be a warranty to the ultimate consumer . . . , despite the absence of privity between the parties. Similarly, it was held . . . that the representations made by the manufacturer of a home permanent lotion in its advertisements, on which the plaintiff relied, constituted an express warranty for breach of which the plaintiff could maintain her action, although there was no contractual relationship between her and the manufacturer. . . .

These cases, and others of similar import, rely on the original concept of an action for breach of warranty, that is, that it sounds in tort and is based on the plaintiff's reliance on deceitful appearances or representations rather than on a promise. . . . The recognition of such a right of action rested on the public policy of protecting an innocent buyer from harm rather than on the insuring of any contractual rights. . . . With the development of the merchandising concepts of the past quarter of a century, the ultimate consumer rarely has the opportunity to inspect the goods offered for sale. . . .

The neighborhood storekeeper who called all of his customers by their first names and measured or weighed out the desired amount of the commodity ordered before packaging it has practically disappeared from the commercial world. Where one occasionally survives, his method of displaying and dispensing his wares has radically changed. The shelves and showcases in his store contain, for the most part, packages and containers which have been packed and sealed by the manufacturer or by a producer who puts out as his own the products made by another. Neither the retailer nor the consumer can sample or otherwise examine the product. The maxim "caveat emptor" has become a millstone around the necks of dealer and customer. While the customer may maintain an action . . . against the retailer for breach of implied warranty, the dealer in turn must sue his supplier to recoup his damages and costs where the customer prevails. Eventually, after several separate and distinct pieces of costly litigation by those in the chain of title, the manufacturer is finally obliged to shoulder the responsibility which should have been his in the first instance.

The supermarkets and other retail outlets of our day dispense with the need for clerks behind counters to wait on customers. The goods are displayed on shelves and counters lining the aisles, and the customer, as he searches for a product, is bewitched, bewildered, and bedeviled by the glittering packaging in riotous color and the alluring enticement of the products' qualities as depicted on labels. The item selected is apt to be the one which was so glowingly described by a glamorous television artist on the housewife's favorite program, just preceding the shopping trip. Or the media of advertising might have been radio, magazine, billboard or newspaper. All are widely used in the appeal directed to the ultimate consumer. There appears to be no sound reason for depriving a plaintiff of the right to maintain an action against the manufacturer where the plaintiff alleges that he was induced to purchase the product by the representations in the manufacturer's advertising and that he sustained harm when the product failed to measure up to the express or implied representations. . . .

The manufacturer or producer who puts a commodity for personal use or consumption on the market in a sealed package or other closed container should be held to have impliedly warranted to the ultimate consumer that the product is reasonably fit for the purpose intended and that it does not contain any harmful and deleterious ingredient of which due and ample warning has not been given. . . . Where the manufacturer or producer makes representations in his advertisements or by the labels on his products as an inducement to the ultimate purchaser, the manufacturer or producer should be held to strict accountability to any person who buys the product in reliance on the representations and later suffers injury because the product fails to conform to them. . . . Lack of privity is not a bar to suit under these circumstances. . . .

[Judgment reversed and action remanded.]

Code Comment: The decision would be the same under the UCC since the UCC does not establish any rule as to privity of contract beyond that of allowing the members of the buyer's family or household, and his guests, to sue for personal injuries resulting from breach of a warranty made by the immediate seller. § 2-318. This is not a statutory declaration that privity should be retained in other cases, because point 3 of the official UCC comment to that section states "beyond this, the section is neutral and is not intended to enlarge or restrict the developing case law on whether the seller's warranties, given to his buyer who resells, extend to other persons in the distributive chain."

Sams v Ezy-Way Foodliner Company

157 Maine 10, 170 A2d 160 (1961)

Sams purchased some frankfurts at Ezy-Way's Self Service Food supermarket. They were contained in a sealed plastic bag labeled "Jordan's Hot Dogs." The manufacturer had a good reputation and there was no evidence of any negligence. In eating one of the hot dogs, Sams was cut by pieces of glass which it contained. He sued Ezy-Way for his damages. From a judgment in favor of the supermarket, Sams appealed.

WILLIAMSON, C.J. . . . The controlling issue in this action of a plaintiff purchaser-consumer against a defendant-retailer is whether there is a "sealed container exception" from the implied warranty of merchantability. . . .

A "hot dog" containing glass is, of course, not fit to eat and is therefore not of merchantable quality. . . .

The fact that the frankfurts were sold in a self-service market does not affect the result. The sign, or label, effectively described the goods in the market and in the package. The printed word was the silent salesman. . . . Compare Mead v Coca Cola Bottling Co., [329 Mass. 440, 108 NE2d 757] holding a warranty of merchantability . . . attached to the sale of coca cola in an automatic vending machine. . . .

We come to the issue of whether the retailer of food in a sealed container is insulated from an implied warranty of merchantability. . . . We make no distinction between [a] can of asparagus . . . , [a] package of macaroni . . . , bread wrapped in paper and sealed [referring to cases involving such containers], and the "hot dogs" in the sealed plastic bag. In each instance we have a sealed container or an original package effectively preventing inspection by the retailer at any time and by the purchaser until the container is opened. The basis of the "sealed container exception" is that the purchaser could not have placed reliance upon the retailer's skill or judgment in determining that the contents were fit to eat. . . .

Vast changes have taken place in the manufacture and distribution of food products. . . . The purchase of food in a can, jar, package, or sealed bag under brand or trade name is commonplace. The pantry shelf, the refrigerator, and the "deep freeze" evidence the fact. Sales are made over the counter, at self-service markets, and by vending machines. Inspection of such products which will uncover the defect within the container, as the defective asparagus, or the pin in the bread, is impossible as a practical matter until at least the container is opened, or in many instances, as here, until the product is eaten. . . .

If the frankfurts here had not been sold in a sealed bag, inspection would not have disclosed the glass within the edible casing. . . .

[Judgment for defendant reversed and action remanded.]

Code Comment: The same conclusion would be made under the UCC. The considerations which persuaded the court in the Sams case would be equally persuasive under the UCC.

This is particularly true since, to introduce an exception that is not found in the UCC, would tend to defeat the purposes and policies of the UCC and to destroy uniformity throughout the country.

Webster v Blue Ship Tea Room

347 Mass 421, 198 NE2d 309 (1964)

Webster ordered a bowl of fish chowder in the Blue Ship Tea Room. She was injured by a fish bone in the chowder. She sued the Tea Room for breach of warranty. From a judgment in her favor, the Tea Room appealed.

REARDON, J. . . . We must decide whether a fish bone lurking in a fish chowder, about the ingredients of which there is no other complaint, constitutes a breach of implied warranty under applicable provisions of the Uniform Commercial Code. . . .

The defendant asserts that here was a native New Englander eating fish chowder in a "quaint" Boston dining place where she had been before; that "fish chowder, as it is served and enjoyed by New Englanders, is a hearty dish, originally designed to satisfy the appetites of our seamen and fishermen"; that "this court knows well that we are not talking of some insipid broth as is customarily served to convalescents." We are asked to rule in such fashion that no chef is forced "to reduce the pieces of fish in the chowder to miniscule size in an effort to ascertain if they contained any pieces of bone." "In so ruling," we are told (in the defendant's brief), "the court will not only uphold its reputation for legal knowledge and acumen, but will, as loyal sons of Massachusetts, save our world-renowned fish chowder from degenerating into an insipid broth containing the mere essence of its former stature as a culinary masterpiece." Notwithstanding these passionate entreaties, we are bound to examine with detachment the nature of fish chowder and what might happen to it under varying interpretations of the Uniform Commercial Code.

Chowder is an ancient dish preëxisting even "the appetites of our seamen and fishermen." It was perhaps the common ancestor of the "more refined cream soups, purées, and bisques." . . . The word "chowder" comes from the French "chaudière," meaning a "cauldron" or "pot." "In the fishing villages of Brittany . . . 'faire la chaudière' means to supply a cauldron in which is cooked a mess of fish and biscuit with some savoury condiments, a hodgepodge contributed by the fishermen themselves, each of whom in return receives his share of the prepared dish. The Breton fishermen probably carried the custom to Newfoundland, long famous for its chowder, whence it has spread to Nova Scotia, New Brunswick, and New England." . . . Our literature over the years abounds in references not only to the delights of chowder but also to its manufacture. A namesake of the plaintiff, Daniel Webster, had a recipe for fish chowder which has survived into a number of modern cookbooks and in which the removal of fish bones is not mentioned at all. One old time recipe recited in the New English Dictionary study defines chowder as "A dish made of fresh fish (esp. cod) or clams, stewed with slices of pork or bacon, onions, and biscuit. . . ." The recitation of these ancient formulae suffices to indicate that in the construction of chowders . . . , worries about fish bones played no role whatsoever. This broad outlook . . . has persisted in . . . modern cookbooks. . . .

Thus, we consider a dish which for many long years, if well made, has been made generally as outlined above. It is not too much to say that a person sitting down in New England to consume a good New England fish chowder embarks on a gustatory adventure which may entail the removal of some fish bones from his bowl as he proceeds. We are not inclined to tamper with age-old recipes by any amendment reflecting the plaintiff's view of the effect of the Uniform Commercial Code upon them. We are aware of the heavy body of case law involving foreign substances in food, but we sense a strong distinction between them and those relative to unwholesomeness of the food itself, e.g., tainted mackerel. . . . In any event, we consider that the joys of life in New England include the ready availability of fresh fish chowder. We should be prepared to cope with the hazards of fish bones, the occasional presence of which in chowders is, it seems to us, to be anticipated, and which, in the light of a hallowed tradition, do not impair their fitness or merchantability.

[Judgment reversed.]

Hunt v Perkins Machinery Co., Inc.

352 Mass 535, 226 NE2d 228 (1967)

Hunt purchased a diesel engine for a fishing boat from the Perkins Machinery Company. He claimed that the company was liable for breach of implied warranty of merchantability because the engine smoked continuously. Perkins raised the defense that the written contract of sale had disclaimed all warranties. The front of the contract which Hunt had signed was a printed form and he had signed the front of the first sheet of a pad of such forms. The face of the forms stated in boldface type: "WARRANTIES. SELLER MAKES NO WARRANTIES (INCLUDING . . . ANY WARRANTIES AS TO MERCHANTABILITY OR FITNESS) EITHER EXPRESS OR IMPLIED WITH RESPECT TO THE PROPERTY UNLESS ENDORSED HEREON IN WRITING. BUYER SHALL BE LIMITED TO THE WARRANTIES OF THE RESPECTIVE MANUFACTURERS OF THE PRODUCTS SOLD." On the back of the form "terms and conditions" were set forth in the same boldface type of all capitals. This was followed by 11 paragraphs of print. The third paragraph was in capital letters and stated "BOTH THIS ORDER AND ITS ACCEPTANCE ARE SUBJECT TO 'TERMS AND CONDITIONS' STATED IN THIS ORDER." Perkins claimed that this third paragraph disclaimed the implied warranty of merchantability.

CUTTER, J. . . . Hunt concedes that Perkin's disclaimer of warranties would have been effective if the disclaimer language in the "Terms and Conditions" . . . , instead of being on the back of the contract form had been (a) on the face of the purchase order, or (b) had been referred to on the face of the order by words such as "see other side" or "as stated on the reverse hereof." The first question for decision is whether the disclaimer of the warranties on the back of this purchase order was "conspicuous."

Some light is shed upon the meaning of "conspicuous" in § 1-201(10) by the official comment on the subsection, which says in part, "This is intended to indicate some of the methods of making a term attention-calling. But the test is whether attention can reasonably be expected to be called to it." . . .

The decided cases are not controlling. In Boeing Airplane Co. v O'Malley, 329 F2d 585, 593 (8th Cir), a disclaimer "merely in the same color and size of other type used for the other provisions" was treated as not conspicuous. In Minikes v Admiral Corp., 48 Misc2d 1012, 1013, 266 NYS2d 461, 462 (Dist Ct), a "disclaimer . . . smaller, not larger, than the rest of the purchase order" was held not conspicuous. In Roto-Lith, Ltd. v F. P. Bartlett & Co., 297 F2d 497, 498-500 (1st Cir), effect was given to a disclaimer in type "still conspicuous" on the back of the acceptance of an order, which was referred to on the front of the order in the following terms, "All goods sold without warranties, express or implied, and subject to the terms on reverse side." . . .

Under § 2-316(2) read with the last sentence of § 1-201(10), it is a question of law for the court whether a provision is conspicuous. We are in as good a position to decide that issue as the trial judge, for a photographic copy of both sides of the purchase order is before us. We decide the issue by applying the statutory test under § 1-201(10) of what is conspicuous, viz. whether "a reasonable person against whom . . . [the disclaimer] is to operate ought to have noticed it."

In the language of the official comment . . . the bold face printing on the front of the purchase order (although adequate in size and contrast with the rest of the printing on the form) was not in words sufficient to call attention to the language on the back of the form. That language would naturally be concealed because the forms were part of a pad of paper when Hunt signed the paper. There was no reference whatsoever on the front of the order to the "Terms and Conditions" as being on the back of the order, and the quoted words "Terms and Conditions" might have been thought to apply to other small type provisions on the front of the order unless Hunt had happened to turn over the form and look at the back of the order. His first reasonable opportunity to do this was when the executed form was returned to him.

In the opinion of a majority of the court, the provisions on the front of the purchase order did not make adequate reference to the provisions on the back of the order to draw attention to the latter. Hence the provisions on the back of the order cannot be said to be conspicuous although printed in an adequate size and style of type. The disclaimer was not effective. . . .

[Judgment affirmed.]

Kassab v Central Soya

432 Pa 217, 246 A2d 848 (1968)

The Kassabs, cattle breeders, purchased a cattle feed from Pritts, an ingredient of which was a supplement called "Cattle Blend," which was manufactured by Central Soya. Through some mistake in the packaging of the feed, the Cattle Blend that was sold to Pritts contained a drug which caused cows to abort and bulls to become sterile. The label on the Cattle Blend purchased by Pritts did not indicate that this drug was present in the cattle feed. When the feed containing this supplement which Pritts sold to the Kassabs caused harm to their cattle, the Kassabs sued Pritts and Central Soya for breach of warranty. Central Soya raised the defense of lack of privity of contract between it and the Kassabs. The lower court entered judgment in favor of the defendants, from which the Kassabs appealed.

ROBERTS, J. . . . There is, of course, no doubt that the feed supplied by Central Soya failed to meet the requirements of merchantability. Section 2-314 of the Code lists, inter alia, the following requirements that goods must meet to be merchantable: they must be "fit for the ordinary purposes for which such goods are used" and must be "adequately contained, packaged, and labeled as the agreement may require." It was properly found . . . that the Cattle Blend supplied by Central Soya was *not* fit for the ordinary purpose of feeding to breed cattle and was *not* properly labeled. But Soya disclaims liability because appellants purchased the feed from Pritts and cannot therefore maintain an action in assumpsit against Soya, a remote manufacturer.

Indeed, were we to continue to adhere to the requirement that privity of contract must exist between plaintiff and defendant in order to maintain an action in assumpsit for injuries caused by a breach of implied warranty, there would be no doubt that Soya could escape liability. . . . This court is now of the opinion that Pennsylvania should join the fast growing list of jurisdictions that have eliminated the privity requirement in assumpsit suits by purchasers against remote manufacturers for breach of implied warranty. . . .

As far back as 1931, the seeds of discontent were sown in the field of privity when Justice Cardozo said in Ultramares Corp. v Touche, 255 NY 170, 174 NE 441, 445 (1931): "The assault upon the citadel of privity is proceeding in these days apace." Since that historic decision the citadel has all but crumbled to dust in this area of product liability. Courts and scholars alike have recognized that the typical consumer does not deal at arm's length with the party whose product he buys. Rather, he buys from a retail merchant who is usually little more than an economic conduit. It is not the merchant who has defectively manufactured the product. Nor is it usually the merchant who advertises the product on such a large scale as to attract consumers. We have in our society literally scores of large, financially responsible manufacturers who place their wares in the stream of commerce not only with the realization, but with the avowed purpose, that these goods will find their way into the hands of the consumer. Only the consumer will use these products; and only the consumer will be injured by them should they prove defective. Yet the law in Pennsylvania continued to permit these manufacturers to escape contractual liability for harm caused consumers by defective merchandise simply because the manufacturer technically did not *sell* directly to the consumer. There was no privity of contract between them. No one denied the *existence* of absolute liability under the Code for breach of implied warranty. But this warranty ran not to the injured party, but rather to the middleman who merely sold to the injured party, thus ignoring commercial reality and encouraging multiplicity of litigation. . . .

[This] court in Miller [v. Preitz, 422 Pa. 383, 221 A2d 320] nevertheless retreated from the modern view because of a belief that § 2-318 of the Uniform Commercial Code requires privity in suits against a remote manufacturer. We no longer adhere to such a belief for we are convinced that, on this issue, the Code must be co-extensive with Restatement Section 402A in the case of [strict tort] product liability. . . .

[UCC] § 2-318 does not cover problems of vertical privity. Merely to *read* the language is to demonstrate that the Code simply fails to treat this problem. Therefore, just as is the rule for any area of contract law not covered by the Code, general principles of law control. See § 1-103. There thus is nothing to prevent this court from joining in the growing number of jurisdictions which, although bound by the Code, have nevertheless judicially abolished vertical privity in breach of warranty cases. . . .

[Judgment reversed and action remanded.]

QUESTIONS AND CASE PROBLEMS

1. An automobile manufacturer was sued for negligence in the construction of the automobile which injured the plaintiff. The manufacturer raised the defense that it had sold the automobile "as is." Was this a good defense? [Fleming v Stoddard Wendle Motor Co., 70 Wash 2d 465, 423 P2d 926]
2. Epstein went to the beauty parlor operated by Giannattasio. The hair coloring used by the beauty shop operator caused harm to Epstein. She brought suit claiming that there was a breach of the implied warranty of fitness for the intended purpose. Was she correct? [Epstein v Giannattasio, 25 Conn Supp 109, 197 A2d 342]
3. Frank purchased a used automobile from the McCafferty Ford Co. The person who sold the auto to McCafferty was not the owner, and the true owner successfully reclaimed it from Frank. Frank then sued McCafferty although McCafferty had said nothing about the title to the automobile. Was McCafferty liable to Frank? [Frank v McCafferty Ford Co., 192 Pa Super 435, 161 A2d 896]
4. Wetzel was a dealer. He purchased a poultry feed additive called Gro-factor Poultry Supplement from Bingman Laboratories. The public did not buy the supplement. When Bingman sued Wetzel for the purchase price, he claimed that there was a breach of warranty of merchantability because the goods did not sell. Was he correct? [Wetzel v Bingman Lab., Inc., 39 Ala App 506, 104 So2d 452]
5. Scanlon was a factory employee. At lunch he purchased from a cart vendor, Food Crafts, a hard roll sandwich. It was later shown that the roll was stale and unfit for human consumption. Because of the hardness of the roll, Scanlon broke a tooth. He then sued Food Crafts for the dental bill. Food Crafts denied liability and claimed that the plaintiff's tooth had broken because it was weak. Decide. [Scanlon v Food Crafts, Inc., 2 Conn Cir 3, 193 A2d 610]
6. Queen ordered goods by sample from Loomis Bros. Corp., a dealer in that kind of goods. The goods that were delivered conformed to the sample but were not fit for the normal intended use. Loomis claimed that it had fully performed its contract since it was only required to deliver goods that conformed to the sample. Was it correct? [Loomis Bros. Corp. v Queen, (Pa) 17 D&C 2d 482, 46 Del County 79]

7. Filler was a member of the high school baseball team. The coach had purchased sunglasses manufactured by Rayex Corp. for use by the team members. The glasses were advertised and the package described them as "professional" glasses for baseball as "sports-world's finest sunglasses" and that they gave "instant eye protection." Unknown to everyone, the glasses were very thin, with the lens ranging from 1.2 to 1.5 millimeters. Because of this thinness, the glasses, when struck by a baseball, shattered into fine splinters and injured Filler's right eye. He sued Rayex Corp., claiming that there was a breach of implied warranty of fitness for a particular purpose. Rayex denied liability and raised the defense of lack of privity. Decide. [Filler v Rayex Corp., (CA7 Ind) 435 F2d 336]

8. The Yamaha Motor Co. sold a motorcycle to a dealer, Harley Davidson of Essex, New Jersey. The motorcycle was partly assembled, and Yamaha depended upon Harley Davidson to assemble it and make it ready to use. Sabloff purchased a motorcycle made by Yamaha from Harley Davidson. He was injured while riding when the front wheel locked for no apparent reason. He sued Yamaha. It raised the defense that Sabloff had been harmed because Harley Davidson had not assembled the motorcycle in a proper manner. Decide. [Sabloff v Yamaha Motor Co., 113 NJ Super 270, 273 A2d 606]

9. Bennet was a passenger in a taxi in Kentucky. When she reached her destination, the driver shot her with a pistol which he had purchased through the mail from a New York dealer. She sued the taxi company and the dealer. She asserted that the dealer was liable for (1) negligence and (2) strict tort. Was the dealer liable? [Bennet v Cincinnati Checker Cab. Co., Inc., (DC ED Ky) 353 F Supp 1206]

10. Eli Lilly manufactured a weed killer called Treflan. Casey purchased some Treflan from a local dealer. It did not kill the weeds. Casey sued Lilly for the damage to his crops resulting from the weeds. Was he entitled to recover? [Eli Lilly & Co. v Casey, (Tex Civ App) 472 SW2d 598]

11. Page purchased a camper from Camper City. While driving in the camper, the seat broke and Page was injured. She went immediately to Camper City and reported what had happened. After several years, she sued Camper City. It asserted that it was not liable because written notice of the defect had not been given to it. Was this a valid defense? [Page v Camper City & Mobile Home Sales, — Ala —, 297 So2d 810]

12. Farrior purchased a Ford automobile from Courtesy Ford Sales, Inc. She received a copy of the manufacturer's warranty. When the car proved defective, she brought suit against Courtesy Ford and the Ford Motor Company claiming that they were jointly liable for the breach of the manufacturer's warranty. Was she correct? [Courtesy Ford Sales, Inc. v Farrior, (Ala Civ App) 298 So2d 26]

27 Remedies for Breach of Sales Contract

STATUTE OF LIMITATIONS

Judicial remedies are ordinarily subject to a time limitation which bars resort to the courts after the expiration of a particular period of time. The Uniform Commercial Code supplies the statute of limitations for sales of goods except when suit is brought on a theory of tort, such as negligence, fraud, or strict tort.

§ **27:1. Code Claim.** An action for a breach of a sales contract must be commenced within four years after the cause of action arises, regardless of when the aggrieved party learned that he had a cause of action.[1] In the case of a warranty, the breach occurs when tender of delivery is made to the buyer even though no defect then appears and no harm is sustained until a later date.[2] When the warranty covers the continuing performance of the goods, however, the cause of action does not arise until the time when the breach is, or should have been, discovered in making such subsequent use.[3] For example, when a mechanical device is sold with a lifetime warranty against accidental starting, there is a warranty as to continuing performance of the goods. The buyer's cause of action for a breach of warranty, arising when the device improperly started by itself, runs from the time when the buyer discovered or should have discovered the breach of warranty; not from the time when the goods were delivered.[4]

In applying the foregoing principles, no distinction is made as to the nature of the harm sustained. That is, a claim for personal injury or for property damage resulting from a breach of a sales contract is governed by the four-year statute of limitations.[5]

(1) Future Performance Warranty. When a warranty relates to performance that is to begin in the future, the statute of limitations does not begin to run at the time of the sale but only when the time for the performance would begin. The result is that when a heating system was installed in

[1] UCC § 2-725(1),(2).
[2] Wolverine Insurance Co. v Tower Iron Works, (CA1 Mass) 370 F2d 700.
[3] UCC § 2-725(2).
[4] Rempe v General Electric Co., 28 Conn Supp 160, 254 A2d 577.
[5] Gardiner v Philadelphia Gas Works, 413 Pa 415, 197 A2d 612.

midsummer under a warranty that it would heat to a certain degree in subzero weather, the cause of action for the breach of warranty did not arise until subzero weather existed. Hence, the statute of limitations did not begin to run in the summer when the heater was sold or installed but later in the winter when the heating system was found to be inadequate.[6]

(2) Notice of Defect. In addition to bringing suit within four years under the UCC statute of limitations, the plaintiff suing the person from whom he purchased the goods for damages claimed because of a breach of the sales contract must have given the seller notice of such breach within a reasonable time after he discovered or should have discovered it.[7] This notice is not required when the plaintiff sues on a non-Code theory of tort liability and does not apply when the plaintiff sues a remote party, such as the manufacturer, for breach of warranty.[8]

§ 27:2. Non-Code Claims. The four-year statute of limitations applies only to claims based upon the Uniform Commercial Code. When the plaintiff sues on a non-Code theory, even though it relates to goods, the UCC statute of limitations does not apply. Thus, when the plaintiff sues a remote manufacturer on the basis of strict tort liability, the action is subject to the general tort statute of limitations and not the UCC four-year statute.[9] The problem relating to non-Code claims is further complicated by the fact that when the claim is not based upon the UCC but upon a tort concept, the statute of limitations ordinarily does not begin to run until harm is sustained,[10] in contrast with the UCC provision under which the statute ordinarily runs from the time when tender of delivery is made, even though the breach is then unknown and no harm has yet been sustained.

REMEDIES OF THE SELLER

The seller of goods has a number of remedies. He may also have additional remedies because the sale was structured as a secured transaction, as discussed in Chapters 35 and 36.

§ 27:3. Seller's Lien. In the absence of an agreement for the extension of credit to the purchaser, the seller has a lien on the goods, that is, the right to retain possession of the goods until he is paid for them. Even when the goods are sold on credit, the seller has a lien on the goods if the buyer becomes insolvent or if the credit period expires while the goods are in the seller's possession.

[6] Perry v Augustine, (Pa) 37 D&C 2d 416.

[7] UCC § 2-607(3)(a).

[8] Wights v Staff Jennings, Inc., 241 Ore 301, 405 P2d 624.

[9] Abate v Barkers of Wallingford, Inc., 27 Conn Supp 46, 229 A2d 366. Also see Mendel v Pittsburgh Plate Glass Co., 57 Misc 2d 45, 291 NYS2d 94, holding that the strict tort liability cause of action of a consumer against the manufacturer should arise at the same time as that of a buyer against his seller for breach of warranty. To hold otherwise would make a manufacturer liable for the harm ad infinitum, whereas a buyer would be limited to the statutory period as against the seller.

[10] Rosenau v New Brunswick, 93 NJ Super 49, 224 A2d 689.

The seller's lien is a specific lien, which attaches to the particular goods and only for the purchase price due on them. It cannot be exercised by the seller for the purpose of collecting any other debt or charge owed him by the purchaser.

The seller's lien may be lost by (a) waiver, as by a later extension of credit, (b) delivery of the goods to a carrier or other bailee, without a reservation of title or possession, for the purpose of delivery to the buyer, (c) acquisition of the property by the buyer or his agent by lawful means, (d) payment or tender of the price by the buyer.

The lien of the seller is not lost when possession is unlawfully or fraudulently obtained by the buyer. Hence, the lien is not lost when the seller delivers the goods to the buyer upon receipt of a bad check which the buyer assured the seller was "good as gold." [11]

Delivery of part of the goods to the buyer does not bar a lien on the remainder of the goods unless the parties intended that it should have that effect. Moreover, if the buyer is insolvent, the seller may refuse to deliver any further goods unless paid for in cash, not only for those goods but also for any previously supplied under the contract.[12]

§ 27:4. Completion or Salvage of Repudiated Contract. It may be that the buyer repudiates or otherwise breaches the contract while the seller has some or all of the goods in his possession in either a finished and ready-to-deliver stage or in a partially manufactured stage. If the seller has in his possession goods that satisfy or conform to the contract with the buyer, he may identify those goods to the contract which the buyer has broken.[13] This will enable the seller to sue the buyer for the purchase price and to make a resale of the goods, holding the buyer responsible for any loss thereon.

If the goods intended for the buyer are in an unfinished state, the seller must exercise reasonable commercial judgment to determine whether (a) to sell them for scrap or salvage or (b) to complete their manufacture, then identify them to the buyer's contract, and resell them.[14] In any case the buyer is liable for the loss sustained by the seller if the latter has acted properly. (See p. 559, Detroit Power Screwdriver Co. v Ladney.)

§ 27:5. Stopping Delivery by Carrier or Other Bailee. The goods may be in transit on their way to the buyer. They also may be in the hands of a non-carrier bailee who is to surrender them to the buyer. The seller may stop delivery of the goods to the buyer, without regard to the quantity involved, if the buyer is insolvent.[15] In addition, the seller may stop delivery if the

---

[11] McAuliffe & Burke Co. v Gallagher, 258 Mass 215, 154 NE 755.

[12] UCC § 2-702(1).

[13] § 2-704(1)(a).

[14] § 2-704(1)(b),(2).

[15] A person is insolvent when he has ceased to pay his debts in the ordinary course of business, or cannot pay his debts as they become due, or is insolvent within the meaning of the federal Bankruptcy Law. UCC § 1-201(23).

quantity involved is a carload, truckload, or planeload, or more, whenever the buyer has repudiated the contract or failed to make a payment due before delivery or if for any reason the seller would have the right to retain or reclaim the goods.[16]

Except for a carrier's lien for transportation or a bailee's lien for storage charges, the right to stop delivery is superior to other claims. Thus, when the creditors of the buyer attach the goods en route, their claims are subject to the right of the seller.

After the seller regains possession of the goods by stopping delivery, he is in the same legal position as though he had not placed them on the carrier or delivered them to the bailee and may assert against them a seller's lien. When the seller reserves title or the right to possession, the seller need not invoke the right to stop delivery since he can withhold the property from the buyer by virtue of such reservation.

(1) Exercise of the Right. The seller exercises the right to stop delivery by notifying the carrier or bailee that the goods are to be returned to or held for him. If the seller gives the carrier or bailee proper notice in sufficient time so that through the exercise of due diligence it can stop delivery, the carrier or bailee must obey the seller's order. Any additional cost involved must be borne by the seller. If the carrier or bailee fails to act, it is liable to the seller for any loss he sustains.

After proper notice has been given to it, the carrier or bailee must follow the instructions of the seller as to the disposal of the goods. When a negotiable document of title for the goods is in circulation, however, the carrier or bailee is not obliged to deliver the goods until the document is surrendered. The holder of such a document may defeat the seller's right of stopping delivery.[17]

(2) Termination of Right to Stop Delivery. The seller's right to stop delivery is terminated or lost, even though a proper notification is given, when (1) the goods have been delivered to the buyer, (2) the carrier acknowledges the right of the buyer by reshipping at his direction or by agreeing to hold for him as a warehouseman, (3) the bailee in possession acknowledges that he holds the goods for the buyer, or (4) a negotiable document of title covering the goods has been negotiated to the buyer.[18]

§ 27:6. Reclamation of Goods Received by Insolvent Buyer. The buyer may have obtained goods from the seller on credit when, unknown to the seller, the buyer was insolvent. If the buyer made a false written statement to the seller that he was solvent and received the goods within three months after that time, the seller may at any time demand and reclaim the goods sold to the buyer on credit.[19] If the buyer never made a false written

[16] § 2-705(1).
[17] § 2-705(3)(c).
[18] § 2-705(2).
[19] § 2-702(2).

statement of solvency, or if he made it more than three months before he received the goods, the seller, in order to reclaim the goods, must demand the return of the goods within ten days after they are received by the buyer.[20]

§ 27:7. Resale by Seller. When the buyer has broken the contract by wrongfully rejecting the goods, wrongfully revoking his acceptance, failing to pay, or repudiating the contract, the seller may resell the goods or the balance of them remaining in his possession, or the goods over which he has reacquired possession as by stopping delivery. After the resale, the seller is not liable to the original buyer upon the contract or for any profit obtained by him on the resale. On the other hand, if the proceeds are less than the contract price, the seller may recover the loss from the original buyer.[21]

Unless otherwise agreed, the resale may be made either as a public or private sale, or as an auction sale, as long as the method followed is commercially reasonable. Certain formalities for the resale are prescribed; but a person who purchases in good faith acquires the goods free of all claims of the original buyer, even though the resale was irregular because the seller did not follow the procedure prescribed for such a sale.[22]

Reasonable notice must be given to the original buyer of the intention to make a private sale. Such notice must be given him of a public sale unless the goods are perishable in character or threaten to decline speedily in value. Notice of a public sale must also be given to the general public in such manner as is commercially reasonable under the circumstances.

§ 27:8. Cancellation by Seller. When the buyer wrongfully rejects the goods, wrongfully revokes an acceptance of the goods, repudiates the contract, or fails to make a payment due on or before delivery, the seller may cancel the contract.[23] Such action puts an end to the contract, discharging all obligations on both sides that are still unperformed, but the seller retains any remedy with respect to the breach by the buyer.[24] Cancellation necessarily revests the seller with title to the goods.

§ 27:9. Seller's Action for Damages. If the buyer wrongfully refuses to accept the goods or if he repudiates the contract, the seller may sue him for the damages that the seller sustains. In the ordinary case the amount of damages is to be measured by the difference between the market price at the time and place of the tender of the goods and the contract price.[25]

If this measure of damages does not place the seller in the position in which he would have been placed by the buyer's performance, recovery may be permitted of lost profits, together with an allowance for overhead.[26] (See

[20] § 2-702(2).
[21] § 2-706(1),(6).
[22] § 2-706(5).
[23] § 2-703(f).
[24] § 2-106(4).
[25] § 2-708(1); Iverson v Schnack, 263 Wis 266, 57 NW2d 400.
[26] UCC § 2-708(2).

p. 558, Anchorage Centennial Development Co. v Van Wormer & Rodrigues.) The seller may in any case recover as incidental damages any commercially reasonable charges, expenses, or commissions incurred in enforcing his remedy, such as those sustained in stopping delivery; in the transportation, care, and custody of the goods after the buyer's breach; and in the return or resale of the goods.[27] Such incidental damages are recovered in addition to any other damages that may be recovered by the seller.

When a tailor's customer stopped payment on his check and the tailor, who had already cut cloth for the customer's suit, stopped further work on the suit, he was entitled to recover only the damages that he had sustained; he was not entitled to recover the full contract price of a finished suit.[28]

§ 27:10. Seller's Action for the Purchase Price. The seller may bring an action to recover the purchase price, together with incidental damages as described in connection with the action for damages, if (a) the goods have been accepted and there has not been any rightful revocation of acceptance; (b) conforming goods were damaged or destroyed after the risk of loss passed to the buyer; or (c) the seller has identified proper goods to the contract but after the buyer's breach has been or will be unable to resell them at a reasonable price.[29] In consequence of these limitations, the right to sue for the contract price, as distinguished from a suit for damages for breach, is a remedy that is not ordinarily available to the seller.

§ 27:11. Repossession of Goods by Seller. The fact that the seller has not paid does not give him any right to take back or repossess the goods. In modern commercial practice, however, when goods are sold on credit, a provision will ordinarily be included in the contract expressly giving the seller the right to repossess the goods if the buyer defaults in payment,[30] but the mere fact that a sale is made on credit or is an installment sale does not confer any right of repossession.[31]

REMEDIES OF THE BUYER

The buyer has a number of remedies provided by Article 2 of the Uniform Commercial Code.

§ 27:12. Rejection of Improper Delivery. If the goods or the tender made by the seller do not conform to the contract in any respect, the buyer may reject the goods. (See p. 560, Zabriskie Chevrolet v Smith.) The buyer has the choice (a) of rejecting the entire quantity tendered, (b) of accepting the entire tender, or (c) of accepting any one or more commercial units and rejecting the rest.[32] Delivery of the goods to a carrier is not an "acceptance"

---

[27] UCC § 2-710.

[28] Rowland Meledandi, Inc. v Kohn, (NY Civil Court) 7 UCCRS 34.

[29] UCC § 2-709(1).

[30] In addition, a security agreement will ordinarily be executed by the buyer, thus giving rise to a secured transaction, as discussed in Chapters 35 and 36.

[31] Miami Air Conditioning Co. v Rood, (Fla App) 223 So2d 78 (pre-Code).

[32] UCC § 2-601.

of the goods by the buyer.[33] The rejection must be made within a reasonable time after the delivery or tender, and the buyer must notify the seller of his action.[34] A two-month delay bars rejection when several times during this interval the buyer visited the building in which the purchased goods were kept and took away with him several small articles.[35]

After rejecting the goods, the buyer may not exercise any right of ownership as to the goods but must hold them awaiting instructions from the seller. When the goods are perishable or threaten to decline in value rapidly, the buyer is required to make reasonable efforts to sell the goods if he is a merchant and the seller does not have any agent or place of business in the market of rejection.[36] In any case, if the seller does not furnish the buyer any instructions, the buyer has the option of reshipping the goods to the seller at the seller's expense, or of storing or reselling them for the seller's account.[37]

§ 27:13. Revocation of Acceptance. The buyer may revoke his acceptance of the goods when they do not conform to the contract to such an extent that the defect substantially impairs their value to him,[38] provided (a) he accepted the goods without knowledge of the nonconformity, because it could not be reasonably discovered or because the seller had assured him that the goods were conforming; or (b) he accepted the goods with knowledge of the nonconformity but reasonably believed that the defect would be cured by the seller.[39] The buyer may not revoke his acceptance merely because the goods do not conform to the contract unless such nonconformity substantially impairs their value to him.[40] Revocation of acceptance may be made not only with respect to the entire quantity of goods but also with respect to any lot or commercial unit that is nonconforming. A buyer who revokes his acceptance stands in the same position as though he had rejected the goods when they had been originally tendered.

When a buyer, in driving an automobile home, discovers defects that substantially impair the value of the car and he immediately complains to the seller, the buyer may revoke his acceptance even though he had made such use of the car and had signed a contract stating that he had accepted the car "in good order." [41]

---

[33] Johnson & Dealaman v Hegarty, 93 NJ Super 14, 224 A2d 510 (recognizing that prior law is continued by the UCC).

[34] UCC § 2-602(1). The failure to specify the particular ground for rejection may bar the buyer from proving it in a subsequent action. § 2-605. As to the right of the seller to cure the default, see § 2-508.

[35] Campbell v Pollack, 101 RI 223, 221 A2d 615.

[36] UCC § 2-603(1).

[37] § 2-604.

[38] The UCC requires "substantial impairment of value" in order to bar revocation of acceptance for trivial matters that may be easily corrected; Rozmus v Thompson's Lincoln-Mercury Co., 209 Pa Super 120, 224 A2d 782.

[39] UCC § 2-608(1).

[40] Hays Merchandise, Inc. v Dewey, 78 Wash 2d 343, 474 P2d 270.

[41] Rozmus v Thompson's Lincoln-Mercury Co., 209 Pa Super 120, 224 A2d 782.

(1) Notice of Revocation. The acceptance of goods cannot be revoked unless the buyer gives the seller a notice of revocation. This notice must be given within a reasonable time after the buyer discovers that the goods do not conform or after he should have discovered it. The notice must also be given before there has been any substantial change in the condition of the goods, apart from the change resulting from their own defective condition.[42]

A revocation of acceptance is effective when the buyer notifies the seller. It is not necessary that the buyer make an actual return of the goods in order to make his revocation effective.[43]

(2) Time for Revocation. A buyer is not required to notify the seller of his intention to revoke his acceptance until the buyer is reasonably certain that the nonconformity of the goods substantially impairs the value of the goods. Thus, the mere fact that the buyer suspects that the goods do not conform and that such nonconformity substantially impairs the value of the contract does not in itself require that he immediately give notice.[44]

A seller has a reasonable time to attempt to correct defects in the goods, and a buyer is not barred from revoking his acceptance of the goods because he has delayed until the attempts of the seller to correct the defects proved unsuccessful. For example, when an automobile had to be taken to the dealer's shop for repairs for some 40 or 50 days of the first year after the sale and the defects were not remedied, the buyer was not barred from revoking his acceptance. Likewise, he was under no obligation to continue indefinitely to allow the seller to attempt to remedy the defects.[45]

§ 27:14. Possession of Goods on Seller's Insolvency. The buyer may have paid in advance for the goods that are still in the seller's possession. Assuming that the seller then becomes insolvent, can the buyer claim the goods from the possession of the seller or is he limited to making a general claim for the refund of the amount paid for them? If the goods have been identified to the contract by either or both the buyer and seller, and the seller becomes insolvent within ten days after receipt of the first installment of the price, the buyer is entitled to recover the goods. The buyer who makes a partial payment has a similar right of reclamation if the seller becomes insolvent within ten days after the first payment is made, but he must pay the balance due.[46]

§ 27:15. Buyer's Action for Damages for Nondelivery. If the seller fails to deliver as required by the contract or repudiates the contract, or if the buyer properly rejects tendered goods or revokes his acceptance as to such goods,

---

[42] UCC § 2-608(2).
[43] Campbell v Pollack, 101 RI 223, 221 A2d 615.
[44] Lanners v Whitney, 247 Ore 223, 428 P2d 398.
[45] Tiger Motor Co. v McMurtry, 284 Ala 283, 224 So2d 638.
[46] UCC § 2-502.

the buyer is entitled to sue the seller for damages for breach of contract. The buyer is entitled to recover the difference between the market price at the time the buyer learned of the breach and the contract price.[47]

Within a reasonable time after the seller's breach, the buyer may *cover,* that is, procure the same or similar goods elsewhere. If the buyer acts in good faith, the measure of damages for the seller's nondelivery or repudiation is then the difference between the cost of cover and the contract price.[48]

The buyer is not under any duty to cover as far as direct damages are concerned, but he may not recover for consequential damages that could have been avoided by reasonably effecting cover.[49] For example, when a trucker cannot haul freight for his customers because the truck purchased from the seller is defective, he may recover damages equal to the difference between the value of the truck as it was and as it should have been. If the buyer does not cover by purchasing or renting a truck from another source, he is barred from recovering the lost profits that he could have obtained had he been able to use the original truck in hauling freight for his customers.

In any case, the buyer is entitled to recover incidental damages, but he must give the seller credit for expenses saved as a result of the seller's breach.

§ 27:16. Action for Breach of Warranty.

(1) Notice of Breach. If the buyer has accepted goods that do not conform to the contract or as to which there is a breach of warranty, he must notify the seller of the breach within a reasonable time after he discovers or should have discovered the breach. Otherwise he is not entitled to complain.[50] If the buyer has given the necessary notice of breach, he may recover damages measured by the loss resulting in the normal course of events from the breach. The purpose of the requirement for notice of defects is to enable the seller to minimize damages in some way, as by correcting the defect, and to give him protection from stale or old claims.[51] The notice is not required to set forth a money demand or to threaten that suit will be brought.

When the manufacturer has a local agent, the notice of the defect in accepted goods may be given to such agent and when such notice is seasonably given to the local agent, the buyer satisfies the UCC's requirement without regard to whether the notice thereafter given to the manufacturer was given within a reasonable time.[52]

---

[47] § 2-713(1). In the case of anticipatory breach, as when the seller states in advance of the delivery date that he will not perform, the buyer has the option of waiting until the performance date or of treating such repudiation as a breach fixing damages as of that time, unless the buyer effects cover. § 2-610.

[48] § 2-712(2).

[49] § 2-712(3).

[50] San Antonio v Warwick Ginger Ale Co., 104 RI 700, 248 A2d 778.

[51] L. A. Green Seed Co. v Williams, 246 Ark 454, 438 SW2d 717.

[52] Kopet v Klein, 275 Minn 525, 148 NW2d 385.

It is not necessary that the buyer give formal notice of a breach of warranty. It is sufficient that the seller be informed in some manner. The content of the notice need only let the seller know that a claim has arisen because of a transaction which involves him, and it is not necessary to include a clear statement of all of the buyer's objections.[53] Hence, when the buyer sent periodic reports to the seller from which it was apparent that the product was not performing as warranted, the seller had "notice" of the breach.[54]

The requirement of notice of breach of warranty is limited to the single situation where a buyer sues the person from whom he directly made the purchase and sues on theory of breach of warranty.

When the seller delivers nonconforming goods, he is liable for the breach of his contract without regard to whether he had knowledge of the nonconformity.[55]

(2) Measure of Damages. If suit is brought for breach of warranty, the measure of damages is the difference between the value of the goods as they were when accepted and the value that they would have had if they had been as warranted.

If the buyer has made a substantial use of the goods, such as having driven an automobile over 8,000 miles, he cannot claim that the goods had no value whatever and recover the entire purchase price paid by him.[56] He may only recover the difference between the contract price and the actual value of the goods.

The buyer may recover as damages for breach of warranty the loss directly and naturally resulting from that breach. In other words, he may recover for the loss proximately resulting from the failure to deliver the goods as warranted.[57]

In all cases the buyer may recover any incidental or consequential damages sustained.[58] For example, if the merchant seller sells a preservative that he knows will be used by the buyer in the process of preserving other goods, the merchant seller is liable for the destruction of the other goods if the preservative he supplies is not fit for that purpose.

Whenever the buyer is entitled to recover damages from the seller, he may deduct the amount of them from any balance remaining due on the purchase price provided he notifies the seller that he intends to do so.[59] When the buyer who has accepted the goods is sued for the contract price, he may counterclaim damages for breach of warranty even though the time for revoking the acceptance or rejecting the goods has passed.[60]

---

[53] Nugent v Popular Markets, 353 Mass 45, 228 NE2d 91.
[54] Babcock Poultry Farm v Shook, 204 Pa Super 141, 203 A2d 399.
[55] Johnson v Daniels Motors, Inc., (Colo App) 470 P2d 588.
[56] Holz v Coates Motor Co., 206 Va 894, 147 SE2d 152.
[57] W & W Livestock Enterprises v Dennler, (Iowa) 179 NW2d 484.
[58] UCC § 2-714(3).
[59] § 2-717.
[60] Marbelite Co. v Philadelphia, 208 Pa Super 256, 222 A2d 443.

Ordinarily the damages are only such as will compensate the plaintiff for the loss that he has sustained; punitive damages are not recoverable. To illustrate, the manufacturer of a truck will not be held liable for punitive damages when the manufacturer's conduct was merely negligence or stubbornness in failing to issue a proper warning and to withdraw the product sooner from the market. Punitive damages may only be awarded when there is an intention to cause harm or when there is reckless indifference or wantonness short of criminality; and such conduct must be clearly shown, any doubts being resolved against such liability, particularly when many suits would or might be brought against the manufacturer and the total possible claims could aggregate millions of dollars.[61]

*(3) **Notice of Third-Party Action Against Buyer.*** The buyer may be sued in consequence of the seller's breach of warranty, as when the buyer's customers sue him because of the condition of the goods which he has resold to them. In such a case it is optional with the buyer whether or not he gives the seller notice of the action against him and requests the seller to defend the action.[62] The buyer may also be sued by a third person because of patent infringement. In this case he must give notice of the action to the seller. Moreover, the seller can demand that the buyer turn over the defense of that action to him.[63]

When the seller is given notice of a suit against the buyer but fails to defend the buyer, the seller cannot dispute the facts shown in that action when he in turn is sued by the buyer.

In any case a buyer has the burden of proving that the goods were not as represented or warranted when he so alleges, whether as a claim in a suit against the seller or as a defense when sued by the seller.

§ 27:17. Cancellation by Buyer. The buyer may cancel or rescind the contract if the seller fails to deliver the goods or if he repudiates the contract, or if the buyer has rightfully rejected tendered goods or revoked his acceptance of the goods. When the buyer cancels, he is entitled to recover as much of the purchase price as he has paid, including the value of property given as a trade-in as part of the purchase price. The fact that the buyer cancels the contract does not destroy his cause of action against the seller for breach of the contract. The buyer may therefore recover from the seller not only any payment made on the purchase price [64] but, in addition, damages for the breach of the contract. The damages represent the difference between the contract price and the market price, or the difference between the contract price and the cost of cover if the buyer has purchased other goods.[65]

---

61 Roginsky v Richardson-Merrell, Inc., (CA2 NY) 378 F2d 832.

62 UCC § 2-607(5)(a).

63 § 2-607(3)(b),(5)(b).

64 Lanners v Whitney, 247 Ore 223, 428 P2d 398.

65 UCC § 2-712(1),(2). In any case, the buyer is entitled to recover incidental damages.

The fact that the goods are returned by the buyer does not in itself establish that there has been a cancellation, since a return of the goods may be merely a revocation of acceptance of the goods with an intent to preserve the contract and receive other goods in exchange.

If the return of the goods to the seller would work a great hardship on the buyer, it may be possible for the buyer to commence an action to obtain a decree of court directing cancellation while retaining the goods until the decree has been entered, rather than putting the buyer to the hardship of doing without such goods.

The right of the buyer to cancel or rescind the sales contract may be lost by a delay in exercising that right. A buyer loses the right when he refuses to permit the seller to attempt to make normal adjustments to remedy the defect; with the consequence that when the buyer refused to permit the seller to take the new television set to the shop to determine why the red color was not functioning properly, the buyer was acting unreasonably and lost the right to cancel.[66]

A buyer cannot cancel when with full knowledge of defects in the goods he makes partial payments and performs acts of dominion inconsistent with any intent to cancel. (See p. 561, Barnes v Chester Burnham Chevrolet.)

The mere fact that a written sales contract was not completed before signing does not entitle a buyer who has received delivery of the goods to cancel the contract,[67] although consumer protection legislation may sometimes prohibit the signing of a sales contract in blank and give the buyer the right to cancel the sale when he has done so.

The fact that the buyer cancels the sale does not destroy his liability on commercial paper which he had already given the seller when such paper is held by a holder in due course or a person having the rights of such a holder.

The buyer's return of the goods to the seller does not release the buyer from liability on a check that he gave as a down payment, even though a retail installment sales act provides that when the seller has regained possession of the goods but does not resell them, "all obligation of the buyer under the agreement, shall be discharged. . . ." This statutory provision relates only to the obligation of the buyer under the sales contract and does not affect liability on a check given as a down payment.[68]

§ **27:18. Buyer's Resale of Goods.** When the buyer has possession of the goods that he has rightfully rejected or as to which he has revoked his acceptance, he is treated the same as a seller in possession of goods after the default of a buyer. That is, he has a security interest in the goods for his claim against the other party and may resell the goods as though he were a seller. From the proceeds of the sale he is entitled to deduct for himself any payments made on the price and any expenses reasonably incurred in the

[66] Wilson v Scampoli, (Dist Col App) 228 A2d 848.
[67] Woods v Van Wallis Trailer Sales Co., 77 NMex 121, 419 P2d 964.
[68] Webb v Chevy Chase Cars, Inc., 259 Md 284, 269 A2d 810.

inspection, receipt, transportation, care and custody, and resale of the goods.[69] (See p. 562, Walter E. Heller & Co. v Hammond Appliance Co.)

§ 27:19. Action for Conversion or Recovery of Goods. When, as a result of the sales agreement, ownership passes to the buyer and the seller wrongfully refuses or neglects to deliver the goods, the buyer may maintain any action allowed by law to the owner of goods wrongfully converted or withheld. Hence, a buyer having the right to immediate possession may bring an action of replevin to recover possession of the goods wrongfully withheld, or he may bring an action to recover the value of the goods on the ground of conversion. Likewise, the buyer may replevy the goods when he satisfies any security interest of the seller in the goods but delivery to the buyer is refused.

The buyer is also given the right of replevin when the seller has identified the goods to the contract and the circumstances are such that similar goods cannot be reasonably procured by the buyer in the open market.[70] Here it is immaterial whether the title has passed to the buyer, and the action of replevin is in effect an action of specific performance granted to protect the buyer from a harm which would follow from the fact that he is not able to obtain similar goods in the market if he does not obtain them from the seller.

The obligation of the seller to deliver proper goods may be enforced by an order for specific performance when the goods are "unique or in other proper circumstances." [71] This permits the buyer to obtain specific performance, not only when the goods have a peculiar or special quality that makes them unique, but also when it would be a hardship on the buyer to deny him that right. Accordingly, a contract calling for the sale of the seller's output or the supplying of the buyer's requirements may present circumstances where specific performance will be required to permit the buyer to obtain the benefit of his contract.

The fact that the contract price is unusually low does not establish that the goods are unique so as to entitle the buyer to specific performance. If the buyer is required to pay more for the goods elsewhere, he will be adequately compensated by recovering the difference between the contract and such price when he claims damages from the seller.[72]

§ 27:20. Remedies for Fraud of Seller. Independently of the preceding remedies, the buyer has the right to sue the seller for damages for the latter's fraud or to cancel the transaction on that ground.[73] As these remedies for fraud exist independently of the provisions of the UCC, the buyer may assert such remedies even when he is barred by the UCC from exercising any remedy for a breach of warranty.

---

[69] UCC § 2-715(1).

[70] § 2-716(3).

[71] § 2-716(1).

[72] Hilmor Sales Co. v Helen Neushaefer, (NY) 6 UCCRS 325.

[73] UCC § 1-103. As to what constitutes fraud, see Chapter 13. As to the expansion of the damages recoverable, see UCC § 2-721.

The general principles of agency law remain in force under the UCC and a seller will be held liable for the fraud of his agent in effecting a sale.[74]

Suit for fraud is generally not a satisfactory solution for the consumer because of the difficulty of proving the existence of fraud. Likewise, some courts require him to show fraud by clear and convincing proof; and it is not sufficient to prove the existence of fraud by a mere preponderance of evidence, although that ordinarily is a sufficient degree of proof in civil litigation.

CONTRACT PROVISIONS ON REMEDIES

The UCC permits the parties to modify or limit by the terms of their contract the remedies which they would otherwise possess.

§ **27:21. Limitation of Damages.** The parties may in their sales contract specify that in the event of breach by either party the damages are to be limited to a certain amount. If this amount is unreasonably large, it is void as a penalty. If the amount is reasonable, the injured party is limited to recovering that amount. Whether the limitation is reasonable is determined in the light of the actual harm that would be caused by breach, the difficulty of proving the amount of such loss, and the inconvenience and impracticality of suing for damages or enforcing other remedies for breach.[75]

§ **27:22. Down Payments and Deposits.** The buyer may have made a deposit with the seller or an initial or down payment at the time of making the contract. If the contract contains a valid liquidation-of-damages provision and the buyer defaults, the seller must return any part of the down payment or deposit in excess of the amount specified by the liquidated damages clause. In the absence of such a clause, and in the absence of proof of greater damages sustained by him, the seller's damages are computed as 20 percent of the purchase price or $500, whichever is the smaller. The extent to which the down payment exceeds such amount must be returned to the buyer.[76]

The rule just stated applies to payments made by the buyer in goods as well as in cash as, for example, by making a trade-in. Such goods given in payment are assigned a dollar value for the purpose of determining the payment made by the buyer. If the goods have been resold, their value is the proceeds of the resale; if not, it is the reasonable value of such goods.[77]

§ **27:23. Limitation on Remedies.** The parties may validly limit the remedies. (See p. 563, Dow Corning Corp. v Capitol Aviation, Inc.) Thus, a seller may specify that the only remedy of the buyer for breach of warranty shall be the repair or replacement of the goods, or that the buyer shall be limited to returning the goods and obtaining a refund of the purchase price. How

---

[74] Fitzsimmons v Honaker, (Colo App) 485 P2d 923.

[75] § 2-718(1).

[76] § 2-718(2).

[77] § 2-718(4). If the seller has notice of the buyer's breach before resale is made, the seller must observe the same standards that apply to the ordinary seller who resells upon breach by the buyer. See § 27:7.

much further the restrictions may go is not clear, but the limitation is not binding if it is unreasonable or unconscionable.

The limitation of consequential damages for personal injuries caused by defective goods is prima facie unconscionable, and therefore prima facie not binding, when the goods are sold for consumption by the buyer.[78] Thus, the warranty-defendant cannot rely on an exclusion of warranties provision in such a case unless the defendant meets the burden of showing that the limitation of liability is commercially reasonable and fair rather than oppressive and surprising. That is, the warranty-defendant cannot defend by the limitation provision against a claim for personal injuries unless he can prove that the limitation is not unconscionable.[79] Moreover, when the seller would be liable to his buyer for a breach of warranty, the seller cannot exclude liability for personal injuries to members of the buyer's family, his household, or his guests.[80] When the seller knows that the failure of the product, such as a harvester, to perform will cause serious economic loss, a limitation of damages for breach to the return of the purchase price is void as unconscionable.[81]

§ **27:24. Waiver of Defenses.** A buyer may be barred from objecting to a breach of the contract by the seller because the buyer has waived his right to do so.

(1) Express Waiver. When sales are made on credit, the seller will ordinarily plan to assign the sales contract to a bank or other financer and thereby convert into immediate cash his customer's obligations to pay in the future. To make the transaction more attractive to banks and financers, the credit seller will generally include in the sales contract with each buyer a *waiver of defense* clause. By this clause the buyer agrees that he will not assert against the seller's assignee any defense which he has against the seller. For example, if the television set does not work properly, the buyer agrees that he will only complain to the seller. He will not complain to the seller's assignee but will continue to pay the assignee just as though everything were satisfactory.

(2) Implied Waiver. When the buyer executes a promissory note as part of the credit transaction described above, he automatically waives with respect to the seller's assignee any defense which he could not raise against a holder in due course of the note. This will be considered in greater detail in the chapters on commercial paper. What it means in the ordinary everyday situation is that when the buyer signs a promissory note for the balance due he cannot assert against the finance company or the bank the defense

---

78 § 2-719(3).

79 Walsh v Ford Motor Co., 59 Misc 2d 241, 298 NYS2d 538.

80 UCC § 2-318.

81 Steele v Case Co., 197 Kan 554, 419 P2d 902 (pre-Code but citing § 2-719(3) "as evidencing a trend of modern thought").

that he never got the goods called for by the contract, that the goods were defective and did not work, or that he had entered into the contract because of fraudulent misstatements of the seller.

(3) Validity. Consumer protection statutes commonly nullify the waiver of defenses by providing that the buyer may assert against the seller's transferee any defense which he might have against the seller. Under some statutes the buyer must give notice of his defense within a specified number of days after being notified of the assignment. Some courts extend consumer protection beyond the scope of the statute by ignoring a time limitation on the giving of notice of defenses.[82]

[82] Star Credit Corp. v Molina, 59 Misc 2d 290, 298 NYS2d 570.

CASES FOR CHAPTER 27

Anchorage Centennial Development Co. v Van Wormer & Rodrigues

(Alaska) 443 P2d 596 (1968)

In connection with a centennial celebration of the purchase of Alaska from Russia, the Anchorage Centennial Commission contracted with Van Wormer & Rodrigues to make and sell to the Commission 50,000 goldcolored metal anniversary coins. When the contract had been partially performed, the Commission canceled the contract. Van Wormer sued the Commission for damages caused by the breach and for the profit that would have been made on the canceled portion of the contract. The undisputed evidence showed that the profit would have been 3 cents a coin. The lower court entered judgment in favor of Van Wormer for damages but did not allow a recovery of loss of profits. The Commission appealed from the award of damages against it. Van Wormer filed a cross-appeal from the court's refusal to allow the recovery of lost profits.

RABINOWITZ, J. . . . The trial court correctly found that at the time the Commission purported to cancel its order for 50,000 coins, 29,000 coins had already been manufactured. Using the 29,000 figure at the agreed cost of 15 cents per coin, Van Wormer was awarded judgment in the amount of $4,350.

Examination of the record in this cause fails to reveal any basis for the trial court's conclusion that Van Wormer was not entitled to recover its loss of profits in regard to the 21,000 coins which had been ordered by the Commission, but had not been manufactured at the time of the Commission's repudiation of the contract. . . . "In awarding damages for breach of contract, an effort is made to put the injured party in as good a position as he would have been had the contract been fully performed."

In the case at bar we are in accord with Van Wormer's argument to the effect that since there is no market for these made-to-order coins, the proper measure of damages is governed by . . . [UCC § 2-708] which provides: "If the measure of damages provided in (a) [difference between market price and contract price] of this section is inadequate to put the seller in as good a position as performance would have done, then the measure of damages is the profit (including reasonable overhead) which the seller would have made from full performance by the buyer, together with any incidental damages provided in . . . [UCC § 2-710], due allowance for costs reasonably incurred, and due credit for payments or proceeds of resale."

We, therefore, conclude that the judgment entered . . . should be modified to include an award to Van Wormer for its loss of profits on the remaining 21,000 coins under the contract. . . .

The judgment entered, . . . as modified in accordance with the foregoing, is affirmed.

Detroit Power Screwdriver Co. v Ladney

25 Mich App 478, 181 NW2d 848 (1970)

The Detroit Power Screwdriver Company made a contract to manufacture a very complicated stud-driving machine for Ladney. The machine was to be made to Ladney's specifications and was not like the machines made by Detroit. When the manufacturing of the machine was nearly completed, Ladney notified Detroit that he would not take the machine. Detroit stopped production and sued Ladney. From a judgment for Ladney, Detroit appealed.

LESENSKI, J. . . . The trial court held that a contract existed and that defendant breached the contract. The court also held, however, that plaintiff had failed to prove damages with sufficient certainty to permit a recovery. . . .

The disposition of the instant case is clearly governed by the Uniform Commercial Code. However, due to the differences between various sections providing remedies to sellers, it is necessary to make a preliminary determination of which sections of the Code control the final outcome.

The Code is, of course, a highly integrated statute, the sections of which must be read together. Accurate application of the Code rarely involves reference to only one section.

. . . Plaintiff places principal reliance on [UCC § 2-709(1)]. . . . Since the machine was not completed, § 2-709(1) is inapplicable. . . .

Since plaintiff is not entitled to the price under § 2-709(1), its right to recovery is controlled by § 2-708.

The measure of damages under § 2-708(1) is: "[T]he measure of damages for nonacceptance or repudiation by the buyer is the difference between the market price at the time and place for tender and the unpaid contract price together with any incidental damages . . . but less expenses saved in consequence of the buyer's breach."

However, § 2-708(2) provides: "If the measure of damages provided in subsection (1) is inadequate to put the seller in as good a position as performance would have done then the measure of damages is the profit (including reasonable overhead) which the seller would have made from full performance by the buyer, together with any incidental damages . . . , due allowance for costs reasonably incurred and due credit for payments or proceeds of resale." . . .

. . . A formula basing damages on the difference between market price and contract price is without meaning in the context of a contract for a specialty item which has no market.

Thus, the question of whether or not the machine in the instant case is a specialty item within the meaning of the Code must be determined in order to know which measure of damages applies. The question, however, also has significance in the instant case beyond the correct measure of damages.

[UCC § 2-610] provides in part: "When either party repudiates the contract with respect to a performance not yet due the loss of which will substantially impair the value of the contract to the other, the aggrieved party may . . . (b) resort to any remedy for breach . . . even though he has notified the repudiating party that he would await the latter's performance and has urged retraction; and (c) in either case suspend his own performance or proceed in accordance with the provisions of this article on the seller's right to identify goods to the contract notwithstanding breach or to salvage unfinished goods . . . ."

The right to suspend performance . . ., however, must be read in light of [UCC § 2-704(2)] . . . which states: "Where the goods are unfinished an aggrieved seller may in the exercise of reasonable commercial judgment for the purposes of avoiding loss and of effective realization either complete the manufacture and wholly identify the goods to the contract or cease manufacture and resell for scrap or salvage value or proceed in any other reasonable manner."

Whether plaintiff's decision not to complete the machine in the instant case was the result of the "exercise of reasonable commercial judgment" thus also depends, at least in part, on whether a market exists for the finished product.

We now return to the initial question of whether the trial court erred in ruling that plaintiff failed to prove damages under the Code.

The record below includes plaintiff's invoice in the amount of $12,017 dated May 11, 1967 for work completed up to April 11th, the date of defendant's stop order. Evidence was also introduced to show that the scrap salvage value of the machine was $1,500.

. . . Plaintiff's invoice was clearly intended to cover expected profits and costs incurred during the work done. That amount would then be reduced by the salvage value of $1,500.

Yet, § 2-708(2) applies only "if the measure of damages provided in subsection (1) is inadequate to put the seller in as good a position as performance would have done." As noted above, however, § 2-708(1) does not apply where the contract is found to involve a specialty item without a reasonably accessible market. Such a finding is crucial since it determines whether § 2-708(1) or § 2-708(2) controls the measure of damages. The determination of which paragraph of § 2-708 controls is, in turn, important since plaintiff has proven its loss under paragraph (2) but has not proven the amount of its loss under paragraph (1).

The ruling of the court below did not include a factual determination of whether the machine here involved is a specialty item without a reasonably accessible market. . . .

We therefore remand the case for further findings. If the trial court finds that the machine is a specialty item without a reasonably accessible market, then it shall award damages pursuant to § 2-708(2). If it does not so hold, the trial court shall dismiss the action due to plaintiff's failure to proof under § 2-708(1). . . .

[Action remanded.]

Zabriskie Chevrolet v Smith

99 NJ Super 441, 240 A2d 195 (1968)

Smith bought a new automobile from Zabriskie Chevrolet. It was represented that the car was a brand-new one that would operate perfectly. Smith's wife drove it from the showroom to their home. Within seven-tenths of a mile the transmission ceased to function properly and the car would only drive with the transmission set at "low low." Because of this defect, Smith stopped payment on the check which he had given for the purchase price. Zabriskie sued Smith for the purchase price. Smith asserted that there had been a breach of warranty because of which he revoked acceptance of the automobile and canceled the purchase. Zabriskie claimed that the acceptance of the automobile could not be revoked.

DOAN, J.D.C. . . . It is clear that a buyer does not accept goods until he has had a "reasonable opportunity to inspect." Defendant sought to purchase a new car. He assumed what every new car buyer has a right to assume and, indeed, has been led to assume by the high-powered advertising techniques of the auto industry—that his new car, with the exception of very minor adjustments, would be mechanically new and factory-furnished, operate perfectly, and be free of substantial defects. The vehicle delivered to defendant did not measure up to these representations. Plaintiff contends that defendant had "reasonable opportunity to inspect" by the privilege to take the car for a typical "spin around the block" before signing the purchase order. If by this contention plaintiff equates a spin around the block with "reasonable opportunity to inspect," the contention is illusory and unrealistic. To the layman, the complicated mechanisms of today's automobiles are a complete mystery. To have the automobile inspected by someone with sufficient expertise to dissemble the vehicle in order to discover latent defects before the contract is signed is assuredly impossible and highly impractical. . . . Consequently, the first few miles of driving become even more significant to the excited new car buyer. This is the buyer's first reasonable opportunity to enjoy his new vehicle to see if it conforms to what it was represented to be and whether he is getting what he bargained for. How long the buyer may drive the new car under the guise of inspection of new goods is not an issue in the present case. It is clear that defendant discovered the nonconformity within 7/10 of a mile and minutes after leaving plaintiffs showroom. Certainly this was well within the ambit of "reasonable opportunity to inspect." . . .

. . . The dealer is in an entirely different position from the layman. The dealer with his staff of expert mechanics and modern equipment knows or should know of substantial defects in the new automobile which it sells. There was offered into evidence the dealer's inspection and adjustment schedule containing over 70 alleged items that plaintiff caused to be inspected, including the transmission. According to that schedule the automobile in question had been checked by the seller for the satisfaction of the buyer, and such inspection included a road test. The fact that the automobile underwent a tortured operation for about 2½ miles from the showroom to defendant's residence demonstrates the inherent serious deficiencies in this vehicle which were present when the so-called inspection was made by plaintiff, and hence plaintiff was aware (or should have been) that the vehicle did not conform to the bargain the parties had made, and plaintiff had no reasonable right to expect that the vehicle in that condition would be accepted.

There having been no acceptance, the next issue presented is whether defendant properly rejected under the Code. . . .

[UCC §] 2-602 indicates that one can reject after taking possession. Possession, therefore, does not mean acceptance and the corresponding loss of the right of rejection. . . .

[UCC §] 2-106 . . . defines conforming goods as follows: "(2) Goods or conduct including any part of a performance are 'conforming' or conform to the contract when they are in accordance with the obligations under the contract." . . .

There was no evidence at the trial concerning any "custom or usage," although plaintiff in its brief argued that it is the usage of the automobile trade that a buyer accept a new automobile, although containing defects of manufacture, if such defects can be and are seasonably cured by the seller. Perhaps this represents prevailing views in the automobile industry which have, over the years, served to blanket injustices and inequities committed upon buyers who demurred in the light of the unequal positions of strength between the parties. . . . In the present case we are not dealing with a situation such as was present in Adams v Tramontin Motor Sales, 42 NJSuper 313, 126 A2d 358 (AppDiv 1956). In that case, brought for breach of implied warranty of merchantability, the court held that minor defects, such as adjustment of the motor, tightening of loose elements, fixing of locks and dome light, and a correction of rumbling noise, were not remarkable defects, and therefore there was no breach. Here the breach was substantial. The new car was practically inoperable and endowed with a defective transmission. This was a "remarkable defect" and justified rejection by the buyer. . . .

[Judgment for defendant.]

Barnes v Chester Burnham Chevrolet

(Miss) 217 So2d 630 (1969)

Barnes purchased a used car on credit from Chester Burnham Chevrolet. He made some payments and a dispute then arose over the making of repairs. The seller refused to provide free repairs. Nine months later, Barnes returned the car to Chester. When Chester sued Barnes for the balance of the purchase price, Barnes raised the defense that he had rescinded or cancelled the sale and claimed that Chester had breached a repair warranty. Judgment was entered for Chester Burnham, and Barnes appealed.

GILLESPIE, P.J. . . . The warranty is in the following language: "The used car you have bought is guaranteed under the following conditions: (1) Only the motor, brakes, transmission and rear axle are guaranteed. (2) The above parts are guaranteed for 30 days on a 50-50 basis. (3) On all repairs you must pay half the cost and Chester Burnham Chevrolet Co. will pay the other half. . . ."

Barnes testified that he took the car back to Burnham about two weeks after the date of purchase because it had a blown head gasket, was overheating, and the motor was stopping. The trouble was not corrected and he took it back a second and third time, but the car still had the same trouble in that it had no power, oil ran down the manifold, and it would overheat and stop. Thereafter Burnham's foreman told Barnes that it could not be fixed and refused to do any more work on a 50-50 basis. Burnham never repaired the defects in the motor. Barnes had paid his part of the repairs attempted by Burnham. Barnes had the car examined by a mechanic when he bought it and the mechanic testified that two of the six cylinders lacked sufficient pressure when the motor was warmed up; that the motor did not have adequate power; and that it would get hot and the engine leaked. After Barnes had it repaired at Burnham's he again tested it and the same defects existed as before. He estimated that the motor would require overhauling or rebuilding to correct the trouble and that this would cost from $150 to $275.

The express warranty covered the motor and it was the obligation of Burnham to repair the motor so as to eliminate the defects testified about and to bear half the cost. According to Barnes' testimony, Burnham failed and refused to repair the motor in accordance with the express warranty. . . .

. . . The contention of Barnes that he rescinded the sale by return of the car is without merit. He kept the car for a period of nine months after he knew Burnham would not repair it. He did not elect to return the car and rescind the sale within a reasonable time after determining that Burnham would not repair it. Barnes did not state that he was rescinding the contract when he returned the car. We hold that Barnes did not return the car within a reasonable time so as to constitute a rescission, nor did Barnes give Burnham any notice that he was rescinding the sale. . . .

[Reversed and remanded to permit the jury to consider Barnes' claim for damages for breach of the repair warranty.]

Walter E. Heller & Co. v Hammond Appliance Co.

29 NJ 589, 151 A2d 537 (1959)

The Peerless Corporation sold 50 appliances to a dealer, the Hammond Appliance Co. The seller then assigned its contract to Walter E. Heller & Co. When Heller sued Hammond for the purchase price, the latter showed that following the purchase the seller and it had agreed that the goods were defective and had mutually rescinded the contract. In spite of this, the seller never came to pick up the goods although Hammond repeatedly requested it to do so. After about a year Hammond began repairing the appliances and finally sold 27 of the 50, still having possession of the remaining 23 at the time of the trial. At the trial, in addition to denying liability, Hammond made a counterclaim for the cost of repairing the appliances, the cost of their storage while waiting for the seller to retake them, and the cost of moving the appliances from one store to another in the effort to sell them. From a judgment against the assignee, Heller appealed. The Appellate Division held that the defendant buyer had waived the rescission by making repairs and sales and was therefore liable for the total purchase price. He appealed to the state supreme court.

PER CURIAM. . . . Upon the happening of the rescission, defendant became a bailee of the goods . . . and the title reverted to the seller. However, the seller, having undertaken to reassume possession, was under a duty to do so within a reasonable time. Not only did failure to perform that duty create a liability for reasonable storage charges, but defendant was not obliged to retain possession indefinitely. . . . He was entitled to undertake a good faith sale without further notice and to hold the proceeds for the benefit of the seller subject to certain rightful credits. . . .

. . . "When the seller of goods persistently refuses to take them back, after being notified of the rescission of the sale by the purchaser for sufficient cause, it is proper, if not obligatory, for the purchaser to take such measures as are expedient to save unnecessary loss to the seller, and if the best method of accomplishing this end is to sell the property (as, in the case of perishable goods), he may sell it 'for account' of the vendor for the best price obtainable, and retain out of the proceeds enough to reimburse him for necessary expenses, and hold the balance subject to the vendor's demand. . . . But one selling property for account of another in this manner must act with reasonable promptness. He will be entitled to storage charges and other expenses only for a reasonable length of time, and whether he has waited an unreasonable time or incurred unreasonable expense, before selling the property, is a question of fact for the jury."

Accordingly, we are of the view that because of the unreasonable delay of the seller and the plaintiff assignee in retaking the goods, defendant was legally justified in selling them. And out of the proceeds he is entitled to retain such sum as represents reasonable storage charges, the reasonable cost of moving and transporting the goods from one store to another (as the proof indicates was done), and the reasonable cost of putting the appliances in a fit condition for sale in the market. . . .

The unsold appliances which have remained in defendant's possession during the pendency of this litigation are still the property of the plaintiff. They may be reclaimed, subject to reasonable storage charges. But if this is not done within a reasonable time after judgment in this court, defendant may dispose of them by bona fide sale. . . .

The judgment of the Appellate Division is modified and the matter is remanded for trial of the issues outlined. . . .

Code Comment: The same decision would be made under the Code. Since the right of the parties to rescind the sales contract and the effect of such rescission are not affected by the Code, the prior law continues. Sec. 1-103. Even without the mutual agreement of the parties, the buyer under the Code would have been entitled to revoke his acceptance of the goods because of their defective condition, cancel the contract, resell the goods, and recover the damages sustained. UCC § 2-711.

Dow Corning Corp. v Capitol Aviation, Inc.

(CA7) Ill) 411 F2d 622 (1969)

Dow Corning contracted to purchase an airplane from Capitol Aviation with delivery to be made in August, 1965. Both parties knew that the plane was being developed experimentally by Aero-Commander, Inc., and Capitol contracted to purchase the plane from Aero. Delivery of the plane was not made to Dow; and when Dow sued Capitol for breach of contract, Capitol sued Aero for breach of its contract with Aero. Aero defended on the ground that this latter contract limited its liability for nondelivery to a return of any payment made by Capitol on the purchase price. Capitol claimed that such limitation was void under the Code. The trial court held that the limitation was not binding and entered judgment for Capitol against Aero. Aero appealed.

DUFFY, J. . . . The District Court entered judgment for Dow against Capitol for $64,000, [and] ruled Aero should reimburse Capitol for the $64,000, and further found Capitol should recover an additional sum of $43,865 for lost profits, making a total judgment for Capitol against Aero of $107,865. . . .

In the fall of 1964, at an aircraft industry convention in Miami which was attended by personnel from Dow and Capitol, Aero announced it would offer for sale a twin-engine turbine-powered executive-type passenger aircraft which it hoped to have available in about a year. . . .

On November 17, 1964, Capitol placed its written order with Aero for one of these new type aircraft at wholesale price of $260,000 with standard equipment. In an appropriate blank on the order with reference to a delivery date was a typewritten insertion TBD (to be determined). Also typed on the order was the recital "Specifications to be supplied at a later date." On February 19, 1965, Aero accepted Capitol's order.

On February 10, 1965, Capitol ordered from Aero two more Turbo-Commanders and a conventional piston type aircraft. As to delivery dates, these three orders also contained the letters TBD (to be determined). These three orders were accepted on February 18 and 19, 1965.

On February 25, 1965, Capitol's sales manager, at Dow's request and without prior consultation with Aero, wrote to Dow's Administrative

Service Manager, Coultrip, advising that Aero's "target delivery date" for Turbo-Commander 1552-12 was "the end of August, 1965," and enclosed several alternative purchase orders. No delivery date was set. Dow took the information from one of the orders and placed it upon its own order form and submitted it to Capitol. However, Dow, without consultation with Aero, and although a delivery date had not been fixed between Aero and Capitol, inserted August, 1965, as the date of shipment. Capitol executed the order committing itself to the August, 1965, date. Later, Aero was informed by Capitol that it had sold a plane to Dow but no details were given. . . .

Consistent with industry custom and practice, there were valid reasons for the contract to provide for an open delivery date. All parties concerned knew that the aircraft which Aero proposed to construct was in an experimental stage of development; that on November 17, 1964, the date of Capitol's order, a prototype of that aircraft had not been flown; and further, that the plane had not been type certified, and no airworthiness certification had been issued for a turbo-commander type aircraft. Both certificates were necessary prerequisites to the delivery of aircraft to a distributor for redelivery to a customer.

Furthermore, it was well known by all concerned in the transaction before us, that Aero was dependent on other suppliers for engines, brakes, landing gear and avionics.

Certain it is that Capitol, at no time, indicated any objection to the open delivery date. . . .

There is no breach of promise here because Aero undertook the obligation of delivery of a plane then in experimental stages, at such time as it could be flown safely. Aero could not furnish and would not be permitted by the Federal Aviation [Administration] to deliver a plane that would not fly safely.

Our conclusion in this respect is, in itself, a reason for a reversal but in the alternative, it is our view that the trial court erred in holding that Paragraph 4 of the purchase order signed by Capitol was not an exclusive remedy and that it was unconsionable and an unreasonable attempt to limit liability under the Uniform Commercial Code. . . .

The trial court pointed out that Section 2-719(1)(b) of the Code provides that a remedy as provided is optional unless it is "expressly agreed to be exclusive." It is true that nowhere does the clause use the word exclusive, but the clear import is that there shall be no remedy other than the return of the deposit. The clause speaks in terms of liability rather than remedies, but it is clear that the parties expressly agreed that this was to be the only recourse. To hold otherwise would be to introduce a new requirement that certain words be used to express the intent of the parties lest they later be found not to have limited their remedies.

As an affirmative defense of the cross claim of Capitol, Aero relied on Paragraph 4 of the purchase order signed by Capitol, to-wit: "Aero Commander, Inc. shall not be liable for failure or delay in making delivery for any cause whatsoever. If delivery of the products covered by this order is not made within thirty (30) days of the 'Specified Delivery Date,' or of the 'Revised Specified Delivery Date,' Purchaser may cancel this order and have the full deposit refunded, provided that such nondelivery is not caused by act of God, war, riot, strikes, or unavoidable casualty." . . .

The case before us is not one where a seller wantonly disregards his obligations to the buyer and sells to another simply for his financial advantage. Here, Aero was desperately trying to construct a new type of aircraft that would be safe to fly. Furthermore, it had been careful not to commit itself to any penalty for late delivery. Under the circumstances of this case, such a provision was reasonable.

The trial court alternatively relied upon Section 2-718 combined with Section 2-302. Section 2-718 provides that an unreasonably large liquidated damage is void as a penalty, and the Comment speculates that an unreasonably small amount might be stricken under the section on unconscionable contracts or clauses. Although it is something of a misnomer to call the return of a deposit a liquidated damage, we will assume the section is available to the appellee.

Section 2-302 makes clear that the unconscionability of a clause is to be judged not in the abstract, but rather in its commercial setting. Here, Aero was constructing what was at least for itself a new type of airplane construction. The plane was to be turbine powered rather than piston powered. Capitol was aware of this. Aero began by making a prototype. This was successful but later effort with production engines proved hazardous. There was an account of a hair-raising trip which revealed substantial difficulty. Aero points out that it is common to the industry not to promise delivery dates, and to obtain a release from liability in the event of failure to deliver. In fact, Aero pointed out that when Dow bought another plane from Aero's competitor, it accepted the same terms as it now claims are unconscionable.

We hold that under the circumstances of this case, Paragraph 4 was not unreasonable or unconscionable. . . .

We hold that Aero, at no time, promised to deliver an aircraft to Capitol on a specified date. We further hold that in any event Aero successfully limited its liability by including Paragraph 4. Therefore, we reverse the judgment Capitol has obtained against Aero.

QUESTIONS AND CASE PROBLEMS

1. *B* purchased a television set from *S*. There was something wrong with the color, and *S*'s serviceman was not able to correct the defect in *B*'s home. The serviceman told *B* that the defect could be corrected if he took the set to his shop. *B* refused to allow this and declared that he canceled the sale. Was he entitled to do so? [Wilson v Scampoli, (Dist Col App) 228 A2d 848]
2. After a sales contract was made, the seller's factory was destroyed by fire. The seller and the buyer then agreed to cancel the contract. Thereafter the seller's factory was rebuilt, and the buyer demanded that the seller perform the contract. Was the seller required to do so? [Goddard v Ishikawajima-Harima Heavy Industries Co., 29 App Div 2d 754, 287 NYS2d 901]
3. A seller sold goods to a buyer on credit. The buyer did not pay for the goods. The seller claimed that the title to the goods revested in him because of the buyer's default. Was he correct? [Jordan v Butler, 182 Neb 626, 156 NW2d 778]
4. Carta bought from Barker, a dealer, a bicycle that was manufactured by the Union Cycle Co. He took it home for his minor daughter. Sandra, a guest at the Carta home, was injured while using the bicycle. Suit was brought against the town of Cheshire, claiming that it had defectively maintained the road, and against the manufacturer, claiming that the bicycle was defectively constructed. The manufacturer, Union Cycle, defended on the ground that Sandra had not given it notice of the defect in the bicycle as required by UCC § 2-607. Decide. [Tomczuk v Town of Cheshire, 26 Conn Supp 219, 217 A2d 71]
5. Wolosin purchased a vegetable and dairy refrigerator case from the Evans Manufacturing Corp. Evans sued Wolosin for the purchase price. Wolosin raised as a defense a claim for damages for breach of warranty. The sales contract provided that Evans would replace defective parts free of charge for one year and that "this warranty is in lieu of any and all other warranties stated or inferred, and of all other obligations on the part of the manufacturer, which neither assumes nor authorizes anyone to assume for it any other obligations or liability in connection with the sale of its products." Evans claimed that it was only liable for replacement of parts. Wolosin claimed that the quoted clause was not sufficiently specific to satisfy the requirement of UCC § 2-719. Decide. [Evans Mfg. Corp. v Wolosin, (Pa) 47 Luzerne County Leg Reg 238]

6. The buyer of a truck noticed on the first day he drove it that the speed control was defective and that the truck used excessive oil. He continued to use the truck and made several payments. Five months later he demanded that the seller take the truck back. Decide. [Hudspeth Motors, Inc. v Wilkinson, 238 Ark 410, 382 SW2d 191; Marbelite Co. v Philadelphia, 208 Pa Super 256, 222 A2d 443]
7. The buyer of goods at an auction sale did not pay for and take the goods. The auctioneer sued the buyer for the amount of the buyer's bid. Was the buyer liable for that amount? [French v Sotheby & Co., (Okla) 470 P2d 318]
8. McInnis purchased a tractor and scraper as new equipment of current model from the Western Tractor & Equipment Co. The written contract stated that the seller disclaimed all warranties and that no warranties existed except as were stated in the contract. Actually, the equipment was not the current model but that of the prior year. Likewise, the equipment was not new but had been used for 68 hours as a demonstrator model and then the hour meter had been reset to zero. The buyer sued the seller for damages. The latter defended on the ground that all liability for warranties had been disclaimed. Was this defense valid? [McInnis v Western Tractor & Equipment Co., 63 Wash 2d 652, 388 P2d 562]
9. Skopes Rubber Corp. purchased skin-diving suits from the United States Rubber Co. The sale was made on the basis of a sample on which the vinyl coating on the suits had been hand applied and was smooth. The suits that were delivered were wrinkled because the vinyl had been machine applied. In use, the suits split at the wrinkle lines. Skopes returned the first installment of the suits because of this defect. He then sued United States Rubber Co. for breach of warranty. It raised the defense that by returning the first installment, Skopes had rescinded the contract and could not thereafter sue for damages. Was this correct? [Skopes Rubber Corp. v United States Rubber Co., (CA1 Mass) 299 F2d 584]
10. Chaplin purchased a walk-in hardening box from Bessire & Co. for approximately $7,000. In effect, it was an insulated room for the storage of ice cream and similar products. It was especially manufactured for Chaplin and installed in the fall of 1957. It developed leaks at once, and Bessire made repairs and guaranteed that it would work properly, which it did during that winter, but in the summer of 1958 it developed other defects which required a modification of the corrective repairs that had been made the fall before. The box worked through the cold months of 1958 and 1959, but in the spring it developed leaks again. In May, 1959, a fuse blew, and within a few hours the temperature of the box rose 30 degrees causing the contents to spoil. Bessire refused to take the box back. Chaplin sued Bessire for breach of warranty, claiming the right to rescind the contract, to recover payments paid on the contract, and to recover special damages for lost merchandise. During the course of the lawsuit, Chaplin made unsuccessful attempts to sell the box. Bessire defended on the ground that Chaplin had delayed too long before seeking to rescind and that, by attempting to sell the box, he lost any right of rescission. Decide. [Chaplin v Bessire & Co., (Ky App) 361 SW2d 293]

28 Nature, Kinds, and Parties

§ **28:1. Definition.** *Commercial paper* includes written promises (such as promissory notes) or orders to pay money (such as checks or drafts) that may be transferred by the process of negotiation. Much of the importance of commercial paper lies in the fact that it is more readily transferred than ordinary contract rights and that the transferee of commercial paper may acquire greater rights than would an ordinary assignee. A person who acquires a commercial paper may therefore be subject to less risk.

§ **28:2. Functions of Commercial Paper.** Commercial paper often serves as a substitute for money. (See p. 573, Kensil v Ocean City.) When a person pays a debt by check, he is using a commercial paper. He might have paid in cash, but for convenience and possibly for safety, he used commercial paper. Such payment is usually conditional upon the instrument being paid.[1]

Commercial paper may create credit. If a debtor gives his creditor a promissory note by which he agrees to pay him in 60 days, that is the same as an agreement that the creditor willl not attempt to collect the claim until 60 days later.

§ **28:3. Kinds of Commercial Paper.** Commercial paper falls into four categories: (1) promissory notes, (2) drafts or bills of exchange, (3) checks, and (4) certificates of deposit.

(1) Promissory Notes. A *negotiable promissory note* is an unconditional promise in writing made by one person to another, signed by the maker, engaging to pay on demand or at a definite time a sum certain in money to order or to bearer.[2] It may be described more simply as a transferable written promise by one person, the *maker*, to pay money to another, the *payee*.

If the promissory note is payable "on demand," that is, immediately, it may be used as a substitute for money. If it is not payable until a future time, the payee in effect extends credit to the maker of the note for the period of time until payment is due.

Special types of promissory notes include secured notes and judgment notes. A *mortgage note* is secured by a mortgage on property that can be foreclosed if the note is not paid when due. A *collateral note* is accompanied by collateral security given to the payee by the borrower. Thus, a

---

[1] UCC § 3-802(1); Makel Textiles v Dolly Originals, (NYS) 4 UCCRS 95.
[2] UCC § 3-104(1).

person borrowing money might give the lender certain property, such as stocks or bonds, to hold as security for the payment of the note.

A *judgment note* contains a clause which gives the holder the right to enter a judgment against the maker if the note is not paid when due. Most states either prohibit or limit their use.[3]

(2) ***Drafts.*** A *negotiable draft* or *bill of exchange* is an unconditional order in writing addressed by one person to another, signed by the person giving it, requiring the person to whom it is addressed to pay on demand or at a definite time a sum certain in money to order or to bearer.[4] In effect,

$ 300 00 Albany, New York June 14 1975
one year after date I promise to pay to
the order of Clifford Thomas
Three hundred Dollars
Payable at Community State Bank
with interest at 6 %.
No. 17 Due June 14, 1976 James Dexter

Promissory Note

Parties: maker (buyer, borrower, or debtor)—James Dexter; payee (seller, lender, or creditor)—Clifford Thomas.

$ 500.00 Des Moines, Iowa March 6 1975
Thirty days after date PAY TO THE
ORDER OF Freedom National Bank
Five hundred DOLLARS
VALUE RECEIVED AND CHARGE TO ACCOUNT OF
TO John R. Nolan
No. 12 Iowa City, Iowa Lorraine C. Scott

Draft (Bill of Exchange)

Drawer (seller or creditor)—Scott; drawee (buyer or debtor)—Nolan; payee (seller's or creditor's bank)—Freedom National Bank.

---

[3] The power to confess judgment is prohibited by the UCCC in consumer transactions, §§ 2.415, 3.408. It is also likely that the doctrine of Sniadach v Family Finance Corp., 395 US 337, prohibiting the prejudgment attachment of wages, will be expanded to prohibit powers to confess judgment, at least with respect to consumer transactions. If that should occur, powers to confess judgment would be invalid everywhere as a matter of constitutional law without regard to whether the UCCC had been adopted.

[4] UCC § 3-104(1).

it is an order by one person upon a second person to pay a sum of money to a third person. The person who gives the order is called the *drawer* and is said to draw the bill. The person on whom the order to pay is drawn is the *drawee*. The person to whom payment is to be made is the payee. The drawer may designate himself as the payee.

The drawee who is ordered to pay the money is not bound to do so unless he accepts the order. After he accepts, he may be identified as the *acceptor*. From the practice of "accepting" a bill of exchange, the term "acceptance" is sometimes applied to these instruments.

(a) SIGHT AND TIME DRAFTS. A *sight draft* is one that is payable on sight or when the holder presents it to the drawee for payment. A *time draft* is payable at a stated time after sight, such as "30 days after sight" or "30 days after acceptance," or at a stated time after a certain date, such as "30 days after date" (of instrument).

(b) DOMESTIC AND INTERNATIONAL BILLS. If a draft is drawn and payable in the same state, or is drawn in one state and payable in another, it is a *domestic bill*. If it appears on the face of the instrument that it was drawn in one nation but is payable in another, it is an *international bill of exchange* or a foreign draft.

(c) TRADE ACCEPTANCES. A time draft may be sent by a seller of goods to the buyer, as drawee, with the understanding that the buyer will accept the draft, thereby assuming primary liability for its payment. This type of paper is a *trade acceptance*. Its advantage to the seller lies in the fact that he can "sell" or discount the trade acceptance. He can thus convert his contract claim against the buyer into money more readily than he could assign his account receivable against the buyer. Generally the seller or the seller's agent retains possession of a bill of lading, warehouse receipt, or other document that is necessary to obtain possession of the goods, such document being delivered to the buyer when he "accepts" the trade acceptance. The advantage to the buyer in the trade acceptance lies in the fact that he, in effect, buys on credit since he obtains the goods on the strength of his signature on the trade acceptance.

(3) Checks. A *check* is a draft drawn on a bank payable on demand.[5] It is an order by a depositor (the drawer) upon his bank (the drawee) to pay a sum of money to the order of another person (the payee). A check is always drawn upon a bank as drawee and is always payable upon demand.

(a) CASHIER'S CHECKS. A *cashier's check* is drawn by a bank upon itself, ordering itself to pay the stated sum of money to the depositor or to the person designated by him. The depositor requests his bank to issue a

---

[5] § 3-104(2)(b).

cashier's check for a given amount, which amount either the depositor pays the bank or the bank charges against the depositor's account. The depositor then forwards the cashier's check, instead of his own, to the seller or creditor.

(b) BANK DRAFTS. A *bank draft* is in effect a check drawn by one bank upon another bank in which the first bank has money on deposit, in the same way that a depositor draws a check upon his own bank. It is commonly used for the same purpose as a cashier's check.[6]

(4) Certificates of Deposit. A *certificate of deposit* is an instrument issued by a bank that acknowledges the deposit of a specific sum of money and promises to pay the holder of the certificate that amount, usually with interest, when the certificate is surrendered.[7]

§ 28:4. Parties to Commercial Paper. A note has two original parties—the maker and the payee; and a draft or a check has three original parties—the drawer, the drawee, and the payee. In addition to these original parties, a commercial paper may have one or more of the parties described under (4) through (9) of this section.

(1) Maker. The *maker* is the person who writes out and creates a promissory note. If the paper is not a promissory note this person has a different name, as the drawer of a check. It is essential to bear in mind the distinction between a maker and a drawer for the reason that the liability of the maker is primary while that of a drawer is secondary.

(2) Drawer. The *drawer* is the person who writes out and creates a draft. This includes bills of exchange, trade acceptances, and checks. The liability of a drawer is secondary.

(3) Payee. The *payee* is the person named on the face of the paper to receive payment. In "pay to the order of John Jones," the named person, John Jones, is the payee.

A payee has no rights in the paper until it is delivered to him. He is not liable on the paper in any way until he transfers the paper or receives payment.

(4) Indorser.[8] A person who owns a commercial paper may transfer it to another person by signing his name on the back of the instrument and delivering it to the other person. When he does so, he is an *indorser.* Thus, if a check is made payable to the order of *P* to pay a bill owed to him, *P* may indorse it to *E* to pay a debt that *P* owes *E*. In such a case *P*, who

[6] Perry v West, 110 NH 351, 266 A2d 849.

[7] A certificate of deposit "is an acknowledgment by a bank of receipt of money with an engagement to repay it," as distinguished from a note, which "is a promise other than a certificate of deposit." UCC § 3-104(2)(c),(d).

[8] The form *endorse* is commonly used in business. The form *indorse* is used in the UCC.

was the payee of the check since it was originally made payable to him, is now also an indorser.

*(5) **Indorsee.*** The person to whom an indorsement is made is called an *indorsee.* He in turn may indorse the instrument; in that case he is also an indorser.

*(6) **Bearer.*** The person in physical possession of a commercial paper which is payable to bearer is called a *bearer.*

*(7) **Holder.*** A *holder* is a person in possession of a commercial paper which is payable at that time either to him, as payee or indorsee, or to bearer. A holder may be (a) an ordinary holder, (b) a holder for value, or (c) a holder in due course.

(a) HOLDER FOR VALUE. Ordinarily a commercial paper is given to a person in the course of business in return for or in payment for something. If the holder gives consideration for the instrument or takes it in payment of a debt, he is a *holder for value.* Thus, if an employee is paid wages by check, he is a holder for value of the check since he received it in payment of wages earned and due. If he indorses the check to his landlord to pay the rent, the landlord becomes the holder for value.

A person may receive a commercial paper without giving anything for it. Thus, when an aunt gives her niece a check for $100 as a birthday present, the niece becomes the owner or holder, but she has not given anything for the check and she is not a holder for value.

(b) HOLDER IN DUE COURSE. A person who becomes a holder of the paper under certain circumstances is given a favored standing and is immune from certain defenses. He is termed a *holder in due course.* A person becoming the holder of an instrument at any time after it was once held by a holder in due course is described as a *holder through a holder in due course.* He is ordinarily given the same special rights as a holder in due course.

*(8) **Accommodation Party.*** A person who becomes a party to a commercial paper in order to add the strength of his name to the paper is called an *accommodation party.* If he is a maker, he is called an accommodation maker; if an indorser, an accommodation indorser. For example, *M* applies to a bank for a loan and is willing to give the bank a promissory note naming it as payee. The bank may be unwilling to lend money to *M* on the strength of his own promise. It may be that *C,* who has a satisfactory credit standing, will sign the note as a comaker with *M.* If *C* does this for the purpose of bolstering *M's* credit, he signs for accommodation and is an accommodation maker.

An accommodation party is liable for payment of the paper regardless of whether he signs the paper merely as a friend or because he is paid for doing so.[9] When the paper is taken for value before it is due, the accommodation party is liable in the capacity in which he signed, even though the holder knows of his accommodation character.[10]

The accommodation party (*C*) is not liable to the party accommodated (*M*).[11] If the accommodation party is required to pay the instrument, he may recover the amount of the payment from the person accommodated. (See p. 573, Simson v Bilderbeck.)

(9) Guarantor. A *guarantor* is a person who signs a commercial paper and adds a statement that he will pay the instrument under certain circumstances. Ordinarily this is done by merely adding "payment guaranteed" or "collection guaranteed" to the signature of the guarantor on the paper.

The addition of "payment guaranteed" or similar words means that the guarantor will pay the instrument when due even though the holder of the paper has not sought payment from any other party. "Collection guaranteed" or similar words means that the guarantor will not pay the paper until after the holder has sought to collect payment from the maker or acceptor and has been unable to do so. In such a case the holder must first obtain a judgment against the maker or acceptor, which judgment remains unpaid because the sheriff cannot find sufficient property of the debtor in question to pay it, or the debtor must be insolvent.[12]

When a guarantor makes a guarantee of payment, he is liable upon his guarantee and it is immaterial that payment was not demanded from the primary debtor nor that the debtor had sufficient assets to pay the paper.[13]

If the meaning of the guaranty is not clear, it is construed as a guaranty of payment. For example, when an indorser adds a statement that the paper is "guaranteed" or adds the word "guarantor" after his signature without specifying whether it is payment or collection which is guaranteed, the indorser is deemed to be a guarantor of payment, with the consequence that the holder of the paper may proceed directly against such guarantor without first proceeding against any other party on the paper.[14]

The liability of a guarantor is as extensive as that of the original debtor.

§ 28:5. Liability of Parties. A person who by the terms of the instrument is absolutely required to pay is primarily liable. For a note, the maker is primarily liable; for a draft, the acceptor (the drawee who has accepted) is primarily liable. A guarantor of payment is primarily liable in any case. Other parties are either secondarily or conditionally liable, as in the case of

---

[9] UCC § 3-415(1).

[10] Seaboard Finance Co. v Dorman, 4 Conn Cir 154, 227 A2d 441.

[11] UCC § 3-415(5). United Refrigerator Co. v Applebaum, 410 Pa 210, 189 A2d 253.

[12] UCC § 3-416(1)(2). The guaranty written on the commercial paper is binding without regard to the requirements of a local statute of frauds. § 3-416(6).

[13] Hartung v Architects Hartung/Odle/Burke, Inc., — Ind App —, 301 NE2d 240.

[14] Sadler v Kay, 120 Ga App 758, 172 SE2d 202.

an indorser, or they are not liable in any capacity. A person who transfers the paper but does not sign it is not liable for its payment.[15]

§ **28:6. Interest and Discount.** When a commercial paper is used as a credit device, it may provide for the payment of interest. For example, a six-month note dated March 1 for a loan of $1,000 may specify 7 percent interest. Payment on September 1 would be $1,035 ($1,000 principal plus $35 interest). Interest that is deducted in advance is known as *discount.* When there is discount, the borrower receives $965 ($1,000 less discount of $35) and then repays $1,000 at maturity.

[15] § 3-401(1). Such a person, however, may be bound by certain warranties that bind any person who transfers commercial paper.

CASES FOR CHAPTER 28

Kensil v Ocean City

89 NJ Super 342, 215 A2d 43 (1965)

Stainton bid at a public auction of public lands conducted by Ocean City, New Jersey. Kensil, the second highest bidder, brought suit against Ocean City and Stainton to set aside the sale on the ground that Stainton did not comply with the statute which required that a deposit of 20 percent of the bid be "paid" by the successful bidder. He based his claim on the fact that Stainton delivered to Ocean City an uncertified check drawn on an account which was insufficient to meet the check at that moment, although the check was thereafter honored by the drawee bank. From an adverse decision, Kensil appealed.

FOLEY, J.A.D. . . . A check can be a negotiable instrument without constituting immediate payment. Under the Code, and even at common law, . . . a check is not payment until presented and paid, unless the parties agree otherwise. Since there was no such agreement here, the conclusion is inescapable that the check was not payment at the time of sale, but a promise of future payment at the time of presentation. . . .

Despite the conclusion that the deposit technically was not paid at the time of the sale, the record shows that payment was made when the check was duly presented. This fact reveals plaintiff's entire argument as an objection, at best, to a technical defect in defendant's compliance, which the city could waive since the check did not in any way affect fair competitive bidding which is the fundamental objective of a bidding statute. It is well settled in this State that minor and inconsequential variations and technical omissions may be the subject of waiver. . . .

Moreover, we are satisfied that defendant city soundly exercised its discretion in accepting defendants' bid. The plain fact is that the city obtained exactly what it sought, namely, the highest bid in open competitive bidding, payment of a required deposit upon presentation of a check therefor in the ordinary course of business, and full and final settlement within the time period specified in the notice of sale. In these circumstances we would ill serve the public interests which the bidding statutes unrelentingly seek to protect if we were to strike down defendants' bid and reinstate bid of plaintiff as he requests, at the expense of depriving the taxpayers of Ocean City of $50,000.

[Judgment affirmed.]

Simson v Bilderbeck, Inc.

76 NMex 667, 417 P2d 803 (1966)

Bilderbeck, Inc., borrowed money from a bank. As part of the transaction, it signed a

promissory note for the amount of the loan, which note was signed by Simson as an accommodation maker. When the note was due, Bilderbeck failed to make payment. The note was paid by Simson, who then sued Bilderbeck for reimbursement of the amount that he had paid. From a decision in Simson's favor, Bilderbeck appealed.

WOOD, J. . . . The trial court found that plaintiff signed the note as an accommodation maker. Appellants [Bilderbeck and other parties] assert that in his capacity as accommodation maker plaintiff is primarily liable on the note. . . . Being primarily liable, they contend that when he paid the note he paid his own obligation. They contend that this payment discharged the note. . . .

When plaintiff paid the note, under [UCC] § 3-415(5) . . . he had a right of recourse against Bilderbeck, Inc. on the note. Under [§] 3-603(2) . . . plaintiff could pay the note and obtain the right of a transferee upon surrender of the note to him. Under [§] 3-201(1) . . . plaintiff had the rights of the transferor bank, there being no issue as to fraud or illegality on the part of plaintiff or that plaintiff was a prior holder. Thus, as to the note, plaintiff succeeded to the bank's rights and could sue Bilderbeck, Inc. on the note. By the terms of our statutes, the note was not discharged when paid by plaintiff, the accommodation maker. . . .

Thus, in answer to appellants' contention, as between plaintiff and Bilderbeck, Inc., plaintiff was not principally liable. As between those two parties, when plaintiff paid the note to the bank, he [acquired] the bank's rights against Bilderbeck, Inc.

[Judgment affirmed.]

QUESTIONS AND CASE PROBLEMS

1. Cortner and Wood, in payment for certain sheep, executed and delivered an instrument whereby they promised to pay $2,000 to the order of W. C. Thomas. Thomas signed his name on the back and delivered the note to Fox, at the latter's bank in Lewisburg, Tennessee. Who of the foregoing parties, if any, are properly described as (a) payee, (b) maker, (c) drawer, (d) indorser, (e) acceptor, (f) drawee, and (g) indorsee? [Fox v Cortner, 145 Tenn 482, 239 SW 1069]
2. Kay was the holder of a note. Sadler indorsed the note and added "Guarantor" after his name. When Kay demanded payment, Sadler claimed that he was not required to pay until Kay had first obtained a judgment against the primary party. Was he correct? [Sadler v Kay, 120 Ga App 758, 172 SE2d 202]
3. Herbert Simms owed money to Personal Finance, Inc., on a note signed only by him. Personal Finance brought a lawsuit against both Herbert and Katie, his wife. What liability, if any, did she have on the note? [Personal Finance, Inc. v Simms, (La App) 123 So2d 646]
4. Herdlicka and Thieda executed a promissory note as makers. The latter was, in fact, an accommodation party. Subsequently Kratovil, the holder of the note, agreed with Herdlicka to extend the time for paying the note and to reduce the monthly payments that were to be made. When the note was not paid in full, Kratovil sued Thieda who claimed that he was released by the fact that the obligation of Herdlicka had been changed by the extension of time, which was made without Thieda's consent. Decide. [Kratovil v Thieda, 62 Ill App 2d 234, 210 NE2d 819]
5. *B* wished to pay a bill that he owed to *C* but did not have sufficient money in his bank. He drew a postdated check on his bank account and gave it to

A. *A* then gave *B* a check drawn on *A*'s bank account for the amount of *B*'s check. When *A* was sued on his check by *C*, *A* claimed that he was an accommodation party. Was he correct? [Midtown Commercial Corp. v Kelner, 29 App Div 2d 349, 288 NYS2d 122]

6. McCornick & Co. brought suit against the Gem State Oil Co. on an instrument that bore the following notation in the margin:

> The obligation of the acceptor of this bill arises out of the purchase of goods from the drawer. Upon the acceptor hereof suspending payment, giving a chattel mortgage, suffering a fire loss, [or] disposing of his business, . . . this [instrument], at the option of the holder, shall immediately become due and payable.

What kind of an instrument was this? [McCornick & Co. v Gem State Oil & Products Co., 38 Idaho 470, 222 P 286]

7. Fowler, Allen, and Flanagan signed a promissory note as makers. When Majors sued them on the note, Flanagan claimed that he had signed for the accommodation of the other parties and therefore was only liable as a surety (undertaking to become primarily liable for the obligation), and that his liability was therefore not determined under the law governing negotiable instruments. Was he correct? [Flanagan v Majors, 85 Ga App 31, 67 SE2d 786]

8. Montgomery Ward & Co. brought suit against Newman upon the following writing:

> Rutland, Vt.
>
> A. Newman
> Dear Sir:
>
> Please pay Montgomery Ward & Co. ($800.00) Eight Hundred Dollars and charge to my account.
>
> This is the second payment on plumbing and heating for three houses, 82-84 Killington Avenue, 15 Vernon Street.
>
> C. W. Young

Does this writing meet the tests of a commercial paper as stated in the definitions of a promissory note, a draft, or a check? [Montgomery Ward & Co. v Newman, 104 Vt 115, 157 A 824]

9. Ruth Laudati obtained a loan from Brown University and signed a promissory note for the repayment of the loan. Her mother, Josephine, guaranteed payment of the note. When the note was not paid, Brown University sued Josephine. She raised the defense that Brown had not sued Ruth. Was this a valid defense? [Brown University v Laudati, — RI —, 320 A2d 609]

29 Negotiability

§ 29:1. Requirements of Negotiability. In order to be negotiable, an instrument must be (1) in writing and (2) signed by the maker or drawer; it must contain (3) a promise or order (4) of an unconditional character (5) to pay in money (6) a sum certain; (7) it must be payable on demand or at a definite time; and (8) it must be payable to order or bearer.[1] (9) If one of the parties is a drawee, he must be identified with reasonable certainty.

In addition to these formal requirements, the instrument usually must be delivered or issued by the maker or drawer to the payee or the latter's agent with the intent that it be effective and create a legal obligation.

If an instrument is not negotiable, the rights of the parties are governed by the general body of contract law.[2] (See p. 584, Frank v Hershey Nat. Bank.)

Thus, a letter to a creditor by which the three signers of the letter guarantee the debt of a third person is not a negotiable instrument within Article 3, and the liability of the signers is not governed by UCC § 3-118.[3]

(1) Writing. A commercial paper must be in writing. Writing includes handwriting, typing, printing, and any other method of setting words down. The use of a pencil is not wise because such writing is not as durable as ink and the instrument may be more easily altered. A commercial paper may be partly printed and partly typewritten with a handwritten signature.

(a) PAROL EVIDENCE. As the commercial paper is in writing, the parol evidence rule applies. This rule prohibits modifying the instrument by proving the existence of a conflicting oral agreement alleged to have been made before or at the time of the execution of the commercial paper. Thus, an instrument payable on a certain date cannot be shown by parol evidence to be payable at a later date, nor can parol evidence be introduced to prove the existence of an option to renew the instrument.

Likewise, parol evidence is not admissible to contradict the unconditional promise of a note by showing that repayment was to be made only from the

[1] UCC § 3-104(1).

[2] Business Aircraft Corp. v Electronic Communications, (Tex Civ App) 391 SW 2d 70. Note, however, that if the nonnegotiability results from the fact that the instrument is not payable to order or bearer, it is governed by Article 3 of the Code with the limitation that there cannot be a holder in due course of such paper. UCC § 3-805.

[3] United States Gypsum Co. v Sampson, (Tex Civ App) 496 SW2d 687.

profits of a particular enterprise.[4] Similarly, parol evidence is not admissible to show by an oral agreement that demand paper is not payable on demand.[5]

(2) Signature. The instrument must be signed by the maker or drawer. His signature usually appears at the lower right-hand corner of the face of the instrument, but it is immaterial where the signature is placed. If the signature is placed on the instrument in such a manner that it does not in itself clearly indicate that the signer was the maker, drawer, or acceptor, however, he is held to be only an indorser.

The signature itself may consist of the full name or of any symbol adopted for that purpose. It may consist of initials, figures, or a mark.[6] A person signing a trade or an assumed name is liable to the same extent as though he signed his own name.[7]

In the absence of a local statute that provides otherwise, the signature may be made by pencil, by typewriter, by print, or by stamp, as well as by pen.[8]

(a) AGENT. A signature may be made for a person by his authorized agent.[9] No particular form of authorization to an agent to execute or sign a commercial paper is required.

An agent signing should indicate that he acts in a representative capacity, and he should disclose his principal. When he does both, the agent is not liable if he has acted within the scope of his authority.[10] The representative capacity of an officer of an organization is sufficiently shown when he signs his name and the title of his office either before or after the organization name.[11]

(b) NONDISCLOSURE OF AGENCY. If a person who signs a commercial paper in a representative capacity, such as an officer or other agent of a corporation, executes the instrument in such a way as to make it appear that it is his own act, he is personally bound with respect to subsequent holders, regardless of whether he intended it to be his own act or an act in his representative capacity. (See p. 585, Seale v Nichols.) As to subsequent holders, parol evidence is not admissible to show that it was not intended that the representative or agent be bound or to show that it was intended

---

[4] Venuto v Strauss, (Tex Civ App) 415 SW2d 543.

[5] Eggers v Eggers, 79 SD 233, 110 NW2d 339.

[6] When a signature consists of a mark made by a person who is illiterate or physically incapacitated, it is commonly required that the name of the person be placed upon the instrument by someone else, who may be required to sign the instrument as a witness. Any form of signature is sufficient in consequence of the definition of "signed" as including any symbol executed or adopted by a party with the present intention to authenticate a writing. UCC § 1-201(39).

[7] § 3-401(2).

[8] Katz v Teicher, 98 Ga App 842, 107 SE2d 250.

[9] § 3-403(1).

[10] § 3-403; Childs v Hampton, 80 Ga App 748, 57 SE2d 291.

[11] UCC § 3-403(3).

to bind the undisclosed principal. Such evidence is admissible, however, against the person with whom the officer or agent had dealt.

Thus, parol evidence is admissible as between the immediate parties to show that an individual cosigning with a corporate maker had intended to sign in a representative capacity.[12]

When the representative is personally bound because he fails to disclose his representative capacity, he is jointly and severally liable with the principal. For example, when the name of the corporation appears as maker with the name of its treasurer signed immediately below but without any notation indicating a representative capacity, the treasurer is jointly and severally liable with the corporation.[13]

(c) PARTIAL DISCLOSURE OF AGENCY. The instrument may read or the agent may sign in a way that either identifies his principal or discloses the agent's representative capacity; but both are not done. In such a case, the agent is personally liable on the instrument to third persons acquiring the instrument; but if sued by the person with whom he dealt, he may prove that it was intended that the principal should be bound.[14]

(3) Promise or Order to Pay. A promissory note must contain a promise to pay money.[15] No particular form of promise is required; the intention as gathered from the face of the instrument controls. If the maker uses such phrases as "I certify to pay" or "the maker obliges himself to pay," a promise is implied; but a mere acknowledgment of a debt, such as a writing stating "I.O.U.," is not a commercial paper.

A draft or check must contain an order or command to pay money.[16] As in the case of a promise in a note, no particular form of order or command is required.

(4) Unconditional. The promise or order to pay must be unconditional. For example, when an instrument makes the duty to pay dependent upon the completion of the construction of a building or upon its placement in a particular location, the promise is conditional and the instrument is nonnegotiable. A promise to pay "when able" is generally interpreted as being conditional.[17]

The use of a term of politeness, such as "please," before an otherwise unconditional order to pay does not destroy the effect of the order within the meaning of the requirements for negotiability. But if the effect of the provision

[12] Speer v Friedland, (Fla App) 276 So2d 84.
[13] Perez v Janota, 107 Ill App 2d 90, 246 NE2d 42; UCC § 3-118(e).
[14] UCC § 3-403(2)(b).
[15] § 3-104(1)(b).
[16] § 3-104(1)(b).
[17] A minority of states regard such a promise as requiring payment within a reasonable time and as therefore being an absolute promise. Mock v First Baptist Church, 252 Ky 243, 67 SW2d 9.

is only to seek payment of money or to request it if certain facts are true, the "order" to pay is conditional and the instrument is nonnegotiable.

Whether a promise or an order to pay is conditional or unconditional is determined from an examination of the instrument itself. An unconditional or absolute promise in an instrument cannot be shown to be conditional by a provision found in a separate written agreement or as part of an oral agreement.

An order for the payment of money out of a particular fund, such as ten dollars from next week's salary, is conditional.[18] If, however, the instrument is based upon the general credit of the drawer and the reference to a particular fund is merely to indicate a source of reimbursement for the drawee, such as "charge my expense account," the order is considered to be absolute.[19]

A promise or order that is otherwise unconditional is not made conditional by the fact that it "is limited to payment out of a particular fund or the proceeds of a particular source, if the instrument is issued by a government or governmental agency or unit; or is limited to payment out of the entire assets of a partnership, unincorporated association, trust, or estate by or on behalf of which the instrument is issued." [20]

(5) Payment in Money. A commercial paper must call for payment in *money*, that is, any circulating medium of exchange which is legal tender at the place of payment. It is immaterial, as far as negotiability is concerned, whether it calls for payment in a particular kind of current money. If the order or promise is not for money, the instrument is not negotiable. For example, an instrument which requires the holder to take stock or goods in lieu of money is nonnegotiable.

An instrument is also nonnegotiable when the promise or order to pay money is coupled with an agreement by the maker or drawee to do something else, unless that agreement will make it easier for the holder of the instrument to collect the money due on the instrument. A provision of the latter type does not impair negotiability because the effect of its inclusion is to make the paper more attractive to a purchaser and thus it encourages the exchange or transfer of the commercial paper.

(6) Sum Certain. The instrument must not only call for payment in money but also for a sum certain. (See p. 586, Universal C.I.T. Credit Corp. v Ingel.) Unless the instrument is definite on its face as to how much is to be paid, there is no way of determining how much the instrument is worth.

When there is a discrepancy between the amount of money as written in words and the amount as set forth in figures on the face of the instrument, the former is the sum to be paid. If the words that indicate the amount are ambiguous or uncertain, reference may be made to the amount in figures to

---

[18] UCC § 3-105(2)(b).

[19] § 3-105(1)(f); Rubio Savings Bank v Acme Farm Products Co., 240 Iowa 547, 37 NW2d 16.

[20] UCC § 3-105(1)(g),(h).

determine the amount intended.[21] When there is an uncertainty of this type in connection with a check, a bank officer or teller may telephone the drawer in order to learn just what amount was intended before payment.

The fact that the instrument may require certain payments in addition to the amount specified as due does not make the instrument nonnegotiable when such additional amounts come within any of the following categories:

(a) INTEREST. A provision for the payment of interest does not affect the certainty of the sum, even though the interest rate increases upon default in payment.[22] In contrast, a note payable "with interest at bank rates" is not for a sum certain because bank rates of interest are not constant, and a paper calling for payment of bank rate interest is therefore not negotiable.[23]

(b) INSTALLMENTS. A provision for payment in installments does not affect certainty. Nor is certainty affected when the installment provision is coupled with a provision for acceleration of the date of payment for the total amount upon default in any payment.

(c) EXCHANGE. A provision for the addition of exchange charges does not affect the certainty of the sum payable since its object is in effect to preserve the constancy of the value involved. In this connection, the fact that the money due on the instrument is stated in a foreign currency does not make the instrument nonnegotiable.[24]

(d) COLLECTION COSTS AND ATTORNEY'S FEES. The certainty of the sum is not affected by a provision adding collection costs and attorney's fees to the amount due, although general principles of law may place a limit upon the amount that can be recovered for such items.

(e) DISCOUNT AND ADDITION. The certainty of the sum and the negotiability of the instrument are not affected by a provision that allows a discount if earlier payment is made or which increases the amount due if late payment is made.[25]

(7) Time of Payment. A commercial paper must be payable on demand or at a definite time. If it is payable "when convenient," the instrument is nonnegotiable because the day of payment may never arrive. (See p. 587, Williams v Cooper.) An instrument payable only upon the happening of a particular event that may never happen is not negotiable. For example, a provision to pay when a person marries is not payable at a definite time

[21] § 3-118(c).
[22] § 3-106(1)(b).
[23] A. Alport & Son, Inc. v Hotel Evans, Inc., 65 Misc 2d 374, 317 NYS2d 937.
[24] § 3-107(2). The UCC follows banking practice in stating that an instrument payable in a foreign currency calls for the payment of a sum certain of money which, in the absence of contrary provision, is the number of dollars that the foreign currency will purchase at the buying sight rate on the due date or demand date of the instrument.
[25] UCC § 3-106(1)(c).

since that particular event may never occur. It is immaterial whether the contingency in fact has happened, because from an examination of the instrument alone it still appears to be subject to a condition that may never happen.

(a) DEMAND. An instrument is payable on demand when it is expressly specified to be payable "on demand;" or at sight or upon presentation, that is, whenever the holder tenders the instrument to the party required to pay and demands payment; or when no time for payment is specified.[26] (See p. 587, Davis v Dennis.) To illustrate the last point, when a note is completely executed except that the time for payment and the lines indicating payment by installments are left blank, the full amount of the note is payable on demand, as opposed to the contention that no amount is payable.[27]

(b) DEFINITE TIME. The time of payment is definite if it can be determined from the face of the instrument. An instrument satisfies this requirement when it is payable (1) on or before a stated date (see p. 588, Ferri v Sylvia), (2) at a fixed period after a stated date, (3) at a fixed period after sight, (4) at a definite time subject to any acceleration, (5) at a definite time subject to extension at the option of the holder, (6) at a definite time subject to extension to a further definite date at the option of the maker or acceptor, or (7) at a definite time subject to an extension to a further definite date automatically upon or after the occurrence of a specified act or event.[28]

An instrument payable in relation to an event which though certain to happen will happen on an uncertain date, such as a specified time after death, is not negotiable.[29]

(8) Order or Bearer. A commercial paper must be payable to order or bearer.[30] This requirement is met by such expressions as "Pay to the order of John Jones," "Pay to John Jones or order," "Pay to bearer," and "Pay to John Jones or bearer." [31] The use of the phrase "to the order of John Jones" or "to John Jones or order" is important in showing that the person executing the instrument is indicating that he does not intend to restrict payment of the instrument to John Jones and that he does not object to paying anyone to whom John Jones orders the paper to be paid. Similarly, if the person executing the instrument originally states that it will be paid "to

---

[26] § 3-108.

[27] Master Homecraft Co. v Zimmerman, 208 Pa Super 401, 222 A2d 440.

[28] UCC § 3-109(1).

[29] § 3-109(2).

[30] Henry v Powers, (Tex Civ App) 447 SW2d 738. While an instrument not payable to order or bearer is not commercial paper, it is nevertheless governed by Article 3 of the UCC, except that there cannot be a holder in due course. UCC § 3-805.

[31] It is not necessary that the instrument actually use the word "order" or "bearer." Any other words indicating the same intention are sufficient. It has been held that the words "pay to holder" could be used in place of "order" or "bearer" without affecting the negotiability of the instrument. UCC §§ 3-110, 3-111.

bearer" or "to John Jones or bearer," he is not restricting the payment of the instrument to the original payee. If the instrument is payable "to John Jones," however, the instrument is not negotiable.

A money order which bears the printed words "payable to," after which the name of the payee is to be written, is not a negotiable instrument because it is payable to a specified or named payee and not to the order of a named payee or bearer.[32]

(a) ORDER PAPER. An instrument is *payable to order* when by its terms it is payable to the order or assignee of any person specified therein with reasonable certainty (Pay to the order of H. F. Rousch), or to a person so described or his order (Pay to H. F. Rousch or his order).[33]

(b) BEARER PAPER. An instrument is *payable to bearer* when by its terms it is payable (1) to bearer or the order of bearer, (2) to a specified person or bearer, or (3) to "cash," or "the order of cash," or any other designation that does not purport to identify a person.[34]

An instrument payable to order and indorsed in blank becomes payable to bearer and may be negotiated by delivery alone until specially indorsed.[35]

(9) Drawee. In the case of a draft or check, the drawee must be named or described in the instrument with reasonable certainty.[36] This requirement, which is based upon practical expediency, is designed to enable the holder of the instrument to know to whom he must go for payment.

When there are two or more drawees, they may be either joint drawees (*A* and *B*) or alternative drawees (*A* or *B*).[37]

§ 29:2. Effect of Provisions for Additional Powers or Benefits. Certain provisions in an instrument that give the holder certain additional powers and benefits may or may not affect negotiability.[38]

(1) Collateral. The inclusion of a power to sell collateral security, such as corporate stocks and bonds, upon default does not impair negotiability. An instrument secured by collateral contains as absolute a promise or order as an unsecured instrument. Negotiability is not affected by a promise or power to maintain or protect collateral or to give additional collateral,[39] or to make the entire debt due, if the additional collateral is not supplied.

---

[32] Nation-Wide Check Corp. v Banks, (Dist Col App) 260 A2d 367.

[33] An instrument is also payable to order when it is conspicuously designated on its face as "exchange" or the like, and names a payee. UCC § 3-110(1).

[34] UCC § 3-111.

[35] § 3-204(2).

[36] § 3-102(1)(b).

[37] § 3-102(1)(b). The instrument is nonnegotiable if there are successive drawees. *Successive drawees* exist when, if one drawee fails to pay, the holder is required to go to the next drawee for payment rather than proceed at once against secondary parties.

[38] UCC § 3-112.

[39] § 3-112(1)(c).

*(2) **Acceleration.*** A power to accelerate the due date of an instrument upon a default in the payment of interest or of any installment of the principal, or upon the failure to maintain or provide collateral does not affect the negotiability of an instrument. However, a power to accelerate "at will" or when a person "deems himself insecure" must be exercised in good faith.[40]

*(3) **Confession of Judgment.*** Negotiability is not affected by a provision authorizing the entry of a judgment by confession upon a default. If the holder of the instrument is authorized to confess judgment at any time, whether before maturity or not, however, the instrument is generally nonnegotiable.[41]

*(4) **Waiver of Statutory Benefit.*** State statutes commonly provide that when a person is sued for a debt, a certain amount or kind of his property is exempt from the claim. If the party who executes a commercial paper promises to waive his rights under such a statute in order that it will be a little easier to collect the amount due, negotiability is ordinarily not affected. A waiver of this kind is void in some states, however.

*(5) **Requirement of Another Act.*** A provision authorizing the holder to require an act other than the payment of money, such as the delivery of goods, makes the instrument nonnegotiable.[42]

§ 29:3. Additional Documents. The fact that a separate document is executed that gives the creditor additional protection, as by a mortgage on real estate or the right to repossess goods sold to the maker of the instrument, does not impair the negotiability of the commercial paper.

§ 29:4. Immaterial Provisions. The addition or omission of certain other provisions has no effect upon the negotiability of a commercial paper that is otherwise negotiable.

A commercial paper is not affected by the omission of the date. In such case it is regarded as carrying the date of the day on which it was executed and delivered to the payee. If the date is essential to the operation of the instrument, as when the instrument is payable a stated number of days or months "after date," any holder who knows the true date may insert that date.

When a commercial paper is dated, the date is deemed prima facie to be the true date, whether the date was originally inserted or was thereafter added.[43] A commercial paper may be antedated or postdated, provided that

---

40 § 1-208.

41 Bittner v McGrath, 186 Pa Super 477, 142 A2d 323. See p. 568.

42 UCC § 3-104(1)(b).

43 § 3-114(3). If the wrong date is inserted, the true date can be proved unless the holder is a holder in due course or a holder through a holder in due course, in which case the date, even though wrong, cannot be contradicted.

is not done to defraud anyone. The holder acquires title as of the date of delivery without regard to whether this is the date stated in the instrument.

It is immaterial so far as negotiability is concerned (1) whether an instrument bears a seal; (2) whether it fails to state that value has been given; or (3) whether it recites the giving of value without stating its nature or amount, although local law may require such a recital.

Some forms of checks provide a special space in which the drawer can note the purpose for which the check is given or set forth the items discharged by the check. Some statutes require that certain instruments state the purpose for which they are given in order to help avoid fraud. The Uniform Commercial Code does not repeal any statute requiring the nature of the consideration to be stated in the instrument.[44] The fact that a trade acceptance recites that "the transaction which gives rise to this instrument is the purchase of goods by the acceptor from the drawer" does not affect its negotiability.[45]

Negotiability is not affected by a provision that by indorsing or cashing the instrument, the person receiving it takes it in full settlement of a specified claim or of all claims against the drawer.[46]

---

[44] Compare UCC § 3-112(1)(a),(2).
[45] Federal Factors Inv. v Wellbanks, 241 Ark 44, 406 SW2d 712.
[46] UCC § 3-112(1)(f).

CASES FOR CHAPTER 29

Frank v Hershey National Bank

269 Md App 138, 306 A2d 207 (1973)

The East Penn Broadcasting Company borrowed money from the Hershey National Bank. A promissory note representing the loan was executed "payable to the Hershey National Bank." The note authorized the confession of judgment at any time. The note was signed with the typewritten name of the borrowing corporation and the handwritten signatures of three individuals. One of these was Frank. When the loan was not paid, the bank sued him and the others on the note. They raised certain defenses under the Uniform Commercial Code. The bank claimed that the UCC was not applicable. From a judgment for the bank, Frank and the others appealed.

DIGGES, J. . . . The parties have proceeded . . . on the assumption that these notes were negotiable and therefore governed by the provisions of the UCC. We find the notes to be non-negotiable and the UCC to be inapplicable. Therefore, the liability of the parties is determined as a matter of simple contract law. . . .

. . . To be negotiable, an instrument must, among other requirements, "be payable to order or to bearer." (§ 3-104(1)(d)) The absence of these magic words renders a note non-negotiable. Here, the notes in question contain just a "promise to pay to the Hershey National Bank" the amount due. However, § 3-805 entitled "instruments not payable to order or to bearer" specifies that: "This subtitle *applies* to any instrument whose terms do not preclude transfer and *which is otherwise negotiable within this subtitle* but which is not payable to order or to bearer, except that there can be no holder in due course of such an instrument." . . . The official comments to this section indicate that: "This section covers the 'non-negotiable instrument.' As it has been used by most courts, this term has been a technical one of art. It does not refer to a writing, such as a note containing an express condition, which is not negotiable and is entirely outside of the scope of this Subtitle and to be treated as a simple contract. It refers to a particular type of instrument which meets all requirements as to form of a negotiable instrument except that it is not payable to order or to bearer."

Thus, while these notes could still be governed by the Code even though they lack words of negotiability, they must meet all other "requirements as to form of a negotiable instrument" except for that. The notes here do not conform to this standard. The UCC § 3-112(1)(d) provides that the negotiability of an instrument is not affected by "a term authorizing confession of judgment on the instrument if it is not paid when due." We held in Stankovich v Lehman, 230 Md 426, 187 A2d 309 (1963), a case decided under the Negotiable Instruments Act, that the authorization to confess judgment "as of any term" permitted entry of judgment at any time prior to the maturity of the note and therefore destroyed negotiability. . . . "It would seem logical that if the statute, as it does, preserves negotiability only if the confession of judgment is at or after maturity, the warrant to confess must expressly, or by necessary implication, restrict its exercise to that time if the note is to be negotiable, and that if the warrant is silent as to the time when it can be exercised, the reasonable implication must be that it can be done at any time. Most of the cases involving this general area of the law have arisen in Pennsylvania, and the Courts of that State have held that notes containing stipulations for confession of judgment without specification or limitation as to time are, like those expressly authorizing judgment prior to maturity, non-negotiable." . . .

Since these non-negotiable notes are not governed by the UCC, their effect is, as already noted, determined under principles of simple contract law.

[Judgment affirmed.]

Seale v Nichols

(Tex) 505 SW2d 251 (1974)

Nichols was the president of Mr. Carl's Fashions, Inc. The corporation did business under the name of The Fashion Beauty Salon. Nichols executed a promissory note which appeared to be signed by The Fashion Beauty Salon and by Nichols. There was nothing on the note to indicate that he signed in a representative capacity. When Seale sued Nichols on the note, the latter raised the defense that he had signed as president of the corporation. The defense was sustained and Seale appealed.

GREENHILL, C.J. . . . The promissory note in question is on a printed form and begins, "I, we or either of us, promise to pay [to Seale]." It is signed as follows:

THE FASHION BEAUTY SALON
Carl V. Nichols (typewritten)
Carl V. Nichols (handwritten)

. . .

. . . Nichols filed the following affidavit: "My name is Carl V. Nichols, and I served as President of Mr. Carl's Fashion, Inc., a Texas corporation, doing business as the Fashion Beauty Salon at 2115 Sherry Lane, Dallas, Texas, from the date of its incorporation, January 14, 1960, and I signed the promissory note attached to Plaintiff's Original Petition marked Exhibit 'A' in the capacity of officer of such corporation and in behalf of such corporation and not in my personal capacity.". . .

[UCC § 3-403 provides:] (b) An authorized representative who signs his own name to an instrument (1) is personally obligated if the instrument neither names the *person represented* nor shows that the representative *signed in a representative capacity;* (2) *except as otherwise established between the immediate parties,* is personally obligated if the instrument names the person represented but does not show that the representative signed in a representative capacity, or if the instrument does not name the person represented but does show that the representative signed in a representative capacity. . . .

Nichols asserts that his signature comes within the meaning of subsection (b)(2) in that the person he represented *was* named (though with an assumed name), but the note did not expressly show his representative capacity. He contends that this subsection, therefore, entitles him to prove his representative capacity by parol evidence. . . .

Nichols' asserted defense is that he signed the note, not as an individual, but as a representative of Mr. Carl's Fashion, Inc. . . .

Section (2) of subsection (b) Article 3.403 says that "except as otherwise established" between the parties, the person (the maker here) "is personally obligated. . . ." And Section (c) of the same article being, "Except as otherwise established. . . ." It might well be contended that to avoid personal responsibility under Section (2) above, the person resisting a summary judgment should be required to come forward with summary judgment proof of facts which would "otherwise establish" his representative capacity, such as prior dealings of the parties, or some understanding between both parties to the instrument. The summary judgment proof of the maker Nichols here is only that *he* intended to sign, and did sign, in a representative capacity. He does not suggest, in his affidavit, that it was "understood between the parties," or "it was agreed between the parties," or that prior dealings between the parties established "circumstances otherwise." Neither does his affidavit say that he disclosed his representative capacity to Seale. If an agent discloses his representative capacity to the payee of the note, and the payee then accepts the note, it is our opinion that this might be sufficient summary judgment proof to raise an issue of fact to "otherwise establish" his representative capacity and defeat the payee's motion for summary judgment. If the holder of the note then desires to negative any "circumstances otherwise," he could bring forward such proof.

The . . . Code does not speak to these matters; and in such event, the prior Texas law should be applied. Texas law provides that in order for an agent to avoid liability for his signature on a contract, he must *disclose* his intent to sign as a representative to the other contracting party. Uncommunicated intent will not suffice. . . .

Again viewing Nichols' affidavit broadly, it states that he signed the note as president of the corporation, thus clearly indicating his subjective intent to sign as an agent. However, nowhere does Nichols say that he disclosed his intent to Seale. Nor does his statement ". . . I signed the promissory note . . . in the capacity of officer of such corporation and in behalf of such corporation and not in my personal capacity," intimate that this intended capacity was communicated to Seale. . . .

[Judgment reversed.]

Universal C.I.T. Credit Corp. v Ingel

347 Mass 119, 196 NE2d 847 (1964)

Ingel made a contract with Allied Aluminum Associates for the installation of aluminum siding on his home. He signed a promissory note which stated that group credit life insurance would be obtained by the holder of the note without additional charge to the customer. Later the note was transferred to a finance company, Universal C.I.T. Credit Corp. When it brought suit against Ingel, he claimed that the note was nonnegotiable because of the above insurance provision and also because the note provided for the payment of "interest after maturity at the highest lawful rate." From a judgment in favor of Universal, Ingel appealed.

SPIEGEL, J. . . . The defendants contend that the note was non-negotiable as a matter of law and, therefore, any defense which could be raised against Allied may also be raised against the plaintiff. They argue that the note contained a promise other than the promise to pay, [and] failed to state a sum certain. . . .

It appears that the note was a form note drafted by the plaintiff. . . . We are . . . satisfied that the insurance clause in the note does not affect negotiability under [UCC] § 3-104(1)(b) since it is clear that the "no other promise" provision refers only to promises by the maker.

The provision in the note for "interest after maturity at the highest lawful" rate does not render the note nonnegotiable for failure to state a sum certain as required by [UCC] § 3-104(1)(b). We are of [the] opinion that after maturity the interest rate is that indicated [by general statute] since in this case there is no agreement in writing for any other rate after default. This being the case, we do not treat this note differently from one payable "with interest." The latter note would clearly

be negotiable under . . . [UCC] § 3-118(d). . . .
[Judgment affirmed.]

Williams v Cooper

(Tex Civ App) 504 SW2d 564 (1973)

Williams gave Cooper a promissory note which stated that he would pay him a stated sum of money "at the earliest possible time after date." Cooper sued Williams on the note. Williams raised the defense that the note was a negotiable demand note, in which case Cooper's suit was barred by a four-year statute of limitations. Cooper claimed that the writing was not a demand note and was not negotiable and therefore a different and longer statute of limitations applied and the suit was not barred. The lower court entered judgment for Cooper. Williams appealed.

BROWN, J. . . . The language "at the earliest possible time" precludes the instrument from being one payable at a definite time. Therefore, for the instrument to be negotiable, it must be payable on demand. The instrument not being payable at sight or on presentation it could only be payable on demand if the legal effect of "at the earliest possible time" is the same as if no time for payment was stated in the instrument. . . .

We hold "at the earliest possible time" is not equivalent to no time for payment being stated in the instrument. Such phrases as "as soon as circumstances will permit me"; "when he was able"; "as soon as he could" have been held conditions upon which the promise to pay depends. . . . "It is quite elementary that an instrument payable upon a condition which does not import an absolute liability is not payable until that condition has happened. . . ."

We overrule Williams' contention that the instrument is a demand note. . . .

[Judgment affirmed.]

Davis v Dennis

(Tex Civ App) 448 SW2d 495 (1969)

Dennis brought suit against Davis on a promissory note. The latter raised the defense that the suit was barred by the statute of limitations. The trial judge held that the action was not barred and Davis appealed.

McKAY, J. . . . Appellee [Dennis] brought suit against appellant [Davis] on September 2, 1966, on a note dated March 25, 1961. The portion of the note we are concerned with was as follows:

"$3,000.00 Palestine, Texas, March 25 A. D. 1961.

"For Value Received, I, we, or either of us, the undersigned, promise to pay to Archie A. Dennis or Archie A. Dennis, Jr. or order, the sum of Three Thousand and no/one-hundred Dollars, with interest from date at the rate of nine (9) percent per annum, interest payable biweekly both principal and interest payable at South Texas Producers Association, Houston, Texas.

"This note is payable in Seventy-eight (78) installments of Thirty-eight dollars and forty-six cents (38.46) each. *This is the note mentioned in the mortgage covering 15 head of dairy cows bearing the same date. . . .*"

The trial court entered judgment for appellee in the total amount of $3,168.79, which amount included unpaid principal of $2,115.72, interest of $765, and attorney's fees of $288.07.

In his findings of fact, the trial court found (1) that said note did not mature until June 25, 1964; (2) that it was due and payable in 78 biweekly installments of $38.46 each, the first payment to be due on or before April 10, 1961, and each two weeks thereafter; (3) that defendant made payments on said note in the approximate time and dates of said note up until November 25, 1963, and made a lump sum payment on that date leaving a balance due of $2,150.72; (4) that had all payments been made on said installment note, the final installment would have matured on November 10, 1964.

The court's conclusions of law were that (1) limitation would not have begun to run until four years after November 10, 1964, and (2) that plaintiff filed his suit less than two years after the maturity of the final installment on said installment note. Appellant excepted and objected to the court's findings and conclusions on the grounds of no evidence or insufficient evidence.

Appellant's points 1 through 6 are directed to the trial court's findings and conclusions. Points 7 and 8 are directed to appellant's plea of the four-year Statute of Limitation. We believe the case may be decided upon the limitation question.

The note does not provide for any fixed time of payment. It provides "interest payable biweekly" and "This note is payable in Seventy-eight (78) installments of Thirty-eight dollars and forty-six cents (38.46) each." Section 3-108, Uniform Commercial Code, . . . provides: "Instruments payable on demand include those payable at sight or on presentation and *those in which no time for payment is stated.*" (Emphasis added.) This Act was effective September 1, 1967, but Article 5932, Section 7, V.A.T.S., in effect prior to the Uniform Commercial Code and Negotiable Instruments Act had a like provision. It has been held from early Texas cases that if no time for payment is stated in a note, it becomes a demand note. . . . If it was a demand note, it was payable on demand and actionable immediately without demand. . . .

Since the note provided "interest payable biweekly," the question arises whether that language makes the note payable at a fixed time. We believe it does not.

In 10 C.J.S. § 247, page 743, we find this statement: ". . . The fact that notes indicating no time of payment are expressed to be payable with interest annually does not prevent them from being payable on demand. . . ."

In another paragraph on the same page, it is stated: "Paper is none the less payable on demand because it contains a provision as to interest, as where it is payable 'on demand' with interest after a specified time, of 'after maturity,' with interest 'annually,' 'with interest within six months from date,' 'without interest,' or 'without interest during the life of the promisor.' " . . .

We are also of the opinion that the language "this note is payable in Seventy-eight (78) installments of Thirty-eight dollars and forty-six cents (38.46) each . . ." does not affect the demand character of the note because there is no maturity date or dates or fixed time of payment of any installment.

The note being a demand note, the four-year Statute of Limitation would begin to run from the date of its execution or delivery. The note in this case, executed March 25, 1961, was barred by the Statute of Limitation on September 2, 1966, the date suit was filed. . . .

The judgment of the trial court is reversed and judgment is here rendered for appellant.

Ferri v Sylvia

100 RI 270, 214 A2d 470 (1965)

Ferri made a note payable to the order of Sylvia "within ten years after date." Within less than that time Sylvia sued for the money due, claiming that the note was uncertain and therefore parol evidence could be admitted to show that she could have the money any time she needed it. From a judgment in Sylvia's favor, Ferri appealed.

JOSLIN, J. . . . The payment provisions of the note are not uncertain nor are they incomplete.

At the law merchant it was generally settled that a promissory note or a bill of exchange payable "on or before" a specified date fixed with certainty the time of payment. . . . The same rule has been fixed by statute first under the negotiable instruments law . . . and now pursuant to the Uniform Commercial Code. The Code in § 3-109(1) reads as follows: "An instrument is payable at a definite time if by its terms it is payable (a) on or before a stated date or at a fixed period after a stated date. . . ."

" 'Within' a certain period, 'on or before' a day named, and 'at or before' a certain day are equivalent terms, and the rules of construction apply to each alike."

We . . . equate the word "within" with the phrase "on or before." So construed, it fixes both the beginning and the end of a period, and insofar as it means the former it is applicable to the right of a maker to prepay, and insofar as it means the latter it is referable to the date the instrument matures. We hold that the payment provision of a negotiable instrument payable "within" a stated period is certain as well as complete on its face and that such an instrument does not mature until the time fixed arrives.

For the foregoing reasons it is clear that the parties unequivocally agreed that the plaintiff could not demand payment of the note until the expiration of the ten-year period. It is likewise clear that any prior or contemporaneous oral agreements of the parties relevant to its due date were so merged and integrated within the writing as to prevent its being explained or supplemented by parol evidence. . . .

[Judgment reversed.]

QUESTIONS AND CASE PROBLEMS

1. *A* borrowed $1,000 from *B* and gave *B* a promissory note which required *A* to repay the aomunt in monthly installments of $100. The note further provided that upon any default by *A*, *B* could accelerate the unpaid balance of the note which would thereupon become due. After *A* had paid two monthly installments, he missed the third installment. *B* then sued *A* for the balance due on the note. *A* raised the defense that *B* had not notified him that he accelerated the debt, and therefore *B* could only recover $100. Was *A* correct? [Smith v Davis, (Tex Civ App) 453 SW2d 340]

2. Nation-Wide Check Corp. sold money orders through local agents. A customer would purchase a money order by paying an agent the amount of the desired money order plus a fee. The customer would then sign his name on the money order as the remitter or sender and would fill in the name of the person who was to receive the money following the printed words "Payable to." In a lawsuit between Nation-Wide and Banks, a payee on some of these orders, the question was raised whether these money orders were negotiable. Decide. [Nation-Wide Check Corp. v Banks, (Dist Col App) 260 A2d 367]

3. A contractor signed a note promising to pay to the order of the holder $10,000 payable from "jobs now under construction." Was the note negotiable? [Webb & Sons, Inc. v Hamilton, 30 App Div 2d 597, 290 NYS2d 122]

4. A depositor sent a telegram to his bank directing it to pay a specified amount to the order of a named person. The bank made the payment as directed. Later it was claimed that the bank had acted improperly because a printed bank check was not used. Decide. [United Milk Products v Lawndale National Bank, (CA7 Ill) 392 F2d 876]

5. James G. Dornan was the treasurer and vice-president of Chet B. Earle, Inc. On behalf of the corporation he executed a promissory note that was signed in the following manner:

Corporate	Chet B. Earle, Inc.	(Seal)
Seal	James G. Dornan	(Seal)

The holder of the note, an indorsee, sued Dornan on the ground that he was personally liable as a comaker. He defended on the ground that he was merely an agent for the corporation and was not personally liable. Was this defense valid? [Bell v Dornan, 203 Pa Super 562, 201 A2d 324]

6. Snowden signed a note as maker for $10,000 and delivered it to the Franklin National Bank, directing the bank to loan $10,000 to a corporation, which was then done by the bank. When the bank sued Snowden on the note, he objected on the ground that he had signed the note to accommodate the corporation which had received the loan and that the bank had assured

him that since the corporation had adequate collateral for the loan of $10,000, the bank would never look to Snowden for payment of his note. Was Snowden liable? [Snowden v Franklin National Bank, (CA5 Tex) 338 F2d 995]

7. Mar obtained a cashier's check from the Washington Mutual Savings Bank. Apparently the check was lost by Mar. It was claimed that the check was not negotiable because it had been lost before it had been negotiated. Was this correct? [Mar v Washington Mutual Savings Bank, 64 Wash 2d 793, 394 P2d 367]

8. Cortis made a contract for storm windows and gave the seller a promissory note in payment. The note promised to pay $3,400 in installments as set forth in the schedule of payments stated in the note. The schedule of payments, however, was left blank. Was the note void? [Liberty Aluminum Products Co. v Cortis, (Pa) 14 D&C 2d 624, 38 Wash County 223]

9. Deegan drew a check payable to the order of Eslava in the amount of $6.80. Thereafter Nelson was prosecuted for forgery on the ground that she had altered this check to make the figures read $66.80. No change was made to the amount of the check stated in words. Was Nelson guilty of forgery? [Iowa v Nelson, 248 Iowa 915, 82 NW2d 724]

10. Mr. and Mrs. Gulas took care of Dulak. When the latter desired to draw checks, Mr. Gulas would prepare the checks and Dulak would sign them. Six days before Dulak died, he told Mr. and Mrs. Gulas that he was obligated to their two sons for $3,000 each, requested his checkbook, and directed Gulas to prepare a check for each son for $3,000. Dulak then signed each check, and the two checks were torn from the checkbook but were not separated from each other. The checks were replaced in the checkbook, which was then put in the dresser drawer in Dulak's room where it was usually kept. After his death, Mrs. Gulas showed the checkbook and the checks to the executors under Dulak's will, and they kept possession of the checks. The two sons then sued to enforce the payment of the checks. Decide. [Dulak's Will, 209 NYS2d 928]

11. Von Dolcke gave Gross a promissory note payable on or before a fixed date. Gross wrote and signed a notation on the instrument that if the amount could not be paid in full when due, "a partial payment will be acceptable of any amount available and the note extended from time to time until it can be paid in full." Was this a negotiable instrument? [Gross v Von Dolcke, 313 Mich 132, 20 NW2d 838].

30 Transfer

NEGOTIATION

The method of negotiating an instrument depends upon the terms of the instrument or its indorsement. If it is order paper, it can be negotiated only by both indorsement and delivery. If it is bearer paper, it may be negotiated by transfer of possession alone.

§ 30:1. Methods of Negotiation.

(1) Negotiation of Order Paper. An instrument payable to order may be negotiated only by the indorsement of the person to whom it is payable at the time and delivery by him or with his authorization. The indorsement must be placed on the instrument by the person to whom it is then payable.

(a) MULTIPLE PAYEES AND INDORSERS. Ordinarily one person is named as payee by the instrument, but two or more payees may be named. In that case, the instrument may specify that it is payable to any one or more of them or that it is payable to all jointly. If nothing is specified, the instrument is payable to all of the payees [1] and they are *joint payees*. For example, if the instrument is made payable "to the order of *A* and *B*," the two persons named are joint payees. The importance of this kind of designation is that it requires the indorsement of both *A* and *B* to negotiate the instrument further. (See p. 602, State National Bank v Sumco Engineering, Inc.) This protects *A* against the action of *B*, and vice versa. Each knows that the other cannot secretly negotiate the instrument and pocket the proceeds. This rule does not apply, however, when the payees are partners or when one person is authorized to act for all and he indorses for all.

Joint payees or joint indorsees who indorse are deemed to indorse jointly and severally.[2] If the instrument is payable to *alternate payees* or if it has been negotiated to alternate indorsees, as *A* or *B*, it may be indorsed and delivered by either of them.

The UCC declares only the rights of joint payees with respect to the paper. Non-Code principles would determine the rights of the joint payees as between themselves. Thus, a check payable to husband and wife is initially "their" property but when it is a check for a refund of income taxes for a year in which the husband alone produced the income on which the tax had

---

1 UCC § 3-116.
2 § 3-118(e).

been paid, the husband is entitled to the proceeds of the check to the exclusion of the wife.[3]

(b) AGENT OR OFFICER AS PAYEE. The instrument may be made payable to the order of an officeholder. For example, a check may read, "Pay to the order of the Receiver of Taxes." Such a check may be received and negotiated by the person who at the time is the Receiver of Taxes. This is a matter of convenience since the person writing the instrument is not required to find out the name of the Receiver of Taxes at that time.

If the instrument is drawn in favor of a person as "Cashier" or some other fiscal officer of a bank or corporation, it is prima facie payable to the bank or corporation of which he is such an officer, and may be negotiated by the indorsement of either the bank or corporation, or of the named officer.[4] If drawn in favor of an agent, it may similarly be negotiated by the agent or his principal.[5]

(c) PARTIAL NEGOTIATION. A negotiation of part of the amount cannot be made.[6] The entire instrument must be negotiated to one person or to the same persons. If the instrument has been partly paid, however, the unpaid balance may be transferred by indorsement. This is proper since the entire amount then due, although it is only a portion of the original amount due, is being transferred.

(d) MISSING INDORSEMENT. Although order paper cannot be negotiated without indorsement, it can be assigned to another without indorsement. In such a case, the transferee has the same rights as the transferor; and if he gave value for the paper, he also has the right to require that the transferor indorse the instrument unqualifiedly to him and thereby effect the negotiation of the instrument.

(2) Negotiation of Bearer Paper. Any commercial paper payable to bearer may be negotiated by merely transferring possession, that is, by handing it over to another person.[7] (See p. 603, Westerly Hospital v Higgins.) This is true not only when the instrument expressly states that it is payable to bearer, but also when the law interprets it as being payable to bearer, as in the case of a check payable to the order of "Cash."

Although bearer paper may be negotiated by such transfer, the one to whom it is delivered may insist that the bearer indorse the paper so as to impose upon him the liability of an indorser. This situation most commonly arises when a check payable to "Cash" is presented to a bank for payment.

---

[3] In re Boudreau, (DC Conn) 350 F Supp 644 (husband's trustee in bankruptcy held entitled to check).

[4] § 3-117(a).

[5] § 3-117.

[6] § 3-202(3). The partial negotiation is not a nullity but is given the effect of a partial assignment.

[7] UCC § 3-202(1).

Because bearer paper can be negotiated by a transfer alone, a thief, a finder, or an unauthorized agent can pass title as though he owned or had the right to negotiate the instrument. This means that the use of bearer paper should be avoided whenever possible.

(3) Time for Determining Character of Paper. The character of the paper is determined as of the time when the negotiation is about to take place, without regard to what it was originally or at any intermediate time. Accordingly, when the last indorsement is special, the paper is order paper without regard to whether it was bearer paper originally or at any intermediate time, and the holder cannot ignore or strike out intervening indorsements, or otherwise treat it as bearer paper because it had once been bearer paper.

§ 30:2. Forged and Unauthorized Indorsements. A forged or unauthorized indorsement is by definition no indorsement of the person by whom it appears to have been made and, accordingly, the possessor of the paper is not the holder when the indorsement of that person was necessary for effective negotiation of the paper to the possessor.

If payment of commercial paper is made to one claiming under or through a forged indorsement, the payor is ordinarily liable to the person who was the rightful owner of the paper (see p. 604, Gast v American Casualty Co.), unless such person is estopped or barred by his negligence or other conduct from asserting any claim against the payor.

§ 30:3. The Impostor Rule. The "forgery" of the payee's name in an indorsement is as effective as if the payee had made or authorized the "signature" when the case comes within one of the three impostor situations: (1) an impostor has induced the maker or drawer to issue the instrument to him or a confederate in the name of the payee; (2) the person signing as, or on behalf of, the drawer intends that the named payee shall have no interest in the paper; or (3) an agent or employee of the drawer has given the drawer the name used as the payee intending that the latter should not have any interest in the paper.

The impostor rule does not apply when there is a "valid" check to an actual creditor for a correct amount owed by the drawer and someone thereafter forges the payee's name, even though the forger is an employee of the drawer.[8]

The first situation is present when a person impersonates the holder of a savings account and, by presenting a forged withdrawal slip to the savings bank, gets the bank to issue a check payable to the bank's customer but which it hands to the impersonator in the belief that he is the customer.[9]

---

[8] Snug Harbor Realty Co. v First National Bank, 105 NJ Super 572, 253 A2d 581, affirmed 54 NJ 95, 253 A2d 545.

[9] Fidelity and Deposit Co. v Manufacturers Hanover Trust Co., (NY Civil Court) 63 Misc 2d 960, 313 NYS2d 823.

The second situation arises when the owner of a checking account, who wishes to conceal the true purpose of his taking money from the bank, makes out a check purportedly in payment of a debt which in fact does not exist.

The last situation is illustrated by the case of the employee who fraudulently causes his employer to sign a check made to a customer or other person, whether existing or not, but the employee does not intend to send it to that person but rather intends to forge the latter's indorsement, to cash the check, and to keep the money for himself.

The impostor rule applies when the person whose name is forged is a co-payee of the paper as well as when he is the sole payee.[10]

These impostor case provisions are based upon the social desire to place the loss upon the party who could have prevented it through the exercise of greater care to protect subsequent holders of an instrument who have no reason to know of any wrongdoing.

Even when the impostor's indorsement is effective, he is subject to civil or criminal liability for making such an indorsement.[11]

§ 30:4. Effect of Incapacity or Misconduct on Negotiation. A negotiation is effective even though (1) it is made by a minor or any other person lacking capacity; (2) it is an act beyond the powers of a corporation; (3) it is obtained by fraud, duress, or mistake of any kind; (4) or the negotiation is part of an illegal transaction or was made in breach of duty. Under general principles of law apart from the UCC, the transferor in such cases may be able to set aside the negotiation or to obtain some other form of legal relief. If, however, the instrument has in the meantime been acquired by a holder in due course, the negotiation can no longer be set aside.[12]

§ 30:5. Lost Paper. The effect of losing commercial paper depends upon who is suing or demanding payment from whom and whether the paper was order paper or bearer paper when it was lost. If the paper is order paper, the finder does not become the holder because the paper, by definition, is not indorsed and delivered by the person to whom it was then payable. The former holder who lost it is still the rightful owner of the paper, although technically he is not the holder because he is not in possession of the paper.

In some instances the practical solution is for the loser to inform the party who wrote the paper and ask that another commercial paper be drawn or written. Thus, an employee losing his paycheck could request his employer to write another paycheck. Ordinarily the employer would write another check and would notify the bank to stop payment on the first check, which was lost. The drawer may require the person requesting a second

---

[10] Philadelphia Title Insurance Co. v Fidelity-Philadelphia Trust Co., 419 Pa 78, 212 A2d 222.

[11] UCC § 3-405. The rule stated in the text likewise applies to promissory notes although ordinarily the situation arises in connection with checks.

[12] UCC § 3-207.

check to sign an agreement to indemnify the drawer should he sustain any loss by virtue of a demand made on the first check.

If the lost paper is a promissory note, it is less likely that the maker will oblige by executing a new promissory note. In any event, the owner of the lost paper may bring suit on it against any party liable thereon. There is, of course, the practical difficulty of proving just what the lost paper provided and explaining the loss of the paper. The court may also require that the plaintiff suing on the lost instrument furnish the defendant with security to indemnify the defendant in case of his loss by reason of any claim on the lost instrument.[13]

If the paper is in bearer form when it is lost, the finder becomes the holder of the paper, since he is in possession of bearer paper and, as holder, is entitled to enforce payment.

Regardless of the form of the paper, the true owner of the paper can recover its value from the finder if the finder refuses to return it on demand or if he has negotiated it or transferred it to another person, because such act of transferring or negotiating constitutes an unlawful exercise of dominion over the paper that was owned by the prior holder. In the event that the finder is able to collect the amount due on the paper, the rightful owner of the paper is entitled to collect that amount from the finder, by proceeding on the theory that the finder was acting as agent for the true owner in obtaining payment of the paper. The rightful owner has the same right with respect to a thief.

INDORSEMENTS

Commercial paper may be transferred by negotiation or assignment. When a commercial paper is transferred by negotiation, an indorsement is usually necessary.

§ 30:6. Introduction. The person to whom an instrument is payable either on its face or by indorsement or the person in possession of bearer paper may indorse it for the purpose of negotiating it by merely signing his name on it, or he may add certain words or statements as part of his indorsement. By definition, an indorsement is properly written on the back of the instrument.

An indorsement must be written on the commercial paper itself, or, if necessary, on a paper attached to it called an allonge.[14] If there is no space on the paper, the indorsement may be written on another piece of paper provided it is so firmly attached to the commercial paper that it becomes part of it. A signature on a separate paper which is stapled, pinned, or clipped to the commercial paper is not effective as an indorsement.

§ 30:7. Kinds of Indorsements.

(1) Blank Indorsement. When the indorser signs only his name, the indorsement is called a *blank indorsement* since it does not indicate the person

[13] § 3-804.
[14] UCC § 3-202(2).

to whom the instrument is to be paid, that is, the indorsee. A person who is in possession of paper on which the last indorsement is blank is the holder and may sue thereon without proving ownership of the paper.[15] This is the most common form of indorsement because it is the simplest and the easiest to write. It may be a dangerous form, however, since it has the effect of making the instrument payable to bearer and it thereafter can be negotiated by delivery by anyone, even a finder or a thief. Such an indorsement usually may be made with safety on a check when the holder is in a bank where he intends to deposit or cash the check.

The holder of an instrument on which the last indorsement is blank may protect himself by writing above the signature of the blank indorser a statement that the instrument is made payable to him.[16] This is called "completing" the indorsement or "converting" the blank indorsement to a special indorsement by specifying the identity of the indorsee.

Negotiation by a blank indorsement does three things: (a) it passes the ownership of the instrument; (b) it makes certain warranties; and (c) it imposes upon the indorser a secondary liability to pay the amount of the instrument if the maker or drawee fails to do so and certain conditions are then satisfied by the holder.

(a) Liability of Successive Indorsers. Unless they otherwise agree, indorsers are liable to each other in the order in which they indorse, which is presumed to be the order in which their signatures appear on the paper.[17]

This rule of liability of successive indorsers may be overcome, however, by proof that the indorsers had all indorsed as part of one transaction and intended to be co-sureties for the paper, who as between themselves would each be liable for only a proportionate share of the liability.[18]

(2) Special Indorsement. A *special indorsement* consists of the signature of the indorser and words specifying the person to whom the indorser

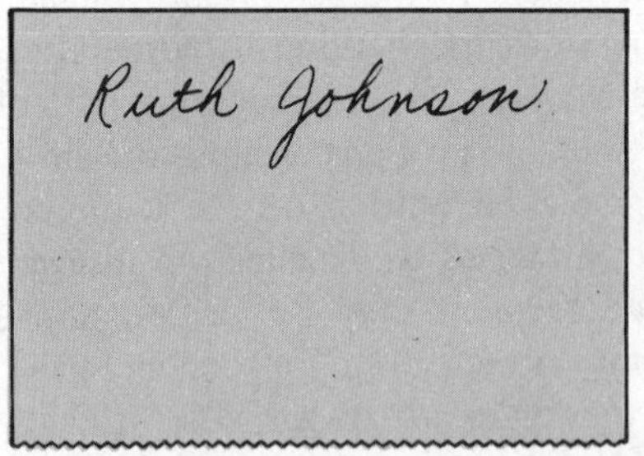

Blank Indorsement

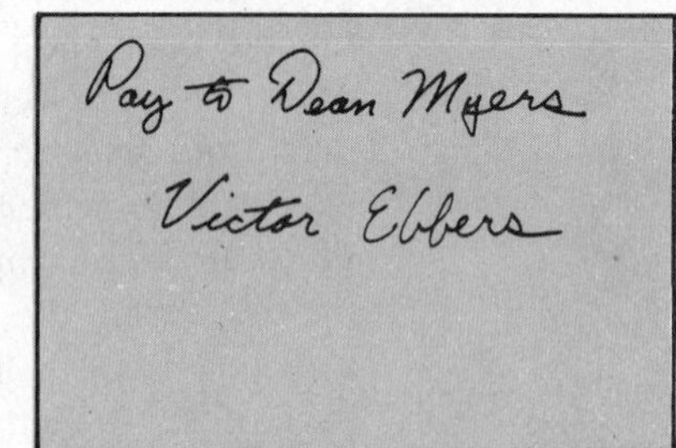

Special Indorsement

[15] First Securities Co. v Schroeder, 351 Ill App 173, 114 NE2d 426.
[16] UCC § 3-204(3).
[17] UCC § 3-414(2).
[18] Gulf Nat. Bank of Lake Charles v Computer Analysis, Inc., (La App) 278 So2d 827 (non-Code).

makes the instrument payable, that is, the indorsee. Common forms of this type of indorsement are "Pay to the order of Robert Hicks, E. S. Flynn" and "Pay to Robert Hicks or order, E. S. Flynn." It is not necessary that the indorsement contain the words "order" or "bearer." Thus, a commercial paper indorsed in the form "Pay to Robert Hicks, E. S. Flynn" continues to be negotiable and may be negotiated further. In contrast, an instrument which on its face reads "Pay to E. S. Flynn" is not negotiable.

When the last indorsement on the instrument is special, both an indorsement and a delivery by or on behalf of the last indorsee is required for further negotiation.[19]

As in the case of the blank indorsement, a special indorsement transfers title to the instrument and results in the making of certain warranties and in imposing a secondary liability upon the indorser to pay the amount of the instrument under certain conditions.

*(3) **Qualified Indorsement.*** A *qualified indorsement* is one that qualifies the effect of a blank or a special indorsement by disclaiming or destroying the liability of the indorser to answer for the default of the maker or drawee. This may be done by including the words "without recourse" in the body of the indorsement, or by using any other words that indicate an intention to destroy the indorser's secondary liability for the default of the maker or drawee.[20]

The qualifying of an indorsement does not affect the passage of title or the negotiable character of the instrument. It merely limits the indorser's liability to the extent of the qualification. Consequently, where an automobile dealer was payee and indorsed his customer's note without recourse, the note was not an obligation of the dealer; and therefore when it was dishonored, the person who guaranteed that the dealer would pay "his obligation" was not liable on the guaranty.[21]

This form of indorsement is most commonly used when the qualified indorser is admittedly a person who has no personal interest in the transaction, as in the case of an attorney or an agent who is merely indorsing to his

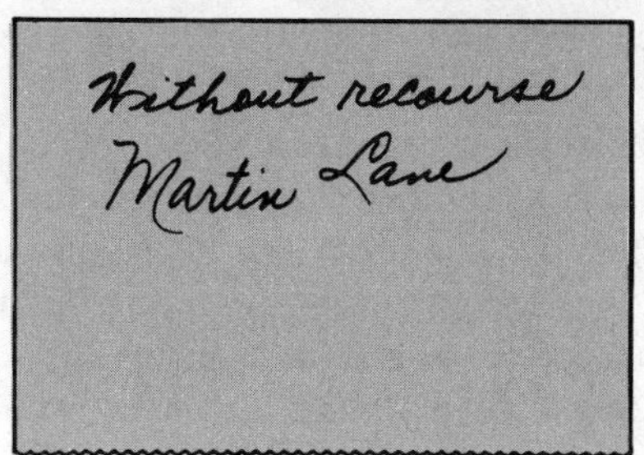

Qualified Indorsement

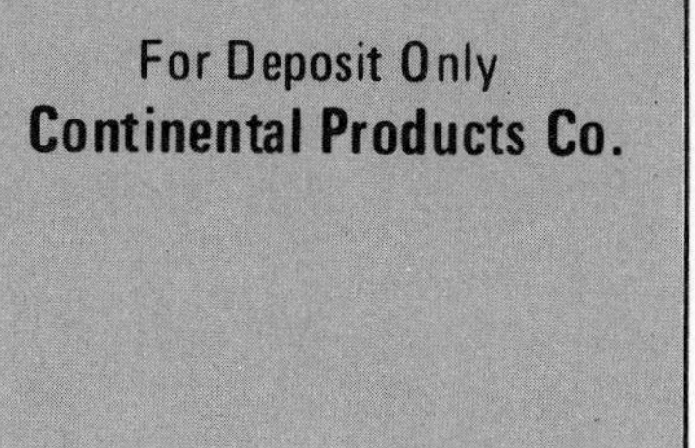

Restrictive Indorsement

[19] UCC § 3-204(1).
[20] § 3-414(1).
[21] Universal C.I.T. Credit Corp. v Love, (La) 279 So2d 182.

client or principal a check made payable to him by a third person. Here the transferee recognizes that the transferor is not a party to the transaction and therefore is not in a position where he should be asked to vouch for the payment of the paper.

*(4) **Restrictive Indorsements.*** A *restrictive indorsement* specifies the purpose of the indorsement or the use to be made of the paper. Restrictive indorsements may be of the following types:

(a) INDORSEMENT FOR DEPOSIT. This indorsement indicates an intent that the instrument be deposited, such as "For deposit only," "For deposit only to the account of John Sacuto" and "Pay to the Springfield National Bank for deposit only." [22]

(b) INDORSEMENT FOR COLLECTION. This indorsement indicates an intention that the instrument be received by the indorsee, usually for the purpose of effecting the collection of the instrument. "For collection only" or "Pay to any bank or banker" [23] are examples of this type of indorsement.

(c) INDORSEMENT PROHIBITING FURTHER NEGOTIATION. The indorsement, "Pay to Harold Singer only," indicates an intent that no further negotiation should occur and is therefore restrictive.[24]

(d) AGENCY OR TRUST INDORSEMENT. An indorsement that makes the indorsee the agent of the indorser, such as "Pay to (indorsee, agent) on account of (indorser, principal)," or which makes the indorsee the owner subject to a trust for another person, such as "Pay to (indorsee, mother) to hold for use of (third person, son)," are restrictive indorsements in that they state that the indorsement is for the benefit of the indorser or another person.[25]

(e) CONDITION AS A PART OF THE INDORSEMENT. An indorsement which indicates that it is to become effective only upon the satisfaction of a particular condition, such as "Pay to Calvin Nash upon completion of Contract #83," is a restrictive indorsement.[26]

A restrictive indorsement does not have the effect of prohibiting further negotiation even though it expressly attempts to do so.[27] In all cases the transferee may therefore be a holder, just as is true under a nonrestrictive indorsement. A bank may ignore and is not affected by the restrictive indorsement of any person except the holder transferring the instrument to the bank or the person presenting it to the bank for payment. However, a *depositary*

[22] § 3-205(c).
[23] § 3-205(c).
[24] § 3-205(b).
[25] § 3-205(d).
[26] § 3-205(a).
[27] § 3-206(1). As to effect of the indorsement, "Pay any bank" or "For deposit," see § 4-201(2).

bank, that is, the one in which the customer deposits the item, and persons not in the bank collection process must recognize the restrictive indorsement to the extent of applying any value given in a manner consistent with the indorsement.[28]

An indorsement "without recourse" is a qualified but not a restrictive indorsement.[29]

§ 30:8. Irregular Kinds of Indorsements. The indorser may make an indorsement that does not fall into any of the standard categories of indorsements. For example, he may write, "I hereby assign all my right, title, and interest in the within note," and then sign his name. The signature in such a case is effective as an indorsement in spite of the added words, on the theory that the indorser actually intended to indorse and was merely attempting to make certain that he transferred his interest.[30]

§ 30:9. Correction of Name by Indorsement. Sometimes the name of the payee or indorsee to a commercial paper is improperly spelled. Thus, H. A. Price may receive a paycheck which improperly is payable to the order of "H. O. Price." If this was a clerical error and the check was intended for H. A. Price, the employee may ask his employer to write a new check payable to him in his proper name.

The payee or indorsee whose name is misspelled may indorse the wrong name, his correct name, or both. A person giving or paying value for the instrument may require both.[31]

This correction of name by indorsement may only be used when it was intended that the instrument should be payable to the person making the corrective indorsement. If there were in fact two employees, one named H. A. Price and the other H. O. Price, it would be illegal as a forgery for one to take the check intended for the other and by indorsing it obtain for himself the benefit or proceeds of the check.

The fact that an irregularity in the name of a party has not been corrected does not destroy the validity of the negotiation, and irregularities in the names are to be ignored unless it is shown that different persons were in fact identified by the different names, as contrasted with the different names merely standing for the one person. Thus, a note had been properly negotiated when it was indorsed "Greenlaw & Sons by George M. Greenlaw," although made payable to "Greenlaw & Sons Roofing & Siding Co.," and there was nothing to show that the two enterprises were not the same firm.[32]

§ 30:10. Bank Indorsements. In order to simplify the transfer of commercial paper from one bank to another in the process of collecting items, "any

---

28 § 3-206(2). Additional limitations are imposed in the case of collection and conditional indorsements, § 3-206(3), and trust indorsements, § 3-206(4).

29 Catalanotto v Associates Discount, (La App) 207 So2d 180.

30 UCC § 3-202(4).

31 § 3-203.

32 Watertown Federal Savings & Loan Ass'n v Spanks, 346 Mass 398, 193 NE2d 333.

agreed method which identifies the transferor bank is sufficient for the item's further transfer to another bank." [33] Thus, a bank may indorse with its Federal Reserve System number instead of using its name.

Likewise, when a customer has deposited an instrument with a bank but has failed to indorse it, the bank may make an indorsement for him unless the instrument expressly requires the payee's personal indorsement. Furthermore the mere stamping or marking on the item of any notation showing that it was deposited by the customer or credited to his account is as effective as an indorsement by the customer would have been.[34] In this way the annoyance and loss of time of returning the instrument to the customer for his indorsement are eliminated.

A personal indorsement is commonly required, however, in the case of paychecks issued by governments and also by some corporations.

ASSIGNMENT OF COMMERCIAL PAPER

In addition to transfer by negotiation, a commercial paper may be transferred by assignment.

§ 30:11. Assignment by Act of the Parties. A commercial paper is regarded as assigned when a person whose indorsement is required on the instrument transfers it without indorsing it. (See p. 608, Waters v Waters.) In such a case the transferee has only the rights of an assignee, and he is subject to all defenses existing against the assignor prior to notice of the assignment. He is entitled, however, to require that the transferor indorse the instrument.[35] If the indorsement is obtained, then the transferee is deemed a holder but only as of the time when the indorsement is made.

§ 30:12. Assignment by Operation of Law. An assignment by operation of law occurs when by virtue of the law the title of one person is vested in another. If the holder of a commercial paper becomes a bankrupt or dies, the title to the instrument vests automatically in the trustee in bankruptcy or in the personal representative of the estate.

WARRANTIES OF TRANSFEROR

The transferor of commercial paper may make an express guarantee. Whether he does so or not, certain warranties are implied.

§ 30:13. Introduction. The transferor, by the act of making the transfer, warrants the existence of certain facts. The warranties of the transferor are not always the same but vary according to the nature of the indorsement he makes or whether he transfers the instrument without indorsement. A distinction is made between warranties arising in connection with acceptance or payment and those arising in connection with transfer. In the case of

---

[33] UCC § 4-206.

[34] § 4-205(1).

[35] § 3-201(3). The indorsement can only be required if the transferee gave value for the paper.

transfer by indorsement, the warranty may run to a subsequent holder; in the case of transfer by delivery only, to the immediate transferee.

§ **30:14. Warranties of Unqualified Indorser.** When the holder of a commercial paper negotiates it by an unqualified indorsement, and receives consideration, the transferor warrants that:

(1) He has a good title, which includes the genuineness of all indorsements necessary to his title to the instrument, or that he is authorized to act for one who has such good title.[36]

(2) His act of transferring the instrument is rightful, independent of the question of his title or authority to act.[37]

(3) The signatures on the instrument are genuine or executed by authorized agents.[38]

(4) The instrument has not been materially altered.[39]

(5) He has no knowledge of the existence or commencement of any insolvency proceeding against the maker or acceptor of the instrument, or against the drawer of an unaccepted draft or bill of exchange.[40]

(6) No defense of any party is good as against him.[41]

These warranties made by the unqualified indorser pass to his transferee and to any subsequent holder who acquires the instrument in good faith.[42]

When the holder presents a check to the drawee bank for payment, his indorsement of the check does not give rise to any warranty that the account of the drawer in the drawee bank is sufficient to cover the check. Consequently, when the drawee bank mistakenly makes payment to the payee who presents and indorses a check of its depositor, the drawee bank cannot recover such payment from the payee when it later learns that the drawer's account was not sufficient. (See p. 605, Kirby v First & Merchants National Bank.)

When an item has been paid to the possessor on the basis of a forged indorsement, a collecting bank which sustains loss by being required to pay the true owner of the paper or a prior collecting bank may recover its loss from its customer because of the customer's warranty of the genuineness of prior signatures when the customer deposited the item with the collecting bank. This right of recovery may be enforced in an ordinary lawsuit or by charging back the account of the customer or of a collecting bank to which the proceeds of the item had been paid. When the bank claiming the right of recovery or charge-back has delayed unreasonably under the circumstances, its right to recover or charge-back is barred by such delay if the other

---

[36] § 3-417(2)(a).
[37] § 3-417(2)(a).
[38] § 3-417(2)(b).
[39] § 3-417(2)(c).
[40] § 3-417(2)(e).
[41] § 3-417(2)(d).
[42] § 3-417(2).

party has sustained loss because of the delay. (See p. 606, First Federal Savings & Loan Ass'n v Branch Banking & Trust Co.)

§ 30:15. Warranties of Other Parties.

(1) Qualified Indorser. The qualified indorser makes the same warranties as an unqualified indorser except that warranty as to "no defenses" (6) is limited to a warranty that the indorser does not have knowledge of any defense, rather than that no such defense exists.[43] The warranties of a qualified indorser run to the same persons as those of an unqualified indorser.

(2) Transferor by Delivery. The warranties made by one who transfers a commercial paper by delivery are the same as those made by an unqualified indorser except that they run only to the immediate transferee and then only if he has given consideration for the transfer.[44] Subsequent holders cannot enforce such warranties against this prior transferor by delivery regardless of the status or character of such holders.

(3) Selling Agent or Broker. A selling agent or broker who discloses the fact that he is acting as such only warrants his good faith and authority to act. One who does not disclose such capacity is subject to the warranties of an ordinary transferor who transfers in the manner employed by him.[45]

---

[43] UCC § 3-417(3). The qualified indorsement does not exclude other warranties unless it is specified to be "without warranties."

[44] UCC § 3-417(2).

[45] § 3-417(4).

CASES FOR CHAPTER 30

State National Bank v Sumco Engineering

46 Ala App 244, 240 So2d 366 (1970)

A check was drawn by Calument and Hecla, Inc. on the State National Bank payable to Sumco Engineering and Madison Construction and Supply Company. Madison presented the check to the drawee bank for payment. The bank paid Madison the full amount of the check although it had not been indorsed by Sumco. Suit was then brought against the drawee bank by Sumco. From a judgment in Sumco's favor the bank appealed.

PER CURIAM . . . The issue, as we see it, is whether the appellant drawee bank was obligated to the drawer of the check to pay the face amount of it to the two payees listed thereon or not.

". . . The contract of the bank with each depositor is to pay the money deposited on demand made at its banking house, in such sums, at such times, and to such persons as the depositor may direct. Under such contract, the bank is not warranted in paying out the money of its depositor except in strict accordance with his order, and it has an absolute obligation in this respect which is not fulfilled merely by the exercise of reasonable diligence." . . .

". . . Where a check is payable to two or more persons as payees, or to their order, the amount of the check must be paid to both payees or upon the order of both. Payment to one of the payees or to the order of one payee without the authority of the other payee does not discharge the drawee bank of its liability for the amount of the check, unless the payees are partners."

In the case at bar the drawer made the check payable to two joint payees, and the payees had a right to believe that they possessed a valuable instrument with such commercial character that title thereto could not pass or that payment thereof could not be made by the drawee without the endorsements of both of them appearing thereon.

But in this case payment was made by the drawee bank with the endorsement of only one of the two payees appearing thereon. Obviously then, the drawee did not pay the face amount of the check to the two payees whose names also appeared on the face of the check, which is contrary to the directions given to the drawee bank by the drawer as embodied in the terms of the instrument explicitly set out on the face thereof.

The rule requiring the drawee bank to strictly abide by the directions of the drawer as set out on the face of the check is based on sound principles. . . .

. . . In a situation such as the one now before us, the unpaid payee should be allowed to recover as against the drawee for the face amount of the check absent any effort to allege and prove a lesser interest in the face amount of said check. . . .

To hold otherwise, would have the effect of thwarting the expressed intent of the drawer—as spelled out on the face of the check—communicated to the drawee bank, to pay to the order of the joint payees, Madison Construction and Supply Company and Sumco Engineering, Inc., the amount of $5,907.74.

The drawer had a right to expect the drawee bank to carry out his instructions to the letter, and the payees designated on the check had a right to expect that payment would be made to both of them in the absence of a direction by one of them to the contrary.

[Judgment affirmed.]

Code Comment: This case was decided under the NIL before the effective date of the Code subsequently adopted in Alabama, but the same decision would be made under the Code.

Westerly Hospital v Higgins

106 RI 155, 256 A2d 506 (1969)

Higgins, who owed a bill to the Westerly Hospital, gave it an installment note for the amount of the debt. The note required him to make 18 monthly installments. The hospital negotiated the note to the Industrial National Bank by an indorsement which consisted of the name of the hospital and a guarantee by the hospital that payment of the note would be made by the maker. Higgins made three payments on the note and then stopped, whereupon the bank wrote on the bàck of the note an indorsement to the hospital and delivered the note to the hospital. The hospital sued Higgins on the note. He raised the defense that the hospital could not sue because it was not the holder, contending that the indorsement by the bank was not effective on the theory that the person who wrote the indorsement on behalf of the bank did not have authority to make such indorsement. The trial court rejected this defense and entered a summary judgment in favor of the hospital, from which Higgins appealed.

Roberts, C.J. . . . The defendant contends that the trial justice's ruling granting summary judgment to plaintiff was error because a genuine issue existed as to whether Westerly Hospital or Industrial was in fact the proper party to bring the instant action on the note. We cannot agree with this contention. In our opinion, the face of the instrument discloses as a matter of law that Westerly Hospital is the holder of the note in question and, therefore, a proper party to bring this action. The face of the instrument reveals that Westerly Hospital was the payee of the note made by defendant and his wife as comakers. It further discloses that an indorsement of guarantee was executed in blank by an authorized representative of plaintiff hospital. The note was then delivered to Industrial. The pertinent provisions of the Uniform Commercial Code . . . provide that where, as in the instant case, there has been a blank indorsement, mere delivery is sufficient to constitute the transferee a holder thereof and is sufficient to make the transfer a valid negotiation. [UCC §] 3-202; [UCC §] 3-204. Thereafter, when defendant defaulted, Industrial delivered the note to plaintiff in return for the payment of the remaining amount of defendant's obligation that had been guaranteed by plaintiff hospital.

The defendant argues that this delivery of the note back to plaintiff was not sufficient to constitute a valid negotiation. He argues that the attempted special indorsement by Industrial to Westerly Hospital was invalid for the lack of the signature of a duly authorized representative of Industrial and thereby Westerly Hospital was precluded from becoming a holder of the instrument. Thus, according to defendant, Industrial was the proper party to bring the action on this note. It seems rather obvious that had the transfer of the note from Westerly Hospital to Industrial been other than in blank, this argument would have merit, it being true that an authorized signature of an agent of Industrial would be necessary to negotiate the instrument.

However, [§] 3-204(2) of the Uniform Commercial Code states, in pertinent part, that "An instrument payable to order and indorsed in blank becomes payable to bearer and may be negotiated by delivery alone until specially indorsed." . . . Instead, a blank indorsement, one specifying no particular indorsee, was made. The legal effect of such an indorsement and delivery was to authorize Industrial as the transferee and holder of the note to further negotiate the note without indorsement but by mere delivery alone. It is clear that any attempt on its part to achieve negotiation by indorsing the note to plaintiff would have been mere surplusage.

In our opinion, then, the redelivery of the note in question by Industrial to Westerly Hospital accomplished a negotiation of the instrument, and the fact that a purported special indorsement to Westerly Hospital was not legally executed is of no consequence and does not affect plaintiff's status as the holder of the note. . . .

[Judgment affirmed.]

Gast v American Casualty Co.

99 NJ Super 538, 240 A2d 682 (1968)

The Gasts owned a building which they contracted to sell to the Hannas. The building was insured against fire with the American Casualty Co. Thereafter, when the house was damaged by fire, a settlement was reached with the insurance company through Sidney Rosenbaum, a public fire adjuster. In order to make payment for the loss, the insurance company drew a draft on itself payable to the Hannas, the Gasts, and to Sidney Rosenbaum. Apparently the Hannas indorsed the draft, forged the names of the other payees as indorsers, cashed the draft, and then disappeared. Thereafter the Gasts sued the American Casualty Co. From a judgment in favor of the insurance company, the Gasts appealed.

GARTON, J.A.D. . . . Defendant [American Casualty Co.] denied that it had any liability by reason of the forgery of the indorsements on the draft and, in addition, alleged that plaintiffs [Gasts] had contributed to the forgery by their negligence and were thus precluded from recovery. . . . The trial judge instructed the jury that . . . "A drawee is liable for payment to a person whose name had been forged unless the person was subsequently negligent in contributing to the forgery. *Therefore, the factual problem, members of the jury, in this problem reduces itself to one of alleged negligence on the part of the defendant, in their manner of payment and, too, the alleged contributory negligence on the part of the plaintiffs under the facts of this case, and these factual issues, of course, will be for your determination. . . .*" (emphasis supplied)

We conclude that the charge as given was erroneous, both on the issue of defendant's liability as drawer-drawee to plaintiffs on the forged indorsements and on the issue of plaintiffs' contributory negligence.

The [italicized] language is a misconception of the law regarding the elements of defendant's liability. The draft was drawn upon defendant and was executed by defendant. As both drawer and drawee, defendant had the responsibility to make payment to the named payees on the instrument. . . .

The nature of defendant's obligation is set forth in the statute. It is not grounded upon negligence. [UCC §] 3-419 provides in pertinent part:

"(1) An instrument is converted when . . . (c) It is paid on a forged indorsement.

"(2) In an action against a drawee under subsection (1) the measure of the drawee's liability is the face amount of the instrument. In any other action under subsection (1) the measure of liability is presumed to be the face amount of the instrument."

The statute created an absolute right to recover in favor of plaintiffs (absent negligence on their part as discussed below) upon proof that the draft was paid on the forged indorsements. Plaintiffs' indorsements were concededly forged. It follows that defendant, having paid the draft, was rendered liable for the conversion in the face amount.

Comment 3 to [UCC §] 3-419, by the draftsmen of the Uniform Commercial Code, makes it clear that the above analysis is correct. That comment states: "Subsection (1)(c) is new. It adopts the prevailing view of decisions holding that payment on a forged indorsement is not an acceptance, but that *even though made in good faith, it is an exercise of dominion and control over the instrument* inconsistent with the rights of the owner, *and results in liability for conversion.*" (emphasis added)

. . . It was therefore error to instruct the jury that plaintiffs were required to show that defendant was negligent.

[Judgment reversed and action remanded.]

Kirby v First & Merchants National Bank

210 Va 88, 168 SE2d 273 (1969)

Neuse Engineering & Dredging Co. delivered a check for $2,500 payable to the order of the Kirbys, drawn on its account in the First & Merchants National Bank. The Kirbys indorsed the check and took it to the bank, which gave them $200 in cash and a deposit credit of $2,300 in an account which Mrs. Kirby had in the same bank. Thereafter the bank notified the Kirbys that the Neuse account was insufficient to pay its $2,500 check. The Kirbys stated that they would come to the bank to cover the deficit, but did not do so; whereupon the bank charged Mrs. Kirby's account with the $2,500, causing an overdraft of $543.47, for which the bank then sued the Kirbys. From a decision in favor of the bank, the Kirbys appealed.

GORDON, J. . . . The trial court apparently decided that Mr. and Mrs. Kirby were liable to the Bank because they had indorsed the Neuse check. But under UCC Section 3-414(1) an indorser contracts to pay an instrument only if the instrument is dishonored. And, as we have pointed out, the Bank did not dishonor the Neuse check, but paid the check in cash when Mrs. Kirby presented it.

As a practical matter, the contract of an indorser under [UCC §] 3-414(1) does not run to a drawee bank. That contract can be enforced by a drawee bank only if it dishonors a check; and if the bank dishonors the check, it has suffered no loss.

The warranties that are applicable in this case are set forth in UCC §§ 3-417(1) and 4-207(1): warranties made to a drawee bank by a presenter and prior transferors of a check. Those warranties are applicable because Mrs. Kirby presented the Neuse check to the Bank for payment. UCC § 3-504(1). . . . And those warranties do not include a warranty that the drawer of a check has sufficient funds on deposit to cover the check.

The rule that a drawee who mistakenly pays a check has recourse only against the drawer was firmly established before adoption of the Uniform Commercial Code. . . .

Virginia followed the same rule. . . .

Nevertheless, First & Merchants contends that under the terms of its deposit contract with Mrs. Kirby, the settlement was provisional and therefore subject to revocation whether or not the Neuse check was paid in cash. . . .* It contends that in this regard the deposit contract changes the rule set forth in the Uniform Commercial Code. But in providing that "all items are credited subject to final payment," the contract recognizes that settlement for an item is provisional only until the item is finally paid. Since the deposit contract does not change the applicable rule as set forth in the Uniform Commercial Code, we do not decide whether a bank can provide by deposit contract that payment of a check in cash is provisional.

Even if the Bank's settlement for the Neuse check had been provisional, the Bank had the right to charge that item back to Mrs. Kirby's account only if it complied with UCC §§ 4-212(3) and 4-301. Those sections authorize the revocation of a settlement if, before the "midnight deadline," the bank "(a) returns the item; or (b) sends written notice of dishonor or nonpayment if the item is held for protest or is otherwise unavailable for return." UCC § 4-301. The Bank concedes that it neither sent written notice of dishonor nor returned the Neuse check before the "midnight deadline." So the Bank had no right to charge the item back to Mrs. Kirby's account.

For the reasons set forth, the trial court erred in entering judgment for First & Merchants against Mr. and Mrs. Kirby.

[Reversed and final judgment.]

* The depositor's contract provides:

"Items received for deposit or collection are accepted on the following terms and conditions. *This bank acts only as depositor's collecting agent and assumes no responsibility beyond its exercise of due care. All items are credited subject to final payment and to receipt of proceeds of final payment in cash or solvent credits by this bank at its own office.* This bank may forward items to correspondents and shall not be liable for default or negligence of correspondents selected with due care nor for losses in transit, and each correspondent shall not be liable except for its own negligence. Items and their proceeds may be handled by any Federal Reserve bank in accordance with applicable Federal Reserve rules, and by this bank or any correspondent, in accordance with any common bank usage, with any practice or procedure that a Federal Reserve bank may use or permit another bank to use, or with any other lawful means. *This bank may charge back, at any time prior to midnight on its business day next following the day of receipt, any item drawn on this bank which is ascertained to be drawn against insufficient funds or otherwise not good or payable. An item received after this bank's regular afternoon closing hour shall be deemed received the next business day.*

"This bank reserves the right to post all deposits, including deposits of cash and of items drawn on it, not later than midnight of its next business day after their receipt at this office during regular banking hours, and shall not be liable for damages for nonpayment of any presented item resulting from the exercise of this right."

First Federal Savings & Loan Ass'n v Branch Banking & Trust Co.

282 NC 44, 191 SE2d 683 (1972)

Hanover Insurance Company drew a draft payable to Geraldine Stallings and Winter Park Federal Savings & Loan Association. The draft bearing the forged indorsement of Winter Park was deposited by Stallings with First Federal Savings & Loan Association. First Federal then sent it to Branch Banking and Trust Company which sent it to Chase Manhattan Bank which presented the draft to and was paid by Hanover. When the forgery was discovered, Hanover paid Winter Park the amount of the draft and that amount was then charged back against Chase which charged it back against Branch Banking which charged it against First Federal. This was done approximately 27 months after the draft had originally been paid by Hanover. Meanwhile Stallings had already withdrawn from her First Federal account all of the proceeds of the draft. First Federal sued Branch Banking for the amount of the draft. The lower court entered judgment for Branch Banking and First Federal appealed.

LAKE, J. . . . The plaintiff took the draft upon the indorsement of one of the payees and the forged indorsement of the other. Such transfer conferred upon the plaintiff the interest of Geraldine M. Stallings in the draft, and no more. . . .

The plaintiff alleges and Hanover admits that, thereafter, Hanover caused Branch to charge back to the plaintiff's account the full amount so paid by Hanover on the draft when it was presented for payment. If, as the plaintiff alleges, Geraldine M. Stallings, at the time of her indorsement to the plaintiff, was entitled to any part of the proceeds of the draft, this right passed to the plaintiff, and the plaintiff was entitled to retain that portion of the proceeds so paid by Hanover upon the presentment of the draft for payment. If, on the other hand, Winter Park was entitled to the full amount of the draft, as Hanover seems to imply in its allegation that, since the discovery of the forgery of the indorsement, it has paid the full amount to Winter Park, then the plaintiff, who succeeded to none of the rights of Winter Park, would have no right to retain any portion of the proceeds of the draft. . . .

Assuming . . . that Geraldine M. Stallings had no right to retain any portion of the proceeds of the draft at the time of her indorsement to the plaintiff, we turn to the right of the drawee, Hanover, to charge the draft back to the collecting bank, and, through it, to the plaintiff, approximately 27 months after the draft was paid by Hanover. [UCC §] 3-417 provides that any person who obtains payment of an instrument, and any prior transferor thereof, warrants to a person who pays it in good faith that he has a good title to the instrument or is authorized to obtain payment on behalf of one who has a good title to it. This warranty is broken if such person claims through the forged instrument of a joint payee having any interest in the proceeds of the paper.

Article 4 of the Uniform Commercial Code, Chapter 25 of the General Statutes, is applicable to drafts forwarded for collection through a bank or banks. [UCC §] 4-207(1) provides that each customer or collecting bank who obtains payment of such paper, and each prior customer and collecting bank, "warrants to the payor bank *or other payor*," who in good faith pays the paper, that he has a good title to it or is authorized to obtain payment on behalf of one who has a good title thereto. With reference to the transaction involved in this action, Hanover is such "other payor," Chase was the collecting bank who obtained payment, Branch was such prior collecting bank and the plaintiff was such prior customer. Paragraph (4) of [UCC §] 4-207 provides: "Unless a claim for breach of warranty under this section is made within a reasonable time after the person claiming learns of the breach, the person liable is discharged to the extent of any loss caused by the delay in making claim." If, under this statute, or under [UCC §] 3-407, Hanover was entitled to proceed directly against the plaintiff for reimbursement of the amount paid by Hanover upon the draft, Hanover would not be liable to the plaintiff in this action for having caused Branch to make the chargeback against the plaintiff's account with Branch.

[UCC §] 4-406, relating to the duty of a customer of a bank to discover and report to his bank unauthorized signatures and alterations, has no application to the right of Hanover to proceed against the plaintiff for the recovery of the amount paid by Hanover upon this draft. . . .

"It is generally recognized that the right of a maker or drawee to recover a payment made on a forged indorsement may be lost if he is guilty of negligence or laches whereby the position of the person receiving payment is changed to the damage of such person. Thus, it is held that a drawee may recover if, after discovery of the forgery, he is guilty of no negligence that is injurious to the person receiving payment. But delay in discovering a forged indorsement ordinarily is not negligence and does not preclude recovery, particularly where no injury to the holder results.

"In order for a drawee or other person to recover a payment made upon a forged indorsement it is a general requisite that he give timely notice after discovery of the forgery. Prompt notice of the discovery of the forgery is not a condition precedent to suit, but if it is shown that the drawee or other payor on learning that an indorsement was forged did not give prompt notice of it, and that damage resulted, recovery of the payment by such person is barred. . . . But the damage occasioned by the delay must be established, and not left to conjecture."

The drawee of a draft is not held to know the signature of an indorser, whether the payee or an intermediate indorser. He is under no duty to examine the draft to determine the genuineness of an indorsement, but may rely upon the warranty made to him by the person receiving payment that such person has title to the instrument. When, however, the drawee learns that an indorsement, necessary to the title of the person who has received payment, is forged, the drawee must then act with reasonable promptness or his right to recover from the person receiving payment, or a prior indorser, will be barred, to the extent of any loss which such person sustains by reason of the drawee's delay. . . .

. . . There is no rule of law establishing the time within which the drawee must notify the person receiving payment, or a prior indorser, that such person's title to the draft was defective by reason of a forged indorsement. A reasonable time for such action depends upon the circumstances in each case.

[Judgment reversed and action remanded.]

Waters v Waters

(Tex Civ App) 498 SW2d 236 (1973)

Jerry Waters and his wife Patsy entered into a property settlement agreement as part of a divorce proceeding. By the agreement, it was agreed that a demand note which had been signed by Jerry payable to the order of Jim Still, who was Patsy's father, should be "transferred to Patsy . . . in the future." Jim delivered the note to Patsy without any indorsement or writing. Jim thereafter died. Patsy sued Jerry on the note. He raised the defense that she was not entitled to sue on the note because she was not the owner of the note. Judgment was entered in favor of Patsy. Jerry appealed.

DUNAGAN, C.J. . . . Appellant [Jerry] contends that there was no evidence . . . that the appellee [Patsy] is the owner of said note. The note does not bear the endorsement of Jim Still. However, the appellee . . . testified that her father gave her the note with the statement that it was hers and she could collect same. The evidence shows that she was in possession of the note.

This evidence is . . . undisputed. This evidence shows a fulfillment of the provisions of the settlement contract "that the note is presently payable to Jim Still, but will be transferred to Patsy A. Waters (appellee) in the future." The settlement contract did not set out or provide in what manner the note was to be transferred to the appellee. . . .

A promissory note can lawfully be transferred without a written assignment or an endorsement of the legal owner and holder thereof. . . . [The Official Code Comment to UCC § 3-201 on the transfer of paper states that] "the section applies to any transfer, whether by a holder or not. Any person who transfers an instrument transfers whatever rights he has in it. The transferee acquires those rights even though they do not amount to 'title.' The transfer of rights is not limited to transfers for value. An instrument may be transferred as a gift, and the donee acquires whatever rights the donor had." . . .

Delivery by a donor to donee of a promissory note payable to donor with intent to invest the donee with ownership is an effective gift of the note and transfer thereof. The gift to appellee from her father did not require a written transfer. Appellant by the settlement agreement and contract agreed for the note to be transferred to appellee and knew that such transfer was to be made and that no particular method for such transfer was provided. Title passes by oral gift. . . .

In Anderson's Uniform Commercial Code, Vol. 2, sec. 3.201:10, p. 752, . . . we find these statements: "Under the pre-Code law there was uncertainty as to the nature of the title received by the transferee of a negotiable instrument without indorsement; that is, as to whether he received a legal title or merely the equitable title to the paper. It is believed that, although the Code does not make any express determination of this issue, the transferee acquires legal title because the 'transfer of an instrument vests in the transferee such rights as the transferor has therein. . . . [UCC § 3-201(1)]. The fact that the transferee for value is given a specifically enforceable right to obtain the missing indorsement should not lead to the conclusion that prior to that time the transferee necessarily has merely equitable title. The only conclusion that must necessarily be drawn from the right to obtain the indorsement is that prior to obtaining the indorsement the transferee is not the 'holder,' for, as stated, 'negotiation takes effect only when the indorsement is made and until that time there is no presumption that the transferee is the owner.' This statement is merely that the transferee is not the holder and must affirmatively prove that he is the 'owner.' There is no statement that he is not the owner nor that he is not the owner of the rights of the transferor, namely, ownership of the legal title to the paper."

Sec. 201:12 reads as follows: "The fact that a transferee lacking a necessary indorsement is not the holder does not mean that the transferee cannot establish his right as assignee and enforce the obligation. To the contrary, a transferee although he has neglected to obtain the indorsement necessary to make him a holder may enforce a note, foreclose on collateral, and obtain a deficiency judgment against the debtor."

Upon a careful review of the entire record, we find ample, competent and legal evidence which supports the trial court's . . . judgment. . . .

[Judgment affirmed.]

QUESTIONS AND CASE PROBLEMS

1. A check given in settlement of a lawsuit was drawn to the order of "*A*, attorney for *B*." Could *A* indorse the check? [Maber, Inc. v Factor Cab Corp., 19 App Div 2d 500, 244 NYS2d 768]
2. The Snug Harbor Realty Co. had a checking account in the First National Bank. When construction work was obtained by the Snug Harbor Realty Co., its superintendent, Magee, would examine the bills submitted for labor and materials. He would instruct the bookkeeper as to what bills were approved, and checks were then prepared by the bookkeeper in accordance with such instructions. After the checks were signed by the proper official of Snug Harbor, they were picked up by Magee for delivery. Instead of delivering certain checks, he forged the signatures of the respective payees as indorsers and cashed the checks. The drawee bank then debited the Snug Harbor account with the amount of these checks. Snug Harbor claimed that this was improper and sued the bank for the amount of such checks. Was Snug Harbor entitled to recover such amount? [Snug Harbor Realty Co. v First National Bank, 105 NJ Super 572, 253 A2d 581, affirmed 54 NJ 95, 253 A2d 545]
3. Kavlick hired Rothman to do construction work and paid him by a note. Rothman indorsed the note "without recourse" to the Eastern Acceptance Corp. The corporation sued Kavlick on the note. He defended on the ground that the consideration for the note had failed and that this defense was available against the corporation because it could not be a holder in due course on account of the form of the indorsement. Decide. [Eastern Acceptance Corp. v Kavlick, 10 NJ Super 253, 77 A2d 49]
4. Searcy executed and delivered a promissory note payable to the order of the Bank of Ensley. A later holder, the First National Bank of Birmingham, sued Searcy on the note. A dispute arose as to whether the First National Bank was the holder of the instrument on January 10, before the closing of the Ensley Bank on January 11. The First National Bank proved that on January 10 the note was indorsed to it by the Ensley Bank. Did this prove that the First National Bank was the holder on January 10? [First National Bank of Birmingham v Searcy, 31 Ala App 553, 19 So2d 559]
5. Benton, as agent for Savidge, received an insurance settlement check from the Metropolitan Life Insurance Co. He indorsed it "For deposit" and

deposited it in the Bryn Mawr Trust Company in the account of Savidge. What was the nature and effect of this indorsement? [Savidge v Metropolitan Life Insurance Co., 380 Pa 205, 110 A2d 730]

6. Humphrey drew a check for $100. It was stolen and the payee's name forged as an indorser. The check was then negotiated to Miller who had no knowledge of these facts. Miller indorsed the check to the Citizens Bank. Payment of the check was voided on the ground of the forgery. The Citizens Bank then sued Miller as indorser. Decide. [Citizens Bank of Hattiesburg v Miller, 194 Miss 557, 11 So2d 457]

7. Fred Klomann held three notes of Sol K. Graff & Sons. He specially indorsed the notes to his daughter, Candace, and delivered the notes to her. She handed them back to Fred so that he could collect them. Thereafter, Fred crossed out Candace's name and substituted the name of his wife, Georgia. Georgia demanded payment from Sol K. Graff & Sons. They refused to pay on the ground that Georgia had no interest in or right to enforce the notes. She brought suit against Sol K. Graff & Sons. Is she entitled to recover? [Klomann v Sol K. Graff & Sons, — Ill App —, 317 NE2d 608]

8. The New Mexico Pipe Trades Welfare Trust Fund had a checking account in the Albuquerque National Bank. The signature card specified that two signatures were required on all checks and stated that the officers of the fund named on the card were authorized to sign checks and to indorse checks for deposit. In an action brought against the bank by Cooper and other trustees of the Welfare Fund, the question arose as to the validity of indorsements made on certain checks. They had been indorsed with two rubber stamps, one reading "New Mexico Pipe Trades Welfare Trust Fund" and the other, "Pay to the order of Albuquerque National Bank . . . For deposit only." No signature of any authorized officer appeared thereon, although the stamps had in fact been put on by one of the named officers. Were the indorsements valid? [Cooper v Albuquerque National Bank, 75 NMex 295, 404 P2d 125]

9. The Feldman Construction Company made a contract with Interstate Steel Corporation for construction work. General Pipe & Supply furnished building materials to Interstate. Feldman drew a check on its bank, the Union Bank, payable to the order of "Interstate Steel Corp. General Pipe & Supply." Interstate indorsed the check and Union Bank then paid the check. Feldman sued Union Bank for the amount of the check because it had not been properly indorsed. Union Bank claimed that the check was payable in the alternative and therefore the indorsement of one of the payees was sufficient. Was the bank correct? [Feldman Constr. Co. v Union Bank, 28 Cal App 3d 731, 104 Cal Rptr 912]

31 Presentment of Paper for Acceptance and Payment

PRESENTMENT OF NOTES FOR PAYMENT

§ 31:1. Introduction. A promissory note is a two-party commercial paper, which means that originally only the maker and payee are involved. The maker is liable for payment on the due date specified in the note or on demand if the note is a demand instrument. If the maker dishonors the note when it is presented to him for payment, the indorsers, if there are any, may become liable for payment of the paper.

This chapter considers the rules of law that must be followed in order to enforce the liability of a party to a note. It must be remembered that even though these rules have been satisfied, a plaintiff will lose in a given case if he is not the holder as discussed in Chapter 28 or if the defendant has a defense that may be asserted against the plaintiff as discussed in Chapter 33.

The procedures for presenting a promissory note for payment and for giving notice of dishonor, which are explained in this chapter, apply also to other types of commercial paper, that is, drafts and checks.

§ 31:2. Liability of Maker. The liability of a maker of a promissory note is primary. This means that payment may be demanded of him and that he may be sued by the holder as soon as the debt is due, but not before that time. (See p. 623, Bertolet v Burke.) The maker is under the duty to pay the note at the time and at the place named, if any place is specified by the note, unless he can set up a defense that is valid against the holder.

By the very act of signing the promissory note, the maker deprives himself of two possible defenses. He admits (1) the existence of the payee named in the instrument and (2) the payee's capacity at that time to indorse the paper.[1] Consequently, when the payee of a note is a minor or a bankrupt, the maker cannot deny the validity of the title of a subsequent holder of the instrument on the ground that the payee lacked capacity to transfer title.

When a note is issued in payment of a debt, the original obligation is suspended until the instrument is due or until presentment for payment in the case of demand paper. If the note is dishonored by nonpayment, the holder may sue either on the note or on the underlying obligation.[2]

---

[1] UCC § 3-413(3).
[2] UCC § 3-802(1)(b).

In addition to the liability of the maker on the note, other persons may be liable for the underlying debt or obligation as a matter of general contract law. This occurs when one person borrows money and gives the lender the promissory note of another person as security. (See p. 624, In re Eton Furniture Co.)

§ 31:3. Need for Presentment for Payment. The holder of a promissory note need not present the instrument to the maker for payment in order to hold the latter liable on the note.[3] If the note is payable at a definite time, the maker is under a duty to pay the holder the amount due on the instrument as soon as that date is reached. The liability of the maker continues until barred by the statute of limitations.

If the note is demand paper, no special demand for payment is required. The holder may even begin a lawsuit against the maker without first making a demand for payment since the act of bringing suit is regarded as the making of a demand. If the note is payable at a definite time, the holder may bring suit on or after the due date without making a prior demand upon the maker.

An unqualified indorser is secondarily liable for the payment of the instrument, which means that he must pay the amount of the instrument to the holder under certain circumstances. Generally this duty arises only if (1) the instrument was presented for payment to the primary party on the due date or at maturity, (2) the primary party defaulted by failing to pay the amount of the instrument to the holder, and (3) the secondary party in question was given proper notice of the primary party's default.

A qualified indorser or a former holder of bearer paper who negotiates the instrument without indorsing it is not liable for payment. However, such parties, as well as an unqualified indorser, who does have a secondary liability, may be liable for a breach of warranty.

§ 31:4. Presentment for Payment. When presentment for payment of notes and other commercial paper is required, the following rules apply:

(1) Person Making Presentment. Presentment for payment must be made by the holder of the paper or by one authorized to act and receive payment for him.

(2) Manner of Presentment. Demand for payment in any manner is sufficient. The party to whom the demand is made may require, however, that greater formality be observed, such as by requiring (a) reasonable identification of the person making presentment and evidence of his authority if he acts for another; (b) production of the instrument for payment at a place specified in it or, if there be none, at any place reasonable in the circumstances; and (c) a signed receipt on the instrument for any partial or

[3] § 3-501(1), Official Comment, point 4.

full payment and its surrender upon full payment. If the party presenting the instrument does not comply with such requests at the time of making presentment, he is allowed a reasonable time within which to do so; but if he does not so comply, the presentment has no effect.[4]

The presentment must make a clear demand for payment and a mere inquiry as to whether payment would be made in the future is not sufficient.[5]

In addition to a presentment for payment made directly between the parties, presentment may be made by sending the paper through the mail to the debtor, or by sending it through a clearinghouse.[6] A collecting bank may also make presentment for payment by sending merely a notice to the nonbank party to whom the demand for payment is made.[7] If the party so notified fails to act within a specified time, his inaction is treated as a dishonor of the note.[8]

(3) On Whom Presentment Is Made. Presentment for payment must be made to the party primarily liable, that is, the maker of the promissory note, or to a person who has authority to make or refuse payment on his behalf.[9] In the case of two or more makers presentment may be made upon any one of them.[10] If the instrument is payable at a bank, it must be presented to a proper person in the bank who is authorized to make payment of the note.[11]

(4) Place of Making Presentment. Presentment for payment is properly made at the place that is specified in the instrument. When a place of payment is not specified, presentment of the instrument is to be made at the place of business or the residence of the person from whom payment is to be demanded.[12]

§ 31:5. Time of Making Presentment. A note payable at a stated date must be presented for payment on that date.[13] If the time for paying the balance due on the note has been accelerated, presentment must be made within a reasonable time after the default in a scheduled payment of principal or interest.[14] For the purpose of determining the secondary liability of any party, presentment for payment must be made within a reasonable time after such person became liable on the instrument.[15]

---

4 UCC § 3-505.

5 Kohlhepp's Estate v Mason, 25 Utah 2d 155, 478 P2d 339.

6 § 3-504(2)(a),(b).

7 § 4-210(1). This provision is not applicable if the paper is payable by, through, or at a bank.

8 UCC § 4-210(2).

9 § 3-504(3).

10 § 3-504(3)(a).

11 § 3-504(4).

12 § 3-504(2)(c).

13 § 3-503(1)(c).

14 § 3-503(1)(d).

15 § 3-503(1)(e).

Presentment must be made at a reasonable time, and if made at a bank, must be made during its banking day.[16]

(1) Computation of Time. In determining the date of maturity of an instrument, the starting day is excluded and the day of payment is included. Thus, an instrument dated July 3 (which leaves 28 days in July) and payable 30 days from date is due on August 2.[17]

(2) Instrument Due on Legal or Business Holiday. When the presentment of the paper is due on a day that is not a full business day, presentment is due on the following full business day. This rule is applied when the due day is not a full business day either because it is a legal holiday or merely because the bank or other person required to make payment on the instrument, as a matter of its business practice, is closed all day or for a half day.[18]

This rule is also applied when the due date is a business holiday for either party, that is, if either the person required to present the instrument or the person who is required to pay upon presentment is not open for a full business day on the due date. The date for presentment is extended to the first day that is a full business day for both of them.[19]

(3) Excuse for Delay in Making Presentment. Failure to present an instrument for payment at the proper time will be excused when the delay is caused by circumstances beyond the control of the holder. It must not, however, be caused by his misconduct, negligence, or fault. Mere inconvenience, such as that arising from inclement weather, is not a valid excuse for delay. When the circumstances that excuse the delay are removed, presentment must be made within a reasonable time.[20]

(4) Effect of Delay. An unexcused delay in any necessary presentment for payment discharges an indorser's liability for payment of the paper. If the note is *domiciled,* that is, payable at a bank, the delay may also operate to discharge the maker. The UCC provides as to such paper that "any . . . maker of a note payable at a bank who because the . . . payor bank becomes insolvent during the delay is deprived of funds maintained with the . . . payor bank to cover the instrument may discharge his liability by written assignment to the holder of his rights against the . . . payor bank in respect of such funds, but such . . . maker is not otherwise discharged." [21]

---

[16] § 3-503(4).

[17] In business practice, when the time is expressed in terms of months rather than days, such as 2 months after date, the date of maturity is the same date in the month of maturity. For example, when the date of the paper is October 15 and the time is 2 months, the date of maturity is December 15.

[18] UCC § 3-503(3).

[19] § 3-503(3).

[20] § 3-511(1). Delay is also excused when the holder does not know that the instrument is due, UCC § 3-511(1), as could occur if the date had been accelerated by a prior holder.

[21] UCC § 3-502(1)(b).

§ 31:6. When Presentment for Payment Is Excused or Unnecessary.

(1) Waiver. Presentment for payment is not required if it has been waived by an express or implied agreement of the secondary party in question.[22] A waiver of presentment is binding upon all parties if it appears on the face of the original note. If the waiver is part of an indorsement, however, it binds only that indorser.[23]

(2) Inability. Presentment for payment is not required if it cannot be made in spite of the exercise of due diligence, as when presentment is attempted at the place where payment is to be made but neither the person who is to make payment nor anyone authorized to act for him can be found at that place.[24] A holder is not required to ask the payee where the primary party lives.[25]

(3) Death or Insolvency. Presentment for payment is not required if the maker of the note has died or if he has gone into insolvency proceedings after he had issued the note.[26]

(4) Refusal to Pay. The holder is not required to make presentment upon the maker if he has already refused to pay the note for no reason, or for any reason other than an objection that proper presentment was not made.[27]

(5) Belief or Conduct of Secondary Party. The secondary party cannot demand that presentment be made if he has no reason to expect that the instrument will be paid and no right to require that payment be made.[28] This situation could arise when the maker executed the note for the benefit of the secondary party but the latter has breached the agreement with the maker and therefore has no right to expect or require that the maker perform his agreement by paying the note.[29]

§ 31:7. Dishonor of Note. If the maker fails or refuses to pay the note when it is properly presented to him, he has dishonored the instrument by nonpayment. The fact that the maker does not make immediate payment of the note when it is presented to him may not dishonor the note. He has the right to withhold making payment until he has made a reasonable examination to determine that the note is properly payable to the holder. He cannot, however, delay payment beyond the close of business on the day of presentment.[30]

---

22 § 3-511(2)(a).
23 § 3-511(6); Gerrity Co. v Padalino, 51 Misc 2d 928, 273 NYS2d 994.
24 UCC §§ 3-504(2), 3-511(2)(c).
25 Cuddy v Sarandrea, 52 RI 465, 161 A 297.
26 § 3-511(3)(a). Insolvency proceedings are defined by § 1-201(22).
27 § 3-511(3)(b).
28 § 3-511(2)(b).
29 § 3-511, Official Comment, point 4.
30 § 3-506(2).

§ 31:8. Notice of Dishonor. If commercial paper is dishonored by nonpayment, any secondary party who is not given proper notice thereof is released from liability, unless the giving of notice is excused.[31] It is only necessary that a party be given notice once because a notice operates for the benefit of all parties who have rights on the instrument against the party notified.[32]

(1) Who May Give Notice. The notice of dishonor is ordinarily given by the holder who has been refused payment or by his agent. If the agent made the presentment for payment, he of course may give notice of the dishonor to his principal who in turn may give it to the secondary party in question. When any person who is liable on the paper receives notice of its dishonor, he may in turn give notice to other secondary parties.[33]

(2) Person Notified. The notice of dishonor may be given to any party who is liable on the instrument. Notice to one partner is notice to all, even though the firm has been dissolved. When the party to be notified is dead or incompetent, notice may be sent to his last-known address or be given to his personal representative. If insolvency proceedings were begun against a party after the note was issued, the notice may be given to him or to the representative of his estate.[34]

(3) Form of Notice. Notice may be given in any reasonable manner. It may be oral or written, and it may be sent by mail. It may have any terms as long as it identifies the instrument and states that it has been dishonored. A misdescription that does not mislead the party notified does not nullify or vitiate the notice. Notice may be effected by sending the instrument itself, with a stamp, ticket, or writing attached thereto, stating that payment has been refused or by sending a notice of debit with respect to the paper.[35] Although not required, it is a sound precaution to give a signed, dated, written notice, and to keep a copy.

(4) Place of Notice. The UCC does not specify a place to which notice is to be given, but it provides that notice generally shall be deemed given whenever such steps have been taken as may be reasonably required to inform the other person, whether or not he actually comes to know of it. Furthermore, a person is deemed to receive notice or notification whenever the matter comes to his attention, or when the notice is delivered at the place of business through which the contract was made or at any other place held out by him as the place for the receipt of such communications.[36]

---

[31] §3-501(2)(a). In the case of a "domiciled" note payable at a bank, the maker must be given notice that the note was not paid when presented at the bank and, if notice is not so given, the maker is released to the same extent already noted in connection with the effect of failure to present at the bank. UCC § 3-501(2)(b).

[32] § 3-508(8).

[33] § 3-508(1).

[34] § 3-508(1),(5),(6),(7).

[35] § 3-508(3).

[36] § 1-201(26).

The duty to exercise reasonable diligence requires that the holder look in the current city directory of the city in which a party to be notified resides.[37]

(5) Time of Notice. Notice must be given before midnight of the third business day after dishonor. If the notice is given following the receipt of notice of dishonor from another party, it must be given before midnight of the third business day after receiving such notice. When required of a bank, notice of dishonor must be given before midnight of the banking day following the banking day on which the note is dishonored or the bank receives notice of such dishonor.[38] A written notice of dishonor is effective when sent. Hence, a notice sent by mail is sufficient even though it is never received, provided it was properly addressed, bore the necessary postage, and was properly mailed.[39]

The sending of notice by ordinary first-class mail is sufficient. A notice sent by certified mail is also sufficient even though such mail is not forwarded to a new address.[40]

If notice is not given within the required time and the delay in or absence of notice is not excused, the person entitled to notice cannot be held liable for the payment of the paper. (See p. 625, Hane v Exten.)

§ 31:9. Excuse for Delay or Absence of Notice of Dishonor. Delay in giving notice of dishonor is excused under the same circumstances as delay in making presentment for payment.[41]

The absence of any notice of dishonor is excused for three of the reasons considered as excusing the absence of presentment; namely (a) waiver, (b) inability to give notice in spite of due diligence, and (c) the fact that the party not notified did not have any reason to believe that the instrument would be paid nor any right to require payment.[42] When an indorser has such knowledge or so participates in the affairs of the primary party that the indorser knows the commercial paper will not be honored by the primary party, it is not required that the holder go through the useless gesture of making a presentment and of notifying the secondary party in order to hold him liable.[43]

Delay by a bank in returning a dishonored item is excused by equipment failure. (See p. 626, Port City State Bank v American National Bank.)

The requirements as to notice of dishonor are not applicable in determining the rights of co-obligors as between themselves. For example, when two indorsers are jointly liable and one pays the full amount, he is entitled to recover one half of such payment by way of contribution from his

---

[37] Bank of America National T. & S. Association v Century L. & W. Co., 19 Cal App 2d 197, 65 P2d 110.

[38] §§ 3-508(2), 4-104(1)(h).

[39] § 3-508(4).

[40] Durkin v Siegel, 340 Mass 445, 165 NE2d 81.

[41] UCC § 3-511.

[42] § 3-511(2).

[43] Makel Textiles v Dolly Originals, (NY Supreme Ct) 4 UCCRS 95.

coindorser without regard to whether the holder had given the coindorser proper notice of dishonor.

§ **31:10. Proof of Dishonor.** Since the liability of the secondary party depends upon whether certain steps were taken within the proper time, it is important for the holder to be able to prove that he has complied with the requirements of the law. In order to aid him in proving such essential facts, certain documents and records are considered evidence of dishonor and of any notice recited therein. The trier of fact must accept such evidence in the absence of proof to the contrary.[44] These documents and records include (1) protests, (2) bank stamps and memorandums, and (3) bank records.

(1) Protests. A *protest* is a memorandum or certificate executed by a notary public, or certain other public officers, upon information satisfactory to him, which sets forth that the particular identified instrument has been dishonored. It may also recite that notice of dishonor was given to all parties or to specified parties.[45]

(2) Bank Stamps and Memorandums. If the stamp put on the paper by a bank or the memorandum attached to the note by the bank is consistent with or suggests a dishonor, it is evidence of that fact. For example, a notation "Not sufficient funds" or "Payment stopped" indicates a dishonor or nonpayment of the instrument and therefore comes within this rule. On the other hand, a notation of "Indorsement missing" is not consistent with dishonor and is therefore not admissible as evidence of a dishonor.[46]

(3) Bank Records. Bank records kept in the usual course of business are admissible as evidence of dishonor even though it cannot be shown who made the entry in the books.[47]

PRESENTMENT OF DRAFTS

§ **31:11. Introduction.** This part considers the rules of law that must be followed in order to enforce the liability of a party to a draft. It must be remembered that even though these rules have been satisfied, a plaintiff will lose in a given case if he is not the holder as discussed in Chapter 28 or if the defendant has a defense which may be asserted against the plaintiff as discussed in Chapter 33.

A note must be presented for payment in order to hold secondary parties liable; under certain circumstances a draft must be presented for acceptance as well as for payment to accomplish that purpose.

If the drawer names himself as drawee, the paper is effective as a promissory note.[48] In such a case, the drawer is the primary party and procedures peculiar to drafts, such as presentment for acceptance, are eliminated.

[44] UCC §§ 3-510, 1-201(31).
[45] §§ 3-509, 3-510(a).
[46] § 3-510(b), Official Comment, point 2.
[47] § 3-510(c).
[48] UCC § 3-118(a).

§ 31:12. Liability of Drawee.

(1) Before Acceptance. An *acceptance* is the written assent of the drawee to the order of the drawer. Before a drawee accepts a draft, he is not liable for its payment. In the absence of a prior contract to accept the draft, the drawee is not under any duty to do so. His act of refusing to accept the draft does not give the holder any right to sue him on the paper, even though he may thereby break a contract with the drawer or some other party that he would accept the bill. Neither does the draft operate as an assignment of any money, even though the drawee has in his possession funds of the drawer.[49]

(2) After Acceptance. When the drawee accepts a draft, he is an acceptor and becomes primarily liable for its payment.[50] By the acceptance he also admits (a) the existence of the payee and (b) the payee's capacity at the time to indorse the draft.[51]

If the drawee pays the instrument to a person who claims it through a forged indorsement, the drawee must bear the loss of such payment.

§ 31:13. Liability of Drawer. The drawer has a secondary liability. By executing the draft, he undertakes to pay the amount of the draft to the holder if, when the instrument is presented to the drawee for acceptance or payment, it is dishonored and proper proceedings are taken by the holder. (See p. 628, Gill v Yoes.)

The drawer, however, may insert in the draft a provision to exclude or limit his own liability as by adding "without recourse" above his signature.[52]

The drawer admits two things by the act of drawing the draft. He admits (1) the existence of the payee, and (2) the payee's capacity at the time to transfer the instrument. The effect of these statutory admissions is the same as in the case of the maker of a promissory note or the acceptor of a draft.[53]

When the drawer executes and delivers to the payee a draft in payment of a debt, the original obligation is suspended until the draft is due, or until presentment for payment if it is demand paper. If the paper is dishonored, the holder may sue either on the paper or on the underlying obligation.[54]

§ 31:14. Liability of Indorser. The liability of an unqualified indorser of a draft is broader than that of an unqualified indorser of a promissory note. Any unqualified indorser is under a secondary liability for the nonpayment of the instrument when due. In addition, the unqualified indorser of a draft is under a secondary liability for the refusal of the drawee to accept the instrument when it is thereafter presented to him for acceptance.

---

[49] UCC § 3-409(1); Aiken Bag Corp. v McLeod, 89 Ga App 737, 81 SE2d 215.

[50] Legal Discount Corp. v Martin Hardware Co., 199 Wash 476, 91 P2d 1010.

[51] UCC § 3-413(3).

[52] § 3-413(2).

[53] § 3-413(3).

[54] UCC § 3-802(1)(b). Special provisions apply when a bank is the drawer. § 3-802(1)(a).

In order to charge the unqualified indorser of the draft for either nonacceptance or nonpayment, it is necessary to prove that a presentment to the drawee had been properly made and due notice given to the indorser of the drawee's failure to accept or pay.

§ 31:15. Necessity of Presentment for Acceptance. The best way for the holder to find out whether the drawee will pay a time draft when it becomes due is to present it to the drawee for acceptance. If the drawee is not willing to pay the instrument according to its terms, he will reject it, that is, dishonor it by nonacceptance. If he is willing to pay it when it becomes due, he will accept it.[55]

Any draft may be presented to the drawee for acceptance. A presentment for acceptance must be made if (1) it is necessary in order to fix the date of maturity of the draft, such as when the instrument is payable a specified number of days after sight; (2) the draft expressly states that it must be presented for acceptance; or (3) the draft is made payable elsewhere than at the residence or place of business of the drawee.[56]

§ 31:16. Manner of Presenting for Acceptance. Presentment of a draft for acceptance is made in the same manner as the presentment of a note for payment,[57] with the obvious difference that the presentment is made upon the drawee rather than upon the maker.

(1) Time for Presentment for Acceptance. Unless a different time is specified in the draft, presentment for acceptance must be made on or before the date on which the instrument is payable by its express provisions. If it is payable after sight, it must be presented for acceptance or negotiated within a reasonable time after its date or issue, whichever is later. With respect to the liability of any secondary party on any other form of instrument, presentment for acceptance must be made within a reasonable time after that party became liable for it.[58]

The time for presentment of a draft for acceptance with respect to the hour and day or the effect of holidays is the same as in the case of presentment of a note for payment.

(2) Delay or Absence of Presentment for Acceptance. Delay in a necessary presentment of a draft for acceptance and the failure to make any presentment are excused under the same circumstances as in the case of the presentment of a note for payment.[59]

---

[55] § 3-410(1).
[56] § 3-501(1)(a).
[57] § 3-504.
[58] § 3-503(1)(a),(b),(e).
[59] § 3-511(1),(2),(3),(6). A minor qualification must be made in that in the case of a draft, it is the death or insolvency proceedings relating to the acceptor or drawee which is material, rather than the death or insolvency of a maker. See also § 3-511(3)(a).

An unexcused delay in making any necessary presentment for acceptance discharges an indorser's liability for payment of the paper.[60] If the draft is domiciled, that is, payable at a bank, the drawer or acceptor is discharged under the circumstances that discharge the maker of a note for dishonor by nonpayment.[61]

(3) Time Allowed for Acceptance. It is not necessary that the drawee accept or dishonor the draft immediately upon its presentment to him. In order to afford him an opportunity of determining from his records whether he should accept, he may postpone making a decision, without thereby dishonoring the draft, until the close of the next business day following the presentment of the draft. Likewise, the holder may allow the postponement of acceptance for an additional business day when he acts in good faith in the hope that he will be able to obtain an acceptance. If the holder agrees to such additional postponement, the liability of the secondary parties is not affected and the draft is not thereby dishonored.[62]

§ 31:17. Kinds of Acceptances.

(1) General Acceptance. A *general acceptance* (or simply an "acceptance") is one in which the acceptor agrees without qualification to pay according to the order of the drawer.

(2) Draft-varying Acceptance. A *draft-varying acceptance* is one in which the acceptor agrees to pay but not exactly in conformity with the order of the draft.[63] An acceptance varies the draft when it changes the time or place of payment, when it agrees to pay only a part of the amount of the draft, or when it sets up a condition that must be satisfied before the acceptance is effective.

An acceptance to pay at a particular bank or place in the United States is a general acceptance, unless the draft expressly states that it is to be paid there only and not elsewhere. In the latter case the acceptance varies the draft.[64]

If the holder does not wish to take the varying acceptance, he may reject it and treat the draft as dishonored by nonacceptance. After giving due notice, he can proceed at once against secondary parties.

If the holder assents to the draft-varying acceptance, however, he in effect consents to the execution of a new instrument; and each drawer and indorser is released from liability unless he affirmatively assents to such

---

60 § 3-502(1)(a).

61 § 3-502(1)(b). See § 31:5(4).

62 § 3-506(1). The time allowed the drawee to determine whether to accept is distinct from any right of re-presentment after dishonor when authorized by the paper. § 3-507(4).

63 § 3-412(1).

64 § 3-412(2).

acceptance. The fact that a secondary party fails to object is not sufficient to prevent his release from liability.

§ 31:18. Form of Acceptance. An acceptance is the drawee's notation on the draft itself that he will make payment as directed thereby. It may be merely his signature, but customarily it will be the word "Accepted," and his signature, and generally the date. In any case, however, the acceptance must be written on the draft itself.[65] Usually it is written across the face of the instrument.

An acceptance cannot be oral, nor can it be contained in some other writing. Thus, a bank is not bound by its oral promise to pay a draft drawn upon it.[66] The fact that the drawee is not liable on the draft because he has not accepted it does not necessarily prevent his being liable because of other obligations or principles of law. (See p. 629, Home Saving Bank v General Finance Corp.)

There can be no acceptance by misconduct. The refusal to return the draft or its destruction by the drawee does not constitute an "acceptance." If the drawee retains the draft and refuses to return it, he is guilty of conversion.[67] The measure of damages is the face amount of the instrument.[68]

§ 31:19. Dishonor by Nonacceptance. When a draft that is presented for acceptance is not accepted within the allowed time, the person presenting it must treat the draft as dishonored by nonacceptance.[69] If he fails to do so, the secondary parties are released from liability.

When a draft is dishonored by nonacceptance, the holder must give the same notice of dishonor as in the case of dishonor of paper by nonpayment. If the draft on its face appears to be drawn or payable outside of the United States, its territories, and the District of Columbia, it is also necessary to protest the dishonor in order to charge the drawer and the indorsers.[70]

§ 31:20. Presentment of Draft for Payment. The requirements and limitations upon the necessity of presentment of a draft for payment are the same as in the case of a promissory note, with the circumstances excusing delays or failure to make presentment of a note likewise excusing delay or failure to make presentment of a draft for payment. The failure to present for payment is likewise excused with respect to a party who has countermanded payment of the draft.[71]

Furthermore, when a draft has been dishonored by nonacceptance, a later presentment for payment is excused unless the instrument has since been accepted.[72]

---

[65] § 3-410(1).

[66] Womack v Durrett, (Tex Civ App) 24 SW2d 463.

[67] § 3-419(1)(a).

[68] § 3-419(2).

[69] § 3-507(1)(a).

[70] § 3-501(3).

[71] § 3-511(1),(2),(3).

[72] § 3-511(4).

The provisions governing notice of dishonor of a draft by nonpayment are the same as those for a note.[73]

§ 31:21. Protest of Dishonor. A protest of dishonor of a draft by nonacceptance or nonpayment is not necessary unless the draft appears on its face to be drawn or payable outside of the United States, its territories, or the District of Columbia. The holder, however, may protest the dishonor of any instrument.[74] Delay in protesting dishonor or the absence of a protest are excused under the same circumstances that apply in the case of a note dishonored by nonpayment.[75]

(1) Waiver of Protest. A *waiver of protest* is effective to excuse the absence of an otherwise required protest. Protest is commonly waived, particulary in the case of out-of-town instruments, because protesting does involve an additional cost and some inconvenience. Frequently, therefore, the instrument will contain a clause stating that protest is waived, or it may be stamped with the words, "Protest waived" or "No Protest." A waiver of protest is a waiver of the requirement of presentment and notice of dishonor as well as of the protest itself even though protest is not required.[76]

When words of guaranty, such as "payment guaranteed" or "collection guaranteed," are used, presentment, notice of dishonor, and protest are not necessary to charge the person using such language.[77]

73 §§ 3-501(2), 3-508. See § 31:8.
74 § 3-501(3).
75 § 3-511(1),(2).
76 § 3-511(5).
77 § 3-416(5).

CASES FOR CHAPTER 31

Bertolet v Burke

(DC Virgin Islands) 295 F Supp 1176 (1969)

Burke executed a promissory note. He later informed Bertolet, the holder of the note, that he would not make payment on the note when it became due. Bertolet immediately sued Burke. The defendant moved for summary judgment.

STALEY, C.J. . . . The issue presented by this motion for summary judgment is whether a cause of action can be sustained on a promissory note before maturity if it appears that the maker has declared his intention not to pay.

Plaintiff, W. M. Bertolet, brought this action against Frank G. Burke, . . . alleging that Burke informed him in writing that he does not intend to make good on a promissory note, payable to plaintiff, which is due to mature on October 1, 1969. The note was executed on October 1, 1966, and bears the face amount of $18,729, with interest at the rate of 6 percent per annum. At this point in time, the contract for the payment of money represented by the promissory note is a unilateral one, since plaintiff has fully performed, and he asks only that he be paid now or be otherwise secured for that which is owed him.

According to [UCC] § 3-122(1)(a), a cause of action against the maker of a time instrument does not accrue until the day after maturity. We are aware of no provision under Article 3 of . . . (Uniform Commercial Code), entitled "Commercial Paper," which permits an action on a promissory note for anticipatory breach. Nor are we aware of any other statute or Virgin Islands case law which would support such an action. This being the case, we must refer to the Restatement, since V.I.C. § 4 provides: "The rules of the common law, as expressed in the restatements of the law approved by the American Law Institute, and to the extent not so expressed, as generally understood and applied in the United States, shall be the rules of decision in the courts of the Virgin Islands in cases to which they apply, in the absence of local laws to the contrary."

Restatement of Contracts § 318 (1932) covers those situations constituting an anticipatory repudiation and a total breach of contract. Comment *e* of § 318 states that: "The doctrine of anticipatory breach is not extended to unilateral contracts unless the promisor's duty is conditional on some future performance by the promisee. It is immaterial whether the contract was originally thus unconditionally unilateral or has become so by the performance of one party. In neither case can a breach arise before the time fixed in the contract for the performance. There must be some dependency of performances in order to make anticipatory breach possible."

Illustration 10 of § 318 presents a factual situation quite analogous to the instant case. There it is said: "*A*, in consideration of $10,000 then paid to him by *B*, promises *B* to transfer Blackacre to *B* on the first day of the following May. Before that day *A* tells *B* that he will not transfer the land as promised. Since the contract is unilateral, *A* has not committed an anticipatory breach of contract."

Our research reveals that the case law is in overwhelming concurrence with the position adopted by the Restatement. . . . In view of the great weight of authority on this issue, we are of the opinion that plaintiff's action cannot be sustained.

[Plaintiff's complaint dismissed.]

In re Eton Furniture Company

(CA3 Pa) 286 F2d 93 (1961)

Huntington was the general manager of the Eton Furniture Co. From time to time he borrowed money from the bank on behalf of Eton but would give his individual note to the bank and sometimes would pledge his own automobile as security. When Eton's checking account in the bank would have on deposit an amount greater than the loan to Eton, the bank would deduct the amount of the loan with interest from Eton's account. Eton was declared a bankrupt, and the trustee in bankruptcy demanded that the bank return the amounts which it had deducted from Eton's account. From a decision in favor of the bank, the trustee in bankruptcy appealed.

BIGGS, C.J. . . . The trustee asserted that the loans negotiated by Huntington from the Bank, and for which he gave his personal notes to the Bank were loans to him and not to Eton. It was argued that Eton received the proceeds of the loans from Huntington and not from the Bank, and that therefore the satisfaction of the obligations from Eton's account with the Bank constituted an unjustified appropriation of Eton's funds by the Bank to pay the debts of another.

. . . Huntington testified that when Eton was short of funds and not in a position to borrow from the Bank, he would procure a loan for Eton on the strength of his personal note, sometimes putting up his car as additional collateral. He stated that these loans were negotiated by him on behalf of Eton and that his notes which he gave to the Bank were collateral security for primary obligations of Eton. . . . "The course of dealing between Huntington and the Bank renders it clear that each understood that when Huntington borrowed money and credited the proceeds to Eton's account, Huntington was acting for the account of and in the interest of Eton, his principal." . . .

The single issue which this court must determine is whether Eton was indebted to the Bank in the amounts of the loans negotiated by Huntington, its general manager. The trustee makes two arguments which we must consider. First, relying on Section 3-401(1) of the Uniform Commercial Code, . . . , he contends that since Huntington's signature alone appears on the notes given by him to the Bank, Huntington alone can be held liable by the Bank for repayment of the loans. Second, he argues that Huntington was not authorized to borrow money for Eton and that, therefore, regardless of any understanding that may have existed between Huntington and the Bank, Eton, not being bound, could not be liable for repayment of the loans.

. . . We . . . start with the premise that Huntington's notes were intended to be collateral security, that all of the parties so understood the transaction, and that the money was in fact used by Eton for its own benefit.

Section 3-401(1) provides that "No person is liable on an instrument unless his signature appears thereon." On the basis of this provision the trustee contends that Eton, not having signed the notes given to the Bank, cannot be held liable for repayment of the loans. This argument finds no support in the words of the statute which provides merely that one who does not sign a note cannot be liable on the note. Contrary to the trustee's argument, the provision quoted cannot be read to mean that no person is liable on a debt whose signature does not appear on a note given as collateral security for that debt. Indeed, it has long been settled in Pennsylvania and elsewhere that the one to whom money is loaned or property advanced is liable for the debt regardless of the fact that his name may not appear on the security taken if that security was regarded by the parties purely as collateral. That Section 3-401(1) was not intended to change this rule is demonstrated clearly by the comment to that section which states in pertinent part: "Nothing in this section is intended to prevent any liability arising apart from the instrument itself. The party who does not sign may still be liable on the original obligation for which the instrument was given. . . ." . . .

In the present case, the evidence of Huntington, adopted "as verity" by the referee, similarly shows that the loans were for Eton's use, that the Bank, Eton, and Huntington understood this to be so, and that the money was in fact used by the Company for its own benefit. We hold that the finding of the referee and that of the court . . . that the debts were incurred by Eton is supported by the evidence and that their rulings are in accordance with the applicable law.

The trustee's contention that Huntington had no authority to incur debts on behalf of the corporation also is without merit. Even if it be assumed that Huntington did not have the authority to borrow money on behalf of Eton the actual receipt and use of the money by Eton constituted ratification of Huntington's acts. . . .

[Judgment affirmed.]

Hane v Exten

255 Md 668, 259 A2d 290 (1969)

Theta Electronic Laboratories executed a promissory note payable to Thomson and his wife, which was indorsed by Exten, O'Neil, and James Hane and their wives. The Thomsons assigned it to John Hane. The note was not paid when due. John Hane took judgment by confession against Theta and the prior indorsers. The judgment against the Extens was vacated, and John Hane appealed.

SINGLEY, J. . . . John B. Hane is the assignee of the note of Theta Electronic Laboratories, Inc. (Theta) in the stated amount of $15,377.07, with interest at 6 percent per annum. The note was dated 10 August 1964; stipulated that the first monthly payment of $320.47 would be due five months from date, or on 10 January 1965; and that "In the event of the failure to pay the interest or principal, as the same becomes due on this Note, the entire debt represented hereby shall at the end of thirty (30) days become due and demandable. . . ." The note was assigned without recourse to Hane by George B. and Marguerite F. Thomson, the original payees, on 26 November 1965. A default having occurred in the making of the monthly payments, Hane took judgments by confession in the Circuit Court for Montgomery County on 7 June 1967 against Theta and three individuals, Gerald M. Exten, Emil L. O'Neil, and James W. Hane, and their wives, who had indorsed Theta's note. On motion of the Extens, the judgment was vacated as to them and the case came on for trial on the merits before the court without a jury. From a judgment for the Extens for costs. Hane has appealed.

This case raises the familiar question: Must Hane show that the Extens were given notice of presentment and dishonor before he can hold them on their indorsement?

The court below, in finding for the Extens, relied on the provisions of Uniform Commercial Code. . . . § 3-414(1) provides:

"Unless the indorsement otherwise specifies (as by such words as 'without recourse') every indorser engages that upon dishonor and any necessary notice of dishonor and protest he will pay the instrument according to its tenor at the time of his indorsement to the holder or to any subsequent indorser who takes it up, even though the indorser who takes it up was not obligated to do so."

§ 3-501(1)(b) provides that "Presentment for payment is necessary to charge any indorser" and § 3-501(2)(a) that "Notice of any dishonor is necessary to charge any indorser," in each case subject, however, to the provisions of § 3-511 which recite the circumstances under which notice of dishonor may be waived or excused, none of which is here present. § 3-502 (1)(a) makes it clear that unless presentment or notice of dishonor is waived or excused, unreasonable delay will discharge an indorser. . . .

There was testimony from which the trier of facts could find as he did that presentment and notice of dishonor were unduly delayed.

It is clear that Hane held the note from November, 1965, until some time in April, 1967, before he made demand for payment. UCC § 3-503(1)(d) provides that "Where an instrument is accelerated, presentment for payment is due within a reasonable time after the acceleration." "Reasonable time" is not defined in § 3-503, except that § 3-503(2) provides, "A reasonable time for presentment is determined by the nature of the instrument, any usage of banking or trade, and the facts of the particular case." But § 1-204(2) characterizes it: "What is a reasonable time for taking any action depends on the nature, purpose, and circumstances of such action."

Reasonableness is primarily a question for the fact finder. Vanderberg & Sons, N. V. v Siter, 204 Pa Super 392, 204 A2d 494 (1964); . . . 1 Anderson's Uniform Commercial Code, Commentary, § 1-204:3. . . . We see no reason to disturb the lower court's finding that Hane's delay of almost 18 months in presenting the note "was unreasonable from any viewpoint." . . .

As regards notice of dishonor, § 3-508(2) requires that notice be given by persons other than banks "before midnight of the third business day after dishonor or receipt of notice of dishonor." Exten, called as an adverse witness by Hane, testified that his first notice that the note had not been paid was the entry of the confessed judgment on 7 June 1967. Hane's brother testified that demand had been made about 15 April 1967. He was uncertain as to when he had given Exten notice of dishonor, but finally conceded that it was "within a week." The lower court found that the ambiguity of this testimony, coupled with Exten's denial that he had received *any* notice before 7 June fell short of meeting the three-day notice requirement of the UCC. The date of giving notice of dishonor is a question of fact, solely for determination by the trier of facts. . . . We cannot say that the court erred in its finding.

In the absence of evidence that presentment and notice of dishonor were waived or excused, Hane's unreasonable delay discharged the Extens, § 3-502(1)(a). . . .

[Judgment affirmed, costs to be paid by appellant.]

Port City State Bank v American National Bank

(CA10 Okla) 486 F2d 196 (1973)

Port City State Bank received two checks for collection. It sent them to American National Bank, the drawee bank. The drawee bank returned the checks as dishonored for insufficient funds after the midnight deadline. Port City sued American National, basing liability on the late return. American National raised the defense that its computer had broken down. Judgment was entered for American National and Port City State Bank appealed.

HILL, C.J. . . . It was stipulated that [the] check was [not] dishonored before the applicable deadline.

These facts establish a prima facie case for the application of 12 C.F.R. 210.12 and [UCC §] 4-302(a), both concerning the necessity of fulfilling the midnight deadline, and thus it became the obligation of appellee at the trial to prove an excuse from these provisions under 12 C.F.R. 210.14 and [UCC §] 4-108(2) [which] prevent the operation of the midnight deadline in cases when the delay by the payor bank is caused by the interruption of communication facilities, suspension of payments by another bank, war, emergency condition or other circumstances beyond the control of the bank provided it exercises such diligence as the circumstances require.

In furtherance of its contention, American National presented evidence that prior to December 1, 1969, it had performed its bookkeeping functions by machine posting, a so-called manual system. During 1969, however, a decision was made to implement a computer bookkeeping operation, and a rental agreement was entered into with a large computer company. That lease provided that all repairs and maintenance were the obligation of the computer firm, and American National was not authorized to undertake any such tasks. After the installation of the computer, American National paralleled its manual system with computer operations for approximately two weeks. Finally the decision was made to change over to computer processing beginning on December 1. A last manual posting was made on Saturday, November 29, and the manual bookkeeping equipment was removed from the bank during that weekend.

At approximately 10:00 a.m. on December 1, the first day for use of computer operations, the American National computer developed a "memory error" which rendered it unusable. Though the computer manufacturer indicated repairs would not take "too long," they lasted until late Monday night and the testing procedure extended into the early hours of Tuesday, December 2.

In reliance upon the belief that the computer would be repaired without prolonged delay, American National took no extraordinary steps to process Monday's business during the business day. However, when it became apparent that evening that the computer was not going to be ready immediately, American National decided to utilize an identical computer in a bank which was a trip of some 2½ hours away, in accord with a backup agreement they had made with the other banking institution. Thus at about 11:30 p.m. personnel from American National and the computer company began processing Monday's business on the backup computer and continued processing through the night. This work had proceeded to the point of capturing the items on discs when, because the backup computer was required by its owner and because they were informed their own computer was operational, the American National personnel returned to their bank to complete the work on their own machine. After returning to American National, the work was processed to the point of completing the printing of the trial balances when another memory error developed which again rendered the computer unusable. No further use could be made of the appellee's computer until a new memory module was installed on Thursday, December 4.

Because of the second failure, American National was forced to utilize the backup computer both Wednesday and Thursday during times it was not required by its owner. Monday's business was completed and work was begun on Tuesday's items the evening of Tuesday, December 2. Tuesday's items were not completed until either Wednesday, the third, or Thursday, the fourth. When the second check arrived in Tuesday's business, it was held to determine if a later deposit had balanced the account. Through the use of the backup computer and then its own computer during the next weekend, American National was fully "caught up" by Monday, December 8.

Based upon this evidence, the trial court held that the computer malfunction suffered by American National was the cause of its failure to meet its required midnight deadline on the checks, and that such malfunction constituted both an emergency condition and a circumstance beyond the control of the bank as outlined in 12 C.F.R. 210.14 and [UCC §] 4-108(2). The court further held that the reaction to the situation by American National fulfilled the requirements of diligence imposed by those regulations, and therefore the court entered judgment for American National. . . .

. . . Appellant contends that a computer failure, as a matter of law, is not an event which [requires] the application of [UCC §]

4-108(2). In our opinion, such a determination is a mixed question of fact and law; however, neither treatment justifies the reversal of the trial court's determination in this case. Factually, it was in no way erroneous to conclude that the malfunction created an emergency condition in the bank and was also a condition beyond the control of the bank. Appellant's argument that in law this malfunction is not included within the prescribed contingencies of § 4-108(2) is without foundation. The statute is clear and unambiguous on its face. . . .

Port City next alleges that the trial court erred in its determination that American National exercised "such diligence" as the circumstances required. Basically, appellant asserts [there were] alternative procedures that American National could have employed, and asserts that if any of these alternatives would have resulted in meeting the deadline, then appellee did not exercise diligence under the circumstances. As the trial court correctly concluded, the statute does not require perfection on the part of appellee, and American National's performance should not be judged on the basis of 20-20 hindsight.

It must first be noted that appellee quickly notified the computer firm of the breakdown, and that company began an immediate repair effort. Further, there was evidence to indicate that such computer breakdowns are generally repaired very quickly. Thus it would appear that appellee was justified in its initial delay in adopting emergency procedures based on its belief such measures would prove unnecessary. Additionally, we must agree with the trial court that appellee's duty under these circumstances was much broader than one requiring merely that it meet its midnight deadline. It was further obligated to keep the bank open and to serve its customers. To abandon the orderly day by day process of bookkeeping to adopt radical emergency measures would have likely prolonged the delay in returning the bank to normal operations.

As to appellant's assertion that appellee should have returned to manual posting, it was shown that the equipment for this procedure was no longer in the bank. Further, no clear evidence was presented to indicate such a procedure would have allowed appellee to fulfill its deadlines if the procedure had been implemented. Any decision to return to manual posting would have to have been made very soon after the discovery of the initial failure. At that time, because of their own experience with computers and the industry history, and also because the manufacturer did not foresee the serious nature of the repairs, American National was justified in believing its computer would be back in service soon. Their delay in commencing emergency operations was reasonable, and these facts prevented a return to manual posting in time to fulfill the deadlines.

As to the possibility of utilizing another backup computer at the regional headquarters of the computer leasing firm, we must agree with the trial court that there was no evidence that this alternative would have proved any more successful than the method actually employed by appellee. . . .

[Judgment affirmed.]

Gill v Yoes

(Okla) 360 P2d 506 (1961)

Gill sold his airplane to Hobson for $8,000. The purchase price was paid by delivering to Gill a draft drawn by Yoes on the Phoenix Savings & Loan Company to the order of Gill. Yoes had no money in the savings and loan association but had applied to it for a loan. The loan application was rejected; and when the draft was presented to the association, it refused to pay it. Gill then sued Yoes on the draft. From a judgment for Yoes, Gill appealed.

PER CURIAM . . . The defendant claimed that she had nothing to do with the purchase of the plane except that she did sign the draft for $8,000 to pay for it; that she knew nothing about the dealings between Hobson and plaintiff; that she had no need for a plane and that she did not buy it. . . .

. . . [NIL Sec. 61] specifically deals with the liability of a drawer of the instrument. It provides in part, "The drawer by drawing the instrument . . . engages that on due presentment the instrument will be accepted and paid or both, according to its tenor. . . ."

The defendant by her answer injected into this case the proposition that the draft given for the plane was for the benefit of a third party, one Hobson. It is really immaterial whether the draft was given for the purchase of the plane by either Hobson or the defendant just so long as it was given. . . .

Defendant represented that she was putting the $8,000 into the transaction and she cannot avoid liability simply because the draft was not honored. . . .

[Judgment reversed.]

Code Comment: The same decision would be made under the Uniform Commercial Code. The substance of NIL § 61 on which the decision is based is restated in UCC § 3-413(2).

Home Savings Bank v General Finance Corp.

10 Wis 2d 417, 103 NW2d 117 (1960)

Schenk's Motor Sales had a checking account in the Home Savings Bank. The bank certified a check drawn by Schenk in reliance on the oral promise of the General Finance Corp. to accept a draft drawn on General by Schenk that had just been deposited in Schenk's account. The certified check was paid by the bank, but General refused to pay the draft on the ground that its oral acceptance was not binding. The bank sued General for the amount of the certified check. From a judgment in favor of General, the Bank appealed.

FAIRCHILD, J. . . . Plaintiff bank points out that it is not attempting to recover from General Finance upon an accepted bill of exchange. . . . "The acceptance must be in writing and signed by the drawee." . . . Plaintiff bank does claim, however, that General Finance orally promised to accept the draft if the bank would certify the $9,700 check payable to General Finance; that the bank did so, and thereby accepted the offer and furnished consideration for the promise . . . .

The essential elements of quasi contract are a benefit conferred upon the defendant by the plaintiff, appreciation by the defendant of such benefit, and acceptance and retention by the defendant of such benefit under circumstances such that it would be inequitable to retain the benefit without payment of the value thereof. . . . The conferring of the benefit and appreciation by defendant are clear.

It also seems clear that at least as to a part of the money, retention by General Finance is inequitable. It is beyond belief that General Finance could have obtained cash for the $9,700 check in any way except by persuading the bank president that the draft would be honored. No matter how gullible or careless it may have been for the president to rely upon an oral acceptance, the retention of the bank's money after refusal to honor the draft as promised cannot be considered equitable.

$3,080.56 was the balance in Schenk's account when the check was certified. The record does not disclose the payment of any checks by the bank after that except the one for $9,700. We think the amount which General Finance cannot equitably retain is the difference between $9,700 and $3,080.56, or $6,619.44. . . .

It has been suggested that since an acceptance of a bill must be in writing in order to be enforceable, it is against public policy to grant restitution in the situation here present. This question is considered in Restatement, Contracts, sec. 355. In comment *a* of subsec. 1, it is said: "The parties to a contract that is rendered unenforceable by the Statute of Frauds or some similar statute very frequently act in reliance on it by rendering the agreed performance, in part or in whole, or by making improvements on land that is the subject matter of the contract. In such cases, the refusal of all judicial remedy would result in harm to one party and unjust enrichment of the other. Therefore, restitution is enforced even though the Statute makes other remedies unavailable.". . .

[Judgment for defendant reversed.]

Code Comment: The same decision would be made under the Uniform Commercial Code because the principles on which the case was decided are general principles that are not displaced by the Code. UCC § 1-103.

QUESTIONS AND CASE PROBLEMS

1. Four promissory notes were executed by Continental Diamond Mines, Inc. payable to the order of M. Kopp. The notes were thereafter indorsed to M. Kopp, Inc. and then to Rafkin. Rafkin was the holder on the due date. Was it necessary for him to make a presentment of the notes to Continental Diamond Mines in order to hold it liable on the notes? [Rafkin v Continental Diamond Mines, Inc., 33 Misc 2d 156, 228 NYS2d 317]
2. *A* indorsed a promissory note on the back. At the top of the back, above all indorsements, there were printed the words "Notice of protest waived." The note was not paid when due. The holder sent *A* notice that the note was not paid, but *A* did not receive the notice because it was sent to a former address at which he no longer lived. *A* denied liability because he had not been properly notified. Decide. [Lizza Asphalt Construction Co. v Greenvale Construction Co., (NY Sup Ct) 4 UCCRS 954]
3. *X* was the principal officer and ran the business of the *X* Corporation. *X* Corporation issued its promissory note payable to *A*. *X* indorsed the note as an accommodation indorser, although he knew that *X* Corporation would not be able to pay the note on the due date. The note was not paid on the due date. *A* sued *X*. *X* raised the defense that *A* had not presented the note to *X* Corporation on the due date. Was this defense valid? [A. J. Armstrong Co. v Janburt Embroidery Corp., 97 NJ Super 246, 234 A2d 737; Makel Textiles v Dolly Originals, (NY Sup Ct) 4 UCCRS 95]
4. Dubinsky borrowed money from the Columbian National Life Insurance Co. He sold his house to Cohen who promised to pay this debt to the insurance company and gave it a promissory note. Later Dubinsky gave the company a renewal note. In a suit upon the renewal note Dubinsky claimed that he was an accommodation maker. Decide. [Columbian National Life Insurance Co. v Dubinsky, 349 Mo 299, 160 SW2d 727]
5. *H* was the holder of a note on which *M* was the maker. *H* owed money to *I* and indorsed *M*'s note to *I* in payment of his debt. Thereafter *M* failed to pay his note to *I*. When *I* demanded that *H* pay his original debt to *I*, *H* raised the defense that *I* had taken *M*'s note in payment of that debt so that it no longer existed. Decide. [Central Stone Co. v John Ruggiero, Inc., 49 Misc 2d 622, 268 NYS2d 172]
6. The *X* Bank sold money orders in which it was the drawer and by which it ordered itself to pay the amount of the money order through the *Z* Bank to the person designated by the purchaser of the money order. (a) Assuming that the instruments were negotiable, what kind of commerial paper were the money orders? (b) Was the *X* Bank or the *Z* Bank the drawee? [Comet Check Cashing Service v Hanover Insurance Group, (NY Civ Ct) 5 UCCRS 852]
7. The Perfection Curing Co. gave the First National Bank of Winnfield a sight draft drawn by it on the Citizens' Bank of Campti. The First National Bank sent the sight draft to the Citizens' Bank for acceptance and payment. The Citizens' Bank received the draft on September 28. On October 11 the Citizens' Bank returned the draft to the First National Bank without either accepting or rejecting the draft. The First National Bank sued the Citizens' Bank on the draft. Can it recover? [First National Bank of Winnfield v Citizens' Bank of Campti, 163 La 919, 113 So 147]

8. Lowe & Myers were contractors doing construction work for the Druid Realty Co. In order to pay for their materials they drew a draft on the realty company directing it to pay $2,000 to the order of the Crane Co. The realty company, through its president, wrote on the instrument that it accepted the instrument and agreed to pay it within 30 days after the completion of the work, provided Crane Company continued to furnish materials to Lowe & Myers. What was the effect of the action by the realty company? [Crane Co. v Druid Realty Co., 137 Md 324, 112 A 621]

9. Fuller Brothers, as the holder, brought an action against Bovay, as indorser. It was shown that the notice of default of the primary party was given to Bovay by a letter addressed "Jonesboro Rice Mill Co., Jonesboro, Ark., Attention Mr. Bovay." Was this a proper notice? [Bovay v Fuller, (CA8 Ark) 63 F2d 280]

10. Drummond executed a draft on the Webb Packing Co. to pay for cattle purchased from Hales. The Webb Packing Co. refused to accept or to pay the draft. Hales gave proper notice to Drummond and then sued him on the draft. Drummond raised the defense that he had been acting merely as the agent of the Webb Packing Co. and that it was understood with Hales that Drummond should not be personally liable on the instrument. Was this a good defense? [Drummond v Hales, (CA10 Okla) 191 F2d 972]

11. De Lise was secondarily liable on a note held by the First Pennsylvania Banking & Trust Co. When sued on the note, De Lise claimed that he was not liable because notice of the maker's default had been given by telephone. Was this a valid defense? [First Pennsylvania Banking & Trust Co. v De Lise, 186 Pa Super 398, 142 A2d 401]

12. In an action brought by Hughes against a corporation that had indorsed a promissory note, the latter claimed that notice of protest had not been properly given. It was shown that the notice had been left at the company's office during business hours after the holder was unable to find any of the officers of the corporation. Was sufficient notice given? [Hughes v Rankin Realty Co., 108 NJL 185, 158 A 487]

13. Mellen-Wright Lumber Co., the holder of a note, sued McNett, as maker, and Kendall, as indorser. The latter claimed that he had not received notice of the dishonor of the note by the maker. The holder proved that he had sent the following letter, dated June 10, to Kendall:

> Dear Sir: We hold note for $2,000 with interest at 7 percent signed by Earl P. McNett and Anna J. McNett, his wife, on which you indorsed guaranteeing payment.
>
> This note will be due June 12 and we are going to ask that you arrange to pay same promptly. We would appreciate this being paid by not later than Friday, June 18.
>
> Kindly advise if you wish to make payment at our office or at one of our local banks.
>
> We are enclosing stamped envelope for reply.

Was Kendall liable? [Mellen-Wright Lumber Co. v McNett, 242 Mich 369, 218 NW 709]

32 Checks and Bank Collections

Of the various types of commercial paper in use today, by far the most common is the check. By means of checks it is possible to make payment safely and conveniently without the need of safeguarding a shipment of money. The checkbook stub and the canceled check make a written record which may be used at a later date to show that a payment was made.

§ 32:1. **Nature of a Check.** A check is a particular kind of draft. The following features of a check distinguish it from other drafts or bills of exchange: [1]

(1) The drawee of a check is always a bank.

(2) As a practical matter, the check is drawn on the assumption that the bank has on deposit in the drawer's account an amount sufficient to pay the check. In the case of a draft, there is no assumption that the drawee has any of the drawer's money with which to pay the instrument. Actually, the rights of the parties are not affected by the fact that the depositor does not have funds on deposit with the bank sufficient to pay the check.

If a draft is dishonored, the drawer is civilly liable; but if a check is drawn with intent to defraud the person to whom it is delivered, the drawer is also subject to criminal prosecution [2] in most states under what are known as *bad check laws*. Most states provide that if the check is not made good within a stated period, such as 10 days, it will be presumed that the check was originally issued with the intent to defraud.

(3) A check is demand paper. A draft may be payable either on demand or at a future date. The standard form of check does not specify when it is payable, and it is therefore automatically payable on demand. This eliminates the need for an acceptance since the holder of the check will merely present it for payment.

One exception arises when a check is postdated, that is, when the check shows a date later than the actual date of execution and delivery. Here the check is not payable until that date arrives. This, in effect, changes the check

---

[1] Checks are governed by both Article 3 of the UCC relating to commercial paper and Article 4 governing bank deposits and collections.

[2] State v De Nicola, 163 Ohio 140, 126 NE2d 62.

to time paper without expressly stating so. (See p. 642, Pennsylvania v Kelinson.)

The delivery of a check is not regarded as an assignment of the money on deposit. It therefore does not automatically transfer the rights of the depositor against his bank to the holder of the check, and there is no duty on the part of the drawee bank to pay the holder the amount of the check.[3]

If a creditor of the depositor attaches or garnishees the bank account before a check drawn on that account has been paid by the bank, the creditor takes priority over the payee of a check which had been earlier drawn on that account.[4]

§ 32:2. Indication of Purpose. Although not required by law, a notation on a check of the purpose for which it is delivered is desirable. It serves to identify the payment in case the purpose is questioned later. Customary notations are "Payment of invoice No. 3924," "Painting house, 1972," or "Fees, drafting of will." If a payee cashes a check bearing such a notation, he is estopped from denying that the payment was made and received for the purpose stated.

A common form of notation is the statement "In full payment (or settlement) of the claim of. . . ." When a check with such a notation is accepted by the payee, the claim referred to is probably discharged without regard to whether the amount of the check was the full amount of the claim or only a part, and without regard to whether there was any dispute as to the actual amount due.

A special form of check, known as a *voucher check,* is used by some businesses. This form is larger than an ordinary check. The additional space is used for stating the purpose of the check or for listing the items of an invoice for which the check is issued in payment. When the payee receives a voucher check, he detaches the voucher portion of the form and keeps it in his files as a record of the payment that he has received.

§ 32:3. Liability of Drawer. If the check is presented for payment and paid, no liability of the drawer arises. If the bank refuses to make payment, the drawer is then subject to a liability similar to that in the case of the nonpayment of an ordinary draft. If proper notice of dishonor is not given the drawer of the check, he may be discharged from liability to the same extent as a drawer of an ordinary draft.

§ 32:4. Duties of Drawee Bank. It is necessary to distinguish between the status of the drawer with respect to his check and his relationship with his bank on the contract of deposit.

(1) Privacy. The bank owes the depositor the duty of maintaining secrecy concerning information which the bank acquires in connection with the depositor-bank relationship.

---

[3] UCC § 3-409(1).

[4] State Bank of Southern Utah v Stallings, 19 Utah 2d 146, 427 P2d 744.

(2) Payment. The bank is under a general contractual duty to its depositor to pay on demand [5] all of his checks to the extent of the funds deposited to his credit. When the bank breaches this contract, it is liable to the drawer for damages.[6] In the case of a draft, there is ordinarily no duty on the drawee to accept it, or to make payment if he has not accepted it.

Although the drawee bank is liable for improperly refusing to pay a check, this liability runs in favor of the drawer alone. Even though the holder of the check or the payee may be harmed when the bank refuses to pay the check, the holder or payee has no right to sue the bank. A holder other than the payee is limited to proceeding on the check against the secondary parties. The payee may also proceed against the drawer on the original obligation, which has not been discharged because the check was not paid.[7]

A bank acting in good faith may pay a check presented more than six months after its date (commonly known as a *stale check*); but, unless the check is certified, it is not required to do so.[8] The fact that a bank may refuse to pay a check which is more than six months old does not mean that it must pay a check which is less than six months old or that it is not required to exercise reasonable care in making payment of any check.[9]

§ 32:5. Stopping Payment. The drawer has the power of stopping payment of a check. After the check is issued, he can notify the drawee bank not to pay it when it is presented for payment. This is a useful device when a check is lost or mislaid. A duplicate check can be written and, to make sure that the payee does not receive payment twice or that an improper person does not receive payment on the first check, payment on the first check can be stopped. Likewise, if payment is made by check and then the payee defaults on his contract so that the drawer would have a claim against him, payment on the check can be stopped, assuming that the payee has not cashed it.

The *stop-payment order* may be either oral or written. If oral, however, it is only binding on the bank for 14 calendar days unless confirmed in writing within that time. A written order is not effective after 6 months unless renewed in writing.[10]

If the bank makes payment of a check after it has been properly notified to stop payment, it is liable to the depositor for the loss he sustains, in the absence of a valid limitation of the bank's liability. The burden of establishing the loss resulting in such case rests upon the depositor.[11] (See p. 643, Tusso v Security National Bank.) Thus, the bank does not become automatically liable for the amount of the check paid in violation of the stop-payment order. The bank is only liable to the extent that it is shown that

---

[5] Petition of Leon Keyser, 98 NH 198, 96 A2d 551.

[6] Collins v City National Bank & Trust Co., 131 Conn 167, 38 A2d 582.

[7] UCC § 3-802(1)(b).

[8] § 4-404.

[9] W. P. Harlin Construction Co. v Continental Bank & Trust Co., 23 Utah 2d 422, 464 P2d 585.

[10] UCC § 4-403(2).

[11] § 4-403(3).

the payment has caused loss to the depositor through the making of a payment on a claim which the depositor was not legally obligated to pay.[12]

The act of stopping payment may in some cases make the depositor liable to the holder of the instrument. If the depositor has no proper ground for stopping payment, he is liable to the payee to whom he has delivered the check. In any case, he is liable for stopping payment with respect to any holder in due course [13] or other party having the rights of a holder in due course, unless he stops payment for a reason that may be asserted against such holder as a defense. The fact that the bank refuses to make payment because of the drawer's instruction does not make the case any different from any other instance in which the drawee refuses to pay.

Generally payment is stopped only when the drawer has good cause with respect to the payee. For example, the purchaser of goods may give the seller a check in advance payment for the goods. The seller may then declare that he is not going to deliver the goods. The purchaser is within his lawful rights if he stops payment on the check since the seller has no right to the check if he does not perform his part of the sales contract. Thus, the payee could not sue the drawer-purchaser for stopping payment on the check. If the check has been negotiated to a subsequent holder who is a holder in due course, the purchaser cannot assert this defense. That is, such a favored holder can hold the drawer liable on the dishonored check.

When the depositor does not give the bank the stop-payment notice in person but makes use of a means of communication such as the telegraph, he cannot hold the bank liable if the notice is delayed in reaching the bank which makes payment before receiving the notice. If negligence on the part of the telegraph company can be established, however, the depositor can sue that company.

It is to the advantage of the seller to require either a certified check of the buyer or a cashier's check from the buyer's bank payable to the order of the seller, for with respect to either check neither the buyer nor the buyer's bank can stop payment to the seller.[14]

§ 32:6. Time of Presentment of Check for Payment. In order to charge a secondary party to demand paper, presentment for payment must generally be made upon the primary party to the instrument within a reasonable time after that secondary party signs it. Reasonable time is determined by the nature of the instrument, by commercial usage, and by the facts of the particular case.[15]

Failure to make such timely presentment discharges all prior indorsers of the instrument. It also discharges the drawer, if the draft is payable at a bank, to the extent that he has lost, through the bank's failure, money which he had on deposit at the bank to meet the payment of the instrument.[16]

---

[12] Cicci v Lincoln National Bank and Trust Co., 46 Misc 2d 465, 260 NYS2d 100.
[13] Illinois v Lombardi, 13 Ill App 3d 754, 301 NE2d 70.
[14] Malphrus v Home Savings Bank, 44 Misc 2d 705, 254 NYS2d 980.
[15] UCC § 3-503(1)(e),(2).
[16] § 3-502(1).

As a modification to the foregoing principles, the UCC establishes two presumptions as to what is a reasonable time in which to present a check for payment.[17] If the check is not certified and is both drawn and payable within the United States, it is presumed as to the drawer that 30 days after the date of the check or the date of its issuance, whichever is later, is the reasonable period in which to make presentment for payment. In the case of an indorser, it is presumed to be 7 days after his indorsement.[18]

(1) Bank's Liability to Drawer. The contract between the drawer-depositor and the drawee-bank obligates the latter to pay in accordance with the orders of its depositor as long as there is sufficient money on deposit to make such payment. If the bank improperly refuses to make payment, it is liable to the drawer for damages which he sustains in consequence of such dishonor. (See p. 644, Allison v First National Bank.)

(2) Bank's Liability to Holder. If the check has not been certified, the holder has no claim against the bank for the dishonor of the check, regardless of the fact that the bank had acted in breach of its contract with its depositor. If the bank had certified the check, it is liable to the holder when it dishonors the check as the certification imposes upon the bank a primary liability to pay the face amount of the check.

Regardless of whether the holder has any right against the bank, he may proceed against the secondary parties, the drawer, and any unqualified indorsers.

§ 32:7. Dishonor of Check. When a check is dishonored by nonpayment, the holder must follow the same procedure of notice to each of the secondary parties as in the case of a draft or bill of exchange if he wishes to hold them liable for payment. As in the case of any drawer of a draft or bill of exchange who countermands payment, notice of dishonor need not be given to the drawer who has stopped payment on a check. Notice is also excused under any circumstances that would excuse notice in the case of a promissory note. For example, no notice need be given a drawer or an indorser who knows that sufficient funds to cover the check are not on deposit, since such party has no reason to expect that the check will be paid by the bank.[19]

A check that is dishonored by nonpayment may be presented to the drawee bank at a later time in the hope that by the later date there will be sufficient funds in the account of the drawer so that the drawee bank will be able to make payment. Although there is this right to make a subsequent presentation for payment, it is essential that notice be given secondary parties after the dishonor of the instrument upon the first presentation. If they are

---

[17] A presumption means that the trier of fact is bound by the presumption in the absence of evidence that supports a contrary conclusion. UCC § 1-201(31).

[18] § 3-503(2).

[19] § 3-511(2)(b).

not duly notified at that time, they are discharged and no new rights can be acquired against them by making a subsequent presentment and then notifying the secondary parties of the second dishonor.

When a check is sent in the course of the collection process to the bank on which it is drawn, that bank must either pay or promptly return the check as unpaid, or send notice of its dishonor, as by returning the check unpaid for "insufficient funds." If the drawee bank does not act before the midnight of the business day on which it received the check, it automatically becomes liable for the face of the instrument.[20]

Oral notice of dishonor is sufficient; and once notice of dishonor is given, subsequent notice is not required when the check is represented and again dishonored. (See p. 645, Leaderbrand v Central State Bank.)

§ 32:8. Setoff of Bank Loan Against Deposit. When a depositor borrows money from his bank, the loan agreement generally specifies that the bank may deduct the amount due on the loan from the customer's deposit account. The loan agreement may specify that the bank may make such a setoff even though the loan is not due. In effect, this is a form of acceleration of the loan or of acceleration when the holder deems himself insecure. In the absence of an express provision permitting the bank to set off a loan before it is due, however, no such right exists.[21]

§ 32:9. Liability of Bank for Improper Payment of Check. A bank that honors a check after the depositor has stopped payment is liable to the depositor for the loss he sustains. In addition, the bank is generally liable if it makes payment under the following circumstances:

(1) Payment on Forged Signature of Drawer. The bank is liable to the depositor (drawer) if it pays a check on which his signature has been forged since a forgery ordinarily has no effect as a signature.[22] A *forgery* of the signature occurs when the name of the depositor has been signed by another person without authority to do so and with the intent to defraud by making it appear that the check was signed by the depositor.[23] The burden of knowing the signatures of all its depositors is thus placed on the bank. Accordingly, upon opening an account in a bank, the depositor is required to sign a card in the way in which he will sign his checks. This signature card remains on file in the bank and is used to make a comparison to determine whether checks presented to the bank for payment have been signed by the depositor.

---

[20] §§ 4-302, 4-104(1)(h); Rock Island Auction Sales v Empire Packing, 32 Ill 2d 269, 204 NE2d 721.

[21] Faber, Coe & Gregg, Inc. v First National Bank, 107 Ill App 2d 204, 246 NE2d 96 (non-Code).

[22] § 3-404(1).

[23] A forgery as thus defined is to be distinguished from a changing of the instrument as originally executed, which constitutes an alteration when done by a party to the instrument and a spoilation when done by a stranger to the instrument. See § 34:8.

Although the bank has no right to pay a check on which the drawer's signature is forged, the drawer may be barred from objecting that his signature was a forgery. If the drawer's negligence contributed substantially to the forging of his signature, he cannot assert that it was forged when the drawee bank makes payment of the check while acting in good faith and conforming to reasonable commercial standards.[24] For example, if the drawer signs his checks with a mechanical writer, he must exercise reasonable care to prevent unauthorized persons from making use of it to forge or "sign" his name with such device. If the depositor's negligence enables a third person to make such improper use of it, the depositor is barred from objecting to the payment of the check by the bank.

When the depositor fails to examine his bank statement and canceled checks with reasonable care and promptness and fails to notify the bank promptly of any forgery, the depositor cannot hold the bank responsible if, in making payment on the forged instrument, it had used ordinary care. Even when the bank failed to exercise care, the depositor cannot object to the forgery of his signature unless he acts within one year.[25]

When a check is presented to the drawee bank for payment, it alone is responsible for determining whether the signature of the drawer, its customer, is a forgery. Prior indorsers do not warrant that the signature of the drawer is genuine; and, if the bank pays money or gives a cashier's check in payment of the depositor's check, it cannot thereafter recover the money paid or defend against payment on the cashier's check on the ground that the drawer's signature had been forged.[26]

A bank is not required to verify the validity of intermediate indorsers because "it would be commercially unreasonable to expect payor banks to undertake foolproof efforts to verify ostensibly valid indorsements." [27]

(2) Payment on Forged Indorsement. A bank that pays a check on a forged indorsement may be liable for conversion.[28] The true owner of an instrument collected on a forged indorsement may recover in a direct suit against a collecting bank even though the bank had acted in good faith and with the highest degree of care and even though it had remitted the amount of the instrument to a prior party.[29] (See p. 646, Jett v Lewis State Bank.)

A bank that has dealt with an instrument or the proceeds of it for an indorsee who was not the true owner is only partly liable to the true owner if the bank had acted in good faith and in accordance with the reasonable commercial standards applicable to a bank. In the latter case, the liability of the bank is limited to surrendering the instrument or the proceeds of it to the true owner if the bank still has either in its possession.[30]

---

[24] §§ 3-404(1), 4-406.

[25] § 4-406.

[26] Citizens Bank of Booneville v National Bank of Commerce, (CA10 Okla) 334 F2d 257.

[27] Cooper v Union Bank, 9 Cal 3d 123, 107 Cal Rptr 1, 507 P2d 609.

[28] UCC § 3-419(1)(c).

[29] Cooper v Union Bank, 9 Cal 3d 123, 107 Cal Rptr 1, 507 P2d 609.

[30] § 3-419(3).

The failure to make an inquiry may constitute a failure to act in accordance with reasonable commercial standards, as where the employee's bank was charged with notice of a breach of fiduciary duty from the fact that a check payable to the order of the employer was indorsed by the employee and deposited in the employee's personal bank account but the employee's bank made no inquiry, the court holding that as a matter of law the failure to make inquiry under these circumstances constituted a failure to act in accordance with reasonable commercial standards.[31]

When a drawee bank pays a check to a collecting bank on the basis of a forged indorsement of the payee's name and is held liable therefor, the drawee bank may recover for its loss from the collecting bank which obtained payment of the check.[32]

(3) Payment on Missing Indorsement. A drawee bank is liable for the loss when it pays a check that lacks an essential indorsement. In such a case, the instrument has not been properly presented; and by definition the person presenting the check for payment is not the holder of the instrument and is not entitled to demand or receive payment. It is a defense to the bank, however, that although the person to whom payment was made was not the holder of the instrument, he was in fact the person whom the drawer or the last holder of the check intended should be paid.

When a person deposits a check in his bank but neglects to indorse it, the bank may make an indorsement for him unless the check contains a statement that it must be signed personally by that person. Even if the bank does not indorse, there is an effective negotiation from the customer to his bank when the check is stamped by the bank to indicate that it was deposited by the customer or was credited to his account.[33]

(4) Alteration of Check. If the face of the check has been altered so that the amount to be paid has been increased, the bank is liable to the drawer for the amount of the increase when it makes payment for the greater amount. The bank has the opportunity of examining the check when it is presented for payment and, if it fails to detect the alteration, it is responsible for the loss.

The drawer may be barred from claiming that there was an alteration by virtue of his conduct with respect to writing the check or his conduct after receiving the canceled check from the bank. As to the former, he is barred if in writing the check he was negligent and that negligence substantially contributed to the making of the material alteration and the bank honored the check in good faith and observed reasonable commercial standards in so doing.[34] For example, the drawer is barred when he leaves blank spaces on his check so that it is readily possible to change "four" to "four hundred,"

---

[31] Von Gohren v Pacific National Bank, 8 Wash App 245, 505 P2d 267.

[32] Birmingham Trust Nat. Bank v Central Bank & Trust Co., 49 Ala App 630, 275 So2d 148.

[33] § 4-205(1).

[34] § 3-406.

and the drawee bank pays out the latter sum without any cause to know of the alteration. The careful person will therefore write figures and words close together and run a line through or cross out any blank spaces.

To avoid possible mistake or confusion, a check that is incorrectly drawn should be rewritten and the first check destroyed or canceled by writing "Void" across its face. If a correction on the original check is attempted, it is likely that the bank will question whether the change was made by the drawer prior to delivery and this may delay the payment of the check.

The drawer of the check may also be barred from objecting to the alteration by his failure to inform the bank after receiving his canceled checks and bank statement. In such a case he is barred under the same conditions as determine when he is barred from objecting to the drawee bank that his signature on the check is a forgery.

(5) Payment After Depositor's Death. The effectiveness of a check ordinarily ceases with the death of a drawer. The death of the drawer, however, does not revoke the agency of the bank until it has knowledge of the death and has had reasonable opportunity to act. Even with such knowledge, the bank may continue for 10 days to pay or certify checks drawn by the drawer unless ordered to stop payment by a person claiming an interest in the account.[35]

§ 32:10. Certified Checks. The drawee bank may certify a check drawn on it, which has the same legal consequence as the acceptance of a draft.[36] The effect of the certification is to set aside in a special account maintained by the bank as much of the depositor's account as is needed to pay the amount of the certified check. With respect to the holder of the check, the certification is an undertaking by the bank that when the check is presented for payment, it will make payment according to the terms of the check without regard to the standing of the depositor's account at that time.

By statute, certified checks are frequently required for payments made at sheriffs' sales and as filing fees sent to government agencies for various purposes. They are also commonly used when property is sold to a buyer who is not well known or who is deemed an unsatisfactory credit risk.

As in the case of an acceptance, any writing on the check showing an intention to certify a check is sufficient. Ordinarily a certification is made by stamping or printing on the check the word "Certified," the name of the bank, the signature and title of the officer making the certification, and the date.

A check may be certified by a bank upon the request of the drawer or the holder. In the latter case all prior indorsers and the drawer are automatically released from liability.[37] Since the holder could have received payment, as the bank was willing to certify the check, and since the holder did

---

[35] § 4-405.
[36] § 3-411(1).
[37] § 3-411(1).

not take the payment but chose to take the certification, the prior secondary parties are released from liability. When the certification is obtained by the drawer, there is no release of the secondary parties.

While, as a practical matter, the certification of a check by a bank makes it "as good as money," it must be remembered that the check is still a check, and that even a certified check is not money.[38]

§ 32:11. Agency Status of Collecting Bank. When a person deposits a commercial paper in a bank, he is ordinarily making it his agent to collect or obtain the payment of the paper. Unless the contrary intent clearly appears, a bank receiving an item is deemed to take it as agent for the depositor rather than as becoming the purchaser of the paper from him. This presumption is not affected by the form of the indorsement nor by the absence of any indorsement. The bank is also regarded as being merely an agent even though the depositor has the right to make immediate withdrawals against the deposited item.[39] In consequence of the agency status, the depositor remains the owner of the item and is therefore subject to the risks of ownership involved in its collection, in the absence of fault on the part of any collecting bank.[40]

When a bank cashes a check deposited by its customer or cashes the customer's check drawn on the strength of a deposited check, it is a holder of the customer's check and may sue the parties thereon, even though as between the customer and the bank the latter is an agent for collection and has the right to charge back the amount of the deposited check if it cannot be collected. When the bank receives final settlement for an item taken for collection, the agency status ends and the bank is merely a debtor of its customer just as though the customer had made an ordinary cash deposit in the bank.[41]

With respect to matters outside the area of bank collections, a bank is governed by the general law that would be applicable in the case of any other person. Thus, if the bank is a party to a sale of goods, it stands as a buyer or seller within Article 2 of the UCC. When it is a party to a transaction not regulated by the UCC, the general law apart from the UCC applies.[42] For example, if a bank promises to pay a debt of another, the ordinary statute of frauds applicable to such promises made by anyone is applicable.[43]

§ 32:12. Liability of Bank for Improper Collection of Check. Although a bank acts as agent for its customer in obtaining payment of a check deposited with it by its customer, it may be liable to a third person when the act of its

---

[38] Olin v Weintraub, (NY Supreme Ct) 2 UCCRS 623.
[39] UCC § 4-201(1).
[40] § 4-202.
[41] Cooper v Union Bank, 9 Cal 3d 123, 107 Cal Rptr 1, 507 P2d 609; Official Code Comment to § 4-213, point 9.
[42] § 1-103.
[43] First National Bank v Haas Drilling Co., (Tex Civ App) 446 SW2d 29.

customer is unauthorized or unlawful with respect to the third person. That is, if the customer has no authority to deposit the check, the bank, in obtaining payment from the drawee of the check and thereafter depositing the proceeds of the check in the account of its customer, may be liable for conversion of the check to the person lawfully entitled to the check and its proceeds. (See p. 647, Salsman v National Community Bank.)

CASES FOR CHAPTER 32

Pennsylvania v Kelinson

199 Pa Super 135, 184 A2d 374 (1962)

Kelinson was president of the Barkel Meat Packing Co., a wholesale meat packer. On February 2 a shipment of meat was delivered to the company. Kelinson gave the driver a check in payment for the full amount but dated it February 4. Approximately thirty checks given in payment of prior shipments had also been postdated. All prior checks had been paid, but the check of February 2 (dated February 4) was not paid. Kelinson was prosecuted for the offenses of passing a worthless check and of obtaining money by false pretenses. From a conviction for both crimes, he appealed.

WATKINS, J. . . . The Commonwealth bases its case upon the issuance of the check in the amount of $8,453.44, which was returned for want of sufficient funds and has never been paid. Because of the nature of its business every check drawn by Barkel to this supplier was postdated. The instant check was the only one not paid.

The Act of 1939 . . . known as the "Worthless Check Act," provides inter alia: "Whoever, with intent to defraud, makes, draws, utters, or delivers any check, draft, or order for the payment of money, upon any bank . . . or other depository, knowing, at the time of such making, drawing, uttering, or delivering, that the maker or drawer has not sufficient funds in, or credit with, such bank, banking institution, trust company, or other depository, for the payment of such check, . . . is guilty of a misdemeanor. . . ."

The defendant contends that postdated checks do not come within the purview of the "worthless check act." . . .

The courts generally, in the more recent cases, have taken the view that such a check is not within the contemplation of "bad check" statutes, such as ours. . . . "By the terms of the act intent to defraud at the time of making or delivering the check is an essential element of the crime. This was a postdated check. As such, it differed from an ordinary check in that it carried on its face implied notice that there was no money presently on deposit available to meet it, with the implied assurance that there would be such funds on the day it became due. At most it amounted to a promise that on the day it became due the drawer would have in the bank a sufficient deposit to meet it." . . .

"What the drawer undertakes is that on a day named he will have the amount of the check to his credit in the bank. In the meantime he wants the full and free use of his entire deposit."

A postdated check is one that is made and delivered at some time prior to the day of its date. It is generally held to be payable at sight or upon presentation at the bank at any time on or after the day of its date. It differs from any ordinary check in that it has on its face implied notice that there is no money presently on deposit available to meet it, with the implied assurance that there will be such funds on the day it becomes due. It is a familiar and useful form of negotiable paper and plays an important part in the role of commerce. Ordinarily its purpose is to obtain an extension of credit. . . .

The law in Pennsylvania is clear that the acceptance of a postdated check amounts to a delivery on credit and the remedies for the nonpayment of such checks are set forth in the Uniform Commercial Code. "Where the instrument offered by the buyer is not a payment but a credit instrument such as a note or a check postdated by even one day, the seller's acceptance of the instrument insofar as third parties are concerned, amounts to a delivery on credit and his remedies are set forth in the section on buyer's insolvency. As between the buyer and the seller, however, the matter turns on the present subsection and the section on conditional delivery, and subsequent dishonor of the instrument gives the seller rights on it as well as for breach of the contract for sale." [UCC §] 2-511, . . . , Comment No. 6. . . .

The appellant also contends that his conviction of obtaining money under false pretense cannot stand because the evidence does not support it. To bring this case within the provisions of the law defining cheating by false pretenses, . . . "there must be found to coexist three separate elements: (1) a false pretense, as a false assertion of existing fact; (2) obtaining property or something of value thereby; (3) an intent to defraud." . . . A mere promise for future conduct does not suffice to constitute a false pretense even though the promisor never intended to perform. . . .

A postdated check is not a present promise; is not a false representation of a present existing fact that there are funds on deposit to pay the check. A postdated check declares boldly on its face that it is nothing more than a promise to pay in the future on or after the date appearing on the face of the instrument.

The Commonwealth has failed to establish by the evidence, as a matter of law, the offenses for which this defendant stands convicted. . . .

[Judgment arrested and the defendant discharged.]

Code Comment: Since the Uniform Commercial Code regulates only civil rights and liabilities, reference must be made to the criminal law of the state in which a person has acted in order to determine whether he has committed a crime. It is therefore possible that in some Uniform Commercial Code states the delivery of a postdated check will be held to be a violation of the bad check law or the obtaining of money by false pretenses. This likelihood is increased when the drawer draws the postdated check with no intention of ever depositing sufficient funds to meet the check.

Tusso v Security National Bank

349 NYS2d 914 (1973)

Tusso sent a check for $600 drawn on the Security National Bank to the Adamson Construction Company. He then realized that he had already paid Adamson. At 9:00 a.m. the next morning he notified the bank to stop payment. Later that morning the check was brought to the bank and at 10:40 a.m. the bank certified the check and charged it to Tusso's account. Tusso sued the bank to recover the amount so charged. The bank claimed that he was required to prove that the bank had been negligent.

COLANERI, J. . . . The bank's . . . defense is incorrect. [UCC §] 4-403(1) entitles a bank customer to stop payment on his check by giving notice to that effect "at such time and in such manner as to afford the bank a reasonable opportunity to act on it prior to any action by the bank with respect to the item . . ." The statute does not place any other affirmative burden of proof upon the plaintiff with respect to the stop payment order other than the "burden of establishing the fact and amount of loss resulting from the payment of an item contrary to a binding stop payment order . . ." (UCC § 4-403(3)). . . .

To read into this statute the additional requirement that the drawer prove the commission of a negligent act by the bank in order to recover would, in effect, alter the statute in a manner not intended by the legislature. . . . In the absence of a contractual provision limiting the bank's liability, a valid stop payment order received by the bank prior to payment or certification renders subsequent payment wrongful, whether or not the bank was shown to be negligent in making such payments. . . .

The plaintiff in this case has the burden of proving that the stop payment order was received by the bank at such time as to afford it a reasonable opportunity to act on such order . . . . The facts as presented support this contention and therefore the court finds in favor of the plaintiff and against the defendant bank.

It has been held that a bank which improperly paid a check on which payment had been stopped may recover from the one who received payment, if such payee was not a holder for value. . . . The facts developed in this case indicate that the defendant construction corporation was already fully paid for its services. Therefore the construction corporation has no right to retain the additional funds improperly paid by the bank, and the court finds that the bank is entitled to judgment against the third party defendant for the amount of the improperly certified check.

Accordingly, judgment for the plaintiff against the defendant (Security National Bank) in the sum of $600.00 with interest thereon from July 25, 1972, together with the costs and disbursements of this action, and, further, the defendant and third-party plaintiff (Security National Bank) may have judgment over and against the third party defendant (Adamson Construction Corporation) in the sum of $600.00 with interest thereon from July 25, 1972, together with the costs and disbursements of this action.

Allison v First National Bank

85 NMex 283, 511 P2d 769 (1973)

Allison obtained cashier's checks from the First National Bank which he sent to a bank in Mexico. First National notified the Mexican bank that the cashier's checks would not be paid and that it had requested the return of the checks for cancellation. First National refused to honor the cashier's checks when presented thereafter for payment. Because of this, assets of Allison were seized by legal process in order to satisfy his debt to the Mexican bank, his reputation was damaged, and he was threatened with criminal prosecution. He sued First National for damages for wrongful dishonor. The bank denied liability for the harm which followed the dishonor of the checks. The lower court entered judgment for Allison but refused to award damages for the consequences which followed the dishonor. The bank appealed on the issue of liability for dishonor. Allison filed a cross-appeal on the issue of consequential damages.

SUTIN, J. . . . *Plaintiff was entitled to damages for defendant's wrongful dishonor of plaintiff's checks.* The trial court made the following findings of fact: That on September 30, 1968, defendant bank refused to honor the above numbered cashier's checks.

That defendant's dishonor of said checks was *wrongful* in that the checks had not been paid and were not void. . . .

The plaintiff has not shown any consequential loss or damage resulting to him by reason of the refusal of First National Bank in Albuquerque to pay in 1968 the cashier's checks issued to him in March, 1953, and is entitled to actual damages of $5,000.00.

[UCC §] 4-402, . . . is entitled "Bank's liability to customer for wrongful dishonor."

A payor bank is liable to its customer for damages proximately caused by the wrongful dishonor of an item. When the dishonor occurs through mistake liability is limited to actual damages proved. *If so proximately caused and proved damages may include* damages for an arrest or prosecution of the customer or other *consequential damages.* Whether any consequential damages are proximately caused by the wrongful dishonor is a question of fact to be determined in each case. . . .

"Wrongful dishonor" has not been defined by the Code. Official comment states that the above ". . . section does not attempt to specify a theory. . . ." It is different from ". . . failure to exercise ordinary care in handling an item . . ." It ". . . excludes any permitted or justified dishonor. . . ." Uniform Commercial Code, § 4-402, Comments 2, 3 and 4.

Wrongful dishonor means a dishonor done in a wrong manner, unjustly, unfair, in a manner contrary to justice. . . . It excludes negligence or permitted or justified dishonor.

"Mistaken dishonor" means a dishonor done erroneously, unintentionally, a state of mind that is not in accord with the facts. . . .

This section does not deal with "intentional or wilful or malicious dishonor." This type of dishonor permits an award of punitive damages. . . .

In the instant case, on three separate occasions, from September 30, 1968 through January 6, 1969, the defendant dishonored the checks (1) by informing a Mexico bank that the checks were not outstanding; (2) that the checks had been paid by reissuance of new cashier's checks and requested the cashier's checks held by plaintiff be returned for cancellation; (3) against returning the checks unpaid. The bank failed to prove the reasons for its dishonor. This dishonor was not permitted or justified. . . . The trial court correctly found the dishonor was wrongful.

"Consequential damages" are not defined in terms in the Uniform Commercial Code, but are used in the sense given them by the leading cases on the subject. 1 Anderson, Uniform Commercial Code, 2nd Ed., p. 48.

In 3 Anderson, Uniform Commerical Code, 2nd Ed., p. 306, the author makes this comment with reference to § 50A-4-402:

Damages for Wrongful Dishonor. A payor bank is liable to its customer for the damages proximately caused by the wrongful dishonor of an item. The damages may include consequential damages (such as those sustained in connection with an arrest and prosecution), provided they are proximate damages. Whether the consequential damages are proximately related to the wrongful dishonor is a question of fact and not of law.

" 'Consequential damage' is defined in Black's Law Dictionary, Third Edition, as: 'Such damage, loss or injury as does not flow directly and immediately from the act of the party, but only from the consequences or results of such act.' " . . . "Consequential damage" includes injuries to credit as a result of wrongful dishonor. . . . It includes ". . . *any* . . . consequential harm, loss or injury proximately caused by a wrongful dishonor. . . ." . . .

As a consequence of the dishonor (1) An attachment lien was filed against 54 items of personalty of the plaintiff in Mexico seizing all his personal assets for purposes of satisfying his debts owed to the Mexican bank. (2) Plaintiff was personally threatened with imprisonment if the checks were invalid. (3) His credit standing was ruined. (4) He was placed under a cloud of suspicion in his Mexican community. Plaintiff had an excellent professional reputation.

Plaintiff is entitled to reasonable and temperate damages determined by the sound discretion and dispassionate judgment of the trial court. . . .

Plaintiff's judgment is affirmed. Plaintiff's cross-appeal is sustained. This cause is remanded to the trial court solely to determine the amount of consequential damages plaintiff is entitled to. . . .

Authors' Comment: The Allison case was reversed on appeal on the ground that the statute of limitations had run. 85 NMex 511, 514 P2d 30. This does not impair the opinion of the Court of Appeals as to the damages otherwise recoverable.

Leaderbrand v Central State Bank

202 Kan 450, 450 P2d 1 (1969)

Lyon gave Leaderbrand a check drawn on Lyon's account in the Central State Bank to pay for goods purchased from Leaderbrand's employer. The check was payable to the order of the employer. On March 15 and again a few days later, Leaderbrand presented the check to the Central State Bank but was informed both times that there were not sufficient funds in Lyon's account to pay the check. On March 21 Leaderbrand deposited the check in his account in the First State Bank. The bank took the check for collection but informed Leaderbrand that he could not draw against the amount of the deposit before the check was collected. First State Bank mailed the check directly to Central State Bank for collection. The latter received the check on March 21 or 22. On April 5, Lyon having stopped payment on this check, Central State Bank returned it to the First State Bank. Leaderbrand claimed that the Central State Bank was liable to him for the amount of the check because of its delay in returning the check and in giving notice of dishonor. The trial court entered a summary judgment in favor of Central State Bank on the theory that Leaderbrand was not the proper

party to sue on the check since the check was payable to his employer. Leaderbrand appealed.

SCHROEDER, J. . . . It should be noted this is not an action upon a check but is an action to hold the payor bank accountable for the amount of a check under [UCC §] 4-302. . . .

Under [UCC §] 4-302 . . . the payor bank is required to handle a demand item promptly, and upon failure to do so is made accountable for the amount of the item to the person presenting it.

Under the previous section of the Uniform Commercial Code ([§] 4-301), a demand item received by the payor bank for credit on its books may be returned or notice of dishonor sent if it acts before its midnight deadline. Subparagraph (3) of this section reads: "(3) *Unless previous notice of dishonor has been sent,* an item is dishonored at the time when for purposes of dishonor it is returned or notice sent in accordance with this section." (Emphasis added.) . . .

" 'Midnight deadline' with respect to a bank is midnight on its next banking day following the banking day on which it receives the relevant item or notice or from which the time for taking action commences to run, whichever is later." [UCC § 4-104(h)]

Under the provision of [UCC §] 3-508(3) notice of dishonor may be given in any reasonable manner. It may be *oral* or written and in any terms which identify the instrument and state that it has been dishonored.

Under the admitted facts and circumstances of the instant case, the check in question came to the Central State Bank of Wichita, the payor bank, for collection, after having been twice orally dishonored by the payor when the appellant presented the check over the counter at such bank for payment.

[UCC §] 3-511(4) reads: "Where a draft has been dishonored by nonacceptance, a later presentment for payment and any notice of dishonor and protest for nonpayment are excused unless in the meantime the instrument has been accepted."

A writing which complies with the requirements of [UCC §] 3-104 is a "draft" if it is an order, and a "check" if it is a draft drawn on a bank and payable on demand.

It thus appears from the foregoing sections of the Uniform Commercial Code that the failure of the payor bank to give notice of dishonor before its "midnight deadline," asserted by the appellant to make the payor bank accountable for the amount of the check, was excused. . . .

[Judgment affirmed.]

Jett v Lewis State Bank

(Fla App) 277 So2d 37 (1973)

Jett wrote a check for $12,000 as a loan payable to the order of a newly-formed corporation, National Giant Portable Fun Slide, Inc. The three officers and sole stockholders of the corporation took the check to another bank, Lewis State Bank, to open a corporate account. The check was indorsed "for deposit only to account of within named payee." In spite of this, the Lewis Bank was directed to credit only $7,000 to the account of the corporation and to pay $5,000 cash to one of the three officers. National Giant went out of business and Jett sued Lewis Bank for diverting $5,000 from the corporate account. From a judgment for Lewis, Jett appealed.

JOHNSON, J. . . . The drawer or maker of a check has no right of direct action against banks, other than the drawee bank, which honor the check on a forged or unauthorized endorsement. The theory behind this rule is that, in an action for conversion against a collecting bank, the essential elements of conversion would be lacking in that the drawer does not have the right to immediate possession of the check because the beneficial ownership of the check is in the payee, not in the drawer. . . .

In an action sounding in both contract, for moneys had and received, and in tort, for conversion, the drawer of a check has been denied recovery against the collecting bank upon the grounds that the collecting bank had no money in its hands which belonged to the drawer, that the drawer had no right in the proceeds of its own check payable to the payee, and that, not being a holder in due course or an agent for such holder, the drawer could not have presented its check to the drawee bank for payment. The value of the drawer's rights in the check is limited to the physical paper on which it is written and is not measured by its payable amount. The amounts a collecting bank receives from a drawee bank for the check cashed by the collecting bank are the drawee bank's funds and not those of the drawer; and whether the drawer is rightfully or wrongfully deprived of a credit is a matter between the drawer and the drawee bank. In short, the drawer's recourse is limited to an action against the drawee bank, for the only harm which befalls the drawer is the charging of its account by the drawee bank. . . .

It has also been held that a drawer of a check cannot recover against a collecting bank which honors a check bearing a faulty endorsement upon the contractual theory of warranty of prior endorsements. A guaranty of prior endorsements is only for the benefit of subsequent holders in due course, and not for the drawer of a check. There is no privity of contract between the drawer of a check and a collecting bank. . . . Once again, the drawer's recourse is against the drawee bank which may be entitled to recover from the collecting bank on the basis of its warranty of prior endorsements.*

We recognize that there have been other cases adopting different theories than those set out above. See 99 ALR2d 638-651. Nevertheless, we feel that the better rule is that the drawer of a check, in this case the appellant, has no right of direct action against a collecting bank, in this case the appellee, which honors a check even if the check bore a faulty endorsement. We note with interest that many of the cases allowing recovery were cases in which the drawer of the check was also the drawee; the drawer was suing the drawee bank; the plaintiff in the case was the payee, rather than the drawer, of the check (as in those cases cited in Judge Spector's dissenting opinion hereto), or the collecting bank was put on notice because the unauthorized endorser immediately deposited the funds in his own personal account. . . .

[Judgment affirmed.]

* For a contrary holding on the theory of warranty of prior endorsements, see Allied Concord F. Corp. v Bank of Amer. Nat. T & S Ass'n, 275 Cal App 2d 1, 80 Cal Rptr 622 (1969), though this case also recognizes that drawer has no right of action for conversion against a collecting bank.

Salsman v National Community Bank

102 NJ Super 482, 246 A2d 162 (1968); affirmed 105 NJ Super 164, 251 A2d 460 (1969)

Arthur Odgers died. His widow, Elizabeth Odgers, thereafter Salsman by remarriage, retained Breslow as the attorney for her husband's estate. She received a check payable to her order drawn on the First National City Bank, which Breslow told her should be deposited in her huband's "estate." She signed an indorsement "Pay to the order of Estate of Arthur J. Odgers." Breslow then deposited this check in his "trustee" account in the National Community Bank. National Community collected the amount of the check from the drawee, the First National City Bank. Thereafter the widow, as administrator of Arthur's estate, sued the Community Bank for collecting this check and crediting Breslow's trustee account with the proceeds.

BOTTER, J.S.C. . . . Mr. Breslow wrote on the back of the . . . check, "Pay to the order of Estate of Arthur J. Odgers." He requested Mrs. Odgers to indorse the check in this fashion, and she did so. Under this special indorsement, when he was no longer in the presence of Mrs. Odgers, Breslow wrote, "Estate of Arthur J. Odgers—for deposit Harold Breslow, Trustee." Under this purported indorsement Breslow's secretary then wrote "For deposit Harold Breslow Trustee." Mrs. Odgers had no knowledge of the subsequent indorsements. The check was then sent by mail to defendant National Community Bank of Rutherford for collection, and the proceeds were collected and deposited in Breslow's general trustee account. Defendant bank did not inquire into the authority of Breslow to indorse the checks for the estate. There was no estate account in defendant's bank. . . .

The bank advised [Mrs. Odgers] that there was no record of an account for the estate of Arthur J. Odgers. Mrs. Odgers then contacted another attorney, and he assisted her in further investigation. . . . Breslow confessed to Mrs. Odgers and her present husband, Mr. Salsman, that he had appropriated the funds to his own use. . . . They immediately took Breslow to defendant bank where he paid over to Mrs. Odgers funds which were still in his account. Later that day Mrs. Odgers and Mr. Salsman went to Mr. Salsman's attorney who called defendant concerning the matter. Attached to exhibit DN-1 is a copy of a letter dated April 1, 1966, sent by an attorney on behalf of Mrs. Odgers to defendant demanding reimbursement of the funds received on collection of the check. Mrs. Odgers was also advised to file a criminal complaint against Breslow, and she did so promptly. Mr. Breslow has since pleaded guilty to the charge of embezzlement and misappropriation of funds . . . and is presently serving a prison sentence. He also resigned from the New Jersey Bar. In April, 1966, Mrs. Odgers started an action against Breslow and on June 3, 1966, obtained a judgment in her favor. Some monies were recovered by execution on that judgment. The balance not yet recovered is $117,437.43.

Defendant bank contends that it is not liable under any provision of the Uniform Commercial Code [for the proceeds of the check], that Mrs. Odgers was negligent, that she ratified the acts of Mr. Breslow and that NJS 3A:41-7 exonerates the bank for any misapplication of funds by Breslow. Defendant bank contends that Breslow had the power to negotiate the check as agent or fiduciary under [UCC §] 3-117, that defendant bank became a holder in due course of the check and that [UCC §] 3-406 bars recovery because of the alleged negligence of Mrs. Odgers in substantially contributing to the making of an unauthorized indorsement. Defendant bank also relies on [UCC §] 3-404 to claim that Mrs. Odgers ratified the unauthorized signature of Breslow. . . .

In the absence of defenses such as negligence, estoppel, or ratification, the payee of a check is entitled to recover against a bank making collection from the drawee based upon a forged or unauthorized indorsement of a check. . . . This has been the established law throughout the country and continues to be the rule in states which have adopted the Uniform Commercial Code. . . .

The check in question was indorsed by the payee, Mrs. Odgers, to the order of the Estate of Arthur J. Odgers. There was no valid indorsement thereafter by the Estate of Arthur J. Odgers. [UCC §] 3-110[(1)](e) provides that an instrument may be payable to the order of "an estate, trust, or fund, in which case it is payable to the order of the representative of such estate, trust, or fund. . . ." The check was not indorsed by the administratrix of the estate, the only person who had authority in law to indorse the check. Harold Breslow was not a trustee of the estate, and the purported indorsement for the estate by "Harold Breslow, Trustee" was authorized and ineffective. Mr. Breslow testified that he never told plaintiff that he would act as her agent. His purported indorsement was not authorized as the agent for the administratrix nor as a representative of the estate. . . .

The check in question could not be negotiated without an authorized indorsement of the special indorsee, the Estate of Arthur J. Odgers. [UCC §] 3-202(1) and 204(1). [UCC §] 3-404(1) provides that "Any unauthorized signature is wholly inoperative as that of the person whose name is signed unless he ratifies it or is precluded from denying it. . . ." There is no evidence in this case which shows a ratification by Mrs. Odgers of the conduct of Breslow; there has been nothing shown to preclude her from denying the indorsements in question; and there is no evidence of any negligence on her part which contributed to the misapplication of the funds. . . . To constitute ratification, the person to be bound must, with full knowledge of all the material facts, express an intent to ratify the unauthorized acts of transactions. Upon discovery of his fraud Mrs. Odgers took prompt action against Breslow and gave prompt notice to the bank. Ratification has not been shown here. . . .

Mrs. Odgers had relied upon an attorney who was then reputable. She followed his instructions and was not negligent in assuming that the check would be deposited into the estate account after she had indorsed it to the order of the estate. Mrs. Odgers was educated and intelligent. From this, however, we cannot infer that she knew that the check would be indorsed by the attorney on behalf of herself as administratrix of the estate. [UCC §] 4-205 empowers a bank to supply a missing indorsement of its customer in order to deposit a check in the account of that customer. Under that section a check is deemed indorsed when a depositary bank states on the check that it was deposited by a customer or credited to his account. Although she had not signed signature cards as administratrix in order to open such an account, Mrs. Odgers cannot be held negligent on the theory that she should have suspected that the check might not have been deposited in an estate account. Mrs. Odgers made repeated inquiries concerning the funds and was given various explanations by Breslow as to their disposition and as to her inability to deal with them at that stage in the administration of the estate. Her conduct was not unreasonable or imprudent.

Receiving the funds without a proper indorsement and crediting the funds to one not entitled thereto constitutes a conversion of the funds. A holder is one who receives an instrument which is indorsed to his order or in blank. . . . The bank cannot be a holder, or a holder in due course, . . . without a valid indorsement of this check by the Estate of Arthur J. Odgers. [UCC §] 3-419(1)(c) provides that an instrument is converted when it is paid on a forged indorsement. [UCC §] 1-201(43) provides that an unauthorized signature or indorsement is one made without authority (actual, implied, or apparent) and includes a forgery. . . . "There is no substantial difference between an unauthorized indorsement and a forged indorsement, the result being the same insofar as concerns the passing of title." The use of the word "forged indorsement" as constituting a conversion under [UCC §] 3-419(1) does not preclude the finding of conversion where the unauthorized signature does not constitute a forgery in the strict sense. If the Uniform Commercial Code fails expressly to include unauthorized indorsements other than forgeries in this conversion section, the law may reach the same result by implication from the code and by general principles. See [UCC §] 1-103 which provides: "Unless displaced by the particular provisions of this Act, the principles of law and equity, including the law merchant . . . or other validating or invalidating cause shall supplement its provisions." . . . See also 1 Anderson's Uniform Commercial Code, § 3-419.3, 688 (1961) where the author states that the enumeration by the code of specific acts constituting a conversion is not exclusive and the general principles of law relating to conversion of property remain in force, citing § 1-103. . . .

In the present case there are sufficient facts to justify the conclusion that defendant bank is liable regardless of how we view the conduct of Mrs. Odgers in giving the check to Breslow. The bank was negligent in allowing funds to be deposited in Breslow's attorney's trust account without inquiry as to his authority to indorse the check as trustee on behalf of the estate. There were no circumstances to suggest any apparent authority in Breslow to do this. Moreover, the indorsement purportedly made on behalf of the estate was a "for deposit" indorsement, a restrictive indorsement [UCC §] 3-205 (c). This is another fact which should have alerted the bank to a misapplication of the funds.

[Judgment for plaintiff.]

QUESTIONS AND CASE PROBLEMS

1. *A* drew a check payable to the order of *B*. The bank on which it was drawn refused to pay the check. *B* sued *A* for the amount of the check. *A* raised the defense that *B* had not shown that he sustained any damages by reason of the refusal of the bank to pay. Was this defense valid? [Duncan v Baskin, 8 Mich App 509, 154 NW2d 617]

2. Doodan, who owed money to Szawlinsky, delivered a check for the amount due Szawlinsky, but the latter never cashed the check. Doodan claimed that the continued retention of the check discharged the debt. Decide. [Doodan v Szawlinsky, 197 Pa Super 623, 179 A2d 661]

3. Berg, who had a checking account in the Central National Bank, drew a check on that bank payable to the order of Anschutz. Colucci obtained the check from Berg by fraudulent misrepresentation and forged the name of Anschutz as an indorsement. The check was subsequently negotiated several times and then presented by a subsequent holder to the Central National Bank for payment. The bank, without knowing that the payee's indorsement was a forgery, paid the amount of the check to the apparent holder. Thereafter Anschutz sued the bank for the amount of the check. Was the bank liable? [Anschutz v Central National Bank, 173 Neb 60, 112 NW2d 545]

4. Stone & Webster drew a check on the First National Bank of Boston payable to the order of Westinghouse in payment of a debt. Before the check could be mailed to Westinghouse, an employee of Stone & Webster forged the indorsement of Westinghouse and cashed the check at the First National Bank & Trust Company of Greenfield. The Greenfield bank then presented the check for payment to the drawee bank, the First National Bank of Boston. The latter paid the Greenfield bank the amount of the check and then debited the account of Stone & Webster with the amount of the check. Stone & Webster then sued the Greenfield bank for the amount of the check. Was the plaintiff entitled to recover? [Stone & Webster Eng. Co. v First National Bank of Greenfield, 345 Mass 1, 184 NE2d 358]

5. Silver, an attorney, had an account labeled "special account" in the Commonwealth Trust Co. Part of the fund on deposit was money belonging to his client, Goldstein. Silver drew a check on this account for his own use. Goldstein sued the bank, claiming that it had no right to honor the check because the bank should have known that the account included the money of third persons and that the attorney was making improper use of the money. Decide. [Goldstein v Commonwealth Trust Co., 19 NJ Super 39, 87 A2d 555]

6. The Virginia Salvage Co. drew a check on the National Mechanics Bank and had the bank certify the check. The check was indorsed by the payee, and a subsequent holder. Schmelz National Bank, demanded payment of the check from the National Mechanics Bank. The latter defended on the ground that the salvage company by that time owed the bank more than the amount of the certified check. Was this a valid defense? [National Mechanics Bank v Schmelz National Bank, 136 Va 33, 116 SE 380]

7. Bogash drew a check on the National Safety Bank and Trust Co. payable to the order of the Fiss Corp. At the request of the corporation, the bank certified the check. The bank later refused to make payment on the check because there was a dispute between Bogash and the corporation as to the amount due the corporation. The corporation sued the bank on the check. Decide. [Fiss Corp. v National Safety Bank and Trust Co., 191 Misc 397, 77 NYS2d 293]

8. Moats, acting with intent to defraud, forged the drawer's name on a check which did not state any amount or name any payee. Was he guilty of forgery? [Illinois v Moats, 8 Ill App 3d 944, 291 NE2d 285]

9. A depositor drew a check and delivered it to the payee. Fourteen months later the check was presented to the drawee bank for payment. The bank did not have any knowledge that anything was wrong and paid the check. The depositor then sued the person receiving the money and the bank. The depositor claimed that the bank could not pay a stale check without asking the depositor whether payment should be made. Was the depositor correct? [Advanced Alloys, Inc. v Sergeant Steel Corp., 340 NYS2d 266]

10. Steinbaum executed and delivered a check payable to the order of the White Way Motors, the name under which DiFranco was doing business. Before the check was paid, Steinbaum stopped payment on the check. DiFranco sued Steinbaum on the check. Decide. [DiFranco v Steinbaum, (Mo App) 177 SW2d 697]

11. Pflaum mailed a check for $5,000 to the Laura Baker School and stated in the accompaning letter that it was a gift to the school which it could use for any purpose. Before the check was presented to the bank for payment, Pflaum stopped payment on it. The school then sued on the check. Decide. [Laura Baker School v Pflaum, 225 Minn 181, 30 NW2d 290]

12. Goldsmith told his employee to draw a check on the Atlantic National Bank to the employee's order for $10.10. The employee wrote the check in his own hand, leaving space to the left of the amount. After Goldsmith signed the check, the employee filled in the spaces to the left of the amount, thus raising the check to $2,110.10. The employee presented the check to the bank, which made payment of the raised amount. Goldsmith sued the bank for the raised amount. Decide. [Goldsmith v Atlantic National Bank, (Fla) 55 So2d 804]

13. Raiton indorsed a promissory note as an accommodation indorser. The face of the note waived presentment, notice, and protest. The maker of the note stopped making payments on the note. The holder of the note, the First State Bank, then demanded payment of the note from Raiton. He defended on the ground that the bank had not demanded additional collateral from the maker. Was this a valid defense? [First State Bank v Raiton, (DC ED Pa) 377 F Supp 859]

33 Rights of Holders and Defenses

RIGHTS AND SPECIAL CLASSES OF HOLDERS

§ 33:1. **Favored and Ordinary Holders.** The law gives certain holders of commercial paper a preferred standing by protecting them from the operation of certain defenses in lawsuits to collect payment. If the holder is not one of these favored holders, he has only the same standing as an ordinary assignee and is subject to all defenses to which an ordinary assignee would be subject.[1]

A holder, whether favored or not, or an assignee, is the only person who has the right to demand payment or to sue on the instrument.[2] Whether he recovers depends upon whether the person sued is liable to him and whether any defense may be asserted against the holder.

Ordinarily a holder may sue any one or more prior parties on the paper without regard to the order in which such persons may be liable to each other.

The holder or assignee is the only one who may grant a discharge of or cancel the liability of another party on the instrument.

§ **33:2. Holder in Due Course.** In order to have the preferred status of a holder in due course, a person must first be a holder. (See p. 664, Northside Building & Investment Co. v Finance Co.) This means that he must be in possession of bearer paper, or in possession of order paper made or issued to him or properly indorsed to him.

(1) Necessary Elements. In addition to being a holder, the holder in due course must meet certain conditions that pertain to (a) value, (b) good faith, (c) ignorance of paper overdue or dishonored, and (d) ignorance of defenses and adverse claims.[3]

(a) VALUE. Since the law of commercial paper is fundamentally a merchant's or businessman's law, it favors only the holders who have given value for the paper. For example, since a legatee under a will does not give value, a person receiving bonds as a legacy is not a holder in due course.[4] The courts do not measure or appraise the value given.

---

1 See § 17:10.
2 UCC § 3-301.
3 UCC § 3-302(1).
4 Wyatt v Mount Airy Cemetery, 209 Pa Super 250, 224 A2d 787.

A person has taken an instrument for value (1) when he has performed the act for which the instrument was given, such as delivering the goods for which the check is sent in payment; (2) when he has acquired a security interest in the paper, such as when it has been pledged with him as security for another obligation; or (3) when he has taken the instrument in payment or as security for a debt.[5]

A promise not yet performed, although sufficient as consideration for a contract, ordinarily does not constitute value to satisfy this requirement for a holder in due course. (See p. 665, Korzenik v Supreme Radio.)

(b) GOOD FAITH. The element of good faith requires that the taker of commercial paper has acted honestly in the acquisition of the instrument.[6] Bad faith may sometimes be indicated by the small value given. This does not mean that the transferee must give full value, but that a gross inadequacy of consideration may be evidence of bad faith. Bad faith is established by proof that the transferee had knowledge of such facts as rendered it improper for him to acquire the instrument under the circumstances.

If the transferee takes the instrument in good faith, it is immaterial whether his transferor acted in good faith. The fact that the transferee is negligent and fails to conform to industry standards or to its own house rules does not establish that the transferee did not act in good faith, as good faith means only that the transferee acted with honesty.[7]

(c) IGNORANCE OF PAPER OVERDUE OR DISHONORED. Commercial paper may be negotiated even though (1) it has been dishonored, whether by nonacceptance or nonpayment; or (2) the paper is overdue, whether because of lapse of time or the acceleration of the due date; or (3) demand paper has been outstanding more than a reasonable time. In other words, ownership may still be transferred. Nevertheless, the fact that the paper is circulating at a late date or after it has been dishonored is a suspicious circumstance that is deemed to put the person acquiring the paper on notice that there is some adverse claim or defense. A person who acquires title to the paper under such circumstances therefore cannot be a holder in due course.

If the fact that the paper is overdue or has been dishonored is not apparent from the paper itself, the new holder is not affected unless he otherwise had knowledge or notice of that fact.

The purchaser of a commercial paper has notice that the instrument is overdue if he has reasonable grounds to believe "(a) that any part of the principal amount is overdue or that there is an uncured default in payment of another instrument of the same series; or (b) that acceleration of the instrument has been made; or (c) that he is taking a demand instrument after

[5] UCC § 3-303. It is also provided that there is a taking for value when another commercial paper is given in exchange or when the taker makes an irrevocable commitment to a third person as by providing a letter of credit. § 3-303(c).

[6] Norman v World Wide Distributors, Inc., 202 Pa Super 53, 195 A2d 115.

[7] Industrial Nat. Bank v Leo's Used Car Exchange, Inc., (Mass) 291 NE2d 603.

demand has been made or more than a reasonable length of time after its issue. A reasonable time for acquiring a check drawn and payable within the states and territories of the United States and the District of Columbia is presumed to be 30 days." [8]

(d) IGNORANCE OF DEFENSES AND ADVERSE CLAIMS. Prior parties on the paper may have defenses which they could raise if sued by the person with whom they had dealt. For example, the drawer of a check, if sued by the payee of the check, might have the defense that the merchandise delivered by the payee was defective. In addition to defenses, third persons, whether prior parties or not, may be able to assert that the instrument belongs to them and not to the holder or to his transferor. A person cannot be a holder in due course if he acquires the commercial paper with notice or knowledge that any party might have a defense or that there is any adverse claim to the ownership of the instrument. Thus, he cannot be a holder in due course when he has knowledge of a failure of consideration in an earlier transaction involving the instrument.

The fact that the payee, subsequent to the paying of value, learns of a defense does not operate retroactively to destroy his character as a holder in due course.[9] When the transferee makes payment for the transfer of the paper in installments and learns of a defense after he has paid in part, he can be a holder in due course as to the payments made before, but not as to payments made after, learning of the existence of the defense. Knowledge acquired by the taker after acquiring the paper has no effect on his status as a holder in due course, so that the fact that the taker learned of a defense before he deposited a check in his account or did anything to collect the check was immaterial.[10]

Knowledge of certain facts constitutes notice to the person acquiring a commercial paper that there is a defense or an adverse claim. The holder or purchaser of the paper is deemed to have notice of a claim or defense (1) if the instrument is so incomplete, bears such visible evidence of forgery or alteration, or is otherwise so irregular as to call into question its validity, terms, or ownership, or to create an ambiguity as to the party who is required to pay; or (2) if the purchaser has notice that the obligation of any party is voidable in whole or in part, or that all parties to the paper have been discharged. For example, if the subsequent holder knows that a note given for home improvement work in fact covers both the improvements and a loan and that the transaction is usurious because excessive costs were charged to conceal the usurious interest, the subsequent holder is not a holder in due course.[11] The purchaser has notice of a claim of ownership of another person to the instrument if he has knowledge that a fiduciary has negotiated the paper in breach of his trust.[12]

---

[8] UCC § 3-304(3).
[9] Waterbury Savings Bank v Jaroszewski, 4 Conn Cir 620, 238 A2d 446.
[10] Kemp Motor Sales v Statham, 120 Ga App 515, 171 SE2d 389.
[11] Mutual Home Dealers Corp. v Alves, 23 App Div 2d 791, 258 NYS2d 786.
[12] UCC § 3-304(2).

In general, a holder is deemed to have notice when he has knowledge of facts which would put a reasonable man upon inquiry, that is, which would make him curious to investigate further, which investigation, if made, would reveal the existence of the defenses.[13]

A holder does not have notice or knowledge of a defense or adverse claim merely because he knows (1) that the instrument is antedated or post-dated; (2) that it was issued or negotiated in return for an executory promise or accompanied by a separate agreement, unless the purchaser has notice that a defense or claim has arisen from the terms thereof; (3) that any party has signed for accommodation; (4) that an incomplete instrument has been completed, unless the purchaser has notice of any improper completion; (5) that any person negotiating the instrument is or was an employee or a fiduciary; or (6) that there has been a default in payment of interest on the instrument or in payment of any other instrument, except one of the same series. (See p. 665, Richardson v First National Bank in Dallas.) The fact that a document related to the instrument has been filed or recorded does not constitute notice which will prevent a person from being a holder in due course.[14]

The fact that a holder knows that the payee had a fluctuating financial record does not prevent his becoming a holder in due course.[15] The fact that the payee negotiates a large volume of commercial paper, such as the notes received in the course of the week, does not put the indorsee on notice of any defect or defense.[16]

The fact that there is a standing business relationship between the seller and his assignee, and that to facilitate such relationship the assignee supplied printed forms bearing its name, does not bar the assignee from being a holder in due course.[17]

The fact that a bank has notice of an employee's misconduct as to one check does not color another transaction as to another check which does not bear any suspicious elements. The circumstances as to one check should not enter into a consideration of another unless there is some evidence which shows that the two checks were handled as one transaction or as related transactions.[18]

The duty of inquiry is greater when consumer transactions are involved and the payee has followed a known general pattern of exploitation and deception. "Where lenders facilitate consumer credit financing they must be held to a high standard of inquiry to make certain their services are not being misused by unscrupulous merchandisers." Thus, it has been held that the transferee of commercial paper of a home improvement company did not take in good faith and was not a holder in due course when the transferee knew that the improvement company was taking advantage of

---

[13] Anderson v Lee, 103 Cal App 2d 24, 228 P2d 613.
[14] UCC §§ 3-304(4), (5).
[15] Texico State Bank v Hullinger, 75 Ill App 2d 212, 220 NE2d 248.
[16] Pugatch v David's Jewelers, 53 Misc 2d 327, 278 NYS2d 759.
[17] Talcott v Shulman, 82 NJ Super 438, 198 A2d 98.
[18] Von Gohren v Pacific National Bank, 8 Wash App 245, 505 P2d 467.

persons of limited economic means and education and that the company did not make any inquiries as to defenses even though it took a substantial quantity of paper from the improvement company and knew that the broker who dealt with the public was in fact acting for the improvement company although he pretended to act for the individual home owners.[19]

(2) Who May Be a Holder in Due Course. Any person may be a holder in due course. This includes the payee of the instrument provided he satisfies the necessary elements. Ordinarily the payee deals directly with the drawer and therefore would have knowledge of any defense that the latter might raise. But the payee becomes a holder in due course when he acts through an intermediary so that in fact he did not deal with the drawer but acquired the paper from the intermediary, even though the paper was made payable to his order. The net result is the same as though the drawer has made the check payable to the intermediary who in turn indorsed it to the payee.

Certain types of purchases of commercial paper do not make the purchaser a holder in due course although he otherwise satisfies all the elements here considered. Such sales are not of an ordinary commercial nature, and therefore the buyer need not be given the protection afforded a holder in due course. Thus, a person is not a holder in due course when he acquires the paper by means of a judicial sale, a sale of the assets of an estate, or a bulk sale not in the regular course of business of the transferor.[20]

(a) SELLER'S ASSIGNEE. The seller of goods on credit frequently assigns the sales contract and his buyer's promissory note to the manufacturer who made the goods, or to a finance company or a bank. In such a case, the assignee of the seller will be a holder in due course of the buyer's commercial paper if the paper is properly negotiated and the transferee satisfies all the elements of being a holder in due course. When there is no evidence of any defense, it is immaterial whether the plaintiff is only a holder or is a holder in due course.[21] The transferee, however, may take such an active part in the sale to the seller's customer or may be so related to the seller that it is proper to conclude that the transferee was in fact a party to the original transaction and had notice or knowledge of any defense of the buyer against the seller, which conclusion automatically bars holding that the transferee is a holder in due course. (See p. 666, Jones v Approved Bancredit Corp.)

(3) Proof of Status as Holder in Due Course. The status of the holder does not become important until a person sued by the holder raises a defense that can be asserted against an ordinary holder but not against a

---

[19] Slaughter v Jefferson Federal Savings & Loan Association, (DC Dist Col) 361 F Supp 590.

[20] UCC § 3-302(3).

[21] Persson v McCormick, (Okla) 412 P2d 619.

holder in due course or a holder through a holder in due course. Initially the plaintiff in the action is entitled to recover as soon as the commercial paper is put in evidence and the signatures on it are admitted to be genuine. If the genuine character of any signature is specifically denied, the burden is then on the plaintiff to prove that the signature is genuine.[22] Once the signatures are admitted or established, the plaintiff-holder is entitled to recover [23] unless the defendant establishes a defense. In the latter situation, the plaintiff has the burden of establishing that he is a holder in due course, or a holder through a holder in due course, in order to avoid such defense.[24]

§ 33:3. Holder Through a Holder in Due Course. Those persons who become holders of the instrument after a holder in due course are given the same protection as the holder in due course provided they are not parties to fraud or illegality that would affect the instrument.

This means that if an instrument is indorsed from *A* to *B* to *C* to *D* and that if *B* is a holder in due course, both *C* and *D* will enjoy the same rights as *B*. If *C* received the instrument as a gift or with knowledge of failure of consideration or other defense, or if *D* took the instrument after maturity, they could not themselves be holders in due course. Nevertheless, they are given the same protection as a holder in due course because they took the instrument through such a holder, namely, *B*. It is not only *C*, the person taking directly from *B*, but also *D*, who takes indirectly through *B*, who is given this extra protection.

DEFENSES

§ 33:4. Classification of Defenses. The importance of being a holder in due course or a holder through a holder in due course is that those holders are not subject to certain defenses when they demand payment or bring suit upon a commercial paper. These may be described as *limited defenses.* Another class of defenses, *universal defenses,* may be asserted against any holder without regard to whether he is an assignee, an ordinary holder, a holder in due course, or a holder through a holder in due course. A holder who is neither a holder in due course nor a holder through a holder in due course is subject to every defense just as though the instrument were not negotiable.

The defenses that cannot be raised against a holder in due course are likewise barred with respect to any instrument which is executed to renew or extend the original instrument.

§ 33:5. Defenses Available Against an Assignee. An assignee of commercial paper is subject to all the defenses to which an assignee of an ordinary

---

[22] UCC § 3-307(1). The plaintiff is aided by a presumption that the signature is genuine or authorized except where the action is to enforce the obligation of a signer who has died or become incompetent. § 3-307(1)(b). Carr Estate, 436 Pa 47, 258 A2d 628.

[23] Altex Aluminum Supply Co. v Asay, 72 NJ Super 582, 178 A2d 636.

[24] UCC § 3-307(3). If the defense is one that may be asserted against any holder, it is immaterial whether the plaintiff is a holder in due course.

contract right is subject. It is immaterial whether the assignment is by voluntary act of a former holder of the paper or whether the assignment occurs by operation of law.

§ 33:6. Defenses Available Against an Ordinary Holder. When suit is brought by the original payee, he is subject to every defense that the defendant may possess, unless he qualifies as a holder in due course. An ordinary holder is also subject to any defense of the defendant.

The fact that a person cannot recover on a commercial paper does not necessarily mean that he is not entitled to recover in another action or against another party. He may be able to recover on a contract that was part of the transaction in which the instrument was given. It is also possible that he may be able to hold a party to the instrument liable for breach of an implied warranty or to recover from a person expressly guaranteeing payment of the instrument.

§ 33:7. Limited Defenses—Not Available Against a Holder in Due Course. Neither a holder in due course nor one having the rights of such a holder is subject to any of the following defenses.[25] They are limited defenses. These defenses, which are also called personal defenses, are barred with respect to any instrument that is executed to renew or extend the original instrument.

(1) Ordinary Contract Defenses. In general terms the defenses that could be raised against a suit on an ordinary contract cannot be raised against the holder in due course.[26] He is not subject to defenses based on defects in the underlying contract.[27] Accordingly, the defendant cannot assert against the holder in due course the defense of lack, failure,[28] or illegality of consideration with respect to the transaction between the defendant and the person with whom he dealt. (See p. 669, Illinois Valley Acceptance Corp. v Woodard.)

(2) Incapacity of Defendant. The incapacity of the defendant may not be raised against a holder in due course unless by general principles of law that incapacity, such as insanity of a person for whom a guardian has been appointed by a court, makes the instrument a nullity.[29]

(3) Fraud in the Inducement. When a person knows that he is executing a commercial paper and knows its essential terms but is persuaded or induced to execute it because of false statements or representations, he cannot defend against a holder in due course or a holder through a holder in due course on the ground of such fraud.[30] As an illustration, *M* is persuaded

[25] UCC § 3-305.
[26] Wyatt v Mount Airy Cemetery, 209 Pa Super 250, 224 A2d 787.
[27] Brown v Kenron Aluminum and Glass Corp., (CA8 Iowa) 477 F2d 526.
[28] Federal Factors, Inc. v Wellbanks, 241 Ark 44, 406 SW2d 712.
[29] UCC § 3-305(2)(b).
[30] Meadow Brook National Bank v Rogers, 44 Misc 2d 250, 253 NYS2d 501.

to purchase an automobile because of *P's* statement concerning its condition. *M* gives *P* a note, which is negotiated until it reaches *H,* who is a holder in due course. *M* meanwhile learns that the car is not as represented and that *P's* statements were fraudulent. When *H* demands payment of the note, *M* cannot refuse to pay him on the ground of *P's* fraud. He must pay the instrument and then recover his loss from *P.*

Likewise, the buyer of goods which in fact are stolen cannot claim as against a subsequent holder in due course of the check which he gave in payment for the goods that he had been defrauded in the sale as such fraud was merely fraud as to the inducement and therefore could not be raised against a holder in due course.[31]

(4) Prior Payment or Cancellation. When a commercial paper is paid before maturity, the person making the payment should demand the surrender of the instrument. If he fails to obtain the instrument, it is possible for the holder to continue to negotiate it. Another person may thus become the holder of the instrument. When the new holder demands payment of the instrument, the defense cannot be raised that payment had been made to a former holder, if the new holder is a holder in due course. The fact that the person making the payment obtained a receipt from the former holder does not affect the application of this principle.

When the holder and the party primarily liable have agreed to cancel the instrument but the face of the instrument does not show any sign of cancellation, the defense of cancellation cannot be asserted against a holder in due course. Similarly, an order to stop payment of a check cannot be raised as a defense by the drawer of a check against a holder in due course.

(a) OVERPAYMENT. The fact that the maker or the drawer of the paper has overpaid the payee is a simple contract defense. Thus, it may not be asserted against a holder in due course but may be asserted against anyone who does not have the rights of a holder in due course. To illustrate the latter, an employer is required by law to deduct from the pay of his employees a specified percentage which is remitted by the employer to the federal government as an advance payment on the federal income tax of the employees. If the employer by mistake makes out a note or check for the gross amount of an employee's wages, the employer may assert that amount as a setoff when sued by the employee for the face of the paper. That is, the employee cannot recover the full face amount of the paper but only the net amount which he should have received after the federal taxes were deducted from that gross amount.[32]

(5) Nondelivery of an Instrument. A person may make out a commercial paper or indorse an existing instrument and leave it on his desk for

---

[31] Star Provision Co. v Sears, Roebuck & Co., 93 Ga App 799, 92 SE2d 835.
[32] Lukens v Goit, (Wyo) 430 P2d 607.

future delivery. At that moment the instrument or the indorsement is not effective because there has been no delivery.

Assume that through the negligence of an employee or through the theft of the instrument, it comes into the hands of another person. If the instrument is in such form that it can be negotiated, as when it is payable to bearer, a subsequent receiver of the instrument may be a holder in due course or a holder through a holder in due course. As against him, the person who made out the instrument or indorsed it cannot defend on the ground that he did not deliver it.

(6) Conditional or Specified Purpose Delivery. As against a favored holder, a person who would be liable on the instrument cannot show that the instrument which is absolute on its face was in fact delivered subject to a condition that had not been performed, or that it was delivered for a particular purpose but was not so used. Assume *A* makes out a check to the order of *B* and hands it to *C* with the understanding that *C* shall not deliver the check to *B* until *B* delivers certain merchandise. If *C* should deliver the check to *B* before the condition is satisfied and *B* then negotiates the check, a holder in due course or a holder through a holder in due course may enforce the instrument.

Similarly, if the instrument is itself restrictively indorsed to subject it to a condition, the defendant may not raise against the holder in due course the defense that payment to him would be inconsistent with the restriction.

Somewhat similar to the defense of a conditional delivery is the defense that delivery was made subject to a particular oral agreement or understanding. As against a holder in due course, a defendant-indorser cannot assert that he has negotiated the instrument to his indorsee under an oral agreement that the negotiation should be without recourse as to him.

(7) Duress Consisting of Threats. The defense that a person signed or executed a commercial paper under threats of harm or violence may not be raised as a defense against a holder in due course when the effect of such duress is merely to make the contract voidable at the election of the victim of the duress. Such duress is not present when the maker of the note had business experience, dealt at arm's length with the party alleged to have been guilty of duress, acted with the advice of counsel, and delayed a month before signing the note.[33]

(8) Unauthorized Completion. If a maker or drawer signs a commercial paper and leaves blank the name of the payee, or the amount, or any other term, and then hands the instrument to another to be completed, the defense of an improper completion cannot be raised when payment is demanded or suit brought by a subsequent holder in due course or a holder through a holder in due course. That is, he may enforce the instrument as completed.[34]

---

[33] Hastain v Greenbaum, 205 Kan 475, 470 P2d 741.

[34] UCC § 3-407(3).

This situation arises when an employer gives a signed blank check to an employee with instructions to make certain purchases and to fill in the name of the seller and the amount when these are determined. If the employee fills in the name of a friend and a large amount and then the employee and the friend negotiate the instrument, the employer cannot defend against a subsequent holder in due course or a holder through a holder in due course on the ground that the completion had been without the authority of the employer.

(9) Theft. As a matter of definition, a holder in due course will not have acquired the paper through theft and any defense of theft therefore must relate to the conduct of a prior party. Assuming that the theft of the paper does not result in a defect in the chain of necessary indorsements, the defense that the instrument had been stolen cannot be asserted against a holder in due course.[35]

§ 33:8. Universal Defenses—Available Against All Holders. Certain defenses are regarded as so basic that the social interest in preserving them outweighs the social interest of giving commercial paper the free-passing qualities of money. Accordingly, such defenses are given universal effect and may be raised against all holders, whether ordinary holders, holders in due course, or holders through a holder in due course. Such defenses are therefore appropriately called universal defenses. They are also called real defenses.

(1) Fraud as to the Nature or Essential Terms of the Paper. If a person signs a commercial paper because he has been fraudulently deceived as to its nature or essential terms, he has a defense available against all holders. This is the situation when an experienced businessman induces an illiterate person to sign a note by falsely representing that it is a contract for repairs. This defense, however, cannot be raised when it is the negligence of the defending party that prevented him from learning the true nature and terms of the instrument. (See p. 670, Burchett v Allied Concord Financial Corp.)

(2) Forgery or Lack of Authority. The defense that a signature was forged or signed without authority may be raised against any holder unless the person whose name was signed ratified it or is estopped by his conduct or negligence from denying it.[36]

When a person receives by mistake a check which is intended for another person having the same name, it is forgery when the recipient of the check indorses the check with the name of the payee. Even though it is the indorser's own name, the indorser does not intend to designate himself by the indorsement but intends to represent that the indorsement has been made by the person intended by the drawer.[37]

---

[35] § 3-305(1).
[36] UCC § 3-404(1); Cohen v Lincoln Savings Bank, 275 NY 399, 10 NE2d 475.
[37] Fulton National Bank v United States, (CA5 Ga) 197 F2d 763.

The fact that the drawer may have been lax and unbusinesslike in issuing the check to a named payee does not constitute negligence which under UCC § 3-406 bars the assertion that the signature of the payee was a forgery.[38]

*(3) **Duress Depriving Control.*** When a person executes or indorses a commercial paper in response to a force of such a nature that under general principles of law there is duress which makes the transaction a nullity, rather than merely voidable, such duress may be raised as a defense against any holder.[39]

*(4) **Incapacity.*** The fact that the defendant is a minor who under general principles of contract law may avoid his obligation is a matter that may be raised against any kind of holder. Other kinds of incapacity may only be raised as a defense if the effect of the incapacity is to make the instrument a nullity.[40]

*(5) **Illegality.*** If the law declares that an instrument is void when executed in connection with certain conduct, such as gambling or usury, that defense may be raised against any holder. Similarly, when contracts of a corporate seller are a nullity because its charter has been forfeited for nonpayment of taxes, a promissory note given to it by a buyer is void and that defense may be raised as against a holder in due course.[41] If the law merely makes the transaction illegal but does not make the instrument void, the defense cannot be asserted against a holder in due course or a holder through a holder in due course.[42]

*(6) **Alteration.*** The fact that an instrument has been altered may be raised against any holder. Unlike other defenses, however, it is only a partial defense as against a holder in due course. That is, the latter holder may enforce the instrument according to its original terms prior to its alteration.[43] Moreover, if the person sued by the holder in due course has substantially contributed by his negligence to making the alteration possible, that defendant is precluded from asserting the defense of alteration.

An alteration does not have any effect unless it is both material and fraudulently made. An alteration is material when it changes the contract of any party in any way, as by changing the date, place of payment, rate of interest, or any other term. It also includes any modification that changes the number or the relationship of the parties to the paper, by adding new terms, or by cutting off a part of the paper itself.[44]

---

[38] East Gadsden Bank v First City National Bank, (Ala Civ App) 281 So2d 431.
[39] UCC § 3-305(2)(b).
[40] § 3-305(2)(b).
[41] Universal Acceptance Corp. v Burks, (Dist Col General Sessions) 7 UCCRS 39.
[42] UCC § 3-305(2)(b).
[43] § 3-407(3).
[44] UCC § 3-407(1).

While a seal has no effect upon the negotiability of paper, the addition of a seal to an unsealed note constitutes a material alteration because it removes the paper from the ordinary statute of limitations applicable to promissory notes or simple contracts and permits suit to be brought within the longer period of time allowed with respect to suits on contracts under seal.[45]

Conversely, the adding or crossing out of words on the instrument which do not affect the contract of any party is not material. Likewise, there is no "alteration," because there is no fraud, when a pencil line is run through the amount of the note after part payment has been made and the current balance is written in pencil, or when a red line is drawn across the face of the note to indicate that the bank examiner had examined the note.[46] Similarly, there is no alteration when the final payment due on a note is changed from $41,000 to $42,000 if the balance of the note showed that this was the correct amount and that the changed figure ($41,000) had been a mistake.[47]

An alteration must be made to the instrument itself. An oral or a collateral written agreement between the holder and one of the parties that modifies the obligation of the party is not an "alteration" within the sense just discussed, even though the obligation of the party is changed or altered thereby.

By definition an alteration is a change made by a party to the instrument. A change of the instrument made by a stranger has no effect, and recovery on the instrument is the same as though the change had not been made provided it can be proved what the instrument had been in its original form.

§ 33:9. Adverse Claims to the Paper. Distinct from a defense which a defendant may raise against a plaintiff as a reason why he should not be required to pay the instrument is a claim of a third person that he and not the possessor of the paper is the owner of the paper. Assume that a check was made to the order of *A*; that thereafter blank indorsements are made by *B*, *C*, and *D*; and that *E* in possession of the check appears to be the holder. *B* might then claim and show, if such be the case, that he indorsed the check because he was fraudulently deceived by *C*; that he avoids his indorsement because of such fraud; and that accordingly the check still belongs to him. *B* in such case is making an adverse claim to the instrument.

A holder in due course holds commercial paper free and clear from all adverse claims of any other person to the paper, including both equitable and legal interests of third persons, and the right of a former holder to rescind his negotiation.[48] In contrast, such adverse claims may be asserted against a holder who is not a holder in due course,[49] which means that the adverse claimant may bring such action against the holder since the law generally provides for the recovery of property by the owner from anyone else.

---

45 Baumer v Du Pont, 338 Pa 193, 12 A2d 566.

46 Bank of New Mexico v Rice, 78 NMex 170, 429 P2d 368.

47 National State Bank v Kleinberg, (NY Supreme Ct) 4 UCCRS 100.

48 UCC §§ 3-305(1), 3-207(2).

49 § 3-306(a), (d).

Ordinarily a defendant when sued by a holder cannot raise against the holder the defense that the holder's ownership is subject to an adverse claim. This may be done only when the adverse claimant has also become a party to the action or is defending the action on behalf of the defendant.[50] Otherwise it would be unfair to the adverse claimant to pass upon the merits of his claim in his absence, as well as being undesirable in opening the door to perjury by giving any defendant the opportunity of beclouding the issues by raising a false claim that a third person has an adverse interest.

§ 33:10. Consumer Protection. Consumer protection legislation frequently provides that when the debtor executes a commercial paper which is negotiated thereafter by the creditor, the transferee cannot be a holder in due course. This protects the debtor by permitting him to raise against the transferee, such as the seller's finance company, the same defenses that the debtor could raise against his creditor, the seller.[51]

---

[50] § 3-306(d).

[51] Randolph National Bank v Vail, — Vt —, 308 A2d 588. The UCCC proposes two alternative rules: one which would abolish the holder in due course protection of the creditor's transferee in practically all cases; the other which would preserve it to the extent of barring the consumer from asserting against a good faith assignee not related to the assignor a defense which he failed to raise within three months after being notified of the assignment. UCCC § 2.404. The Federal Trade Commission is studying the formulation of a regulation on the preservation of buyers' claims and defenses in consumer installment sales.

CASES FOR CHAPTER 33

Northside Building & Investment Co. v Finance Co.

119 Ga App 131, 166 SE2d 608 (1969)

Stockbridge Investment Corp. borrowed money from the Finance Company. As security for the loan, it delivered to Finance Company a number of notes held by it but without indorsing them. Thereafter Finance Company brought suit on one of these notes against its maker, the Northside Building & Investment Co. The latter raised the defense of payment, which could not be raised against a holder in due course. Finance Company claimed that it was a holder in due course and not subject to the defense. Northside claimed that Finance Company was not a holder in due course because the note had not been indorsed to it. From a judgment in favor of Finance Company, Northside appealed.

QUILLIAN, J. . . . Was the Finance Company a holder in due course? For if so, the defense of payment raised by the defendant would be effectively negated unless the plaintiff had notice of the payment within the meaning of [UCC §] 3-602. . . .

While a transfer for value of an instrument gives the transferee the specifically enforceable right to have the unqualified indorsement of the transferor, "negotiation takes effect only when the indorsement is made and until that time there is no presumption that the transferee is the owner." [UCC §] 3-201. . . . "Negotiation is the transfer of an instrument in such form that the transferee becomes a holder." [UCC §] 3-202. . . .

Under the provisions of the Commercial Code, now in effect, in order to be a "holder" in due course, one must first be a "holder" within the meaning of the Act. A holder is defined as a "person who is in possession of a document of title or an instrument or an investment security drawn, issued, or indorsed to him or to his order or to bearer or in blank." [UCC §] 1-201(20) . . . Thus, it is apparent that . . . the Finance Company was not a holder since there had been no indorsement to it of the note in question.

However, under the provisions of [UCC §] 3-201 the Finance Company as transferee would acquire the same rights as its transferor had. In this case Stockbridge was the transferor, but there was no showing that it was a holder in due course. Where it is shown that a defense exists, the plaintiff may seek to cut off such defense by establishing itself as a holder in due course or that it has acquired the rights of a prior holder in due course under [UCC §] 3-201. But in doing so, the plaintiff must sustain the burden of proof by a preponderance of evidence. There was no showing made to sustain this burden, that anyone through whom the plaintiff had acquired its rights was a holder in due course. . . .

[Judgment reversed.]

Korzenik v Supreme Radio

347 Mass 309, 197 NE2d 702 (1964)

Southern New England Distributing Corporation, which held two notes of Supreme Radio, indorsed them to Korzenik, an attorney, and his partner "as a retainer for services to be performed." When Korzenik sued Supreme Radio on the notes, it raised the defense of fraud in the procurement. Korzenik claimed that he was a holder in due course. From a decision against him, Korzenik appealed.

WHITTEMORE, J. . . . Decisive of the case . . . is the correct ruling that the plaintiffs are not holders in due course under [UCC] § 3-302; they have not shown to what extent they took for value under § 3-303. That section provides: "A holder takes the instrument for value (a) to the extent that the agreed consideration has been performed or that he acquires a security interest in or a lien on the instrument otherwise than by legal process; or (b) when he takes the instrument in payment of or as security for an antecedent claim against any person whether or not the claim is due; or (c) when he gives a negotiable instrument for it or makes an irrevocable commitment to a third person." . . .

The Uniform Laws Comment to § 3-303 points out that . . . "value is divorced from consideration" and that except as provided in paragraph (c) "an executory promise to give value is not . . . value. . . . The underlying reason of policy is that when the purchaser learns of a defense . . . he is not required to enforce the instrument, but is free to rescind the transaction for breach of the transferor's warranty."

. . . § 3-307(3), provides: "After it is shown that a defense exists, a person claiming the rights of a holder in due course has the burden of establishing that he or some person under whom he claims is in all respects a holder in due course." The defense of fraud having been established, this section puts the burden on the plaintiffs. The plaintiffs have failed to show "the extent . . . [to which] the agreed consideration . . . [had] been performed." . . .

[Judgment affirmed.]

Richardson Co. v First National Bank in Dallas

(Tex Civ App) 504 SW2d 812 (1974)

Auman was employed by the Richardson Company. She purchased an automobile on credit and the claim for the unpaid balance was held by the First National Bank. Auman gave the bank a check to pay the balance. The check was drawn by the Richardson Company and made payable to the First National Bank. The bank received the check for this purpose and released the security interest in the car which the bank held to secure payment of the unpaid balance. The Richardson Company sued the First National Bank on the theory that the bank knew or should have known of the misconduct of Auman and was guilty of conversion in applying the company's check to the discharge of Auman's personal debt. From a judgment for the bank, the Richardson Company appealed.

DUNAGAN, C.J. . . . Edwin L. Cunningham, an officer of the First National Bank, the appellee, in his affidavit stated that the bank received the check from Mrs. Auman . . . "with information that the check represented compensation from Mrs. Auman's employer and was to be applied to discharge her indebtedness to the bank. . . ." . . .

The Richardson Company, appellant, argues that the bank had "notice" of the appellant's claim because the bank had knowledge of some fiduciary relationship existing between Mrs. Auman and her employer and therefore the bank is not a holder in due course under the Texas Business and Commerce Code. The appellant filed no affidavit proof or otherwise averred that a fiduciary relationship existed between Mrs. Auman and her employer. No allegation or summary judgment proof has been made that Mrs. Auman was responsible for the disbursement of the appellant's funds or that Mrs. Auman's relationship to her employer was of such a confidential nature that she was a "fiduciary." Furthermore, The Richardson Company had not controverted statements in the affidavits supporting the bank's motion for summary judgment that it had no knowledge concerning Mrs. Auman's relationship with her employer, The Richardson Company, other than that it was provided in financial statements given to merchants from whom the bank purchased installment contracts. Such information is insufficient as a matter of law to constitute "notice" of a fiduciary relationship. Notice of a "fiduciary" relationship is specifically stated not to be notice of a "claim" to an instrument under the Texas Business and Commerce Code, § 3-304, which, in part, provides:

"(d) Knowledge of the following facts does not of itself give the purchaser notice of a defense or claim . . .
(5) that any person negotiating the instrument is or was a fiduciary; . . ."

Therefore, the information provided in Mrs. Auman's application for financing, even if sufficient to provide First National Bank knowledge of a "fiduciary relationship" between The Richardson Company and Mrs. Auman, would be insufficient knowledge to place First National on "notice" of a claim or defense to the check. . . .

. . . Even if a bank has notice that a person is a fiduciary, the bank is safe in assuming proper conduct: "It is the law of this state that there is a presumption that a trustee or fiduciary will legally perform their functions." . . .

"Good faith" is defined in [UCC §] 1-201(19) . . . to mean: "honesty in fact in the conduct or transaction concerned." The test for "good faith" under the [UCC] is not diligence or negligence; and it is immaterial that appellee may have had notice of such facts as would put a reasonable prudent person on inquiry which would lead to discovery, unless appellee had actual knowledge of facts and circumstances that amounted to bad faith. . . .

We . . . hold . . . as a matter of law, that appellee was a holder in due course and did change its position in good faith reliance on payment of the check. . . .

[Judgment affirmed.]

Jones v Approved Bancredit Corp.

(Del) 256 A2d 739 (1969)

Jones made a contract to purchase a prefabricated home on credit from Albee Dell Homes. She signed a promissory note and mortgage for the purchase price. These papers were transferred by Albee Dell Homes to Approved Bancredit Corp. When Jones stopped making payments on the note, she was sued by Bancredit. She raised certain defenses. Bancredit moved for a summary judgment on the ground that the defenses were not available against it because it was a holder in due course. From a decision that Bancredit was a holder in due course, Jones appealed.

HERRMANN, J. . . . The defendant, Myrtle V. Jones, owned a lot of land in Delaware and wished to have a house built on it. She responded to a newspaper advertisement by Albee Dell Homes, Inc. (hereinafter "Dell"), a sales agency for precut homes in Elkton, Maryland. After selecting a type of house from various plans presented, Mrs. Jones signed a purchase order contract and credit application and made a deposit. Several weeks later, Dell's representative presented to Mrs. Jones for signature a series of documents evidencing an obligation of $3,250 * to be paid by Mrs. Jones in monthly installments over a period of years for the house. The documents evidencing the obligation included the following papers: a mortgage; a judgment bond and warrant; a promissory note; a construction contract; a request for insurance; an affidavit that the masonry work and foundation were completed and paid for (when in fact none of the work had been commenced); and an affidavit that no materials were delivered or work started as of the date of the mortgage.

Mrs. Jones demurred to the signing of the mass of documents thus placed before her and stated that she would like to consult her attorney before signing because she did not understand the documents. Dell's representative objected, stating that it was not necessary for Mrs. Jones to have an attorney; that it would be a waste of money to do so; that he would advise her. Although Mrs. Jones reiterated her wish for an attorney several times, Dell's representative insisted upon her signing the papers then and there, stating that it was necessary to do so if the work was to start seasonably. He assured her that Dell would take care of the entire situation to her satisfaction. Mrs. Jones finally acquiesced and signed all the documents. Immediately thereafter, the paper was indorsed and assigned by Dell to the plaintiff, Approved Bancredit Corp. (hereinafter "Bancredit"), which paid Dell $2,250 for the $3,250 note.

During the construction, an employee of the builder drove a bulldozer into the side of the partially completed house and knocked it off its foundations. Thereafter, the builder refused to go forward with the work. Dell disclaimed responsibility on the ground that the damage to the structure was the result of a "cave-in" and was "a work of God." The structure was left in a dangerous condition with the water-filled basement constituting an attractive nuisance to children. The County authorities demanded that this unsafe condition be rectified. Mrs. Jones consulted an attorney who notified Dell and Bancredit that Mrs. Jones would be obliged to remove the remnants of the building and fill the basement, in order to make the area safe, unless another satisfactory course of action was suggested. There was no reply and the demolition was accomplished at Mrs. Jones' expense. Later, Dell closed its office and terminated its business except for the servicing of certain contracts through a representative in Delaware. . . .

Dell and Bancredit were both wholly owned subsidiaries of Albee Homes, Inc. (hereinafter "Homes"). The business of the parent corporation was to process precut lumber and to sell precut homes. It had between 50 and 70 sales agencies in 19 states; Dell was its Maryland sales agency. Ninety-nine percent of Bancredit's business came from Dell and the other wholly owned sales agency subsidiaries of Homes; it was organized for this purpose. Bancredit examined into the laws of the various states in which the sales agencies operated and prescribed the forms of contracts and financing documents to be used by each agency, including Dell, in concluding a transaction. Homes and Bancredit had the same officers and directors; Homes named the directors and officers of Dell. Checks of Bancredit, issued to consummate a financing transaction like that entered into by Mrs. Jones and Dell, were countersigned by Homes. During the construction of a house, Bancredit routinely requested and received progress reports. Specifically, the manager of Bancredit testified on deposition that Bancredit was a "finance department" of Homes; that each transaction of Dell, like the transactions of each of the other sales agencies, was approved in advance by Bancredit; that the first paper received was the application of the purchaser for extension of credit which was reviewed and passed upon in advance by Bancredit, with directions back to Dell as to any special condition to be imposed upon the purchaser in connection with the loan under consideration. Bancredit had the exclusive power of approval, condition, or rejection of a transaction tendered by the sales agency. . . .

In dealing with the holder in due course status, a basic problem has been recognized by

* The principle amount of the obligation was $2,500. The balance consisted of "charges."

the courts in cases involving the financing of installment sales, especially of consumer goods and household improvements. The problem arises from the increasingly apparent need for a balancing of the interest of the commercial community in the unrestricted negotiability of commercial papers, on the one hand, against the interest of the installment buyers of the community, on the other hand, in the preservation of their normal remedy of withholding payment whenever there has been misrepresentation, failure of consideration, or other valid reason for refusal to pay. This problem and this need have given rise to this concept: the more the holder knows about the underlying transaction which is the source of the paper, the more he controls or participates in it, the less he fits the role of good faith purchaser for value; and the less justification there is for according to him the protected status of holder in due course considered necessary for the free flow of paper in the commercial world.

The rule, balancing the needs of the installment-buying community and the commercial community, has evolved in various ways. Many courts have solved the problem by denying holder in due course status to the finance company where it maintains a close business relationship with the dealer whose paper it buys; where the financer is closely connected with the particular credit transaction under scrutiny; or where the financer prescribes to the dealer the forms of the papers, the buyer signs the purchase agreement and the note concurrently, and the dealer indorses the note and assigns the contract immediately thereafter. In such situations, many courts look upon the transaction as a species of tripartite transaction; and the tenor of the cases is that the finance company, in such situation, should not be permitted to hide behind "the fictional fence" of the UNIL or the UCC and thereby achieve an unfair advantage over the purchaser. . . .

And in Unico v Owen, 50 NJ 101, 232 A2d 405 [4 UCC Rep. 452] (1967), wherein the finance company was formed expressly to handle the financing of sales by the dealer exclusively, the Supreme Court of New Jersey summarized its position on the question before us as follows: "For purposes of consumer goods transactions, we hold that where the seller's performance is executory in character and when it appears from the totality of the arrangements between dealer and financer that the financer has had a substantial voice in setting standards for the underlying transaction, or has approved the standards established by the dealer, and has agreed to take all or a predetermined or substantial quantity of the negotiable paper which is backed by such standards, the financer should be considered a participant in the original transaction and therefore not entitled to holder in due course status. . . ." The factual situation in the Unico case is especially analogous to the instant case.

The divergent line of cases, reflecting an underlying conflict in policy considerations, accords determinative importance to the maintenance of a free flow of credit. These cases protect the finance company from purchaser defenses on the ground that this is an overriding consideration in order to assure easy negotiability of commercial paper and the resultant availability of the rapid financing methods required by our present-day economy. . . .

Under the totality of facts and circumstances of this case, we hold that the rule of balance should be adopted and applied; that it should operate in favor of the installment buyer for the reason that, in our opinion, Bancredit was so involved in the transaction that it may not be treated as a subsequent purchaser for value. By reason of its sister corporation relationship to Dell and the established course of dealing between them, Bancredit was more nearly an original party to the transaction than a subsequent purchaser of the paper; and, for the reasons of fairness and balance stated in the foregoing authorities, Bancredit should be denied the protected status of holder in due course which would prevent Mrs. Jones from having her day in court on the defenses she would have otherwise had against Dell.

The rule we here adopt must be applied carefully because of the delicate balance of the interests of the installment buying community and the commercial community. But the need for special care in application should not foreclose the adoption of the rule and its application in a proper case. In this day of demonstrated need for emphasis upon consumer protection and truth in lending, special consideration must be given to preventing the misuse of negotiable instruments to deprive installment purchasers of legitimate defenses. In a proper case, such as the one before us, this becomes the controlling consideration.

For the reasons stated, we conclude that the Superior Court erred in holding that Bancredit was a holder in due course. Accordingly, the judgment below is reversed and the cause remanded for further proceedings consistent herewith.

Code Comment: The Jones decision was governed by the NIL since the note was executed in 1963 and the Uniform Commercial Code did not become effective in Delaware until 1967. The same decision, however, would be made under the UCC because the decision does not depend upon any statutory provision but rather on an appraisal of a fact situation and the desire of the court to afford consumer protection. That no distinction exists in the mind of this court between the UCC and the pre-Code law is seen from its criticism of the " 'fictional fence' of the UNIL or the UCC. . . ."

The trend of decisions under the Code appears to favor the maker of a promissory note as against a finance company where consumer goods are involved. Unico v Owen, 50 NJ 101, 232 A2d 405; American Plan Corp. v Woods, 16 Ohio App 2d 1, 240 NE2d 886.

Illinois Valley Acceptance Corp. v Woodard

— Ind App —, 304 NE2d 859 (1973)

At various times Woodard purchased goods from the Moody Manufacturing Company. In 1968 he made a purchase and arranged for its payment by accepting a trade acceptance drawn on him. He accepted it although the amount was blank because it had not yet been determined what goods he would be purchasing from Moody. An amount was later filled in and thereafter Moody assigned the acceptance to Illinois Valley Acceptance Corp. Illinois sued Woodard on the trade acceptance. He raised the defenses that there had been fraud, that he had never received the goods, and that the trade acceptance had been accepted with the amount in blank. Judgment was entered for Woodard and Illinois Valley appealed.

ROBERTSON, P.J. . . . Whether the trial court erred . . . is tied to Acceptance's classification as a holder in due course of the questioned trade acceptance. . . .

Acceptance's acknowledged status as a holder was not sufficient for it to recover because Woodard raised the defenses of fraud and failure of consideration, each a valid defense under [UCC §] 3-306. . . . These defenses, however, may have been cut off if Acceptance was a holder in due course. The holder in due course takes the instrument "free from all defenses of any party to the instrument with whom the holder has not dealt," subject to several exceptions. [UCC §] 3-305(2) . . . To avail itself of this "super-plaintiff" status, Acceptance had the burden of establishing by a preponderance of the evidence that it was "in all respects a holder in due course." [UCC §] 3-307(3). . . . "In all respects" means that Acceptance had to establish the existence of each of the elements set forth in IC 1971, 26-1-3-302, Ind.Ann.Stat. § 19-3-302 (Burns 1964). It provides: "(1) A holder in due course is a holder who takes the instrument (a) for value; and (b) in good faith; and (c) without notice that it is overdue or has been dishonored or of any defense against or claim to it on the part of any person."

The evidence, when examined with the foregoing requisites in mind, establishes Acceptance as a holder in due course. Briefly summarized that evidence shows the trade acceptance being endorsed over to Acceptance by Moody. Moody in turn received a draft for 85% of the face value of the trade acceptance. There was nothing irregular with the appearance of the trade acceptance and the transaction was similar to other prior transactions between the parties. At that time Acceptance had no knowledge that the trade acceptance had been signed in blank and that the goods had not been delivered.

A portion of Woodard's arguments appears to be directed to the questions of good faith and notice. Both are statutorily defined: "(19) 'Good faith' means honesty in fact in the conduct or transaction concerned." [UCC §] 26-1-1-201, Ind.Ann.Stat. § 19-1-201 (Burns 1964) Notice, insofar as applicable, is defined as: "(1) The purchaser has notice of a claim or defense if (a) the instrument is so incomplete, bears such visible evidence of forgery or alteration, or is otherwise so irregular as to call into question its validity, terms or ownership or to create an ambiguity as to the party to pay; or (b) the purchaser has notice that the obligation of any party is voidable in whole or in part, or that all parties have been discharged." [UCC §] 3-304. . . .

The gist of Woodard's cross examination of Acceptance's vice-president was directed to when Acceptance became aware of Moody's bankruptcy and to the Finance Agreement between Moody and Acceptance. We believe that the bankruptcy has no relevancy because of its nonexistence at the time the trade acceptance was endorsed over to Acceptance. The Finance Agreement, introduced into evidence by Woodard, may have been an attempt to establish something akin to the doctrine of close connectedness, characterized by Woodard as the lack of an arms-length transaction, for the purpose of showing that Acceptance was so closely related to Moody commercially that it knew, or should have known, either Moody was in poor financial shape or that it had not delivered the goods represented by the trade acceptance. Acceptance's summary judgment affidavit as well as the testimony given at the trial belies such a relationship.

Woodard further argues that there was no value given for the trade acceptance and that the Finance Agreement between Moody and Acceptance was merely a borrowing agreement. The evidence shows that Acceptance paid Moody 85% of the face value of trade acceptance and held the remainder in reserve. There can be little question that the value concept was satisfied. [UCC §] 3-303. . . . Nor does the designation of the Finance Agreement as a borrowing arrangement standing alone serve to frustrate the taking of value. The issuance of the draft by Acceptance and the holding in reserve of the remaining 15% eliminates any question regarding unused credit. . . .

Woodard's affirmative defense of want of consideration is not available against a holder in due course. [UCC §] 3-408. . . .

Turning next to the question of fraud [UCC §] 3-305(2)(c) . . . allows a defense against a holder in due course based upon "such misrepresentation as has induced the party to sign the instrument with neither knowledge nor reasonable opportunity to obtain knowledge of its character or its essential terms." The comments subsequent to this statute state that fraud in the essence or fraud in the factum is a valid defense against a holder in due course with the theory being that the "signature is ineffective because he did not intend to sign such an instrument at all." Woodard's past conduct in signing blank trade acceptances for Moody negates a defense based on the foregoing. Woodard testified he was familiar with the forms and knew they constituted a promise to pay. . . .

It is our conclusion that the evidence conclusively demonstrated Acceptance to be a holder in due course. We, accordingly, reverse and remand for judgment to be entered for the plaintiff-appellant Illinois Valley Acceptance Corp., and against the defendant-appellee Robert Woodard.

[Judgment reversed and remanded.]

Burchett v Allied Concord Financial Corp.

74 NMex 575, 396 P2d 186 (1964)

Kelly was an agent selling aluminum siding for Consolidated Products. He persuaded Mr. and Mrs. Burchett to have aluminum siding put on their house, which would be used for advertising purposes as a "show house" and the Burchetts were to receive a $100 credit on the contract price for every other customer buying in a specified area. The Burchetts understood that by this method they would receive the improvements for nothing. The same proposal was made to their neighbors, the Beevers. Kelly then

gave both families papers to sign, which in fact were notes promising to pay the price stated and mortgages on their houses to secure the payment of the notes. Nothing was said in the signed papers as to receiving credits on other sales. The Burchetts and the Beevers then brought an action against the Allied Concord Financial Corporation, to which the notes and mortgages had been transferred, to set them aside on the ground that they were fraudulently procured. From a judgment in their favor, Allied Concord appealed.

CARMODY, J. . . . Following the explanation by Kelly, both families agreed to the offer and were given a form of a printed contract to read. While they were reading the contract, Kelly was filling out blanks in other forms. After the appellees had read the form of the contract submitted to them, they signed, *without reading,* the form or forms filled out by Kelly, assuming them to be the same as that which they had read and further assuming that what they signed provided for the credits which Kelly assured them they would receive. Needless to say, what appellees signed were notes and mortgages on the properties to cover the cost of the aluminum siding, and contracts containing no mention of credits for advertising or other sales. . . .

Within a matter of days after the contracts were signed, the aluminum siding was installed, although in neither case was the job completed to the satisfaction of appellees. Some time later, the appellees received letters from appellant, informing them that appellant had purchased the notes and mortgages which had been issued in favor of Consolidated Products and that appellees were delinquent in their first payment. Upon the receipt of these notices, appellees discovered that mortgages had been recorded against their property and they immediately instituted these proceedings. . . .

The trial court found that the notes and mortgages, although signed by the appellees, were fraudulently procured. . . .

We believe that the official comments following § 3-305(2)(c), Comment No. 7, provide an excellent guideline. . . .

"7. Paragraph (c) of subsection (2) is new. It follows the great majority of the decisions under the original Act in recognizing the defense of 'real' or 'essential' fraud, sometimes called fraud in the essence or fraud in the factum, as effective against a holder in due course. The common illustration is that of the maker who is tricked into signing a note in the belief that it is merely a receipt or some other document. The theory of the defense is that his signature on the instrument is ineffective because he did not intend to sign such an instrument at all. Under this provision the defense extends to an instrument signed with knowledge that it is a negotiable instrument, but without knowledge of its essential terms. . . .

We observe that the inclusion of Subsection (2)(c) in § 3-305 of the Uniform Commercial Code was an attempt to codify or make definite the rulings of many jurisdictions on the question as to the liability to a holder in due course of a party who either had knowledge, or a reasonable opportunity to obtain the knowledge, of the essential terms of the instrument, before signing. Many courts [have been] called upon to determine this question under the Uniform Negotiable Instruments Law. Almost all of the courts that were called upon to rule on this question required a showing of freedom from negligence, in order to constitute a good defense against a bona fide holder of negotiable paper. . . .

The reason for the rule . . . is that when one of two innocent persons must suffer by the act of a third, the loss must be borne by the one who enables the third person to occasion it. . . .

The facts and circumstances surrounding each particular case, both under the Negotiable Instruments Law and the Uniform Commercial Code, require an independent determination. . . .

Applying the elements of the test to the case before us, Mrs. Burchett was 47 years old and had a ninth grade education, and Mr. Burchett was approximately the same age, but his education does not appear. Mr. Burchett was foreman of the sanitation department of the city of Clovis and testified that he was familiar with some legal documents. Both the Burchetts understood English, and there was no showing that they lacked ability to read. Both were able to understand the original form of contract which was submitted to them. As to the Beevers, Mrs. Beevers was 38 years old and had been through the ninth grade. Mr. Beevers had approximately the same education, but his age does not appear. However, he had been working for the same firm for about nine years and knew a little something about mortgages, at least to the extent of having one upon his property. Mrs. Beevers was employed in a supermarket, and it does not appear that either of the Beevers had any difficulty with the English language and they made no claim that they were unable to understand it. Neither the Beevers nor the Burchetts had ever had any prior association with Kelly and the papers were signed upon the very day that they first met him. There was no showing of any reason why they should rely upon Kelly or have confidence in him. The occurrences took place in the homes of appellees, but other than what appears to be Kelly's "chicanery," no reason was given which would warrant a reasonable person in acting as hurriedly as was done in this case. None of the appellees attempted to obtain any independent information either with respect to Kelly or Consolidated Products, nor did they seek out any other person to read or explain the instruments to them. As a matter of fact, they apparently didn't believe this was necessary because, like most people, they wanted to take advantage of "getting something for nothing." There is no dispute but that the appellees did not have actual knowledge of the nature of the instruments which they signed, at the time they signed them. Appellant urges that appellees had a reasonable opportunity to obtain such knowledge but failed to do so, were therefore negligent, and that their defense was precluded.

We recognize that the reasonable opportunity to obtain knowledge may be excused if the maker places reasonable reliance on the representations. The difficulty in the instant case is that the reliance upon the representations of a complete stranger (Kelly) was not reasonable, and all of the parties were of sufficient age, intelligence, education, and business experience to know better. In this connection, it is noted that the contracts clearly stated, on the same page which bore the signatures of the various appellees, the following:

"No one is authorized on behalf of this company to represent this job to be 'A SAMPLE HOME OR A FREE JOB.' " . . .

The finding of the trial court that Burchetts were not guilty of negligence is not supported by substantial evidence and must fall. We determine under these facts as a matter of law that both the Burchetts and the Beevers had a reasonable opportunity to obtain knowledge of the character or the essential terms of the instruments which they signed, and therefore appellant as a holder in due course took the instruments free from the defenses claimed . . . .

[Judgment reversed.]

QUESTIONS AND CASE PROBLEMS

1. *H* was the holder of a promissory note. When he sued *M*, the maker of the note, *M* raised as a defense the objection that *H* was not a holder in due course. Can *H* recover? [Brock v Adams, 79 NMex 17, 439 P2d 234]
2. *D* drew a check to the order of *P*. It was later claimed that *P* was not a holder in due course because the check was postdated and because *P* knew that *D* was having financial difficulties and that the particular checking account on which this check was drawn had been frequently overdrawn. Do these circumstances prevent *P* from being a holder in due course? [Citizens Bank, Booneville v National Bank of Commerce, (CA Okla) 334 F2d 257; Franklin National Bank v Sidney Gotowner, (NY Sup Ct) 4 UCCRS 953]
3. Statham drew a check. The payee indorsed it to the Kemp Motor Sales. Statham then stopped payment on the check on the ground that there was a

failure of consideration for the check. Kemp sued Statham on the check. When Statham raised the defense of failure of consideration, Kemp replied that it was a holder in due course. Statham claimed that Kemp could not recover because it learned of his defense before it deposited the check in its bank account. Decide. [Kemp Motor Sales v Statham, 120 Ga App 515, 171 SE2d 389]

4. Henry executed and delivered a check to Jesse Farley in payment of an automobile. On the face of the check was written "Car to be free and clear of liens." The check was indorsed and delivered by Farley to the Zachry Company. When the latter sued Henry, Henry raised the defense of fraud in the inducement and failure of consideration, and claimed that Zachry was not a holder in due course because the words "Car to be free and clear of liens" gave notice of defenses. Was Henry correct? [C. D. Henry v A. L. Zachry Co., 93 Ga App 536, 92 SE2d 225]
5. Vanella sold his automobile to Blackburn Motors by falsely representing that there were no liens on the car. Blackburn paid Vanella with a check that was cashed by the Marine Midland Trust Co. When Blackburn learned of Vanella's fraud, it stopped payment on the check. Midland then sued Blackburn to enforce its secondary liability as drawer. Blackburn raised the defense of Vanella's fraud. Was this defense available to it? [Marine Midland Trust Co. v Blackburn, 50 Misc 2d 954, 271 NYS2d 388]
6. Wolsky executed a promissory note payable to the order of Green. Green indorsed it "Pay to the order of M. E. Grasswick, (signed) Albert E. Green" and delivered it to Grasswick. Grasswick then indorsed and delivered it to McGuckin, a holder in due course. When the note was not paid, McGuckin sued Wolsky and the indorsers. Green claimed that the negotiation by him to Grasswick was agreed between them to be without recourse. Was this a valid defense? [McGuckin v Wolsky, 78 ND 921, 53 NW2d 852]
7. Ten negotiable notes were negotiated to the First National Bank, which paid for them with a draft on another bank. The First National Bank then learned that the notes had been procured by fraud. Thereafter the bank on which the draft of the First National Bank had been drawn made payment. When the bank sued the maker, Motors Acceptance Corp., the latter claimed that the bank was not a holder in due course because it had not "paid" for the notes before it learned of the defense. Decide. [First National Bank of Waukesha v Motors Acceptance Corp., 15 Wis 2d 44, 112 NW2d 381]
8. Rocchio executed and delivered a note payable to the order of Berta. When Berta sued Rocchio on the note, the latter offered parol evidence to show that the note had been given as payment for a business and its inventory and that less inventory had been delivered than had been agreed upon. Berta claimed that the obligation of the instrument could not be modified by parol evidence. Was he correct? [Berta v Rocchio, 149 Colo 325, 369 P2d 51]
9. *A* and *B* were negotiating for the sale of land. *A* paid *B* in advance with a postdated check. When *A* and *B* could not agree on a final contract, *A* stopped payment of the check. Was *B* a holder in due course? [Briand v Wild, 110 NH 373, 268 A2d 896]
10. In an action on a promissory note it was claimed that there had been a material change of the note. Was this a sufficient defense? [Mandel v Sedrish, (NY) 3 UCCRS 526]

34 Discharge of Parties and Paper

DISCHARGE OF INDIVIDUAL PARTIES

A party to a commercial paper who would otherwise be liable on it may be discharged either individually or by some act that has discharged all parties to the paper at one time. The nature of the transaction or occurrence determines which takes place.

§ 34:1. Manner of Discharge. A party is discharged from liability to any other party (1) with whom he enters into an agreement for his discharge, or (2) with whom he enters into a transaction which under the law of contracts is effective to discharge liability on an ordinary contract for the payment of money.[1] Accordingly, there may be a discharge by accord and satisfaction, a novation, a convenant not to sue, rescission, or the substitution of another instrument. The liability may also be barred by operation of law as in the case of a discharge in bankruptcy, the operation of the statute of limitations, or by the merger of liability into a judgment in favor of the holder when an action has been brought on the instrument.

§ 34:2. Discharge by Payment. The obligation of a particular party on commercial paper is discharged when he pays the amount of the instrument to the holder[2] or to his authorized agent. Payment to anyone else, even though in physical possession of the instrument, is not effective. (See p. 680, First National Bank v Gorman.)

If the holder consents, payment may be made by a third person, even a total stranger to the paper; and surrender of the paper to such a person gives him the rights of a transferee of the instrument.[3]

By definition, a commercial paper provides for the payment of a sum of money. Any party liable on the instrument and the holder thereof may, however, agree that the transfer or delivery of other kinds of property shall operate as payment. Sometimes a new instrument may be executed or delivered to the holder of the original instrument. In the absence of proof of an agreement to the contrary, a delivery of a subsequent instrument, without the destruction or other act to discharge the first, is regarded as merely the giving

---

[1] UCC § 3-601(2); Reagan v National Bank of Commerce, (Tex Civ App) 418 SW2d 593.

[2] UCC § 3-603(1).

[3] § 3-603(2).

of additional security for the payment of the original instrument but not as being a payment or discharge of the first.[4]

(1) Knowledge of Adverse Claim to the Paper. When the payment of the amount of the paper is made to the holder, the party making payment may know that some other person claims an interest in or ownership of the paper. The knowledge that there is an adverse claimant does not prevent making a payment to the holder, and such payment is still a discharge of the obligation of the party making payment. Specifically, an adverse claim may thus be disregarded unless (1) the adverse claimant furnishes the payor with indemnity to protect him in the event that he, the payor, does not pay because the adverse claim proves to be worthless or (2) the adverse claimant obtains a court injunction against making payment.[5]

The purpose of this provision is to give commercial paper greater acceptance since the person writing such paper knows that he will be able to discharge the instrument by making payment in the ordinary case to the holder without the risk of deciding whether an adverse claim is valid.

(2) Satisfaction. The principles governing payment apply to a satisfaction entered into with the holder of the instrument.[6] Instead of paying the holder in full in money, a payment of less than all is accepted as full payment, or some service is rendered or property is given by the party discharged.

(3) Tender of Payment. A party who is liable may offer to the holder the full payment when or after the instrument is due. If the holder refuses such payment, the party making the tender of payment is not discharged from his liability for the amount then due; but the holder cannot hold him liable for any interest that accrues after that date. Likewise, in the event that the holder sues the person making the tender, the holder cannot recover legal costs from him nor attorney's fees.[7]

If the holder refuses a proper tender, his refusal may discharge third persons even though it does not affect the liability of the person making the tender. Specifically, any party to the paper who would have a right, if he made payment, to recover that amount from the person making the tender is discharged if the tender is not accepted.[8] For example, if the paper is negotiated through the unqualified indorsers *A*, *B*, and *C*, to the holder *D*, and if *B* or *C* is required to pay *D*, he would have the right to sue *A*, the prior indorser, to recover from him the amount paid the holder *D*. In such a case, if *A* makes a proper tender of payment which *D* refuses, *B* and *C* are discharged from any liability to *D*.

---

[4] Farmers Union Oil Co. v Fladeland, 287 Minn 315, 178 NW2d 254.

[5] § 3-603(1). Certain exceptions are made to this rule when payment is made in bad faith on a stolen instrument or when the instrument is restrictively indorsed.

[6] § 3-601(1).

[7] § 3-604(1).

[8] § 3-604(2).

(4) Payment by Secondary Party. When a party secondarily liable pays, such payment does not discharge the paper or prior parties but merely transfers the rights of the holder to the party making the payment. This is so even though there is no assignment or transfer of the paper from the paid holder to the secondary party.[9]

§ 34:3. Cancellation. The holder of an instrument, with or without consideration, may discharge the liability of a particular party by cancellation by a notation on the paper which makes that intent apparent, or by destroying, mutilating, or striking out the party's signature on the paper. Even though this cancels an indorsement necessary to the chain of title of the holder, his title to the paper is not affected,[10] since the paper had been properly negotiated.

A cancellation is not effective if it is made by a person who is not the holder or who is not acting by his authority or when the physical destruction of the instrument is made by accident or mistake. The party who claims that an apparent cancellation should not take effect has the burden of proof.

§ 34:4. Renunciation. The holder of an instrument, with or without consideration, may discharge the liability of a particular party by renunciation. This is effected either (1) by surrendering the instrument to the party to be discharged, or (2) by executing a signed written renunciation which is then delivered to the party to be discharged.[11] (See p. 681, White System v Lehmann.) If the holder surrenders the instrument in effecting the renunciation, he ceases to be the holder and thereafter cannot hold any party liable on the paper, although such other parties are not themselves discharged with respect to the person to whom the paper was surrendered or any other subsequent holder thereof. There is no renunciation when the written renunciation is not delivered but is retained by the holder. (See p. 682, Greene v Cotton.)

By definition, a renunciation can only be made by the person who is the owner of the paper, or his authorized agent. When not so made, the renunciation has no effect and the person making the renunciation may be liable for the tort of conversion of the paper to any person whose joinder in the renunciation was required. For example, one payee who surrenders the paper without the indorsement of the other copayee and a bank accepting the surrender without the missing indorsement are liable to such other copayee for conversion. (See p. 681, Gillespie v Riley Management Corp.)

§ 34:5. Impairment of Right of Recourse. In most instances there is at least one party to commercial paper who, if required to pay, will have a right of recourse, or a right to obtain indemnity, from some other party. For example, in the least complicated situation the payee of a note has indorsed

[9] K & S International, Inc. v Howard, 249 Ark 901, 462 SW2d 458.
[10] § 3-605.
[11] § 3-605(1).

it without qualification to the present holder. If the holder obtains payment from the indorsing payee, the latter has a right of recourse against the maker of the note. If the holder, without the indorser's consent, discharges the liability of the maker, extends the time for payment, or agrees not to sue him, the indorser is also discharged unless he consented thereto, on the theory that his right of recourse has been impaired.[12]

This same principle applies to other parties, as when the holder releases or agrees not to sue an indorser subsequent to the payee, since other parties might have a right to recourse against a prior indorser so released.

Courts are reluctant to hold that secondary parties are discharged by an extension or renewal of commercial paper when the secondary party had knowledge of, or participated in obtaining, the extension. The conduct of the secondary party, however, must rise to the level of "consent" or it does not prevent his discharge.

§ 34:6. Impairment of Collateral. When commercial paper is executed, the maker may give the holder property, such as stocks or bonds, to hold as security for the payment of the instrument. Likewise, any other party liable on the instrument may give collateral as security to the holder for the same purpose. This collateral security benefits all parties who might be liable on the paper because to the extent that payment is obtained from the security, they are not required to make payment. Conversely, if the collateral security is impaired or harmed in any way that reduces its value, the parties who are liable are harmed since the possibility that they will be required to pay increases. Accordingly, a particular party is discharged if the holder unjustifiably impairs collateral security provided by that party or by any person against whom such party has a right of recourse.[13]

A party claiming that he is discharged by impairment of collateral has to show to what extent the collateral has in fact been impaired. If he does not do this, he remains liable for the full amount of the paper.[14]

The collateral right involved in the "no impairment" rule may be a thing such as property given to the holder to hold as a pledge or it may be the right which one person has to recover from another in the event that he sustains loss or is subjected to liability.

(1) Reservation of Rights. When a creditor releases a debtor, such release may constitute an impairment of collateral. The creditor may prevent his release from discharging another party by making an express reservation of his right to proceed against such other party. (See p. 683, Hallowell v Turner.)

---

12 § 3-606(1)(a). Note that this is similar to the situation where a holder refuses to accept a proper tender of payment from the maker in which case an indorser is discharged. The operation of this rule is avoided, and the other party not released, if the holder executes a reservation of his right against the other party at the time when he discharges the party subject to the latter's right of recourse. § 3-606(2).

13 § 3-606(1)(b).

14 Christensen v McAtee, 256 Ore 233, 473 P2d 659.

§ 34:7. Reacquisition of Paper by Intermediate Party. Commercial paper is sometimes reacquired by a party who had been an earlier holder. This occurs most commonly when that earlier party pays the then existing holder the amount due, thereby in effect purchasing the paper from that holder. When this occurs, the prior party may cancel all indorsements subsequent to his and then reissue or further negotiate the paper. Then the intervening indorsers subsequent to him whose indorsements have been canceled are discharged as to the reacquirer and all subsequent holders.[15]

§ 34:8. Alteration. When an instrument is materially and fraudulently altered by the holder, any party whose obligation on the paper is changed thereby is discharged, unless he had assented to the alteration or is barred by his conduct from asserting that he is discharged.[16] The effect of the discharge by alteration is limited, however; for, if the altered instrument is held by a holder in due course, he may enforce it according to its original terms.[17]

A notice by a lending bank to the borrower that the bank has increased the rate of interest on his loan does not constitute an "alteration" of the note which the borrower had executed when he obtained the loan, since there is no changing of the terms of the note itself and since the intent of the bank in giving such notice is not "fraudulent."[18]

§ 34:9. Discharge for Miscellaneous Causes. In addition to the discharge of a party as discussed in the preceding sections, the conduct of certain parties with respect to the commercial paper or the enforcement of rights thereunder may release some of the parties to the paper. This occurs (1) when a check has been certified on the application of the holder; (2) when the holder accepts an acceptance that varies the terms of the draft; and (3) when a presentment, notice of dishonor, or protest, when required, is delayed beyond the time permitted or is absent and such delay or absence is not excused.

In addition, federal or local statutes may provide for the discharge of a party by bankruptcy proceedings or by local laws declaring certain obligations not enforceable because they violate particular statutes.[19]

DISCHARGE OF ALL PARTIES

In contrast with conduct which discharges individual parties to paper, some actions release everyone from liability.

§ 34:10. Discharge of Party Primarily Liable. The primary party on an instrument, that is, the maker of a note or the acceptor of a draft,[20] has

---

[15] § 3-208.
[16] § 3-407(2)(a).
[17] § 3-407(3). See § 35:8(6).
[18] New Britan National Bank v Baugh, 31 App Div 2d 898, 297 NYS2d 872.
[19] UCC § 3-601, Official Comment, point 1.
[20] An accommodated payee is in effect also a primary party since the accommodating party, if required to pay an indorsee, has a right of recourse against such payee.

no right of recourse against any party on the paper. Conversely, every other party who may be held liable on the paper has a right of recourse against persons primarily liable. If the holder discharges in any way a party who is primarily liable, all parties to the instrument are discharged, since the discharge of the primary party discharges the persons who had a right of recourse against him.[21]

§ 34:11. Primary Party's Reacquisition of Paper. When a party primarily liable on the paper reacquires it in his own right at any time, whether before or after it is due, the instrument is then held by one who has no right to sue any other party on the paper. Such reacquisition therefore discharges the liability of all intervening parties to the instrument.[22] Moreover, as reacquisition requires a lawful transfer, it necessarily involves the negotiation or surrender by the person who was then the holder of the right against that party, and no party thereafter remains liable on the paper. The reacquisition by the party who has no right of action or recourse against anyone else on the paper therefore discharges the liability of all parties on it.[23]

EFFECT OF DISCHARGE ON HOLDER IN DUE COURSE

An ordinary holder or an assignee of paper is subject to any discharge. A holder in due course may or may not be subject to a prior discharge.

§ 34:12. Discharge of Individual Party. The fact that a party has been discharged of liability, and even that a new holder of the paper knows of it, does not prevent the new holder from being a holder in due course as to any party remaining liable on the paper.[24] If the holder in due course does not have notice or knowledge of a discharge of a party obtained before he acquired the paper, he is not bound by the discharge and may enforce the obligation of the discharged party as though he had never been discharged.[25] In order to protect himself, a party securing his own discharge should have a notation of it made on the paper so that any subsequent holder would necessarily have notice of that fact.

§ 34:13. Discharge of All Parties. The fact that the liabilities of all parties to a commercial paper have been discharged does not destroy the negotiable character nor the existence of the commercial paper. If it should thereafter be negotiated to a person who qualifies as a holder in due course, the latter may enforce the liability of any party on the paper, although otherwise discharged, of whose discharge the holder in due course had no notice or knowledge.[26]

---

[21] UCC § 3-601(3). In some instances this rule is modified by § 3-606.

[22] § 3-208.

[23] § 3-601(3)(a).

[24] § 3-305(2)(e).

[25] § 3-602. As an exception to this rule, the holder in due course is bound by a prior discharge in insolvency proceedings, such as bankruptcy, whether he had notice thereof or not. § 3-305(2)(d).

[26] § 3-601, Official Comment, point 3.

CASES FOR CHAPTER 34

First National Bank v Gorman

45 Wyo 519, 21 P2d 549 (1933)

Gorman executed and delivered a promissory note to the First National Bank. After several payments, the note was stolen from the bank. Subsequently, Gorman paid the remainder to one representing himself to be Richardson, who previously had been connected with the payee bank. In an action brought by the bank to collect the remainder of the note from Gorman, the latter pleaded payment and produced the note marked paid by the impostor. From a judgment for the plaintiff, the defendant appealed.

BLUME, J. . . . Counsel for the appellant [defendant] claims that defendant's possession of the note raises a presumption that it has been paid; that this presumption has not been overcome; that the plaintiff should have been more careful in not letting the note in question get out of its possession; that that carelessness made it possible for someone to hold himself out as the agent of the defendant; and that it is now estopped to claim that payment was made to one not authorized. Counsel relies partially upon cases which hold that where two innocent parties must suffer, that one should suffer who has made the loss possible. . . . There is some slight authority to sustain the position that mere possession of a note, though not indorsed, entitles the holder to collect the money due thereon. . . . Daniel on Negotiable Instruments . . . in commenting on the point under consideration . . . says:

"If the instrument be payable to a particular party or order, and unindorsed by him, it has been held that a payment to any person in actual possession will still be valid because, although he may have no legal title, he may be the agent of the actual owner. But this doctrine, it seems to us, goes too far. Such person in actual possession may perhaps be presumed to be agent of the holder prima facie. But even this is doubtful, and to us seems wrong, for nothing is more common than to indorse negotiable instruments to agents for collection; and if the bill or note be unindorsed . . it might be that the owner had withheld his indorsement for the very purpose of preventing collection by a person not entitled to receive the money; and if this were so, the presumption of agency (if, indeed, it be at all admitted) would be rebutted. The contrary doctrine destroys a great and salutary safeguard to the rights of proprietors of negotiable instruments and to a large degree breaks down the distinction between those payable to order and those payable to bearer." The authorities generally are in full accord with this statement. . . .

In the case of Anderson v Wm. H. Moore Dry Goods Company, . . . payment was made of an unindorsed note to one without authority to collect. Instead of contending in that case that the person who received payment was the apparent agent of the owner, counsel claimed that he was the holder of the note within the meaning of the Negotiable Instruments Law . . . , reading that "payment is made in due course when it is made at or after the maturity of the instrument to the holder thereof in good faith and without notice that his title is defective." The court, however, held that the term "holder" means the person who is legally in possession of the instrument, either by indorsement or delivery or both, and who is entitled to receive payment from the drawer or acceptor or maker of the note, and does not include a person in actual possession who has no right to such possession. . . . Thus we have arrived at the same conclusion by two different methods of reasoning. When the note was presented for payment by a stranger without a legal transfer, the presumption was that it was lost or purloined or otherwise improperly got into circulation. . . . The defendant took the risk of making payment to him, without being able to show that he had authority to collect. Moreover, he had other ample means by which he could have fully protected himself, namely, by obtaining a draft or check payable to the plaintiff bank. . . .

[Judgment for plaintiff affirmed.]

Code Comment: The same decision would be made under the Uniform Commercial Code since the requirements of the Uniform Negotiable Instruments Law as to who is the holder of an instrument and the necessity for proper indorsements are continued under the UCC.

White System v Lehmann

(La App) 144 So2d 122 (1962)

White System sued Lehmann on a promissory note which he had executed as maker. Lehmann defended on the ground that the holder had renounced or canceled the obligation when, after Lehmann's default, it carried the note in its profit and loss account. From a judgment in favor of White System, Lehmann appealed.

MILLER, J. pro tem. . . . The primary defense is that the plaintiff, by transferring the obligation to the Profit & Loss Account in his bookkeeping records, has in effect renounced or canceled the debt and therefore the obligation is fully discharged. This defense is untenable. In order to renounce his rights, the holder must so expressly state in writing or must surrender or deliver the instrument to the person primarily liable thereon. . . . There is no evidence whatever to establish that the plaintiff executed such a written renouncement, and the fact that the note was attached to his petition clearly refutes that he surrendered or delivered it to the defendant. Obviously there was no renouncement of the debt.

Counsel for defendant in support of his contention that the transfer of the defendant's obligation to the Profit & Loss Account by the plaintiff constituted a discharge of the instrument, cites (LSA) R.S. 7:119 (Pars. 3, 4) which respectively provide that a negotiable instrument is discharged by the intentional cancellation by the holder or by any other act which will discharge a simple contract for the payment of money.

The sections of the Statutes cited . . . are not applicable to the facts of this case. The action of the plaintiff in placing the obligation in the Profit & Loss Account, after its default, is merely an internal bookkeeping entry, utilized by the holder, who was apparently motivated by either recognized accounting principles or for income tax purposes. Unquestionably he could have transferred the defendant's indebtedness to any other account if he so desired, no approval of, nor communication to, the debtor being required. The fact that he carried the account on his books, even though in a substandard classification, clearly negatived any intentional cancellation of the obligation; otherwise his action would have been useless and in vain. The modes of discharging a negotiable instrument, as set forth above, could only be interpreted as meaning that the action of the holder is of such a definite or certain nature that there could be no question of his intention to discharge the obligation arising out of the negotiable instrument. Such were not the facts in this matter. . . .

[Judgment affirmed.]

Code Comment: The same decision would be made under the Uniform Commercial Code. There was no act done to the face or back of the paper itself, it was not surrendered to the party claiming that he was discharged, nor was any written renunciation delivered to him. In the absence of any of these, there could be no cancellation or renunciation. UCC § 3-605.

Gillespie v Riley Management Corp.

13 Ill App 3d 988, 301 NE2d 506 (1973)

As part of a sales transaction Riley Management obtained a cashier's check payable to the order of it and Gillespie, the other party to the transaction. The transaction was abandoned and William Riley, the president of the corporation, took the cashier's check to the National City Bank, indorsed it "not used for purpose issued" and surrendered it in return for two other checks payable to the order of Riley Management. Gillespie then sued Riley Management and the bank for conversion of the cashier's check on the theory that Gillespie as copayee had an ownership interest in the cashier's check which had been destroyed by Riley's intentionally surrendering the check without Gillespie's indorsement. Judgment was entered for Riley and Gillespie appealed.

MORAN, J. . . . Plaintiff's position is that the cashier's check issued when defendant placed its signature on the instrument and handed it to Riley, that, at this point in time, a debtor-creditor relationship was created between the defendant and the named payees (plaintiff and Riley Management Corporation), that Riley's status as purchaser ceased and he became one of two payees, that delivery to one of two or more payees is delivery to all, and that under § 3-116 of the Uniform Commercial Code (UCC), it was necessary that both payees negotiate the check to legally discharge the defendant from liability. . . .

A cashier's check is defined as bill of exchange drawn by a bank upon itself and accepted in advance by the act of issuance. When a purchaser has paid the consideration and the bank has transferred the cashier's check to the purchaser, for delivery to the payee, the contract between the bank and purchaser has become executed, a debtor-creditor relationship takes place and, by definition, the check issues. . . . This same contract . . . contemplates a delivery of the cashier's check by the purchaser to the named payee. Until delivery, the purchaser retains ownership of the check and is entitled to return it for cancellation. . . . Once there is delivery, actual or constructive, of a cashier's check to a payee, the rule, with limited exceptions, is that it is not subject to countermand by either its purchaser or the issuing bank. . . .

Complications arise in attempting to apply the pronounced rules to the instant case, for in various stages of events Riley acted in two differing capacities: he was agent-purchaser for the Corporation and agent-payee of the Corporation. He could not simultaneously act in both capacities. At the time defendant issued the original cashier's check Riley ceased to function as agent-purchaser and assumed the role of agent-payee. . . . The transfer thus became a delivery to one of two payees. Delivery to one of two payees is tantamount to delivery to both. . . .

An instrument payable to the order of two or more payees not in the alternative is payable to all payees and may be negotiated, discharged or enforced only by all of them. (UCC, § 3-116.) Having found the cashier's check issued and delivered, the defendant could neither countermand nor discharge its liability without the endorsement of both payees. . . .

[Judgment reversed.]

Greene v Cotton

(Ky) 457 SW2d 493 (1970)

Cotton executed a promissory note promising to pay Jones a sum of money. Jones died; Greene and Foree were appointed his executors. Among the papers of Jones was found a writing stating that if Cotton was alive at the time of Jones' death and if any balance on the note remained unpaid, such balance should be released. The note was partly paid at the time of Jones' death. Cotton brought an action against the executors to obtain a declaration that the balance of the note was discharged. From a judgment in Cotton's favor, an appeal was taken by Greene and Foree.

DAVIS, C. . . . On August 17, 1955, the Cottons executed and delivered to S. R. Jones their promissory note in the sum of $72,000 bearing 5% interest and secured by mortgage on real estate in Grant County owned by the Cottons. Various payments on the note had reduced the principal due to $38,400 at the date of the death of Jones on May 2, 1967.

The appellants, executors of the will of Jones, found among Jones' effects a key to a lockbox at Citizens Bank of Dry Ridge. Upon inspecting the contents of that lockbox, they found an envelope bearing the typewritten address:

> "To admrs. of my estate
>
> "S. R. Jones"

Within the envelope was found a typewritten paper signed by S. R. Jones, which recited:

> "I, S. R. Jones hereby request that if B. C. Cotton be living at the time of my death and if there is an unpaid balance on his note and mortgage to me that same be released and the note and mortgage returned to him marked paid.
>
> Dated July 7, 1966.
>
> /s/ S. R. Jones"

B. C. Cotton was president of Citizens Bank of Dry Ridge, and there was evidence that Cotton knew that Jones had executed a paper purporting to cancel the note. However, Cotton never received physical possession of the paper, nor did he (or anyone other than Jones) have a key to Jones' lockbox. It appears that the last credit on the note was made on July 7, 1966, the date of the purported release. It also appears that Jones kept the typed release in his own office until Tuesday, April 28, 1967, on which date he placed it in the lockbox at Dry Ridge. His death ensued on Saturday, May 2, 1967.

Pursuant to a finding by an advisory jury, and in overruling appellants' motion to set aside the findings reported by the jury, the trial judge recited as one finding of fact:

> "S. R. Jones intended to renounce the note and his right, title and interest therein, without the necessity of actually relinquishing control of the note itself."

That finding, so far as it is considered as a *factual* finding, is obviously not clearly erroneous, so it will not be disturbed. . . .

But, that finding of fact does not lead to the trial court's conclusion of law that the *intended* release legally accomplished its purpose. It is manifest that the release was an "iffy" thing. By its own terms it noted its applicability only "if" B. C. Cotton were alive at the time of Jones' death and "if" there then remained an unpaid balance due to Jones on the note. It is not contended, as it could not be, that the release was executed with the formality required for a will.

Patently, Jones was mindful when the release was typed that Cotton might make further payments on the note—indeed that it might be fully paid. Clearly, he did not purport to remit the debt except on the contingency that Jones should die before the death of B. C. Cotton. Most importantly, Jones never delivered the release to Cotton and never parted with dominion over it. Nobody but Jones, or his qualified personal representatives at his death, had any right to enter the lockbox. If Jones had elected to sue on the note, Cotton could not have interposed the release as a defense. If Jones had changed his mind, he could have destroyed the release or modified it, and Cotton would have had no recourse. In short, we agree with the trial judge that Jones thought he had done all that was legally required but that fact, without more, did not accomplish the intended result.

[UCC §] 3-605(1)(b), in treating the legal requirements for cancellation and renunciation of a note, provides that the result may be achieved: "(b) by renouncing his rights by a writing signed *and delivered* or by surrender of the instrument to the party to be discharged." . . .

. . . Since there is no claim of a contract to release supported by consideration, the release must stand or fall as a gift. It falls.

. . . "It may be stated as a general rule that a mere statement, declaration, or memorandum by the creditor to the effect that he gives, has given, or intends to give the debt to the debtor, that he does not desire or intend that the debt shall be paid or collected or that the amount remaining unpaid at his death is to be forgiven, is ineffectual for such purpose." . . .

Despite the *intention* of a donor to effect a transfer of a bank account, the failure to comply with legal requirements cannot be supplied merely by noting the abortive attempt to carry out an intention. . . .

The judgment is reversed for proceedings consistent with the opinion.

Hallowell v Turner

95 Idaho 392, 509 P2d 1313 (1973)

Kohntopp and Turner signed a promissory note as makers. Hallowell held the note. In consideration of a payment of $2,500 to him made by Kohntopp, Hallowell executed an agreement not "to execute" against Kohntopp. This agreement expressly reserved Hallowell's rights against Turner. Turner did not know of the existence of this agreement and thus did not consent to it. Later Hallowell sued Turner on the note. The defense was raised that the agreement not to execute against Kohntopp operated as a discharge of Turner. From a judgment for Turner, an appeal was taken by Hallowell.

McQUADE, J. . . . [UCC §] 3-606 provides: "*Impairment of recourse or of collateral.*

(1) The holder discharges any party to the instrument to the extent that without such party's consent the holder

(a) without express reservation of rights releases or agrees not to sue any person against whom the party has to the knowledge of the holder a right of recourse or agrees to suspend the right to enforce against such person the instrument or collateral or otherwise discharges such person, except that failure or delay in effecting any required presentment, protest or notice of dishonor with respect to any such person does not discharge any party as to whom presentment, protest or notice of dishonor is effective or unnecessary; or

(b) unjustifiably impairs any collateral for the instrument given by or on behalf of the party or any person against whom he has a right of recourse.

"(2) By express reservation of rights against a party with a right of recourse the holder preserves

(a) all his rights against such party as of the time when the instrument was originally due; and

(b) the right of the party to pay the instrument as of that time; and

(c) all rights of such party to recourse against others."

Under the above cited provisions, the requirements for a discharge were not met.

Notification to the party against whom rights are reserved is not a prerequisite to the validity of a reservation of rights. Respondent [Turner] cites paragraph 4 of the official comment to [UCC §] 3-606 as indicative of the need for notice. This comment is misleading in its allusion to a requirement of notice, since it refers to a subsection (3). There is no subsection (3) in [UCC §] 3-606 as finally adopted by the Commissioners on Uniform State Laws and enacted in Idaho. The part of paragraph 4 of the official comment to [UCC §] 3-606 referring to subsection (3) should be disregarded.

The express reservation of rights by appellant in the "agreement not to execute" was valid. Under [UCC §] 3-606 there must be consent *or* an express reservation of rights to prevent a discharge. Thus, consent is not necessary where the obligee makes an express reservation of rights.

Both appellant [Hallowell] and respondent discuss whether there was a right of recourse by respondent against Kohntopp. No evidence to support a finding that appellant Hallowell knew of Noble Turner's role of surety, if indeed he was a surety, appears in the record. Paragraph 3 of the official comment to [UCC §] 3-606 reads as follows: "The words 'to the knowledge of the holder' exclude the latent surety, as for example the accommodation maker where there is nothing on the instrument to show that he has signed for accommodation and the holder is ignorant of that fact. In such a case the holder is entitled to proceed according to what is shown by the face of the paper or what he otherwise knows, and does not discharge the surety when he acts in ignorance of the relation." In this case Ralph Kohntopp and Noble Turner appear on the face of the note to be co-makers. Under [UCC §] 3-118,* this would mean their liability on the face of the note would be joint and several. Even if respondent does have a right of recourse against Kohntopp, appellant still would have avoided discharging respondent by making the express reservation of rights.

It is not necessary on this appeal to decide what affect the "agreement not to execute" has on the obligations of Ralph Kohntopp. However, (2)(c) of [UCC §] 3-606 should be noted in relation to such obligations, reading as follows: "(2) By express reservation of rights against a party with a right of recourse the holder preserves . . . (c) all rights of such party to recourse against others." As already noted,

* [UCC §] 3-118 provides in part: "*Ambiguous terms and rules of construction.*—The following rules apply to every instrument: . . . (e) Unless the instrument otherwise specifies two (2) or more persons who sign as maker, acceptor or drawer or indorser and as a part of the same transaction, are jointly and severally liable even though the instrument contains such words as 'I promise to pay.' "

the reservation of rights was effective and respondent's obligation to appellant was not discharged by the "agreement not to execute."... [Judgment reversed.]

QUESTIONS AND CASE PROBLEMS

1. *H* was the holder of a note on which *M* was the maker. *H* owed money to *C* and indorsed *M*'s note to *C* in payment of his debt. Thereafter *M* failed to pay his note to *C*. When *C* demanded that *H* pay his original debt to *C*, *H* raised the defense that *C* had taken *M*'s note in payment of that debt so that it no longer existed. Decide. [Central Stone Co. v John Ruggiero, Inc., 49 Misc 2d 622, 268 NYS2d 172]
2. *H* was the holder of a promissory note made by *M*. The note was payable in 12 months. After preliminary discussion between the parties in the eleventh month with respect to refinancing, *H* telephoned *M* that he "canceled" the note. The next day, *H* changed his mind and negotiated the note to *C* who satisfied the requirements of being a holder in due course. When *C* demanded payment of *M*, *M* asserted that he was not liable because he had been discharged when *H* canceled the note. Was he correct? [Citizens Fidelity Bank & Trust Co. v Stark, (Ky) 431 SW2d 722; Bihlmire v Hahn, (DC Wis) 43 FRD 503]
3. The Citizens State Bank issued a cashier's check payable to the order of Donovan. He indorsed it to Denny, who did business as the Houston Aircraft Co., and included in the indorsement a recital that it was "in full [payment of] any and all claims of any character whatever." Denny crossed out this quoted phrase and wrote Donovan and the bank that he had done so. The Houston Aircraft Co. sued the Citizens National Bank on the check. Was the bank liable? [Houston Aircraft Co. v Citizens State Bank, (Tex Civ App) 184 SW2d 335]
4. Satek authorized his agent to execute a mortgage with Fortuna as mortgagor. Fortuna executed a note secured by the mortgage. Later Fortuna made a part payment on the note to the agent. This payment was made before maturity, and the agent at the time did not have possession of the note. Satek later sued to foreclose the mortgage. The court refused to allow Fortuna credit for the payment made to the agent. Why? [Satek v Fortuna, 324 Ill App 523, 58 NE2d 464]
5. Burg executed and delivered a promissory note for $1,060 payable to Liesemer. When the note was due, Burg paid $893 and demanded credit for the remainder of the amount due because of the boarding expense incurred by Liesemer's daughter. Liesemer gave Burg the note so that he could compute the amount due. Burg refused to give credit for Liesemer's claim and kept the note. When Liesemer brought an action to recover the remainder of the note, it appeared that Burg had written across the face of the note, "Paid February 9th." It was contended that the note had been discharged by cancellation. Do you agree? [Liesemer v Burg, 106 Mich 124, 63 NW 999]
6. C. Neal executed and delivered a promissory note payable to the order of A. Neal, who indorsed the instrument to his wife, Mary Neal, a holder in due course. Before maturity, the maker paid the amount of the note to the payee. After maturity, Mary, who had divorced A. Neal and resumed her maiden name of Fogarty, brought an action against C. Neal to recover on

the note. Neal contended that the note had been discharged by payment. Do you agree with this contention? [Fogarty v Neal, 201 Ky 85, 255 SW 1049]

7. Twombly, who owned negotiable bonds of the Muskogee Electric Traction Co., was advised by her financial agent, the State Street Trust Co., that the bonds had no value. Acting on this belief, Twombly burned the bonds. Some years later it was found that the bonds had some value, and the trust company, on behalf of Twombly, demanded payment on the bonds. Was it entitled to payment? [State Street Trust Co. v Muskogee Electric Traction Co., (CA10 Okla) 204 F2d 920]
8. As part of a business plan Schwald executed and delivered a note to Montgomery. The parties then made a new business arrangement, and Montgomery intentionally tore up the note and threw it into the wastebasket. It was subsequently contended that this note had been canceled. Do you agree? [Montgomery v Schwald, 117 Mo App 75, 166 SW 831]
9. Henry and Herbert Mordecai were partners doing business under the name of the Southern Cigar Co. They indorsed a promissory note executed by the firm to Henry Mordecai and delivered it to the District National Bank. They also delivered as security a certificate for certain stock in the Monumental Cigar Co. After maturity of the note, the indorsers made an assignment of a claim against the United States to the bank, which accepted it in satisfaction of its rights on the note. Was the note discharged? [District National Bank v Mordecai, 133 Md 419, 105 A 586]

35 Secured Consumer Credit Sales

GENERAL PRINCIPLES

§ 35:1. Nature of a Secured Credit Sale. Various devices have been developed to provide the credit seller of goods with protection beyond his right to sue the buyer for the purchase price. Today such devices, and others discussed in Chapter 36, are known as *secured transactions* and are governed by Article 9 of the UCC.[1]

A *secured credit sale* is a sale in which the possession and the risk of loss pass to the buyer but the seller retains a security interest in the goods until he has been paid in full. In some instances the seller retains the title until paid, but this is not essential. The seller's security interest entitles him to repossess the goods when the buyer fails to make payment as required or when he commits a breach of the purchase contract in any other way. This right is in addition to the right to sue for the purchase price.

Forerunners of this credit device include: (1) a *conditional sale,* where the seller retained title until the condition of payment in full had been satisfied; (2) a *bailment lease,* under which transaction the buyer rented the property and, after the payment of sufficient rentals to equal the purchase price, could elect to take title to the property; and (3) a *chattel mortgage,* by which the buyer, upon taking title from the seller, in turn gave the seller a mortgage on the property for the amount of the unpaid balance of the purchase price. The laws pertaining to these three types of transactions have been replaced by the secured transaction provisions of the UCC.[2]

The Uniform Commercial Code is not designed solely to aid sellers. The provisions of Article 9 increase the protection given to buyers over that available to them under the former law. Special consumer protection statutes

---

[1] This book is based on the 1962 version of the Uniform Commercial Code which is set forth in the Code Appendix. In 1972 amendments to the 1962 version were approved by the UCC sponsors and, thus far, have been adopted in Arkansas, Illinois, Nebraska, Nevada, North Dakota, Oregon, Texas, and Virginia. The changes made by the 1972 amendments to the UCC are confined mainly to Article 9 on secured transactions. Some of the changes made thereto are indicated in the footnotes.

[2] The UCC, however, has not abolished these transactions nor made them illegal. The parties may still enter into a conditional sale, bailment lease, or chattel mortgage; but if they do, the transaction must satisfy the requirements of the secured transaction under the Code. Thus, the UCC establishes certain minimum requirements applicable to all types of security devices employed by the credit seller. An instrument that is called a "chattel mortgage" will be interpreted as a "security agreement." Strevell-Patterson Finance Co. v May, 77 NMex 331, 422 P2d 366.

designed to protect buyers, in addition to the UCC, may also be in force within a given state.[3]

§ **35:2. Creation of Security Interest.** A security interest for the protection of the seller of goods to a buyer arises as soon as the seller and buyer agree that the buyer shall have property rights in particular goods and that the seller shall have a security interest in them.[4] It is immaterial whether or not the sales agreement provides for the passage of title to the buyer prior to his payment for the goods in full, as the location of title to the property involved, called *collateral,* is immaterial.[5]

(1) Security Agreement. The agreement of the seller and buyer that the seller shall have a security interest in the goods must be evidenced by a written [6] *security agreement* which is signed by the buyer and which describes the collateral.[7] This description need only reasonably identify the collateral.[8] It is not necessary that the goods be described specifically, as by serial number or by manufacturer's model.[9] A description is sufficient when it would enable a third person aided by inquiries made to others to determine what goods were involved.[10]

The description in the security agreement must be sufficiently broad to include all property which the parties intended to include. The creditor does not have any security interest in property which is not included in the description of the collateral in the security agreement. This concept applies to all collateral, whether consumer goods, farm products, inventory, or equipment. (See p. 697, Jones & Laughlin Supply v Dugan Production Corp.)

Whether the agreement between the parties is a security agreement depends upon its construction or interpretation. Hence, a buyer cannot claim that an outright sale was made to him when the contract is conspicuously entitled as a "conditional sales contract" and states that the sale is made "subject to the terms and conditions set forth below and upon the reverse side hereof," when the conditional sale provisions were specified on the reverse side but the buyer apparently neglected to read the reverse side.[11] The fact that a financing statement has been filed does not eliminate the requirement of a security agreement.[12]

---

[3] Such laws continue in effect under UCC §§ 9-201, 9-203(2) and supplement its provisions.

[4] § 9-204(1).

[5] § 9-202.

[6] American Card Co. v H.M.H. Co., 97 RI 159, 196 A2d 150.

[7] UCC § 9-203(1)(b).

[8] Cain v Country Club Delicatessen, 25 Conn Supp 327, 203 A2d 441.

[9] UCC § 9-110.

[10] The term "accounts receivable" is sufficient to cover future accounts receivable since the quoted words adequately put third persons on notice as to the interest of the creditor in accounts receivable: In re Platt, (DC ED Pa) 257 F Supp 478.

[11] General Motors Acceptance Corp. v Blanco, 181 Neb 562, 149 NW2d 516.

[12] Kaiser Aluminum & Chemical Sales, Inc., v Hurst, (Iowa) 176 NW2d 166.

(2) Future Transactions. The security agreement may contemplate future action by extending to goods not in existence that are to be acquired and delivered to the buyer at a future date. In general the security interest does not attach to future goods until the buyer has rights in such goods.[13]

§ 35:3. Consumer Goods. *Consumer goods* are those which are used or bought for use primarily for personal, family, or household purposes.[14] It is the intended use rather than the nature of the article which determines its character. For example, goods purchased by a buyer for resale to ultimate consumers are not consumer goods in the hands of such middleman but constitute a part of his inventory.

A mobile home in the possession of the person making use thereof is a consumer good. An automobile is a consumer good when purchased by the buyer to go to and from work. Equipment used in business is not a consumer good. Hence, a tractor purchased by a construction contractor is not a consumer good,[15] but equipment. Likewise, a musical instrument used by a nightclub entertainer is equipment.[16]

In this chapter secured credit sales relating to consumer goods are considered. In Chapter 36, attention will be given to secured credit sales of inventory and equipment, and to secured loan transactions.

In many states security interests in automobiles in the hands of the ultimate consumer are governed by special installment sale or consumer protection statutes. As to automobiles which constitute a dealer's inventory, security interests are governed by Article 9 of the Uniform Commercial Code.[17]

RIGHTS OF PARTIES INDEPENDENT OF DEFAULT

In a secured credit sale of consumer goods, both the seller and the buyer have rights independent of default by either party.

§ 35:4. Rights of the Seller of Consumer Goods Independent of Default. The seller stands in a dual position of being both a seller, having rights under Article 2 of the UCC governing sales, and a secured creditor, having rights under Article 9 of the UCC regulating secured transactions.[18]

The seller may transfer or assign his interest under the sales contract and under the security agreement to a third person, and the assignee acquires all the rights and interest of the seller. The rights of the assignee may rise

---

13 UCC § 9-204(1)(2).

14 § 9-109(1).

15 Beam v John Deere Co., 240 Ark 107, 398 SW2d 218.

16 Strevell-Patterson Finance Co. v May, 77 NMex 331, 422 P2d 366.

17 Guy Martin Buick, Inc. v Colorado Springs National Bank, — Colo —, 511 P2d 912.

18 UCC § 9-113. No civil liability rests upon the seller for harm sustained by third persons as a result of acts or omissions of the debtor or in consequence of the existence of the secured transaction. § 9-317.

higher than those of the seller to the extent that there is a defense or claim valid against the seller which is not effective against the assignee because the buyer has waived such a right as against an assignee.

The secured credit seller of consumer goods has rights that are effective not only against the buyer but also against purchasers of the property from the buyer as soon as the security agreement is executed with respect to goods in which the buyer has acquired an interest. From that moment on, the seller's interest is generally effective against third persons [19] and is described as a *perfected security interest.* Whether a security interest is perfected is immaterial, however, when the question is the effect of the security agreement as between the creditor and the debtor.[20]

(1) Filing Not Required. In an ordinary sale of consumer goods under a secured transaction, no filing in any government office is required in order to perfect the secured seller's interest. Such a seller is protected against purchasers from and creditors of the buyer who may acquire the property thereafter.[21]

As an exception to the rule that the seller of such goods has a perfected security interest as soon as the agreement is executed and the buyer has an interest in the property, the seller's security interest is not perfected, and filing is required to perfect it, if the goods purchased are to be attached to buildings or land as a fixture, or if they consist of farm equipment sold for a purchase price of over $2,500. A security interest in a motor vehicle required to be licensed is not perfected unless the vehicle is licensed with a notation of the security interest made in the title certificate, if such is required by law, or if not so required, unless there is a filing under the UCC.[22]

(2) Interstate Security Interests. The UCC regulates not only transactions within the state but also the effect to be given security interests in property brought into the state from another state. If the interest of the secured party was perfected in the other state, his interest will be regarded as perfected by the state into which the property is brought. Within the second state, however, it is necessary to file within four months in order to keep the security interest continuously perfected.

If the secured party's interest in the goods was unperfected when they were brought into the second state, that interest may be perfected therein,[23] in which case the perfection of the security interest dates from such perfection in the second state.[24]

If title to the property, such as an automobile, is represented by a title certificate, the law of the state which issued the certificate determines

---

[19] § 9-201.

[20] Anderson v First Jacksonville Bank, 243 Ark 977, 423 SW2d 273.

[21] UCC § 9-302(1)(d). The UCC makes detailed provisions as to the priority of conflicting security interests with respect to fixtures, accessions, and commingled and processed goods. § 9-313 et seq.

[22] § 9-302(1)(c), (d), (3), (4).

[23] § 9-103(3).

[24] § 9-103(3).

whether an interest is perfected. Accordingly, if the law of the certificate-issuing state requires that a security interest be noted on the title certificate in order to be binding, that requirement is the exclusive means of perfecting the interest of the secured creditor.[25]

(3) Repair and Storage Lien. In most states, persons making repairs to or storing property have a right to assert a lien against the property for the amount of their charges. A question of priority arises when the customer bringing the goods for repair or storage is not the absolute owner and there is an outstanding security interest in the goods. In such a case, the lien for repairs or storage charges prevails over the outstanding security interest.[26] The contrary result is reached, however, when the lien for repairs or storage is based on a statute which expressly states that the lien shall be subordinate or inferior to the interest of the secured creditor.[27]

§ 35:5. Rights of the Buyer of Consumer Goods Independent of Default. The buyer in a secured transaction, like the seller, has a double status under the UCC. By virtue of Article 2 he has certain rights because he is a buyer, and by virtue of Article 9 he has certain rights because he is a debtor in a secured transaction.

(1) Rights as a Buyer. The secured credit sale of consumer goods remains fundamentally a sale that is governed by Article 2, and therefore the debtor-buyer has the same rights as an ordinary buyer under that article.[28] (See p. 698, L. & N. Sales Co. v Stuski.)

The buyer has certain rights of ownership in the collateral. It is not material whether technically he is the owner of the title. Whatever interest he owns he may transfer voluntarily, and his creditors may reach it by the process of law as fully as though there were no security agreement.[29] Such third persons generally cannot acquire any greater rights than the buyer, and therefore they hold the property subject to the security interest of the seller.

It is common practice for credit sellers to seek to protect themselves by prohibiting the buyer from reselling the property. Such a provision has no effect and does not prevent an effective resale, even though the security agreement in addition to prohibiting such resale also expressly makes it a default or breach of the contract to make a resale.[30]

(2) Rights as a Debtor. The secured transaction buyer is a debtor to the extent that there is a balance due on the purchase price. In order for the

---

[25] § 9-103(4). This provision does not apply to an automobile which was purchased originally in a state that did not provide for the notation of a security interest on the certificate of title, although it was thereafter brought into a state which had such a notation requirement. First National Bank v Stamper 93 NJ Super 150, 225 A2d 162.

[26] UCC § 9-310.

[27] Bond v Dudley, 244 Ark 568, 426 SW2d 780.

[28] UCC § 9-206(2).

[29] § 9-311; Bloom v Hilty, 210 Pa Super 255, 232 A2d 26.

[30] UCC § 9-311.

buyer to know just how much he owes and to check with his own records what the seller claims to be due, the buyer has the right to compel the seller to state what balance is owed and also to specify in which collateral the seller claims a security interest. This is done by the buyer's sending the seller a statement of the amount which he believes to be due, or a statement of the collateral which he believes to be subject to the security agreement, with the request that the seller approve or correct the statement. The seller must so indicate; and if he has assigned the contract and the security interest to a third person, he must furnish the buyer with the name and address of such successor in interest.[31]

*(3) **Waiver of Defenses.*** It is common practice for finance companies that have a standing agreement to purchase sales contracts from a credit seller to provide him with forms to be signed by the buyer. These forms generally specify that the buyer waives, as against the assignee of the sales contract and security agreement, any right that he would have against the seller. In addition to an express agreement waiving his defenses, a buyer who, as part of the purchase transaction, signs both a commercial paper and a security agreement is deemed as a matter of law to waive such defenses, even though nothing is said as to any waiver.

Both express and implied waivers are valid and bind the buyer if the assignee takes his assignment for value, in good faith, and without notice or knowledge of any claim or defense of the buyer.[32] Consequently, when a construction contractor purchases a tractor on credit under a security agreement which states that he will not assert against an assignee of the seller any claim available to the contractor against the seller, such statement is binding and bars proof by the buyer when sued by the assignee that the tractor was older and of less value than represented by the seller.[33]

The validity of any waiver of defense is subject to two limitations: (a) those defenses which could be raised against the holder in due course of commercial paper cannot be waived; (b) the waiver is not effective if a statute or decision establishes a different rule for buyers of consumer goods.[34] (See p. 699, Household Finance Corp. v Mowdy.)

§ **35:6. Defined Default.** A *default* by the debtor is merely his failure to pay the money as due. In order to provide greater protection to the creditor, the modern financing agreement will expand the definition of default to include matters which are not directly related to nonpayment. Thus, it will be specified that if the debtor moves away without notifying the creditor, such conduct is a default. This is merely a shorthand way of saying that although moving away is not a default, the creditor shall be entitled to exercise the same remedies when the debtor moves away as though he had

---

31 § 9-208.
32 § 9-206(1), (2).
33 Beam v John Deere Co., 240 Ark 107, 398 SW2d 218.
34 UCC § 9-206(1); see § 29:24.

defaulted in payment of the debt. When a security agreement states that the debtor's bankruptcy shall constitute a default, such bankruptcy is given the effect of a default within the meaning of Uniform Commercial Code § 9-504(1), so that upon the debtor's bankruptcy the creditor may exercise the rights which the UCC states may be exercised upon default.[35]

§ 35:7. Protection of Subpurchaser. When the seller of consumer goods sells on credit, his security interest in the goods is perfected even though the buyer is given possession of the goods and the seller does not file a financing statement. When no financing statement is filed, however, a resale by the consumer to another consumer will destroy the seller's security interest in the goods if the second buyer does not have knowledge of the security interest of the original seller and buys for his own personal, family, or household use.[36] In order for a sale to destroy a security interest, it is necessary that the security interest has been created by the seller who has sold the goods to the consumer who resold them to another consumer. The security interest is not destroyed if it was created by a former seller or owner.[37] (See p. 702, Balon v Cadillac Automobile Co.)

RIGHTS OF PARTIES AFTER DEFAULT

When the buyer defaults by committing a breach of contract, the secured creditor and the buyer have additional rights.

§ 35:8. Secured Seller's Repossession and Resale of Collateral. Upon the buyer's default the secured party is entitled to take the collateral or purchased property from the buyer.[38] If he can do so without causing a breach of the peace, the seller may repossess the property without legal proceedings.[39] In any case he may use legal proceedings if he desires.[40]

---

[35] Borochoff Properties, Inc. v Howard Lumber Co., 115 Ga App 691, 155 SE2d 651.

[36] § 9-307(2). The same provision applies to farm equipment having an original purchase price not in excess of $2,500 other than fixtures when the purchase by the subpurchaser is for his own farming operations.

[37] Baker Production Credit Ass'n v Long Creek Meat Co., — Ore —, 513 P2d 1129.

[38] If the seller has assigned the sales contract, the assignee is entitled to exercise the rights of the seller upon default. Consequently, if the buyer returns the goods for repair to the seller but the seller surrenders them on demand to the assignee of the sales contract, the seller is not guilty of a conversion when the assignee is entitled to possession of the goods because of the buyer's default. N. J. Scott Excavating & Wrecking v Rosencrantz, 107 NH 422, 223 A2d 522.

[39] A breach of the peace within the UCC provision is to be defined in terms of the common-law offense of a "disturbance of public order by an act of violence, or by an act likely to produce violence, or which, by causing consternation and alarm, disturbs the peace and quiet of the community." Cherno v Bank of Babylon, 54 Misc 2d 277, 282 NYS2d 114.

[40] UCC § 9-503. When a court action is brought for repossession of the collateral, the debtor must be given notice and a hearing must be held to determine whether there has been a default. Fuentes v Shevin, 407 US 67. In contrast, when the creditor repossesses the collateral without court action, a notice and hearing are not required. Repossession without judicial action under UCC § 9-503 is held not to constitute "state action" and is therefore valid when authorized by the security agreement, even though the debtor is not afforded notice and hearing before the collateral is repossessed. Giglio v Bank of Delaware, — Del Ch —, 307 A2d 816.

The seller who has repossessed the goods may resell them at a private or public sale at any time and place and on any terms. He must, however, act in good faith and in a manner that is commercially reasonable.[41] The seller must give the buyer reasonable advance notice of a resale unless the goods are perishable, or unless they threaten to decline speedily in value, or unless they are of a type customarily sold on a recognized market.[42] The seller's resale destroys all interest of the buyer in the goods.

If the secured creditor is the highest bidder or the only bidder at a public sale, the creditor may purchase the collateral even though such a sale is conducted in the creditor's office.[43]

(1) Compulsory Resale. If the buyer has paid 60 percent or more of the cash price of the consumer goods, the seller must resell them within 90 days after repossession, unless the buyer, after default, has signed a written statement surrendering the right to require the resale. If the seller does not resell within the time specified, the buyer may sue him for conversion of the collateral or proceed under the UCC provision applicable to failure to comply with the UCC.[44]

(2) Notice. Ordinarily notice must be given of the sale of collateral. The UCC does not specify the form of notice, and any form of notice that is reasonable is sufficient.[45] A letter to the debtor can satisfy this requirement. If a public sale is made, the notice must give the time and place of the sale. If a private sale is made, it is sufficient to give reasonable notice of the time after which the private sale will be made. No notice is required when the collateral is perishable or is threatening to decline rapidly in value or is sold on a recognized market or exchange.[46] Notice must be given of the resale of an automobile that is collateral because there is no "recognized market" for the sale of used cars.[47]

When notice is given to the public, it should be sufficiently explicit to enable a third person to form a basis for evaluating the collateral so that he can determine whether he wishes to bid at the sale.[48] A warning that if payments are not made, the collateral will be put up for public sale is not a sufficient notice of the sale to satisfy the requirement of the UCC, because there is no notice of the time and place of the sale.[49] Likewise, a declaration by the creditor after repossession that the collateral will be sold to the

---

[41] § 9-504(1)(3).

[42] § 9-504(3).

[43] American Plan Corp. v Eiseman, 4 Ohio App 2d 385, 33 OO2d 486, 212 NE2d 824.

[44] UCC § 9-507(1).

[45] Third National Bank v Stagnaro, 25 Mass App Dec 58.

[46] UCC § 9-504(3).

[47] Norton v National Bank of Commerce, 240 Ark 143, 398 SW2d 538.

[48] Westbury Electronic Corp. v Anglo-American Totalisator Co., 52 Misc 2d 1060, 277 NYS2d 553 (pre-Code pledge decision stating general principles applicable under the Code. UCC § 1-103).

[49] Braswell v American National Bank, 117 Ga App 699, 161 SE2d 420.

highest bidder is not sufficient notice of sale when there is no statement as to the time or place of the sale.[50]

(3) Redemption of Collateral. If the buyer acts in time, he may redeem or obtain the return to him of the goods by tendering to the secured party the amount that is owed him, including expenses and any legal costs that have been incurred. The right to redeem is destroyed if the seller has made a resale or entered into a binding contract for resale.[51]

(4) Manner of Resale. Upon the debtor's default the creditor may sell the collateral at public or private sale or he may lease it to a third person, as long as he acts in a manner that is commercially reasonable.[52] The UCC does not require any particular kind of sale but only that the disposition be "commercially reasonable." [53] The fact that higher offers are received after the making of a contract for the resale of the collateral does not show that the contract was not "commercially reasonable." [54]

(5) Accounting After Resale. When the secured party makes a resale of the goods, the proceeds of the sale are applied in the following order to pay (a) reasonable costs of repossession, storage, and resale of the goods; (b) the balance due, including interest and any proper additions such as attorney's fees; and (c) subsequent security interests in the property that are discharged by the sale.[55]

If any balance remains after the payment of these claims, the buyer is entitled to the surplus. Conversely, if the net proceeds of sale are insufficient to pay the costs and the debt due the seller, the buyer is liable to him for such deficiency unless it has been otherwise agreed by the parties.[56]

(6) Priority as to Other Creditors. When a creditor holds a perfected security interest, he is entitled to exercise his rights with respect to the collateral as against (a) a creditor having an unperfected security interest, (b) a general creditor having no security interest, and (c) the debtor's trustee in bankruptcy. If the collateral is claimed by another creditor having a perfected security interest in the same collateral and both creditors have perfected by filing, the one first filing prevails over the other creditor.[57]

§ 35:9. Secured Seller's Retention of Collateral to Discharge Obligation. If a compulsory disposition of the collateral is not required, the secured party may propose in writing that he keep the collateral in payment of the debt

---

[50] Barker v Horn, 245 Ark 315, 432 SW2d 21.
[51] UCC § 9-506.
[52] § 9-504(1).
[53] Brody v James, 92 NJ Super 254, 223 A2d 35.
[54] Old Colony Trust Co. v Penn Rose Industries Corp., (CA3 Pa) 398 F2d 310.
[55] UCC § 9-504(1).
[56] § 9-504(2).
[57] § 9-312(5)(a). Other provisions regulate priorities in other circumstances.

If the buyer does not object to this proposal, the secured party may do so and the secured obligation is automatically discharged. If written objection to the retention of the collateral by the secured party is made within 30 days, he must then proceed to dispose of it by resale or other reasonable manner.[58]

§ 35:10. Buyer's Remedies for Violation of UCC by Secured Party. The UCC authorizes both injunctive and money-damage relief against the secured party who violates the provisions of the UCC applicable upon default. The remedies provided by the UCC are not exclusive, and the buyer may also invoke any remedies authorized by any other statute applicable to the particular transaction.

When the sales contract is not executed in the manner required by a statute relating to installment sales, the contract is generally voidable at the election of the buyer and the seller is subject to some form of penalty, such as a criminal fine or loss of financing charges.[59]

Local statutes, such as motor vehicle retail installment sales acts, may impose notice requirements upon a creditor repossessing collateral and subject him to a penalty for failing to give the required notice.[60]

The buyer is entitled to recover the damages caused him by the secured party's failure to comply with the UCC. In the absence of proof of a greater amount of damages, the buyer is entitled to recover not less than the credit service charge together with 10 percent of the principal amount of the debt or the time price differential plus 10 percent of the cash price.[61]

If a resale has not yet been made nor a binding contract therefore entered into, the buyer may obtain a court order or injunction requiring the seller to comply with the UCC provisions.

If the creditor repossesses the collateral when the debtor is not in default or takes other property in which he has no security interest, the creditor commits a conversion. The debtor may recover damages from the creditor for the conversion representing the value of his interest in the goods. If the creditor has acted recklessly and with willful indifference to the rights of the debtor, the latter may also recover punitive damages. (See p. 704, Beggs v Universal C.I.T. Credit Corp.)

When the creditor makes a sale of the collateral without giving the debtor notice, the creditor deprives the debtor of his opportunity to bid at the sale and to retain the property. Consequently, the creditor will not be allowed to recover from the debtor any loss sustained or expenses incurred at such sale.[62] Thus, the creditor who has not given the debtor sufficient notice of the sale of the collateral is barred from obtaining a deficiency judgment against the debtor when the collateral is resold for less than the

---

58 § 9-505(2).

59 Keyes v Brown, 155 Conn 409, 232 A2d 486.

60 Yates v General Motors Acceptance Corp., 356 Mass 580, 254 NE2d 785.

61 UCC § 9-507(1).

62 Skeels v Universal C.I.T. Credit Corp., (DC WD Pa) 222 F Supp 696.

amount due the creditor.[63] (See p. 705, Turk v St. Petersburg Bank and Trust Company.)

[63] Some courts hold that the failure to give notice does not bar the creditor but merely raises a presumption that the collateral was actually of the value of the balance of the debt and that unless the creditor can show otherwise there is no liability for a deficiency judgment. In most cases this presumption has the same effect as a flat prohibition of a deficiency judgment.

CASES FOR CHAPTER 35

Jones & Laughlin Supply v Dugan Production Corp.

85 NMex 51, 508 P2d 1348 (1973)

Jones & Laughlin Supply held a security interest in certain drilling equipment of the Lucky Drilling Company. Property of that company was sold at sheriff's sale and purchased by Dugan Production Corporation and McDonald. J & L claimed that the property purchased by them was subject to its security interest. The security agreement did not include the items in question but a filed unsigned financing statement and oral testimony showed that the disputed items were to have been subject to the security interest. J & L brought an action to recover the disputed items. From a judgment for the plaintiff, the defendants appealed.

LOPEZ, J. . . . The [issue is] whether a Whealand rotary table and a Waukesha gasoline engine were included in a certain security agreement executed between Lucky Drilling Company as debtor and plaintiff as secured party. . . .

. . . At the sheriff's sale, Dugan Production Corporation . . . purchased the Whealand rotary table. . . . The defendant, George McDonald, purchased the Waukesha gasoline engine. Prior to the sheriff's sale, Lucky Drilling Company mortgaged certain equipment to plaintiff and plaintiff took a security agreement and mortgage on March 31, 1970. A review of the record reveals that this security agreement, together with an unsigned financing statement with exhibits was filed on April 27, 1970 in the office of the County Clerk of San Juan County, New Mexico and on April 24, 1970 in the office of the New Mexico Secretary of State.

. . . The two items in question were not specifically described in the security agreement or in the financing statement. . . . The financing statement was not signed by the debtor or the secured party as required by [UCC §] 9-402. . . .

The financing statement contains the wording: ". . . all hand tools, drill collars, drill pipe, equipment, accessories, parts, exchanges, substitutions, additions, accretions, betterments, supplies and items that Debtor may now have or hereafter acquire and use with or as part of such collateral or in connection therewith. . . ." The financing statement further contains the wording: "Debtor's seven complete rotary drilling rigs identified as No. 1 . . ." through "No. 7 . . . , including all components as described on Exhibit 'A' and Exhibit 'B' attached hereto. . . ." This financing statement is not signed by the debtor or the mortgagee.

The security agreement which is signed by all the parties contains the wording: "Debtor's seven rotary drilling rigs Nos. 1 thru 7 including all components as described on Exhibit 'A' (6 pages) and Exhibit 'B' (7 pages), both of which are attached hereto and made a part hereof by this reference, . . . , together with all hand tools, drill collars, drill pipe and together with all equipment, accessories, parts, exchanges, additions, betterments, and appliances that Debtor may hereafter acquire and use with or as a part of the above described goods. . . ." The security agreement does not contain the language "equipment, parts, supplies and items which the Debtor may now have" as does the financing statement.

The undisputed testimony is that the Whealand rotary table in question had been bought with Rig No. 2 originally and prior to the giving of the security agreement has been replaced by a Brewster rotary table. The Whealand rotary table was returned to the parts inventory in the Bloomfield yard and never used again. The inventory mentioned in the Exhibits "A" and "B" lists the Brewster rotary table as a component part of Rig No. 2. In respect to the V-12 gasoline Waukesha engine, the testimony reveals that this engine was purchased with Rig No. 3 and later on was replaced by V-12 Waukesha diesel engine before the security agreement was executed. The inventory mentioned in the Exhibits "A" and "B" shows the V-12 diesel engine as a component of Rig No. 3 and not the engine in question. . . .

. . . There is a conflict in the language of the security agreement and the financing of the statement. We follow the reasoning in the Anderson Uniform Commercial Code, Vol. 4 at 124 (2d Ed. 1971) referring to Uniform Commercial Code which states: "§ 9-110:17.—Conflicting descriptions in security agreement and financing statement. "When there is a conflict between the financing statement on file and the security agreement as to the property involved, the latter prevails for the reason that no security interest can exist in the absence of a security agreement, and therefore a financing statement which goes beyond the scope of the agreement has no effect to that extent." . . .

Plaintiff contends the disputed items were included within the security agreement because they were reasonably described therein. [UCC §] 9-110. . . . Plaintiff contends this reasonable description is provided by "external evidence." This "external evidence" consists of the unsigned financing statement and evidence at trial to the effect that Lucky Drilling Company mortgaged and plaintiff took, pursuant to the mortgage, security on *all* of the equipment of Lucky Drilling Company.

Plaintiff relies on Mountain Credit v Michiana Lumber & Supply, Inc., 498 P2d 967 (Colo 1972) and Security Bank & Trust Co. v Blaze Oil Company, 463 P2d 495 (Wyo 1970). Neither decision aids plaintiff because in each case the security agreement contained general language which reasonably described the items in dispute. In *Mountain Credit* the disputed item was a log-loader; the security agreement covered logging equipment and machinery used in logging operations. In *Security Bank & Trust Co.* the disputed items were miscellaneous items; the security agreement covered *all* machinery and equipment owned or subsequently acquired. In our case the security agreement does not contain expansive language as does the security agreement in the above two cited cases. Plaintiff's security agreement neither refers to "now owned equipment" or to "all" equipment of Lucky Drilling Company.

A security agreement is effective according to *its* terms. . . . A security interest is not effective against third parties unless the debtor has signed a security agreement which contains a description of the collateral. . . . The disputed items cannot be included within the security agreement by the "outside evidence" relied on by plaintiff because the disputed items are not described in the security agreement.

It is true, as the trial court found, that the filing of the financing statement was sufficient to put defendants on inquiry as to plaintiff's security interest. This avails plaintiff nothing when the security agreement did not cover the disputed items. We hold that the security agreement did not cover the two disputed items. . . .

[Judgment reversed and action remanded.]

L. & N. Sales Co. v Stuski

188 Pa Super 117, 146 A2d 154 (1958)

Stuski purchased 123 beverage pourers from L. & N. Sales Co., which was the sales outlet for the manufacturer. Four writings were signed: (1) a purchase contract on September 28, 1955, which did not release or limit any warranties of the seller; (2) an express written warranty of merchantability given on September 28, 1955, which stated that it was in place of any other warranty express or implied and all other liabilities or obligations of the seller; (3) a purchase money security agreement, in the nature of a conditional sales contract executed on October 5, 1955, to secure the purchase price due the seller, the latter reciting that no warranties, guarantees, or representations of any kind were made; and (4) a judgment note authorizing the

seller to confess judgment against the buyer on default. The buyer thereafter refused to make payments because the pourers did not work. The sales company then entered a judgment on the note against Stuski. He filed a petition to open the judgment to permit him to make a defense and to rescind the purchase. From the refusal of the court to open the judgment, Stuski appealed.

WATKINS, J. . . . The defendant [buyer], according to the uncontradicted testimony, experienced difficulty with the pourers shortly after their installation in that the meters did not register accurately, the drinks poured were not consistent in that one would be large, another small, and that it was impossible to have any control over the business or inventory under these circumstances. The seller's serviceman attempted to correct the defects and prevent the mechanism from sticking by use of lubricating oil and other means, but was apparently unsuccessful. The defendant after making one monthly payment defaulted and judgment was confessed for the unpaid balance, plus collection fees. . . .

The conditional sales contract, although being a purchase money security interest . . . the sale being controlled by the [Code] article on sales, is still a security agreement and its force and effect controlled by Art. 9, Sec. 206(3) which expressly prohibits such an agreement from limiting or modifying warranties made in the original contract of sale, as follows: "(3) When a seller retains a purchase money security interest in goods, the sale is governed by the Article on Sales (Article 2) and a security agreement cannot limit or modify warranties made in the original contract of sale." Therefore, the conditional sales contract, regardless of language contained therein, under the present circumstances cannot be considered as limiting or releasing plaintiff from liability on any warranty made by the seller at the time the sales contract was executed, since the security agreement was executed subsequent thereto for the purpose of securing the credit extended to the defendant.

The express written warranty of merchantability also could not exclude or modify the warranty of fitness for a particular purpose because these warranties are not inconsistent, and the warranty of fitness is expressly saved from such exclusion by Art. 2, § 317(c) of the Code, as follows: "(c) Express warranties displace inconsistent implied warranties other than an implied warranty of fitness for a particular purpose." . . .

The time within which a contract of sale must be rescinded must be within a reasonable time under the existing circumstances. In the present case rescission was attempted a month and a half after the pourers were first used. The defendant, according to his uncontradicted testimony, was very desirous that the pourers should work properly, and gave the manufacturer every opportunity to make them work, which appears reasonable. That the manufacturer guaranteed the quality of material and offered to service or replace all the pourers, did not deprive the defendant of his right to rescind as soon as he was satisfied that the pourers could not be made to work satisfactorily.

[Judgment reversed.]

Code Comment: This decision was made under the 1952 text of the Uniform Commercial Code as adopted in Pennsylvania. The same decision would be made under the 1962 text of the Code, which has since been adopted in Pennsylvania. The amendments are not applicable.

Household Finance Corp. v Mowdy

13 Ill App 3d 822, 300 NE2d 863 (1973)

The Mowdys made a contract with Diversified Industries for the installation of a swimming pool, made a down payment of $500, and executed a promissory note for the balance. Diversified sold the note and contract to Household Finance Corporation. The Mowdys stopped paying on the contract. HFC sued them for the balance due. They raised the defenses that the contract had been obtained by fraud and improper practices, that they had defenses valid against Diversified, that all such defenses could be raised against HFC by virtue of the Illinois Consumer Fraud Act, Section 2D, and demanded the return of their deposit of

$500 by HFC. Judgment was entered in favor of HFC. The Mowdys appealed.

SEIDENFELD, J. . . . Plaintiff relies on its status as a holder in due course, and contends that section 2D of the Consumer Fraud Act was satisfied by a notice provision in the contract. Further, HFC claims that evidence showing fraudulent inducement was based on inadmissible hearsay. . . .

Section 2D . . . provides: If a consumer in a retail installment sales transaction gives the seller a negotiable instrument in part or full payment for the merchandise which is the subject of a purchase order, retail charge agreement or retail installment sales contract before that merchandise is delivered or furnished to him, the assignment of that agreement or contract or the transfer of that negotiable instrument does not bar that consumer from asserting against the assignee or transferee any defense or right of action he may have against the seller unless (1) the contract or agreement contains, in at least 10-point bold type, the following notice:

"NOTICE TO BUYER

You have the right to give the assignee named (or if no assignee is named, to give the seller) written notice of any defense or right of action which you may have against the seller within 5 days of delivery of the merchandise described herein. If a notice is not received within that time, you may not assert such defense or right of action against the assignee."; and (2) such a notice is not given within the time period stated. Notice is received with the meaning of this Section if the seller or assignee has refused to accept delivery by certified or registered mail of such a notice. . . .

HFC relies upon a notice contained in the contract which provides that the buyer may cancel the agreement if it has been signed at a place other than the seller's place of business by giving a notice within three days after the signing of the agreement. However, this notice is pursuant to another statute (Ill Rev Stat 1971, ch. 121½, par. 262B), is designed for a different purpose, and does not fulfill the requirements of section 2D.

Section 2D is unequivocal in its requirement. The statute is designed to combat a specific evil and is remediable in nature. It therefore should be liberally construed to effect its purpose of providing aggrieved buyers in explicit terms a method whereby they may communicate their complaints following delivery of purchased merchandise so as to preserve their claims and defenses against an assignee to whom payments will have to be made. Assuming that defendants did not advise HFC of possible defenses within a reasonable time by waiting 60 days following installation before giving written notice of cancellation, such fact would not obviate the requirement of inserting proper notice in the contract so that defendants would be informed of their rights under the Consumer Fraud Act.

While we hold that section 2D of the Consumer Fraud Act was not complied with in the installment contract assigned to HFC, we must also consider whether or not an express or implied clause in the contract which in substance purports to waive the buyer's defenses and claims against an assignee prevents the purchasers from asserting defenses against the assignee, HFC, even though they did not receive the notice required under section 2D.

UCC § 9-206(1) makes waiver of defense clauses valid subject to any statute or decision which establishes a different rule. Section 17 of the Retail Installment Sales Act . . . specifically validates agreements between buyer and seller not to assert against the assignee of retail installment contracts who takes for value, in good faith and without notice of defenses, any claim or defense the buyer may have against the seller.

Whether the language of paragraph four on the reverse side of the contract stating, "Assignee shall not be chargeable with any obligations or liabilities of seller" operates to waive the buyers' right to assert defenses against HFC need not be decided here. Even in the absence of an express waiver clause UCC § 9-206(1) implies an agreement not to assert defenses, if as part of one transaction, the buyer signs both a negotiable instrument and security agreement. . . . The implied waiver would thus operate in the transaction before us, unless there is an overriding consideration of public policy as expressed in section 2D of the Consumer Fraud Act.

We have held, prior to the enactment of section 2D, that a contractual waiver of certain defenses, such as are involved here, will be given effect, regardless of whether a negotiable note is taken in connection with the installment contract sale. . . . However, giving primacy to a waiver of defense clause would circumvent the remedy provided in section 2D so that dissatisfied consumer-buyers would not be able to preserve their claims and defenses against assignees to whom payments will have to be made. To avoid the operation of section 2D sellers would need merely to insert a waiver clause in their form contracts, which the average consumer-buyer may not read or understand. . . . The circumvention becomes even more blatant, when, as in the instant case, the waiver of defense clause is implied by UCC § 9-206(1) without need for mention of it in the contract itself.

Second, the use of a waiver of defense clause has the effect of imparting the attributes of negotiability to an otherwise nonnegotiable document. . . . In transactions in which either a negotiable note or a contract containing a waiver of defense clause evidences the buyer's obligation, the practical effect on the buyer is much the same. He is deprived of his ability to assert defenses he has on the contract against the seller's assignee. Thus the reasons for enacting section 2D to apply in consumer installment transactions in which a negotiable instrument is taken in payment are equally applicable to contracts which contain a waiver of defense clause, express or implied.

We therefore hold the waiver of defense clause implied in the instant installment contract does not nullify the requirements of section 2D. By our holding, the validity of waiver of defense clauses allowed by statute . . . is not destroyed, but only limited as is required by section 2D of the Consumer Fraud Act. If the notice provision as specified is complied with, and no claims or defenses are brought to the seller's or assignee's attention within the time and in the manner designated, then a waiver of defense clause would be effective to cut off later claims or defenses the buyer might seek to assert against an assignee.

We therefore conclude that the trial court erred in holding that the plaintiff took the contract free of defenses defendants may have had against the original seller. Since the trial court did not pass upon the sufficiency of defendants' grounds for relief, the extent of the damage, if any, or the appropriateness of rescission or revocation of acceptance, the case will be remanded. . . .

[An] issue which might have to be considered on remand if any of defendants' claims or defenses are sustained is whether section 2D authorizes recovery from HFC of moneys paid to Diversified as down payment before the assignment. Defendants rely on the language of section 2D which states that "any defense or *right of action*" that the consumer has against the seller may be asserted against the assignee if the required notice to buyer is not inserted in the contract. Plaintiff argues that such an operation of section 2D would be inequitable.

We believe the buyer's ability to assert "rights of action" against the assignee provided by section 2D is limited by the amount of the debt assigned as indicated by the negotiable instrument or instruments taken by the assignee. The statute is designed only to operate in the context of an assignment of a negotiable instrument which was given as payment by a consumer on a retail installment sales contract. As such it is really the debt assigned which is subject to the buyer's defenses and rights of action, although it is against the assignee who holds the instrument acknowledging the debt that the buyer must assert his claims.

Moreover, in our view, the rights of the buyers in the instant case under section 2D are similar to those provided buyers by virtue of UCC § 3-306, which describes the rights of one not a holder in due course. A reasonable reading of UCC § 3-306 indicates the buyer's rights against the holder are limited by the amount of the note or instrument transferred. Thus the authority of buyers to assert defenses and rights of action should be construed as a right to set off these claims against the assignee's right to collect on the note he is holding. Such a construction of section 2D is in accord with the law generally regarding assignments of contract rights. . . .

[Judgment reversed and action remanded.]

Balon v Cadillac Automobile Co.

— NH —, 303 A2d 194 (1973)

Balon and Gibert each purchased a Cadillac for personal use from Saia, a private owner. They did not know that each car was subject to an unfiled security interest in favor of the original seller, the Cadillac Automobile Company of Boston. Balon and Gibert claimed that they owned their cars free of the security interest of Cadillac. Cadillac contended that Balon and Gibert did not believe that they were purchasing a clear title and were subject to its unfiled security interests. Cadillac repossessed the cars. Balon and Gibert sued Cadillac. From judgment in their favor, Cadillac appealed.

LAMPRON, J. . . . The issue to be decided is whether the trial court properly found and ruled that Balon and Gibert each had clear title to his automobile by virtue of § 9-307 of the Uniform Commercial Code. . . .

On September 28, 1965, Charles Pernokas was a salesman for Cadillac Automobile in Boston, Massachusetts. He had previously worked for another employer as a car salesman with Russell Saia. On that day Saia came to Cadillac Automobile looking for a convertible for a customer. Pernokas showed him two cars and Saia said he would hear from him shortly. He telephoned soon thereafter saying that his customer, Peter J. Russell, would take one of the Cadillac convertibles and gave the required credit information and references. On the next day, Saia telephoned Pernokas again and told him another customer, Joseph P. DeLuca, would take the other convertible and gave credit information on him.

Pernokas testified that in each instance he delivered the car to Saia's place and that Saia and another person, supposedly Russell in one instance and DeLuca in the other, identified himself and signed the security agreements. The selling price, $5300 for each car, was paid by a $1000 cash down payment on each and the balance financed on a conditional sale agreement.

At about that time, an individual named Arthur Freije told Balon in Manchester that "somebody" had a "friend" who could get a good deal on Cadillacs. "Somebody" was Fred Sarno who had accompanied Saia on his visit to the Cadillac garage after which the two cars in question were bought. The "friend" was Russell Saia. Balon passed the information along to his stepfather, Gibert, and eventually both Balon and Gibert purchased a Cadillac convertible through Freije for $4300 each.

The October and November payments on these Cadillacs were not made to Cadillac Automobile. As a result of these defaults, Simons, its credit manager, made an investigation and concluded that Peter J. Russell and Joseph P. DeLuca, the apparent purchasers, did not exist and decided that "both of these were two straw deals." There was evidence that payments on these cars were made at the garage in December by Russell Saia or with his knowledge. After the cars were repossessed from Balon and Gibert a meeting was arranged at the Cadillac garage to straighten out the matter. When they had waited there about two hours for someone to come, Simon made a telephone call and a man arrived who was overheard to say he was Peter Russell. In a later conversation with Balon and Gibert the man identified himself as Russell Peters. When asked for credentials by Simon, this same person showed him a license made out to Russell Saia and said that Peter Russell was an alias he used. There was evidence that the address given as that of Peter Russell on the credit statement and security agreement in conjunction with the car purchased in his name was listed in the city directory as the residence of "Mrs. Jean Saia." The trial court properly found on the evidence that the two Cadillac automobiles in question were purchased by Russell Saia and that he was the principal in their sale to Balon and Gibert.

[UCC §] 9-307 . . . reads as follows: (1) "A buyer in the ordinary course of business . . . takes free of a security interest created by his seller even though the security interest is perfected and even though the buyer knows of its existence. (2) In the case of consumer goods

. . . a buyer takes free of a security interest even though perfected if he buys without knowledge of the security interest, for value and for his own personal, family or household purposes . . . unless prior to the purchase the secured party has filed a financing statement covering such goods." . . . The secured interest of Cadillac Automobile was perfected when the agreement of the parties was executed. . . . However the security agreements covering these two automobiles were never filed. . . .

The buyer protected by § 9-307(1) is one who purchases in the ordinary course of business from a person in the business of selling goods of the kind involved. § 1-201(9). Hence § 9-307(1) applies primarily to purchases from the inventory of a dealer in the type of goods sold. 4 Anderson, Uniform Commercial Code 323:24 (2d ed. 1971); *see* National Shawmut Bank v Jones, 108 NH 386, 236 A2d 484 (1967). The buyer protected under § 9-307(2) is one who purchases goods for consumer use, that is, for personal, family or household purposes, from a consumer seller. In order to fall within the protection of this section the goods must be consumer goods in the hands of both the buyer and the seller. . . .

The categorization of these automobiles at the time of the execution of the security agreement with Cadillac Automobile is an important factor in determining whether they were inventory or consumer goods in the hands of Saia when he sold them. . . . This classification of the goods remains unchanged in the controversy between Balon, Gibert, and Cadillac Automobile when it seeks to enforce its security agreement. Simon, Cadillac's credit manager, testified that it is company policy to record security agreements except when the buyer is an individual consumer as determined by the contract. Their security agreement provides that if the car is purchased for business purposes the address of the buyer's place of business must appear as the address on the front of the contract. There was evidence that the address on the front of the Peter Russell contract was listed in the Boston directory as the residence of Mrs. Jean Saia. Simon also testified that as far as the seller was concerned these sales were made to two private consumers for their personal, family and household use. Accordingly, following its policy with respect to consumer purchasers, the security agreements were not filed.

We hold that the trial court properly found and ruled that Russell Saia was a dishonest consumer purchaser of these automobiles. We further hold that these cars remained consumer goods in his hands at the time of the sales to Balon and Gibert who are protected by [UCC §] 9-307(2) if they were good faith consumer buyers for value without knowledge of Cadillac's security interest.

The company maintains, however, that the only conclusion which can be reached on the evidence is that Balon and Gibert "could not have conceivably held honest convictions that these transactions were legitimate." In support it cites § 1-201(19) which provides: "'Good faith' means honesty in fact in the conduct or transaction concerned." By its terms this is a subjective standard of good faith, that is, whether the particular purchaser believed he was in good faith, not whether anyone else would have held the same belief. The test is what the particular person did or thought in the given situation and whether or not he was honest in what he did. . . .

There was evidence that Gibert had known Freije, who made the approaches which culminated in these sales, in a social way for about fifteen years. His wife had known him all her life. Balon knew him also and had purchased a 1963 Cadillac from him without any untoward incidents. Balon and Gibert learned from inquiries made to dealers known to them that the asking price of $4300 was consistent with prices at which such cars could be bought. The explanation advanced that these convertibles sold in September, when the new models were due, could be found by them plausible reasons for the price quoted. Simon testified that when Balon and Gibert came to Boston after their cars were taken they seemed genuinely concerned [in] trying to figure out what happened. There was no evidence that they had actual knowledge of the status of the title to these cars. The fact that others might have acted differently, made more inquiries, or been more suspicious does not require a conclusion that they lacked good faith when they purchased these cars. . . . The evidence is clear that they paid value and bought for personal, family, or household purposes.

We hold that the trial court properly found and ruled that Balon and Gibert were good faith consumer buyers for value from a consumer seller without knowledge of Cadillac Automobile's security interest which had not been filed. . . . Consequently they were entitled to the protection of [UCC §] 9-307(2). . . .

[Judgment affirmed.]

Beggs v Universal C.I.T. Credit Corp.

(Mo) 409 SW2d 719 (1966)

Beggs owned two tractors. Universal C.I.T. Credit Corporation held a security interest in a 1959 tractor. Beggs became delinquent and Universal sent an agent to repossess the tractor which was subject to its security interest. The agent took a 1958 tractor although Beggs informed the agent that it was the wrong tractor and the agent did nothing to verify the identity of the collateral. The towing company hired by the agent damaged the tractor. Beggs sued Universal for damages for the harm caused the tractor and for punitive damages. From a judgment for Beggs allowing the damages claimed, Universal appealed.

HOUSER, J. . . . Plaintiff owned two Diamond T tractors. Defendant had a mortgage on one of them. . . . Defendant's agent Price took possession of the tractor on which defendant did not have a mortgage. When recovered it needed extensive repairs. . . .

Actual damages: We find substantial evidence to support the verdict of $1,800 actual damages. There was believable testimony that defendant's agent called a towing service which towed the tractor through the streets without "pulling the axles" or lifting the rear wheels off the street, thereby extensively damaging the transmission and power train. . . .

Punitive damages: We find substantial evidence justifying the submission of the question of punitive damages.

There was testimony from which the jury could have believed the following facts: Plaintiff owned two Diamond T tractors. One was mortgaged to the defendant and the other was mortgaged to a bank. . . . Although both vehicles were red in color, trimmed in white, there were distinctive differences in appearance between the two. . . .

Defendant's collection manager Price was assigned to find Beggs, find the unit for which the defendant had been looking, a 1959 Diamond T diesel tractor, and bring the account current or make other arrangements, namely, "store" the tractor until the account should be brought to date. As an adjuster it was Price's duty "to get the money or get the truck." . . .

. . . Price knew that the only [tractor] owned by Beggs on which defendant had a mortgage was a 1959 Diamond T diesel. Price had in his possession the information as to the serial number of the 1959 Diamond T diesel, but he did not check the serial number on the tractor which he ordered towed away. Price did not ask Beggs if the tractor on the lot was a 1959 Diamond T diesel. . . . Price claimed to be "under the impression" from an interoffice memo that this was the right [tractor]. He had no previous experience with Diamond T [tractors] and did not know the difference between 1958 and 1959 models. . . . He did not know that the tractor he caused to be towed away was a 1958 model until the next morning when he went to his office. When he found out he did not make any effort to call Beggs and tell him he was sorry and that he had made a mistake. He said it was then out of his hands; that he had "done his job," that he did not know what Beggs' telephone number was and that he really "could [not] have cared less."

The test to be applied in determining whether malice existed as a basis for the award of punitive damages is whether the defendant did a wrongful act intentionally and without just cause or excuse. "This means that defendant not only intended to do the act which is ascertained to be wrongful but that he knew it was wrongful when he did it. There must be, in order to justify punitive damages, some element of wantonness or bad motive, but if one intentionally does a wrongful act and knows at the time that it is wrongful he does it wantonly and with a bad motive." . . .

The jury could properly believe that in taking possession of the 1958 tractor under the circumstances of this case defendant was doing a wrongful act intentionally and without just cause or excuse. The only pretense under which defendant could have claimed the right to take possession of plaintiff's 1958 Diamond T tractor was under and by virtue of a mortgage on that particular tractor. Its authorized agent, however, was plainly and repeatedly informed of a fact which if true completely destroyed its claim. Twice Price was told that his company had no lien on the vehicle which he proposed to take. He was further informed that "the bank" had a mortgage on it. In spite of this notice, Price made no effort to identify the tractor on the lot as the tractor covered by defendant's mortgage, notwithstanding he had been trained to make such a check before repossessing property. With actual notice that the vehicle in question was not the vehicle for which he was looking, and without taking the elementary precaution of checking the serial number of the intended vehicle against the serial number stated in the records in his possession, defendant's agent forcibly took possession of the wrong vehicle over the repeated protests of the rightful owner. Price's conduct, for which defendant is responsible, demonstrated a callous disregard for and a studied indifference to the known rights and interests of the plaintiff.

. . . On the question of the size of the award for punitive damages defendant claims that $14,000 is so enormous under the circumstances that the jury must have misjudged the penalty necessary as a deterrent to future actions of this kind, and is so excessive that it shows bias and prejudice on the part of the jury.

Punitive damages are awarded for the purpose of inflicting punishment for wrongdoing, and as an example and deterrent to similar conduct. . . . The amount to be awarded lies wholly within the sound discretion of the jury and a court will not interfere with the jury's assessment of punitive damages unless there is an abuse of discretion . . . or the size of the award is indicative of passion, prejudice or bias. . . . Ordinarily abuse of discretion in this reference means so out of all proper proportion to the factors involved as to reveal improper motives or a clear absence of the honest exercise of judgment. . . . There is no fixed relation between the amount of actual damages and the amount of punitive damages that may be awarded, . . . and no fixed standard by which they can be measured, . . . but generally, punitive damages must bear some relation to the injury inflicted and the cause thereof. The jury should take into consideration the attendant circumstances, . . . including the mitigating and aggravating circumstances. . . . The defendant's worth or financial condition (shown here to be $49,000,000) is a consideration.

There is nothing to indicate that the managing officials of the defendant were guilty of wrongdoing, such as conspiring to tie up Beggs' operations, or instructing their agent Price to take any of Beggs' property he might find. Price was instructed to take the 1959 tractor *on which the company had a lien,* if he could not get the money. If the managing officials themselves were at fault it was in putting too much pressure on Price to get results. Under all of the facts and circumstances of this case, in the light of the general principles of law and the decided cases, we have concluded that the award of $14,000 punitive damages is excessive by $6,500.

It is therefore ordered that if plaintiff will within fifteen days enter in this Court a remittitur of $6,500 from the award of punitive damages as of the date of the judgment, the judgment will be affirmed in the sum of $1,800 actual and $7,500 punitive damages; otherwise, the judgment will be reversed and the cause remanded.

Turk v St. Petersburg Bank and Trust Co.

(Fla App) 281 So2d 534 (1973)

Turk was president of Bob King, Inc., which sold automobiles. In order to finance the obtaining of inventory for Bob King, Turk borrowed money from the St. Petersburg Bank. The loan was represented by a note which was secured by the inventory of Bob King. The bank repossessed the collateral and resold it without giving notice of the sale to Turk. The amount obtained by the sale was substantially less than the balance due on the debt and the

bank sued Turk for that deficiency. Judgment was entered for the bank and Turk appealed.

LILES, A.C.J.* . . . We believe that the verdict should be reversed. . . .

. . . This transaction was governed by the Uniform Commercial Code, and particularly [§ 9-504(3)] which reads as follows: "(3) Disposition of the collateral may be by public or private proceedings and may be made by way of one or more contracts. Sale or other disposition may be as a unit or in parcels and at any time and place and on any terms but every aspect of the disposition including the method, manner, time, place and terms must be commercially reasonable. Unless collateral is perishable or threatens to decline speedily in value or is of a type customarily sold on a recognized market, reasonable notification of the time and place of any public sale or reasonable notification of the time after which any private sale or other intended disposition is to be made shall be sent by the secured party to the debtor, and except in the case of consumer goods to any other person who has a security interest in the collateral and who has duly filed a financing statement indexed in the name of the debtor in this state or who is known by the secured party to have a security interest in the collateral. The secured party may buy at any public sale and if the collateral is of a type customarily sold in a recognized market or is of a type which is the subject of widely distributed standard price quotations he may buy at private sale."

. . . Before a secured party (in this instance the bank) can obtain a deficiency against a debtor (in this instance Turk) the debtor must be given notice of what is about to occur. This is as it should be because the debtor in this instance, Turk, could have done many things. He could have purchased the automobiles himself; he could have paid the extent of the liability, i.e., $20,000; he could have secured purchasers for the automobiles. He was not afforded the opportunity to do anything. If the bank in this instance wanted to dispose of the collateral without judicial process or notice to the debtor as the statute provides, it may do so; but it is not then entitled to a deficiency against any debtor not so notified. The record reflects that notice was given to Bob King, Inc., but the statute prevents the bank from securing a deficiency against Irving Turk.

There are exceptions to the rule as will be noted in the statute. However, automobile auctions should not be construed as a "recognized market" under [UCC § 9-504(3)]. Although such auctions do not present some of the evils intended to be prevented by the statute, it seems reasonable to limit the definition of "recognized market" to widely recognized stock and commodity exchanges which are regulated in some substantial way. This will prevent nearly all of the evils while imposing only a slight notice burden on creditors in order to obtain their deficiency judgments.

In the absence of a required notice by the secured creditor . . . the creditor forfeits his right to any deficiency against any debtor not so notified. We hereby adopt the reasoning of the New York Court in Leasco Data Processing Equipment Corporation v Atlas Shirt Company, Inc., 66 Misc2d 1089, 323 NYS2d 13 (NY Civ 1971) to the effect that since deficiency judgments after repossession of collateral are in derogation of the common law, any right to a deficiency accrues only after strict compliance with the relevant statutes. . . .

[Judgment reversed.]

* Acting Chief Judge.

QUESTIONS AND CASE PROBLEMS

1. Hull-Dobbs sold an automobile to Mallicoat and then assigned the sales contract to the Volunteer Finance & Loan Corp. Later Volunteer repossessed the automobile and sold it. When Volunteer sued Mallicoat for the deficiency between the contract price and the proceeds on resale, Mallicoat raised the defense that he had not been properly notified of the resale. The loan manager of the finance company testified that Mallicoat had been sent a registered

letter stating that the car would be sold. He did not state whether the letter merely declared in general terms that the car would be sold or specified a date for its resale. He admitted that the letter never was delivered to Mallicoat and was returned to the finance company "unclaimed." The loan manager also testified that the sale was advertised by posters, but on cross examination he admitted that he was not able to state when or where it was thus advertised. It was shown that Volunteer knew where Mallicoat and his father lived and where Mallicoat was employed. Mallicoat claimed that he had not been properly notified. Volunteer asserted that sufficient notice had been given. Was the notice of the resale sufficient? [Mallicoat v Volunteer Finance & Loan Corp., 57 Tenn App 106, 415 SW2d 347]

2. Allen, who operated a trailer park, rented a trailer, which at all times remained in the park, to Cady under a lease which gave Cady the option to purchase the trailer. The lease stated that the cash price of the trailer plus various charges was $5,800, of which the down payment was $1,934, and specified that $17 of each weekly payment of $32 was to be applied to the down payment. The lease was for 24 months so that the total payments, if the trailer was not purchased, would be $3,578, or 62 percent of the price of the trailer. Cady became bankrupt and Cohen, his trustee in bankruptcy, claimed that the interest of Allen in the trailer was void because the transaction was a conditional sale and there had not been any recording of the sales contract. Was Allen's claim to the trailer binding? [Allen v Cohen, (CA2 NY) 310 F2d 312]
3. Bailey purchased a freezer-and-food plan from Pen Del Farms on the installment plan. The latter sold its rights under the contract to the Associated Acceptance Corp. and gave it a copy of the original contract. When Associated sued Bailey, he claimed that the transaction was void under the Maryland Retail Installment Sales Act because the copy of the contract that had been given him had not been fully signed on behalf of the seller. Associated replied that the copy which it had received had been fully executed and that it contained the statement of Bailey that "purchaser acknowledges receipt of true, executed copy of this contract at time of execution hereof." Was Bailey's defense valid? [Associated Acceptance Corp. v Bailey, 226 Md 550, 174 A2d 440]
4. Hileman purchased a washer from the Maytag Rice Co. on credit and executed a chattel mortgage. The mortgage gave the seller authority "to make use of such force as may be necessary to enter upon, with or without breaking into any premises, where the [goods] may be found." Maytag assigned the contract and mortgage to the Harter Bank & Trust Company. When Hileman failed to pay the installment due, Harter Bank had its employees remove a screen in Hileman's house and enter through a window for the purpose of removing the mortgaged washer. Hileman sued the Harter Bank for unlawfully trespassing upon his property. Was he entitled to damages? [Hileman v Harter Bank & Trust Co., 174 Ohio 95, 186 NE2d 853]
5. *A* rented a compressor to *B* for use in operating pneumatic equipment in construction work. The compressor ordinarily sold at $5,000. The lease ran for one year with monthly rentals of $500, with an option given to *B* to

purchase the compressor at the end of the year for the payment of $1. After the lease had run five months, *B* went into bankruptcy. *A* filed a petition in the proceeding to recover the compressor. The trustee in bankruptcy claimed the lease was a secured transaction. Was he correct? [In re Merkel, Inc., 45 Misc 2d 753, 258 NYS2d 118]

6. Sam's Furniture & Appliance Stores sold furniture and home appliances to the public. Sam went bankrupt. At that time, Sam had in his store various items that had been repossessed from customers. Were such goods inventory or consumer goods? [In re Sam's Furniture & Appliance Stores, (DC WD Pa Ref Bankruptcy) 1 UCCRS 422]

7. The National Bank had a perfected security interest in South Dakota in property of Welker. Without the knowledge of the bank, he brought the property to Pennsylvania. A year later he went into bankruptcy and the trustee in bankruptcy claimed the property. The National Bank claimed the property on the ground that it had a security interest. The trustee in bankruptcy asserted that the perfection of such security interest had been lost because there had been no filing in Pennsylvania within four months after the property was brought into Pennsylvania, or at any time thereafter. The National Bank claimed that it was not bound by any requirement of filing in Pennsylvania because it did not know that the goods had been brought to Pennsylvania. Decide. [In re Welker, (DC WD Pa Ref Bankruptcy) 2 UCCRS 169]

8. Little Brown Jug, Inc., purchased goods from L. & N. Sales Co. Little Brown Jug later claimed that it was not bound by the conditional sales contract because its representative had been too busy to read it and thought that he was merely signing an order form. Was that a valid defense? [L. & N. Sales Co. v Little Brown Jug, Inc., (Pa) 12 D&C 2d 469]

9. Cook sold to Martin a new tractor truck for approximately $13,000 with a down payment of approximately $3,000 and the balance to be paid in 30 monthly installments. The sales agreement provided that upon default in any payment Cook could take "immediate possession of the property . . . without notice or demand. For this purpose vendor may enter upon any premises the property may be." Martin failed to pay the installments when due, and Cook notified him that the truck would be repossessed. Martin had the tractor truck, attached to a loaded trailer, locked on the premises of a company in Memphis. Martin intended to drive to the West Coast as soon as the trailer was loaded. When Cook located the tractor truck, no one was around. In order to disconnect the trailer from the truck, as Cook had no right to the trailer, Cook removed the wire screen over a ventilator hole by unscrewing it from the outside with his penknife. He next reached through the ventilator hole with a stick and unlocked the door of the tractor truck. He then disconnected the trailer and had the truck towed away. Martin sued Cook for unlawfully repossessing the truck by committing a breach of the peace. Decide. [Martin v Cook, 237 Miss 267, 114 So2d 669]

36 Other Secured Transactions, Suretyship, and Letters of Credit

SECURED CREDIT SALES OF INVENTORY

§ 36:1. Nature of Transaction. In contrast with one who buys personal property for his own use, the buyer may be a merchant or dealer who intends to resell the goods. The goods which such a merchant or dealer buys are classified as *inventory*. The financing of the purchase of inventory may involve a third person, rather than the seller, as creditor. For example, a third person, such as a bank or finance company, may loan the dealer the money with which to make the purchase and to pay the seller in full. In such a case the security interest in the goods may be given by the buyer to the third person and not to the seller.[1] Accordingly, the terms "creditor" and "secured party" as used in this chapter may refer to a seller who sells on credit or to a third person who finances the purchase of goods.

In general, the provisions regulating a secured transaction in inventory follow the same pattern as is applicable to the secured credit sale of consumer goods. Variations recognize the differences in the commercial settings of the two transactions.

Initially there must be a security agreement to give rise to the security interest. (See p. 721, Mosley v Dallas Entertainment Co.) If perfection of the interest is desired, there must also be a filing of a financing statement or the creditor must hold possession of the collateral.

§ 36:2. Use of Property and Extent of Security Interest. A secured transaction relating to inventory will generally give the buyer full freedom to deal with the collateral goods as though he were the absolute owner and the goods were not subject to a security interest. Thus, the parties may agree that the buyer-dealer may mingle the goods with his own existing inventory, resell the goods, take goods back and make exchanges, and so on, without being required to keep any records of just what became of the goods covered by the security agreement, or to replace the goods sold with other goods, or to account for the proceeds from the resale of the original goods.[2]

---

[1] Prior to the adoption of the UCC, security was frequently provided the person financing the purchase of inventory by the device of a trust receipt, under which the purchaser-merchant would declare that he held the inventory in trust for the creditor. This device was regulated by the Uniform Trust Receipts Act (UTRA).

[2] UCC § 9-205. The 1972 amendments to the Code contain a section expressly governing security interests when there has been a consignment of the goods. UCC § 9-114.

(1) After-Acquired Property. The security agreement may expressly provide that the security interest of the creditor shall bind after-acquired property, that is, other goods, whether inventory or equipment, thereafter acquired by the buyer. (See p. 723, Galleon Industries, Inc. v Lewyn Machinery Co., Inc.) The combination of the buyer's freedom to use and dispose of the collateral and the subjecting of after-acquired goods to the interest of the secured creditor permits the latter to have a *floating lien* on a changing or shifting stock of goods of the buyer. Conversely stated, the UCC rejects the common-law concept that the security interest was lost if the collateral was not maintained and accounted for separately and that a floating lien upon the buyer's property was void as a fraud against the latter's creditors.

The security interest in inventory covered as after-acquired property has priority over claims of subsequent creditors and third persons, except buyers in the ordinary course of business and sellers to the debtor holding perfected purchase money security interests in the goods sold the debtor.[3]

(2) Proceeds of Resale. The security agreement also may expressly cover proceeds resulting from the resale of the goods.[4] If the financing statement covers the proceeds, the secured party's security interest, together with any perfection thereof, continues in the proceeds obtained by the buyer on the resale of the goods. If the original financing statement does not cover such proceeds, the perfection of the security interest in the original goods continues for only 10 days unless within that time the secured party perfects his interest in the proceeds by filing or by taking possession of the proceeds.[5]

When the creditor has a security interest in a tractor that is traded in and the financing statement covering his interest also covers "proceeds," the creditor has a security interest in the replacement tractor that the buyer obtains by the new purchase.[6]

The term *proceeds* refers to what is obtained upon a sale or exchange of the collateral. It does not include payments made by way of indemnification by a tort-feasor who damaged the collateral or by an insurance company that made payment under a policy covering the collateral.

---

[3] Rosenberg v Rudnick, (DC Mass) 262 F Supp 635.

[4] UCC § 9-203(1)(b); In re Platt, (DC ED Pa) 257 F Supp 478. Under the 1972 amendment to the UCC, a security agreement automatically covers the proceeds unless the security agreement provides otherwise. UCC § 9-306(2).

Under the 1972 amendment, proceeds of insurance are deemed proceeds of the collateral and are subject to the security interest. UCC § 9-306(1) [1972 amendment].

[5] UCC § 9-306(3). Proceeds includes not only money but also checks and other commercial paper, and the account or debt owed by the subpurchaser. § 9-306(1). Under the 1972 amendment to the UCC, a security interest in proceeds is perfected even though the financing statement did not refer to proceeds, as the filing with respect to the collateral is made a filing for proceeds of the collateral, and the original financing statement remains continuously effective as to identifiable cash proceeds unless there is an express statement that such proceeds are not covered. UCC § 9-306(3)(a) [1972 amendment].

[6] Universal C.I.T. Credit Corp. v Prudential Investment Corp., 101 RI 287, 222 A2d 571.

§ 36:3. Filing of Financing Statement. Filing is usually required to perfect the creditor's interest in inventory or the proceeds therefrom.[7] An exception is made when a statute, such as a motor vehicle statute, requires the security interest to be noted on the title certificate issued for the property.[8] An unperfected security interest is likewise valid as against anyone standing in the position of the debtor or whose rights rise no higher than those of the debtor.

(1) Financing Statement. The paper that is filed is a financial statement and is distinct from the security agreement which was executed by the parties to give rise to the secured transaction.[9] The *financing statement* must be signed by both the debtor and the secured party, and it must give an address of the secured party from which information concerning the security interest may be obtained and a mailing address of the debtor; and it must contain a statement indicating the types, or describing the items, of collateral.[10]

The UCC adopts the system of "notice filing," which requires a filing only of a simple notice which indicates merely that the secured party who has filed may have a security interest in the collateral described.[11] The criterion for the sufficiency of a financing statement is whether anyone searching the records would be misled by the matter of which complaint is made.[12]

Errors in the financing statement have no effect when not misleading, but they nullify the effect of the filing if they are seriously misleading. (See p. 724, John Deere Co. v Pahl.)

A description in the financing statement of the collateral as "all personal property" is not sufficient and therefore its filing does not perfect the security interest.[13]

§ 36:4. Duration and Continuation of Filing. If the debt is due within 5 years, the filing of the financing statement is effective for the entire period until the debt matures and for 60 days thereafter. If the debt is not due

---

[7] A security interest is binding as between the parties even though a financing statement has not been filed. Bloom v Hilty, 210 Pa Super 255, 232 A2d 26; reversed on other grounds, 427 Pa 463, 234 A2d 860.

[8] UCC § 9-302(1),(3),(4). Reference must be made to the UCC as adopted in a particular state as to the place of filing, for the UCC as submitted for adoption gave the states the option of providing as to certain kinds of property for a system of statewide-effective filing with the Secretary of State or of requiring a local county filing. See § 9-401.

[9] § 9-402. However, the security agreement may be filed as a financing statement if it contains the required information and is signed by both parties.

[10] UCC § 9-402(1). The financing statement is insufficient when it does not contain the address of the creditor. Strevell-Patterson Finance Co. v May, 77 NMex 331, 422 P2d 366. The financing statement may be signed only by the secured creditor if the collateral is subject to a security interest arising in a foreign state and the creditor makes a filing in the state into which the collateral is thereafter taken. Likewise, a signing by the secured creditor alone is sufficient if the filing is made to perfect a security interest in proceeds.

[11] In re Platt, (DC ED Pa) 257 F Supp 478.

[12] Plemens v Didde-Glaser, 244 Md 556, 224 A2d 464.

[13] In re Fuqua, (CA10 Kan) 461 F2d 1186.

within 5 years, a filing is effective only for 5 years. At the expiration of the designated period, the perfection of the security interest terminates unless a continuation statement has been filed prior thereto.[14] The *continuation statement* is merely a written declaration by the secured party which identifies the original filing statement by its file number and declares that it is still effective. The filing of the continuation statement continues the perfection of the security interest for a period of 5 years after the last date on which the original filing was effective. The filing of successive continuation statements will continue the perfection indefinitely.[15]

(1) Termination Statement. When the buyer has paid the debt in full, he may make a written demand on the secured party, or the latter's assignee if the security interest has been assigned, to send the buyer a *termination statement* that a security interest is no longer claimed under the specified financing statement. The buyer may then present this statement to the filing officer who marks the record "terminated" and returns to the secured party the various papers which had been filed by him.[16]

(2) Assignments. The secured party may have assigned his interest either before the filing of the financing statement or thereafter. If the assignment was made prior to its filing, the financing statement may include a recital of the assignment and state the name and address of the assignee, or a copy of the assignment may be attached thereto. If the assignment is made subsequent to the filing of the financing statement, a separate written statement of assignment may be filed in the same office.[17]

§ 36:5. Protection of Customer of the Buyer. The customer of the dealer selling from inventory takes the goods free from the security interest of the dealer's supplier. That is, one who buys in the ordinary course of business items of property taken from the original buyer's inventory is free of the secured party's interest, even though that interest was perfected and even though such ultimate customer knew of the secured party's interest.[18] (See p. 726, Taylor Motor Rental, Inc. v Associates Discount Corp.)

The sale to a buyer in ordinary course when not authorized by the secured party does not destroy a security interest, whether perfected or not, which was created by a debtor prior to acquisition of the goods by the buyer's seller.[19] Hence, there is danger in purchasing used items from a dealer of uncertain reputation. The ultimate buyer is subject to a prior security interest in the

---

[14] UCC § 9-403(2). If the obligation is payable on demand, the filing is effective for 5 years from filing. The 1972 amendment provides for a continuation of perfection for 5 years in all cases, without regard to when the obligation matures, thereby eliminating the extra sixty days allowed by the 1962 UCC when the financing statement showed a maturity of less than 5 years. UCC § 9-403(2) [1972 amendment].

[15] § 9-403(3).

[16] § 9-404.

[17] § 9-405.

[18] § 9-307(1).

[19] § 9-306(2).

used goods even though that interest was unperfected at the time of its ultimate purchase. This has the significance that there may be nothing which the ultimate purchaser could do, as by searching the record, to determine whether there was an outstanding security interest held by someone.

A security interest created by a manufacturer is destroyed by a resale of the goods by the dealer to a buyer on the theory that such sale, which was obviously contemplated by the manufacturer, was authorized, and the destruction of the security interest was likewise authorized.

The buyer of consumer goods or of farm equipment not having an original purchase price in excess of $2,500 is subject to a security interest created by a former owner or his seller if it had been perfected by filing prior to the ultimate sale to the buyer. If it had been perfected without filing, the ultimate buyer is not subject to a security interest created by his seller if he buys without knowledge of its existence, for value, and for his own personal, family, or household purposes, or his own farming operations.[20]

§ **36:6. Rights and Remedies After Default.** The rights and remedies of the secured party and the buyer of inventory after a default on the part of the latter are the same as in the case of a secured credit sale of consumer goods. As a partial modification of that pattern, the creditor taking possession of inventory on the buyer's default is not required to make a sale of the goods but may retain them in full discharge of the debt due, unless an objection is made by the buyer to such retention. In the latter case the creditor must then make a sale.[21]

SECURED CREDIT SALES OF EQUIPMENT

§ **36:7. Use of Collateral.** For the purpose of secured transactions, a distinction is made as to the purpose for which the buyer procures the goods. If the ultimate consumer purchases primarily for his personal, family, or household use, the goods are described as *consumer goods*.[22] The consumer's purchase, however, is described as *equipment* if used or purchased for use primarily in a businėss, in farming, or in a profession, or if the goods do not constitute consumer goods, inventory, or farm products.[23]

§ **36:8. Filing.** In general, the equipment secured sale is treated the same as a secured transaction as to inventory, except that the various provisions relating to resale by the buyer and the creditor's rights in proceeds have no practical application because the buyer does not resell the property but makes the purchase with the intention to keep and use or operate it.

Filing is required to perfect a purchase money security interest in equipment, with the exception of farm equipment having a purchase price not in

---

[20] § 9-307(2).

[21] § 9-505(22). In this situation the secured creditor must give notice not only to his debtor but also to any other party who has an interest in the goods and who has properly filed a financing statement.

[22] As to the secured credit sale of consumer goods, see Chapter 35.

[23] UCC § 9-109(2).

excess of $2,500, and motor vehicles which must be licensed under a specific licensing statute.[24]

If the equipment becomes a fixture, the priority between the creditors holding security interests therein and other creditors is determined by UCC § 9-313. Whether equipment becomes a fixture so as to come within the scope of this section is determined by the local non-Code law governing fixtures.

SECURED LOAN TRANSACTIONS

§ 36:9. Nature of Transaction. In Chapter 35 and the first part of this chapter, consideration has been given to secured transactions as a means of protecting sellers or third persons financing the purchase of goods. The secured transaction may also be employed to protect one who lends on credit apart from the making of any sale. In the latter case the secured transaction may be one in which the collateral is delivered to or pledged with the creditor, or it may be one in which the borrower retains possession of the collateral.

§ 36:10. Pledge. A *pledge* is a secured transaction in which the lender is given possession[25] of the personal property or collateral in which he has the security interest. More specifically, a pledge is a bailment created as security for the payment of a debt.[26] Under a pledge, specific property is delivered into the possession of a bailee-creditor with the authority, express or implied, that in the event that the debt is not paid, the property may be sold and the proceeds of the sale applied to discharge the debt secured by the pledge.[27] For example, a person borrowing $1,000 may give his creditor property worth $1,000 or more to hold as security. If the borrower repays the loan, the property is returned to him. If he does not repay the debt, the creditor may sell the property and reduce the debt by the amount of the net proceeds. The notice of the sale must be specific enough to identify the nature of the property to be sold so as to alert persons possibly interested in purchasing.

Although there is no specific rule as to what the notice of a pledgee's sale must contain, it must identify the property. In the case of unlisted stock, it is necessary to indicate the nature of the business of the corporation, the assets and liabilities of the corporation, and what part of the outstanding stock is being sold.[28]

Upon default, the pledgee does not become the owner of the pledge but has merely the right to foreclose upon it or expose it to sale.[29] If the pledgee

---

[24] § 9-302(1)(c),(3).

[25] Greve v Leger, 64 Cal 2d 853, 52 Cal Rptr 9, 415 P2d 824 (holding, however, that a statute prohibiting the "pledge" of a liquor license should not be given this technical definition but, in order to achieve the legislative objective, should extend to any giving of rights to a creditor for his protection).

[26] Bailes v First National Bank, — Ala —, 281 So2d 632.

[27] McAllen State Bank v Texas Bank & Trust Co., (Tex) 433 SW2d 167.

[28] Kiamie's Estate, 309 NY 325, 130 NE2d 745.

[29] Horne v Burress, (Miss) 197 So2d 802.

makes a fictitious sale of the property to himself and then resells the property to a third person at a profit, the pledgor is entitled to damages caused thereby.[30]

In general terms, the rights of the debtor (the *pledgor*) and the creditor (the *pledgee*) under a pledge relationship are the same as the rights of a buyer and seller under a secured credit sale of consumer goods. A distinction arises from the fact that the pledgee is given possession from the commencement of the secured transaction, whereas under a secured credit sale the secured party obtains possession only upon default. After a default occurs, the two transactions may be regarded as the same.

(1) Creation and Perfection. The pledge relation arises as soon as it is agreed that the pledgee shall have a security interest in the property which is delivered to him and on the basis thereof he gives value, such as lending money.[31] Perfection arises from the fact that the collateral is in the possession of the creditor and the filing is not required.[32]

(2) Duties of Pledgee. Because the secured party or pledgee is in possession of the property or collateral, he must use reasonable care in preserving the property and is liable for damage which results from his failure to do so.[33] The pledgee must keep the collateral separate and identified, although fungible goods of the same kind and quality may be commingled.[34] If money, such as dividends, is received by the pledgee by virtue of his holding the collateral, he must apply such money to the reduction of the debt or send it to the debtor.[35]

Commercial paper may be transferred by way of pledge.[36]

§ 36:11. Pawn. The term *pawn* is often used to indicate a pledge of tangible personal property, rather than documents representing property rights. A person engaged in the business of lending money at interest, in which he requires a pawn as security, is known as a *pawnbroker*. In order to avoid usurious loan practices and trafficking in stolen goods, the business of professional pawnbroking is generally regulated by statute. State and municipal regulations commonly require the licensing of pawnbrokers, and regulate the general conduct of the business and the charges that may be made for loans.

---

30 Wade v Markwell Co., 118 Cal App 2d 410, 258 P2d 497.

31 UCC § 9-204(1).

32 §§ 9-302(1)(a), 9-305.

33 § 9-207(1),(3). The reasonable expenses of caring for the collateral, including insurance and taxes, are charged to the debtor and are secured by the collateral. § 9-207(2)(a).

34 § 9-207(2)(d).

35 § 9-207(2)(c).

36 Salem Development Co. v Ross, 251 Cal App 2d 53, 59 Cal Rptr 548. The collection rights of the creditor as respects parties on the paper are defined by UCC § 9-502. As the pledge will ordinarily be accompanied by an indorsing of the paper, the creditor will be a holder of the commercial paper and will have the rights of such.

In most states pawnbrokers are permitted to charge a higher rate of interest on small loans than would otherwise be legal.

§ 36:12. Securing of Debt Without Change of Possession. This situation is illustrated by the owner of a television set who borrows money from the bank and, to protect the latter, gives the bank a security interest in his property. In general terms, the relation between the lender and the borrower is regulated in the same manner as in the case of a secured credit sale of inventory goods. Filing is required whether or not the collateral constitutes consumer goods.[37] When there is a default in the payment of the debt, the lender has the same choice of remedies under such a secured transaction as the secured credit seller of inventory.

§ 36:13. Security Interest in Goods Being Manufactured. A manufacturer may borrow and use as collateral goods that are partly finished or goods not yet manufactured. In such a case, the financing party and the manufacturer execute a security agreement giving the lender a security interest in existing goods and in goods to be manufactured thereafter, and the proceeds of all such goods. In general, this security transaction follows the same pattern as a secured credit sale of inventory.

SURETYSHIP AND GUARANTY

§ 36:14. Definition. The relationship by which one person becomes responsible for the debt or undertaking of another person is used most commonly to insure that a debt will be paid or that a contractor will perform the work called for by his contract. A distinction may be made between the two kinds of such agreements. One kind is called a contract or undertaking of *suretyship,* and the third person is called a *surety*. The other kind is called a contract or undertaking of *guaranty,* and the third person is called a *guarantor*. In both cases the person who owes the money or is under the original obligation to pay or perform is called the *principal,* the principal debtor, or debtor, and the person to whom the debt or obligation is owed is known as the *creditor.*[38]

Suretyship and guaranty undertakings have the common feature of a promise to answer for the debt or default of another; but they have a basic difference. The surety is primarily liable for the debt or obligation of the principal; ordinarily the guarantor is only secondarily liable. This means that the moment the principal is in default, the creditor may demand performance or payment of the surety. He generally cannot do so in the case of the guarantor; he must first attempt to collect from the principal. An exception is an "absolute guaranty" which creates the same obligation as a suretyship. A guaranty of payment creates an absolute guaranty.

---

[37] UCC § 9-302(1).

[38] Unless otherwise stated, "surety" as used in the text includes guarantor as well as surety, and "guaranty" is limited to a conditional guaranty. The word "principal" is also used by the law to identify the person who employs an agent. The "principal" in suretyship must be distinguished from the agent's "principal."

There is frequently confusion in the use of the terms suretyship and guaranty, and it becomes a question of construction to determine what the parties really intended by their contract. In some states a statute provides that an undertaking to answer for the debt of another is to be interpreted as a suretyship agreement in the absence of an express statement that only a guaranty agreement was intended. In some states the distinction is in effect abolished.

§ 36:15. Indemnity Contract. Both suretyship and guaranty differ from an *indemnity contract,* which is an undertaking by one person for a consideration to pay another person a sum of money to indemnify him if he incurs a certain loss. A fire insurance policy is a typical example of an indemnity contract.

§ 36:16. Creation of the Relation. Suretyship and guaranty are ordinarily based upon contract, express or implied. All of the principles applicable to the capacity, formation, validity, and interpretation of contracts are therefore generally applicable to the law of suretyship.[39] The liability of a surety is measured by the terms of his contract or bond, and his obligation is not necessarily as broad as that of his principal.

Generally the ordinary rules of offer and acceptance apply. Notice of the acceptance, however, must sometimes be given by the creditor to the guarantor.

In most states the statute of frauds requires that contracts of guaranty be in writing in order to be enforceable, subject to the exception that no writing is required when the promisor makes the promise primarily for his own benefit.

In the absence of a special statute, no writing is required for contracts of suretyship or indemnity, because they impose primary liability, and not a secondary liability to answer for the debt or default of another. Special statutes or sound business practices, however, commonly require the use of written contracts of both suretyship and indemnity.[40]

§ 36:17. Rights of Surety. The surety has a number of rights to protect him from sustaining loss, to obtain his discharge because of the conduct of others that would be harmful to him, or to recover the money that he had been required to pay because of his contract.

(1) Exoneration. If the surety finds his position threatened with danger, as when the debtor is about to leave the state and take his property with him, the surety may call upon the creditor to take steps to enforce his claim against the debtor while he can still do so. If at that time the creditor could proceed against the debtor and fails to do so, the surety is released or

[39] General Phoenix Corp. v Cabot, 300 NY 87, 89 NE2d 238.

[40] Some courts regard a surety's contract as an undertaking to answer for another's debt and therefore as requiring a writing under the statute of frauds. American Casualty Co. v Devine, 275 Ala 628, 157 So2d 661 (bond furnished by contractor to assure payment of labor and materialmen).

exonerated from liability to the extent that he can show that he has been harmed.

(2) Subrogation. When a surety pays a debt that he is obligated to pay, he automatically acquires the claim and the right of the creditor. This right is known as *subrogation.* That is, once the creditor is paid in full, the surety stands in the same position as the creditor and may sue the debtor, or enforce any security that was available to the creditor, in order to recover the amount that he has paid. The effect is the same as if the creditor, on being paid, made an express assignment of all his rights to the surety.

The right of subrogation, which arises when a surety on a contractor's labor and material bond pays labor and material claimants, is not a security interest and the surety is therefore entitled to recover the payments made even though no filing was made under the UCC.[41]

(3) Indemnity. A surety who has made payment of a claim for which he was liable as surety is entitled to indemnity from the principal, that is, he is entitled to demand from the principal reimbursement of the amount which he has paid.[42]

(4) Contribution. If there are two or more sureties, each is liable to the creditor for the full amount of the debt, until the creditor has been paid in full. As between themselves, however, each is only liable for a proportionate share of the debt. Accordingly, if a surety has paid more than his share of the debt, he is entitled to demand that his cosureties contribute to him in order to share the burden which, in the absence of a contrary agreement, must be done equally.

§ 36:18. Defenses of the Surety. The surety's defenses include not only those that may be raised by a party to any contract but also the special defenses that are peculiar to the suretyship relation.

(1) Ordinary Defenses. Since the relationship of suretyship is based upon a contract, the surety may raise any defense that a party to an ordinary contract may raise, such as lack of capacity of parties, absence of consideration, fraud, or mistake.

Fraud and concealment are common defenses. Since the risk of the principal's default is thrown upon the surety, it is unfair for the creditor to conceal from the surety facts that are material to the surety's risk.

Fraud on the part of the principal that is unknown to the creditor and in which he has not taken part does not ordinarily release the surety.[43]

(a) DISCLOSURE. By common law the creditor was not required to volunterr information to the surety and was not required to disclose that the

[41] Jacobs v Northeastern Corp., 416 Pa 417, 206 A2d 49.
[42] Non-Marine Underwriters v Carrs Fork Coal Co., (Ky App) 421 SW2d 852.
[43] National Union Fire Insurance Co. v Robuck, (Fla App) 203 So2d 204.

principal was insolvent. There is a growing modern view which requires the creditor to inform the surety of matters material to the risk when the creditor has reason to believe that the surety does not possess such information. (See p. 727, Sumitomo Bank v Iwasaki.) Thus, the creditor is under a duty to inform the surety when there is reason to believe that the surety is in effect walking into a trap of which it is not aware. That is, the creditor is required to volunteer information it possesses about the principal when (a) the creditor has reason to believe that those facts materially increase risk beyond that which surety intends to assume; (b) the creditor has reason to believe that the facts are unknown to surety; and (c) the creditor has reasonable opportunity to communicate the facts to the surety.[44]

(2) Suretyship Defenses. In addition to the ordinary defenses that can be raised against any contract, the following defenses are peculiar to the suretyship relation:

(a) Invalidity of original obligation.

(b) Discharge of principal by payment or any other means.

(c) Material modification of the original contract to which the surety does not consent,[45] as by a binding extension of time for performance.

The compensated surety of a building contractor is not discharged when the owner makes payments to the contractor earlier than called for by the contract, unless it can show that it was prejudiced thereby and then it is only discharged to the extent of such prejudice.[46]

To discharge a surety by the granting of an extension, there must be a binding contract to forebear and the mere fact that the creditor accepts two late payments does not establish that there is such a contract to forebear and hence does not discharge the surety.[47]

(d) Loss of securities that had been given the creditor to hold as additional security for the performance of the original contract, to the extent that such loss is caused by the misconduct or negligence of the creditor.

LETTERS OF CREDIT

§ 36:19. Introduction. A letter of credit is a form of agreement that the issuer of the letter will pay drafts drawn on him by the creditor. It is thus a form of advance arranging of finances in that it is known in advance how much money may be obtained from the issuer of the letter. It is likewise a security device because the creditor knows that the draft which he draws will be accepted or paid by the issuer.

Article 5 of the Uniform Commercial Code establishes certain minimum requirements for letters of credit but for the most part they are governed in international trade by Rules of the International Chamber of Commerce.[48]

---

[44] Beverly Hills Nat. Bank v Glynn, 267 Cal App 2d 859, 73 Cal Rptr 808.

[45] Town of Hingham v B. J. Pentabone, Inc., 354 Mass 537, 238 NE2d 534.

[46] Central Towers Apartments, Inc. v Martin, 61 Tenn App 244, 453 SW2d 789.

[47] Fireman's Fund Ins. Co. v Richard, (La App) 209 So2d 95.

[48] Uniform Customs and Practices for Commercial Documentary Credits fixed by the 13th Congress of the International Chamber of Commerce.

The use of letters of credit arose in international trade. While this continues to be the primary area of use, there is a growing use of letters in domestic sales and some evidence of the use of a letter of credit in place of a surety bond.[49]

§ 36:20. Definition, Parties, and Duration.

(1) Definition. A letter of credit is an engagement by its issuer that it will pay or accept drafts drawn on it when the conditions specified in the letter are satisfied. The issuer is usually a bank.

(2) Parties. The parties to a letter of credit are (1) the issuer, (2) the customer who makes the arrangements with the issuer, and (3) the beneficiary who will be the drawer of the drafts which will be drawn under the letter of credit. The beneficiary benefits by the existence of the letter of credit because the letter gives greater assurance that the drafts will be paid. There may also be (4) an advising bank.[50] This will occur when the local issuer of the letter of credit requests its correspondent bank where the beneficiary is located to notify or advise the beneficiary that the letter has been issued.

As an illustration of the above definitions, an American merchant may buy goods from a Spanish merchant. There may be a prior course of dealings between the parties so that the seller is willing to accept the buyer's commercial paper as payment or to accept trade acceptances drawn on the buyer. If the foreign seller is not willing to do this, the American buyer, as customer, may go to his bank, the issuer, and obtain a letter of credit naming the Spanish seller as beneficiary. The American bank's correspondent or advising bank in Spain notifies the Spanish seller that this has been done. The Spanish seller will then draw drafts on the American buyer. By the letter of credit, the issuer is required to accept or pay commercial paper of the seller.

(3) Duration. A letter of credit continues for any time specified in the letter. Generally a maximum amount is stated in the letter so that the letter is exhausted or used up when drafts aggregating that maximum amount have been accepted or paid by the issuer. A letter of credit may be used in installments as the beneficiary chooses. A letter of credit cannot be revoked or modified by the issuer or the customer without the consent of the beneficiary unless that right is expressly reserved in the letter.

§ 36:21. Form. A letter of credit must be in writing and signed by the issuer. Other than this, any form is sufficient. Consideration is not required to establish or to modify a letter of credit.

---

[49] Barclays Bank D.C.O. v The Mercantile National Bank, (CA5 Ga) 481 F2d 1224.

[50] UCC § 5-103(e).

§ **36:22. Duty of Issuer.** The issuer is obligated to honor drafts drawn under the letter of credit if the conditions specified in the letter have been satisfied. Generally this means that the bank must assure itself that all specified papers have been submitted. The issuer has no duty to verify that the papers are properly supported by facts or that the underlying transaction has been performed. It is thus immaterial that the goods sold by the seller in fact do not conform to the contract as long as the seller tenders the documents specified by the letter of credit. (See p. 728, Banco Espanol de Credito v State Street Bank.)

(1) Liability of Issuer for Wrongful Dishonor. If the issuer dishonors a draft without justification, it is liable to its customer for breach of contract. The issuer is also liable to the beneficiary.[51] as though the issuer had accepted the draft and then dishonored it.

§ **36:23. Liability of Beneficiary.** The beneficiary is a drawer and therefore has a drawer's liability with respect to the paper drawn by him. When he presents the paper for acceptance of payment, the beneficiary-drawer becomes subject to the ordinary warranty liabilities specified by Article 3 of the UCC. In addition, he warrants that all necessary conditions specified in the letter of credit have been satisfied.[52]

---

[51] UCC § 5-115(1).
[52] UCC § 5-111(1).

CASES FOR CHAPTER 36

Mosley v Dallas Entertainment Co., Inc.

(Tex Civ App) 496 SW2d 237 (1973)

The Dallas Entertainment Company operated a club, the Music Box, which it sold to Follies Buffet. A cash register was included in the property which was sold. Dallas and Follies Buffet orally agreed that Dallas was to have a security interest in the property which was sold by Dallas and a financing statement was filed covering all property and equipment. The statement did not specifically describe the cash register. No security agreement was executed. Follies Buffet later sold the cash register to Mosley who resold it to another person. Dallas Entertainment sued Mosley for conversion on the theory that Dallas had a security interest in the cash register which was converted by the act of selling the cash register without its consent. Judgment was entered for Dallas. Mosley appealed.

MOORE, J. . . . Appellant, Bill Mosley, was in the business of buying and selling used cash registers and does not dispute the fact that he purchased the cash register from Follies Buffet in December, 1970, and that he subsequently sold the cash register to a customer in the course of his business. It is not contended that appellant had actual knowledge of appellee's alleged security interests in the cash register.

[UCC § 9-203(c)] provides that subject to certain exceptions not applicable here, ". . . a security interest is not enforceable against the debtor or third parties unless . . . (2) the debtor has signed a security agreement which contains a description of the collateral. . . ."

By his first four points appellant attacks the judgment on the ground that there is no evidence or alternatively that the evidence is insufficient to show appellee was a secured party under a Security Agreement executed by the debtor because appellee failed to produce a written security agreement. Appellee does not deny that it was required to prove that it had a written security agreement signed by the debtor describing the cash register and that no such security agreement was introduced in evidence. In reply appellee contends first that there is competent oral testimony to prove the existence of a security agreement and secondly that the financing statement itself amounts to a security agreement.

The only evidence of a security agreement is to be found in the oral testimony of Peggy Foley, appellee's president. When viewed in a light most favorable to the judgment her testimony shows that Dallas Entertainment Company received a note and a security agreement at the time the Music Box was sold to Follies Buffet which was signed by a Dr. Cullen. During the course of her testimony she identified an instrument as the security agreement but when the instrument was offered in evidence counsel for appellant objected on the ground the instrument was not signed. The court sustained the objection and the instrument does not appear in the record. Upon being asked whether she had "an independent recollection that Dallas Entertainment Company, Inc. obtained a security interest in a cash register," she replied "Yes, I do." She was not asked nor did she testify that the cash register involved in this suit was described in the security agreement.

The first question for our determination is whether the judgment of the trial court can be sustained on the theory that a security agreement may be established by parol evidence.

We have been unable to find any Texas case interpreting the applicable provisions of the Uniform Commercial Code and therefore must make our own interpretation of the statute aided by authorities from other jurisdictions having similar statutes.

A "security interest" in personal property means an interest which secures payment or performance of an obligation. § 1-201(37). "Security Agreement" is defined in § 9-105(8) as being the bargain of the parties in fact. The requirement that there must be an agreement, not only in connection with § 1-201(3), but also in connection with § 9-203(a)(2) which requires that security agreements be written.

In paragraph 5 of the Uniform Commercial Code Comment following § 9-203, supra, we find this statement: "The formal requisites stated in this Section are not only conditions to the enforceability of a security interest against third parties. They are in the nature of a Statute of Frauds. Unless the secured party is in possession of the collateral, his security interest, absent a writing which satisfies [the UCC,] is not enforceable even against the debtor, and cannot be made so on any theory of equitable mortgage or the like. . . ."

In American Card Company, Inc. v H. M. H. Co., 196 A2d 150 (RI Sup Ct, 1966), the court specifically rejected the argument that the security agreement could be established by parol, stating that oral assertions were without probative force to supply the absence of a required security agreement in writing. . . .

Since the foregoing statute requires the secured party to show that the debtor has signed a security agreement containing a description of the collateral, we hold that the oral testimony of the secured party is without probative force to establish a security interest for the simple reason that it fails to satisfy the statutory requirement that the security agreement be in writing and signed by the debtor.

This brings us to the question of whether the judgment may be sustained on the theory that the financing statement amounts to a security agreement. The financing statement in this case appears to have been written on the Secretary of State's standard form. As noted above, it recites a general description of the collateral in which a security interest is claimed. It is signed by the creditor, appellee, and by a party alleged to be the agent of Follies, though the character of that signature was never established in the trial of this case. Nowhere in the instrument does it grant the creditor a security interest in the collateral nor does it identify the obligation owed to the creditor.

The code makes no provision for a naked financing statement to be enforced as a security agreement. It merely gives notice of the existence of a security interest but in itself does not create a security interest. Anderson, Uniform Commercial Code, 2d Ed. § 9-402:4. A financing statement cannot serve as a security agreement where it does not grant the creditor an interest in the collateral and does not identify the obligation owed to the creditor. . . . Since the financing statement offered by appellee fails to contain any language showing the alleged debtor granted the creditor (appellee) an interest in the collateral and since appellee was unable to produce a written security agreement signed by appellant, appellee failed to establish a cause of action. . . .

[Judgment reversed.]

Galleon Industries, Inc. v Lewyn Machinery Co., Inc.

— Ala App —, 279 So2d 137 (1973)

In 1969 Galleon borrowed money from the Central Bank and Trust Company. As security for the loan, Galleon gave Central a security interest in the equipment and inventory owned or thereafter acquired by Galleon. Central filed a financing statement and perfected this security interest. Thereafter, in 1970, Lewyn sold equipment to Galleon. The equipment was made by Lancaster and the sale was to be made for cash but, through a mistake, the goods were sent by Lancaster directly to Galleon before it paid for the goods. Lewyn then sent Galleon an invoice stating that payment was to be made "net 30 days." Galleon failed to pay the loan to Central Bank and Trust Company and it took possession of the equipment sold by Lewyn, claiming such equipment under the authority of the after-acquired property clause. Lewyn then sued Galleon and Central Bank to obtain possession of the equipment. From a judgment for Lewyn, Central Bank appealed.

WRIGHT, J. . . . Plaintiff, Lewyn, presented his case on the theory that title to the machine did not pass to Galleon until it had been paid for and since Galleon never paid, the title, and thus the right to possession, remained in Lewyn. We consider that the vesting of rights, as required under § 9-204 of the Uniform Commercial Code, and not the passing of title (§ 2-401) is the question to be determined on this appeal. The provisions of § 2-401 are explicitly subject to the provisions of Article 9—therefore, the question being the effect of Central's after-acquired property clause, we will limit our discussion to whether or not sufficient rights did in fact vest in the buyer Galleon, for Central's perfected security interest to attach.

It is without dispute in the evidence that the machine was shipped by the manufacturer to the buyer, Galleon. Lewyn stated that such shipment was by mistake, and that it was orally agreed between Galleon and Lewyn that delivery was not to be made except upon payment. However, after receiving notice of the shipment Lewyn sent to Galleon an invoice requiring payment "net in 30 days." Thus any prior agreement as to delivery and payment was modified or waived by Lewyn and Galleon became a credit buyer. We do not decide here the application of § 2-201, the Statute of Frauds, to the sales agreement. The effect of delivery, together with the invoice, was to limit any retention of rights or title to an explicit security agreement subject to the provisions of Article 9 of the Uniform Commercial Code as to perfection and priority. . . .

§ 9-202 states "Each provision of this Article with regards to rights, obligations or remedies applies whether title to collateral is in the secured party or in the debtor." It is stated in Anderson, Uniform Commercial Code, 2d Edition, Volume 2, page 26: "If it is the desire of the parties to effect a reservation of title until the purchase price be paid, a secured transaction should be entered into and a proper filing made if required to protect the creditor's interest as against third persons."

§ 9-204 provides for a security agreement covering after-acquired property such as that held by Central. This section also provides the manner in which such security interest shall attach. In the case of the security interest of Central, it attached when the debtor, Galleon, acquired "rights" in the collateral covered by the security agreement. As we have previously stated, the delivery of the machine and the forwarding of the invoice stating "net 30 days" made Galleon a credit buyer. A credit buyer acquires "rights" in the property when possession is received from the seller. . . .

Lewyn, if retaining title until payment, by delivery to a credit buyer reserved only a purchase money security interest, such security interest was never perfected by filing as required by § 9-302. Lewyn could have perfected its purchase money security interest and received priority over the perfected security interest of Central by filing a financing statement at the time of delivery, or within 10 days thereafter. § 9-312(4). According to the evidence, Lewyn learned of the foreclosure and taking of possession by Central eight days after delivery to Galleon. There still remained two days for perfection of its security interest by filing a financing statement. Such filing would have given it priority over the perfected security interest of Central. § 9-312(4).

Since sufficient "rights" had passed to Galleon by delivery and the sending of the invoice, the requirements of § 9-204 were satisfied and the security interest of Central attached to the machine. The failure of Lewyn to perfect its security interest by filing within 10 days after delivery gave Central priority. Thus at the time of the filing of the suit . . . , Central had a superior right to possession.

We reject the argument of appellee that use of the term "equipment" in the after-acquired property clause of Central's security agreement is insufficient to include the machine involved. Under the evidence there is no question that the machine involved was to be used in the business of Galleon, and was placed within the premises as equipment. The sufficiency of a description in a financing statement is measured in terms of notice. Does the designation of "equipment now owned or hereafter acquired" give notice to a seller of a machine to be installed on the premises of an operating business and used in production that it is subject or likely to be subject to a perfected security interest? We hold it does. . . .

. . . Central Bank and Trust Company had a superior right to possession to the property sued for . . . .

[Judgment reversed and action remanded.]

John Deere Co. v Pahl

59 Misc 2d 872, 300 NYS2d 701 (1969)

Ranalli Construction Co. purchased on credit a construction machine, known as a John Deere Crawler Loader, from Melvin Tractor Equipment, Inc. Melvin filed a financing statement to perfect its security interest in the loader. In the statement, the name of the buyer was misspelled as "Ranelli." Ranalli thereafter sold the loader to Anklin, who resold it to Pahl. Melvin assigned the contract to John Deere Co. When Deere sought to recover possession of the loader from Pahl, it was claimed that Deere could not recover possession on the theory that the filing of the financing statement by Melvin had been fatally defective because of the misspelling of the buyer's name. Pahl moved to dismiss the complaint filed in the action of Deere.

CARDAMONE, J. . . . The plaintiff alleges that it has perfected its security interest in this crawler loader and has brought this action demanding possession of the machine. The defendant alleges that it is entitled to possession of the crawler loader free and clear of plaintiff's security interest. The basis of defendant's contention is that the [financing statement] was incorrectly filed because the name "Ranalli" was misspelled and the filing in the Secretary of State's office was under the name "Ranelli Construction, Inc." The defendant has moved to dismiss the plaintiff's complaint on the grounds that since the security interest was not properly perfected, the complaint fails to state a cause of action.

The applicable statute is contained in Article 9 of the Uniform Commerical Code. Under the statute a financing statement must be filed in order to protect a security interest in property not retained by the creditor (§ 9-302); a copy of the security agreement is sufficient as a financing statement if it contains the information which must be included in such a statement and is signed by both parties (§ 9-402(1)); filing consists of the presentation for filing of a financing statement and tender of the filing fee or acceptance of the statement by the filing officer (§ 9-403(1)). The statement is indexed by the filing officer according to the name of the debtor (§ 9-403(4)); a security interest is perfected when all the applicable steps required for perfection have been taken (§ 9-303(1)). The proper place to file in order to perfect a security interest is in the Department of State, and if the original debtor has a place of business in only one County, then in the County in which the place of business is located as well as in the Department of State (§ 9-401(1)(c)).

Formal requisites for financing statements are contained in § 9-402 which provides in subdivision (3) thereof that the debtor's name and address and the secured party's name and address as well as the types of property covered should be set forth in the financing statement. § 9-402(5) provides that "A financing statement substantially complying with the requirements of this section is effective even though it contains minor errors which are not seriously misleading."

§ 9-301 defines those persons who take priority over unperfected security interests, and subdivision (1)(c) defines one to be a buyer not in ordinary course of business to the extent that he gives value and receives delivery of the collateral without knowledge of the security interest and before it is perfected. Knowledge is defined in § 1-201(25) as follows: "a person 'knows' or has 'knowledge' of the fact when he has actual knowledge of it."

The defendant is a buyer in the ordinary course of business who now has no actual knowledge of the security interest of the plaintiff. The only remaining question is whether the filing in the Secretary of State's office was perfected. If it was, the plaintiff's security interest in the equipment is paramount; if it was not, the plaintiff's security interest will be subordinate to the rights of the defendant in possession.

§ 9-402 adopts a system of "notice filing" which merely indicates that the secured party which has filed may have a security interest in the collateral described. The purpose of the filed statement is to give sufficient information necessary to put a searcher on inquiry. The secured party has the duty to make sure of proper filing and indexing. . . .

Subsection (5) of 9-402 was added to make it clear that an immaterial error should not have the devastating effect reached in GMAC v Haley, 329 Mass 559, 109 NE2d 143 (1952), where "E. R. Millen Co." was held to be insufficient to identify "E. R. Millen Co., Inc." A nonmisleading typographical error, subsequently corrected, was held not to invalidate a factors lien. (Matter of Bloch Brothers Paper Co. v Larkin, 198 Misc 669, 102 NYS2d 1003 (1950).) In Bloch the lien was originally filed against "Efficiency Direct Mail Service, Inc." but was subsequently amended so that it read "Efficient Direct Mail Service, Inc." Similarly, the misspelling of a first name of the debtor "Shelia" instead of "Sheila" is not misleading. (See: Beneficial Finance Co. of New York v Kurland Cadillac-Oldsmobile Inc., 57 Misc2d 806, 811, 293 NYS2d 647, 652. . . .

Here, however, an inquiry made by the defendant on October 3, 1968, to the filing officer of the Secretary of State against the name Ranalli Construction Inc., revealed five different financing statements (in all of which "Ranalli" was correctly spelled) no one of which covered the . . . loader which is the subject of this litigation. A similar inquiry made by the plaintiff to the . . . County Clerk's Office on January 17, 1969, revealed the existence of the financing statement (with "Ranalli" correctly spelled) on the 350 crawler loader in question. Obviously, in this day of volume filling, the exact spelling of the debtor's last name is essential since those that are correctly spelled will be revealed by a search and those where an exact spelling is not present on the financing statement may not necessarily be shown on a search. This is particularly true where the statement is indexed by the filing officer according to the name of the debtor (§ 9-403(4)). It is for this reason that "A Guide to Filings" issued by the Secretary of State's Office (September, 1965) in its instructions for filing . . . (Form UCC-1) at page 10 under "Names Address" states: "If a New York corporation: GIVE CORPORATE NAME EXACTLY as in Certificate of Incorporation." . . .

Where the debtor's name was "Kaplan" and it was indexed under "Kaplas," such was held seriously misleading and the financing statement was held not to substantially comply with the requirements of the Code. . . .

Under the circumstances here, the misspelling of the corporation debtor's name is seriously misleading and amounts to no filing at all. The security interest of the plaintiff is, therefore, ineffective as to the defendant in possession.

. . . The defendant's motion to dismiss the plaintiff's complaint is granted.

Taylor Motor Rental, Inc. v Associates Discount Corp.

196 Pa Super 182, 173 A2d 688 (1961)

Associates Discount Corp. held a perfected security interest in an automobile owned by McCurry Motors, Inc. The latter corporation sold the automobile to Taylor Motor Rental, Inc. When payments were not made of the installments due Associates, it repossessed the automobile. Taylor then sued it to recover the automobile. Associates showed that McCurry Motors and Taylor were two corporations that were both managed by Fred McCurry, that the two corporations had common officers, shareholders, and employees, and that Fred McCurry had applied for the state certificate of title in the name of Taylor. From a judgment in favor of Associates, Taylor appealed.

WOODSIDE, J. . . . [Quoting from the opinion of the lower court:] "The precise question in this case is which of the parties was entitled to possession of the automobile. Plaintiff claimed its right to possession by virtue of its purported purchase from McCurry, and the defendant claimed its right to possession of the automobile by virtue of its secured interest.

"There can be no question that the defendant had a valid and perfected security interest in the automobile under the provisions of the Uniform Commercial Code. . . . It gave value for the automobile by its payment of the purchase price to the Studebaker factory, it obtained a security agreement which described the automobile by serial number and it had on file in appropriate offices a properly executed financing statement which described the type of property it was financing for McCurry Motors. . . .

"Defendant's security interest in the automobile was enforceable against everyone, except as otherwise provided in the Commercial Code. . . . Plaintiff claims to be a buyer in the ordinary course of business and relies on (§ 9-307). . . .

"It is clear that plaintiff was not a buyer in the ordinary course of business as defined by the Commercial Code. Both the relationship of plaintiff and McCurry, with their interlocking officers, shareholders, and employees and the fact that both plaintiff corporation and McCurry Motors, Inc., were managed by Fred McCurry negates this. Moreover, Fred McCurry acted for both plaintiff and McCurry Motors, Inc., in applying for the certificate of title in the name of the plaintiff. . . . The purported sale by McCurry Motors, Inc., to the plaintiff was merely a paper transaction for the benefit of Fred McCurry [to obtain] the automobile for which defendant has never been paid." . . .

Only if the appellant were "a buyer in ordinary course of business" would it take free of the appellee's security interest. The facts set forth above clearly support the trial court's finding that the transaction was not in the ordinary course of business. . . .

[Judgment affirmed.]

Code Comment: UCC § 9-307(1) provides "a buyer in ordinary course of business . . . . other than a person buying farm products from a person engaged in farming operations, takes free of a security interest created by his seller even though the security interest is perfected and even though the buyer knows of its existence." A buyer in ordinary course of business is defined as "a person who in good faith and without knowledge that the sale to him is in violation of the ownership rights or security interest of a third party in the goods buys in ordinary course from a person in the business of selling goods of that kind. . . ." UCC § 1-201(9).

Sumitomo Bank v Iwasaki

70 Cal 2d 81, 73 Cal Rptr 564, 447 P2d 956 (1968)

Frank Iwasaki sued the Sumitomo Bank to recover the loans which he had made to the Nagayamas and which the bank had guaranteed. The court held that the bank was not liable as to a "third loan" because Frank had not notified the bank that the loan was made to the Nagayamas in order for them to pay their federal taxes. Frank appealed.

TOBRINER, A.J. . . . This appeal presents an issue of first impression: whether a creditor owes a duty of disclosure to a surety on a continuing guaranty during the course, as well as at the inception, of the suretyship relationship, and if so, the nature and extent of that duty. We shall explain why we adopt the Restatement rule. That rule provides that each time the creditor accepts the continuing offer of a surety on a continuing guaranty by extending further credit to the principal debtor, the creditor owes a duty to the surety to disclose facts known by the creditor if the creditor has reason to believe that those facts materially increase the risk beyond that which the surety intended to assume and that those facts are unknown to the surety. (Rest., Security, § 124, subd. (1), com. *c*, pp. 327-328, 330.) . . .

In all suretyship relations, the creditor owes to the surety a duty of continuous good faith and fair dealing. . . . Thus, the creditor must not misrepresent or conceal facts so as to induce or permit the surety to enter or continue in the relationship in reliance on a false impression as to the nature of the risk. As with other contracts, a creditor's fraud, which may consist of intentional or negligent misrepresentation or active suppression of the truth, will discharge the surety as to any subsequently incurred liability. . . .

Section 124, subdivision (1), of the Restatement of Security prescribes three conditions prerequisite to imposition of a duty on a creditor to disclose facts it knows about the debtor to the surety. Those conditions are: (a) "the creditor has reason to believe" that those facts materially increase the risk "beyond that which the surety intends to assume"; (b) the creditor "has reason to believe that the facts are unknown to the surety"; and (c) the creditor "has a reasonable opportunity to communicate" the facts to the surety. . . . The creditor's failure to disclose such facts to the surety prior to an extension of further credit to the debtor will discharge the surety from liability on the subsequent loan only if all three conditions are satisfied. . . . If the evidence fails to establish any one of the three factors, a judgment discharging a surety from liability because of a breach of a duty of disclosure governed by section 124, subdivision (1), cannot stand. . . .

Although the evidence establishes that plaintiff knew about the Nagayamas' inability to pay their federal taxes without a loan, the evidence cannot establish that (a) plaintiff had reason to believe that this fact materially increased the risk beyond that which defendant intended to assume. The evidence cannot establish condition (a) because no evidence discloses the financial condition of the Nagayamas in July, 1961, when defendant executed the guaranty. As a result, no evidence describes the risk defendant intended to assume, or tells us whether plaintiff had reason to know what risk defendant intended to assume. Thus the evidence cannot support a finding that the Nagayamas' inability to pay their taxes without a loan materially increased defendant's risk. *A fortiori,* it cannot support a finding that *plaintiff had reason to believe* this fact materially increased defendant's risk. Indeed, the practice of borrowing funds to pay taxes and the resort to financial assistance for that purpose is so frequent in American life that its presence here surely does not establish that the creditor had reason to believe that this circumstance materially increased the risk beyond that which the surety intended to assume.

The evidence cannot support a finding that a necessary condition of section 124, subdivision (1), of the Restatement was satisfied.

The judgment, insofar as it rests upon the trial court's conclusion that defendant's performance as obligor on the third loan was excused, and insofar as it denies recovery to plaintiff on said third loan, is reversed. The cause is remanded to the trial court with directions to retry the issue of defendant's liability on said third loan. . . .

Banco Espanol de Credito v State Street Bank & Trust Co.

(Ca1 Mass) 385 F2d 230 (1967)

Lawrence, a Boston merchant, purchased clothing from two manufacturers in Spain. He obtained letters of credit to finance the transactions. The manufacturers were the beneficiaries of the letters and Banco Espanol was named as advising bank. The letters called for the production of a certification by a firm named Supervigilancia that the goods conformed to the "order." A certificate of such conformity, as well as other required documents, were submitted with drafts to Banco Espanol as advising bank. It paid the drafts and then forwarded them to the State Street Bank. The latter refused to pay the drafts on the ground that the certificate of conformity of the goods was not justified because it did not show that the samples used by the inspector for comparison were the original samples on which the contract was based, but rather were samples handed by the sellers to the inspecting agency. Banco Espanol sued State Street Bank. From a judgment for State Street Bank, Banco Espanol appealed.

COFFIN, C.J. . . . The Uniform Commercial Code, . . . § 5-114(1) . . . , provides, in relevant part, that "An issuer must honor a draft or demand for payment which complies with the terms of the relevant credit regardless of whether the goods or documents conform to the underlying contract for sale or other contract between the customer and the beneficiary." This Code provision, however, simply codifies longstanding decisional law and does not assist us here in determining whether the inspection certificate submitted by Supervigilancia complied with the terms of the credit.

We take as a starting point the substantial body of case law which establishes and supports the general rule that documents submitted incident to a letter of credit are to be strictly construed. This is because international financial transactions rest upon the accuracy of documents rather than on the condition of the goods they represent. But we note some leaven in the loaf of strict construction. . . . Some courts now cast their eyes on a wider scene than a single document. We are mindful, also, of the admonition of several legal scholars that the integrity of international transactions (i.e., rigid adherence to material matters) must somehow strike a balance with the requirement of their fluidity (i.e., a reasonable flexibility as to ancillary matters) if the objective of increased dealings to the mutual satisfaction of all interested parties is to be enhanced. . . .

What we face here is a matter of procedure which can, in the first instance, be structured by the purchasing party. How may a buyer in the international market place be assured before payment that his purchase as delivered is of the quality agreed upon by the parties? As buyers become more concerned about quality, this issue is likely to become more important. That there are so few cases or comments addressed to the issue of reasonable precautions to assure quality is indicative of the relatively novel status of the problem, at least so far as courts have dealt with it. We are mindful of the testimony in this case that an official of appellee, a busy bank, engaged in passing upon the issuance of 1,500 to 2,000 letters of credit a year for several decades, has encountered in this case his first experience with a letter of credit calling for a certificate of conformity to the order.

What are the realities of such a requirement on the part of the buyer? It is not enough that he receive the quantity of goods he ordered, nor that he receive goods capable of standard measure or grade. He must also, in such a case as this, receive them cut, tailored, sewn according to a style he has in mind. He must therefore rely on a sample he has seen and liked. Being in a distant part of the globe, the buyer must usually elect one of two alternatives. He may be present during the inspection process to verify the sample or he may select, with his seller's acquiescence, a person or firm in whom he has confidence to represent him. Unless he elects to be present, he is acting on faith—faith that the representative is capable and honest, and faith that the representative has the right samples or criteria to serve as a standard. Even if he mails an approved sample direct to the representative, he must rely on the integrity of the mails. . . .

. . . The buyer here—Lawrence—was striving to assure the delivery of quality goods. . . . When it finally reached agreement with the seller as to an inspecting agency, it neglected to specify precisely how it would conduct the inspection operation, leaving only the bland instruction that the goods must conform to orders. And, so far as the inspecting agency was concerned, the orders merely referred to samples that might very well have been inspected in Spain at some past time.

Consequently when faced on the eve of the shipping deadline both with a barrage of contradictory telegrams from the buyer and with samples which the sellers under oath stated "corresponded" with samples approved earlier by the buyer's representative in Barcelona, Supervigilancia had to act to the dissatisfaction of one of the parties to the basic contract. That it took the word, under oath, of the seller as to the appropriateness of the sample is no more than any inspector must ordinarily do. Unless the buyer is physically present . . . the inspector must take someone's word that he is judging by the proper samples. . . .

We see no significant difference in Supervigilancia being told by the manufacturers that the samples were those approved by the buyer and being told that they "corresponded" to such samples. . . .

To hold otherwise—that a buyer could frustrate an international transaction on the eve of fulfillment by a challenge to authenticity of sample—would make vulnerable many such arrangements where third parties are vested by buyers with inspection responsibilities but where, apart from their own competence and integrity, there is no iron-clad guarantee of the sample itself. . . .

We hold, therefore, that the inspection certificate in this case conformed in all significant respects to the requirements of the letter of credit. . . .

[Judgment reversed and action remanded.]

QUESTIONS AND CASE PROBLEMS

1. King was the president of Magnolia Swift Homes, Inc., a construction company. The corporation purchased building materials from John A. Denies Sons Co. King personally guaranteed that payment would be made for the purchases of Magnolia. Later Magnolia went through bankruptcy and was discharged. John A. Denies then sued King on his guaranty. King claimed that since the debt which he guaranteed had been discharged in bankruptcy, there was nothing for which he was liable. Decide. [King v John A. Denies Sons Co., 56 Tenn App 39, 404 SW2d 580]
2. A. D. Runnels purchased goods from J. R. Watkins Co. He asked Hinds Runnels to sign a paper. This paper was, in fact, an agreement to guarantee that Hinds would pay for whatever A. D. Runnels would purchase from Watkins. When sued on this promise by Watkins, Hinds raised the defense that he signed some paper but did not know what he was signing. Was this a valid defense? [J. R. Watkins Co. v A. D. Runnels, 252 Miss 87, 172 So2d 567]
3. Henry Platt, who did business under the name of Platt Fur Co., owed money to The Finance Company of America. The financing statements filed by the latter to protect its interests described the debtor as Platt Fur Co. When Henry Platt went into bankruptcy, it was claimed that this financing statement was not sufficient because it was not in the name of Henry Platt. Decide. [In re Platt, (DC ED Pa) 257 F Supp 478]
4. The Minneapolis-Moline Co. gave Shepler a dealer's franchise to sell its farm equipment. Shepler went bankrupt and the equipment that he had on hand,

which had come from Minneapolis-Moline, was claimed by the trustee in bankruptcy because Minneapolis-Moline had failed to file to protect its interest in the equipment. The manufacturer claimed that it did not have to file because there is no necessity for filing to perfect "a purchase money security interest in farm equipment." Was this contention valid? [In re Shepler, (DC ED Pa) 54 Berks Col LJ 110, 58 Lanc L Rev 43]

5. The Northwest Recapping Inc. negotiated with Industrial Credit Co. to obtain loans on the security of its accounts receivable. In order to persuade Industrial to enter into such an agreement, Dahmes executed a "guarantee" of the repayment of any such loans. The guarantee stated that the liability of Dahmes was "direct and unconditional" and "may be enforced without requiring lender first to resort to any other right, remedy, or security." Under the applicable local statute, the loans made by Industrial were usurious, but under the same law Northwest Recapping could not raise the defense of usury because a statute prohibited corporations from raising such a defense. Later, when Industrial Credit sued Dahmes, he contended that his undertaking under the "guarantee" was his own personal contract so that he, as an individual, could assert the defense of usury. Decide. [Dahmes v Industrial Credit Company, 261 Minn 26, 110 NW2d 484]

6. Are any of the following statements sufficient for a description of the collateral subject to a security interest:

(a) "Passenger and commercial automobiles financed by Girard Trust Corn Exchange Bank?" [Girard Trust Corn Exchange Bank v Warren Lepley Ford, Inc., No. 2, (Pa) 13 D&C 2d 119]

(b) "All present and future accounts receivable?" [Industrial Packaging Products Co. v Fort Pitt Packaging International, Inc., 399 Pa 643, 161 A2d 19]

(c) A description of an automobile that does not contain a serial number? [Girard Trust Corn Exchange Bank v Warren Lepley Ford, Inc., No. 2, (Pa) 13 D&C 2d 119]

7. Lambert loaned Heaton $25,000 for six months. Heaton gave a promissory note, payable at the end of six months, in the face amount of $30,000, thereby concealing the fact that usurious interest was charged. Under the local statute, the loan contract was, in fact, void, because of the usury. Heaton obtained a bond from the United Bonding Insurance Co., which guaranteed to Lambert that the promissory note would be paid when due. When the note was not paid, Lambert sued Heaton and the bonding company. The latter raised the defense that its obligation was voided because the usurious character of the transaction had not been disclosed to it. Decide. [Lambert v Heaton, (Fla App) 134 So2d 536]

8. McDivitt purchased two trucks from Harris Ford, Inc., under "bailment leases" which provided for the obtaining of title by McDivitt after the "rentals" paid under the leases reached a specified amount. Harris Ford sold its rights under the sales contract and bailment leases to the Universal C.I.T. Credit Corporation. Thereafter, McDivitt failed to pay the installments when due and was notified that if he did not pay up the back installments by a specified date, action would be taken by the finance company to enforce its rights. Subsequent thereto, but before any such action was taken,

McDivitt was fined for having the two trucks driven with excess loads in violation of the Motor Vehicle Code. As the fine was not paid for this offense, the two trucks were put up for sale under the provisions of the local statute. This was proper if McDivitt was the owner of the trucks. The finance company objected that it was the owner and therefore the enforcement proceeding was illegal. Decide. [Commonwealth v Two Ford Trucks, 185 Pa Super 292, 137 A2d 847]

9. Bank *B* loaned money to luncheonette *L*. *B* and *L* executed a security agreement giving *B* a security interest in "all of the contents of the luncheonette including equipment." *B* filed in the proper office a financing statement in which the collateral was described in the same manner as in the security agreement. Thereafter *S* sold *L* a cash register on credit and delivered it on the first of the month. When *L* did not pay the monthly installment on its loan from *B*, *B* took possession of the luncheonette equipment including the cash register. *S* claimed that it was entitled to the cash register. Decide. [National Cash Register Co. v Firestone & Co., 346 Mass 255, 191 NE2d 47]

10. Tiernan Building Corporation contracted with a builder, American Structures, Inc., for the construction of a building. A performance bond was executed by the Equitable First & Marine Insurance Company. The contract between the owner and the contractor stated that the building plans could not be changed without Equitable's consent. The contract specified that General Electric air conditioning units were to be installed. The contractor installed a different brand of units. This was done with Tiernan's consent but without the consent of Equitable. The substitute equipment was not satisfactory and had to be replaced. Tiernan sued Equitable for the cost of substituting new replacement units. Was Equitable liable? [Equitable Fire & Marine Ins. Co. v Tiernan Building Corp., (Fla App) 190 So2d 197]

11. The Girard Trust Corn Exchange Bank financed the purchase of new cars by Warren Lepley Ford, Inc., an automobile dealer. A security agreement was executed between the bank and the dealer, and proper filing was made. Thereafter, the dealer sold the cars that had been purchased as the result of this transaction with the bank and then purchased other cars with the proceeds of the money. Warren Lepley later became insolvent. Girard Trust claimed that it was entitled to a security interest in the subsequently-purchased cars in the hands of the receiver. The receiver contended that the right of the bank did not go beyond the cash proceeds and was lost once the cash proceeds were spent in any way. Decide. [Girard Trust Corn Exchange Bank v Warren Lepley Ford, Inc., No 3, (Pa) 25 D&C 2d 395]

12. Muska borrowed money from the Bank of California. He secured the loan by giving the bank a security interest in equipment and machinery which he had at his place of business. The bank filed a financing statement to perfect this interest. The statement contained all the information required by the Code except that it failed to state the residence address of the debtor. Muska went bankrupt. The trustee in bankruptcy claimed that the security interest of the bank was not perfected on the theory that the omission of the residence address from the financing statement made it defective. Was the bank's interest perfected? [Lines v Bank of California, (CA9 Cal) 467 F2d 1274]

37 Insurance

§ 37:1. Nature of Insurance. *Insurance* is a contract by which a promise is made to pay another a sum of money if the latter sustains a specified loss.[1] Insurance is basically a plan of security against risk by charging losses against a fund created by the *premiums* or payments made by many individuals. The promisor is called the *insurer,* sometimes the underwriter. The person to whom the promise is made is the *insured,* the assured, or the policyholder. The promise of the insurer is generally set forth in a contract called a *policy*.

§ 37:2. The Parties. As the result of statutory regulation, virtually all insurance policies are today written by corporations, fraternal or benefit societies, and national or state governments.

The insured must have the capacity to make a contract. If a minor procures insurance, the policy is generally voidable by him.[2]

Insurance contracts are ordinarily made through an agent or a broker. The agent is an agent of the insurance company, generally working exclusively for one company. For the most part, the ordinary rules of agency law determine the effect of his dealings with the applicant for insurance.

An *insurance broker* is ordinarily an independent contractor. He is not employed by any one insurance company. He is the agent for the insured in obtaining insurance for him. In some instances, however, the broker is regarded as the agent of the insurance company when this will permit the conclusion that the insurance company is bound by the act of the broker. Some state statutes treat the broker as an agent of the insurer, declaring in effect that payments made to him are payments to the insurer.

§ 37:3. Insurable Interest. The insured must have an insurable interest in the subject matter insured. If he does not, he cannot enforce the insurance contract.[3]

---

[1] Barry's Estate, 208 Okla 8, 252 P2d 437.

[2] In an increasing number of states, however, statutes make a minor's contract of insurance binding as though he were an adult. The lowering in most states of the age of majority from 21 to 18 years will in many instances avoid the question of the effect of minority upon an insurance contract as the person will no longer be deemed a minor.

[3] Grider v Twin City Fire Insurance Co., (Mo App) 426 SW2d 698.

(1) Insurable Interest in Property. A person has an insurable interest in property whenever he has any right or interest in the property so that its destruction or damage will cause him a direct pecuniary or money loss.[4]

A partner has an insurable interest in property owned by the partnership, as its destruction would cause him an actual and substantial economic loss.[5] This is so even though with respect to "ownership," it is the partnership which owns the property.

It is immaterial whether the insured is the owner of the legal or equitable title, a lienholder, or a person in possession of the property. Thus, a person who is merely a possessor, such as the innocent purchaser of a stolen automobile, has an insurable interest therein.[6] Likewise, a contractor remodeling a building has an insurable interest in the building to the extent of the money that will be paid him under the contract, because he would not be able to receive that money if the building were destroyed by fire.[7]

In the case of property insurance, the insurable interest must exist at the time the loss occurs.[8] (See p. 739, Universal C.I.T. Credit Corp. v Foundation Reserve Insurance Co.) Except when expressly required by statute, it is not necessary that the interest exist at the time when the policy or contract of insurance was made.

(2) Insurable Interest in Life. Every person has an insurable interest in his own life and may therefore insure his own life and name anyone he chooses as beneficiary.

A person has an insurable interest in the life of another if he can expect to receive pecuniary gain from the continued life of the other person and, conversely, would suffer financial loss from the latter's death. Thus, it is held that a creditor has an insurable interest in the life of his debtor since the death of the debtor may mean that the creditor will not be paid the amount owed him. The creditor may take out insurance in excess of the amount of the debt; but if the amount of the insurance is unreasonably greater than the debt, the policy will generally be void.

A partnership has an insurable interest in the life of each of the partners, for the death of any one of them will dissolve the firm and cause some degree of loss to the partnership. A business enterprise has an insurable interest in the life of an executive or a key employee because his death would inflict a financial loss upon the business to the extent that he could not be replaced or could not readily be replaced.

---

[4] Closuit v Mitby, 238 Minn 274, 56 NW2d 428; Royal Insurance Co. v Sisters of the Presentation, (CA9 Cal) 430 F2d 759.

[5] Georgia Farm Bureau Mut. Ins. Co. v Mikell, 126 Ga App 640, 191 SE2d 557.

[6] Perrotta v Empire Mutual Insurance Co., 62 Misc 2d 925, 310 NYS2d 393; although on appeal it was held that there was no insurable interest because the insured failed to show that he was an innocent purchaser. 35 App Div 2d 961, 317 NYS2d 779. A few states hold that the purchaser does not have an insurable interest.

[7] Reishus v Implement Dealers Mutual Insurance Co., (ND) 118 NW2d 673.

[8] In some jurisdictions this rule is declared by statute. Fenter v General Accident Fire and Life Assurance Corp., 258 Ore 545, 484 P2d 310.

In the case of life insurance the insurable interest must exist at the time the policy is obtained. It is immaterial that the interest no longer exists when the loss is actually sustained. Thus, the fact that the insured husband and wife beneficiary are divorced after the life insurance policy was procured does not affect the validity of the policy.

Whether a person has an insurable interest is a matter to be raised by the insurance company. It cannot be raised by one beneficiary seeking to disqualify another beneficiary.[9]

Where an insurer issues a policy to a beneficiary who has no insurable interest in the insured's life and particularly when it does so without the consent of the insured, it has been held that the insurer is liable for tort damages to the estate of the insured when the beneficiary thereafter kills the insured in order to collect on the insurance.[10]

§ 37:4. The Insurance Contract. The formation of the contract of insurance is governed by the general principles applicable to contracts. Frequently a question arises as to whether advertising material, estimates, and statistical projections constitute a part of the contract. (See p. 738, Martell v National Guardian Life Insurance Company.)

By statute it is now commonly provided that an insurance policy must be written. In order to avoid deception, many statutes also specify the content of certain policies, in whole or in part, and some even specify the size and style of type to be used in printing them. Provisions in a policy in conflict with a statute are generally void.[11]

In the absence of statute or government regulation, an insurer may enter into a contract of insurance on such terms and upon such examination as it deems fit. An insurer that sold air flight insurance through a vending machine was held not liable to surviving heirs of other passengers killed when the insured caused the plane to crash. The fact that the insurer did not screen persons purchasing flight insurance to determine the existence of any suicide or murder potential did not make the insurer liable for negligence.[12]

(1) The Application as Part of the Contract. In many instances the application for insurance is attached to the policy when issued and is made part of the contract of insurance by express stipulation of the policy. When a policy is delivered to an insured, he must examine the policy and the attached application and is bound by any false statement which appears in the application if he retains the policy and attached application without making objection to such statement.[13]

---

[9] Mullenax v National Reserve Life Insurance Co., 29 Colo App 418, 485 P2d 137.

[10] Ramay v Carolina Life Ins. Co., 244 SC 16, 135 SE2d 362.

[11] Herbert L. Farkas Co. v New York Fire Insurance Co., 5 NJ 604, 76 A2d 895.

[12] Galanis v Mercury International Insurance Underwriters, 247 Cal App 2d 690, 55 Cal Rptr 890.

[13] Odom v Insurance Co. of State of Pennsylvania, (Tex) 455 SW2d 195.

§ 37:5. When the Insurance Contract Is Effective. An applicant for insurance may or may not be protected by insurance before a formal written policy is issued to him. Four situations may arise:

(1) When the applicant tells a broker to obtain property or liability insurance, the applicant is merely making the broker his agent.[14] If the broker procures a policy, the customer is insured. If the broker fails to do so, the customer does not have any insurance. But the broker may be personally liable to the customer for the loss.

(2) The person seeking insurance and the insurer or its agent may orally agree that the applicant will be protected by insurance during the interval between the time the application is received and the time when the insurer either rejects the application, or accepts it and issues a policy. This agreement to protect the applicant by insurance during such an interval is binding even though it is oral.[15] Generally, however, when such a preliminary contract is made, the agent will sign a memorandum stating the essential terms of the policy to be executed. This memorandum is a *binder*.[16]

An "oral binder" of insurance is a temporary contract which terminates when the written policy contemplated by it is issued. In some states a maximum duration for an oral contract of insurance is set by statute. (See p. 740, Flester v Ohio Cas. Ins. Co.)

(3) The parties may agree that at a later time a policy will be issued and delivered. In that case the insurance contract is not in effect until the policy is delivered or sent to the applicant. Accordingly, loss sustained after the transaction between the applicant and the insurance agent but before the delivery of the policy is not covered by the policy thereafter delivered.

(4) The parties may agree that a policy of life insurance shall be binding upon the payment of the first premium even though the applicant has not been examined, provided he thereafter passes an examination. Under such an agreement the applicant is ordinarily covered by insurance when he dies before the examination, if it can be shown that he would have passed a fair examination.

When the application clearly states that the policy is not in force until the applicant is approved as a risk by an authorized officer of the insurer, coverage is not effective at the time of paying the first premium and submitting the application to the soliciting agent even though the latter wrongly informs the applicant that he is covered by the policy.[17]

(1) Delivery of Policy. Ordinarily delivery of the policy is not essential to the existence of a contract of insurance. Thus, there may be an interim or temporary oral contract or binder of insurance or a contract based upon the

---

[14] General Accident Assurance Co. v Caldwell, (CA9 Cal) 59 F2d 473.
[15] Overton v Washington National Insurance Co., 106 RI 387, 260 A2d 444.
[16] Altrocchi v Hammond, 17 Ill App 2d 192, 149 NE2d 646.
[17] Elliott v Interstate Life & Accident Insurance Co., 211 Va 240, 176 SE2d 314.

acceptance by the insurer of the insured's written application.[18] As an exception, delivery of the policy may be made an express condition to coverage.

(2) Prepayment of Premiums. Ordinarily a contract of property insurance exists even though the premium due has not been paid. Thus, it is possible to effect property and liability insurance in most cases by an oral binder or agreement, as by a telephone call. In the case of life insurance policies, it is common to require both delivery of the policy to the insured while in a condition of good health and the prepayment of the first premium on the policy.

(3) When Coverage is Effective. Distinct from the question of when is there a contract of insurance is the question of when does the coverage of the risk commence under a contract of insurance. Some policies of insurance do not cover the specified risk until after a certain period of time has elapsed after the policy becomes binding. That is, there is a waiting period before the contract of insurance provides protection. In most kinds of insurance, the coverage is immediately effective so that there is no waiting period once the insurer has accepted the application and there is a contract of insurance. (See p. 741, Metts v Central Standard Life Ins. Co.)

(4) Machine-Vended Insurance. When insurance is sold by a vending machine, as in the case of air flight insurance, it becomes effective when the applicant places the application and the premium in the machine and receives his receipt.

§ 37:6. Modification of Contract Form. In order to make changes or corrections to the policy, it may not be necessary to issue a new policy. An indorsement on the policy or the execution of a separate *rider* is effective for the purpose of changing the policy.

When a provision of an indorsement conflicts with a provision of the policy the indorsement controls.[19]

§ 37:7. Interpretation of Insurance Contract. The contract of insurance is interpreted by the same rules that govern the interpretation of ordinary contracts. Words are to be given their ordinary meaning and interpreted in the light of the nature of the coverage intended. Thus, an employee who had been killed was not regarded as "disabled" within the meaning of a group policy covering employees.[20]

The courts are increasingly recognizing the fact that most persons obtaining insurance are not specially trained, and therefore the contract of insurance is to be read as it would be understood by the average man or the average businessman rather than by one with technical knowledge of the law.

---

[18] Krause v Washington National Insurance Co., 225 Ore 446, 468 P2d 513.
[19] Zurich Insurance Co. v Bouler, (La App) 198 So2d 129.
[20] Marriot v Pacific National Life Assurance Co., 24 Utah 2d 182, 467 P2d 981.

If there is an ambiguity in the policy, the provision is interpreted against the insurer.[21] In some instances courts will give a liberal interpretation to the policy terms in order to favor the insured or the beneficiary on the basis that the insured did not in fact have a free choice.

When there is any uncertainty as to whether a contract of insurance exists before the delivery of the written policy, the uncertainty will be determined against the insurer and it will be concluded that the policy was effective immediately. If the insurer claims that a statement in the application form bars this conclusion, it is necessary that the provision would have been so understood by a person of ordinary intelligence and knowledge. (See p. 742, Klos v Mobil Oil Co.)

§ **37:8. Antidiscrimination.** A number of state statutes prohibit insurers from refusing to write or renew policies of insurance because of the age, residence, occupation, national origin, or race of the applicant or insured and prohibit the cancellation of a policy except for nonpayment of premiums or, in the case of automobile insurance, the insured's loss of his motor vehicle license or registration.[22]

Statutes also commonly prohibit insurance companies from making premium discriminations among members of the same risk class and from making rebates or refunds to particular individuals only.

§ **37:9. Premiums.** Premiums may be paid by check. If the check is not paid, however, the instrument loses its character as payment.

If the premiums are not paid, the policy will ordinarily lapse because of nonpayment, subject to antilapse statutes or provisions.

(1) Return of Premiums. When an insurance policy is canceled according to the terms of the policy before the expiration of the term for which premiums have been paid, the insurer is required to return such part of the premiums as has not been earned.[23]

(2) Nonforfeiture and Antilapse Provisions. As to the payment of premiums due on life insurance policies subsequent to the first premium, the policies now in general use provide or a statute may specify that the policy shall not automatically lapse upon the date the next premium is due if payment is not then made. By policy provision or statute, the insured is also allowed a *grace period* of 30 to 31 days, in which to make payment of the premium due. When there is a default in the payment of a premium by the insured, the insurer may be required by statute (1) to issue a paid-up policy in a smaller amount, (2) to provide extended insurance for a period of time, or (3) to pay the cash surrender value of the policy.

---

[21] Murray v Western Pacific Insurance Co., 2 Wash App 985, 472 P2d 611. This principle is not applied if the provision in question is in the policy because it is required by statute.

[22] Pennsylvania, 40 PS § 1008.1 et seq.

[23] Jorgensen v St. Paul Fire and Marine Insurance Co., 158 Colo 466, 408 P2d 66.

§ 37:10. Extent of Insurer's Liability. In the case of life and disability insurance, the insurer is required to pay the amount called for by the contract of insurance. When the policy is one to indemnify against loss, the liability of the insurer is to pay only to the extent that the insured sustains loss, subject to a maximum amount stated in the contract. Thus, a fire insurer is liable for only $1,000, even though it has written a $20,000 policy, when the fire loss sustained by the insured is in fact only $1,000. If the loss were $22,000, the liability of the insurer would be only $20,000.

§ 37:11. Cancellation. The contract of insurance may expressly declare that it may or may not be canceled. By statute or policy provision, the insurer is commonly required to give a specific number of days' written notice of a cancellation.

Property and liability insurance policies generally reserve to the insurer the right to cancel the policy upon giving a specified number of days' notice. In some states antidiscrimination statutes restrict the right of insurers to cancel. An insurance company may not exercise its right to cancel the policy when it does so to punish the insured because he appeared as a witness in a case against it.[24]

Only the insured is entitled to notice of cancellation unless the policy or an indorsement expressly declares otherwise. The mere fact that a creditor is entitled to the proceeds of the insurance policy in the case of loss does not in itself entitle him to notice of cancellation.[25]

§ 37:12. Coverage of Policy. When an insurance claim is disputed by the insurer, the person bringing suit has the burden of proving that there was a loss, that it occurred while the policy was in force, and that the loss was of a kind which was within the coverage of the policy. The insurer has the burden of proving that there is no coverage because one of the contract exceptions is applicable,[26] or of proving that there is a defense to the claim of liability on the policy.

§ 37:13. Defenses of the Insurer. The insurer may raise any defense that would be valid in an action upon a contract. Some defenses that do not apply to an action on an ordinary contract may also be raised.

---

[24] L'Orange v Medical Protective Co., (CA6 Ohio) 394 F2d 57.

[25] Ford Motor Credit Co. v Commonwealth County Mutual Insurance Co., (Tex Civ App) 420 SW2d 732.

[26] Phoenix Insurance Co. v Branch, (Fla App) 234 So2d 396.

CASES FOR CHAPTER 37

Martell v National Guardian Life Insurance Co.

27 Wis 2d 164, 133 NW2d 721 (1965)

Martell obtained two policies of life insurance from the National Guardian Life Insurance Co. Attached by a paper clip to one of the policies was a specimen value sheet showing that if dividends were left with the company by Martell, the policies would become paid-up endowment policies when he attained the

age of 66. When he attained that age, he sued for the combined face value of the two policies, $10,000. National denied that the policies were paid-up endowments, denied that the specimen value sheet was part of its obligation, and offered to pay only the cash surrender value of the policies with dividends and interest. From a decision in favor of National, Martell appealed.

HALLOWS, J. . . . Each policy provided the attached application, and the policy constituted the entire contract between the parties. . . .

Assuming the specimen value sheet was clipped to one of the policies at the time of delivery as the plaintiff's version has it, we do not find sufficient credible evidence that the parties intended it to be a part of their contract. The specimen value sheet was not issued by the home office of the defendant and was not on the policy when received by Smith, the agent. . . . We construe the language "this policy" to include and refer only to the printed policy issued at the home office. Under this interpretation, the printed policy plus the application by its terms constitute the entire contract between the parties. Any contemporaneous document to be a part of the contract would require thereon the signature of the president, secretary, or treasurer. Here, we have but one specimen value sheet for two policies attached to one only by a paper clip, bearing a date of ten days prior to the date of the printed policy and not signed by a designated officer of the defendant. . . .

The specimen value sheet and the printed policy, considering them contemporaneous documents, are incompatible; and no internal reference in the printed policy is made to or incorporating the specimen value sheet, and likewise no language of incorporation appears in the specimen value sheet. The paper clip hardly performs that function as a matter of law. In addition, the specimen value sheet in effect contradicts the terms of the printed policy. It is argued the specimen value sheet merely particularizes the general language of when the policy matures as an endowment, but this argument assumes the "specimen" is a guaranty. Even if the specimen value sheet were considered a part of the contract, the plaintiff would not be entitled to recovery of the face amount because the language of the specimen value sheet is not promissory in nature but illustrative. . . . In the instant case the sheet plainly states it is a specimen value sheet. No promissory language is to be implied. The data of future values is not guaranteed but illustrates on the basis of assumed facts. . . .

Language in an insurance policy connoting expectancy or illustrative on assumed conditions or facts will not support recovery. . . .

[Judgment affirmed.]

Universal C.I.T. Credit Corp. v Foundation Reserve Insurance Co.

79 NMex 785, 450 P2d 194 (1969)

Norman Bowman purchased an automobile on credit for use by his cousin, Jimmy, but took title in his own name. The Foundation Reserve Insurance Co. issued a policy covering destruction of the car and naming Jimmy as the insured with a clause providing for payment to the finance company. The car was destroyed some time later and the finance company, the Universal C.I.T., sued the insurance company which raised the defense of lack of insurable interest. From a judgment in favor of the insurance company, the finance company appealed.

COMPTON, J. . . . Norman Bowman had purchased the automobile for the benefit of Jimmy Don Bowman, his seventeen-year-old cousin, a student, living with him during the school year 1965-1966, as a means of transportation to and from school and to his work after school. Norman Bowman purchased the vehicle and took title in his name. He alone was liable on the note securing the conditional sales agreement on the automobile.

Appellee's agent with full knowledge that Norman Bowman was the owner of the automobile issued its policy to Jimmy Don Bowman. The agent also knew that Jimmy Don Bowman had no pecuniary interest in the vehicle. A condition of the policy, however, provided that knowledge possessed by the agent would not estop the company from asserting a lack of insurable interest in the named insured.

In May or June, 1966, the school year having ended, Jimmy Don Bowman no longer used the vehicle. He turned it back to Norman

Bowman and returned to the State of Washington to live with his father. He had no intention of ever using the automobile again. In July, 1966, the automobile was totally wrecked in a one-car accident while being driven by a party who had possession of the vehicle with the permission of Norman Bowman for the purpose of "trying it out" as a prospective buyer. . . .

The court concluded that Jimmy Don Bowman had no insurable interest in the automobile. It is argued that Jimmy Don Bowman, the named insured, had an insurable interest in the automobile by virtue of the fact that he might incur liability because of his operation or use of it. . . .

When the insured voluntarily abandoned the use of the vehicle, his insurable interest, if any, ceased to exist. An insurable interest must exist at the time of loss. . . . There was no contractual obligation between Jimmy Don Bowman with anyone. He could not have suffered loss by its destruction. He had no interest in the vehicle and he lost nothing. . . .

[Judgment affirmed.]

Flester v Ohio Casualty Ins. Co.

— Md App —, 307 A2d 663 (1973)

In 1969 Flester obtained an automobile liability policy from the Ohio Casualty Insurance Company covering a 1962 Ford Fairlane and a 1956 Thunderbird. By subsequent indorsement the Thunderbird was removed from the policy and was replaced by a 1967 Mercury Cougar. Three days later the Cougar was damaged and Flester used the Thunderbird in its place. Flester consulted Marton, his insurance broker, and an agreement was reached on August 11, 1969, for temporary insurance covering the Thunderbird. In the following April, 1970, a renewal policy was mailed to Flester covering the Fairlane and the Cougar but saying nothing as to the Thunderbird. No one noticed the identity of the automobiles covered. Flester paid the premium due on the renewal policy and on May 10, 1970, was in a collision with the Thunderbird. He claimed that Ohio Casualty was liable for the damage to the Thunderbird by virtue of the oral contract of insurance which modified the coverage of the original written policy. The insurer denied liability on the oral contract covering the Thunderbird on the ground that the contract had terminated when the renewal policy was issued in April, 1970, and therefore did not provide coverage at the time of the May 10 collision. Judgment was entered for the insurer and Flester appealed.

LEVINE, J. . . . The conversation of August 11, 1969, between Flester and Marton, resulted in a commitment on behalf of Ohio Casualty which, in the parlance of the insurance world, is called a binder. . . . "The term 'binder' has a well-known significance in the parlance of insurance contracts, and a binder or a binding slip is merely a written memorandum of the most important terms of a preliminary contract of insurance intended to give temporary protection pending the investigation of the risk of insurer, or *until the issuance of a formal policy*; a contract is insurance in praesenti, *temporary in its nature,* intended to take the place of an ordinary policy until one can be issued . . . ." . . .

"Frequently, for the purpose of convenience or expediency so that the owner of an automobile may operate it before obtaining the formal policy of insurance, an oral contract of insurance is entered into, or a binding slip, also called a 'binder,' is issued, for the purpose of insuring the vehicle *until the actual issuance and delivery of the policy* to the insured. As in the case of other types of insurance, it is settled generally that such a contract is valid and binds the insurer *until the issuance and delivery of the policy agreed upon.*" . . .

Clearly, what occurred in this case differs from the commonly-accepted situation outlined above. The underlying thrust of Flester's appeal is the contention that the parties—on August 11, 1969—entered into a separate oral contract, not one which was to terminate upon the issuance of a written policy, but rather upon the replacement of a vehicle which was, itself, not covered by the oral agreement. . . .

By its very definition, a binder is intended to be temporary; and some states have even enacted statutes restricting the length of time during which a binder may remain in force. . . . No such statutory period exists in Maryland; nor did the binder in question here specify a termination date. In such situations elsewhere, the binder's coverage has been held to extend until issuance of the formal policy, . . . or until the passage of a reasonable time to investigate the risk and communicate a rejection to the applicant. . . . In 9 Couch on Insurance 2d, [Anderson Edition] § 39:207 (1962), it is stated: "Since parol contracts of insurance *usually cover the time necessarily elapsing between the placing of the insurance and the issuing of the policy,* the duration is ordinarily for such period of time as is a reasonable one under the circumstances for the issuance of a formal policy. The preliminary or temporary contract is therefore effective *until either superseded by a policy,* when issued, or terminated by a rejection of the application, and notice thereof to the insured, or by the expiration of the time specified in the preliminary or temporary contract, or of a reasonable time, when none is specified." . . .

As we have stressed, the outcome of the August 11 discussion between Flester and Marton does not reflect the concept of a typical automobile insurance binder, i.e., temporary insurance designed to afford protection for a relatively brief time span. This period usually covers the interval between the application for the insurance and the issuance of a formal policy. It is in this context that binders are normally regarded as expiring "upon the issuance of the policy." While the agreement in this case may not fit into one of the conventional molds, it is no less a binder. The thread that runs through the various definitions of this term is the *temporary* coverage that is provided by the insurer.

Here, the issuance of a new policy covering the Thunderbird was never intended; the binder was only given "with respect to" the policy already in existence. In other words, the binder was intended by the parties to be effective, as Judge McCullough said, during "a period of time when either the Cougar would have been replaced or repaired." With the passage of the relatively short time period intended for either eventuality, however, and without any word from Flester, the binder's existence terminated upon the expiration of the policy which it had *temporarily* modified. At that point, it was "superseded" by the formal policy issued on April 21, 1970. That Flester failed to note what automobiles were listed in that policy does not defeat its operativeness, and he is bound by its description of the insured vehicles. . . .

Under the view we adopt here, there could not have been an independent insurance contract covering the Thunderbird, to expire on some future date when the *Cougar* was ultimately replaced. That argument is contrary to the concept of temporary coverage inherent in the binder, and would, in effect, establish an oral policy of indefinite duration. As Judge McCullough so aptly observed, under this view "the binder goes on and on and on, it would, in effect, still be in force today." . . .

[Judgment affirmed.]

Metts v Central Standard Life Insurance Co.

142 Cal App 2d 445, 298 P2d 621 (1956)

Metts filled out a printed application form for polio insurance distributed by the Central Standard Life Insurance Co. He mailed the application to the company on May 15. It was received by the company on May 23. On May 21, Metts' son was stricken with polio, of which the insurer was notified on May 28. The company refused to pay on the ground that it had not accepted the application. Metts sued the insurer. From a judgment in favor of Metts, the insurer appealed.

BRAY, J. . . . The application form, on its reverse side, stated: "Infantile Paralysis. Immediate First Day Coverage Automatically Covers Entire Family." "No Waiting Period." "Pays from *First Day* that poliomyelitis manifests itself and thereafter, as provided. . . ."

Plaintiff contends that the application form itself was an offer to contract which was accepted by him; that the above mentioned wording on the back of the form caused him to believe that when he mailed the completed form and premium payment, the contract was then in effect and that he was immediately covered.

Defendant contends that there was no representation that the policy would take effect as of the date of the application, and that the application was an offer by the insured not accepted until a policy was issued. . . .

"Because contracts of insurance are not the result of negotiation and are generally drawn by the insurer, any uncertainties or ambiguities therein are resolved most strongly in favor of the insured. . . ."

Our first task is to determine, then, whether there is any uncertainty or ambiguity in the language of the application. . . . The only language [of the application form] important here is that above quoted appearing on the reverse side: "*Immediate* First Day Coverage *Automatically* Covers Entire Family." (Emphasis added.) The use of the words "immediate" and "automatically" in these phrases is difficult to explain as having any meaning other than that the coverage commences from the date of the application. At least, a reasonable conclusion is, that did these phrases apply to the first day of sickness rather than the first day of coverage, there would be no need for the words "immediate" and "automatically." The policy when issued would state that it covered illness from the first day of illness and covered the entire family. The form further states: "Pays from *First Day* that poliomyelitis manifests itself. . . ." In view of that statement, what is the meaning of the words "immediate First Day Coverage" if not coverage immediately upon signing?

Under the rule above mentioned such words are fairly capable of an interpretation which would afford the greater measure of protection to the insured. A layman could hardly be expected to give any other interpretation. . . . We are therefore required to hold that the application form constituted an offer by defendant of coverage to take effect immediately upon the signing and posting of the application. . . .

[Judgment affirmed.]

Klos v Mobil Oil Co.

55 NJ 117, 259 A2d 889 (1969)

Klos applied for life insurance issued through the Mobil Oil Company to its credit card holders. The company sent an advertising brochure to holders of its credit card soliciting their applications for insurance. The brochure stated that policies would become effective seven days before the next credit card billing date. Klos mailed an application for insurance on October 8. The next billing date for him was October 17, which would make October 10 the effective date of the policy. However, the printed application which he sent for the insurance stated that the coverage was not effective until the policy was issued. The policy was issued to Klos and received by him on October 25 but it specified that it would not be effective until November 10. On October 28 Klos fell at home and died therefrom. The insurance company refused to pay his beneficiary under the policy because the policy specified that it would not be effective until November 10. The beneficiary sued claiming that the policy was in effect on October 28 because it had become effective either on October 10 or on October 25. From a judgment for Mobil Oil, the beneficiary appealed.

PROCTOR, J. . . . Plaintiff's husband, Stanley Klos, . . . was the holder of a Mobil Oil Company credit card. The billing date for charges accruing under the credit card was the 17th of each month. With his September 1964 billing, Klos received a letter, a brochure, and an application form soliciting him, as a Mobil credit cardholder, to purchase an accident insurance policy from American [Home Assurance Company]. . . .

The issue raised by this case is the effective date of the policy coverage. There are a number of possibilities suggested in the various pieces of literature and documents which American issued. The letter accompanying the brochure and the application form did not contain any date of coverage, but the brochure provided that the accident policy "will become effective 7 days prior to your next Mobil billing date following receipt of your application." The brochure also stated that the insured would be given a "10-day right to study policy . . . to be sure the coverage meets your expectations. If you are not satisfied, return it and there will be no charge to you and no obligation on your part."

The application form which Klos signed on October 8 contained the following printed statement immediately above his signature: "I understand that coverage is not effective until policy is issued." Finally, on October 20 the insurance company mailed out the policy to Klos in an envelope on which was printed, "Important—Your Insurance Policy is Enclosed!" The policy contained the same ten-day examination period that appeared in the brochure. On the first page under the caption "Coverage Schedule" the "Effective Date" for coverage was specified as November 10, 1964.

. . . The plaintiff first contended that the policy was effective as of October 10 in accordance with the language of the brochure. She reasoned that the decedent was covered seven days prior to the billing date following American's receipt of the application. . . . In the alternative, she argued that, in accordance with the language of the application, the policy was at least effective as of the date of its issuance on October 20.

The trial court rejected both contentions. It reasoned that the October 10 date could not govern since the clause in the brochure is ambiguous and must be subordinated to the language of the application, particularly since the plaintiff conceded in her affidavit that her husband did not rely on the brochure's clause. The court also rejected the October 20 date and concluded that the specific date of November 10 in the policy should govern. Since the decedent's alleged accident occurred before November 10, the court held that there could be no recovery. The Appellate Division affirmed, substantially for the reasons expressed by the trial court. We disagree with these conclusions and accordingly reverse.

At the outset we note that the techniques used in marketing the insurance we are dealing with here are quite different from the traditional methods and have become widespread through the growing use of credit cards. Companies which issue credit cards, such as Mobil Oil Company, frequently mail out literature soliciting cardholders to purchase various commodities to be billed through their credit facilities. In the present case, the literature, which included a letter, a brochure, and an application, solicited Mobil's cardholders to purchase accident insurance from American. The brochure and the letter provided for "easy payments" to be billed through the cardholder's Mobil account. The letter says that the brochure "fully describes the plan." The brochure reads:

> "YOUR COVERAGE IS ALL-RISK
>
> . . .
>
> There are no restrictions on occupation, age or travel. THERE ARE ONLY TWO POLICY EXCLUSIONS—SUICIDE AND WAR."
>
> "EASY APPLICATION . . .
>
> No physical examinations . . . no health or credit questions. Choose the plan that meets your needs . . . Fill in the enclosed application form . . . Date and sign it . . . Mail it in the postage-paid envelope TODAY!"

The customer is urged to act quickly. He is warned in the brochure that "[e]very 6 minutes someone meets with accidental death" and he is told that there will be "[*n*]o red tape." There are no further steps required of the cardholder after he has mailed in the completed application. The letter says that the defendant insurer "takes pride in *offering* you" its policy, and the brochure commences with the phrase "Now *offered* to you" (emphasis added).

It is true, as American contends, that generally an application for insurance constitutes an offer to the insurer which it may accept or reject. . . . This rule affords an insurer an opportunity to determine whether an application is a desirable risk. But we do not believe the rule is applicable to the present case.

The accident insurance here is available to Mobil credit cardholders irrespective of their age or health. There is no requirement of a physical examination presumably because the policy is limited to death or certain injuries resulting from an accident. Nor are there credit rating questions to be examined by the insurer. Apparently, American is willing to rely on the credit screening techniques employed by Mobil Oil prior to issuing credit cards to its customers. Moreover, the scope of coverage is fully spelled out in the literature accompanying the application. Nothing is left open for future negotiations with reference to the subject matter, parties, rate of premium, amount, or duration of risk. In short, there is nothing for a cardholder or American to do after the application is made other than the latter's purely mechanical operation of processing the matter. In these circumstances we believe that the sending of the letter, brochure, and application form constituted an offer by American which could be accepted by Kløs.

When Klos mailed in his completed application, he accepted American's offer and a contract for insurance was consummated with all of the essential elements agreed upon. . . . To hold otherwise would be to allow an insurance company to postpone the date of the coverage it had promised even though it had nothing more to do than merely process the completed application. . . . Once the contract for insurance was consummated, American was obligated to issue the policy it had promised. . . . ". . . Where . . . the parties agree in writing upon specific terms of the coverage, the Company cannot avoid liability by issuing a policy which does not cover the risk contemplated . . . . It cannot promise one contract and fulfill it with another." . . . Therefore, we conclude that if the date of coverage in the policy varies from the date which the parties agreed upon in their contract for insurance, the date in the policy is not binding on the plaintiff. . . .

American attempts to avoid this conclusion by contending that their solicitation could not constitute an offer because the application form gave the cardholder a choice of coverage. We do not agree. The literature and application form listed four plans of coverage; each of these plans constituted a separate offer to the cardholder which he was free to accept or reject.

It is not enough, however, to conclude that the parties had entered into a contract for insurance. We must still determine whether the date of coverage in the contract differs from that in the policy. As we have said, there are a number of possibilities suggested in the brochure, the application and the policy. The policy specified the effective coverage date as November 10, 1964, subsequent to decedent's alleged accident on October 25. On the other hand, the brochure would seem to suggest that the coverage was effective as of October 10, 1964, prior to the alleged accident. The brochure stated that coverage would become effective seven days prior to the Mobil billing date following receipt of his application. Since the application was received on October 16 and the next billing date was October 17, the brochure, taken alone, would afford coverage as of October 10.

American argues that the brochure cannot be taken alone but must be construed in conjunction with the provision in the application which informed the decedent that coverage would not be effective until the policy issued. It reasons that coverage could not be effective on October 10, since the policy had not yet issued. The next billing date which would permit a full seven day period to elapse after issuance of the policy would be November 17. Therefore, coverage would become effective November 10, the date specified in the policy. We do not believe that the provisions of the brochure and the application can be construed together to arrive at the same date. They are in conflict. The brochure does not refer to the next billing date following *issuance* of the policy; it refers to the billing date following *receipt* of the application. As we have said, taken alone, the brochure suggests an effective coverage date of October 10. At most, this seven day clause is ambiguous and, under well settled principles, should be construed in favor of the insured. . . . Nevertheless, it is unnecessary to rest our decision on this point. The application form which Klos signed informed him that coverage would not be effective until the policy issued. Since the alleged accident occurred after the policy was issued, the conflict of coverage dates between the brochure and the application does not affect the result of this case. Under either of these dates plaintiff would be entitled to recover if her husband's death was accidental.

American contends that the application form did not guarantee coverage *when* the policy was issued, but only cautioned the applicant that he would not be covered *before* the policy was issued. . . . Although the application form in the present case stated that there would be no coverage "until" the policy issued, we believe that the average layman who reads that phrase reasonably expects he will be covered when he receives his policy. That expectation is particularly well founded where, as here, the literature which was issued by American stressed the urgency of procuring coverage as soon as possible. The whole tone of its solicitation was one of speed. It promised that there would be "[*n*]*o* red tape." Moreover, as we have said, neither the applicant nor the insurer had anything more to do, particularly after the policy was issued. In such circumstances, an applicant who actually had the policy in his possession surely would be mystified to learn that for no apparent reason he was not covered until some future date. As we have continually emphasized, members of the public who purchase insurance policies are entitled to the full measures of protection necessary to meet their reasonable expectations. . . .

. . . By affording the insured an inspection period, American hoped that the latter would make his objections known at that time. This assumption is not founded in sound reason. . . . In the present case, Klos was told that he was entitled to inspect the policy for ten days without charge or obligation. Certainly a person receiving this advice would reasonably consider himself covered for the ten day inspection period, and here, plaintiff has alleged that her husband died as the result of an accident incurred within that period.

Finally, the ten day inspection period refutes defendant's argument that Klos was obligated to read the policy and report any deficiencies. There is, of course, no way of knowing for certain whether Klos read his policy after receiving it. Plaintiff's affidavit implies that he did not read it. We think it is immaterial. We need not decide whether Klos would have been obligated to read the policy at some later date for it is clear that, at the least, he was entitled to a full ten day period in which to do so. That he had his alleged accident during this period does not detract from this right which American expressly gave to him. . . .

[Reversed and action remanded.]

QUESTIONS AND CASE PROBLEMS

1. Rebecca Foster obtained a policy of life insurance from the United Insurance Co. insuring the life of Lucille McClurkin and naming herself as beneficiary. Lucille did not live with Rebecca, and Rebecca did not inform Lucille of the existence of the policy. Rebecca paid the premiums on the policy, and on the death of Lucille sued the United Insurance Co. for the amount of the insurance. At the trial, Rebecca testified vaguely that her father had told her that Lucille was her second cousin on his side of the family. Was Rebecca entitled to recover on the policy? [Foster v United Insurance Co., 250 SC 423, 158 SE2d 201]

2. A policy of insurance had the words "double indemnity" across the top imprinted with a rubber stamp. Nothing was said in the policy about double indemnity. When a loss was sustained, the insured claimed that he was entitled to double indemnity. Was he correct? [Niewoehner v Western Life Insurance Co., 149 Mont 57, 422 P2d 644]

3. On October 29, Griffin sent an application for life insurance and the first premium to the Insurance Company of North America. In the application, her son, Carlisle Moore, was named as beneficiary. On November 25 of the same year, Griffin died. On November 26, the company rejected the application and notified the broker who took the application, who in turn notified Moore by letter dated November 30. Moore sued the company for breach of contract. Decide. [Moore v Insurance Co. of North America, 49 Ill App 2d 287, 200 NE2d 1]

4. Lisle applied for life insurance with the Federal Life & Casualty Co. Both Lisle and his wife made false, fraudulent statements to the insurer in connection with the application. The insurer's physician examined Lisle twice but did not ascertain anything that revealed the falsity of those statements. After the insured's death about a year later, the insurer denied liability on the ground of fraud. Lisle's widow claimed that the insurer could not raise the question of fraud since it had examined the insured before accepting his application. Was the insurer liable? [Federal Life & Casualty Co. v Lisle, 140 Ohio 2d 269, 172 NE2d 919]

5. Moore's wife applied for accident insurance on her husband. She paid the premium due. Unknown to her, the application was rejected. However, when she inquired of the agent as to the status of the application, the agent said that he had had no word. When she inquired some time later, the agent said he thought that the policy had come in and, if it had not, she would be notified in a few days. She heard nothing. Two weeks later her husband was killed accidentally. After his death the insurance company informed her that the application had been rejected. She sued the insurance company. Decide. [Moore v Palmetto State Life Insurance Co., 222 SC 492, 73 SE2d 688]
6. Einhorn held warehouse receipts as collateral security for a loan that he had made to the prior holder of the receipts. Einhorn obtained a fire insurance policy from the Firemen's Insurance Co., which insured him against loss of the property by fire to the extent of his interest in the collateral. The property represented by the receipts was destroyed by fire. Einhorn assigned his claim on the policy to Flint Frozen Foods, which then sued the insurer. Was the policy obtained by Einhorn valid? [Flint Frozen Foods v Firemen's Insurance Co., 8 NJ 606, 86 A2d 673]
7. Hicks obtained an automobile collision policy from the Alabama Farm Bureau Mutual Casualty Insurance Co. The policy provided that there was no coverage of loss during the period between the expiration of the term of the policy and the date of the actual payment of a renewal premium. Hicks did not pay the renewal premium until several months after the expiration of the policy. During the noncovered period, he was in a collision. When he paid the renewal premium to the agent-manager at the insurer's local office, he informed him of this collision. He then filed a proof of loss for the damage sustained in the collision. The insurer refused to pay the loss. The insured sued the insurer. Decide. [Alabama Farm Bureau Mutual Cas. Ins. Co. v Hicks, 41 Ala App 143, 133 So2d 217]
8. Bondurant obtained a public liability insurance policy from the United States Fidelity and Guarantee Co. Johnson sustained an injury that came within the coverage of the policy and brought suit against Bondurant and U.S.F.&G. Co. While the action was pending, Bondurant was declared a bankrupt and received his discharge in bankruptcy. Because of such discharge, Johnson could not hold Bondurant liable. U.S.F.&G. Co. thereupon claimed that since Bondurant was not liable to Johnson, it was not liable either since its liability was no greater than that of its insured. Decide. [Johnson v Bondurant, (Kan) 359 P2d 861]

38 Kinds of Insurance

FIRE INSURANCE

A *fire insurance policy* is a contract to indemnify the insured for destruction of or damage to property caused by fire. In almost every state the New York standard fire insurance form is the standard policy.

§ 38:1. Nature of Contract.

(1) Actual, Hostile Fire. In order for fire loss to be covered by fire insurance, there must be an actual flame or burning, and the fire must be hostile. The hostile character is easily determined when the fire is caused by accident, such as a short circuit in electric wiring; but it is often difficult to determine when the fire is intentional, as when it is being used for heating or cooking. A *hostile fire* in the latter case is one which to some extent becomes uncontrollable or escapes from the place in which it is intended to be. To illustrate, when soot is ignited and causes a fire in the chimney, the fire is hostile.[1] On the other hand, a loss caused by the smoke or heat of a fire in its ordinary container, which has not broken out or become uncontrollable, results from a *friendly fire*. Consequently, when property is accidentally thrown into the trash and burned, a fire policy does not cover the loss. (See p. 763, Youse v Employers Fire Insurance Co.) By endorsement, the coverage may be and frequently is extended to include such damage.

Damage from heat alone is not covered, but damage from heat or smoke caused by a hostile fire is covered.

(2) Immediate or Proximate Cause. The fire must be the immediate or proximate cause of the loss. In addition to direct destruction or damage by fire, a fire may set in motion a chain of events that damage the property. When there is a reasonable connection between a fire and the ultimate loss sustained, the insurer is liable for the loss.

The New York standard form of fire insurance policy excludes loss or damage caused directly or indirectly by enemy attack by armed forces, invasion, insurrection, rebellion, revolution, civil war, or usurped power, or by order of any civil authority; or by neglect of the insured to use all

[1] Way v Abington Mutual Fire Insurance Co., 166 Mass 67, 43 NE 1032.

reasonable means to save and preserve the property at and after a fire or when the property is endangered by fire in neighboring premises; or by theft.

Damage by explosion is also excluded unless fire follows, and then the insurer is liable only for that part of the damage caused by the fire. The standard form of fire insurance policy includes protection from lightning damage even though no fire is caused thereby.

§ 38:2. Determination of Insurer's Liability. Basically the insurer is liable for the actual amount of the loss sustained. This liability is limited, however, by the maximum amount stated in the policy or the amount of damages sustained by total destruction of the property, whichever is less.

(1) Amount of Loss. The amount of the loss, in the absence of statute or agreement to the contrary, is the actual cash value at the time of the loss. If the insurer and the insured cannot agree, policies commonly provide for the determination of the amount of loss by appraisers or arbitrators.[2]

(2) Total Loss. A *total loss* does not necessarily mean that the property has been completely destroyed. The loss is regarded as being total if the unconsumed portion is of no value for the purposes for which the property was utilized at the time of the insurance. Consequently, the mere fact that some of the walls and the roof remained after the fire did not prove that the loss was not total.[3]

(3) Replacement by Insurer. Frequently the insurer will stipulate in the policy that it has the right to replace or restore the property to its former condition in lieu of paying the insured the cash value of the loss.

(4) Coinsurance. A *coinsurance clause* requires the insured to maintain insurance on his property up to a certain amount or a certain percent of the value, generally 80 percent. Under such a provision, if the policyholder insures his property for less than the required amount, the insurer is liable only for its proportionate share of the amount of insurance required to be carried. To illustrate, suppose the owner of a building valued at $40,000 insures it against loss to the extent of $24,000, and the policy contains a coinsurance clause requiring that insurance of 80 percent of the value of the property be carried. In case a $16,000 loss is sustained, the insured would not receive $16,000 from the insurer but only $12,000 because the amount of insurance he carries ($24,000) is only three fourths of the amount required ($32,000, that is, 80 percent of $40,000).

The use of a coinsurance clause is not permitted in all states. In some states it is prohibited or is permitted only with the consent of the insured.

---

[2] Saba v Homeland Insurance Co., 159 Ohio 237, 112 NE2d 1.

[3] Home Insurance Co. v Greene, (Miss) 229 So2d 576.

§ 38:3. Assignment of Fire Insurance Policy. Fire insurance is a personal contract, and in the absence of statute or contractual authorization it cannot be assigned before a loss is sustained without the consent of the insurer.[4] In addition, it is commonly provided that the policy shall be voided if an assignment to give a purchaser of the property the protection of the policy is attempted. Such a forfeiture clause applies only when the insured attempts to transfer his entire interest in the policy. It does not apply to equitable assignments. To illustrate, if the policy prohibits an assignment before loss, a pledge of the policy as security for a loan by the insured does not constitute a violation of the provision.

§ 38:4. Mortgage Clause. If the insured property is subject to a mortgage, either or both the mortgagor and mortgagee may take out policies of fire insurance to protect their respective interests in the property. Each has an insurable interest therein.[5] In the absence of a contrary stipulation, the policy taken out by either covers only his own interest. That is, the mortgagor's policy protects only the value of his right of redemption or the value of the property in excess of the mortgage, while the policy of the mortgagee covers only the debt. Neither can claim the benefit of insurance money paid to the other.

It is common, however, for the mortgagee to insist as a condition of making the loan that the mortgagor obtain and pay the premiums on a policy covering the full value of the property and providing that in case of loss the insurance money will be paid to the mortgagor and the mortgagee as their respective interests may appear. As the amount of the mortgage debt is reduced, the interest of the mortgagee in the property becomes less and the share of insurance proceeds that he would receive accordingly becomes less. Such a mortgage clause has the advantage of protecting both the mortgagor and mortgagee by one policy and of providing a flexible method of insuring each of them.[6]

§ 38:5. Extended Coverage. The term *extended coverage* generally refers to protection of property against loss from windstorm, hail, explosions other than those within steam boilers on the premises, riot, civil commotion, aircraft damage, vehicle damage, and smoke damage.

(1) Vandalism. A special form of extended coverage may be obtained to protect property from vandalism. Generally this protects from damage to property which breaks or defaces. If vandals burn a building, fire insurance would provide coverage. Likewise, if the harm occurs as part of a riot, standard extended coverage would afford protection.

---

[4] Shadid v American Druggist Fire Insurance Co., (Okla) 386 P2d 311.

[5] Southwestern Graphite Co. v Fidelity & Guaranty Insurance Corp., (CA5 Tex) 201 F2d 553.

[6] Sisk v Rapuano, 94 Conn 294, 108 A 858.

§ 38:6. Other Provisions. Fire insurance policies commonly prohibit the insured from doing certain acts that will or may increase the hazard or risk involved and provide that the policy is void if the insured commits the prohibited acts.

It is commonly provided that false statements made by the insured when they are known to be false shall avoid the policy. Under such a provision a fraudulent misstatement of the value of the property avoids the policy.

The insured may take out more than one policy on the same property, in the absence of a provision in any of the policies to the contrary; but in the event of loss he cannot recover more than the total loss he sustains. Such a loss is prorated among the insurers.

An insurer is not liable when the damage or destruction of the property is intentionally caused by the insured. The fact that the insured negligently caused a fire is not a defense to the insurer, even when there is a stipulation that the insured shall not change or increase the hazard insured against.

§ 38:7. Cancellation. It is common to provide by statute or by the terms of the policy that under certain circumstances the policy may be terminated or canceled by the act of one party alone. When this is done, the provisions of the statute and the policy must be strictly followed in order to make the cancellation effective.[7]

The provision governing a cancellation of a policy may be waived. Thus, when a policy requires five days' notice by the insurer but it gives only three days' notice, the insured waives the notice requirement if he surrenders the policy for cancellation without objection.[8]

AUTOMOBILE INSURANCE

Associations of insurers, such as the National Bureau of Casualty Underwriters and the National Automobile Underwriters Association, have proposed standard forms of policies that have been approved by their members in virtually all the states.

§ 38:8. Nature of Contract. In the case of insurance to compensate the driver or owner for his own damages, it is immaterial whether his negligence caused or contributed to the harm which had befallen him. In the case of the insurance that protects him from the claims of others, there is no liability on the insurer in favor of those persons unless he has so acted that he would be liable to them without regard to the insurance. If he were not negligent in the operation of his automobile, he would not be liable, ordinarily, for the harm caused, and a person injured by his auto could not hold his insurance company liable since its liability is no greater than his own.

(1) Ownership of Automobile. Basically, liability insurance protects the insured with respect to an automobile which he owns. Whether or not

---

[7] Mobile Fire & Marine Insurance Co. v Kraft, 36 Ala App 684, 63 So2d 34.
[8] Violette v Insurance Co. of Pennsylvania, 92 Wash 685, 161 P 343.

he owns the automobile in question is determined by Article 2 of the Uniform Commercial Code, and it is immaterial whether the steps required by the motor vehicle statute have been taken.

§ 38:9. Financial Responsibility Laws. In a few states and under some no-fault insurance statutes, liability insurance must be obtained before a driver's license will be issued. In other states *financial responsibility laws* require that if a driver is involved in an accident, he must furnish proof of financial responsibility. Under some laws this means that the driver must deposit security sufficient to pay any judgment that may be entered against him with respect to that accident. Under other statutes, it is sufficient that the driver produce a liability policy in a specified amount as to future accidents.

The security form of statute may not protect the victim of the first accident. If the driver is unwilling or unable to deposit the required security, he will forfeit his license; but this does not provide any payment to the victim of the first accident. By definition the second type of law does not protect the victim of the first accident. Moreover, the efficacy of financial responsibility laws has been reduced by the decision that the United States Constitution requires that there be a hearing to establish the probable liability of the driver to the victim before his driver's license can be suspended or revoked; [9] and the requirement of such a hearing has the effect of delaying and making cumbersome what was formerly a relatively simple and swift administrative remedy.

§ 38:10. Liability Insurance. The owner or operator of a motor vehicle may obtain *liability insurance* to protect himself from claims made by third persons for damage to their property (property damage liability) or person (bodily injury liability) arising from the use or operation of an automobile. When the insurer pays under such a policy, it makes the payment directly to the third person and is liable to pay him for the same items as the insured would be required to pay, but for not more than the maximum stated in the policy.

If the insurer is liable for the damage caused a third person or his property, it is likewise liable for cost of repairs, destruction of property, loss of services, and other damages for which the insured himself would be liable.[10]

The terms "use" and "operation" are very liberally interpreted to include events in which there is some involvement of the automobile, although not for the purpose of transportation. For example, where a supermarket bagboy was loading a customer's car and accidentally shut the door on her hand, the insurer was liable as there had been a "use of the automobile" within the coverage of the policy.[11]

The liability of the insured is not affected by the fact that he is insured. This means that if for any reason his policy does not cover the full loss or

[9] Bell v Burson, 402 US 535.

[10] Hayes v Penn Mutual Life Insurance Co., 228 Mass 191, 117 NE 189.

[11] Wrenn & Outlaw v Employers' Liability Assurance Corp., 246 SC 97, 142 SE2d 741.

if the insurance company is not solvent or in business at that time, he is liable for any amount not paid, assuming that he would be liable in the absence of insurance.

*(1) **Person Operating.*** Liability policies ordinarily protect the owner of the auto from liability when it is operated by another person with the permission of the insured,[12] as in the case of an employee or agent of the owner.

Liability insurance may also protect an insured individual or his spouse against liability incurred while operating another person's automobile. This is referred to as *D.O.C.* (drive-other-car) *coverage,* or *temporary replacement coverage.* (See p. 763, State Farm Mutual Auto Insurance Co. v Johnston.)

(a) MEMBERS OF HOUSEHOLD OF INSURED. Automobile liability policies variously extend coverage to members of the insured's household or residence. Such terms are generally liberally construed to reach the conclusion that a given relative is a member of the insured's "household" or "residence."

To illustrate this liberality in interpretation, it has been held that when the insured took title to the automobile and in the following year transferred it to his daughter, aged 20, who took the automobile to another city where she was attending a job training school, the daughter was still a resident of the insured's household, even though her future plans were indefinite and there was no obligation to follow the employment for which she was being trained nor any obligation of the company training her to employ her.[13]

(b) OTHER DRIVER. The automobile liability policy protects the insured when he is driving. If someone else is driving with the insured's permission, the policy protects both the original insured and such other driver. This *omnibus* or *other-driver clause* is generally liberally interpreted so that permission is often found in acquiescence in the other driver's use or in the insured's failing to object or to prevent such use. In the absence of an express prohibition by the insured against the permittee's lending the car to another, a permission by *A* given to *B* to use the car generally includes an implied permission to *B* to permit *C* to drive, in which case the liability of the insurer is the same as though *A* or *B* were driving.[14]

The buyer of an automobile does not come within the scope of an omnibus clause because his operation of the automobile is not based upon the permission of the seller but upon his ownership of the automobile. To avoid litigation, policies commonly expressly exclude buyers from the scope of the omnibus clause. (See p. 766, DeRubbo v Aetna Ins. Co.)

---

[12] West v McNamara, 159 Ohio 187, 111 NE2d 909.

[13] Goodsell v State Automobile and Casualty Underwriters, 261 Iowa 135, 153 NW2d 458.

[14] Some courts interpret the omnibus clause more strictly and refuse to recognize a second permittee when the original insured did not expressly authorize such relending or where the use made by the second permittee was not the same use which the insured contemplated would be made by the first permittee. Hanegan v Horace Mann Mutual Insurance Co., 77 Ill 2d 142, 221 NE2d 669; St. Paul Insurance Co. v Carlyle, (Mo App) 428 SW2d 753.

(2) Exclusions. In liability insurance the insurer may protect itself by excluding damage claims arising out of certain types of causes. Such policies may exclude claims of employees of the owner or claims under the workmen's compensation laws, or liability for claims when the insured admits to the injured third person that the insured is liable and agrees to pay his claim.

In the case of commercial vehicles the insurer may stipulate that it shall only be bound by the policy "provided: (a) the regular and frequent use of the automobile is confined to the area within a fifty mile radius of the limits of the city or town where the automobile is principally garaged . . . , (b) no regular or frequent trips are made by the automobile to any locations beyond such radius." [15]

(3) Notice and Cooperation. A liability policy generally provides that the insurer is not liable unless the insured (a) gives the insurer prompt notice of any serious accident or claim or lawsuit brought against him, (b) furnishes the insurance company with all details of the occurrence, and (c) cooperates with the insurer in the preparation of the defense against a lawsuit brought on the policy and participates at the trial. Notice and cooperation under such a policy are conditions precedent to the liability of the insurer.[16]

These requirements are subject to modification in terms of "reasonableness." Thus, the insured is not required to report a trivial accident when there was no reason to believe that the injured person was going to proceed further with the matter. The notice to the insurer need only be given within a reasonable time after the occurrence, and "reasonable" is determined in the light of all the surrounding circumstances.[17]

(4) Duty to Defend. A liability insurer has the duty to defend any suit brought against its insured on a claim which, if valid, would come within the policy coverage. That is to say, a liability insurer cannot refuse to defend the insured on the ground that it does not believe the claim of the third person. Consequently, when the third person's complaint against the insured states a claim within the policy coverage, a liability insurer cannot refuse to defend on the ground that its investigation shows that the claim is without merit.

If the insurer wrongly refuses to defend and the third person recovers a judgment against the insured in excess of the policy maximum, the insurer is liable to the insured for the full amount of the judgment.[18] Under statutes in some states, the insurer may also be required to pay the insured the amount of his costs and attorney's fees when the insurer refuses in bad faith to settle or defend the action.[19]

---

[15] Bruins v Anderson, 73 SD 620, 47 NW2d 493.

[16] Heimlich v Kees Appliance Co., 256 Wis 356, 41 NW2d 359.

[17] Coolidge v Standard Accident Insurance Co., 114 Cal 355, 300 P 885.

[18] Landie v Century Indemnity Co., (Mo App) 390 SW2d 558.

[19] Pendlebury v Western Casualty & Surety Co., 89 Idaho 456, 406 P2d 129.

§ 38:11. Collision and Upset Insurance. Liability insurance does not indemnify the owner for damage to his own automobile. In order to obtain this protection, the owner of the auto must obtain property insurance to cover damage from collision and upset.

The term "collision" is generally liberally interpreted so that there is insurance coverage whenever there is an unintended striking of another object even though the object is not an automobile or is not moving. For example, there is a "collision" with another "object" within the coverage of the policy when because of the wet surface of the road the insured truck careened off the highway and plunged into a ditch filled with water.[20] Likewise, there is a collision when a wheel comes off of the automobile.

The phrase "struck by automobile" is likewise liberally interpreted so that there is coverage when the insured ran his motor scooter into an automobile, as against the contention that "struck by automobile" required that the automobile run into the insured.[21]

The term "upset" is generally liberally construed to cover an event which destroys the normal balance of the automobile even though it does not turn over. Thus, it has been held that there is an "upset" when a front wheel of a dump truck slips into a rut and the resulting stress causes the frame and hoist of the truck to twist out of shape.[22]

In the case of an accident, if the driver of the other automobile has liability insurance, the first driver may be able to collect the damages to his automobile from the liability insurer of the other car. It is desirable, however, to have property insurance on his car. The reason is that his own insurer must pay him for damage to his car without regard to whether he was negligent, but the liability insurer of the other driver is not required to pay unless the first driver was not negligent and the other driver was negligent.

(1) Exclusions. Although the insurer against loss from collision will ordinarily pay damages without serious dispute, it is not required to pay in every case. It is commonly provided that the insurer is not liable when the automobile is used by a person engaged in violating the law. It may also be stipulated that liability is avoided if the auto is subject to a lien or encumbrance that has not been disclosed. It is common to exclude damages, resulting from collision, for the loss of the use of the auto, depreciation, or for loss of personal property in the auto.

(2) Notice and Cooperation. As in the case of public liability insurance, the auto owner is under a duty to give notice, to inform, and to cooperate with the insurer. He must also give the insurer an opportunity to examine the automobile to determine the extent of damage before making repairs.

---

[20] Washington Fire & Marine Insurance Co. v Ryburn, 228 Ark 930, 311 SW2d 302.
[21] Foundation Reserve Insurance Co. v McCarthy, 77 NMex 118, 419 P2d 963.
[22] Dillehay v Hartford Fire Insurance Co., 91 Idaho 360, 421 P2d 155.

§ 38:12. Uninsured Motorists. Statutes and liability policies commonly provide for special coverage when the insured sustains loss because of an uninsured motorist. Since the *uninsured motorist coverage* is a liability coverage, there is no liability of the insurer in the absence of establishing that the uninsured motorist was negligent so that he would be held liable in a suit brought against him by the insured.[23] Consequently, collision and accident insurance provide greater protection in that under such coverage the insurer is bound by its contract without regard to whether anyone could be held liable to the insured.

Uninsured motorist coverage generally includes the hit-and-run driver who leaves the scene of the collision before he can be identified. Policies commonly require that the collision be reported to the police or other appropriate authorities within 24 hours and that diligent effort be made to locate the hit-and-run driver. These restrictions are imposed in order to guard against the fraud of reporting the other car as "unknown" when its driver was in fact known, or against the fraud of having a one-car accident and then falsely claiming that the damage was the result of a collision with a hit-and-run driver.

This coverage differs from other insurance that the insured could obtain in that only personal injury claims are covered and generally only up to $10,000. Contact with the uninsured or unidentified vehicle is required, so that there is no uninsured motorist coverage when the insured runs off the road to avoid a collision and sustains injury thereby, or when the insured is injured upon striking oil or a substance dropped from the uninsured vehicle.[24]

A policy restriction excluding a driver under the age of 25 from the uninsured motorist coverage has been held void as against public policy.[25]

§ 38:13. No-Fault Insurance. A state statute may require that every automobile liability policy provide for *no-fault coverage*. This means that when the insured is injured while using the insured automobile, the insurer will make a payment to him without regard to whether the other driver was legally liable for the harm. In effect, this is insurance for medical expense and loss of wages that runs in favor of the holder of the liability policy and is in addition to or in lieu of the coverage which the policy provides him with respect to his liability to other persons.

The no-fault insurance statutes generally do not provide for payment for pain and suffering.

If another person is harmed, such as a pedestrian, no-fault insurance statutes generally provide for a similar kind of payment to such third person either by his own auto insurer or by that of the car inflicting the injury. There is authority that no-fault insurance is constitutional, as against the

---

[23] McCrory v Allstate Insurance Co., (La App) 194 So2d 759.

[24] Wynn v Doe, 255 SC 509, 180 SE2d 95.

[25] First National Insurance Co. v Devine, (Fla App) 211 So2d 587.

contention that it violates the guarantees of equal protection and due process. It has been sustained as a carefully studied plan to provide a new remedy to meet the problems caused by the automobile: rising costs of insurance, overloading of courts, and delay in making payment to the injured person.[26] In contrast, other cases have held that no-fault insurance is unconstitutional.

Disputes under no-fault insurance are sometimes determined by arbitration. In addition, some states require the arbitration of small claims of any nature. The concept of no-fault insurance does not have an exact definition because it is still in an evolutionary stage with no uniform pattern of legislation being followed and with frequent amendments changing the statutory pattern.

§ **38:14. Theft Insurance.** The owner of an automobile can secure theft insurance, which will protect him from loss through the theft and from damage to the auto caused by a theft. The standard form of policy covers loss from larceny, robbery, and pilferage as well as theft.

An automobile theft policy does not ordinarily protect against loss of contents. It is common to exclude liability for equipment or personal property taken from the auto, but additional insurance protecting from such theft can be secured. It is common also to exclude liability for loss sustained while a passenger auto is used for commercial transportation or is rented to another.

§ **38:15. Fire, Lightning, and Transportation Insurance.** In this type of insurance the insurer agrees to pay for any loss arising out of damage to or the destruction of a motor vehicle or its equipment caused by fire originating in any manner, by lightning, or by the stranding, sinking, burning, collision, or derailment of any conveyance in or upon which the automobile or the truck is being transported. This type of policy is commonly combined with a policy against theft and pilferage and is usually subject to the same exclusions.

§ **38:16. Comprehensive Insurance.** In many automobile insurance policies, comprehensive material damage coverage, which protects the policyholder against virtually all such risks except collision or upset, replaces fire and theft insurance. The exclusions for this kind of insurance include wear and tear, freezing, mechanical breakdown, and loss of personal effects.

§ **38:17. Nonpolicy Liability of Insurer.** In certain instances an insurer will be liable because of the breach of a nonpolicy duty. These situations arise most commonly against a background of automobile liability insurance, although the principles involved are not necessarily so limited.

(1) Mental Distress of Claimant. When an insurer or its adjuster intentionally subjects a claimant to mental distress, the insurer may be liable

---

[26] Pinnick v Cleary, 271 Mass 592, 271 NE2d 592.

for the tort of intentional infliction of mental distress. Threats and harassment used in the effort to persuade a claimant to accept a settlement may impose such liability. The mere fact that the insurer or its agent has acted in a way which appears unreasonable and unethical, however, does not necessarily impose liability for the mental distress which follows.[27]

(2) Invasion of Privacy. When a person makes a claim against an insurance company he confers a qualified privilege upon the insurer to observe and study his public actions in order to determine the truth of the statement made by the claimant. For example, when a claimant asserts that he has been so injured that he cannot leave his house or work, the insurer may photograph him leaving the house and at work. Such conduct of the insurer does not constitute a violation of the claimant's right of privacy because the activity under surveillance occurs in a public place.

When proper investigation is made of a claimant's activity, the insurer is not liable because the claimant experienced mental distress when he became aware that he was under surveillance.

The right of the insurer to observe public activity does not give it a right to make an invasion of privacy which would not be allowed a private person. For example, while the insurer may photograph a claimant working at his regular place of employment, the insurer's investigator cannot secretly enter the claimant's home and photograph him working inside his house.

LIFE INSURANCE

A contract of *life insurance* requires the insurer to pay a stipulated sum of money upon the death of the insured. It is not a contract of indemnity since the insurer does not undertake to indemnify the beneficiary for the financial loss sustained as the result of the death of the insured.

§ 38:18. Kinds of Life Insurance Policies.

(1) Ordinary Life Insurance. Ordinary life insurance in turn may be subclassified as (a) *straight life insurance,* which requires payments of premiums throughout the life of the insured; (b) *limited payment insurance,* requiring the payment of premiums during a limited period, such as ten, twenty, or thirty years, or until the death of the insured if that should occur before the end of the specified period; (c) *endowment insurance*, under which the insurer undertakes to pay a stipulated sum when the insured reaches a specified age, or upon his death if that occurs; and (d) *term insurance,* under which the insurer undertakes to pay a stipulated sum only in the event of the death of the insured during a specified period, such as one, two, five, or ten years.

Somewhat similar to policies of endowment insurance are *annuity policies* and *retirement income insurance* under which the insured either pays a

[27] Cluff v Farmers Insurance Exchange, 10 Ariz App 560, 460 P2d 666.

lump sum to the insurer and thereafter receives fixed annual payments, or pays periodic premiums to the insurer until a certain date and then receives fixed annual payments.

(2) Group Insurance. *Group life insurance* is insurance of the lives of employees of a particular employer or persons engaged in a particular business or profession. Such policies are usually either term policies or straight life insurance. A medical examination is usually not required.

(3) Industrial Insurance. *Industrial insurance* is in substance ordinary life insurance written for a small amount, usually from $100 to $500. Premiums are generally paid weekly or monthly and are collected from door to door by the agent of the insured. No physical examination is required for industrial insurance. The industrial policy may be either term, straight life, limited payment, or endowment.

(4) Double Indemnity. Many life insurance companies undertake to pay double the amount of the policy, called *double indemnity,* if death is caused by an accident and occurs within ninety days after the accident. A comparatively small, additional premium is charged for this special protection. These policies generally define accidental death as "death resulting from bodily injury effected solely by external, violent, and accidental means, independently and exclusively of all other causes and within ninety days after such injury." In order to avoid the assertion of false claims of accidental death, most policies now require that there be a visible wound on the surface of the body. An exception is made in the case of death by drowning or by asphyxiation.

Double indemnity clauses generally exempt the insurer from liability for a death occurring while the insured is serving in the armed forces, while engaged in riots or insurrections, or when the insured is over 65 years of age.

(5) Disability Insurance. In consideration of the payment of an additional premium, many life insurance companies also provide insurance against total permanent disability of the insured. *Disability* is usually defined in a life insurance policy as any "incapacity resulting from bodily injury or disease to engage in any occupation for remuneration or profit." The policy generally provides that a disability which has continued for a stated minimum period, such as four to six months, will be regarded as a *total permanent disability.*

It has become common for insurers, upon the payment of an additional premium, to include in the policy a clause waiving premiums becoming due during the total or permanent disability of the insured. The effect of such a provision is to prevent the policy from lapsing for nonpayment of premiums during the period of such disability.

(6) Risks Not Covered. Life insurance policies frequently provide that death shall not be within the protection of the policy or that a double indemnity provision shall not be applicable when death is due to or caused by

(1) suicide, (2) narcotics, (3) violation of the law, (4) execution for crime, (5) war activities, or (6) operation of aircraft. For such exclusions to operate, there must be a proximate relationship between the prohibited conduct or condition and the harm sustained in order to relieve the insurer from liability on the policy. (See p. 767, Rivers v Conger Life Insurance Co.) It is generally provided by statute or stated by court decision that a beneficiary who has feloniously killed the insured is not entitled to receive the proceeds of the policy.[28]

§ 38:19. The Beneficiary. The person to whom the proceeds of life insurance policy are payable upon the death of the insured is called the *beneficiary*. He may be a third person, or the beneficiary may be the estate of the insured. There may be more than one beneficiary.

As a practical matter, it is preferable to provide for the payment of insurance money directly to named beneficiaries rather than to one's estate, even though the same persons would receive the proceeds on the distribution of the estate. When the insurance is paid into the estate, the proceeds will be reduced by the administration charges of the estate, such as the fees of the attorneys of the estate and the commissions of the executor or administrator; and the distribution will be subject to the delay required in the formal administration of an estate.

In addition, since the insurance proceeds that pass through the estate of the insured are subject to his debts, it is possible that the proceeds of the insurance policy will be consumed in whole or in part for the payment of debts and thus not be received by the beneficiary. When the policy is payable directly to a named beneficiary, the proceeds of the policy are generally not subject to the debts of the insured.[29]

The beneficiary named in the policy may be barred from claiming the proceeds of the policy because of a prior settlement agreement, by which it was agreed to do otherwise. (See p. 769, Beneficial Life Ins. Co. v Stoddard.)

(1) Primary and Contingent Beneficiaries. It is desirable to name a primary and a contingent beneficiary. Thus, *A* may make his insurance payable to *B*; but if *B* dies before *A*, the insurance shall be payable to *C*. In such cases *B* is the *primary beneficiary*, and *C* is the *contingent beneficiary* because he takes the proceeds as beneficiary only upon the contingency that *B* dies before *A*.

The designation of the contingent beneficiary should not be made conditional only upon the death of the primary beneficiary before the death of the insured. The change should also be effective in case of the death of the insured and the primary beneficiary in a common disaster or under such circumstances that it cannot be determined who died first. For example, if a man's wife is named as the primary beneficiary and their two children as

---

[28] Neff v Massachusetts Mutual Life Insurance Co., 158 Ohio 45, 107 NE2d 100.
[29] Succession of Onorato, 219 La 1, 51 So2d 804.

contingent beneficiaries, the policy should be written so that the proceeds will be payable to the contingent beneficiaries either if the wife dies before the husband does or in the case of the death of the husband and wife in a common disaster, such as an automobile accident.

*(2) **Change of Beneficiary.*** The customary policy provides that the insured reserves the right to change the beneficiary without the latter's consent. When the policy contains such a provision, the beneficiary cannot object to a change that destroys all rights which he had under the policy and which names another as beneficiary in his place.[30]

In the absence of a provision in the policy so authorizing, the beneficiary acquires a vested interest, even though he gave no consideration. The insured, therefore, cannot thereafter change the beneficiary even with the consent of the insurer.[31]

In industrial policies it is customary for the policy to contain a *facility-of-payment clause* under which the insurer is given the option of selecting from a designated class or group anyone whom the insurer deems equitably entitled to receive payment and to make payment to that person. Such a clause enables the insurer to pay the amount of the insurance proceeds directly to any person who pays the debts of the decedent, such as his funeral bills, rather than to a named beneficiary who had not expended any money on behalf of the decedent.

The insurance policy will ordinarily state that in order to change the beneficiary, the insurer must be so instructed in writing by the insured and the policy must then be endorsed by the company with the change of the beneficiary. These provisions are generally liberally construed. If the insured has notified the insurer but dies before the endorsement of the change is made by the company, the change of beneficiary is effective. If the insured has clearly indicated his intention to change the beneficiary, the consent of the insurer to the change is not required.[32]

§ 38:20. Incontestable Clause. Statutes commonly require the inclusion of an incontestable clause in life insurance policies. Ordinarily this clause states that after the lapse of two years the policy cannot be contested by the insurance company. The insurer is free to contest the validity of the policy at any time during the contestable period; but once that period has expired, it must pay the stipulated sum upon the death of the insured and cannot claim that in obtaining the policy the insured had been guilty of misrepresentation, fraud, or any other conduct that would exempt it from liability.

The incontestable clause does not bar matters of defense that arise subsequent to the sustaining of loss. The incontestability clause does not bar proof that the loss was sustained by a risk not covered by the policy. (See

---

[30] Reliance Life Insurance Co. v Jaffe, 121 Cal App 2d 241, 263 P2d 82.

[31] The vested character of the beneficiary's right in such cases is sustained on a variety of theories including that of a third-party beneficiary contract, an irrevocable gift, a trust, or a principal-agent relationship.

[32] Stone v Stephens, 92 Ohio App 53, 110 NE2d 18.

p. 770, National Producers Life Ins. Co. v Rogers.) Generally the incontestable clause is not applicable to double indemnity or disability provisions of the policy.

§ 38:21. Surrender of Policy and Alternatives. Surrender of a life insurance policy is ordinarily made when a person finds that he cannot afford to pay further premiums on the policy or that he needs the surrender value of the policy in money.

*(1) **Cash Surrender Value.*** By modern statute or policy provision, it is commonly provided that if the life insurance policy has been in force a stated number of years, usually two or three, the insured may surrender the policy and the insurer will then make a payment of the cash value of the policy to him.[33] Ordinarily term policies do not have a cash surrender value.

Each year a certain percentage of the premiums is set aside by the insurer to hold as a reserve against the date when payment must be made under the policy. If the policy is surrendered or canceled, the potential liability of the reserve fund is removed and part of the fund can then be released as a payment to the insured. The longer the policy has been in existence, the larger is the cash surrender value.

*(2) **Loan on Policy.*** Sometimes the insured's problem can be solved by borrowing from the insurer. The modern policy contains a definite scale of maximum amounts that can be borrowed depending upon the age of the policy. The insurer is able to make such loans because it has the security of the cash surrender value if the loan is not repaid; or if the insured dies without making repayment, it may deduct the debt from the proceeds payable to the beneficiary.

The loan value of a policy is usually the same amount as the cash surrender value. The policyholder, as a borrower, must pay interest to the insurance company on the loan.

*(3) **Paid-up Policy.*** Under modern statutes or common forms of policies, if the insured can no longer afford the expense of his insurance, he may request the insurer to issue to him a new policy of paid-up insurance. The insured in effect takes out a new paid-up policy of insurance for a smaller amount of protection and pays for that policy through the transfer of the reserve value of the old policy. In some states, when a policy lapses for nonpayment of premiums, the insurer must automatically issue a paid-up policy on the basis of the reserve value of the lapsed policy.

*(4) **Extended Insurance.*** Instead of a paid-up policy for a smaller amount, it is generally possible under modern statutes and policies for the insured to obtain term insurance that provides the original amount of protection. This remains effective until the reserve value of the original policy has been consumed.

---

[33] Blume v Pittsburgh Life & Trust Co., 263 Ill 160, 104 NE 1031.

(5) Reinstatement of Lapsed Policy. When a premium on a policy is not paid within the required period or within the grace period, the insured generally may reinstate the policy within a reasonable time thereafter as long as he is still an insurable risk and provided he pays all premiums that are in arrears.

§ **38:22. Settlement Options.** Although an ordinary life insurance policy will provide for the payment of a specified amount upon the death of the insured, the insured generally may designate one of several plans of distribution of this fund. These plans of distribution are called *settlement options.* When the insured has designated a particular option, the beneficiary generally cannot change it after his death. Sometimes the policy reserves to the beneficiary the right to change the settlement option.

In addition to payment of a lump sum in settlement of all claims against the insurer arising under the policy, the standard form of policy provides the following options: (1) Retention by the insurer of the proceeds of the policy until the death of the beneficiary, during which period the insurer pays interest to the beneficiary at a specified rate; (2) payment of equal monthly installments for a specified number of years; (3) payment of equal monthly installments for a specified number of years or until the beneficiary dies, whichever period is longer; or (4) payment of equal monthly installments in an amount specified by the beneficiary as long as there is a sufficient principal-and-interest fund from which to make payment.

§ **38:23. Rights of Creditors.** If a man takes out insurance on his own life, can his creditors complain? To the extent that he is paying premiums to the insurance company, the amount of his money available to pay creditors is reduced. Can the creditors reach the cash surrender value of the policy or the proceeds upon the insured's death?

If the insured makes the policy payable to his estate, the proceeds become part of the general assets of his estate upon his death and, in the absence of statute, are subject to the claims of his creditors. If the insured makes the policy on his own life payable to another person and if the insured is at all times solvent when he pays the premiums, his creditors cannot reach the policy in payment of their claims, and the beneficiary is entitled to the entire proceeds of the policy.

Between these two extremes are a variety of situations. The insured may have been insolvent during part or all of the life of the policy; or the obtaining of the insurance policy or the assignment of it or the changing of the beneficiary may have been done to defraud the creditors.

If the policy is originally payable to the estate of the insured an assignment by the insured of his interest when made in fraud of creditors will not defeat the rights of his creditors.

If the policy is made payable to a third person as beneficiary but the insured is insolvent, courts differ as to the rights of the insured's creditors.

CASES FOR CHAPTER 38

Youse v Employers Fire Insurance Co.

172 Kan 111, 238 P2d 472 (1951)

Youse owned a ring that was insured with the Employers Fire Insurance Co. against loss, including "all direct loss or damage by fire." The ring was accidentally thrown by Youse into a trash burner and was damaged when the trash was burned. He sued the insurer. From a judgment for the plaintiff, the defendant appealed.

PRICE, J. . . . The company contends . . . that the quoted insuring clause of the policy, "against all direct loss or damage by fire" covers only loss or damage resulting from a hostile fire as distinguished from a friendly fire; that here the fire, being intentionally lighted in and confined to a place or receptacle where it was intended to be, was not a hostile fire within the usual and well-established meaning of the term and therefore no recovery can be had.

The insured argues that he purchased and paid for *fire insurance*—not just for fire insurance to cover loss resulting only from socalled hostile fires; that the direct loss and damage to the ring by fire is undisputed; that the company would have the court write into the policy an unauthorized and unreasonable restriction; that there is no ambiguity in the terms of the policy and therefore it should be enforced according to its literal terms; and that even though there was some uncertainty as to its meaning, the court is bound to construe the policy strictly against the company and favorably to the insured. . . .

"The distinction most commonly made by courts in considering contracts of fire insurance is that drawn between hostile and friendly fires. If the fire burns in a place where it (is) intended to burn, although damages may have resulted where none were intended, the fire is a friendly fire and the insurer is not liable for damages flowing therefrom. A friendly fire refers to one which remains confined within the place intended and refers to a fire in a furnace, stove, or other usual place. A hostile fire, on the other hand, means one not confined to the place intended or one not intentionally started; and it is generally considered to refer to such a fire which, if it had pursued its natural course, would have resulted in a total or partial destruction of the insured property. When a friendly fire escapes from the place it ought to be to some place where it ought not to be, causing damage, it becomes a hostile fire for which the insurer is liable.

"In order to recover for damages sustained, the insured must show that the first was a hostile, rather than a friendly, fire. . . ."

. . . The very great weight of authority appears to be that fires . . . are classified as friendly or hostile in nature, notwithstanding that such distinction is not made in the language of the policy itself. . . .

We think it cannot be denied that in common parlance and everyday usage one has not "had a fire" so long as it has burned only in the place where it was intended to burn, [as] . . . a fire in [a] furnace, cookstove, or fireplace. . . .

In our opinion there can be no question but that the fire which damaged or destroyed the sapphire ring was what in law is known as a friendly fire. It was intentionally lighted, was for the usual and ordinary purpose of burning trash, and was at all times confined to the place where it was intended, and did not escape.

[Judgment for plaintiff reversed.]

State Farm Mut. Auto Ins. Co. v Johnston

9 Cal 3d 270, 107 Cal Rptr 149, 507 P2d 1357 (1973)

Johnston purchased a 1957 automobile for use by his son Billy, under eighteen years of age. Johnston registered the car in his own name and insured it with the State Farm Mutual Automobile Insurance Company. Some time later the car would not run and Billy bought a 1964 car which he registered in his own name. He later sold the 1957 car. He did not insure the 1964 car. When the 1964 car was

involved in an accident, he claimed State Farm was liable on the policy obtained by his father on the theory that the 1964 car was within the "temporary substitute automobile" clause of that policy. State Farm denied liability on the ground that the 1964 automobile was a permanent replacement. State Farm brought a declaratory judgment action to determine whether it was liable. The court held that the 1964 car was a "temporary substitute automobile," and that State Farm was liable on its policy. State Farm appealed.

McComb, J. . . . [The State Farm] policy provided coverage for the "owned automobile" —meaning the described vehicle and including a "temporary substitute automobile," which was defined as "an automobile not owned by the named insured or his spouse while temporarily used with the permission of the owner as a substitute for the described automobile when withdrawn from normal use because of its breakdown, repair, servicing, loss or destruction." This clause commonly found in automobile liability insurance policies is primarily designed for the benefit of the insured. The purpose is not to defeat liability but reasonably to define coverage by limiting the insurer's risk to one operating vehicle at a time for a single premium. (12 Couch on Insurance (2d ed. 1964) [Anderson Edition] § 45.219, p. 261.)

. . . As commonly accepted, "temporary" is an antonym of "permanent." . . . Here, it is unclear whether plaintiff, in its use of the word "temporary," was attempting to put a time limitation on the use of the substitute automobile. Any doubt as to its meaning must be resolved in accord with settled rules for interpreting an insurance contract. . . .

Plaintiff argues that since Billy purchased the 1964 car to use in place of the inoperable 1957 car, and then sold the 1957 car, his use of the 1964 car was not a "temporary substitute" but rather a "permanent replacement." In this regard, plaintiff would limit the coverage of the policy to operation of the substituted automobile during the period of repair until the automobile named in the policy is restored to use. But this argument adds a requirement not found in plaintiff's policy and relates the word "temporarily" to the insured car rather than to use of the substitute car. Certainly, plaintiff's policy contemplated that the insured car might never be restored to use during the term of the policy, for it provided for a "temporary substitute" when the insured car should be withdrawn from normal use because of "breakdown . . . loss or destruction." Here, the breakdown of the 1957 car apparently was such that it did not warrant repair but rather replacement for the remainder of the policy period. The important consideration for coverage under this provision of the policy was not the length of time of use but, rather, the purpose of the substitution and the substantial similarity between the use of the originally insured automobile and its substitute. In short, it is contemplated between the insurer and the insured that the *same* use of the *substitute vehicle* will be made as the one originally insured. . . . Here, Billy used the 1964 car substitute for the same driving needs that he had used the 1957 car; Milton, his father, knew of the substitution and approved of its use for the same purposes as had applied with the 1957 car . . . ; and the sale of the inoperable 1957 car would not preclude coverage for the 1964 car as a "temporary substitute automobile" for the remainder of the policy period. . . .

In Nelson v St. Paul Mercury Insurance Company, 83 SD 32, 153 NW2d 397, at page 400, where substantially the same "temporary substitute automobile" provision was considered, the Supreme Court of South Dakota said: "The word 'temporarily' relates to and is a restriction on the use of the substitute vehicle. The policy does not similarly require that the insured vehicle be 'temporarily' withdrawn from normal use. This phase of the insurance contract is without time limit. . . . Furthermore, the policy does not require the replacement, or an intention to replace, the insured vehicle in use after being withdrawn from normal use. A breakdown, repair, loss or destruction might be permanent in nature. Obviously, there would never be an intention to replace in use an automobile damaged beyond repair, as in the present case, or one that has been lost or destroyed. Nevertheless, the substitute automobile clause is clearly designed to extend coverage to an insured in those cases during the remainder of the policy period. The insured is thereby afforded protection paid for and the insurer's risk is confined to one operating vehicle at a time."

Here, if plaintiff's policy, for which a premium was paid, be held to apply to any risk at all, it could apply only to the operation of the 1964 car operated by Billy when the accident occurred. No other risk existed at that time. Plaintiff's risk with respect to the use and operation of the 1957 car ceased with its breakdown and sale. . . . An insurer charges a premium for assuming a risk covered by the policy. An insurer earns a premium only when there is a risk involved. . . . The risk to plaintiff under the policy was the same whether Billy operated the 1957 car or the later substituted 1964 car for the same basic purposes—only one operating vehicle was covered at the given time. The policy makes clear that its purpose was to extend coverage, without payment of additional premium, to a "temporary substitute automobile" used in place of the insured automobile withdrawn from normal use for reasons stated in the policy. . . .

. . . "In the replacement-automobile cases the courts are usually willing to allow coverage under the policy as long as there is only one operable car. It makes no difference that the replacement car is purchased before the replaced car is sold as long as the replaced car is sold or is not operable at the time of the accident. In this way other users of the highways are protected and the insurance company's liability is limited to the operation of one car by the insured." . . .

While plaintiff's introduction of the word "temporary" into its "substitute automobile" provision appears to have created an ambiguity, it is the plaintiff's language; and plaintiff cannot avoid the effect of its choice of teminology. . . . "The provision for coverage of a substituted vehicle 'is for the insured's benefit' and is to be 'construed liberally in favor of the insured, if any construction is necessary.' " . . . Here, it must be concluded that Billy was using the 1964 car as a "temporary substitute automobile" under the terms of plaintiff's policy.

An argument has been made that the 1964 Chevrolet cannot be regarded as a temporary substitute automobile, because the requirement that the automobile be "temporarily used with the permission of the owner" suggests that the automobile must belong to someone other than the person using it; and Billy owned the 1964 Chevrolet and was using it. Since, however, we must give the policy provisions a liberal interpretation in favor of the insured . . . we find this factor not determinative. Had the 1964 Chevrolet been purchased by Billy's father, the named insured, or the father's spouse, it would clearly have been a newly acquired automobile * and could not be regarded as a temporary substitute automobile, the policy specifically providing that a temporary substitute automobile may not be one owned by the named insured or his spouse. But the 1964 car was not acquired by Billy's father or the father's spouse, as a result of which the provisions regarding a newly acquired automobile are inapplicable. At the same time, since the 1964 Chevrolet was owned by someone other than the named insured or his spouse, it can qualify as a temporary substitute automobile.

Billy was unquestionably given unrestricted permission to use the 1957 Chevrolet in order to go to work and run errands; and, as hereinabove pointed out, the 1964 Chevrolet was acquired for use as a temporary substitute for the 1957 Chevrolet after breakdown of the latter. Under the circumstances, since Billy was using the 1964 Chevrolet for the same purposes for which he had been given permission to use the 1957 Chevrolet, he must be regarded as a permissive user of the 1964 Chevrolet and hence covered as an insured under plaintiff's policy.

[Judgment affirmed.]

---

* Under the policy, "Owned Automobile" includes a newly acquired automobile, which is defined as "an automobile, ownership of which is acquired by the named insured or his spouse, if a resident of the same household, if (1) it replaces an automobile owned by either and covered by this policy . . . and (2) the named insured within 30 days following such delivery date applies to the company for insurance on such newly acquired automobile. . . ."

DeRubbo v Aetna Ins. Co.

16 Conn 388, 288 A2d 430 (1971)

Erardi was an automobile dealer. He obtained a liability insurance policy from the Aetna Insurance Company. Joseph Cannatelli, Jr., purchased an automobile from Erardi and paid for it in cash. Over a month later his father, Joseph Cannatelli, Sr., was driving the automobile and was involved in a collision in which DeRubbo and others were injured. At the time the automobile was still registered in the name of Erardi as dealer because he had not given Cannatelli, Jr., a certificate of title in spite of the latter's repeated demands. DeRubbo and the other persons injured obtained a judgment against Cannatelli and then sued Aetna on the theory that Cannatelli, Sr., was an additional insured under the omnibus clause of Aetna's policy issued to Erardi. Aetna denied liability because Cannatelli, Sr., was using the automobile with the permission of a buyer to whom possession and title had been transferred. A judgment was entered in favor of the plaintiffs and Aetna appealed.

THIM, A.J. . . . The basic issue in this case is whether the policy issued by the defendant to Erardi covered the operation of the vehicle by Cannatelli, Sr. . . .

. . . The plaintiffs claimed that there was coverage under the policy because Cannatelli, Sr., was operating the vehicle with the permission of Erardi. The defendant, however, claimed that Cannatelli, Sr., was not an insured under the provisions of the policy because Erardi had transferred possession of the vehicle to Cannatelli, Jr., pursuant to an agreement. The policy specifically states: "[A]ny person or organization other than the named insured with respect to any automobile . . . possession of which has been transferred to another by the named insured pursuant to an agreement of sale" is not an insured within the terms of the policy. . . .

. . . There is nothing ambiguous about the meaning of the language appearing in the disputed provision of this policy. Erardi transferred physical possession of the car to Cannatelli, Jr., pursuant to an agreement of sale. None of the parties contends to the contrary. The plaintiffs concede that Cannatelli, Jr., paid the full price, together with a sum of money to pay taxes and the registration fee, and he received in return a bill of sale for the car. The only part of the transaction to be completed was delivery of a certificate of title. If "agreement of sale" were construed to mean "fully performed agreement of sale," not only would the language of the policy be distorted but the clause would become a nullity. It would be unjust and inequitable to hold the defendant liable for damages inflicted by a motor vehicle which had been sold by the insured and had completely and irrevocably passed from his right of possession and control, simply because the insured had neglected to comply with a provision of the motor vehicle title and registration law by failing to execute and deliver a muniment of title prior to the occurrence of the accident although the sale and transfer had been completed in every other respect. . . .

Not only had possession been transferred but title had also passed pursuant to the Uniform Commercial Code. "Unless otherwise explicitly agreed title passes to the buyer at the time and place at which the seller completes his performance with reference to the physical delivery of the goods, despite any reservation of a security interest and even though a document of title is to be delivered at a different time or place." [UCC § 2-401(2)]. . . .

In view of the fact that the policy plainly speaks of possession, and since it is uncontested that Cannatelli, Jr., had obtained possession of the car four to six weeks before the accident, the court erred in not charging the jury, as a matter of law, that Cannatelli, Sr., was not an insured under the policy. Further, even if a passing of title were required, which it was not, title had passed under the provisions of the Uniform Commercial Code.

. . . Since, however, this policy ceases to apply to vehicles once there is a transfer of possession, even if the jury found Erardi to be the owner of the vehicle, the policy would not apply, possession having been transferred. . . .

There is no merit to the plaintiffs' claim that the car was being operated, with permission, for garage purposes. Cannatelli, Jr.'s father was using the car to deliver produce for his employer. Assuming, arguendo, that Cannatelli, Sr., had permission from Erardi to use the car, there was still no coverage because possession of and title to the car had been transferred by Erardi to Cannatelli, Jr., pursuant to the agreement of sale. . . .

[Judgment reversed and action remanded.]

Rivers v Conger Life Insurance Co.

(Fla App) 229 So2d 625 (1969)

Jefferson was the insured under a life policy issued by the Conger Life Insurance Co. He died as the result of burns sustained while smoking in bed. The insurer refused to pay on the policy on the ground that the insured had been intoxicated, and the policy excluded from its coverage death of the insured while under the influence of alcohol. When the beneficiary sued on the policy, the jury returned a verdict in favor of the beneficiary; but the trial judge entered a judgment n.o.v.* in favor of the insurer, from which action the beneficiary appealed.

TJOFLAT, A.J. . . . This action was commenced by appellant, Estella Rivers, the named beneficiary of a disability insurance policy issued by the appellee, Conger Life Insurance Company, on the life of one Thomas Jefferson, who died on January 21, 1967, of third degree burns suffered in a fire apparently caused by smoking in bed. The complaint alleged that appellant was entitled to receive the accidental death benefit afforded by the policy and attorney fees incurred because of the company's refusal to pay.

In its answer, the appellee alleged that the fire started because the insured became intoxicated and fell asleep as he smoked. It denied that death was by accidental means as defined in the policy. Alternatively, as an affirmative defense, appellee took the position that there was no liability because the policy excepted from coverage death caused by intentional act or occurring while the insured is under the influence of alcohol.

The evidence adduced at the trial revealed that Jefferson was a 56-year old farm laborer, who lived in Archie Lee Rollins' rooming house in Belle Glade. On the night of January 18, 1967, Rollins saw smoke coming out of Jefferson's window and immediately rushed to his room. He found Jefferson, severely burned and unconscious, lying in bed, and the mattress on fire. Cigarette butts and match stems were on the floor. There was a hole in the center of the mattress where the fire had burned through to the bed springs. The evidence was in dispute as to the presence of two empty wine bottles on the floor by the bed. The investigating police officer, who was called to the scene, described them as wine bottles. Rollins said they were soda bottles. Essie Mae Kennedy, another occupant of the rooming house, saw only a small bottle of rubbing alcohol in the room.

Jefferson was rushed to Glades General Hospital. On admission he was in a state of shock and incoherent. Despite extensive treatment, the case was terminal. His kidneys failed, uremia developed, and he slipped into a deep coma and died within 92 hours.

On the death certificate, the cause of death was indicated as "uremia" due to third degree burns over 30 percent of the body. Other significant conditions, contributing to death but not related to the terminal disease, were noted as: "alcoholic cirrhosis with acute liver failure."

The jury returned a verdict for appellant in the amount of $3,600, the full death benefit. Appellee then moved for judgment notwithstanding the verdict. The motion was granted, and this appeal was taken from the judgment consequently entered for appellee.

The applicable insuring provision of the disability policy states, in part: "Upon receipt of due proof that . . . the Insured has sustained bodily injury resulting in death . . . solely through external, violent, and accidental means, of which . . . there is a visible contusion or wound, on the exterior of the body, death being the direct result thereof, and independent of all other causes, the Company will pay, subject to the Exceptions hereinafter enumerated, to the Beneficiary. . . ."

To recover under this provision, the beneficiary must prove that the insured's death came by accidental means; and we are satisfied that appellant met that burden in this case. . . .

* See Glossary, page 12.

Once the coverage of the policy was sufficiently invoked, the burden was upon the appellee to bring the case within an exception to the coverage in order to avoid liability.

It is appellee's contention on this appeal that the beneficiary's claim is barred by the exception which provides: "The Agreement as to benefit under this Policy shall be null and void if the Insured's death . . . results directly or indirectly, from one of the following causes: (a) . . . while under the influence of alcohol. . . ."

Appellee argues that it is manifest that Jefferson was under the influence of alcohol at the time of the fire, and that the trial judge was therefore obliged to set the verdict aside, even though the evidence did not demonstrate, as a matter of law, that his condition contributed to the fatal injuries. This disposition was indicated because the exception does not expressly require that causal relationship to be shown, and most courts have been reluctant to read the element of proximate cause into the provision. . . .

We cannot accept appellee's rationale. It essentially ignores the following policy exclusion which indicates that coverage cannot be defeated unless it is shown that the insured's death is a proximate result of his intoxication: "INTOXICANTS AND NARCOTICS: The Company shall not be liable for any loss sustained or contracted in consequence of the insured's being intoxicated. . . ." This is the provision required by the Florida Insurance Code to be included in a disability insurance policy if an insurer desires to eliminate coverage where the insured's consumption of alcohol is a circumstance attending his death or disability. The burden of proof implicit in its language is obviously greater than that imposed by the exception cited by appellee. For example, the term "intoxicated" is stronger than the term "under the influence" and describes a person who is under the influence of intoxicating beverages to such an extent that he has lost the normal control of his bodily and mental faculties. The words "in consequence of being intoxicated" mean that a causative connection between intoxication and death must be shown if coverage is to be denied.

As is pointed out in 10 Couch on Insurance, 2d [Anderson ed.], § 41:457: "Where the exception clause is so phrased that the harm is the consequence or sequel of the insured's intoxication or other specified condition, it necessarily follows that in order to avoid liability under the exception the insurer must establish that the intoxication has some causative connection with the death or injury of the insured, where the clause is so phrased as to make the death or injury of the insured a sequel of his intoxication. Thus, it has been held that where a policy does not cover injuries received by the insured as the 'result' or 'in consequence' of being intoxicated, or 'caused' by intoxication, some causal connection must be shown." . . .

In sum, it is obvious that this provision is more favorable to the beneficiary than the exception relied upon by the appellee. Since we are dealing with a form insurance contract, the inconsistency created by these clauses must be resolved in appellant's favor. We therefore hold that, in order to avoid liability in this case, appellee was required to demonstrate a causative connection between Jefferson's intoxication and death.

An examination of the evidence reveals distinct questions of fact as to the insured's intoxication and its association with death. The last witnesses to see Jefferson before the fire was discovered were unequivocal in stating that he was sober and in complete control of himself. They saw him between 4:30 and 5:30 o'clock that evening, and he gave no indication of having been drinking. The record discloses nothing about his whereabouts or activities until the tragedy occurred. The only direct evidence of Jefferson's consumption of intoxicants came in the testimony of Dr. Luis R. Guerrero, a surgeon, who smelled alcohol on his breath at the hospital. However, the doctor was unable to specify the amount of intake, since "one beer smells the same as twenty beers," and a blood-alcohol test was not performed. He thus declined to render an opinion as to whether the insured was intoxicated. Furthermore, he testified that the burns were the direct cause of death. They brought about the irreversible kidney failure and consequent uremia.

On this expert testimony, the evidence disclosed by the death certificate and the testimony of the lay witnesses we have cited, the jury was entitled to return a verdict for appellant. Certainly it cannot be said that the manifest weight and probative force of the evidence required the trial court to grant appellee's motion for judgment notwithstanding the verdict. The granting of the motion was error. Accordingly, we reverse and remand the case for reinstatement of the final judgment for appellant.

Beneficial Life Ins. Co. v Stoddard

95 Idaho 628, 516 P2d 187 (1973)

Stoddard insured his life with the Beneficial Life Insurance Company. His wife Phyllis was named as beneficiary. Thereafter they were divorced. They entered into a property settlement agreement which was approved by the divorce court and made part of the divorce decree. By the settlement agreement the policy was awarded to Stoddard. No change was ever made to the beneficiary designation and on Stoddard's death, Phyllis claimed the proceeds of the policy because she was still named as the beneficiary. The administrator of Stoddard's estate also claimed the proceeds. The insurance company admitted liability and paid the proceeds into court. The court awarded them to the administrator and the ex-wife appealed.

BAKES, J. . . . At the time of the divorce, the parties entered into an extensive property settlement stipulation, subsequently incorporated into the divorce decree, which settled the rights of both parties in all property, community or otherwise. The stipulation awarded to Earl Stoddard "*All life insurance* and savings of the defendant through his Employment Savings Insurance Plan of Nuclear Corporation" and concluded with the following provision: "It is further expressly agreed between the parties hereto that this shall be a full and complete settlement of all property rights, community or otherwise, between the plaintiff and the defendant, and it is further agreed that each party to this action *waives any* and all further demand against the other party of every kind and nature, excepting those expressly set out herein." . . .

The sole issue presented in this appeal is whether a wife's interest as the beneficiary of an insurance policy issued on the life of her then husband, can be defeated by a property settlement agreement incorporated into a divorce decree which awards the life insurance policy to the husband, notwithstanding the fact that at the time of the husband's death, the wife remained the named beneficiary. We answer in the affirmative and affirm the judgment of the trial court.

It is a general rule that when a husband names his wife as the beneficiary in a life insurance policy on his own life, and thereafter they are divorced but no change is made in the beneficiary, the mere fact of divorce does not affect the right of the named beneficiary to the proceeds of the insurance policy. . . .

The weight of competent authority, however, supports the proposition urged by respondent in the instant case that the beneficiary's interest in the policy may be terminated by a property settlement agreement which may reasonably be construed as a relinquishment of the spouse's rights to the insurance. This is true even though the insured does not remove the former spouse as the beneficiary under the policy.

. . . The California cases are agreed that where a wife is named as beneficiary in a life insurance policy on her husband's life, she may, by property settlement agreement, divest herself of all interest as such beneficiary, even though she remains as the named beneficiary at the time of the husband's death. . . .

In the instant case, a property settlement stipulation was incorporated into the divorce decree granting to Earl Stoddard "all life insurance . . . through his Employment Savings Insurance Plan of Nuclear Corporation." . . .

. . . The trial court correctly found that the property settlement stipulation constituted a relinquishment of the appellant's rights to the insurance policy and that respondent was entitled to the proceeds of the policy.

[Judgment affirmed.]

National Producers Life Ins. Co. v Rogers

8 Ariz App 53, 442 P2d 876 (1968)

George Rogers insured his life with the National Producers Life Insurance Company. Ten years later he committed suicide. The insurance company denied liability because the policy stated that death by suicide was excepted. The beneficiary of the policy claimed that the insurer could not raise this defense because the two years specified by the two-year incontestability clause had expired. She sued the insurance company. A judgment was entered in her favor and the insurer appealed.

MALLOY, J. . . . Under the heading "RESTRICTIONS AND EXCEPTIONS," the insurance policy provided:

"This policy does not cover: Suicide, or death occurring as a result of alcoholism of the Insured; Death resulting from army or naval service in time of war, or death occurring by aeronautics unless a fare-paying passenger on a definitely established airline between two fixed points; Death caused by any intentional act of the beneficiary or beneficiaries."

Under the heading "GENERAL PROVISIONS," the policy provided:

"INCONTESTABILITY—This policy shall become incontestable after two years from its date or the date of the last reinstatement except for non-payment of premiums or assessments or for fraud." . . .

" 'In determining whether the incontestable clause is applicable to a given situation a distinction should be noted between matters of defense going to the invalidity of the whole policy on the one hand, and on the other hand provisions relating to excepted risks. . . .' " . . .

. . . The authorities which hold that an incontestability clause bars a defense of suicide after the end of the contestable period are relatively few in number and often subject to criticism or qualification. . . .

We think that the clear weight of the better-reasoned authorities is in accord with the holding in Wright v Philadelphia Life Ins. Co., 25 F2d 514, 515 (DC ED SC 1927), that a provision in a life insurance contract excluding coverage for death by suicide: ". . . is entirely distinct from the incontestable clause, is consistent with it, and the one in no way contradicts the other. The insurance company in this case is not denying in any way the validity of the contract, and therefore is not contesting the policy. Indeed, it stands upon the contract, affirms its validity, and says that, by the terms of the contract itself, the risk was not assumed." . . .

. . . An insurer may, unless prohibited by statute, or public policy, make such contracts and insert such exclusions into its policies as it deems proper. . . . It has long been established that, in the absence of a limiting statute, an exclusion of the risk of death by suicide is not contrary to public policy. . . .

We note that a life insurance policy issued today in the State of Arizona cannot exclude the risk of suicide for more than two years after the date of issuance of the policy. ARS § 20-1226, subsec. A(5). (Section 26, art 12, ch 64, Laws 1954, effective January 1, 1955.) But there was no such statutory limitation in existence when the policy in the present case was issued in 1947, and this statute is not retroactive.

For the same reason, the following statutory provision, which might otherwise be dispositive of the dispute here, is not pertinent:

"A clause in any policy of life insurance providing that the policy shall be incontestable after a specified period *shall preclude only a contest of the validity of the policy, and shall not preclude the assertion at any time of defenses based upon provisions in the policy which exclude or restrict coverage,* whether or not such restrictions or exclusions are excepted in the clause." ARS § 20-1217. . . .

[Judgment reversed.]

QUESTIONS AND CASE PROBLEMS

1. A father told his son that the son could have the father's car but that the son must not drive it. The son had a friend drive the car. The friend ran into another car. The insurer denied liability on the ground that the father had not given permission to the friend to drive the car and that therefore the friend was not an "other driver" within the protection of the omnibus clause. Decide [Esmond v Liscio, 209 Pa Super 200, 224 A2d 793]

2. Harsha had a policy of automobile liability insurance issued by the Fidelity General Insurance Co. that provided coverage as to personal injuries by an "uninsured motorist" to the extent of $10,000. Harsha's son was injured while a passenger when Harsha's automobile collided with Leffard's automobile. The insurance policy carried by Leffard had a liability maximum of $10,000, and his insurer paid $9,500 to Harsha on behalf of her son. Harsha, claiming that her son's injuries were $50,000, sued Fidelity on the theory that Leffard was an uninsured motorist with respect to the $40,000 not covered by his policy. Was she correct? [Harsha v Fidelity General Insurance Co., 11 Ariz App 438, 465 P2d 377]

3. The Hess-Mace Trucking Co. was delivering sand to a contractor, A. Teichert & Son. One of the sand trucks got stuck in a soft ramp. A water truck owned by Marion's Trucking Co. tried to tow the stuck truck. In arranging the tow line, the driver of the sand truck was injured. The insurer of the water truck claimed that the insurer of the sand truck was required to pay for the injury on the theory that the latter's policy covered accidents arising out of the "use" of the sand truck. Decide. [St. Paul Fire & Marine Ins. Co. v Hartford Accident & Indemnity Co., 244 Cal App 2d 826, 53 Cal Rptr 650]

4. Marshall Produce Co. insured its milk and egg processing plant against fire with the St. Paul Fire & Marine Insurance Co. Smoke from a fire near its plant was absorbed by its egg powder. Cans of the powder delivered to the United States Government were rejected as contaminated. Marshall Produce sued the insurance company for a total loss. The insurer contended that there had been no fire involving the insured property and no total loss. Decide. [Marshall Produce Co. v St. Paul Fire & Marine Insurance Co., 256 Minn 404, 98 NW2d 280]

5. A father owned an automobile. He insured it under a policy which also covered temporary substitute and newly-acquired vehicles. Thereafter, when the finance company repossessed the father's car, his son bought a new automobile. Was the son's automobile covered by the father's policy? [Hays v Robertson, 20 Utah 2d 816, 435 P2d 925]

6. The owner of an automobile went to an amusement park. He locked his car with the keys inside. When he went to leave, he requested one of the security guards of the park to break a window of the car. The guard broke a window with his gun, but in so doing, the gun was accidentally discharged and injured one of the persons who had come to the playground with the owner. It was claimed that the injury to the friend was within the coverage of the car owner's policy relating to harm "which arises out of the use" of the car. Was the harm covered? [Cagle v Playland Amusement, Inc., (La App) 202 So2d 396]

7. Sackett insured his automobile with the Farmer's Insurance Exchange against loss by accidental means. A gas station attendant improperly fastened the radiator cap with the result that the water boiled out of the radiator and damaged the engine. The Farmers Insurance Exchange claimed that it was not liable because the harm came within the exception of "mechanical breakdown and failure." Was the insurer correct? [Sackett v Farmers Insurance Exchange, 237 Cal App 2d 899, 47 Cal Rptr 350]

8. The owner of an automobile gave permission to someone else to drive the car. The permittee had insurance with the Government Employees Insurance Co. with a drive-other-car provision. The owner had insurance with the Globe Indemnity Co. with an omnibus clause. The driver had a collision with another person, and the two insurance companies disagreed as to what part of the third person's claim each company should pay. The driver's policy contained an excess insurance clause stating in substance that if the loss arose out of the use by the insured of a nonowned automobile, the policy would be "excess insurance over any other valid and collectible insurance." The owner's policy provided in substance that when the automobile was driven by a permittee, the owner's insurance would be only "excess" insurance. It further stated in effect that the owner's policy would not apply if the permittee had valid and collectible insurance "either primary or excess." What was the liability of the two insurers? [Government Employees Insurance Co. v Globe Indemnity Co., (Ky) 415 SW2d 581]

9. Turner had a policy of life insurance issued by the Equitable Life Assurance Society. His wife was the beneficiary. When she died, Turner changed the beneficiary to Olsen. Thereafter he began drinking heavily and was committed two times to institutions for alcoholism. About two years after he was released the second time, he changed the beneficiary of the policy to Hawkins. When Turner died, Olsen sued Hawkins and the insurance company for the proceeds of the policy, claiming that the change of beneficiary was not valid on the theory that Turner lacked capacity to change the beneficiary. In addition to Turner's confinement to institutions for alcoholism, it was shown that on a number of instances he had been arrested for minor offenses committed while intoxicated, and there was evidence that he was childish and forgetful. Was Olsen entitled to the proceeds of the policy? [Olsen v Hawkins, 90 Idaho 28, 408 P2d 462]

10. Walker obtained a policy of life insurance from the National Life and Accident Insurance Company. The policy reserved the right to change the beneficiary. Walker named his wife as beneficiary, and she paid the premiums on the policy. Later Walker's wife sued the insurance company and claimed that the insured could not change the beneficiary because she had paid the premiums on the policy. Decide. [National Life and Accident Insurance Co. v Walker, (Ky) 246 SW2d 139]

39 Bankruptcy

GENERAL PRINCIPLES The bankruptcy law is based upon federal statutes.

§ 39:1. Nature and the Scope. Our society has provided a system by which the honest debtor can, in substance, pay into court what he has, be relieved of all unpaid debts, and start economic life anew. This is achieved by bankruptcy laws in the case of the federal government and insolvency laws in the case of the states.

Historically these laws were not concerned with benefiting the debtor as much as they were with benefiting creditors. In their origin bankruptcy laws were designed to enable creditors to compel a fraudulent debtor to bring his property into court and to pay it to his creditors, thus preventing him from concealing his property or from paying it only to some of his creditors. Today bankruptcy and insolvency proceedings partake of both features as can be seen from the fact that such a proceeding may be started by the debtor himself or by his creditors.

State insolvency laws have only a limited sphere of operation today because the federal bankruptcy laws have superseded them to a large degree.

§ 39:2. Classification of Bankrupts.

(1) Voluntary Bankrupts. A *voluntary bankrupt* is one who subjects himself to the bankruptcy law. Any person, and in most instances any corporation or an association, may become a voluntary bankrupt. The filing of a voluntary petition automatically operates as an adjudication or determination that the petitioner is bankrupt.

Municipal, railroad, insurance, and banking corporations, and building and loan associations cannot be voluntary bankrupts.[1]

(2) Involuntary Bankrupts. An *involuntary bankrupt* is one who has been subjected to the bankruptcy law upon the petition of his creditors. Under the prescribed circumstances, most natural persons, partnerships, and corporations owing debts that amount to the sum of $1,000 or more may be forced by creditors into bankruptcy. Wage earners [2] and farmers; municipal,

---

[1] 11 United States Code § 22(a).

[2] A "wage earner" for this purpose is defined as an individual who works for wages, salary, or hire, and whose compensation does not exceed $1,500 a year. 11 USC § 1(32).

railroad, insurance, and banking corporations; and building and loan associations cannot be adjudicated involuntary bankrupts.[3]

§ 39:3. Involuntary Proceedings. If there are 12 or more creditors, 3 or more of them must join in the petition. If there are less than 12 creditors, one of them may file the petition.[4]

The petitioning creditor or creditors must have provable claims [5] against the debtor totaling $500 or more. The amount of the claims must be in excess of the value of pledged securities held by the creditors.

In determining the number of creditors of a debtor, small claims, such as are typically owed to the local corner store, are ignored. (See p. 783, In re Okamoto.)

The debtor against whom the petition is filed may appear and oppose the petition.[6] If there are more than 11 creditors when less than 3 filed the petition, the creditors who have not joined in the petition are given an opportunity to join. If the statutory number of creditors do not join in the petition, it will be dismissed.[7]

§ 39:4. Acts of Bankruptcy. An involuntary petition may not be filed unless the debtor has committed an act of bankruptcy within 4 months prior to the filing of the petition.[8]

A debtor commits an act of bankruptcy under federal statute (1) by concealing, removing, or permitting to be concealed or removed, any part of his property with intent to hinder, delay, or defraud his creditors, or any of them; (2) by transferring, while insolvent, any portion of his property to one or more of his creditors with intent to prefer such creditor or creditors over his other creditors; (3) by suffering or permitting, while insolvent, any creditor to obtain a lien upon any of his property through legal proceedings and not having vacated or discharged such lien within 30 days from date thereof or at least 5 days before the date that was set for any sale or other disposition of such property; (4) by making a general assignment for the benefit of his creditors; (5) while insolvent, by permitting or being forced to put a receiver or a trustee in charge of his property; or (6) by admitting in writing his inability to pay his debts and his willingness to be adjudged a bankrupt.[9]

---

[3] Special statutory provision is made for the reorganization and liquidation of such corporations because of the nature of the enterprise and in order to protect the public.

[4] 11 USC § 95(b).

[5] See § 39:14. A claim may be unliquidated as to amount provided that it is not contingent as to liability, although the unliquidated claim may be disqualified if a maximum value cannot be estimated. 11 USC § 95(b).

[6] 11 USC § 41(b).

[7] § 95(d).

[8] § 21(b).

[9] The filing of a voluntary petition in bankruptcy is in itself an act of bankruptcy since the debtor admits in writing his inability to pay his debts and his willingness to be adjudged a bankrupt.

§ 39:5. Insolvency. Insolvency is a necessary element of the second, third, and fifth acts of bankruptcy, but not of the others. The bankruptcy act declares that a person is deemed to be *insolvent* under the provisions of the statute "whenever the aggregate of his property, exclusive of any property which he may have conveyed, transferred, concealed, removed, or permitted to be concealed or removed, with intent to defraud, hinder, or delay his creditors, shall not at a fair valuation be sufficient in amount to pay his debts." [10]

§ 39:6. Bankruptcy Officials. The actual bankruptcy proceeding, apart from that which takes place in court, is under the control of certain officials: (1) the referee, (2) the receiver, and (3) the trustee.

(1) Referee. A *referee* is appointed for a 6-year term to hear the evidence in bankruptcy cases and to submit his findings to the court. He acts in the nature of a special bankruptcy court. A receiver may impose fines for contempt up to $250.[11]

(2) Receiver. On the petition of creditors who fear that the assets of the debtor will be lost, a *receiver* may be appointed as custodian to preserve the assets [12] and turn them over to the trustee when appointed.

(3) Trustee. The creditors of the debtor elect—or if they fail to do so, the court appoints—a trustee. The *trustee* has a double role as owner of the property of the debtor and as holder of the rights of a most favored creditor.

§ 39:7. The Bankruptcy Trustee as Successor to the Debtor. The trustee in bankruptcy automatically becomes by operation of the law the owner of all property of the bankrupt in excess of such property as the bankrupt is entitled to under local state exemption laws.

As the statutory owner or successor to the bankrupt's property, the trustee has only the status of an assignee. That is, the trustee will not be a holder in due course of paper as to which the bankrupt was merely an ordinary holder. (See p. 785, New York Terminal Warehouse Co. v Bullington.)

(1) Payment of Bankrupt's Outstanding Checks. The rule that the title to the property of the bankrupt passes to his trustee in bankruptcy is subject to an exception that a drawee bank in which the bankrupt has a checking account may make payment on a bankrupt's check when it has had no notice or knowledge of his bankruptcy.[13]

---

[10] 11 USC § 1(19).

[11] 1973 Bankruptcy Rule No. 920(a). He may not impose a punishment of imprisonment. If it appears to the referee that conduct warrants a greater fine or imprisonment, he may certify the matter to the district court.

[12] § 11(3).

[13] Bank of Marin v England, 385 US 99.

§ 39:8. The Bankruptcy Trustee as a Favored Creditor. The bankruptcy trustee possesses the rights that are possessed by the most favored creditor of the bankrupt. Specifically, this means that the trustee can avoid certain preferences gained by a judgment against the bankrupt or by a transfer of property, of which a recording or registering is required, within 4 months prior to the filing of the petition or after the filing thereof and before adjudication.[14] He is required by the terms of the bankruptcy act to recover for the benefit of the creditors any of the bankrupt's property that has been transferred within 4 months prior to the filing of the petition, with the intent to hinder, delay, or defraud any creditors, or that is in the hands of a person under a transfer that is void by the laws of any state or that was received by such person with knowledge or reason to know that the debtor was insolvent.[15]

§ 39:9. Voidable Preferences. To constitute a voidable preference, with the consequence that it may be avoided by the debtor's trustee in bankruptcy, there must be (1) transfer of property (2) within four months of bankruptcy (3) to or for the benefit of a creditor (4) which enables him to obtain a greater percentage of his debt than other creditors of the same class, and which is made (5) when the debtor is insolvent and (6) the creditor knows or has reason to know that the debtor is insolvent.[16]

(1) Balance Sheet Test of Insolvency. A debtor is insolvent under the bankruptcy act when his assets, fairly valued, are not sufficient to pay his debts.[17] This contrasts with the equity concept of involvency, which is the inability to pay debts as they become due.[18]

§ 39:10. Avoidance of Liens. The mere adjudication in bankruptcy does not automatically avoid or vacate a lien created within the 4-month period, and the lien remains in force unless avoided by the trustee as a preferential transfer.[19] If the lien is not avoided in the bankruptcy proceeding and if the trustee in bankruptcy sells the assets of the bankrupt that are subject to a judicial lien, the purchaser from the trustee in bankruptcy, in an action in a state court, may avoid the creditor's lien to the same extent as could the trustee in bankruptcy.[20]

When a creditor has an unperfected security interest in personal property of the bankrupt, such security interest cannot be asserted against the trustee

---

[14] § 96(b).

[15] §§ 107(d), 110(e).

[16] Bankruptcy Act § 60, 11 USC § 96.

[17] Arst v First Nat. Bank, 211 Kan 758, 508 P2d 520.

[18] Note that under the UCC both criteria for insolvency are employed. "A person is 'insolvent' who either has ceased to pay his debts in the ordinary course of business or cannot pay his debts as they become due or is insolvent within the meaning of the federal bankruptcy law." UCC § 1-201(23).

[19] Crystal Laundry & Cleaners, Inc. v Continental Finance & Loan Co., 97 Ga App 823, 104 SE2d 654.

[20] Geo. A. Clark & Son, Inc. v Nold, (SD) 185 NW2d 677.

in bankruptcy of the debtor, without regard to whether it would otherwise be preferential within the meaning of the bankruptcy act.[21] If the security interest has been perfected and is not preferential in character, the trustee in bankruptcy and any purchaser of the debtor's assets from the trustee holds such assets subject to the interest of the creditor.[22]

As Article 9 of the UCC has eliminated the significance of title in transactions involving personal property, the determination of whether the creditor prevails over the bankrupt debtor's trustee in bankruptcy is not controlled by the name of the transaction between the creditor and the debtor nor by whether the creditor has or has not reserved title to the collateral.[23] The same conclusion is to be reached when a mortgage of real estate is involved since even in title theory states, the mortgage is merely a lien with respect to third persons even though it purports to transfer title to the mortgagee.

ADMINISTRATION OF THE BANKRUPT'S ESTATE

The federal statutes regulate in detail the manner in which claims against the bankrupt are to be determined and his assets distributed in payment of them.

§ 39:11. Meetings of Creditors. At various times in the administration of the bankruptcy, a meeting of the creditors is held, such as the initial meeting to appoint a trustee, subsequent meetings to pass on particular matters authorized by the bankruptcy act, and a final meeting when the estate is to be closed.[24]

A majority in number and in the amount of claims of all creditors and who are present and whose claims have been allowed is required for any decision by the creditors. Creditors who have priority or security are not entitled to vote, nor are their claims counted in computing the number of creditors or the amounts of their claims, unless the amounts of their claims exceed the values of such priorities or security, and then only for such excess.[25]

§ 39:12. Examination of Persons. Provision is made for the examination of the bankrupt and other persons as to his property and his conduct relating thereto. The wife of the bankrupt may be examined only in respect to business transacted by her or to which she is a party, and to determine whether she has transacted or has been a party to any business of her husband.[26]

§ 39:13. Proof and Allowance of Claims. Each creditor is required to file a sworn statement setting forth his claim and the basis thereof. These claims

---

[21] UCC § 9-301 (applicable to security interests in personal property).

[22] When a security interest in personal property is involved, perfection is governed by Article 9 of the Uniform Commercial Code. If land is involved, the perfection of a security interest therein, such as a mortgage, is governed by non-Code law of the state where the land is located.

[23] In re Yale Express System, Inc., (CA2 NY) 370 F2d 433.

[24] 11 USC § 91(d),(e).

[25] § 92(a),(b).

[26] § 44(a).

are ordinarily passed upon by the referee, although in some instances they may be considered initially by the court. The claim is then allowed or disallowed as in any other lawsuit. A claim must ordinarily be disallowed if not presented until more than six months after the first meeting of creditors.[27]

The six months time limitation on the filing of claims is mandatory and a creditor is not excused from filing within that time by the circumstance that the trustee in bankruptcy in fact knew of the existence of the creditor's claim. (See p. 785, In re Vega Baja Lumber Yard, Inc.)

A creditor who received some preferential payment or transfer of property within four months prior to the filing of the petition in bankruptcy cannot prove his claim unless he surrenders such payment or transfer.[28] If the claim of a creditor is secured, he is also barred from proving his claim except as to that part of his claim in excess of the security.

§ **39:14. Claims that are Provable.** Not all claims may be proven, that is, be permitted to share in the distribution of the assets of the bankrupt debtor. The claims that may be proved are: (a) a debt evidenced by a judgment or an instrument in writing, absolutely owing at the time of the filing of the petition by or against the bankrupt, whether then payable or not; (b) a debt due as costs against a bankrupt who was, at the time of the filing of the petition by or against the bankrupt, the plaintiff in an action that would pass to the trustee and that the trustee, upon notice thereof, declines to prosecute; (c) a debt founded upon a claim for costs, incurred in good faith by a creditor before the filing of the petition, in an action to recover a provable debt; (d) a debt based upon an open account, or upon a contract express or implied; (e) a debt based upon a provable debt reduced to judgment after the filing of the petition and before the consideration of the bankrupt's application for a discharge, less costs and interest after the filing of the petition; (f) an award of workmen's compensation; (g) a right to damages for negligence; (h) contingent debts and contingent contractual liabilities; and (i) claims for anticipatory breach of contract.[29]

(1) Unliquidated Claims. In respect to an *unliquidated claim* of a creditor, that is, a claim for an uncertain or disputed amount, the bankruptcy act provides that upon application to the court of bankruptcy, such a claim shall be liquidated or estimated in such a manner as the court shall direct. If possible to liquidate or estimate the claim within a reasonable time, the claim may be allowed against the bankrupt's estate.[30]

§ **39:15. Sale of Bankrupt's Assets.** In order to pay the debts of the bankrupt, it is necessary to convert his assets into cash and the trustee is accordingly authorized to sell his property. The sale in general may be made in any manner that is in the best interests of the estate. Such sales are under the

---

[27] § 93(n).
[28] §§ 93(g), 96(b), 107.
[29] § 103(a).
[30] §§ 93(d), 103(d).

supervision of the bankruptcy court; and if any property is sold for less than 75 percent of its value, confirmation of the sale by the court is necessary.

§ 39:16. Distribution of Estate. After all of the bankrupt's debts are determined, the assets that have been collected by the trustee are distributed first to those creditors with priorities; then to the general creditors without priorities; and, should any balance remain after all creditors have been paid, the balance to the bankrupt. These payments to creditors, called *dividends,* are made in installments.

The bankruptcy act confers a prior right of payment to (a) costs of administration and expenses necessary to preserve the estate, filing fees paid by creditors in involuntary proceedings, expenses of creditors in recovering property transferred or concealed by the bankrupt, and the reasonable expenses of creditors in opposing a composition that is refused or set aside; (b) wages due to workmen, clerks, traveling or city salesmen, or servants, earned within 3 months preceding the petition, but not to exceed $600 to each person; (c) expenses of creditors in opposing an arrangement or a plan for the discharge of a bankrupt, or in convicting a person of violating the bankruptcy law; (d) taxes owed by the bankrupt, except taxes against property over and above the value of the interest of the bankrupt therein; and (e) debts owed persons, including the United States, who by law are entitled to priority.

Payments due by an employer to a trust for employees are not "wages" within the priority provision where payments from the trust were only made upon retirement, disability, or death. (See p. 786, Joint Industry Board v United States.)

STATUS OF BANKRUPT

When a debtor is adjudicated a bankrupt, an important change takes place in his legal status. When he is thereafter granted a discharge he is released of his ordinary debts.

§ 39:17. Rights and Duties of Bankrupt. The bankruptcy act confers certain rights upon and imposes certain duties on the bankrupt.[31] If the debtor fails to cooperate or if he deceives the court as by the concealment of property which he hopes to save for himself, the law provides specific penalties, in addition to denying the bankrupt the benefits of the statute.

(1) Rights. The debtor has the right to object to being declared or adjudicated a bankrupt. If so adjudicated, he may request a discharge in bankruptcy. He is protected generally from arrest on civil process while within the court district on matters relating to the bankruptcy proceeding. The debtor is given an immunity from criminal prosecution based on his testimony at meetings other than at the hearing on his discharge and other than in a prosecution for perjury.

---

[31] § 25.

(2) Duties. The debtor is required to file statements showing the property he possesses, any claim to an exemption, and the names of his creditors, with detailed information as to their claims. He must also attend meetings of creditors and hearings before the referee and court, and answer all proper questions relating to his estate. He must examine the proofs of claim filed against him to see if he disputes them, and he must obey orders of the bankruptcy court.

§ 39:18. Discharge in Bankruptcy. The decree terminating the bankruptcy proceeding is generally a discharge or release of the debtor from his debts.

(1) Application for Discharge. The adjudication of any individual to be a bankrupt operates automatically as an application for a discharge in bankruptcy. A corporation may file an application for a discharge within six months after it is adjudged to be a bankrupt.[32]

(2) Denial of Discharge. The application for discharge will be denied if the bankrupt has: (a) committed certain offenses punishable by imprisonment as provided in the Act; (b) unjustifiably destroyed, mutilated, falsified, concealed, or failed to keep books of account or records from which his financial status and business transactions might be ascertained; (c) obtained money or property on credit for a business by a false representation in writing concerning financial condition; (d) permitted others, within a year previous to the filing of the petition, to remove, transfer, conceal, or destroy any of his property, with the intent to hinder, delay, or defraud creditors, or has been guilty of this himself; (e) been granted a discharge in bankruptcy within 6 years; (f) refused, during the proceedings, to answer any material question approved by the court, or to obey any lawful order of the court; (g) failed to explain satisfactorily the loss of any assets, or the deficiency of his assets to pay his debts; or (h) failed to pay in full the filing fees required by the bankruptcy act.[33]

A discharge in bankruptcy cannot be refused for any ground not stated in the Bankruptcy Act. Consequently, a discharge cannot be refused because the bankrupt was a gambler.[34]

(a) UNDERLYING TRANSACTION. It is the nature of the claim against the debtor at the time of bankruptcy which is controlling. Consequently, when an agreement is made to settle a claim for embezzlement or conversion and the obligation under the agreement has not been paid at the time of bankruptcy, the liability of the bankrupt is a contract liability on the settlement agreement and the referee may not go back to the underlying tort occurrence so as to bar the discharge of the claim. (See p. 787, In re Kelley.)

---

[32] § 32(a).
[33] § 32(c).
[34] In re Zidoff, (CA7 Ill) 309 F2d 417.

(b) FALSE FINANCIAL STATEMENT. When the debtor has obtained credit by making a false written statement as to financial condition, the claim of the creditor who extended credit in reliance on that statement is not affected by the debtor's discharge in bankruptcy if the misstatement was material and was fraudulently made.[35]

When a debtor has obtained an additional loan on the basis of a fraudulent written misrepresentation as to his financial condition, the debtor's subsequent bankruptcy discharge has no effect as to his total indebtedness.[36]

The obtaining of credit by means of a false financial statement is a bar to a discharge only when the bankrupt is engaged in business.[37] If the bankrupt is a nonbusiness debtor, such as an ordinary consumer, the false financial statement does not bar his discharge in bankruptcy but merely prevents the discharge in bankruptcy from barring the claim of the particular creditor who had extended credit.

A false financial statement does not bar a discharge in bankruptcy unless the creditor had relied thereon and had acted reasonably in so doing. If the surrounding circumstances indicated to a reasonable man that the statement may be false and that further inquiry should be made, a creditor who merely relies or claims to rely on the statement without making any further inquiry cannot raise the falsity of the statement as a bar to the debtor's discharge and the debtor will not be denied a discharge merely because he had made the false financial statement. (See p. 789, Kentile Floors, Inc. v Winham.)

§ 39:19. Effect of Discharge. A discharge in bankruptcy releases the bankrupt from all his provable debts, except debts that: [38] (a) are due as taxes which became due and owing within the 3 years preceding bankruptcy; (b) are liabilities (1) for obtaining property by false pretenses or false representation, (2) for a loan or property obtained on credit or an extension of credit obtained by a materially false written statement by the debtor as to financial condition, (3) for willful and malicious injuries to the person or the property of another,[39] (4) for alimony for the support of a wife or child, (5) for seduction of an unmarried female, (6) for breach of promise accompanied by seduction, and (7) for criminal conversation; (c) have not been listed by the bankrupt in time to be proved, unless the creditor had notice or actual knowledge of the proceedings; (d) are created by the bankrupt's fraud, embezzlement, misappropriation, or defalcation while acting as an officer or in any fiduciary position; (e) are wages due to workmen, clerks, salesmen, or servants, which have been earned within 3 months preceding the petition; or

---

35 11 USC § 35(a)(2).

36 Budget Finance Plan v Haner, 92 Idaho 56, 436 P2d 722.

37 11 USC § 32(c)(3).

38 11 USC § 35.

39 A judgment based on a claim for willful and wanton negligence is within the bankruptcy exception as to "willful and malicious" claims. Bice v Jones, 45 Ala App 709, 236 So2d 718. It is generally held that conduct which is "intentional" is "willful and malicious," although a minority of courts require proof of actual willfulness and malice. Robinson v Early, 248 Cal App 2d 19, 56 Cal Rptr 183.

(f) are due for moneys of an employee received or retained by the bankrupt to secure the faithful performance by such employee of the provisions of the contract of employment.

When a claim is discharged in bankruptcy, it must be ignored for all purposes. For example, when a collision damage judgment entered against the bankrupt is discharged, the judgment ceases to exist, even though in fact it has not been paid. Consequently, neither the bankrupt's motor vehicle registration nor his operator's license may be suspended under a state financial responsibility law because the judgment was not paid.[40]

The discharge in bankruptcy does not destroy the debts but merely gives the debtor a protection from their enforcement. The order discharging the bankrupt, however, expressly declares that a judgment obtained in any other court upon a discharged claim is "null and void" and enjoins all creditors of the bankrupt from bringing suit against him on such obligations.[41]

After a debtor has been discharged in bankruptcy, there are no restraints upon his activities or use of property. If he can obtain necessary capital, he can reengage in any business, including the same business in which he was engaged prior to bankruptcy. The property that he acquires subsequent to his discharge in bankruptcy cannot be reached by prebankruptcy creditors even though their claims had not been paid in full.[42] It is immaterial in what manner the postbankruptcy property is acquired, whether as earnings, gifts, inheritance, or investment gains.

§ 39:20. Liability of Third Persons and Collateral. The fact that a debtor obtains a discharge in bankruptcy does not ordinarily bar a claimant or creditor with respect to third persons or collateral. For example, the bankruptcy of the maker of a promissory note does not discharge the liability of an indorser. Similarly, when an automobile public liability insurer is liable directly to the injured third person, that liability is not affected by the fact that the insured driver has been discharged in bankruptcy.[43] Similarly, if a creditor has a valid security interest in collateral that was perfected more than four months before the filing of the bankruptcy petition, the creditor's security interest is not affected by the debtor's discharge in bankruptcy. Likewise, a tax lien on the bankrupt's property is not affected by the debtor's discharge.

BANKRUPTCY COMPOSITIONS

In addition to the traditional liquidations in bankruptcy, twentieth century amendments to the bankruptcy law permit the parties by agreement to make various reorganizations and compositions.

§ 39:21. Corporate Reorganizations. The provisions for corporate reorganizations [44] permit a corporation, an indenture trustee, or 3 or more creditors

[40] Perez v Campbell, 402 US 637.
[41] 11 USC § 32(f)(2).
[42] Schenker v Demarest, (La App) 195 So2d 346.
[43] Fix v Automobile Club Inter-Insurance Exchange, (Mo) 413 SW2d 194.
[44] 11 USCA §§ 501 to 676, inclusive.

of the corporation with certain claims amounting in the aggregate to $5,000 or over to file a petition for a reorganization. The petition must show among other things that the corporation is insolvent or is unable to pay its debts as they mature and that relief is necessary under the statute. It may also include the proposed scheme of reorganization. The statute directs the court to confirm a plan of reorganization provided that it is fair, equitable, and feasible; that it has been proposed and accepted in good faith; and that all payments made or promised are approved as reasonable.[45]

§ **39:22. Arrangements.** The provisions for arrangements [46] permit any debtor who could become a bankrupt to file a petition for the acceptance of a plan for the settlement, satisfaction, or extension of the time of payment of his unsecured debts. The statute directs the court to confirm the plan if it is satisfied that the plan is fair, equitable, and feasible, that the debtor has done no act which would bar a discharge in bankruptcy, and that the proposal and the acceptance are made in good faith.

§ **39:23. Real Property Arrangements.** The provisions for real property arrangements [47] permit any debtor who could become a bankrupt, except a corporation, to file a petition for the acceptance of a plan for the alteration or the modification of the rights of creditors holding debts secured by real property or a leasehold interest of which the debtor is the legal or equitable owner. The statute stipulates that the court shall confirm a plan that is accepted by the creditors in good faith.

§ **39:24. Wage Earners' Plans.** The provisions for wage earners' plans [48] permit an individual who is insolvent or is unable to pay his debts as they mature and whose principal income is derived from salary, wages, or commissions not exceeding $3,600 a year, to file a petition for the acceptance of a composition or an extension of time, or both, in view of future earnings or salary. The statute directs the court to confirm a plan that is proposed and accepted by the creditors in good faith.

---

[45] SEC v United States Realty and Improvement Co., 310 US 434.
[46] 11 USCA §§ 701 to 799, inclusive.
[47] Ch. 12, §§ 801 to 926, inclusive.
[48] Ch. 13, §§ 1001 to 1086, inclusive.

CASES FOR CHAPTER 39

In re Okamoto

(CA9 Cal) 491 F2d 496 (1974)

Okamoto owed money to Hornblower & Weeks-Hemphill, Noyes. Hornblower filed a petition to have Okamoto declared an involuntary bankrupt. Okamoto moved to dismiss the petition on the ground that he had more than twelve creditors and therefore the petition could not be filed by only one. Hornblower replied that the claims of the other creditors were too small to count and therefore Okamoto did not have more than twelve creditors and the petition could accordingly be filed by one

creditor. The lower court held that every creditor was to be counted and dismissed Hornblower's petition. Hornblower appealed.

ELY, J. . . . Hornblower attempted to proceed as the sole petitioning creditor, pursuant to § 59(b) of the Bankruptcy Act, 11 U.S.C. § 95(b). Okamoto's answer alleged that he was indebted to more than eleven creditors, and the answer was accompanied by a schedule listing twenty-one creditors. The Referee in Bankruptcy conducted a hearing under § 59(d) and found that Okamoto had nineteen unsecured creditors which must be counted. Since a single creditor cannot proceed under § 59(b) unless the total number of claimants is less than twelve, the Referee dismissed Hornblower's petition. On review, the District Court affirmed the Referee's Order of dismissal.

. . . Hornblower attacks the finding of the Bankruptcy Court that Okamoto had more than eleven creditors. Hornblower principally asserts that creditors for relatively small current expenses should be excluded in computing the total number of creditors under § 59(b). Section 59(b) provides in part: "Three or more creditors who have provable claims not contingent as to liability against a person, amounting in the aggregate to $500 in excess of the value of any securities held by them, or, if all of the creditors of the person are less than twelve in number, then one or more of the creditors whose claim or claims equal that amount, may file a petition to have him adjudged a bankrupt. . . ." If less than three creditors join in the petition, § 59(e) furnishes the guidelines for computing the total number of claimants. Although § 59(e) does not provide for the exclusion of creditors with small claims. Hornblower contends that the doctrine of *de minimis non curat lex* [the law does not bother with trifles] should be applied. Since eight of the debts here involved were for amounts less than sixty-five dollars, Hornblower argues that the total number of creditors meets the statutory limit.

In support of its contention, Hornblower cites several early District Court decisions, including In re Blount, 142 F. 263 (E.D. Ark. 1906). At the time of filing its petition, Hornblower recognized that the more recent decisions had disapproved the *Blount* rationale. *See, e.g.,* Grigsby-Grunow Co. v Hieb Radio Supply Co., 71 F2d 113 (8th Cir 1934); In re Colorado Lime Co., 298 F Supp 1053 (D Colo 1969). Subsequent to the decision by the Bankruptcy Court, however, the Fifth Circuit issued its opinion in Denham v Shellman Grain Elevator, Inc., 444 F2d 1376 (5th Cir 1971). In *Denham* the Court adopted a similar contention to that here advanced, holding that creditors claiming insignificant amounts are not to be included in determining the total number of creditors for the purposes of § 59(b). The Court explained: "It is our belief that whether or not a scheme was involved, it was not the intent of Congress to allow recurring bills such as utility bills and the like to create a situation which, by refusal of these small creditors to join in an involuntary petition, can defeat the use of the Bankruptcy Act by a large creditor, as in the subject case. This would be grossly inequitable, and for this reason this Court refuses to follow the *Colorado Lime* decision.". . .

We are not persuaded by *Denham,* for it appears to us that the *Denham* court ignored unambiguous Congressional direction. The Congress has explicitly prescribed the procedure that must be followed when less than three creditors join in the petition. In such circumstances the Act provides that the alleged bankrupt *must* have less than twelve creditors and expressly excludes certain types of creditors from the required computation. Since Congress made no distinction between large and small claims, we cannot arrogate unto ourselves the power to do so and thereby engraft an additional exception to the Act. Hornblower's argument properly should be addressed to the Congress. Our conclusion is reinforced by the fact that Congress has clearly and expressly excluded small claims when it has intended to do so. *See* Bankruptcy Act § 56(c), 11 USC § 92(c).* . . .

Since Okamoto was indebted to more than eleven creditors and only one claimant filed the

* Bankruptcy Act § 56(c), 11 USC § 92(c), provides: "Claims of $50 or less shall not be counted in computing the number of creditors voting or present at creditors' meetings, but shall be counted in computing the amount."

petition under § 59(b), the petition was properly dismissed.

[Judgment affirmed.]

New York Terminal Warehouse Co. v Bullington

(CA5 Tex) 213 F2d 340 (1954)

The Denton Peanut Co. stored peanuts with the New York Terminal Warehouse Co. for which the latter issued negotiable warehouse receipts. These receipts were given as security for a loan from the Commodity Credit Corporation. Later Denton became bankrupt, and Bullington was appointed its trustee in bankruptcy. The bankruptcy court required the Commodity Credit Corporation to surrender the warehouse receipts to Bullington before it would be allowed to prove the full amount of its claim in the bankruptcy court. Bullington then presented the warehouse receipts to the New York Terminal. Terminal refused to deliver any peanuts on the ground that it had already delivered the full quantity to Denton without requiring the production and surrender of the negotiable warehouse receipts. Bullington sued New York Terminal. From a judgment in his favor, Terminal appealed.

RIVES, C.J. . . . Under the bankruptcy act, the trustee succeeds to the title of the bankrupt, and he has certain rights in addition to those possessed by the bankrupt. He has the status of a lien or execution creditor. . . . However, the trustee does not occupy the position of a bona fide purchaser for value without notice of any equity. . . .

We entertain no doubt of the authority of the bankruptcy court to direct the Commodity Credit Corporation to assign its security to the Trustee as a condition precedent to approving its claim. . . .

It does not follow, however, that the Trustee thereby attained the status theretofore occupied by Commodity Credit Corporation of a holder in due course of the negotiable warehouse receipts. To the contrary we think that the rights and title of the trustee are to be measured by the same principles as apply to other property of the bankrupt estate. The rule protecting one holding through a holder in due course . . . "does not apply to cases where the payee or a holder of paper, being so circumstanced at the start that he cannot recover thereon, transfers it to an innocent third party for value, and subsequently purchases it back for value." While the bankruptcy court had authority to require the Commodity Credit Corporation to surrender possession of the warehouse receipts before approving its unsecured claim with priority, the appellant warehouse company . . . had a right to show upon present trial that equity and justice do not require that the Trustee be subrogated to the position of an innocent holder for value of the warehouse receipts formerly held by Commodity Credit Corporation, absolved of all defenses and equities to which the bankrupt would have been subject. Certainly if the bankrupt has had the benefit of the peanuts once, equity does not require a second realization on the same asset by the Trustee. . . .

[Judgment reversed.]

In re Vega Baja Lumber Yard, Inc.

(DC D Puerto Rico) 285 F Supp 143 (1968)

The Vega Baja Lumber Yard owed money to the First City National Bank. The bank sued the lumber yard and attached some of its property. Thereafter bankruptcy proceedings were begun and the lumber yard was adjudicated a bankrupt. The bank filed a claim in bankruptcy. The referee rejected the bank's claim because it had been filed more than six months after the debtor had been adjudicated a bankrupt. The bank claimed that the six-months limitation did not bar it because the trustee knew of its claim.

FERNANDEZ-BADILLO, D.J. . . . The weight of authority considers the six month period . . . as peremptory and immutable. . . .

. . . The Court has no discretion to accept an untimely filing of a claim.

It has been equally established that if there is upon the record in the bankruptcy proceedings, within the six months . . . , anything to show the existence, nature and amount of a claim, it may be amended even after expiration of the period. . . . Courts have been watchful in departing from the general rule of strict interpretation of the statute, and amendments offered after the six months period are closely scrutinized to avoid the filing of an untimely new claim under the guise of an amendment. . . .

The creditor must have shown in some form that he had a demand against the estate and intended to hold the estate liable. The substance of a claim must have been made in some form before the statutory period expired. . . .

There are many cases where the dilatory creditor has done some positive act which was considered tantamount to an assertion or demand against the bankrupt's estate. See, for example: Fyne v Atlas Supply Co. (4th Cir 1957) 245 F2d 107 (amendment allowed where there was a letter from claimant's counsel to trustee, attorney participated in the first meeting of creditors, and the claim in question gave rise to the involuntary petition in bankruptcy, which claim had been reduced to judgment): In re Fant (D.C.S.C. 1927) 21 F2d 182 (creditor's claim was fully set up in the petition for bankruptcy, admission in part by the bankrupt that claim was correct, claimant's action in state court brought into the bankruptcy court a considerable fund); 55 F Supp 532, affirmed in Public Operating Corp. v Schneider, 2 Cir, 145 F2d 830 (attorney's letter to the referee stating client was a creditor of bankrupt, that a claim would be filed as soon as an examination of the records of creditor was completed and asking that the letter be accepted as a notice of claim against the estate to be subsequently amended.) . . .

Regardless of how liberal an approach is had as to what is sufficient to constitute a basis for amendment, the courts have consistently searched the record for an assertion or claim, no matter how informal, that would permit amendment. . . .

. . . Pendency of litigation, in and of itself, is not sufficient basis to permit an amendment. . . . Mere knowledge on the part of the trustee or of the referee in bankruptcy as to the existence of a claim is not sufficient basis for allowing the filing of an amended claim. . . .

There is no claim in the files, informal, defective or inarticulately drawn, by or on behalf of the creditor, that could amount to an original proof of claim.

It is therefore ordered that the denial of the petition for approval of claim be affirmed.

Joint Industry Board v United States

391 US 224 (1968)

An industry-wide collective bargaining contract required employers to make specified contributions to a trust for employees. A & S Electrical Corporation was an employer subject to this contract. It went into bankruptcy. At the time it had not made all the payments due by it to the employee trust. The Joint Board of the Electrical Industry, as trustee of the fund, asserted that the claim for the contributions was entitled to priority as "wages due workmen." This was opposed by the United States. Priority was denied the claim of the trust and the Joint Board appealed.

WHITE, J. . . . Contributions received by the trustees are credited to the account of the individual employees but are "payable to him only as hereinafter provided," namely, upon death, retirement from the industry at age 60, permanent disability, entry into the Armed Forces, or ceasing to be a participant under the plan. Death benefits are paid only out of income, if available, and other benefits, though they may be payable in installments, will at a minimum return to the employee the total of the contributions credited to his name, without interest.

A & S Electric Corporation, an employer liable for contributions to the annuity plan, was adjudicated a bankrupt in 1963. The Joint Industry Board filed a claim which included $5,114 representing payments under the plan which fell due but were unpaid during the three months prior to the commencement of the proceedings. Priority for this amount was asserted under § 64a(2). The United States, with a fourth-class priority claim for unpaid taxes, objected to the allowance of the Joint Board's priority claim. The referee and the courts agreed with the United States, holding that payments due to the Joint Board were not wages due to workmen, relying for this conclusion principally upon United States v Embassy Restaurant, Inc. 359 US 29. . . .

We agree that Embassy Restaurant controls this case. There the claim was for unpaid employer contributions to a welfare fund, the contributions being $8 per month for each full-time employee; the fund provided life insurance, weekly sick benefits, hospital and surgical payments, and other advantages for covered employees. That claim, the Court held, was not entitled to § 64a(2) priority because payments to such a welfare fund did not satisfy the manifest purpose of the priority, which was "to enable employees displaced by bankruptcy to secure, with some promptness, the money directly due to them in back wages, and thus to alleviate in some degree the hardship that unemployment usually brings to workers and their families." . . . The contributions involved there were payable to trustees, not to employees, and were disbursable to employees only on the occurrence of certain events, not including the bankruptcy of the employer. Neither the contributions nor the plan provided any immediate support for workmen during the period of financial distress.

The case before us concerns employer contributions to the welfare fund which are similarly not due the employees and never were; they were payable only to the trustees, who had the exclusive right to hold and manage the fund. Though the contributions were credited to individual employee accounts, nothing was payable to employees except upon the occurrence of certain events. Until death, retirement after age 60, permanent disability, entry into military service, or cessation of participation under the plan, no benefits were payable. Further, as the referee pointed out, the employee could not assign, pledge, or borrow against the contributions, or otherwise use them as his own. Quite obviously the annuity fund was not intended to relieve the distress of temporary unemployment, whether arising from the bankruptcy of the employer or for some other reason. Hence, if Embassy Restaurant is to be followed, the unpaid contributions in this case do not satisfy the fundamental purpose of the § 64a(2) priority for wages due to workmen. . . .

[Judgment affirmed.]

FORTAS, J. (dissenting). . . . I do not agree that United States v Embassy Restaurant, Inc., 359 US 29, . . . controls this case. I believe the employer's unpaid contributions to the employees' annuity plan are "wages . . . due to workmen" within § 64a(2) of the Bankruptcy Act. Those contributions accrued and unpaid within three months before the commencement of the bankruptcy proceedings are entitled to the statutory priority. . . .

It is unmistakably clear (1) that the sums in question were to be paid as part of the wage bargain between employer and employee; (2) that the sum due each employee was specifically related to and measured by his work; (3) that the sum which each employee earned was accounted for separately and individually; he was entitled to the amount paid to the trustee on account of his individual labor; and (4) that inevitably, as sure as death, there was to come a point of time when the sum remitted to the trustee on account of each individual's work would be paid to that individual or his heirs. . . .

But the present case is materially different from Embassy Restaurant. In that case, the employee was never entitled to receive the sums which were paid into the fund on account of his labor. These sums and the sums paid by the employer for all other employees were used to provide life insurance, sick benefits, hospital and surgical payments, and other benefits. An employee was never entitled to demand and receive payment of sums that he had earned. These sums were not credited to him to be paid upon his death or retirement or other contingencies. . . .

In re Kelley

(DC ND Cal) 259 F Supp 297 (1965)

Kelley embezzled money of Century Enterprises, Inc. An agreement was made by which Kelley agreed to make certain repayments to Century. Kelley was thereafter adjudicated a bankrupt. He claimed that his liability under the settlement agreement was discharged by the discharge in bankruptcy. The referee held that it was not barred because it was based upon a willful and malicious injury to the property of another.

SWEIGERT, D.J. . . . The agreement provides that the Bankrupt and his wife, in their individual capacities, and Century Enterprises, Inc., would execute and deliver their promissory note in "the sum of $18,444.13, payable at $500.00 per month or more, including interest at the rate of ten (10%) percent on the declining balance from January 1, 1963, with installments due on the first day of each and every month commencing March 1, 1963." The agreement also contained the following provision, which because of its importance to the case, is set out in full:

> That in consideration of the terms, conditions and covenants of this agreement, First Parties [respondents] do for themselves, their heirs, executors, administrators and assigns, agree with Second Parties [bankrupt, his wife and Century], their heirs, executors, administrators and successors that neither of First Parties will apply or jointly institute any suit, action at law or equity or proceeding against the Second Parties or any of them, nor in any way institute or prosecute any claim, demand, action or cause of action for such claim, damage, loss, recovery or expense of any nature arising out of the transaction between First Parties and Second Parties hereinabove referred to. No provision herein shall, however, in any manner be construed or intended to limit, affect or impair the right of First Parties to act upon the promissory note agreed to be delivered by the terms of this agreement in the event of a failure of the Second Parties to make the payments as provided for therein, including attorney fees and court costs.

Pursuant to the agreement and note of January 10, 1963, the bankrupt made payments of $500.00 per month from March 1, 1963, through July 1, 1963. Thereafter, bankrupt and his wife defaulted on said promissory note, and on November 15, 1963, the respondents commenced an action in the Superior Court of the State of California, in and for the County of Santa Clara, on said promissory note. The bankrupt answered and raised the affirmative defense that the promissory note included interest at a usurious rate, namely 20%. The parties to the action in the Superior Court thereafter entered into a Stipulation for Judgment whereby it was agreed that the bankrupt, his wife and Century have judgment against them for "the sum of $16,842.41 principal, interest from July 1, 1963, to date at 7% per annum amounting to $717.71, $2,500.00 attorney fees and $34.50 costs." On February 11, 1964, judgment was entered in favor of respondents and against bankrupt, his wife and Century for $20,094.62.

The petitioning bankrupt raises a number of issues in his Petition for Review of the Referee's order holding that the $20,094.62 debt was nondischargeable. However, the question that first must be answered is whether the note given pursuant to the agreement of January 10, 1963, was accepted by respondents only as evidence of a pre-existing debt, or whether it was given by the bankrupt and his wife as consideration for a waiver of the antecedent tort action, namely the conversion by bankrupt of respondents' funds.

It is the general rule that if a note is given merely as evidence of a debt, the court may look behind the note to the debt to determine if it was created by "wilful and malicious injury to the . . . property of another" or one of the other excepted causes of § 17a of the Bankruptcy Act . . . .

But, if it is shown that the note, by express agreement is given and received, as a discharge of the original obligation or tort action, then the execution of the note extinguishes the tort action and it would be error for the court to look behind the note . . . .

In the instant case the note and agreement of January 10, 1963, contains express language of novation, namely the substitution of the note for the respondents' agreement not to "institute or prosecute any claim, damage, loss, recovery or expense of any nature arising out of the transaction between First Parties [respondents] and Second Parties [bankrupt, his wife and Century] hereinabove referred to." According to the agreement, the remedy of the respondents is restricted to an action upon the promissory note if the bankrupt defaults. Inasmuch as there is no evidence in the record to support any other interpretation the court concludes that the intent of this agreement was not merely to evidence or suspend the debt, but to discharge the antecedent tort action.

The bankrupt and his wife gave valuable consideration in return for respondents' agreement to waive the tort cause of action. The bankrupt made himself personally liable for what was, in form, a debt of the corporation, Century. Whether bankrupt would have been held personally liable for the debt of Century because of his acts, regardless of the agreement, is a question that need not be decided. Further, the signing of the agreement and note by the bankrupt's wife made her separate property and earnings liable for the debt. . . . In addition, the bankrupt's personal undertaking upon the note may constitute a loss to the bankrupt of the defense that Century had paid a usurious rate of interest to respondents. . . . In light of the foregoing the court concludes that the discharge of the antecedent tort claim of respondents was amply supported by consideration from the bankrupt and his wife.

. . . To allow the respondents to now go behind the note to establish the nondischargeable character of the original indebtedness would destroy the very essence of what the bankrupt bargained for in the agreement of January 10, 1963. It is, therefore, this court's opinion that it was error for the Referee to go behind that agreement, and the note given pursuant thereto.

The decision of the Referee is reversed and it is ordered that the bankrupt's debt to respondents be discharged.

Kentile Floors, Inc. v Winham

(CA9 Ariz) 440 F2d 1128 (1971)

Kentile sold goods over an extended period to Winham. The credit relationship began without Winham's being required to furnish any financial statement. After some time, payments were not regularly made. Kentile requested a financial statement. Winham submitted a statement for the year which had then just ended. Thereafter Kentile requested a second statement. The second statement was false. Kentile continued to extend credit to Winham. Winham was later adjudicated bankrupt. Kentile objected to Winham's discharge in bankruptcy because of the false financial statement. The objection of Kentile was dismissed, the discharge of Winham was granted, and Kentile appealed.

Hamley, C.J. . . . Kentile also objected to a general discharge because Winham's Floor Covering obtained extensions of credit by publishing materially false financial statements. . . . Both the referee and the district court found materially false financial statements were published by the bankrupts as sole proprietors of Winham's Floor Coverings. The referee found that Kentile relied on the statements when it subsequently extended credit. The district court found that Kentile did not rely on the statements, and that Kentile had no right to rely on them.

The record discloses that Mr. Winham intentionally modified the true figures on his statement of financial condition for the purpose of showing a good statement. He acknowledged that he felt that if a correct statement were submitted, his credit would be curtailed. After receiving the statements, Kentile did extend further credit to Mr. Winham. While the law favors discharges in bankruptcy, it will not ordinarily tolerate the bankrupt's intentional departure from honest business practices where there is a reasonable likelihood of prejudice. A bankrupt who admits that he prepared false financial statements in an effort to obtain or retain credit standing, and who thereafter achieves that goal, has a heavy burden to carry in trying to show that the false statement was not, or should not have been, instrumental in the subsequent extensions of credit.

Reliance on the financial statements is necessary to preclude discharge for violation of § 14(c)(3). . . . Notwithstanding the bankrupts' heavy burden of proof, referred to above, we agree with the district court that whatever reliance Kentile placed upon these statements was not reasonable reliance, that Kentile therefore had no right to rely upon the statements in this situation, and that the bankrupts should not, on this ground, be denied a general discharge.

A recitation of the facts surrounding the submission of the financial statements and subsequent extensions of credit is necessary to illustrate why Kentile should have been alerted to the actual financial condition of Winham's Floor

Coverings and why Kentile should not have relied upon the financial statements without further investigation.

As noted above, the bankrupts had been dealing with Kentile, through its distributor, for a period of time before the arrangement for direct purchases from Kentile was consummated early in 1964. The arrangement corresponded somewhat with the bankrupts' entrance into the field of commercial floor coverings. Kentile acknowledged the bankrupts' history of prompt payment prior to 1965. Kentile further acknowledged representatives had been calling on the bankrupts from time to time for the purpose of reviewing the bankrupts' business records. When Kentile began extending credit to the bankrupts, it did not require publication of a statement of financial condition as a prerequisite.

In the spring of 1965 the bankrupts' payments on the account had become sporadic. Kentile's credit manager stated that the payments were "not satisfactory." The record indicates that Kentile was then seriously considering curtailment of Winhams' credit. Kentile was also aware of Winhams' sporadic payments on the account with Kentile's distributor. Kentile was, in fact, aware of many of the difficulties with which the bankrupts were beset in early 1965.

By March 1965, Kentile had begun to insist that the bankrupts supply a statement of financial condition. Before having received any financial statement from the bankrupts, however, Kentile had extended approximately $96,000 in credit. This was the amount due Kentile from the bankrupts when the first financial statement was submitted in April 1965. The statement purported to reflect the financial condition of Winham's Floor Coverings as of December 31, 1964. Kentile was aware of the financial problems the bankrupts had experienced in the interim. Kentile also knew that the total of all Winhams' accounts payable on December 31, 1964, as reflected in the financial statement, was substantially less than the amount Winhams owed Kentile and its distributor when the statement was received in April 1965.

Kentile's credit manager was somewhat equivocal when asked the significance that could be placed on a financial statement such as this. The financial condition reported in the statement seemed, to the credit manager, inconsistent with the manner in which the bankrupts were making payments on the account.

The second financial statement submitted by Winham was received by Kentile in June 1965, and purported to reflect the financial condition as of March 31, 1965. This statement, compared with the first statement, showed an improvement during the first quarter of 1965, contrary to all other information available to Kentile. Credit was curtailed shortly after its receipt. Credit was not curtailed because Kentile discovered the bankrupts' true financial condition, but because the payments on the account were not satisfactory.

Given the lengthy and apparently fairly close business relationship of Kentile and Winham's Floor Coverings, we do not think further investigation by Kentile would have damaged that relationship had Winham's been a going concern. We therefore think Kentile acted unreasonably if it relied upon the first statement in extending credit without any further investigation of the bankrupts' then existing financial condition. While a financial statement is not necessarily unreliable because it reflects the condition as it existed three or four months earlier, Kentile's knowledge of what occurred in the interim was sufficient to require further inquiry. Reliance on the second statement, showing an improvement of condition in the interim, was similarly unjustified.

[Judgment affirmed.]

QUESTIONS AND CASE PROBLEMS

1. Shelton owed money to Winthrop Sales. Shelton went into bankruptcy and was granted a discharge. Later Winthrop Sales sued Shelton although its claim against him had been discharged in bankruptcy. Shelton did not raise any defense with respect to the bankruptcy discharge. A judgment was entered against him. Shelton, on appeal, claimed that the bankruptcy

discharge prevented the suit against him. Decide. [Winthrop Sales Corp. v Shelton, (Mo App) 389 SW2d 70]

2. A Utah statute provides for the revocation of an operator's license if he fails to pay a judgment entered against him because of his negligent operation of an automobile. Kesler's license was revoked under this statute. He thereafter went into bankruptcy and the judgment was discharged. He then claimed that his state license should be restored. The Utah Department of Public Safety refused to restore the license because the Utah statute expressly provided that the revocation of the license shall not be affected by a subsequent discharge in bankruptcy. Kesler claimed that the Utah statute was unconstitutional on the theory that it conflicted with the bankruptcy power of the national government. Decide. [Kesler v Department of Public Safety, 369 US 153]
3. Putman, as executrix of the estate of Fred Putman, obtained a judgment for $10,000 against the Ocean Shore Railway Co. for negligently causing the death of Putman. She and two others filed a petition in bankruptcy against Folger, who had a statutory liability for the debts of the railway corporation. In opposing the petition, he contended that the claim of Mrs. Putman was not a provable debt in bankruptcy. Do you agree? [In re Putman, (DC ND Cal) 193 F 464]
4. De Shazo owed the Household Finance Corporation $349.02. In order to borrow additional money, he submitted a false statement to Household as to the total amount of his debts. Household, relying on this false statement, loaned him $150.98 more and had him sign one note for $500, representing both the unpaid balance of the old loan and the total amount of the new loan. Thereafter De Shazo was discharged in bankruptcy. What effect did the discharge have on the note held by Household Finance and listed in the bankrupt's schedule of indebtedness? [Household Finance Corp. of Seattle v De Shazo, 57 Wash 771, 359 P2d 1044]
5. An involuntary petition in bankruptcy was filed against a merchant doing business in a building leased from Abbot. On the same day a receiver was appointed, and he took possession of the store and the stock of goods. In an action brought by Abbot upon a claim connected with the possession of the building by the receiver, a question arose as to whether the receiver was vested with title to the bankrupt's assets. What is your opinion? [In re Rubel, (DC ED Wis) 166 F 131]
6. At the instigation of Perry, trustee in bankruptcy of Martin, the court directed a referee to decide the validity of claims made by several claimants to a gas and oil leasehold in which the bankrupt had some interest. Chandler and other claimants opposed the proceeding on the ground that the referee did not have power to hear and decide such a question and that it was for a bankruptcy court to decide. Was this contention sound? [Chandler v Perry, (CCA5 Tex) 74 F2d 371]
7. Certain creditors filed a petition in bankruptcy against the Percy Ford Co. An adjudication of bankruptcy followed. At the time of the filing of the petition, the National Shawmut Bank held four notes upon which the bankrupt was absolutely liable, but the notes were not then due and payable. The bank contended that the notes constituted provable debts. Do you agree? [In re Percy Ford Co., (DCD Mass) 199 F 334]

40 Agency—Creation and Termination

NATURE OF THE AGENCY RELATIONSHIP

One of the most common legal relationships is that of agency. When it exists, one person can act for and can stand in the place of another.[1] By virtue of the agency device, one man can make contracts at numerous different places with many different persons at the same time.

§ **40:1. Definition.** *Agency* is a relation based upon an express or implied agreement whereby one person, the *agent*, is authorized to act under the control of and for another, his *principal,* in making contracts with third persons.[2] The acts of the agent obligate the principal to third persons and give the principal rights against the third persons.

Agency is based upon the consent of the parties and, for that reason, it is called a consensual relation.[3] If consideration is present, the relationship is also contractual. The law sometimes imposes an agency relationship.

The term "agency" is frequently used with other meanings. It is sometimes used to denote the fact that one has the right to sell certain products, such as when a dealer is said to possess an automobile agency. In other instances the term is used to mean an exclusive right to sell certain articles within a given territory. In these cases, however, the dealer is not an agent in the sense of representing the manufacturer.[4] The right of the dealer under such arrangements is frequently represented by a franchise which he purchases from the manufacturer or supplier.

§ **40:2. Agent Distinguished.**

(1) Employees and Independent Contractors. An agent is distinguished from an ordinary employee, who is not hired to represent the employer in dealings with third persons. It is possible, however, for the same person to be both an agent and an employee. For example, the driver of a

---

[1] King v Young, (Fla App) 107 So2d 751.

[2] Restatement, Agency, 2d § 1; Rule v Jones, 256 Wis 102, 40 NW2d 580. When the question is the tax liability of an enterprise (see Boise Cascade Corp. v Washington, 3 Wash App 78, 473 P2d 429), the definition of agency may be different than when the question is contract or tort liability, which are the areas of law considered in this part.

[3] Valentine Oil Co. v Powers, 157 Neb 87, 59 NW2d 160.

[4] United Fire & Casualty Co. v Nissan Motor Corp., 164 Colo 42, 433 P2d 769.

milk delivery truck is an agent, as well as an employee,[5] in making contracts between the milk company and its customers, but he is only an employee with respect to the work of delivering milk.

An agent or employee differs from an *independent contractor* in that the principal or employer has control over and can direct an agent or an employee, but the other party to the contract does not have control over the performance of the work by an independent contractor.[6]

A person who appears to be an independent contractor may in fact be so controlled by the other contracting party that he is regarded as the agent of the latter. For example, when all the management decisions of a franchisee are made by the franchisor, the franchisee is held to be the agent of the franchisor, with the consequence that third persons dealing with the franchisee may assert against the franchisor the typical claims of third persons against a principal, as against the contention that the franchisee was an independent contractor and that it alone was liable for such claims as customers of the franchisee might possess.[7]

The fact that the person contracting with a contractor reserves the right to inspect the work or that the owner's architect has the right to require the redoing of work that does not meet contract specifications does not give such control over the independent contractor as to make him merely an employee. That is, the reservation of power to determine and insure compliance with the terms of the contract does not constitute control of how the work is to be done.[8]

A person may be an independent contractor generally but an agent with respect to a particular transaction. Thus, an "agency" or a "broker" rendering personal services to customers is ordinarily an independent contractor, but he may be the agent of a customer when the rendition of a service involves making a contract on behalf of the customer with a third person. (See p. 806, Zak v Fidelity-Phenix Insurance Co.)

(2) Real Estate Agents. In many cases, a real estate broker is merely a middleman who seeks to locate a buyer or seller for his client. In such a case, the broker is not an agent because he does not have authority to make a contract with a third person that will bind his client.[9]

(3) Bailees. When personal property is delivered to another under an agreement that the property will be returned to the deliveror or transferred to a third person, a bailment arises. The person to whom the property is delivered, the bailee, is not an agent because he has no authority to make any contract on behalf of the bailor.

---

[5] In business practice, all employed persons, regardless of the nature of the work performed or the services rendered, are considered as employees.

[6] Jenkins v AAA Heating and Cooling, Inc., 245 Ore 382, 421 P2d 971.

[7] Nichols v Arthur Murray, Inc., 248 Cal App 2d 610, 56 Cal Rptr 728 (see p. 806, Hill v Newman).

[8] Lipka v United States, (CA2 NY) 369 F2d 288.

[9] Batson v Strehlow, 68 Cal 2d 662, 68 Cal Rptr 589, 441 P2d 101.

Situations commonly arise, however, in which the same person is both an agent and a bailee. When a salesman is loaned a company car, he is a bailee with respect to the car; but with respect to making sales contracts, he is an agent.

(4) ***Required Act.*** The mere fact that one person requires another person to do an act does not make the latter person the agent of the former. For example, when a bank directs a borrower to obtain the signature of another person in order to obtain a bank loan, the borrower is not the agent of the bank in contacting the other person and procuring his signature.[10]

A leased farm land from *B* and the lease required *A* to use commercial fertilizers on the land. *A* was not the agent of *B* for the purpose of purchasing fertilizer from *C* and *C* could not proceed against *B* or *B's* land to collect the purchase price due on the fertilizer purchased by *A*.[11]

§ 40:3. Purpose of Agency. Usually an agency may be created to perform any act which the principal himself could lawfully do.[12] The object of the agency may not be criminal, nor may it be contrary to public policy.

Also, some acts must be performed by a person himself and cannot be entrusted or delegated to an agent. Voting, swearing to the truth of documents, testifying in court, and making a will are instances where personal action is required. In the preparation of papers, however, it is proper to employ someone else to prepare the paper which is then signed or sworn to by the employing party. Various forms that are required by statute, such as applications for licenses and tax returns, will in some instances expressly authorize the execution of such forms by an agent as long as the identities of both principal and agent and the latter's representative capacity are clearly shown.

§ 40:4. Who May Be a Principal. Any person, if he is competent to act for himself, may act through an agent. An appointment of an agent by a person lacking capacity is generally regarded as void or voidable to the same extent that a contract made by such person would be. Thus, a minor may act through an agent,[13] and a resulting contract will be voidable to the same extent as though made by the minor.

Groups of persons may also appoint agents to act for them. For example, three men, having formed a partnership, may employ an agent to act for them in the business transactions of the firm. Certain groups of persons, on account of the nature of the organization, must act through agents. Thus, a corporation can only make a contract through an agent since the corporation is not a living person.[14]

---

[10] First National Bank v Caro Constr. Co., Inc., 211 Kan 678, 508 P2d 516.

[11] Landas Fertilizer Co. v Hargreaves, (Iowa) 206 NW2d 675.

[12] Jefferson Standard Life Insurance Co. v Guilford County, 226 NC 441, 38 SE 2d 519.

[13] Smith v Smith, 41 Ala App 403, 139 So2d 345.

[14] Kiel v Frank Shoe Mfg. Co., 245 Wis 292, 14 NW2d 164.

§ **40:5. Who May Be an Agent.** Since a contract made by an agent is in law the contract of the principal, it is immaterial whether or not the agent has legal capacity to make a contract for himself.[15] It is permissible to employ as agents aliens, minors, and others who are under a natural or legal disability.

When a minor purchases an automobile in the name of his parents and the transaction is set up to make it appear that the parents are the buyers and the seller believes that the minor is acting as agent for the parents, the minor is estopped from thereafter seeking to disaffirm the sale on the ground that he was purchasing on his own behalf and not as agent for his parents.[16]

While ordinarily an agent is one person acting for another, an agent may be a partnership or a corporation.

In certain instances the law imposes limitations upon the right to act as an agent. In order to protect the public from loss at the hands of dishonest or untrained "agents," statutes commonly provide that a person must obtain a license from an appropriate government agency or bureau before he can act as an auctioneer, a real estate agent, or a securities broker.

§ **40:6. Classification of Agents.** A *general agent* is authorized by the principal to transact all of his affairs in connection with a particular kind of business or trade, or to transact all of his business at a certain place.[17] To illustrate, a person who is appointed by the owner of a store as manager is a general agent.

A *special agent* is authorized by the principal to handle a definite business transaction or to do a specific act. One who is authorized by another to purchase a particular house for him is a special agent.

A *universal agent* is authorized by the principal to do all acts that can be delegated lawfully to representatives. This form of agency arises when a person in the military service gives another person a "blanket" power of attorney to do anything that must be done while he is in the service.

§ **40:7. Agency Coupled with an Interest.** An agent has an *interest in the authority* when he has given a consideration or has paid for the right to exercise the authority granted to him. To illustrate, when a lender, in return for making a loan of money, is given as security authority to collect rents due to the borrower and to apply those rents to the payment of the debt owed him, the lender becomes the borrower's agent with an interest in the authority given him to collect the rents.[18]

An agent has an *interest in the subject matter* when for a consideration he is given an interest in the property with which he is dealing. Hence, when the agent is authorized to sell certain property of the principal and is given a lien on such property as security for a debt owed to him by the principal, the agent has an interest in the subject matter.[19]

---

[15] R 2d § 21(1).
[16] Jankovsky v Halladay Motors, (Wyo) 482 P2d 129.
[17] State v Rooney, (Mo) 406 SW2d 1.
[18] Halloran-Judge Trust Co. v Heath, 70 Utah 124, 258 P 342.
[19] Cleveland v Bateman, 21 NMex 675, 158 P 648.

CREATING THE AGENCY

An agency may arise by appointment, conduct, ratification, or operation of law.

§ 40:8. Authorization by Appointment. The usual method of creating an agency is by express authorization, that is, a person is appointed to act for and on behalf of another.

In most instances the authorization of the agent may be oral.[20] Some appointments, however, must be made in a particular way. A majority of the states, by statute, require the appointment of an agent to be in writing when the agency is created to acquire or dispose of any interest in land.[21] (See p. 808, Heinrich v Martin.) A written authorization of agency is called a *power of attorney*.

Ordinarily no agency arises from the fact of co-ownership of property or of relationship of the parties. Consequently, when a check was made payable to the order of husband and wife, it was necessary for each to indorse the check because there was no agency by which the husband could indorse the name of his wife and deposit the money in his own account.[22]

§ 40:9. Authorization by Principal's Conduct.

(1) Principal's Conduct as to Agent. Since agency is created by the consent of the parties, any conduct, including words, that gives the agent reason to believe that the principal consents to his acting as agent is sufficient to create an agency.[23] If one person, knowingly and without objection, permits another to act as his agent, the law will find in his conduct an expression of authorization to the agent, and the principal will not be permitted to deny that the agent was in fact authorized.[24] Thus, if the owner of a hotel allows another person to assume the duties of hotel clerk, that person may infer from the owner's conduct that he has authority to act as the hotel clerk.

(2) Principal's Conduct as to Third Persons. In addition to conduct or dealings with the agent which cause him as a reasonable man to believe that he has authority, the principal may have such dealing with third persons as to cause them to believe that the "agent" has authority.[25] Thus, if the owner of a store places another person in charge, third persons may assume that the person in charge is the agent for the owner in that respect. When this occurs, it is said that the agent has *apparent authority* because he appears to be the agent, and the principal is estopped or prevented from contradicting the appearance that he has created.[26] Likewise the "principal" may be bound

---

[20] R 2d § 26; Rowan v Hull, 55 WVa 335, 47 SE 92.

[21] Cano v Tyrral, 256 Cal App 2d 824, 64 Cal Rptr 522; In re Meister's Will, 39 App Div 2d 857, 333 NYS2d 41.

[22] Glasser v Columbia Federal Savings and Loan Ass'n, (Fla) 197 So2d 6.

[23] Silver v Com. Tr. Co., 22 NJ Super 604, 92 A2d 152.

[24] R 2d § 26.

[25] Houtz v General Bonding & Insurance Co., (CA10 NMex) 235 F2d 591.

[26] T. S. McShane Co. v Great Lakes Pipe Line Co., 156 Neb 766, 57 NW2d 778.

by apparent authority when he has permitted the agent to make statements or to do business in such a way as to cause third persons to reasonably believe that he had authority.

When a franchisor permits the franchisee to do business under the name of a franchisor, the latter is estopped from denying that the franchisee has authority to make customary contracts, such as a contract for advertising, and to bind the franchisor by such contracts.[27]

The term "apparent authority" is used only when there is merely the appearance of authority but it in fact does not exist, and the appearance of authority of the agent must be caused by the acts of the principal.[28] This apparent authority extends to all acts that a person of ordinary prudence, familiar with business usages and the particular business, would be justified in assuming that the agent has authority to perform.[29] (See p. 809, Walker v Pacific Mobile Homes.)

The mere placing of property in the possession of another person does not give him either actual or apparent authority to sell the property.[30]

While it is essential to the concept of apparent authority that the third person reasonably believes that the agent has authority, the converse is not to be implied. That is, the mere fact that a third person believes someone has an agent's authority does not give rise to authority or to apparent authority.[31]

The fact that a principal has appointed an agent does not clothe the latter with unlimited apparent authority. To hold the principal responsible for the apparently authorized acts of the agent, it is necessary to show that the principal was responsible for the appearance of authority.[32]

The improbability that the purported agent did in fact possess the necessary authority is a significant factor in determining whether there was apparent authority. For example, where the issue was the authority of a shop foreman to make a contract compensating an employee for improving the employer's product, the employee should recognize that a shop foreman would not have authority to bind the employer to a contract which could cost the employer many thousands of dollars.[33]

(3) Acquiescence by Principal. The conduct of the principal that gives rise to the agent's authority may be acquiescence in or failing to object to acts done by the purported or apparent agent over a period of time. For example, a person collecting payments on a note and remitting the

---

[27] Duluth Herald and News Tribune v Plymouth Optical Co., 286 Minn 495, 176 NW2d 552.

[28] Lumber Mart Co. v Buchanan, 69 Wash 2d 658, 419 P2d 1002.

[29] Berman v Griggs, 145 Maine 258, 75 A2d 365.

[30] Brunette v Idaho Veneer Co., 86 Idaho 193, 384 P2d 233. Although under Uniform Commercial Code, § 2-403, if the entrustee deals in goods of that kind, he has the power but not the right to transfer title to a person buying in good faith in the ordinary course of business.

[31] Automotive Acceptance Corp. v Powell, 45 Ala App 596, 234 So2d 593.

[32] Ford v Unity Hospital, 32 NY2d 464, 346 NYS2d 238, 299 NE2d 659.

[33] Patterson v Page Aircraft Maintenance, Inc., (Ala App), 382 So2d 433.

proper amounts to the holder of the note will be regarded as the latter's agent for collection when this conduct has been followed over a period of years without objection.[34]

Where the drawer's employee drew checks to herself for fourteen months which were debited to the drawer's account and no complaint was made by him, this lack of objection was in effect a communication to the bank that the employee had the authority to draw the checks in question.[35]

§ 40:10. Agency by Ratification. An agent may attempt on behalf of the principal to do an act which he has not been authorized to do. Or a person who is not the agent of another may attempt to act as his agent. Ordinarily a person can ratify any unauthorized act done on his behalf which he could have authorized.[36] The effect is the same as though he had authorized the act in the first place.[37]

When the principal ratifies the act of the unauthorized person purporting to be his authorized agent, such ratification releases the agent from any liability which he would otherwise have as to third persons because of the breach of an implied warranty of authority and from any liability which he may have as to the principal ratifying his act.

Initially, ratification is a question of intention. Just as in the case of authorization, where there is the question of whether or not the principal authorized the agent, so there is the question of whether or not the principal intended to approve or ratify the action of the agent. Ratification may thus be found in conduct indicating an intention to ratify,[38] such as paying for goods ordered by the agent.[39]

Ratification of an earlier loan transaction is shown when the principal executes a renewal note and papers which make an extension of the earlier loan.[40]

If the other requirements of ratification are satisfied, a principal ratifies an agent's acts when, with knowledge of the act, he accepts [41] or retains [42] the benefit of the act, or brings an action to enforce legal rights based upon the act [43] or defends an action by asserting the existence of a right based on the unauthorized transaction, or fails to repudiate the agent's act within a reasonable time.[44] The receipt, acceptance, and deposit of a check by the principal with knowledge that it arises from an unauthorized transaction is a common illustration of ratification by conduct of the unauthorized transaction.[45]

---

[34] Holsclaw v Catalina Savings & Loan Association, 13 Ariz App 362, 476 P2d 883.

[35] Von Gohren v Pacific National Bank, 8 Wash App 245, 505 P2d 467.

[36] R 2d § 84.

[37] Davidson v Farr, (Mo App) 273 SW2d 500; Justheim Petroleum Co. v Hammond, (CA10 Utah) 227 F2d 629.

[38] R 2d § 93.

[39] Southwestern Portland Cement v Beavers, 82 NMex 218, 478 P2d 546.

[40] Doxey-Layton Co. v Holbrook, 25 Utah 2d 194, 479 P2d 348.

[41] Ashland v Lapiner Motor Co., 247 Iowa 596, 75 NW2d 357.

[42] R 2d § 99.

[43] Mattila v Olsevick, 228 Ore 606, 365 P2d 1072.

[44] R 2d § 94.

[45] Timber Structures v Chateau Royale Corp., 49 Ill App 2d 343, 199 NE2d 623.

A principal ratifies the agent's act of installing a vending machine on the premises when the principal complains to the supplier of the machine that it does not work, demands that it be repaired, and finally requests that it be removed.[46]

The fact that the principal rehires an agent does not constitute a ratification of an unauthorized act committed by him during his former period of employment.[47]

(1) Conditions for Ratification. In addition to the intent to ratify, expressed in some instances with certain formality, the following conditions must be satisfied in order that the intention take effect as a ratification:

(1) The agent must have purported to act on behalf of the principal.[48] If the person without authority informed the other person that he was acting as agent for the principal, this requirement is satisfied.

(2) The principal must have been capable of authorizing the act both at the time of the act and at the time when he ratified.[49]

(3) A principal must ratify the entire act of the agent.

(4) The principal must ratify the act before the third person withdraws.[50] If the third person brings an action against the agent because of lack of authority to make the contract, the bringing of the action is equivalent to a withdrawal that prevents the principal from thereafter ratifying the contract.[51]

(5) The act to be ratified must generally be legal.[52]

(6) The principal must have full knowledge of all material facts.[53] If the agent conceals a material fact, the ratification of the principal made in ignorance of such fact is not binding. Of course, there can be no ratification when the principal does not know of the making of the contract by his agent. Consequently, when the owner's agent and a contractor made unauthorized major changes to an installation contract without the knowledge of the principal, the fact that the principal had no knowledge of the matter barred any claim that he had ratified the act of his agent.[54]

It is not always necessary, however, to show that the principal had actual knowledge; for knowledge will be imputed to him if he knows of such other facts as would put a prudent man on inquiry, or if that knowledge can be inferred from the knowledge of other facts or from a course of

---

[46] George F. Mueller & Sons, Inc. v Northern Illinois Gas Co., 12 Ill App 3d 362, 299 NE2d 601.

[47] Gill Truck and Trailer Rental, Inc. v Hunter Truck Lines, Inc., (La App) 283 So2d 509.

[48] State ex rel Olsen v Sundling, 128 Mont 596, 281 P2d 499.

[49] R 2d §§ 84, 86.

[50] LaSalle National Bank v Brodsky, 51 Ill App 2d 260, 201 NE2d 208.

[51] R 2d § 88, Comment (a) and Illustration (4).

[52] § 86.

[53] Pacific Trading Co. v Sun Insurance Office, 140 Ore 314, 13 P2d 616.

[54] Kirk Reid Co. v Fine, 205 Va 778, 139 SE2d 829.

business.[55] Knowledge is likewise not an essential factor when the principal has indicated that he does not care to know the details and is willing to be bound by the contract regardless of his lack of knowledge.[56]

(2) Circumstances Not Affecting Ratification. Ratification is not affected by the fact (a) that the third person has not agreed again to the transaction after it has been ratified; (b) that the principal first repudiated but then changed his mind and ratified the transaction, provided the third party had not withdrawn prior to the ratification; (c) that the agent would be liable to the third person for breach of warranty of his authority or misrepresentation if the principal were not bound; (d) that the agent or the third person knew the agent was unauthorized; (e) that the agent died or lost capacity prior to the ratification; or (f) that the principal did not communicate his ratifying intent to the third person.[57]

§ 40:11. Agency by Operation of Law. In certain instances the courts, influenced by necessity or social desirability, create or find an agency when there is none. For example, a wife may purchase necessaries and charge them to her husband's account when he does not supply them. Here the social policy is the furtherance of the welfare of the neglected wife. The services of an employment agency rendered to a wife have been held not to constitute necessaries, however, so that the husband cannot be held liable therefor as an agent by operation of the law.[58]

As another example of agency by operation of law, a minor may purchase necessaries upon the credit of his father when the latter fails to supply them. If the minor is already adequately supplied by the father, the mother cannot make additional purchases or contracts and charge the father, even though this could have been done if the minor had not been already adequately provided for by the father.[59]

An emergency power of an agent to act under unusual circumstances not covered by his authority is recognized when the agent is unable to communicate with the principal and failure to act will cause the principal substantial loss.[60]

§ 40:12. Proving the Agency Relationship. The burden of proving the existence of an agency relationship rests upon the person who seeks to benefit by such proof.[61] The third person who desires to bind the principal because of the act of an alleged agent has the burden of proving that the latter person was in fact the authorized agent of the principal and possessed the authority to do the act in question.[62] For example, when the buyer asserts that there

---

[55] Van Tassell v Lewis, 118 Utah 356, 222 P2d 350.
[56] City National Bank & Trust Co. v Finch, 205 Okla 340, 237 P2d 869.
[57] R 2d § 92.
[58] Approved Personnel Service v Dallas, (Tex Civ App) 358 SW2d 150.
[59] Watkins v Medical & Dental Finance Bureau, 101 Ariz 580, 422 P2d 696.
[60] R 2d § 47.
[61] Cue Oil Co. v Fornea Oil Co., 208 Miss 810, 45 So2d 230.
[62] Great American Ins. Co. v United States, (Ct Claims) 481 F2d 1298.

has been a breach of an express warranty made by the seller's agent, the buyer must establish that there was an actual or apparent authority to make the warranty.[63] In the absence of sufficient proof, the jury must find that there is no agency.

The existence of an agency cannot be established by proof of the statements that the agent had made to the third person.[64] The fact that the latter told the third person that such relationship existed cannot be shown in evidence to establish that the person so stating was the agent of the principal.[65] The person purporting to act as agent, however, may testify that on a certain day the principal gave him certain instructions and that, in following those instructions, he made a contract with a third person. This is testifying to the facts from which the court may conclude that there was an authorization.[66]

The authority of the agent may be established by circumstantial evidence. For example, a principal made a contract with a landowner to permit subsurface explosions in his land for the purpose of exploratory testing. It was established that the seismograph crew which conducted such testing acted with the authorization of the principal when the truck of the crew bore the same emblem as appeared on a card given to the landowner in order to identify the principal's crew and when the principal paid the landowner for the privilege of conducting the tests.[67]

TERMINATION OF AGENCY

An agency may be terminated by the act of one or both of the parties to the agency agreement, or by operation of law.

§ 40:13. Termination by Act of Parties.

(1) Expiration of Agency Contract. The ordinary agency may expire by the terms of the contract creating it. Thus, the contract may provide that it shall last for a stated period, as five years, or until a particular date arrives, or until the happening of a particular event, such as the sale of certain property. In such a case, the agency is automatically terminated when the specified date arrives or the event on which it is to end occurs.[68] When one appoints another to represent him in his business affairs while he is away, the relation ends upon the return of the principal.[69]

When it is provided that the agency shall last for a stated period of time, it terminates upon the expiration of that period without regard to whether the acts contemplated by the creation of the agency have been performed.[70]

---

[63] Regan Purchase & Sales Corp. v Primavera, (NY Civil Court) 68 Misc 2d 858, 328 NYS2d 490.

[64] Aerovias Panama v Air Carrier Engine Service, (Fla App) 195 So2d 230.

[65] Holbeck v Illinois Bankers Life Assurance Co., 318 Ill App 296, 47 NE2d 721.

[66] Benham v Selected Investment Corp., (Okla) 313 P2d 489.

[67] Bynum v Mandrel Industries, Inc., (Miss) 241 So2d 629.

[68] R 2d §§ 105, 106, 107.

[69] Freed Finance Co. v Preece, 14 Utah 2d 409, 385 P2d 156.

[70] R 2d § 105.

If no period is stated, the agency continues for a reasonable time, but it may be terminated at the will of either party.[71]

(2) Agreement. Since the agency relation is based upon consent, it can be terminated by the consent of the principal and agent.[72]

(3) Option of a Party. An agency agreement may provide that upon the giving of notice or the payment of a specified sum of money, one party may terminate the relationship.

(4) Revocation by Principal. The relationship between principal and agent is terminated whenever the principal discharges the agent even though the agency was stated to be "irrevocable."[73] If the agency was not created for a specified time but was to exist only at will, or if the agent has been guilty of misconduct, the principal may discharge the agent without liability of the principal.[74]

Expressions of dissatisfaction with the work of an agent does not constitute a revocation of his authority. The intent to revoke must be clearly and unequivocally expressed. (See p. 809, Kinmon v J. P. King Auction Co.) But any conduct which manifests an intent to revoke the authority is sufficient, as when the principal takes back from the agent the property which had been entrusted to him for the purpose of the agency or retains another agent to do what the original agent had been authorized to do.[75]

When the agency is based upon a contract to employ the agent for a specified period of time, the principal is liable to the agent for damages if the principal wrongfully discharges the agent. The fact that the principal is liable for damages does not, however, prevent the principal from terminating the agency by discharging the agent. In such a case it is said that the principal has the power to terminate the agency by discharging the agent but he does not have the right to do so.

(5) Renunciation by Agent. The agency relationship is terminated if the agent refuses to continue to act as agent, or when he abandons the object of the agency and acts for himself in committing a fraud upon the principal.[76]

If the relationship is an agency at will, the agent has the right as well as the power to renounce or abandon the agency at any time. In addition, he has the right of renunciation of the relationship in any case if the principal is guilty of making wrongful demands upon him or of other misconduct.

---

[71] Seneca Falls Machine Co. v McBeth, (CA3 Pa) 368 F2d 915.
[72] R 2d § 117.
[73] Shumaker v Hazen, (Okla) 372 P2d 873.
[74] Seattle Times Co. v Murphy, 172 Wash 474, 20 Pd 858.
[75] Tinney v Duckett, (Dist Col App) 141 A2d 192.
[76] New York Casualty Co. v Sazenski, 240 Minn 202, 60 NW2d 368.

If, however, the agency is based upon a contract calling for the continuation of the relationship for a specified or determinable period, that is, until a particular date arrives or a certain event occurs, the agent has no right to abandon or renounce the relationship when the principal is not guilty of wrong.

When the renunciation by the agent is wrongful, the agent is liable to the principal for the damages that the principal sustains.[77] In some states the agent also forfeits his right to receive any compensation for the services rendered but not due prior to the renunciation. In other states he may recover the reasonable value of such services, but not in excess of the contract price minus the damages sustained by the principal. In all states the agent may recover any salary or commission that had become due prior to the renunciation. This remedy is subject, however, to the opposing claim of the principal for damages.

(6) ***Rescission.*** The agency contract may be terminated by rescission to the same extent that any other contract may be so terminated.[78]

§ 40:14. Termination by Operation of Law.

(1) ***Death.*** The death of either the principal [79] or agent ordinarily terminates the authority of an agent automatically,[80] even though the death is unknown to the other. Some state statutes provide that the death of the principal is not a revocation until the agent has notice nor as to third persons who deal with the agent in good faith and are ignorant of the death. Generally, however, these statutes are limited to principals who are members of the armed forces.

For example, when a notary public fills in a blank space in a deed in accordance with the owner's instructions, the notary's act and deed are void where the owner had died before the notary had filled in the blanks, as the owner's death had revoked the authority of the notary to act on his behalf.[81]

The fact that a contract of agency is terminated by death does not impose any liability for damages even though the contract has not been completed.[82] In an attorney-client relationship the death of the client does not terminate the agency if the client had expressly agreed that the attorney should conduct the proceeding to its conclusion.[83]

If the agent has knowledge of the death of the principal but thereafter signs the name of the principal, the agent may be guilty of forgery. Thus, when a daughter indorsed her mother's social security checks after the mother had died, the daughter was guilty of forgery. The court held that

[77] R 2d § 400.
[78] Cutcliffe v Chestnut, 122 Ga App 195, 176 SE2d 607.
[79] Julian v Lawton, 240 NC 436, 82 SE2d 210.
[80] Commercial Nursery Co. v Ivey, 164 Tenn 502, 51 SW2d 238.
[81] Stalting v Stalting, 52 SD 318, 217 NW 390.
[82] R 2d § 450, Comment (b).
[83] Jones v Miller, (CA3 Pa) 203 F2d 131.

even if the daughter had authority from her mother to indorse and cash the social security checks sent to the mother, such authority terminated upon the mother's death, and the subsequent indorsing of the mother's name with knowledge of her death constituted forgery.[84]

*(2) **Insanity.*** The insanity of either the principal or agent ordinarily terminates the agent's authority.[85] If the incapacity of the principal is only temporary, the agent's authority may be merely suspended rather than terminated.

*(3) **Bankruptcy.*** Bankruptcy of the principal [86] or agent usually terminates the relationship. It is generally held, however, that the bankruptcy of an agent does not terminate his power to deal with goods of the principal that are in his possession.

Insolvency, as distinguished from a formal adjudication of bankruptcy, usually does not terminate the agency. In most states accordingly the authority of an agent is not terminated by the appointment of a receiver for the principal's financial affairs.[87]

*(4) **Impossibility.*** The authority of an agent is terminated when it is impossible to perform the agency for any reason, such as the destruction of the subject matter of the agency, the death or loss of capacity of the third person with whom the agent is to contract, or a change in law that makes it impossible to perform the agency lawfully.[88]

*(5) **War.*** When the country of the principal and that of the agent are at war, the authority of the agent is usually terminated or at least suspended until peace is restored. When the war has the effect of making performance impossible, the agency is, of course, terminated. For example, the authority of an agent who is a nonresident enemy alien to sue is terminated because such an alien is not permitted to sue.[89]

*(6) **Unusual Events or Changes of Circumstances.*** The view is also held that the authority of an agent is terminated by the occurrence of an unusual event or a change in value or business conditions of such a nature that the agent should reasonably infer that the principal would not desire the agent to continue to act under the changed circumstances.[90] For example, an agent employed to sell land at a specified price should regard his authority

---

[84] Ross v United States, (CA8 Mo) 374 F2d 97.
[85] R 2d § 122; Sellers' Estate, 154 Ohio 483, 43 OO 425, 96 NE2d 595.
[86] Du Bois v U. S. F. & G. Co., 341 Pa 85, 18 A2d 802.
[87] Chilletti v Missouri, Kansas & Texas Rwy. Co., 102 Kan 297, 171 P 14.
[88] R 2d §§ 116, 124.
[89] Johnson v Eisentrager, 339 US 763.
[90] R 2d §§ 108, 109.

to sell at that price as terminated when the value of the land increases greatly because of the discovery of oil on the land.

§ 40:15. Termination of Agency Coupled with an Interest. If the agency is coupled with an interest in the authority, the agency cannot be terminated by the act of the principal. The Restatement of the Law of Agency adopts the rule that the principal's death does not terminate such an agency.[91] In some states, however, it is held to be terminated by his death.

An agency coupled with an interest in the authority is not revoked by the death of the agent.[92] Thus, when the agent would have the right to receive periodic commissions under a continuing contract between the principal and the third person, the agent's estate, if the agency is coupled with an interest in the authority, may receive the commissions accruing after the agent's death. If not so coupled, the right to receive commissions terminates with the agent's death.

When the agency is coupled with an interest in the subject matter, the principal cannot terminate the agency nor is it terminated or affected by the death or insanity of either the principal or the agent.

§ 40:16. Effect of Termination of Authority. If the agency is revoked by the principal, the authority to act for the principal is not terminated until notice of revocation is given to or received by the agent. As between the principal and agent, the right of the agent to bind his principal to third persons generally ends immediately upon the termination of his authority. Such termination is effective without the giving of notice to third persons.

When the agency is terminated by the act of the principal, notice must be given to third persons. (See p. 810, Record v Wagner.) If such notice is not given, the agent may have the power to make contracts that will bind the principal and third persons. This rule is predicated on the theory that a known agent will have the appearance of still being the agent unless notice to the contrary is given to third persons.

When the law requires the giving of notice in order to end the power of the agent to bind the principal, individual notice must be given or mailed to all persons who had prior dealings with the agent or the principal. Notice to the general public can be given by publishing a statement that the agency has been terminated in a newspaper of general circulation in the affected geographical area.

If a notice is actually received, the power of the agent is terminated without regard to whether the method of giving notice had been proper. Conversely, if proper notice is given, it is immaterial that it did not actually come to the attention of the party notified. Thus, a member of the general public cannot claim that the principal is bound to him on the ground that the

---

[91] § 139(1).
[92] R 2d § 139(1).

third person did not see the newspaper notice stating that the agent's authority had been terminated.

CASES FOR CHAPTER 40

Hill v Newman

126 NJ Super 557, 316 A2d 8 (1973)

Hill purchased furniture from Grant Furniture. When she complained that it was damaged, she was told that they would send someone to fix the damage. An independent contractor, Newman, was sent to fix the furniture. He identified himself as the man from Grant's. The lacquer he put on the furniture exploded and caused serious fire injury to Hill. She sued Newman and Grant. A verdict was returned in favor of the plaintiff against both defendants.

PER CURIAM . . . Grant first argues that Newman was an independent contractor and it was not vicariously liable for his negligence. . . .

New Jersey has recognized the general rule that one who engages a contractor to do work not in itself a nuisance, is not liable for his negligent acts in the performance of the contract. Certain exceptions have been recognized: (1) where the work is in itself a nuisance or inherently dangerous, or (2) where the landowner in fact retains or exercises control over the manner and means of the work, or (3) where he engages an incompetent contractor. . . . The cases cited in defendant's argument support no more than these principles. The "inherently dangerous" exception was ruled out of the case.

Neither the general rule nor the exceptions relate to a situation in which the independent contractor is allowed to become the apparent agent of the employer. There is nothing in the record to show that Grant retained or exercised control of Newman in the work that he did, or that Newman was an incompetent contractor.

There was enough here to establish an apparent agency: Grant's assurance that they would send somebody to repair the furniture when plaintiff phoned to complain of its condition, the phone call for an appointment that she received from Newman who said he was from Grant's, and his identifying himself when he arrived at her apartment that he was the man from Grant's who had come to fix the furniture. . . .

> "One who employs an independent contractor to perform services for another which are accepted in the reasonable belief that the services are being rendered by the employer or by his servants, is subject to liability for physical harm caused by the negligence of the contractor in supplying such services, to the same extent as though the employer were supplying them himself or by his servants."

There is no question under the facts that plaintiff relied upon the manifestation of authority in Newman, thereby constituting an invitation to deal with him and enter into relations with him such as were consistent with the apparent authority.

[Judgment affirmed.]

Zak v Fidelity-Phenix Insurance Co.

58 Ill App 2d 341, 208 NE2d 29 (1965)

Joanne Zak had a policy of automobile liability insurance issued by the Metropolitan Casualty Insurance Co. Zak was involved in an accident and was sued by the persons injured. Metropolitan refused to defend Zak in the action as required by the policy on the ground that the policy had been canceled for nonpayment of premiums. A judgment was entered against Zak. Then Zak sued Metropolitan for the alleged breach of the obligation of the policy by failing to defend Zak in the earlier action. Fidelity-Phenix Insurance Co., which had taken over the business of Metropolitan, defended in the latter action. From a judgment in favor of the insurer, Zak appealed.

MURPHY, J. . . . We have concluded that the determinative issue in this case is the effectiveness, as a matter of law, of the denial by defendant that the premium was paid to them by plaintiff, and of its cancellation of the policy for that reason. . . .

There is no dispute that plaintiff, Joanne Zak, paid the amount of the premium to Nick Kafkis. The defendant contends, however, that the payment of the premium to Kafkis was not equivalent to payment to it. To resolve this question, we must first determine the status of Kafkis. City of Chicago v Barnett, 404 Ill 136, 141, 88 NE2d 477 (1949), employed the following definition of an insurance broker: "An insurance broker is defined in Ballentine's Law Dictionary as follows: 'One who acts as a middleman between the [insured] and the insurer, and who solicits insurance from the public under no employment from any special company; but having secured an order, he either places the insurance with a company selected by the [insured], or in the absence of any selection by him, then with a company selected by such broker. A broker is the agent for the insured, though at the same time for some purposes he may be the agent for the insurer, and his acts and representations within the scope of his authority as such agent are binding on the insured.' "

The Insurance Code of 1937 . . . defines a broker in the following terms: "The term 'broker' means any person, partnership, association, or corporation, who or which acts or aids in any manner in the solicitation or negotiation, for or on behalf of the [insured], with or without compensation, of policies or contracts for insurance covering property or risks in this State of the kinds enumerated in Section 4."

The fact that Kafkis was engaged by plaintiff to act on her behalf to secure an automobile liability policy, the fact that Kafkis was at the time admittedly authorized to solicit insurance in the office of an agent of the company, Tom J. Agres, as well as other undisputed facts concerning the issuance of the instant policy, demonstrate, under the foregoing guidelines, that Kafkis was acting as an "insurance broker." We so hold.

The Insurance Code . . . controls the issue of whether payment of the premium to Kafkis is to be regarded as payment to the insurer [defendant insurance company]. Section 1065. 52 provides: "That portion of all premiums or monies which an agent, broker, or solicitor collects from an insured and which is to be paid to a company, its agents, or his employer because of the assumption of liability through the issuance of policies or contracts for insurance, shall be held by the agent, broker, or solicitor in a fiduciary capacity and shall not be misappropriated or converted to his own use or illegally withheld by the agent, broker or solicitor. Any company which directly or through its agents delivers in this State to any insurance broker a policy or contract for insurance pursuant to the application or request of such broker, acting for an insured other than himself, shall be deemed to have authorized such broker to receive on its behalf payment of any premium which is due on such policy or contract for insurance at the time of its issuance or delivery or which becomes due thereon not more than ninety (90) days thereafter."

The foregoing section was enacted for the benefit of the public . . . , and "it is to safeguard the public and the policyholders." . . . The public and policyholders would not be protected from the misappropriation of funds by brokers if responsibility for the brokers' misappropriation was placed upon the policyholder. The possibility of such misappropriation or conversion, and its effect on the insurance-buying public, appears to be the evil this statutory provision was intended to remedy [when it placed the responsibility for the brokers' misappropriation on the insurance company by authorizing the broker to receive premium payments on its behalf]. If a broker misappropriates or converts a premium to his own use, it is a matter to be resolved between the broker and the insurance company. . . .

The evidence in this case shows that the sole reason for the cancellation of this policy was nonpayment of the premium and that Agres requested the defendant to cancel the policy for that reason, placing the burden on plaintiff of recovering the allegedly misappropriated premium from Kafkis. This was a wrongful use of the privilege of cancellation.

As plaintiff has said, "a fraud would be perpetrated upon the insured if a company were entitled to receive payment of premium and then reject the obligations under its policy by asserting that the premium had not been paid." It is true that "where the privilege of cancellation is exercised under circumstances which would make it operate as a fraud on insured, it is invalid and ineffective." . . . Justice and fair dealing require this court to declare the cancellation void and unenforceable. Therefore, absent cancellation, the policy was in force at the time of the November 14, 1958, occurrence. Defendant having wrongfully refused and failed to assume its policy obligations, it is liable for the amounts of the judgments against plaintiff, which arose out of the November 14, 1958, occurrence. . . .

[Judgment reversed and case remanded.]

Heinrich v Martin

(ND) 134 NW2d 786 (1965)

Martin and his wife owned land which he listed for sale with Schneider, a real estate broker. Schneider agreed to sell the land to Heinrich. Heinrich sued the Martins for specific performance, claiming that the latter failed to perform the contract for the sale of the land. From a judgment in favor of the Martins, Heinrich appealed.

STRUTZ, J. . . . The listing agreement, which the defendant Martin admits signing, was dated, and it listed, among other things, the total acreage, the number of acres under cultivation, the sale price per acre, the required down payment, and the manner in which the balance due should be paid. Nowhere in the listing agreement was the broker given any authority to enter into a contract of sale of the land with any prospective buyer.

After such listing, the broker sought a buyer and, almost one year after the date on the listing agreement, he interested the plaintiff in the defendants' land. It is agreed that the defendant Gottlieb Martin did not sign any memorandum or other writing by which he contracted to sell the land to the plaintiff, but he did write a letter to the plaintiff, agreeing to sell the land to him under certain definite terms and conditions. He also orally told the broker to get the plaintiff to issue a check to the broker and one to the defendant for a part of the down payment to "close the deal." It is the listing agreement which the defendant signed, the defendant's letter to the plaintiff offering to sell the land, and the request for and delivery of such check, that form the basis for the plaintiff's cause of action.

[By statute] . . . certain contracts are invalid unless the contract, or some note or memorandum thereof, is in writing, signed by the party to be charged, or by his agent. Among the contracts that are thus declared to be invalid are agreements for the sale of real property. This section further provides that, if such agreement is made by an agent of the party to be charged, the authority of the agent must be in writing, signed by the party sought to be charged.

Thus a real estate broker, with whom lands are listed for sale by an owner, has no authority to make a contract for sale which is binding on the owner in the absence of written authority, signed by the owner. Any writing which plaintiff might have received from the broker, as defendants' agent, would not be binding on the defendants since the broker had no such written authority.

The listing agreement, which . . . Martin admits having signed and delivered to the broker, is not an agreement to sell the land to the plaintiff. It is merely a written memorandum, signed by the owner, authorizing the broker to secure a buyer for the land. As this court has held, a real estate broker with whom land is listed does not have the power to make a binding contract for sale of such land unless the broker has written authority to make such contract. . . . A writing, signed by an owner, which merely lists the land for sale is not sufficient to satisfy the provision of the Statute of Frauds and empower the prospective buyer to force the owner to convey the property to him. . . .

[Judgment affirmed.]

Walker v Pacific Mobile Homes

68 Wash 2d 347, 413 P2d 3 (1966)

Walker owned a trailer that he wished to sell. He took it to the business premises of Pacific Mobile Homes. The only person on the premises at that time and several other times when Walker was there was Stewart, who identified himself as a salesman of Pacific and who agreed to take possession of Walker's trailer and to attempt to sell it for him. Stewart made out some forms of Pacific Mobile Homes and thereafter wrote some letters on the letterhead of Pacific to Walker. Walker's trailer was sold, but the salesman disappeared with most of the money. Walker sued Pacific for the proceeds of the sale. It denied liability on the ground that Stewart lacked authority to make any sales agreement and that all salesmen of Pacific were expressly forbidden to take used trailers to try to sell them for their owners. From a decision in favor of Walker, Pacific appealed.

HALE, J. . . . The evidence warranted findings and conclusions that Pacific Mobile Homes had clothed Stewart . . . with apparent or ostensible authority to take the trailer onto the lot for sale . . . and to collect the purchase money therefor. The salesman's solitary presence in the company office and about the lot on several occasions, among numerous trailers on display, beneath a sign conspicuously proclaiming the whole to be an enterprise of Pacific Mobile Homes, Inc., and his towing plaintiff's trailer to the trailer lot and putting it on display there, allowed a person of ordinary business prudence to reasonably assume that the salesman had authority from Pacific Mobile Homes, Inc., to buy, sell, receive, and deliver trailers for cash, on credit, consignment, or in exchange. Then, too, the salesman's untrammeled access to and use of his principal's letterhead, stationery, and business forms, and his seeming control of the office and lot, fortify the idea of apparent authority.

Authority to perform particular services for a principal carries with it the implied authority to perform the usual and necessary acts essential to carry out the authorized services. . . . One dealing in good faith with an agent who appears to be acting within the scope of his authority is not bound by undisclosed limitations on the agent's power. . . .

A corporation may be bound by the contracts or agreements of its agent if within the apparent scope of the agent's authority, although the contract may be beyond the scope of his actual authority. . . .

It is also the well-established rule that the apparent or ostensible authority of an agent can be inferred only from acts and conduct of the principal. . . . The extent of an agent's authority cannot be established by his own acts and declarations. . . .

The burden of establishing agency rests upon the one who asserts it. Facts and circumstances are sufficient to establish apparent authority only when a person exercising ordinary prudence, acting in good faith and conversant with business practices and customs, would be misled thereby, and such person has given due regard to such other circumstances as would cause a person of ordinary prudence to make further inquiry. . . .

A principal may be estopped to deny that his agent possesses the authority he assumes to exercise, where the principal knowingly causes or permits him so to act as to justify a third person of ordinarily careful and prudent business habits to believe that he possesses the authority exercised and avails himself of the benefit of the agent's acts. . . .

[Judgment affirmed.]

Kinmon v J. P. King Auction Co., Inc.

290 Ala 323, 276 So2d 569 (1973)

Kinmon owned a summer home which he wanted to sell at auction. He employed the J. P. King Auction Company to make the sale. King sold the property to the highest bidder for $35,000. Kinmon had expected twice that much and refused to convey title to the buyer or to pay commissions to King. King sued Kinmon to collect the commissions. Kinmon raised the defense that he had revoked King's

authority to sell the property. From a judgment for King, Kinmon appealed.

FAULKNER, J. . . . "Bittersweet" is a home in Perdido Beach, Alabama. . . .

On July 29, 1971, George H. Kinmon, the owner, signed a contract with J. P. King Auction Company (King) to sell the property "for the highest price obtainable." Kinmon testified to having "conveyed" to the representatives of King that he expected to realize $103,500 for the property. The latter told Kinmon that Bittersweet would bring what it was worth the day of the sale. The written contract did not incorporate any guaranteed minimum price, referring merely to "the highest price obtainable."

King prepared and distributed a brochure announcing the "absolute auction" of Bittersweet: "This is the place for your Vacation Home or Company Lodge, plenty of room for sleeping and entertaining on Beautiful Soldier Creek just a few minutes by boat to Alabama Point and on out into the Gulf for some of the best fishing in the world. Enjoy swimming and skiing just from your own boathouse or just plain fishing from the pier. There is everything to enjoy at 'Bittersweet.'

Let Today's Investment Be Tomorrow's Security."

"YOUR PRICE IS OUR PRICE."

Kinmon, concerned about the possibility of not realizing an adequate price for his property, protested against the inclusion of the terms "Your Price is Our Price" and "absolute auction." However, preparations for the auction continued. Signs announcing the forthcoming auction and stating "Your Price is Our Price" remained undisturbed by Kinmon.

On August 21, 1971, the day of the auction, Kinmon was "upset." He told King's secretary that he wasn't signing anything. At one point during the bidding, Kinmon went up to King and stated that if Bittersweet did not bring $70,000, "I will take you to Supreme Court." King went ahead with the bidding and sold the property to the highest bidder for $35,000. Kinmon subsequently refused to convey the property or pay King's commission. King sued, and the Circuit Court of Baldwin County held that he was entitled to his commission. Kinmon appealed from this decree.

. . . There is no doubt Kinmon and King could have written a $50,000, $70,000, or $100,000 minimum price for Bittersweet into their auction sale contract. They did not do so. The contract recites that Bittersweet would be sold "for the highest price obtainable." Kinmon may have wished or hoped that the sale would realize $100,000. However, it is elementary that it is the terms of the written contract, not the mental operations of one of the parties, that control its interpretation. . . .

Contracting parties are free to modify their contract by mutual assent. . . . After expressing discontent with the advertised slogan "Your Price is Our Price," Kinmon could have asked King to insert a minimum price guarantee into the contract. He did not do so. Unilateral grumbling cannot modify bilateral contract.

It is the general rule that the agency to sell at auction, whether such auction be "with reserve" or "absolute," may be withdrawn at any time prior to the opening of bids. . . . This withdrawal of authority must be clear and unequivocal. Nowhere in the record is there evidence that Kinmon clearly and unequivocally stated that he no longer wished King to sell his property, that he was revoking King's authority, that he was withdrawing Bittersweet from sale. Being "upset" is not enough; threatening to take King to court if $70,000 were not realized is not enough. . . .

[Judgment affirmed.]

Record v Wagner

100 NH 419, 128 A2d 921 (1957)

Record owned a farm that was operated by his agent, Berry, who lived on the farm. The latter hired Wagner to bale the hay in 1953 and told him to bill Record for this work. He did so and was paid by Record. By the summer of 1954, the agency had been terminated by Record, but Berry remained in possession as tenant of the farm and nothing appeared changed. In 1954 Berry asked Wagner to bale the hay the same as in the prior year and bill Record for the work. He did so, but Record

refused to pay on the ground that Berry was not then his agent. When Wagner sued him and recovered a judgment against him, Record appealed.

DUNCAN, J. . . . "It is a familiar principle of law that the authority of the agent to bind his principal continues, even after an actual revocation, until notice of the revocation is given." . . .

By paying the 1953 bill, the defendant recognized Berry's authority to hire the plaintiff on the former's credit. Berry then resided on the defendant's farm, and was properly found the defendant's agent at that time. In 1954, Berry continued to reside on the main farm, and to all appearances was operating it in the same manner and in the same capacity. If in fact he had ceased to occupy the farm as agent, but did so as a tenant, the defendant made no effort to notify the plaintiff of the change in Berry's status.

It could be found that in the exercise of reasonable diligence the plaintiff was justified as a result of the defendant's conduct in believing that Berry had authority to pledge the defendant's credit in 1954 for the same services which the defendant recognized as a proper charge against himself in 1953. . . . The important fact is that the defendant permitted the outward appearances of Berry's authority to remain unchanged in 1954 from what they were in 1953, and by not notifying the plaintiff of the termination of the agency permitted the plaintiff to be misled. Having done so, he rather than the plaintiff should bear the loss. . . . We do not consider the circumstance that Berry had previously pledged the defendant's credit upon only one occasion . . . to be of controlling importance. . . . The evidence that no question of the agent's authority was raised on the occasion, coupled with the evidence of the misleading circumstances of his continued occupancy and management of the farms and the cattle in the defendant's continued absence, was sufficient to warrant the verdict.

[Judgment for Wagner.]

QUESTIONS AND CASE PROBLEMS

1. What is the objective of each of the following rules of law?
   (a) The burden of proving the existence of an agency relationship rests upon the person who seeks to benefit by such proof.
   (b) If a principal fails to notify third persons when he terminates the agency, his agent may continue to make contracts that are binding on the principal.
2. A daughter was using the family car to buy sweet corn for the family from a roadside stand. When she collided with another driver, the latter claimed that the former was the father's agent and that the father was liable for her tort. Was she the agent of her father? [Grimes v Labreck, 108 NH 26, 226 A2d 787]
3. Whitehead had a policy of hospital insurance. The authority of the agent who had "sold" him the policy and to whom Whitehead paid premiums was terminated by the insurance company, but Whitehead was never notified of this fact. He continued to pay premiums to the former agent. When Whitehead told a hospital that he had an insurance policy, the company confirmed this statement and admitted that the policy was in force. Thereafter the insurer refused to pay any hospital bills on the ground that the former agent to whom premium payments were made had no authority to receive the payments. Was the insurer liable? [American Casualty Co. v Whitehead, (Miss) 206 So2d 838]
4. Bush owned real estate, which he listed with a real estate broker to sell at $26,000 "or at any other price terms acceptable to me." Montone offered

to purchase it for less than $26,000 and so informed the broker; but before Bush had accepted the offer, Montone informed the broker that he revoked his offer. Bush then "accepted" the offer and later sued Montone to enforce the contract. Decide. [Montone v Bush, (Fla App) 167 So2d 884]

5. Through his agent, Davis, Fieschko executed a written agreement to sell his real estate to Herlich. The agreement had been negotiated by Dykstra as Herlich's agent. The contract for the purchase of the land was signed by Dykstra as the agent for Herlich. Thereafter Herlich sent a check for the down payment to Davis. The check did not contain any reference to the sale or the terms of the sale. Herlich did not go through with the sale and, when sued for breach of the contract, he argued that he was not bound by the contract since he had not signed it and Dykstra had not been authorized in writing to sign it. Fieschko claimed that Herlich had ratified the contract when he sent the check for the down payment. Decide. [Fieschko v Herlich, 32 Ill App 2d 280, 177 NE2d 376]

6. Coffin had a liability and property damage insurance policy on his automobile issued by the Farm Bureau Mutual Insurance Co. He purchased a new automobile and wanted to transfer the insurance. He phoned the home office of the insurance company, stated his request, and was transferred to two different girls who each stated that she did not have authority to make such a transfer and finally connected him with Pierson. Coffin stated to Pierson that he wanted to transfer his existing insurance and also to add comprehensive and collision coverage. Pierson told him that the new car was insured as requested from that moment on. Coffin had an accident in his car the next day before any change had been made in his policy. He sued the insurance company, which defended on the ground that no change had ever been made and that Pierson was merely a typing supervisor in the auto underwriters' department who had no authority to make any policy change. Was the new car covered by insurance? [Farm Bureau Mutual Insurance Company v Coffin, 136 Ind App 12, 186 NE2d 180]

7. Fishbaugh employed Scheibenberger to run a farm for him. Scheibenberger was authorized to rent the farm, to collect the rent, to superintend and direct repairs, and to allow the tenant to sell corn for the payment of taxes and fencing. The agent leased the farm to Hinsley, who sold certain crops to Spunaugle. Fishbaugh sued Spunaugle for the value of these crops. The decision turned on whether Scheibenberger was a general agent. What is your opinion? [Fishbaugh v Spunaugle, 118 Iowa 337, 92 NW 58]

8. An automobile was owned by Peterson. He gave possession of the car to his son, Edward, and Edward's wife, Gloria, but retained the title to the car. Edward's daughter, Christine, was sixteen and was driving the car to the city at Gloria's direction in order to buy her younger sister a pair of shoes. Because of Christine's negligent driving, the car struck Johnson who was riding a motorcycle. He sued Christine's mother. He claimed that Christine was the agent of the mother. Could the mother raise the defense that Christine was a minor? [Johnson v Peterson, — Cal App 3d —, 113 Cal Rptr 445]

41 Principal and Agent

AGENT'S AUTHORITY

The fact that one person is the agent of another does not dispose of all questions. It is necessary to determine the scope of the agent's authority.

§ **41:1. Scope of Agent's Authority.** The authority of an agent includes that which is (1) expressly given by the principal; (2) incidental to the authority that is expressly given by the principal; and (3) customary for such an agent to exercise. In addition, an agent may have (4) apparent authority.

(1) Express Authority. If the principal tells the agent to perform a certain act, the agent has *express authority* to do so. Express authority can be indicated by conduct as well as by words. Accordingly, when the agent informs the principal of his intended plans and the principal makes no objection to them, authorization may be indicated by such silence.[1]

(2) Incidental Authority. An agent has implied *incidental authority* to perform any act reasonably necessary to execute the express authority given to him.[2] To illustrate, if the principal authorizes the agent to purchase goods without furnishing funds to the agent to pay for them, the agent has implied incidental authority to purchase the goods on credit.

(3) Customary Authority. An agent has implied *customary authority* to do any act which, according to the custom of the community, usually accompanies the transaction for which he is authorized to act as agent.[3] For example, an agent who has express authority to receive payments from third persons has implied authority to issue receipts.[4]

One authorized to act as general manager has the power to make any contract necessary for the usual and ordinary conduct of business.

An agent with express authority to receive checks in payment does not have implied authority to cash them.[5] An employee's authority to indorse checks payable to an employer does not embrace authority to indorse and deposit those checks into the employee's personal bank account.[6] Authorization to a lawyer to settle a client's claim does not authorize the lawyer to indorse the client's name on a check given in settlement of the claim.[7]

---

1 Boise Payette Lumber Co. v Larsen, (CA9 Idaho) 214 F2d 373.

2 Restatement, Agency, 2d § 35.

3 R 2d § 36.

4 Degen v Acme Brick Co., 228 Ark 1054, 312 SW2d 194.

5 Merchants' & Manufacturers' Association v First National Bank, 40 Ariz 531, 14 P2d 717.

6 Von Gohren v Pacific National Bank, 8 Wash App 245, 505 P2d 467.

7 Zidek v Forbes National Bank, 159 Pa Super 442, 48 A2d 103.

An agent does not have incidental or customary power to release or compromise debts owed to his principal or to settle disputed amounts of debts for smaller sums, even though he is designated as the "field representative" of the principal. Thus, a bank is not bound by an agreement made by its field representative with the owner of a financed automobile that if the owner surrenders the automobile to the representative, the balance of the owner's debt to the bank will be forgiven by the bank.[8]

(4) Apparent Authority. As noted in Chapter 40, a person has apparent authority as an agent when the principal by his words or conduct reasonably leads a third party to believe that such a person has that authority.

The mere possession of property of another does not give rise to any apparent authority of the possessor to act with respect to the property. (See p. 824, Taylor v Equitable Trust Co.)

§ 41:2. Effect of Proper Exercise of Authority. When an agent with authority properly makes a contract with a third person that purports to bind the principal, there is by definition a binding contract between the principal and the third person. The agent is not a party to this contract. Consequently, when the owner of goods is the principal, his agent is not liable for breach of warranty with respect to the goods "sold" by the agent because the owner-principal, not the agent, is the seller in the sales transaction.[9]

Furthermore, even though a transaction between the agent and the third person may be formalized by the execution of subsequent documents, such as a written policy of insurance after an oral agreement has been made with the agent, the later writing does not destroy the rights acquired by the principal or the third person under the agent's informal or oral contract; and parol evidence is admissible to determine the actual agreement that had been made with the agent. (See p. 822, Baker v St. Paul Fire & Marine Ins. Co.)

§ 41:3. Duty to Ascertain Extent of Agent's Authority. A third person who deals with a person claiming to be an agent cannot rely on the statements made by the agent concerning the extent of his authority. If the agent is not authorized to perform the act involved or is not even the agent of the principal, the transaction between the alleged agent and the third person will have no legal effect between the principal and the third person.

When the third person should realize that the agent is merely a soliciting agent of an insurance company with no greater authority than to obtain an application from third persons and transmit it to the insurance company, the insurer is not bound by an agreement which such agent makes with an applicant by which the applicant had been promised unlimited medical expenses coverage, whereas the policy as delivered contained a maximum limitation on such coverage.[10]

---

[8] Peoples First National Bank & Trust Co. v Gaudelli, 177 Pa Super 212, 110 A2d 900.

[9] Gaito v Hoffman, 5 UCCRS 1056.

[10] American National Insurance Co. v Laird, 228 Ark 812, 311 SW2d 313.

(1) Authority Dependent on an Event. If the authority of an agent is contingent upon the happening of some event, one may not ordinarily rely upon the statement of the agent as to the happening of that event. Thus, when an agent is authorized to sell for his principal a given quantity of oranges only in the event of the arrival of a specified ship, one dealing with the agent should ascertain for himself whether the ship has arrived and should not rely on the agent's statement that it has.

An exception to this rule is made in cases in which the happening of the event is peculiarly within the knowledge of the agent and cannot be ascertained easily, if at all, by the party dealing with the agent. As an illustration, if the agent of a railroad issues a bill of lading for goods without actually receiving the goods, the railroad, as principal, is liable to one who accepts the bill in good faith and for value. This exception[11] is justified because, although the authority of the agent to issue bills of lading is dependent upon receiving the goods, persons taking bills of lading have no way of ascertaining whether the agent did receive the goods.

(2) Agent's Acts Adverse to Principal. The third party who deals with an agent is also required to take notice of any acts that are clearly adverse to the interest of the principal. Thus, if the agent is obviously making use of funds of the principal for his own benefit, the person dealing with the agent acts at his peril.[12]

The only certain way that the third person can protect himself is to inquire of the principal whether the agent is in fact the agent of the principal and has the necessary authority. If the principal states that the agent has the authority, the principal cannot later deny this authorization unless the subject matter is such that an authorization must be in writing in order to be binding.[13]

(3) Death of Third Party. The extent of the agent's authority becomes particularly significant when the third person dies after the transaction with the agent but before any action has been taken by the principal. If the agent had authority to contract on behalf of the principal, his agreement with the third person would give rise immediately to a binding contract and the third person's subsequent death would ordinarily not effect that contract. In contrast, if the agent did not have authority to contract but only to transmit an offer from the third person, the death of the third person before the principal had accepted the offer would work a revocation of the offer and the principal could not create a contract by purporting to accept after the death of the third person.[14]

§ 41:4. Limitations on Agent's Authority. A person who has knowledge of a limitation on an agent's authority cannot disregard that limitation. When

[11] UCC § 7-301.
[12] Central West Casualty Co. v Stewart, 248 Ky 137, 58 SW2d 366.
[13] Litchfield v Green, 43 Ariz 509, 33 P2d 290.
[14] Richardson v Ward, (La App) 202 So2d 327.

the third person knows that the authority of the agent depends upon whether financing has been obtained, the principal is not bound by the act of the agent if the financing was not obtained. (See p. 825, Citizens State Bank v Rausch.) If the authority of the agent is based on a writing and the third person knows that there is such a writing, he is charged with knowledge of the limitations contained in it. The third person is likewise charged with such knowledge when the contract submitted to him indicates the existence of a limitation on the agent's authority.

If the agent informs the third person that he lacks authority to do a particular act but that he will endeavor to obtain authorization from his principal, the third person cannot successfully claim that the agent has apparent authority.[15] If the third person enters into a contract on the assumption that the agent will be able to obtain authorization, the third person does so at his risk.

(1) Apparent Limitations. In some situations it will be apparent to the third person that he is dealing with an agent whose authority is limited. When the third person knows that he is dealing with an officer of a private corporation or a representative of a governmental agency, he should recognize that such person will ordinarily not have unlimited authority [16] and that a contract made with him might not be binding unless ratified by his principal.

(2) Secret Limitations. If the principal has clothed his agent with authority to perform certain acts but the principal has given him secret instructions that limit his authority, the third person is allowed to take the authority of the agent at its face value and is not bound by the secret limitations of which he has no knowledge.[17]

§ 41:5. Delegation of Authority by Agent. As a general rule, an agent cannot delegate his authority to another.[18] (See p. 825, Bucholtz v Sirotkin Travel Ltd.) In other words, unless the principal expressly or impliedly consents, an agent cannot appoint *subagents* to carry out his duties.[19] The reason for this rule is that since an agent is usually selected because of some personal qualifications, it would be unfair and possibly injurious to the principal if the authority to act could be shifted by the agent to another. This is particularly true when the agent was originally appointed for the performance of a task requiring discretion or judgment. For example, an agent who is appointed to adjust claims against an insurance company cannot delegate the performance of his duties to another.

An agent, however, may authorize another to perform his work for him in the following instances:

---

[15] Central New York Realty Corp. v Abel, 28 App Div 2d 50, 281 NYS2d 115.
[16] Weil and Associates v Urban Renewal Agency, 206 Kan 405, 479 P2d 875.
[17] South Second Livestores Auction, Inc. v Roberts, 69 NMex 155, 364 P2d 859.
[18] R 2d § 18; Knudsen v Torrington Co., (CA2 Conn) 254 F2d 283.
[19] Bourg v Hebert, 224 La 535, 70 So2d 116.

(1) When the acts to be done involve only mechanical or ministerial duties. Thus, an agent to make application for hail insurance on wheat may delegate to another the clerical act of writing the application. And it may be shown that there is customary authority for a clerk in the office of the insurance agent to sign the agent's name so as to have the effect of a signing by the agent and be binding upon the insurance company, the agent's principal.[20]

(2) When a well-known custom justifies such appointment. To illustrate, if one is authorized to buy or sell a grain elevator, he may do so through a broker when that is the customary method.

(3) When the appointment is justified by necessity or sudden emergency and it is impractical to communicate with the principal, and such appointment of a subagent is reasonably necessary for the protection of the interests of the principal entrusted to the agent.[21] For instance, an agent to collect tolls, who is in charge of a bridge, may appoint another to collect tolls in his place when he is required to be on the bridge making repairs.[22]

(4) When it was contemplated by the parties that subagents would be employed. For example, a bank may now generally use subagents to receive payment of notes that have been left for collection since the parties contemplated that this would be done.

DUTIES AND LIABILITIES OF PRINCIPAL AND AGENT

The creation of the principal-agent relationship gives rise not only to powers but also to duties and liabilities.

§ 41:6. Duties and Liabilities of Agent to Principal. The agent owes to the principal the duties of (1) loyalty, (2) obedience and performance, (3) reasonable care, (4) accounting, and (5) information.

(1) Loyalty. An agent must be loyal or faithful to his principal. He must not obtain any secret profit or advantage from his relationship.[23] To illustrate, if an agent knows that his employer is negotiating for a lease and secretly obtains the lease for himself, the court will compel the agent to surrender the lease to the principal.

Similarly, if a broker is retained to purchase certain property, the broker cannot purchase the property for himself either in his own name or in the name of his wife.[24] Likewise, an agent cannot purchase property of the principal, which the agent was hired to sell, without the principal's express consent.[25] Similarly, an agent's wife cannot purchase in her own name property of the principal which the agent was hired to sell.

---

20 United Bonding Insurance Co. v Banco Suizo-Panameno, (CA5 Fla) 422 F2d 1142.

21 Magenau v Aetna Freight Lines, (CA3 Pa) 257 F2d 445.

22 Ada-Konawa Bridge Co. v Cargo, 163 Okla 122, 21 P2d 1.

23 Doner v Phoenix Joint Stock Land Bank, 381 Ill 106, 45 NE2d 20.

24 Gerhardt v Weiss, 247 Cal App 2d 114, 55 Cal Rptr 425.

25 Kellett v Boynton, 87 Ga App 692, 75 SE2d 292.

If the agent owns property, he cannot purchase it from himself on behalf of his principal without disclosing to the principal his interest in the transaction. If he fails to disclose his interest, the principal may avoid the transaction even if he was not financially harmed by the agent's conduct. Or the principal can approve the transaction and sue the agent for any profit realized by the agent.

An agent cannot act as agent for both parties to a transaction unless both know of the dual capacity and agree to it. If he does so act without the consent of both parties, the transaction is voidable at the election of any principal who did not know of the agent's double status.

An agent must not accept secret gifts or commissions from third persons in connection with his activities as agent. If he does, the principal may sue him for those gifts or commissions. Such practices are condemned because the judgment of the agent may be influenced by the receipt of gifts or commissions. A principal may also recover from his agent any secret profit that the latter has made in violation of his duty of loyalty to his principal. If an agent makes a false report to the principal in order to conceal the agent's interest, the principal is entitled to recover not only the secret profit made and property acquired by the agent but may also be awarded punitive damages by way of punishing and discouraging such wrongdoing.[26] (See p. 827, Kribbs v Jackson.)

An agent violates his duty of loyalty when he uses the name of his principal in perpetrating a fraud upon third persons.[27]

An agent is, of course, prohibited from aiding the competitors of his principal or disclosing to them information relating to the business of the principal. It is also a breach of duty for the agent to deceive his principal with false information.

The principal may authorize his agent to sell certain property for a net price and keep any excess for his compensation. In such a case, it is immaterial who is the buyer of the property, provided the agent does not have a "prohibited" buyer at the time that the principal fixes the net price. For example, the agent violates the duty of loyalty when he first obtains an offer for his principal's property from the agent's mother-in-law, then tells the principal that he has an offer for the property without disclosing the identity or relationship of the offeror, and the principal establishes the net price on the basis of that offer.[28]

(2) Obedience and Performance. An agent is under a duty to obey all lawful instructions given to him. He is required to perform the services specified for the period and in the way specified.[29] If he does not, he is liable to the principal for any harm caused him.[30] For example, if an agent,

---

[26] Bate v Marsteller, 232 Cal App 2d 605, 43 Cal Rptr 149.

[27] Jarboe Bros. Storage Warehouses, Inc. v Allied Van Lines, Inc., (CA4 Md) 400 F2d 743.

[28] Loughlin v Idora Realty Co., 259 Cal App 2d 536, 66 Cal Rptr 747.

[29] R 2d § 383.

[30] Missouri ex rel Algiere v Russell, 359 Mo 800, 223 SW2d 481.

without authority to do so, releases one who is in debt under circumstances that the release is binding upon the principal, the agent is liable to the principal for the loss.

If an agent is instructed to take cash payments only but accepts a check in payment, he is liable for any loss caused by his act, such as that which arises when the check accepted by him is not collectible because it is forged. Likewise, when an insurance broker undertakes to obtain a policy of insurance for his principal that will provide a specified coverage as to workmen's compensation claims but fails to obtain a policy with the proper coverage, the broker must indemnify the principal for the loss caused by the agent's failure to obtain the proper insurance.[31]

If the agent violates his instructions, it is immaterial that he acts in good faith or intends to benefit the principal. It is the fact that he violates the instructions and thereby causes his principal a loss which imposes a liability on the agent. In determining whether the agent has obeyed his instructions, they must be interpreted in the way that a reasonable man would interpret them.[32]

(3) Reasonable Care. It is the duty of an agent to act with the care that a reasonable man would exercise under the circumstances. In addition, if the agent possesses a special skill, as in the case of a broker or an attorney, he must exercise that skill.

(4) Accounting. An agent must account to his principal for all property or money belonging to his principal that comes into the agent's possession.[33] The agent should, within a reasonable time, give notice of collections made and render an accurate account of all receipts and expenditures. The agency agreement may state, of course, at what intervals or on what dates accountings are to be made.

An agent should keep his principal's property and money separate and distinct from his own. If an agent mingles his property with the property of his principal so that the two cannot be identified or separated, the principal may claim all of the commingled mass. Furthermore, when funds of the principal and of the agent are mixed, any loss that occurs must be borne by the agent. For example, when the agent deposits the funds of the principal in a bank account in his own name, he is liable for the amount if the bank should fail.

(5) Information. It is the duty of an agent to keep the principal informed of all facts pertinent to the agency that may enable the principal to protect his interests.[34] In consequence, a principal's promise to pay a bonus to his agent for information secured by the agent in the performance of his

---

[31] Roberson v Knupp Insurance Agency, 125 Ill App 2d 373, 260 NE2d 849.
[32] Smith v Union Savings & Loan Association, 97 Colo 440, 50 P2d 538.
[33] R 2d § 382.
[34] R 2d § 381; Spritz v Brockton Savings Bank, 305 Mass 170, 25 NE2d 155.

duties is unenforceable on the ground that the principal was entitled to the information anyway. The promise is therefore not supported by consideration.

If the agent fails to communicate information to his principal which should have been communicated, and the principal sustains loss because he lacks that information, the principal may recover the amount of such loss from the agent.[35]

§ 41:7. Enforcement of Liability of Agent. When the agent's breach of duty causes harm to the principal, the amount of the loss may be deducted from any compensation due the agent or may be recovered from him in an ordinary lawsuit.

When the agent handles money for the principal, the contract of employment may provide that the amount of any shortages in the agent's account may be deducted from the compensation to which the agent would otherwise be entitled.[36]

If the agent has made a secret profit, the principal may recover the profit from the agent. In any case, the agent may forfeit his right to all compensation, without regard to whether the principal has been benefited by some of the actions of the agent and without regard to whether the principal has actually been harmed.[37]

§ 41:8. Duties and Liabilities of Principal to Agent. The principal is under certain duties to the agent. He must perform the contract, compensate the agent for his services, reimburse him for proper expenditures, and indemnify him for loss under certain circumstances.

(1) Employment According to Terms of Contract. When the contract is for a specified time, the principal is under the obligation to permit the agent to act as such for the term of the contract, in the absence of any just cause or contract provision which permits the principal to terminate the agency sooner. If his principal gives the agent an exclusive right to act as such, the principal cannot give anyone else the authority to act as his agent nor may the principal himself do the act to which the exclusive agent's authority relates. If the principal does so, the exclusive agent is entitled to his compensation as though he had performed the act.

(2) Compensation. The principal must pay the agent the compensation agreed upon. If the parties have not fixed the amount of the compensation by their agreement but intended that the agent should be paid, the agent may recover the customary compensation for such services. If there is no established compensation, he may recover the reasonable value of his services.

When one requests another to perform services under circumstances that reasonably justify the expectation of being paid, a duty to make payment

---

[35] Bliesener v Baird & Warner, Inc., 88 Ill App 2d 383, 232 NE2d 13.
[36] Male v Acme Markets, 110 NJ Super 9, 264 A2d 245.
[37] Allied Securities, Inc. v Clocker, 185 Neb 514, 176 NW2d 914.

arises.[38] For example, when one requests a broker or an attorney to act as an agent in his professional capacity, it is implied that compensation is to be paid.

When the agent is employed on the contingency that he is to be compensated only if he obtains or produces a specified result, the agent is not entitled to compensation or reimbursement if he does not achieve the desired result, regardless of how much time or money he has spent in the effort. Likewise, an agent is not entitled to compensation with respect to transactions canceled by third persons as long as the principal was not at fault. (See p. 828, Eskin v Acheson Manufacturing Co.) In any case an agent may agree to work without compensation; for it is authorization to act, and not compensation for acting, that is the test of agency.

(a) ADVANCE PAYMENT. When agents are compensated on a basis of a percentage of the sales price of goods they sell or the contracts they make, it is customary to allow them to draw a stated amount weekly or monthly subject to adjustment at the end of some longer accounting period in the event that the commissions actually earned should be greater than the sums paid for the drawing account. If the contract between the principal and the agent does not give the principal the right to recover overpayments, the employer does not have such a right. That is, when an agent is allowed to take advances to be charged against future commissions, the principal cannot recover the excess of the advances over the earned commissions in the absence of an express or implied agreement to that effect.[39]

If it is not clear from the agency contract whether the principal has the right to recoup over-advances, the contract is interpreted strictly against the principal and the right to recoup is denied.[40]

(b) REPEATING TRANSACTIONS. In certain industries third persons make repeated transactions with the principal. In such cases the agent who made the original contract with the third person commonly receives a certain compensation or percentage of commissions on all subsequent renewal or additional contracts. In the insurance business, for example, the insurance agent obtaining the policyholder for the insurer receives a substantial portion of the first year's premium and then receives a smaller percentage of the premiums paid by the policyholder in the following years.

Whether an agent or his estate is entitled to receive compensation on repeating transactions, either after the termination of the agent's employment or after the agent's death, depends upon the terms of the agency contract. Frequently it is provided that the right to receive compensation on repeating transactions terminates upon the termination of the agent's authority or employment by the principal.

A provision that an agent's renewal commissions shall terminate if he accepts employment with another insurance company before the expiration

---

[38] R 2d § 441.
[39] Valoco Building Products v Chafee, 4 Conn Cir 322, 231 A2d 101.
[40] Badger v Nu-Tone Products Co., 162 Colo 216, 425 P2d 698.

of a specified period after the termination of his employment is valid. There is no vested right to renewal premiums but only such right as the contract of employment confers. Such a limitation is not a restraint on trade since it is not to be regarded as restraining the agent from following his profession, trade, or business.[41]

(c) POST-AGENCY TRANSACTIONS. An agent is not entitled to compensation in connection with transactions, such as sales or renewals of insurance policies, occurring after the termination of the agency, even though the post-agency transactions are the result of the agent's former activities.[42] Some contracts between a principal and agent expressly give the agent the right to post-termination compensation, however, or they may expressly deny the agent such compensation.

*(3) **Reimbursement.*** The principal is under a duty to reimburse the agent for all disbursements made at the request of the principal and for all expenses necessarily incurred in the lawful discharge of the agency for the benefit of the principal.[43] The agent cannot recover, however, for expenses caused by his own misconduct or negligence. By way of illustration, if the agent transfers title to the wrong person, he cannot recover from the principal the amount of expense incurred in correcting the error.

*(4) **Indemnity.*** It is the duty of the principal to indemnify the agent for any losses or damages suffered without his fault but occurring on account of the agency.[44] For example, when an agent was compelled by law to pay his own money because under the direction of his principal he, without knowing that they belonged to the third person rather than to the principal, had sold certain goods owned by a third person, he was entitled to recover the amount of such payment from his principal.

When the loss sustained is not the result of obedience to the principal's instructions but of the agent's misconduct, or of an obviously illegal act, the principal is not liable for indemnification.

---

[41] Geiss v Northern Insurance Agency, (ND) 153 NW2d 688.

[42] Houseware Associates, Inc. v Crown Products Co., 147 Ind App 504, 262 NE2d 209.

[43] R 2d § 439(a), (b); Differential Steel Car Co. v MacDonald, (CA6 Ohio) 180 F2d 260.

[44] R 2d § 439(c), (d).

CASES FOR CHAPTER 41

Baker v St. Paul Fire & Marine Insurance Co.

(Mo App) 427 SW2d 281 (1968)

Elson, who operated a general insurance agency, represented eight companies. Baker applied to him on January 28 for a major medical expense policy. Baker was injured in an accident on February 19. The policy was issued on February 26 with coverage running from that date. The policy was apparently delivered to Baker while he was still in the hospital. He objected that the policy was to have become

effective as of the date that he had applied for the insurance, and he attempted during the several following months to have the policy changed in this respect. Being unable to do so, he brought suit on the policy. The company raised the defense that his injury had been sustained before the effective date of the policy. Baker offered evidence that Elson had orally agreed when he had received the application on January 28 that Baker was to be covered immediately. From a judgment in favor of Baker, the insurer appealed.

CROSS, J. . . . Plaintiff tried . . . his case on the theory that he was entitled to recover under an oral agreement with defendant's agent that the insurance coverage in question would be effective immediately on receipt of plaintiff's application therefor, accompanied by payment of premium in full, pending issuance and delivery of the policy. It is defendant's position that . . . (1) there was no evidence that defendant's agent had authority to bind the effective date by an oral contract of insurance and (2) any oral agreement as to the effective date of the coverage merged into and was extinguished by the written policy (which was issued and dated to be effective after plaintiff suffered casualty giving rise to medical expenses incurred) and that parol evidence of the oral agreement was not admissible to contradict the terms of the policy. . . .

In contending there was no evidence that Elson had authority to make an oral contract of insurance, defendant admits that Elson's possession of its printed application blank and his signature thereon as "agent" show "an agency relationship of some kind," but argues that evidence is lacking to show the scope and extent of the agency. Specifically, defendant insists that plaintiff has not sustained his burden to prove that Elson had authority from defendant to bind it under an oral contract of insurance. To support its position, defendant cites and relies upon cases which follow the familiar rule that an agent who is authorized merely to solicit insurance, take applications, deliver policies and collect premiums, is without power to make oral contracts of insurance; also the rule that the scope of agency cannot be established by the mere declarations of the alleged agent himself. Defendant concedes that the principal is responsible for the acts of the agent when the agent acts within his *apparent* authority if the principal has clothed its agent with *the appearance* of authority. . . .

In Voss v American Mutual Liability Insurance Co., Mo App 341 SW2d 270, [and] in Chailland v M.F.A. Mutual Insurance Co., Mo Sup., 375 SW2d 78, [a similar agency question was involved]. . . .

It is significant to our present question that in both Voss and Chailland it was determined that documentary evidence emanating from the insurance company itself constituted substantial proof that the agent possessed apparent authority to effect immediate coverage by an oral binder. In the Voss case the probative document was the company's application blank form containing the question addressed to the agent, "Have you bound coverage?" In Chailland the writing was the company's letter admitting the authority of its agents "to execute a written binder on insurance in certain instances." Likewise, there is strikingly analogous documentary evidence in this case to show that agent Elson had actual authority to bind the company for insurance coverage, without limitation as to its effective date, by issuing a written binder. We refer to the clause contained in the printed application blank form used by defendant's agent in taking plaintiff's application, here requoted: "I represent that, to the best of my knowledge and belief, the foregoing statements are full, complete and true, and agree the insurance hereby applied for, *unless effective under the provisions of the binding receipt attached hereto,* shall take effect on the policy date stated in the policy but only then if the policy is delivered and the full first premium is paid while the health of each person proposed for insurance remains as described herein." (Our italics.) . . .

Having determined that agent Elson was authorized to execute *a written binder of insurance,* we progress to the next stage of inquiry. Did he have delegated power to bind the company *by oral contract*? That question has clearly been answered by the Supreme Court in the Chailland case in this language. . . . "An agent authorized to execute a written binder of insurance must be held to have the apparent authority to make an oral contract of binder unless, of course, notice of any restriction against such power is brought home to a person dealing with such agent." And, as was considered to be a pertinent circumstance in the Voss case, there is no evidence in this case that any notice whatsoever was brought to plaintiff's attention indicating there was any restriction against agent Elson's authority to bind his company by an oral contract of insurance. Consequently it is a permissible conclusion that Elson possessed "the apparent authority to make an oral contract of binder." . . .

[Judgment affirmed.]

Taylor v Equitable Trust Co.

269 Md 149, 304 A2d 838 (1973)

The Taylors were depositors of the Equitable Trust Company. In return for their check, Equitable gave them a treasurer's check for $20,000. Thereafter Vittetoe, a loan officer of the bank, received a long-distance telephone call from a person who identified himself as Mr. Taylor and requested that the $20,000 represented by the treasurer's check be transferred to the account of Jody Associates at Irving Trust Company in New York. Vittetoe did not know Mr. Taylor personally and replied that written instructions from Taylor would be required. Sometime later, Frank Terranova appeared at the bank and described himself as the Taylors' agent, surrendered the treasurer's check, and requested that the money represented thereby be transferred to the account of Jody Associates in the Irving Trust Company. Terranova surrendered the treasurer's check which was not indorsed. Terranova also presented a letter which he had signed in his own name, addressed to Vittetoe, in which was repeated the request to transfer the $20,000.

Equitable made the transfer as requested. Taylor denied that Terranova had the authority to request such transfer and sued Equitable for damages. Judgment was entered for Equitable. Taylor appealed.

SINGLEY, J. . . . Subtitle 3 of the UCC . . . is applicable here because the check of a bank treasurer or cashier is regarded as a draft drawn on the drawer bank, treated by UCC 3-118(a) as a note and satisfies the requirements of UCC § 3-104. UCC § 3-403(1) recognizes that the signature of an agent or other representative may be valid. Of course, the power to sign for another may be expressly given, or may be implied, or may rest on apparent authority: otherwise, the signature would be unauthorized under § 1-201(43). . . .

An unauthorized signature is wholly inoperative under § 3-404 unless the person whose signature it purports to be ratifies it or is precluded from denying it. Under § 3-401 an item containing a forged or unauthorized signature is not properly payable. . . .

There is no doubt that Equitable was negligent in not insisting on written instructions from Taylor . . . and in not verifying Terranova's authority to act for Taylor, if it proposed to act in reliance upon it. . . .

Both sides make much of the issue whether Terranova was or was not Taylor's agent. Certainly Taylor is not precluded by § 3-406 from asserting Terranova's lack of authority, because of Equitable's acknowledged failure to act in accordance with reasonable commercial standards, in making a transfer without a written direction from Taylor.

Taylor's statement that Terranova was not authorized to act for him, made in his direct testimony and again when Equitable called him as an adverse witness, went unchallenged. The existence of implied or apparent authority could only be bottomed on Terranova's letter, enclosing the check, which for all Vittetoe knew, might have been stolen. Even if we regard the letter as a representation by Terranova that he was authorized to act for Taylor, Equitable was not entitled to rely on Terranova's statement, without more. . . . In our view, Vittetoe's testimony regarding his telephone call to Miami was not enough to save the day, not only because of his equivocation and uncertainty, but because of his total disregard of even the simplest precautions to make sure that the voice at the other end was that of Taylor, a man whom he did not know.

Two comments seem particularly pertinent here: "A third person dealing with a purported agent should communicate with the principal to verify the agent's authority to sign. A written statement from the principal as to the agent's authority may also aid in avoiding any subsequent dispute as to whether such authority existed, or whether the principal had made any statement as to the authority of the apparent agent." 2 Anderson, Uniform Commercial Code, § 3-404:3 at 922. In Noah v Bowery Sav. Bank, 225 NY 284, 122 NE 235, rev'g 171 App Div 912, 155 NYS 1128 (1919), the court, in discussing the conduct of a savings bank, which permitted a withdrawal by a person other than the depositor who had possession of the passbook, said: "Lack of suspicion cannot always be the determinative factor in paying out a depositor's money. Reasonable care might demand a suspicion where from habitual indifference none in fact existed." 122 NE at 237. . . .

It is certainly true that agency could not be implied simply from Terranova's possession of the check. . . .

Judgment should have been entered in favor of Robert L. Taylor and Zena Taylor against Equitable for $20,000.00 and interest should have been allowed from 26 February 1968. . . .

[Judgment reversed.]

Citizens State Bank v Rausch

9 Ill App 3d 1004, 293 NE2d 678 (1973)

Rausch owned Black Acres Farm, which was subject to a first mortgage. Rausch wanted to refinance the mortgage debt and sent an agent to the Citizens State Bank with authority to make a new loan and to pledge stock as security for the new loan if a second mortgage was obtained on the farm. This condition as to obtaining a second mortgage was known to the bank. The second mortgage was not obtained but the agent and the bank made a new loan agreement, part of which obligated Rausch to deliver certain shares of stock to the bank as security. The bank sued Rausch and his wife to compel them to deliver the stock to it under the second loan agreement. Judgment was entered in their favor and the bank appealed.

Stamos, P.J. . . . The action was initiated by plaintiff's complaint, seeking to compel delivery of stock certificates which were allegedly pledged by defendants in December, 1963 as security for the refinancing of a previous loan to Black Acres Farm, Inc. . . . A Master in Chancery . . . made the . . . recommendation . . . that plaintiff be denied relief upon its complaint, because one condition in the suretyship agreement—that defendants receive a second mortgage on Black Acres Farm as consideration—had not been fulfilled to the actual knowledge of the pledgee Bank. . . .

We . . . conclude that there was sufficient evidence supporting the Master's findings that the December pledge of stock by defendants was conditioned upon their receiving a second mortgage on Black Acres Farm, that plaintiff was actually aware of that condition at the time of the pledge agreement, and that the condition was never fulfilled. Even if we were to accept plaintiff's contention that it was unaware of the condition, a different disposition would not be warranted. The surety agreement was negotiated by a special agent on defendants' behalf. Uncontroverted evidence established that the scope of the agency was limited by the requirement that defendants receive a second mortgage on Black Acres Farm in return for their pledge of shares of stock. Accordingly, the special agent was powerless to bind the defendants to an agreement, unless it contained the consideration demanded by defendants from Black Acres Farm. A principal is bound by the acts of his special agent only insofar as such acts are in accord with the conferred authority. . . . Persons dealing with a special agent are bound, at their peril, to ascertain the nature and extent of the agent's authority. . . . We therefore hold that the Master's finding and the Chancellor's decree denying relief to plaintiff were supported by the evidence. . . .

[Judgment affirmed.]

Bucholtz v Sirotkin Travel Ltd.

74 Misc 2d 180, 343 NYS2d 438 (1973)

Bucholtz made reservations through the Sirotkin Travel Agency for a three-day trip to

Las Vegas. The reservations were in fact not made by the agency and Bucholtz sued the agency for damages for breach of its contract. The agency raised the defense that the mistake was the fault of another travel agency or "wholesaler" through which the agency made reservations on behalf of its client.

DONOVAN, J. . . . This small claim proceeding involves a matter of increasing importance to the traveling public, namely, the responsibility of a travel agency in connection with the sale of a tour.

Claimant engaged the defendant travel agency to make reservations for a three day trip for herself and her husband to Las Vegas. The agency advised the claimant that they would stay at the Aladdin Hotel. Changes were made in the arrival and departure time of their flight from that originally stated. At the airport tags on the plaintiff's baggage were switched so that the baggage was not directed to the Aladdin Hotel. On arrival in Las Vegas the claimant learned that no reservations had been made for herself or her husband at the Aladdin Hotel. They were required to take alternative accommodations at a motel. The motel was a half mile out of town. This created additional expense and inconvenience for the claimant and her husband in traveling to the places of interest in the town.

The law presently lacks clarity with respect to the relationship between the travel agency and its clients. Obviously the travel agency is an agent, but the question comes, whose agent? Is it the agent of a hotel or other innkeeper with whom, or for whom, the agency transacts business? Or the steamship line or airline with whom it does business? Generally the travel agency is neither an agent nor an employee of the common carriers and innkeepers with whom it may do business. . . .

The travel agent deals directly with the traveler. He must be charged with the duty of exercising reasonable care in securing passage on an appropriate carrier and lodging with an innkeeper. The money was paid over by the traveler to the defendant agency for that specific purpose.

News reports are constantly appearing with stories of travelers—many of them quite young—being stranded far from home or having vacation plans ruined because passage or lodging for which they have paid has not been provided. Who is to bear the responsibility? Is it some remote "wholesaler" who is unknown to the traveler, or the traveler himself, or the travel agency in whom the traveler has reposed his confidence?

Sometimes we must go deep into the past to find ancient principles and mold them to take care of new problems. The policy of the common law from ancient times has been to safeguard the traveler. Speaking of the rule at common law which held the innkeeper liable as an insurer of the property left in his custody by a guest, the court, in Hulett v Swift, 33 NY 571 (1865) said: "The considerations of public policy in which the rule had its origin, forbid any relaxation of its rigor. The number of travelers was few, when this custom was established for their protection. The growth of commerce and increased facilities of communication, have so multiplied the class for whose security it was designed, that its abrogation would be the removal of a safeguard against fraud, in which almost every citizen has an immediate interest. The rule is in the highest degree remedial. No public interest would be promoted, by changing the legal effect of the implied contract between the host and the guest, and relieving the former from his common law liability. Innkeepers, like carriers and other insurers, at times find their contracts burdensome; but in the profits they derive from the public, and the privileges accorded to them by the law, they find an ample and liberal compensation. The vocation would be still more profitable if coupled with new immunities; but we are not at liberty to discard the settled rules of the common law, founded on reasons which still operate in all their original force. Open robbery and violence, it is true, are less frequent as civilization advances; but the devices of fraud multiply with the increase of intelligence, and the temptations which spring from opportunity, keep pace with the growth and diffusion of wealth."

As foreseen by the court one hundred years ago, the devices of fraud have indeed multiplied.

In this case nothing was done by the travel agency to verify or confirm either the plane reservations or the hotel reservations. If this duty is the responsibility of the travel agency, then the travel agency is liable in negligence for its failure to exercise reasonable care in making the reservations.

It may be urged that the default in this respect is that of the remote "wholesaler."

Where, as here, the agent is selected because he is supposed to have some special fitness for the performance of the duties to be undertaken, the traveler is entitled to rely on the judgment and discretion of that agent as well as his honesty and financial responsibility. The agent may not evade responsibility by delegating to a subagent the carrying out of the task which has been committed to him. . . . Travel agencies may find it convenient, in the course of transacting their business, to deal with wholesalers. The news reports are so voluminous that we may take judicial notice of the vice inherent in conducting business in so loose a fashion. The wholesaler may fail to pay for accommodations or may even fail to book the accommodations and the traveler is left in a helpless situation. He either has no recourse because of financial insufficiency or he may be required to travel to a distant jurisdiction in order to maintain a suit.

Unless the principal, here the traveler, has expressly or impliedly authorized the travel agency to delegate responsibility to a second agency or "wholesaler," the responsibility must remain on the defendant travel agency. In an area so fraught with danger to the traveler, public policy demands that the travel agency be held responsible to: (a) verify or confirm the reservations and (b) use reasonable diligence in ascertaining the responsibility of any intervening "wholesaler" or tour organizer. . . .

Claimant here did not consent to any delegation of the duty owed to her by the defendant travel agency.

The defendant is liable to the claimant for the breach of its fiduciary responsibility in failing to use reasonable care to confirm the reservations. . . .

[Judgment for plaintiff.]

Kribbs v Jackson

387 Pa 611, 129 A2d 490 (1957)

Kribbs owned real estate that had been rented through his agent, Jackson, at a monthly rental of $275. When this lease terminated, Jackson and a third person, Solomon, made an agreement that if the latter obtained a new tenant for a rental of $500 a month, Jackson would pay Solomon $100 a month. The latter obtained a new tenant who paid a monthly rental of $550. Jackson continued to send Kribbs $275 a month, less his commissions and janitor and utility costs, paid Solomon $100 a month, and kept the balance of the rental for himself. When Kribbs learned of these facts three years later, he sued Jackson and Solomon, claiming from Jackson the money that he had kept for himself and which he had paid Solomon, and claiming from Solomon the money he had received from Jackson. From a judgment in Kribbs' favor on both claims an appeal was taken.

CHIDSEY, J. . . . There can be no doubt that Jackson was guilty of fraud and that he was personally liable to Kribbs for the entire amount fraudulently withheld from him. An agent owes a duty of loyalty to his principal. It is his duty in all dealings affecting the subject matter of his agency, to act with the utmost good faith and loyalty for the furtherance and advancement of the interests of his principal. . . . An agent who makes a profit in connection with transactions conducted by him on behalf of the principal is under a duty to give such profit to the principal. . . . "All profits made and advantage gained by the agent in the execution of the agency belong to the principal. . . ."

It is also the duty of the agent to give to his principal all information relating to the subject matter of his agency coming to the knowledge of the agent while acting as such. . . . Jackson, by deliberately concealing from his principal the amount of rent the [new tenant] agreed to pay under the lease, by intentionally failing to disclose to Kribbs his contract with Solomon, and by refusing to remit to Kribbs all receipts less proper deductions, was . . . plainly guilty of actionable fraud and in violation of his duties as a fiduciary. Therefore he is liable to his principal, not only for the secret profit realized from the transaction, but he is also liable to account to Kribbs for the money which he fraudulently and without authority gave to Solomon. . . .

[Judgment affirmed in both claims.]

Eskin v Acheson Manufacturing Co.

(CA3 Pa) 236 F2d 135 (1956)

Eskin was the sales agent of the Acheson Manufacturing Co. which produced brass products. During World War II, at a time when prices were subject to government control, Eskin obtained large orders. Because of the wartime conditions, these orders could not be filled at once. By the time they could be filled, government price controls were removed. Acheson then informed the customers that because of its increased costs it could not supply the purchases at the original price and would charge the prices existing when the goods were shipped. Acheson informed the customers that they could cancel their orders if they wished. Customers whose orders exceeded one million dollars canceled. Eskin then sued Acheson for the commissions he would have received on the orders if Acheson had not raised the price and caused their cancellation. From a judgment for Acheson, Eskin appealed.

HASTIE, C.J. . . . A manufacturer's agent procured purchase orders which in all their terms, including the price offered, were satisfactory to the manufacturer when and as it received them from the agent. In our view, the arrangement between these parties was such that as each satisfactory order was received a unilateral contract was formed between the principal and the agent. The agent had completed the act which was his part of the bargain. The manufacturer then became bound by a conditional promise to pay the agent a 5 percent commission if and when that order should be filled. This does not mean that any buyer's offer had ripened or would necessarily ripen into a contract of sale. The prospective seller had merely bound himself by a conditional promise to his agent. . . . [While] the condition must be fulfilled precisely as stipulated before the promise can be enforced, . . . [there is a] duty of the maker of the conditional promise not to prevent the fulfillment of the condition by unwarranted conduct. Such a breach of the promisor's implied obligation of reasonable cooperation in connection with the condition will entitle the promisee to the promised performance, despite the unfulfilled condition. . . . But there is no rule of thumb to indicate what frustrating conduct is "unwarranted," or "unreasonable" or "arbitrary" within this conception. . . . [The test] is to be found in the reasonable expectations of the makers of such a bargain in all the circumstances of the given case. . . .

Here we have parties doing business in an abnormal economy. Shortages of materials and resultant long delays in filling orders were the familiar experience of the industry. Prices were controlled, but controls were recognized as temporary. Any member of the business community must have recognized the likelihood that removal of controls in the not distant future would cause rather extreme price fluctuations.

In these circumstances, plaintiff solicited orders understanding that his right to a commission was conditioned upon the filling of the orders at a considerably later date in the uncertainties of an abnormal economy. It may well be that the parties reasonably anticipated that for the duration of stability imposed by the controlled price structure, the manufacturer would not subject orders to price increases after they were received. But it seems to us that reasonable persons contemplating the possibility of decontrol would not expect the manufacturer thereafter to produce and sell goods at the old controlled prices to meet accumulated orders received under basic conditions no longer existing. Indeed, the uncertainties of the abnormal economy and their impact on reasonable business behavior must be viewed as basic qualifying circumstances in this entire procedure of taking orders for filling in the indefinite future. It was not an unreasonable frustration of the agent's expectations for the manufacturer to subject outstanding orders to price increases which fairly reflected the influence of a basic change in our economy on production costs. . . .

[Judgment affirmed.]

QUESTIONS AND CASE PROBLEMS

1. What is the objective of each of the following rules of law?
   (a) A third person who deals with a person claiming to be an agent cannot rely on the statements made by the latter concerning the extent of his authority.
   (b) If the parties have not fixed the amount of the compensation by their agreement but have intended that the agent should be paid, the agent may recover the customary compensation for his services.
2. Can an attorney delegate his authority to represent his client to another attorney with whom he shares the same suite of offices when he does not have the client's approval to do so? [People v Betillo, 53 Misc 2d 540, 279 NYS2d 444]
3. A property owner applied to an insurance agent for insurance on his property. The agent told him that he was protected immediately, and thereafter the policy was issued. The agent backdated the policy to the time of the property owner's application. Between the time when the property owner had applied for the insurance and was told that he was covered and the subsequent time when the policy was issued, the property was damaged by a cause coming within the scope of the policy. The insurance company paid the property owner's claim on the policy and then sued the agent for indemnity on the ground that he did not have authority to backdate a policy. The agent showed that he had repeatedly made oral contracts of insurance and that the insurer then issued the policies on the basis of such oral contracts and that the policies were backdated to the date of the oral contracts. Was the agent liable to the insurer for the loss? [Lewis v Travelers Insurance Co., 51 NJ 244, 239 A2d 4]
4. McKinney requested E. M. Christmas, a real estate broker, to sell McKinney's property. A sale to a purchaser was effected with the contract calling for monthly installment payments by the purchaser, which payments were to be collected by the broker. When the purchaser stopped making the payments, McKinney was not notified of that fact but one of the broker's employees bought out the purchaser's contract. The broker continued making payments to McKinney as though they were being made by the purchaser. Later Christmas, the broker, resold the land to another buyer at a substantial profit. McKinney sued Christmas for this profit. Decide. [McKinney v Christmas, 143 Colo 361, 353 P2d 373]
5. Regional Broadcasters of Michigan, Inc. owned and operated radio station WTRU. Moreschini supplied advertising material to WTRU under contract made with the station manager. When Moreschini sued Regional Broadcasters, it raised the defense that the manager had been instructed not to make any contracts on behalf of the station. Was Regional bound? [Moreschini v Regional Broadcasters, 373 Mich 496, 129 NW2d 859]
6. An insurance company directed its agent to notify the insured under a particular policy that his policy was canceled. The insurance agent instructed his stenographer to notify the insured. She notified the insured. It was later

claimed that this notice was not effective to cancel the policy because it had not been given by the insurer's agent. Decide. [International Service Insurance Co. v Maryland Casualty Co., (Tex Civ App) 421 SW2d 721]

7. Hockett employed Snearly as an agent in connection with the sales made at the Gilette Livestock Exchange operated by Hockett. Snearly was to perform various clerical operations in connection with the agent's work, and to write checks on the account of the principal for the payment of the persons selling their cattle and for the payment of his own salary. By the terms of compensation Snearly was to receive $25 on each sale made at the Exchange up to a certain date and $30 thereafter. According to this rate of compensation, Snearly was entitled to approximately $6,000 for the period in question, but he wrote checks to himself for approximately $27,000. Hockett sued Snearly to recover the excess compensation. Snearly defended on the ground that the additional compensation was taken for extra services rendered by him. The extra work was shown to have a value of approximately $2,000. Snearly also defended on the ground that the principal had waived any right to object to an overpayment by failing to take any action sooner. Decide. [Snearly v Hockett, (Wyo) 352 P2d 230]

8. Promoters were planning the formation of a new corporation. They retained an attorney to obtain a charter for the corporation. The attorney made a contract with Erickson, selling him stock of the new corporation. Did the attorney have the authority to make this contract? [Erickson v Civic Plaza National Bank, (Mo App) 422 SW2d 373]

9. Hihn and Eastland, doing business in California, were authorized to sell certain land in Texas. They in turn employed Maney, of Texas, to sell the land. He made the sale and then sued them for the commissions due him on the sale. Did Hihn and Eastland have authority to employ Maney to make the sale? [Eastland v Maney, 36 Tex Civ App 147, 81 SW 574]

10. Wiles ran a taxi business. Mullinax, an insurance broker, agreed to obtain and keep Wiles continuously covered with workmen's compensation insurance. This was done for a number of years, with Mullinax renewing the policy whenever it expired. The insurance company which had issued the policy to Wiles canceled it, and Mullinax attempted to obtain a policy from other companies. He was unable to do so but did not inform Wiles of his difficulties nor of the fact that Wiles was not covered by insurance. An employee of Wiles was killed, and a workmen's compensation claim for his death was successfully made. Wiles then learned for the first time that there was no insurance to cover this claim. Wiles sued Mullinax for the amount of the workman's compensation claim. Decide. [Wiles v Mullinax, 267 NC 392, 148 SE2d 229]

42 Third Persons in Agency

LIABILITIES OF AGENT TO THIRD PARTY

In agency transactions the third party may have certain rights against the agent because of the manner in which the transaction was conducted or the nature of the agent's acts.

§ 42:1. Authorized Action of Disclosed Agent. If an agent makes a contract with a third person on behalf of a disclosed principal and has proper authority to do so and if the contract is executed properly, the agent has no personal liability on the contract. Whether the principal performs the contract or not, the agent cannot be held liable by the third party.[1] Thus, an insurance agency arranging for the insuring of a customer with a named company is not liable on the policy which the company issues to the insured.[2] If the agent lacks authority, however, or if certain other circumstances exist, he may be liable.

§ 42:2. Unauthorized Action. If a person purports to act as an agent for another but lacks authority to do so, the contract that he makes is not binding on the principal. Similarly, when *A* and *B* had a joint bank account, with each having authority to withdraw but neither having authority to overdraw the account, the bank could not hold *B* liable for the amount of *A*'s overdraft.[3]

If the agent's unauthorized act causes loss to the third person, however, the agent is generally responsible for his loss. When he purports to act as agent for the principal, he makes an implied warranty that he has authority to do so.[4] Under this implied warranty it is immaterial that the agent acted in good faith or misunderstood the scope of his authority. The fact that he was not authorized imposes liability upon him,[5] unless the third person knew that the agent exceeded his authority.

An agent with a written authorization may protect himself from liability on the implied warranty of authority by showing the written authorization to the third person and permitting the third person to determine for himself the scope of the agent's authority. When the third person wrongly decides that the agent has certain authority, the agent has no liability if it is later held by the court that he did not have such authority.[6]

---

1 Restatement, Agency 2d §§ 320, 328; Kelly v Olson, 272 Minn 134, 136 NW2d 621.

2 Isabell v Aetna Ins. Co., (Tenn App) 495 SW2d 821.

3 Nielson v Suburban Trust & Savings Bank, 37 Ill App 2d 224, 185 NE2d 404.

4 Darr Equipment Co. v Owens, (Tex Civ App) 408 SW2d 566.

5 Moser v Kyle Corp., 255 Wis 634, 39 NW2d 587.

6 Fuller v Melko, 5 NJ 554, 76 A2d 683.

§ 42:3. No Principal with Capacity. When a person acts as an agent, he impliedly warrants not only that he has a principal but also that his principal has legal capacity. If there is no principal or if the principal lacks legal capacity, the person acting as an agent is liable for any loss to the third person.

The agent can protect himself from liability on the implied warranty of the existence of a principal with capacity by making known to the third person all material, pertinent facts or by obtaining the agreement of the third person that the agent shall not be liable.

§ 42:4. Undisclosed and Partially Disclosed Principal. An agent becomes liable as a party to the contract, just as though he were acting for himself, when the third person is not told or does not know that the agent is acting for a specific principal, that is, when there is an *undisclosed principal.*[7] The agent is also liable on the contract when the third person is told or knows only that the agent is acting as an agent but the identity of the principal is not known or stated, that is, when the principal is only partially disclosed.[8] (See p. 843, Mawer-Gulden-Annis, Inc. v Brazilian & Colombian Coffee Co.)

When an agent sells goods of his principal without disclosing his principal's identity, the agent is bound by the "seller's" implied warranty of title and is liable to the buyer if the goods were in fact stolen and are taken from the buyer by the police.[9] Likewise, when an auctioneer sells without disclosing the identity of his principal, the auctioneer is bound by an implied warranty of title.[10]

(1) Actual Knowledge of Third Party. An agent is liable as a party to the contract if the third party does not actually know that he is dealing with an agent and does not know the identity of the principal. The fact that sufficient information is disclosed which would enable the third party to inquire further and ascertain the identity of the principal is generally not sufficient to remove the agent from liability for the contract. For example, when a person running a store or a corporation purchases inventory he is personally liable therefor when he does not disclose the identity of the principal. The fact that the third party knows the trade name under which the store is operated is not sufficient to put the third person on notice that the store may be owned by someone else nor charge him with notice or knowledge that the owner is a corporation, even though the third party, by examining the fictitious names registration index, could have discovered the identity of the principal. Consequently, where a store was operated by a corporation under the assumed name of "The Gazebo," the individual running the store as agent for the corporation was personally liable on a contract to purchase

---

[7] Sago v Ashford, 145 Colo 289, 358 P2d 599.

[8] Special Sections, Inc. v Rappaport, 25 App Div 2d 896, 269 NYS2d 319.

[9] Itoh v Kimi Sales, Ltd., (NY Civil Court) 74 Misc 2d 402, 345 NYS2d 416.

[10] Universal C.I.T. Credit Corp. v State Farm Mut. Auto. Ins. Co., (Mo App) 493 SW2d 385.

inventory where no disclosure of agency nor of the identity of the principal was made.[11]

§ 42:5. Wrongful Receipt of Money. If an agent obtains a payment of money from the third person by the use of illegal methods, the agent is liable to the third person.[12]

If the third person makes an overpayment to the agent or a payment when none is due, the agent is also usually liable to the third person for the amount of such overpayment or payment. If the agent has acted in good faith and does not know that the payment is improperly made, however, he is liable to the third person only so long as he still has the payment in his possession or control. If in such a case he has remitted the payment to the principal before the time the third person makes a demand upon him for its return, the agent is not liable.[13] In the latter case the third person's right of action, if he has one, is only against the principal. But payment to the principal does not relieve the agent of liability when the agent knows that the payment was not proper.[14]

§ 42:6. Assumption of Liability. An agent may intentionally make himself liable upon the contract with the third person. This situation frequently occurs when the agent is a well-established local brokerage house or other agency and the principal is located out of town and is not known locally.

§ 42:7. Execution of Contract. A simple contract that would appear to be the contract of the agent only can by oral testimony, if believed, be shown to have been intended as a contract between the principal and the third party. If the intention is established, it will be permitted to contradict the face of the written contract, and the contract as thus modified will be enforced.

To avoid any question of interpretation, James Craig, an agent for B. G. Gray, should execute an instrument by signing either "*B. G. Gray, by James Craig,*" that is, "Principal, by Agent" or "*B. G. Gray, per James Craig,*" that is, "Principal, per Agent." Such a signing is in law a signing by *Gray,* and the agent is therefore not a party to the contract. The signing of the principal's name by an authorized agent without indicating the agent's name or identity is likewise in law the signature of the principal.

If the instrument is ambiguous as to whether the agent has signed in a representative or an individual capacity, parol evidence is admissible, as between the original parties to the transaction, to establish the character in which the agent was acting.[15]

If an agent executes a specialty (that is, a check, note, or draft, or a sealed instrument in those states in which a seal retains its common-law

---

[11] Judith Garden, Inc. v Mapel, (NY Civil Court) 73 Misc 2d 810, 342 NYS2d 486.
[12] R 2d § 343.
[13] United States National Bank v Stonebrink, 200 Ore 176, 265 P2d 238.
[14] Hirning v Federal Reserve Bank, (CA8 Minn) 52 F2d 382.
[15] Emala v Walter G. Coale, Inc., 244 Md 159, 223 A2d 177.

force) and does so without disclosing his agency or the identity of his principal, he is bound and he cannot show that the parties did not intend this result. Because of the formal character of the writing, the liability of the parties is determined from the face of the instrument alone and it cannot be modified or contradicted by proof of intention or other matters not set forth in the writing.

§ 42:8. Failure to Obtain Commitment of Principal. In some situations the agent is in effect a middleman or go-between who has the duty to the third person to see to it that the principal is bound to the third person. For example, when an agent of an insurance company who has authority to write policies of insurance tells a policyholder whose fire policy had been canceled that the agent will look into the matter and that the insured should forget about it unless he hears from the agent, the latter is under an obligation to make reasonable efforts to obtain the reinstatement of the policy or to notify the insured that he could not do so. The agent is liable to the insured for the latter's fire loss if the agent does not obtain the reinstatement of the policy and does not so inform the insured.[16]

§ 42:9. Torts and Crimes. An agent is liable for harm caused the third person by the agent's fraudulent, malicious, or negligent acts. The fact that he is acting as an agent at the time or that he is acting in good faith under the directions of his principal does not relieve him of liability if his conduct would impose liability upon him if he were acting for himself.[17] The fact that he is following instructions does not shield him from liability.

An agent is not excused from complying with the law because he is an agent. Consequently, if an agent violates a civil rights act, it is no defense that he was acting in obedience to instructions of his principal.[18]

If an agent commits a traditional crime, such as stealing from the third person or shooting the third person, the agent is liable for his crime without regard to the fact that he was acting as an agent, and without regard to whether he had acted for his own self-interest or had sought to advance the interest of the principal.

LIABILITIES OF THIRD PARTY TO AGENT

A third party may be liable to the agent because of the manner in which the transaction was conducted or because of the acts of the third party causing harm to the agent.

§ 42:10. Authorized Action of Disclosed Agent. Ordinarily the third party is not liable to the agent for a breach of a contract that the agent has made with the third person on behalf of a disclosed principal.[19] In certain instances, however, the third party may be liable to the agent.

[16] Adkins & Ainley v Busada, (Dist Col App) 270 A2d 135.
[17] R 2d § 343; Dr. Salsbury's Laboratories v Bell, (Tex Civ App) 386 SW2d 341.
[18] Johnson v Harrigan-Peach Land Development Co., 79 Wash 2d 745, 489 P2d 923; Ford v Wisconsin Real Estate Examining Board, 48 Wis 2d 91, 179 NW2d 786.
[19] R 2d § 363.

§ 42:11. Undisclosed and Partially Disclosed Principal. If the agent executed the contract without informing the third person or without the third party's knowing both of the existence of the agency and the identity of the principal, the agent may sue the third party for breach of contract.[20]

In such instances, if the contract was a simple contract, the principal may also sue the third person even though the third person thought that he was contracting only with the agent. The right of the principal to sue the third person is, of course, superior to the right of the agent to do so. If the contract was a specialty, the undisclosed principal, not appearing on the instrument as a party, could not bring an action to enforce the contract.

§ 42:12. Agent Intending to Be Bound. If the third person knew that the agent was acting as an agent but nevertheless the parties intended that the agent should be personally bound by the contract, the agent may sue the third person for breach of contract.

§ 42:13. Execution of Contract. The principles that determine when an agent is liable to the third person because of the way in which he has executed a written contract apply equally in determining when the third person is liable to the agent because of the way in which the contract is executed. If the agent could be sued by the third person, the third person can be sued by the agent. Thus, if the agent executes a sealed instrument in his own name, he alone can sue the third person on that instrument.

§ 42:14. Agent as Transferee. The agent may sue the third person for breach of the latter's obligation to the principal when the principal has assigned or otherwise transferred his claim or right to the agent, whether absolutely for the agent's own benefit or for the purpose of collecting the money and remitting it to the principal.[21]

§ 42:15. Special Interest of Agent. If the agent has a special interest in the subject matter of the contract, he may bring an action against the third party upon the latter's default. For example, a commission merchant has a lien on the principal's goods in his possession for his compensation and expenses. Such a merchant, therefore, has an interest that entitles him to sue the buyer for breaking his contract.

§ 42:16. Torts and Crimes. The third party is liable in tort for fraudulent or other wrongful acts causing injury to the agent.[22] If the third party by slander or other means wrongfully causes the principal to discharge the agent, the latter may recover damages from the third party. The agent may also bring an action in tort against the third person for wrongful injuries to his person or property. If the agent has possession of the principal's property, he may sue any third person whose acts injure that property.

---

20 § 364; Eppenauer v Davis, (Tex Civ App) 272 SW2d 934.
21 R 2d § 365.
22 § 374.

If the third party commits any crime with respect to the agent or property of the agent, the criminal liability of the third party is the same as though no agency were involved.

LIABILITIES OF PRINCIPAL TO THIRD PARTY

The principal is liable to the third person for the properly authorized and executed contracts of his agent and, in certain circumstances, for his agent's unauthorized contracts and torts as well.

§ **42:17. Agent's Contracts.** When there is a principal with contractual capacity who had authorized or ratified the agent's action and when the agent properly executed the contract as an agency transaction, a contract exists between the principal and the third person on which each usually can be sued by the other in the event of a breach. At common law, if the contract is under seal, an undisclosed principal cannot sue or be sued.[23] If the contract is a simple contract, the third person may sue the principal whether or not the principal was disclosed. Since the agent acts for the principal, the third person may sue the principal directly even though his existence was not disclosed or was unknown and the third person therefore contracted with the agent alone.[24] If the third person thereafter learns of the existence of the undisclosed principal, the third person may sue the principal.[25]

The right to sue the undisclosed principal on a simple contract is subject to two limitations. First, the third person cannot sue the principal if in good faith the principal has settled his account with the agent with respect to the contract. Some states refuse to apply this limitation, however, unless the third person reasonably has led the principal to believe that the account between the agent and the third person had been settled. (See p. 844, Poretta v Superior Dowel Co.)

As a second limitation, the third person cannot sue the principal if the third person has elected to hold the agent and not the principal.[26] To constitute such an election, the third person, with knowledge of the existence of the principal, must express an intention to hold the agent liable or he must secure a judgment against the agent. In those jurisdictions which permit the third person to join the principal and agent as codefendants, the third party, although he may sue both in one action, must choose at the end of the trial the party from whom to collect, thus discharging the other.[27]

This rule as to election does not apply when the principal is partially disclosed, for in that case the right of the third person is not to be regarded as alternatively against either the agent or the principal but as concurrent—

---

[23] McMullen v McMullen, (Fla App) 145 So2d 568.

[24] An undisclosed principal may enforce warranty liability arising under the Uniform Commercial Code when the sales contract was made by his authorized agent. Pendarvis v General Motors Corp., (NY) 6 UCCRS 457.

[25] Menveg v Fishbaugh, 123 Cal App 460, 11 P2d 438.

[26] R 2d § 210(1); Murphy v Hutchinson, 93 Miss 643, 48 So 178.

[27] R 2d § 210A; Hospelhorn v Poe, 174 Md 242, 198 A 582.

that is, a right against both—and therefore the third person may recover a judgment against either without discharging the other.[28]

The principal is not liable upon a contract made by the agent in his individual capacity, even though the agent makes the contract in order to further the business of his principal. (See p. 845, Investment Properties of Asheville, Inc. v Allen.) Likewise, the undisclosed principal is not liable on commercial paper executed by the agent in the agent's own name. (See p. 847, Ness v Greater Arizona Realty, Inc.)

§ 42:18. Payment to Agent. When the third person makes payment to an authorized agent, such payment is deemed as made to the principal. The result is that the principal must give the third person full credit for such payment, even though in fact the agent never remits or delivers the payment to the principal, if the third person made the payment in good faith and had no reason to know that the agent would be guilty of such misconduct.[29]

§ 42:19. Agent's Statements. A principal is bound by a statement made by his agent while transacting business within the scope of his authority.[30] This means that the principal cannot thereafter contradict the statement of his agent and show that it is not true. Statements or declarations of an agent, in order to bind the principal, must be made at the time of performing the act to which they relate or shortly thereafter.

§ 42:20. Agent's Knowledge. The principal is bound by knowledge or notice of any fact that is acquired by his agent while acting within the scope of his authority.[31]

Conversely, if the subject matter is outside the scope of the agent's authority, the agent is under no duty to inform the principal of knowledge acquired by him. For example, when an agent is authorized and employed only to collect rents, his knowledge of the unsatisfactory condition of the premises is not imputed to the landlord-principal, since the reporting of such information is not part of the agent's collection duties.

The rule that the agent's knowledge is imputed to the principal is extended in some cases to knowledge gained prior to the creation of the agency relationship. The notice and knowledge in any case must be based on reliable information. Thus, when the agent hears only rumors of acts or facts, the principal is not charged with notice.[32]

---

[28] R 2d § 184. An exception would arise when the contract makes the obligation the joint obligation of the partially disclosed principal and the agent. In such a case, a judgment against the one would discharge the liability of the other under principles of contract law.

[29] This general rule of law is restated in some states by § 2 of the Uniform Fiduciaries Act, which is expressly extended by § 1 thereof to agents, partners, and corporate officers. Similar statutory provisions are found in a number of other states.

[30] R 2d § 284.

[31] R 2d § 272; Capron v State, 247 Cal App 2d 212, 55 Cal Rptr 330.

[32] Stanley v Schwalby, 162 US 255.

When the principal employs an agent having specialized knowledge, the principal is charged with the knowledge of the agent. Thus, a church employing a professional engineer in connection with the construction of a building is charged with the engineer's knowledge of the custom and usages of the trade.[33]

(1) Exceptions. When the agent knows that a third person's statements are false, the principal is charged with such knowledge and cannot hold the third person liable for such falsity. In such a case the principal is barred from asserting that he has been deceived as the principal is deemed to possess the agent's knowledge.[34] Thus, when the agent of the transferee of a warehouse receipt knew that the receipt had been issued without the delivery of the goods described therein, the warehouseman was not liable to the transferee for the loss caused by the false bill.[35]

The principal is not responsible for the knowledge of his agent, that is, he is not charged with having knowledge of what is known by his agent, under the following circumstances: (a) when the agent is under a duty to another principal to conceal his knowledge; (b) when the agent is acting adversely to his principal's interest; or (c) when the third party acts in collusion with the agent for the purpose of cheating the principal. In such cases it is not likely that the agent would communicate his knowledge to the principal. The principal is therefore not bound by the knowledge of the agent.[36]

(2) Communication to Principal. As a consequence of regarding the principal as possessing the knowledge of his agent, when the law requires that a third person communicate with the principal, that duty may be satisfied by communicating with the agent. Thus, an offeree effectively communicates the acceptance of the offer when he makes such communication to the offeror's agent,[37] and an offeror effectively communicates the revocation of his offer to the offeree by communicating the revocation to the offeree's agent.[38]

§ 42:21. Agent's Torts. The principal is liable to third persons for the wrongful acts of his agent committed while acting within the scope of the agent's employment.[39] These acts are usually acts of negligence. By the common-law view a principal was not liable for the willful torts of his agent. The modern decisions hold that the principal is liable for intentional torts committed for the purpose of furthering the principal's business. Thus, the

---

[33] Fifteenth Avenue Christian Church v Moline Heating and Construction Co., 13 Ill App 3d 766, 265 NE2d 405.

[34] Adam Miguez Funeral Home v First National Life Insurance Co., (La App) 234 So2d 496.

[35] Lawrence Warehouse Co. v Dove Creek State Bank, 172 Colo 90, 470 P2d 838.

[36] Melgard v Moscow Idaho Seed Co., 73 Idaho 265, 251 P2d 546.

[37] Dobson & Johnson, Inc. v Waldron, 47 Tenn App 121, 336 SW2d 313.

[38] Hogan v Aluminum Lock Shingle Corp., 214 Ore 218, 329 P2d 271.

[39] Oman v United States, (CA10 Utah) 179 F2d 738.

principal is liable for the fraudulent acts or the misrepresentations of the agent made within the scope of his authority. (See p. 847, Oddo v Interstate Bakeries.)

To illustrate, when an agent in the routine of his authorized agency issues false stock certificates, the principal is liable. In some states the principal is not liable for his agent's fraud if he did not authorize or know of the fraud of the agent at the time of the agent's fraudulent statement or misrepresentation.[40] When the principal's agent induces the buyer to make a purchase because of the agent's fraudulent misrepresentations, the buyer may cancel the sale.[41]

When the activity of the agent is not directly employment-related, the fact that one of the motives of the agent is to find customers for the principal's product does not in itself bring the agent's activity within the scope of his agency so as to impose vicarious liability upon the principal for the tort of the agent.

When a salesman goes driving to engage in a social activity, he is not acting within the scope of his agency and his principal is not liable for the agent's negligence in driving, even though the agent hopes that he might meet someone who will be a customer but does not have any specific person in mind.[42]

When the agent's conduct is outside the scope of his authority, the principal is not liable for the loss caused the third party, even though it was the fact that the agent was the principal's agent which gave him the opportunity to meet the third person or to do the act which caused harm to the third person. (See p. 848, Gandy v Cole.)

In determining whether the principal is liable for the wrongful actions of his agent, it is immaterial that the principal did not personally benefit by those acts.

Ordinarily the principal is liable only for compensatory damages for the tort of the agent. If, however, the agent's act is of so offensive or extreme a character that the agent would be liable for punitive or exemplary damages, some courts hold that such damages may be recovered from the principal.[43] An insurance company that employs an agent to collect premiums is liable for compensatory and punitive damages when the agent, in the effort to collect premiums, threatens the insured with a pistol.[44]

When the tort is committed by a person while driving an automobile, some states expand the liability of the supplier of the automobile so as to impose liability for the act of the driver as though the driver were his agent or employee. This has the same effect as imposing agency liability by operation of law and arises in some states in the case of (1) the license-sponsor rule or (2) the family-purpose doctrine.

---

[40] Littler v Dunbar, 365 Pa 277, 74 A2d 650.

[41] Morris Chevrolet, Inc. v Pitzer, (Okla) 479 P2d 958.

[42] Morgan v Collier County Motors, (Fla App) 193 So2d 35.

[43] State ex rel. v Hartford Accident & Indemnity Co., 44 Tenn App 405, 314 SW2d 161.

[44] Clemmons v Life Insurance Co. of Georgia, 274 NC 416, 163 SE2d 761.

(1) License-Sponsor Rule. In a number of states, when a minor under a specified age applies for an automobile operator's license, his parent or a person standing in the position of his parent, is required to sign his license application as a sponsor. In some states the *license-sponsor rule* makes the sponsor jointly and severally liable with the minor for the latter's negligence in driving, although some statutes relieve the sponsor of liability if either he or the minor has filed proof of financial responsibility.

(2) Family-Purpose Doctrine. In about half of the states, a person who owns or supplies an automobile that he permits members of his family to use for their own purposes is vicariously liable for harm caused by the negligent operation of the vehicle by any such member of the family. The *family-purpose doctrine* is repudiated in nearly half of the states as illogical and contrary to the general principles of agency law. Even when recognized, the doctrine is not applicable if the use of the vehicle is not with the permission of the owner or if the use is outside of the scope of that contemplated.

The family-purpose doctrine is not limited to cases involving minors nor to the children of the providing parent. That is, a person may be liable for providing an automobile to an adult; and the person so provided may be any family member, however related to the person providing the car. In some jurisdictions that person may even be one who is not related to the provider, as long as he is a bona fide member of the household of the provider, such as a servant who is provided with or allowed to use the car for his own benefit.

Under the family-purpose doctrine it is not essential that the provider of the car be the owner of it. The essential element is that he is the one who has control of it and has the power to grant or deny permission to use it so that its use at any particular time is with his permission. Hence, the doctrine, when recognized, is applicable to impose liability upon the father who has control of the use of the car that the child has purchased but which is used by the family when and to the extent that the father permits.

(3) Civil Rights. When the tortious act of an agent or employee is a violation of civil rights legislation, the principal is liable to the same extent as vicarious liability is imposed for any other tort. The federal civil rights legislation is interpreted as only imposing liability on natural persons so that when a policeman without justification beats a person being questioned at a police station, the city employing the policeman is not vicariously liable under the federal civil rights legislation.[45]

§ **42:22. Agent's Crimes.** The principal is liable for the crimes of the agent committed at the principal's direction.[46] When not authorized, however, the principal is ordinarily not liable for the crime of his agent merely because it

[45] Monroe v Pape, 365 US 167.
[46] Miller v Com., 240 Ky 346, 42 SW2d 518.

was committed while otherwise acting within the scope of the latter's authority or employment.

Some states impose liability on the principal when the agent has in the course of his employment violated liquor sales laws, pure food laws, and laws regulating prices or prohibiting false weights. Thus, by some courts a principal may be held criminally responsible for the sale by his agent or employee of liquor to a minor in violation of the liquor law, even though the sale was not known to the principal and violated his instructions to his agent.[47]

LIABILITIES OF THIRD PARTY TO PRINCIPAL

The third party may be liable to the principal either in contract or in tort, or he may be required to make restitution of property of the principal.

§ 42:23. Third Person's Contracts. If the principal is bound by a contract to the third person, the third person is usually bound to the principal. The third person is accordingly liable to the principal on a properly authorized contract that is properly executed as a principal-third party contract. The third person is likewise liable on an unauthorized contract that the principal has ratified. He is also liable to the principal even though the principal was not disclosed,[48] except when the agent has made a sealed contract or a commercial paper, such as a check or note, in which case only the parties to the instrument can sue or be sued on it. In the case of a commercial paper, however, the undisclosed principal may sue on the contract out of which the instrument arose.

Although the third person is liable to the principal on the contract made by the agent without disclosing any agency, the third person, when sued by the principal, is entitled to assert against the principal any defense that he could have asserted against the agent.[49]

§ 42:24. Torts of Third Person. The third party is liable to the principal for injuries caused by the third party's wrongful acts against the principal's interests or property in the care of the agent.[50] He is also responsible to the principal in some cases for causing the agent to fail in the performance of his agreement.[51] Thus, when an agent is willfully persuaded and induced to leave an employment to which he is bound by contract for a fixed term, the principal may bring an action for damages against the party causing the contract to be violated. So, also, one who colludes with an agent to defraud his principal is liable to the principal for damages.[52]

---

[47] In contrast, note the restatement of the traditional rule by the New York Penal Code, § 20.20(c) imposing corporate liability only as to offenses "engaged in by an agent of the corporation while acting within the scope of his employment and in behalf of the corporation."

[48] Southern Industries, Inc. v US, (CA9 Ariz) 326 F2d 221.

[49] Huntsberry's v Du Bonnet Shoe Co., (Dist Col App) 143 A2d 92.

[50] R 2d §§ 314, 315.

[51] § 312.

[52] Leimkuehler v Wessendorf, 323 Mo 64, 18 SW2d 445.

If the third person dealing with the agent acts in good faith and does not know that the agent is violating his duty to his principal, the third party is not liable to the principal for the agent's misconduct. Consequently, the third person is not liable to the principal for secret profit made by the agent where the third person did not know nor have reason to know that he was assisting the agent in unlawfully making a secret profit, but he believed that the agent was acting as he was authorized to do.[53]

In contrast, if an agent sells personal property of the principal to a third person which the agent has no authority to sell, the third person must surrender the property to the principal and pay damages for its conversion, regardless of his good faith or ignorance of the agent's misconduct.

§ **42:25. Restitution of Property.** When property of the principal has been transferred to a third person by an agent lacking authority to do so, the principal may ordinarily recover the property from the third person.

TRANSACTIONS WITH SALESMEN

Many transactions with salesmen do not result in contracts between the employer of the salesman and the third person with whom the salesman deals.

§ **42:26. Non-agent.** The giving of an order to a salesman does not give rise to a contract with his employer when the salesman had authority only to solicit and receive orders from third persons; and the employer of the salesman is not bound by a contract until the employer accepts the order.

(1) Reason for Limitation on Authority of Salesmen. The limitation on the authority of the salesman is commonly based upon the fact that credit may be involved in the transaction, and the employer of the salesman does not wish to permit its soliciting agent to make decisions as to the sufficiency of the credit of the buyer but wishes all of these matters to be handled by the credit management department of the home office.

Even when sales are made on a cash basis, the employer of the salesman may want control of the order so as to avoid the danger of overselling its existing and obtainable inventory. For example, if each salesman could bind the employer by an absolute obligation to deliver certain items and if all of the salesmen in the aggregate sold more than the seller had in inventory or could obtain at the same price at which the items in stock were purchased, the selling success of the salesmen would be an economic disaster for the employer. He would lose money obtaining the goods at higher prices in order to fill the orders or would find that he had lawsuits on his hands by buyers seeking to recover damages for nondelivery of goods.

To avoid these difficulties, it is common to limit the authority of a salesman to that of merely a soliciting agent accepting and transmitting orders to the employer. To make this clear to buyers, order forms signed by the customer, who is given a copy, generally state that the salesman's

---

[53] Martin Co. v Commercial Chemists, Inc., (Fla App) 213 So2d 477.

authority is limited in this manner and that there is no "contract" with the employer until the order is approved by the home office.

(2) Withdrawal of Customer. From the fact that the customer giving a salesman an order does not ordinarily have a binding contract with the employer of the salesman until the employer approves the order, it necessarily follows that the customer is not bound by any contract until the employer approves the order. Prior to that time the "buyer" may withdraw from the transaction. His withdrawal under such circumstances is not a breach of contract, for by definition there is no contract to be broken. Likewise, if the buyer had given the salesman any money deposit, down payment, or part payment on the purchase price, the customer, on withdrawing from the transaction, is entitled to a refund of all of his payment.

(3) Contrast with True Agent. In contrast with the consequences described when the salesman is only a soliciting agent, if the person with whom the buyer deals is a true agent of the seller, there is, by definition, a binding contract between the principal and the customer from the moment that the agent agrees with the customer, that is, when he accepts the customer's order. Should the customer seek to withdraw from the contract thereafter, he must base his action on a ground which justifies his unilateral repudiation or rejection of the contract. If he has no such justification, his action of withdrawing is a breach of his contract and he is liable for damages which the seller sustains because of his breach of contract. If the buyer has made any down payment, prepayment, or deposit, the seller may deduct his damages from the amount thereof before refunding any excess to the buyer. When the transaction relates to the sale of goods, the seller is entitled to retain from such advance payment either $500 or 20 percent of the purchase price, whichever is less, unless the seller can show that greater damages were in fact sustained by him.[54]

[54] UCC § 2-718(2)(b). See § 8:6(2) as to rescission based on consumer protection legislation.

CASES FOR CHAPTER 42

Mawer-Gulden-Annis, Inc. v Brazilian & Colombian Coffee Co.

49 Ill App 2d 400, 199 NE2d 222 (1964)

Brazilian & Colombian Co. ordered 40 barrels of olives from Mawer-Gulden-Annis, Inc. but did not disclose that it was acting for its principal, Pantry Queen. Mawer billed and later sued Brazilian for the payment of the contract price. From a judgment in Mawer's favor, Brazilian appealed.

KLUCYNSKI, J. . . . In the instant case the trial court, upon hearing and weighing the evidence, and passing upon the credibility of the witnesses, found that Brazilian did not disclose the name of its principal at the time of contracting. We cannot hold that these findings were against the manifest weight of the evidence, especially when in its letter of June 20, 1961, . . . eight days after the confirmation and delivery, Brazilian, through Weinshenk, its president, writes, "The writer tried to contact you several times by phone and vice versa to give you the name of the buyer, but as your B/L #OZ 3990 (the bill of lading) indicates, you delivered these goods to our customers, Pantry Queen Food Products Company, and therefore you should have invoiced them for this merchandise directly." . . .

"It is a settled rule in [oral] contracts, if the agent does not disclose his agency and name his principal, he binds himself and becomes subject to all liabilities, express and implied, created by the contract and transaction, in the same manner as if he were the principal in interest. . . . And the fact that the agent is known to be a commission merchant, auctioneer, or other professional agent, makes no difference. . . ."

The duty is upon the agent, who wishes to avoid liability, to disclose the name or identity of his principal clearly and in such a manner as to bring such adequately to the actual notice of the other party, and it is not sufficient that the third person has knowledge of facts and circumstances which would, if reasonably followed by inquiry, disclose the identity of the principal. . . . "The necessity for disclosing . . . principals [is] to give the contracting party the opportunity to make inquiry as to the fact, and then to determine whether he is satisfied that such persons are the principals of the agent, and if they are, then whether such party is willing to extend credit to such principals."

The defendant's argument that the plaintiff is chargeable with knowledge of the principal from the fact that the carrier allegedly called and spoke to the shipping clerk regarding the olives and that the bill of lading made out by the shipping clerk showed Pantry Queen as the consignee, when taken together with the fact that defendant is generally known as a broker, is untenable.

Even if we assume plaintiff, from the above circumstances, had learned the identity of the principal, such information was not so timely as to relieve defendant of liability. To avoid personal liability, disclosure of the principal must be made at the time of contracting, otherwise either the agent or the subsequently disclosed principal may be held. . . . Disclosure of the principal's existence and identity subsequently has no bearing upon the relationship created at the time of the transaction. Defendant, not having informed plaintiff of the customer for whom it was purchasing, therefore, contracted as a principal, and cannot now complain if it is held liable as such. . . .

[Judgment affirmed.]

Poretta v Superior Dowel Co.

153 Maine 308, 137 A2d 361 (1957)

Poretta sold wood to Young who was in fact acting for the Superior Dowel Co., an undisclosed principal. When Poretta learned of that fact, he sued Superior Dowel for the purchase price. The latter defended on the ground that it had paid Young the amount of the purchase price. From a judgment in favor of Poretta, Superior appealed.

DUBORD, J. . . . "Is an undisclosed principal absolved from liability to his agent's vendor who has sold goods to the agent upon the credit of the agent who has received payment or advances, or a settlement of accounts, from his undisclosed principal before discovery of the undisclosed principal by the agent's vendor?"

There are two different rules bearing upon the issue. The first one, which appears to be supported by the weight of authority is that an undisclosed principal is generally relieved of his liability for his agent's contracts to the extent that he has settled with his agent prior to the discovery of the agency. The other rule is, that an undisclosed principal is discharged only where he has been induced to settle with the agent by conduct on the part of the third person leading him to believe that such person has settled with the agent.

The decisions appear to be in a state of hopeless confusion. "The rule that an undisclosed principal, when discovered, may be held liable upon a contract made in his behalf will not be enforced for the advantage of a third party if it will work injustice to the principal. An undisclosed principal may be relieved from liability by reason of a changed state of accounts between him and the agent, the rule formerly laid down in England and now very generally followed in the United States being that, where the principal, acting in good faith, has settled with the agent so that he would be subjected to loss were he compelled to pay the third person, he is relieved from liability to the latter, and this doctrine is, in at least one jurisdiction, in effect prescribed by statute. This doctrine is now held in England, and in a few cases in the United States, to be too broad, and the better rule is stated to be that the principal is discharged only where he has been induced to settle with the agent by conduct on the part of the third person leading him to believe that such person has settled with the agent or has elected to hold the latter. . . .

The American Law Institute . . . adopted and promulgated the following rule:

"An undisclosed principal is discharged from liability to the other party to the contract if he has paid or settled accounts with an agent reasonably relying upon conduct of the other party, not induced by the agent's misrepresentations, which indicates that the agent has paid or otherwise settled the account." 1 Am. Law. Inst. Restatement of Agency, § 208. . . .

We cite § 292, 1 Williston on Contracts, Rev. Ed.:

"There is considerable confusion of authority in regard to the question whether settlement by the principal with his agent before the person with whom the agent dealt makes a claim upon the principal is a defense to the latter. The decision of the controversy depends upon whether the liability of an undisclosed principal is to be regarded as an absolute right of one who deals with the agent although confessedly the credit of the agent has been exclusively relied upon, or whether, on the other hand, a person who thus deals with an agent is to be given only such limited right against the undisclosed principal as is consistent with equity. If the first of these theories is sound, the person dealing with the agent cannot be deprived of his right against the principal unless in some way he has subjected himself to an estoppel by misleading the principal. If, however, the second theory is sound, the mere fact that the principal has innocently put himself in a situation where hardship will be caused by holding him liable on the agent's contract should be a defense. . . ."

Mr. Mechem in his Treatise on the Law of Agency, [in] . . . arriving at his conclusion that the law as now set forth in the Restatement was the correct law, . . . has this to say: . . .

"If the principal sends an agent to buy goods for him and on his account, it is not unreasonable that he should see that they are paid for. Although the seller may consider the agent to be the principal, the actual principal knows better. He can easily protect himself by insisting upon evidence that the goods have been paid for or that the seller with full knowledge of the facts has elected to rely upon the responsibility of the agent, and if he does not, but, except where misled by some action of the seller, voluntarily pays the agent without knowing that he has paid the seller, there is no hardship in requiring him to pay again. If the other party has the right, within a reasonable time, to charge the undisclosed principal upon his discovery,—and this right seems to be abundantly settled in the law of agency—it is difficult to see how this right of the other party can be defeated, while he is not himself in fault, by dealings between the principal and the agent, of which he had no knowledge, and to which he was not a party."

The Restatement may be regarded both as the product of expert opinion and as the expression of the law by the legal profession. . . .

We, therefore, adopt the rule as laid down in the Restatement of the Law of Agency. . . .

[Judgment affirmed.]

Investment Properties of Asheville, Inc. v Allen

283 NC 277, 196 SE2d 262 (1973)

Investment Properties of Asheville negotiated with Allen for a long-term lease of her Acton property on which they desired to build a motel complex. Allen was represented by an agent, Norburn. Investment Properties was represented by its agent Robertson. After the lease was obtained, Investment Properties spent approximately $20,000 in preparing the land for the proposed motel. It sued Allen to recover this amount. It claimed that Norburn had agreed that Allen would reimburse Investment Properties for this amount and that he would make such payment if she did not. Allen refused to pay the amount on the ground that if Norburn had made any promise to pay for the grading,

she was not bound thereby. From a judgment for Investment Properties, Allen appealed.

SHARP, J. . . . When plaintiffs rested their case against Mrs. Allen the evidence tended to show: At plaintiffs' request on 10 May 1965 Dr. Norburn had procured Mrs. Allen's signature to a contract in which she leased her Acton property to Investment Properties, Inc., for a term of 50 years at a specified monthly rental to begin not later than 10 May 1966, or earlier if plaintiffs began to receive any income from the property. The contract gave plaintiffs carte blanche in grading, reshaping, and developing the property, but it contained no agreement that defendant would subject her land to the lien of a construction loan if plaintiffs required borrowed money to develop the premises. Dr. Norburn had previously made it quite clear to Dr. Robertson, who was acting for plaintiffs, that he was not interested in subordinating his sister's interest in the land, and plaintiffs had accepted the lease with that understanding. Shortly thereafter, however, Dr. Robertson told Dr. Norburn that plaintiffs would not be able to finance construction of the motel complex they had planned to put on the property unless they could give the lender a first lien on the premises.*

After consulting counsel and learning the possible consequences of such a concession Dr. Norburn told Dr. Robertson that he would not try to persuade his sister to subordinate her interest in the leased premises unless plaintiffs gave her a guarantee which would save her harmless in the event the construction loan was not paid. . . .

. . . However, plaintiffs were never willing to give a guarantee satisfactory to Dr. Norburn, and he never approved any proposition which they presented to him. Neither he nor they ever submitted any of these proposals to Mrs. Allen. She never agreed to subordinate her property, and she never signed another contract of any kind with plaintiffs.

The fact that Dr. Norburn, at plaintiffs' instance, had obtained his sister's signature to the lease dated 10 May 1965 did not clothe him with apparent authority to re-negotiate the lease, and all the evidence tends to show he had no actual authority to do so. Further, the evidence tends to show that throughout their negotiations with Dr. Norburn plaintiffs were fully aware (1) that they could not secure a construction loan for their motel project unless Mrs. Allen executed a new contract in which she agreed to give the lending institution a first lien on the leased premises; (2) that without a new contract they expended funds and graded her property at their own risk; (3) that until they could agree with Dr. Norburn upon a guarantee which he believed would protect Mrs. Allen he would not attempt to get her signature on a new lease; and (4) that even if they satisfied Dr. Norburn, he might not be able to procure her signature. Notwithstanding, plaintiffs continued to go forward with preparations to construct the motel. They cleared defendant's property of all growth and did extensive grading on it as a site for a motel. . . .

The only explanation of plaintiffs' course of conduct is the testimony of plaintiff Taylor that, "we had a guarantee for the work from a person we thought would pay." This person was certainly not Mrs. Allen. She never agreed to pay plaintiffs anything and the record contains no suggestion that she knew anyone else had done so.

Plaintiff Taylor testified that "they" charged the work done on Mrs. Allen's property to Dr. Norburn and, sometime later, he billed him for the $19,456.88—the bill for which they have sued . . . Mrs. Allen.

---

* *Authors' Note:* If the tenant's creditor was not given a first lien and the tenant defaulted, the creditor would be able to sell the interest of the tenant in the land. This would not have much value because it is likely that the financial difficulty which led to the sale to pay the creditor would also cause the tenant to stop paying rent which would then enable the lessor to terminate the lease, so that a purchaser of the lease would in effect be getting nothing for his money. In contrast, if the lessor had agreed that his ownership of the land would be subordinated or made inferior to the tenant's creditor, thus giving the creditor a first lien on the land, a sale by the creditor would sell the entire interest in the property, the interests of both the lessor-owner and the tenant. This totality of interests would not be destroyed or affected by the tenant's nonpayment of rent and would have a much greater market value than that of the leasehold interest. Hence, a creditor would be willing to lend the tenant much more money if the greater value stood as security for the debt.

It is in evidence from Dr. Norburn's unrestricted testimony as a witness for the defense that, on 17 June 1965, when Dr. Robertson threatened to abandon the motel project unless plaintiffs got a new lease, Dr. Norburn told him if plaintiffs would put up one-third of the cost of the construction he felt certain his sister would execute a new contract; that, if she did not, he would pay for the grading done in the meantime. . . .

Without Dr. Norburn's testimony there is no evidence in the Allen case from which the jury could find that either she or he ever promised to pay for the grading. This testimony, however, does not help plaintiffs' case for it shows (1) that Dr. Norburn made the promise upon a condition which was not met and (2) that he made the agreement with plaintiffs in his personal capacity and not as the agent of Allen. In making his promise of 17 June 1965 to Dr. Robertson, Dr. Norburn did not profess to be acting for Mrs. Allen. He acted in his own name and pledged his credit only. Dr. Robertson understood this and was then satisfied to have it so. Plaintiffs did no grading on Mrs. Allen's property in reliance upon any obligation on her part to pay for it. . . . When a party contracts with a known agent personally on his own credit alone, he will not be allowed afterwards to charge the principal. Having dealt with the agent as a principal he cannot set up an agent's apparent authority, on which he did not rely, so as to establish rights against a principal. . . .

We now hold, therefore, that the evidence admitted against Mrs. Allen is insufficient to establish that she or anyone purporting to act for her promised to pay for the work done on her property by Asheville Contracting Company. That being so, no question of ratification arises since "ratification is not possible unless the person making the contract, in doing so, purported to act as the agent of the person . . . claimed to be the principal.". . .

[Judgment reversed.]

Ness v Greater Arizona Realty, Inc.

21 Ariz App 231, 517 P2d 1278 (1974)

Berth Ness signed a promissory note in his own name payable to the order of Greater Arizona Realty, Inc. Subsequently Greater Arizona sued Louise Ness and three corporations on the theory that when Berth Ness signed the note in his own name he was in fact acting as agent for Louise Ness and the three corporations and therefore they were all liable for the payment of the note. Judgment was entered in favor of Greater Arizona and the defendants appealed.

HOWARD, J. . . . [UCC § 3-403] provides: "A. No person is liable on an instrument unless his signature appears thereon. B. A signature is made by use of any name, including any trade or assumed name, upon an instrument, or by any word or marker used in lieu of a written signature."

The official comment on the above mentioned statute found in Uniform Laws Annotated—Uniform Commercial Code § 3-401 provides: "1. No one is liable on an instrument unless and until he has signed it. The chief application of the rule has been in cases holding that a principal whose name does not appear on an instrument signed by his agent is not liable on the instrument even though the payee knew when it was issued that it was intended to be the obligation of one who did not sign. . . ."

Nowhere in appellee's complaint does it appear that the names of appellants appeared on the note. Nor is it alleged that the note in any way discloses that Berth Ness signed in any capacity other than for himself individually. A suit may not be maintained or judgment obtained on a promissory note against an undisclosed principal whose signature does not appear thereon. . . .

The appellee could have sued appellants on the underlying obligation for which the note was given but this was not done. . . .

[Judgment reversed.]

Oddo v Interstate Bakeries, Inc.

(CA8 Mo) 271 F2d 417 (1959)

Oddo purchased baked goods from Interstate Bakeries for sale in his store. Cooley, the delivery man for Interstate, falsely altered the slips showing the daily deliveries to Oddo. In consequence, Interstate billed Oddo for more than

was delivered. Each time after Oddo paid his current bill to Cooley, Cooley would embezzle the amount by which Oddo had been overcharged. When Oddo learned of the overcharges, he sued Interstate, which claimed that it was not liable because Cooley had embezzled the money. From a judgment in favor of Interstate, Oddo appealed.

WOODROUGH, C.J. . . . [The lower court held] that the fraud which the agent Cooley practiced in falsely recording and reporting the quantities of bakery products he delivered to plaintiff was the kind of fraud from which he alone profited and from which his employer did not benefit. It has been held as to such transactions . . . that the money the agent himself thus obtains wrongfully from a customer could not be recovered from the agent's principal. We do not express opinion as to such cases because it seems clear that the fraud Cooley practiced on plaintiff in this case was one from which defendant did directly receive a benefit. Here Cooley did not obtain any money or any goods from plaintiff by means of his fraud. It was the defendant that adopted Cooley's false reports to it and defendant wrongfully obtained plaintiff's money by the misrepresentations it made to the plaintiff and by overcharging him. . . . The defendant suffered its loss when its agent Cooley made off with the proceeds of its goods. But that was a transaction with which the plaintiff had nothing to do. There is no basis for connecting plaintiff with it and it affords no justification for defendant to retain plaintiff's money. Defendant has no right to say to plaintiff, "True, I overcharged you and obtained your money without consideration upon false representations of what you owed me, but I lost the same amount when my agent embezzled from me and therefore I will keep your money." There is no basis on which it can use that loss to offset what it owes the plaintiff for overcharging him.

It appears from the court's summarizing of conclusions that the decision to deny plaintiff any relief resulted largely from applying to the case the principle that where one of two equally innocent parties must suffer the consequences of the fraud of a third party, he who made the fraud possible must bear the loss.

In respect to this principle, it appeared to the court that defendant was an "innocent" party as to the loss it suffered. That loss occurred, as pointed out, when its agent Cooley failed to account to it for the goods confided to him. But the evidence was that in the course of the business through the years defendant never required Cooley to present any record of what he did with any of the goods turned over to him to sell except as to the part he sold on credit. As to all the goods confided to him, he was charged in gross when he went out in the morning and credited when he came back with the charges and the cash he brought in. If defendant had required signed delivery sheets and duplicate receipts in respect to all sales, the particular fraud Cooley practiced would have been more difficult for him.

On the other hand, . . . when Cooley appeared at the store, his deliveries of bread sold to plaintiff were counted and found to accord with his delivery slip, and that slip was duly signed by plaintiff's authority and the bills that came to plaintiff to be paid were computed on the figures over plaintiff's authorized signature. . . . There was no proof that it was an unusual and careless method on plaintiff's part. . . .

Plaintiff was deceived into believing the representation of the billings to be true by the willful fraud of the only agent of defendant that defendant sent to him to transact its business with him. That a principal is liable for the fraud of his agent committed in the very business in which the agent was appointed to act seems to be too elemental a proposition for serious discussion. . . .

[Judgment reversed.]

Gandy v Cole

35 Mich App 695, 193 NW2d 58 (1971)

Gandy claimed that she was defrauded by Webb, that Webb was the agent of Cole, and that the latter was liable for Webb's fraud. Cole denied liability on the ground that no fraud was committed within the scope of Webb's authority. Gandy sued Cole. Judgment was entered for Cole and Gandy appealed.

DANHOF, P.J. . . . Allen L. Cole operated a business known as Allen L. Cole & Associates.

This business provided various services to gas station operators and was limited solely to gas station operators. Cole's employees, referred to as field men, would call at the gas stations and examine the operation. They would do such things as check the inventory and the bookkeeping and make out tax returns. At regular intervals the gas station operator would receive a statement containing advice on how to improve his operation. The only time that the field men handled money was when they collected the fees that were owed to Cole.

Plaintiff's husband was a subscriber to Cole's services and William Webb was the field man assigned to his gas station. In 1965 plaintiff's husband was killed in an automobile accident and from that time on Webb took an active part in the management of the plaintiff's finances. At about the time of the death of plaintiff's husband. Webb gave plaintiff a business card that indicated that he was employed by Allen L. Cole & Associates, business counsellors.

Webb soon took over the management of most of the plaintiff's money, including the proceeds of the sale of the gas station and the proceeds of a life insurance policy on plaintiff's husband. Until the sale of the station the Gandy's service station bank account was continued in the names of the plaintiff and Webb. Webb wrote a check payable to Allen L. Cole & Associates on this account. The check was in payment for the services rendered by Cole.

Webb continued to control the plaintiff's finances for a considerable time. During this time Webb invested in some race horses, in partnership with Cole, and in some gas stations. It appears that at the present time these investments are without value. Webb undertook the management of the plaintiff's funds with the understanding that he would pay her $300 per month out of these funds. For a time Webb made the $300 payments but later he decreased them to $100 per month. Plaintiff became dissatisfied and made numerous phone calls to Webb seeking an explanation. In late 1965 Webb had ceased to be employed as a field man but he still maintained an office in Cole's establishment. At no time did the plaintiff contact, or attempt to contact Cole or any of his employees regarding her finances. In 1967 the plaintiff sought legal advice and this action was commenced. About the time of the commencement of this action William Webb disappeared and as of the date of trial his whereabouts were unknown.

The plaintiff argues that Cole placed Webb in a position where he was able to defraud her, and therefore, Cole must be held liable. The law . . . is stated in 1 Restatement Agency, 2d, §§ 261, 262, pp. 570, 571, . . . "A principal who puts a servant or other agent in a position which enables the agent, while apparently acting within his authority, to commit a fraud upon third persons is subject to liability to such third persons for the fraud. A person who otherwise would be liable to another for the misrepresentations of one apparently acting for him is not relieved from liability by the fact that the servant or other agent acts entirely for his own purposes, unless the other has notice of this."

For Cole to be liable it must be found that he placed Webb in a position where he could defraud the plaintiff while apparently acting within his authority. The trial court found that Cole had not placed Webb in such a position and we agree.

The business operated by Cole was not one of the general management of an individual's business affairs. It was highly specialized, providing certain services for gas stations only. These services were limited to things such as bookkeeping, preparing tax returns, and providing advice regarding the management of the business. At no time did Allen L. Cole & Associates undertake to manage their clients' financial affairs in general. Nor, did they ever take possession of their clients' funds, and at no time did they hold themselves out as being willing to undertake such activities.

The plaintiff places heavy emphasis on the fact that Webb gave her a business card that indicated he was associated with Allen L. Cole & Associates, business counsellors. We do not believe that merely by allowing an agent to use the designation "business counsellor" Allen L. Cole placed the agent in a position which gave him the opportunity to defraud the plaintiff.

We also agree with the finding of the trial court that regardless of the position in which Cole placed Webb the plaintiff did not place any reliance on Allen L. Cole, but relied entirely on

Webb in his personal capacity and not as an agent of Cole. Even in a case where an agent has been placed in a position of trust, his principal will not be liable for fraudulent acts from which he received no benefit if the agent was dealt with in a personal capacity and not as an agent. This is true even if the agent being employed by the principal is one of the things that inspires confidence in him. . . . :

> "It would seem to be clear that if the agent is purporting to act as an agent and doing the things which such agents normally do, and the third person has no reason to know that the agent is acting on his own account, the principal should be liable because he has invited third persons to deal with the agent within the limits of what, to such third persons, would seem to be the agent's authority. To go beyond this, however, and to permit the third persons to recover in every case where the agent takes advantage of the standing and position of his principal to perpetrate a fraud would seem to be going too far. Thus, undoubtedly, the fact that a person is a bank cashier causes third persons to trust him; but the bank should not be liable to third persons defrauded by the cashier merely because the position he occupied more readily inspired the belief that he was trustworthy. If he is dealt with as an agent of the bank but merely as a trusted person because of his position in the bank, there should be no more liability than for any other act of an agent or servant not done within the scope of the employment."

The trial court's conclusion that the plaintiff did not rely on Cole has ample support in the record. The plaintiff had no contact with Cole, she paid Cole no fee, and when she became suspicious she did not attempt to contact Cole. Therefore, it is reasonable to conclude that she did not rely on Cole. . . .

The plaintiff argues that the fact that a payment from Gandy's service station was made by a check signed by William Webb was sufficient notice to inform Cole that Webb was involved in the plaintiff's finances. We cannot agree. It would indeed be a heavy burden on a businessman to require that he examine every check that he receives to determine who had signed it.

The plaintiff contends that Cole ratified Webb's acts by retaining benefits that were received as a result of Webb's fraud after he had learned of the fraud. Plaintiff's argument is based on the fact that in 1965 Cole received $1,040 from Webb and in 1966 Webb loaned Cole $2000. The loan was subsequently repaid and the $1,040 was received in payment for money that Webb owed Cole. The trial court found that Cole did not have knowledge that he was receiving the plaintiff's money. . . .

. . . In order to find ratification we must first find that the acts complained of were done or professedly done on the account of the principal. . . . As we have previously stated the trial court found that Webb did not deal with the plaintiff as an agent of Cole, but rather acted in his personal capacity. Since Webb was not acting or professedly acting on Cole's account, Cole cannot be held to have ratified Webb's acts. . . .

[Judgment affirmed.]

O'HARA, J. (dissenting). . . . When, as in this case, a principal permits an agent to present to potential customers a business card proclaiming to all and sundry that he, the principal, is a "business counselor" and that the card bearer is his representative, the principal had better make it his business to know what "counseling" is done, particularly when the counseling results in doing a customer of the principal out of some $15,000.

A faultless principal has no defense against dishonesty, but it does not follow that this accords a principal the right to limitless gullibility. When his employee begins dealing in race horses, lends his principal money, and gives him a check signed by the principal's customer far in excess of any amount that could possibly accrue for legitimate services rendered, I would hold as a matter of law there was an obligation upon the principal to inform himself of his agent's doings [at once].

QUESTIONS AND CASE PROBLEMS

1. A corporation entered into a secured transaction. On its default, the secured creditor proceeded to sell the collateral and gave notice of the sale to the president of the corporation. The corporation claimed that the notice was not sufficient because it was merely given to the president and not to the corporation. Was it correct? [A. J. Armstrong Co. v Janburt Embroidery Corp., 97 NJ Super 246, 234 A2d 737]

2. An agent received in the mail stock certificates intended for his principal. The agent forged on the certificates an indorsement from the original owner of the certificates to himself. In a lawsuit by the owner of the certificates against the principal, the owner claimed that the principal knew what the agent had done. Was he correct? [Hartford Accident & Indemnity Co. v Walston & Co., 21 NY2d 219, 287 NY2d 58, 234 NE2d 230; adhered to 22 NY2d 672, 291 NYS2d 366, 238 NE2d 754]

3. Buchanan was a candidate for a political office. His campaign treasurer made a false report of the expenses of the campaign. A statute required the filing of such reports and made it a criminal offense to make a false report. Buchanan was prosecuted for the false report made by his campaign treasurer. Was he guilty of a statutory criminal offense? [Florida v Buchanan, (Fla App) 189 So2d 270]

4. Arnold Israel, acting as authorized agent for an undisclosed principal, Unified Consultants, made an authorized contract on their behalf with Tabloid Lithographers. Unified did not perform its part of the contract, and Tabloid sued both Israel and Unified. Tabloid obtained a judgment in the action against Unified, whereupon Israel claimed that he was released from any liability. Was this correct? [Tabloid Lithographers v Israel, 87 NJ Super 358, 209 A2d 364]

5. Sawday, the local salesman and representative of the Sunset Milling and Grain Co., executed a contract with Anderson by the terms of which Sunset was to deliver certain goods. The contract was signed by Sawday as "C. Trevor Sawday, representative of the Sunset Milling and Grain Co." Anderson sued Sunset, which defended on the ground that it was not bound because of the form of execution of the contract. Decide. [Sunset Milling and Grain Co. v Anderson, 39 Cal 2d 773, 249 P2d 24]

6. Blanche Trembley stated that she was agent for Trembley, Inc., and in the name of that corporation she made a contract with the Puro Filter Corp. of America. There was no corporation by the name of Trembley, Inc. The Puro Filter Corp. brought an action against Trembley to recover on the contract. Was it entitled to recover? [Puro Filter Corp. v Trembley, 266 App Div 750, 41 NYS2d 472]

7. Smith made a contract with Hal Anderson for architectural services. Some payments were made with checks bearing the name Hal Anderson, Inc. Payment was not made in full, and Smith sued Anderson for the balance. He defended on the ground that once Smith had received the corporate checks, Smith was put on notice of the fact that Hal was acting as an agent for an identified principal and thereafter could hold only the principal liable. Was this correct? [Anderson v Smith, (Tex Civ App) 398 SW2d 635]

8. Weeks was a collection agent for the Life Insurance Co. of Georgia. Clemmons held a policy in the company. When Weeks called for the premium at her home, Clemmons did not have the money. Weeks angrily drew a pistol and pointed it at her saying, "I will shoot." He then walked away, stating that she better have the money the next time he called. Clemmons sued the insurance company for damages. It contended that it was not liable for willful assault by its employee. Was this a valid defense? [Clemmons v Life Insurance Co., 274 NC 416, 163 SE2d 761]

9. Peterson was the agent of Federal Auto Systems. Kost wished to be franchised by Federal and gave Peterson an application for a franchise and a check. It was understood that Peterson would have the check certified and forward it with the application to Federal. It was also agreed that if Federal would not grant the franchise, the check would be returned. Peterson obtained a bank money order for the amount of the check instead of having it certified, and sent the application and the bank money order to Federal. Federal did not grant the franchise to Kost but did not return the money paid by him. Kost sued Peterson for breaking the agreement to return the check. Was he liable? [Kost v Peterson, 292 Minn 46, 193 NW2d 291]

10. Tongue gave Real Estate Exchange & Investors, Inc., a real estate broker, an exclusive right to sell his property at a specified price in return for a payment by Tongue of specified commissions on any sale. The Exchange offered to purchase the property from Tongue at the specified price. Tongue refused to sell it to the Exchange. The Exchange then sued Tongue for the commissions specified in the contract. Was it entitled? [Real Estate Exchange & Investors, Inc. v Tongue, 17 NC App 575, 194 SE2d 873]

11. Arley wished to insure his property in Nevada against fire. He went to Nelson, an insurance broker, and discussed the matter with Chaney, a solicitor for Nelson. It was agreed that a policy would be obtained from the Union Pacific Insurance Company and Arley was told that he was "covered." The policy was not obtained. Arley's property was destroyed by fire several months later. When he notified Nelson of his loss, the latter then obtained a policy of insurance but the insurance company cancelled the policy when it learned that the property had been destroyed before the property was insured. Arley sued Chaney and Nelson. The defense was raised that they could not be liable because they had disclosed the principal and had authority to write contracts binding the principal. Was this defense valid? [Arley v Chaney, 262 Ore 69, 496 P2d 202]

12. Weisz purchased a painting at an auction sale in the Parke-Burnett Galeries. It was later shown that the painting was a forgery. When Weisz sued Parke-Burnett for breach of warranty, it raised the defense that it was making the sale for the owner and therefore any warranty suit must be brought against the owner. Was it correct? [Weisz v Parke-Burnett Galeries, Inc., (NY Civil Court) 325 NYS2d 576]

43 Employment

THE EMPLOYMENT RELATION

The law of employment is similar to that of agency. There are material differences, however, and the relationship has become subject to regulation by statute generally described as labor legislation.

§ 43:1. Nature of Relationship. The relationship of an employer and an employee exists when, pursuant to an express or implied agreement of the parties,[1] one person, the *employee*, undertakes to perform services or to do work under the direction and control of another, the *employer*. In the older cases this was described as the master-servant relationship.

An employee without agency authority is hired only to work under the control of the employer, as contrasted with (1) an agent, who is to make contracts with third persons on behalf of and under control of the principal, by whom he may or may not be employed, and with (2) an independent contractor, who is to perform a contract independent of, or free from, control by the other party.

§ 43:2. Creation of the Employment Relation. The contract upon which the employment relationship is based is subject to all of the principles applicable to contracts generally. The relation of the employer and employee can be created only by consent of both parties. A person cannot be required to work against his will, nor can he become an employee without the consent of the employer.[2]

The contract of employment may be implied, as when the employer accepts services which, as a reasonable man, he knows are rendered with the expectation of receiving compensation. Thus, when a minor worked with his father under the supervision of the company's agent, the company impliedly assented to the relationship of employer and employee, even though the minor's name was not on the payroll.[3]

As a result of the rise of labor unions, large segments of industrial life are now covered by *union contracts*. This means that the union and the employer agree upon a basic pattern or set of terms of employment. For example, a union contract will state that all workers performing a specified class of work shall receive a certain hourly wage. Once the contract has been made between the employer and the union, the employee has the right

[1] Pioneer Casualty Co. v Bush, (Tex Civ App) 457 SW2d 165.
[2] Taylor v Baltimore etc. R.R. Co., 108 Va 817, 62 SE 798.
[3] Tennessee Coal etc. R.R. Co. v Hayes, 97 Ala 201, 12 So 98.

to receive the rate of pay specified therein and the union cannot surrender this right without the employee's consent.[4]

(1) Volunteered Services. In various shopping centers and parking lots, persons perform services for customers of the enterprise, such as loading packages in their cars. These persons are not employees of the enterprise, and tips from customers are the only remuneration they receive. The fact that they perform a service which might be rendered by employees of the enterprise does not make them employees. Likewise, they are not employees of the customer. This is important because it means that when the volunteer is negligent and causes injury to another person, the third person cannot recover damages from the enterprise or the customer. Thus, when a volunteer at a parking lot was negligent in driving the customer's car from the place where it was parked to the exit of the lot and, in so doing, damaged a third person's car, the third person could not hold the customer responsible for the harm caused by the volunteer.[5]

(2) Borrowed Employee. When the regular employer loans his employee to someone else, the other person is the employer both for the purpose of determining tort liability to a third person because of a wrongful act of the employee, and for the purpose of determining workmen's compensation liability to the employee because of an injury sustained while doing the work of the temporary employer. For example, when a hotel as a favor to one of its guests who operated a nearby restaurant permitted the hotel handyman to do odd jobs at the guest's restaurant, the handyman, while working at the restaurant making minor repairs, was an employee of the guest for the purpose of determining workmen's compensation liability.[6]

(3) Self-Service. The fact that customers wait on themselves in a self-service store does not make them employees of the store so as to make the store responsible to a customer injured by falling on debris dropped on the floor by another customer.[7]

§ 43:3. Terms of Employment. Basically the parties are free to make an employment contract on any terms they wish. The employment contemplated must, of course, be lawful; and by statute it is subject to certain limitations. Thus, persons under a certain age may not be employed at certain kinds of labor. Statutes commonly specify minimum wages and maximum hours which the employer must observe, and they require employers to provide many safety devices. A state may also require employers to pay employees for the time that they are away from work while voting.[8]

---

[4] Eversole v La Combe, 125 Mont 87, 231 P2d 945.

[5] McClellan v Allstate Insurance Co., (Dist Col App) 247 A2d 58.

[6] Winchester v Seay, 219 Tenn 321, 409 SW2d 378 (also rejecting the defense that the handyman was not covered by workmen's compensation insurance because his employment by the guest was "casual").

[7] Cameron v Bohack, 27 App Div 2d 362, 280 NYS2d 483.

[8] State v International Harvester Co., 241 Minn 367, 63 NW2d 547.

Historically, wages constituted the sole reward of labor. Today in many fields of employment additional benefits are conferred upon the worker, either by virtue of the contract of employment or by federal and state statutory provision.[9]

§ 43:4. Duties and Rights of the Employee. The duties and rights of an employee are determined primarily by his contract of employment with the employer. The law also implies certain provisions.

(1) Services. The employee is under a duty to perform or hold himself in readiness to perform such services as may be required by the contract of employment. If the employee holds himself in readiness to comply with his employer's directions, he has discharged his obligation and he will not forfeit his right to compensation because the employer has withheld directions and has thus kept him idle.

The employee impliedly agrees to serve his employer honestly and faithfully. He also impliedly agrees to serve him exclusively during his hours of employment. The employee may do other work, however, if the time and nature of the employment are not inconsistent with his duties to the first employer and if the contract of employment with the first employer does not contain any provision against it.

An employee must obey reasonable regulations and requirements adopted by the employer. Thus, an employer may require a cashier to agree to be fingerprinted in order to eliminate her as a suspect when the premises have been burglarized by an unidentified person.[10]

The employee impliedly purports that, in performing his duties, he will exercise due care and ordinary diligence in view of the nature of the work. When skill is required, the employee need exercise only ordinary skill,[11] unless the employee had held himself out as possessing a special skill required by the work.

When the contract of employment specifies that the employer is to be the judge of the value, utility, or satisfactory character of the employee's services, the employer must act in good faith in exercising the rights which the contract gives him when dissatisfied. If the employer may terminate the contract upon the occurrence of a specified condition, the employer has the burden of proving that such condition has occurred when he seeks to terminate the contract on that ground. (See p. 867, Fitzmaurice v Van Vlaanderen Machine Co.)

When the employee's misconduct has imposed liability upon the employer, the employee can be required to indemnify the employer for the loss which the employee has caused.

---

[9] See Chapter 5 as to various statutory regulations of labor, such as those relating to fair labor standards, hours of service, fair employment practices, and labor-management relations.

[10] Martin v Santora, (Miss) 199 So2d 63.

[11] Strickland v Perrucio, 5 Conn Cir 142, 246 A2d 810.

*(2) **Trade Secrets.*** An employee may be given confidential trade secrets by his employer. He is under a duty not to disclose such knowledge. It is immaterial that the contract of employment did not stipulate against such disclosures. If he violates this obligation, the employer may enjoin the use of such information.

Former employees who are competing with their former employer may be enjoined by him from utilizing information as to suppliers and customers which they had obtained while employees where such information is of vital importance to the employer's business.[12] A court will not, however, enjoin an ex-employee from soliciting some customers of his former employer where the number solicited is a small percentage of the former employer's customers and anyone could have identified the customers as prospective buyers without having any "inside" information based on having worked for the former employer. (See p. 867, Silfen v Cream.)

The employee is under no duty to refrain from divulging general information of the particular business in which he is employed. Nor is he under a duty not to divulge the information of the particular business when the relation between employer and employee is not considered confidential.[13] Mere knowledge and skill obtained through experience are not in themselves trade secrets, and employees may use the fruits of their experience in later employment or in working for themselves.[14]

*(3) **Inventions.*** In the absence of an express or implied agreement to the contrary, the inventions of an employee belong to him, even though he used the time and property of the employer in their discovery, provided that he was not employed for the express purpose of inventing the things or the process which he discovered. The employer has the burden of proving that he is entitled to the invention of a process discovered by an employee in the course of employment.[15]

If the invention is discovered during working hours and with the employer's materials and equipment, the employer has the right to use the invention without charge in the operation of his business. If the employee has obtained a patent for the invention, he must grant the employer a nonexclusive license to use the invention without the payment of royalty. This *shop right* of the employer does not give him the right to make and sell machines that embody the employee's invention; it only entitles him to use the invention in the operation of his plant.

When an employee employed as a tinsmith by a shipbuilder devised a better way of installing beds in ships, the employer was entitled to use the employee's idea without compensating him where no express agreement for payment had been made.[16]

---

[12] Harry R. Defler Corp. v Kleenan, 19 App Div 2d 396, 243 NYS2d 930.
[13] Abbott Laboratories v Norse Chemical Co., 33 Wis 2d 445, 147 NW2d 529.
[14] Lessner Dental Laboratories, Inc. v Kidney, 16 Ariz App 159, 492 P2d 39.
[15] Bandag, Inc. v Morenings, 259 Iowa 998, 146 NW2d 916.
[16] Kinkade v New York Shipbuilding Corp., 21 NJ 362, 122 A2d 360.

When the employee is employed in order to secure certain results from experiments to be conducted by him, the inventions belong to the employer on the ground that there is a trust relation or that there is an implied agreement by the employee to make an assignment of the inventions to the employer.[17]

In any case an employee may expressly agree that his inventions made during his employment will be the property of the employer. If such a contract is not clear and specific, the courts are inclined to rule against the employer. The employee may also agree to assign to the employer inventions made after the term of employment.

A provision which requires an employee to turn over to his employer all ideas relating to the employer's business which occur to the employee within one year after the termination of employment is too broad and will not be enforced, although such a provision would be valid if limited to ideas based on trade secrets or confidential information of the employer.[18]

(4) Compensation. The rights of an employee with respect to compensation are governed in general by the same principles that apply to the compensation of an agent.

In the absence of an agreement to the contrary, when an employee is discharged, whether for cause or not, the employer must pay his wages down to the expiration of the last pay period. The express terms of employment or union contracts, or custom, frequently provide for payment of wages for fractional terminal periods, however, and they may even require a severance pay equal to the compensation for a full period of employment. Provisions relating to deferred compensation under a profit-sharing trust for employees are liberally construed in favor of employees.[19]

An employee is not constitutionally entitled to a hearing on the question of the computation of his pay and the making of deductions therefrom.[20]

(5) Employee's Lien or Preference. Most states protect an employee's claim for compensation either by a lien or a preference over other claimants of payment out of the proceeds from the sale of the employer's property. These statutes vary widely in their terms. They are usually called *laborers'* or *mechanics' lien laws*. Sometimes the statutes limit the privilege to the workmen of a particular class, such as plasterers or bricklayers. Compensation for the use of materials or machinery is not protected by such statutes.

§ 43:5. Pension Plans. Many employers have established pension plans to benefit their employees after they retire. In addition to providing the employee with the obvious payment benefits, a plan which is approved or

---

[17] US v Dubilier Condenser Corp., 289 US 178.

[18] Armorlite Lens Co. v Campbell, (DC SD Cal) 340 F Supp 273.

[19] Russell v Princeton Laboratories, Inc., 50 NJ 30, 231 A2d 800.

[20] Los Angeles County Employees Union v County of Los Angeles Board of Supervisors, 33 Cal App 3d 269, 109 Cal Rptr 46 (county employer).

qualified by the Internal Revenue Service also benefits both the employer and his employees by reducing their federal income tax liability. Up to a certain limit the employer may treat as an income tax deduction the contributions which he makes to the pension fund. The money which is held in the pension fund for the employees is not subject to federal income tax until payments are made by the fund to the employee. This enables the fund to grow faster and the employee's tax which is paid upon receiving the pension payments will be lower because they are received in years when the employee's gross income is less.

(1) Pension Reform Act of 1974. This federal statute, also known as the Employees Retirement Income Security Act (ERISA),[21] was adopted to provide protection for the pension interests of employees. The statute does this by provisions relating to:

(a) FIDUCIARY STANDARDS AND REPORTING. Persons administering a pension fund must handle it so as to protect the interest of the employees. The fact that an employer contributed all or part of the money does not entitle him to use the fund as though it were still his own. Persons administering pension plans must make detailed reports to the Secretary of Labor.

(b) EARLY VESTING. The Reform Act requires the early vesting of rights of an employee.

(c) PENSION PORTABILITY. The Pension Act provides a system of voluntary participation to provide pension portability so that an employee does not lose his credits for years of services with one employer when he goes to work for another.

(d) ACTUARIAL FUNDING. The Reform Act requires that contributions be made by employers to their pension funds on a basis which is actuarially determined so that the pension fund will be sufficiently large to make the payments which will be required of it.

(e) TERMINATION INSURANCE. The Act establishes an insurance plan to protect employees when the employer goes out of business. To provide this protection, the statute creates a Pension Benefit Guaranty Corporation. In effect this corporation guarantees that the employee will receive his benefits in much the same pattern as the Federal Deposit Insurance Corporation protects bank depositors. The Guaranty Corporation is financed by small payments made by employers for every employee covered by a pension plan.

(f) SECRETARY OF LABOR. The Act gives the Secretary of Labor extensive powers in the operation and supervision of the pension plan.

---

[21] PL 93-406.

(g) ENFORCEMENT. The Act authorizes the Secretary of Labor and employees to bring court actions to compel the observance of the statutory requirements.

(h) CRIMINAL OFFENSES. The Act makes it a crime to fire, discriminate against, or threaten any employee who exercises any right conferred by the federal statute.

EMPLOYER'S LIABILITY FOR EMPLOYEE'S INJURIES

For most kinds of employment, workmen's compensation statutes govern. They provide that the injured employee is entitled to compensation for accidents occurring in the course of his employment from a risk involved in that employment.

In some employment situations, however, common-law principles apply. Under them the employer is not an insurer of the employee's safety.[22] It is necessary, therefore, to consider the duties and defenses of an employer apart from statute.

§ 43:6. Common-Law Status of Employer.

(1) Duties. The employer is under the common-law duty to furnish an employee with a reasonably safe place in which to work,[23] (see p. 870, Dawes v McKenna) reasonably safe tools and appliances, and a sufficient number of competent fellow employees for the work involved; and to warn the employee of any unusual dangers peculiar to the employer's business.[24] Statutes also commonly require employers to provide a safe working place or safe working conditions. Under the federal Occupational Safety and Health Act of 1970, the Secretary of the Department of Labor is authorized to set safety standards for places of employment.[25] State laws continue in force as to matters not regulated by the federal statutes.

(2) Defenses. At common law the employer is not liable to an injured employee, regardless of the employer's negligence, if the employee was guilty of contributory negligence, or if he was harmed by the act of a fellow employee,[26] or if he was harmed by an ordinary hazard of the work, because he assumed such risks.

§ 43:7. Statutory Changes. The rising incidence of industrial accidents, due to the increasing use of more powerful machinery and the growth of the industrial labor population, led to a demand for statutory modification of common-law rules relating to liability of employers for industrial accidents.

---

[22] Workmen's compensation statutes by their terms generally do not apply to agricultural, domestic, or casual employment. In addition, in some states the plan of workmen's compensation is optional with the employer or the employee.

[23] Phillips Oil Co. v Linn, (CA5 Tex) 194 F2d 903.

[24] Restatement, Agency 2d § 510.

[25] PL 91-596; 84 Stat 1590, 29 USC §§ 651 et seq. The federal statute also creates a National Institute of Occupational Health and Safety.

[26] R 2d § 475.

(1) Modification of Employer's Common-Law Defenses. One type of change by statute was to modify the defenses which an employer could assert when sued by an employee for damages. Under statutes that apply to common carriers engaged in interstate commerce,[27] the plaintiff must still bring an action in a court and prove the negligence of the employer or of his employees,[28] but the burden of proving his case is made lighter by limitations on the employer's defenses.

Under the Federal Employers' Liability Act contributory negligence is a defense only in mitigation of damages; assumption of risk is not a defense.[29]

In many states the common-law defenses of employers whose employees are engaged in hazardous types of work have also been modified by statute.

(2) Workmen's Compensation. A more sweeping development was made by the adoption of workmen's compensation statutes in every state. With respect to certain industries or businesses, these statutes provide that an employee or certain relatives of a deceased employee are entitled to recover damages for the injury or death of the employee whenever the injury arose within the course of the employee's work from a risk involved in that work. In such a case compensation is paid without regard to whether the employer or the employee was negligent, although generally no compensation is allowed for a willfully self-inflicted injury or one sustained while intoxicated.

There has been a gradual widening of the workmen's compensation statutes, so that compensation today is generally recoverable for accident-inflicted injuries and occupational diseases.[30] In some states compensation for occupational diseases is limited to those specified in the statute by name, such as silicosis, lead poisoning, or injury to health from radioactivity. In other states any disease arising from an occupation is compensable.

Workmen's compensation proceedings are brought before a special administrative agency or workmen's compensation board. In contrast, a common-law action for damages or an action for damages under an employer's liability statute is brought in a court of law.

Workmen's compensation statutes do not bar an employee from suing another employee for the injury caused him. Likewise, an employee may sue the employer when liability is based upon some principle not related to the employment relationship. For example, when an employee is harmed by a product purchased from his employer, liability is determined by the law of product liability and not the law of employment or workmen's compensation. (See p. 870, Panagos v North Detroit General Hospital.)

LIABILITY FOR INJURIES OF THIRD PERSONS

When an employee causes injury to a third person, a question arises as to whether the employee, the employer, or both, are liable to the third person.

---

[27] Federal Employer's Liability Act, 45 USC §§ 1 et seq. and the Federal Safety Appliance Act, 49 USC §§ 1 et seq.

[28] Moore v Chesapeake & Ohio Railway, 340 US 573.

[29] Shenker v Baltimore and Ohio R.R., 374 US 1.

[30] Webb v New Mexico Publishing Co., 47 NMex 279, 141 P2d 333.

§ 43:8. Employee's Liability to Third Persons for Injuries. Whenever the employee injures another person, either another employee or an outsider, the liability of the employee is determined by the same principles that would apply if the employee were not employed.

§ 43:9. Employer's Liability to Third Persons for Injuries. An employer is liable to a third person for the harm done him by the act of his employee (1) when the employer expressly directed the act; (2) when the harm was due to the employer's fault in not having competent employees, or in failing to give them proper instructions, or a similar fault; (3) when the act by the employee was within the course of his employment; [31] or (4) when the act was done by the employee without authority but the employer ratified or assented to it.

The third basis upon which the employer is made liable for acts of his employees committed within the scope of his employment [32] is known as the *doctrine of respondeat superior*. (See p. 872, United States v Romitti.) If the act by the employee is not within the scope of his employment, the employer is not liable under this doctrine.[33] Consequently, when an employer lends an employee the employer's truck or car for the employee's personal use after working hours, the employer is ordinarily not liable for harm caused by the employee to a third person through his negligent operation of the vehicle.[34]

(1) Nature of Act. Historically the act for which liability would be imposed under the doctrine of respondeat superior was a negligent act. While it was necessary that the act was in the course of employment, an act did not cease to be within the course of employment merely because it was not expressly authorized nor even because it was committed in violation of instructions. Ordinarily an employer is not liable for a willful, unprovoked assault committed by an employee upon a third person or customer of the employer,[35] but the employer is sometimes held liable for wanton and malicious conduct of an employee on the theory that it is within the scope of employment when the employee inflicts such harm in the belief that he is furthering the employer's interest.[36]

There is a trend toward widening the employer's liability for the tort of his employee. When the employee is hired to retake property of the principal, as in the case of an employee of a finance company hired to

---

[31] Bryce v Jackson Diners, 80 RI 327, 96 A2d 637.

[32] R 2d declares acts within the scope of the servant's employment to be acts of the kind that the employee was employed to perform; occurring substantially within the authorized time and space limits; and actuated, at least in part, by a purpose to serve the employer. It also requires for this purpose that if force is intentionally used against another, its use was not unexpectable by the employer. § 228(1).

[33] Parry v Davison-Paxon Co., 87 Ga App 51, 73 SE2d 59.

[34] Adams v Quality Service Laundry & Dry Cleaners, 253 Wisc 334, 34 NW2d 148.

[35] Nettles v Thornton, (Fla App) 198 So2d 44.

[36] R 2d § 231; Bremen State Bank v Hartford Accident & Indemnity Co., (CA7 Ill) 427 F2d 425. Some courts follow the older rule that the employer is never liable for a willful or malicious act by his employee regardless of its purpose.

repossess automobiles on which installments have not been paid, the employer is generally liable for the unlawful force used by the employee in retaking the property or in committing an assault upon the buyer. In contrast, the majority of court decisions do not impose liability on an employer for an assault committed by his bill collector upon the debtor.

(2) Insurance. The fact that the employer is insured does not affect the employer's liability, because the insurer's liability is the same as the employer's.

(3) Borrowed Employee. In holding an employer liable for the act of an employee, it is immaterial whether the employee is a permanent employee or a borrowed or temporary employee. Hence, it is no defense to the liability of a repairman for the negligent repair of automobile brakes that the actual work was done by a borrowed employee.[37]

(4) Employee of United States. The Federal Tort Claims Act declares that the United States shall be liable vicariously whenever a federal employee driving a motor vehicle in the course of his employment causes harm under such circumstances that a private employer would be liable.[38] This statute further provides, and here reverses the ordinary rule, that the employee driver in such case shall not be liable to the injured person.[39]

(5) Employee's Automobile. When the employee uses his own automobile, there is authority that the employer is not liable for the negligent driving of the employee unless it is determined that the employer expressly or in fact authorized the employee's use of the automobile; and the mere fact that the employee was doing work for the employer at the time does not impose liability upon the employer. If the employee is involved in a collision or causes negligent harm while driving in his own car to or from work, the employer is ordinarily not liable to the injured person. Likewise, the employer is not liable when harm is caused to a third person while the employee is driving to or from meals or an employees' banquet.[40]

§ 43:10. Supervisory Liability. Historically an employer was liable for the wrongful act of an employee only when the latter was acting in the course of his employment. Conversely, if the harm was done by the employee after working hours or for his own personal benefit, there was no liability of the employer.

This concept is being eroded by the application of a concept of supervisory liability that, in effect, makes the employer liable simply because it was his employee who did the wrong. Sometimes this conclusion is explained in terms that the employer was in the better position to have avoided the harm through a more careful screening of his employees. This is ordinarily

---

[37] Irianne v Diamond T, 94 NJ Super 148, 227 A2d 335.

[38] 28 USC §§ 1346, 1504, 2401, 2402, 2671-2680.

[39] Fancher v Baker, 240 Ark 288, 399 SW2d 280.

[40] Barr v Colorado Interstate Gas Co., (CA5 Tex) 217 F2d 85.

mere lip service to the concept that there must be fault as the basis for liability, because ordinarily it would be impossible for the employer to have screened so carefully and so prophetically as to have avoided the harm that resulted. The *doctrine of supervisory liability* has rather limited application, primarily because it is virtually a form of absolute liability, that is, imposing liability because harm has happened without regard to whether any fault was involved.

In the field of tort law, the concept of supervisory liability is found primarily in the case of hotels. In one case the hotel was liable when a bellboy after his working hours stole the keys to a guest's automobile and removed the automobile from the private parking garage to which another bellboy had taken it.

(1) Employer's Liability for Assault by Third Person. Assume that an employee while engaged in the course of his employment is injured by the act of a third person, such as an angry customer, a picket, or a rioter. When the employee sustains injury caused by a third person, the employer is not liable therefor to the employee unless it can be shown that the employer was in some way negligent and that such negligence made it possible for the employee to be harmed.[41]

§ 43:11. Owner's Liability for Injuries Caused by Independent Contractor. If work is done by an independent contractor rather than by an employee, the owner is not liable for harm caused by the contractor to third persons or their property. Likewise, the owner is ordinarily not liable for harm caused third persons by the negligence of the independent contractor's employees. For example, the owner of an automobile leaving it for repairs is not liable to a person injured by the repairman while making a road test of the car, because the repairman is not the employee of the owner, even though the road test had been made at the request of the owner.[42]

There is, however, a trend toward imposing liability on the owner even in such a case when the work undertaken is especially hazardous in nature. That is, the law is taking the position that if the owner wishes to engage in a particular activity, he must be responsible for the harm it causes and cannot insulate himself from such liability by the device of hiring an independent contractor to do the work. For example, when a person engaged a detective agency to provide plant guards, that person was liable for malicious prosecution by an employee of the agency. The guard duties entrusted to the agency were of such a personal nature that they could not be assigned or delegated so as to free the agency's customer from liability.[43]

The use of independent contractors will not insulate an owner from liability when he retains control of the work. Consequently, when the owner made "subcontracts" directly with contractors and retained control and

---

[41] Hopkins v Hacker, 105 NH 150, 195 A2d 587.
[42] Nawrocki v Cole, 41 Wash 2d 474, 249 P2d 969.
[43] Hendricks v Leslie Fay, 273 NC 59, 159 SE2d 362.

supervision of the construction work, he was legally in possession; and when an employee of one of the contractors fell because of a defective catwalk, the owner could be held liable and could not rely on the defense that the employee's employer was an independent contractor.[44]

§ 43:12. Employer's Indemnity Agreement. When the employer performs extensive or dangerous work on the premises of a customer, the contract between the employer and the customer will commonly contain a clause by which the employer expressly agrees to indemnify the customer for any harm occurring in the performance of the work. For example, a contractor installing heavy equipment in an industrial plant may agree to indemnify the plant for any loss sustained by the plant in the course of the installation. In view of the fact that such agreements are generally made between persons who are "in business" and therefore know the significance of what they are doing, the agreements usually are literally enforced.

Depending upon the financial position of the contractor and the respective bargaining powers of the parties, the contractor may find it necessary to furnish the plant with an indemnity bond issued by an insurance company or to deposit certain assets with a bank to hold as a fund from which to pay the plant for any proper claim.

§ 43:13. Enforcement of Claim by Third Person. When a third person is injured by an employee, he may have a cause of action or an enforceable claim against both the employee and the employer. In most states and in the federal courts, the injured person may sue either or both in one action. If the injured person sues both, he may obtain judgment against both of them but he can only collect the full amount of the judgment once.

If the employee was at fault and if his wrongful conduct was not in obedience to his employer's directions, the employer may recover indemnity from the employee for the loss that the employer sustained when he was required to make payment to the third person. When an employee acting at the direction of his employer uproots shrubbery on what the employer erroneously believes is the employer's side of the boundary line but which in fact is on the neighboring land, the employee is entitled to be indemnified by his employer to the extent that the employee pays the judgment obtained by the third person.

§ 43:14. Notice to Employer of Danger. In a number of situations one person must give notice or warning of danger to another person and is liable for the harm that befalls the other person because of a failure to give such notice or warning. When the persons who will be exposed to the foreseeable danger are employees of a particular person, notice to the employer is generally sufficient. As a matter of practical expediency, the law assumes that the employer can be more certain of reaching each of his employees than an outsider could, and it further assumes that the employer will relay

---

[44] Jackson v Beasley Construction Co., 76 Ill App 2d 282, 222 NE2d 209.

any warning to his employees in order to protect them. Thus, the manufacturer of a dangerous instrumentality satisfies the requirement of giving warning of its dangerous quality if he informs his purchaser, and an employee of the purchaser cannot bring suit against the manufacturer on the ground that the manufacturer did not give him personal warning.[45] Likewise, when a landowner owes "invitee" protection to employees of an independent contractor working on the premises, the owner discharges his duty to inform the employees of an unknown danger by informing the independent contractor.[46]

In some product liability cases involving powerful equipment, it is held that a warning to the employer is not sufficient, and that the manufacturer must attach a warning tag or sign on the equipment.

TERMINATION OF EMPLOYMENT CONTRACT

A contract of employment may, in general, be terminated in the same manner as contracts of any other kind. If a definite duration is not specified in the contract, it is terminable at will and either party may terminate the contract by giving the other reasonable notice of his intention.[47] Local statutes and union contracts commonly regulate the period of notice which the employer must give to the employee.

The employment contract may stipulate that the employer may terminate the relationship if he is not satisfied with the services of the employee. In such cases the employer is generally considered the sole judge of his reason provided that he acts in good faith.

§ 43:15. Justifiable Discharge by Employer. In the absence of a contract or statutory provision to the contrary, an employer may discharge an employee for any reason or for no reason if the employment is at will.[48] When the employment may not be terminated at will, the employer will be liable for damages if he discharges the employee without justification. The employer is justified in discharging an employee because of the employee's (1) nonperformance of duties, (2) misrepresentation or fraud in obtaining the employment, (3) disobedience to proper directions,[49] (4) disloyalty, (5) wrongful misconduct, (6) incompetency, or (7) disability. (See p. 873, Fisher v Church of St. Mary.)

§ 43:16. Remedies of Employee Wrongfully Discharged. An employee who has been wrongfully discharged may bring against the employer an action for (1) wages, (2) breach of contract,[50] or (3) value of services already rendered. In certain instances he may also bring (4) an action that results in

---

[45] West v Hydro-Test, Inc., (La App) 196 So2d 598.
[46] Delhi-Taylor Corp. v Henry, (Tex) 416 SW2d 390.
[47] Plaskitt v Black Diamond Trailer Co., 209 Va 460, 164 SE2d 645.
[48] Odell v Humble Oil & Refining Co., (CA10 NMex) 201 F2d 123.
[49] NLRB v American Thread Co., (CA5 NLRB) 210 F2d 381.
[50] Olsen v Arabian American Oil Co., (CA2 NY) 194 F2d 477.

performance of the employment contract, or (5) a proceeding under a federal or state labor relations statute.

§ 43:17. Justifiable Abandonment by Employee. The employee cannot be compelled to perform his contract of employment. Hence, he can at any time end the relationship by a refusal to perform the services for which he was engaged. If the contract is not terminable at will, his refusal to carry out his part of the contract may or may not make him liable for damages, depending upon the reason for leaving his employment.

The employment relationship may be abandoned by the employee for (1) nonpayment of wages, (2) wrongful assault by the employer, (3) requirement of services not contemplated, (4) employer's refusal to permit employee's performance, and (5) injurious conditions of employment.

§ 43:18. Remedies of the Employer for Wrongful Abandonment. When an employee wrongfully abandons his employment, the employer may bring (1) an action for breach of contract; and in certain circumstances he may also bring (2) an action against a third person maliciously inducing the breach of contract, (3) an action to enjoin the employee from working for another employer, or (4) a proceeding under a federal or state labor relations statute.

§ 43:19. Attachment and Garnishment of Wages. It is generally provided that a creditor may require a third person who owes money to his debtor to pay such amount to the creditor to satisfy the creditor's claim against the debtor. That is, if *A* has a valid claim for $100 against *B*, and *C* owes *B* $100, *A* can require *C* to pay him $100, which thereby satisfies both *C*'s debt to *B* and *B*'s debt to *A*. The necessary legal procedure generally requires the third person to pay the money into court or to the sheriff rather than directly to the original creditor. The original creditor may also by this process usually reach tangible property belonging to his debtor which is in the custody or possession of a third person. This procedure is commonly called *attachment* and the third person is called a *garnishee.*

Under the federal Truth in Lending Act (Title I of the Federal Consumer Credit Protection Act) only a certain portion of an employee's pay can be garnisheed. Ordinarily, the amount that may be garnisheed may not exceed (a) 25 percent of the employee's weekly take-home pay or (b) the amount by which the weekly take-home pay exceeds 30 times the federal minimum wage, whichever is less.[51] The federal statute also prohibits an employer from discharging an employee because his wages have been garnisheed for any one indebtedness.

---

[51] CCPA § 303. Under the UCCC, where adopted, this second alternative has been increased to 40 times the federal weekly minimum pay. UCCC § 5.105(2)(b). Prejudgment attachment of wages without notice and hearing is invalid. Sniadach v Family Finance Corp., 395 US 337.

CASES FOR CHAPTER 43

Fitzmaurice v Van Vlaanderen Machine Co.

110 NJ Super 159, 264 A2d 740 (1970)

The Van Vlaanderen Machine Co., a printing press manufacturer, made a contract with Fitzmaurice, a management consultant. The contract called for Fitzmaurice to render consulting services for one year but provided that the machine company could terminate the contract at the end of three months "if at that time you do not find my work profitable." At the end of three months, the representative of the machine company told Fitzmaurice that the machine company was "unsatisfied" and wanted "to call it off." Fitzmaurice sued the machine company for breach of contract. From a judgment in his favor, the machine company appealed.

PER CURIAM. . . . Defendant urges that (1) the contract between the parties was one for personal satisfaction, and therefore defendant was not required to show a reasonable basis for its decision to terminate its relationship with plaintiff; (2) the court erred in charging the jury that the burden rested upon defendant to prove that the contract was not profitable. . . .

Defendant argues that the contract was one of personal satisfaction, which permitted it unilaterally to cancel. Not so. The contract created an employment relationship covering a one year period, but subject to termination, at defendant's option, three months after its date if defendant did not find plaintiff's services to be profitable. The right to dissolve the contractual relationship was thus a conditional one. A personal satisfaction contract, so called, generally involves a subject matter which concerns the personal taste, fancy, or feeling of another, who is thus made the sole judge of the quality of the performance. . . . However, contracts which promise performance in the form of results to the satisfaction of another are in a different category and, as to them, the New Jersey rule is that the party claiming dissatisfaction must act honestly and in good faith. . . . This comports with the majority rule. . . .

The contract here evidenced an intent that the continuation of plaintiff's relationship with defendant was not to be subject to the sole and unbridled discretion of defendant's officers but was to be cancelable only if they found plaintiff's services not to be "profitable." Whether or not such services were profitable would appear to be measurable by commercial standards. Defendant's decision thereon was, of course, subject to the test of good faith and reasonableness. . . . Such a construction gives due weight to the language employed by the parties, considered in the context of their dealings, imposes the least hardship upon either of the parties and cannot be said to be unfair or unreasonable. . . . Thus the jury was properly instructed that the test was whether defendant's conclusion that plaintiff's services were not profitable, on which it based its termination of the agreement, could fairly and reasonably have been reached under the proofs adduced. . . .

Defendant argues that the court erred in charging that the burden of establishing facts justifying defendant's termination of the contract rested with defendant. Not so. Plaintiff did not obligate himself to perform to the satisfaction of defendant, but rather agreed to render business diagnosis and management services for the term of one year. Only upon the establishment of a contingency, i.e., the failure of defendant to find his work to be profitable, did he agree to release defendant from its obligation. Where a party seeks to avoid a contractual obligation by reason of the happening of an event or condition stipulated in a contract, the burden of establishing the occurrence of the condition rests upon the party asserting it. . . .

[Judgment affirmed.]

Leo Silfen, Inc. v Cream

29 NY2d 387, 328 NYS2d 423, 278 NE2d 636 (1972)

Cream was an officer and employee of Leo Silfen, Inc. He was discharged and then went into business and solicited former customers of

his ex-employer. The latter sought to enjoin him from so doing and to recover damages. An associated corporation, Formula 33 Corporation, joined in the action as a co-plaintiff. A judgment was entered in favor of the corporations and against Cream. He appealed.

BREITEL, J. . . . Plaintiffs have failed to prove a physical appropriation or copying of confidential information, or wrongful disclosure or use of a trade secret. In particular, no trade secret protection is warranted since plaintiffs' customers are likely, if not known, users of the employers' merchandise and engaged in business at advertised locations.

Plaintiff corporations are engaged in selling building maintenance supplies to industrial and commercial users. Plaintiffs purchase their inventory from independent supply houses and then, at a substantial markup, resell to customers under their own label. Plaintiff Silfen sells soaps, polishes, waxes, finishers, and disinfectants, while plaintiff Formula 33 Corporation specializes in ice and snow melting compounds.

In 1949 defendant Cream joined Silfen, then engaged only in the paper and twine business. Cream was assigned and became solely responsible for the development of a cleaning and maintenance chemical supply division. During its formative years Cream interviewed and hired salesmen, developed products, and found suppliers. Initial customer solicitation consisted of direct contact and media advertising. Meeting little success he employed the services of mailing houses which provided lists of prospects to whom brochures and business reply cards were forwarded. Eventually, an average of one million mailings were made annually with a reply rate of 0.6%. Of those replying 25% became customers at an average cost per new customer in 1967 of $45. Over the years, some 15,000 customers were obtained.

For each customer a separate file was kept containing: name of purchasing agent and other personnel at customer's office; temperament of purchasing agent; gratuities given; particular requirements; and past purchases. In 1961 these customer profiles were consolidated into a central filing system and measures were taken to insure that each salesman had access only to that portion of the files containing his customers.

So concerned were plaintiffs in the protection of this information that in the employment agreement with each salesman hired after 1961 it was provided: "[The salesman] acknowledges that the list of the Corporations' customers is a unique asset of their respective businesses, and . . . will not, during or after the term of his employment, appropriate to his own use or disclose to others for any purpose, any names on such list or any confidential information obtained by him during his employment." Vigilance is also demonstrated by a form required to be signed by each salesman after contact with a customer: "The names of all the company customers ever called by me, and those appearing on the face of this telephone report sheet, were obtained from leads furnished by the company and remain the property of the company and will not be disclosed to any unauthorized persons in violation of the trust placed in me by the company."

In 1965, on the death of the principal of Silfen and the taking of control by his widow, Cream was named executive vice-president and general manager of plaintiff corporations for a term of 12 years. The written agreement between the parties provided for a base salary of $26,000 plus 25% of the aggregate net profits. The corporations reserved the right to discharge Cream if the aggregate net profits in any one year failed to exceed $35,000. If was also provided that if Cream terminated the agreement he would "not, for one year thereafter . . . engage in the sale to the corporations' customers of any products competing with the corporations' products." Since Cream was discharged this restriction is not controlling. The agreement contained no comparable provision to cover Cream's discharge.

On November 17, 1967, Cream was discharged purportedly because of a decline of net profits. Cream, however, urges that he was discharged in order to make room for the new husband of the widow, the former Mrs. Silfen. Thirteen days after his discharge he set up Real Estate Maintenance Chemical Specialty Corporation and engaged in the same business as plaintiffs except limited to building owners and building managers. About three months later, in March, 1968, plaintiffs brought this action to enjoin defendants' solicitation of plaintiffs' customers. The complaint alleged that defendants had been soliciting plaintiffs' customers, that Cream had made copies of plaintiffs' secret and confidential customer files, and was using such information in his solicitation. Cream admits that of a list of 1,100 customers submitted by plaintiffs defendants had solicited 47. Defendants, however, contend that the names of these customers were procured from available commercial lists compiled by commercial list houses. Defendants allege in their answer and assert in their testimony that the customers are openly engaged in business at advertised locations and their names are well known to plaintiffs' competitors.

Notably, plaintiffs did not attempt to sustain their allegation that Cream had made copies of plaintiffs' secret and confidential files, or used the recorded detail in those files with respect to each customer's "profile". The solicitation of plaintiffs' customers was at most the product of casual memory, or, as defendants would have the court believe, coincidence.* If there has been a physical taking or studied copying, the court may in a proper case enjoin solicitation, not necessarily as a violation of a trade secret, but as an egregious breach of trust and confidence while in plaintiffs' service. . . . Nor is there any allegation or evidence of other wrongful or fraudulent tactics employed by Cream in connection with the solicitation of plaintiffs' customers. If there had been, a court might award damages and enjoin further similar conduct as constituting unfair competition. . . . All that remains, therefore, on the theory alleged in the complaint or developed on the trial is whether plaintiffs' customer list, exclusive of the recorded detail about each customer, classifies as a trade secret rendering defendants' solicitation of customers on that list improper, sufficient to warrant injunction and damages.

Generally, where the customers are readily ascertainable outside the employer's business as prospective users or consumers of the employer's services or products, trade secret protection will not attach and courts will not enjoin the employee from soliciting his employer's customers. . . . Conversely, where the customers are not known in the trade or are discoverable only by extraordinary efforts courts have not hesitated to protect customer lists and files as trade secrets. This is especially so where the customers' patronage had been secured by years of effort and advertising effected by the expenditure of substantial time and money . . . .

The customers solicited by defendants, as apparently found by the trial court, are openly engaged in business in advertised locations and their names and addresses may readily be found by those engaged in the trade. . . .

In the absence of express agreement to that effect between the parties, or a demonstration that a customer list has the several attributes of a trade secret, courts, without more, should not enjoin an ex-employee from engaging in fair and open competition with his former employer. The limiting effects upon the former employee with respect to his ability to earn a living are marked and obvious. . . . Moreover, the issuance of the permanent injunction in the present case has an untoward consequence. By discharging Cream plaintiffs obtained greater protection than they would have had under their agreement with him, if he had terminated the employment. It was observed earlier that the 1965 employment agreement provided that Cream would not solicit plaintiffs' customers for one year following his termination of the employment. This provision suggests that the parties considered Cream's role as a future competitor, and, more important, were satisfied to provide protection for only one year.

In concluding, it may be stated expressly what was earlier implied, namely, that if defendants had been shown to have appropriated by copying, studied memory, or by some other manner which does not now come to mind, the detailed information in the customer files there would be a case quite different from this. The record shows no such appropriation with respect

---

* In passing it should be noted that defendants do not argue that otherwise protectible information might be exempted if it is shown that the employee's appropriation was the result of experience or memory and not physical taking or copying. There are authorities which suggest that an employee may use in competition with his former employer the names, even lists, of customers retained in his memory. . . .

to a single customer, let alone many customers to an extent barring reliance on casual memory. Instead, it shows that defendants solicited 47 of the 1,100 customers submitted on a list prepared by plaintiffs from its confidential files. The point is that in the circumstances described names of customers alone involved no trade secret and there was no wrongful conduct by defendants. If trade secrets there were, they consisted of the data in the carefully secured and segregated files.

[Judgment reversed.]

Dawes v McKenna

100 RI 317, 215 A2d 235 (1965)

Dawes did cleaning for Mr. and Mrs. McKenna two days a week. While carrying trash to an incinerator in the backyard, she fell on an icy walk and was injured. She sued the McKennas. From a verdict in favor of Dawes, the McKennas appealed.

ROBERTS, J. . . . The common-law principles governing the liability of an [employer] for injury sustained by his servants are applicable generally to cases involving injury to domestic servants, and accordingly an [employer] is required to exercise reasonable care to provide such servants with reasonably safe places in which to work. . . . An employer of a domestic servant may be liable for the injury of such servant when it results from his failure to exercise reasonable care for the servant's safety while engaged in the scope of the employment, so long as the servant has not assumed the risk of the danger in question and is not guilty of negligence that contributes to his injury.

While there is authority to the contrary, it is our opinion that in appropriate circumstances the obligation to furnish a reasonably safe place in which the servant may work extends to outside walks or passages rendered dangerous by accumulations of ice or snow. Many cases which upon examination appear to hold to the contrary are distinguishable in that the walks or passages where the snow or ice accumulated were not in fact areas within which the servant was required to work, usually being walks used for ingress and egress or other incidental purposes not work connected.

In the instant case, however, the walk upon which plaintiff fell was part of defendants' premises within which her duties were to be performed, in part at least. Therefore, it was the duty of defendants to keep it reasonably safe for such use. . . . That plaintiff may not have been required to empty the basket in times of inclement weather is not material here, the fact being that she made use of the walk in the performance of her duties at the time she was injured by the fall. If that fall was a result of defendants' failure to act reasonably to keep the walk safe for such use, they are liable for her injury unless she had assumed the risk of that condition as being part of her employment or was so negligent in using the walk as to contribute to her own injury. . . .

The defendants' contention that plaintiff was contributorily negligent as a matter of law rests upon her action in using the walk, knowing of its icy condition. This, they contend, was not the action of a reasonably prudent person in the same circumstances. Primary reliance is placed upon plaintiff's testimony that as she entered the yard to go to the incinerator, she saw the icy pavement and noticed that it was not sanded. She testified also: "I had been over it before and I thought I could go over it again because I was doing my work." When asked if at that moment she had "decided to take a chance," she replied: "I didn't think it was going to be a chance, I thought I was going to get through." We cannot accept the contention that this establishes that plaintiff was contributorily negligent as a matter of law.

[Judgment directed in favor of plaintiff.]

Panagos v North Detroit General Hospital

35 Mich App 554, 192 NY2d 542 (1971)

Ruth Panagos was employed by the North Detroit General Hospital. While eating lunch in the hospital cafeteria, she cut her mouth on a foreign particle contained in a piece of pie which she had purchased in the cafeteria. She sued the hospital for damages. The defendant moved to dismiss the claim on the theory that any claim of the plaintiff could only be asserted as a workmen's compensation claim. The trial court refused to dismiss the action. Judgment

was entered for the plaintiff. The defendant appealed.

BURNS, P.J. . . . Did the trial court err in denying the motion to dismiss which was based on the ground that the Workmen's Compensation Department has exclusive original jurisdiction to determine whether an injury arose out of and in the course of employment with defendant?

MCLA § 412.1 (Stat Ann 1968 Rev § 17.151) provides in part: "Section 1. An employee, who receives a personal injury arising out of and in the course of his employment by an employer who is at the time of such injury subject to the provisions of this act, shall be paid compensation in the manner and to the extent hereinafter provided."

Defendant contends that the Workmen's Compensation Department has exclusive jurisdiction to determine whether an injury arose "out of and in the course of" plaintiff's employment. Thus, contends defendant, it is the Department which determines whether any given injury is within the purview of the Workmen's Compensation Act.

In Herman v Theis (1968), 10 Mich App 684, 160 NW2d 365, plaintiff was injured when he fell asleep while driving home. He brought a tort action against his employer contending that the employer was negligent in overworking the plaintiff. The court stated:

"Plaintiff states in his brief to this Court that the injuries may have arisen 'out of' his employment by defendant, but denies that they were 'in the course of' his employment and reminds us that defendant also denied this in his answer. This Court will not engage in this evaluation of the facts of any of the merits of the claim, as such issues were not decided by a lower court or board, and we find that plaintiff's 'opinion' is mere conjecture, unsupported by any decision which we could re-examine. Jurisdiction for the determination of those issues concerning exclusiveness and conditions of liability initially must lie with the compensation department and plaintiff may not waive such jurisdiction by filing an action at law and merely stating that C.L.S. 1961, § 412.1 (Stat. Ann. 1960 Rev. § 17.151) does not apply to his situation. Rather, the workmen's compensation department is the forum which properly considers questions of employment relationship, injury, and compensation (C.L. 1948, § 413.16 [Stat. Ann. 1960 Rev. § 17.190]), and it must determine whether its jurisdiction is proper, based on findings of 'exclusiveness' and 'conditions of liability,' the decision concerning the jurisdiction then being appealable to the appeal board and the courts, if plaintiff disagrees, as he does here. The question as to 'out of and in the course of' is one of fact, and not of law, and it is the function of the department to consider the facts and circumstances in determining 'exclusive' jurisdiction. . . .

'Based upon the bare allegations of plaintiff's declaration we cannot and should not venture an answer as to whether or not such arose out of and in the course of employment. This is more properly a matter for determination of the workmen's compensation department, if such forum is yet available to plaintiff.' " Herman v Theis, supra, at 689, 690, 160 NW 2d at 368.

Defendant contends that the above language by this Court stands for the proposition that the question of whether a given injury arose "out of and in the course of employment" must first be decided by the Workmen's Compensation Board before any resort to the courts may be had. However, the Court stated at p 691, 160 NW2d at p 369:

"To accept plaintiff's argument would be to deny the employer the right to have his liability *as an employer* determined by the forum established by statute to determine it whenever the plaintiff believed that the department might not agree that such a relationship existed. Thus, we have found that a plaintiff's remedy against an employer based on an injury allegedly arising out of an employment relationship properly belongs within the Workmen's Compensation Department for initial determination as to jurisdiction and liability."

In Herman, plaintiff's cause of action was based upon the employment relationship. Plaintiff contended that defendant overworked the plaintiff thus causing him to fall asleep while driving his car and to injure himself.

In the case at bar plaintiff's cause of action is not based upon the fact that she was employed by the defendant hospital. The case is based entirely upon the fact that there was deleterious material in a piece of pie which she had purchased in her employer's cafeteria.

The court in Herman quoted the following from a concurring opinion in Totten v Detroit Aluminum & Brass Corporation (1955), 344 Mich 414, 419, 73 NW2d 882:

" 'It is also conceivable that there are circumstances under which an employee may recover damages based on the negligence of his employer, or his workmen, entirely unrelated to the relationship of employee which the claimant bears to the defendant employer.' " Herman v Theis, supra, p 691, 160 NW2d p 369.

Plaintiff's present case is based upon the vendor-vendee relationship. The whole theory of the cause of action has nothing to do with the fact that plaintiff also happened to be employed by the defendant. We see no need for plaintiff to first seek relief from the Workmen's Compensation Department when it is clear that the employee-employer relationship is unrelated to the cause of action. Nor do we find any statutory mandate which would require a plaintiff to first appear before the Workmen's Compensation Department just because the defendant is also the plaintiff's employer. . . .

[Judgment affirmed.]

United States v Romitti

(CA9 Cal) 363 F2d 662 (1966)

Moore was an electronics engineer employed by the United States. While traveling under a work assignment from one air base to another, he ran into and injured Romitti, who then sued the United States under the Federal Tort Claims Act. The United States defended on the ground that Moore was not acting within the course of his employment while driving to the new job assignment and that accordingly the United States was not liable as an employer. From a judgment in favor of Romitti, the government appealed.

BROWNING, J. . . . All agree that the question presented is whether under the doctrine of respondeat superior as applied in California (where Mr. Moore's negligent act occurred) a private employer would be liable for plaintiff's injuries in the circumstances of this case. . . .

The evidence was as follows. Mr. Moore was employed by the United States as an electronics engineer assigned to Edwards Air Force Base, Kern County, California. Edwards Air Force Base maintained a secondary facility for parachute testing near El Centro, California, about 240 miles away. Mr. Moore and two other government employees . . . were ordered to travel from the Kern County base to the El Centro base "to support physiological jump tests for Dyna Soar Program," and then to return to the base in Kern County. They were authorized to travel by government or commercial carrier, either air or surface, or by privately owned automobile. Travel by private automobile was "authorized between Edwards Air Force Base, California and El Centro, California, and return, only," and was to be reimbursed at the rate of 10 cents per mile. Per diem was authorized in the amount of $16 per day, including travel time. The total cost attributable to travel was not to exceed what the cost would have been if first-class rail transportation were used.

After working at their regular duty stations during the morning of July 11, 1962, the three men left their office building about noon to drive to the El Centro facility in Mr. Moore's car. They took with them, for use in the scheduled parachute test, two electronic devices (valued at $6,600 each) and certain hand tools, all belonging to the government. They drove directly to El Centro, arrived about 5:00 p.m., and checked in at a local motel. There they met with the parachutist and with representatives of the manufacturer of the electronic equipment which was to be tested. The test could not be held the next day because of bad weather; on the second morning the men drove to the test site with the equipment and the test was conducted. Mr. Moore's car was used in carrying the men and their equipment about the base—a proper and compensable use of the vehicle under the employer's orders.

The men then returned to the motel, packed, and began the return trip to the Kern County base, transporting the electronic equipment, the hand tools, and the test data recorded on two rolls of magnetic tape and one roll of graph tape. They started the return journey between 10:30 and 11:00 a.m. The accident occurred at 1:30 p.m. on the direct route between the El Centro and the Kern County bases. There was testimony that if the men had arrived late in the afternoon, they could have proceeded directly to their homes, but their vacation time would have been reduced by the number of hours remaining in the workday. Mr. Rathburn, the only one of the three men who survived the accident, testified that they intended to return directly to the Kern County base, as indeed their orders appeared to require, and that they expected to arrive during regular duty hours.

To summarize, the trier of fact had before it evidence that Mr. Moore was traveling on direct orders of his employer and for the sole purpose of serving his employer's business; that he was transporting property of the employer and fellow employees (including his supervisor), both necessary to the performance of that business; that he was traveling on the most direct route between two of his employer's work locations; that he was using an expressly authorized means of transportation; that he was driving during regular working hours; and that he was being paid his regular salary plus per diem, plus costs of transportation. This was enough to support a finding that Moore's negligence occurred "in the transaction of the business of the agency," and therefore to justify the conclusion that a private employer would be liable under California law. . . .

We are satisfied that the trial court could properly conclude that when the accident occurred during the return trip to the Kern County base, Mr. Moore was serving the business of his employer. . . ; that he was engaged in his employer's work, and not in going to or coming from it. . . ; and that his employer was therefore liable for his negligent acts.

[Judgment affirmed.]

Fisher v Church of St. Mary

(Wyo) 497 P2d 882 (1972)

Fisher was employed by the St. Mary's school as a teacher. Her employment was terminated because of physical disability. She sued the school for breach of contract. The case was tried without a jury. The trial court found in favor of the employer. Fisher appealed from the judgment.

McIntyre, C.J. . . . According to the contract in question, Mrs. Fisher agreed to teach in Saint Mary's school system for ten months commencing August 31, 1970. She was to be paid a salary of $5,800 for the year, payable in ten monthly installments. She performed under the contract to November 12, 1970, at which time she suffered a cerebral hemorrhage and underwent surgery. As a result, Mrs. Fisher was hospitalized until December 13, 1970. She was again hospitalized from December 18 to December 28, 1970.

The plaintiff was paid her full salary through the month of November. For December and January she was paid the difference between her full salary and that of a substitute teacher. There is no dispute concerning any of these months. The school then hired a full-time replacement for Mrs. Fisher commencing February 1, 1971, and plaintiff's salary was terminated as of that date.

Plaintiff acknowledges she was unable to resume her teaching duties prior to April 1, 1971, but she claims she announced to defendant her intention and readiness to resume teaching as of that time. Therefore, she asserts, without qualification, her right to damages equal to her full salary for April, May and June of 1971. She suggests, apparently with some doubts about her right thereto, that she should also receive the difference between her salary and the amount paid for a substitute for the months of February and March, 1971. . . .

. . . [Was] the trial court . . . justified in finding, from the evidence before it, that plaintiff had failed to perform a sufficient portion of her contract to warrant termination on account of illness; and did the defendant in fact terminate the contract?

. . . Contracts to perform personal acts are considered as made on the implied condition that the party shall be alive and capable of performing the contract, so that death or disability, including sickness, will operate as a discharge, termination of the contract, or excuse for nonperformance.

. . . Until illness has continued long enough to be material, a contract for personal services cannot be terminated.

However, after the breach has become material or the prospective incapacity is such as to justify termination, the employer has an election to continue the contract or to terminate it. . . .

. . . If the [employment] agreement is silent on the subject, temporary disability of short duration as compared with the term of service contemplated does not of itself warrant termination of the contract. However, illness of long duration whereby the employee is rendered unable to substantially perform his duties permits the employer to treat the agreement as terminated.

. . . There is no fixed or certain formula by which it may always be determined whether the illness constitutes sufficient justification for the employer to terminate. The nature of the business and duties required by the contract, the character and possible duration of the illness, the necessities of the employer, to what extent the duties can for a time be performed by another and many other circumstances may enter into and materially influence the right to terminate.

. . . Whether justification exists for termination of a contract, under the facts and circumstances of a particular case, is usually a question of fact for the fact finder. . . .

. . . We must conclude: Whether Mrs. Fisher's employment for a ten-month period could be rightly terminated by Saint Mary's School on account of her illness and disability was a matter dependent upon such factors as length of the term, nature of the services, length of illness and nature of disability; and, while a mere temporary illness ordinarily is not sufficient reason for termination of her contract, illness and disability for such length of time as to cause serious inconvenience or injury to the school would be sufficient reason for termination of her contract.

. . . It was a question of fact for the trier to decide whether Mrs. Fisher's inability to perform was for a sufficient duration, under the circumstances of this case, to warrant termination of her contract because of illness.

It is apparent that one of the considerations in deciding what action the school would take was the length of service Mrs. Fisher had rendered and the future services she could be expected to render. Thus, the school indicated its willingness to continue plaintiff's tenure through the 1970-1971 school year if her services would be available for the following school year. On March 16, 1971, however, Mrs. Fisher advised she would not teach for Saint Mary's in the 1971-1972 school year. The school then advised plaintiff, by a letter dated March 30, 1971, that the relationship between them was terminated in all respects.

It is undisputed that Mrs. Fisher had taught two months and 12 days on her ten-month contract when she suffered her cerebral hemorrhage. She agrees she could not have returned to work before April 1, 1971. Thus, admittedly, she would have had to be absent from her duties because of illness four months and 18 days. We cannot say as a matter of law that the trial court was wrong in treating an absence of four months and 18 days a sufficient portion of the ten-month contract to materially inconvenience and injure the school and to justify termination. . . .

[Judgment affirmed.]

QUESTIONS AND CASE PROBLEMS

1. An employer provided an annual outing for his employees, which was held on a working day. Any employee not attending the outing was required to report to work as usual. An employee was killed on the outing. Was his death covered by workmen's compensation? [Lybrand, Ross Bros. & Montgomery v Industrial Commission, 36 Ill 2d 410, 223 NE2d 150]
2. Faunce was employed by the Boost Co., which manufactured a soft drink. After some years he left its employ and began manufacturing a different soft

drink. The company claimed that he was using trade secrets learned while he was in its employ and sought to enjoin him. It was proved that the soft drink made by the defendant was not the same as that made by the plaintiff; that the difference between one soft drink and another was primarily due to the one percent of the volume that represented flavoring; and that the drink made by the defendant could be made by anyone in the soft drink business on the basis of general knowledge of the trade. Was Boost entitled to an injunction? [Boost Co. v Faunce, 17 NJ Super 458, 86 A2d 283]

3. Thouron did part-time housework in Acree's home in return for an hourly pay and free transportation to and from her home in Acree's automobile driven by Acree's full-time chauffeur. While she was being driven to Acree's house to work, there was a collision because of the chauffeur's negligence. Thouron sued Acree for damages caused by the negligence of the latter's chauffeur. The workmen's compensation law was not applicable since it excluded domestic employees. The liability of the employer was thus governed by common law. Decide. [Thouron v Acree, 54 Del 117, 174 A2d 702]

4. Complitano was an employee of Steel & Alloy Tank Co. The city in which the plant was located sponsored a softball league. Complitano and other employees of Steel & Alloy formed a team which represented the employer in the league. All games were played after hours and off the premises and were managed and controlled in all respects by the employees. Steel Alloy made a financial contribution to the support of the team but had no other interest in it. Complitano was injured while playing in one of the games and filed a claim for workmen's compensation on the theory that the activity was of mutual benefit to the employer and the claimant. Decide. [Complitano v Steel & Alloy Tank Co., 63 NJ Super 444, 164 A2d 792]

5. Baugh was employed by the Lummus Cotton Gin Co. The contract of employment stated that his employment was "conditional on . . . conduct and service being satisfactory to us, we to be the sole judge. . . ." After some time the company discharged Baugh solely because it could not afford to employ him longer. Baugh sued the company. Was it liable for breach of contract? [Lummus Cotton Gin Co. v Baugh, 29 Ga App 498, 116 SE 51]

6. Buffo was employed by the Baltimore & Ohio Railroad Co. With a number of other workers he was removing old brakes from railroad cars and replacing them with new brakes. In the course of the work, rivet heads and scrap from the brakes accumulated on the tracks under the cars, but these were removed only occasionally when the men had time. Buffo, while holding an air hammer in both arms, was crawling under a car when his foot slipped on scrap on the ground, which caused him to strike and injure his knee. He sued the railroad for damages under the Federal Employers' Liability Act. Decide. [Buffo v Baltimore & Ohio Railroad Co., 364 Pa 437, 72 A2d 593]

7. The Central Lumber Co. furnished material to Schroeder for the construction of certain buildings. It also loaned her $465 to enable her to pay the men working in the construction. A mechanics' lien law gave a lien to persons furnishing materials, machinery, or fixtures for the construction of buildings. Was the company entitled to a lien for the $465? [Central Lumber Co. v Schroeder, 164 La 759, 114 So 644]

44 Creation and Termination

NATURE AND CREATION

Modern partnership law shows traces of Roman law, the law merchant, and the common law of England. A Uniform Partnership Act (UPA) has been adopted in most states.[1]

§ 44:1. Definition. The single proprietorship is the most common form of business organization, but many larger businesses have two or more owners. The partnership is a common type of multiple ownership.

A *partnership* or copartnership is a legal relationship created by the voluntary "association of two or more persons to carry on as co-owners a business for profit."[2] The persons so associated are called *partners*.

§ 44:2. Characteristics of a Partnership. A partnership can be described in terms of its characteristics:

(1) A partnership is a voluntary contractual relation; it is not imposed by law. Because of the intimate and confidential nature of the partnership relation, courts do not attempt to thrust a partner upon anyone.

(2) The relation of partnership usually involves contributions by the members of capital, labor, or skill, or a combination of these.

(3) The parties are associated as co-owners and principals to transact the business of the firm.

(4) A partnership is organized for the pecuniary profit of its members. If profit is not its object, the group will commonly be an unincorporated association.

The trend of the law is to treat a partnership as a separate legal person,[3] although historically and technically it is merely a group of individuals with each partner being the owner of a fractional interest in the common enterprise.

When a bank accepts a partnership as a depositor, the bank must treat the deposit as belonging to the partnership and cannot treat it as property of the individual partners.[4] Some courts also regard a partnership as distinct

[1] This Act has been adopted in all states except Georgia, Louisiana, and Mississippi; and it is in force in the District of Columbia, Guam, and the Virgin Islands.

[2] Uniform Partnership Act, § 6(1); Carle v Carle Tool & Engineering Co., 33 NJ Super 469, 110 A2d 568.

[3] Mendonca Dairy v Mauldin, (Okla) 420 P2d 552.

[4] Loucks v Albuquerque National Bank, 76 NMex 735, 418 P2d 191.

from the individual partners so that a partnership cannot claim the benefit of a personal immunity possessed by an individual partner. (See p. 887, Mathews v Wosek.)

Since a partnership is based upon the agreement of the parties, the characteristics and attributes of the partnership relationship are initially a matter of the application of general principles of contract law, upon which the principles of partnership law are superimposed.

§ 44:3. Purposes of a Partnership. A partnership, whether it relates to the conduct of a business or a profession, may be formed for any lawful purpose. A partnership cannot be formed to carry out immoral or illegal acts, or acts that are contrary to public policy. When there is an illegal purpose, the partners cannot sue on the contracts that involve the illegality. Moreover, in such cases the partners cannot seek the aid of courts to settle their affairs among themselves. In addition, if the conduct of the partnership constitutes a crime, all persons involved in the commission of the crime are subject to punishment.

§ 44:4. Classification of Partnerships. Ordinary partnerships are classified as general and special partnerships, and as trading and nontrading partnerships.

(1) General and Special Partnerships. A *general partnership* is created for the general conduct of a particular kind of business, such as a hardware business or a manufacturing business.[5] A *special partnership* is formed for a single transaction, such as the purchase and resale of a certain building.

(2) Trading and Nontrading Partnerships. A *trading partnership* is organized for the purpose of buying and selling, such as a firm engaged in the retail grocery business. A *nontrading partnership* is one organized for a purpose other than engaging in commerce, such as the practice of law or medicine.

§ 44:5. Firm Name. In the absence of a statutory requirement, a partnership need not have a firm name, although it is customary to have one. The partners may, as a general rule, adopt any firm name they desire. They may use a fictitious name or even the name of a stranger. There are, however, certain limitations upon the adoption of a firm name:

(1) The name cannot be the same as or deceptively similar to the name of another firm for the purpose of attracting its patrons.

(2) Some states prohibit the use of the words "and company" unless they indicate an additional partner.

(3) Most states require the registration of a fictitious partnership name.

---

[5] A general partnership has been held to be an "association" within a statute specifying the county in which lawsuits were to be brought against a "private corporation, an association, or a joint stock company." Hudgens v Bain Equipment & Tube Sales, Inc., (Tex Civ App) 459 SW2d 873.

§ 44:6. Classification of Partners. (1) A *general partner* is one who publicly and actively engages in the transaction of firm business.

(2) A *nominal partner* holds himself out as a partner or permits others to hold him out as such. He is not in fact a partner, but in some instances he may be held liable as a partner.

(3) A *silent partner* is one who, although he may be known to the public as a partner, takes no active part in the business.

(4) A *secret partner* is one who takes an active part in the management of the firm but who is not known to the public as a partner.

(5) A *dormant partner* is one who takes no active part in transacting the business and who remains unknown to the public.

§ 44:7. Who May Be Partners. In the absence of statutory provisions to the contrary, persons who are competent to contract may form a partnership. A minor may become a partner, but he may avoid the contract of partnership and withdraw.

In general, the capacity of an insane person to be a partner is similar to that of a minor, except that an adjudication of insanity usually makes subsequent agreements void rather than merely voidable. An enemy alien may not be a partner, but other aliens may enter into the relation. A corporation, unless expressly authorized by statute or its certificate of incorporation, may not act as a partner. The modern statutory trend, however, is to permit corporations to become partners.

§ 44:8. Creation of Partnership. A partnership is a voluntary association and exists because the parties agree to be in partnership. If there is no agreement, there is no partnership. If the parties agree that the legal relationship between them shall be such that they in fact operate a business for profit as co-owners, a partnership is created even though the parties may not have labeled their new relationship a "partnership."[6] The law is concerned with the substance of what is done rather than the name. Conversely, a partnership does not arise if the parties do not agree to the elements of a partnership, even though they call it a partnership. Thus, the fact that an agreement described the signers as constituting a "partnership" did not make them a partnership when in fact they were not operating a business as co-owners for profit.[7]

The manner in which an enterprise is described in a tax return or an application for a license is significant in determining whether it is a partnership as against a person making the return or the application. The mere fact that the enterprise is described as a partnership is not controlling or binding, however, as against a person named in the return or the application as a partner if he did not know of its preparation, did not sign it, and did not know what it said.[8] When the parties are in fact employer and employee, there is

[6] Kaufnan-Brown Potato Co. v Long, (CA9 Cal) 182 F2d 594.
[7] Havens v Woodfill, 148 Ind App 366, 266 NE2d 221.
[8] Bates v Morris, (Mo App) 467 SW2d 286.

no partnership (see p. 888, Chaiken v Employment Security Commission), even though the employer had filed a partnership form of income tax return.[9]

§ 44:9. Partnership Agreement. As a general rule, partnership agreements need not be in writing.[10] A partnership agreement must be in writing, however, if it is within the provision of the statute of frauds that a contract which cannot be performed within one year must be in writing. In some situations the agreement may come under the provision of the statute that requires a transfer of interest in land to be in writing. Generally, however, the agreement need not be written solely because the partnership is formed to engage in the business of buying and selling real estate.

Even when unnecessary, it is always desirable to have the partnership agreement in writing to avoid subsequent controversies as to mutual rights and duties. The formal document that is prepared to evidence the contract of the parties is termed a *partnership agreement, articles of partnership,* or *articles of copartnership.*

§ 44:10. Determining Existence of Partnership. Whether a partnership exists is basically a matter of proving the intention of the parties.[11]

As in the case of agency, the burden of proving the existence of a partnership is upon the person who claims that one exists.[12] Thus, a son has the burden of proving that he is a partner and not the employee of his father and brother who run a family business.[13]

When the parties have not clearly indicated the nature of their relationship, the law has developed the following guides to aid in determining whether the parties have created a partnership:

(1) Control. The presence or absence of control of a business enterprise is significant in determining whether there is a partnership and whether a particular person is a partner.

(2) Sharing Profits and Losses. The fact that the parties share profits and losses is strong evidence of a partnership.

(3) Sharing Profits. An agreement that does not provide for sharing losses but does provide for sharing profits is evidence that the parties are united in partnership, since it is assumed that they will also share losses.[14] The UPA provides that sharing profits is prima facie evidence of a partnership; but a partnership is not to be inferred when profits are received in payment (a) of a debt, (b) of wages, (c) of rent, (d) of an annuity to a deceased partner's widow or representative, (e) of interest, or (f)

---

[9] Terry v Slidell Refrigerating & Heating, Inc., (La App) 271 So2d 536.
[10] First National Bank v Chambers, (Tex Civ App) 398 SW2d 313.
[11] Jaworsky v LeBlanc, (La App) 239 So2d 176.
[12] Jewell v Harper, 199 Ore 223, 258 P2d 115.
[13] Falkner v Falkner, 24 Mich App 633, 180 NW2d 491.
[14] Bengston v Shain, 42 Wash 2d 404, 255 P2d 892.

for the goodwill of the business.[15] The fact that one doctor receives one half of the net income does not establish that he is a partner of another doctor where he was guaranteed a minimum annual amount and federal income tax and social security contributions were deducted, thus indicating that the relationship was employer and employee.[16] If there is no evidence of the reason for receiving the profits, a partnership of the parties involved exists.

(4) Gross Returns. The sharing of gross returns is of itself very slight, if any, evidence of partnership. To illustrate, in a case in which one party owned a show that was exhibited upon land owned by another under an agreement to divide the gross proceeds, no partnership was proved because there was no co-ownership or community of interest in the business. Similarly, it was not established that there was a partnership when it was shown that a farmer rented his airplane to a pilot to do aerial chemical spraying under an arrangement by which the pilot would pay the farmer, as compensation for the use of the plane, a share of the fees which the pilot received.[17]

(5) Co-ownership. Neither the co-ownership of property nor the sharing of profits or rents from property which two or more persons own creates a partnership.

(6) Contribution of Property. The fact that all persons have not contributed property to the enterprise does not establish that the enterprise is not a partnership. A partnership may be formed even though some of its members furnish only skill or labor.[18]

(7) Fixed Payment. When a person who performs continuing service for another person receives a fixed payment for his services, not dependent upon the existence of profits and not affected by losses, he is not a partner.[19]

§ 44:11. Partners as to Third Persons. In some instances a person who is in fact not a partner or a member of a partnership may be held accountable to third persons as though he were a partner. This liability arises when a person conducts himself in such a manner that third persons are reasonably led to believe that he is a partner and to act in reliance on that belief to their injury.[20] The person who incurs such a liability is termed a nominal partner, a partner by estoppel, or an ostensible partner.

Partnership liability may arise by estoppel when a person who in fact is not a partner is described as a partner in a document filed with the government, provided the person so described has in some way participated in the filing of the document and the person claiming the benefit of the estoppel had

---

15 UPA § 7(4).
16 Moscatelli v Nordstrom, 40 App Div 2d 903, 337 NYS2d 575.
17 Ward Brothers v Crowe, (La App) 240 So2d 797.
18 Watson v Watson, 231 Ind 385, 108 NE2d 893.
19 Odess v Taylor, 282 Ala 389, 211 So2d 805.
20 UPA § 16(1).

knowledge of that document and relied on the statement. For example, suppose that the partnership of *A* and *B*, in registering its fictitious name, names *A*, *B*, and *C* as partners and the registration certificate is signed by all of them. If a creditor who sees this registration statement extends credit to the firm in reliance in part on the fact that *C* is a partner, *C* has a partner's liability insofar as that creditor is concerned.

Conversely, no estoppel arises when the creditor does not know of the existence of the registration certificate and consequently does not rely thereon in extending credit to the partnership.[21] Likewise, such liability does not arise when *C* does not know that he was described as a partner.

(1) Effect of Estoppel. The existence of a partnership by estoppel means only that the fact of nonpartnership cannot be raised as a defense against a third person in whose favor the estoppel operates. That is, when creditor *C* sues *A* and claims that *A* is liable for the debt of the partnership because *A* is a partner, *A* cannot show that he is not a partner or that there is no partnership. In contrast, this estoppel does not make the apparent partner a member of a partnership when in fact there is no partnership. Consequently, the fact that the third person is protected does not entitle the apparent partner to a share of profits earned by the other persons who appear to be his partners, because the fact remains that the apparent partner and the others are not partners. (See p. 890, Smith v Kelley.)

§ 44:12. Partnership Property. In general, partnership property consists of all the property contributed by the partners or acquired for the firm or with its funds.[22] There is usually no limitation upon the kind and amount of property that a partnership may acquire. The firm may own real as well as personal property, unless it is prohibited from doing so by statute or by the partnership agreement.

The parties may agree that real estate owned by one of the partners should become partnership property. When this intent exists, the particular property constitutes partnership property even though it is still in the name of the original owner.[23]

(1) Title to Personal Property in Firm Name. A partnership may hold and transfer the title to personal property in the firm name, whether the name is fictitious or consists of the names of living people. Thus, a partnership may hold a mortgage on personal property in the firm name, such as "Keystone Cleaners."

(2) Title to Real Property in Firm Name. A majority of states now permit a partnership to hold or transfer the title to real property in the firm name alone, without regard to whether or not that name is fictitious.[24]

---

[21] Reisen Lumber & Millwork Co. v Simonelli, 98 NJ Super 335, 237 A2d 303.
[22] UPA § 8; All Florida Sand v Lawler Construction Co., 209 Ga 720, 75 SE2d 559.
[23] Cyrus v Cyrus, 242 Minn 180, 64 NW2d 538.
[24] UPA § 8(3), (4).

(3) Transferees of Firm's Real Property. In order for a transfer of a firm's real property to be technically correct, (a) it must have been made by a partner or agent with the authority to make the transfer and (b) it must have been made in the name of the holder of the title. When both conditions have been satisfied, the transferee has legal title as against the partnership.

If the transfer was authorized but was not made in the name of the title holder, the transferee acquires equitable title to the property and the right to have a proper instrument of conveyance executed. When the transfer of the partnership property was not authorized, the firm may recover the property from the transferee if he knew that it was firm property or if he did not purchase it for value. When the title to the firm property is recorded but not in the name of the firm, a person who purchases from the record holder in good faith, for value, and without notice or knowledge of the partnership title, may keep the property.

A conveyance by a partner of partnership property, even though without authority, cannot be recovered by the partnership where it has been conveyed by the grantee to a holder for value and without notice or knowledge that the partner, in making the conveyance, had exceeded his authority.[25]

(4) Title to Partnership Property in Name of Individual Partner. Frequently property that in fact is partnership property appears of record as owned by one of the partners. This may arise when the property in question was owned by that individual before the partnership was formed and, while he contributed the property to the partnership when it was organized, he never went through the formality of transferring title to the partnership. The situation may also arise when a member of an existing partnership uses partnership funds to acquire property and, either through a clerical mistake or in order to deceive his partners, takes title in his own name. In such cases the partner holding the title will be treated as a trustee holding the property for the benefit and use of the partnership,[26] just as though the property were held in the name of the firm.

§ 44:13. Tenancy in Partnership. Partners hold firm property by *tenancy in partnership.*[27] The characteristics of such a tenancy are:

(1) In the absence of contrary agreement, all partners have equal right to use firm property for partnership purposes.

(2) A partner possesses no interest in any specific portion of the partnership property that he can sell, assign, or mortgage.[28] The partner has no right in any specific property that he can transfer to a third person, although he may transfer his interest in specific property to his sole surviving partner.

---

[25] Turner v Turner, 131 Vt 253, 305 A2d 592.
[26] Henderson v Henderson, 219 Ga 310, 133 SE2d 251.
[27] UPA § 25(1); Williams v Dovell, 202 Md 646, 96 A2d 484.
[28] Cook v Lauten, 1 Ill App 2d 255, 117 NE2d 414.

(3) In most states the creditors of a partner cannot levy on and sell his interest in specific partnership property.[29] (See p. 891, Tom Nakamura, Inc. v G & G Produce Company, Inc.)

(4) The interest of a deceased partner in specific firm property vests in the surviving partners only for partnership purposes.

(5) A partner's interest in specific property is not subject on his death to any rights of his surviving spouse.

This distinct form of tenure is sometimes confused with joint tenancies and tenancies in common. The ordinary joint tenant has full beneficial ownership upon the death of the cotenant, whereas a surviving partner does not. A cotenant may transfer his interest, putting another in his place, but a partner cannot do so.

DISSOLUTION AND TERMINATION

§ 44:14. Effect of Dissolution. Dissolution ends the right of the partnership to exist as a going concern. It is followed by a winding-up period, upon the conclusion of which the partnership's legal existence is terminated.

§ 44:15. Dissolution by Act of Parties.

(1) Agreement. A partnership may be dissolved in accordance with the terms of the original agreement of the parties, as by the expiration of the period for which the relation was to continue or by the performance of the object for which it was organized.[30] The relation may also be dissolved by subsequent agreement, as when the partners agree to dissolve the firm before the lapse of the time specified in the articles of partnership or before the attainment of the object for which the firm was created. The sale or assignment by one partner of his interest to the remaining partners does not in itself dissolve the partnership.

(2) Withdrawal. A partner has the power to withdraw at any time; but if his withdrawal violates his agreement, he becomes liable to his copartners for damages for breach of contract. When the relation is for no definite purpose or time, a partner may withdraw without liability at any time,[31] unless a sudden withdrawal would do irreparable damage to the firm.

(3) Expulsion. A partnership is dissolved by the expulsion of any partner from the business bona fide in accordance with such a power conferred by the agreement between the partners.

(4) Alienation of Interest. Under the UPA neither a voluntary sale[32] nor an involuntary sale for the benefit of creditors[33] works a dissolution of the partnership. A minority of states follow the contrary rule of the common law under which such sales dissolve the firm.

---

[29] UPA § 25(2)(c).
[30] § 31(1)(a).
[31] Butler v Thomasson, (Tex Civ App) 256 SW2d 936.
[32] UPA § 27.
[33] § 28.

§ 44:16. Dissolution by Operation of Law.

(1) Death. An ordinary partnership is dissolved immediately upon the death of any partner,[34] even when the agreement provides for the continuance of the business. Thus, when the executor of a deceased partner carries on the business with the remaining partner, there is legally a new firm.

(2) Bankruptcy. Bankruptcy of the firm or of one of the partners causes the dissolution of the firm; insolvency alone does not.

(3) Illegality. A partnership is dissolved "by any event which makes it unlawful for the business of the partnership to be carried on or for the members to carry it on in partnership." [35] To illustrate, when it is made unlawful by statute for judges to engage in the practice of law, a law firm is dissolved when one of its members becomes a judge.

(4) War. A firm is ordinarily dissolved when there is war between the governments to which the different partners owe allegiance.

§ 44:17. Dissolution by Decree of Court. When a partnership is to continue for a certain time, there are several situations in which one partner is permitted to obtain its dissolution through a decree of court. A court will not order the dissolution for trifling causes or temporary grievances that do not involve a permanent harm or injury to the partnership.

(1) Insanity. A partner may obtain a decree of dissolution when his partner has been judicially declared a lunatic or when it is shown that he is of unsound mind.

(2) Incapacity. A decree of dissolution will be granted when one partner becomes in any way incapable of performing the terms of the partnership agreement. For example, a serious injury to one partner making it physically impossible for him to do his part is a ground for dissolution.

(3) Misconduct. A partner may obtain a decree of dissolution when his partner has been guilty of conduct that substantially tends to affect prejudicially the continuance of the business. The habitual drunkenness of a partner is a sufficient cause for judicial dissolution.

(4) Impracticability. A partner may obtain a decree of dissolution when another partner habitually or purposely commits a breach of the partnership contract or so conducts himself in matters relating to the partnership business that it is not reasonably practicable to carry on the business in partnership with him. Dissolution will be granted where dissensions are so serious and persistent as to make continuance impracticable, or where all confidence and cooperation between the parties have been destroyed.[36]

---

[34] Hurley v Hurley, 33 Del Ch 231, 91 A2d 674; Lamp v Lempfert, 259 Iowa 902, 146 NW2d 241.

[35] UPA § 31(3).

[36] First Western Mortgage Co. v Hotel Gearhart, 260 Ore 196, 488 P2d 450.

(5) Lack of Success. A decree of dissolution will be granted when the partnership cannot be continued except at a loss.

(6) Equitable Circumstances. A decree of dissolution will be granted under any other circumstances that equitably call for a dissolution. A situation of this kind, for example, is present when one partner has been induced by fraud to enter into partnership.

§ 44:18. Notice of Dissolution. The rule that dissolution terminates the authority of the partners to act for the firm requires some modification. Under some circumstances one partner may continue to possess the power to make a binding contract.

(1) Notice to Partners. When the firm is dissolved by an act of a partner, notice must be given to the other partners unless his act clearly shows an intent to withdraw from or to dissolve the firm. If he acts without notice to his partners, he is bound as between them upon contracts created for the firm. The UPA declares that "where the dissolution is caused by the act, death, or bankruptcy of a partner, each partner is liable to his co-partners for his share of any liability created by any partner acting for the partnership as if the partnership had not been dissolved unless (a) the dissolution being by act of any partner, the partner acting for the partnership had knowledge of the dissolution, or (b) the dissolution being by the death or bankruptcy of a partner, the partner acting for the partnership had knowledge or notice of the death or bankruptcy." [37]

(2) Notice to Third Persons. When dissolution is caused by the act of a partner or of the partners, notice must be given to third parties.[38] A notice should expressly state that the partnership has been dissolved. Circumstances from which a termination may be inferred are generally not sufficient notice. Thus, the fact that the partnership checks added "Inc." after the partnership name is not sufficient notice that the partnership does not exist and that the business had been incorporated.[39] (See p. 893, Phillip Lithographing Co. v Babich.)

Actual notice of dissolution must be given to persons who have dealt with the firm. To persons who know of the relation but have had no dealings with the firm, a publication of the fact is sufficient. Such notice may be by newspaper publication, by posting a placard in a public place, or by any similar method. Failure to give proper notice continues the power of each partner to bind the others in respect to third persons on contracts within the scope of the business.

When dissolution has been caused by operation of law, notice to third persons is not required. As between the partners, however, the UPA requires knowledge or notice of dissolution by death and bankruptcy. And it

---

[37] § 34.

[38] Adkins v Hash, 190 Va 86, 56 SE2d 60.

[39] Conner v Steel, Inc., 28 Colo App 1, 470 P2d 71.

has been held that when the third party dealing with the partnership is not informed of the death of a partner, the surviving partners and the firm are bound by a notice sent by the third person to the deceased partner.[40]

§ 44:19. Winding Up Partnership Affairs. In the absence of an express agreement permitting continuation of the business by the surviving partners, they must wind up the business and account for his share to any partner who has withdrawn, been expelled, or has died. If the remaining partners continue the business and use that partner's distributive share in so doing, he is entitled to such share together with interest or the profit earned thereon.

Although the partners have no authority after dissolution to create new obligations, they retain authority for acts necessary to wind up the business. (See p. 894, King v Stoddard.) With a few exceptions, all partners have the right to participate in the winding up of the business.[41]

When the firm is dissolved by the death of one partner, the partnership property vests in the surviving partners for the purpose of administration. They must collect and preserve the assets, pay the debts, and with reasonable promptness make an accounting to the representative of the deceased partner's estate. In connection with these duties, the law requires the highest degree of integrity. A partner in performing these acts cannot sell to himself any of the partnership property without the consent of the other partners.

§ 44:20. Distribution of Assets. Creditors of the firm have first claim on the assets of the partnership. Difficulty arises when there is a contest between the creditors of the firm and the creditors of the individual partners. The general rule is that firm creditors have first claim on assets of the firm, and the individual creditors share in the remaining assets, if there are any.

Conversely, creditors of the individual partners have priority in the distribution of the individual assets; the claims of the firm creditors may be satisfied out of the individual partner's assets only after claims of individual creditors are settled.

After the firm liabilities to nonpartners have been paid, the assets of the partnership are distributed as follows: (1) Each partner is entitled to a refund of advances made to or for the firm; (2) contributions to the capital of the firm are then returned; (3) the remaining assets, if any, are divided equally as profits among the partners unless there is some other agreement. If the partnership has sustained a loss, the partners share it equally in the absence of a contrary agreement.

A provision in a partnership agreement that on the death of a partner his interest shall pass to the deceased partner's widow is valid and takes effect as against the contention that it is not valid because it does not satisfy the requirements applicable to wills.[42]

---

[40] Childers v United States, (CA5 Tex) 442 F2d 1299.
[41] UPA § 37.
[42] Hillowitz Estate, 22 NY2d 107, 291 NYS2d 325, 238 NE2d 723.

§ 44:21. Continuation of Partnership Business. As a practical matter, the business of the partnership is commonly continued after dissolution and winding up. In all cases, however, there is a technical dissolution, winding up, and a termination of the life of the original partnership. If the business continues, either with the surviving partners, or with them and additional partners, it is a new partnership. Again, as a practical matter, the liquidation of the old partnership may in effect be merely a matter of bookkeeping entries with all parties in interest recontributing or relending to the new business any payment to which they would be entitled from the liquidation of the original partnership.

If any dispute arises, however, it must be determined on the basis that the original partnership had ceased to exist and that the parties in interest had reached a new partnership agreement. Thus, the executor of a deceased partner has no rights in running or winding up the business in the absence of the consent of the other partners either contained in the original partnership agreement or obtained upon the death of the partner in question. The right of such executor is limited to demanding an accounting from the surviving partners upon the completion of the winding up of the partnership affairs. Consequently, a representative of the individual estate of a deceased partner does not have any right to complete a contract between a third person and the partnership.[43]

[43] Niagara Mohawk Power Corp. v Silbergeld, 58 Misc 2d 285, 294 NYS2d 975.

CASES FOR CHAPTER 44

Mathews v Wosek

44 Mich App 706, 205 NW2d 813 (1973)

Wosek Delivery Service was a partnership composed of Richard and his wife, Kathleen. Richard was driving a partnership automobile. Mathews was a passenger in the automobile when it was struck by a train. Mathews and Wosek were acting within the scope of their employment by Love Brothers, Inc. By virtue of the appropriate workmen's compensation act, Richard Wosek as a fellow servant of Mathews could not be sued by Mathews. Mathews sued the Wosek partnership which raised the defense that as Mathews could not have sued Wosek individually, Mathews could not sue the Wosek partnership. From a judgment against him, Mathews appealed.

LEVIN, J. . . . Section 13 of the Uniform Partnership Act, reads: ". . . (Partnership bound by partner's wrongful act). Where, by any wrongful act or omission of any partner acting in the ordinary course of the business or the partnership, or with the authority of his copartners, loss or injury is caused to any person not being a partner in the partnership, or any penalty is incurred, the partnership is liable therefor *to the same extent as the partner* so acting or omitting to act." . . .

In Caplan v. Caplan, 268 N.Y. 445, 198 N.E. 23, 101 A.L.R. 1223 (1935), a wife, injured in an automobile collision caused by her husband's negligence, commenced an action against a partnership of which her husband was a member. The collision had occurred while her husband was driving on partnership business. The New York Court of Appeals ruled that the interspousal immunity of the husband also immunized the partnership from liability.

The reasoning of the New York Court focused on the nature of a partnership. The Court declared that a partnership is not a "separate entity." It stressed that the mutual liability of the partners resulted from agreement. The Court reasoned that when a tortfeasor partner is free of personal liability, and thus liability could not be truly mutual in fact, it would be anomalous to hold the other partners liable. . . .

In Eule v. Eule Motor Sales, 34 N.J. 537, 170 A2d 241 (1961), the New Jersey Supreme Court . . . ruled, on facts similar to those in the New York case of Caplan v. Caplan, *supra,* that a partnership was subject to liability. . . .

Starting from the premise that the immunity of an agent would not save a *corporation* from liability (a premise with which the New York Court also began), the New Jersey Court was unable to find any distinction "of practical significance" between these two classes of enterprise organization.

The New Jersey Court viewed the partnership as an entity in itself, not merely the aggregate of the various partners. The plaintiff in the New Jersey case sought to hold the partnership as an entity, not the individual partners: "The action is against the partnership as such, and a judgment for plaintiff accordingly would bind the partnership assets and not the partners individually." . . .

The New Jersey Court declared . . . that the tort-feasor partner's obligation "to contribute if partnership assets should be insufficient to meet partnership liabilities" is not a bar to the imposition of liability against the partnership because . . . "[p]artners contemplate liability for negligent operation of their vehicles, and either expect to share it or to provide against it by insurance. Surely partners do not contemplate a different approach with respect to injuries to the spouse of one of them merely because the agency of the hurt happens to be the husband rather than some other partnership representative. In terms of what men expect, the wife's claim is no different from any other."

In saying that a partnership is liable "to the same extent as the partner," the draftsmen of the Uniform Partnership Act may have either intended to limit liability or, . . . have intended affirmatively to state the common-law obligation to make compensation. Either interpretation would be consistent with the language employed.

The question presented is not free of doubt. We must choose one of two arguably sound positions. We choose the result reached by the New Jersey Supreme Court. An immunity from liability should be given a strict construction. . . . In many instances, including the one presently before us, the immunity arises out of a particular relationship between the litigants or some of them. Persons frequently act concurrently in more than one role. Where litigants have a dual relationship, one of which is consistent with the imposition of liability, we see no compelling reason to prefer the relationship which bars recovery.

The tendency of the law of partnership has been to emphasize to a greater extent than at earlier stages of the law's development the entity aspects of a partnership. . . . This may explain, at least in part, the difference in the approaches of the New York Court in 1935 and the New Jersey Court in 1961. It would be a step backward to hold that an action against a partnership—an action seeking to reach partnership assets—cannot be maintained because a partnership may also be viewed as an aggregation of individuals.

We agree with the New Jersey Court that insofar as assessment of tort liability is concerned there is no reasonable basis for distinguishing between the enterprise liability of a corporation and a partnership. This does not necessarily mean that if partnership assets are insufficient the tortfeasor partner, or indeed other partners, are personally liable for the excess—that is a separate question which we need not now decide. . . .

[Judgment reversed and action remanded.]

Chaiken v Employment Security Commission

— Del Super —, 274 A2d 707 (1971)

Chaiken and two others ran a barber shop. The Delaware Employment Security Commission claimed that the other two persons were employees of Chaiken and that Chaiken had failed

to pay the unemployment compensation tax assessed against employers. He defended on the ground that he had not "employed" the other two and that all three were partners. From a decision that they were employees, Chaiken appealed.

STOREY, J. . . . Chaiken contends that he and his "partners":

(1) properly registered the partnership name and names of partners in the Prothonotary's office, . . .
(2) properly filed federal partnership information returns and paid federal taxes quarterly on an estimated basis, and
(3) duly executed partnership agreements.

Of the three factors, the last is most important. Agreements of "partnership" were executed between Chaiken and Mr. Strazella, a barber in the shop, and between Chaiken and Mr. Spitzer, similarly situated. The agreements were nearly identical. The first paragraph declared the creation of a partnership and the location of business. The second provided that Chaiken would provide barber chair, supplies, and licenses, while the other partner would provide tools of the trade. The paragraph also declared that upon dissolution of the partnership, ownership of items would revert to the party providing them. The third paragraph declared that the income of the partnership would be divided 30% for Chaiken, 70% for Strazella; 20% for Chaiken and 80% for Spitzer. The fourth paragraph declared that all partnership policy would be decided by Chaiken, whose decision was final. The fifth paragraph forbade assignment of the agreement without permission of Chaiken. The sixth paragraph required Chaiken to hold and distribute all receipts. The final paragraph stated hours of work for Strazella and Spitzer and holidays.

The mere existence of an agreement labelled "partnership" agreement and the characterization of signatories as "partners" does not conclusively prove the existence of a partnership. Rather, the intention of the parties, as explained by the wording of the agreement, is paramount. . . .

A partnership is defined as an association of two or more persons to carry on as co-owners a business for profit. . . . As co-owners of a business, partners have an equal right in the decision making process. 6 Del.C. § 1518 (5). But this right may be abrogated by agreement of the parties without destroying the partnership concept, provided other partnership elements are present. . . .

Thus, while paragraph four reserves for Chaiken all right to determine partnership policy, it is not standing alone, fatal to the partnership concept. Co-owners should also contribute valuable consideration for the creation of the business. Under paragraph two, however, Chaiken provides the barber chair (and implicitly the barber shop itself), mirror, licenses and linen, while the other partners merely provide their tools and labor—nothing more than any barber-employee would furnish. Standing alone, however, mere contribution of work and skill can be valuable consideration for a partnership agreement. . . .

Partnership interests may be assignable, although it is not a violation of partnership law to prohibit assignment in a partnership agreement. . . . Therefore, paragraph five on assignment of partnership interests does not violate the partnership concept. On the other hand, distribution of partnership assets to the partners upon dissolution is only allowed after all partnership liabilities are satisfied. . . . But paragraph two of the agreement, in stating the ground rules for dissolution, makes no declaration that the partnership assets will be utilized to pay partnership expenses before reversion to their original owners. This deficiency militates against a finding in favor of partnership intent since it is assumed Chaiken would have inserted such provision had he thought his lesser partners would accept such liability. Partners do accept such liability, employees do not.

Most importantly, co-owners carry on "a business for profit." The phrase has been interpreted to mean that partners share in the profits and the losses of the business. The intent to divide the profits is an indispensable requisite of partnership. . . . Paragraph three of the agreement declares that each partner shall share in the income of the business. There is no sharing of the profits, and as the agreement is drafted, there are no profits. Merely sharing the gross returns does not establish a partnership. . . . Nor is the sharing of profits prima facie evidence of a partnership where the profits received are in payment of wages. . . .

The failure to share profits therefore is fatal to the partnership concept here.

Evaluating Chaiken's agreement in the light of the elements implicit in a partnership, no partnership intent can be found. The absence of the important right of decision making or the important duty to share liabilities upon dissolution individually may not be fatal to a partnership. But when both are absent, coupled with the absence of profit sharing, they become strong factors in discrediting the partnership argument. . . .

In addition, the total circumstances of the case taken together indicate the employer-employee relationship between Chaiken and his barbers. The agreement set forth the hours of work and days off—unusual subjects for partnership agreements. The barbers brought into the relationship only the equipment required of all barber shop operators. And each barber had his own individual "partnership" with Chaiken. Furthermore, Chaiken conducted all transactions with suppliers, and purchased licenses, insurance, and the lease for the business property in his own name. Finally, the name "Richard's Barber Shop" continued to be used after the execution of the so-called partnership agreements.

It is the conclusion of this Court that Chaiken did not carry the burden of proving the existence of partnerships with Spitzer and Strazella. . . . Since . . . no partnership at law exists, the facts support the Commission's finding. . . .

[Judgment affirmed.]

Smith v Kelley

(Ky App) 465 SW2d 39 (1971)

Kelley and Galloway were accountants doing business as a partnership. Smith was employed by them until he left in 1968. When he left the firm, he claimed that as a partner he was entitled to a twenty percent share of the profits. The partnership denied that he was a partner and claimed that he was merely an employee. Smith showed that the partnership had represented to third persons and governmental agencies that he was a partner in their firm. Smith sued the partnership. Judgment was entered against Smith and he appealed.

CLAY, C.*. . . Appellant brought this suit for a partnership accounting. The Chancellor adjudged no partnership existed and dismissed appellant's claim. Appellant contends on appeal that the judgment is "erroneous."

With one exception, there is little dispute about the facts. In 1964 appellees Kelley and Galloway were partners in an accounting business. Appellant left another firm and came to work for them. For three and one-half years appellant drew $1,000 a month, plus $100 a month for travel expenses. At the end of each year he was paid a relatively small additional sum as a bonus out of the profits of the business. Not until appellant left the Kelley-Galloway firm in 1968 did he make any claims that he was entitled to a fixed percentage of the profits. In this lawsuit he asserts he had a twenty-percent interest therein.

There was no writing evidencing a partnership agreement. However, during the years appellant worked for the firm he was held out to the public as a partner. In a contract entered into between Kelley, Galloway, appellant and a third party, appellant was designated a partner. Partnership tax returns listed him as such; so did a statement filed with the Kentucky Board of Accountancy. In a suit filed in the circuit court against a third party he was designated a partner.

On the other hand, Kelley, Galloway and another employee of the firm testified there was no agreement that Smith would be a partner or have a right to share in the profits; he made no contribution to the assets of the partnership; he took no part in the management; he had no authority to hire or fire employees or to make purchases for the firm; he did not sign any

* Commissioner.

notes when the firm was borrowing money; and he was not obligated to stand any losses of the firm.

A partnership is a contractual relationship and the intention to create it is necessary. . . . As to third parties, a partnership may arise by estoppel . . . but our question is whether the parties intended to and did create such a relationship as would entitle appellant to share in the profits.

The Chancellor found that the original partners had at no time agreed that appellant would be entitled to share in a percentage of the profits. This was a matter of credibility and the Chancellor, who heard the evidence, chose to believe appellees. His finding on this point was not clearly erroneous and would seem to be dispositive of the case. In addition however, the conduct of the parties over a three-and-one-half-year period confirms the conclusion that, though appellant was held out to the public as a partner, between themselves a partnership relationship was not intended to be and was not created. We find no error in the court's findings of fact or conclusions of law. . . .

[Judgment affirmed.]

Tom Nakamura, Inc. v G & G Produce Company, Inc.

93 Idaho 183, 457 P2d 422 (1969)

Garrison and Lehman as partners were growing a potato crop. The G & G Produce Company was owned by members of Garrison's family. The corporation owed money to Tom Nakamura, Inc. Nakamura sued G & G and attached the potato crop on the theory that Garrison was personally liable for the debt of G & G and that the potato crop could be attached to satisfy this debt. Garrison filed a counterclaim asserting that the attachment of the partnership property was wrongful because the liability of a partner could not be enforced in this way. Nakamura claimed that Garrison had stated that the crop was owned by the G & G Corporation or by him personally. The court entered judgment against Nakamura and also dismissed the counterclaim for damages for the wrongful attachment. Appeals were taken by the plaintiff from the judgment against him and by the partnership from the dismissal of the counterclaim.

SHEPARD, J. . . . The Nakamura suit was instituted not only against G & G corporation, but against Lonnie Garrison and Max Lehman, individually, and against the Garrison-Lehman partnership. Nakamura's theory, insofar as the same can be determined, was that the G & G corporation was indebted to Nakamura and that the Garrisons were the alter ego of the corporation, and that the corporation was, in fact, a fictitious entity used to shield the Garrisons from personal liability. They also theorized that Lonnie Garrison used corporate funds from G & G Produce to pay his share of the expenses in raising the partnership potato crop, and they conclude therefrom that the Garrison-Lehman partnership became in effect a three-way partnership in which the G & G corporation was the third partner. The Warnock theory of suit against those other than the G & G corporation was essentially the same as that of Nakamura except that, as above indicated, Lonnie and June Garrison had executed a note in favor of Warnock not only as officers of the corporation, but as individuals. The trial court rendered judgment in favor of each of the plaintiffs against G & G corporation for said amounts. The trial court also rendered judgment in favor of Warnock against Lonnie and June Garrison, as individuals, for the amount of the note which they had executed as individuals. From said judgments of the trial court no appeal was taken.

The trial court dismissed the Nakamura action against Lonnie and June Garrison, as individuals, against the Garrison-Lehman partnership, and as against Lehman as an individual. The court also dismissed the Warnock action against the Garrison-Lehman partnership and as against Lehman as an individual. Appellants Nakamura and Warnock appeal this ruling of the district court and argue that under the facts as established we should pierce the corporate veil, disregard the corporate entity, and attach personal liability to Lonnie and June Garrison, who they allege are the alter ego of G & G Produce Co., Inc. They further argue that liability for the corporate indebtedness should also be attached to the Garrison-Lehman partnership and to Max Lehman as an individual, since G & G Produce Co., Inc. contributed funds to the partnership venture and in effect thus became a third partner in the venture.

We hold that the judgment of the trial court dismissing the actions as to Lonnie and June Garrison, as individuals, was erroneous and such portion of the trial court's decision is reversed. . . .

. . . [UPA § 24] provides the property rights of a partner are:

> "1. His rights in specific partnership property.
> 2. His interest in the partnership.
> 3. His right to participate in the management."

[UPA § 25] provides in pertinent part:

> "1. A partner is coowner with his partners of specific partnership property, holding as a tenant in partnership.
> 2. The incidents of this tenancy are such that: . . . c. A partner's right in specific partnership property is not subject to attachment or execution, except on a claim against the partnership. . . ."

[UPA § 28] provides in pertinent part:

> "1. On due application to a competent court by any judgment creditor of a partner, the court which entered the judgment, order, or decree, or any other court, may charge the interest of the debtor partner with payment of the unsatisfied amount of such judgment debt with interest thereon: . . ."

The record before us conclusively shows that the statutory procedure hereinabove enumerated was not complied with by either of plaintiffs in this action. We, therefore, affirm that portion of the judgment of the district court dismissing the partnership as a defendant in the action.

We come then to the final question presented, the alleged unlawful attachment. Prior to the institution of these suits, Tom Nakamura had numerous telephone conversations with Lonnie Garrison requesting payments on the overdue accounts. Garrison told him on various occasions that he, Garrison, would have additional income from the proceeds of a potato crop in Hammett, Idaho, and that the overdue accounts would be paid therefrom. Evidently, both Nakamura and Warnock gained the impression that the potato crop belonged to Garrison and his wife as individuals, or belonged to the G & G corporation. On October 15, 1964, a writ of attachment was issued in the Nakamura case directed to the sheriff of Elmore County requiring him to attach the potato crop in Hammett, Idaho, which was then in the process of being harvested. The sheriff went to the premises, ordered all harvesting stopped, and ordered that no potatoes should be removed from the premises. He, however, never took possession of the potatoes nor did he post written notice of the attachment on the premises. It is undisputed, however, that all harvesting work stopped at that point. Shortly after the institution of the Warnock suit, an attachment was also issued upon the same potato crop in Hammett, Idaho, and by the same sheriff executed in like fashion.

The partnership of Garrison and Lehman, and Garrison and Lehman as individuals, counterclaimed in the original action claiming a wrongful attachment since the potato crop was owned by the partnership of Garrison and Lehman. . . .

. . . [UPA § 25] provides a specific prohibition against attaching a partner's right in specific partnership property, and [UPA § 28] provides the mechanics necessary to reach a partner's interests in partnership property through the medium of a charging order. It is undisputed that no such charging order was acquired and we conclude, therefore, that the attachment was wrongful as against the partnership and it may recover damages therefor. We hold, therefore, that the trial court erred in dismissing the cause of action of the partner for wrongful attachment.

In remanding this matter for the consideration of liability on the claim for wrongful attachment, we deem it advisable to remind the lower court that [UPA § 4(2)] applies the law of estoppel to Idaho partnership law. It is unclear from the record before us precisely what representations, if any, were made by Lonnie Garrison . . . concerning the ownership of the potato crop. Whether the representations were such as to induce . . . Nakamura to levy attachment upon the potato crop under the belief that they were owned by either Lonnie Garrison, individually, or G & G corporation, is likewise unclear from the record before us. In the event that such representations were made by Garrison and in fact, did induce the actions of Nakamura . . . this could result in an estoppel from asserting the claim for wrongful attachment or act in mitigation of the damages for wrongful attachment. If such representations were made, it would be inequitable, of course, to permit Garrison to make the representations inducing the attachment and then sue for wrongful attachment. If suit were allowed for wrongful attachment, Garrison would be profiting from his wrongdoing and misrepresentations even though such profit might accrue to him as a member of the partnership. . . .

[Judgment as to counterclaim reversed and action remanded.]

Philipp Lithographing Co. v Babich

27 Wis 2d 645, 135 NW2d 343 (1965)

Paul Babich ran a business under the name of "House of Paul." The latter became a partnership between Babich, Dyson, and Schnepp but continued under the same name. The partners arranged for printing of advertising material with Philipp Lithographing Co., making contracts on three separate occasions for such printing. During the course of these dealings the "House of Paul" became a corporation. When the printing bills were not paid in full, Philipp sued the partners as individuals. They claimed they were not liable on the theory that the corporation had made the contracts. From a decision adverse to them, the partners appealed.

WILKIE, J. . . . Negotiations for the first printing contract began before the "House of Paul" was incorporated. Respondent [Philipp] claims that appellants continued to hold themselves out as partners during negotiations for the last contract. Appellants counter that by this time respondent had notice of the change in form of the business from a partnership to a corporation. The general rule is that partners who continue to hold themselves out as such after the formation of a corporation cannot escape responsibility for contracts entered into after the change in business status without adequate notice that the partnership has been dissolved. This is especially true when the corporation operates under the same name and circumstances as the partnership. The trial court found that respondent "received no actual notice of said incorporation" from appellants and that appellants "continued to deal with [respondent] as partners." These findings will not be upset unless against the great weight and clear preponderance of the evidence.

Appellants gave no formal notice of the alteration of the business status. Thus, if there was notice, it must necessarily have arisen from the particular circumstances in the case. It is significant that the Dun & Bradstreet report received August 19, 1960—three months after the actual incorporation—described Schnepp and Babich as partners and went on to declare that the partners "may incorporate in the near future." Respondent, through Boesel, relied on this report. Appellants question the reliability of these statements because they were conclusions of the Dun & Bradstreet reporter. But the information upon which the report was based was obtained in an interview with appellants Babich and Schnepp. If a trained investigator could not learn of the incorporation as a result of an interview with two corporate officers, the trial court could reasonably have found that such knowledge was unavailable to respondent.

In response to a demand for payment, respondent's president, Frederick Glantz, received a letter from appellant Schnepp on August 1, 1961. This letter was on "House of Paul" stationery, was signed by Schnepp in a personal rather than a corporate capacity, and explained that payments had ceased because "*we* had to put the major portion of *our* income back into stock in order to continue *our* growth." (Emphasis added.) Schnepp continued that on the basis of "*our* sales, I feel confident that *we*" can make regular payments "on *our* account and liquidate *our* debt." (Emphasis added.) The form and substance of this letter indicate that appellants were still holding themselves out as partners well after the contract was even entered into.

The payment on the first two contracts and the three part payments made on the last one were made by "House of Paul, Inc." checks. Appellants contend that this was sufficient to put respondent's officers or agents on notice that "House of Paul" had been incorporated. However, testimony discloses that respondent's accounts receivable were handled by a bookkeeper-employee, and that the officers of the company did not see any of the checks or learn that payment was actually made by corporate check. Nor, under the circumstances, can appellants escape liability because the bookkeeper saw the corporate checks. This is because she was completely unaware of the negotiations between the parties, and could not be expected to attach any significance whatsoever to the fact that the account was paid by corporate check.

We conclude, therefore, that the disputed findings of the trial court are not against the great weight and clear preponderance of the evidence.

[Judgment affirmed.]

King v Stoddard

28 Cal App 3d 708, 104 Cal Rptr 903 (1972)

The Stoddard family, father, mother, and son, were a partnership which published a newspaper, the Walnut Kernel. The parents died and the son kept running the paper. King performed accounting services for the paper. When he was not paid, he sued the son and the executors of the estates of the deceased partners, the parents, claiming that his bill was a partnership liability for which each was liable. The executors defended on the ground that the son as surviving partner did not have authority to employ an accountant but was only authorized to wind up the partnership business. To this defense it was answered that the newspaper was continued in order to preserve its asset value as a going concern, so that it could be sold, and that the running of the paper was therefore part of the winding up process, which, if true, would give the surviving partner the authority to employ the accountant. From a judgment in favor of the accountant, the executors appealed.

Brown, A.J. . . . The operation of the business continued after the death of Lyman E. Stoddard, Sr.; Lyman E. Stoddard, Jr., operated it as the sole surviving partner. . . .

For approximately 10 years prior to the death of Alda S. Stoddard, the respondents, King and White, and their predecessors had been accountants for the Walnut Kernel. They continued to do the accounting after the deaths of Alda and Lyman, Sr. The appellants were aware that respondents were continuing their work. One of the respondents, King, testified that he understood that respondents would be paid at such time as the estates were in a liquid condition allowing payment and that he would not have continued to render the services had he known that the estates would not be responsible.

John L. Stoddard and Nancy Gans, the executors, did not individually participate in the operation of the partnership business in any manner. The court concluded they were not individually liable.

The court found the estate of Alda S. Stoddard liable for the accounting services rendered by appellants during the period of time following her death—1963 to 1968. The court also found the estate of Lyman E. Stoddard, Sr., jointly liable with the estate of Alda S. Stoddard for the accounting services rendered by appellants following his death—1964 to 1968. The court disallowed any claim rendered prior to the deaths of Lyman E. Stoddard, Sr., or Alda S. Stoddard as no claims were filed in those estates as required by section 700 et seq. of the Probate Code. The estate's liability was predicated upon the court's finding that the services were rendered during the process of winding up the partnership operation of the Walnut Kernel newspaper. We have concluded that the trial court erred and that the continuation of the business was not a winding up of the affairs of the partnership.

The partnership was dissolved by operation of law upon the deaths of Alda and Lyman E. Stoddard, Sr. . . . "In general a dissolution operates only with respect to future transactions; as to everything past the partnership continues until all pre-existing matters are terminated." . . .

. . . [UPA § 35] provides that "[a]fter dissolution a partner can bind the partnership . . .

(a) By any act appropriate for winding up partnership affairs . . . ."

It is this latter provision upon which the court based its decision that the estates of the deceased partners were liable for the accounting services performed after dissolution. The court found that "LYMAN STODDARD, JR.'S continuation of the WALNUT KERNEL business was an appropriate act for winding up the partnership, since the assets of the business would have substantial value only if it was a going business. It was to the advantage of the partnership that the business be maintained as a going business."

Respondents, as accountants, had performed services both before and after the dissolution. The services, however, were a continuation of the accounting services pursuant to the ordinary course of the operation of the business. Respondent King testified that he was ". . . doing work for the activity of the newspaper, the financial activity of the newspaper" and that he was doing the same type of work as he had always performed for the Walnut Kernel. The exhibits which support his bill for services indicate that he did not, or was not able to, break down his services into categories which would separate ordinary accounting services from those related to a winding up of the partnership. The court, however, found that the continuation of the business itself was an "act appropriate for winding up partnership affairs."

We disagree with this finding. It is probably true that there might have been advantages to the partnership to sell the business as a going business, but the indefinite continuation of the partnership business is contrary to the requirement for winding up of the affairs upon dissolution. In Harvey v Harvey, 90 Cal App 2d 549, 554, 203 P2d 112, 115-116, the court disapproved a finding that the business and assets of a partnership were of such character as to render its liquidation impracticable and inadvisable until a purchaser could be found. The court stated: "In effect it [the finding] authorizes the indefinite continuation of the partnership after the death of a partner, a procedure not in accordance with section 571 of the Probate Code. Respondents counter with the argument that the business is such that it cannot be wound up profitably, and the estate given its share. But this argument overlooks the distinction between winding up a business and winding up the partnership interest in that business." . . .

Even if we assume that a situation might exist where continuation of the business for a period would be appropriate to winding up the partnership interest, such a situation did not exist here. The record reflects the fact that the surviving partner was not taking action to wind up the partnership as was his duty . . . nor did the estates consent in any way to a delay. Rather, their insistence on winding up took the form of an effort to sell the business and a suit to require an accounting. There is nothing in the record upon which to base the argument made by respondents that appellants consented to their continued employment. The fact that they did not object is of no relevance. They had no right to direct and did not participate in the operation of the business. Therefore, the determination that the acts of the accountants were rendered during a winding up process is not based upon substantial evidence. . . .

We conclude that the services of respondents were rendered after the dissolution resulting from the deaths of the partners, Lyman, Sr., and Alda Stoddard, and do not constitute services during the "winding up" processes of the partnership. . . .

[Judgment reversed.]

QUESTIONS AND CASE PROBLEMS

1. Bates and Huffman formed a partnership to run a shoe business. In a lawsuit between the partners, Huffman claimed that the partnership agreement was void because Bates was a minor. Was he correct? [Huffman v Bates, (Mo App) 348 SW2d 363]

2. Gordon Elliot was a member of a partnership. He withdrew from the partnership. Subsequently he was divorced from his wife, and the divorce decree awarded to his wife his interest in the partnership assets. Did this make her a partner? [Elliot v Elliot, 88 Idaho 81, 396 P2d 719]
3. A suit was brought by the heirs of members of a partnership to determine the right to the proceeds of sale of certain real estate. The real estate had been purchased by the partnership with partnership money and in the partnership name. The real estate was not used in the partnership business but was held only for investment purposes. It was claimed by the heirs that this real estate was not subject to the provisions of the Uniform Partnership Act governing tenancy by partnership because it was not used in the business. Were they correct? [Brown v Brown, 45 Tenn App 78, 320 SW2d 721]
4. The Consolidated Loan Co. was owned and operated by three partners. After the death of two of the partners, the surviving partner, Salabes, made an agreement with the estates of the other two to continue the partnership. Thereafter Salabes brought an action for a decree that she "is now the sole remaining partner in, or the sole proprietress of, Consolidated Loan Company" subject to the interests of the estates of the deceased partners. Was she the sole owner of the enterprise? [Miller v Salabes, 225 Md 53, 169 A2d 671]
5. The Weidlich Sterling Spoon Co., a partnership owned by three brothers, was dissolved. By agreement, one of the brothers was designated as liquidating partner. After he completed liquidation, he filed an account which related only to certain legal charges and expenses that had been incurred. Was this a proper accounting? [Weidlich v Weidlich, 147 Conn 160, 157 A2d 910]
6. Williams owned and operated a bakery business. His two sons were employed in the business and from time to time received a share of the profits as a bonus. The father and one of the sons died. The administrator of the son's estate, the First National Bank, then sued the estate of the father for an accounting, claiming that the father and the two sons were a partnership and that the deceased son's estate was therefore entitled to a one-third share. Decide. [First National Bank v Williams, 142 Ore 648, 20 P2d 222]
7. The National Acceptance Co., a partnership, entered into a contract obligating it to make certain payments to the General Machinery & Supply Co. Later, General Machinery claimed that it was not bound by the contract because some of the partners of National were minors and could avoid their contract. Was this a valid defense for General Machinery? [General Machinery & Supply Co. v National Acceptance Co., (Colo App) 472 P2d 735]
8. A lease was executed by which *L* rented a property to *I*. Thereafter *C* claimed that *L* and *I* were in fact partners and that the agreement between *L* and *I* was drawn in the form of a lease so as to shield *L* from the liability to which he would be subject as a partner. Was such evidence admissible? [Goodpasture Grain & Milling Co. v Buck, 77 NMex 609, 426 P2d 586]
9. Simpson and Balaban, as partners, owned and operated the Desert Cab Company. Simpson died. The administrator of his estate obtained a court order authorizing the sale of Simpson's interest in the partnership and in the physical assets of the partnership. Was this order proper? [Balaban v Bank of Nevada, 86 Nev 862, 477 P2d 860]

45 Authority of Partners

§ 45:1. Authority of Majority of Partners. When there are more than two partners in a firm, the decision of the majority prevails in matters involving the manner in which the ordinary functions of the business will be conducted. To illustrate, a majority of the partners of a firm decide to increase the firm's advertising and enter into a contract for that purpose. The transaction is valid and binds the firm and all of the partners.

The act of the majority is not binding if it contravenes the partnership agreement. For such matters unanimous action is required.[1] Thus, the majority of the members cannot change the nature of the business against the protests of the minority.

When there are two or any other even number of partners, there is the possibility of an even division on a matter that requires majority approval. In such a case no action can be taken, and the partnership is deadlocked. When the partners are evenly divided on any question, one partner has no authority to act. (See p. 901, Summers v Dooley.) If the division is over a basic issue and the partners persist in the deadlock so that it is impossible to continue the business, any one of the partners may petition the court to order the dissolution of the firm.[2]

§ 45:2. Express Authority of Individual Partners. An individual partner may have express authority to do certain acts, either because the partnership agreement so declares or because a sufficient number of partners have agreed thereto. In addition, he has authority to do those acts which are customary for a member of such a partnership. As in the case of an agent, the acts of a partner in excess of his authority do not ordinarily bind the partnership.

In his relations with third persons, a partner's authority to act for the firm is similar to that of an agent to act for his principal.

§ 45:3. Customary Authority of Individual Partners. A partner, by virtue of the fact that he is a comanager of the business, customarily has certain powers necessary and proper to carry out that business. In the absence of express limitation the law will therefore imply that he has such powers. The scope of such powers varies with the nature of the partnership and also with the business customs and usages of the area in which the partnership operates.

---

[1] Uniform Partnership Act, § 18(h).

[2] Mayhew v McGlothlin, 269 Ky 184, 106 SW2d 643.

The following are the more common of the customary or implied powers of individual partners:

(1) Contracts. A partner may make any contract necessary to the transaction of firm business. He cannot make a contract of guaranty, however, merely to induce a third person to purchase from the partnership.

When the plaintiff sues on a promissory note or other contract executed by a partner who does not possess express authority to enter into such transaction, the plaintiff has the burden of proving that the making of the contract or the giving of commercial paper was "usual" for a business of the character of the partnership. (See p. 902, Burns v Gonzalez.)

(2) Sales. A partner may sell the firm's goods in the regular course of business and make the usual warranties incidental to such sales. This authority, however, is limited to the goods kept for sale.

(3) Purchases. A partner may purchase any kind of property within the scope of the business, and for this purpose he may pledge the credit of the firm. This authority is not affected by the fact that he subsequently misuses or keeps the goods.

(4) Loans. A partner in a trading firm may borrow money for partnership purposes. In doing so, he may execute commercial paper in the firm name or give security, such as a mortgage or a pledge of the personal property of the firm. (See p. 903, Reid v Linder.) If the third person acts in good faith, the transaction is binding even though the partner misappropriates the money.[3] A partner in a nontrading partnership does not ordinarily possess the power to borrow.

(5) Insurance. A partner may insure the firm property, cancel a policy of insurance, or make proof and accept settlement for the loss.

(6) Employment. A partner may engage such employees and agents as are necessary to carry out the purpose of the enterprise.

(7) Claims Against Firm. A partner has the authority to compromise, adjust, and pay bona fide claims against the partnership. He may pay debts out of firm funds, or he may pay them by transferring firm property. Although he has no power to pay his own debts from firm assets, his creditors are protected if they receive such payments in good faith and without knowledge that it comes from firm assets.

(8) Claims of Firm. A partner may adjust, receive payment of, and release debts and other claims of the firm. He may take money or commercial paper but, as a rule, cannot accept goods in payment. One who makes

[3] Zander v Larsen, 41 Wash 2d 503, 250 P2d 531.

a proper payment is protected even though the partner to whom payment is made fails to account to the firm for the payment.

(9) Admissions. A partner may bind the firm by admissions or statements that are adverse to the interests of the partnership if they are made in regard to firm affairs and in the pursuance of firm business.

(10) Notice. A partner may receive notice of matters affecting the partnership affairs, and such notice, in the absence of fraud, is binding on the others.[4]

§ 45:4. Limitations on Authority. The partners may agree to limit the normal powers of each partner. When a partner, contrary to such an agreement, negotiates a contract for the firm with a third person, the firm is bound if the third person was unaware of the agreement. In such a case, the partner violating the agreement is liable to his partners for any loss caused by the breach of his contract. If the third person knew of the limitation, however, the firm would not be bound.[5]

A third person cannot assume that the partner has all the authority which he purports to have. If there is anything that would put a reasonable man on notice that the partner's customary powers are limited, the third person is bound by the limitation.

The third person must be on the alert for the following situations in particular, as they serve to notify him that the partner with whom he deals either has restricted authority or no authority at all:

(1) Nature of Business. A third person must take notice of limitations arising out of the nature of the business. A partnership may be organized for a particular kind of business, trade, or profession, and third persons are presumed to know the limitations commonly laid upon partners in such an enterprise. Thus, an act of a partner that would ordinarily bind a commercial firm, such as the issuance of a note, would not bind a partnership engaged in a profession.[6] A partner in a trading partnership has much greater powers than one in a nontrading firm.[7]

(2) Scope of Business. A third person must recognize and act in accordance with limitations that arise from the scope of the business. A partner cannot bind the firm to a third person in a transaction not within the scope of the firm's business unless he has express authority to do so. Thus, when a partner in a dental firm speculates in land or when a partner in a firm dealing in automobiles buys television sets for resale, the third person, in the absence of estoppel or express authority, cannot hold the other partners liable on such a contract. The scope of the business is a question of fact to be

---

[4] UPA § 12.

[5] § 9(4).

[6] Livingston v Roosevelt, (NY) 4 Johns 51.

[7] Marsh v Wheeler, 77 Conn 449, 59 A 410.

determined by the jury from the circumstances of each case. In general, it means the activities commonly recognized as a part of a given business at a given place and time. The usual scope, however, may be enlarged by agreement or by conduct.

(3) Termination of Partnership. A third person must watch for the termination of the partnership relation, either when the partnership is terminated under conditions requiring no notice or when notice of the termination has been properly given.

(4) Adverse Interest. A third person must take notice of an act of a partner that is obviously against the interest of the firm. To illustrate, if a partner issues a promissory note in the firm name and delivers it to his creditor in payment of a personal obligation, the latter acts at his peril because such an act may be a fraud upon the firm.

§ 45:5. Prohibited Transactions. There are certain transactions into which a partner cannot enter on behalf of the partnership unless he is expressly authorized to do so. A third person entering into such a transaction therefore acts at his peril when the partner has not been so authorized. In such a case, the third person should check with the other partners to determine whether the transaction is authorized.

The following are prohibited transactions:

(1) Cessation of Business. A partner cannot bind the firm by a contract that would make it impossible for the firm to conduct its usual business.

A partner does not have implied authority to sell the business, goodwill, and assets of a partnership business. (See p. 904, Feingold v Davis.)

(2) Suretyship. A partner has no implied authority to bind the firm by contracts of surety, guaranty, or indemnity for purposes other than the firm business.

(3) Arbitration. A partner in most states cannot submit controversies of his firm to arbitration. The UPA expressly denies this power "unless authorized by the other partners or unless they have abandoned the business."[8]

(4) Confession of Judgment. A partner cannot confess judgment against the firm upon one of its obligations, because all partners should have an opportunity to defend in court. This power is expressly denied by the UPA, except when the other partners consent or when "they have abandoned the business."[9]

(5) Assignment for Creditors. A partner cannot ordinarily make a general assignment of firm property for the benefit of creditors. Exceptions

[8] UPA § 9(3)(e).
[9] § 9(3)(d).

are usually made in cases of bona fide acts in an emergency. The exceptions appear to be limited by the UPA, which provides that "unless authorized by the other partners or unless they have abandoned the business, one or more but less than all the partners have no authority to assign the partnership property in trust for creditors or on the assignee's promise to pay the debts of the partnership." [10]

(6) Personal Obligations. A partner cannot discharge his personal obligations or claims of the firm by interchanging them in any way.

(7) Sealed Instruments. Instruments under seal are binding upon the firm when they are made in the usual course of business. In a minority of the states, however, a partner cannot bind his copartners by an instrument under seal.

[10] § 9(3)(a).

CASES FOR CHAPTER 45

Summers v Dooley

94 Idaho 87, 481 P2d 318 (1971)

Summers and Dooley formed a partnership to collect trash. Summers became unable to work and he hired a third man to do his work and paid him out of his personal funds. Summers suggested to Dooley that the third man be paid from the partnership funds but Dooley refused to do so. Finally Summers sued Dooley for reimbursement for the money he had spent to pay the third man. From a judgment for Dooley, Summers appealed.

DONALDSON, J. . . . Summers continued to operate the business using the third man and in October of 1967 instituted suit in the district court for $6,000 against his partner, the gravamen of the complaint being that Summers has been required to pay out more than $11,000 in expenses, incurred in the hiring of the additional man, without any reimbursement from either the partnership funds or his partner. After trial before the court, sitting without a jury, Summers was granted only partial relief and he has appealed. He urges in essence that the trial court erred by failing to conclude that he should be reimbursed for expenses and costs connected in the employment of extra help in the partnership business.

The principal thrust of appellant's contention is that in spite of the fact that one of the two partners refused to consent to the hiring of additional help, nonetheless, the non-consenting partner retained profits earned by the labors of the third man and therefore the non-consenting partner should be estopped from denying the need and value of the employee, and has by his behavior ratified the act of the other partner who hired the additional man.

The issue presented for decision by this appeal is whether an equal partner in a two man partnership has the authority to hire a new employee in disregard of the objection of the other partner and then attempt to charge the dissenting partner with the costs incurred as a result of his unilateral decision.

The State of Idaho has enacted specific statutes with respect to the legal concept known as "partnership." Therefore any solution of partnership problems should logically begin with an application of the relevant code provision.

In the instant case the record indicates that although Summers requested his partner Dooley to agree to the hiring of a third man, such requests were not honored. In fact Dooley made it clear that he was "voting no" with regard to the hiring of an additional employee.

An application of the relevant statutory provisions and pertinent case law to the factual situation presented by the instant case indicates that the trial court was correct in its disposal of the issue since a majority of the partners did not consent to the hiring of the third man. I.C. § 53-318(8) provides: "Any difference arising as to ordinary matters connected with the partnership business may be decided by a *majority of the partners*. . . ." It is the opinion of this Court that the preceding statute is of a mandatory rather than permissive nature. . . .

A careful reading of the statutory provision indicates that subsection 5 bestows *equal rights in the management and conduct of the partnership business* upon all of the partners. The concept of equality between partners with respect to management of business affairs is a central theme and recurs throughout the Uniform Partnership law. . . . Business differences must be decided by a majority of the partners.

". . . If the partners are equally divided, those who forbid a change must have their way." . . .

In the case at bar one of the partners continually voiced objection to the hiring of the third man. He did not sit idly by and acquiesce in the actions of his partner. Under these circumstances it is manifestly unjust to permit recovery of an expense which was incurred individually and not for the benefit of the partnership but rather for the benefit of one partner.

[Judgment affirmed.]

Burns v Gonzalez

(Tex Civ App) 439 SW2d 128 (1969)

Gonzalez and Bosquez were partners under the name of International American Advertising Agency. The business of the partnership was selling radio broadcasting time on commission. Representing himself as acting on behalf of the partnership, Bosquez executed a promissory note payable to Burns in his own name and the name of the partnership. Burns sued the partners on the note individually and as partners. The defense was made on behalf of Gonzalez and the partnership that Bosquez lacked authority to execute the promissory note and that there was no evidence that the execution of such a note was the usual way of conducting a partnership engaged in the business of selling broadcasting time. From a judgment entered in favor of the partnership and Gonzalez, an appeal was taken by Burns.

CADENA, J. . . . The sole business of the partnership was the sale, on a commission basis, of broadcast time on XERF, a radio station located in Ciudad Acuna, Mexico, and owned and operated by a Mexican corporation, Compania Radiodifusora de Coahuila, S.A. (herein called "Radiodifusora"). Bosquez and Gonzalez each owned 50% of the Radiodifusora stock, with Bosquez acting as president of the corporation. . . .

Under Sec. 9(1), U. P. A. "Every partner is an agent of the partnership for the purpose of its business, and the act of every partner, including the execution in the partnership name of any instrument, *for apparently carrying on in the usual way the business of the partnership* of which he is a member binds the partnership, unless the partner so acting has in fact no authority to act for the partnership in the particular matter, and the person with whom he is dealing has knowledge of the fact that he has no such authority." (Emphasis added.) In this case, in fact, Bosquez had no authority to bind the partnership by executing a negotiable instrument. But, since this express limitation on the authority of Bosquez was unknown to Burns, then, under the language of Sec. 9(1), his act in executing the note would bind the partnership if such act can be classified as an act "for apparently carrying on in the usual way the business of the partnership."

As we interpret Sec. 9(1), the act of a partner binds the firm, absent an express limitation of authority known to the party dealing with such partner, if such act is for the purpose of "apparently carrying on" the business of the partnership in the way in which other firms engaged in the same business in the locality usually transact business, or in the way in which the particular partnership usually transacts its business. In this case, there is no evidence relating to the manner in which firms engaged in the sale of advertising time on radio stations usually transact business. Specifically, there is no evidence as to whether or not the borrowing of money, or the execution of negotiable instruments, was incidental to the transaction of business, "in the usual way," by other advertising agencies or by this partnership, Inter-American Advertising Agency. It becomes important, therefore, to determine the location of the burden of proof concerning the "usual way" of transacting business by advertising agencies.

Sec. 9(1) states that the act of a partner "for apparently carrying on in the usual way the business of the partnership" binds the firm. This language does not place the burden of proof on the non-participating partner to establish the non-existence of the facts which operate to impose liability on the firm. If the Legislature had intended to place the burden of proof on the non-participating partner, it could have done so easily. The statute could have been drafted to declare that the act of a partner binds the firm "unless it is shown that such act was not for apparently carrying on in the usual way the business of the partnership." Actually, the liability-imposing language of Sec. 9(1) indicates that the burden of proof is on the person seeking to hold the non-participating partner accountable. It is not couched in terms appropriate for the establishment of a presumption, "administrative" or otherwise. The language relating to carrying on in the usual way the business of the partnership is no more than a statement of the rule concerning vicarious liability based on "apparent" authority. . . .

. . . The burden of proving the "usual way" in which advertising agencies transact business was upon Burns.

Our conclusion is supported by the fact that the liability of partners with respect to third persons is largely determined by reference to the principles of the law of agency. . . . One who asserts that the particular act of an agent is within the scope of the agent's authority has the burden of proving the extent of such authority. . . . We recognize, of course, that there are aspects in which the partner-agent differs from the "ordinary" agent. But we know of no distinction which compels application of different rules concerning the burden of proof in connection with establishment of the extent of the agent's power. . . .

. . . The power of a partner to issue commercial paper arises not from the existence of the partnership, but from the nature of the partnership business and the manner in which such business is usually conducted. This is the plain meaning of Sec. 9(1).

The only thing we know of the nature of the partnership here is that it was restricted to the sale of broadcast time over XERF on a commission basis. There is nothing to show that the transaction of such business required "periodical or continuous or frequent purchasing" or made "frequent resort to borrowing a necessity, not existing by reason of embarrassments, or on account of some fortuitous event, but for the advantageous prosecution of even a prosperous business." . . .

Since the evidence does not disclose that Bosquez, in executing the 1962 note, was performing an act "for apparently carrying on in the usual way the business of the partnership," there is no basis for holding that the note sued on was a partnership obligation. . . .

[Judgment affirmed.]

Reid v Linder

77 Mont 406, 251 P 157 (1926)

Wilcomb, Linder, and Darnutzer were partners engaged in a farming and stock-raising business under the name of Trout Creek Land Co. One of the partners executed and delivered four promissory notes, each signed "Trout Creek Land Co., by A. J. Wilcomb." Reid, as receiver of the Bank of Twin Bridges, Montana, a corporation, brought an action against the members of the partnership to recover on the notes. Wilcomb's partners, as a defense, alleged that he had no authority to bind his partners on a firm note. From a judgment for the plaintiff, the defendants, other than Wilcomb, appealed.

MATTHEWS, J. . . . It is contended that the firm was a nontrading copartnership. The question is important, as in such a partnership a partner has no implied power to borrow money and give firm mercantile paper therefor. . . .

"The test of the character of the partnership is buying and selling. If it buys and sells, it is commercial and trading; if it does not buy or sell, it is one of employment or occupation." . . .

The firm engaged in buying and selling cattle, as well as farming and selling grain, and . . . it required capital and the use of credit; in fact, it operated from the beginning on credit alone, and established a custom within itself long prior to the issuance of the notes in question. . . . It appears that the issuance of negotiable paper was justified by custom and necessity of the firm as well as by the fact that the firm engaged in trading. . . .

As the firm was a trading partnership, each member of the firm was the agent for the partnership in the transaction of its business and had authority to do what was necessary to carry on such business in the ordinary manner, and for that purpose could bind the partnership by an agreement in writing . . . ; and notes executed by one of the partners for the benefit of the firm became partnership obligations, binding upon all the members of the firm, in the absence of bad faith on the part of the contracting parties and knowledge thereof on the part of the payee. . . .

But it is contended that Wilcomb used the firm credit for the purpose of playing the wheat market, without authority from the other members of the firm, and, in this, acted with bad faith toward his copartners. Even though this be admitted to be true, the borrowing was ostensibly authorized; and, if the bank was a bona fide lender, it was entitled to recover on the notes, even though the partner borrowing was actually obtaining the money for his own use. . . .

[Judgment for plaintiff affirmed.]

Feingold v Davis

444 Pa 399, 282 A2d 291 (1971)

William and Charlotte Davis, husband and wife, conducted the Davis Nursing Home as a partnership. William made a contract to sell the home and all its assets and goodwill to Feingold. Charlotte refused to recognize the contract. Feingold sued William and Charlotte to obtain a decree of specific performance of the sales contract. Judgment was entered against the plaintiff and he appealed.

POMEROY, J. . . . Under Section 10(4) of the Uniform Partnership Act, . . . a conveyance by one partner of real estate (and by the same token an agreement to make a conveyance) titled in the names of all the partners, passes the equitable interest of the partnership, subject, however, to an important proviso, viz., that the act is within the authority of paragraph (1) of Section 9 of the Partnership Act. Section 9(1) makes a partner an agent of the partnership *"for the purpose of its business,"* and makes the act of a partner "for apparently carrying on in the usual way the business of the partnership" binding on a partnership unless in fact the partner has no such authority, and the person with whom he is dealing knows he has not. The transaction here involved was manifestly not the carrying on in the usual way of the business of the partnership, but the converse; it was the sale of the business, including good will and apparently all other assets, except cash. Under paragraph (2) of the same Section 9, such a transaction is not binding on the partnership unless authorized by all partners. Similarly, paragraph (3) provides that all partners must authorize, *inter alia,* the disposition of the good will of the business or the doing of "any other act which would make it impossible to carry on the ordinary business of the partnership."

. . . At least insofar as the contemplated conveyance relates to real estate, the non-signing partner's authorization to the one purporting to act for the partnership must be in writing in order to be binding. Nothing in Section 9 of the Partnership Act dealing with the extent of a partner's agency relationship with the firm provides or suggests that the requisite authority of the partners for whom one partner is acting can be less than written authority where real estate is involved. There is no reason to suppose that the unequivocal and long-standing requirement of the Statute of Frauds that an agent to sell real estate must be authorized to do so in writing in order to charge his principal is not applicable to a partnership agent, and we hold that the authority must be so evidenced. . . . In the case at bar no partnership articles or any other writing evidencing the authority of William Davis was produced. His co-partner and the firm were therefore not bound by the binder agreement. . . .

[Judgment affirmed.]

QUESTIONS AND CASE PROBLEMS

1. O'Bryan, Sullivan, and Davis were partners engaged in operating freight steamers on the Yukon River. Sullivan purchased in the firm name and received from Merrill certain lumber for the construction of firm warehouses at terminal points for the storage of freight. In an action on the contract of sale brought by Merrill against the members of the firm, it was contended that some of the partners had no power to bind the firm on this kind of contract. Do you agree with this contention? [Merrill v O'Bryan, 48 Wash 415, 93 P 917]
2. Milton Smith, Maude Smith, and Warren Ten Brook were partners doing business as "Greenwood Sales & Service." Pretending to act on behalf of the partnership, Ten Brook borrowed $6,000 from Holloway, giving her a note that was signed: "Greenwood Sales & Service, by Warren Ten Brook, Partner." In fact, Ten Brook borrowed the $6,000 so that he could make his capital contribution to the partnership. The check so obtained from Holloway was payable to the order of the partnership and was in fact deposited by Ten Brook in the partnership account. When the note was not paid, Holloway sued all of the partners. The other partners claimed that neither the partnership nor they were bound by Ten Brook's unauthorized act committed for his personal gain. Was this defense valid? [Holloway v Smith, 197 Va 334, 88 SE2d 909]
3. Wilke, President of the Commercial Bank of Webster City, Iowa, and Wright entered into a farming and stock-raising partnership. The business was conducted under the name of Wilke and Wright Farm Co. The agreement stipulated that Wilke was "to have control and management of said business." Thereafter, Wright sold some partnership cattle to Gross and Gidley, cattle buyers, who resold the cattle to Simon. In an action brought against Simon to recover the cattle, Wilke alleged that Wright had no authority to sell them. Decide. [Wilke v Simon, 46 SD 422, 193 NW 666]
4. Elrod and Hansford were partners under the name of Walter Elrod & Co. Hansford purchased on credit from the firm of Dawson Blakemore & Co. certain merchandise for the firm. Before the sale, Elrod had notified Dawson Blakemore & Co. that he would not be bound to pay for any purchase for the firm made on credit by Hansford. Thereafter Dawson Blakemore & Co. brought an action against the members of Walter Elrod & Co. to recover the price of the goods. Elrod contended that he was not bound by the contract made by Hansford. Decide. [Dawson Blakemore & Co. v Elrod, 105 Ky 624, 49 SW 465]
5. Petrikis, Ellis, and others, who were partners, signed an agreement stating: "We, the undersigned, hereby agree to sell our interests in the partnership business. If and when the sale takes place and after all bills are accounted for, the remainder of the money is to be divided according to the share each

partner now attains in the said business." Petrikis then began negotiations to sell the business to Hanges and finally made a contract selling the business to him for $17,500. Ellis, one of the partners, refused to accept the terms of the contract. Hanges then notified the partners that he called the deal off, whereupon the partners brought suit against him for breach of contract. Was Hanges liable for breach of contract? [Petrikis v Hanges, 111 Cal App 2d 734, P2d 39]

6. Damsker and Carey, partners, entered into a contract with Goldberg for the construction of a building. The construction contract provided that disputes arising thereunder would be submitted to arbitration. A dispute arose relating to extra work, and Damsker gave notice that arbitration was requested on behalf of the partnership. Goldberg opposed the entry of an order to arbitrate on the ground that the application for arbitration was not made by both partners. Decide. [Application of Damsker, 283 App Div 719, 127 NYS2d 355]

46 Duties, Rights, Remedies, and Liabilities

§ 46:1. **Duties of Partners.** In many respects the duties and responsibilities of a partner are the same as those of an agent.

(1) Loyalty and Good Faith. Each partner owes a duty of loyalty to the firm, which requires him to devote himself to the firm's business and bars him from making any secret profit at the expense of the firm,[1] or from using the firm's funds for his personal benefit, or from making a secret gain in connection with business opportunities within the field of the business of the partnership.[2] A partner must always act with strict fidelity to the interests of the firm. He must use his powers and the firm's property for the benefit of the partners and not for his personal gain. His duties to the firm must be observed above the furtherance of his own interests. To illustrate, when one partner in his own name renewed a lease on the premises occupied by the firm, he was compelled to hold the lease for the firm on the ground that his conduct was contrary to the good faith required of partners.

A partner, in the absence of an agreement to the contrary, is required to give his undivided time and energy to the development of the business of the partnership. Even when a partner is not required to give all of his time to the firm's business, he cannot promote a competing business. If he does so, he is liable for damages to the partnership. To illustrate, two persons form a partnership for the purpose of making and selling hats, and one of them, unknown to the other, engages in an individual enterprise of the same nature. The latter, not having given his assent, may compel the former to account for the profits of the competing business.

The obligation of a partner to refrain from competing with the partnership continues after the termination of the partnership if the partnership agreement contains a valid anticompetitive covenant. (See p. 915, Grund v Wood.) In the absence of any such restriction, or if the restriction agreed upon is held invalid, a partner is free to compete with the remaining partners, even though they continue the partnership business.

---

[1] Baum v McBride, 152 Neb 152, 40 NW2d 649.

[2] Stark v Reingold, 18 NJ 251, 113 A2d 379.

*(2) **Obedience.*** Each partner is under an obligation to do all that is required of him by the partnership agreement. Duties and restrictions are frequently imposed upon certain members by the partnership agreement. To illustrate, if a partner agrees to take no part in the business and a loss is suffered because of his violation of the agreement, he must indemnify his partners.

In addition, each partner must observe any limitations imposed by a majority of the partners with respect to the ordinary details of the business. If a majority of the partners operating a retail store decide that no sales shall be made on credit, a partner who is placed in charge of the store must observe this limitation. If a third person does not know of this limitation of authority, the managing partner will have the power to make a binding sale on credit to the third person. If the third person does not pay the bill and the firm thereby suffers loss, the partner who violated the "no-credit" limitation is liable to the firm for the loss caused by his disobedience.

*(3) **Reasonable Care.*** A partner must use reasonable care in the transaction of the business of the firm. He is liable for any loss resulting from his failure to do so. He is not liable, however, for honest mistakes or errors of judgment. Nor is he liable when the complaining partner likewise failed in his duty to do or not to do the same act. Thus, when one partner failed to use reasonable care in collecting the debts owed to the firm, the other partner who was equally at fault in not making the collection was not justified in complaining, unless the former, as managing partner, had been entrusted with general control of the partnership affairs.

*(4) **Information.*** A partner has the duty to inform the partnership of matters relating to the partnership. He must "render on demand true and full information of all things affecting the partnership to any partner or the legal representative of any deceased partner or partner under legal disability." [3]

The obligation to inform embraces matters relating to the liquidation of the partnership or the purchase by one partner of the interest of another. (See p. 916, Moser v Williams.)

*(5) **Accounting.*** A partner must make and keep, or turn over to the proper person, correct records of all business that he has transacted for the firm. When the partners are equally at fault in not making and keeping proper records, however, none can complain. Thus, if a firm employs a bookkeeper who commits serious errors, one partner cannot complain against another partner unless the latter was in some way responsible for the errors.

One partner may be assigned the task of maintaining the books and accounts of the firm. In such a case he has, of course, the duty to maintain proper records. If it is shown that he has been guilty of improper conduct, he

---

[3] Uniform Partnership Act, § 20.

has the burden of proving the accuracy of his records. Any doubt will be resolved against him; that is, if it is not clear whether he has or has not accounted for a particular item, it will be assumed that he has not and he will be liable to the firm for the item.[4]

§ 46:2. Rights of Partners as Owners. Each partner, in the absence of a contrary agreement, has the following rights, which stem from the fact that he is a co-owner of the partnership business:

(1) Management. Each partner has a right to take an equal part in transacting the business of the firm. To illustrate, three persons enter into a partnership. The first contributes $10,000 in cash; the second, property valued at $7,500; and the third, his skill and labor. All possess equal rights to participate in the conduct of the partnership business.[5] It is immaterial that one partner contributed more than another to the firm.

As an incident of the right to manage the partnership, each partner has the right to possession of the partnership property for the purposes of the partnership.

(2) Inspection of Books. All partners are equally entitled to inspect the books of the firm. "The partnership books shall be kept, subject to any agreement between the partners, at the principal place of business of the partnership, and every partner shall at all times have access to and may inspect and copy any of them." [6]

(3) Share of Profits. Each partner is entitled to a share of the profits. The partners may provide, if they so wish, that profits shall be shared in unequal proportions. In the absence of such a provision in the partnership agreement, each partner is entitled to an equal share of the profits without regard to the extent of his capital contribution to the partnership or to the extent of his services.

The right to profits is regarded as personal property regardless of the nature of the partnership property. Upon the death of a partner, his right to sue for profits and an accounting passes to his executor or administrator.

(4) Compensation. Although one partner performs more duties or renders more valuable services than the others, he is not entitled to compensation for these extra services in the absence of an agreement to that effect.[7] To illustrate, when one partner becomes seriously ill and the other partners transact all of the firm's business, they are not entitled to compensation for these services, because the sickness of a partner is considered a risk assumed in the relation. No agreement can be implied that the active partner

---

[4] Wilson v Moline, 234 Minn 174, 47 NW2d 865.

[5] Katz v Brewington, 71 Md 79, 20 A 139; UPA § 18(e).

[6] UPA § 19.

[7] Lewis v Hill, (Tex Civ App) 409 SW2d 946.

is to be compensated,[8] even though the services rendered by the active partner are such that ordinarily they would be rendered in the expectation of receiving compensation.

As an exception, "a surviving partner is entitled to reasonable compensation for his services in winding up the partnership affairs." [9] A minority of states, however, deny compensation even to the surviving partner.

(5) Repayment of Loans. A partner is entitled to have returned to him any money advanced to or for the firm. These amounts, however, must be separate and distinct from original or additional contributions to the capital of the firm.

(6) Payment of Interest. In the absence of an agreement to the contrary, contributions to capital do not draw interest. The theory is that the profits constitute sufficient compensation. A partner may, therefore, receive interest only on the capital contributed by him from the date when repayment should have been made.[10] The partners, of course, may agree to pay interest on the capital contributions.

A majority of courts treat advances in the form of loans just as if they were made by a stranger. The Uniform Partnership Act provides that "a partner, who in aid of the partnership makes any payment or advance beyond the amount of capital which he agrees to contribute, shall be paid interest from the date of the payment or advance." [11]

When one partner embezzles or unlawfully withholds partnership property or money, the other partner may recover interest thereon when he sues for a dissolution of the partnership and the recovery of his proportionate share of the assets embezzled or withheld.[12]

(7) Contribution and Indemnity. A partner who pays more than his share of the debts of the firm has a right to contribution from his copartners. Under this principle, if an employee of a partnership negligently injures a third person while acting within the scope of his employment and the injured party collects damages from one partner, the latter may enforce contribution from the copartners.

The UPA states that "the partnership must indemnify every partner in respect of payments made and personal liabilities reasonably incurred by him in the ordinary and proper conduct of its business or for the preservation of its business or property." [13] The partner has no right, however, to indemnity or reimbursement when he (a) acts in bad faith, (b) negligently causes the necessity for payment, or (c) has previously agreed to bear the expense alone.

---

[8] Conrad v Judson, (Tex Civ App) 465 SW2d 819.

[9] UPA § 18(f).

[10] § 18(d).

[11] § 18(c).

[12] Luchs v Ormsby, 171 Cal App 2d 377, 340 P2d 702.

[13] UPA § 18(b).

(8) Distribution of Capital. Each partner is entitled to receive a share of the firm property upon dissolution after the payment of all creditors and the repayment of loans made to the firm by partners. Unless otherwise stated in the partnership agreement, each partner is entitled to the return of his capital contribution.

After such distribution is made, each partner is the sole owner of the fractional part distributed to him, rather than a co-owner of all the property as he was during the existence of the partnership.

§ 46:3. Remedies of Partners. The remedies available to the members of a firm are, in some instances, limited because of the peculiar relation to the partners and because of the nature of their claims. In the following discussion the distinction between actions at law and actions in equity is preserved, although in most states and in the federal courts there is today only a civil action.[14]

(1) Actions at Law. An action on a partnership claim can only be brought in the partnership name.[15] A partner cannot maintain an action at law against the firm upon a claim against the partnership. A partnership cannot bring an action at law against one of its members on claims that the firm holds against him. In the absence of statute a partnership cannot maintain an action against another firm when they have partners in common.

One partner cannot maintain an action at law against another on claims involving partnership transactions.[16] There are two exceptions to this general rule: (a) when the claim has been distinguished from the firm dealings by agreement; and (b) when the firm accounts have been balanced and show the amount to be due.

Partners may sue each other at law in those cases in which there is no necessity of investigating the partnership accounts. Situations of this kind exist when a partner dissolves the relation in violation of his agreement, when a partner fails to furnish capital or services agreed, or when a partner wrongfully causes injuries to his copartner that in no way involve the partnership.

(2) Actions in Equity. The proper tribunal to settle all controversies growing out of partnership transactions is a court of equity. For example, an action by a partner to recover his share of profits should be brought in equity. The powers and the procedure of this court are such as to enable it to settle fully problems that arise in winding up the affairs of the firm.

In many instances an accounting is sought in connection with the dissolution of the firm. The Uniform Partnership Act states that a partner is entitled to an accounting (a) if he is wrongfully excluded from the partnership business or possession of its property by his copartners; (b) if the right

---

[14] See § 1:4(1).
[15] Apex Sales Co. v Abraham, (La App) 201 So2d 184.
[16] Catron v Watson, 12 Ariz App 132, 468 P2d 399.

exists under the terms of any agreement; (c) if he is a trustee; or (d) if other circumstances render an accounting just and reasonable.[17]

§ **46:4. Partner's Liability as to Particular Acts.** Just as a principal is not liable for every act of his agent, so the partnership and the members of the partnership are not liable for every act of each partner. Just as an agent's act binds the principal only when it is within the agent's scope of authority, real or apparent, so a partner's act binds the firm and other partners only when it is within the scope of the partner's authority, real or apparent.

(1) Contracts. All members of the firm are liable on contracts made by a partner for the partnership and in its name if they were made within the scope of his real or apparent authority. This is true even though the partners may be unknown to the third persons. Thus, a dormant partner, when discovered, is bound with the others.

When a partner, acting on behalf of the partnership, makes an authorized, simple contract in his own name, the other members of the firm are liable as undisclosed prinicpals.

When a partner with necessary authority executes commercial paper in the name of the firm, each partner is bound thereby, even though he had not individually signed the paper. (See p. 916, McCollum v Steitz.) If a partner signs a commercial paper in his own name, the partnership, as undisclosed principal, cannot sue or be sued thereon.[18]

When a borrowing partner gives the lender a promissory note which is his personal obligation, the partnership and the other partners cannot be held liable thereon even though the borrowing partner used the money for the benefit of the partnership.[19]

The fact that a partner has either express or implied authority to bind the partnership does not in itself establish that a contract made by him is a partnership contract. As in the case of agency situations generally, a contract between the third person and the principal, here the partnership, only arises when that is the intention of the parties. Consequently, where a third person and a partner contract intending to bind the partner individually rather than the partnership, no contract liability of the partnership is created.[20] Care must be taken to distinguish this situation from that in which the partnership is not disclosed and in which only the third person has the intention of dealing with the partner only, as in such cases the partnership may be bound or have rights under the rules governing undisclosed principals who act through authorized agents.

(2) Torts. All partners are liable for torts, such as fraud, trespass, negligence, and deceit, committed by one partner while transacting firm

---

[17] UPA § 22.
[18] The signing by the partner in such case is governed by the UCC § 3-403.
[19] Edwards Feed Mill v Johnson, (Tex Civ App) 302 SW2d 151.
[20] Ogallala Fertilizer Co. v Salsberry, 186 Neb 537, 184 NW2d 729.

business.[21] The members of a firm are also liable for breach of trust by a partner in respect to goods or money of a third person held by the firm.

When a partner is guilty of fraud in dealing with a third person, the partnership is liable for the consequences even though the commission of fraud was not within the scope of the partner's authority. (See p. 917, Zemelman v Boston Ins. Co.)

When one partner is guilty of misconduct with respect to a third person, the partnership and the other partners may be vicariously liable for such misconduct. The circumstances may be such that the other partners are themselves liable for acts of their own in failing to take steps to protect the third person's interest. The partnership is not liable for a tort that has no relation to the partnership business. This is so even though the partnership had been informed of the partner's conduct but had not taken any action thereon.[22]

(3) Crimes. The partners of a firm and the partnership itself are liable for certain crimes committed by a partner in the course of the business, such as selling goods without obtaining a necessary vendor's license or selling in violation of a statute prohibiting sale. If carrying on the firm business does not necessarily involve the commission of the act constituting a crime, the firm and the partners not participating in the commission of a crime or authorizing its commission generally are not criminally liable. This exception is not recognized in some cases, such as the making of prohibited sales to minors or sales of adulterated products.

As a practical matter, the criminal liability of a partnership is limited to the imposition of a fine because it is not possible to imprison the partnership.

§ 46:5. Nature of Partner's Liability. By virtue of local statutes, partners are jointly liable on all firm contracts in some states; they are jointly and severally liable in other states.[23] They are jointly and severally liable for all torts committed by an employee or one of the partners in the scope of the partnership business.[24]

When partners are liable for the wrongful injury caused a third person, the latter may sue all or any number of the members of the firm.

§ 46:6. Extent of Partner's Liability. Each member of the firm is individually and unlimitedly liable for the debts of the partnership regardless of his investment or his interest in its management. Moreover, the individual property of a partner may be sold in satisfaction of a judgment, even before the firm property has been exhausted.

(1) Liability for Breach of Duty. When a partner violates a duty owed to the partnership, his liability is determined by the general principles of law applicable to such conduct.

---

[21] UPA § 13.
[22] Kelsey-Seybold Clinic v Maclay, (Tex) 466 SW2d 716.
[23] Roberts v White, 117 Vt 573, 97 A2d 245.
[24] Morse v Mayberry, 183 Neb 89, 157 NW2d 881.

When one partner commits a fraud upon his partner, the injured partner may recover both compensatory and exemplary damages from the wrongdoing partner. (See p. 918, Morgan v Arnold.)

(2) Liability of New Partners. At common law a new partner entering an old firm is liable only for obligations arising thereafter. He may, however, expressly or impliedly assume the existing liabilities. When a new firm takes over the assets of an old firm, there is often an agreement that the new firm will pay existing obligations.

The UPA states that a "person admitted as a partner into an existing partnership is liable for all the obligations of the partnership arising before his admission as though he had been a partner when such obligations were incurred, except that this liability shall be satisfied only out of partnership property."[25] Thus, his liability does not extend to his individual property.

(3) Effect of Dissolution on Partner's Liability. A partner remains liable after dissolution unless the creditors expressly release him or unless the claims against the firm are satisfied. The UPA states the following rules: "(1) The dissolution of the partnership does not of itself discharge the existing liability of any partner. (2) A partner is discharged from any existing liability upon dissolution of the partnership by an agreement to that effect between himself, the partnership creditor, and the person or partnership continuing the business; and such agreement may be inferred from the course of dealing between the creditor having knowledge of the dissolution and the person or partnership continuing the business. (3) Where a person agrees to assume the existing obligations of a dissolved partnership, the partners whose obligations have been assumed shall be discharged from any liability to any creditor of the partnership who, knowing of the agreement, consents to a material alteration in the nature or time of payment of such obligations. (4) The individual property of a deceased partner shall be liable for all obligations of the partnership incurred while he was a partner but subject to the prior payment of his separate debts."[26]

§ 46:7. Enforcement of Partner's Liability. The manner in which the civil liability of a partner may be enforced depends upon the form of the lawsuit brought by the creditor. The firm may have been sued in the name of all the individual partners doing business as the partnership, as "Plaintiff v. *A*, *B*, and *C*, doing business as the Ajax Warehouse." In such a case, those partners named are bound by the judgment against the firm if they have been properly served in the suit. Partners either not named or not served are generally not bound by the judgment.[27]

When there is a dispute on the point, the question of whether one partner was acting in the scope of the partnership business at a particular time is a question to be submitted to the jury. (See p. 919, Phillips v Cook.)

---

[25] UPA § 17; also see §§ 41(1) and (7).
[26] § 36.
[27] Denver National Bank v Grimes, 97 Colo 158, 47 P2d 862.

If the judgment binds an individual partner, the creditor may enforce the judgment against that partner before, at the same time, or after he seeks to enforce the judgment against the firm or other partners who are also bound by the judgment. If a partner is not bound by the judgment, the creditor must bring another lawsuit against the partner in which he establishes that the defendant is a partner in the particular partnership and that a judgment was entered against the partnership for a partnership liability. When this is established, a judgment is entered in favor of the creditor against the particular partner. The creditor may then have execution on this judgment against the property of the partner.

§ 46:8. Suit in the Firm Name. At common law a partnership could not sue or be sued in the firm name on the theory that there was no legal person by that name. If the partnership was composed of *A, B,* and *C,* it was necessary for them to sue or be sued as *A, B,* and *C.* If the firm name was "The X Bakery," some states required that they appear in the action as "*A, B,* and *C,* trading as The X Bakery." By statute or court rule, this principle of the common law has been abolished in many states, and a partnership may sue or be sued either in the names of the partners or in the firm name.[28]

The identity of the parties to an action is determined by the nature of the obligation on which the action is brought. If the action is brought on a commercial paper held by one partner, the action must be brought in his name, although he could readily change this situation by indorsing the instrument to the firm.

[28] Lewis Manufacturing Co. v Superior Court, 140 Cal App 2d 245, 295 P2d 145.

CASES FOR CHAPTER 46

Grund v Wood

Colo App, 490 P2d 955 (1971)

Grund, Wood, and others were partners in a medical partnership. Paragraph 10.5 of the partnership agreement stated that a partner withdrawing from the partnership would not practice medicine within a five-mile radius of the partnership clinic for a period of two years after his withdrawal. It was further stated that if a withdrawing partner violated this covenant, he would forfeit $1,300 for every month that he had been a partner, not to exceed $15,600. The agreement further recited, "Such amount shall be deemed to be liquidated damages." Grund withdrew from the medical partnership. He sued to obtain his share of the partnership assets. Wood claimed that Grund had violated the anticompetitive covenant and held back $15,600. The lower court awarded the plaintiff his share of assets less $15,600. Grund appealed.

PIERCE, J. . . . Plaintiff [assigns as] error . . . the trial court's finding that paragraph 10.5 of the partnership agreement was a valid and enforceable liquidated damage provision rather than an unenforceable penalty or forfeiture. We cannot agree with plaintiff's contention.

Where a contract has been made not to engage in a particular profession within a stated area, it has been the policy of courts to construe such an agreement as being for liquidated damages rather than a penalty when the evidence shows that the stipulated amount of damages is reasonable and is not unjust, oppressive, or disproportionate to the damage that would result from the breach of such a covenant. . . . In

Farthing v San Mateo Clinic, 143 Cal App 2d 385, 299 P2d 977, a noncompetition agreement providing for liquidated damages was upheld where a retiring partner's rights to his unpaid partnership interest would be forfeited upon his resumption of practice within a proscribed area. The liquidated damages provision there was similarly based upon a scale determined by the length of time a withdrawing partner had been a member of the partnership. Therein, the court stated:

> "There is no way of calculating the future loss that will be suffered through the loss of this group of patients. . . . It is obvious that the measure selected is reasonably related to the anticipated loss. The interest in accounts receivable of a partner who was nearing parity would be much greater than that of one at the bottom of the scale, and a better established partner usually would take a much greater share of business from the clinic than would a partner who was not as well established."

. . . The trial court found . . . that it was the intention of the parties to provide for liquidated damages in the agreement and the method for assessing those damages was reasonable. [We] hold its determination that paragraph 10.5 was a valid and enforceable liquidated damages provision was proper. . . .

[Judgment affirmed.]

Moser v Williams

(Mo App) 443 SW2d 212 (1969)

Williams and Moser formed a partnership to sell a six-acre tract of land. On February 12, 1960, Williams made a contract in the name of the partnership to sell the land to a buyer at a substantial profit. Later, on February 12, Moser offered to sell his half interest in the partnership to Williams. Williams accepted the offer but did not inform Moser that he had made a contract to sell the partnership land. The sale of Moser's interest was made on the basis of a valuation which ignored the profit made on the undisclosed sale. When Moser later learned of that sale, he sued Williams for one-half the profit which the partnership would have made thereby. Judgment was entered for Moser and Williams appealed.

DOERNER, C. . . . The parties were partners, and as such a fiduciary relationship existed between them. . . . Accordingly, defendant was under the duty to exercise the utmost good faith in his relations with plaintiff. . . . As defendant himself testified, he entered into a contract with [third party] to sell the partnership property, at a profit, on the same day he accepted plaintiff's offer to sell his interest in the partnership land. Defendant admitted that he did not, either at that or any subsequent time, inform plaintiff of his contract with [third party] by which defendant stood to make a profit. Certainly, under those circumstances, suspicious on their face, the burden was on defendant to show that he had, in good faith, accepted plaintiff's offer before he was aware of or actually entered into the contract he made with the [third party]. Defendant, . . . on cross-examination revealed that the [third party], through a broker, before February 12, 1960, had made repeated offers to defendant, none of which . . . were communicated by defendant to plaintiff. . . .

Furthermore, while the case was tried below and decided on the issue of which contract was made first, we are of the opinion that plaintiff was entitled to prevail in any event. While defendant's acceptance of plaintiff's offer occurred on February 12, 1960, defendant did not seriously attempt to complete the purchase of plaintiff's interest until April 18, 1960, after defendant closed his sale to [third party] on April 15, 1960. In the interim . . . defendant never at any time disclosed to plaintiff that he had agreed to sell the partnership land . . . at a profit. . . .

[Judgment affirmed.]

McCollum v Steitz

261 Cal App 2d 76, 67 Cal Rptr 703 (1968)

Steitz and Hamrick were partners operating a restaurant, the Desert Inn. On behalf of the partnership, Hamrick borrowed money from McCollum and signed a promissory note which read, "For value received — promise to pay." The note was signed by Hamrick and under his

name he wrote the name "The Desert Inn" and its address. The note was not paid. McCollum sued Steitz on the theory that the note was a partnership obligation and therefore Steitz was liable although not a party thereto. Steitz claimed that the note was signed by Hamrick as an individual note and therefore did not bind the partnership, in which case Steitz would not be liable for its payment. Judgment was entered for McCollum and Steitz appealed.

CONLEY, P.J. . . . A general partner is the agent of the partnership and may bind the partnership. . . .

Appellant cites Bank of America v Kumle, 70 Cal App 2d 362, 160 P2d 875, in his argument that respondents did not meet their burden of proof. However, that case is distinguishable. In that case, the notes in question were not executed in the partnership name but in an individual name, and they were not executed for the purpose of furthering or meeting the obligations of the partnership business, for at that time there was no partnership, and obviously a partnership was not then carrying on the business. Here, the partnership had been in existence and operating the "Desert Inn" for many years; appellant knew of the debt before the execution of this note; the partner of appellant testified the note was intended to be that of the "Desert Inn" as did Mrs. Hey . . . .

The principal contention made by the appellant is that the promissory note was not executed in compliance with the requirements of the Commercial Code so as to bind Mr. Steitz as a partner. Over objection, evidence came in that Mr. and Mrs. Hey had at one time made a loan to the "Desert Inn" in the total sum of $20,000 to buy stock and pay taxes. . . .

Sections 3401 and 3403 of the Commercial Code declare the signature and form thereof required in executing a negotiable instrument such as the one in this suit. Section 3401 reads as follows: "(1) No person is liable on an instrument unless his signature appears thereon. (2) A signature is made by use of any name, including any trade or assumed name, upon an instrument, or by any word or mark used in lieu of a written signature."

Section 3403 of the Commercial Code provides in part: "A signature may be made by an agent or other representative, and his authority to make it may be established as in other cases of representation. No particular form of appointment is necessary to establish such authority."

. . . While no person is liable on an instrument unless his signature appears on it, . . . a partnership is liable on a note executed on behalf of the partnership . . . , and all partners are jointly liable for the obligation. . . .

. . . The name "Desert Inn" is on the note. One may be liable under a trade name even though one's own name is not on the instrument. . . .

The "Desert Inn" was a well-known business. Section 3403, subdivision (3), of the Commercial Code states, in part, that the name of an organization *preceded or followed* by the name of the authorized person is the signature made in a representative capacity. Here, Hamrick's name came before that of the "Desert Inn." The address "2445 Whites Bridge Rd." is set forth twice on the note. . . . The note was properly executed by Mr. Hamrick, who was the manager of the partnership business, and . . . in writing "Desert Inn" under his own name with two statements of the address, he properly included the necessary factors to make the partnership liable.

[Judgment affirmed.]

Zemelman v Boston Ins. Co.

4 Cal App 3d 15, 84 Cal Rptr 206 (1970)

Zemelman and others did business as a partnership under the name of Art Seating Company. The partnership obtained a fire insurance policy from the Boston Insurance Company. There was a fire loss and a claim was filed under the policy. The claim was prepared by one of the partners, Irving Zemelman. The insurance company asserted that false statements were made by Irving and, consequently, the insurer was not liable on the policy because the policy contained an express provision stating that it was void if a false claim was made. The partnership replied that it was not bound by any

fraudulent statements of Irving, as the making of fraudulent statements was not within the scope of his authority. Judgment was entered for the insurance company, and the partnership appealed.

REPPY, A.J. . . . "All the partners will be bound by the fraud of one of the partners in contracts relating to the partnership made with innocent third parties. That is to say, all are responsible for the injury occasioned by the fraud, . . . whether they were cognizant of the fraud or not. The rule is the same as it is in respect to the responsibility of the principal for the fraud of his agent, while acting within the scope of his authority; and, indeed, a partner becomes liable for the fraud of his co-partner, because of the relation each bears to the other of agent in the partnership business." . . .

If it can be said that Irving's acts were done within the scope of his authority as a copartner, then the partnership is bound to accept the legal consequences of such acts. . . . Acts within the scope of authority of a copartner are generally considered to be those which are ". . . for apparently carrying on in the usual way the business of the partnership of which he is a member . . . ." . . .

Appellents take the position that Irving's acts were *not* within the scope of his authority as a copartner, relying on Nuffer v Insurance Co. of North America, 236 Cal App 2d 349, 45 Cal Rptr 918. Such reliance is misplaced. In *Nuffer* an agent had a power of attorney and willfully burned down premises insured under certain fire insurance policies. The appellate court ruled (at page 357) that a principal is not foreclosed from collecting the proceeds of insurance policies because his agent committed *arson,* an act not within that agent's apparent authority. In doing so, the court cited certain decisions which held that a principal is responsible for the results of his agent's filing of a false insurance claim even without the principal's knowledge, and distinguished them because in each the *false filing* was done with apparent authority. . . .

Because the partnership is bound by the acts of Irving, . . . the insurance contracts were voided and the partnership was foreclosed from receiving any part of their proceeds. . . .

[Judgment affirmed.]

Morgan v Arnold

(Tex Civ App) 441 SW2d 897 (1969)

Arnold and Morgan were partners. They voluntarily dissolved the partnership on the basis of a financial statement prepared by Morgan. In this statement he knowingly undervalued the assets of the partnership so that Arnold received approximately $13,000 less than he was entitled to. Subsequent to the dissolution, Arnold learned of the deception and sued Morgan for damages. The jury awarded Arnold compensatory damages of approximately $13,000 and exemplary damages of $25,000. Morgan appealed.

WILLIAMS, J. . . . Fraud is one of the grounds for an award of exemplary damages. . . . In essence it is the purpose or intention of the defendant which is determinative of his liability for exemplary damages. . . . Aggravating circumstances may authorize such exemplary damages as, in the jury's opinion, the defendant's conduct justifies. . . .

"It has been said that as a prerequisite to the recovery of exemplary damages, it must appear that the representations forming the basis of the fraud action were false, that they were willfully made with full knowledge that they were false and with intent to injure the other party, and that the other party was injured as a result of the representations." . . .

Evidence of willfulness on the part of the defendant may be implied from actual wrongful acts and conduct of the defendant. . . .

The jury had before them and considered all of the facts, both direct and circumstantial, dealing with the question of falsity of the representation concerning the value of the partnership interest and the reason and motive possessed by Morgan in making such false representation. We conclude from our review of the evidence that it cannot be said, as contended by appellant, that there is no evidence to support the answer of the jury . . . nor can we say that the answer of the jury thereto is clearly erroneous.

It must be borne in mind that we are not here dealing with an arm's length transaction between strangers but, on the contrary, we are confronted with the relationship between partners who had fiduciary relationship with each other. . . . Partners have a fiduciary relationship and . . . when persons enter into a partnership, "each consents, as a matter of law, to have his conduct towards the other measured by the standards of the finer loyalties exacted by courts of equity." It has been held that failure to inform a co-owner of material facts breaches the fiduciary duty between partners and that such omission results in a "legal fraud." . . .

Exemplary damages, by their very nature are unliquidated and the amount to be awarded rests largely in the discretion of the jury. Unless the award is so large as to indicate that it is the result of passion, prejudice or corruption, or that evidence has been disregarded, the verdict of the jury is conclusive and will not be set aside as excessive, either by the trial court or on appeal. . . .

[Judgment affirmed.]

Phillips v Cook

239 Md 215, 210 A2d 743 (1965)

Phillips and Harris were partners selling automobiles. While driving a partnership car on partnership business, Harris collided with Cook. The Cooks sued Phillips and Harris. The trial judge submitted to the jury whether Harris was in fact operating the automobile in the scope of the partnership business at the time of the collision. The jury found that he was and returned a verdict in favor of the plaintiffs against both defendants. Judgment was entered thereon and Phillips appealed.

MARBURY, J. . . . In October 1959, Harris and Phillips entered into a partnership on an equal basis under the name of "Dan's Used Cars" for the purpose of buying and selling used automobiles. Phillips owned the lot and a gas station adjacent to it. He went into the partnership with Harris because the latter had the experience and money which he did not have to put into the business. This partnership agreement was oral and it was agreed between the partners that each would have an equal voice in the conduct and management of the business.

Neither of the partners owned a personal automobile or had one titled in his individual name. It was agreed as a part of the partnership arrangement that Harris would use a partnership vehicle for transportation to and from his home. Under this agreement, he was authorized to demonstrate and sell such automobiles, call on dealers for the purpose of seeing and purchasing used cars, or go to the Department of Motor Vehicles on partnership business after leaving the lot in the evening and before returning the next day. Both Harris and Phillips could use a partnership automobile as desired. Such vehicles were for sale at any time during the day or night and at various times and places they had "for sale" signs on the windshields. Harris had no regular hours to report to the used car lot but could come and go as he saw fit. Phillips testified that it was essential that Harris have a partnership automobile for his transportation to and from his home, and that it was the most practical way to operate. It is also significant to note that both Harris and Phillips testified at the trial that each paid for the gasoline used in the partnership automobiles they drove. However, Phillips said at the time of the taking of his deposition, which was admitted in evidence, that the gasoline used came out of the used car business and was for cars that were for sale on the lot. He admitted that the Mercury sedan involved in the collision was for sale and had been sitting on the lot. This car was titled in the name of the partnership and Phillips could have used it if he wanted to. After the accident, he objected to Harris using the dealer's tags because "he didn't want to get in any more accidents." About a week later, the partnership was terminated and Harris left the business. . . .

. . . Appellant contends that because Harris was on his way home from the used car lot at the time of the accident the evidence was insufficient to support a finding by the jury that he was acting within the scope of the partnership arrangement or that such use of the vehicle was of benefit to the partnership.

In a case involving a partnership, the contract of partnership constitutes all of its members as agents of each other and each partner acts both as a principal and as the agent of the others in regard to acts done within the apparent scope of the business, purpose and agreement of the partnership or for its benefit. It is clear that the partnership is bound by the partner's wrongful act if done within the scope of the partnership's business. . . .

The test of the liability of the partnership and of its members for the torts of any one partner is whether the wrongful act was done within what may reasonably be found to be the scope of the business of the partnership and for its benefit. The extent of the authority of a partner is determined essentially by the same principles as those which measure the scope of an agent's authority. . . . Partnership cases may differ from principal and agent and master and servant relationships because in the non-partnership cases, the element of control or authorization is important. This is not so in the case of a partnership for a partner is also a principal. . . .

In the past, we have held both in workmen's compensation cases and others that where an employer authorizes or furnishes the employee transportation to and from his work as an incident to his employment, or as a benefit to the employer, the employee is considered in the course of his employment when so traveling. This is so whether it be to his place to eat, sleep or to the employee's home. . . .

Here, the fact that the defendant partners were in the used car business; that the very vehicle involved in the accident was one of the partnership assets for sale at all times, day or night, at any location; that Harris was on call by Phillips or customers at his home—he went back to the lot two or three times after going home; that he had no set time and worked irregular hours, coupled with the fact that he frequently stopped to conduct partnership business on the way to and from the lot; drove partnership vehicles to the Department of Motor Vehicles, and to dealers in Baltimore to view and buy used cars while on his way to or from his home; that one of the elements of the partnership arrangement was that each partner could have full use of the vehicles; that the use of the automobile by Harris for transportation to and from his home was admittedly "essential" to the partnership arrangement and the most practical and convenient way to operate; and that Harris conducted partnership business both at the used car lot and from his home requires that the question of whether the use of the automobile at the time of the accident was in the partnership interest and for its benefit be submitted to the jury. We find that the lower court did not err . . . .

[Judgment affirmed.]

QUESTIONS AND CASE PROBLEMS

1. Delay and Foster entered into a partnership. Thereafter Foster wrongfully dissolved the partnership. Delay brought an action at law against Foster to recover damages arising out of the wrongful dissolution and breach of the partnership agreement. The defendant contended that the plaintiff was not entitled to bring an action at law but should have brought an action in equity. Do you agree? [Delay v Foster, 34 Idaho 691, 203 P 461]
2. The St. John Transportation Co., a corporation, made a contract with the firm of Bilyeu & Herstel, contractors, by which the latter was to construct a ferryboat. Herstel, a member of the firm of contractors, executed a contract in the firm name with Benbow for certain materials and labor in connection with the construction of the ferryboat. In an action brought by Benbow to enforce a lien against the ferryboat, called The James Johns, it was contended that all members of the firm were bound by the contract made by Herstel. Do you agree? [Benbow v The James Johns, 56 Ore 554, 108 P 634]
3. Kittilsby and Vevelstad were partners doing work on a mining claim known as the Sea Level Claim. Kittilsby did the assessment work for one year and then went to Seattle, upon the promise of Vevelstad to do the work for the

following year. Vevelstad did not do the work, and the claim became open to location. Vevelstad procured Singleton, who was to act for him, to locate and prove a claim covering the same district. After Singleton had conveyed the claim to him for a nominal consideration, Vevelstad sold the claim to the Juneau Sea Level Copper Mines. Thereafter Kittilsby brought an action against Vevelstad to recover half of the proceeds of the sale. Was he entitled to judgment? [Kittilsby v Vevelstad, 103 Wash 126, 173 P 744]

4. Martinoff brought a suit against Triboro Roofing Co. and a partnership named Renray Realty Co. The plaintiff named the partnership in its firm name as a defendant and also each of the seven partners. Service of process was made on only one of the partners, namely David Raynes. What liabilities of the firm and the individual partners could be enforced in this action? [Martinoff v Triboro Roofing Co., 228 NYS2d 139]

5. Henslee and Boyd formed a partnership to operate a sawmill business. As part of the agreement, Henslee agreed to sell timber to the partnership at the prevailing market prices. Boyd later sued Henslee to set aside the agreement on the ground of fraud and breach of partnership duties. One of the objections made by Boyd was that Henslee had refused to sell timber to the partnership as required by the agreement. Henslee replied that he had refused to sell because the partnership could not pay in cash. Boyd then answered that Henslee should not have insisted on a cash sale since that would use up the partnership's ready cash. Was Henslee guilty of a breach of his partnership duty? [Henslee v Boyd, 235 Ark 369, 360 SW2d 505]

6. A partnership agreement specified that the partners who worked as full-time employees "shall draw a salary for their work in such amounts as may be agreed on from time to time by unanimous consent and agreement of all the partners." In a dispute between Horn, one of the partners, and the partnership, it was claimed by Horn that this agreement entitled him to compensation for the life of the partnership, and could not be terminated by a vote of the other partners. Was he correct? [Horn v Builders Supply Co., (Tex Civ App) 401 SW2d 143]

47 Special Ventures

GENERAL PRINCIPLES

New forms of business organizations are evolving to meet the modern business and investment needs.

§ **47:1. Introduction.** No one questions the statement that man's way of life and his pattern of doing business are continually changing. As man undertakes new activities he is faced with the problem of organization. How should he structure the enterprise? This has both a positive and a negative aspect. As to the positive, it is necessary to employ that form of structure or organization which will permit the doing of the desired work or the attainment of the desired goal in the most efficient manner. As to the negative, how can the enterprise and the participants be protected from the hazards that may arise?

Initially the entrepreneur and society tend to follow existing patterns. This is due in part to the fact that the old familiar patterns and devices have been working reasonably well. It is also due to the inability of man to imagine a new structure. Slowly, however, discontent arises with some aspect of the old patterns and man attempts a slight modification. After a while the modifications become so dominant that it can be recognized that the structure is no longer the old pattern modified but is in effect a new pattern. A number of these variant patterns are considered in this chapter. Some of them are of interest today primarily as a matter of legal and societal history. Others are very much in use.

§ **47:2. Purpose of Special Venture.** Today's special venture may be either permanent or temporary. Down to the middle of this century, persons organizing a business generally hoped to stay in that business the rest of their lives or for many years. Today it is common to form temporary ventures.

These are sometimes temporary because the subject matter or life of the contemplated enterprise is not continuing. For example, when several contractors pool their resources for the purpose of constructing a highway, that particular venture is terminated when the highway is completed. Had the contractors so agreed, a permanent continuing relationship could have been formed. Structurally it would probably be a partnership or a corporation. In view of the one-project lifespan of the venture above described, the contractors would probably not adopt a formal organization but would have a loose working arrangement or joint venture.

In many instances the special venture is merely a new way of doing old operations in order to obtain a particular advantage, generally a tax advantage. Thus, we have limited partnerships formed, not for the purpose of investing and obtaining a money return on the limited partner's investment, but for the purpose of obtaining tax shelter benefits for the limited partner. Likewise, a general partnership may be formed not for the purpose of staying in business but for the purpose of effecting a sale of a single proprietorship. Here instead of *A*, a single proprietor, selling his business to *B*, *A* and *B* will form a partnership which will be immediately liquidated with the assets being distributed to *B*. This has the same ownership transferring effect as though the business had been sold by *A* directly to *B* but *A* will have in some instances a better tax position than in a direct sale. Sometimes the owner of property wishes to continue to use it but desires to sell it to obtain certain advantages. In such a case, the owner may sell the property to a buyer who will then lease it back to the seller. When the sales price and lease rentals are properly adjusted, this can result in a tax saving.

In this chapter a number of patterns for special ventures are considered. In addition to these, the enterprise may be based upon an agency, a partnership, or a corporation.

FRANCHISES

The use of franchises has expanded rapidly in recent years as a method of controlling and financing operations by the franchisor and as a method of investment and participation for the franchisee.

§ 47:3. Definition. A *franchise* has been defined by the Federal Trade Commission for the purpose of one of its investigations as "an arrangement in which the owner of a trademark, tradename, or copyright licenses others, under specified conditions or limitations, to use the trademark, tradename, or copyright in purveying goods or services." The franchise has developed in the American economy as a means by which a business can expand through numerous outlets and maintain control of operations, but shift to someone else the burdens and problems of actual operation. To the *franchisee* (the holder of the franchise), the franchise has the attraction of permitting him to operate as a single proprietor or one-man business or a small corporation, yet not stand alone in the economic world because he has the advantages of being associated with the *franchisor* (the grantor of the franchise) or of selling the franchisor's nationally advertised product or service.

§ 47:4. The Franchisor and the Franchisee. Theoretically the relationship between the franchisor and the franchisee is an arm's length relationship between two independent contractors, their respective rights being determined by the contract existing between them.

(1) Prices and Standards. The franchise device is frequently used as a means of maintaining prices or standards, or both. Depending upon the nature of the business, the franchisor may be content to charge the franchisee according to the franchisor's established price scale or contract and is not concerned with the prices or charges of the franchisee in dealing with its customers. If the franchisor is not content with letting the franchisee fix his own prices, the franchisor might be able to require a price maintenance under fair trade acts [1] or by the device of selling on consignment.[2] If the franchise involves licensing the franchisee to use a trademark or formula of the franchisor, the latter may be able to exercise greater control over the franchisee than otherwise.

Ordinarily there should be no question of the validity of provisions seeking to maintain standards since a franchisor has a legitimate interest in maintaining standards in order to protect his name and reputation.

(2) Purchase of Materials and Supplies. Ordinarily the franchise carries with it an obligation of the franchisee to deal exclusively with the franchisor and thus provides the franchisor with an outlet for his goods and services. When the franchise relates to a product-selling business, the exclusive dealings provision imposes upon the seller the duty "to use best efforts to supply the goods and [upon] the buyer to use best efforts to promote their sale." [3] Exclusive dealings provisions will in some cases be held invalid, however, under the federal antitrust law. For example, when the franchisee is tied to exclusive purchasing of requirements from the franchisor, there may be a violation of the federal antitrust law.[4]

(3) Payment for Franchise. The franchise holder will ordinarily pay a flat initial fee for the privilege of being granted the franchise. Commonly there will be a percentage scale clause so that additional payments are made to the franchisor of a stated percentage of the amount of sales or the volume of business of the franchisee. The franchise agreement may also require the franchisee to pay a percentage of advertising costs of the franchisor.

(4) Penalty Powers. Franchise contracts contain various provisions by which the grantor of the franchise can enforce the terms of the franchise contract without going to court. When the terms relate to service operations, such as the operation of a hotel or motel, the franchise contract may provide for inspections by the franchisor and may give him the right, at the franchisee's

---

[1] Since the only persons involved are the franchisor and the franchisee, who are the parties to the price maintenance agreement, no question arises as to nonsigners (see § 5:4) although a fair trade act may be inapplicable because the transaction does not relate to a commodity within the scope of the statutes.

[2] Such agreements may violate the federal antitrust law, however, when placed in an economically coercive setting. See Simpson v Union Oil Co., 377 US 13.

[3] UCC § 2-306(2).

[4] Siegel v Chicken Delight, Inc., (CA9) 448 F2d 43.

expense, to place an employee of the franchisor in charge of the franchisee's business in the event that the franchise contract terms are not met. More drastic penalties may be provided in the form of the reservation of the power of the franchisor to suspend or revoke the franchise. Such remedies are commonly employed when the franchise holder does not meet "production" or sales quotas.

When the relationship between the franchisor and a franchisee is designed primarily to effect the sale of products manufactured by the franchisor, the relationship is governed by Article 2 of the Uniform Commercial Code and the fundamental "selling" characteristic of the relationship is not to be obscured by provisions in the contract relating to franchising and services.[5]

In some instances the grantor of the franchise has acted in an arbitrary manner or has made unreasonable demands upon the franchise holder. There is no general rule of law protecting franchise holders, although it is possible that in time the concept of unconscionability [6] will be extended by the courts so as to monitor or police the terms and operation of a franchise contract. At present, federal legislation is the greatest protection to the franchise holder, the antitrust law protecting him from certain oppressive practices, with the Automobile Dealer's Day in Court Act [7] protecting the holders of automobile dealership franchises.

By federal statute an automobile dealer holding a franchise from a manufacturer may sue the manufacturer for damages arising from the manufacturer's failure to act in "good faith" in complying with any terms or provisions of franchise, or in terminating, cancelling, or not renewing the dealer's franchise.[8]

(5) ***Duration.*** The franchise may run as long as the parties agree. Generally it will run a short period, such as a year, so that the franchise holder is well aware that if he wants to stay in business under the franchise, he must adhere to the terms of the contract and keep the franchise grantor satisfied. Franchise contracts generally contain an additional provision permitting termination of the franchise upon notice. The fact that the franchise holder has spent much time and money on the assumption that he would continue to have the franchise does not bar the franchisor from terminating the franchise agreement when so authorized by its terms, although some courts will bar a termination without cause until the franchise has run sufficiently long to enable the franchisee to recapture his capital investment.

When a lease and dealership contract are executed by a gasoline company and a gas station operator as parts of the same transaction, the gasoline

---

[5] Warner Motors, Inc. v Chrysler Motors Corp., (DC ED Pa) 5 UCCRS 365; compare Division of the Triple T Service, Inc. v Mobil Oil Corp., 60 Misc 2d 720; 304 NYS2d 191.

[6] See § 15:6.

[7] See § 15:6.

[8] 15 USC § 1222. Several states have similar statutes. As to the meaning of good faith, see § 15:5.

company can only terminate the lease when it would be allowed to terminate the dealership agreement. Consequently, where by statute it could only terminate the dealership for cause, it could not terminate the lease without cause although the lease expressly gave the right to terminate on ten days' notice. (See p. 934, Shell Oil Co. v Marinello.)

(6) Statutory Regulation. There are several statutory reform movements, both at the federal and the state levels, to provide general protection for the franchise holder. In one sense, this is merely another effort on the part of society to equalize the bargaining positions of the parties, who in theory are bargaining equals but who in actual practice are not. Viewed in this light, the modern movement for consumer protection[9] and the movement for the protection of franchise holders are closely related.

Protective regulation of franchisees generally relates to problems of fraud in the sale of the franchise and protecting the franchisee from unreasonable demands and termination by the franchisor. The sale of franchises is often fraudulent with the franchisor misrepresenting the "get rich quick" aspects and the scope of the enterprise. Members of the small consumer class are particularly vulnerable to the sales appeal of the franchisor for the franchise is sold as a way to obtain financial independence and to "be your own boss." Too often the franchise operation exists only on paper so that the individual franchise is worth substantially less than the price the franchisee pays for it. In such circumstances the franchisee is in the same unfortunate position as the defrauded buyer of stock of a corporation. Because of this similarity, a number of states have proceeded against the fraudulent vendor of franchises by applying the law regulating the sale of securities. Other courts refuse to hold that the statute governing the sale of securities is applicable to the sale of a franchise. (See p. 936, Brown v Computer Credit System, Inc.)

Franchise promotion plans which pay a franchisee a bonus for each new recruit which he obtains have been condemned in some states as an illegal lottery.[10]

(a) THE FOREIGN FRANCHISOR. One of the big problems facing a franchisee is that the franchisor is often a foreign enterprise. This imposes a substantial burden on a franchisee who seeks to bring suit against the franchisor. To facilitate suing the foreigner, most states have in recent years adopted long-arm statutes.[11] Under such a statute the franchisee may bring suit against the franchisor in the state of the franchisee's residence or place of business. When the franchisor conducted a selling campaign within the forum state and was obligated to render certain services, there is a sufficient contact with the forum to justify the application of the long-arm statute

---

[9] See Ch. 8.
[10] Bond v Koscot Interplanetary, Inc., (Fla App) 276 So2d 198.
[11] See Appendix 1.

as to local contracts and to permit suit by the forum franchisee against the nonresident franchisor.[12]

§ 47:5. The Franchisor and Third Persons. Generally the franchisor is not liable in any way to a third person dealing with or affected by the franchise holder. This freedom from liability, while at the same time maintaining control over the general pattern of operations, is one of the reasons why franchisors grant franchises. If the negligence of the franchisee causes harm to a third person, the franchisor is not liable because the franchisee is regarded as an independent contractor. (See p. 937, Quijada Corp. v General Motors Corp.) When the franchisee makes a contract with a third person, the franchisor is not liable on the contract since the franchisee is not the agent of the franchisor and does not have authority to bind the franchisor by contract.

(1) Actual Control. An exception is made to the foregoing rules when the franchisor exercises such actual control over the operations of the franchise holder that the latter is not to be regarded as an independent contractor but rather as an employee or agent of the franchisor. This conclusion is likely to be reached when the franchisee makes contracts in the name of the franchisor, the franchisor controls the hiring and firing of employees of the franchisee, and the franchisor alone can adjust customer complaints. Likewise, when a franchisee is so controlled by a franchisor that it is in fact the alter ego of the franchisor, the franchisor will be liable to a customer of the franchisee where a consumer protection statute seeks to protect consumers from exploitation by being charged for unused instructions, services, or goods.[13]

(2) Product Liability. When the franchise involves the resale of goods manufactured or obtained by the franchisor and supplied by him to the franchisee, there is the growing likelihood that if the product causes harm to the franchisee's customers, the franchisor will be liable to the customer on theories of warranty [14] or strict tort [15] liability.

Similarly, when a franchisor establishes the standards under which franchisees make products, the franchisor is liable to an injured person as though he were a manufacturer or seller,[16] even though the manufacturing franchisee is an independent contractor.[17]

---

[12] Doug Sanders Gold Intercontinental v American Manhattan Industries, Inc., (DC ED Wis) 359 F Supp 918.

[13] Weil v Arthur Murray, Inc., (NY Civil Court) 67 Misc 2d 417, 324 NYS2d 381.

[14] UCC §§ 2-313 and 2-314.

[15] See § 28:18.

[16] Carter v Joseph Bancroft & Sons Co., (DC ED Pa) 360 F Supp 1103.

[17] It would be more accurate to describe the franchisee as an independent user, as he does not contract "to do" but basically merely "to use." In many instances the franchisee is under an obligation to maintain a specified quota, in which case he may more properly be called an independent contractor.

§ 47:6. The Franchisee and Third Persons. When the franchise holder has any contract relationship or contact with a third person, the contract or tort liability of the franchisee is the same as though there were no franchise. For example, if the franchise is to operate a restaurant, the franchise holder is liable to a customer for breach of an implied warranty of the fitness of the food for human consumption to the same extent as though the franchise holder were running his own restaurant under his own name. If the franchise holder negligently causes harm to a third person, as by running over him with a truck used in the enterprise, the conclusion is the same and the tort liability of the franchise holder is determined by the principles which would be applicable if no franchise existed. The franchise holder is liable on the contract that he makes in his own name.

Conversely stated, the fact that there is a franchise does not add to or subtract from the liability which the franchisee would have in the same situation had there been no franchise.

SPECIAL VENTURE ORGANIZATIONS

When joint or common participation is sought, a special venture organization might be formed instead of a decentralized structure, such as that in a franchise system, or a standard organization, such as a corporation.

§ 47:7. Limited Partnership. A common form of modified partnership is the limited partnership. This form of partnership is solely a creature of statute; that is, it cannot be created in the absence of a statute authorizing it. Most of the states have adopted the Uniform Limited Partnership Act (ULPA).[18]

In a *limited partnership* certain members contribute capital without assuming personal liability for firm debts beyond the loss of their investment.[19] These members are known as *special* or *limited partners*. The members who manage the business and assume full personal liability for firm debts are *general partners*. A limited partnership can be formed under the ULPA by "one or more general partners and one or more limited partners." [20]

Unlike a general partnership, this special form can be created only by executing and swearing to a certificate setting forth the essential details of the partnership and the relative rights of the partners. The certificate, when executed, must be recorded in the office of the official in charge of public records, such as the Recorder of Deeds, of the county in which the principal place of business of the partnership is located.

The limited partner contributes cash or property, but not services. With certain exceptions, his name cannot appear in the firm name. His rights are limited to receiving his share of the profits and a return of capital upon dissolution; he cannot exercise any control over the business. If improper

---

[18] This Act has been adopted in all states except Alabama, Delaware, and Louisiana, and is in force in the District of Columbia and the Virgin Islands.

[19] Lichtyger v Franchard Corp., 18 NY2d 528, 277 NYS2d 377, 223 NE2d 869.

[20] Uniform Limited Partnership Act, § 1.

use is made of his name, giving the public the impression that he is an active partner, or if he exercises a control over the business, he becomes liable as a general partner. In any case, a limited partner cannot withdraw his capital contribution when it is needed to pay creditors.

While a limited partner cannot take part in the actual operation of the partnership without subjecting himself to liability as a general partner, he may give general management advice in seeking to salvage a failing enterprise without thereby losing the benefit of his "limited" status with respect to a general partner. That is, a general partner cannot require the limited partner to share in the losses of the enterprise. (See p. 938, Weil v Diversified Properties.)

The dissolution and winding up of limited partnerships is governed by the same principles applicable to general partnerships.[21] In many respects the ULPA follows the general pattern of the UPA.

A general partner is not to be deemed the agent of the limited partner so that the conducting of the business by the general partner within the forum state does not constitute the doing of business by the foreign limited partner.[22]

Although the limited partner is in fact making an investment in the enterprise, statutes regulating the making of investments by the purchase of securities do not apply to the formation of a limited partnership.[23]

§ 47:8. Joint Venture. A *joint venture,* or joint adventure, is a relationship in which two or more persons combine their labor or property for a single undertaking and share profits and losses equally,[24] or as otherwise agreed. Where several contractors pool all their assets in order to construct one tunnel, their relationship is a joint venture.[25]

The statute of frauds does not apply to a joint venture agreement even though the object of the adventure is a real estate operation.[26]

A joint venture is similar in many respects to a partnership, but it differs primarily in that the joint venture relates to the prosecution of a single venture or transaction, although its accomplishment may require several years, while a partnership is generally a continuing business or enterprise. This is not an exact definition because a partnership may be expressly created for a single transaction. Because this distinction is so insubstantial, many courts hold that a joint venture is subject to the same principles of law as partnerships.[27] Thus, the duties owed by the joint venturers to each other are the same as in the case of partnerships, with the result that when the joint venturers agree to acquire and develop a certain tract of land but some of

---

[21] Oil & Gas Ventures, Inc. v Cheyenne Oil Corp., 41 Del Ch 596, 202 A2d 282.
[22] Lynn v Cohen, (DC SD NY) 359 F Supp 565.
[23] Garbo v Hilleary Franchise Systems, Inc., (Mo App) 479 SW2d 491.
[24] Burbank v Sinclair Prairie Oil Co., 304 Ky 833, 202 SW2d 420.
[25] Wheatley v Halvorson, 213 Ore 228, 323 P2d 49.
[26] Yonofsky v Wernick, (DC SD NY) 362 F Supp 1005.
[27] Pedersen v Manitowac Co., NYS2d 412, 306 NYS2d 903, 255 NE2d 146.

the venturers secretly purchase the land in their own names, the other joint venturers are entitled to damages for this breach of the duty of loyalty.[28]

An agreement for farming operations that provides for sharing expenses and profits, or an agreement to purchase real estate for development and resale, will often be regarded as a joint venture.

It is essential that there be a community of interest or purpose and that each coadventurer have an equal right to control the operations or activities of the undertaking. The actual control of the operations may be entrusted to one of the joint adventurers. Thus, the fact that one joint adventurer is placed in control of the farming and livestock operations of the undertaking and appears to be the owner of the land does not destroy the joint adventure relationship.[29]

As in the case of partnerships, a minor may be a member of a joint venture.

It is generally essential that the joint venture be for a business or commercial purpose.[30] (See p. 940, Edlebeck v Hooten.)

The fact that there is a common business objective or goal does not establish that the persons seeking that objective or goal are engaged in a joint venture. The relationship may be merely a contract to employ an independent contractor or an employee, or a sales contract.[31] In determining whether a relationship is one of employment or a joint venture, it is often important to determine whether one person carries workmen's compensation insurance with respect to the other, whether Social Security taxes are paid with respect to him, and whether federal withholding tax deductions are made from the share of profits received by any of the persons.[32] Persons who are joint venturers will ordinarily have unlimited joint and several liability with respect to obligations of the enterprise, without respect to whether they have signed any agreement or commercial paper executed on behalf of the venture.

When the joint venture agreement states the time for which the venture is to last, such specification will be given effect. In the absence of a fixed duration provision, a joint venture is ordinarily terminable at the will of any participant,[33] except that when the joint venture clearly relates to a particular transaction, such as the construction of a particular bridge, the joint venture ordinarily lasts until the particular transaction or project is completed or becomes impossible to complete.

When there is joint activity by an owner and a prospective buyer, such activity may be a joint venture so that the negligence of the one is imputed to the other. For example, where an owner of an airplane and a person who contemplated buying a fractional interest in the plane were

---

[28] Boyd v Bevilacqua, 247 Cal App 2d 272, 55 Cal Rptr 610.
[29] McAnelly's Estate, 127 Mont 158, 258 P2d 741.
[30] Bach v Liberty Mutual Fire Insurance Co., 36 Wis 2d 72, 152 NW2d 911.
[31] Knisely v Burke Concrete Accessories, 2 Wash App 533, 468 P2d 717.
[32] Mutual Creamery Insurance Co. v Gaylord, 290 Minn 47, 186 NW2d 176.
[33] Maimon v Telman, 40 Ill 2d 535, 240 NE2d 652.

taking turns flying the plane, such use of the plane was a joint venture and the negligence of the owner piloting the plane is therefore imputed to the prospective buyer so that when he brought suit against a third person, an electric company maintaining a power line into which the plane crashed, the buyer was barred by the negligence of the owner.[34]

Joint venture is a term which is descriptive of the relationship rather than the structure. For example, there may be a corporation through which the joint venture is conducted, as when *A* and *B*, the joint venturers, form a corporation to conduct the venture with each probably owning one half of its stock.

Sight is frequently lost of this distinction between relationship and structure for the reason that many joint ventures have no formal structure and therefore the relationship is the concept which attracts attention.

§ 47:9. Mining Partnership. A *mining partnership* is an association formed for the purpose of conducting mining operations. In some states it is declared by statute that a mining partnership exists when two or more persons engage in working a mine claim. Apart from statute, the formation of such a partnership is a matter of intention, as in the case of an ordinary partnership, evidenced by words or conduct of the parties. The intent to create a mining partnership must be shown.

In many respects the mining partnership is governed by the same principles as an ordinary partnership. The authority of a mining partner to bind the mining partnership, however, is more limited than in the case of a general partnership. Ordinarily that authority is limited to matters that are necessary and proper or usual for the purpose of working the mine. Moreover, the interest of a partner is transferable, and his transferee becomes a partner in the firm in his place without regard to the wishes of the other partners. Similarly, there is no dissolution when the interest of a partner passes to another person by operation of law, or when a partner becomes bankrupt or dies. Profits and losses, unless otherwise stipulated, are shared proportionately according to the contributions made or shares held by each partner.

§ 47:10. Syndicate. A *syndicate* is generally defined as an association of persons formed to conduct a particular business transaction, generally of a financial nature. Thus, a syndicate may be formed by which its members agree to contribute sufficient money to purchase the control of a railroad. One of the common types of this form of business is the *underwriting syndicate,* which is an organization of investment banks for the purpose of marketing large issues of stocks or bonds.

A syndicate may be incorporated, in which case it has the attributes of an ordinary corporation. If it is not incorporated, it is treated in many respects the same as a general partnership, although it is held that, as in the case of the mining partnership, the personal factor or relationship between

[34] Walker v Texas Electric Service Co., (Tex Civ App) 499 SW2d 20.

the partners is not important. When this is so held, it also follows that the interest of each member is freely transferable and that his transferee succeeds to his rights and membership in the syndicate.

§ 47:11. Unincorporated Association. An *unincorporated association* is a combination of two or more persons for the furtherance of a common nonprofit purpose. No particular form of organization is required, and any conduct or agreement indicating an attempt to associate or work together for a common purpose is sufficient. Social clubs, fraternal associations, and political parties are common examples of unincorporated associations.

Generally the members of an unincorporated association are not liable for the debts or liabilities of the association by the mere fact that they are members. It is generally required to show that they authorized or ratified the act in question. If either authorization or ratification by a particular member can be shown, he is unlimitedly liable as in the case of a general partner.

Except when otherwise provided by statute, an unincorporated association does not have any legal existence, such as has a corporation, apart from the members who compose it.[35] Thus, an unincorporated association cannot sue or be sued in its own name.[36]

§ 47:12. Cooperative. A *cooperative* consists of a group of two or more independent persons or enterprises which cooperate with respect to a common objective or function. Thus, farmers may pool their farm products and sell them as a group. Consumers may likewise pool their orders and purchase goods in bulk.

(1) Incorporated Cooperative. Statutes commonly provide for the special incorporation of cooperative enterprises. Such statutes often provide that any excess of payments over costs of operation shall be refunded to each participant member in direct proportion to the volume of business which he has done with the cooperative.[37] This contrasts with the payment of a dividend by an ordinary business corporation in which the payment of dividends is proportional to the number of shares held by the stockholder and is unrelated to the extent of his business activities with the enterprise. The fact that a cooperative is incorporated does not convert it into a corporation for all purposes and it retains its fundamental characteristic of an association designed to render services to its members. (See p. 941, Lambert v Fisherman's Dock Cooperative.)

As the agreement by the members of sellers' cooperatives that all products shall be sold at a common price is an agreement to fix prices, the sellers' cooperative is basically an agreement in restraint of trade. The Capper-Volstead Act of 1922 expressly exempts normal selling activities of farmers'

---

[35] Harker v McKissock, 12 NJ 310, 96 A2d 660.

[36] Kansas Private Club Association v Londerholm, 196 Kan 319, 410 P2d 429.

[37] Allied Supermarkets, Inc. v Grocer's Dairy Co., 45 Mich App 310, 206 NW 2d 490.

and dairymen's cooperatives from the operation of the federal Sherman Antitrust Act as long as they engage in normal cooperative practices and do not conspire with outsiders to fix prices.

§ 47:13. Business Trust. A *business trust, common-law trust,* or *Massachusetts trust* arises when the owners of property transfer the ownership to one or more persons, called *trustees,* to be managed for business purposes by the trustees for the benefit of the original owners. In addition to the transfer of the legal title to the trustee or trustees, *trust certificates* or *trust shares* are issued to the former owners as evidence of their interest, and the profits are divided proportionately among the holders of the certificates.

Like shares in a corporation, shares in a business trust may be transferred. Unlike a corporation, the holders of the shares do not have control of the trustees running the business, as do shareholders of the board of directors of a corporation. Some courts hold that the business trust is merely a trust and the fact that it is designed for business operations, rather than to pay money for the support of certain persons or institutions, does not prevent the ordinary trust relationship law from applying.

Other courts hold that for the purpose of taxation or the regulation of the business, the business trust is to be classified as a corporation.[38]

One of the objectives of the business trust is to achieve a limited liability for the members or holders of trust certificates. In most jurisdictions the certificate holders are not liable for the debts of the business trust if they have relinquished all control over management to the trustees. The same conclusion is reached if a clause in the agreement establishing the trust states that the certificate holders shall not be liable, at least with respect to persons dealing with the trust with knowledge or notice of such a limitation. In order to bring knowledge of such a limitation to third persons it is common for the stationery of the business trust to state that such a limitation exists.

§ 47:14. Joint-Stock Company. *Joint-stock companies* are of common-law origin, although in a number of states they are now regulated by statute. This form of association has features resembling both a partnership and a corporation, or a business trust. Like a corporation, the shares of its members are transferable. The contract of the members provides that any member may transfer his share and that the person to whom the share is transferred shall be accepted as a member. The management of the company is generally delegated to designated persons because as a general rule the membership is much larger than that of an ordinary partnership. The business is usually conducted under an impersonal name.

§ 47:15. Expansion of Participant Liability. The fact that the relationship between persons is not a partnership, a joint venture, or a similar organization does not necessarily establish that a member of the enterprise is not

---

[38] Rubens v Costello, 75 Ariz 5, 251 P2d 306.

liable to third persons. There is a judicial trend in favor of imposing liability on persons participating in an enterprise or economic activity when it may be reasonably foreseen that harm may be caused third persons. This concept is distinct from the supervisory and vicarious liability of an employer for the acts of his employee, or the product liability of a manufacturer or seller, but the same underlying force of protecting the third person or the consumer may be seen at work.

For example, under this new view it has been held that a savings and loan association financing a home construction project owed a duty to purchasers of the homes to see that the houses were not defectively constructed; and when cutting corners on construction costs made the homes defective but private buyers could not determine this fact for themselves, the savings and loan association was liable on a negligence basis to the purchasers even though there was no privity of contract between them, and the failure in duty of the governmental building inspectors did not relieve the association of such liability.[39]

As an aspect of participant liability, the character of one participant may affect the status of another. For example, where a state government and a private enterprise are joint venturers or partners in a profit-making venture, the discriminatory conduct of the private enterprise may be deemed "state action" within the meaning of the constitutional guarantee of equal protection.[40]

---

[39] Connor v Great Western Savings and Loan Ass'n, 69 Cal 2d 850, 73 Cal Rptr 369, 447 P2d 609 (a dissenting opinion was filed on the ground that the financer had no control over the construction work and that any duty owed by the financer was to its shareholders and not to the purchasers of the homes). California Civil Code § 3434 was amended after the Connor decision so as to limit the Connor doctrine by prohibiting liability of a lender to third persons for the negligent construction work of a borrower as long as the lender does not engage in any nonlending activity and is not a party to any misrepresentations. Bradley v Craig, 274 Cal App 2d 466, 79 Cal Rptr 401, refused to apply the Connor concept in an individual construction loan transaction when the lender was deemed to do nothing more than lend money.

[40] Burton v Wilmington Parking Authority, 365 US 715. See also Lucas v Wisconsin Electric Power Company, (CA7 Wis) 466 F2d 638 cert den 409 US 1114.

CASES FOR CHAPTER 47

Shell Oil Co. v Marinello

63 NJ 402, 307 A2d 598 (1973)

Shell Oil Company leased a gas station to Marinello and executed a dealership agreement with him for the operation of the station. The lease gave Shell the right to terminate the lease on ten days' notice. Some time later, Shell notified Marinello that it was terminating the lease. He objected on the ground that there was no "cause" for termination in that he had properly performed his obligations under the dealership agreement. He claimed that Shell was terminating the lease to retaliate against him for not selling sufficient tires, batteries, and accessories, and for requesting a price reduction in gasoline. Shell claimed that it could terminate the lease without cause. Marinello brought a lawsuit to prevent the termination of his lease. Judgment was entered in his favor and Shell appealed.

SULLIVAN, J. . . . Shell, a major oil company, is a supplier of motor vehicle fuels and automotive lubricants under the trade name "Shell." It also supplies tires, batteries and accessories (TBA) to its dealers for resale. Its products are sold in hundreds of Shell service stations throughout the State. Many of the service station locations are controlled by Shell through long-term leases. In the past, Shell's practice has been not to operate these stations itself, but to lease the station premises to an operator with whom it enters into a dealer or franchise agreement.

Shell argues that its lease of the service station premises to Marinello is independent of its dealer agreement with him, and that its legal rights as a landlord under the lease are absolute and cannot be restricted. This is pure sophistry. The two contractual documents are but part of an integrated business relationship. . . .

These instruments, and the business relationship created thereby, cannot be viewed in the abstract. Shell is a major oil company. It not only controls the supply, but, in this case, the business site. The record shows that while the product itself and the location are prime factors in the profitability of a service station, the personality and efforts of the operator and the good will and clientele generated thereby are of major importance. The amount . . . a station will sell is directly related to courtesy, service, cleanliness and hours of operation, all dependent on the particular operator.

Marinello testified that when the station was offered to him in 1959 he was told by the Shell representative that the station was run down, but that a good operator could make money and that if he built up the business his future would be in the station. Shell's own witnesses admitted that it was Shell's policy not to terminate its relationship with a lessee-dealer except for good cause, which was described as not running the station in a good and business-like manner.

Viewing the combined lease and franchise against the foregoing background, it becomes apparent that Shell is the dominant party and that the relationship lacks equality in the respective bargaining positions of the parties. For all practical purposes Shell can dictate its own terms. The dealer, particularly if he has been operating the station for a period of years and built up its business and clientele, when the time for renewal of the lease and dealer agreement comes around, cannot afford to risk confrontation with the oil company. He just signs on the dotted line.

When there is grossly disproportionate bargaining power, the principle of freedom to contract is non-existent and unilateral terms result. In such a situation courts will not hesitate to declare void as against public policy grossly unfair contractual provisions which clearly tend to the injury of the public in some way. . . .

> "Courts and legislatures have grown increasingly sensitive to imposition, conscious or otherwise, on members of the public by persons with whom they deal, who through experience, specialization, licensure, economic strength or position, or membership in associations created for their mutual benefit and education, have acquired such expertise or monopolistic or practical control in the business transaction involved as to give them an undue advantage. . . . Grossly unfair contractual obligations resulting from the use of such expertise or control by the one possessing it, which result in assumption by the other contracting party of a burden which is at odds with the common understanding of the ordinary and untrained member of the public, are considered unconscionable and therefore unenforceable. . . . The perimeter of public policy is an ever increasing one. Although courts continue to recognize that persons should not be unnecessarily restricted in their freedom to contract, there is an increasing willingness to invalidate unconscionable contractual provisions which clearly tend to injure the public in some way. . . ."

. . . It is clear that the provisions of the lease and dealer agreement giving Shell the right to terminate its business relationship with Marinello, almost at will, are the result of Shell's disproportionate bargaining position and are grossly unfair. That the public is affected in a direct way is beyond question. We live in a motor vehicle age. Supply and distribution of motor vehicle fuels are vital to our economy. In fact the Legislature has specifically concluded that the distribution and sale of motor fuels within this State is affected with a public interest. N.J.S.A. 56:6-19(c).

It is a fallacy to state that the right of termination is bilateral. The oil company can always get another person to operate the station. It is the incumbent dealer who has everything to lose since, even if he had another location to go to, the going business and trade he built up would remain with the old station.

The relationship between Shell and Marinello is basically that of franchise. The lease is an integral part of that same relationship. Our Legislature in enacting the Franchise Practices Act, has declared that distribution and sales through franchise arrangements in New Jersey vitally affect the general economy of the State, the public interest and the public welfare. N.J.S. A. 56:10-2. The Act prohibits a franchisor from terminating, cancelling or failing to renew a franchise without good cause which is defined as the failure by the franchisee to substantially comply with the requirements imposed on him by the franchise. N.J.S.A. 56:10-5.

. . . The Act reflects the legislative concern over long-standing abuses in the franchise relationship, particularly provisions giving the franchisor the right to terminate, cancel or fail to renew the franchise. To that extent the provisions of the Act merely put into statutory form the extant public policy of this State. . . .

The trial court found that Marinello had substantially performed his obligations in a satisfactory manner and had not given Shell any just cause to terminate the lease and franchise. The record amply supports this finding and conclusion. We will not disturb it.

We hold (1) that the lease and dealer agreement herein are integral parts of a single business relationship, basically that of a franchise (2) that the provision giving Shell the absolute right to terminate on 10 days notice is void as against the public policy of this State, (3) that said public policy requires that there be read into the existing lease and dealer agreement, and all future lease and dealer agreements which may be negotiated in good faith between the parties, the restriction that Shell not have the unilateral right to terminate, cancel or fail to renew the franchise, including the lease, in absence of a showing that Marinello has failed to substantially perform his obligations under the lease and dealer agreement, *i.e.,* for good cause, and (4) that good cause for termination has not been shown in this case.

[Judgment affirmed on termination issue.]

Brown v Computer Credit System, Inc.

128 Ga App 429, 197 SE2d 165 (1973)

Computer Credit System operated a computerized credit card system. Brown paid $10,000 as a fee for a franchise to sell membership in the system to local stores. Brown sued to recover the $10,000, basing his claim on the local statute which provided that the purchaser of unregistered securities could sue the seller to recover the purchase price. From a judgment for Computer, Brown appealed.

EBERHARDT, P.J. . . . Brown appeals, raising the sole question of whether the agreement is a "security" subject to the provisions of the Securities Act. . . .

In Georgia Market Centers, Inc. v Fortson, 225 Ga 854, 171 SE2d 620, the Supreme Court held that a similar agreement was not a security within the ambit of the [Georgia] Securities Act . . . . The test adopted there . . . is that an "investment contract" . . . is a security if the scheme involves an investment of money in a common enterprise with profits to come solely from the efforts of others, provided that the person investing capital supplies no more than token participation. There, however, as here, the investor is entitled to no return under the agreement except through his own efforts. In the instant case the agreement provides that the only way for Brown to realize profits is to sell the company's services within his territory, and that he has no right to participate in the company's profits or losses except to the extent of profits derived from business produced by his sales activities. He may, of course, procure the assistance of others in selling the service to merchants. Hence, under the test laid down in the *Market Centers* case . . . we hold that the "Master Franchise Agreement" involved here is not a "security" within the meaning of the Securities Act.

It is urged that the test [above] set forth . . . is not adequate to meet the ever increasing flood of "franchise" systems which are being sold across the country, and that the test of an "investment contract" should be expanded to include the consideration of whether the franchisee's money is being used as risk capital by the franchisor. However, we are bound by the ruling in *Market Centers* that where the contract promises no return to the franchisee except in connection with his own efforts, the contract is not a "security" within the meaning of the Securities Act. . . .

[Judgment affirmed.]

Quijada Corp. v General Motors Corp.

(Dist Col App) 253 A2d 538 (1969)

Quijada Corp. owned a diesel engine bus manufactured by General Motors. The bus was driven in Wisconsin, Illinois, Indiana, and Virginia. From November, 1963, to January, 1964, it was taken to various distributors of General Motors located in those states for extensive engine repairs. Quijada claimed that the repairs were negligently made, because of which the bus was damaged, and sued General Motors for such negligence. From a judgment in favor of General Motors, Quijada appealed.

FICKLING, A.J. . . . After a trial on the sole issue of agency, the court found that no agency relationship existed between appellee [General Motors] and its distributors and entered a judgment for appellee. . . .

Unless it could be established that the distributors were appellee's agents, appellant had no cause of action against appellee. . . .

[We do not] find any merit in appellant's contention that the trial court erred in holding that appellant had failed to show an agency relationship between General Motors and the distributors. The distributorship system has given rise to much litigation involving the issue of whether distributors are independent contractors or agents of the corporation whose products they sell. Although each case must be decided on its facts, the determining factor is the corporation's right to control the day-to-day operations of the distributor.

In the instant case, the agreements between appellee and the distributors gave the distributors the nonexclusive right to sell and service Detroit Diesel products and parts in their territories. The distributors were required to: prepare monthly reports of retail sales and inventory; prepare periodic financial and operating statements; send their employees to Detroit Diesel training schools; erect and maintain advertising signs at their expense; maintain the business hours customary in the trade; maintain satisfactory business facilities; and obtain the consent of appellee before changing the location of their businesses. Appellee agreed to create a demand for its products through advertisements. Although these requirements may be some indicia of control, courts have held similar requirements to be consistent with the distributor's status as an independent contractor. These requirements only affect the end result to be achieved—the sale and servicing of Detroit Diesel products and parts—and in no way control the method by which this is accomplished.

By comparison, the functions specifically left to the sole discretion of the distributors were those which directly pertained to the manner in which the distributors performed the work contemplated by the distributorship arrangement. The agreement gave the distributors full responsibility for the servicing and installation of Detroit Diesel products and parts, and provided that the distributors were to *purchase* the Detroit Diesel parts. Thus, appellee did not retain any legal title to the parts which were sold. Testimony at trial and depositions introduced into evidence established that: appellee had no control over the hiring, firing, or supervision of the distributors' employees; appellee's representatives visited the distributors and made suggestions, but the distributors were under no obligation to adopt them; and the distributors were not obligated to make repairs in accordance with the manuals supplied by appellee. In addition, the distributorship agreement specifically stated that the distributors were not agents of appellee and did not have the authority to create any obligation in the name of appellee or to bind appellee in any manner. These factors strongly indicate that the distributors were independent contractors and, on the record before us, we hold that the trial court did not err in finding no liability on the part of appellee for any alleged damages caused by the distributors.

[Judgment affirmed.]

Weil v Diversified Properties

(DC Dist Col) 319 F Supp 778 (1970)

Diversified Properties was organized as a limited partnership. Weil was the general partner. He brought an action seeking to hold the limited partners liable as general partners on the theory that they had taken such part in the management of the business that they had become general partners.

GESELL, D.J. . . . Diversified Properties is a limited partnership organized effective January 2, 1967, with varying degrees of ownership in several garden-type apartments and other real estate . . . . Weil had been managing and dealing in real estate and had varying participations in several properties. He needed capital and approached defendant Baer with a view to placing some of his real estate interests in a limited partnership to be formed. Baer, a CPA, had several clients looking for tax shelter and mainly through his auspices a group of limited partners was assembled . . . . Weil was the only general partner.

All parties agree the limited partners remained strictly in that status until about May 1, 1968. By April, however, the partnership was hard pressed for cash . . . and the projected cash flow was very inadequate. Weil, who had been managing the properties from a partnership office at one of the apartment projects, looked for other employment and at a meeting of the partners on April 24 offered to discontinue his salary and close up the partnership office, steps which would effect a saving of something in the neighborhood of $75,000. This was a gloomy and revealing meeting. Weil's proposal was accepted with little consideration of what, if anything, Weil would do in the future. By the time of the next partnership meeting a week later, two individuals—Rubenstein and Tempchin—had been selected to manage one or more of the properties on a commission basis in accordance with a general proposal Weil had advanced. The partnership books and records had been transferred to Baer's office, the official business address of the partnership, and Weil commenced working for another real estate company as vice president. From then on the partners were involved in refinancing and meeting further capital demands. Although they put more money into the venture money pressures increased and the partnership remained very short of cash with early foreclosures threatening. All partners hoped to sell some properties and thus keep others afloat. Weil's name still appeared on various obligations which in fact had been assigned to the partnership. As general partner he had also naturally made numerous business commitments for the partnership. Creditors therefore turned to him with persistent demands for payment which could not be met. The limited partners had no obligation or willingness to come forward with still more capital sufficient to meet these demands.

It is against this general background that the activities and relationships of the partners must be analyzed in more detail. Weil argues that the limited partners took control of the enterprise within the meaning of [ULPA § 7], which provides: A limited partner shall not become liable as a general partner unless, in addition to the exercise of his rights and powers as a limited partner, he takes part in the control of the business.

Weil contends that after his withdrawal from a salaried position on May 1, 1968, he was supposed to continue as general partner, keeping an eye on the business, but that he was ignored. He claims that meetings of the other partners were held in his absence and without notice, and that Rubenstein and Tempchin not only refused to follow his instructions but took orders from the limited partners, particularly Baer, Kaye, Steinberg and Jerome Snider. He points to various isolated episodes suggesting interference by certain individual limited partners with matters Weil contends he should have handled as general partner. The limited partners by categorical testimony strenuously deny these charges and the over-all inferences that Weil seeks to draw from various incidents.

The only significant independent witness, Rubenstein, who was brought into the enterprise on the recommendation of Weil, had managed three properties for the partnership, had no detailed knowledge of the partnership operations and could testify mainly only to impressions. He did not follow intermittent suggestions or instructions from Weil concerning disbursement of the limited funds available. In the first place, there was not enough money. Also, he felt he should consult all partners because he was not sure of Weil's status. Throughout he had difficulty communicating with the other partners and also with Weil. It does appear that both Rubenstein and Tempchin had been told by Baer that they could consult him on any matters of business judgment, and they did this on occasion. Baer's office had the books and records. Under the agreement, Baer could sign checks and he had probably the best over-all understanding of the partnership's complex and somewhat uncertain obligations. Rubenstein also was occasionally in contact with Steinberg, Kaye, Jerome Snider and Weil. All limited partners categorically deny that they ever gave explicit orders or instructions to either Rubenstein or Tempchin. The partnership was not well managed by anyone, and existed mainly through improvisation from crisis to crisis. Rubenstein gave little concrete testimony as to any directions he received and Tempchin was not called to testify by either side. Most of the witnesses, including Weil, reconstructed the confusing events of the post-May period from the vantage of hindsight with a considerable element of self-interest.

Cases relating to whether or not limited partners have taken part in control of the business and are thus to be treated as general partners involve claims by creditors against the partners. . . . No case has been found where a general partner has invoked § 7 of the Act against his own limited partners. The purpose of § 7 is to protect creditors: "The Act proceeds on the assumption that no public policy requires a person who contributes to the capital of a business, acquires an interest in its profits, and some degree of control over the conduct of the business to become bound for the obligations of the business, provided creditors have no reason to believe that when their credits were extended that such persons were so bound." . . . "The statute, in fixing this liability on account of noncompliance with its provisions, does not change his special partnership into a general one, but simply makes him liable as a general partner to creditors. All his relations to his copartners, and their obligations growing out of their relation to him as a special partner, remain unimpaired." . . .

The remedy of a general partner who faces interference from his limited partners is to dissolve the partnership under § 31 of the Uniform Partnership Act . . . . So long as the partnership continues, he is in a relationship of trust with his colleagues. . . . He may not invoke the provisions of the Act to enlarge the liability of his partners.

. . . As between themselves, partners may make any agreement they wish which is not barred by prohibitory provisions of statutes, by common law, or by consideration of public policy. . . . Whatever may be the obligations of the limited partners as against creditors or third parties, Weil may not prevail against them if they have not breached the terms of the agreement. Having entered into the partnership agreement with advice of counsel, an agreement made largely for his own benefit in a field where he was especially experienced, he is bound by its terms. Accordingly, the initial inquiry must be to determine whether the limited partners have in any way violated the terms of the written agreement. . . .

Weil has not by a preponderance of the evidence established any violation by the limited partners of terms of the agreement with him. . . . Since the partnership agreement was not violated by the limited partners, Weil has no cause of action and his request for the appointment of a receiver and an accounting will be denied.

The provisions of the Limited Partnership Act are primarily designed to protect creditors. So long as the provisions of the agreement were followed, no partner can complain. Weil's complaint is dismissed.

[Judgment for limited partners.]

Edlebeck v Hooten

20 Wis 2d 83, 121 NW2d 240 (1963)

Edlebeck was injured when his father's car was struck by a car driven by Clarence Hooten in which the latter's brother, Robert, was riding. Edlebeck sued both of the Hooten brothers claiming they were engaged in a joint venture and that accordingly, Robert was liable for any negligence of Clarence. The Hooten brothers were returning from a deer hunting trip at the time. The car being driven by Clarence was his wife's car, and he paid for the gasoline; each brother brought his own lunch; each brother was hunting on his own, although they operated from the car as a base and would assist each other in bringing home any deer that either had killed; and any deer killed was butchered by the father and the meat divided among the brothers. From a judgment for Edlebeck, Hooten appealed.

HALLOWS, J. . . . The terms "joint adventure" and "joint enterprise" have been used interchangeably by this and other courts. The terms are often used to describe a special business arrangement of less dignity but partaking of some essentials of a partnership and governed by the laws applicable thereto and sometimes to describe or characterize the relationship of a driver of an automobile and his passengers to determine the imputation of negligence. . . . "Essentially there is little difference between a partnership and a joint adventure; the latter as a rule being more limited, and confined in its scope principally to a single transaction." . . .

Joint adventures are of modern origin, creatures of American courts, not recognized at early common law apart from partnerships, but now considered to be a status created by persons combining their properties or services in the conduct of an enterprise without forming a formal partnership. . . . At least as between the parties, the association must be with intent to engage in a single business adventure for joint profit for which purpose the participants combine their efforts, property, skill, or knowledge. Each must agree expressly or impliedly to a community of interest as to the purpose of the undertaking and to stand in the relation of agent as well as principal to the other coadventurers with equal right of control of the means employed to carry out the common purpose. . . .

Four requisites have generally been recognized by the courts to be essential to the existence of a joint adventure: (1) Contribution of money or services but not necessarily in equal proportion by each of the parties, (2) joint proprietorship and mutual control over the subject matter of the venture, (3) an agreement to share profits though not necessarily the losses, and (4) a contract express or implied establishing the relationship. . . .

A distinction may be made between cases involving the use of an automobile in the carrying on of a joint adventure from cases in which the use of the automobile is of itself the joint enterprise. In the former cases the use is incidental to or only a part of the carrying out of the purpose of the joint adventure, while in the latter cases it is of the essence. The importance of the existence of a joint enterprise is, in this case, to impute the negligence of the driver Clarence Hooten to the defendant Robert Hooten, a passenger, by the application of the rules governing partnership since the automobile was used in carrying out the hunting venture. In theory at least, if such a joint adventure exists, it should not make any difference for the purpose of imputation of negligence whether a participant in the joint adventure was a passenger in the car or not if the operation of the auto at the time of the accident was within the scope and in furtherance of the purpose of the joint adventure. If in this case the predominant purpose was not hunting for pleasure but commercial hunting for meat and profit, we might have a joint adventure which would be the basis for the imputation of negligence.

A venture to constitute a joint adventure must be for profit in a financial or commercial sense. . . . A husband and wife were not joint adventurers in traveling together in an auto from Wisconsin to Iowa to make their home and to seek separate positions. . . . "In one sense, husbands and wives in their journey through life are always engaged in joint enterprises, sometimes successful, sometimes disastrous." It may be that in a romantic sense marriage is a joint adventure, but not in a legal sense. Unless other facts exist, a joint adventure will not be grounded upon the marital relationship. . . .

In Van Gilder v Gugel (1936), 220 Wis 612, 265 NW 706, 165 ALR 824, we held that where two persons were returning home in an automobile after assisting each other in wood cutting on their respective woodlots, no joint adventure existed, pointing out that the journey was not part of any business or enterprise in which they were jointly or mutually interested financially although each had a similar purpose in making the trip. . . .

There is a line of cases based on joint ownership of an automobile which could be argued as authority for holding that a joint adventure does apply to social as well as commercial relationships. . . .

The use of the term "joint adventure" was incorrect to characterize the imputation of negligence of the driver of the auto to the passenger which in fact rested upon the joint ownership of the car and joint use thereof for a common purpose and is withdrawn. In such cases a joint control or a right to equal control of the automobile exists giving rise to a mutual agency. . . . Essentially such cases are governed by the principles of agency as are cases of an owner allowing another to drive his car for his benefit or their common benefit. In the non-joint-ownership cases, ownership of a car by a passenger raises a rebuttable presumption of the agency of the driver. . . . These cases of joint ownership and of agency are not applicable to the facts of this case, nor do they require a business basis for the imputation of negligence.

Human nature being what it is, it is probably true the cases involving the relationship of driver and the passenger where there is joint ownership or joint purpose will be referred to as joint enterprises or joint adventures used in a popular sense. If so, these cases should not be confused with those involving the legal concept of joint enterprise as used in this opinion. . . . The concept of joint adventure or enterprise should be confined to business enterprises for the purpose of imputation of negligence based upon the relationship of the parties. . . .

[Judgment reversed.]

Lambert v Fisherman's Dock Cooperative, Inc.

115 NJ Super 424, 280 A2d 193 (1971)

Lambert was a member of the Fisherman's Dock Cooperative, Inc. The cooperative changed its bylaws to provide that when a shareholder's membership in the cooperative was terminated, he was to receive what he had paid for his shares rather than the book value of his shares. Lambert's membership was terminated and he claimed that he was entitled to the book value of the shares in spite of the contrary bylaw. Lambert sued Fisherman's Dock and a judgment was entered in his favor. Fisherman's Dock appealed.

LABRECQUE, J.A.D. . . . Defendant is a fishermen's cooperative organized July 1, 1953 pursuant to N.J.S.A. 34:17-1 et seq. governing cooperative societies of working men. Briefly, its purposes were to provide a ready market for the sale of aquatic products . . . produced by its members, provide docking and other facilities for members and patrons, and generally to benefit its members through a more efficient and economical method of marketing their produce. Its capital stock was divided into 2,000 shares, each with a par value of $50. Each member could cast but one vote, regardless of his share holdings. . . .

. . . Stock in the association was to be transferred only with the consent of [the Board of Directors] to those eligible to hold the same. The board was vested with power to cancel permanently the membership of a stockholder for good and sufficient cause upon tender to him of the fair book value of the shares held by him, as determined by the board, together with any other sums due and unpaid and less any amount due the association. In the event of the proposed cancellation of membership or expulsion of a member he was to be informed in writing of the charges against him at least ten days before the meeting at which the board was to pass upon his proposed cancellation or expulsion, at which time he was to be afforded an opportunity to be heard.

Under article II of the bylaws the association's stock certificates were to contain the foregoing restrictions on membership and transfer of stock, and a further provision that:

> When the board of directors of the association is of the opinion that the association has sufficient working capital to enable the association to do so, certificates of stock shall be retired at their cost to the holder, in the order in which issued, except that each member shall continue to hold at least two shares of the stock. This association shall have the right to purchase any of its stock at its par or book value, whichever is less, in the event the owner thereof is not engaged in the production of fishery products. *This stock is also subject to all the other terms and conditions stated in the articles of incorporation and the bylaws of this association.* [Emphasis added]

The articles of association and bylaws were subject to amendment.

Plaintiff William M. Lambert had been in the real estate and insurance business for 22 years. He became a shareholder in the association when he purchased two shares of its stock, allegedly for $125, in 1957.* During the next two years he was engaged in commercial fishing and sold his catch through the cooperative. For these years he received patronage dividends (more accurately described as patronage refunds) representing his share of the profit derived from the operations of the association, based upon the dollar amount of fish products which it handled for him during those years.

In 1959 plaintiff gave up the fishing business and began to engage in clamming. At first he sought to sell his clams through the association, but the volume was too great for the latter to handle and it was then agreed that plaintiff would market his catch himself, but would use the association's docking, processing and storage facilities, upon payment of a fee. This fee was originally 15 cents a (bushel) basket of clams; it was later reduced to ten, then to eight cents, then increased to ten. An additional $65 per month was paid as rental for space used for maintenance and storage. Besides this plaintiff purchased fuel and supplies for his boats from the association at what was less than the general retail price. This practice continued until plaintiff withdrew from the clamming business and sold his boats sometime in 1964. Thereafter he no longer patronized the association, and in July 1965, after notice, his membership was terminated.

During the period plaintiff engaged in clamming he received no patronage dividends even though the dividends paid to others included profits derived from goods and services bought by him from the association. The court found that between the years 1960 and 1963 defendant had reduced its charges to plaintiff from ten cents to eight cents a basket after pressure by plaintiff to pay him a patronage dividend based on the amount of business he was doing with defendant. . . .

Briefly stated, plaintiff's theory of recovery was that when he purchased his two shares of the association's stock he was purchasing a "growth" stock; since the net worth of the association increased substantially in value thereafter, his interest had increased in proportion; thus he should be paid an amount equal to the net worth of the association, regardless of its liquidity. He argued that by changing the bylaws the association destroyed the "growth potential" of his shares, and thus breached its contract with him as a shareholder.

The court below appears to have accepted plaintiff's theory as to the nature of his relationship with the association. It held that the provision in the bylaws fixing the amount to be paid an expelled member for his stock

---

* Defendant offered proof that the price paid was $57 a share.

constituted a contract between plaintiff and defendant and vested in plaintiff certain rights which could not be altered without his assent, even though all of the other shareholders, acting in concert, agreed. He ruled that it made no difference whether the corporation was one formed under Title 34 of the Revised Statutes or one formed under Title 14; that the association's stock bore all of the essential characteristics of stock issued by corporations formed primarily for profit. We find ourselves in disagreement.

A cooperative association is a unique institution, differing in many of its essentials from a corporation organized for profit. The relationship between such an association and one of its members is in many respects the antithesis of that which exists between a corporation organized under the General Corporation Act and its stockholders. The latter exists for the purpose of making a profit for its stockholders and its activities are geared to the accomplishment of that end. The amount of dividends paid each stockholder, as well as the number of votes he may cast, depend upon the number of shares held by him. One may be a stockholder though he has never purchased the corporation's product or availed himself of its services—and never intends to. With certain exceptions not here relevant, the stock of such a corporation may be purchased, held and transferred without restriction and without the necessity of corporate approval.

A cooperative association, on the other hand, has been defined as a democratic association of persons organized to furnish themselves an economic service under a plan that eliminates entrepreneur profit and that provides for substantial equality of ownership and control. . . . In general, each shareholder has equal ownership and exercises an equal share in the control of the association, regardless of the number of shares of stock he holds. . . . By its very nature a cooperative is not designed to make a profit, and the return on capital, if authorized, is limited. . . . Usually, such profits as may be realized from the association's activities are proportionately divided among the shareholders on the basis of the amount of their patronage during the period the profit was earned. . . .

A significant characteristic of a cooperative is the right of the association to restrict ownership of its shares to those availing themselves of its services, to restrict the number of shares held by a member and to prohibit or limit transfers of stock. . . .

A cooperative may also specify how members may withdraw or otherwise be separated from membership, and the amount to be paid them upon such withdrawal or separation. . . .

From the foregoing it is clear that a cooperative association exists primarily for the purpose of furnishing services for its members. It is intended to continue to function, notwithstanding the withdrawal or expulsion of individual members. Unless and until liquidation takes place, individual members have no present possessory interest in the association's assets and may be required to surrender their shares to the association upon receipt of such consideration as may be fixed by the bylaws. A growth stock would be a rank misnomer for such a security.

With these principles in mind we proceed to consideration of the merits. It appears clear that ample justification existed for the termination of plaintiff's membership and that the procedure laid down in the bylaws was followed in bringing it to an end. The sole questions remaining are (1) the amount to be paid plaintiff upon surrender of his stock, and (2) whether he was entitled to patronage dividends.

Plaintiff contends that upon the cancellation of his stock he was entitled to receive its fair book value as prescribed by the appropriate section of the bylaws in effect at the time the stock was issued to him. Defendant contends that the section of the bylaws which was in effect at the time plaintiff's membership was terminated governs; hence he is entitled to receive no more than the cost of acquisition of his stock. Plaintiff counters that the amended bylaws could not affect his rights under the original bylaws in the absence of his assent to the new bylaws.

We hold that the amended bylaws controlled the redemption of defendant's shares in 1965, and that he thereby became entitled to receive only the price he had paid for his shares. Defendant had no vested right to his proportionate share of the "full book value" of the assets of the cooperative, regardless of how that term might be defined. To permit a member who voluntarily withdraws or who is no longer eligible to membership, to take with him a share of the association's assets based upon his stock holdings, would not only pose the possibility of financial ruin to such an association but would run contrary to the very principles which govern its existence. . . .

[Judgment reversed.]

QUESTIONS AND CASE PROBLEMS

1. Ettelsohn, Allen, and Levinson formed a limited partnership. The proceedings for the formation of the limited partnership complied with requirements of the statute except that Ettelsohn, the limited partner, contributed goods instead of cash as specified by the statute. In an action brought by Claflin, a creditor of the firm, it was claimed that Ettelsohn was a general partner. Decide. [Claflin v Sattler, 41 Minn 430, 43 NW 382]
2. Merrilees, Hopkins, Mayer, and Adams formed a limited partnership but did not record their partnership agreement until 49 days after the partnership business began operations. Stowe, a creditor, claimed that a general partnership had been created because of the delay in filing the agreement. Decide. [Stowe v Merrilees, 6 Cal App 2d 217, 44 P2d 368]
3. Simpson and Saunders each had a used car dealer's license. They made an agreement to run their businesses independently but to share a lot, the building thereon, the furnishings, and the use of a telephone. Bates sued both Simpson and Saunders claiming that they were joint venturers and therefore both were liable for the fraudulent conduct of Simpson. Was Saunders liable? [Bates v Simpson, 121 Utah 165, 239 P2d 749]
4. In 1955 Booth, an experienced broker and trader in oil properties, and Wilson, who had been a jewelry merchant, made an oral agreement to work together in acquiring and trading in oil, gas, and mineral leases as a joint venture. As each lease was dealt in and disposed of, the two would take out whatever profit there was, divide it equally between themselves, and treat that operation as closed. In 1958 Booth and Wilson attempted to arrange a lease transaction with Gilbert but were unable to do so because of defects in the title. Booth then told Gilbert to revoke the contract, that he and Wilson did not have the money to go through with the deal, and that Gilbert should try to make the best deal with anyone else that he could. Thereafter, Wilson and Rector took a lease from Gilbert in their names. Booth then sued Wilson and Rector, claiming that he was entitled to share therein. Was he correct? [Booth v Wilson, (Tex Civ App) 339 SW2d 388]
5. Brenner was in the scrap iron business. Almost daily Plitt loaned Brenner money with which to purchase scrap iron. The agreement of the parties was that when the scrap was sold, Plitt would be repaid and would receive an additional sum as compensation for making the loan. The loans were to be repaid in any case, without regard to whether Brenner made a profit. A dispute arose as to the relationship between the two men. Plitt claimed that it was a joint venture. Decide. [Brenner v Plitt, 182 Md 348, 34 A2d 853]

48 Nature and Classes

§ **48:1. Definition of a Corporation.** A *corporation* is an entity, an artificial legal being, created by government grant and endowed with certain powers. That is, the corporation exists in the eyes of the law as a person, separate and distinct from the people who own the corporation. (See p. 953, Branmar Theatre Co. v Branmar, Inc.)

This concept means that property of the corporation is not owned by the persons who own shares in the corporation, but by the corporation.[1] Debts of the corporation are debts of this artificial person and not of the people running the corporation or owning shares of stock in it. The corporation can sue and be sued in its own name with respect to corporate rights and liabilities, but the shareholders cannot sue or be sued as to those rights and liabilities. Furthermore, a parent corporation and its wholly-owned subsidiary corporation are regarded as separate entities.

A corporation is formed by obtaining approval of a *certificate of incorporation, articles of incorporation,* or a *charter* from the state or national government.[2] The persons who develop the idea of forming a corporation and who induce others to join in the enterprise are called *promoters.* The persons who make the application to the government for the charter are called *incorporators.*

The corporation is one of the most important forms of business organization. To the large-scale enterprise it offers an easier way to finance itself

[1] Wells v Hiskett, (Tex Civ App) 288 SW2d 257.

[2] In speaking of corporate matters, one is likely to become confused by the use of the terms "charter," "articles of incorporation," and "certificate of incorporation." Originally, when a piece of paper was given to the individual corporation by the crown or the state governor, it was called a charter, deriving its name from the Latin word traveling through Norman French to show that it was something which was written. Under the modern statute the word "charter" is generally replaced with "certificate of incorporation." That is, an application is filed for a certificate of incorporation rather than requesting or petitioning the government to grant or issue a charter. The application for a certificate of incorporation is accompanied by the blueprint of the proposed corporation or its articles of incorporation. The approval of the application in effect makes "official" the right of the corporation to exist and to follow the pattern or blueprint of the articles of incorporation.

It is necessary to bear in mind that any rule governing the granting of a charter applies equally to the approving of an application for a certificate of incorporation. Similarly, a rule stated in terms of the provisions of articles of incorporation is likewise applicable to the provisions of a charter.

by means of dividing its ownership into many small units that can be sold to a wide economic range of purchasers. In addition to assisting financing operations, the corporate device offers a limited liability to the persons interested in the enterprise and a perpetual succession not affected by the death of any particular owner or by the transfer of his interest. Because of its limited liability, the corporation is also popular with many smaller businesses.

§ 48:2. Evolution of the Corporation. The business corporation arose in the law to meet the economic needs of the modern world. The law was unwilling to permit single proprietors and partnerships to have the attributes that are today possessed by a business corporation; but since society needed those attributes, it created a new legal person, the corporation, and the law was willing to endow it with the attributes that were denied to individuals or partnerships. Various organizations, such as colonial trading companies, municipal and religious corporations, joint stock companies, and limited partnerships contributed to the development of the modern corporation. The evolutionary process continues because of the growing recognition that some corporations have such a specialized function or nature that they should be treated differently than business corporations generally.

The corporation is formed by obtaining government approval. Originally this was in the form of a charter expressly given to the incorporators—at first, by the British Crown, and then, after the American Revolution, by the governor or legislature of the particular state. While the corporation has an older ancestry, the business corporation of the twentieth century can be said to date from the British companies formed in the sixteenth and seventeenth centuries for the purpose of discovering new territory and trading and governing such territories. The Tudor rulers of England, hard put for cash, in effect farmed out or franchised out the right to explore and rule the undiscovered world.

By the beginning of the twentieth century, American society responded to the increasing demand for incorporation by applying the assembly-line technique to the granting of corporate charters. Obtaining a charter was made a cut-and-dried procedure similar to obtaining most licenses. The promoters filed an application and paid a fee and, if the application was properly filled out, it would be merely a routine operation to get the charter.

§ 48:3. Classifications of Corporations.

(1) Public, Private, and Quasi-Public Corporations. A *public corporation* is one established for governmental purposes and for the administration of public affairs. A city is a public or municipal corporation acting under authority granted it by the state.

A *private corporation* is one established by private interests, whether for charitable and benevolent purposes or for purposes of finance, industry, and commerce. Private corporations are often called "public" in business circles when their stock is sold to the public.

A *quasi-public corporation,* which is also known as a public service corporation or a public utility, is a private corporation furnishing services upon which the public is particularly dependent. Examples of this class of corporations are those operating railroads, canals, and bridges or those supplying gas, electricity, and water. Such corporations are usually given special franchises and powers, such as the power of eminent domain.

(2) Domestic and Foreign Corporations. If a corporation has been created under the law of a particular state or nation, it is called a *domestic corporation* with respect to that state or nation. Any other corporation going into that state or nation is called a *foreign corporation.* Thus, a corporation holding a Texas charter is a domestic corporation in Texas but a foreign corporation in all other states and nations. This distinction becomes important in considering the extent of control that may be exercised by a government over corporations operating within its territorial boundaries. Whether a corporation is domestic is determined without regard to the residence of its shareholders or incorporators, or the state in which it conducts business.[3] A corporation created under the law of one nation is classified as an *alien corporation* in other nations.

(3) Special Service Corporations. Corporations formed for transportation, banking, insurance, savings and loan operations, and similar specialized functions are subject to separate codes or statutes with regard to their organization. In addition, federal and state laws and administrative agencies regulate in detail the manner in which their business is conducted.

(4) Close Corporations. There is no requirement that an enterprise must be big before it can incorporate. Many corporations are small firms, which in the last century would have operated as single proprietorships or partnerships but which are today incorporated either to obtain the advantages of limited liability or a tax benefit, or both. Such a corporation may have only a small number of outstanding shares and these are owned by the person who formerly would have been the single proprietor or by him and his family or friends. Such stock is closely held by this man or group, from whence comes the name of *close corporation.* Such stock is not traded publicly.

It would be foolish to require a close corporation to follow the same procedure as a large corporation; and statutes adopted within the last decade have in many states liberalized the corporation law when close corporations are involved, such as by permitting their incorporation by a smaller number of persons, allowing them to have a one-man board of directors, and authorizing the skipping of meetings.[4]

---

[3] Omaha National Bank v Jensen, 157 Neb 22, 58 NW2d 582.

[4] This distinction between big and little corporations is part of the same current of legal development that in the Uniform Commercial Code has given rise to the distinction between the merchant seller or buyer, on the one hand, and the casual seller or buyer, on the other.

A number of states have separate *small* or *close corporation codes.*[5] These commonly require that there be no more than a stated number of shareholders, that the stock not be sold publicly, and that the stock be subject to certain transfer restrictions. When a corporation qualifies under such a statute, it is permitted to have a simpler structure than would be possible for a standard corporation, as by eliminating the board of directors, and to function in a simpler manner, as by conducting business in the manner of a partnership[6] rather than a corporation. In some states the general business corporation code has provisions contemplating the possible concentration of corporate ownership and control in one person.[7]

(5) Professional Corporations. In every state a corporation may be organized for the purpose of conducting a profession. Thus, several doctors may form a corporation for the purpose of rendering medical care to patients, who are now the patients of the corporation rather than of the individual doctors.[8] In general a professional corporation is formed and will follow the pattern of the ordinary business corporation.

The fact that professional men may form a corporation does not permit a converse conclusion that any corporation may render professional services. (See p. 955, Kansas v Zales Jewelry Co.) To some extent a corporation may supply professional services to its members.[9]

(6) Nonprofit Corporations. A *nonprofit corporation* (or an eleemosynary corporation) is one that is organized for charitable or benevolent purposes, such as certain hospitals, homes, and universities.[10] Special procedure for incorporation is sometimes prescribed, with provision being made for a detailed examination and hearing as to the purpose, function, and methods of raising money for the enterprise.

§ 48:4. Power to Create a Corporation. Since by definition a corporation is created by government grant, the right to be a corporation must be obtained from the proper government.[11]

---

[5] See, for example, 8 Delaware Code Ann §§ 341-356.

[6] North Carolina, Gen Stats §§ 55-73(b).

[7] See, for example, New York Business Corporation Law §§ 401, 404, 615, 702.

[8] Under some statutes the organization is called an "association," but it has the attributes of a corporation. See Ronald A. Anderson, *Running a Professional Corporation* (Philadelphia, Pennsylvania: The Littoral Development Company, 1971), § 2:2.

[9] A labor union has a constitutional right to employ a lawyer on a salary basis to provide free legal services for union members. United Mine Workers v Illinois State Bar Association, 389 US 217. A union may also recommend to its members individual attorneys for the purpose of suing under the federal Employers' Liability Act and may obtain the commitment of such attorneys that they will not charge more than 25 percent of any recovery. United Transportation Union v State Bar of Michigan, 401 US 576.

[10] Gilbert v McLeod Infirmary, 219 SC 174, 64 SE2d 524. The Committee on Corporate Laws of the American Bar Association has prepared a Model Non-Profit Corporation Act as a companion to the Model Business Association Act. The Non-Profit Corporation Act has formed the basis for nonprofit corporation statutes in Alabama, Iowa, Nebraska, North Carolina, North Dakota, Ohio, Oregon, Texas, Virginia, Washington, Wisconsin, and the District of Columbia.

[11] Lloyds of Texas, (DC Tex) 43 F2d 383.

(1) Federal Power. The federal government may create corporations whenever appropriate to carry out the powers expressly granted to it.

(2) State Power. Generally a state by virtue of its police power may create any kind of corporation for any purpose. Most states have a *general corporation code* that lists certain requirements, and anyone who satisfies the requirements and files the necessary papers with the government may automatically become a corporation. The American Bar Association has proposed a Model Business Corporation Act (ABA MBCA).[12] There is no uniform corporation act.

§ **48:5. Regulation of Corporations.** In addition to determining whether a corporate power exists, it is necessary to consider whether there is any government regulation imposed upon the exercise of that power. Both the federal and state governments, by virtue of their power to create corporations, can exercise control over them.

Domestic corporations are regulated by the provisions of the Code or general statutes under which they are organized and also by the tax laws and general laws of the state of their origin. A foreign corporation is also subject to regulation and taxation in every state in which it does business, except as later noted. Generally a foreign corporation must register to do business within the state.

(1) Constitutional Limitations. In regulating a corporation, both state and national governments must observe certain limitations because corporations come within the protection of certain constitutional guarantees.

(a) THE CORPORATION AS A PERSON. The Constitution of the United States prohibits the national government and the state governments from depriving any "person" of life, liberty, or property without due process of law. Many state constitutions contain a similar limitation upon their respective state governments. A corporation is regarded as a "person" within the meaning of such provisions.

The federal Constitution prohibits a state from denying to any "person" within its jurisdiction the equal protection of the laws. No such express limitation is placed upon the federal government, although the due process clause binding the federal government is liberally interpreted so that it prohibits substantial inequality of treatment.

While a corporation is regarded as a "person" with respect to rights and liabilities, a corporation is not regarded as a person within a statute which uses the term to refer to natural persons. For example, a corporation cannot

---

[12] This Act or its 1969 revision has been adopted, or has influenced local legislation, in a substantial number of states. The American Bar Association Model Act of 1950 was revised as of July 1, 1969. References to the Model Act are to the 1969 revision unless otherwise indicated.

claim that its lawsuit should be given priority at trial because a state statute grants such a priority to a "person" 65 years old or over.[13]

Likewise, a corporation is not a person within the meaning of statutes designed to protect indigent persons if its shareholders are not indigent. (See p. 956, S.O.U.P., Inc. v FTC.) Similarly, a corporation is not a "person" within the scope of a statute authorizing any "person" to prepare the legal papers for a transaction to which he is a party.[14]

(b) THE CORPORATION AS A CITIZEN. For certain purposes, such as determining the right to bring a lawsuit in a federal court, a corporation is today deemed a "citizen" of any state in which it has been incorporated and of the state where it has its principal place of business, without regard to the actual citizenship of the individual persons owning the stock of the corporation. Thus, a corporation incorporated in New York is a New York corporation even though its shareholders are citizens of many other states. Likewise, a Delaware corporation having its principal place of business in New York is deemed a citizen of New York as well as Delaware.[15] An environmental protection law authorizing any "citizen" to bring suit to prevent pollution permits a corporation to bring such a suit.[16]

The federal Constitution prohibits states from abridging "the privileges or immunities of citizens of the United States." A corporation, however, is not regarded as a "citizen" within this clause. Thus, with one exception, a foreign corporation has no constitutional right to do business in another state if that other state wishes to exclude it. For example, Pennsylvania can deny a New York corporation the right to come into Pennsylvania to do business. As a practical matter, most states do not exclude foreign corporations but seize upon this power as justifying special regulation or taxation. On this basis it is commonly provided that a foreign corporation must register or even take out a domestic charter, file copies of its charter, pay certain taxes, or appoint a resident agent before it can do business within the state.

As an exception to the power of a state, a state cannot require a license or registration of a foreign interstate commerce corporation or impose a tax on the right to engage in such a business.

A corporation cannot be made a death beneficiary of a United States bond as such designation is limited to natural persons.[17]

The citizenship of a corporation is ordinarily not affected by the fact that it acquires the stock or assets of another corporation. (See p. 957, John Mohr & Sons v Apex Terminal Warehouses.)

---

[13] County of New Haven v Porter, 22 Conn Supp 154, 164 A2d 236.

[14] Kentucky State Bar Association v Tussey, (Ky) 476 SW2d 177 (holding that the preparation of mortgage papers for use by the bank constituted the unauthorized practice of law, even though the bank made no charge against the borrowers for so doing).

[15] 28 USC § 1332(c).

[16] Orange County Audubon Society, Inc. v Hold, (Fla App) 276 So2d 542.

[17] Freedland's Estate, 38 Mich App 592, 197 NW2d 143.

(2) Multiple Regulation. Government regulation of corporations becomes complicated when the corporation engages in business in several states, and the problem arises as to what extent it must comply with the regulation of each state. In some instances the interstate character of the corporate business brings it within the scope of the federal interstate commerce power and the corporation must therefore comply with both state and federal regulations.[18] Thus, an interstate dealer in food will generally be required to satisfy state laws with respect to his product as well as the federal Food, Drug, and Cosmetic Act.[19]

§ 48:6. Ignoring the Corporate Entity. In some instances the corporate entity is ignored, however, and rights and liabilities are determined as though there were no corporation and as though the shareholders were the persons doing the act performed by the corporation, meaning that they do not obtain the various advantages of being a corporation.

(1) Prevention of Fraud or Illegality. When the corporation is formed to perpetrate a fraud or conceal illegality,[20] a court will ordinarily ignore the corporate entity, or as it is figuratively called, "pierce the corporate veil." [21] (See p. 959, Casanova Guns, Inc. v Connally.) For example, if enemy aliens are not eligible to purchase or own particular kinds of property, they cannot organize an American corporation and purchase the property in the name of the corporation. In such a case a court would look behind the corporation to see that the alien enemies were really the persons involved and would not allow them to defeat the law by the device of forming a corporation. Similarly, a buyer under a requirements contract remains liable even though he incorporates the business in order to evade the contract obligation.[22]

When a person engages in business and uses the corporation as a mask by which to hide from a person he is defrauding, the law will ignore the separate corporate entity and will hold such person liable for the acts of the corporation on the theory that it is the alter ego of the person.[23]

(2) Functional Reality. When a corporation is in effect merely a department of a large enterprise, as when a large manufacturer incorporates the marketing department, it is likely that the separate corporate character of the incorporated department will be ignored.

In some instances a court will hold that there is such an identity between a local subsidiary corporation doing business within the state and the foreign

---

[18] In case of an inconsistency or conflict, a federal regulation displaces or supersedes a state regulation.

[19] 21 USC §§ 301-392.

[20] Central Fibre Products Co. v Lorenz, 246 Iowa 384, 66 NW2d 30.

[21] It is likely that the enforcement of the obligation of good faith imposed by UCC § 1-203 will result in ignoring a corporate entity in some cases. Thompson v United States, (CA8 Tex) 408 F2d 1075.

[22] Western Oil & Fuel Co. v Kemp, (CA8 Minn) 245 F2d 633.

[23] Kirk v H.G.P. Corp., 208 Kan 777, 494 P2d 1087.

parent corporation that the latter may be regarded as doing business within the state.[24] For example, where the question was whether the parent corporation was doing business within the state, it was concluded that since the marketing corporation was admittedly doing business within the state and since it was merely a department or branch of the parent holding corporation, the holding corporation was to be deemed doing business within the state; as opposed to the contention that the corporation doing business within the state was a different legal person distinct from the parent holding corporation.

When a corporation is merely a department of another enterprise, it is probable that its separate corporate identity will be ignored when liability of the enterprise to third persons is involved. For example, when a manufacturer owns all of the stock of a corporate distributor which distributes only the product of that manufacturer, the distributor is in effect merely the marketing department of the manufacturer. On this rationale, when a consumer sues the distributor corporation because he had been injured by a product made by the manufacturer, he may recover from the distributing corporation on the basis of evidence showing that the manufacturing corporation was negligent.[25] That is, the distributor cannot say that the manufacturer who was negligent was a different and independent legal person.

All of this is contrary to the ordinary rule that when the various phases of an enterprise are organized as separate corporations, each of such corporations is a separate person, even though the stock may be owned and they may be managed by the same persons.[26]

It is not possible to state a specific rule to predict when the individual entities of the economically related corporations will be ignored. The fact that one corporation controls another, or that a parent or holding company and a subsidiary company have officers and directors or shareholders in common, is not sufficient ground for ignoring the separate corporate entity of each corporation.[27] The fact that two corporations have identical shareholders does not justify a court in regarding the two corporations as being only one.[28]

The fact that there is a close working relationship between two corporations does not in itself constitute any basis for ignoring their separate corporate entities when they in fact are separately run enterprises.[29]

When a sale of goods is made between a corporation and its wholly-owned subsidiary, the separate entities of the two corporations will not be ignored for the purpose of reaching the conclusion that no sales tax is due on the theory that the subsidiary was in fact merely a department of the parent corporation so that the transfer was not a taxable "sale." [30]

---

[24] Hill v Zale Corp., 25 Utah 2d 357, 482 P2d 332.

[25] Moore v Jewel Tea Co., 46 Ill 2d 288, 263 NE2d 103.

[26] Gordon Chemical Co. v Aetna Casualty & Surety Co., 358 Mass 632, 266 NE 2d 653.

[27] Bell Oil & Gas Co. v Allied Chemical Corp., (Tex) 431 SW2d 336.

[28] Schusterman v Appeal Bd., 336 Mich 246, 57 NY2d 869.

[29] Crowell Corp. v Merrie Paper Co., 35 App Div 2d 803, 315 NYS2d 762.

[30] Superior Coal Co. v Department of Finance, 377 Ill 282, 36 NE2d 354.

In the absence of proof of any fraud a court will not ignore the corporate entity, even though the same person owned the stock and controlled the corporation.[31] Similarly, a parent corporation will be regarded as distinct from its subsidiary when each corporation is operated by its own management which makes its decisions independently of the other.

(3) Preservation of Privilege. When a parent corporation has a right or a privilege, it is possible that a subsidiary corporation, which is merely a branch of the parent corporation, will be entitled to the privilege of the parent corporation. To illustrate, a number of hospitals cooperated to form a laundry corporation to do the laundry work for the hospitals. The tax assessor claimed that this laundry corporation should pay the same kind of tax as was assessed against commercial laundries generally. The court held that although the laundry was a distinct corporation, it was in effect merely the cooperating hospitals doing their laundry work at a central plant which happened to be organized in the corporate form. Consequently, it was not an ordinary commercial laundry subject to tax but retained the same tax exemption as the hospitals would have if they were doing the laundry work.[32]

(4) Advantages of Corporate Existence. The court will not go behind the corporate identity merely because the corporation has been formed to obtain tax savings or to obtain limited liability for its shareholders. Likewise, the corporate entity will not be ignored merely because the corporation does not have sufficient assets to pay the claims against it.[33]

The fact that recognizing the corporate entity has the effect of preventing creditors of the corporation from reaching assets which would otherwise be held by the shareholders, in whose hands they would be subject to the claims of the creditors, is not in itself a ground for refusing to recognize the corporate entity.[34] Because a corporation is a separate entity, its property is separately owned by it and cannot be added to the property owned by a shareholder in order to determine the shareholder's financial rights for the purpose of imposing taxes or fixing alimony. It is immaterial that the individual is the only shareholder in the corporation.[35]

---

[31] Russell v Gans, (Fla App) 275 So2d 270.

[32] Children's Hospital Medical Center v Board of Assessors, 353 Mass 35, 227 NE2d 908.

[33] Walkovszky v Carlton, 18 NY2d 414, 276 NYS2d 585, 223 NE2d 6.

[34] In re Guptill Holding Corporation, 33 App Div 2d 362, 307 NYS2d 970.

[35] Quinn v Quinn, 11 Md App 638, 276 A2d 425.

CASES FOR CHAPTER 48

Branmar Theatre Co. v Branmar, Inc.

(Del Ch) 264 A2d 526 (1970)

The Branmar Theatre Co., a family corporation, leased a theatre from Branmar, Inc. The lease prohibited it from transferring the theatre. The holders of the stock of Branmar Theatre Co. sold their stock to the Schwartzes. The lessor (Branmar, Inc.) claimed that this was a violation of the antiassignment provision and

threatened to cancel the lease. Branmar Theatre Co. thereafter brought an action for a declaratory judgment to enjoin the cancellation of the lease.

SHORT, V.C. . . . Plaintiff was incorporated under the laws of Delaware on June 7, 1967. The owners of its outstanding capital stock were the Robert Rappaport family of Cleveland, Ohio. On June 9, 1967, plaintiff and defendant entered into a lease agreement for a motion picture theatre in the Branmar Shopping Center, New Castle County, Delaware. The lease, 16 pages in length, recites that the lessor is to erect a theatre building in the shopping center. It provides for the payment of rent by the lessee to the lessor of $27,500 per year plus a percentage of gross admissions receipts, plus 5 percent of any amounts paid to the lessee by refreshment concessionaires. The percentage of admissions figure is regulated by the type of attractions in the theatre, the minimum being 5 percent and the maximum 10. The lease provides for a 20-year term with an option in the lessee to renew for an additional 10 years. The lessee is to provide the lessor with a loan of $60,000, payable in installments, to be used for construction. The lessee is to provide, at its cost, whatever fixtures and equipment are necessary to operate the theatre. Paragraph 12 of the lease, the focal point of this lawsuit, provides:

"Lessee [tenant] shall not sublet, assign, transfer or in any manner dispose of the said premises or any part thereof, for all or any part of the term hereby granted, without the prior written consent of the Lessor [landlord], such consent shall not be unreasonably withheld."

Joseph Luria, the principal for Branmar Shopping Center testified at trial that he negotiated the lease agreement with Isador Rappaport; that he made inquiries about Rappaport's ability to manage a theatre and satisfied himself that Rappaport had the competence and the important industry connections to successfully operate the theatre. It appears that Rappaport and his son operate a successful theatre in Cleveland, Ohio, and have owned and operated theatres elsewhere.

Following execution of the lease, the Rappaports were approached by Muriel Schwartz and Reba Schwartz, operators of 10 theatres in the Delaware and neighboring Maryland area, with an offer to manage the theatre for the Rappaports who had no other business interests in the Wilmington area. This offer was not accepted, but the Schwartzes subsequently agreed with the Rappaports to purchase the lease from plaintiff and have it assigned to them. An assignment was executed by plaintiff to the Schwartzes. Defendant rejected the assignment under the power reserved in Paragraph 12 of the lease. On May 29, 1969, the Schwartzes purchased the outstanding shares of plaintiff from the Rappaports. Upon receipt of notice of the sale, defendant advised plaintiff that it considered the sale of the shares to the Schwartzes to be a breach of Paragraph 12 of the lease and the lease to be null and void.

The theatre building is now substantially completed and ready for occupancy. The Schwartzes are ready and willing to perform under the lease agreement. Defendant intends to substitute a new tenant, Sameric Theatres, for the corporate plaintiff, contending that Sameric is a better qualified operator than the Schwartzes.

Defendant argues that the sale of stock was in legal effect an assignment of the lease by the Rappaports to the Schwartzes, was in breach of Paragraph 12 of the lease, and that it was therefore justified in terminating plaintiff's leasehold interest. That in the absence of fraud, and none is charged here, transfer of stock of a corporate lessee is ordinarily not a violation of a clause prohibiting assignment is clear from the authorities. . . . Defendant contends, however, that this is not the ordinary case. Here, it says, due to the nature of the motion picture business, the performance required was by the Rappaports personally. But while defendant's negotiations were with a member of the Rappaport family when the lease was executed, it chose to let the theatre to a corporation whose stock might foreseeably be transferred by the then stockholders. In the preparation of the lease, a document of 16 pages, defendant was careful to spell out in detail the rights and duties of the parties. It did not, however, see fit to provide for forfeiture in the event the stockholders sold their shares. Had this been the intent, it would have been a simple matter to have so provided. . . . "When plaintiff chose to deal with a corporation as its tenant, it must also have known that shares of stock therein might be owned by different stockholders and were subject to assignment to others in the ordinary course of business. The inhibitions against assignment run as to the lease itself and not to the stock in the lessee corporation. . . . Had the parties to the lease intended that the sale and transfer by one or more stockholders in the lessee corporation . . . of their shares of stock therein was to be deemed to be an assignment or attempted assignment of the lease itself, such fact should have been expressed in the lease in clear and unequivocal language." . . .

Defendant suggests that since "the Rappaports" could not assign the lease without its consent, they should not be permitted to accomplish the same result by transfer of their stock. But the rule that precludes a person from doing indirectly what he cannot do directly has no application to the present case. The attempted assignment was not by the Rappaports but by plaintiff corporation, the sale of stock by its stockholders. Since defendant has failed to show circumstances to justify ignoring the corporation's separate existence, reliance upon the cited rule is misplaced.

I find that the sale of stock by the Rappaports to the Schwartzes was not an assignment within the terms of Paragraph 12 of the lease and that the [lease] remains in full force and effect. . . .

[Judgment for plaintiff.]

Kansas v Zale Jewelry Co.

179 Kan 628, 298 P2d 283 (1956)

The State of Kansas, on the complaint of the attorney general, brought an original action in the Supreme Court of Kansas against the Zale Jewelry Co., a corporation, to order it to stop the practice of optometry and to forfeit its charter for engaging therein. The State claimed that Dr. Marks, who practiced optometry in one part of the store, and the Douglas Optical Company, which also did business in part of the store, were in fact employees of the Zale Co., which, as their employer, was therefore engaging in optometry.

SMITH, C.J. . . . Defendant relies in the main on two leases . . . to establish that the relationship between it and Marks and it and Douglas was strictly that of lessor and lessee. . . . The two leases . . . each had the provision about defendant handling the business and financial affairs of both Marks and Douglas Optical. A reasonable inference is that such provision was in the lease so as to permit defendant to exercise control over both.

Rowe v Standard Drug Co., 132 Ohio St. 629, 9 NE2d 609, 612, was a case where a drug company was charged with . . . practicing optometry. The arrangement between the drug company was somewhat analogous to what we have here. The drug company relied on leases between it and an optical company to establish the relationship of lessor and lessee. The court said:

"The court, however, is not limited by the terms of the lease, but will consider the manner in which the optical business was conducted and the extent to which the corporation participated in transactions involving optometrists. . . ."

". . . A lease, valid on its face, may be a mere sham or device to cover up the real transaction; but such a subterfuge will not be permitted to become a cloak for illegal practices. The courts will always pierce the veil to discover the real relationship. Where a corporation directly or indirectly engages in the practice of optometry, the lease will afford no protection on a proper challenge of the illegality." . . .

Besides the feature of the leases, . . . there is the fact that at first the neon sign near the stairway to the balcony read until this action was commenced "Optical Dept." [The] inference is that the business on the balcony was a part of the business of defendant. Even though it be held to refer to Douglas Optical and not Dr. Marks, still without Dr. Marks, the optical business would not have done well. . . . All Dr. Marks' prescriptions were filled by Douglas

Optical. When glasses were charged, the account was carried in the name of defendant. . . .

The relationship between defendant and Dr. Marks is that of employer and employee. Dr. Marks is practicing optometry. He is employed to do so by defendant—hence defendant is practicing optometry, which it cannot do.

Judgment is in favor of plaintiff ousting defendant from the practice of optometry in the state. Plaintiff asks us to order the dissolution of defendant and the appointment of a receiver to wind it up. We find the record does not warrant such a drastic measure.

S.O.U.P., Inc. v FTC

(CA Dist Col) 449 F2d 1142 (1971)

A federal statute permits a person to proceed in court without paying court costs if he is unable to do so.* A corporation, Students Opposing Unfair Practices, Inc. (S.O.U.P.) claimed that it was a "person" within the meaning of this statute and that it could therefore proceed without the payment of costs to seek a review of the decision of the Federal Trade Commission.

PER CURIAM . . . At the request of members of the Court, a financial statement of each of the small number of members of the corporation was filed. . . . We think it would be inconsistent with the congressional intent to hold that this corporation should be allowed to proceed in that manner in view of the financial data submitted since it is likely that the costs of proceeding would not exceed $100.00. We think we would not comply with the statute, properly construed in the situation presented, if we granted the application, although in so deciding we appreciate the good faith of applicants and their public interest motivation. . . .

Statement of Senior Circuit Judge FAHY in support of the order of the court, in which Circuit Judge WILKEY concurs.

SOUP is not prevented by our order from proceeding with the litigation. It can easily arrange for the small item of costs by assessment or voluntary contribution of its members. The corporate form is a convenient, organizational vehicle, but its convenience does not justify turning it into a vehicle also for avoiding the costs involved in a lawsuit as if it were a pauper. The public interest motivating SOUP's members, which I join in applauding, does not help make the corporation "a person . . . unable to pay such costs or give security therefor." 28 USC § 1915(a).

The text of the statute reflects the congressional intent and purpose to enable "person[s]" to obtain exemption, not corporations formed by persons who themselves do not come within the exemption. The statute has the salutary purpose of opening the doors of the courts to poor persons on a basis of equality with the more well-to-do, not to open the doors to "poor" corporations formed by nonpoor members as a convenient form by which to organize and litigate. . . .

BAZELON, C.J. (dissenting). This case presents an important question concerning the right of a corporation to sue without prepayment of costs under 28 USC § 1915(a). . . .

Students Opposing Unfair Practices, Inc. (SOUP) is a private, non-profit corporation designed primarily to assist the Federal Trade Commission in "more vigorously protecting the consumers' rights to fair and honest advertising." Pursuant to this goal, SOUP attempted to intervene in an FTC proceeding against the Campbell Soup Company. The case is now before this Court on SOUP's petition for review of an FTC order accepting a consent decree against Campbell. Petitioner challenges both the adequacy of the decree as a remedy for alleged violations of the Federal Trade Commission Act, and the agency's refusal to grant SOUP full rights to intervene in the proceeding before it.

Section 1915(a) provides that a federal court may authorize litigation without prepayment of costs "by a *person* who makes affidavit that he is unable to pay such costs or give security therefor." . . . The statute's reference to "person" does not indicate, however, that the section has no application to corporations. . . .

* This is described as proceeding in forma pauperis.

But my conclusion that § 1915(a) applies to corporations rests on more than this admittedly formal approach to the statute's interpretation. The purpose of the in forma pauperis statute is to insure that indigent parties will not be precluded from litigating significant questions merely because they are unable to pay a relatively small fee. Like an individual, a corporation may lack the means to meet this threshold expense, and thus it too may be barred from the courtroom without regard to the merits of its claim. I can find no reason to believe that Congress's concern for the obstacles facing an indigent litigant extended only to natural persons, and I would therefore hold the statute applicable to corporations. . . .

The real difficulty with SOUP's motion, it seems, concerns the assertion of indigency. SOUP is conceded to lack the *corporate* resources to pay the costs of proceeding in this Court. Indeed, the FTC not only accepts the corporation's claim of indigency, but itself permitted SOUP to proceed in forma pauperis before the agency. Nevertheless, this Court has apparently concluded that a corporation cannot be indigent for purposes of § 1915(a) so long as its members have the personal means to pay the costs of the proceeding. This approach, which disregards the petitioner's corporate form and treats it as a collection of individual litigants, imposes unnecessary administrative burdens on this Court and may effectively discourage litigation by certain corporations.

Instead of resolving the question of indigency on the basis of a single affidavit from a corporate officer, it is now apparently necessary for us to evaluate affidavits from each of the "members" of the corporation. In this case the corporation comprises only five persons. But if "members" refers to shareholders, the problem of evaluating these affidavits could in some cases be staggering. For us to undertake this time-consuming responsibility as a means of collecting about $100 in court costs strikes me as remarkably poor economics. It is also inconsistent with Congress's evident intention of simplifying the inquiry into indigency.

Moreover, by looking behind the corporation to the individuals it represents, today's order may have the unfortunate effect of deterring the use of corporations as vehicles for raising issues of great public importance. By measuring the corporation's indigency in terms of the assets of its wealthiest member, we may discourage non-indigent individuals from joining corporations that intend to bring law suits on behalf of the public. If these persons are forced to commit their personal resources to the cause, they may prefer to sue as individuals. Yet it seems clear that in this type of law suit a corporation or association is often a more valuable party than an individual. Furthermore, if these persons refuse to assume personal liability for the costs of litigation, issues of great importance may fail to reach a judicial hearing. For these reasons I cannot accept the Court's approach to the determination of indigency of corporations under § 1915(a) in these circumstances. Nothing in this record indicates that SOUP's effort to proceed in forma pauperis is in any way offensive to the public interest. Nor does anyone assert that its application is a sham or an abuse of this Court. Since a decision in favor of SOUP would in no sense deprive us of the ability to forestall any possibility of abuse in subsequent cases, I would grant petitioner's application.

[Petition denied.]

John Mohr & Sons v Apex Terminal Warehouses, Inc.

(CA7 Ind) 422 F2d 638 (1970)

John Mohr & Sons, an Illinois corporation, purchased the Lafayette Grain Terminal, Inc. (LGT, Inc.), an Indiana corporation. It later leased the warehouse facilities of LGT, Inc. to Apex Terminal Warehouse, an Indiana corporation. Martin, the president and owner of Apex, guaranteed the payment of the rent. When the rent was not paid, John Mohr brought suit against Apex and Martin in a federal district court, claiming that it was entitled to do so because of the diversity of citizenship that existed between the parties. The defendants denied that there was a diversity of citizenship. From a decision in favor of John Mohr, the defendants appealed.

MAJOR, J. . . . Lafayette Grain Terminal, Inc. (hereinafter LGT, Inc.), an Indiana corporation, owned the terminal in question in 1961. LGT, Inc. was owned one half by a Mr. Barnes and his family and one half by plaintiff, which acquired its interest in 1961. At that time, Barnes and his son were two of the four directors. In 1963, Barnes and his son resigned and two officers of plaintiff were elected to the board of directors. It appears that holding these two directorships was sufficient to control the affairs of the corporation. When plaintiff's officers were elected, an employee of plaintiff was assigned to Lafayette to manage the terminal.

In 1964, mortgagees of the terminal buildings instituted foreclosure proceedings against LGT, Inc. An insurance company held the first mortgage and plaintiff the second. Plaintiff was the successful bidder at a United States marshal's foreclosure sale and became the record owner of the warehouse on September 8, 1964, by virtue of a marshal's deed. Plaintiff took, however, subject to the insurance company's first mortgage. After the foreclosure but before the lease of the warehouse to Apex, plaintiff operated it as "LGT, Inc., a Division of John Mohr & Sons."

Since the foreclosure in 1964, LGT, Inc. has been dormant, The day after the sale, it had no assets except a few accounts receivable, and the accounts payable exceeded the value of these assets. Plaintiff assumed these assets and paid the liabilities. LGT, Inc. has not subsequently earned any income.

On the basis of these facts, defendants assert that the court is without jurisdiction. Their position is that plaintiff, an Illinois corporation, and LGT, Inc. effected a type of "merger" so that the Indiana citizenship of LGT, Inc. must be attributed to plaintiff with the result that diversity is destroyed. More specifically, the defendants urge that a *de facto* merger took place or that LGT, Inc. should be regarded as the mere *alter ego* of the plaintiff. The court finds that under neither of these theories urged upon it is it proper to find that diversity is absent.

As defendants contend, a consolidated corporation may, under certain circumstances, be found to have the citizenship of each of the preconsolidation, separate, corporate components. . . . However, the instant case does not permit such a conclusion. . . . There is absolutely no evidence that plaintiff or LGT, Inc. ever intended to or took any steps to accomplish a merger.

Neither is there any merit to defendants' urging that the *alter ego* doctrine be applied. To support the defendants' contention, the court would be required to disregard the plaintiff and look to LGT, Inc., the Indiana citizen. Yet LGT, Inc. has been dormant for nearly four years. To look *through* LGT, Inc. to the plaintiff would be more plausible, but this would not help the defendants because plaintiff is clearly an Illinois corporation.

More fundamentally, this is simply not an appropriate occasion to apply *alter ego* reasoning. Before the doctrine may be applied, ". . . it must be shown that the stockholders' disregard of the corporate entity made it a mere instrumentality for the transaction of their own affairs; that there is such unity of interest and ownership that the separate personalities of the corporation and the owners no longer exist; and to adhere to the doctrine of corporate entity would promote injustice or protect fraud."

. . . It cannot be said that LGT, Inc. has been such an instrumentality for plaintiff. LGT, Inc. has been totally inactive for four years and has not been an instrumentality for anyone. While it is true that the two corporations had interlocking directorates and management before the foreclosure in 1964, the affairs of the two firms were kept separate. For example, before the foreclosure, the employee that plaintiff sent to manage the warehouse was paid by LGT, Inc. After foreclosure, he was paid by LGT, Division of John Mohr & Sons. There was a similar change in bank accounts.

The distinction between LGT, Inc. and its principal asset, the terminal, must be kept clear. The fact that plaintiff acquired this asset does not mean that the affairs of the two corporations became intermingled. Plaintiff acquired the terminal through an arm's length transaction at a United States marshal's sale. At all times plaintiff's interest in the property, either as a lien holder or as record owner, was subject to the rights of a first mortgagee.

Finally, it cannot be said that treating the two corporations as separate entities would promote injustice or fraud. This would be a much different case if, for example, LGT, Inc. had created the plaintiff solely for the purpose of creating diversity. . . . This is not the situation here.

[Judgment affirmed.]

Casanova Guns, Inc. v Connally

(CA7 Wis) 454 F2d 1320 (1972)

Casanova Guns, Inc., applied for a license under the Federal Gun Control Act. It was denied a license because of its close relationship to Casanova's, Inc., which had been convicted of violating the federal law. Casanova Guns brought an action against Connally, as Secretary of the Treasury of the United States, to review the refusal of the application.

PER CURIAM. . . . The district court upheld the commissioner's decision.

The license was denied because of Casanova Guns' relationship with Casanova's, Inc. (Casanova's), a convicted felon. The Gun Control Act prohibits the issuance of federal firearms licenses to convicted felons and to companies directed or controlled by convicted felons. 18 USC § 923(d)(1)(B). Based upon their findings that Casanova's controlled or had the power to control Casanova Guns, the commissioner and the district court found the appellant ineligible for a renewal license. We are asked to review the finding that Casanova's controlled Casanova Guns.

An understanding of the commissioner's decision requires an examination of the history of the respective corporations. Casanova's, although incorporated in 1959 by Clarence Casanova, has been in the sporting goods and gun business in Milwaukee for 39 years. The president and major stockholder of Casanova's, Clarence Casanova, held approximately 350 of the 500 shares. Other members of the Casanova family held the remainder of the shares and acted as minor officers in the corporation. In 1966 Casanova's was indicted for the possession of unregistered firearms. Two years later the corporation pleaded guilty and was fined the minimum amount imposed by the statute. That conviction rendered Casanova's ineligible under § 923 for renewal of its federal license.

Casanova Guns was organized in March 1967, subsequent to the indictment of Casanova's but prior to the conviction. The president and sole shareholder of Casanova Guns was John Casanova, Clarence Casanova's son and a shareholder of Casanova's. The other family members, who continued to direct Casanova's, became officers and directors of Casanova Guns. In February 1967 Casanova Guns applied for and received a federal firearms license. After the license was obtained, Casanova Guns took over the first company's entire gun business. Casanova's continued in the general sporting goods business.

On April 16, 1969, Casanova Guns purchased the entire inventory of firearms of Casanova's. In exchange for the inventory, Casanova Guns gave an unsecured promissory note for $424,000. John Casanova ran Casanova Guns in the same building and used the same display area as Casanova's. There was an informal arrangement by which Casanova Guns leased floor space and storage facilities from Casanova's. Separate books and accounts were kept for the two corporations, but John, who considered himself the sole employee of Casanova Guns, was paid his $32,710 salary by Casanova's.

In January 1969, Casanova Guns had applied for a renewal of its federal license. That renewal application was refused on May 29, 1969.

. . . The applicant's employer, Casanova Guns, Inc., is a corporate successor in interest directly related to a corporation, Casanova's Inc., which is a convicted felon. The business operations of Casanova Guns, Inc., are substantially the same as the operations of its related predecessor. Furthermore, the officers of Casanova Guns, Inc., were the persons responsible for the operations of Casanova's, Inc. Therefore, Casanova Guns, Inc., being a related successor to a convicted felon, is prohibited from receiving, possessing or transporting firearms in commerce or affecting commerce under Title VII of the Omnibus Crime Control and Safe Streets Act of 1968. . . .

The appellant urges that Casanova Guns is not a convicted felon and therefore should not be denied a license on the basis of the felon status of Casanova's. That view ignores the express language of the licensing act. The statute explicitly prohibits the issuance of a license to a convicted felon or to a corporation, partnership or association over which a convicted felon exercises or could exercise control. Additionally, it is well settled that the fiction of a corporate entity must be disregarded whenever it has been adopted or used to circumvent the provisions of a statute. . . .

It is apparent from the record that a substantial purpose for the incorporation of Casanova Guns was the circumvention of the statute restricting issuance of firearms licenses to convicted felons. Casanova Guns was formed after Casanova's was under federal indictment. Indeed, the testimony of John Casanova at the administrative hearing is a reluctant admission that the second corporation was formed to insure the continuation of the gun business.

Further, there is a significant unity of interest between the officers and stockholders of the two corporations and the business operations were closely integrated. The four officers of each corporation were the same, the only difference being that Clarence Casanova was the president of Casanova's and John Casanova was the president of Casanova Guns. Casanova Guns operated from the same building as Casanova's and was dependent on Casanova's for light, heat, telephone, bookkeeping and additional personnel when necessary. Casanova's provided these services on an informal "fee" arrangement, but the nature of that arrangement does not destroy the interlocking relationship between the management personnel and practices of the two companies.

In addition, the total assets of Casanova Guns derived from the inventory purchased from Casanova's. That inventory was purchased on a $424,000 unsecured note which is payable on demand. We believe a debt of this nature and magnitude warrants the inference that Casanova's possessed a substantial degree of control over Casanova Guns. That belief is bolstered by the admission of Clarence Casanova that he exercised some control over Casanova Guns in order to protect his investment. That control was made possible by the fact that the two corporations operated out of the same building; also, Clarence Casanova's daughter was the bookkeeper for both corporations.

[Decision affirmed.]

QUESTIONS AND CASE PROBLEMS

1. Several shareholders of a corporation borrowed money from the bank in which the corporation had its bank account. When the shareholders did not pay the loans back to the bank, the bank deducted the amount of the loans from the bank account of the corporation on the theory that the shareholders had used the money for the benefit of the corporation. Was the bank entitled to make this deduction? [Potts v First City Bank, 7 Cal App 3d 341, 86 Cal Rptr 552]
2. An action was brought by Alabama Tank Lines and other carriers against the Martin Truck Line, claiming that the truck line was operating without the necessary certificate of the state Public Service Commission. It was shown that Martin Truck Line had obtained a certificate at a time when all of its stock was owned by Thornbury, Cook, and Edwards. The stock was thereafter sold to Houghland and Page. No approval of the transfer of stock to them was obtained from the Public Service Commission. Was Martin Truck Line entitled to continue to do business under the certificate that had been originally issued? [Martin Truck Line v Alabama Tank Lines, 261 Ala 163, 73 So2d 756]

3. The Meridian Life Insurance Co., an Indiana corporation, obtained permission to transact business in South Dakota. In order to obtain this permission, it agreed that in any action brought against it in South Dakota on an insurance policy, service of the process in the suit could be made upon the Insurance Commissioner of South Dakota with the same effect as though the corporation were actually served. Thomson was the beneficiary of a policy issued by the company in Texas to a Texas resident. Thomson sued on the policy in South Dakota and made service on the Insurance Commissioner. The company objected that a state could not constitutionally compel a foreign corporation to appoint the Insurance Commissioner as its agent for service with respect to lawsuits brought on foreign causes of action. Was the corporation correct? [Thomson v Meridian Life Insurance Co., 38 SD 570, 162 NW 373]

4. A corporation was formed for the purpose of doing the laundry work for a cooperating group of hospitals. The local tax assessors claimed that the laundry corporation was required to pay the same taxes as any other laundry corporation. The hospitals claimed that the laundry corporation had the same "charitable" status as the hospitals, which, if true, would exempt it from the taxes in question. Was it exempt? [Children's Hospital Medical Center v Board of Assessors, 353 Mass 35, 227 NE2d 908]

5. Riesberg was the president and sole shareholder of the Carson Steel Co. His wife, driving an automobile owned by the corporation, collided at a grade crossing with a train of the Pittsburgh & Lake Erie Railroad. Riesberg sued the railroad for damage to the automobile. Was he entitled to recover? [Riesberg v Pittsburgh & Erie RR, 407 Pa 434, 180 A2d 575]

6. North Gate Corporation leased property to National Food Stores. The lease contained a provision that neither the corporation nor its "beneficiaries" would engage in a competing business within a specified radius. Some shareholders of North Gate Corporation engaged in such a business within the prohibited area. National Food Stores claimed that the restriction on "beneficiaries" applied to "shareholders" of North Gate. Were the shareholders bound by the anticompetitive covenant? [North Gate Corporation v National Food Stores, Inc., 30 Wis 2d 317, 140 NW2d 744]

7. Erlich and his wife owned all the stock of the West Coast Poultry Co. Erlich claimed that Glasner and others had caused the corporation to be prosecuted for food law violations; that these prosecutions were unsuccessful; that the conduct of the defendants was a violation of the federal Civil Rights Act; that, by interfering with the conduct of the corporation's business, the actions of the defendant in turn were "a direct interference with plaintiff's right to operate his business and earn a livelihood for himself and his family"; and that he accordingly was entitled to recover damages under the federal Civil Rights Act. Was he correct? [Erlich v Glasner, (CA9 Cal) 418 F2d 226]

8. The Drackett Co. manufactured a bathroom fixture cleaner named "Vanish." All of the products of this company were sold by its wholly owned subsidiary, "The Drackett Products Co." The subsidiary had no other business, and all of the income of the parent company was obtained from the subsidiary company's sales. Shirley purchased a can of Vanish. When she used it, chemical fumes caused extreme damage to her lungs. She sued Drackett Products Co., claiming that it was negligent. It defended on the ground that it did not make

the product, that it was not negligent because it had no reason to foresee that any harm would result, and that it could not be liable for any fault of the manufacturing corporation. Was this a valid defense? [Shirley v The Drackett Products Co., 26 Mich App 644, 182 NW2d 726]

9. Greenberg organized the PSG Company in order to obtain certain tax advantages. He owned all of the stock of the corporation and was its principal officer. El Salto sued PSG Co. and Greenberg, claiming that the corporation was liable for damages for discriminatory price practices and that Greenberg was also liable for such damages on the theory that PSG was the alter ego of Greenberg. Is Greenberg liable to El Salto on the facts above stated? [El Salto v PSG Co., (CA9 Ore) 444 F2d 477]

10. Robinson was a salesman of the Realty Investment Consultants, Inc. (R.I.C., Inc.). Kramer was president, treasurer, and director of the corporation and owned all of its stock. Robinson contacted Ferrarell in answer to the latter's letter of inquiry in response to a newspaper ad of R.I.C. Robinson executed a contract with Ferrarell on behalf of R.I.C. and signed the contract as agent for that corporation. Subsequently, Ferrarell sued Robinson and Kramer for breach of the contract by R.I.C. Were they liable? [Ferrarell v Robinson, 11 Ariz App 473, 465 P2d 610]

49 Creation and Termination

A corporation receives its authority from government. Statutory law specifies the requirements that must be met for creating a corporation and the manner in which a corporation can be dissolved or terminated.

CREATION OF THE CORPORATION

All states have general laws governing the creation of corporations by persons who comply with the provisions of the statutes.

§ 49:1. Promoters. The promoters are the persons who plan the corporation and sell the idea to others. They may also file the necessary papers with the government to create the corporation. They are independent operators. They are not regarded as agents of the corporation since the corporation is not yet in existence.

A promoter, in the absence of statutory authority, cannot bind the corporation [1] or give it rights by a preincorporation contract even though he purports to act for it. The corporation, upon coming into existence, may become a party to such a contract, however, by assignment or by novation. Moreover, when the corporation knowingly accepts the benefits of the promoter's contract, it becomes liable on that contract.[2]

The promoter is personally liable for all contracts made in behalf of the corporation before its existence unless he is exempted by the terms of the agreement or by the circumstances surrounding it.[3] (See p. 973, Quaker Hill v Parr.) A promoter is not personally bound, even though he signs as "president," when the other contracting party was informed that the corporation was not yet in existence and such future officer refused to execute a contract naming him as a party individually.[4] When a promoter makes a contract on behalf of a corporation to be formed thereafter, he is liable thereon if the corporation is not formed, in the absence of agreement that he should not be so liable.[5]

A promoter is also liable for all torts that he commits in connection with his activities. Although the corporation is not ordinarily liable for the torts of the promoter, it may become so by its conduct after incorporation. Thus, when a corporation, with actual or implied notice of the fraud of the

---

[1] Mankin v Bryant, 206 Ga 120, 56 SE2d 447.
[2] Frye & Smith v Foote, 113 Cal App 2d 907, 247 P2d 825.
[3] Tucker v Colorado Indoor Trap Shoot, Inc., (Okla) 471 P2d 912.
[4] Stewart Realty Co., Inc. v Keller, 118 Ohio App 49, 24 OO2d 473, 193 NE2d 179.
[5] King Features Syndicate v Courrier, 241 Iowa 870, 43 NW2d 718.

promoter, assumes responsibility for the promoter's contract, it is liable for the promoter's fraud to induce the other party to enter into the contract.

A promoter stands in a fiduciary relation to the corporation and to stock subscribers.[6] He cannot make secret profits at their expense. Accordingly, if a promoter makes secret profits on a sale of land to a corporation, he must account to the corporation for those profits, that is, he must surrender the profits to it. He may be held guilty of embezzlement if he converts to his own benefit property that should have gone to the corporation.[7]

The corporation is not liable in most states for the expenses and services of the promoter unless it subsequently promises to pay for them or unless its charter or a statute imposes such liability upon it.

§ **49:2. Incorporators.** The statutes often require three applicants who possess the capacity to contract. A few states require that the incorporators or a specified percentage of the incorporators be citizens of the state or of the United States.

The requirement that there be three incorporators has frequently, in the case of the small business, merely had the result that the single proprietor obtains the cooperation of two dummy or nominal incorporators. The ABA Model Act therefore takes the direct approach and, in common with many modern statutes, permits the formation of a corporation by one incorporator.[8]

As the result of the historical accident that corporations were formed by natural persons, the rule developed that a corporation could not be an incorporator. In recent decades it has been common for a corporation to be the actual moving party in the organizing of another corporation. The Model Act recognizes this by permitting a domestic or foreign corporation to be an incorporator,[9] and many statutes make a similar provision when the new corporation is a consolidation of existing corporations.

§ **49:3. Application for Incorporation.** The organizers must apply for a certificate of incorporation and file certain documents, such as the proposed articles of incorporation.

The modern trend of statutes simplifies the mechanics of incorporating by providing that the incorporators send to a designated state official two copies of the articles of incorporation; and provides that when the designated official determines that the articles satisfy the statutory requirements, he indorses "approved" or "filed" or similar words and the date on each copy. The officer then retains one copy for his records and returns the other copy to the corporation.[10]

Statutes may require incorporators to give some form of public notice, such as by advertisement in a newspaper, of the intention to form the corporation.

---

[6] Arent v Bray, (CA4 Va) 371 F2d 571.
[7] May v Mississippi, 240 Miss 361, 127 So2d.
[8] American Bar Association Model Business Corporation Act, § 53.
[9] ABA MBCA § 53.
[10] § 55.

(1) Name of Proposed Corporation. Subject to certain limitations, the incorporators may select any name.

(2) Object of Proposed Corporation. A corporation may be formed for any lawful purpose.

When the applicants for a charter satisfy the statutory requirements, they are entitled to a charter and cannot be refused a charter for a ground not stated in the statute.[11]

Some states also require a statement of the means to be used to attain the object of the corporation. This is particularly common in the case of nonprofit or charitable corporations.

(3) Capital Stock. The amount of capital stock to be authorized and the number and value of the shares into which it is divided must be specified.

The ABA Model Business Corporation Act requires that the articles of incorporation contain a description of the classes of shares, the number of shares in each class, and the relative rights of each class.[12] Other statutes have similar requirements. A number of states require that the incorporators state that the corporation will not begin to do business until a specified amount has been paid into the corporation,[13] but the trend in corporation legislation is to abandon this requirement.[14]

(4) Place of Business. The location of the principal office or place of business of the proposed corporation must be stated.

(5) Duration. The period during which the proposed corporation is to exist must be set forth. In a number of states limitations are imposed upon the number of years a corporation may exist, the maximum ranging from 20 to 100 years. Commonly, provision is made for a renewal or extension of corporate life. Many states permit the incorporators to select perpetual life for the corporation.

(6) Directors and Officers. In half of the states the number of directors or the names and addresses of directors for the first year must be stated. Sometimes additional information regarding the directors is required. In some instances the names and addresses of the officers for the first year must also be stated.

The purpose of requiring the naming of the first board of directors is to provide the corporation with a body to govern or manage the corporation

---

[11] Gay Activists Alliance v Lomenzo, 31 NY2d 965, 341 NYS2d 108, 293 NE2d 255 (Secretary of State may not refuse charter because the purposes are violative of "public policy" and the corporate name is "not appropriate").

[12] § 54.

[13] When a corporation begins business without the stated paid-in capital having been paid in, liability may be imposed on shareholders or officers for the corporate debts even though they exceed the amount of capital that should have been paid in. Tri-State Developers, Inc. v Moore, (Ky) 343 SW2d 812.

[14] Such a provision was included in the original Model Act, § 48, but has been omitted from the current revision of that Act.

during the interval from the moment that the corporate life begins until the organization meeting of the shareholders is held. In some states that do not require the naming of the first board of directors in this manner, the incorporators have the power of management during this period.

(7) Incorporators. The names and addresess of the incorporators must be given, along with the number of shares subscribed by each. Sometimes the method of payment for those shares must also be stated.

(8) Registered Office and Agent. The trend of current statutes is to require a corporation to give a specific office address and the name of an agent, which are described as the "registered" office and the "registered" agent.[15] The object of such provisions is to provide information to the world as to where someone can be found, to whom to give notice, or where to effect legal service upon the corporation.[16]

§ 49:4. The Charter. After the application for a certificate of incorporation or a charter is filed, the fee paid, and other conditions precedent fulfilled, usually an administrative official, such as the secretary of state, examines the papers. If the requirements of the law have been met, a certificate of incorporation, license, or charter is issued and recorded or filed, as specified by the terms of the local statute.

Under the Model Business Corporation Act corporate existence begins upon the issuance of the certificate of incorporation by the state official.[17] In some states corporate existence does not begin until an organization meeting is held under the charter to put the corporation in operation, and in others, not until a report on the organization meeting is made. The statute may declare that the charter shall be void if the certificate of organization is not properly filed within the prescribed time. In a few states there is an additional requirement of a local recording of the certificate of incorporation.[18]

The charter not only creates the corporation but also confers contractual rights and imposes contractual duties as between the state, the corporation, and the shareholders.[19] In theory it is required that the corporation accept the charter which is given to it; but unless expressly required by statute, it is not necessary for the corporation to inform any state officer that the charter is accepted. The acceptance can be inferred from conduct, such as holding an organization meeting or doing business under the charter.[20]

---

[15] ABA MBCA § 12.

[16] The fact that a corporation does not designate such an agent does not mean that it cannot be sued or given notice. Most statutes provide that in such case the service may be made upon or the notice given to a specified state official, such as the secretary of state. In addition, a plaintiff suing a foreign corporation that has not appointed a person upon whom service can be made may in many instances effect service under a "long-arm" statute when the foreign defendant has engaged in local business or committed a local wrong or breach within the terms of such statute. See Gray v American Radiator & Standard Sanitary Corp., 22 Ill 2d 432, 176 NE2d 761.

[17] ABA MBCA § 56.

[18] 8 Delaware Code Ann § 103(c).

[19] Petition of Collins-Doan Co., 3 NJ 382, 70 A2d 159.

[20] Bank of U.S. v Dandridge, 12 Wheat (US) 64.

Since the charter is regarded as a contract, the corporation is protected from subsequent change or modification by the clause of the federal Constitution that prohibits states from impairing the obligation of contracts.[21] This does not mean that in no case can the rights given by a charter be modified. Under many statutes it is expressly provided that the charter granted by the state is subject to the power reserved by the state to change the charter should it desire to do so. Independently of such a reservation, the rule has developed that permits the state, under the exercise of its police power, to modify existing contracts, including corporate charters, to further the public health, safety, morals, or general welfare.

§ 49:5. Proper and Defective Incorporation. If the legal procedure for incorporation has been followed, the corporation has a perfect legal right to exist. It is then called a *corporation de jure*, meaning that it is a corporation by virtue of law.

In some cases everything is not done exactly as it should be and the question then arises as to the consequence of the defect. This problem becomes less and less important as time goes on because (1) with the great number of corporations being formed, it becomes increasingly clear just what should be done to form a corporation so that the likelihood of the corporation's attorney or anyone else making a mistake is increasingly less; (2) standardized incorporation has eliminated a great deal of uncertainty that existed when each corporation was formed by a separately granted charter; and (3) the probability of a corporation's coming into existence with some defect is less because of the pattern of having a full-time government official examine the application and accompanying papers, thereby assuring that if there is any significant mistake, it will probably be noted by the government expert before the application for the certificate is approved.

Assume, however, that there is still some defect in the corporation which is formed. If the defect is not a material one, the law usually will overlook the defect and hold that the corporation is a corporation de jure.

The ABA MBCA abolishes objections to irregularities and defects in incorporating. It provides that the "certificate of incorporation shall be conclusive evidence that all conditions required to be performed by the incorporators have been complied with and that the corporation has been incorporated under this Act." [22] State statutes generally follow this pattern. Such an approach is based upon the practical consideration that when countless people are purchasing shares of stock and entering into business transactions with thousands of corporations, it becomes an absurdity to expect that

---

[21] Dartmouth College Case, 4 Wheat (US) 518.

[22] ABA MBCA § 56. The Model Act expressly excepts "a proceeding to cancel or revoke the certificate of incorporation or for involuntary dissolution of the corporation." The provision would likewise not be operative when the original corporate existence was for a specified number of years which had expired, the corporation then becoming a de facto corporation if it continued to do business without obtaining an extension of its corporate life.

anyone is going to make the detailed search that would be required to determine whether a given corporation is a de jure corporation.[23]

(1) De facto Corporation. The defect in the incorporation may be so substantial that the law cannot ignore it and will not accept the corporation as a de jure corporation. Yet there may be sufficient compliance so that the law will recognize that there is a corporation. When this occurs, the association is called a *de facto corporation.* It exists in fact but not by right, and the state may bring proceedings to have the corporate charter revoked because of the defect.[24] If, however, the state does not take proceedings against the defective corporation, the de facto corporation has all the rights and privileges of a regular lawful or de jure corporation, and third persons contracting with it cannot avoid their contracts on the ground that the corporation was merely a de facto corporation. The de facto corporation is, in a sense, like a voidable contract. It can be set aside by the state; but unless the state acts, the corporation is lawful with respect to the entire world. The shareholders of a de facto corporation generally have limited liability.

Although there is conflict among the authorities, most courts hold that a de facto corporation must meet four tests: (a) there must be a valid law under which the corporation could have been properly incorporated; (b) the attempt to organize the corporation must have been made in good faith; (c) the attempt to organize must result in colorable compliance with the requirements of the statute; and (d) there must be a use of the corporate powers.

(2) Partnership v Corporation by Estoppel. The defect in incorporation may be so great that the law will not accept the corporation even as a de facto corporation, let alone as a de jure corporation. In such a case, in the absence of a statute making the incorporation conclusive, there is no corporation. If the incorporators proceed to run the business in spite of such irregularity, they may be held liable as partners.[25]

The partnership liability rule is sometimes not applied when the third person dealt with the business as though it were a corporation. In such instances it is stated that the third person is estopped from denying that the "corporation" with which he did business has legal existence. In effect there is a *corporation by estoppel* with respect to that creditor.

---

[23] This trend and the reasons therefor may be compared to those involved in giving rise to the concept of the negotiability of commercial paper. Note the similar protection from defenses given to the person purchasing shares for value and without notice. Uniform Commercial Code § 8-202.

[24] Colonial Investment Co. v Cherrydale Cement Block Co., 194 Va 454, 73 SE 2d 419.

[25] In a minority of states the court will not hold the individuals liable as partners, but will hold liable the person who committed the act on behalf of the business on the theory that he was an agent who acted without authority and is therefore liable for breach of the implied warranties of the existence of a principal possessing capacity and of the proper authorization. Doggrell v Great Southern Box Co., (CA6 Tenn) 206 F2d 671.

The doctrine of corporation by estoppel is not always applied, and it is difficult to bring one's case within the rule by showing that the third person dealt with the defective corporation as a corporation. The doctrine is applied when one of the promoters or incorporators attempts to deny that there is a corporation. Here it is held that having attempted to create the corporation or having purported to do so, the promoter or incorporator cannot deny that a corporation was created.

(3) Abandoning Incorporation. At times a project to form a corporation is abandoned and the corporation is never formed and never engages in any business. In such a case those persons who had actively participated up to that point are regarded as joint venturers with the result that each has the power of an agent or partner to dispose of property held in the name of the corporation that was never formed.

If the incorporators have failed to obtain a charter and have not done business, neither the corporation by estoppel nor the partnership rule will be applied.

DISSOLUTION OR TERMINATION

A corporation may be dissolved or terminated by agreement, insolvency, reorganization proceedings, consolidation, merger, or forfeiture of charter. Some statutes provide for the dissolution of corporations by court decree.

§ 49:6. Dissolution by Agreement.

(1) Expiration of Time. If the incorporators have selected a corporate life of a stated number of years, the corporate existence automatically terminates upon the expiration of that period.

(2) Surrender of Charter. The shareholders may terminate the corporate existence by surrendering the charter to the government. The surrender is not effective until the state accepts the charter. The state's acceptance of a surrender of the charter ends the corporate existence and generally extinguishes the liability of the corporation for debts.

§ 49:7. Insolvency, Bankruptcy, and Reorganization.

(1) Insolvency. The insolvency of a corporation does not in itself terminate the corporate existence. Statutes in some states, however, provide that when the corporation is insolvent, creditors may commence proceedings to dissolve the corporation. Sometimes the statute merely dissolves the corporation as to creditors. This situation is sometimes called a *de facto dissolution* or *quasi dissolution.*

The appointment of a receiver for the corporation does not in itself dissolve the corporation, although the administration of the property by the receiver may result in the practical termination of the corporation. In some states the appointment of liquidators to wind up an insolvent corporation automatically dissolves the corporation.[26] In the absence of statute, a court cannot appoint a receiver for a solvent corporation and order its dissolution.[27]

(2) Bankruptcy. When a corporation is adjudicated bankrupt, a sale of all its assets will be ordered. This leaves the corporation without any assets with which to do business unless there should be a surplus above the amount required to pay off the debts of the corporation. The bankruptcy proceeding does not, however, terminate the legal existence of the corporation.

(3) Reorganization. When a reorganization of a corporation occurs under the federal bankruptcy laws, the corporate existence is not terminated. If the reorganization is successful, the result is the same as though the corporation merely exchanged obligations and securities. Under state law, however, reorganization proceedings generally result in the formation of a new corporation.

§ 49:8. Forfeiture of Charter. The government that granted the charter may forfeit or revoke the charter for good cause. Sometimes the legislature provides in a general statute that the charter of any corporation shall be automatically forfeited when certain acts are committed or omitted.

Common grounds for forfeiture are fraudulent incorporation; *willful nonuser*, that is, failure to exercise powers; or *misuser*, that is, abuse of corporate powers and franchises. When it is claimed that a corporation has abused its privileges, such acts must be willful, serious, and injurious to the public. The action against the corporation to forfeit its charter must be brought by and in the name of the government, meaning ordinarily an action by the attorney general of the state.[28] Forfeiture of a charter is an extreme penalty. Because of its severity, it is rarely used.

In a number of states when a corporation does not pay its taxes, its power to do business is suspended. (See p. 974, Bank of America National Trust and Savings Ass'n v Morse.) Some states impose personal liability upon the officers and directors for such taxes.

§ 49:9. Judicial Dissolution. In some states provision is made for the judicial dissolution of a corporation when its management is deadlocked and the deadlock cannot be broken by the shareholders.[29] In some states a "custodian" may be appointed for a corporation when the shareholders are unable to break a deadlock in the board of directors and irreparable harm is threatened or sustained by the corporation because of the deadlock.[30]

Arbitration may, in some instances, be a solution for the problem of the corporation in which management control is deadlocked, and in some

---

[26] Brown & Son v Wholesalers, Inc., (La App) 52 So2d 321.
[27] Hepner v Miller, 130 Colo 243, 274 P2d 818.
[28] Petition of Collins-Doan Co., 3 NJ 382, 70 A2d 159.
[29] Laskey v L. & L. Manchester Drive-In, Inc., (Maine) 216 A2d 310.
[30] Slotsky v Geller, 49 Pa D&C 2d 255.

instances, arbitrators have given one corporate faction or group the right to buy out the stock of the other at a price fixed by the arbitrators.[31]

CONSOLIDATIONS, MERGERS, AND CONGLOMERATES

Two or more corporations may be combined to form a new structure. This may be a consolidation, a merger, or the formation of a conglomerate.

§ 49:10. Definitions.

(1) Consolidation. In a *consolidation* of two or more corporations, the separate corporate existences cease, and a new corporation with the property and assets of the old corporations comes into being.[32]

When a consolidation is effected, the new corporation ordinarily succeeds to the rights, powers, and immunities of its component parts.[33] Limitations, however, may be prescribed by certificate of incorporation, constitution, or statute. As a general rule, the consolidated corporation is subject to all the liabilities of the constituent corporations.[34]

(2) Merger. Merger differs from consolidation in that, when two corporations merge, one absorbs the other. One corporation preserves its original charter and identity and continues to exist, and the other disappears and its corporate existence terminates.

Simplified merger procedure is authorized in some states under *short merger statutes* when there is a merger of a parent corporation and its subsidiary. Under most merger statutes a dissenting shareholder has the right to require the enterprise to purchase his shares from him.

(a) DE FACTO COMBINATION. The procedure for merger and consolidation is specifically and minutely regulated in most jurisdictions. If two corporations have not complied with the specified procedure, there is no merger or consolidation. In some instances, however, two corporations have become so combined in fact that it has been held that there was a de facto merger. (See p. 975, Pratt v Ballman-Cummings Furniture Co.)

(3) Conglomerate. Conglomerate is the term describing the relationship of a parent corporation to subsidiary corporations engaged in diversified fields of activity unrelated to the field of activity of the parent corporation. For example, a wire manufacturing corporation that owns all the stock of a newspaper corporation and of a drug manufacturing corporation would be described as a conglomerate. In contrast, if the wire manufacturing company owned a mill to produce the metal used in making the wire and owned a mine which produced the ore that was used by the mill, the relationship

---

[31] Colletti v Mesh, 23 App Div 2d 245, 260 NYS2d 130; affirmed 17 NYS2d 460, 266 NYS2d 814, 213 NE2d 894.

[32] Freeman v Hiznay, 349 Pa 89, 36 A2d 509.

[33] ABA MBCA § 69.

[34] Teague v Home Mortgage & Investment Co., 250 Ark 322, 465 SW2d 312.

would probably be described as an *integrated industry* rather than as a conglomerate. This is merely a matter of usage, rather than of legal definition. Likewise, when the parent company is not engaged in production or the rendering of services, it is customary to call it a holding company.[35]

Without regard to whether the enterprise is a holding company, or whether the group of businesses constitute a conglomerate or an integrated industry, each part is a distinct corporation to which the ordinary corporation law applies. In some instances additional principles apply because of the nature of the relationship existing between the several corporations involved. In some instances the entity of one of the corporations in the conglomerate group may be ignored.

The increase in conglomerates during the last two decades has been the result of a number of factors. The conglomerate may be formed to obtain a tax advantage; or to avoid the application of the federal antitrust law, which would be applicable if one business acquired a similar business; or to diversify the character of hazards to which the overall "enterprise" or "investment" is subjected, as in the case of a conglomerate formed by a casualty insurance and a life insurance company, the latter company being the more likely to have a large surplus and less likely to be subject to relatively unpredictable losses.

§ 49:11. Legality. Consolidations, mergers, and asset acquisitions between enterprises are often prohibited by federal antitrust legislation on the ground that the effect is to lessen competition in interstate commerce. A business corporation may not merge with a charitable corporation because this would divert the assets of the respective corporations to purposes not intended by their shareholders.[36]

Conglomerates are lawful; but there is a movement to amend or interpret the antimerger provision, Section 7 of the Clayton Act, so as to subject conglomerates to the same limitations as apply to consolidations and mergers.

§ 49:12. Liability of Enterprise.

(1) Liability of Successor Enterprise. Generally the enterprise engaging in or continuing the business after a merger or consolidation will be subject to the contract obligations and debts of the original corporations.

The corporation which absorbs another corporation by merger is generally liable for the contracts of the corporation which was absorbed and it is no defense that the third party does not have any contract with the absorbing corporation. (See p. 977, Gaswint v Case.)

The liability of a successor corporation on a contract of the earlier corporation may arise from conduct showing a novation or agreement that the

---

[35] See § 50:2(10)(b).

[36] Stevens Bros. Foundation, Inc. v Commissioner of Internal Revenue, (CA8 Tax Ct) 324 F2d 633, cert den 376 US 969, reh den 377 US 920.

successor be substituted for the earlier corporation. To illustrate, where there was a supply contract between corporations *A* and *B*, and corporation *C* became the successor to corporation *B*, and thereafter *A* and *C* did business just as though *C* were *B*, it will be concluded that there was an agreement and that *C* should have all the rights and liabilities of *B* under the original *A-B* contract.[37]

However, the mere fact that one corporation acquires the business or purchases the assets of another corporation does not make the purchasing corporation liable for the debts of the selling corporation where there is no consolidation or merger of the two corporations, nor an assumption of debts by the purchasing corporation nor any design to defraud the creditors of the selling corporation. (See p. 977, Comstock v Great Lakes Distributing Co.)

(2) *Liability of Component Enterprise.* An existing business may be acquired by another corporation under a variety of circumstances. How does the acquisition affect the rights and liabilities of the business that is acquired? For example, when corporation *A* buys out corporation *B*, what becomes of the rights and liabilities of corporation *B*?

When there is a formal consolidation or merger, statutes commonly provide expressly for the transfer of rights and liabilities to the surviving corporation or the new corporation. The contract of sale or agreement between corporation *A* and corporation *B* will ordinarily expressly assign *B*'s rights to *A* and contain an assumption by *A* of the liabilities of *B*. In accord with general principles of contract law, *A* can sue an assignee on the assigned rights and third persons can sue on the transferred liabilities on the theory that they are third party beneficiaries of such assumption.

Liability on the part of the acquiring corporation does not, however, follow in all cases. (See p. 979, McKee v Harris-Seybold Co.)

---

[37] Automatic Retailers of America v Evans Cigarette Service Co., 269 Md 101, 304 A2d 581.

CASES FOR CHAPTER 49

Quaker Hill v Parr

148 Colo 45, 364 P2d 1056 (1961)

Quaker Hill made a contract for the sale of plants to the "Denver Memorial Nursery, Inc." The contract was signed by Parr as Denver's president. Quaker Hill knew that the corporation was not yet formed and the contract so stated, but Quaker Hill had insisted that the contract be executed in this manner rather than wait until the corporation was organized. The corporation was never formed, and Quaker Hill sued Parr and other promoters of the corporation. From a judgment in the promoters' favor, Quaker Hill appealed.

DOYLE, J. . . . The general principle which plaintiff urges as applicable here is that promoters are personally liable on their contracts, though made on behalf of a corporation to be formed. . . . A well recognized exception to this general rule, however, is that if the contract is made on behalf of the corporation and the other party agrees to look to the corporation and not to the promoters for payment, the promoters incur no personal liability.

In the present case, according to the trial court's findings, the plaintiff . . . was well aware of the fact that the corporation was not formed and nevertheless urged that the contract be made in the name of the proposed corporation. . . . The entire transaction contemplated the corporation as the contracting party. Personal liability does not arise under such circumstances. . . .

The curious form of this transaction is undoubtedly explainable on the basis of the . . . great rush to complete it, the heavy emphasis on completion of the sale rather than on securing payment or a means of payment. No effort was made to expressly obligate the . . . defendants and this present effort must be regarded as pure afterthought.

[Judgment for defendants affirmed.]

Bank of America National Trust and Savings Ass'n v Morse

— Ore —, 508 P2d 194 (1973)

Morse Bros. Painting and Weatherproofing, a corporation, failed to pay its taxes to the state of California. Because of this the state suspended its authority to do business. Thereafter its president, J. L. Morse, and its secretary, Doris Morse, borrowed money from the Bank of America. The note was signed: "Morse Bros. Painting and Weatherproofing, a Corporation By /s/ J. L. Morse President By /s/ Doris N. Morse Secretary." When the loan was made, neither the bank nor the Morses knew that the authority of the corporation had been suspended. The bank sued Doris Morse on the note after the death of her husband. From a judgment in favor of the bank, Doris appealed.

MCALLISTER, J. . . . The corporation ceased to do business in January, 1970, shortly after the death of J. L. Morse. So far as it appears, however, the corporation has never been formally dissolved.

The bank contends that defendant is personally liable on two alternative theories: (1) The suspension of the corporation's "powers, rights and privileges" imposed, as a matter of law, personal liability for corporate debts upon the officers and directors. (2) Defendant is liable on the note because, although purporting to sign as an officer on behalf of the corporation, she was without authority to do so. . . .

. . . The statute upon which plaintiff relies does not in terms make the corporation's officers or directors liable for debts incurred during suspension, but provides only for the suspension of the corporation's "powers, rights and privileges," [when taxes due by the corporation have not been paid]. Among the powers suspended is the power to borrow money and issue notes. . . . The purpose of the statute is to bring pressure upon the corporation to pay the tax. . . . To this end the Revenue and Taxation Code also provides. . . . "Every contract made in violation of this article is hereby declared to be voidable, at the instance of any party other than the taxpayer." . . .

. . . The . . . statute does not make the note void, but only voidable at the instance of the bank. The bank has made no attempt to avoid the transaction. Moreover, under the statute, the corporation remained in existence although its powers and privileges were suspended. It apparently continued to do business, and had assets, until after the note's maturity date, October 29, 1969. . . .

The California statute, providing for suspension rather than forfeiture of corporate powers is apparently unusual. A Michigan statute provides for suspension of corporate powers upon failure to pay license fees or to file required annual reports with the state. That statute, unlike the California provision, expressly makes corporate officers liable for corporate debts contracted during the period of default. . . . It is not unusual for state law to impose personal liability on officers or directors for debts contracted while the corporation is in default under the statutes requiring the filing of reports. . . . It has been held that this liability is purely statutory, and that the statutes are to be strictly construed. . . .

Unlike the above statutes, which are intended to enforce the duty to file reports which provide the public with information about the corporation's affairs, the California statute is designed only to aid the state in its collection of revenue. There is no purpose to protect individuals as potential creditors of investors. There is no compelling reason why a corporation's tax delinquency should result in its officers being individually liable for corporate debts. In the absence of any indication in the statute that the legislature intended that result, this court will not construe the California statute as imposing liability on defendant.

Plaintiff's other theory is that defendant is personally liable on the note by virtue of her signature. . . . (UCC § 3-404) provides: "(1) Any unauthorized signature is wholly inoperative as that of the person whose name is signed unless he ratifies it or is precluded from denying it; but it operates as the signature of the unauthorized signer in favor of any person who in good faith pays the instrument or takes it for value." . . .

Plaintiff contends that when the corporation's powers were suspended, it was deprived not only of the power to borrow money and issue notes, . . . but also of the power to authorize defendant to do so on its behalf. Her signature on the note, therefore, was an "unauthorized signature" within the meaning of § 3-404 and as a result she is personally liable on the instrument. In Black, Sivalls & Bryson, Inc. v Connell, 149 Kan 118, 86 P2d 545 (1939), decided under the Uniform Negotiable Instruments Law, the corporation's charter had been forfeited under a state statute. After this forfeiture, the corporation's president executed a corporate note. He was held personally liable by virtue of his signature on the instrument. Plaintiff relies on this case, but we agree with defendant that it is distinguishable. The corporation in that case had lost its charter; the court characterized its status as follows: ". . . Upon the forfeiture of the charter of a corporation it ceases to exist. . . . The title to its assets vests in the stockholders. It has no power thereafter to do anything, or to authorize anyone to do things for it. . . . The situation has been compared to that of the death of an individual whose ability to do things, or to authorize anyone to do things for him, necessarily has ceased. . . ." . . . Under the California suspension statute, the corporation has no right to exercise its powers, but it continues to exist. Moreover, the statutes recognize the possibility that the corporation may continue to do business in violation of the suspension, and § 23-304 makes contracts entered during the suspension period voidable at the option of the other parties. From this it follows that such contracts may be enforced against the corporation, and that the California statutes recognize the corporation's power to authorize agents to make commitments on its behalf during the period of suspension. If plaintiff had sought to enforce the note against the corporation, the corporation could not have defended on the ground that the note was unauthorized, as the statute makes contracts entered in violation of the suspension "voidable at the instance of any party other than the [corporate] taxpayer." Under the Uniform Commercial Code the unauthorized signer of a note can be held liable only if the purported principal is not bound. The holder is not entitled to a choice between the agent and his principal.

The trial court's judgment for plaintiff is incorrect on the law. . . .

[Judgment reversed.]

Pratt v Ballman-Cummings Furniture Co.

— Ark —, 495 SW2d 509 (1973)

Ballman-Cummings Furniture Company and Ft. Smith Chair Company formed a partnership. Pratt owned stock in Ballman-Cummings Furniture Company. He claimed that the partnership agreement was in fact a merger of the two corporations and that he therefore had the statutory right to be paid the value of his shares because he dissented from such merger. From a judgment for the corporation, Pratt appealed.

BROWN, J. . . . The appellants are minority stockholders of Ballman-Cummings Furniture Company of Ft. Smith. They claim that by a vote of the majority stockholders of [Ballman-] Cummings, the corporation, under the pretext of forming a partnership with Ft. Smith Chair Company, Inc., accomplished a de facto merger or consolidation of the two corporations. If the arrangement is in fact a partnership it is authorized by Ark.Stat.Ann. § 64-104 . . . ; if the arrangement constitutes a merger then the appellants, protesting minority stockholders, are entitled to be paid by the succeeding corporation, the fair value of their stock. Ark.Stat. Ann. § 64-707 . . . .

At the close of plaintiffs' (appellants') case the chancellor sustained a challenge to the sufficiency of the evidence, making this finding: "Not only have plaintiffs failed to establish factually or as a matter of law a statutory merger or consolidation, sale or exchange, but they have also failed as well by their proof to establish even a de facto change to support their theory of entitlement to recovery herein. A difference of opinion with or over management alone is not sufficient."

The Ayers family of Ft. Smith, by virtue of its stock holdings, is in control of both corporations and the corporations have interlocking directors.

The partnership agreement was executed in November 1967. It provided that the partnership would consist of two partners, naming the two corporations. The name of the partnership was designated Ayers Furniture Industries. Each partner would contribute $1500 to the initial capital of the partnership. It was agreed that each corporation would sell its merchandise to the partnership. The partnership would be responsible for all merchandising functions in connection with the promotion and sale of furniture. It would also handle billing and collection of accounts receivable. The partnership would also assume the responsibility for the delivery of furniture to customers. (It was explained by witness John Ayers, ownership of the furniture by the partnership made it possible to load furniture produced by both factories in a single trailer which otherwise was not permitted by ICC regulations.) It was also explained by the same witness that the partnership would eliminate the duplication of expenses of billing and collections. It was also provided that the partners would designate one individual as a general manager of the partnership who would be fully authorized to conduct the business and affairs of the partnership.

It would be most difficult to say that the partnership arrangement, as exemplified by the agreement which we have briefly described, constituted in and of itself a merger of the two corporations. We gather, particularly from oral argument, that appellants recognize this as a fact. On the other hand, there are well recognized in the law, de facto mergers—an association under the guise of a partnership whereby one of the corporations loses its identity as such and is actually controlled by the management of the partnership. When a particular corporate combination "is in legal effect a merger or a consolidation, even though the transaction may be otherwise labeled by the parties, the courts treat the transaction as a de facto merger or consolidation so as to confer upon dissenting stockholders the right to receive cash payment for their shares." . . .

Mr. John Ayers is the chief officer of Ballman-Cummings, of Ft. Smith Chair, and of the partnership. It is the position of appellants, while asserting that they do not accuse Mr. Ayers of fraud, that under his executive direction, Ballman-Cummings has lost its long standing identity in the market place. That development, so they say, has resulted in consistent annual losses by the corporation of thousands of dollars, while the profits of Ft. Smith Chair remained stable. The evidence shows that Ballman-Cummings is in the process of liquidation.

In holding as we do, we do not mean to insinuate that appellants preponderantly established a case for relief, but we do say that they made a prima facie case. Having done so it was error for the court to grant appellees' motion at the close of appellants' case, particularly when giving the evidence its strongest probative force in favor of appellants. . . .

According to appellants the events which brought about the alleged destruction of Ballman-Cummings are summarized in their brief and their argument, and absent any other explanation, are persuasive:

> Not only is the separate identity of the merging corporations as marketing entities replaced by the image of a separate and new entity, but Article 2, Section 5 (Articles of Partnership) provides: "The partners

shall designate one individual as a General Manager of the partnership who will be fully authorized to conduct the business and affairs of the partnership."

Furthermore, the management, sales and bookkeeping functions of the two corporations were entirely merged together, with a single officer, not the one elected by the directors of each corporation, in charge of each function. John Ayers became the General Manager of both corporations and the partnership, or more properly of both corporations in the partnership. Prior to the merger each corporation had a sales manager, after the merger Gene Rapley who had been sales manager for Ballman-Cummings became sales manager for the combined operations, while Tom Condren who had been sales manager for Chair Company became the designer for the combined operations. The controller for one corporation, Mr. Layman, was placed in charge of the accounting processes for the combined operations, while the controller for the other corporation, Mr. Thompson, took over the credit collection and customer service activities of the combined operation. Dale Keller, who had been purchasing agent for Ballman-Cummings, became purchasing agent for the combined operations, while Mr. Keller who had been with Chair Company became the chief assistant in the purchasing department.

Whether there is a correlation between the shifting of the described responsibilities and the resultant folding of Ballman-Cummings is not the question; the question is whether a prima facie case was made. We think it was. We might add that no solid reason was given by Mr. Ayers for Ballman-Cummings' collapse. There was only a general statement that it was due to economic reasons. Mr. Ayers said he had no explanation why the loss of Ballman-Cummings rose so severely except "apparently loss cycles that we had been experiencing, the problems we had been experiencing in production were pyramiding on us during that year." Appellees are also burdened by the fact that the partnership was proposed on the basis that it would increase profits, which of course it did not do. . . .

[Judgment reversed and action remanded.]

Gaswint v Case

— Ore —, 509 P2d 19 (1973)

Gaswint was employed by an Oregon corporation, Amigo Motor Homes, Inc. The stock of the corporation was acquired by Black Diamond Enterprises, Inc. Some time thereafter Gaswint was discharged. He sued Case and the two corporations for damages for breach of contract. Black Diamond asserted that it was not liable to the plaintiff because it had never made any contract with him. A judgment was entered in favor of Gaswint, from which judgment an appeal was taken.

TONGUE, J. . . . Defendants contend that Black Diamond, a Tennessee corporation, was entitled to a judgment of nonsuit because there was no evidence that it was a party to the agreement dated August 14, 1969, and that there was no evidence that it agreed to employ plaintiff for a period of one year or that it had agreed to assume the liabilities of Amigo.

There was evidence, however, that there had been a merger between Black Diamond and Amigo and that Black Diamond had acquired all of the capital stock of Amigo.

Under 8A Tenn Code Ann, § 48-905(e) and also under ORS 57.480(5), Black Diamond, as the "surviving" corporation in the merger, was responsible and liable for the obligations of Amigo, including its obligations under the agreement of August 14, 1969. . . . Therefore, plaintiff was not required to prove an express agreement by Black Diamond to hire plaintiff or to assume the liabilities of Amigo. . . .

[Judgment affirmed.]

Comstock v Great Lakes Distributing Company

209 Kan 306, 496 P2d 1308 (1972)

Comstock was injured when an automobile jack collapsed. The jack had been manufactured

by the Vulcan Manufacturing Company. In 1963, subsequent to the manufacturing of this particular jack, the controlling interest in Vulcan passed from its then existing shareholders and was acquired by a new investor, Verplank. Vulcan was not able to pay its debts and stopped doing business in 1965. Its assets were then sold at a sheriff's public auction sale. The equipment of Vulcan which had been purchased at the sheriff's sale was resold two times thereafter and a substantial part was ultimately purchased by Great Lakes. Great Lakes rented space from the owner of the building in which the Vulcan business had been conducted and began repairing and manufacturing automobile jacks.

Comstock sued Vulcan, Great Lakes, and others to recover damages for his injury. From a judgment for the defendants, Comstock appealed.

KAUL, J. . . . The basis of plaintiff's action against Great Lakes is that it is merely a continuation of Vulcan, or in the alternative there was a de facto merger of Vulcan and Great Lakes. In order to support his claim, plaintiff attempts to compare the corporate composition of Vulcan prior to 1963 with the corporate makeup of Great Lakes, which did not exist until 1965. Plaintiff ignores the complete change in Vulcan's corporate composition during the period 1963-1965 due to the intervening acquisition by Verplank. At the time of the alleged continuation or merger, the parties who were stockholders, officers and directors of Vulcan prior to 1963 no longer had such status. The continuation or merger into Great Lakes, claimed by plaintiff, must be considered with reference to Vulcan as it was composed under the Verplank operation when the jack in question was manufactured and when Vulcan ceased doing business, not as it was in 1963 when acquired by Verplank. In other words, June 8, 1965, when Vulcan ceased doing business, serves as the point of reference for the consideration of the issue of continuance or merger.

. . . Both parties accept the general rule of nonliability of a transferee corporation for the prior debts of the transferor and the exceptions thereto: . . . "Generally where one corporation sells or otherwise transfers all of its assets to another corporation, the latter is not liabile for the debts and liabilities of the transferor, except: (1) where the purchaser expressly or impliedly agrees to assume such debts; (2) where the transaction amounts to a consolidation or merger of the corporation; (3) where the purchasing corporation is merely a continuation of the selling corporation; and (4) where the transaction is entered into fraudulently in order to escape liability for such debts." . . .

Plaintiff admits the rule of nonliability, which we have quoted, is the law of this jurisdiction, but attempts to impose liability on Great Lakes on the theory of consolidation or merger under exception (2), or in the alternative on the theory that Great Lakes was merely a continuation of Vulcan under exception (3). The record does not support either theory.

We shall first direct our attention to the claim of consolidation or merger. . . . "Strictly speaking, a consolidation signifies such a union as necessarily results in the creation of a new corporation and the termination of the constituent ones, whereas a merger signifies the absorption of one corporation by another, which retains its name and corporate identity with the added capital, franchises and powers of a merged corporation." . . .

In the instant case there is no evidence of direct dealing between Vulcan and Great Lakes. Vulcan never sold, transferred or delivered anything to Great Lakes. Some of the equipment and machinery formerly owned by Vulcan is now owned by Great Lakes. The testimony of Judge Plunkett, which is undisputed, was that the machinery and equipment were sold at a sheriff's auction to a Dale Thule and L. L. Hurst, Jr., after competitive bidding by several bidders. Thule was described as the owner of an automotive equipment business and Hurst as owner of the Edwards Manufacturing Company. Thereafter, the First Heartland Investment Company, to protect its investment, bid in the machinery and equipment within the statutory time. Later part of the machinery and equipment was sold to Great Lakes and the remainder to Lakes Center Switch Company of Winona, Minnesota. . . .

There is no evidence that any assets, tangible or intangible, passed directly from Vulcan to Great Lakes. Nor is there any evidence that any of the original purchasers of Vulcan's property at foreclosure sales acted as "strawmen" to accomplish a transfer of ownership from Vulcan to Great Lakes.

The portion of the machinery and equipment formerly owned by Vulcan, which eventually came into the hands of Great Lakes, passed through first and second purchasers following a foreclosure sale before acquisition by Great Lakes. . . . "When a corporation purchases the franchises and property of another corporation at a sale under a decree foreclosing a mortgage thereon, or other judicial sale, or where natural persons purchase at such sale and afterwards transfer to a corporation, the new corporation is not liable for the debts of the old company, provided they are not prior liens on the property, and provided their payment has not been assumed, nor their payment imposed by the foreclosure decree or by statute. So where an individual purchases the assets of a corporation at a foreclosure sale and then resells to a new company composed largely of the members of the company whose assets were sold, and there is no fraud, the new company is not liable for the debts of the old. . . ." . . .

By the undisputed evidence, Great Lakes acquired the machinery and equipment as a bona fide purchaser; it does not own any interest in the building formerly owned by Vulcan, but only occupies a part of it as a tenant. Other assets of Vulcan were purchased or acquired by other parties. The acquisition of some Vulcan property by Great Lakes, under the circumstances described, does not tend to show a consolidation, merger or mere continuation as those terms have been defined.

Is there any evidence tending to show that Great Lakes was merely a continuation or reincarnation of Vulcan? None of the incorporators of Great Lakes were stockholders or officers of Vulcan at the time Great Lakes was chartered in February of 1965. Vulcan was a going business under the control of, and operated by, Verplank at that time and continued as a corporate entity. There was testimony that the directors or stockholders of Vulcan held a meeting as late as October 1965. Great Lakes did not come into being as a result of a reincorporation of Vulcan or by amendment of the Vulcan corporate charter. . . .

. . . There is no evidence in the instant case of any direct dealings between the two corporations—no transfer of capital stock, assets, contracts or franchises and no evidence of any agreement or understanding between the two corporations. . . .

[Judgment affirmed.]

McKee v Harris-Seybold Co.

109 NJ Super 555, 264 A2d 98 (1970)

McKee was injured while working with a paper cutting machine which had been manufactured in 1916 by Seybold Machine Co. In 1926 Seybold made a contract to sell its assets to Harris Automatic Press, which agreed to assume certain Seybold liabilities. This contract was assigned to a new corporation, Harris-Seybold-Potter Co., which thereafter changed its name to Harris-Seybold Co. McKee sued Harris-Seybold, claiming that it was liable to him because of the harm he sustained in using the cutter which had been made by Seybold Machine Co. Harris-Seybold moved for summary judgment in its favor.

BRESLIN, J. . . . Defendant Harris-Seybold . . . contends that it did not assume any contingent liability of the Seybold Machine Company arising out of (1) the alleged negligent design and manufacture of the machine in question by Seybold, (2) any express or implied warranties arising out of said sale, or (3) the defective design or manufacture of the machine. . . .

It is the general rule that where one company sells or otherwise transfers all its assets to another company, the latter is not liable for the debts and liabilities of the transferor, including those arising out of the latter's tortious conduct, except where: (1) the purchaser expressly or impliedly agrees to assume such debts; (2) the transaction amounts to a consolidation or merger of the seller and purchaser;

(3) the purchasing corporation is merely a continuation of the selling corporation, or (4) the transaction is entered into fraudulently in order to escape liability for such debts. . . . A fifth exception, sometimes incorporated as an element of one of the above exceptions, is the absence of adequate consideration for the sale or transfer. . . .

Liability cannot be impressed upon the movant under the first exception. The contract in question provided that the purchaser and its successors, i.e., the movant assume certain liabilities of the seller (Seybold) enumerated in the contract. These specific liabilities were open accounts for purchasers, accrued water bills, local taxes, payroll accounts, past federal taxes owing, if any, certain sales representative contracts, and current obligations of the seller for purchase of materials and supplies and for the delivery of manufactured goods. These liabilities were in existence at the time the balance sheet attached to the contract was prepared. Since the contract was not to be consummated until February 1, 1927, it was also provided that the purchaser assume the liabilities incurred by Seybold "in the usual course of its manufacturing business, but not otherwise" subsequent to June 30, 1926— the date the balance sheet was prepared. (Seybold's earnings from that date were to be assigned to the buyer.) In paragraph eight of the contract Seybold warranted that there were "no undisclosed or contingent obligations" of Seybold not specified in the contract, and that Seybold would hold the purchaser harmless from such undisclosed or contingent obligations.

A contract must be construed as a whole and the language employed must be given its ordinary meaning, in the absence of anything to show that the language was used in a different sense. . . . Provisions of a contract must be interpreted, if possible, so as to give effect to the general purpose and intention of the parties. . . . It is clear that there was no express assumption by the purchaser of any liabilities except those designated in the contract. It is equally manifest that the purchaser's assumption of those obligations incurred by the seller in the "usual course of manufacturing" subsequent to June 30, 1926, does not include the type of contingent liability herein sought to be imposed. "Usual" is variously defined to mean that which happens in the ordinary course of events, that which is customary or according to common practice. . . . The liabilities incurred by Seybold prior to June 30, 1926, expressly assumed by the purchaser, were those incident to regular upkeep of manufacturing operations, e.g., obligations for materials and supplies purchased. The liabilities incurred by Seybold in the usual course of manufacturing subsequent to June 30, 1926, which were also expressly assumed by the purchaser, were not intended to be of an all-inclusive nature, but rather of the same type as those incurred prior to the above date. This is so especially in view of the restrictive language that appears immediately after "in the usual course of manufacturing business," i.e., "but not otherwise." There was no contractual express or implied assumption of contingent tort liability.

Plaintiff also asserts that the transaction in dispute was not a mere sale of assets but a de facto merger or consolidation which would render the movant liable for the torts of Seybold. . . .

In the present case, Seybold sold all its assets, including its physical assets, patents, and its goodwill and the right to use its name. It cannot be argued that it was not a complete transfer. . . . The consideration paid to Seybold for the transfer was almost $2 million in cash and 5,500 shares of the vendee's common stock. It was not a transfer for securities alone. The shares paid as consideration amounted, in fact, to only a negligible part of the total purchase price. Since the overwhelming portion of the consideration was cash, there was little, if any, continuity of stockholder interest in the purchasing corporation. . . .

Furthermore, there is here no broad assumption of liabilities such as is usually present in de facto merger situations, and, on the face of the contract and the exhibits offered, there is nothing that can be remotely construed as evidence of an intent [by] the contracting parties to effectuate a merger or consolidation rather than a sale of assets.

It may be argued that since the purchaser caused a new corporation to come into existence and succeed to the former's rights under the contract, a consolidation was in reality accomplished. However, although the new corporation, "Harris-Seybold-Potter," did take over the operations of the purchaser and those sold to it by Seybold, the Seybold corporate entity still enjoyed its separate and distinct identity after the transfer. Moreover, the new corporation was brought into being solely through the efforts of the purchaser, not through any activity of Seybold.

The transfer in question was not a de facto merger or consolidation so as to render the movant liable for Seybold's torts.

[Motion granted.]

QUESTIONS AND CASE PROBLEMS

1. *A* made a contract with *B* on behalf of *X* Corporation. *B* knew that *X* Corporation was not yet formed. Thereafter *X* Corporation was properly organized, but *B* refused to perform its contract on the ground that *X* had not been in existence when the contract was made. Was this a valid defense? [330 Michigan Avenue, Inc. v Cambridge Hotel, Inc., (Fla App) 183 So2d 725]
2. The Maid of the Mist Steamboat Co. was organized for operating sight-seeing steamships on the Niagara River. It had a fifty-year charter which expired in 1942. No one realized that fact until 1947. In that year an application was made under the New York law to renew the charter of the corporation. During the intervening period from 1942 to 1947 the corporation had continued to do business as usual. What kind of corporation was it during that period? [Garzo v Maid of the Mist Steamboat Co., 303 NY 516, 104 NE2d 882]
3. The Vincent Drug Co., a single proprietorship, took steps to incorporate. On January 2, articles of incorporation for Vincent Drug Co., Inc., were filed with the secretary of state, together with the firm's check for filing and license fees. The firm after that date conducted its business as a corporation pursuant to the articles. Although retaining the fees, the state later returned the articles to the firm's counsel because of a failure to include, as required by statute, the street addresses of the firm's incorporators and directors. Corrected articles showing such addresses were filed and recorded in May. Later the state tax commission questioned the firm's franchise tax return recitation that it had commenced business as a corporation as of January, the commission contending that the corporation did not exist before May. Was the commission correct? [Vincent Drug Co., Inc. v Utah State Tax Commission, 17 Utah 2d 202, 407 P2d 683]
4. Adams and two other persons were promoters for a new corporation, the Aldrehn Theaters Co. The promoters retained Kridelbaugh to perform legal services in connection with the incorporation of the new business and promised to pay him $1,500. The corporation was incorporated through Kridelbaugh's services, and the promoters became its only directors. Kridelbaugh attended a meeting of the board of directors at which he was told that he should obtain a permit for the corporation to sell stock because the directors wished to pay him for his prior services. The promoters failed to pay Kridelbaugh, and he sued the corporation. Was the corporation liable? [Kridelbaugh v Aldrehn Theaters Co., 195 Iowa 147, 191 NW 803]

5. Akel and his wife organized and incorporated the Akel Corporation. Prior to the actual incorporation, they obtained from Dooley a lease of property in which the Akel Corporation was named as the tenant. Dooley had no information as to whether the corporation was in existence. The corporation was in fact incorporated prior to the commencement of the lease. Later Dooley sued Akel and his wife for the rent. They claimed that they were not liable as individuals because the corporation was the tenant. Decide. [Akel v Dooley, (Fla App) 185 So2d 491]
6. A labor union made a collective bargaining agreement with Interscience Publishers, Inc. The contract made no provision that it was binding on successors of the contracting parties. Later, for general business reasons and not as an antilabor measure, Interscience merged with and disappeared into another publishing corporation, John Wiley & Sons, Inc. The former's employees, with a few exceptions, worked for Wiley. Thereafter the labor union claimed that Wiley was required to submit to arbitration, in accordance with the terms of the contract with Interscience, certain questions relating to employees who had worked for Interscience but were working for Wiley after the merger. Wiley claimed that it was not bound by the arbitration agreement with Interscience. Decide. [John Wiley & Sons v Livingston, 376 US 543]
7. Corporation *A* owed money to *B*. The debt was guaranteed by *C*. Corporation *A* merged with Corporation *D*, with *D* being the surviving corporation. *D* failed to pay the debt to *B*, who then sued *C* on the guarantee. *C* denied liability on the ground that he had guaranteed the debt of Corporation *A* and that as Corporation *A* was no longer in existence, he, *C*, was not bound by any guarantee. Was this defense valid? [Essex International, Inc. v Clamage, (CA7 Ill) 440 F2d 547]

50 Corporate Powers

§ 50:1. Nature of Corporate Powers. Some of the powers possessed by a corporation are the same as those powers held by a natural person, such as the right to own property. Others are distinct powers not possessed by ordinary persons, such as the power to exist perpetually.

All corporations do not have the same powers. For example, those that operate banks, insurance companies, savings and loan associations, and railroads generally have special powers.

Except for limitations in the federal Constitution or the state's own constitution, a state may grant to a corporation any powers that it chooses. In addition, a corporation has certain powers that are incidental to corporate existence. These powers are implied because they are reasonably necessary to carry out and make effective the expressly granted powers. Moreover, in exercising their powers, corporations have a choice of employing any lawful means.[1] The ABA MBCA broadly authorizes a corporation "to have and exercise all powers necessary or convenient to effect its purpose." [2] Many state statutes make a similar "catchall" grant of powers.

In view of the broad sweep that is characteristic of these statutes, the question seldom arises today whether a corporation has a particular power. Today's problem will be whether the president of the corporation had the authority to make a contract on behalf of the corporation rather than the question of did the corporation have the power to authorize the president to make such a contract. That is, today's question relating to power is more likely to be who can exercise the corporate power rather than does the corporation possess the power.

Statutes defining the powers of a corporation are to be interpreted liberally and not as being limited to the pattern of commerce or the state of science at the time the statute was adopted.

(1) Limitations on Corporate Powers. If a power is expressly prohibited to a corporation, the corporation cannot exercise that power. In addition, certain other powers cannot be implied and therefore cannot be exercised in the absence of express authorization. It is generally held that there is no implied power to lend credit, to enter a partnership, to consolidate, or to merge.

---

[1] Greenwich Water Co. v Adams, 145 Conn 535, 144 A2d 323.

[2] American Bar Association Model Business Corporation Act § 53.

§ 50:2. Particular Powers.

(1) Perpetual Succession. One of the distinctive features of a corporation is its perpetual succession or continuous life—the power to continue as a unit forever or for a stated period of time regardless of changes in stock ownership. If no period is fixed for its duration, the corporation will exist indefinitely unless it is legally dissolved. When the period is limited, the corporation may in many states extend the period by meeting additional requirements of the statute. In view of such power of extension, a corporation may make a long-term contract running beyond the termination date of its certificate of incorporation.[3]

(2) Corporate Name. A corporation must have a name to identify it. As a general rule it may select any name for this purpose. It may not, however, select for its exclusive use a name that all may lawfully use, such as a descriptive name, or one that another firm has the exclusive right to use.

Most statutes require that the corporate name contain some word indicating the corporate character [4] and that it shall not be the same as or deceptively similar to the name of another corporation. Some statutes likewise prohibit the use of a name which is likely to mislead the public. The ABA MBCA states that the corporate name "shall not contain any word or phrase which indicates or implies that it is organized for any purpose other than one or more of the purposes contained in its articles of incorporation." [5] Under such a provision it would be improper to include in the corporate name the word "electronic" or "computerized" when such a word had no relation to the actual work of the corporation and the purpose of including such word in the corporate name is to take advantage of the current popularity of those words and thus attract investors to purchase the corporate stock or customers to deal with the corporation. In some states a name similar to one in use may be rejected even though the similarity is not so extreme as to be deceptive [6] but is merely confusing.[7]

A number of states permit persons planning to form a corporation to reserve the name contemplated by filing an appropriate application with a state official. Such reservation is effective for a period generally ranging from 60 to 120 days.

Even when the practice of imitating another's name is not prohibited by the statutes of a particular state, the imitation may still be prohibited as

---

[3] Milton Frank Allen Publications, Inc. v Georgia Ass'n of Petroleum Retailers, Inc., 219 Ga 665, 135 SE2d 330.

[4] American Bar Association Model Business Corporation Act § 8(a) declares that the corporate name must contain the word "corporation," "company," "incorporated," "limited," or an abbreviation of one of such words.

With respect to a professional corporation, there may be some additional requirement that the name indicate the nature of the services rendered in addition to the fact that it is a corporation. For example, it may be necessary to have the name of "Jones Accounting Associates, Inc." rather than merely "Jones Associates, Inc."

[5] ABA MBCA § 8(b).

[6] Steakely v Braden, (Tex Civ App) 322 SW2d 363.

[7] New York Business Corporation Law § 301(a)(2).

unfair competition. Under this principle, the Mount Hope Cemetery Association could prevent a rival corporation from using New Mount Hope Cemetery Association as its corporate name.[8]

(3) ***Corporate Seal.*** A corporation may have a distinctive seal. However, a corporation need not use a seal in the transaction of business unless it is required by statute to use a seal or unless a natural person in transacting that business would be required to use a seal.

(4) ***Bylaws.*** The shareholders of a corporation have inherent power to make bylaws to supplement the charter of the corporation, but the right to do so is commonly expressed by statute.

Bylaws are adopted by the action of the shareholders, but some statutes provide for the adoption of bylaws by the directors unless otherwise provided. Action by the state or an amendment of the corporation charter is not required to make the bylaws effective. The difference between bylaws and provisions of a charter is a practical consideration. The charter represents provisions that should endure throughout the life of the corporation. The *bylaws* represent provisions for governing the corporation but which might become undesirable in the course of events, and therefore they should not be given the same permanence as the charter. This distinction is not always observed, and there is frequently a tendency to put much detail into the charter. No actual harm is done by so doing, except that it makes the charter unnecessarily long and also makes a change more difficult since state approval is required to amend the charter, while bylaws can be changed by corporate action.

The bylaws are subordinate to the general law of the state, including the statute under which the corporation is formed, as well as to the charter of the corporation. Bylaws that conflict with such superior authority or which are in themselves unreasonable are invalid. Bylaws that are valid are binding upon all shareholders regardless of whether they know of the existence of those bylaws or were among the majority which consented to their adoption. Bylaws are not binding upon third persons, however, unless they have notice or knowledge of them.

Statutes commonly provide for the adoption of emergency bylaws by the board of directors in case of war.[9] A few statutes provide for emergency bylaws in time of civil disorder.[10]

---

[8] Mount Hope Cemetery Association v New Mount Hope Cemetery Association, 246 Ill 416, 92 NE 912.

[9] ABA MBCA § 27A [Optional] provides that the board of directors "may adopt emergency bylaws . . . operative during any emergency in the conduct of the business of the corporation resulting from an attack on the United States or any nuclear or atomic disaster. . . ."

[10] The problem faced by the corporation when a civil disorder or other emergency is present would ordinarily be solved by a person or persons, such as the executive committee, taking the initiative and performing such acts as they believe were required by the exigency of the situation. Thereafter, when normal times returned, a meeting of either the directors or the shareholders would be held and a resolution adopted ratifying the action that had been taken.

(5) Stock. A corporation may issue stock and certificates representing such stock.[11]

(6) Borrowing Money. Corporations have the implied power to borrow money in carrying out their authorized business purposes. For example, a fire insurance company may borrow money to pay losses due on its policies. Statutes commonly prohibit corporations from raising the defense of usury.

(7) Execution of Commercial Paper. The power to issue or indorse commercial paper, or to accept drafts, is implied when the corporation has the power to borrow money and when such means are appropriate and ordinarily used to further the authorized objectives of the corporation.

Such transactions, however, are unauthorized when they are not related to, or if they are detrimental to, the furtherance of the corporate business. For example, it is beyond the power of a corporation to be an accommodation party on a note given by someone buying its stock and a building used for the corporate business.[12] In such a case the corporation would be giving up assets and in return would be obligated to pay itself the purchase price which the buyer promised to pay.

(8) Bonds. A corporation having the power to borrow money has the implied power to issue various types of bonds.

The bonds issued by a corporation are subject to Article 8 of the Uniform Commercial Code. If the bonds satisfy the requirements of UCC § 3-104, they are governed by Article 3 of the Code on commercial paper as far as negotiation is concerned.

Ordinarily conditions inserted in the corporate bonds for the protection of the bondholders have the effect of making the bonds nonnegotiable and therefore not within the scope of Article 3 of the Uniform Commercial Code, and only Article 8 applies to them.

(9) Transferring Property. The corporate property may be leased, assigned for the benefit of creditors, or sold. (See p. 992, Wilmington Memorial Co., Inc. v Silverbrook Cemetery Co.) In many states, however, a solvent corporation may not transfer all of its property except with the consent of all or a substantial majority of its shareholders. In any case, the sale must be for a fair price.

A corporation, having power to incur debts, may mortgage or pledge its property as security for those debts. This rule does not apply to franchises of public service companies, such as street transit systems and gas and electric companies.

(10) Acquisition of Property. Although the power to acquire and hold property is usually given in the charter, a corporation always has the implied

---

[11] Statutes in approximately one half of the states authorize a corporation to issue stock rights and warrants. See, for example, 8 Delaware Code § 157.

[12] Haynie v Milan Exchange, Inc., 62 Tenn App 36, 458 SW2d 23.

power to acquire and hold such property as is reasonably necessary for carrying out its express powers. In some states the power of a corporation to hold property is restricted as to the method of acquiring it, or is limited as to the quantity or the value of the property or the period of time for which it may be held. Restrictions on holding real estate are also imposed upon corporations by the constitutions of some states. (See p. 993, Oklahoma v International Paper Co.)

(a) INVESTMENTS. Modern corporation codes generally provide that a corporation may acquire the stock of other corporations.

(b) HOLDING COMPANIES. A corporation owning stock of another corporation may own such a percentage of the stock of the other company that it controls the latter's operations. In such a case the first company is commonly called a *holding company*. Sometimes a holding company is organized solely for the purpose of controlling other companies called *operating* or *subsidiary companies.*

The device of a holding company may be socially desirable or undesirable depending upon the circumstances under which it operates. If it is merely a device to coordinate different phases of an economic activity, the holding company is a proper device. If its object is to eliminate competition between the operating companies whose stock is held, it may be illegal under state or federal antitrust laws.[13] If a holding company that operates in interstate commerce holds stock of electric or gas public utility companies, it may be ordered dissolved when it is found by the Securities and Exchange Commission to serve no economically useful purpose.[14] It is no objection, however, that the subsidiary company engages in a business in which the holding company could not lawfully engage. (See p. 994, Connecticut General Life Insurance Co. v Superintendent of Insurance.)

The fact that one corporation owns its subsidiary does not give it an unlimited right to control the subsidiary. Some degree of restriction is placed on the parent corporation in requiring "fairness" in its dealings with the subsidiary.[15]

(11) Acquisition of Own Stock. Generally a corporation may purchase its own stock, if it is solvent at the time and the purchase is made from surplus so that capital is not impaired.[16] Sometimes a more precise standard is specified.[17] The Model Act permits a corporation to acquire its own shares

---

[13] Northern Securities Co. v U.S., 193 US 197.

[14] American Power and Light Co. v S.E.C., 329 US 90.

[15] Getty Oil Co. v Skelly Oil Co., (Del) 267 A2d 883.

[16] In re Brown's Estate, 130 Ill App 2d 514, 264 NE2d 287.

[17] A corporation may not purchase its own shares "if . . . the present fair value of the remaining assets . . . would be less than one and one fourth . . . times the amount of its liabilities to creditors." Arkansas Business Corporation Act § 5; Ark Stat Ann § 64-105.

". . . only to the extent of unreserved and unrestricted earned surplus available therefor. . . ."[18] In a few states corporations are denied implied power to purchase their own stock, but they are permitted to receive it as a gift, in payment of a debt, or as security for a debt.

Stock which is reacquired by the corporation that issued it is commonly called *treasury stock*. Ordinarily the treasury stock is regarded as still being issued or outstanding stock.[19] As such, the shares are not subject to the rule that original shares cannot be issued for less than par. They can be sold by the corporation at any price.[20] Under the Model Act, "treasury shares may be disposed of by the corporation for such consideration expressed in dollars as may be fixed from time to time by the board of directors."[21]

Although treasury stock retains the character of outstanding stock, it has an inactive status while it is held by the corporation. Thus, the treasury shares cannot be voted[22] nor can dividends be declared on them.

The reacquisition by a corporation of its shares and the holding of them as treasury shares is to be distinguished from what occurs upon the redemption of shares. When shares are redeemed, they are automatically canceled.[23]

Stock which is surrendered is not deemed outstanding without regard to whether it is retained as treasury shares or is formally cancelled. (See p. 995, Jack Cole-Dixie Highway Co. v Red Ball Motor Freight, Inc.)

The purchase of shares by the corporation frequently has the objective of buying out dissenting shareholders who would otherwise challenge the actions of corporate management. In a number of cases it has been held that this purpose is not improper.[24]

(12) Business in Another State. A corporation has the inherent power and generally is expressly authorized to engage in business in other states. This grant of power by the incorporating state does not exempt the corporation, however, from satisfying the restrictions imposed by the foreign state in which it seeks to do business.

(13) Participation in Enterprise. Corporations may generally participate in an enterprise to the same extent as individuals. They may enter into joint ventures. The modern statutory trend is to permit a corporation to be a

---

[18] ABA MBCA § 6.

[19] When a corporation reacquires its own shares, it has the choice of "retiring" them and thus restoring them to the status of authorized but unissued shares or to treat them as still issued and available for retransfer. It is the latter which are described as treasury shares.

[20] State ex rel Weede v Bechtel, 244 Iowa 785, 56 NW2d 173.

[21] ABA MBCA § 18.

[22] Atterbury v Consolidated Coppermines Corp., 26 Del Ch 1, 20 A2d 743. Likewise, a subsidiary corporation holding shares of stock of the parent corporation by which it is controlled cannot vote such shares of the parent corporation. Italo Petroleum Corp. v Producers' Oil Corp., 20 Del Ch 283, 174 A 276.

[23] ABA MBCA § 67.

[24] Kors v Carey, 39 Del Ch 47, 158 A2d 136.

member of a partnership. A corporation may be a limited partner.[25] The Model Act authorizes a corporation "to be a promoter, partner, member, associate, or manager of any partnership, joint venture, trust or other enterprise." [26]

When the power to be a participant in an enterprise is not expressly granted to a corporation, there is a conflict as to whether it has implied authority to be a participant. When the relationship is of a permanent character or is of such a nature as to subject the corporation to the control of the outside enterprise, it is likely that the courts will refuse to imply a power to be a participant. For example, in the absence of express statutory authorization to be a partner, a corporation cannot be a member of a general partnership. Many modern corporation codes expressly grant this power.

In addition to the question of corporate power to participate in an enterprise, such participation is subject to and may be illegal under the federal antitrust legislation.[27]

(14) Employee Benefit and Aid. The ABA MBCA empowers a corporation "to pay pensions and establish pension plans, pension trusts, profit sharing plans, stock bonus plans, stock option plans, and other incentive plans for any or all of its directors, officers, and employees." [28]

Corporations have such power under most state codes either by express provision or by judicial decision. Such power is possessed by a professional corporation, and the existence of such power is a major reason for the forming of a professional corporation. The various employee benefit plans enable either the professional corporation or its members or both to obtain an advantage in the computation of federal income tax liability that would not otherwise be open to them as individuals or as partners.

The Model Act recognizes the common rule permitting a corporation to assist its employees financially by stating that each corporation shall have power "to lend money and use its credit to assist its employees." [29] A few states expressly authorize the directors to lend money to employees and directors if such action will benefit the corporation.[30] Some statutes prohibit loans that are secured by a pledge of shares of the corporation. Under the Model Act, the directors can make loans to an employee and to an employee-director, but consent of the shareholders is required for a loan to a director who is not an employee.[31]

(15) Charitable Contributions. The Model Act authorizes a corporation without any limitation "to make donations for the public welfare or for

---

[25] Port Arthur Trust Co. v Muldrow, 155 Tex 612, 291 SW2d 312.
[26] ABA MBCA § 4(p).
[27] United States v Penn-Olin Chemical Co., 378 US 158.
[28] ABA MBCA § 4(o).
[29] § 4(f).
[30] New Jersey, NJ Stat Ann § 14A:6-11.
[31] ABA MBCA § 47.

charitable, scientific, or educational purposes." [32] In some states some limitation is imposed upon the amount that can be donated for charitable purposes. The federal income tax law tends to set a limitation on charitable contributions, since corporations ordinarily will not make contributions in an amount greater than may be claimed as a deduction for the purpose of federal income tax computation.

Modern courts are more willing to take for granted that a corporation may spend its money for a charitable purpose, as opposed to the earlier theory that the money of a corporation was a fund to be held in trust for the furtherance of the business purpose for which the corporation was created. This transition in theory has been encouraged by the rise of the concept that business has a responsibility for the general welfare of society and may therefore properly spend corporate money for societal betterment.

(16) Civic Improvement. The Model Act also authorizes a corporation "to transact any lawful business which the board of directors shall find will be in aid of governmental policy." [33] Under such broad authorization a corporation may aid in a military war, in a war on poverty, and take part in measures to prevent civil strife.

§ 50:3. Ultra Vires Acts. When a corporation acts in excess of or beyond the scope of the powers granted by its charter and the statute under which it was organized, then the corporation's act is described as *ultra vires.* (See p. 996, Lurie v Arizona Fertilizer & Chemical Co.) Such an act is improper because it is a violation of the obligation of the corporation to the state. It is also improper with respect to shareholders and creditors of the corporation because corporate funds have been diverted to unauthorized uses.

As an illustration of the latter point, assume that a corporation is created and authorized to manufacture television sets. Various persons purchase stock in the corporation, lend it money, or sell to it on credit because of their estimate of the worth of the television business in general and of the corporation as a television manufacturing company in particular. Assume that the corporation has funds that it uses for the ultra vires purpose of lending to persons to buy homes. Many of the shareholders and creditors would probably never have become associated with the corporation if it had been organized for that purpose. The fact that the ultra vires use of the money may be better economically or socially than the authorized use does not alter the fact that the shareholders' and the creditors' money is not used the way they intended.

(1) Ultra Vires Acts and Illegality Distinguished. Although it is not lawful for a corporation to perform ultra vires acts, the objection to the commission of such acts is distinct from the objection of illegality.[34] (See

---

[32] § 4(m).
[33] § 4(n).
[34] Healy v Geilfuss, 37 Del Ch 502, 146 A2d 5.

p. 998, Ladd Estate Co. v Wheatley.) In the case of illegality, the act would be wrong regardless of the nature of the person or the association committing it. The fact that an act is ultra vires merely means that this particular corporation does not have permission from the state to do the act. Thus, it would ordinarily be beyond the powers of a business corporation, and therefore ultra vires, to engage in a charitable enterprise, such as the building of a church or college. But the activity would hardly be termed illegal.

§ 50:4. Effect of Ultra Vires Contracts. There is some conflict in the law as to the effect of an ultra vires act. Under the modern statutory trend ultra vires cannot be raised to attack the validity of any act, contract, or transfer of property,[35] except as noted under § 50:5. This trend is recognized by the Model Act which declares that "no act of a corporation and no conveyance or transfer of real or personal property to or by a corporation shall be invalid by reason of the fact that the corporation was without capacity or power to do such an act or to make or receive such a conveyance or transfer. . . ." [36]

In the absence of statute, most courts recognize ultra vires as a defense but refuse to apply it in a particular case if it would be inequitable and work a hardship. The courts also refuse to recognize it as a defense against the holder of a commercial paper on which the corporation, without authority, became an accommodation party. Likewise, a transfer of real or personal property cannot be set aside on the ground that it is ultra vires. Here the object of the law is to preserve the security of titles even though the result is to permit the wrongful act of the corporation to stand.

In most states if the ultra vires contract has been completely performed, neither party can rescind the contract on the ground that it was originally ultra vires.[37] Conversely, if neither party to the ultra vires contract has performed his part, the court will neither enforce the contract nor hold either party liable for a breach of the contract. A person who has benefited by the ultra vires act cannot refuse to pay for the value which he has received on the ground that the transaction was ultra vires.[38]

§ 50:5. Remedies for Ultra Vires Acts. In all states (a) a shareholder may obtain an injunction to stop the board of directors or other persons involved from entering into an ultra vires transaction; (b) the corporation or a shareholder acting on behalf of the corporation may sue the persons who made or approved the contract to recover damages for the loss caused the corporation by the ultra vires act; and (c) an action may be brought by the attorney general of the state to revoke the charter on the ground of its serious or repeated violation.

---

[35] ABA MBCA § 7; Inter-Continental Corp. v Moody, (Tex Civ App) 411 SW2d 578.

[36] ABA MBCA § 7.

[37] Anderson v Rexroad, 175 Kan 676, 266 P2d 320.

[38] Marshall v Webster, 287 Ky 692, 155 SW2d 13.

(1) Proof of Damages. When an action is brought to enjoin or set aside corporate action on the ground that it is ultra vires, there is no requirement that the plaintiffs show that the corporation or they are in any way harmed, as each stockholder has a right to see that his corporation does not do an act which is not authorized.[39] Similarly, when the attorney general brings an action to forfeit the corporate charter because of ultra vires acts there is no requirement of proof of damage to the corporation; as a practical matter, a court is more likely to forfeit the charter if harm to the community can be shown.

In contrast, when stockholders bring a derivative action to recover damages on behalf of the corporation for the harm caused by the ultra vires acts, the plaintiffs must necessarily show the extent to which the corporation has been harmed. However, the stockholders are not required to prove what individual harm they have sustained.

---

[39] Central New York Bridge Association, Inc. v American Contract Bridge League, Inc., 72 Misc 2d 271, 339 NYS2d 438.

CASES FOR CHAPTER 50

Wilmington Memorial Co., Inc. v Silverbrook Cemetery Co.

(Del Ch) 287 A2d 405 (1972)

The Silverbrook Cemetery Company sold bronze grave markers. The Wilmington Memorial Company also sold bronze grave markers and claimed that the cemetery company did not have authority to make such sales. The charter of the cemetery company gave it power to sell "personal estate of every kind" and a general power to make all contracts and do all acts necessary for the conducting of the cemetery. Wilmington Memorial brought an action for a declaratory judgment against the cemetery. The cemetery moved for summary judgment in its favor.

SHORT, V.C. . . . The cemetery itself comprises sixty acres of land upon which an office building, a crematorium and two garages have been constructed. The burial grounds are divided into two distinct sections: a traditional stone monument area and a memorial park area in which all graves are marked by flat bronze memorials set in the ground flush to the surface.

Defendant's sale of bronze markers is the subject of this action. Up to this time it has never sold any stone monuments. Defendant has been selling bronze markers since 1950 and during the years 1966, 1967 and 1968 averaged between fifty and sixty individual sales per year. These sales accounted for ninety-five per cent of the total bronze markers installed in the cemetery. No sales have been made by defendant to customers who have not purchased burial lots in the cemetery. Marker sales are usually conducted in the main office in which sample memorials are on display, or by letter to the customer sometime after a burial. The standard 24 inch by 12 inch marker is sold for $135 including the cost of installation. Though there is no requirement that lot owners purchase markers exclusively from defendant, it requires that all bronze markers purchased from third parties must be installed by defendant at a charge of $50 for the standard size marker. The cost of installation is charged to the third party dealer. In contrast, outside monument dealers are permitted to install stone monuments in the traditional cemetery section. Defendant readily admits that installation does not require skilled labor. It also admits that a substantial part of the installation charge represents profit.

Plaintiff company, incorporated in 1960 under the General Corporation Law, has been in the monument business since 1937. Its place of doing business is located in the proximate vicinity of defendant's cemetery. A major portion of its business is in the sale of granite monuments. However, it has been selling bronze markers in competition with defendant since 1950.

Plaintiff contends that defendant's sale of markers is in violation of its charter. The charter does not expressly provide for the sale of markers. However, it does expressly carry the broad general powers "to purchase . . . personal estate of every kind and the same to . . . sell . . . ," and "to enter into any and all contracts . . . proper to be in the conduct of its business [as a cemetery company]." These provisions clearly indicate the legislative intent to grant to Silverbrook the power to engage in activities related to the business of operating a cemetery. Burial of and memorializing the dead are certainly related activities. As the court said in Clagett v Vestry of Rock Creek Parish, DC, 241 F Supp 950: "grave and marker . . . are so initmately related to the extent that the suggestion of one suggests the other." See also, People ex rel. Guettler v Mount Olive Cemetery Ass'n, 26 Ill 2d 156, 186 NE2d 39 (markers and monuments); State v Lakewood Cemetery Ass'n, 93 Minn 191, 101 NW 161 (greenhouse); Wing v Forest Lawn Cemetery Ass'n, 15 Cal 2d 472, 101 P2d 1099 (mortuary). I am satisfied that Silverbrook's charter, by necessary implication, confers the power to sell grave markers.

Plaintiff charges that defendant's tax exempt status permits it to compete unfairly with its taxable competitors. Under Silverbrook's charter the "cemetery grounds, with the buildings" are exempt from taxation. At the present time bronze markers are on display in a corner of Silverbrook's office building and a garage on the grounds is being used, among other things, for storing and assembling markers. Since Silverbrook pays no taxes on the cemetery grounds or any of its buildings, plaintiff argues that it is afforded an unfair economic advantage. Assuming, without deciding, that plaintiff has standing to raise this issue, I am satisfied that it must be resolved in defendant's favor. The selling of markers having been found to be an activity authorized by Silverbrook's charter the exemption of its property from taxes does not qualify its right to exercise all the privileges granted thereby. Daily Monument Co. v Crown Hill Cemetery Ass'n, 114 Ohio App 143, 176 NE2d 268. Moreover, the only advantage occasioned to defendant of which plaintiff can complain would be the exemption from taxes on that portion of cemetery property which is used to display and store markers. On the evidence adduced this advantage, if any, is de minimis.

Plaintiff contends that defendant's well-developed relationship with the purchasers of grave lots enables it to unfairly approach the same customers for the sale of markers. Defendant admits that it "is in the inevitable enviable position of having the first opportunity to approach the purchasers." However, it is not unusual in our economic system that such a relationship produces an advantage over competitors. I see nothing unfair or inequitable in such an advantage. And this is particularly so where, as here, there is no showing that defendant's sale of markers is tied directly or indirectly by contract to the sale of grave lots. . . .

. . . Defendants' motion for summary judgment is granted.

Oklahoma v International Paper Co.

(Okla) 342 P2d 565 (1959)

The State of Oklahoma sued the International Paper Company for the statutory penalty for unlawfully owning rural land in violation of the state constitutional provision that no corporation should own rural land "except such as shall be necessary and proper for carrying on the business for which it was chartered." The paper company claimed that the rural land it owned was being reforested by it. From a decision in the company's favor, the State appealed.

PER CURIAM. . . . [The defendant's charter authorized it, among other things, to] acquire, own, occupy, use and develop and dispose of timber lands, timber, timber rights, cut-over lands, or other lands for the purpose of manufacture of lumber, timber, articles of lumber, and wood products. [The defendant claimed] that the lands in controversy were purchased and held and used for said purposes and that said lands were also owned and held for growing and producing timber under a reforesting program and that the timber therefrom has been and will be harvested and cut and converted into lumber and wood products. . . .

In Texas Company v State ex rel. Coryell, 198 Okla 565, 180 P2d 631, 632, this court . . . said: "The words 'necessary and proper' used in the Constitution as expressive of the extent of the right of a corporation to acquire and hold land, do not import that which is indispensably necessary, but do import that which is proper, useful, and suitable and thus conducive to the accomplishment of the purposes of the corporation, which implies actual need therefor in contradistinction to mere preference." . . .

In the case now before us the evidence reflects the source of supply of timber for lumber, poles, and pulp for paper has for some years past been decreasing to the point where companies engaged in that business have, in order to assure a constant supply of timber, been compelled to engage in a program of reforesting on cut-over and other suitable lands and for that purpose have acquired considerable tracts of land; that an assured constant and sufficient supply of timber is required before such concerns can justify expenditure of large sums of money for the construction of processing plants for the carrying on of the business for which such companies were formed and to supply the demand for wood and paper products; that a period of time from 40 to 70 years is required to establish and bring to rotation a reforesting program complete with cutting and replacement and therefore requires the acquisition of [land] to assure a uniform and efficient program and operation. . . .

The . . . acquisition of the [land] was . . . proper, useful, and suitable, and thus conducive to the proper carrying on of a lawful enterprise within the legitimate purposes provided for in the articles in incorporation. . . .

[Judgment for defendant affirmed.]

BERRY, J., dissenting. . . . The ownership of land by corporations tend[s] to create a perpetuity and thereby give corporations special privileges not enjoyed by all; tend[s] to permit concentration of wealth in the hands of a few and . . . to take real estate off the market and thus prevent[s] individuals from acquiring [it] for use [as] homes. . . .

Connecticut General Life Insurance Co. v Superintendent of Insurance

10 NY2d 42, 217 NYS2d 39, 176 NE2d 63 (1961)

Connecticut General Life Insurance Co. is a Connecticut insurance company which obtained a license to write life insurance policies in New York. It thereafter proposed to acquire 80 percent or more of the common stock of the National Fire Insurance Co. of Hartford, a fire and casualty insurance company licensed to write policies in New York. The New York State Superintendent of Insurance brought an action for a declaratory judgment to have the Connecticut company prohibited from writing life policies in New York if it acquired such stock because, through its subsidiary, it would then be writing fire and casualty insurance in New York. From a decision in favor of the Superintendent, the insurance company appealed.

FOSTER, J. . . . Undoubtedly [the New York statutes] forbid a foreign life insurance company licensed in this State from engaging in the business of writing fire or casualty insurance. . . . The real issue involved in this case is whether or not, by purchasing controlling interest in a fire or casualty company, the parent life insurance company actually is engaging in that business. . . . As appellant [insurance company] appropriately points out, the Legislature, in the Insurance Law, has used express language to prohibit certain activity through or by subsidiaries when that was its intention. [The Court then listed the specific sections of the statute expressly applying to holding companies and subsidiaries.]

The Insurance Law is replete with additional express references to subsidiaries and affiliates. . . . From these . . . and from the absence of express references to subsidiaries in [the sections here applicable], we may infer properly that the Legislature did not intend that the limitations [here applicable] be extended by implication to cover parent-subsidiary situations. This is a well-established canon of statutory construction. . . .

Such a construction, of course, is consistent with the general rule . . . that in no legal sense can the business of a corporation be said to be that of its stockholders . . . or the business of a subsidiary corporation be said to be that of a parent. . . . It is consistent also with the settled rule that a subsidiary corporation may engage in a business forbidden to its parent, unless the subsidiary entity is used as a cloak to cover for fraud or illegality. . . . On this issue we agree with the dissent below that the Superintendent may not presuppose, "without justification, that the plaintiff will utilize a fire or casualty subsidiary as a mere agent or tool to evade the provisions of said sections," and that "We are bound to assume that the mandate of the statute will be respected and that a subsidiary or plaintiff doing a fire or casualty business will carry on in the usual way, namely, as an independent corporate entity." Appellant, in seeking to purchase a controlling interest in a fire insurance company, admittedly desires to improve its competitive position, and to enable its agents to offer to the public both life insurance and casualty and fire insurance. This does not, as the Superintendent argues, mean that appellant desires to engage in the fire or casualty insurance business. If the time comes that appellant, through the guise of a subsidiary, actually engages in that business, that will be time enough to refuse to renew appellant's license.

No public policy would be offended by consummation of the proposed acquisition. Appellant's admitted assets, capital, and surplus apparently are sufficient to insure against insolvency and to protect policyholders in this State. . . .

[Judgment reversed.]

DESMOND, C.J., (dissenting). . . . The majority opinion says: "No public policy would be offended by consummation of the proposed acquisition." We think this State's policy of protecting the trustheld funds of life insurers from any and all diversions is plain, compelling, and essential and that it positively forbids what petitioner is trying to do. . . .

A life insurance company holds its policyholders' funds in trust for the protection of their beneficiaries against want. Those trust funds, conservatively and prudently invested to serve the high trust purpose on the happening of the inevitable event insured against, should not be subjected even in the most remote way to the hazards of other kinds of insurance. Nor should the life insurer's trusteed funds be, by investment in other insurance stocks, indirectly subjected to the other company's less restrictive investment policies. If any further explanation of the public policy is sought, it can be found in the Armstrong Committee Reports of 1906 (see Vol. 10, p. 385 et seq.) which described the life insurance companies of that day as transacting through stock ownership "the business of banks and trust companies," reminded us of the life companies' duty of conservatism in investment, rejected the idea that life companies should be allowed to make more money by speculation, and warned that a life insurer which gets control of companies in other business will end up by managing those other companies and thus engaging in their separate businesses. . . .

[DYE and BURKE, JJ., concur in the dissent.]

Jack Cole—Dixie Highway Co. v Red Ball Motor Freight, Inc.

(Miss) 254 So2d 734 (1971)

As part of a business purchase and reorganization, it was agreed that all preferred stock of Dixie Highway should be surrendered and thereafter the Jack Cole—Dixie Highway Co. would have only common stock. An amendment to a corporate charter was prepared which declared that there should only be common stock. This amendment was agreed to on January 22, 1965. The amendment declared that it would be effective when filed for record, which occurred in one county on January 23 and in another county on January 27, 1965. A lawsuit was brought in which the question arose as to

the date on which the preferred stock was cancelled, as this determined whether the preferred stock should be classified as outstanding securities.

BRADY, J. . . . The effective date of the amendment is of no consequence to the disposition of this case since the amendment itself was not required for the cancellation of the corporation's preferred stock. There is a wide distinction between the authorized capital stock of a corporation and its actual capital stock. While an amendment to the articles of incorporation would be required to increase or decrease the amount of the "authorized" capital stock of the company, no amendment was required to reduce the amount of actual stock outstanding, this being a matter solely for agreement between the stockholders and the corporation. Whenever a stockholder surrenders his stock to the corporation, the stock is no longer outstanding, regardless of whether the corporation cancels the stock or simply retains the stock as treasury stock; and further, in either event, such stock no longer constitutes a present liability of the corporation. . . .

The intent of Dixie . . . is especially apparent from Dixie's federal income tax return for the year 1965, which reported the surrender and cancellation of all the preferred stock of the corporation on January 22, 1965. . . . There are many other instances where various reports, financial statements, and applications reflected this same intent.

The trial court held that the aforesaid acts constituted a valid surrender and cancellation of the 5,500 shares of preferred stock on January 22, 1965, and that the preferred stock could no longer be considered as constituting outstanding securities, debts or obligations of Dixie. . . .

[Judgment affirmed.]

Lurie v Arizona Fertilizer & Chemical Co.

101 Ariz 482, 421 P2d 330 (1966)

Members of the Lurie family controlled and were directors of Allied Yuma Farms, Inc. Chapman, a neighboring farmer, persuaded the Luries to engage in a joint farming venture. Arizona Fertilizer and Chemical Company sold fertilizers to the joint venture. When it was not paid it sued the Luries. They raised the defense that they were not liable because they had acted for the corporation, Allied Yuma Farms, Inc. The plaintiff replied that the forming of the joint venture was ultra vires and therefore the Luries, as directors of Allied, were personally liable for the contracts made in the course of the ultra vires activity. From a judgment for Arizona, the Luries appealed.

MCFARLAND, J. . . . The theory on which plaintiff seeks to hold the Luries personally liable is that the contract for plaintiff's fertilizer was ultra vires as to Allied Yuma Farms, Inc., and the directors of the corporation—the Luries—should be held personally liable for their ultra vires acts.

The proposition that the contract was ultra vires is based on the corporation's actions in entering into a joint venture and into farming operations generally, where neither act was within the powers granted by the articles of incorporation.

Although it has not been decided in this jurisdiction, the general rule is, in the absence of statute or charter provision, that a corporation is without legal authority to enter into a partnership. . . . A joint venture differs from a partnership principally in that while a partnership is usually formed for the transaction of a general business of a particular kind, a joint venture is usually, but not necessarily, limited to a single transaction, although the business of conducting it may continue for a number of years. . . .

Plaintiff cites the case of Brand v Fernandez (Tex Civ App) 91 SW2d 932, as authority for its contention that joint ventures should be treated as partnerships insofar as the validity of corporate involvement is concerned. The Brand case found a joint-venture agreement resulting in the surrender of control of a substantial part of the corporation's assets to be invalid, reasoning that the agreement deprived the corporate officers of their elected authority. In that case, however, the corporation was a bank, and its affairs were more closely connected with the public interest than in the instant case.

The legal effect of corporate embarkation on a joint venture should be distinguished from entry into a partnership. Although the corporation may subject itself to debts other than those contracted by its directors and officers, the directors divest themselves of their sole controlling authority only as to one transaction in a joint venture, and not of the entire corporate business as in a partnership. The prevailing view is to hold corporate joint ventures valid, either directly . . . or by implication. . . .

As applied to corporate entry into partnerships and joint ventures, the doctrine of ultra vires is designed to protect the shareholders' interest. In the instant case, the shareholders were all directors, and were cognizant of the joint venture. The entire assets of the corporation were not committed to the venture, but only a portion thereof, and the co-adventurer had no control over those assets left out of the venture other than the power to subject them to the venture's debts. The claim of ultra vires is not being brought on behalf of the shareholders or any one with a genuine interest in the retention of director control, but by a creditor who placed no reliance on the corporate structure. The doctrine of ultra vires, and its resultant legal effect, should not be applied on this ground.

The other theory on which plaintiff seeks to invoke the doctrine is that the articles of incorporation of Allied Yuma Farms, Inc., do not expressly authorize the business of farming. The articles of incorporation provide for construction and management of hotels, dwellings, etc., the acquisition and sale or lease of personal and real property, and to further engage in any and all general business or activities as are permitted corporations under the laws of the State of Washington. That these articles may be more broadly interpreted under the Washington law is of no import, as Art. 14, § 5, of the constitution of Arizona, ARS, provides that foreign corporations may stand in no better position than Arizona corporations when doing business in Arizona.

The law of Arizona relating to scope of corporate business is set out in Article 14, § 4 of the constitution of Arizona, which provides: "No corporation shall engage in any business other than that expressly authorized in its charter or by the law under which it may have been or may hereafter be organized."

This provision is implemented by ARS § 10-171, which states: "No corporation shall engage in any business other than that expressly authorized in its articles of incorporation or by the law under which it is organized."

These limitations were thoroughly considered by this court in Trico Electric Cooperative v Ralston, 67 Ariz 358, 196 P2d 470, wherein it was held that a corporation could not lawfully contract outside the object of its creation as defined in the law of its organization. . . . "A corporation has only such powers as are expressly or impliedly conferred by its charter. Unlike a natural person, if [sic] may not do all things not expressly or impliedly prohibited, but must draw from its charter the power to act in any given respect, and can do only that which is expressly or impliedly authorized therein. A corporate charter is the index to the objects for which it was created and to the powers with which it has been endowed. The enumeration of certain powers operates as a limitation on such objects only as are embodied therein, and is an implied prohibition of the exercise of other and distinct powers, except such incidental powers as are reasonably necessary to accomplish the purposes for which it was organized. . . . The charter of a corporation organized under general legislation consists of the provisions of the state constitution, the particular statute under which it is organized, and all other general laws which are made applicable to the corporation formed thereunder and its articles of incorporation. . . . With respect to matters to which statutes do not apply, the articles of incorporation of the corporation control and are its fundamental and organic law. . . . But in respect to those matters to which the statute does not apply the articles of incorporation govern. . . .

Although the Luries argue that farming may be necessarily incident to the charter power to acquire and sell real property, they do not contend that this property was held for resale or that it was acquired for a valid charter purpose. In the absence of any evidence showing farming to be an incidental business reasonably necessary under the charter powers, we find the farming transaction and the contract for fertilizer which arose from it to be ultra vires.

The contract being ultra vires, it is plaintiff's contention, and presumably the theory on which the trial court granted the directed verdict, that the Luries should be personally liable as directors. The proposition that the directors will be held personally liable for acts done in behalf of the corporation which were outside of its charter powers finds support in the case of Mandeville v Courtright, 3 Cir, 142 F 97, 6 LRA, NS, 1003, cert denied Mayer v Mandeville, 202 US 615, 26 SCt 764, 50 LEd 1172. In that case, the corporation was incorporated in New Jersey, and practiced dentistry in Pennsylvania under the corporate name. The corporation was forbidden by Pennsylvania law to so practice. The plaintiff was a dental patient who was injured by improper treatment. The Circuit Court of Appeals, 3d Circuit, held the directors and managing officers liable for the tortious acts of their agents, reasoning that the directors could not act under the guise of their corporate entity when that corporation could not conduct such a business and they knew it.

In the instant case, Allied Yuma Farms, Inc., was not permitted to carry on farming operations nor to enter into the fertilizer contract under the law of Arizona as implemented by the corporate charter. There were only four stockholders, all of whom were directors in the corporation and knew the nature of the business in which the corporation was engaged. The corporation was undercapitalized, and funds were diverted to it from other Lurie corporations and the Lurie partnership, as needed. The corporation had no separate officers, no stationery, and little other outward indicia of corporate existence. These facts tend to point up to the conclusion that the corporation was merely a means of avoiding personal liability while using the financial standing and good will of the Luries as individuals in their dealings with others.

Plaintiff did not know the Luries intended to engage in the joint venture solely through their corporation, and was led to believe by Chapman that they were acting as individuals. It was never made clear to their co-adventurers that the Luries intended to act only as a corporation, as the venture agreement was not reduced to writing, and it was only after the venture had failed and the liabilities accrued that the corporate entity was brought out. . . .

The Luries, in this ultra vires act, were attempting to use the corporation to make money as individuals without incurring individual liability. . . . As set forth herein, the acts of the Luries were ultra vires in that they were not within the reason and purpose for which the corporation was ostensibly formed and were clearly for the purpose of their own personal benefit. In the light of the Luries' total disregard of the corporate entity, both in their actions and representations in conducting this venture, and in disregard of the charter which they now attempt to stand behind, the law and equity must intervene to protect the rights of third persons as the corporate fiction has been urged to an extent not within its reason and purpose. . . .

These considerations, taken in conjunction with the premise that the Luries were bound by law to know the invalidity of their ultra vires transactions, prohibited by the law of the corporation which they now attempt to stand behind, are sufficient to warrant the personal liability imposed by the trial court.

[Judgment affirmed.]

Ladd Estate Company v Wheatley

246 Ore 627, 426 P2d 878 (1967)

The Ladd Estate Company brought suit on a promissory note made by Wheatley and guaranteed by Westover Tower, Inc. Westover claimed that its guaranty of the note was not binding because Wheatley was a director of the corporation when the guaranty was made and the guaranty was therefore ultra vires and illegal as it violated a statute prohibiting loans to directors. The lower court entered judgment for Ladd and Westover appealed.

LUSK, J. . . . The claim that the giving of the guaranty was an illegal act is based upon ORS 57.226, which reads: "No loans shall be made by a corporation to its officers or directors, and no loans shall be made by a corporation secured by its shares." The court found that Wheatley was a director at the time the guaranty was given. . . . An act of a corporation in contravention of a statute specifically prohibiting it is illegal and unenforceable. . . . We think, however, that the transaction, though admittedly ultra vires, is not denounced by ORS 57.226. That statute prohibits the making of "loans" by a corporation to its officers or directors. Concededly, the guaranty in question was not a loan. Counsel for Westover characterize it in their brief as "an executory agreement to make a loan to an officer and director." It was not even that, for it was only a conditional agreement. "The guarantee of a loan is not a loan. To guarantee a loan is to undertake to pay a debt or perform a duty, in case of the failure of another person primarily liable for such payment or performance. Ball Electric Light Co. v Child, 68 Conn 522, 525, 37 A 391. The making of a loan creates an absolute obligation: the guaranteeing a loan a conditional obligation. . . ." . . . .

[Judgment affirmed.]

QUESTIONS AND CASE PROBLEMS

1. In an action by the Federal Savings State Bank as the holder of a note against Grimes, the maker of the note, the authority of the corporate payee, the Industrial Mutual Life Insurance Co., to accept the note from the maker was questioned. It was argued that the corporate payee possessed the power because there was no statute expressly prohibiting the exercise of that power. Was this argument valid? [Federal Savings State Bank v Grimes, 156 Kan 55, 131 P2d 894]
2. A husband, *H*, borrowed money from bank *B*. *B* promised to insure the loan so that if *H* died before the debt was repaid, the proceeds of the insurance policy would pay off the debt. *B* failed to obtain the insurance, and *H* died owing a balance on the debt. *H*'s widow sued the bank to cancel the balance remaining on the theory that if *B* had obtained the insurance as it had promised to do, there would not be any balance. *B* defended on the ground that it could not have obtained the insurance because it would have been ultra vires for it to have done so. Was this defense valid? [Robichaud v Athol Credit Union, 352 Mass 351, 225 NE2d 347]
3. The H & R Construction Corporation entered into a contract for construction work, and the Seaboard Surety Co. executed a bond assuring that the contract would be performed. The Seaboard Surety Co. was required to pay damages when the contractor did not perform the contract. It then sued the construction corporation and also the H. C. Nelson Investment Co. to recover the money it had so paid. Its suit against the Nelson Investment Co. was based on the theory that the construction corporation and the investment company were partners. Was there a partnership? [Nelson v Seaboard Surety Co., (CA8 Ill) 262 F2d 189]
4. An employee of the Archer Pancoast Co., a corporation, was killed as the result of falling through a hatchway in a building occupied by the company as a factory. Hoffman, superintendent of the factory, called Noll, an undertaker, and arranged for the funeral. Hoffman agreed to pay Noll $100 for his services. After performing the work, Noll brought an action against the Archer Pancoast Co. to recover the agreed sum. The defendant raised the defense of ultra vires. Decide. [Noll v Archer Pancoast Co., 60 App Div 414, 69 NYS 1007]
5. A bylaw of the Coleman Realty Co. provided that the corporation could not sell its stock to a person not a shareholder without first offering to sell it

at its book value to the corporation or to the remaining shareholders in proportion to their interests. This bylaw was later repealed at a shareholders' meeting by the vote of Mrs. Ludgate who owned a majority of the stock. Bechtold, a minority shareholder, brought an action to declare that the repeal of the bylaw was invalid and had no effect. Was the repeal of the bylaw effective? [Bechtold v Coleman Realty Co., 367 Pa 208, 79 A2d 661]

6. The Columbia Chemical Co. was incorporated under the laws of New York for the purpose of manufacturing and selling chemicals. Thereafter a group of persons filed incorporation papers in the same state for an organization with the name of Columbian Chemical Co. It was contended that the second company had no right to adopt such a name. Do you agree? [New York v O'Brien, 101 App Div 296, 91 NYS 649]

7. The Philadelphia Electric Co. was incorporated "for the purpose of supplying heating, lighting, and power by electricity to the public." The company supplied electricity but in addition began to sell electrical appliances. An action of quo warranto was brought by the attorney general against the corporation to forfeit its charter for engaging in ultra vires acts. Decide. [Commonwealth of Pennsylvania ex rel. Baldrige, Attorney General v Philadelphia Electric Co., 300 Pa 577, 151 A 344]

8. The Central Mutual Auto Insurance Co. was a Michigan corporation. A foreign corporation, the Central Mutual Insurance Co., was granted a license to do business in Michigan. Central Mutual Auto Insurance Co. brought an action to prevent the foreign corporation from doing business within Michigan under that name. Decide. [Central Mutual Auto Insurance Co. v Central Mutual Insurance Co., 275 Mich 554, 267 NW 733]

9. A corporation wished to borrow money. A plan was arranged with the lender by which the corporation would issue a block of stock which the lender would hold as collateral to secure the repayment of the loan. A shareholder objected on the ground that a corporation may only issue its stock to one who will become its owner and that it could only be issued for payment and not as security. Could the corporation issue the stock as proposed? [Costabile v Essex Linoleum and Carpet Co., 98 NJ Super 224, 236 A2d 625]

51 Corporate Stock and Shareholders

CORPORATE STOCK

The ownership of a fractional part of a corporation is the share or stock of the shareholder or stockholder. "Share" and "stock" have the same meaning. Stock is the older term and share is more commonly used in modern statutes.

§ **51:1. Nature of Stock.** Membership in a corporation is usually based upon ownership of one or more shares of stock of the corporation. Each share represents a fractional interest in the total property possessed by the corporation. Each share confers the right to receive the dividends, when declared, and the right to participate in a distribution of capital upon the dissolution of the corporation. The shareholder does not own or have an interest in any specific property of the corporation; the corporation is the owner of all of its property.

(1) Capital and Capital Stock. *Capital* refers to the net assets of the corporation. It signifies the actual worth of the corporation. It is the aggregate of the sums subscribed and paid in by the shareholders, together with all gains or profits arising from the business, less losses that have been incurred.

Capital stock refers to the declared money value of the outstanding stock of the corporation.[1] Thus, in a corporation that has issued 10,000 shares of $100 par value stock, the capital stock of the corporation is $1 million. Modern corporation codes generally provide for changing the amount of the capital stock.

(2) Valuation of Stock. Corporate stock commonly has a specified *par value.* This means that the person subscribing to the stock and acquiring it from the corporation must pay that amount. When stock is issued by the corporation for a price greater than the par value, some statutes provide that only the par value amount is to be treated as stated capital, the excess being allocated to surplus.[2]

Shares may be issued with no par value. In such a case no amount is stated in the certificate, and the amount that the subscriber pays the corporation is determined by the board of directors.

---

[1] Burton v Burton, 161 Cal App 2d 572, 326 P2d 855.

[2] California Corporations Code, § 1901.

The value found by dividing the value of the corporate assets by the number of shares outstanding is the *book value* of the shares. The *market value* of a share of stock is the price at which it can be voluntarily bought or sold.

§ 51:2. Certificate of Stock. The corporation ordinarily issues a *certificate of stock* or share certificate as evidence of the shareholder's ownership of stock. Although the issuance of such certificates is not essential either to the existence of a corporation or to the ownership of its stock, it is an almost universal practice since it is a convenient method of proving ownership and since it makes transfer of ownership easier.

Any form of certificate that identifies the interest owned by a person in the corporation is sufficient. The ABA Model Business Corporation Act requires that the certificate include (1) the state of incorporation; (2) the name of the person to whom issued; (3) the number and the class of shares represented and the designation of the series, if any; (4) the par value of each share or a statement that there is no par value; and (5) if there is more than one class of shares, a summary of the rights or restrictions of each class or a statement that such information will be furnished on request.[3]

§ 51:3. Kinds of Stock. The stock of a corporation may be divided into two or more classes.

(1) Preferences. *Common stock* is ordinary stock that has no preferences. Each share usually entitles the holder to one vote and to a share of the profits in the form of dividends, when declared, and to participate in the distribution of capital upon dissolution of the corporation.[4]

Preferred stock has a priority over common stock. The priority may be with respect to dividends. Thus, shares of "6% preferred stock of $100 par value" means that the holders of such shares are entitled to receive annual dividends of $6 for each share before any dividends are paid to the holders of the common stock. Preferred stock may also have a priority over common stock in the distribution of capital upon dissolution of the corporation. Preferred stock is ordinarily nonvoting.

(a) CUMULATIVE PREFERRED STOCK. Ordinarily the right to receive dividends is dependent upon the declaration of dividends by the board of directors for that particular period of time. If there is no fund from which the dividends may be declared or if the directors do not declare them from an available fund, the shareholder has no right to dividends. The fact that a shareholder has not received dividends for the current year does not in itself give him the right to accumulate or carry over into the next year a claim for those dividends.

---

[3] ABA MBCA § 23. The issuance of a certificate before the shares represented by it have been paid in full is prohibited.

[4] Storrow v Texas Consolidated Compress & Mfg. Association, (CA5 Tex) 87 F 612.

It is sufficient that the articles of incorporation manifest an intent that the preferred stock be cumulative, as where it was stated that no dividends could be paid upon the common stock until unpaid dividends for all preceding years had been paid to the preferred shareholders. It was immaterial that the articles did not expressly state that the right to dividends was "cumulative" or that the dividends were not guaranteed.[5]

In the absence of a statement that the right to dividends is noncumulative, it is frequently held that preferred stock has the right to cumulate dividends,[6] particularly with respect to each year in which there was a surplus available for dividend declaration.

If the right to dividends on preferred stock does not accumulate, it is possible for the directors to defeat the rights of preferred shareholders in favor of the common shareholders. To illustrate, assume that in a corporation in which there are equal amounts of outstanding common and preferred stock, a surplus is available in each of five years for the declaration of a 6 percent dividend on the preferred stock of $100 par value but that nothing is available for the common stock. If the board of directors declared no dividends until the fifth year and if the preferred shareholders were not permitted to accumulate their preferences for the prior years, they would receive only 6 percent of $6 a share in the fifth year and the holders of common stock could receive the balance, whereas the common shareholders would have received nothing had dividends of $6 been declared annually on the preferred stock.

(b) PARTICIPATING PREFERRED STOCK. Sometimes the preferred stock is given the right of participation. After the common shares receive dividends or a capital distribution equal to that first received by the preferred stock, both kinds share equally in the balance.

(2) Duration of Shares. Ordinarily shares continue to exist for the life of the corporation. Under modern statutes, however, any kind of shares, whether common or preferred, may be made terminable at an earlier date.

(a) REDEEMABLE SHARES. *Redeemable shares* are surrendered to the corporation, which pays the shareholder the par value of the shares or such amount as is stated in the redemption agreement. In substance, the transaction is similar to the corporation's buying out the shareholder's interest. The transaction goes further in that the redeemed shares ordinarily cease to exist after redemption, as distinguished from being owned by the corporation as treasury stock.

(b) CONVERTIBLE SHARES. *Convertible shares* entitle the shareholder to exchange his shares for a different type of share or for bonds of the corporation. In current corporate financing practice, convertible unsecured bonds

---

[5] Arizona Power Co. v Stuart, (CA9 Ariz) 212 F2d 535.

[6] Hazel Atlas Glass Co. v Van Dyk & Reeves, (CA2 NY) 8 F2d 716.

that may be converted into stock are more common than shares which may be converted into bonds.

When the corporate securities are convertible, the security holder generally has the option of determining when he wishes to convert, subject to a time limitation within which he must so elect. Conversion is thus carried out on an individual basis.

(3) Fractional Shares. Modern statutes expressly authorize a corporation to issue fractional shares or to issue scrip or certificates representing such fractional shares that can be sold or combined for the acquisition of whole shares.[7] In some states the holder of a fractional share is entitled to vote, to receive dividends, and to participate in the distribution of corporate assets upon liquidation.[8]

(4) Shares in Series. Under some statutes the shares of stock within a given class may be subdivided into "series." [9]

ACQUISITION OF SHARES

Shares of stock may be acquired by (1) subscription, either before or after the corporation is organized, or (2) transfer of existing shares from a shareholder or from the corporation.

§ 51:4. Subscription. A *stock subscription* is a contract or an agreement to buy a specific number and kind of shares of stock when they are issued. As in the case of any other contract, the agreement to subscribe to shares of a corporation is subject to avoidance for fraud.[10]

(1) Formality. By the great weight of authority, a contract to subscribe for shares of a corporation not yet formed or for unissued shares of stock of an existing corporation is not within the statute of frauds and need not be evidenced by a writing. In contrast, a contract for the transfer of existing corporate stock is subject to a statute of frauds provision similar to that applicable in the case of goods, except that the security provision applies without regard to the amount involved. Thus, any contract for the sale of a security must be evidenced by a writing to be enforceable or to be available as a defense.[11] This requirement of a writing extends to contracts relating to rights, such as a contract for the sale of stock purchase warrants.[12]

The requirement of a writing does not apply to an oral contract when there has been delivery or payment under the contract, a failure by one

[7] Delaware Code Ann § 155; ABA MBCA § 24.
[8] Massachusetts Annotated Laws, Ch 156B § 28.
[9] ABA MBCA § 16.
[10] Cumberland Co-op. Bakeries v Lawson, 91 WVa 245, 112 SE 568.
[11] UCC § 8-319.
[12] Mortimer B. Burnside & Co. v Havener Securities Corp., 25 App Div 2d 373, 269 NYS2d 724.

party to repudiate a written confirmation by the other party of the oral contract, or an admission in court of the existence of the contract.[13]

The writing which is required by the statute of frauds must show that there has been a contract for the sale of a stated quantity of described securities at a defined or stated price.[14] The writing must be signed in the manner required of a writing for the sale of goods.

No writing is required for instructions between a customer and his broker because, although such instructions contemplate the subsequent making of a sale, the giving of the instructions does not constitute a contract of sale. (See p. 1025, Lindsey v Stein Brothers & Boyce, Inc.)

Occasionally a special statute requires a writing for a stock subscription, or stipulates that the subscription be accompanied by a cash payment or that the original subscribers sign the articles of incorporation. Some states require that any preincorporation subscription be in writing.[15]

(2) Subscription Before Incorporation. In many states a preincorporation subscription of shares is regarded as an offer to the corporation. By this view it is necessary for the corporation to accept the subscription offer either expressly or by conduct. A few states hold that such subscriptions automatically become binding contracts when the organization has been completed.

In some states the preincorporation subscription is irrevocable for a stated period.[16] The ABA MBCA provides that "a subscription for shares of a corporation to be organized shall be irrevocable for a period of six months, unless otherwise provided by the terms of the subscription agreement or unless all of the subscribers consent to the revocation of such subscription."[17] As in the case of any contract, there may be a rescission upon proper grounds.

Generally a subscriber is not entitled to receive his share certificate until he has paid for the shares it represents.[18]

(3) Subscription After Incorporation. Subscriptions may be made after incorporation. In that event the transaction is like any other contract with the corporation. The offer of the subscription may come from the subscriber or from the corporation, but in either case there must be an acceptance. Upon acceptance the subscriber immediately becomes a shareholder with all the rights, privileges, and liabilities of a shareholder even though the subscriber has not paid any of the purchase price. The transaction, however, may only be a contract for the future issue of shares rather than a present subscription.

---

[13] UCC § 8-319(b),(c),(d).
[14] § 8-319(a).
[15] New York Business Corporation Law § 503(b).
[16] New York Business Corporation Law § 503(a).
[17] ABA MBCA § 17.
[18] Cornhusker Development & Investment Group v Knecht, 180 Neb 873, 146 NW2d 567.

§ 51:5. Transfer of Shares. In the absence of a valid restriction, a shareholder may transfer his shares to anyone he chooses.

(1) Restrictions on Transfer. Restrictions on the transfer of stock are valid provided they are not unreasonable.[19] In order to prevent its stock from going into the hands of strangers, it is lawful for a corporation to require the first right to purchase stock before a shareholder may sell it to an outsider.[20] The provision of the ABA Model Business Corporation Act has been followed in many states to authorize "any provision . . . for the regulation of the internal affairs of the corporation, including any provision restricting the transfer of shares." [21] There is, however, some statutory authority for declaring void a bylaw restriction on the transfer of shares.[22]

There is a conflict of authority as to the validity of a provision that no transfers may be made of shares without the approval of the directors or the other shareholders. The trend is to sustain such a provision when the shareholders are the owner-tenants of an incorporated cooperative apartment house.[23] In any case a restriction on transfer is interpreted in favor of transferability. For example, a restriction on the transfer by a retiring employee of the corporation was held not applicable to an employee who was discharged, and a restriction on the "sale" of shares was held not to bar a gift inter vivos or a bequest by will.[24]

Restrictions on transfers of stock designed to preserve the character or eligibility of the corporation as a professional corporation or a pseudo corporation, or to qualify under special corporation or tax laws, are valid.

A restriction upon the right to transfer is not valid as against a purchaser of the certificate unless the restriction is conspicuously noted on the certificate or unless the transferee has actual knowledge of the restriction.[25]

(2) Interest Transferred. The transfer of shares may be absolute, that is, it may divest all ownership and make the transferee the full owner, or it may be merely for security, as when stock is pledged to secure the repayment of a loan. Since it is an essential element of a pledge transaction that the pledgee be able to sell the pledged property upon default, a pledge of stock requires the delivery to the pledgee of the stock certificate together with a separate assignment of or indorsement on the stock certificate in favor of the pledgee or bearer. When this is done, the pledgee will be able to transfer title to the shares in case of default.

Directors and officers of a corporation may purchase stock held by shareholders of the corporation.[26]

---

[19] Tracey v Franklin, 31 Del Ch 477, 67 A2d 56.
[20] Lawson v Household Finance Corp., 17 Del Ch 1, 147 A 312.
[21] ABA MBCA § 54(h).
[22] New Hampshire Rev Stats Ann § 296:14.
[23] Gale v York Center Community Co-op., Inc., 21 Ill 2d 86, 171 NE2d 30.
[24] Stern v Stern, 79 Dist Col App 340, 146 F2d 870.
[25] UCC § 8-204.
[26] Taylor v Wright, 69 Cal App 2d 371, 159 P2d 980.

§ 51:6. Mechanics of Transfer. The ownership of shares is transferred by the delivery of the certificate of stock indorsed by its owner in blank, or to a specified person; or by the delivery of the certificate by such person accompanied by a separate assignment or power of attorney executed by him.[27] A transfer made in this manner is effective as between the parties even though the corporate charter or bylaws specify that shares cannot be transferred until a transfer is made on the books of the corporation or the records of a corporate transfer agent.

A delivery from the owner of the shares directly to his transferee is not required. There is a sufficient delivery when the owner of the shares indorses them with his name and mails them to the corporation with the request that a new certificate be issued in the name of the transferee and be sent directly to him.[28]

A physical transfer of the certificate without a necessary indorsement is effective as between the parties because indorsement is only necessary to make a transferee a "bona fide" purchaser as against third parties.[29]

In the absence of a delivery of the certificate or an assignment, there can be no effective transfer of ownership of the shares. Hence, the fact that the decedent indorsed stock certificates in blank did not establish a gift when he died in possession of the certificates apparently without having made any delivery of them.[30]

Conversely, when the alleged donee has possession of shares which were never indorsed by the alleged donor and which are registered on the corporate books in the name of the alleged donor, the alleged donee has the burden of proving the alleged gift by clear and convincing evidence.[31]

In general, the transfer agent stands in the same position as the corporation with respect to its stock and must make a formal transfer whenever the corporation would itself be required to recognize a transfer. When a corporation or its transfer agent wrongfully refuses to register a transfer of shares of stock, the new owner of the shares may bring suit for damages sustained and in some states may sue for the face value of the shares on the theory of conversion.[32] (See p. 1025, Welland Investment Corp. v First National Bank.)

Possession of the certificate is also essential to an involuntary transfer by execution of judicial process.[33]

§ 51:7. Effect of Transfer.

(1) Validity of Transfer. As a transfer of shares is a transfer of ownership, the transfer must in general satisfy the requirements governing any other

---

[27] UCC § 8-309. The second alternative of a delivery of an unindorsed certificate is designed to keep the certificate "clean," as when the transfer is for a temporary or special purpose as in the case of a pledge of the certificate as security for a loan.

[28] Kintzinger v Millin, 254 Iowa 173, 117 NW2d 68.

[29] Jorgensen's Estate, 70 Ill App 2d 398, 217 NE2d 290.

[30] Donsavage's Estate v Mockler, 420 Pa 587, 218 A2d 112.

[31] First Security Bank v Hall, 29 Utah 2d 24, 504 P2d 995.

[32] Wagoner v Mail Delivery Service, Inc., 193 Kan 470, 394 P2d 119 (pre-Code).

[33] UCC § 8-317.

transfer of property or agreement to transfer property. As between the parties, a transfer may be set aside for any ground that would warrant similar relief under property law. If the transfer of stock has been obtained by duress, the transferor may obtain a rescission of the transfer.[34]

*(2) **Negotiability.*** Under the common law the transferee of shares of stock had no greater right than the transferor because the certificate and the shares represented by the certificate were nonnegotiable. By statute the common-law rule has been changed by imparting negotiability to the certificate. Just as various defenses cannot be asserted against the holder in due course of a commercial paper, it is provided that similar defenses cannot be raised against the person acquiring the certificate in good faith and for value. As against such a person, the defenses cannot be raised that his transferor did not own the shares, that he did not have authority to deliver the certificate, or that the transfer was made in violation of a restriction upon transfer not known to such person and not noted conspicuously on the certificate. A former owner cannot object as against a subsequent purchaser for value and in good faith that his transferee obtained the certificate from him by fraud, duress, mistake, or did not give him any consideration.[35] Conversely, if the purchaser of stock knows that his vendor holds the title subject to the claims of other persons, such as a divorced wife claiming an interest therein, the purchaser is subject to the rights of such third persons.[36]

This concept of negotiability is also recognized as against corporate lien claims on the stock. Although modern statutes commonly give the corporation a lien upon stock for a debt owed it by the shareholder, the corporation cannot assert a lien against a purchaser of the shares unless the right of the corporation to the lien is noted conspicuously on the certificate.[37]

The fact that corporate stock has the quality of negotiability does not make it commercial paper within Article 3 of the Uniform Commercial Code. Shares of stock are classified under the UCC as investment securities; and Article 8, as supplemented by the continuing non-Code law which has not been displaced,[38] is the source of the law governing the rights of the parties to the transaction involving such securities[39] although courts may look to Article 3 for guidance when a question regarding an investment security cannot be resolved on the basis of the language in Article 8 alone.

---

[34] Pierce v Haverlah Estate, (Tex Civ App) 428 SW2d 422 (holding that if transfer of stock had been made to prevent a threatened prosecution for theft of the stock, there was "duress" which would justify a rescission of the transfer since the significant element was the effect of the threat upon the victim's mind and not whether the victim was guilty of the crime charged).

[35] §§ 8-301, 8-311, 8-315.

[36] Blanton v Austin, (Tex Civ App) 392 SW2d 140.

[37] UCC § 8-103.

[38] § 1-103.

[39] E. F. Hutton & Co. v Manufacturers National Bank, (DC ED Mich) 259 F Supp 513.

*(3) **Secured Transaction.*** Corporate stock is frequently delivered to a creditor as security for a debt owed by the shareholder. Thus, a debtor borrowing money from a bank may deliver shares of stock to the bank as collateral security for the repayment of the loan, or a broker's customer purchasing stock on margin may leave the stock in the possession of the broker as security for the payment of any balance due. The delivery of the security to the creditor or his retention of possession gives rise to a perfected security interest without any filing by the creditor. In itself the pledge does not make the pledgee of the corporate stock the owner of the stock nor of any of the assets of the corporation.[40]

*(4) **Effect of Transfer on Corporation.*** Until there is a transfer on its books, the corporation is entitled to treat as the owner the person whose name is on the books.[41] The corporation may properly refuse to recognize the transferee when the corporation is given notice or has knowledge that the transfer is void or in breach of trust. In such a case the corporation properly refuses to effect a transfer until the rights of the parties have been determined.

The corporation may also refuse to register the transfer of shares when the outstanding certificate is not surrendered to it, in the absence of satisfactory proof that it had been lost, destroyed, or stolen.

§ 51:8. Lost, Destroyed, and Stolen Securities. Although for some purposes the negotiable character of a security makes the paper stand for the security, the loss, destruction, or theft of the paper does not destroy the owner's rights. Subject to certain limitations, he may obtain from the issuer of the security a new paper evidencing his ownership, that is, a new share certificate. Two limitations on this right of replacement are expressly stated in the Uniform Commercial Code, and a third is recognized.

*(1) **Time.*** The owner of the security must make the request to the issuer or its transfer agent before the missing security has been acquired by a bona fide purchaser and the issuer has notice of that fact or has entered on its book a transfer of ownership to such purchaser.[42] Ordinarily this can only occur if the security was in "bearer" form, for otherwise a third person could not qualify as a "purchaser" and the issuer's registration of the transfer to him would in itself be wrongful.

*(2) **Bond.*** The applicant for the replacement security must furnish the issuer with "a sufficient indemnity bond" [43] to protect the issuer from loss should it issue a replacement security and a bona fide purchaser thereafter present the original security.

---

40 Southern Arizona Bank v United States, (Court of Claims) 386 F2d 1002.
41 UCC § 8-207.
42 UCC § 8-405(1),(2)(a).
43 § 8-405(2)(b).

The UCC does not specify the amount and terms of such a bond, but the duty to act in good faith [44] will in turn require that the bond terms be commercially reasonable.

(3) Additional Requirements. In addition to the two limitations above noted, the UCC permits the issuer to impose "any other reasonable requirements." [45] Ordinarily this will take the form of an affidavit setting forth the facts with respect to the ownership; to the loss, destruction, or theft of the original security; and to the efforts made to find or recover the lost or stolen security.

§ 51:9. Protection of the Public.

(1) Blue-Sky Laws. In order to protect the public from the sale of securities of nonexistent or worthless corporations, many states have adopted regulations called *blue-sky laws.* The statutes vary in detail. Some impose a criminal penalty for engaging in fraudulent practices, while others require the licensing of dealers in securities and approval by a government agency before a given security can be sold to the public.[46]

A salesman selling stock as representative of a corporation is deemed a "seller" within the operation of a blue-sky law imposing liability on the "seller" of unregistered securities, as opposed to the contention that the seller subjected to statutory control must be the corporation or owner of the stock.[47] Some states impose liability for the purchase price on directors and corporate agents taking part in an illegal sale of securities.[48]

Under some statutes the officers and directors of a corporation are held liable for the illegal sale of its shares. While the sale is technically made by the corporation and not by them, they are nevertheless regarded as being in control of running the corporation and should therefore be held liable for the loss caused by the corporation to the buyer of the shares.[49]

The extensive federal regulation of corporate securities does not displace the operation of state blue-sky laws as to intrastate transactions.[50]

(2) Federal Securities Act. The state blue-sky laws are subject to the very important limitation that they can apply only to intrastate transactions

---

44 § 1-203.

45 § 8-405(2)(c).

46 Uniformity of blue-sky laws has been achieved in one half of the states through the adoption of the Uniform Securities Act, as amended in 1958. This act has been adopted in Alabama, Alaska, Arkansas, Colorado, Hawaii, Idaho, Indiana, Kansas, Kentucky, Maryland, Massachusetts, Michigan, Missouri, Montana, Nebraska, Nevada, New Jersey, New Mexico, Oklahoma, Oregon, South Carolina, Utah, Virginia, Washington, Wisconsin, Wyoming, and is in force in the District of Columbia and Puerto Rico.

47 Spears v Lawrence Securities, Inc., 239 Ore 583, 399 P2d 348.

48 Weidner v Engelhart, (ND) 176 NW2d 509.

49 Davis v Walker, 170 Neb 891, 104 NW2d 479.

50 15 USC § 77r.

and cannot apply to sales made in interstate commerce. To meet this defect the Federal Securities Act of 1933 was adopted. This Act requires the filing of a *registration statement* that gives the public certain information.

The registration statement is filed with the Securities and Exchange Commission (SEC). The only object is to provide the interested investor with a place where he can learn certain facts about the security and the enterprise. There is nothing which constitutes an approval by the government that the investment is sound nor is there any guarantee that the investor will not lose his money.

(a) APPLICABILITY. The statute applies to the issuing of stocks and bonds and any other form of investment security.

(b) REGISTRATION STATEMENT EXEMPTION. The issuing of some securities is exempt from the requirement of a registration statement. Registration is not required for issues of less than one-half million dollars nor to issues by government and nonprofit corporations. The statute does not apply to transactions between private investors nor to private offerings to a limited number of persons who would have access to the kinds of information set forth in the registration statement.[51]

(c) LIABILITY FOR FRAUD. The federal act imposes civil liability and criminal penalties for fraudulent statements in connection with the issuance of securities whether or not exempt from the registration statement requirements. Civil and criminal liability is also imposed for false statements made in the registration statement and for the omission of material matter therefrom. The same liability applies to fraudulent statements in and omissions from a stock prospectus (selling circular).

Any investor who sustains loss because of the false statements or omissions of the registration statement may sue to recover damages.

A defendant sued for damages may defend on the ground that he had exercised due diligence in determining the facts and that after reasonable investigation did not know nor have reason to believe that any statement in the registration statement was false or that any material fact had been omitted. The Act declares it unlawful for any issuer, underwriter, or dealer in securities to send either the securities or a prospectus for them in interstate commerce or the mails without having first registered the issue with the Securities and Exchange Commission.

(d) CRIMINAL PENALTIES. A criminal penalty is imposed for failure to register or for making false statements to the Commission. The Commission may enjoin any practice that violates the act, and persons injured may bring suit for civil damages against the violator.

---

[51] Securities Act Amendment of 1964, PL 88-467, 78 Stat 565, 15 USC § 781 (g)(1)(B).

(3) Federal Securities Exchange Act. In addition to the evils connected with the issuing and floating of securities, a number of evils arose from practices at security exchanges. Dealers in security transactions in the interstate market are now subject to the Federal Securities Exchange Act of 1934. Exchanges, brokers, and dealers who deal in the securities traded in interstate commerce or on any national security exchange must register if they have assets of $1 million or more and 500 or more shareholders.

A registrant is required to file periodic reports in order to keep the registration information up-to-date. The Federal Securities Exchange Act of 1934 declares it unlawful for any broker, dealer, or exchange, directly or indirectly, to make use of the mails or any means of communication for the purpose of using the facilities of an exchange to effect any transaction in a security, unless such exchange is registered as a national securities exchange with the Securities and Exchange Commission or unless it is exempt from registration.

Various practices that were used in market manipulation are declared unlawful and prohibited by the Act. Wash sales, matched orders, and circulation of false rumors and tips are made unlawful and prohibited. These devices attempt to create the impression of great trading activity in a particular stock, thus tending to increase the price that the public is willing to pay for it.

Other practices that can be used either for a lawful trading or an unlawful manipulating purpose are not prohibited by the Act but are subject to the regulation of the Securities and Exchange Commission so that the Commission may see that they are used for a legitimate purpose. Speculative activity on exchanges is restricted by giving the Board of Governors of the Federal Reserve System power to fix the margin on which trading can be conducted and to restrict the extent to which money can be borrowed to finance stock transactions.

Control of corporations by insiders is checked to some extent by the Act by requiring that solicitations for proxies state the identity and interest of the solicitor and what action is to be passed upon at the corporate meeting for which the proxy is solicited. Corporate insiders are also prohibited under certain circumstances from making a profit on the basis of information that they have but that the general public could not have.

(4) Holding Company Regulation. Later statutes provide for the registration of interstate electric or gas utility holding companies with the Securities and Exchange Commission and authorize the Federal Power Commission to regulate the rates on interstate shipments of natural gas and electric power. In registering, the holding company must file detailed information concerning its corporate structure and financing.

Authority is given to the Securities and Exchange Commission to order the dissolution of holding companies if they were created merely for the purpose of corporate manipulation. If a holding company does not register as required by law, it is illegal for it to engage in interstate transactions. A holding company that has registered is subject to various restrictions as to financing and security issues, and the Commission is given supervisory powers over the company's financial records.

RIGHTS OF SHAREHOLDERS

The control of the shareholders over the corporation is indirect. Periodically, ordinarily once a year, the shareholders elect directors and through this means can control the corporation. At other times, however, the shareholders have no right or power to control the corporate activity so long as it is conducted within lawful channels.

§ 51:10. Ownership Rights.

(1) Certificate of Stock. A shareholder has the right to have issued to him a properly executed certificate as evidence of his ownership of shares.

(2) Transfer of Shares. Subject to certain valid restrictions, a shareholder has the right to transfer his shares as he chooses. He may sell the shares at any price or transfer them as a gift.

§ 51:11. Right to Vote. The right to vote means the right to vote at shareholders' meetings for the election of directors and on such other special matters as must be passed upon by the shareholders. As an illustration of the latter, a proposal to change the capital stock structure of the corporation or a proposal to sell all or substantially all of the assets of the corporation must be approved by the shareholders.[52]

A shareholder may vote his shares as he pleases for the protection of his own interests, as against the contention that he owes a duty to the corporation or other shareholders to act in a way which will be for their interest. The fact that a shareholder is also a director of the corporation does not restrict his freedom of voting his shares nor disqualify him from voting on any issue on which other shareholders are entitled to vote.[53] Likewise, the fact that the action of the majority stockholders may reduce the value of the shares of stock does not in itself entitle minority stockholders to recover damages from the majority stockholders. (See p. 1026, McDaniel v Painter.)

(1) Who May Vote. Ordinarily only those common shareholders in whose names the stock appears on the books of the corporation are entitled to vote. Generally the directors may fix a date for determining the shareholders who may vote.[54]

When a shareholder has pledged his shares as security, he may generally continue to vote the shares and the pledgee is not entitled to vote the shares until a transfer of the shares is made to the pledgee by the corporation.[55]

---

[52] Good v Lackawanna Leather Co., 96 NJ Super 439, 233 A2d 201.
[53] Beutelspacher v Spokane Savings Bank, 164 Wash 227, 2 P2d 729.
[54] ABA MBCA § 30.
[55] ABA MBCA § 33.

The requirement that a person be a shareholder of record in order to vote excludes a person not so recorded even though he might be entitled to be registered as the shareholder. Thus, a pledgee may not vote shares that are not registered in his name even though, because of the pledgor's default, the pledgee was entitled to have the shares transferred to his name.[56]

The more recent corporation statutes recognize that there may be a conflict of interest between the holders of the voting stock and the holders of a particular class of stock not entitled to vote. In order to protect the interests of the nonvoting stock, some statutes require that action, such as the amendment of the certificate or articles of incorporation that could affect the nonvoting class, must be voted upon and approved by that class as a class, in addition to being approved by the required majority of the voting shares.[57]

A substantial number of state statutes provide that shares called for redemption cannot be voted after the shareholder has been given notice of redemption and the corporation has made an irrevocable deposit with a bank or trust company of money sufficient to pay for the redeemed shares.

(2) Number of Votes. Each shareholder is ordinarily entitled to one vote for each voting share. In some states, however, the number of votes allowed to each shareholder is limited by statute. There is a conflict of authority whether a shareholder may vote a fractional share.[58] Whole shares may only be voted as whole shares and cannot be voted as fractional shares and divided between candidates.[59]

In most states cumulative voting in the election of directors may be provided for or automatically exists when the contrary is not stated in the charter or articles of incorporation.[60] In nearly half of the states cumulative voting is mandatory, being imposed by either constitution or statute. A few states prohibit cumulative voting.

Under a *cumulative voting* plan each shareholder has as many votes as the number of shares he owns multiplied by the number of directors to be elected, and he can distribute them as he sees fit. To illustrate, if a person owns 30 shares and 10 directors are to be elected, he is entitled to cast 300 votes. For example, he could cast 30 votes for each of 10 nominees, 60 votes for each of 5, 100 for each of 3, or 300 votes for 1.

There is a conflict of authority as to the validity of a provision for the election of the directors by classes, as when directors serve for three years and one third of the directors are elected each year. In some jurisdictions such a provision is held invalid as impairing the right of cumulative voting.

---

[56] Beraksa v Stardust Records, Inc., 215 Cal App 2d 708, 30 Cal Rptr 504.

[57] See, for example, ABA MBCA § 60, which confers upon nonvoting shares the right to vote as a class on the adoption of 10 specified types of amendments affecting their interest.

[58] Com. ex rel Cartwright v Cartwright, 350 Pa 638, 40 A2d 30.

[59] Garnier v Garnier, 248 Cal App 2d 255, 56 Cal Rptr 247.

[60] ABA MBCA § 33.

In other jurisdictions such a system is valid, and cumulative voting is exercised as to the directors within each class to be elected at each election. (See p. 1027, Bohannan v The Corporation Commission.)

(3) Voting by Proxy. A shareholder has the right to authorize another to vote for him.[61] This is known as *voting by proxy.* In the absence of restrictions to the contrary, any person, even one who is not a shareholder, may act as a proxy. Ordinarily authority to act as a proxy may be conferred by an informal written instrument.[62] The corporation law of a particular state may expressly require that a proxy be signed although, in the absence of such a requirement, a stamped facsimile signing has been held sufficient.[63] There is also some statutory recognition of the visual transmission of proxies, as in the case of a "photogram appearing to have been transmitted by a shareholder." [64]

Statutes may limit the period for which a proxy continues as authorization. In the absence of an express limitation, the proxy may specify that it continues indefinitely until canceled by the shareholder.[65] Ordinarily a proxy is revoked by the death of the shareholder. This rule may be modified by a statute permitting the proxy holder to vote in spite of the death or incompetence of the proxy donor if the corporate officer responsible for maintaining the list of shareholders has not been given written notice of the death or incompetence.[66]

When proxy solicitation statements are false and misleading, a shareholder has the right to bar the action contemplated or to recover damages because of action taken [67] on the basis of the proxy vote.

(4) Voting Agreements and Trusts. Shareholders, as a general rule, are allowed to enter into an agreement by which they concentrate their voting strength for the purpose of controlling the management.

A *voting trust* exists when by agreement a group of shareholders, or all of the shareholders, transfer their shares in trust to one or more persons as trustees who are authorized to vote the stock during the life of the trust agreement. In general, such agreements have been upheld if their object is lawful. In some jurisdictions such trusts cannot run beyond a specified number of years. There are some signs of a relaxation as to this matter. Several states have abandoned any time limitation, several have extended the

---

[61] § 33.

[62] See, for example, the regulations of the Securities and Exchange Commission, Rule X-14A-4. By statute it has been declared in at least one jurisdiction that "a telegram . . . is a sufficient writing." In a few states an oral proxy is valid.

[63] Schott v Climax Molybdenum Co., 38 Del Ch 450, 154 A2d 221.

[64] North Carolina Gen Stat § 55-68(a).

[65] Booker v First Federal Savings and Loan Ass'n, 215 Ga 277, 110 SE2d 360, cert den 361 US 916.

[66] New York Business Corporation Law § 609(c). Notice the similar practical approach to the problem made in the case of the death or incompetence of the drawer of a check. UCC § 4-405.

[67] J. I. Case Co. v Borak, 377 US 426.

time limitation, and many states provide for an extension or renewal of the agreement.

In view of the practical impossibility of determining future events, it is likely that a voting trust will be held valid even though no purpose is declared. This view has been sustained when the trust agreement merely stated that the depositing shareholders "deem it for the best interests of themselves and of the Corporation to unite the voting power held by them as holders of Common Stock." [68] The trustee of a voting trust occupies a fiduciary position similar to that of an ordinary trustee and must deal fairly with the rights of all shareholders he represents.[69]

(5) Sale of Vote. In order to prevent abuses in corporate management some states prohibit a shareholder from selling his vote. When an absolute sale of stock is made, the transaction is not a prohibited "sale of a vote" merely because payment and delivery are deferred until after the date of issuance of a proxy statement, and the seller is required by the contract to deliver forthwith to the buyer an irrevocable proxy enabling the buyer to vote the shares at all meetings prior to the delivery date.[70]

§ 51:12. Preemptive Offer of Shares. If the capital stock of a corporation is increased, each shareholder ordinarily has the preemptive right to subscribe to such percentage of the new shares as his old shares bore to the former total of capital stock. This right is given in order to enable each shareholder to maintain his relative interest in the corporation.[71]

The existence of a preemptive right may make impossible the concluding of a transaction in which the corporation is to transfer a block of stock as consideration. Moreover, practical difficulties arise as to how stock should be allocated among shareholders of different classes. For these reasons the trend of corporation statutes has been toward the abolition of the preemptive right and court decisions have made many exceptions to the requirement.[72] Statutes in half the states provide that there is no preemptive right with respect to shares sold to employees of the corporation. In many states the certificate of incorporation may expressly prohibit preemptive rights.

§ 51:13. Inspection of Books. A shareholder has the right to inspect the books of his corporation. The shareholder must ask for the examination in

[68] Holmes v Sharretts, 228 Md 358, 180 A2d 302.

[69] Jesser v Mayfair Hotel, Inc., (Mo) 316 SW2d 465.

[70] Lurie v Kaplan, 31 App Div 2d 93, 295 NYS2d 493 (also holding that it was immaterial that the sale price was above the market price).

[71] Gord v Iowana Farms Milk Co., 245 Iowa 1, 60 NW2d 820.

[72] ABA MBCA § 26. The Model Act in effect takes a neutral position by proposing one section that declares that shareholders have no preemptive right, except as expressly stated in the articles of incorporation; and an alternative provision declaring that they have such right, except to the extent expressly denied by the articles or by the alternative section. In recognition of the necessity that the corporation have a free hand in using a block as payment, even the latter alternative section declares that the preemptive right does not exist as to "any shares sold otherwise than for cash."

good faith, for proper motives, and at a reasonable time and place.[73] The Model Act authorizes inspection of corporate records "for any proper purpose." [74]

The purpose of inspection must be reasonably related to the shareholder's interest as a shareholder.[75] A shareholder is entitled to inspect the records to determine the financial condition of the corporation, the quality of its management, and any matters relating to his rights or interest in the corporate business,[76] such as the value of his stock; to obtain information needed for a lawsuit against the corporation or its directors or officers; or in order to organize the other shareholders into an "opposition" party to remove the board of directors at the next election.

Inspection has frequently been refused when it was sought merely from idle curiosity or for "speculative purposes." Inspection has sometimes been denied on the ground that it was merely sought to obtain a mailing list of persons who would be solicited to buy products of another enterprise. Inspection has also been refused where the object of the stockholder was to advance his political or social beliefs without regard to the economic welfare of the corporation. (See p. 1028, Minnesota ex rel Pillsbury v Honeywell, Inc.)

Many cases deny the right of inspection when it would be harmful to the corporation or is sought only for the purpose of annoying, harassing, or causing vexation, or for the purpose of aiding competitors of the corporation. In contrast, the right of inspection is so broadly recognized in some states that the fact that the shareholder may make an improper use of the information obtained does not bar inspection.

A provision of the articles of incorporation or bylaws seeking to restrict the right of inspecting corporate books conferred by statute may be held invalid. Thus, a provision in the certificate of incorporation requiring 25 percent stock ownership in order to examine the corporate books is void as contrary to the statute which gave the right to inspect to each shareholder; and the limitation may not be sustained on the theory that the shareholders had surrendered such statutory right of inspection by agreeing that only a 25 percent shareholder should have the right.[77]

The purpose of the inspecting stockholder may be to learn the names and addresses of other shareholders so that he can buy their stock from them. This is a proper reason for inspection as it enables a shareholder to protect his interest in the corporation by increasing his ownership and voting power. A contrary rule would be particularly undesirable as it would give management complete control of such information, which it could use to further its control by proxy solicitation or purchase of outstanding shares.[78]

---

[73] Sanders v Pacific Gamble Robinson Co., 250 Minn 265, 84 NW2d 919.

[74] ABA MBCA § 52.

[75] Willard v Harrworth Corp., (Del Ch) 258 A2d 914.

[76] Sawers v American Phenolic Corp., 404 Ill 440, 89 NE2d 374.

[77] Loew's Theatres, Inc. v Commercial Credit Co., (Del Ch) 243 A2d 78.

[78] Florida Telephone Corp. v Florida ex rel Peninsular Telephone Co., (Fla App) 111 So2d 677.

The ABA MBCA seeks to prevent the abuse of the power to inspect corporate books by limiting the right of inspection to persons who have owned the stock for not less than 6 months or who own not less than 5 percent of all the outstanding shares of the corporation. As a further safeguard, the Model Act requires that the request for inspection be made by "written demand stating the purpose thereof." [79]

Inspection need not be made personally. A shareholder may employ an accountant or an attorney to examine the records for him. The Model Act declares that the shareholder "shall have the right to examine, in person, or by agent or attorney, at any reasonable time or times, for any proper purpose its relevant books and records of account, minutes, and record of shareholders and to make extracts therefrom." [80]

(1) Form of Books. There are generally no legal requirements as to the form of corporate books and records. The Model Act recognizes that corporate books and records may be stored in modern data storage systems. "Any books, records, and minutes may be in written form or in any other form capable of being converted into written form within a reasonable time." [81]

(2) Financial Statements. In recognition of the widespread practice of corporations preparing formal financial statements, the Model Act requires a corporation to send such a statement to a shareholder upon request. It provides that "upon the written request of any shareholder . . . , the corporation shall mail to such shareholder . . . its most recent financial statements showing in reasonable detail its assets and liabilities, and the results of its operations." [82] A number of states have similar provisions.[83]

§ 51:14. Dividends. A shareholder has the right to receive his proportion of dividends as they are declared, subject to the relative rights of other shareholders to preferences, accumulation of dividends, and participation. However, there is no absolute right to receive dividends.[84]

(1) Funds Available for Declaration of Dividends. Statutes commonly provide that no dividends may be declared unless there is a "surplus" for their payment. This surplus is generally calculated as the amount of the corporate assets in excess of all outstanding liabilities and outstanding shares of the corporation.[85] Thus, if a corporation owed $50,000 and had issued stock of $200,000, there could not be a fund for the declaration of dividends until the corporate assets were in excess of $250,000. The theory is that there must be preserved intact such a fund as will pay off all creditors of

---

[79] ABA MBCA § 52.
[80] § 52.
[81] § 52.
[82] § 52.
[83] New Jersey Stat Ann § 14A:5-28.
[84] Wabash R. Co. v Barclay, 280 US 197.
[85] Randall v Bailey, 288 NY 280, 43 NE2d 43.

the corporation and return to each shareholder his capital investment before any dividends can be paid. The effect of this rule is to deny a corporation a right to declare dividends from current net profits if there is a deficit from prior years.

Dividends may be paid from paid-in surplus. This is the amount that is paid for a subscription to stock in excess of its par value, if it is par-value stock, and of the amount designated by the board of directors as payment for shares having no par value.

A book surplus may be created by decreasing the capital stock or increasing the value of the corporate assets. A cash dividend cannot be declared from a surplus based on such an unrealized appreciation of corporate assets. That is, a corporation cannot increase the valuation of its property on its books and then declare a cash dividend from the resulting paper surplus.

Conversely, for the purpose of dividend declaration, a corporation should write down its assets when because of their risk, nature, or depreciation they are in effect overvalued.

As an exception to these rules, a wasting assets corporation may pay dividends out of current net profits without regard to the preservation of the corporate assets. *Wasting assets corporations* include those enterprises that are designed to exhaust or use up the assets of the corporation (as by extracting oil, coal, iron, and other ores), as compared with a manufacturing plant where the object is to preserve the plant as well as to continue to manufacture. A wasting assets corporation may also be formed for the purpose of buying and liquidating a bankrupt's stock of merchandise.

In some states statutes provide that dividends may be declared from current net profits, without regard to the existence of a deficit from former years, or from surplus.

If dividends are about to be declared from an unlawful source, an injunction can be obtained to stop their declaration or payment. If the payment has already been made, the directors responsible for the action may be sued individually and be made to indemnify the corporation for the loss they have caused it by the improper payment if they acted negligently or in bad faith in declaring the dividends.

(2) Discretion of Directors. Assuming that a fund is available for the declaration of dividends, it is then a matter primarily within the discretion of the board of directors whether a dividend shall be declared. The fact that there is a surplus which could be used for dividends does not determine that they must be declared.[86] This rule is not affected by the nature of the shares. Thus, the fact that the shareholders hold cumulative preferred shares does not give them any right to demand a declaration of dividends or to interfere with an honest exercise of discretion by the directors.[87]

The fact that a wasting assets corporation may declare dividends from current earnings does not require the directors to do so, and they have the

---

[86] Agnew v American Ice Co., 2 NJ 291, 66 A2d 330.

[87] Treves v Menzies, 37 Del Ch 330, 142 A2d 520.

same discretionary power with respect to dividend declaration as directors of an ordinary business corporation.[88] A very important factor encouraging the declaration of dividends is the federal penalty surtax to which accumulated earnings of a corporation in excess of $100,000 may be subject.[89]

In general, a court will refuse to substitute its judgment for the judgment of the directors and will interfere only when it is shown that their conduct is harmful to the welfare of the corporation or its shareholders.[90] The courts, however, will compel the declaration of a dividend when it is apparent that the directors have amassed a surplus beyond any practical business need.

Once dividends are duly declared, a debtor-creditor relation exists between the corporation and the shareholders as to those dividends. The shareholder may accordingly sue the corporation to recover the amount of his lawfully declared dividends if it fails to pay them.[91]

(3) Form of Dividends. Customarily, a dividend is paid in money; but it may be paid in property, such as a product manufactured by the corporation, in shares of other corporations held by the corporation, or in shares of the corporation itself. In the last case, referred to as a *stock dividend,* the result is the same as though the directors paid a cash dividend and all the shareholders then purchased additional stock in amounts proportionate to their original holdings. The corporation merely capitalizes or transfers to the capital account earnings or earned surplus in an amount equal to the par or stated value of the stock dividend.[92] The result is that the stock dividend does not change the proportionate interest of each shareholder but only the evidence which represents that interest. He now has a greater number of shares, but his total shares represent the same proportionate interest in the corporation as before.[93]

It is necessary to distinguish between stock splits and stock dividends. In spite of the common interchangeable use of these terms they represent distinct legal concepts.[94] When a corporation splits its shares in two, the number of outstanding shares is doubled and consequently each share then stands for only one half of the interest in the corporation represented by an original share. Although a holder of one share receives an additional share, the additional share merely offsets the 50 percent dilution of the value of his original stock resulting from doubling the number of outstanding shares.

(4) Effect of Transfer of Shares. In determining who is entitled to dividends, it is immaterial when the surplus from which the distribution is made was earned. As between the transferor and the transferee, if the

---

[88] Moskowitz v Bantrell, 41 Del Ch 177, 190 A2d 749.

[89] 26 USC §§ 531-537. This penalty was not enforced during the wage-price-dividend freeze that was initiated in 1971.

[90] Gordon v Elliman, 306 NY 456, 119 NE2d 331.

[91] Crellin's Estate v Com. of Internal Revenue, (CA9) 203 F2d 812.

[92] Fosdick Trust, 4 NY2d 646, 176 NYS2d 966, 152 NE2d 228.

[93] Merritt-Chapman and Scott Corp. v N.Y. Trust Co., (CA2 NY) 184 F2d 954.

[94] Ketter Industries, Inc. v Fineberg, (Fla App) 203 So2d 644.

dividend is in cash or property other than the shares of the corporation declaring the dividend, the person who was the owner on the date the dividend was declared is entitled to the dividend. Thus, if a cash dividend is declared before a transfer is made, the transferor is entitled to it. If the transfer was made before the declaration date, the transferee is entitled to it. In applying this rule, it is immaterial when distribution of the dividend is made.

The rule that the date of declaration determines the right to a cash dividend is subject to modification by the corporation. The board of directors in declaring the dividend may state that it will be payable to those who will be the holders of record on a later specified date.

If the dividend consists of shares in the corporation declaring the dividend, ownership is determined by the date of distribution. Whichever party is the owner of the shares when the stock dividend is distributed is entitled to the stock dividend. The reason for this variation from the cash dividend rule lies in the fact that the declaration of a stock dividend has the effect of diluting the existing corporate assets among a larger number of shares. The value of the holding represented by each share is accordingly diminished. Unless the person who owns the stock on the date when distribution is made receives a proportionate share of the stock dividend, the net effect will be to lessen his holding.

The transferor and transferee may enter into any agreement they choose with respect to dividends.

These rules determine the right to dividends as between transferor and transferee. Regardless of what those rights may be, the corporation is generally entitled to continue to recognize the transferor as a shareholder until it has been notified that a transfer has been made and the corporate records are accordingly changed.[95] If the corporation, believing that the transferor is still the owner of the shares, sends him a dividend to which the transferee is entitled, the transferee cannot sue the corporation. In that case, the remedy of the transferee is to sue the transferor for the money or property that the latter has received.

§ 51:15. Capital Distribution. Upon the dissolution of the corporation, the shareholders are entitled to receive any balance of the corporate assets that remains after the payment of all creditors. Certain classes of stock may have a preference or priority in this distribution.

§ 51:16. Shareholders' Actions. When the corporation has the right to sue its directors or officers or third persons for damages caused by them to the corporation or for breach of contract, one or more shareholders may bring such action if the corporation refuses to do so. This is a *derivative* (secondary) *action* in that the shareholder enforces only the cause of action of the corporation, and any money recovery is paid into the corporate treasury.

---

[95] Davis v Fraser, 307 NY 433, 121 NE2d 406.

An action cannot be brought by minority shareholders, however, if the action of the corporate directors or officers has been ratified by a majority of the shareholders acting in good faith and if the matter is of such a nature that had such majority originally authorized the acts of the directors or officers, there would not have been any wrong.[96]

Shareholders may also intervene or join in an action brought against the corporation when the corporation refuses to defend the action against it or is not doing so in good faith. Otherwise the shareholders may take no part in an action by or against [97] the corporation.

Shareholders in a deadlocked corporation may bring an action to obtain a dissolution of the corporation. (See p. 1030, Goldstein v Studley.)

LIABILITIES OF SHAREHOLDERS

The shareholder is ordinarily protected from liability for the acts of the corporation. Some exceptions are made by statute.

§ 51:17. Limited Liability. The liability of a shareholder is generally limited. This means that he is not personally responsible for the debts and liabilities of the corporation. The capital contributed by the shareholders may be exhausted by the claims of creditors, but he has no personal liability for any unpaid balance. The risk of the shareholder is thus limited to losing the original capital invested by him. By way of comparison, if a partnership had debts of $1 million, any partner would be liable without limitation for the total amount of the debt. In the case of a corporation owing $1 million, no shareholder is personally liable for any part of that debt. The explanation for this rule is that the corporation is a distinct, legal person.

§ 51:18. Exceptions to Limited Liability. Liability may be imposed upon a shareholder as though there were no corporation when either the court ignores the corporate entity because of the particular circumstances of the case, or when the corporation is so defectively organized that it is deemed not to exist.

(1) Wage Claims. Statutes sometimes provide that the shareholders shall be unlimitedly liable for the wage claims of corporate employees. This principle has been abandoned in some states in recent years or has been confined to the major shareholders of corporations of which the stock is not sold publicly.

(2) Unpaid Subscriptions. Most states prohibit the issuance of par value shares for less than par or except for "money, labor done, or property actually received." Whenever shares issued by a corporation are not fully paid for, the original subscriber receiving the shares or any transferee who

[96] Claman v Robertson, 164 Ohio 61, 128 NE2d 429.

[97] Ingalls Iron Works Co. v Ingalls Foundation, 266 Ala 656, 98 So2d 30.

does not give value, or who knows that the shares were not fully paid, may be liable for the unpaid balance if the corporation is insolvent and the money is required to pay the debts of creditors.[98]

If the corporation has issued the shares as fully paid, or has given them as a bonus, or has agreed to release the subscriber for the unpaid balance, the corporation cannot recover that balance. The fact that the corporation is thus barred does not prevent the creditors of the corporation from bringing an action to compel payment of the balance.[99] The same rules are applied when stock is issued as fully paid in return for property or services which are overvalued so that the stock is not actually paid for in full. There is a conflict of authority, however, as to whether the shareholder is liable from the mere fact that the property or service he gave for the shares was in fact overvalued by the directors or whether in addition it must be shown that the directors had acted in bad faith in making the erroneous valuation. The trend of modern statutes is to prohibit disputing the valuation placed by the corporation on services or property in the absence of proof of fraud.[100]

If a statute makes void the shares issued for less than par, they may be canceled upon suit of the corporation.

*(3) **Unauthorized Dividends.*** If dividends are improperly paid out of capital, the shareholders generally are liable to creditors to the extent of such depletion of capital. In some states the liability of the shareholder depends on whether the corporation was insolvent at the time, whether the debts were existing at the time, and whether the shareholders had notice of the source of the dividend.

*(4) **Insider Information.*** A person who has knowledge of inside information about a corporation, such as a discovery which it has made or action with respect to dividends, and who takes advantage of another person who lacks that information, as by inducing him to sell his stock at a low price, is liable for the amount of the damages caused the other party.[101]

*(5) **Short-Swing Profits.*** The Act of 1934 permits a corporation to recover from a major shareholder the profit which he has made on a short-swing sale. Specifically any security holder who owns and sells more than 10% of the securities of the corporation within a six-months' period after he purchases them must pay to the corporation the profit which he made on such sale. This provision also applies to directors and officers of corporations whose securities are registered, without regard to the percentage of stock owned by such director or officer.

---

[98] Under ABA MBCA § 25, the transferee is protected if he acts in good faith without knowledge or notice that the shares were not fully paid.

[99] Strong v Crancer, 335 Mo 1209, 76 SW2d 383.

[100] Haselbush v Alsco, 161 Colo 138, 421 P2d 113.

[101] Securities Act of 1934, § 10(b), Rule 10b-5.

The statute authorizes the recovery of a short-swing profit without regard to whether there is any fraudulent intent or conduct which is improper by general principles of law.[102]

§ 51:19. The Professional Corporation. The liability of a shareholder in a professional corporation is limited to the same degree as that of a shareholder in an ordinary business corporation. Several fact situations may arise:

(1) Act of Shareholder in Creating Liability. If a shareholder in a professional corporation negligently drives the company car in going to attend a patient, or personally obligates himself on a contract made for the corporation, or is guilty of malpractice, he is liable without limit for the liability that has been created. This is the same rule of law that applies in the case of the ordinary business corporation. Professional corporation statutes generally repeat the rule with respect to malpractice liability by stating that the liability of a shareholder for malpractice is not affected by the fact of incorporation.

(2) Malpractice of an Associate. The liability of a shareholder in a professional corporation for the malpractice of an associate is not clear. If Doctors *A, B,* and *C* are a partnership, each is unlimitedly liable for any malpractice liability incurred by the others. Assume that Doctors *A, B,* and *C* are a professional corporation, will *A* be liable for the malpractice of *C*? If the orthodox rule applicable to business corporations applies here, the answer is "no liability." The statutory reference to malpractice liability is generally not very clear, and it is possible that a conservative court will interpret the statutory preservation of malpractice liability as preserving the liability of one professional man for the act of his associates when such liability would exist if they were a partnership.

(3) Ordinary Torts. If an ordinary tort, meaning one not related to malpractice, is committed, each shareholder is protected from liability for the acts of others. For example, assume that in order to aid a patient, a medical corporation sends its secretary after hours with medicine to a patient's home. In the course of the trip the secretary negligently runs over a pedestrian. In such a case both the secretary and the corporation would be liable for the harm caused the pedestrian. Would a shareholder be liable?

It should be concluded that a shareholder would not be liable. Here the ordinary rule of limited liability for a shareholder should apply. Since the situation described does not involve "malpractice," there is no possibility of concluding that there is a liability of a shareholder under a malpractice exception to the general rule of limited liability. Consequently, in the absence of an express contrary statement in the professional corporation statute, a shareholder in the professional corporation is shielded from liability in the case of ordinary torts of others.

---

[102] Securities Act of 1934, § 16(a), 16(b).

CASES FOR CHAPTER 51

Lindsey v Stein Brothers & Boyce, Inc.

222 Tenn 149, 433 SW2d 669 (1968)

Lindsey owned shares of stock. He telephoned Brooks, a member of the brokerage firm of Stein Brothers & Boyce, to sell his shares when the market reached $85 a share. Brooks agreed to make the sale but failed to do so. The stock was not sold until the market price had fallen to $64 a share. Lindsey sued Stein Brothers for breach of the agreement to sell the shares at $85 a share. Stein Brothers raised the defense that there was no writing to satisfy the Statute of Frauds with respect to that agreement. From a judgment in favor of the defendants, Lindsey appealed.

BURNETT, C.J. . . . The stockbroker . . . filed an amended demurrer which in effect alleged that the contract was not in writing signed by the parties against whom enforcement was sought sufficient to indicate a sale for a stated quantity of described securities at a definite or stated price as required by UCC § 8-319. . . .

Obviously the question presented is whether or not the contract between a stockbroker and his customer whereby the broker is engaged on a commission basis to sell stock for the customer is subject to this Statute of Frauds. . . .

. . . Where one contracts with a broker to act as his agent in purchasing stock for him, such a contract is one of agency rather than for the sale of goods, wares, or merchandise. Such contract of agency is not within the Statute of Frauds." . . .

[UCC §] 8-219 establishes that "A contract for the sale of securities is not enforceable by way of action or defense unless . . ." one of four stated conditions is met. The language of this section of the Code indicates that only contracts involving a sale of securities must meet the Statute of Fraud requirements. The issue to be decided may be disposed of by determining whether the contract between broker and customer is one for the sale of securities. To reach the preceding issue, one must define the word "sale." [UCC §] 2-106 states that "A 'sale' consists in the passing of title from the seller to the buyer for a price." Obviously, the contract sued on in the present case does not in any way allege a sale. All that is alleged is the simple instruction to a stockbroker by the owner of the stock to take his stock and sell it at a certain price. These facts establish not a sale but only an agency relationship.

. . . The definition of a sale found in [UCC §] 2-106 . . . is specifically applicable only to Article 2 of the UCC dealing with sales. However, the definition can certainly be adopted to apply to [UCC §] 8-319 since Article 8 contains no definition of sale. If the definition of "sale" contained in [UCC §] 2-106, above quoted, is adopted to apply to [UCC §] 8-319, . . . the most important fact involved in determining whether the case presently before the court involves a contract of sale is whether title passes from the customer to the broker and then to the ultimate purchaser, whether the broker was merely a conduit, the title never vesting in him but passing directly from the seller to the customer.

It seems . . . this . . . is logically sound and clearly was within the purpose of the UCC as expressed in [UCC §] 1-102(2), which is to bring the law governing commercial transactions into accord with actual commercial practice.

. . . It is easy . . . to see how from a practical standpoint it would be impossible for one to call a stockbroker and tell him to buy or sell some shares of this or that and to have any writing to substantiate the telephone conversation. . . .

[Judgment reversed and action remanded.]

Welland Investment Corp. v First National Bank

81 NJ Super 180, 195 A2d 210 (1963)

Lane borrowed money from the Welland Investment Corp. pledging as security several certificates representing shares of common stock of Mercury Photo Corp., a Delaware corporation. Lane defaulted on his loan, entitling the Welland Investment Corp. to dispose of the collateral. It presented the stock certificates to Mercury's local transfer agent, the First National Bank, and requested the making of a

transfer of the stock to it. The First National Bank refused to do so without the approval of Mercury. Mercury took no action and the transfer was not made. Welland Investment Corp. then sued First National Bank to compel it to make the transfer and to obtain damages for its refusal.

MATTHEWS, J. . . . The bank . . . has ignored subsection (a) of [UCC §] 8-406(1) . . . as follows:

"(1) Where a person acts as authenticating trustee, transfer agent, registrar, or other agent for an issuer in the registration of transfers of its securities or in the issue of new securities or in the cancellation of surrendered securities, (a) he is under a duty to the issuer to exercise good faith and due diligence in performing his functions; and (b) he has with regard to the particular functions he performs the same obligation to the holder or owner of the security and has the same rights and privileges as the issuer has in regard to those functions."

When subsection (b) is read in conjunction with subsection (a), . . . it is at once apparent that the intent of the entire subsection (1) is to equate the obligation of a transfer agent toward the holder of a security with that of the obligation of the issuer. The net effect of this is to abolish the artificial concept formerly found in our law to the effect that an agent could not be held personally liable toward third parties for acts constituting mere nonfeasance. . . . Proper construction of [UCC §] 8-406 . . . dictates that the obligations of the transfer agent are the same as that of the issuer. Thus, the net effect of these two sections is to establish that the issuer and any of its transfer agents have equal obligations to security holders. . . .

[Action set down for hearing as to facts.]

McDaniel v Painter

(CA10 Kan) 418 F2d 545 (1969)

The Painters owned the majority of stock of the First National Bank. McDaniel and two others owned a minority of the shares. The Painters contracted to sell their stock to Danehower for more than its book value and the buyer agreed to employ one of the Painters in the bank. The minority stockholders brought an action against the Painters and Danehower to recover damages for the reduction caused by the sale in the value of the stock held by them. A judgment was entered for the defendants. The plaintiffs appealed.

HILL, C.J. . . . Appellants urge that a fiduciary relationship existed between majority and minority stockholders of the banking corporation, which obligation was breached by the act of selling and purchasing, . . . by failing to inform minority shareholders of the offer to purchase, and by the sale of stock by insiders at a price not available to minority stockholders. . . .

. . . The controversy centers around and was precipitated by a sale of controlling interest stock in The First National Bank of Chanute, Kansas, on March 2, 1966. Prior to the sale, Dale and R. D. Painter owned 5157 of the 10,000 outstanding shares of capital stock in the Chanute bank; appellants cumulatively control 770 shares. During the preceding ten years very little trading was done in the bank's capital stock, with the per share book value fluctuating upwards from $46.40 in 1955 to approximately $98.00 in 1966. Early in 1965, Dale Painter, with the aid of a disinterested bank, evaluated the worth of the Painter family's interest in the Chanute bank. Several banks in the vicinity were informed of the Painters' willingness to sell to a qualified buyer and requested those banks, in a confidential manner, to refer prospective purchasers to Dale. Ultimately, appellee Danehower was directed to the Chanute bank and, following several months of negotiation and investigation, in March, 1966, bought the Painters' fifty-one percent interest for $690,000 consideration. Included in the sales contract was provision for assignment of a credit life insurance agency and its assets as well as an agreement that Dale would be retained on the bank's staff for five years at an annual salary of $10,000, personally guaranteed by Danehower in the event the bank released Dale. Of the Painter family, only Dale remains, serving as Chairman of the Board; Danehower is now bank president. After the election of new officers, Dale and Danehower entered into another agreement, the substance of which was that Dale would be retained as a bank employee for five years at $10,000 per annum, to provide the bank his knowledge, experience and business acumen. Since the sale of controlling stock, there is absolutely no indication in the record that the bank has suffered from the change in ownership. . . .

The cornerstone of appellants' case proposed that a fiduciary duty exists regarding the sale of corporate stock by dominant stockholders and that a breach of that obligation may be redressed by individual stockholder suits. . . . "[E]very stockholder, including a majority holder, is at liberty to dispose of his shares at any time and for any price to which he may agree without being liable to other stockholders . . . as long as he does not dominate, interfere with, or mislead other stockholders in exercising the same rights." In other words, a dominant or majority stockholder does not become a fiduciary for other shareholders by reason of mere ownership of stock. It is only when one steps out of the role as a stockholder and acts in the corporate management, with disregard for the interests and welfare of the corporation and its stockholders that he assumes the burden of fiducial responsibility. Thus, when transferring control of the corporation, the managing majority are dutybound not to sell controlling interest to outsiders if the circumstances surrounding the proposed transfer would alert suspicion in a prudent man that the purchasers are an irresponsible group who will mismanage and loot the corporate assets.

The fact that controlling stock sells for more than book value, as it did here, is not evidence of fraud since it is generally recognized that majority stock is more valuable than minority stock. Neither is there merit in the argument that appellees, as dominant shareholders, must refrain from receiving a premium which reflects the control potential of the stock. . . .

The cases relied upon by appellants graphically illustrate the imposition of a fiduciary duty in a multiplicity of situations involving stock sales. Notwithstanding, while each stands for a well stated principle, their rules are inapposite to the facts of this case. In those decisions in which recovery had been granted, the sales involved elements of fraud, misuse of confidential information, looting, siphoning off for personal gain of a business advantage rightfully belonging to the corporation and shareholders in common, or wrongfully appropriating corporate assets. The inappropriateness of these cases is highlighted by appellants' admissions that they know of no specific misconduct on the part of the new management other than the propriety of the loan and the employment contract with Dale Painter.

The sale to Danehower appears in all respects to be fair, free of secret or undisclosed arrangements which could create a suspicious atmosphere, and was consummated in the utmost of good faith. The confidential nature of the transaction and the continued employment of Dale Painter are not indicative of a plot to loot and mismanage the bank but rather reflect the high concern of all parties that the transition period be as smooth and business-like as possible. There is not even a scintilla of evidence to the contrary. To condemn the kind of transaction involved in this case would tend strongly to discourage stock investments and would be a menace to the efficient management of corporate business.

The general rule in Kansas provides that "shares of stock of a corporation are personal property, and may be transferred like any other property, unless the transfer is restrained by the charter or articles of association . . . ." . . . No mention has been made about restraints on alienation within the corporate charter or articles of incorporation. The spirit and letter of the law have not been violated by parties to the sale. Appellees were free to sell their ownership in the bank to persons who, upon satisfactory investigation, proved to be of sufficient financial worth and good character.

[Judgment affirmed.]

Bohannan v The Corporation Commission

82 Ariz 299, 313 P2d 379 (1957)

Bohannan and others presented the articles of a new corporation to the Arizona Corporation

Commission for filing. The Commission refused to accept the charter for filing on the ground that the cumulative voting provision of the state constitution was violated by the articles in creating a nine-member elective board of directors, three of whom were to be elected each year. Bohannan brought an action to compel the Commission to accept and file the charter. From a judgment in favor of the Commission, Bohannan appealed.

STRUCKMEYER, J. . . . Article 14, Section 10, of the Arizona Constitution provides:

"In all elections for directors or managers of any corporation, each shareholder shall have the right to cast as many votes in the aggregate as he shall be entitled to vote in same company under its charter multiplied by the number of directors or managers to be elected at such election; and each shareholder may cast the whole number of votes, either in person or by proxy, for one candidate, or distribute such votes among two or more such candidates; and such directors or managers shall not be elected otherwise." . . .

Any scheme, plan, or device which completely denies the effectiveness of cumulative voting must necessarily fall. . . .

It is urged by appellees that the general effect of staggering directors by terms is to reduce the number of directors which can be elected by minority stockholders. . . . If this argument has any validity, it must be predicated on the proposition that the Constitution demands that minority stockholders be represented on corporate boards in proportion to or at least somewhat in the ratio to the number of shares owned or controlled by such minority. . . . If we are unable to find that the Constitution either by direct expression or fair implication requires proportionate representation, we will be compelled to render a construction which is consistent with the normal and ordinary meaning of the words. Such a construction merely guarantees that a means be provided whereby it is possible for some minority entitled to participate in the elections to secure representation on the board and would not guarantee to a minority stockholder or any particular percentage less than 49 percent a director of his or their choosing.

In Wolfson v Avery, [6 Ill2d 78, 126 NE 2d 710] the Illinois court [held invalid the election of directors by staggered terms and] found that the phrase . . . "to be elected" [a provision of the Illinois constitution similar to that of Arizona], expressed a recognition that the number of directors varied as between corporations and did not contemplate the possibility that less than the whole number of directors might be elected at any particular annual meeting. . . . In the dissenting opinion it was pointed out that there was no express prohibition in the Constitution against classification and the staggering of directors when the words of the Constitution are taken in their ordinary signification. We have examined both arguments advanced . . . and can say that each has some element of logical plausibility. We are more inclined to agree with the dissenting justice, but do not expressly base our conclusions on this alone. Rather to the extent that Article 14, Section 10, is susceptible of two possible interpretations in that reasonable men may differ as to the import of its language, we find it to be ambiguous.

We will, therefore, look beyond the article for assistance in determining its meaning. . . . And in so doing examine into, ascertain, and give effect to the intent and purpose of the framers of the Constitution. . . . In this we are unable to conclude, as did the Illinois court, that it was the intention of the framers of the Constitution to require that minority shareholders be represented on corporate boards in proportion to the percent of shares controlled by them, [as the statements made at the Constitutional Convention referred only to *some* representation of minority stockholders.]

[Judgment reversed.]

Minnesota ex rel Pillsbury v Honeywell, Inc.

291 Minn 322, 191 NW2d 406 (1971)

Pillsbury was opposed to the war in Vietnam. He learned that Honeywell was manufacturing anti-personnel fragmentation bombs to be used in that war. He purchased 100 shares

of stock of Honeywell so that he could inspect its books and ascertain just what was being done. Honeywell refused to permit the inspection of its books. He began a lawsuit in the name of the state against Honeywell in order to compel inspection of the corporate books. Judgment was entered against him and he appealed.

KELLY, J. . . . Petitioner [Pillsbury] appeals from an order and judgment . . . denying . . . a petition to compel respondent, Honeywell, . . . to produce its original shareholder ledger, current shareholder ledger, and all corporate records dealing with weapons and munitions manufacture. . . .

The issues raised by petitioner are as follows: . . . (2) whether petitioner, who bought shares in respondent corporation for the purpose of changing its policy of manufacturing war munitions, had a proper purpose germane to a shareholder's interest. . . .

. . . While inspection will not be permitted for purposes of curiosity, speculation, or vexation, adverseness to management and a desire to gain control of the corporation for economic benefit does not indicate an improper purpose.

Several courts agree with petitioner's contention that a mere desire to communicate with other shareholders is . . . a proper purpose. . . . This would seem to confer an almost absolute right to inspection. We believe that a better rule would allow inspections only if the shareholder has a proper purpose for such communication. This rule was applied in McMahon v Dispatch Printing Co., 101 NJL 470, 129 A 425 (1925), where inspection was denied because the shareholder's objective was to discredit politically the president of the company, who was also the New Jersey secretary of state.

The act of inspecting a corporation's shareholder ledger and business records must be viewed in its proper perspective. In terms of the corporate norm, inspection is merely the act of the concerned owner checking on what is in part his property. In the context of the large firm, inspection can be more akin to a weapon in corporate warfare. The effectiveness of the weapon is considerable: "Considering the huge size of many modern corporations and the necessarily complicated nature of their bookkeeping, it is plain that to permit their thousands of stockholders to roam at will through their records would render impossible not only any attempt to keep their records efficiently, but the proper carrying on of their businesses." . . . Because the power to inspect may be the power to destroy, it is important that only those with a bona fide interest in the corporation enjoy that power. . . .

Petitioner had utterly no interest in the affairs of Honeywell before he learned of Honeywell's production of fragmentation bombs. Immediately after obtaining this knowledge, he purchased stock in Honeywell for the sole purpose of asserting ownership privileges in an effort to force Honeywell to cease such production. . . . But for his opposition to Honeywell's policy, petitioner probably would not have bought Honeywell stock . . . and would not desire to communicate with Honeywell's shareholders. His avowed purpose in buying Honeywell stock was to place himself in a position to try to impress his opinions . . . upon Honeywell management and its other shareholders. Such a motivation can hardly be deemed a proper purpose germane to his economic interest as a shareholder.

. . . Petitioner had already formed strong opinions on the immorality and the social and economic wastefulness of war long before he bought stock in Honeywell. His sole motivation was to change Honeywell's course of business because that course was incompatible with his political views. If unsuccessful, petitioner indicated that he would sell the Honeywell stock.

We do not mean to imply that a shareholder with a bona fide investment interest could not bring this suit if motivated by concern with the long- or short-term economic effects on Honeywell resulting from the production of war munitions. Similarly, this suit might be appropriate when a shareholder has a bona fide concern about the adverse effects of abstention from profitable war contracts on his investment in Honeywell.

In the instant case, however, the trial court, in effect, has found from all the facts that petitioner was not interested in even the long-term well-being of Honeywell or the enhancement of the value of his shares. His sole purpose was to persuade the company to adopt his social and political concerns, irrespective of any economic benefit to himself or Honeywell. This puropse on the part of one buying into the corporation does not entitle the petitioner to inspect Honeywell's books and records.

Petitioner argues that he wishes to inspect the stockholder ledger in order that he may correspond with other shareholders with the hope of electing to the board one or more directors who represent his particular viewpoint. . . . While a plan to elect one or more directors is specific and the election of directors normally would be a proper purpose, here the purpose was not germane to petitioner's or Honeywell's economic interest. Instead, the plan was designed to further petitioner's political and social beliefs. Since the requisite propriety of purpose germane to his or Honeywell's economic interest is not present, the allegation that petitioner seeks to elect a new board of directors is insufficient to compel inspection. . . .

[Judgment affirmed.]

Goldstein v Studley

(Mo App) 452 SW2d 75 (1970)

Marvin and Betty Goldstein were shareholders of the Missouri Machinery and Engineering Company. They owned one half of its stock. The other half was owned by James and Eileen Studley. The two families held all the corporate offices. They could not agree on how the corporation should be run. The Goldsteins brought a derivative action to obtain the appointment of a receiver for the corporation and to liquidate the corporation. The relief requested was refused and the Goldsteins appealed.

RICKHOFF, J. . . . The business of Missouri Machinery and Engineering Co. consists of the sale and service of pumps, motors, compressors, and supplying accompanying engineering and installation services. Mr. Studley and Mr. Goldstein are both active in the business, Mr. Goldstein being responsible, in general, for "outside" work and Mr. Studley being generally responsible for "inside" work. Mr. Goldstein's duties relate primarily to sales and direct contacts with customers of the company. Mr. Studley's duties relate primarily to operation of the shop and supervision of the shop employees. There was in actual practice a certain amount of overlapping in the performance of the respective duties of the two men and also certain duties for the performance of which the responsibility was not clear. Mr. Goldstein complained that Mr. Studley did not properly supervise the shop employees, did not schedule work properly, and failed to keep adequate time records on jobs. Mr. Studley complained that Mr. Goldstein failed to collect the company's accounts receivable and interfered with and harassed Mr. Studley in his work.

Prior to 1967, Mr. Goldstein had taken the company's inventory and the corporation's tax returns were prepared on the basis of the inventories taken by him. In 1967, Mr. Studley objected to the inventory valuations used by Mr. Goldstein and the latter refused to take an inventory for the end of the year 1967. Mr. Studley took an inventory, but the company's bookkeeper felt the figures were inflated and declined to prepare a 1967 income tax return based on those inventory figures. Mr. Goldstein refused to take an inventory, and neither Mr. Studley nor Mr. Goldstein would sign a tax return based on the inventory figures supplied by Mr. Studley, and at the time of trial, in November 1968, no 1967 income tax return had been filed. In prior years it had been the practice for the company's bookkeeper to prepare monthly financial statements, but he testified he had been unable to do so during 1968 since he had been unable to close the books for 1967 because Mr. Goldstein and Mr. Studley were unable to agree upon the inventory. It is apparent that the inventory made by Mr. Studley was based upon the selling price of the articles comprising the inventory, whereas in prior years the cost price had been used.

The gross amount of the corporation's sales for the years prior to 1964 were not shown, but for the years 1964 through 1966 there was an increase in sales from $119,942.83 to $126,648.59. The sales for 1967 were not shown, but for the first nine months of 1968, sales were only $4,842.69.

Although Mr. Goldstein and Mr. Studley each blame the other for their numerous, and for the most part, petty disagreements, it is apparent that they are unable to cooperate in the management of the corporation's business. They have not even been able to discuss their problems and attempt to resolve them. Whether the failure to prepare an inventory at the end of 1967 is the fault of Mr. Goldstein for refusing to perform the task he had performed in previous years, or is the fault of Mr. Studley for criticizing the valuation methods used by Mr. Goldstein in the past and then preparing an inventory which even the firm's bookkeeper refused to use in preparing a tax return, is immaterial. The important fact is that as a result of their disagreement, it had not been possible at the time of the trial, in November 1968, to prepare and file the corporation's income tax return which was due months earlier. The same comment is applicable to the inability of the principals to work out a method for keeping records of time spent on performing the company's orders, with resultant loss in billings to the company's customers, and to all of the other wrangles of the principals. It no doubt would have been to the best interests of the parties to come to an agreement, and perhaps individuals acting in a more reasonable manner would have accommodated themselves to each other to their mutual profit. But it is not the province of this court to decide whether parties should work in harmony or whether it would be advantageous for them to do so. The duty of this court is to determine whether, in fact, the directors are deadlocked in the management of the corporate affairs, whether the shareholders are unable to break that deadlock, and whether, as a result, irreparable injury to the corporation is being suffered or is threatened.

We find that the directors are deadlocked and that the shareholders are unable to break the deadlock. The directors are apparently unable to agree upon any action. Since this is a four member board of directors and the shares are evenly divided, there is no possibility of either side electing a majority of the directors even if an election could be conducted. It appears that the shareholders are unable to progress to the point of selecting a chairman for a shareholders' meeting, much less transact any business.

. . . Irreparable damage is threatened the corporation by reason of the deadlock in management. . . . The drastic situation in which the corporation will soon find itself if events continue according to the recent pattern is suggested by the drop in sales during 1968. For the first nine months of that year sales amounted to only $4,842.69, whereas for the last prior year for which figures were shown (1966) sales were $126,648.59. Accounts receivable due the company have accumulated for lack of proper attention to collection. If the corporation is unable to perform essential functions such as filing tax returns and collecting accounts receivable, and if its sales are to continue at a minimal rate, it is apparent that its insolvency is only a matter of time. We believe it necessary for the protection of all who may ultimately be affected by that eventuality that the process be halted at this time. . . .

[Judgment reversed and action remanded.]

QUESTIONS AND CASE PROBLEMS

1. Graham was a shareholder of Commercial Credit Co. As a result of a stock split, he became entitled to additional shares. A certificate representing these shares was sent by registered mail to his home in Baltimore. At the time he was in California. The envelope containing the share certificate was received and receipted for by one servant in his house and was placed in a basket of mail by another servant, awaiting his return. The stock certificate apparently disappeared thereafter. Graham demanded that the corporation issue a new certificate to him for the missing certificate. When this was refused unless he would furnish indemnity against loss should the original certificate be found, Graham refused to furnish security and brought suit claiming that the shares had never been issued to him on the theory that

the domestic servant had no authority to receive the stock certificate and to sign a receipt for it. Was he correct? [Graham v Commercial Credit Co., 41 Del Ch 580, 200 A2d 828]

2. Elizabeth Szabo, who owned stock of the American Telephone & Telegraph Co., was notified by the company that there had been a three-for-one split of the company's stock effective as of April 24, 1959, and that on May 29, 1959, the company would prepare and mail to her an additional stock certificate representing twice the number of shares already held by her. Upon receiving the notice from the company, Szabo indorsed on her certificate a transfer to herself and her son as joint tenants with the right of survivorship. She delivered the indorsed certificate to the stock transfer agent of the corporation but directed him to hold up the transfer of the stock until the new certificate for the split shares was available. The stock transfer agent was also notified to have the new certificate made out to Szabo and her son as joint tenants with the right of survivorship. Three days before the new certificate for the stock split was issued, Szabo died. Her son claimed the original shares of stock from her estate and the new shares issued on the stock split. Was he entitled to all these shares? [Szabo's Estate, 10 NY2d 123, 217 NYS2d 593, 176 NE2d 395]

3. Smallwood made a contract to purchase stock of the Re-Mark Chemical Co. from Moretti. Moretti did not deliver the stock certificate to Smallwood but gave him a written assignment of 5,000 shares and directed the company to issue 5,000 shares to Smallwood. There was a delay in issuing the certificate because of certain stock registration problems. Meanwhile four dividends were declared on the stock. They were received by Moretti, who paid them to Smallwood, who accepted them without question. Shortly thereafter the Re-Mark Co. went into bankruptcy reorganization, and Smallwood then sought to set aside the purchase from Moretti. He claimed that the purchase was not effective because no stock certificate had been issued to him and therefore he had not been given the legal title to the stock. Was he entitled to set the sale aside? [Smallwood v Moretti, (Fla App) 128 So2d 628]

4. The Skinner Packing Co., which was incorporated under the laws of Maine, was authorized to do business in Nebraska where it had its principal place of business. The company sent an agent to Excelsior Springs, Mo., where he made a contract for the sale of 100 shares of stock in the company to Rhines. Within a year thereafter, Rhines concluded that he had been swindled and brought an action against the company to recover the purchase price of the stock. He based his claim upon a violation of the Missouri Blue-Sky Law. The defendant asserted that the transaction was not governed by the Missouri statute. Do you agree? [Rhines v Skinner Packing Co., 108 Neb 105, 187 NW 874]

5. A bylaw of the Coleman Realty Co. provided that the corporation could not sell its stock to a person not a shareholder without first offering to sell it at its book value to the corporation or to the remaining shareholders in proportion to their interests. This bylaw was later repealed at a shareholders' meeting by the vote of Mrs. Ludgate who owned a majority of the stock. Bechtold, a minority shareholder, brought an action to declare that the repeal of the bylaw was invalid and had no effect. Was the repeal of the bylaw effective? [Bechtold v Coleman Realty Co., 367 Pa 208, 79 A2d 661]

6. A dealer sold goods to a corporation. When the corporation failed to pay him, he sued *X* who owned a block of shares of the corporation and had been active in organizing the corporation. Was *X* liable? [Blond Lighting Fixture Supply Co. v Funk, (Tex Civ App) 392 SW2d 586]
7. Lehman was a shareholder of the National Benefit Insurance Co., which had been incorporated under the laws of Iowa. He brought an action to compel the corporation to permit him to inspect and copy records and documents of the corporation. It was admitted that he had the right to inspect the papers. Did he have a right to make copies of them? [Lehman v National Benefit Insurance Co., 243 Iowa 1348, 53 NW2d 872]
8. Siebrecht organized a corporation called the Siebrecht Realty Co. and then transferred his building to the corporation in exchange for its stock. The corporation rented different parts of the building to different tenants. Elenkrieg, an employee of one of the tenants, fell and was injured because of the defective condition of a stairway. She sued Siebrecht individually on the ground that the corporation had been formed by him for the purpose of securing limited liability. Decide. [Elenkrieg v Siebrecht, 238 NY 254, 144 NE 519]
9. Chandler owned stock in a corporation. The stock was taxed by the town of New Gloucester as property owned by Chandler. Sweetsir, the proper official, sued Chandler for the taxes due. Chandler defended on the ground that the stock should be taxed as evidence of a debt, the same as a bond, and that the tax as assessed was therefore unlawful. Was his contention valid? [Sweetsir v Chandler, 98 Maine 145, 56 A584]
10. The stock of *X* Corporation was subject to certain transfer restrictions. When *X* Corporation was dissolved, *A*, a shareholder, then sold his stock to *B* but did not comply with the stock transfer restrictions. It was claimed that *B* had not acquired any of the rights of *A* by such transfer. Was this correct? [Mischer v Burke, (Tex Civ App) 456 SW2d 550]

52 Management of Corporations

§ **52:1. Introduction.** A corporation is managed, directly or indirectly, by its shareholders, board of directors, and officers.

Since the shareholders elect the directors, they indirectly determine the management policies of the business.[1] Without express authorization by the corporation, however, a shareholder cannot bind it by contract.

§ **52:2. Meetings of Shareholders.** To have legal effect, action by the shareholders must be taken at a regular or special meeting.

(1) Regular Meetings. The time and place of regular or stated meetings are usually prescribed by the articles of incorporation or bylaws. Notice to shareholders of such meetings is ordinarily not required, but it is usually given as a matter of good business practice. Some statutes require that notice be given of all meetings, and generally notice must be given specifying the subject matter when the meeting is of an unusual character.

(2) Special Meetings. Unless otherwise prescribed, special meetings are called by the directors. It is sometimes provided that a special meeting may be called by a certain percentage of shareholders.[2] The purpose of this alternative method is to prevent a board of directors from ruling the corporation with an iron hand. Statutes conferring upon designated persons the privilege of calling a special meeting must be followed, and persons not designated by the statute may not call a meeting.[3]

Notice of the day, hour, and the place of a special meeting must be given to all shareholders. The notice must also include a statement of the nature of the business to be transacted. No other business may be transacted at such a meeting.

If proper notice is not given, the defect may be cured at a properly held meeting by ratification of the action taken by the earlier meeting or the defect may be waived by those entitled to notice.[4]

---

[1] When the voting stock of a large corporation is widely held by small shareholders scattered over an extensive geographic area, this indirect control is not very effective and management tends to determine the policies of the corporation.

[2] New York Business Corporation Law § 603.

[3] Smith v Upshaw, 217 Ga 703, 124 SE2d 751.

[4] Camp v Shannon, 162 Tex 515, 348 SW2d 517.

(3) Quorum. A valid meeting requires the presence of a quorum of the voting shareholders. In order to constitute a quorum, usually a specified number of shareholders or a number authorized to vote a stated proportion of the voting stock must attend.[5] If a quorum is present, a majority of those present may act with respect to any matter, unless there is an express requirement of a greater affirmative vote.

When a meeting opens with a quorum, the quorum generally is not thereafter broken if shareholders leave the meeting and those remaining are not sufficient to constitute a quorum. This principle is designed to prevent obstructionist tactics by dissenting shareholders.

(4) No Meeting Action. A number of statutes provide for corporate action by shareholders without holding a meeting. The ABA MBCA provides that "Any action required by this Act to be taken at a meeting of the shareholders of a corporation, or any action which may be taken at a meeting of the shareholders, may be taken without a meeting if they consent in writing, setting forth the action so taken [and] signed by all of the shareholders entitled to vote with respect to the subject matter thereof." [6] Such provisions give flexibility of operation, which is needed by the small or close corporation.

§ 52:3. Directors. The management of a corporation is usually entrusted to a board of directors who are elected by the shareholders. Most states now permit the number of directors to be fixed by the bylaws.

Most states specify that the board of directors shall consist of not less than three directors. A few states authorize one or more directors.[7] Professional corporation legislation often authorizes or is interpreted as authorizing a one- or two-man board of directors.[8]

Statutory provisions for the classification of directors are common. The Model Act provides that when the board consists of nine or more members, the directors may be divided "into either two or three classes, each class to be as nearly equal in number as possible." [9]

(1) Qualifications. Eligibility for membership on a board of directors is determined by statute, certificate of incorporation, or bylaw. In the absence of a contrary provision, any person is eligible for membership, including a nonresident, a minor, or even a person who is not a shareholder.

Bylaws commonly require a director to own stock in the corporation, although ordinarily this requirement is not imposed by law. If a director is also a shareholder, he has a dual capacity and has rights both as a director and as a shareholder.

---

[5] The American Bar Association Model Business Corporation Act provides that unless stated in the articles of incorporation, a majority of the voting shares constitutes a quorum and that, in specifying the quorum in the articles, it cannot be set at less than one third of the shares entitled to vote at the particular meeting. ABA MBCA § 32.

[6] § 145.

[7] 8 Delaware Code Ann § 141(b). See also ABA MBCA § 36.

[8] Christian v Shideler, (Okla) 382 P2d 129.

[9] ABA MBCA § 37.

(2) Powers of Directors. The board of directors has authority to manage the corporation. The court will not interfere with its discretion in the absence of illegal conduct or fraud harming the rights of creditors, shareholders, or the corporation.

The board of directors may enter into any contract or transaction necessary to carry out the business for which the corporation was formed. The board may appoint officers and other agents to act for the company, or it may delegate authority to one or more of its members to do so. For example, it may appoint several of its own members as an executive committee to act for the board between board meetings.

Knowledge of a director of a corporation is knowledge of the corporation when the director acquires such knowledge while acting in the course of his employment and in the scope of his authority. Knowledge learned by a director while acting in his own interest, however, is not imputed to the corporation.

(3) Conflict of Interests. Directors may be involved in contracts or transactions with the corporation or may have a financial interest in a business which has such transactions or contracts. Frequently such a situation creates a conflict of interests in that the loyalty owed by the director to the corporation is in conflict with his personal economic interest or that of the other business in which he has an interest. A director is disqualified from taking part in corporate action with respect to a matter in which he has a conflicting interest. Since it cannot be known how the other directors would have voted if they had known of the conflict of interest, the corporation generally may avoid any transaction because of the director's conflict of interest when the directors did not know of the director's disqualification. Thus, a director who performs special services for his corporation cannot vote at a directors' meeting on a resolution to give him special compensation for such services.[10] In small corporations a person owning a substantial interest in the business will often have himself made a director and his attorney another director. When the situation is such that the owner-director is disqualified because of conflicting interest, the attorney-director is likewise disqualified.[11]

A director is not disqualified when the matter in question does not affect him personally.

A director is not disqualified from voting on a matter in which a near relative is interested, as the nearness of the relative is not regarded as an "interest" of the director so as to disqualify him from voting.[12]

A number of states provide by statute that the conflict of interest of a director does not impair the transaction or contract entered into or authorized

---

[10] Indurated Concrete Corp. v Abbott, 195 Md 496, 74 A2d 17.
[11] Sarner v Fox Hill, Inc., 151 Conn 437, 199 A2d 6.
[12] Rocket Mining Corp. v Gill, 25 Utah 2d 434, 483 P2d 897.

by the board of directors if the disqualified director discloses his interest and the contract or transaction is fair and reasonable with respect to the corporation.

§ 52:4. Meetings of Directors. Theoretically, action by directors can only be taken at a proper meeting of the board. Bylaws sometimes require the meeting to be held at a particular place. Most states expressly provide that the directors may meet either in or outside of the state of incorporation. Directors who participate without objection in a meeting irregularly held as to place or time other than as specified in the bylaws cannot object later.

Generally a director is not allowed to vote by proxy. The theory underlying the general rule is that he must attend personally to the affairs of the corporation. Similarly the directors as a board cannot delegate their duty to others. The general pattern is to require meetings of directors because of the advantage flowing from the interchange of ideas at such meetings, although most statutes make some provision permitting the skipping of such meetings.

(1) No Meeting Action. Most states permit action to be taken by the board of directors without the holding of an actual meeting.[13] It is commonly provided when such action is taken that it be set forth in writing and signed by all the directors. Moreover, when the directors and shareholders are the same persons, there is no objection to running a corporation in an informal manner. It is not necessary that the board of directors then act by means of a formal meeting.[14]

§ 52:5. Liability of Directors. Directors are fiduciaries entrusted with the management of the corporation. Corporate directors must exercise due care in the management of corporate affairs and are liable for loss sustained by the corporation when their negligence results in the selection of improper employees or officers who embezzle money from the corporation. Likewise, directors can be held liable for resulting loss when they have turned over to the president the control which the directors should have retained over management and permitted the president to make large unsecured loans to companies owned and controlled by him and failed to examine financial reports that would have disclosed such misconduct.[15]

Directors must manage the corporation for the good of all shareholders and may not ignore the interest or viewpoint of some of the shareholders merely because they constitute only a minority.[16]

While the fiduciary concept imposes liability upon directors for mismanagement, it also protects them as long as they act in a reasonable manner

---

[13] New Jersey Stat Ann § 14A:6-7(2).
[14] Remillong v Schneider, (ND) 185 NW2d 493.
[15] Nesse v Brown, 218 Tenn 686, 405 SW2d 577.
[16] Grognet v Fox Valley Trucking Service, 45 Wis 2d 235, 172 NW2d 812.

within the scope of their authority. They are not liable merely because, when viewed from the standpoint of later events, it would have been to the advantage of the corporation to have taken different action than the directors had taken.

Directors are not liable for losses resulting from their management when they have acted in good faith and with due diligence, and have exercised reasonable care. For willful or negligent acts, however, they are held strictly accountable, and they are bound by all rules that the law imposes on those in a fiduciary position. The exact degree to which a director will be deemed to hold a fiduciary position is not clear, however, and a director is not barred from purchasing for himself a controlling block of shares of the stock of the corporation in which he is director.[17]

The Model Act imposes liability upon the directors for the illegal payment of dividends, the illegal purchase by the corporation of its own shares, and illegal distributions of the assets of the corporation upon liquidation.[18]

Directors of a corporation are not personally liable for wrongs committed by the corporation merely by virtue of the fact that they are directors. It must be shown that they have authorized or ratified the improper conduct or have in some way participated therein. (See p. 1049, Wrigley v Nottingham.)

(1) Director's Liability for Conflict of Interests. When a director violates the rule prohibiting conflicting interests, the corporation may recover from him any secret profit that he has made. The ordinary rule of agency law as to loyalty determines his liability. When the corporation has sustained loss because it has taken the action advocated by the disqualified director, it will generally be able to hold him liable for the loss by applying the agency principles of loyalty and duty to inform of matters relevant to the transaction, namely, his interest.

(2) Action Against Director. Actions against directors should be brought by the corporation. If the corporation fails to act, as is the case when the directors alleged to be liable control the corporation, one or more shareholders may bring the action in a representative capacity for the corporation.

(3) Removal of Directors. Ordinarily directors are removed by the vote of the shareholders. In some states the board of directors may remove a director and elect his successor on the ground that the director removed (a) did not accept office; (b) failed to satisfy the qualifications for office; (c) was continuously absent from the state without a leave of absence granted by the board, generally for a period of six months or more; (d) was adjudicated a bankrupt; (e) was convicted of a felony; (f) was unable to

[17] Vulcanized Rubber & Plastics Co. v Scheckter, 400 Pa 405, 162 A2d 400.

[18] ABA MBCA § 48. The earlier version of the Model Act also imposed liability upon directors for loans made to officers and directors and for the amount of capital not paid into the corporation if it commenced doing business before it obtained $1,000. These two provisions were deleted from the present version of the Model Act, although they are found in a number of state statutes which have followed the earlier Model Act.

perform his duties as director because of any illness or disability, generally for a period of six months or more; or (g) has been judicially declared of unsound mind.[19]

The Model Act provides for removal of directors "with or without cause" by a majority vote of the shareholders.[20]

(4) Resignation of Directors. The fact that a director resigns does not wipe out any liability which he may have incurred because of his conduct. Consequently, when a director could be liable to a corporation because of self-interest arising from his being the vice-president of another corporation, the director is not shielded from liability by the fact that he resigned from the first corporation before the plan to which objection is made was carried through to completion; it is sufficient that he was a director when the plan was initiated or begun.[21] As a practical matter, however, it may be that the protesting shareholders will be content to drop the claim against the director once he has resigned. If they have already brought a class action against the director, court approval is commonly required in order to discontinue the action.

§ 52:6. Officers of the Corporation. Corporations will generally have a president, at least one vice-president, a secretary, and a treasurer. Corporation codes generally expressly permit the same person to be both secretary and treasurer. In larger corporations there will often be a recording secretary and a corresponding secretary.

(1) Appointment. Sometimes the officers are elected by the shareholders, but usually they are appointed by the board of directors. The Model Act follows the general pattern of providing for the selection of officers by the board of directors.[22] Ordinarily no particular formality need be observed in making such appointments. There are seldom particular qualifications required of officers. Unless prohibited, a director may hold an executive office. The Model Act and state statutes commonly provide that one person may hold two or more corporate offices. In some instances a limitation is imposed, as by the Model Act, which prohibits the same person from being both president and secretary of the corporation.[23]

§ 52:7. Powers of Officers. The officers of a corporation are its agents but the scope of their authority varies. Consequently, their powers are controlled by the laws of agency. As in the case of any other agency, the third person has the burden of proving that a particular officer has the authority which he purports to have. Moreover, if the third person knows that a particular act

---

[19] See California Corporations Code § 807, recognizing grounds (a), (b), (e), and (g).

[20] ABA MBCA § 39.

[21] Bentz v Vardaman Mfg., (Miss) 210 So2d 35.

[22] ABA MBCA § 50.

[23] § 50.

requires the adoption of a resolution by the board of directors, he cannot rely on the apparent authority of the president or other corporate officer to perform the act.[24]

(1) ***President.*** It is sometimes held that in the absence of some limitation upon his authority, the president of a corporation has, by virtue of his office, authority to act as agent on behalf of the corporation within the scope of the business in which the corporation is empowered to engage. It has been held, however, that the president has such broad powers only when he is the general manager of the corporation and then such powers stem from the office of general manager and not from that of president. In any event, the president does not have authority by virtue of his office to make a contract which because of its unusual character would require action by the board of directors. The president, therefore, cannot make a contract to fix the compensation to be paid a director of the corporation, to make long-term or unusual contracts of employment, to bind the corporation as a guarantor, to release a claim of the corporation, or to promise that the corporation will later repurchase shares which are issued to a subscriber.

It is ordinarily held that the president of a business corporation is not authorized to execute commercial paper in the name of the corporation merely because he is president, although he may do so if he is authorized by the board of directors to borrow money for the corporation.[25]

Generally the president cannot by virtue of his office purchase an unrelated business on behalf of the corporation, that is, make a conglomerate-pattern acquisition. Thus, when the president of a drug company entered into a contract by which the corporation purchased an unrelated business at a cost of over $100,000, the contract was outside of the president's authority and was not binding upon the corporation, even though the general counsel for the corporation had incorrectly stated in the presence of the seller that the president did not require special authorization to enter into such a contract and even though the contract was not thereafter repudiated by the board of directors of the drug company.[26]

(2) ***Other Officers and Employees.*** The authority of corporate employees and other officers, such as secretary or treasurer, is generally limited to the duties of their offices. Their authority may, however, be extended by the conduct of the corporation, in accordance with the general principles governing apparent authority based on the conduct of the principal. An unauthorized act may, of course, be ratified. The authority of a general manager of the corporation is determined by principles of ordinary agency law. (See p. 1046, Cote Brothers, Inc. v Granite Lake Realty Corp.)

---

[24] In re Westec Corporation, (CA5 Tex) 434 F2d 195.

[25] Goodride Tire Co. v Albert-Harris, 114 Ohio App 276, 19 OO2d 173, 181 NE 2d 719.

[26] North American Sales Alliance v Carrtone Laboratories, (La App) 214 So2d 167.

§ 52:8. Liability of Officers. The relation of the officers to the corporation, like that of the directors, is a fiduciary relationship. For this reason, the officers are liable for secret profits made in connection with or at the expense of the business of the corporation. The rule of loyalty which prohibits corporate officers from obtaining personal benefit by diverting corporate opportunities to themselves applies to small or close corporations.[27]

As an aspect of the corporate officer's fiduciary position, he must not make any profit that is not disclosed to the corporation. If an officer diverts a corporate opportunity to himself, the corporation may recover from the officer the profit of which the corporation had been deprived. (See p. 1047, Abbott Redmont Thinlite Corp. v Redmont.) This is an application of the prohibition against secret profits applicable to ordinary agents. Thus, the president of a contracting corporation must account to the corporation for a secret profit which he or a member of his family made on the letting of a subcontract.[28]

Officers are also liable for willful or negligent acts that cause a loss to the corporation. On the other hand, they are not liable for mere errors in judgment committed while exercising their discretion, provided they have acted with reasonable prudence and care.

§ 52:9. Agents and Employees of Corporation. The authority, rights, and liabilities of an agent of a corporation are governed by the same rules applicable when the principal is a natural person.

The authority of corporate employees is governed by general agency principles.[29] The construction foreman of a construction corporation does not have implied authority to modify the terms of the contract between the corporation and a supplier of building materials.[30]

§ 52:10. Indemnification of Officers, Directors, Employees, and Agents. While performing what they believe to be their duty, officers, directors, employees, and agents of corporations may commit acts for which they are later sued or criminally prosecuted. At common law the expense or loss involved in defending such actions and prosecutions or in making out-of-court settlements was borne by the individual. He had no right to obtain any money from the corporation to indemnify him for such loss. The trend of modern statutes is to authorize or to require the board of directors to make indemnity in such cases.[31] The Model Act broadly authorizes the corporation to indemnify such a person "if he acted in good faith and in a manner he

---

[27] Seaboard Industries, Inc. v Monaco, 442 Pa 256, 276 A2d 305.

[28] Voss Oil Co. v Voss, (Wyo) 367 P2d 977.

[29] Weaver Construction Co. v Farmers National Bank, 253 Iowa 1280, 115 NW 2d 804.

[30] Tri-City Concrete Co., Inc. v A.L.A. Construction Co., 343 Mass 425, 179 NE2d 319.

[31] Professional Insurance Co. v Barry, 60 Misc 2d 424, 303 NYS2d 556.

reasonably believed to be in or not opposed to the best interests of the corporation and, with respect to any criminal action or proceeding, had no reasonable cause to believe his conduct was unlawful. . . ." [32]

In some states statutory provision is made requiring the corporation to indemnify directors and officers for reasonable expenses incurred by them in defending unwarranted suits brought against them by shareholders.[33] Such statutes have been adopted to induce responsible persons to accept positions of corporate responsibility.[34]

Some corporation codes expressly authorize the corporation to purchase insurance to indemnify its directors and officers from liability because of their corporate acts.

§ **52:11. Corporate Minutes.** Minutes are ordinarily kept of meetings of the shareholders and of the directors of a corporation. The keeping of accurate minutes is important not only for the purpose of preserving continuity in management policies but also because of the consequence that the action taken may have with respect to the liability of individual persons, with respect to tax liability of individual persons, or with respect to tax liability of the corporation. The minutes are not conclusive, however, and they may be supplemented or contradicted by parol evidence.[35]

§ **52:12. Computers and Corporate Management.** The advent of the age of computers has not changed the basic principles of law determining the liability of management, but it gives rise to new situations to which the old principles will be applied. Is management liable for failing to use computers? Generally this will not raise a legal question, as the courts will feel that it is a matter for the business judgment of management to determine whether the benefits to be derived offset the costs and any possible hazards. It may well be that in a given case the use of computers would provide better information on which management decisions could be made or provide better inventory and product-quality controls. In such a case, the argument could be made that management was negligent in failing to use computers in much the same way that management would ordinarily be regarded as negligent in using water power instead of electricity to run machinery.

When computers are used, management may be liable for failure to exercise proper care in their use. Thus, management must exercise due care in selecting proper equipment and qualified personnel; in protecting the physical equipment, such as machines, tapes, and cards, from fire, atmospheric, and similar hazards; in maintaining safeguards against error; in protecting from misuse of the computers to defraud or embezzle; and in protecting the interests of the company by procuring proper protection through

[32] ABA MBCA § 5(a).
[33] Fletcher v A. J. Industries, 266 Cal App 2d 313, 72 Cal Rptr 146.
[34] Merritt-Chapman & Scott Corp. v Wolfson, (Del) 264 A2d 358.
[35] Lano v Rochester Germicide Co., 261 Minn 556, 113 NW2d 460.

copyrights and antidisclosure agreements with employees, service companies, and customers.

§ 52:13. Liability of Management to Third Persons. Ordinarily the management of a corporation—meaning its directors, officers, and executive employees—is not liable to third persons for the effect upon such third persons of their management or unsound advice. The liability of a director or officer for misconduct ordinarily is a liability that may be enforced only by the corporation or by shareholders bringing a derivative action on behalf of the corporation. Ordinarily a director or officer is not liable to a third person for loss caused by the negligent performance of his duties as director or officer, even though because of such negligence the corporation is in turn liable to the third person to whom the corporation owed the duty to use care or was under a contract obligation to render a particular service.

Officers and managers of a corporation are not liable for the economic consequence of their advice upon third persons, even though they caused the corporation to refuse to deal with or to break its contract with such third persons, as long as the officers and managers had acted in good faith to advance the interests of the corporation. (See p. 1050, Wampler v Palmerton.) Thus, a person who has a contract with the corporation which is not renewed because of the adverse vote of the directors cannot sue the directors for damages even though they had been "wrong" in their decision as such a matter was merely an error in judgment for which there is no tort liability. This differs from the situation in which a person intentionally or maliciously interferes with a contract or the economic expectations of another person.[36]

As exceptions to the above rule, a director or officer may be directly liable to an injured third person when the director or officer commits a tort or directs the commission of a tort upon the third person, as when he takes an active part in causing the corporation to conspire to enter into a monopoly or trust agreement to the detriment of the third person. When a corporate officer, director, or employee is liable to a third person for his misconduct, it is no defense that the corporation may also be liable to the third person.[37]

If a director or an officer makes a contract in his individual capacity, he is personally liable thereon to the other person and is not protected from liability by the fact that his motive was to act on behalf of the corporation. Ordinarily when a contract is made on behalf of the corporation, the officer or director is not personally liable in case of breach of the contract.[38]

§ 52:14. Insiders. A person holding an office or a position within a corporation, whether or not a director or shareholder, may be held accountable for any advantage obtained by him from the use of information known to him by virtue of his position. Thus, if a director sells his stock or buys the stock of a

---

[36] Wilson v McClenny, 262 NC 121, 136 SE2d 569.

[37] Wrigley v Nottingham, 111 Ga App 404, 141 SE2d 859.

[38] A. B. Corporation v Futrovsky, 250 Md 65, 267 A2d 130.

shareholder without disclosing to such person matters materially affecting the value of the stock, which matters are known to the insider, redress may be obtained. If the action of the insider constitutes fraud, the injured person may sue for money damages. Whether or not the elements of actual fraud are present, an action may be brought by the Securities and Exchange Commission to redress the wrong caused the other party.[39]

In some instances it is unlawful for a shareholder to act without disclosing to the other contracting party information he possesses by virtue of his position within the corporation. For example, it is unlawful for a majority shareholder to purchase the stock of a minority shareholder without disclosing material facts affecting the value of the stock known to the majority shareholder by virtue of his position of power within the corporation and not known to the selling minority shareholder.[40] Similarly, directors selling their stock to outsiders without disclosing the fact that the next earnings statement of the corporation would show a drop in corporate income can be held liable to the corporation for the profit which they make on such a sale.[41]

The concept of disclosure of inside information is a twentieth century manifestation of the social forces which seek to prevent exploitation, hardship, and oppression. The exact boundaries of the concept are not yet clear, and difficulty is encountered in determining where to draw the line between superior information which a person has the right to keep to himself and information that he cannot utilize because he might gain an advantage over the other party to the transaction who does not possess such knowledge.

§ 52:15. Criminal Liability. Officers and directors, as in the case of agents generally, are personally responsible for any crimes committed by them even when they act in behalf of the corporation. At the local level they may be criminally responsible for violation of ordinances relating to sanitation, safety, and hours of closing. At the state level they may be criminally liable for conducting a business without obtaining necessary licenses or after the corporate certificate of incorporation was forfeited for failing to file reports [42] or pay taxes. At the national level they may be prosecuted for violation of the federal antitrust laws.[43]

A number of states impose criminal liability upon the person, corporate officer, or agent who conducts local business on behalf of a foreign corporation that has not qualified to engage in such business.[44]

§ 52:16. Corporate Debts and Taxes. As the corporation is a separate legal person, debts and taxes owed by the corporation are ordinarily the obligations

---

[39] S.E.C. v Capital Gains Research Bureau, 375 US 180; S.E.C. v Texas Gulf Sulphur Co., (DC SD NY) 258 F Supp 262.

[40] Sherman v Baker, 2 Wash App 845, 472 P2d 589.

[41] Diamond v Oreamuno, 29 App Div 2d 285, 287 NYS2d 300.

[42] Bremer v Equitable Construction & Mortgage Corp., 26 Mich App 204, 182 NW2d 69.

[43] United States v Wise, 370 US 405.

[44] California Corporation Code § 6803.

of the corporation only. Consequently, neither directors nor officers are individually liable for the corporate debts or taxes, even though it may have been their acts which gave rise to the debts or their neglect which resulted in the failure to pay the taxes. As an exception to this general principle, statutes in some states impose upon corporate officers liability for taxes, such as sales taxes, owed by the corporation.

In some states civil liability for corporate debts is imposed upon the officers and directors of the corporation when it improperly engages in business. (See p. 1052, Eberts Cadillac Co. v Miller.)

§ 52:17. Protection from Abuse. Various devices and limitations have developed to protect shareholders both from misconduct by management and from the action of the majority of the shareholders. Shareholders may protect themselves by voting for new directors, and also officers if the latter are elected, at the next annual election; or they may take special remedial action at a special meeting of shareholders called for that purpose. Even if the objecting shareholders represent only a minority so that they could not control an election, they may bring a legal action when the management misconduct complained of constitutes a legal wrong.[45]

In some cases dissenting shareholders are permitted to require the corporation to buy out their interests even though no legal wrong has been committed. For example, even though a merger or consolidation is otherwise proper, it is commonly provided that a dissenting shareholder may require the corporation to buy his stock from him. In some instances the dissenting shareholder may even be able to prevent the merger or consolidation on the ground that it violates basic principles of fairness[46] or that it is forbidden by amended Section 7 of the Clayton Act.

§ 52:18. Irregular Procedure. There is a strong judicial tendency to ignore the effect of a procedural error or irregularity when the circumstances are such that it can be concluded that all or substantially all of the shareholders have agreed to or waived any objection to the procedure which was followed.[47] (See p. 1052, Coastal Pharmaceutical Co. v Goldman.) Thus, irregularities with respect to the place and notice of a meeting of the board of directors will be ignored in the case of a closely held corporation when all of the directors attended and participated in the meeting or acquiesced in action taken at such meeting.[48] A third person sued by the corporation cannot challenge the right of the corporation to sue on the ground that

---

[45] If the wrong complained of is a wrong to the objecting shareholder, he will sue in his own name and any money recovered in the action will be for his benefit. If the wrong complained of is a wrong against the corporation, the objecting shareholder may at best bring only a derivative action, and any money recovered in the action is paid to the corporation and thus only indirectly benefits the objecting shareholder.

[46] Sterling v Mayflower Hotel Corp., 33 Del Ch 20, 89 A2d 862 affirmed 33 Del Ch 293, 93 A2d 107.

[47] Nadler v S.E.C., (CA2 SEC) 296 F2d 63, cert den 369 US 849.

[48] Freeman v King Pontiac Co., 236 SC 335, 114 SE2d 478.

corporate procedural requirements have not been observed. Similarly, a third person cannot defend against a claim held by a corporation on the ground that the corporation, if it had been sued by the person from whom it acquired the claim, could have raised the defense of the statute of frauds. Thus, when a right under a contract to purchase land from a third person was assigned to the corporation, the third person could not raise the defense that the assignment did not satisfy the requirements of the statute of frauds.[49]

Likewise, when the corporation has received the benefit of a transaction, it will be estopped from claiming that there was some irregularity in the corporate procedure followed. For example, a corporation cannot refuse to pay the corporation manager for services actually performed by him on the ground that the meeting of the directors at which he was hired was irregular because proper notice of the meeting had not been given to the directors as required by the corporate bylaws.[50]

As in the case of agency generally, a corporation may ratify acts of its officers or directors that were otherwise unauthorized. Likewise, a corporation's pattern of conduct may be such as to estop it from raising the question of lack of authority. For example, when a corporate resolution required a signature and countersignature on all corporate checks and notes, the corporation was estopped from challenging a note on the ground that it bore only one signature when the corporation had paid to the same holder 15 prior one-signature notes and checks without protest.[51] Contrary to the rule that shareholders cannot act for the corporation, some courts are recognizing as binding on the corporation a contract entered into on behalf of the corporation by the holders of all of the corporate stock.[52]

---

[49] Community Land Corp. v Stuenkel, (Mo) 436 SW2d 11.

[50] Clyserol Laboratories, Inc. v Smith, (Okla) 362 P.2d 99.

[51] Berdane Furs, Inc. v First Pennsylvania Banking & Trust Co., 190 Pa Super 639, 155 A2d 465.

[52] Brewer v First National Bank, 202 Va 807, 120 SE2d 273; Popperman v Rest Haven Cemetery, Inc., 162 Tex 255, 345 SW2d 715.

CASES FOR CHAPTER 52

Cote Brothers, Inc. v Granite Lake Realty Corp.

105 NH 111, 193 A2d 884 (1963)

Cote Brothers sold bakery products to the Granite Lake Camp which was run by the Granite Lake Realty Corp. and an allied corporation, Granite Lake Camp Associates, Inc. Both corporations were owned, operated, and managed by the same three individuals who were the stockholders, officers, and directors. Liability of the corporations for the plaintiff's bill was denied on the ground that no officer of the corporations had been authorized to purchase the bakery products. From a judgment for the plaintiff, the defendants appealed.

KENISON, C.J. . . . The defendant corporation and its allied corporation Granite Lake Camp Associates, Inc. were both small close corporations which were organized, operated and managed by the same three individuals as stockholders, officers and directors. The issue in this case is whether the defendant is liable on a mercantile claim for merchandise delivered which, it is argued, no officer of the corporation was authorized to purchase. The guide lines for deciding this issue were set forth in Holman-Baker Co. v Pre-Design Co., 104 NH 116, 117-118, 179 A2d 454, 455 as follows: "In the world of credit there is emerging a rule, consistent with modern business practices, under which a principal is bound by the promise of his general agent, whether or not authorized, when such promise is made within the scope of the agent's power. . . . The rationale of the rule is not based on express authority, implied authority, apparent authority or estoppel 'but [is derived] solely from the agency relation and exists for the protection of persons harmed by or dealing with a servant or other agent' and is described as 'inherent agency power.' Restatement, Second, Agency, s. 8 A."

The defendant owned the premises known as Granite Lake Camp which was leased to and operated by another corporation, Granite Lake Camp Associates, Inc. The corporations were organized by three individuals for the purpose of acquiring and operating Granite Lake Camp as "a summer camp." The same three individuals (Chester Gusick, Charles Gusick and Milton Lubow) were the sole stockholders, officers and directors of both corporations. One of the three stockholders, directors and officers, "Milton Lubow, was the man who handled the finances." At the beginning of their operation a letter was circularized to prospective merchants and suppliers signed by Milton Lubow as secretary-treasurer of Granite Lake Camp Associates, Inc. The letter, which was admitted as an exhibit over the defendants' objection, stated that the three individuals named above were the only persons authorized to order merchandise for Granite Lake Camp and that "we operate our business through Granite Lake Camp Associates, Inc. and Granite Lake Realty Corporation." During the period of time when the plaintiff's bill was due and owing rental payments were made by Granite Lake Camp Associates, Inc. to the defendant. From 1959 to 1962 the mortgage on the real estate in the original amount of $127,500 was reduced to "approximately seventy thousand dollars."

While both Chester Gusick and Charles Gusick testified that they had no knowledge of the letter sent to prospective merchants and that it was not authorized by them, it is evident that the letter was written in furtherance of the everyday business of the corporations and that it was done by Milton Lubow who was selected by the Gusick brothers as "the man who handled the finances." . . . "Commercial convenience requires that the principal should not escape liability where there have been deviations from the usually granted authority by persons who are such essential parts of his business enterprise. In the long run it is of advantage to business, and hence to employers as a class, that third persons should not be required to scrutinize too carefully the mandates of permanent or semi-permanent agents who do no more than what is usually done by agents in similar positions." It is reasonably clear that Lubow as a stockholder, officer and financial manager of two allied close corporations had inherent agency power to purchase ordinary supplies for the business conducted through the two corporations. . . . In view of this result it is unnecessary to consider whether the Court's ruling could be sustained on another ground by disregarding the corporate entity to prevent inequity or hardship to mercantile creditors. . . .

[Judgment affirmed.]

Abbott Redmont Thinlite Corp. v Redmont

(CA2 NY) 475 F2d 85 (1973)

Redmont was the president of Abbott Redmont Thinlite Corporation. He left that corporation and ran the Circle Redmont Corporation in competition with his former employer. In so doing, it was claimed that he diverted five contracts from his former employer to his company. The former employer sued Redmont and Circle Redmont Corporation to recover the profit of which the former employer was deprived. Judgment was entered for the employer as to part of its claim and it appealed.

OAKES, C.J. . . . The issue here presented is whether the appellees, Rudolph R. Redmont and Circle Redmont Corporation, deprived the appellant, Abbott Redmont Thinlite Corporation, of a business opportunity in which it had a "tangible expectancy," and thereby violated

Redmont's obligations as a former officer-employee of appellant. . . .

Appellee Redmont, who had previously worked in the glass block business, joined appellant Abbott in 1960 as president of Abbott Redmont Thinlite Corporation. Abbott Redmont's business consisted of furnishing and installing glass block skylights, including toplights (glass blocks set in aluminum grids, generally used in schools) and rooflights (glass blocks set in anti-corrosive concrete grids, generally used in sewage plants). The method used to sell these lights was to discover through trade journals and other sources what construction projects were in the course of design. Once aware of this, Abbott would contact the architect who was in the process of working up the designs for those projects, and attempt to convince him to write into the design the use of skylights and other specifications which Abbott's products line would fulfill. Part of appellee Redmont's job was to contact such architects and to convince them of the advisability of employing Abbott's products in their final design. As of the time in question, up to and including the date when Redmont quit his employ with Abbott and began his own company, Circle Redmont Corporation (Circle), Abbott was the sole distributor in the metropolitan New York area for the particular products with which this action is concerned. Therefore, once the proper requirements were, or named product was, written into the architect's specifications, to all intents and purposes Abbott was assured of the required subcontract. Once Abbott's products had been incorporated into the plans and specifications by the architect, the projects were then in the regular course put out for bid to general contractors. When the general contractor was chosen Abbott would enter into a formal subcontract with the general contractor to furnish and install the Abbott product.

There are five projects here involved.* Appellee Redmont, while in the employ of Abbott, had proceeded to contact the architects for each of these five projects and to write Abbott product specifications into each of the projects. In each case Redmont had also prepared a bid for submission to the general contractor who had been successful in obtaining the general construction contract (or the owner himself if the owner chose to build without a general contractor). Redmont concededly retained knowledge of the amounts of the bids which he had prepared while in Abbott's employ after his employment ceased.

In early 1966 Owens-Illinois, the producer of the glass block used in all of Abbott's products, announced that it was discontinuing the production of glass block. Soon afterward, in February, 1966, Products Research Corporation (PRC), which made the aluminum grids for the toplights and inserted the Owens-Illinois glass block in the grids and from which Abbott purchased the complete toplight sections, informed Abbott that as a result of Owens-Illinois' action, it was leaving the glass block business. . . . Redmont . . . left Abbott on April 1, 1966. . . .

Redmont, meanwhile, had established his own company, Circle, and had found another source of supply for rooflights and toplights. On the dates given below, Redmont, acting by and for Circle, entered into contracts for toplight and rooflight work on projects for which he had persuaded the architects to write in Abbott product specifications while working for Abbott:

Job	*Date of Redmont's Contract*
Plainfield Public Library	4/18/66
Oakland High School	6/ 2/66
Junior High School 144	7/20/66
Riverdale Girls School	8/ 5/66
Manhattan Pumping Station	8/ 5/66

As stated, the central questions for determination here are whether Abbott Redmont Thinlite Corporation had a "tangible expectancy," . . . in the five contracts listed above and whether Redmont violated his fiduciary duty by diverting that expectancy to his own profit. Although Redmont had left the employ of Abbott at the time he contracted with the general contractors for these projects, he was taking advantage of

---

*

Job	*Type*
Plainfield Library	Toplight
Oakland High School	Toplight
Junior High School 144	Toplight
Riverdale Girls School	Toplight
Manhattan Pumping Station	Rooflight

a corporate opportunity which he had helped obtain for Abbott and which would have almost certainly been Abbott's but for Redmont's departure. Redmont, we believe, had an obligation which carried over after he left Abbott not to exploit projects which would have clearly brought profits to Abbott but for his competition. . . . Once Abbott's specifications were written into the achitect's plans it was almost a certainty that Abbott would get the final subcontract to install its lights. While occasionally the architect's specifications would be changed, the record shows that this happened very rarely. Thus, it was not merely an "expectancy," but almost a certainty that Redmont's work on these five deals would secure the final contract for Abbott. . . . Redmont did take business which, but for his entry into direct competition with Abbott, would have been Abbott's if Redmont had not departed. . . .

The degree of likelihood of realization from the opportunity is, however, the key to whether an expectancy is tangible. . . .

The high degree of likelihood that, but for Redmont's competition, Abbott would have been awarded these contracts is combined here with the fact that Redmont benefited by information as a result of his employment at Abbott —knowledge of the details of the specifications, knowledge of the contractor's requirements, knowledge of Abbott's probable costs—which made Abbott peculiarly vulnerable to his competition on the specific deals here in question. While this is not the kind of information that, like customers' lists, is "confidential" in the sense of the term that might in and of itself create liability on use, . . . it was information obtained in the course of his employment. A former employee may, of course, go into competition with his ex-employer and can use general information concerning the method of business and names of customers of his ex-employer in his new venture. . . . But he cannot, as here, utilize specific information he obtained during his employment to deprive his ex-employer of customers with whom he knows a deal is in the process of completion. The use of specific information on deals in progress obtained while in Abbott's employ, and the *degree of likelihood* that but for Redmont's competition Abbott would have been awarded the contract, dictate our holding that Redmont violated his fiduciary obligations to Abbott by submitting competing bids.

But Abbott had a "tangible expectancy" in the four toplight contracts only until June 7, 1966, when PRC cancelled Abbott's toplight orders, leaving Abbott without a source of supply. Abbott had ample warning from PRC that these orders would be cancelled if Abbott did not submit shop drawings to PRC by June 6, 1966. Abbott's failure to submit the requested drawings constitutes intentional abandonment . . . of its contract rights in the toplight projects on which contracts were signed after that, *i.e.*, the Junior High School 144 project and the Riverdale Girls School project. It is not clear from the record how long Abbott retained its supply of glass blocks for rooflights for the Manhattan Pumping Station, the one rooflight project after Owens-Illinois went out of the glass block business. Absent any such supply, Abbott cannot complain of any loss by misappropriation of its "opportunity" since it would have abandoned the opportunity in any event. On this the record is not clear.

We reverse as to the Plainfield Public Library and Oakland High School projects, affirm as to the Junior High School 144 and Riverdale Girls School projects, and remand for further findings in respect to the Manhattan Pumping Station project and for the award of damages in accordance with this opinion.

Wrigley v Nottingham

111 Ga App 404, 141 SE2d 859 (1965)

Nottingham was employed by a corporation. The corporation broke this contract by firing him. He claimed that the breach had been caused by the malicious conduct of Wrigley, Jr., the majority shareholder, and other directors of the corporation. Nottingham sued Wrigley, Jr., and other directors for damages for the tort of maliciously inducing the breach of the contract. From a judgment in favor of Nottingham, the defendants appealed.

BELL, P.J. . . . It is charged that Wrigley, Jr., could control the corporate acts by reason of his ownership of all the voting stock coupled with his family relationship with members of the board. . . . The petition asserts . . . that the breach was procured maliciously and without justifiable cause. . . .

A corporation is nothing more than a robot, created by the law, possessing only that sensibility which its management and agents bring to it. Most corporate liabilities do not attach personally to its stockholders, officers, or agents. The corporation, however, is not so fortunate, as it is often subjected to liability through the tortious misconduct of its management and agents when the wrongs are done in the scope of the agency relationship. This imposition of corporate liability for the acts of its agents does not ipso facto in the eyes of the law relieve the agents from personal accountability for their torts. In actions based on torts committed by corporate agents, the choice of naming the defendant against a possible imposition of ultimate liability frequently rests with the one wronged. The plaintiff may name in his action as a party the corporation alone, or he may name the corporation and the agents, or the agent alone. . . .

In the case before us, the plaintiff could have sued the company for breach of contract he alleges was induced by its agents. The fact that he chose to sue in tort . . . naming as defendants the individuals allegedly responsible for procuring the breach is an election which the plaintiff was authorized to make. . . .

[Judgment affirmed.]

Note: On further appeal the judgment was reversed on other grounds. 221 Ga 386, 144 SE2d 749.

Wampler v Palmerton

250 Ore 65, 439 P2d 601 (1968)

Diamond Lake Lumber Co. operated sawmills. Newman was the president and managing officer, and Palmerton was a business advisor of the corporation. Diamond Lake made a logging contract with Wampler. It was contemplated that it would take five years to complete this contract. Diamond Lake failed to make payments to Wampler as required by the contract. Because of this breach of the contract, Wampler went into bankruptcy and then sued Newman and Palmerton, claiming that they had caused the corporation to break its contract with him and were liable for such interference with his contract rights. From a judgment in favor of Wampler, the defendants appealed.

HOLMAN, J. . . . Before it can be determined whether plaintiff's proof was sufficient, it is first necessary to establish the nature and elements of a cause of action in tort for interference with a contract, which is the cause of action plaintiff insists he has. The modern action results from the process by which the reach of several ancient remedies was extended. An ancestor of the cause of action is thought to have been the principle of Roman law which permitted the head of a family to sue for harm done by physical violence to a member of his family or his slave. The principle was carried over into early English common law. According to Bracton, an action against the person who injured an attendant or serf was given to a lord to protect his interest in not being deprived of the servant's services. Further protection of this sort of interest was deemed necessary when the bubonic plague in the Fourteenth Century created a scarcity of workers. The Ordinance of Laborers was enacted, upon which a cause of action was based for the enticing away of another's servants or workmen regardless whether violence was employed. Gradually, any distinction between the common-law action and the statutory action disappeared. The remedy was limited to recovery for enticement of a dependent member of another's household until 1853 when the case of Lumley v Gye decided that the defendant who persuaded an opera singer to break her contract with an opera company was liable. In 1893, in Temperton v Russell, the cause of action was extended to cover contracts other than those of employment. The defendant in Temperton induced by threats the breach of a contract to furnish building materials.

The interest protected by the interference with contract action is the interest of the individual in the security and integrity of the contractual relations into which he has entered. Economic relations are controlled by contract, and the public also has an interest in maintaining the security of such transactions. Therefore the law provides protection. To be actionable, an interference must be a knowing and not an inadvertent or incidental invasion of plaintiff's contractual interests.

The relief granted is of the broad type available in intentional tort actions and includes recompense for mental suffering, damage to reputation, and punitive damages. It therefore affords the relief which would have been recoverable from the party breaching the contract and also for the less tangible personal harms such as those sought in the instant case. . . .

A person who interferes with a contract is not always responsible for the resultant injury. If he is promoting an interest which is equal or superior in social value to that with which he interferes, his actions are said to be privileged or justified. The purpose or motive of the interferor may be the controlling factor in the determination of the existence of justification since it usually discloses the interest involved.

In the usual interference with a contract situation, the person interfering is a complete stranger to the contractual relationship. A complicating ingredient is added where the party induced to breach its contract is a corporation and the third person who induces the breach is not a stranger, but is a person who, by reason of his position with the corporation, owes a duty of advice and action to the corporation. In the instant case, one defendant—Newman—was the President, and the other defendant—Palmerton—was employed as a business adviser of the corporation that was the party to the contract.

A corporation can only act upon the advice of officers or employes and through the actions of agents. Doing business through corporate structures is a recognized and necessary incident of business life. A party is usually able to abandon a disadvantageous but valid contract and be responsible for breach of contract only. Corporations would substantially be prevented from similarly abandoning disadvantageous but valid contracts, and from securing related business advice, if the officers and employes who advised and carried out the breach had to run the risk of personal responsibility in an action for interference with contract. Therefore, courts have tended to shield such persons from responsibility for inducing breach of the corporate contract, often saying that they are not liable if the action was taken in "good faith" and for the benefit of the corporation.

It is obvious that if the action or advice is to serve other interests than those of the corporation, there can be no immunity because it is not rendered for the purpose which gives birth to the immunity.

The immunity of a corporate officer or employee, who is acting within the scope of his employment and for benefit of the corporation, to interfere with a corporate contract is often spoken of as "privilege." It might well be viewed as a lack of any duty of noninterference on the part of the corporate agent. The person contracting with the corporation cannot reasonably have any contractual expectancy that does not take into consideration the fact that the corporation may be advised to breach the contract, in accordance with its interests, by a person whose duty it is to do so.

In the present case, the action of defendants clearly was taken to benefit the corporation. Plaintiff alleges that the defendants intended, by inducing the corporate breach of contract, to enrich the corporation and thereby indirectly to improve their own financial conditions. We are then faced with the question whether lack of "good faith" exists where the selfish motivation of the corporate official or employe for inducing the corporate breach is to secure derivative benefits from the improved financial condition of the corporation.

Most corporate officers or employes have some sort of personal interest in the financial welfare of their principal, even though it may only be a hope of an increase in salary. If "good faith" is equated with the lack of any such selfish interest in enhancing the financial condition of the corporation, most officers or employes would not dare to give the business advice it is their duty to render. We do not believe that "good faith" as used here can reasonably mean anything more than an intent to benefit the corporation.

Since the plaintiff alleges that the defendants were acting to benefit the corporation, the motivation attributed to them establishes privilege and is insufficient to render them liable for the tort of interference with a contract. Such is the case even though plaintiff argues that the defendants intended to cause the corporation to take an unfair advantage of the plaintiff by means of the breach of contract. So long as the officer or employe acts within the general range of his authority intending to benefit the corporation, the law identifies his actions with the corporation. In such a situation the officer is not liable for interfering with a contract of the corporation any more than the corporation could be liable in tort for interfering with it. The words "good faith" should not be employed to render a corporate officer or employe liable for engaging in morally questionable activities upon behalf of his principal that nevertheless would not be tortious if he were acting for himself as the party to the contract.

The interest protected by the interference with contract action is the interest of the plaintiff in not having his contract rights interfered with by intermeddling strangers. However, so long as the person inducing the breach of a corporate contract is an officer or employe acting for the benefit of the corporation and within the scope of his authority, the plaintiff cannot show that this interest was invaded and therefore cannot maintain an interference with contract action.

[Judgment reversed.]

Eberts Cadillac Co. v Miller

10 Mich App 370, 159 NW2d 217 (1968)

Miller was president and Holcomb was treasurer of Chewning Motors, a Michigan corporation. After 1958 they had nothing to do with the business, no corporate meetings were held, and the corporation did not file the annual reports required by statute. Eberts Cadillac Co. was owed money by Chewning Motors. It sued Miller and Holcomb on the basis that a Michigan statute imposed liability on corporate officers in such cases. The statute provided with respect to the annual reports that "any officer . . . of such corporation so in default who has neglected or refused to join in making such report . . . shall be liable for all debts of such corporation contracted during the period of such neglect or refusal." From a judgment for Miller, the defendants appealed.

HOLBROOK, P.J. . . . Are corporate officers and directors who take no steps to terminate their status as such, but simply abandon the corporation by ceasing to attend meetings and ceasing to perform the duties of their office, for whom no successors are elected, liable under the statute when the corporation subsequently is in default for failure to file its annual report?

"The answer must be yes. A position of corporate trust . . . is not terminated merely by leaving the tent. Adequate protection of the myriad rights and interests involved in the sophisticated world of modern commerce requires something more . . . . To insure orderliness, as well as to locate corporate responsibility with certainty, a corporate officer or director retains his office until properly replaced by his successor, (barring, perhaps, some particular bylaw peculiarly bearing on the problem). . . . Among the responsibilities of corporate offices is the duty to see that the office is properly transferred into other hands. . . .

The trial judge held that the defendants were officers of the corporation prior to April 1, 1958, and that they were not replaced at that time or at any time thereafter at a meeting of the shareholders or board of directors. . . . Corporate officers hold over in their positions until replaced at a new election. . . . The defendants being officers of the corporation at the time of default when the indebtedness was incurred, became liable under the statute by their neglecting to file the report required. . . .

[Judgment affirmed.]

Coastal Pharmaceutical Co. v Goldman

213 Va 831, 195 SE2d 848 (1973)

Goldman brought an action to rescind a contract with Coastal Pharmaceutical Company on the ground that the contract had never been authorized nor ratified by Coastal.

Goldman owned the stock of Ghent Arms Corp. which operated a nursing home. Because

of its poor financial condition, Goldman contracted to transfer his stock to Coastal Pharmaceutical Co., which would make the Ghent Corp. a wholly-owned subsidiary of Coastal. Thereafter Goldman learned that Coastal was on the verge of bankruptcy and sought to rescind the contract on the ground that the contract had never been expressly authorized nor ratified by Coastal. Judgment was entered for Goldman and Coastal appealed.

POFF, J. . . . The crucial question involved is whether the chancellor was correct in his ruling that because Coastal never authorized execution of the agreement by formal corporate action or ratified it by timely corporate action or by implication, the agreement "never became a valid mutually binding and enforceable contract." . . .

We consider first Goldman's argument that neither the board of directors nor the stockholders [of Coastal] formally authorized Gay [who acted as agent of Coastal] to execute the contract and that the contract was therefore null and void.

This court has held that a corporation cannot escape liability for commercial commitments made by its officers in the name of the corporation by asserting a lack of *de jure* authorization by its board of directors. . . .

Necessarily, the converse is also true; a corporation cannot be required to assume liabilities of such a contract and be denied its benefits. If implied or *de facto* authorization is sufficient to bind the corporation and its stockholders to obligations, it is sufficient to validate their rights.

Corporations are creatures of statutory law. The same law which creates them provides procedures for the conduct of their affairs. Ordinarily, corporate conduct must conform to those procedures. But the total complex of corporate law acknowledges that all corporations are not alike and recognizes that strict statutory conformity, seldom practiced faithfully by the largest and most sophisticated corporations, is impractical if not impossible for others. For the law to close its eyes to the differences and attempt to compress all corporations into a neat little mold would be to forsake realism for legalism and often to sacrifice justice for standardization. As we said in Brewer v First Nat'l Bank, 202 Va 807, 812-813, 120 SE2d 273, 278 (1961): "While it is salutary, and in some instances mandatory, that these rules be followed, it is generally recognized that where there is a family, or close corporation, such as the one involved in this case, in which the stockholders, officers and directors ignore the requirements of the statutes and corporate by-laws, and conduct its business in an informal manner, the actions so taken may, nonetheless, be binding upon the corporation. . . . In this case, the agreement of January 17, 1955, was not authorized at a formal meeting of the board of directors of the corporation, nor was the writing executed in the proper manner. However, it is clear from the actions of the parties, from the circumstances surrounding and subsequent to the execution of the agreement, and from the agreement itself, that it was intended, by all concerned, to be the *act of the corporation*." . . .

. . . Under the facts of this case, Gay was vested by Coastal with *de facto* authority to execute the contract as an "act of the corporation" within the spirit of the rule in *Brewer*.

The dispositive facts of this case, as distinguished from facts not relevant to the specific basis of the Chancellor's decree, are not in dispute. For a period of more than a year preceding execution of the contract, Coastal and Ghent Arms were negotiating some form of combination. Goldman was the sole owner of one corporation and part owner of the other. The physical combination between the two corporations began originally in December 1969 when, under a $3,500.00 loan from Coastal to Ghent Arms, Gay, Coastal's managing director, went on Ghent Arms' payroll to serve both corporations. The combination took further form after Gay became Coastal's president a month later and, with other Coastal employees, assumed managerial authority over the nursing home. During 1970, with the home's financial condition improving, Coastal's stockholders, moribund for seven years, held three meetings, all of which Goldman attended. Although the minutes of these meetings were inartistically drafted and did not record conventional resolutions or categorical votes on informal motions, they clearly reflect a corporate purpose to authorize Coastal's officers to pursue the steps preliminary to corporate acquisition of the nursing home.

On January 17, 1971, Coastal's stockholders met again. That meeting and its date are both significant. At that point in time, an attorney was preparing a written contract to incorporate the oral agreement reached by Gay and Goldman a few days before; five days later, the written contract would be signed and pre-dated to January 17, 1971.

At that meeting, Coastal's stockholders treated Ghent Arms as their own. After hearing Gay's report of Ghent Arms' financial status, they proceeded to elect a board of directors for Ghent Arms Corporation for the year 1971, and they closed the meeting with a standing ovation commending Gay's management of the affairs of the corporation. In light of the preparatory action taken at earlier meetings, this exercise of dominion over the nursing home and the endorsement of Gay's conduct can be interpreted only as a corporate affirmation of the oral agreement Gay had made with Goldman and an implied authority for Gay to validate that agreement by signing the written contract.

Goldman contends that since this authority did not spring from the action of the board of directors, execution of the contract cannot be an "act of the corporation." True, directors normally conduct the business of the corporation. True, the several meetings in which the contract was authorized were called "stockholders' meetings." But, except for the minutes of the March 31, 1970 meeting (which did not record those present), the minutes show that all members of the board of directors attended all meetings. Nothing in these minutes indicates an objection by any director or any of the sixty-six stockholders. So far as the record discloses, until Goldman decided on March 9, 1971 to rescind the contract, approval was unanimous, enthusiastic, and uninterrupted from beginning to end. . . .

[Judgment reversed and action remanded.]

QUESTIONS AND CASE PROBLEMS

1. Ponder was the president of the Long Beach Motel Hotel Corporation. He requested a quotation from General Electric on air conditioners for the hotel. He was sent a quotation, on the basis of which he sent in a purchase order on behalf of the corporation. General Electric rejected this order made in the name of the corporation and in effect stated that it would only sell to Ponder personally. A new purchase order was sent to Ponder which showed him individually as the buyer. He signed his name but then added "Pres." When General Electric sued him for the purchase price, he claimed that he had signed on behalf of the corporation and that General Electric knew that it was dealing with the corporation. Was he bound by the contract? [General Electric Co. v Ponder, (La App) 234 So2d 786]

2. The directors of the American Founders Life Insurance Co. made a contract with the Colorado Management Corp. for certain services. American Founders later sued for the return of the money paid to Colorado on the ground that the contract could be set aside because it had been approved by American Founders at a board of directors' meeting at which only six of the eight directors were present and three of these directors were also directors of Colorado and two of them were also officers of Colorado. The bylaws of American Founders required a majority, which was five, to constitute a quorum for a directors' meeting. Was American Founders entitled to recover? [Colorado Management Corp. v American Founders Life Insurance Co., 145 Colo 413, 359 P2d 665]

3. Heyl and others were directors of Western Inn Corporation. The corporation desired to construct a motel but financial difficulties developed. Outside financing did not prove possible, and finally Heyl and several other directors loaned the money to the corporation. At the time of each loan, all details were made known to, and approved by, the board of directors and the shareholders. As part of the loan agreement with Heyl and the others, a mortgage on the corporation's hotel property was given to them. Thereafter the corporation defaulted on the loan agreement, and Heyl and the other directors who had loaned the corporation the money foreclosed on the mortgage and purchased the hotel property at the foreclosure sale. The Western Inn Corporation sued Heyl and the directors on the theory that they had committed a breach of their fiduciary duty as directors by purchasing the corporation property for themselves at the foreclosure sale and that they therefore held the property as constructive trustees for the corporation. Was the corporation correct? [Western Inn Corp. v Heyl, (Tex Civ App) 452 SW2d 752]

4. The president of the Atlantic & North Carolina Railroad Co. published in one newspaper a notice of a special meeting of stockholders to be held in Newbern, North Carolina. After the stockholders assembled, they adjourned to meet in Morehead City on the same day. After reassembling, the stockholders voted to authorize a lease of the corporate property to the Howland Improvement Co. Twenty days later the regular annual meeting of the corporation was held. A resolution was then introduced by Foy, at the instance of Hill, instructing the proper officers to bring a suit to set the lease aside. The stockholders' meeting voted to take no action on this resolution and voted that it be tabled. On behalf of himself and other stockholders, Hill then brought a suit against the railroad company to have the lease annulled. He contended that the lease was not properly authorized because the notice of the meeting had not been given as required by the bylaws and because the meeting had not been held at the place of call. Was the special meeting properly held? [Hill v Atlantic & North Carolina Railroad Co., 143 NC 539, 55 SE 854]

5. Anthony Yee was the president of the Waipahu Auto Exchange, a corporation. As part of his corporate duties, he arranged financing for the company. The Federal Services Finance Corporation drew twelve checks payable to the order of the Waipahu Auto Exchange. These were then indorsed by its president: "Waipahu Auto Exchange, Limited, by Anthony Yee, President," and were cashed at two different banks. The Bishop National Bank of Hawaii, on which the checks were drawn, charged its depositor, Federal Services, with the amount of these checks. Federal Services then sued Bishop National Bank to restore to its account the amount of these twelve checks on the theory that Bishop National Bank had improperly made payment on the checks because Anthony Yee had no authority to cash them. Did Yee have authority to indorse and cash the checks? [Federal Services Finance Corp. v Bishop National Bank of Hawaii, (CA9 Haw) 190 F2d 442]

6. Sacks claimed that when he was a salesman for Helene Curtis Industries, its president, Stein, made an oral contract with him to the effect that Sacks was to act as the sales manager of the corporation at a compensation of a straight

salary and a percentage of the increased volume of the corporation's sales. The corporation later refused to pay compensation on this basis and asserted that it had never been informed of any such agreement. The corporation denied that the contract had in fact been made and asserted that the president had no authority to make such an agreement. Was the agreement binding on the corporation? [Sacks v Helene Curtis Industries, 340 Ill App 76, 91 NE2d 127]

7. Frushour, a director of Kidd Island Bay Development Corp., undertook to acquire for Kidd two parcels of Day's land which Kidd desired, either by exchanging for the two parcels a tract of land owned by Kidd or by money purchase. Instead, Frushour exchanged the Kidd tract for the two Day parcels to which he took title in his own name, while telling other Kidd directors and officers that Day would not exchange but would only buy the Kidd tract. Accordingly, Kidd deeded the 15-acre tract to Day, and a check came to Kidd from a realty company where Frushour worked. Knutsen, also a Kidd director, upon learning what had transpired, brought a shareholder's derivative action against Frushour to have the Day parcels held in trust for Kidd. Frushour's defense was that a director may engage in personal business activities and that Kidd had not forbidden its directors to engage in outside real estate transactions on their own account. Decide. [Knutsen v Frushour, 92 Idaho 37, 436 P2d 521]

8. Cholfin and his wife were two of the three directors of the Allied Freightways Corporation. Cholfin ran the business, and his wife and the other director took no active part in its management. Cholfin unlawfully used $16,587.25 of the corporate funds to pay his own debts and $3,086.39 of the corporate funds to pay those of his wife. Allied Freightways brought suit to recover from the Cholfins the money improperly spent from the corporation. Allied Freightways claimed that each of the defendants was liable for the full amount of all improper expenditures. Was this correct? [Allied Freightways v Cholfin, 325 Mass 630, 91 NE2d 765]

53 Real Property—Deeds

NATURE AND TRANSFER OF REAL PROPERTY

The law of real property is technical and to a large extent uses a vocabulary drawn from the days of feudalism. Much of the earlier law of real property is no longer of practical importance in the modern business world. The following discussion is therefore a simplified, modern presentation of the subject.

§ 53:1. Definitions. *Real property* includes (1) land, (2) buildings and fixtures, and (3) rights in the land of another.

(1) Land. *Land* means more than the surface of the earth. It embraces the soil and all things of a permanent nature affixed to the ground, such as herbs, grass, or trees, and other growing, natural products. The term also includes the waters upon the ground and things that are embedded beneath the surface. For example, coal, oil, and marble embedded beneath the surface form part of the land.

Technically, land is considered as extending downward to the earth's center and upward indefinitely. The Uniform Aeronautics Act states that the owner of land owns the space above, subject to the right of aircraft in flight which does not interfere with the use of the land and is not dangerous to persons or property lawfully on the land.[1]

(2) Buildings and Fixtures. A *building* includes any structure placed on or beneath the surface of land, without regard to its purpose or use. A *fixture* is personal property that has been attached to the earth or placed in a building in such a way or under such circumstances that it is deemed part of the real property.[2]

(3) Rights in the Land of Another. These rights include *easements,* such as the right to cross another's land, and *profits,* such as the right to take coal from another's land.

---

[1] The Uniform Aeronautics Act (UAA) has been adopted in Arizona, Delaware, Georgia, Hawaii, Idaho, Indiana, Maryland, Minnesota, Missouri, Montana, Nevada, New Jersey, North Carolina, North Dakota, Pennsylvania, South Carolina, South Dakota, Tennessee, Utah, Vermont, and Wisconsin, but was withdrawn by the Commissioners on Uniform State Laws in 1943.

[2] See § 53:21.

§ 53:2. Antidiscrimination. The owner of land cannot discriminate in the sale or renting of real estate because of race or color,[3] nor generally because of creed, national origin, or ancestry.[4] A provision in a deed limiting the right of the buyer to resell cannot be enforced when the effect of enforcement would be to make a prohibited discrimination.[5] Likewise, a state may not provide that an owner of real estate may sell or rent or refuse to sell or rent to any person as he sees fit. (See p. 1077, Reitman v Mulkey.)

§ 53:3. Easements. An *easement* is not only a right in the land of another, but it is a right that belongs to the land which is benefited. The benefited land is called the *dominant tenement,* and the subject land is called the *servient tenement.*

An easement is an interest in land and therefore an oral promise to create an easement is not binding because of the state of frauds.[6]

(1) Creation of Easement. An easement may be created by:

(1) Deed.

(2) Implication when one conveys part of his land that has been used as a dominant estate in relation to the part retained. To illustrate, if water or drain pipes run from the part alienated through the part retained, there is an implied right to have such use continued. In order that an easement will be implied in such a case, the use must be apparent, continuous, and reasonably necessary.

A contractor's use of a driveway for his construction equipment while a house was being built is obviously a temporary use and the house owner cannot claim the right to use the driveway thereafter on the theory that such use by the contractor gave rise to an easement by implication.[7]

(3) Implication when it is necessary to the use of the land alienated. This ordinarily arises when one sells land to which no entry can be made, except over the land retained or over the land of a stranger. The right to use the land retained for the purpose of going to and from the land is known as a *way of necessity.*

(4) Estoppel, as when the grantor states that the plot conveyed is bounded by a street. If, in such a case, the grantor owns the adjoining plot, he cannot deny the public the right to use the area which he has described as a street.

(5) Prescription by adverse use for a prescribed period.[8] (See p. 1078, Cramer v Jenkins.) A cattleman did not obtain an easement by prescription to drive his cattle across a neighbor's land, where such crossing was not

---

[3] 42 USC § 1982; Jones v Alfred H. Mayer Co., 392 US 409.
[4] Davis v Vesta Co., 45 NJ 301, 212 A2d 345.
[5] Shelley v Kraemer, 334 US 1; Barrows v Jackson, 346 US 249.
[6] Katcher v Sans Souci Co., (Fla App) 200 So2d 826.
[7] Fones v Fagan, 214 Va 87, 196 SE2d 916.
[8] See § 53:6(6).

adverse because the cattleman always requested permission from the neighbor before he drove his cattle across the land.[9]

*(2) **Termination of Easement.*** Once an easement has been granted it cannot be destroyed by the act of the grantor. A "revocation" attempted by him, without the easement owner's consent has no effect.[10]

An easement may be lost by nonuse when there are surrounding circumstances which show an intent to abandon the easement. For example, where a surface transit system had an easement to maintain trolley tracks, it could be found that there was an abandonment of the easement when the tracks were removed and all surface transportation was discontinued.[11] Likewise, where the owner of the easement planted a flower bed on his land across the end of the path of the easement, it was evident that he intended to abandon the easement.[12]

§ 53:4. Liens. Real property may be subject to liens that arise by the voluntary act of the owner of the land, such as the lien of a mortgage[13] which is created when the owner voluntarily borrows money and the land is made security for the repayment of the debt. Liens may also arise involuntarily as in the case of tax liens, judgment liens, and mechanics' liens. In the case of taxes and judgments, the liens provide a means for enforcing the obligations of the owner of the land to pay the taxes or the judgment.

Mechanics' liens give persons furnishing labor and materials in the improvement of real estate the right to proceed against the real estate for the collection of the amounts due them. If the owner had dealt directly with such persons, the mechanics' lien is a remedy in addition to the right to enforce the contract of the owner. If the claimant did not have a contract directly with the owner, as in the case of a person furnishing labor or materials to the contractor who dealt with the owner, the claimant has no contract claim against the owner. Mechanics' liens are created by statutes which regulate in detail the kinds of claims for which liens may be imposed and the procedure to be followed.

§ 53:5. Duration and Extent of Ownership. The interest held by a person in real property may be defined in terms of the period of time for which he will remain the owner. He may have (1) a fee simple estate or (2) a life estate. These estates are termed *freehold estates.* In addition, either of these estates may be subject to a condition or may expire or terminate upon the happening of a specified contingency. Although a person may own property

---

[9] Yeckel v Connell, — Wyo —, 508 P2d 1200.

[10] Austin Lake Estates Recreation Club, Inc. v Gilliam, (Tex Civ App) 493 SW 2d 343.

[11] DC Transit System, Inc. v State Roads Commission, 265 Md 546, 290 A2d 807.

[12] Kelly v Smith, 58 Misc 2d 883, 296 NYS2d 451.

[13] See § 54:2.

for a specified number of years, this interest is not regarded as a freehold estate, but is a *leasehold estate* and is subject to rules of law different from those applicable to freehold estates.[14]

(1) Fee Simple Estate. An *estate in fee*, a *fee simple* or a *fee simple absolute,* is the largest estate known to our law. The owner of such fee has the absolute and entire property in the land. The important characteristics of this estate are as follows: (a) it is alienable during life; (b) it is alienable by will; (c) it descends to heirs generally if not devised (transferred by will); (d) it is subject to rights of the owner's surviving spouse; and (e) it is liable for debts of the owner before or after death.

Statutes commonly declare that a deed conveying property will be held to convey a fee simple estate if nothing is expressly stated that limits the grantee to a lesser estate.[15]

(2) Life Estate. A *life estate* (or life tenancy), as its name indicates, lasts only during the life of a person, ordinarily its owner. Upon his death no interest remains to pass to his heirs or by his will.

§ 53:6. Transferring Real Property.

(1) Deed. The most common form of transfer of title to real property is by the delivery of a deed by the owner.[16]

(2) Public Grant or Patent. Real property may be acquired directly from the government. The method of transfer in such a case may be by legislative grant or by patent, which has been commonly used by the federal government under the homestead laws.

(3) Dedication. Any person possessing a legal or equitable interest in land may appropriate it to the use of the public. This is known as a *dedication.* The real property must be set apart with the intention to surrender it to the use of the public. An acceptance is usually necessary on the part of the municipality or the state.

(4) Eminent Domain.[17] Two important questions are involved in the transfer of property by this method; namely, whether there is a taking of property and whether the property is intended for public use. In respect to the first, it is not necessary that one be physically deprived of his land. It is sufficient if he is denied the normal use of his property. It is not necessary that the public actually use the land. It is sufficient that it is appropriated for the public benefit.

---

[14] See § 54:1.
[15] Slaten v Loyd, 282 Ala 485, 213 So2d 219.
[16] See § 53:7.
[17] See § 21:3(1).

It is held immaterial that the exercise of the power of eminent domain would benefit a competitor, as where the ultimate result would be the building of a highway which would facilitate motor traffic to a more remote competitor. The law finds a public purpose in the taking of the property to construct a highway as the public will travel on the finished highway and the law is not concerned with why the public would want to travel on the highway or whether its so doing will benefit a particular private interest.[18]

(5) Accretion. The owner of land acquires or loses title to land that is added or taken away by the imperceptible action of water upon his property. An increase of land caused by the action of water upon its borders is known as *accretion.* This gain or increase may result from alluvion or dereliction. *Alluvion* occurs when soil or sand is washed up by the water and becomes attached to the land. *Dereliction* occurs when the water recedes, leaving bare land which was formerly a part of its bed. Thus, when the boundary line between two farms is the middle of a stream, gradual changes in the course of the stream add to the land on one side and take away from the land on the other.

There is no change of title in the case of *avulsion,* which occurs when a boundary river shifts suddenly or violently, as in the case of a storm or a channel breakthrough, resulting in land being on the other side of the river from the side where it had been.[19]

(6) Adverse Possession. Title to land may be acquired by holding it adversely to the true owner for a certain period of time. In such a case one gains title by *adverse possession.* If such possession is maintained, the possessor automatically becomes the owner of the property even though he admittedly had no lawful claim to the land before.

In order to acquire title in this manner, possession must be (a) actual, (b) visible and notorious, (c) exclusive, (d) hostile, and (e) continuous for a required period of time.

The period during which land must be held adversely in order to gain title varies in the different states. In many states the statute prescribes twenty or twenty-one years, whereas in others the period is shorter.

Occupation of land in the mistaken belief that one is the owner is a "hostile" possession.[20] When a property owner occupies more land than he actually owns, as when he wrongfully believes that he owns down to a particular fence but the fence is actually on the adjoining land, such owner adversely occupies the strip between his land and the fence as he occupies it as owner to the exclusion of the rest of the world, and it is immaterial that he would not have done so if he had known that he did not own the strip.[21]

---

[18] In re Legislative Route 62214, 425 Pa 349, 229 A2d 1.
[19] Olsen v Jones, (Okla) 412 P2d 162.
[20] Port of Portland v Maxwell, 9 Ore App 105, 496 P2d.
[21] Bradt v Giovannone, 35 App Div 2d 322, 315 NYS2d 961.

Occasional or intermittent acts, such as driving cattle across land or cutting timber, do not show a sufficient continuity of use to give rise to title by adverse possession.[22]

(7) ***Prescription.*** The right to use another's land for some purpose, as in the case of an easement, may be acquired by adverse use. This is known as *prescription.* The elements requisite to the acquiring of rights by prescription are practically the same as in adverse possession, except that the use need not be exclusive of others and continuous use is not literally required.

(8) ***Marriage.*** In most states if the deceased spouse did not leave a will, the surviving spouse is given absolute ownership of a fractional share of all property owned by the other spouse at the date of death. Provision is generally made for varying the share inversely to the number of children or other heirs, for rejecting the provisions of a will that deprive the surviving spouse of the statutory share,[23] and sometimes for permitting a spouse to claim an interest in property conveyed during the deceased spouse's lifetime without the consent of the surviving spouse.

(9) ***Abandonment.*** Unlike personal property,[24] title to real estate generally cannot be lost or transferred by abandonment.

(10) ***Boundary Line Agreement.*** When there is a bona fide dispute between neighboring landowners as to the common boundary line, an agreement as to the location of the line is binding upon them. Theoretically it has the effect of transferring title to any strip of land between the agreed boundary line and a different true boundary line.[25]

DEEDS

Although many of the technical limitations of the feudal and earlier common-law days have disappeared, much of the law relating to the modern deed originated in those days. For this reason the drawing of a deed to transfer the title to land should be entrusted only to one who knows exactly what must be done.

§ 53:7. Definition. A *deed* is an instrument or writing by which an owner or *grantor* transfers or conveys an interest in land to a new owner called a *grantee* or transferee. In some states that have retained the influence of the common law, the deed must be sealed.

Unlike a contract, no consideration is required to make a deed effective. Real property, as in the case of personal property, may either be sold or given as a gift. Although consideration is not required to make a valid deed or transfer of title by deed, the absence of consideration may be evidence

[22] Powell v Hopkins, 288 Ala 466, 262 So2d 289.
[23] See § 39:12.
[24] See § 21:12(2).
[25] Roman v Ries, 259 Cal App 2d 65, 66 Cal Rptr 120.

to show that the transfer was made by the owner in fraud of his creditors who may then be able to set aside the transfer. A deed is necessary to transfer title to land, even though it is a gift.[26]

§ 53:8. Classification of Deeds. Deeds may be classified in terms of the interest conveyed as (1) a *quitclaim deed,* which transfers merely whatever interest, if any, the grantor may have in the property, without specifying that interest in any way, and (2) a *warranty deed,* which purports to transfer a specified interest and which warrants or guarantees that such interest is transferred.

A deed may also be classified as (1) a statutory deed or (2) a common-law deed. The *common-law deed* is a long form that sets forth the details of the transaction. The *statutory deed* in substance merely recites that a named person is making a certain conveyance to a named grantee. It is generally held that the existence of a statute authorizing a short form of deed does not preclude the use of the common-law form.

§ 53:9. Grantor's Warranties.

(1) Warranties of Title. In the common-law deed the grantor may expressly warrant or make certain covenants as to the title conveyed. The statutes authorizing a short form of deed provide that unless otherwise stated in the deed, the grantor shall be presumed to have made certain warranties of title.

The more important of the covenants or warranties of title which the grantor may make are: (a) *covenant of seizin,* or guarantee that the grantor owns the exact estate which he has purported to convey; (b) *covenant of right to convey,* or guarantee that the grantor, if he is not the owner, as in the case of an agent, has the right or authority to make the conveyance; (c) *covenant against encumbrances,* or guarantee that the land is not subject to any right or interest of a third person, such as a lien or easement; (d) *covenant for quiet enjoyment,* or covenant by the grantor that the grantee's possession of the land shall not be disturbed either by the grantor, in the case of a limited covenant, or by the grantor or any person claiming title under him, in the case of a general covenant; and (e) *covenant for further assurances,* or promise by the grantor that he will execute any additional document that may be required to perfect the title of the grantee.

(2) Nontitle Warranties. Distinct from the warranties of title, a grantor may make any warranty or guaranty he chooses, although such other obligations are more likely to be found in the sales contract, such as an undertaking to deliver the house in "new house condition." [27] A buyer acts at his peril when the warranty or guaranty in the contract is not repeated in the deed, for in many instances the deed will supersede or take the place of the

[26] Proctor v Forsythe, 4 Wash App 238, 480 P2d 511.
[27] Smith v Millwood Construction Corp., 260 Md 319, 272 A2d 19.

prior written sales contract. Thus, if the warranty or guaranty is only in the prior contract, the silence of the deed will bar proof of that prior sales contract provision.

*(3) **Fitness for Use.*** In the absence of an express warranty in the deed, no warranty as to fitness arises under the common law in the sale or conveyance of real estate. Thus, by the common law there is no implied warranty that a house is reasonably fit for habitation,[28] even though it is a new house sold by the builder.[29]

When a home is purchased directly from the builder, many courts imply a warranty that it was constructed in a good workmanlike manner [30] but do not go so far as to impose a warranty that the house is fit to use or free from defects. Similarly, a buyer may have some protection against defects due to poor design of the building when he purchases his home from the contractor who prepared the building plans and specifications. In such a case the contractor may be held liable if, because of a defect in the plans and specifications, the building when constructed is not fit for the purpose for which it was constructed.[31] And a builder is liable for fraud when he intentionally conceals defects in the construction which the buyer could not discover by inspection.[32]

A growing number of courts, in approximately half of the states, hold that when a builder or real estate developer sells a new house to a home buyer, he makes an implied warranty that the house and foundation are fit for occupancy or use, without regard to whether the house was purchased before, during, or after completion of construction.[33] (See p. 1079, Humber v Morton.)

There is likewise authority that strict tort liability may be applied to the developer or vendor of the new home for personal injuries sustained by the buyer or a member of his family.[34] There is also a trend of authority by which a seller is required to inform the buyer of any respect in which government approval has not been obtained and to hold a seller liable for fraud when, knowing the truth, he remains silent. No warranty of fitness arises when the seller is a casual seller as when an owner sells his house to a buyer.[35]

The warranty of habitability is not a guaranty with respect to neighboring property. Thus, a builder is not liable for breach of warranty when the

---

[28] Amos v McDonald, 123 Ga App 509, 181 SE2d 515.

[29] Mitchem v Johnson, 7 Ohio 2d 66, 218 NE2d 594. No warranty arises under the Sales Article of the UCC since its provisions apply only to sales of "goods." Vernali v Centrella, 28 Conn Supp 476, 266 A2d 200. The provision of the UCC requiring that a buyer give his seller notice of a defect is not applicable to the case of a defect in a house. Pollard v Saxe & Yolles Development Co., 32 Cal App 3d 390, 108 Cal Rptr 174.

[30] Shiffers v Cunningham Shepherd Builders Co., 28 Colo App 29, 470 P2d 593.

[31] Rosell v Silver Crest Enterprises, 7 Ariz App 137, 436 P2d 915.

[32] Reynolds v Wilson, 121 Ga App 153, 173 SE2d 256.

[33] Weeks v Slavick Builders, 24 Mich App 621, 180 NW2d 503; Rothberg v Olenik, 128 Vt 295, 262 A2d 461.

[34] Schipper v Levitt & Sons, 44 NJ 70, 207 A2d 314.

[35] Gallegos v Graff, — Colo App —, 508 P2d 798.

improving of neighboring land, coupled with heavy rains, causes water to stand on the property improved and sold by him.[36]

Akin to widening the seller's warranty liability is a widening of fraud liability to include unverified false statements made in selling. Thus, a real estate broker and his surety were held liable for fraud when the broker assured the purchaser that there was no water seepage problem and the statement proved false. It was immaterial whether or not the broker at the time he made the statement had knowledge that it was false.[37] When a seller in good faith represented the building as sound, when in fact it was infested by termites, the seller was liable for damages to the buyer although no express statement had been made as to termites and even though the buyer had examined the house but did not know what to look for and did not detect the presence of termites.[38]

There appears to be developing a concept of contractor's liability similar to a warranty or enterprise liability concept.[39]

(4) Damages for Breach of Grantor's Warranty. When the grantor has broken a warranty, he is liable for damages caused the grantee but he is not liable for damages greater than the loss actually sustained. For example, when a grantor broke his warranty of title in that the true boundary lines did not run up to the fences on the land but the grantee was able to acquire the "missing" strips between the boundary lines and the fences from the neighbors for a nominal cost, the grantor was liable to the grantee only for such nominal damages.[40]

§ 53:10. Execution of Deeds. Ordinarily a deed must be signed, by signature or mark, and sealed by the grantor. In order to have the deed recorded, statutes generally require that two or more witnesses sign the deed and that the grantor then acknowledge his deed before a notary public or other officer. In the interest of legibility, it is frequently required that the signatures of the parties be followed by their printed or typewritten names.

In many states the statute that authorizes a short or simplified form of deed also declares that no seal is required to make effective a writing which purports to convey an interest in land.[41]

A deed must be executed and delivered by a person having capacity. It may be set aside by the grantor on the ground of the fraud of the grantee provided that innocent third persons have not acquired rights in the land.[42]

---

[36] Burger v Hector, (Fla App) 278 So2d 636.

[37] Sawyer v Tildahl, 275 Minn 457, 148 NW2d 131.

[38] Maser v Lind, 181 Neb 365, 148 NW2d 831.

[39] Wurst v Pruyn, 250 La 1109, 202 So2d 268. Some courts take an intermediate position, holding that a buyer may rescind a sales contract when there is a defect in the building that could not have been disclosed by reasonable investigation, but refusing to imply a warranty against such defect. Davey v Brownson, 3 Wash App 820, 478 P2d 258.

[40] Creason v Peterson, 24 Utah 2d 305, 470 P2d 403.

[41] Woodell v Hollywood Homes, 105 RI 280, 252 A2d 28.

[42] Bicknell v Jones, 203 Kan 196, 453 P2d 127.

The deed remains binding as between the grantor and his grantee even though it has not been acknowledged or recorded.

Deeds were originally strictly interpreted according to rules of feudal origin. Many courts today are turning away from the past and are interpreting deeds in the same way as ordinary contracts, namely they are seeking to ascertain the intent of the parties.

The parol evidence rule is applied to a deed and thus excludes proof of prior or contemporaneous oral agreements with respect to the property conveyed. In addition, the provisions of a prior contract of sale, even though in writing, are generally held to be "merged" in the deed. In other words, if there is any inconsistent term in a prior written contract, such term is displaced by the later deed which omits or contradicts the earlier term. Thus, when a deed omitted a particular tract of land, it could not be shown that the prior written agreement had included such tract in the description of the land conveyed when there was not sufficient proof that the omission from the deed was the result of fraud, misrepresentation, or mistake.[43]

§ **53:11. Delivery.** A deed has no effect and title does not pass until the deed has been delivered. Delivery is a matter of intent as shown by both words and conduct; no particular form of ceremony is required. The essential intent in delivering a deed is not merely that the grantor intends to hand over physical control and possession of the paper on which the deed is written, but that he intends thereby to divest himself of ownership of the property described in the deed. That is, he must deliver the deed with the intent that it should take effect as a deed and convey an interest in the property. (See p. 1081, Shroyer v Shroyer.)

A deed is ordinarily made effective by handing it to the grantee with the intention that he should thenceforth be the owner of the property described in the deed. A delivery may also be made by placing the deed, addressed to the grantee, in the mail or by giving it to a third person with directions to hand it to the grantee. Where the grantor mailed the deed to the grantee, there was a valid delivery by the act of mailing and the grantee's interest was not affected by the fact that the grantor committed suicide later that day and the deed was not received by the grantee until after the grantor's death.[44]

When the grantor at the direction of the grantee sends a deed to the grantee's attorney, there is a delivery of the deed and a transfer of title to the grantee.[45] Likewise, an actual delivery of the deed from the grantor to the grantee is not required where the grantor takes the deed to the appropriate government office and has the deed recorded.[46]

When a deed is delivered to a third person for the the purpose of delivery by him to the grantee upon the happening of some event or contingency,

---

[43] Duncan v McAdams, 222 Ark 143, 257 SW2d 568.
[44] Allgood v Allgood, 230 Ga 312, 196 SE2d 888.
[45] Capozzella v Capozzella, 213 Va 820, 196 SE2d 67.
[46] Turner v Close, 125 Kan 485, 264, P 1047.

the transaction is called a *delivery in escrow.* No title passes until the fulfillment of the condition or the happening of the event or contingency.

An effective delivery of a deed may be made symbolically as by delivering to the grantee the key to a locked box and informing the grantee that the deed to him of the property is in the box.[47]

§ 53:12. Acceptance. Generally there must be an acceptance by the grantee. In all cases, however, an acceptance is presumed, but the grantee may disclaim the transfer if he acts within a reasonable time after learning that the transfer has been made.

§ 53:13. Cancellation of Deeds. A deed, although delivered, acknowledged, and recorded, may be set aside or canceled by the grantor upon proof of such circumstances as would warrant the setting aside of a contract. For example, when a conveyance is made in consideration of a promise to support the grantor, the failure of the grantee to perform will ordinarily justify cancellation of the deed.

§ 53:14. Recording of Deeds. If the owner of the land desires to do so, he may record his deed in the office of a public official sometimes called a recorder or commissioner of deeds. The recording is not required to make the deed effective to pass title, but it is done so that the public will know that the grantee is the present owner and thereby to prevent the former owner from making any other transaction relating to the property. The recording statutes provide that a person purchasing land from the last holder of record will take title free of any unrecorded claim to the land of which the purchaser does not have notice or knowledge.

The fact that a deed is recorded charges everyone with knowledge of its existence even though they in fact do not know of it because they have neglected to examine the record. The recording of a deed, however, is only such notice if the deed was properly executed. Likewise, the grantee of land cannot claim any protection by virtue of the recording of a deed when (1) an adverse claim is made by one whose title is superior to that of the owner of record; (2) the grantee had notice or knowledge of the adverse claim when he acquired title; (3) a person acting under a hostile claim was then in possession of the land; (4) the grantee received the land as a gift; or (5) the transfer to the grantee was fraudulent.

§ 53:15. Additional Protection of Buyers. Apart from the protection given to buyers and third persons by the recorded title to property, a buyer may generally also protect himself by procuring title insurance or an *abstract of title,* which is a summarized report of the title to the property as shown by the records, together with a report of all judgments, mortgages, and similar claims against the property that have also been recorded.

---

[47] Agrelius v Mohesky, 208 Kan 790, 494 P2d 1095.

§ 53:16. Donees and Purchasers with Notice. Donees or persons who do not give value and persons who have knowledge or notice of outstanding claims always take title to property subject to any claims, such as unrecorded deeds and equitable or statutory liens on the land.

§ 53:17. Creditors of Grantor. The transfer of title under a deed may be defeated in some instances by creditors of the grantor.

(1) Fraudulent Conveyances. Following an English statute,[48] it is held in most states that a conveyance for the purpose of hindering, delaying, or defrauding creditors is voidable as against such creditors. The rule is applicable in the case of subsequent creditors, as well as those existing at the time of the conveyance. For example, when one, just before entering into debt, makes a conveyance that he knows is likely to render him unable to pay his obligations, subsequent creditors may avoid the conveyance. Likewise, where the owner of land conveyed it for nothing to his mother as soon as a creditor obtained a judgment against him for $7,000, it was clear that the conveyance was made with the intent of defeating the right of the creditor and the deed to the mother would therefore be set aside.[49] When the transfer is made to a bona fide purchaser without notice, the title passes under a deed free from the demands or claims of either existing or subsequent creditors. In any case the person who claims that a transfer of title has been made in fraud of creditors has the burden of proving that fact.

Under the Uniform Fraudulent Conveyance Act [50] conveyances in certain situations are classified as being in fraud of creditors. If the claim of a defrauded creditor of the grantor is due, he ordinarily may have the fraudulent conveyance set aside or he may disregard the conveyance and attach or levy execution upon the property conveyed.

(2) Federal Bankruptcy Act. Another situation in which the claims of creditors may defeat the passing of title is that in which the conveyance violates a provision of the Federal Bankruptcy Act. Under the provisions of that statute a conveyance that operates to give a preference to one creditor as against another may be set aside if the conveyance was made within four months prior to the time when the grantor was adjudged a bankrupt. The trustee in bankruptcy is also authorized to avoid any conveyance that is a fraud upon creditors.[51]

§ 53:18. Grantee's Covenants. In a deed the grantee may undertake to do or to refrain from doing certain acts. Such an agreement becomes a binding

---

[48] Statute 13 Elizabeth Ch. 5.

[49] Stoner v Farber, 207 Okla 641, 263 P2d 159.

[50] This Act has been adopted in Arizona, California, Delaware, Idaho, Maryland, Massachusetts, Michigan, Minnesota, Montana, Nevada, New Hampshire, New Jersey, New Mexico, New York, North Dakota, Ohio, Oklahoma, Pennsylvania, South Dakota, Tennessee, Utah, Washington, Wisconsin, Wyoming, and the Virgin Islands.

[51] See § 39:9.

contract between the grantor and the grantee. The grantor may sue the grantee for its breach. When the covenant of the grantee relates directly to the property conveyed, such as an agreement to maintain fences on the property or that the property shall be used only for residential purposes, it is said not only that the covenant is binding between the grantor and the grantee but also that it *runs with the land*. This means that anyone acquiring the grantee's land from the grantee is also bound by the covenant of the grantee, even though this subsequent owner had not made any such agreement with anyone.

The right to enforce the covenant also runs with the land owned by the grantor to whom the promise was made. Thus, if *A* owns adjoining tracts of land and conveys one of them to *B* and *B* covenants to maintain the surface drainage on the land so that it will not flood *A*'s land, the benefit of this covenant will run with the land retained by *A*. If *A* sells his remaining tract of land to *C*, *B* is bound to perform his covenant so as to benefit the neighboring tract even though it is now owned by *C*.

A covenant which provides that the grantee shall refrain from certain conduct is termed a *restrictive* (or negative) *covenant*. It runs with the land in the same manner as a covenant that calls for the performance of an act, that is, an *affirmative covenant*.

§ 53:19. Scope of Grantee's Restrictive Covenants. A restrictive covenant may impose both a limitation on the kind of structure that can be erected on the land and the nature of the use which may be made.

A covenant restricting the owner to one single-family private dwelling bars the owner from building a duplex apartment.[52]

(1) General Building Scheme. When a tract of land is developed and individual lots or homes are sold to separate purchasers, it is common to use the same restrictive covenants in all deeds in order to impose uniform restrictions and patterns on the property. Any person acquiring a lot within the tract is bound by the restrictions if they are in his deed or a prior recorded deed, or if he has notice or knowledge of such restrictions. Any person owning one of the lots in the tract may bring suit against another lot owner to enforce the restrictive covenant.[53] The effect is to create a zoning code based upon the agreement of the parties in their deeds, as distinguished from one based upon government regulation.

(2) Restraints on Alienation. The covenants of the grantee may restrict him when he seeks to sell his property. It is lawful to provide that the grantor shall have the option to purchase the property, or that if the grantee offers to sell it to anyone, the grantor will be given an opportunity to match the price that a third person is willing to pay. Restrictions on the grantee's right to sell the property are not enforceable when the restriction discriminates against

---

[52] Easterly v Hall, 256 SC 336, 182 SE2d 671.

[53] Hagan v Sabal Palms, (Fla App) 186 So2d 302.

potential buyers because of race, color, creed, or national origin. Thus, a covenant that the grantee will only resell to a member of the Caucasian race cannot be enforced.[54] A restraint on alienation that specifies that the grantee will not sell the property to anyone or that he will not sell to anyone other than the grantor or his heirs or representatives [55] is contrary to public policy.

§ 53:20. Interpretation of Restrictive Covenants. Restrictive covenants of a grantee are generally interpreted strictly so as to impose the least restraint upon the grantee consistent with the letter of the covenant.

(1) Parol Evidence. A covenant must be expressed in a deed; it cannot be established by parol evidence. Consequently, when the deed did not so specify, if could not be shown by parol evidence that the grantor and the grantee had agreed that the land conveyed would be used only as a baseball park.[56]

(2) Enforcement of Grantee's Covenants. A grantee's covenant may be enforced by the grantor or by a neighboring property owner intended to be benefited by the covenant. The grantee's covenant may be enforced in an action at law for damages. In the case of restrictive or negative covenants, the complaining person may also obtain the aid of a court with equity jurisdiction to grant an injunction compelling the owner of the land to comply with the terms of the covenant. Equitable relief is generally denied, however, in the case of affirmative covenants. A declaratory judgment can often be obtained to determine the validity or meaning of both negative and affirmative covenants.

Relief, whether at law or in equity, will not be afforded when enforcement of the restriction would amount to a discrimination prohibited by the Fourteenth Amendment of the Constitution of the United States, or when the circumstances and neighborhood have so changed that it would be absurd to continue to enforce the restriction. Thus, restrictions in deeds delivered 50 years ago stipulating that no private automobile garages could be erected or maintained have frequently been held invalid in recent years because the auto is now so essential that its exclusion would be ridiculous and would now make the ownership of the property less valuable. Restrictions requiring that premises be used only for residential purposes may often be ignored when stores and other commercial or industrial enterprises have entered the neighborhood in such a large number that the character of the neighborhood is no longer predominantly residential. (See p. 1083, Cochran v Long.)

Every change in character of a neighborhood does not warrant abandoning a restrictive covenant. The change must be so radical or complete as to make it clear that the restriction has outlined its usefulness.[57]

---

[54] Shelley v Kraemer, 334 US 1; Barrows v Jackson, 346 US 249.

[55] Braun v Klug, 335 Mich 691, 57 NW2d 299.

[56] McCarthy's St. Louis Park Cafe, Inc. v Minneapolis Baseball & Athletic Association, 258 Minn 447, 104 NW2d 895.

[57] Chevy Chase Village v Jaggers, 261 Md 275 A2d 167.

The fact that the public may benefit by a departure from a restriction is not necessarily a sufficient ground for ignoring a restriction.

FIXTURES

By the concept of fixtures, personal property changes to real property and third persons and creditors may acquire rights therein.

§ 53:21. Definition. A *fixture* includes personal property that is attached to the earth or placed in a building in such a way or under such circumstances that it is deemed part of the real property.

A person buys a refrigerator, an air conditioner, or a furnace, or some other item that is used in a building. He then has the item installed. The question whether the item is a fixture and therefore part of the building can arise in a variety of situations. (1) The real estate tax assessor assesses the building and adds in the value of the item on the theory that it is part of the building. (2) The buyer of the item owns the building and then sells the building, and his buyer claims that the item stays with the building. (3) The buyer has a mortgage on the building, and the mortgagee claims that the item is bound by the mortgage. (4) The buyer does not own the building in which he puts the item, and the landlord claims that the item must stay in the building when the tenant leaves. (5) The buyer did not pay in full for the item, and the seller of the item has a security interest that he asserts against the buyer of the item or against the landlord of the building in which the buyer installed the item. The seller of the item may be asserting his claim against the mortgagee of the building or against the buyer of the building.[58]

The determination of the rights of these parties depends upon the common law of fixtures, as occasionally modified by statute.[59]

§ 53:22. Tests of a Fixture. In the absence of an agreement between the parties, the courts apply three tests [60] to determine whether the personal property has become a fixture:

(1) Annexation. Generally the personal property becomes a fixture if it is so attached to the realty that it cannot be removed without materially damaging the realty or destroying the personal property itself. If the property is so affixed as to lose its specific identity, such as bricks in a wall, it becomes part of the realty. Where railroad tracks are so placed as to be immovable they are to be deemed fixtures.[61]

An air conditioner is a fixture when it is set in an opening in an apartment wall and is permanently fastened by screws and rubber seals, and

---

[58] Whether an addition to property is subject to a mechanics' lien is also frequently governed by whether it has become a "fixture." Boone v Smith, 79 NMex 614, 447 P2d 23.

[59] The UCC regulates the priority of security interests in fixtures, UCC § 9-313, but does not determine when an item is a fixture.

[60] Merchants & Mechanics Federal Savings & Loan Ass'n v Herald, 120 Ohio App 115, 201 NE2d 237.

[61] American Creosote Co., Inc. v Springer, 257 La 116, 241 So2d 510.

considerable force is required to remove it and removal would damage the sleeves in which it was set or the walls of the building.[62]

*(2) **Adaptation.*** Personal property especially adapted or suited to the building may constitute a fixture. By the *institutional* or *industrial plant doctrine,* machinery reasonably necessary for the operation of an industrial plant usually becomes part of the realty when installed, without regard to whether it is physically attached or not.[63] This principle does not apply to office equipment and trucks used in the operation of the enterprise.

*(3) **Intent.*** The true test is the intention of the person affixing the property at the time it was affixed.[64]

In the absence of direct proof, it is necessary to resort to the nature of the property, the method of its attachment, and all the surrounding circumstances to determine what the intent was. (See p. 1084, Premonstratensian Fathers v Badger Mutual Fire Ins. Co.) Generally, when a tenant installs equipment for the operation of a store or business, the equipment is regarded as personal property or *trade fixtures* which the tenant may remove when he leaves the rented premises. As against third persons, the mere intention to make personal property a part of the realty may be insufficient when the property has not been attached or is not adapted in such a way as to indicate that it is part of the realty.

The fact that machinery installed in a plant would be very difficult and expensive to move and so delicate that the moving would cause damage and unbalancing is significant in reaching the conclusion that the owner of the plant had installed the equipment as a permanent addition and thus had the intent which would make the equipment become fixtures.[65] When the floors in a large apartment house are of concrete which is covered with a thin sheet of plywood to which is stapled wall to wall carpeting, the carpeting constitutes a fixture which cannot be removed from the building as removal would probably destroy the carpeting, it had been cut to size, and the carpeting was necessary to make the building livable as an apartment.[66]

§ 53:23. Movable Machinery and Equipment. Machinery and equipment that is movable is ordinarily held not to constitute fixtures, even though, in order to move it, it is necessary to unbolt it from the floor or to disconnect electrical wires or water pipes.[67]

---

[62] State Automobile Mut. Ins. Co. v Trautwein, (Ky) 414 SW2d 587.

[63] United Laundries, Inc. v Board of Property Assessment, 359 Pa 195, 58 A2d 833.

[64] Del-Tan Corporation v Wilmington Housing Authority, (Del) 269 A2d 209.

[65] Wilmington Housing Authority v Parcel of Land, 59 Del 278, 219 A2d 148.

[66] Exchange Leasing Corp. v Aegen, 7 Ohio App 2d 11, 218 NE2d 633, (noting that the owner had installed carpeting so that the public would rent, which distinguished the case from one in which the tenant puts carpeting on the floor and the landlord claims that he has acquired title to the carpeting).

[67] Belinky v New York, 24 App Div 2d 908, 264 NYS2d 401.

It is ordinarily held that refrigerators and freezers, and gas and electric ranges [68] are not fixtures and do not lose their character as personal property when they are readily removable upon disconnecting pipes or unplugging wires. A portable window air conditioner which rests on a rack which is fixed to the window sill by two screws and is connected directly to the building only by an electric cord plug is not a fixture but remains personal property.[69]

The mere fact that an item may be "unplugged," however, does not establish that it is not a fixture. For example, a computer and its related hardware constituted "fixtures" when there was such a mass of wires and cables under the floor that the installation gave the impression of permanence.[70]

§ 53:24. Trade Fixtures. Equipment which is attached to a rented building by a tenant for use by him in his trade or business is ordinarily removable by him when he leaves the premises.[71] Such equipment is commonly called a *trade fixture.*[72] In some states the trade fixture is taxed as real estate, which would be normal if it were a true fixture, but the tax is assessed against the tenant,[73] which would not be the case if it were a true fixture.

Where a tenant is required to leave the premises in their original condition when the lease is terminated, it is likely that things installed by him will be regarded as retaining their character as personal property so that he may remove such property when he leaves.[74]

Pumping equipment used in coal mines is ordinarily a trade fixture when installed by a tenant and does not become part of the realty.[75]

CO-OWNERSHIP OF PROPERTY

All interests in particular real property may be held in severalty, that is, by one person alone. As explained in Chapter 20, ownership in severalty also exists when title is held in the form of "*A* or *B*."

§ 53:25. Multiple Ownership. Several persons may have concurrent interests in the same real property. The forms of multiple ownership for real property are the same as those for personal property. These have been discussed in Chapter 20.

When cotenants sell property, they hold the proceeds of sale by the same type of tenancy as they held the original property.

---

[68] Elliott v Tallmadge, 207 Ore 428, 297 P2d 310.

[69] Lafleur v Foret, (La App) 213 So2d 141.

[70] Bank of America v Los Angeles County, 224 Cal App 2d 108, 36 Cal Rptr 413.

[71] Pearson v Harper, 87 Idaho 245, 392 P2d 687.

[72] This is a misnomer because personal property is not a fixture when the intent is that it will be removed and taken away.

[73] County of Ventura v Channel Islands State Bank, 251 Cal App 2d 240, 59 Cal Rptr 404 (assessment against tenant is proper as he is the owner).

[74] Phoenix v Linsenmeyer, 78 Ariz 378, 280 P2d 698.

[75] Howe Coal Co. v Prairie Coal Co., (DC WD Ark) 362 F Supp 1117.

§ 53:26. Condominiums. A *condominium* is a combination of co-ownership and ownership in severalty. As a factual detail, real estate will be involved. For example, persons owning an office building or an apartment house by condominium are co-owners of the land and of the halls, lobby, elevators, stairways, and exits; yards, gardens, and surrounding land; incinerator, laundry rooms, and other areas used in common; but each person individually owns his own apartment or office in the building.[76]

(1) Control and Expenses. In some states the owners of the various units in the condominium have equal voice in the management and share an equal part of its expenses. In others, control and liability for expenses are shared by a unit owner in the same ratio that the value of his unit bears to the value of the entire condominium project. In all states the unit owners have an equal right to use the common areas.

The owner of each condominium unit makes repairs and improvements at his own expense. Generally he will be prohibited from making any major change which would impair or damage the safety or value of an adjoining unit. Any changes or improvements made to outside walls must ordinarily be consistent with the existing pattern of the building.

(a) COLLECTION OF EXPENSES FROM UNIT OWNER. When a unit owner fails to pay his share of taxes, operating expenses, and repairs, it is commonly provided that a lien be entered against his unit for the amount which is due by him. If payment is not then made, some condominium statutes authorize the association to shut off the unit's water, gas, electricity, and heat, and eventually to sell the delinquent owner's rights in the unit.

(2) Tort Liability. Most condominium projects fail to make provision as to the liability of unit owners for a tort occurring in the common areas. A few states expressly provide that when a third person is injured in the common areas, his suit may only be brought against the condominium association and any judgment recovered is a charge against the association to be paid off as a common expense.[77]

When the condominium association is incorporated, the same result should be obtained by applying ordinary principles of corporation law under which liability for torts occurring on the premises of the corporation are not the liability of the individual shareholders.

§ 53:27. Advantages of Condominium Ownership.

(1) Freedom from Enterprise Liability. The owner of a unit is not liable personally for an enterprise liability nor may his unit be taken from

---

[76] The great majority of states have adopted statutes authorizing condominium ownership in order to obtain the low cost Federal Housing Administration insurance of condominium mortgages which was authorized by the National Housing Act of 1961 in states in which condominium ownership was recognized. 12 USC § 234, PL 87-70, 75 Stat 161.

[77] Alaska Stat Ann (1963 Supplement) § 34.07.20.

him for such a liability. For example, even though the total enterprise be sold for taxes or to pay a tort judgment in favor of a third person injured on the common premises, each unit owner is still the owner of his unit just as before.

(2) Transferability of Unit. The condominium unit is property which the unit owner can transfer as freely as any other kind of property. Generally he must give the other unit owners a first offer to purchase his unit. Otherwise he can sell or transfer as he chooses.

Because of this transferability of the unit, it is easier for the unit owner to raise money by mortgaging his unit than would be the case if the enterprise were run as an apartment house or cooperative and the unit owner would have merely a fractional interest or a leasehold interest to put up as security.

(3) Tax Deductions. The owner of a unit in a condominium may write off on his personal income tax return a proportionate share of the operating expenses, insurance, taxes, and losses of the condominium. Over a period of time the unit owner can thus effect a savings in his taxes which in effect will lower the cost to him of the condominium unit. If he merely leased an apartment, he would not obtain this advantage.

(4) Stability of Restrictions. If a housing project is organized as a cooperative it is sometimes uncertain as to whether restrictions voluntarily assumed by the present unit owner or tenants will be binding upon others who acquire the units from them by sale or assignment. In the case of the condominium unit, any restriction which is binding on the original owner will remain binding on any subsequent owner of the unit.

LIABILITY TO THIRD PERSONS FOR CONDITION OF REAL PROPERTY

In the case of real estate, liability is ordinarily based upon occupancy. That is, the person in possession may be liable for harm to the third person caused by a condition of the premises, even though the occupier is not the owner but is merely a tenant renting the premises.

§ 53:28. Status-of-plaintiff Common-law Rule. Under the common law the liability to a person injured on the premises was controlled by his status, that is, whether he was a trespasser, a licensee, or an invitee. A different duty was owed to each of these three categories.

(1) Trespassers. As to *trespassers,* the occupier ordinarily owes only the duty of refraining from causing intentional harm once the presence of the trespasser is known; but he is not under any duty to warn of dangers or to make the premises safe to protect the trespasser from harm. The most significant exception to this rule arises in the case of small children who, although trespassers, are generally afforded greater protection through the *attractive nuisance doctrine.* For example, the owner of a private residential swimming

pool was liable for the drowning of a 5-year old child when the owner did not maintain adequate fencing around the pool, since the placing of such fencing would not have imposed a great burden upon him.[78]

(2) Licensees. As to *licensees,* who are on the premises with the permission of the occupier, the latter owes the duty of warning of nonobvious dangers that are known to the licensor. The licensor, however, is not required to take any steps to learn of the presence of dangers.

(3) Invitees. As to *invitees,* whose presence is sought to further the economic interest of the occupier, such as his customers, there is the duty to take reasonable steps to discover any danger and the duty to warn the invitee or to correct the danger. For example, a store must make a reasonable inspection of the premises to determine that there is nothing on the floor that would be dangerous, such as a slippery substance that might cause a patron to fall, and must either correct the condition or appropriately rope off the danger area or give suitable warning. If the occupier of the premises fails to conform to the degree of care described and harm results to an invitee on the premises, the occupier is liable to him for such harm.

In most states the courts have expanded the concept of invitees beyond the category of those persons whose presence will economically benefit the occupier so that it includes members of the public who are invited when it is apparent that such persons cannot be reasonably expected to make an inspection of the premises before making use of them and that they would not be making repairs to correct any dangerous condition. Some courts have also made minor inroads into the prior law by treating a recurring licensee, such as a mailman, as an invitee.[79]

§ 53:29. Negligence Rule. Several courts have begun what will probably become a new trend in ignoring these distinctions and holding the occupier liable according to ordinary negligence standards; that is, when the occupier as a reasonable man should foresee from the circumstances that harm would be caused a third person, the occupier has the duty to take reasonable steps to prevent such harm without regard to whether the potential victim would be traditionally classified as a trespasser, a licensee, or an invitee.[80]

Under this rule, the occupier of a parking lot who knows that people customarily cut across the lot to patronize a neighboring coffee shop is liable to such a pedestrian who is injured by falling down the edge of the parking lot where a retaining wall had fallen away, when such occupier knew or should have known that pedestrians would cross the lot during the night and a reasonably prudent man would foresee that in the dark the condition of the lot made harm to such persons probable or foreseeable.[81]

---

[78] Giacona v Tapley, 5 Ariz App 494, 428 P2d 439.
[79] Haffey v Lemieux, 154 Conn 185, 224 A2d 551.
[80] Rowland v Christian, 69 Cal 2d 108, Cal Rptr 97, 443 P2d 561.
[81] Ward v Enevold, (Colo) 504 P2d 1108.

§ 53:30. Intermediate Rule. Some courts have taken an intermediate position and have merely abolished the distinction between licensees and invitees so that the occupier owes the same duty of care to all lawful visitors, and whether one is a licensee or an invitee is merely a circumstance to be considered by the jury in applying the ordinary rule of negligence.[82] On this basis it has been held that a policeman may recover from the occupier of premises when he fell and was injured on accumulated ice on the premises, although he had entered for the purpose of serving a parking violation summons.[83]

In some states the distinction between licensees and invitees has been retained in name but destroyed in fact by requiring a licensor to warn the licensee of dangers which the licensor knew or in the exercise of reasonable care should have known.[84]

In some states a tolerated trespasser will be regarded as a licensee and the property occupier required to give warning of hidden dangers, such as a steel cable strung about four feet above ground.[85]

In some states a land occupier is held liable to a licensee when the occupier has maintained a negligent or *qualified nuisance* on the property.[86] This view in effect makes a partial abolition of the licensee-invitee distinction.

---

[82] The same position is taken by the British Occupiers' Liability Act 1957 5 & 6 Eliz 2 c 31.

[83] Mounsey v Ellard, — Mass —, 297 NE2d 43, 51 ("the special immunity which the licensee rule affords landowners cannot be justified in an urban industrial society. . . . The problem of allocating the costs and risks of human injury is far too complex to be decided solely by the status of the entrant, especially where the status question often prevents the jury from ever determining the fundamental question whether the defendant has acted reasonably in light of all the circumstances in the particular case.").

[84] Texas v Tennison, (Tex Civ App) 496 SW2d 219.

[85] Fitzsimmons v New York, 42 App Div 2d 636, 345 NYS2d 171.

[86] Rothfuss v Hamilton Masonic Temple, 34 Ohio 2d 176, 297 NE2d 105.

CASES FOR CHAPTER 53

Reitman v Mulkey

387 US 369 (1967)

Article I, § 26, of the California Constitution was added in 1964 by a statewide election. It provided that "neither the State nor any subdivision or agency thereof shall deny, limit, or abridge, directly or indirectly, the right to any person, who is willing or desires to sell, lease or rent any part or all of his real property, to decline to sell, lease or rent such property to such person or persons as he, in his absolute discretion chooses." It was claimed that this provision was in violation of the Equal Protection Clause of the Fourteenth Amendment of the United States Constitution.

WHITE, J. . . . The California Supreme Court . . . held that Art. I, § 26, [Proposition 14] was invalid as denying the equal protection of the laws guaranteed by the Fourteenth Amendment. . . .

There is no sound reason for rejecting this judgment. Petitioners [landlords] contend that the California court has misconstrued the Fourteenth Amendment since the repeal of any statute prohibiting racial discrimination, which is constitutionally permissible, may be said to "authorize" and "encourage" discrimination because it makes legally permissible that which was formerly proscribed. But as we understand the California court, it did not posit a constitutional violation on the mere repeal of the Unruh and Rumford Acts. It did not read either our cases or the Fourteenth Amendment as establishing an automatic constitutional barrier to the repeal of an existing law prohibiting racial discriminations in housing; nor did the court rule that a State may never put in statutory form an existing policy of neutrality with respect to private discriminations. What the court below did was first to reject the notion that the State was required to have a statute prohibiting racial discriminations in housing. Second, it held the purpose and intent of § 26 was to authorize private racial discriminations in the housing market, to repeal the Unruh and Rumford Acts and to create a constitutional right to discriminate on racial grounds in the sale and leasing of real property. Hence, the court dealt with § 26 as though it expressly authorized and constitutionalized the private right to discriminate. Third, the court assessed the ultimate impact of § 26 in the California environment and concluded that the section would encourage and significantly involve the State in private racial discrimination contrary to the Fourteenth Amendment.

The California court could very reasonably conclude that § 26 would and did have wider impact than a mere repeal of existing statutes. Section 26 mentioned neither the Unruh nor Rumford Acts in so many words. Instead, it announced the constitutional right of any person to decline to sell or lease his real property to anyone to whom he did not desire to sell or lease. Unruh and Rumford were thereby pro tanto repealed. But the section struck more deeply and more widely. Private discriminations in housing were now not only free from Rumford and Unruh but they also enjoyed a far different status than was true before the passage of those statutes. The right to discriminate, including the right to discriminate on racial grounds, was now embodied in the State's basic charter, immune from legislative, executive, or judicial regulation at any level of the state government. Those practicing racial discriminations need no longer rely solely on their personal choice. They could now invoke express constitutional authority, free from censure or interference of any kind from official sources. . . .

. . . The California Supreme Court believes that the section will significantly encourage and involve the State in private discriminations. We have been presented with no persuasive considerations indicating that this judgment should be overturned.

[Judgment affirmed.]

Cramer v Jenkins

(Mo) 339 SW2d 15 (1966)

Cramer had used a path across certain land for a number of years. This land was later purchased by Jenkins. Some time thereafter, Jenkins started to farm the land and attempted to prevent its use by Cramer. Cramer brought an action to establish his right to cross the land. From a judgment in favor of Cramer, Jenkins appealed.

HYDE, P.J. . . . Defendant's brief admits that plaintiff "has used this way for the statutory period and if he satisfies this court as to the other elements of prescription, he has acquired the way he claims." However, defendant claims plaintiff's possession was not hostile. Defendant cites Gates v Roberts, Mo Sup, 350 SW2d 729, 732, saying: " 'Hostile possession' means possession opposed and antagonistic to the claims of all others . . . and imports the occupation of land by the possessor with the intent to possess the land as his own." However, the Gates case was not an easement case; but involved a claim of title to an entire city lot. . . . It is said: "[T]he principal difference being in the character of the claim and use" in easement cases. . . . The claimant of an easement only claims a right to make a certain use of land and does not claim to possess the whole title and exclude the owner from it for all purposes.

The American Law Institute Restatement of the Law of Property, . . . "The satisfaction of the above stated prerequisites for 'adversity,' namely, that the use has not been made in subordination to the rights of the claimed servient owner, but, rather, has been made under claim of right is commonly inferred, rather than directly proved. Thus proof that a particular use of another's land has in fact occurred normally justifies, in most states, a finding that the use has been adverse until this presumption is challenged by rebutting evidence." . . . Defendant's own testimony . . . would warrant a finding that plaintiff's use of this roadway was not in subordination to defendant because plaintiff's use began long before defendant became the owner of the land and, although such use was known to defendant when he bought the land, he neither said anything about it nor made any objection to it until 1954, when he decided it would be more convenient to him to plow over it. We consider that plaintiff's evidence made a prima facie case which the court properly could decide was not overcome by defendant's evidence.

Defendant, arguing the use was permissive and not under a claim of right, says that when plaintiff's use began in 1919, the land now owned by defendant was in prairie grass, unenclosed, not farmed by the owner, and that anyone could cross it at any point. Defendant says the land was not plowed to the drainage ditch until 1937 or 1938 and that all of it was not plowed until defendant became the owner. Defendant's position seems to be that plaintiff's use of the way could not have been adverse when part of the land was swampy, in prairie grass, and not farmed or plowed by the owner and that, when defendant began to farm it, plaintiff had to do something more than continue the use he had been making to give defendant knowledge that his use was adverse to defendant's title. . . . Even though some of this land was swampy, nevertheless the ground along the drainage ditch appears to have always been a good place for a road and that was its location throughout the entire period. There were visible markings of the roadway and plaintiff worked it "with the blade on the back of a Ford tractor." Moreover, plaintiff used this way for the statutory period after the land owned by defendant was being cultivated. Furthermore, defendant's land was not unsettled territory. . . .

Defendant further argues that plaintiff's possession of the way was not exclusive, pointing out that defendant himself used it and that the evidence showed others owning or farming land beyond plaintiff's land used it. We know of no case holding that to obtain an easement of right of way the user must prevent the owner of the land from using it. . . . On the contrary, it is said: "The adverse user must be exclusive in the sense that the right does not depend for its enjoyment on similar rights in others. . . . The use may be exclusive in the required sense even though it is participated in by the owner of the servient tenement, or by owners of adjoining land." . . . "The requirement of 'exclusive,' as regards acquirement of an easement of way by prescription, does not mean that the claimant shall have been the sole user, or the only one who could or might enjoy the same or a similar right over the same land, but simply that the individual right shall not depend for its enjoyment upon a similar right in others, being, by virtue of some distinction of its own, independent of all others."

Although this way was not fenced, it was in a well defined location, continuously used by plaintiff as his means of ingress and egress from 1919 to 1954 "without a word said or a finger lifted in antagonism to it" until defendant after having seen plaintiff use it over this period (and from 1941 to 1954 while defendant was farming the land) asserted a hostile right to plow this roadway and prevent plaintiff from using it. Our conclusion is that the evidence warranted a finding of an easement by prescription in plaintiff to this roadway and that the court reached the correct result in ruling plaintiff had an easement for ingress and egress to his land over this roadway. . . .

[Judgment affirmed.]

Humber v Morton

(Tex) 426 SW2d 554 (1968)

Humber purchased a new house from Morton who was in the business of building and selling new houses. The first time that she lit a fire in the fireplace, the house caught on fire because of a defect in the fireplace and the house was partially damaged. She sued Morton who defended in part on the theory that the rule of caveat emptor, or "Let the buyer beware," barred the suit.

NORVELL, J. . . . We are of the opinion that the courts erred in holding as a matter of law that Morton was not liable to Mrs. Humber because the doctrine of caveat emptor applied to the sale of a new house by a "builder-vendor" and consequently no implied warranty that the house was fit for human habitation arose from the sale. Accordingly, we reverse the judgments of the courts below and remand the cause to the district court for a . . . trial upon the merits. . . .

It is undisputed that Morton built the house and then sold it as a new house. Did he thereby impliedly warrant that such house was constructed in a good workmanlike manner and was suitable for human habitation? We hold that he did. Under such circumstances, the law raises an implied warranty. . . .

Does the doctrine of caveat emptor apply to the sale of a new house by a builder-vendor?

Originally, the two great systems of jurisprudence applied different doctrines to sales of both real and personal property. The rule of the common law—caveat emptor—was fundamentally based upon the premise that the buyer and seller dealt at arm's length, and that the purchaser had means and opportunity to gain information concerning the subject matter of the sale which were equal to those of the seller. . . .

In 1884, the Supreme Court of the United States applied the doctrine of implied warranty, the antithesis of caveat emptor, to a real property situation involving false work and pilings driven into the bed of the Maumee River. . . .

While in numerous common-law jurisdictions, the caveat emptor doctrine as applied to the vendor-builder, new-house situation has overstayed its time, it was said by way of dicta in a Texas Court of Civil Appeals case in 1944 that: "By offering the (new) house for sale as a new and complete structure, appellant impliedly warranted that it was properly constructed and of good material and specifically that it had a good foundation. . . ."

This decision has been described as "a preview of things to come." . . . See also, Williston on Contracts (3rd Ed Jaeger) § 926A, wherein it is said: "It would be much better if this enlightened approach (implied warranty, Jones v Gatewood, 381 P2d 158 [Okla]) were generally adopted with respect to the sale of new houses for it would tend to discourage much of the sloppy work and jerry-building that has become perceptible over the years." . . .

The Glisan case (Glisan v Smolenske), 153 Colo 274, 387 P2d 260 (1963), was factually similar to the hypothetical example heretofore set out in this opinion. Smolenske had agreed to purchase a house from Glisan while it was under construction. The court propounded and answered the implied warranty question, thusly:

"Was there an implied warranty that the house, when completed, would be fit for habitation? There is a growing body of law on this question, which, if followed, requires an answer in the affirmative. . . ."

While it is not necessary for us to pass upon a situation in which the vendor-purchaser relationship is absent, the case of Schipper v Levitt & Sons, 44 NJ 70, 207 A2d 314 (1965), is important as much of the reasoning set forth in the opinion is applicable here. The Supreme Court of New Jersey . . . placed emphasis upon the close analogy between a defect in a new house and a manufactured chattel. The opinion states:

"The law should be based on current concepts of what is right and just and the judiciary should be alert to the never-ending need for keeping its common-law principles abreast of the times. Ancient distinctions which make no sense in today's society and tend to discredit the law should be readily rejected. . . .

If at one time in Texas the rule of caveat emptor had application to the sale of a new house by a vendor-builder, that time is now past. The decisions and legal writings herein referred to afford numerous examples and situations illustrating the harshness and injustice of the rule when applied to the sale of new houses by a builder-vendor. . . . Obviously, the ordinary purchaser is not in a position to ascertain when there is a defect in a chimney flue, or vent of a heating apparatus, or whether the plumbing work covered by a concrete slab foundation is faulty. . . .

The caveat emptor rule as applied to new houses is an anachronism patently out of harmony with modern home buying practices. It does a disservice not only to the ordinary prudent purchaser but to the industry itself by lending encouragement to the unscrupulous, fly-by-night operator and purveyor of shoddy work.

The judgments of the courts below are reversed and the cause remanded for trial in accordance with this opinion.

Shroyer v Shroyer

(Mo) 425 SW2d 214 (1968)

Jennie Shroyer executed a deed transferring her farm to Wayne and Wesley, the sons of her deceased brother. By her will, Jennie left the same farm to Jessie, the widow of her deceased brother. After Jennie's death, an action was brought to determine who owned Jennie's farm. The evidence showed that after Jennie executed the deed, it was acknowledged before a notary public and shown to Wayne, who looked at it and returned it to Jennie. Thereafter she remained in possession of the land and acted in all respects as though she still owned it. However, Jennie told other persons that the boys were the owners of the farm and that she was merely holding the deed for safekeeping. An action was brought by Jessie to cancel the deed on the ground that it was not effective because it had never been delivered. From a decision in favor of Jessie, the nephews appealed.

HOUSER, C. . . . Jennie Peters was a strong-willed woman with a mind of her own. "You just didn't tell her what to do." . . . She was "in the habit of making up deeds" and would dispose of her property, change her mind and make another disposition of her property, then change her mind again. In the six years before her death she made three different dispositions of her property. Jennie preferred secrecy about her property affairs and wanted to keep peace in the family. After executing the will dated October 15, 1960 Jennie turned it over to her niece Betty Daily with the request that Betty put it in her bank box and "not ever say anything about it." Jennie said she thought it would "keep down trouble in the family" if nobody knew about it. The will remained in Betty's safety deposit box in Peoples Bank of Mercer until Jennie died. After giving Betty possession of the will Jennie did not thereafter discuss the will with Betty, or request of Betty that she return the will or destroy it. After Virgil's death Wayne and Wesley would come out to Jennie's farm about once a week. They would chop ice and perform other chores, such as throwing hay down for the cattle, cleaning out the barn, repairing fences, etc. . . .

The only question is whether there was a delivery of the deed. The controlling element in determining this question, a mixed question of law and fact, is the intention of the parties, particularly the intention of the grantor. . . . The vital inquiry with respect to the grantor is whether she intended a complete transfer; whether she parted with dominion over the instrument with the intention of relinquishing all dominion and control over the conveyance and of making it presently effective and operative as a conveyance of the title to the land. . . . It is not necessary, in order to constitute a delivery of a deed, that the instrument actually be handed over to the grantee, or to another person for the grantee. . . . A valid delivery once having taken place is not rendered ineffectual by the act of the grantee in giving the deed into the custody of the grantor for safekeeping. . . . It is all a question of the intention of the parties, which may be manifested by words or acts or both. . . .

The burden of proof of nondelivery of a deed is upon the party who seeks to invalidate the conveyance on the ground of nondelivery. . . . In this case plaintiff, Jessie Shroyer, has the burden of proof of nondelivery.

. . . This deed was not recorded at the time of the grantor's death. . . .

. . . There is a presumption of *nondelivery,* in view of the conceded fact that the deed was in grantor's possession at the time of her death and that the deed was not then recorded. . . .

This . . . placed upon grantees, defendants Wesley and Wayne Shroyer, the burden of going forward with the evidence to rebut plaintiff's prima facie case. . . . To sustain this burden defendants introduced George and Beulah Shroyer's testimony.

In reviewing the evidence in this case we are conscious of the fact that the determination of delivery . . . depends to a large extent upon the credibility of George and Beulah

Shroyer and the interpretation of their testimony. In weighing their testimony as well as all of the rest of the testimony in the case, and in making our own independent findings, we are aided and assisted by the findings and judgment of the chancellor, who heard and observed the demeanor of the witnesses and was in by far the best position to judge of their credibility and reliability. So armed and informed, and with due deference to the chancellor's findings, it is our conclusion that grantees-defendants Wesley and Wayne Shroyer have not met and sustained the burden of rebutting plaintiff's prima facie case of nondelivery.

We find that Jennie, under the false impression that her will of October 15, 1960 had been destroyed, made a warranty deed on December 1, 1964 and executed it one week later, by which she intended and undertook to convey her 80-acre homeplace to her nephews Wesley and Wayne Shroyer, but that she did not deliver, or intend to deliver, the deed to Wayne with the intention of relinquishing all dominion and control over the conveyance or of transferring title to Wesley and Wayne *in praesenti*; that in December, 1964 she wanted her nephews to eventually become the owners of the farm; that her attempts to effect such a transfer of title by the deed in question were ineffective for lack of delivery; that the deed never became operative and was properly cancelled and set aside by the chancellor and defendants properly called to account for the royalties received from the operation of the rock quarry. . . .

George Shroyer's testimony that Jennie told him that she handed the deed to Wayne is not conclusive that delivery was intended. What Jennie is supposed to have said at the time is not necessarily indicative of that intent but is subject to the interpretation that she was merely exhibiting the deed to Wayne to inform him of the fact that she intended the boys to have the farm at her death and to permit him to read the instrument, but that she was reserving control over the deed. It is a reasonable inference that if she handed the deed to Wayne it was ". . . merely for temporary convenience at the time, and [her] continued possession of the instrument afterwards indicated an intention to retain control of it." . . .

That she intended to retain control over the farm is confirmed by her subsequent exercise of acts of ownership over the farm, continuing to live there and operate it, and receiving and keeping the royalty payments for her own use and benefit. The fact that defendants were not placed in possession of the farm is yet another indication that Jennie did not intend to pass title presently.

George Shroyer's testimony relative to Jennie's exhibition of the deed to Wayne, and the theory of delivery, is detracted from by the testimony suggesting that neither Wesley nor Wayne, prior to Jennie's death, seemed to know anything about Jennie's estate or of the existence of a deed, and that after Jennie's death, when the family gathered at the probate office for the reading of the will, Wesley and Wayne did not speak up, or claim the property by virtue of a deed, or suggest the existence of a deed from Jennie to them.

In addition to the foregoing reasons, the conclusion that the deed was not delivered at the time it was executed and acknowledged is buttressed by the writing of July 5, 1966 (some 19 months after the deed was executed) in which Jennie by a purported will in her own handwriting plainly demonstrated that she did not consider that the deed had been delivered so as to pass title in December, 1964. Although she recited that she *had deeded* her home of 80 acres to the boys, and gave her reasons, the wording used strongly indicates her intention that they were to take in the future. The boys "*shall* have a good deed to the farm." The rock contract "*shall* go with the deed to Wesley and Wayne." The royalties were to be used to pay her funeral expenses and other obligations (still retaining control over the proceeds of the quarry) and *after all accounts are settled* the deed and lease "*shall* be turned over to the owners of the farm Wesley and Wayne Shroyer." (Our emphasis.) This is not the language of a grantor who considered that she had previously transferred and relinquished all right, title and interest in a farm, by making and delivering a deed to the grantees. This "voice from the grave," so to speak, weighs heavily in our determination that Jennie did not deliver the deed, and that as late as approximately three months prior to her death Jennie did not consider that she had already delivered the deed and given up the property to her intended beneficiaries, but rather considered it yet necessary to make a will providing for the postmortem delivery of the deed.

[Judgment affirmed.]

Cochran v Long

(Ky) 294 SW2d 503 (1956)

Long owned real estate in what was designated as Block #2 of Harrodsburg, Kentucky. All lots in this block were subject to a restrictive covenant that they could only be used for residential purposes. A state highway was relocated so that it ran through Block #2, and from 400 to 500 motor vehicles passed on the highway per hour. A number of commercial enterprises had been built outside of but near Block #2. Long and others brought an action against Cochran and others owning property in Block #2 to determine whether this change of conditions released their land from the covenant that it be used only for residential purposes. From a judgment that the covenant was not binding, Cochran appealed.

STEWART, J. . . . The decisive issue in this case is whether there has been such a radical change in the status of lots 1, 2, 3, 4, 5, and 28 in Block 2, affected by the restrictive covenant, as to relieve them of the burden of this covenant. . . .

"A change of conditions which will . . . annul . . . a restrictive covenant is a change of such a character as to make it impossible longer to secure in a substantial degree the benefits sought to be realized through the performance of a promise respecting the use of the land. If it is still possible, despite a change in conditions, to secure the anticipated benefit in a substantial, though lessened, degree, the change of conditions will not alone be sufficient to warrant the refusal of injunctive relief against breach of the obligation arising from the promise." . . .

The problem before us is simply one of deciding whether the facts in this case disclose there has been such a basic change in the character of the restricted property as to cause the covenant in question to be inapplicable to what appellees claim is a new situation. . . .

The chancellor, in finding for appellees [Long and others], held there had been such a complete change in the territory under scrutiny that the restriction as to residential use applicable to lots 1 through 5 and to lot 28 in Block 2 was no longer of any substantial value to these lots. This conclusion was reached primarily, because of the location of the new highway through this block, over which much traffic proceeds and from which considerable noise ensues. For this reason, it was believed the trend is toward a business district in this area, although in Block 2 only two commercial establishments have been built since the completion of the highway. It is true there was testimony to the effect that some distance to the north and outside of Block 2, particularly at a street intersection about a block distant, several business places have been located within the last year or so, but we do not believe this changes the basic picture at the present time.

It does not follow that the mere presence of a highway that has become one of the principal arteries of travel through the city of Harrodsburg automatically alters the character of property involved here to the extent that this property is released from the restrictions that adhere to it. . . .

Nor are we convinced that the evidence in this record shows there has been such a transition over to business in Block 2 and the surrounding area as to interfere in any material respect with the enjoyment by appellant lot owners of the benefit of the neighborhood as a place of residence. This is especially true where, as here, the restricted property, though it be small in extent, has not been invaded. Appellants do not claim that the approach of business on either side of the restricted lots along the highway has affected the restricted area's desirability for residential purposes or materially changed its character as a residential district. . . .

[Judgment reversed and action remanded.]

Premonstratensian Fathers v Badger Mutual Fire Ins. Co.

46 Wis 2d 362, 175 NW2d 337 (1970)

In 1958 a supermarket was constructed and owned by Jacobs Realty Corporation. The market contained five large walk-in coolers or refrigerators. Title to the market was thereafter transferred to the Premonstratensian Fathers and was insured against fire by Badger Mutual Insurance Company. The building was severely damaged by fire and the insurer paid approximately $80,000 for the building damage. The Fathers claimed an additional $20,000 for the destruction of the coolers. The insurer refused to pay this amount and asserted that the coolers were not owned by the Fathers. From a judgment for the Fathers, the insurer appealed.

HANSE, N.J. . . . If the coolers are determined to be common-law fixtures, and were such at the time of the construction of the building and the installation of the coolers, then they would have passed to the Fathers under the warranty deed of March 7, 1960, and they would be insured under the terms of the policy. The issue then is whether these coolers constitute fixtures.

The rule which has developed . . . as to what constitutes a fixture is not really a comprehensive definition, but rather a statement of the factors which are to be applied to the fact and circumstances of a particular case to determine whether or not the property in question does constitute a fixture. . . .

ANNEXATION

. . . An object will not acquire the status of a fixture unless it is in some manner or means . . . attached or affixed, either actually or constructively, to the realty." . . . The trial court ably pointed out the physical facts which led to its conclusion that there is indeed annexation in this case. The more important of these are as follows: (1) The exterior walls of the cooler, in four instances, constituted the interior wall of another room. (2) In the two meat coolers, a meat hanging and tracking system was built into the coolers. These tracks were used to move large cuts of meats from the cooler area into the meat preparation areas, and were suspended from the steel girders of the building structure by means of large steel bolts. These bolts penetrated through the roof of the cooler supporting wooden beams, which, in turn, supported the tracking system. The tracking in the coolers was a part of a system of tracking throughout the rear portion of the supermarket. (3) The coolers were attached to hardwood plank which was, in turn, attached to the concrete floor of the supermarket. The attachment of the plank to the floor was accomplished through the use of a ramsetting gun. The planks were laid on the floor, and the bolts were driven through them into the concrete floor, where they then exploded, firmly fixing the coolers into place. There was a material placed on the planks which served both as an adhesive and as an insulation. (4) The floor of the coolers was specially sloped during the construction of the building so that the slope would carry drainage into a specially constructed drain in the concrete. In addition, four of the coolers were coated with a protective coating to seal the floors. In the freezer, a special concrete buildup was constructed in the nature of a trough, the purpose of which was to carry away moisture as frozen chickens melted. (5) A refrigeration unit was built into each cooler. The unit was suspended from the ceiling of the cooler, and tubing was run through the wall of the cooler to compressors located elsewhere in the store. (6) Electric lights and power receptacles were built into each cooler and were connected by electrical wiring through the walls and the ceiling of the cooler to the store's electrical power supply. (7) The walls of the cooler were interlocked, and set into the splines, the hardwood planks ramset into the concrete floor, in tongue and groove fashion.

These factors adequately support the conclusion that the coolers were indeed physically annexed to the premises. The insurers argue that the coolers were removable without material injury to the premises, which detracts from the annexation. There was a dispute in the evidence introduced at the trial, with the insurers' expert testifying that this type of cooler was easily severable from the building, while one of the members of the Jacobs family testified that when he removed some of the bolts from the floor following the fire, large sections of concrete would crack on the floor. This was a conflict for resolution by the trial court. In any event, the element of removability without material damage to the building no longer enjoys the position of prominence in the law of fixtures which it once held. It is now only one of the factors which is to be considered by the trial court. . . .

ADAPTATION

Adaptation refers to the relationship between the chattel and the use which is made of the realty to which the chattel is annexed. The use of the realty was that of a retail grocery, commonly known as a supermarket. This was the intent of the parties at the time of the construction of the building, and the intent of the parties throughout the entire history of the business. The fact of operation has borne out this intent. In a business which carries fresh foods, frozen foods, produce, meats and butter, coolers used for storage and handling of these perishables are patently related to the use of the building. In fact, it would be hard to picture any equipment more closely related to the operation of a supermarket, where large quantities of perishables must, of necessity, be purchased for storage and processing.

The insurers raise a number of points to dispute this finding. They state: The coolers were not custom made; the coolers are useful not to the building, but to the use to which the building is put; the coolers could have been used anywhere; other coolers could have been used. There is no requirement that the coolers be custom made, but only that they be adapted to the use to which the building is put. The test here is not the adaptability to the building, but the adaptability to the use to which the building is put. The fact that other coolers could have been used, or that these coolers could have been used elsewhere, does not alter the fact that there was a close connection between these coolers and the retail grocery business conducted on the property. . . .

INTENT

This court has repeatedly held that intent is the primary determinant of whether a certain piece of property has become a fixture. The relevant intent is that of the party making the annexation. At the time of the construction of the supermarket and the installation of the coolers, both the Jacobs Realty Corporation and the Jacobs Brothers Stores, Inc., were in existence as separate legal entities. The title to the land in question was registered in the name of the Jacobs Realty Corporation, but the exact status of Jacobs Brothers Stores, Inc., is unclear at that date. There is no definitive evidence which demonstrates whether it was the Jacobs Realty Corporation or the Jacobs Brothers Stores, Inc., which purchased the coolers and caused them to be installed on the premises. The invoice from the manufacturer was sent to the "Jacobs Bros. Super Market," a nonexistent legal entity. The evidence introduced at the trial as to who paid for the coolers consisted of the testimony of Henry Jacobs. He did not remember which of the corporations issued the check in payment of the coolers; many of their records were burned; John, Norbert and Henry Jacobs paid for them through one of the corporations; and he was inclined to think it was Jacobs Realty Corporation that purchased them. Thus, there is no evidence from which it can be positively asserted that either Jacobs Realty Corporation or Jacobs Brothers Stores, Inc., purchased the coolers.

In its decision, the trial court found, as a reasonable and legitimate inference from all the facts and circumstances surrounding the placement of the coolers onto the realty, that there was an intention that the coolers become a permanent accession to the realty; that when Jacobs Realty Corporation conveyed the land together with all buildings and improvements thereon to Jacobs Brothers Stores, Inc., the intention still prevailed that the coolers were a permanent accession to the realty; and that the same intention still prevailed when Jacobs Brothers Stores, Inc., conveyed the building and improvements to the plaintiff, and when the plaintiff leased the premises (the land, with all buildings and improvements thereon) back to the corporation as lessee. . . .

The coolers were fixtures when installed; passed to Jacobs Brothers Stores, Inc., through the warranty deed; subsequently passed to the Fathers through that warranty deed; and are in fact fixtures within the meaning of the coverage clause of the insurance policy in this case. . . .

[Judgment affirmed.]

QUESTIONS AND CASE PROBLEMS

1. The land for the Mira Loma Subdivision had been conveyed by the Enfield Realty Co. to Hallie Houston by a deed which stated, "No mercantile business of any kind shall ever be carried on, on the premises hereby conveyed; . . . it being understood that all improvements to be created on said premises shall be built and used for residence purposes only, excepting such improvements as may be proper for use in connection with a residence." By subsequent conveyances MacDonald and Merritt acquired three lots in the subdivision, and title to 27 other lots was conveyed to other owners. MacDonald and Merritt brought an action against the other lot owners to obtain a decree declaring that they could subdivide their three lots and erect duplex homes. Were they entitled to such a decree? [MacDonald v Painter, (Tex) 441 SW2d 179]
2. Miller executed a deed to real estate, naming Mary Zieg as grantee. He placed the deed in an envelope on which was written, "To be filed at my death," and put the envelope and deed in a safe deposit box in the National Bank. The box had been rented in the names of Miller and Mary Zieg. After his death Mary removed the deed from the safe deposit box. Moseley, as executor under Miller's will, brought an action against Mary to declare the deed void. Decide. [Moseley v Zieg, 180 Neb 810, 146 NW2d 72]
3. Price sued Whisnant, as guardian for McRary, who had cut and removed trees from certain land. Price claimed title on the basis that he owned the land by adverse possession. He proved that for a period of more than 20 years he had from time to time entered on the land and cut and removed logs. Was Price the owner of the land? [Price v Whisnant, 236 NC 381, 72 SE2d 851]
4. Wyatt owned Crow Island in the White River. By the government land surveys of 1826 and 1854, the river separated the island from land to the east owned by Wycough. The river abruptly changed its course and cut a new channel to the east, with the result that part of the Wycough land was no longer separated by water from Crow Island. Wyatt brought a suit against Wycough, claiming that he now owned that portion of land which had been joined to his as a result of the movement of the river channel. Was he correct? [Wyatt v Wycough, 232 Ark 760, 341 SW2d 18]
5. Digirolamo owned a tract of land near the Philadelphia Gun Club. During shooting contests held by the club, buckshot from the contestants' guns sometimes fell on his land. He sued the club to compel it to stop. The club claimed that as it had held these contests for over 21 years, it had acquired an easement to do so. Decide. [Digirolamo v Philadelphia Gun Club, 371 Pa 40, 89 A2d 357]

6. Castlewood Terrace is a residential district which by the original deed of 1896 could only be used for single-family residences. Pashkow wanted to build a high-rise apartment in the area. Paschen brought an action for a declaratory judgment that Pashkow could not do so. Pashkow claimed that the restrictive covenant was no longer binding because a school had been built in the area and that the value of his land would be more than doubled if used for a high-rise apartment than if used for a single-family dwelling. Was the covenant binding? [Paschen v Pashkow, 63 Ill App 2d 56, 211 NE2d 576]

7. Smikahl sold to Hansen a tract of land on which there were two houses and four trailer lots equipped with concrete patios and necessary connections for utility lines. The tract purchased by Hansen was completely surrounded by the land owned by Smikahl and third persons. In order to get onto the highway, it was necessary to cross the Smikahl tract. Several years later, Smikahl put a barbed wire fence around his land. Hansen sued to prevent obstruction to travel between his land and the highway over the Smikahl land. Smikahl defended on the ground that no such right of travel had been given to Hansen. Was he correct? [Hansen v Smikahl, 173 Neb 309, 113 NW2d 210]

8. Henry Lile owned a house. When the land on which it was situated was condemned for a highway, he removed the house to the land of his daughter, Sarah Crick. In the course of construction work, blasting damaged the house and Sarah Crick sued the contractors, Terry & Wright. They claimed that Henry should be joined in the action as a plaintiff and that Sarah could not sue by herself because it was Henry's house. Were the defendants correct? [Terry & Wright v Crick, (Ky) 418 SW2d 217]

9. Davis Store Fixtures sold certain equipment on credit to Head, who installed it in a building which was later used by the Cadillac Club. When payment was not made, Davis sought to repossess the equipment. If the equipment constituted fixtures, this could not be done. The equipment consisted of a bar for serving drinks, a bench, and a drainboard. The first two were attached to the floor or wall with screws, and the drainboard was connected to water and drainage pipes. Did the equipment constitute fixtures? [Davis Store Fixtures v Cadillac Club, 60 Ill App 2d 106, 207 NE2d 711]

10. By a sealed writing, called a "lease," *A* declared that his neighbor *B* had the right to drive over a driveway in the rear of *A*'s house. *B* later claimed that he had an easement. *A* denied this and contended that *B* had a "lease." Was *A* correct? [Rice v Reich, 51 Wis 2d 205, 186 NW2d 269]

54 Leases

CREATION AND TERMINATION

A lease is generally created and terminated by the agreement of the parties. In some cases the conduct of the parties takes the place of an express agreement.

The person who owns the real property and permits the occupation of the premises is known as the *landlord* or *lessor*. The *tenant* or *lessee* is the one who occupies the property. A *lease* establishes the relationship of landlord and tenant. It is in effect a conveyance of a leasehold estate in land. The term "lease" is also used to designate the paper that is evidence of this transfer of interest.

§ **54:1. Definition.** The relation of landlord and tenant exists whenever one person holds possession of the real property of another under an express or implied agreement.

§ **54:2. Essential Elements.** The following elements are necessary in the establishment of the relation of landlord and tenant:

(1) The occupying of the land must be with the express or implied consent of the landlord.

(2) The tenant must occupy the premises in subordination to the rights of the landlord.

(3) A reversionary interest in the land must remain in the landlord. That is, the landlord must be entitled to retake the possession of the land upon the expiration of the lease.

(4) The tenant must have an estate of present possession in the land. This means that he must have a right that entitles him to be in possesion of the land now.

The requirement that a tenant have possession distinguishes the tenant's interest from the other interests in the land. For example, a person may receive permission from the owner of land to erect and maintain a billboard on the owner's land. This does not create a leasehold interest because a licensee does not have any right to stay in possession of the land. Similarly, a person having a right of way, or a right to cross over his neighbor's land is not in possession of that land. He has merely an easement and is not a tenant of the neighbor. A tenant also differs from a *sharecropper,* for the latter is in substance the employee of the landlord and is paid by a share of the crops he raises.

A tenant is not the agent of the landlord,[1] so that a notice or information given to a tenant does not constitute notice or information given to the landlord. Statutes may, however, provide that service of particular notices upon a person occupying or in possession of property shall be deemed a sufficient service upon the owner of the property.

§ 54:3. Classification of Tenancies.

(1) Tenancy for Years. A *tenancy for years* is one under which the tenant has an estate of definite duration. The term "for years" is used to describe such a tenancy even though the duration of the tenancy is for only one year or for less than a year.

(2) Tenancy from Year to Year. A *tenancy from year to year* is one under which a tenant, holding an estate in land for an indefinite period of duration, pays an annual, monthly, or weekly rent. A distinguishing feature of this tenancy is the fact that it does not terminate at the end of a year, month, or week except upon proper notice.

In almost all states a tenancy from year to year is implied if the tenant holds over after a tenancy for years with the consent of the landlord, as shown by his express statement or by conduct such as continuing to accept rent.[2] The lease will frequently state that a holding over shall give rise to a tenancy from year to year unless written notice to the contrary be given, or will expressly provide for an extension or renewal of the lease.

(3) Tenancy at Will. When land is held for an indefinite period, which may be terminated at any time by the landlord, or by the landlord and the tenant acting together, a *tenancy at will* exists. A person who enters into possession of land for an indefinite period with the owner's permission but without any reservation of rent is a tenant at will. An agreement that a person can move into an empty house and live there until he finds a home to buy creates a tenancy at will.

Statutes in some states and decisions in others require advance notice of termination of this type of tenancy.

(4) Tenancy by Sufferance. When a tenant holds over without permission of the landlord, the latter may treat him as a trespasser or as a tenant. Until the landlord elects to do one or the other, a *tenancy by sufferance* exists.

§ 54:4. Antidiscrimination. Statutes in many states prohibit an owner who rents his property for profit from discriminating against prospective tenants

---

[1] Gillentine v Illinois Wesleyan University, (CA5 Ill) 194 F2d 970.

[2] In some jurisdictions, when rent is accepted from a tenant holding over after the expiration of the term of his lease and there is no agreement to the contrary, there results only a periodic tenancy from month to month rather than a tenancy from year to year. Bay West Realty Co. v Christy, (NY Civil Court) 61 Misc 2d 891, 310 NYS2d 348.

on the basis of race, color, religion, or national origin. Enforcement of such statutes is generally entrusted to an administrative agency.[3]

§ **54:5. Creation of the Relation.** The relation of landlord and tenant is created by an express or implied contract. An oral lease is valid at common law, but statutes in most states require written leases for certain tenancies. Many statutes follow the English Statute of Frauds, by providing that a lease for a term exceeding three years must be in writing. Statutes in other states require written leases when the term exceeds one year.

§ **54:6. Covenants and Conditions.** Some obligations of the parties in the lease are described as covenants. Thus, a promise by the tenant to make repairs is called a *covenant to repair*. Sometimes it is provided that the lease shall be forfeited or terminated upon a breach of a promise, and the provision is then called a *condition* rather than a covenant.

§ **54:7. Termination of Lease.** A lease is generally not terminated by the death, insanity, or bankruptcy of either party, except in the case of a tenancy at will. Provisions in a lease giving the landlord the right to terminate the lease under certain conditions are generally strictly construed against him.

When the landlord has the right to terminate the lease upon giving notice to the tenant, it is ordinarily immaterial what his motive is for so doing.

In an ordinary lease between private persons, each party has unlimited freedom to terminate the lease in accordance with its terms and to refuse to renew the lease. In the case of government-controlled housing, the tenant has a right to a hearing on the question of whether his lease should be renewed.[4] Laws adopted to regulate housing, to impose rent controls, or to prevent discrimination may restrict the landlord in exercising his power to terminate leases.

Leases may be terminated in the following ways:

(1) Expiration of Term in a Tenancy for Years. When a tenancy for years exists, the relation of landlord and tenant ceases upon the expiration of the agreed term, without any requirement that one party give the other any notice of termination. Express notice to end the term may be required of either or both parties by provisions in the lease, except when a statute prohibits imposing such a requirement.

(2) Notice in a Tenancy from Year to Year. In the absence of an agreement of the parties, notice is now usually governed by statutes. Thirty or sixty days' notice is generally required to end a tenancy from year to year. As to tenancies for periods of less than a year, the provisions of the statute may require only one week.

---

[3] In re Williams, 4 Ore App 482, 479 P2d 513.
[4] Tompkins Square Neighbors, Inc. v Zaragoza, 73 Misc 2d 126, 341 NYS2d 627.

(3) Release. The relation of landlord and tenant is terminated if the landlord makes a release or conveyance of his interest in the land to the tenant. A tenant may at any time purchase the rented property if the landlord and the tenant agree. In addition, the lease may give the tenant the option of purchasing at a stated time or at a stated price.

An option clause that gives the tenant the right to require the landlord to sell the property to him is to be distinguished from a preemption or "first offering" clause, under which the tenant cannot require the landlord to sell but the landlord, should he decide to sell the property, must give the tenant the first chance to buy it.[5]

(4) Merger. If the tenant acquires the landlord's interest in any manner, as by inheritance or purchase, the leasehold interest is said to disappear by merger into the title to the land now held by the former tenant. The result is the same if the tenant has an estate for years and inherits a life estate in the same premises.

(5) Surrender. A surrender or giving up by the tenant of his estate to the landlord terminates the tenancy if the surrender is accepted by the latter. A surrender may be made expressly or impliedly.

An express surrender must, under the Statute of Frauds, be in writing and signed by the person making the surrender or by his authorized agent.

A surrender by operation of law occurs only when the acts of the parties clearly show that both consider that the premises have been surrendered, as when the premises have been adbandoned by the tenant and their return has been accepted by the landlord. An acceptance may be inferred from the conduct of the landlord, but such conduct must clearly indicate an intention to accept.

(6) Forfeiture. The landlord may terminate the tenancy by forfeiting the relation because of the tenant's misconduct or breach of a condition, if a term of the lease or a statute so provides. In the absence of such a provision the landlord may only make a claim for damages. This method of terminating the relation is not favored by courts.

(7) Destruction of Property. If a lot and the building on it are leased, either an express provision in the lease or a statute generally releases the tenant from his liability when the building is destroyed or reduces the amount of rent in proportion to the loss sustained. Such statutes do not impose upon the landlord any duty to repair or restore the property to its former condition.

When the lease covers rooms or an apartment in a building, a destruction of the leased premises terminates the lease.

(8) Fraud. Since a lease is based on a contract, a lease may be avoided when circumstances are such that a contract may be avoided for fraud.

---

[5] Weintz v Bumgarner, 150 Mont 306, 434 P2d 712.

(9) Transfer of the Tenant. Residential leases commonly contain a provision for termination upon the tenant's being transferred by his employer to another city or the tenant's being called into military service. Since such provisions are often strictly construed against the tenant, he should exercise care to see that the provision is sufficiently broad to cover the situations that may arise.

When the parties specify a particular condition subsequent which will terminate the lease, the occurrence of a different event has no effect. For example, when the lease specified that the tenant, who was a member of the Peace Corps, would be released if transferred from the city by the Peace Corps, such clause had no effect when the tenant left the city to take employment with another government agency in India and was not transferred as a member of the Peace Corps.[6]

§ 54:8. Notice of Termination. When notice of termination is required, no particular words are necessary to constitute a sufficient notice, provided the words used clearly indicate the intention of the party. The notice, whether given by the landlord or the tenant, must be definite. For example, when the tenant merely stated that he "guessed he would have to give up the house," there was insufficient notice.[7] Statutes sometimes require that the notice be in writing. In the absence of such a provision, however, oral notice is generally held to be sufficient.

The parties may agree to a specific method of giving notice. Thus, they may agree that the sending of a notice by registered or certified mail shall constitute sufficient notice. In such a case a notice mailed within the proper time is sufficient even though the notice is not received until after the period for giving notice has expired.[8]

Tenants in government housing projects who pay the required rental may generally remain in possession indefinitely.[9] When a notice to terminate is necessary, the mere fact that the tenant knows that the landlord wants him to leave does not take the place of a notice.[10] Under some statutes it is held that the notice by which the landlord seeks to terminate a lease must expressly declare that he terminates the lease and that it is not sufficient to direct the tenant to "remove from the apartment you occupy." [11]

When the landlord had the right to terminate the lease by giving notice to the tenant, it was immaterial at common law what his motive was for so doing. Consequently, when the landlord had the right to terminate upon notice, it was immaterial that he may have been motivated by the desire to retaliate against the tenant for having made justified complaints as to the condition of the premises to the appropriate housing authority.

---

[6] Satin v Buckley, (Dist Col App) 246 A2d 778.

[7] Hunter v Karcher, 8 SD 554, 67 NW 621.

[8] Trust Co. v Shea, 3 Ill App 2d 368, 122 NE2d 292.

[9] Oyala v Delgado, (NY Civil Court) 64 Misc 2d 727, 315 NYS2d 666.

[10] 28 Mott Street Co. v Summit Import Corp., (NY Civil Court) 64 Misc 2d 860, 316 NYS2d 259.

[11] Garsen v Hohenleitner, 73 Misc 2d 192, 341 NYS2d 181.

By modern cases such "retaliatory eviction" is prohibited.[12] There is likewise authority that a franchisor cannot exercise a power to terminate a lease without cause when this would evade a franchisee-protection statute which prohibits the termination of franchises except upon cause.

§ 54:9. Renewal of Lease. When a lease terminates for any reason, it is ordinarily a matter for the landlord and the tenant to enter into a new agreement if they so wish to extend or renew the lease. The modern lease form generally gives the tenant the option to renew the lease. The power to renew the lease may be stated negatively by declaring that the lease runs indefinitely, as from year to year, subject to being terminated by either party by his giving written notice a specified number of days or months before the proposed date. If it is not clear whether a renewal provision gives the tenant only the right to renew for one more term of the lease or whether it gives him the right to renew indefinitely for an unlimited number of times, the law will interpret the lease strictly as permitting only one additional term. (See p. 1106, Kilbourne v Forester.)

When the landlord is a state or local government, as in the case of the low-cost housing project, the landlord cannot refuse to renew the lease for a reason that would constitute a discrimination prohibited by the federal Constitution. This concept also applies when the landlord obtains financing from government funds. Likewise, a private landlord could not refuse to renew a lease in retaliation for a tenant's exercise of rights guaranteed by the First Amendment of the federal Constitution, when the landlord had acquired the property by purchase from a municipal housing authority and had entered into a detailed agreement with the authority as to the standards to be observed by the landlord.[13]

In some instances the option will expressly state that the rental to be paid under the renewal term is to be renegotiated. By the common law this destroyed the option because it was not definite. By the modern view the option is binding, obligating the tenant to pay and obligating the lessor to accept what would be a reasonable rental value of the premises when used for the purpose for which the tenant has leased them.

§ 54:10. Purchase by Tenant. A lease of an entire building frequently gives the tenant the option to purchase the building either at a price specified in the lease or at the appraised value of the property at the time of the exercise of the option.

RIGHTS AND DUTIES OF THE PARTIES

The rights and duties of the landlord and tenant are based upon principles of real estate law and contract law. With the rising tide of consumer protectionism, the tendency is increasing to treat the relationship as merely a contract and to govern the rights and duties of the parties by general principles of contract law.

---

[12] See § 54:11(4).
[13] McQueen v Druker, (CA1 Mass) 438 F2d 781.

§ 54:11. Possession. Possession involves both the right to acquire possession at the beginning of the lease and the right to retain possession until the lease is ended. The modern lease commonly provides that if the lessor is late in making the premises available to the tenant, the commencement of the lease shall be postponed until the lessor notifies the tenant that occupancy is ready and the lease then runs for its original term. Such a provision is particularly attractive to the lessor where the rented premises is an apartment in a new building which is under construction at the time the lease is executed. In this way the landlord protects himself from losing his tenants when there is a construction delay.

Such a provision may be held not binding because it is unconscionable where its effect is not explained to the tenant and the provision is lost in a maze of fine print and technical terms.[14]

(1) Tenant's Right to Acquire Possession. By making a lease, the landlord impliedly covenants that he will give possession of the premises to the tenant at the agreed time. If the landlord rents a building which is being constructed, there is an implied covenant that it will be ready for occupancy at the commencement of the term of the lease.

(2) Tenant's Right to Retain Possession. After the tenant has entered into possession, he has exclusive possession and control of the premises as long as the lease continues and so long as he is not in default under the lease, unless the lease otherwise provides. Thus, the tenant can refuse to allow the landlord to enter the property for the purpose of showing it to prospective customers, although today many leases expressly give this right to the landlord.

If the landlord interferes with this possession by evicting the tenant, he commits a wrong for which the tenant is afforded legal redress. An *eviction* exists when the tenant is deprived of the possession, use, and enjoyment of the premises by the interference of the landlord or one acting under him. If the landlord wrongfully deprives the tenant of the use of one room when he is entitled to the use of the whole building, there is a *partial eviction.*

(a) COVENANT FOR QUIET ENJOYMENT. Most written leases today contain an express promise by the landlord to respect the possession of the tenant, called a *covenant for quiet enjoyment.* Such a provision protects the tenant from interference with his possession by the landlord, but it does not impose liability upon the landlord for the unlawful acts of third persons. Thus, such a covenant does not require the landlord to protect a tenant from damage by a rioting mob.[15]

---

[14] Seabrook v Commuter Housing Co., Inc., (NY Civil Court) 72 Misc 2d 6, 338 NYS2d 67.

[15] New Rochelle Mall v Docktor Pet Centers Realty, 65 Misc 2d 503, 317 NYS2d 404.

(3) Constructive Eviction. An eviction may be actual or constructive. It is a *constructive eviction* when some act or omission of the landlord substantially deprives the tenant of the use and enjoyment of the premises. It is essential in a constructive eviction that the landlord intend to deprive the tenant of the use and enjoyment of the premises. This intent may, however, be inferred from the results of his conduct. A tenant cannot claim that he has been constructively evicted by a particular condition unless he in fact has abandoned the occupancy of the premises because of that condition. If he continues to occupy the premises for more than a reasonable time after the acts claimed to constitute a constructive eviction, he is deemed to waive the eviction. He cannot thereafter abandon the premises and claim that he has been evicted.

A landlord commits a constructive eviction when he intentionally drives the tenant out of the property by shutting off the heat, gas, or water supply, or keeps him from entering the property by refusing to operate the elevators.

The landlord's failure to repair the roof which resulted in water leaking on some eight square feet out of a total of 2,500 square feet of rented area was not sufficient to amount to a partial constructive eviction.[16] The fact that a governmental housing authority does not provide adequate police protection for the safety of tenants in a government housing project does not constitute a constructive eviction of such tenants.[17]

(4) Retaliatory Eviction. A landlord may not evict a tenant or refuse to renew a lease in order to retaliate against the tenant because the tenant has exercised his statutory or constitutional rights. (See p. 1107, Toms Point Apartments v Goudzward.)

§ 54:12. Use of Premises. The lease generally specifies the use to which the tenant may put the property and authorizes the landlord to adopt regulations with respect to the use of the premises that are binding upon the tenant as long as they are reasonable, lawful, and not in conflict with the terms of the lease. In the absence of express or implied restrictions, a tenant is entitled to use the premises for any purpose for which they are adapted or for which they are ordinarily employed, or in a manner contemplated by the parties in executing the lease. He is under an implied duty to use the premises properly even when the lease is silent as to the matter. What constitutes proper use of the premises depends, in the first place, upon the wording of the lease and, secondly, upon the nature of the property.

The tenant is under an implied duty to refrain from willful or permissive waste. At common law the tenant of farm land is entitled to cut sufficient timber for fuel and for repairs to fences, buildings, and farm implements. This rule is extended in many jurisdictions to allow the tenant to clear timber to a reasonable degree so that he may put the land under cultivation. If this

---

[16] Norwich Realty Affiliates v Rappaport, 29 App Div 2d 814, 287 NYS2d 310.
[17] New York City Housing Authority v Medlin, 57 Misc 2d 145, 291 NYS2d 672.

would involve any substantial area, it is likely that the lease would define the rights of the parties in this respect.

Ordinarily a landlord is not responsible for the nature of the use to which the tenants put the property. However, if the landlord knows that the tenant will use the premises unlawfully, as for the purpose of running a gambling operation, the landlord may be subject to criminal prosecution. A landlord is not deemed to take part in the tenant's business. Consequently, when a department store makes a bona fide lease of space to an optometrist, it is not unlawfully practicing optometry even though the rent is based on a percentage of "sales" of the optometrist and his accounts receivable are assigned to the store, when in fact the store does not exercise any control over the professional activities of the optometrist.[18]

(1) Change of Use. The modern lease will in substance make a change of use a condition subsequent so that if the tenant uses the property for any purpose other than the one specified, the landlord has the option of declaring the lease terminated.

Other clauses of the lease frequently restrict the tenant in making a change of use. For example, if alterations to the building would be required for the new use, the tenant would ordinarily find that a clause of the lease required permission of the landlord to make alterations,[19] with the consequence that the tenant might be unable to make the alterations necessary for a different use.

The fact that the tenant may make a different use of the premises either properly or improperly is recognized in many modern leases by specifying that should a change of use by the tenant increase or affect the insurance cost of the landlord, the tenant is liable to the landlord for the additional premiums which the landlord must pay on his insurance or for the loss sustained by the landlord should his insurance be avoided because of actions of the tenant.

In general, courts are inclined to permit the tenant to make any use of the premises that is otherwise lawful and not prohibited by the lease and which can be made without any damage to or alteration of the premises.

(2) Continued Use of Property. With the increased danger of damage to the premises by vandalism or fire when the building is vacant and because of the common insurance provision making a fire insurance policy void when a vacancy continues for a specified time,[20] the modern lease will ordinarily require the tenant to give the landlord notice of nonuse or vacancy of the premises. Likewise, in many situations, it is important to the landlord that the tenant operate a particular business. For example, when the landlord operated a truck stop station and rented an adjacent diner to a tenant, the operation of the diner during reasonable hours was an essential part of the

---

[18] Arizona v Sears, Roebuck & Co., 102 Ariz 175, 427 P2d 126.
[19] See § 54:15.
[20] As to property insurance generally, see Ch. 38.

transaction.[21] Hence, there may be a duty on the tenant to make use of the premises as a counterpart of his right to possession.

(3) Rules. The modern lease generally contains a blanket agreement by the tenant to abide by the provisions of rules and regulations adopted by the landlord. These rules are generally binding on the tenant whether they exist at the time the lease was made or were thereafter adopted. As an exception, a rule adopted by the landlord is void when it restrains trade, as when it prohibits delivery of milk to the tenants by any truck unless the landlord gives permission to make deliveries.[22] Moreover, a provision in a lease relating to rules will generally be strictly construed so as to favor the tenant.

(4) Restriction of Animals. A restriction in a lease prohibiting the keeping of animals for pets is valid.[23]

§ 54:13. Rent. The tenant is under a duty to pay rent as compensation to the landlord.[24] In times of emergency, war, and recovery from war, however, government may impose maximum limitations on rents that are charged. When a business is conducted on the leased premises, it is quite common to provide for both a base rent and an additional rent that is computed as a percentage of the sales made by the tenant.

The lease may provide for the payment of additional rent when the tenant's profits exceed a specified minimum, in which case there is no liability for additional rent until the minimum is exceeded.[25]

The time of payment of rent is ordinarily fixed by the lease. When the lease does not control, rent generally is not due until the end of the term. Statutes or custom, however, may require rent to be paid in advance when the agreement of the parties does not regulate the point. Rent that is payable in crops is generally payable at the end of the term.

If the lease is assigned, the assignee is liable to the landlord for the rent. The assignment, however, does not in itself discharge the tenant from his obligations under the lease. The landlord may bring an action for the rent against either the tenant or the assignee, or both, but he is entitled to only one satisfaction. A sublessee ordinarily is not liable to the original lessor for rent, unless he assumes such liability or unless the liability is imposed by statute.

(1) Rent Escalation. Where a lease contains an escalation clause which increases the rent by a specified formula when wages paid the landlord's elevator operators increase, the tenant is required to pay the additional rent

---

[21] Tooley's Truck Stop v Chrisanthopouls, 55 NJ 231, 260 A2d 845.

[22] Southland Development Corp. v Ehrler's Dairy, Inc., (Ky) 468 SW2d 284.

[23] Linden Hill #2 Co-operative v Leskowitz, 41 App Div 2d 741, 341 NYS2d 317.

[24] For the effect of destruction of the premises on the duty to pay rent, see § 54:7(7).

[25] River View Associates v Sheraton Corporation, 33 App Div 2d 187, 306 NYS 2d 153.

as computed by the application of the formula, and the fact that this increase is greater than the net increase in wages does not make the provision illegal, unconscionable, nor contrary to the public policy.[26]

§ 54:14. Repairs and Condition of Premises. In the absence of an agreement to the contrary, the tenant has the duty to make those repairs that are necessary to prevent waste and decay of the premises, and he is liable for *permissive waste* if he fails to do so. When the landlord leases only a portion of the premises, or leases the premises to different tenants, he is under a duty to make repairs in connecting parts, such as halls, basements, elevators, and stairways, which are under his control. Some statutes require that a landlord who leases a building for dwelling purposes must keep it in condition fit for habitation. In some states a warranty is implied as to the fitness of residential premises whether furnished or unfurnished.[27]

When an apartment in a multiple unit apartment complex is rented, there is an implied warranty of habitability.[28]

By the modern view that there is an implied warranty of habitability, a tenant can claim damages for the breach of this warranty and offset them against the landlord's claim for rent, with the result that if the damages exceed the rent, no rent is due and therefore the landlord cannot obtain repossession of the premises for nonpayment of rent.[29] (See p. 1109, Green v Superior Court.)

Some courts have given such recognition to the implied warranty of habitability as to permit the tenant to set off against the landlord's claim for rent the damages of the tenant for nonhabitability even though the lease expressly declares that the tenant will not assert any setoff or counterclaim in any action brought against him by the lessor.[30]

Most states deny the landlord the right to enter the leased premises to inspect them for waste and need of repairs except when the right is expressly reserved in the lease. It is customary for leases of apartments and commercial property to reserve to the landlord the right to enter to inspect the premises and to make repairs. When the landlord makes repairs by special permission of the tenant or under such a reserved power, he must exercise the care

---

[26] Rich v Don-Ron Trouser Corp., (NY Civil Court) 74 Misc 2d 259, 343 NYS2d 684.

[27] Lund v MacArthur, 51 Haw 473, 462 P2d 482.

[28] Jack Spring, Inc. v Little, 50 Ill 2d 351, 280 NE2d 208. "Modern case law is now finding an implied warranty of habitability by a landlord to his tenant. 'In a modern society one cannot be expected to live in a multi-storied apartment building without heat, hot water, garbage disposal, or elevator service. Failure to supply such things is a breach of the implied covenant of habitability.' " Theis v Heuer, — Ind —, 280 NE 2d 300.

[29] Jack Spring, Inc. v Little, 50 Ill 2d 351, 280 NE2d 208.

[30] Steinberg v Carreras, (NY Civil Court) 74 Misc 2d 32, 344 NYS2d 136. "The rule accepted until recently that separated the landlords' right to rent from their duty to provide services as required by law has been thoroughly sapped of vitality. . . . The product of a peculiar complex of historical circumstances, it is obviously inappropriate to contemporary urban realities, and is utterly discordant with the almost universal rule in our society based upon the interdependence of rights and duties."

which a reasonable man would exercise to make the repairs in a proper manner but he is not automatically liable as an insurer if the tenant is injured after the landlord has made the repairs.[31]

Various laws protect tenants, as by requiring landlords to observe specified safety, health, and fire prevention standards.

In order to protect tenants from unsound living conditions, it is constitutional for a statute to provide that the tenant is not required to pay the rent as long as the premises are not fit to live in. (See p. 1112, Farrell v Drew.) As a compromise, some states require that the tenant continue to pay the rent but authorize him to pay it into an escrow or agency account from which it is paid to the landlord on proof that he has made necessary repairs to the premises.

Leases commonly require the tenant to obey local ordinances and laws relating to the care and use of the premises. If compliance with a law requires the making of repairs, such a provision imposes upon the tenant the duty to make the repairs necessary to comply with the law.[32]

§ 54:15. Improvements. In the absence of special agreement, neither the tenant nor the landlord is under a duty to make improvements, as contrasted with repairs. Either party may, however, make a covenant for improvements, in which case a failure to perform will render him liable in an action for damages for breach of contract brought by the other party. In the absence of an agreement to the contrary, improvements that are attached to the land become part of the realty and belong to the landlord.[33]

(1) Removal of Fixtures. When the tenant has the right to remove trade fixtures, he must usually exercise the right of removal within the term of the lease, in the absence of a contrary provision in the lease. Some courts allow the tenant a reasonable time after the expiration of the lease in which to make such removal or allow the tenant to make the removal after the expiration of the lease but before the premises have been surrendered to the landlord.

§ 54:16. Taxes and Assessments. In the absence of an agreement to the contrary, the landlord and not the tenant is usually under a duty to pay taxes or assessments. If the tax or assessment, however, is chargeable to improvements made by the tenant that do not become a part of the property, the tenant is liable.

If the tenant pays taxes or assessments to protect his interest, he may recover the amount, including damages, from the landlord, or withhold the amount from the rent.

When the premises are assigned by the tenant, the assignee is bound by any covenants of the tenant to pay taxes and assessments. Such covenants

[31] Kowinko v Salecky, 5 Conn Cir 657, 260 A2d 892.

[32] Lindsay Brothers, Inc. v Milwaukee Cold Storage Co., 58 Wis 2d 658, 207 NW2d 639.

[33] As to the removal of improvements as trade fixtures, see § 53:22(3).

are said to "run with the land." The fact that the assignee is bound by the covenants does not, however, discharge the tenant from liability.

A sublessee is not bound by the covenants of the tenant, but he may expressly assume them. In the latter case, however, the tenant is not discharged from his covenants.

§ 54:17. Tenant's Deposit.

(1) Custody. In some states protection is given the tenant who is required to make a payment to the landlord as a "deposit" to insure compliance by the tenant with the terms of the lease. It is sometimes provided that the landlord hold such a payment as a trust fund, that he must inform the tenant of any bank in which the money is deposited, and that he is subject to a penalty if he uses the money as his own before the tenant has breached the lease.[34]

(2) Refund. A landlord may require a tenant to make a deposit to protect the landlord from any default on the part of the tenant. Once paid by the tenant, it frequently happens that the landlord will keep the entire deposit, even though it is in excess of any claim against the tenant, and tenants will not bring suit because the amount involved is too small to justify an action. Tenant protection statutes sometimes remedy this situation by requiring the landlord to refund any part of the deposit in excess of the amount actually needed to compensate him. Under such a statute, it is immaterial that the tenant had agreed that the deposit was nonrefundable.[35]

When such a provision is combined with authorization to bring a class action on behalf of a group of tenants, it becomes economically feasible to bring a lawsuit against the landlord provided there is a significant number of tenants of the same landlord who have the same complaint of deposit withholding. If there are not a sufficient number of tenants involved, the practical aspects of litigation will generally bar any action by the tenant.

§ 54:18. Remedies of Landlord.

(1) Landlord's Lien. In the absence of an agreement or statute [36] so providing, the landlord does not have a lien upon the personal property or crops of the tenant for money due him for rent. The parties may create by express or implied contract, however, a lien in favor of the landlord for rent, and also for advances, taxes, or damages for failure to make repairs.

In the absence of a statutory provision, the lien of the landlord is superior to the claims of all other persons, except prior lienors and bona fide purchasers without notice.

---

[34] Purfield v Kathrane, (NY Civil Court) 73 Misc 2d 194, 341 NYS2d 376.

[35] Bauman v Islay Investments, 30 Cal App 3d 752, 106 Cal Rptr 889.

[36] The landlord's lien is not affected by the UCC. Universal C.I.T. Credit Corp. v Congressional Motors, Inc., 246 Md 380, 228 A2d 463.

(2) Suit for Rent. Whether or not the landlord has a lien for unpaid rent, he may sue the tenant on the latter's contract to pay rent as specified in the lease or, if payment of rent is not specified, he may enforce a quasi-contractual obligation to pay the reasonable value of the occupation and use of the property. In some jurisdictions the landlord is permitted to bring a combined action in which he recovers the possession of the land and the overdue rent at the same time.

(3) Distress. The common law devised a speedy remedy to aid the landlord in collecting his rent. It permitted him to seize personal property found on the premises and to hold it until the arrears were paid. The right was known as *distress*. It was not an action against the tenant for rent but merely a right to retain the property as security until the rent was paid. Statutes have generally either abolished or greatly modified the right of distress.[37]

(4) Recovery of Possession. The lease commonly provides that upon the breach of any of its provisions by the tenant, such as the failure to pay rent, the lease shall terminate or the landlord may, at his option, declare it terminated. When the lease is terminated for any reason, the landlord then has the right to evict the tenant and retake possession of the property.

At common law the landlord, when entitled to possession, may regain it without resorting to legal proceedings. This *right of reentry* is available in many states even when the employment of force is necessary. Other states deny the right to use force.[38]

Modern cases hold that a landlord cannot lock out a tenant for overdue rent and must employ legal process to regain possession even though the lease expressly gives the landlord the right of self-help.[39]

A state statute permitting a landlord to lock out a tenant and hold his property for nonpayment of rent is unconstitutional as a denial of due process where the landlord may so act without any prior notice to the tenant nor judicial hearing, and the statute is not cured by the fact that the tenant can obtain his property by filing a bond for double the amount of the landlord's claim.[40]

The landlord may resort to legal process to evict the tenant in order to enforce his right to possession of the premises. The action of ejectment is ordinarily used. In addition to common-law remedies, statutes in many states provide a summary remedy to recover possession that is much more efficient than the slow common-law remedies. Unless expressly stated, a statutory

---

[37] There is authority that the due process clause of the United States Constitution requires that a hearing be held to determine whether the tenant is in default even though a state statute authorizes the sale of distrained property without a hearing. Santiago v McElroy, (DC ED Pa) 319 F Supp 284; Dielen v Levine, (DC Neb) 344 F Supp 823.

[38] Bachinsky v Federal Coal etc. Co., 78 WVa 721, 90 SE 227.

[39] Brooks v LaSalle National Bank, 11 Ill App 3d 791, 298 NE2d 262.

[40] MacQueen v Lambert, (DC Fla) 348 F Supp 1334.

remedy does not replace those of the common law, but is merely cumulative.[41] In many states today the landlord brings an action of trespass or a civil action to recover possession.

LIABILITY FOR INJURIES ON PREMISES

When the tenant, a member of his family, or a third person is injured by a condition of the premises, the question arises as to who is liable for the damages sustained by the injured person.

§ 54:19. Landlord's Liability to Tenant. In the absence of a covenant to keep the premises in repair, the landlord is ordinarily not liable to the tenant for the latter's personal injuries caused by the defective condition of the premises that are placed under the control of the tenant by the lease. Likewise, the landlord is not liable for the harm caused by an obvious condition that was known to the tenant at the time the lease was made. For example, he is not liable for the fatal burning of a tenant whose clothing was set on fire by an open-faced radiant gas heater.[42]

Likewise, where the backyard of an apartment house ended with a sharp drop into a ravine and there was no protecting fence or other barrier to prevent anyone from falling into the ravine, the landlord was not liable for the injury sustained when a tenant's child fell down into the ravine, as the danger was obvious to anyone renting an apartment.[43]

The landlord is liable to the tenant for injuries caused by latent or non-apparent defects of which the landlord had knowledge.[44]

When the landlord retains control of part of his building or land that is rented to others, he is liable to a tenant who is injured because of the defective condition of such retained portion if the condition was the result of the landlord's failure to exercise the proper degree of care.

In a number of states, by decision or statute, a landlord is liable to a tenant or a child or guest of the tenant where there is a defect which makes the premises dangerously defective, even though the landlord did not have any knowledge of the defect. By this view, a tenant's guest who sat on a railing which collapsed may recover for strict tort liability.[45] Other states refuse to apply the strict tort liability concept and the landlord is then not liable for harm caused by a latent defect which could not have been reasonably discovered by him.[46]

(1) Crimes of Third Persons. Ordinarily the landlord is not liable to the tenant for crimes committed on the premises by third persons, as when a

---

[41] Chicago Great West Railway Co. v Illinois Central Railway Co., 142 Iowa 459, 119 NW 261.

[42] Tillotson v Abbott, 295 Kan 706, 472 P2d 240.

[43] Golf Club Co. v H. I. Rothstein, 97 Ga App 128, 102 SE2d 654.

[44] Hacker v Nitschle, 310 Mass 754, 39 NE2d 644.

[45] Krennerich v WCG Investment Corp., (La App) 278 So2d 842. (The court rejected the contention that the guest had been negligent in making an abnormal use of the railing.)

[46] Dwyer v Skyline Apartments, Inc., 123 NJ Super 48, 301 A2d 463 (plumbing within the wall corroded causing scalding water to gush out and injure tenant).

third person enters the premises and commits larceny or murder. The landlord is not required to establish any security system to protect the tenant from crimes of third persons. Housing regulations apply only to the physical characteristics and use of the premises. They do not impose any duty on the landlord to maintain a security system to protect tenants from unlawful acts of third persons.[47] When a landlord does not maintain the security system that existed when the lease was entered into, however, he may be liable for the harm sustained by the tenant by the illegal acts of third persons whose misconduct was foreseeable.

Thus, the landlord of a large apartment complex had the duty of taking reasonable steps to protect against the entry of third persons onto the premises and the commission of crimes by them when such crimes were being repeatedly committed and the landlord had eliminated a doorman and a garage attendant who had performed security duties when the tenant first moved into the apartment building.[48]

(2) Limitation of Liability. A provision in a lease excusing or exonerating the landlord from liability is generally valid, regardless of the cause of the tenant's loss.[49] A number of courts, however, have restricted the landlord's power to limit his liability in the case of residential, as distinguished from commercial, leasing; so that a provision in a residential lease that the landlord shall not be liable for damage caused by water, snow, or ice is void.[50] A modern trend holds that clauses limiting liability of the landlord are void with respect to harm caused by the negligence of the landlord when the tenant is a residential tenant generally or is a tenant in a government low-cost housing project. (See p. 1113, Crowell v Housing Authority.)

Third persons on the premises, even though with the consent of the tenant, are generally not bound by such a clause and may therefore sue the landlord when they sustain injuries. Thus, it has been held that members of the tenant's family,[51] employees, and guests, are not bound where they do not sign the lease, although there is authority to the contrary.

(3) Indemnification of Lessor. The modern lease commonly contains a provision declaring that the tenant will indemnify the landlord for any liability of the landlord to a third person which arises in connection with the rented premises. These provisions will generally be worded so broadly that the tenant must indemnify the landlord even when the harm to the third person was caused by the negligence or fault of the landlord. Such indemnity clauses are valid although some states have adopted statutes declaring them invalid with respect to harm caused by the landlord's fault.[52]

---

[47] Williams v William J. Davis, Inc., (Dist Col App) 275 A2d 231.

[48] Kline v 1500 Massachusetts Avenue Apartment Corporation, (CA Dist Col) 439 F2d 477.

[49] Home Indemnity Co. v Basiliko, 245 Md 412, 226 A2d 258.

[50] Feldman v Stein Building & Lumber Co., 6 Mich App 180, 148 NW2d 544.

[51] Harper v Vallejo Housing Authority, 104 Cal App 2d 621, 232 P2d 262.

[52] Rigger v Baltimore County, 269 Md 306, 305 A2d 128.

§ 54:20. Landlord's Liability to Third Persons. The landlord is ordinarily not liable to third persons injured because of the condition of the premises when the landlord is not in possession of the premises. If the landlord retains control over a portion of the premises, such as hallways or stairways, however, he is liable for injuries to third persons caused by his failure to exercise proper care in connection with that part of the premises. The modern trend of cases imposes liability on the landlord when a third person is harmed by a condition that the landlord had contracted with the tenant to correct.

§ 54:21. Tenant's Liability to Third Persons. A tenant in complete possession has control of the property and is therefore liable when his failure to use due care under the circumstances causes harm to (a) licensees, such as a person allowed to use his telephone, and (b) invitees, such as customers entering his store. With respect to both classes, the liability of the tenant is the same as an owner in possession of his property.[53] It is likewise immaterial whether the property is used for residential or business purposes, provided the tenant has control of the area where the injury occurs.

The liability of the tenant to third persons is not affected by the fact that the landlord may have contracted in the lease to make repairs which, if made, would have avoided the injury. The tenant can protect himself, however, in the same manner that the landlord can, by procuring public liability insurance to indemnify him for loss from claims of third persons.

Both the landlord and the tenant may be liable to third persons for harm caused by the condition of the leased premises. For example, if the landlord maintains unhealthy or dangerous conditions amounting to a nuisance[54] and then leases the property to a tenant who continues the nuisance, both parties may be liable, the one for creating and the other for maintaining the nuisance. In some states no liability is imposed upon a tenant in such circumstances unless the person injured by the nuisance first requests the tenant to stop or abate the nuisance and the tenant refuses to do so.

TRANSFER OF RIGHTS

Both the landlord and the tenant have property and contract rights with respect to the lease. When either makes a transfer of them, questions arise as to the rights and liabilities of the transferee.

§ 54:22. Transfer of Landlord's Reversionary Interest. The reversionary interest of the landlord may be transferred voluntarily by his act, or involuntarily by a judicial or execution sale. The tenant then becomes the tenant of the new owner of the reversionary interest, and the new owner is bound by the terms of the lease.[55]

When the landlord assigns his reversion, the assignee is, in the absence of an agreement to the contrary, entitled to subsequent accruals of rent. The

---

[53] Mitchell v Thomas, 91 Mont 370, 8 P2d 639.

[54] South Carolina v Turner, 198 SC 499, 18 SE2d 376.

[55] Bender v Kaelin, 257 Ky 783, 79 SW2d 250.

rent may, however, be reserved in an assignment of a reversion. The landlord also has the right to assign the lease independent of the reversion, or to assign the rent independent of the lease.

(1) Obligations of Lessor. When the lessor transfers his reversionary interests, his transferee, the new landlord, becomes bound by the obligations specified in the lease, such as a covenant to repair. He is not liable, however, for damages for the prior breach of any such covenants committed by the former landlord unless he has expressly assumed liability for them.[56]

§ 54:23. Tenant's Assignment of Lease and Sublease. An *assignment of a lease* is a transfer by the tenant of his entire interest in the premises to a third person. A tenancy for years may be assigned by the tenant unless he is restricted from doing so by the terms of the lease or by statute.[57] A *sublease* is a transfer of any part of the premises by the tenant to a third person, the *sublessee,* for a period less than the term of the lease.[58]

Whether the transaction between the tenant and a third person is a sublease or an assignment is determined by the effect of the transaction. If the entire interest of the tenant is transferred to the third person, the transaction is an assignment of the lease, without regard to whether the parties have described the transaction as a sublease or an assignment. In contrast, if there is some interest left over after the interest of the third person expires, the relationship is a sublease.[59]

(1) Limitations on Rights. The lease may contain provisions denying the right to assign or sublet or imposing specified restrictions on the privilege of assigning or subletting. Such restrictions are enforceable in order to enable the landlord to protect himself from tenants who would damage the property or be financially irresponsible.

Restrictions in the lease are construed liberally in favor of the tenant. An ineffectual attempt to assign or sublet does not violate a provision prohibiting such acts. This is equally true when the tenant merely permits someone else to use the land.

As a provision restricting the right of the tenant to assign the lease or requiring the landlord's written consent thereto is for the benefit of the landlord, it may be waived by him. In the case of commercial leasing, when the difference between tenants relates primarily to financial standing rather than the way in which the property will be used, the landlord may be under the duty to waive the no-assignment clause and to accept a financially sound subtenant in order to reduce his claim against the original tenant for rent. (See p. 1114, Scheinfeld v Muntz TV, Inc.)

---

[56] Plaza Investment Co. v Abel, 8 Mich App 153 NW2d 379.
[57] MacFadden-Deauville Hotel v Murrell, (CA5 Fla) 182 F2d 537.
[58] Spears v Canon de Carnue Land Grant, 80 NMex 766, 461 P2d 415.
[59] Jensen v O. K. Investment Corp., 29 Utah 2d 231, 507 P2d 713.

(2) Effect of Assignment or Sublease. An express covenant or promise by the sublessee is necessary to impose liability upon him. In contrast with a sublease, when the lease is assigned and the assignee takes possession of the property, he becomes bound by the terms of the lease.

Neither the act of subletting nor the landlord's agreement to it releases the original tenant from liability under the terms of the original lease.

When a lease is assigned, the original tenant remains liable for the rent which becomes due thereafter. If the assignee renews or extends the lease by virtue of an option contained therein, the original tenant is likewise liable for the rent for such extended period [60] in the absence of a contrary agreement or novation by which the lessor agreed that the assignee shall be deemed substituted as tenant and the original tenant shall be released from further liability.

It is customary and desirable for the tenant to require the sublessee to covenant or promise that he will perform all obligations under the original lease and that he will indemnify the tenant for any loss caused by default of the sublessee. An express covenant or promise by the sublessee is necessary to impose liability upon him. The fact that the sublease is made "subject" to the terms of the original lease merely recognizes the superiority of the original lease, but does not impose any duty upon the sublessee to perform the tenant's obligations under the original lease. If the sublessee promises the tenant that he will assume the obligation of the original lease, the landlord, as a third-party beneficiary, may sue the sublessee for breach of the provisions of the original lease.

---

[60] Kornblum v Mangles, (Fla App) 167 So2d 16.

CASES FOR CHAPTER 54

Kilbourne v Forester

(Mo App) 464 SW2d 770 (1971)

In June, 1966, Forester leased an apartment to Kilbourne for one year. The lease stated, "The lease is renewable at the end of the year period." Kilbourne renewed the lease for the year 1967-1968. She again gave notice of renewal for the year 1968-1969 but Forester refused to recognize such renewal and brought an action to recover possession of the premises. From a judgment for Forester, Kilbourne appealed.

SHANGLER, P.J. . . . [The lease which was] concededly for a term of one year from . . . July 7, 1966, vested in appellant the right to renew, a right which she maintains . . . was "exercisable by her at the end of every yearly period" [by] notice and by her continued performance under its terms. . . .

. . . The lease contract between the parties was for a definite term, fixed at one year. It was made no less certain by any possibility that the provision: "The lease is renewable at the end of the year period" authorized a perpetuity of leases (as appellant contends) rather than only a second lease by one renewal, as it plainly means. Because the law discourages perpetuities, and does not favor covenants for continued renewals, "a covenant which does not plainly imply or express a perpetual renewal will not be construed to give this right." . . . The renewal provision of the lease between these parties is in general terms; it contains none of the language customarily used to express an intention for perpetual renewals, and certainly none can be implied. Such a general provision will be construed as authorizing but one renewal of all the terms of the old lease except that of the option of renewal itself. . . . By the explicit terms of the lease, therefore, the certain end of appellant's estate and tenancy was no later than July 6, 1968. "When the term of a lease is to end on a precise day, there is no occasion for a notice to quit previously to bringing an ejectment, because both parties are equally apprised of the determination of the term" . . . which relieves the necessity for notice to quit from or to a tenant whose term is to end at a certain time adopts this rationale and expresses the common law rule in so doing. . . .

[Judgment affirmed.]

Toms Point Apartments v Goudzward

72 Misc 2d 629, 339 NYS2d 281 (1972)

Goudzward was a tenant in the Toms Point Apartments. She held a meeting with other tenants to consider the possibility of forming an organization to deal with the landlord respecting their grievances. Thereafter the landlord refused to renew Goudzward's lease. She refused to leave the premises and the landlord brought a court action against her to recover possession.

DIAMOND, J. . . . At the trial, the tenant raised the affirmative defense of "retaliatory eviction." She claimed that the landlord's refusal to renew her lease was solely in retaliation for her actions with her fellow tenants in opposing the landlord. The landlord contends that the tenant has failed to sustain the burden of proof required and, further, that the defense of retaliatory eviction does not apply in this case.

Tenant seeks to dismiss the action and have the Court order the landlord to renew the lease on terms equal to those offered other tenants.

The Court has before it the question whether a landlord has the right to pick his tenants and refuse to renew the tenancy of a person he finds undesirable for any reason, or whether that right is affected by the defense of retaliatory eviction.

The defense of retaliatory eviction . . . is a comparatively new one. Retaliatory eviction has been defined in many ways. In Markese v Cooper, Co. Ct., 333 NYS2d 63, the Court stated that retaliatory eviction is the nomenclature that has developed to define the action of a landlord who evicts his tenant because of the tenant's reporting of a housing code violation. The Court in that case went on to say that it might have been called anything, "vengeful eviction" or, simply, "getting even." The Court in Hosey v Club Van Cortlandt, DC, 299 F Supp 501, described retaliatory eviction as an act by a landlord evicting a tenant when the overriding reason was to retaliate against the tenant for exercising his constitutional right.

The defense of retaliatory eviction in a holdover proceeding was not available at common law, nor do we in New York have any statutes specifically prohibiting retaliatory eviction. A few states have recently enacted such statutes. Illinois has declared it to be against public policy for a landlord to "terminate or refuse to renew a lease or tenancy of property used as a residence on the ground that the tenant has complained to any government authority of a bona fide violation of any applicable building code, health ordinance, or similar regulation." Ill SHS ch 80 § 71 (1966). Rhode Island and Michigan allow a tenant-defendant, in an action based upon termination of a lease, to interpose the defense that the alleged termination was intended as a penalty for the tenant reporting a violation of any health or safety code, or any ordinance. Maryland has provided that retaliatory action will be stayed for a period of six months after a tenant has reported a major defect in the premises. California's new Civil Code Section 1942.5 states that a landlord, whose dominant purpose is retaliation against a lessee for complaining to a government agency or for exercising other rights, "may not recover possession of a dwelling in any action or proceeding, cause the lesssee to quit involuntarily, increase the rent, or decrease any services, within 60 days." New Jersey provides for criminal punishment of any landlord who takes reprisals against a tenant for reporting violations of any health or building code. . . .

The cases in New York are not in complete agreement on the interpretation of retaliatory eviction. Some New York cases have recognized it as a proper defense in holdover proceedings. . . . The Federal courts have also recognized the defense. The Court in Hosey v Club Van Cortlandt, DC, 299 FSupp 501, held that "The 14th amendment prohibits a state court from evicting a tenant when the overriding reason the landlord is seeking the eviction is to retaliate against the tenant for an exercise of his constitutional rights." Also see Edwards v Habib, 130 US App DC 126, 397 F2d 687.

The tenant in her Memorandum of Law places great emphasis upon Hosey v Club Van Cortlandt in support of her argument against granting the petition. She also requests an order by the Court for a mandatory renewal of the lease. The Court points out the fact that the judges' decision in the Hosey v Club Van Cortlandt case wrote, 299 FSupp p. 505, "The right of a landlord to pick his tenants and to refuse to renew the tenancy of a person he finds undesirable for any reason is not in issue here." The Court in the herein matter deems that issue to be the major issue.

The law in New York is well settled that in the absence of a covenant in the lease, or some agreement therefor, there is no way, legal or equitable, of compelling a renewal of a lease. . . . Therefore, when the term of a lease has expired, the landlord, in the absence of a contract to renew, is at liberty to refuse to do so, and anyone with whom he sees fit to deal may become his tenant. . . .

There is no dispute between the parties that absent the defense of retaliatory eviction the Court must grant the landlord's petition of eviction. Testimony at the trial indicates that the tenant did hold a meeting of the tenants in her apartment and that she had testified at a hearing concerning the dismissal of the landlord's custodian. There was some testimony that the tenant had concerned herself with such matters as lack of services, rent increases and inequities in rent. The tenant testified that she complained to the Attorney General's Office regarding the failure of the landlord to pay interest on rent security deposits and that she appeared at a "hearing" of the superintendent who was fired by the landlord. The landlord during the trial neither admitted nor denied the testimony of the tenant regarding these activities.

. . . The Court rejects tenant's argument that if the Court finds a retaliatory eviction it should grant the remedy of ordering a new lease. There seems to be no authority, public policy or any other justification for disturbing the well settled law in New York that there is no way, legal or equitable, to compel a renewal of a lease.

In reviewing the New York, Federal, and out of state cases discussed above, the Court finds that the basis for accepting the defense of retaliatory eviction is as follows:

A tenant has the constitutional right such as to discuss the conditions of the building he is living in with his co-tenants; to encourage them to use legal means to remedy improper conditions; hold meetings; form tenants' associations; and inform public officials of their complaints. These rights would for all practical purposes be meaningless if the threat of eviction would coerce the most justifiable complaints into a submissive silence.

Failure to recognize the defense of retaliatory eviction might result in the continuation of undesirable housing conditions contrary to the strong public policy of creating and/or maintaining proper housing . . . . Our Court should not by the granting of an eviction of a complaining tenant encourage the landlord to evade his responsibility to abide by the law.

The Court is in accord with the reasoning behind the acceptance of the defense of retaliatory eviction in an action by a landlord to recover possession. Once having accepted that concept, the Court is faced with the problem as to what elements are necessary to create a valid retaliatory eviction defense. . . .

It seems to this Court that *all* of the following should be present for the tenant to prevail:

1. The tenant must have exercised a constitutional right in the action he undertook.

2. The grievance complained of by the tenant must be bona fide, reasonable, serious in nature, and have a foundation in fact. However, the grievance need not have been adjudicated by the agency reviewing the complaint.

3. The tenant did not create the condition upon which the complaint is based.

4. The grievance complained of must be present at the time the landlord commences his proceeding.

5. The overriding reason the landlord is seeking the eviction is to retaliate against the tenant for exercising his constitutional rights.

Applying the facts in the present case to the above criteria, the Court finds that at the time the landlord commenced this action and, at the present time, none of the original grievances existed. The tenant testified that the tenants' association never came into being; that the tenants had collected the interest due them; that the problem with the superintendent had been resolved. Moreover, the tenant failed to show any current complaint against the landlord.

In Edwards v Habib, 130 US App DC 126, 397 F2d 687, 702, the Court cautioned that even if a tenant can prove a retaliatory defense, he would not be entitled to remain in possession in perpetuity. "If this illegal purpose is dissipated, the landlord can, in the absence of legislation or a binding contract, evict his tenants or raise their rents for economic or other legitimate reasons, or even for no reason at all."

The Court finds that the tenant has failed to prove the elements necessary to sustain the alleged retaliatory eviction defense. Accordingly, the decision of the Court is as follows:

Final Judgment in favor of the landlord against the tenant. . . .

Green v Superior Court

10 Cal 3d 616, 111 Cal Rptr 704, 517 P2d 1168 (1974)

Sumski rented an apartment to Green. Green did not pay the rent because the apartment was not fit to live in. Sumski claimed that Green was unlawfully in the premises without paying rent and brought an action of unlawful detainer against him. The Superior Court entered judgment for Sumski. Green then filed a petition in the Supreme Court to compel the Superior Court to vacate or set aside the judgment for Sumski.

TOBRINER, J. . . . Under traditional common law doctrine, long followed in California, a landlord was under no duty to maintain leased dwellings in habitable condition during the term of the lease. In the past several years, however, the highest courts of a rapidly growing number of states and the District of Columbia have reexamined the bases of the old common law rule and have uniformly determined that it no longer corresponds to the realities of the modern urban landlord-tenant relationship. Accordingly, each of these jurisdictions has discarded the old common law rule and has adopted an implied warranty of habitability for residential leases. . . .

. . . Continued adherence to the time-worn doctrine conflicts with the expectations and demands of the contemporary landlord-tenant relationship and with modern legal principles in analogous fields. . . .

Second, . . . the statutory "repair and deduct" provisions of Civil Code . . . do not preclude this development in the common law, for such enactments were never intended to be the exclusive remedy for tenants but have always been viewed as complementary to existing common law rights.

Finally, we have concluded that a landlord's breach of this warranty of habitability may be raised as a defense in an unlawful detainer action. Past California cases have established that a defendant in an unlawful detainer action may raise any affirmative defense which, if established, will preserve the tenant's possession of the premises. . . . A landlord's breach of a warranty of habitability directly relates to whether any rent is "due and owing" by the tenant; hence, such breach may be determinative of whether the landlord or tenant is entitled to possession of the premises upon nonpayment of rent. Accordingly, the tenant may properly raise the issue of warranty of habitability in an unlawful detainer action. . . .

At common law, the real estate lease developed in the field of real property law, not contract law. Under property law concepts, a lease was considered a conveyance or sale of the premises for a term of years, subject to the ancient doctrine of caveat emptor. Thus, under traditional common law rules, the landlord owed no duty to place leased premises in a habitable condition and no obligation to repair the premises. . . . These original common law precepts perhaps suited the agrarianism of the early Middle Ages which was their matrix; at such time, the primary value of a lease lay in the land itself and whatever simple living structures may have been included in the leasehold were of secondary importance and were readily repairable by the typical "jack-of-all-trades" lessee farmer. Furthermore, because the law of property crystallized before the development of mutually dependent covenants in contract law, a lessee's covenant to pay rent was considered at common law as independent of the lessor's covenants. Thus even when a lessor expressly covenanted to make repairs, the lessor's breach did not justify the lessee's withholding of the rent. . . .

The recent decisions recognize initially that the geographic and economic conditions that characterized the agrarian lessor-lessee transaction have been entirely transformed in the modern urban landlord-tenant relationship. We have suggested that in the Middle Ages, and, indeed, until the urbanization of the industrial revolution, the land itself was by far the most important element of a lease transaction; this predominance explained the law's treatment of such leases as conveyances of interests in land. In today's urban residential leases, however, land as such plays no comparable role. The typical city dweller, who frequently leases an apartment several stories above the actual plot of land on which an apartment building rests, cannot realistically be viewed as acquiring an interest in land; rather, he has contracted for a place to live. . . . "When American city dwellers, both rich and poor, seek, 'shelter' today, they seek a well known package of goods and services—a package which includes not merely walls and ceilings, but also adequate heat, light and ventilation, serviceable plumbing facilities, secure windows and doors, proper sanitation, and proper maintenance."

. . . Similarly, leading legal scholars in the field have long stressed the propriety of a more contractually oriented analysis of lease agreements. . . . Our holding in this case reflects our belief that the application of contract principles, including the mutual dependency of covenants, is particularly appropriate in dealing with residential leases of urban dwelling units.

Modern urbanization has not only undermined the validity of utilizing general property concepts in analyzing landlord-tenant relations, but it has also significantly altered the factual setting directly relevant to the more specific duty of maintaining leased premises. As noted above, at the inception of the common law rule, any structure on the leased premises was likely to be of the most simple nature, easily inspected by the lessee to determine if it fit his needs, and easily repairable by the typically versatile tenant farmer. Contemporary urban housing and the contemporary urban tenant stand in marked contrast to this agrarian model.

First, the increasing complexity of modern apartment buildings not only renders them much more difficult and expensive to repair than the living quarters of earlier days, but also makes adequate inspection of the premises by a prospective tenant a virtual impossibility; complex heating, electrical and plumbing systems are hidden from view, and the landlord, who has had experience with the building, is certainly in a much better position to discover and to cure dilapidations in the premises. Moreover, in a multiple-unit dwelling repair will frequently require access to equipment and areas solely in the control of the landlord.

Second, unlike the multi-skilled lessee of old, today's city dweller generally has a single, specialized skill unrelated to maintenance work. Furthermore, whereas an agrarian lessee frequently remained on a single plot of land for his entire life, today's urban tenant is more mobile than ever; a tenant's limited tenure in a specific apartment will frequently not justify efforts at extensive repairs. Finally, the expense of needed repairs will often be outside the reach of many tenants for "[l]ow and middle income tenants, even if they were interested in making repairs, would be unable to obtain any financing for major repairs since they have no long-term interest in the property." . . .

In addition to these significant changes, urbanization and population growth have wrought an enormous transformation in the contemporary housing market, creating a scarcity of adequate low cost housing in virtually every urban setting. This current state of the housing market is by no means unrelated to the common law duty to maintain habitable premises. For one thing, the severe shortage of low and moderate cost housing has left tenants with little bargaining power through which they might gain express warranties of habitability from landlords, and thus the mechanism of the "free market" no longer serves as a viable means for fairly allocating the duty to repair leased premises between landlord and tenant. For another, the scarcity of adequate housing has limited further the adequacy of the tenant's right to inspect the premises; even when defects are apparent the low income tenant frequently has no realistic alternative but to accept such housing with the expectation that the landlord will make the necessary repairs. Finally, the shortage of available low cost housing has rendered inadequate the few remedies that common law courts previously have developed to ameliorate the harsh consequences of the traditional "no duty to repair" rule.

These enormous factual changes in the landlord-tenant field have been paralleled by equally dramatic changes in the prevailing legal doctrines governing commerical transactions. Whereas the traditional common law "no duty to maintain or repair" rule was steeped in the caveat emptor ethic of an earlier commercial era . . . modern legal decisions have recognized that the consumer in an industrial society should be entitled to rely on the skill of the supplier to assure that goods and services are of adequate quality. In seeking to protect the reasonable expectations of consumers, judicial decisions, discarding the caveat emptor approach, have for some time implied a warranty of fitness and merchantability in the case of the sale of goods. . . . In recent years, moreover, . . . courts have increasingly recognized the applicability of this implied warranty theory to real estate transactions; prior cases have found a warranty of fitness implied by law with respect to the construction of new housing units. . . .

In most significant respects, the modern urban tenant is in the same position as any other normal consumer of goods. . . . Through a residential lease, a tenant seeks to purchase "housing" from his landlord for a specified period of time. The landlord "sells" housing, enjoying a much greater opportunity, incentive and capacity than a tenant to inspect and maintain the condition of his apartment building. A tenant may reasonably expect that the product he is purchasing is fit for the purpose for which it is obtained, that is, a living unit. Moreover, since a lease contract specifies a designated period of time during which the tenant has a right to inhabit the premises, the tenant may legitimately expect that the premises will be fit for such habitation for the duration of the term of the lease. It is just such reasonable expectations of consumers which the modern "implied warranty" decisions endow with formal, legal protection. . . .

The crucial issue in this case thus becomes whether a landlord's breach of a warranty of habitability directly relates to the issue of possession. Holding that such breach was irrelevant to the question of possession, early California cases refused to permit a defense that the landlord had breached a covenant to repair premises. . . . These decisions, however, rested primarily upon the ancient property doctrine of "independent covenants," under which a tenant's obligation to pay rent was viewed as a continuing obligation which was not excused by the landlord's failure to fulfill any covenant of repair he may have assumed. As indicated earlier in this opinion, the entire foundation of the "independent covenants" doctrine rested on the central role played by land in the lease transaction of the Middle Ages; the doctrine simply reflected the fact that in those early times covenants regarding the maintenance of buildings were generally "incidental" to the furnishing of land, and did not go to the root of the consideration for the lease. In that setting, a landlord's breach of such an "incidental" covenant to repair was reasonably considered insufficient to justify the tenant's refusal to pay rent, the tenant's main obligation under the lease.

The transformation which the residential lease has undergone since the Middle Ages, however, has completely eroded the underpinnings of the "independent covenant" rule. Today the habitability of the dwelling unit has become the very essence of the residential lease; the landlord can as materially frustrate the purpose of such a lease by permitting the premises to become uninhabitable as by withdrawing the use of a portion of the premises. . . . Thus, in keeping with the contemporary trend to analyze urban residential leases under modern contractual principles, we now conclude that the tenant's duty to pay rent is "mutually dependent" upon the landlord's fulfillment of his implied warranty of habitability. . . .

Once we recognize that the tenant's obligation to pay rent and the landlord's warranty of habitability are mutually dependent, it becomes clear that the landlord's breach of such warranty may be directly relevant to the issue of possession. If the tenant can prove such a breach by the landlord, he may demonstrate that his nonpayment of rent was justified and that no rent is in fact "due and owing" to the landlord. Under such circumstances, of course, the landlord would not be entitled to possession of the premises. . . .

We have concluded that a warranty of habitability is implied by law in residential leases in this state and that the breach of such a warranty may be raised as a defense in an unlawful detainer action. Under the implied warranty which we recognize, a residential landlord covenants that premises he leases for living quarters will be maintained in a habitable state for the duration of the lease. This implied warranty of habitability does not require that a landlord ensure that leased premises are in perfect, aesthetically pleasing condition, but it does mean that "bare living requirements" must be maintained. . . .

. . . We must remand this case to the trial court so that it may determine whether the landlord has breached the implied warranty of habitability as defined in this opinion.

If the trial court does find a breach of implied warranty, the court must then determine the extent of the damages flowing from this breach. Recent decisions have suggested that in these circumstances the "tenant's damages shall be measured by the difference between the fair rental value of the premises if they had been as warranted and the fair rental value of the premises as they were during occupancy by the tenant in the unsafe or unsanitary condition." . . .

[Judgment vacated and action remanded.]

Farrell v Drew

19 NY2d 486, 281 NYS2d 1, 227 NE2d 824 (1967)

A New York statute provided that the rent owed by any tenant receiving welfare funds should "abate" if there was a "violation of law . . . dangerous, hazardous, or detrimental to life or health." Drew and two others, who were tenants of Farrell, received welfare funds. When Farrell brought an action to evict them for nonpayment of rent, they claimed that they were not required to pay the rent because there was a dangerous and hazardous condition in the building rendering it unsafe for occupants. From a judgment in favor of the tenants, Farrell appealed.

FULD, C.J. . . . The legislature made clear, by its "Declaration of purpose and necessity" . . . that it was prompted to pass section 143-b of the Social Welfare Law in order to alleviate "certain [existing] evils and abuses . . . which have caused many tenants, who are welfare recipients, to suffer untold hardships, deprivation of services and deterioration of housing facilities because certain landlords have been exploiting such tenants by failing to make necessary repairs and by neglecting to afford necessary services."

The legislation, designed to operate as an effective weapon in the fight against slum housing in general . . . , was adopted only after it became apparent that existing sanctions, including criminal sanctions, were inadequate to cope with the problems of building law enforcement. . . .

In the cases before us, the landlord does not challenge the Legislature's power to require that building law violations be corrected. Her attack is directed solely against the sanction chosen by the Legislature to attain its objective of safe housing. Specifically, her contention is that the rent abatement provided by section 143-b works a denial of equal protection of the laws, a deprivation of property without due process, and an unconstitutional impairment of contractual rights.

Although the landlord lacks standing to complain that the statute discriminates in favor of *tenants* who are welfare recipients, . . . she is entitled to urge that it denies equal protection of the laws on the ground that it is aimed only at *landlords* of welfare recipients. However, it is settled that such legislation is not unconstitutional as long as a "reasonable basis" exists for differentiating among the members of the same class. . . . As we wrote in the Durham Realty Corp. case, which involved a statute barring eviction of tenants who paid a "reasonable" rent . . . , "One class of landlords is selected for regulation because one class conspicuously offends; one class of tenants has protection because all who seek homes cannot be provided with places to sleep and eat. Those who are out of possession, willing to pay exorbitant rentals, or unable to pay any rentals whatever, have been left to shift for themselves. But such classifications deny to no one the equal protection of the laws. The distinction between the groups is real and rests on a substantial basis."

In the situation presented by the cases before us, it is the landlords of welfare recipients who, the Legislature found, "conspicuously offend." To be sure, they are not the only landlords who fail to make repairs in slum dwellings. But welfare recipients have even less freedom than other tenants of deteriorated buildings in selecting a place to live . . . and the landlords of welfare recipients, secure in their receipt of rents directly from public funds, have even less incentive than other landlords to make repairs. Under circumstances such as these, if the Legislature chooses to select one class of landlords and impose a special sanction against them, the equal protection clause does not forbid it. . . .

It is likewise clear that the State may, in the exercise of its police power, provide for the curtailment of rent payments to landlords as a means of inducing them to eliminate dangerous housing conditions. . . . We have, in the past, upheld and applied statutes or regulations, not too unlike the one before us, which provide for (1) rent reduction . . . , (2) partial rent abatement . . . , and (3) rent receivership. . . .

[Judgment affirmed.]

Crowell v Housing Authority

(Tex) 495 SW2d 887 (1973)

Crowell rented an apartment from the Housing Authority of the City of Dallas. The gas heater in the apartment was defective and carbon monoxide from the heater killed Crowell. His son, Lewis, sued the Housing Authority under the Texas Survival Statute to recover medical expenses and damages for the pain and suffering of his father. The Housing Authority raised the defense that the lease expressly declared that the Authority would not be liable for any damages. The lower court held that this provision barred the action. Crowell appealed.

WALKER, J. [The lease between the respondent, the Housing Authority, and Crowell declared:]

> ". . . nor shall the Landlord nor any of its representatives or employees be liable for any damage to person or property of the Tenant, his family, or his visitors, which might result from the condition of these or other premises of the Landlord, from theft or from any cause whatsoever."

A somewhat similar provision was upheld in Manius v Housing Authority of City of Pittsburg, 350 Pa 512, 39 A2d 614. The courts of two other jurisdictions concluded that it is contrary to public policy to allow a housing authority to exempt itself by contract from liability to its own tenants for negligence in the performance of its duty to provide safe and sanitary housing for persons of low income. Thomas v Housing Authority of City of Bremerton, 71 Wash 2d 69, 426 P2d 836; Housing Authority of Birmingham Dist v Morris, 244 Ala 557, 14 So2d 527. We approve and adopt the latter view.

Agreements exempting a party from future liability for negligence are generally recognized as valid and effective except where, because of the relationship of the parties, the exculpatory provision is contrary to public policy or the public interest. If the contract is between private persons who bargain from positions of substantially equal strength, the agreement is ordinarily enforced by the courts. The exculpatory agreement will be declared void, however, where one party is at such disadvantage in bargaining power that he is practically compelled to submit to the stipulation. It is generally held, for example, that a contract exempting an employer from all liability for negligent injury of his employees in the course of their employment is void as against public policy. The same rule applies to agreements exempting public utilities from liability for negligence in the performance of their duty of public service. . . .

The rules applicable to public utilities have been applied by some courts to innkeepers and public warehousemen. . . . There is a definite tendency to extend the same rules to other professional bailees such as garagemen and owners of parking lots and parcel checkrooms. These bailees are under no public duty, but they deal with the public and the indispensable need for their services deprives the customer of any real bargaining power. . . .

The same considerations lead us to the conclusion that the exculpatory agreement in the present case is contrary to public policy. Respondent [Housing Authority] is a public body organized for the declared public purpose, among others, of providing safe and sanitary dwelling accommodations to persons of low income. It may lease accommodations only to families or persons who lack sufficient income to enable them, without financial assistance, to live in decent, safe and sanitary dwellings without overcrowding. . . . As pointed out by the court in *Thomas,* the situation of respondent and its tenants presents a classic example of unequal bargaining power. The terms of the contract are dictated by respondent, and a prospective tenant has no choice but to accept them if he and his family are to enjoy decent housing accommodations not otherwise available to them. We hold that the exculpatory provision quoted above is contrary to public policy and void in so far as it purports to affect respondent's liability in the present case. . . .

[Judgment reversed and action remanded.]

Scheinfeld v Muntz TV, Inc.

67 Ill App 2d 8, 214 NE2d 506 (1966)

Scheinfeld, doing business as Greenleaf Investors, leased a warehouse to Muntz TV, Inc. Thereafter, with Greenleaf's written consent, Muntz sublet the warehouse to Breuer Electric Mfg. Co. Muntz TV later decided to sublet to Calumet Mfg. Co., but Greenleaf refused to consent thereto. Breuer vacated the premises. Scheinfeld then proceeded against Muntz TV for the full rent. Muntz TV claimed that it was only liable for the difference between the full rent and the rent that Calumet would have paid. From a decision in favor of Scheinfeld, Muntz appealed.

DEMPSEY, J. . . . The controlling question is whether a lessor has the duty to mitigate damages if a suitable subtenant is secured and tendered by the lessee. . . .

. . . Application of the mitigation of damages rule is consistent with the landlord-tenant relationship; for example: the property relations between Greenleaf and Muntz and between Muntz and Breuer would not have been affected had the Calumet sublease been consented to; Greenleaf could still have looked solely to Muntz and Muntz solely to Breuer for performance of the covenants of the lease and sublease. . . .

The argument that the landlord's duty to mitigate arises only if the lease so provides is relevant where the provisions of the lease cover the landlord's duty to mitigate damages; where, however, there is no provision in the lease expressing the intent of the parties on this specific subject matter, it is the law of contracts which implies that duty. . . . Since neither the prime lease nor the sublease in the instant-case provides that the respective landlords shall have no duty to mitigate damages, this court would not be eliminating any of the express provisions of either lease in applying the mitigation rule.

We reaffirm, therefore, our holding . . . that the contractual rule compelling mitigation of damages applies to leases. In doing so, we emphasize the validity of the provisions of the lease and sublease in the present case prohibiting assignment and subletting without the landlord's consent and giving the landlord the option to rerent on such terms as he sees fit is not in question. We do not mean that the landlord must accept any subtenant submitted by the lessee, that he must grant a new lease to the proposed subtenant, that he must release the lessee from further responsibility for rent, or that he must rent his property for a purpose which might damage it. The landlord's duty to mitigate damages does not prevent him from exercising his choice of tenants in rerenting the premises. But when the duty to mitigate is raised by the tender of a suitable sublessee, the option of the landlord lies between consenting to the sublease or crediting the tenant with the amount which would have been paid by the sublessee had he been accepted. The landlord may not arbitrarily reject a suitable sublessee and yet continue to hold the tenant liable for the whole rental in default. Thus, in the case at bar, Breuer should be credited on its indebtedness to Muntz with the rental it could have received from Calumet, and Muntz should receive like credit on its indebtedness to Greenleaf, if it is established that Calumet would have been a reputable and responsible tenant. . . .

[Judgment reversed and case remanded.]

QUESTIONS AND CASE PROBLEMS

1. Dawson Enterprises was developing a shopping center. It rented one of the stores to Acme Markets by a lease which gave Acme the right to terminate the lease if Dawson did not make certain improvements by a specified date. The shopping center was a commercial failure, apparently because of the competition of a nearby center, and Dawson could not obtain any other tenants. Because the lease to Acme was outstanding, Dawson was not able to sell the land. Dawson brought an action against Acme to have the lease declared void on the theory that (a) it was not binding because of Acme's option to terminate, and (b) the lease could be avoided because of economic frustration in that it was impossible to develop the shopping center as had been contemplated. Could the lease to Acme be set aside? [Acme Markets v Dawson Enterprises, 253 Md 76, 251 A2d 839]
2. Clay, who owned a tract of land, permitted Hartney to occupy a cabin on the land. There was no agreement as to the length of time that it could be occupied, and either could terminate the relationship when he chose. There was no provision for rent. Hartney died. The next day Clay closed up the cabin and put Hartney's possessions outside the door. Paddock, who was appointed the executor under Hartney's will, claimed the right to occupy the cabin. Was he entitled to do so? [Paddock v Clay, 138 Mont 541, 357 P2d 1]
3. Joy White rented an apartment in an apartment house operated by Ridgleawood, Inc. After some discussion, she gave her apartment over to Allan and took a more expensive apartment in the same apartment house. Ridgleawood accepted rent from both White and Allan for the respective apartments. When Allan damaged his apartment, Ridgleawood sued White on the ground she was liable for the conduct of her assignee. Decide. [Ridgleawood, Inc. v White, (Tex Civ App) 380 SW2d 766]
4. Thompson rented property to Fletcher. Thompson sold the property to Bryan in February. Thereafter Thompson refused to accept Fletcher's offer of rent payments for March and April, but Fletcher did not know that the property had been sold. In April, Bryan declared the lease forfeited for nonpayment of rent. Decide. [Fletcher v Bryan, 76 NMex 221, 413 P2d 885]

5. Spears owned a building. On the first floor he rented space to a dry cleaner and a barber shop. The center door, which was at the top of an open stairway leading down into the basement, gave the appearance of a part of a double door leading into the dry cleaner's. There was no warning sign over the center door, and the door was unlocked. Trimble wanted to enter the dry cleaner's as a customer and by mistake opened the center door. Before she could realize her mistake, she fell down the stairs and was injured. When she sued Spears, he denied liability and further claimed that Trimble was guilty of contributory negligence. Decide. [Trimble v Spears, 182 Kan 406, 320 P2d 1029]
6. Martin leased a building for a 5-year period to a new tenant after making repairs to the building to fit it for the tenant and after having paid approximately $1,000 as commissions to a real estate agent to obtain the tenant. Under the lease the tenant was required to pay the last five months' rent in advance, or approximately $3,000. During the term of the lease the tenant defaulted in the payment of rent and Martin, acting within the terms of the lease, terminated it. Lochner, the receiver who was thereafter appointed for the tenant, sued for the return of the advance rent on the ground that there could be no "rent" due for an unexpired portion of a lease which had been terminated by the landlord and the landlord would be unjustly enriched if he were allowed to retain the advance payment. Decide. [Lochner v Martin, 218 Md 519, 147 A2d 749]
7. Stockham owned certain real estate. For a consideration he gave to the Borough Bill Posting Co. the exclusive privilege of erecting and using a signboard to be located on the land for bill posting purposes. He reserved the right, in case the property was sold or required for building purposes, to cancel all privileges upon returning to the company, a pro rata amount of the consideration. In an action brought by Stockham against the company, it was contended that a landlord-tenant relationship had been created. Do you agree? [Stockham v Borough Bill Posting Co., 144 App Div 642, 129 NYS 745]
8. Catanese leased premises for use as a drug store from Saputa. Catanese moved his store to another location but continued to pay the rent to Saputa. Saputa entered the premises without the permission of Catanese and made extensive alterations to the premises to suit two physicians who had agreed to rent the premises from Saputa. Catanese informed Saputa that he regarded the making of the unauthorized repairs as ground for canceling the lease. Saputa then sued Catanese for the difference between the rent Catanese agreed to pay and the rent the doctors agreed to pay for the remainder of the term of the Catanese lease. Was Catanese liable for such rent? [Saputa v Catanese, (La App) 182 So2d 826]
9. *A* leased property to *B*. The lease declared that *A* should pay the taxes assessed against the property because of any "improvements" while *B* would pay the portion of taxes assessed against the property because of trade fixtures installed by him. Certain changes were made to the building by *B*. A dispute arose as to whether these were "improvements" or "trade fixtures." Who pays the additional real estate taxes assessed because of such changes if it cannot be determined whether they are improvements or trade fixtures? [Allied Stores Corp. v North West Bank, 2 Wash App 2d 778, 469 P2d 993]

Appendix 1
COURTS

A *court* is a tribunal established by government to hear and decide matters properly brought before it, giving redress to the injured or enforcing punishment against wrongdoers, and to prevent wrongs. A *court of record* is one whose proceedings are preserved in an official record. A *court not of record* has limited judicial powers; its proceedings are not recorded, at least not officially.

Each court has inherent power to establish rules necessary to preserve order in the court and to transact the business of the court. An infraction of these rules or the disobedience of any other lawful order, as well as a willful act contrary to the dignity of the court or tending to pervert or obstruct justice, may be punished as *contempt of court.*

Jurisdiction of Courts

Each court is empowered to decide certain types or classes of cases. This power is called *jurisdiction.* A court may have original or appellate jurisdiction, or both. A court with *original jurisdiction* has the authority to hear a controversy when it is first brought into court. A court having *appellate jurisdiction* has authority to review the judgment of a lower court.

The jurisdiction of a court may be general as distinguished from limited or special. A court having *general jurisdiction* has power to hear and decide all controversies involving legal rights and duties. A court of *limited* (or special) *jurisdiction* has authority to hear and decide only those cases that fall within a particular class, or only certain cases within a class, such as cases in which the amounts involved are below a specified sum.

Courts are frequently classified in terms of the nature of their jurisdiction. A *civil court* is authorized to hear and decide issues involving private rights and duties, such as libel or infringement of a trademark. A *criminal court* is one that is established for the trial of cases involving offenses against the public, such as forgery or embezzlement. In a like manner courts are classified into juvenile courts, probate courts, and courts of domestic relations upon the basis of their limited jurisdiction.

Officers of the Court

The *judge* is the primary officer of the court. He is either elected or appointed. *Attorneys* or counselors at law are also officers of the court. They are usually selected by the parties to the controversy—but in some cases by the judge—to present the issues of a case to the court.

The *clerk* of the court is appointed in some of the higher courts, but he is usually elected to office in the lower courts. His principal duties are to enter cases upon the court calendar, to keep an accurate record of the proceedings, to attest the same, and, in some instances, to approve bail bonds and to compute the amount of costs involved.

The *sheriff* is the chief executive of a county. In addition to the duty of maintaining peace and order within the territorial limits of a county, he has many other duties in connection with the administration of justice in county courts of record. His principal duties consist of summoning witnesses, taking charge of the jury, preserving order in court, serving writs, carrying out judicial sales, and executing judgments. The *marshals* of the United States perform these duties in the federal courts. In county courts not of record, such as the courts of justices of the peace, these duties, when appropriate, are performed by a *constable.* Some of the duties of the sheriff are now performed by persons known as *court criers,* or by deputy sheriffs, known as *bailiffs.*

The Jury

The *jury* is a body of citizens sworn by a court to try to determine by verdict the issues of fact submitted to them. A trial jury consists of not more than twelve persons. The first step in forming a jury is to make a *jury list.* This step consists of the preparation by the proper officers or board of a list of qualified persons from which a jury may be drawn.

A certain number of persons drawn from the jury list constitute the *jury panel.* A trial jury is selected from members of the panel.

Federal Courts

The federal system of courts includes the following:

(1) Supreme Court of the United States. The Supreme Court is the only federal court expressly established by the Constitution. Congress is authorized by the Constitution to create other federal courts.

The Supreme Court has original jurisdiction in all cases affecting ambassadors, other public ministers, and consuls, and in those cases in which a state is a party. Except as regulated by Congress, it has appellate jurisdiction in all cases that may be brought into the federal courts in accordance with the terms of the Constitution. The Supreme Court also has appellate jurisdiction of certain cases that have been decided by the supreme courts of the states. Over 4,000 cases are filed with this court in a year.

(2) Courts of Appeals. The United States, including the District of Columbia, is divided into 11 judicial circuits. Each of the circuits has a court of appeals. These courts are courts of record.

A court of appeals has appellate jurisdiction only and is empowered to review the final decisions of the district courts, except in cases that may be taken directly to the Supreme Court. The decisions of the courts of appeal are final in most cases. An appeal may be taken on certain constitutional questions. Otherwise, review depends on the discretion of the Supreme Court and, in some cases, of the court of appeals.

(3) District Courts. The United States, including the District of Columbia, is divided into a number of judicial districts. Some states form a single district, whereas others are divided into two or more districts. District courts are also located in the territories.

The district courts have original jurisdiction in practically all cases that may be maintained in the federal courts. They are the trial courts for civil and criminal cases.

Civil cases that may be brought in these district courts are (a) civil suits brought by the United States; (b) actions brought by citizens of different states claiming land under grants by different states; (c) proceedings under the bankruptcy, internal revenue, postal, copyright, and patent laws; (d) civil cases of admiralty and maritime jurisdiction; (e) actions against national banking associations; and (f) cases between citizens of different states or between citizens of one state and of a foreign state involving $10,000 or more that arise under the federal Constitution, or laws and treaties made thereunder.

(4) Other Federal Courts. In addition to the Supreme Court, the court of appeals, and the district courts, the following tribunals have been created by Congress to determine other matters as indicated by their titles: Customs Court, Court of Customs and Patent Appeals, Court of Claims, Tax Court,[1] Court of Military Appeals, and the territorial courts.

State Courts

The system of courts in the various states is organized along lines similar to the federal court system, although differing in details, such as the number of courts, their names, and jurisdiction.

(1) State Supreme Court. The highest court in most states is known as the Supreme Court. In a few states it may have a different name, such as "Court of Appeals" in New York. The jurisdiction of a supreme court is ordinarily appellate, although in a few instances it is origi-

[1] This court was created originally as a Board of Tax Appeals with the status of an independent agency in the executive branch of the federal government. The Tax Reform Act of 1969 established the official name as United States Tax Court with the status of a court of record under Article 1 of the Constitution of the United States.

nal. In some states the supreme court is required to render an opinion on certain questions that may be referred to it by the legislature or by the chief executive of the state. The decision of the state supreme court is final in all cases not involving the federal Constitution, laws, and treaties.

(2) Intermediate Courts. In some states intermediate courts have original jurisdiction in a few cases but, in the main, they have appellate jurisdiction of cases removed for review from the county or district courts. They are known as superior, circuit, or district appellate courts. As a general rule, their decisions may be reviewed by the highest state court.

(3) County and District Courts. These courts of record have appellate jurisdiction of cases tried in the justice and police courts, as well as general original jurisdiction of criminal and civil cases. They also have jurisdiction of wills and guardianship matters, except when, as in some states, the jurisdiction of such cases has been given to special orphans', surrogate, or probate courts.

(4) Other State Courts. In addition to the foregoing, the following, which are ordinarily not courts of record, have jurisdiction as indicated by their titles: city or municipal courts, police courts, traffic courts, small claims courts, and justice of the peace courts.

Appendix 2
COURT PROCEDURE

Detailed laws specify how, when, and where a legal dispute can be brought to court. These rules of procedure are necessary in order to achieve an orderly, fair determination of litigation and in order to obtain, as far as humanly possible, the same decisions on the same facts. It is important to remember, however, that there is no uniform judicial procedure. While there are definite similarities, the law of each state may differ from the others. For the most part the uniform laws that have been adopted do not regulate matters of procedure.

Steps in a Lawsuit

(1) Parties. In a lawsuit the person suing is the *plaintiff*, and the person against whom he makes his claim is the *defendant*. There may be more than one plaintiff and more than one defendant. If *A* and *B* jointly own an automobile which is damaged by *C*, both *A* and *B* must join in an action against *C*. It is improper for *A* or *B* to sue alone since it is "their" and not "his" car.

In some instances several persons, such as shareholders or taxpayers, may bring a *class action* on behalf of themselves and all other persons having the same or similar interest. In other cases a defendant has the right to bring another person into an action on the ground that such person also has a claim against him. For example, an insurance company, by the procedure of *interpleader*, may require a person claiming to be entitled to the proceeds of a policy to come into an action brought by another person as beneficiary on the same policy.

By another procedure a seller sued by a customer for product liability may join the manufacturer as an additional defendant.

(2) Commencement of Action. In the common-law courts an action was commenced by filing an order with the keeper of the court records to issue a writ to the sheriff. This writ of summons ordered the sheriff to inform the defendant to appear before the court on a particular date. This method of commencing an action is still followed in many states.

By way of contrast, an action in a court of equity was begun when the plaintiff filed with the court a *complaint* in which he stated the facts about which he complained. No writ was issued, but a copy of the complaint was served on the defendant. In many states and in the federal courts, the reforms of recent years have extended this equity practice to all legal actions. Such actions are today commenced by the filing of the plaintiff's complaint. Some states still preserve the former distinction between law and equity, while others give the plaintiff the option of commencing the action by either method.

(3) Service of Process. The defendant must be served with *process* (a writ, notice, or summons; or the complaint itself) to inform him that the action is pending against him and to subject him to the power of the court.

(4) Pleadings. After process has been served on the defendant, the plaintiff is ready to proceed. If he has not filed with the clerk of the court a written statement of his claim or complaint, he will now do so. After the complaint is filed, a copy is served on the defendant. The defendant must make some reply, generally within 15 or 20 days. If he does not, the plaintiff ordinarily wins the case by default and a judgment is entered in his favor.

Before answering the plaintiff's complaint, the defendant may make certain preliminary objections. He may assert, for example, that the action was brought in the wrong court, or that he had not been properly served. If the objection is sustained, the case may be ended, depending upon the nature of the objection, or the plaintiff may be allowed to correct his mistake. The defendant may also raise the objection, sometimes called a *motion to dismiss* or *demurrer*, that even if the plaintiff's complaint is accepted as true, he is still not entitled to any relief.

If the defendant loses on his objection, he must file an *answer*, which either admits or denies some or all of the facts averred by the plaintiff. For example, if the plaintiff declared that the defendant made a contract on a certain date, the defendant may either admit that he made the contract or deny that he did so. The fact that he admits making the contract does not end the case, for the defendant may then plead defenses, for example, that at a later date the plaintiff and the defendant agreed to set the contract aside.

Without regard to whether he pleads such new matter, the defendant may generally assert a *counterclaim* or *cross complaint* against the plaintiff. Thus, he may contend that the plaintiff owes him money or damages and that this liability should be offset against any claim which the plaintiff may have.

After the defendant files his answer, the plaintiff may generally file preliminary objections to the answer. Just as the defendant could raise objections, the plaintiff may, in certain instances, argue that the counterclaim cannot be asserted in the court in which the case is pending, that the answer is fatally defective in form, or that it is not a legally sufficient answer. Again the court must pass upon the preliminary objections. When these are disposed of, the pleading stage is ordinarily over.

Generally, all of the pleadings in an action may raise only a few or perhaps one question of law, or a question of fact, or both. Thus, the whole case may depend on whether a letter admittedly written by the defendant amounted to an acceptance of the plaintiff's offer, thereby constituting a contract. If this question of law is answered in favor of the plaintiff, a judgment will be entered for the plaintiff; otherwise, for the defendant. By way of contrast, it may be admitted that a certain letter would be an acceptance if it had been written; but the defendant may deny that he ever wrote it. Here the question is one of fact, and the judgment is entered for the plaintiff if it is determined that the fact happened as he claimed. Otherwise the judgment is entered for the defendant.

If the only questions involved are questions of law, the court will decide the case on the pleadings alone since there is no need for a trial to determine the facts. If questions of fact are involved, then there must be a trial to determine what the facts really were.

(5) Pretrial Procedure. Many states and the federal courts have adopted other procedural steps that may be employed before the trial, with the purpose of eliminating the need for a trial, simplifying the issues to be tried, or giving the parties information needed for preparation for trial.

(a) MOTION FOR JUDGMENT ON THE PLEADINGS. After the pleadings are closed, many courts permit either party to move for a *judgment on the pleadings*. When such a motion is made, the court examines the record and may then enter a judgment according to the merits of the case as shown by the record.

(b) MOTION FOR SUMMARY JUDGMENT. In most courts a party may shorten a lawsuit by bringing into court sworn statements and affidavits which show that a claim or defense is false or a sham. This procedure cannot be used when there is substantial dispute of fact concerning the matters to be proved by the use of the affidavits.

(c) PRETRIAL CONFERENCE. In many courts either party may request the court to call a *pretrial conference*, or the court may take the initiative in doing so. This conference is in substance a round-table discussion by a judge of the court and the attorneys in the case. The object of the conference is to eliminate matters that are not in dispute and to determine what issues remain for litigation.

The pretrial conference is not intended as a procedure to compel the parties to settle their case. It not infrequently results, however, that when the attorneys discuss the matter with the court, they recognize that the differences between the conflicting parties are not so great as contemplated or that one side has less merit than was at first believed; in consequence, a settlement of the case is agreed upon.

(d) DISCOVERY. The Federal Rules of Civil Procedure and similar rules in a large number of states now permit one party to inquire of the adverse party and of all witnesses about anything relating to the action. This includes asking the adverse party the names of witnesses; asking the adverse party and the witnesses what they know about the case; examining, inspecting, and photographing books, records, buildings, and machines; and making an examinaiton of the physical or mental condition of a party when it has a bearing on the action. These procedures are classed as *discovery*.

Under the prior practice, except for the relatively unusual situation in which a party could obtain information before trial by filing a bill for discovery in equity, a party never knew what witnesses would appear in court for the adverse party or what they would say, or what documentary evidence would be produced.

(e) DEPOSITIONS. Ordinarily a witness testifies in court at the time of the trial. In some instances it may be necessary or desirable to take his testimony out of court before the time of the trial. It may be that he is aged or infirm or is about to leave the state or country and will not be present when the trial of the action is held. In such a case the interested party is permitted to have the testimony, called a *deposition*, of the witness taken outside of the court.

(6) Determination of Facts.

(a) THE TRIER OF FACTS. If the legal controversy is one which in the common-law days would have been tried by a jury, either party to the action has the constitutional right today to demand that the action be tried before a jury. If all parties agree, however, the case may be tried by the court or judge alone without a jury, and in some instances referred to a master or a referee appointed by the court to hear the matter.

In equity, although there is no constitutional right to a jury trial, the chancellor or equity judge may submit questions to a jury. There is the basic difference that in such cases the verdict or decision of the jury is only advisory to the chancellor; that is, he seeks it for his own information but is free to ignore it if he wants to do so. In contrast, the verdict of a jury in an action at law is binding on the court unless a basic error is present.

When new causes of action are created by statute, such as the right of an employee to obtain workmen's compensation for an injury arising in the course of his employment without regard to whether the employer is negligent, there is no constitutional right to a trial by jury. The trier of facts may accordingly be a judge without a jury, or a special administrative board or agency, such as a Workmen's Compensation Board.

(b) BASIS FOR DECISION. The trier of fact, whether a jury, a judge, a referee, or a board, can only decide questions of fact on the basis of evidence presented before it. Each party offers evidence in support of his claim. The evidence usually consists of the answers of persons to questions in court. Their answers are called *testimony*. The evidence may also include some *real evidence*, that is tangible things, such as papers, books, and records. It is immaterial whether the records are kept in ordinary ledger books or stored on computer tapes because a computer printout of data made for trial is admissible as evidence of the information contained in the computer.[2] In some cases, such as a damage action for improper construction of a building, the trier of fact may be taken to view the building so that a better understanding can be obtained.

The witness who testifies in court is usually a person who had some direct contact with the facts in the case, such as a person who saw the events occur or who heard one of the parties say something. In some instances it is also proper to offer the testimony of persons who have no connection with the case when they have expert knowledge and their opinions as experts are desired.

A witness who refuses to appear in court may be ordered to do so by a *subpoena*. He may also be compelled to bring relevant papers with him to court by a *subpoena duces tecum*. If he fails to obey the subpoena, the witness may be arrested for contempt of court. In some states the names of the order upon the witness and the procedure for contempt have been changed, but the substance remains the same.

(7) Conduct of the Trial. The conduct of a trial will be discussed in terms of a jury trial. Generally a case is one of several assigned for trial on a certain day or during a certain trial period. When the turn of the case is called, the opposing counsel seat themselves at tables in front of the judge and the jury is drawn. After the jury is sworn, the attorneys usually make *opening addresses* to the jury. Details vary in different jurisdictions, but the general pattern is that each attorney tells the jury what he intends to prove. When this step has been completed, the presentation of the evidence by both sides begins.

The attorney for the plaintiff starts with his first witness and asks him all the questions that he desires and that are proper. This is called the *direct examination* of the witness since it is made by the attorney calling his own witness. After the direct examination has been finished, the opposing counsel asks the same witness such questions as he desires in an effort to disprove his story. This is called *cross-examination.*

After the cross-examination has been completed, the attorney for the plaintiff may ask the same witness other questions to overcome the effect of the cross-examination. This is called *redirect examination.* This step in turn may be followed by further examination by the defendant's attorney, called *recross-examination.*

After the examination of the plaintiff's first witness has been concluded, the plaintiff's second witness takes the witness stand and is subjected to an examination in the same way as the first. This continues until all of the plaintiff's witnesses have been called. Then the plaintiff rests his case, and the defendant calls his first witness. The pattern of examination of witnesses is repeated, except that now the defendant is calling his own witnesses and his attorney conducts the direct and redirect examination, while the questioning by the plaintiff's attorney is cross- or recross-examination.

After the witnesses of both parties have been examined and all the evidence has been presented, each attorney makes another address, a *summation,* to the jury in which he sums up the case and suggests that a verdict be returned for his client.

(8) Charge to the Jury and the Verdict. The summation by the attorneys is followed by the *charge* of the judge to the jury. This charge is a résumé of what has happened at the trial and an explanation of the applicable law. At its conclusion, the judge instructs the jury to retire and study the case in the light of his charge and then return a *verdict*. By his instructions, the judge leaves to the jury the problem of determining the facts but states the law that they must apply to such facts as they may find. The jury then retires to secret deliberation in the jury room.

---

[2] Transport Indemnity Co. v Seib, 178 Neb 253, 132 NW2d 871.

(9) Taking the Case from the Jury and Attacking the Verdict. At several points during the trial or immediately after, a party may take a step to end the case or to set aside the verdict.

(a) VOLUNTARY NONSUIT. If the plaintiff is dissatisfied with the progress of his case, he may wish to stop the trial and begin again at a later date. In most jurisdictions he can do so by taking a *voluntary nonsuit.*

(b) COMPULSORY NONSUIT. After the plaintiff has presented the testimony of all his witnesses, the defendant may request the court to enter a nonsuit on the ground that the case presented by the plaintiff does not entitle him to recover.

(c) MISTRIAL. When necessary to avoid great injustice, the trial court may declare that there has been a mistrial and thereby terminate the trial and postpone it to a later date. While either party may move the court to enter a mistrial, it is discretionary with the court whether it does so. A mistrial is commonly entered when the evidence has been of a highly prejudicial character and the trial judge does not believe that the jury can ignore it even when instructed to do so, or when a juror has been guilty of misconduct.

(d) DIRECTED VERDICT. After the presentation of all the evidence at the trial, either party may request the court to direct the jury to return a verdict in his favor. When the plaintiff would not be entitled to recover even though all the testimony in the plaintiff's favor were believed, the defendant is entitled to have the court direct the jury to return a verdict for the defendant. The plaintiff is entitled to a verdict in his favor when, even if all the evidence on behalf of the defendant were believed, the jury would still be required to find for the plaintiff. In some states the defendant may make such a motion at the close of the plaintiff's proof.

(e) NEW TRIAL. After the verdict has been returned by the jury, a party may move for a new trial if he is not satisfied with the verdict or with the amount of damages that has been awarded. If it is clear that the jury has made a mistake or if material evidence that could not have been discovered sooner is available, the court will award a new trial and the case will be tried again before another jury.

(f) JUDGMENT N.O.V. If the verdict returned by the jury is clearly wrong as a matter of law, the court may set aside the verdict and enter a judgment contrary to the verdict. This in some states is called a *judgment non obstante veredicto* (notwithstanding the verdict), or as it is abbreviated, a judgment n.o.v.

(10) Judgment and Costs. The court enters a judgment conforming to the verdict unless a new trial has been granted, a mistrial declared after the return of the verdict, or a judgment n.o.v. entered. Generally whoever is the winning party will also be awarded costs in the action. In equity actions or those that had their origin in equity, and in certain statutory proceedings, the court has discretion to award costs to the winner, to divide them between the parties, or to have each party bear his own.

Costs ordinarily include the costs of filing papers with the court, the cost of having the sheriff or other officers of the court take official action, the statutory fees paid to the witnesses, the cost of a jury fee, if any, and the cost of printing the record when this is required on appeal. They do not include compensation for the time spent by the party in preparing his case or in being present at the trial, the expense in going to his attorney or to the court, the time lost from work because of the case, or the fee paid by him to his attorney. Sometimes when a special statutory action is brought, the statute authorizes recovery of a small attorney's fee. Thus, a mechanic's lien statute may authorize the recovery of an attorney's fee of 10 percent of the amount recovered, or a "reasonable attorney's fee." As a general rule, the costs that a party recovers represent only a part of the total expenses actually sustained in the litigation.

(11) Appeal. After a judgment has been entered, the party who is aggrieved thereby may appeal. This means that a party who wins the judgment but is not awarded as much as he had hoped, as well as a party who loses the case, may take an appeal.

The appellate court does not hear witnesses. It examines the record of the proceedings before the lower court, that is, the file of the case containing all the pleadings, the testimony of witnesses, and the judge's charge, to see if there was error of law. To assist the court, the attorneys for the parties file arguments or briefs and generally make their arguments orally before the court.

If the appellate court does not agree with the application of the law made by the lower court, it generally sets aside or modifies the action of the lower court and enters such judgment as it concludes the lower court should have entered. It may set aside the action of the lower court and send the case back to the lower court with directions to hold a new trial or with directions to enter a new judgment in accordance with the opinion that is filed by the appellate court.

(12) Execution. After a judgment has been entered or after an appeal has been decided, the losing party generally will comply with the judgment of the court. If he refuses to do so, the winning party may then take steps to execute or carry out the judgment.

If the judgment is for the payment of a sum of money, the plaintiff may direct the sheriff or other judicial officer to sell as much of the property of the defendant as is necessary to pay the plaintiff's judgment and the costs of the proceedings and of the execution. Acting under this authorizaiton, the sheriff may make a public sale of the defendant's property and apply the proceeds to the payment of the plaintiff's judgment. In most states the defendant is allowed an exemption of several hundred dollars and certain articles, such as personal clothing and tools of his trade.

If the judgment is for the recovery of specific property, the judgment will direct the sheriff to deliver the property to the plaintiff.

If the judgment directs the defendant to do or to refrain from doing an act, it is commonly provided that his failure to obey the order is a contempt of court punishable by fine or imprisonment.

Declaratory Judgment

In this century a new court procedure for settling disputes, authorized by statute, has made its appearance. This is the *declaratory judgment* procedure. Under it a person, when confronted with the early prospect of an actual controversy, may petition the court to decide the question before loss is actually sustained. A copy of the petition is served on all parties. They may file answers. After all the pleadings have been filed the court then decides the questions involved just as though a lawsuit had been brought.

Appendix 3
HOW TO FIND THE LAW

In order to determine what the law on a particular question or issue is, it may be necessary to examine (1) compilations of constitutions, treaties, statutes, executive orders, proclamations, and administrative regulations; (2) reports of state and federal court decisions; (3) digests of opinions; (4) treatises on the law; and (5) loose-leaf services.

Compilations

In the consideration of a legal problem in business it is necessary to determine whether the matter is affected or controlled by the Constitution, national or state; by a national treaty; by an act of Congress or a state legislature, or by a city ordinance; by a decree or proclamation of the President of the United States, a governor, or a mayor; or by a regulation of a federal, state, or local administrative agency.

Each body or person that makes laws, regulations, or ordinances usually will compile and publish at the end of each year or session all of the matter that it has adopted. In addition to the periodical or annual volumes, it is common to compile all the treaties, statutes, regulations, or ordinances in separate volumes. To illustrate, the federal Anti-Injunction Act may be cited as the Act of March 23, 1932, 47 Stat. 70, 29 USC Sections 101 et seq. This means that this law was enacted on March 23, 1932, and that this law can be found at page 70 in Volume 47 of the reports that contain all of the statutes adopted by the Congress.

The second part of the citation, 29 USC Sections 101 et seq., means that in the collection of all of the federal statutes, which is known as the United States Code, the full text of the statute can be found in the sections of the 29th title beginning with Section 101.

Court Decisions

For complicated or important legal cases or when an appeal is to be taken, a court will generally write an *opinion*, which explains why the court made the decision. Appellate courts as a rule write opinions. The great majority of these decisions, particularly in the case of the appellate courts, are collected and printed. In order to avoid confusion, the opinions of each court will ordinarily be printed in a separate set of reports, either by official reporters or private publishers.

In the reference "Pennoyer v. Neff, 95 U.S. 714, 24 L.Ed. 565," the first part states the names of the parties. It does not necessarily tell who was the plaintiff and who was the defendant. When an action is begun in a lower court, the first name is that of the plaintiff and the second name that of the defendant. When the case is appealed, generally the name of the person taking the appeal appears on the records of the higher court as the first one and that of the adverse party as the second. Sometimes, therefore, the original order of the names of the parties is reversed.

The balance of the reference consists of two citations. The first citation, 95 U.S. 714, means that the opinion which the court filed in the case of Pennoyer and Neff may be found on page 714 of the 95th volume of a series of books in which are printed officially the opinions of the United States Supreme Court. Sometimes the same opinion is printed in two different sets of volumes. In the example, 24 L.Ed. 565 means that in the 24th volume of another set of books, called *Lawyers' Edition*, of the United States Supreme Court Reports, the same opinion begins on page 565.

In opinions by a state court there are also generally two citations, as in the case of "Morrow v. Corbin, 122 Tex. 553, 62 S.W.2d 641." This means that the opinion in the lawsuit between Morrow and Corbin may be found in the 122d volume of the reports of the highest court of Texas, beginning on page 553; and also in Volume 62 of the *Southwestern Reporter*, Second Series, at page 641.

The West Publishing Company publishes a set of sectional reporters covering the entire United States. They are called sectional because each reporter, instead of being limited to a particular court or a particular state, covers the decisions of the courts of a particular section of the country. Thus the decisions of the courts of Arkansas, Kentucky, Missouri, Tennessee, and Texas are printed by the West Publishing Company as a group in a sectional reporter called the *Southwestern Reporter*.[1] Because of the large number of decisions involved, generally

[1] The sectional reporters are: Atlantic—A. (Connecticut, Delaware, District of Columbia, Maine, Maryland, New Hampshire, New Jersey, Pennsylvania, Rhode Island, Vermont); Northeastern—N.E. (Illinois, Indiana, Massachusetts, New York, Ohio); Northwestern—N.W. (Iowa, Michigan, Minnesota, Nebraska, North Dakota, South Dakota, Wisconsin); Pacific—P. (Alaska, Arizona, California, Colorado, Hawaii, Idaho, Kansas, Montana, Nevada, New Mexico, Oklahoma, Oregon, Utah, Washington, Wyoming); Southeastern—S.E. (Georgia, North Carolina, South Carolina, Virginia, West Virginia); Southwestern—S.W. (Arkansas, Kentucky, Missouri, Tennessee, Texas); and Southern—So. (Alabama, Florida, Louisiana, Mississippi). There is also a special New York State reporter known as the New York Supplement and a special California State reporter known as the California Reporter.

only the opinions of the state appellate courts are printed. A number of states [2] have discontinued publication of the opinions of their courts, and those opinions are now found only in the West reporters.

The reason for the "Second Series" in the Southwestern citation is that when there were 300 volumes in the original series, instead of calling the next volume 301, the publisher called it Volume 1, Second Series. Thus 62 S.W.2d Series really means the 362d volume of the *Southwestern Reporter*. Six to eight volumes appear in a year for each geographic section.

In addition to these state reporters, the West Publishing Company publishes a *Federal Supplement*, which primarily reports the opinions of the Federal District Courts; the *Federal Reporter*, which primarily reports the decisions of the United States Courts of Appeals; and the *Supreme Court Reporter,* which reports the decisions of the United States Supreme Court. The Supreme Court decisions are also reported in a separate set called the *Lawyers' Edition*, published by the Lawyers Co-operative Publishing Company.

The reports published by the West Publishing Company and Lawyers Co-operative Publishing Company are unofficial reports, while those bearing the name or abbreviation of the United States or of a state, such as "95 U.S. 714" or "122 Tex. 553" are official reports. This means that in the case of the latter, the particular court, such as the United States Supreme Court, has officially authorized that its decisions be printed and that by federal statute such official printing is made. In the case of the unofficial reporters, the publisher prints the decisions of a court on its own initiative. Such opinions are part of the public domain and not subject to any copyright or similar restriction.

Digests of Opinions

The reports of court decisions are useful only if one has the citation, that is, the name and volume number of the book and the page number of the opinion he is seeking. For this reason, digests of the decisions have been prepared. These digests organize the entire field of law under major headings, which are then arranged in alphabetic order. Under each heading, such as "Contracts," the subject is divided into the different questions that can arise with respect to that field. A master outline is thus created on the subject. This outline includes short paragraphs describing what each case holds and giving its citaiton.

Treatises and Restatements

Very helpful in finding a case or a statute are the treatises on the law. These may be special books, each written by an author on a particular subject, such as *Williston on Contracts, Bogert on Trusts, Fletcher on Corporations*, or they may be general encyclopedias, as in the case of *American Jurisprudence, American Jurisprudence, Second*, and *Corpus Juris Secundum.*

Another type of treatise is found in the restatements of the law prepared by the American Law Institute. Each restatement consists of one or more volumes devoted to a particular phase of the law, such as the *Restatement of the Law of Contracts, Restatement of the Law of Agency*, and *Restatement of the Law of Property*. In each restatement the American Law Institute, acting through special committees of judges, lawyers, and professors of law, has set forth what the law is; and in many areas where there is no law or the present rule is regarded as unsatisfactory, the restatement specifies what the Institute deems to be the desirable rule.

Loose-Leaf Services

A number of private publishers, notably Commerce Clearing House and Prentice-Hall, publish loose-leaf books devoted to particular branches of the law. Periodically the publisher sends to the purchaser a number of pages that set forth any decision, regulation, or statute made or adopted since the prior set of pages was prepared. Such services are unofficial.

---

[2] See, for example, Alaska, Florida, Kentucky, Louisiana, Maine, Mississippi, Missouri, North Dakota, Oklahoma, Texas, and Wyoming.

GLOSSARY

A

abandon: give up or leave employment; relinquish possession of personal property with intent to disclaim title.

abate: put a stop to a nuisance; reduce or cancel a legacy because the estate of the testator is insufficient to make payment in full.

ab initio: from the beginning.

abrogate: recall or repeal; make void or inoperative.

absolute liability: liability for an act that causes harm even though the actor was not at fault.

absolute privilege: protection from liability for slander or libel given under certain circumstances to statements regardless of the fact that they are false or maliciously made.

abstract of title: history of the transfers of title to a given piece of land, briefly stating the parties to and the effect of all deeds, wills, and judicial proceedings relating to the land.

acceleration clause: provision in a contract or any legal instrument that upon a certain event the time for the performance of specified obligations shall be advanced; for example, a provision making the balance due upon debtor's default.

acceptance: unqualified assent to the act or proposal of another; as the acceptance of a draft (bill of exchange), of an offer to make a contract, of goods delivered by the seller, or of a gift or a deed.

accession: acquisition of title to property by a person by virtue of the fact that it has been attached to property that he already owned or was the offspring of an animal he owned.

accessory after the fact: one who after the commission of a felony knowingly assists the felon.

accessory before the fact: one who is absent at the commission of the crime but who aided and abetted its commission.

accident: an event that occurs even though a reasonable man would not have foreseen its occurrence, because of which the law holds no one legally responsible for the harm caused.

accommodation party: a person who signs a commercial paper to lend credit to another.

accord and satisfaction: an agreement to substitute a different performance for that called for in the contract and the performance of that substitute agreement.

accretion: the acquisition of title to additional land when the owner's land is built up by gradual deposits made by the natural action of water.

acknowledgment: an admission or confirmation, generally of an instrument and usually made before a person authorized to administer oaths, as a notary public; the purpose being to declare that the instrument was executed by the person making the instrument, or that it was his free act, or that he desires that it be recorded.

action: a proceeding brought to enforce any right.

action in personam: an action brought to impose a personal liability upon a person, such as a money judgment.

action in rem: an action brought to declare the status of a thing, such as an action to declare the title to property to be forfeited because of its illegal use.

action of assumpsit: a common-law action brought to recover damages for breach of a contract.

action of ejectment: a common-law action brought to recover the possession of land.

action of mandamus: a common-law action brought to compel the performance of a ministerial or clerical act by an officer.

action of quo warranto: a common-law action brought to challenge the authority of an officer to act or to hold office.

action of replevin: a common-law action brought to recover the possession of personal property.

action of trespass: a common-law action brought to recover damages for a tort.

act of bankruptcy: any of the acts specified by the national bankruptcy law which, when committed by the debtor within the four months preceding the filing of the petition in bankruptcy, is proper ground for declaring the debtor a bankrupt.

act of God: a natural phenomenon that is not reasonably foreseeable.

administrative agency: a governmental commission or board given authority to regulate particular matters.

administrator — administratrix: the person (man—woman) appointed to wind up and settle the estate of a person who has died without a will.

adverse possession: the hostile possession of real estate, which when actual, visible, notorious, exclusive, and continued for the required time, will vest the title to the land in the person in such adverse possession.

advisory opinion: an opinion that may be rendered in a few states when there is no actual controversy before the court and the matter is submitted by private persons, or in some instances by the governor of the state, to obtain the court's opinion.

affidavit: a statement of facts set forth in written form and supported by the oath or affirmation of the person making the statement, setting forth that such facts are true to his knowledge or to his information and belief. The affidavit is executed before a notary public or other person authorized to administer oaths.

affinity: the relationship that exists by virtue of marriage.

affirmative covenant: an express undertaking or promise in a contract or deed to do an act.

agency: the relationship that exists between a person identified as a principal and another by virtue of which the latter may make contracts with third persons on behalf of the principal. (Parties—principal, agent, third person)

agency coupled with an interest in the authority: an agency in which the agent has given a consideration or has paid for the right to exercise the authority granted to him.

agency coupled with an interest in the subject matter: an agency in which for a consideration the agent is given an interest in the property with which he is dealing.

agency shop: a union contract provision requiring that nonunion employees pay to the union the equivalent of union dues in order to retain their employment.

agent: one who is authorized by the principal or by operation of law to make contracts with third persons on behalf of the principal.

allonge: a paper securely fastened to a commercial paper in order to provide additional space for indorsements.

alluvion: the additions made to land by accretion.

alteration: any material change of the terms of a writing fraudulently made by a party thereto.

ambulatory: not effective and therefore may be changed, as in the case of a will that is not final until the testator has died.

amicable action: an action that all parties agree should be brought and which is begun by the filing of such an agreement, rather than by serving the adverse parties with process. Although the parties agree to litigate, the dispute is real, and the decision is not an advisory opinion.

amicus curiae: literally, a friend of the court; one who is appointed by the court to take part in litigation and to assist the court by furnishing an opinion in the matter.

annexation: attachment of personal property to realty in such a way as to make it become real property and part of the realty.

annuity: a contract by which the insured pays a lump sum to the insurer and later receives fixed annual payments.

anomalous indorser: a person who signs a commercial paper but is not otherwise a party to the instrument.

anticipatory breach: the repudiation by a promisor of the contract prior to the time he is required to perform when such repudiation is accepted by the promisee as a breach of the contract.

anti-injunction acts: statutes prohibiting the use of injunctions in labor disputes except under exceptional circumstances; notably the federal Norris-La Guardia Act of 1932.

Anti-Petrillo Act: a federal statute that makes it a crime to compel a radio broadcasting station to hire musicians not needed, to pay for services not performed, or to refrain from broadcasting music of school children or from foreign countries.

antitrust acts: statutes prohibiting combinations and contracts in restraint of trade, notably the federal Sherman Antitrust Act of 1890, now generally inapplicable to labor union acitvity.

appeal: taking the case to a reviewing court to determine whether the judgment of the lower court or administrative agency was correct. (Parties—appellant, appellee)

appellate jurisdiction: the power of a court to hear and decide a given class of cases on appeal from another court or administrative agency.

arbitration: the settlement of disputed questions, whether of law or fact, by one or more arbitrators by whose decision the parties agree to be bound. Increasingly used as a procedure for labor dispute settlement.

assignment: transfer of a right. Generally used in connection with personal property rights, as rights under a contract, commercial paper, an insurance policy, a mortgage, or a lease. (Parties—assignor, assignee)

assumption of risk: the common-law rule that an employee could not sue the employer for injuries caused by the ordinary risks of employment on the theory that he had assumed such risks by undertaking the work. The rule has been abolished in those areas governed by workmen's compensation laws and most employers' liability statutes.

attachment: the seizure of property of, or a debt owed to, the debtor by the service of process upon a third person who is in possession of the property or who owes a debt to the debtor.

attractive nuisance doctrine: a rule imposing liability on a landowner for injuries sustained by small children playing on his land when the landowner permits a condition to exist or maintains equipment that he should realize would attract small children who could not realize the danger. The rule does not apply if an unreasonable burden would be imposed on the landowner in taking steps to protect the children.

authenticate: make or establish as genuine, official, or final, as by signing, countersigning, sealing, or any other act indicating approval.

B

bad check laws: laws making it a criminal offense to issue a bad check with intent to defraud.

baggage: such articles of necessity or personal convenience as are usually carried for personal use by passengers of common carriers.

bail: variously used in connection with the release of a person or property from the custody of the law, referring (a) to the act of releasing or bailing, (b) to the persons who assume liability in the event that the released person does not appear or it is held that the property should not be released, and (c) to the bond or sum of money that such persons furnish the court or other official as indemnity for nonperformance of the obligation.

bailee's lien: a specific, possessory lien of the bailee on the goods for work done to them. Commonly extended by statute to any bailee's claim for compensation and eliminating the necessity of retention of possession.

bailment: the relation that exists when personal property is delivered into the possession of another under an agreement, express or implied, that the identical property will be returned or will be delivered in accordance with the agreement. (Parties—bailor, bailee)

bankruptcy: a procedure by which one unable to pay his debts may be declared a bankrupt, after which all his assets in excess of his exemption claim are surrendered to the court for administration and distribution to his creditors, and the debtor is given a discharge that releases him from the unpaid balance due on most debts.

bearer: the person in physical possession of commercial paper payable to bearer, a document of title directing delivery to bearer, or an investment security in bearer form.

beneficiary: the person to whom the proceeds of a life insurance policy are payable, a person for whose benefit property is held in trust, or a person given property by a will.

bequest: a gift of personal property by will.

bill of exchange (draft): an unconditional order in writing by one person upon another, signed by the person giving it, and ordering the person to whom it is directed to pay on demand or at a definite time a sum certain in money to order or to bearer.

bill of lading: a document issued by a carrier reciting the receipt of goods and the terms of the contract of transportation. Regulated by the federal Bills of Lading Act or the Uniform Commercial Code.

bill of sale: a writing signed by the seller reciting that he has sold to the buyer the personal property therein described.

binder: a memorandum delivered to the insured stating the essential terms of a policy to be executed in the future, when it is agreed that the contract of insurance is to be effective before the written policy is executed.

blank indorsement: an indorsement that does not name the person to whom the paper, document of title, or investment security is negotiated.

blue-sky laws: state statutes designed to protect the public from the sale of worthless stocks and bonds.

boardinghouse keeper: one regularly engaged in the business of offering living accommodations to permanent lodgers or boarders.

bona fide: in good faith; without any fraud or deceit.

bond: an obligation or promise in writing and sealed, generally of corporations, personal representatives, trustees; fidelity bonds.

boycott: a combination of two or more persons to cause harm to another by refraining from patronizing or dealing with such other person in any way or inducing others to so refrain; commonly an incident of labor disputes.

bulk sales acts: statutes to protect creditors of a bulk seller by preventing him from obtaining cash for his goods and then leaving the state. Notice must be given creditors, and the bulk sale buyer is liable to the seller's creditors if the statute is not satisfied. Expanded to "bulk transfers" under the Code.

business trust: a form of business organization in which the owners of the property to be devoted to the business transfer the title of the property to trustees with full power to operate the business.

C

cancellation: a crossing out of a part of an instrument or a destruction of all legal effect of the instrument, whether by act of party, upon breach by the other party, or pursuant to agreement or decree of court.

capital: net assets of a corporation.

capital stock: the declared money value of the outstanding stock of the corporation.

cash surrender value: the sum that will be paid the insured if he surrenders his policy to the insurer.

cause of action: the right to damages or other judicial relief when a legally protected right of the plaintiff is violated by an unlawful act of the defendant.

caveat emptor: let the buyer beware. This maxim has been restricted by warranty and strict tort liability concepts.

certificate of protest: a written statement by a notary public setting forth the fact that the holder had presented the commercial paper to the primary party and that the latter had failed to make payment.

cestui que trust: the beneficiary or person for whose benefit the property is held in trust.

charter: the grant of authority from a government to exist as a corporation. Generally replaced today by a certificate of incorporation approving the articles of incorporation.

chattel mortgage: a security device by which the owner of personal property transfers the title to a creditor as security for the debt owed by the owner to the creditor. Replaced under the Uniform Commercial Code by a secured transaction. (Parties—chattel mortgagor, chattel mortgagee)

chattels personal: tangible personal property.

chattels real: leases of land and buildings.

check: an order by a depositor on his bank to pay a sum of money to a payee; a bill of exchange drawn on a bank and payable on demand.

chose in action: intangible personal property in the nature of claims against another, such as a claim for accounts receivable or wages.

chose in possession: tangible personal property.

circumstantial evidence: relates to circumstances surrounding the facts in dispute from which the trier of fact may deduce what had happened.

civil action: in many states a simplified form of action combining all or many of the former common-law actions.

civil court: a court with jurisdiction to hear and determine controversies relating to private rights and duties.

closed shop: a place of employment in which only union members may be employed. Now generally prohibited.

codicil: a writing by one who has made a will which is executed with all the formality of a will and is treated as an addition to or modification of the will.

coinsurance: a clause requiring the insured to maintain insurance on his property up to a stated amount and providing that to the extent that he fails to do so the insured is to be deemed a coinsurer with the insurer so that the latter is liable only for its proportionate share of the amount of insurance required to be carried.

collateral note: a note accompanied by collateral security.

collective bargaining: the process by which the terms of employment are agreed upon through negotiations between the employer or employers within a given industry or industrial area and the union or the bargaining representative of the employees.

collective bargaining unit: the employment area within which employees are by statute authorized to select a bargaining representative, who is then to represent all the employees in bargaining collectively with the employer.

collusion: an agreement between two or more persons to defraud the government or the courts, as by obtaining a divorce by collusion when no grounds for a divorce exist, or to defraud third persons of their rights.

color of title: circumstances that make a person appear to be the owner when he in fact is not the owner, as the existence of a deed appearing to convey the property to a given person gives him color of title although the deed is worthless because it is in fact a forgery.

commission merchant: a bailee to whom goods are consigned for sale.

common carrier: a carrier that holds out its facilities to serve the general public for compensation without discrimination.

common law: the body of unwritten principles originally based on the usages and customs of the community which were recognized and enforced by the courts.

common stock: stock that has no right or priority over any other stock of the corporation as to dividends or distribution of assets upon dissolution.

common trust fund: a plan by which the assets of small trust estates are pooled into a common fund, each trust being given certificates representing its proportionate ownership of the fund, and the pooled fund is then invested in investments of large size.

community property: the cotenancy held by husband and wife in property acquired during their marriage under the law of some of the states, principally in the southwestern United States.

complaint: the initial pleading filed by the plaintiff in many actions which in many states may be served as original process to acquire jurisdiction over the defendant.

composition of creditors: an agreement among creditors that each shall accept a part payment as full payment in consideration of the other creditors doing the same.

concealment: the failure to volunteer information not requested.

conditional estate: an estate that will come into being upon the satisfaction of a condition precedent or that will be terminated upon the satisfaction of a condition subsequent, provided in the latter case that the grantor or his heirs re-enter and retake possession of the land.

conditional sale: a credit transaction by which the buyer purchases on credit and promises to pay the purchase price in installments, while the seller retains the title to the goods, together with the right of repossession upon default, until the condition of payment in full has been satisfied. The conditional sale is replaced under the Uniform Commercial Code by a secured transaction.

confidential relationship: a relationship in which, because of the legal status of the parties or their respective physical or mental conditions or knowledge, one party places full confidence and trust in the other and relies upon him entirely for guidance.

conflict of laws: the body of law that determines the law of which state is to apply when two or more states are involved in the facts of a given case.

confusion of goods: the mixing of goods of different owners that under certain circumstances results in one of the owners becoming the owner of all the goods.

consanguinity: relationship by blood.

consideration: the promise or performance that the promisor demands as the price of his promise.

consignment: a bailment made for the purpose of sale by the bailee. (Parties—consignor, consignee)

consolidation of corporations: a combining of two or more corporations in which the corporate existence of each one ceases and a new corporation is created.

constructive: an adjective employed to indicate that the noun which is modified by it does not exist but the law disposes of the matter as though it did; as a constructive bailment or a constructive trust.

contingent beneficiary: the person to whom the proceeds of a life insurance policy are payable in the event that the primary beneficiary dies before the insured.

contract: a binding agreement based upon the genuine assent of the parties, made for a lawful object, between competent parties, in the form required by law, and generally supported by consideration.

contract carrier: a carrier who transports on the basis of individual contracts that it makes with each shipper.

contract to sell: a contract to make a transfer of title in the future as contrasted with a present transfer.

contribution: the right of a co-obligor who has paid more than his proportionate share to demand that the other obligor pay him the amount of the excess payment he has made.

contributory negligence: negligence of the plaintiff that contributes to his injury and at common law bars him from recovery from the defendant although the defendant may have been more negligent than the plaintiff.

conveyance: a transfer of an interest in land, ordinarily by the execution and delivery of a deed.

cooling-off period: a procedure designed to avoid strikes by requiring a specified period of delay before the strike may begin during which negotiations for a settlement must continue.

cooperative: a group of two or more persons or enterprises that act through a common agent with respect to a common objective, as buying or selling.

copyright: a grant to an author of an exclusive right to publish and sell his work for a period of 28 years, renewable for a second period of 28 years.

corporation: an artificial legal person or being created by government grant, which for many purposes is treated as a natural person.

cost plus: a method of determining the purchase price or contract price by providing for the payment of an amount equal to the costs of the seller or contractor to which is added a stated percentage as his profit.

costs: the expenses of suing or being sued, recoverable in some actions by the successful party, and in others, subject to allocation by the court. Ordinarily they do not include attorney's fees or compensation for loss of time.

counterclaim: a claim that the defendant in an action may make against the plaintiff.

covenants of title: covenants of the grantor contained in a deed that guarantee such matters as his right to make the conveyance, his ownership of the property, the freedom of the property from encumbrances, or that the grantee will not be disturbed in the quiet enjoyment of the land.

crime: a violation of the law that is punished as an offense against the state or government.

cross complaint: a claim that the defendant may make against the plaintiff.

cross-examination: the examination made of a witness by the attorney for the adverse party.

cumulative voting: a system of voting for directors in which each shareholder has as many votes as the number of voting shares he owns multiplied by the number of directors to be elected, which votes he can distribute for the various candidates as he desires.

cy-pres doctrine: the rule under which a charitable trust will be carried out as nearly as possible in the way the settlor desired, when for any reason it cannot be carried out exactly in the way or for the purposes he had expressed.

D

damages: a sum of money recovered to redress or make amends for the legal wrong or injury done.

damnum absque injuria: loss or damage without the violation of a legal right, or the mere fact that a person sustains a loss does not mean that his legal rights have been violated or that he is entitled to sue someone.

declaratory judgment: a procedure for obtaining the decision of a court on a question before any action has been taken or loss sustained. It differs from an advisory opinion in that there must be an actual, imminent controversy.

dedication: acquisition by the public or a government of title to land when it is given over by its owner to use by the public and such gift is accepted.

deed: an instrument by which the grantor (owner of land) conveys or transfers the title to a grantee.

de facto: existing in fact as distinguished from as of right, as in the case of an officer or a corporation purporting to act as such without being elected to the office or having been properly incorporated.

deficiency judgment: a personal judgment for the amount still remaining due the mortgagee after foreclosure, which is entered against any person liable on the mortgage debt. Statutes generally require the mortgagee to credit the fair value of the property against the balance due when the mortgagee has purchased the property. Also, a similar judgment entered by a creditor against a debtor in a secured transaction under Article 9 of the UCC.

del credere agent: an agent who sells goods for the principal and who guarantees to the principal that the buyer will pay for the goods.

delegation: the transfer to another of the right and power to do an act.

de minimis non curat lex: a maxim that the law is not concerned with trifles. Not always applied, as in the case of the encroachment of a building over the property line, in which case the law will protect the landowner regardless of the extent of the encroachment.

demonstrative evidence: evidence that consists of visible, physical objects, as a sample taken from the wheat in controversy or a photograph of the subject matter involved.

demonstrative legacy: a legacy to be paid or distributed from a specified fund or property.

demurrage: a charge made by the carrier for the unreasonable detention of cars by the consignor or consignee.

demurrer: a pleading that may be filed to attack the sufficiency of the adverse party's pleading as not stating a cause of action or a defense.

dependent relative revocation: the doctrine recognized in some states that if a testator revokes or cancels a will in order to replace it with a later will, the earlier will is to be deemed revived if for any reason the later will does not take effect or no later will is executed.

deposition: the testimony of a witness taken out of court before a person authorized to administer oaths.

devise: a gift of real estate made by will.

directed verdict: a direction by the trial judge to the jury to return a verdict in favor of a specified party to the action.

directors: the persons vested with control of the corporation, subject to the elective power of the shareholders.

discharge in bankruptcy: an order of the bankruptcy court discharging the bankrupt debtor from the unpaid balance of most of the claims against him.

discharge of contract: termination of a contract by performance, agreement, impossibility, acceptance of breach, or operation of law.

discovery: procedures for ascertaining facts prior to the time of trial in order to eliminate the element of surprise in litigation.

dishonor by nonacceptance: the refusal of the drawee to accept a draft (bill of exchange).

dishonor by nonpayment: the refusal to pay a commercial paper when properly presented for payment.

dismiss: a procedure to terminate an action by moving to dismiss on the ground that the plaintiff has not pleaded a cause of action entitling him to relief.

disparagement of goods: the making of malicious, false

statements as to the quality of the goods of another.

distress for rent: the common-law right of the lessor to enter the premises when he was not paid the rent and to seize all personal property found on the premises. Statutes have modified or abolished this right in many states.

distributive share: the proportionate part of the estate of the decedent that will be distributed to an heir or legatee, and also as devisee in those jurisdictions in which real estate is administered as part of the decedent's estate.

domestic bill of exchange: a draft drawn in one state and payable in the same or another state.

domestic corporation: a corporation that has been incorporated by the state as opposed to incorporation by another state.

domicile: the home of a person or the state of incorporation of a corporation, to be distinguished from a place where a person lives but which he does not regard as his home, or a state in which a corporation does business but in which it was not incorporated.

dominant tenement: the tract of land that is benefited by an easement to which another tract, or servient tenement, is subject.

double indemnity: a provision for payment of double the amount specified by the insurance contract if death is caused by an accident and occurs under specified circumstances.

double jeopardy: the principle that a person who has once been placed in jeopardy by being brought to trial at which the proceedings progressed at least as far as having the jury sworn cannot thereafter be tried a second time for the same offense.

draft: see bill of exchange.

draft-varying acceptance: one in which the acceptor's agreement to pay is not exactly in conformity with the order of the instrument.

due care: the degree of care that a reasonable man would exercise to prevent the realization of harm, which under all the circumstances was reasonably forseeable in the event that such care were not taken.

due process of law: the guarantee by the 5th and 14th amendments of the federal Constitution and of many state constitutions that no person shall be deprived of life, liberty, or property without due process of law. As presently interpreted, this prohibits any law, either state or federal, that sets up an unfair procedure or the substance of which is arbitrary or capricious.

duress: conduct that deprives the victim of his own free will and which generally gives the victim the right to set aside any transaction entered into under such circumstances.

E

easement: a permanent right that one has in the land of another, as the right to cross another's land or easement of way.

eleemosynary corporation: a corporation organized for a charitable or benevolent purpose.

embezzlement: a statutory offense consisting of the unlawful conversion of property entrusted to the wrongdoer with respect to which he owes the owner a fiduciary duty.

eminent domain: the power of a government and certain kinds of corporations to take private property against the objection of the owner, provided the taking is for a public purpose and just compensation is made therefor.

encumbrance: a right held by a third person in or a lien or charge against property, as a mortgage or judgment lien on land.

equity: the body of principles that originally developed because of the inadequacy of the rules then applied by the common-law courts of England.

erosion: the loss of land through a gradual washing away by tides or currents, with the owner losing title to the lost land.

escheat: the transfer to the state of the title to a decedent's property when he dies intestate not survived by anyone capable of taking the property as his heir.

escrow: a conditional delivery of property or of a deed to a custodian or escrow holder, who in turn makes final delivery to the grantee or transferee when a specified condition has been satisfied.

estate: the extent and nature of one's interest in land; the assets constituting a decedent's property at the time of his death, or the assets of a bankrupt.

estate in fee simple: the largest estate possible in which the owner has the absolute and entire property in the land.

estoppel: the principle by which a person is barred from pursuing a certain course of action or of disputing the truth of certain matters when his conduct has been such that it would be unjust to permit him to do so.

evidence: that which is presented to the trier of fact as the basis on which the trier is to determine what happened.

exception: an objection, as an exception to the admission of evidence on the ground that it was hearsay; a clause excluding particular property from the operation of a deed.

ex contractu: a claim or matter that is founded upon or arises out of a contract.

ex delicto: a claim or matter that is founded upon or arises out of a tort.

execution: the carrying out of a judgment of a court, generally directing that property owned by the defendant be sold and the proceeds first used to pay the execution or judgment creditor.

exemplary damages: damages in excess of the amount needed to compensate for the plaintiff's injury, which are awarded in order to punish the defendant for his malicious or wanton conduct so as to make an example of him; also punitive.

exoneration: an agreement or provision in an agreement that one party shall not be held liable for loss; the right of the surety to demand that those primarily liable pay the claim for which the surety is secondarily liable.

expert witness: one who has acquired special knowledge in a particular field through practical experience, or study, or both, which gives him a superior knowledge so that his opinion is admissible as an aid to the trier of fact.

ex post facto law: a law making criminal an act that was lawful when done or that increases the penalty for an act which was subject to a lesser penalty when done. Such laws are generally prohibited by constitutional provisions.

extraordinary bailment: a bailment in which the bailee is subject to unusual duties and liabilities, as a hotelkeeper or common carrier.

F

facility-of-payment clause: a provision commonly found in an industrial policy permitting the insurer to make payment to any member of a designated class or to any person the insurer believes equitably entitled thereto.

factor: a bailee to whom goods are consigned for sale.

factors' acts: statutes protecting persons who buy in good faith for value from a factor although the goods had not been delivered to the factor with the consent or authorization of their owner.

fair employment practice acts: statutes designed to eliminate discrimination in employment in terms of race, religion, natural origin, or sex.

fair labor standards acts: statutes, particularly the federal statute, designed to prevent excessive hours of employment and low pay, the employment of young children, and other unsound practices.

fair trade acts: statutes that authorize resale price maintenance agreements as to trademark and brand name articles, and generally provide that all persons in the industry are bound by such an agreement whether they have signed it or not although such provision is often invalid.

featherbedding: the exaction of money for services not performed, which is made an unfair labor practice generally and a criminal offense in connection with radio broadcasting.

Federal Securities Act: a statute designed to protect the public from fraudulent securities.

Federal Securities Exchange Act: a statute prohibiting improper practices at and regulating security exchanges.

Federal Trade Commission Act: a statute prohibiting unfair methods of competition in interstate commerce.

fellow-servant rule: a common-law defense of the employer that barred an employee from suing an employer for injuries caused by a fellow employee.

felony: a criminal offense that is punishable by confinement in prison or by death, or that is expressly stated by statute to be a felony.

financial responsibility laws: statutes that require a driver involved in an automobile accident to prove his financial responsibility in order to retain his license, which responsibility may be shown by procuring public liability insurance in a specified minimum amount.

financing factor: one who lends money to manufacturers on the security of goods to be manufactured thereafter.

firm offer: an offer stated to be held open for a specified time, which must be so held in some states even in the absence of an option contract, or under the Code, with respect to merchants.

fixture: personal property that has become so attached to or adapted to real estate that it has lost its character as personal property and is part of the real estate.

Food, Drug, and Cosmetic Act: a federal statute prohibiting the interstate shipment of misbranded or adulterated foods, drugs, cosmetics, and therapeutic devices.

forbearance: refraining from doing an act.

foreclosure: procedure for enforcing a mortgage resulting in the public sale of the mortgaged property and less commonly in merely barring the right of the mortgagor to redeem the property from the mortgage.

foreign (international) bill of exchange: a bill of exchange made in one nation and payable in another.

foreign corporation: a corporation incorporated under the laws of another state.

forgery: the fraudulent making or altering of an instrument that apparently creates or alters a legal liability of another.

franchise: (a) a privilege or authorization, generally exclusive, to engage in a particular activity within a particular geographic area, as a government franchise to operate a taxi company within a specified city, or a private franchise as the grant by a manufacturer of a right to sell his products within a particular territory or for a particular number of years; (b) the right to vote.

fraud: the making of a false statement of a past or existing fact with knowledge of its falsity or with reckless indifference as to its truth with the intent to cause another to rely thereon, and he does rely thereon to his injury.

freight forwarder: one who contracts to have goods transported and, in turn, contracts with carriers for such transportation.

fructus industriales: crops that are annually planted and raised.

fructus naturales: fruits from trees, bushes, and grasses growing from perennial roots.

fungible goods: goods of a homogenous nature of which any unit is the equivalent of any other unit or is treated as such by mercantile usage.

future advance mortgage: a mortgage given to secure additional loans to be made in the future as well as an original loan.

G

garnishment: the name given in some states to attachment proceedings.

general creditor: a creditor who has a claim against the debtor but does not have any lien on any of the debtor's property, whether as security for his debt or by way of a judgment or execution upon a judgment.

general damages: damages that in the ordinary course of events follow naturally and probably from the injury caused by the defendant.

general legacy: a legacy to be paid out of the assets generally of the testator without specifying any particular fund or source from which the payment is to be made.

general partnership: a partnership in which the partners conduct as co-owners a business for profit, and each partner has a right to take part in the management of the business and has unlimited liability.

gift causa mortis: a gift made by the donor because he believed he faced immediate and impending death, which gift is revoked or is revocable under certain circumstances.

grace period: a period generally of 30 or 31 days after the due date of a premium of life insurance in which the premium may be paid.

grand jury: a jury not exceeding 23 in number that considers evidence of the commission of crime and prepares indictments to bring offenders to trial before a petty jury.

grant: convey real property; an instrument by which such property has been conveyed, particularly in the case of a government.

gratuitous bailment: a bailment in which the bailee does not receive any compensation or advantage.

grievance settlement: the adjustment of disputes relating to the administration or application of existing contracts as compared with disputes over new terms of employment.

guarantor: one who undertakes the obligation of guaranty.

guaranty: an undertaking to pay the debt of another if the creditor first sues the debtor and is unable to recover the debt from the debtor or principal. (In some instances the liability is primary, in which case it is the same as suretyship.)

H

hearsay evidence: statements made out of court which are offered in court as proof of the information contained in the statements, which, subject to many exceptions, are not admissible in evidence.

hedging: the making of simultaneous contracts to purchase and to sell a particular commodity at a future date with the intention that the loss on one transaction will be offset by the gain on the other.

heirs: those persons specified by statute to receive the estate of a decedent not disposed of by will.

holder: the person in possession of a commercial paper payable to him as payee or indorsee, or the person in possession of a commercial paper payable to bearer.

holder in due course: the holder of a commercial paper under such circumstances that he is treated as favored and is given an immunity from certain defenses.

holder through a holder in due course: a person who is not himself a holder in due course but is a holder of the paper after it was held by some prior party who was a holder in due course, and who is given the same rights as a holder in due course.

holographic will: a will written by the testator in his own hand.

hotelkeeper: one regularly engaged in the business of offering living accommodations to all transient persons.

hung jury: a petty jury that has been unable to agree upon a verdict.

I

ignorantia legis non excusat: ignorance of the law is not an excuse.

implied contract: a contract expressed by conduct or implied or deduced from the facts. Also used to refer to a quasi-contract.

imputed: vicariously attributed to or charged to another, as the knowledge of an agent obtained while acting in the scope of his authority is imputed to his principal.

incidental authority: authority of an agent that is reasonably necessary to execute his express authority.

incontestable clause: a provision that after the lapse of a specified time the insurer cannot dispute the policy on the ground of misrepresentation or fraud of the insured or similar wrongful conduct.

in custodia legis: in the custody of the law.

indemnity: the right of a person secondarily liable to require that a person primarily liable pay him for his loss when the secondary party discharges the obligation which the primary party should have discharged; the right of an agent to be paid the amount of any loss or damage sustained by him without his fault because of his obedience to the principal's instructions; an undertaking by one person for a consideration to pay another person a sum of money to indemnify him when he incurs a specified loss.

independent contractor: a contractor who undertakes to perform a specified task according to the terms of a contract but over whom the other contracting party has no control except as provided for by the contract.

indictment: a formal accusation of crime made by a grand jury which accusation is then tried by a petty or trial jury.

inheritance: the interest which passes from the decedent to his heirs.

injunction: an order of a court of equity to refrain from doing (negative injunction) or to do (affirmative or mandatory injunction) a specified act. Its use in labor disputes has been greatly restricted by statute.

in pari delicto: equally guilty; used in reference to a transaction as to which relief will not be granted to either party because both are equally guilty of wrongdoing.

insolvency: an excess of debts and liabilities over assets.

insurable interest: an interest in the nonoccurrence of the risk insured against, generally because such occurrence would cause financial loss, although sometimes merely because of the close relationship between the insured and the beneficiary.

insurance: a plan of security against risks by charging the loss against a fund created by the payments made by policyholders.

intangible personal property: an interest in an enterprise, such as an interest in a partnership or stock of a corporation, and claims against other persons, whether based on contract or tort.

interlineation: a writing between the lines or adding to the provisions of a document, the effect thereof depending upon the nature of the document.

interlocutory: an intermediate step or proceeding that does not make a final disposition of the action and from which ordinarily no appeal may be taken.

international bill of exchange: a bill or draft made in one nation and payable in another.

interpleader: a form of action or proceeding by which a person against whom conflicting claims are made may bring the claimants into court to litigate their claims between themselves, as in the case of a bailor when two persons each claim to be the owner of the bailed property, or an insurer when two persons each claim to be the beneficiary of the insurance policy.

inter se: among or between themselves, as the rights of partners inter se or as between themselves.

inter vivos: any transaction which takes place between living persons and creates rights prior to the death of any of them.

intestate: the condition of dying without a will as to any property.

intestate succession: the distribution made as directed by statute of property owned by the decedent of which he did not effectively dispose by will.

ipso facto: by the very act or fact in itself without any further action by any one.

irrebuttable presumption: a presumption which cannot be rebutted by proving that the facts are to the contrary; not a true presumption but merely a rule of law described in terms of a presumption.

irreparable injury to property: an injury that would be of such a nature or inflicted upon such an interest that it would not be reasonably possible to compensate the injured party by the payment of money damages because the property in question could not be purchased in the open market with the money damages which the defendant could be required to pay.

J

joint and several contract: a contract in which two or more persons are jointly and severally obligated or are jointly and severally entitled to recover.

joint contract: a contract in which two or more persons are jointly liable or jointly entitled to performance under the contract.

joint stock company: an association in which the shares of the members are transferable and control is delegated to a group or board.

joint tenancy: the estate held by two or more jointly with the right of survivorship as between them, unless modified by statute.

joint venture: a relationship in which two or more persons combine their labor or property for a single undertaking and share profits and losses equally unless otherwise agreed.

judgment: the final sentence, order, or decision entered into at the conclusion of the action.

judgment note: a promissory note containing a clause authorizing the holder of the note to enter judgment against the maker of the note if it is not paid when due. Also called cognovit note.

judgment n.o.v.: a judgment which may be entered after verdict upon the motion of the losing party on the ground that the verdict is so wrong that a judgment should be entered the opposite of the verdict, or non obstante veredicto (notwithstanding the verdict).

judgment on the pleadings: a judgment which may be entered after all the pleadings are filed when it is clear from the pleadings that a particular party is entitled to win the action without proceeding any further.

judicial sale: a sale made under order of court by an officer appointed to make the sale or by an officer having such authority as incident to his office. The sale may have the effect of divesting liens on the property.

jurisdiction: the power of a court to hear and determine a given class of cases; the power to act over a particular defendant.

jurisdictional dispute: a dispute between rival labor unions which may take the form of each claiming that particular work should be assigned to it.

justifiable abandonment by employee: the right of an employee to abandon his employment because of nonpayment of wages, wrongful assault, the demand for the performance of services not contemplated, or injurious working conditions.

justifiable discharge of employee: the right of an employer to discharge an employee for nonperformance of duties, fraud, disobedience, disloyalty, or incompetence.

L

laches: the rule that the enforcement of equitable rights will be denied when the party has delayed so long that rights of third persons have intervened or the death or disappearance of witnesses would prejudice any party through the loss of evidence.

land: earth, including all things imbedded in or attached thereto, whether naturally or by act of man.

last clear chance: the rule that if the defendant had the last clear chance to have avoided injuring the plaintiff, he is liable even though the plaintiff had also been contributorily negligent. In some states also called the humanitarian doctrine.

law of the case: matters decided in the course of litigation which are binding on the parties in the subsequent phases of litigation.

leading questions: questions which suggest the desired answer to the witness, or assume the existence of a fact which is in dispute.

lease: an agreement between the owner of property and a tenant by which the former agrees to give possession of the property to the latter in consideration of the payment of rent. (Parties—landlord or lessor, tenant or lessee)

leasehold: the estate or interest which the tenant has in land rented to him.

legacy: a gift of personal property made by will.

legal tender: such form of money as the law recognizes as lawful and declares that a tender thereof in the proper amount is a proper tender which the creditor cannot refuse.

letters of administration: the written authorization given to an administrator as evidence of his appointment and authority.

letters testamentary: the written authorization given to an executor as evidence of his appointment and authority.

levy: a seizure of property by an officer of the court in execution of a judgment of the court, although in many states it is sufficient if the officer is physically in the presence of the property and announces the fact that he is "seizing" it, although he then allows the property to remain where he found it.

lex loci: the law of the place where the material facts occurred as governing the rights and liabilities of the parties.

lex loci contractus: the law of the place where the contract was made as governing the rights and liability of the parties to a contract with respect to certain matters.

lex loci fori: the law of the state in which the action is brought as determining the rules of procedure applicable to the action.

lex loci sitae rei: the law of the place where land is located as determining the validity of acts done relating thereto.

libel: written or visual defamation without legal justification.

license: a personal privilege to do some act or series of acts upon the land of another, as the placing of a sign thereon, not amounting to an easement or a right of possession.

lien: a claim or right against property existing by virtue of the entry of a judgment against its owner or by the entry of a judgment and a levy thereunder on the property, or because of the relationship of the claimant to the particular property, such as an unpaid seller.

life estate: an estate for the duration of a life.

limited jurisdiction: a court with power to hear and determine cases within certain restricted categories.

limited liability: loss of contributed capital or investment as maximum liability.

limited partnership: a partnership in which at least one partner has a liability limited to the loss of the capital contribution that he has made to the partnership, and such a partner neither takes part in the management of the partnership nor appears to the public to be a partner.

lineal consanguinity: the relationship that exists when one person is a direct descendant from the other.

liquidated damages: a provision stipulating the amount of damages to be paid in event of default or breach of contract.

liquidation: the process of converting property into money whether of particular items of property or all the assets of a business or an estate.

lis pendens: the doctrine that certain types of pending actions are notice to everyone so that if any right is acquired from a party to that action, the transferee takes that right subject to the outcome of the pending action.

lobbying contract (illegal): a contract by which one party agrees to attempt to influence the action of a legislature or Congress, or any members thereof, by improper means.

lottery: any plan by which a consideration is given for a chance to win a prize.

lucri causa: with the motive of obtaining gain or pecuniary advantage.

M

majority: of age, as contrasted with being a minor; more than half of any group, as a majority of stockholders.

malice in fact: an intention to injure or cause harm.

malice in law: a presumed intention to injure or cause harm when there is no privilege or right to do the act in question, which presumption cannot be contradicted or rebutted.

maliciously inducing breach of contract: the wrong of inducing an employee to break his contract with his employer or inducing the breach of any other kind of contract with knowledge of its existence and without justification.

malum in se: an offense that is criminal because contrary to the fundamental sense of a civilized community, as murder.

malum prohibitum: an offense that is criminal not because inherently wrong but is prohibited for the convenience of society, as overtime parking.

marshalling assets: the distribution of a debtor's assets in such a way as to give the greatest benefit to all of his creditors.

martial law: government exercised by a military commander over property and persons not in the armed forces, as contrasted with military law which governs the military personnel.

mechanics' lien: protection afforded by statute to various types of laborers and persons supplying materials, by giving them a lien on the building and land that has been improved or added to by them.

mens rea: the mental state that must accompany an act to make the act a crime. Sometimes described as the "guilty mind," although appreciation of guilt is not required.

merger by judgment: the discharge of a contract through being merged into a judgment which is entered in a suit on the contract.

merger of corporations: a combining of corporations by which one absorbs the other and continues to exist, preserving its original charter and identity while the other corporation ceases to exist.

mesne: intermediate or intervening, as mesne profits, which are the fruits or income from the land received in between the time that the true owner was wrongfully dispossessed and the time that he recovers the land.

misdemeanor: a criminal offense which is neither treason nor a felony.

misrepresentation: a false statement of fact although made innocently without any intent to deceive.

mobilia sequuntur personam: the maxim that personal property follows the owner and in the eyes of the law is located at the owner's domicile.

moratorium: a temporary suspension by statute of the

enforcement of debts or the foreclosure of mortgages.

mortgage: an interest in land given by the owner to his creditor as security for the payment to the creditor of a debt, the nature of the interest depending upon the law of the state where the land is located. (Parties—mortgagor, mortgagee)

multiple insurers: insurers who agree to divide a risk so that each is only liable for a specified portion.

N

National Labor Management Relations Act: the federal statute, also known as the Taft-Hartley Act, designed to protect the organizational rights of labor and to prevent unfair labor practices by management or labor.

natural and probable consequences: those ordinary consequences of an act which a reasonable man would foresee.

negative covenant: an undertaking in a deed to refrain from doing an act.

negligence: the failure to exercise due care under the circumstances in consequence of which harm is proximately caused to one to whom the defendant owed a duty to exercise due care.

negligence per se: an action which is regarded as so improper that it is declared by law to be negligent in itself without regard to whether due care was otherwise exercised.

negotiable instruments: drafts, promissory notes, checks, and certificates of deposit in such form that greater rights may be acquired thereunder than by taking an assignment of a contract right; called negotiable commercial paper by the Code.

negotiation: the transfer of a commercial paper by indorsement and delivery by the person to whom then payable in the case of order paper, and by physical transfer in the case of bearer paper.

nominal damages: a nominal sum awarded the plaintiff in order to establish that his legal rights have been violated although he in fact has not sustained any actual loss or damages.

nominal partner: a person who in fact is not a partner but who holds himself out as a partner or permits others to do so.

Norris-LaGuardia Anti-Injunction Act: a federal statute prohibiting the use of the injunction in labor disputes, except in particular cases.

notice of dishonor: notice given to parties secondarily liable that the primary party to the instrument has refused to accept the instrument or to make payment when it was properly presented for that purpose.

novation: the discharge of a contract between two parties by their agreeing with a third person that such third person shall be substituted for one of the original parties to the contract, who shall thereupon be released.

nudum pactum: a mere promise for which there is no consideration given and which therefore is ordinarily not enforceable.

nuisance: any conduct that harms or prejudices another in the use of his land or which harms or prejudices the public.

nuisance per se: an activity which is in itself a nuisance regardless of the time and place involved.

nuncupative will: an oral will made and declared by the testator in the presence of witnesses to be his will and generally made during the testator's last illness.

O

obiter dictum: that which is said in the opinion of a court in passing or by the way, but which is not necessary to the determination of the case and is therefore not regarded as authoritative as though it were actually involved in the decision.

obliteration: any erasing, writing upon, or crossing out that makes all or part of a will impossible to read, and which has the effect of revoking such part when done by the testator with the intent of effecting a revocation.

occupation: taking and holding possession of property; a method of acquiring title to personal property after it has been abandoned.

open-end mortgage: a mortgage given to secure additional loans to be made in the future as well as the original loan.

operation of law: the attaching of certain consequences to certain facts because of legal principles that operate automatically, as contrasted with consequences which arise because of the voluntary action of a party designed to create those consequences.

opinion evidence: evidence not of what the witness himself observed but the conclusion which he draws from what he observed, or in the case of an expert witness, also from what he is asked or what he has heard at the trial.

option contract: a contract to hold an offer to make a contract open for a fixed period of time.

P

paper title: the title of a person evidenced only by deeds or matter appearing of record under the recording statutes.

parol evidence rule: the rule that prohibits the introduction in evidence of oral or written statements made prior to or contemporaneously with the execution of a complete written contract, deed, or instrument, in the absence of clear proof of fraud, accident, or mistake causing the omission of the statement in question.

passive trust: a trust that is created without imposing any duty to be performed by the trustee and is therefore treated as an absolute transfer of the title to the trust beneficiary.

past consideration: something that has been performed in the past and which therefore cannot be consideration for a promise made in the present.

patent: the grant to an inventor of an exclusive right to make and sell his invention for a nonrenewable period of 17 years; a deed to land given by a government to a private person.

pawn: a pledge of tangible personal property rather than of documents representing property rights.

pecuniary legacy: a general legacy of a specified amount of money without indicating the source from which payment is to be made.

per autre vie: limitation of an estate. An estate held by *A* during the lifetime of *B*, is an estate of *A* per autre vie.

per curiam opinion: an opinion written "by the court" rather than by a named judge when all the judges of the court are so agreed on the matter that it is not deemed to merit any discussion and may be simply disposed of.

perpetual succession: a phrase describing the continuing life of the corporation unaffected by the death of any stockholder or the transfer by stockholders of their stock.

perpetuities, rule against: a rule of law that prohibits the creation of an interest in property which will not become definite or vested until a date further away than 21 years after the death of persons alive at the time the owner of the property attempts to create the interest.

per se: in, through, or by itself.

person: a term that includes both natural persons, or living people, and artificial persons, as corporations which are created by act of government.

personal defenses: limited defenses that cannot be asserted by the defendant against a holder in due course. This term is not expressly used in Uniform Commercial Code.

per stirpes: according to the root or by way of representation. Distribution among heirs related to the decedent in different degrees, the property being divided into lines of descent from the decedent and the share of each line then divided within the line by way of representation.

petty jury: the trial jury of twelve. Also petit jury.

picketing: the placing of persons outside of places of employment or distribution so that by words or banners they may inform the public of the existence of a labor dispute.

pleadings: the papers filed by the parties in an action in order to set forth the facts and frame the issues to be tried, although under some systems, the pleadings merely give notice of a general indication of the nature of the issues.

pledge: a bailment given as security for the payment of a debt or the performance of an obligation owed to the pledgee. (Parties—pledgor, pledgee)

police power: the power to govern; the power to adopt laws for the protection of the public health, welfare, safety, and morals.

policy: the paper evidencing the contract of insurance.

polling the jury: the process of inquiring of each juror individually in open court as to whether the verdict announced by the foreman of the jury was agreed to by him.

possession: exclusive dominion and control of property.

possessory lien: a right to retain possession of property of another as security for some debt or obligation owed the lienor which right continues only as long as possession is retained.

possibility of reverter: the nature of the interest held by the grantor after conveying land outright but subject to a condition or provision that may cause the grantee's interest to become forfeited and the interest to revert to the grantor or his heirs.

postdate: to insert or place a later date on an instrument than the actual date on which it was executed.

power of appointment: a power given to another, commonly a beneficiary of a trust, to designate or appoint who shall be beneficiary or receive the fund upon his death.

power of attorney: a written authorization to an agent by the principal.

precatory words: words indicating merely a desire or a wish that another use property for a particular purpose but which in law will not be enforced in the absence of an express declaration that the property shall be used for the specified purpose.

pre-emptive offer of shares: the right, subject to many exceptions, that each shareholder has that whenever the capital stock of the corporation is increased he will be allowed to subscribe to such a percentage of the new shares as his old shares bore to the former total capital stock.

preferred creditor: a creditor who by some statute is given the right to be paid first or before other creditors.

preferred stock: stock that has a priority or preference as to payment of dividends or upon liquidation, or both.

preponderance of evidence: the degree or quantum of evidence in favor of the existence of a certain fact when from a review of all the evidence it appears more probable that the fact exists than that it does not. The actual number of witnesses involved is not material nor is the fact that the margin of probability is very slight.

prescription: the acquisition of a right to use the land of another, as an easement, through the making of hostile, visible, and notorious use of the land, continuing for the period specified by the local law.

presumption: a rule of proof which permits the existence of a fact to be assumed from the proof that another fact exists when there is a logical relationship between the two or when the means of disproving the assumed fact are more readily within the control or knowledge of the adverse party against whom the presumption operates.

presumption of death: the rebuttable presumption which arises that a person has died when he has been continuously absent and unheard of for a period of 7 years.

presumption of innocence: the presumption of fact that a person accused of crime is innocent until it is shown that he in fact is guilty of the offense charged.

presumption of payment: a rebuttable presumption that one performing continuing services which would normally be paid periodically, as weekly or monthly, has in fact been paid when a number of years have passed without any objection or demand for payment having been made.

presumptive heir: a person who would be the heir if the ancestor should die at that moment.

pretrial conference: a conference held prior to the trial at which the court and the attorneys seek to simplify the issues in controversy and eliminate matters not in dispute.

price: the consideration for a sale of goods.

prima facie: such evidence as by itself would establish the claim or defense of the party if the evidence were believed.

primary beneficiary: the person designated as the first one to receive the proceeds of a life insurance policy, as distinguished from a contingent beneficiary who will receive the proceeds only if the primary beneficiary dies before the insured.

primary liability: the liability of a person whose act or omission gave rise to the cause of action and who in all fairness should therefore be the one to pay the victim of his wrong, even though others may also be liable for his misconduct.

principal: one who employs an agent to act on his behalf; the person who as between himself and the surety is primarily liable to the third person or creditor.

principal in the first degree: one who actually engages

in the commission or perpetration of a crime.

principal in the second degree: one who is actually or constructively present at the commission of the crime and who aids and abets in its commission.

private carrier: a carrier owned by the shipper, such as a company's own fleet of trucks.

privileged communication: information which the witness may refuse to testify to because of the relationship with the person furnishing the information, as husband-wife, attorney-client.

privilege from arrest: the immunity from arrest of parties, witnesses, and attorneys while present within the jurisdiction for the purpose of taking part in other litigation.

privity: a succession or chain of relationship to the same thing or right, as privity of contract, privity of estate, privity of possession.

probate: the procedure for formally establishing or proving that a given writing is the last will and testament of the person purporting to have signed it.

product liability: liability imposed upon the manufacturer or seller of goods for harm caused by a defect in the goods, embracing liability for (1) negligence, (2) fraud, (3) breach of warranty, and (4) strict tort.

profit à prendre: the right to take a part of the soil or produce of another's land, such as timber or water.

promissory estoppel: the doctrine that a promise will be enforced although it is not supported by consideration when the promisor should have reasonably expected that his promise would induce action or forbearance of a definite and substantial character on the part of the promisee, and injustice can only be avoided by enforcement of the promise.

promissory note: an unconditional promise in writing made by one person to another, signed by the maker, engaging to pay on demand, or at a definite time, a sum certain in money to order or to bearer. (Parties—maker, payee)

promissory representation: a representation made by the applicant to the insurer as to what is to occur in the future.

promissory warranty: a representation made by the applicant to the insurer as to what is to occur in the future which the applicant warrants will occur.

promoters: the persons who plan the formation of the corporation and sell or promote the idea to others.

proof: the probative effect of the evidence; the conclusion drawn from the evidence as to the existence of particular facts.

property: the rights and interests one has in anything subject to ownership.

pro rata: proportionately, or divided according to a rate or standard.

protest: the formal certification by a notary public or other authorized person that proper presentment of a commercial paper was made to the primary party and he defaulted, the certificate commonly also including a recital that notice was given to secondary parties.

proximate cause: the act which is the natural and reasonably foreseeable cause of the harm or event which occurs and injures the plaintiff.

proximate damages: damages which in the ordinary course of events are the natural and reasonably foreseeable result of the defendant's violation of the plaintiff's rights.

proxy: a written authorization by a shareholder to another person to vote the stock owned by the shareholder; the person who is the holder of such a written authorization.

public charge: a person who because of a personal disability or lack of means of support is dependent upon public charity or relief for sustenance.

public domain: public or government owned lands.

public easement: a right of way for use by members of the public at large.

public policy: certain objectives relating to health, morals, and integrity of government that the law seeks to advance by declaring invalid any contract which conflicts with those objectives even though there is no statute expressly declaring such contract illegal.

punitive damages: damages in excess of those required to compensate the plaintiff for the wrong done, which are imposed in order to punish the defendant because of the particularly wanton or willful character of his wrongdoing; also exemplary.

purchase-money mortgage: a mortgage given by the

purchaser of land to the seller to secure the seller for the payment of the unpaid balance of the purchase price, which the seller purports to lend the purchaser.

purchaser in good faith: a person who purchases without any notice or knowledge of any defect of title, misconduct, or defense.

Q

qualified acceptance: an acceptance of a draft that varies the order of the bill in some way.

qualified indorsement: an indorsement that includes words such as "without recourse" evidencing the intent of the indorser that he shall not be held liable for the failure of the primary party to pay the instrument.

quantum meruit: an action brought for the value of the services rendered the defendant when there was no express contract as to the payment to be made.

quantum valebant: an action brought for the value of goods sold the defendant when there was no express contract as to the purchase price.

quasi: as if, as though it were, having the characteristics of; a modifier employed to indicate that the subject is to be treated as though it were in fact the noun which follows the word "quasi:" as in quasi contract, quasi corporation, quasi public corporation.

quid pro quo: literally "what for what." An early form of the concept of consideration by which an action for debt could not be brought unless the defendant had obtained something in return for his obligation.

quitclaim deed: a deed by which the grantor purports only to give up whatever right or title he may have in the property without specifying or warranting that he is transferring any particular interest.

quorum: the minimum number of persons, shares represented, or directors who must be present at a meeting in order that business may be lawfully transacted.

R

ratification by minor: the approval of a contract given by a minor after attaining majority.

ratification of agency: the approval of the unauthorized act of an agent or of a person who is not an agent for any purpose after the act has been done, which has the same effect as though the act had been authorized before it was done.

ratio decidendi: the reason or basis for deciding the case in a particular way.

ratio legis: the reason for a principle or rule of law.

real defenses: certain defenses (universal) that are available against any holder of a commercial paper regardless of his character, although this term is not expressly used by the Uniform Commercial Code.

real evidence: tangible objects that are presented in the courtroom for the observation of the trier of fact as proof of the facts in dispute or in support of the theory of a party.

real property: land and all rights in land.

reasonable care: the degree of care that a reasonable man would take under all the circumstances then known.

rebate: a refund made by the seller or the carrier of part of the purchase price or freight bill. Generally illegal as an unfair method of competition.

rebuttable presumption: a presumption which may be overcome or rebutted by proof that the actual facts were different than those presumed.

receiver: an impartial person appointed by a court to take possession of and manage property for the protection of all concerned.

recognizance: an obligation entered into before a court to do some act, such as to appear at a later date for a hearing. Also called a contract of record.

redemption: the buying back of one's property, which has been sold because of a default, upon paying the amount which had been originally due together with interest and costs.

referee: an impartial person selected by the parties or appointed by a court to determine facts or decide matters in dispute.

referee in bankruptcy: a referee appointed by a bankruptcy court to hear and determine various matters relating to bankruptcy proceedings.

reformation: a remedy by which a written instrument is corrected when it fails to express the actual intent of both parties because of fraud, accident, or mistake.

registration of titles: a system generally known as the Torrens system of permanent registration of title to all land within the state.

reimbursement: the right of one paying money on behalf of another which such other person should have himself paid to recover the amount of the payment from him.

release of liens: an agreement or instrument by which the holder of a lien on property, such as a mortgage lien, releases the property from the lien although the debt itself is not released.

remedy: the action or procedure that is followed in order to enforce a right or to obtain damages for injury to a right.

remote damages: damages which were in fact caused by the defendant's act but the possibility that such damages should occur seemed so improbable and unlikely to a reasonable man that the law does not impose liability for such damages.

renunciation of duty: the repudiation of one's contractual duty in advance of the time for performance, which repudiation may be accepted by the adverse party as an anticipatory breach.

renunciation of right: the surrender of a right or privilege as the right to act as administrator or the right to receive a legacy under the will of a decedent.

reorganization of corporation: procedure devised to restore insolvent corporations to financial stability through readjustment of debt and capital structure either under the supervision of a court of equity or of bankruptcy.

repossession: any taking again of possession although generally used in connection with the act of a secured seller in taking back the property upon the default of the credit buyer.

representations: statements, whether oral or written, made to give the insurer the information which it needs in writing the insurance, and which if false and relating to a material fact will entitle the insurer to avoid the contract.

representative capacity: action taken by one not on his own behalf but on behalf of another, as an executor acting on behalf of the decedent's estate, or action taken both on one's behalf and on behalf of others, as a stockholder bringing a representative action.

resale price maintenance agreement: an agreement that the buyer will not resell a trademark or brand name article below a stated minimum price which agreement, by virtue of fair trade laws, is valid not only as between the contracting parties but in some states may also bind other persons in the trade who know of the agreement although they did not sign it.

rescission upon agreement: the setting aside of a contract by the action of the parties as though the contract had never been made.

rescission upon breach: the action of one party to a contract to set the contract aside when the other party is guilty of a breach of the contract.

reservation: the creation by the grantor of a right that did not exist before, which he reserves or keeps for himself upon making a conveyance of property.

residuary estate: the balance of the testator's estate available for distribution after all administrative expenses, exemptions, debts, taxes, and specific, pecuniary, and demonstrative legacies have been paid.

res inter alios acta: the rule that transactions and declarations between strangers having no connection with the pending action are not admissible in evidence.

res ipsa loquitur: the permissible inference that the defendant was negligent in that the thing speaks for itself when the circumstances are such that ordinarily the plainitff could not have been injured had the defendant not been at fault.

res judicata: the principle that once a final judgment is entered in an action between the parties, it is binding upon them and the matter cannot be litigated again by bringing a second action.

respondeat superior: the doctrine that the principal or employer is vicariously liable for the unauthorized torts committed by his agent or employee while acting within the scope of his agency or the course of his employment, respectively.

restraints on alienation: limitations on the ability of the owner to convey freely as he chooses. Such limitations are generally regarded as invalid.

restrictive covenants: covenants in a deed by which

the grantee agrees to refrain from doing specified acts.

restrictive indorsement: an indorsement that prohibits the further transfer, constitutes the indorsee the agent of the indorser, vests the title in the indorsee in trust for or to the use of some other person, is conditional, or is for collection or deposit.

resulting trust: a trust that is created by implication of law to carry out the presumed intent of the parties.

retaliatory statute: a statute that provides that when a corporation of another state enters the state it shall be subject to the same taxes and restrictions as would be imposed upon a corporation from the retaliating state if it had entered the other state. Also called reciprocity statutes.

reversible error: an error or defect in court proceedings of so serious a nature that on appeal the appellate court will set aside the proceedings of the lower court.

reversionary interest: the interest that a lessor has in property which is subject to an outstanding lease.

revival of judgment: the taking of appropriate action to preserve a judgment, in most instances to continue the lien of the judgment that would otherwise expire after a specified number of years.

revival of will: the restoration by the testator of a will which he had previously revoked.

rider: a slip of paper executed by the insurer and intended to be attached to the insurance policy for the purpose of changing it in some respect.

riparian rights: the right of a person through whose land runs a natural watercourse to use the water free from unreasonable pollution or diversion by upper riparian owners and blocking by lower riparian owners.

risk: the peril or contingency against which the insured is protected by the contract of insurance.

Robinson-Patman Act: a federal statute designed to eliminate price discrimination in interstate commerce.

run with the land: the concept that certain covenants in a deed to land are deemed to "run" or pass with the land so that whoever owns the land is bound by or entitled to the benefit of the covenants.

S

sale or return: a sale in which the title to the property passes to the buyer at the time of the transaction but he is given the option of returning the property and restoring the title to the seller.

scienter: knowledge, referring to those wrongs or crimes which require a knowledge of wrong in order to constitute the offense.

scope of employment: the area within which the employee is authorized to act with the consequence that a tort committed while so acting imposes liability upon the employer.

seal: at common law an impression on wax or other tenacious material attached to the instrument. Under modern law, any mark not ordinarily part of the signature is a seal when so intended, including the letters "L. S." and the word "seal," or a pictorial representation of a seal, without regard to whether they had been printed or typed on the instrument before its signing.

sealed verdict: a verdict that is rendered when the jury returns to the courtroom during an adjournment of the court, the verdict then being written down and sealed and later affirmed before the court when the court is in session.

seaman's will: an oral or informal written will made by a seaman to dispose of his personal property.

secondary evidence: copies of original writings or testimony as to the contents of such writings which are admissible when the original cannot be produced and the inability to do so is reasonably explained.

secret partner: a partner who takes an active part in the management of the partnership but is not known to the public as a partner.

secured transaction: a credit sale of goods or a secured loan that provides special protection for the creditor.

settlor: one who settles property in trust or creates a trust estate.

severable contract: a contract the terms of which are such that one part may be separated or severed from the other, so that a default as to one part is not necessarily a default as to the entire contract.

several contracts: separate or independent contracts made by different persons undertaking to perform the same obligation.

severalty: sole ownership of property by one person.

severed realty: real property that has been cut off and made moveable, as by cutting down a tree, and which thereby loses its character as real property and becomes personal property.

shareholder's action: an action brought by one or more shareholders on behalf of the shareholders generally and of the corporation to enforce a cause of action of the corporation against third persons.

sheriff's deed: the deed executed and delivered by the sheriff to the purchaser at a sale conducted by the sheriff in his official capacity.

Sherman Antitrust Act: a federal statute prohibiting combinations and contracts in restraint of interstate trade, now generally inapplicable to labor union activity.

shop right: the right of an employer to use in his business without charge an invention discovered by an employee during working hours and with the employer's material and equipment.

sight draft: a draft or bill of exchange payable on sight or when presented for payment.

silent partner: a partner who takes no active part in the business, without regard to whether he is known to the public as a partner.

sitdown strike: a strike in which the employees remain in the plant and refuse to allow the employer to operate it.

slander: defamation of character by spoken words or gestures.

slander of title: the malicious making of false statements as to a seller's title.

slander per se: certain words deemed slanderous without requiring proof of damages to the victim, as words charging a crime involving moral turpitude and an infamous punishment, a disease which would exclude from society, or words which tend to injure the victim in his business, profession, or occupation.

slowdown: a slowing down of production by employees without actual stopping of work.

social security acts: statutes providing for assistance for the aged, blind, unemployed, and similar classes of persons in need.

soldier's will: an oral or informal written will made by a soldier to dispose of his personal estate.

special agent: an agent authorized to transact a specific transaction or to do a specific act.

special damages: damages that do not necessarily result from the injury to the plaintiff but at the same time are not so remote that the defendant should not be held liable therefor provided that the claim for special damages is properly made in the action.

special indorsement: an indorsement that specifies the person to whom the instrument is indorsed.

special jurisdiction: a court with power to hear and determine cases within certain restricted categories.

specific (identified) goods: goods which are so identified to the contract that no other goods may be delivered in performance of the contract.

specific lien: the right of a creditor to hold particular property or assert a lien on particular property of the debtor because of the creditor's having done work on or having some other association with the property; as distinguished from having a lien generally against the assets of the debtor merely because the debtor is indebted to him.

specific performance: an action brought to compel the adverse party to perform his contract on the theory that merely suing him for damages for its breach will not be an adequate remedy.

spendthrift trust: a trust, which to varying degrees, provides that creditors of the beneficiary shall not be able to reach the principal or income held by the trustee and that the beneficiary shall not be able to assign his interest in the trust.

spoliation: an alteration or change made to a written instrument by a person who has no relationship to or interest in the writing. It has no effect as long as the terms of the instrument can still be ascertained.

stare decisis: the principle that the decision of a court should serve as a guide or precedent and control the decision of a similar case in the future.

status quo ante: the original positions of the parties to a contract prior to the making of the contract or the doing of some other act.

Statute of Frauds: a statute, which in order to prevent fraud through the use of perjured testimony, requires that certain types of transactions be evidenced in writing in order to be binding or enforceable.

Statute of Limitations: a statute that restricts the period of time within which an action may be brought.

stop delivery: the right of an unpaid seller under certain conditions to prevent a carrier or a bailee from delivering goods to the buyer.

stop payment: an order by a depositor to his bank to refuse to make payment of his check when presented for payment.

strict tort liability: a product liability theory which imposes liability on the manufacturer, seller, or distributor of goods for harm caused by goods which are dangerously defective.

sublease: a transfer of the premises by the lessee to a third person, the sublessee or subtenant, for a period less than the term of the original lease.

subpoena: a court order directing a person to appear as a witness. In some states also it is the original process that is to be served on the defendant in order to give the court jurisdiction over his person.

subrogation: the right of a party secondarily liable to stand in the place of the creditor after he has made payment to the creditor and to enforce the creditor's right against the party primarily liable in order to obtain indemnity from him.

subsidiary corporation: a corporation that is controlled by another corporation through the ownership by the latter of a controlling amount of the voting stock of the former.

subsidiary term: a provision of a contract that is not fundamental or does not go to the root of the contract.

substantial performance: the equitable doctrine that a contractor substantially performing a contract in good faith is entitled to recover the contract price less damages for noncompletion or defective work.

substantive law: the law that defines rights and liabilities.

substitution: discharge of contracts by substituting another in its place.

subtenant: one who rents the leased premises from the original tenant for a period of time less than the balance of the lease to the original tenant.

sui generis: in a class by itself, or its own kind.

sui juris: legally competent, possessing capacity.

summary judgment: a judgment entered by the court when no substantial dispute of fact is present, the court acting on the basis of affidavits or depositions which show that the claim or defense of a party is a sham.

summons: a writ by which an action was commenced under the common law.

superior servant rule: an exception to the fellow-servant rule that is made when the injured servant is under the control of the servant whose conduct caused him injury.

supersedeas: a stay of proceedings pending the taking of an appeal or an order entered for the purpose of effecting such a stay.

surcharge: a money judgment entered against a fiduciary for the amount of loss which his negligence or misconduct has caused the estate under his control.

suretyship: an undertaking to pay the debt or be liable for the default of another.

surrender: the yielding up of the tenant's leasehold estate to the lessor in consequence of which the lease terminates.

survival acts: statutes which provide that causes of action shall not terminate on death but shall survive and may be enforced by or against a decedent's estate.

survivorship: the right by which a surviving joint tenant or tenant by the entireties acquires the interest of the predeceasing tenant automatically upon his death.

symbolic delivery: the delivery of goods by delivery of the means of control, as a key or relevant document of title, as a negotiable bill of lading.

syndicate: an association of individuals formed to conduct a particular business transaction, generally of a financial nature.

T

tacking: adding together successive periods of adverse possession of persons in privity with each other in order to constitute a sufficient period of continuous adverse possession to vest title thereby.

Taft-Hartley Act: popular name for the National Labor Management Relations Act of 1947.

tenancy at sufferance: the holding over by a tenant after his lease has expired of the rented land without the permission of the landlord and prior to the time that the landlord has elected to treat him as a trespasser or a tenant.

tenancy at will: the holding of land for an indefinite period that may be terminated at any time by the landlord or by the landlord and tenant acting together.

tenancy for years: a tenancy for a fixed period of time, even though the time is less than a year.

tenancy from year to year: a tenancy which continues indefinitely from year to year until terminated.

tenancy in common: the relation that exists when two or more persons own undivided interests in property.

tenancy in partnership: the ownership relation that exists between partners under the Uniform Partnership Act.

tender of payment: an unconditional offer to pay the exact amount of money due at the time and place specified by the contract.

tender of performance: an unconditional offer to perform at the time and in the manner specified by the contract.

tentative trust: a trust which arises when money is deposited in a bank account in the name of the depositor "in trust for" a named person.

terminable fee: an estate that terminates upon the happening of a contingency without any entry by the grantor or his heirs, as a conveyance for "so long as" the land is used for a specified purpose.

testamentary: designed to take effect at death, as by disposing of property or appointing an executor.

testate: the condition of leaving a will upon death.

testate succession: the distribution of an estate in accordance with the will of the decedent.

testator—testatrix: a man—woman who makes a will.

testimonium clause: a concluding paragraph in a deed, contract, or other instrument, reciting that the instrument has been executed on a specified date by the parties.

testimony: the answers of witnesses under oath to questions given at the time of the trial in the presence of the trier of fact.

theory of the case: the rule that when a case is tried on the basis of one theory, the appellant in taking an appeal cannot argue a different theory to the appellate court.

third-party beneficiary: a third person whom the parties to a contract intend to benefit by the making of the contract and to confer upon him the right to sue for breach of the contract.

tie-in sale: the requirement imposed by the seller that the buyer of particular goods or equipment also purchase certain other goods from the seller in order to obtain the original property desired.

time draft: a bill of exchange payable at a stated time after sight or at a definite time.

title insurance: a form of insurance by which the insurer insures the buyer of real property against the risk of loss should the title acquired from the seller be defective in any way.

toll the statute: stop the running of the period of the Statute of Limitations by the doing of some act by the debtor.

Torrens System: see registration of titles.

tort: a private injury or wrong arising from a breach of a duty created by law.

trade acceptance: a draft or bill of exchange drawn by the seller of goods on the purchaser at the time of sale and accepted by the purchaser.

trade fixtures: articles of personal property which have been attached to the freehold by a tenant and which are used for or are necessary to the carrying on of the tenant's trade.

trademark: a name, device, or symbol used by a manufacturer or seller to distinguish his goods from those of other persons.

trade name: a name under which a business is carried on and, if fictitious, it must be registered.

trade secrets: secrets of any character peculiar and important to the business of the employer that have been communicated to the employee in the course of confidential employment.

treason: an attempt to overthrow or betray the government to which one owes allegiance.

treasury stock: stock of the corporation which the corporation has reacquired.

trier of fact: in most cases a jury, although it may be the judge alone in certain classes of cases, as in equity, or in any case when jury trial is waived, or an administrative agency or commission is involved.

trust: a transfer of property by one person to another with the understanding or declaration that such property be held for the benefit of another, or the holding of property by the owner in trust for another, upon his declaration of trust, without a transfer to another person. (Parties—settlor, trustee, beneficiary.)

trust corpus: the fund or property that is transferred to the trustee or held by the settlor as the body or subject matter of the trust.

trust deed: a form of deed which transfers the trust property to the trustee for the purposes therein stated, particularly used when the trustee is to hold the title to the mortgagor's land in trust for the benefit of the mortgage bondholders.

trustee de son tort: a person who is not a trustee but who has wrongly intermeddled with property of another and rather than proceed against him for the tort, the law will require him to account for the property as though he were such a trustee.

trustee in bankruptcy: an impartial person elected to administer the bankrupt's estate.

trust receipt: a credit security device under which the wholesale buyer executes a receipt stating that he holds the purchased goods in trust for the person financing the purchase by lending him money. The trust receipt is replaced by the secured transaction under the UCC.

U

uberrima fides: utmost good faith, a duty to exercise the utmost good faith which arises in certain relationships, as that between an insurer and the applicant for insurance.

ultra vires: an act or contract which the corporation does not have authority to do or make.

underwriter: an insurer.

undisclosed principal: a principal on whose behalf an agent acts without disclosing to the third person the fact that he is an agent nor the identity of the principal.

undue influence: the influence that is asserted upon another person by one who dominates that person.

unfair competition: the wrong of employing competitive methods that have been declared unfair by statute or an administrative agency.

unfair labor practice acts: statutes that prohibit certain labor practices and declare them to be unfair labor practices.

unincorporated association: a combination of two or more persons for the furtherance of a common nonprofit purpose.

union contract: a contract between a labor union and an employer or group of employers prescribing the general terms of employment of workers by the latter.

union shop: under present unfair labor practice statutes, a place of employment where nonunion men may be employed for a trial period of not more than 30 days after which the nonunion worker must join the union or be discharged.

universal agent: an agent authorized by the principal to do all facts that can lawfully be delegated to a representative.

usury: the lending of money at greater than the maximum rate allowed by law.

V

vacating of judgment: the setting aside of a judgment.

valid: legal.

verdict: the decision of the trial or petty jury.

vice-principal rule: the rule that persons performing supervisory functions or acting as vice employers are not to be regarded as fellow servants of those under their authority for the purpose of determining the liability of the employer for the injuries of the employee at common law.

void: of no legal effect and not binding on anyone.

voidable: a transaction that may be set aside by one party thereto because of fraud or similar reason but which is binding on the other party until the injured party elects to avoid.

voidable preference: a preference given by the bankrupt

to one of his creditors, but which may be set aside by the trustee in bankruptcy.

voir dire examination: the preliminary examination of a juror or a witness to ascertain that he is qualified to act as such.

volenti non fit injuria: the maxim that the defendant's act cannot constitute a tort if the plaintiff had consented thereto.

voluntary nonsuit: a means of the plaintiff's stopping a trial at any time by moving for a voluntary nonsuit.

voting trust: the transfer by two or more persons of their shares of stock of a corporation to a trustee who is to vote the shares and act for such shareholders.

W

waiver: the release or relinquishment of a known right or objection.

warehouse receipt: a receipt issued by the warehouseman for goods stored with him. Regulated by the Uniform Commercial Code, which clothes the receipt with some degree of negotiability.

warehouseman: a person regularly engaged in the business of storing the goods of others for compensation. If he holds himself out to serve the public without discrimination, he is a public warehouseman.

warranties of indorser of commercial paper: the implied covenants made by an indorser of a commercial paper distinct from any undertaking to pay upon the default of the primary party.

warranties of insured: statements or promises made by the applicant for insurance which he guarantees to be as stated and which if false will entitle the insurer to avoid the contract of insurance in many jurisdictions.

warranties of seller of goods: warranties consisting of express warranties that relate to matters forming part of the basis of the bargain; warranties as to title and right to sell; and the implied warranties which the law adds to a sale depending upon the nature of the transaction.

warranty deed: a deed by which the grantor conveys a specific estate or interest to the grantee and covenants that he has transferred the estate or interest by making one or more of the covenants of title.

warranty of authority: an implied warranty of an agent that he has the authority which he purports to possess.

warranty of principal: an implied warranty of an agent that he is acting for an existing principal who has capacity to contract.

watered stock: stock issued by a corporation as fully paid when in fact it is not.

way: an easement to pass over the land of another.

will: an instrument executed with the formality required by law, by which a person makes a disposition of his property to take effect upon his death or appoints an executor.

willful: intentional as distinguished from accidental or involuntary. In penal statutes, with evil intent or legal malice, or without reasonable ground for believing one's act to be lawful.

witness: a person who has observed the facts to which he testifies or an expert witness who may testify on the basis of observation, the testimony presented in the court, or hypothetical questions put to him by the attorneys in the case.

Wool Products Labeling Act: a federal statute prohibiting the misbranding of woolen fabrics.

workmen's compensation: a system providing for payments to workmen because they have been injured from a risk arising out of the course of their employment while they were employed at their employment or have contracted an occupational disease in that manner, payment being made without consideration of the negligence of any party.

works of charity: in connection with Sunday laws, acts involved in religious worship or aiding persons in distress.

works of necessity: in connection with Sunday laws, acts that must be done at the particular time in order to be effective in saving life, health, or property.

Y

year and a day: the common-law requirement that death result within a year and a day in order to impose criminal liability for homicide.

Z

zoning restrictions: restrictions imposed by government on the use of property for the advancement of the general welfare.

Uniform Commercial Code

TITLE

AN ACT

To be known as the Uniform Commercial Code, Relating to Certain Commercial Transactions in or regarding Personal Property and Contracts and other Documents concerning them, including Sales, Commercial Paper, Bank Deposits and Collections, Letters of Credit, Bulk Transfers, Warehouse Receipts, Bills of Lading, other Documents of Title, Investment Securities, and Secured Transactions, including certain Sales of Accounts, Chattel Paper, and Contract Rights; Providing for Public Notice to Third Parties in Certain Circumstances; Regulating Procedure, Evidence and Damages in Certain Court Actions Involving such Transactions, Contracts or Documents; to Make Uniform the Law with Respect Thereto; and Repealing Inconsistent Legislation.

ARTICLE 1

GENERAL PROVISIONS

PART 1

SHORT TITLE, CONSTRUCTION, APPLICATION AND SUBECT MATTER OF THE ACT

Section 1—101. Short Title.

This Act shall be known and may be cited as Uniform Commercial Code.

Section 1—102. Purposes; Rules of Construction; Variation by Agreement.

(1) This Act shall be liberally construed and applied to promote its underlying purposes and policies.

(2) Underlying purposes and policies of this Act are

(a) to simplify, clarify and modernize the law governing commercial transactions;

(b) to permit the continued expansion of commercial practices through custom, usage and agreement of the parties;

(c) to make uniform the law among the various jurisdictions.

(3) The effect of provisions of this Act may be varied by agreement, except as otherwise provided in this Act and except that the obligations of good faith, diligence, reasonableness and care prescribed by this Act may not be disclaimed by agreement but the parties may by agreement determine the standards by which the performance of such obligations is to be measured if such standards are not manifestly unreasonable.

(4) The presence in certain provisions of this Act of the words "unless otherwise agreed" or words of similar import does not imply that the effect of other provisions may not be varied by agreement under subsection (3).

(5) In this Act unless the context otherwise requires

(a) words in the singular number include the plural, and in the plural include the singular;

(b) words of the masculine gender include the feminine and the neuter, and when the sense so indicates words of the neuter gender may refer to any gender.

Section 1—103. Supplementary General Principles of Law Applicable.

Unless displaced by the particular provisions of this Act, the principles of law and equity, including the law merchant and the law relative to capacity to contract, principal and agent, estoppel, fraud, misrepresentation, duress, coercion, mistake, bankruptcy, or other validating or invalidating cause shall supplement its provisions.

Section 1—104. Construction Against Implicit Repeal.

This Act being a general act intended as a unified coverage of its subject matter, no part of it shall be deemed to be impliedly repealed by subsequent legislation if such construction can reasonably be avoided.

Section 1—105. Territorial Application of the Act; Parties' Power to Choose Applicable Law.

(1) Except as provided hereafter in this section, when a transaction bears a reasonable relation to this state and also to another state or nation, the parties may agree that the law either of this state or of such other state or nation shall govern their rights and duties. Failing such agreement this Act applies to transactions bearing an appropriate relation to this state.

(2) Where one of the following provisions of this Act specifies the applicable law, that provision governs and a contrary agreement is effective only to the extent permitted by the law (including the conflict of laws rules) so specified:

Rights of creditors against sold goods. Section 2—402.

Applicability of the Article on Bank Deposits and Collections. Section 4—102.

Bulk transfers subject to the Article on Bulk Transfers. Section 6—102.

Applicability of the Article on Investment Securities. Section 8—106.

Policy and scope of the Article on Secured Transactions. Sections 9—102 and 9—103.

Section 1—106. Remedies to Be Liberally Administered.

(1) The remedies provided by this Act shall be liberally administered to the end that the aggrieved party may be put in as good a position as if the other party had fully performed, but neither consequential or special nor penal damages may be had except as specifically provided in this Act or by other rule of law.

(2) Any right or obligation declared by this Act is enforceable by action unless the provision declaring it specifies a different and limited effect.

Section 1—107. Waiver or Renunciation of Claim or Right After Breach.

Any claim or right arising out of an alleged breach can be discharged in whole or in part without consideration by a written waiver or renunciation signed and delivered by the aggrieved party.

Section 1—108. Severability.

If any provision or clause of this Act or application thereof to any person or circumstances is held invalid, such invalidity shall not affect other provisions or applications of the Act which can be given effect without the invalid provision or application, and to this end the provisions of this Act are declared to be severable.

Section 1—109. Section Captions.

Section captions are parts of this Act.

PART 2

GENERAL DEFINITIONS AND PRINCIPLES OF INTERPRETATION

Section 1—201. General Definitions.

Subject to additional definitions contained in the subsequent Articles of this Act which are applicable to specific Articles or Parts thereof, and unless the context otherwise requires, in this Act:

(1) "Action" in the sense of a judicial proceeding includes recoupment, counterclaim, set-off, suit in equity and any other proceedings in which rights are determined.

(2) "Aggrieved party" means a party entitled to resort to a remedy.

(3) "Agreement" means the bargain of the parties in fact as found in their language or by implication from other circumstances including course of dealing or usage of trade or course of performance as provided in this Act (Sections 1—205 and 2—208). Whether an agreement has legal consequences is determined by the provisions of this Act, if applicable; otherwise by the law of contracts (Section 1—103). (Compare "Contract".)

(4) "Bank" means any person engaged in the business of banking.

(5) "Bearer" means the person in possession of an instrument, document of title, or security payable to bearer or indorsed in blank.

(6) "Bill of lading" means a document evidencing the receipt of goods for shipment issued by a person engaged in the business of transporting or forwarding goods, and includes an airbill. "Airbill" means a document serving for air transportation as a bill of lading does for marine or rail transportation, and includes an air consignment note or air waybill.

(7) "Branch" includes a separately incorporated foreign branch of a bank.

(8) "Burden of establishing" a fact means the burden of persuading the triers of fact that the existence of the fact is more probable than its nonexistence.

(9) "Buyer in ordinary course of business" means a person who in good faith and without knowledge that the sale to him is in violation of the ownership rights or security interest of a third party in the goods buys in ordinary course from a person in the business of selling goods of that kind but does not include a pawnbroker. "Buying" may be for cash or by exchange of other property or on secured or unsecured credit and includes receiving goods or documents of title under a preexisting contract for sale but does not include a transfer in bulk or as security for or in total or partial satisfaction of a money debt.

(10) "Conspicuous": A term or clause is conspicuous when it is so written that a reasonable person against whom it is to operate ought to have noticed it. A printed heading in capitals (as: NON-NEGOTIABLE BILL OF LADING) is conspicuous. Language in the body of a form is "conspicuous" if it is in larger or other contrasting type or color. But in a telegram any stated term is "conspicuous." Whether a term or clause is "conspicuous" or not is for decision by the court.

(11) "Contract" means the total legal obligation which results from the parties' agreement as affected by this Act and any other applicable rules of law. (Compare "Agreement".)

(12) "Creditor" includes a general creditor, a secured creditor, a lien creditor and any representative of creditors, including an assignee for the benefit of creditors, a trustee in bankruptcy, a receiver in equity and an executor or administrator of an insolvent debtor's or assignor's estate.

(13) "Defendant" includes a person in the position of defendant in a crossaction or counterclaim.

(14) "Delivery" with respect to instruments, documents of title, chattel paper or securities means voluntary transfer of possession.

(15) "Document of title" includes bill of lading, dock warrant, dock receipt, warehouse receipt or order for the delivery of goods, and also any other document which in the regular course of business or financing is treated as adequately evidencing that the person in possession of it is entitled to receive, hold and dispose of the document and the goods it covers. To be a document of title a document must purport to be issued by or addressed to a bailee and purport to cover goods in the bailee's possession which are either identified or are fungible portions of an identified mass.

(16) "Fault" means wrongful act, omission or breach.

(17) "Fungible" with respect to goods or securities means goods or securities of which any unit is, by nature or usage of trade, the equivalent of any other like unit. Goods which are not fungible shall be deemed fungible for

the purposes of this Act to the extent that under a particular agreement or document unlike units are treated as equivalents.

(18) "Genuine" means free of forgery or counterfeiting.

(19) "Good faith" means honesty in fact in the conduct or transaction concerned.

(20) "Holder" means a person who is in possession of a document of title or an instrument or an investment security drawn, issued or indorsed to him or to his order or to bearer or in blank.

(21) To "honor" is to pay or to accept and pay, or where a credit so engages to purchase or discount a draft complying with the terms of the credit.

(22) "Insolvency proceedings" includes any assignment for the benefit of creditors or other proceedings intended to liquidate or rehabilitate the estate of the person involved.

(23) A person is "insolvent" who either has ceased to pay his debts in the ordinary course of business or cannot pay his debts as they become due or is insolvent within the meaning of the federal bankruptcy law.

(24) "Money" means a medium of exchange authorized or adopted by a domestic or foreign government as a part of its currency.

(25) A person has "notice" of a fact when

(a) he has actual knowledge of it; or

(b) he has received a notice or notification of it; or

(c) from all the facts and circumstances known to him at the time in question he has reason to know that it exists.

A person "knows" or has "knowledge" of a fact when he has actual knowledge of it. "Discover" or "learn" or a word or phrase of similar import refers to knowledge rather than to reason to know. The time and circumstances under which a notice or notification may cease to be effective are not determined by this Act.

(26) A person "notifies" or "gives" a notice or notification to another by taking such steps as may be reasonably required to inform the other in ordinary course whether or not such other actually comes to know of it. A person "receives" a notice or notification when

(a) it comes to his attention; or

(b) it is duly delivered at the place of business through which the contract was made or at any other place held out by him as the place for receipt of such communications.

(27) Notice, knowledge or a notice or notification received by an organization is effective for a particular transaction from the time when it is brought to the attention of the individual conducting that transaction, and in any event from the time when it would have been brought to his attention if the organization had exercised due diligence. An organization exercises due diligence if it maintains reasonable routines for communicating significant information to the person conducting the transaction and there is reasonable compliance with the routines. Due diligence does not require an individual acting for the organization to communicate information unless such communication is part of his regular duties or unless he has reason to know of the transaction and that the transaction would be materially affected by the information.

(28) "Organization" includes a corporation, government or governmental subdivision or agency, business trust, estate, trust, partnership or association, two or more persons having a joint or common interest, or any other legal or commercial entity.

(29) "Party", as distinct from "third party," means a person who has engaged in a transaction or made an agreement within this Act.

(30) "Person" includes an individual or an organization (See Section 1—102).

(31) "Presumption" or "presumed" means that the trier of fact must find the existence of the fact presumed unless and until evidence is introduced which would support a finding of its nonexistence.

(32) "Purchase" includes taking by sale, discount, negotiation, mortgage, pledge, lien, issue or re-issue, gift or any other voluntary transaction creating an interest in property.

(33) "Purchaser" means a person who takes by purchase.

(34) "Remedy" means any remedial right to which an aggrieved party is entitled with or without resort to a tribunal.

(35) "Representative" includes an agent, an officer of a corporation or association, and a trustee, executor or administrator of an estate, or any other person empowered to act for another.

(36) "Rights" includes remedies.

(37) "Security interest" means an interest in personal property or fixtures which secures payment or performance of an obligation. The retention or reservation of title by a seller of goods notwithstanding shipment or delivery to buyer (Section 2—401) is limited in effect to a reservation of a "security interest." The term also includes any interest of a buyer of accounts, chattel paper, or contract rights which is subject to Article 9. The special property interest of a buyer of goods on identification of such goods to a contract for sale under Section 2—401 is not a "security interest," but a buyer may also acquire a "security interest" by complying with Article 9. Unless a lease or consignment is intended as security, reservation of title thereunder is not a "security interest" but a consignment is in any event subject to the provisions on consignment sales (Section 2—326). Whether a lease is intended as security is to be determined by the facts of each case; however, (a) the inclusion of an option to purchase does not of itself make the lease one intended for security, and (b) an agreement that upon compliance with the terms of the lease the lessee shall become or has the option to become the owner of the property for no additional consideration or for a nominal consideration does make the lease one intended for security.

(38) "Send" in connection with any writing or notice means to deposit in the mail or deliver for transmission by any other usual means of communication with postage or cost of transmission provided for and properly addressed and in the case of an instrument to an address specified thereon or otherwise agreed, or if there be none to any address reasonable under the circumstances. The receipt of any writing or notice within the time at which it would have arrived if properly sent has the effect of a proper sending.

(39) "Signed" includes any symbol executed or adopted by a party with present intention to authenticate a writing.

(40) "Surety" includes guarantor.

(41) "Telegram" includes a message transmitted by radio, teletype, cable, any mechanical method of transmission, or the like.

(42) "Term" means that portion of an agreement which relates to a particular matter.

(43) "Unauthorized" signature or indorsement means one made without actual, implied or apparent authority and includes a forgery.

(44) "Value." Except as otherwise provided with respect to negotiable instruments and bank collections (Sections 3—303, 4—208 and 4—209) a person gives "value" for rights if he acquires them

- (a) in return for a binding commitment to extend credit or for the extension of immediately available credit whether or not drawn upon and whether or not a charge-back is provided for in the event of difficulties in collection; or
- (b) as security for or in total or partial satisfaction of a pre-existing claim; or
- (c) by accepting delivery pursuant to a pre-existing contract for purchase; or
- (d) generally, in return for any consideration sufficient to support a simple contract.

(45) "Warehouse receipt" means a receipt issued by a person engaged in the business of storing goods for hire.

(46) "Written" or "writing" includes printing, typewriting or any other intentional reduction to tangible form.

Section 1—202. Prima Facie Evidence by Third Party Documents.

A document in due form purporting to be a bill of lading, policy or certificate of insurance, official weigher's or inspector's certificate, consular invoice, or any other document authorized or required by the contract to be issued by a third party shall be prima facie evidence of its own authenticity and genuineness and of the facts stated in the document by the third party.

Section 1—203. Obligation of Good Faith.

Every contract or duty within this Act imposes an obligation of good faith in its performance or enforcement.

Section 1—204. Time; Reasonable Time; "Seasonably."

(1) Whenever this Act requires any action to be taken within a reasonable time, any time which is not manifestly unreasonable may be fixed by agreement.

(2) What is a reasonable time for taking any action depends on the nature, purpose and circumstances of such action.

(3) An action is taken "seasonably" when it is taken at or within the time agreed or if no time is agreed at or within a reasonable time.

Section 1—205. Course of Dealing and Usage of Trade.

(1) A course of dealing is a sequence of previous conduct between the parties to a particular transaction which is fairly to be regarded as establishing a common basis of understanding for interpreting their expressions and other conduct.

(2) A usage of trade is any practice or method of dealing having such regularity of observance in a place, vocation or trade as to justify an expectation that it will be observed with respect to the transaction in question. The existence and scope of such a usage are to be proved as facts. If it is established that such a usage is embodied in a written trade code or similar writing, the interpretation of the writing is for the court.

(3) A course of dealing between parties and any usage of trade in the vocation or trade in which they are engaged or of which they are or should be aware give particular meaning to and supplement or qualify terms of an agreement.

(4) The express terms of an agreement and an applicable course of dealing or usage of trade shall be construed wherever reasonable as consistent with each other; but when such construction is unreasonable, express terms control both course of dealing and usage of trade and course of dealing controls usage of trade.

(5) An applicable usage of trade in the place where any part of performance is to occur shall be used in interpreting the agreement as to that part of the performance.

(6) Evidence of a relevant usage of trade offered by one party is not admissible unless and until he has given the other party such notice as the court finds sufficient to prevent unfair surprise to the latter.

Section 1—206. Statute of Frauds for Kinds of Personal Property Not Otherwise Covered.

(1) Except in the cases described in subsection (2) of this section, a contract for the sale of personal property is not enforceable by way of action or defense beyond five thousand dollars in amount or value of remedy unless there is some writing which indicates that a contract for sale has been made between the parties at a defined or stated price, reasonably identifies the subject matter, and is signed by the party against whom enforcement is sought or by his authorized agent.

(2) Subsection (1) of this section does not apply to contracts for the sale of goods (Section 2—201) nor of securities (Section 8—319) nor to security agreements (Section 9—203).

Section 1—207. Performance or Acceptance Under Reservation of Rights.

A party who with explicit reservation of rights performs or promises performance or assents to performance in a manner demanded or offered by the other party does not thereby prejudice the rights reserved. Such words as "without prejudice", "under protest" or the like are sufficient.

Section 1—208. Option to Accelerate at Will.

A term providing that one party or his successor in interest may accelerate payment or performance or require collateral or additional collateral "at will" or "when he deems himself insecure" or in words of similar import shall be construed to mean that he shall have power to do so only if he in good faith believes that the prospect of payment or performance is impaired. The burden of establishing lack of good faith is on the party against whom the power has been exercised.

ARTICLE 2

SALES

PART 1

SHORT TITLE, GENERAL CONSTRUCTION AND SUBJECT MATTER

Section 2—101. Short Title.

This Article shall be known and may be cited as Uniform Commercial Code—Sales.

Section 2—102. Scope; Certain Security and Other Transactions Excluded from This Article.

Unless the context otherwise requires, this Article applies to transactions in goods; it does not apply to any transaction which although in the form of an unconditional contract to sell or present sale is intended to operate only as a security transaction nor does this Article impair or repeal any statute regulating sales to consumers, farmers or other specified classes of buyers.

Section 2—103. Definitions and Index of Definitions.

(1) In this Article unless the context otherwise requires

(a) "Buyer" means a person who buys or contracts to buy goods.

(b) "Good faith" in the case of a merchant means honesty in fact and the observance of reasonable commercial standards of fair dealing in the trade.

(c) "Receipt" of goods means taking physical possession of them.

(d) "Seller" means a person who sells or contracts to sell goods.

(2) Other definitions applying to this Article or to specified Parts thereof, and the sections in which they appear are:

"Acceptance". Section 2—606.
"Banker's credit". Section 2—325.
"Between merchants". Section 2—104.
"Cancellation". Section 2—106(4).
"Commercial unit". Section 2—105.
"Confirmed credit". Section 2—325.
"Conforming to contract". Section 2—106.
"Contract for sale". Section 2—106.
"Cover". Section 2—712.
"Entrusting". Section 2—403.
"Financing agency". Section 2—104.
"Future goods". Section 2—105.
"Goods". Section 2—105.
"Identification". Section 2—501.
"Installment contract". Section 2—612.
"Letter of Credit". Section 2—325.
"Lot". Section 2—105.
"Merchant". Section 2—104.
"Overseas". Section 2—323.
"Person in position of seller". Section 2—707.
"Present sale". Section 2—106.
"Sale". Section 2—106.
"Sale on approval". Section 2—326.
"Sale or return". Section 2—326.
"Termination". Section 2—106.

(3) The following definitions in other Articles apply to this Article:

"Check". Section 3—104.
"Consignee". Section 7—102.
"Consignor". Section 7—102.
"Consumer goods". Section 9—109.
"Dishonor". Section 3—507.
"Draft". Section 3—104.

(4) In addition Article 1 contains general definitions and principles of construction and interpretation applicable throughout this Article.

Section 2—104. Definitions: "Merchant"; "Between Merchants"; "Financing Agency".

(1) "Merchant" means a person who deals in goods of the kind or otherwise by his occupation holds himself out as having knowledge or skill peculiar to the practices or goods involved in the transaction or to whom such knowledge or skill may be attributed by his employment of an agent or broker or other intermediary who by his occupation holds himself out as having such knowledge or skill.

(2) "Financing agency" means a bank, finance company or other person who in the ordinary course of business makes advances against goods or documents of title or who by arrangement with either the seller or the buyer intervenes in ordinary course to make or collect payment due or claimed under the contract for sale, as by purchasing or paying the seller's draft or making advances against it or by merely taking it for collection whether or not documents of title accompany the draft. "Financing agency" includes also a bank or other person who similarly intervenes between persons who are in the position of seller and buyer in respect to the goods (Section 2—707).

(3) "Between merchants" means in any transaction with respect to which both parties are chargeable with the knowledge or skill of merchants.

Section 2—105. Definitions: Transferability; "Goods"; "Future" Goods; "Lot"; "Commercial Unit".

(1) "Goods" means all things (including specially manufactured goods) which are movable at the time of identification to the contract for sale other than the money in which the price is to be paid, investment securities (Article 8) and things in action. "Goods" also includes the unborn young of animals and growing crops and other identified things attached to realty as described in the section on goods to be severed from realty (Section 2—107).

(2) Goods must be both existing and identified before any interest in them can pass. Goods which are not both existing and identified are "future" goods. A purported present sale of future goods or of any interest therein operates as a contract to sell.

(3) There may be a sale of a part interest in existing identified goods.

(4) An undivided share in an identified bulk of fungible goods is sufficiently identified to be sold although the quantity of the bulk is not determined. Any agreed proportion of such a bulk or any quantity thereof agreed upon by number, weight or other measure may to the extent of the seller's interest in the bulk be sold to the buyer who then becomes an owner in common.

(5) "Lot" means a parcel or a single article which is the subject matter of a separate sale or delivery, whether or not it is sufficient to perform the contract.

(6) "Commercial unit" means such a unit of goods as by commercial usage is a single whole for purposes of sale and division of which materially impairs its character or value on the market or in use. A commercial unit may be a single article (as a machine) or a set of articles (as a suite of furniture or an assortment of sizes) or a quantity (as a bale, gross, or carload) or any other unit treated in use or in the relevant market as a single whole.

Section 2—106. Definitions: "Contract"; "Agreement"; "Contract for Sale"; "Sale"; "Present Sale"; "Conforming to Contract"; "Termination"; "Cancellation".

(1) In this Article unless the context otherwise requires, "contract" and "agreement" are limited to those relating to the present or future sale of goods. "Contract for sale" includes both a present sale of goods and a contract to sell goods at a future time. A "sale" consists in the passing of title from the seller to the buyer for a price (Section 2—401). A "present sale" means a sale which is accomplished by the making of the contract.

(2) Goods or conduct including any part of a performance are "conforming" or conform to the contract when they are in accordance with the obligations under the contract.

(3) "Termination" occurs when either party pursuant to a power created by agreement or law puts an end to the contract otherwise than for its breach. On "termination" all obligations which are still executory on both sides are discharged but any right based on prior breach or performance survives.

(4) "Cancellation" occurs when either party puts an end to the contract for breach by the other and its effect is the same as that of "termination" except that the cancelling party also retains any remedy for breach of the whole contract or any unperformed balance.

Section 2—107. Goods to Be Severed from Realty: Recording.

(1) A contract for the sale of timber, minerals or the like or a structure or its materials

to be removed from realty is a contract for the sale of goods within this Article if they are to be severed by the seller, but until severance a purported present sale thereof which is not effective as a transfer of an interest in land is effective only as a contract to sell.

(2) A contract for the sale apart from the land of growing crops or other things attached to realty and capable of severance without material harm thereto but not described in subsection (1) is a contract for the sale of goods within this Article whether the subject matter is to be severed by the buyer or by the seller even though it forms part of the realty at the time of contracting, and the parties can by identification effect a present sale before severance.

(3) The provisions of this section are subject to any third party rights provided by the law relating to realty records, and the contract for sale may be executed and recorded as a document transferring an interest in land and shall then constitute notice to third parties of the buyer's rights under the contract for sale.

PART 2

FORM, FORMATION AND READJUSTMENT OF CONTRACT

Section 2—201. Formal Requirements; Statute of Frauds.

(1) Except as otherwise provided in this section, a contract for the sale of goods for the price of $500 or more is not enforceable by way of action or defense unless there is some writing sufficient to indicate that a contract for sale has been made between the parties and signed by the party against whom enforcement is sought or by his authorized agent or broker. A writing is not insufficient because it omits or incorrectly states a term agreed upon but the contract is not enforceable under this paragraph beyond the quantity of goods shown in such writing.

(2) Between merchants if within a reasonable time a writing in confirmation of the contract and sufficient against the sender is received and the party receiving it has reason to know its contents, it satisfies the requirements of subsection (1) against such party unless written notice of objection to its contents is given within ten days after it is received.

(3) A contract which does not satisfy the requirements of subsection (1) but which is valid in other respects is enforceable

(a) if the goods are to be specially manufactured for the buyer and are not suitable for sale to others in the ordinary course of the seller's business and the seller, before notice of repudiation is received and under circumstances which reasonably indicate that the goods are for the buyer, has made either a substantial beginning of their manufacture or commitments for their procurement; or

(b) if the party against whom enforcement is sought admits in his pleading, testimony or otherwise in court that a contract for sale was made, but the contract is not enforceable under this provision beyond the quantity of goods admitted; or

(c) with respect to goods for which payment has been made and accepted or which have been received and accepted (Section 2—606).

Section 2—202. Final Written Expression: Parol or Extrinsic Evidence.

Terms with respect to which the confirmatory memoranda of the parties agree or which are otherwise set forth in a writing intended by the parties as a final expression of their agreement with respect to such terms as are included therein may not be contradicted by evidence of any prior agreement or of a contemporaneous oral agreement but may be explained or supplemented

(a) by course of dealing or usage of trade (Section 1—205) or by course of performance (Section 2—208); and

(b) by evidence of consistent additional terms unless the court finds the writing to have been intended also as a complete and exclusive statement of the terms of the agreement.

Section 2—203. Seals Inoperative.

The affixing of a seal to a writing evidencing a contract for sale or an offer to buy or sell goods does not constitute the writing a sealed instrument, and the law with respect to sealed instruments does not apply to such a contract or offer.

Section 2—204. Formation in General.

(1) A contract for sale of goods may be made in any manner sufficient to show agreement, including conduct by both parties which recognizes the existence of such a contract.

(2) An agreement sufficient to constitute a contract for sale may be found even though the moment of its making is undetermined.

(3) Even though one or more terms are left open, a contract for sale does not fail for indefiniteness if the parties have intended to make a contract and there is a reasonably certain basis for giving an appropriate remedy.

Section 2—205. Firm Offers.

An offer by a merchant to buy or sell goods in a signed writing which by its terms gives assurance that it will be held open is not revocable, for lack of consideration, during the time stated or if no time is stated for a reasonable time, but in no event may such period of irrevocability exceed three months; but any such term of assurance on a form supplied by the offeree must be separately signed by the offeror.

Section 2—206. Offer and Acceptance in Formation of Contract.

(1) Unless otherwise unambiguously indicated by the language or circumstances

(a) an offer to make a contract shall be construed as inviting acceptance in any manner and by any medium reasonable in the circumstances;

(b) an order or other offer to buy goods for prompt or current shipment shall be construed as inviting acceptance either by a prompt promise to ship or by the prompt or current shipment of conforming or non-conforming goods, but such a shipment of non-conforming goods does not constitute an acceptance if the seller seasonably notifies the buyer that the shipment is offered only as an accommodation to the buyer.

(2) Where the beginning of a requested performance is a reasonable mode of acceptance, an offeror who is not notified of acceptance within a reasonable time may treat the offer as having lapsed before acceptance.

Section 2—207. Additional Terms in Acceptance or Confirmation.

(1) A definite and seasonable expression of acceptance or a written confirmation which is sent within a reasonable time operates as an acceptance even though it states terms additional to or different from those offered or agreed upon, unless acceptance is expressly made conditional on assent to the additional or different terms.

(2) The additional terms are to be construed as proposals for addition to the contract. Between merchants such terms become part of the contract unless

(a) the offer expressly limits acceptance to the terms of the offer;

(b) they materially alter it; or

(c) notification of objection to them has already been given or is given within a reasonable time after notice of them is received.

(3) Conduct by both parties which recognizes the existence of a contract is sufficient to establish a contract for sale although the writings of the parties do not otherwise establish a contract. In such case the terms of the particular contract consist of those terms on which the writings of the parties agree, together with any supplementary terms incorporated under any other provisions of this Act.

Section 2—208. Course of Performance or Practical Construction.

(1) Where the contract for sale involves repeated occasions for performance by either party with knowledge of the nature of the performance and opportunity for objection to it by the other, any course of performance accepted or acquiesced in without objection shall be relevant to determine the meaning of the agreement.

(2) The express terms of the agreement and any such course of performance, as well as any course of dealing and usage of trade, shall be construed whenever reasonable as consistent with each other; but when such construction is unreasonable, express terms shall control course of performance and course of performance shall control both course of dealing and usage of trade (Section 1—205).

(3) Subject to the provisions of the next section on modification and waiver, such course of performance shall be relevant to show a waiver or modification of any term inconsistent with such course of performance.

Section 2—209. Modification, Rescission and Waiver.

(1) An agreement modifying a contract within this Article needs no consideration to be binding.

(2) A signed agreement which excludes modification or rescission except by a signed writing cannot be otherwise modified or rescinded, but except as between merchants such a requirement on a form supplied by the merchant must be separately signed by the other party.

(3) The requirements of the statute of frauds section of this Article (Section 2—201) must be satisfied if the contract as modified is within its provisions.

(4) Although an attempt at modification or rescission does not satisfy the requirements of subsection (2) or (3) it can operate as a waiver.

(5) A party who has made a waiver affecting an executory portion of the contract may retract the waiver by reasonable notification received by the other party that strict performance will be required of any term waived, unless the retraction would be unjust in view of a material change of position in reliance on the waiver.

Section 2—210. Delegation of Performance; Assignment of Rights.

(1) A party may perform his duty through a delegate unless otherwise agreed or unless the other party has a substantial interest in having his original promisor perform or control the acts required by the contract. No delegation of performance relieves the party delegating of any duty to perform or any liability for breach.

(2) Unless otherwise agreed all rights of either seller or buyer can be assigned except where the assignment would materially change the duty of the other party, or increase materially the burden or risk imposed on him by his contract, or impair materially his chance of obtaining return performance. A right to damages for breach of the whole contract or a right arising out of the assignor's due performance of his entire obligation can be assigned despite agreement otherwise.

(3) Unless the circumstances indicate the contrary, a prohibition of assignment of "the contract" is to be construed as barring only the delegation to the assignee of the assignor's performance.

(4) An assignment of "the contract" or of "all my rights under the contract" or an assignment in similar general terms is an assignment of rights and unless the language or the circumstances (as in an assignment for security) indicate the contrary, it is a delegation of performance of the duties of the assignor and its acceptance by the assignee constitutes a promise by him to perform those duties. The promise is enforceable by either the assignor or the other party to the original contract.

(5) The other party may treat any assignment which delegates performance as creating reasonable grounds for insecurity and may without prejudice to his rights against the assignor demand assurances from the assignee (Section 2—609).

PART 3

GENERAL OBLIGATION AND CONSTRUCTION OF CONTRACT

Section 2—301. General Obligations of Parties.

The obligation of the seller is to transfer and deliver and that of the buyer is to accept and pay in accordance with the contract.

Section 2—302. Unconscionable Contract or Clause.

(1) If the court as a matter of law finds the contract or any clause of the contract to

have been unconscionable at the time it was made, the court may refuse to enforce the contract, or it may enforce the remainder of the contract without the unconscionable clause, or it may so limit the application of any unconscionable clause as to avoid any unconscionable result.

(2) When it is claimed or appears to the court that the contract or any clause thereof may be unconscionable, the parties shall be afforded a reasonable opportunity to present evidence as to its commercial setting, purpose and effect to aid the court in making the determination.

Section 2—303. Allocation or Division of Risks.

Where this Article allocates a risk or a burden as between the parties "unless otherwise agreed", the agreement may not only shift the allocation but may also divide the risk or burden.

Section 2—304. Price Payable in Money, Goods, Realty, or Otherwise.

(1) The price can be made payable in money or otherwise. If it is payable in whole or in part in goods, each party is a seller of the goods which he is to transfer.

(2) Even though all or part of the price is payable in an interest in realty, the transfer of the goods and the seller's obligations with reference to them are subject to this Article, but not the transfer of the interest in realty or the transferor's obligations in connection therewith.

Section 2—305. Open Price Term.

(1) The parties if they so intend can conclude a contract for sale even though the price is not settled. In such a case the price is a reasonable price at the time for delivery if

(a) nothing is said as to price; or
(b) the price is left to be agreed by the parties and they fail to agree; or
(c) the price is to be fixed in terms of some agreed market or other standard as set or recorded by a third person or agency and it is not so set or recorded.

(2) A price to be fixed by the seller or by the buyer means a price for him to fix in good faith.

(3) When a price left to be fixed otherwise than by agreement of parties fails to be fixed through fault of one party, the other may at his option treat the contract as cancelled or himself fix a reasonable price.

(4) Where, however, the parties intend not to be bound unless the price be fixed or agreed and it is not fixed or agreed, there is no contract. In such a case the buyer must return any goods already received or if unable so to do must pay their reasonable value at the time of delivery and the seller must return any portion of the price paid on account.

Section 2—306. Output, Requirements and Exclusive Dealings.

(1) A term which measures the quantity by the output of the seller or the requirements of the buyer means such actual output or requirements as may occur in good faith, except that no quantity unreasonably disproportionate to any stated estimate or in the absence of a stated estimate to any normal or otherwise comparable prior output or requirements may be tendered or demanded.

(2) A lawful agreement by either the seller or the buyer for exclusive dealing in the kind of goods concerned imposes unless otherwise agreed an obligation by the seller to use best efforts to supply the goods and by the buyer to use best efforts to promote their sale.

Section 2—307. Delivery in Single Lot or Several Lots.

Unless otherwise agreed all goods called for by a contract for sale must be tendered in a single delivery and payment is due only on such tender, but where the circumstances give either party the right to make or demand delivery in lots the price if it can be apportioned may be demanded for each lot.

Section 2—308. Absence of Specified Place for Delivery.

Unless otherwise agreed

(a) the place for delivery of goods is the seller's place of business or if he has none his residence; but
(b) in a contract for sale of identified goods which to the knowledge of

the parties at the time of contracting are in some other place, that place is the place for their delivery; and

(c) documents of title may be delivered through customary banking channels.

Section 2—309. Absence of Specific Time Provisions; Notice of Termination.

(1) The time for shipment or delivery or any other action under a contract if not provided in this Article or agreed upon shall be a reasonable time.

(2) Where the contract provides for successive performances but is indefinite in duration it is valid for a reasonable time but unless otherwise agreed may be terminated at any time by either party.

(3) Termination of a contract by one party except on the happening of an agreed event requires that reasonable notification be received by the other party and an agreement dispensing with notification is invalid if its operation would be unconscionable.

Section 2—310. Open Time for Payment or Running of Credit; Authority to Ship Under Reservation.

Unless otherwise agreed

(a) payment is due at the time and place at which the buyer is to receive the goods even though the place of shipment is the place of delivery; and

(b) if the seller is authorized to send the goods he may ship them under reservation, and may tender the documents of title, but the buyer may inspect the goods after their arrival before payment is due unless such inspection is inconsistent with the terms of the contract (Section 2—513); and

(c) if delivery is authorized and made by way of documents of title otherwise than by subsection (b) then payment is due at the time and place at which the buyer is to receive the documents regardless of where the goods are to be received; and

(d) where the seller is required or authorized to ship the goods on credit the credit period runs from the time of shipment but post-dating the invoice or delaying its dispatch will correspondingly delay the starting of the credit period.

Section 2—311. Options and Cooperation Respecting Performance.

(1) An agreement for sale which is otherwise sufficiently definite (subsection (3) of Section 2—204) to be a contract is not made invalid by the fact that it leaves particulars of performance to be specified by one of the parties. Any such specification must be made in good faith and within limits set by commercial reasonableness.

(2) Unless otherwise agreed specifications relating to assortment of the goods are at the buyer's option and except as otherwise provided in subsections (1) (c) and (3) of Section 2—319 specifications or arrangements relating to shipment are at the seller's option.

(3) Where such specification would materially affect the other party's performance but is not seasonably made or where one party's cooperation is necessary to the agreed performance of the other but is not seasonably forthcoming, the other party in addition to all other remedies

(a) is excused for any resulting delay in his own performance; and

(b) may also either proceed to perform in any reasonable manner or after the time for a material part of his own performance treat the failure to specify or to cooperate as a breach by failure to deliver or accept the goods.

Section 2—312. Warranty of Title and Against Infringement; Buyer's Obligation Against Infringement.

(1) Subject to subsection (2) there is in a contract for sale a warranty by the seller that

(a) the title conveyed shall be good, and its transfer rightful; and

(b) the goods shall be delivered free from any security interest or other

deals with merchants not casual seller

lien or encumbrance of which the buyer at the time of contracting has no knowledge.

(2) A warranty under subsection (1) will be excluded or modified only by specific language or by circumstances which give the buyer reason to know that the person selling does not claim title in himself or that he is purporting to sell only such right or title as he or a third person may have.

(3) Unless otherwise agreed a seller who is a merchant regularly dealing in goods of the kind warrants that the goods shall be delivered free of the rightful claim of any third person by way of infringement or the like, but a buyer who furnishes specifications to the seller must hold the seller harmless against any such claim which arises out of compliance with the specifications.

Section 2—313. Express Warranties by Affirmation, Promise, Description, Sample.

(1) Express warranties by the seller are created as follows:

(a) Any affirmation of fact or promise made by the seller to the buyer which relates to the goods and becomes part of the basis of the bargain creates an express warranty that the goods shall conform to the affirmation or promise.

(b) Any description of the goods which is made part of the basis of the bargain creates an express warranty that the goods shall conform to the description.

(c) Any sample or model which is made part of the basis of the bargain creates an express warranty that the whole of the goods shall conform to the sample or model.

(2) It is not necessary to the creation of an express warranty that the seller use formal words such as "warrant" or "guarantee" or that he have a specific intention to make a warranty, but an affirmation merely of the value of the goods or a statement purporting to be merely the seller's opinion or commendation of the goods does not create a warranty.

Section 2—314. Implied Warranty: Merchantability; Usage of Trade.

(1) Unless excluded or modified (Section 2—316), a warranty that the goods shall be merchantable is implied in a contract for their sale if the seller is a merchant with respect to goods of that kind. Under this section the serving for value of food or drink to be consumed either on the premises or elsewhere is a sale.

(2) Goods to be merchantable must be at least such as

(a) pass without objection in the trade under the contract description; and

(b) in the case of fungible goods, are of fair average quality within the description; and

(c) are fit for the ordinary purposes for which such goods are used; and

(d) run, within the variations permitted by the agreement, of even kind, quality and quantity within each unit and among all units involved; and

(e) are adequately contained, packaged, and labeled as the agreement may require; and

(f) conform to the promises or affirmations of fact made on the container or label if any.

(3) Unless excluded or modified (Section 2—316) other implied warranties may arise from course of dealing or usage of trade.

Section 2—315. Implied Warranty: Fitness for Particular Purpose.

Where the seller at the time of contracting has reason to know any particular purpose for which the goods are required and that the buyer is relying on the seller's skill or judgment to select or furnish suitable goods, there is unless excluded or modified under the next section an implied warranty that the goods shall be fit for such purpose.

Section 2—316. Exclusion or Modification of Warranties.

(1) Words or conduct relevant to the creation of an express warranty and words or conduct tending to negate or limit warranty shall be construed wherever reasonable as consistent

with each other; but subject to the provisions of this Article on parol or extrinsic evidence (Section 2—202) negation or limitation is inoperative to the extent that such construction is unreasonable.

(2) Subject to subsection (3), to exclude or modify the implied warranty of merchantability or any part of it the language must mention merchantability and in case of a writing must be conspicuous, and to exclude or modify any implied warranty of fitness the exclusion must be by a writing and conspicuous. Language to exclude all implied warranties of fitness is sufficient if it states, for example, that "There are no warranties which extend beyond the description on the face hereof."

(3) Notwithstanding subsection (2)

(a) unless the circumstances indicate otherwise, all implied warranties are excluded by expressions like "as is", "with all faults" or other language which in common understanding calls the buyer's attention to the exclusion of warranties and makes plain that there is no implied warranty; and

(b) when the buyer before entering into the contract has examined the goods or the sample or model as fully as he desired or has refused to examine the goods, there is no implied warranty with regard to defects which an examination ought in the circumstances to have revealed to him; and

(c) an implied warranty can also be excluded or modified by course of dealing or course of performance or usage of trade.

(4) Remedies for breach of warranty can be limited in accordance with the provisions of this Article on liquidation or limitation of damages and on contractual modification of remedy (Sections 2—718 and 2—719).

Section 2—317. Cumulation and Conflict of Warranties Express or Implied.

Warranties whether express or implied shall be construed as consistent with each other and as cumulative, but if such construction is unreasonable the intention of the parties shall determine which warranty is dominant. In ascertaining that intention the following rules apply:

(a) Exact or technical specifications displace an inconsistent sample or model or general language of description.

(b) A sample from an existing bulk displaces inconsistent general language of description.

(c) Express warranties displace inconsistent implied warranties other than an implied warranty of fitness for a particular purpose.

Section 2—318. Third Party Beneficiaries of Warranties Express or Implied.

A seller's warranty whether express or implied extends to any natural person who is in the family or household of his buyer or who is a guest in his home if it is reasonable to expect that such person may use, consume or be affected by the goods and who is injured in person by breach of the warranty. A seller may not exclude or limit the operation of this section.

Section 2—319. F.O.B. and F.A.S. Terms.

(1) Unless otherwise agreed the term F.O.B. (which means "free on board") at a named place, even though used only in connection with the stated price, is a delivery term under which

(a) when the term is F.O.B. the place of shipment, the seller must at that place ship the goods in the manner provided in this Article (Section 2—504) and bear the expense and risk of putting them into the possession of the carrier; or

(b) when the term is F.O.B. the place of destination, the seller must at his own expense and risk transport the goods to that place and there tender delivery of them in the manner provided in this Article (Section 2—503);

(c) when under either (a) or (b) the term is also F.O.B. vessel, car or other vehicle, the seller must in addition at his own expense and risk load the goods on board. If the term is F.O.B. vessel, the buyer must name the vessel and in an appropriate case the seller must comply with the provisions of this Article on the form of bill of lading (Section 2—323).

(2) Unless otherwise agreed the term F.A.S. vessel (which means "free alongside") at a named port, even though used only in connection with the stated price, is a delivery term under which the seller must

(a) at his own expense and risk deliver the goods alongside the vessel in the manner usual in that port or on a dock designated and provided by the buyer; and

(b) obtain and tender a receipt for the goods in exchange for which the carrier is under a duty to issue a bill of lading.

(3) Unless otherwise agreed in any case falling within subsection (1) (a) or (c) or subsection (2) the buyer must seasonably give any needed instructions for making delivery, including when the term is F.A.S. or F.O.B. the loading berth of the vessel and in an appropriate case its name and sailing date. The seller may treat the failure of needed instructions as a failure of cooperation under this Article (Section 2—311). He may also at his option move the goods in any reasonable manner preparatory to delivery or shipment.

(4) Under the term F.O.B. vessel or F.A.S. unless otherwise agreed the buyer must make payment against tender of the required documents and the seller may not tender nor the buyer demand delivery of the goods in substitution for the documents.

Section 2—320. C.I.F. and C. & F. Terms.

(1) The term C.I.F. means that the price includes in a lump sum the cost of the goods and the insurance and freight to the named destination. The term C. & F. or C.F. means that the price so includes cost and freight to the named destination.

(2) Unless otherwise agreed and even though used only in connection with the stated price and destination, the term C.I.F. destination or its equivalent requires the seller at his own expense and risk to

(a) put the goods into the possession of a carrier at the port for shipment and obtain a negotiable bill or bills of lading covering the entire transportation to the named destination; and

(b) load the goods and obtain a receipt from the carrier (which may be contained in the bill of lading) showing that the freight has been paid or provided for; and

(c) obtain a policy or certificate of insurance, including any war risk insurance, of a kind and on terms then current at the port of shipment in the usual amount, in the currency of the contract, shown to cover the same goods covered by the bill of lading and providing for payment of loss to the order of the buyer or for the account of whom it may concern; but the seller may add to the price the amount of the premium for any such war risk insurance; and

(d) prepare an invoice of the goods and procure any other documents required to effect shipment or to comply with the contract; and

(e) forward and tender with commercial promptness all the documents in due form and with any indorsement necessary to perfect the buyer's rights.

(3) Unless otherwise agreed the term C. & F. or its equivalent has the same effect and imposes upon the seller the same obligations and risks as a C.I.F. term except the obligation as to insurance.

(4) Under the term C.I.F. or C. & F. unless otherwise agreed the buyer must make payment against tender of the required documents and the seller may not tender nor the buyer demand delivery of the goods in substitution for the documents.

Section 2—321. C.I.F. or C. & F.: "Net Landed Weights"; "Payment on Arrival"; Warranty of Condition on Arrival.

Under a contract containing a term C.I.F. or C. & F.

(1) Where the price is based on or is to be adjusted according to "net landed weights", "delivered weights", "out turn" quantity or quality or the like, unless otherwise agreed the seller must reasonably estimate the price. The payment due on tender of the documents called for by the contract is the amount so estimated, but after final adjustment of the price a settlement must be made with commercial promptness.

(2) An agreement described in subsection (1) or any warranty of quality or condition of the goods on arrival places upon the seller the risk of ordinary deterioration, shrinkage and the like in transportation but has no effect on the place or time of identification to the contract for sale or delivery or on the passing of the risk of loss.

(3) Unless otherwise agreed, where the contract provides for payment on or after arrival of the goods, the seller must before payment allow such preliminary inspection as is feasible; but if the goods are lost, delivery of the documents and payment are due when the goods should have arrived.

Section 2—322. Delivery "Ex-Ship".

(1) Unless otherwise agreed a term for delivery of goods "ex-ship" (which means from the carrying vessel) or in equivalent language is not restricted to a particular ship and requires delivery from a ship which has reached a place at the named port of destination where goods of the kind are usually discharged.

(2) Under such a term unless otherwise agreed

(a) the seller must discharge all liens arising out of the carriage and furnish the buyer with a direction which puts the carrier under a duty to deliver the goods; and

(b) the risk of loss does not pass to the buyer until the goods leave the ship's tackle or are otherwise properly unloaded.

Section 2—323. Form of Bill of Lading Required in Overseas Shipment; "Overseas".

(1) Where the contract contemplates overseas shipment and contains a term C.I.F. or C. & F. or F.O.B. vessel, the seller unless otherwise agreed must obtain a negotiable bill of lading stating that the goods have been loaded on board or, in the case of a term C.I.F. or C. & F., received for shipment.

(2) Where in a case within subsection (1) a bill of lading has been issued in a set of parts, unless otherwise agreed if the documents are not to be sent from abroad the buyer may demand tender of the full set; otherwise only one part of the bill of lading need be tendered. Even if the agreement expressly requires a full set

(a) due tender of a single part is acceptable within the provisions of this Article on cure of improper delivery (subsection (1) of Section 2—508); and

(b) even though the full set is demanded, if the documents are sent from abroad the person tendering an incomplete set may nevertheless require payment upon furnishing an indemnity which the buyer in good faith deems adequate.

(3) A shipment by water or by air or a contract contemplating such shipment is "overseas" insofar as by usage of trade or agreement it is subject to the commercial, financing or shipping practices characteristic of international deep water commerce.

Section 2—324. "No Arrival, No Sale" Term.

Under a term "no arrival, no sale" or terms of like meaning, unless otherwise agreed,

(a) the seller must properly ship conforming goods and if they arrive by any means he must tender them on arrival, but he assumes no obligation that the goods will arrive unless he has caused the non-arrival; and

(b) where without fault of the seller the goods are in part lost or have so deteriorated as no longer to conform to the contract or arrive after the contract time, the buyer may proceed as if there had been casualty to identified goods (Section 2—613).

Section 2—325. "Letter of Credit" Term; "Confirmed Credit".

(1) Failure of the buyer seasonably to furnish an agreed letter of credit is a breach of the contract for sale.

(2) The delivery to seller of a proper letter of credit suspends the buyer's obligation to pay. If the letter of credit is dishonored, the seller may on seasonable notification to the buyer require payment directly from him.

(3) Unless otherwise agreed the term "letter of credit" or "banker's credit" in a contract for sale means an irrevocable credit issued by a financing agency of good repute and, where the shipment is overseas, of good international repute. The term "confirmed credit" means that the credit must also carry the direct obligation of such an agency which does business in the seller's financial market.

Section 2—326. Sale on Approval and Sale or Return; Consignment Sales and Rights of Creditors.

(1) Unless otherwise agreed, if delivered goods may be returned by the buyer even though they conform to the contract, the transaction is

(a) a "sale on approval" if the goods are delivered primarily for use, and

(b) a "sale or return" if the goods are delivered primarily for resale.

(2) Except as provided in subsection (3), goods held on approval are not subject to the claims of the buyer's creditors until acceptance; goods held on sale or return are subject to such claims while in the buyer's possession.

(3) Where goods are delivered to a person for sale and such person maintains a place of business at which he deals in goods of the kind involved, under a name other than the name of the person making delivery, then with respect to claims of creditors of the person conducting the business the goods are deemed to be on sale or return. The provisions of this subsection are applicable even though an agreement purports to reserve title to the person making delivery until payment or resale or uses such words as "on consignment" or "on memorandum". However, this subsection is not applicable if the person making delivery

(a) complies with an applicable law providing for a consignor's interest or the like to be evidenced by a sign, or

(b) establishes that the person conducting the business is generally known by his creditors to be substantially engaged in selling the goods of others, or

(c) complies with the filing provisions of the Article on Secured Transactions (Article 9).

(4) Any "or return" term of a contract for sale is to be treated as a separate contract for sale within the statute of frauds section of this Article (Section 2—201) and as contradicting the sale aspect of the contract within the provisions of this Article on parol or extrinsic evidence (Section 2—202).

Section 2—327. Special Incidents of Sale on Approval and Sale or Return.

(1) Under a sale on approval unless otherwise agreed

(a) although the goods are identified to the contract, the risk of loss and the title do not pass to the buyer until acceptance; and

(b) use of the goods consistent with the purpose of trial is not acceptance but failure seasonably to notify the seller of election to return the goods is acceptance, and if the goods conform to the contract acceptance of any part is acceptance of the whole; and

(c) after due notification of election to return, the return is at the seller's risk and expense but a merchant buyer must follow any reasonable instructions.

(2) Under a sale or return unless otherwise agreed

(a) the option to return extends to the whole or any commercial unit of the goods while in substantially their original condition, but must be exercised seasonably; and

(b) the return is at the buyer's risk and expense.

Section 2—328. Sale by Auction.

(1) In a sale by auction if goods are put up in lots each lot is the subject of a separate sale.

(2) A sale by auction is complete when the auctioneer so announces by the fall of the hammer or in other customary manner. Where a bid is made while the hammer is falling in acceptance of a prior bid, the auctioneer may in his discretion reopen the bidding or declare the goods sold under the bid on which the hammer was falling.

(3) Such a sale is with reserve unless the goods are in explicit terms put up without reserve. In an auction with reserve the auctioneer may withdraw the goods at any time until he announces completion of the sale. In an auction without reserve, after the auctioneer calls for bids on an article or lot, that article or lot cannot be withdrawn unless no bid is made within a reasonable time. In either case a bidder may retract his bid until the auctioneer's announcement of completion of the sale, but a bidder's retraction does not revive any previous bid.

(4) If the auctioneer knowingly receives a bid on the seller's behalf or the seller makes or procures such a bid, and notice has not been given that liberty for such bidding is reserved, the buyer may at his option avoid the sale or take the goods at the price of the last good faith bid prior to the completion of the sale. This subsection shall not apply to any bid at a forced sale.

PART 4

TITLE, CREDITORS AND GOOD FAITH PURCHASERS

Section 2—401. Passing of Title; Reservation for Security; Limited Application of This Section.

Each provision of this Article with regard to the rights, obligations and remedies of the seller, the buyer, purchasers or other third parties applies irrespective of title to the goods except where the provision refers to such title. Insofar as situations are not covered by the other provisions of this Article and matters concerning title become material the following rules apply:

(1) Title to goods cannot pass under a contract for sale prior to their identification to the contract (Section 2—501), and unless otherwise explicitly agreed the buyer acquires by their identification a special property as limited by this Act. Any retention or reservation by the seller of the title (property) in goods shipped or delivered to the buyer is limited in effect to a reservation of a security interest. Subject to these provisions and to the provisions of the Article on Secured Transactions (Article 9), title to goods passes from the seller to the buyer in any manner and on any conditions explicitly agreed on by the parties.

(2) Unless otherwise explicitly agreed, title passes to the buyer at the time and place at which the seller completes his performance with reference to the physical delivery of the goods, despite any reservation of a security interest and even though a document of title is to be delivered at a different time or place; and in particular and despite any reservation of a security interest by the bill of lading

(a) if the contract requires or authorizes the seller to send the goods to the buyer but does not require him to deliver them at destination, title passes to the buyer at the time and place of shipment; but

(b) if the contract requires delivery at destination, title passes on tender there.

(3) Unless otherwise explicitly agreed where delivery is to be made without moving the goods,

(a) if the seller is to deliver a document of title, titles passes at the time when and the place where he delivers such documents; or

(b) if the goods are at the time of contracting already identified and no documents are to be delivered, title passes at the time and place of contracting.

(4) A rejection or other refusal by the buyer to receive or retain the goods, whether or not justified, or a justified revocation of acceptance

revests title to the goods in the seller. Such re-vesting occurs by operation of law and is not a "sale".

Section 2—402. Rights of Seller's Creditors Against Sold Goods.

(1) Except as provided in subsections (2) and (3), rights of unsecured creditors of the seller with respect to goods which have been identified to a contract for sale are subject to the buyer's rights to recover the goods under this Article (Sections 2—502 and 2—716).

(2) A creditor of the seller may treat a sale or an identification of goods to a contract for sale as void if as against him a retention of possession by the seller is fraudulent under any rule of law of the state where the goods are situated, except that retention of possession in good faith and current course of trade by a merchant-seller for a commercially reasonable time after a sale or identification is not fraudulent.

(3) Nothing in this Article shall be deemed to impair the rights of creditors of the seller

(a) under the provisions of the Article on Secured Transactions (Article 9); or

(b) where identification to the contract or delivery is made not in current course of trade but in satisfaction of or as security for a pre-existing claim for money, security or the like and is made under circumstances which under any rule of law of the state where the goods are situated would apart from this Article constitute the transaction a fraudulent transfer or voidable preference.

Section 2—403. Power to Transfer; Good Faith Purchase of Goods; "Entrusting".

(1) A purchaser of goods acquires all title which his transferor had or had power to transfer except that a purchaser of a limited interest acquires rights only to the extent of the interest purchased. A person with voidable title has power to transfer a good title to a good faith purchaser for value. When goods have been delivered under a transaction of purchase, the purchaser has such power even though

(a) the transferor was deceived as to the identity of the purchaser, or

(b) the delivery was in exchange for a check which is later dishonored, or

(c) it was agreed that the transaction was to be a "cash sale", or

(d) the delivery was procured through fraud punishable as larcenous under the criminal law.

(2) Any entrusting of possession of goods to a merchant who deals in goods of that kind gives him power to transfer all rights of the entruster to a buyer in ordinary course of business.

(3) "Entrusting" includes any delivery and any acquiescence in retention of possession regardless of any condition expressed between the parties to the delivery or acquiescence and regardless of whether the procurement of the entrusting or the possessor's disposition of the goods have been such as to be larcenous under the criminal law.

(4) The rights of other purchasers of goods and of lien creditors are governed by the Articles on Secured Transactions (Article 9), Bulk Transfers (Article 6) and Documents of Title (Article 7).

PART 5

PERFORMANCE

Section 2—501. Insurable Interest in Goods; Manner of Identification of Goods.

(1) The buyer obtains a special property and an insurable interest in goods by identification of existing goods as goods to which the contract refers even though the goods so identified are nonconforming and he has an option to return or reject them. Such identification can be made at any time and in any manner explicitly agreed to by the parties. In the absence of explicit agreement identification occurs

(a) when the contract is made if it is for the sale of goods already existing and identified;

(b) if the contract is for the sale of future goods other than those described in paragraph (c), when goods are shipped, marked or otherwise designated by the seller as goods to which the contract refers;

(c) when the crops are planted or otherwise become growing crops or the young are conceived if the contract is for the sale of unborn young to be born within twelve months after contracting or for the sale of crops to be harvested within twelve months or the next normal harvest season after contracting whichever is longer.

(2) The seller retains an insurable interest in goods so long as title to or any security interest in the goods remains in him, and where the identification is by the seller alone he may, until default or insolvency or notification to the buyer that the identification is final, substitute other goods for those identified.

(3) Nothing in this section impairs any insurable interest recognized under any other statute or rule of law.

Section 2—502. Buyer's Right to Goods on Seller's Insolvency.

(1) Subject to subsection (2) and even though the goods have not been shipped, a buyer who has paid a part or all of the price of goods in which he has a special property under the provisions of the immediately preceding section may on making and keeping good a tender of any unpaid portion of their price recover them from the seller if the seller becomes insolvent within ten days after receipt of the first installment on their price.

(2) If the identification creating his special property has been made by the buyer, he acquires the right to recover the goods only if they conform to the contract for sale.

Section 2—503. Manner of Seller's Tender of Delivery.

(1) Tender of delivery requires that the seller put and hold conforming goods at the buyer's disposition and give the buyer any notification reasonably necessary to enable him to take delivery. The manner, time and place for tender are determined by the agreement and this Article, and in particular

(a) tender must be at a reasonable hour, and if it is of goods they must be kept available for the period reasonably necessary to enable the buyer to take possession; but

(b) unless otherwise agreed the buyer must furnish facilities reasonably suited to the receipt of the goods.

(2) Where the case is within the next section respecting shipment, tender requires that the seller comply with its provisions.

(3) Where the seller is required to deliver at a particular destination, tender requires that he comply with subsection (1) and also in any appropriate case tender documents as described in subsections (4) and (5) of this section.

(4) Where goods are in the possession of a bailee and are to be delivered without being moved

(a) tender requires that the seller either tender a negotiable document of title covering such goods or procure acknowledgment by the bailee of the buyer's right to possession of the goods; but

(b) tender to the buyer of a nonnegotiable document of title or of a written direction to the bailee to deliver is sufficient tender unless the buyer seasonably objects, and receipt by the bailee of notification of the buyer's rights fixes those rights as against the bailee and all third persons; but risk of loss of the goods and of any failure by the bailee to honor the nonnegotiable document of title or to obey the direction remains on the seller until the buyer has had a reasonable time to present the document or direction, and a refusal by the bailee to honor the document or to obey the direction defeats the tender.

(5) Where the contract requires the seller to deliver documents

(a) he must tender all such documents in correct form, except as provided in this Article with respect to bills of lading in a set (subsection (2) of Section 2—323); and

(b) tender through customary banking channels is sufficient and dishonor of a draft accompanying the documents constitutes non-acceptance or rejection.

Section 2—504. Shipment by Seller.

Where the seller is required or authorized to send the goods to the buyer and the contract does not require him to deliver them at a particular destination, then unless otherwise agreed he must

(a) put the goods in the possession of such a carrier and make such a contract for their transportation as may be reasonable having regard to the nature of the goods and other circumstances of the case; and

(b) obtain and promptly deliver or tender in due form any document necessary to enable the buyer to obtain possession of the goods or otherwise required by the agreement or by usage of trade; and

(c) promptly notify the buyer of the shipment.

Failure to notify the buyer under paragraph (c) or to make a proper contract under paragraph (a) is a ground for rejection only if material delay or loss ensues.

Section 2—505. Seller's Shipment Under Reservation.

(1) Where the seller has identified goods to the contract by or before shipment:

(a) his procurement of a negotiable bill of lading to his own order or otherwise reserves in him a security interest in the goods. His procurement of the bill to the order of a financing agency or of the buyer indicates in addition only the seller's expectation of transferring that interest to the person named.

(b) a non-negotiable bill of lading to himself or his nominee reserves possession of the goods as security but except in a case of conditional delivery (subsection (2) of Section 2—507) a non-negotiable bill of lading naming the buyer as consignee reserves no security interest even though the seller retains possession of the bill of lading.

(2) When shipment by the seller with reservation of a security interest is in violation of the contract for sale, it constitutes an improper contract for transportation within the preceding section but impairs neither the rights given to the buyer by shipment and identification of the goods to the contract nor the seller's powers as a holder of a negotiable document.

Section 2—506. Rights of Financing Agency.

(1) A financing agency by paying or purchasing for value a draft which relates to a shipment of goods acquires to the extent of the payment or purchase and in addition to its own rights under the draft and any document of title securing it any rights of the shipper in the goods including the right to stop delivery and the shipper's right to have the draft honored by the buyer.

(2) The right to reimbursement of a financing agency which has in good faith honored or purchased the draft under commitment to or authority from the buyer is not impaired by subsequent discovery of defects with reference to any relevant document which was apparently regular on its face.

Section 2—507. Effect of Seller's Tender; Delivery on Condition.

(1) Tender of delivery is a condition to the buyer's duty to accept the goods and, unless otherwise agreed, to his duty to pay for them. Tender entitles the seller to acceptance of the goods and to payment according to the contract.

(2) Where payment is due and demanded on the delivery to the buyer of goods or documents of title, his right as against the seller to retain or dispose of them is conditional upon his making the payment due.

Section 2—508. Cure by Seller of Improper Tender or Delivery; Replacement.

(1) Where any tender or delivery by the seller is rejected because non-conforming and the time for performance has not yet expired, the seller may seasonably notify the buyer of his intention to cure and may then within the contract time make a conforming delivery.

(2) Where the buyer rejects a non-conforming tender which the seller had reasonable grounds to believe would be acceptable with or without money allowance, the seller may if he seasonably notifies the buyer have a further reasonable time to substitute a conforming tender.

Section 2—509. Risk of Loss in the Absence of Breach.

(1) Where the contract requires or authorizes the seller to ship the goods by carrier

(a) if it does not require him to deliver them at a particular destination, the risk of loss passes to the buyer when the goods are duly delivered to the carrier even though the shipment is under reservation (Section 2—505); but

(b) if it does require him to deliver them at a particular destination and the goods are there duly tendered while in the possession of the carrier, the risk of loss passes to the buyer when the goods are there duly so tendered as to enable the buyer to take delivery.

(2) Where the goods are held by a bailee to be delivered without being moved, the risk of loss passes to the buyer

(a) on his receipt of a negotiable document of title covering the goods; or

(b) on acknowledgment by the bailee of the buyer's right to possession of the goods; or

(c) after his receipt of a non-negotiable document of title or other written direction to deliver, as provided in subsection (4) (b) of Section 2—503.

(3) In any case not within subsection (1) or (2), the risk of loss passes to the buyer on his receipt of the goods if the seller is a merchant; otherwise the risk passes to the buyer on tender of delivery.

(4) The provisions of this section are subject to contrary agreement of the parties and to the provisions of this Article on sale on approval (Section 2—327) and on effect of breach on risk of loss (Section 2—510).

Section 2—510. Effect of Breach on Risk of Loss.

(1) Where a tender or delivery of goods so fails to conform to the contract as to give a right of rejection, the risk of their loss remains on the seller until cure or acceptance.

(2) Where the buyer rightfully revokes acceptance, he may to the extent of any deficiency in his effective insurance coverage treat the risk of loss as having rested on the seller from the beginning.

(3) Where the buyer as to conforming goods already identified to the contract for sale repudiates or is otherwise in breach before risk of their loss has passed to him, the seller may to the extent of any deficiency in his effective insurance coverage treat the risk of loss as resting on the buyer for a commercially reasonable time.

Section 2—511. Tender of Payment by Buyer; Payment by Check.

(1) Unless otherwise agreed tender of payment is a condition to the seller's duty to tender and complete any delivery.

(2) Tender of payment is sufficient when made by any means or in any manner current in the ordinary course of business unless the seller demands payment in legal tender and gives any extension of time reasonably necessary to procure it.

(3) Subject to the provisions of this Act on the effect of an instrument on an obligation (Section 3—802), payment by check is conditional and is defeated as between the parties by dishonor of the check on due presentment.

Section 2—512. Payment by Buyer Before Inspection.

(1) Where the contract requires payment before inspection, non-conformity of the goods does not excuse the buyer from so making payment unless

(a) the non-conformity appears without inspection; or

(b) despite tender of the required documents the circumstances would justify injunction against honor under the provisions of this Act (Section 5—114).

(2) Payment pursuant to subsection (1) does not constitute an acceptance of goods or impair the buyer's right to inspect or any of his remedies.

Section 2—513. Buyer's Right to Inspection of Goods.

(1) Unless otherwise agreed and subject to subsection (3), where goods are tendered or delivered or identified to the contract for sale, the buyer has a right before payment or acceptance to inspect them at any reasonable place and time and in any reasonable manner. When the seller is required or authorized to send the goods to the buyer, the inspection may be after their arrival.

(2) Expenses of inspection must be borne by the buyer but may be recovered from the seller if the goods do not conform and are rejected.

(3) Unless otherwise agreed and subject to the provisions of this Article on C.I.F. contracts (subsection (3) of Section 2—321), the buyer is not entitled to inspect the goods before payment of the price when the contract provides

(a) for delivery "C.O.D." or on other like terms; or

(b) for payment against documents of title, except where such payment is due only after the goods are to become available for inspection.

(4) A place or method of inspection fixed by the parties is presumed to be exclusive, but unless otherwise expressly agreed it does not postpone identification or shift the place for delivery or for passing the risk of loss. If compliance becomes impossible, inspection shall be as provided in this section unless the place or method fixed was clearly intended as an indispensable condition failure of which avoids the contract.

Section 2—514. When Documents Deliverable on Acceptance; When on Payment.

Unless otherwise agreed documents against which a draft is drawn are to be delivered to the drawee on acceptance of the draft if it is payable more than three days after presentment; otherwise, only on payment.

Section 2—515. Preserving Evidence of Goods in Dispute.

In furtherance of the adjustment of any claim or dispute

(a) either party on reasonable notification to the other and for the purpose of ascertaining the facts and preserving evidence has the right to inspect, test and sample the goods including such of them as may be in the possession or control of the other; and

(b) the parties may agree to a third party inspection or survey to determine the conformity or condition of the goods and may agree that the findings shall be binding upon them in any subsequent litigation or adjustment.

PART 6

BREACH, REPUDIATION AND EXCUSE

Section 2—601. Buyer's Rights on Improper Delivery.

Subject to the provisions of this Article on breach in installment contracts (Section 2—612) and unless otherwise agreed under the sections on contractual limitations of remedy (Sections 2—718 and 2—719), if the goods or the tender of delivery fail in any respect to conform to the contract, the buyer may

(a) reject the whole; or

(b) accept the whole; or

(c) accept any commercial unit or units and reject the rest.

Section 2—602. Manner and Effect of Rightful Rejection.

(1) Rejection of goods must be within a reasonable time after their delivery or tender. It is ineffective unless the buyer seasonably notifies the seller.

(2) Subject to the provisions of the two following sections on rejected goods (Sections 2—603 and 2—604),

(a) after rejection any exercise of ownership by the buyer with respect to any commercial unit is wrongful as against the seller; and

(b) if the buyer has before rejection taken physical possession of goods in which he does not have a security interest under the provisions of this Article (subsection (3) of Section 2—711), he is under a duty after rejection to hold them with reasonable care at the seller's disposition for a time sufficient to permit the seller to remove them; but

(c) the buyer has no further obligations with regard to goods rightfully rejected.

(3) The seller's rights with respect to goods wrongfully rejected are governed by the provisions of this Article on Seller's remedies in general (Section 2—703).

Section 2—603. Merchant Buyer's Duties as to Rightfully Rejected Goods.

(1) Subject to any security interest in the buyer (subsection (3) of Section 2—711), when the seller has no agent or place of business at the market of rejection, a merchant buyer is under a duty after rejection of goods in his possession or control to follow any reasonable instructions received from the seller with respect to the goods and in the absence of such instructions to make reasonable efforts to sell them for the seller's account if they are perishable or threaten to decline in value speedily. Instructions are not reasonable if on demand indemnity for expenses is not forthcoming.

(2) When the buyer sells goods under subsection (1), he is entitled to reimbursement from the seller or out of the proceeds for reasonable expenses of caring for and selling them, and if the expenses include no selling commission then to such commission as is usual in the trade or if there is none to a reasonable sum not exceeding ten per cent on the gross proceeds.

(3) In complying with this section the buyer is held only to good faith, and good faith conduct hereunder is neither acceptance nor conversion nor the basis of an action for damages.

Section 2—604. Buyer's Options as to Salvage of Rightfully Rejected Goods.

Subject to the provisions of the immediately preceding section on perishables, if the seller gives no instructions within a reasonable time after notification of rejection, the buyer may store the rejected goods for the seller's account or reship them to him or resell them for the seller's account with reimbursement as provided in the preceding section. Such action is not acceptance or conversion.

Section 2—605. Waiver of Buyer's Objections by Failure to Particularize.

(1) The buyer's failure to state in connection with rejection a particular defect which is ascertainable by reasonable inspection precludes him from relying on the unstated defect to justify rejection or to establish breach

(a) where the seller could have cured it if stated seasonably; or

(b) between merchants when the seller has after rejection made request in writing for a full and final written statement of all defects on which the buyer proposes to rely.

(2) Payment against documents made without reservation of rights precludes recovery of the payment for defects apparent on the face of the documents.

Section 2—606. What Constitutes Acceptance of Goods.

(1) Acceptance of goods occurs when the buyer

(a) after a reasonable opportunity to inspect the goods signifies to the seller that the goods are conforming or that he will take or retain them in spite of their non-conformity; or

(b) fails to make an effective rejection (subsection (1) of Section 2—602), but such acceptance does not occur until the buyer has had a reasonable opportunity to inspect them; or

(c) does any act inconsistent with the seller's ownership; but if such act is wrongful as against the seller it is an acceptance only if ratified by him.

(2) Acceptance of a part of any commercial unit is acceptance of that entire unit.

Section 2—607. Effect of Acceptance; Notice of Breach; Burden of Establishing Breach After Acceptance; Notice of Claim or Litigation to Person Answerable Over.

(1) The buyer must pay at the contract rate for any goods accepted.

(2) Acceptance of goods by the buyer precludes rejection of the goods accepted and, if made with knowledge of a non-conformity, cannot be revoked because of it unless the acceptance was on the reasonable assumption that the non-conformity would be seasonably cured, but acceptance does not of itself impair any other remedy provided by this Article for non-conformity.

(3) Where a tender has been accepted

(a) the buyer must within a reasonable time after he discovers or should have discovered any breach notify the seller of breach or be barred from any remedy; and

(b) if the claim is one for infringement or the like (subsection (3) of Section 2—312) and the buyer is sued as a result of such a breach, he must so notify the seller within a reasonable time after he receives notice of the litigation or be barred from any remedy over for liability established by the litigation.

(4) The burden is on the buyer to establish any breach with respect to the goods accepted.

(5) Where the buyer is sued for breach of a warranty or other obligation for which his seller is answerable over

(a) he may give his seller written notice of the litigation. If the notice states that the seller may come in and defend and that if the seller does not do so he will be bound in any action against him by his buyer by any determination of fact common to the two litigations, then unless the seller after seasonable receipt of the notice does come in and defend he is so bound.

(b) if the claim is one for infringement or the like (subsection (3) of Section 2—312) the original seller may demand in writing that his buyer turn over to him control of the litigation including settlement or else be barred from any remedy over and if he also agrees to bear all expense and to satisfy any adverse judgment, then unless the buyer after seasonable receipt of the demand does turn over control the buyer is so barred.

(6) The provisions of subsections (3), (4) and (5) apply to any obligation of a buyer to hold the seller harmless against infringement or the like (subsection (3) of Section 2—312).

Section 2—608. Revocation of Acceptance in Whole or in Part.

(1) The buyer may revoke his acceptance of a lot or commercial unit whose non-conformity substantially impairs its value to him if he has accepted it

(a) on the reasonable assumption that its non-conformity would be cured and it has not been seasonably cured; or

(b) without discovery of such non-conformity if his acceptance was reasonably induced either by the difficulty of discovery before acceptance or by the seller's assurances.

(2) Revocation of acceptance must occur within a reasonable time after the buyer discovers or should have discovered the ground for it and before any substantial change in condition of the goods which is not caused by their own defects. It is not effective until the buyer notifies the seller of it.

(3) A buyer who so revokes has the same rights and duties with regard to the goods involved as if he had rejected them.

Section 2—609. Right to Adequate Assurance of Performance.

(1) A contract for sale imposes an obligation on each party that the other's expectation of receiving due performance will not be impaired. When reasonable grounds for insecurity

arise with respect to the performance of either party, the other may in writing demand adequate assurance of due performance and until he receives such assurance may if commercially reasonable suspend any performance for which he has not already received the agreed return.

(2) Between merchants the reasonableness of grounds for insecurity and the adequacy of any assurance offered shall be determined according to commercial standards.

(3) Acceptance of any improper delivery or payment does not prejudice the aggrieved party's right to demand adequate assurance of future performance.

(4) After receipt of a justified demand failure to provide within a reasonable time not exceeding thirty days such assurance of due performance as is adequate under the circumstances of the particular case is a repudiation of the contract.

Section 2—610. Anticipatory Repudiation.

When either party repudiates the contract with respect to a performance not yet due the loss of which will substantially impair the value of the contract to the other, the aggrieved party may

(a) for a commercially reasonable time await performance by the repudiating party; or

(b) resort to any remedy for breach (Section 2—703 or Section 2—711), even though he has notified the repudiating party that he would await the latter's performance and urged retraction; and

(c) in either case suspend his own performance or proceed in accordance with the provisions of this Article on the seller's right to identify goods to the contract notwithstanding breach or to salvage unfinished goods (Section 2—704).

Section 2—611. Retraction of Anticipatory Repudiation.

(1) Until the repudiating party's next performance is due he can retract his repudiation unless the aggrieved party has since the repudiation cancelled or materially changed his position or otherwise indicated that he considers the repudiation final.

(2) Retraction may be by any method which clearly indicates to the aggrieved party that the repudiating party intends to perform, but must include any assurance justifiably demanded under the provisions of this Article (Section 2—609).

(3) Retraction reinstates the repudiating party's rights under the contract with due excuse and allowance to the aggrieved party for any delay occasioned by the repudiation.

Section 2—612. "Installment Contract"; Breach.

(1) An "installment contract" is one which requires or authorizes the delivery of goods in separate lots to be separately accepted, even though the contract contains a clause "each delivery is a separate contract" or its equivalent.

(2) The buyer may reject any installment which is non-conforming if the non-conformity substantially impairs the value of that installment and cannot be cured or if the non-conformity is a defect in the required documents; but if the non-conformity does not fall within subsection (3) and the seller gives adequate assurance of its cure the buyer must accept that installment.

(3) Whenever non-conformity or default with respect to one or more installments substantially impairs the value of the whole contract there is a breach of the whole. But the aggrieved party reinstates the contract if he accepts a non-conforming installment without seasonably notifying of cancellation or if he brings an action with respect only to past installments or demands performance as to future installments.

Section 2—613. Casualty to Identified Goods.

Where the contract requires for its performance goods identified when the contract is made, and the goods suffer casualty without fault of either party before the risk of loss passes to the buyer, or in a proper case under a "no arrival, no sale" term (Section 2—324) then

(a) if the loss is total the contract is avoided; and

(b) if the loss is partial or the goods have so deteriorated as no longer to conform to the contract, the buyer may nevertheless demand inspection and at his option either treat the contract as avoided or accept the goods with due allowance from the contract price for the deterioration or the deficiency in quantity but without further right against the seller.

Section 2—614. Substituted Performance.

(1) Where without fault of either party the agreed berthing, loading, or unloading facilities fail or an agreed type of carrier becomes unavailable or the agreed manner of delivery otherwise becomes commercially impracticable but a commercially reasonable substitute is available, such substitute performance must be tendered and accepted.

(2) If the agreed means or manner of payment fails because of domestic or foreign governmental regulation, the seller may withhold or stop delivery unless the buyer provides a means or manner of payment which is commercially a substantial equivalent. If delivery has already been taken, payment by the means or in the manner provided by the regulation discharges the buyer's obligation unless the regulation is discriminatory, oppressive or predatory.

Section 2—615. Excuse by Failure of Presupposed Conditions.

Except so far as a seller may have assumed a greater obligation and subject to the preceding section on substituted performance:

(a) Delay in delivery or non-delivery in whole or in part by a seller who complies with paragraphs (b) and (c) is not a breach of his duty under a contract for sale if performance as agreed has been made impracticable by the occurrence of a contingency the non-occurrence of which was a basic assumption on which the contract was made or by compliance in good faith with any applicable foreign or domestic governmental regulation or order whether or not it later proves to be invalid.

(b) Where the causes mentioned in paragraph (a) affect only a part of the seller's capacity to perform, he must allocate production and deliveries among his customers but may at his option include regular customers not then under contract as well as his own requirements for further manufacture. He may so allocate in any manner which is fair and reasonable.

(c) The seller must notify the buyer seasonably that there will be delay or non-delivery and, when allocation is required under paragraph (b), of the estimated quota thus made available for the buyer.

Section 2—616. Procedure on Notice Claiming Excuse.

(1) Where the buyer receives notification of a material or indefinite delay or an allocation justified under the preceding section he may by written notification to the seller as to any delivery concerned, and where the prospective deficiency substantially impairs the value of the whole contract under the provisions of this Article relating to breach of installment contracts (Section 2—612), then also as to the whole,

(a) terminate and thereby discharge any unexecuted portion of the contract; or

(b) modify the contract by agreeing to take his available quota in substitution.

(2) If after receipt of such notification from the seller the buyer fails so to modify the contract within a reasonable time not exceeding thirty days, the contract lapses with respect to any deliveries affected.

(3) The provisions of this section may not be negated by agreement except in so far as the seller has assumed a greater obligation under the preceding section.

PART 7

REMEDIES

Section 2—701. Remedies for Breach of Collateral Contracts Not Impaired.

Remedies for breach of any obligation or promise collateral or ancillary to a contract for sale are not impaired by the provisions of this Article.

Section 2—702. Seller's Remedies on Discovery of Buyer's Insolvency.

(1) Where the seller discovers the buyer to be insolvent he may refuse delivery except for cash including payment for all goods theretofore delivered under the contract, and stop delivery under this Article (Section 2—705).

(2) Where the seller discovers that the buyer has received goods on credit while insolvent he may reclaim the goods upon demand made within ten days after the receipt, but if misrepresentation of solvency has been made to the particular seller in writing within three months before delivery the ten day limitation does not apply. Except as provided in this subsection, the seller may not base a right to reclaim goods on the buyer's fraudulent or innocent misrepresentation of solvency or of intent to pay.

(3) The seller's right to reclaim under subsection (2) is subject to the rights of a buyer in ordinary course or other good faith purchaser or lien creditor under this Article (Section 2—403). Successful reclamation of goods excludes all other remedies with respect to them.

Section 2—703. Seller's Remedies in General.

Where the buyer wrongfully rejects or revokes acceptance of goods or fails to make a payment due on or before delivery or repudiates with respect to a part or the whole, then with respect to any goods directly affected and, if the breach is of the whole contract (Section 2—612), then also with respect to the whole undelivered balance, the aggrieved seller may

(a) withhold delivery of such goods;
(b) stop delivery by any bailee as hereafter provided (Section 2—705);
(c) proceed under the next section respecting goods still unidentified to the contract;
(d) resell and recover damages as hereafter provided (Section 2—706);
(e) recover damages for non-acceptance (Section 2—708) or in a proper case the price (Section 2—709);
(f) cancel.

Section 2—704. Seller's Right to Identify Goods to the Contract Notwithstanding Breach or to Salvage Unfinished Goods.

(1) An aggrieved seller under the preceding section may

(a) identify to the contract conforming goods not already identified if at the time he learned of the breach they are in his possession or control;
(b) treat as the subject of resale goods which have demonstrably been intended for the particular contract even though those goods are unfinished.

(2) Where the goods are unfinished an aggrieved seller may in the exercise of reasonable commercial judgment for the purposes of avoiding loss and of effective realization either complete the manufacture and wholly identify the goods to the contract or cease manufacture and resell for scrap or salvage value or proceed in any other reasonable manner.

Section 2—705. Seller's Stoppage of Delivery in Transit or Otherwise.

(1) The seller may stop delivery of goods in the possession of a carrier or other bailee when he discovers the buyer to be insolvent (Section 2—702) and may stop delivery of carload, truckload, planeload or larger shipments of express or freight when the buyer repudiates or fails to make a payment due before delivery or if for any other reason the seller has a right to withhold or reclaim the goods.

(2) As against such buyer the seller may stop delivery until

(a) receipt of the goods by the buyer; or
(b) acknowledgment to the buyer by any bailee of the goods except a carrier that the bailee holds the goods for the buyer; or
(c) such acknowledgment to the buyer by a carrier by reshipment or as warehouseman; or

(d) negotiation to the buyer of any negotiable document of title covering the goods.

(3) (a) To stop delivery the seller must so notify as to enable the bailee by reasonable diligence to prevent delivery of the goods.

(b) After such notification the bailee must hold and deliver the goods according to the directions of the seller, but the seller is liable to the bailee for any ensuing charges or damages.

(c) If a negotiable document of title has been issued for goods, the bailee is not obliged to obey a notification to stop until surrender of the document.

(d) A carrier who has issued a non-negotiable bill of lading is not obliged to obey a notification to stop received from a person other than the consignor.

Section 2—706. Seller's Resale Including Contract for Resale.

(1) Under the conditions stated in Section 2—703 on seller's remedies, the seller may resell the goods concerned or the undelivered balance thereof. Where the resale is made in good faith and in a commercially reasonable manner the seller may recover the difference between the resale price and the contract price together with any incidental damages allowed under the provisions of this Article (Section 2—710), but less expenses saved in consequence of the buyer's breach.

(2) Except as otherwise provided in subsection (3) or unless otherwise agreed, resale may be at public or private sale including sale by way of one or more contracts to sell or of identification to an existing contract of the seller. Sale may be as a unit or in parcels and at any time and place and on any terms but every aspect of the sale including the method, manner, time, place and terms must be commercially reasonable. The resale must be reasonably identified as referring to the broken contract, but it is not necessary that the goods be in existence or that any or all of them have been identified to the contract before the breach.

(3) Where the resale is at private sale the seller must give the buyer reasonable notification of his intention to resell.

(4) Where the resale is at public sale

(a) only identified goods can be sold except where there is a recognized market for a public sale of futures in goods of the kind; and

(b) it must be made at a usual place or market for public sale if one is reasonably available and except in the case of goods which are perishable or threaten to decline in value speedily the seller must give the buyer reasonable notice of the time and place of the resale; and

(c) if the goods are not to be within the view of those attending the sale, the notification of sale must state the place where the goods are located and provide for their reasonable inspection by prospective bidders; and

(d) the seller may buy.

(5) A purchaser who buys in good faith at a resale takes the goods free of any rights of the original buyer even though the seller fails to comply with one or more of the requirements of this section.

(6) The seller is not accountable to the buyer for any profit made on any resale. A person in the position of a seller (Section 2—707) or a buyer who has rightfully rejected or justifiably revoked acceptance must account for any excess over the amount of his security interest, as hereinafter defined (subsection (3) of Section 2—711).

Section 2—707. "Person in the Position of a Seller".

(1) A "person in the position of a seller" includes as against a principal an agent who has paid or become responsible for the price of goods on behalf of his principal or anyone who otherwise holds a security interest or other right in goods similar to that of a seller.

(2) A person in the position of a seller may as provided in this Article withhold or stop delivery (Section 2—705) and resell (Section 2—706) and recover incidental damages (Section 2—710).

Section 2—708. Seller's Damages for Non-acceptance or Repudiation.

(1) Subject to subsection (2) and to the provisions of this Article with respect to proof of market price (Section 2—723), the measure of damages for non-acceptance or repudiation by the buyer is the difference between the market price at the time and place for tender and the unpaid contract price together with any incidental damages provided in this Article (Section 2—710), but less expenses saved in consequence of the buyer's breach.

(2) If the measure of damages provided in subsection (1) is inadequate to put the seller in as good a position as performance would have done, then the measure of damages is the profit (including reasonable overhead) which the seller would have made from full performance by the buyer, together with any incidental damages provided in this Article (Section 2—710), due allowance for costs reasonably incurred and due credit for payments or proceeds of resale.

Section 2—709. Action for the Price.

(1) When the buyer fails to pay the price as it becomes due the seller may recover, together with any incidental damages under the next section, the price

(a) of goods accepted or of conforming goods lost or damaged within a commercially reasonable time after risk of their loss has passed to the buyer; and

(b) of goods identified to the contract if the seller is unable after reasonable effort to resell them at a reasonable price or the circumstances reasonably indicate that such effort will be unavailing.

(2) Where the seller sues for the price he must hold for the buyer any goods which have been identified to the contract and are still in his control except that if resale becomes possible he may resell them at any time prior to the collection of the judgment. The net proceeds of any such resale must be credited to the buyer and payment of the judgment entitles him to any goods not resold.

(3) After the buyer has wrongfully rejected or revoked acceptance of the goods or has failed to make a payment due or has repudiated (Section 2—610), a seller who is held not entitled to the price under this section shall nevertheless be awarded damages for non-acceptance under the preceding section.

Section 2—710. Seller's Incidental Damages.

Incidental damages to an aggrieved seller include any commercially reasonable charges, expenses or commissions incurred in stopping delivery, in the transportation, care and custody of goods after the buyer's breach, in connection with return or resale of the goods or otherwise resulting from the breach.

Section 2—711. Buyer's Remedies in General; Buyer's Security Interest in Rejected Goods.

(1) Where the seller fails to make delivery or repudiates or the buyer rightfully rejects or justifiably revokes acceptance then with respect to any goods involved, and with respect to the whole if the breach goes to the whole contract (Section 2—612), the buyer may cancel and whether or not he has done so may in addition to recovering so much of the price as has been paid

(a) "cover" and have damages under the next section as to all the goods affected whether or not they have been identified to the contract; or

(b) recover damages for non-delivery as provided in this Article (Section 2—713).

(2) Where the seller fails to deliver or repudiates the buyer may also

(a) if the goods have been identified recover them as provided in this Article (Section 2—502); or

(b) in a proper case obtain specific performance or replevy the goods as provided in this Article (Section 2—716).

(3) On rightful rejection or justifiable revocation of acceptance a buyer has a security interest in goods in his possession or control for any payments made on their price and any expenses reasonably incurred in their inspection,

receipt, transportation, care and custody and may hold such goods and resell them in like manner as an aggrieved seller (Section 2—706).

Section 2—712. "Cover"; Buyer's Procurement of Substitute Goods.

(1) After a breach within the preceding section the buyer may "cover" by making in good faith and without unreasonable delay any reasonable purchase of or contract to purchase goods in substitution for those due from the seller.

(2) The buyer may recover from the seller as damages the difference between the cost of cover and the contract price together with any incidental or consequential damages as hereinafter defined (Section 2—715), but less expenses saved in consequence of the seller's breach.

(3) Failure of the buyer to effect cover within this section does not bar him from any other remedy.

Section 2—713. Buyer's Damages for Non-Delivery or Repudiation.

(1) Subject to the provisions of this Article with respect to proof of market price (Section 2—723), the measure of damages for non-delivery or repudiation by the seller is the difference between the market price at the time when the buyer learned of the breach and the contract price together with any incidental and consequential damages provided in this Article (Section 2—715), but less expenses saved in consequence of the seller's breach.

(2) Market price is to be determined as of the place for tender or, in cases of rejection after arrival or revocation of acceptance, as of the place of arrival.

Section 2—714. Buyer's Damages for Breach in Regard to Accepted Goods.

(1) Where the buyer has accepted goods and given notification (subsection (3) of Section 2—607) he may recover as damages for any non-conformity of tender the loss resulting in the ordinary course of events from the seller's breach as determined in any manner which is reasonable.

(2) The measure of damages for breach of warranty is the difference at the time and place of acceptance between the value of the goods accepted and the value they would have had if they had been as warranted, unless special circumstances show proximate damages of a different amount.

(3) In a proper case any incidental and consequential damages under the next section may also be recovered.

Section 2—715. Buyer's Incidental and Consequential Damages.

(1) Incidental damages resulting from the seller's breach include expenses reasonably incurred in inspection, receipt, transportation and care and custody of goods rightfully rejected, any commercially reasonable charges, expenses on commissions in connection with effecting cover and any other reasonable expense incident to the delay or other breach.

(2) Consequential damages resulting from the seller's breach include

(a) any loss resulting from general or particular requirements and needs of which the seller at the time of contracting had reason to know and which could not reasonably be prevented by cover or otherwise; and

(b) injury to person or property proximately resulting from any breach of warranty.

Section 2—716. Buyer's Right to Specific Performance or Replevin.

(1) Specific performance may be decreed where the goods are unique or in other proper circumstances.

(2) The decree for specific performance may include such terms and conditions as to payment of the price, damages, or other relief as the court may deem just.

(3) The buyer has a right of replevin for goods identified to the contract if after reasonable effort he is unable to effect cover for such goods or the circumstances reasonably indicate that such effort will be unavailing or if the goods have been shipped under reservation and satisfaction of the security interest in them has been made or tendered.

Section 2—717. Deduction of Damages From the Price.

The buyer on notifying the seller of his intention to do so may deduct all or any part of the damages resulting from any breach of the contract from any part of the price still due under the same contract.

Section 2—718. Liquidation or Limitation of Damages; Deposits.

(1) Damages for breach by either party may be liquidated in the agreement but only at an amount which is reasonable in the light of the anticipated or actual harm caused by the breach, the difficulties of proof of loss, and the inconvenience or non-feasibility of otherwise obtaining an adequate remedy. A term fixing unreasonably large liquidated damages is void as a penalty.

(2) Where the seller justifiably withholds delivery of goods because of the buyer's breach, the buyer is entitled to restitution of any amount by which the sum of his payments exceeds

(a) the amount to which the seller is entitled by virtue of terms liquidating the seller's damages in accordance with subsection (1), or

(b) in the absence of such terms, twenty per cent of the value of the total performance for which the buyer is obligated under the contract or $500, whichever is smaller.

(3) The buyer's right to restitution under subsection (2) is subject to offset to the extent that the seller establishes

(a) a right to recover damages under the provisions of this Article other than subsection (1), and

(b) the amount or value of any benefits received by the buyer directly or indirectly by reason of the contract.

(4) Where a seller has received payment in goods their reasonable value or the proceeds of their resale shall be treated as payments for the purposes of subsection (2); but if the seller has notice of the buyer's breach before reselling goods received in part performance, his resale is subject to the conditions laid down in this Article on resale by an aggrieved seller (Section 2—706).

Section 2—719. Contractual Modification or Limitation of Remedy.

(1) Subject to the provisions of subsections (2) and (3) of this section and of the preceding section on liquidation and limitation of damages,

(a) the agreement may provide for remedies in addition to or in substitution for those provided in this Article and may limit or alter the measure of damages recoverable under this Article, as by limiting the buyer's remedies to return of the goods and repayment of the price or to repair and replacement of non-conforming goods or parts; and

(b) resort to a remedy as provided is optional unless the remedy is expressly agreed to be exclusive, in which case it is the sole remedy.

(2) Where circumstances cause an exclusive or limited remedy to fail of its essential purpose, remedy may be had as provided in this Act.

(3) Consequential damages may be limited or excluded unless the limitation or exclusion is unconscionable. Limitation of consequential damages for injury to the person in the case of consumer goods is prima facie unconscionable, but limitation of damages where the loss is commercial is not.

Section 2—720. Effect of "Cancellation" or "Rescission" on Claims for Antecedent Breach.

Unless the contrary intention clearly appears, expressions of "cancellation" or "rescission" of the contract or the like shall not be construed as a renunciation or discharge of any claim in damages for an antecedent breach.

Section 2—721. Remedies for Fraud.

Remedies for material misrepresentation or fraud include all remedies available under this Article for non-fraudulent breach. Neither rescission of the contract for sale nor rejection or return of the goods shall bar or be deemed inconsistent with a claim for damages or other remedy.

Section 2—722. Who Can Sue Third Parties for Injury to Goods.

Where a third party so deals with goods which have been identified to a contract for sale as to cause actionable injury to a party to that contract

(a) a right of action against the third party is in either party to the contract for sale who has title to or a security interest or a special property or an insurable interest in the goods; and if the goods have been destroyed or converted, a right of action is also in the party who either bore the risk of loss under the contract for sale or has since the injury assumed that risk as against the other;

(b) if at the time of the injury the party plaintiff did not bear the risk of loss as against the other party to the contract for sale and there is no arrangement between them for disposition of the recovery, his suit or settlement is, subject to his own interest, as a fiduciary for the other party to the contract;

(c) either party may with the consent of the other sue for the benefit of whom it may concern.

Section 2—723. Proof of Market Price: Time and Place.

(1) If an action based on anticipatory repudiation comes to trial before the time for performance with respect to some or all of the goods, any damages based on market price (Section 2—708 or Section 2—713) shall be determined according to the price of such goods prevailing at the time when the aggrieved party learned of the repudiation.

(2) If evidence of a price prevailing at the times or places described in this Article is not readily available, the price prevailing within any reasonable time before or after the time described or at any other place which in commercial judgment or under usage of trade would serve as a reasonable substitute for the one described may be used, making any proper allowance for the cost of transporting the goods to or from such other place.

(3) Evidence of a relevant price prevailing at a time or place other than the one described in this Article offered by one party is not admissible unless and until he has given the other party such notice as the court finds sufficient to prevent unfair surprise.

Section 2—724. Admissibility of Market Quotations.

Whenever the prevailing price or value of any goods regularly bought and sold in any established commodity market is in issue, reports in official publications or trade journals or in newspapers or periodicals of general circulation published as the reports of such market shall be admissible in evidence. The circumstances of the preparation of such a report may be shown to affect its weight but not its admissibility.

Section 2—725. Statute of Limitations in Contracts for Sale.

(1) An action for breach of any contract for sale must be commenced within four years after the cause of action has accrued. By the original agreement the parties may reduce the period of limitation to not less than one year but may not extend it.

(2) A cause of action accrues when the breach occurs, regardless of the aggrieved party's lack of knowledge of the breach. A breach of warranty occurs when tender of delivery is made, except that where a warranty explicitly extends to future performance of the goods and discovery of the breach must await the time of such performance the cause of action accrues when the breach is or should have been discovered.

(3) Where an action commenced within the time limited by subsection (1) is so terminated as to leave available a remedy by another action for the same breach, such other action may be commenced after the expiration of the time limit and within six months after the termination of the first action unless the termination resulted from voluntary discontinuance or from dismissal for failure or neglect to prosecute.

(4) This section does not alter the law on tolling of the statute of limitations nor does it apply to causes of action which have accrued before this Act becomes effective.

ARTICLE 3

COMMERCIAL PAPER

PART 1

SHORT TITLE, FORM AND INTERPRETATION

Section 3—101. Short Title.

This Article shall be known and may be cited as Uniform Commercial Code—Commercial Paper.

Section 3—102. Definitions and Index of Definitions.

(1) In this Article unless the context otherwise requires

(a) "Issue" means the first delivery of of an instrument to a holder or a remitter.

(b) An "order" is a direction to pay and must be more than an authorization or request. It must identify the person to pay with reasonable certainty. It may be addressed to one or more such persons jointly or in the alternative but not in succession.

(c) A "promise" is an undertaking to pay and must be more than an acknowledgment of an obligation.

(d) "Secondary party" means a drawer or endorser.

(e) "Instrument" means a negotiable instrument.

(2) Other definitions applying to this Article and the sections in which they appear are:

"Acceptance". Section 3—410.
"Accommodation party". Section 3—415.
"Alteration". Section 3—407.
"Certificate of deposit". Section 3—104
"Certification". Section 3—411.
"Check". Section 3—104.
"Definite time". Section 3—109.
"Dishonor". Section 3—507.
"Draft". Section 3—104.
"Holder in due course". Section 3—302.
"Negotiation". Section 3—202.
"Note". Section 3—104.
"Notice of dishonor". Section 3—508.
"On demand". Section 3-108.
"Presentment". Section 3—504.
"Protest". Section 3—509.
"Restrictive Indorsement". Section 3—205.
"Signature". Section 3—401.

(3) The following definitions in other Articles apply to this Article:

"Account". Section 4—104.
"Banking Day". Section 4—104.
"Clearing house". Section 4—104.
"Collecting bank". Section 4-105.
"Customer". Section 4—104.
"Depositary Bank". Section 4—105.
"Documentary Draft". Section 4—104.
"Intermediary Bank". Section 4—105.
"Item". Section 4-104.
"Midnight deadline". Section 4—104.
"Payor bank". Section 4-105.

(4) In addition Article 1 contains general definitions and principles of construction and interpretation applicable throughout this Article.

Section 3—103. Limitations on Scope of Article.

(1) This Article does not apply to money, documents of title or investment securities.

(2) The provisions of this Article are subject to the provisions of the Article on Bank Deposits and Collections (Article 4) and Secured Transactions (Article 9).

Section 3—104. Form of Negotiable Instruments; "Draft"; "Check"; "Certificate of Deposit"; "Note".

(1) Any writing to be a negotiable instrument within this Article must

(a) be signed by the maker or drawer; and

(b) contain an unconditional promise or order to pay a sum certain in money and no other promise, order, obligation or power given by the maker or drawer except as authorized by this Article; and

(c) be payable on demand or at a definite time; and

(d) be payable to order or to bearer.

(2) A writing which complies with the requirements of this section is

(a) a "draft" ("bill of exchange") if it is an order;

(b) a "check" if it is a draft drawn on a bank and payable on demand;

(c) a "certificate of deposit" if it is an acknowledgment by a bank of receipt of money with an engagement to repay it;

(d) a "note" if it is a promise other than a certificate of deposit.

(3) As used in other Articles of this Act, and as the context may require, the terms "draft", "check", "certificate of deposit" and "note" may refer to instruments which are not negotiable within this Article as well as to instruments which are so negotiable.

Section 3—105. When Promise or Order Unconditional.

(1) A promise or order otherwise unconditional is not made conditional by the fact that the instrument

(a) is subject to implied or constructive conditions; or

(b) states its consideration, whether performed or promised, or the transaction which gave rise to the instrument, or that the promise or order is made or the instrument matures in accordance with or "as per" such transaction; or

(c) refers to or states that it arises out of a separate agreement or refers to a separate agreement for rights as to prepayment or acceleration; or

(d) states that it is drawn under a letter of credit; or

(e) states that it is secured, whether by mortgage, reservation of title or otherwise; or

(f) indicates a particular account to be debited or any other fund or source from which reimbursement is expected; or

(g) is limited to payment out of a particular fund or the proceeds of a particular source, if the instrument is issued by a government or governmental agency or unit; or

(h) is limited to payment out of the entire assets of a partnership, unincorporated association, trust or estate by or on behalf of which the instrument is issued.

(2) A promise or order is not unconditional if the instrument

(a) states that it is subject to or governed by any other agreement, or

(b) states that it is to be paid only out of a particular fund or source except as provided in this section.

Section 3—106. Sum Certain.

(1) The sum payable is a sum certain even though it is to be paid

(a) with stated interest or by stated installments; or

(b) with stated different rates of interest before and after default or a specified date; or

(c) with a stated discount or addition if paid before or after the date fixed for payment; or

(d) with exchange or less exchange, whether at a fixed rate or at the current rate; or

(e) with costs of collection or an attorney's fee or both upon default.

(2) Nothing in this section shall validate any term which is otherwise illegal.

Section 3—107. Money.

(1) An instrument is payable in money if the medium of exchange in which it is payable is money at the time the instrument is made. An instrument payable in "currency" or "current funds" is payable in money.

(2) A promise or order to pay a sum stated in a foreign currency is for a sum certain in money and, unless a different medium of payment is specified in the instrument, may be satisfied by payment of that number of dollars

which the stated foreign currency will purchase at the buying sight rate for that currency on the day on which the instrument is payable or, if payable on demand, on the day of demand. If such an instrument specifies a foreign currency as the medium of payment, the instrument is payable in that currency.

Section 3—108. Payable on Demand.

Instruments payable on demand include those payable at sight or on presentation and those in which no time for payment is stated.

Section 3—109. Definite Time.

(1) An instrument is payable at a definite time if by its terms it is payable

(a) on or before a stated debt or at a fixed period after a stated date; or

(b) at a fixed period after sight; or

(c) at a definite time subject to any acceleration; or

(d) at a definite time subject to extension at the option of the holder, or to extension to a further definite time at the option of the maker or acceptor or automatically upon or after a specified act or event.

(2) An instrument which by its terms is otherwise payable only upon an act or event uncertain as to time of occurrence is not payable at a definite time even though the act or event has occurred.

Section 3—110. Payable to Order.

(1) An instrument is payable to order when by its terms it is payable to the order or assigns of any person therein specified with reasonable certainty, or to him or his order, or when it is conspicuously designed on its face as "exchange" or the like and names a payee. It may be payable to the order of

(a) the maker or drawer; or

(b) the drawee; or

(c) a payee who is not maker, drawer or drawee; or

(d) two or more payees together or in the alternative; or

(e) an estate, trust or fund, in which case it is payable to the order of the representative of such estate, trust or fund or his successors; or

(f) an office, or an officer by his title as such in which case it is payable to the principal, but the incumbent of the office or his successors may act as if he or they were the holder; or

(g) a partnership or unincorporated association, in which case it is payable to the partnership or association and may be indorsed or transferred by any person thereto authorized.

(2) An instrument not payable to order is not made so payable by such words as "payable upon return of this instrument properly indorsed."

(3) An instrument made payable both to order and to bearer is payable to order unless the bearer words are handwritten or typewritten.

Section 3—111. Payable to Bearer.

An instrument is payable to bearer when by its terms it is payable to

(a) bearer or the order of bearer; or

(b) a specified person or bearer; or

(c) "cash" or the order of "cash", or any other indication which does not purport to designate a specific payee.

Section 3—112. Terms and Omissions Not Affecting Negotiability.

(1) The negotiability of an instrument is not affected by

(a) the omission of a statement of any consideration or of the place where the instrument is drawn or payable; or

(b) a statement that collateral has been given to secure obligations either on the instrument or otherwise of an obligor on the instrument or that in case of default on those obligations the holder may realize on or dispose of the collateral; or

(c) a promise or power to maintain or protect collateral or to give additional collateral; or

(d) a term authorizing a confession of judgment on the instrument if it is not paid when due; or

(e) a term purporting to waive the benefit of any law intended for the advantage or protection of any obligor; or

(f) a term in a draft providing that the payee by indorsing or cashing it acknowledges full satisfaction of an obligation of the drawer; or

(g) a statement in a draft drawn in a set of parts (Section 3—801) to the effect that the order is effective only if no other part has been honored.

(2) Nothing in this section shall validate any term which is otherwise illegal.

Section 3—113. Seal.

An instrument otherwise negotiable is within this Article even though it is under a seal.

Section 3-114. Date, Antedating, Postdating.

(1) The negotiability of an instrument is not affected by the fact that it is undated, antedated or postdated.

(2) Where an instrument is antedated or postdated the time when it is payable is determined by the stated date if the instrument is payable on demand or at a fixed period after date.

(3) Where the instrument or any signature thereon is dated, the date is presumed to be correct.

Section 3—115. Incomplete Instruments.

(1) When a paper whose contents at the time of signing show that it is intended to become an instrument is signed while still incomplete in any necessary respect, it cannot be enforced until completed, but when it is completed in accordance with authority given it is effective as completed.

(2) If the completion is unauthorized, the rules as to material alteration apply (Section 3—407), even though the paper was not delivered by the maker or drawer; but the burden of establishing that any completion is unauthorized is on the party so asserting.

Section 3—116. Instruments Payable to Two or More Persons.

An instrument payable to the order of two or more persons

(a) if in the alternative is payable to any one of them and may be negotiated, discharged or enforced by any of them who has possession of it;

(b) if not in the alternative is payable to all of them and may be negotiated, discharged or enforced only by all of them.

Section 3—117. Instruments Payable With Words of Description.

An instrument made payable to a named person with the addition of words describing him

(a) as agent or officer of a specified person is payable to his principal, but the agent or officer may act as if he were the holder;

(b) as any other fiduciary for a specified person or purpose is payable to the payee and may be negotiated, discharged or enforced by him;

(c) in any other manner is payable to the payee unconditionally and the additional words are without effect on subsequent parties.

Section 3—118. Ambiguous Terms and Rules of Construction.

The following rules apply to every instrument:

(a) Where there is doubt whether the instrument is a draft or a note the holder may treat it as either. A draft drawn on the drawer is effective as a note.

(b) Handwritten terms control typewritten and printed terms, and typewritten control printed.

(c) Words control figures except that if the words are ambiguous, figures control.

(d) Unless otherwise specified, a provision for interest means interest at the judgment rate at the place of payment from the date of the instrument, or if it is undated from the date of issue.

(e) Unless the instrument otherwise specifies, two or more persons who sign as maker, acceptor or drawer or indorser and as a part of the same transaction are jointly and severally liable even though the instrument contains such words as "I promise to pay."

(f) Unless otherwise specified, consent to extension authorizes a single extension for not longer than the original period. A consent to extension, expressed in the instrument, is binding on secondary parties and accommodation makers. A holder may not exercise his option to extend an instrument over the objection of a maker or acceptor or other party who in accordance with Section 3—604 tenders full payment when the instrument is due.

Section 3—119. Other Writings Affecting Instrument.

(1) As between the obligor and his immediate obligee or any transferee the terms of an instrument may be modified or affected by any other written agreement executed as a part of the same transaction, except that a holder in due course is not affected by any limitation of his rights arising out of the separate written agreement if he had no notice of the limitation when he took the instrument.

(2) A separate agreement does not affect the negotiability of an instrument.

Section 3—120. Instruments "Payable Through" Bank.

An instrument which states that it is "payable through" a bank or the like designates that bank as a collecting bank to make presentment but does not of itself authorize the bank to pay the instrument.

Section 3—121. Instruments Payable at Bank.

Note: *If this Act is introduced in the Congress of the United States, this section should be omitted.*
(States to select either alternative)

Alternative A—

A note or acceptance which states that it is payable at a bank is the equivalent of a draft drawn on the bank payable when it falls due out of any funds of the maker or acceptor in current account or otherwise available for such payment.

Alternative B—

A note or acceptance which states that it is payable at a bank is not of itself an order or authorization to the bank to pay it.

Section 3—122. Accrual of Cause of Action.

(1) A cause of action against a maker or an acceptor accrues

(a) in the case of a time instrument on the day after maturity;

(b) in the case of a demand instrument upon its date or, if no date is stated, on the date of issue.

(2) A cause of action against the obligor of a demand or time certificate of deposit accrues upon demand, but demand on a time certificate may not be made until on or after the date of maturity.

(3) A cause of action against a drawer of a draft or an indorser of any instrument accrues upon demand following dishonor of the instrument. Notice of dishonor is a demand.

(4) Unless an instrument provides otherwise, interest runs at the rate provided by law for a judgment

(a) in the case of a maker, acceptor or other primary obligor of a demand instrument, from the date of demand;

(b) in all other cases from the date of accrual of the cause of action.

PART 2

TRANSFER AND NEGOTIATION

Section 3—201. Transfer: Right to Indorsement.

(1) Transfer of an instrument vests in the transferee such rights as the transferor has therein, except that a transferee who has himself been a party to any fraud or illegality

affecting the instrument or who as a prior holder had notice of a defense or claim against it cannot improve his position by taking from a later holder in due course.

(2) A transfer of a security interest in an instrument vests the foregoing rights in the transferee to the extent of the interest transferred.

(3) Unless otherwise agreed, any transfer for value of an instrument not then payable to bearer gives the transferee the specifically enforceable right to have the unqualified indorsement of the transferor. Negotiation takes effect only when the indorsement is made and until that time there is no presumption that the transferee is the owner.

Section 3—202. Negotiation.

(1) Negotiation is the transfer of an instrument in such form that the transferee becomes a holder. If the instrument is payable to order, it is negotiated by delivery with any necessary indorsement; if payable to bearer, it is negotiated by delivery.

(2) An indorsement must be written by or on behalf of the holder and on the instrument or on a paper so firmly affixed thereto as to become a part thereof.

(3) An indorsement is effective for negotiation only when it conveys the entire instrument or any unpaid residue. If it purports to be of less, it operates only as a partial assignment.

(4) Words of assignment, condition, waiver, guaranty, limitation or disclaimer of liability and the like accompanying an indorsement do not affect its character as an indorsement.

Section 3—203. Wrong or Misspelled Name.

Where an instrument is made payable to a person under a misspelled name or one other than his own he may indorse in that name or his own or both; but signature in both names may be required by a person paying or giving value for the instrument.

Section 3—204. Special Indorsement; Blank Indorsement.

(1) A special indorsement specifies the person to whom or to whose order it makes the instrument payable. Any instrument specially indorsed becomes payable to the order of the special indorsee and may be further negotiated only by his indorsement.

(2) An indorsement in blank specifies no particular indorsee and may consist of a mere signature. An instrument payable to order and indorsed in blank becomes payable to bearer and may be negotiated by delivery alone until specially indorsed.

(3) The holder may convert a blank indorsement into a special indorsement by writing over the signature of the indorser in blank any contract consistent with the character of the indorsement.

Section 3—205. Restrictive Indorsements.

An indorsement is restrictive which either

(a) is conditional; or

(b) purports to prohibit further transfer of the instrument; or

(c) includes the words "for collection", "for deposit", "pay any bank", or like terms signifying a purpose of deposit or collection; or

(d) otherwise states that it is for the benefit or use of the indorser or of another person.

Section 3—206. Effect of Restrictive Indorsement.

(1) No restrictive indorsement prevents further transfer or negotiation of the instrument.

(2) An intermediary bank, or a payor bank which is not the depositary bank, is neither given notice nor otherwise affected by a restrictive indorsement of any person except the bank's immediate transferor or the person presenting for payment.

(3) Except for an intermediary bank, any transferee under an indorsement which is conditional or includes the words "for collection", "for deposit", "pay any bank", or like terms (subparagraphs (a) and (c) of Section 3—205) must pay or apply any value given by him for or on the security of the instrument consistently with the indorsement, and to the extent that he does so he becomes a holder for value. In addiion such transferee is a holder in due course

if he otherwise complies with the requirements of Section 3—302 on what constitutes a holder in due course.

(4) The first taker under an indorsement for the benefit of the indorser or another person (subparagraph (d) of Section 3—205) must pay or apply any value given by him for or on the security of the instrument consistently with the indorsement, and to the extent that he does so he becomes a holder for value. In addition such taker is a holder in due course if he otherwise complies with the requirements of Section 3—302 on what constitutes a holder in due course. A later holder for value is neither given notice nor otherwise affected by such restrictive indorsement unless he has knowledge that a fiduciary or other person has negotiated the instrument in any transaction for his own benefit or otherwise in breach of duty (subsection (2) of Section 3—304).

Section 3—207. Negotiation Effective Although It May Be Rescinded.

(1) Negotiation is effective to transfer the instrument although the negotiation is

(a) made by an infant, a corporation exceeding its powers, or any other person without capacity; or

(b) obtained by fraud, duress or mistake of any kind; or

(c) part of an illegal transaction; or

(d) made in breach of duty.

(2) Except as against a subsequent holder in due course such negotiation is in an appropriate case subject to rescission, the declaration of a constructive trust or any other remedy permitted by law.

Section 3—208. Reacquisition.

Where an instrument is returned to or reacquired by a prior party he may cancel any indorsement which is not necessary to his title and reissue or further negotiate the instrument, but any intervening party is discharged as against the reacquiring party and subsequent holders not in due course and if his indorsement has been canceled is discharged as against subsequent holders in due course as well.

PART 3

RIGHTS OF A HOLDER

Section 3—301. Rights of a Holder.

The holder of an instrument whether or not he is the owner may transfer or negotiate it and, except as otherwise provided in Section 3—603 on payment or satisfaction, discharge it or enforce payment in his own name.

Section 3—302. Holder in Due Course.

(1) A holder in due course is a holder who takes the instrument

(a) for value; and

(b) in good faith; and

(c) without notice that it is overdue or has been dishonored or of any defense against or claim to it on the part of any person.

(2) A payee may be a holder in due course.

(3) A holder does not become a holder in due course of an instrument:

(a) by purchase of it at judicial sale or by taking it under legal process; or

(b) by acquiring it in taking over an estate; or

(c) by purchasing it as part of a bulk transaction not in regular course of business of the transferor.

(4) A purchaser of a limited interest can be a holder in due course only to the extent of the interest purchased.

Section 3—303. Taking for Value.

A holder takes the instrument for value

(a) to the extent that the agreed consideration has been performed or that he acquires a security interest in or a lien on the instrument otherwise than by legal process; or

(b) when he takes the instrument in payment of or as security for an antecedent claim against any person whether or not the claim is due; or

(c) when he gives a negotiable instrument for it or makes an irrevocable commitment to a third person.

Section 3—304. Notice to Purchaser.

(1) The purchaser has notice of a claim or defense if

(a) the instrument is so incomplete, bears such visible evidence of forgery or alteration, or is otherwise so irregular as to call into question its validity, terms or ownership or to create an ambiguity as to the party to pay; or

(b) the purchaser has notice that the obligation of any party is voidable in whole or in part, or that all parties have been discharged.

(2) The purchaser has notice of a claim against the instrument when he has knowledge that a fiduciary has negotiated the instrument in payment of or as security for his own debt or in any transaction for his own benefit or otherwise in breach of duty.

(3) The purchaser has notice that an instrument is overdue if he has reason to know

(a) that any part of the principal amount is overdue or that there is an uncured default in payment of another instrument of the same series; or

(b) that acceleration of the instrument has been made; or

(c) that he is taking a demand instrument after demand has been made or more than a reasonable length of time after its issue. A reasonable time for a check drawn and payable within the states and territories of the United States and the District of Columbia is presumed to be thirty days.

(4) Knowledge of the following facts does not of itself give the purchaser notice of a defense or claim

(a) that the instrument is antedated or postdated;

(b) that it was issued or negotiated in return for an executory promise or accompanied by a separate agreement, unless the purchaser has notice that a defense or claim has arisen from the terms thereof;

(c) that any party has signed for accommodation;

(d) that an incomplete instrument has been completed, unless the purchaser has notice of any improper completion;

(e) that any person negotiating the instrument is or was a fiduciary;

(f) that there has been default in payment of interest on the instrument or in payment of any other instrument, except one of the same series.

(5) The filing or recording of a document does not of itself constitute notice within the provisions of this Article to a person who would otherwise be a holder in due course.

(6) To be effective notice must be received at such time and in such manner as to give a reasonable opportunity to act on it.

Section 3—305. Rights of a Holder in Due Course.

To the extent that a holder is a holder in due course he takes the instrument free from

(1) all claims to it on the part of any person; and

(2) all defenses of any party to the instrument with whom the holder has not dealt except

(a) infancy, to the extent that it is a defense to a simple contract; and

(b) such other incapacity, or duress, or illegality of the transaction, as renders the obligation of the party a nullity; and

(c) such misrepresentation as has induced the party to sign the instrument with neither knowledge nor reasonable opportunity to obtain knowledge of its character or its essential terms; and

(d) discharge in insolvency proceedings; and

(e) any other discharge of which the holder has notice when he takes the instrument.

Section 3—306. Rights of One Not Holder in Due Course.

Unless he has the rights of a holder in due course, any person takes the instrument subject to

(a) all valid claims to it on the part of any person; and

(b) all defenses of any party which would be available in an action on a simple contract; and

(c) the defenses of want or failure of consideration, nonperformance of any condition precedent non-delivery, or delivery for a special purpose (Section 3—408); and

(d) the defense that he or a person through whom he holds the instrument acquired it by theft, or that payment or satisfaction to such holder would be inconsistent with the terms of a restrictive indorsement. The claim of any third person to the instrument is not otherwise available as a defense to any party liable thereon unless the third person himself defends the action for such party.

Section 3—307. Burden of Establishing Signatures, Defenses and Due Course.

(1) Unless specifically denied in the pleadings each signature on an instrument is admitted. When the effectiveness of a signature is put in issue

(a) the burden of establishing it is on the party claiming under the signature; but

(b) the signature is presumed to be genuine or authorized except where the action is to enforce the obligation of a purported signer who has died or become incompetent before proof is required.

(2) When signatures are admitted or established, production of the instrument entitles a holder to recover on it unless the defendant establishes a defense.

(3) After it is shown that a defense exists a person claiming the rights of a holder in due course has the burden of establishing that he or some person under whom he claims is in all respects a holder in due course.

PART 4

LIABILITY OF PARTIES

Section 3—401. Signature.

(1) No person is liable on an instrument unless his signature appears thereon.

(2) A signature is made by use of any name, including any trade or assumed name, upon an instrument, or by any word or mark used in lieu of a written signature.

Section 3—402. Signature in Ambiguous Capacity.

Unless the instrument clearly indicates that a signature is made in some other capacity, it is an indorsement.

Section 3—403. Signature by Authorized Representative.

(1) A signature may be made by an agent or other representative, and his authority to make it may be established as in other cases of representation. No particular form of appointment is necessary to establish such authority.

(2) An authorized representative who signs his own name to an instrument

(a) is personally obligated if the instrument neither names the person represented nor shows that the representative signed in a representative capacity;

(b) except as otherwise established between the immediate parties, is personally obligated if the instrument names the person represented but does not show that the representative signed in a representative capacity, or if the instrument does not name the person represented but does show that the representative signed in a representative capacity.

(3) Except as otherwise established, the name of an organization preceded or followed by the name and office of an authorized individual is a signature made in a representative capacity.

Section 3—404. Unauthorized Signatures.

(1) Any unauthorized signature is wholly inoperative as that of the person whose name is signed unless he ratifies it or is precluded from denying it; but it operates as the signature of the unauthorized signer in favor of any person who in good faith pays the instrument or takes it for value.

(2) Any unauthorized signature may be ratified for all purposes of this Article. Such ratification does not of itself affect any rights of the person ratifying against the actual signer.

Section 3—405. Impostors; Signature in Name of Payee.

(1) An indorsement by any person in the name of a named payee is effective if

(a) an impostor by use of the mails or otherwise has induced the maker or drawer to issue the instrument to him or his confederate in the name of the payee; or

(b) a person signing as or on behalf of a maker or drawer intends the payee to have no interest in the instrument; or

(c) an agent or employee of the maker or drawer has supplied him with the name of the payee intending the latter to have no such interest.

(2) Nothing in this section shall affect the criminal or civil liability of the person so indorsing.

Section 3—406. Negligence Contributing to Alteration or Unauthorized Signature.

Any person who by his negligence substantially contributes to a material alteration of the instrument or to the making of an unauthorized signature is precluded from asserting the alteration or lack of authority against a holder in due course or against a drawee or other payor who pays the instrument in good faith and in accordance with the reasonable commercial standards of the drawee's or payor's business.

Section 3—407. Alteration.

(1) Any alteration of an instrument is material which changes the contract of any party thereto in any respect, including any such change in

(a) the number or relations of the parties; or

(b) an incomplete instrument, by completing it otherwise than as authorized; or

(c) the writing as signed, by adding to it or by removing any part of it.

(2) As against any person other than a subsequent holder in due course

(a) alteration by the holder which is both fraudulent and material discharges any party whose contract is thereby changed unless that party assents or is precluded from asserting the defense;

(b) no other alteration discharges any party and the instrument may be enforced according to its original tenor, or as to incomplete instruments according to the authority given.

(3) A subsequent holder in due course may in all cases enforce the instrument according to its original tenor, and when an incomplete instrument has been completed, he may enforce it as completed.

Section 3—408. Consideration.

Want or failure of consideration is a defense as against any person not having the rights of a holder in due course (Section 3—305), except that no consideration is necessary for an instrument or obligation thereon given in payment of or as security for an antecedent obligation of any kind. Nothing in this section shall be taken to displace any statute outside this Act under which a promise is enforceable notwithstanding lack or failure of consideration. Partial failure of consideration is a defense pro tanto whether or not the failure is in an ascertained or liquidated amount.

Section 3—409. Draft Not an Assignment.

(1) A check or other draft does not of itself operate as an assignment of any funds in the

hands of the drawee available for its payment, and the drawee is not liable on the instrument until he accepts it.

(2) Nothing in this section shall affect any liability in contract, tort or otherwise arising from any letter of credit or other obligation or representation which is not an acceptance.

Section 3—410. Definition and Operation of Acceptance.

(1) Acceptance is the drawee's signed engagement to honor the draft as presented. It must be written on the draft and may consist of his signature alone. It becomes operative when completed by delivery or notification.

(2) A draft may be accepted although it has not been signed by the drawer or is otherwise incomplete or is overdue or has been dishonored.

(3) Where the draft is payable at a fixed period after sight and the acceptor fails to date his acceptance, the holder may complete it by supplying a date in good faith.

Section 3-411. Certification of a Check.

(1) Certification of a check is acceptance. Where a holder procures certification the drawer and all prior indorsers are discharged.

(2) Unless otherwise agreed a bank has no obligation to certify a check.

(3) A bank may certify a check before returning it for lack of proper indorsement. If it does so, the drawer is discharged.

Section 3—412. Acceptance Varying Draft.

(1) Where the drawee's proffered acceptance in any manner varies the draft as presented, the holder may refuse the acceptance and treat the draft as dishonored in which case the drawee is entitled to have his acceptance cancelled.

(2) The terms of the draft are not varied by an acceptance to pay at any particular bank or place in the United States, unless the acceptance states that the draft is to be paid only at such bank or place.

(3) Where the holder assents to an acceptance varying the terms of the draft, each drawer and indorser who does not affirmatively assent is discharged.

Section 3—413. Contract of Maker, Drawer and Acceptor.

(1) The maker or acceptor engages that he will pay the instrument according to its tenor at the time of his engagement or as completed pursuant to Section 3—115 on incomplete instruments.

(2) The drawer engages that upon dishonor of the draft and any necessary notice of dishonor or protest he will pay the amount of the draft to the holder or to any indorser who takes it up. The drawer may disclaim this liability by drawing without recourse.

(3) By making, drawing or accepting the party admits as against all subsequent parties including the drawee the existence of the payee and his then capacity to indorse.

Section 3—414. Contract of Indorser; Order of Liability.

(1) Unless the indorsement otherwise specifies (as by such words as "without recourse") every indorser engages that upon dishonor and any necessary notice of dishonor and protest he will pay the instrument according to its tenor at the time of his indorsement to the holder or to any subsequent indorser who takes it up, even though the indorser who takes it up was not obligated to do so.

(2) Unless they otherwise agree, indorsers are liable to one another in the order in which they indorse, which is presumed to be the order in which their signatures appear on the instrument.

Section 3—415. Contract of Accommodation Party.

(1) An accommodation party is one who signs the instrument in any capacity for the purpose of lending his name to another party to it.

(2) When the instrument has been taken for value before it is due, the accommodation party is liable in the capacity in which he has signed even though the taker knows of the accommodation.

(3) As against a holder in due course and without notice of the accommodation, oral proof of the accommodation is not admissible to give the accommodation party the benefit of discharges dependent on his character as such. In

other cases the accommodation character may be shown by oral proof.

(4) An indorsement which shows that it is not in the chain of title is notice of its accommodation character.

(5) An accommodation party is not liable to the party accommodated, and if he pays the instrument has a right of recourse on the instrument against such party.

Section 3—416. Contract of Guarantor.

(1) "Payment guaranteed" or equivalent words added to a signature mean that the signer engages that if the instrument is not paid when due he will pay it according to its tenor without resort by the holder to any other party.

(2) "Collection guaranteed" or equivalent words added to a signature mean that the signer engages that if the instrument is not paid when due he will pay it according to its tenor, but only after the holder has reduced his claim against the maker or acceptor to judgment and execution has been returned unsatisfied, or after the maker or acceptor has become insolvent or it is otherwise apparent that it is useless to proceed against him.

(3) Words of guaranty which do not otherwise specify guarantee payment.

(4) No words of guaranty added to the signature of a sole maker or acceptor affect his liability on the instrument. Such words added to the signature of one or two or more makers or acceptors create a presumption that the signature is for the accommodation of the others.

(5) When words of guaranty are used, presentment, notice of dishonor and protest are not necessary to charge the user.

(6) Any guaranty written on the instrument is enforcible notwithstanding any statute of frauds.

Section 3—417. Warranties on Presentment and Transfer.

(1) Any person who obtains payment or acceptance and any prior transferor warrants to a person who in good faith pays or accepts that

(a) he has a good title to the instrument or is authorized to obtain payment or acceptance on behalf of one who has a good title; and

(b) he has no knowledge that the signature of the maker or drawer is unauthorized, except that this warranty is not given by a holder in due course acting in good faith

(i) to a maker with respect to the maker's own signature; or

(ii) to a drawer with respect to the drawer's own signature, whether or not the drawer is also the drawee; or

(iii) to an acceptor of a draft if the holder in due course took the draft after the acceptance or obtained the acceptance without knowledge that the drawer's signature was unauthorized; and

(c) the instrument has not been materially altered, except that this warranty is not given by a holder in due course acting in good faith

(i) to the maker of a note; or

(ii) to the drawer of a draft whether or not the drawer is also the drawee; or

(iii) to the acceptor of a draft with respect to an alteration made prior to the acceptance if the holder in due course took the draft after the acceptance, even though the acceptance provided "payable as originally drawn" or equivalent terms; or

(iv) to the acceptor of a draft with respect to an alteration made after the acceptance.

(2) Any person who transfers an instrument and receives consideration warrants to his transferee and, if the transfer is by indorsement, to any subsequent holder who takes the instrument in good faith that

(a) he has a good title to the instrument or is authorized to obtain payment or acceptance on behalf of one who has a good title and the transfer is otherwise rightful; and

(b) all signatures are genuine or authorized; and

(c) the instrument has not been materially altered; and

(d) no defense of any party is good against him; and

(e) he has no knowledge of any insolvency proceeding instituted with respect to the maker or acceptor or the drawer of an unaccepted instrument.

(3) By transferring "without recourse" the transferor limits the obligation stated in subsection (2) (d) to a warranty that he has no knowledge of such a defense.

(4) A selling agent or broker who does not disclose the fact that he is acting only as such gives the warranties provided in this section, but if he makes such disclosure warrants only his good faith and authority.

Section 3—418. Finality of Payment or Acceptance.

Except for recovery of bank payments as provided in the Article on Bank Deposits and Collections (Article 4) and except for liability for breach of warranty on presentment under the preceding section, payment or acceptance of any instrument is final in favor of a holder in due course, or a person who has in good faith changed his position in reliance on the payment.

Section 3—419. Conversion of Instrument; Innocent Representative.

(1) An instrument is converted when

(a) a drawee to whom it is delivered for acceptance refuses to return it on demand; or

(b) any person to whom it is delivered for payment refuses on demand either to pay or to return it; or

(c) it is paid on a forged indorsement.

(2) In an action against a drawee under subsection (1) the measure of the drawee's liability is the face amount of the instrument. In any other action under subsection (1) the measure of liability is presumed to be the face amount of the instrument.

(3) Subject to the provisions of this Act concerning restrictive indorsements a representative, including a depositary or collecting bank, who has in good faith and in accordance with the reasonable commercial standards applicable to the business of such representative dealt with an instrument or its proceeds on behalf of one who was not the true owner is not liable in conversion or otherwise to the true owner beyond the amount of any proceeds remaining in his hands.

(4) An intermediary bank or payor bank which is not a depositary bank is not liable in conversion solely by reason of the fact that proceeds of an item indorsed restrictively (Sections 3—205 and 3—206) are not paid or applied consistently with the restrictive indorsement of an indorser other than its immediate transferor.

PART 5

PRESENTMENT, NOTICE OF DISHONOR AND PROTEST

Section 3—501. When Presentment, Notice of Dishonor, and Protest Necessary or Permissible.

(1) Unless excused (Section 3—511) presentment is necessary to charge secondary parties as follows:

(a) presentment for acceptance is necessary to charge the drawer and indorsers of a draft where the draft so provides, or is payable elsewhere than at the residence or place of business of the drawee, or its date of payment depends upon such presentment. The holder may at his option present for acceptance any other draft payable at a stated date;

(b) presentment for payment is necessary to charge any indorser;

(c) in the case of any drawer, the acceptor of a draft payable at a bank or the maker of a note payable at a bank, presentment for payment is necessary, but failure to make presentment discharges such drawer, acceptor or maker only as stated in Section 3—502(1)(b).

(2) Unless excused (Section 3—511)

(a) notice of any dishonor is necessary to charge any indorser;

(b) in the case of any drawer, the acceptor of a draft payable at a bank or the maker of a note payable at a bank, notice of any dishonor is necessary, but failure to give such notice discharges such drawer, acceptor or maker only as stated in Section 3—502(1)(b).

(3) Unless excused (Section 3—511), protest of any dishonor is necessary to charge the drawer and indorsers of any draft which on its face appears to be drawn or payable outside of the states and territories of the United States and the District of Columbia. The holder may at his option make protest of any dishonor of any other instrument and in the case of a foreign draft may on insolvency of the acceptor before maturity make protest for better security.

(4) Notwithstanding any provision of this section, neither presentment nor notice of dishonor nor protest is necessary to charge an indorser who has indorsed an instrument after maturity.

Section 3—502. Unexcused Delay; Discharge.

(1) Where without excuse any necessary presentment or notice of dishonor is delayed beyond the time when it is due

(a) any indorser is discharged; and

(b) any drawer or the acceptor of a draft payable at a bank or the maker of a note payable at a bank who, because the drawee or payor bank becomes insolvent during the delay, is deprived of funds maintained with the drawee or payor bank to cover the instrument may discharge his liability by written assignment to the holder of his rights against the drawee or payor bank in respect of such funds, but such drawer, acceptor or maker is not otherwise discharged.

(2) Where without excuse a necessary protest is delayed beyond the time when it is due, any drawer or indorser is discharged.

Section 3—503. Time of Presentment.

(1) Unless a different time is expressed in the instrument, the time for any presentment is determined as follows:

(a) where an instrument is payable at or a fixed period after a stated date, any presentment for acceptance must be made on or before the date it is payable;

(b) where an instrument is payable after sight, it must either be presented for acceptance or negotiated within a reasonable time after date or issue whichever is later;

(c) where an instrument shows the date on which it is payable, presentment for payment is due on that date;

(d) where an instrument is accelerated, presentment for payment is due within a reasonable time after the acceleration;

(e) with respect to the liability of any secondary party presentment for acceptance or payment of any other instrument is due within a reasonable time after such party becomes liable thereon.

(2) A reasonable time for presentment is determined by the nature of the instrument, any usage of banking or trade and the facts of the particular case. In the case of an uncertified check which is drawn and payable within the United States and which is not a draft drawn by a bank the following are presumed to be reasonable periods within which to present for payment or to initiate bank collection:

(a) with respect to the liability of the drawer, thirty days after date or issue whichever is later; and

(b) with respect to the liability of an indorser, seven days after his indorsement.

(3) Where any presentment is due on a day which is not a full business day for either the person making presentment or the party to pay or accept, presentment is due on the next following day which is a full business day for both parties.

(4) Presentment to be sufficient must be made at a reasonable hour, and if at a bank during its banking day.

Section 3—504. How Presentment Made.

(1) Presentment is a demand for acceptance or payment made upon the maker, acceptor,

drawee or other payor by or on behalf of the holder.

(2) Presentment may be made

(a) by mail, in which event the time of presentment is determined by the time of receipt of the mail, or

(b) through a clearing house; or

(c) at the place of acceptance of payment specified in the instrument or if there be none at the place of business or residence of the party to accept or pay. If neither the party to accept or pay nor anyone authorized to act for him is present or accessible at such place, presentment is excused.

(3) It may be made

(a) to any one of two or more makers, acceptors, drawees or other payors; or

(b) to any person who has authority to make or refuse the acceptance or payment.

(4) A draft accepted or a note made payable at a bank in the United States must be presented at such bank.

(5) In the cases described in Section 4—210 presentment may be made in the manner and with the result stated in that section.

Section 3—505. Rights of Party to Whom Presentment Is Made.

(1) The party to whom presentment is made may without dishonor require

(a) exhibition of the instrument; and

(b) reasonable identification of the person making presentment and evidence of his authority to make it if made for another; and

(c) that the instrument be produced for acceptance or payment at a place specified in it, or if there be none at any place reasonable in the circumstances; and

(d) a signed receipt on the instrument for any partial or full payment and its surrender upon full payment.

(2) Failure to comply with any such requirement invalidates the presentment, but the person presenting has a reasonable time in which to comply and the time for acceptance or payment runs from the time of compliance.

Section 3—506. Time Allowed for Acceptance or Payment.

(1) Acceptance may be deferred without dishonor until the close of the next business day following presentment. The holder may also in a good faith effort to obtain acceptance and without either dishonor of the instrument or discharge of secondary parties allow postponement of acceptance for an additional business day.

(2) Except as a longer time is allowed in the case of documentary drafts drawn under a letter of credit, and unless an earlier time is agreed to by the party to pay, payment of an instrument may be deferred without dishonor pending reasonable examination to determine whether it is properly payable, but payment must be made in any event before the close of business on the day of presentment.

Section 3—507. Dishonor; Holder's Right of Recourse; Term Allowing Re-Presentment.

(1) An instrument is dishonored when

(a) a necessary or optional presentment is duly made and due acceptance or payment is refused or cannot be obtained within the prescribed time or in case of bank collections the instrument is seasonably returned by the midnight deadline (Section 4—301); or

(b) presentment is excused and the instrument is not duly accepted or paid.

(2) Subject to any necessary notice of dishonor and protest, the holder has upon dishonor an immediate right of recourse against the drawers and indorsers.

(3) Return of an instrument for lack of proper indorsement is not dishonor.

(4) A term in a draft or an indorsement thereof allowing a stated time for re-presentment in the event of any dishonor of the draft by nonacceptance if a time draft or by nonpayment if a sight draft gives the holder as against any secondary party bound by the term an option to waive the dishonor without affecting the liability

of the secondary party, and he may present again up to the end of the stated time.

Section 3—508. Notice of Dishonor.

(1) Notice of dishonor may be given to any person who may be liable on the instrument by or on behalf of the holder or any party who has himself received notice, or any other party who can be compelled to pay the instrument. In addition an agent or bank in whose hands the instrument is dishonored may give notice to his principal or customer or to another agent or bank from which the instrument was received.

(2) Any necessary notice must be given by a bank before its midnight deadline and by any other person before midnight of the third business day after dishonor or receipt of notice of dishonor.

(3) Notice may be given in any reasonable manner. It may be oral or written, and in any terms which identify the instrument and state that it has been dishonored. A misdescription which does not mislead the party notified does not vitiate the notice. Sending the instrument bearing a stamp, ticket or writing stating that acceptance or payment has been refused or sending a notice of debit with respect to the instrument is sufficient.

(4) Written notice is given when sent although it is not received.

(5) Notice to one partner is notice to each although the firm has been dissolved.

(6) When any party is in insolvency proceedings instituted after the issue of the instrument, notice may be given either to the party or to the representative of his estate.

(7) When any party is dead or incompetent, notice may be sent to his last known address or given to his personal representative.

(8) Notice operates for the benefit of all parties who have rights on the instrument against the party notified.

Section 3—509. Protest; Noting for Protest.

(1) A protest is a certificate of dishonor made under the hand and seal of a United States consul or vice consul or a notary public or other person authorized to certify dishonor by the law of the place where dishonor occurs. It may be made upon information satisfactory to such person.

(2) The protest must identify the instrument and certify either that due presentment has been made or the reason why it is excused and that the instrument has been dishonored by nonacceptance or nonpayment.

(3) The protest may also certify that notice of dishonor has been given to all parties or to specified parties.

(4) Subject to subsection (5) any necessary protest is due by the time that notice of dishonor is due.

(5) If, before protest is due, an instrument has been noted for protest by the officer to make protest, the protest may be made at any time thereafter as of the date of the noting.

Section 3—510. Evidence of Dishonor and Notice of Dishonor.

The following are admissible as evidence and create a presumption of dishonor and of any notice of dishonor therein shown:

(a) a document regular in form as provided in the preceding section which purports to be a protest;

(b) the purported stamp or writing of the drawee, payor bank or presenting bank on the instrument or accompanying it stating that acceptance or payment has been refused for reasons consistent with dishonor;

(c) any book or record of the drawee, payor bank, or any collecting bank kept in the usual course of business which shows dishonor, even though there is no evidence of who made the entry.

Section 3—511. Waived or Excused Presentment, Protest or Notice of Dishonor or Delay Therein.

(1) Delay in presentment, protest or notice of dishonor is excused when the party is without notice that it is due or when the delay is caused by circumstances beyond his control and he exercises reasonable diligence after the cause of the delay ceases to operate.

(2) Presentment or notice or protest as the case may be is entirely excused when

(a) the party to be charged has waived it expressly or by implication either before or after it is due; or

(b) such party has himself dishonored the instrument or has countermanded payment or otherwise has no reason to expect or right to require that the instrument be accepted or paid; or

(c) by reasonable diligence the presentment or protest cannot be made or the notice given.

(3) Presentment is also entirely excused when

(a) the maker, acceptor or drawee of any instrument except a documentary draft is dead or in insolvency proceedings instituted after the issue of the instrument; or

(b) acceptance or payment is refused but not for want of proper presentment.

(4) Where a draft has been dishonored by nonacceptance, a later presentment for payment and any notice of dishonor and protest for nonpayment are excused unless in the meantime the instrument has been accepted.

(5) A waiver of protest is also a waiver of presentment and of notice of dishonor even though protest is not required.

(6) Where a waiver of presentment or notice or protest is embodied in the instrument itself, it is binding upon all parties; but where it is written above the signature of an indorser it binds him only.

PART 6

DISCHARGE

Section 3—601. Discharge of Parties.

(1) The extent of the discharge of any party from liability on an instrument is governed by the sections on

(a) payment or satisfaction (Section 3—603); or

(b) tender of payment (Section 3—604); or

(c) cancellation or renunciation (Section 3—605); or

(d) impairment of right of recourse or of collateral (Section 3—606); or

(e) reacquisition of the instrument by a prior party (Section 3—208); or

(f) fraudulent and material alteration (Section 3—407); or

(g) certification of a check (Section 3—411); or

(h) acceptance varying a draft (Section 3—412); or

(i) unexcused delay in presentment or notice of dishonor or protest (Section 3—502).

(2) Any party is also discharged from his liability on an instrument to another party by any other act or agreement with such party which would discharge his simple contract for the payment of money.

(3) The liability of all parties is discharged when any party who has himself no right of action or recourse on the instrument

(a) reacquires the instrument in his own right; or

(b) is discharged under any provision of this Article, except as otherwise provided with respect to discharge for impairment of recourse or of collateral (Section 3—606).

Section 3—602. Effect of Discharge Against Holder in Due Course.

No discharge of any party provided by this Article is effective against a subsequent holder in due course unless he has notice thereof when he takes the instrument.

Section 3—603. Payment or Satisfaction.

(1) The liability of any party is discharged to the extent of his payment or satisfaction to the holder even though it is made with knowledge of a claim of another person to the instrument unless prior to such payment or satisfaction the person making the claim either supplies indemnity deemed adequate by the party seeking the discharge or enjoins payment or satisfaction by order of a court of competent jurisdiction in an action in which the adverse claimant and the holder are parties. This subsection does not, however, result in the discharge of the liability

(a) of a party who in bad faith pays or satisfies a holder who acquired the instrument by theft or who (unless having the rights of a holder in due course) holds through one who so acquired it; or

(b) of a party (other than an intermediary bank or a payor bank which is not a depositary bank) who pays or satisfies the holder of an instrument which has been restrictively indorsed in a manner not consistent with the terms of such restrictive indorsement.

(2) Payment or satisfaction may be made with the consent of the holder by any person including a stranger to the instrument. Surrender of the instrument to such a person gives him the rights of a transferee (Section 3—201).

Section 3—604. Tender of Payment.

(1) Any party making tender of full payment to a holder when or after it is due is discharged to the extent of all subsequent liability for interest, costs and attorney's fees.

(2) The holder's refusal of such tender wholly discharges any party who has a right of recourse against the party making the tender.

(3) Where the maker or acceptor of an instrument payable otherwise than on demand is able and ready to pay at every place of payment specified in the instrument when it is due, it is equivalent to tender.

Section 3—605. Cancellation and Renunciation.

(1) The holder of an instrument may even without consideration discharge any party

(a) in any manner apparent on the face of the instrument or the indorsement, as by intentionally cancelling the instrument or the party's signature by destruction or mutilation, or by striking out the party's signature; or

(b) by renouncing his rights by a writing signed and delivered or by surrender of the instrument to the party to be discharged.

(2) Neither cancellation nor renunciation without surrender of the instrument affects the title thereto.

Section 3—606. Impairment of Recourse or of Collateral.

(1) The holder discharges any party to the instrument to the extent that without such party's consent the holder

(a) without express reservation of rights releases or agrees not to sue any person against whom the party has to the knowledge of the holder a right of recourse or agrees to suspend the right to enforce against such person the instrument or collateral or otherwise discharges such person, except that failure or delay in effecting any required presentment, protest or notice of dishonor with respect to any such person does not discharge any party as to whom presentment, protest or notice of dishonor is effective or unnecessary; or

(b) unjustifiably impairs any collateral for the instrument given by or on behalf of the party or any person against whom he has a right of recourse.

(2) By express reservation of rights against a party with a right of recourse the holder preserves

(a) all his rights against such party as of the time when the instrument was originally due; and

(b) the right of the party to pay the instrument as of that time; and

(c) all rights of such party to recourse against others.

PART 7

ADVICE OF INTERNATIONAL SIGHT DRAFT

Section 3—701. Letter of Advice of International Sight Draft.

(1) A "letter of advice" is a drawer's communication to the drawee that a described draft has been drawn.

(2) Unless otherwise agreed, when a bank receives from another bank a letter of advice of an international sight draft, the drawee bank may immediately debit the drawer's account and stop the running of interest pro tanto. Such a debit and any resulting credit to any account covering outstanding drafts leaves in the drawer full power to stop payment or otherwise dispose of the amount and creates no trust or interest in favor of the holder.

(3) Unless otherwise agreed and except where a draft is drawn under a credit issued by the drawee, the drawee of an international sight draft owes the drawer no duty to pay an unadvised draft but if it does so and the draft is genuine, may appropriately debit the drawer's account.

PART 8

MISCELLANEOUS

Section 3—801. Drafts in a Set.

(1) Where a draft is drawn in a set of parts, each of which is numbered and expressed to be an order only if no other part has been honored, the whole of the parts constitutes one draft, but a taker of any part may become a holder in due course of the draft.

(2) Any person who negotiates, indorses or accepts a single part of a draft drawn in a set thereby becomes liable to any holder in due course of that part as if it were the whole set, but as between different holders in due course to whom different parts have been negotiated the holder whose title first accrues has all rights to the draft and its proceeds.

(3) As against the drawee the first presented part of a draft drawn in a set is the part entitled to payment, or if a time draft to acceptance and payment. Acceptance of any subsequently presented part renders the drawee liable thereon under subsection (2). With respect both to a holder and to the drawer payment of a subsequently presented part of a draft payable at sight has the same effect as payment of a check notwithstanding an effective stop order (Section 4—407).

(4) Except as otherwise provided in this section, where any part of a draft in a set is discharged by payment or otherwise the whole draft is discharged.

Section 3—802. Effect of Instrument on Obligation for Which It Is Given.

(1) Unless otherwise agreed, where an instrument is taken for an underlying obligation

(a) the obligation is pro tanto discharged if a bank is drawer, maker or acceptor of the instrument and there is no recourse on the instrument against the underlying obligor; and

(b) in any other case the obligation is suspended pro tanto until the instrument is due or if it is payable on demand until its presentment. If the instrument is dishonored, action may be maintained on either the instrument or the obligation; discharge of the underlying obligor on the instrument also discharges him on the obligation.

(2) The taking in good faith of a check which is not postdated does not of itself so extend the time on the original obligation as to discharge a surety.

Section 3—803. Notice to Third Party.

Where a defendant is sued for breach of an obligation for which a third person is answerable over under this Article, he may give the third person written notice of the litigation, and the person notified may then give similar notice to any other person who is answerable over to him under this Article. If the notice states that the person notified may come in and defend and that if the person notified does not do so he will in any action against him by the person giving the notice be bound by any determination of fact common to the two litigations, then unless after seasonable receipt of the notice the person notified does come in and defend he is so bound.

Section 3—804. Lost, Destroyed or Stolen Instruments.

The owner of an instrument which is lost, whether by destruction, theft or otherwise, may maintain an action in his own name and recover from any party liable thereon upon due proof of his ownership, the facts which prevent his production of the instrument and its terms. The court may require security indemnifying the defendant against loss by reason of further claims on the instrument.

Section 3—805. Instruments Not Payable to Order or to Bearer.

This Article applies to any instrument whose terms do not preclude transfer and which is otherwise negotiable within this Article but which is not payable to order or to bearer, except that there can be no holder in due course of such an instrument.

ARTICLE 4

BANK DEPOSITS AND COLLECTIONS

PART 1

GENERAL PROVISIONS AND DEFINITIONS

Section 4—101. Short Title.

This Article shall be known and may be cited as Uniform Commercial Code—Bank Deposits and Collections.

Section 4—102. Applicability.

(1) To the extent that items within this Article are also within the scope of Articles 3 and 8, they are subject to the provisions of those Articles. In the event of conflict the provisions of this Article govern those of Article 3, but the provisions of Article 8 govern those of this Article.

(2) The liability of a bank for action or non-action with respect to any item handled by it for purposes of presentment, payment or collection is governed by the law of the place where the bank is located. In the case of action or non-action by or at a branch or separate office of a bank, its liability is governed by the law of the place where the branch or separate office is located.

Section 4—103. Variation by Agreement; Measure of Damages; Certain Action Constituting Ordinary Care.

(1) The effect of the provisions of this Article may be varied by agreement except that no agreement can disclaim a bank's responsibility for its own lack of good faith or failure to exercise ordinary care or can limit the measure of damages for such lack or failure; but the parties may by agreement determine the standards by which such responsibility is to be measured if such standards are not manifestly unreasonable.

(2) Federal Reserve regulations and operating letters, clearing house rules, and the like, have the effect of agreements under subsection (1), whether or not specifically assented to by all parties interested in items handled.

(3) Action or non-action approved by this Article or pursuant to Federal Reserve regulations or operating letters constitutes the exercise of ordinary care and, in the absence of special instructions, action or non-action consistent with clearing house rules and the like or with a general banking usage not disapproved by this Article, prima facie constitutes the exercise of ordinary care.

(4) The specification or approval of certain procedures by this Article does not constitute disapproval of other procedures which may be reasonable under the circumstances.

(5) The measure of damages for failure to exercise ordinary care in handling an item is the amount of the item reduced by an amount which could not have been realized by the use of ordinary care, and where there is bad faith it includes other damages, if any, suffered by the party as a proximate consequence.

Section 4—104. Definitions and Index of Definitions.

(1) In this Article unless the context otherwise requires

(a) "Account" means any account with a bank and includes a checking, time, interest or savings account;

(b) "Afternoon" means the period of a day between noon and midnight;

(c) "Banking day" means that part of any day on which a bank is open to the public for carrying on substantially all of its banking functions;
(d) "Clearing house" means any association of banks or other payors regularly clearing items;
(e) "Customer" means any person having an account with a bank or for whom a bank has agreed to collect items and includes a bank carrying an account with another bank;
(f) "Documentary draft" means any negotiable or non-negotiable draft with accompanying documents, securities or other papers to be delivered against honor of the draft;
(g) "Item" means any instrument for the payment of money even though it is not negotiable but does not include money;
(h) "Midnight deadline" with respect to a bank is midnight on its next banking day following the banking day on which it receives the relevant item or notice or from which the time for taking action commences to run, whichever is later;
(i) "Properly payable" includes the availability of funds for payment at the time of decision to pay or dishonor;
(j) "Settle" means to pay in cash, by clearing house settlement, in a charge or credit or by remittance, or otherwise as instructed. A settlement may be either provisional or final;
(k) "Suspends payments" with respect to a bank means that it has been closed by order of the supervisory authorities, that a public officer has been appointed to take it over or that it ceases or refuses to make payments in the ordinary course of business.

(2) Other definitions applying to this Article and the sections in which they appear are:

"Collecting bank" Section 4—105.
"Depositary bank" Section 4—105.
"Intermediary bank" Section 4—105.
"Payor bank" Section 4—105.
"Presenting bank" Section 4—105.
"Remitting bank" Section 4—105.

(3) The following definitions in other Articles apply to this Article:

"Acceptance" Section 3—410.
"Certificate of deposit" Section 3—104.
"Certification" Section 3—411.
"Check" Section 3—104.
"Draft" Section 3—104.
"Holder in due course" Section 3—302.
"Notice of dishonor" Section 3—508.
"Presentment" Section 3—504.
"Protest" Section 3—509.
"Secondary party" Section 3—102.

(4) In addition Article 1 contains general definitions and principles of construction and interpretation applicable throughout this Article.

Section 4—105. "Depositary Bank"; "Intermediary Bank"; "Collecting Bank"; "Payor Bank"; "Presenting Bank"; "Remitting Bank".

In this Article unless the context otherwise requires:

(a) "Depositary bank" means the first bank to which an item is transferred for collection even though it is also the payor bank;
(b) "Payor bank" means a bank by which an item is payable as drawn or accepted;
(c) "Intermediary bank" means any bank to which an item is transferred in course of collection except the depositary or payor bank;
(d) "Collecting bank" means any bank handling the item for collection except the payor bank;
(e) "Presenting bank" means any bank presenting an item except a payor bank;
(f) "Remitting bank" means any payor or intermediary bank remitting for an item.

Section 4—106. Separate Office of a Bank.

A branch or separate office of a bank [maintaining its own deposit ledgers] is a separate bank for the purpose of computing the time within which and determining the place at or to which action may be taken or notices or orders shall be given under this Article and under Article 3.

Section 4—107. Time of Receipt of Items.

(1) For the purpose of allowing time to process items, prove balances and make the necessary entries on its books to determine its position for the day, a bank may fix an afternoon hour of two P.M. or later as a cut-off hour for the handling of money and items and the making of entries on its books.

(2) Any item or deposit of money received on any day after a cut-off hour so fixed or after the close of the banking day may be treated as being received at the opening of the next banking day.

Section 4—108. Delays.

(1) Unless otherwise instructed, a collecting bank in a good faith effort to secure payment may, in the case of specific items and with or without the approval of any person involved, waive, modify or extend time limits imposed or permitted by this Act for a period not in excess of an additional banking day without discharge of secondary parties and without liability to its transferor or any prior party.

(2) Delay by a collecting bank or payor bank beyond time limits prescribed or permitted by this Act or by instructions is excused if caused by interruption of communication facilities, suspension of payments by another bank, war, emergency conditions or other circumstances beyond the control of the bank provided it exercises such diligence as the circumstances require.

Section 4—109. Process of Posting.

The "process of posting" means the usual procedure followed by a payor bank in determining to pay an item and in recording the payment including one or more of the following or other steps as determined by the bank:

(a) verification of any signature;

(b) ascertaining that sufficient funds are available;

(c) affixing a "paid" or other stamp;

(d) entering a charge or entry to a customer's account;

(e) correcting or reversing an entry or erroneous action with respect to the item.

PART 2

COLLECTION OF ITEMS: DEPOSITARY AND COLLECTING BANKS

Section 4—201. Presumption and Duration of Agency Status of Collecting Banks and Provisional Status of Credits; Applicability of Article; Item Indorsed "Pay Any Bank".

(1) Unless a contrary intent clearly appears and prior to the time that a settlement given by a collecting bank for an item is or becomes final (subsection (3) of Section 4—211 and Sections 4—212 and 4—213) the bank is an agent or sub-agent of the owner of the item and any settlement given for the item is provisional. This provision applies regardless of the form of indorsement or lack of indorsement and even though credit given for the item is subject to immediate withdrawal as of right or is in fact withdrawn; but the continuance of ownership of an item by its owner and any rights of the owner to proceeds of the item are subject to rights of a collecting bank such as those resulting from outstanding advances on the item and valid rights of setoff. When an item is handled by banks for purposes of presentment, payment and collection, the relevant provisions of this Article apply even though action of parties clearly establishes that a particular bank has purchased the item and is the owner of it.

(2) After an item has been indorsed with the words "pay any bank" or the like, only a bank may acquire the rights of a holder

(a) until the item has been returned to the customer initiating collection; or

(b) until the item has been specially indorsed by a bank to a person who is not a bank.

Section 4—202. Responsibility for Collection; When Action Seasonable.

(1) A collecting bank must use ordinary care in

(a) presenting an item or sending it for presentment; and

(b) sending notice of dishonor or nonpayment or returning an item other than a documentary draft to the bank's transferor [or directly to the depositary bank under subsection (2) of Section 4—212] (*see note to Section 4—212*) after learning that the item has not been paid or accepted, as the case may be; and

(c) settling for an item when the bank receives final settlement; and

(d) making or providing for any necessary protest; and

(e) notifying its transferor of any loss or delay in transit within a reasonable time after discovery thereof.

(2) A collecting bank taking proper action before its midnight deadline following receipt of an item, notice or payment acts seasonably; taking proper action within a reasonably longer time may be seasonable but the bank has the burden of so establishing.

(3) Subject to subsection (1) (a), a bank is not liable for the insolvency, neglect, misconduct, mistake or default of another bank or person or for loss or destruction of an item in transit or in the possession of others.

Section 4—203. Effect of Instructions.

Subject to the provisions of Article 3 concerning conversion of instruments (Section 3—419) and the provisions of both Article 3 and this Article concerning restrictive indorsements, only a collecting bank's transferor can give instructions which affect the bank or constitute notice to it and a collecting bank is not liable to prior parties for any action taken pursuant to such instructions or in accordance with any agreement with its transferor.

Section 4—204. Methods of Sending and Presenting; Sending Direct to Payor Bank.

(1) A collecting bank must send items by reasonably prompt method taking into consideration any relevant instructions, the nature of the item, the number of such items on hand, and the cost of collection involved and the method generally used by it or others to present such items.

(2) A collecting bank may send

(a) any item direct to the payor bank;

(b) any item to any non-bank payor if authorized by its transferor; and

(c) any item other than documentary drafts to any non-bank payor, if authorized by Federal Reserve regulation or operating letter, clearing house rule or the like.

(3) Presentment may be made by a presenting bank at a place where the payor bank has requested that presentment be made.

Section 4—205. Supplying Missing Indorsement; No Notice from Prior Indorsement.

(1) A depositary bank which has taken an item for collection may supply any indorsement of the customer which is necessary to title unless the item contains the words "payee's indorsement required" or the like. In the absence of such a requirement a statement placed on the item by the depositary bank to the effect that the item was deposited by a customer or credited to his account is effective as the customer's indorsement.

(2) An intermediary bank, or payor bank which is not a depositary bank, is neither given notice nor otherwise affected by a restrictive indorsement of any person except the bank's immediate transferor.

Section 4—206. Transfer Between Banks.

Any agreed method which identifies the transferor bank is sufficient for the item's further transfer to another bank.

Section 4—207. Warranties of Customer and Collecting Bank on Transfer or Presentment of Items; Time for Claims.

(1) Each customer or collecting bank who obtains payment or acceptance of an item and each prior customer and collecting bank warrants to the payor bank or other payor who in good faith pays or accepts the item that

(a) he has a good title to the item or is authorized to obtain payment or acceptance on behalf of one who has a good title; and

(b) he has no knowledge that the signature of the maker or drawer is unauthorized, except that this warranty is not given by any customer or collecting bank that is a holder in due course and acts in good faith

(i) to a maker with respect to the maker's own signature; or
(ii) to a drawer with respect to the drawer's own signature, whether or not the drawer is also the drawee; or
(iii) to an acceptor of an item if the holder in due course took the item after the acceptance or obtained the acceptance without knowledge that the drawer's signature was unauthorized; and

(c) the item has not been materially altered, except that this warranty is not given by any customer or collecting bank that is a holder in due course and acts in good faith
(i) to the maker of a note; or
(ii) to the drawer of a draft whether or not the drawer is also the drawee; or
(iii) to the acceptor of an item with respect to an alteration made prior to the acceptance if the holder in due course took the item after the acceptance, even though the acceptance provided "payable as originally drawn" or equivalent terms; or
(iv) to the acceptor of an item with respect to an alteration made after the acceptance.

(2) Each customer and collecting bank who transfers an item and receives a settlement or other consideration for it warrants to his transferee and to any subsequent collecting bank who takes the item in good faith that

(a) he has a good title to the item or is authorized to obtain payment or acceptance on behalf of one who has a good title and the transfer is otherwise rightful; and
(b) all signatures are genuine or authorized; and
(c) the item has not been materially altered; and
(d) no defense of any party is good against him; and
(e) he has no knowledge of any insolvency proceeding instituted with respect to the maker or acceptor or the drawer of an unaccepted item.

In addition each customer and collecting bank so transferring an item and receiving a settlement or other consideration engages that upon dishonor and any necessary notice of dishonor and protest he will take up the item.

(3) The warranties and the engagement to honor set forth in the two preceding subsections arise notwithstanding the absence of indorsement or words of guaranty or warranty in the transfer or presentment and a collecting bank remains liable for their breach despite remittance to its transferor. Damages for breach of such warranties or engagement to honor shall not exceed the consideration received by the customer or collecting bank responsible plus finance charges and expenses related to the item, if any.

(4) Unless a claim for breach of warranty under this section is made within a reasonable time after the person claiming learns of the breach, the person liable is discharged to the extent of any loss caused by the delay in making claim.

Section 4—208. Security Interest of Collecting Bank in Items, Accompanying Documents and Proceeds.

(1) A bank has a security interest in an item and any accompanying documents or the proceeds of either

(a) in case of an item deposited in an account to the extent to which credit given for the item has been withdrawn or applied;
(b) in case of an item for which it has given credit available for withdrawal as of right, to the extent of the credit given whether or not the credit is drawn upon and whether or not there is a right of charge-back; or
(c) if it makes an advance on or against the item.

(2) When credit which has been given for several items received at one time or pursuant to a single agreement is withdrawn or applied

in part, the security interest remains upon all the items, any accompanying documents or the proceeds of either. For the purpose of this section, credits first given are first withdrawn.

(3) Receipt by a collecting bank of a final settlement for an item is a realization on its security interest in the item, accompanying documents and proceeds. To the extent and so long as the bank does not receive final settlement for the item or give up possession of the item or accompanying documents for purposes other than collection, the security interest continues and is subject to the provisions of Article 9 except that

(a) no security agreement is necessary to make the security interest enforceable (subsection (1) (b) of Section 9—203); and

(b) no filing is required to perfect the security interest; and

(c) the security interest has priority over conflicting perfected security interests in the item, accompanying documents or proceeds.

Section 4—209. When Bank Gives Value for Purposes of Holder in Due Course.

For purposes of determining its status as a holder in due course, the bank has given value to the extent that it has a security interest in an item provided that the bank otherwise complies with the requirements of Section 3—302 on what constitutes a holder in due course.

Section 4—210. Presentment by Notice of Item Not Payable by, Through or at a Bank; Liability of Secondary Parties.

(1) Unless otherwise instructed, a collecting bank may present an item not payable by, through or at a bank by sending to the party to accept or pay a written notice that the bank holds the item for acceptance or payment. The notice must be sent in time to be received on or before the day when presentment is due and the bank must meet any requirement of the party to accept or pay under Section 3—505 by the close of the bank's next banking day after it knows of the requirement.

(2) Where presentment is made by notice and neither honor nor request for compliance with a requirement under Section 3—505 is received by the close of business on the day after maturity or in the case of demand items by the close of business on the third banking day after notice was sent, the presenting bank may treat the item as dishonored and charge any secondary party by sending him notice of the facts.

Section 4—211. Media of Remittance; Provisional and Final Settlement in Remittance Cases.

(1) A collecting bank may take in settlement of an item

(a) a check of the remitting bank or of another bank on any bank except the remitting bank; or

(b) a cashier's check or similar primary obligation of a remitting bank which is a member of or clears through a member of the same clearing house or group as the collecting bank; or

(c) appropriate authority to charge an account of the remitting bank or of another bank with the collecting bank; or

(d) if the item is drawn upon or payable by a person other than a bank, a cashier's check, certified check or other bank check or obligation.

(2) If before its midnight deadline the collecting bank properly dishonors a remittance check or authorization to charge on itself or presents or forwards for collection a remittance instrument of or on another bank which is of a kind approved by subsection (1) or has not been authorized by it, the collecting bank is not liable to prior parties in the event of the dishonor of such check, instrument or authorization.

(3) A settlement for an item by means of a remittance instrument or authorization to charge is or becomes a final settlement as to both the person making and the person receiving the settlement

(a) if the remittance instrument or authorization to charge is of a kind approved by subsection (1) or has not been authorized by the person receiving the settlement and in either case the person receiving the settlement acts seasonably before its midnight deadline in presenting, forwarding for collection or paying the instrument or authorization,—at the time the remittance instrument or authorization is finally paid by the payor by which it is payable;

(b) if the person receiving the settlement has authorized remittance by a non-bank check or obligation or by a cashier's check or similar primary obligation of or a chcek upon the payor or other remitting bank which is not of a kind approved by subsection (1) (b),—at the time of the receipt of such remittance check or obligation; or

(c) if in a case not covered by subparagraphs (a) or (b) the person receiving the settlement fails to seasonably present, forward for collection, pay or return a remittance instrument or authorization to it to charge before its midnight deadline,—at such midnight deadline.

Section 4—212. Right of Charge-Back or Refund.

(1) If a collecting bank has made provisional settlement with its customer for an item and itself fails by reason of dishonor, suspension of payments by a bank or otherwise to receive a settlement for the item which is or becomes final, the bank may revoke the settlement given by it, charge back the amount of any credit given for the item to its customer's account or obtain refund from its customer whether or not it is able to return the items if by its midnight deadline or within a longer reasonable time after it learns the facts it returns the item or sends notification of the facts. These rights to revoke, charge-back and obtain refund terminate if and when a settlement for the item received by the bank is or becomes final (subsection (3) of Section 4—211 and subsections (2) and (3) of Section 4—213).

[(2) Within the time and manner prescribed by this section and Section 4—301, an intermediary or payor bank, as the case may be, may return an unpaid item directly to the depositary bank and may send for collection a draft on the depositary bank and obtain reimbursement. In such case, if the depositary bank has received provisional settlement for the item, it must reimburse the bank drawing the draft and any provisional credits for the item between banks shall become and remain final.]

Note: *Direct returns is recognized as an innovation that is not yet established bank practice, and therefore, Paragraph 2 has been bracketed. Some lawyers have doubts whether it should be included in legislation or left to development by agreement.*

(3) A depositary bank which is also the payor may charge-back the amount of an item to its customer's account or obtain refund in accordance with the section governing return of an item received by a payor bank for credit on its books (Section 4—301).

(4) The right to charge-back is not affected by

(a) prior use of the credit given for the item; or

(b) failure by any bank to exercise ordinary care with respect to the item, but any bank so failing remains liable.

(5) A failure to charge-back or claim refund does not affect other rights of the bank against the customer or any other party.

(6) If credit is given in dollars as the equivalent of the value of an item payable in a foreign currency, the dollar amount of any charge-back or refund shall be calculated on the basis of the buying sight rate for the foreign currency prevailing on the day when the person entitled to the charge-back or refund learns that it will not receive payment in ordinary course.

Section 4—213. Final Payment of Item by Payor Bank; When Provisional Debits and Credits Become Final; When Certain Credits Become Available for Withdrawal.

(1) An item is finally paid by a payor bank when the bank has done any of the following, whichever happens first:

(a) paid the item in cash; or

(b) settled for the item without reserving a right to revoke the settlement and without having such right under statute, clearing house rule or agreement; or

(c) completed the process of posting the item to the indicated account of the drawer, maker or other person to be charged therewith; or

(d) made a provisional settlement for the item and failed to revoke the settlement in the time and manner permitted by statute, clearing house rule or agreement.

Upon a final payment under subparagraphs (b) (c) or (d) the payor bank shall be accountable for the amount of the item.

(2) If provisional settlement for an item between the presenting and payor banks is made through a clearing house or by debits or credits in an account between them, then to the extent that provisional debits or credits for the item are entered in accounts between the presenting and payor banks or between the presenting and successive prior collecting banks seriatim, they become final upon final payment of the item by the payor bank.

(3) If a collecting bank receives a settlement for an item which is or becomes final (subsection (3) of Section 4—211, subsection (2) of Section 4—213) the bank is accountable to its customer for the amount of the item and any provisional credit given for the item in an account with its customer becomes final.

(4) Subject to any right of the bank to apply the credit to an obligation of the customer, credit given by a bank for an item in an account with its customer becomes available for withdrawal as of right

(a) in any case where the bank has received a provisional settlement for the item,—when such settlement becomes final and the bank has had a reasonable time to learn that the settlement is final;

(b) in any case where the bank is both a depositary bank and a payor bank and the item is finally paid,—at the opening of the bank's second banking day following receipt of the item.

(5) A deposit of money in a bank is final when made but, subject to any right of the bank to apply the deposit to an obligation of the customer, the deposit becomes available for withdrawal as of right at the opening of the bank's next banking day following receipt of the deposit.

Section 4-214. Insolvency and Preference.

(1) Any item in or coming into the possession of a payor or collecting bank which suspends payment and which item is not finally paid shall be returned by the receiver, trustee or agent in charge of the closed bank to the presenting bank or the closed bank's customer.

(2) If a payor bank finally pays an item and suspends payments without making a settlement for the item with its customer or the presenting bank which settlement is or becomes final, the owner of the item has a preferred claim against the payor bank.

(3) If a payor bank gives or a collecting bank gives or receives a provisional settlement for an item and thereafter suspends payments, the suspension does not prevent or interfere with the settlement becoming final if such finality occurs automatically upon the lapse of certain time or the happening of certain events (subsection (3) of Section 4—211, subsections (1) (d), (2) and (3) of Section 4—213).

(4) If a collecting bank receives from subsequent parties settlement for an item which settlement is or becomes final and suspends payments without making a settlement for the item with its customer which is or becomes final, the owner of the item has a preferred claim against such collecting bank.

PART 3

COLLECTION OF ITEMS: PAYOR BANKS

Section 4—301. Deferred Posting; Recovery of Payment by Return of Items; Time of Dishonor.

(1) Where an authorized settlement for a demand item (other than a documentary draft) received by a payor bank otherwise than for immediate payment over the counter has been made before midnight of the banking day of

receipt, the payor bank may revoke the settlement and recover any payment if before it has made final payment (subsection (1) of Section 4—213) and before its midnight deadline it

(a) returns the item; or

(b) sends written notice of dishonor or nonpayment if the item is held for protest or is otherwise unavailable for return.

(2) If a demand is received by a payor bank for credit on its books, it may return such item or send notice of dishonor and may revoke any credit given or recover the amount thereof withdrawn by its customer, if it acts within the time limit and in the manner specified in the preceding subsection.

(3) Unless previous notice of dishonor has been sent, an item is dishonored at the time when for purposes of dishonor it is returned or notice sent in accordance with this section.

(4) An item is returned:

(a) as to an item received through a clearing house, when it is delivered to the presenting or last collecting bank or to the clearing house or is sent or delivered in accordance with its rules; or

(b) in all other cases, when it is sent or delivered to the bank's customer or transferor or pursuant to his instructions.

Section 4—302. Payor Bank's Responsibility for Late Return of Item.

In the absence of a valid defense such as breach of a presentment warranty (subsection (1) of Section 4—207), settlement effected or the like, if an item is presented on and received by a payor bank the bank is accountable for the amount of

(a) a demand item other than a documentary draft whether properly payable or not if the bank, in any case where it is not also the depositary bank, retains the item beyond midnight of the banking day of receipt without settling for it or, regardless of whether it is also the depositary bank, does not pay or return the item or send notice of dishonor until after its midnight deadline; or

(b) any other properly payable item unless within the time allowed for acceptance or payment of that item the bank either accepts or pays the item or returns it and accompanying documents.

Section 4—303. When Items Subject to Notice, Stop-Order, Legal Process or Setoff; Order in Which Items May Be Charged or Certified.

(1) Any knowledge, notice or stop-order received by, legal process served upon or setoff exercised by a payor bank, whether or not effective under other rules of law to terminate, suspend or modify the bank's right or duty to pay an item or to charge its customer's account for the item, comes too late to so terminate, suspend or modify such right or duty if the knowledge, notice, stop-order or legal process is received or served and a reasonable time for the bank to act thereon expires or the setoff is exercised after the bank has done any of the following:

(a) accepted or certified the item;

(b) paid the item in cash;

(c) settled for the item without reserving a right to revoke the settlement and without having such right under statute, clearing house rule or agreement;

(d) completed the process of posting the item to the indicated account of the drawer, maker or other person to be charged therewith or otherwise has evidenced by examination of such indicated account and by action its decision to pay the item; or

(e) become accountable for the amount of the item under subsection (1) (d) of Section 4—213 and Section 4—302 dealing with the payor bank's responsibility for late return of items.

(2) Subject to the provisions of subsection (1) items may be accepted, paid, certified or charged to the indicated account of its customer in any order convenient to the bank.

PART 4

RELATIONSHIP BETWEEN PAYOR BANK AND ITS CUSTOMER

Section 4—401. When Bank May Charge Customer's Account.

(1) As against its customer, a bank may charge against his account any item which is otherwise properly payable from that account even though the charge creates an overdraft.

(2) A bank which in good faith makes payment to a holder may charge the indicated account of its customer according to

(a) the original tenor of his altered item; or

(b) the tenor of his completed item, even though the bank knows the item has been completed unless the bank has notice that the completion was improper.

Section 4—402. Bank's Liability to Customer for Wrongful Dishonor.

A payor bank is liable to its customer for damages proximately caused by the wrongful dishonor of an item. When the dishonor occurs through mistake, liability is limited to actual damages proved. If so proximately caused and proved, damages may include damages for an arrest or prosecution of the customer or other consequential damages. Whether any consequential damages are proximately caused by the wrongful dishonor is a question of fact to be determined in each case.

Section 4—403. Customer's Right to Stop Payment; Burden of Proof of Loss.

(1) A customer may by order to his bank stop payment of any item payable for his account but the order must be received at such time and in such manner as to afford the bank a reasonable opportunity to act on it prior to any action by the bank with respect to the item described in Section 4—303.

(2) An oral order is binding upon the bank only for fourteen calendar days unless confirmed in writing within that period. A written order is effective for only six months unless renewed in writing.

(3) The burden of establishing the fact and amount of loss resulting from the payment of an item contrary to a binding stop payment order is on the customer.

Section 4—404. Bank Not Obligated to Pay Check More Than Six Months Old.

A bank is under no obligation to a customer having a checking account to pay a check, other than a certified check, which is presented more than six months after its date, but it may charge its customer's account for a payment made thereafter in good faith.

Section 4—405. Death or Incompetence of Customer.

(1) A payor or collecting bank's authority to accept, pay or collect an item or to account for proceeds of its collection if otherwise effective is not rendered ineffective by incompetence of a customer of either bank existing at the time the item is issued or its collection is undertaken if the bank does not know of an adjudication of incompetence. Neither death nor incompetence of a customer revokes such authority to accept, pay, collect or account until the bank knows of the fact of death or of an adjudication of incompetence and has reasonable opportunity to act on it.

(2) Even with knowledge a bank may for ten days after the date of death pay or certify checks drawn on or prior to that date unless ordered to stop payment by a person claiming an interest in the account.

Section 4—406. Customer's Duty to Discover and Report Unauthorized Signature or Alteration.

(1) When a bank sends to its customer a statement of account accompanied by items paid in good faith in support of the debit entries or holds the statement and items pursuant to a request or instructions of its customer or otherwise in a reasonable manner makes the statement and items available to the customer, the customer must exercise reasonable care and promptness to examine the statement and items to discover his unauthorized signature or any alteration on an item and must notify the bank promptly after discovery thereof.

(2) If the bank establishes that the customer failed with respect to an item to comply with the duties imposed on the customer by subsection (1) the customer is precluded from asserting against the bank

(a) his unauthorized signature or any alteration on the item if the bank also establishes that it suffered a loss by reason of such failure; and

(b) an unauthorized signature or alteration by the same wrongdoer on any other item paid in good faith by the bank after the first item and statement was available to the customer for a reasonable period not exceeding fourteen calendar days and before the bank receives notification from the customer of any such unauthorized signature or alteration.

(3) The preclusion under subsection (2) does not apply if the customer establishes lack of ordinary care on the part of the bank in paying the item(s).

(4) Without regard to care or lack of care of either the customer or the bank, a customer who does not within one year from the time the statement and items are made available to the customer (subsection (1)) discover and report his unauthorized signature or any alteration on the face or back of the item or does not within three years from that time discover and report any unauthorized indorsement is precluded from asserting against the bank such unauthorized signature or indorsement or such alteration.

(5) If under this section a payor bank has a valid defense against a claim of a customer upon or resulting from payment of an item and waives or fails upon request to assert the defense, the bank may not assert against any collecting bank or other prior party presenting or transferring the item a claim based upon the unauthorized signature or alteration giving rise to the customer's claim.

Section 4—407. Payor Bank's Right to Subrogation on Improper Payment.

If a payor bank has paid an item over the stop payment order of the drawer or maker or otherwise under circumstances giving a basis for objection by the drawer or maker, to prevent unjust enrichment and only to the extent necessary to prevent loss to the bank by reason of its payment of the item, the payor bank shall be subrogated to the rights

(a) of any holder in due course on the item against the drawer or maker; and

(b) of the payee or any other holder of the item against the drawer or maker either on the item or under the transaction out of which the item arose; and

(c) of the drawer or maker against the payee or any other holder of the item with respect to the transaction out of which the item arose.

PART 5

COLLECTION OF DOCUMENTARY DRAFTS

Section 4—501. Handling of Documentary Drafts; Duty to Send for Presentment and to Notify Customer of Dishonor.

A bank which takes a documentary draft for collection must present or send the draft and accompanying documents for presentment and upon learning that the draft has not been paid or accepted in due course, must seasonably notify its customer of such fact even though it may have discounted or bought the draft or extended credit available for withdrawal as of right.

Section 4—502. Presentment of "On Arrival" Drafts.

When a draft or the relevant instructions require presentment "on arrival", "when goods arrive" or the like, the collecting bank need not present until in its judgment a reasonable time for arrival of the goods has expired. Refusal to pay or accept because the goods have not arrived is not dishonor; the bank must notify its transferor of such refusal but need not present the draft again until it is instructed to do so or learns of the arrival of the goods.

Section 4—503. Responsibility of Presenting Bank for Documents and Goods; Report of Reasons for Dishonor; Referee in Case of Need.

Unless otherwise instructed and except as provided in Article 5 a bank presenting a documentary draft

(a) must deliver the documents to the drawee on acceptance of the draft if it is payable more than three days after presentment; otherwise, only on payment; and

(b) upon dishonor, either in the case of presentment for acceptance or presentment for payment, may seek and follow instructions from any referee in case of need designated in the draft or, if the presenting bank does not choose to utilize his services, it must use diligence and good faith to ascertain the reason for dishonor, must notify its transferor of the dishonor and of the results of its effort to ascertain the reasons therefor and must request instructions.

But the presenting bank is under no obligation with respect to goods represented by the documents except to follow any reasonable instructions seasonably received; it has a right to reimbursement for any expense incurred in following instructions and to prepayment of or indemnity for such expenses.

Section 4—504. Privilege of Presenting Bank to Deal With Goods; Security Interest for Expenses.

(1) A presenting bank which, following the dishonor of a documentary draft, has seasonably requested instructions but does not reecive them within a reasonable time may store, sell, or otherwise deal with the goods in any reasonable manner.

(2) For its reasonable expenses incurred by action under subsection (1) the presenting bank has a lien upon the goods or their proceeds, which may be foreclosed in the same manner as an unpaid seller's lien.

ARTICLE 5

LETTERS OF CREDIT

Section 5—101. Short Title.

This Article shall be known and may be cited as Uniform Commercial Code—Letters of Credit.

Section 5—102. Scope.

(1) This Article applies

(a) to a credit issued by a bank if the credit requires a documentary draft or a documentary demand for payment; and

(b) to a credit issued by a person other than a bank if the credit requires that the draft or demand for payment be accompanied by a document of title; and

(c) to a credit issued by a bank or other person if the credit is not within subparagraphs (a) or (b) but conspicuously states that it is a letter of credit or is conspicuously so entitled.

(2) Unless the engagement meets the requirements of subsection (1), this Article does not apply to engagements to make advances or to honor drafts or demands for payment, to authorities to pay or purchase, to guarantees or to general agreements.

(3) This Article deals with some but not all of the rules and concepts of letters of credit as such rules or concepts have developed prior to this act or may hereafter develop. The fact that this Article states a rule does not by itself require, imply or negate application of the same or a converse rule to a situation not provided for or to a person not specified by this Article.

Section 5—103. Definitions.

(1) In this Article unless the context otherwise requires

(a) "Credit" or "letter of credit" means an engagement by a bank or other person made at the request of a customer and of a kind within the scope of this Article (Section 5—102) that the issuer will honor drafts or other demands for payment upon compliance with the conditions specified in the credit. A credit may be either revocable or irrevocable. The engagement may be either an agreement to honor or a statement that the bank or other person is authorized to honor.

(b) A "documentary draft" or a "documentary demand for payment" is one honor of which is conditioned upon the presentation of a document or documents. "Document" means any paper including document of title, security, invoice, certificate, notice of default and the like.

(c) An "issuer" is a bank or other person issuing a credit.

(d) A "beneficiary" of a credit is a person who is entitled under its terms to draw or demand payment.

(e) "An "advising bank" is a bank which gives notification of the issuance of a credit by another bank.

(f) A "confirming bank" is a bank which engages either that it will itself honor a credit already issued by another bank or that such a credit will be honored by the issuer or a third bank.

(g) A "customer" is a buyer or other person who causes an issuer to issue a credit. The term also includes a bank which procures issuance or confirmation on behalf of that bank's customer.

(2) Other definitions applying to this Article and the sections in which they appear are:

"Notation of Credit". Section 5—108.
"Presenter". Section 5—112(3).

(3) Definitions in other Articles applying to this Article and the sections in which they appear are:

"Accept" or "Acceptance". Section 3—410.
"Contract for sale". Section 2—106.
"Draft". Section 3—104.
"Holder in due course". Section 3—302.
"Midnight deadline". Section 4—104.
"Security". Section 8—102.

(4) In addition, Article 1 contains general definitions and principles of construction and interpretation applicable throughout this Article.

Section 5—104. Formal Requirements; Signing.

(1) Except as otherwise required in subsection (1) (c) of Section 5—102 on scope, no particular form of phrasing is required for a credit. A credit must be in writing and signed by the issuer and a confirmation must be in writing and signed by the confirming bank. A modification of the terms of a credit or confirmation must be signed by the issuer or confirming bank.

(2) A telegram may be a sufficient signed writing if it identifies its sender by an authorized authentication. The authentication may be in code and the authorized naming of the issuer in an advice of credit is a sufficient signing.

Section 5—105. Consideration.

No consideration is necessary to establish a credit or to enlarge or otherwise modify its terms.

Section 5—106. Time and Effect of Establishment of Credit.

(1) Unless otherwise agreed a credit is established

(a) as regards the customer as soon as a letter of credit is sent to him or the letter of credit or an authorized written advice of its issuance is sent to the beneficiary; and

(b) as regards the beneficiary when he receives a letter of credit or an authorized written advice of its issuance.

(2) Unless otherwise agreed, once an irrevocable credit is established as regards the customer, it can be modified or revoked only with the consent of the customer, and once it is established as regards the beneficiary it can be modified or revoked only with his consent.

(3) Unless otherwise agreed, after a revocable credit is established it may be modified or revoked by the issuer without notice to or consent from the customer or beneficiary.

(4) Notwithstanding any modification or revocation of a revocable credit, any person authorized to honor or negotiate under the terms of the original credit is entitled to reimbursement for or honor of any draft or demand for payment duly honored or negotiated before receipt of notice of the modification or revocation and the issuer in turn is entitled to reimbursement from its customer.

Section 5—107. Advice of Credit; Confirmation; Error in Statement of Terms.

(1) Unless otherwise specified an advising bank by advising a credit issued by another bank does not assume any obligation to honor drafts drawn or demands for payment made under the credit, but it does assume obligation for the accuracy of its own statement.

(2) A confirming bank by confirming a credit becomes directly obligated on the credit to the extent of its confirmation as though it were its issuer and acquires the rights of an issuer.

(3) Even though an advising bank incorrectly advises the terms of a credit it has been authorized to advise, the credit is established as against the issuer to the extent of its original terms.

(4) Unless otherwise specified the customer bears as against the issuer all risks of transmission and reasonable translation or interpretation of any message relating to a credit.

Section 5—108. "Notation Credit"; Exhaustion of Credit.

(1) A credit which specifies that any person purchasing or paying drafts drawn or demands for payment made under it must note the amount of the draft or demand on the letter or advice of credit is a "notation credit".

(2) Under a notation credit

(a) a person paying the beneficiary or purchasing a draft or demand for payment from him acquires a right to honor only if the appropriate notation is made and, by transferring or forwarding for honor the documents under the credit, such a person warrants to the issuer that the notation has been made; and

(b) unless the credit or a signed statement that an appropriate notation has been made accompanies the draft or demand for payment, the issuer may delay honor until evidence of notation has been procured which is satisfactory to it, but its obligation and that of its customer continue for a reasonable time not exceeding thirty days to obtain such evidence.

(3) If the credit is not a notation credit

(a) the issuer may honor complying drafts or demands for payment presented to it in the order in which they are presented and is discharged pro tanto by honor of any such draft or demand;

(b) as between competing good faith purchasers of complying drafts or demands the person first purchasing has priority over a subsequent purchaser even though the later purchased draft or demand has been first honored.

Section 5—109. Issuer's Obligation to Its Customer.

(1) An issuer's obligation to its customer includes good faith and observance of any general banking usage but unless otherwise agreed does not include liability or responsibility

(a) for performance of the underlying contract for sale or other transaction between the customer and the beneficiary; or

(b) for any act or omission of any person other than itself or its own branch or for loss or destruction of a draft, demand or document in transit or in the possession of others; or

(c) based on knowledge or lack of knowledge of any usage of any particular trade.

(2) An issuer must examine documents with care so as to ascertain that on their face they appear to comply with the terms of the credit but unless otherwise agreed assumes no liability or responsibility for the genuineness, falsification or effect of any document which appears on such examination to be regular on its face.

(3) A non-bank issuer is not bound by any banking usage of which it has no knowledge.

Section 5—110. Availability of Credit in Portions; Presenter's Reservation of Lien or Claim.

(1) Unless otherwise specified a credit may be used in portions in the discretion of the beneficiary.

(2) Unless otherwise specified a person by presenting a documentary draft or demand for payment under a credit relinquishes upon its honor all claims to the documents, and a person by transferring such draft or demand or causing such presentment authorizes such relinquishment. An explicit reservation of claim makes the draft or demand noncomplying.

Section 5—111. Warranties on Transfer and Presentment.

(1) Unless otherwise agreed the beneficiary by transferring or presenting a documentary draft or demand for payment warrants to all interested parties that the necessary conditions of the credit have been complied with. This is in addition to any warranties arising under Articles 3, 4, 7 and 8.

(2) Unless otherwise agreed a negotiating, advising, confirming, collecting or issuing bank presenting or transferring a draft or demand for payment under a credit warrants only the matters warranted by a collecting bank under Article 4, and any such bank transferring a document warrants only the matters warranted by an intermediary under Articles 7 and 8.

Section 5—112. Time Allowed for Honor or Rejection; Withholding Honor or Rejection by Consent; "Presenter".

(1) A bank to which a documentary draft or demand for payment is presented under a credit may without dishonor of the draft, demand or credit

(a) defer honor until the close of the third banking day following receipt of the documents; and

(b) further defer honor if the presenter has expressly or impliedly consented thereto.

Failure to honor within the time here specified constitutes dishonor of the draft or demand and of the credit [except as otherwise provided in subsection (4) of Section 5—114 on conditional payment].

Note: *The bracketed language in the last sentence of subsection (1) should be included only if the optional provisions of Section 5—114(4) and (5) are included.*

(2) Upon dishonor the bank may unless otherwise instructed fulfill its duty to return the draft or demand and the documents by holding them at the disposal of the presenter and sending him an advice to that effect.

(3) "Presenter" means any person presenting a draft or demand for payment for honor under a credit even though that person is a confirming bank or other correspondent which is acting under an issuer's authorization.

Section 5—113. Indemnities.

(1) A bank seeking to obtain (whether for itself or another) honor, negotiation or reimbursement under a credit may give an indemnity to induce such honor, negotiation or reimbursement.

(2) An indemnity agreement inducing honor, negotiation or reimbursement

(a) unless otherwise explicitly agreed applies to defects in the documents but not in the goods; and

(b) unless a longer time is explicitly agreed, expires at the end of ten business days following receipt of the documents by the ultimate customer unless notice of objection is sent before such expiration date. The ultimate customer may send notice of objection to the person from whom he received the documents, and any bank receiving such notice is under a duty to send notice to its transferor before its midnight deadline.

Section 5—114. Issuer's Duty and Privilege to Honor; Right to Reimbursement.

(1) An issuer must honor a draft or demand for payment which complies with the terms of the relevant credit regardless of whether the goods or documents conform to the underlying contract for sale or other contract between the customer and the beneficiary. The issuer is not excused from honor of such a draft or demand by reason of an additional general term that all documents must be satisfactory to the issuer, but an issuer may require that specified documents must be satisfactory to it.

(2) Unless otherwise agreed, when documents appear on their face to comply with the terms of a credit but a required document does not in fact conform to the warranties made on negotiation or transfer of a document of title (Section 7—507) or of a security (Section 8—306) or is forged or fraudulent or there is a fraud in the transaction

(a) the issuer must honor the draft or demand for payment if honor is demanded by a negotiating bank or other holder of the draft or demand which has taken the draft or demand under the credit and under circumstances which would make it a holder in due course (Section 3—302) and in an appropriate case would make it a person to whom a document of title has been duly negotiated (Section 7—502) or a bona fide purchaser of a security (Section 8—302); and

(b) in all other cases as against its customer, an issuer acting in good faith may honor the draft or demand for payment despite notification from the customer of fraud, forgery or other defect not apparent on the face of the documents, but a court of appropriate jurisdiction may enjoin such honor.

(3) Unless otherwise agreed an issuer which has duly honored a draft or demand for payment is entitled to immediate reimbursement of any payment made under the credit and to be put in effectively available funds not later than the day before maturity of any acceptance made under the credit.

[(4) When a credit provides for payment by the issuer on receipt of notice that the required documents are in the possession of a correspondent or other agent of the issuer

(a) any payment made on receipt of such notice is conditional; and

(b) the issuer may reject documents which do not comply with the credit if it does so within three banking days following its receipt of the documents; and

(c) in the event of such rejection, the issuer is entitled by charge back or otherwise to return of the payment made.]

[(5) In the case covered by subsection (4) failure to reject documents within the time specified in sub-paragraph (b) constitutes acceptance of the documents and makes the payment final in favor of the beneficiary.]

Note: *Subsections (4) and (5) are bracketed as optional. If they are included, the bracketed language in the last sentence of Section 5—112(1) should also be included.*

Section 5—115. Remedy for Improper Dishonor or Anticipatory Repudiation.

(1) When an issuer wrongfully dishonors a draft or demand for payment presented under a credit, the person entitled to honor has with respect to any documents the rights of a person in the position of a seller (Section 2—707) and may recover from the issuer the face amount of the draft or demand together with incidental damages under Section 2—710 on seller's incidental damages and interest but less any amount realized by resale or other use or disposition of the subject matter of the transaction. In the

event no resale or other utilization is made the documents, goods or other subject matter involved in the transaction must be turned over to the issuer on payment of judgment.

(2) When an issuer wrongfully cancels or otherwise repudiates a credit before presentment of a draft or demand for payment drawn under it, the beneficiary has the rights of a seller after anticipatory repudiation by the buyer under Section 2—610 if he learns of the repudiation in time reasonably to avoid procurement of the required documents. Otherwise the beneficiary has an immediate right of action for wrongful dishonor.

Section 5—116. Transfer and Assignment.

(1) The right to draw under a credit can be transferred or assigned only when the credit is expressly designated as transferable or assignable.

(2) Even though the credit specifically states that it is nontransferable or nonassignable, the beneficiary may before performance of the conditions of the credit assign his right to proceeds. Such an assignment is an assignment of a contract right under Article 9 on Secured Transactions and is governed by that Article except that

(a) the assignment is ineffective until the letter of credit or advice of credit is delivered to the assignee which delivery constitutes perfection of the security interest under Article 9; and

(b) the issuer may honor drafts or demands for payment drawn under the credit until it receives a notification of the assignment signed by the beneficiary which reasonably identifies the credit involved in the assignment and contains a request to pay the assignee; and

(c) after what reasonably appears to be such a notification has been received the issuer may without dishonor refuse to accept or pay even to a person otherwise entitled to honor until the letter of credit or advice of credit is exhibited to the issuer.

(3) Except where the beneficiary has effectively assigned his right to draw or his right to proceeds, nothing in this section limits his right to transfer or negotiate drafts or demands drawn under the credit.

Section 5—117. Insolvency of Bank Holding Funds for Documentary Credit.

(1) Where an issuer or an advising or confirming bank or a bank which has for a customer procured issuance of a credit by another bank becomes insolvent before final payment under the credit and the credit is one to which this Article is made applicable by paragraphs (a) or (b) of Section 5—102(1) on scope, the receipt or allocation of funds or collateral to secure or meet obligations under the credit shall have the following results:

(a) to the extent of any funds or collateral turned over after or before the insolvency as indemnity against or specifically for the purpose of payment of drafts or demands for payment drawn under the designated credit, the drafts or demands are entitled to payment in preference over depositors or other general creditors of the issuer or bank; and

(b) on expiration of the credit or surrender of the beneficiary's rights under it unused, any person who has given such funds or collateral is similarly entitled to return thereof; and

(c) a change to a general or current account with a bank if specifically consented to for the purpose of indemnity against or payment of drafts or demands for payment drawn under the designated credit falls under the same rules as if the funds had been drawn out in cash and then turned over with specific instructions.

(2) After honor or reimbursement under this section the customer or other person for whose account the insolvent bank has acted is entitled to receive the documents involved.

ARTICLE 6

BULK TRANSFERS

Section 6—101. Short Title.

This Article shall be known and may be cited as Uniform Commercial Code—Bulk Transfers.

Section 6—102. "Bulk Transfers"; Transfers of Equipment; Enterprises Subject to This Article; Bulk Transfers Subject to This Article.

(1) A "bulk transfer" is any transfer in bulk and not in the ordinary course of the transferor's business of a major part of the materials, supplies, merchandise or other inventory (Section 9—109) of an enterprise subject to this Article.

(2) A transfer of a substantial part of the equipment (Section 9—109) of such an enterprise is a bulk transfer if it is made in connection with a bulk transfer of inventory, but not otherwise.

(3) The enterprises subject to this Article are all those whose principal business is the sale of merchandise from stock, including those who manufacture what they sell.

(4) Except as limited by the following section all bulk transfers of goods located within this state are subject to this Article.

Section 6—103. Transfers Excepted from This Article.

The following transfers are not subject to this Article:

(1) Those made to give security for the performance of an obligation;

(2) General assignments for the benefit of all the creditors of the transferor, and subsequent transfers by the assignee thereunder;

(3) Transfers in settlement or realization of a lien or other security interest;

(4) Sales by executors, administrators, receivers, trustees in bankruptcy, or any public officer under judicial process;

(5) Sales made in the course of judicial or administrative proceedings for the dissolution or reorganization of a corporation and of which notice is sent to the creditors of the corporation pursuant to order of the court or administrative agency;

(6) Transfers to a person maintaining a known place of business in this State who becomes bound to pay the debts of the transferor in full and gives public notice of that fact, and who is solvent after becoming so bound;

(7) A transfer to a new business enterprise organized to take over and continue the business, if public notice of the transaction is given and the new enterprise assumes the debts of the transferor and he receives nothing from the transaction except an interest in the new enterprise junior to the claims of creditors;

(8) Transfers of property which is exempt from execution.

Public notice under subsection (6) or subsection (7) may be given by publishing once a week for two consecutive weeks in a newspaper of general circulation where the transferor has its principal place of business in this state an advertisement including the names and addresses of the transferor and transferee and the effective date of the transfer.

Section 6—104. Schedule of Property, List of Creditors.

(1) Except as provided with respect to auction sales (Section 6—108), a bulk transfer subject to this Article is ineffective against any creditor of the transferor unless:

(a) The transferee requires the transferor to furnish a list of his existing creditors prepared as stated in this section; and

(b) The parties prepare a schedule of the property transferred sufficient to identify it; and

(c) The transferee preserves the list and schedule for six months next following the transfer and permits inspection of either or both and copying therefrom at all reasonable hours by any creditor of the transferor, or files the list and schedule in (a public office to be here identified).

(2) The list of creditors must be signed and sworn to or affirmed by the transferor or his agent. It must contain the names and business addresses of all creditors of the transferor, with the amounts when known, and also the names of all persons who are known to the transferor to assert claims against him even though such claims are disputed. If the transferor is the obligor of an outstanding issue of bonds, debentures or the like as to which there is an indenture trustee, the list of creditors need include only the name and address of the indenture trustee and the aggregate outstanding principal amount of the issue.

(3) Responsibility for the completeness and accuracy of the list of creditors rests on the transferor, and the transfer is not rendered ineffective by errors or omissions therein unless the transferee is shown to have had knowledge.

Section 6—105. Notice to Creditors.

In addition to the requirements of the preceding section, any bulk transfer subject to this Article except one made by auction sale (Section 6—108) is ineffective against any creditor of the transferor unless at least ten days before he takes possession of the goods or pays for them, whichever happens first, the transferee gives notice of the transfer in the manner and to the persons hereafter provided (Section 6—107).

[Section 6—106. Application of the Proceeds.

In addition to the requirements of the two preceding sections:

(1) Upon every bulk transfer subject to this Article for which new consideration becomes payable, except those made by sale at auction, it is the duty of the transferee to assure that such consideration is applied so far as necessary to pay those debts of the transferor which are either shown on the list furnished by the transferor (Section 6—104) or filed in writing in the place stated in the notice (Section 6—107) within thirty days after the mailing of such notice. This duty of the transferee runs to all the holders of such debts, and may be enforced by any of them for the benefit of all.

(2) If any of said debts are in dispute, the necessary sum may be withheld from distribution until the dispute is settled or adjudicated.

(3) If the consideration payable is not enough to pay all of the said debts in full, distribution shall be made pro rata.]

Note: *This section is bracketed to indicate division of opinion as to whether or not it is a wise provision, and to suggest that this is a point on which State enactments may differ without serious damage to the principle of uniformity.*

In any State where this section is omitted, the following parts of sections, also bracketed in the text, should also be omitted, namely:

Section 6—107(2)(e).
6—108(3)(c).
6—109(2).

In any State where this section is enacted, these other provisions should be also.

Optional Subsection (4)

[(4) The transferee may within ten days after he takes possession of the goods pay the consideration into the (specify court) in the county where the transferor had its principal place of business in this state and thereafter may discharge his duty under this section by giving notice by registered or certified mail to all the persons to whom the duty runs that the consideration has been paid into that court and that they should file their claims there. On motion of any interested party, the court may order the distribution of the consideration to the persons entitled to it.]

Note: *Optional subsection (4) is recommended for those states which do not have a general statute providing for payment of money into court.*

Section 6—107. The Notice.

(1) The notice to creditors (Section 6-105) shall state:

(a) that a bulk transfer is about to be made; and

(b) the names and business addresses of the transferor and transferee, and all other business names and addresses used by the transferor within three years last past so far as known to the transferee; and

(c) whether or not all the debts of the transferor are to be paid in full as they fall due as a result of the transaction, and if so, the address to which creditors should send their bills.

(2) If the debts of the transferor are not to be paid in full as they fall due or if the transferee is in doubt on that point, then the notice shall state further:

(a) the location and general description of the property to be transferred and the estimated total of the transferor's debts;

(b) the address where the schedule of property and list of creditors (Section 6—104) may be inspected;

(c) whether the transfer is to pay existing debts and if so the amount of such debts and to whom owing;

(d) whether the transfer is for new consideration and if so the amount of such consideration and the time and place of payment; [and]

[(e) if for new consideration the time and place where creditors of the transferor are to file their claims.]

(3) The notice in any case shall be delivered personally or sent by registered or certified mail to all the persons shown on the list of creditors furnished by the transferor (Section 6—104) and to all other persons who are known to the transferee to hold or assert claims against the transferor.

Note: *The words in brackets are optional.*

Section 6—108. Auction Sales; "Auctioneer".

(1) A bulk transfer is subject to this Article even though it is by sale at auction, but only in the manner and with the results stated in this section.

(2) The transferor shall furnish a list of his creditors and assist in the preparation of a schedule of the property to be sold, both prepared as before stated (Section 6—104).

(3) The person or persons other than the transferor who direct, control or are responsible for the auction are collectively called the "auctioneer". The auctioneer shall:

(a) receive and retain the list of creditors and prepare and retain the schedule of property for the period stated in this Article (Section 6—104);

(b) give notice of the auction personally or by registered or certified mail at least ten days before it occurs to all persons shown on the list of creditors and to all other persons who are known to him to hold or assert claims against the transferor; [and]

[(c) assure that the net proceeds of the auction are applied as provided in this Article (Section 6—106).]

(4) Failure of the auctioneer to perform any of these duties does not affect the validity of the sale or the title of the purchasers, but if the auctioneer knows that the auction constitutes a bulk transfer such failure renders the auctioneer liable to the creditors of the transferor as a class for the sums owing to them from the transferor up to but not exceeding the net proceeds of the auction. If the auctioneer consists of several persons, their liability is joint and several.

Note: *The words in brackets are optional.*

Section 6—109. What Creditors Protected; [Credit for Payment to Particular Creditors].

(1) The creditors of the transferor mentioned in this Article are those holding claims based on transactions or events occurring before the bulk transfer, but creditors who become such after notice to creditors is given (Sections 6—105 and 6—107) are not entitled to notice.

[(2) Against the aggregate obligation imposed by the provisions of this Article concerning the application of the proceeds (Section 6—106 and subsection (3) (c) of 6-108) the transferee or auctioneer is entitled to credit for sums paid to particular creditors of the transferor, not exceeding the sums believed in good faith at the time of the payment to be properly payable to such creditors.]

Section 6—110. Subsequent Transfers.

When the title of a transferee to property is subject to a defect by reason of his non-compliance with the requirements of this Article, then:

(1) a purchaser of any of such property from such transferee who pays no value or who takes with notice of such non-compliance takes subject to such defect, but

(2) a purchaser for value in good faith and without such notice takes free of such defect.

Section 6—111. Limitation of Actions and Levies.

No action under this Article shall be brought nor levy made more than six months after the date on which the transferee took possession of the goods unless the transfer has been concealed. If the transfer has been concealed, actions may be brought or levies made within six months after its discovery.

Note to Article 6: *Section 6—106 is bracketed to indicate division of opinion as to whether or not it is a wise provision, and to suggest that this is a point on which State enactments may differ without serious damage to the principle of uniformity.*

In any State where Section 6—106 is not enacted, the following parts of sections, also bracketed in the text, should also be omitted, namely:

Section 6—107(2)(e).
6—108(3)(c).
6—109(2).

In any State where Section 6—106 is enacted, these other provisions should be also.

ARTICLE 7

WAREHOUSE RECEIPTS, BILLS OF LADING AND OTHER DOCUMENTS OF TITLE

PART 1

GENERAL

Section 7—101. Short Title.

This Article shall be known and may be cited as Uniform Commercial Code—Documents of Title.

Section 7—102. Definitions and Index of Definitions.

(1) In this Article, unless the context otherwise requires:

(a) "Bailee" means the person who by a warehouse receipt, bill of lading or other document of title acknowledges possession of goods and contracts to deliver them.

(b) "Consignee" means the person named in a bill to whom or to whose order the bill promises delivery.

(c) "Consignor" means the person named in a bill as the person from whom the goods have been received for shipment.

(d) "Delivery order" means a written order to deliver goods directed to a warehouseman, carrier or other person who in the ordinary course of business issues warehouse receipts or bills of lading.

(e) "Document" means document of title as defined in the general definitions in Article 1 (Section 1—201).

(f) "Goods" means all things which are treated as movable for the purposes of a contract of storage or transportation.

(g) "Issuer" means a bailee who issues a document except that in relation to an unaccepted delivery order it means the person who orders the possessor of goods to deliver. Issuer includes any person for whom an agent or employee purports to act in issuing a document if the agent or employee has real or apparent authority to issue documents, notwithstanding that the issuer received no goods or that the goods were misdescribed or that in any other respect the agent or employee violated his instructions.

(h) "Warehouseman" is a person engaged in the business of storing goods for hire.

(2) Other definitions applying to this Article or to specified Parts thereof, and the sections in which they appear are:

"Duly negotiate". Section 7—501.

"Person entitled under the document". Section 7—403(4).

(3) Definitions in other Articles applying to this Article and the sections in which they appear are:

"Contract for sale". Section 2—106.

"Overseas". Section 2—323.

"Receipt" of goods. Section 2—103.

(4) In addition Article 1 contains general definitions and principles of construction and interpertation applicable throughout this Article.

Section 7—103. Relation of Article to Treaty, Statute, Tariff, Classification or Regulation.

To the extent that any treaty or statute of the United States, regulatory statute of this State or tariff, classification or regulation filed or issued pursuant thereto is applicable, the provisions of this Article are subject thereto.

Section 7—104. Negotiable and Non-Negotiable Warehouse Receipt, Bill of Lading or Other Document of Title.

(1) A warehouse receipt, bill of lading or other document of title is negotiable

(a) if by its terms the goods are to be delivered to bearer or to the order of a named person; or

(b) where recognized in overseas trade, if it runs to a named person or assigns.

(2) Any other document is nonnegotiable. A bill of lading in which it is stated that the goods are consigned to a named person is not made negotiable by a provision that the goods are to be delivered only against a written order signed by the same or another named person.

Section 7—105. Construction Against Negative Implication.

The omission from either Part 2 or Part 3 of this Article of a provision corresponding to a provision made in the other Part does not imply that a corresponding rule of law is not applicable.

PART 2

WAREHOUSE RECEIPTS: SPECIAL PROVISIONS

Section 7—201. Who May Issue a Warehouse Receipt; Storage Under Government Bond.

(1) A warehouse receipt may be issued by any warehouseman.

(2) Where goods including distilled spirits and agricultural commodities are stored under a statute requiring a bond against withdrawal or a license for the issuance of receipts in the nature of warehouse receipts, a receipt issued for the goods has like effect as a warehouse receipt even though issued by a person who is the owner of the goods and is not a warehouseman.

Section 7—202. Form of Warehouse Receipt; Essential Terms; Optional Terms.

(1) A warehouse receipt need not be in any particular form.

(2) Unless a warehouse receipt embodies within its written or printed terms each of the following, the warehouseman is liable for damages caused by the omission to a person injured thereby:

(a) the location of the warehouse where the goods are stored;

(b) the date of issue of the receipt;

(c) the consecutive number of the receipt;

(d) a statement whether the goods received will be delivered to the bearer, to a specified person, or to a specified person or his order;

(e) the rate of storage and handling charges, except that where goods are stored under a field warehousing arrangement a statement of that fact is sufficient on a non-negotiable receipt;

(f) a description of the goods or of the packages containing them;

(g) the signature of the warehouseman, which may be made by his authorized agent;

(h) if the receipt is issued for goods of which the warehouseman is owner, either solely or jointly or in common with others, the fact of such ownership; and

(i) a statement of the amount of advances made and of liabilities incurred for which the warehouseman claims a lien or security interest (Section 7—209). If the precise amount of such advances made or of such liabilities incurred is, at the time of the issue of the receipt, unknown to the warehouseman or to his agent who issues it, a statement of the fact that advances have been made or liabilities incurred and the purpose thereof is sufficient.

(3) A warehouseman may insert in his receipt any other terms which are not contrary to the provisions of this Act and do not impair his obligation of delivery (Section 7—403) or his duty of care (Section 7—204). Any contrary provisions shall be ineffective.

Section 7—203. Liability for Non-Receipt or Misdescription.

A party to or purchaser for value in good faith of a document of title other than a bill of lading relying in either case upon the description therein of the goods may recover from the issuer damages caused by the non-receipt or misdescription of the goods, except to the extent that the document conspicuously indicates that the issuer does not know whether any part or all of the goods in fact were received or conform to the description, as where the description is in terms of marks or labels or kind, quantity or condition, or the receipt or description is qualified by "contents, condition and quality unknown", "said to contain" or the like, if such indication be true, or the party or purchaser otherwise has notice.

Section 7—204. Duty of Care; Contractual Limitation of Warehouseman's Liability.

(1) A warehouseman is liable for damages for loss of or injury to the goods caused by his failure to exercise such care in regard to them as a reasonably careful man would exercise under like circumstances but, unless otherwise agreed, he is not liable for damages which could not have been avoided by the exercise of such care.

(2) Damages may be limited by a term in the warehouse receipt or storage agreement limiting the amount of liability in case of loss or damage, and setting forth a specific liability per article or item, or value per unit of weight, beyond which the warehouseman shall not be liable; provided, however, that such liability may on written request of the bailor at the time of signing such storage agreement or within a reasonable time after receipt of the warehouse receipt be increased on part or all of the goods thereunder, in which event increased rates may be charged based on such increased valuation, but that no such increase shall be permitted contrary to a lawful limitation of liability contained in the warehouseman's tariff, if any. No such limitation is effective with respect to the warehouseman's liability for conversion to his own use.

(3) Reasonable provisions as to the time and manner of presenting claims and instituting actions based on the bailment may be included in the warehouse receipt or tariff.

(4) This section does not impair or repeal . . .

Note: *Insert in subsection (4) a reference to any statute which imposes a higher responsibility upon the warehouseman or invalidates contractual limitations which would be permissible under this Article.*

Section 7—205. Title Under Warehouse Receipt Defeated in Certain Cases.

A buyer in the ordinary course of business of fungible goods sold and delivered by a warehouseman who is also in the business of buying and selling such goods takes free of any claim under a warehouse receipt even though it has been duly negotiated.

Section 7—206. Termination of Storage at Warehouseman's Option.

(1) A warehouseman may on notifying the person on whose account the goods are held and any other person known to claim an interest in the goods require payment of any charges and removal of the goods from the warehouse at the termination of the period of storage fixed by the document, or, if no period is fixed, within a stated period not less than thirty days after the notification. If the goods are not removed before the date specified in the notification, the warehouseman may sell them in accordance with the provisions of the section on enforcement of a warehouseman's lien (Section 7—210).

(2) If a warehouseman in good faith believes that the goods are about to deteriorate or decline in value to less than the amount of his lien within the time prescribed in subsection (1) for notification, advertisement and sale, the warehouseman may specify in the notification any reasonable shorter time for removal of the goods and in case the goods are not removed, may sell them at public sale held not less than one week after a single advertisement or posting.

(3) If as a result of a quality or condition of the goods of which the warehouseman had no notice at the time of deposit the goods are a hazard to other property or to the warehouse or to persons, the warehouseman may sell the goods at public or private sale without advertisement on reasonable notification to all persons known to claim an interest in the goods. If the warehouseman after a reasonable effort is unable to sell the goods, he may dispose of them in any lawful manner and shall incur no liability by reason of such disposition.

(4) The warehouseman must deliver the goods to any person entitled to them under this Article upon due demand made at any time prior to sale or other disposition under this section.

(5) The warehouseman may satisfy his lien from the proceeds of any sale or disposition under this section but must hold the balance for delivery on the demand of any person to whom he would have been bound to deliver the goods.

Section 7—207. Goods Must Be Kept Separate; Fungible Goods.

(1) Unless the warehouse receipt otherwise provides, a warehouseman must keep separate the goods covered by each receipt so as to permit at all times identification and delivery of those goods except that different lots of fungible goods may be commingled.

(2) Fungible goods so commingled are owned in common by the persons entitled thereto and the warehouseman is severally liable to each owner for that owner's share. Where because of overissue a mass of fungible goods is insufficient to meet all the receipts which the warehouseman has issued against it, the persons entitled include all holders to whom overissued receipts have been duly negotiated.

Section 7—208. Altered Warehouse Receipts.

Where a blank in a negotiable warehouse receipt has been filled in without authority, a purchaser for value and without notice of the want of authority may treat the insertion as authorized. Any other unauthorized alteration leaves any receipt enforceable against the issuer according to its original tenor.

Section 7—209. Lien of Warehouseman.

(1) A warehouseman has a lien against the bailor on the goods covered by a warehouse receipt or on the proceeds thereof in his possession for charges for storage or transportation (including demurrage and terminal charges), insurance, labor, or charges present or future in relation to the goods, and for expenses necessary for preservation of the goods or reasonably incurred in their sale pursuant to law. If the person on whose account the goods are held is liable for like charges or expenses in relation to other goods whenever deposited and it is stated in the receipt that a lien is claimed for charges and expenses in relation to other goods, the warehouseman also has a lien against him for such charges and expenses whether or not the other goods have been delivered by the warehouseman. But against a person to whom a negotiable warehouse receipt is duly negotiated, a warehouseman's lien is limited to charges in

an amount or at a rate specified on the receipt or if no charges are so specified then to a reasonable charge for storage of the goods covered by the receipt subsequent to the date of the receipt.

(2) The warehouseman may also reserve a security interest against the bailor for a maximum amount specified on the receipt for charges other than those specified in subsection (1), such as for money advanced and interest. Such a security interest is governed by the Article on Secured Transactions (Article 9).

(3) A warehouseman's lien for charges and expenses under subsection (1) or a security interest under subsection (2) is also effective against any person who so entrusted the bailor with possession of the goods that a pledge of them by him to a good faith purchaser for value would have been valid but is not effective against a person as to whom the document confers no right in the goods covered by it under Section 7—503.

(4) A warehouseman loses his lien on any goods which he voluntarily delivers or which he unjustifiably refuses to deliver.

Section 7—210. Enforcement of Warehouseman's Lien.

(1) Except as provided in subsection (2), a warehouseman's lien may be enforced by public or private sale of the goods in block or in parcels, at any time or place and on any terms which are commercially reasonable, after notifying all persons known to claim an interest in the goods. Such notification must include a statement of the amount due, the nature of the proposed sale and the time and place of any public sale. The fact that a better price could have been obtained by a sale at a different time or in a different method from that selected by the warehouseman is not of itself sufficient to establish that the sale was not made in a commercially reasonable manner. If the warehouseman either sells the goods in the usual manner in any recognized market therefor, or if he sells at the price current in such market at the time of his sale, or if he has otherwise sold in conformity with commercially reasonable practices among dealers in the type of goods sold, he has sold in a commercially reasonable manner. A sale of more goods than apparently necessary to be offered to insure satisfaction of the obligation is not commercially reasonable except in cases covered by the preceding sentence.

(2) A warehouseman's lien on goods other than goods stored by a merchant in the course of his business may be enforced only as follows:

(a) All persons known to claim an interest in the goods must be notified.

(b) The notification must be delivered in person or sent by registered or certified letter to the last known address of any person to be notified.

(c) The notification must include an itemized statement of the claim, a description of the goods subject to the lien, a demand for payment within a specified time not less than ten days after receipt of the notification, and a conspicuous statement that unless the claim is paid within that time the goods will be advertised for sale and sold by auction at a specified time and place.

(d) The sale must conform to the terms of the notification.

(e) The sale must be held at the nearest suitable place to that where the goods are held or stored.

(f) After the expiration of the time given in the notification, an advertisement of the sale must be published once a week for two weeks consecutively in a newspaper of general circulation where the sale is to be held. The advertisement must include a description of the goods, the name of the person on whose account they are being held, and the time and place of the sale. The sale must take place at least fifteen days after the first publication. If there is no newspaper of general circulation where the sale is to be held, the advertisement must be posted at least ten days before the sale in not less than six conspicuous places in the neighborhood of the proposed sale.

(3) Before any sale pursuant to this section any person claiming a right in the goods may pay the amount necessary to satisfy the lien and the reasonable expenses incurred under this section. In that event the goods must not be sold, but must be retained by the warehouseman subject to the terms of the receipt and this Article.

(4) The warehouseman may buy at any public sale pursuant to this section.

(5) A purchaser in good faith of goods sold to enforce a warehouseman's lien takes the goods free of any rights of persons against whom the lien was valid, despite noncompliance by the warehouseman with the requirements of this section.

(6) The warehouseman may satisfy his lien from the proceeds of any sale pursuant to this section but must hold the balance, if any, for delivery on demand to any person to whom he would have been bound to deliver the goods.

(7) The rights provided by this section shall be in addition to all other rights allowed by law to a creditor against his debtor.

(8) Where a lien is on goods stored by a merchant in the course of his business, the lien may be enforced in accordance with either subsection (1) or (2).

(9) The warehouseman is liable for damages caused by failure to comply with the requirements for sale under this section and in case of willful violation is liable for conversion.

PART 3

BILLS OF LADING: SPECIAL PROVISIONS

Section 7—301. Liability for Non-Receipt or Misdescription; "Said to Contain"; Shipper's Load and Count"; Improper Handling.

(1) A consignee of a non-negotiable bill who has given value in good faith or a holder to whom a negotiable bill has been duly negotiated relying in either case upon the description therein of the goods, or upon the date therein shown, may recover from the issuer damages caused by the misdating of the bill or the non-receipt or misdescription of the goods, except to the extent that the document indicates that the issuer does not know whether any part or all of the goods in fact were received or conform to the description, as where the description is in terms of marks or labels or kind, quantity, or condition or the receipt or description is qualified by "contents or conditions of contents of packages unknown", "said to contain", "shipper's weight, load and count" or the like, if such indication be true.

(2) When goods are loaded by an issuer who is a common carrier, the issuer must count the packages of goods if package freight and ascertain the kind and quantity if bulk freight. In such cases "shipper's weight, load and count" or other words indicating that the description was made by the shipper are ineffective except as to freight concealed by packages.

(3) When bulk freight is loaded by a shipper who makes available to the issuer adequate facilities for weighing such freight, an issuer who is a common carrier must ascertain the kind and quantity within a reasonable time after receiving the written request of the shipper to do so. In such cases "shipper's weight" or other words of like purport are ineffective.

(4) The issuer may by inserting in the bill the words "shipper's weight, load and count" or other words of like purport indicate that the goods were loaded by the shipper; and if such statement be true, the issuer shall not be liable for damages caused by the improper loading. But their omission does not imply liability for such damages.

(5) The shipper shall be deemed to have guaranteed to the issuer the accuracy at the time of shipment of the description, marks, labels, number, kind, quantity, condition and weight, as furnished by him; and the shipper shall indemnify the issuer against damage caused by inaccuracies in such particulars. The right of the issuer to such indemnity shall in no way limit his responsibility and liability under the contract of carriage to any person other than the shipper.

Section 7—302. Through Bills of Lading and Similar Documents.

(1) The issuer of a through bill of lading or other document embodying an undertaking to be performed in part by persons acting as its agents or by connecting carriers is liable to anyone entitled to recover on the document for

any breach by such other persons or by a connecting carrier of its obligation under the document, but to the extent that the bill covers an undertaking to be performed overseas or in territory not contiguous to the continental United States or an undertaking including matters other than transportation this liability may be varied by agreement of the parties.

(2) Where goods covered by a through bill of lading or other document embodying an undertaking to be performed in part by persons other than the issuer are received by any such person, he is subject with respect to his own performance while the goods are in his possession to the obligation of the issuer. His obligation is discharged by delivery of the goods to another such person pursuant to the document, and does not include liability for breach by any other such persons or by the issuer.

(3) The issuer of such through bill of lading or other document shall be entitled to recover from the connecting carrier, or such other person in possession of the goods when the breach of the obligation under the document occurred, the amount it may be required to pay to anyone entitled to recover on the document therefor, as may be evidenced by any receipt, judgment, or transcript thereof, and the amount of any expense reasonably incurred by it in defending any action brought by anyone entitled to recover on the document therefor.

Section 7—303. Division; Reconsignment; Change of Instructions.

(1) Unless the bill of lading otherwise provides, the carrier may deliver the goods to a person or destination other than that stated in the bill or may otherwise dispose of the goods on instructions from

(a) the holder of a negotiable bill; or

(b) the consignor on a non-negotiable bill notwithstanding contrary instructions from the consignee; or

(c) the consignee on a non-negotiable bill in the absence of contrary instructions from the consignor, if the goods have arrived at the billed destination or if the consignee is in possession of the bill; or

(d) the consignee on a non-negotiable bill if he is entitled as against the consignor to dispose of them.

(2) Unless such instructions are noted on a negotiable bill of lading, a person to whom the bill is duly negotiated can hold the bailee according to the original terms.

Section 7—304. Bills of Lading in a Set.

(1) Except where customary in overseas transportation, a bill of lading must not be issued in a set of parts. The issuer is liable for damages caused by violation of this subsection.

(2) Where a bill of lading is lawfully drawn in a set of parts, each of which is numbered and expressed to be valid only if the goods have not been delivered against any other part, the whole of the parts constitute one bill.

(3) Where a bill of lading is lawfully issued in a set of parts and different parts are negotiated to different persons, the title of the holder to whom the first due negotiation is made prevails as to both the document and the goods even though any later holder may have received the goods from the carrier in good faith and discharged the carrier's obligation by surrender of his part.

(4) Any person who negotiates or transfers a single part of a bill of lading drawn in a set is liable to holders of that part as if it were the whole set.

(5) The bailee is obliged to deliver in accordance with Part 4 of this Article against the first presented part of a bill of lading lawfully drawn in a set. Such delivery discharges the bailee's obligation on the whole bill.

Section 7—305. Destination Bills.

(1) Instead of issuing a bill of lading to the consignor at the place of shipment a carrier may at the request of the consignor procure the bill to be issued at destination or at any other place designated in the request.

(2) Upon request of anyone entitled as against the carrier to control the goods while in transit and on surrender of any outstanding bill of lading or other receipt covering such goods, the issuer may procure a substitute bill to be issued at any place designated in the request.

Section 7—306. Altered Bills of Lading.

An unauthorized alteration or filling in of a blank in a bill of lading leaves the bill enforceable according to its original tenor.

Section 7—307. Lien of Carrier.

(1) A carrier has a lien on the goods covered by a bill of lading for charges subsequent to the date of the receipt of the goods for storage or transportation (including demurrage and terminal charges) and for expenses necessary for preservation of the goods incident to their transportation or reasonably incurred in their sale pursuant to law. But against a purchaser for value of a negotiable bill of lading, a carrier's lien is limited to charges stated in the bill or the applicable tariffs, or if no charges are stated then to a reasonable charge.

(2) A lien for charges and expenses under subsection (1) on goods which the carrier was required by law to receive for transportation is effective against the consignor or any person entitled to the goods unless the carrier had notice that the consignor lacked authority to subject the goods to such charges and expenses. Any other lien under subsection (1) is effective against the consignor and any person who permitted the bailor to have control or possession of the goods unless the carrier had notice that the bailor lacked such authority.

(3) A carrier loses his lien on any goods which he voluntarily delivers or which he unjustifiably refuses to deliver.

Section 7—308. Enforcement of Carrier's Lien.

(1) A carrier's lien may be enforced by public or private sale of the goods, in bloc or in parcels, at any time or place and on any terms which are commercially reasonable, after notifying all persons known to claim an interest in the goods. Such notification must include a statement of the amount due, the nature of the proposed sale and the time and place of any public sale. The fact that a better price could have been obtained by a sale at a different time or in a different method from that selected by the carrier is not of itself sufficient to establish that the sale was not made in a commercially reasonable manner. If the carrier either sells the goods in the usual manner in any recognized market therefor or if he sells at the price current in such market at the time of his sale or if he has otherwise sold in conformity with commercially reasonable practices among dealers in the type of goods sold, he has sold in a commercially reasonable manner. A sale of more goods than apparently necessary to be offered to ensure satisfaction of the obligation is not commercially reasonable except in cases covered by the preceding sentence.

(2) Before any sale pursuant to this section any person claiming a right in the goods may pay the amount necessary to satisfy the lien and the reasonable expenses incurred under this section. In that event the goods must not be sold, but must be retained by the carrier subject to the terms of the bill and this Article.

(3) The carrier may buy at any public sale pursuant to this section.

(4) A purchaser in good faith of goods sold to enforce a carrier's lien takes the goods free of any rights of persons against whom the lien was valid, despite noncompliance by the carrier with the requirements of this section.

(5) The carrier may satisfy his lien from the proceeds of any sale pursuant to this section but must hold the balance, if any, for delivery on demand to any person to whom he would have been bound to deliver the goods.

(6) The rights provided by this section shall be in addition to all other rights allowed by law to a creditor against his debtor.

(7) A carrier's lien may be enforced in accordance with either subsection (1) or the procedure set forth in subsection (2) of Section 7—210.

(8) The carrier is liable for damages caused by failure to comply with the requirements for sale under this section and in case of willful violation is liable for conversion.

Section 7—309. Duty of Care; Contractual Limitation of Carrier's Liability.

(1) A carrier who issues a bill of lading whether negotiable or non-negotiable must exercise the degree of care in relation to the goods which a reasonably careful man would exercise under like circumstances. This subsection does not repeal or change any law or rule of law which imposes liability upon a common carrier for damages not caused by its negligence.

(2) Damages may be limited by a provision that the carrier's liability shall not exceed a value stated in the document if the carrier's rates are dependent upon value and the consignor by the carrier's tariff is afforded an opportunity to declare a higher value or a value as lawfully provided in the tariff, or where no tariff is filed he is otherwise advised of such opportunity; but no such limitation is effective with respect to the carrier's liability for conversion to its own use.

(3) Reasonable provisions as to the time and manner of presenting claims and instituting actions based on the shipment may be included in a bill of lading or tariff.

PART 4

WAREHOUSE RECEIPTS AND BILLS OF LADING: GENERAL OBLIGATIONS

Section 7—401. Irregularities in Issue of Receipt or Bill or Conduct of Issuer.

The obligations imposed by this Article on an issuer apply to a document of title regardless of the fact that

(a) the document may not comply with the requirements of this Article or of any other law or regulation regarding its issue, form or content; or

(b) the issuer may have violated laws regulating the conduct of his business; or

(c) the goods covered by the document were owned by the bailee at the time the document was issued; or

(d) the person issuing the document does not come within the definition of warehouseman if it purports to be a warehouse receipt.

Section 7—402. Duplicate Receipt or Bill; Overissue.

Neither a duplicate nor any other document of title purporting to cover goods already represented by an outstanding document of the same issuer confers any right in the goods, except as provided in the case of bills in a set, overissue of documents for fungible goods and substitutes for lost, stolen or destroyed documents. But the issuer is liable for damages caused by his overissue or failure to identify a duplicate document as such by conspicuous notation on its face.

Section 7—403. Obligation of Warehouseman or Carrier to Deliver; Excuse.

(1) The bailee must deliver the goods to a person entitled under the document who complies with subsections (2) and (3), unless and to the extent that bailee establishes any of the following:

(a) delivery of the goods to a person whose receipt was rightful as against the claimant;

(b) damage to or delay, loss or destruction of the goods for which the bailee is not liable [but the burden of establishing negligence in such cases is on the person entitled under the document];

Note: *The brackets in (1)(b) indicate that State enactments may differ on this point without serious damage to the principle of uniformity.*

(c) previous sale or other disposition of the goods in lawful enforcement of a lien or on warehouseman's lawful termination of storage;

(d) the exercise by a seller of his right to stop delivery pursuant to the provisions of the Article on Sales (Section 2—705);

(e) a diversion, reconsignment or other disposition pursuant to the provisions of this Article (Section 7—303) or tariff regulating such right;

(f) release, satisfaction or any other fact affording a personal defense against the claimant;

(g) any other lawful excuse.

(2) A person claiming goods covered by a document of title must satisfy the bailee's lien where the bailee so requests or where the bailee is prohibited by law from delivering the goods until the charges are paid.

(3) Unless the person claiming is one against whom the document confers no right under Sec. 7—503 (1), he must surrender for cancellation or notation of partial deliveries any

outstanding negotiable document covering the goods, and the bailee must cancel the document or conspicuously note the partial delivery thereon or be liable to any person to whom the document is duly negotiated.

(4) "Person entitled under the document" means holder in the case of a negotiable document, or the person to whom delivery is to be made by the terms of or pursuant to written instructions under a non-negotiable document.

Section 7—404. No Liability for Good Faith Delivery Pursuant to Receipt or Bill.

A bailee who in good faith including observance of reasonable commercial standards has received goods and delivered or otherwise disposed of them according to the terms of the document of title or pursuant to this Article is not liable therefor. This rule applies even though the person from whom he received the goods had no authority to procure the document or to dispose of the goods and even though the person to whom he delivered the goods had no authority to receive them.

PART 5

WAREHOUSE RECEIPTS AND BILLS OF LADING: NEGOTIATION AND TRANSFER

Section 7—501. Form of Negotiation and Requirements of "Due Negotiation".

(1) A negotiable document of title running to the order of a named person is negotiated by his indorsement and delivery. After his indorsement in blank or to bearer any person can negotiate it by delivery alone.

(2) (a) A negotiable document of title is also negotiated by delivery alone when by its original terms it runs to bearer.

(b) When a document running to the order of a named person is delivered to him, the effect is the same as if the document had been negotiated.

(3) Negotiation of a negotiable document of title after it has been indorsed to a specified person requires indorsement by the special indorsee as well as delivery.

(4) A negotiable document of title is "duly negotiated" when it is negotiated in the manner stated in this section to a holder who purchases it in good faith without notice of any defense against or claim to it on the part of any person and for value, unless it is established that the negotiation is not in the regular course of business or financing or involves receiving the document in settlement or payment of a money obligation.

(5) Indorsement of a non-negotiable document neither makes it negotiable nor adds to the transferee's rights.

(6) The naming in a negotiable bill of a person to be notified of the arrival of the goods does not limit the negotiability of the bill nor constitute notice to a purchaser thereof of any interest of such person in the goods.

Section 7—502. Rights Acquired by Due Negotiation.

(1) Subject to the following section and to the provisions of Section 7—205 on fungible goods, a holder to whom a negotiable document of title has been duly negotiated acquires thereby:

(a) title to the document;

(b) title to the goods;

(c) all rights accruing under the law of agency or estoppel, including rights to goods delivered to the bailee after the document was issued; and

(d) the direct obligation of the issuer to hold or deliver the goods according to the terms of the document free of any defense or claim by him except those arising under the terms of the document or under this Article. In the case of a delivery order the bailee's obligation accrues only upon acceptance, and the obligation acquired by the holder is that the issuer and any indorser will procure the acceptance of the bailee.

(2) Subject to the following section, title and rights so acquired are not defeated by any stoppage of the goods represented by the document or by surrender of such goods by the

bailee, and are not impaired even though the negotiation or any prior negotiation constituted a breach of duty or even though any person has been deprived of possession of the document by misrepresentation, fraud, accident, mistake, duress, loss, theft or conversion, or even though a previous sale or other transfer of the goods or document has been made to a third person.

Section 7—503. Document of Title to Goods Defeated in Certain Cases.

(1) A document of title confers no right in goods against a person who before issuance of the document had a legal interest or a perfected security interest in them and who neither

(a) delivered or entrusted them or any document of title covering them to the bailor or his nominee with actual or apparent authority to ship, store or sell or with power to obtain delivery under this Article (Section 7—403) or with power of disposition under this Act (Sections 2—403 and 9—307) or other statute or rule of law; nor

(b) acquiesced in the procurement by the bailor or his nominee of any document of title.

(2) Title to goods based upon an unaccepted delivery order is subject to the rights of anyone to whom a negotiable warehouse receipt or bill of lading covering the goods has been duly negotiated. Such a title may be defeated under the next section to the same extent as the rights of the issuer or a transferee from the issuer.

(3) Title to goods based upon a bill of lading issued to a freight forwarder is subject to the rights of anyone to whom a bill issued by the freight forwarder is duly negotiated; but delivery by the carrier in accordance with Part 4 of this Article pursuant to its own bill of lading discharges the carrier's obligation to deliver.

Section 7—504. Rights Acquired in the Absence of Due Negotiation; Effect of Diversion; Seller's Stoppage of Delivery.

(1) A transferee of a document, whether negotiable or non-negotiable, to whom the document has been delivered but not duly negotiated, acquires the title and rights which his transferor had or had actual authority to convey.

(2) In the case of a non-negotiable document, until but not after the bailee receives notification of the transfer, the rights of the transferee may be defeated

(a) by those creditors of the transferor who could treat the sale as void under Section 2—402; or

(b) by a buyer from the transferor in ordinary course of business if the bailee has delivered the goods to the buyer or received notification of his rights; or

(c) as against the bailee by good faith dealings of the bailee with the transferor.

(3) A diversion or other change of shipping instructions by the consignor in a non-negotiable bill of lading which causes the bailee not to deliver to the consignee defeats the consignee's title to the goods if they have been delivered to a buyer in ordinary course of business and in any event defeats the consignee's rights against the bailee.

(4) Delivery pursuant to a non-negotiable document may be stopped by a seller under Section 2—705, and subject to the requirement of due notification there provided. A bailee honoring the seller's instructions is entitled to be indemnified by the seller against any resulting loss or expense.

Section 7—505. Indorser Not a Guarantor for Other Parties.

The indorsement of a document of title issued by a bailee does not make the indorser liable for any default by the bailee or by previous indorsers.

Section 7—506. Delivery Without Indorsement; Right to Compel Indorsement.

The transferee of a negotiable document of title has a specifically enforceable right to have his transferor supply any necessary indorsement, but the transfer becomes a negotiation only as of the time the indorsement is supplied.

Section 7—507. Warranties on Negotiation or Transfer of Receipt or Bill.

Where a person negotiates or transfers a document of title for value otherwise than as a mere intermediary under the next following section, then unless otherwise agreed he warrants to his immediate purchaser only in addition to any warranty made in selling the goods

(a) that the document is genuine; and

(b) that he has no knowledge of any fact which would impair its validity or worth; and

(c) that his negotiation or transfer is rightful and fully effective with respect to the title to the document and the goods it represents.

Section 7—508. Warranties of Collecting Bank as to Documents.

A collecting bank or other intermediary known to be entrusted with documents on behalf of another or with collection of a draft or other claim against delivery of documents warrants by such delivery of the documents only its own good faith and authority. This rule applies even though the intermediary has purchased or made advances against the claim or draft to be collected.

Section 7—509. Receipt or Bill: When Adequate Compliance With Commercial Contract.

The question whether a document is adequate to fulfill the obligations of a contract for sale or the conditions of a credit is governed by the Articles on Sales (Article 2) and on Letters of Credit (Article 5).

PART 6

WAREHOUSE RECEIPTS AND BILLS OF LADING: MISCELLANEOUS PROVISIONS

Section 7—601. Lost and Missing Documents.

(1) If a document has been lost, stolen or destroyed, a court may order delivery of the goods or issuance of a substitute document and the bailee may without liability to any person comply with such order. If the document was negotiable, the claimant must post security approved by the court to indemnify any person who may suffer loss as a result of non-surrender of the document. If the document was not negotiable, such security may be required at the discretion of the court. The court may also in its discretion order payment of the bailee's reasonable costs and counsel fees.

(2) A bailee who without court order delivers goods to a person claiming under a missing negotiable document is liable to any person injured thereby, and if the delivery is not in good faith becomes liable for conversion. Delivery in good faith is not conversion if made in accordance with a filed classification or tariff or, where no classification or tariff is filed, if the claimant posts security with the bailee in an amount at least double the value of the goods at the time of posting to indemnify any person injured by the delivery who files a notice of claim within one year after the delivery.

Section 7—602. Attachment of Goods Covered by a Negotiable Document.

Except where the document was originally issued upon delivery of the goods by a person who had no power to dispose of them, no lien attaches by virtue of any judicial process to goods in the possession of a bailee for which a negotiable document of title is outstanding unless the document be first surrendered to the bailee or its negotiation enjoined, and the bailee shall not be compelled to deliver the goods pursuant to process until the document is surrendered to him or impounded by the court. One who purchases the document for value without notice of the process or injunction takes free of the lien imposed by judicial process.

Section 7—603. Conflicting Claims; Interpleader.

If more than one person claims title or possession of the goods, the bailee is excused from delivery until he has had a reasonable time to ascertain the validity of the adverse claims or to bring an action to compel all claimants to interplead and may compel such interpleader, either in defending an action for non-delivery of the goods, or by original action, whichever is appropriate.

ARTICLE 8

INVESTMENT SECURITIES

PART 1

SHORT TITLE AND GENERAL MATTERS

Section 8—101. Short Title.

This Article shall be known and may be cited as Uniform Commercial Code—Investment Securities.

Section 8—102. Definitions and Index of Definitions.

(1) In this Article unless the context otherwise requires

(a) A "security" is an instrument which
   (i) is issued in bearer or registered form; and
   (ii) is of a type commonly dealt in upon securities exchanges or markets or commonly recognized in any area in which it is issued or dealt in as a medium for investment; and
   (iii) is either one of a class or series or by its terms is divisible into a class or series of instruments; and
   (iv) evidences a share, participation or other interest in property or in an enterprise or evidences an obligation of the issuer.

(b) A writing which is a security is governed by this Article and not by Uniform Commercial Code-Commercial Paper even though it also meets the requirements of that Article. This Article does not apply to money.

(c) A security is in "registered form" when it specifies a person entitled to the security or to the rights it evidences and when its transfer may be registered upon books maintained for that purpose by or on behalf of an issuer or the security so states.

(d) A security is in "bearer form" when it runs to bearer according to its terms and not by reason of any indorsement.

(2) A "subsequent purchaser" is a person who takes other than by original issue.

(3) A "clearing corporation" is a corporation all of the capital stock of which is held by or for a national securities exchange or association registered under a statute of the United States such as the Securities Exchange Act of 1934.

(4) A "custodian bank" is any bank or trust company which is supervised and examined by state or federal authority having supervision over banks and which is acting as custodian for a clearing corporation.

(5) Other definitions applying to this Article or to specified Parts thereof and the sections in which they appear are:

"Adverse claim".	Section 8—301.
"Bona fide purchaser".	Section 8—302.
"Broker".	Section 8—303.
"Guarantee of the signature".	Section 8—402.
"Intermediary bank".	Section 4—105.
"Issuer".	Section 8—201.
"Overissue".	Section 8—104.

(6) In addition Article 1 contains general definitions and principles of construction and interpretation applicable throughout this Article.

Section 8—103. Issuer's Lien.

A lien upon a security in favor of an issuer thereof is valid against a purchaser only if the right of the issuer to such lien is noted conspicuously on the security.

Section 8—104. Effect of Overissue; "Overissue."

(1) The provisions of this Article which validate a security or compel its issue or reissue do not apply to the extent that validation, issue or reissue would result in overissue; but

(a) if an identical security which does not constitute an overissue is reasonably available for purchase, the person entitled to issue or validation may compel the issuer to purchase and deliver such a security to him against surrender of the security, if any, which he holds; or

(b) if a security is not so available for purchase, the person entitled to issue or validation may recover from the issuer the price he or the last purchaser for value paid for it with interest from the date of his demand.

(2) "Overissue" means the issue of securities in excess of the amount which the issuer has corporate power to issue.

Section 8—105. Securities Negotiable; Presumptions.

(1) Securities governed by this Article are negotiable instruments.

(2) In any action on a security

(a) unless specifically denied in the pleadings, each signature on the security or in a necessary indorsement is admitted;

(b) when the effectiveness of a signature is put in issue, the burden of establishing it is on the party claiming under the signature but the signature is presumed to be genuine or authorized;

(c) when signatures are admitted or established, production of the instrument entitles a holder to recover on it unless the defendant establishes a defense or a defect going to the validity of the security; and

(d) after it is shown that a defense or defect exists, the plaintiff has the burden of establishing that he or some person under whom he claims is a person against whom the defense or defect is ineffective (Section 8—202).

Section 8—106. Applicability.

The validity of a security and the rights and duties of the issuer with respect to registration of transfer are governed by the law (including the conflict of laws rules) of the jurisdiction of organization of the issuer.

Section 8—107. Securities Deliverable; Action for Price.

(1) Unless otherwise agreed and subject to any applicable law or regulation respecting short sales, a person obligated to deliver securities may deliver any security of the specified issue in bearer form or registered in the name of the transferee or indorsed to him or in blank.

(2) When the buyer fails to pay the price as it comes due under a contract of sale, the seller may recover the price

(a) of securities accepted by the buyer; and

(b) of other securities if efforts at their resale would be unduly burdensome or if there is no readily available market for their resale.

PART 2

ISSUE—ISSUER

Section 8—201. "Issuer."

(1) With respect to obligations on or defenses to a security, "issuer" includes a person who

(a) places or authorizes the placing of his name on a security (otherwise than as authenticating trustee, registrar, transfer agent or the like) to evidence that it represents a share, participation or other interest in his property or in an enterprise or to evidence his duty to perform an obligation evidenced by the security; or

(b) directly or indirectly creates fractional interests in his rights or property which fractional interests are evidenced by securities; or

(c) becomes responsible for or in place of any other person described as an issuer in this section.

(2) With respect to obligations on or defenses to a security, a guarantor is an issuer to the extent of his guaranty whether or not his obligation is noted on the security.

(3) With respect to registration of transfer (Part 4 of this Article) "issuer" means a person on whose behalf transfer books are maintained.

Section 8—202. Issuer's Responsibility and Defenses; Notice of Defect or Defense.

(1) Even against a purchaser for value and without notice, the terms of a security include those stated on the security and those made part of the security by reference to another instrument, indenture or document or to a constitution, statute, ordinance, rule, regulation, order or the like to the extent that the terms so referred to do not conflict with the stated terms. Such a reference does not of itself charge a purchaser for value with notice of a defect going to the validity of the security even though the security expressly states that a person accepting it admits such notice.

(2) (a) A security other than one issued by a government or governmental agency or unit, even though issued with a defect going to its validity, is valid in the hands of a purchaser for value and without notice of the particular defect unless the defect involves a violation of constitutional provisions in which case the security is valid in the hands of a subsequent purchaser for value and without notice of the defect.

(b) The rule of subparagraph (a) applies to an issuer which is a government or governmental agency or unit only if either there has been substantial compliance with legal requirements governing the issue or the issuer has received a substantial consideration for the issue as a whole or for the particular security and a stated purpose of the issue is one for which the issuer has power to borrow money or issue the security.

(3) Except as otherwise provided in the case of certain unauthorized signatures on issue (Section 8—205), lack of genuineness of a security is a complete defense even against a purchaser for value and without notice.

(4) All other defenses of the issuer including nondelivery and conditional delivery of the security are ineffective against a purchaser for value who has taken without notice of the particular defense.

(5) Nothing in this section shall be construed to affect the right of a party to a "when, as and if issued" or a "when distributed" contract to cancel the contract in the event of a material change in the character of the security which is the subject of the contract or in the plan or arrangement pursuant to which such security is to be issued or distributed.

Section 8—203. Staleness as Notice of Defects or Defenses.

(1) After an act or event which creates a right to immediate performance of the principal obligation evidenced by the security or which sets a date on or after which the security is to be presented or surrendered for redemption or exchange, a purchaser is charged with notice of any defect in its issue or defense of the issuer

(a) if the act or event is one requiring the payment of money or the delivery of securities or both on presentation or surrender of the security and such funds or securities are available on the date set for payment or exchange and he takes the security more than one year after that date; and

(b) if the act or event is not covered by paragraph (a) and he takes the security more than two years after the date set for surrender or presentation or the date on which such performance became due.

(2) A call which has been revoked is not within subsection (1).

Section 8—204. Effect of Issuer's Restrictions on Transfer.

Unless noted conspicuously on the security a restriction on transfer imposed by the issuer, even though otherwise lawful, is ineffective except against a person with actual knowledge of it.

Section 8—205. Effect of Unauthorized Signature on Issue.

An unauthorized signature placed on a security prior to or in the course of issue is ineffective except that the signature is effective in favor of a purchaser for value and without notice of the lack of authority if the signing has been done by

(a) an authenticating trustee, registrar, transfer agent or other person entrusted by the issuer with the signing of the security or of similar securities or their immediate preparation for signing; or

(b) an employee of the issuer or of any of the foregoing entrusted with responsible handling of the security.

Section 8—206. Completion or Alteration of Instrument.

(1) Where a security contains the signatures necessary to its issue or transfer but is incomplete in any other respect

(a) any person may complete it by filling in the blanks as authorized; and

(b) even though the blanks are incorrectly filled in, the security as completed is enforceable by a purchaser who took it for value and without notice of such incorrectness.

(2) A complete security which has been improperly altered even though fraudulently remains enforceable but only according to its original terms.

Section 8—207. Rights of Issuer With Respect to Registered Owners.

(1) Prior to due presentment for registration of transfer of a security in registered form, the issuer or indenture trustee may treat the registered owner as the person exclusively entitled to vote, to receive notifications and otherwise to exercise all the rights and powers of an owner.

(2) Nothing in this Article shall be construed to affect the liability of the registered owner of a security for calls, assessments or the like.

Section 8—208. Effect of Signature of Authenticating Trustee, Registrar or Transfer Agent.

(1) A person placing his signature upon a security as authenticating trustee, registrar, transfer agent or the like warrants to a purchaser for value without notice of the particular defect that

(a) the security is genuine; and

(b) his own participation in the issue of the security is within his capacity and within the scope of the authorization received by him from the issuer; and

(c) he has reasonable grounds to believe that the security is in the form and within the amount the issuer is authorized to issue.

(2) Unless otherwise agreed, a person by so placing his signature does not assume responsibility for the validity of the security in other respects.

PART 3

PURCHASE

Section 8—301. Rights Acquired by Purchaser; "Adverse Claim"; Title Acquired by Bona Fide Purchaser.

(1) Upon delivery of a security the purchaser acquires the rights in the security which his transferor had or had actual authority to convey except that a purchaser who has himself been a party to any fraud or illegality affecting the security or who as a prior holder had notice of an adverse claim cannot improve his position by taking from a later bona fide purchaser. "Adverse claim" includes a claim that a transfer was or would be wrongful or that a particular adverse person is the owner of or has an interest in the security.

(2) A bona fide purchaser in addition to acquiring the rights of a purchaser also acquires the security free of any adverse claim.

(3) A purchaser of a limited interest acquires rights only to the extent of the interest purchased.

Section 8—302. "Bona Fide Purchaser."

A "bona fide purchaser" is a purchaser for value in good faith and without notice of any adverse claim who takes delivery of a security in bearer form or of one in registered form issued to him or indorsed to him or in blank.

Section 8—303. "Broker."

"Broker" means a person engaged for all or part of his time in the business of buying and selling securities, who in the transaction concerned acts for, or buys a security from or sells a security to a customer. Nothing in this Article determines the capacity in which a person acts for purposes of any other statute or rule to which such person is subject.

Section 8—304. Notice to Purchaser of Adverse Claims.

(1) A purchaser (including a broker for the seller or buyer but excluding an intermediary bank) of a security is charged with notice of adverse claims if

(a) the security whether in bearer or registered form has been indorsed "for collection" or "for surrender" or for some other purpose not involving transfer; or

(b) the security is in bearer form and has on it an unambiguous statement that it is the property of a person other than the transferor. The mere writing of a name on a security is not such a statement.

(2) The fact that the purchaser (including a broker for the seller or buyer) has notice that the security is held for a third person or is registered in the name of or indorsed by a fiduciary does not create a duty of inquiry into the rightfulness of the transfer or constitute notice of adverse claims. If, however, the purchaser (excluding an intermediary bank) has knowledge that the proceeds are being used or that the transaction is for the individual benefit of the fiduciary or otherwise in breach of duty, the purchaser is charged with notice of adverse claims.

Section 8—305. Staleness as Notice of Adverse Claims.

An act or event which creates a right to immediate performance of the principal obligation evidenced by the security or which sets a date on or after which the security is to be presented or surrendered for redemption or exchange does not of itself constitute any notice of adverse claims except in the case of a purchase

(a) after one year from any date set for such presentment or surrender for redemption or exchange; or

(b) after six months from any date set for payment of money against presentation or surrender of the security if funds are available for payment on that date.

Section 8—306. Warranties on Presentment and Transfer.

(1) A person who presents a security for registration of transfer or for payment or exchange warrants to the issuer that he is entitled to the registration, payment or exchange. But a purchaser for value without notice of adverse claims who receives a new, reissued or reregistered security on registration of transfer warrants only that he has no knowledge of any unauthorized signature (Section 8—311) in a necessary indorsement.

(2) A person by transferring a security to a purchaser for value warrants only that

(a) his transfer is effective and rightful; and

(b) the security is genuine and has not been materially altered; and

(c) he knows no fact which might impair the validity of the security.

(3) Where a security is delivered by an intermediary known to be entrusted with delivery of the security on behalf of another or with collection of a draft or other claim against such delivery, the intermediary by such delivery warrants only his own good faith and authority even though he has purchased or made advances against the claim to be collected against the delivery.

(4) A pledgee or other holder for security who redelivers the security received, or after payment and on order of the debtor delivers that security to a third person, makes only the warranties of an intermediary under subsection (3).

(5) A broker gives to his customer and to the issuer and a purchaser the warranties provided in this section and has the rights and privileges of a purchaser under this section. The warranties of and in favor of the broker acting as an agent are in addition to applicable warranties given by and in favor of his customer.

Section 8—307. Effect of Delivery Without Indorsement; Right to Compel Indorsement.

Where a security in registered form has been delivered to a purchaser without a necessary indorsement, he may become a bona fide purchaser only as of the time the indorsement is supplied, but against the transferor the transfer is complete upon delivery and the purchaser has a specifically enforceable right to have any necessary indorsement supplied.

Section 8—308. Indorsement, How Made; Special Indorsement; Indorser Not a Guarantor; Partial Assignment.

(1) An indorsement of a security in registered form is made when an appropriate person signs on it or on a separate document an assignment or transfer of the security or a power to assign or transfer it or when the signature of such person is written without more upon the back of the security.

(2) An indorsement may be in blank or special. An indorsement in blank includes an indorsement to bearer. A special indorsement specifies the person to whom the security is to be transferred, or who has power to transfer it. A holder may convert a blank indorsement into a special indorsement.

(3) "An appropriate person" in subsection (1) means

(a) the person specified by the security or by special indorsement to be entitled to the security; or

(b) where the person so specified is described as a fiduciary but is no longer serving in the described capacity,—either that person or his successor; or

(c) where the security or indorsement so specifies more than one person as fiduciaries and one or more are no longer serving in the described capacity,—the remaining fiduciary or fiduciaries, whether or not a successor has been appointed or qualified; or

(d) where the person specified is an individual and is without capacity to act by virtue of death, incompetence, infancy or otherwise,—his executor, administrator, guardian or like fiduciary; or

(e) where the security or indorsement so specifies more than one person as tenants by the entirety or with right of survivorship and by reason of death all cannot sign,—the survivor or survivors; or

(f) a person having power to sign under applicable law or controlling instrument; or

(g) to the extent that any of the foregoing persons may act through an agent,—his authorized agent.

(4) Unless otherwise agreed the indorser by his indorsement assumes no obligation that the security will be honored by the issuer.

(5) An indorsement purporting to be only of part of a security representing units intended by the issuer to be separately transferable is effective to the extent of the indorsement.

(6) Whether the person signing is appropriate is determined as of the date of signing and an indorsement by such a person does not become unauthorized for the purposes of this Article by virtue of any subsequent change of circumstances.

(7) Failure of a fiduciary to comply with a controlling instrument or with the law of the state having jurisdicition of the fiduciary relationship, including any law requiring the fiduciary to obtain court approval of the transfer, does not render his indorsement unauthorized for the purpose of this Article.

Section 8—309. Effect of Indorsement Without Delivery.

An indorsement of a security whether special or in blank does not constitute a transfer until delivery of the security on which it appears or, if the indorsement is on a separate document, until delivery of both the document and the security.

Section 8—310. Indorsement of Security in Bearer Form.

An indorsement of a security in bearer form may give notice of adverse claims (Section 8—304) but does not otherwise affect any right to registration the holder may possess.

Section 8—311. Effect of Unauthorized Indorsement.

Unless the owner has ratified an unauthorized indorsement or is otherwise precluded from asserting its ineffectiveness

(a) he may assert its ineffectiveness against the issuer or any purchaser other than a purchaser for value and without notice of adverse claims who has in good faith received a new, reissued or re-registered security on registration of transfer; or

(b) an issuer who registers the transfer of a security upon the unauthorized indorsement is subject to liability for improper registration (Section 8—404).

Section 8—312. Effect of Guaranteeing Signature or Indorsement.

(1) Any person guaranteeing a signature of an indorser of a security warrants that at the time of signing

(a) the signature was genuine; and

(b) the signer was an appropriate person to indorse (Section 8—308); and

(c) the signer had legal capacity to sign.

But the guarantor does not otherwise warrant the rightfulness of the particular transfer.

(2) Any person may guarantee an indorsement of a security and by so doing warrants not only the signature (subsection 1) but also the rightfulness of the particular transfer in all respects. But no issuer may require a guarantee of indorsement as a condition to registration of transfer.

(3) The foregoing warranties are made to any person taking or dealing with the security in reliance on the guarantee and the guarantor is liable to such person for any loss resulting from breach of the warranties.

Section 8—313. When Delivery to the Purchaser Occurs; Purchaser's Broker as Holder.

(1) Delivery to a purchaser occurs when

(a) he or a person designated by him acquires possession of a security; or

(b) his broker acquires possession of a security specially indorsed to or issued in the name of the purchaser; or

(c) his broker sends him confirmation of the purchase and also by book entry or otherwise identifies a specific security in the broker's possession as belonging to the purchaser; or

(d) with respect to an identified security to be delivered while still in the possession of a third person when that person acknowledges that he holds for the purchaser; or

(e) appropriate entries on the books of a clearing corporation are made under Section 8—320.

(2) The purchaser is the owner of a security held for him by his broker but is not the holder except as specified in subparagraphs (b), (c) and (e) of subsection (1). Where a security is part of a fungible bulk, the purchaser is the owner of a proportionate property interest in the fungible bulk.

(3) Notice of an adverse claim received by the broker or by the purchaser after the broker takes delivery as a holder for value is not effective either as to the broker or as to the purchaser. However, as between the broker and the purchaser the purchaser may demand delivery of an equivalent security as to which no notice of an adverse claim has been received.

Section 8—314. Duty to Deliver, When Completed.

(1) Unless otherwise agreed, where a sale of a security is made on an exchange or otherwise through brokers

(a) the selling customer fulfills his duty to deliver when he places such a security in the possession of the selling broker or of a person designated by the broker or if requested causes an acknowledgment to be made to the selling broker that it is held for him; and

(b) the selling broker including a correspondent broker acting for a selling customer fulfills his duty to deliver by placing the security or a like security in the possession of the buying broker or a person designated by him or by effecting clearance of the sale in accordance with the rules of the exchange on which the transaction took place.

(2) Except as otherwise provided in this section and unless otherwise agreed, a transferor's duty to deliver a security under a contract of purchase is not fulfilled until he places the security in form to be negotiated by the purchaser in the possession of the purchaser or of a person designated by him or at the purchaser's request causes an acknowledgment to be made to the purchaser that it is held for him. Unless made on an exchange a sale to a broker purchasing for his own account is within this subsection and not within subsection (1).

Section 8—315. Action Against Purchaser Based Upon Wrongful Transfer.

(1) Any person against whom the transfer of a security is wrongful for any reason, including his incapacity, may against anyone except a bona fide purchaser reclaim possession of the security or obtain possession of any new security evidencing all or part of the same rights or have damages.

(2) If the transfer is wrongful because of an unauthorized indorsement, the owner may also reclaim or obtain possession of the security or new security even from a bona fide purchaser if the ineffectiveness of the purported indorsement can be asserted against him under the provisions of this Article on unauthorized indorsements (Section 8—311).

(3) The right to obtain or reclaim possession of a security may be specifically enforced and its transfer enjoined and the security impounded pending the litigation.

Section 8—316. Purchaser's Right to Requisites for Registration of Transfer on Books.

Unless otherwise agreed the transferor must on due demand supply his purchaser with any proof of his authority to transfer or with any other requisite which may be necessary to obtain registration of the transfer of the security, but if the transfer is not for value, a transferor need not do so unless the purchaser furnishes the necessary expenses. Failure to comply with a demand made within a reasonable time gives the purchaser the right to reject or rescind the transfer.

Section 8—317. Attachment or Levy Upon Security.

(1) No attachment or levy upon a security or any share or other interest evidenced thereby which is outstanding shall be valid until the security is actually seized by the officer making the attachment or levy, but a security which has been surrendered to the issuer may be attached or levied upon at the source.

(2) A creditor whose debtor is the owner of a security shall be entitled to such aid from courts of appropriate jurisdiction, by injunction or otherwise, in reaching such security or in satisfying the claim by means thereof as is allowed at law or in equity in regard to property which cannot readily be attached or levied upon by ordinary legal process.

Section 8—318. No Conversion by Good Faith Delivery.

An agent or bailee who in good faith (including observance of reasonable commercial standards if he is in the business of buying, selling or otherwise dealing with securiites) has received securities and sold, pledged or delivered them according to the instructions of his principal is not liable for conversion or for participation in breach of fiduciary duty although the principal had no right to dispose of them.

Section 8—319. Statute of Frauds.

A contract for the sale of securities is not enforceable by way of action or defense unless

(a) there is some writing signed by the party against whom enforcement is sought or by his authorized agent or broker sufficient to indicate that a contract has been made, for sale of a stated quantity of described securities at a defined or stated price; or

(b) delivery of the security has been accepted or payment has been made but the contract is enforceable under this provision only to the extent of such delivery or payment; or

(c) within a reasonable time a writing in confirmation of the sale or purchase and sufficient against the sender under paragraph (a) has been received by the party against whom enforcement is sought and he has failed to send written objection to its contents within ten days after its receipt; or

(d) the party against whom enforcement is sought admits in his pleading, testimony or otherwise in court that a contract was made for sale of a stated quantity of described securities at a defined or stated price.

Section 8—320. Transfer or Pledge within a Central Depository System.

(1) If a security

(a) is in the custody of a clearing corporation or of a custodian bank or a nominee of either subject to the instructions of the clearing corporation; and

(b) is in bearer form or indorsed in blank by an appropriate person or registered in the name of the clearing corporation or custodian bank or a nominee of either; and

(c) is shown on the account of a transferor or pledgor on the books of the clearing corporation;

then, in addition to other methods, a transfer or pledge of the security or any interest therein may be effected by the making of appropriate entries on the books of the clearing corporation reducing the account of the transferor or pledgor and increasing the account of the transferee or pledgee by the amount of the obligation or the number of shares or rights transferred or pledged.

(2) Under this section entries may be with respect to like securities or interests therein as a part of a fungible bulk and may refer merely to a quantity of a particular security without reference to the name of the registered owner, certificate or bond number or the like and, in appropriate cases, may be on a net basis taking into account other transfers or pledges of the same securty.

(3) A transfer or pledge under this section has the effect of a delivery of a security in bearer form or duly indorsed in blank (Section 8—301) representing the amount of the obligation or the number of shares or rights transferred or pledged. If a pledge or the creation of a security interest is intended, the making of entries has the effect of a taking of delivery by the pledgee or a secured party (Sections 9—304 and 9—305). A transferee or pledgee under this section is a holder.

(4) A transfer or pledge under this section does not constitute a registration of transfer under Part 4 of this Article.

(5) That entries made on the books of the clearing corporation as provided in subsection (1) are not appropriate does not affect the validity or effect of the entries nor the liabilities or obligations of the clearing corporation to any person adversely affected thereby.

PART 4

REGISTRATION

Section 8—401. Duty of Issuer to Register Transfer.

(1) Where a security in registered form is presented to the issuer with a request to register transfer, the issuer is under a duty to register the transfer as requested if

(a) the security is indorsed by the appropriate person or persons (Section 8—308); and

(b) reasonable assurance is given that those indorsements are genuine and effective (Section 8—402); and

(c) the issuer has no duty to inquire into adverse claims or has discharged any such duty (Section 8—403); and

(d) any applicable law relating to the collection of taxes has been complied with; and

(e) the transfer is in fact rightful or is to a bona fide purchaser.

(2) Where an issuer is under a duty to register a transfer of a security, the issuer is also liable to the person presenting it for registration or his principal for loss resulting from any unreasonable delay in registration or from failure or refusal to register the transfer.

Section 8—402. Assurance That Indorsements Are Effective.

(1) The issuer may require the following assurance that each necessary indorsement (Section 8—308) is genuine and effective

(a) in all cases, a guarantee of the signature (subsection (1) of Section 8—312) of the person indorsing; and
(b) where the indorsement is by an agent, appropriate assurance of authority to sign;
(c) where the indorsement is by a fiduciary, appropriate evidence of appointment or incumbency;
(d) where there is more than one fiduciary, reasonable assurance that all who are required to sign have done so;
(e) where the indorsement is by a person not covered by any of the foregoing, assurance appropriate to the case corresponding as nearly as may be to the foregoing.

(2) A "guarantee of the signature" in subsection (1) means a guarantee signed by or on behalf of a person reasonably believed by the issuer to be responsible. The issuer may adopt standards with respect to responsibility provided such standards are not manifestly unreasonable.

(3) "Appropriate evidence of appointment or incumbency" in subsection (1) means

(a) in the case of a fiduciary appointed or qualified by a court, a certificate issued by or under the direction or supervision of that court or an officer thereof and dated within sixty days before the date of presentation for transfer; or
(b) in any other case, a copy of a document showing the appointment or a certificate issued by or on behalf of a person reasonably believed by the issuer to be responsible or, in the absence of such a document or certificate, other evidence reasonably deemed by the issuer to be appropriate. The issuer may adopt standards with respect to such evidence provided such standards are not manifestly unreasonable. The issuer is not charged with notice of the contents of any document obtained pursuant to this paragraph (b) except to the extent that the contents relate directly to the appointment or incumbency.

(4) The issuer may elect to require reasonable assurance beyond that specified in this section but if it does so and for a purpose other than that specified in subsection 3(b) both requires and obtains a copy of a will, trust, indenture, articles of co-partnership, by-laws or other controlling instrument, it is charged with notice of all matters contained therein affecting the transfer.

Section 8—403. Limited Duty of Inquiry.

(1) An issuer to whom a security is presented for registration is under a duty to inquire into adverse claims if

(a) a written notification of an adverse claim is received at a time and in a manner which affords the issuer a reasonable opportunity to act on it prior to the issuance of a new, reissued or re-registered security and the notification identifies the claimant, the registered owner and the issue of which the security is a part and provides an address for communications directed to the claimant; or
(b) the issuer is charged with notice of an adverse claim from a controlling instrument which it has elected to require under subsection (4) of Section 8—402.

(2) The issuer may discharge any duty of inquiry by any reasonable means, including notifying an adverse claimant by registered or certified mail at the address furnished by him or if there be no such address at his residence or regular place of business that the security has been presented for registration of transfer by a named person, and that the transfer will be registered unless within thirty days from the date of mailing the notification, either

(a) an appropriate restraining order, injunction or other process issues from a court of competent jurisdiction; or
(b) an indemnity bond sufficient in the issuer's judgment to protect the issuer and any transfer agent, registrar or other agent of the issuer involved, from any loss which it or

they may suffer by complying with the adverse claim is filed with the issuer.

(3) Unless an issuer is charged with notice of an adverse claim from a controlling instrument which it has elected to require under subsection (4) of Section 8—402 or receives notification of an adverse claim under subsection (1) of this section, where a security presented for registration is indorsed by the appropriate person or persons the issuer is under no duty to inquire into adverse claims. In particular

(a) an issuer registering a security in the name of a person who is a fiduciary or who is described as a fiduciary is not bound to inquire into the existence, extent, or correct description of the fiduciary relationship; and thereafter the issuer may assume without inquiry that the newly registered owner continues to be the fiduciary until the issuer receives written notice that the fiduciary is no longer acting as such with respect to the particular security;

(b) an issuer registering transfer on an indorsement by a fiduciary is not bound to inquire whether the transfer is made in compliance with a controlling instrument or with the law of the state having jurisdiction of the fiduciary relationship, including any law requiring the fiduciary to obtain court approval of the transfer; and

(c) the issuer is not charged with notice of the contents of any court record or file or other recorded or unrecorded document even though the document is in its possession and even though the transfer is made on the indorsement of a fiduciary to the fiduciary himself or to his nominee.

Section 8—404. Liability and Non-Liability for Registration.

(1) Except as otherwise provided in any law relating to the collection of taxes, the issuer is not liable to the owner or any other person suffering loss as a result of the registration of a transfer of a security if

(a) there were on or with the security the necessary indorsements (Section 8—308); and

(b) the issuer had no duty to inquire into adverse claims or has discharged any such duty (Section 8—403).

(2) Where an issuer has registered a transfer of a security to a person not entitled to it, the issuer on demand must deliver a like security to the true owner unless

(a) the registration was pursuant to subsection (1); or

(b) the owner is precluded from asserting any claim for registering the transfer under subsection (1) of the following section; or

(c) such delivery would result in overissue, in which case the issuer's liability is governed by Section 8—104.

Section 8—405. Lost, Destroyed and Stolen Securities.

(1) Where a security has been lost, apparently destroyed or wrongfully taken and the owner fails to notify the issuer of that fact within a reasonable time after he has notice of it and the issuer registers a transfer of the security before receiving such a notification, the owner is precluded from asserting against the issuer any claim for registering the transfer under the preceding section or any claim to a new security under this section.

(2) Where the owner of a security claims that the security has been lost, destroyed or wrongfully taken, the issuer must issue a new security in place of the original security if the owner

(a) so requests before the issuer has notice that the security has been acquired by a bona fide purchaser; and

(b) files with the issuer a sufficient indemnity bond; and

(c) satisfies any other reasonable requirements imposed by the issuer.

(3) If, after the issue of the new security, a bona fide purchaser of the original security

presents it for registration of transfer, the issuer must register the transfer unless registration would result in overissue, in which event the issuer's liability is governed by Section 8—104. In addition to any rights on the indemnity bond, the issuer may recover the new security from the person to whom it was issued or any person taking under him except a bona fide purchaser.

Section 8—406. Duty of Authenticating Trustee, Transfer Agent or Registrar.

(1) Where a person acts as authenticating trustee, transfer agent, registrar, or other agent for an issuer in the registration of transfers of its securities or in the issue of new securities or in the cancellation of surrendered securities

(a) he is under a duty to the issuer to exercise good faith and due diligence in performing his functions; and

(b) he has with regard to the particular functions he performs the same obligation to the holder or owner of the security and has the same rights and privileges as the issuer has in regard to those functions.

(2) Notice to an authenticating trustee, transfer agent, registrar or other such agent is notice to the issuer with respect to the functions performed by the agent.

ARTICLE 9

SECURED TRANSACTIONS; SALES OF ACCOUNTS, CONTRACT RIGHTS AND CHATTEL PAPER

PART 1

SHORT TITLE, APPLICABILITY AND DEFINITIONS

Section 9—101. Short Title.

This Article shall be known and may be cited as Uniform Commercial Code—Secured Transactions.

Section 9—102. Policy and Scope of Article.

(1) Except as otherwise provided in Section 9—103 on multiple state transactions and in Section 9—104 on excluded transactions, this Article applies so far as concerns any personal property and fixtures within the jurisdiction of this state

(a) to any transaction (regardless of its form) which is intended to create a security interest in personal property or fixtures including goods, documents, instruments, general intangibles, chattel papers, accounts or contract rights; and also

(b) to any sale of accounts, contract rights or chattel paper.

(2) This Article applies to security interests created by contract including pledge, assignment, chattel mortgage, chattel trust, trust deed, factor's lien, equipment trust, conditional sale, trust receipt, other lien or title retention contract and lease or consignment intended as security. This Article does not apply to statutory liens except as provided in Section 9—310.

(3) The application of this Article to a security interest in a secured obligation is not affected by the fact that the obligation is itself secured by a transaction or interest to which this Article does not apply.

Note: *The adoption of this Article should be accompanied by the repeal of existing statutes dealing with conditional sales, trust receipts, factor's liens where the factor is given a non-possessory lien, chattel mortgages, crop mortgages, mortgages on railroad equipment, assignment of accounts and generally statutes regulating security interests in personal property.*

Where the state has a retail installment selling act or small loan act, that legislation should be carefully examined to determine what changes in those acts are needed to conform them to this Article. This Article primarily sets out rules defining rights of a secured party against persons dealing with the debtor; it does not prescribe regulations and controls which may be necessary to curb abuses arising in the small loan business or in the financing of consumer purchases on credit. Accordingly there is no intention to repeal existing regulatory acts in those fields. See Section 9—203(2) and the Note thereto.

Section 9—103. Accounts, Contract Rights, General Intangibles and Equipment Relating to Another Jurisdiction; and Incoming Goods Already Subject to a Security Interest.

(1) If the office where the assignor of accounts or contract rights keeps his records concerning them is in this state, the validity and perfection of a security interest therein and the possibility and effect of proper filing is governed by this Article; otherwise by the law (including the conflict of laws rules) of the jurisdiction where such office is located.

(2) If the chief place of business of a debtor is in this state, this Article governs the validity and perfection of a security interest and the possibility and effect of proper filing with regard to general intangibles or with regard to goods of a type which are normally used in more than one jurisdiction (such as automotive equipment, rolling stock, airplanes, road building equipment, commercial harvesting equipment, construction machinery and the like) if such goods are classified as equipment or classified as inventory by reason of their being leased by the debtor to others. Otherwise, the law (including the conflict of laws rules) of the jurisdiction where such chief place of business is located shall govern. If the chief place of business is located in a jurisdiction which does not provide for perfection of the security interest by filing or recording in that jurisdiction, then the security interest may be perfected by filing in this state. [For the purpose of determining the validity and perfection of a security interest in an airplane, the chief place of business of a debtor who is a foreign air carrier under the Federal Aviation Act of 1958, as amended, is the designated office of the agent upon whom service of process may be made on behalf of the debtor.]

(3) If personal property other than that governed by subsections (1) and (2) is already subject to a security interest when it is brought into this state, the validity of the security interest in this state is to be determined by the law (including the conflict of laws rules) of the jurisdiction where the property was when the security interest attached. However, if the parties to the transaction understood at the time that the security interest attached that the property would be kept in this state and it was brought into this state within 30 days after the security interest attached for purposes other than transportation through this state, then the validity of the security interest in this state is to be determined by the law of this state. If the security interest was already perfected under the law of the jurisdiction where the property was when the security interest attached and before being brought into this state, the security interest continues perfected in this state for four months and also thereafter if within the four month period it is perfected in this state. The security interest may also be perfected in this state after the expiration of the four month period; in such case perfection dates from the time of perfection in this state. If the security interest was not perfected under the law of the jurisdiction where the property was when the security interest attached and before being brought into this state, it may be perfected in this state; in such case perfection dates from the time of perfection in this state.

(4) Notwithstanding subsections (2) and (3), if personal property is covered by a certificate of title issued under a statute of this state or any other jurisdiction which requires indication on a certificate of title of any security interest in the property as a condition of perfection, then the perfection is governed by the law of the jurisdiction which issued the certificate.

[(5) Notwithstanding subsection (1) and Section 9—302, if the office where the assignor of accounts or contract rights keeps his records concerning them is not located in a jurisdiction which is a part of the United States, its territories or possessions, and the accounts or contract rights are within the jurisdiction of this state or the transaction which creates the security interest otherwise bears an appropriate relation to this state, this Article governs the validity and perfection of the security interest and the security interest may only be perfected by notification to the account debtor.]

Note: *The last sentence of subsection (2) and subsection (5) are bracketed to indicate optional enactment. In states engaging in financing of airplanes of foreign carriers and of international open accounts receivable, bracketed language will be of value. In other states not engaging in financing of this type, the bracketed language may not be considered necessary.*

Section 9—104. Transactions Excluded from Article.

This Article does not apply

(a) to a security interest subject to any statute of the United States such as the Ship Mortgage Act, 1920, to the extent that such statute governs the rights of parties to and third parties affected by transactions in particular types of property; or

(b) to a landlord's lien; or

(c) to a lien given by statute or other rules of law for services or materials except as provided in Section 9—310 on priority of such liens; or

(d) to a transfer of a claim for wages, salary or other compensation of an employee; or

(e) to an equipment trust coverning railway rolling stock; or

(f) to a sale of accounts, contract rights or chattel paper as part of a sale of the business out of which they arose, or an assignment of accounts, contract rights or chattel paper which is for the purpose of collection only, or a transfer of a contract right to an assignee who is also to do the performance under the contract; or

(g) to a transfer of an interest or claim in or under any policy of insurance; or

(h) to a right represented by a judgment; or

(i) to any right of set-off; or

(j) except to the extent that provision is made for fixtures in Section 9—313, to the creation or transfer of an interest in or lien on real estate, including a lease or rents thereunder; or

(k) to a transfer in whole or in part of any of the following: any claim arising out of tort; any deposit, savings, passbook or like account maintained with a bank, savings and loan association, credit union or like organization.

Section 9—105. Definitions and Index of Definitions.

(1) In this Article unless the context otherwise requires:

(a) "Account debtor" means the person who is obligated on an account, chattel paper, contract right or general intangible;

(b) "Chattel paper" means a writing or writings which evidence both a monetary obligation and a security interest in or a lease of specific goods. When a transaction is evidenced both by such a security agreement or a lease and by an instrument or a series of instruments, the group of writings taken together constitutes chattel paper;

(c) "Collateral" means the property subject to a security interest, and includes accounts, contract rights and chattel paper which have been sold;

(d) "Debtor" means the person who owes payment or other performance of the obligation secured, whether or not he owns or has rights in the collateral, and includes the seller of accounts, contract rights or chattel paper. Where the debtor and the owner of the collateral are not the same person, the term "debtor" means the owner of the collateral in any provision of the Article dealing with the collateral, the obligor in any provision dealing with the obligation, and may include both where the context so requires;

(e) "Document" means document of title as defined in the general definitions of Article 1 (Section 1—201);

(f) "Goods" includes all things which are movable at the time the security interest attaches or which are fixtures (Section 9—313), but does not include money, documents, instruments, accounts, chattel paper, general intangibles, contract rights and other things in action. "Goods" also include the unborn young of animals and growing crops;

(g) "Instrument" means a negotiable instrument (defined in Section 3—104), or a security (defined in Section 8—102) or any other writing which evidences a right to the payment of money and is not itself a security agreement or lease and is of a type which is in ordinary course of business transferred by delivery with any necessary indorsement or assignment;

(h) "Security agreement" means an agreement which creates or provides for a security interest;

(i) "Secured party" means a lender, seller or other person in whose favor there is a security interest, including a person to whom accounts, contract rights or chattel paper have been sold. When the holders of obligations issued under an indenture of trust, equipment trust agreement or the like are represented by a trustee or other person, the representative is the secured party.

(2) Other definitions applying to this Article and the sections in which they appear are:

"Account". Section 9—106.
"Consumer goods". Section 9—109(1).
"Contract right". Section 9—106.
"Equipment". Section 9—109(2).
"Farm products". Section 9—109(3).
"General intangibles". Section 9—106.
"Inventory". Section 9—109(4).
"Lien creditor". Section 9—301(3).
"Proceeds". Section 9—306(1).
"Purchase money security interest". Section 9—107.

(3) The following definitions in other Articles apply to this Article:

"Check". Section 3—104.
"Contract for sale". Section 2—106.
"Holder in due course". Section 3—302.
"Note". Section 3—104.
"Sale". Section 2—106.

(4) In addition Article 1 contains general definitions and principles of construction and interpretation applicable throughout this Article.

Section 9—106. Definitions: "Account"; "Contract Right"; "General Intangibles".

"Account" means any right to payment for goods sold or leased or for services rendered which is not evidenced by an instrument or chattel paper. "Contract right" means any right to payment under a contract not yet earned by performance and not evidenced by an instrument or chattel paper. "General intangibles" means any personal property (including things in action) other than goods, accounts, contract rights, chattel paper, documents and instruments.

Section 9—107. Definitions: "Purchase Money Security Interest".

A security interest is a "purchase money security interest" to the extent that it is

(a) taken or retained by the seller of the collateral to secure all or part of its price; or

(b) taken by a person who by making advances or incurring an obligation gives value to enable the debtor to acquire rights in or the use of collateral if such value is in fact so used.

Section 9—108. When After-Acquired Collateral Not Security for Antecedent Debt.

Where a secured party makes an advance, incurs an obligation, releases a perfected security interest, or otherwise gives new value which is to be secured in whole or in part by after-acquired property, his security interest in the after-acquired collateral shall be deemed to be taken for new value and not as security for an antecedent debt if the debtor acquires his rights in such collateral either in the ordinary course of his business or under a contract of purchase made pursuant to the security agreement within a reasonable time after new value is given.

Section 9—109. Classification of Goods; "Consumer Goods"; "Equipment"; "Farm Products"; "Inventory".

Goods are

(1) "consumer goods" if they are used or bought for use primarily for personal, family or household purposes;

(2) "equipment" if they are used or bought for use primarily in business (including farming or a profession) or by a debtor who is a non-profit organization or a governmental subdivision or agency or if the goods are not included in the definitions of inventory, farm products or consumer goods;

(3) "farm products" if they are crops or livestock or supplies used or produced in farming operations or if they are products of crops or livestock in their unmanufactured states (such as ginned cotton, wool-clip, maple syrup, milk and eggs), and if they are in the possession of a debtor engaged in raising, fattening, grazing or other farming operations. If goods are farm products, they are neither equipment nor inventory;

(4) "inventory" if they are held by a person who holds them for sale or lease or to be furnished under contracts of service or if he has so furnished them, or if they are raw materials, work in process or materials used or consumed in a business. Inventory of a person is not to be classified as his equipment.

Section 9—110. Sufficiency of Description.

For the purposes of this Article any description of personal property or real estate is sufficient whether or not it is specific if it reasonably identifies what is described.

Section 9—111. Applicability of Bulk Transfer Laws.

The creation of a security interest is not a bulk transfer under Article 6 (see Section 6—103).

Section 9—112. Where Collateral Is Not Owned by Debtor.

Unless otherwise agreed, when a secured party knows that collateral is owned by a person who is not the debtor, the owner of the collateral is entitled to receive from the secured party any surplus under Section 9—502(2) or under Section 9—504(1), and is not liable for the debt or for any deficiency after resale, and he has the same right as the debtor

(a) to receive statements under Section 9—208;

(b) to receive notice of and to object to a secured party's proposal to retain the collateral in satisfaction of the indebtedness under Section 9—505;

(c) to redeem the collateral under Section 9—506;

(d) to obtain injunctive or other relief under Section 9—507(1); and

(e) to recover losses caused to him under Section 9—208(2).

Section 9—113. Security Interests Arising Under Article on Sales.

A security interest arising solely under the Article on Sales (Article 2) is subject to the provisions of this Article except that to the extent that and so long as the debtor does not have or does not lawfully obtain possession of the goods

(a) no security agreement is necessary to make the security interest enforceable; and

(b) no filing is required to perfect the security interest; and

(c) the rights of the secured party on default by the debtor are governed by the Article on Sales (Article 2).

PART 2

VALIDITY OF SECURITY AGREEMENT AND RIGHTS OF PARTIES THERETO

Section 9—201. General Validity of Security Agreement.

Except as otherwise provided by this Act a security agreement is effective according to its terms between the parties, against purchasers of the collaterial and against creditors. Nothing in this Article validates any charge or practice illegal under any statute or regulation thereunder governing usury, small loans, retail installment sales, or the like, or extends the application of any such statute or regulation to any transaction not otherwise subject thereto.

Section 9—202. Title to Collateral Immaterial.

Each provision of this Article with regard to rights, obligations and remedies applies whether title to collateral is in the secured party or in the debtor.

Section 9—203. Enforceability of Security Interest; Proceeds, Formal Requisites.

(1) Subject to the provisions of Section 4—208 on the security interest of a collecting bank and Section 9—113 on a security interest arising under the Article on Sales, a security interest is not enforceable against the debtor or third parties unless

(a) the collateral is in the possession of the secured party; or

(b) the debtor has signed a security agreement which contains a description of the collateral and in addition, when the security interest covers crops or oil, gas or minerals to be extracted or timber to be cut, a description of the land concerned. In describing collateral, the word "proceeds" is sufficient without further description to cover proceeds of any character.

(2) A transaction, although subject to this Article, is also subject to ....-......*, and in the case of conflict between the provisions of this Article and any such statute, the provisions of such statute control. Failure to comply with any applicable statute has only the effect which is specified therein.

Note: *At * in subsection (2) insert reference to any local statute regulating small loans, retail installment sales and the like.*

The foregoing subsection (2) is designed to make it clear that certain transactions, although subject to this Article, must also comply with other applicable legislation.

This Article is designed to regulate all the "security" aspects of transactions within its scope. There is, however, much regulatory legislation, particularly in the consumer field, which supplements this Article and should not be repealed by its enactment. Examples are small loan acts, retail installment selling acts and the like. Such acts may provide for licensing and rate regulation and may prescribe particular forms of contract. Such provisions should remain in force despite the enactment of this Article. On the other hand if a Retail Installment Selling Act contains provisions on filing, rights on default, etc., such provisions should be repealed as inconsistent with this Article.

Section 9—204. When Security Interest Attaches; After-Acquired Property; Future Advances.

(1) A security interest cannot attach until there is agreement (subsection (3) of Section 1—201) that it attach and value is given and the debtor has rights in the collateral. It attaches as soon as all of the events in the preceding sentence have taken place unless explicit agreement postpones the time of attaching.

(2) For the purposes of this section the debtor has no rights

(a) in crops until they are planted or otherwise become growing crops, in the young of livestock until they are conceived;

(b) in fish until caught, in oil, gas or minerals until they are extracted, in timber until it is cut;

(c) in a contract right until the contract has been made;

(d) in an account until it comes into existence.

(3) Except as provided in subsection (4) a security agreement may provide that collateral, whenever acquired, shall secure all obligations covered by the security agreement.

(4) No security interest attaches under an after-acquired property clause

(a) to crops which become such more than one year after the security agreement is executed, except that a security interest in crops which is given in conjunction with a lease or a land purchase or improvement transaction evidenced by a contract, mortgage or deed of trust may if so agreed attach to crops to be grown on the land concerned during the period of such real estate transaction;

(b) to consumer goods other than accessions (Section 9—314) when given as additional security unless the debtor acquires rights in them within ten days after the secured party gives value.

(5) Obligations covered by a security agreement may include future advances or other value whether or not the advances or value are given pursuant to commitment.

Section 9—205. Use or Disposition of Collateral Without Accounting Permissible.

A security interest is not invalid or fraudulent against creditors by reason of liberty in the debtor to use, commingle or dispose of all or part of the collateral (including returned or repossessed goods) or to collect or compromise accounts, contract rights or chattel paper, or to accept the return of goods or make repossessions, or to use, commingle or dispose of proceeds, or by reason of the failure of the secured party to require the debtor to account for proceeds or replace collateral. This section does not relax the requirements of possession where perfection of a security interest depends upon possession of the collateral by the secured party or by a bailee.

Section 9—206. Agreement Not to Assert Defenses Against Assignee; Modification of Sales Warranties Where Security Agreement Exists.

(1) Subject to any statute or decision which establishes a different rule for buyers or lessees of consumer goods, an agreement by a buyer or lessee that he will not assert against an assignee any claim or defense which he may have against the seller or lessor is enforceable by an assignee who takes his assignment for value, in good faith and without notice of a claim or defense, except as to defenses of a type which may be asserted against a holder in due course of a negotiable instrument under the Article on Commercial Paper (Article 3). A buyer who as part of one transaction signs both a negotiable instrument and a security agreement makes such an agreement.

(2) When a seller retains a purchase money security interest in goods the Article on Sales (Article 2) governs the sale and any disclaimer, limitation or modification of the seller's warranties.

Section 9—207. Rights and Duties When Collateral Is in Secured Party's Possession.

(1) A secured party must use reasonable care in the custody and preservation of collateral in his possession. In the case of an instrument or chattel paper reasonable care includes taking necessary steps to preserve rights against prior parties unless otherwise agreed.

(2) Unless otherwise agreed, when collateral is in the secured party's possession

(a) reasonable expenses (including the cost of any insurance and payment of taxes or other charges) incurred in the custody, preservation, use or operation of the collateral are chargeable to the debtor and are secured by the collateral;

(b) the risk of accidental loss or damage is on the debtor to the extent of any deficiency in any effective insurance coverage;

(c) the secured party may hold as additional security any increase or profits (except money) received from the collateral, but money so received, unless remitted to the debtor, shall be applied in reduction of the secured obligation;

(d) the secured party must keep the collateral identifiable but fungible collateral may be commingled;

(e) the secured party may repledge the collateral upon terms which do not impair the debtor's right to redeem it.

(3) A secured party is liable for any loss caused by his failure to meet any obligation imposed by the preceding subsection but does not lose his security interest.

(4) A secured party may use or operate the collateral for the purpose of preserving the collateral or its value or pursuant to the order of a court of appropriate jurisdiction or, except in the case of consumer goods, in the manner and to the extent provided in the security agreement.

Section 9—208. Request for Statement of Account or List of Collateral.

(1) A debtor may sign a statement indicating what he believes to be the aggregate amount of unpaid indebtedness as of a specified date and may send it to the secured party with a request that the statement be approved or corrected and returned to the debtor. When the security agreement or any other record kept by the secured party identifies the collateral, a debtor may similarly request the secured party to approve or correct a list of the collateral.

(2) The secured party must comply with such a request within two weeks after receipt by sending a written correction or approval. If the secured party claims a security interest in all of a particular type of collateral owned by the debtor, he may indicate that fact in his reply and need not approve or correct an itemized list of such collateral. If the secured party without reasonable excuse fails to comply, he is liable for any loss caused to the debtor thereby; and if the debtor has properly included in his request a good faith statement of the obligation or a list of the collateral or both, the secured party may claim a security interest only as shown in the statement against persons misled by his failure to comply. If he no longer has an interest in the obligation or collateral at the time the request is received, he must disclose the name and address of any successor in interest known to him and he is liable for any loss caused to the debtor as a result of failure to disclose. A successor in interest is not subject to this section until a request is received by him.

(3) A debtor is entitled to such a statement once every six months without charge. The secured party may require payment of a charge not exceeding $10 for each additional statement furnished.

PART 3

RIGHTS OF THIRD PARTIES; PERFECTED AND UNPERFECTED SECURITY INTERESTS; RULES OF PRIORITY

Section 9—301. Persons Who Take Priority Over Unperfected Security Interests; "Lien Creditor".

(1) Except as otherwise provided in subsection (2), an unperfected security interest is subordinate to the rights of

(a) persons entitled to priority under Section 9—312;

(b) a person who becomes a lien creditor without knowledge of the security interest and before it is perfected;

(c) in the case of goods, instruments, documents, and chattel paper, a person who is not a secured party and who is a transferee in bulk or other buyer not in ordinary course of business to the extent that he gives value and receives delivery of the collateral without knowledge of the security interest and before it is perfected;

(d) in the case of accounts, contract rights, and general intangibles, a person who is not a secured party and who is a transferee to the extent that he gives value without knowledge of the security interest and before it is perfected.

(2) If the secured party files with respect to a purchase money security interest before or within ten days after the collateral comes into possession of the debtor, he takes priority over

the rights of a transferee in bulk or of a lien creditor which arise between the time the security interest attaches and the time of filing.

(3) A "lien creditor" means a creditor who has acquired a lien on the property involved by attachment, levy or the like and includes an assignee for benefit of creditors from the time of assignment, and a trustee in bankruptcy from the date of the filing of the petition or a receiver in equity from the time of appointment. Unless all the creditors represented had knowledge of the security interest, such a representative of creditors is a lien creditor without knowledge even though he personally has knowledge of the security interest.

Security 9—302. When Filing Is Required to Perfect Security Interest; Security Interests to Which Filing Provisions of This Article Do Not Apply.

(1) A financing statement must be filed to perfect all security interests except the following:

(a) a security interest in collateral in possession of the secured party under Section 9—305;

(b) a security interest temporarily perfected in instruments or documents without delivery under Section 9—304 or in proceeds for a 10 day period under Section 9—306;

(c) a purchase money security interest in farm equipment having a purchase price not in excess of $2500; but filing is required for a fixture under Section 9—313 or for a motor vehicle required to be licensed;

(d) a purchase money security interest in consumer goods; but filing is required for a fixture under Section 9—313 or for a motor vehicle required to be licensed;

(e) an assignment of accounts or contract rights which does not alone in conjunction with other assignments to the same assignee transfer a significant part of the outstanding accounts or contract rights of the assignor;

(f) a security interest of a collecting bank (Section 4—208) or arising under the Article on Sales (see Section 9—113) or covered in subsection (3) of this section.

(2) If a secured party assigns a perfected security interest, no filing under this Article is required in order to continue the perfected status of the security interest against creditors of and transferees from the original debtor.

(3) The filing provisions of this Article do not apply to a security interest in property subject to a statute

(a) of the United States which provides for a national registration or filing of all security interests in such property; or

Note: *States to select either alternative A or Alternative B.*

Alternative A—

(b) of this state which provides for central filing of, or which requires indication on a certificate of title of, such security interests in such property.

Alternative B—

(b) of this state which provides for central filing of security interests in such property, or in a motor vehicle which is not inventory held for sale for which a certificate of title is required under the statutes of this state if a notation of such a security interest can be indicated by a public official on a certificate or a duplicate thereof.

(4) A security interest in property covered by a statute described in subsection (3) can be perfected only by registration or filing under that statute or by indication of the security interest on a certificate of title or a duplicate thereof by a public official.

Section 9—303. When Security Interest Is Perfected; Continuity of Perfection.

(1) A security interest is perfected when it has attached and when all of the applicable steps required for perfection have been taken. Such

steps are specified in Sections 9—302, 9—304, 9—305 and 9—306. If such steps are taken before the security interest attaches, it is perfected at the time when it attaches.

(2) If a security interest is originally perfected in any way permitted under this Article and is subsequently perfected in some other way under this Article, without an intermediate period when it was unperfected, the security interest shall be deemed to be perfected continuously for the purposes of this Article.

Section 9—304. Perfection of Security Interest in Instruments, Documents, and Goods Covered by Documents; Perfection by Permissive Filing; Temporary Perfection Without Filing or Transfer of Possession.

(1) A security interest in chattel paper or negotiable documents may be perfected by filing. A security interest in instruments (other than instruments which constitute part of chattel paper) can be perfected only by the secured party's taking possession, except as provided in subsections (4) and (5).

(2) During the period that goods are in the possession of the issuer of a negotiable document therefor, a security interest in the goods is perfected by perfecting a security interest in the document, and any security interest in the goods otherwise perfected during such period is subject thereto.

(3) A security interest in goods in the possession of a bailee other than one who has issued a negotiable document therefor is perfected by issuance of a document in the name of the secured party or by the bailee's receipt of notification of the secured party's interest or by filing as to the goods.

(4) A security interest in instruments or negotiable documents is perfected without filing or the taking of possession for a period of 21 days from the time it attaches to the extent that it arises for new value given under a written security agreement.

(5) A security interest remains perfected for a period of 21 days without filing where a secured party having a perfected security interest in an instrument, a negotiable document or goods in possession of a bailee other than one who has issued a negotiable document therefor

(a) makes available to the debtor the goods or documents representing the goods for the purpose of ultimate sale or exchange or for the purpose of loading, unloading, storing, shipping, manufacturing, processing or otherwise dealing with them in a manner preliminary to their sale or exchange; or

(b) delivers the instrument to the debtor for the purpose of ultimate sale or exchange or of presentation, collection, renewal or registration of transfer.

(6) After the 21 day period in subsections (4) and (5) perfection depends upon compliance with applicable provisions of this Article.

Section 9—305. When Possession by Secured Party Perfects Security Interest Without Filing.

A security interest in letters of credit and advices of credit (subsection (2)(a) of Section 5—116), goods, instruments, negotiable documents or chattel paper may be perfected by the secured party's taking possession of the collateral. If such collateral other than goods covered by a negotiable document is held by a bailee, the secured party is deemed to have possession from the time the bailee receives notification of the secured party's interest. A security interest is perfected by possession from the time possession is taken without relation back and continues only so long as possession is retained, unless otherwise specified in this Article. The security interest may be otherwise perfected as provided in this Article before or after the period of possession by the secured party.

Section 9—306. "Proceeds"; Secured Party's Rights on Disposition of Collateral.

(1) "Proceeds" includes whatever is received when collateral or proceeds is sold, exchanged, collected or otherwise disposed of. The term also includes the account arising when the right to payment is earned under a contract right. Money, checks and the like are "cash proceeds". All other proceeds are "non-cash proceeds".

(2) Except where this Article otherwise provides, a security interest continues in collateral notwithstanding sale, exchange or other disposition thereof by the debtor unless his action was authorized by the secured party in the security agreement or otherwise, and also continues in any identifiable proceeds including collections received by the debtor.

(3) The security interest in proceeds is a continuously perfected security interest if the interest in the original collateral was perfected, but it ceases to be a perfected security interest and becomes unperfected ten days after receipt of the proceeds by the debtor unless

(a) a filed financing statement covering the original collateral also covers proceeds; or

(b) the security interest in the proceeds is perfected before the expiration of the ten day period.

(4) In the event of insolvency proceedings instituted by or against a debtor, a secured party with a perfected security interest in proceeds has a perfected security interest

(a) in identifiable non-cash proceeds;

(b) in identifiable cash proceeds in the form of money which is not commingled with other money or deposited in a bank account prior to the insolvency proceedings;

(c) in identifiable cash proceeds in the form of checks and the like which are not deposited in a bank account prior to the insolvency proceedings; and

(d) in all cash and bank accounts of the debtor, if other cash proceeds have been commingled or deposited in a bank account, but the perfected security interest under this paragraph (d) is

(i) subject to any right of set-off; and

(ii) limited to an amount not greater than the amount of any cash proceeds received by the debtor within ten days before the institution of the insolvency proceedings and commingled or deposited in a bank account prior to the insolvency proceedings less the amount of cash proceeds received by the debtor and paid over to the secured party during the ten day period.

(5) If a sale of goods results in an account or chattel paper which is transferred by the seller to a secured party, and if the goods are returned to or are repossessed by the seller or the secured party, the following rules determine priorities:

(a) If the goods were collateral at the time of sale for an indebtedness of the seller which is still unpaid, the original security interest attaches again to the goods and continues as a perfected security interest if it was perfected at the time when the goods were sold. If the security interest was originally perfected by a filing which is still effective, nothing further is required to continue the perfected status; in any other case, the secured party must take possession of the returned or repossessed goods or must file.

(b) An unpaid transferee of the chattel paper has a security interest in the goods against the transferor. Such security interest is prior to a security interest asserted under paragraph (a) to the extent that the transferee of the chattel paper was entitled to priority under Section 9—308.

(c) An unpaid transferee of the account has a security interest in the goods against the transferor. Such security interest is subordinate to a security interest asserted under paragraph (a).

(d) A security interest of an unpaid transferee asserted under paragraph (b) or (c) must be perfected for protection against creditors of the transferor and purchasers of the returned or repossessed goods.

Section 9—307. Protection of Buyers of Goods.

(1) A buyer in ordinary course of business (subsection (9) of Section 1—201) other than a person buying farm products from a person engaged in farming operations takes free of a security interest created by his seller even though the security interest is perfected and even though the buyer knows of its existence.

(2) In the case of consumer goods and in the case of farm equipment having an original purchase price not in excess of $2500 (other than fixtures, see Section 9—313), a buyer takes free of a security interest even though perfected if he buys without knowledge of the security interest, for value and for his own personal, family or household purposes or his own farming operations, unless prior to the purchase the secured party has filed a financing statement covering such goods.

Section 9—308. Purchase of Chattel Paper and Non-Negotiable Instruments.

A purchaser of chattel paper or a non-negotiable instrument who gives new value and takes possession of it in the ordinary course of his business and without knowledge that the specific paper or instrument is subject to a security interest has priority over a security interest which is perfected under Section 9—304 (permissive filing and temporary perfection). A purchaser of chattel paper who gives new value and takes possession of it in the ordinary course of his business has priority over a security interest in chattel paper which is claimed merely as proceeds of inventory subject to a security interest (Section 9—306), even though he knows that the specific paper is subject to the security interest.

Section 9—309. Protection of Purchasers of Instruments and Documents.

Nothing in this Article limits the rights of a holder in due course of a negotiable instrument (Section 3—302) or a holder to whom a negotiable document of title has been duly negotiated (Section 7—501) or a bona fide purchaser of a security (Section 8—301) and such holders or purchasers take priority over an earlier security interest even though perfected. Filing under this Article does not constitute notice of the security interest to such holders or purchasers.

Section 9—310. Priority of Certain Liens Arising by Operation of Law.

When a person in the ordinary course of his business furnishes services or materials with respect to goods subject to a security interest, a lien upon goods in the possession of such person given by statute or rule of law for such materials or services takes priority over a perfected security interest unless the lien is statutory and the statute expressly provides otherwise.

Section 9—311. Alienability of Debtor's Rights; Judicial Process.

The debtor's rights in collateral may be voluntarily or involuntarily transferred (by way of sale, creation of a security interest, attachment, levy, garnishment or other judicial process) notwithstanding a provision in the security agreement prohibiting any transfer or making the transfer constitute a default.

Section 9—312. Priorities Among Conflicting Security Interests in the Same Collateral.

(1) The rules of priority stated in the following sections shall govern where applicable: Section 4—208 with respect to the security interest of collecting banks in items being collected, accompanying documents and proceeds; Section 9—301 on certain priorities; Section 9—304 on goods covered by documents; Section 9—306 on proceeds and repossessions; Section 9—307 on buyers of goods; Section 9—308 on possessory against non-possessory interests in chattel paper or non-negotiable instruments; Section 9—309 on security interests in negotiable instruments, documents or securities; Section 9—310 on priorities between perfected security interests and liens by operation of law; Section 9—313 on security interests in fixtures as against interests in real estate; Section 9—314 on security interests in accessions as against interest in goods; Section 9—315 on conflicting security interests where goods lose their identity or become part of a product; and Section 9—316 on contractual subordination.

(2) A perfected security interest in crops for new value given to enable the debtor to produce the crops during the production season

and given not more than three months before the crops become growing crops by planting or otherwise takes priority over an earlier perfected security interest to the extent that such earlier interest secures obligations due more than six months before the crops become growing crops by planting or otherwise, even though the person giving new value had knowledge of the earlier security interest.

(3) A purchase money security interest in inventory collateral has priority over a conflicting security interest in the same collateral if

(a) the purchase money security interest is perfected at the time the debtor receives possession of the collateral; and

(b) any secured party whose security interest is known to the holder of the purchase money security interest or who, prior to the date of the filing made by the holder of the purchase money security interest, had filed a financing statement covering the same items or type of inventory, has received notification of the purchase money security interest before the debtor receives possession of the collateral covered by the purchase money security interest; and

(c) such notification states that the person giving the notice has or expects to acquire a purchase money security interest in inventory of the debtor, describing such inventory by item or type.

(4) A purchase money security interest in collateral other than inventory has priority over a conflicting security interest in the same collateral if the purchase money security interest is perfected at the time the debtor receives possession of the collateral or within ten days thereafter.

(5) In all cases not governed by other rules stated in this section (including cases of purchase money security interests which do not qualify for the special priorities set forth in subsections (3) and (4) of this section), priority between conflicting security interests in the same collateral shall be determined as follows:

(a) in the order of filing if both are perfected by filing, regardless of which security interest attached first under Section 9—204(1) and whether it attached before or after filing;

(b) in the order of perfection unless both are perfected by filing, regardless of which security interest attached first under Section 9—204(1) and, in the case of a filed security interest, whether it attached before or after filing; and

(c) in the order of attachment under Section 9—204(1) so long as neither is perfected.

(6) For the purpose of the priority rules of the immediately preceding subsection, a continuously perfected security interest shall be treated at all times as if perfected by filing if it was originally so perfected and it shall be treated at all times as if perfected otherwise than by filing if it was originally perfected otherwise than by filing.

Section 9—313. Priority of Security Interests in Fixtures.

(1) The rules of this section do not apply to goods incorporated into a structure in the manner of lumber, bricks, tile, cement, glass, metal work and the like and no security interest in them exists under this Article unless the structure remains personal property under applicable law. The law of this state other than this Act determines whether and when other goods become fixtures. This Act does not prevent creation of an encumbrance upon fixtures or real estate pursuant to the law applicable to real estate.

(2) A security interest which attaches to goods before they become fixtures takes priority as to the goods over the claims of all persons who have an interest in the real estate except as stated in subsection (4).

(3) A security interest which attaches to goods after they become fixtures is valid against all persons subsequently acquiring interests in the real estate except as stated in subsection (4) but is invalid against any person with an interest in the real estate at the time the security

interest attaches to the goods who has not in writing consented to the security interest or disclaimed an interest in the goods as fixtures.

(4) The security interests described in subsections (2) and (3) do not take priority over

(a) a subsequent purchaser for value of any interest in the real estate; or
(b) a creditor with a lien on the real estate subsequently obtained by judicial proceedings; or
(c) a creditor with a prior encumbrance of record on the real estate to the extent that he makes subsequent advances

if the subsequent purchase is made, the lien by judicial proceedings is obtained, or the subsequent advance under the prior encumbrance is made or contracted for without knowledge of the security interest and before it is perfected. A purchaser of the real estate at a foreclosure sale other than an encumbrancer purchasing at his own foreclosure sale is a subsequent purchaser within this section.

(5) When under subsections (2) or (3) and (4) a secured party has priority over the claims of all persons who have interests in the real estate, he may, on default, subject to the provisions of Part 5, remove his collateral from the real estate; but he must reimburse any encumbrancer or owner of the real estate who is not the debtor and who has not otherwise agreed for the cost of repair of any physical injury, but not for any diminution in value of the real estate caused by the absence of the goods removed or by any necessity for replacing them. A person entitled to reimbursement may refuse permission to remove until the secured party gives adequate security for the performance of this obligation.

Section 9—314. Accessions.

(1) A security interest in goods which attaches before they are installed in or affixed to other goods takes priority as to the goods installed or affixed (called in this section "accessions") over the claims of all persons to the whole except as stated in subsection (3) and subject to Section 9—315(1).

(2) A security interest which attaches to goods after they become part of a whole is valid against all persons subsequently acquiring interests in the whole except as stated in subsection (3) but is invalid against any person with an interest in the whole at the time the security interest attaches to the goods who has not in writing consented to the security interest or disclaimed an interest in the goods as part of the whole.

(3) The security interests described in subsections (1) and (2) do not take priority over

(a) a subsequent purchaser for value of any interest in the whole; or
(b) a creditor with a lien on the whole subsequently obtained by judicial proceedings; or
(c) a creditor with a prior perfected security interest in the whole to the extent that he makes subsequent advances

if the subsequent purchase is made, the lien by judicial proceedings obtained or the subsequent advance under the prior perfected security interest is made or contracted for without knowledge of the security interest and before it is perfected. A purchaser of the whole at a foreclosure sale other than the holder of a perfected security interest purchasing at his own foreclosure sale is a subsequent purchaser within this section.

(4) When under subsections (1) or (2) and (3) a secured party has an interest in accessions which has priority over the claims of all persons who have interests in the whole, he may, on default, subject to the provisions of Part 5, remove his collateral from the whole; but he must reimburse any encumbrancer or owner of the whole who is not the debtor and who has not otherwise agreed for the cost of repair of any physical injury but not for any diminution in value of the whole caused by the absence of the goods removed or by any necessity for replacing them. A person entitled to reimbursement may refuse permission to remove until the secured party gives adequate security for the performance of this obligation.

Section 9—315. Priority When Goods Are Commingled or Processed.

(1) If a security interest in goods was perfected and subsequently the goods or a part

thereof have become part of a product or mass, the security interest continues in the product or mass if

(a) the goods are so manufactured, processed, assembled or commingled that their identity is lost in the product or mass; or

(b) a financing statement covering the original goods also covers the product into which the goods have been manufactured, processed or assembled.

In a case to which paragraph (b) applies, no separate security interest in that part of the original goods which has been manufactured, processed or assembled into the product may be claimed under Section 9—314.

(2) When under subsection (1) more than one security interest attaches to the product or mass, they rank equally according to the ratio that the cost of the goods to which each interest originally attached bears to the cost of the total product or mass.

Section 9—316. Priority Subject to Subordination.

Nothing in this Article prevents subordination by agreement by any person entitled to priority.

Section 9—317. Security Party Not Obligated on Contract of Debtor.

The mere existence of a security interest or authority given to the debtor to dispose of or use collateral does not impose contract or tort liability upon the secured party for the debtor's acts or omissions.

Section 9—318. Defenses Against Assignee; Modification of Contract After Notification of Assignment; Term Prohibiting Assignment Ineffective; Identification and Proof of Assignment.

(1) Unless an account debtor has made an enforceable agreement not to assert defenses or claims arising out of a sale as provided in Section 9—206 the rights of an assignee are subject to

(a) all the terms of the contract between the account debtor and assignor and any defense or claim arising therefrom; and

(b) any other defense or claim of the account debtor against the assignor which accrues before the account debtor receives notification of the assignment.

(2) So far as the right to payment under an assigned contract right has not already become an account, and notwithstanding notification of the assignment, any modification of or substitution for the contract made in good faith and in accordance with reasonable commercial standards is effective against an assignee unless the account debtor has otherwise agreed, but the assignee acquires corresponding rights under the modified or substituted contract. The assignment may provide that such modification or substitution is a breach by the assignor.

(3) The account debtor is authorized to pay the assignor until the account debtor receives notification that the account has been assigned and that payment is to be made to the assignee. A notification which does not reasonably identify the rights assigned is ineffective. If requested by the account debtor, the assignee must seasonably furnish reasonable proof that the assignment has been made and unless he does so the account debtor may pay the assignor.

(4) A term in any contract between an account debtor and an assignor which prohibits assignment of an account or contract right to which they are parties is ineffective.

PART 4

FILING

Section 9—401. Place of Filing; Erroneous Filing; Removal of Collateral.

First Alternative Subsection (1)

(1) The proper place to file in order to perfect a security interest is as follows:

(a) when the collateral is goods which at the time the security interest attaches are or are to become fixtures, then in the office where a mortgage on the real estate concerned would be filed or recorded;

(b) in all other cases, in the office of the [Secretary of State].

Second Alternative Subsection (1)

(1) The proper place to file in order to perfect a security interest is as follows:

(a) when the collateral is equipment used in farming operations, or farm products, or accounts, contract rights or general intangibles arising from or relating to the sale of farm products by a farmer, or consumer goods, then in the office of the ...... in the county of the debtor's residence or if the debtor is not a resident of this state then in the office of the ...... in the county where the goods are kept, and in addition when the collateral in crops in the office of the ...... in the county where the land on which the crops are growing or to be grown is located;

(b) when the collateral is goods which at the time the security interest attaches are or are to become fixtures, then in the office where a mortgage on the real estate concerned would be filed or recorded;

(c) in all other cases, in the office of the [Secretary of State].

Third Alternative Subsection (1)

(1) The proper place to file in order to perfect a security interest is as follows:

(a) when the collateral is equipment used in farming operations, or farm products, or accounts, contract rights or general intangibles arising from or relating to the sale of farm products by a farmer, or consumer goods, then in the office of the ...... in the county of the debtor's residence or if the debtor is not a resident of this state then in the office of the ...... in the county where the goods are kept, and in addition when the collateral is crops in the office of the ...... in the county where the land on which the crops are growing or to be grown is located;

(b) when the collateral is goods which at the time the security interest attaches are or are to become fixtures, then in the office where a mortgage on the real estate concerned would be filed or recorded;

(c) in all other cases, in the office of the [Secretary of State] and in addition, if the debtor has a place of business in only one county of this state, also in the office of ...... of such county, or, if the debtor has no place of business in this state, but resides in the state, also in the office of ...... of the county in which he resides.

Note: *One of the three alternatives should be selected as subsection (1).*

(2) A filing which is made in good faith in an improper place or not in all of the places required by this section is nevertheless effective with regard to any collateral as to which the filing complied with the requirements of this Article and is also effective with regard to collateral covered by the financing statement against any person who has knowledge of the contents of such financing statement.

(3) A filing which is made in the proper place in this state continues effective even though the debtor's residence or place of business or the location of the collateral or its use, whichever controlled the original filing, is thereafter changed.

Alternative Subsection (3)

[(3) A filing which is made in the proper county continues effective for four months after a change to another county of the debtor's residence or place of business or the location of the collateral, whichever controlled the original filing. It becomes ineffective thereafter unless a copy of the financing statement signed by the secured party is filed in the new county within said period. The security interest may also be perfected in the new county after the expiration of the four-month period; in such case perfection dates from the time of perfection in the new county. A change in the use of the collateral does not impair the effectiveness of the original filing.]

(4) If collateral is brought into this state from another jurisdiction, the rules stated in Section 9—103 determine whether filing is necessary in this state.

Section 9—402. Formal Requisites of Financing Statement; Amendments.

(1) A financing statement is sufficient if it is signed by the debtor and the secured party, gives an address of the secured party from which information concerning the security interest may be obtained, gives a mailing address of the debtor and contains a statement indicating the types, or describing the items, of collateral. A financing statement may be filed before a security agreement is made or a security interest otherwise attaches. When the financing statement covers crops growing or to be grown or goods which are or are to become fixtures, the statement must also contain a description of the real estate concerned. A copy of the security agreement is sufficient as a financing statement if it contains the above information and is signed by both parties.

(2) A financing statement which otherwise complies with subsection (1) is sufficient although it is signed only by the secured party when it is filed to perfect a security interest in

(a) collateral already subject to a security interest in another jurisdiction when it is brought into this state. Such a financing statement must state that the collateral was brought into this state under such circumstances.

(b) proceeds under Section 9—306 if the security interest in the original collateral was perfected. Such a financing statement must describe the original collateral.

(3) A form substantially as follows is sufficient to comply with subsection (1):

Name of debtor (or assignor) ....
....
Address ....
....
Name of secured party (or assignee)
....
Address ....
....

1. This financing statement covers the following types (or items) of property:
   (Describe) ....
   ....
2. (If collateral is crops) The above described crops are growing or are to be grown on:
   (Describe Real Estate) ....
   ....
3. (If collateral is goods which are or are to become fixtures) The above described goods are affixed or to be affixed to:
   (Describe Real Estate) ....
   ....
4. (If proceeds or products of collateral are claimed) Proceeds—Products of the collateral are also covered.

Signature of Debtor (or Assignor)
....
Signature of Secured Party (or Assignee) ....

(4) The term "financing statement" as used in this Article means the original financing statement and any amendments but if any amendment adds collateral, it is effective as to the added collateral only from the filing date of the amendment.

(5) A financing statement substantially complying with the requirements of this section is effective even though it contains minor errors which are not seriously misleading.

Section 9—403. What Constitutes Filing; Duration of Filing; Effect of Lapsed Filing; Duties of Filing Officer.

(1) Presentation for filing of a financing statement and tender of the filing fee or acceptance of the statement by the filing officer constitutes filing under this Article.

(2) A filed financing statement which states a maturity date of the obligation secured of five years or less is effective until such maturity date and thereafter for a period of sixty days. Any other filed financing statement is effective for a period of five years from the date of filing. The effectiveness of a filed financing statement lapses on the expiration of such sixty day period after a stated maturity date or on the expiration

of such five year period, as the case may be, unless a continuation statement is filed prior to the lapse. Upon such lapse the security interest becomes unperfected. A filed financing statement which states that the obligation secured is payable on demand is effective for five years from the date of filing.

(3) A continuation statement may be filed by the secured party (i) within six months before and sixty days after a stated maturity date of five years or less, and (ii) otherwise within six months prior to the expiration of the five year period specified in subsection (2). Any such continuation statement must be signed by the secured party, identify the original statement by file number and state that the original statement is still effective. Upon timely filing of the continuation statement, the effectiveness of the original statement is continued for five years after the last date to which the filing was effective whereupon it lapses in the same manner as provided in subsection (2) unless another continuation statement is filed prior to such lapse. Succeeding continuation statements may be filed in the same manner to continue the effectiveness of the original statement. Unless a statute on disposition of public records provides otherwise, the filing officer may remove a lapsed statement from the files and destroy it.

(4) A filing officer shall mark each statement with a consecutive file number and with the date and hour of filing and shall hold the statement for public inspection. In addition the filing officer shall index the statements according to the name of the debtors and shall note in the index the file number and the address of the debtor given in the statement.

(5) The uniform fee for filing, indexing and furnishing filing data for an original or a continuation statement shall be $..............

Section 9—404. Termination Statement.

(1) Whenever there is no outstanding secured obligation and no commitment to make advances, incur obligations or otherwise give value, the secured party must on written demand by the debtor send the debtor a statement that he no longer claims a security interest under the financing statement, which shall be identified by file number. A termination statement signed by a person other than the secured party of record must include or be accompanied by the assignment or a statement by the secured party of record that he has assigned the security interest to the signer of the termination statement. The uniform fee for filing and indexing such an assignment or statement thereof shall be $......... If the affected secured party fails to send such a termination statement within ten days after proper demand therefor, he shall be liable to the debtor for one hundred dollars, and in addition for any loss caused to the debtor by such failure.

(2) On presentation to the filing officer of of such a termination statement he must note it in the index. The filing officer shall remove from the files, mark "terminated" and send or deliver to the secured party the financing statement and any continuation statement, statement of assignment or statement of release pertaining thereto.

(3) The uniform fee for filing and indexing a termination statement including sending or delivering the financing statement shall be $.........

Section 9—405. Assignment of Security Interest; Duties of Filing Officer; Fees.

(1) A financing statement may disclose an assignment of a security interest in the collateral described in the statement by indication in the statement of the name and address of the assignee or by an assignment itself or a copy thereof on the face or back of the statement. Either the original secured party or the assignee may sign this statement as the secured party. On presentation to the filing officer of such a financing statement the filing officer shall mark the same as provided in Section 9—403(4). The uniform fee for filing, indexing and furnishing filing data for a financing statement so indicating an assignment shall be $........

(2) A secured party may assign of record all or a part of his rights under a financing statement by the filing of a separate written statement of assignment signed by the secured party of record and setting forth the name of the secured party of record and the debtor, the file number and the date of filing of the financing statement and the name and address of the

assignee and containing a description of the collateral assigned. A copy of the assignment is sufficient as a separate statement if it complies with the preceding sentence. On presentation to the filing officer of such a separate statement, the filing officer shall mark such separate statement with the date and hour of the filing. He shall note the assignment on the index of the financing statement. The uniform fee for filing, indexing and furnishing filing data about such a separate statement of assignment shall be $.........

(3) After the disclosure or filing of an assignment under this section, the assignee is the secured party of record.

Section 9—406. Release of Collateral; Duties of Filing Officer; Fees.

A secured party of record may by his signed statement release all or a part of any collateral described in a filed financing statement. The statement of release is sufficient if it contains a description of the collateral being released, the name and address of the debtor, the name and address of the secured party, and the file number of the financing statement. Upon presentation of such a statement to the filing officer, he shall mark the statement with the hour and date of filing and shall note the same upon the margin of the index of the filing of the financing statement. The uniform fee for filing and noting such a sattement of release shall be $.........

Section 9—407. Information from Filing Officer.

(1) If the person filing any financing statement, termination statement, statement of assignment, or statement of release, furnishes the filing officer a copy thereof, the filing officer shall upon request note upon the copy the file number and date and hour of the filing of the original and deliver or send the copy to such person.

(2) Upon request of any person, the filing officer shall issue his certificate showing whether there is on file on the date and hour stated therein, any presently effective financing statement naming a particular debtor and any statement of assignment thereof and if there is, giving the date and hour of filing of each such statement and the names and addresses of each secured party therein. The uniform fee for such a certificate shall be $........ plus $........ for each financing statement and for each statement of assignment reported therein. Upon request the filing officer shall furnish a copy of any filed financing statement or statement of assignment for a uniform fee of $......... per page.

> **Note:** *This new section is proposed as an optional provision to require filing officers to furnish certificates. Local law and practices should be consulted with regard to the advisability of adoption.*

PART 5

DEFAULT

Section 9—501. Default; Procedure When Security Agreement Covers Both Real and Personal Property.

(1) When a debtor is in default under a security agreement, a secured party has the rights and remedies provided in this Part and, except as limited by subsection (3), those provided in the security agreement. He may reduce his claim to judgment, foreclose or otherwise enforce the security interest by any available judicial procedure. If the collateral is documents, the secured party may proceed either as to the documents or as to the goods covered thereby. A secured party in possession has the rights, remedies and duties provided in Section 9—207. The rights and remedies referred to in this subsection are cumulative.

(2) After default, the debtor has the rights and remedies provided in this Part, those provided in the security agreement and those provided in Section 9—207.

(3) To the extent that they give rights to the debtor and impose duties on the secured party, the rules stated in the subsections referred to below may not be waived or varied except as provided with respect to compulsory disposition of collateral (subsection (1) of Section 9—505) and with respect to redemption of collateral (Section 9—506) but the parties may by agreement determine the standards by which the fulfillment of these rights and duties is to

be measured if such standards are not manifestly unreasonable:

(a) subsection (2) of Section 9—502 and subsection (2) of Section 9—504 insofar as they require accounting for surplus proceeds of collateral;

(b) subsection (3) of Section 9—504 and subsection (1) of Section 9—505 which deal with disposition of collateral;

(c) subsection (2) of Section 9—505 which deals with acceptance of collateral as discharge of obligation;

(d) Section 9—506 which deals with redemption of collateral; and

(e) subsection (1) of Section 9—507 which deals with the secured party's liability for failure to comply with this Part.

(4) If the security agreement covers both real and personal property, the secured party may proceed under this Part as to the personal property or he may porceed as to both the real and the personal property in accordance with his rights and remedies in respect of the real property in which case the provisions of this Part do not apply.

(5) When a secured party has reduced his claim to judgment, the lien of any levy which may be made upon his collateral by virtue of any execution based upon the judgment shall relate back to the date of the perfection of the security interest in such collateral. A judicial sale, pursuant to such execution, is a foreclosure of the security interest by judicial procedure within the meaning of this section, and the secured party may purchase at the sale and thereafter hold the collateral free of any other requirements of this Article.

Section 9—502. Collection Rights of Secured Party.

(1) When so agreed and in any event on default, the secured party is entitled to notify an account debtor or the obligor on an instrument to make payment to him whether or not the assignor was theretofore making collections on the collateral, and also to take control of any proceeds to which he is entitled under Section 9—306.

(2) A secured party who by agreement is entitled to charge back uncollected collateral or otherwise to full or limited recourse against the debtor and who undertakes to collect from the account debtors or obligors must proceed in a commercially reasonable manner and may deduct his reasonable expenses of realization from the collections. If the security agreement secures an indebtedness, the secured party must account to the debtor for any surplus, and unless otherwise agreed, the debtor is liable for any deficiency. But, if the underlying transaction was a sale of accounts, contract rights, or chattel paper, the debtor is entitled to any surplus or is liable for any deficiency only if the security agreement so provides.

Section 9—503. Secured Party's Right to Take Possession After Default.

Unless otherwise agreed a secured party has on default the right to take possession of the collateral. In taking possession a secured party may proceed without judicial process if this can be done without breach of the peace or may proceed by action. If the security agreement so provides, the secured party may require the debtor to assemble the collateral and make it available to the secured party at a place to be designated by the secured party which is reasonably convenient to both parties. Without removal a secured party may render equipment unusable, and may dispose of collateral on the debtor's premises under Section 9—504.

Section 9—504. Secured Party's Right to Dispose of Collateral After Default; Effect of Disposition.

(1) A secured party after default may sell, lease or otherwise dispose of any or all of the collateral in its then condition or following any commercially reasonable preparation or processing. Any sale of goods is subject to the Article on Sales (Article 2). The proceeds of disposition shall be applied in the order following to

(a) the reasonable expenses of retaking, holding, preparing for sale, selling and the like and, to the extent provided for in the agreement and not prohibited by law, the reasonable attorneys' fees and legal expenses incurred by the secured party;

(b) the satisfaction of indebtedness secured by the security interest under which the disposition is made;

(c) the satisfaction of indebtedness secured by any subordinate security interest in the collateral if written notification of demand therefor is received before distribution of the proceeds is completed. If requested by the secured party, the holder of a subordinate security interest must seasonably furnish reasonable proof of his interest, and unless he does so, the secured party need not comply with his demand.

(2) If the security interest secures an indebtedness, the secured party must account to the debtor for any surplus, and, unless otherwise agreed, the debtor is liable for any deficiency. But if the underlying transaction was a sale of accounts, contract rights, or chattel paper, the debtor is entitled to any surplus or is liable for any deficiency only if the security agreement so provides.

(3) Disposition of the collateral may be by public or private proceedings and may be made by way of one or more contracts. Sale or other disposition may be as a unit or in parcels and at any time and place and on any terms, but every aspect of the disposition including the method, manner, time, place and terms must be commercially reasonable. Unless collateral is perishable or threatens to decline speedily in value or is of a type customarily sold on a recognized market, reasonable notification of the time and place of any public sale or reasonable notification of the time after which any private sale or other intended disposition is to be made shall be sent by the secured party to the debtor, and except in the case of consumer goods to any other person who has a security interest in the collateral and who has duly filed a financing statement indexed in the name of the debtor in this state or who is known by the secured party to have a security interest in the collateral. The secured party may buy at any public sale and if the collateral is of a type customarily sold in a recognized market or is of a type which is the subject of widely distributed standard price quotations, he may buy at private sale.

(4) When collateral is disposed of by a secured party after default, the disposition transfers to a purchaser for value all of the debtor's rights therein, discharges the security interest under which it is made and any security interest or lien subordinate thereto. The purchaser takes free of all such rights and interests even though the secured party fails to comply with the requirements of this Part or of any judicial proceedings.

(a) in the case of a public sale, if the purchaser has no knowledge of any defects in the sale and if he does not buy in collusion with the secured party, other bidders or the person conducting the sale ;or

(b) in any other case, if the purchaser acts in good faith.

(5) A person who is liable to a secured party under a guaranty, indorsement, repurchase agreement or the like and who receives a transfer of collateral from the secured party or is subrogated to his rights has thereafter the rights and duties of the secured party. Such a transfer of collateral is not a sale or disposition of the collateral under this Article.

Section 9—505. Compulsory Disposition of Collateral; Acceptance of the Collateral as Discharge of Obligation.

(1) If the debtor has paid sixty per cent of the cash price in the case of a purchase money security interest in consumer goods or sixty per cent of the loan in the case of another security interest in consumer goods, and has not signed after default a statement renouncing or modifying his rights under this Part, a secured party who has taken possession of collateral must dispose of it under Section 9—504 and if he fails to do so within ninety days after he takes possession, the debtor at his option may recover in conversion or under Section 9—507 (1) on secured party's liability.

(2) In any other case involving consumer goods or any other collateral a secured party in possession may, after default, propose to retain the collateral in satisfaction of the

obligation. Written notice of such proposal shall be sent to the debtor and except in the case of consumer goods to any other secured party who has a security interest in the collateral and who has duly filed a financing statement indexed in the name of the debtor in this state or is known by the secured party in possession to have a security interest in it. If the debtor or other person entitled to receive notification objects in writing within thirty days from the receipt of the notification or if any other secured party objects in writing within thirty days after the secured party obtains possession, the secured party must dispose of the collateral under Section 9—504. In the absence of such written objection the secured party may retain the collateral in satisfaction of the debtor's obligation.

Section 9—506. Debtor's Right to Redeem Collateral.

At any time before the secured party has disposed of collateral or entered into a contract for its disposition under Section 9—504 or before the obligation has been discharged under Section 9—505(2) the debtor or any other secured party may unless otherwise agreed in writing after default redeem the collateral by tendering fulfillment of all obligations secured by the collateral as well as the expenses reasonably incurred by the secured party in retaking, holding and preparing the collateral for disposition, in arranging for the sale, and to the extent provided in the agreement and not prohibited by law, his reasonable attorney's fees and legal expenses.

Section 9—507. Secured Party's Liability for Failure to Comply with This Part.

(1) If it is established that the secured party is not proceeding in accordance with the provisions of this Part, disposition may be ordered or restrained on appropriate terms and conditions. If the disposition has occurred, the debtor or any person entitled to notification or whose security interest has been made known to the secured party prior to the disposition has a right to recover from the secured party any loss caused by a failure to comply with the provisions of this Part. If the collateral is consumer goods, the debtor has a right to recover in any event an amount not less than the credit service charge plus ten per cent of the principal amount of the debt or the time price differential plus ten per cent of the cash price.

(2) The fact that a better price could have been obtained by a sale at a different time or in a different method from that selected by the secured party is not of itself sufficient to establish that the sale was not made in a commercially reasonable manner. If the secured party either sells the collateral in the usual manner in any recognized market therefor or if he sells at the price current in such market at the time of his sale or if he has otherwise sold in conformity with reasonable commercial practices among dealers in the type of property sold, he has sold in a commercially reasonable manner. The pirnciples stated in the two preceding sentences with respect to sales also apply as may be appropriate to other types of disposition. A disposition which has been approved in any judicial proceeding or by any bona fide creditors' committee or representative of creditors shall conclusively be deemed to be commercially reasonable, but this sentence does not indicate that any such approval must be obtained in any case nor does it indicate that any disposition not so approved is not commercially reasonable.

ARTICLE 10

EFFECTIVE DATE AND REPEALER

Section 10—101. Effective Date.

This Act shall become effective at midnight on December 31st following its enactment. It applies to transactions entered into and events occurring after that date.

Section 10—102. Specific Repealer; Provision for Transition.

(1) The following acts and all other acts and parts of acts inconsistent herewith are hereby repealed:

(Here should follow the acts to be specifically repealed including the following:

Uniform Negotiable Instruments Act
Uniform Warehouse Receipts Act
Uniform Sales Act
Uniform Bills of Lading Act
Uniform Stock Transfer Act
Uniform Conditional Sales Act
Uniform Trust Receipts Act

Also any acts regulating:

Bank collections
Bulk sales
Chattel mortgages
Conditional sales
Factor's lien acts
Farm storage of grain and similar acts
Assignment of accounts receivable)

(2) Transactions validly entered into before the effective date specified in Section 10—101 and the rights, duties and interests flowing from them remain valid thereafter and may be terminated, completed, consummated or enforced as required or permitted by any statute or other law amended or repealed by this Act as though such repeal or amendment had not occurred.

Note

Subsection (1) should be separately prepared for each state. The foregoing is a list of statutes to be checked.

Section 10—103. General Repealer.

Except as provided in the following section, all acts and parts of acts inconsistent with this Act are hereby repealed.

Section 10—104. Laws Not Repealed.

[(1)] The Article on Documents of Title (Article 7) does not repeal or modify any laws prescribing the form or contents of documents of title or the services or facilities to be afforded by bailees, or otherwise regulating bailees' businesses in respects not specifically dealt with herein; but the fact that such laws are violated does not affect the status of a document of title which otherwise complies with the definition of a document of title (Section 1—201).

[(2) This Act does not repeal .... *, cited as the Uniform Act for the Simplification of Fiduciary Security Transfers, and if in any respect there is any inconsistency between that Act and the Article of this Act on investment securities (Article 8) the provisions of the former Act shall control.]

Note: *At * in subsection (2) insert the statutory references to the Uniform Act for the Simplification of Fiduciary Security Transfers if such Act has previously been enacted. If it has not been enacted, omit subsection (2).*

INDEX OF CASES

A*

B

* Page references for definitions are indicated in italic type.

C

D

E

F

G

SUBJECT INDEX

B

C

D

E

F

G

H

I

J

L

M

N

Q

R

S

V

W

Z